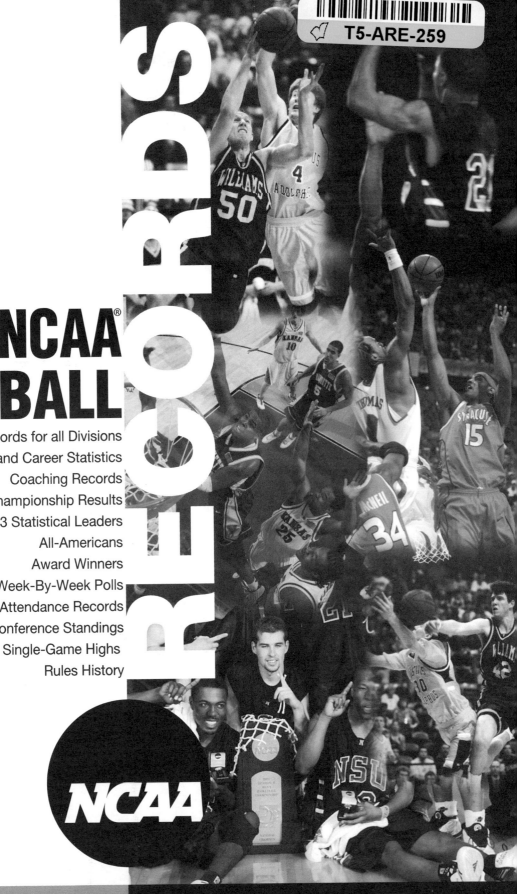

NCAA® BASKETBALL

RECORDS

Individual and Team Records for all Divisions

Includes Single-Game, Season and Career Statistics

Coaching Records

Championship Results

2003 Statistical Leaders

All-Americans

Award Winners

Week-By-Week Polls

Attendance Records

2003 Conference Standings

Single-Game Highs

Rules History

NCAA

THE NATIONAL COLLEGIATE ATHLETIC ASSOCIATION
P.O. Box 6222, Indianapolis, Indiana 46206-6222
317/917-6222
http://www.ncaa.org

October 2003

Compiled By:
Gary K. Johnson, *Senior Assistant Director of Statistics.*
Sean W. Straziscar, *Assistant Director of Statistics.*

Edited By:
Marty Benson, *Assistant Director of Publishing.*

Production By:
Toi Davis, *Production Designer II.*

Cover Design By:
Wayne Davis, *Associate Director of Graphics.*

Cover Photography By:
Clarkson and Associates.

Distributed to sports information directors and conference publicity directors.

NCAA, NCAA logo and National Collegiate Athletic Association are registered marks of the Association and use in any manner is prohibited unless prior approval is obtained from the Association.

Contents

Name-Change Key

The following players changed their names after their collegiate careers ended. They are listed throughout the book by the names under which they played in college (those listed at the left). Their current names are listed below. In addition, various schools have changed their name. The current school name is listed along with other names by which the schools have been referred.

PLAYER name changes

Name as a collegian:	Changed to:
Lew Alcindor (UCLA)	Kareem Abdul-Jabbar
Walt Hazzard (UCLA)	Mahdi Abdul-Rahmad
Chris Jackson (LSU)	Mahmoud Abdul-Rauf
Akeem Olajuwon (Houston)	Hakeem Olajuwon
Keith Wilkes (UCLA)	Jamaal Wilkes
Jason Williams (Duke)	Jay Williams

SCHOOL name changes

Current school name:	Changed from:
Albertson	Col. of Idaho
Alcorn St.	Alcorn A&M
Alliant Int'l	U.S. Int'l; Cal Western
Arcadia	Beaver
Arizona St.	Tempe St.
Ark.-Pine Bluff	Arkansas AM&N
Armstrong Atlantic	Armstrong St.
Auburn	Alabama Poly
Augusta St.	Augusta
Bemidji St.	Bemidji Teachers
Benedictine (Ill.)	Ill. Benedictine
Bradley	Bradley Tech
UC Davis	California Aggies
Cal St. Fullerton	Orange County State College; Orange St.
Cal St. L.A.	Los Angeles St.
Cal St. Northridge	San Fernando Valley St.
Carnegie Mellon	Carnegie Tech
Case Reserve	Case Institute of Technology
Central Okla.	Central St. (Okla.)
Charleston So.	Baptist (S.C.)
Charleston (W.Va.)	Morris Harvey
Charlotte	UNC Charlotte
Chattanooga	Tenn.-Chatt.
Cleveland St.	Fenn
Colorado St.	Colorado A&M
Colorado St.-Pueblo	Southern Colo.
Columbus St.	Columbus
Concordia (Calif.)	Christ College-Irvine
Concordia (Ill.)	Concordia Teachers
Crown	St. Paul Bible
DeSales	Allentown
Detroit	Detroit Mercy; Detroit Tech
Dist. of Columbia	D.C. Teachers; Federal City
Dominican	Rosary
Drexel	Drexel Tech
Duke	Trinity (N.C.)
Eastern Mich.	Michigan Normal
Emporia St.	Kansas St. Normal
FDU-Florham	FDU-Madison
Farmington St.	Maine-Farmington
Fresno St.	Fresno Pacific
Ga. Southern	Georgia Teachers
Ill.-Chicago	Ill.-Chicago Circle
Illinois St.	Illinois St. Normal; Illinois Normal
Indiana (Pa.)	Indiana St. (Pa.)
Indianapolis	Indiana Central
Iowa	State University of Iowa
Iowa St.	Ames
James Madison	Madison
Kansas St.	Kansas Aggies
Kent St.	Kent
La Sierra	Loma Linda
Lamar	Lamar Tech
Liberty	Lynchburg Baptist; Liberty Baptist
La.-Lafayette	Southwestern La.
La.-Monroe	Northeast La.
Loyola Marymount	Loyola U. of L.A.
Lynn	College of Boca Raton
Lyon	Arkansas College
Maritime (N.Y.)	N.Y. Maritime
Martin Luther	Northwestern (Wis.)
Marycrest Int'l	Teikyo Marycrest
Md.-East. Shore	Maryland St.

Current school name:	Changed from:
Massachusetts	Massachusetts St.; Massachusetts Agriculture Col.
Mass. Liberal Arts	North Adams St.
Mass.-Dartmouth	Southeastern Mass.
Mass.-Lowell	Lowell; Lowell St.; Lowell Tech
McDaniel	Western Md.
Memphis	Memphis St.
Minn. St. Mankato	Mankato Teachers; Mankato St.
Minn. St. Moorhead	Moorhead St.; Moorhead Teachers
Mont. St.-Billings	Eastern Montana
Montana St.-Northern	Northern Montana
Murray St.	Murray Teachers
Neb.-Kearney	Kearney St.
Neb.-Omaha	Omaha
New England U.	St. Francis (Me.)
New Jersey City	Jersey City St.
N.J. Inst. of Tech.	Newark Engineering
New Mexico St.	New Mexico A&M
New Orleans	Louisiana St. (N.O.)
North Ala.	Florence St.
N.C. Central	North Caro. College
UNC Pembroke	Pembroke St.
North Central Texas	Cooke County
North Texas	North Tex. St.
Northeastern St.	Northeastern Okla. St.
Northern Ariz.	Arizona St.-Flagstaff; Flagstaff Teachers
Northern Colo.	Colorado St. College
Northern Iowa	Iowa Teachers
Oklahoma St.	Oklahoma A&M
Old Dominion	William & Mary (Norfolk)
Pepperdine	George Pepperdine
Philadelphia U.	Philadelphia Textile
Polytechnic (N.Y.)	New York Poly; Brooklyn Poly
Rhodes	Southwestern (Tenn.)
Rice	Rice Institute
Richard Stockton	Stockton St.
Rochester Inst.	Mechanics Institute
Rowan	Glassboro St.
Southern Ind.	Indiana St.-Evansville
Southern Me.	Maine Portland-Gorham; Gorham St. (Me.)
Southern Miss.	Mississippi Southern College; Mississippi Normal
Southern N.H.	New Hamp. Col.
Southern U.	Southern B.R.
Southwest Minn. St.	Southwest St.
Stevens Institute	Stevens Tech
Taylor-Ft. Wayne	Summit Christian
TCNJ	Trenton St.
Tex. A&M-Commerce	East Texas St.
Tex. A&M-Kingsville	Texas A&I
Tex.-Pan American	Pan American
Texas St.	Southwest Tex. St.
Towson	Towson St.
Truman	Northeast Mo. St.; Truman St.
Tulsa	Henry Kendall
UCF	Florida Tech
UNLV	Nevada Southern
UTEP	Texas Western
Washburn	Lincoln College
Washington St.	Washington Agricultural College
West Ala.	Livingston
West Tex. A&M	West Texas St.
Western Mich.	Western State Teachers
Western N. M.	New Mexico Western
Western Ore.	Oregon Tech; Oregon College of Education
Western St.	Colo. Western; Colorado Normal
Westmar	Western Union College; Teikyo Westmar
Wichita St.	Fairmount
Widener	Pennsylvania Military College
Wm. Paterson	Paterson St.
Wis.-Eau Claire	Eau Claire Teachers
Wis.-La Crosse	La Crosse Teachers
Wis.-River Falls	River Falls Teachers
Wis.-Superior	Superior Normal; Superior St. Teachers
Xavier	St. Xavier

SCHOOLS also known as

Current school name:	Also known as:
Air Force	U.S. Air Force Academy
Apprentice School	Newport News
Army	U.S. Military Academy; West Point
Baruch	Bernard M. Baruch
Case Reserve	Case Western Reserve

Current school name:	Also known as:
CCNY	City College of New York
Coast Guard	U.S. Coast Guard Academy
GC&SU	Georgia College & State
Hawthorne	Nathaniel Hawthorne
IPFW	Indiana/Purdue-Ft. Wayne
IUPUI	Indiana/Purdue-Indianapolis
Lehman	Herbert H. Lehman
Lipscomb	David Lipscomb
Long Island	LIU-Brooklyn
LSU	Louisiana St.
Merchant Marine	King's Point; U.S. Merchant Marine Academy
MIT	Massachusetts Institute of Technology
Navy	U.S. Naval Academy
NYCCT	New York City Tech
NYIT	New York Institute of Technology; New York Tech
Rochester Inst.	RIT
Sewanee	University of the South
TCNJ	The Col. of New Jersey (was Trenton St.)
TCU	Texas Christian
UAB	Ala.-Birmingham
UCF	Central Fla. (was Florida Tech)
UCLA	University of California, Los Angeles
UMBC	Md.-Balt. County
UMKC	Mo.-Kansas City
UNLV	Nevada-Las Vegas (was Nevada Southern)
UTEP	Texas-El Paso (was Texas Western)
VMI	Va. Military
WPI	Worcester Poly Inst.

SCHOOL MERGERS

Current school name:	Two Schools Merged & Year:
Case Reserve	Case Tech & Western Reserve; 1971-72
Mass.-Lowell	Lowell St. & Lowell Tech; 1975-76

Division I Records

Individual Records

Basketball records are confined to the "modern era," which began with the 1937-38 season, the first without the center jump after each goal scored. Except for the school's all-time won-lost record or coaches' records, only statistics achieved while an institution was an active member of the NCAA are included in team or individual categories. Official weekly statistics rankings in scoring and shooting began with the 1947-48 season; individual rebounds were added for the 1950-51 season, although team rebounds were not added until 1954-55. Assists were added in 1983-84, blocked shots and steals were added in 1985-86 and three-point field goals were added in 1986-87. Scoring, rebounding, assists, blocked shots and steals are ranked on total number and on per-game average; shooting, on percentage. In statistical rankings, the rounding of percentages and/or averages may indicate ties where none exist. In these cases, the numerical order of the rankings is accurate. In 1973, freshmen became eligible to compete on the varsity level.

Scoring

POINTS
Game
100—Frank Selvy, Furman vs. Newberry, Feb. 13, 1954 (41 FGs, 18 FTs)
Season
1,381—Pete Maravich, LSU, 1970 (522 FGs, 337 FTs, 31 games)
Career
3,667—Pete Maravich, LSU, 1968-70 (1,387 FGs, 893 FTs, 83 games)

POINTS VS. DIVISION I OPPONENT
Game
72—Kevin Bradshaw, U.S. Int'l vs. Loyola Marymount, Jan. 5, 1991

AVERAGE PER GAME
Season
44.5—Pete Maravich, LSU, 1970 (1,381 in 31)
Career
44.2—Pete Maravich, LSU, 1968-70 (3,667 in 83)

COMBINED POINTS, TWO TEAMMATES
Game
125—Frank Selvy (100) and Darrell Floyd (25), Furman vs. Newberry, Feb. 13, 1954

COMBINED POINTS, TWO TEAMMATES VS. DIVISION I OPPONENT
Game
92—Kevin Bradshaw (72) and Isaac Brown (20), U.S. Int'l vs. Loyola Marymount, Jan. 5, 1991

COMBINED POINTS, TWO OPPOSING PLAYERS ON DIVISION I TEAMS
Game
115—Pete Maravich (64), LSU and Dan Issel (51), Kentucky, Feb. 21, 1970

GAMES SCORING AT LEAST 50 POINTS
Season
10—Pete Maravich, LSU, 1970
Season—Consecutive Games
3—Pete Maravich, LSU, Feb. 10 to Feb. 15, 1969
Career
28—Pete Maravich, LSU, 1968-70

GAMES SCORING AT LEAST 40 POINTS
Career
56—Pete Maravich, LSU, 1968-70

GAMES SCORING IN DOUBLE FIGURES
Career
132—Danny Manning, Kansas, 1985-88

CONSECUTIVE GAMES SCORING IN DOUBLE FIGURES
Career
115—Lionel Simmons, La Salle, 1987-90

Field Goals

FIELD GOALS
Game
41—Frank Selvy, Furman vs. Newberry, Feb. 13, 1954 (66 attempts)
Season
522—Pete Maravich, LSU, 1970 (1,168 attempts)
Career
1,387—Pete Maravich, LSU, 1968-70 (3,166 attempts)

CONSECUTIVE FIELD GOALS
Game
16—Doug Grayson, Kent St. vs. North Carolina, Dec. 6, 1967 (18 of 19)
Season
25—Ray Voelkel, American, 1978 (during nine games, Nov. 24-Dec. 16)

FIELD-GOAL ATTEMPTS
Game
71—Jay Handlan, Wash. & Lee vs. Furman, Feb. 17, 1951 (30 made)
Season
1,168—Pete Maravich, LSU, 1970 (522 made)
Career
3,166—Pete Maravich, LSU, 1968-70 (1,387 made)

FIELD-GOAL PERCENTAGE
Game
(Min. 15 made) 100%—Clifford Rozier, Louisville vs. Eastern Ky., Dec. 11, 1993 (15 of 15)
(Min. 20 made) 95.5%—Bill Walton, UCLA vs. Memphis, March 26, 1973 (21 of 22)
*Season
74.6%—Steve Johnson, Oregon St., 1981 (235 of 315)

*Based on qualifiers for national championship.

Career
(Min. 400 made and 4 made per game) 67.8%—Steve Johnson, Oregon St., 1976-81 (828 of 1,222)

Three-Point Field Goals

THREE-POINT FIELD GOALS
Game
15—Keith Veney, Marshall vs. Morehead St., Dec. 14, 1996 (25 attempts)
Season
158—Darrin Fitzgerald, Butler, 1987 (362 attempts)
Career
413—Curtis Staples, Virginia, 1995-98 (1,079 attempts)

THREE-POINT FIELD GOALS MADE PER GAME
Season
5.6—Darrin Fitzgerald, Butler, 1987 (158 in 28)
Career
(Min. 200 made) 4.6—Timothy Pollard, Mississippi Val., 1988-89 (256 in 56)

CONSECUTIVE THREE-POINT FIELD GOALS
Game
11—Gary Bossert, Niagara vs. Siena, Jan. 7, 1987
Season
15—Todd Leslie, Northwestern, 1990 (during four games, Dec. 15-28)

CONSECUTIVE GAMES MAKING A THREE-POINT FIELD GOAL
Season
38—Steve Kerr, Arizona, Nov. 27, 1987, to April 2, 1988
Career
88—Cory Bradford, Illinois, Nov. 10, 1998 to Feb. 10, 2001

THREE-POINT FIELD-GOAL ATTEMPTS
Game
27—Bruce Seals, Manhattan vs. Canisius, Jan. 31, 2000 (9 made)
Season
362—Darrin Fitzgerald, Butler, 1987 (158 made)
Career
1,079—Curtis Staples, Virgina, 1995-98 (413 made)

THREE-POINT FIELD-GOAL ATTEMPTS PER GAME
Season
12.9—Darrin Fitzgerald, Butler, 1987 (362 in 28)
Career
9.1—Keith Veney, Lamar & Marshall, 1993-94, 1996-97 (1,014 in 111)

THREE-POINT FIELD-GOAL PERCENTAGE
Game
(Min. 9 made) 100%—Mark Poag, Old Dominion vs. VMI, Nov. 25, 1997 (9 of 9); Markus Wilson, Evansville vs. Tenn.-Martin, Nov. 18, 1998 (9 of 9)
(Min. 12 made) 85.7%—Gary Bossert, Niagara vs. Siena, Jan. 7, 1987 (12 of 14)
Season
(Min. 50 made) 63.4%—Glenn Tropf, Holy Cross, 1988 (52 of 82)
(Min. 100 made) 57.3%—Steve Kerr, Arizona, 1988 (114 of 199)
Career
(Min. 200 made and 2.0 made per game) 49.7%—Tony Bennett, Wis.-Green Bay, 1989-92 (290 of 584)
(Min. 300 made) 45.5%—Shawn Respert, Michigan St., 1992-95 (331 of 728)

Free Throws

FREE THROWS
Game
30—Pete Maravich, LSU vs. Oregon St., Dec. 22, 1969 (31 attempts)
Season
355—Frank Selvy, Furman, 1954 (444 attempts)
Career
(3 yrs.) 893—Pete Maravich, LSU, 1968-70 (1,152 attempts)
(4 yrs.) 905—Dickie Hemric, Wake Forest, 1952-55 (1,359 attempts)

CONSECUTIVE FREE THROWS MADE
Game
24—Arlen Clark, Oklahoma St. vs. Colorado, March 7, 1959 (24 of 24)
Season
73—Gary Buchanan, Villanova, 2000-01 (during 21 games, Nov. 17-Feb. 12)
Career
85—Darnell Archey, Butler, 2001-03 (during 57 games, Feb. 15, 2001-Jan. 18, 2003)

FREE THROWS
Game
36—Ed Tooley, Brown vs. Amherst, Dec. 4, 1954 (23 made)
Season
444—Frank Selvy, Furman, 1954 (355 made)
Career
(3 yrs.) 1,152—Pete Maravich, LSU, 1968-70 (893 made)
(4 yrs.) 1,359—Dickie Hemric, Wake Forest, 1952-55 (905 made)

FREE-THROW PERCENTAGE
Game
(Min. 24 made) 100%—Arlen Clark, Oklahoma St. vs. Colorado, March 7, 1959 (24 of 24)
*Season
95.9%—Craig Collins, Penn St., 1985 (94 of 98)

*Based on qualifiers for national championship.

Career
(Min. 300 made and 2.5 made per game) 91.3%—Gary Buchanan, Villanova, 2000-03 (324 of 355)
(Min. 600 made) 88.5%—Ron Perry, Holy Cross, 1976-80 (680 of 768)

(Min. 2.5 made per game) 92.3%—Dave Hildahl, Portland St., 1979-81 (131 of 142)

Rebounds

REBOUNDS
Game
51—Bill Chambers, William & Mary vs. Virginia, Feb. 14, 1953
(Since 1973) 35—Larry Abney, Fresno St. vs. Southern Methodist, Feb. 17, 2000
Season
734—Walt Dukes, Seton Hall, 1953 (33 games)
(Since 1973) 597—Marvin Barnes, Providence, 1974 (32 games)
Career
(3 yrs.) 1,751—Paul Silas, Creighton, 1962-64 (81 games)
(4 yrs.) 2,201—Tom Gola, La Salle, 1952-55 (118 games)
(Since 1973) 1,570—Tim Duncan, Wake Forest, 1994-97 (128 games)

AVERAGE PER GAME
Season
25.6—Charlie Slack, Marshall, 1955 (538 in 21)
(Since 1973) 20.4—Kermit Washington, American, 1973 (511 in 25)
Career
(Min. 800) 22.7—Artis Gilmore, Jacksonville, 1970-71 (1,224 in 54)
(4 yrs.) 21.8—Charlie Slack, Marshall, 1953-56 (1,916 in 88)
(Since 1973) 15.2—Glenn Mosley, Seton Hall, 1974-77 (1,263 in 83)

Assists

ASSISTS
Game
22—Tony Fairley, Charleston So. vs. Armstrong Atlantic, Feb. 9, 1987; Avery Johnson, Southern U. vs. Texas Southern, Jan. 25, 1988; Sherman Douglas, Syracuse vs. Providence, Jan. 28, 1989
Season
406—Mark Wade, UNLV, 1987 (38 games)
Career
1,076—Bobby Hurley, Duke, 1990-93 (140 games)

AVERAGE PER GAME
Season
13.3—Avery Johnson, Southern U., 1988 (399 in 30)

Career
(Min. 600) 12.0—Avery Johnson, Southern U., 1987-88 (732 in 61)
(4 yrs.) 8.4—Chris Corchiani, North Carolina St., 1988-91 (1,038 in 124)

Blocked Shots

BLOCKED SHOTS
Game
14—David Robinson, Navy vs. UNC Wilmington, Jan. 4, 1986; Shawn Bradley, Brigham Young vs. Eastern Ky., Dec. 7, 1990; Roy Rogers, Alabama vs. Georgia, Feb. 10, 1996; Loren Woods, Arizona vs. Oregon, Feb. 3, 2000
Season
207—David Robinson, Navy, 1986 (35 games)
Career
535—Wojciech Myrda, La.-Monroe, 1999-2002 (115 games)

AVERAGE PER GAME
Season
6.4—Adonal Foyle, Colgate, 1997 (180 in 28)
Career
(Min. 225) 5.9—Keith Closs, Central Conn. St., 1995-96 (317 in 54)
(4 yrs.) 4.7—Wojciech Myrda, La.-Monroe, 1999-2002 (535 in 115)

Steals

STEALS
Game
13—Mookie Blaylock, Oklahoma vs. Centenary (La.), Dec. 12, 1987; and vs. Loyola Marymount, Dec. 17, 1988
Season
160—Desmond Cambridge, Alabama A&M, 2002 (29 games)
Career
385—John Linehan, Providence, 1998-2002 (122 games)

AVERAGE PER GAME
Season
5.5—Desmond Cambridge, Alabama A&M, 2002 (160 in 29)
Career
(Min. 225) 3.9—Desmond Cambridge, Alabama A&M, 1999-2002 (330 in 84)

(4 yrs.) 3.2—Eric Murdock, Providence, 1988-91 (376 in 117)

Fouls

SHORTEST PLAYING TIME BEFORE BEING DISQUALIFIED
Game
1:38—Mike Pflugner, Butler vs. Ill.-Chicago, March 2, 1996

Games

GAMES PLAYED (SINCE 1947-48)
Season
40—Mark Alarie, Tommy Amaker, Johnny Dawkins, Danny Ferry and Billy King, Duke, 1986; Larry Johnson, UNLV, 1990; Anthony Epps, Jamaal Magloire, Ron Mercer and Wayne Turner, Kentucky, 1997
Career
151—Wayne Turner, Kentucky, 1996-99

General

ACHIEVED 2,000 POINTS AND 2,000 REBOUNDS
Career
Tom Gola, La Salle, 1952-55 (2,462 points and 2,201 rebounds)
Joe Holup, George Washington, 1953-56 (2,226 points and 2,030 rebounds)

AVERAGED 20 POINTS AND 20 REBOUNDS
Career
Bill Russell, San Francisco, 1954-56 (20.7 points and 20.3 rebounds)
Paul Silas, Creighton, 1962-64 (20.5 points and 21.6 rebounds)
Julius Erving, Massachusetts, 1970-71 (26.3 points and 20.2 rebounds)
Artis Gilmore, Jacksonville, 1970-71 (24.3 points and 22.7 rebounds)
Kermit Washington, American, 1971-73 (20.1 points and 20.2 rebounds)

Team Records

Note: Where records involve both teams, each team must be an NCAA Division I member institution.

SINGLE-GAME RECORDS

Scoring

POINTS
186—Loyola Marymount vs. U.S. Int'l (140), Jan. 5, 1991

POINTS BY LOSING TEAM
150—U.S. Int'l vs. Loyola Marymount (181), Jan. 31, 1989

POINTS, BOTH TEAMS
331—Loyola Marymount (181) vs. U.S. Int'l (150), Jan. 31, 1989

MARGIN OF VICTORY
117—Long Island (179) vs. Medgar Evers (62), Nov. 26, 1997

MARGIN OF VICTORY VS. DIVISION I OPPONENT
91—Tulsa (141) vs. Prairie View (50), Dec. 7, 1995

POINTS IN A HALF
98—Long Island vs. Medgar Evers, Nov. 26, 1997 (2nd)

POINTS IN A HALF VS. DIVISION I OPPONENT
97—Oklahoma vs. U.S. Int'l, Nov. 29, 1989 (1st)

POINTS IN A HALF, BOTH TEAMS
172—Loyola Marymount (86) vs. Gonzaga (86), Feb. 18, 1989 (2nd)

LEAD BEFORE OPPONENT SCORES AT START OF A GAME
34-0—Seton Hall vs. Kean, Nov. 29, 1998

LEAD BEFORE DIVISION I OPPONENT SCORES AT START OF A GAME
32-0—Connecticut vs. New Hampshire, Dec. 12, 1990

DEFICIT OVERCOME TO WIN GAME
32—Duke (74) vs. Tulane (72), Dec. 30, 1950 (trailed 22-54 with 2:00 left in the first half)

SECOND-HALF DEFICIT OVERCOME TO WIN GAME
31—Duke (74) vs. Tulane (72), Dec. 30, 1950 (trailed 27-58 with 19:00 left in the second half); Kentucky (99) vs. LSU (95), Feb. 15, 1994 (trailed 37-68 with 15:34 left in the second half)

HALFTIME DEFICIT OVERCOME TO WIN GAME
29—Duke (74) vs. Tulane (72), Dec. 30, 1950 (trailed 27-56 at halftime)

DEFICIT BEFORE SCORING OVERCOME TO WIN GAME
28—New Mexico St. (117) vs. Bradley (109), Jan. 27, 1977 (trailed 0-28 with 13:49 left in first half)

FEWEST POINTS ALLOWED (Since 1938)
6—Tennessee (11) vs. Temple, Dec. 15, 1973; Kentucky (75) vs. Arkansas St., Jan. 8, 1945

FEWEST POINTS ALLOWED (Since 1986)
21—Coastal Caro. (61) vs. Georgia So., Jan. 2, 1997

**FEWEST POINTS, BOTH TEAMS
(SINCE 1938)**
17—Tennessee (11) vs. Temple (6), Dec. 15, 1973

Field Goals

FIELD GOALS
76—Long Island vs. Medgar Evers, Nov. 26, 1997 (124 attempts)

FIELD GOALS VS. DDIVISION I OPPONENT
74—Houston vs. Valparaiso, Feb. 24, 1968 (112 attempts)

FIELD GOALS, BOTH TEAMS
130—Loyola Marymount (67) vs. U.S. Int'l (63), Jan. 31, 1989

FIELD GOALS IN A HALF
42—Oklahoma vs. U.S. Int'l, Nov. 29, 1989 (90 attempts) (1st half)

FIELD-GOAL ATTEMPTS
147—Oklahoma vs. U.S. Int'l, Nov. 29, 1989 (70 made)

FIELD-GOAL ATTEMPTS, BOTH TEAMS
245—Loyola Marymount (124) vs. U.S. Int'l (121), Jan. 7, 1989

FIELD-GOAL ATTEMPTS IN A HALF
90—Oklahoma vs. U.S. Int'l, Nov. 29, 1989 (42 made) (1st half)

FEWEST FIELD GOALS (SINCE 1938)
2—Duke vs. North Carolina St., March 8, 1968 (11 attempts); Arkansas St. vs. Kentucky, Jan. 8, 1945

FEWEST FIELD-GOAL ATTEMPTS (SINCE 1938)
9—Pittsburgh vs. Penn St., March 1, 1952 (3 made)

FIELD-GOAL PERCENTAGE
(Min. 15 made) 83.3%—Maryland vs. South Carolina, Jan. 9, 1971 (15 of 18)
(Min. 30 made) 81.4%—New Mexico vs. Oregon St., Nov. 30, 1985 (35 of 43)

FIELD-GOAL PERCENTAGE, HALF
94.1%—North Carolina vs. Virginia, Jan. 7, 1978 (16 of 17) (2nd half)

Three-Point Field Goals

THREE-POINT FIELD GOALS
28—Troy St. vs. George Mason, Dec. 10, 1994 (74 attempts)

THREE-POINT FIELD GOALS, BOTH TEAMS
44—Troy St. (28) vs. George Mason (16), Dec. 10, 1994

CONSECUTIVE THREE-POINT FIELD GOALS MADE WITHOUT A MISS
11—Niagara vs. Siena, Jan. 7, 1987; Eastern Ky. vs. UNC Asheville, Jan. 14, 1987

THREE-POINT FIELD-GOAL ATTEMPTS WITHOUT MAKING ONE
22—Canisius vs. St. Bonaventure, Jan. 21, 1995

NUMBER OF DIFFERENT PLAYERS TO SCORE A THREE-POINT FIELD GOAL, ONE TEAM
9—Dartmouth vs. Boston College, Nov. 30, 1993

THREE-POINT FIELD-GOAL ATTEMPTS
74—Troy St. vs. George Mason, Dec. 10, 1994 (28 made)

THREE-POINT FIELD-GOAL ATTEMPTS, BOTH TEAMS
108—Troy St. (74) vs. George Mason (34), Dec. 10, 1994

THREE-POINT FIELD-GOAL PERCENTAGE
(Min. 10 made) 91.7%—Drexel vs. Delaware, Dec. 3, 2000 (11 of 12)
(Min. 15 made) 83.3%—Eastern Ky. vs. UNC Asheville, Jan. 14, 1987 (15 of 18)

THREE-POINT FIELD-GOAL PERCENTAGE, BOTH TEAMS
(Min. 10 made) 83.3%—Lafayette (7 of 8) vs. Marist (3 of 4), Dec. 6, 1986 (10 of 12)

Free Throws

(Min. 15 made) 76.2%—Florida (10 of 14) vs. California (6 of 7), Dec. 27, 1986 (16 of 21)
(Min. 20 made) 72.4%—Princeton (12 of 15) vs. Brown (9 of 14), Feb. 20, 1988 (21 of 29)

FREE THROWS MADE
56—TCU vs. Eastern Mich., Dec. 21, 1999 (70 attempts)

FREE THROWS MADE, BOTH TEAMS
88—Morehead St. (53) vs. Cincinnati (35), Feb. 11, 1956 (111 attempts)

FREE-THROW ATTEMPTS
79—Northern Ariz. vs. Arizona, Jan. 26, 1953 (46 made)

FREE THROWS, BOTH TEAMS
130—Northern Ariz. (79) vs. Arizona (51), Jan. 26, 1953 (78 made)

FEWEST FREE THROWS MADE
0—Many teams

FEWEST FREE THROWS
0—Many teams

FREE-THROW PERCENTAGE
(Min. 32 made) 100.0%—UC Irvine vs. Pacific (Cal.), Feb. 21, 1981 (34 of 34); Samford vs. UCF, Dec. 20, 1990 (34 of 34)
(Min. 35 made) 97.2%—Vanderbilt vs. Mississippi St., Feb. 26, 1986 (35 of 36); Butler vs. Dayton, Feb. 21, 1991 (35 of 36); Marquette vs. Memphis, Jan. 23, 1993 (35 of 36)
(Min. 40 made) 95.5%—UNLV vs. San Diego St., Dec. 11, 1976 (42 of 44)

FREE-THROW PERCENTAGE, BOTH TEAMS
100%—Purdue (25 of 25) vs. Wisconsin (22 of 22), Feb. 7, 1976 (47 of 47)

Rebounds

REBOUNDS
108—Kentucky vs. Mississippi, Feb. 8, 1964

REBOUNDS, BOTH TEAMS
152—Indiana (95) vs. Michigan (57), March 11, 1961

REBOUND MARGIN
84—Arizona (102) vs. Northern Ariz. (18), Jan. 6, 1951

Assists

ASSISTS (INCLUDING OVERTIMES)
44—Colorado vs. George Mason, Dec. 2, 1995 (ot)

ASSISTS (REGULATION)
41—North Carolina vs. Manhattan, Dec. 27, 1985; Weber St. vs. Northern Ariz., March 2, 1991

ASSISTS, BOTH TEAMS (INCLUDING OVERTIMES)
67—Colorado (44) vs. George Mason (23), Dec. 2, 1995 (ot)

ASSISTS, BOTH TEAMS (REGULATION)
65—Dayton (34) vs. UCF (31), Dec. 3, 1988

Blocked Shots

BLOCKED SHOTS
21—Georgetown vs. Southern (N.O.), Dec. 1, 1993

BLOCKED SHOTS, BOTH TEAMS
29—Rider (17) vs. Fairleigh Dickinson (12), Jan. 9, 1989

Steals

STEALS
39—Long Island vs. Medgar Evers, Nov. 26, 1997

STEALS VS. DIVISION I OPPONENT
34—Oklahoma vs. Centenary (La.), Dec. 12, 1987

STEALS, BOTH TEAMS
44—Oklahoma (34) vs. Centenary (La.) (10), Dec. 12, 1987

Fouls

FOULS
50—Arizona vs. Northern Ariz., Jan. 26, 1953

FOULS, BOTH TEAMS
84—Arizona (50) vs. Northern Ariz. (34), Jan. 26, 1953

PLAYERS DISQUALIFIED
8—St. Joseph's vs. Xavier, Jan. 10, 1976

PLAYERS DISQUALIFIED, BOTH TEAMS
12—UNLV (6) vs. Hawaii (6), Jan. 19, 1979 (ot); Arizona (7) vs. West Tex. A&M (5), Feb. 14, 1952

Overtimes

OVERTIME PERIODS
7—Cincinnati (75) vs. Bradley (73), Dec. 21, 1981

POINTS IN ONE OVERTIME PERIOD
26—Vermont vs. Hartford, Jan. 24, 1998

POINTS IN ONE OVERTIME PERIOD, BOTH TEAMS
45—Va. Commonwealth (23) vs. Texas A&M (22), Dec. 2, 2000

POINTS IN OVERTIME PERIODS
49—Middle Tenn. vs. Tennessee Tech, Feb. 12, 2000 (4 ot)

POINTS IN OVERTIME PERIODS, BOTH TEAMS
94—Middle Tenn. (49) vs. Tennessee Tech (45), Feb. 12, 2000 (4 ot)

WINNING MARGIN IN OVERTIME GAME
21—Nicholls St. (86) vs. Sam Houston St. (65), Feb. 4, 1999 (23-2 in the ot)

SEASON RECORDS

Scoring

POINTS
4,012—Oklahoma, 1988 (39 games)

POINTS PER GAME
122.4—Loyola Marymount, 1990 (3,918 in 32)

SCORING MARGIN AVERAGE
30.3—UCLA, 1972 (94.6 offense, 64.3 defense)

GAMES AT LEAST 100 POINTS
28—Loyola Marymount, 1990

CONSECUTIVE GAMES AT LEAST 100 POINTS
12—UNLV, 1977; Loyola Marymount, 1990

Field Goals

FIELD GOALS
1,533—Oklahoma, 1988 (3,094 attempts)

FIELD GOALS PER GAME
46.3—UNLV, 1976 (1,436 in 31)

FIELD-GOAL ATTEMPTS
3,094—Oklahoma, 1988 (1,533 made)

FIELD-GOAL ATTEMPTS PER GAME
98.5—Oral Roberts, 1973 (2,659 in 27)

FIELD-GOAL PERCENTAGE
57.2%—Missouri, 1980 (936 of 1,635)

Three-Point Field Goals

THREE-POINT FIELD GOALS
407—Duke, 2001 (1,057 attempts)

THREE-POINT FIELD GOALS PER GAME
11.1—Troy St., 1996 (300 in 27)

THREE-POINT FIELD-GOAL ATTEMPTS
1,057—Duke, 2001 (407 made)

THREE-POINT FIELD-GOAL ATTEMPTS PER GAME
34.0—Mississippi Val., 1997 (985 in 29)

THREE-POINT FIELD-GOAL PERCENTAGE
(Min. 100 made) 50.8%—Indiana, 1987 (130 of 256)
(Min. 150 made) 50.0%—Mississippi Val., 1987 (161 of 322)
(Min. 200 made) 49.2%—Princeton, 1988 (211 of 429)

CONSECUTIVE GAMES SCORING A THREE-POINT FIELD GOAL (MULTIPLE SEASONS)
539—UNLV, Nov. 26, 1986, to present

Free Throws

FREE THROWS MADE
865—Bradley, 1954 (1,263 attempts)

FREE THROWS MADE PER GAME
28.9—Morehead St., 1956 (838 in 29)

CONSECUTIVE FREE THROWS MADE
49—Indiana St., 1991 (during two games, Feb. 13-18)

FREE THROWS
1,263—Bradley, 1954 (865 made)

FREE-THROW ATTEMPTS PER GAME
41.0—Bradley, 1953 (1,107 in 27)

FREE-THROW PERCENTAGE
82.2%—Harvard, 1984 (535 of 651)

Rebounds

REBOUNDS
2,109—Kentucky, 1951 (34 games)

REBOUNDS PER GAME
70.0—Connecticut, 1955 (1,751 in 25)

REBOUND MARGIN AVERAGE
25.0—Morehead St., 1957 (64.3 offense, 39.3 defense)
(Since 1973) 18.5—Manhattan, 1973 (56.5, 38.0)

Assists

ASSISTS
926—UNLV, 1990 (40 games)

ASSISTS PER GAME
24.7—UNLV, 1991 (863 in 35)

Blocked Shots

BLOCKED SHOTS
309—Georgetown, 1989 (34 games)

BLOCKED SHOTS PER GAME
9.1—Georgetown, 1989 (309 in 34)

Steals

STEALS
486—Oklahoma, 1988 (39 games)

STEALS PER GAME
14.9—Long Island, 1998 (478 in 32)

Fouls

FOULS
966—Providence, 1987 (34 games)

FOULS PER GAME
29.3—Indiana, 1952 (644 in 22)

FEWEST FOULS
253—Air Force, 1962 (23 games)

FEWEST FOULS PER GAME
11.0—Air Force, 1962 (253 in 23)

Defense

LOWEST SCORING AVERAGE PER GAME ALLOWED (SINCE 1982)
(Since 1938) 25.7—Oklahoma St., 1939 (693 in 27)
(Since 1948) 32.5—Oklahoma St., 1948 (1,006 in 31)
(Since 1965) 47.1—Fresno St., 1982 (1,412 in 30)

LOWEST FIELD-GOAL PERCENTAGE ALLOWED (Since 1978)
35.2—Stanford, 2000 (667 of 1,893)

Overtimes

OVERTIME GAMES
8—Western Ky., 1978 (won 5, lost 3); Portland, 1984 (won 4, lost 4); Valparaiso, 1993 (won 4, lost 4)

CONSECUTIVE OVERTIME GAMES
4—Jacksonville, 1982 (won 3, lost 1); Illinois St., 1985 (won 3, lost 1); Dayton, 1988 (won 1, lost 3)

OVERTIME WINS
6—Chattanooga, 1989 (6-0); Wake Forest, 1984 (6-1)

OVERTIME HOME WINS
5—Cincinnati, 1967 (5-0)

OVERTIME ROAD WINS
4—Delaware, 1973 (4-0); Arizona St., 1981 (4-0); Cal St. Fullerton, 1989 (4-0); New Mexico St., 1994 (4-0)

OVERTIME PERIODS
14—Bradley, 1982 (3-3)

CONSECUTIVE OVERTIME WINS—ALL-TIME
11—Louisville, Feb. 10, 1968-March 29, 1975; Massachusetts, March 21, 1991-Feb. 28, 1996; Virginia, Dec. 5, 1991-Feb. 8, 1996

General Records

GAMES IN A SEASON
45—Oregon, 1945 (30-15)

GAMES IN A SEASON (Since 1948)
40—Duke, 1986 (37-3); UNLV, 1990 (35-5); Kentucky, 1997 (35-5)

VICTORIES IN A SEASON
37—Duke, 1986 (37-3) & 1999 (37-2); UNLV, 1987 (37-2)

VICTORIES IN FIRST SEASON IN DIVISION I
29—Seattle, 1953 (29-4)

WON-LOST PERCENTAGE IN FIRST SEASON IN DIVISION I
.931—Md.-East. Shore, 1974 (27-2)

VICTORIES IN A PERFECT SEASON
32—North Carolina, 1957; Indiana, 1976

CONSECUTIVE VICTORIES IN A SEASON
34—UNLV, 1991 (34-1)

CONSECUTIVE VICTORIES
88—UCLA, from Jan. 30, 1971, through Jan. 17, 1974 (ended Jan. 19, 1974, at Notre Dame, 71-70; last UCLA defeat before streak also came at Notre Dame, 89-82)

CONSECUTIVE HOME-COURT VICTORIES
129—Kentucky, from Jan. 4, 1943, to Jan. 8, 1955 (ended by Georgia Tech, 59-58)

CONSECUTIVE REGULAR-SEASON VICTORIES (National Postseason Tournaments Not Included)
76—UCLA, 1971-74

DEFEATS IN A SEASON
30—Grambling, 2000 (1-30)

CONSECUTIVE DEFEATS IN A SEASON
28—Prairie View, 1992 (0-28)

CONSECUTIVE DEFEATS
33—Grambling, from Dec. 6, 1999, to Dec. 16, 2000

CONSECUTIVE HOME-COURT DEFEATS
32—New Hampshire, from Feb. 9, 1988, to Feb. 2, 1991 (ended vs. Holy Cross, 72-56)

CONSECUTIVE ROAD DEFEATS (including only games at the opponents' home sites)
64—Tex.-Pan American, from Nov. 25, 1995, to Jan. 8, 2000 (ended vs. Oral Roberts, 79-62)

CONSECUTIVE NON-HOME DEFEATS (including games at the opponents' home sites and at neutral sites)
56—Sacramento St., from Nov. 22, 1991, to Jan. 5, 1995 [ended at Loyola (Ill.), 68-56]

CONSECUTIVE 30-WIN SEASONS
3—Kentucky, 1947-49 and 1996-98

CONSECUTIVE 25-WIN SEASONS
10—UCLA, 1967-76; UNLV, 1983-92

CONSECUTIVE 20-WIN SEASONS
31—North Carolina, 1971-2001

CONSECUTIVE WINNING SEASONS
54—UCLA, 1949-2002

CURRENT CONSECUTIVE WINNING SEASONS
33—Indiana, 1971-2003; Syracuse, 1971-2003

CONSECUTIVE NON-LOSING SEASONS (Includes .500 Record)
60—Kentucky, 1928-52, 54-88# (2 .500 seasons)
#Kentucky did not play basketball during the 1953 season.

CONSECUTIVE NON-LOSING SEASONS (Includes .500 Record)-CURRENT
34—Syracuse, 1970-2003 (one .500 season)

UNBEATEN TEAMS (Since 1938; Number of Victories In Parenthesis)
1939 Long Island (24)†
1940 Seton Hall (19)††
1944 Army (15)††
1954 Kentucky (25)††
1956 San Francisco (29)*
1957 North Carolina (32)*
1964 UCLA (30)*
1967 UCLA (30)*
1972 UCLA (30)*
1973 UCLA (30)*
1973 North Carolina St. (27)††
1976 Indiana (32)*
*NCAA champion; †NIT champion; ††not in either tournament

UNBEATEN IN REGULAR SEASON BUT LOST IN NCAA (*) OR NIT (†)
1939 Loyola (Ill.) (20; 21-1)†
1941 Seton Hall (19; 20-2)†
1951 Columbia (21; 21-1)*
1961 Ohio St. (24; 27-1)*
1968 Houston (28; 31-2)*
1968 St. Bonaventure (22; 23-2)*
1971 Marquette (26; 28-1)*
1971 Pennsylvania (26; 28-1)*
1975 Indiana (29; 31-1)*
1976 Rutgers (28; 31-2)*
1979 Indiana St. (27; 33-1)*
1979 Alcorn St. (25; 28-1)†
1991 UNLV (30; 34-1)*

30-GAME WINNERS (SINCE 1938)
37—Duke, 1986 & 1999; UNLV, 1987.
36—Kentucky, 1948.
35—Arizona, 1988; Duke, 2001; Georgetown, 1985; Kansas, 1986 & 1998; Kentucky, 1997 & 1998; Massachusetts, 1996; UNLV, 1990; Oklahoma, 1988.

34—Arkansas, 1991; Connecticut, 1999; Duke, 1992; Georgetown, 1984; Kansas, 1997; Kentucky, 1947 & 1996; UNLV, 1991; North Carolina, 1993 & 1998.

33—Indiana St., 1979; Louisville, 1980; Michigan St., 1999; UNLV, 1986.

32—Arkansas, 1978 & 1995; Bradley, 1950, 1951 & 1986; Connecticut, 1996 & 1998; Duke, 1991 & 1998; Houston, 1984; Indiana, 1976; Iowa St., 2000; Kentucky, 1949, 1951, 1986 & 2003; Louisville, 1983 & 1986; Marshall, 1947;

Maryland, 2002; Michigan St., 2000; North Carolina, 1957, 1982 & 1987; Temple, 1987 & 1988; Tulsa, 2000.

31—Arkansas, 1994; Cincinnati, 2002; Connecticut, 1990; Duke, 2002; Houston, 1968 & 1983; Illinois, 1989; Indiana, 1975 & 1993; LSU, 1981; Memphis, 1985; Michigan, 1993; Minnesota, 1997; Oklahoma, 1985 & 2002; Oklahoma St., 1946; Rutgers, 1976; St. John's (N.Y.), 1985 & 1986; Seton Hall, 1953 & 1989; Stanford, 2001; Syracuse, 1987; UCLA, 1995; Wyoming, 1943.

30—Arizona, 1998; Arkansas, 1990; California, 1946; Georgetown, 1982; Indiana, 1987; Iowa, 1987; Kansas, 1990 & 2003; Kentucky, 1978 & 1993; La Salle, 1990; Massachusetts, 1992; Michigan, 1989; Navy, 1986; North Carolina, 1946; North Carolina St., 1951 & 1974; Oklahoma, 1989; Oregon, 1945; Stanford 1998; Syracuse, 1989 & 2003; Texas Tech, 1996; UCLA, 1964, 1967, 1972 & 1973; Utah, 1991 & 1998; Virginia, 1982; Western Ky., 1938.

All-Time Individual Leaders

Single-Game Records

SCORING HIGHS VS. DIVISION I OPPONENT

Pts.	Player, Team vs. Opponent	Date
72	Kevin Bradshaw, U.S. Int'l vs. Loyola Marymount	Jan. 5, 1991
69	Pete Maravich, LSU vs. Alabama	Feb. 7, 1970
68	Calvin Murphy, Niagara vs. Syracuse	Dec. 7, 1968
66	Jay Handlan, Wash. & Lee vs. Furman	Feb. 17, 1951
66	Pete Maravich, LSU vs. Tulane	Feb. 10, 1969
66	Anthony Roberts, Oral Roberts vs. N.C. A&T	Feb. 19, 1977
65	Anthony Roberts, Oral Roberts vs. Oregon	Mar. 9, 1977
65	Scott Haffner, Evansville vs. Dayton	Feb. 18, 1989
64	Pete Maravich, LSU vs. Kentucky	Feb. 21, 1970
63	Johnny Neumann, Mississippi vs. LSU	Jan. 30, 1971
63	Hersey Hawkins, Bradley vs. Detroit	Feb. 22, 1988
62	Darrell Floyd, Furman vs. Citadel	Jan. 14, 1956
62	Oscar Robertson, Cincinnati vs. North Texas	Feb. 6, 1960
62	Askia Jones, Kansas St. vs. Fresno St.	Mar. 24, 1994
61	Lew Alcindor, UCLA vs. Washington St.	Feb. 25, 1967
61	Pete Maravich, LSU vs. Vanderbilt	Dec. 11, 1969
61	Rick Mount, Purdue vs. Iowa	Feb. 28, 1970
61	Austin Carr, Notre Dame vs. Ohio	Mar. 7, 1970
61	Wayman Tisdale, Oklahoma vs. Texas-San Antonio	Dec. 28, 1983
61	Eddie House, Arizona St. vs. California (2 ot)	Jan. 8, 2000
60	Elgin Baylor, Seattle vs. Portland	Jan. 30, 1958
60	Billy McGill, Utah vs. Brigham Young	Feb. 24, 1962
60	John Mengelt, Auburn vs. Alabama	Feb. 14, 1970
60	Johnny Neumann, Mississippi vs. Baylor	Dec. 29, 1970
59	Pete Maravich, LSU vs. Alabama	Feb. 17, 1968
59	Ernie Fleming, Jacksonville vs. St. Peter's	Jan. 29, 1972
59	Kevin Bradshaw, U.S. Int'l vs. Florida Int'l	Jan. 14, 1991

Oscar Robertson of Cincinnati left his mark on all scoring lists that were kept during his career.

Photo by Rich Clarkson/NCAA Photos

SCORING HIGHS VS. NON-DIVISION I OPPONENT

Pts.	Player, Team vs. Opponent	Date
100	Frank Selvy, Furman vs. Newberry	Feb. 13, 1954
85	Paul Arizin, Villanova vs. Philadelphia NAMC	Feb. 12, 1949
81	Freeman Williams, Portland St. vs. Rocky Mountain	Feb. 3, 1978
73	Bill Mlkvy, Temple vs. Wilkes	Mar. 3, 1951
71	Freeman Williams, Portland St. vs. Southern Ore.	Feb. 9, 1977
67	Darrell Floyd, Furman vs. Morehead St.	Jan. 22, 1955
66	Freeman Williams, Portland St. vs. George Fox	Jan. 13, 1978
65	Bob Zawoluk, St. John's (N.Y.) vs. St. Peter's	Mar. 30, 1950
63	Sherman White, Long Island vs. John Marshall	Feb. 1950
63	Frank Selvy, Furman vs. Mercer	Feb. 11, 1953
62	Elvin Hayes, Houston vs. Valparaiso	Feb. 24, 1968
61	Matt Teahan, Denver vs. Neb. Wesleyan	Feb. 26, 1979
60	Bob Pettit, LSU vs. Louisiana College	Dec. 7, 1953
60	Harry Kelly, Texas Southern vs. Jarvis Christian	Feb. 23, 1983
60	Dave Jamerson, Ohio vs. Col. of Charleston	Dec. 21, 1989
59	Rick Barry, Miami (Fla.) vs. Rollins	1965
58	Frank Selvy, Furman vs. Wofford	Feb. 23, 1954
57	David Thompson, North Carolina St. vs. Buffalo St.	Dec. 5, 1974
57	Calvin Murphy, Niagara vs. Villa Madonna	Dec. 6, 1967
56	Stan Davis, Appalachian St. vs. Carson-Newman	Jan. 24, 1974
56	Tim Roberts, Southern U. vs. Faith Baptist	Dec. 12, 1994
55	Rick Barry, Miami (Fla.) vs. Tampa	1965
55	Elvin Hayes, Houston vs. Texas St.	Feb. 12, 1966
55	Wayman Tisdale, Oklahoma vs. Texas St.	Dec. 10, 1984
54	Rick Barry, Miami (Fla.) vs. Florida Southern	1965

FIELD-GOAL PERCENTAGE
(Minimum 12 field goals made)

Pct.	Player, Team vs. Opponent (FG-FGA)	Date
100	Clifford Rozier, Louisville vs. Eastern Ky. (15 of 15)	Dec. 11, 1993
100	Dan Henderson, Arkansas St. vs. Ga. Southern (14 of 14)	Feb. 26, 1976
100	Cornelius Holden, Louisville vs. Southern Miss. (14 of 14)	Mar. 3, 1990
100	Dana Jones, Pepperdine vs. Boise St. (14 of 14)	Nov. 30, 1991
100	Ted Guzek, Butler vs. Michigan (13 of 13)	Dec. 15, 1956
100	Rick Dean, Syracuse vs. Colgate (13 of 13)	Feb. 14, 1966
100	Gary Lechman, Gonzaga vs. Portland St. (13 of 13)	Jan. 21, 1967
100	Kevin King, Charlotte vs. South Ala. (13 of 13)	Feb. 20, 1978
100	Vernon Smith, Texas A&M vs. Alas. Anchorage (13 of 13)	Nov. 26, 1978
100	Steve Johnson, Oregon St. vs. Hawaii-Hilo (13 of 13)	Dec. 5, 1979
100	Antoine Carr, Wichita St. vs. Abilene Christian (13 of 13)	Nov. 28, 1980
100	Doug Hashley, Montana St. vs. Idaho St. (13 of 13)	Feb. 5, 1982
100	Brad Daugherty, North Carolina vs. UCLA (13 of 13)	Nov. 24, 1985
100	Ricky Butler, UC Irvine vs. Cal St. Fullerton (13 of 13)	Feb. 21, 1991
100	Rafael Solis, Brooklyn vs. Wagner (13 of 13)	Dec. 11, 1991
100	Ben Handlogten, Western Mich. vs. Toledo (13 of 13)	Jan. 27, 1996
100	Mate Milisa, Long Beach St. vs. Cal St. Monterey (13 of 13)	Dec. 22, 1999
100	Leon Roberts, Northern Ill. vs. Rockford (13 of 13)	Dec. 6, 2000
100	Calvin Ento, Montana St. vs. Dickinson St. (13 of 13)	Dec. 10, 2002
100	George Faerber, Purdue vs. Iowa (12 of 12)	Mar. 13, 1971
100	Jeff Tropf, Central Mich. vs. Northern Ill. (12 of 12)	Jan. 4, 1978
100	Durand Macklin, LSU vs. Mississippi St. (12 of 12)	Jan. 5, 1980
100	Ron Charles, Michigan St. vs. Michigan (12 of 12)	Jan. 24, 1980
100	Ricky Frazier, Missouri vs. Oklahoma St. (12 of 12)	Feb. 26, 1980
100	Bryan Warrick, St. Joseph's vs. Charlotte (12 of 12)	Jan. 16, 1982
100	David Robinson, Navy vs. East Caro. (12 of 12)	Mar. 7, 1985
100	Michael Ansley, Alabama vs. New Mexico St. (12 of 12)	Nov. 27, 1987
100	Mike Doktorczyk, UC Irvine vs. Pacific (Cal.) (12 of 12)	Jan. 21, 1989
100	Brian Parker, Chicago St. vs. Eastern Ill. (12 of 12)	Jan. 30, 1989
100	Alan Ogg, UAB vs. Mo. Western St. (12 of 12)	Dec. 30, 1989
100	Samuel Hines, South Ala. vs. Auburn (12 of 12)	Dec. 21, 1991
100	Jarrell Evans, Mississippi vs. Abilene Christian (12 of 12)	Nov. 29, 1993

Pct.	Player, Team vs. Opponent (FG-FGA)	Date
100	John Whorton, Kent St. vs. Akron (12 of 12)	Feb. 28, 1998
100	Anthony Glover, St. John's (N.Y.) vs. Hofstra (12 of 12)	Dec. 22, 1999
100	Tyson Patterson, Appalachian St. vs. Western Caro. (12 of 12)	Jan. 24, 2000
100	Mike Vukovich, UC Santa Barb. vs. Pacific (Cal.) (12 of 12)	Feb. 3, 2001
100	Ashley Champion, Chattanooga vs. Samford (12 of 12)	Nov. 22, 2002

THREE-POINT FIELD GOALS MADE

3FG	Player, Team vs. Opponent	Date
15	Keith Veney, Marshall vs. Morehead St.	Dec. 14, 1996
14	Dave Jamerson, Ohio vs. Col. of Charleston	Dec. 21, 1989
14	Askia Jones, Kansas St. vs. Fresno St.	Mar. 24, 1994
14	Ronald Blackshear, Marshall vs. Akron	Mar. 1, 2002
12	Gary Bossert, Niagara vs. Siena	Jan. 7, 1987
12	Darrin Fitzgerald, Butler vs. Detroit	Feb. 9, 1987
12	Alex Dillard, Arkansas vs. Delaware St.	Dec. 11, 1993
12	Mitch Taylor, Southern U. vs. La. Christian	Dec. 1, 1994
12	David McMahan, Winthrop vs. Coastal Caro.	Jan. 15, 1996
12	Clarence Gilbert, Missouri vs. Colorado	Feb. 23, 2002
12	Terrence Woods, Florida A&M vs. Coppin St.	Mar. 1, 2003
11	Jeff Hodson, Augusta St. vs. Armstrong Atlantic	Jan. 28, 1986
11	Dennis Scott, Georgia Tech vs. Houston	Dec. 28, 1988
11	Scott Haffner, Evansville vs. Dayton	Feb. 18, 1989
11	Bobby Phills, Southern U. vs. Alcorn St.	Feb. 3, 1990
11	Dave Jamerson, Ohio vs. Kent St.	Feb. 24, 1990
11	Jeff Fryer, Loyola Marymount vs. Michigan	Mar. 18, 1990
11	Doug Day, Radford vs. Central Conn. St.	Dec. 12, 1990
11	Brent Price, Oklahoma vs. Loyola Marymount	Dec. 15, 1990
11	Bobby Phills, Southern U. vs. Manhattan	Dec. 28, 1990
11	Terry Brown, Kansas vs. North Carolina St.	Jan. 5, 1991
11	Marc Rybczyk, Central Conn. St. vs. Long Island	Nov. 26, 1991
11	Mark Alberts, Akron vs. Wright St.	Feb. 8, 1992
11	Mike Alcorn, Youngstown St. vs. Pitt.-Bradford	Feb. 24, 1992
11	Doug Day, Radford vs. Morgan St.	Dec. 9, 1992
11	Lindsey Hunter, Jackson St. vs. Kansas	Dec. 27, 1992
11	Keith Veney, Lamar vs. Prairie View	Feb. 2, 1993
11	Keith Veney, Lamar vs. Ark.-Little Rock	Feb. 11, 1993
11	Scott Neely, Campbell vs. Coastal Caro.	Jan. 29, 1994
11	Chris Brown, UC Irvine vs. New Mexico St.	Mar. 13, 1994
11	Randy Rutherford, Oklahoma St. vs. Kansas	Mar. 5, 1995
11	Troy Hudson, Southern Ill. vs. Hawaii-Hilo	Dec. 29, 1995
11	Seth Chadwick, Wofford vs. Mercer	Feb. 15, 1997
11	Cory Schwab, Northern Ariz. vs. Cal Poly	Dec. 2, 2000
11	Ron Williamson, Howard vs. Georgetown	Dec. 16, 2000
11	T.J. Sorrentine, Vermont vs. Northeastern	Jan. 17, 2002
11	Ron Williamson, Howard vs. N.C. A&T	Jan. 21, 2003
11	Terrence Woods, Florida A&M vs. N.C. A&T	Feb. 1, 2003

THREE-POINT FIELD-GOAL PERCENTAGE
(Minimum 7 three-point field goals made)

Pct.	Player, Team vs. Opponent (3FG-FGA)	Date
100	Mark Poag, Old Dominion vs. VMI (9 of 9)	Nov. 25, 1997
100	Marcus Wilson, Evansville vs. Tenn.-Martin (9 of 9)	Nov. 18, 1998
100	Tomas Thompson, San Francisco vs. Loyola Marymount (8 of 8)	Mar. 7, 1992
100	Shawn Haughn, Dayton vs. St. Louis (8 of 8)	Feb. 13, 1994
100	James Singleton, Murray St. vs. Eastern Ill. (8 of 8)	Feb. 13, 2003
100	John Goldsberry, UNC Wilmington vs. Maryland (8 of 8)	Mar. 21, 2003
100	Kelvin Collins, Northeast La. vs. Nevada (7 of 7)	Dec. 30, 1986
100	Wally Lancaster, Virginia Tech vs. San Francisco St. (7 of 7)	Jan. 3, 1987
100	Ramon Trice, St. Louis vs. Butler (7 of 7)	Feb. 16, 1987
100	Juan Sanchez, Temple vs. Rhode Island (7 of 7)	Feb. 16, 1997
100	DeMar Moore, Bowling Green vs. Western Mich. (7 of 7)	Jan. 3, 1998
100	Senque Carey, Washington vs. Old Dominion (7 of 7)	Dec. 4, 1999
100	Okechi Egbe, Tenn.-Martin vs. Bethel (7 of 7)	Nov. 20, 2000
100	Justin Brown, Montana St. vs. Western Ill. (7 of 7)	Dec. 6, 2000
100	Lionel Armstead, West Virginia vs. Ark.-Monticello (7 of 7)	Dec. 1, 2001
100	Bronski Dockery, St. Francis (N.Y.) vs. Central Conn. St. (7 of 7)	Dec. 3, 2001
100	Nick Moore, Toledo vs. Akron (7 of 7)	Feb. 13, 2002
100	Felton Freeman, Sam Houston St. vs. TCU (7 of 7)	Nov. 22, 2002
100	Matt Walsh, Florida vs. Miami (Fla.) (7 of 7)	Dec. 21, 2002
100	Ezra Williams, Georgia vs. LSU (7 of 7)	Jan. 5, 2003
100	Tyrone Green, N.C. A&T vs. N.C. Central (7 of 7)	Jan. 19, 2003
90.0	Jarminca Resse, Air Force vs. Doane (9 of 10)	Nov. 22, 1997
90.0	Cory Schwab, Northern Ariz. vs. Southern Ore. (9 of 10)	Dec. 28, 1999
90.0	Aki Palmer, Colorado St. vs. Michigan (9 of 10)	Jan. 2, 2000
90.0	Eric Perry, Oral Roberts vs. Chicago St. (9 of 10)	Feb. 3, 2000
90.0	Aaron Bond, Northern Ariz. vs. Tenn.-Martin (9 of 10)	Dec. 21, 2002
90.0	Jason Kapono, UCLA vs. Washington St. (9 of 10)	Jan. 4, 2003

FREE-THROW PERCENTAGE
(Minimum 12 free throws made)

Pct.	Player, Team vs. Opponent (FT-FTA)	Date
100	Arlen Clark, Oklahoma St. vs. Colorado (24 of 24)	Mar. 7, 1959
100	York Larese, North Carolina vs. Duke (21 of 21)	Dec. 29, 1959
100	Steve Nash, Santa Clara vs. St. Mary's (Cal.) (21 of 21)	Jan. 7, 1995
100	Paul Renfro, Texas-Arlington vs. Lafayette (20 of 20)	Feb. 11, 1979
100	Anthony Peeler, Missouri vs. Iowa St. (20 of 20)	Jan. 31, 1990
100	Donyell Marshall, Connecticut vs. St. John's (N.Y.)	Jan 15, 1994
100	Jeron Roberts, Wyoming vs. UTEP (20 of 20)	Feb. 7, 1998
100	Skip Chappelle, Maine vs. Massachusetts (19 of 19)	1961
100	Gene Phillips, Southern Methodist vs. Texas A&M (19 of 19)	Feb. 2, 1971
100	Jim Kennedy, Missouri vs. Hawaii (19 of 19)	Dec. 22, 1975
100	Kevin Smith, Michigan St. vs. Indiana (19 of 19)	Jan. 7, 1982
100	Sidney Goodman, Coppin St. vs. N.C. A&T (19 of 19)	Feb. 18, 1995
100	Geno Ford, Ohio vs. Eastern Mich. (19 of 19)	Feb. 12, 1997
100	Eddie Benton, Vermont vs. New Hampshire (19 of 19)	Feb. 18, 1993
100	Tommy Boyer, Arkansas vs. Texas Tech (18 of 18)	Feb. 19, 1963
100	Ted Kitchel, Indiana vs. Illinois (18 of 18)	Jan. 10, 1981
100	Eric Rhodes, Stephen F. Austin vs. Texas St. (18 of 18)	Feb. 21, 1987
100	Todd Lichti, Stanford vs. UC Santa Barb. (18 of 18)	Dec. 28, 1987
100	Lionel Simmons, La Salle vs. American (18 of 18)	Feb. 2, 1988
100	Jeff Webster, Oklahoma vs. Southern Methodist (18 of 18)	Jan. 2, 1994
100	Anquell McCollum, Western Caro. vs. Marshall (18 of 18)	Feb. 5, 1996
100	Keith Van Horn, Utah vs. TCU (18 of 18)	Feb. 13, 1997
100	Edwin Young, Dayton vs. Northeast La. (18 of 18)	Dec. 18, 1997
100	Rayford Young, Texas Tech vs. Kansas (18 of 18)	Feb 13, 1999
100	Lynn Greer, Temple vs. St. Joseph's (18 of 18)	Feb. 2, 2002
100	Gabe Martin, Liberty vs. Fla. Atlantic (18 of 18)	Dec. 20, 2002

REBOUNDS

Reb.	Player, Team vs. Opponent	Date
51	Bill Chambers, William & Mary vs. Virginia	Feb. 14, 1953
43	Charlie Slack, Marshall vs. Morris Harvey	Jan. 12, 1954
42	Tom Heinsohn, Holy Cross vs. Boston College	Mar. 1, 1955
40	Art Quimby, Connecticut vs. Boston U.	Jan. 11, 1955
39	Maurice Stokes, St. Francis (Pa.) vs. John Carroll	Jan. 28, 1955
39	Dave DeBusschere, Detroit vs. Central Mich.	Jan. 30, 1960
39	Keith Swagerty, Pacific (Cal.) vs. UC Santa Barb.	Mar. 5, 1965
38	Jerry Koch, St. Louis vs. Bradley	Mar. 5, 1954
38	Charlie Tyra, Louisville vs. Canisius	Dec. 10, 1955
38	Steve Hamilton, Morehead St. vs. Florida St.	Jan. 2, 1957
38	Paul Silas, Creighton vs. Centenary (La.)	Feb. 19, 1962
38	Tommy Woods, East Tenn. St. vs. Middle Tenn.	Mar. 1, 1965
36	Herb Neff, Tennessee vs. Georgia Tech	Jan. 26, 1952
36	Dickie Hemric, Wake Forest vs. Clemson	Feb. 4, 1955
36	Swede Halbrook, Oregon St. vs. Idaho	Feb. 15, 1955
36	Wilt Chamberlain, Kansas vs. Iowa St.	Feb. 15, 1958
36	Jim Barnes, UTEP vs. Western N.M.	Jan. 4, 1964
35	Ronnie Shavlik, North Carolina St. vs. Villanova	Jan. 29, 1955
35	Bill Ebben, Detroit vs. Brigham Young	Dec. 28, 1955
35	Larry Abney, Fresno St. vs. Southern Methodist	Feb. 17, 2000
34	Bob Burrow, Kentucky vs. Temple	Dec. 10, 1955
34	Ronnie Shavlik, North Carolina St. vs. South Carolina	Feb. 11, 1955
34	Fred Cohen, Temple vs. Connecticut	Mar. 16, 1956
34	Bailey Howell, Mississippi St. vs. LSU	Feb. 1, 1957
34	David Vaughn, Oral Roberts vs. Brandeis	Jan. 8, 1973

(Since 1973)

Reb.	Player, Team vs. Opponent	Date
35	Larry Abney, Fresno St. vs. Southern Methodist	Feb. 17, 2000
34	David Vaughn, Oral Roberts vs. Brandeis	Jan. 8, 1973
32	Durand Macklin, LSU vs. Tulane	Nov. 26, 1976
32	Jervaughn Scales, Southern U. vs. Grambling	Feb. 7, 1994
31	Jim Bradley, Northern Ill. vs. Wis.-Milwaukee	Feb. 19, 1973
31	Calvin Natt, Northeast La. vs. Ga. Southern	Dec. 29, 1976
30	Marvin Barnes, Providence vs. Assumption	Feb. 3, 1973
30	Brad Robinson, Kent St. vs. Central Mich.	Feb. 9, 1974
30	Monti Davis, Tennessee St. vs. Alabama St.	Feb. 8, 1979
29	Lionel Garrett, Southern U. vs. Bishop	Feb. 16, 1979
29	Donald Newman, Ark.-Little Rock vs. Centenary (La.)	Jan. 24, 1984
29	Hank Gathers, Loyola Marymount vs. U.S. Int'l	Jan. 31, 1989
28	Alvan Adams, Oklahoma vs. Indiana St.	Nov. 27, 1972
28	Cliff Robinson, Southern California vs. Portland St.	Jan. 20, 1978
28	Eric McArthur, UC Santa Barb. vs. New Mexico St.	Jan. 11, 1990
28	Marcus Mann, Mississippi Val. vs. Jackson St.	Mar. 1, 1996
28	David Bluthenthal, Southern California vs. Arizona St.	Jan. 20, 2000
27	Andy Hopson, Oklahoma St. vs. Missouri	Jan. 30, 1973
27	Henry Ray, McNeese St. vs. Texas-Arlington	1974
27	Bill Walton, UCLA vs. Loyola (Ill.)	Jan. 25, 1973
27	Bill Walton, UCLA vs. Maryland	Dec. 1, 1973
27	Rick Kelley, Stanford vs. Kentucky	Dec. 22, 1974
27	Kerry Davis, Cal St. Fullerton vs. Central Mich.	Dec. 15, 1975
27	Hank Gathers, Loyola Marymount vs. U.S. Int'l	Dec. 7, 1989
27	Dikembe Mutombo, Georgetown vs. Connecticut	Mar. 8, 1991
27	Reginald Slater, Wyoming vs. Troy St.	Dec. 14, 1991
27	Ervin Johnson, New Orleans vs. Lamar	Feb. 18, 1993
27	Willie Fisher, Jacksonville vs. Louisiana Tech	Dec. 4, 1993
27	Kareem Carpenter, Eastern Mich. vs. Western Mich.	Feb. 8, 1995

Reb.	Player, Team vs. Opponent	Date
27	Amien Hicks, Morris Brown vs. Clark Atlanta	Jan. 14, 2002
27	Andre Brown, DePaul vs. TCU	Feb. 6, 2002

ASSISTS

Ast.	Player, Team vs. Opponent	Date
22	Tony Fairley, Charleston So. vs. Armstrong Atlantic	Feb. 9, 1987
22	Avery Johnson, Southern U. vs. Texas Southern	Jan. 25, 1988
22	Sherman Douglas, Syracuse vs. Providence	Jan. 28, 1989
21	Mark Wade, UNLV vs. Navy	Dec. 29, 1986
21	Kelvin Scarborough, New Mexico vs. Hawaii	Feb. 13, 1987
21	Anthony Manuel, Bradley vs. UC Irvine	Dec. 19, 1987
21	Avery Johnson, Southern U. vs. Alabama St.	Jan. 16, 1988
20	Grayson Marshall, Clemson vs. Md.-East. Shore	Nov. 25, 1985
20	James Johnson, Middle Tenn. vs. Freed-Hardeman	Jan. 2, 1986
20	Avery Johnson, Southern U. vs. Texas Southern	Mar. 6, 1987
20	Avery Johnson, Southern U. vs. Mississippi Val.	Feb. 8, 1988
20	Howard Evans, Temple vs. Villanova	Feb. 10, 1988
20	Jasper Walker, St. Peter's vs. Holy Cross	Feb. 11, 1989
20	Chris Corchiani, North Carolina St. vs. Maryland	Feb. 27, 1991
20	Drew Henderson, Fairfield vs. Loyola (Md.)	Jan. 25, 1992
20	Dana Harris, UMBC vs. St. Mary's	Dec. 12, 1992
20	Sam Crawford, New Mexico St. vs. Sam Houston St.	Dec. 21, 1992
20	Ray Washington, Nicholls St. vs. McNeese St.	Jan. 28, 1995
20	Mateen Cleaves, Michigan St. vs. Michigan	Mar. 4, 2000
19	Frank Nardi, Wis.-Green Bay vs. Northern Iowa	Feb. 24, 1986
19	Avery Johnson, Southern U. vs. Tex. A&M-Kingsville	Dec. 6, 1986
19	Avery Johnson, Southern U. vs. Jackson St.	Jan. 16, 1987
19	Andre Van Drost, Wagner vs. Long Island	Feb. 25, 1987
19	Todd Lehmann, Drexel vs. Liberty	Feb. 5, 1990
19	Greg Anthony, UNLV vs. Pacific (Cal.)	Dec. 29, 1990
19	Keith Jennings, East Tenn. St. vs. Appalachian St.	Feb. 2, 1991
19	Nelson Haggerty, Baylor vs. Oral Roberts	Feb. 27, 1993

BLOCKED SHOTS

Blk.	Player, Team vs. Opponent	Date
14	David Robinson, Navy vs. UNC Wilmington	Jan. 4, 1986
14	Shawn Bradley, Brigham Young vs. Eastern Ky.	Dec. 7, 1990
14	Roy Rogers, Alabama vs. Georgia	Feb. 10, 1996
14	Loren Woods, Arizona vs. Oregon	Feb. 3, 2000
13	Kevin Roberson, Vermont vs. New Hampshire	Jan. 9, 1992
13	Jim McIlvaine, Marquette vs. Northeastern Ill.	Dec. 9, 1992
13	Keith Closs, Central Conn. St. vs. St. Francis (Pa.)	Dec. 21, 1994
13	D'or Fischer, Northwestern St. vs. Texas St.	Jan. 22, 2001
13	Kyle Davis, Auburn vs. Miami (Fla.)	Mar. 14, 2001
13	Wojciech Myrda, La.-Monroe vs. Texas-San Antonio	Jan. 17, 2002
12	David Robinson, Navy vs. James Madison	Jan. 9, 1986
12	Derrick Lewis, Maryland vs. James Madison	Jan. 28, 1987
12	Rodney Blake, St. Joseph's vs. Cleveland St.	Dec. 2, 1987
12	Walter Palmer, Dartmouth vs. Harvard	Jan. 9, 1988
12	Alan Ogg, UAB vs. Florida A&M	Dec. 16, 1988
12	Dikembe Mutombo, Georgetown vs. St. John's (N.Y.)	Jan. 23, 1989
12	Shaquille O'Neal, LSU vs. Loyola Marymount	Feb. 3, 1990
12	Cedric Lewis, Maryland vs. South Fla.	Jan. 19, 1991
12	Ervin Johnson, New Orleans vs. Texas A&M	Dec. 29, 1992
12	Kurt Thomas, TCU vs. Texas A&M	Feb. 25, 1995
12	Keith Closs, Central Conn. St. vs. Troy St.	Jan. 20, 1996
12	Adonal Foyle, Colgate vs. Fairfield	Nov. 26, 1996
12	Adonal Foyle, Colgate vs. Navy	Feb. 5, 1997
12	Tarvis Williams, Hampton vs. N.C. A&T	Jan. 9, 1999
12	Darrick Davenport, TCU vs. Alas. Fairbanks	Nov. 20, 1999
12	Tarvis Williams, Hampton vs. Delaware St.	Jan. 13, 2001
12	D'or Fischer, Northwestern St. vs. Siena	Nov. 21, 2001

STEALS

Stl.	Player, Team vs. Opponent	Date
13	Mookie Blaylock, Oklahoma vs. Centenary (La.)	Dec. 12, 1987
13	Mookie Blaylock, Oklahoma vs. Loyola Marymount	Dec. 17, 1988
12	Kenny Robertson, Cleveland St. vs. Wagner	Dec. 3, 1988
12	Terry Evans, Oklahoma vs. Florida A&M	Jan. 27, 1993
12	Richard Duncan, Middle Tenn. vs. Eastern Ky.	Feb. 20, 1999
12	Greedy Daniels, TCU vs. Ark.-Pine Bluff	Dec. 30, 2000
12	Jehiel Lewis, Navy vs. Bucknell	Jan. 12, 2002
11	Darron Brittman, Chicago St. vs. McKendree	Jan. 24, 1986
11	Darron Brittman, Chicago St. vs. St. Xavier	Feb. 8, 1986
11	Marty Johnson, Towson vs. Bucknell	Feb. 17, 1988
11	Aldwin Ware, Florida A&M vs. Tuskegee	Feb. 24, 1988
11	Mark Macon, Temple vs. Notre Dame	Jan. 29, 1989
11	Carl Thomas, Eastern Mich. vs. Chicago St.	Feb. 20, 1991
11	Ron Arnold, St. Francis (N.Y.) vs. Mt. St. Mary's	Feb. 4, 1993
11	Tyus Edney, UCLA vs. George Mason	Dec. 22, 1995
11	Philip Huler, Fla. Atlantic vs. Campbell	Jan. 18, 1997
11	Ali Ton, Davidson vs. Tufts	Nov. 29, 1997
11	Chris Thomas, Notre Dame vs. New Hampshire	Nov. 16, 2001

Stl.	Player, Team vs. Opponent	Date
11	Drew Schifino, West Virginia vs. Ark.-Monticello	Dec. 1, 2001
11	John Linehan, Providence vs. Rutgers	Jan. 22, 2002
11	Travis Demanby, Fresno St. vs. Oklahoma St.	Feb. 10, 2002
10	31 tied	

Season Records

POINTS

Player, Team	Season	G	FG	3FG	FT	Pts.
Pete Maravich, LSU	†1970	31	522	—	337	1,381
Elvin Hayes, Houston	†1968	33	519	—	176	1,214
Frank Selvy, Furman	†1954	29	427	—	355	1,209
Pete Maravich, LSU	†1969	26	433	—	282	1,148
Pete Maravich, LSU	1968	26	432	—	274	1,138
Bo Kimble, Loyola Marymount	†1990	32	404	92	231	1,131
Hersey Hawkins, Bradley	†1988	31	377	87	284	1,125
Austin Carr, Notre Dame	1970	29	444	—	218	1,106
Austin Carr, Notre Dame	†1971	29	430	—	241	1,101
Otis Birdsong, Houston	†1977	36	452	—	186	1,090
Dwight Lamar, La.-Lafayette	†1972	29	429	—	196	1,054
Kevin Bradshaw, U.S. Int'l	†1991	28	358	60	278	1,054
Glenn Robinson, Purdue	†1994	34	368	79	215	1,030
Hank Gathers, Loyola Marymount	†1989	31	419	0	177	1,015
Oscar Robertson, Cincinnati	†1960	30	369	—	273	1,011
Freeman Williams, Portland St.	1977	26	417	—	176	1,010
Billy McGill, Utah	†1962	26	394	—	221	1,009
Rich Fuqua, Oral Roberts	1972	28	423	—	160	1,006
Oscar Robertson, Cincinnati	†1958	28	352	—	280	984
Oscar Robertson, Cincinnati	†1959	30	331	—	316	978
Rick Barry, Miami (Fla.)	†1965	26	340	—	293	973
Larry Bird, Indiana St.	†1979	34	376	—	221	973
Dennis Scott, Georgia Tech	1990	35	336	137	161	970
Freeman Williams, Portland St.	†1978	27	410	—	149	969
Chris Jackson, LSU	1989	32	359	84	163	965

SCORING AVERAGE

Player, Team	Season	G	FG	3FG	FT	Pts.	Avg.
Pete Maravich, LSU	†1970	31	522	—	337	1,381	44.5
Pete Maravich, LSU	†1969	26	433	—	282	1,148	44.2
Pete Maravich, LSU	†1968	26	432	—	274	1,138	43.8
Frank Selvy, Furman	†1954	29	427	—	355	1,209	41.7
Johnny Neumann, Mississippi	†1971	23	366	—	191	923	40.1
Freeman Williams, Portland St.	†1977	26	417	—	176	1,010	38.8
Billy McGill, Utah	†1962	26	394	—	221	1,009	38.8
Calvin Murphy, Niagara	1968	24	337	—	242	916	38.2
Austin Carr, Notre Dame	1970	29	444	—	218	1,106	38.1
Austin Carr, Notre Dame	1971	29	430	—	241	1,101	38.0
Kevin Bradshaw, U.S. Int'l	†1991	28	358	60	278	1,054	37.6
Rick Barry, Miami (Fla.)	†1965	26	340	—	293	973	37.4
Elvin Hayes, Houston	1968	33	519	—	176	1,214	36.8
Marshall Rogers, Tex.-Pan American	†1976	25	361	—	197	919	36.8
Howard Komives, Bowling Green	†1964	23	292	—	260	844	36.7
Dwight Lamar, La.-Lafayette	†1972	29	429	—	196	1,054	36.3
Hersey Hawkins, Bradley	†1988	31	377	87	284	1,125	36.3
Darrell Floyd, Furman	†1955	25	344	—	209	897	35.9
Rich Fuqua, Oral Roberts	1972	28	423	—	160	1,006	35.9
Freeman Williams, Portland St.	†1978	27	410	—	149	969	35.9
Rick Mount, Purdue	1970	20	285	—	138	708	35.4
Bo Kimble, Loyola Marymount	†1990	32	404	92	231	1,131	35.3
Oscar Robertson, Cincinnati	†1958	28	352	—	280	984	35.1
Anthony Roberts, Oral Roberts	1977	28	402	—	147	951	34.0
Dan Issel, Kentucky	1970	28	369	—	210	948	33.9
William Averitt, Pepperdine	†1973	25	352	—	144	848	33.9

†national leader

FIELD-GOAL PERCENTAGE
(Based on qualifiers for annual championship)

Player, Team	Season	G	FG	FGA	Pct.
Steve Johnson, Oregon St.	†1981	28	235	315	74.6
Dwayne Davis, Florida	†1989	33	179	248	72.2
Keith Walker, Utica	†1985	27	154	216	71.3
Steve Johnson, Oregon St.	†1980	30	211	297	71.0
Adam Mark, Belmont	†2002	26	150	212	70.8
Oliver Miller, Arkansas	†1991	38	254	361	70.4
Alan Williams, Princeton	†1987	25	163	232	70.3
Mark McNamara, California	†1982	27	231	329	70.2
Warren Kidd, Middle Tenn.	1991	30	173	247	70.0
Pete Freeman, Akron	1991	28	175	250	70.0
Joe Senser, West Chester	†1977	25	130	186	69.9
Lee Campbell, Southwest Mo. St.	†1990	29	192	275	69.8
Stephen Scheffler, Purdue	1990	30	173	248	69.8

Player, Team	Season	G	FG	FGA	Pct.
Brendan Haywood, North Carolina	†2000	36	191	274	69.7
Mike Atkinson, Long Beach St.	†1994	26	141	203	69.5
Lester James, St. Francis (N.Y.)	1991	29	149	215	69.3
Micheal Bradley, Villanova	†2001	31	254	367	69.2
Murray Brown, Florida St.	†1979	29	237	343	69.1
Joe Senser, West Chester	†1978	25	135	197	68.5
Charles Outlaw, Houston	†1992	31	156	228	68.4
Shane Kline-Ruminski, Bowling Green	†1995	26	181	265	68.3
Marcus Kennedy, Eastern Mich.	1991	33	240	352	68.2
Felton Spencer, Louisville	1990	35	188	276	68.1
Tyrone Howard, Eastern Ky.	1987	30	156	230	67.8
Todd MacCulloch, Washington	†1997	28	163	241	67.6
Ron Charles, Michigan St.	1980	27	169	250	67.6

†national leader

THREE-POINT FIELD GOALS MADE

Player, Team	Season	G	3FG
Darrin Fitzgerald, Butler	†1987	28	158
Freddie Banks, UNLV	1987	39	152
Randy Rutherford, Oklahoma St.	†1995	37	146
Terrence Woods, Florida A&M	†2003	28	139
Dennis Scott, Georgia Tech	†1990	35	137
Demon Brown, Charlotte	2003	29	137
Rashad Phillips, Detroit	†2001	35	136
Troy Hudson, Southern Ill.	†1997	30	134
Timothy Pollard, Mississippi Val.	†1988	28	132
Jason Williams, Duke	2001	39	132
Dave Jamerson, Ohio	1990	28	131
Sydney Grider, La.-Lafayette	1990	29	131
Keith Veney, Marshall	1997	29	130
Curtis Staples, Virginia	†1998	30	130
Kyle Korver, Creighton	2003	34	129
Lazelle Durden, Cincinnati	1995	34	127
Jeff Fryer, Loyola Marymount	†1989	31	126
Timothy Pollard, Mississippi Val.	1989	28	124
Shane Battier, Duke	2001	39	124
Bobby Phills, Southern U.	†1991	28	123
Sydney Grider, La.-Lafayette	1989	29	122
Andy Kennedy, UAB	1989	34	122
Mark Alberts, Akron	1990	28	122
Chris Brown UC Irvine	†1994	26	122
Darren McLinton, James Madison	†1996	30	122
William Fourche, Southern U.	1997	27	122

THREE-POINT FIELD GOALS MADE PER GAME
(Based on qualifiers for annual championship)

Player, Team	Season	G	3FG	Avg.
Darrin Fitzgerald, Butler	†1987	28	158	5.64
Terrence Woods, Florida A&M	†2003	28	139	4.96
Demon Brown, Charlotte	2003	29	137	4.72
Timothy Pollard, Mississippi Val.	†1988	28	132	4.71
Chris Brown, UC Irvine	†1994	26	122	4.69
Dave Jamerson, Ohio	†1990	28	131	4.68
William Fourche, Southern U.	†1997	27	122	4.52
Sydney Grider, La.-Lafayette	1990	29	131	4.52
Keith Veney, Marshall	1997	29	130	4.48
Troy Hudson, Southern Ill.	1997	30	134	4.47
Timothy Pollard, Mississippi Val.	†1989	28	124	4.43
Keke Hicks, Coastal Caro.	1994	26	115	4.42
Bobby Phills, Southern U.	†1991	28	123	4.39
Mitch Taylor, Southern U.	†1995	25	109	4.36
Mark Alberts, Akron	1990	28	122	4.36
Curtis Staples, Virginia	†1998	30	130	4.33
Jeff Fryer, Loyola Marymount	1990	28	121	4.32
Shawn Respert, Michigan St.	1995	28	119	4.25
Sydney Grider, La.-Lafayette	1989	29	122	4.21
Bernard Haslett, Southern Miss.	†1993	26	109	4.19
Stevin Smith, Arizona St.	1993	27	113	4.19
Tim Roberts, Southern U.	1995	26	108	4.15
Dominick Young, Fresno St.	†1996	29	120	4.14
Mark Alberts, Akron	1993	26	107	4.12
Lazelle Durden, Cincinnati	1994	25	102	4.08

†national leader

THREE-POINT FIELD-GOAL PERCENTAGE
(Based on qualifiers for annual championship)

Player, Team	Season	G	3FG	3FGA	Pct.
Glenn Tropf, Holy Cross	†1988	29	52	82	63.4
Sean Wightman, Western Mich.	†1992	30	48	76	63.2
Keith Jennings, East Tenn. St.	†1991	33	84	142	59.2
Dave Calloway, Monmouth	†1989	28	48	82	58.5
Steve Kerr, Arizona	1988	38	114	199	57.3

Player, Team	Season	G	3FG	3FGA	Pct.
Reginald Jones, Prairie View	†1987	28	64	112	57.1
Jim Cantamessa, Siena	†1998	29	66	117	56.4
Joel Tribelhorn, Colorado St.	1989	33	76	135	56.3
Mike Joseph, Bucknell	1988	28	65	116	56.0
Brian Jackson, Evansville	†1995	27	53	95	55.8
Amory Sanders, Southeast Mo. St.	†2001	24	53	95	55.8
Christian Laettner, Duke	1992	35	54	97	55.7
Reginald Jones, Prairie View	1988	27	85	155	54.8
Eric Rhodes, Stephen F. Austin	1987	30	58	106	54.7
Dave Orlandini, Princeton	1988	26	60	110	54.5
David Falknor, Akron	2001	22	47	87	54.0
Mike Joseph, Bucknell	1989	31	62	115	53.9
John Bays, Towson	1989	29	71	132	53.8
Jeff Anderson, Kent St.	†1993	26	44	82	53.7
Jay Edwards, Indiana	1988	23	59	110	53.6
Anthony Davis, George Mason	1987	27	45	84	53.6
Mark Anglavar, Marquette	1989	28	53	99	53.5
Scot Dimak, Stephen F. Austin	1987	30	46	86	53.5
Matt Lapin, Princeton	†1990	27	71	133	53.4
Michael Charles, UAB	1988	28	63	118	53.4

†national leader

FREE-THROW PERCENTAGE
(Based on qualifiers for annual championship)

Player, Team	Season	G	FT	FTA	Pct.
Craig Collins, Penn St.	†1985	27	94	98	95.9
Steve Drabyn, Belmont	†2003	29	78	82	95.1
Rod Foster, UCLA	1982	27	95	100	95.0
Clay McKnight, Pacific (Cal.)	†2000	24	74	78	94.9
Matt Logie, Lehigh	2003	28	91	96	94.8
Carlos Gibson, Marshall	†1978	28	84	89	94.4
Danny Basile, Marist	†1994	27	84	89	94.4
Jim Barton, Dartmouth	1986	26	65	69	94.2
Gary Buchanon, Villanova	†2001	31	97	103	94.2
Jack Moore, Nebraska	1982	27	123	131	93.9
Rob Robbins, New Mexico	†1990	34	101	108	93.5
Dandrea Evans, Troy St.	1994	27	72	77	93.5
Tommy Boyer, Arkansas	†1962	23	125	134	93.3
Damon Goodwin, Dayton	1986	30	95	102	93.1
Brent Jolly, Tennesee Tech	2001	29	95	102	93.1
Ryan Mendez, Stanford	2001	34	94	101	93.1
Brian Magid, George Washington	†1980	26	79	85	92.9
Mike Joseph, Bucknell	1990	29	144	155	92.9
Hollis Price, Oklahoma	2003	34	130	140	92.9
Steve Kaplan, Rutgers	†1970	23	102	110	92.7
Dave Hildahl, Portland St.	1981	21	76	82	92.7
Mike Dillard, Sam Houston St.	†1996	25	63	68	92.6
Casey Schmidt, Valparaiso	1994	25	75	81	92.6
Greg Starrick, Southern Ill.	†1972	26	148	160	92.5
Steve Henson, Kansas St.	†1988	34	111	120	92.5
Randy Nesbit, Citadel	1980	27	74	80	92.5
Robert Smith, UNLV	†1977	32	98	106	92.5
Matthew Hildebrand, Liberty	1994	30	149	161	92.5
Michael Smith, Brigham Young	†1989	29	160	173	92.5

†national leader

REBOUNDS

Player, Team	Ht.	Season	G	Reb.
Walt Dukes, Seton Hall	6-10	†1953	33	734
Leroy Wright, Pacific (Cal.)	6-8	†1959	26	652
Tom Gola, La Salle	6-6	†1954	30	652
Charlie Tyra, Louisville	6-8	†1956	29	645
Paul Silas, Creighton	6-7	†1964	29	631
Elvin Hayes, Houston	6-8	†1968	33	624
Artis Gilmore, Jacksonville	7-2	†1970	28	621
Tom Gola, La Salle	6-6	†1955	31	618
Ed Conlin, Fordham	6-5	1953	26	612
Art Quimby, Connecticut	6-5	1955	25	611
Bill Russell, San Francisco	6-9	1956	29	609
Jim Ware, Oklahoma City	6-8	†1966	29	607
Joe Holup, George Washington	6-6	1956	26	604
Artis Gilmore, Jacksonville	7-2	†1971	26	603
Elton Tuttle, Creighton	6-5	1954	30	601
Marvin Barnes, Providence	6-9	†1974	32	597
Bill Russell, San Francisco	6-9	1955	29	594
Art Quimby, Connecticut	6-5	1954	26	588
Ed Conlin, Fordham	6-5	1955	27	578
Marvin Barnes, Providence	6-9	†1973	30	571
Bill Spivey, Kentucky	7-0	†1951	33	567
Bob Pelkington, Xavier	6-7	1964	26	567
Paul Silas, Creighton	6-7	†1962	25	563
Elgin Baylor, Seattle	6-6	†1959	29	559
Paul Silas, Creighton	6-7	†1963	27	557

†national leader

Connecticut's Emeka Okafor led the nation in blocked shots last season.

Photo by Connecticut Sports Information

Player, Team	Ht.	Season	G	Reb.	Avg.
Spencer Haywood, Detroit	6-8	†1969	22	472	21.5
Ed Conlin, Fordham	6-5	1955	27	578	21.4
Tom Heinsohn, Holy Cross	6-7	1956	26	549	21.1
Bill Russell, San Francisco	6-9	1956	29	609	21.0
Toby Kimball, Connecticut	6-8	†1965	23	483	21.0

†national leader; ††From 1956 through 1962, individual champions were determined by percentage of all recoveries; Holup led in percentage of recoveries and Slack led in average In 1956.

(Since 1973)

Player, Team	Ht.	Season	G	Reb.	Avg.
Kermit Washington, American	6-8	†1973	25	511	20.4
Marvin Barnes, Providence	6-9	1973	30	571	19.0
Marvin Barnes, Providence	6-9	†1974	32	597	18.7
Pete Padgett, Nevada	6-8	1973	26	462	17.8
Jim Bradley, Northern Ill.	6-10	1973	24	426	17.8
Bill Walton, UCLA	6-11	1973	30	506	16.9
Larry Kenon, Memphis	6-9	1973	30	501	16.7
Glenn Mosley, Seton Hall	6-8	†1977	29	473	16.3
John Irving, Hofstra	6-9	1977	27	440	16.3
Carlos McCullough, Tex.-Pan American	6-7	1974	22	358	16.3
Brad Robinson, Kent St.	6-7	1974	26	423	16.3
Monti Davis, Tennessee St.	6-7	†1979	26	421	16.2
Sam Pellom, Buffalo	6-8	†1976	26	420	16.2
Robert Elmore, Wichita St.	6-10	1977	28	441	15.8
Bill Cartwright, San Francisco	7-1	1979	29	455	15.7
Bill Champion, Manhattan	6-10	1973	26	402	15.5
Bill Champion, Manhattan	6-10	1974	27	419	15.5
Lionel Garrett, Southern U.	6-9	1979	28	433	15.5
Dwayne Barnett, Samford	6-6	1976	23	354	15.4
John Irving, Hofstra	6-9	†1975	21	323	15.4
Cornelius Cash, Bowling Green	6-8	1973	26	396	15.2
Pete Padgett, Nevada	6-8	1974	26	395	15.2
Jimmie Baker, UNLV	6-9	1973	28	424	15.1
Larry Smith, Alcorn St.	6-8	†1980	26	392	15.1
Charles McKinney, Baylor	6-6	1974	25	375	15.0
Lewis Lloyd, Drake	6-6	1980	27	406	15.0

†national leader

ASSISTS

Player, Team	Season	G	Ast.
Mark Wade, UNLV	†1987	38	406
Avery Johnson, Southern U.	†1988	30	399
Anthony Manuel, Bradley	1988	31	373
Avery Johnson, Southern U.	1987	31	333
Mark Jackson, St. John's (N.Y.)	†1986	32	328
Sherman Douglas, Syracuse	†1989	38	326
Greg Anthony, UNLV	†1991	35	310
Sam Crawford, New Mexico St.	†1993	34	310
Reid Gettys, Houston	†1984	37	309
Carl Golston, Loyola (Ill.)	†1985	33	305
Craig Neal, Georgia Tech	1988	32	303
Keith Jennings, East Tenn. St.	1991	33	301
Doug Gottlieb, Oklahoma St.	†1999	34	299
Chris Corchiani, North Carolina St.	1991	31	299
Keith Jennings, East Tenn. St.	†1990	34	297
Howard Evans, Temple	1988	34	294
Ahlon Lewis, Arizona St.	†1998	32	294
Doug Gottlieb, Oklahoma St.	†2000	34	293
Danny Tarkanian, UNLV	1984	34	289
Sherman Douglas, Syracuse	1987	38	289
Bobby Hurley, Duke	1991	39	289
Greg Anthony, UNLV	1990	39	289
Sherman Douglas, Syracuse	1988	35	288
Bobby Hurley, Duke	1990	38	288
Marcus Carr, Cal St. Northridge	†2001	32	286
Steve Blake, Maryland	†2002	36	286

†national leader

ASSIST AVERAGE

Player, Team	Season	G	Ast.	Avg.
Avery Johnson, Southern U.	†1988	30	399	13.30
Anthony Manuel, Bradley	1988	31	373	12.03
Avery Johnson, Southern U.	†1987	31	333	10.74
Mark Wade, UNLV	1987	38	406	10.68
Nelson Haggerty, Baylor	†1995	28	284	10.14
Glenn Williams, Holy Cross	†1989	28	278	9.92
Chris Corchiani, North Carolina St.	†1991	31	299	9.65
Tony Fairley, Charleston So.	1987	28	270	9.64
Tyrone Bogues, Wake Forest	1987	29	276	9.52
Ron Weingard, Hofstra	†1985	24	228	9.50
Craig Neal, Georgia Tech	1988	32	303	9.47
Craig Lathan, Ill.-Chicago	†1984	29	274	9.45

(Since 1973)

Player, Team	Ht.	Season	G	Reb.
Marvin Barnes, Providence	6-9	†1974	32	597
Marvin Barnes, Providence	6-9	†1973	30	571
Kermit Washington, American	6-8	1973	25	511
Bill Walton, UCLA	6-11	1973	30	506
Larry Bird, Indiana St.	6-9	†1979	34	505
Larry Kenon, Memphis	6-9	†1973	30	501
Akeem Olajuwon, Houston	7-0	†1984	37	500
Glenn Mosley, Seton Hall	6-8	†1977	29	473
Popeye Jones, Murray St.	6-8	†1991	33	469
Pete Padgett, Nevada	6-8	†1973	26	462
Xavier McDaniel, Wichita St.	6-8	†1985	31	460
Larry Johnson, UNLV	6-7	†1990	40	457
Tim Duncan, Wake Forest	6-11	†1997	31	457
Anthony Bonner, St. Louis	6-8	1990	33	456
Bill Cartwright, San Francisco	7-1	1979	29	455
David Robinson, Navy	6-11	†1986	35	455
Benoit Benjamin, Creighton	7-0	1985	32	451
Jerome Lane, Pittsburgh	6-6	†1987	33	444
Robert Elmore, Wichita St.	6-10	1977	28	441
John Irving, Hofstra	6-9	1977	27	440
Lionel Garrett, Southern U.	6-9	1979	28	433
Popeye Jones, Murray St.	6-8	†1992	30	431
Jim Bradley, Northern Ill.	6-10	1973	24	426
Hank Gathers, Loyola Marymount	6-7	†1989	31	426
Jimmie Baker, UNLV	6-9	1973	28	424

†national leader

REBOUND AVERAGE

Player, Team	Ht.	Season	G	Reb.	Avg.
Charlie Slack, Marshall	6-5	†1955	21	538	25.6
Leroy Wright, Pacific (Cal.)	6-8	†1959	26	652	25.1
Art Quimby, Connecticut	6-5	1955	25	611	24.4
Charlie Slack, Marshall	6-5	1956	22	520	23.6
Ed Conlin, Fordham	6-5	†1953	26	612	23.5
Joe Holup, George Washington	6-6	††1956	26	604	23.2
Artis Gilmore, Jacksonville	7-2	†1971	26	603	23.2
Art Quimby, Connecticut	6-5	†1954	26	588	22.6
Paul Silas, Creighton	6-7	1962	25	563	22.5
Leroy Wright, Pacific (Cal.)	6-8	†1960	17	380	22.4
Walt Dukes, Seton Hall	6-10	1953	33	734	22.2
Charlie Tyra, Louisville	6-8	1956	29	645	22.2
Charlie Slack, Marshall	6-5	1954	21	466	22.2
Artis Gilmore, Jacksonville	7-2	†1970	28	621	22.2
Bill Chambers, William & Mary	6-4	1953	22	480	21.8
Bob Pelkington, Xavier	6-7	†1964	26	567	21.8
Dick Cunningham, Murray St.	6-10	†1967	22	479	21.8
Paul Silas, Creighton	6-7	1964	29	631	21.8
Tom Gola, La Salle	6-6	1954	30	652	21.7
Jerry Harper, Alabama	6-8	1956	24	517	21.5

Player, Team	Season	G	Ast.	Avg.
Curtis McCants, George Mason	1995	27	251	9.30
Andre Van Drost, Wagner	1987	28	260	9.29
Todd Lehmann, Drexel	†1990	28	260	9.29
Danny Tirado, Jacksonville	1991	28	259	9.25
Carl Golston, Loyola (Ill.)	1985	33	305	9.24
Ahlon Lewis, Arizona St.	†1998	32	294	9.19
Terrell Lowery, Loyola Marymount	1991	31	283	9.13
Keith Jennings, East Tenn. St.	1991	33	301	9.12
Sam Crawford, New Mexico St.	†1993	34	310	9.12
Mark Jackson, St. John's (N.Y.)	†1986	36	328	9.11
Aaron Mitchell, La.-Lafayette	1990	29	264	9.10
Jason Kidd, California	†1994	30	272	9.07
Mark Dickel, UNLV	†2000	31	280	9.03

†national leader

BLOCKED SHOTS

Player, Team	Season	G	Blk.
David Robinson, Navy	†1986	35	207
Adonal Foyle, Colgate	†1997	28	180
Keith Closs, Central Conn. St.	†1996	28	178
Shawn Bradley, Brigham Young	†1991	34	177
Wojciech Myrda, La.-Monroe	†2002	32	172
Alonzo Mourning, Georgetown	†1989	34	169
Adonal Foyle, Colgate	1996	29	165
Ken Johnson, Ohio St.	†2000	30	161
Alonzo Mourning, Georgetown	†1992	32	160
Shaquille O'Neal, LSU	1992	30	157
Roy Rogers, Alabama	1996	32	156
Emeka Okafor, Connecticut	†2003	33	156
Dikembe Mutombo, Georgetown	1991	32	151
Adonal Foyle, Colgate	†1995	30	147
Tarvis Williams, Hampton	†2001	32	147
Theo Ratliff, Wyoming	1995	28	144
David Robinson, Navy	†1987	32	144
Wojciech Myrda, La.-Monroe	2000	28	144
Cedric Lewis, Maryland	1991	28	143
Jim McIlvaine, Marquette	†1994	33	142
Alvin Jones, Georgia Tech	†1998	33	141
Shaquille O'Neal, LSU	1991	28	140
Calvin Booth, Penn St.	1998	32	140
Keith Closs, Central Conn. St.	1995	26	139
Kevin Roberson, Vermont	1992	28	139

†national leader

BLOCKED-SHOT AVERAGE

Player, Team	Season	G	Blk.	Avg.
Adonal Foyle, Colgate	†1997	28	180	6.43
Keith Closs, Central Conn. St.	†1996	28	178	6.36
David Robinson, Navy	†1986	35	207	5.91
Adonal Foyle, Colgate	1996	29	165	5.69
Wojciech Myrda, La.-Monroe	†2002	32	172	5.38
Ken Johnson, Ohio St.	†2000	30	161	5.37
Keith Closs, Central Conn. St.	†1995	26	139	5.35
Shaquille O'Neal, LSU	†1992	30	157	5.23
Shawn Bradley, Brigham Young	†1991	34	177	5.21
Theo Ratliff, Wyoming	1995	28	144	5.14
Wojciech Myrda, La.-Monroe	2000	28	144	5.14
Cedric Lewis, Maryland	1991	28	143	5.11
Shaquille O'Neal, LSU	1991	28	140	5.00
Alonzo Mourning, Georgetown	1992	32	160	5.00
Tarvis Williams, Hampton	†1999	27	135	5.00
Alonzo Mourning, Georgetown	†1989	34	169	4.97
Kevin Roberson, Vermont	1992	28	139	4.96
Adonal Foyle, Colgate	1995	30	147	4.90
Roy Rogers, Alabama	1996	32	156	4.88
Lorenzo Coleman, Tennessee Tech	1997	28	134	4.79
Kenny Green, Rhode Island	†1990	26	124	4.77
Emeka Okafor, Connecticut	†2003	33	156	4.73
Dikembe Mutombo, Georgetown	1991	32	151	4.72
Jerome James, Florida A&M	†1998	27	125	4.63
Tarvis Williams, Hampton	†2001	32	147	4.59
Pascal Fleury, UMBC	1995	27	124	4.59

†national leader

STEALS

Player, Team	Season	G	Stl.
Desmond Cambridge, Alabama A&M	†2002	29	160
Mookie Blaylock, Oklahoma	†1988	39	150
Aldwin Ware, Florida A&M	1988	29	142
Darron Brittman, Chicago St.	†1986	28	139
John Linehan, Providence	2002	31	139
Nadav Henefeld, Connecticut	†1990	37	138
Mookie Blaylock, Oklahoma	†1989	35	131

Player, Team	Season	G	Stl.
Ronn McMahon, Eastern Wash.	1990	29	130
Marty Johnson, Towson	1988	30	124
Allen Iverson, Georgetown	†1996	37	124
Eric Coley, Tulsa	†2000	37	123
Jim Paguaga, St. Francis (N.Y.)	1986	28	120
Shawn Griggs, La.-Lafayette	†1994	30	120
Pointer Williams, McNeese St.	1996	27	118
Tony Fairley, Charleston So.	†1987	28	114
Scott Burrell, Connecticut	†1991	31	112
Kenny Robertson, Cleveland St.	1989	28	111
Lance Blanks, Texas	1989	34	111
Eric Murdock, Providence	1991	32	111
Jason Kidd, California	†1993	29	110
Johnny Rhodes, Maryland	1996	30	110
Robert Dowdell, Coastal Caro.	1990	29	109
Keith Jennings, East Tenn. St.	1991	33	109
Mark Woods, Wright St.	1993	30	109
Gerald Walker, San Francisco	1994	28	109

†national leader

STEAL AVERAGE

Player, Team	Season	G	Stl.	Avg.
Desmond Cambridge, Alabama A&M	†2002	29	160	5.52
Darron Brittman, Chicago St.	†1986	28	139	4.96
Aldwin Ware, Florida A&M	†1988	29	142	4.90
John Linehan, Providence	2002	31	139	4.48
Ronn McMahon, Eastern Wash.	†1990	29	130	4.48
Pointer Williams, McNeese St.	1996	27	118	4.37
Greedy Daniels, TCU	†2001	25	108	4.32
Jim Paguaga, St. Francis (N.Y.)	1986	28	120	4.29
Marty Johnson, Towson	1988	30	124	4.13
Tony Fairley, Charleston So.	†1987	28	114	4.07
Shawn Griggs, La.-Lafayette	†1994	30	120	4.00
Kenny Robertson, Cleveland St.	†1989	28	111	3.96
Alexis McMillan, Stetson	†2003	22	87	3.95
Gerald Walker, San Francisco	1994	28	109	3.89
Mookie Blaylock, Oklahoma	1988	39	150	3.85
Carl Williams, Liberty	†2000	28	107	3.82
Desmond Cambridge, Alabama A&M	2001	28	107	3.82
Jason Kidd, California	†1993	29	110	3.79
Jay Goodman, Utah St.	1993	27	102	3.78
Andre Cradle, Long Island	1994	21	79	3.76
Robert Dowdell, Coastal Caro.	1990	29	109	3.76
Mookie Blaylock, Oklahoma	1989	35	131	3.74
Johnny Rhodes, Maryland	1996	30	110	3.67
Roderick Taylor, Jackson St.	1996	29	106	3.66
Mark Woods, Wright St.	1993	30	109	3.63

†national leader

Top Season Performances by Class

SCORING AVERAGE

Class	Player, Team	Season	G	FG	3FG	FT	Pts.	Avg.
Senior	Pete Maravich, LSU	1970	31	522	—	337	1,381	44.5
Junior	Pete Maravich, LSU	1969	26	433	—	282	1,148	44.2
Sophomore	Pete Maravich, LSU	1968	26	432	—	274	1,138	43.8
Freshman	Chris Jackson, LSU	1989	32	359	84	163	965	30.2

FIELD-GOAL PERCENTAGE

Class	Player, Team	Season	G	FG	FGA	Pct.
Senior	Steve Johnson, Oregon St.	1981	28	235	315	74.6
Junior	Steve Johnson, Oregon St.	1980	30	211	297	71.0
Sophomore	Dwayne Davis, Florida	1989	33	179	248	72.2
Freshman	Sidney Moncrief, Arkansas	1976	28	149	224	66.5

THREE-POINT FIELD GOALS MADE PER GAME

Class	Player, Team	Season	G	3FG	Avg.
Senior	Darrin Fitzgerald, Butler	1987	28	158	5.64
Junior	Terrence Woods, Florida A&M	2003	28	139	4.96
Sophomore	Mark Alberts, Akron	1990	28	122	4.36
Freshman	Keith Veney, Lamar	1993	27	106	3.93

THREE-POINT FIELD-GOAL PERCENTAGE

Class	Player, Team	Season	G	3FG	3FGA	Pct.
Senior	Keith Jennings, East Tenn. St.	1991	33	84	142	59.2
Junior	Glenn Tropf, Holy Cross	1988	29	52	82	63.4
Sophomore	Dave Calloway, Monmouth	1989	28	48	82	58.5
Freshman	Jay Edwards, Indiana	1988	23	59	110	53.6

FREE-THROW PERCENTAGE

Class	Player, Team	Season	G	FT	FTA	Pct.
Senior	Craig Collins, Penn St.	1985	27	94	98	95.9
Junior	Steve Drabyn, Belmont	2003	29	78	82	95.1
Sophomore	Danny Basile, Marist	1994	27	84	89	94.4
Freshman	Jim Barton, Dartmouth	1986	26	65	69	94.2

REBOUND AVERAGE

Class	Player, Team	Season	G	Reb.	Avg.
Senior	Art Quimby, Connecticut	1955	25	611	24.4
Junior	Charlie Slack, Marshall	1955	21	538	25.6
Sophomore	Ed Conlin, Fordham	1953	26	612	23.5
Freshman	Pete Padgett, Nevada	1973	26	462	17.8

ASSIST AVERAGE

Class	Player, Team	Season	G	Ast.	Avg.
Senior	Avery Johnson, Southern U.	1988	30	399	13.30
Junior	Anthony Manuel, Bradley	1988	31	373	12.03
Sophomore	Curtis McCants, George Mason	1995	27	251	9.30
Freshman	Omar Cook, St. John's (N.Y.)	2001	29	252	8.69

BLOCKED-SHOT AVERAGE

Class	Player, Team	Season	G	Blk.	Avg.
Senior	Wojciech Mydra, La.-Monroe	2002	32	172	5.38
Junior	Adonal Foyle, Colgate	1997	28	180	6.43
Sophomore	Keith Closs, Central Conn. St.	1996	28	178	6.36
Freshman	Keith Closs, Central Conn. St.	1995	26	139	5.35

STEAL AVERAGE

Class	Player, Team	Season	G	Stl.	Avg.
Senior	Desmond Cambridge, Alabama A&M	2002	29	160	5.52
Junior	Kenny Robertson, Cleveland St.	1989	28	111	3.96
Sophomore	Gerald Walker, San Francisco	1994	28	109	3.89
Freshman	Jason Kidd, California	1993	29	110	3.79

Top Season Performances by a Freshman

POINTS

Player, Team	Season	G	FG	3FG	FT	Pts.
Chris Jackson, LSU	1989	32	359	84	163	965
James Williams, Austin Peay	1973	29	360	—	134	854
Jason Conley, VMI	2002	28	285	79	171	820
Wayman Tisdale, Oklahoma	1983	33	338	—	134	810
Alphonso Ford, Mississippi Val.	1990	27	289	104	126	808

SCORING AVERAGE

Player, Team	Season	G	FG	3FG	FT	Pts.	Avg.
Chris Jackson, LSU	1989	32	359	84	163	965	30.2
Alphonso Ford, Mississippi Val.	1990	27	289	104	126	808	29.9
James Williams, Austin Peay	1973	29	360	—	134	854	29.4
Jason Conley, VMI	2002	28	285	79	171	820	29.3
Harry Kelly, Texas Southern	1980	26	313	—	127	753	29.0

FIELD-GOAL PERCENTAGE

Player, Team	Season	G	FG	FGA	Pct.
Sidney Moncrief, Arkansas	1976	28	149	224	66.5
Gary Trent, Ohio	1993	27	194	298	65.1
Ed Pinckney, Villanova	1982	32	169	264	64.0
David Harrison, Colorado	2002	27	139	218	63.8
Jimmy Lunsford, Alabama St.	1993	22	142	223	63.7

THREE-POINT FIELD GOALS MADE

Player, Team	Season	G	3FG
Keydren Clark, St. Peter's	2003	29	109
Keith Veney, Lamar	1993	27	106
Alphonso Ford, Mississippi Val.	1990	27	104
Tony Ross, San Diego St.	1987	28	104
Ronnie McCollum, Centenary (La.)	1998	30	101

THREE-POINT FIELD GOALS MADE PER GAME

Player, Team	Season	G	3FG	Avg.
Keith Veney, Lamar	1993	27	106	3.93
Alphonso Ford, Mississippi Val.	1990	27	104	3.85
Keydren Clark, St. Peter's	2003	29	109	3.76
Tony Ross, San Diego St.	1987	28	104	3.71
Donnie Carr, La Salle	1997	27	99	3.67

THREE-POINT FIELD-GOAL PERCENTAGE

Player, Team	Season	G	3FG	3FGA	Pct.
Jay Edwards, Indiana	1988	23	59	110	53.6
Ross Richardson, Loyola Marymount	1991	25	61	116	52.6

Player, Team	Season	G	3FG	3FGA	Pct.
Lance Barker, Valparaiso	1992	26	61	117	52.1
Ed Peterson, Yale	1989	28	53	104	51.0
Ross Land, Northern Ariz.	1997	28	64	126	50.8
Willie Brand, Texas-Arlington	1988	29	65	128	50.8

FREE-THROW PERCENTAGE

Player, Team	Season	G	FT	FTA	Pct.
Jim Barton, Dartmouth	1986	26	65	69	94.2
J.J. Redick, Duke	2003	33	102	111	91.9
Steve Alford, Indiana	1984	31	137	150	91.3
Gerry McNamara, Syracuse	2003	35	90	99	90.9
Jay Edwards, Indiana	1988	23	69	76	90.8

REBOUNDS

Player, Team	Season	G	Reb.
Pete Padgett, Nevada	1973	26	462
Kenny Miller, Loyola (Ill.)	1988	29	395
Shaquille O'Neal, LSU	1990	32	385
Ralph Sampson, Virginia	1980	34	381
Adonal Foyle, Colgate	1995	30	371

REBOUND AVERAGE

Player, Team	Season	G	Reb.	Avg.
Pete Padgett, Nevada	1973	26	462	17.8
Glenn Mosley, Seton Hall	1974	21	299	14.2
Ira Terrell, Southern Methodist	1973	25	352	14.1
Kenny Miller, Loyola (Ill.)	1988	29	395	13.6
Bob Stephens, Drexel	1976	23	307	13.3

ASSISTS

Player, Team	Season	G	Ast.
Bobby Hurley, Duke	1990	38	288
Kenny Anderson, Georgia Tech	1990	35	285
T.J. Ford, Texas	2002	33	273
Andre LaFleur, Northeastern	1984	32	252
Omar Cook, St. John's (N.Y.)	2001	29	252
Chris Thomas, Notre Dame	2002	33	252

ASSIST AVERAGE

Player, Team	Season	G	Ast.	Avg.
Omar Cook, St. John's (N.Y.)	2001	29	252	8.69
T.J. Ford, Texas	2002	33	273	8.27
Orlando Smart, San Francisco	1991	29	237	8.17
Kenny Anderson, Georgia Tech	1990	35	285	8.14
Taurence Chisholm, Delaware	1985	28	224	8.00

BLOCKED SHOTS

Player, Team	Season	G	Blk.
Shawn Bradley, Brigham Young	1991	34	177
Alonzo Mourning, Georgetown	1989	34	169
Adonal Foyle, Colgate	1995	30	147
Alvin Jones, Georgia Tech	1998	33	141
Keith Closs, Central Conn. St.	1995	26	139

BLOCKED-SHOT AVERAGE

Player, Team	Season	G	Blk.	Avg.
Keith Closs, Central Conn. St.	1995	26	139	5.35
Shawn Bradley, Brigham Young	1991	34	177	5.21
Alonzo Mourning, Georgetown	1989	34	169	4.97
Adonal Foyle, Colgate	1995	30	147	4.90
Richard Lugo, St. Francis (N.Y.)	1997	28	125	4.46

STEALS

Player, Team	Season	G	Stl.
Nadav Henefeld, Connecticut	1990	37	138
Jason Kidd, California	1993	29	110
Kellii Taylor, Pittsburgh	1997	32	101
Ben Larson, Cal Poly	1996	29	100
Five tied with 90			

STEAL AVERAGE

Player, Team	Season	G	Stl.	Avg.
Jason Kidd, California	1993	29	110	3.79
Nadav Henefeld, Connecticut	1990	37	138	3.73
Ben Larson, Cal Poly	1996	29	100	3.45
Eric Murdock, Providence	1988	28	90	3.21
Pat Baldwin, Northwestern	1991	28	90	3.21
Joel Hoover, Md.-East. Shore	1997	28	90	3.21

Career Records

POINTS

Player, Team	Ht.	Last Season	Yrs.	G	FG	3FG#	FT	Pts.
Pete Maravich, LSU	6-5	1970	3	83	1,387	—	893	3,667
Freeman Williams, Portland St.	6-4	1978	4	106	1,369	—	511	3,249
Lionel Simmons, La Salle	6-7	1990	4	131	1,244	56	673	3,217
Alphonso Ford, Mississippi Val.	6-2	1993	4	109	1,121	333	590	3,165
Harry Kelly, Texas Southern	6-7	1983	4	110	1,234	—	598	3,066
Hersey Hawkins, Bradley	6-3	1988	4	125	1,100	118	690	3,008
Oscar Robertson, Cincinnati	6-5	1960	3	88	1,052	—	869	2,973
Danny Manning, Kansas	6-10	1988	4	147	1,216	10	509	2,951
Alfredrick Hughes, Loyola (Ill.)	6-5	1985	4	120	1,226	—	462	2,914
Elvin Hayes, Houston	6-8	1968	3	93	1,215	—	454	2,884
Larry Bird, Indiana St.	6-9	1979	3	94	1,154	—	542	2,850
Otis Birdsong, Houston	6-4	1977	4	116	1,176	—	480	2,832
Kevin Bradshaw, Bethune-Cookman & U.S. Int'l	6-6	1991	4	111	1,027	132	618	2,804
Allan Houston, Tennessee	6-5	1993	4	128	902	346	651	2,801
Hank Gathers, Southern California & Loyola Marymount	6-7	1990	4	117	1,127	0	469	2,723
Reggie Lewis, Northeastern	6-7	1987	4	122	1,043	30(1)	592	2,708
Daren Queenan, Lehigh	6-5	1988	4	118	1,024	29	626	2,703
Byron Larkin, Xavier	6-3	1988	4	121	1,022	51	601	2,696
David Robinson, Navy	7-1	1987	4	127	1,032	1	604	2,669
Wayman Tisdale, Oklahoma	6-9	1985	3	104	1,077	—	507	2,661
Troy Bell, Boston College	6-1	2003	4	122	761	300	810	2,632
Michael Brooks, La Salle	6-7	1980	4	114	1,064	—	500	2,628
Calbert Cheaney, Indiana	6-6	1993	4	132	1,018	148	429	2,613
Mark Macon, Temple	6-5	1991	4	126	980	246	403	2,609
Don MacLean, UCLA	6-10	1992	4	127	943	11	711	2,608
Joe Dumars, McNeese St.	6-3	1985	4	116	941	(5)	723	2,605
Henry Domercant, Eastern Ill.	6-4	2003	4	120	861	285	595	2,602
Terrance Bailey, Wagner	6-2	1987	4	110	985	42	579	2,591
Dickie Hemric, Wake Forest	6-6	1955	4	104	841	—	905	2,587
Calvin Natt, La.-Monroe	6-5	1979	4	108	1,017	—	547	2,581
Derrick Chievous, Missouri	6-7	1988	4	130	893	30	764	2,580
Skip Henderson, Marshall	6-2	1988	4	125	1,000	133	441	2,574
Austin Carr, Notre Dame	6-3	1971	3	74	1,017	—	526	2,560
Sean Elliott, Arizona	6-8	1989	4	133	896	140	623	2,555
Rodney Monroe, North Caro. St.	6-3	1991	4	124	885	322	459	2,551
Calvin Murphy, Niagara	5-10	1970	3	77	947	—	654	2,548
Keith Van Horn, Utah	6-9	1997	4	122	891	206	554	2,542
Frank Selvy, Furman	6-3	1954	3	78	922	—	694	2,538
Johnny Dawkins, Duke	6-2	1986	4	133	1,026	(19)	485	2,537
Willie Jackson, Centenary (La.)	6-6	1984	4	114	995	(18)	545	2,535
Steve Rogers, Alabama St.	6-5	1992	4	113	817	187	713	2,534
Steve Burtt, Iona	6-2	1984	4	121	1,003	—	528	2,534
Shawn Respert, Michigan St.	6-3	1995	4	118	866	331	468	2,531
Joe Jakubick, Akron	6-5	1984	4	108	973	(53)	584	2,530
Andrew Toney, La.-Lafayette	6-3	1980	4	107	996	—	534	2,526
Ron Perry, Holy Cross	6-2	1980	4	109	922	—	680	2,524
Ronnie McCollum, Centenary (La.)	6-4	2001	4	113	822	345	535	2,524
Mike Olliver, Lamar	6-1	1981	4	122	1,130	—	258	2,518
Bryant Stith, Virginia	6-5	1992	4	131	856	114	690	2,516
Bill Bradley, Princeton	6-5	1965	3	83	856	—	791	2,503
Jeff Grayer, Iowa St.	6-5	1988	4	125	974	27	527	2,502
Elgin Baylor, Albertson & Seattle	6-6	1958	3	80	956	—	588	2,500

#Listed is the number of three-pointers scored since it became the national rule in 1987; the number in the parenthesis is number scored before 1987—these counted as three points in the game but counted as two-pointers in the national rankings. The three-pointers in the parenthesis are not included in total points.

2,000-POINT SCORERS

A total of 397 players in Division I history have scored at least 2,000 points over their careers. The first was Jim Lacy, Loyola (Md.), with 2,154 over four seasons ending in 1949. The first to reach 2,000 in a three-season career was Furman's Frank Selvy, 2,538 through 1954. The 397 come from 207 different colleges. Duke leads with eight 2,000-pointers: Jim Spanarkel (last season was 1979), Mike Gminski (1980), Gene Banks (1981), Mark Alarie (1986), Johnny Dawkins (1986), Danny Ferry (1989), Christian Laettner (1992) and Jason Williams (2002). Next are Georgia Tech and La Salle with six, followed by Indiana, Michigan, Murray State, North Carolina, Notre Dame, Oklahoma, Tennessee, Villanova and Wake Forest with five apiece.

SCORING AVERAGE

(Minimum 1,400 points)

Player, Team	Last Season	Yrs.	G	FG	3FG	FT	Pts.	Avg.
Pete Maravich, LSU	1968	3	83	1,387	—	893	3,667	44.2
Austin Carr, Notre Dame	1971	3	74	1,017	—	526	2,560	34.6
Oscar Robertson, Cincinnati	1960	3	88	1,052	—	869	2,973	33.8

Player, Team	Season	Yrs.	G	FG	3FG	FT	Pts.	Avg.
Calvin Murphy, Niagara	1970	3	77	947	—	654	2,548	33.1
Dwight Lamar, La.-Lafayette	†1973	2	57	768	—	326	1,862	32.7
Frank Selvy, Furman	1954	3	78	922	—	694	2,538	32.5
Rick Mount, Purdue	1970	3	72	910	—	503	2,323	32.3
Darrell Floyd, Furman	1956	3	71	868	—	545	2,281	32.1
Nick Werkman, Seton Hall	1964	3	71	812	—	649	2,273	32.0
Willie Humes, Idaho St.	1971	2	48	565	—	380	1,510	31.5
William Averitt, Pepperdine	1973	2	49	615	—	311	1,541	31.4
Elgin Baylor, Albertson & Seattle	1958	3	80	956	—	588	2,500	31.3
Elvin Hayes, Houston	1968	3	93	1,215	—	454	2,884	31.0
Freeman Williams, Portland St.	1978	4	106	1,369	—	511	3,249	30.7
Larry Bird, Indiana St.	1979	3	94	1,154	—	542	2,850	30.3
Bill Bradley, Princeton	1965	3	83	856	—	791	2,503	30.2
Rich Fuqua, Oral Roberts	†1973	2	54	692	—	233	1,617	29.9
Wilt Chamberlain, Kansas	1958	2	48	503	—	427	1,433	29.9
Rick Barry, Miami (Fla.)	1965	3	77	816	—	666	2,298	29.8
Doug Collins, Illinois St.	1973	3	77	894	—	452	2,240	29.1
Alphonso Ford, Mississippi Val.	1993	4	109	1,121	333	590	3,165	29.0
Chris Jackson, LSU	1990	2	64	664	172	354	1,854	29.0
Dave Schellhase, Purdue	1966	3	74	746	—	582	2,074	28.8
Dick Wilkinson, Virginia	1955	3	78	783	—	665	2,233	28.6
James Williams, Austin Peay	1974	2	54	632	—	277	1,541	28.5

†Each played two years of non-Division I competition (Lamar—four years, 3,493 points and 31.2 average; Fuqua—four years, 3,004 points and 27.1 average).

FIELD-GOAL PERCENTAGE

(Minimum 400 field goals made and 4 field goals made per game)

Player, Team	Ht.	Last Season	Yrs.	G	FG	FGA	Pct.
Steve Johnson, Oregon St.	6-10	1981	4	116	828	1,222	67.8
Michael Bradley, Kentucky & Villanova	6-10	2001	3	100	441	651	67.7
Murray Brown, Florida St.	6-8	1980	4	106	566	847	66.8
Lee Campbell, Middle Tenn. & Southwest Mo. St.	6-7	1990	3	88	411	618	66.5
Warren Kidd, Middle Tenn.	6-9	1993	3	83	496	747	66.4
Todd MacCulloch, Washington	7-0	1999	4	115	702	1,058	66.4
Joe Senser, West Chester	6-5	1979	4	96	476	719	66.2
Kevin Magee, UC Irvine	6-8	1982	2	56	552	841	65.6
Orlando Phillips, Pepperdine	6-7	1983	2	58	404	618	65.4
Bill Walton, UCLA	6-11	1974	3	87	747	1,147	65.1
William Herndon, Massachusetts	6-3	1992	4	100	472	728	64.8
Larry Stewart, Coppin St.	6-8	1991	3	91	676	1,046	64.6
Larry Johnson, UNLV	6-7	1991	2	75	612	952	64.3
Dwayne Davis, Florida	6-7	1991	4	124	572	892	64.1
Lew Alcindor, UCLA	7-2	1969	3	88	943	1,476	63.9
Akeem Olajuwon, Houston	7-0	1984	3	100	532	833	63.9
Brendan Haywood, North Carolina	7-0	2001	4	141	541	849	63.7
Oliver Miller, Arkansas	6-9	1992	4	137	680	1,069	63.6
Mike Coleman, Liberty	6-7	1992	4	105	421	663	63.5
Jeff Ruland, Iona	6-10	1980	3	89	717	1,130	63.5
Mark McNamara, California	6-10	1982	4	107	709	1,119	63.4
Dan McClintock, Northern Ariz.	7-0	2000	4	115	542	858	63.2
Cherokee Rhone, Centenary (La.)	6-8	1982	3	63	421	667	63.1
Carlos Boozer, Duke	6-9	2002	3	101	554	878	63.1
Bobby Lee Hurt, Alabama	6-9	1985	4	126	646	1,024	63.1

THREE-POINT FIELD GOALS

Player, Team	Ht.	Last Season	Yrs.	G	3FG
Curtis Staples, Virginia	6-3	1998	4	122	413
Keith Veney, Lamar & Marshall	6-3	1997	4	111	409
Doug Day, Radford	6-1	1993	4	117	401
Ronnie Schmitz, UMKC	6-3	1993	4	112	378
Mark Alberts, Akron	6-1	1993	4	107	375
Brett Blizzard, UNC Wilmington	6-4	2003	4	125	371
Kyle Korver, Creighton	6-7	2003	4	128	371
Pat Bradley, Arkansas	6-2	1999	4	132	366
Bryce Drew, Valparaiso	6-3	1998	4	121	364
Jeff Fryer, Loyola Marymount	6-2	1990	4	112	363
Dennis Scott, Georgia Tech	6-8	1990	3	99	351
Rashad Phillips, Detroit	5-10	2001	4	129	348
Allan Houston, Tennessee	6-5	1993	4	128	346
Jobey Thomas, Charlotte	6-4	2002	4	130	346
Ronnie McCollum, Centenary (La.)	6-4	2001	4	113	345
Trajan Langdon, Duke	6-4	1999	4	136	342
Louis Bullock, Michigan	6-2	1999	4	132	339
Jeff Boschee, Kansas	6-3	2002	4	137	338
Gary Buchanan, Villanova	6-3	2003	4	122	337
Alphonso Ford, Mississippi Val.	6-2	1993	4	109	333
Tim Gill, Oral Roberts	6-2	1998	4	112	333
Pete Lisicky, Penn St.	6-4	1998	4	118	332
Brian Merriweather, Tex.-Pan American	6-3	2001	3	84	332
Clarence Gilbert, Missouri	6-2	2002	4	128	332
Shawn Respert, Michigan St.	6-3	1995	4	118	331

Player, Team	Ht.	Last Season	Yrs.	G	3FG
Demond Mallet, McNeese St.	6-1	2001	5	117	331
Monty Mack, Massachusetts	6-3	2001	4	123	331

THREE-POINT FIELD GOALS PER GAME
(Minimum 200 three-point field goals made)

Player, Team	Ht.	Last Season	Yrs.	G	3FG	Avg.
Timothy Pollard, Mississippi Val.	6-3	1989	2	56	256	4.57
Sydney Grider, La.-Lafayette	6-3	1990	2	58	253	4.36
Brian Merriweather, Tex.-Pan American	6-3	2001	3	84	332	3.95
Josh Heard, Tennessee Tech	6-2	2000	2	55	210	3.82
Kareem Townes, La Salle	6-3	1995	3	81	300	3.70
Keith Veney, Lamar & Marshall	6-3	1997	4	111	409	3.68
Dave Mooney, Coastal Caro.	6-4	1988	2	56	202	3.61
Dennis Scott, Georgia Tech	6-8	1990	3	99	351	3.55
Mark Alberts, Akron	6-1	1993	4	107	375	3.50
Doug Day, Radford	6-1	1993	4	117	401	3.43
Curtis Staples, Virginia	6-3	1998	4	122	413	3.39
Ronnie Schmitz, UMKC	6-3	1993	4	112	378	3.38
Jeff Fryer, Loyola Marymount	6-2	1990	4	112	363	3.24
Dana Barros, Boston College	5-11	1989	3	91	291	3.20
Tony Ross, San Diego St.	6-3	1989	3	85	270	3.18
Randy Woods, La Salle	6-0	1992	3	88	278	3.16
Dominick Young, Fresno St.	5-10	1997	3	89	279	3.13
Wally Lancaster, Virginia Tech	6-5	1989	3	82	257	3.13
David Sivulich, St. Mary's (Cal.)	5-10	1998	3	76	238	3.13
Jim Barton, Dartmouth	6-4	1989	3	78	242	3.10
Alan Barkside, Colorado & Ark.-Little Rock	6-4	2001	4	86	264	3.07
Alphonso Ford, Mississippi Val.	6-2	1993	4	109	333	3.06
Ronnie McCollum, Centenary (La.)	6-4	2001	4	113	345	3.05
Charles Jones, Rutgers & Long Island	6-3	1998	4	108	329	3.05
Keke Hicks, Coastal Caro.	6-4	1995	4	93	282	3.03

THREE-POINT FIELD-GOAL PERCENTAGE
(Minimum 200 three-point field goals made and 2.0 three-point field goals made per game)

Player, Team	Ht.	Last Season	Yrs.	G	3FG	3FGA	Pct.
Tony Bennett, Wis.-Green Bay	6-0	1992	4	118	290	584	49.7
David Olson, Eastern Ill.	6-4	1992	4	111	262	562	46.6
Ross Land, Northern Ariz.	6-5	2000	4	117	308	664	46.4
Dan Dickau, Washington & Gonzaga	6-0	2002	4	97	215	465	46.2
Sean Jackson, Ohio & Princeton	5-11	1992	4	104	243	528	46.0
Barry Booker, Vanderbilt	6-3	1989	3	98	246	535	46.0
Kevin Booth, Mt. St. Mary's	6-0	1993	5	110	265	577	45.9
Dave Calloway, Monmouth	6-3	1991	4	115	260	567	45.9
Tony Ross, San Diego St.	6-3	1992	3	85	270	589	45.8
Jason Matthews, Pittsburgh	6-3	1991	4	123	259	567	45.7
Corey Reed, Radford	6-6	1998	4	104	232	510	45.5
Jim Barton, Dartmouth	6-4	1989	3	78	242	532	45.5
Shawn Respert, Michigan St.	6-3	1995	4	118	331	728	45.5
Kyle Korver, Creighton	6-7	2003	4	128	371	819	45.3
Carlton Becton, N.C. A&T	6-6	1989	3	84	209	462	45.2
Eric Channing, New Mexico St.	6-4	2002	4	124	283	627	45.1
Ray Allen, Connecticut	6-5	1996	3	101	233	520	44.8
Curtis Shelton, Southeast Mo. St.	5-9	1994	4	107	215	480	44.8
Jeff McCool, New Mexico St.	6-5	1989	3	92	201	450	44.7
Jason Kapono, UCLA	6-8	2003	4	127	317	710	44.6
Scott Neely, Campbell	6-3	1996	4	115	244	553	44.1
Wesley Person, Auburn	6-6	1994	4	108	262	594	44.1
Tim Gill, Oral Roberts	6-2	1998	4	112	333	757	44.0
Mark Alberts, Akron	6-1	1993	4	107	375	853	44.0
John Rillie, Gonzaga	6-5	1995	3	88	230	524	43.9
Scott Hartzell, UNC Greensboro	6-0	1996	4	113	309	704	43.9
Andy Kennedy, North Carolina St. & UAB	6-8	1991	4	121	330	752	43.9

FREE-THROW PERCENTAGE
(Minimum 300 free throws made and 2.5 free throws made per game)

Player, Team		Last Season	Yrs.	G	FT	FTA	Pct.
Gary Buchanan, Villanova		2003	4	122	324	355	91.3
Greg Starrick, Kentucky & Southern Ill.		1972	4	72	341	375	90.9
Jack Moore, Nebraska		1982	4	105	446	495	90.1
Steve Henson, Kansas St.		1990	4	127	361	401	90.0
Steve Alford, Indiana		1987	4	125	535	596	89.8
Bob Lloyd, Rutgers		1967	3	77	543	605	89.8
Jim Barton, Dartmouth		1989	4	104	394	440	89.5
Tommy Boyer, Arkansas		1963	3	70	315	353	89.2
Kyle Korver, Creighton		2003	4	128	312	350	89.1
Brent Jolly, Tennessee Tech		2003	4	123	347	391	88.7
Marcus Wilson, Evansville		1999	4	119	455	513	88.7
Joe Crispin, Penn St.		2001	4	127	448	506	88.5
Ron Perry, Holy Cross		1980	4	109	680	768	88.5

Player, Team		Last Season	Yrs.	G	FT	FTA	Pct.
Joe Dykstra, Western Ill.		1983	4	117	587	663	88.5
Mike Joseph, Bucknell		1990	4	115	397	449	88.4
Kyle Macy, Purdue & Kentucky		1980	5	125	416	471	88.3
Matt Hildebrand, Liberty		1994	4	117	398	451	88.2
Jimmy England, Tennessee		1971	3	81	319	362	88.1
Rod Foster, UCLA		1983	4	113	309	351	88.0
Michael Smith, Brigham Young		1989	4	122	431	491	87.8
Jason Matthews, Pittsburgh		1991	4	123	481	548	87.8
Mike Iuzzolino, Penn St. & St. Francis (Pa.)		1991	4	102	402	458	87.8
Rick Suder, Duquesne		1986	4	105	342	390	87.7
Bill Bradley, Princeton		1965	3	83	791	903	87.6
William Lewis, Monmouth		1992	4	112	317	362	87.6

REBOUNDS

Player, Team	Ht.	Last Season	Yrs.	G	Reb.
Tom Gola, La Salle	6-6	1955	4	118	2,201
Joe Holup, George Washington	6-6	1956	4	104	2,030
Charlie Slack, Marshall	6-5	1956	4	88	1,916
Ed Conlin, Fordham	6-5	1955	4	102	1,884
Dickie Hemric, Wake Forest	6-6	1955	4	104	1,802
Paul Silas, Creighton	6-7	1964	3	81	1,751
Art Quimby, Connecticut	6-5	1955	4	80	1,716
Jerry Harper, Alabama	6-8	1956	4	93	1,688
Jeff Cohen, William & Mary	6-7	1961	4	103	1,679
Steve Hamilton, Morehead St.	6-7	1958	4	102	1,675
Charlie Tyra, Louisville	6-8	1957	4	95	1,617
Bill Russell, San Francisco	6-9	1956	3	79	1,606
Elvin Hayes, Houston	6-8	1968	3	93	1,602
Ron Shavlik, North Carolina St.	6-8	1956	3	95	1,598
Marvin Barnes, Providence	6-9	1974	3	89	1,592
Tim Duncan, Wake Forest	6-11	1997	4	128	1,570
Elgin Baylor, Albertson & Seattle	6-6	1958	3	80	1,559
Ernie Beck, Pennsylvania	6-4	1953	3	82	1,557
Dave DeBusschere, Detroit	6-5	1962	3	80	1,552
Wes Unseld, Louisville	6-8	1968	3	82	1,551
Derrick Coleman, Syracuse	6-9	1990	4	143	1,537
Malik Rose, Drexel	6-7	1996	4	120	1,514
Ralph Sampson, Virginia	7-4	1983	4	132	1,511
Chris Smith, Virginia Tech	6-6	1961	4	88	1,508
Keith Swagerty, Pacific (Cal.)	6-7	1967	3	82	1,505

(For careers beginning in 1973 or after)

Player, Team	Ht.	Last Season	Yrs.	G	Reb.
Tim Duncan, Wake Forest	6-11	1997	4	128	1,570
Derrick Coleman, Syracuse	6-9	1990	4	143	1,537
Malik Rose, Drexel	6-7	1996	4	120	1,514
Ralph Sampson, Virginia	7-4	1983	4	132	1,511
Pete Padgett, Nevada	6-8	1976	4	104	1,464
Lionel Simmons, La Salle	6-7	1990	4	131	1,429
Anthony Bonner, St. Louis	6-7	1990	4	133	1,424
Tyrone Hill, Xavier	6-9	1990	4	126	1,380
Popeye Jones, Murray St.	6-8	1992	4	123	1,374
Michael Brooks, La Salle	6-7	1980	4	114	1,372
Xavier McDaniel, Wichita St.	6-7	1985	4	117	1,359
John Irving, Arizona & Hofstra	6-9	1977	4	103	1,348
Sam Clancy, Pittsburgh	6-6	1981	4	116	1,342
Keith Lee, Memphis	6-10	1985	4	128	1,336
Larry Smith, Alcorn St.	6-8	1980	4	111	1,334
Clarence Weatherspoon, Southern Miss.	6-7	1992	4	117	1,320
Michael Cage, San Diego St.	6-9	1984	4	112	1,317
Bob Stephens, Drexel	6-7	1979	4	99	1,316
Patrick Ewing, Georgetown	7-0	1985	4	143	1,316
David Robinson, Navy	7-1	1987	4	127	1,314
Wayne Rollins, Clemson	7-1	1977	4	110	1,311
David West, Xavier	6-9	2003	4	126	1,309
Bob Warner, Maine	6-6	1976	4	96	1,304
Ervin Johnson, New Orleans	6-11	1993	4	123	1,287
Calvin Natt, La.-Monroe	6-5	1979	4	108	1,285

REBOUND AVERAGE
(Minimum 800 rebounds)

Player, Team	Ht.	Last Season	Yrs.	G	Reb.	Avg.
Artis Gilmore, Jacksonville	7-2	1971	2	54	1,224	22.7
Charlie Slack, Marshall	6-5	1956	4	88	1,916	21.8
Paul Silas, Creighton	6-7	1964	3	81	1,751	21.6
Leroy Wright, Pacific (Cal.)	6-8	1960	3	67	1,442	21.5
Art Quimby, Connecticut	6-5	1955	4	80	1,716	21.5
Walt Dukes, Seton Hall	6-10	1953	2	59	1,247	21.1
Bill Russell, San Francisco	6-9	1956	3	79	1,606	20.3
Kermit Washington, American	6-8	1973	3	73	1,478	20.2
Julius Erving, Massachusetts	6-6	1971	2	52	1,049	20.2
Joe Holup, George Washington	6-6	1956	4	104	2,030	19.5

Player, Team	Ht.	Last Season	Yrs.	G	Reb.	Avg.
Elgin Baylor, Albertson & Seattle	6-6	1958	3	80	1,559	19.5
Dave DeBusschere, Detroit	6-5	1962	3	80	1,552	19.4
Ernie Beck, Pennsylvania	6-4	1953	3	82	1,557	19.0
Wes Unseld, Louisville	6-8	1968	3	82	1,551	18.9
Tom Gola, La Salle	6-6	1955	4	118	2,201	18.7
Ed Conlin, Fordham	6-5	1955	4	102	1,884	18.5
Keith Swagerty, Pacific (Cal.)	6-7	1967	3	82	1,505	18.4
Wilt Chamberlain, Kansas	7-0	1958	2	48	877	18.3
Jerry Harper, Alabama	6-8	1956	4	93	1,688	18.2
Dick Cunningham, Murray St.	6-10	1968	3	71	1,292	18.2
Marvin Barnes, Providence	6-9	1974	3	89	1,592	17.9
Jim Barnes, UTEP	6-8	1964	2	54	965	17.9
Alex Ellis, Niagara	6-5	1958	3	77	1,376	17.9
Dickie Hemric, Wake Forest	6-6	1955	4	104	1,802	17.3
Elvin Hayes, Houston	6-8	1968	3	93	1,602	17.2

(For careers beginning in 1973 or after; minimum 800 rebounds)

Player, Team	Ht.	Last Season	Yrs.	G	Reb.	Avg.
Glenn Mosley, Seton Hall	6-8	1977	4	83	1,263	15.2
Bill Campion, Manhattan	6-10	1975	3	74	1,070	14.6
Pete Padgett, Nevada	6-8	1976	4	104	1,464	14.1
Bob Warner, Maine	6-6	1976	4	96	1,304	13.6
Shaquille O'Neal, LSU	7-1	1992	3	90	1,217	13.5
Cornelius Cash, Bowling Green	6-8	1975	3	79	1,068	13.5
Ira Terrell, Southern Methodist	6-8	1976	3	80	1,077	13.5
Bob Stephens, Drexel	6-7	1979	4	99	1,316	13.3
Larry Bird, Indiana St.	6-9	1979	3	94	1,247	13.3
Bernard King, Tennessee	6-7	1977	3	76	1,004	13.2
John Irving, Arizona & Hofstra	6-9	1977	4	103	1,348	13.1
Carey Scurry, Long Island	6-9	1985	3	79	1,013	12.8
Adonal Foyle, Colgate	6-10	1997	3	87	1,103	12.7
Warren Kidd, Middle Tenn.	6-6	1993	3	83	1,048	12.6
Malik Rose, Drexel	6-7	1996	4	120	1,514	12.6
Jervaughn Scales, Southern U.	6-6	1994	3	88	1,099	12.5
Tim Duncan, Wake Forest	6-11	1997	4	128	1,570	12.3
Michael Brooks, La Salle	6-7	1980	4	114	1,372	12.0
Larry Smith, Alcorn St.	6-8	1980	4	111	1,334	12.0
Wayne Rollins, Clemson	7-1	1977	4	110	1,311	11.9
Calvin Natt, La.-Monroe	6-5	1979	4	108	1,285	11.9
Ed Lawrence, McNeese St.	7-0	1976	4	102	1,212	11.9
Michael Cage, San Diego St.	6-9	1984	4	112	1,317	11.8
Xavier McDaniel, Wichita St.	6-7	1985	4	117	1,359	11.6
John Rudd, McNeese St.	6-6	1978	4	102	1,181	11.6
Sam Clancy, Pittsburgh	6-6	1981	4	116	1,342	11.6
Larry Stewart, Coppin St.	6-6	1991	3	91	1,052	11.6
Reggie Jackson, Nicholls St.	6-6	1995	4	110	1,271	11.6

ASSISTS

Player, Team	Ht.	Last Season	Yrs.	G	Ast.
Bobby Hurley, Duke	6-0	1993	4	140	1,076
Chris Corchiani, North Carolina St.	6-1	1991	4	124	1,038
Ed Cota, North Carolina	6-2	2000	4	138	1,030
Keith Jennings, East Tenn. St.	5-7	1991	4	127	983
Steve Blake, Maryland	6-3	2003	4	138	972
Sherman Douglas, Syracuse	6-0	1989	4	138	960
Tony Miller, Marquette	6-0	1995	4	123	956
Greg Anthony, Portland & UNLV	6-1	1991	4	138	950
Doug Gottlieb, Notre Dame & Oklahoma St.	6-1	2000	4	124	947
Gary Payton, Oregon St.	6-2	1990	4	120	939
Orlando Smart, San Francisco	6-0	1994	4	116	902
Andre LaFleur, Northeastern	6-3	1987	4	128	894
Chico Fletcher, Arkansas St.	5-6	2000	4	114	893
Jim Les, Bradley	5-11	1986	4	118	884
Frank Smith, Old Dominion	6-0	1988	4	120	883
Taurence Chisholm, Delaware	5-7	1988	4	110	877
Grayson Marshall, Clemson	6-2	1988	4	122	857
Anthony Manuel, Bradley	5-11	1989	4	108	855
Pooh Richardson, UCLA	6-1	1989	4	122	833
Butch Moore, Southern Methodist	5-10	1986	4	125	828
Mateen Cleaves, Michigan St.	6-3	2000	4	123	816
Drafton Davis, Marist	6-0	1988	4	115	804
Jacque Vaughn, Kansas	6-1	1997	4	126	804
Marc Brown, Siena	5-11	1991	4	123	796
Brandin Knight, Pittsburgh	6-0	2003	4	127	785

ASSIST AVERAGE

(Minimum 550 assists)

Player, Team	Ht.	Last Season	Yrs.	G	Ast.	Avg.
Avery Johnson, Southern U.	5-11	1988	2	61	732	12.00
Sam Crawford, New Mexico St.	5-8	1993	2	67	592	8.84
Mark Wade, Oklahoma & UNLV	6-0	1987	3	79	693	8.77
Chris Corchiani, North Carolina St.	6-1	1991	4	124	1,038	8.37
Taurence Chisholm, Delaware	5-7	1988	4	110	877	7.97

Player, Team	Ht.	Last Season	Yrs.	G	Ast.	Avg.
Van Usher, Tennessee Tech	6-0	1992	3	85	676	7.95
Anthony Manuel, Bradley	5-11	1989	4	108	855	7.92
Chico Fletcher, Arkansas St.	5-6	2000	4	114	893	7.83
Gary Payton, Oregon St.	6-2	1990	4	120	938	7.82
Orlando Smart, San Francisco	6-0	1994	4	116	902	7.78
Tony Miller, Marquette	6-0	1995	4	123	956	7.77
Keith Jennings, East Tenn. St.	5-7	1991	4	127	983	7.74
Bobby Hurley, Duke	6-0	1993	4	140	1,076	7.69
Doug Gottlieb, Notre Dame & Oklahoma St.	6-1	2000	4	124	947	7.63
Chuck Evans, Old Dominion & Mississippi St.	5-11	1993	3	85	648	7.62
Jim Les, Bradley	5-11	1986	4	118	884	7.49
Ed Cota, North Carolina	6-2	2000	4	138	1,030	7.46
Curtis McCants, George Mason	6-0	1998	3	81	598	7.38
Frank Smith, Old Dominion	6-0	1988	4	120	883	7.36
Doug Wojcik, Navy	6-1	1987	3	99	714	7.21
Mark Woods, Wright St.	6-1	1993	4	113	811	7.18
Nelson Haggerty, Baylor	6-0	1995	4	98	699	7.13
Steve Blake, Maryland	6-3	2003	4	138	972	7.04
Grayson Marshall, Clemson	6-2	1988	4	122	857	7.02
Drafton Davis, Marist	6-0	1988	4	115	804	6.99

BLOCKED SHOTS

Player, Team	Ht.	Last Season	Yrs.	G	Blk.
Wojciech Mydra, La.-Monroe	7-2	2002	4	115	535
Adonal Foyle, Colgate	6-10	1997	3	87	492
Tim Duncan, Wake Forest	6-11	1997	4	128	481
Alonzo Mourning, Georgetown	6-10	1992	4	120	453
Tarvis Williams, Hampton	6-9	2001	4	114	452
Ken Johnson, Ohio St.	6-11	2001	4	127	444
Lorenzo Coleman, Tennessee Tech	7-1	1997	4	113	437
Calvin Booth, Penn St.	6-11	1999	4	114	428
Theo Ratliff, Wyoming	6-10	1995	4	111	425
Troy Murphy, Notre Dame	6-9	2001	3	94	425
Etan Thomas, Syracuse	6-9	2000	4	122	424
Rodney Blake, St. Joseph's	6-8	1988	4	116	419
Shaquille O'Neal, LSU	7-1	1992	3	90	412
Kevin Roberson, Vermont	6-7	1992	4	112	409
Jim McIlvaine, Marquette	7-1	1994	4	118	399
Tim Perry, Temple	6-9	1988	4	130	392
Jason Lawson, Villanova	6-11	1997	4	131	375
Pervis Ellison, Louisville	6-9	1989	4	136	374
Peter Aluma, Liberty	6-10	1997	4	119	366
Acie Earl, Iowa	6-10	1993	4	116	365
Jerome James, Florida A&M	7-1	1998	3	81	363

Xavier's David West, Nick Collison of Kansas and Brandon Hunter of Ohio are the only players of the 21st century to register 2,000 career points and 1,000 career rebounds.

Photo by Xavier Sports Information

Player, Team	Ht.	Last Season	Yrs.	G	Blk.
Melvin Ely, Fresno St.	6-10	2002	4	124	361
Dikembe Mutombo, Georgetown	7-2	1991	3	96	354
David Robinson, Navy	6-11	1987	2	67	351
Charles Smith, Pittsburgh	6-10	1988	4	122	346
Brian Skinner, Baylor	6-10	1998	4	103	346

BLOCKED-SHOT AVERAGE
(Minimum 225 blocked shots)

Player, Team	Ht.	Last Season	Yrs.	G	Blk.	Avg.
Keith Closs, Central Conn. St.	7-2	1996	2	54	317	5.87
Adonal Foyle, Colgate	6-10	1997	3	87	492	5.66
David Robinson, Navy	6-11	1987	2	67	351	5.24
Wojciech Mydra, La.-Monroe	7-2	2002	4	115	535	4.65
Shaquille O'Neal, LSU	7-1	1992	3	90	412	4.58
Troy Murphy, Notre Dame	6-9	2001	3	94	425	4.52
Jerome James, Florida A&M	7-1	1998	3	81	363	4.48
Justin Rowe, Maine	7-0	2003	2	55	226	4.11
Tarvis Williams, Hampton	6-9	2001	4	114	452	3.96
Lorenzo Coleman, Tennessee Tech	7-1	1997	4	113	437	3.87
Theo Ratliff, Wyoming	6-10	1995	4	111	425	3.83
Alonzo Mourning, Georgetown	6-10	1992	4	120	453	3.78
Tim Duncan, Wake Forest	6-11	1997	4	128	481	3.76
Calvin Booth, Penn St.	6-11	1999	4	114	428	3.75
Lorenzo Williams, Stetson	6-9	1991	2	63	234	3.71
Dikembe Mutombo, Georgetown	7-2	1991	3	96	354	3.69
Marcus Camby, Massachusetts	6-11	1996	3	92	336	3.65
Kevin Roberson, Vermont	6-7	1992	4	112	409	3.65
Rodney Blake, St. Joseph's	6-8	1988	4	116	419	3.61
Ken Johnson, Ohio St.	6-11	2001	4	127	444	3.50
Etan Thomas, Syracuse	6-9	2000	4	122	424	3.48
Kelvin Cato, South Ala. & Iowa St.	6-11	1997	3	79	274	3.47
Jim McIlvaine, Marquette	7-1	1994	4	118	399	3.38
Brian Skinner, Baylor	6-10	1998	4	103	346	3.36
Rik Smits, Marist	7-4	1988	4	107	345	3.22

STEALS

Player, Team	Ht.	Last Season	Yrs.	G	Stl.
John Linehan, Providence	5-9	2002	5	122	385
Eric Murdock, Providence	6-2	1991	4	117	376
Pepe Sanchez, Temple	6-0	2000	4	116	365
Cookie Belcher, Nebraska	6-4	2001	5	131	353
Kevin Braswell, Georgetown	6-2	2002	4	128	349
Bonzi Wells, Ball St.	6-5	1998	4	116	347
Gerald Walker, San Francisco	6-1	1996	4	111	344
Johnny Rhodes, Maryland	6-6	1996	4	122	344
Michael Anderson, Drexel	5-11	1988	4	115	341
Kenny Robertson, Cleveland St.	6-0	1990	4	119	341
Keith Jennings, East Tenn. St.	5-7	1991	4	127	334
Juan Dixon, Maryland	6-3	2002	4	141	333
Desmond Cambridge, Alabama A&M	6-1	2002	3	84	330
Greg Anthony, Portland & UNLV	6-1	1991	4	138	329
Jason Hart, Syracuse	6-3	2000	4	132	329
Chris Corchiani, North Carolina St.	6-1	1991	4	124	328
Gary Payton, Oregon St.	6-2	1990	4	120	321
Chris Garner, Memphis	5-10	1997	4	123	321
Tim Winn, St. Bonaventure	5-10	2000	4	108	319
Mark Woods, Wright St.	6-1	1993	4	113	314
Pointer Williams, Tulane & McNeese St.	6-0	1996	4	115	314
Scott Burrell, Connecticut	6-7	1993	4	119	310
Clarence Ceasar, LSU	6-7	1995	4	112	310
Shawnta Rogers, George Washington	5-4	1999	4	114	310
Elliot Perry, Memphis	6-0	1991	4	126	304

STEAL AVERAGE
(Minimum 225 steals)

Player, Team	Ht.	Last Season	Yrs.	G	Stl.	Avg.
Desmond Cambridge, Alabama A&M	6-1	2002	3	84	330	3.93
Mookie Blaylock, Oklahoma	6-0	1989	2	74	281	3.80
Ronn McMahon, Eastern Wash.	5-9	1990	3	64	225	3.52
Eric Murdock, Providence	6-2	1991	4	117	376	3.21
Van Usher, Tennessee Tech	6-0	1992	3	85	270	3.18
John Linehan, Providence	5-9	2002	5	122	385	3.16
Pepe Sanchez, Temple	6-0	2000	4	116	365	3.15
Gerald Walker, San Francisco	6-1	1996	4	111	344	3.10
Bonzi Wells, Ball St.	6-5	1998	4	116	347	2.99
Michael Anderson, Drexel	5-11	1988	4	115	341	2.97
Tim Winn, St. Bonaventure	5-10	2000	4	108	319	2.95
Haywoode Workman, Oral Roberts	6-3	1989	3	85	250	2.94
Shawn Griggs, LSU & La.-Lafayette	6-6	1994	3	89	260	2.92
Morris Scott, Florida A&M	6-0	2001	4	87	252	2.90
Kenny Robertson, Cleveland St.	6-0	1990	4	119	341	2.87
Jason Rowe, Loyola (Md)	5-10	2000	4	95	272	2.86

Player, Team	Ht.	Last Season	Yrs.	G	Stl.	Avg.
Darnell Mee, Western Ky.	6-3	1993	3	91	259	2.85
Pat Baldwin, Northwestern	6-1	1994	4	96	272	2.83
Johnny Rhodes, Maryland	6-6	1996	4	122	344	2.82
Mark Woods, Wright St.	6-1	1993	4	113	314	2.78
Clarence Ceasar, LSU	6-7	1995	4	112	310	2.77
Aldwin Ware, Florida A&M	6-2	1988	4	110	301	2.74
Jarion Childs, American	6-0	2000	4	108	295	2.73
Pointer Williams, Tulane & McNeese St.	6-0	1996	4	115	314	2.73
Kevin Braswell, Georgetown	6-2	2002	4	128	349	2.73

GAMES PLAYED

Player, Team	Last Season	Yrs.	G
Wayne Turner, Kentucky	1999	4	151
Christian Laettner, Duke	1992	4	148
Danny Manning, Kansas	1988	4	147
Shane Battier, Duke	2001	4	146
Stacey Augmon, UNLV	1991	4	145
Jamaal Magloire, Kentucky	2000	4	145
Patrick Ewing, Georgetown	1985	4	143
Danny Ferry, Duke	1989	4	143
Derrick Coleman, Syracuse	1990	4	143
Jared Prickett, Kentucky	1997	4	143
Ryan Robertson, Kansas	1999	4	142
Nick Collison, Kansas	2003	4	142
Brian Davis, Duke	1992	4	141
Anthony Epps, Kentucky	1997	4	141
Brendan Haywood, North Carolina	2001	4	141
Juan Dixon, Maryland	2002	4	141
Kirk Hinrich, Kansas	2003	4	141
Kevin Freeman, Connecticut	2000	4	140
Charlie Bell, Michigan St.	2001	4	140
Ralph Beard, Kentucky	1949	4	139
Lee Mayberry, Arkansas	1992	4	139
Kevin Pritchard, Kansas	1990	4	139
Ademola Okulaja, North Carolina	1999	4	139
Eric Chenowith, Kansas	2001	4	139
Dante Swanson, Tulsa	2003	4	139

2,000 POINTS & 1,000 REBOUNDS

Player, Team	Ht.	Last Season	Yrs.	G	Pts.	Reb.
Lionel Simmons, La Salle	6-7	1990	4	131	3,217	1,429
Harry Kelly, Texas Southern	6-7	1983	4	110	3,066	1,085
Oscar Robertson, Cincinnati	6-5	1960	3	88	2,973	1,338
Danny Manning, Kansas	6-10	1988	4	147	2,951	1,187
Elvin Hayes, Houston	6-8	1968	3	93	2,884	1,602
Larry Bird, Indiana St.	6-9	1979	3	94	2,850	1,247
Hank Gathers, Southern California & Loyola Marymount	6-7	1990	4	117	2,723	1,128
Daren Queenan, Lehigh	6-5	1988	4	118	2,703	1,013
David Robinson, Navy	7-1	1987	4	127	2,669	1,314
Wayman Tisdale, Oklahoma	6-9	1985	3	104	2,661	1,048
Michael Brooks, La Salle	6-7	1980	4	114	2,628	1,372
Dickie Hemric, Wake Forest	6-6	1955	4	104	2,587	1,802
Calvin Natt, La.-Monroe	6-5	1979	4	108	2,581	1,285
Keith Van Horn, Utah	6-9	1997	4	122	2,542	1,074
Willie Jackson, Centenary (La.)	6-6	1984	4	114	2,535	1,013
Bill Bradley, Princeton	6-5	1965	3	83	2,503	1,008
Elgin Baylor, Albertson & Seattle	6-6	1958	3	80	2,500	1,559
Tom Gola, La Salle	6-6	1955	4	118	2,462	2,201
Christian Laettner, Duke	6-11	1992	4	148	2,460	1,149
Keith Lee, Memphis	6-11	1985	4	128	2,408	1,336
Phil Sellers, Rutgers	6-5	1976	4	114	2,399	1,115
Byron Houston, Oklahoma St.	6-7	1992	4	127	2,379	1,190
Ron Harper, Miami (Ohio)	6-6	1986	4	120	2,377	1,119
Bryant Reeves, Oklahoma St.	7-0	1995	4	136	2,367	1,152
Lew Alcindor, UCLA	7-2	1969	3	88	2,325	1,367
Mike Gminski, Duke	6-11	1980	4	122	2,323	1,242
Billy McGill, Utah	6-9	1962	3	86	2,321	1,106
Adam Keefe, Stanford	6-9	1992	4	125	2,319	1,119
Jerry West, West Virginia	6-3	1960	3	93	2,309	1,240
Tunji Awojobi, Boston U.	6-5	1997	4	114	2,308	1,237
Jonathan Moore, Furman	6-8	1980	4	117	2,299	1,242
Rick Barry, Miami (Fla.)	6-7	1965	3	77	2,298	1,274
Gary Winton, Army	6-5	1978	4	105	2,296	1,168
Kenneth Lyons, North Texas	6-7	1983	4	111	2,291	1,020
Tom Davis, Delaware St.	6-6	1991	4	95	2,274	1,013
Nick Werkman, Seton Hall	6-3	1964	3	71	2,273	1,036
Jim McDaniels, Western Ky.	7-0	1971	3	81	2,238	1,118
Joe Holup, George Washington	6-6	1956	4	104	2,226	2,030
Ralph Sampson, Virginia	7-4	1983	4	132	2,225	1,511
Patrick Ewing, Georgetown	7-0	1985	4	143	2,184	1,316
Doug Smith, Missouri	6-10	1991	4	128	2,184	1,054

Player, Team	Ht.	Last Season	Yrs.	G	Pts.	Reb.
Jenny Sanders, George Mason	6-5	1989	4	107	2,177	1,026
Joe Barry Carroll, Purdue	7-1	1980	4	123	2,175	1,148
Reggie King, Alabama	6-6	1979	4	118	2,168	1,279
Len Chappell, Wake Forest	6-8	1962	3	87	2,165	1,213
Danny Ferry, Duke	6-10	1989	4	143	2,155	1,003
Xavier McDaniel, Wichita St.	6-7	1985	4	117	2,152	1,359
Derrick Coleman, Syracuse	6-9	1990	4	143	2,143	1,537
Joe Binion, N.C. A&T	6-8	1984	4	116	2,143	1,194
Pervis Ellison, Louisville	6-9	1989	4	136	2,143	1,149
Dan Issel, Kentucky	6-9	1970	3	83	2,138	1,078
Jesse Arnelle, Penn St.	6-5	1955	4	102	2,138	1,238
Sam Perkins, North Carolina	6-10	1984	4	135	2,133	1,167
David West, Xavier	6-9	2003	4	126	2,132	1,309
Bob Elliott, Arizona	6-10	1977	4	114	2,131	1,083
Clarence Weatherspoon, Southern Miss.	6-7	1992	4	117	2,130	1,320
Reggie Jackson, Nicholls St.	6-6	1995	4	110	2,124	1,271
Greg Grant, Utah St.	6-7	1986	4	115	2,124	1,003
John Wallace, Syracuse	6-8	1996	4	127	2,119	1,065
Tim Duncan, Wake Forest	6-11	1997	4	128	2,117	1,570
Odell Hodge, Old Dominion	6-9	1997	5	128	2,117	1,086
Bill Cartwright, San Francisco	6-11	1979	4	111	2,116	1,137
Bob Harstad, Creighton	6-6	1991	4	128	2,110	1,126
Gary Trent, Ohio	6-8	1995	3	93	2,108	1,050
Nick Collison, Kansas	6-9	2003	4	142	2,097	1,143

Player, Team	Ht.	Last Season	Yrs.	G	Pts.	Reb.
B.B. Davis, Lamar	6-8	1981	4	119	2,084	1,122
Durand Macklin, LSU	6-7	1981	5	123	2,080	1,276
Ralph Crosthwaite, Western Ky.	6-9	1959	4	103	2,076	1,309
Sidney Green, UNLV	6-9	1983	4	119	2,069	1,276
Bob Lanier, St. Bonaventure	6-11	1970	3	75	2,067	1,180
Raef LaFrentz, Kansas	6-11	1998	4	131	2,066	1,186
Fred West, Texas Southern	6-9	1990	4	118	2,066	1,136
Sidney Moncrief, Arkansas	6-4	1979	4	122	2,066	1,015
Popeye Jones, Murray St.	6-8	1992	4	123	2,057	1,374
Danya Abrams, Boston College	6-7	1997	4	122	2,053	1,029
Mark Acres, Oral Roberts	6-11	1985	4	110	2,038	1,051
Fred Hetzel, Davidson	6-8	1965	3	79	2,032	1,094
Bailey Howell, Mississippi St.	6-7	1959	3	75	2,030	1,277
Malik Rose, Drexel	6-7	1996	4	120	2,024	1,514
Larry Krystkowiak, Montana	6-9	1986	4	120	2,017	1,105
Greg Kelser, Michigan St.	6-7	1979	4	115	2,014	1,092
Brandon Hunter, Ohio	6-7	2003	4	119	2,012	1,103
Herb Williams, Ohio St.	6-10	1981	4	114	2,011	1,111
Stacey Augmon, UNLV	6-8	1991	4	145	2,011	1,005
Jeff Cohen, William & Mary	6-7	1961	4	103	2,003	1,679
Tyrone Hill, Xavier	6-9	1990	4	126	2,003	1,380
Alonzo Mourning, Georgetown	6-10	1992	4	120	2,001	1,032
Josh Grant, Utah	6-9	1993	5	131	2,000	1,066

Annual Individual Champions

Scoring Average

Season	Player, Team	Ht.	Cl.	G	FG	FT	Pts.	Avg.
1948	Murray Wier, Iowa	5-9	Sr.	19	152	95	399	21.0
1949	Tony Lavelli, Yale	6-3	Sr.	30	228	215	671	22.4
1950	Paul Arizin, Villanova	6-3	Sr.	29	260	215	735	25.3
1951	Bill Mlkvy, Temple	6-4	Sr.	25	303	125	731	29.2
1952	Clyde Lovellette, Kansas	6-9	Sr.	28	315	165	795	28.4
1953	Frank Selvy, Furman	6-3	Jr.	25	272	194	738	29.5
1954	Frank Selvy, Furman	6-3	Sr.	29	427	*355	1,209	41.7
1955	Darrell Floyd, Furman	6-1	Jr.	25	344	209	897	35.9
1956	Darrell Floyd, Furman	6-1	Sr.	28	339	268	946	33.8
1957	Grady Wallace, South Carolina	6-4	Sr.	29	336	234	906	31.2
1958	Oscar Robertson, Cincinnati	6-5	So.	28	352	280	984	35.1
1959	Oscar Robertson, Cincinnati	6-5	Jr.	30	331	316	978	32.6
1960	Oscar Robertson, Cincinnati	6-5	Sr.	30	369	273	1,011	33.7
1961	Frank Burgess, Gonzaga	6-1	Sr.	26	304	234	842	32.4
1962	Billy McGill, Utah	6-9	Sr.	26	394	221	1,009	38.8
1963	Nick Werkman, Seton Hall	6-3	Jr.	22	221	208	650	29.5
1964	Howard Komives, Bowling Green	6-1	Sr.	23	292	260	844	36.7
1965	Rick Barry, Miami (Fla.)	6-7	Sr.	26	340	293	973	37.4
1966	Dave Schellhase, Purdue	6-4	Sr.	24	284	213	781	32.5
1967	Jim Walker, Providence	6-3	Sr.	28	323	205	851	30.4
1968	Pete Maravich, LSU	6-5	So.	26	432	274	1,138	43.8
1969	Pete Maravich, LSU	6-5	Jr.	26	433	282	1,148	44.2
1970	Pete Maravich, LSU	6-5	Sr.	31	*522	337	*1,381	*44.5
1971	Johnny Neumann, Mississippi	6-6	So.	23	366	191	923	40.1
1972	Dwight Lamar, La.-Lafayette	6-1	Jr.	29	429	196	1,054	36.3
1973	William Averitt, Pepperdine	6-1	Sr.	25	352	144	848	33.9
1974	Larry Fogle, Canisius	6-5	So.	25	326	183	835	33.4
1975	Bob McCurdy, Richmond	6-7	Sr.	26	321	213	855	32.9
1976	Marshall Rodgers, Tex.-Pan American	6-2	Sr.	25	361	197	919	36.8
1977	Freeman Williams, Portland St.	6-4	Jr.	26	417	176	1,010	38.8
1978	Freeman Williams, Portland St.	6-4	Sr.	27	410	149	969	35.9
1979	Lawrence Butler, Idaho St.	6-3	Sr.	27	310	192	812	30.1
1980	Tony Murphy, Southern U.	6-3	Sr.	29	377	178	932	32.1
1981	Zam Fredrick, South Carolina	6-2	Sr.	27	300	181	781	28.9
1982	Harry Kelly, Texas Southern	6-7	Jr.	29	336	190	862	29.7
1983	Harry Kelly, Texas Southern	6-7	Sr.	29	333	169	835	28.8
1984	Joe Jakubick, Akron	6-5	Sr.	27	304	206	814	30.1
1985	Xavier McDaniel, Wichita St.	6-8	Sr.	31	351	142	844	27.2
1986	Terrance Bailey, Wagner	6-2	Jr.	29	321	212	854	29.4
1987	Kevin Houston, Army	5-11	Sr.	29	311	268	953	32.9

Season	Player, Team	Ht.	Cl.	G	FG	3FG	FT	Pts.	Avg.
1988	Hersey Hawkins, Bradley	6-3	Sr.	31	377	87	284	1,125	36.3
1989	Hank Gathers, Loyola Marymount	6-7	Jr.	31	419	0	177	1,015	32.7
1990	Bo Kimble, Loyola Marymount	6-5	Sr.	32	404	92	231	1,131	35.3
1991	Kevin Bradshaw, U.S. Int'l	6-6	Sr.	28	358	60	278	1,054	37.6
1992	Brett Roberts, Morehead St.	6-8	Sr.	29	278	66	193	815	28.1
1993	Greg Guy, Tex.-Pan American	6-1	Jr.	19	189	67	111	556	29.3
1994	Glenn Robinson, Purdue	6-8	Jr.	34	368	79	215	1,030	30.3
1995	Kurt Thomas, TCU	6-9	Sr.	27	288	3	202	781	28.9
1996	Kevin Granger, Texas Southern	6-3	Sr.	24	194	30	230	648	27.0
1997	Charles Jones, Long Island	6-3	Jr.	30	338	109	118	903	30.1
1998	Charles Jones, Long Island	6-3	Sr.	30	326	116	101	869	29.0
1999	Alvin Young, Niagara	6-3	Sr.	29	253	65	157	728	25.1
2000	Courtney Alexander, Fresno St.	6-6	Sr.	27	252	58	107	669	24.8
2001	Ronnie McCollum, Centenary (La.)	6-4	Sr.	27	244	85	214	787	29.1
2002	Jason Conley, VMI	6-5	Fr.	28	285	79	171	820	29.3
2003	Ruben Douglas, New Mexico	6-5	Sr.	28	218	94	253	783	28.0

*record

Field-Goal Percentage

Season	Player, Team	Cl.	G	FG	FGA	Pct.
1948	Alex Peterson, Oregon St.	Jr.	27	89	187	47.6
1949	Ed Macauley, St. Louis	Sr.	26	144	275	52.4
1950	Jim Moran, Niagara	Jr.	27	98	185	53.0
1951	Don Meineke, Dayton	Jr.	32	240	469	51.2
1952	Art Spoelstra, Western Ky.	So.	31	178	345	51.6
1953	Vernon Stokes, St. Francis (N.Y.)	Sr.	24	147	247	59.5
1954	Joe Holup, George Washington	So.	26	179	313	57.2
1955	Ed O'Connor, Manhattan	Sr.	23	147	243	60.5
1956	Joe Holup, George Washington	Sr.	26	200	309	64.7
1957	Bailey Howell, Mississippi St.	So.	25	217	382	56.8
1958	Ralph Crosthwaite, Western Ky.	Jr.	25	202	331	61.0
1959	Ralph Crosthwaite, Western Ky.	Sr.	26	191	296	64.5
1960	Jerry Lucas, Ohio St.	So.	27	283	444	63.7
1961	Jerry Lucas, Ohio St.	Jr.	27	256	411	62.3
1962	Jerry Lucas, Ohio St.	Sr.	28	237	388	61.1
1963	Lyle Harger, Houston	Sr.	26	193	294	65.6
1964	Terry Holland, Davidson	Sr.	26	135	214	63.1
1965	Tim Kehoe, St. Peter's	Sr.	19	138	209	66.0
1966	Julian Hammond, Tulsa	Sr.	29	172	261	65.9
1967	Lew Alcindor, UCLA	So.	30	346	519	66.7
1968	Joe Allen, Bradley	Sr.	28	258	394	65.5
1969	Lew Alcindor, UCLA	Sr.	30	303	477	63.5
1970	Willie Williams, Florida St.	Sr.	26	185	291	63.6
1971	John Belcher, Arkansas St.	Jr.	24	174	275	63.3
1972	Kent Martens, Abilene Christian	Sr.	21	136	204	66.7

Season	Player, Team	Cl.	G	FG	FGA	Pct.
1973	Elton Hayes, Lamar	Sr.	24	146	222	65.8
1974	Al Fleming, Arizona	So.	26	136	204	66.7
1975	Bernard King, Tennessee	Fr.	25	273	439	62.2
1976	Sidney Moncrief, Arkansas	Fr.	28	149	224	66.5
1977	Joe Senser, West Chester	So.	25	130	186	69.9
1978	Joe Senser, West Chester	Jr.	25	135	197	68.5
1979	Murray Brown, Florida St.	Jr	29	237	343	69.1
1980	Steve Johnson, Oregon St.	Jr.	30	211	297	71.0
1981	Steve Johnson, Oregon St.	Sr.	28	235	315	*74.6
1982	Mark McNamara, California	Sr.	27	231	329	70.2
1983	Troy Lee Mikel, East Tenn. St.	Sr.	29	197	292	67.5
1984	Akeem Olajuwon, Houston	Jr.	37	249	369	67.5
1985	Keith Walker, Utica	Sr.	27	154	216	71.3
1986	Brad Daugherty, North Carolina	Sr.	34	284	438	64.8
1987	Alan Williams, Princeton	Sr.	25	163	232	70.3
1988	Arnell Jones, Boise St.	Sr.	30	187	283	66.1
1989	Dwayne Davis, Florida	So.	33	179	248	72.2
1990	Lee Campbell, Southwest Mo. St.	Sr.	29	192	275	69.8
1991	Oliver Miller, Arkansas	Jr.	38	254	361	70.4
1992	Charles Outlaw, Houston	Jr.	31	156	228	68.4
1993	Charles Outlaw, Houston	Sr.	30	196	298	65.8
1994	Mike Atkinson, Long Beach St.	Jr.	26	141	203	69.5
1995	Shane Kline-Ruminski, Bowling Green	Sr.	26	181	265	68.3
1996	Quadre Lollis, Montana St.	Sr.	30	212	314	67.5
1997	Todd MacCulloch, Washington	So.	28	163	241	67.6
1998	Todd MacCulloch, Washington	Jr.	30	225	346	65.0
1999	Todd MacCulloch, Washington	Sr.	29	210	317	66.2
2000	Brendan Haywood, North Carolina	Jr.	36	191	274	69.7
2001	Michael Bradley, Villanova	Jr.	31	254	367	69.2
2002	Adam Mark, Belmont	So.	26	150	212	70.8
2003	Adam Mark, Belmont	Jr.	28	199	297	67.0

*record

Three-Point Field Goals Made Per Game

Season	Player, Team	Cl.	G	3FG	Avg.
1987	Darrin Fitzgerald, Butler	Sr.	28	158	*5.64
1988	Timothy Pollard, Mississippi Val.	Jr.	28	132	4.71
1989	Timothy Pollard, Mississippi Val.	Sr.	28	124	4.43
1990	Dave Jamerson, Ohio	Sr.	28	131	4.68
1991	Bobby Phills, Southern U.	Sr.	28	123	4.39
1992	Doug Day, Radford	Jr.	29	117	4.03
1993	Bernard Haslett, Southern Miss.	Jr.	26	109	4.19
1994	Chris Brown, UC Irvine	Jr.	26	122	4.69
1995	Mitch Taylor, Southern U.	Jr.	25	109	4.36
1996	Dominick Young, Fresno St.	Jr.	29	120	4.14
1997	William Fourche, Southern U.	Sr.	27	122	4.52
1998	Curtis Staples, Virginia	Sr.	30	130	4.33
1999	Brian Merriweather, Tex.-Pan American	So.	27	110	4.07
2000	Brian Merriweather, Tex.-Pan American	Jr.	28	114	4.07
2001	DeWayne Jefferson, Mississippi Val.	Sr.	27	107	3.96
2002	Cain Doliboa, Wright St.	Sr.	28	104	3.71
2003	Terrence Woods, Florida A&M	Jr.	28	139	4.96

*record

Three-Point Field-Goal Percentage

Season	Player, Team	Cl.	G	3FG	3FGA	Pct.
1987	Reginald Jones, Prairie View	Jr.	28	64	112	57.1
1988	Glenn Tropf, Holy Cross	Jr.	29	52	82	*63.4
1989	Dave Calloway, Monmouth	So.	28	48	82	58.5
1990	Matt Lapin, Princeton	Sr.	27	71	133	53.4
1991	Keith Jennings, East Tenn. St.	Sr.	33	84	142	59.2
1992	Sean Wightman, Western Mich.	Jr.	30	48	76	63.2
1993	Jeff Anderson, Kent St.	Jr.	26	44	82	53.7
1994	Brent Kell, Evansville	So.	29	62	123	50.4
1995	Brian Jackson, Evansville	Jr.	27	53	95	55.8
1996	Joe Stafford, Western Caro.	Jr.	30	58	110	52.7
1997	Kent McCausland, Iowa	So.	29	70	134	52.2
1998	Jim Cantamessa, Siena	So.	29	66	117	56.4
1999	Rodney Thomas, IUPUI	Jr.	26	59	113	52.2
2000	Jonathan Whitworth, Middle Tenn.	Jr.	28	50	99	50.5
2001	Amory Sanders, Southeast Mo. St.	Sr.	24	53	95	55.8
2002	Dante Swanson, Tulsa	Jr.	33	73	149	49.0
2003	Jeff Schiffner, Pennsylvania	Jr.	28	74	150	49.3

*record

Free-Throw Percentage

Season	Player, Team	Cl.	G	FT	FTA	Pct.
1948	Sam Urzetta, St. Bonaventure	So.	22	59	64	92.2
1949	Bill Schroer, Valparaiso	So.	24	59	68	86.8
1950	Sam Urzetta, St. Bonaventure	Sr.	22	54	61	88.5
1951	Jay Handlan, Wash. & Lee	Jr.	22	148	172	86.0
1952	Sy Chadroff, Miami (Fla.)	Sr.	22	99	123	80.5
1953	John Weber, Yale	Sr.	24	117	141	83.0
1954	Dick Daugherty, Arizona St.	Sr.	23	75	86	87.2
1955	Jim Scott, West Tex. A&M	Sr.	23	153	171	89.5
1956	Bill Von Weyhe, Rhode Island	Jr.	25	180	208	86.5
1957·	Ernie Wiggins, Wake Forest	Sr.	28	93	106	87.7
1958	Semi Mintz, Davidson	Sr.	24	105	119	88.2
1959	Arlen Clark, Oklahoma St.	Sr.	25	201	236	85.2
1960	Jack Waters, Mississippi	Jr.	24	103	118	87.3
1961	Stew Sherard, Army	Jr.	24	135	154	87.7
1962	Tommy Boyer, Arkansas	Jr.	23	125	134	93.3
1963	Tommy Boyer, Arkansas	Sr.	24	147	161	91.3
1964	Rick Park, Tulsa	Jr.	25	121	134	90.3
1965	Bill Bradley, Princeton	Sr.	29	273	308	88.6
1966	Bill Blair, Providence	Sr.	27	101	112	90.2
1967	Bob Lloyd, Rutgers	Sr.	29	255	277	92.1
1968	Joe Heiser, Princeton	Sr.	26	117	130	90.0
1969	Bill Justus, Tennessee	Sr.	28	133	147	90.5
1970	Steve Kaplan, Rutgers	So.	23	102	110	92.7
1971	Greg Starrick, Southern Ill.	Jr.	23	119	132	90.2
1972	Greg Starrick, Southern Ill.	Sr.	26	148	160	92.5
1973	Don Smith, Dayton	Jr.	26	111	122	91.0
1974	Rickey Medlock, Arkansas	Jr.	26	87	95	91.6
1975	Frank Oleynick, Seattle	Sr.	26	135	152	88.8
1976	Tad Dufelmeier, Loyola (Ill.)	Jr.	25	71	80	88.8
1977	Robert Smith, UNLV	Sr.	32	98	106	92.5
1978	Carlos Gibson, Marshall	Jr.	28	84	89	94.4
1979	Darrell Mauldin, Campbell	Jr.	26	70	76	92.1
1980	Brian Magid, George Washington	Sr.	26	79	85	92.9
1981	Dave Hildahl, Portland St.	Sr.	21	76	82	92.7
1982	Rod Foster, UCLA	Jr.	27	95	100	95.0
1983	Rob Gonzalez, Colorado	Sr.	28	75	82	91.5
1984	Steve Alford, Indiana	Fr.	31	137	150	91.3
1985	Craig Collins, Penn St.	Sr.	27	94	98	*95.9
1986	Jim Barton, Dartmouth	Fr.	26	65	69	94.2
1987	Kevin Houston, Army	Sr.	29	268	294	91.2
1988	Steve Henson, Kansas St.	So.	34	111	120	92.5
1989	Michael Smith, Brigham Young	Sr.	29	160	173	92.5
1990	Rob Robbins, New Mexico	Jr.	34	101	108	93.5
1991	Darin Archbold, Butler	Jr.	29	187	205	91.2
1992	Don MacLean, UCLA	Sr.	32	197	214	92.1
1993	Josh Grant, Utah	Sr.	31	104	113	92.0
1994	Danny Basile, Marist	So.	27	84	89	94.4
1995	Greg Bibb, Tennessee Tech	Jr.	27	106	117	90.6
1996	Mike Dillard, Sam Houston St.	Jr.	25	63	68	92.6
1997	Aaron Zobrist, Bradley	Sr.	30	77	85	90.6
1998	Matt Sundblad, Lamar	Jr.	27	96	104	92.3
1999	Lonnie Cooper, Louisiana Tech	Sr.	25	70	76	92.1
2000	Clay McKnight, Pacific (Cal.)	Sr.	24	74	78	94.9
2001	Gary Buchanan, Villanova	So.	31	97	103	94.2
2002	Cary Cochran, Nebraska	Sr.	28	71	77	92.2
2003	Steve Drabyn, Belmont	Jr.	29	78	82	95.1

*record

Rebound Average

Season	Player, Team	Ht.	Cl.	G	Reb.	Avg.
1951	Ernie Beck, Pennsylvania	6-4	So.	27	556	20.6
1952	Bill Hannon, Army	6-3	So.	17	355	20.9
1953	Ed Conlin, Fordham	6-5	So.	26	612	23.5
1954	Art Quimby, Connecticut	6-5	Jr.	26	588	22.6
1955	Charlie Slack, Marshall	6-5	Jr.	21	538	*25.6
1956	Joe Holup, George Washington	6-6	Sr.	26	604	†.256
1957	Elgin Baylor, Seattle	6-6	Jr.	25	508	†.235
1958	Alex Ellis, Niagara	6-5	Sr.	25	536	†.262
1959	Leroy Wright, Pacific (Cal.)	6-8	Jr.	26	652	†.238
1960	Leroy Wright, Pacific (Cal.)	6-8	Sr.	17	380	†.234
1961	Jerry Lucas, Ohio St.	6-8	Jr.	27	470	†.198
1962	Jerry Lucas, Ohio St.	6-8	Sr.	28	499	†.211
1963	Paul Silas, Creighton	6-7	Sr.	27	557	20.6

Season	Player, Team	Ht.	Cl.	G	Reb.	Avg.
1964	Bob Pelkington, Xavier	6-7	Sr.	26	567	21.8
1965	Toby Kimball, Connecticut	6-8	Sr.	23	483	21.0
1966	Jim Ware, Oklahoma City	6-8	Sr.	29	607	20.9
1967	Dick Cunningham, Murray St.	6-10	Jr.	22	479	21.8
1968	Neal Walk, Florida	6-10	Jr.	25	494	19.8
1969	Spencer Haywood, Detroit	6-8	So.	22	472	21.5
1970	Artis Gilmore, Jacksonville	7-2	Jr.	28	621	22.2
1971	Artis Gilmore, Jacksonville	7-2	Sr.	26	603	23.2
1972	Kermit Washington, American	6-8	Jr.	23	455	19.8
1973	Kermit Washington, American	6-8	Sr.	22	439	20.0
1974	Marvin Barnes, Providence	6-9	Sr.	32	597	18.7
1975	John Irving, Hofstra	6-9	So.	21	323	15.4
1976	Sam Pellom, Buffalo	6-8	So.	26	420	16.2
1977	Glenn Mosley, Seton Hall	6-8	Sr.	29	473	16.3
1978	Ken Williams, North Texas	6-7	Sr.	28	411	14.7
1979	Monti Davis, Tennessee St.	6-7	Jr.	26	421	16.2
1980	Larry Smith, Alcorn St.	6-8	Sr.	26	392	15.1
1981	Darryl Watson, Mississippi Val.	6-7	Sr.	27	379	14.0
1982	LaSalle Thompson, Texas	6-10	Jr.	27	365	13.5
1983	Xavier McDaniel, Wichita St.	6-7	So.	28	403	14.4
1984	Akeem Olajuwon, Houston	7-0	Jr.	37	500	13.5
1985	Xavier McDaniel, Wichita St.	6-8	Sr.	31	460	14.8
1986	David Robinson, Navy	6-11	Jr.	35	455	13.0
1987	Jerome Lane, Pittsburgh	6-6	So.	33	444	13.5
1988	Kenny Miller, Loyola (Ill.)	6-9	Fr.	29	395	13.6
1989	Hank Gathers, Loyola Marymount	6-7	Jr.	31	426	13.7
1990	Anthony Bonner, St. Louis	6-8	Sr.	33	456	13.8
1991	Shaquille O'Neal, LSU	7-1	So.	28	411	14.7
1992	Popeye Jones, Murray St.	6-8	Sr.	30	431	14.4
1993	Warren Kidd, Middle Tenn.	6-9	Sr.	26	386	14.8
1994	Jerome Lambert, Baylor	6-8	Jr.	24	355	14.8
1995	Kurt Thomas, TCU	6-9	Sr.	27	393	14.6
1996	Marcus Mann, Mississippi Val.	6-8	Sr.	29	394	13.6
1997	Tim Duncan, Wake Forest	6-11	Sr.	31	457	14.7
1998	Ryan Perryman, Dayton	6-7	Sr.	33	412	12.5
1999	Ian McGinnis, Dartmouth	6-8	So.	26	317	12.2
2000	Darren Phillip, Fairfield	6-7	Sr.	29	405	14.0
2001	Chris Marcus, Western Ky.	7-1	Jr.	31	374	12.1
2002	Jeremy Bishop, Quinnipiac	6-6	Jr.	29	347	12.0
2003	Brandon Hunter, Ohio	6-7	Sr.	30	378	12.6

record; †From 1956 through 1962, championship was determined on highest individual recoveries out of total by both teams in all games.

Assist Average

Season	Player, Team	Cl.	G	Ast.	Avg.
1984	Craig Lathen, Ill.-Chicago	Jr.	29	274	9.45
1985	Rob Weingard, Hofstra	Sr.	24	228	9.50
1986	Mark Jackson, St. John's (N.Y.)	Jr.	36	328	9.11
1987	Avery Johnson, Southern U.	Jr.	31	333	10.74
1988	Avery Johnson, Southern U.	Sr.	30	399	*13.30
1989	Glenn Williams, Holy Cross	Sr.	28	278	9.93
1990	Todd Lehmann, Drexel	Sr.	28	260	9.29
1991	Chris Corchiani, North Carolina St.	Sr.	31	299	9.65
1992	Van Usher, Tennessee Tech	Sr.	29	254	8.76
1993	Sam Crawford, New Mexico St.	Sr.	34	310	9.12
1994	Jason Kidd, California	So.	30	272	9.07
1995	Nelson Haggerty, Baylor	Sr.	28	284	10.14

Season	Player, Team	Cl.	G	Ast.	Avg.
1996	Raimonds Miglinieks, UC Irvine	Sr.	27	230	8.52
1997	Kenny Mitchell, Dartmouth	Sr.	26	203	7.81
1998	Ahlon Lewis, Arizona St.	Sr.	32	294	9.19
1999	Doug Gottlieb, Oklahoma St.	Jr.	34	299	8.79
2000	Mark Dickel, UNLV	Sr.	31	280	9.03
2001	Markus Carr, Cal St. Northridge	Jr.	32	286	8.94
2002	T.J. Ford, Texas	Fr.	33	273	8.27
2003	Martell Bailey, Ill.-Chicago	Jr.	30	244	8.13

*record

Blocked-Shot Average

Season	Player, Team	Cl.	G	Blk.	Avg.
1986	David Robinson, Navy	Jr.	35	207	5.91
1987	David Robinson, Navy	Sr.	32	144	4.50
1988	Rodney Blake, St. Joseph's	Sr.	29	116	4.00
1989	Alonzo Mourning, Georgetown	Fr.	34	169	4.97
1990	Kenny Green, Rhode Island	Sr.	26	124	4.77
1991	Shawn Bradley, Brigham Young	Fr.	34	177	5.21
1992	Shaquille O'Neal, LSU	Jr.	30	157	5.23
1993	Theo Ratliff, Wyoming	Jr.	28	124	4.43
1994	Grady Livingston, Howard	Jr.	26	115	4.42
1995	Keith Closs, Central Conn. St.	Fr.	26	139	5.35
1996	Keith Closs, Central Conn. St.	So.	28	178	*6.36
1997	Adonal Foyle, Colgate	Jr.	28	180	6.43
1998	Jerome James, Florida A&M	Sr.	27	125	4.63
1999	Tarvis Williams, Hampton	So.	27	135	5.00
2000	Ken Johnson, Ohio St.	Sr.	30	161	5.37
2001	Tarvis Williams, Hampton	Sr.	32	147	4.59
2002	Wojciech Myrda, La.-Monroe	Sr.	32	172	5.38
2003	Emeka Okafor, Connecticut	So.	33	156	4.73

*record

Steal Average

Season	Player, Team	Cl.	G	Stl.	Avg.
1986	Darron Brittman, Chicago St.	Sr.	28	139	*4.96
1987	Tony Fairley, Charleston So.	Sr.	28	114	4.07
1988	Aldwin Ware, Florida A&M	Sr.	29	142	4.90
1989	Kenny Robertson, Cleveland St.	Jr.	28	111	3.96
1990	Ronn McMahon, Eastern Wash.	Sr.	29	130	4.48
1991	Van Usher, Tennessee Tech	Jr.	28	104	3.71
1992	Victor Snipes, Northeastern Ill.	So.	25	86	3.44
1993	Jason Kidd, California	Fr.	29	110	3.79
1994	Shawn Griggs, La.-Lafayette	Sr.	30	120	4.00
1995	Roderick Anderson, Texas	Sr.	30	101	3.37
1996	Pointer Williams, McNeese St.	Sr.	27	118	4.37
1997	Joel Hoover, Md.-East. Shore	Fr.	28	90	3.21
1998	Bonzi Wells, Ball St.	Sr.	29	103	3.55
1999	Shawnta Rogers, George Washington	Sr.	29	103	3.55
2000	Carl Williams, Liberty	Sr.	28	107	3.82
2001	Greedy Daniels, TCU	Jr.	25	108	4.32
2002	Desmond Cambridge, Alabama A&M	Sr.	29	160	5.52
2003	Alexis McMillan, Stetson	Sr.	22	87	3.95

*record

All-Time Team Leaders

Single-Game Records

SCORING HIGHS

Pts.	Team vs. Opponent (Opp. Pts.)	Date
186	Loyola Marymount vs. U.S. Int'l (140)	Jan. 5, 1991
181	Loyola Marymount vs. U.S. Int'l (150)	Jan. 31, 1989
179	Long Island vs. Medgar Evers (62)	Nov. 26, 1997
173	Oklahoma vs. U.S. Int'l (101)	Nov. 29, 1989
172	Oklahoma vs. Loyola Marymount (112)	Dec. 15, 1990
166	Arkansas vs. U.S. Int'l (101)	Dec. 9, 1989
164	UNLV vs. Hawaii-Hilo (111)	Feb. 19, 1976
164	Loyola Marymount vs. Azusa-Pacific (138)	Nov. 28, 1988
162	Loyola Marymount vs. U.S. Int'l (144)	Jan. 7, 1989

Pts.	Team vs. Opponent (Opp. Pts.)	Date
162	Loyola Marymount vs. Chaminade (129)	Nov. 25, 1990
162	Oklahoma vs. Angelo St. (99)	Dec. 1, 1990
162	Drake vs. Grinnell (110)	Dec. 11, 2002
159	Southern U. vs. Texas College (65)	Dec. 6, 1990
159	LSU vs. Northern Ariz. (86)	Dec. 28, 1991
157	Loyola Marymount vs. San Francisco (115)	Feb. 5, 1990
156	Southern U. vs. Baptist Christian (91)	Dec. 14, 1992
156	South Ala. vs. Prairie View (114)	Dec. 2, 1994
155	Oral Roberts vs. Union (Tenn.) (113)	Feb. 24, 1972
155	Southern U. vs. Prairie View (91)	Feb. 22, 1993
154	Texas-Arlington vs. Huston-Tillotson (85)	Nov. 29, 1990
154	Southern U. vs. Patten (57)	Nov. 26, 1993

Pts.	Team vs. Opponent (Opp. Pts.)	Date
153	TCU vs. Tex.-Pan American (87)	Nov. 29, 1997
152	Jacksonville vs. St. Peter's (106)	Dec. 3, 1970
152	Oklahoma vs. Centenary (La.) (84)	Dec. 12, 1987
152	Oklahoma vs. Oral Roberts (122)	Dec. 10, 1988
152	Loyola Marymount vs. U.S. Int'l (137)	Dec. 7, 1989
152	Northeastern vs. Loyola Marymount (123)	Nov. 24, 1990

SCORING HIGHS BY LOSING TEAM

Pts.	Team vs. Opponent (Opp. Pts.)	Date
150	U.S. Int'l vs. Loyola Marymount (181)	Jan. 31, 1989
144	U.S. Int'l vs. Loyola Marymount (162)	Jan. 7, 1989
141	Loyola Marymount vs. LSU (148) (ot)	Feb. 3, 1990
140	Utah St. vs. UNLV (142) (3 ot)	Jan. 2, 1985
140	U.S. Int'l vs. Loyola Marymount (186)	Jan. 5, 1991
140	Long Island vs. St. Francis (N.Y.) (142) (2 ot)	Feb. 22, 2003
137	U.S. Int'l vs. Loyola Marymount (152)	Dec. 7, 1989
136	Gonzaga vs. Loyola Marymount (147)	Feb. 18, 1989
132	Troy St. vs. George Mason (148)	Dec. 10, 1994
127	Pepperdine vs. Loyola Marymount (142)	Feb. 20, 1988
127	Troy St. vs. George Mason (142)	Nov. 28, 1995
126	Western Mich. vs. Marshall (127)	Dec. 20, 1999
125	Nevada vs. Loyola Marymount (130)	Dec. 30, 1988
123	San Francisco vs. Loyola Marymount (137)	Feb. 9, 1990
123	Loyola Marymount vs. Pepperdine (148)	Feb. 17, 1990
123	Loyola Marymount vs. Northeastern (152)	Nov. 24, 1990
123	Sam Houston St. vs. Texas-Arlington (125)	Dec. 28, 1998
122	Oral Roberts vs. Oklahoma (152)	Dec. 10, 1988
121	Loyola Marymount vs. LSU (148) (ot)	Feb. 3, 1990
121	Loyola Marymount vs. Oklahoma (136)	Dec. 23, 1989

SCORING HIGHS BOTH TEAMS COMBINED

Pts.	Team (Pts.) vs. Team (Pts.)	Date
331	Loyola Marymount (181) vs. U.S. Int'l (150)	Jan. 31, 1989
326	Loyola Marymount (186) vs. U.S. Int'l (140)	Jan. 5, 1991
306	Loyola Marymount (162) vs. U.S. Int'l (144)	Jan. 7, 1989
289	Loyola Marymount (152) vs. U.S. Int'l (137)	Dec. 7, 1989
289	LSU (148) vs. Loyola Marymount (141) (ot)	Feb. 3, 1990
284	Oklahoma (172) vs. Loyola Marymount (112)	Dec. 15, 1990
283	Loyola Marymount (147) vs. Gonzaga (136)	Feb. 18, 1989
282	UNLV (142) vs. Utah St. (140) (3 ot)	Jan. 2, 1985
282	St. Francis (N.Y.) (142) vs. Long Island (140) (2 ot)	Feb. 22, 2003
280	George Mason (148) vs. Troy St. (132)	Dec. 10, 1994
275	Northeastern (152) vs. Loyola Marymount (123)	Nov. 24, 1990
274	Oklahoma (152) vs. Oral Roberts (122)	Dec. 10, 1988
274	Oklahoma (173) vs. U.S. Int'l (101)	Nov. 29, 1989
272	Loyola Marymount (157) vs. San Francisco (115)	Feb. 4, 1990
269	Loyola Marymount (142) vs. Pepperdine (127)	Feb. 20, 1988
269	Loyola Marymount (150) vs. St. Mary's (Cal.) (119)	Feb. 1, 1990
269	George Mason (142) vs. Troy St. (127)	Nov. 28, 1995

MARGIN OF VICTORY

Pts.	Team (Pts.) vs. Opponent (Opp. Pts.)	Date
117	Long Island (179) vs. Medgar Evers (62)	Nov. 26, 1997
101	Texas (102) vs. San Marcos Baptist (1)	Jan. 10, 1916
97	Southern U. (154) vs. Patten (57)	Nov. 26, 1993
96	Purdue (112) vs. Indiana St. (6)	Jan. 10, 1911
96	Western Ky. (103) vs. Adairville Independents (7)	Jan. 10, 1923
95	Oklahoma (146) vs. Northeastern Ill. (51)	Dec. 2, 1989
94	Southern U. (159) vs. Texas College (65)	Dec. 6, 1990
93	Washington (100) vs. Puget Sound (7)	Jan. 14, 1921
92	Villanova (117) vs. Philadelphia NAMC (25)	Feb. 12, 1949
91	LSU (124) vs. Rhodes (33)	Dec. 8, 1952
91	Tennessee St. (148) vs. Fisk (57)	Dec. 6, 1993
91	Tulsa (141) vs. Prairie View (50)	Dec. 7, 1995
89	Northwestern La. (129) vs. LeTourneau (51)	Jan. 20, 1992
89	Nicholls St. (140) vs. Faith Baptist (51)	Dec. 17, 1994
88	Southern U. (132) vs. Faith Baptist (44)	Dec. 12, 1994
88	Prairie View (129) vs. Oklahoma Baptist (41)	Jan. 21, 1997
87	Canisius (107) vs. St. Ann's (20)	Dec. 8, 1907
86	Ohio St. (88) vs. Ohio (2)	Feb. 6, 1903
84	Rhode Island (118) vs. Fort Varnum (34)	Nov. 20, 1943
83	Texas (89) vs. Texas St. (6)	Feb. 11, 1919
82	Navy (126) vs. McDaniel (44)	Dec. 3, 1952
82	Morehead St. (130) vs. Asbury (48)	Nov. 30, 1996
81	Rhode Island (119) vs. Mass. Maritime (38)	1945
81	Oklahoma (146) vs. Florida A&M (65)	Jan. 27, 1993
80	Dayton (80) vs. Cedarville (0)	Jan. 23, 1907
80	Syracuse (106) vs. Oswego St. (26)	1945
80	Rhode Island (124) vs. Quonset Naval (44)	Dec. 12, 1946
80	Minnesota (80) vs. Alabama St. (34)	Dec. 23, 1996

MARGIN OF VICTORY VS. DIVISION I OPPONENT (SINCE 1938)

Pts.	Team (Pts.) vs. Opponent (Opp. Pts.)	Date
91	Tulsa (141) vs. Prairie View (50)	Dec. 7, 1995
81	Oklahoma (146) vs. Florida A&M (65)	Jan. 27, 1993
80	Minnesota (80) vs. Alabama St. (34)	Dec. 23, 1996
77	Kentucky (143) vs. Georgia (66)	Feb. 27, 1956
75	Maryland (132) vs. North Texas (57)	Dec. 23, 1998
74	Kentucky (124) vs. Tenn.-Martin (50)	Nov. 26, 1994
73	LSU (159) vs. Northern Ariz. (86)	Dec. 28, 1991
72	Iowa (103) vs. Chicago (31)	Feb. 5, 1944
72	Oklahoma (173) vs. U.S. Int'l (101)	Nov. 29, 1989
72	Ohio St. (116) vs. Chicago St. (44)	Nov. 30, 1991
72	Missouri (117) vs. Chicago St. (45)	Dec. 2, 1995
72	Texas Tech (107) vs. Nicholls (35)	Dec. 7, 2002
71	Ohio St. (109) vs. Delaware (38)	Jan. 11, 1960
71	New Mexico (71) vs. Dartmouth (36)	Dec. 29, 1972
71	Dayton (109) vs. Bowling Green (38)	Dec. 11, 1954
70	Massachusetts (108) vs. Maine (38)	Feb. 23, 1974
70	Kansas (115) vs. Brown (45)	Jan. 3, 1989
70	Connecticut (116) vs. Central Conn. St. (46)	Jan. 23, 1996
69	Kentucky (98) vs. Vanderbilt (29)	Feb. 27, 1947
69	Lamar (126) vs. Sam Houston St. (57)	Dec. 30, 1991
68	Oklahoma (152) vs. Centenary (La.) (84)	Dec. 12, 1987
68	Oklahoma (132) vs. Southern Utah St. (64)	Dec. 20, 1988
68	Connecticut (115) vs. Central Conn. St. (47)	Jan. 10, 1991
68	Kansas (140) vs. Oral Roberts (72)	Jan. 14, 1993
68	Southern Utah (140) vs. South Ala. (72)	Dec. 10, 1994

SCORING HIGHS IN A HALF

Pts.	Team vs. Opponent (Half)	Date
98	Long Island vs. Medgar Evers (2nd)	Nov. 26, 1997
97	Oklahoma vs. U.S. Int'l (1st)	Nov. 29, 1989
96	Southern U. vs. Texas College (2nd)	Dec. 6, 1990
94	Loyola Marymount vs. U.S. Int'l (1st)	Jan. 31, 1989
94	Oklahoma vs. Northeastern Ill. (2nd)	Dec. 2, 1989
94	Loyola Marymount vs. U.S. Int'l (1st)	Jan. 5, 1991
93	Loyola Marymount vs. U.S. Int'l (1st)	Jan. 7, 1989
93	Oklahoma vs. Loyola Marymount (2nd)	Dec. 15, 1990
92	Loyola Marymount vs. U.S. Int'l (2nd)	Jan. 5, 1991
92	Alabama St. vs. Grambling (2nd)	Jan. 21, 1991
91	Oklahoma vs. Angelo St. (2nd)	Dec. 1, 1990
87	Oklahoma vs. Oral Roberts (2nd)	Dec. 10, 1988
87	Loyola Marymount vs. U.S. Int'l (2nd)	Jan. 31, 1989
86	Jacksonville vs. St. Peter's (2nd)	Dec. 3, 1970
86	Lamar vs. Portland St. (2nd)	Jan. 12, 1980
86	Loyola Marymount vs. Gonzaga (2nd)	Feb. 18, 1989
86	Gonzaga vs. Loyola Marymount (2nd)	Feb. 18, 1989
86	Kentucky vs. LSU (1st)	Jan. 16, 1996

SCORING HIGHS IN A HALF BOTH TEAMS COMBINED

Pts.	Team (Pts.) vs. Team (Pts.) (Half)	Date
172	Loyola Marymount (86) vs. Gonzaga (86) (2nd)	Feb. 18, 1989
170	Loyola Marymount (94) vs. U.S. Int'l (76) (1st)	Jan. 31, 1989
164	Loyola Marymount (94) vs. U.S. Int'l (70) (1st)	Jan. 5, 1991
162	Loyola Marymount (92) vs. U.S. Int'l (70) (2nd)	Jan. 5, 1991
161	Loyola Marymount (93) vs. U.S. Int'l (68) (1st)	Jan. 7, 1989
161	Loyola Marymount (87) vs. U.S. Int'l (74) (2nd)	Jan. 31, 1989
160	Oklahoma (87) vs. Oral Roberts (73) (2nd)	Dec. 10, 1988

FEWEST POINTS SCORED IN A GAME SINCE 1938

Pts.	Team vs. Opponent (Opp. Pts.)	Date
6	Temple vs. Tennessee (11)	Dec. 15, 1974
9	Pittsburgh vs. Penn St. (24)	Mar. 1, 1952
10	Duke vs. North Carolina St. (12)	Mar. 8, 1968
11	Oklahoma vs. Oklahoma St. (14)	Feb. 19, 1944
11	Tennessee vs. Temple (6)	Dec. 15, 1974
11	Cincinnati vs. Kentucky (24)	Dec. 20, 1983
12	Marquette vs. Creighton (57)	Dec. 16, 1940
12	Pittsburgh vs. Penn St. (15)	Jan. 15, 1944
12	North Carolina St. vs. Duke (10)	Mar. 8, 1968
13	Pittsburgh vs. Penn St. (32)	Feb. 20, 1943
13	Illinois vs. Purdue (23)	Feb. 7, 1938
14	Virginia vs. Navy (36)	Jan. 12, 1938
14	Michigan St. vs. Michigan (42)	Dec. 7, 1940
14	Kansas St. vs. Missouri (38)	Mar. 4, 1944
14	Oklahoma St. vs. Oklahoma (11)	Feb. 19, 1944
14	Alabama vs. Tennessee (23)	1945
15	Alabama vs. Tennessee (37)	1942
15	Arkansas vs. Oklahoma St. (17)	Jan. 28, 1944

Pts.	Team vs. Opponent (Opp. Pts.)	Date
15	Penn St. vs. Pittsburgh (12)	Jan. 15, 1944
15	Creighton vs. Oklahoma St. (35)	Feb. 9, 1948
15	Charleston So. vs. Col. of Charleston (18)	Feb. 6, 1980
16	Vanderbilt vs. Tennessee Tech (21)	1938
16	Miami (Ohio) vs. Marshall (22)	Feb. 19, 1938
16	South Carolina vs. Clemson (38)	Feb. 10, 1939
16	South Carolina vs. Clemson (43)	Feb. 18, 1939
16	Stanford vs. Oregon St. (18)	Jan. 28, 1980

FEWEST POINTS SCORED IN A GAME SINCE 1986

Pts.	Team vs. Opponent (Opp. Pts.)	Date
21	Ga. Southern vs. Coastal Caro. (61)	Jan. 2, 1997
23	Miami (Ohio) vs. Dayton (60)	Dec. 29, 2001
24	Nicholls St. vs. LSU (68)	Nov. 22, 2002
25	Texas-Pan American vs. North Carolina St. (75)	Jan. 7, 1997
25	Valparaiso vs. Wis.-Green Bay (69)	Mar. 2, 1992
26	UC Santa Barb. vs. Fresno St. (46)	Feb. 26, 1986
26	Northwestern vs. Evansville (48)	Nov. 26, 1999
27	New Hampshire vs. Providence (56)	Dec. 5, 1992
27	Yale vs. Princeton (55)	Jan. 11, 1991
27	Bucknell vs. Princeton (68)	Dec. 9, 1998
28	Dartmouth vs. Princeton (66)	Feb. 10, 1990
28	Wofford vs. North Carolina St. (57)	Dec. 3, 1996
28	Winthrop vs. North Carolina St. (57)	Dec. 3, 1996
29	Long Beach St. vs. UNLV (49)	Mar. 9, 1991
29	Texas-Pan American vs. Iowa (85)	Dec. 4, 1992
29	Loyola (Ill.) vs. Wisconsin (66)	Nov. 14, 1998
30	Columbia vs. Dartmouth (54)	Jan. 14, 1989
30	Akron vs. Northern Ill. (48)	Jan. 26, 1991
30	Morris Brown vs. Tulane (88)	Jan. 4, 2003
31	Tex.-Arlington vs. Southern Methodist (36)	Dec. 16, 1989
31	Cornell vs. Princeton (48)	Feb. 8, 1992
31	UMBC vs. Maryland (67)	Dec. 4, 1996
31	Jacksonville vs. South Ala. (52)	Jan. 29, 1998
32	Charleston So. vs. Alabama (63)	Dec. 18, 1989
32	New Hampshire vs. Connecticut (85)	Dec. 12, 1990
32	Appalachian St. vs. St. Bonaventure (76)	Jan. 7, 1995
32	Morehead St. vs. Kentucky (96)	Dec. 16, 1995
32	Lehigh vs. Miami (Fla.) (68)	Dec. 30, 1996
32	Brigham Young vs. New Mexico (74)	Feb. 3, 1997
32	Fordham vs. Virginia Tech (50)	Feb. 8, 1997
32	New Orleans vs. South Ala. (54)	Jan. 18, 1999

FIELD-GOAL PERCENTAGE

Pct.	Team (FG-FGA) vs. Opponent	Date
83.3	Maryland (15-18) vs. South Carolina	Jan. 9, 1971
81.4	New Mexico (35-43) vs. Oregon St.	Nov. 30, 1985
81.0	Fresno St. (34-42) vs. Portland St.	Dec. 3, 1977
81.0	St. Peter's (34-42) vs. Utica	Dec. 4, 1984
80.5	Fordham (33-41) vs. Fairfield	Feb. 27, 1984
80.0	Holy Cross (32-40) vs. Vermont	Nov. 30, 1981
80.0	Oklahoma St. (28-35) vs. Tulane	Mar. 22, 1992
80.0	Long Beach St. (56-70) vs. Cal St. Monterey	Dec. 22, 1999
79.4	Arkansas (27-34) vs. Texas Tech	Feb. 20, 1979
79.4	Columbia (27-34) vs. Dartmouth	Mar. 2, 1984
79.0	North Carolina (49-62) vs. Loyola Marymount	Mar. 19, 1988
78.6	Villanova (22-28) vs. Georgetown	Apr. 1, 1985
78.6	St. Peter's (22-28) vs. Army	Jan. 9, 1982
78.4	Western Ky. (29-37) vs. Dayton	Jan. 24, 1979
78.1	Army (25-32) vs. Manhattan	Jan. 20, 1979
78.0	Southern Utah (32-41) vs. Montana Tech	Dec. 19, 2002
77.8	Samford (35-45) vs. Loyola (La.)	Dec. 12, 1992
77.5	Nicholls St. (31-40) vs. Samford	Dec. 30, 1983
77.4	Richmond (24-31) vs. Citadel	Feb. 8, 1976
77.2	Stephen F. Austin (44-57) vs. LeTourneau	Nov. 26, 2002
77.0	Purdue (47-61) vs. Long Island	Nov. 14, 1997

THREE-POINT FIELD GOALS

3FG	Team vs. Opponent	Date
28	Troy St. vs. George Mason	Dec. 10, 1994
24	Cincinnati vs. Oakland	Dec. 5, 1998
23	Lamar vs. Louisiana Tech	Feb. 28, 1993
23	Kansas St. vs. Fresno St.	Mar. 24, 1994
23	Troy St. vs. George Mason	Nov. 28, 1995
23	Sanford vs. Troy St.	Jan. 13, 2001
22	Gonzaga vs. San Francisco	Feb. 23, 1995
21	Kentucky vs. North Carolina	Dec. 27, 1989
21	Loyola Marymount vs. Michigan	Mar. 18, 1990
21	UNLV vs. Nevada	Dec. 8, 1990
21	Troy St. vs. Loyola (La.)	Dec. 22, 1993
21	Cal Poly vs. Cal Baptist	Dec. 3, 1996
21	Mississippi Val. vs. Troy St.	Dec. 6, 1996
21	Arkansas vs. Troy St.	Dec. 10, 1996

3FG	Team vs. Opponent	Date
21	Long Island vs. Robert Morris	Feb. 3, 1997
20	Navy vs. Mt. St. Mary's	Nov. 26, 1990
20	Lamar vs. Prairie View	Feb. 3, 1993
20	Arkansas vs. Texas Southern	Dec. 29, 1993
20	Baylor vs. TCU	Feb. 14, 1995
20	Southern California vs. Oregon St.	Jan. 29, 2000
20	Northern Ariz. vs. Cal Poly	Dec. 2, 2000
20	Nicholls St. vs. Troy St.	Dec. 17, 2001
20	Missouri vs. Colorado	Feb. 23, 2002
20	Arkansas St. vs. Lyon	Dec. 7, 2002
19	19 tied	

THREE-POINT FIELD GOALS ATTEMPTED

3FGA	Team vs. Opponent	Date
74	Troy St. vs. George Mason	Dec 10, 1994
67	Mississippi Val. vs. Troy St.	Dec. 6, 1996
58	Cal Poly vs. Cal Baptist	Dec. 3, 1996
53	Kentucky vs. La.-Lafayette	Dec. 23, 1989
51	Texas-Arlington vs. New Mexico	Nov. 23, 1990
51	Arizona St. vs. Brigham Young	Dec. 1, 1992
50	Morehead St. vs. George Mason	Dec. 3, 1996
50	Cal Poly vs. Air Force	Dec. 5, 1997
48	Kentucky vs. North Carolina	Dec. 27, 1989
48	Cincinnati vs. Oakland	Dec. 5, 1998
47	Kentucky vs. Furman	Dec. 19, 1989
47	Charleston So. vs. Clemson	Dec. 1, 1993
47	Centenary (La.) vs. UCF	Jan. 11, 1993
46	UNLV vs. Nevada	Dec. 8, 1990
46	Georgetown vs. Boston College	Feb. 26, 1994
45	Loyola Marymount vs. LSU	Feb. 3, 1990
45	Houston vs. St. Louis	Dec. 15, 1990
45	Drake vs. Iowa	Nov. 29, 1994
45	Mississippi Valley vs. Loyola Marymount	Nov. 14, 2001
44	Cal St. Northridge vs. Colorado	Nov. 23, 1990
44	Central Conn. St. vs. Colorado	Dec. 8, 1990
44	Kentucky vs. LSU	Feb. 2, 1992
44	North Texas vs. Texas-Arlington	Jan. 9, 1993
44	Kentucky vs. LSU	Mar. 14, 1993
44	Samford vs. Mercer	Feb. 18, 1995
44	Fresno St. vs. Cal St. Northridge	Nov. 30, 1999
44	St. Bonaventure vs. Richmond	Mar. 7, 2002

THREE-POINT FIELD-GOAL PERCENTAGE
(Minimum 10-three point field goals made)

Pct.	Team (3FG-3FGA) vs. Opponent	Date
91.7	Drexel (11-12) vs. Delaware	Dec. 3, 2000
90.9	Duke (10-11) vs. Clemson	Feb. 1, 1988
90.9	Hofstra (10-11) vs. Rhode Island	Jan. 16, 1993
87.5	Stetson (14-16) vs. Centenary (La.)	Jan. 13, 1996
85.7	Western Ill. (12-14) vs. Valparaiso	Jan. 13, 1992
84.6	Murray St. (11-13) vs. Southeast Mo. St.	Jan. 16, 1993
83.3	Eastern Ky. (15-18) vs. UNC Asheville	Jan. 14, 1987
83.3	Princeton (10-12) vs. Pennsylvania	Jan. 6, 1990
83.3	Evansville (10-12) vs. Butler	Feb. 9, 1991
83.3	Southern Utah (10-12) vs. Cal St. Northridge	Mar. 1, 1991
83.3	Wis.-Milwaukee (10-12) vs. Eastern Mich.	Feb. 19, 1992
83.3	Purdue (10-12) vs. Michigan	Feb. 7, 1993
83.3	UNLV (10-12) vs. William & Mary	Feb. 11, 1995
83.3	Evansville (10-12) vs. Southern Ill.	Feb. 24, 1996
83.3	Wis.-Green Bay (10-12) vs. Miami (Ohio)	Dec. 5, 1998
81.3	Niagara (13-16) vs. Siena	Jan. 7, 1987
80.0	Marshall (12-15) vs. Wyoming	Dec. 7, 1991
80.0	Washington St. (12-15) vs. Princeton	Dec. 29, 1992
80.0	Princeton (12-15) vs. Columbia	Feb. 13, 1993
80.0	Niagara (12-15) vs. Iona	Feb. 17, 1995
80.0	Marquette (12-15) vs. Tulane	Jan. 27, 2001
78.9	Ohio (15-19) vs. Col. of Charleston	Dec. 21, 1989
78.9	San Francisco (15-19) vs. Gonzaga	Feb. 9, 2001
78.6	Toledo (11-14) vs. Akron	Jan. 20, 1993
78.6	UMBC (11-14) vs. Charleston So.	Jan. 23, 1993
78.6	Ohio (11-14) vs. Youngstown St.	Dec. 20, 1993
78.6	Ga. Southern (11-14) vs. Appalachian St.	Jan. 18, 1997
78.6	UCF (11-14) vs. South Carolina St.	Nov. 28, 1999

FREE-THROW PERCENTAGE
(Minimum 30 free throws made)

Pct.	Team (FT-FTA) vs. Opponent	Date
100	UC Irvine (34-34) vs. Pacific (Cal.)	Feb. 21, 1981
100	Samford (34-34) vs. UCF	Dec. 20, 1990
100	Marshall (31-31) vs. Davidson	Dec. 17, 1979
100	Indiana St. (31-31) vs. Wichita St.	Feb. 18, 1991
97.2	Vanderbilt (35-36) vs. Mississippi St.	Feb. 26, 1986
97.2	Butler (35-36) vs. Dayton	Feb. 21, 1991

Pct.	Team (FT-FTA) vs. Opponent	Date
97.2	Marquette (35-36) vs. Memphis	Jan. 23, 1993
97.0	Miami (Fla.) (32-33) vs. Creighton	Feb. 10, 1964
97.0	Toledo (32-33) vs. Old Dominion	Dec. 9, 1995
97.0	Hawaii (32-33) vs. New Mexico	Feb. 24, 1996
96.8	Oregon St. (30-31) vs. Memphis	Dec. 19, 1990
96.8	Niagara (30-31) vs. Fairfield	Jan. 31, 1998
95.5	UNLV (42-44) vs. San Diego St.	Dec. 11, 1976
94.7	Southwest Mo. St. (36-38) vs. Evansville	Dec. 30, 2001
94.6	TCU (35-37) vs. Tex.-Arlington	Dec. 23, 1996
94.4	Eastern Mich. (34-36) vs. Jackson St.	Dec. 20, 1994
93.8	North Carolina St. (30-32) vs. North Carolina	Feb. 21, 1998
93.8	Brigham Young (30-32) vs. Weber St.	Dec. 28, 2000
93.7	Mount St. Mary's (30-32) vs. Robert Morris	Feb. 6, 1990

REBOUNDS

Reb.	Team vs. Opponent	Date
108	Kentucky vs. Mississippi	Feb. 8, 1964
103	Holy Cross vs. Boston College	Mar. 1, 1956
102	Arizona vs. Northern Ariz.	Jan. 6, 1951
101	Weber St. vs. Idaho St.	Jan. 22, 1966
100	William & Mary vs. Virginia	Feb. 14, 1954
95	Indiana vs. Michigan	Mar. 11, 1961
95	Murray St. vs. MacMurray	Jan. 2, 1967
92	Santa Clara vs. St. Mary's (Cal.)	Feb. 15, 1971
92	Oral Roberts vs. Brandeis	Jan. 8, 1973
91	Notre Dame vs. St. Norbert	Dec. 7, 1965
91	Southern Miss. vs. Tex.-Pan American	Feb. 9, 1970
91	Houston vs. Rice	Mar. 7, 1974
90	Vanderbilt vs. Sewanee	Dec. 4, 1954

ASSISTS

Ast.	Team vs. Opponent	Date
44	Colorado vs. George Mason (ot)	Dec. 2, 1995
43	TCU vs. Central Okla.	Dec. 12, 1998
41	North Carolina vs. Manhattan	Dec. 27, 1985
41	Weber St. vs. Northern Ariz.	Mar. 2, 1991
40	New Mexico vs. Texas-Arlington	Nov. 23, 1990
40	Loyola Marymount vs. U.S. Int'l	Jan. 5, 1991
40	Southern Utah vs. Texas Wesleyan	Jan. 25, 1992
40	Lamar vs. Prairie View	Feb. 2, 1993
40	TCU vs. North Texas	Dec. 1, 1998
39	Southern Miss. vs. Virginia Tech	Jan. 16, 1988
39	UNLV vs. Pacific (Cal.)	Feb. 8, 1990
39	UNLV vs. Rutgers	Feb. 3, 1991
39	Davidson vs. Warren Wilson	Dec. 9, 1991
39	TCU vs. Midwestern St.	Nov. 30, 1994
39	Arizona St. vs. Delaware St.	Dec. 1, 1997
39	TCU vs. Central Okla.	Dec. 9, 2000
38	New Mexico vs. U.S. Int'l	Dec. 3, 1985
38	Pepperdine vs. U.S. Int'l	Jan. 7, 1986
38	UCLA vs. Loyola Marymount	Dec. 2, 1990
38	Arizona vs. Northern Ariz.	Dec. 18, 1991
38	Tex.-Pan American vs. Concordia Lutheran	Dec. 4, 1993
38	LSU vs. George Mason	Dec. 3, 1994
38	Arizona vs. Morgan St.	Nov. 20, 1997
38	TCU vs. Ark.-Pine Bluff	Dec. 30, 2000
37	15 tied	

BLOCKED SHOTS

Blk.	Team vs. Opponent	Date
21	Georgetown vs. Southern (N.O.)	Dec. 1, 1993
20	Iona vs. Northern Ill.	Jan. 7, 1989
20	Georgia vs. Bethune-Cookman	Dec. 7, 1993
20	Massachusetts vs. West Virginia	Jan. 3, 1995
19	Seton Hall vs. Norfolk St.	Dec. 4, 2000
18	North Carolina vs. Stanford	Dec. 20, 1985
17	Maryland vs. Md.-East. Shore	Feb. 27, 1987
17	Rider vs. Fairleigh Dickinson	Jan. 9, 1989
17	Georgetown vs. Providence	Feb. 22, 1989
17	Georgetown vs. Hawaii-Loa	Nov. 23, 1990
17	Brigham Young vs. Eastern Ky.	Dec. 7, 1990
17	Northwestern St. vs. Ouachita Baptist	Nov. 30, 1991
17	New Orleans vs. Texas A&M	Dec. 29, 1992
17	Massachusetts vs. Hartford	Dec. 28, 1993
17	Louisville vs. Kentucky	Jan. 1, 1995
17	William & Mary vs. George Mason	Feb. 26, 1996
17	Miami (Fla.) vs. Hartford	Dec. 13, 1996
17	Fairleigh Dickinson vs. Hartford	Nov. 11, 1997
17	Kentucky vs. Morehead St.	Nov. 20, 1997
17	Duke vs. Virginia	Jan. 10, 1999
17	La.-Monroe vs. Lamar	Feb. 3, 2000
17	Georgetown vs. Southern-N.O.	Feb. 10, 2000
16	UTEP vs. Fort Lewis	Nov. 26, 1988
16	Maryland vs. Md.-East. Shore	Dec. 1, 1988

Blk.	Team vs. Opponent	Date
16	Oklahoma St. vs. Oklahoma	Feb. 14, 1989
16	Clemson vs. Radford	Dec. 9, 1989
16	Villanova vs. Drexel	Dec. 16, 1989
16	LSU vs. Texas	Jan. 2, 1990
16	UCLA vs. UC Irvine	Nov. 23, 1990
16	Kentucky vs. Georgia	Feb. 3, 1991
16	Rutgers vs. St. Bonaventure	Jan. 16, 1992
16	William & Mary vs. Marymount (Va.)	Nov. 29, 1995
16	Kentucky vs. Morehead St.	Dec. 16, 1995
16	Old Dominion vs. American	Jan 16, 1999
16	La.-Monroe vs. Ark.-Monticello	Dec. 4, 1999
16	TCU vs. Rice	Mar. 3, 2000
16	Seton Hall vs. St. Peter's	Nov. 27, 2000

STEALS

Stl.	Team vs. Opponent	Date
39	Long Island vs. Medgar Evers	Nov. 26, 1997
34	Oklahoma vs. Centenary (La.)	Dec. 12, 1987
34	Northwestern St. vs. LeTourneau	Jan. 20, 1992
33	Connecticut vs. Pittsburgh	Jan. 6, 1990
32	Manhattan vs. Lehman	Dec. 14, 1987
32	Oklahoma vs. Angelo St.	Dec. 1, 1990
32	Long Island vs. Medgar Evers	Nov. 29, 1994
32	La.-Lafayette vs. Baptist Christian	Nov. 25, 1995
30	Southern U. vs. Baptist Christian	Dec. 14, 1992
30	Cal Poly vs. Notre Dame (Cal.)	Nov. 25, 1995
30	TCU vs. Ark.-Pine Bluff	Dec. 30, 2000
29	Cleveland St. vs. Canisius	Dec. 28, 1986
29	Oklahoma vs. U.S. Int'l	Nov. 19, 1989
29	Centenary (La.) vs. East Texas Baptist	Dec. 12, 1992
29	TCU vs. Delaware St.	Dec. 3, 1997
28	Oklahoma vs. Morgan St.	Dec. 21, 1991
28	Memphis vs. Southeastern La.	Jan. 11, 1993
28	Oklahoma vs. Florida A&M	Jan. 27, 1993
27	Oregon St. vs. Hawaii-Loa	Dec. 22, 1985
27	Cal St. Fullerton vs. Lamar	Nov. 24, 1989
27	Texas-San Antonio vs. Samford	Jan. 19, 1991
27	Iowa St. vs. Bethune-Cookman	Dec. 31, 1992
27	San Francisco vs. Delaware St.	Nov. 27, 1993
27	Charleston So. vs. Warner Southern	Dec. 11, 1993
27	Georgetown vs. Southern (N.O.)	Feb. 13, 1999
27	TCU vs. Alabama St.	Nov. 20, 2000

Season Records

VICTORIES

Team	Season	Won	Lost	Pct.
UNLV	†1987	37	2	.949
Duke	†1999	37	2	.949
Duke	†1986	37	3	.925
Kentucky	†1948	36	3	.923
Massachusetts	†1996	35	2	.946
Georgetown	†1985	35	3	.921
Arizona	†1988	35	3	.921
Kansas	1986	35	4	.897
Oklahoma	†1988	35	4	.897
Kansas	†1998	35	4	.897
Kentucky	†1998	35	4	.897
Duke	†2001	35	4	.897
UNLV	1990	35	5	.875
Kentucky	†1997	35	5	.875
UNLV	†1991	34	1	.971
Duke	†1992	34	2	.944
Kentucky	1996	34	2	.944
Kansas	1997	34	2	.944
Connecticut	1999	34	2	.944
Kentucky	†1947	34	3	.919
Georgetown	†1984	34	3	.919
Arkansas	†1991	34	4	.895
North Carolina	†1993	34	4	.895
North Carolina	1998	34	4	.895
Indiana St.	†1979	33	1	.971
Louisville	†1980	33	3	.917
Kansas	†2002	33	4	.892
UNLV	1986	33	5	.868
Michigan St.	1999	33	5	.868

VICTORIES IN FIRST SEASON IN DIVISION I

Team	Season	Won	Lost	Pct.
Seattle	1953	29	4	.879
Md.-East. Shore	1974	27	2	.931

Team	Season	Won	Lost	Pct.
Oral Roberts	1972	26	2	.929
Old Dominion	1977	25	4	.862
Long Beach St.	1970	24	5	.828
La.-Lafayette	1972	23	3	.885
Southern U.	1978	23	5	.821
Hawaii	1971	23	5	.821
Alabama St.	1983	22	6	.786
Alcorn St.	1978	22	7	.759
Stephen F. Austin	1987	22	8	.733
Idaho St.	1959	21	7	.750
McNeese St.	1974	20	5	.800
Memphis	1956	20	7	.741
Loyola (La.)	1952	20	14	.588
Jackson St.	1978	19	5	.792
Northeastern	1973	19	7	.731
Ga. Southern	1974	19	7	.731
Miami (Fla.)	1949	19	8	.704
Col. of Charleston	1992	19	8	.704
Morehead St.	1956	19	10	.655
New Mexico St.	1951	19	14	.576
New Orleans	1976	18	8	.692
Florida A&M	1979	18	9	.667
Alabama A&M	2000	18	10	.643

†national leader

WON-LOST PERCENTAGE

Team	Season	Won	Lost	Pct.
North Carolina	†1957	32	0	1.000
Indiana	†1976	32	0	1.000
UCLA	†1964	30	0	1.000
UCLA	†1967	30	0	1.000
UCLA	†1972	30	0	1.000
UCLA	†1973	30	0	1.000
San Francisco	†1956	29	0	1.000
North Carolina St.	1973	27	0	1.000
Kentucky	†1954	25	0	1.000
Long Island	†1939	24	0	1.000
Seton Hall	†1940	19	0	1.000
Army	†1944	15	0	1.000
UNLV	†1991	34	1	.971
Indiana St.	†1979	33	1	.971
Indiana	†1975	31	1	.969
North Carolina St.	†1974	30	1	.968
UCLA	†1968	29	1	.967
UCLA	†1969	29	1	.967
UCLA	†1971	29	1	.967
San Francisco	†1955	28	1	.966
UTEP	†1966	28	1	.966
Marquette	1971	28	1	.966
Pennsylvania	1971	28	1	.966
Alcorn St.	1979	28	1	.966
Ohio St.	†1961	27	1	.964

†national leader

WON-LOST PERCENTAGE IN FIRST SEASON IN DIVISION I

Team	Season	Won	Lost	Pct.
Md.-East. Shore	1974	27	2	.931
Oral Roberts	1972	26	2	.929
Seattle#	1953	29	4	.879
La.-Lafayette#	1972	25	4	.862
Old Dominion	1977	25	4	.862
Long Beach St.#	1970	24	5	.828
Southern U.	1978	23	5	.821
Hawaii	1971	23	5	.821
McNeese St.	1974	20	5	.800
Jackson St.	1978	19	5	.792
Alabama St.	1983	22	6	.786
Alcorn St.	1978	22	7	.759
Idaho St.#	1959	21	7	.750
Memphis#	1956	20	7	.741
Air Force	1958	17	6	.739
Stephen F. Austin	1987	22	8	.733
Northeastern	1973	19	7	.731
Ga. Southern	1974	19	7	.731
Va. Commonwealth	1974	17	7	.708
Miami (Fla.)	1949	19	8	.704
Col. of Charleston	1992	19	8	.704
New Orleans	1976	18	8	.692
Weber St.	1964	17	8	.680
George Mason	1979	17	8	.680
Florida A&M	1979	18	9	.667
Mercer	1974	16	8	.667
Tennessee Tech	1956	14	7	.667

Team	Season	Won	Lost	Pct.
American	1967	16	8	.667
Fairfield	1965	14	7	.667

#appeared in NCAA tournament

MOST-IMPROVED TEAMS
(Since 1974)

Team	Season	W-L Record	Previous Yr. W-L	Games Up
Mercer	†2003	23-6	6-23	17
N.C. A&T	†1978	20-8	3-24	16½
Murray St.	†1980	23-8	4-22	16½
Liberty	†1992	22-7	5-23	16½
North Texas	†1976	22-4	6-20	16
Ohio State	†1999	27-9	8-22	16
Tulsa	†1981	26-7	8-19	15
Utah St.	†1983	20-9	4-23	15
Radford	†1991	22-7	7-22	15
Boston College	†2001	27-5	11-19	15
Western Mich.	1992	21-9	5-22	14½
Tennessee St.	†1993	19-10	4-24	14½
Central Mich.	2001	20-8	6-23	14½
Fresno St.	1978	21-6	7-20	14
James Madison	†1987	20-10	5-23	14
Loyola Marymount	†1988	28-4	12-16	14
Cal Poly	†1996	16-13	1-26	14
Northern Ariz.	†1997	21-7	6-20	14
McNeese St.	2001	22-9	6-21	14
Central Mich.	2003	25-7	9-19	14
Michigan St.	1978	25-5	10-17	13½
Loyola (Md.)	†1994	17-13	2-25	13½
Texas-San Antonio	†1998	16-11	3-25	13½
Iowa St.	†2000	32-5	15-15	13½
Ark.-Little Rock	2001	18-11	4-24	13½

†national leader

POINTS

Team	Season	G	Pts.
Oklahoma	†1988	39	4,012
Loyola Marymount	†1990	32	3,918
Arkansas	†1991	38	3,783
UNLV	1990	40	3,739
Oklahoma	†1989	36	3,680
UNLV	†1987	39	3,612
Duke	†1999	39	3,581
Duke	†2001	39	3,538
Loyola Marymount	1988	32	3,528
Loyola Marymount	1989	31	3,486
Houston	†1977	37	3,482
UNLV	†1976	31	3,426
UNLV	1977	32	3,426
Duke	1991	39	3,421
UNLV	1991	35	3,420
Arkansas	†1995	39	3,416
Syracuse	1989	38	3,410
Michigan	1989	37	3,393
Duke	1990	38	3,386
Kansas	†2002	37	3,365
Oklahoma	1991	35	3,363
Arkansas	1990	35	3,345
North Carolina	1989	37	3,331
Oklahoma	†1985	37	3,328
Kentucky	†1997	40	3,325

†national leader

SCORING OFFENSE

Team	Season	G	Pts.	Avg.
Loyola Marymount	†1990	32	3,918	122.4
Loyola Marymount	†1989	31	3,486	112.5
UNLV	†1976	31	3,426	110.5
Loyola Marymount	†1988	32	3,528	110.3
UNLV	†1977	32	3,426	107.1
Oral Roberts	†1972	28	2,943	105.1
Southern U.	†1991	28	2,924	104.4
Loyola Marymount	1991	31	3,211	103.6
Oklahoma	1988	39	4,012	102.9
Oklahoma	1989	36	3,680	102.2
Oklahoma	1990	32	3,243	101.3
Southern U.	†1994	27	2,727	101.0
Jacksonville	†1970	28	2,809	100.3
Jacksonville	1971	26	2,598	99.9
Arkansas	1991	38	3,783	99.6
Southern U.	1990	31	3,078	99.3
Syracuse	†1966	28	2,773	99.0
Iowa	1970	25	2,467	98.7

Team	Season	G	Pts.	Avg.
Miami (Fla.)	†1965	26	2,558	98.4
Houston	1966	29	2,845	98.1
La.-Lafayette	1972	29	2,840	97.9
U.S. Int'l	1990	28	2,738	97.8
Houston	†1968	33	3,226	97.8
UNLV	1991	35	3,420	97.7
Md.-East. Shore	†1974	29	2,831	97.6
Troy St.	1994	27	2,634	97.6
Oklahoma City	1966	29	2,829	97.6

†national leader

SCORING DEFENSE

Team	Season	G	Pts.	Avg.
Oklahoma St.	†1948	31	1,006	32.5
Oklahoma St.	†1949	28	985	35.2
Oklahoma St.	†1950	27	1,059	39.2
Alabama	1948	27	1,070	39.6
Creighton	1948	23	925	40.2
Wyoming	1948	27	1,101	40.8
Wyoming	1950	36	1,491	41.4
Siena	1948	28	1,161	41.5
St. Bonaventure	1948	22	921	41.9
Siena	1949	29	1,215	41.9
Tulane	1948	26	1,102	42.4
Wyoming	1949	35	1,509	43.1
Texas	1948	25	1,079	43.2
Utah	1948	20	868	43.4
Minnesota	1949	21	912	43.4
Washington (Mo.)	1948	21	915	43.6
St. Bonaventure	1949	26	1,137	43.7
St. Louis	1948	27	1,183	43.8
Kentucky	1949	34	1,492	43.9
Washington St.	1949	30	1,317	43.9
Texas A&M	†1951	29	1,275	44.0
Kentucky	1948	39	1,730	44.4
Baylor	1949	24	1,068	44.5
Tulsa	1950	23	1,027	44.7
Hamline	1948	31	1,389	44.8

†national leader

(Since 1965)

Team	Season	G	Pts.	Avg.
Fresno St.	†1982	30	1,412	47.1
Princeton	†1992	28	1,349	48.2
Princeton	†1991	27	1,320	48.9
North Carolina St.	1982	32	1,570	49.1
Princeton	1982	26	1,277	49.1
Princeton	†1984	28	1,403	50.1
St. Peter's	†1980	31	1,563	50.4
Fresno St.	†1981	29	1,470	50.7
Princeton	†1990	27	1,378	51.0
Princeton	1981	28	1,438	51.4
Princeton	†1998	29	1,491	51.4
St. Peter's	1981	26	1,338	51.5
Wyoming	1982	30	1,545	51.5
Princeton	†1977	26	1,343	51.7
Princeton	†1996	29	1,498	51.7
Princeton	†1983	29	1,507	52.0
James Madison	1982	30	1,559	52.0
Fresno St.	†1978	27	1,417	52.5
Princeton	†1999	30	1,581	52.7
Princeton	†1976	27	1,427	52.9
Columbia	1982	26	1,375	52.9
Princeton	†1989	27	1,430	53.0
Fresno St.	†1985	32	1,696	53.0
Princeton	†1997	28	1,496	53.4
UTEP	1982	28	1,497	53.5
Georgetown	1982	37	1,979	53.5
Army	†1969	28	1,498	53.5

†national leader

SCORING MARGIN

Team	Season	Off.	Def.	Mar.
UCLA	†1972	94.6	64.3	30.3
North Carolina St.	†1948	75.3	47.2	28.1
Kentucky	†1954	87.5	60.3	27.2
Kentucky	†1952	82.3	55.4	26.9
UNLV	†1991	97.7	71.0	26.7
UCLA	†1968	93.4	67.2	26.2
UCLA	†1967	89.6	63.7	25.9
Houston	1968	97.8	72.5	25.3
Duke	†1999	91.8	67.2	24.7
Kentucky	1948	69.0	44.4	24.6
Kentucky	†1949	68.2	43.9	24.3

Team	Season	Off.	Def.	Mar.
Bowling Green	1948	70.5	46.7	23.8
Loyola (Ill.)	†1963	91.8	68.1	23.7
Charlotte	†1975	88.9	65.2	23.7
Arizona St.	†1962	90.1	67.6	22.5
St. Bonaventure	†1970	88.4	65.9	22.5
Kentucky	†1951	74.7	52.5	22.2
Indiana	1975	88.0	65.9	22.1
Kentucky	†1996	91.4	69.4	22.1
Cincinnati	†1960	86.7	64.7	22.0
Oklahoma	†1988	102.9	81.0	21.9
North Carolina St.	†1973	92.9	71.1	21.8
Jacksonville	1970	100.3	78.5	21.8
UNLV	†1976	110.5	89.0	21.5
Duke	†1998	85.6	64.1	21.5

†national leader

FIELD-GOAL PERCENTAGE

Team	Season	FG	FGA	Pct.
Missouri	†1980	936	1,635	57.2
Michigan	†1989	1,325	2,341	56.6
Oregon St.	†1981	862	1,528	56.4
UC Irvine	†1982	920	1,639	56.1
Michigan St.	†1986	1,043	1,860	56.1
North Carolina	1986	1,197	2,140	55.9
Kansas	1986	1,260	2,266	55.6
Kentucky	†1983	869	1,564	55.6
Notre Dame	1981	824	1,492	55.2
Houston Baptist	†1984	797	1,445	55.2
Maryland	1980	985	1,789	55.1
Idaho	1981	816	1,484	55.0
UC Irvine	1981	934	1,703	54.8
Navy	†1985	946	1,726	54.8
Stanford	1983	752	1,373	54.8
Maryland	†1975	1,049	1,918	54.7
New Orleans	1983	937	1,714	54.7
Georgia Tech	1986	1,008	1,846	54.6
Arkansas	†1978	1,060	1,943	54.6
Michigan	†1988	1,198	2,196	54.6
New Mexico	1989	992	1,819	54.5
Southern U.	1978	1,107	2,031	54.5
Arkansas	†1977	849	1,558	54.5
Arizona	1988	1,147	2,106	54.5
Pepperdine	1983	900	1,653	54.4
Oregon St.	1980	943	1,732	54.4
Ohio St.	†1970	831	1,527	54.4
UNC Wilmington	1977	816	1,500	54.4
Davidson	†1964	894	1,644	54.4

†national leader

FIELD-GOAL PERCENTAGE DEFENSE
(Since 1978)

Team	Season	FG	FGA	Pct.
Stanford	†2000	667	1,893	35.2
Marquette	†1994	750	2,097	35.8
Marquette	†1997	628	1,735	36.2
Temple	2000	633	1,747	36.2
Wake Forest	1997	667	1,832	36.4
UNLV	†1992	628	1,723	36.5
Wis.-Green Bay	1997	499	1,368	36.5
Georgetown	†1991	680	1,847	36.8
Temple	†1994	621	1,686	36.8
Princeton	2000	577	1,558	37.0
Kansas St.	†1999	729	1,963	37.1
St. Joseph's	†2003	609	1,639	37.2
Detroit	1999	590	1,583	37.2
Northwestern	1999	577	1,548	37.3
Texas St.	1999	597	1,601	37.3
Wis.-Green Bay	1994	664	1,777	37.4
Va. Commonwealth	†2002	767	2,052	37.4
Cincinnati	2002	761	2,035	37.4
Alabama	†1995	771	2,048	37.6
Col. of Charleston	2002	663	1,762	37.6
Old Dominion	1999	797	2,116	37.7
Illinois	2003	657	1,741	37.7
Maryland	2003	704	1,864	37.8
Wisconsin	1997	502	1,329	37.8
Kansas	1995	768	2,032	37.8
Ohio St.	2000	654	1,730	37.8
Kansas	†2001	782	2,069	37.8

†national leader

THREE-POINT FIELD GOALS MADE

Team	Season	G	3FG
Duke	†2001	39	407
Arkansas	†1995	39	361
Kentucky	†1993	34	340
Missouri	†2002	36	326
Kentucky	†1992	36	317
St. Bonaventure	2002	30	314
Samford	†2000	32	313
Troy St.	†2003	32	312
Long Island	†1998	32	310
Ball St.	2002	35	310
UNLV	†1987	39	309
Mississippi Val.	†1997	29	309
Col. of Charleston	2003	33	308
Charlotte	2001	33	305
Oregon	2002	35	304
East Tenn. St.	†1991	33	301
Arkansas	†1994	34	301
Kentucky	1994	34	301
Long Island	1997	30	301
New Mexico	1998	32	301
Duke	2002	35	301
New Mexico	1994	31	300
Troy St.	†1996	27	300
Mississippi Val.	2003	29	299
Loyola Marymount	†1990	32	298
Temple	2002	34	298

†national leader

THREE-POINT FIELD GOALS MADE PER GAME

Team	Season	G	3FG	Avg.
Troy St.	†1996	27	300	11.11
Mississippi Val.	†1997	29	309	10.66
Troy St.	†1995	27	287	10.63
St. Bonaventure	†2002	30	314	10.47
Duke	†2001	39	407	10.44
Samford	1995	27	279	10.33
Mississippi Val.	†2003	29	299	10.31
Belmont	2001	28	288	10.29
Marshall	1996	28	284	10.14
Lamar	†1993	27	271	10.04
St. Bonaventure	2003	27	271	10.04
Kentucky	†1990	28	281	10.04
Long Island	1997	30	301	10.03
Kentucky	1993	34	340	10.00
Tennessee Tech	†2000	28	279	9.96
Davidson	2003	27	269	9.96
Vermont	1995	27	268	9.93
Florida	†1998	29	285	9.83
Samford	2001	29	284	9.79
Samford	2000	32	313	9.78
Belmont	2000	28	273	9.75
Troy St.	2003	32	312	9.75
Dartmouth	2002	27	263	9.74
Troy St.	†1994	27	262	9.70
Long Island	1998	32	310	9.69

†national leader

THREE-POINT FIELD-GOAL PERCENTAGE
(Minimum 100 three-point field goals made)

Team	Season	G	3FG	3FGA	Pct.
Indiana	†1987	34	130	256	50.8
Mississippi Val.	1987	28	161	322	50.0
Stephen F. Austin	1987	30	120	241	49.8
Princeton	†1988	26	211	429	49.2
Prairie View	1988	27	129	266	48.5
Kansas St.	1988	34	179	370	48.4
Arizona	1988	38	254	526	48.3
Indiana	†1989	35	121	256	47.3
Bucknell	1988	28	154	328	47.0
Holy Cross	1988	29	158	337	46.9
Michigan	1989	37	196	419	46.8
Wis.-Green Bay	†1992	30	204	437	46.7
Citadel	1989	28	153	328	46.6
Niagara	1987	31	128	275	46.5
Eastern Mich.	1987	29	144	310	46.5
Wis.-Green Bay	†1991	31	189	407	46.4
Colorado St.	1989	33	141	305	46.2
Bucknell	1989	31	160	347	46.1
Illinois	1987	31	112	243	46.1
Illinois St.	1987	32	110	240	45.8
Jacksonville	1987	30	188	412	45.6
Rider	1987	28	151	331	45.6
Davidson	1987	30	138	303	45.5
New Mexico St.	1988	32	143	314	45.5
Gonzaga	1989	28	119	262	45.4
Indiana	†1994	30	182	401	45.4

†national leader

FREE-THROW PERCENTAGE

Team	Season	FT	FTA	Pct.
Harvard	†1984	535	651	82.2
Brigham Young	†1989	527	647	81.5
Harvard	†1985	450	555	81.1
Ohio St.	†1970	452	559	80.9
Siena	†1998	574	715	80.3
Vanderbilt	†1974	477	595	80.2
Michigan St.	†1986	490	613	79.9
Butler	†1988	413	517	79.9
Miami (Fla.)	†1965	642	807	79.6
Tulane	†1963	390	492	79.3
Tennessee	†1971	538	679	79.2
Auburn	†1966	476	601	79.2
Oklahoma St.	†1958	488	617	79.1
Duke	†1978	665	841	79.1
Utah	†1993	476	602	79.1
Gonzaga	1989	485	614	79.0
Western Ky.	†1997	342	433	79.0
Montana St.	†2000	481	609	79.0
Oral Roberts	†1980	481	610	78.9
Marshall	1958	479	608	78.8
Bucknell	1989	590	749	78.8
Manhattan	†2003	560	711	78.8
Alabama	†1987	521	662	78.7
Siena	†1999	672	854	78.7
Butler	†1991	725	922	78.6
Western Ill.	†1982	447	569	78.6

†national leader

REBOUNDS

Team	Season	G	Reb.
Kentucky	†1951	34	2,109
North Carolina St.	1951	37	2,091
Houston	†1968	33	2,074
Columbia	†1957	24	2,016
Fordham	†1953	27	1,879
North Carolina St.	†1955	32	1,864
Houston	†1967	31	1,862
Fordham	†1952	29	1,859
Kentucky	1952	32	1,817
West Virginia	†1959	34	1,810
Western Ky.	†1954	32	1,810
Creighton	†1964	29	1,803
North Carolina St.	1952	34	1,782
Dayton	1955	29	1,738
North Carolina St.	1954	35	1,735
Notre Dame	†1965	27	1,722
Dayton	†1956	29	1,713
New Mexico St.	1970	31	1,713
Seton Hall	1953	33	1,706
La Salle	1955	31	1,697
LSU	†1970	32	1,691
Middle Tenn.	†1969	26	1,685
Kansas	†1998	39	1,682
Kentucky	1955	26	1,680
St. John's (N.Y.)	1952	31	1,678

†national leader

REBOUND MARGIN
(Since 1973)

Team	Season	Off.	Def.	Mar.
Manhattan	†1973	56.5	38.0	18.5
American	1973	56.7	40.3	16.4
Alcorn St.	†1978	52.3	36.0	16.3
Oral Roberts	1973	66.9	50.3	15.6
Alcorn St.	†1980	49.2	33.8	15.4
Michigan St.	†2001	42.5	27.1	15.4
UCLA	1973	49.0	33.9	15.1
Houston	1973	54.7	40.8	13.9
Massachusetts	†1974	44.5	30.7	13.8
Alcorn St.	†1979	50.1	36.3	13.8
Minnesota	1973	49.0	36.0	13.0
Va. Commonwealth	1974	55.1	42.1	13.0
Northeastern	†1981	44.9	32.0	12.9
Stetson	†1975	47.1	34.7	12.4

Wake Forest's Vytas Danelius, the ACC's top returning rebounder, helped the Demon Deacons lead the country in rebounding.

Team	Season	Off.	Def.	Mar.
Notre Dame	†1976	46.3	34.1	12.2
Harvard	1973	53.5	41.3	12.2
Tennessee St.	1980	46.5	34.3	12.2
Tennessee St.	1979	49.7	37.9	11.8
Buffalo	1976	51.5	39.7	11.8
Southern U.	1978	43.1	31.4	11.7
Wyoming	1981	42.0	30.3	11.7
Michigan St.	†2000	39.0	27.3	11.7
Alabama	1973	50.9	39.3	11.6
Mississippi Val.	†1996	48.3	36.8	11.6
Iowa	†1987	43.1	31.5	11.5

†national leader

ASSISTS

Team	Season	G	Ast.
UNLV	†1990	40	926
UNLV	†1991	35	863
Oklahoma	†1988	39	862
UNLV	†1987	39	853
Oklahoma	†1985	37	828
Arkansas	1991	38	819
Kansas	†1986	39	814
North Carolina	1986	34	800
North Carolina	†1989	37	788
Southern Methodist	1988	35	786
Kentucky	†1996	36	783
North Carolina	1987	36	782
Kentucky	†1997	40	776
Kansas	†2002	37	767
Loyola Marymount	1990	32	763
Kansas	1990	35	762
Kansas	†1998	39	746
Oklahoma	1989	36	743
Arkansas	†1995	39	721
Maryland	2002	36	714
Duke	†2001	39	701
North Carolina	1991	35	699
North Carolina	1998	38	699
North Carolina	†1993	38	698
Maryland	2001	36	692

†national leader

ASSISTS PER GAME

Team	Season	G	Ast.	Avg.
UNLV	†1991	35	863	24.7
Loyola Marymount	†1990	32	762	23.8
North Carolina	†1986	34	800	23.5
UNLV	1990	40	926	23.2
Southern Methodist	†1987	29	655	22.6
Southern Methodist	†1988	35	786	22.5
Oklahoma	†1985	37	828	22.4
Oklahoma	1988	39	862	22.1
Northwestern St.	†1993	26	570	21.9
UNLV	1987	39	853	21.9
Kansas	1990	35	763	21.8

Team	Season	G	Ast.	Avg.
Kentucky	†1996	36	783	21.8
North Carolina	1987	36	782	21.7
Iowa St.	1988	32	694	21.7
Arkansas	1991	38	819	21.6
North Carolina	†1989	37	788	21.3
Georgia Tech	1988	32	680	21.3
Montana St.	1996	30	627	20.9
Montana St.	†1995	29	606	20.9
Montana St.	†1998	30	624	20.8
Kansas	†2002	37	767	20.7
TCU	†1999	32	650	20.3
Arkansas	†1994	34	687	20.2
Fresno St.	1998	34	685	20.2
Montana St.	1999	29	583	20.1
UNLV	†2000	31	623	20.1

†national leader

BLOCKED SHOTS

Team	Season	G	Blk.
Georgetown	†1989	34	309
Massachusetts	†1995	34	273
UNLV	†1991	35	266
Connecticut	†2003	33	253
Old Dominion	†1999	34	248
Syracuse	2003	35	247
Brigham Young	1991	34	246
Duke	1999	39	245
Kentucky	†1998	39	240
Seton Hall	†2001	31	236
Connecticut	†2002	34	236
Clemson	†1990	35	235
Georgetown	1991	32	235
Central Conn. St.	†1996	28	235
Maryland	†2000	35	235
Navy	†1986	35	233
Georgetown	1990	31	233
Old Dominion	†1997	33	233
Massachusetts	1996	37	232
Arkansas	1991	38	229
Syracuse	1999	33	229
Georgetown	2000	34	226
LSU	1990	32	225
Alabama	†1992	35	223
Cincinnati	2000	33	223

†national leader

BLOCKED SHOTS PER GAME

Team	Season	G	Blk.	Avg.
Georgetown	†1989	34	309	9.09
Central Conn. St.	†1996	28	235	8.39
Massachusetts	†1995	34	273	8.03
Colgate	†1997	28	217	7.75
Connecticut	†2003	33	253	7.67
Seton Hall	†2001	31	236	7.61
UNLV	†1991	35	266	7.60
Georgetown	†1990	31	233	7.52
Central Conn. St.	1995	26	194	7.46
La.-Monroe	†2000	28	207	7.39
Georgetown	1991	32	235	7.34
Florida A&M	1996	27	198	7.33
Iona	†1999	30	220	7.33
Old Dominion	1999	34	248	7.29
Brigham Young	1991	34	246	7.24
Old Dominion	1997	33	233	7.06
Syracuse	2003	35	247	7.06
LSU	1990	32	225	7.03
Iona	2000	31	216	6.97
Syracuse	1999	33	229	6.94
Connecticut	†2002	34	236	6.94
Rutgers	2002	31	215	6.94
Mississippi Val.	1999	27	187	6.93
Fairfield	2002	29	199	6.86
Vermont	†1992	29	198	6.83
Navy	2000	29	198	6.83

†national leader

STEALS

Team	Season	G	Stl.
Oklahoma	†1988	39	486
Connecticut	†1990	37	484
Kentucky	†1997	40	480
Long Island	†1998	32	478
Cleveland St.	†1987	33	473

Team	Season	G	Stl.
Arkansas	†1991	38	467
Texas	†1994	34	453
Loyola Marymount	1990	32	450
Arkansas	†1995	39	445
Cleveland St.	†1986	33	436
Kentucky	†1996	36	435
Tulsa	†2000	37	433
Georgetown	1996	37	431
Maryland	†1999	34	431
Texas-San Antonio	1991	29	430
Duke	†2001	39	411
West Virginia	1998	33	407
Oklahoma	†1993	32	405
UNLV	1991	35	399
Long Island	1997	30	396
Florida A&M	1988	30	395
Alabama A&M	†2002	27	395
Kentucky	1994	34	394
Syracuse	2002	36	394
UAB	†2003	34	394

†national leader

STEALS PER GAME

Team	Season	G	Stl.	Avg.
Long Island	†1998	32	478	14.94
Texas-San Antonio	†1991	29	430	14.83
Cleveland St.	†1987	33	473	14.33
Centenary (La.)	†1993	27	380	14.07
Loyola Marymount	†1990	32	450	14.06
Alabama A&M	†2002	27	395	13.62
Liberty	†2000	28	376	13.43
Texas	†1994	34	453	13.32
Cleveland St.	†1986	33	436	13.21
Long Island	†1997	30	396	13.20
Florida A&M	†1988	30	395	13.17
Connecticut	1990	37	484	13.08
Alabama A&M	2000	28	366	13.07
Charlotte	1991	28	363	12.96
Northeastern Ill.	†1992	28	358	12.79
Maryland	†1999	34	431	12.68
Oklahoma	1993	32	405	12.66
Southern U.	1991	28	352	12.57
Cleveland St.	1988	30	376	12.53
Nicholls St.	†1995	30	376	12.53
Tulane	1992	31	388	12.52
Southern U.	1993	31	387	12.48
Drake	1994	27	337	12.48
West Virginia	1998	33	407	12.33
McNeese St.	†1996	27	330	12.22

†national leader

MOST GAMES PLAYED
(Since 1947-48)

Team	Season	W	L	G
Duke	†1986	37	3	40
UNLV	†1990	35	5	40
Kentucky	†1997	35	5	40
Kentucky	†1948	36	3	39
Kansas	†1986	35	4	39
Louisville	†1986	32	7	39
UNLV	†1987	37	2	39
LSU	†1987	24	15	39
Oklahoma	†1988	35	4	39
Duke	†1991	32	7	39
Arkansas	†1995	32	7	39
Kansas	†1998	35	4	39
Kentucky	†1998	35	4	39
Duke	†1999	37	2	39
Michigan St.	†2000	32	7	39
Duke	†2001	35	4	39
Georgetown	†1985	35	3	38
UNLV	1986	33	5	38
LSU	1986	26	12	38
Syracuse	1987	31	7	38
Western Ky.	1987	29	9	38
Kansas	1988	27	11	38
Arizona	1988	35	3	38
Seton Hall	†1989	31	7	38
Syracuse	†1989	30	8	38
Duke	1990	29	9	38
Arkansas	1991	34	4	38
North Carolina	†1993	34	4	38
Syracuse	†1996	29	9	38

Team	Season	W	L	G
North Carolina	1998	34	4	38
Michigan St.	1999	33	5	38
Kansas	†2003	30	8	38

†national leader

Annual Team Champions

Won-Lost Percentage

Season	Team	Won	Lost	Pct.
1948	Western Ky.	28	2	.933
1949	Kentucky	32	2	.941
1950	Holy Cross	27	4	.871
1951	Columbia	21	1	.956
1952	Kansas	26	2	.929
1953	Seton Hall	31	2	.939
1954	Kentucky	25	0	1.000
1955	San Francisco	28	1	.966
1956	San Francisco	29	0	1.000
1957	North Carolina	32	0	1.000
1958	West Virginia	26	2	.929
1959	Mississippi St.	24	1	.960
1960	California	28	2	.933
	Cincinnati	28	2	.933
1961	Ohio St.	27	1	.964
1962	Mississippi St.	24	1	.960
1963	Loyola (Ill.)	29	2	.935
1964	UCLA	30	0	1.000
1965	UCLA	28	2	.933
1966	UTEP	28	1	.966
1967	UCLA	30	0	1.000
1968	UCLA	29	1	.967
1969	UCLA	29	1	.967
1970	UCLA	28	2	.933
1971	UCLA	29	1	.967
1972	UCLA	30	0	1.000
1973	UCLA	30	0	1.000
	North Carolina St.	27	0	1.000
1974	North Carolina St.	30	1	.968
1975	Indiana	31	1	.969
1976	Indiana	32	0	1.000
1977	San Francisco	29	2	.935
1978	Kentucky	30	2	.938
1979	Indiana St.	33	1	.971
1980	Alcorn St.	28	2	.933
1981	DePaul	27	2	.931
1982	North Carolina	32	2	.941
1983	Houston	31	3	.912
1984	Georgetown	34	3	.919
1985	Georgetown	35	3	.921
1986	Duke	37	3	.925
1987	UNLV	37	2	.949
1988	Temple	32	2	.941
1989	Ball St.	29	3	.906
1990	La Salle	30	2	.938
1991	UNLV	34	1	.971
1992	Duke	34	2	.944
1993	North Carolina	34	4	.895
1994	Arkansas	31	3	.912
1995	UCLA	31	2	.939
1996	Massachusetts	35	2	.946
1997	Kansas	34	2	.944
1998	Princeton	27	2	.931
1999	Duke	37	2	.949
2000	Cincinnnati	29	4	.879
2001	Stanford	31	3	.912
2002	Kansas	33	4	.892
2003	Kentucky	32	4	.889

Most-Improved Teams

Season	Team	W-L Record	Previous Yr. W-L	Games Up
1974	Kansas	23-7	8-18	13
1975	Holy Cross	20-8	8-18	11
1976	North Texas	22-4	6-20	16

Photo by Rich Clarkson/NCAA Photos

Arizona's Jason Gardner helped the Wildcats lead the country in points per game in 2002-03.

Season	Team	W-L Record	Previous Yr. W-L	Games Up
1977	La.-Lafayette	21-8	7-19	12½
1978	N.C. A&T	20-8	3-24	16½
1979	Wagner	21-7	7-19	13
1980	Murray St.	23-8	4-22	16½
1981	Tulsa	26-7	8-19	15
1982	Cal St. Fullerton	18-14	4-23	11½
1983	Utah St.	20-9	4-23	15
1984	Northeastern	27-5	13-15	12
	Loyola (Md.)	16-12	4-24	12
1985	Cincinnati	17-14	3-25	12½
1986	Bradley	32-3	17-13	12½
1987	James Madison	20-10	5-23	14
1988	Loyola Marymount	28-4	12-16	14
1989	Ball St.	29-3	14-14	13
1990	South Fla.	20-11	7-21	11½
	George Washington	14-17	1-27	11½
1991	Radford	22-7	7-22	15
1992	Liberty	22-7	5-23	16½
1993	Tennessee St.	19-10	4-24	14½
1994	Loyola (Md.)	17-13	2-25	13½
1995	Western Ill.	20-8	7-20	12½
1996	Cal Poly	16-13	1-26	14
1997	Northern Ariz.	21-7	6-20	14
1998	Texas-San Antonio	16-11	3-25	13½
1999	Ohio St.	27-9	8-22	16
2000	Iowa St.	32-5	15-15	13½
2001	Boston College	27-5	11-19	15
2002	Fla. Atlantic	19-12	7-24	12
	Texas Tech	23-9	9-19	12
2003	Mercer	23-6	6-23	17

Scoring Offense

Season	Team	G	W-L	Pts.	Avg.
1948	Rhode Island	23	17-6	1,755	76.3
1949	Rhode Island	22	16-6	1,575	71.6
1950	Villanova	29	25-4	2,111	72.8
1951	Cincinnati	22	18-4	1,694	77.0
1952	Kentucky	32	29-3	2,635	82.3
1953	Furman	27	21-6	2,435	90.2
1954	Furman	29	20-9	2,658	91.7
1955	Furman	27	17-10	2,572	95.3
1956	Morehead St.	29	19-10	2,782	95.9
1957	Connecticut	25	17-8	2,183	87.3
1958	Marshall	24	17-7	2,113	88.0
1959	Miami (Fla.)	25	18-7	2,190	87.6
1960	Ohio St.	28	25-3	2,532	90.4
1961	St. Bonaventure	28	24-4	2,479	88.5
1962	Loyola (Ill.)	27	23-4	2,436	90.2
1963	Loyola (Ill.)	31	29-2	2,847	91.8
1964	Detroit	25	14-11	2,402	96.1
1965	Miami (Fla.)	26	22-4	2,558	98.4
1966	Syracuse	28	22-6	2,773	99.0
1967	Oklahoma City	26	16-10	2,496	96.0
1968	Houston	33	31-2	3,226	97.8
1969	Purdue	28	23-5	2,605	93.0
1970	Jacksonville	28	26-2	2,809	100.3
1971	Jacksonville	26	22-4	2,598	99.9
1972	Oral Roberts	28	26-2	2,943	105.1
1973	Oral Roberts	27	21-6	2,626	97.3
1974	Md.-East. Shore	29	27-2	2,831	97.6
1975	South Ala.	26	19-7	2,412	92.8
1976	UNLV	31	29-2	3,426	110.5
1977	UNLV	32	29-3	3,426	107.1
1978	New Mexico	28	24-4	2,731	97.5
1979	UNLV	29	21-9	2,700	93.1
1980	Alcorn St.	30	28-2	2,729	92.0
1981	UC Irvine	27	17-10	2,332	86.4
1982	Long Island	30	20-10	2,605	86.8
1983	Boston College	32	25-7	2,697	84.3
1984	Tulsa	31	27-4	2,816	90.8
1985	Oklahoma	37	31-6	3,328	89.9
1986	U.S. Int'l	28	8-20	2,542	90.8
1987	UNLV	39	37-2	3,612	92.6
1988	Loyola Marymount	32	28-4	3,528	110.3
1989	Loyola Marymount	31	20-11	3,486	112.5
1990	Loyola Marymount	32	26-6	3,918	*122.4
1991	Southern U.	28	19-9	2,924	104.4
1992	Northwestern St.	28	15-13	2,660	95.0
1993	Southern U.	31	21-10	3,011	97.1
1994	Southern U.	27	16-11	2,727	101.0
1995	TCU	27	16-11	2,529	93.7
1996	Troy St.	27	11-16	2,551	94.5
1997	Long Island	30	21-9	2,746	91.5
1998	TCU	33	27-6	3,209	97.2
1999	Duke	39	37-2	3,581	91.8
2000	Duke	34	29-5	2,992	88.0
2001	TCU	31	20-11	2,902	93.6
2002	Kansas	37	33-4	3,365	90.9
2003	Arizona	32	28-4	2,725	85.2

*record

Scoring Defense

Season	Team	G	W-L	Pts.	Avg.
1948	Oklahoma St.	31	27-4	1,006	*32.5
1949	Oklahoma St.	28	23-5	985	35.2
1950	Oklahoma St.	27	18-9	1,059	39.2
1951	Texas A&M	29	17-12	1,275	44.0
1952	Oklahoma St.	27	19-8	1,228	45.5
1953	Oklahoma St.	30	23-7	1,614	53.8
1954	Oklahoma St.	29	24-5	1,539	53.1
1955	San Francisco	29	28-1	1,511	52.1
1956	San Francisco	29	29-0	1,514	52.2
1957	Oklahoma St.	26	17-9	1,420	54.6
1958	San Francisco	27	25-2	1,363	50.5
1959	California	29	25-4	1,480	51.0
1960	California	30	28-2	1,486	49.5
1961	Santa Clara	27	18-9	1,314	48.7
1962	Santa Clara	25	19-6	1,302	52.1
1963	Cincinnati	28	26-2	1,480	52.9
1964	San Jose St.	24	14-10	1,307	54.5
1965	Tennessee	25	20-5	1,391	55.6
1966	Oregon St.	28	21-7	1,527	54.5
1967	Tennessee	28	21-7	1,511	54.0
1968	Army	25	20-5	1,448	57.9
1969	Army	28	18-10	1,498	53.5
1970	Army	28	22-6	1,515	54.1
1971	Fairleigh Dickinson	23	16-7	1,236	53.7
1972	Minnesota	25	18-7	1,451	58.0
1973	UTEP	26	16-10	1,460	56.2
1974	UTEP	25	18-7	1,413	56.5
1975	UTEP	26	20-6	1,491	57.3
1976	Princeton	27	22-5	1,427	52.9
1977	Princeton	26	21-5	1,343	51.7
1978	Fresno St.	27	21-6	1,417	52.5
1979	Princeton	26	14-12	1,452	55.8
1980	St. Peter's	31	22-9	1,563	50.4
1981	Fresno St.	29	25-4	1,470	50.7
1982	Fresno St.	30	27-3	1,412	47.1
1983	Princeton	29	20-9	1,507	52.0
1984	Princeton	28	18-10	1,403	50.1
1985	Fresno St.	32	23-9	1,696	53.0

Season	Team	G	W-L	Pts.	Avg.
1986	Princeton	26	13-13	1,429	55.0
1987	Southwest Mo. St.	34	28-6	1,958	57.6
1988	Ga. Southern	31	24-7	1,725	55.6
1989	Princeton	27	19-8	1,430	53.0
1990	Princeton	27	20-7	1,378	51.0
1991	Princeton	27	24-3	1,320	48.9
1992	Princeton	28	22-6	1,349	48.2
1993	Princeton	26	15-11	1,421	54.7
1994	Princeton	26	18-8	1,361	52.3
1995	Princeton	26	16-10	1,501	57.7
1996	Princeton	29	22-7	1,498	51.7
1997	Princeton	28	24-4	1,496	53.4
1998	Princeton	29	27-2	1,491	51.4
1999	Princeton	30	22-8	1,581	52.7
2000	Princeton	30	19-11	1,637	54.6
2001	Wisconsin	29	18-11	1,641	56.6
2002	Columbia	28	11-17	1,596	57.0
2003	Air Force	28	12-16	1,596	57.0

*record

Scoring Margin

Season	Team	G	Off.	Def.	Mar.
1949	Kentucky	34	68.2	43.9	24.3
1950	Holy Cross	31	72.6	55.4	17.2
1951	Kentucky	34	74.7	52.5	22.2
1952	Kentucky	32	82.3	55.4	26.9
1953	La Salle	28	80.1	61.8	18.3
1954	Kentucky	25	87.5	60.3	27.2
1955	Utah	28	79.0	59.9	19.1
1956	San Francisco	29	72.2	52.2	20.0
1957	Kentucky	28	84.2	69.4	14.8
1958	Cincinnati	28	86.5	65.9	20.6
1959	Idaho St.	28	74.2	53.7	20.5
1960	Cincinnati	30	86.7	64.7	22.0
1961	Memphis	23	85.0	64.2	20.8
1962	Arizona St.	27	90.1	67.6	22.5
1963	Loyola (Ill.)	31	91.8	68.1	23.7
1964	Davidson	26	89.3	70.5	18.8
1965	Connecticut	26	85.1	66.5	18.6
1966	Loyola (Ill.)	25	97.5	76.6	20.9
1967	UCLA	30	89.6	63.7	25.9
1968	UCLA	30	93.4	67.2	26.2
1969	UCLA	30	84.7	63.8	20.9
1970	St. Bonaventure	28	88.4	65.9	22.5
1971	Jacksonville	26	99.9	79.0	20.9
1972	UCLA	30	94.6	64.3	*30.3
1973	North Carolina St.	27	92.9	71.1	21.8
1974	Charlotte	26	90.2	69.4	20.8
1975	Charlotte	26	88.9	65.2	23.7
1976	UNLV	31	110.5	89.0	21.5
1977	UNLV	32	107.1	87.7	19.4
1978	UCLA	28	85.3	67.4	17.9
1979	Syracuse	30	88.7	71.5	17.2
1980	Alcorn St.	30	91.0	73.6	17.4
1981	Wyoming	30	73.6	57.5	16.1
1982	Oregon St.	27	69.6	55.0	14.6
1983	Houston	34	82.4	64.9	17.4
1984	Georgetown	37	74.3	57.9	16.4
1985	Georgetown	38	74.3	57.3	17.1
1986	Cleveland St.	33	88.9	69.6	19.3
1987	UNLV	39	92.6	75.5	17.1
1988	Oklahoma	39	102.9	81.0	21.9
1989	St. Mary's (Cal.)	30	76.1	57.6	18.5
1990	Oklahoma	32	101.3	80.4	21.0
1991	UNLV	35	97.7	71.0	26.7
1992	Indiana	34	83.4	65.8	17.6
1993	North Carolina	38	86.1	68.3	17.8
1994	Arkansas	34	93.4	75.6	17.9
1995	Kentucky	33	87.4	69.0	18.4
1996	Kentucky	36	91.4	69.4	22.1
1997	Kentucky	40	83.1	62.8	20.3
1998	Duke	36	85.6	64.1	21.5
1999	Duke	39	91.8	67.2	24.7
2000	Stanford	31	78.9	59.7	19.3
2001	Duke	39	90.7	70.5	20.2
2002	Duke	35	88.9	69.2	19.7
2003	Kansas	38	82.7	66.9	15.8

*record

Field-Goal Percentage

Season	Team	FG	FGA	Pct.
1948	Oregon St.	668	1,818	36.7
1949	Muhlenberg	593	1,512	39.2
1950	TCU	476	1,191	40.0
1951	Maryland	481	1,210	39.8
1952	Boston College	787	1,893	41.6
1953	Furman	936	2,106	44.4
1954	George Washington	744	1,632	45.6
1955	George Washington	867	1,822	47.6
1956	George Washington	725	1,451	50.0
1957	Manhattan	679	1,489	45.6
1958	Fordham	693	1,440	48.1
1959	Auburn	593	1,216	48.8
1960	Auburn	532	1,022	52.1
1961	Ohio St.	939	1,886	49.8
1962	Florida St.	709	1,386	51.2
1963	Duke	984	1,926	51.1
1964	Davidson	894	1,644	54.4
1965	St. Peter's	579	1,089	53.2
1966	North Carolina	838	1,620	51.7
1967	UCLA	1,082	2,081	52.0
1968	Bradley	927	1,768	52.4
1969	UCLA	1,027	1,999	51.4
1970	Ohio St.	831	1,527	54.4
1971	Jacksonville	1,077	2,008	53.6
1972	North Carolina	1,031	1,954	52.8
1973	North Carolina	1,150	2,181	52.7
1974	Notre Dame	1,056	1,992	53.0
1975	Maryland	1,049	1,918	54.7
1976	Maryland	996	1,854	53.7
1977	Arkansas	849	1,558	54.5
1978	Arkansas	1,060	1,943	54.6
1979	UCLA	1,053	1,897	55.5
1980	Missouri	936	1,635	*57.2
1981	Oregon St.	862	1,528	56.4
1982	UC Irvine	920	1,639	56.1
1983	Kentucky	869	1,564	55.6
1984	Houston Baptist	797	1,445	55.2
1985	Navy	946	1,726	54.8
1986	Michigan St.	1,043	1,860	56.1
1987	Princeton	601	1,111	54.1
1988	Michigan	1,198	2,196	54.6
1989	Michigan	1,325	2,341	56.6
1990	Kansas	1,204	2,258	53.3
1991	UNLV	1,305	2,441	53.5
1992	Duke	1,108	2,069	53.6
1993	Indiana	1,076	2,062	52.2
1994	Auburn	854	1,689	50.6
1995	Washington St.	902	1,743	51.7
1996	UCLA	897	1,698	52.8
1997	UCLA	932	1,791	52.0
1998	North Carolina	1,131	2,184	51.8
1999	Northern Ariz.	783	1,497	52.3
2000	Samford	825	1,649	50.0
2001	Stanford	953	1,865	51.1
2002	Kansas	1,259	2,487	50.6
2003	Morehead St.	854	1,674	51.0

*record

Field-Goal Percentage Defense

Season	Team	FG	FGA	Pct.
1977	Minnesota	766	1,886	40.6
1978	Delaware St.	733	1,802	40.7
1979	Illinois	738	1,828	40.4
1980	Penn St.	543	1,309	41.5
1981	Wyoming	637	1,589	40.1
1982	Wyoming	584	1,470	39.7
1983	Wyoming	599	1,441	41.6
1984	Georgetown	799	2,025	39.5
1985	Georgetown	833	2,064	40.4
1986	St. Peter's	574	1,395	41.1
1987	San Diego	660	1,645	40.1
1988	Temple	777	1,981	39.2
1989	Georgetown	795	1,993	39.9
1990	Georgetown	713	1,929	37.0
1991	Georgetown	680	1,847	36.8
1992	UNLV	628	1,723	36.4

Season	Team	FG	FGA	Pct.
1993	Marquette	634	1,613	39.3
1994	Marquette	750	2,097	35.8
1995	Alabama	771	2,048	37.6
1996	Temple	670	1,741	38.5
1997	Marquette	628	1,735	36.2
1998	Miami (Fla.)	634	1,672	37.9
1999	Kansas St.	729	1,963	37.1
2000	Stanford	667	1,893	*35.2
2001	Kansas	782	2,069	37.8
2002	Va. Commonwealth	767	2,052	37.4
2003	St. Joseph's	609	1,639	37.2

*record

Three-Point Field Goals Made Per Game

Season	Team	G	3FG	Avg.
1987	Providence	34	280	8.24
1988	Princeton	26	211	8.12
1989	Loyola Marymount	31	287	9.26
1990	Kentucky	28	281	10.04
1991	Texas-Arlington	29	265	9.14
1992	La Salle	31	294	9.48
1993	Lamar	27	271	10.04
1994	Troy St.	27	262	9.70
1995	Troy St.	27	287	10.63
1996	Troy St.	27	300	*11.11
1997	Mississippi Val.	29	309	10.66
1998	Florida	29	285	9.83
1999	Cal Poly	27	255	9.44
2000	Tennessee Tech	28	279	9.96
2001	Duke	39	407	10.44
2002	St. Bonaventure	30	314	10.47
2003	Mississippi Val.	29	299	10.31

*record

Three-Point Field-Goal Percentage

Season	Team	G	3FG	3FGA	Pct.
1987	Indiana	34	130	256	*50.8
1988	Princeton	26	211	429	49.2
1989	Indiana	35	121	256	47.3
1990	Princeton	27	208	460	45.2
1991	Wis.-Green Bay	31	189	407	46.4
1992	Wis.-Green Bay	30	204	437	46.7
1993	Valparaiso	28	214	500	42.8
1994	Indiana	30	182	401	45.4
1995	Southern Utah	28	244	571	42.7
1996	Weber St.	30	245	577	42.5
1997	Northern Ariz.	28	221	527	41.9
1998	Northern Ariz.	29	254	591	43.0
1999	Northern Ariz.	29	243	546	44.5
2000	Colorado St.	30	255	579	44.0
2001	Akron	28	189	436	43.3
2002	Marshall	30	252	595	42.4
2003	Illinois St.	29	188	427	44.0

*record

Free-Throw Percentage

Season	Team	FT	FTA	Pct.
1948	Texas	351	481	73.0
1949	Davidson	347	489	71.0
1950	Temple	342	483	70.8
1951	Minnesota	287	401	71.6
1952	Kansas	491	707	69.4
1953	George Washington	502	696	72.1
1954	Wake Forest	734	1,010	72.7
1955	Wake Forest	709	938	75.6
1956	Southern Methodist	701	917	76.4
1957	Oklahoma St.	569	752	75.7
1958	Oklahoma St.	488	617	79.1
1959	Tulsa	446	586	76.1
1960	Auburn	424	549	77.2
1961	Tulane	459	604	76.0
1962	Arkansas	647	502	77.6
1963	Tulane	390	492	79.3
1964	Miami (Fla.)	593	780	76.0
1965	Miami (Fla.)	642	807	79.6
1966	Auburn	476	601	79.2
1967	West Tex. A&M	400	518	77.2

Season	Team	FT	FTA	Pct.
1968	Vanderbilt	527	684	77.0
1969	Jacksonville	574	733	78.3
1970	Ohio St.	452	559	80.9
1971	Tennessee	538	679	79.2
1972	Lafayette	656	844	77.7
1973	Duke	496	632	78.5
1974	Vanderbilt	477	595	80.2
1975	Vanderbilt	530	692	76.6
1976	Morehead St.	452	577	78.3
1977	Utah	499	638	78.2
1978	Duke	665	841	79.1
1979	St. Francis (Pa.)	350	446	78.5
1980	Oral Roberts	481	610	78.9
1981	Connecticut	487	623	78.2
1982	Western Ill.	447	569	78.6
1983	Western Ill.	526	679	77.5
1984	Harvard	535	651	*82.2
1985	Harvard	450	555	81.1
1986	Michigan St.	490	613	79.9
1987	Alabama	521	662	78.7
1988	Butler	413	517	79.9
1989	Brigham Young	527	647	81.5
1990	Lafayette	461	588	78.4
1991	Butler	725	922	78.6
1992	Northwestern	497	651	76.3
1993	Utah	476	602	79.1
1994	Colgate	511	665	76.8
1995	Brigham Young	617	798	77.3
1996	Utah	649	828	78.4
1997	Western Ky.	342	433	79.0
1998	Siena	574	715	80.3
1999	Siena	672	854	78.7
2000	Montana St.	481	609	79.0
2001	Brigham Young	651	835	78.0
2002	Morehead St.	485	619	78.4
2003	Manhattan	560	711	78.8

*record

Rebounding

Season	Team	G	Reb.	Pct.
1955	Niagara	26	1,507	.624
1956	George Washington	26	1,451	.616
1957	Morehead St.	27	1,735	.621
1958	Manhattan	26	1,437	.591
1959	Mississippi St.	25	1,012	.589
1960	Iona	18	1,054	.607
1961	Bradley	26	1,330	.592
1962	Cornell	25	1,463	.590
1963	UTEP	26	1,167	.591
1964	Iona	20	1,071	.640
1965	Iona	23	1,191	.628
1966	UTEP	29	1,430	.577
1967	Florida	25	1,275	.600
1968	Houston	33	2,074	62.8
1969	Middle Tenn.	26	1,685	64.8
1970	Florida St.	26	1,451	55.8
1971	Pacific (Cal.)	28	1,643	58.7
1972	Oral Roberts	28	1,686	60.2

Season	Team	G	Off.	Def.	Mar.
1973	Manhattan	26	56.5	38.0	*18.5
1974	Massachusetts	26	44.5	30.7	13.8
1975	Stetson	26	47.1	34.7	12.4
1976	Notre Dame	29	46.3	34.1	12.2
1977	Notre Dame	29	42.4	31.6	10.8
1978	Alcorn St.	29	52.3	36.0	16.3
1979	Alcorn St.	29	50.1	36.3	13.8
1980	Alcorn St.	30	49.2	33.8	15.4
1981	Northeastern	30	44.9	32.0	12.9
1982	Northeastern	30	41.2	30.8	10.4
1983	Wichita St.	28	42.4	33.6	8.8
1984	Northeastern	32	40.1	30.3	9.8
1985	Georgetown	38	39.6	30.5	9.1
1986	Notre Dame	29	36.4	27.8	8.6
1987	Iowa	35	43.1	31.5	11.5
1988	Notre Dame	29	36.0	26.2	9.9
1989	Iowa	33	41.4	31.8	9.6
1990	Georgetown	31	44.8	34.0	10.8
1991	New Orleans	31	41.7	32.4	9.3
1992	Delaware	31	42.1	33.8	8.3
1993	Massachusetts	31	43.9	32.8	11.2
1994	Utah St.	27	38.4	29.8	8.6
1995	Navy	29	40.6	29.6	11.0
1996	Mississippi Val.	29	48.3	36.8	11.6
1997	Utah St.	29	37.4	26.6	10.9

Season	Team	G	Off.	Def.	Mar.
1998	Utah	34	37.0	27.1	10.0
1999	Navy	27	43.6	33.7	10.0
2000	Michigan St.	39	39.0	27.3	11.7
2001	Michigan St.	33	42.5	27.1	15.4
2002	Gonzaga	33	41.5	32.6	8.9
2003	Wake Forest	31	41.7	32.0	9.6

Note: From 1955 through 1967, the rebounding champion was determined by highest team recoveries out of the total by both teams in all games. From 1968 through 1972, the champion was determined by rebound average per game. Beginning with the 1973 season, the champion is determined by rebounding margin.

*record

Assists

Season	Team	G	Ast.	Avg.
1984	Clemson	28	571	20.4
1985	Oklahoma	37	828	22.4
1986	North Carolina	34	800	23.5
1987	Southern Methodist	29	655	22.6
1988	Southern Methodist	35	786	22.5
1989	North Carolina	37	788	21.3
1990	Loyola Marymount	32	762	23.8
1991	UNLV	35	863	*24.7
1992	Arkansas	34	674	19.8
1993	Northwestern St.	26	570	21.9
1994	Arkansas	34	687	20.2
1995	Montana St.	29	606	20.9
1996	Kentucky	36	783	21.8
1997	Kentucky	40	776	19.4
1998	Montana St.	30	624	20.8
1999	TCU	32	650	20.3
2000	UNLV	31	623	20.1
2001	Kansas	33	641	19.4
2002	Kansas	37	767	20.7
2003	Maryland	31	573	18.5

*record

Blocked Shots

Season	Team	G	Blk.	Avg.
1986	Navy	35	233	6.66
1987	Siena	29	188	6.48

Season	Team	G	Blk.	Avg.
1988	Siena	29	193	6.66
1989	Georgetown	34	309	*9.09
1990	Georgetown	31	233	7.52
1991	UNLV	35	266	7.60
1992	Vermont	29	198	6.83
1993	Wyoming	28	184	6.57
1994	Howard	27	179	6.63
1995	Massachusetts	34	273	8.03
1996	Central Conn. St.	28	235	8.39
1997	Colgate	28	217	7.75
1998	Texas	31	203	6.55
1999	Iona	30	220	7.33
2000	La.-Monroe	28	207	7.39
2001	Seton Hall	31	236	7.61
2002	Connecticut	34	236	6.94
2003	Connecticut	33	253	7.67

*record

Steals

Season	Team	G	Stl.	Avg.
1986	Cleveland St.	33	436	13.2
1987	Cleveland St.	33	473	14.3
1988	Florida A&M	30	395	13.2
1989	Arkansas	32	372	11.6
1990	Loyola Marymount	32	450	14.1
1991	Texas-San Antonio	29	430	14.8
1992	Northeastern Ill.	28	358	12.8
1993	Centenary (La.)	27	380	14.1
1994	Texas	34	453	13.3
1995	Nicholls St.	30	376	12.5
1996	McNeese St.	27	330	12.2
1997	Long Island	30	396	13.2
1998	Long Island	32	478	*14.9
1999	Maryland	34	431	12.7
2000	Liberty	28	376	13.4
2001	Alabama A&M	28	339	12.1
2002	Alabama A&M	29	395	13.6
2003	UAB	34	394	11.6

*record

Statistical Trends

Year	Teams	Games	FG Made	FG Att.	Pct.	FT Made	FT Att.	Pct.	PF	Pts.
1948	160	24.7	20.3	69.4	29.3	12.7	21.1	59.8	18.5	53.3
1949	148	25.3	20.7	67.4	30.8	13.4	21.7	61.6	19.4	54.8
1950	145	25.2	21.6	68.4	31.6	14.4	23.3	61.8	19.5	57.6
1951	153	26.0	22.8	68.9	33.1	15.1	24.1	62.8	21.4	60.7
1952	156	25.7	23.8	*70.3	33.7	15.8	25.3	62.6	*22.5	63.3
1953	158	23.8	24.0	69.1	34.7	21.1	*32.9	64.0	21.3	69.1
1954	160	24.6	24.4	67.8	35.4	21.0	32.2	65.2	21.0	69.0
1955	162	23.6	25.6	69.3	36.9	*21.6	32.4	66.5	19.0	72.7
1956	166	24.7	26.1	69.5	37.5	21.2	31.7	66.8	18.9	73.3
1957	167	24.6	25.8	67.6	38.2	20.4	30.3	67.3	18.3	72.0
1958	173	24.0	25.8	67.1	38.4	16.8	25.3	66.4	18.2	68.4
1959	174	24.3	25.9	66.2	39.1	17.0	25.4	67.1	18.2	68.7
1960	175	24.5	26.3	66.2	39.8	17.4	25.8	68.4	18.4	70.0
1961	173	24.5	26.7	65.6	40.7	17.4	25.5	68.2	18.2	70.7
1962	178	24.4	27.0	67.3	40.2	16.5	24.3	67.9	18.1	70.5
1963	178	23.5	26.6	63.8	41.7	16.3	23.9	68.2	18.2	69.5
1964	179	24.3	28.7	67.4	42.5	17.1	25.1	68.3	19.1	74.4
1965	182	24.8	29.2	67.7	43.1	17.4	25.2	69.0	19.3	75.7
1966	182	21.9	30.0	68.8	43.6	17.5	25.3	69.2	19.2	77.5
1967	185	24.9	28.9	66.0	43.8	17.2	24.9	69.0	19.2	74.9
1968	189	25.1	29.1	66.6	43.7	17.4	25.1	69.1	19.0	75.5
1969	193	25.3	29.1	66.4	43.8	17.4	25.4	68.4	19.0	75.6
1970	196	25.4	30.0	67.8	44.2	17.7	25.7	68.7	19.3	77.6
1971	203	25.8	30.1	67.8	44.4	17.5	25.7	68.1	19.3	*77.7
1972	210	25.7	30.1	67.2	44.8	17.5	25.6	68.6	19.2	*77.7
1973	216	25.8	31.2	69.6	44.8	13.1	19.2	68.4	19.2	75.5
1974	233	26.0	31.0	68.3	45.4	12.8	18.7	68.4	19.2	74.8
1975	235	26.2	*31.5	68.4	46.0	13.7	19.9	69.0	20.2	76.6
1976	235	26.6	31.0	66.3	46.7	13.8	19.9	69.2	20.2	75.7
1977	245	27.2	30.4	64.9	46.7	14.2	20.5	69.4	20.1	74.9

Brett Blizzard of UNC Wilmington led the nation in three-point field goals made last season.

Photo by UNC Wilmington Sports Information

With his move from Kansas to North Carolina, Roy Williams (left), shaking hands with mentor and long-time former Tar Heels' coach Dean Smith, will have coached two of the top three programs in history.

Year	Teams	Games	FG Made	FG Att.	Pct.	3FG Made	3FG Att.	Pct.	FT Made	FT Att.	Pct.	PF	Pts.
1978	254	27.2	30.1	63.6	47.3				14.3	20.7	69.2	20.2	74.5
1979	257	27.7	29.6	62.1	47.7				14.8	21.1	*69.7	20.6	74.0
1980	261	28.0	28.6	59.7	47.9				14.9	21.3	69.6	20.2	72.0
1981	264	28.1	27.8	58.0	48.0				14.5	21.0	68.9	20.1	70.1
1982	273	28.0	26.7	55.6	47.9				14.3	20.8	68.6	19.4	67.6
1983	274	29.0	27.2	57.0	47.7				14.5	21.2	68.5	19.9	69.3
1984	276	29.1	26.7	55.6	*48.1				14.8	21.4	68.9	20.0	68.2
1985	282	29.3	27.3	57.0	47.9				14.7	21.3	68.9	19.7	69.2
1986	283	29.5	27.4	57.3	47.7				14.7	21.3	69.1	19.6	69.4

Year	Teams	Games	FG Made	FG Att.	Pct.	3FG Made	3FG Att.	Pct.	FT Made	FT Att.	Pct.	PF	Pts.
1987	290	29.6	27.2	58.7	46.4	3.5	9.2	*38.4	14.9	21.5	69.1	19.7	72.8
1988	290	29.6	27.6	58.4	47.3	4.0	10.4	38.3	15.2	22.0	68.9	19.7	74.4
1989	293	29.6	28.1	59.4	47.3	4.4	11.8	37.8	15.6	22.6	69.1	20.1	76.2
1990	292	29.6	27.5	59.5	46.2	4.7	12.8	36.8	15.6	22.6	68.9	19.8	75.3
1991	295	29.6	27.9	60.6	46.1	5.0	13.8	36.2	15.9	23.2	68.6	19.6	76.7
1992	298	29.5	26.7	58.4	45.7	5.0	14.0	35.6	15.9	23.3	68.1	20.0	74.2
1993	298	28.6	26.5	58.6	45.2	5.3	14.9	35.4	15.4	22.8	67.7	19.6	73.6
1994	301	28.7	26.8	60.6	44.3	5.7	16.5	34.5	15.6	23.2	67.1	19.9	75.0
1995	302	28.7	26.5	59.7	44.4	5.9	17.2	34.5	15.3	22.6	67.6	19.7	74.2
1996	305	28.7	25.8	58.5	44.1	5.9	17.1	34.3	15.1	22.4	67.4	19.4	72.5
1997	305	28.8	25.0	57.3	43.7	5.8	17.1	34.1	14.8	21.9	69.1	19.3	70.6
1998	306	29.1	25.3	57.7	43.9	6.0	17.4	34.4	14.9	22.0	67.5	19.4	71.4
1999	310	29.1	24.8	57.0	43.6	5.9	17.4	34.2	14.7	21.6	67.8	19.0	70.3
2000	318	30.0	25.0	57.4	43.5	6.1	17.7	34.4	14.5	21.2	68.1	18.9	70.5
2001	318	29.8	25.0	56.8	44.0	6.1	17.7	34.6	15.4	22.4	68.5	19.9	71.4
2002	321	*30.2	25.1	57.2	43.8	*6.3	*18.3	34.6	14.8	21.5	69.0	19.2	71.3
2003	*325	29.7	24.8	56.4	44.0	*6.3	18.1	34.8	14.4	20.7	69.4	19.1	70.2

Year	Teams	Games	Reb.	Ast.	Blk.	St.	TO
1993	298	28.6	36.1	*14.5	3.2	7.6	15.8
1994	301	28.7	*37.8	*14.5	3.3	*7.8	15.9
1995	302	28.7	37.2	*14.5	3.3	7.5	15.8
1996	305	28.7	36.7	14.1	3.2	7.4	15.6
1997	305	28.8	36.1	13.9	3.2	7.5	15.7
1998	306	29.1	36.4	14.0	3.2	7.6	15.9
1999	310	29.1	36.1	13.9	*3.4	*7.8	*16.0
2000	318	30.0	36.3	14.0	*3.4	7.6	15.8
2001	318	29.8	35.9	13.9	3.3	7.1	15.2
2002	321	*30.2	35.9	13.9	*3.4	7.3	15.1
2003	*325	29.7	35.1	13.8	3.3	7.2	14.9

*all-time high

All-Time Winningest Teams

Victories

(Minimum 25 years in Division I)

No.	Team	First Season	Yrs.	Won	Lost	Tied	Pct.
1.	Kentucky	1903	100	1,849	572	1	.764
2.	North Carolina	1911	93	1,808	666	0	.731
3.	Kansas	1899	105	1,801	753	0	.705
4.	Duke	1906	98	1,706	775	0	.688
5.	St. John's (N.Y.)	1908	96	1,662	763	0	.685
6.	Temple	1895	107	1,608	874	0	.648
7.	Syracuse	1901	102	1,602	737	0	.685
8.	Pennsylvania	1897	103	1,555	876	2	.640
9.	Indiana	1901	103	1,540	825	0	.651
10.	Notre Dame	1898	98	1,529	838	1	.646
11.	UCLA	1920	84	1,520	672	0	.693
12.	Oregon St.	1902	102	1,517	1,067	0	.587
13.	Utah	1909	95	1,492	775	0	.658
14.	Princeton	1901	103	1,475	896	0	.622
15.	Western Ky.	1915	84	1,466	723	0	.670
16.	Illinois	1906	98	1,458	798	0	.646
17.	Purdue	1897	105	1,453	849	0	.631
18.	Washington	1896	101	1,444	980	0	.596
19.	Cincinnati	1902	102	1,440	835	0	.633
20.	Arizona	1905	98	1,438	788	0	.646
21.	Louisville	1912	89	1,431	778	0	.648
22.	North Carolina St.	1913	91	1,419	846	0	.626
23.	Texas	1906	97	1,412	881	0	.616
23.	West Virginia	1904	94	1,412	901	0	.610
25.	Bradley	1903	99	1,409	910	0	.608
26.	Arkansas	1924	80	1,377	742	0	.650
27.	Ohio St.	1899	104	1,375	952	0	.591
28.	Fordham	1903	100	1,367	1,082	0	.558
29.	Alabama	1913	90	1,365	823	1	.624
30.	Oklahoma	1908	96	1,364	880	0	.608
31.	Villanova	1921	83	1,361	788	0	.633
32.	Montana St.	1902	101	1,360	1,050	0	.564
33.	Iowa	1902	102	1,358	923	0	.595
34.	St. Joseph's	1910	94	1,353	897	0	.601
35.	Washington St.	1902	102	1,352	1,259	0	.518
36.	Southern California	1907	97	1,349	960	0	.584
37.	Georgetown	1907	95	1,347	858	0	.611
37.	Missouri	1907	97	1,347	936	0	.590
39.	Connecticut	1901	100	1,341	793	0	.628
40.	Oklahoma St.	1908	94	1,339	962	0	.582
41.	Minnesota	1896	108	1,325	1,003	4	.569
42.	Brigham Young	1918	86	1,318	875	0	.601
43.	Kansas St.	1903	99	1,317	961	0	.578
44.	Tennessee	1909	94	1,316	853	2	.607
45.	Oregon	1903	98	1,315	1,159	0	.532
46.	Michigan St.	1899	104	1,302	936	0	.582
47.	Dayton	1904	98	1,299	932	0	.582
48.	Vanderbilt	1901	101	1,296	946	0	.578

No.	Team	First Season	Yrs.	Won	Lost	Tied	Pct.
49.	California	1908	94	1,292	973	0	.570
50.	Marquette	1917	86	1,290	814	0	.613

Percentage

(Minimum 25 years in Division I)

No.	Team	First Season	Yrs.	Won	Lost	Tied	Pct.
1.	Kentucky	1903	100	1,849	572	1	.764
2.	North Carolina	1911	93	1,808	666	0	.731
3.	UNLV	1959	45	928	363	0	.719
4.	Kansas	1899	105	1,801	753	0	.705
5.	UCLA	1920	84	1,520	672	0	.693
6.	Duke	1906	98	1,706	775	0	.688
7.	St. John's (N.Y.)	1908	96	1,662	763	0	.685
8.	Syracuse	1901	102	1,602	737	0	.685
9.	Western Ky.	1915	84	1,466	723	0	.670
10.	Utah	1909	95	1,492	775	0	.658
11.	Indiana	1901	103	1,540	825	0	.651
12.	Arkansas	1924	80	1,377	742	0	.650
13.	Temple	1895	107	1,608	874	0	.648
14.	Louisville	1912	89	1,431	778	0	.648
15.	Weber St.	1963	41	756	413	0	.647
16.	Chattanooga	1978	26	501	274	0	.646
17.	Illinois	1906	98	1,458	798	0	.646
18.	Arizona	1905	98	1,438	788	0	.646
19.	Notre Dame	1898	98	1,529	838	1	.646
20.	Pennsylvania	1897	103	1,555	876	2	.640
21.	DePaul	1924	80	1,258	716	0	.637
22.	Villanova	1921	83	1,361	788	0	.633
23.	Cincinnati	1902	102	1,440	835	0	.633
24.	Murray St.	1926	78	1,274	744	0	.631
25.	Purdue	1897	105	1,453	849	0	.631
26.	Connecticut	1901	100	1,341	793	0	.628
27.	North Carolina St.	1913	91	1,419	846	0	.626
28.	Alabama	1913	90	1,365	823	1	.624
29.	Princeton	1901	103	1,475	896	0	.622
30.	New Orleans	1970	34	602	368	0	.621
31.	Texas	1906	97	1,412	881	0	.616
32.	Marquette	1917	86	1,290	814	0	.613
33.	La Salle	1931	73	1,157	731	0	.613
34.	Illinois St.	1972	32	574	365	0	.611
35.	Georgetown	1907	95	1,347	858	0	.611
36.	West Virginia	1904	94	1,412	901	0	.610
37.	Providence	1927	76	1,176	754	0	.609
38.	Va. Commonwealth	1969	35	594	383	0	.608
39.	Oklahoma	1908	96	1,364	880	0	.608
40.	Memphis	1921	82	1,188	767	0	.608
41.	Bradley	1903	99	1,409	910	0	.608
42.	Tennessee	1909	94	1,316	853	2	.607
43.	Navy	1907	97	1,198	778	0	.606
44.	Holy Cross	1901	84	1,164	756	0	.606
45.	UTEP	1947	57	936	613	0	.604
46.	Old Dominion	1966	38	671	442	0	.603
47.	Houston	1946	58	975	645	0	.602
48.	San Francisco	1924	76	1,138	754	0	.601
49.	St. Joseph's	1910	94	1,353	897	0	.601
50.	Brigham Young	1918	86	1,318	875	0	.601

All-Time Won-Lost Records

(No Minimum Seasons of Competition)

Team	First Season	Yrs.	Won	Lost	Tied	Pct.
Air Force	1957	47	503	713	0	.414
Akron	1902	102	1,259	845	0	.598
Alabama	1913	90	1,365	823	1	.624
Alabama A&M	1987	17	353	150	0	.702
Alabama St.	1983	21	302	296	0	.505
Albany (N.Y.)	1910	94	995	709	0	.584
Alcorn St.	1978	26	389	365	0	.516
American	1927	77	957	886	0	.519
Appalachian St.	1920	78	998	865	0	.536
Arizona	1905	98	1,438	788	0	.646
Arizona St.	1912	87	1,076	956	0	.530
Ark.-Little Rock	1979	25	422	308	0	.578
Ark.-Pine Bluff	1996	8	40	171	0	.190
Arkansas	1924	80	1,377	742	0	.650
Arkansas St.	1971	33	489	435	0	.529
Army	1903	101	1,040	966	0	.518

Team	First Season	Yrs.	Won	Lost	Tied	Pct.
Auburn	1906	95	1,094	933	1	.540
Austin Peay	1930	72	942	833	0	.531
Ball St.	1972	32	529	390	0	.576
Baylor	1907	97	1,032	1,165	0	.470
Belmont	1953	51	775	676	0	.534
Bethune-Cookman	1962	41	498	607	0	.451
Binghamton	1947	57	512	714	0	.418
Birmingham-So.	1908	83	1,199	685	0	.636
Boise St.	1972	32	476	418	0	.532
Boston College	1905	70	933	748	0	.555
Boston U.	1902	94	905	907	0	.499
Bowling Green	1916	88	1,145	919	0	.555
Bradley	1903	99	1,409	910	0	.608
Brigham Young	1918	86	1,318	875	0	.601
Brown	1901	96	835	1,249	0	.401
Bucknell	1896	108	1,126	1,032	0	.522
Buffalo	1915	84	888	894	0	.498
Butler	1897	105	1,223	960	0	.560
Cal Poly	1995	9	106	148	0	.417
Cal St. Fullerton	1961	43	525	641	0	.450
Cal St. Northridge	1959	45	583	628	0	.481
California	1908	94	1,292	973	0	.570
Campbell	1978	26	298	418	0	.416
Canisius	1904	99	1,086	982	0	.525
Centenary (La.)	1946	53	686	764	0	.473
Central Conn. St.	1935	67	906	671	0	.575
Central Mich.	1974	30	373	450	0	.453
Charleston So.	1966	38	438	583	0	.429
Charlotte	1966	38	599	479	0	.556
Chattanooga	1978	26	501	274	0	.646
Chicago St.	1985	19	131	394	0	.250
Cincinnati	1902	102	1,440	835	0	.633
Citadel	1913	90	835	1,034	0	.447
Clemson	1912	92	1,022	1,087	2	.485
Cleveland St.	1973	31	444	420	0	.514
Coastal Caro.	1975	29	388	432	0	.473
Col. of Charleston	1979	25	597	167	0	.781
Colgate	1901	103	1,075	1,116	0	.491
Colorado	1902	100	1,033	974	0	.515
Colorado St.	1902	100	1,005	1,022	0	.496
Columbia	1901	103	1,076	1,067	0	.502
Connecticut	1901	100	1,341	793	0	.628
Coppin St.	1986	18	296	231	0	.562
Cornell	1899	105	1,043	1,196	0	.466
Creighton	1917	85	1,215	857	0	.586
Dartmouth	1901	102	1,150	1,203	0	.489
Davidson	1909	94	1,106	1,048	0	.513
Dayton	1904	98	1,299	932	0	.582
Delaware	1906	98	975	1,023	2	.488
Delaware St.	1974	30	324	498	0	.394
Denver	1904	100	1,054	1,072	0	.496
DePaul	1924	80	1,258	716	0	.637
Detroit	1906	96	1,193	954	0	.556
Drake	1907	97	1,005	1,210	0	.454
Drexel	1895	104	1,026	888	0	.536
Duke	1906	98	1,706	775	0	.688
Duquesne	1914	87	1,185	846	0	.583
East Caro.	1932	71	878	858	0	.506
East Tenn. St.	1928	73	959	797	0	.546
Eastern Ill.	1982	22	326	312	0	.511
Eastern Ky.	1926	77	917	882	1	.510
Eastern Mich.	1974	30	408	448	0	.477
Eastern Wash.	1984	20	210	339	0	.383
Elon	2000	4	47	66	0	.416
Evansville	1978	26	421	315	0	.572
Fairfield	1949	54	686	694	0	.497
Fairleigh Dickinson	1968	35	502	442	0	.532
Fla. Atlantic	1989	15	147	274	0	.349
Florida	1916	83	1,013	942	0	.518
Florida A&M	1979	25	292	418	0	.411
Florida Int'l	1982	22	272	346	0	.440
Florida St.	1948	56	877	653	0	.573
Fordham	1903	100	1,367	1,082	0	.558
Fresno St.	1922	81	1,076	891	0	.547
Furman	1946	58	776	800	0	.492
Ga. Southern	1974	30	433	409	0	.514
George Mason	1979	25	361	347	0	.510
George Washington	1907	86	1,063	916	0	.537
Georgetown	1907	95	1,347	858	0	.611
Georgia	1906	98	1,142	1,049	0	.521
Georgia St.	1964	40	365	694	0	.345
Georgia Tech	1906	87	1,109	981	0	.531
Gonzaga	1908	96	1,209	1,020	0	.542

Team	First Season	Yrs.	Won	Lost	Tied	Pct.
Grambling	1978	26	293	436	0	.402
Hampton	1953	51	732	600	0	.550
Hartford	1958	46	564	613	0	.479
Harvard	1901	92	882	1,129	0	.439
Hawaii	1971	33	482	459	0	.512
High Point	1928	76	1,156	834	0	.581
Hofstra	1937	65	967	730	0	.570
Holy Cross	1901	84	1,164	756	0	.606
Houston	1946	58	975	645	0	.602
Howard	1974	30	384	457	0	.457
Idaho	1906	98	1,133	1,210	0	.484
Idaho St.	1927	76	1,001	912	0	.523
Ill.-Chicago	1948	56	645	691	0	.483
Illinois	1906	98	1,458	798	0	.646
Illinois St.	1972	32	574	365	0	.611
Indiana	1901	103	1,540	825	0	.651
Indiana St.	1924	80	1,109	880	0	.558
Iona	1941	60	895	639	0	.583
Iowa	1902	102	1,358	923	0	.595
Iowa St.	1908	96	1,063	1,106	0	.490
IPFW	1974	30	342	472	0	.420
IUPUI	1973	31	438	472	0	.481
Jackson St.	1978	26	362	386	0	.484
Jacksonville	1958	46	635	605	0	.512
Jacksonville St.	1926	72	1,074	559	0	.658
James Madison	1970	34	554	389	0	.587
Kansas	1899	105	1,801	753	0	.705
Kansas St.	1903	99	1,317	961	0	.578
Kent St.	1914	87	890	1,049	0	.459
Kentucky	1903	100	1,849	572	1	.764
La Salle	1931	73	1,157	731	0	.613
La.-Lafayette	1912	87	1,178	868	0	.576
La.-Monroe	1952	52	806	594	0	.576
Lafayette	1901	93	1,133	982	0	.536
Lamar	1952	52	767	635	0	.547
Lehigh	1902	102	824	1,200	0	.407
Liberty	1973	31	433	457	0	.487
Long Beach St.	1951	53	767	664	0	.536
Long Island	1929	69	1,021	722	2	.586
Louisiana Tech	1974	30	495	360	0	.579
Louisville	1912	89	1,431	778	0	.648
Loyola (Ill.)	1914	85	1,082	912	1	.543
Loyola (Md.)	1909	92	1,063	1,039	0	.506
Loyola Marymount	1907	80	850	991	0	.462
LSU	1909	95	1,264	965	0	.567
Maine	1905	83	809	898	0	.474
Manhattan	1905	97	1,129	991	1	.533
Marist	1982	22	323	305	0	.514
Marquette	1917	86	1,290	814	0	.613
Marshall	1907	92	1,247	865	2	.590
Maryland	1924	80	1,206	822	0	.595
Massachusetts	1902	93	1,028	920	0	.528
McNeese St.	1974	30	430	416	0	.508
Md.-East. Shore	1982	22	181	427	0	.298
Memphis	1921	82	1,188	767	0	.608
Mercer	1974	30	376	458	0	.451
Miami (Fla.)	1927	53	727	553	0	.568
Miami (Ohio)	1906	98	1,145	935	0	.550
Michigan	1909	82	1,138	785	0	.592
Michigan St.	1899	104	1,302	936	0	.582
Middle Tenn.	1914	80	917	937	0	.513
Minnesota	1896	108	1,325	1,003	4	.569
Mississippi	1909	93	1,005	1,093	0	.479
Mississippi St.	1909	91	1,117	976	0	.534
Mississippi Val.	1980	24	302	373	0	.447
Missouri	1907	97	1,347	936	0	.590
Monmouth	1984	20	277	289	0	.489
Montana	1906	95	1,184	1,054	0	.529
Montana St.	1902	101	1,360	1,050	0	.564
Morehead St.	1930	74	913	861	0	.515
Morgan St.	1985	19	152	383	0	.284
Mount St. Mary's	1909	94	1,304	843	0	.607
Murray St.	1926	78	1,274	744	0	.631
N.C. A&T	1974	30	467	375	0	.555
Navy	1907	97	1,198	778	0	.606
Nebraska	1897	107	1,240	1,115	0	.527
Nevada	1913	90	1,000	1,005	0	.499
New Hampshire	1903	99	740	1,192	0	.383
New Mexico	1900	100	1,189	937	0	.559
New Mexico St.	1905	94	1,193	900	2	.570
New Orleans	1970	34	602	368	0	.621
Niagara	1906	97	1,225	981	1	.555
Nicholls St.	1981	23	260	370	0	.413

Team	First Season	Yrs.	Won	Lost	Tied	Pct.
Norfolk St.	1954	50	970	419	0	.698
North Carolina	1911	93	1,808	666	0	.731
North Carolina St.	1913	91	1,419	846	0	.626
North Texas	1917	85	895	1,082	0	.453
Northeastern	1921	82	930	899	0	.510
Northern Ariz.	1910	86	931	972	0	.489
Northern Ill.	1968	36	464	511	0	.476
Northern Iowa	1904	95	970	943	0	.507
Northwestern	1905	98	834	1,262	1	.398
Northwestern St.	1977	27	309	438	0	.414
Notre Dame	1898	98	1,529	838	1	.646
Oakland	1968	36	508	476	0	.516
Ohio	1908	96	1,227	931	0	.569
Ohio St.	1899	104	1,375	952	0	.591
Oklahoma	1908	96	1,364	880	0	.608
Oklahoma St.	1908	94	1,339	962	0	.582
Old Dominion	1966	38	671	442	0	.603
Oral Roberts	1972	37	637	445	0	.589
Oregon	1903	98	1,315	1,159	0	.532
Oregon St.	1902	102	1,517	1,067	0	.587
Pacific (Cal.)	1911	93	1,010	1,036	0	.494
Penn St.	1897	107	1,235	909	1	.576
Pennsylvania	1897	103	1,555	876	2	.640
Pepperdine	1939	65	1,043	785	0	.571
Pittsburgh	1906	96	1,248	988	0	.558
Portland	1923	79	973	1,038	0	.484
Portland St.	1947	42	550	543	0	.503
Prairie View	1981	23	140	490	0	.222
Princeton	1901	103	1,475	896	0	.622
Providence	1927	76	1,176	754	0	.609
Purdue	1897	105	1,453	849	0	.631
Quinnipiac	1952	52	724	641	0	.530
Radford	1985	19	304	244	0	.555
Rhode Island	1907	95	1,215	901	0	.574
Rice	1917	87	865	1,110	0	.438
Richmond	1913	91	1,089	968	0	.529
Rider	1968	36	503	498	0	.502
Robert Morris	1977	27	328	429	0	.433
Rutgers	1907	91	1,030	932	0	.525
Sacramento St.	1949	55	604	841	0	.418
Sacred Heart	1966	38	640	439	0	.593
Sam Houston St.	1932	68	872	841	0	.509
Samford	1973	31	368	487	0	.430
San Diego	1956	48	673	623	0	.519
San Diego St.	1922	82	1,089	945	0	.535
San Francisco	1924	76	1,138	754	0	.601
San Jose St.	1910	89	1,003	1,042	0	.490
Santa Clara	1918	84	1,174	796	0	.596
Seton Hall	1904	91	1,220	858	2	.587
Siena	1939	62	863	705	0	.550
South Ala.	1969	35	563	418	0	.574
South Carolina	1909	95	1,143	1,013	1	.530
South Carolina St.	1958	46	736	523	0	.585
South Fla.	1972	32	450	455	0	.497
Southeast Mo. St.	1982	22	399	253	0	.612
Southeastern La.	1981	22	229	376	0	.379
Southern California	1907	97	1,349	960	0	.584
Southern Ill.	1968	36	576	455	0	.559
Southern Methodist	1917	87	1,061	988	0	.518
Southern Miss.	1913	84	989	834	1	.543
Southern U.	1978	26	429	312	0	.579
Southern Utah	1969	35	529	412	0	.562
Southwest Mo. St.	1909	91	1,390	752	0	.649
St. Bonaventure	1920	83	1,129	782	0	.591
St. Francis (N.Y.)	1902	84	1,009	1,000	0	.502
St. Francis (Pa.)	1946	58	758	732	1	.509
St. John's (N.Y.)	1908	96	1,662	763	0	.685
St. Joseph's	1910	94	1,353	897	0	.601
St. Louis	1916	87	1,143	974	0	.540
St. Mary's (Cal.)	1926	76	890	1,035	0	.462
St. Peter's	1931	70	876	803	0	.522
Stanford	1914	88	1,214	946	0	.562
Stephen F. Austin	1925	77	1,144	773	0	.597
Stetson	1972	32	447	435	0	.507
Stony Brook	1961	43	550	489	0	.529
Syracuse	1901	102	1,602	737	0	.685
TCU	1914	90	979	1,101	0	.471
Temple	1895	107	1,608	874	0	.648
Tenn.-Martin	1952	52	585	693	0	.458
Tennessee	1909	94	1,316	853	2	.607
Tennessee St.	1978	26	306	407	0	.429
Tennessee Tech	1926	78	885	858	1	.508
Tex. A&M-Corp. Chris.	2000	4	53	57	0	.482

Team	First Season	Yrs.	Won	Lost	Tied	Pct.
Tex.-Pan American	1969	35	432	511	0	.458
Texas	1906	97	1,412	881	0	.616
Texas A&M	1913	91	1,099	1,072	0	.506
Texas Southern	1978	26	374	359	0	.510
Texas St.	1985	19	245	290	0	.458
Texas Tech	1926	78	1,142	860	0	.570
Texas-Arlington	1960	44	462	716	0	.392
Texas-San Antonio	1982	22	334	288	0	.537
Toledo	1917	86	1,195	826	0	.591
Towson	1980	24	293	390	0	.429
Troy St.	1951	53	836	606	0	.580
Tulane	1913	84	962	964	0	.499
Tulsa	1908	92	1,163	933	0	.555
UAB	1979	25	489	300	0	.620
UC Irvine	1966	38	520	540	0	.491
UC Riverside	1955	49	784	588	0	.571
UC Santa Barb.	1938	63	867	797	0	.521
UCF	1971	33	499	409	0	.550
UCLA	1920	84	1,520	672	0	.693
UMBC	1969	35	389	538	0	.420
UMKC	1970	33	470	461	0	.505
UNC Asheville	1965	39	562	556	0	.503
UNC Greensboro	1968	36	408	503	0	.448
UNC Wilmington	1977	27	425	347	0	.551
UNLV	1959	45	928	363	0	.719
Utah	1909	95	1,492	775	0	.658
Utah St.	1909	90	1,219	911	0	.572
UTEP	1947	57	936	613	0	.604
Va. Commonwealth	1969	35	594	383	0	.608
Valparaiso	1918	86	1,059	1,009	0	.512
Vanderbilt	1901	101	1,296	946	0	.578
Vermont	1901	89	899	960	0	.484
Villanova	1921	83	1,361	788	0	.633
Virginia	1906	98	1,283	991	1	.564
Virginia Tech	1909	95	1,172	987	0	.543
VMI	1911	93	692	1,241	0	.358
Wagner	1977	27	329	423	0	.438
Wake Forest	1906	97	1,269	980	0	.564
Washington	1896	101	1,444	980	0	.596
Washington St.	1902	102	1,352	1,259	0	.518
Weber St.	1963	41	756	413	0	.647
West Virginia	1904	94	1,412	901	0	.610
Western Caro.	1977	27	329	423	0	.438
Western Ill.	1982	22	287	334	0	.462
Western Ky.	1915	84	1,466	723	0	.670
Western Mich.	1914	90	1,056	970	0	.521
Wichita St.	1906	96	1,192	1,046	0	.533
William & Mary	1906	98	1,008	1,132	0	.471
Winthrop	1979	25	384	363	0	.514
Wis.-Green Bay	1974	30	512	364	0	.584
Wis.-Milwaukee	1897	106	1,092	1,024	0	.516
Wisconsin	1899	105	1,214	1,056	0	.535
Wofford	1952	52	729	734	0	.498
Wright St.	1971	33	548	366	0	.600
Wyoming	1905	98	1,281	923	0	.581
Xavier	1920	82	1,112	831	0	.572
Yale	1896	108	1,218	1,266	0	.490
Youngstown St.	1928	73	919	850	0	.520

Winningest Teams by Decade

The 1930s

Rk.	Team	Won	Lost	Pct.
1.	Long Island	198	38	.839
2.	Kentucky	162	34	.827
3.	St. John's (N.Y.)	181	40	.819
4.	Kansas	153	37	.805
5.	Syracuse	143	37	.794
6.	Purdue	148	39	.791
7.	Western Ky.	197	52	.791
8.	Rhode Island	142	39	.785
9.	Notre Dame	170	49	.776
10.	CCNY	120	35	.774
11.	Washington	206	63	.766
12.	DePaul	142	44	.763
13.	Arkansas	167	57	.746
14.	Duquesne	143	50	.741
15.	Wyoming	147	52	.739
16.	Navy	108	40	.730
17.	North Carolina	163	61	.728
18.	George Washington	129	50	.721
19.	New York U.	124	49	.717
20.	Western Mich.	123	50	.711

The 1940s

Rk.	Team	Won	Lost	Pct.
1.	Kentucky	239	42	.851
2.	Oklahoma St.	237	55	.812
3.	Rhode Island	178	44	.802
4.	Eastern Ky.	145	40	.784
5.	Western Ky.	222	66	.771
6.	Tennessee	152	46	.768
7.	Bowling Green	204	66	.756
8.	Notre Dame	162	55	.747
9.	Toledo	176	65	.730
10.	St. John's (N.Y.)	162	60	.730
11.	North Carolina	196	75	.723

Rk.	Team	Won	Lost	Pct.
12.	West Virginia	157	59	.727
13.	Illinois	150	57	.725
14.	DePaul	180	69	.723
15.	Bradley	144	56	.720
16.	New York U.	150	60	.714
17.	Utah	159	68	.700
18.	Wyoming	163	70	.700
19.	Texas	168	73	.697
20.	CCNY	133	62	.682

Played only seven seasons:

	Team	Won	Lost	Pct.
	Seton Hall	128	22	.853
	Duquesne	118	32	.787
	George Washington	117	47	.713

The 1950s

Rk.	Team	Won	Lost	Pct.
1.	Kentucky	224	33	.872
2.	North Carolina St.	240	65	.787
3.	Seattle	233	69	.772
4.	La Salle	209	65	.763
5.	Dayton	228	71	.763
6.	Holy Cross	199	65	.754
7.	Kansas St.	179	63	.740
8.	Connecticut	187	67	.736
9.	West Virginia	205	74	.735
10.	Louisville	202	77	.724
11.	Illinois	165	64	.721
12.	Western Ky.	205	82	.714
13.	UCLA	193	78	.712
14.	Duquesne	187	76	.711
15.	Kansas	171	74	.698
16.	St. John's (N.Y.)	176	77	.696
17.	Cincinnati	175	80	.686
18.	Oklahoma St.	192	88	.686
19.	Lafayette	171	81	.679
20.	St. Louis	185	88	.678

The 1960s

Rk.	Team	Won	Lost	Pct.
1.	UCLA	234	52	.818
2.	Cincinnati	214	63	.773
3.	Providence	204	64	.761
4.	Duke	213	67	.761
5.	Kentucky	197	69	.741
6.	Ohio St.	188	69	.732
7.	St. Joseph's	201	74	.731
8.	Dayton	207	77	.729
9.	Bradley	197	74	.727
10.	Princeton	188	71	.726
11.	Vanderbilt	182	69	.725
12.	North Carolina	184	72	.719
13.	St. Bonaventure	172	69	.714
14.	Villanova	193	79	.710
15.	Houston	198	82	.707
16.	St. John's (N.Y.)	185	79	.701
17.	Miami (Fla.)	183	82	.691
18.	West Virginia	197	89	.689
19.	Temple	183	83	.688
20.	UTEP	177	81	.686

Played only seven seasons:

	Weber St.	147	36	.803

The 1970s

Rk.	Team	Won	Lost	Pct.
1.	UCLA	273	27	.910
2.	Marquette	251	41	.860
3.	Pennsylvania	223	56	.799
4.	North Carolina	239	65	.786
5.	Kentucky	223	69	.764
6.	Louisville	224	70	.762
7.	Syracuse	213	69	.755
8.	Long Beach St.	209	71	.746
9.	Indiana	208	75	.735
10.	Florida St.	201	74	.731
11.	UNLV	203	78	.722
12.	North Carolina St.	208	80	.722
13.	San Francisco	202	79	.719
14.	Houston	210	84	.714
15.	Providence	209	84	.713
16.	South Carolina	198	80	.712
17.	St. John's (N.Y.)	205	85	.707
18.	Maryland	199	85	.701
19.	Rutgers	193	84	.697
20.	Notre Dame	202	89	.694

Played only eight seasons:

	Oral Roberts	161	59	.732

The 1980s

Rk.	Team	Won	Lost	Pct.
1.	North Carolina	281	63	.817
2.	UNLV	271	65	.807
3.	Georgetown	269	69	.796
4.	DePaul	235	67	.778
5.	Temple	225	78	.743
6.	Syracuse	243	87	.736
7.	UTEP	227	82	.735
8.	Oklahoma	245	90	.731

Rk.	Team	Won	Lost	Pct.
9.	Kentucky	233	86	.730
10.	St. John's (N.Y.)	228	85	.728
11.	Indiana	228	86	.726
12.	Oregon St.	212	80	.726
13.	Louisville	250	96	.723
14.	Illinois	233	90	.721
15.	Memphis	225	89	.717
16.	Northeastern	213	86	.712
17.	Chattanooga	215	89	.707
18.	Arkansas	218	92	.703
19.	Missouri	227	99	.696
20.	West Virginia	217	95	.696

The 1990s

Rk.	Team	Won	Lost	Pct.
1.	Kansas	286	60	.827
2.	Kentucky	282	63	.817
3.	Arizona	256	67	.793
4.	Duke	271	78	.777
5.	North Carolina	270	78	.776
6.	Connecticut	259	75	.775
7.	Utah	250	76	.767
8.	Princeton	210	66	.761
9.	Arkansas	260	83	.758
10.	UCLA	240	79	.752
11.	Cincinnati	246	83	.748
12.	Xavier	217	86	.716
13.	Syracuse	232	92	.716
14.	Massachusetts	237	94	.716
15.	Murray St.	219	88	.713
16.	Indiana	229	94	.709
17.	New Mexico St.	219	91	.706
18.	Wis.-Green Bay	211	90	.701
19.	Purdue	222	96	.698
20.	New Mexico	224	97	.698

Played only eight seasons:

	Col. of Charleston	191	42	.820

The 2000s

Rk.	Team	Won	Lost	Pct.
1.	Duke	121	20	.858
2.	Oklahoma	111	26	.810
3.	Stanford	102	26	.797
4.	Kansas	113	29	.796
5.	Arizona	107	29	.787
6.	Gonzaga	105	29	.784
7.	Butler	100	28	.781
8.	Utah St.	103	29	.780
9.	Cincinnati	102	30	.773
10.	Tulsa	108	33	.766
11.	Syracuse	104	33	.759
12.	Florida	100	32	.758
13.	Creighton	99	32	.756
14.	Col. of Charleston	92	30	.754
15.	Kentucky	101	34	.748
16.	Maryland	103	35	.746
17.	Illinois	100	34	.746
18.	Xavier	94	32	.746
19.	Kent St.	98	34	.742
20.	Michigan St.	101	37	.732

Winningest Teams Over Periods of Time

Victories Over a Two-Year Period

Team	First Year	Last Year	Won	Lost
Montana St.	1928	1929	72	4
Kentucky	1947	1948	70	6
UNLV	1986	1987	70	7
Kentucky	1997	1998	70	9
Georgetown	1984	1985	69	6
UNLV	1990	1991	69	6
Kansas	1997	1998	69	6
Duke	1998	1999	69	6
Kentucky	1996	1997	69	7
Kentucky	1948	1949	68	5
Connecticut	1998	1999	66	7
Duke	1999	2000	66	7
Duke	2001	2002	66	8
Montana St.	1927	1928	66	9
Duke	1991	1992	66	9
Oklahoma	1988	1989	65	10
Michigan St.	1999	2000	65	12
UNLV	1987	1988	65	8
Temple	1987	1988	64	6
Arizona	1988	1989	64	7
Massachusetts	1995	1996	64	7
Arkansas	1990	1991	64	9
Duke	2000	2001	64	9
Bradley	1950	1951	64	11
UNLV	1989	1990	64	13

Victories Over a Three-Year Period

Team	First Year	Last Year	Won	Lost
Kentucky	1996	1998	104	11
Kentucky	1947	1949	102	8
Montana St.	1927	1929	102	11
Duke	1999	2001	101	11
Kentucky	1946	1948	98	8
Kansas	1996	1998	98	11
Duke	1998	2000	98	11
UNLV	1985	1987	98	11
UNLV	1986	1988	98	13
UNLV	1989	1991	98	14
Kentucky	1997	1999	98	18
Kentucky	1995	1997	97	12
UNLV	1990	1992	95	8
Duke	2000	2002	95	13
Duke	1990	1992	95	18
UNLV	1987	1989	94	16
Kentucky	1948	1950	93	10
Montana St.	1928	1930	93	14
Georgetown	1984	1986	93	14
Duke	1997	1999	93	15
Michigan St.	1999	2001	93	17
Massachusetts	1994	1996	92	14
Oklahoma	1988	1990	92	15
Duke	2001	2003	92	15
Kansas	1997	1999	92	16
UNLV	1988	1990	92	19

Victories Over a Four-Year Period

Team	First Year	Last Year	Won	Lost
Duke	1998	2001	133	15
Duke	1999	2002	132	15
Kentucky	1995	1998	132	16
Kentucky	1996	1999	132	20
Kentucky	1946	1949	130	10
UNLV	1987	1990	129	21
Kentucky	1947	1950	127	13
UNLV	1984	1987	127	17
UNLV	1986	1989	127	21
UNLV	1985	1988	126	17
UNLV	1988	1991	126	20
Kentucky	1948	1951	125	12
UNLV	1989	1992	124	16

Team	First Year	Last Year	Won	Lost
Kentucky	1994	1997	124	19
Kansas	1995	1998	123	17
Montana St.	1927	1930	123	21
Duke	1989	1992	123	26
Georgetown	1984	1987	122	19
Duke	1997	2000	122	20
Montana St.	1926	1929	122	23
Duke	2000	2003	121	20
Kansas	1996	1999	121	21
Georgetown	1982	1985	121	23
Kentucky	1997	2000	121	28
Kentucky	1945	1948	120	12

Winning Percentage Over a Two-Year Period

(Minimum 40 games)

Team	First Year	Last Year	Won	Lost	Pct.
UCLA	1972	1973	60	0	1.000
Indiana	1975	1976	63	1	.984
UCLA	1967	1968	59	1	.983
UCLA	1971	1972	59	1	.983
North Carolina St.	1973	1974	57	1	.983
North Carolina	1923	1924	41	1	.976
UCLA	1964	1965	58	2	.967
UCLA	1968	1969	58	2	.967
Long Island	1935	1936	49	2	.961
St. John's (N.Y.)	1930	1931	46	2	.958
UNLV	1991	1992	60	3	.952
Seton Hall	1940	1941	39	2	.951
Arkansas	1928	1929	38	2	.950
Notre Dame	1926	1927	38	2	.950
UCLA	1969	1970	57	3	.950
UCLA	1970	1971	57	3	.950
Alcorn St.	1978	1979	56	3	.949
Montana St.	1928	1929	72	4	.947
Long Island	1936	1937	53	3	.946
Pennsylvania	1970	1971	53	3	.946
Ohio St.	1961	1962	53	3	.946
Long Island	1934	1935	50	3	.943
Kentucky	1954	1955	48	3	.941
St. John's (N.Y.)	1929	1930	46	3	.939
Pennsylvania	1920	1921	43	3	.935

Winning Percentage Over a Three-Year Period

(Minimum 60 games)

Team	First Year	Last Year	Won	Lost	Pct.
UCLA	1971	1973	89	1	.989
UCLA	1967	1969	88	2	.978
UCLA	1970	1972	87	3	.967
Long Island	1934	1936	75	3	.962
UCLA	1968	1970	86	4	.956
UCLA	1969	1971	86	4	.956
UCLA	1972	1974	86	4	.956
St. John's (N.Y.)	1929	1931	67	4	.944
Long Island	1935	1937	77	5	.939
Pennsylvania	1919	1921	58	4	.935
Indiana	1974	1976	86	6	.935
Ohio St.	1960	1962	78	6	.929
Pennsylvania	1970	1972	78	6	.929
Kentucky	1947	1949	102	8	.927
Kentucky	1946	1948	98	8	.925
Kentucky	1951	1953	61	5	.924
Cincinnati	1960	1962	84	7	.923
UCLA	1973	1975	84	7	.923
UNLV	1990	1992	95	8	.922
Pennsylvania	1970	1972	78	6	.929
Cincinnati	1961	1963	82	7	.921
North Carolina St.	1973	1975	79	7	.919
DePaul	1980	1982	79	7	.917
Arkansas	1926	1928	56	5	.918
Pennsylvania	1920	1922	67	6	.918
St. John's (N.Y.)	1930	1932	66	6	.917

Team	First Year	Last Year	Won	Lost	Pct.
Seton Hall	1940	1942	55	5	.917
Kentucky	1949	1951	89	9	.908
Marquette	1970	1972	79	8	.908
Kentucky	1996	1998	104	11	.904
Kentucky	1945	1947	84	9	.903

Team	First Year	Last Year	Won	Lost	Pct.
Long Island	1934	1937	103	6	.945
UCLA	1972	1975	114	7	.942
Kentucky	1946	1949	130	10	.929
Kentucky	1952	1955	77	6	.928
Pennsylvania	1918	1921	76	6	.927
Arkansas	1926	1929	75	6	.929
Long Island	1936	1939	99	8	.925
Cincinnati	1960	1963	110	9	.924
Pennsylvania	1919	1922	82	7	.921
St. John's (N.Y.)	1929	1932	89	8	.918
St. John's (N.Y.)	1928	1931	85	8	.914
UCLA	1964	1967	106	10	.914
UCLA	1966	1969	106	10	.914
Kentucky	1948	1951	125	12	.912
Long Island	1939	1942	92	9	.911
UCLA	1973	1976	112	11	.911
Long Island	1935	1938	100	10	.909
Kentucky	1945	1948	120	12	.909
Cincinnati	1959	1962	110	11	.909

Winning Percentage Over a Four-Year Period

(Minimum 80 games)

Team	First Year	Last Year	Won	Lost	Pct.
UCLA	1970	1973	117	3	.975
UCLA	1967	1970	116	4	.967
UCLA	1969	1972	116	4	.967
UCLA	1968	1971	115	5	.958
UCLA	1971	1974	115	5	.958
Kentucky	1951	1954	86	5	.945

Winning Streaks

Full Season

Wins	Team	Seasons	Ended By	Score
88	UCLA	1971-74	Notre Dame	71-70
60	San Francisco	1955-57	Illinois	62-33
47	UCLA	1966-68	Houston	71-69
45	UNLV	1990-91	Duke	79-77
44	Texas	1913-17	Rice	24-18
43	Seton Hall	1939-41	Long Island	49-26
43	Long Island	1935-37	Stanford	45-31
41	UCLA	1968-69	Southern California	46-44
39	Marquette	1970-71	Ohio St.	60-59
37	Cincinnati	1962-63	Wichita St.	65-64
37	North Carolina	1957-58	West Virginia	75-64
36	North Carolina St.	1974-75	Wake Forest	83-78
35	Arkansas	1927-29	Texas	26-25

Home Court

Wins	Team	Seasons	Ended By	Score
129	Kentucky	1943-55	Georgia Tech	59-58
99	St. Bonaventure	1948-61	Niagara	87-77
98	UCLA	1970-76	Oregon	65-45
86	Cincinnati	1957-64	Bradley	87-77
81	Arizona	1945-51	Kansas St.	76-57
81	Marquette	1967-73	Notre Dame	71-69
80	Lamar	1978-84	Louisiana Tech	68-65
75	Long Beach St.	1968-74	San Francisco	94-84
72	UNLV	1974-78	New Mexico	102-98
71	Arizona	1987-92	UCLA	89-87
68	Cincinnati	1972-78	Georgia Tech	59-56
67	Western Ky.	1949-55	Xavier	(ot) 82-80

Regular Season

(Does not include national postseason tournaments)

Wins	Team	Seasons	Ended By	Score
76	UCLA	1971-74	Notre Dame	71-70
57	Indiana	1975-77	Toledo	59-57
56	Marquette	1970-72	Detroit	70-49
54	Kentucky	1952-55	Georgia Tech	59-58
51	San Francisco	1955-57	Illinois	62-33
48	Pennsylvania	1970-72	Temple	57-52
47	Ohio St.	1960-62	Wisconsin	86-67
44	Texas	1913-17	Rice	24-18
43	UCLA	1966-68	Houston	71-69
43	Long Island	1935-37	Stanford	45-31
42	Seton Hall	1939-41	Long Island	49-26

Current Home Court

Wins	Team	Wins	Team
39	Western Ky.	15	Sam Houston St.
28	Duke	15	Texas
27	Southern Ill.	15	Wis.-Milwaukee
22	Pittsburgh	14	Stephen F. Austin
18	Butler	13	Wisconsin
18	Weber St.	12	Colorado
17	Creighton	12	Holy Cross
17	Illinois	11	Kentucky
17	Syracuse	10	Delaware St.
17	Wake Forest	10	Wagner
15	Austin Peay		

Rivalries

Consecutive Years

Years	Opponents	First Year	Last Year
102	Columbia vs. Yale	1902	2003
102	Princeton vs. Yale	1902	2003
101	Pennsylvania vs. Princeton	1903	2003
100	Columbia vs. Pennsylvania	1904	2003
100	Cornell vs. Pennsylvania	1904	2003
99	Maine vs. New Hampshire	1905	2003
98	Idaho vs. Washington St.	1906	2003
97	Kansas vs. Kansas St.	1907	2003
97	Kansas vs. Missouri	1907	2003
96	Kansas St. vs. Nebraska	1908	2003

Games Played

Games	Opponents	First Year	Last Year
318	Oregon vs. Oregon St.	1903	2003
271	Oregon St. vs. Washington	1904	2003
271	Oregon vs. Washington	1904	2003
266	Oregon St. vs. Washington St.	1907	2003
261	Oregon vs. Washington St.	1908	2003
254	Washington vs. Washington St.	1910	2003
253	Kansas vs. Kansas St.	1907	2003
247	Kansas vs. Missouri	1907	2003
241	California vs. Stanford	1912	2003
232	Brigham Young vs. Utah	1909	2003

Victories for One Opponent

W-L	Opponents	First Year	Last Year
176-142	Oregon St. vs. Oregon	1903	2003
173- 97	Washington vs. Oregon	1904	2003
165- 88	Kansas vs. Kansas St.	1907	2003
163- 91	Washington vs. Washington St.	1910	2003
157- 91	Kansas vs. Missouri	1907	2003
156- 56	Kansas vs. Iowa St.	1908	2003
156-110	Oregon St. vs. Washington St.	1909	2003
153- 70	Kansas vs. Nebraska	1900	2003
150-107	Washington St. vs. Idaho	1906	2003
146-61	North Carolina vs. Wake Forest	1911	2003

Consecutive Victories

Won	Opponents	First Year	Last Year
52	UCLA vs. California	1961	1985
41	Southern California vs. UCLA	1932	1943
39	Kentucky vs. Mississippi	1929	1972
39	Rhode Island vs. Maine	1924	1952
38	Providence vs. Brown	1959	1978
38	Syracuse vs. Cornell	1963	†2003
36	Arizona vs. Washington St.	1986	†2003
35	Connecticut vs. New Hampshire	1939	1961

Won	Opponents	First Year	Last Year
35	South Carolina vs. Citadel	1945	1988
34	Marquette vs. Wis.-Milwaukee	1917	†1999

†active streak

Current Consecutive Victories

Won	Opponents	First Year	Last Year
38	Syracuse vs. Cornell	1963	2003
36	Arizona vs. Washington St.	1986	2003
34	Marquette vs. Wis.-Milwaukee	1917	1999
33	North Carolina vs. VMI	1922	1997
26	Kansas vs. Kansas St.	1994	2003
26	Ohio St. vs. Northwestern	1990	2003
25	Kentucky vs. Xavier	1942	1968

Consecutive Home Victories

Won	Opponents	First Year	Last Year
52	Princeton vs. Brown	1929	2002
49	North Carolina vs. Clemson	1926	†2003
47	UCLA vs. Washington St.	1950	†2003
41	Kentucky vs. Mississippi	1929	1996
37	Southern California vs. UCLA	1932	1944
34	Kentucky vs. Georgia	1930	1984
33	Rhode Island vs. Northeastern	1917	1988
32	Rhode Island vs. New Hampshire	1937	1973
32	UCLA vs. California	1961	1989
31	Marquette vs. Wis.-Milwaukee	1920	†1999
31	North Carolina vs. Virginia	1921	1972
31	Providence vs. Brown	1955	1978

†active streak

Current Consecutive Home Victories

Won	Opponents	First Year	Last Year
49	North Carolina vs. Clemson	1926	2003
47	UCLA vs. Washington St.	1950	2003
31	Marquette vs. Wis.-Milwaukee	1920	1999
30	Indiana vs. Northwestern	1969	2003
29	Kentucky vs. Vanderbilt	1975	2003
20	Oklahoma St. vs. Drake	1931	1958

Victories for One Opponent in One Year

W-L	Opponents	Year
5-0	Kansas vs. Nebraska	1909
5-0	Kansas vs. Kansas St.	1935
4-0	by many	

A.P. Poll Records

Full Season At No. 1

1956, San Francisco, 14 weeks
1960, Cincinnati, 12 weeks
1961, Ohio St., 13 weeks
1962, Ohio St., 14 weeks
1963, Cincinnati, 16 weeks
1967, UCLA, 15 weeks
1969, UCLA, 15 weeks
1972, UCLA, 16 weeks
1973, UCLA, 16 weeks
1976, Indiana, 17 weeks
1991, UNLV, 17 weeks
1992, Duke, 18 weeks

Most Consecutive Weeks At No. 1

46, UCLA, Feb. 9, 1971 to Jan. 15, 1974
27, Ohio St., Dec. 13, 1960 to March 13, 1962
23, UCLA, Preseason Nov. 1966 to Jan. 16, 1968
19, San Francisco, Feb. 8, 1955 to March 6, 1956
18, Duke, Preseason Nov. 1991 to March 16, 1992
17, Indiana, Preseason Nov. 1975 to March 16, 1976
17, UNLV, Preseason Nov. 1990 to March 12, 1991
16, Cincinnati, Preseason Nov. 1962 to March 12, 1963
15, UCLA, Preseason Nov. 1968 to March 4, 1969
15, North Carolina, Dec. 6, 1983 to March 13, 1984
15, Kansas, Dec. 3, 1996 to March 11, 1997

Preseason No. 1 To Not Rank No. 1 The Rest of the Season

1970, South Carolina
1978, North Carolina
1981, Kentucky
1986, Georgia Tech
1988, Syracuse
1990, UNLV
2000, Connecticut

Biggest Jump To No. 1 From Previous Week

8th, West Virginia, Dec. 17 to Dec. 24, 1957
6th, Duke, Dec. 7 to Dec. 14, 1965
5th, Holy Cross, Jan. 10 to Jan. 17, 1950
5th, Kansas St., Dec. 23 to Dec. 30, 1952
5th, Indiana, Dec. 21 to Dec. 28, 1982
5th, UCLA, Jan. 11 to Jan. 18, 1983
5th, Temple, Feb. 2 to Feb. 9, 1988
5th, Oklahoma, Feb. 7 to Feb. 14, 1989
5th, Oklahoma, Feb. 27 to March 6, 1990
4th, 13 tied

Biggest Jump From Not Rated the Previous Week

(at least 20 rated)
4th, Kansas, Preseason to Nov. 27, 1989
5th, St. Louis, Dec. 26, 1950 to Jan. 3, 1951
5th, Cincinnati, Jan. 31 to Feb. 7, 1961
6th, Notre Dame, Jan. 12 to Jan. 19, 1954
6th, Missouri, Dec. 7 to Dec. 14, 1954
6th, Maryland, Dec. 10 to Dec. 17, 1957
6th, Oklahoma St., Jan. 21 to Jan. 28, 1958
7th, Bradley, Mar. 9 to Mar. 23, 1954
7th, Oklahoma City, Jan. 14 to Jan. 21, 1958
7th, Iowa, Dec. 27, 1960 to Jan. 3, 1961
7th, Wake Forest, Jan. 30 to Feb. 6, 1976
7th, North Carolina St., Preseason to Nov. 29, 1983

Biggest Jump From Not Rated the Previous Week

(at least 25 rated)
4th, Kansas, Preseason to Nov. 27, 1989
8th, Arizona, Preseason to Nov. 20, 2001

10th, Notre Dame, Dec. 3 to Dec. 10, 2002
12th, Arizona St., Nov. 21 to Nov. 28, 1994
12th, Duke, Nov. 20 to Nov. 27, 1995
12th, North Carolina, Nov. 26 to Dec. 3, 2002
13th, Wake Forest, Jan. 25 to Feb. 1, 1993
13th, Oregon, Jan. 29 to Feb. 5, 2002
14th, Iowa, Jan. 9 to Jan. 16, 2001
14th, Pittsburgh, Feb. 5 to Feb. 12, 2002

Biggest Drop From No. 1 From Previous Week

9th, UNLV, Feb. 22 to Mar. 1, 1983
8th, UCLA, Dec. 7 to Dec. 14, 1965
8th, South Carolina, Preseason Nov. to Dec. 9, 1969
8th, Duke, Jan. 17 to Jan. 24, 1989
8th, Connecticut, Preseason Nov. to Nov. 16, 1999
7th, St. John (N.Y.), Dec. 18 to Dec. 26, 1951
7th, UCLA, Jan. 25 to Feb. 1, 1983
7th, Cincinnati, March 7 to March 14, 2000
6th, Michigan St., Jan. 9 to Jan. 16, 1979
6th, Memphis, Jan. 11 to Jan. 18, 1983
6th, UNLV, Preseason Nov. 1989 to Nov. 27, 1989
6th, Syracuse, Jan. 2 to Jan. 9, 1990
6th, Michigan, Nov. 30 to Dec. 7, 1992
6th, Kentucky, Nov. 29 to Dec. 6, 1993

Biggest Drop To Not Rated From The Previous Week

(at least 20 rated)
2nd, Louisville, Preseason to Dec. 2, 1986
4th, Indiana, Dec. 27, 1960, to Jan. 3, 1961
5th, Kansas, Dec. 8 to Dec. 15, 1953
6th, Iowa, Dec. 27, 1955, to Jan. 3, 1956
6th, Louisville, Preseason to Nov. 29, 1983
7th, Indiana, Dec. 14 to Dec. 21, 1954
7th, Missouri, Dec. 21 to Dec. 28, 1954
7th, Utah, Dec. 27, 1955, to Jan. 3, 1956
7th, Kansas, Dec. 9 to Dec. 16, 1958
7th, Duquesne, Dec. 9 to Dec. 16, 1969
7th, Ohio St., Dec. 16 to Dec. 23, 1980

Biggest Drop To Not Rated From The Previous Week

(at least 25 rated)
11th, Indiana, Dec. 21 to Dec. 28, 1994
14th, UCLA, Nov. 26 to Dec. 3, 2002
15th, St. John's (N.Y.), Nov. 15 to Nov. 23, 1999
15th, UCLA, Nov. 21 to Nov. 28, 2000
15th, St. Joseph's, Dec. 18 to Dec. 25, 2001
16th, Oklahoma, Feb. 1 to Feb. 8, 1993
16th, Duke, Jan. 9 to Jan. 16, 1995
16th, Minnesota, Dec. 19 to Dec. 26, 1994
16th, Arkansas, Preseason to Nov. 20, 1995
16th, Temple, Dec. 8 to Dec. 15, 1998
17th, Eight tied

Lowest Ranking To Rise To No. 1 During Season

(does not include 1962-69 when only 10 ranked)
NR, Indiana St., Dec. 5, 1978 to Feb. 13, 1979 (only 20 ranked)
20th, UNLV, Preseason Nov. 1982 to Feb. 15, 1983
20th, Kentucky, Dec. 31, 2002 to March 18, 2003
19th, Indiana, Dec. 16, 1952 to March 3, 1953
19th, Houston, Jan. 4 to March 1, 1983
19th, Connecticut, Preseason Nov. 1994 to Feb. 13, 1995
18th, North Carolina, Jan. 4 to Feb. 1, 1983
18th, Duke, Nov. 16, 1999 to March 14, 2000
17th, San Francisco, Dec. 21, 1954 to Feb. 8, 1955
17th, Arizona, Preseason Nov. to Dec. 22, 1987
17th, Oklahoma, Nov. 27, 1989 to March 6, 1990
17th, UCLA, Jan. 24 to March 17, 1994

Lowest Ranking To Drop From No. 1 During Season

(does not include 1962-69 when only 10 ranked)
NR, St. John's (N.Y.), Dec. 18, 1951 to Jan. 15, 1952 (only 20 ranked)
NR, Duke, Jan. 8 to Feb. 26, 1980 (only 20 ranked)
NR, Alabama, Dec. 31, 2002 to Feb. 11, 2003
24th, Connecticut, Preseason Nov. 1999 to Feb. 29, 2000
21st, Arizona, Nov. 21, 2000 to Jan. 9, 2001
20th, Indiana, Dec. 11, 1979 to Feb. 5, 1980
17th, Memphis, Jan. 11 to March 1, 1983
17th, Syracuse, Preseason Nov. 1987 to Jan. 26, 1988
16th, North Carolina, Preseason Nov. 1977 to March 13, 1978
16th, North Carolina, Dec. 17, 1957 to Feb. 18, 1958

Most Teams At No. 1 In One Season

7, 1983 (Houston, Indiana, Memphis, UNLV, North Carolina, UCLA and Virginia)
6, 1993 (Duke, Indiana, Kansas, Kentucky, Michigan and North Carolina)
6, 1994 (Arkansas, Duke, Kansas, Kentucky, North Carolina and UCLA)
6, 1995 (Arkansas, Connecticut, Kansas, Massachusetts, North Carolina and UCLA)
5, 1979 (Duke, Indiana, Michigan St., Notre Dame and UCLA)
5, 1990 (Kansas, Missouri, UNLV, Oklahoma and Syracuse)
5, 2001 (Arizona, Duke, Michigan St., North Carolina and Stanford)
5, 2003 (Alabama, Arizona, Duke, Florida and Kentucky)
4, eight tied

Most Consecutive Weeks With Different No. 1

7, Jan. 3 to Feb. 14, 1994 (in order: Arkansas, North Carolina, Kansas, UCLA, Duke, North Carolina and Arkansas)
5, Jan. 17 to Feb. 14, 1989 (in order: Duke, Illinois, Oklahoma, Arizona and Oklahoma)
5, Feb. 6 to March 6, 1990 (in order: Missouri, Kansas, Missouri, Kansas and Oklahoma)
5, Jan. 30 to Feb. 27, 1995 (in order: Massachusetts, North Carolina, Connecticut, Kansas and UCLA)
4, Dec. 11, 1951 to Jan. 2, 1952 [in order: Kentucky, St. John's (N.Y.), Kentucky and Kansas]
4, Feb. 17 to March 10, 1970 (in order: UCLA, Kentucky, UCLA and Kentucky)
4, Feb. 7 to Feb. 28, 1978 (in order: Kentucky, Arkansas, Marquette and Kentucky)
4, Feb. 6 to Feb. 27, 1979 (in order: Notre Dame, Indiana St., UCLA and Indiana St.)
4, Jan. 13 to Feb. 3, 1987 (in order: UNLV, Iowa, North Carolina and UNLV)

Largest Point Margin in Defeating No. 1

41, No. 2 Kentucky (81) vs. No. 1 St. John's (N.Y.), Lexington, KY, Dec. 17, 1951
32, No. 2 UCLA (101) vs. No. 1 Houston (69), Los Angeles (NSF), Mar. 22, 1968
24, No. 3 Massachusetts (104) vs. No. 1 Arkansas (80), Springfield, MA, Nov. 25, 1994
24, No. 2 North Carolina (97) vs. No. 1 Duke (73), Chapel Hill, NC, Feb. 5, 1998
23, No. 15 Villanova (96) vs. No. 1 Connecticut (73), Storrs, CT, Feb. 18, 1995
22, Tied No. 5 Oklahoma (100) vs. No. 1 Kansas (78), Norman, OK, Feb. 27, 1990
20, No. 5 Arizona St. (87) vs. No. 1 Oregon St. (67), Corvallis, OR, Mar. 7, 1981
20, No. 13 North Carolina (91) vs. No. 1 Duke (71), Durham, NC, Jan. 18, 1989
20, No. 17 Georgia Tech (89) vs. No. 1 North Carolina (69), Atlanta, Jan. 12, 1994

Largest Point Margin for an Unranked Opponent Defeating No. 1

19, Wisconsin (86) vs. Ohio St. (67), Madison, WI, Mar. 3, 1962
19, Villanova (93) vs. Syracuse (74), Greensboro, NC, Jan. 6, 1990
18, Maryland (69) vs. North Carolina (51), College Park, MD, Feb. 21, 1959
16, Alabama (78) vs. Kentucky (62), Tuscaloosa, AL, Jan. 23, 1978
16, Nebraska (67) vs. Missouri (51), Columbia, MO, Feb. 6, 1982
15, Vanderbilt (101) vs. Kentucky (86), Nashville, TN, Jan. 13, 1993
15, Long Beach St. (64) vs. Kansas (49), Lawrence, KS, Jan. 25, 1993
15, California (85) vs. UCLA (70), Oakland, CA, Jan. 30, 1994
14, Cincinnati (66) vs. Duquesne (52), Cincinnati, Feb. 25, 1954
14, Kansas (91) vs. UNLV (77), New York, Nov. 22, 1989
14, North Carolina St. (86) vs. North Carolina (72), Chapel Hill, NC, Feb. 21, 1998

Most Weeks At No. 1 - All-Time

(Complete List)
128, UCLA, 1964-95
92, Duke, 1966-2003
84, North Carolina, 1957-2001
80, Kentucky, 1949-2003
45, Cincinnati, 1959-2000
44, Indiana, 1953-93
39, Kansas, 1952-2002
32, UNLV, 1983-91
29, Arizona, 1988-2003
28, San Francisco, 1955-77
27, Ohio St., 1961-62
21, Michigan, 1965-93
16, Kansas St., 1952-59
15, DePaul, 1980-81
15, Massachusetts, 1995-96
13, North Carolina St., 1975
12, Arkansas, 1978-95
12, Connecticut, 1995-2000
12, Georgetown, 1985
12, Stanford, 2000-01
12, Virginia, 1981-83
11, Houston, 1968-83
8, St. John's (N.Y.), 1950-85
8, West Virginia, 1958
7, Syracuse, 1988-90
6, Missouri, 1982-90
6, Seton Hall, 1953
6, Temple, 1988
5, Bradley, 1950-51
5, Holy Cross, 1950
5, Notre Dame, 1974-79
5, Oklahoma, 1989-90
5, Oregon St., 1981
4, Indiana St., 1979
4, La Salle, 1953-55
4, Loyola (Ill.), 1964
4, Michigan St., 1979-2001
3, Marquette, 1971-78
2, Alabama, 2003
2, Duquesne, 1954
2, Illinois, 1952-89
2, St. Louis, 1949
1, Florida, 2003
1, Georgia Tech, 1986
1, Iowa, 1987
1, Memphis, 1983
1, Oklahoma St., 1951
1, South Carolina, 1970
1, Wichita St., 1965

Most Times Defeating No. 1

(Complete List)
10, UCLA, 1965-2003
9, North Carolina, 1959-98
8, Duke, 1958-97
8, Maryland, 1959-2003
7, Oklahoma, 1951-2002
6, Georgia Tech, 1955-94
6, Kentucky, 1951-2003
6, Notre Dame, 1971-87
6, Ohio St., 1965-93
5, Cincinnati, 1954-98
5, Indiana, 1984-2002
5, Kansas, 1953-94
5, St. John's (N.Y.), 1951-85
5, Vanderbilt, 1951-93
4, Arizona, 1987-2001
4, Missouri, 1989-97
4, North Carolina St., 1983-98
4, Villanova, 1983-95
4, Wake Forest, 1975-92
3, Alabama, 1978-94
3, DePaul, 1950-52
3, Massachusetts, 1993-95
3, Minnesota, 1951-89
3, Nebraska, 1958-82
3, St. Louis, 1951-2000
3, Stanford, 1988-2003

DIVISION I

3, Utah, 1954-2002
3, West Virginia, 1957-83
2, California, 1960-94
2, CCNY, 1950
2, Clemson, 1980-2001
2, Dayton, 1953-54
2, George Washington, 1995-96
2, Georgetown, 1963-85
2, Houston, 1968-78
2, Iowa, 1965-99
2, Kansas St., 1990-94
2, Louisville, 1953-86
2, Loyola (Ill.), 1949-63
2, LSU, 1978-2002
2, Michigan, 1964-97
2, Mississippi St., 1959-96
2, Oklahoma St., 1949-89
2, Oregon, 1970-74
2, Oregon St., 1953-74
2, Purdue, 1979-2000
2, Southern California, 1969-70
2, Syracuse, 1985-99
2, Temple, 1995-2000
2, Xavier, 1996-99
1, Arizona St., 1981
1, Arkansas, 1984
1, Auburn, 1988
1, Boston College, 1994
1, Bradley, 1960
1, Cal St. Fullerton, 1983
1, Chaminade, 1982
1, Charlotte, 1977
1, Connecticut, 1999
1, Detroit, 1951
1, Florida, 2000
1, Florida St., 2002
1, Illinois, 1979
1, Iowa St., 1957
1, Jacksonville, 1970

1, Long Beach St., 1993
1, Manhattan, 1958
1, Marquette, 2003
1, Michigan St., 1979
1, New Mexico, 1988
1, Old Dominion, 1981
1, Providence, 1976
1, St. Joseph's, 1981
1, Tennessee, 1969
1, Texas, 1980
1, UNLV, 1989
1, UTEP, 1966
1, Virginia, 1986
1, Virginia Tech, 1983
1, Washington, 1979
1, Wichita St., 1963
1, Wisconsin, 1962

Notes About No. 1

No. 1 has been defeated 214 times.
No. 1 has been defeated eight times in overtime.
No. 1 has been defeated 30 times by one point.
No. 1 has been defeated 109 times by a non-ranked opponent.

Chaminade is the only non-Division I team to upset the nation's top team. It happened in Honolulu on December 24, 1982 when Chaminade defeated No. 1 Virginia, 77-72.

California, CCNY, Louisville, Maryland, UTEP and Villanova have never ranked No. 1 despite winning the NCAA championship.

The following men's and women's programs from the same school have been ranked No. 1 at the same time:
Connecticut, Feb. 13, 1995
Connecticut, Nov. 30, 1998
Duke, Jan. 7-14, 2003

The last time No. 1 met No. 2 in the Final Four was 1996. No. 2 Kentucky beat No. 1 Massachusetts in the semifinal, then won the championship two days later.

No. 1 vs. No. 2

Date	No. 1, Score	W-L	No. 2, Score	Site
Mar. 26, 1949	Kentucky 46	W	Oklahoma St. 36	Seattle (CH)
Dec. 17, 1951	St. John's (N.Y.) 40	L	Kentucky 81	Lexington, KY
Dec. 21, 1954	Kentucky 70	W	Utah 65	Lexington, KY
Mar. 23, 1957	North Carolina 54	W	Kansas 53	Kansas City, MO (CH)
Mar. 18, 1960	Cincinnati 69	L	California 77	San Francisco (NSF)
Mar. 25, 1961	Ohio St. 65	L (ot)	Cincinnati 70	Kansas City, MO (CH)
Mar. 24, 1962	Ohio St. 59	L	Cincinnati 71	Louisville, KY (CH)
Dec. 14, 1964	Wichita St. 85	L	Michigan 87	Detroit
Mar. 20, 1965	Michigan 80	L	UCLA 91	Portland, OR (CH)
Mar. 18, 1966	Kentucky 83	W	Duke 79	College Park, MD (NSF)
Jan. 20, 1968	UCLA 69	L	Houston 71	Houston
Mar. 22, 1968	Houston 69	L	UCLA 101	Los Angeles (NSF)
Dec. 15, 1973	UCLA 84	W	North Carolina St. 66	St. Louis
Jan. 19, 1974	UCLA 70	L	Notre Dame 71	South Bend, IN
Jan. 26, 1974	Notre Dame 75	L	UCLA 94	Los Angeles
Mar. 25, 1974	North Carolina St. 80	W	UCLA 77	Greensboro, NC (NSF)
Mar. 31, 1975	UCLA 92	W	Kentucky 85	San Diego (CH)
Nov. 29, 1975	Indiana 84	W	UCLA 64	St. Louis
Mar. 22, 1976	Indiana 65	W	Marquette 56	Baton Rouge, LA
Dec. 26, 1981	North Carolina 82	W	Kentucky 69	East Rutherford, NJ
Jan. 9, 1982	North Carolina 65	W	Virginia 60	Chapel Hill, NC
April 2, 1983	Houston 94	W	Louisville 81	Albuquerque, NM (NSF)
Dec. 15, 1984	Georgetown 77	W	DePaul 57	Landover, MD
Jan. 26, 1985	Georgetown 65	L	St. John's (N.Y.) 66	Washington, DC
Feb. 27, 1985	St. John's (N.Y.) 69	L	Georgetown 85	New York
Mar. 9, 1985	Georgetown 92	W	St. John's (N.Y.) 80	New York
Feb. 4, 1986	North Carolina 78	W (ot)	Georgia Tech 77	Atlanta
Mar. 29, 1986	Duke 71	W	Kansas 67	Dallas (NSF)
Feb. 13, 1990	Kansas 71	L	Missouri 77	Lawrence, KS
Mar. 10, 1990	Oklahoma 95	W	Kansas 77	Kansas City, MO
Feb. 10, 1991	UNLV 112	W	Arkansas 105	Fayetteville, AR
Feb. 3, 1994	Duke 78	L	North Carolina 89	Chapel Hill, NC
Mar. 30, 1996	Massachusetts 74	L	Kentucky 81	East Rutherford, NJ (NSF)
Feb. 5, 1998	Duke 73	L	North Carolina 97	Chapel Hill, NC

Schools Defeating No. 1

Date	Rank	School	No. 1 Team	Score	Site
Jan. 20, 1949	3	Oklahoma St.	St. Louis	29-27	Stillwater, OK
Mar. 14, 1949	16	Loyola (Ill.)	Kentucky	67-56	New York
Jan. 17, 1950	NR	DePaul	St. John's (N.Y.)	74-68	New York
Mar. 18, 1950	NR	CCNY	Bradley	69-61	New York
Mar. 28, 1950	NR	CCNY	Bradley	71-68	New York (CH)
Dec. 29, 1950	NR	St. Louis	Kentucky	43-42	New Orleans
Jan. 11, 1951	11	St. John's (N.Y.)	Bradley	68-59	New York
Jan. 15, 1951	NR	Detroit	Bradley	70-65	Peoria, IL
Jan. 20, 1951	NR	Oklahoma	Oklahoma St.	44-40	Norman, OK
Mar. 3, 1951	NR	Vanderbilt	Kentucky	61-57	Louisville, KY
Dec. 13, 1951	NR	Minnesota	Kentucky	61-57	Minneapolis
Dec. 17, 1951	2	Kentucky	St. John's (N.Y.)	81-40	Lexington, KY
Dec. 29, 1951	12	St. Louis	Kentucky	61-60	New Orleans
Jan. 28, 1952	NR	DePaul	Illinois	69-65	Chicago
Mar. 22, 1952	10	St. John's (N.Y.)	Kentucky	64-57	Raleigh, NC (RF)
Dec. 27, 1952	NR	DePaul	La Salle	63-61	Chicago
Jan. 17, 1953	15	Kansas	Kansas St.	80-66	Lawrence, KS
Mar. 1, 1953	NR	Dayton	Seton Hall	70-65	Dayton, OH
Mar. 2, 1953	18	Louisville	Seton Hall	73-67	Louisville, KY
Mar. 7, 1953	NR	Minnesota	Indiana	65-63	Minneapolis
Dec. 22, 1953	12	Oregon St.	Indiana	67-51	Eugene, OR
Feb. 25, 1954	NR	Cincinnati	Duquesne	66-52	Cincinnati
Feb. 27, 1954	16	Dayton	Duquesne	64-54	Dayton, OH
Dec. 18, 1954	15	Utah	La Salle	79-69	New York
Jan. 31, 1955	NR	Georgia Tech	Kentucky	65-59	Atlanta
Jan. 14, 1957	9	Iowa St.	Kansas	39-37	Ames, IA
Dec. 21, 1957	8	West Virginia	North Carolina	75-64	Lexington, KY
Jan. 27, 1958	NR	Duke	West Virginia	72-68	Durham, NC
Mar. 3, 1958	NR	Nebraska	Kansas St.	55-48	Lincoln, NE
Mar. 8, 1958	10	Kansas	Kansas St.	61-44	Manhattan, KS
Mar. 11, 1958	NR	Manhattan	West Virginia	89-84	New York
Jan. 6, 1959	NR	Vanderbilt	Kentucky	75-66	Nashville, TN
Jan. 14, 1959	3	North Carolina	North Carolina St.	72-68	Raleigh, NC
Feb. 9, 1959	10	Mississippi St.	Kentucky	66-58	Mississippi State, MS
Feb. 21, 1959	NR	Maryland	North Carolina	69-51	College Park, MD
Mar. 14, 1959	5	Cincinnati	Kansas St.	85-75	Lawrence, KS (RF)
Jan. 16, 1960	4	Bradley	Cincinnati	91-90	Peoria, IL
Mar. 18, 1960	2	California	Cincinnati	77-69	San Francisco (NSF)
Mar. 25, 1961	2	Cincinnati	Ohio St.	70-65 (ot)	Kansas City, MO (CH)
Mar. 3, 1962	NR	Wisconsin	Ohio St.	86-67	Madison, WI
Mar. 24, 1962	2	Cincinnati	Ohio St.	71-59	Louisville, KY (CH)
Feb. 16, 1963	NR	Wichita St.	Cincinnati	65-64	Wichita, KS
Mar. 23, 1963	3	Loyola (Ill.)	Cincinnati	60-58	Louisville, KY
Dec. 28, 1963	NR	Georgetown	Loyola (Ill.)	69-58	Philadelphia
Jan. 4, 1964	NR	Georgia Tech	Kentucky	76-67	Atlanta
Jan. 6, 1964	6	Vanderbilt	Kentucky	85-83	Nashville, TN
Dec. 12, 1964	NR	Nebraska	Michigan	74-73	Lincoln, NE
Dec. 14, 1964	2	Michigan	Wichita St.	87-85	Detroit
Jan. 2, 1965	NR	St. John's (N.Y.)	Michigan	75-74	New York
Jan. 29, 1965	NR	Iowa	UCLA	87-82	Chicago
Mar. 8, 1965	NR	Ohio St.	Michigan	93-85	Columbus, OH
Mar. 20, 1965	2	UCLA	Michigan	91-80	Portland, OR (CH)
Dec. 10, 1965	6	Duke	UCLA	82-66	Durham, NC
Dec. 11, 1965	6	Duke	UCLA	94-75	Charlotte, NC
Feb. 7, 1966	NR	West Virginia	Duke	94-90	Morgantown, WV
Mar. 19, 1966	3	UTEP	Kentucky	72-65	College Park, MD (CH)
Jan. 20, 1968	2	Houston	UCLA	71-69	Houston
Mar. 22, 1968	2	UCLA	Houston	101-69	Los Angeles (NSF)
Mar. 23, 1968	NR	Ohio St.	Houston	89-85	Los Angeles (N3rd)
Mar. 8, 1969	NR	Southern California	UCLA	46-44	Los Angeles
Dec. 6, 1969	NR	Tennessee	South Carolina	55-54	Columbia, SC
Feb. 21, 1970	NR	Oregon	UCLA	78-65	Eugene, OR
Mar. 6, 1970	NR	Southern California	UCLA	87-86	Los Angeles
Mar. 14, 1970	4	Jacksonville	Kentucky	106-100	Columbus, OH (RF)
Jan. 23, 1971	9	Notre Dame	UCLA	89-82	South Bend, IN
Jan. 19, 1974	2	North Dame	UCLA	71-70	South Bend, IN
Jan. 26, 1974	2	UCLA	Notre Dame	94-75	Los Angeles
Feb. 15, 1974	NR	Oregon St.	UCLA	61-57	Corvallis, OR
Feb. 16, 1974	NR	Oregon	UCLA	56-51	Eugene, OR
Jan. 3, 1975	NR	Wake Forest	North Carolina St.	83-78	Greensboro, NC
Mar. 22, 1975	5	Kentucky	Indiana	92-90	Dayton, OH (RF)
Dec. 29, 1976	NR	Providence	Michigan	82-81 (2ot)	Providence, RI
Mar. 1, 1977	NR	Notre Dame	San Francisco	93-82	South Bend, IN
Mar. 19, 1977	17	Charlotte	Michigan	75-68	Lexington, KY (RF)
Jan. 23, 1978	NR	Alabama	Kentucky	78-62	Tuscaloosa, AL
Feb. 11, 1978	NR	LSU	Kentucky	95-94	Baton Rouge, LA
Feb. 18, 1978	NR	Houston	Arkansas	84-75	Houston
Feb. 26, 1978	9	Notre Dame	Marquette	65-59	South Bend, IN
Dec. 29, 1978	NR	Ohio St.	Duke	90-84	New York
Dec. 30, 1978	NR	St. John's (N.Y.)	Duke	69-66	New York

Robert Jackson and Marquette knocked off No. 1 Kentucky last season on the Golden Eagles' road to the Final Four.

UTEP, then known as Texas Western, knocked off No. 1 Kentucky for the 1966 Championship. Bobby Joe Hill helped lead the Miners.

Photo by Marquette Sports Information

Photo by Rich Clarkson/NCAA Photos

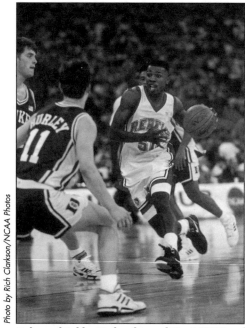

Duke and Bobby Hurley downed No. 1 UNLV and Greg Anthony (with ball) in the semifinals before beating Kansas for the 1991 championship.

Photo by Rich Clarkson/NCAA Photos

Date	Rank	School	No. 1 Team	Score	Site
Jan. 11, 1979	4	Illinois	Michigan St.	57-55	Champaign, IL
Jan. 13, 1979		Purdue	Michigan St.	52-50	West Lafayette, IN
Jan. 27, 1979	NR	Maryland	Notre Dame	67-66	College Park, MD
Feb. 11, 1979	4	UCLA	Notre Dame	56-52	South Bend, IN
Feb. 22, 1979	NR	Washington	UCLA	69-68	Seattle
Mar. 26, 1979	3	Michigan St.	Indiana St.	75-64	Salt Lake City
Dec. 18, 1979	5	Kentucky	Indiana	69-58	Lexington, KY
Jan. 9, 1980	18	Clemson	Duke	87-82	Clemson, SC
Jan. 12, 1980	15	North Carolina	Duke	82-67	Durham, NC
Mar. 9, 1980	NR	UCLA	DePaul	77-71	Tempe, AZ (2nd)
Dec. 13, 1980	NR	Texas	DePaul	65-63	Austin, TX
Jan. 10, 1981	NR	Old Dominion	DePaul	63-62	Chicago
Feb. 22, 1981	11	Notre Dame	Virginia	57-56	Chicago
Mar. 7, 1981	5	Arizona St.	Oregon St.	87-67	Corvallis, OR
Mar. 14, 1981	NR	St. Joseph's	DePaul	49-48	Dayton, OH (1st)
Jan. 21, 1982	NR	Wake Forest	North Carolina	55-48	Chapel Hill, NC
Feb. 6, 1982	NR	Nebraska	Missouri	67-51	Columbia, MO
Feb. 27, 1982	NR	Maryland	Virginia	47-46 (ot)	College Park, MD
Dec. 24, 1982	NR	Chaminade	Virginia	77-72	Honolulu
Jan. 8, 1983	NR	Ohio St.	Indiana	70-67	Columbus, OH
Jan. 10, 1983	NR	Virginia Tech	Memphis	64-56	Blacksburg, VA
Jan. 28, 1983	NR	Alabama	UCLA	70-67	Los Angeles
Feb.13, 1983	12	Villanova	North Carolina	56-53	Chapel Hill, NC
Feb. 24, 1983	NR	Cal St. Fullerton	UNLV	86-78	Fullerton, CA
Feb. 27, 1983	NR	West Virginia	UNLV	87-78	Morgantown, WV
Apr. 4, 1983	16	North Carolina St.	Houston	54-52	Albuquerque, NM (CH)
Feb. 12, 1984	NR	Arkansas	North Carolina	65-64	Pine Bluff, NC
Mar. 10, 1984	16	Duke	North Carolina	77-75	Greensboro, NC
Mar. 22, 1984	NR	Indiana	North Carolina	72-68	Atlanta (RSF)
Jan. 26, 1985	2	St. John's (N.Y.)	Georgetown	66-65	Washington, DC
Jan. 28, 1985	11	Syracuse	Georgetown	65-63	Syracuse, NY
Feb. 27, 1985	2	Georgetown	St. John's (N.Y.)	85-69	New York
Apr. 1, 1985	NR	Villanova	Georgetown	66-64	Lexington, KY
Jan. 30, 1986	NR	Virginia	North Carolina	86-73	Charlottesville, VA
Feb. 20, 1986	NR	Maryland	North Carolina	77-72	Chapel Hill, NC
Feb. 23, 1986	20	North Carolina St.	North Carolina	76-65	Raleigh, NC
Mar. 31, 1986	7	Louisville	Duke	72-69	Dallas (CH)
Dec. 1, 1986	NR	UCLA	North Carolina	89-84	Los Angeles
Jan. 17, 1987	16	Oklahoma	UNLV	89-88	Norman, OK
Jan. 24, 1987	NR	Ohio St.	Iowa	80-76	Iowa City, IA
Feb. 1, 1987	NR	Notre Dame	North Carolina	60-58	South Bend, IN
Mar. 28, 1987	3	Indiana	UNLV	97-93	New Orleans (NSF)
Nov. 21, 1987	3	North Carolina	Syracuse	96-93	Springfield, MA
Nov. 30, 1987	17	Arizona	Syracuse	80-69	Anchorage, AK
Dec. 5, 1987	NR	Vanderbilt	North Carolina	78-76	Nashville, TN
Jan. 2, 1988	NR	New Mexico	Arizona	61-59	Albuquerque, NM
Jan. 9, 1988	NR	Auburn	Kentucky	53-52	Lexington, KY
Feb. 4, 1988	NR	Stanford	Arizona	82-74	Palo Alto, CA
Mar. 26, 1988	5	Duke	Temple	63-53	East Rutherford, NJ (RF)
Jan. 18, 1989	13	North Carolina	Duke	91-71	Durham, NC
Jan. 21, 1989	NR	Wake Forest	Duke	75-71	Winston-Salem, NC
Jan. 26, 1989	NR	Minnesota	Illinois	69-62	Minneapolis
Feb. 4, 1989	NR	Oklahoma St.	Oklahoma	77-73	Stillwater, OK
Feb. 12, 1989	5	Oklahoma	Arizona	82-80	Norman, OK
Feb. 25, 1989	7	Missouri	Oklahoma	97-84	Columbia, MO
Mar. 23, 1989	15	UNLV	Arizona	68-67	Denver (RSF)
Nov. 22, 1989	NR	Kansas	UNLV	91-77	New York
Jan. 6, 1990	NR	Villanova	Syracuse	93-74	Greensboro, NC
Jan. 20, 1990	4	Missouri	Kansas	95-87	Columbia, MO
Feb. 8, 1990	NR	Kansas St.	Missouri	65-58	Manhattan, KS
Feb. 13, 1990	2	Missouri	Kansas	77-71	Lawrence, KS
Feb. 25, 1990	10	Oklahoma	Missouri	107-90	Norman, OK
Feb. 27, 1990	T5	Oklahoma	Kansas	100-78	Norman, OK
Mar. 17, 1990	NR	North Carolina	Oklahoma	79-77	Austin, TX (2nd)
Mar. 30, 1991	6	Duke	UNLV	79-77	Indianapolis (NSF)
Feb. 5, 1992	9	North Carolina	Duke	75-73	Chapel Hill, NC
Feb. 23, 1992	NR	Wake Forest	Duke	72-68	Winston-Salem, NC
Dec. 5, 1992	4	Duke	Michigan	79-68	Durham, NC
Jan. 10, 1993	10	Georgia Tech	Duke	80-79	Atlanta
Jan. 13, 1993	NR	Vanderbilt	Kentucky	101-86	Nashville, TN
Jan. 25, 1993	NR	Long Beach St.	Kansas	64-49	Lawrence, KS
Feb. 23, 1993	NR	Ohio St.	Indiana	81-77 (ot)	Columbus, OH
Mar. 14, 1993	NR	Georgia Tech	North Carolina	77-75	Charlotte, NC
Mar. 27, 1993	9	Kansas	Indiana	83-77	St. Louis (RF)
Nov. 24, 1993	18	Massachusetts	North Carolina	91-86 (ot)	New York
Dec. 4, 1993	21	Indiana	Kentucky	96-84	Indianapolis
Jan. 8, 1994	NR	Alabama	Arkansas	66-64	Tuscaloosa, AL
Jan. 12, 1994	17	Georgia Tech	North Carolina	89-69	Atlanta
Jan. 17, 1994	NR	Kansas St.	Kansas	68-64	Lawrence, KS
Jan. 30, 1994	NR	California	UCLA	85-70	Oakland, CA
Feb. 3, 1994	2	North Carolina	Duke	89-78	Chapel Hill, NC
Feb. 12, 1994	NR	Georgia Tech	North Carolina	96-89	Chapel Hill, NC
Mar. 12, 1994	10	Kentucky	Arkansas	90-78	Memphis, TN
Mar. 20, 1994	NR	Boston College	North Carolina	75-72	Landover, MD (2nd)
Nov. 25, 1994	3	Massachusetts	Arkansas	104-80	Springfield, MA

Date	Rank	School	No. 1 Team	Score	Site
Dec. 3, 1994	7	Kansas	Massachusetts	81-75	New York
Jan. 4, 1995	NR	North Carolina St.	North Carolina	80-70	Raleigh, NC
Feb. 4, 1995	NR	George Washington	Massachusetts	78-75	Washington, DC
Feb. 7, 1995	8	Maryland	North Carolina	86-73	College Park, MD
Feb. 18, 1995	15	Villanova	Connecticut	96-73	Storrs, CT
Feb. 20, 1995	25	Oklahoma	Kansas	76-73	Norman, OK
Nov. 28, 1995	5	Massachusetts	Kentucky	92-82	Auburn Hills, MI
Dec. 22, 1995	NR	Temple	Kansas	75-66	East Rutherford, NJ
Feb. 24, 1996	NR	George Washington	Massachusetts	86-76	Amherst, MA
Mar. 10, 1996	NR	Mississippi St.	Kentucky	84-73	New Orleans
Mar. 30, 1996	2	Kentucky	Massachusetts	81-74	East Rutherford, NJ (NSF)
Nov. 26, 1996	NR	Xavier	Cincinnati	71-69	Cincinnati
Feb. 4, 1997	NR	Missouri	Kansas	96-94	Columbia, MO
Mar. 21, 1997	15	Arizona	Kansas	85-82	Birmingham, AL (RSF)
Nov. 26, 1997	3	Duke	Arizona	95-87	Lahaina, HI
Dec. 13, 1997	NR	Michigan	Duke	81-73	Ann Arbor, MI
Jan. 14, 1998	NR	Maryland	North Carolina	89-83 (ot)	College Park, MD
Feb. 5, 1998	2	North Carolina	Duke	97-73	Chapel Hill, NC
Feb. 21, 1998	NR	North Carolina St.	North Carolina	86-72	Chapel Hill, NC
Mar. 8, 1998	4	North Carolina	Duke	83-68	Greensboro, NC
Mar. 28, 1998	7	Utah	North Carolina	65-59	San Antonio, TX (NSF)
Nov. 28, 1998	15	Cincinnati	Duke	77-75	Anchorage, AK
Feb. 1, 1999	17	Syracuse	Connecticut	59-42	Hartford, CT
Mar. 29, 1999	3	Connecticut	Duke	77-74	St. Petersburg, FL (CH)
Nov. 11, 1999	NR	Iowa	Connecticut	70-68	New York
Nov. 18, 1999	NR	Xavier	Cincinnati	66-64	Cincinnati
Jan. 8, 2000	5	Arizona	Stanford	68-65	Palo Alto, CA
Feb. 12, 2000	15	Temple	Cincinnati	77-69	Cincinnati
Mar. 4, 2000	NR	UCLA	Stanford	94-93 (ot)	Palo Alto, CA
Mar. 9, 2000	NR	St. Louis	Cincinnati	68-58	Memphis, TN
Mar. 24, 2000	11	Florida	Duke	87-78	Syracuse, NY (RSF)
Nov. 25, 2000	NR	Purdue	Arizona	72-69	Indianapolis
Dec. 21, 2000	3	Stanford	Duke	84-83	Oakland, CA
Jan. 7, 2001	NR	Indiana	Michigan St.	59-58	Bloomington, IN
Feb. 3, 2001	NR	UCLA	Stanford	79-73	Palo Alto, CA
Feb. 18, 2001	NR	Clemson	North Carolina	75-65	Clemson, SC
Mar. 8, 2001	8	Arizona	Stanford	76-75	Palo Alto, CA
Jan. 6, 2002	NR	Florida St.	Duke	77-76	Tallahasee, FL
Jan. 12, 2002	11	UCLA	Kansas	87-77	Los Angeles
Feb. 17, 2002	3	Maryland	Duke	87-73	College Park, MD
Mar. 10, 2002	4	Oklahoma	Kansas	64-55	Kansas City, MO
Mar. 21, 2002	NR	Indiana	Duke	74-73	Lexington, KY (RSF)
Dec. 21, 2002	NR	LSU	Arizona	66-65	Baton Rouge, LA
Dec. 30, 2002	NR	Utah	Alabama	51-49	Salt Lake City
Jan. 18, 2003	17	Maryland	Duke	87-72	College Park, MD
Jan. 30, 2003	24	Stanford	Arizona	82-77	Tucson, AZ
Feb. 4, 2003	6	Kentucky	Florida	70-55	Lexington, KY
Mar. 13, 2003	NR	UCLA	Arizona	96-89 (ot)	Los Angeles
Mar. 29, 2003	9	Marquette	Kentucky	83-69	Minneapolis (RF)

NR=Not Rated
NCAA Tournament Abbreviations After Site:
NF=National Final or Championship Game
NSF=National Semifinal
N3rd= NCAA National Consolation Game
RF=Regional Final
RSF=Regional Semifinal
2nd=Second-Round Game
1st=First-Round Game

Connecticut's Rickey Moore, a member of the 1999 all-tournament team, helped lead the Huskies over No. 1 Duke in the championship game. It was the first time since 1986 that the No. 1 team fell in the title game.

Week-by-Week A.P. Polls

REGULAR-SEASON POLLS

The Associated Press began its basketball poll on January 20, 1949. The following are those polls, year by year and week by week. Starting in the 1961-62 season, A.P. provided a preseason (PS) poll. A.P. did a post-tournament poll in 1953, 1954, 1974 and 1975.

1948-49

	Jan 18	Jan 25	Feb 1	Feb 8	Feb 15	Feb 22	Mar 1	Mar 8
Arkansas	-	-	-	-	-	-	20	-
Baylor	-	18	-	-	-	-	-	-
Bowling Green	15	-	14	14	10	9	9	10
Bradley	16	19	18	-	12	10	10	7
Butler	19	17	16	16	11	11	11	18
Cincinnati	13	-	-	-	-	-	-	-
DePaul	-	16	-	-	17	-	-	-
Duquesne	-	-	-	20	20	17	-	-
Eastern Ky.	-	-	20	-	-	-	-	-
Hamline	8	7	8	5	9	15	16	19
Holy Cross	14	20	19	15	-	-	-	-
Illinois	7	6	4	4	4	4	4	4
Kentucky	2	2	1	1	1	1	1	1
Loyola (Ill.)	12	13	13	11	13	12	14	16
Minnesota	4	5	5	7	6	5	5	6
North Carolina St.	-	15	17	-	18	-	15	13
New York U.	20	-	15	-	-	-	-	-
Ohio St.	-	-	-	18	-	18	19	20
Oklahoma	-	-	-	-	16	-	-	-
Oklahoma St.	5	3	3	3	3	3	2	2
San Francisco	6	9	10	9	8	8	8	8
Southern California	-	-	-	-	-	19	-	-
St. Louis	1	1	2	2	2	2	3	3
Stanford	17	11	9	10	20	-	-	-
Texas	-	-	-	-	-	20	-	-
Tulane	11	12	11	8	5	6	7	9
UCLA	-	-	-	-	-	-	-	15
Utah	10	10	12	12	14	16	13	12
Villanova	9	8	7	13	15	-	17	14
Western Ky.	3	4	6	6	7	7	6	5
Washington St.	18	14	-	17	-	-	-	-
Wyoming	-	-	-	19	19	14	12	17
Yale	-	-	-	-	20	13	18	11

1949-50

	Jan 5	Jan 10	Jan 17	Jan 24	Jan 31	Feb 7	Feb 14	Feb 21	Feb 28	Mar 7
Arizona	-	-	-	-	-	18	17	19	15	15
Bowling Green	19	-	-	-	-	-	-	-	-	-
Bradley	3	6	4	6	3	2	2	1	1	1
CCNY	14	7	7	8	10	14	13	20	-	-
Cincinnati	-	12	20	-	-	-	-	-	-	-
Duquesne	8	8	6	2	2	3	7	4	5	6
Hamline	-	-	-	-	-	20	-	-	-	-
Holy Cross	6	5	1	1	1	1	1	2	3	4
Illinois	16	-	-	20	-	-	-	-	-	-
Indiana	5	4	8	9	12	16	-	17	-	20
Kansas	-	-	-	-	-	-	-	-	-	19
Kansas St.	20	-	13	12	11	10	14	13	12	14
Kentucky	2	2	5	4	6	7	5	5	4	3
La Salle	18	13	10	7	8	9	11	12	9	10
Long Island	4	3	3	3	4	6	6	10	14	13
Louisville	-	-	19	-	15	13	-	-	-	-
Minnesota	10	11	16	18	-	-	-	-	-	-
Missouri	12	16	-	-	-	-	-	-	-	-
Nebraska	-	-	-	-	-	-	-	-	16	-
North Carolina St.	7	9	12	10	9	8	8	9	8	5
Notre Dame	-	-	-	-	16	-	-	-	-	-
Ohio St.	-	15	11	13	7	4	3	3	2	2
Oklahoma	17	19	-	-	-	-	-	-	-	-
Oklahoma St.	-	-	-	-	19	-	-	-	-	-
St. John's (N.Y.)	1	1	2	5	5	4	4	6	10	9
St. Louis	11	-	-	-	-	19	18	15	-	-
San Francisco	-	-	-	-	-	15	12	11	13	12
San Jose St.	-	-	-	-	-	-	-	18	19	17
Siena	-	18	-	-	-	-	-	-	-	-
Southern California	-	-	-	-	-	19	16	-	-	-
Tennessee	-	-	17	-	-	-	-	-	-	-
Toledo	-	-	-	-	-	-	-	14	17	-
Tulane	-	-	15	-	-	-	-	-	-	-
UCLA	9	10	9	11	13	12	10	7	6	7
Vanderbilt	-	-	-	-	18	-	20	-	20	-
Villanova	13	17	18	19	-	-	15	-	11	11
Washington	-	20	-	16	-	-	-	-	-	-
Washington St.	-	-	-	-	17	16	-	-	-	18
Western Ky.	-	14	14	17	14	11	9	8	7	8
Wisconsin	15	-	-	15	17	-	-	-	-	16
Wyoming	-	-	-	14	20	-	-	-	18	-

1950-51

	Dec 19	Dec 26	Jan 3	Jan 9	Jan 16	Jan 23	Jan 30	Feb 6	Feb 13	Feb 20	Feb 27	Mar 7
Arizona	-	-	16	-	14	15	13	16	11	12	-	12
Beloit	-	-	-	-	-	-	-	-	18	20	16	-
Bradley	2	2	1	1	3	4	5	5	8	7	5	6
Brigham Young	15	-	-	-	19	12	14	12	12	11	-	11
CCNY	6	11	-	-	-	-	-	-	-	-	-	-
Cincinnati	17	17	17	-	16	15	16	11	15	18	-	17
Columbia	-	8	14	8	7	7	6	6	4	3	3	3
Cornell	19	18	14	-	-	-	-	-	-	-	-	-
Dayton	-	-	-	-	-	-	-	18	17	14	14	13
Duquesne	-	-	13	15	20	-	-	-	-	-	-	-
Illinois	-	20	-	14	14	16	14	16	11	10	6	5
Indiana	4	5	6	6	6	5	3	6	4	7	7	7
Kansas	11	10	20	17	-	17	20	-	-	-	-	-
Kansas St.	20	-	9	9	10	9	7	4	3	5	4	4
Kentucky	1	1	3	3	2	1	1	1	1	1	1	1
La Salle	-	16	-	19	-	17	-	-	-	-	-	-
Long Island	7	4	4	4	2	4	12	19	16	-	-	-
Louisville	-	-	-	-	-	-	-	-	17	14	-	-
Missouri	8	9	-	-	-	-	-	-	-	-	-	-
Murray St.	-	-	-	-	-	-	-	-	-	-	20	16
North Carolina St.	3	6	7	7	9	8	8	10	9	9	8	8
Notre Dame	14	-	-	-	-	-	-	-	-	-	-	-
Oklahoma	16	-	-	-	-	18	18	-	17	-	-	-
Oklahoma St.	5	3	2	1	3	2	2	2	2	2	2	2
Princeton	-	-	18	20	-	-	-	-	-	-	-	-
St. Bonaventure	-	-	-	-	17	-	-	-	-	-	-	-
St. John's (N.Y.)	13	12	11	11	5	6	9	7	7	8	9	9
St. Louis	-	-	5	5	8	10	10	8	5	6	10	10
Seattle	-	-	-	-	-	-	-	-	-	20	-	-
Siena	-	-	-	-	18	13	-	19	-	-	-	18
Southern California	-	-	-	13	19	12	13	15	13	13	18	19
Toledo	10	13	19	18	12	-	20	-	-	-	13	14
UCLA	9	-	-	-	-	19	-	-	17	-	-	-
Villanova	18	7	8	16	11	11	11	9	10	15	15	20
Washington	12	15	12	12	15	-	-	-	-	19	19	15
West Virginia	-	19	-	-	-	-	-	-	-	-	-	-
Wyoming	-	14	10	10	13	20	-	-	-	-	-	-

1951-52

	Dec 10	Dec 17	Dec 25	Jan 1	Jan 8	Jan 15	Jan 22	Jan 29	Feb 5	Feb 12	Feb 19	Feb 26	Mar 4
Dayton	-	-	-	-	20	19	16	14	11	11	11	11	11
DePaul	-	-	-	-	-	-	-	19	-	18	-	-	11
Duke	12	19	-	-	-	-	-	-	-	-	-	15	12
Duquesne	-	-	-	-	16	7	10	7	5	3	3	4	4
Eastern Ky.	19	-	-	-	-	-	-	-	-	-	-	-	-
Fordham	-	-	-	-	-	-	20	-	-	-	-	-	-
Holy Cross	-	17	-	-	20	11	17	-	19	17	17	-	13
Illinois	3	3	2	2	2	1	3	3	6	5	-	2	2
Indiana	11	6	5	5	4	14	20	13	18	20	-	-	-
Iowa	-	-	-	12	10	4	4	8	9	5	4	7	7
Kansas	8	7	4	1	1	1	2	4	6	9	7	8	8
Kansas St.	5	5	8	9	7	9	7	2	2	2	2	3	3
Kentucky	1	2	1	4	3	3	3	1	1	1	1	1	1
La Salle	9	12	17	13	-	15	18	-	19	-	20	-	-
Louisville	17	-	-	15	13	14	12	13	15	15	13	-	17
Michigan St.	-	-	-	20	19	-	-	-	-	-	-	-	-
Minnesota	-	-	15	-	-	-	-	-	-	-	-	-	-
Murray St.	-	-	-	-	-	18	16	-	-	-	-	-	-
North Carolina St.	10	9	19	17	-	17	-	-	-	-	-	-	-
Notre Dame	14	20	9	14	-	-	-	-	-	-	-	-	-
New York U.	20	11	6	6	13	-	-	-	-	-	-	-	-
Oklahoma St.	13	13	-	-	-	-	-	-	16	-	-	-	-
Oklahoma City	-	-	-	-	-	-	15	18	18	-	16	15	13
Penn St.	-	-	-	-	-	-	-	-	-	14	17	13	-
St. Bonaventure	-	-	-	-	-	10	8	5	5	4	10	12	15
St. John's (N.Y.)	2	1	7	8	12	-	15	6	5	5	4	9	10
St. Louis	4	4	12	7	5	5	8	6	7	7	9	5	5
Seattle	-	-	-	-	-	-	-	-	-	-	16	-	18
Seton Hall	7	10	10	11	9	12	13	11	17	12	14	14	14

	December			January					February				March
	10	17	25	1	8	15	22	29	5	12	19	26	4
Siena	-	-	-	-	17	11	19	18	-	16	18	20	-
Stanford	16	-	13	-	-	-	-	-	-	-	-	-	-
Texas St.	-	-	-	-	-	-	-	-	-	-	-	-	20
Syracuse	-	-	20	19	14	-	-	-	-	-	-	-	-
TCU	-	-	-	-	-	15	12	-	-	-	-	-	-
UCLA	-	-	16	-	-	-	-	-	-	-	-	-	19
Utah	-	-	15	18	-	-	17	-	-	-	-	-	-
Vanderbilt	18	-	-	-	-	-	-	-	-	-	-	-	-
Villanova	15	18	14	-	-	-	-	-	-	-	-	19	-
Washington	6	8	3	3	6	8	6	9	8	8	6	6	6
West Virginia	-	-	-	-	11	10	9	10	12	14	12	10	9
Western Ky.	-	16	11	-	-	-	-	-	20	-	-	18	-
Wyoming	-	14	-	-	-	-	-	-	-	-	19	16	16

1952-53

	December			January				February				March		
	16	23	30	6	13	20	27	3	10	17	24	3	10	24
California	18	-	-	20	-	14	-	14	19	19	-	-	-	-
Colorado	-	18	-	-	-	-	-	-	-	-	-	-	-	-
DePaul	-	-	14	-	-	-	10	7	7	14	15	-	-	19
Duke	-	-	-	-	-	-	-	-	-	18	-	-	-	-
Duquesne	-	-	-	-	-	-	-	-	-	-	19	18	11	9
Eastern Ky.	-	-	-	-	-	18	15	-	-	-	20	17	-	-
Fordham	-	-	-	8	7	10	7	13	16	-	-	-	-	-
Georgetown	-	-	-	-	20	-	-	-	-	-	-	-	-	-
Holy Cross	8	4	6	14	17	-	-	17	-	-	-	20	-	13
Idaho	-	20	-	18	-	-	-	-	-	-	-	-	-	-
Illinois	3	2	4	4	4	6	6	6	5	5	10	10	13	11
Indiana	19	15	12	7	6	2	2	2	2	2	2	1	1	1
Kansas	20	-	-	-	15	9	14	18	14	10	5	6	5	3
Kansas St.	2	5	1	1	1	4	5	5	10	8	9	8	8	12
La Salle	1	1	3	3	3	5	4	4	4	4	4	2	3	6
LSU	10	8	17	11	14	14	11	10	8	6	6	5	7	5
Louisville	-	-	-	-	-	-	-	-	17	16	18	14	14	-
Manhattan	-	-	-	-	-	20	19	19	15	13	16	-	20	-
Miami (Ohio)	-	-	-	-	-	-	-	-	-	-	12	16	-	-
Minnesota	16	17	9	19	-	19	-	-	-	-	-	-	-	-
Murray St.	-	-	-	-	-	-	-	-	-	17	-	-	-	-
Navy	20	13	-	15	-	-	16	-	-	-	-	18	19	-
Niagara	-	-	-	-	-	-	-	20	17	-	-	-	-	-
North Carolina	-	-	-	-	-	-	18	12	-	-	-	-	-	-
North Carolina St.	6	6	11	9	8	8	12	15	12	15	13	12	18	18
Notre Dame	7	11	19	13	11	16	17	-	-	-	17	13	17	10
Oklahoma St.	5	9	7	5	9	7	8	9	6	7	7	7	6	8
Oklahoma City	13	19	16	-	18	17	-	16	13	12	11	11	10	-
St. Bonaventure	14	12	15	-	-	-	-	-	-	-	-	-	-	-
St. John's (N.Y.)	-	-	-	-	-	-	-	-	-	-	-	-	20	7
St. Louis	17	-	-	-	-	-	-	-	-	-	-	-	-	-
Santa Clara	-	-	-	-	-	-	-	-	-	-	-	-	-	16
Seattle	-	15	13	16	16	13	13	11	11	11	14	15	14	14
Seton Hall	4	3	2	2	2	1	1	1	1	1	1	3	4	2
Southern California	-	-	-	12	12	-	-	-	-	-	-	-	-	-
Southwest Mo. St.	-	-	-	-	-	-	-	-	-	-	-	-	-	20
Toledo	-	-	18	-	-	-	-	-	-	-	-	-	-	-
Tulsa	15	14	8	17	13	11	20	-	19	-	-	-	-	-
UCLA	12	20	-	-	19	-	-	-	-	-	-	-	-	-
Villanova	-	-	-	-	-	-	-	-	-	19	-	-	-	-
Wake Forest	-	-	-	-	-	-	-	-	-	-	-	-	12	15
Washington	9	7	5	6	5	3	3	3	3	3	3	4	2	4
Wayne St. (Mich.)	-	-	20	-	-	-	-	-	-	-	-	-	-	-
Western Ky.	11	10	10	10	10	12	9	8	9	9	8	9	9	17
Wyoming	-	-	-	-	-	-	-	-	-	-	-	-	16	-

1953-54

	December				January				February				March		
	8	15	22	29	5	12	19	26	2	9	16	23	2	9	23
Bradley	-	-	-	-	-	-	-	-	18	-	-	-	-	-	7
Brigham Young	-	-	-	19	-	-	-	-	-	-	-	-	-	-	-
California	17	15	-	-	-	-	15	14	15	14	-	-	-	-	-
Colorado A&M	-	-	-	-	-	18	-	-	-	-	19	18	-	19	-
Connecticut	-	-	-	-	-	-	-	18	-	-	-	-	19	-	-
Dayton	15	-	16	-	14	17	-	18	-	-	17	16	14	15	-
Duke	-	13	-	-	8	9	13	20	8	15	14	10	11	18	15
Duquesne	3	3	3	2	2	2	2	2	2	2	1	1	4	3	5
Fordham	-	9	7	10	-	-	-	-	-	-	-	-	-	-	-
George Washington	-	-	-	-	12	7	10	10	11	10	8	8	9	7	12
Holy Cross	19	14	10	12	7	6	8	7	10	9	9	7	13	9	3
Idaho	-	-	20	17	-	20	-	-	-	-	-	-	-	-	-
Illinois	9	4	4	8	15	19	20	-	-	-	-	20	-	-	19
Indiana	1	1	1	3	3	3	3	3	3	3	3	3	2	2	4
Iowa	-	-	-	-	-	-	-	-	-	-	10	20	16	16	13
Kansas	5	-	-	-	16	11	17	17	19	20	-	17	15	13	18
Kansas St.	8	-	-	-	-	-	-	-	-	-	-	-	-	-	-
Kentucky	2	2	2	1	1	1	1	1	1	1	2	2	1	1	1
La Salle	6	20	16	13	-	-	19	12	9	7	12	13	8	12	2
LSU	10	5	14	18	-	16	12	14	17	17	13	12	7	8	14
Louisville	-	-	-	-	-	-	-	-	20	-	-	-	20	-	-
Maryland	-	-	-	-	-	-	14	13	13	11	11	11	17	14	20
Minnesota	12	6	8	6	6	10	9	8	12	12	18	-	-	-	-
Navy	-	-	-	-	18	-	-	-	-	16	20	-	-	-	-
Niagara	-	18	-	-	12	13	18	-	-	-	-	-	-	-	16
North Carolina St.	7	8	9	9	20	-	-	-	-	19	-	-	18	10	-
Notre Dame	-	16	19	-	-	-	6	6	7	6	6	6	5	6	6
Oklahoma St.	4	7	5	5	4	4	5	4	5	4	5	5	6	5	10
Oklahoma City	19	12	15	11	9	8	7	9	16	13	16	15	-	-	-
Oregon St.	13	11	12	4	10	-	-	-	-	-	-	-	-	16	-
Penn St.	-	-	-	-	-	-	-	-	-	-	-	-	-	-	9
Rice	-	-	11	16	11	15	-	-	-	-	-	-	-	-	-
St. Louis	18	-	-	-	-	-	-	-	-	-	-	-	-	-	-
Santa Clara	16	-	-	-	-	-	-	-	-	-	-	-	-	-	-
Seattle	-	-	-	15	16	14	16	11	6	8	7	9	10	11	17
Siena	-	19	-	-	-	-	-	-	-	-	-	-	-	-	-
Southern California	-	-	-	-	-	-	-	-	-	-	-	-	-	-	11
UCLA	-	17	13	14	-	-	-	-	-	-	-	19	-	-	-
Vanderbilt	-	-	20	20	19	-	-	-	-	-	-	-	-	-	-
Western Ky.	11	10	6	7	5	5	4	4	4	5	4	4	3	4	8
Wichita St.	-	-	-	-	-	11	11	16	14	18	15	14	12	20	-
Wisconsin	-	-	18	-	-	-	-	-	-	-	-	-	-	-	-
Wyoming	14	-	-	20	-	-	-	-	-	-	-	-	-	-	-

1954-55

	December				January				February				March	
	7	14	21	28	4	11	18	25	1	8	15	22	1	8
Alabama	-	-	19	12	20	16	12	14	13	13	17	12	11	12
Auburn	-	-	-	-	-	20	-	-	-	-	-	-	-	-
Cincinnati	-	-	-	-	-	-	-	-	-	17	12	17	-	-
Colorado	-	-	-	-	-	-	-	-	-	-	-	-	-	15
Dayton	7	5	6	4	10	12	18	15	15	16	13	11	10	9
Duke	17	-	-	18	17	-	-	-	-	-	-	-	-	-
Duquesne	3	9	9	8	2	3	5	4	4	4	4	4	8	6
George Washington	-	11	8	9	6	8	9	6	7	6	5	10	13	14
Holy Cross	5	19	-	-	-	-	16	13	14	-	-	-	-	-
Illinois	14	3	3	6	12	7	7	10	10	10	14	13	17	18
Indiana	6	7	-	-	-	-	-	-	-	-	-	-	-	-
Iowa	4	13	20	19	14	19	19	19	-	15	15	16	12	5
Kansas	-	-	20	16	-	-	-	-	-	-	-	-	-	-
Kentucky	2	2	1	1	1	1	1	1	1	2	2	2	2	2
La Salle	1	1	4	3	4	4	4	5	3	3	3	3	3	3
Louisville	-	12	14	13	16	20	-	-	-	-	-	-	-	-
Marquette	-	-	-	-	-	-	15	11	9	9	6	5	4	8
Maryland	-	-	-	-	11	11	6	8	12	11	11	17	18	-
Memphis	-	-	-	-	-	-	-	-	-	-	-	15	19	-
Minnesota	-	-	-	11	13	14	14	-	11	12	8	7	6	11
Missouri	-	6	7	-	9	6	8	12	17	14	-	20	20	-
Niagara	8	10	10	10	15	15	20	20	16	-	-	-	-	-
North Carolina St.	10	4	5	2	3	2	2	3	6	7	7	6	5	4
Northwestern	-	-	-	-	-	-	-	16	-	-	-	-	-	-
Notre Dame	9	20	-	-	20	-	-	-	-	-	-	-	-	-
Ohio St.	-	14	11	20	-	-	-	-	-	-	-	-	-	-
Oklahoma St.	11	-	-	-	-	-	-	-	-	-	-	-	-	-
Oregon St.	-	-	-	-	-	-	-	-	19	18	16	-	14	10
Penn St.	19	-	-	-	-	-	-	-	-	-	-	-	-	-
Pennsylvania	-	-	16	17	19	-	-	-	-	-	-	-	-	-
Purdue	-	-	-	-	-	17	-	-	-	-	-	-	-	-
Richmond	-	-	-	-	-	13	13	17	-	-	-	-	-	-
St. John's (N.Y.)	-	16	-	-	-	-	-	-	-	-	-	-	-	-
St. Louis	12	-	-	-	-	-	-	-	-	-	-	-	-	20
San Francisco	-	-	17	5	5	5	3	2	2	1	1	1	1	1
Seton Hall	-	-	-	-	-	20	-	-	-	-	-	-	-	-
Southern California	-	-	13	14	-	18	-	-	-	-	-	-	-	-
Tennessee	-	-	-	-	-	-	-	-	-	-	18	-	-	-
TCU	-	-	-	-	-	-	20	-	-	-	-	-	-	-
Tulsa	-	-	-	-	-	-	-	-	-	-	19	19	15	16
UCLA	13	8	17	15	7	10	10	9	8	8	9	9	9	13
Utah	16	15	2	7	8	9	10	7	5	5	10	8	7	7
Vanderbilt	-	-	-	-	-	-	17	18	20	20	20	14	16	17
Villanova	-	-	-	-	17	-	-	-	17	19	-	-	-	-
Wake Forest	17	17	-	-	-	-	-	-	-	-	-	-	-	-
West Virginia	-	-	12	-	-	-	-	-	-	-	-	-	-	19
Western Ky.	20	-	-	-	-	-	-	-	-	-	-	-	-	-
Wichita St.	15	17	14	-	-	-	-	-	-	-	-	-	-	-

1955-56

	December				January					February				March
	6	13	20	27	3	10	17	24	31	7	14	21	28	6
Alabama	6	5	16	19	17	19	13	12	12	10	8	7	4	4
Brigham Young	10	8	5	20	-	-	-	-	-	-	-	-	-	-
Cincinnati	-	14	-	-	20	-	-	14	-	20	-	-	-	-
Dayton	7	7	4	2	3	2	2	2	2	2	2	4	3	3
Duke	-	-	14	8	11	6	7	10	10	8	11	11	11	19

	December				January					February				March
	6	13	20	27	3	10	17	24	31	7	14	21	28	6
Duquesne	9	6	20	-	-	-	-	-	-	-	-	-	-	-
George Washington	13	13	11	12	7	14	-	-	-	19	-	19	-	-
Holy Cross	11	10	7	14	14	11	12	11	14	13	16	17	15	12
Houston	-	-	-	-	-	-	-	-	-	-	18	14	18	17
Illinois	8	-	17	9	9	8	6	5	6	6	3	2	2	7
Indiana	-	19	18	-	13	12	-	-	-	-	-	-	-	-
Iowa	4	4	10	6	-	-	20	13	19	17	15	13	10	5
Iowa St.	-	-	-	-	8	15	-	-	-	-	-	20	-	-
Kansas	-	18	-	-	-	-	-	-	-	-	-	-	-	-
Kansas St.	-	-	-	-	-	-	-	-	-	-	-	-	17	-
Kentucky	2	12	9	13	6	5	4	3	8	7	7	8	12	9
La Salle	18	-	-	-	-	-	-	-	-	-	-	-	-	-
Louisville	-	-	-	11	-	13	10	9	5	5	4	3	6	6
Marquette	14	-	13	-	-	-	-	-	-	-	-	-	-	-
Marshall	-	-	-	-	-	-	-	-	18	-	-	-	-	-
Memphis	-	-	18	-	12	17	15	19	16	-	19	-	-	-
Michigan St.	-	-	-	16	20	-	-	-	-	-	-	-	-	-
Minnesota	20	-	-	-	-	-	-	-	-	-	-	-	-	-
North Carolina	-	16	6	4	5	9	9	8	9	12	10	9	8	15
North Carolina St.	3	2	2	3	2	3	3	4	4	4	5	6	5	2
Ohio St.	16	-	-	15	10	7	11	-	-	-	-	-	-	-
Oklahoma St.	-	-	-	-	-	20	-	20	-	-	-	-	-	-
Oklahoma City	12	20	15	10	-	16	14	16	15	14	14	18	16	16
Rice	-	-	-	17	18	-	-	-	-	-	-	-	-	-
St. Francis (N.Y.)	-	-	-	-	-	-	-	15	13	16	13	16	-	-
St. Louis	-	17	-	-	-	-	17	17	11	11	17	-	19	-
San Francisco	1	1	1	1	1	1	1	1	1	1	1	1	1	1
Southern Methodist	-	-	-	-	-	-	19	18	17	15	12	12	9	8
Stanford	19	-	-	-	-	-	-	-	-	-	-	-	-	-
Temple	-	11	12	17	16	10	8	6	7	9	9	10	14	13
Tulsa	-	-	-	-	15	-	-	-	-	-	-	-	-	-
UCLA	16	-	-	-	-	-	18	-	20	18	20	15	13	10
Utah	5	3	3	7	-	20	16	-	-	-	-	-	-	20
Vanderbilt	-	9	8	5	4	4	5	7	3	3	6	5	7	11
Wake Forest	-	-	-	-	-	18	-	-	-	-	-	-	20	18
West Virginia	14	15	-	-	19	-	-	-	-	-	-	-	-	14

1956-57

	December			January					February				March	
	11	18	26	2	8	15	22	29	5	12	19	26	5	12
Alabama	9	17	-	-	-	-	-	-	-	-	-	-	-	-
Bradley	-	-	-	-	-	12	10	10	8	5	5	7	13	19
California	-	-	-	-	-	19	19	15	19	12	15	-	14	13
Canisius	10	18	17	15	14	14	14	12	14	14	-	-	-	20
Dayton	15	-	-	-	-	-	-	-	-	-	-	-	-	-
Duke	-	13	9	-	15	16	15	19	-	17	16	-	-	-
Idaho St.	-	-	20	-	-	-	-	17	20	-	-	15	15	16
Illinois	7	5	6	5	10	8	9	7	15	16	-	-	-	-
Indiana	-	-	-	-	-	-	-	-	-	18	11	10	-	-
Iowa St.	17	14	14	7	7	9	3	8	9	9	9	16	17	-
Kansas	1	1	1	1	1	1	2	2	2	2	2	2	2	2
Kansas St.	14	10	-	-	-	-	-	-	-	-	17	12	-	-
Kentucky	3	7	3	3	3	4	5	4	3	3	3	3	3	3
Louisville	4	6	8	6	5	5	4	3	6	8	7	8	6	6
Manhattan	-	-	-	13	-	-	-	-	-	-	-	-	-	-
Memphis	-	-	-	20	-	-	-	-	16	-	20	19	19	12
Michigan St.	-	-	-	-	-	-	-	-	-	-	-	-	8	11
Minnesota	-	-	-	-	19	-	-	-	-	-	-	-	-	-
Mississippi St.	-	-	-	-	-	-	-	-	-	-	19	20	18	15
Niagara	16	-	-	-	-	-	-	-	-	-	-	-	-	-
North Carolina	6	3	2	2	2	2	1	1	1	1	1	1	1	1
North Carolina St.	8	19	-	-	-	-	-	-	-	-	-	-	-	-
Notre Dame	-	-	-	-	-	-	-	-	-	-	-	-	-	17
Ohio St.	11	11	-	-	-	17	12	11	12	-	-	-	-	-
Oklahoma City	18	15	11	17	11	13	16	16	13	13	13	18	10	9
Oklahoma St.	19	12	10	11	12	19	-	20	-	-	-	17	16	20
Purdue	-	-	-	-	-	-	-	-	17	-	-	-	-	-
St. John's (N.Y.)	-	15	-	-	-	-	-	-	-	-	-	-	-	-
St. Louis	-	9	5	16	17	-	-	-	-	20	-	14	12	10
San Francisco	2	2	19	-	-	-	-	-	-	-	-	-	-	-
Seattle	20	-	18	10	9	7	8	9	7	4	4	5	5	5
Southern Methodist	5	4	7	4	4	3	6	6	4	6	6	4	4	4
Tennessee	-	-	12	12	16	-	-	-	-	-	-	-	-	-
Tulane	-	-	16	-	-	-	18	14	-	-	-	-	-	-
UCLA	-	-	-	8	8	6	7	5	5	7	8	6	7	14
Vanderbilt	-	-	12	9	6	10	13	-	18	18	10	9	9	8
Wake Forest	-	-	-	18	13	11	11	13	10	11	12	13	20	18
West Virginia	13	8	4	19	18	15	17	18	11	10	14	11	11	7
West Va. Tech	-	-	-	-	-	-	-	-	-	15	18	-	-	-
Western Ky.	12	20	15	14	20	18	20	-	-	-	-	-	-	-

1957-58

	December				January				February				March	
	10	17	24	31	7	14	21	28	4	11	18	25	4	11
Arkansas	-	-	-	-	-	-	20	17	18	-	-	-	-	-
Auburn	-	-	-	-	-	-	-	-	-	-	-	20	16	16
Bradley	4	11	11	12	10	10	10	12	11	13	15	14	11	14
California	-	-	-	19	-	-	-	-	-	-	-	19	-	-
Cincinnati	19	4	5	5	7	5	4	3	3	3	2	3	3	2
Dartmouth	-	-	-	-	-	19	18	19	20	-	19	-	-	-
Dayton	-	-	-	-	-	-	17	16	14	14	11	10	8	11
Duke	-	-	-	-	-	-	-	-	13	8	7	6	6	10
Georgia Tech	-	-	-	-	-	-	-	-	19	-	-	-	-	-
Illinois	-	-	-	-	17	-	-	-	-	-	-	-	-	-
Indiana	-	-	-	-	-	-	-	-	-	-	-	-	-	12
Iowa St.	-	-	20	-	-	-	-	-	-	-	-	-	-	-
Kansas	2	2	2	2	2	3	2	2	2	4	4	7	10	7
Kansas St.	5	3	3	3	4	2	3	4	4	1	1	1	1	3
Kentucky	3	5	9	10	9	9	9	8	12	12	13	12	9	9
La Salle	-	-	-	20	-	-	-	-	-	-	-	-	-	-
Maryland	-	6	6	7	11	8	6	9	8	9	14	17	17	6
Memphis	20	-	-	-	18	-	-	-	-	-	-	-	-	-
Michigan St.	7	9	8	8	14	18	15	15	15	19	12	15	12	17
Minnesota	11	10	-	-	-	-	-	-	-	-	-	-	-	-
Mississippi St.	-	18	10	9	5	11	14	14	17	18	18	16	15	15
North Carolina	1	1	4	4	3	6	8	7	7	11	16	9	13	13
North Carolina St.	12	20	13	11	13	20	12	10	9	10	9	11	14	20
Notre Dame	15	-	-	-	-	-	-	-	-	17	10	8	7	8
Oklahoma	-	-	-	-	-	14	-	-	-	20	-	-	-	-
Oklahoma St.	18	16	14	14	8	7	7	6	6	6	8	13	18	19
Oregon St.	-	17	-	18	15	16	-	20	-	-	-	-	-	-
Rice	16	14	-	-	-	-	-	-	-	-	-	-	-	-
Richmond	-	19	17	-	-	-	-	-	-	-	-	-	-	-
St. Bonaventure	-	-	-	-	-	-	-	-	-	-	-	-	20	-
St. John's (N.Y.)	-	-	19	17	16	15	13	13	-	-	-	-	-	-
St. Louis	9	-	18	-	-	-	-	-	-	-	-	-	-	-
San Francisco	6	7	7	6	6	4	5	5	5	5	5	4	4	4
Seattle	14	12	15	-	20	-	-	-	16	16	17	18	19	18
Syracuse	17	-	-	-	-	-	-	-	-	-	-	-	-	-
Temple	10	-	-	13	12	12	11	11	10	7	6	5	5	5
Tennessee	-	-	-	-	-	13	16	-	-	15	20	-	-	-
TCU	-	-	-	16	-	-	-	-	-	-	-	-	-	-
UCLA	13	13	-	-	-	-	-	-	-	-	-	-	-	-
Utah	-	15	12	15	19	-	-	-	-	-	-	-	-	-
West Virginia	8	8	1	1	1	1	1	1	1	2	3	2	2	1
Western Ky.	-	-	16	-	-	-	-	-	-	-	-	-	-	-
Wichita St.	-	-	-	-	20	17	19	18	-	-	-	-	-	-

1958-59

	December				January				February				March	
	9	16	23	30	6	13	20	27	3	10	17	24	2	9
Auburn	12	13	8	9	6	5	5	4	4	4	2	6	7	8
Bradley	-	11	13	10	9	7	9	9	8	7	10	9	9	4
California	-	15	14	20	-	20	-	20	19	18	15	12	11	11
Cincinnati	1	1	2	2	7	6	6	5	5	5	6	4	3	5
Dayton	-	-	20	-	-	-	-	-	-	-	-	-	-	-
Illinois	-	-	-	-	20	-	-	18	-	-	-	-	-	-
Indiana	19	-	-	-	-	19	-	-	-	15	19	-	-	-
Kansas	7	-	-	-	-	-	-	-	-	-	-	-	-	-
Kansas St.	3	3	4	3	4	4	3	3	3	3	4	2	2	1
Kentucky	2	2	1	1	1	2	1	1	1	1	3	1	1	2
Louisville	-	-	-	-	-	-	-	17	-	-	-	-	-	-
Marquette	17	-	17	15	15	13	12	12	12	11	13	13	13	20
Memphis	-	-	18	-	-	-	-	-	-	-	-	-	-	-
Michigan St.	15	11	9	7	5	8	8	8	7	12	9	8	6	7
Mississippi St.	8	8	7	8	12	12	11	11	11	10	5	5	4	3
North Carolina	13	10	3	4	3	3	2	2	2	2	1	3	5	9
North Carolina St.	5	4	6	5	2	1	4	6	6	6	6	7	10	6
Northwestern	10	6	12	6	8	11	18	-	-	-	-	-	-	-
Notre Dame	11	-	-	-	-	-	-	-	-	-	-	-	-	-
Oklahoma City	-	-	-	17	13	17	15	14	13	14	18	15	14	17
Oklahoma St.	20	-	-	-	-	-	-	-	-	-	-	-	-	-
Pittsburgh	-	18	-	-	-	-	-	-	-	-	-	-	-	-
Portland	-	-	-	-	-	18	17	-	-	-	-	19	-	-
Purdue	-	-	-	18	-	-	-	-	-	20	20	-	-	-
St. Bonaventure	-	-	-	-	-	14	13	16	18	-	14	18	19	19
St. John's (N.Y.)	20	-	-	13	10	9	7	7	15	19	-	17	18	-
St. Joseph's	-	14	-	12	-	-	-	-	20	-	-	-	20	14
St. Louis	9	17	16	16	14	15	14	15	9	8	8	11	12	12
St. Mary's (Cal.)	14	-	-	-	-	-	-	-	-	-	-	20	17	15
Seattle	-	16	-	-	16	16	16	13	14	13	12	16	-	13
Southern Methodist	18	20	-	-	-	-	-	-	-	-	-	-	-	-
Tennessee	6	5	11	14	17	-	-	-	-	-	-	-	-	-

DIVISION I

(1958-59, continued)

Team	Dec 9	16	23	30	Jan 6	13	20	27	Feb 3	10	17	24	Mar 2	9
Texas A&M	-	-	-	-	19	-	-	-	-	-	-	-	-	-
TCU	-	-	-	19	-	-	-	19	17	16	16	14	15	16
UCLA	-	19	-	-	-	-	-	-	-	-	-	-	-	-
Utah	-	-	-	-	-	-	-	20	-	16	17	17	16	18
Villanova	-	-	15	-	18	-	19	-	-	-	-	-	-	-
Washington	-	-	19	-	-	-	-	-	-	-	-	-	-	-
West Virginia	4	7	5	11	11	10	10	10	10	9	11	10	8	10
Xavier	16	9	10	-	-	-	-	-	-	-	-	-	-	-

1959-60

Team	Dec 22	29	Jan 5	12	19	26	Feb 2	9	16	23	Mar 1	8
Auburn	-	-	-	-	-	-	-	17	17	13	11	11
Bradley	5	9	4	4	2	2	2	2	3	3	4	4
California	4	3	2	2	3	3	3	3	3	4	3	2
Cincinnati	1	1	1	1	1	1	1	1	1	1	1	1
Dayton	-	-	-	19	19	-	13	15	-	-	-	-
DePaul	-	20	-	-	-	-	-	-	-	-	-	-
Detroit	17	11	15	20	20	14	14	19	-	-	-	-
Duke	16	18	-	-	-	-	-	-	-	-	-	18
Georgia Tech	8	10	6	6	6	6	6	6	6	6	7	13
Holy Cross	-	-	-	-	-	-	16	13	17	-	20	16
Illinois	10	8	9	14	13	-	19	20	20	-	-	-
Indiana	9	7	11	-	-	-	-	-	-	20	12	7
Iowa	19	14	-	-	15	-	-	-	-	-	-	-
Kansas St.	-	-	-	-	-	-	15	-	-	-	-	-
Kentucky	13	13	-	17	16	15	-	-	-	-	-	-
La Salle	14	-	-	19	-	-	-	-	-	-	-	-
Miami (Fla.)	-	15	14	15	11	11	11	10	10	9	8	10
Michigan St.	11	-	-	-	-	-	-	-	-	-	-	-
New York U.	12	12	-	-	-	-	-	-	-	14	14	12
North Carolina	-	-	19	16	12	12	17	13	19	-	16	-
Ohio	-	-	-	-	-	-	-	-	18	-	-	-
Ohio St.	3	5	7	5	5	5	4	4	4	2	2	3
Providence	-	-	-	-	-	20	16	14	16	15	15	14
St. Bonaventure	-	-	-	-	-	-	19	-	14	10	9	9
St. John's (N.Y.)	-	-	-	-	-	-	-	-	15	11	19	20
St. Louis	7	6	12	11	18	16	18	18	-	16	13	15
Southern California	20	-	10	10	14	18	-	-	-	-	-	-
Texas A&M	18	-	13	8	10	10	10	12	11	18	-	-
Toledo	-	16	20	18	17	13	12	11	12	19	-	-
Utah	6	4	5	7	7	7	7	9	8	5	6	6
Utah St.	-	-	17	12	9	9	9	7	7	8	10	8
Villanova	15	17	16	9	8	8	8	8	9	12	17	17
Virginia Tech	-	-	-	-	-	17	-	-	-	-	-	-
Wake Forest	-	19	8	13	-	20	-	-	-	-	18	19
West Virginia	2	2	3	3	4	4	5	5	5	7	5	5
Western Ky.	-	-	18	-	-	-	-	-	-	-	-	-

1960-61

Team	Dec 13	20	27	Jan 3	10	17	24	31	Feb 7	14	21	28	Mar 7
Auburn	11	9	9	10	-	-	-	-	-	-	-	-	-
Bradley	2	2	2	2	2	3	3	3	4	5	4	4	6
Cincinnati	-	-	-	-	-	-	-	-	5	4	3	3	2
Colorado	-	15	-	-	-	-	-	-	-	-	-	-	-
Dayton	20	-	-	-	-	-	-	-	-	-	-	-	-
DePaul	-	-	-	-	7	-	-	-	-	-	-	-	-
Detroit	3	8	13	-	-	-	-	-	-	-	-	-	-
Drake	-	20	14	-	-	-	-	-	-	-	-	-	-
Duke	8	7	6	8	8	8	5	4	3	3	6	9	10
Georgia Tech	15	-	-	-	-	-	-	-	-	-	-	-	-
Illinois	19	-	-	-	-	-	-	-	-	-	-	-	-
Indiana	4	4	4	-	-	-	-	-	-	-	-	-	-
Iowa	-	-	-	7	6	4	6	9	9	5	6	-	8
Kansas	16	20	-	-	-	-	-	-	-	-	-	-	-
Kansas St.	20	12	12	-	9	10	-	10	7	6	8	7	4
Kentucky	20	-	19	-	-	-	-	-	-	-	-	-	-
Louisville	9	5	5	4	4	5	8	8	10	-	-	-	-
Maryland	12	-	-	-	-	-	-	-	-	-	-	-	-
Memphis	-	-	19	-	-	-	-	-	-	-	-	-	-
North Carolina	5	10	11	6	7	6	4	5	6	7	7	5	5
North Carolina St.	10	10	10	-	-	-	-	-	-	-	-	-	-
Ohio St.	1	1	1	1	1	1	1	1	1	1	1	1	1
Providence	-	13	15	-	-	-	-	-	-	-	-	-	-
Purdue	-	-	-	-	-	-	10	-	-	-	-	-	-
St. Bonaventure	6	3	3	3	3	2	2	2	2	2	2	3	3
St. John's (N.Y.)	7	6	7	5	5	9	7	7	-	-	-	-	-
St. Louis	-	16	8	-	-	-	-	-	-	-	-	-	-
Southern California	-	-	-	-	-	9	9	8	8	10	10	-	7
UCLA	13	14	16	9	10	-	-	-	-	-	-	-	-
Utah	18	18	-	-	-	-	-	-	-	-	-	-	-
Utah St.	-	14	-	-	-	-	-	-	-	-	-	-	-
Vanderbilt	-	17	16	-	-	-	-	-	-	-	-	-	-
Wake Forest	-	19	-	-	-	-	-	-	-	-	-	-	-
West Virginia	-	-	-	-	-	-	-	-	-	10	9	8	9
Wichita St.	16	-	18	-	-	-	-	-	-	-	-	-	-

1961-62

Team	PS	Dec 19	26	Jan 2	9	16	23	30	Feb 6	13	20	27	Mar 6	13
Arizona St.	-	10	-	-	-	-	-	-	-	-	-	-	-	-
Bowling Green	-	-	-	10	9	8	8	8	8	10	7	7	8	8
Bradley	-	-	-	-	-	9	9	9	7	5	6	6	6	5
Cincinnati	2	2	2	2	2	3	3	3	3	2	2	2	2	2
Colorado	-	-	-	-	-	-	-	-	-	9	9	-	-	9
Duke	7	-	10	8	10	7	7	6	5	7	8	8	9	10
Duquesne	-	7	3	7	8	5	6	7	6	9	-	-	-	-
Kansas St.	8	4	5	4	5	4	4	4	4	4	4	3	3	6
Kentucky	-	-	6	3	3	2	2	2	2	2	3	4	4	3
Loyola (Ill.)	-	-	-	-	-	-	-	-	-	-	-	-	10	-
Mississippi St.	-	-	-	9	7	10	10	10	9	8	5	5	5	4
Ohio St.	1	1	1	1	1	1	1	1	1	1	1	1	1	1
Oregon St.	-	-	-	-	-	-	-	-	10	6	10	-	-	-
Providence	5	3	-	-	-	-	-	-	-	-	-	-	-	-
Purdue	6	8	9	-	-	-	-	-	-	-	-	-	-	-
St. Bonaventure	-	9	-	-	-	-	-	-	-	-	-	-	-	-
St. John's (N.Y.)	9	-	-	-	-	-	-	-	-	-	-	-	-	-
Seattle	10	10	-	-	-	-	-	-	-	-	-	-	-	-
Southern California	4	6	4	6	4	6	5	5	-	-	-	-	-	-
Utah	-	-	-	-	-	-	-	-	-	-	10	-	7	7
Villanova	-	-	-	5	6	-	-	-	-	-	-	-	-	-
Wake Forest	3	-	-	-	-	-	-	-	-	-	-	-	-	-
West Virginia	-	5	7	-	-	-	-	-	-	-	-	-	-	-
Wichita St.	-	8	-	-	-	-	-	-	-	-	-	-	-	-

1962-63

Team	PS	Dec 4	11	18	25	Jan 1	8	15	22	29	Feb 5	12	19	26	Mar 5	12
Arizona St.	-	-	-	-	6	4	3	4	5	5	5	5	4	4	4	4
Auburn	-	-	-	-	-	10	-	-	-	-	-	9	-	-	-	-
Cincinnati	1	1	1	1	1	1	1	1	1	1	1	1	1	1	1	1
Colorado	-	-	8	6	-	-	-	-	8	-	7	7	-	-	-	10
Duke	2	2	2	2	8	7	6	5	4	3	3	3	2	2	2	2
Georgia Tech	-	-	-	-	-	-	7	6	7	6	6	10	-	10	-	-
Illinois	8	-	10	8	4	3	5	3	3	4	4	6	6	8	8	8
Indiana	-	8	-	-	-	-	-	-	-	-	-	-	-	-	-	-
Kentucky	3	9	-	9	5	6	-	-	-	-	-	-	-	-	-	-
Loyola (Ill.)	4	4	4	4	3	2	2	2	2	2	2	2	3	3	5	3
Mississippi St.	6	5	5	5	10	-	-	9	9	-	8	6	8	7	7	6
New York U.	-	-	-	-	-	-	-	-	-	-	-	-	10	9	-	9
North Carolina	-	-	-	-	-	-	-	-	10	-	-	-	-	-	-	-
Ohio St.	-	-	-	3	3	2	5	4	8	-	-	9	5	5	3	7
Oregon St.	7	2	7	9	-	-	10	-	-	-	-	-	-	-	-	-
Providence	-	-	-	-	-	-	-	-	-	-	-	-	-	-	10	-
St. Bonaventure	9	-	-	-	-	-	-	-	-	-	-	-	-	-	-	-
Seattle	-	-	-	10	-	-	-	-	-	-	-	-	-	-	-	-
Southern California	-	-	-	-	-	-	-	7	-	-	-	-	-	-	-	-
Stanford	-	-	-	-	-	-	-	-	-	9	10	7	10	8	9	-
UCLA	-	-	-	-	-	9	-	-	-	-	-	-	-	-	-	-
West Virginia	5	3	6	7	-	-	9	-	6	-	-	-	-	-	-	-
Wichita St.	-	10	-	-	-	8	8	7	8	10	9	-	7	8	6	5
Wisconsin	10	6	7	-	-	-	-	-	-	-	-	-	-	-	-	-

1963-64

Team	PS	Dec 10	17	24	31	Jan 7	14	21	28	Feb 4	11	18	25	Mar 3	10
Arizona St.	6	4	-	-	-	-	-	-	-	-	-	-	-	-	-
Cincinnati	3	6	4	5	4	8	8	-	-	-	-	-	-	-	-
Davidson	-	-	10	7	7	5	5	4	3	5	4	8	7	10	10
DePaul	-	-	-	-	-	-	-	9	9	10	10	9	9	8	9
Drake	-	-	-	-	-	-	-	-	-	-	-	10	-	-	-
Duke	4	3	5	8	9	9	10	8	8	7	5	4	4	4	3
Kansas	-	10	-	-	-	-	-	-	-	-	-	-	-	-	-
Kentucky	9	5	2	2	1	2	4	5	4	3	3	3	2	3	4
Loyola (Ill.)	1	1	1	1	3	3	2	3	10	9	-	10	-	9	8
Michigan	8	7	3	3	5	4	3	2	2	2	2	2	3	2	2
New York U.	2	2	7	10	-	-	-	-	-	-	-	-	-	-	-
Ohio St.	7	-	-	-	-	-	-	-	-	-	-	-	-	-	-
Oregon St.	10	9	-	9	8	6	7	10	-	-	9	7	6	6	6
Toledo	-	-	9	-	-	-	-	-	-	-	-	-	-	-	-
UCLA	-	6	4	2	1	1	1	1	1	1	1	1	1	1	1
Vanderbilt	-	-	8	6	6	7	6	6	5	8	7	-	-	-	-
Villanova	-	-	-	10	10	9	7	6	6	8	5	8	-	7	7
Wichita St.	5	-	-	-	-	-	10	7	-	4	6	6	5	5	5

1964-65

	PS	December				January				February				March	
		8	15	22	29	5	12	19	26	2	9	16	23	2	9
Bradley	14	-	-	-	-	-	-	-	-	-	-	-	-	-	-
Brigham Young	19	-	-	-	-	-	-	-	-	-	-	-	-	10	9
Davidson	4	-	-	10	-	10	8	7	6	5	5	5	6	7	6
DePaul	20	-	-	-	-	-	-	-	-	-	-	-	-	-	-
Duke	5	8	6	6	8	6	10	10	10	6	6	6	5	8	10
Illinois	-	-	-	7	6	-	-	-	-	-	10	-	-	-	-
Indiana	-	-	-	8	7	2	5	5	9	7	8	7	7	-	-
Kansas	18	-	-	-	-	-	-	-	-	-	-	-	-	-	-
Kansas St.	8	-	-	-	-	-	-	-	-	-	-	-	-	-	-
Kentucky	11	9	8	-	-	-	-	-	-	-	-	-	-	-	-
Michigan	1	1	2	1	1	3	2	2	2	1	1	1	1	1	1
Minnesota	11	6	4	3	3	-	-	-	-	-	-	9	8	6	7
New Mexico	-	-	-	-	-	-	-	-	-	-	-	-	10	-	-
North Carolina	13	-	-	-	-	-	-	-	-	-	-	-	-	-	-
Notre Dame	17	-	-	-	-	-	-	-	-	-	-	-	-	-	-
Providence	-	-	-	-	-	9	6	6	4	4	4	4	4	4	4
St. John's (N.Y.)	10	10	7	-	-	7	7	8	7	-	-	-	-	-	-
St. Joseph's	-	-	-	-	10	4	4	3	3	3	3	3	3	3	3
St. Louis	-	4	10	9	9	-	-	-	-	-	-	-	-	-	-
San Francisco	9	5	3	5	5	8	9	9	8	10	-	-	-	-	-
Seattle	15	-	-	-	-	-	-	-	-	-	-	-	-	-	-
Syracuse	7	-	-	-	-	-	-	-	-	-	-	-	-	-	-
Tennessee	-	-	-	-	-	-	-	-	-	-	-	8	-	-	-
UCLA	2	7	5	4	4	1	1	1	1	2	2	2	2	2	2
Vanderbilt	6	3	9	-	-	-	-	-	-	9	7	-	9	5	5
Villanova	16	-	-	-	-	-	-	-	-	-	-	-	-	9	8
Wichita St.	3	2	1	2	2	5	3	4	5	8	9	10	-	-	-

1965-66

	PS	December				January				February				March	
		7	14	21	28	4	11	18	25	1	8	15	22	1	8
Bradley	9	9	9	5	3	5	5	7	-	-	-	-	-	-	-
Brigham Young	-	-	-	-	6	8	7	-	-	-	-	-	-	-	-
Cincinnati	-	-	-	-	-	-	-	-	8	10	-	-	-	10	7
Duke	3	6	1	1	1	1	1	1	1	1	2	2	2	3	2
Iowa	-	-	-	9	4	7	-	-	-	-	-	-	-	-	-
Kansas	8	7	4	-	-	-	10	6	9	7	7	7	6	6	4
Kansas St.	10	-	-	-	-	-	-	-	-	-	-	-	-	-	-
Kentucky	-	-	-	10	5	2	2	2	2	2	1	1	1	1	1
Loyola (Ill.)	-	-	-	-	-	-	-	9	7	5	3	4	4	4	6
Michigan	2	2	3	3	7	-	-	-	-	9	10	10	10	-	9
Minnesota	7	5	6	6	9	-	-	-	-	-	-	-	-	-	-
Nebraska	-	-	-	-	-	-	-	-	-	-	9	9	8	9	-
Providence	6	8	7	7	10	6	6	4	3	4	6	6	9	8	-
St. Joseph's	4	3	2	2	8	4	4	3	5	8	8	8	7	7	5
South Carolina	-	10	-	-	-	-	-	-	-	-	-	-	-	-	-
UTEP	-	-	-	-	-	9	8	8	6	6	4	3	3	2	3
UCLA	1	1	8	-	-	10	9	10	10	-	-	-	-	-	-
Vanderbilt	5	4	5	4	2	3	3	5	4	3	5	5	5	5	8
Western Ky.	-	-	-	-	-	-	-	-	-	-	-	-	-	-	10
Wichita St.	-	-	10	8	-	-	-	-	-	-	-	-	-	-	-

1966-67

	PS	December				January					February				March
		6	13	20	27	3	10	17	24	31	7	14	21	28	7
Boston College	-	-	-	-	-	-	-	-	-	-	10	-	-	10	9
Bradley	-	-	-	-	-	10	-	-	-	-	-	-	-	-	-
Brigham Young	-	9	7	-	-	-	-	-	-	-	-	-	-	-	-
Cincinnati	10	10	10	7	7	8	-	-	-	-	-	-	-	-	-
Duke	4	7	-	-	-	-	-	-	-	-	-	-	-	-	-
Florida	-	-	-	-	-	-	10	8	-	-	-	-	-	-	-
Houston	7	5	9	8	6	5	4	3	3	6	5	7	7	7	7
Kansas	-	-	-	9	-	9	8	7	7	7	7	6	4	4	3
Kentucky	3	3	4	-	-	-	-	-	-	-	-	-	-	-	-
Louisville	5	4	3	2	2	2	2	2	4	3	3	2	2	2	2
Michigan St.	-	-	8	5	10	-	-	-	-	-	-	-	-	-	-
Mississippi St.	-	-	-	-	-	10	-	-	-	-	-	-	-	-	-
New Mexico	6	6	5	6	5	4	3	9	-	-	-	-	-	-	-
North Carolina	9	8	6	3	3	3	5	4	2	2	2	4	5	3	4
Princeton	-	-	-	-	-	-	7	5	5	5	4	3	6	5	5
Providence	-	-	-	-	-	7	9	10	10	10	9	-	-	-	-
St. John's (N.Y.)	-	-	-	-	8	-	-	-	-	-	-	-	-	-	-
Syracuse	-	-	-	-	-	-	-	-	-	-	-	10	8	-	-
Tennessee	-	-	-	-	-	-	-	-	-	-	-	-	9	8	8
UTEP	2	2	2	4	4	6	6	6	6	4	8	8	10	9	10
UCLA	1	1	1	1	1	1	1	1	1	1	1	1	1	1	1
Vanderbilt	-	-	-	10	9	-	-	-	9	9	-	9	-	-	-
Western Ky.	8	-	-	-	-	-	-	-	8	8	6	5	3	6	6

1967-68

	PS	December				January					February				March	
		5	12	19	26	2	9	16	23	30	6	13	20	27	5	12
Boston College	7	10	6	8	10	-	-	-	-	-	-	-	-	-	-	-
Bradley	-	-	-	10	-	-	-	-	-	-	-	-	-	-	-	-
Columbia	-	-	-	-	-	-	10	10	8	8	7	6	6	6	8	7
Davidson	10	-	8	6	8	-	-	-	-	-	-	-	-	-	10	8
Dayton	6	6	-	-	-	-	-	-	-	-	-	-	-	-	-	-
Duke	-	-	-	-	-	-	-	-	-	9	-	10	8	10	6	10
Houston	2	2	2	2	2	2	2	2	1	1	1	1	1	1	1	1
Indiana	-	-	9	5	3	-	-	-	-	-	-	-	-	-	-	-
Kansas	5	4	-	-	-	-	-	-	-	-	-	-	-	-	-	-
Kentucky	-	9	4	7	6	5	4	8	9	10	8	8	5	5	4	5
Louisville	3	3	5	-	-	-	-	-	-	-	-	-	-	9	9	9
Marquette	-	-	-	-	-	-	-	-	-	-	-	-	10	8	-	-
New Mexico	-	-	-	-	-	10	9	6	4	4	6	5	7	7	7	6
New Mexico St.	-	-	-	-	-	-	-	-	-	-	10	-	-	-	-	-
North Carolina	4	5	7	4	5	3	3	3	3	3	3	3	3	3	5	4
Oklahoma City	-	-	-	-	-	8	-	-	-	-	-	-	-	-	-	-
Princeton	8	-	10	-	-	-	-	-	-	-	-	-	-	-	-	-
Purdue	-	7	-	-	-	-	-	-	-	-	-	-	-	-	-	-
St. Bonaventure	-	-	-	-	-	9	7	7	5	5	4	4	4	4	3	3
Tennessee	-	-	-	9	4	6	5	4	6	6	5	7	-	-	-	-
UCLA	1	1	1	1	1	1	1	1	2	2	2	2	2	2	2	2
Utah	-	-	-	-	7	7	6	5	10	-	-	-	-	-	-	-
Vanderbilt	9	8	3	3	9	4	8	9	7	7	9	9	9	-	-	-

1968-69

	PS	December					January				February				March
		3	10	17	24	31	7	14	21	28	4	11	18	25	4
Baylor	-	-	-	-	-	-	-	18	-	-	-	19	-	-	-
Boston College	-	-	-	-	-	-	-	-	-	-	-	-	-	20	16
California	-	19	18	15	-	-	-	-	-	-	-	-	-	-	-
Cincinnati	14	9	6	6	10	10	19	19	-	-	-	-	-	-	-
Colorado	-	-	-	-	-	-	-	20	17	17	20	14	18	-	18
Columbia	-	-	-	-	-	-	-	-	19	18	14	-	-	-	-
Davidson	6	6	3	3	3	2	6	4	4	4	6	6	5	5	5
Dayton	-	-	-	-	-	-	-	-	20	20	19	17	-	-	-
Detroit	18	15	14	13	11	7	13	-	-	-	-	-	-	-	-
Drake	-	-	-	-	-	-	18	-	-	-	-	-	-	-	11
Duke	17	16	9	-	-	-	-	-	-	-	-	-	-	-	-
Duquesne	-	-	-	-	-	15	15	12	10	11	15	13	8	10	9
Florida	19	-	-	-	-	-	-	-	-	-	-	-	-	-	-
Houston	8	6	12	20	-	-	-	-	-	-	-	-	-	-	-
Illinois	-	-	-	-	12	8	4	8	8	7	10	10	19	15	20
Iowa	-	20	19	-	-	-	-	-	-	-	-	-	-	-	-
Kansas	5	4	11	11	8	5	5	10	13	15	13	12	16	13	19
Kentucky	3	3	4	4	4	3	7	5	5	5	4	4	6	6	7
La Salle	-	-	20	16	17	11	11	11	9	9	7	5	4	3	2
Louisville	-	-	-	19	14	14	14	-	-	-	-	20	13	11	15
Marquette	15	20	-	-	-	-	20	15	16	16	17	18	20	18	14
New Mexico	9	8	5	5	6	18	-	-	-	-	18	-	-	-	-
New Mexico St.	-	-	-	14	15	12	10	7	7	8	16	15	15	16	12
North Carolina	2	2	2	2	2	4	2	2	2	2	2	2	3	2	4
Northwestern	-	-	-	-	-	19	12	17	-	-	-	-	-	-	-
Notre Dame	4	5	7	7	7	16	17	16	15	-	-	-	-	-	17
Ohio St.	12	13	17	17	16	13	16	13	12	12	12	16	10	14	-
Purdue	10	14	13	12	18	-	-	-	18	14	9	8	9	9	6
St. Bonaventure	7	11	10	9	13	20	-	-	-	-	-	-	-	-	-
St. John's (N.Y.)	-	-	-	-	-	17	8	6	6	6	5	9	7	7	8
Santa Clara	-	18	16	10	9	6	3	3	3	3	3	3	2	4	3
South Carolina	-	-	-	-	-	-	-	-	-	19	-	-	12	8	13
Tennessee	20	20	-	-	20	-	-	-	-	-	-	-	17	17	-
Tulsa	-	-	-	-	-	-	-	14	14	13	11	7	14	19	-
UCLA	1	1	1	1	1	1	1	1	1	1	1	1	1	1	1
Vanderbilt	13	12	-	-	-	-	-	-	-	-	-	-	-	-	-
Villanova	11	10	8	8	5	9	9	9	11	10	8	11	11	12	10
Western Ky.	16	17	15	18	-	-	-	-	-	-	-	-	-	-	-
Wyoming	-	-	-	-	19	-	-	-	-	-	-	-	-	-	-

1969-70

	PS	December				January				February				March	
		9	16	23	30	6	13	20	27	3	10	17	24	3	10
Cincinnati	-	-	-	-	-	-	-	-	-	-	-	-	-	19	-
Colorado	10	17	16	-	20	-	-	-	-	-	-	-	-	-	-
Columbia	-	-	-	-	15	17	13	-	17	17	19	-	18	-	-
Davidson	5	4	4	9	11	8	8	11	11	15	13	9	11	10	15
Drake	19	-	-	-	-	-	-	-	16	13	11	17	16	14	14
Duke	-	-	-	-	-	19	19	16	-	-	-	-	-	-	-
Duquesne	11	7	-	-	-	-	-	-	-	-	-	-	-	-	-
Florida St.	-	-	-	-	-	-	-	-	18	12	9	8	10	11	11
Georgia	-	-	-	-	-	-	-	-	-	-	20	-	-	-	-
Houston	20	-	19	8	8	11	9	7	12	16	15	15	15	13	12
Illinois	-	-	-	15	-	-	17	12	10	14	-	-	-	-	-
Iowa	-	-	-	-	-	-	-	18	20	20	14	11	9	8	7
Jacksonville	-	18	18	13	10	7	6	6	6	8	7	6	6	6	4
Kansas	-	-	-	16	-	-	-	-	-	-	-	-	-	-	-
Kansas St.	-	-	-	-	-	-	-	17	19	18	-	18	17	16	-
Kentucky	2	1	1	1	1	2	2	2	2	3	3	2	1	2	1

WEEK-BY-WEEK A.P. POLLS—1969-70

57

DIVISION I

		December				January				February				March	
	PS	9	16	23	30	6	13	20	27	3	10	17	24	3	10
Long Beach St.	-	-	-	-	-	-	-	-	-	-	-	-	-	-	19
Louisville	15	11	14	14	-	20	18	18	-	-	-	19	-	-	-
LSU	-	-	15	-	-	-	-	-	-	-	-	-	-	-	-
Marquette	8	12	17	-	18	13	10	8	7	9	12	10	8	9	8
New Mexico St.	6	3	3	7	7	6	5	5	5	6	6	5	5	5	5
Niagara	-	-	-	-	-	15	12	-	-	-	-	-	-	-	17
North Carolina	7	5	7	4	4	4	7	9	9	7	10	13	19	-	-
North Carolina St.	-	-	-	-	15	10	11	10	8	5	5	12	14	19	10
Notre Dame	13	10	6	11	13	-	-	20	-	-	16	14	13	15	9
Ohio St.	18	16	-	-	-	-	-	-	-	-	-	-	-	-	-
Ohio	-	19	10	5	5	9	14	13	13	-	-	-	-	17	-
Oklahoma	-	-	-	-	-	16	-	-	-	-	-	-	-	-	-
Pennsylvania	-	-	-	17	14	18	15	14	14	10	8	7	7	7	13
Purdue	3	14	12	18	17	-	-	-	-	-	-	-	-	-	-
St. Bonaventure	17	20	-	19	12	5	4	4	3	4	4	3	3	4	3
St. John's (N.Y.)	14	-	-	-	-	-	-	-	-	-	-	-	-	-	-
Santa Clara	12	15	11	-	-	-	-	-	-	-	-	20	-	-	-
South Carolina	1	8	5	3	3	3	3	3	4	2	2	4	4	3	6
Southern California	16	6	13	12	19	-	20	15	15	11	18	-	-	-	20
Tennessee	-	9	8	6	6	12	-	-	-	-	-	-	-	-	-
UCLA	4	2	2	2	2	1	1	1	1	1	1	1	2	1	2
Utah St.	-	-	-	-	-	-	-	-	-	-	-	-	20	18	16
Villanova	9	12	9	20	-	-	-	-	-	19	-	-	-	-	-
Western Ky.	-	-	-	-	-	-	-	-	-	-	17	16	12	12	18
Washington	-	-	20	10	9	14	15	-	-	-	-	-	-	-	-

1970-71

		December				January				February				March		
	PS	8	15	22	29	5	12	19	26	2	9	16	23	2	9	16
Army	-	14	-	-	-	-	-	-	-	-	-	-	-	-	-	-
Brigham Young	-	-	-	-	-	-	-	-	-	-	-	-	-	-	-	20
Drake	10	7	9	9	7	16	-	-	-	-	-	-	-	-	-	18
Duke	13	-	-	-	-	-	-	-	-	-	-	-	-	-	19	-
Duquesne	-	-	-	-	-	-	-	-	17	14	12	10	8	11	11	15
Florida St.	-	-	17	-	-	-	-	-	-	-	-	-	-	-	-	-
Fordham	-	-	-	-	-	18	14	17	-	-	20	18	11	10	10	9
Houston	17	-	-	-	-	-	-	-	-	18	15	-	-	15	18	14
Illinois	-	-	-	-	-	-	-	-	18	15	-	-	-	-	-	-
Indiana	16	11	13	11	14	12	11	18	-	-	-	-	-	18	-	-
Jacksonville	4	3	5	4	9	7	7	6	6	6	6	6	6	9	9	11
Kansas	14	11	12	8	12	8	8	5	5	5	5	5	5	4	5	4
Kentucky	3	5	3	7	8	11	10	12	11	8	8	12	10	8	8	8
La Salle	-	-	-	-	-	-	-	15	14	10	13	11	14	19	-	-
Long Beach St.	18	-	-	-	-	-	-	-	-	-	-	-	20	17	17	16
LSU	-	-	-	-	18	-	-	-	-	-	-	-	-	-	-	-
Louisville	-	20	-	-	17	13	16	-	-	-	-	19	15	-	-	-
Marquette	6	4	4	3	3	3	2	2	1	1	2	2	2	2	2	2
Memphis	-	-	-	-	-	-	19	-	-	-	-	-	-	-	-	-
Miami (Ohio)	-	-	-	-	-	-	-	-	-	-	-	-	-	-	20	-
Michigan	-	-	-	-	-	-	-	-	-	20	16	16	12	-	-	-
Murray St.	-	-	-	-	-	-	-	-	19	19	17	17	-	-	-	-
New Mexico St.	15	15	17	20	-	-	-	-	-	-	-	-	-	-	-	-
North Carolina	-	-	20	17	-	20	15	20	20	16	11	8	13	12	13	13
North Caro. St.	19	-	-	-	-	-	-	-	-	-	-	-	-	-	-	-
Notre Dame	5	6	7	14	15	9	9	9	7	12	9	14	19	16	14	12
Ohio St.	-	-	-	-	-	-	-	-	-	-	-	20	18	13	12	10
Oregon	-	18	16	17	16	-	-	16	13	-	-	-	-	-	-	-
Oregon St.	-	-	-	-	-	-	20	-	-	-	-	-	-	-	-	-
Pennsylvania	11	8	6	5	6	5	4	4	4	4	4	4	4	5	4	3
Purdue	-	-	-	16	20	19	-	-	-	-	-	-	-	-	-	-
St. Bonaventure	-	19	19	15	13	10	12	10	-	-	-	-	-	-	-	-
St. John's (N.Y.)	-	-	-	19	-	-	-	-	-	-	-	-	-	-	-	-
Southern California	7	9	8	6	4	4	3	3	3	2	3	3	3	3	3	5
South Carolina	2	2	2	2	2	2	6	11	10	7	10	7	7	6	6	6
Tennessee	-	17	14	12	10	17	18	8	8	11	14	13	17	14	15	17
UCLA	1	1	1	1	1	1	1	1	2	3	1	1	1	1	1	1
Utah St.	12	16	15	-	19	15	17	12	9	13	19	15	16	20	16	-
Villanova	8	10	10	13	11	14	13	14	16	17	18	-	-	-	-	19
Virginia	-	-	-	-	-	-	-	19	15	-	-	-	-	-	-	-
Western Ky.	9	13	11	10	5	6	5	7	12	9	7	9	9	7	7	7

1971-72

		December				January					February				March	
	PS	7	14	21	28	4	11	18	25	1	8	15	22	29	7	14
Arizona St.	-	17	-	-	-	-	-	-	-	-	-	-	-	-	-	-
Brigham Young	19	15	6	7	8	18	14	13	13	10	10	11	7	7	8	9
Duquesne	-	-	-	-	-	-	-	-	-	-	20	-	-	-	-	-
Florida St.	-	18	9	14	-	20	12	11	10	12	14	14	11	10	14	10
Hawaii	-	-	-	-	18	16	19	18	15	14	18	16	17	15	12	-
Houston	7	12	20	-	-	-	-	-	-	-	-	-	16	13	19	-
Illinois	-	-	-	-	-	-	16	-	-	-	-	-	-	-	-	-
Indiana	-	-	12	8	7	5	17	-	-	-	-	-	-	-	20	17
Jacksonville	11	8	14	16	-	-	-	-	-	17	16	-	-	-	-	-
Kansas	14	-	-	-	-	-	-	-	-	-	-	-	-	-	-	-
Kentucky	10	7	7	11	12	19	15	-	-	-	-	17	18	-	-	18
Long Beach St.	8	6	13	9	10	8	7	4	5	5	8	9	6	6	5	5
Louisville	9	16	17	19	15	7	5	6	4	3	4	4	3	2	4	4
La.-Lafayette	-	-	16	12	13	15	13	12	12	13	13	12	10	11	9	8
Marquette	4	2	2	2	2	2	2	2	2	2	2	2	2	5	7	7
Marshall	-	-	-	20	17	13	20	16	14	11	11	10	8	9	10	12
Maryland	6	5	15	15	16	12	-	-	18	-	-	19	12	18	13	14
Memphis	-	-	-	-	-	-	-	-	-	-	15	18	19	20	11	13
Michigan	13	9	-	-	-	-	-	-	-	20	-	-	-	16	-	-
Minnesota	-	-	-	-	-	-	-	17	16	19	19	-	-	-	16	11
Missouri	-	-	-	-	-	-	18	-	20	15	17	15	14	19	18	-
New Mexico	16	-	-	-	-	-	-	-	-	-	-	-	-	-	-	-
North Carolina	2	3	4	4	4	3	3	3	3	4	3	3	5	3	3	2
North Caro. St.	-	20	-	-	-	-	-	-	-	-	-	-	-	-	-	-
Northern Ill.	-	-	-	-	-	-	-	20	19	-	-	-	-	-	-	-
Ohio	-	-	-	17	-	-	-	-	-	-	-	-	-	-	-	-
Ohio St.	5	4	10	6	6	10	9	7	6	9	7	8	15	14	-	19
Oklahoma	20	-	-	-	-	-	-	-	-	-	-	-	-	-	-	-
Oral Roberts	-	-	-	-	-	-	-	-	-	-	-	-	20	17	17	16
Pennsylvania	15	10	5	13	14	6	6	10	9	6	5	5	4	4	2	3
Princeton	-	-	18	-	-	-	-	14	17	-	-	-	-	-	-	-
Providence	-	-	-	-	-	-	-	-	-	16	12	13	-	-	-	-
St. John's (N.Y.)	17	14	8	10	9	17	-	-	-	-	-	-	-	-	-	-
South Carolina	12	11	3	3	3	4	4	5	11	8	9	7	9	8	6	6
Southern California	3	13	10	5	5	11	10	8	7	18	-	-	-	-	-	-
Tennessee	-	-	-	-	20	-	-	19	-	-	-	20	-	-	-	-
UCLA	1	1	1	1	1	1	1	1	1	1	1	1	1	1	1	1
Villanova	18	18	-	-	-	14	11	15	-	-	-	-	-	-	-	15
Virginia	-	-	19	18	11	9	8	9	8	7	6	6	13	12	15	20
West Virginia	-	-	-	-	19	-	-	-	-	-	-	-	-	-	-	-

1972-73

		December				January					February				March	
	PS	5	12	19	26	2	9	16	23	30	6	13	20	27	6	13
Alabama	-	-	-	-	18	14	14	11	9	6	10	17	18	-	-	-
Arizona St.	-	-	-	-	-	-	-	-	-	-	-	-	-	-	-	16
Austin Peay	-	-	-	-	-	-	-	-	-	-	-	-	-	-	-	19
Brigham Young	12	-	17	15	14	15	-	-	-	-	-	20	-	-	-	-
Florida St.	2	2	2	7	12	19	18	19	-	-	-	-	-	-	-	-
Houston	15	20	16	14	13	10	10	12	11	11	11	7	9	8	7	13
Indiana	-	-	15	9	15	20	16	16	6	5	4	11	10	12	9	6
Jacksonville	-	-	-	-	-	-	15	15	13	15	16	13	20	18	16	-
Kansas St.	17	16	20	17	16	18	17	14	18	18	18	15	13	16	11	9
Kentucky	13	8	-	-	-	-	-	-	-	-	-	-	-	-	19	17
Long Beach St.	6	7	7	6	6	5	6	5	5	4	3	3	3	4	4	3
La.-Lafayette	7	10	8	8	9	8	13	13	12	13	13	14	12	11	14	7
Louisville	20	-	-	-	-	-	20	20	-	-	-	-	-	-	-	-
Marquette	5	5	4	3	3	3	4	7	10	10	7	5	5	5	6	5
Maryland	3	3	3	2	2	2	2	3	4	3	9	10	8	9	10	8
Memphis	11	11	19	-	-	-	-	-	17	17	15	16	14	10	15	12
Michigan	19	18	18	-	-	-	-	-	-	-	-	-	-	-	-	-
Minnesota	4	4	5	5	5	6	8	6	8	9	5	4	4	3	3	10
Missouri	-	-	12	10	7	7	5	8	7	7	8	12	16	13	12	15
New Mexico	-	-	-	-	-	16	-	-	19	-	20	18	15	15	-	-
North Carolina	-	13	11	13	11	9	7	4	3	8	6	6	6	7	8	11
North Carolina St.	8	6	6	4	4	4	3	2	2	2	2	2	2	2	2	2
Ohio St.	10	15	-	-	-	-	-	-	-	-	-	-	-	-	-	-
Oklahoma	-	-	-	19	19	-	-	-	-	-	-	-	-	-	-	-
Oral Roberts	18	12	10	16	-	-	-	-	-	19	19	-	-	-	-	-
Pennsylvania	9	9	9	11	8	17	-	-	-	-	-	-	-	-	-	18
Providence	-	19	14	18	17	13	11	9	14	12	12	8	7	6	5	4
Purdue	-	-	-	-	-	-	-	-	20	-	-	-	17	20	-	-
St. John's (N.Y.)	-	-	-	-	-	-	18	17	15	14	14	9	11	17	17	-
St. Joseph's	-	-	-	-	-	-	-	-	-	-	-	-	-	-	18	-
San Francisco	-	-	-	-	20	12	12	10	16	16	17	-	-	-	19	20
Santa Clara	-	-	-	20	-	-	-	-	-	-	-	-	-	-	-	-
South Carolina	16	-	-	-	-	-	-	-	-	-	-	-	-	19	-	-
Southern California	20	17	-	-	-	-	-	-	-	20	-	-	-	-	-	-
Syracuse	-	-	-	-	-	-	-	-	-	-	-	-	-	14	13	14
Tennessee	14	14	-	-	-	-	-	-	-	-	-	-	-	-	-	-
UCLA	1	1	1	1	1	1	1	1	1	1	1	1	1	1	1	1
Vanderbilt	-	-	13	12	10	11	9	18	-	-	-	-	-	-	-	-
Virginia Tech	-	-	-	-	-	-	-	-	-	-	-	19	19	-	-	-

1973-74

		December				January					February				March			
	PS	4	11	18	25	2	8	15	22	29	5	12	19	26	5	12	19	27
Alabama	18	18	13	10	13	7	12	10	9	8	8	8	8	7	12	11	13	14
Arizona	15	15	14	14	12	15	-	-	-	-	-	20	-	18	-	-	-	-
Arizona St.	-	-	-	-	-	-	-	-	20	-	-	-	-	-	-	-	-	-
Austin Peay	-	-	-	-	20	20	-	-	-	-	-	-	-	-	-	-	-	-
Centenary (La.)	-	-	-	-	-	-	-	-	18	-	-	-	-	-	-	-	-	-
Cincinnati	-	-	-	20	-	-	-	20	-	-	-	-	-	-	-	-	-	-
Creighton	-	-	-	-	-	-	-	-	-	-	-	17	15	16	19	19	-	-

		December				January					February				March			
	PS	4	11	18	25	2	8	15	22	29	5	12	19	26	5	12	19	27
Dayton	-	-	-	-	-	-	-	-	-	-	-	-	-	-	-	20	16	20
Hawaii	-	-	-	-	-	-	20	-	-	-	-	-	-	-	-	-	-	-
Houston	14	14	-	-	-	-	-	-	-	-	-	-	-	-	-	-	-	-
Indiana	3	3	3	7	7	8	13	12	11	12	12	12	10	9	13	10	11	9
Jacksonville	17	17	19	19	-	-	-	-	-	-	-	-	-	-	-	-	-	-
Kansas	13	-	-	-	-	-	-	-	-	18	17	16	16	15	15	14	6	7
Kansas St.	-	13	15	13	18	-	-	-	-	-	-	-	18	-				
Kentucky	10	10	-	-	-	-	-	-	-	-	-	-	-	-	-	-	-	-
Long Beach St.	12	12	12	11	10	9	9	9	10	10	9	10	13	13	9	9	9	10
Louisville	9	9	9	8	8	13	11	16	14	15	15	18	20	20	18	16	-	-
Marquette	7	7	7	6	6	6	7	6	6	5	6	9	9	8	11	7	3	3
Maryland	4	4	4	2	2	3	3	4	5	6	7	6	5	5	4	4	4	4
Md.-East. Shore	-	-	-	-	-	-	-	-	-	-	20	-	-	-	-	-	-	-
Memphis	20	10	12	16	18	19	-	-	-	-	-	-	-	-	-	-	-	-
Michigan	-	-	-	-	-	-	18	14	15	20	16	15	19	17	16	12	7	6
Missouri	-	-	-	-	-	-	-	18	-	-	-	-	-	-	-	-	-	-
UNLV	19	19	-	-	19	15	16	-	-	-	-	-	-	-	-	-	-	-
New Mexico	-	-	-	-	17	12	8	15	19	17	-	-	-	19	17	17	20	-
North Carolina	5	5	5	4	4	4	5	5	4	4	4	4	6	4	6	8	10	12
North Carolina St.	2	2	2	5	5	5	4	3	3	2	2	2	1	1	1	1	1	1
Notre Dame	8	8	6	3	3	2	2	2	1	3	3	3	2	2	2	3	5	5
Oral Roberts	-	-	-	-	-	-	-	-	-	19	19	-	-	-	20	-	18	18
Penn	16	16	11	-	-	-	-	-	-	-	-	-	-	-	-	-	-	-
Pittsburgh	-	-	-	-	-	-	-	17	16	13	10	7	7	11	14	13	15	16
Providence	6	6	8	9	9	14	10	7	8	9	11	11	11	12	8	5	8	8
Purdue	-	-	-	-	-	-	-	-	-	-	-	-	-	-	-	-	18	11
San Francisco	11	11	17	-	-	-	-	-	-	-	-	-	-	-	-	-	-	-
South Carolina	-	-	16	15	-	-	15	11	13	14	13	14	14	14	10	18	17	19
Southern California	-	-	20	16	14	11	17	13	12	11	14	13	12	10	7	15	14	17
Syracuse	-	-	18	18	15	19	-	-	-	-	-	-	-	-	-	-	-	-
UTEP	-	-	-	-	-	-	-	-	18	-	-	-	-	-	-	-	-	-
UCLA	1	1	1	1	1	1	1	1	2	1	1	1	3	3	3	2	2	2
Utah	-	-	-	-	-	-	-	-	-	-	-	19	17	-	-	-	-	15
Vanderbilt	-	-	-	17	11	10	6	8	7	7	5	5	4	6	5	6	11	13
Wisconsin	-	-	-	-	-	17	13	19	17	16	-	-	-	-	-	-	-	-

1974-75

		December					January				February				March				April
	PS	3	10	17	24	31	7	14	21	28	4	11	18	25	4	11	18	25	2
Alabama	9	11	10	8	7	6	8	7	6	9	7	7	5	8	7	10	11	11	10
Arizona	19	18	17	13	10	14	10	13	13	15	17	19	15	19	19	-	-	-	-
Arizona St.	-	-	-	-	-	16	12	9	10	12	10	8	8	9	9	8	7	7	8
Auburn	-	-	-	-	-	-	-	-	20	14	-	-	-	-	-	-	-	-	-
Centenary (La.)	-	-	-	-	-	-	-	-	-	-	-	-	18	-	-	17	19	18	-
Cincinnati	-	-	-	-	-	-	-	-	-	-	-	-	-	-	-	17	12	12	13
Clemson	-	-	-	-	-	-	-	-	-	-	16	18	16	11	14	14	-	-	-
Creighton	-	-	-	-	-	-	-	-	-	-	18	20	14	13	13	-	-	-	-
Drake	-	-	-	-	-	-	-	-	-	-	-	-	-	-	-	-	14	16	16
Houston	-	20	-	-	-	-	-	-	-	-	-	-	-	-	-	-	-	-	-
Indiana	3	3	3	2	2	2	1	1	1	1	1	1	1	1	1	1	1	3	3
Kansas	6	7	9	18	-	-	-	-	18	20	-	-	-	-	-	-	-	-	-
Kansas St.	-	-	-	-	-	-	-	-	-	-	-	-	-	-	-	-	17	15	15
Kentucky	16	15	-	20	17	9	7	10	11	5	5	4	7	4	6	6	5	2	2
La Salle	-	-	-	-	-	-	14	11	9	7	13	12	17	-	-	-	-	-	-
Louisville	8	6	4	4	4	4	3	3	2	3	3	6	6	3	3	3	3	4	4
Marquette	5	8	7	6	14	13	13	12	12	13	11	9	9	6	5	5	10	10	11
Maryland	4	4	5	5	5	7	5	5	3	8	4	3	3	2	2	4	4	5	5
Memphis	15	16	14	11	16	19	-	-	-	-	-	-	-	-	-	-	-	-	-
Michigan	17	19	16	-	-	17	11	19	-	-	-	-	-	-	-	-	-	19	19
Minnesota	18	-	-	-	-	-	17	16	17	-	-	-	-	-	-	-	-	-	-
UNLV	-	-	-	-	-	-	-	-	-	-	-	-	-	-	-	-	16	20	17
North Carolina	11	9	8	10	8	8	15	14	14	10	12	11	13	14	12	7	6	9	9
North Carolina St.	1	1	1	1	1	1	4	4	5	2	6	5	4	7	8	9	8	8	7
Notre Dame	12	13	11	12	13	19	-	-	-	16	14	16	11	16	16	12	9	14	14
Oklahoma	-	-	19	17	18	-	-	-	-	-	-	-	-	-	-	-	-	-	-
Oregon	-	-	18	19	19	11	9	8	8	11	9	13	-	-	-	-	-	-	-
Oregon St.	-	-	-	-	-	-	-	-	-	-	-	17	20	17	15	15	13	-	18
Penn	20	14	12	9	9	12	-	-	-	-	20	14	12	10	10	11	15	17	-
Princeton	-	-	-	-	-	-	-	-	-	-	-	-	-	-	-	-	-	13	12
Providence	14	17	20	16	12	10	19	15	16	-	-	-	-	-	-	-	-	-	20
Purdue	13	12	15	15	15	18	-	-	20	-	-	-	-	-	-	-	-	-	-
Rutgers	-	-	-	-	20	-	-	17	19	-	19	-	-	-	20	16	-	-	-
South Carolina	7	5	13	14	11	15	16	20	-	19	-	-	-	-	-	-	-	-	-
Southern California	10	10	6	7	6	5	6	6	7	6	8	10	10	12	11	13	18	-	-
Stanford	-	-	-	-	-	-	-	-	15	17	-	-	-	-	-	-	-	-	-
Syracuse	-	-	-	-	-	-	-	-	-	-	-	-	-	-	-	-	20	6	6
Tennessee	-	-	-	-	-	-	18	18	-	18	15	-	-	-	-	-	-	-	-
UTEP	-	-	-	-	-	-	-	-	-	-	-	-	-	15	18	17	-	-	-
Tex.-Pan American	-	-	-	-	-	-	-	-	-	-	-	15	19	18	17	20	-	-	-
UCLA	2	2	2	3	3	3	2	2	4	4	2	2	2	5	4	2	2	1	1
Wake Forest	-	-	-	-	-	-	19	-	-	-	-	-	-	-	-	-	-	-	-
Washington	-	-	-	-	-	-	-	-	-	-	-	-	-	20	-	-	-	-	-

1975-76

		December					January				February				March		
	PS	2	9	16	23	30	6	13	20	27	3	10	17	24	2	9	16
Alabama	12	14	11	8	8	8	10	11	12	11	14	11	10	7	16	8	6
Arizona	11	11	10	-	-	-	-	-	-	-	-	-	-	-	-	18	15
Arizona St.	18	19	19	19	-	-	-	-	-	-	-	-	-	-	-	-	-
Auburn	-	17	17	17	-	-	-	-	-	-	-	-	-	-	-	-	-
Centenary (La.)	-	-	-	-	19	18	-	18	-	19	18	19	20	19	20	20	19
Charlotte	19	-	-	-	-	-	-	-	-	-	-	-	-	-	-	18	17
Cincinnati	10	10	9	7	6	7	15	14	16	18	16	13	13	18	13	15	12
DePaul	-	-	-	-	-	-	-	-	-	-	-	-	-	-	-	-	17
Florida St.	-	-	-	-	-	-	-	-	-	-	-	-	-	-	18	-	-
Indiana	1	1	1	1	1	1	1	1	1	1	1	1	1	1	1	1	1
Kansas St.	14	18	-	-	-	-	-	-	-	-	-	-	-	-	-	-	-
Kentucky	6	7	14	20	18	-	-	-	-	-	-	-	-	-	-	-	-
La Salle	-	-	-	-	-	20	-	-	-	-	-	-	-	-	-	-	-
Louisville	8	6	6	10	11	11	16	-	-	-	-	-	19	-	-	-	-
Marquette	4	3	3	3	7	6	4	3	3	2	2	2	2	2	2	2	2
Maryland	3	2	2	2	2	2	2	2	2	7	5	4	7	10	9	12	11
Memphis	19	-	-	-	-	-	-	-	-	-	-	-	-	-	-	-	-
Michigan	16	16	18	16	16	17	19	16	17	15	16	16	15	13	11	14	9
Minnesota	-	-	-	-	20	16	17	-	-	-	-	-	-	-	-	-	-
Missouri	-	-	20	-	-	-	-	20	-	13	13	14	14	12	15	10	14
UNLV	-	-	16	13	12	10	5	4	4	3	3	7	6	5	5	4	3
North Carolina	5	4	4	4	3	3	6	7	5	4	4	3	3	4	4	5	8
North Carolina St.	13	13	13	9	9	9	11	13	11	8	10	12	12	15	17	-	-
North Texas	-	-	-	-	-	-	-	-	-	-	20	20	-	-	-	-	-
Notre Dame	7	9	8	5	5	5	13	15	15	10	11	10	8	6	8	7	7
Oregon	-	-	-	-	-	-	-	-	-	-	-	-	-	17	-	-	-
Oregon St.	-	-	-	-	-	-	-	17	13	16	-	-	-	-	-	-	-
Pepperdine	-	-	-	-	-	-	-	-	-	-	-	-	-	-	-	-	20
Princeton	-	-	-	-	-	-	-	-	-	17	15	-	-	-	-	-	-
Providence	17	15	-	-	-	-	-	-	-	-	-	-	-	-	-	-	-
Rutgers	-	-	-	15	15	14	12	10	7	5	7	5	4	3	3	3	4
St. John's (N.Y.)	-	-	-	18	17	15	14	12	9	14	12	17	16	14	16	17	-
San Francisco	15	12	12	14	14	19	20	-	-	-	-	-	-	-	-	-	-
Southern California	-	-	-	-	-	-	18	-	-	-	-	-	-	-	-	-	-
Syracuse	20	-	-	-	-	-	-	-	-	-	-	-	-	-	-	-	-
Tennessee	9	8	7	11	10	12	9	9	10	9	8	8	9	11	12	9	13
Texas A&M	-	-	-	-	-	-	-	-	-	-	-	-	-	20	19	-	-
Texas Tech	-	-	-	-	-	-	-	-	-	-	-	-	-	-	-	19	16
UCLA	2	5	5	6	4	4	3	8	6	12	9	6	5	9	7	6	5
Virginia	-	-	-	-	-	-	-	-	-	-	-	-	-	-	-	13	18
Virginia Tech	-	-	-	-	-	-	-	-	-	-	19	18	18	-	-	-	-
VMI	-	-	-	-	-	-	-	-	20	-	-	-	-	-	-	-	-
Wake Forest	-	-	-	-	-	-	7	5	14	-	-	-	-	-	-	-	-
Washington	-	20	15	12	13	13	8	6	8	6	6	9	11	8	10	11	-
West Tex. A&M	-	-	-	-	-	-	-	19	19	20	-	-	-	-	-	-	-
Western Mich.	-	-	-	-	-	-	-	-	-	-	17	15	17	16	14	16	10
Wisconsin	-	-	-	-	-	-	-	-	18	-	-	-	-	-	-	-	-

1976-77

		Nov.	December				January				February				March		
	PS	30	7	14	21	28	4	11	18	25	1	8	15	22	1	8	15
Alabama	13	13	10	7	5	4	4	4	3	3	8	7	4	8	12	12	11
Arizona	10	11	9	8	14	13	11	10	16	16	19	18	17	20	17	20	-
Arkansas	-	-	-	19	18	17	18	16	17	15	14	13	11	6	7	8	18
Auburn	-	-	-	-	-	20	-	-	-	-	-	-	-	-	-	-	-
Charlotte	19	-	-	-	-	-	-	-	-	-	-	-	-	-	-	18	17
Cincinnati	12	12	8	6	4	5	2	3	2	12	12	12	10	14	14	11	-
Clemson	-	-	16	13	11	10	16	17	-	19	16	15	18	19	18	-	-
DePaul	18	18	19	-	-	-	-	-	-	-	-	-	-	-			
Detroit	-	-	-	-	-	-	-	-	-	-	20	19	15	16	15	17	12
Indiana	5	4	13	16	-	-	-	-	-	-	-	-	-	-	-	-	-
Kansas St.	-	-	-	-	-	-	-	-	-	-	-	-	-	-	-	-	16
Kentucky	6	5	4	3	7	6	3	2	6	6	3	3	2	2	2	6	3
Louisville	9	7	14	17	13	14	14	13	12	11	9	6	8	10	10	14	19
Marquette	2	2	2	2	6	12	12	11	8	9	6	9	9	18	19	16	7
Maryland	8	16	17	14	15	16	15	14	13	-	-	-	-	-	-	-	-
Memphis	-	-	-	-	-	-	20	18	18	20	-	-	-	-	-	-	-
Michigan	1	1	1	1	1	1	5	6	5	2	7	5	5	3	3	1	1
Minnesota	-	-	-	-	20	15	13	9	11	13	10	8	12	13	9	9	13
Missouri	20	-	-	-	-	-	-	-	-	-	-	-	-	-	-	-	-
UNLV	7	6	5	12	12	11	9	8	7	5	4	10	6	4	5	5	4
North Carolina	3	9	12	11	10	9	6	5	4	4	13	14	13	9	6	4	5
North Carolina St.	15	-	-	-	-	-	-	-	-	-	-	-	-	-	-	-	-
Notre Dame	14	8	7	4	2	2	8	19	-	-	-	-	-	-	-	-	-
Oregon	-	-	-	-	-	-	-	20	-	-	-	-	-	17	-	-	-
Providence	-	-	-	-	-	-	17	15	15	14	15	16	16	12	8	13	-
Purdue	-	-	-	-	-	-	-	-	19	18	18	-	-	-	-	-	-
Rutgers	17	19	-	-	-	-	-	-	-	-	-	-	-	-	-	-	-
St. John's (N.Y.)	-	-	-	20	-	-	-	-	-	-	-	-	-	-	-	-	-
San Francisco	11	10	6	5	3	3	1	1	1	1	1	1	1	1	1	3	8
Southern Ill.	-	17	18	18	-	-	-	-	-	-	-	-	-	-	-	-	-
Syracuse	-	-	20	15	17	18	19	-	20	17	17	17	20	15	13	10	6
Tennessee	16	15	15	-	19	-	-	-	14	7	11	11	14	7	11	7	15
UCLA	4	3	3	9	8	8	7	12	10	8	2	2	3	5	4	2	2

	PS	Nov. 30	Dec. 7	Dec. 14	Dec. 21	Dec. 28	Jan. 4	Jan. 11	Jan. 18	Jan. 25	Feb. 1	Feb. 8	Feb. 15	Feb. 22	Mar. 1	Mar. 8	Mar. 15
Utah	-	-	-	-	16	19	-	-	-	-	-	-	-	-	20	19	14
VMI	-	-	-	-	-	-	-	-	-	-	-	20	19	-	-	-	20
Wake Forest	-	14	11	10	9	7	10	7	9	10	5	4	7	11	16	-	9

1977-78

	PS	Nov. 29	Dec. 6	Dec. 13	Dec. 20	Dec. 27	Jan. 3	Jan. 10	Jan. 17	Jan. 24	Jan. 31	Feb. 7	Feb. 14	Feb. 21	Feb. 28	Mar. 6	Mar. 13
Alabama	15	15	-	-	18	-	-	-	-	-	-	-	-	-	-	-	-
Arkansas	7	7	6	4	4	3	3	3	6	4	2	2	1	4	4	7	5
Cincinnati	9	8	7	6	12	11	12	19	-	-	-	-	-	-	-	-	-
DePaul	-	-	-	-	-	-	-	20	18	19	13	11	8	7	6	4	3
Detroit	19	19	17	16	15	20	-	-	-	-	-	17	19	16	16	19	18
Duke	-	-	-	-	-	-	-	-	17	11	17	-	20	13	15	8	7
Florida St.	-	-	-	-	-	18	-	-	-	17	15	16	14	12	11	13	15
Georgetown	-	-	-	-	-	-	20	17	19	16	14	-	18	18	17	-	-
Holy Cross	18	17	15	13	12	16	13	14	-	-	-	-	-	-	-	-	-
Houston	-	-	-	-	-	-	-	-	-	-	-	-	-	-	-	14	-
Illinois St.	-	-	-	-	-	-	-	-	-	20	19	15	15	15	13	17	-
Indiana	-	-	-	-	-	15	11	18	-	-	-	-	-	-	-	-	13
Indiana St.	-	-	11	7	6	6	6	6	4	13	-	-	-	-	-	-	-
Kansas	-	-	19	20	16	17	14	10	8	8	8	8	6	6	5	9	10
Kansas St.	-	-	-	19	-	-	-	-	-	-	-	-	-	-	-	-	-
Kentucky	2	1	1	1	1	1	1	1	1	1	1	1	3	2	1	1	1
Louisville	10	9	16	10	8	7	10	9	9	12	9	9	9	20	20	12	9
Marquette	3	4	4	3	2	5	4	4	2	2	3	3	2	1	3	3	8
Maryland	14	14	12	18	20	14	15	-	-	-	-	-	-	-	-	-	-
Miami (Ohio)	-	-	-	-	-	-	-	-	-	-	-	-	-	-	-	-	19
Michigan	13	13	9	15	-	-	-	-	-	-	-	-	-	-	-	-	-
Michigan St.	-	-	-	-	-	-	18	12	10	7	7	10	10	10	9	6	4
Minnesota	16	-	-	-	-	-	-	-	-	-	-	-	-	19	-	-	-
Nebraska	-	-	-	-	-	-	-	-	-	-	-	19	-	-	-	-	-
UNLV	8	10	10	9	9	9	9	11	16	-	-	-	-	-	-	-	-
New Mexico	-	-	-	-	-	-	-	-	20	14	10	6	5	5	8	5	12
North Carolina	1	2	2	5	3	2	2	2	5	3	6	7	11	8	10	11	16
North Carolina St.	-	-	-	-	-	-	-	16	-	-	-	-	-	-	-	-	-
Notre Dame	4	3	3	2	5	4	5	5	7	5	4	4	7	9	7	10	6
Pennsylvania	-	-	-	-	-	-	-	-	-	-	-	-	-	-	-	-	20
Providence	-	-	20	14	14	13	17	14	12	9	16	20	13	11	18	-	-
Purdue	12	11	-	17	-	-	-	-	-	-	-	-	-	-	-	-	-
St. John's (N.Y.)	20	16	13	-	-	-	-	-	-	-	-	-	-	-	-	-	-
San Francisco	5	5	8	11	11	19	19	-	-	-	20	-	-	-	-	20	11
Syracuse	11	12	18	12	10	10	8	8	11	10	18	18	16	17	14	18	-
Texas	-	-	-	-	-	-	-	-	15	15	12	12	12	14	12	16	17
UCLA	6	6	5	8	7	8	7	7	3	6	5	5	4	3	2	2	2
Utah	-	20	14	-	17	-	-	-	-	-	-	-	-	-	19	15	14
Virginia	-	-	-	-	19	16	13	15	13	18	11	13	17	-	-	-	-
Wake Forest	17	18	-	-	-	-	-	-	-	-	-	14	-	-	-	-	-

1978-79

	PS	Nov. 28	Dec. 5	Dec. 12	Dec. 19	Dec. 26	Jan. 3	Jan. 9	Jan. 16	Jan. 23	Jan. 30	Feb. 6	Feb. 13	Feb. 20	Feb. 27	Mar. 6	Mar. 13
Alabama	19	-	-	-	-	-	-	-	18	18	15	16	20	-	-	-	-
Arkansas	-	-	-	-	-	20	14	10	11	15	14	14	11	10	9	7	5
DePaul	-	-	-	-	-	-	-	-	-	-	-	-	-	20	15	8	6
Detroit	-	-	-	-	-	-	-	-	-	-	-	-	18	16	18	17	-
Duke	1	1	1	1	1	1	5	7	8	7	3	3	5	6	5	6	11
Georgetown	-	-	20	16	14	15	12	14	10	11	17	18	16	17	16	11	-
Illinois	-	-	-	18	15	6	4	4	4	8	19	20	-	-	-	-	-
Indiana	10	20	-	-	-	-	-	-	-	-	-	-	-	-	-	-	-
Indiana St.	-	-	-	20	16	11	11	9	5	3	2	2	1	2	1	1	1
Iowa	-	-	-	-	-	-	-	-	-	-	18	15	14	12	11	14	20
Kansas	5	4	5	8	7	18	19	15	20	-	-	-	-	-	-	-	-
Kentucky	11	10	10	6	11	13	9	17	-	-	-	-	-	-	-	-	-
Long Beach St.	-	-	-	-	-	17	15	19	-	-	-	-	-	-	-	-	-
LSU	14	11	12	11	10	7	7	5	9	9	9	8	6	5	8	9	7
Louisville	4	5	7	4	12	10	16	12	7	5	5	5	9	13	13	18	13
Marquette	18	17	16	14	13	16	17	13	13	13	10	9	13	9	10	12	10
Maryland	-	19	19	-	-	-	20	-	19	-	-	-	-	-	-	-	-
Michigan	8	8	6	9	9	8	13	16	-	-	-	-	-	-	-	-	-
Michigan St.	7	7	4	3	5	4	1	1	6	4	4	10	8	7	4	4	3
Mississippi St.	-	-	-	-	-	-	18	-	-	-	-	-	-	-	-	-	-
UNLV	20	18	15	15	18	14	-	-	-	-	-	-	-	-	-	-	-
North Carolina	16	14	14	13	6	5	3	3	2	2	7	6	4	4	7	3	9
North Carolina St.	12	6	8	7	4	9	8	8	14	20	-	-	-	-	-	-	-
Notre Dame	3	3	3	2	2	2	2	2	1	1	1	1	3	3	2	5	4
Ohio St.	-	-	-	-	-	-	-	-	16	10	13	13	17	14	17	-	-
Oklahoma	-	-	-	-	-	-	-	-	-	-	-	-	-	-	-	-	16
Pennsylvania	-	-	-	-	-	-	-	-	-	-	-	-	-	-	-	-	14
Purdue	-	-	-	-	-	-	-	-	-	-	-	-	13	18	19	16	15
Rutgers	15	16	18	-	-	-	-	-	-	-	-	-	-	-	-	-	18
St. John's (N.Y.)	-	-	-	-	-	-	-	-	-	-	-	-	-	-	-	-	17
San Francisco	17	15	17	19	-	-	-	-	-	-	-	-	-	-	20	19	12
Southern California	13	12	11	12	20	-	-	-	-	-	-	-	-	-	-	-	-
Syracuse	9	9	9	10	8	19	-	20	12	12	8	7	7	8	6	10	8
Temple	-	-	-	-	-	-	-	18	17	16	20	19	15	15	12	13	-
Tennessee	-	-	-	-	-	-	-	-	-	-	-	-	-	-	-	20	-
Texas	6	13	13	17	19	-	-	-	-	17	11	12	12	11	14	15	-
Texas A&M	-	-	-	-	17	12	10	11	15	14	12	11	-	-	-	-	-
Toledo	-	-	-	-	-	-	-	-	-	-	-	-	-	-	-	-	19
UCLA	2	2	2	5	3	3	6	6	3	6	6	4	2	1	3	2	2
Vanderbilt	-	-	-	-	-	-	-	-	-	19	16	17	19	19	-	-	-

1979-80

	PS	Dec. 4	Dec. 11	Dec. 18	Dec. 26	Jan. 2	Jan. 8	Jan. 15	Jan. 22	Jan. 29	Feb. 5	Feb. 12	Feb. 19	Feb. 26	Mar. 4
Arizona St.	-	-	-	-	-	-	-	-	-	-	19	18	18	15	18
Arkansas	-	-	20	20	19	-	-	-	-	-	-	-	-	-	-
Brigham Young	15	18	18	18	20	19	17	18	20	19	14	13	14	12	12
Clemson	-	-	-	-	-	-	18	17	12	16	16	10	12	17	-
DePaul	9	10	11	6	4	3	2	1	1	1	1	1	1	1	1
Duke	3	2	2	1	1	1	1	5	3	5	10	16	17	-	14
Georgetown	19	17	16	17	17	18	20	-	-	-	-	-	-	20	11
Illinois	-	-	-	-	-	20	-	-	-	-	-	-	-	-	-
Indiana	1	1	1	5	10	11	19	19	16	18	20	-	19	13	7
Iona	-	-	-	-	-	-	-	-	-	-	-	-	-	-	19
Iowa	-	20	17	13	11	10	12	13	-	-	-	20	-	-	-
Kansas	20	19	-	-	-	-	-	-	-	-	-	-	-	-	-
Kansas St.	-	-	-	-	-	-	-	-	-	20	-	19	-	-	-
Kentucky	2	5	5	3	2	2	4	6	5	3	6	5	3	2	4
LSU	7	6	6	7	5	4	6	14	11	10	7	6	5	5	3
Louisville	10	14	12	11	12	15	11	7	7	7	3	3	2	4	2
Marquette	18	16	-	-	-	-	-	-	-	-	-	-	-	-	-
Maryland	-	-	-	-	-	-	-	-	15	12	5	8	9	7	8
Missouri	-	-	19	16	13	12	13	15	10	14	15	14	13	11	16
North Carolina	6	8	8	8	6	6	15	9	13	11	11	11	8	10	15
North Carolina St.	-	-	-	-	-	-	-	16	-	-	-	-	-	19	-
Notre Dame	5	4	4	4	3	7	7	8	8	8	9	12	10	14	9
Ohio St.	4	3	3	2	7	5	3	2	4	6	13	9	11	9	10
Oregon St.	17	15	14	19	18	14	9	4	2	2	4	4	6	6	5
Purdue	11	12	9	9	8	8	10	11	14	17	12	15	15	18	20
St. John's (N.Y.)	16	9	15	15	15	17	14	10	9	9	8	7	7	8	13
Syracuse	12	11	10	10	9	9	5	3	6	4	2	2	4	3	6
Tennessee	-	-	-	-	-	-	-	20	19	-	-	-	-	-	-
Texas A&M	14	-	-	-	-	-	-	-	-	-	-	-	-	-	-
UCLA	8	7	7	14	16	16	16	-	-	-	-	-	-	-	-
Virginia	13	13	13	12	14	13	8	12	17	13	18	-	-	-	-
Washington St.	-	-	-	-	-	-	-	-	-	-	-	-	20	-	-
Weber St.	-	-	-	-	-	-	-	-	18	15	17	17	16	16	17

1980-81

	PS	Dec. 2	Dec. 9	Dec. 16	Dec. 23	Dec. 30	Jan. 6	Jan. 13	Jan. 20	Jan. 27	Feb. 3	Feb. 10	Feb. 17	Feb. 24	Mar. 3	Mar. 10
Arizona St.	-	-	15	14	11	13	14	12	7	5	5	5	7	5	5	3
Arkansas	20	11	17	19	17	-	-	-	-	-	-	-	-	18	15	20
Brigham Young	18	19	19	18	20	19	17	15	18	15	16	15	17	15	18	16
Clemson	-	-	-	-	-	-	20	19	19	-	-	-	-	-	-	-
Connecticut	-	-	-	-	-	-	-	-	20	20	-	-	-	-	-	-
DePaul	2	1	1	1	1	1	1	4	T3	3	3	3	3	4	2	1
Georgetown	16	19	-	-	-	-	-	-	-	-	-	-	-	-	-	-
Illinois	-	-	-	17	18	16	12	18	15	-	18	17	15	14	16	19
Indiana	5	5	7	11	15	15	-	-	-	-	17	20	16	16	14	9
Iowa	14	12	16	16	14	14	11	14	9	13	15	14	12	8	8	13
Kansas	-	-	-	-	-	-	-	-	-	18	-	-	-	-	-	-
Kentucky	1	2	2	2	2	5	4	3	6	7	6	11	10	9	7	8
Lamar	-	-	-	-	-	-	-	-	-	-	-	-	19	-	-	-
LSU	12	15	11	10	10	10	9	6	5	4	4	4	4	2	3	4
Louisville	3	8	-	20	-	-	-	-	-	-	-	-	-	20	17	12
Maryland	4	4	4	9	9	9	8	10	10	14	13	19	20	17	20	18
Michigan	-	-	18	15	13	12	10	9	16	17	14	13	18	-	-	-
Minnesota	-	-	-	-	-	-	19	20	-	19	-	-	-	-	-	-
Missouri	11	17	14	-	-	-	-	-	-	-	-	-	-	-	-	-
North Carolina	13	10	10	8	6	6	16	17	17	12	11	10	13	11	12	6
Notre Dame	10	13	9	6	8	4	5	7	13	8	9	12	11	6	6	7
Ohio St.	9	9	8	7	-	-	-	-	-	-	-	-	-	-	-	-
Oregon St.	7	6	5	4	4	2	2	1	1	T1	2	2	2	1	1	2
St. John's (N.Y.)	17	16	-	-	-	-	-	-	-	-	-	-	-	-	-	-
South Ala.	-	-	-	-	16	17	15	13	11	16	20	18	-	-	-	-
Syracuse	19	18	20	-	-	-	-	-	-	-	-	-	-	-	-	-
Tennessee	-	-	-	-	-	18	13	11	8	11	10	9	8	10	10	15
Texas A&M	15	14	12	13	12	11	-	-	-	-	-	-	-	-	-	-
UCLA	6	3	3	3	3	7	7	8	12	10	12	8	6	13	13	10
Utah	-	-	-	-	19	20	18	16	14	9	7	6	9	7	9	14
Virginia	8	7	6	5	5	3	3	2	2	T1	1	1	1	3	4	5
Wake Forest	-	-	13	12	7	8	6	5	T3	6	8	7	5	12	11	11
Wichita St.	-	-	-	-	-	-	-	-	-	-	19	16	14	19	-	-
Wyoming	-	-	-	-	-	-	-	-	-	-	-	-	-	-	19	17

1981-82

		December					January				February				March	
	PS	1	8	15	22	29	5	12	19	26	2	9	16	23	2	9
Alabama	20	17	16	14	12	12	16	13	16	13	8	10	19	17	18	13
UAB	14	11	9	16	19	-	-	-	-	-	-	-	-	-	20	17
Arkansas	18	13	11	9	6	5	11	9	15	12	14	8	17	15	14	12
Brigham Young	-	15	-	-	-	-	-	-	-	-	-	-	-	-	-	-
DePaul	8	7	7	7	13	8	5	4	4	4	4	3	3	3	2	2
Fresno St.	-	-	-	-	-	-	-	-	-	19	17	18	15	14	12	11
Georgetown	5	20	20	19	17	17	13	8	13	-	-	20	13	12	8	6
Georgia	16	-	-	-	-	-	-	-	-	-	-	-	-	-	-	-
Houston	-	-	-	-	18	18	14	10	19	-	-	-	-	-	-	-
Idaho	-	-	-	-	-	-	18	14	8	11	15	13	11	9	6	8
Indiana	12	12	10	13	11	11	-	-	-	-	-	-	20	-	-	-
Iowa	9	6	6	6	10	10	7	5	6	6	5	5	7	11	11	16
Kansas St.	-	-	-	-	-	-	-	-	18	14	T19	15	18	-	17	-
Kentucky	3	2	2	2	2	4	3	6	9	7	9	12	10	7	15	15
LSU	17	-	-	-	-	-	-	-	-	-	-	-	-	-	-	-
La.-Lafayette	-	-	18	15	-	-	-	-	-	-	-	-	-	-	-	-
Louisville	4	3	3	3	8	14	12	17	17	-	-	-	-	-	-	20
Memphis	-	-	-	-	-	-	-	-	-	-	T19	14	12	10	13	9
Minnesota	10	10	8	8	5	9	6	11	5	10	6	9	8	13	7	7
Missouri	15	16	13	11	9	7	4	2	2	1	1	4	4	5	5	5
UNLV	-	18	15	-	-	-	-	-	-	-	-	-	-	-	-	-
North Carolina	1	1	1	1	1	1	1	1	1	2	2	2	2	2	1	1
North Carolina St.	-	-	-	-	-	20	15	12	14	17	-	-	-	-	-	-
Notre Dame	19	-	-	-	-	-	-	-	-	-	-	-	-	-	-	-
Oregon St.	-	-	19	20	16	15	17	15	12	8	10	6	5	4	4	4
St. John's (N.Y.)	-	-	-	-	-	-	20	-	-	-	-	-	-	-	-	-
San Francisco	-	14	12	10	7	6	8	7	11	9	7	17	16	16	-	-
Tennessee	-	-	-	-	-	-	-	-	20	15	16	-	-	19	-	-
Texas	-	-	-	-	-	-	-	19	7	5	12	-	-	-	-	-
Tulsa	11	9	14	12	14	13	10	18	10	16	11	7	6	8	10	10
UCLA	2	8	17	17	15	16	19	-	-	-	-	-	-	20	19	19
Villanova	-	-	-	18	20	19	-	-	-	20	-	-	-	-	-	-
Virginia	7	5	5	5	4	3	2	3	3	3	3	1	1	1	3	3
Virginia Tech	-	-	-	-	-	-	-	20	-	-	-	-	-	-	-	-
Wake Forest	13	-	-	-	-	-	-	-	-	18	13	16	14	18	16	18
Washington	-	-	-	-	-	-	-	-	-	-	-	19	-	-	-	-
West Virginia	-	-	-	-	-	-	-	-	-	-	18	11	9	6	9	14
Wichita St.	6	4	4	4	3	2	9	16	-	-	-	-	-	-	-	-

1982-83

		Nov.	December				January				February				March		
	PS	30	7	14	21	28	4	11	18	25	1	8	15	22	1	8	15
Alabama	12	13	11	10	8	6	5	10	-	-	-	-	-	-	-	-	-
Arkansas	17	16	15	13	12	11	10	7	4	12	9	8	7	6	5	6	9
Auburn	-	-	-	-	-	-	-	-	20	-	-	-	-	-	-	-	-
Boston College	-	-	-	-	-	-	-	-	-	-	-	-	18	19	15	14	11
Chattanooga	-	-	-	-	-	-	-	-	-	-	-	-	-	-	19	18	15
Georgetown	2	2	3	T5	11	10	17	-	19	15	14	14	14	18	16	15	20
Georgia	-	-	-	-	-	-	-	-	-	-	19	-	-	-	-	-	18
Houston	14	11	9	14	19	18	19	16	14	9	8	6	4	2	1	1	1
Illinois St.	-	-	-	-	-	-	-	-	-	17	16	17	-	-	-	-	-
Indiana	9	8	6	T5	5	1	1	4	2	2	6	4	2	4	11	7	5
Iowa	11	10	7	7	10	9	8	12	10	14	13	20	16	17	-	-	-
Kentucky	4	3	2	2	2	3	3	6	11	10	15	13	11	10	7	10	12
Louisville	8	7	13	12	14	13	13	9	9	8	12	11	9	5	3	3	2
Marquette	18	17	16	-	-	-	-	-	-	-	-	-	-	-	-	-	-
Memphis	6	5	4	3	4	2	2	1	6	5	4	9	13	14	17	17	17
Minnesota	-	-	-	-	-	-	-	17	16	16	17	19	-	-	-	-	-
Missouri	15	9	8	8	6	12	15	14	12	13	10	10	12	T15	13	12	10
UNLV	T20	19	18	18	17	15	11	8	5	4	2	2	1	1	9	9	6
North Carolina	3	15	17	17	-	-	18	11	3	3	1	1	3	11	8	5	8
North Carolina St.	16	18	18	15	15	17	16	19	-	-	-	-	-	-	-	-	16
Ohio St.	-	-	-	-	-	-	-	20	-	-	-	-	20	T15	14	16	-
Oklahoma	T20	-	-	-	-	-	-	-	-	-	-	19	-	-	-	19	-
Oklahoma St.	-	-	-	-	-	-	-	-	18	20	-	-	-	-	-	-	19
Oregon St.	10	19	-	-	-	-	-	-	-	-	-	-	-	-	-	-	-
Purdue	-	-	20	-	-	-	20	-	-	-	-	18	-	-	20	-	-
St. John's (N.Y.)	19	12	12	9	7	7	7	3	8	7	5	7	6	9	10	8	3
Syracuse	-	-	-	16	13	14	9	13	15	18	20	15	17	13	18	20	-
Tennessee	13	14	14	11	9	8	12	18	-	-	-	-	-	20	-	-	-
Tulsa	-	-	-	-	20	19	-	-	-	-	-	-	-	-	-	-	-
UCLA	7	6	5	4	3	5	6	5	1	1	7	5	10	8	6	4	7
Villanova	5	4	10	19	18	16	14	15	13	11	11	12	8	7	4	13	13
Virginia	1	1	1	1	1	4	4	2	7	6	3	3	5	3	2	2	4
Virginia Tech	-	-	-	-	-	-	-	-	17	-	-	-	-	-	-	-	-
Wake Forest	-	-	-	-	-	-	-	-	-	19	-	-	-	-	-	-	-
Washington St.	-	-	-	-	-	-	-	-	-	-	18	-	-	-	-	-	-
West Virginia	-	-	-	20	16	20	-	-	-	-	-	-	-	-	-	-	-
Wichita St.	-	-	-	-	-	-	-	-	-	-	-	16	15	12	12	11	14

1983-84

		Nov.	December				January					February				March	
	PS	29	6	13	20	27	3	10	17	24	31	7	14	21	28	6	13
Arkansas	14	14	15	-	-	-	-	-	-	16	-	-	14	11	12	8	8
Auburn	-	-	-	-	-	-	-	-	-	-	19	16	-	19	-	-	-
Boston College	15	15	12	8	6	12	17	18	16	-	-	-	-	-	-	-	-
DePaul	18	16	13	4	4	4	3	3	2	2	2	2	3	5	5	4	4
Duke	-	-	-	-	-	-	-	-	-	-	-	-	19	14	15	16	14
Fresno St.	13	17	20	-	-	-	16	13	17	-	-	-	-	-	-	-	-
Georgetown	4	3	3	5	5	5	4	4	6	4	4	3	2	2	4	2	2
Georgia	16	13	10	12	14	11	11	15	-	18	-	-	-	-	-	-	-
Georgia Tech	-	-	-	-	-	-	-	-	-	-	18	18	-	-	-	-	-
Houston	3	8	6	3	3	3	7	7	4	7	6	5	4	3	2	5	5
Illinois	-	-	-	-	-	20	14	9	10	9	8	8	7	6	10	7	6
Indiana	19	-	-	-	-	-	-	-	-	-	-	-	T17	-	-	-	-
Iowa	7	5	5	18	19	-	-	-	-	-	-	-	-	-	-	-	-
Kansas	17	-	-	-	-	-	-	-	-	-	-	-	-	-	-	-	-
Kentucky	2	1	2	2	2	2	2	2	3	3	3	6	6	4	3	3	3
LSU	11	12	9	10	11	9	9	11	15	10	14	20	T17	-	-	-	-
Louisville	6	-	-	16	10	14	-	-	-	14	17	15	-	-	-	18	-
Maryland	8	6	11	9	8	6	5	5	7	5	10	13	-	-	19	14	11
Memphis	5	4	4	T6	16	17	19	19	18	13	9	9	8	12	14	17	16
Michigan	-	-	-	-	20	15	-	-	-	-	-	-	-	-	-	-	-
Michigan St.	12	11	17	17	-	-	-	-	-	-	-	-	-	-	-	-	-
UNLV	-	-	-	-	-	-	18	14	8	6	5	4	5	7	7	10	13
North Carolina	1	2	1	1	1	1	1	1	1	1	1	1	1	1	1	1	1
North Carolina St.	-	7	8	T6	13	13	12	-	-	-	-	-	-	-	-	-	-
Oklahoma	20	-	-	-	-	-	-	17	20	11	12	10	9	8	6	6	7
Oregon St.	10	10	18	14	15	19	15	16	11	-	-	-	-	20	20	20	17
Purdue	-	-	19	11	7	18	-	-	19	-	16	11	11	13	11	11	10
St. John's (N.Y.)	-	19	16	13	12	8	13	10	14	-	-	-	-	-	-	-	-
Syracuse	-	-	-	-	-	-	-	-	-	20	13	19	16	16	16	-	18
Temple	-	-	-	-	-	-	-	-	-	-	-	-	20	17	18	15	20
UTEP	-	-	-	20	18	16	10	8	5	8	7	7	10	9	8	9	9
Tulsa	-	-	-	-	-	-	-	20	13	12	11	12	12	10	9	12	12
UCLA	9	9	7	15	9	7	6	6	9	15	20	-	-	-	-	-	-
Virginia	-	-	-	-	-	-	20	-	-	19	-	-	-	-	-	-	-
Va. C'wealth	-	20	-	-	-	-	-	-	-	-	-	-	-	-	-	-	-
Wake Forest	-	-	-	19	17	10	8	12	12	17	15	14	13	15	17	19	19
Washington	-	-	-	-	-	-	-	-	-	-	-	17	15	18	13	13	15
Wichita St.	-	18	14	-	-	-	-	-	-	-	-	-	-	-	-	-	-

1984-85

		Nov.	December				January					February				March	
	PS	27	4	11	18	25	1	8	15	22	29	5	12	19	26	5	12
UAB	-	13	18	17	-	-	-	-	-	-	20	-	19	-	-	-	-
Arizona	-	-	-	-	-	-	-	-	-	-	-	-	-	-	19	-	-
Arkansas	16	17	-	-	-	-	-	-	-	-	-	-	-	-	-	-	-
Boston College	-	-	-	-	-	-	-	12	15	-	-	-	-	20	-	-	-
DePaul	3	2	2	2	5	9	10	13	10	7	13	18	-	-	-	-	-
Duke	6	4	4	3	2	2	2	2	2	5	6	5	7	6	5	7	10
Georgetown	1	1	1	1	1	1	1	1	1	1	2	2	2	2	2	1	1
Georgia	-	-	-	-	-	-	-	-	-	-	-	-	-	18	14	17	19
Georgia Tech	20	18	15	12	13	10	8	9	17	16	8	10	6	8	10	9	6
Illinois	2	7	7	6	4	8	6	15	11	6	5	9	17	16	18	14	12
Indiana	4	12	11	16	16	15	12	11	8	13	-	-	-	-	-	-	-
Iowa	-	-	-	-	-	-	-	19	-	-	-	12	11	14	-	-	-
Kansas	19	†20	19	18	15	12	11	10	9	15	19	13	10	15	11	10	13
Kentucky	18	-	-	-	-	-	-	-	-	-	-	-	-	-	-	-	-
LSU	14	16	13	19	19	18	14	-	-	-	-	-	-	-	-	19	20
Louisiana Tech	-	-	-	-	20	19	18	14	12	12	15	14	12	10	7	8	8
Louisville	17	6	6	14	12	20	-	-	-	-	-	-	-	-	-	-	-
Loyola (Ill.)	-	-	-	-	-	-	-	-	-	-	-	-	-	-	20	16	14
Maryland	-	-	-	-	-	-	19	-	-	-	17	20	20	-	-	-	-
Memphis	8	5	5	5	3	3	3	6	5	4	3	3	5	4	4	5	5
Michigan	-	-	-	20	18	13	16	-	-	18	10	8	3	3	3	3	2
Michigan St.	-	-	-	-	-	-	-	17	19	-	-	-	-	-	-	-	-
UNLV	11	†20	20	-	-	-	-	-	-	20	16	11	14	11	9	11	9
North Carolina	-	19	16	13	10	7	9	5	6	8	11	15	13	13	8	6	7
North Carolina St.	13	11	10	9	14	14	17	-	-	-	-	-	-	-	16	18	16
Oklahoma	5	10	17	15	11	17	13	8	13	9	7	7	4	5	6	4	4
Oregon St.	-	-	-	-	-	-	-	20	14	10	14	16	18	19	-	-	-
Southern Methodist		10	9	8	7	6	4	7	4	3	2	4	4	9	9	13	20
St. John's (N.Y.)	7	3	3	4	8	5	4	3	4	2	1	1	1	1	1	2	3
Syracuse	12	14	12	10	9	6	5	7	7	11	9	6	8	7	12	13	15
Texas Tech	-	-	-	-	-	-	-	-	-	-	-	-	-	-	-	-	17
Tulsa	-	-	-	-	-	-	-	-	20	17	12	17	15	12	15	15	18
Va. C'wealth	-	-	-	-	-	-	20	18	16	19	-	-	-	17	17	12	11
Virginia Tech	15	15	14	11	17	16	-	-	-	-	-	-	-	-	-	-	-
Villanova	-	-	-	-	-	-	-	16	18	14	18	19	16	-	-	-	-
Washington	9	8	9	8	7	11	15	-	-	-	-	-	-	-	-	-	-

1985-86

		Nov.	December					January				February				March	
	PS	26	3	10	17	24	31	7	14	21	28	4	11	18	25	4	11
Alabama	-	-	-	-	-	-	-	-	-	-	-	20	18	-	-	-	-
UAB	16	20	17	16	14	14	16	14	12	18	-	-	-	-	-	-	-
Auburn	10	19	†19	-	-	-	-	-	-	-	-	-	-	-	-	-	-
Bradley	-	-	-	-	-	-	-	-	20	17	13	13	13	12	11	9	14

		Nov.	December					January				February				March	
	PS	26	3	10	17	24	31	7	14	21	28	4	11	18	25	4	11
DePaul	-	-	-	19	18	20	-	-	-	-	-	-	-	-	-	-	-
Duke	6	6	3	3	3	3	3	3	3	2	5	4	2	2	1	1	1
Georgetown	8	8	6	†5	5	5	11	13	15	12	12	11	9	13	15	14	13
Georgia Tech	1	2	5	†5	7	7	6	5	5	4	3	2	5	5	4	6	6
Illinois	7	7	12	10	15	16	14	18	-	-	-	-	-	-	-	19	19
Indiana	-	-	†19	18	17	17	15	-	-	-	15	18	16	15	16	16	16
Iowa	-	-	18	-	-	-	-	-	-	-	-	-	-	-	-	-	-
Kansas	5	5	7	7	6	6	5	9	8	7	4	6	3	3	2	2	2
Kentucky	11	10	9	9	13	13	12	11	11	11	8	12	11	8	5	3	3
LSU	14	12	11	11	9	9	8	8	14	14	17	-	-	-	-	-	-
Louisville	9	9	16	15	16	15	18	17	18	13	18	16	19	16	13	11	7
Maryland	†19	17	-	-	-	-	-	-	-	-	-	-	-	-	-	-	-
Memphis	15	14	13	12	10	10	9	6	6	3	2	3	4	4	7	10	12
Michigan	3	3	2	2	2	2	2	2	2	6	9	7	10	7	10	7	5
Michigan St.	-	-	-	-	-	-	-	-	-	-	-	-	-	19	17	17	18
Navy	†19	-	-	-	-	-	-	-	-	-	-	-	-	17	19	18	17
UNLV	18	16	14	13	12	12	13	12	10	10	10	9	6	11	9	13	11
North Carolina	2	1	1	1	1	1	1	1	1	1	1	1	1	1	3	4	8
North Carolina St.	17	15	-	-	-	-	-	-	-	-	-	-	17	20	18	20	-
Notre Dame	12	11	10	17	19	18	17	16	13	16	14	14	14	14	12	12	10
Ohio St.	-	-	-	20	-	-	-	-	-	-	-	-	-	-	-	-	-
Oklahoma	13	13	8	8	8	8	7	7	7	5	6	5	8	10	14	15	15
Purdue	-	-	-	-	-	-	-	20	19	15	-	-	-	-	20	-	-
Richmond	-	-	-	-	-	-	-	-	-	-	20	-	-	-	-	-	-
St. John's (N.Y.)	-	18	15	14	11	11	10	10	9	8	7	10	7	6	8	5	4
Syracuse	4	4	4	4	4	4	4	4	4	9	11	8	12	9	6	8	9
UTEP	-	-	-	-	-	-	19	15	17	19	19	17	15	-	-	-	20
Virginia Tech	-	-	-	-	20	19	20	19	16	20	16	15	20	18	-	-	-
Western Ky.	-	-	-	-	-	-	-	-	-	-	-	19	-	-	-	-	-

1986-87

		December					January				February				March	
	PS	2	9	16	23	30	6	13	20	27	3	10	17	24	3	10
Alabama	13	8	18	-	-	-	-	15	13	9	9	14	12	10	9	9
Arizona	19	20	-	-	-	-	-	-	-	-	-	-	-	-	-	-
Arkansas	-	-	20	-	-	-	-	-	-	-	-	-	-	-	-	-
Auburn	12	7	7	6	5	5	13	10	17	18	20	-	-	-	-	-
Clemson	-	-	-	-	-	-	20	12	10	14	12	12	10	13	13	13
Cleveland St.	20	-	-	-	-	-	-	-	-	-	-	-	-	-	-	-
DePaul	-	-	-	19	17	15	7	7	6	8	5	5	4	4	5	5
Duke	-	-	-	-	-	20	17	14	12	13	16	15	17	17	14	17
Florida	-	-	-	-	20	-	-	-	-	19	-	19	18	18	-	-
Georgetown	18	16	13	10	10	8	16	9	15	11	10	13	11	8	7	4
Georgia Tech	6	15	16	16	19	18	-	-	-	-	-	-	-	-	-	-
Illinois	14	9	6	5	9	16	12	8	9	12	14	11	14	14	12	11
Indiana	3	3	2	8	8	6	4	4	3	†4	2	2	2	3	4	3
Iowa	10	5	4	3	3	3	2	2	1	2	4	4	7	7	6	6
Kansas	8	6	14	13	13	12	19	20	-	20	18	17	15	16	-	20
Kentucky	11	13	19	18	18	11	9	-	-	-	-	-	-	-	-	-
Louisville	2	-	-	-	-	-	-	-	-	-	-	-	-	-	-	-
Missouri	-	-	-	-	-	-	-	-	-	-	-	-	-	-	19	14
Navy	9	10	10	11	12	9	15	19	18	-	-	-	-	-	-	-
UNLV	5	2	1	1	1	1	1	1	4	3	1	1	1	1	1	1
New Orleans	-	-	-	-	-	-	-	-	-	-	-	-	-	19	16	16
North Carolina	1	1	5	4	4	4	3	3	2	1	3	3	3	2	2	2
North Carolina St.	17	18	15	12	11	19	18	17	20	-	-	-	-	-	-	-
Northeastern	-	19	-	-	-	-	-	-	-	-	-	-	-	-	-	-
Notre Dame	-	-	-	-	-	-	-	-	-	-	-	-	-	-	20	18
Oklahoma	7	11	9	7	6	13	11	16	11	10	8	8	13	12	17	-
Pittsburgh	16	12	17	14	14	17	14	18	16	17	13	10	8	9	11	12
Providence	-	-	-	-	-	-	-	-	-	-	17	20	19	20	-	-
Purdue	4	4	3	2	2	2	6	6	5	†4	7	7	6	6	3	7
St. John's (N.Y.)	-	-	-	15	15	10	10	13	14	15	19	16	20	-	-	-
Syracuse	15	17	12	9	7	7	5	5	7	6	11	9	9	11	10	10
Temple	-	-	-	20	16	14	8	11	8	7	6	6	5	5	8	8
TCU	-	-	-	-	-	-	-	-	19	16	15	18	16	15	15	19
UCLA	-	-	11	17	-	-	-	-	-	-	-	-	-	-	18	15
Western Ky.	-	14	8	-	-	-	-	-	-	-	-	-	-	-	-	-

1987-88

		December					January				February				March		
	PS	1	8	15	22	29	5	12	19	26	2	9	16	23	1	8	15
Arizona	17	9	4	2	1	1	3	1	1	1	1	3	3	3	3	3	2
Auburn	-	-	-	-	-	-	-	19	-	-	-	-	-	-	-	-	-
Bradley	-	-	-	-	-	-	-	-	-	-	18	15	17	14	14	12	11
Brigham Young	-	-	-	-	-	-	-	-	12	7	4	†8	7	11	15	17	19
DePaul	20	-	-	-	-	-	-	-	-	-	-	-	-	-	-	-	-
Duke	15	13	10	10	9	9	9	7	9	5	3	†8	6	5	9	8	5
Florida	14	7	12	11	8	8	15	-	-	14	19	-	-	-	-	-	-
Georgia Tech	18	-	-	-	-	-	-	-	-	-	-	-	-	20	13	18	-
Georgetown	16	17	14	18	19	18	14	11	15	15	14	-	-	-	-	-	-
Illinois	-	-	-	-	-	-	19	20	13	13	17	-	-	-	-	19	16
Indiana	6	5	6	5	13	13	12	15	-	-	-	19	-	-	-	-	-
Iowa	11	6	3	7	14	14	16	17	19	16	13	13	13	13	11	15	17
Iowa St.	-	-	-	20	16	16	17	14	10	12	16	-	-	-	-	-	-
Kansas	7	16	18	17	18	17	18	16	16	-	-	-	-	-	-	-	-
Kansas St.	-	-	-	-	-	-	-	-	-	-	-	14	-	-	-	-	20
Kentucky	5	2	1	1	2	2	1	5	4	9	10	10	9	12	8	6	6
Louisville	13	14	-	-	-	20	-	-	-	-	-	-	-	-	-	-	-
Loyola Marymount	-	-	-	-	-	-	-	-	-	-	-	-	20	19	18	16	15
Memphis	-	20	20	19	20	19	-	-	-	-	-	-	-	-	-	-	-
Michigan	9	15	15	13	11	12	11	10	7	8	11	12	10	7	10	10	10
Missouri	8	8	9	16	17	-	-	-	-	-	-	-	15	15	-	-	-
UNLV	-	19	17	15	15	15	13	13	8	4	2	7	11	8	5	7	12
New Mexico	-	-	-	-	-	-	-	18	-	-	-	-	-	-	-	-	-
North Carolina	3	1	5	4	4	4	4	2	2	3	8	6	5	9	6	9	7
North Carolina St.	-	-	-	-	-	-	-	-	20	-	-	-	-	-	16	11	14
Notre Dame	-	-	19	-	-	-	-	-	-	-	-	-	-	-	-	-	-
Oklahoma	19	18	16	14	12	10	8	3	11	10	7	4	4	4	4	4	4
Pittsburgh	4	4	2	3	3	3	2	6	6	11	9	5	8	6	7	5	8
Purdue	2	11	13	12	10	11	10	8	5	2	6	2	2	2	2	2	3
St. John's (N.Y.)	-	-	-	-	-	-	20	-	-	-	20	-	-	-	-	-	-
Southern Miss.	-	-	-	-	-	-	-	-	-	20	-	16	14	18	-	-	-
Syracuse	1	3	8	9	7	7	7	9	14	17	12	11	12	10	12	13	9
Temple	12	12	11	8	6	6	6	4	3	6	5	1	1	1	1	1	1
UTEP	-	-	-	-	-	-	-	-	18	18	-	-	-	-	-	-	-
Vanderbilt	-	-	-	-	-	-	-	-	-	-	15	17	16	17	19	-	-
Villanova	-	-	-	-	-	-	-	-	-	19	-	20	-	-	-	-	-
Wyoming	10	10	7	6	5	5	5	12	17	-	-	18	19	16	17	14	13
Xavier	-	-	-	-	-	-	-	-	-	-	-	-	-	-	20	20	18

1988-89

		Nov.		December				January					February				March	
	PS	22	29	6	13	20	27	3	10	17	24	31	7	14	21	28	7	14
Alabama	-	-	-	-	-	-	-	-	-	-	-	-	-	-	-	-	-	20
Arizona	11	10	11	10	9	9	8	8	12	9	6	4	1	2	2	1	1	1
Ball St.	-	-	-	-	-	-	-	-	-	-	-	-	-	-	20	19	19	18
Connecticut	-	-	-	-	18	-	-	-	-	-	-	-	-	-	-	-	-	-
Duke	1	1	1	1	1	1	1	1	1	1	8	12	14	11	9	9	7	9
Florida	15	15	19	-	-	-	-	-	-	-	-	-	-	-	-	-	-	-
Florida St.	16	17	14	13	12	11	10	15	14	14	11	8	12	7	12	16	14	16
Georgia Tech	13	14	12	12	11	16	17	19	19	-	-	-	20	-	-	-	-	-
Georgetown	2	2	3	4	5	6	5	5	7	3	2	6	2	4	3	2	3	2
Georgia	-	-	-	-	-	-	-	-	20	-	-	-	-	-	-	-	-	-
Illinois	9	9	7	7	6	5	4	3	2	2	1	2	7	5	10	8	4	3
Indiana	-	20	-	-	-	-	-	-	-	19	16	17	13	9	4	3	6	8
Iowa	7	7	6	5	4	4	9	9	5	7	12	9	8	15	14	11	15	14
Kansas	-	-	-	-	-	-	20	20	18	16	17	18	-	-	-	-	-	-
LSU	-	-	-	-	-	-	-	-	-	-	-	-	19	-	20	-	-	-
Louisville	4	12	13	15	15	14	14	13	9	4	3	7	4	10	8	14	16	12
Michigan	3	3	2	2	2	2	2	7	6	6	10	11	10	13	13	10	8	10
Missouri	14	13	8	11	10	10	11	11	10	8	5	5	3	3	7	7	10	6
UNLV	10	8	9	9	13	13	12	12	11	10	13	16	19	18	18	18	18	15
North Carolina St.	18	18	16	19	18	17	18	16	15	15	15	13	17	19	17	20	17	19
North Carolina	6	5	10	8	8	8	7	6	8	13	7	3	6	8	5	5	9	5
Notre Dame	-	-	-	-	-	19	-	-	-	-	-	-	-	-	-	-	-	-
Ohio St.	17	16	15	14	14	12	15	14	18	16	17	17	16	16	-	-	-	-
Oklahoma	5	4	5	6	7	7	6	4	3	5	4	1	5	1	1	4	2	4
Providence	-	-	-	-	-	-	-	-	-	20	-	20	-	-	-	-	-	-
St. Mary's (Cal.)	-	-	-	-	-	-	-	-	-	-	-	-	-	-	-	19	17	20
Seton Hall	-	-	-	20	17	15	13	10	13	12	9	10	11	12	15	12	11	11
South Carolina	-	-	-	-	-	-	18	16	-	-	-	-	-	-	-	-	-	-
Stanford	20	-	-	-	-	-	-	-	-	20	19	20	18	17	16	13	12	13
Syracuse	8	6	4	3	3	3	3	2	4	11	14	14	9	6	6	6	5	7
Temple	19	19	17	-	-	-	-	-	-	-	-	-	-	-	-	-	-	-
Tennessee	-	-	-	20	16	16	19	19	17	17	18	-	-	-	-	-	-	-
UCLA	-	-	-	-	-	20	-	-	-	-	-	-	-	-	-	-	-	-
Villanova	12	11	18	17	-	-	-	-	-	-	-	-	-	-	-	-	-	-
West Virginia	-	-	-	-	-	-	-	-	-	-	-	18	15	14	11	15	13	17

1989-90

		Nov.	December				January					February				March	
	PS	27	5	12	19	26	2	9	16	23	30	6	13	20	27	6	13
Alabama	-	-	21	19	20	22	22	24	25	24	-	-	-	-	-	-	23
Arizona	6	2	20	20	22	21	19	18	23	19	24	22	20	21	23	15	14
Arkansas	9	11	10	7	10	11	14	12	12	6	3	3	8	13	12	9	7
Clemson	-	-	-	-	-	-	-	-	-	-	-	-	-	23	20	17	17
Connecticut	-	-	-	-	-	-	-	-	-	20	13	8	10	6	4	8	4
Duke	10	7	6	12	12	13	13	10	8	8	5	4	6	3	†5	12	15
Florida	23	24	25	24	-	-	-	-	-	-	-	-	-	-	-	-	-
Georgetown	5	3	3	3	3	3	3	2	2	3	6	5	3	5	7	5	8
Georgia	-	-	-	-	-	-	-	-	-	-	-	-	-	-	25	25	-
Georgia Tech	22	21	18	15	14	14	12	9	11	13	17	16	13	8	11	14	9
Illinois	8	8	7	5	5	4	4	8	7	10	11	12	15	†19	18	20	18
Indiana	14	14	14	11	11	10	9	13	14	12	22	25	-	25	-	-	-
Iowa	-	-	-	21	16	18	20	-	-	-	-	-	-	-	-	-	-
Kansas	-	4	2	2	2	2	2	1	1	2	2	2	1	2	1	2	5
La Salle	-	-	-	-	23	20	17	21	17	18	15	14	14	14	13	11	12
LSU	2	9	9	9	8	9	11	14	13	16	14	11	9	12	15	16	19

	PS	Nov. 27	December 5	12	19	26	January 2	9	16	23	30	February 6	13	20	27	March 6	13
Louisville	12	13	11	10	9	8	8	11	10	4	10	15	18	16	21	18	16
Loyola Marymount	-	-	-	-	-	-	25	23	21	22	20	20	19	22	22	21	21
Memphis	24	22	16	17	17	15	21	20	-	-	-	-	-	-	-	-	-
Michigan	4	10	8	6	6	5	5	3	6	7	4	7	5	7	8	13	13
Michigan St.	-	-	-	25	25	-	-	-	-	-	-	23	21	15	14	7	3
Minnesota	20	-	-	-	-	25	24	16	22	21	19	17	17	18	17	19	20
Missouri	11	5	4	4	4	7	7	5	4	1	1	1	2	1	3	6	11
UNLV	1	6	5	14	13	12	10	7	9	5	12	9	7	4	2	3	2
New Mexico St.	-	-	-	-	-	-	-	-	-	-	-	-	25	24	24	23	24
North Carolina	7	12	17	-	-	24	-	-	-	-	25	-	-	-	-	-	-
North Carolina St.	19	25	19	16	15	19	18	17	19	-	-	-	-	-	-	-	-
Notre Dame	17	19	-	-	-	-	-	-	-	-	-	-	-	-	-	-	-
Oklahoma St.	21	23	-	22	24	-	-	-	-	-	-	-	-	-	-	-	-
Oklahoma	16	17	12	8	7	6	6	4	3	9	9	13	11	10	†5	1	1
Oregon St.	-	-	24	23	21	23	23	22	18	17	21	18	16	17	16	22	22
Pittsburgh	18	18	22	-	-	-	-	-	-	-	-	-	-	-	-	-	-
Purdue	-	-	-	-	-	-	-	-	24	13	8	10	12	9	9	10	10
St. John's (N.Y.)	25	20	15	18	19	17	16	15	15	15	18	24	24	-	-	-	-
Syracuse	3	1	1	1	1	1	1	6	5	11	7	6	4	11	10	4	6
Temple	15	16	23	-	-	-	-	-	-	-	-	-	-	-	-	-	-
UCLA	13	15	13	13	18	16	15	19	16	23	16	19	23	-	-	-	-
Xavier	-	-	-	-	-	-	-	25	20	25	23	21	22	†19	19	24	25

1990-91

	PS	Nov. 27	December 4	11	18	25	January 1	8	15	22	29	February 5	12	19	26	March 5	12
Alabama	7	6	12	20	-	-	-	-	-	-	-	-	-	24	-	24	19
Arizona	3	2	2	4	4	4	4	6	6	5	6	5	6	9	7	9	8
Arkansas	2	3	3	2	2	2	2	2	2	2	2	2	3	3	3	5	2
Connecticut	17	15	14	16	15	13	12	9	13	19	-	-	-	-	-	-	-
DePaul	-	-	-	-	-	-	-	-	-	-	-	-	-	-	-	25	24
Duke	6	8	5	10	9	8	8	14	12	9	7	6	5	7	8	6	6
East Tenn. St.	-	-	-	24	21	20	17	16	15	12	16	13	10	13	19	15	17
Georgetown	9	9	6	5	12	16	15	15	19	21	18	20	18	25	-	-	-
Georgia	21	17	13	11	17	17	-	-	-	-	-	-	-	-	-	-	-
Georgia Tech	16	14	20	23	-	-	24	24	-	-	23	-	-	-	-	-	-
Indiana	8	10	7	7	6	5	5	3	3	3	4	4	4	4	5	3	3
Iowa	-	-	-	-	-	23	22	22	24	-	-	-	-	-	-	-	-
Kansas	-	-	-	-	-	-	-	-	-	-	24	18	11	8	10	12	12
Kentucky	-	-	25	18	18	18	16	11	9	8	10	10	16	12	13	10	9
LSU	14	20	18	12	10	15	14	20	20	16	14	19	20	19	18	16	22
Louisville	23	25	-	-	-	-	-	-	-	-	-	-	-	-	-	-	-
Michigan St.	4	5	19	21	24	25	25	-	-	22	-	25	-	-	-	-	-
Mississippi St.	-	-	-	-	-	-	-	-	-	-	-	-	23	21	23	18	21
Missouri	20	23	-	-	-	-	-	-	-	-	-	-	-	-	-	-	-
Nebraska	-	-	-	-	22	22	19	18	17	14	11	15	17	14	15	13	11
UNLV	1	1	1	1	1	1	1	1	1	1	1	1	1	1	1	1	1
New Mexico St.	-	-	-	-	-	24	23	23	21	23	20	16	12	15	11	11	15
New Orleans	-	-	-	-	-	-	-	-	-	24	22	21	-	-	-	-	-
North Carolina	5	4	10	9	8	7	7	5	5	7	9	9	8	6	4	7	4
Ohio St.	10	11	9	8	7	6	6	4	4	4	3	3	2	2	2	2	5
Oklahoma	15	18	16	13	11	14	13	12	11	13	21	23	-	-	-	-	-
Oklahoma St.	-	-	-	-	-	-	-	-	-	-	-	22	21	16	12	12	14
Pittsburgh	12	13	11	15	14	11	11	17	16	17	19	24	22	23	22	-	-
Princeton	-	-	-	-	25	-	-	-	-	-	-	-	25	23	21	19	18
Seton Hall	-	-	-	-	-	-	-	-	25	-	25	-	-	24	20	21	13
South Carolina	-	-	†21	17	16	12	20	21	22	25	-	-	-	-	-	-	-
Southern Miss.	24	19	15	22	20	21	21	19	18	15	17	12	9	11	14	22	25
St. John's (N.Y.)	25	21	17	14	13	9	9	10	10	10	5	8	13	18	17	20	20
Syracuse	13	7	4	3	3	3	3	8	8	6	8	7	7	5	6	4	7
Temple	19	-	24	-	-	-	-	-	-	-	-	-	-	-	-	-	-
Texas	22	22	23	25	23	-	-	-	-	-	-	-	24	-	-	23	23
UTEP	-	-	-	-	-	-	-	25	-	-	-	-	-	-	-	-	-
UCLA	11	12	8	6	5	10	10	7	7	11	12	14	15	17	16	17	16
Utah	-	-	-	-	-	-	-	-	23	20	13	17	14	10	9	8	10
Villanova	-	24	-	-	-	-	-	-	-	-	-	-	-	-	-	-	-
Virginia	18	16	†21	19	19	19	18	13	14	18	15	11	19	20	25	-	-

1991-92

	PS	Nov. 25	December 2	9	16	23	30	January 6	13	20	27	February 3	10	17	24	March 2	9	16
Alabama	17	16	15	20	20	20	19	16	9	15	22	18	16	14	16	20	17	13
Arizona St.	24	25	-	-	-	-	-	-	-	-	-	-	-	-	-	-	-	-
Arizona	5	3	3	2	2	6	6	6	7	11	9	7	7	5	5	4	2	10
Arkansas	3	2	11	19	19	15	16	13	12	9	7	5	11	10	9	7	6	9
Charlotte	-	-	-	24	24	25	21	22	18	19	17	20	22	-	-	-	-	-
Cincinnati	-	-	-	-	-	-	-	-	-	-	-	-	24	19	19	14	12	12
Connecticut	15	15	12	8	7	5	5	5	8	7	6	10	18	21	24	-	-	-
DePaul	18	20	20	-	-	-	-	-	-	-	-	-	-	-	21	15	19	24
Duke	1	1	1	1	1	1	1	1	1	1	1	1	1	1	1	1	1	1
Florida St.	-	-	-	-	-	-	-	-	-	-	23	23	23	16	22	19	18	20
Georgetown	16	17	18	23	23	24	22	-	22	-	-	-	-	25	18	17	21	22
Georgia Tech	23	18	17	†13	13	13	15	14	16	18	20	24	-	-	-	-	-	-
Indiana	2	10	9	†13	14	10	10	10	5	4	4	6	4	7	2	2	4	5
Iowa	21	21	21	16	22	23	-	-	-	-	-	-	-	-	-	-	-	-
Iowa St.	-	-	-	-	-	-	-	-	24	-	-	-	-	23	-	-	-	-
Kansas	12	12	10	7	6	4	4	4	6	5	5	3	4	3	3	3	3	2
Kentucky	4	13	14	9	8	17	17	15	10	8	14	19	19	13	11	10	9	6
LSU	6	9	16	25	-	-	-	-	-	-	-	22	20	-	-	23	23	25
Louisville	25	-	-	-	25	21	24	-	25	20	24	-	-	-	-	-	-	-
Massachusetts	-	-	-	-	-	-	-	25	-	-	-	-	-	-	-	25	22	17
Michigan	20	23	25	18	15	11	11	11	15	16	15	15	17	20	17	18	14	15
Michigan St.	-	-	22	†13	12	9	9	9	11	14	13	11	12	11	12	13	16	14
Missouri	-	-	-	21	17	16	13	12	13	12	8	12	9	9	6	11	13	16
Nebraska	-	-	-	-	-	-	-	-	-	-	-	-	-	-	25	-	-	-
UNLV	-	-	24	-	-	-	-	-	-	25	21	17	15	12	7	6	7	7
North Carolina	8	6	5	5	9	8	8	8	14	10	11	9	6	4	10	16	20	18
Ohio St.	7	5	4	4	4	7	7	7	4	6	10	8	8	6	8	5	5	3
Oklahoma	19	19	19	17	16	14	14	21	23	17	18	21	-	-	-	-	24	23
Oklahoma St.	13	11	8	6	5	3	3	3	3	3	3	2	2	8	14	12	11	11
Pittsburgh	-	24	-	-	-	-	-	-	-	-	-	-	-	-	-	-	-	-
St. John's (N.Y.)	10	8	7	11	10	18	18	17	17	22	-	-	-	24	20	-	25	-
Seton Hall	9	7	6	12	11	12	12	18	21	-	-	-	25	22	-	22	15	19
Southern California	-	-	-	-	-	-	25	23	-	-	25	16	13	15	13	8	10	8
Stanford	-	-	-	-	-	-	-	-	-	24	-	-	-	-	-	-	-	-
Syracuse	-	-	-	-	-	-	23	20	20	13	12	13	10	17	22	24	-	21
UTEP	-	-	-	-	-	-	-	-	-	23	19	25	21	-	-	-	-	-
Tulane	-	-	-	-	-	-	-	24	19	21	16	14	14	18	15	21	-	-
UCLA	11	4	2	3	3	2	2	2	2	2	2	4	3	2	4	9	8	4
Utah	14	14	13	10	18	19	-	-	-	-	-	-	-	-	-	-	-	-
Wake Forest	22	22	23	22	21	22	20	19	-	-	-	-	-	-	-	-	-	-

1992-93

	PS	Nov. 23	30	December 7	14	21	28	January 4	11	18	25	February 1	8	15	22	March 1	8	15
Arizona	10	10	9	14	15	14	22	20	12	11	8	8	5	4	4	3	6	5
Arkansas	-	-	-	16	12	10	9	13	9	8	16	17	14	13	15	13	14	12
Boston College	-	-	-	-	-	-	-	-	22	-	-	-	21	-	-	-	-	-
Brigham Young	-	-	-	-	-	-	25	-	-	-	-	-	-	-	23	21	25	-
California	-	-	-	-	25	21	19	-	-	-	-	-	-	-	-	-	-	-
Cincinnati	21	23	22	19	19	23	21	16	11	9	6	4	8	8	10	12	11	7
Connecticut	16	16	25	-	24	22	23	19	15	17	22	-	-	-	-	-	-	-
Duke	3	3	4	1	1	1	1	1	3	6	7	5	3	7	9	6	8	10
Florida St.	9	7	11	10	10	18	18	23	-	-	19	12	10	9	6	11	10	11
Georgia Tech	14	14	13	17	17	16	14	10	8	16	18	22	-	-	-	-	-	18
Georgetown	12	13	14	†11	11	11	10	17	20	18	21	23	-	-	-	-	-	-
Houston	-	-	-	-	-	-	-	-	-	-	25	-	-	-	-	-	-	-
Indiana	4	4	2	4	4	4	4	5	6	2	2	1	1	1	1	2	2	1
Iowa	11	11	10	8	8	8	8	8	13	14	11	9	13	20	18	15	17	13
Iowa St.	19	24	-	-	-	-	-	-	-	-	-	-	-	-	-	-	-	-
Kansas	2	2	3	2	2	2	2	4	4	1	1	3	7	6	7	8	7	9
Kansas St.	-	-	-	-	-	-	-	-	-	-	-	-	23	-	-	-	-	-
Kentucky	5	5	5	3	3	3	3	2	1	4	4	2	2	2	2	5	4	2
Long Beach St.	-	-	-	-	-	-	-	-	-	25	-	-	-	-	-	-	-	-
Louisville	13	12	12	9	21	-	-	-	-	-	-	-	-	22	-	22	16	15
Marquette	-	-	-	-	-	-	-	-	-	-	24	20	15	24	20	-	-	-
Massachusetts	23	20	19	23	-	-	-	22	-	-	-	-	22	19	21	23	20	14
Memphis	8	9	8	21	-	-	-	-	-	-	-	-	-	-	-	-	-	-
Michigan	1	1	1	6	6	6	6	3	2	5	5	7	4	5	5	4	3	3
Michigan St.	20	18	18	24	23	20	17	14	23	21	-	25	-	-	-	-	-	-
Minnesota	-	-	-	-	-	-	-	-	19	-	-	-	-	-	-	-	-	-
Nebraska	25	25	-	25	20	17	20	-	-	-	-	-	-	-	-	-	-	-
UNLV	22	22	23	22	22	19	16	12	18	15	10	10	12	15	13	16	19	25
New Mexico	-	-	-	-	-	-	-	-	-	-	-	-	-	-	-	-	-	21
New Mexico St.	-	-	21	-	-	-	-	-	-	-	-	-	-	-	-	-	24	24
New Orleans	-	-	-	-	-	-	-	-	-	-	-	-	25	21	19	17	13	17
North Carolina	7	8	7	5	5	5	5	6	5	3	3	6	6	3	3	1	1	4
Ohio St.	-	-	-	-	-	-	-	-	21	24	-	-	-	-	-	-	-	-
Oklahoma	15	15	15	†11	9	9	15	11	10	12	20	16	-	-	-	-	-	-
Oklahoma St.	-	-	-	-	-	-	-	-	-	-	-	-	-	-	-	19	21	23
Pittsburgh	-	-	-	-	-	-	-	24	-	20	13	15	17	17	25	-	-	-
Purdue	-	-	24	18	16	15	13	9	17	13	14	19	18	14	17	24	18	22
Seton Hall	6	6	6	7	7	7	7	7	7	10	9	14	19	16	14	10	9	6
St. John's (N.Y.)	-	-	-	-	-	-	-	-	-	-	-	-	-	25	-	25	-	-
Syracuse	18	17	17	15	14	13	12	21	24	-	-	-	-	-	-	-	-	-
Tulane	17	19	20	20	18	24	-	-	-	-	23	18	20	18	16	20	23	-
UCLA	24	21	16	13	13	12	11	15	16	23	-	-	-	-	-	-	-	-
Utah	-	-	-	-	-	-	-	-	25	22	17	21	16	12	11	9	15	19
Vanderbilt	-	-	-	-	-	25	24	18	-	19	11	11	11	11	8	7	5	8
Virginia	-	-	-	-	-	-	-	25	14	7	15	24	24	23	22	-	-	-
Western Ky.	-	-	-	-	-	-	-	-	-	-	-	-	-	-	-	-	-	20
Wake Forest	-	-	-	-	-	-	-	-	-	-	-	13	9	10	12	14	12	16
Xavier	-	-	-	-	-	-	-	-	-	-	-	-	-	-	24	18	22	-

1993-94

	PS	Nov. 22	29	December 6	13	20	27	January 3	10	17	24	31	February 7	14	21	28	March 7	14
UAB	-	-	-	-	-	-	-	-	22	18	20	17	19	21	-	24	22	-
Arizona	18	19	19	14	13	13	12	9	6	9	13	12	16	15	9	8	7	9
Arkansas	3	3	2	1	1	1	1	1	4	3	5	6	3	1	1	1	1	2

WEEK-BY-WEEK A.P. POLLS—1993-94 63

DIVISION I

	PS	Nov. 22	Nov. 29	Dec. 6	Dec. 13	Dec. 20	Dec. 27	Jan. 3	Jan. 10	Jan. 17	Jan. 24	Jan. 31	Feb. 7	Feb. 14	Feb. 21	Feb. 28	Mar. 7	Mar. 14
Boston College	-	-	-	-	20	18	23	20	20	-	-	-	-	-	21	23	-	-
California	6	12	13	25	-	-	-	24	19	21	-	19	18	19	17	20	16	16
Cincinnati	19	22	23	20	17	20	18	17	21	19	-	25	-	23	-	-	-	25
Connecticut	-	-	-	21	16	15	14	16	14	10	6	5	6	3	5	4	2	4
Duke	4	4	6	4	3	3	3	3	2	5	2	1	2	6	2	2	5	6
Florida	-	-	-	-	-	-	-	-	-	-	-	24	20	17	16	19	17	14
Florida St.	25	-	-	-	-	-	-	-	-	-	-	-	-	-	-	-	-	-
Geo. Washington	24	23	22	24	23	23	21	23	-	-	-	-	-	-	-	-	-	-
Georgetown	15	15	25	-	-	-	-	-	-	-	-	-	-	-	-	-	-	-
Georgia Tech	14	13	17	18	14	14	15	12	17	17	21	-	-	25	23	-	-	-
Illinois	17	17	16	16	19	19	22	21	-	-	-	-	24	-	-	-	-	-
Indiana	12	11	21	12	12	12	13	14	11	8	11	14	12	16	12	17	18	18
Kansas	9	6	3	7	6	6	6	5	3	1	3	3	5	4	10	13	11	13
Kentucky	2	2	1	6	5	5	5	4	8	7	9	7	4	11	7	7	10	7
LSU	-	-	-	-	25	-	-	-	-	-	-	-	-	-	-	-	-	-
Louisville	7	7	11	10	10	11	11	11	15	13	12	9	7	5	13	10	14	10
Marquette	-	-	-	-	-	24	24	25	-	-	22	-	22	22	22	22	19	21
Maryland	-	-	-	-	-	-	-	-	-	25	18	21	-	-	-	-	-	-
Massachusetts	22	18	9	8	8	8	9	8	7	6	8	11	13	10	11	11	9	8
Michigan	5	5	5	3	7	7	7	13	10	15	15	13	11	7	3	3	8	11
Minnesota	10	9	15	17	15	16	16	19	18	20	17	22	23	20	20	18	20	23
Missouri	-	-	-	-	-	-	-	-	t25	-	24	20	15	12	6	6	3	5
Nebraska	-	-	-	-	-	-	-	-	-	-	-	-	-	-	-	-	-	22
New Mexico St.	-	-	-	-	-	-	-	-	-	-	25	23	-	-	25	-	-	-
North Carolina	1	1	4	2	2	2	2	2	1	4	4	2	1	2	4	5	4	1
Oklahoma St.	11	10	8	15	22	22	20	-	-	-	-	-	-	-	24	21	23	19
Pennsylvania	-	-	-	-	-	-	-	-	-	-	-	-	-	-	-	25	24	-
Purdue	21	21	14	11	11	10	10	10	9	12	7	8	10	9	14	9	6	3
St. Louis	-	-	-	-	-	-	-	-	-	23	23	18	17	18	19	16	21	24
Syracuse	20	20	18	13	21	21	19	18	16	16	14	15	14	14	18	14	13	15
Temple	8	8	7	5	4	4	4	7	13	11	10	10	8	13	8	12	12	12
Texas	-	-	-	-	-	-	-	-	-	-	-	-	-	-	-	-	25	20
UCLA	13	14	10	9	9	9	8	6	5	2	1	4	9	8	15	15	15	17
Vanderbilt	23	24	20	23	24	-	-	22	24	-	-	-	-	-				
Virginia	16	16	12	22	-	-	-	-	-	-	-	-	-	-	-	-	-	-
West Virginia	-	-	-	-	-	-	-	-	23	24	19	-	-	-	-	-	-	-
Western Ky.	-	-	-	-	-	25	25	-	-	-	-	-	-	-	-	-	-	-
Wisconsin	-	25	24	19	18	17	17	15	12	14	16	16	21	24	-	-	-	-
Xavier	-	-	-	-	-	-	-	-	t25	22	-	-	25	-	-	-	-	-

1994-95

Team	PS	Nov. 21	Nov. 28	Dec. 5	Dec. 12	Dec. 19	Dec. 26	Jan. 2	Jan. 9	Jan. 16	Jan. 23	Jan. 30	Feb. 6	Feb. 13	Feb. 20	Feb. 27	Mar. 6	Mar. 13
Alabama	18	25	-	-	-	-	-	-	-	-	-	20	23	18	20	21	20	20
Arizona	5	5	9	8	7	6	10	9	13	11	12	12	9	12	13	12	12	15
Arizona St.	-	-	12	16	13	15	16	15	12	13	13	16	14	13	15	15	18	16
Arkansas	1	1	4	3	4	3	3	3	5	9	9	8	12	10	8	7	5	6
California	-	-	-	-	-	24	14	17	20	-	-	-	-	-	-	-	-	-
Cincinnati	13	12	10	13	17	13	20	-	-	23	19	23	-	-	-	-	-	-
Clemson	-	-	-	-	-	-	-	-	18	-	-	-	-	-	-	-	-	-
Connecticut	19	16	16	10	10	10	8	6	2	2	2	4	3	1	4	4	6	8
Duke	8	8	6	9	9	9	7	11	16	-	-	-	-	-	-	-	-	-
Florida	10	10	8	6	8	8	13	13	15	24	23	25	-	-	-	-	-	-
Georgetown	15	14	19	18	15	12	12	12	10	10	14	13	20	-	-	23	24	22
Georgia Tech	23	22	20	17	14	18	17	24	22	22	21	21	18	20	24	-	-	-
Illinois	25	-	-	-	-	23	-	-	-	20	-	-	-	-	-	-	-	-
Indiana	9	11	-	-	-	-	24	21	-	-	-	-	-	-	-	-	-	-
Iowa	-	-	-	-	-	-	-	22	19	-	-	-	-	-	-	-	-	-
Iowa St.	-	-	-	-	-	25	21	16	23	14	11	11	19	21	23	24	-	24
Kansas	11	9	7	4	3	7	6	5	3	7	7	3	2	3	1	3	2	5
Kentucky	4	4	3	7	6	5	5	8	7	5	5	6	5	4	6	5	3	2
Maryland	7	7	11	11	12	11	9	7	9	8	8	5	8	7	7	6	10	10
Massachusetts	3	3	1	5	5	4	4	4	1	1	1	1	4	5	5	8	8	7
Michigan	16	13	17	23	25	-	-	-	-	-	-	-	-	-	-	-	-	-
Michigan St.	20	17	18	15	18	17	15	14	11	12	10	9	7	8	12	10	9	11
Minnesota	-	-	15	12	11	16	-	-	-	-	-	-	-	24	22	-	-	-
Mississippi St.	-	-	-	-	-	-	-	-	-	-	-	-	21	23	16	14	15	18
Missouri	-	-	-	-	-	-	-	-	17	16	20	18	13	9	14	19	17	23
Nebraska	-	-	-	-	-	-	23	19	-	-	-	-	-	-	-	-	-	-
New Mexico St.	-	-	25	22	24	21	22	20	24	19	24	-	-	-	-	-	-	-
North Carolina	2	2	2	1	1	1	1	1	4	3	3	2	1	2	3	2	4	4
Ohio	-	23	14	21	19	-	-	-	-	-	-	-	-	-	-	-	-	-
Oklahoma	-	-	-	-	-	-	-	-	-	-	25	24	-	-	25	16	16	17
Oklahoma St.	21	19	-	-	-	-	-	-	-	-	-	-	24	22	18	18	19	14
Oregon	-	-	-	-	-	-	-	-	25	17	18	22	22	19	-	-	25	-
Pennsylvania	-	-	-	-	-	-	-	25	21	25	-	-	-	-	-	-	-	-
Purdue	-	-	-	-	-	-	-	-	-	-	-	-	25	25	21	17	14	12
St. John's (N.Y.)	-	-	-	-	-	-	25	-	-	-	-	-	-	-	-	-	-	-
Stanford	-	-	-	-	-	-	-	23	-	21	17	17	15	17	19	20	-	-
Syracuse	12	18	22	19	16	14	11	10	8	6	6	10	10	11	17	22	21	25
UCLA	6	6	5	2	2	2	2	2	6	4	4	7	6	6	2	1	1	1
Utah	-	-	-	-	-	-	-	-	-	-	-	-	-	-	-	-	22	19
Villanova	22	21	24	24	22	-	-	-	-	-	22	19	16	15	9	11	13	9
Virginia	14	20	23	20	23	22	-	-	-	18	15	15	17	16	11	13	11	13
Wake Forest	24	24	21	25	21	19	18	18	14	15	16	14	11	14	10	9	7	3
Western Ky.	-	-	-	-	-	-	-	-	-	-	-	-	-	-	-	-	23	21
Wisconsin	17	15	13	14	20	20	19	-	-	-	-	-	-	-	-	-	-	-
Xavier	-	-	-	-	-	-	-	-	-	-	-	-	-	-	-	25	-	-

1995-96

Team	PS	Nov. 20	Nov. 27	Dec. 4	Dec. 11	Dec. 18	Dec. 26	Jan. 2	Jan. 8	Jan. 15	Jan. 22	Jan. 29	Feb. 5	Feb. 12	Feb. 19	Feb. 26	Mar. 5	Mar. 12
Arizona	19	4	4	4	3	9	9	18	18	13	14	16	13	13	13	11	11	11
Arkansas	16	-	25	-	-	-	-	-	-	-	-	-	-	-	-	-	-	-
Auburn	-	-	-	-	-	-	-	-	-	23	21	22	-	-	-	-	-	-
Boston College	-	-	-	-	-	-	-	24	-	24	20	21	22	21	20	-	-	-
California	25	-	-	-	-	24	-	-	-	-	25	-	-	-	-	-	-	-
Cincinnati	21	21	21	17	12	9	5	5	4	3	5	5	5	6	6	7	8	7
Clemson	-	-	-	-	-	-	24	22	16	19	18	24	-	-	-	-	-	-
Connecticut	6	6	9	9	8	8	7	7	6	5	4	4	4	3	3	4	3	3
Duke	-	-	12	18	21	20	20	19	-	-	-	-	-	-	-	-	-	-
Eastern Mich.	-	-	-	-	-	-	-	-	-	-	-	23	24	23	-	-	-	-
Geo. Washington	-	-	-	-	-	-	-	-	-	-	-	-	-	-	-	24	-	-
Georgetown	5	5	6	6	7	6	6	6	5	8	6	9	8	14	11	8	6	4
Georgia	-	-	-	-	-	18	16	14	19	22	-	-	-	-	-	-	-	-
Georgia Tech	-	25	20	16	19	21	-	-	-	-	-	25	-	-	23	18	18	13
Illinois	-	-	-	21	16	14	12	13	21	-	-	-	-	-	-	-	-	-
Indiana	23	23	-	-	-	-	-	-	-	-	-	-	-	-	-	-	-	-
Iowa	8	10	11	12	9	10	10	10	11	16	T22	16	19	19	18	20	19	21
Iowa St.	-	-	-	-	-	-	-	-	-	-	-	-	21	22	22	23	23	17
Kansas	2	2	2	1	1	1	4	4	3	4	3	3	3	5	5	3	5	6
Kentucky	1	1	1	5	5	4	2	2	2	2	2	2	2	2	2	1	1	2
Louisville	12	13	18	23	20	25	-	-	-	-	-	-	20	24	21	21	22	24
Marquette	-	-	-	-	-	-	-	-	-	-	-	24	-	-	-	-	21	20
Maryland	15	14	19	20	-	-	-	-	-	-	-	-	-	-	-	-	-	-
Massachusetts	7	7	5	3	3	2	1	1	1	1	1	1	1	1	1	2	2	1
Memphis	13	12	7	7	6	5	3	3	9	9	12	11	15	15	19	14	14	16
Michigan	17	16	24	22	18	17	19	21	23	20	16	20	23	-	-	-	-	-
Mississippi St.	9	9	8	8	15	16	17	17	12	21	-	-	-	25	-	-	-	-
Missouri	14	15	13	11	14	15	18	-	-	-	-	-	-	-	-	-	-	-
New Mexico	-	-	-	-	-	-	-	25	25	-	-	-	-	-	-	-	-	23
North Carolina	20	20	17	13	10	11	11	16	10	10	11	8	12	17	17	19	20	25
Penn St.	-	-	-	-	-	-	-	-	20	14	14	10	10	9	14	12	16	18
Purdue	24	24	-	-	-	-	-	-	22	17	19	17	14	11	7	5	4	5
Santa Clara	-	-	-	25	22	-	-	-	-	-	-	-	-	-	-	-	-	-
Stanford	18	18	16	24	-	-	-	-	24	-	-	-	25	20	24	25	-	-
Syracuse	-	-	-	-	25	19	13	11	14	12	17	18	18	16	15	15	13	15
Texas	-	-	-	-	-	-	-	23	-	-	-	-	-	-	-	-	-	-
Texas Tech	-	-	-	-	-	-	-	-	-	25	T22	15	13	12	9	9	7	8
Tulsa	-	-	-	-	-	-	25	-	-	-	-	-	-	-	-	-	-	-
UCLA	4	4	23	-	24	-	23	20	17	13	15	19	17	18	16	17	17	14
Utah	10	8	14	14	13	13	15	15	13	15	10	7	7	7	8	10	10	12
Villanova	3	3	3	2	2	7	8	8	7	7	7	6	6	4	4	6	9	10
Virginia	19	17	15	15	23	23	22	-	-	-	-	-	-	-	-	-	-	-
Virginia Tech	22	22	22	19	17	22	21	18	15	11	8	13	11	10	12	16	15	22
Wake Forest	11	11	10	10	11	12	14	12	8	6	9	12	9	8	10	13	12	9
Wis.-Green Bay	-	-	-	-	-	-	-	-	-	-	-	-	-	-	25	22	24	-

1996-97

Team	PS	Nov. 19	Nov. 26	Dec. 3	Dec. 10	Dec. 17	Dec. 24	Dec. 31	Jan. 7	Jan. 14	Jan. 21	Jan. 28	Feb. 4	Feb. 11	Feb. 18	Feb. 25	Mar. 4	Mar. 11
Alabama	-	-	-	-	24	20	19	-	-	-	-	-	-	-	-	-	-	-
Arizona	19	19	11	15	8	6	9	9	7	6	11	10	14	11	13	15	12	15
Arkansas	13	16	16	22	20	19	22	22	-	-	-	-	-	-	-	-	-	-
Boston College	21	21	23	20	25	-	25	25	23	19	22	-	-	-	-	-	-	23
California	-	-	-	-	-	-	-	-	-	-	-	-	-	-	25	-	-	-
Col. of Charleston	-	-	-	-	-	-	-	-	-	-	-	-	-	25	22	20	17	16
Cincinnati	1	1	1	4	7	7	7	6	6	4	9	8	12	8	11	9	10	10
Clemson	20	12	10	12	10	8	6	5	5	3	2	7	10	7	8	12	13	14
Colorado	-	-	-	-	-	-	-	-	-	-	18	18	15	15	21	19	18	24
Duke	10	10	6	10	14	11	12	13	10	13	10	12	8	6	6	7	7	8
Fresno St.	14	14	15	13	16	21	-	-	-	-	-	-	-	-	-	-	-	-
Geo. Washington	24	24	25	-	-	-	-	-	-	-	-	-	-	-	-	-	-	-
Georgia	-	-	-	-	-	-	-	-	24	21	-	-	-	-	-	-	24	17
Illinois	-	-	-	-	-	-	-	24	25	-	-	-	-	20	23	21	15	19
Indiana	-	22	20	8	12	13	13	12	15	17	21	17	24	-	24	22	25	-
Iowa	23	25	-	-	-	-	-	-	-	-	-	-	25	-	-	-	-	-
Iowa St.	11	11	9	9	6	5	5	4	4	8	14	11	6	9	7	13	16	18
Kansas	2	2	2	1	1	1	1	1	1	1	1	1	1	1	1	1	1	1
Kentucky	3	8	8	6	3	3	3	3	3	5	3	3	3	4	3	3	6	5
Louisville	-	-	-	-	22	18	16	14	14	10	6	9	11	17	15	17	20	25
Marquette	25	-	-	-	-	-	-	-	-	-	25	24	-	-	-	-	-	-
Maryland	-	-	-	-	-	25	21	19	19	11	7	5	7	10	14	16	22	22
Massachusetts	15	15	17	-	-	-	-	-	-	-	-	-	-	-	-	-	-	-
Michigan	9	9	7	7	5	4	4	8	16	18	13	16	13	14	18	24	-	-
Minnesota	22	23	24	16	17	16	15	15	11	7	8	6	4	3	2	2	2	3
Mississippi	-	-	-	-	-	-	-	-	-	20	-	-	-	-	-	-	-	-
New Mexico	17	18	19	11	15	15	14	16	18	12	15	13	9	13	10	11	14	11

Team	PS	Nov. 19	26	Dec. 3	10	17	24	31	Jan. 7	14	21	28	Feb. 4	11	18	25	Mar. 4	11
North Carolina	8	7	14	14	11	12	11	11	13	22	19	19	20	16	12	8	5	4
Oregon	-	-	-	-	-	-	24	20	17	24	-	-	-	-	-	-	-	-
St. Joseph's	-	-	-	-	-	-	-	-	-	-	-	-	-	-	-	23	19	12
South Carolina	-	-	-	-	-	-	-	-	-	-	-	25	19	12	9	6	4	6
Stanford	18	20	21	24	21	22	23	21	21	15	17	15	18	22	20	25	23	21
Syracuse	12	13	12	19	-	-	-	-	-	-	-	-	-	-	-	-	-	-
Texas	16	17	18	18	13	14	18	18	22	23	23	23	-	-	-	-	-	-
Texas Tech	-	-	-	-	18	23	-	23	20	25	20	22	23	21	-	-	-	-
Tulane	-	-	-	-	-	-	-	-	-	-	-	-	21	23	-	-	-	-
Tulsa	-	-	22	21	-	-	-	-	-	-	24	21	22	-	-	-	-	-
UCLA	5	5	13	17	23	24	-	-	-	-	-	-	-	24	17	10	9	7
Utah	6	4	4	3	9	9	8	7	9	9	5	4	5	5	5	4	3	2
Villanova	7	6	5	5	4	10	10	10	8	16	12	14	16	18	19	18	21	20
Virginia	-	-	-	25	-	-	-	-	-	-	-	-	-	-	-	-	-	-
Wake Forest	4	3	3	2	2	2	2	2	2	2	4	2	2	2	4	5	8	9
Xavier	-	-	-	23	19	17	17	17	12	14	16	20	17	19	16	14	11	13

PS=preseason

1997-98

Team	PS	Nov. 18	25	Dec. 2	9	16	23	30	Jan. 6	13	20	27	Feb. 3	10	17	24	Mar. 3	10
Arizona	1	1	1	4	6	5	5	8	5	5	6	6	4	3	3	2	2	4
Arkansas	-	-	-	18	15	13	12	23	22	22	18	15	14	12	16	12	16	17
Charlotte	18	17	25	-	-	-	-	-	-	-	-	-	-	-	-	-	-	-
Cincinnati	-	-	-	-	-	-	-	-	-	-	21	18	20	19	17	17	14	9
Clemson	5	5	13	17	17	-	21	21	24	-	25	-	-	-	-	-	-	-
Connecticut	12	12	11	13	13	12	11	10	8	10	8	9	7	6	7	6	6	6
Duke	3	3	3	1	1	3	3	3	2	2	1	1	1	2	2	1	1	3
Florida St.	-	-	-	19	16	17	17	15	13	17	20	-	-	-	-	-	-	-
Fresno St.	13	13	12	16	18	-	-	-	-	-	-	-	-	-	-	-	-	-
Geo. Washington	-	-	-	-	-	-	-	-	-	-	-	-	22	17	24	-	-	-
Georgia	19	25	22	21	23	20	-	-	-	-	-	-	-	-	-	-	-	-
Georgia Tech	-	-	-	22	24	-	-	-	-	-	-	-	-	-	-	-	-	-
Hawaii	-	-	-	-	-	-	-	-	21	24	24	-	-	-	-	-	-	-
Illinois	-	-	-	-	-	-	-	-	-	-	-	-	-	-	23	22	18	22
Illinois St.	-	24	-	-	-	-	-	-	-	-	-	-	-	-	-	-	-	-
Indiana	17	23	21	-	-	-	-	-	-	-	-	25	-	-	-	-	-	-
Iowa	15	14	14	10	10	15	15	14	11	13	10	16	24	-	-	-	-	-
Kansas	2	2	2	2	3	2	2	2	4	3	3	5	3	4	4	4	4	2
Kentucky	8	9	8	7	4	4	4	6	6	6	7	7	8	7	8	7	7	5
Louisville	25	22	19	-	-	-	-	-	-	-	-	-	-	-	-	-	-	-
Marquette	-	-	-	-	-	-	-	25	20	23	-	-	-	-	-	-	-	-
Maryland	-	-	24	23	19	22	20	20	-	-	-	23	25	24	25	-	21	20
Massachusetts	-	-	-	-	-	-	-	-	-	-	-	-	23	20	18	20	-	-
Michigan	-	-	-	-	-	21	-	18	17	19	16	19	18	21	22	21	17	12
Michigan St.	-	-	-	-	-	-	-	-	-	-	-	22	16	13	14	10	12	16
Mississippi	23	21	17	14	21	18	16	16	14	11	13	12	17	18	15	13	10	13
Murray St.	-	-	-	-	-	-	-	-	-	-	-	-	-	-	-	-	-	25
New Mexico	11	11	10	8	14	14	14	12	12	T15	17	14	12	11	11	16	20	18
North Carolina	4	4	4	3	2	1	1	1	1	1	2	2	2	1	1	3	4	1
Oklahoma	20	19	18	-	-	-	-	-	-	-	-	-	-	-	-	-	-	-
Oklahoma St.	-	-	-	-	-	-	-	-	-	25	-	-	-	-	-	25	25	-
Princeton	-	-	-	25	22	19	18	17	15	12	11	11	11	10	9	9	8	8
Purdue	9	8	6	6	8	8	7	5	9	9	12	10	10	8	5	11	9	11
Rhode Island	21	20	23	-	-	-	22	24	23	20	22	21	-	25	-	-	-	-
South Carolina	7	6	5	5	5	6	10	11	16	14	14	13	13	15	13	14	15	14
Stanford	14	15	15	12	11	9	8	7	7	7	5	4	9	14	10	8	11	10
Syracuse	-	-	-	-	-	25	19	19	18	T15	15	20	19	23	21	23	22	21
Temple	24	18	20	20	20	16	24	-	-	-	-	-	-	-	-	24	24	24
Texas	22	-	-	-	-	-	-	-	-	-	-	-	-	-	-	-	-	-
TCU	-	-	-	-	-	24	25	-	-	-	-	-	-	22	19	15	13	15
UCLA	6	7	7	15	12	11	9	9	10	8	9	8	6	9	12	18	19	19
Utah	16	16	16	11	9	7	6	4	3	4	4	3	5	5	6	5	5	7
Wake Forest	-	-	-	24	25	23	-	-	-	-	-	-	-	-	-	-	-	-
West Virginia	-	-	-	-	-	-	23	22	25	21	23	17	15	16	20	19	23	-
Xavier	10	10	9	9	7	10	13	13	19	18	19	24	21	-	-	-	-	23

PS=Preseason

1998-99

Team	PS	Nov. 17	24	Dec. 1	8	15	22	29	Jan. 5	12	19	26	Feb. 2	9	16	23	Mar. 2	9
Arizona	18	12	11	13	8	T8	8	6	11	7	9	13	10	10	8	7	13	12
Arkansas	19	19	21	19	23	20	19	20	18	24	22	21	23	-	-	-	22	17
Auburn	-	-	-	-	-	19	18	17	14	8	6	7	6	3	3	2	4	4
Charlotte	-	-	-	-	-	-	-	-	-	-	-	-	-	-	-	-	-	24
Col. of Charleston	-	-	-	-	-	-	-	-	-	-	-	-	22	20	18	17	16	16
Cincinnati	15	17	15	6	4	4	4	3	3	3	5	5	3	4	9	9	7	11
Clemson	-	24	22	24	17	16	16	14	20	25	-	-	-	-	-	-	-	-
Connecticut	2	2	2	1	1	1	1	1	1	1	1	1	1	2	2	4	3	3
Duke	1	1	1	4	3	2	2	2	2	2	2	2	2	1	1	1	1	1
Florida	-	-	-	-	-	-	-	-	-	-	-	25	-	23	23	19	21	23
Indiana	22	21	17	16	11	10	10	8	13	23	18	20	21	17	19	20	17	19
Iowa	-	-	-	-	-	25	21	21	19	12	14	16	14	19	20	18	20	21
Kansas	8	8	8	7	10	13	13	18	16	15	19	22	-	24	-	-	-	22
Kentucky	4	4	4	8	5	3	3	7	5	6	7	6	5	8	6	13	14	8
Louisville	-	-	-	-	-	-	-	-	-	-	24	-	-	-	-	-	-	-
Maryland	6	6	5	2	2	5	5	4	6	5	4	4	7	7	5	5	5	5
Massachusetts	24	23	-	-	-	-	-	-	-	-	-	-	-	-	-	-	-	-
Miami (Fla.)	-	-	-	-	-	-	-	-	-	-	25	23	25	16	15	11	9	10
Miami (Ohio)	-	-	24	22	-	-	-	-	-	-	-	-	-	-	25	-	-	-
Michigan St.	5	5	7	9	14	14	15	13	12	14	11	8	8	5	4	3	2	2
Minnesota	-	-	-	-	24	17	17	16	17	19	17	19T	18	22	-	-	23	-
Missouri	-	-	-	-	-	-	-	-	-	-	-	-	24	-	22	-	24	-
New Mexico	T20	20	20	17	12	11	11	15	15	16	12	18	17	25	24	21	25	25
North Carolina	11	10	9	3	7	7	7	9	10	9	10	10	12	12	14	14	15	13
Ohio St.	-	-	-	-	-	-	-	-	25	21	-	15	15	13	11	10	11	14
Oklahoma	-	-	-	-	-	24	23	-	-	-	-	-	-	-	-	-	-	-
Oklahoma St.	13	13	12	11	19	18	25	25	22	22	23	-	-	-	-	-	-	-
Pittsburgh	-	-	-	20	20	22	24	23	-	-	-	-	-	-	-	-	-	-
Purdue	16	15	14	14	9	T8	9	11	7	13	16	14T	18	21	17	23	-	-
Rhode Island	23	25	-	-	-	-	-	-	-	-	-	-	-	-	-	-	-	-
St. John's (N.Y.)	-	-	23	25	18	15	14	12	9	11	8	9	9	11	10	8	10	9
Stanford	3	3	3	5	6	6	6	5	4	4	3	3	4	6	7	6	6	7
Syracuse	T20	22	19	12	13	21	22	22	21	18	20	17	16	18	21	T24	-	-
Temple	7	7	6	10	16	-	-	-	-	-	-	-	-	-	-	T24	-	-
Tennessee	9	18	25	-	21	-	-	-	-	-	-	-	-	-	-	-	18	20
Texas	-	-	-	-	-	-	-	-	-	-	-	-	-	-	-	22	-	-
TCU	25	-	-	-	-	-	-	24	24	20	21	24	-	-	-	-	-	-
UCLA	12	11	10	18	15	12	12	10	8	10	13	11	13	9	16	15	12	15
Utah	10	9	18	21	25	-	-	-	-	-	-	-	20	14	12	12	8	6
Washington	14	14	16	15	22	-	-	-	-	-	-	-	-	-	-	-	-	-
Wisconsin	-	-	-	-	-	23	20	19	23	17	15	12	11	15	13	16	19	18
Xavier	17	16	13	23	-	-	-	-	-	-	-	-	-	-	-	-	-	-

PS=preseason

1999-2000

Team	PS	Nov. 16	23	30	Dec. 7	14	21	28	Jan. 4	11	18	25	Feb. 1	8	15	22	29	Mar. 7	14
Arizona	9	10	8	4	2	4	3	5	5	2	2	5	9	7	4	4	3	9	4
Auburn	4	3	2	7	8	6	7	4	4	4	4	7	10	9	12	11	19	-	24
Cincinnati	2	1	1	1	1	1	4	3	3	1	1	1	1	1	1	3	2	1	7
Connecticut	1	8	7	5	6	3	2	2	2	5	8	6	7	13	18	22	24	21	20
DePaul	20	20	18	22	20	19	24	24	23	21	23	-	-	-	-	-	-	-	-
Duke	10	18	16	17	14	11	10	9	8	6	5	3	3	3	3	2	4	3	1
Florida	8	7	6	11	9	9	8	6	6	10	9	10	12	12	11	9	8	11	13
Gonzaga	24	25	25	25	24	22	22	-	-	-	-	-	-	-	-	-	-	-	-
Illinois	16	17	15	16	22	20	15	20	19	22	-	-	-	-	-	-	25	25	21
Indiana	-	-	-	23	15	21	20	12	10	9	11	14	11	10	10	16	14	18	22
Iowa	-	22	23	-	-	-	-	-	-	-	-	-	-	-	-	-	-	-	-
Iowa St.	-	-	-	-	-	-	-	-	-	-	-	-	20	17	14	17	10	7	6
Kansas	11	11	10	6	5	8	12	10	9	8	7	12	15	20	24	23	23	24	-
Kentucky	14	14	11	13	23	-	-	-	25	20	18	16	14	11	19	18	22	16	19
LSU	-	-	-	-	-	-	-	-	21	24	-	-	22	25	16	15	12	10	10
Louisville	-	-	-	-	-	-	-	-	-	25	-	-	-	-	-	-	-	-	-
Maryland	-	-	24	24	21	16	17	14	12	18	24	22	25	23	22	19	17	20	17
Miami (Fla.)	25	-	-	-	-	-	-	-	-	-	-	-	-	-	-	-	-	23	23
Michigan St.	3	2	3	8	4	5	5	8	11	11	10	9	8	6	6	5	7	5	2
North Carolina	6	5	4	2	7	7	6	13	14	13	21	-	-	-	-	-	-	-	-
North Carolina St.	-	-	-	-	-	-	25	-	-	-	-	21	-	-	-	-	-	-	-
Ohio St.	5	4	12	15	13	12	16	15	13	17	13	8	5	5	7	6	6	4	8
Oklahoma	-	-	-	-	-	23	21	22	20	16	17	18	18	16	20	20	21	15	12
Oklahoma St.	22	23	21	21	17	14	13	11	16	14	12	15	13	14	8	10	13	17	14
Oregon	-	-	-	-	-	-	-	-	-	-	-	-	23	24	-	-	-	-	-
Purdue	23	24	22	19	25	24	-	-	-	-	-	-	-	-	25	21	20	22	25
St. John's (N.Y.)	18	15	-	-	-	-	-	-	-	-	19	25	-	-	-	-	18	19	9
Seton Hall	-	-	-	-	-	-	-	-	-	-	-	-	-	-	23	-	-	-	-
Southern California	-	-	-	-	-	-	-	-	-	-	-	23	-	-	-	-	-	-	-
Stanford	13	9	9	3	3	2	1	1	1	3	3	2	2	2	2	1	1	2	3
Syracuse	17	13	14	14	12	10	9	7	7	7	6	4	4	4	9	13	9	12	16
Temple	7	6	5	10	19	17	19	17	-	23	-	23	21	19	15	8	5	6	5
Tennessee	19	19	17	18	16	13	11	16	15	12	16	11	6	8	5	7	11	8	11
Texas	21	21	20	9	10	15	14	18	17	15	14	17	16	18	17	14	16	13	15
Tulsa	-	-	-	-	-	-	-	25	22	19	15	13	17	15	13	12	15	14	18
UCLA	12	12	13	12	11	18	18	23	24	-	25	-	-	-	-	-	-	-	-
Utah	15	16	19	20	-	-	-	21	18	-	22	19	19	21	21	25	-	-	-
Vanderbilt	-	-	-	-	-	-	-	-	-	-	20	20	24	22	-	24	-	-	-
Wake Forest	-	-	-	-	18	25	23	19	-	-	-	-	-	-	-	-	-	-	-

2000-01

Team	PS	Nov. 14	21	28	Dec. 5	12	19	26	Jan. 2	9	16	23	30	Feb. 6	13	20	27	Mar. 6	13
Alabama	-	-	-	-	23	18	17	20	18	16	T15	18	17	18	21	14	20	-	-
Arizona	1	1	1	5	5	7	10	12	16	21	17	12	7	11	8	8	9	8	5
Arkansas	T15	15	24	25	21	25	25	-	-	-	-	-	-	-	-	-	-	-	-
Boston College	-	-	-	-	-	-	-	-	-	24	25	23	20	17	9	10	11	10	7
Cincinnati	18	17	16	22	18	17	22	19	25	-	-	-	-	-	-	-	-	-	-
Connecticut	14	13	12	16	15	11	11	10	10	13	T15	24	-	-	-	-	-	-	-
Dayton	-	-	-	24	-	-	-	-	-	-	-	-	-	-	-	-	-	-	-
DePaul	21	22	21	-	-	-	-	-	-	-	-	-	-	-	-	-	-	-	-
Duke	2	2	2	1	1	1	1	3	3	2	2	2	2	3	3	4	2	3	1

DIVISION I

2000-01

Team	PS	N14	N21	N28	D5	D12	D19	D26	J2	J9	J16	J23	J30	F6	F13	F20	F27	M6	M13
Florida	11	11	11	10	8	8	7	5	5	8	7	14	13	8	11	7	6	5	8
Fresno St.											22	19	23	20			25		
Georgetown					24	23	21	19	12	9	10	14	15	18	21	21	18	21	
Georgia													25						
Illinois	8	8	8	9	9	5	5	9	9	7	11	7	6	7	4	3	5	4	4
Indiana																			20
Iowa							22	19	23		14	21	18	14	25				24
Iowa St.	25				25			25	23	18	23	17	15	12	7	6	8	7	10
Kansas	7	4	3	2	3	10	9	7	7	5	5	4	3	5	6	11	10	9	12
Kentucky	12	20	22												22	13	15	15	9
Maryland	5	6	6	13	19	20	20	18	17	14	12	8	9	13	17	20	16	11	11
Michigan St.	3	3	4	3	2	2	2	1	1	3	3	3	5	4	5	5	3	2	3
Mississippi					23	24	24	22	20	21	19		25	16	12	14	14	14	
Missouri											20								
North Carolina	6	7	7	6	14	15	15	14	13	9	6	5	4	1	1	2	4	6	6
Notre Dame	T15	16	14	11	10	21	21	22	21	25			23	20	14	18	13	19	19
Ohio St.																			24
Oklahoma	22	21	19	14	20	19	18	17	15	22	22	-	24	21	13	16	17	16	13
Providence																25			
St. John's (N.Y.)		24	23	19	24														
St. Joseph's																23	18	21	22
Seton Hall	10	10	10	8	7	9	8	11	11	15	18	16	22						
Southern Cal	23	23	20	15	12	13	13	16	20	19	24	25	21	22					
Stanford	4	5	5	4	4	3	3	2	2	1	1	1	1	2	2	1	1	1	2
Syracuse				20	13	12	12	15	14	11	8	11	12	9	10	17	19	17	17
Temple				17															
Tennessee	9	9	9	7	6	4	4	6	6	4	4	6	8	10	15	22			
Texas									24	23		20					24	20	18
UCLA	17	14	15												24	15	12	13	15
Utah	13	12	13	18	22														
Virginia	24	25	25	21	16	14	14	8	8	10	13	13	11	6	12	9	7	12	16
Wake Forest	20	18	17	12	11	6	6	4	4	6	10	9	16	19	23	24	23	22	23
Wisconsin	19	19	18	23	17	16	16	13	12	17	19	15	10	16	19	19	22	23	25
Xavier																24		25	

2001-02

Team	PS	N20	N27	D4	D11	D18	D25	J1	J8	J15	J22	J29	F5	F12	F19	F26	M5	M12
Alabama	24	22	21	16	22	23	21	18	T14	16	14	7	5	7	5	6	8	8
Arizona		8	4	7	6	11	14	15	20	15	10	19	11	9	14	14	15	7
Ball St.				16	15	20	21											
Boston College	17	17	15	13	11	10	11	11	16	22								
Butler						23	20	24										
California													21	25				
Cincinnati						25	17	13	10	7	4	4	6	5	4	4	5	5
Connecticut								25	17						23	19	10	
Duke	1	1	1	1	1	1	1	2	1	1	1	1	1	1	1	3	3	3
Florida	6	7	6	6	5	4	3	3	2	5	6	8	6	8	11	15		
Fresno St.		23	24	21														
Georgetown	14	16	18	19	18	16	20	24										
Georgia										20	15	16	17	21	18	16	17	23
Gonzaga				25	24	22	22	18	13	16	11	9	8	7	7	6		25
Hawaii																		25
Illinois	3	2	2	5	10	9	7	7	9	11	9	12	21	18	16	15	10	13
Indiana	22	20			21					25			22	23	25	23		
Iowa	9	9	7	12	15	12	9	9	13	17								
Kansas	7	4	8	4	4	3	2	2	1	4	2	2	2	2	1	1	1	2
Kentucky	4	10	13	11	9	7	6	6	8	12	8	10	7	10	12	11	12	16
Marquette			23	17	14	14	19	25				18	11	9	9	13	12	
Maryland	2	6	5	3	3	2	8	8	4	3	3	3	3	2	2	2	2	4
Memphis	12	12	20	22														
Miami (Fla.)							24	21	21	24	22	15	12	13	17	22	20	21
Michigan St.	15	13	22	24	23	17	13	19	25									
Mississippi St.									22									17
Missouri	8	5	3	2	8	10	17	21	18	22	22							
North Carolina	19																	
North Caro. St.													24					
Ohio St.											20	25	16	23	19	18	21	14
Oklahoma	25				24	22	12	10	5	5	6	6	4	4	6	5	4	3
Oklahoma St.	18	15	14	10	8	6	5	5	6	6	11	9	14	16	13	12	14	20
Oregon										23	19		13	17	15	13	9	11
Pittsburgh									23			21		14	11	10	7	9
St. Joseph's	10	19	19	18	16	15												
Southern Cal	20	24								18	23	23	25	25	T20	19	22	18
Stanford	13	14	11	14	12	13	16	12	T14	19	17	18	20	12	10	17	16	24
Syracuse	21	18	12	9	13	18	18	16	12	8	12	14	23					
Temple	16	25																
Texas	23								24									
Texas Tech										20	24							
UCLA	5	3	10	20	17	19	15	14	11	9	13	13	15	20	25			
Virginia	11	11	9	8	5	4	4	7	10	7	8	10	15	22				
Wake Forest			25	23	19	20	25	23	19	14	21	22	19	T20	24			
Western Ky.		21	17	25											24	20	18	19
Xavier																	24	22

2002-03

Team	PS	N19	N26	D3	D10	D17	D24	D31	J7	J14	J21	J28	F4	F11	F18	F25	M4	M11	M18
Alabama	8	4	4	3	2	2	1	1	4	9	15	23	22						
Arizona	1	1	1	1	1	1	4	4	2	2	1	1	2	1	1	1	1	1	1
Auburn									24										
California										25	20		22	18	23	22	24		
Col. of Charleston				25															
Cincinnati	23	23	21		23														
Connecticut	15	14	12	11	9	8	6	5	3	T6	11	14	18	23	-	-	-	-	23
Creighton				20	18	15	16	13	10	16	13	12	17	19	19	15			
Dayton															25	25	21	22	16
Duke	6	6	6	4	3	3	3	1	1	3	5	9	8	8	6	10	12	7	
Florida	7	8	7	8	14	13	12	12	11	T6	5	4	1	4	7	4	3	7	10
Georgia	16	18	17						20	20	19	15	17	20	22	21	25	21	25
Gonzaga	22	21	20																
Illinois				25	15	12	7	11	10	8	18	13	16	14	20	18	14	13	11
Indiana	21	22	19	10	7	6	10	17	15	18	14	19							
Kansas	2	2	2	14	20	19	19	18	14	12	6	12	12	9	6	7	6	4	6
Kentucky	17	17	15	18	12	18	14	20	18	16	8	7	6	3	2	2	2	2	1
LSU							24	21		23									
Louisville								24	19	15	9	8	5	2	4	11	15	20	14
Marquette	18	16	13	13	16	14	13	13	24	21	20	18	15	11	11	10	8	8	9
Maryland	13	T12	11	9	18	24	23	22	T21	17	12	10	8	16	13	14	13	14	17
Memphis															24	18	16	19	
Michigan St.	9	9	9	21	21	15	15	14	25										
Minnesota	24	24	24	20		25													
Mississippi St.	12	T12	23	24	24	16	16	8	7	14	22	21	23	19	20	23		20	
Missouri	19	20	18	15	11	11	17	16	13	11	21	25	21	21					24
North Carolina				12	22	22													
Notre Dame				10	9	8	6	5	10	16	11	10	10	12	9	16	17	22	
Oklahoma	3	7	8	6	6	7	5	10	9	5	7	6	7	5	5	3	5	6	3
Oklahoma St.											24	13	9	11	13	16	16	20	23
Oregon	11	10	10	7	5	5	11	9	12	22	23	22							
Pittsburgh	5	5	5	5	4	4	2	2	6	3	2	2	4	7	9	8	7	5	4
Purdue													24		24				
St. Joseph's																25		25	
Stanford			17	19	17								25	24	21	19	17	15	18
Syracuse										25		24	19	17	15	15	12	11	13
Texas	4	3	3	2	8	10	9	7	8	4	4	3	3	6	3	5	4	3	5
Texas Tech								25	23										
Tulsa	25	25	22	19	17	22	20												
UCLA	14	15	14																
Utah																	23	22	
Virginia								22											
Wake Forest							25	23	17	19	17	17	14	15	10	12	9	9	8
Western Ky.	20	19																	
Wisconsin			25	23													24	18	21
Xavier	10	11	16	16	13	21	21	19	T21	-	-	20	18	14	13	11	10	12	

PS=preseason
(Note: AP does not do a post-tournament poll)

Final Season Polls

Final Regular-Season Polls

The Helms Foundation of Los Angeles selected the national college men's basketball champions from 1942-82 and researched retroactive picks from 1901-41. The Helms winners are listed in this section to the time The Associated Press (AP) poll started in 1949. The AP is the writers' poll, while the UPI and USA Today/CNN and USA Today/NABC polls are the coaches' polls.

HELMS

1901	Yale	1913	Navy	1925	Princeton	1937	Stanford
1902	Minnesota	1914	Wisconsin	1926	Syracuse	1938	Temple
1903	Yale	1915	Illinois	1927	Notre Dame	1939	Long Island
1904	Columbia	1916	Wisconsin	1928	Pittsburgh	1940	Southern California
1905	Columbia	1917	Washington St.	1929	Montana St.	1941	Wisconsin
1906	Dartmouth	1918	Syracuse	1930	Pittsburgh	1942	Stanford
1907	Chicago	1919	Minnesota	1931	Northwestern	1943	Wyoming
1908	Chicago	1920	Pennsylvania	1932	Purdue	1944	Army
1909	Chicago	1921	Pennsylvania	1933	Kentucky	1945	Oklahoma St.
1910	Columbia	1922	Kansas	1934	Wyoming	1946	Oklahoma St.
1911	St. John's (N.Y.)	1923	Kansas	1935	New York U.	1947	Holy Cross
1912	Wisconsin	1924	North Carolina	1936	Notre Dame	1948	Kentucky

1949
AP
1. Kentucky
2. Oklahoma St.
3. St. Louis
4. Illinois
5. Western Ky.
6. Minnesota
7. Bradley
8. San Francisco
9. Tulane
10. Bowling Green
11. Yale
12. Utah
13. North Carolina St.
14. Villanova
15. UCLA
16. Loyola (Ill.)
17. Wyoming
18. Butler
19. Hamline
20. Ohio St.

1950
AP
1. Bradley
2. Ohio St.
3. Kentucky
4. Holy Cross
5. North Carolina St.
6. Duquesne
7. UCLA
8. Western Ky.
9. St. John's (N.Y.)
10. La Salle
11. Villanova
12. San Francisco
13. Long Island
14. Kansas St.
15. Arizona
16. Wisconsin
17. San Jose St.
18. Washington St.
19. Kansas
20. Indiana

1951
AP
1. Kentucky
2. Oklahoma St.
3. Columbia
4. Kansas St.
5. Illinois
6. Bradley
7. Indiana
8. North Carolina St.
9. St. John's (N.Y.)
10. St. Louis
11. Brigham Young
12. Arizona
13. Dayton
14. Toledo
15. Washington
16. Murray St.
17. Cincinnati
18. Siena
19. Southern California
20. Villanova

UPI
1. Kentucky
2. Oklahoma St.
3. Kansas St.
4. Illinois
5. Columbia
6. Bradley
7. North Carolina St.
8. Indiana
9. St. John's (N.Y.)
10. Brigham Young
11. St. Louis
12. Arizona
13. Washington
14. Beloit
14. Villanova
16. UCLA
17. Cincinnati
18. Dayton
18. St. Bonaventure
18. Texas A&M

1952
AP
1. Kentucky
2. Illinois
3. Kansas St.
4. Duquesne
5. St. Louis
6. Washington
7. Iowa
8. Kansas
9. West Virginia
10. St. John's (N.Y.)
11. Dayton
12. Duke
13. Holy Cross
14. Seton Hall
15. St. Bonaventure
16. Wyoming
17. Louisville
18. Seattle
19. UCLA
20. Texas St.

UPI
1. Kentucky
2. Illinois
3. Kansas
4. Duquesne
5. Washington
6. Kansas St.
7. St. Louis
8. Iowa
9. St. John's (N.Y.)
10. Wyoming
11. St. Bonaventure
12. Seton Hall
13. TCU
14. West Virginia
15. Holy Cross
16. Western Ky.
17. La Salle
18. Dayton
19. Louisville
20. UCLA
20. Indiana

1953
AP
1. Indiana
2. Seton Hall
3. Kansas
4. Washington
5. LSU
6. La Salle
7. St. John's (N.Y.)
8. Oklahoma St.
9. Duquesne
10. Notre Dame
11. Illinois
12. Kansas St.
13. Holy Cross
14. Seattle
15. Wake Forest
16. Santa Clara
17. Western Ky.
18. North Carolina St.
19. DePaul
20. Southwest Mo. St.

UPI
1. Indiana
2. Seton Hall
3. Washington
4. La Salle
5. Kansas
6. LSU
7. Oklahoma St.
8. North Carolina St.
9. Kansas St.
10. Illinois
11. Western Ky.
12. California
13. Notre Dame
14. DePaul
14. Wyoming
16. St. Louis
17. Holy Cross
18. Oklahoma City
19. Brigham Young
20. Duquesne

1954
AP
1. Kentucky
2. La Salle
3. Holy Cross
4. Indiana
5. Duquesne
6. Notre Dame
7. Bradley
8. Western Ky.
9. Penn St.
10. Oklahoma St.
11. Southern California
12. George Washington
13. Iowa
14. LSU
15. Duke
16. Niagara
17. Seattle
18. Kansas
19. Illinois
20. Maryland

UPI
1. Indiana
2. Kentucky
3. Duquesne
4. Oklahoma St.
5. Notre Dame
6. Western Ky.
7. Kansas
8. LSU
9. Holy Cross
10. Iowa
11. La Salle
12. Illinois
13. Colorado St.
14. North Carolina St.
14. Southern California
16. Oregon St.
17. Seattle
17. Dayton
19. Rice
20. Duke

1955
AP
1. San Francisco
2. Kentucky
3. La Salle
4. North Carolina St.
5. Iowa
6. Duquesne
7. Utah
8. Marquette
9. Dayton
10. Oregon St.
11. Minnesota
12. Alabama
13. UCLA
14. George Washington
15. Colorado
16. Tulsa
17. Vanderbilt
18. Illinois
19. West Virginia
20. St. Louis

UPI
1. San Francisco
2. Kentucky
3. La Salle
4. Utah
5. Iowa
6. North Carolina St.
7. Duquesne
8. Oregon St.
9. Marquette
10. Dayton
11. Colorado
12. UCLA
13. Minnesota
14. Tulsa
15. George Washington
16. Illinois
17. Niagara
18. St. Louis
19. Holy Cross
20. Cincinnati

DIVISION I

1956

AP
1. San Francisco
2. North Carolina St.
3. Dayton
4. Iowa
5. Alabama
6. Louisville
7. Southern Methodist
8. UCLA
9. Kentucky
10. Illinois
11. Oklahoma City
12. Vanderbilt
13. North Carolina
14. Holy Cross
15. Temple
16. Wake Forest
17. Duke
18. Utah
19. Oklahoma St.
20. West Virginia

UPI
1. San Francisco
2. North Carolina St.
3. Dayton
4. Iowa
5. Alabama
6. Southern Methodist
7. Louisville
8. Illinois
9. UCLA
10. Vanderbilt
11. North Carolina
12. Kentucky
13. Utah
14. Temple
15. Holy Cross
16. Oklahoma St.
16. St. Louis
18. Seattle
18. Duke
18. Canisius

1957

AP
1. North Carolina
2. Kansas
3. Kentucky
4. Southern Methodist
5. Seattle
6. Louisville
7. West Virginia
8. Vanderbilt
9. Oklahoma City
10. St. Louis
11. Michigan St.
12. Memphis
13. California
14. UCLA
15. Mississippi St.
16. Idaho St.
17. Notre Dame
18. Wake Forest
19. Canisius
19. Oklahoma St.

UPI
1. North Carolina
2. Kansas
3. Kentucky
4. Southern Methodist
5. Seattle
6. California
7. Michigan St.
8. Louisville
9. UCLA
9. St. Louis
11. West Virginia
12. Dayton
13. Bradley
14. Brigham Young
15. Indiana
16. Vanderbilt
16. Xavier
16. Oklahoma City
19. Notre Dame
20. Kansas St.

1958

AP
1. West Virginia
2. Cincinnati
3. Kansas St.
4. San Francisco
5. Temple
6. Maryland
7. Kansas
8. Notre Dame
9. Kentucky
10. Duke
11. Dayton
12. Indiana
13. North Carolina
14. Bradley
15. Mississippi St.
16. Auburn
17. Michigan St.
18. Seattle
19. Oklahoma St.
20. North Carolina St.

UPI
1. West Virginia
2. Cincinnati
3. San Francisco
4. Kansas St.
5. Temple
6. Maryland
7. Notre Dame
8. Kansas
9. Dayton
10. Indiana
11. Bradley
12. North Carolina
13. Duke
14. Kentucky
15. Oklahoma St.
16. Oregon St.
16. North Carolina St.
18. St. Bonaventure
19. Michigan St.
19. Wyoming
19. Seattle

1959

AP
1. Kansas St.
2. Kentucky
3. Mississippi St.
4. Bradley
5. Cincinnati
6. North Carolina St.
7. Michigan St.
8. Auburn
9. North Carolina
10. West Virginia
11. California
12. St. Louis
13. Seattle
14. St. Joseph's
15. St. Mary's (Cal.)
16. TCU
17. Oklahoma City
18. Utah
19. St. Bonaventure
20. Marquette

UPI
1. Kansas St.
2. Kentucky
3. Michigan St.
4. Cincinnati
5. North Carolina St.
6. North Carolina
6. Mississippi St.
8. Bradley
9. California
10. Auburn
11. West Virginia
12. TCU
13. St. Louis
14. Utah
15. Marquette
16. Tennessee Tech
17. St. John's (N.Y.)
18. Navy
18. St. Mary's (Cal.)
20. St. Joseph's

1960

AP
1. Cincinnati
2. California
3. Ohio St.
4. Bradley
5. West Virginia
6. Utah
7. Indiana
8. Utah St.
9. St. Bonaventure
10. Miami (Fla.)
11. Auburn
12. New York U.
13. Georgia Tech
14. Providence
15. St. Louis
16. Holy Cross
17. Villanova
18. Duke
19. Wake Forest
20. St. John's (N.Y.)

UPI
1. California
2. Cincinnati
3. Ohio St.
4. Bradley
5. Utah
6. West Virginia
7. Utah St.
8. Georgia Tech
9. Villanova
10. Indiana
11. St. Bonaventure
12. New York U.
13. Texas
14. North Carolina
15. Duke
16. Kansas St.
17. Auburn
18. Providence
19. St. Louis
20. Dayton

1961

AP
1. Ohio St.
2. Cincinnati
3. St. Bonaventure
4. Kansas St.
5. North Carolina
6. Bradley
7. Southern California
8. Iowa
9. West Virginia
10. Duke
11. Utah
12. Texas Tech
13. Niagara
14. Memphis
15. Wake Forest
16. St. John's (N.Y.)
17. St. Joseph's
18. Drake
19. Holy Cross
20. Kentucky

UPI
1. Ohio St.
2. Cincinnati
3. St. Bonaventure
4. Kansas St.
5. Southern California
6. North Carolina
7. Bradley
8. St. John's (N.Y.)
9. Duke
10. Wake Forest
11. Iowa
12. West Virginia
13. Utah
14. St. Louis
15. Louisville
16. St. Joseph's
17. Dayton
18. Kentucky
18. Texas Tech
20. Memphis

1962

AP
1. Ohio St.
2. Cincinnati
3. Kentucky
4. Mississippi St.
5. Bradley
6. Kansas St.
7. Utah
8. Bowling Green
9. Colorado
10. Duke
11. Loyola (Ill.)
12. St. John's (N.Y.)
13. Wake Forest
14. Oregon St.
15. West Virginia
16. Arizona St.
17. Duquesne
18. Utah St.
19. UCLA
20. Villanova

UPI
1. Ohio St.
2. Cincinnati
3. Kentucky
4. Mississippi St.
5. Kansas St.
6. Bradley
7. Wake Forest
8. Colorado
9. Bowling Green
10. Utah
11. Oregon St.
12. St. John's (N.Y.)
13. Duke
13. Loyola (Ill.)
15. Arizona St.
16. West Virginia
17. UCLA
18. Duquesne
19. Utah St.
20. Villanova

1963

AP
1. Cincinnati
2. Duke
3. Loyola (Ill.)
4. Arizona St.
5. Wichita St.
6. Mississippi St.
7. Ohio St.
8. Illinois
9. New York U.
10. Colorado

UPI
1. Cincinnati
2. Duke
3. Arizona St.
4. Loyola (Ill.)
5. Illinois
6. Wichita St.
7. Mississippi St.
8. Ohio St.
9. Colorado
10. Stanford
11. New York U.
12. Texas
13. Providence
14. Oregon St.
15. UCLA
15. St. Joseph's
17. West Virginia
18. Bowling Green
19. Kansas St.
19. Seattle

1964

AP
1. UCLA
2. Michigan
3. Duke
4. Kentucky
5. Wichita St.
6. Oregon St.
7. Villanova
8. Loyola (Ill.)
9. DePaul
10. Davidson

UPI
1. UCLA
2. Michigan
3. Kentucky
4. Duke
5. Oregon St.
6. Wichita St.
7. Villanova
8. Loyola (Ill.)
9. UTEP
10. Davidson
11. DePaul
12. Kansas St.
13. Drake
13. San Francisco
15. Utah St.
16. Ohio St.
16. New Mexico
16. Texas A&M
19. Arizona St.
19. Providence

1965

AP
1. Michigan
2. UCLA
3. St. Joseph's
4. Providence
5. Vanderbilt
6. Davidson
7. Minnesota
8. Villanova
9. Brigham Young
10. Duke

UPI
1. Michigan
2. UCLA
3. St. Joseph's
4. Providence
5. Vanderbilt
6. Brigham Young
7. Davidson
8. Minnesota
9. Duke
10. San Francisco
11. Villanova
12. North Carolina St.
13. Oklahoma St.
14. Wichita St.
15. Connecticut
16. Illinois
17. Tennessee
18. Indiana
19. Miami (Fla.)
20. Dayton

1966

AP
1. Kentucky
2. Duke
3. UTEP
4. Kansas
5. St. Joseph's
6. Loyola (Ill.)
7. Cincinnati
8. Vanderbilt
9. Michigan
10. Western Ky.

UPI
1. Kentucky
2. Duke
3. UTEP
4. Kansas
5. Loyola (Ill.)
6. St. Joseph's
7. Michigan
8. Vanderbilt
9. Cincinnati
10. Providence
11. Nebraska
12. Utah
13. Oklahoma City
14. Houston
15. Oregon St.
16. Syracuse
17. Pacific (Cal.)
18. Davidson
19. Brigham Young
19. Dayton

1967

AP
1. UCLA
2. Louisville
3. Kansas
4. North Carolina
5. Princeton
6. Western Ky.
7. Houston
8. Tennessee
9. Boston College
10. UTEP

UPI
1. UCLA
2. Louisville
3. North Carolina
4. Kansas
5. Princeton
6. Houston
7. Western Ky.
8. UTEP
9. Tennessee
10. Boston College
11. Toledo
12. St. John's (N.Y.)
13. Tulsa
14. Vanderbilt
14. Utah St.
16. Pacific (Cal.)
17. Providence
18. New Mexico
19. Duke
20. Florida

1968

AP
1. Houston
2. UCLA
3. St. Bonaventure
4. North Carolina
5. Kentucky
6. New Mexico
7. Columbia
8. Davidson
9. Louisville
10. Duke

UPI
1. Houston
2. UCLA
3. St. Bonaventure
4. North Carolina
5. Kentucky
6. Columbia
7. New Mexico
8. Louisville
9. Davidson
10. Marquette
11. Duke
12. New Mexico St.
13. Vanderbilt
14. Kansas St.
15. Princeton
16. Army
17. Santa Clara
18. Utah
19. Bradley
20. Iowa

1969

AP
1. UCLA
2. La Salle
3. Santa Clara
4. North Carolina
5. Davidson
6. Purdue
7. Kentucky
8. St. John's (N.Y.)
9. Duquesne
10. Villanova
11. Drake
12. New Mexico St.
13. South Carolina
14. Marquette
15. Louisville
16. Boston College
17. Notre Dame
18. Colorado
19. Kansas
20. Illinois

UPI
1. UCLA
2. North Carolina
3. Davidson
4. Santa Clara
5. Kentucky
6. La Salle
7. Purdue
8. St. John's (N.Y.)
9. New Mexico St.
10. Duquesne
11. Drake
12. Colorado
13. Louisville
14. Marquette
15. Villanova
15. Boston College
17. Weber St.
18. Wyoming
19. Colorado St.
20. South Carolina
20. Kansas

1970

AP
1. Kentucky
2. UCLA
3. St. Bonaventure
4. Jacksonville
5. New Mexico St.
6. South Carolina
7. Iowa
8. Marquette
9. Notre Dame
10. North Carolina St.
11. Florida St.
12. Houston
13. Pennsylvania
14. Drake
15. Davidson
16. Utah St.
17. Niagara
18. Western Ky.
19. Long Beach St.
20. Southern California

UPI
1. Kentucky
2. UCLA
3. St. Bonaventure
4. New Mexico St.
5. Jacksonville
6. South Carolina
7. Iowa
8. Notre Dame
9. Drake
10. Marquette
11. Houston
12. North Carolina St.
13. Pennsylvania
14. Florida St.
15. Villanova
15. Long Beach St.
17. Western Ky.
17. Utah St.
17. Niagara
20. Cincinnati
20. UTEP

1971

AP
1. UCLA
2. Marquette
3. Pennsylvania
4. Kansas
5. Southern California
6. South Carolina
7. Western Ky.
8. Kentucky
9. Fordham
10. Ohio St.
11. Jacksonville
12. Notre Dame
13. North Carolina
14. Houston
15. Duquesne
16. Long Beach St.
17. Tennessee
18. Villanova
19. Drake
20. Brigham Young

UPI
1. UCLA
2. Marquette
3. Pennsylvania
4. Kansas
5. Southern California
6. South Carolina
7. Western Ky.
8. Kentucky
9. Fordham
10. Ohio St.
11. Jacksonville
11. Brigham Young
13. North Carolina
14. Notre Dame
14. Long Beach St.
16. Drake
17. Villanova
18. Duquesne
18. Houston
20. Weber St.

1972

AP
1. UCLA
2. North Carolina
3. Pennsylvania
4. Louisville
5. Long Beach St.
6. South Carolina
7. Marquette
8. La.-Lafayette
9. Brigham Young
10. Florida St.
11. Minnesota
12. Marshall
13. Memphis
14. Maryland
15. Villanova
16. Oral Roberts
17. Indiana
18. Kentucky
19. Ohio St.
20. Virginia

UPI
1. UCLA
2. North Carolina
3. Pennsylvania
4. Louisville
5. South Carolina
6. Long Beach St.
7. Marquette
8. La.-Lafayette
9. Brigham Young
10. Florida St.
11. Maryland
12. Minnesota
13. Memphis
14. Kentucky
15. Villanova
16. Kansas St.
17. UTEP
18. Marshall
19. Missouri
19. Weber St.

1973

AP
1. UCLA
2. North Carolina St.
3. Long Beach St.
4. Providence
5. Marquette
6. Indiana
7. La.-Lafayette
8. Maryland
9. Kansas St.
10. Minnesota
11. North Carolina
12. Memphis
13. Houston
14. Syracuse
15. Missouri
16. Arizona St.
17. Kentucky
18. Pennsylvania
19. Austin Peay
20. San Francisco

UPI
1. UCLA
2. North Carolina St.
3. Long Beach St.
4. Marquette
5. Providence
6. Indiana
7. La.-Lafayette
7. Kansas St.
9. Minnesota
10. Maryland
11. Memphis
12. North Carolina
13. Arizona St.
14. Syracuse
15. Kentucky
16. South Carolina
17. Missouri
18. Weber St.
18. Houston
20. Pennsylvania

1974

AP
1. North Carolina St.
2. UCLA
3. Marquette
4. Maryland
5. Notre Dame
6. Michigan
7. Kansas
8. Providence
9. Indiana
10. Long Beach St.
11. Purdue
12. North Carolina
13. Vanderbilt
14. Alabama
15. Utah
16. Pittsburgh
17. Southern California
18. Oral Roberts
19. South Carolina
20. Dayton

UPI
1. North Carolina St.
2. UCLA
3. Notre Dame
4. Maryland
5. Marquette
6. Providence
7. Vanderbilt
8. North Carolina
9. Indiana
10. Kansas
11. Long Beach St.
12. Michigan
13. Southern California
14. Pittsburgh
15. Louisville
16. South Carolina
17. Creighton
18. New Mexico
19. Alabama
19. Dayton

1975

AP
1. UCLA
2. Kentucky
3. Indiana
4. Louisville
5. Maryland
6. Syracuse
7. North Carolina St.
8. Arizona St.
9. North Carolina
10. Alabama
11. Marquette
12. Princeton
13. Cincinnati
14. Notre Dame
15. Kansas St.
16. Drake
17. UNLV
18. Oregon St.
19. Michigan
20. Pennsylvania

UPI
1. Indiana
2. UCLA
3. Louisville
4. Kentucky
5. Maryland
6. Marquette
7. Arizona St.
8. Alabama
9. North Carolina St.
10. North Carolina
11. Pennsylvania
12. Southern California
13. Utah St.
14. UNLV
14. Notre Dame
16. Creighton
17. Arizona
18. New Mexico St.
19. Clemson
20. UTEP

1976

AP
1. Indiana
2. Marquette
3. UNLV
4. Rutgers
5. UCLA
6. Alabama
7. Notre Dame
8. North Carolina
9. Michigan
10. Western Mich.
11. Maryland
12. Cincinnati
13. Tennessee
14. Missouri
15. Arizona
16. Texas Tech
17. DePaul
18. Virginia
19. Centenary (La.)
20. Pepperdine

UPI
1. Indiana
2. Marquette
3. Rutgers
4. UNLV
5. UCLA
6. North Carolina
7. Alabama
8. Notre Dame
9. Michigan
10. Washington
11. Missouri
12. Arizona
13. Maryland
14. Tennessee
15. Virginia
16. Cincinnati
17. Florida St.
18. St. John's (N.Y.)
19. Western Mich.
19. Princeton

1977

AP
1. Michigan
2. UCLA
3. Kentucky
4. UNLV
5. North Carolina
6. Syracuse
7. Marquette
8. San Francisco
9. Wake Forest
10. Notre Dame
11. Alabama
12. Detroit
13. Minnesota
14. Utah
15. Tennessee
16. Kansas St.
17. Charlotte
18. Arkansas
19. Louisville
20. VMI

UPI
1. Michigan
2. San Francisco
3. North Carolina
4. UCLA
5. Kentucky
6. UNLV
7. Arkansas
8. Tennessee
9. Syracuse
10. Utah
11. Kansas St.
12. Cincinnati
13. Louisville
14. Marquette
15. Providence
16. Indiana St.
17. Minnesota
18. Alabama
19. Detroit
20. Purdue

1978

AP
1. Kentucky
2. UCLA
3. DePaul
4. Michigan St.
5. Arkansas
6. Notre Dame
7. Duke
8. Marquette
9. Louisville
10. Kansas
11. San Francisco
12. New Mexico
13. Indiana
14. Utah
15. Florida St.
16. North Carolina
17. Texas
18. Detroit
19. Miami (Ohio)
20. Pennsylvania

UPI
1. Kentucky
2. UCLA
3. Marquette
4. New Mexico
5. Michigan St.
6. Arkansas
7. DePaul
8. Kansas
9. Duke
10. North Carolina
11. Notre Dame
12. Florida St.
13. San Francisco
14. Louisville
15. Indiana
16. Houston
17. Utah St.
18. Utah
19. Texas
20. Georgetown

1979

AP
1. Indiana St.
2. UCLA
3. Michigan St.
4. Notre Dame
5. Arkansas
6. DePaul
7. LSU
8. Syracuse
9. North Carolina
10. Marquette
11. Duke
12. San Francisco
13. Louisville
14. Pennsylvania
15. Purdue
16. Oklahoma
17. St. John's (N.Y.)
18. Rutgers
19. Toledo
20. Iowa

UPI
1. Indiana St.
2. UCLA
3. North Carolina
4. Michigan St.
5. Notre Dame
6. Arkansas
7. Duke
8. DePaul
9. LSU
10. Syracuse
11. Iowa
12. Georgetown
13. Marquette
14. Purdue
15. Texas
16. Temple
17. San Francisco
18. Tennessee
19. Louisville
20. Detroit

1980

AP
1. DePaul
2. Louisville
3. LSU
4. Kentucky
5. Oregon St.
6. Syracuse
7. Indiana
8. Maryland
9. Notre Dame
10. Ohio St.
11. Georgetown
12. Brigham Young
13. St. John's (N.Y.)
14. Duke
15. North Carolina
16. Missouri
17. Weber St.
18. Arizona St.
19. Iona
20. Purdue

UPI
1. DePaul
2. LSU
3. Kentucky
4. Louisville
5. Oregon St.
6. Syracuse
7. Indiana
8. Maryland
9. Ohio St.
10. Georgetown
11. Notre Dame
12. Brigham Young
13. St. John's (N.Y.)
14. Missouri
15. North Carolina
16. Duke
17. Weber St.
18. Texas A&M
19. Arizona St.
20. Kansas St.

1981

AP
1. DePaul
2. Oregon St.
3. Arizona St.
4. LSU
5. Virginia
6. North Carolina
7. Notre Dame
8. Kentucky
9. Indiana
10. UCLA
11. Wake Forest
12. Louisville
13. Iowa
14. Utah
15. Tennessee
16. Brigham Young
17. Wyoming
18. Maryland
19. Illinois
20. Arkansas

UPI
1. DePaul
2. Oregon St.
3. Virginia
4. LSU
5. Arizona St.
6. North Carolina
7. Indiana
8. Kentucky
9. Notre Dame
10. Utah
11. UCLA
12. Iowa
13. Louisville
14. Wake Forest
15. Tennessee
16. Wyoming
17. Brigham Young
18. Illinois
19. Kansas
20. Maryland

1982

AP
1. North Carolina
2. DePaul
3. Virginia
4. Oregon St.
5. Missouri
6. Georgetown
7. Minnesota
8. Idaho
9. Memphis
10. Tulsa
11. Fresno St.
12. Arkansas
13. Alabama
14. West Virginia
15. Kentucky
16. Iowa
17. UAB
18. Wake Forest
19. UCLA
20. Louisville

UPI
1. North Carolina
2. DePaul
3. Virginia
4. Oregon St.
5. Missouri
6. Minnesota
7. Georgetown
8. Idaho
9. Memphis
10. Fresno St.
11. Tulsa
12. Alabama
13. Arkansas
14. Kentucky
15. Wyoming
16. Iowa
17. West Virginia
18. Kansas St.
19. Wake Forest
20. Louisville

1983

AP
1. Houston
2. Louisville
3. St. John's (N.Y.)
4. Virginia
5. Indiana
6. UNLV
7. UCLA
8. North Carolina
9. Arkansas
10. Missouri
11. Boston College
12. Kentucky
13. Villanova
14. Wichita St.
15. Chattanooga
16. North Carolina St.
17. Memphis
18. Georgia
19. Oklahoma St.
20. Georgetown

UPI
1. Houston
2. Louisville
3. St. John's (N.Y.)
4. Virginia
5. Indiana
6. UNLV
7. UCLA
8. North Carolina
9. Arkansas
10. Kentucky
11. Villanova
12. Missouri
13. Boston College
14. North Carolina St.
15. Georgia
16. Chattanooga
17. Memphis
18. Illinois St.
19. Oklahoma St.
20. Georgetown

1984

AP
1. North Carolina
2. Georgetown
3. Kentucky
4. DePaul
5. Houston
6. Illinois
7. Oklahoma
8. Arkansas
9. UTEP
10. Purdue
11. Maryland
12. Tulsa
13. UNLV
14. Duke
15. Washington
16. Memphis
17. Oregon St.
18. Syracuse
19. Wake Forest
20. Temple

UPI
1. North Carolina
2. Georgetown
3. Kentucky
4. DePaul
5. Houston
6. Illinois
7. Arkansas
8. Oklahoma
9. UTEP
10. Maryland
11. Purdue
12. Tulsa
13. UNLV
14. Duke
15. Washington
16. Memphis
17. Syracuse
18. Indiana
19. Auburn
20. Oregon St.

1985

AP
1. Georgetown
2. Michigan
3. St. John's (N.Y.)
4. Oklahoma
5. Memphis
6. Georgia Tech
7. North Carolina
8. Louisiana Tech
9. UNLV
10. Duke
11. Va. Commonwealth
12. Illinois
13. Kansas
14. Loyola (Ill.)
15. Syracuse
16. North Carolina St.
17. Texas Tech
18. Tulsa
19. Georgia
20. LSU

UPI
1. Georgetown
2. Michigan
3. St. John's (N.Y.)
4. Memphis
5. Oklahoma
6. Georgia Tech
7. North Carolina
8. Louisiana Tech
9. UNLV
10. Illinois
11. Va. Commonwealth
12. Duke
13. Kansas
14. Tulsa
15. Syracuse
16. Texas Tech
17. Loyola (Ill.)
18. North Carolina St.
19. LSU
20. Michigan St.

1986

AP
1. Duke
2. Kansas
3. Kentucky
4. St. John's (N.Y.)
5. Michigan
6. Georgia Tech
7. Louisville
8. North Carolina
9. Syracuse
10. Notre Dame
11. UNLV
12. Memphis
13. Georgetown
14. Bradley
15. Oklahoma
16. Indiana
17. Navy
18. Michigan St.
19. Illinois
20. UTEP

UPI
1. Duke
2. Kansas
3. St. John's (N.Y.)
4. Kentucky
5. Michigan
6. Georgia Tech
7. Louisville
8. North Carolina
9. Syracuse
10. UNLV
11. Notre Dame
12. Memphis
13. Bradley
14. Indiana
15. Georgetown
16. UTEP
17. Oklahoma
18. Michigan St.
19. Alabama
20. Illinois

1987

AP
1. UNLV
2. North Carolina
3. Indiana
4. Georgetown
5. DePaul
6. Iowa
7. Purdue
8. Temple
9. Alabama
10. Syracuse
11. Illinois
12. Pittsburgh
13. Clemson
14. Missouri
15. UCLA
16. New Orleans
17. Duke
18. Notre Dame
19. TCU
20. Kansas

UPI
1. UNLV
2. Indiana
3. North Carolina
4. Georgetown
5. DePaul
6. Purdue
7. Iowa
8. Temple
9. Alabama
10. Syracuse
11. Illinois
12. Pittsburgh
13. UCLA
14. Missouri
15. Clemson
16. TCU
17. Wyoming
18. Notre Dame
19. New Orleans
19. Oklahoma
19. UTEP

1988

AP
1. Temple
2. Arizona
3. Purdue
4. Oklahoma
5. Duke
6. Kentucky
7. North Carolina
8. Pittsburgh
9. Syracuse
10. Michigan
11. Bradley
12. UNLV
13. Wyoming
14. North Carolina St.
15. Loyola Marymount
16. Illinois
17. Iowa
18. Xavier
19. Brigham Young
20. Kansas St.

UPI
1. Temple
2. Arizona
3. Purdue
4. Oklahoma
5. Duke
6. Kentucky
7. Pittsburgh
8. North Carolina
9. Syracuse
10. Michigan
11. UNLV
12. Bradley
13. North Carolina St.
14. Wyoming
15. Illinois
16. Loyola Marymount
17. Brigham Young
18. Iowa
19. Indiana
20. Kansas St.

1989

AP
1. Arizona
2. Georgetown
3. Illinois
4. Oklahoma
5. North Carolina
6. Missouri
7. Syracuse
8. Indiana
9. Duke
10. Michigan
11. Seton Hall
12. Louisville
13. Stanford
14. Iowa
15. UNLV
16. Florida St.
17. West Virginia
18. Ball St.
19. North Carolina St.
20. Alabama

UPI
1. Arizona
2. Georgetown
3. Illinois
4. North Carolina
5. Oklahoma
6. Indiana
7. Duke
8. Missouri
9. Syracuse
10. Michigan
11. Seton Hall
12. Stanford
13. Louisville
14. UNLV
15. Iowa
16. Florida St.
17. Arkansas
18. North Carolina St.
19. West Virginia
20. Alabama

1990

AP
1. Oklahoma
2. UNLV
3. Connecticut
4. Michigan St.
5. Kansas
6. Syracuse
7. Arkansas
8. Georgetown
9. Georgia Tech
10. Purdue
11. Missouri
12. La Salle
13. Michigan
14. Arizona
15. Duke
16. Louisville
17. Clemson
18. Illinois
19. LSU
20. Minnesota
21. Loyola Marymount
22. Oregon St.
23. Alabama
24. New Mexico St.
25. Xavier

UPI
1. Oklahoma
2. UNLV
3. Connecticut
4. Michigan St.
5. Kansas
6. Syracuse
7. Georgia Tech
8. Arkansas
9. Georgetown
10. Purdue
11. Missouri
12. Arizona
13. La Salle
14. Duke
15. Michigan
16. Louisville
17. Clemson
18. Illinois
19. Alabama
20. New Mexico St.

1991

AP
1. UNLV
2. Arkansas
3. Indiana
4. North Carolina
5. Ohio St.
6. Duke
7. Syracuse
8. Arizona
9. Kentucky
10. Utah
11. Nebraska
12. Kansas
13. Seton Hall
14. Oklahoma St.
15. New Mexico St.
16. UCLA
17. East Tenn. St.
18. Princeton
19. Alabama
20. St. John's (N.Y.)
21. Mississippi St.
22. LSU
23. Texas
24. DePaul
25. Southern Miss.

UPI
1. UNLV
2. Arkansas
3. Indiana
4. North Carolina
5. Ohio St.
6. Duke
7. Arizona
8. Syracuse
9. Nebraska
10. Utah
11. Seton Hall

12. Kansas
13. Oklahoma St.
14. UCLA
15. East Tenn. St.
16. Alabama
17. New Mexico St.
18. Mississippi St.
19. St. John's (N.Y.)
20. Princeton
21. LSU
22. Michigan St.
23. Georgetown
24. North Carolina St.
25. Texas

1992
AP
1. Duke
2. Kansas
3. Ohio St.
4. UCLA
5. Indiana
6. Kentucky
7. UNLV
8. Southern California
9. Arkansas
10. Arizona
11. Oklahoma St.
12. Cincinnati
13. Alabama
14. Michigan St.
15. Michigan
16. Missouri
17. Massachusetts
18. North Carolina
19. Seton Hall
20. Florida St.
21. Syracuse
22. Georgetown
23. Oklahoma
24. DePaul
25. LSU

UPI
1. Duke
2. Kansas
3. UCLA
4. Ohio St.
5. Arizona
6. Indiana
7. Southern California
8. Arkansas
9. Kentucky
10. Oklahoma St.
11. Michigan St.
12. Missouri
13. Alabama
14. Cincinnati
15. North Carolina
16. Florida St.
17. Michigan
18. Seton Hall
19. Georgetown
20. Syracuse
21. Massachusetts
22. Oklahoma
23. DePaul
24. St. John's (N.Y.)
25. Tulane

1993
AP
1. Indiana
2. Kentucky
3. Michigan
4. North Carolina
5. Arizona
6. Seton Hall
7. Cincinnati
8. Vanderbilt
9. Kansas
10. Duke
11. Florida St.
12. Arkansas
13. Iowa

14. Massachusetts
15. Louisville
16. Wake Forest
17. New Orleans
18. Georgia Tech
19. Utah
20. Western Ky.
21. New Mexico
22. Purdue
23. Oklahoma St.
24. New Mexico St.
25. UNLV

USA TODAY/CNN
1. Indiana
2. North Carolina
3. Kentucky
4. Michigan
5. Arizona
6. Seton Hall
7. Cincinnati
8. Kansas
9. Vanderbilt
10. Duke
11. Florida St.
12. Arkansas
13. Iowa
14. Louisville
15. Wake Forest
16. Utah
17. Massachusetts
18. New Orleans
19. UNLV
20. Georgia Tech
21. Purdue
22. Virginia
23. Oklahoma St.
24. New Mexico St.
25. Western Ky.

1994
AP
1. North Carolina
2. Arkansas
3. Purdue
4. Connecticut
5. Missouri
6. Duke
7. Kentucky
8. Massachusetts
9. Arizona
10. Louisville
11. Michigan
12. Temple
13. Kansas
14. Florida
15. Syracuse
16. California
17. UCLA
18. Indiana
19. Oklahoma St.
20. Texas
21. Marquette
22. Nebraska
23. Minnesota
24. St. Louis
25. Cincinnati

USA TODAY/CNN
1. Arkansas
2. North Carolina
3. Connecticut
4. Purdue
5. Missouri
6. Duke
7. Massachusetts
8. Kentucky
9. Louisville
10. Arizona
11. Michigan
12. Temple
13. Kansas
14. Syracuse
15. Florida
16. UCLA
17. California

18. Indiana
19. Oklahoma St.
20. Minnesota
21. St. Louis
22. Marquette
23. UAB
24. Texas
25. Cincinnati

1995
AP
1. UCLA
2. Kentucky
3. Wake Forest
4. North Carolina
5. Kansas
6. Arkansas
7. Massachusetts
8. Connecticut
9. Villanova
10. Maryland
11. Michigan St.
12. Purdue
13. Virginia
14. Oklahoma St.
15. Arizona
16. Arizona St.
17. Oklahoma
18. Mississippi St.
19. Utah
20. Alabama
21. Western Ky.
22. Georgetown
23. Missouri
24. Iowa St.
25. Syracuse

USA TODAY/NABC
1. UCLA
2. Kentucky
3. Wake Forest
4. Kansas
5. North Carolina
6. Arkansas
7. Massachusetts
8. Connecticut
9. Michigan St.
10. Maryland
11. Purdue
12. Villanova
13. Arizona
14. Oklahoma St.
15. Virginia
16. Arizona St.
17. Utah
18. Iowa St.
19. Mississippi St.
20. Oklahoma
21. Alabama
22. Syracuse
23. Missouri
24. Oregon
25. Stanford

1996
AP
1. Massachusetts
2. Kentucky
3. Connecticut
4. Georgetown
5. Kansas
6. Purdue
7. Cincinnati
8. Texas Tech
9. Wake Forest
10. Villanova
11. Arizona
12. Utah
13. Georgia Tech
14. UCLA
15. Syracuse
16. Memphis
17. Iowa St.
18. Penn St.
19. Mississippi St.

20. Marquette
21. Iowa
22. Virginia Tech
23. New Mexico
24. Louisville
25. North Carolina

USA TODAY/NABC
1. Massachusetts
2. Kentucky
3. Connecticut
4. Purdue
5. Georgetown
6. Cincinnati
7. Texas Tech
8. Kansas
9. Wake Forest
10. Utah
11. Arizona
12. Villanova
13. UCLA
14. Syracuse
15. Georgia Tech
16. Iowa St.
17. Memphis
18. Penn St.
19. Iowa
20. Mississippi St.
21. Virginia Tech
22. Marquette
23. Louisville
24. North Carolina
25. Stanford

1997
AP
1. Kansas
2. Utah
3. Minnesota
4. North Carolina
5. Kentucky
6. South Carolina
7. UCLA
8. Duke
9. Wake Forest
10. Cincinnati
11. New Mexico
12. St. Joseph's
13. Xavier
14. Clemson
15. Arizona
16. Col. of Charleston
17. Georgia
18. Iowa St.
19. Illinois
20. Villanova
21. Stanford
22. Maryland
23. Boston College
24. Colorado
25. Louisville

USA TODAY/NABC
1. Kansas
2. Utah
3. Minnesota
4. Kentucky
5. North Carolina
6. South Carolina
7. UCLA
8. Duke
9. Wake Forest
10. Cincinnati
11. New Mexico
12. Clemson
13. Arizona
14. Xavier
15. St. Joseph's
16. Villanova
17. Iowa St.
18. Col. of Charleston
19. Maryland
20. Boston College
21. Stanford
22. Georgia
23. Colorado

20. Marquette
21. Iowa
22. Virginia Tech
23. New Mexico
24. Louisville
25. North Carolina

1998
AP
1. North Carolina
2. Kansas
3. Duke
4. Arizona
5. Kentucky
6. Connecticut
7. Utah
8. Princeton
9. Cincinnati
10. Stanford
11. Purdue
12. Michigan
13. Mississippi
14. South Carolina
15. TCU
16. Michigan St.
17. Arkansas
18. New Mexico
19. UCLA
20. Maryland
21. Syracuse
22. Illinois
23. Xavier
24. Temple
25. Murray St.

USA TODAY/NABC
1. North Carolina
2. Kansas
3. Duke
4. Arizona
5. Connecticut
6. Kentucky
7. Utah
8. Princeton
9. Purdue
10. Stanford
11. Cincinnati
12. Michigan
13. South Carolina
14. Mississippi
15. Michigan St.
16. TCU
17. Arkansas
18. New Mexico
19. Syracuse
20. UCLA
21. Xavier
22. Maryland
23. Illinois
24. Temple
25. Oklahoma

1999
AP
1. Duke
2. Michigan St.
3. Connecticut
4. Auburn
5. Maryland
6. Utah
7. Stanford
8. Kentucky
9. St. John's (N.Y.)
10. Miami (Fla.)
11. Cincinnati
12. Arizona
13. North Carolina
14. Ohio St.
15. UCLA
16. Col. of Charleston
17. Arkansas
18. Wisconson
19. Indiana
20. Texas
21. Iowa
22. Kansas
23. Florida
24. Charlotte
25. New Mexico

24. Illinois
25. Louisville

USA TODAY/NABC
1. North Carolina
2. Kansas
3. Duke
4. Arizona
5. Kentucky
6. Connecticut
7. Utah
8. Princeton
9. Cincinnati
10. Stanford
11. Cincinnati
12. Michigan
13. South Carolina
14. Mississippi
15. Michigan St.
16. TCU
17. Arkansas
18. New Mexico
19. Syracuse
20. UCLA
21. Xavier
22. Maryland
23. Illinois
24. Temple
25. Oklahoma

2000
AP
1. Duke
2. Michigan St.
3. Stanford
4. Arizona
5. Temple
6. Iowa St.
7. Cincinnati
8. Ohio St.
9. St. John's (N.Y.)
10. LSU
11. Tennessee
12. Oklahoma
13. Florida
14. Oklahoma St.
15. Texas
16. Syracuse
17. Maryland
18. Tulsa
19. Kentucky
20. Connecticut
21. Illinois
22. Indiana
23. Miami (Fla.)
24. Auburn
25. Purdue

USA TODAY/NABC
1. Duke
2. Michigan St.
3. Stanford
4. Arizona
5. Temple
6. Cincinnati
7. Iowa St.
8. Ohio St.
9. LSU
10. Tennessee
11. Florida
12. St. John's (N.Y.)
13. Oklahoma
14. Syracuse
15. Oklahoma St.
16. Maryland
17. Indiana
18. Texas
19. Tulsa
20. Kentucky
21. Connecticut
22. Auburn
23. Illinois
24. Purdue
25. Miami (Fla.)

2001

AP
1. Duke
2. Stanford
3. Michigan St.
4. Illinois
5. Arizona
6. North Carolina
7. Boston College
8. Florida
9. Kentucky
10. Iowa St.
11. Maryland
12. Kansas
13. Oklahoma
14. Mississippi
15. UCLA
16. Virginia
17. Syracuse
18. Texas
19. Notre Dame
20. Indiana
21. Georgetown
22. St. Joseph's
23. Wake Forest
24. Iowa
25. Wisconsin

USA TODAY/NABC
1. Duke
2. Stanford
3. Michigan St.
4. Arizona
5. North Carolina
6. Illinois
7. Boston College
8. Florida
9. Iowa St.
10. Kentucky
11. Maryland
12. Kansas
13. Mississippi
14. Oklahoma
15. Virginia
16. Syracuse
17. Texas
18. UCLA
19. Notre Dame
20. Georgetown
21. Indiana
22. Wake Forest
23. St. Joseph's
24. Wisconsin
25. Iowa

2002

AP
1. Duke
2. Kansas
3. Oklahoma
4. Maryland
5. Cincinnati
6. Gonzaga
7. Arizona
8. Alabama
9. Pittsburgh
10. Connecticut
11. Oregon
12. Marquette
13. Illinois
14. Ohio St.
15. Florida
16. Kentucky
17. Mississippi St.
18. Southern California
19. Western Ky.
20. Oklahoma St.
21. Miami (Fla.)
22. Xavier
23. Georgia
24. Stanford
25. Hawaii

USA TODAY/ESPN
1. Duke
2. Kansas
3. Oklahoma
4. Maryland
5. Cincinnati
6. Gonzaga
7. Pittsburgh
8. Alabama
9. Arizona
10. Marquette
11. Oregon
12. Ohio St.
13. Connecticut
14. Florida
15. Kentucky
16. Illinois
17. Southern California
18. Mississippi St.
19. Xavier
20. Western Ky.
21. Miami (Fla.)
22. Oklahoma St.
23. Stanford
24. Hawaii
25. North Carolina St.

2003

AP
1. Kentucky
2. Arizona
3. Oklahoma
4. Pittsburgh
5. Texas
6. Kansas
7. Duke
8. Wake Forest
9. Marquette
10. Florida
11. Illinois
12. Xavier
13. Syracuse
14. Louisville
15. Creighton
16. Dayton
17. Maryland
18. Stanford
19. Memphis
20. Mississippi St.
21. Wisconsin
22. Notre Dame
23. Connecticut
24. Missouri
25. Georgia

USA TODAY/ESPN
1. Kentucky
2. Arizona
3. Oklahoma
4. Pittsburgh
5. Texas
6. Kansas
7. Duke
8. Florida
9. Wake Forest
10. Illinois
11. Marquette
12. Syracuse
13. Louisville
14. Xavier
15. Creighton
16. Stanford
17. Maryland
18. Dayton
19. Wisconsin
20. Notre Dame
21. Mississippi St.
22. Memphis
23. Oklahoma St.
24. Connecticut
25. Missouri

Final Post-Tournament Polls

1994

USA TODAY/CNN
1. Arkansas
2. Duke
3. Arizona
4. Florida
5. Purdue
6. Missouri
7. Connecticut
8. Michigan
9. North Carolina
10. Louisville
11. Boston College
12. Kansas
13. Kentucky
14. Syracuse
15. Massachusetts
16. Indiana
17. Marquette
18. Temple
19. Tulsa
20. Maryland
21. Oklahoma St.
22. UCLA
23. Minnesota
24. Texas
25. Pennsylvania

1995

USA TODAY/NABC
1. UCLA
2. Arkansas
3. North Carolina
4. Oklahoma St.
5. Kentucky
6. Connecticut
7. Massachusetts
8. Virginia
9. Wake Forest
10. Kansas
11. Maryland
12. Mississippi St.
13. Arizona St.
14. Memphis
15. Tulsa
16. Georgetown
17. Syracuse
18. Missouri
19. Purdue
20. Michigan St.
21. Alabama

22. Utah
23. Villanova
24. Texas
25. Arizona

1996

USA TODAY/NABC
1. Kentucky
2. Massachusetts
3. Syracuse
4. Mississippi St.
5. Kansas
6. Cincinnati
7. Georgetown
8. Connecticut
9. Wake Forest
10. Texas Tech
11. Arizona
12. Utah
13. Georgia Tech
14. Louisville
15. Purdue
16. Georgia
17. Villanova
18. Arkansas
19. UCLA
20. Iowa St.
21. Virginia Tech
22. Iowa
23. Marquette
24. North Carolina
25. New Mexico

1997

USA TODAY/NABC
1. Arizona
2. Kentucky
3. Minnesota
4. North Carolina
5. Kansas
6. Utah
7. UCLA
8. Clemson
9. Wake Forest
10. Louisville
11. Duke
12. Stanford
13. Iowa St.
14. South Carolina
15. Providence
16. Cincinnati

17. St. Joseph's
18. California
19. New Mexico
20. Texas
21. Col. of Charleston
22. Xavier
23. Boston College
24. Michigan
25. Colorado

1998

USA TODAY/NABC
1. Kentucky
2. Utah
3. North Carolina
4. Stanford
5. Duke
6. Arizona
7. Connecticut
8. Kansas
9. Purdue
10. Michigan St.
11. Rhode Island
12. UCLA
13. Syracuse
14. Cincinnati
15. Maryland
16. Princeton
17. Michigan
18. West Virginia
19. South Carolina
20. Mississippi
21. New Mexico
22. Arkansas
23. Valparaiso
24. Washington
25. TCU

1999

USA TODAY/NABC
1. Connecticut
2. Duke
3. Michigan St.
4. Ohio St.
5. Kentucky
5. St. John's (N.Y.)
7. Auburn
8. Maryland
9. Stanford
10. Utah
11. Cincinnati
12. Gonzaga
12. Miami (Fla.)
14. Temple
15. Iowa
16. Arizona
17. Florida
18. North Carolina

19. Oklahoma
20. Miami (Ohio)
21. UCLA
22. Purdue
23. Kansas
24. Southwest Mo. St.
25. Arkansas

2000

USA TODAY/NABC
1. Michigan St.
2. Florida
3. Iowa St.
4. Duke
5. Stanford
5. Oklahoma St.
7. Cincinnati
8. Arizona
9. Tulsa
10. Temple
11. North Carolina
12. Syracuse
12. LSU
14. Tennessee
15. Purdue
16. Wisconsin
17. Ohio St.
18. St. John's (N.Y.)
19. Oklahoma
20. Miami (Fla.)
21. Texas
22. Kentucky
23. UCLA
24. Gonzaga
25. Maryland

2001

USA TODAY/NABC
1. Duke
2. Arizona
3. Michigan St.
4. Maryland
5. Stanford
6. Illinois
7. Kansas
8. Kentucky
9. Mississippi
10. North Carolina
11. Boston College
12. UCLA
13. Florida
14. Southern California
15. Iowa St.
16. Temple
17. Georgetown
18. Syracuse
19. Oklahoma
20. Gonzaga

21. Virginia
22. Cincinnati
23. Notre Dame
24. St. Joseph's
25. Penn St.

2002

USA/ESPN
1. Maryland
2. Kansas
3. Indiana
4. Oklahoma
5. Duke
6. Connecticut
7. Oregon
8. Cincinnati
9. Pittsburgh
10. Arizona
11. Illinois
12. Kent St.
13. Kentucky
14. Alabama
15. Missouri
16. Gonzaga
17. Ohio St.
18. Marquette
18. Texas
20. UCLA
21. Mississippi St.
22. Southern Ill.
23. Florida
24. Xavier
25. North Carolina St.

2003

USA/ESPN
1. Syracuse
2. Kansas
3. Texas
4. Kentucky
5. Arizona
6. Marquette
7. Oklahoma
8. Pittsburgh
9. Duke
10. Maryland
11. Connecticut
12. Wake Forest
13. Illinois
13. Wisconsin
15. Notre Dame
16. Florida
17. Xavier
18. Michigan St.
19. Louisville
20. Stanford
21. Butler
22. Missouri

23. Creighton
24. Oklahoma St.
25. Dayton

American Sports Wire Poll

The following poll ranks the top historically black institutions of the NCAA as selected by American Sports Wire and compiled by Dick Simpson.

Year	Team	Coach	Won	Lost
1992	Howard	Butch Beard	17	14
1993	Jackson St.	Andy Stoglin	25	9
1994	Texas Southern	Robert Moreland	19	11
1995	Texas Southern	Robert Moreland	22	7
1996	South Carolina St.	Cy Alexander	22	8
1997	Coppin St.	Fang Mitchell	22	9
1998	South Carolina St.	Cy Alexander	22	8
1999	Alcorn St.	Davey L. Whitney	23	7
2000	South Carolina St.	Cy Alexander	20	14
2001	Hampton	Steve Merfeld	25	7
2002	Hampton	Steve Merfeld	25	7
2003	South Carolina St.	Cy Alexander	20	11

Division II Records

Individual Records

Basketball records are confined to the "modern era," which began with the 1937-38 season, the first without the center jump after each goal scored. Official weekly statistics rankings in scoring and shooting begun with the 1947-48 season. Individual rebounds were added for the 1950-51 season, while team rebounds were added for the 1959-60 season. Assists were added for the 1988-89 season. Blocked shots and steals were added for the 1992-93 season. Scoring and rebounding are ranked on per-game average; shooting, on percentage. Beginning with the 1967-68 season, Division II rankings were limited only to NCAA members. The 1973-74 season was the first under a three-division reorganization plan adopted by the special NCAA Convention of August 1973. In statistical rankings, the rounding of percentages and/or averages may indicate ties where none exist. In these cases, the numerical order of the rankings is accurate.

Scoring

POINTS
Game
113—Clarence "Bevo" Francis, Rio Grande vs. Hillsdale, Feb. 2, 1954
Season
1,329—Earl Monroe, Winston-Salem, 1967 (32 games)
Career
4,045—Travis Grant, Kentucky St., 1969-72 (121 games)

AVERAGE PER GAME
Season
†46.5—Clarence "Bevo" Francis, Rio Grande, 1954 (1,255 in 27)
Career
(Min. 1,400) 33.4—Travis Grant, Kentucky St., 1969-72 (4,045 in 121)

†Season and career figures for Francis limited only to his 39 games (27 in 1954) against four-year colleges.

GAMES SCORING AT LEAST 50 POINTS
Season
†8—Clarence "Bevo" Francis, Rio Grande, 1954
Career
†14—Clarence "Bevo" Francis, Rio Grande, 1953-54

†Season and career figures for Francis limited only to his 39 games (27 in 1954) against four-year colleges.

MOST GAMES SCORING IN DOUBLE FIGURES
Career
130—Lambert Shell, Bridgeport, 1989-92

Field Goals

FIELD GOALS
Game
38—Clarence "Bevo" Francis, Rio Grande vs. Alliance, Jan. 16, 1954 (71 attempts) and vs. Hillsdale, Feb. 2, 1954 (70 attempts)
Season
539—Travis Grant, Kentucky St., 1972 (869 attempts)
Career
1,760—Travis Grant, Kentucky St., 1969-72 (2,759 attempts)

CONSECUTIVE FIELD GOALS
Game
20—Lance Berwald, North Dakota St. vs. Augustana (S.D.), Feb. 17, 1984
Season
28—Don McAllister, Hartwick, 1980 (during six games, Jan. 26-Feb. 9); Lance Berwald, North Dakota St., 1984 (during three games, Feb. 13-18)

FIELD-GOAL ATTEMPTS
Game
71—Clarence "Bevo" Francis, Rio Grande vs. Alliance, Jan. 16, 1954 (38 made)
Season
925—Jim Toombs, Stillman, 1965 (388 made)
Career
3,309—Bob Hopkins, Grambling, 1953-56 (1,403 made)

FIELD-GOAL PERCENTAGE
Game
(Min. 20 made) 100%—Lance Berwald, North Dakota St. vs. Augustana (S.D.), Feb. 17, 1984 (20 of 20)
***Season**
75.2%—Todd Linder, Tampa, 1987 (282 of 375)

*based on qualifiers for annual championship

Career
(Min. 400 made) 70.8%—Todd Linder, Tampa, 1984-87 (909 of 1,284)

Three-Point Field Goals

THREE-POINT FIELD GOALS
Game
16—Markus Hallgrimson, Mont. St.-Billings vs. Western N.M., Feb. 12, 2000 (28 attempts)
Season
167—Alex Williams, Sacramento St., 1988 (369 attempts)
Career
442—Steve Moyer, Gannon, 1996-99 (1,026 attempts)

THREE-POINT FIELD GOALS MADE PER GAME
Season
6.2—Markus Hallgrimson, Mont. St.-Billings, 2000 (160 in 26)
Career
4.7—Antonio Harris, LeMoyne-Owen, 1998-99 (245 in 52)

CONSECUTIVE THREE-POINT FIELD GOALS
Game
10—Duane Huddleston, Mo.-Rolla vs. Truman, Jan. 23, 1988
Season
18—Dan Drews, Le Moyne (during 11 games, Dec. 11, 1993 to Feb. 2, 1994)

CONSECUTIVE GAMES MAKING A THREE-POINT FIELD GOAL
Season
34—Roger Powers, St. Rose, Nov. 8, 1996 to March 8, 1997
Career
93—Daniel Parke, Rollins, Jan. 26, 1994, to Feb. 28, 1997

THREE-POINT FIELD-GOAL ATTEMPTS
Game
34—Markus Hallgrimson, Mont. St.-Billings vs. Western N.M., Feb. 26, 2000 (13 made)
Season
382—Markus Hallgrimson, Mont. St.-Billings, 2000 (160 made)
Career
1,047—Tony Smith, Pfeiffer, 1989-92 (431 made)

THREE-POINT FIELD-GOAL ATTEMPTS PER GAME
Season
14.7—Markus Hallgrimson, Mont. St.-Billings, 2000 (382 in 26)
Career
11.3—Markus Hallgrimson, Mont. St.-Billings, 1997-00 (927 in 82)

THREE-POINT FIELD-GOAL PERCENTAGE
Game
(Min. 9 made) 100%—Steve Divine, Ky. Wesleyan vs. Wayne St. (Mich.), March 14, 1992 (9 of 9)
***Season**
(Min. 35 made) 65.0%—Ray Lee, Hampton, 1988 (39 of 60)

(Min. 50 made) 60.3%—Aaron Fehler, Oakland City, 1995 (73 of 121)
(Min. 100 made) 56.7%—Scott Martin, Rollins, 1991 (114 of 201)
(Min. 150 made) 45.3%—Alex Williams, Sacramento St., 1988 (167 of 369)

*based on qualifiers for annual championship

Career
(Min. 200 made) 51.3%—Scott Martin, Rollins, 1988-91 (236 of 460)

Free Throws

FREE THROWS
Game
37—Clarence "Bevo" Francis, Rio Grande vs. Hillsdale, Feb. 2, 1954 (45 attempts)
Season
401—Joe Miller, Alderson-Broaddus, 1957 (496 attempts)
Career
1,130—Joe Miller, Alderson-Broaddus, 1954-57 (1,460 attempts)

CONSECUTIVE FREE THROWS
Game
23—Carl Hartman, Alderson-Broaddus vs. Salem, Dec. 6, 1954
Season
94—Paul Cluxton, Northern Ky., 1997 (during 34 games, Nov. 8-Mar. 20)

FREE-THROW ATTEMPTS
Game
45—Clarence "Bevo" Francis, Rio Grande vs. Hillsdale, Feb. 2, 1954 (37 made)
Season
†510—Clarence "Bevo" Francis, Rio Grande, 1954 (367 made)
Career
1,460—Joe Miller, Alderson-Broaddus, 1954-57 (1,130 made)

†Season figure for Francis limited to 27 games against four-year colleges.

FREE-THROW PERCENTAGE
Game
(Min. 20 made) 100%—Milosh Pujo, Lewis vs. Mt. St. Clare, Dec. 30, 1997 (20 of 20); Forrest "Butch" Meyeraan, Minn. St. Mankato vs. Wis.-River Falls, Feb. 21, 1961 (20 of 20)
***Season**
100%—Paul Cluxton, Northern Ky., 1997 (94 of 94)

*based on qualifiers for annual championship

Career
(Min. 250 made) 93.5%—Paul Cluxton, Northern Ky., 1994-97 (272 of 291)
(Min. 500 made) 87.9%—Steve Nisenson, Hofstra, 1963-65 (602 of 685)

Rebounds

REBOUNDS
Game
46—Tom Hart, Middlebury vs. Trinity (Conn.), Feb. 5, 1955, and vs. Clarkson, Feb. 12, 1955
Season
799—Elmore Smith, Kentucky St., 1971 (33 games)
Career
2,334—Jim Smith, Steubenville, 1955-58 (112 games)

AVERAGE PER GAME
Season
29.5—Tom Hart, Middlebury, 1956 (620 in 21)
Career
(Min. 900) 27.6—Tom Hart, Middlebury, 1953, 55-56 (1,738 in 63)

Assists

ASSISTS
Game
25—Ali Baaqar, Morris Brown vs. Albany St. (Ga.), Jan. 26, 1991; Adrian Hutt, Metro St. vs. Sacramento St., Feb. 9, 1991
Season
400—Steve Ray, Bridgeport, 1989 (32 games)
Career
1,044—Demetri Beekman, Assumption, 1990-93 (119 games)

AVERAGE PER GAME
Season
12.5—Steve Ray, Bridgeport, 1989 (400 in 32)
Career
(Min. 550) 12.1—Steve Ray, Bridgeport, 1989-90 (785 in 65)

Blocked Shots

BLOCKED SHOTS
Game
15—Mark Hensel, Pitt.-Johnstown vs. Slippery Rock, Jan. 22, 1994
Season
157—James Doyle, Concord, 1998 (30 games)
Career
416—James Doyle, Concord, 1995-98 (120 games)

AVERAGE PER GAME
Season
5.3—Antonio Harvey, Pfeiffer, 1993 (155 in 29)
Career
4.00—Derek Moore, S.C.-Aiken, 1996-99 (408 in 102)

Steals

STEALS
Game
17—Antonio Walls, Alabama A&M vs. Albany St. (Ga.), Jan. 5, 1998

Season
139—J.R. Gamble, Queens (N.C.), 2001 (32 games)
Career
383—Eddin Santiago, Mo. Southern St., 1999-02, (117 games)

AVERAGE PER GAME
Season
5.0—Wayne Copeland, Lynn, 2000 (129 in 26)
Career
4.46—Wayne Copeland, Lynn, 1999-00 (254 in 57)

Games

GAMES PLAYED
Season
37—Michael Alcock, Lee Barlow, John Bynun, Rashawn Fulcher, Kane Oakley, Metro St., 2000; Antonio Garcia, Dana Williams, Patrick Critchelow, Leroy John, Chris Haskin, and Adam Mattingly, Ky. Wesleyan, 1999
Career
133—Gino Bartolone, Ky. Wesleyan, 1998-01; Pat Morris, Bridgeport, 1989-92

DIVISION II

Team Records

Note: Where records involve both teams, each team must be an NCAA Division II member institution.

SINGLE-GAME RECORDS

Scoring

POINTS
258—Troy St. vs. DeVry (Ga.) (141), Jan. 12, 1992
POINTS VS. DIVISION II TEAM
169—Stillman vs. Miles (123), Feb. 17, 1966
POINTS BY LOSING TEAM
146—Mississippi Col. vs. West Ala. (160), Dec. 2, 1969
POINTS, BOTH TEAMS
306—West Ala. (160) and Mississippi Col. (146), Dec. 2, 1969
POINTS IN A HALF
135—Troy St. vs. DeVry (Ga.), Jan. 12, 1992
FEWEST POINTS ALLOWED (Since 1938)
4—Albion (76) vs. Adrian, Dec. 12, 1938; Tennessee St. (7) vs. Oglethorpe, Feb. 16, 1971
FEWEST POINTS, BOTH TEAMS (Since 1938)
11—Tennessee St. (7) and Oglethorpe (4), Feb. 16, 1971
WIDEST MARGIN OF VICTORY
118—Mississippi Col. (168) vs. Dallas Bible (50), Dec. 9, 1971

Field Goals

FIELD GOALS
102—Troy St. vs. DeVry (Ga.), Jan. 12, 1992 (190 attempts)
FIELD-GOAL ATTEMPTS
190—Troy St. vs. DeVry (Ga.), Jan. 12, 1992 (102 made)
FEWEST FIELD GOALS (Since 1938)
0—Adrian vs. Albion, Dec. 12, 1938 (28 attempts)
FEWEST FIELD-GOAL ATTEMPTS
7—Mansfield vs. West Chester, Dec. 8, 1984 (4 made)
FIELD-GOAL PERCENTAGE
81.6%—Youngstown St. vs. Northern Iowa, Jan. 26, 1980 (31 of 38)

FIELD-GOAL PERCENTAGE, HALF
95.0%—Abilene Christian vs. Cameron, Jan. 21, 1989 (19 of 20)

Three-Point Field Goals

THREE-POINT FIELD GOALS
51—Troy St. vs. DeVry (Ga.), Jan. 12, 1992 (109 attempts)
THREE-POINT FIELD GOALS, BOTH TEAMS
39—Columbus St. (22) vs. Troy St. (17), Feb. 14, 1991
CONSECUTIVE THREE-POINT FIELD GOALS MADE WITHOUT A MISS
12—Southwest St. vs. Bemidji St., Jan. 22, 2000; Catawba vs. Wingate, Feb. 28, 1998; Pace vs. Medgar Evers, Nov. 27, 1991
NUMBER OF DIFFERENT PLAYERS TO SCORE A THREE-POINT FIELD GOAL, ONE TEAM
10—Troy St. vs. DeVry (Ga.), Jan. 12, 1992
THREE-POINT FIELD-GOAL ATTEMPTS
109—Troy St. vs. DeVry (Ga.), Jan. 12, 1992 (51 made)
THREE-POINT FIELD-GOAL ATTEMPTS, BOTH TEAMS
95—Columbus St. (52) vs. Troy St. (43), Feb. 14, 1991
THREE-POINT FIELD-GOAL PERCENTAGE
(Min. 10 made) 90.9%—Philadelphia U. vs. Spring Garden, Nov. 24, 1987 (10 of 11); Armstrong Atlantic vs. Columbus St., Feb. 24, 1990 (10 of 11); Norfolk St. vs. Clark Atlanta, Dec. 26, 1992 (10 of 11)
HIGHEST THREE-POINT FIELD-GOAL PERCENTAGE, BOTH TEAMS
(Min. 10 made) 83.3%—Tampa (9 of 10) vs. St. Leo (1 of 2), Jan. 21, 1987 (10 of 12)
(Min. 20 made) 75.9%—Indiana (Pa.) (11 of 15) vs. Cheyney (11 of 14), Jan. 26, 1987 (22 of 29)

Free Throws

FREE THROWS MADE
64—Wayne St. (Mich.) vs. Grand Valley St., Feb. 13, 1993 (79 attempts); Baltimore vs. Washington (Md.), Feb. 9, 1955 (84 attempts)
FREE THROWS MADE, BOTH TEAMS
89—Southern Ind. (50) vs. Northern St. (39), Nov. 15, 1997 (3ot); Baltimore (64) and Washington (Md.) (25), Feb. 9, 1955

CONSECUTIVE FREE THROWS MADE
37—Southern Ind., January 23-30, 2003 (three games)
FREE-THROW ATTEMPTS
84—Baltimore vs. Washington (Md.), Feb. 9, 1955 (64 made)
FREE-THROW ATTEMPTS, BOTH TEAMS
142—Southern Ind. (80) vs. Northern St. (62), Nov. 15, 1997 (3 ot) (89 made)
FREE-THROW PERCENTAGE
(Min. 31 made) 100%—Dowling vs. Southampton, Feb. 6, 1985 (31 of 31)
FREE-THROW PERCENTAGE, BOTH TEAMS
(Min. 30 made) 97.0%—Hartford (17 of 17) vs. Bentley (15 of 16), Feb. 22, 1983 (32 of 33)

Rebounds

REBOUNDS
111—Central Mich. vs. Alma, Dec. 7, 1963
REBOUNDS, BOTH TEAMS
141—Loyola (Md.) (75) vs. McDaniel (66), Dec. 6, 1961; Concordia (Ill.) (72) vs. Concordia (Neb.) (69), Feb. 26, 1965
REBOUND MARGIN
65—Moravian (100) vs. Drew (35), Feb. 18, 1969

Assists

ASSISTS
65—Troy St. vs. DeVry (Ga.), Jan. 12, 1992
ASSISTS, BOTH TEAMS
65—Central Okla. (34) vs. Stonehill (31), Dec. 29, 1990

Personal Fouls

PERSONAL FOULS
51—Northern St. vs. Southern Ind., Nov. 15, 1997 (3 ot)
PERSONAL FOULS, BOTH TEAMS (Including Overtimes)
91—Northern St. (51) vs. Southern Ind. (40), Nov. 15, 1997 (3 ot)
PERSONAL FOULS, BOTH TEAMS (Regulation Time)
74—Bentley (36) vs. Mass.-Boston (38), Jan. 23, 1971

PLAYERS DISQUALIFIED
7—Northern St. vs. Southern Ind., Nov. 15, 1997 (3 ot); Illinois Col. vs. Illinois Tech, Dec. 13, 1952; Steubenville vs. West Liberty, 1952; Washington (Md.) vs. Baltimore, Feb. 9, 1955; Colorado St.-Pueblo vs. Air Force, Jan. 12, 1972; Edinboro vs. Calif. (Pa.) (5 ot), Feb. 4, 1989

PLAYERS DISQUALIFIED, BOTH TEAMS
12—Alfred (6) and Rensselaer (6), Jan. 9, 1971

Overtimes

OVERTIME PERIODS
7—Yankton (79) vs. Black Hills (80), Feb. 18, 1956

POINTS IN ONE OVERTIME PERIOD
27—Southern Ind. vs. Central Mo. St., Jan. 5, 1985

POINTS IN ONE OVERTIME PERIOD, BOTH TEAMS
46—North Dakota St. (25) vs. St. Cloud St. (21), Jan. 16, 1999; North Dakota St. (25) vs. South Dakota (21), Jan. 9, 1999

POINTS IN OVERTIME PERIODS
60—Calif. (Pa.) vs. Edinboro (5 ot), Feb. 4, 1989

POINTS IN OVERTIME PERIODS, BOTH TEAMS
114—Calif. (Pa.) (60) vs. Edinboro (54) (5 ot), Feb. 4, 1989

WINNING MARGIN IN OVERTIME GAME
22—Pfeiffer (72) vs. Belmont Abbey (50), Dec. 8, 1960

SEASON RECORDS

Scoring

POINTS
3,566—Troy St., 1993 (32 games); Central Okla., 1992 (32 games)

AVERAGE PER GAME
121.1—Troy St., 1992 (3,513 in 29)

AVERAGE SCORING MARGIN
31.4—Bryan, 1961 (93.8 offense, 62.4 defense)

GAMES AT LEAST 100 POINTS
25—Troy St., 1993 (32-game season)

CONSECUTIVE GAMES AT LEAST 100 POINTS
17—Norfolk St., 1970

Field Goals

FIELD GOALS
1,455—Kentucky St., 1971 (2,605 attempts)

FIELD GOALS PER GAME
46.9—Lincoln (Mo.), 1967 (1,267 in 27)

FIELD-GOAL ATTEMPTS
2,853—Ark.-Pine Bluff, 1967 (1,306 made)

FIELD-GOAL ATTEMPTS PER GAME
108.2—Stillman, 1968 (2,814 in 26)

FIELD-GOAL PERCENTAGE
62.4%—Kentucky St., 1976 (1,093 of 1,753)

Three-Point Field Goals

THREE-POINT FIELD GOALS
444—Troy St., 1992 (1,303 attempts)

THREE-POINT FIELD GOALS PER GAME
15.3—Troy St., 1992 (444 in 29)

THREE-POINT FIELD-GOAL ATTEMPTS
1,303—Troy St., 1992 (444 made)

THREE-POINT FIELD-GOAL ATTEMPTS PER GAME
44.9—Troy St., 1992 (1,303 in 29)

THREE-POINT FIELD-GOAL PERCENTAGE
(Min. 90 made) 53.8%—Winston-Salem, 1988 (98 of 182)
(Min. 200 made) 50.2%—Oakland City, 1992 (244 of 486)

CONSECUTIVE GAMES SCORING A THREE-POINT FIELD GOAL (Multiple Seasons)
537—Ky. Wesleyan, Nov. 22, 1986-Present

Free Throws

FREE THROWS MADE
896—Ouachita, 1965 (1,226 attempts)

FREE THROWS MADE PER GAME
36.1—Baltimore, 1955 (686 in 19)

FREE-THROW ATTEMPTS
1,226—Ouachita, 1965 (896 made)

FREE-THROW ATTEMPTS PER GAME
49.6—Baltimore, 1955 (943 in 19)

FREE-THROW PERCENTAGE
82.5%—Gannon, 1998 (473 of 573)

Rebounds

REBOUNDS
1,667—Norfolk St., 1973 (31 games)

AVERAGE PER GAME
65.8—Bentley, 1964 (1,513 in 23)

AVERAGE REBOUND MARGIN
24.4—Mississippi Val., 1976 (63.9 offense, 39.5 defense)

Assists

ASSISTS
736—Southern N.H., 1993 (33 games)

AVERAGE PER GAME
25.6—Quincy, 1994 (716 in 28)

Personal Fouls

PERSONAL FOULS
947—Seattle, 1952 (37 games)

PERSONAL FOULS PER GAME
29.9—Shaw, 1987 (748 in 25)

FEWEST PERSONAL FOULS
184—Sewanee, 1962 (17 games)

FEWEST PERSONAL FOULS PER GAME
10.0—Ashland, 1969 (301 in 30)

Defense

LOWEST POINTS PER GAME ALLOWED
20.2—Alcorn St., 1941 (323 in 16)

LOWEST POINTS PER GAME ALLOWED (Since 1948)
29.1—Miss. Industrial, 1948 (436 in 15)

LOWEST FIELD-GOAL PERCENTAGE ALLOWED (Since 1978)
35.8—Tarleton St., 2002 (657 of 1,837)

Overtimes

MOST OVERTIME GAMES
8—Belmont Abbey, 1983 (won 4, lost 4)

MOST CONSECUTIVE OVERTIME GAMES
3—10 times, most recent: Pace, 1996 (won 3, lost 0)

MOST MULTIPLE-OVERTIME GAMES
5—Cal St. Dom. Hills, 1987 (four 2 ot, one 3 ot; won 2, lost 3)

General Records

GAMES IN A SEASON
39—Regis (Colo.), 1949 (36-3)

VICTORIES IN A SEASON
36—Regis (Colo.), 1949 (36-3)

VICTORIES IN A PERFECT SEASON
34—Fort Hays St., 1996

CONSECUTIVE VICTORIES
52—Langston (from 1943-44 opener through fifth game of 1945-46 season)

CONSECUTIVE 30-WIN SEASONS
5—Ky. Wesleyan, 1998 (30); 1999 (35); 2000 (31); 2001 (31); 2002 (31)

CONSECUTIVE HOME-COURT VICTORIES
80—Philadelphia U. (from Jan. 8, 1991 to Nov. 21, 1995)

CONSECUTIVE REGULAR-SEASON VICTORIES (Postseason Tournaments Not Included)
52—Langston (from 1943-44 opener through fifth game of 1945-46 season)

DEFEATS IN A SEASON
28—UNC Pembroke, 2003 (0-28)

CONSECUTIVE DEFEATS IN A SEASON
28—UNC Pembroke, 2003 (0-28)

CONSECUTIVE DEFEATS
46—Olivet, Feb. 21, 1959, to Dec. 4, 1961; Southwest Minn. St., Dec. 11, 1971, to Dec. 1, 1973

CONSECUTIVE WINNING SEASONS
35—Norfolk St., 1963-97

CONSECUTIVE NON-LOSING SEASONS
35—Norfolk St., 1963-97

††UNBEATEN TEAMS (Since 1938; Number Of Victories In Parentheses)
1938 Glenville St. (28)
1941 Milwaukee St. (16)
1942 Indianapolis (16)
1942 Rochester (16)
1944 Langston (23)
1945 Langston (24)
1948 West Virginia St. (23)
1949 Tennessee St. (24)
1956 Rochester Inst. (17)
1959 Grand Canyon (20)
1961 Calvin (20)
1964 Bethany (W. Va.) (18)
1965 Central St. (Ohio) (30)
1965 Evansville (29)#
1993 Cal St. Bakersfield (33)#
1996 Fort Hays St. (34)#

††at least 15 victories; #NCAA Division II champion

All-Time Individual Leaders

Single-Game Records

SCORING HIGHS

Pts.	Player, Team vs. Opponent	Season
113	Clarence "Bevo" Francis, Rio Grande vs. Hillsdale	1954
84	Clarence "Bevo" Francis, Rio Grande vs. Alliance	1954
82	Clarence "Bevo" Francis, Rio Grande vs. Bluffton	1954
80	Paul Crissman, Southern California Col. vs. Pacific Christian	1966
77	William English, Winston-Salem vs. Fayetteville St.	1968
75	Travis Grant, Kentucky St. vs. Northwood	1970
72	Nate DeLong, Wis.-River Falls vs. Winona St.	1948
72	Lloyd Brown, Aquinas vs. Cleary	1953
72	Clarence "Bevo" Francis, Rio Grande vs. Calif. (Pa.)	1953
72	John McElroy, Youngstown St. vs. Wayne St. (Mich.)	1969
71	Clayborn Jones, L.A. Pacific vs. L.A. Baptist	1965
70	Paul Wilcox, Davis & Elkins vs. Glenville St.	1959
70	Bo Clark, UCF vs. Fla. Memorial	1977

Season Records

SCORING AVERAGE

Player, Team	Season	G	FG	FT	Pts.	Avg.
Clarence "Bevo" Francis, Rio Grande	†1954	27	444	367	1,255	*46.5
Earl Glass, Miss. Industrial	†1963	19	322	171	815	42.9
Earl Monroe, Winston-Salem	†1967	32	509	311	*1,329	41.5
John Rinka, Kenyon	†1970	23	354	234	942	41.0
Willie Shaw, Lane	†1964	18	303	121	727	40.4
Travis Grant, Kentucky St.	†1972	33	*539	226	1,304	39.5
Thales McReynolds, Miles	†1965	18	294	118	706	39.2
Bob Johnson, Fitchburg St.	1963	18	213	277	703	39.1
Roger Kuss, Wis.-River Falls	†1953	21	291	235	817	38.9
Florindo Vieira, Quinnipiac	1954	14	191	138	520	37.1

†national champion; *record

FIELD-GOAL PERCENTAGE
(Based on qualifiers for annual championship)

Player, Team	Season	G	FG	FGA	Pct.
Todd Linder, Tampa	†1987	32	282	375	*75.2
Maurice Stafford, North Ala.	†1984	34	198	264	75.0
Matthew Cornegay, Tuskegee	†1982	29	208	278	74.8
Brian Moten, West Ga.	†1992	26	141	192	73.4
Ed Phillips, Alabama A&M	†1968	22	154	210	73.3
Ray Strozier, Central Mo. St.	†1980	28	142	195	72.8
Harold Booker, Cheyney	†1965	24	144	198	72.7
Chad Scott, Calif. (Pa.)	†1994	30	178	245	72.7
Tom Schurfranz, Bellarmine	†1991	30	245	339	72.3
Marv Lewis, Southampton	†1969	24	271	375	72.3
Louis Newsome, North Ala.	†1988	29	192	266	72.2
Ed Phillips, Alabama A&M	†1971	24	159	221	71.9
Gregg Northington, Alabama St.	1971	26	324	451	71.8

†national champion; *record

THREE-POINT FIELD GOALS

Player, Team	Season	G	3FG
Alex Williams, Sacramento St.	1988	30	167
Markus Hallgrimson, Mont. St.-Billings	2000	26	160
Eric Kline, Northern St.	1995	30	148
Eric Kline, Northern St.	1994	33	148
Shawn Pughsley, Central Okla.	1998	32	139
Jed Bedford, Columbus St.	2003	32	135
Reece Gliko, Mont. St.-Billings	1997	28	135
Ray Gutierrez, Calif. (Pa.)	1993	27	135
Jason Garrow, Augustana (S.D.)	1992	27	135
Markus Hallgrimson, Mont. St.-Billings	1999	28	133
Shawn Williams, Central Okla.	1991	29	129
Tarvoris Uzoigwe, Henderson St.	2003	35	128
Robert Martin, Sacramento St.	1988	30	128
Steve Brown, West Ala.	2000	26	126
Antonio Harris, LeMoyne-Owen	1999	26	126
Tommie Spearman, Columbus	1995	29	126
Kwame Morton, Clarion	1994	26	126
Damien Blair, West Chester	1994	28	125
Steve Moyer, Gannon	1999	28	124
John Boyd, LeMoyne-Owen	1992	26	123

THREE-POINT FIELD GOALS PER GAME

Player, Team	Season	G	3FG	Avg.
Markus Hallgrimson, Mont. St.-Billings	†2000	26	160	*6.2
Alex Williams, Sacramento St.	†1988	30	*167	5.6
Jason Garrow, Augustana (S.D.)	†1992	27	135	5.0
Eric Kline, Northern St.	†1995	30	148	4.9
Ray Gutierrez, Calif. (Pa.)	†1993	29	142	4.9
Steve Brown, West Ala.	2000	26	126	4.8
Antonio Harris, LeMoyne-Owen	†1999	26	126	4.8
Kwame Morton, Clarion	†1994	26	126	4.8
Reece Gliko, Mont. St.-Billings	†1997	28	135	4.8
Markus Hallgrimson, Mont. St.-Billings	1999	28	133	4.8
John Boyd, LeMoyne-Owen	1992	26	123	4.7
Duane Huddleston, Mo.-Rolla	1988	25	118	4.7
Antonio Harris, LeMoyne-Owen	†1998	26	119	4.6
Ricardo Watkins, Tuskegee	2000	24	110	4.6
Eric Kline, Northern St.	1994	33	148	4.5
Robbie Waldrop, Lees-McRae	2001	25	112	4.5
Damien Blair, West Chester	1994	28	125	4.5
Eric Carpenter, Cal St. San B'dino	1994	26	116	4.5
Shawn Williams, Central Okla.	†1991	29	129	4.4
Stephen Hamrick, Eastern N.M.	1994	27	120	4.4
Steve Moyer, Gannon	1999	28	124	4.4

†national champion; *record

THREE-POINT FIELD-GOAL PERCENTAGE
(Based on qualifiers for annual championship)

Player, Team	Season	G	3FG	3FGA	Pct.
Ray Lee, Hampton	†1988	24	39	60	*65.0
Steve Hood, Winston-Salem	1988	28	42	67	62.7
Mark Willey, Fort Hays St.	†1990	29	49	81	60.5
Aaron Fehler, Oakland City	†1995	26	73	121	60.3
Aaron Baker, Mississippi Col.	†1989	27	69	117	59.0
Walter Hurd, Johnson Smith	1989	27	49	84	58.3
Matt Hopson, Oakland City	†1996	31	84	145	57.9
Jon Bryant, St. Cloud St.	1996	27	54	94	57.4
Adam Harness, Oakland City	†1997	26	39	68	57.4
Scott Martin, Rollins	†1991	28	114	201	56.7
Charles Byrd, West Tex. A&M	†1987	31	95	168	56.5
Aaron Buckoski, Michigan Tech	1997	26	39	69	56.5
Jay Nolan, Bowie St.	1987	27	70	124	56.5
Kris Kidwell, Oakland City	1996	28	44	78	56.4
Tony Harris, Dist. Columbia	1987	30	79	141	56.0
Rickey Barrett, Ala.-Huntsville	1987	26	63	113	55.8
Quinn Murphy, Drury	1995	27	45	81	55.6
Erik Fisher, San Fran. St.	1991	28	80	144	55.6
Mike Doyle, Philadelphia U.	1988	30	82	149	55.0

†national champion; *record

FREE-THROW PERCENTAGE
(Based on qualifiers for annual championship)

Player, Team	Season	G	FT	FTA	Pct.
Paul Cluxton, Northern Ky.	†1997	35	94	94	*100.0
Tomas Rimkus, Pace	1997	25	65	68	95.6
C. J. Cowgill, Chaminade	†2001	22	113	119	95.0
Billy Newton, Morgan St.	†1976	28	85	90	94.4
Kent Andrews, McNeese St.	†1968	24	85	90	94.4
Mike Sanders, Northern Colo.	†1987	28	82	87	94.3
Curtis Small, Southampton	†2002	29	109	116	94.0
Brent Mason, St. Joseph's (Ind.)	2001	31	125	133	94.0
Aaron Farley, Harding	†2003	30	137	146	93.8
Travis Starns, Colorado Mines	†1999	26	87	93	93.5
Jay Harrie, Mont. St.-Billings	†1994	26	86	92	93.5
Joe Cullen, Hartwick	†1969	18	96	103	93.2
Dan Shanks, Coker	1997	27	119	128	93.0
Charles Byrd, West Tex. A&M	†1988	27	92	99	92.9
Jeremy Kudera, South Dakota	2001	28	78	84	92.9
Brian Koephick, Minn. St. Mankato	1988	28	104	112	92.9
Jon Hagen, Minn. St. Mankato	†1963	25	76	82	92.7
Paul Cluxton, Northern Ky.	†1996	32	100	108	92.6
Jim Borodawka, Mass.-Lowell	†1995	27	74	80	92.5
Carl Gonder, Augustana (S.D.)	†1982	27	86	93	92.5

†national champion; *record

REBOUNDS (SINCE 1973)

Player, Team	Season	G	Reb.
Marvin Webster, Morgan St.	1974	33	740
Major Jones, Albany St. (Ga.)	1975	27	608
Earl Williams, Winston-Salem	1974	26	553
Antonio Garcia, Ky. Wesleyan	1999	37	540

DIVISION II

Player, Team	Season	G	Reb.
Charles Oakley, Virginia Union	1985	31	535
Larry Johnson, Prairie View	1974	23	519
Andre Means, Sacred Heart	1977	32	516
Major Jones, Albany St. (Ga.)	1975	25	513
Harvey Jones, Alabama St.	1974	28	503
Andre Means, Sacred Heart	1978	30	493
Colin Ducharme, Longwood	2001	31	490
Rick Mahorn, Hampton	1980	31	490
Rob Roesch, Staten Island	1989	31	482
Leonard Robinson, Tennessee St.	1974	28	478
Major Jones, Albany St. (Ga.)	1976	24	475

REBOUND AVERAGE

Player, Team	Season	G	Reb.	Avg.
Tom Hart, Middlebury	†1956	21	620	*29.5
Tom Hart, Middlebury	†1955	22	649	29.5
Frank Stronczek, American Int'l	†1966	26	717	27.6
R.C. Owens, Albertson	†1954	25	677	27.1
Maurice Stokes, St. Francis (Pa.)	1954	26	689	26.5
Roman Turmon, Clark Atlanta	1954	23	602	26.2
Pat Callahan, Lewis	1955	20	523	26.2
Hank Brown, Mass.-Lowell	1966	19	496	26.1
Maurice Stokes, St. Francis (Pa.)	1955	28	726	25.9

†national champion; *record

(SINCE 1973)

Player, Team	Season	G	Reb.	Avg.
Larry Johnson, Prairie View	1974	23	519	22.6
Major Jones, Albany St. (Ga.)	1975	27	608	22.5
Marvin Webster, Morgan St.	1974	33	740	22.4
Earl Williams, Winston-Salem	1974	26	553	21.3
Major Jones, Albany St. (Ga.)	1974	25	513	20.5
Larry Gooding, St. Augustine's	1974	22	443	20.1
Major Jones, Albany St. (Ga.)	1976	24	475	19.8
Calvin Robinson, Mississippi Valley	1976	23	432	18.8
Scott Mountz, Calif. (Pa.)	1978	24	431	18.0
Howard Shockley, Salisbury	1975	23	406	17.7
Charles Oakley, Virginia Union	1985	31	535	17.3
Marvin Webster, Morgan St.	1975	27	458	17.0
Larry Johnson, Ark.-Little Rock	1976	24	402	16.8
Keith Smith, Shaw	1979	20	329	16.5
Andre Means, Sacred Heart	1978	30	493	16.4
Donnie Roberts, St. Paul's	1975	25	406	16.2
Andre Means, Sacred Heart	1977	32	516	16.1
Dan Donahue, SIU Edwardsville	1975	26	419	16.1
Lorenzo Poole, Albany St. (Ga.)	1995	26	417	16.0
David Binion, N.C. Central	1983	25	400	16.0

ASSISTS

Player, Team	Season	G	Ast.
Steve Ray, Bridgeport	†1989	32	*400
Steve Ray, Bridgeport	†1990	33	385
Tony Smith, Pfeiffer	†1992	35	349
Rob Paternostro, Southern N.H.	1995	33	309
Jim Ferrer, Bentley	1989	31	309
Brian Gregory, Oakland	1989	28	300
Charles Jordan, Erskine	1992	34	298
Ernest Jenkins, N.M. Highlands	†1995	27	291
Pat Chambers, Philadelphia U.	1994	30	290
Craig Lottie, Alabama A&M	1995	32	287
Adrian Hutt, Metro St.	†1991	28	285
Javar Cheatham, Gannon	†2001	30	283
Patrick Boen, Stonehill	1989	32	278
Ernest Jenkins, N.M. Highlands	†1994	27	277
Clayton Smith, Metro St.	†2003	33	274
Adam Kaufman, Edinboro	1998	34	273
Darnell White, Calif. (Pa.)	1994	30	273
Demetri Beekman, Assumption	1992	32	271
Tyrone Tate, Southern Ind.	1994	32	270
Gallagher Driscoll, St. Rose	1991	29	267

†national champion; *record

ASSIST AVERAGE

Player, Team	Season	G	Ast.	Avg.
Steve Ray, Bridgeport	†1989	32	*400	*12.5
Steve Ray, Bridgeport	†1990	33	385	11.7
Demetri Beekman, Assumption	†1993	23	264	11.5
Ernest Jenkins, N.M. Highlands	†1995	27	291	10.8
Brian Gregory, Oakland	1989	28	300	10.7
Brent Schremp, Slippery Rock	1995	25	259	10.4
Ernest Jenkins, N.M. Highlands	†1994	27	277	10.3
Adrian Hutt, Metro St.	†1991	28	285	10.2
Tony Smith, Pfeiffer	†1992	35	349	10.0

Player, Team	Season	G	Ast.	Avg.
Jim Ferrer, Bentley	1989	31	309	10.0
Todd Chappell, Texas Wesleyan	†2000	27	263	9.7
Pat Chambers, Philadelphia U.	1994	30	290	9.7
Marcus Talbert, Colo. Christian	1994	27	261	9.7
Paul Beaty, Miles	1992	26	248	9.5
Lawrence Jordan, IPFW	1990	28	266	9.5
Hal Chambers, Columbus St.	1993	24	227	9.5
Javar Cheatham, Gannon	†2001	30	283	9.4
Rob Paternostro, Southern N.H.	1995	33	309	9.4
Gallagher Driscoll, St. Rose	1991	29	267	9.2
David Daniels, Colo. Christian	1993	29	264	9.1
Darnell White, Calif. (Pa.)	1994	30	273	9.1

†national champion; *record

BLOCKED SHOTS

Player, Team	Season	G	Blk.
James Doyle, Concord	†1998	30	*157
Antonio Harvey, Pfeiffer	†1993	29	155
John Burke, Southampton	†1996	28	142
Vonzell McGrew, Mo. Western St.	†1995	31	132
Colin Ducharme, Longwood	2001	31	130
Corey Johnson, Pace	1995	30	130
Derek Moore, S.C.-Aiken	1998	30	129
Johnny Tyson, Central Okla.	†1994	27	126
Garth Joseph, St. Rose	†1997	34	124
Kino Outlaw, Mount Olive	1995	28	124
Kino Outlaw, Mount Olive	1996	27	117
Moustapha Diouf, Queens (N.C.)	2003	33	116
Ben Wallace, Virginia Union	1996	31	114
Mark Hensel, Pitt.-Johnstown	1994	27	113
Ben Wallace, Virginia Union	1995	31	111
Elwood Vines, Bloomsburg	1993	27	107
Horacio Llamas, Grand Canyon	1996	29	106
Coata Malone, Alabama A&M	1995	32	106
Eugene Haith, Philadelphia U.	1993	31	105
Bilal Salaam, Kutztown	2003	28	104

†national champion; *record

BLOCKED-SHOT AVERAGE

Player, Team	Season	G	Blk.	Avg.
Antonio Harvey, Pfeiffer	†1993	29	155	*5.34
James Doyle, Concord	†1998	30	*157	5.23
John Burke, Southampton	†1996	28	142	5.07
Johnny Tyson, Central Okla.	†1994	27	126	4.66
Kino Outlaw, Mount Olive	†1995	28	124	4.43
Kino Outlaw, Mount Olive	1996	27	117	4.33
Corey Johnson, Pace	1995	30	130	4.33
Derek Moore, S.C.-Aiken	1998	30	129	4.30
Vonzell McGrew, Mo. Western St.	1995	31	132	4.26
Jason Roseto, Edinboro	†2001	23	97	4.22
Colin Ducharme, Longwood	2001	31	130	4.19
Mark Hensel, Pitt.-Johnstown	1994	27	113	4.19
Aaron Davis, Southern Conn. St.	†2003	25	103	4.12
Victorius Payne, Lane	1996	25	101	4.04
Elwood Vines, Bloomsburg	1993	27	107	3.96
George Bailey, Lock Haven	†2002	20	79	3.95
Lawrence Williams, San Fran. St.	1995	27	103	3.81
Derek Moore, S.C.-Aiken	1996	26	97	3.73
Bilal Salaam, Kutztown	2003	28	104	3.71
Ben Wallace, Virginia Union	1996	31	114	3.68

†national champion; *record

STEALS

Player, Team	Season	G	Stl.
J.R. Gamble, Queens (N.C.)	†2001	32	*139
Wayne Copeland, Lynn	†2000	26	129
Wayne Copeland, Lynn	†1999	31	125
Terrance Gist, S.C.-Spartanburg	†1998	29	122
Devlin Herring, Pitt.-Johnstown	†1997	27	122
Oronn Brown, Clarion	1997	29	120
Devlin Herring, Pitt.-Johnstown	1998	29	118
David Clark, Bluefield St.	†1996	31	118
Tyrone McDaniel, Lenoir-Rhyne	†1993	32	116
Ken Francis, Molloy	†1994	27	116
Darnell White, Calif. (Pa.)	1994	30	115
Eddin Santiago, Mo. Southern St.	2001	30	114
Tracy Gross, High Point	1997	29	114
Robert Campbell, Armstrong Atlantic	2001	33	113
Joe Newton, Central Okla.	1993	32	110
Peron Austin, Colorado St.-Pueblo	1997	28	110
Marcus Stubblefield, Queens (N.C.)	1993	28	110
Shannon Holmes, NYIT	†1995	30	110

Player, Team	Season	G	Stl.
Terrence Baxter, Pfeiffer	2000	31	109
Terryl Woolery, Cal Poly Pomona	1997	27	109

†national champion; *record

STEAL AVERAGE

Player, Team	Season	G	Stl.	Avg.
Wayne Copeland, Lynn	†2000	26	129	*4.96
John Morris, Bluefield St.	1994	23	104	4.52
Devlin Herring, Pitt.-Johnstown	†1997	27	122	4.52
J.R. Gamble, Queens (N.C.)	†2001	32	*139	4.34
Ken Francis, Molloy	†1994	27	116	4.29
Terrance Gist, S.C.-Spartanburg	†1998	29	122	4.21
Oronn Brown, Clarion	1997	29	120	4.14
Devlin Herring, Pitt.-Johnstown	1998	29	118	4.07
Michael Dean, Cal St. Hayward	1998	26	105	4.04
Terryl Woolery, Cal Poly Pomona	1997	27	109	4.04
Wayne Copeland, Lynn	†1999	31	125	4.03
Kevin Nichols, Bemidji St.	1994	26	104	4.00
Tracy Gross, High Point	1997	29	114	3.93
Peron Austin, Colorado St.-Pueblo	1997	28	110	3.93
Marcus Stubblefield, Queens (N.C.)	1993	28	110	3.93
Demetri Beekman, Assumption	1993	23	89	3.87
Darnell White, Calif. (Pa.)	1994	30	115	3.83
J.R. Gamble, Queens (N.C.)	2000	28	107	3.82
David Clark, Bluefield St.	†1996	31	118	3.81
Eddien Santiago, Mo. Southern St.	2001	30	114	3.80

†national champion; *record

Career Records

POINTS

Player, Team	Seasons	Pts.
Travis Grant, Kentucky St.	1969-72	*4,045
Bob Hopkins, Grambling	1953-56	3,759
Tony Smith, Pfeiffer	1989-92	3,350
Earnest Lee, Clark Atlanta	1984-87	3,298
Joe Miller, Alderson-Broaddus	1954-57	3,294
Henry Logan, Western Caro.	1965-68	3,290
John Rinka, Kenyon	1967-70	3,251
Dick Barnett, Tennessee St.	1956-59	3,209
Willie Scott, Alabama St.	1966-69	3,155
Johnnie Allen, Bethune-Cookman	1966-69	3,058
Bennie Swain, Texas Southern	1955-58	3,008
Lambert Shell, Bridgeport	1989-92	3,001
Carl Hartman, Alderson-Broaddus	1952-55	2,959
Earl Monroe, Winston-Salem	1964-67	2,935

*record

SCORING AVERAGE
(Minimum 1,400 points)

Player, Team	Seasons	G	FG	3FG	FT	Pts.	Avg.
Travis Grant, Kentucky St.	1969-72	121	*1,760	—	525	*4,045	*33.4
John Rinka, Kenyon	1967-70	99	1,261	—	729	3,251	32.8
Florindo Vieira, Quinnipiac	1954-57	69	761	—	741	2,263	32.8
Willie Shaw, Lane	1961-64	76	960	—	459	2,379	31.3
Mike Davis, Virginia Union	1966-69	89	1,014	—	730	2,758	31.0
Henry Logan, Western Caro.	1965-68	107	1,263	—	764	3,290	30.7
Willie Scott, Alabama St.	1966-69	103	1,277	—	601	3,155	30.6
Carlos Knox, IUPUI	1995-98	85	832	208	684	2,556	30.1
George Gilmore, Chaminade	1991-92	51	485	174	387	1,531	30.0
Brett Beeson, Moorhead St.	1995-96	54	551	92	421	1,615	29.9
Bob Hopkins, Grambling	1953-56	126	1,403	—	953	3,759	29.8
Rod Butler, Western New Eng.	1968-70	59	697	—	331	1,725	29.2
Gregg Northington, Alabama St.	1970-72	75	894	—	403	2,191	29.2
Isaiah Wilson, Baltimore	1969-71	67	731	—	471	1,933	28.9

*record

FIELD-GOAL PERCENTAGE
(Minimum 400 field goals made)

Player, Team	Seasons	G	FG	FGA	Pct.
Todd Linder, Tampa	1984-87	122	909	1,284	*70.8
Tom Schurfranz, Bellarmine	1987-88, 91-92	112	742	1,057	70.2
Chad Scott, Calif. (Pa.)	1991-94	115	465	664	70.0
Ed Phillips, Alabama A&M	1968-71	95	610	885	68.9
Ulysses Hackett, S.C.-Spartanburg	1990-92	90	824	1,213	67.9
Larry Tucker, Lewis	1981-83	84	677	999	67.8
Otis Evans, Wayne St. (Mich.)	1989-92	106	472	697	67.7
Matthew Cornegay, Tuskegee	1979-82	105	524	783	66.9
Ray Strozier, Central Mo. St.	1978-81	110	563	843	66.8
Dennis Edwards, Fort Hays St.	1994-95	59	666	998	66.7

Player, Team	Seasons	G	FG	FGA	Pct.
James Morris, Central Okla.	1990-93	76	532	798	66.7
Lance Berwald, North Dakota St.	1983-84	58	475	717	66.2
Harold Booker, Cheyney	1965-67, 69	108	662	1,002	66.1

*record

THREE-POINT FIELD GOALS MADE

Player, Team	Seasons	G	3FG
Steve Moyer, Gannon	1996-99	112	*442
Tony Smith, Pfeiffer	1989-92	126	431
Kwame Morton, Clarion	1991-94	105	411
Gary Duda, Merrimack	1989-92	122	389
Markus Hallgrimson, Mont. St.-Billings	1998-00	82	371
Columbus Parker, Johnson Smith	1990-93	115	354
Gary Paul, Indianapolis	1987-90	111	354
Matt Miller, Drury	1999-02	106	351
Travis Tuttle, North Dakota	1994-97	108	350
Mike Ziegler, Colorado Mines	1987-90	118	344
Chris Brown, Tuskegee	1993-96	104	339
Stephen Hamrick, Eastern N.M.	1993-96	107	339
Mike Kuhens, Queens (N.Y.)	1995-98	104	334
Jesse Ogden, Edinboro	1995-98	110	334
Brent Kincaid, Calif. (Pa.)	1993-96	115	325
Damien Blair, West Chester	1992-95	109	317
Ryan Stefanski, Calif. (Pa.)	2000-03	104	314
Matt Van Leeuwen, Merrimack	1998-01	112	312
Cliff DuBois, Barry	1996-99	112	311
Brad Joens, Wayne St. (Neb.)	1998-01	117	310
Michael Shue, Lock Haven	1994-97	92	308
Jon Cronin, Stonehill	1989-92	117	308
Wil Pierce, Western St.	1993-96	114	307
Roger Powers, St. Rose	1994-97	123	305

*record

THREE-POINT FIELD GOALS MADE PER GAME
(Minimum 200 three-point field goals made)

Player, Team	Seasons	G	3FG	Avg.
Antonio Harris, LeMoyne-Owen	1998-99	52	245	*4.71
Markus Hallgrimson, Mont. St.-Billings	1998-00	82	371	4.52
Alex Williams, Sacramento St.	1987-88	58	247	4.26
Tommie Spearman, Columbus St.	1994-95	56	233	4.16
Reece Gliko, Mont. St.-Billings	1996-97	56	231	4.13
Danny Phillips, Mont. St.-Billings	2001-02	55	222	4.03
Steve Moyer, Gannon	1996-99	112	*442	3.95
Kwame Morton, Clarion	1991-94	105	411	3.91
Zoderick Green, Central Okla.	1993-95	57	212	3.72
Shawn Williams, Central Okla.	1989-91	57	212	3.72
Mike Sinclair, Bowie St.	1987-89	82	299	3.65
Tai Crutchfield, Philadelphia U.	2000-01	58	210	3.62
Nate Allen, Western St.	1996-97	57	205	3.60
Robert Martin, Sacramento St.	1987-89	85	294	3.46
Tony Smith, Pfeiffer	1989-92	126	431	3.42
Michael Shue, Lock Haven	1994-97	92	308	3.35
Matt Miller, Drury	1999-02	106	351	3.31
Chris Brown, Tuskegee	1993-96	104	339	3.26
Travis Tuttle, North Dakota	1994-97	108	350	3.24
Mike Kuhens, Queens (N.Y.)	1995-98	104	334	3.21
Gary Paul, Indianapolis	1987-90	111	354	3.19
Gary Duda, Merrimack	1989-92	122	389	3.19
Stephen Hamrick, Eastern N.M.	1993-96	107	339	3.17
Rod Harris, Southampton	1987-89	78	241	3.09

*record

THREE-POINT FIELD-GOAL PERCENTAGE
(Minimum 200 three-point field goals made)

Player, Team	Seasons	G	3FG	3FGA	Pct.
Scott Martin, Rollins	1988-91	104	236	460	*51.3
Todd Woelfle, Oakland City	1995-98	103	210	412	51.0
Matt Markle, Shippensburg	1989-92	101	202	408	49.5
Paul Cluxton, Northern Ky.	1994-97	122	303	619	48.9
Lance Gelnett, Millersville	1989-92	109	266	547	48.6
Antonio Harris, LeMoyne-Owen	1998-99	52	245	510	48.0
Mark Willey, Fort Hays St.	1989-92	117	224	478	46.9
Todd Bowden, Randolph-Macon	1987-89	84	229	491	46.6
Gary Paul, Indianapolis	1987-90	111	354	768	46.1
Matt Ripaldi, Southern N.H.	1993-96	123	277	604	45.9
Alex Williams, Sacramento St.	1987-88	58	247	541	45.7
Jason Bullock, Indiana (Pa.)	1993-96	119	287	637	45.1
Boyd Printy, Truman	1990-92	77	201	447	45.0
Lance Luitjens, Northern St.	1994-96	95	275	614	44.8
Buck Williams, North Ala.	1987-89	84	238	535	44.5

*record

DIVISION II

FREE-THROW PERCENTAGE
(Minimum 250 free throws made)

Player, Team	Seasons	G	FT	FTA	Pct.
Paul Cluxton, Northern Ky.	1994-97	122	272	291	*93.5
Kent Andrews, McNeese St.	1967-69	67	252	275	91.6
Jon Hagen, Minn. St. Mankato	1963-65	73	252	280	90.0
Dave Reynolds, Davis & Elkins	1986-89	107	383	429	89.3
Michael Shue, Lock Haven	1994-97	92	354	400	88.5
Tony Budzik, Mansfield	1989-92	107	367	416	88.2
Terry Gill, New Orleans	1972-74	79	261	296	88.2
Bryan Vacca, Randolph-Macon	1980-83	94	262	298	87.9
Steve Nisenson, Hofstra	1963-65	83	602	685	87.9
Jeff Gore, St. Rose	1991-93	91	333	379	87.9
Jack Sparks, Bentley	1976-80	99	253	288	87.8
Dan Shanks, Coker	1994-97	102	467	533	87.6
Troy Nesmith, Gannon	1997-98	54	274	313	87.5
Wayne Profitt, Lynchburg	1965-67	57	482	551	87.5
Clyde Briley, McNeese St.	1962-65	101	561	642	87.4
Jason Sempsrott, South Dakota St.	1994-97	110	462	529	87.3
Foy Ballance, Armstrong Atlantic	1978-81	108	351	402	87.3
Jehu Brabham, Mississippi Col.	1969-71	72	452	518	87.3
Pete Chambers, West Chester	1966-68	67	267	306	87.3

*record

REBOUNDS
(For careers beginning in 1973 or after)

Player, Team	Seasons	G	Reb.
Major Jones, Albany St. (Ga.)	1973-76	105	2,052
Clemon Johnson, Florida A&M	1975-78	109	1,494
Wayne Robertson, Southern N.H.	1991-94	127	1,487
Carlos Terry, Winston-Salem	1975-78	117	1,467
James Hector, American Int'l	1991-94	115	1,446
Jeff Covington, Youngstown St.	1975-78	106	1,381
John Ebeling, Fla. Southern	1979-82	127	1,362
Kelvin Hicks, NYIT	1977-80	94	1,258
John Edwards, Fla. Southern	1973	94	1,214
John Fox, Millersville	1984-87	118	1,214
Dave Vonesh, North Dakota	1988-91	122	1,207
Marvin Webster, Morgan St.	1975-76	60	1,198
Ramzee Statnton, West Chester	2000-03	111	1,142
Mark Tetzlaff, South Dakota St.	1982-85	118	1,132
Chris Bowles, Southern Ind.	1991-94	114	1,129
Steve O'Neill, American Int'l	1977-81	108	1,093
Bob Stanley, Mo.-Rolla	1974-77	95	1,049
Ernie DeWitt, Bryant	1978-81	107	1,036
Gerald Lavender, North Ala.	1977-80	118	1,033
Walt Whitakere, Minn. St. Moorhead	1979-82	107	1,017
Andre Means, Sacred Heart	1977-78	62	1,009
Leo Parent, Mass.-Lowell	1987-89	92	1,001
Mario Elie, American Int'l	1982-85	120	1,001

Jed Bedford of Columbus State led the country in three-point shots made last season.

Photo by Columbus St. Sports Information

REBOUND AVERAGE
(Minimum 800 rebounds)

Player, Team	Seasons	G	Reb.	Avg.
Tom Hart, Middlebury	1953, 55-56	63	1,738	*27.6
Maurice Stokes, St. Francis (Pa.)	1953-55	72	1,812	25.2
Frank Stronczek, American Int'l	1965-67	62	1,549	25.0
Bill Thieben, Hofstra	1954-56	76	1,837	24.2
Hank Brown, Mass.-Lowell	1965-67	49	1,129	23.0
Elmore Smith, Kentucky St.	1969-71	85	1,917	22.6
Charles Wrinn, Trinity (Conn.)	1951-53	53	1,176	22.2
Roman Turmon, Clark Atlanta	1952-54	60	1,312	21.9
Tony Missere, Pratt	1966-68	62	1,348	21.7
Ron Horton, Delaware St.	1966-68	64	1,384	21.6

*record

(For careers beginning in 1973 or after; minimum 800 rebounds)

Player, Team	Seasons	G	Reb.	Avg.
Marvin Webster, Morgan St.	1975-76	60	1,198	20.0
Major Jones, Albany St. (Ga.)	1973-76	105	2,052	19.5
Howard Shockley, Salisbury	1975-76	49	817	16.7
Andre Means, Sacred Heart	1977-78	62	1,009	16.3
Antonio Garcia, Ky. Wesleyan	1998-99	70	997	14.2
Clemon Johnson, Florida A&M	1975-78	109	1,494	13.7
Larry Johnson, Ark.-Little Rock	1976-78	69	944	13.7
Kelvin Hicks, NYIT	1977-80	94	1,258	13.4
John Edwards, Fla. Southern	1973-76	94	1,214	12.9
James Hector, American Int'l	1991-94	115	1,446	12.6
Wayne Robertson, Southern N.H.	1991-94	127	1,487	11.7
Wayne Armstrong, Armstrong Atlantic	1975-77	78	897	11.5
Bob Stanley, Mo.-Rolla	1974-77	95	1,049	11.0
Leo Parent, Mass.-Lowell	1987-89	92	1,011	11.0

ASSISTS

Player, Team	Seasons	G	Ast.
Demetri Beekman, Assumption	1990-93	119	*1,044
Adam Kaufman, Edinboro	1998-01	116	936
Rob Paternostro, Southern N.H.	1992-95	129	919
Gallagher Driscoll, St. Rose	1989-92	121	878
Tony Smith, Pfeiffer	1989-92	126	828
Jamie Stevens, Mont. St.-Billings	1996-99	110	805
Steve Ray, Bridgeport	1989-90	65	785
Dan Ward, St. Cloud St.	1992-95	100	774
Jordan Canfield, Washburn	1994-97	126	756
Charles Jordan, Erskine	1989-92	119	727
Donald Johnson, Franklin Pierce	1998-01	114	722
Patrick Chambers, Philadelphia U.	1991-94	123	709
Lamont Jones, Bridgeport	1992-95	119	708
Ernest Jenkins, N.M. Highlands	1992-95	84	699
Antoine Campbell, Ashland	1995-98	113	697
Pat Madden, Jacksonville St.	1989-91	88	688
Nate Tibbetts, South Dakota	1998-01	112	678
Candice Pickens, Calif. (Pa.)	1993-96	121	675
Mark Benson, Tex. A&M-Kingsville	1989-91	86	674
Craig Lottie, Alabama A&M	1992-95	93	673

*record

ASSIST AVERAGE
(Minimum 550 assists)

Player, Team	Seasons	G	Ast.	Avg.
Steve Ray, Bridgeport	1989-90	65	785	*12.1
Demetri Beekman, Assumption	1990-93	119	*1,044	8.8
Ernest Jenkins, N.M. Highlands	1992-95	84	699	8.3
Adam Kaufman, Edinboro	1998-01	116	936	8.1
Mark Benson, Tex. A&M-Kingsville	1989-91	86	674	7.8
Pat Madden, Jacksonville St.	1989-91	88	688	7.8
Dan Ward, St. Cloud St.	1992-95	100	774	7.7
Jamie Stevens, Mont. St.-Billings	1996-99	110	805	7.3
Gallagher Driscoll, St. Rose	1989-92	121	878	7.3
Craig Lottie, Alabama A&M	1992-95	93	673	7.2
Rob Paternostro, Southern N.H.	1992-95	129	919	7.1
Eddin Santiago, Mo. Southern St.	1999-02	117	804	6.9
Tony Smith, Pfeiffer	1989-92	126	828	6.6
Donald Johnson, Franklin Pierce	1998-01	114	722	6.3
Mike Buscetto, Quinnipiac	1990-93	99	624	6.3
Patrick Herron, Winston-Salem	1992-95	97	604	6.2
Pat Delaney, St. Anselm	1999-02	118	731	6.2
Antoine Campbell, Ashland	1995-98	113	697	6.2
Charles Jordan, Erskine	1989-92	119	727	6.1
Nate Tibbetts, South Dakota	1998-01	112	678	6.1

*record

BLOCKED SHOTS

Player, Team	Seasons	G	Blk.
James Doyle, Concord	1995-98	120	*416
Derek Moore, S.C.-Aiken	1996-99	102	408
Rich Edwards, Adelphi	1999-02	123	305
Kino Outlaw, Mount Olive	1994-96	81	305
Garth Joseph, St. Rose	1995-97	89	300
Sylvere Bryan, Tampa	1999-02	116	294
Kerwin Thompson, Eckerd	1993-96	116	284
Aaron Davis, Southern Conn. St.	2000-03	94	269
Jeff Weirsma, Erskine	2000-03	109	268
Eugene Haith, Philadelphia U.	1993-95	86	267
John Tomsich, Le Moyne	1996-99	114	264
Chandar Bingham, Virginia Union	1997-00	106	261
Coata Malone, Alabama A&M	1994-96	90	243
Alonzo Goldston, Fort Hays St.	1995-97	96	240
Damon Reed, St. Rose	1997-00	128	236
Ben Wallace, Virginia Union	1995-96	62	225
Antwain Smith, St. Paul's	1996-99	105	222
Eric Watson, Calif. (Pa.)	1996-99	119	214
Vonzell McGrew, Mo. Western St.	1993-95	57	211
Corey Johnson, Pace	1993-95	58	210
John Burke, Southampton	1995-96	54	205
Adrian Machado, Stonehill	1993-96	108	196
Steve Schutz, Fort Lewis	1994-97	96	195
Allen Wilson, Francis Marion/S.C.-Aiken	1995,97-99	110	194

*record

BLOCKED-SHOT AVERAGE
(Minimum 175 blocked shots)

Player, Team	Seasons	G	Blk.	Avg.
Derek Moore, S.C.-Aiken	1996-99	102	408	4.00
John Burke, Southampton	1995-96	54	205	3.80
Kino Outlaw, Mount Olive	1994-96	81	305	3.77
Vonzell McGrew, Mo. Western St.	1993-95	57	211	3.70
Tihomir Juric, Wis.-Parkside	1993-94	53	193	3.64
Ben Wallace, Virginia Union	1995-96	62	225	3.63
Corey Johnson, Pace	1993-95	58	210	3.62
James Doyle, Concord	1995-98	120	*416	3.47
Mark Hensel, Pitt.-Johnstown	1993-94	53	180	3.40
Garth Joseph, St. Rose	1995-97	89	300	3.37
Eugene Haith, Philadelphia U.	1993-95	86	267	3.10
Aaron Davis, Southern Conn. St.	2000-03	94	269	2.86
Coata Malone, Alabama A&M	1994-96	90	243	2.70
Sylvere Bryan, Tampa	1999-02	116	294	2.53
Alonzo Goldston, Fort Hays St.	1995-97	96	240	2.50
Rich Edwards, Adelphi	1999-02	123	305	2.48
Chandar Bingham, Virginia Union	1997-00	106	261	2.46
Jeff Weirsma, Erskine	2000-03	109	268	2.46
Kerwin Thompson, Eckerd	1993-96	116	284	2.45
Merriel Jenkins, Hawaii-Hilo	1997-99	77	188	2.44
John Tomsich, Le Moyne	1996-99	114	264	2.32
Lawrence Williams, San Fran. St.	1993-95	79	176	2.23

*record

STEALS

Player, Team	Seasons	G	Stl.
Eddin Santiago, Mo. Southern St.	1999-02	117	383
Oronn Brown, Clarion	1994-97	106	361

Player, Team	Seasons	G	Stl.
Robert Campbell, Armstrong Atlantic	1998-01	118	357
Marcus Best, Winston-Salem	1999-02	119	345
Devlin Herring, Pitt.-Johnstown	1995-98	106	333
Rolondo Hall, Davis & Elkins	1998-01	106	314
Terrence Baxter, Pfeiffer	1998-01	108	281
David Clark, Bluefield St.	1994-96	83	278
Terrance Gist, S.C.-Spartanburg	1994-97	112	276
Omar Kasi, Molloy	1997-00	109	272
Sotirios Karapostolou, Southern N.H.	2000-03	107	271
DeMarcos Anzures, Metro St.	1997-00	125	271
Mike Hancock, Neb.-Kearney	1995-98	121	271
Lorinza Harrington, Wingate	1999-02	121	263
Patrick Herron, Winston-Salem	1993-95	78	263
Ken Francis, Molloy	1993-95	81	260
Brandon Hughes, Newberry	1997-00	88	259
Lamont Jones, Bridgeport	1993-95	84	256
Deartrus Goodmon, Alabama A&M	1993-96	126	255
Wayne Copeland, Lynn	1999-00	57	254
Clayton Smith, Metro St.	2000-03	127	251
J.R. Gamble, Queens (N.C.)	2000-01	60	246
Donald Johnson, Franklin Pierce	1998-01	114	243
Keith Linson, Central Mo. St.	1994-97	116	241

*record

STEAL AVERAGE
(Minimum 150 steals)

Player, Team	Seasons	G	Stl.	Avg.
Wayne Copeland, Lynn	1999-00	57	254	4.46
J.R. Gamble, Queens (N.C.)	2000-01	60	246	4.10
John Morris, Bluefield St.	1994-95	50	185	3.70
Oronn Brown, Clarion	1994-97	106	*361	3.41
Patrick Herron, Winston-Salem	1993-95	78	263	3.37
David Clark, Bluefield St.	1994-96	83	278	3.35
Peron Austin, Colorado St.-Pueblo	1997-98	58	190	3.28
Eddin Santiago, Mo. Southern St.	1999-02	117	*383	3.27
Darnell White, Calif. (Pa.)	1993-94	59	192	3.25
Rudy Berry, Cal St. Stanislaus	1993-94	51	164	3.21
Ken Francis, Molloy	1993-95	81	260	3.21
Bob Cunningham, NYIT	1995-96	55	175	3.18
Devlin Herring, Pitt.-Johnstown	1995-98	106	333	3.14
Craig Fergeson, Columbus St.	1995-96	61	191	3.13
Bryan Heaps, Abilene Christian	1993-94	56	171	3.05
Lamont Jones, Bridgeport	1993-95	84	256	3.05
Kelly Mann, Concord	1997-98	62	185	2.98
Javar Cheatham, Gannon	2000-01	58	172	2.97
Rolondo Hall, Davis & Elkins	1998-01	106	314	2.96
Brandon Hughes, Newberry	1997-00	88	259	2.94
Malcolm Turner, Sonoma St.	1995-96	52	152	2.92
Tullius Pate, Coker	1994-95	55	158	2.87
Aaron Johnson, C.W. Post	1993-94	56	160	2.86
Steve St. Martin, Assumption	1995-98	72	205	2.85

*record

DIVISION II

Annual Individual Champions

Scoring Average

Season	Player, Team	G	FG	FT	Pts.	Avg.
1948	Nate DeLong, Wis.-River Falls	22	206	206	618	28.1
1949	George King, Charleston (W.Va.)	26	289	179	757	29.1
1950	George King, Charleston (W.Va.)	31	354	259	967	31.2
1951	Scott Seagall, Millikin	31	314	260	888	28.6
1952	Harold Wolfe, Findlay	22	285	101	671	30.5
1953	Roger Kuss, Wis.-River Falls	21	291	235	817	38.9
1954	Clarence "Bevo" Francis, Rio Grande	27	444	367	1,255	*46.5
1955	Bill Warden, North Central	13	162	127	451	34.7
1956	Bill Reigel, McNeese St.	36	425	370	1,220	33.9
1957	Ken Hammond, West Va. Tech	27	334	274	942	34.9
1958	John Lee Butcher, Pikeville	27	330	210	870	32.2

Season	Player, Team	G	FG	FT	Pts.	Avg.
1959	Paul Wilcox, Davis & Elkins	23	289	195	773	33.6
1960	Don Perrelli, Southern Conn. St.	22	263	168	694	31.5
1961	Lebron Bell, Bryant	14	174	114	462	33.0
1962	Willie Shaw, Lane	18	239	115	593	32.9
1963	Earl Glass, Miss. Industrial	19	322	171	815	42.9
1964	Willie Shaw, Lane	18	303	121	727	40.4
1965	Thales McReynolds, Miles	18	294	118	706	39.2
1966	Paul Crissman, Southern Cal College	23	373	90	836	36.3
1967	Earl Monroe, Winston-Salem	32	509	311	*1,329	41.5
1968	Mike Davis, Virginia Union	25	351	206	908	36.3
1969	John Rinka, Kenyon	26	340	202	882	33.9
1970	John Rinka, Kenyon	23	354	234	942	41.0
1971	Bo Lamar, La.-Lafayette	29	424	196	1,044	36.0
1972	Travis Grant, Kentucky St.	33	*539	226	1,304	39.5

Season	Player, Team	G	FG	FT	Pts.	Avg.
1973	Claude White, Elmhurst	18	248	101	597	33.2
1974	Aaron James, Grambling	27	366	137	869	32.2
1975	Ron Barrow, Southern U.	23	296	115	707	30.7
1976	Ron Barrow, Southern U.	27	318	136	772	28.6
1977	Ed Murphy, Merrimack	28	369	158	896	32.0
1978	Harold Robertson, Lincoln (Mo.)	28	408	149	965	34.5
1979	Bo Clark, UCF	23	315	97	727	31.6
1980	Bill Fennelly, Central Mo. St.	28	337	189	863	30.8
1981	Gregory Jackson, St. Paul's	26	267	183	717	27.6
1982	John Ebeling, Fla. Southern	32	286	284	856	26.8
1983	Danny Dixon, Alabama A&M	27	379	152	910	33.7
1984	Earl Jones, Dist. Columbia	22	215	200	630	28.6
1985	Earnest Lee, Clark Atlanta	29	380	230	990	34.1
1986	Earnest Lee, Clark Atlanta	28	314	191	819	29.3

Season	Player, Team	G	FG	3FG	FT	Pts.	Avg.
1987	Earnest Lee, Clark Atlanta	29	326	35	174	861	29.7
1988	Daryl Cambrelen, Southampton	25	242	32	170	686	27.4
1989	Steve deLaveaga, Cal Lutheran	28	278	79	151	786	28.1
1990	A.J. English, Virginia Union	30	333	65	270	1,001	33.4
1991	Gary Mattison, St. Augustine's	26	277	53	159	766	29.5
1992	George Gilmore, Chaminade	28	280	82	238	880	31.4
1993	Darrin Robinson, Sacred Heart	26	313	75	130	831	32.0
1994	Kwame Mortin, Clarion	26	264	126	191	845	32.5
1995	Carlos Knox, IUPUI	29	284	39	218	825	28.4
1996	Brett Beeson, Moorhead St.	27	305	58	232	900	33.3
1997	Dan Sancomb, Wheeling Jesuit	27	295	11	125	726	26.9
1998	Carlos Knox, IUPUI	26	238	96	209	781	30.0
1999	Eddie Robinson, Central Okla.	26	305	24	95	729	28.0
2000	David Evans, BYU-Hawaii	28	300	48	134	782	27.9
2001	Marlon Dawson, Central Okla.	26	206	101	155	668	25.7
2002	Angel Figueroa, Dowling	25	216	79	143	654	26.2
2003	Ron Christy, Teikyo Post	29	295	64	134	788	27.2

*record

Field-Goal Percentage

Season	Player, Team	G	FG	FGA	Pct.
1949	Vern Mikkelson, Hamline	30	203	377	53.8
1950	Nate DeLong, Wis.-River Falls	29	287	492	58.3
1951	Johnny O'Brien, Seattle	33	248	434	57.1
1952	Forrest Hamilton, Southwest Mo. St.	30	147	246	59.8
1953	Bob Buis, Carleton	21	149	246	60.6
1954	Paul Lauritzen, Augustana (Ill.)	19	158	251	62.9
1955	Jim O'Hara, UC Santa Barb.	24	140	214	65.4
1956	Logan Gipe, Ky. Wesleyan	22	134	224	59.8
1957	John Wilfred, Winston-Salem	30	229	381	60.1
1958	Bennie Swain, Texas Southern	35	363	587	61.8
1959	Dick O'Meara, Babson	18	144	225	64.0
1960	Edwin Cox, Howard Payne	26	126	194	64.9
1961	Tony Solomon, St. Paul's	20	94	149	63.1
1962	Tom Morris, St. Paul's	17	108	168	64.3
1963	Howard Trice, Howard Payne	26	168	237	70.9
1964	Robert Springer, Howard Payne	24	119	174	68.4
1965	Harold Booker, Cheyney	24	144	198	72.7
1966	Harold Booker, Cheyney	27	170	240	70.8
1967	John Dickson, Arkansas St.	24	214	308	69.5
1968	Edward Phillips, Alabama A&M	22	154	210	73.3
1969	Marvin Lewis, Southampton	24	271	375	72.3
1970	Travis Grant, Kentucky St.	31	482	688	70.1
1971	Edward Phillips, Alabama A&M	24	159	221	71.9
1972	Don Manley, Otterbein	23	146	207	70.5
1973	Glynn Berry, Southampton	26	191	302	63.2
1974	Kirby Thurston, Western Caro.	25	242	367	65.9
1975	Gerald Cunningham, Kentucky St.	29	280	411	68.1
1976	Thomas Blue, Elizabeth City St.	24	270	388	69.6
1977	Kelvin Hicks, NYIT	24	161	232	69.4
1978	Ron Ripley, Wis.-Green Bay	32	162	239	67.8
1979	Carl Bailey, Tuskegee	27	210	307	68.4
1980	Ray Strozier, Central Mo. St.	28	142	195	72.8
1981	Matthew Cornegay, Tuskegee	26	177	247	71.7
1982	Matthew Cornegay, Tuskegee	29	208	278	74.8
1983	Rudy Burton, Elizabeth City St.	24	142	201	70.6
1984	Maurice Stafford, North Ala.	34	198	264	75.0
1985	Todd Linder, Tampa	31	219	306	71.6
1986	Todd Linder, Tampa	28	204	291	70.1
1987	Todd Linder, Tampa	32	282	375	*75.2
1988	Louis Newsome, North Ala.	29	192	266	72.2
1989	Tom Schurfranz, Bellarmine	28	164	240	68.2
1990	Ulysses Hackett, S.C.-Spartanburg	32	301	426	70.7
1991	Tom Schurfranz, Bellarmine	30	245	339	72.3
1992	Brian Moten, West Ga.	26	141	192	73.4
1993	Chad Scott, Calif. (Pa.)	28	173	245	70.6

Season	Player, Team	G	FG	FGA	Pct.
1994	Chad Scott, Calif. (Pa.)	30	178	245	72.7
1995	John Pruett, SIU Edwardsville	26	138	193	71.5
1996	Kyle Kirby, IPFW	26	133	195	68.2
1997	Andy Robertson, Fla. Southern	32	183	269	68.0
1998	Anthony Russell, West Fla.	28	191	284	67.3
1999	DaVonn Harp, Kutztown St.	27	140	205	68.3
2000	Shaun Bass, Drury	28	156	237	65.8
2001	Charles Ward, St. Augustine's	27	159	243	65.4
2002	Brett Barnard, Le Moyne	27	141	211	66.8
2003	Anthony Greenup, Shaw	30	172	242	71.1

*record

Three-Point Field Goals Made Per Game

Season	Player, Team	G	3FG	Avg.
1987	Bill Harris, Northern Mich.	27	117	4.3
1988	Alex Williams, Sacramento St.	30	*167	5.6
1989	Robert Martin, Sacramento St.	28	118	4.2
1990	Gary Paul, Indianapolis	28	110	3.9
1991	Shawn Williams, Central Okla.	29	129	4.4
1992	Jason Garrow, Augustana (S.D.)	27	135	5.0
1993	Ray Gutierrez, Calif. (Pa.)	29	142	4.9
1994	Kwame Morton, Clarion	26	126	4.8
1995	Eric Kline, Northern St.	30	148	4.9
1996	Daren Alix, Merrimack	28	114	4.1
1997	Reece Gliko, Mont. St.-Billings	28	135	4.8
1998	Antonio Harris, LeMoyne-Owen	26	119	4.6
1999	Antonio Harris, LeMoyne-Owen	26	126	4.8
2000	Markus Hallgrimson, Mont. St.-Billings	26	160	*6.2
2001	Blake Johnson, Edinboro	28	111	4.0
2002	Danny Phillips, Mont. St.-Billings	28	120	4.3
2003	Jed Bedford, Columbus St.	32	135	4.2

*record

Three-Point Field-Goal Percentage

Season	Player, Team	G	3FG	3FGA	Pct.
1987	Charles Byrd, West Tex. A&M	31	95	168	56.5
1988	Ray Lee, Hampton	24	39	60	*65.0
1989	Aaron Baker, Mississippi Col.	27	69	117	59.0
1990	Mark Willey, Fort Hays St.	29	49	81	60.5
1991	Scott Martin, Rollins	28	114	201	56.7
1992	Jeff Duvall, Oakland City	30	49	91	53.8
1993	Greg Wilkinson, Oakland City	32	82	152	53.9
1994	Todd Jones, Southern Ind.	29	56	105	53.3
1995	Aaron Fehler, Oakland City	26	73	121	60.3
1996	Matt Hopson, Oakland City	31	84	145	57.9
1997	Adam Harness, Oakland City	26	39	68	57.4
1998	Todd Woelfe, Oakland City	27	87	162	53.7
1999	John Cabanilla, Oakland City	29	46	85	54.1
2000	Jasen Gast, Incarnate Word	26	39	72	54.2
2001	Bobby Hoegh, Southwest Baptist	23	72	147	49.0
2002	Jared Ramirez, Northern Colo.	27	60	115	52.2
2003	Ben Nemmers, North Dakota St.	30	83	159	52.2

*record

Free-Throw Percentage

Season	Player, Team	G	FT	FTA	Pct.
1948	Frank Cochran, Delta St.	22	36	43	83.7
1949	Jim Walsh, Spring Hill	25	62	75	82.7
1950	Dean Ehlers, Central Methodist	33	186	213	87.3
1951	Jim Hoverder, Central Mo. St.	23	75	85	88.2
1952	Jim Fenton, Akron	24	104	121	86.0
1953	Dick Parfitt, Central Mich.	22	93	105	88.6
1954	Bill Parrott, David Lipscomb	24	174	198	87.9
1955	Pete Kovacs, Monmouth (Ill.)	20	175	199	87.9
1956	Fred May, Loras	22	127	146	87.0
1957	Jim Sutton, South Dakota St.	22	127	138	92.0
1958	Arnold Smith, Allen	22	103	113	91.2
1959	Bill Reece, Lenoir-Rhyne	27	84	92	91.3
1960	Ron Slaymaker, Emporia St.	20	80	88	90.9
1961	Harvey Rosen, Wilkes	22	105	115	91.3
1962	Wayne Mahone, Stephen F. Austin	26	76	84	90.5
1963	Jon Hagen, Minn. St. Mankato	25	76	82	92.7
1964	Steve Nisenson, Hofstra	28	230	252	91.3
1965	Jon Hagen, Minn. St. Mankato	23	103	112	92.0
1966	Jack Cryan, Rider	25	182	198	91.9
1967	Kent Andrews, McNeese St.	22	101	110	91.8

Season	Player, Team	G	FT	FTA	Pct.
1968	Kent Andrews, McNeese St.	24	85	90	94.4
1969	Joe Cullen, Hartwick	18	96	103	93.2
1970	John Rinka, Kenyon	23	234	263	89.0
1971	Ed Roeth, Defiance	26	138	152	90.8
1972	Jeff Kuntz, St. Norbert	25	142	155	91.6
1973	Bob Kronisch, Brooklyn	30	93	105	88.6
1974	Terry Gill, New Orleans	30	97	105	92.4
1975	Clarence Rand, Alabama St.	29	91	101	90.1
1976	Billy Newton, Morgan St.	28	85	90	94.4
1977	Emery Sammons, Philadelphia U.	28	145	157	92.4
1978	Dana Skinner, Merrimack	28	142	154	92.2
1979	Jack Sparks, Bentley	28	76	84	90.5
1980	Grey Giovanine, Central Mo. St.	28	75	83	90.4
1981	Ted Smith, SIU Edwardsville	26	67	73	91.8
1982	Carl Gonder, Augustana (S.D.)	27	86	93	92.5
1983	Joe Sclafani, New Haven	28	86	98	87.8
1984	Darrell Johnston, Southern N.H.	29	74	81	91.4
1985	Tom McDonald, South Dakota St.	33	88	97	90.7
1986	Todd Mezzulo, Alas. Fairbanks	27	114	125	91.2
1987	Mike Sanders, Northern Colo.	28	82	87	94.3
1988	Charles Byrd, West Tex. A&M	29	92	99	92.8
1989	Mike Boschee, North Dakota	28	71	77	92.2
1990	Mike Morris, Ala.-Huntsville	28	114	125	91.2
1991	Ryun Williams, South Dakota	30	114	125	91.2
1992	Hal McManus, Lander	28	110	119	92.4
1993	Jason Williams, New Haven	27	115	125	92.0
1994	Jay Harrie, Mont. St.-Billings	26	86	92	93.5
1995	Jim Borodawka, Mass.-Lowell	27	74	80	92.5
1996	Paul Cluxton, Northern Ky.	32	100	108	92.6
1997	Paul Cluxton, Northern Ky.	35	94	94	*100.0
1998	Troy Nesmith, Gannon	27	146	158	92.4
1999	Travis Starns, Colorado Mines	26	87	93	93.5
2000	Jason Kreider, Michigan Tech	31	84	91	92.3
2001	C.J. Cowgill, Chaminade	22	113	119	95.0
2002	Curtis Small, Southampton	29	109	116	94.0
2003	Aaron Farley, Harding	30	137	146	93.8

*record

Rebound Average

Season	Player, Team	G	Reb.	Avg.
1951	Walter Lenz, Frank. & Marsh.	17	338	19.9
1952	Charley Wrinn, Trinity (Conn.)	19	486	25.6
1953	Ellerbe Neal, Wofford	23	609	26.5
1954	R.C. Owens, Albertson	25	677	27.1
1955	Tom Hart, Middlebury	22	649	29.5
1956	Tom Hart, Middlebury	21	620	*29.5
1957	Jim Smith, Steubenville	26	651	25.0
1958	Marv Becker, Widener	18	450	25.0
1959	Jim Davis, King's (Pa.)	17	384	22.6
1960	Jackie Jackson, Virginia Union	19	424	†.241
1961	Jackie Jackson, Virginia Union	26	641	24.7
1962	Jim Ahrens, Buena Vista	28	682	24.4
1963	Gerry Govan, St. Mary's (Kan.)	18	445	24.7
1964	Ernie Brock, Virginia St.	24	597	24.9
1965	Dean Sandifer, Lakeland	23	592	25.7
1966	Frank Stronczek, American Int'l	26	717	27.6
1967	Frank Stronczek, American Int'l	25	602	24.1
1968	Ron Horton, Delaware St.	23	543	23.6
1969	Wilbert Jones, Albany St. (Ga.)	28	670	23.9
1970	Russell Jackson, Southern U.	22	544	24.7
1971	Tony Williams, St. Francis (Me.)	24	599	25.0
1972	No rankings			
1973	No rankings			
1974	Larry Johnson, Prairie View	23	519	22.6
1975	Major Jones, Albany St. (Ga.)	27	608	22.5
1976	Major Jones, Albany St. (Ga.)	24	475	19.8
1977	Andre Means, Sacred Heart	32	516	16.1
1978	Scott Mountz, Calif. (Pa.)	24	431	18.0
1979	Keith Smith, Shaw	20	329	16.5
1980	Ricky Mahorn, Hampton	31	490	15.8
1981	Earl Jones, Dist. Columbia	25	333	13.3
1982	Donnie Carter, Tuskegee	29	372	12.8
1983	David Binion, N.C. Central	25	400	16.0
1984	Jerome Kersey, Longwood	27	383	14.2
1985	Charles Oakley, Virginia Union	31	535	17.3

Season	Player, Team	G	Reb.	Avg.
1986	Raheem Muhammad, Wayne St. (Mich.)	31	428	13.8
1987	Andre Porter, Southampton	23	309	13.4
1988	Anthony Ikeobi, Clark Atlanta	27	380	14.1
1989	Toby Barber, Winston-Salem	24	327	13.6
1990	Leroy Gasque, Morris Brown	24	375	15.6
1991	Sheldon Owens, Shaw	27	325	12.0
1992	David Allen, Wayne St. (Neb.)	28	362	12.9
1993	James Hector, American Int'l	28	389	13.9
1994	Pat Armour, Jacksonville St.	25	363	14.5
1995	Lorenzo Poole, Albany St. (Ga.)	26	417	16.0
1996	J.J. Sims, West Ga.	28	374	13.4
1997	Kebu Stewart, Cal St. Bakersfield	33	442	13.4
1998	Antonio Garcia, Ky. Wesleyan	33	457	13.8
1999	Antonio Garcia, Ky. Wesleyan	37	540	14.6
2000	Howard Jackson, Lincoln Memorial	24	321	13.4
2001	Colin Duchacme, Longwood	31	490	15.8
2002	Danny Jones, Tarleton St.	33	416	13.0
2003	Billy McDaniel, Ark.-Monticello	27	345	12.8

*record; †Championship determined by highest individual recoveries out of total by both teams in all games.

Assist Average

Season	Player, Team	G	Ast.	Avg.
1989	Steve Ray, Bridgeport	32	*400	*12.5
1990	Steve Ray, Bridgeport	33	385	11.7
1991	Adrian Hutt, Metro St.	28	285	10.2
1992	Tony Smith, Pfeiffer	35	349	10.0
1993	Demetri Beekman, Assumption	23	264	11.5
1994	Ernest Jenkins, N.M. Highlands	27	277	10.3
1995	Ernest Jenkins, N.M. Highlands	27	291	10.8
1996	Bobby Banks, Metro St.	27	244	9.0
1997	Emanuel Richardson, Pitt.-Johnstown	27	235	8.7
1998	Emanuel Richardson, Pitt.-Johnstown	29	260	9.0
1999	Shawn Brown, Merrimack	27	223	8.3
2000	Todd Chappell, Texas Wesleyan	27	263	9.7
2001	Javar Cheatham, Gannon	30	283	9.4
2002	Pat Delany, St. Anselm	30	234	7.8
2003	Clayton Smith, Metro St.	33	274	8.3

*record

Blocked-Shot Average

Season	Player, Team	G	Blk.	Avg.
1993	Antonio Harvey, Pfeiffer	29	155	*5.3
1994	Johnny Tyson, Central Okla.	27	126	4.7
1995	Kino Outlaw, Mount Olive	28	124	4.4
1996	John Burke, Southampton	28	142	5.1
1997	Garth Joseph, St. Rose	34	124	3.6
1998	James Doyle, Concord	30	*157	5.2
1999	Chandar Bingham, Virginia Union	27	95	3.5
2000	Josh Stanhiser, Columbia Union	25	87	3.5
2001	Jason Roseto, Edinboro	23	97	4.2
2002	George Bailey, Lock Haven	20	79	4.0
2003	Aaron Davis, Southern Conn. St.	25	103	4.1

*record

Steal Average

Season	Player, Team	G	Stl.	Avg.
1993	Marcus Stubblefield, Queens (N.C.)	28	110	3.9
1994	Ken Francis, Molloy	27	116	4.3
1995	Shannon Holmes, NYIT	30	110	3.7
1996	David Clark, Bluefield St.	31	118	3.8
1997	Devlin Herring, Pitt.-Johnstown	27	122	4.5
1998	Terrance Gist, S.C.-Spartanburg	29	122	4.2
1999	Wayne Copeland, Lynn	31	125	4.0
2000	Wayne Copeland, Lynn	26	*129	*5.0
2001	J.R. Gamble, Queens (N.C.)	32	139	4.3
2002	Shahar Golan, Assumption	30	106	3.5
2003	Gerry McNair, C.W. Post	30	103	3.4

*record

DIVISION II

Annual Team Champions

Won-Lost Percentage

Season	Team	Won	Lost	Pct.
1968	Monmouth	27	2	.931
1969	Alcorn St.	26	1	.963
1970	Central Wash.	31	2	.939
1971	Kentucky St.	31	2	.939
1972	Olivet	22	1	.957
1973	Coe	24	1	.960
1974	West Ga.	29	4	.879
1975	Bentley	23	2	.920
1976	Philadelphia U.	25	3	.893
1977	Clarion	27	3	.900
	Kentucky St.	27	3	.900
	Towson	27	3	.900
1978	Wis.-Green Bay	30	2	.938
1979	Roanoke	25	3	.893
1980	Alabama St.	32	2	.941
1981	Mt. St. Mary's	28	3	.903
1982	Cheyney	28	3	.903
1983	Dist. Columbia	29	3	.906
1984	Norfolk St.	29	2	.935
1985	Jacksonville St.	31	1	.969
	Virginia Union	31	1	.969
1986	Wright St.	28	3	.903
1987	Norfolk St.	28	3	.903
1988	Fla. Southern	31	3	.912
1989	UC Riverside	30	4	.882
1990	Ky. Wesleyan	31	2	.939
1991	Southwest Baptist	29	3	.906
1992	Calif. (Pa.)	31	2	.939
1993	Cal St. Bakersfield	33	0	1.000
1994	Philadelphia U.	29	2	.935
1995	Jacksonville St.	24	1	.960
1996	Fort Hays St.	34	0	1.000
1997	Fort Hays St.	29	2	.935
1998	UC Davis	31	2	.939
1999	Ky. Wesleyan	35	2	.946
2000	Fla. Southern	32	2	.941
2001	Adelphi	31	1	.969
2002	Cal St. San B'dino	28	2	.933
	Northeastern St.	28	2	.933
2003	Northeastern St.	32	3	.914

Scoring Offense

Season	Team	G	W-L	Pts.	Avg.
1948	St. Anselm	19	12-7	1,329	69.9
1949	Charleston (W.Va.)	26	18-8	2,023	77.8
1950	Charleston (W.Va.)	31	22-9	2,477	79.9
1951	Beloit	23	18-5	1,961	85.3
1952	Lambuth	22	17-5	1,985	90.2
1953	Arkansas Tech	21	20-1	1,976	94.1
1954	Montclair St.	22	18-4	2,128	96.7
1955	West Va. Tech	20	15-5	2,150	107.5
1956	West Va. Tech	22	16-6	2,210	100.5
1957	West Va. Tech	29	26-3	2,976	102.6
1958	West Va. Tech	29	24-5	2,941	101.4
1959	Grambling	29	28-1	2,764	95.3
1960	Mississippi Col.	19	15-4	2,169	114.2
1961	Lawrence Tech	25	19-6	2,409	96.4
1962	Troy St.	25	20-5	2,402	96.1
1963	Miles	21	17-4	2,011	95.8
1964	Benedict	27	19-8	2,730	101.1
1965	Ark.-Pine Bluff	26	22-4	2,655	102.1
1966	Southern Cal College	23	15-8	2,480	107.8
1967	Lincoln (Mo.)	27	24-3	2,925	108.3
1968	Stillman	26	17-9	2,898	111.5
1969	Norfolk St.	25	21-4	2,653	106.1
1970	Norfolk St.	26	19-7	2,796	107.5
1971	Savannah St.	29	18-11	3,051	105.2
1972	Florida A&M	28	18-10	2,869	102.5
1973	Md.-East. Shore	31	26-5	2,974	95.9
1974	Texas Southern	28	15-13	2,884	103.0
1975	Prairie View	26	16-10	2,774	106.7
1976	Southern U.	27	13-14	2,637	97.7
1977	Virginia Union	30	25-5	2,966	98.9
1978	Merrimack	28	22-6	2,606	93.1
1979	Armstrong Atlantic	27	21-6	2,626	97.3
1980	Ashland	27	11-16	2,514	93.1
1981	Virginia St.	31	20-11	2,761	89.1
1982	Alabama St.	28	22-6	2,429	86.8
1983	Virginia St.	29	19-10	2,802	96.6
1984	Southern N.H.	29	18-11	2,564	88.4
1985	Alabama A&M	31	21-10	2,881	92.9
1986	Alabama A&M	32	23-9	2,897	90.5
1987	Alabama A&M	30	23-7	2,826	94.2
1988	Oakland	28	19-9	2,685	95.9
1989	Stonehill	32	23-9	3,244	101.4
1990	Jacksonville St.	29	24-5	2,872	99.0
1991	Troy St.	30	22-8	3,259	108.6
1992	Troy St.	29	23-6	3,513	*121.1
1993	Central Okla.	29	23-6	3,293	113.6
1994	Central Okla.	27	17-10	2,782	103.0
1995	Central Okla.	30	23-7	3,219	107.3
1996	Central Okla.	29	19-10	2,933	101.1
1997	Mont. St.-Billings	28	22-6	2,904	103.7
1998	Mont. St.-Billings	28	21-7	2,945	105.2
1999	Central Okla.	27	16-11	2,657	98.4
2000	Mont. St.-Billings	26	17.9	2,460	94.6
2001	Mont. St.-Billings	27	18-9	2,648	98.1
2002	Mont. St.-Billings	28	21-7	2,559	91.4
2003	Pfeiffer	31	22-9	2,926	94.4

*record

Scoring Defense

Season	Team	G	W-L	Pts.	Avg.
1948	Miss. Industrial	15	13-2	436	‡29.1
1949	Gordon	20	16-4	655	32.8
1950	Tex. A&M-Corp. Chris.	26	25-1	1,030	39.6
1951	St. Martin's	24	11-13	1,137	47.4
1952	Truman	19	12-7	876	46.1
1953	Sacramento St.	26	18-8	1,381	53.1
1954	Sacramento St.	18	9-9	883	49.1
1955	Amherst	22	16-6	1,233	56.0
1956	Amherst	22	16-6	1,277	58.0
1957	Stephen F. Austin	26	23-3	1,337	51.4
1958	McNeese St.	23	19-4	1,068	46.4
1959	Humboldt St.	23	14-9	1,166	50.7
1960	Wittenberg	24	22-2	1,122	46.8
1961	Wittenberg	29	25-4	1,270	43.8
1962	Wittenberg	26	21-5	1,089	41.9
1963	Wittenberg	28	26-2	1,285	45.9
1964	Wittenberg	23	18-5	1,186	51.6
1965	Cheyney	25	24-1	1,393	55.7
1966	Chicago	16	12-4	894	55.9
1967	Ashland	24	21-3	1,025	42.7
1968	Ashland	30	23-7	1,164	38.8
1969	Ashland	30	26-4	1,017	33.9
1970	Ashland	27	23-4	1,118	41.4
1971	Ashland	28	25-3	1,523	54.4
1972	Chicago	20	16-4	1,132	56.6
1973	Steubenville	29	22-7	1,271	43.8
1974	Steubenville	26	14-12	1,336	51.4
1975	Cal Poly	26	15-11	1,590	61.2
1976	Wis.-Green Bay	29	21-8	1,768	61.0
1977	Wis.-Green Bay	29	26-3	1,682	58.0
1978	Wis.-Green Bay	32	30-2	1,682	52.6
1979	Wis.-Green Bay	32	24-8	1,612	50.4
1980	Wis.-Green Bay	27	15-12	1,577	58.4
1981	San Fran. St.	26	17-9	1,463	56.3
1982	Cal Poly	29	23-6	1,537	53.0
1983	Cal Poly	28	18-10	1,553	55.5
1984	Cal Poly	28	20-8	1,458	52.1
1985	Cal Poly	27	16-11	1,430	53.0
1986	Lewis	30	24-6	1,702	56.7
1987	Denver	29	20-9	1,844	63.6
1988	N.C. Central	29	26-3	1,683	58.0
1989	N.C. Central	32	28-4	1,791	56.0
1990	Humboldt St.	31	20-11	1,831	59.1
1991	Minn. Duluth	32	27-5	1,899	59.3
1992	Pace	30	23-7	1,517	50.6
1993	Philadelphia U.	32	30-2	1,898	59.3
1994	Pace	29	19-10	1,715	59.1
1995	Armstrong Atlantic	31	20-11	1,929	62.2
1996	Coker	26	16-10	1,592	61.2

Season	Team	G	W-L	Pts.	Avg.
1997	Fort Hays St.	31	29-2	1,837	59.3
1998	Presbyterian	28	16-12	1,704	60.9
1999	Incarnate Word	30	28-2	1,727	57.6
2000	Wingate	30	26-4	1,775	59.2
2001	Henderson St.	32	22-10	1,919	60.0
2002	Tusculum	28	15-13	1,600	57.1
2003	Barry	28	18-10	1,490	53.2

‡ record since 1948

Scoring Margin

Season	Team	Off.	Def.	Mar.
1950	Montana	77.4	57.7	19.7
1951	Eastern Ill.	84.7	57.9	26.8
1952	Southwest Tex. St.	77.4	48.9	28.5
1953	Arkansas Tech	94.7	74.3	20.4
1954	Texas Southern	89.2	63.3	25.9
1955	Mt. St. Mary's	95.2	73.3	21.9
1956	Western Ill.	92.5	72.1	20.4
1957	West Va. Tech	102.6	77.2	25.4
1958	Tennessee St.	88.7	64.1	24.6
1959	Grambling	95.3	73.3	22.0
1960	Mississippi Col.	114.2	92.9	21.3
1961	Bryan	93.8	62.4	*31.4
1962	Mansfield	87.6	64.7	22.9
1963	Gorham St.	94.7	69.7	25.0
1964	Central Conn. St.	94.5	67.7	26.8
1965	Cheyney	80.7	55.7	25.0
1966	Cheyney	90.0	64.4	25.6
1967	Lincoln (Mo.)	108.3	82.2	26.1
1968	Western New Eng.	104.7	76.8	27.9
1969	Indiana (Pa.)	88.6	64.5	24.1
1970	Husson	106.1	79.0	27.1
1971	Kentucky St.	103.5	78.2	25.3
1972	Brockport St.	93.8	70.3	23.5
1973	Wis.-Green Bay	71.2	52.1	19.1
1974	Alcorn St.	96.9	79.8	17.1
1975	Bentley	95.2	78.7	16.5
1976	UCF	94.8	78.4	16.4
1977	Texas Southern	88.4	71.9	16.5
1978	Wis.-Green Bay	68.8	52.6	16.2
1979	Roanoke	77.8	60.8	17.0
1980	UCF	91.7	72.1	19.6
1981	West Ga.	88.5	70.2	18.3
1982	Minn. Duluth	81.7	64.8	16.9
1983	Minn. Duluth	84.8	69.8	15.0
1984	Chicago St.	85.9	70.2	15.7
1985	Virginia Union	87.6	67.8	19.8
1986	Mt. St. Mary's	80.0	65.7	14.3
1987	Ky. Wesleyan	92.4	72.9	19.8
1988	Fla. Southern	89.6	70.5	19.1
1989	Virginia Union	88.2	69.6	18.6
1990	Ky. Wesleyan	97.3	76.8	20.5
1991	Ashland	99.8	78.2	21.6
1992	Oakland City	99.5	77.1	22.4
1993	Philadelphia U.	78.8	59.3	19.4
1994	Oakland City	87.8	65.5	22.3
1995	Jacksonville St.	101.2	77.6	23.6
1996	Fort Hays St.	92.1	70.2	21.9
1997	Fort Hays St.	84.1	59.3	24.8
1998	Oakland City	85.8	64.1	21.7
1999	Incarnate Word	78.5	57.6	21.0
2000	Metro St.	87.0	67.9	19.1
2001	Adelphi	85.3	65.7	19.7
2002	Ky. Wesleyan	91.3	72.7	18.6
2003	Ky. Wesleyan	88.9	72.7	16.3

* record

Field-Goal Percentage

Season	Team	FG	FGA	Pct.
1948	Tex. A&M-Commerce	445	1,119	39.8
1949	Southwest Mo. St.	482	1,106	43.6
1950	Tex. A&M-Corp. Chris.	555	1,290	43.0
1951	Beloit	773	1,734	44.6
1952	Southwest Mo. St.	890	1,903	46.8
1953	Lebanon Valley	637	1,349	47.2
1954	San Diego St.	675	1,502	44.9
1955	UC Santa Barb.	672	1,383	48.6
1956	UC Santa Barb.	552	1,142	48.3
1957	Alderson-Broaddus	1,006	2,094	48.0
1958	N.C. A&T	552	1,072	51.5
1959	Grambling	1,048	2,048	51.2
1960	William Carey	708	1,372	51.6
1961	Virginia Union	908	1,735	52.3
1962	West Va. Tech	871	1,575	55.3
1963	Lenoir-Rhyne	869	1,647	52.8
1964	LeMoyne-Owen	844	1,520	55.5
1965	Southern U.	1,036	1,915	54.1
1966	Howard Payne	932	1,710	54.5
1967	Alabama St.	874	1,555	56.2
1968	South Carolina St.	588	1,010	58.2
1969	Southampton	846	1,588	53.3
1970	Savannah St.	1,145	1,969	58.2
1971	Alabama St.	1,196	2,100	57.0
1972	Florida A&M	1,194	2,143	55.7
1973	Wis.-Green Bay	929	1,700	54.6
1974	Kentucky St.	1,252	2,266	55.3
1975	Kentucky St.	1,121	1,979	56.6
1976	Kentucky St.	1,093	1,753	*62.4
1977	Merrimack	1,120	2,008	55.8
1978	Wis.-Green Bay	840	1,509	55.6
1979	Morris Brown	980	1,763	55.6
1980	UNC Pembroke	849	1,544	55.0
1981	Bellarmine	851	1,561	54.5
1982	Fla. Southern	943	1,644	57.4
1983	Lewis	807	1,448	55.7
1984	Lewis	851	1,494	57.0
1985	Virginia Union	1,132	1,967	57.5
1986	Tampa	856	1,546	55.4
1987	Johnson Smith	995	1,817	54.8
1988	Fla. Southern	1,118	2,026	55.2
1989	Millersville	1,119	2,079	53.8
1990	S.C.-Spartanburg	954	1,745	54.7
1991	S.C.-Spartanburg	923	1,631	56.6
1992	S.C.-Spartanburg	898	1,664	54.0
1993	Cal St. Bakersfield	1,002	1,849	54.2
1994	Southern Ind.	1,171	2,142	54.7
1995	High Point	862	1,603	53.8
1996	Fort Hays St.	1,158	2,145	54.0
1997	Oakland City	961	1,821	52.8
1998	West Tex. A&M	953	1,841	51.8
1999	South Dakota	835	1,631	51.2
2000	Mo. Western St.	845	1,621	52.1
2001	Southern Ind.	1,014	1,937	52.3
2002	Neb.-Kearney	899	1,762	51.0
2003	Michigan Tech	920	1,740	52.9

* record

Field-Goal Percentage Defense

Season	Team	FG	FGA	Pct.
1978	Wis.-Green Bay	681	1,830	37.2
1979	Wis.-Green Bay	639	1,709	37.4
1980	Wis.-Parkside	688	1,666	41.3
1981	Central St. (Ohio)	675	1,724	39.2
1982	Minn. St. Mankato	699	1,735	40.3
1983	Central Mo. St.	746	1,838	40.6
1984	Norfolk St.	812	1,910	42.5
1985	Central Mo. St.	683	1,660	41.1
1986	Norfolk St.	782	1,925	40.6
1987	Denver	691	1,709	40.4
1988	Minn. Duluth	702	1,691	41.5
1989	N.C. Central	633	1,642	38.6
1990	Central Mo. St.	696	1,757	39.6
1991	Southwest Baptist	758	1,942	39.0
1992	Virginia Union	766	2,069	37.0
1993	Pfeiffer	767	2,028	37.8
1994	Virginia Union	705	1,966	35.9
1995	Virginia Union	723	1,973	36.6
1996	Virginia Union	718	1,944	36.9
1997	St. Rose	887	2,409	36.8
1998	Delta St.	705	1,930	36.5
1999	Delta St.	610	1,652	36.9
2000	Fla. Southern	702	1,887	37.2
2001	Tampa	631	1,723	36.6
2002	Tarleton St.	657	1,837	*35.8
2003	Tarleton St.	655	1,757	37.3

* record

DIVISION II

Three-Point Field Goals Made Per Game

Season	Team	G	3FG	Avg.
1987	Northern Mich.	27	187	6.9
1988	Sacramento St.	30	303	10.1
1989	Central Okla.	27	280	10.4
1990	Stonehill	27	259	9.6
1991	Hillsdale	27	318	11.8
1992	Troy St.	29	*444	*15.3
1993	Hillsdale	28	366	13.1
1994	Hillsdale	25	315	12.6
1995	Hillsdale	29	330	11.4
1996	Mont. St.-Billings	28	304	10.9
1997	Mont. St.-Billings	28	394	14.1
1998	Mont. St.-Billings	28	375	13.4
1999	Mont. St.-Billings	28	355	12.7
2000	Mont. St.-Billings	26	294	11.3
2001	Mont. St.-Billings	27	284	10.5
2002	St. Anselm	30	301	10.0
2003	Bemidji St.	29	338	11.7

*record

Three-Point Field-Goal Percentage

Season	Team	G	3FG	3FGA	Pct.
1987	St. Anselm	30	97	189	51.3
1988	Winston-Salem	28	98	182	*53.8
1989	Mississippi Col.	27	144	276	52.2
1990	Shaw	27	74	143	51.7
1991	Rollins	28	278	585	47.5
1992	Oakland City	30	244	486	50.2
1993	Oakland City	32	215	465	46.2
1994	Oakland City	28	225	495	45.5
1995	Oakland City	30	256	561	45.6
1996	Oakland City	31	260	537	48.4
1997	Oakland City	30	311	651	47.8
1998	Michigan Tech	31	267	613	43.6
1999	South Dakota	29	258	577	44.7
2000	Eckerd	28	156	366	42.6
2001	Mesa St.	27	152	346	43.9
2002	Michigan Tech	30	216	499	43.3
2003	Michigan Tech	32	252	581	43.4

*record

Free-Throw Percentage

Season	Team	FT	FTA	Pct.
1948	Charleston (W.Va.)	446	659	67.7
1949	Linfield	276	402	68.7
1950	Jacksonville St.	452	613	73.7
1951	Millikin	603	846	71.3
1952	Eastern Ill.	521	688	75.7
1953	Upsala	513	69	74.0
1954	Central Mich.	376	509	73.9
1955	Mississippi Col.	559	733	76.3
1956	Wheaton (Ill.)	625	842	74.2
1957	Wheaton (Ill.)	689	936	73.6
1958	Wheaton (Ill.)	517	689	75.0
1959	Wabash	418	545	76.7
1960	Allen	225	297	75.8
1961	Southwest Mo. St.	453	605	74.9
1962	Lenoir-Rhyne	477	599	79.6
1963	Hampden-Sydney	442	559	79.1
1964	Western Caro.	492	621	79.2
1965	Mississippi Col.	529	663	79.8
1966	Athens St.	631	802	78.7
1967	Northwestern St.	528	678	77.9
1968	Kenyon	684	858	79.7
1969	Kenyon	583	727	80.2
1970	Wooster	571	714	80.0
1971	South Ala.	422	518	81.5
1972	Clark Atlanta	409	520	78.7
1973	Rockford (Ill.)	367	481	76.3
1974	New Orleans	537	701	76.6
1975	Alabama St.	456	565	80.7
1976	Alabama St.	451	576	78.3
1977	Puget Sound	495	637	77.7
1978	Merrimack	508	636	79.9
1979	Bentley	506	652	77.6
1980	Philadelphia U.	436	549	79.4
1981	Coppin St.	401	514	78.0
1982	Fla. Southern	726	936	77.6
1983	Transylvania	463	606	76.4
1984	Transylvania	491	639	76.8
1985	Minn. St. Mankato	349	445	78.4
1986	Southern N.H.	507	672	75.4
1987	Columbus St.	339	433	78.3
1988	Rollins	631	795	79.4
1989	Rollins	477	607	78.6
1990	Rollins	449	582	77.1
1991	Lenoir-Rhyne	441	564	78.2
1992	Adams St.	397	512	77.5
1993	Philadelphia U.	491	630	77.9
1994	West Liberty St.	473	602	78.6
1995	Western St.	469	603	77.8
1996	South Dakota	501	648	77.3
1997	Hawaii-Hilo	471	606	77.7
1998	Gannon	473	573	*82.5
1999	Minn. Duluth	430	547	78.6
2000	Bemidji St.	386	492	78.5
2001	Morningside	383	485	79.0
2002	St. Cloud St.	461	587	78.5
2003	South Dakota	452	566	79.9

*record

Rebound Margin

Season	Team	Off.	Def.	Mar.
1976	Mississippi Val.	63.9	39.5	*24.4
1977	Philadelphia U.	38.7	24.1	14.6
1978	Mass.-Lowell	49.0	37.5	11.5
1979	Dowling	48.2	32.6	15.6
1980	Ark.-Pine Bluff	40.3	25.9	14.4
1981	Wis.-Green Bay	40.6	26.5	14.1
1982	Central St. (Ohio)	48.0	37.2	10.8
1983	Hampton	50.2	38.5	11.8
1984	Calif. (Pa.)	46.4	33.1	13.3
1985	Virginia Union	44.1	32.0	12.1
1986	Tampa	39.9	28.0	11.8
1987	Millersville	44.7	33.8	10.9
1988	Clark Atlanta	44.7	32.5	12.1
1989	Hampton	46.7	36.3	10.3
1990	Fla. Atlantic	41.0	29.4	11.6
1991	Calif. (Pa.)	44.6	32.0	12.6
1992	Oakland City	43.4	31.8	11.6
1993	Metro St.	45.5	32.0	13.5
1994	Oakland City	44.0	33.7	10.3
1995	Jacksonville St.	47.7	35.2	12.5
1996	Virginia Union	48.0	36.1	11.9
1997	Southern Conn. St.	41.6	32.3	9.3
1998	South Dakota St.	46.5	35.9	10.6
1999	Ky. Wesleyan	44.8	32.6	12.2
2000	Salem Int'l	44.2	32.1	12.1
2001	Salem Int'l	42.6	31.3	11.4
2002	Tarleton St.	43.0	32.0	11.1
2003	South Dakota St.	44.1	32.5	11.6

*record

2003 Most-Improved Teams

School (Coach)	2003	2002	Games Improved
1. Alas. Fairbanks (Al Sokaitis)	20-8	4-23	15½
2. Cal St. Chico (Prescott Smith)	18-9	6-21	12
2. Colorado Mines (Pryor Orser)	18-10	5-21	12
4. Presbyterian (Gregg Nibert)	27-9	12-16	11
5. Kutztown (Bernie Driscoll)	18-10	6-19	10½
5. Lenoir-Rhyne (John Lentz)	22-8	10-17	10½
5. Okla. Panhandle (Charles Terry)	15-11	5-22	10½
8. Christian Bros. (Mike Nienaber)	18-11	7-19	9½
8. C.W. Post (Tom Galeazzi)	25-8	13-15	9½
10. Francis Marion (John Schweitz)	13-14	4-23	9

School (Coach)	2003	2002	Games Improved
11. Emporia St. (David Moe)	16-12	7-19	8
11. Mercy (Steve Kelly)	10-16	2-24	8
11. Queens (N.C.) (Bart Lundy)	29-4	19-10	8
14. Bridgeport (Mike Ruane)	23-8	14-14	7½
14. Bryant (Max Good)	17-14	7-19	7½
14. Central Okla. (Terry Evans)	19-10	10-16	7½
14. Mars Hill (Terry Rogers)	13-15	4-21	7½
14. Saginaw Valley (Dean Lockwood)	13-14	5-21	7½

To determine games improved, add the difference in victories between the two seasons to the difference in losses, then divide by two.

All-Time Winningest Teams

Includes records as a senior college only; minimum 10 seasons of competition. Postseason games are included.

Percentage

Team	Yrs.	Won	Lost	Pct.
1. Cal St. Bakersfield	32	656	268	.710
2. Lynn	10	200	86	.699
3. Philadelphia U.	79	1,115	486	.696
4. Queens (N.C.)	14	281	128	.687
5. Cheyney	40	759	350	.684
6. Virginia Union	78	1,251	596	.677
7. Southern N.H.	40	765	366	.676
8. Metro St.	19	377	183	.673
9. Fla. Southern	47	895	436	.672
10. LeMoyne-Owen	44	814	398	.672
11. Ky. Wesleyan	92	1,373	676	.670
12. Fort Hays St.	85	1,225	643	.656
13. Incarnate Word	20	376	203	.649
14. St. Rose	29	549	299	.647
15. Gannon	59	981	546	.642
16. Southern Ind.	34	608	340	.641
17. Northern St.	84	1,229	693	.639
18. Carson-Newman	45	869	492	.639
19. Fairmont St.	80	1,292	741	.636
20. Grand Canyon	55	907	539	.627
21. Bentley	40	661	398	.624
22. North Dakota	98	1,348	817	.623
23. Bloomsburg	100	1,159	710	.620
24. West Tex. A&M	82	1,255	773	.619
25. Central Ark.	81	1,286	793	.619
26. Alas. Anchorage	26	467	288	.619
27. Indiana (Pa.)	74	1,013	628	.617
28. C.W. Post	47	742	460	.617
29. Millersville	73	1,016	634	.616
30. Central Mo. St.	98	1,347	848	.614

*Includes one tie.

Victories

Team	Yrs.	Won	Lost	Pct.
1. Ky. Wesleyan	92	1,373	676	.670
2. North Dakota	98	1,348	817	.623
3. Central Mo. St.	98	1,347	848	.614
4. Washburn	97	1,343	956	.584
5. North Dakota St.	105	1,320	940	.584
6. Fairmont St.	80	1,292	741	.636
7. Central Ark.	81	1,286	793	.619
8. Drury	94	1,276	807	.613
9. West Tex. A&M	82	1,255	773	.619
10. Virginia Union	78	1,251	596	.677
11. Northern St.	84	1,229	693	.639
12. Fort Hays St.	85	1,225	643	.656
13. South Dakota St.	95	1,215	810	.600
14. Pittsburg St.	92	1,197	973	.552
15. Emporia St.	97	1,174	970	.548

Team	Yrs.	Won	Lost	Pct.
16. Bloomsburg	100	1,159	710	.620
17. Neb.-Kearney	95	1,144	796	.590
18. Cal St. Chico	90	1,142	992	.535
19. Lenoir-Rhyne	82	1,121	886	.559
20. Philadelphia U.	79	1,115	486	.696
21. East Central	76	1,110	743	.599
22. Indianapolis	78	1,109	765	.592
23. Northwest Mo. St.	87	1,107	827	.572
24. Tex. A&M-Commerce	88	1,091	889	.551
25. Northern Mich.	97	1,084	746	.592
26. Catawba	77	1,071	909	.541
26. St. Cloud St.	80	1,071	685	.610
28. Henderson St.	88	1,068	811	.568
29. Wayne St. (Neb.)	88	1,058	899	.541
30. Arkansas Tech	80	1,050	831	.558

Winningest Teams of the 2000s

PERCENTAGE
(Minimum 3 seasons as NCAA member)

Team	Yrs.	Won	Lost	Pct.
1. Ky. Wesleyan	4	119	12	.908
2. Northeastern St.	4	107	17	.863
3. Adelphi	4	104	20	.839
4. Cal St. San B'dino	4	98	19	.838
5. Metro St.	4	113	22	.837
6. Salem Int'l	4	106	21	.835
7. Fla. Southern	4	101	23	.815
8. Southern Ind.	4	98	25	.797
9. Northwest Mo. St.	4	98	26	.790
9. Washburn	4	98	26	.790
11. Michigan Tech	4	95	26	.785
12. Wingate	4	95	27	.779
13. Charleston (W.Va.)	4	97	28	.776
13. Northern Ky.	4	97	28	.776
15. Neb.-Kearney	4	92	27	.773
16. St. Cloud St.	4	90	27	.769
16. Tampa	4	90	27	.769
18. Seattle Pacific	4	88	27	.765
19. South Dakota St.	4	91	29	.758
20. Henderson St.	4	96	32	.750
20. Mass.-Lowell	4	93	31	.750
22. Winston-Salem	4	88	30	.746
23. Mo. Southern St.	4	90	31	.744
24. Incarnate Word	4	81	28	.743
25. Gannon	4	86	30	.741
26. Calif. (Pa.)	4	88	31	.739
27. Fort Hays St.	4	85	30	.739
28. South Dakota	4	82	29	.739
29. Findlay	3	65	23	.739
30. Queens (N.C.)	4	90	32	.738

VICTORIES

Team	Yrs.	Won	Lost	Pct.
1. Ky. Wesleyan	4	119	12	.908
2. Metro St.	4	113	22	.837

Team	Yrs.	Won	Lost	Pct.
3. Northeastern St.	4	107	17	.863
4. Salem Int'l.	4	106	21	.835
5. Adelphi	4	104	20	.839
6. Fla. Southern	4	101	23	.815
7. Cal St. San B'dino	4	98	19	.838
7. Northwest Mo. St.	4	98	26	.790
7. Southern Ind.	4	98	25	.797
7. Washburn	4	98	26	.790
11. Charleston (W.Va.)	4	97	28	.776
11. Northern Ky.	4	97	28	.776
13. Henderson St.	4	96	32	.750
14. Michigan Tech	4	95	26	.785
14. Wingate	4	95	27	.779
16. Mass.-Lowell	4	93	31	.750
17. Neb.-Kearney	4	92	27	.773
18. South Dakota St.	4	91	29	.758
19. St. Cloud St.	4	90	27	.769
19. Tampa	4	90	27	.769
19. Mo. Southern St.	4	90	31	.744
19. Queens (N.C.)	4	90	32	.738
23. Seattle Pacific	4	88	27	.765
23. Winston-Salem	4	88	30	.746
23. Calif. (Pa.)	4	88	31	.739
26. Gannon	4	86	30	.741
26. Eckerd	4	86	32	.729
26. Indiana (Pa.)	4	86	34	.717
26. Johnson Smith	4	86	35	.711
30. Fort Hays St.	4	85	30	.739

All-Time Won-Lost Records

(No Minimum Seasons of Competition)

Team	First Year	Yrs.	Won	Lost	Pct.
Abilene Christian	1920	80	983	888	.525
Adelphi	1946	56	847	647	.567
Ala.-Huntsville	1974	30	412	445	.481
Alas. Anchorage	1978	26	467	288	.619
Alas. Fairbanks	1953	47	486	586	.453
Alderson-Broaddus	1936	65	974	843	.536
American Int'l	1934	69	817	818	.500
Anderson (S.C.)	1999	5	56	58	.491
Angelo St.	1966	38	526	508	.509
Arkansas Tech	1914	80	1,050	831	.558
Armstrong Atlantic	1967	37	555	478	.537
Ashland	1922	82	973	834	.538
Assumption	1924	74	954	741	.563
Augusta St.	1966	38	567	487	.538
Augustana (S.D.)	1928	73	793	894	.470
Barry	1985	19	245	275	.471
Bellarmine	1952	53	459	410	.528
Bemidji St.	1922	77	778	867	.473
Bentley	1964	40	661	398	.624
Bloomsburg	1902	100	1,159	710	.620
Bryant	1963	41	524	561	.483
UC Davis	1910	91	875	1029	.460
UC San Diego	1966	28	487	484	.502
Cal Poly Pomona	1948	56	760	745	.505
Cal St. Bakersfield	1972	32	656	268	.710
Cal St. Chico	1914	90	1,142	992	.535
Cal St. Dom. Hills	1978	26	346	349	.498
Cal St. L.A.	1949	55	696	729	.488
Cal St. San B'dino	1985	19	300	208	.591
Cal St. Stanislaus	1967	37	411	490	.456
Carson-Newman	1959	45	869	492	.639
Catawba	1927	77	1,071	909	.541
Central Ark.	1921	81	1,297	793	.621
Central Mo. St.	1906	98	1,347	848	.614
Central Okla.	1921	76	1,023	831	.552
Chadron St.	1922	78	934	887	.513
Chaminade	1977	27	420	343	.550
Cheyney	1964	40	759	350	.684
Clayton St.	1990	14	176	192	.478
Colorado Mines	1910	94	621	1110	.359
Columbus St.	1967	36	569	402	.586
C.W. Post	1956	47	742	460	.617
Delta St.	1928	73	1,034	677	.604
Drury	1909	94	1,276	807	.613
East Central	1928	76	1,110	743	.599
East Stroudsburg	1927	76	803	863	.482
Eckerd	1964	40	556	442	.557
Edinboro	1929	73	904	651	.581

Team	First Year	Yrs.	Won	Lost	Pct.
Emporia St.	1902	97	1,174	970	.548
Erskine	1914	78	941	849	.526
Fairmont St.	1917	80	1,292	741	.636
Ferris St.	1926	74	860	805	.517
Fla. Southern	1957	47	895	436	.672
Florida Tech	1965	39	414	596	.410
Fort Hays St.	1917	85	1,225	643	.656
Fort Lewis	1963	41	483	579	.455
Francis Marion	1970	33	434	482	.474
Franklin Pierce	1964	40	636	410	.608
Gannon	1945	59	981	546	.642
GC&SU	1970	34	466	449	.509
Grand Canyon	1949	55	907	539	.627
Grand Valley St.	1967	37	595	420	.586
Harding	1958	46	589	678	.465
Hawaii-Hilo	1977	27	471	339	.581
Henderson St.	1911	88	1,068	811	.568
Humboldt St.	1924	80	630	822	.434
Incarnate Word	1984	20	376	203	.649
Indiana (Pa.)	1927	74	1,013	628	.617
Indianapolis	1923	78	1,109	765	.592
Johnson Smith	1929	63	916	648	.586
Kennesaw St.	1986	18	285	236	.547
Ky. Wesleyan	1908	92	1,373	676	.670
Lake Superior St.	1947	56	779	607	.562
Lander	1969	35	584	458	.560
Le Moyne	1949	55	769	586	.568
LeMoyne-Owen	1960	44	814	398	.672
Lenoir-Rhyne	1920	82	1,121	886	.559
Lewis	1949	54	868	572	.603
Lincoln Memorial	1981	23	399	275	.592
Longwood	1977	27	394	334	.541
Lynn	1994	10	200	86	.699
Mansfield	1918	76	815	689	.542
Mass.-Lowell	1976	28	398	385	.508
Mercyhurst	1972	32	434	434	.500
Merrimack	1950	54	677	672	.502
Metro St.	1985	19	377	183	.673
Michigan Tech	1920	81	701	856	.450
Midwestern St.	1947	57	1,042	695	.600
Millersville	1929	73	1,016	634	.616
Minn. Duluth	1930	72	1,034	675	.605
Minn. St. Mankato	1921	78	966	736	.568
Mo.-Rolla	1910	91	703	1018	.408
Mo.-St. Louis	1967	37	464	502	.480
Mo. Southern St.	1969	35	551	462	.544
Mo. Western St.	1970	34	612	392	.610
Mont. St.-Billings	1927	74	888	737	.546
Morehouse	1911	92	993	900	.525
Neb.-Kearney	1906	95	1,144	796	.590
Neb.-Omaha	1911	88	908	959	.486
New Haven	1962	40	590	481	.551
N.J. Inst. Of Tech	1954	50	658	494	.571
N.M. Highlands	1924	77	793	909	.466
NYIT	1959	42	571	449	.560
Newberry	1913	88	878	1119	.440
North Ala.	1949	55	883	711	.554
N.C. Central	1928	69	961	730	.568
UNC-Pembroke	1940	64	814	758	.518
North Dakota	1905	98	1,348	817	.623
North Dakota St.	1898	105	1,320	940	.584
North Fla.	1993	11	124	175	.415
Northern Colo.	1902	102	948	986	.490
Northern Ky.	1972	32	535	368	.592
Northern Mich.	1906	97	1,084	746	.592
Northern St.	1920	84	1,229	693	.639
Northwest Mo. St.	1917	87	1,107	827	.572
Oakland City	1923	62	752	681	.525
Pace	1948	56	687	680	.503
Philadelphia U.	1920	79	1,115	486	.696
Pittsburg St.	1912	92	1,197	973	.552
Pitt.-Johnstown	1970	34	397	463	.462
Presbyterian	1914	90	1,030	982	.512
Queens (N.C.)	1990	14	281	128	.687
Quincy	1940	64	934	712	.567
Regis (Colo.)	1945	56	791	680	.538
Saginaw Valley	1970	34	493	449	.523
St. Anselm	1935	69	872	662	.568
St. Cloud St.	1923	80	1,071	685	.610
St. Joseph's (Ind.)	1906	91	917	869	.513
St. Leo	1966	38	394	581	.404
St. Michael's	1921	83	956	853	.528

Team	First Year	Yrs.	Won	Lost	Pct.	Team	First Year	Yrs.	Won	Lost	Pct.
St. Rose	1974	29	549	299	.647	Tampa	1950	41	639	476	.573
Seattle Pacific	1943	59	883	660	.572	Tex. A&M-Commerce	1916	88	1,091	889	.551
Shepherd	1950	54	705	678	.510	Tex. A&M-Kingsville	1926	74	778	947	.451
Slippery Rock	1926	73	804	798	.502	Truman	1920	84	996	877	.532
Sonoma St.	1964	34	367	491	.428	Valdosta St.	1955	53	680	508	.572
S.C.-Aiken	1991	13	170	192	.470	Virginia Union	1926	78	1,251	596	.677
S.C.-Spartanburg	1975	29	492	339	.592	Washburn	1905	97	1,343	956	.584
South Dakota	1908	93	1,025	900	.532	Wayne St. (Mich.)	1942	62	815	941	.464
South Dakota St.	1906	95	1,215	810	.600	Wayne St. (Neb.)	1912	88	1,058	899	.541
Colorado St.-Pueblo	1964	40	673	429	.611	West Ala.	1957	46	531	633	.456
Southern Conn. St.	1968	36	481	445	.519	West Chester	1928	76	888	806	.524
SIU Edwardsville	1968	36	450	466	.491	West Fla.	1968	19	285	221	.563
Southern Ind.	1970	34	608	340	.641	West Ga.	1957	46	691	503	.579
Southern N.H.	1964	40	765	366	.676	West Tex. A&M	1921	82	1,255	773	.619
Southwest Baptist	1966	38	541	479	.530	Wheeling Jesuit	1958	47	581	621	.483
Southwest St.	1967	37	396	576	.407	Winona St.	1916	88	824	986	.455
Stonehill	1949	54	756	615	.551						

DIVISION II

Division III Records

Individual Records

Division III men's basketball records are based on the performances of Division III teams since the three-division re-organization plan was adopted by the special NCAA Convention in August 1973. Assists were added for the 1988-89 season; blocked shots and steals were added for the 1992-93 season. In statistical rankings, the rounding of percentages and/or averages may indicate ties where none exist. In these cases, the numerical order of the rankings is accurate.

Scoring

POINTS
Game
77—Jeff Clement, Grinnell vs. Illinois Col., Feb. 18, 1998
Season
1,044—Greg Grant, TCNJ, 1989 (32 games)
Career
2,940—Andre Foreman, Salisbury, 1988-89, 91-92 (109 games)

AVERAGE PER GAME
Season
37.3—Steve Diekmann, Grinnell, 1995 (745 in 20)
Career
(Min. 1,400) 32.8—Dwain Govan, Bishop, 1974-75 (1,805 in 55)

POINTS SCORED WITH NO TIME ELAPSING
Game
24—Rob Rittgers, UC San Diego vs. Menlo, Jan. 16, 1988 (made 24 consecutive free throws due to 12 bench technical fouls)

CONSECUTIVE POINTS SCORED
Game
25—Andy Panko, Lebanon Valley vs. Frank. & Marsh., Jan. 19, 1998

GAMES SCORING AT LEAST 50 POINTS
Season
3—Jeff Clement, Grinnell, 1998
Career
4—Jeff Clement, Grinnell, 1996-99; Steve Diekmann, Grinnell, 1993-95

GAMES SCORING IN DOUBLE FIGURES
Career
116—Lamont Strothers, Chris. Newport, 1988-91

CONSECUTIVE GAMES SCORING IN DOUBLE FIGURES
Career
116—Lamont Strothers, Chris. Newport, from Nov. 20, 1987, to March 8, 1991

Field Goals

FIELD GOALS
Game
29—Shannon Lilly, Bishop vs. Southwest Assembly of God, Jan. 31, 1983 (36 attempts)
Season
394—Dave Russell, Shepherd, 1975 (687 attempts)
Career
1,140—Andre Foreman, Salisbury, 1988-89, 91-92 (2,125 attempts)

CONSECUTIVE FIELD GOALS
Game
18—Jason Light, Emory & Henry vs. King (Tenn.), Dec. 2, 1995
Season
24—Todd Richards, Mount Union, 2000 (during five games)

FIELD-GOAL ATTEMPTS
Game
68—Jeff Clement, Grinnell vs. Illinois Col., Feb. 18, 1998 (26 made)
Season
742—Greg Grant, TCNJ, 1989 (387 made)
Career
2,149—Lamont Strothers, Chris. Newport, 1988-91 (1,016 made)

FIELD-GOAL PERCENTAGE
Game
(Min. 18 made) 100%—Jason Light, Emory & Henry vs. King (Tenn.), Dec. 2, 1995 (18 of 18)
*Season
76.6—Travis Weiss, St. John's (Minn.), 1994 (160 of 209)
*Based on qualifiers for annual championship.
Career
(Min. 400 made) 73.6—Tony Rychlec, Mass. Maritime, 1981-83 (509 of 692)

Three-Point Field Goals

THREE-POINT FIELD GOALS
Game
19—Jeff Clement, Grinnell vs. Illinois Col., Feb. 18, 1998
Season
186—Jeff Clement, Grinnell, 1998 (511 attempts)
Career
516—Jeff Clement, Grinnell, 1996-99 (1,532 attempts)

THREE-POINT FIELD GOALS MADE PER GAME
Season
8.5—Jeff Clement, Grinnell, 1998 (186 in 22)
Career
5.7—Jeff Clement, Grinnell, 1996-99 (516 in 91)

CONSECUTIVE THREE-POINT FIELD GOALS
Game
10—Josh Richter, Simpson vs. Dubuque, Feb. 22, 2003; Brad Block, Aurora vs. Rockford, Feb. 20, 1988; Jim Berrigan, Framingham St. vs. Western New Eng., Feb. 27, 1988
Season
16—John Richards, Sewanee (during five games, Feb. 10 to Feb. 25, 1990)

CONSECUTIVE GAMES MAKING A THREE-POINT FIELD GOAL
Season
31—Troy Greenlee, DePauw, Nov. 17, 1989, to March 17, 1990
Career
75—Chris Carideo, Widener, 1992-95

THREE-POINT FIELD-GOAL ATTEMPTS
Game
52—Jeff Clement, Grinnell vs. Illinois Col., Feb. 18, 1998 (19 made)
Season
511—Jeff Clement, Grinnell, 1998 (186 made)
Career
1,532—Jeff Clement, Grinnell, 1996-99 (516 made)

THREE-POINT FIELD-GOAL ATTEMPTS PER GAME
Season
23.2—Jeff Clement, Grinnell, 1998 (511 in 22)
Career
16.8—Jeff Clement, Grinnell, 1996-99 (1,532 in 91)

THREE-POINT FIELD-GOAL PERCENTAGE
Game
(Min. 11 made) 100%—Joe Goldin, Randolph-Macon vs. Emory & Henry, Feb. 16, 1997 (11 of 11)
Season
(Min. 40 made) 67.0%—Reggie James, N.J. Inst. of Tech., 1989 (59 of 88)
(Min. 90 made) 56.9%—Eric Harris, Bishop, 1987 (91 of 160)

Career
(Min. 200 made) 51.3%—Jeff Seifriz, Wis.-Whitewater, 1987-89 (217 of 432)

Free Throws

FREE THROWS
Game
30—Rob Rittgers, UC San Diego vs. Menlo, Jan. 16, 1988 (30 attempts)
Season
249—Dave Russell, Shepherd, 1975 (293 attempts)
Career
792—Matt Hancock, Colby, 1987-90 (928 attempts)

CONSECUTIVE FREE THROWS MADE
Game
30—Rob Rittgers, UC San Diego vs. Menlo, Jan. 16, 1988
Season
59—Mike Michelson, Coast Guard (during 13 games, Jan. 16 to Feb. 27, 1990)
Career
84—Dirk Rhinehart, Kalamazoo (16 games, Jan. 3, 2001 to Dec. 17, 2001)

FREE THROWS ATTEMPTED
Game
30—Rob Rittgers, UC San Diego vs. Menlo, Jan. 16, 1988 (30 made)
Season
326—Moses Jean-Pierre, Plymouth St., 1994 (243 made)
Career
928—Matt Hancock, Colby, 1987-90 (792 made)

FREE-THROW PERCENTAGE
Game
(Min. 30 made) 100%—Rob Rittgers, UC San Diego vs. Menlo, Jan. 16, 1988 (30 of 30)
*Season
96.3%—Korey Coon, Ill. Wesleyan, 2000 (157 of 163)
*based on qualifiers for annual championship
Career
(Min. 250 made) 92.5%—Andy Enfield, Johns Hopkins, 1988-91 (431 of 466)
(Min. 500 made) 86.2%—Brad Clark, Wis.-Oshkosh, 1997-00 (535 of 621)

Rebounds

REBOUNDS
Game
36—Mark Veenstra, Calvin vs. Colorado St.-Pueblo., Feb. 3, 1976; Clinton Montford, Methodist vs. Warren Wilson, Jan. 21, 1989
Season
579—Joe Manley, Bowie St., 1976 (29 games)
Career
917—Tennyson Whitted, Ramapo, 2000-03 (108 games)

AVERAGE PER GAME
Season
20.0—Joe Manley, Bowie St., 1976 (579 in 29)
Career
(Min. 900) 17.4—Larry Parker, Plattsburgh St., 1975-78 (1,482 in 85)

Assists

ASSISTS
Game
26—Robert James, Kean vs. N.J. Inst. of Tech., March 11, 1989

Season
391—Robert James, Kean, 1989 (29 games)
Career
917—Tennyson Whitted, Ramapo, 2000-03 (108 games)

AVERAGE PER GAME
Season
13.5—Robert James, Kean, 1989 (391 in 29)
Career
(Min. 550) 8.6—Phil Dixon, Shenandoah, 1993-96 (889 in 103)

Blocked Shots

BLOCKED SHOTS
Game
16—Tory Black, N.J. Inst. of Tech. vs. Polytechnic (N.Y.), Feb. 5, 1997
Season
198—Tory Black, N.J. Inst. of Tech., 1997 (26 games)
Career
576—Ira Nicholson, Mt. St. Vincent, 1994-97 (100 games)

AVERAGE PER GAME
Season
7.6—Tory Black, N.J. Inst. of Tech., 1997 (198 in 26)

Career
6.1—Neil Edwards, York (N.Y.), 1998-00 (337 in 55)

Steals

STEALS
Game
17—Matt Newton, Principia vs. Harris-Stowe, Jan. 4, 1994
Season
189—Moses Jean-Pierre, Plymouth St., 1994 (30 games)
Career
448—Tennyson Whitted, Ramapo, 2000-03 (108 games)

AVERAGE PER GAME
Season
6.3—Moses Jean-Pierre, Plymouth St., 1994 (189 in 30)

Career
5.5—Moses Jean-Pierre, Plymouth St., 1993-94 (303 in 55 games)

Games

GAMES PLAYED
Season
34—Thane Anderson, Matt Benedict, Tim Blair, Lanse Carter, Mike Johnson, Todd Oehrlein, Mike Prasher and Derrick Shelton, Wis.-Eau Claire, 1990
Career
119—Steve Honderd, Calvin, 1990-93; Chris Finch, Frank. & Marsh., 1989-92; Chris Fite, Rochester, 1989-92; Jim Clausen, North Park, 1978-81

Team Records

Note: Where records involve both teams, each team must be an NCAA Division III member institution.

SINGLE-GAME RECORDS

Scoring

POINTS
168—Bishop vs. Southwest Assembly of God (76), Jan. 31, 1983

POINTS BY LOSING TEAM
149—Lawrence vs. Grinnell (150), Jan. 25, 2003; Grinnell vs. Illinois Col. (157), Feb. 18, 1994

POINTS, BOTH TEAMS
315—Simpson (167) vs. Grinnell (148), Nov. 19, 1994

POINTS IN A HALF
92—Wis.-Platteville vs. Mt. St. Clare, Dec. 14, 1989 (first)

POINTS SCORED WITH NO TIME ELAPSING OFF OF THE CLOCK
24—UC San Diego vs. Menlo, Jan. 16, 1988 (made 24 consecutive free throws due to 12 bench technical fouls)

FEWEST POINTS ALLOWED
6—Dickinson (15) vs. Muhlenberg, Feb. 3, 1982

FEWEST POINTS ALLOWED IN A HALF
0—Dickinson (2) vs. Muhlenberg (first), Feb. 3, 1982

FEWEST POINTS, BOTH TEAMS
21—Dickinson (15) vs. Muhlenberg (6), Feb. 3, 1982

FEWEST POINTS, HALF, BOTH TEAMS
2—Dickinson (2) vs. Muhlenberg (0) (first), Feb. 3, 1982

MARGIN OF VICTORY
112—Eureka (149) vs. Barat (37), Nov. 29, 1989

Field Goals

FIELD GOALS
78—Bishop vs. Southwest Assembly of God, Jan. 31, 1983 (103 attempts)

FIELD-GOAL ATTEMPTS
135—Grinnell vs. Simpson, Nov. 25, 1995 (52 made)

FEWEST FIELD GOALS
3—Muhlenberg vs. Dickinson, Feb. 3, 1982 (11 attempts)

FEWEST FIELD-GOAL ATTEMPTS
11—Muhlenberg vs. Dickinson, Feb. 3, 1982 (3 made)

FIELD-GOAL PERCENTAGE
89.8%—St. Norbert vs. Grinnell, Jan. 28, 2000

FIELD-GOAL PERCENTAGE, HALF
95.7—Beloit vs. Grinnell, Jan. 27, 2001 (22 of 23)

Three-Point Field Goals

THREE-POINT FIELD GOALS
32—Grinnell vs. Clarke, Dec. 3, 1997 (78 attempts)

THREE-POINT FIELD GOALS, BOTH TEAMS
35—Grinnell (30) vs. Colorado Col. (5), Nov. 17, 1995; Manhattanville (25) vs. St. Joseph's (N.Y.) (10), Dec. 10, 1994; Beloit (21) vs. Carthage (14), Nov. 23, 1993

CONSECUTIVE THREE-POINT FIELD GOALS MADE WITHOUT A MISS
11—Willamette vs. Western Baptist, Jan. 8, 1987

NUMBER OF DIFFERENT PLAYERS TO SCORE A THREE-POINT FIELD GOAL, ONE TEAM
13—Grinnell vs. Monmouth (Ill.), Feb. 14, 1998

THREE-POINT FIELD-GOAL ATTEMPTS
86—Grinnell vs. Pillsbury, Dec. 7, 1999 (31 made)

THREE-POINT FIELD-GOAL ATTEMPTS, BOTH TEAMS
97—Grinnell (79) vs. Colorado Col. (18), Nov. 17, 1995

THREE-POINT FIELD-GOAL PERCENTAGE
(Min. 10 made) 100%—Willamette vs. Western Baptist, Jan. 8, 1987 (11 of 11); Kean vs. Ramapo, Feb. 11, 1987 (10 of 10)
(Min. 15 made) 89.5%—Simpson vs. Dubuque, Feb. 22, 2003 (17 of 19)

THREE-POINT FIELD-GOAL PERCENTAGE, BOTH TEAMS
(Min. 10 made) 92.9%—Luther (8 of 8) vs. Wartburg (5 of 6), Feb. 14, 1987 (13 of 14)

(Min. 15 made) 75.0%—Anna Maria (4 of 6) vs. Nichols (11 of 14), Feb. 10, 1987 (15 of 20)
(Min. 20 made) 62.9%—Simpson (17 of 19) vs. Dubuque (5 of 16), Feb. 22, 2003 (22 of 35)

Free Throws

FREE THROWS MADE
53—UC San Diego vs. Menlo, Jan. 16, 1988 (59 attempts)

FREE THROWS MADE, BOTH TEAMS
93—Grinnell (50) vs. Beloit (43), Jan. 10, 1998

FREE THROWS ATTEMPTED
71—Earlham vs. Oberlin, Dec. 5, 1992 (46 made)

FREE THROWS ATTEMPTED, BOTH TEAMS
105—Earlham (71) vs. Oberlin (34), Dec. 5, 1992

FEWEST FREE THROWS MADE
0—Many teams

FEWEST FREE-THROW ATTEMPTS
0—Many teams

FREE-THROW PERCENTAGE
(Min. 28 made) 100.0%—Albany (N.Y.) vs. Potsdam St., Feb. 19, 1994 (28 of 28)
(Min. 30 made) 97.2%—Ill. Wesleyan vs. North Park, Feb. 19, 2003 (35 of 36)
(Min. 45 made) 92.6%—Grinnell vs. Beloit, Jan. 10, 1998 (50 of 54)

FREE-THROW PERCENTAGE, BOTH TEAMS
(Min. 20 made) 95.5%—Baldwin-Wallace (13 of 13) vs. Muskingum (8 of 9), Dec. 29, 1977 (21 of 22)
(Min. 30 made) 94.9%—Muskingum (30 of 31) vs. Ohio Wesleyan (7 of 8), Jan. 10, 1981 (37 of 39)

Rebounds

REBOUNDS
98—Alma vs. Marion, Dec. 28, 1973

REBOUNDS, BOTH TEAMS
124—Ill. Wesleyan (62) vs. North Central (62), Feb. 8, 1977; Rochester Inst. (72) vs. Thiel (52), Nov. 18, 1988

DIVISION III

REBOUND MARGIN
  56—MIT (74) vs. Emerson-MCA (18), Feb. 21, 1990

Assists

ASSISTS
  53—Simpson vs. Grinnell, Nov. 25, 1995

ASSISTS, BOTH TEAMS
  79—Simpson (53) vs. Grinnell (26), Nov. 25, 1995

Personal Fouls

PERSONAL FOULS
  47—Concordia (Ill.) vs. Trinity Christian, Feb. 26, 1988

PERSONAL FOULS, BOTH TEAMS
  80—Grinnell (46) vs. St. Norbert (34), Jan. 28, 2000

PLAYERS DISQUALIFIED
  6—Thomas More vs. Franklin, Feb. 2, 2002; Union (N.Y.) vs. Rochester, Feb. 15, 1985; Haverford vs. Drew, Jan. 10, 1990; Manhattanville vs. Drew, Jan. 11, 1992; Roger Williams vs Curry, Jan. 14, 1995

PLAYERS DISQUALIFIED, BOTH TEAMS
  11—Union (N.Y.) (6) vs. Rochester (5), Feb. 15, 1985

Overtimes

OVERTIME PERIODS
  5—Babson (115) vs. Wheaton (Mass.)(107), Feb. 18, 1999; Capital (86) vs. Muskingum (89), Jan. 5, 1980; Carnegie Mellon (81) vs. Allegheny (76), Feb. 12, 1983; Rochester (99) vs. Union (N.Y.) (98), Feb. 15, 1985

POINTS IN ONE OVERTIME PERIOD
  31—Marymount (Va.) vs. Catholic, Jan. 30, 1999

POINTS IN ONE OVERTIME PERIOD, BOTH TEAMS
  51—Wash. & Lee (28) vs. Mary Washington (23), Jan. 9, 1995

POINTS IN OVERTIME PERIODS
  50—Babson (50) vs. Wheaton (Mass.) (5 ot), Feb. 18, 1999

POINTS IN OVERTIME PERIODS, BOTH TEAMS
  92—Babson (50) vs. Wheaton (Mass.) (42) (5 ot), Feb. 18, 1999

SEASON RECORDS

Scoring

POINTS
  3,119—Grinnell, 2003 (25 games)

AVERAGE PER GAME
  124.9—Grinnell, 2002 (2,997 in 24)

AVERAGE SCORING MARGIN
  31.1—Husson, 1976 (98.7 offense, 67.6 defense)

GAMES AT LEAST 100 POINTS
  23—Grinnell, 2002 (24-game season)

CONSECUTIVE GAMES AT LEAST 100 POINTS
  19—Grinnell, from Nov. 23, 2002, to Feb. 8, 2003

CONSECUTIVE GAMES AT LEAST 100 POINTS (Multiple Seasons)
  28—Grinnell, from Jan. 25, 2002, to Feb. 8, 2003

Field Goals

FIELD GOALS
  1,323—Shepherd, 1975 (2,644 attempts)

FIELD GOALS PER GAME
  42.5—Mercy, 1977 (1,062 in 25)

FIELD-GOAL ATTEMPTS
  2,644—Shepherd, 1975 (1,323 made)

FIELD-GOAL ATTEMPTS PER GAME
  98.4—Grinnell, 2002 (2,361 in 24)

FIELD-GOAL PERCENTAGE
  60.0—Stony Brook, 1978 (1,033 of 1,721)

Three-Point Field Goals

THREE-POINT FIELD GOALS
  522—Grinnell, 2003 (1,546 attempts)

THREE-POINT FIELD GOALS PER GAME
  20.9—Grinnell, 2003 (522 in 25)

THREE-POINT FIELD-GOAL ATTEMPTS
  1,546—Grinnell, 2003 (522 made)

THREE-POINT FIELD-GOAL ATTEMPTS PER GAME
  62.4—Grinnell, 1999 (1,373 in 22)

THREE-POINT FIELD-GOAL PERCENTAGE
  (Min. 100 made) 62.0%—N.J. Inst. of Tech., 1989 (124 of 200)
  (Min. 150 made) 49.1%—Eureka, 1994 (317 of 646)

CONSECUTIVE GAMES SCORING A THREE-POINT FIELD GOAL
  424—Salisbury, Nov. 25, 1986-Present

Free Throws

FREE THROWS MADE
  698—Ohio Wesleyan, 1988 (888 attempts)

FREE THROWS MADE PER GAME
  23.7—Grinnell, 1995 (498 in 21)

FREE-THROW
  930—Queens (N.Y.), 1981 (636 made)

FREE-THROW PER GAME
  33.2—Grinnell, 1995 (698 in 21)

FREE-THROW PERCENTAGE
  81.8%—Wis.-Oshkosh, 1998 (516 of 631)

Rebounds

REBOUNDS
  1,616—Keene St., 1976 (29 games)

AVERAGE PER GAME
  56.3—Mercy, 1977 (1,408 in 25)

AVERAGE REBOUND MARGIN
  17.0—Hamilton, 1991 (49.6 offense, 32.5 defense)

Assists

ASSISTS
  861—Salisbury, 1991 (29 games)

AVERAGE PER GAME
  31.2—Me.-Farmington, 1991 (748 in 24)

Fouls

FOULS
  801—McMurry, 2001 (28 games)

FOULS PER GAME
  30.9—Grinnell, 1998 (679 in 22)

FEWEST FOULS
  177—Caltech, 1997 (20 games)

FEWEST FOULS PER GAME
  8.9—Caltech, 1997 (177 in 20)

Defense

FEWEST POINTS PER GAME ALLOWED
  47.5—Wis.-Platteville, 1997 (1,283 in 27)

LOWEST FIELD-GOAL PERCENTAGE ALLOWED (Since 1978)
  36.3—Grove City, 1999 (533 of 1,469)

Overtimes

OVERTIME GAMES
  7—McMurry, 2003 (won 7, lost 0); Albany (N.Y.), 1981 (won 5, lost 2); TCNJ, 1982 (won 6, lost 1); St. John's (Minn.), 1983 (won 4, lost 3); New Jersey City, 1994 (won 4, lost 3)

CONSECUTIVE OVERTIME GAMES
  3—McMurry, 2003 (won 3, lost 0); Albright, 1997 (won 3, lost 0); Buffalo St., 1997 (won 2, lost 1); Ferrum, 1997 (won 1, lost 2); Ithaca, 1987 (won 3, lost 0); Cortland St., 1989 (won 1, lost 2); Oberlin, 1989 (won 1, lost 2); Susquehanna, 1989 (won 3, lost 0)

OVERTIME WINS
  7—McMurry, 2003 (7-0)

OVERTIME HOME WINS
  5—McMurry, 2003 (5-0)

General Records

GAMES PLAYED IN A SEASON
  34—LeMoyne-Owen, 1980 (26-8); Wis.-Eau Claire, 1990 (30-4)

VICTORIES IN A SEASON
  32—Potsdam St., 1986 (32-0)

CONSECUTIVE VICTORIES
  60—Potsdam St. (from first game of 1985-86 season to March 14, 1987)

CONSECUTIVE HOME-COURT VICTORIES
  62—North Park (from Feb. 8, 1984, to Feb. 3, 1988)

CONSECUTIVE REGULAR SEASON VICTORIES
  59—Potsdam St. (from Nov. 22, 1985, to Dec. 12, 1987)

DEFEATS IN A SEASON
  26—Otterbein, 1988 (1-26); Maryville (Mo.), 1991 (0-26)

CONSECUTIVE DEFEATS IN A SEASON
  26—Maryville (Mo.), 1991 (0-26)

CONSECUTIVE DEFEATS
  117—Rutgers-Camden (from Jan. 22, 1992, to Jan. 3, 1997; ended with 77-72 win vs. Bloomfield on Jan. 7, 1997)

CONSECUTIVE WINNING SEASONS
  35—Wittenberg, 1969-2003

CONSECUTIVE NON-LOSING SEASONS
  47—Wittenberg, 1957-2003

UNBEATEN TEAMS (NUMBER OF VICTORIES IN PARENTHESES)
  1986 Potsdam St. (32); 1995 Wis.-Platteville (31); 1998 Wis.-Platteville (30)

All-Time Individual Leaders

Single-Game Records

SCORING HIGHS

Pts.	Player, Team vs. Opponent	Season
77	Jeff Clement, Grinnell vs. Illinois Col.	1998
69	Steve Diekmann, Grinnell vs. Simpson	1995
63	Joe DeRoche, Thomas vs. St. Joseph's (Me.)	1988
62	Shannon Lilly, Bishop vs. Southwest Assembly of God	1983
61	Josh Metzger, Wis.-Lutheran vs. Grinnell	2001
61	Steve Honderd, Calvin vs. Kalamazoo	1993
61	Dana Wilson, Husson vs. Ricker	1974
60	Ed Brands, Grinnell vs. Ripon	1996
60	Steve Diekmann, Grinnell vs. Coe	1994
59	Ed Brands, Grinnell vs. Chicago	1996
59	Steve Diekmann, Grinnell vs. Monmouth (Ill.)	1995
58	Andy Panko, Lebanon Valley vs. Juniata	1999
58	Jeff Clement, Grinnell vs. Clarke	1998
57	David Otte, Simpson vs. Grinnell	1995
56	Scott Wilson, Grinnell vs. Martin Luther	1998
56	Steve Diekmann, Grinnell vs. Illinois Col.	1994
56	Kyle Price, Illinois Col. vs. Grinnell	1994
56	Shay DeLaney, Coe vs. Grinnell	1994
56	Mark Veenstra, Calvin vs. Adrian	1976
55	Jeff Clement, Grinnell vs. Lawrence	1998
55	Eric Ochel, Sewanee vs. Emory	1995
55	Dwain Govan, Bishop vs. Texas Southern	1975

Season Records

SCORING AVERAGE

Player, Team	Season	G	FG	3FG	FT	Pts.	Avg.
Steve Diekmann, Grinnell	†1995	20	223	137	162	745	*37.3
Rickey Sutton, Lyndon St.	†1976	14	207	—	93	507	36.2
Shannon Lilly, Bishop	†1983	26	345	—	218	908	34.9
Dana Wilson, Husson	†1974	20	288	—	122	698	34.9
Rickey Sutton, Lyndon St.	†1977	16	223	—	112	558	34.9
Steve Diekmann, Grinnell	†1994	21	250	117	106	723	34.4
Ed Brands, Grinnell	†1996	24	260	158	136	814	33.9
Jeff Clement, Grinnell	†1998	22	238	*186	84	746	33.9
Dwain Govan, Bishop	†1975	29	392	—	179	963	33.2
Clarence Caldwell, Greensboro	1976	22	306	—	111	723	32.8
Jeff Clement, Grinnell	†1999	22	217	166	121	721	32.8
Greg Grant, TCNJ	†1989	32	387	76	194	*1,044	32.6
Dave Russell, Shepherd	1975	32	*394	—	*249	1,037	32.4
Dwain Govan, Bishop	1974	26	358	—	126	842	32.4
Ron Stewart, Otterbein	1983	24	297	—	166	760	31.7

†national champion; *record

FIELD-GOAL PERCENTAGE
(Based on qualifiers for annual championship)

Player, Team	Season	G	FG	FGA	Pct.
Travis Weiss, St. John's (Minn.)	†1994	26	160	209	*76.6
Pete Metzelaars, Wabash	†1982	28	271	360	75.3
Tony Rychlec, Mass. Maritime	†1981	25	233	311	74.9
Tony Rychlec, Mass. Maritime	1982	20	193	264	73.1
Russ Newnan, Menlo	1991	26	130	178	73.0
Ed Owens, Hampden-Sydney	†1979	24	140	192	72.9
Scott Baxter, Capital	†1991	26	164	226	72.6
Maurice Woods, Potsdam St.	1982	30	203	280	72.5
Earl Keith, Stony Brook	1979	24	164	227	72.2
Pete Metzelaars, Wabash	1981	25	204	283	72.1
Jon Rosner, Yeshiva	1991	22	141	196	71.9
Pete Metzelaars, Wabash	1979	24	122	170	71.8
Anthony Farley, Miles	1982	26	168	235	71.5

†national champion; *record

THREE-POINT FIELD GOALS MADE

Player, Team	Season	G	3FG
Jeff Clement, Grinnell	1998	22	*186
Jeff Clement, Grinnell	1999	22	166
Ed Brands, Grinnell	1996	24	158
Chris Peterson, Eureka	1994	31	145
Steve Nordlund, Grinnell	2002	24	137
Steve Diekmann, Grinnell	1995	20	137
Chris Jans, Loras	1991	25	133
Eric Burdette, Wis.-Whitewater	1996	28	130
Ed Brands, Grinnell	1995	20	129
Tommy Doyle, Salem St.	1996	28	124

Player, Team	Season	G	3FG
Everett Foxx, Ferrum	1992	29	124
Kirk Anderson, Augustana (Ill.)	1993	30	123
Jeff deLaveaga, Cal Lutheran	1992	28	122
Dave Stantial, Keene St.	2002	27	120
David Bailey, Concordia (Ill.)	1994	24	120
Steve Nordlund, Grinnell	2003	25	119
Woody Piirto, Grinnell	1999	22	117
Steve Matthews, Emerson	1999	25	117
Steve Diekmann, Grinnell	1994	21	117
Jeff Seifriz, Wis.-Whitewater	1989	31	114
Jermaine Woods, Chris. Newport	2003	29	113
Steve Matthews, Emerson	2000	27	113
Jeff Clement, Grinnell	1997	22	113
Chris Carideo, Widener	1995	27	113

*record

THREE-POINT FIELD GOALS MADE PER GAME

Player, Team	Season	G	3FG	Avg.
Jeff Clement, Grinnell	†1998	22	*186	*8.5
Jeff Clement, Grinnell	†1999	22	166	7.5
Steve Diekmann, Grinnell	†1995	20	137	6.9
Ed Brands, Grinnell	†1996	24	158	6.6
Ed Brands, Grinnell	1995	29	129	6.5
Steve Nordlund, Grinnell	†2002	24	137	5.7
Steve Diekmann, Grinnell	†1994	21	117	5.6
Chris Jans, Loras	†1991	25	133	5.3
Woody Piirto, Grinnell	1999	22	117	5.3
Jeff Clement, Grinnell	†1997	22	113	5.1
Mark Bedell, Fisk	1997	19	97	5.1
David Bailey, Concordia (Ill.)	1994	24	120	5.0
Steve Nordlund, Grinnell	†2003	25	119	4.8
Steve Matthews, Emerson	1999	25	117	4.7
Chris Peterson, Eureka	1994	31	145	4.7
Eric Burdette, Wis.-Whitewater	1996	28	130	4.6
Chris Geruschat, Bethany (W.Va.)	1991	24	111	4.6
Chris Carideo, Widener	1994	24	110	4.6
Luke Madsen, Wis.-River Falls	1996	22	98	4.5
Dave Stantial, Keene St.	2002	27	120	4.4
Tommy Doyle, Salem St.	1996	28	124	4.4
Mark Van Winkle, Eureka	1998	25	110	4.4
Ernie Bray, UC Santa Cruz	1994	24	105	4.4
Jeff deLaveaga, Cal Lutheran	†1992	28	122	4.4

†national champion; *record

THREE-POINT FIELD-GOAL PERCENTAGE
(Based on qualifiers for annual championship)

Player, Team	Season	G	3FG	3FGA	Pct.
Reggie James, N.J. Inst. of Tech.	†1989	29	59	88	*67.0
Chris Miles, N.J. Inst. of Tech.	†1987	26	41	65	63.1
Chris Miles, N.J. Inst. of Tech.	1989	29	46	75	61.3
Matt Miota, Lawrence	†1990	22	33	54	61.1
Mike Bachman, Alma	†1991	26	46	76	60.5
Ray Magee, Richard Stockton	†1988	26	41	71	57.7
Keith Orchard, Whitman	1988	26	42	73	57.5
Brian O'Donnell, Rutgers-Camden	1988	24	65	114	57.0
Eric Harris, Bishop	1987	26	91	160	56.9
Rick Brown, Muskingum	1988	30	71	125	56.8
Jamie Eichel, Fredonia St.	1989	24	51	90	56.7

†national champion; *record

FREE-THROW PERCENTAGE
(Based on qualifiers for annual championship)

Player, Team	Season	G	FT	FTA	Pct.
Korey Coon, Ill. Wesleyan	†2000	25	157	163	*96.3
Nick Wilkins, Coe	†2003	26	66	69	95.7
Chanse Young, Manchester	†1998	25	65	68	95.6
Andy Enfield, Johns Hopkins	†1991	29	123	129	95.3
Chris Carideo, Widener	†1992	26	80	84	95.2
Yudi Teichman, Yeshiva	†1989	21	119	125	95.2
Brett Davis, Wis.-Oshkosh	1998	27	72	76	94.7
Mark Giovino, Babson	†1997	28	86	91	94.5
Mike Scheib, Susquehanna	†1977	22	80	85	94.1
Jason Prenevost, Middlebury	†1994	22	60	64	93.8
Derrick Rogers, Averett	†2001	27	72	77	93.5
Jerry Prestier, Baldwin-Wallace	†1978	25	125	134	93.3
Charlie Nanick, Scranton	†1996	25	96	103	93.2
Jeff Bowers, Southern Me.	†1988	29	95	102	93.1
Eric Jacobs, Scranton	1986	29	81	87	93.1
Jim Durrell, Colby-Sawyer	†1993	25	67	72	93.1
Joe Purcell, King's (Pa.)	†1979	26	66	71	93.0

Player, Team	Season	G	FT	FTA	Pct.
Todd Reinhardt, Wartburg	†1990	26	91	98	92.9
Reiner Kolodinski, Occidental	1979	24	65	70	92.9
Shannon Lilly, Bishop	†1982	22	142	153	92.8
Matt Freesemann, Wartburg	†1995	24	128	138	92.8

†national champion; *record

REBOUND AVERAGE

Player, Team	Season	G	Reb.	Avg.
Joe Manley, Bowie St.	†1976	29	*579	*20.0
Fred Petty, Southern N.H.	†1974	22	436	19.8
Larry Williams, Pratt	†1977	24	457	19.0
Charles Greer, Thomas	1977	17	318	18.7
Larry Parker, Plattsburgh St.	†1975	23	430	18.7
John Jordan, Southern Me.	†1978	29	536	18.5
Keith Woolfolk, Upper Iowa	1978	26	479	18.4
Michael Stubbs, Trinity (Conn.)	†1990	22	398	18.1
Mike Taylor, Pratt	1978	23	414	18.0
Walt Edwards, Husson	1976	26	467	18.0
Dave Kufeld, Yeshiva	†1979	20	355	17.8

†national champion; *record

ASSISTS

Player, Team	Season	G	Ast.
Robert James, Kean	†1989	29	*391
Tennyson Whitted, Ramapo	†2002	29	319
Ricky Spicer, Wis.-Whitewater	1989	31	295
Joe Marcotte, N.J. Inst. of Tech.	†1995	30	292
Andre Bolton, Chris. Newport	†1996	30	289
Ron Torgalski, Hamilton	1989	26	275
Albert Kirchner, Mt. St. Vincent	†1990	24	267
Steve Artis, Chris. Newport	1991	29	262
Phil Dixon, Shenandoah	1996	27	258
Tennyson Whitted, Ramapo	†2003	30	253
Phil Dixon, Shenandoah	†1994	26	253
Steve Artis, Chris. Newport	1990	28	251
David Genovese, Mt. St. Vincent	1994	27	248
Russell Springman, Salisbury	1990	27	246
Michael Crotty, Williams	2003	32	245
Tom Genco, Manhattanville	1990	26	244
Andre Bolton, Chris. Newport	1995	28	243
Mark Cottom, Ferrum	1991	25	242
Tim Lawrence, Maryville (Tenn.)	1992	29	241

†national champion; *record

ASSIST AVERAGE

Player, Team	Season	G	Ast.	Avg.
Robert James, Kean	†1989	29	*391	*13.5
Albert Kirchner, Mt. St. Vincent	†1990	24	267	11.1
Tennyson Whitted, Ramapo	†2002	29	319	11.0
Ron Torgalski, Hamilton	1989	26	275	10.6
Louis Adams, Rust	1989	22	227	10.3
Eric Johnson, Coe	†1991	24	238	9.9
Joe Marcotte, N.J. Inst. of Tech.	†1995	30	292	9.7
Phil Dixon, Shenandoah	†1994	26	253	9.7
Mark Cottom, Ferrum	1991	25	242	9.7
Andre Bolton, Chris. Newport	†1996	30	289	9.6
Phil Dixon, Shenandoah	1996	27	258	9.6
Ricky Spicer, Wis.-Whitewater	1989	31	295	9.5
David Rubin, Hobart	†1998	25	237	9.5
Pat Heldman, Maryville (Tenn.)	1989	25	236	9.4
Deshone Bond, Stillman	†1997	25	235	9.4
Tom Genco, Manhattanville	1990	26	244	9.4
Justin Culhane, Suffolk	1992	24	225	9.4

†national champion; *record

BLOCKED SHOTS

Player, Team	Season	G	Blk.
Tory Black, N.J. Inst. of Tech.	†1997	26	*198
Neil Edwards, York (N.Y.)	†2000	26	193
Ira Nicholson, Mt. St. Vincent	†1995	28	188
Ira Nicholson, Mt. St. Vincent	†1996	27	163
Ira Nicholson, Mt. St. Vincent	1997	24	151
Antoine Hyman, Keuka	1997	26	148
Matt Cusano, Scranton	†1993	29	145
Neil Edwards, York (N.Y.)	†1999	26	144
Johnny Woods, Wesley	2000	24	132
Antoine Hyman, Keuka	1996	25	131
Andrew South, N.J. Inst. of Tech.	†1994	27	128
Mike Mientus, Allentown	1995	25	118
Roy Woods, Fontbonne	1995	25	117
Eric Lidecis, Maritime (N.Y.)	1994	26	116
Antonio Ramos, Clarke	2001	25	114
Joe Henderson, Hunter	1999	22	112
Mike Mientus, Allentown	1997	26	112
Andrew South, N.J. Inst. of Tech.	1993	26	111
Jeremy Putman, Dubuque	1995	25	110
Steve Juskin, Frank. & Marsh.	†2003	30	108
Robert Clyburn, Kean	1995	27	108

†national champion; *record

BLOCKED-SHOT AVERAGE

Player, Team	Season	G	Blk.	Avg.
Tory Black, N.J. Inst. of Tech.	†1997	26	*198	*7.62
Neil Edwards, York (N.Y.)	†2000	26	193	7.42
Ira Nicholson, Mt. St. Vincent	†1995	28	188	6.71
Ira Nicholson, Mt. St. Vincent	1997	24	151	6.29
Ira Nicholson, Mt. St. Vincent	†1996	27	163	6.04
Antoine Hyman, Keuka	1997	26	148	5.69
Neil Edwards, York (N.Y.)	†1999	26	144	5.54
Johnny Woods, Wesley	2000	24	132	5.50
Antoine Hyman, Keuka	1996	25	131	5.24
Joe Henderson, Hunter	1999	22	112	5.09
Matt Cusano, Scranton	†1993	29	145	5.00
Andrew South, N.J. Inst. of Tech.	†1994	27	128	4.74
Roy Woods, Fontbonne	1995	25	117	4.68
Johnny Woods, Wesley	†2001	22	101	4.59
Antonio Ramos, Clarke	2001	25	114	4.56
Erik Lidecis, Maritime (N.Y.)	1994	26	116	4.46
Jeremy Putman, Dubuque	1995	25	110	4.40
Mike Mientus, Allentown	1995	27	118	4.37
Mike Mientus, Allentown	1997	26	112	4.31
Kyle McNamar, Curry	†2002	25	107	4.28

†national champion; *record

STEALS

Player, Team	Season	G	Stl.
Moses Jean-Pierre, Plymouth St.	†1994	30	*189
Daniel Martinez, McMurry	†2000	29	178
Purvis Presha, Stillman	†1996	25	144
Tennyson Whitted, Ramapo	†2002	29	138
Matt Newton, Principia	1994	25	138
John Gallogly, Salve Regina	†1997	24	137
Greg Dean, Concordia-M'head	1997	23	126
Scott Clarke, Utica	†1995	24	126
Deron Black, Allegheny	1996	27	123
David Brown, Westfield St.	1994	25	122
Ricky Hollis, Brockport St.	2000	27	121
John Gallogly, Salve Regina	†1998	23	121
Barry Aranoff, Yeshiva	1995	22	121
Horace Jenkins, Wm. Paterson	2001	31	120
Brian Meehan, Salve Regina	1995	28	120
Tennyson Whitted, Ramapo	†2003	30	118
Scott Clarke, Utica	1996	26	118
Darrel Lewis, Lincoln (Pa.)	1997	26	115
Mario Thompson, Occidental	†1999	24	114
Moses Jean-Pierre, Plymouth St.	†1993	25	114
Keith Darden, Concordia-Austin	†2001	24	111
Shawn McCartney, Hunter	1995	28	111
Gerald Garlic, Goucher	1995	29	111

†national champion; *record

STEAL AVERAGE

Player, Team	Season	G	Stl.	Avg.
Moses Jean-Pierre, Plymouth St.	†1994	30	*189	*6.30
Daniel Martinez, McMurry	†2000	29	178	6.14
Purvis Presha, Stillman	†1996	25	144	5.76
John Gallogly, Salve Regina	†1997	24	137	5.71
Matt Newton, Principia	1994	25	138	5.52
Barry Aranoff, Yeshiva	†1995	22	121	5.50
Greg Dean, Concordia-M'head	1997	23	126	5.48
John Gallogly, Salve Regina	†1998	23	121	5.26
Scott Clarke, Utica	1995	24	126	5.25
Joel Heckendorf, Martin Luther	1996	17	84	4.94
David Brown, Westfield St.	1994	25	122	4.88
Ivo Moyano, Polytechnic (N.Y.)	1994	19	91	4.78
Tennyson Whitted, Ramapo	†2002	29	138	4.76
Mario Thompson, Occidental	†1999	24	114	4.75
Keith Darden, Concordia-Austin	†2001	24	111	4.63
Moses Jean-Pierre, Plymouth St.	†1993	25	114	4.56
Deron Black, Allegheny	1996	27	123	4.55
Scott Clarke, Utica	1996	26	118	4.54
Ricky Hollis, Brockport St.	2000	27	121	4.48
Darrel Lewis, Lincoln (Pa.)	1997	26	115	4.42

†national champion; *record

Career Records

POINTS

Player, Team	Seasons	Pts.
Andre Foreman, Salisbury	1988-89, 91-92	*2,940
Willie Chandler, Misericordia	2000-03	2,898
Lamont Strothers, Chris. Newport	1988-91	2,709
Matt Hancock, Colby	1987-90	2,678
Scott Fitch, Geneseo St.	1990-91, 93-94	2,634
Greg Grant, TCNJ	1987-89	2,611
Rick Hughes, Thomas More	1993-96	2,605
Wil Peterson, St. Andrews	1980-83	2,553
Ron Stewart, Otterbein	1980-83	2,549
Andy Panko, Lebanon Valley	1996-99	2,515
Scott Tedder, Ohio Wesleyan	1985-88	2,501
Moses Jean-Pierre, Plymouth St.	1991-94	2,483
Steve Honderd, Calvin	1990-93	2,469
Herman Alston, Kean	1988-91	2,457
Dick Hempy, Otterbein	1984-87	2,439
John Patraitis, Anna Maria	1995-98	2,434
Kevin Moran, Curry	1983-86	2,415
Alex Butler, Rhode Island Col.	1994-97	2,398
Rickey Sutton, Lyndon St.	1976-79	2,379
Frank Wachlarowicz, St. John's (Minn.)	1975-79	2,357
Henry Shannon, Maryville (Mo.)	1996-99	2,352
Cedric Oliver, Hamilton	1976-79	2,349
Dana Janssen, Neb. Wesleyan	1983-86	2,333
Kevin Brown, Emory & Henry	1984-87	2,322
Carl Howell, St. Joseph's (Me.)	1996-99	2,319
Nick Gutman, Otterbein	1991-94	2,306

*record

SCORING AVERAGE
(Minimum 1,400 points)

Player, Team	Seasons	G	FG	3FG	FT	Pts.	Avg.
Dwain Govan, Bishop	1974-75	55	750	—	305	1,805	*32.8
Dave Russell, Shepherd	1974-75	60	710	—	413	1,833	30.6
Rickey Sutton, Lyndon St.	1976-79	80	960	—	459	2,379	29.7
John Atkins, Knoxville	1976-78	70	845	—	322	2,012	28.7
Steve Peknik, Windham	1974-77	76	816	—	467	2,099	27.6
Clarence Caldwell, Greensboro	1975-77	70	802	—	299	1,903	27.2
Andre Foreman, Salisbury	1988-89, 91-92	109	1,140	68	592	*2,940	27.0
Darrel Lewis, Lincoln (Pa.)	1996-99	86	796	265	409	2,267	26.4
Willie Chandler, Misericordia	2000-03		1,005	346	542	2,898	26.3
Matt Hancock, Colby	1987-90	102	844	198	*792	2,678	26.3
Terrence Dupree, Polytechnic (N.Y.)	1990-92	70	700	22	407	1,829	26.1
Steve Diekmann, Grinnell	1992-95	85	741	371	365	2,218	26.1
Rick Hughes, Thomas More	1993-96	101	1,039	13	514	2,605	25.8
Mark Veenstra, Calvin	1974-77	89	960	—	341	2,261	25.4
Ron Swartz, Hiram	1984-87	90	883	78	408	2,252	25.0
Clarence Caldwell, Greensboro	1974-77	93	971	—	363	2,309	24.8
James Rehnquist, Amherst	1975-77	61	614	—	284	1,512	24.8

*record

FIELD-GOAL PERCENTAGE
(Minimum 400 field goals made)

Player, Team	Seasons	G	FG	FGA	Pct.
Tony Rychlec, Mass. Maritime	1981-83	55	509	692	*73.6
Pete Metzelaars, Wabash	1979-82	103	784	1,083	72.4
Maurice Woods, Potsdam St.	1980-82	93	559	829	67.4
Earl Keith, Stony Brook	1975-76, 78-79	94	777	1,161	66.9
Dan Rush, Bridgewater (Va.)	1992-95	102	712	1,069	66.6
Wade Gugino, Hope	1989-92	97	664	1,010	65.7
David Otte, Simpson	1992-95	76	549	840	65.4
Rick Batt, UC San Diego	1989-92	106	558	855	65.2
Kevin Ryan, TCNJ	1987-90	102	619	955	64.8
Greg Kemp, Aurora	1991-94	102	680	1,051	64.7
Scott Baxter, Capital	1988-91	104	505	782	64.6
Paul Rich, Geneseo St.	1978-81	88	452	700	64.6
Nate Thomas, Neb. Wesleyan	1995-98	98	497	772	64.4
Tod Hart, Ithaca	1980-83	97	726	1,133	64.1
Tony Seay, Averett	1989-90	55	465	726	64.0
John Ellenwood, Wooster	1997-00	98	442	692	63.9
Jeff Gibbs, Otterbein	1999-02	109	758	1,188	63.8
Dick Hempy, Otterbein	1984-87	112	923	1,447	63.8
John Wassenbergh, St. Joseph's (Me.)	1993-96	108	815	1,281	63.6
Jason Nickerson, Va. Wesleyan	1996-99	79	614	967	63.5
Mike Johnson, Wis.-Eau Claire	1989-91	89	402	636	63.2

*record

THREE-POINT FIELD GOALS MADE

Player, Team	Seasons	G	3FG
Jeff Clement, Grinnell	1996-99	91	*516
Chris Carideo, Widener	1992-95	103	402
Steve Diekmann, Grinnell	1992-95	85	371
Matt Garvey, Bates	1994-97	95	361
Ray Wilson, UC Santa Cruz	1989-92	100	354
Ed Brands, Grinnell	1993-96	78	347
Willie Chandler, Misericordia	2000-03	110	346
Steve Nordlund, Grinnell#	2001-03	73	335
Steve Matthews, Emerson/Wentworth Inst.	1998-00	81	334
Chris Hamilton, Blackburn	1988-91	101	334
Scott Fitch, Geneseo St.	1990-91, 93-94	109	332
Billy Collins, Nichols	1992-95	92	331
John Estelle, Wabash	1997-00	109	328
Mark Bedell, Fisk	1994-97	94	321
Jason Valant, Colorado Col.	1990-93	103	315
Everett Foxx, Ferrum	1989-92	104	315
Nevada Smith, Bethany (W.Va.)	1999-02	105	313
Aaron Lee, Mass.-Dartmouth	1992-95	115	313
Steve Chase, St. Joseph's (Me.)	1990-93	119	311
Jim Durrell, Colby-Sawyer	1991-94	100	308
Chris Geruschat, Bethany (W.Va.)	1989-92	89	307
Tommy Doyle, Salem St.	1993-96	110	304
Ryan Knuppel, Elmhurst	1998-01	102	303
Burt Paddock, Manchester	1994-97	109	302

*record; #active player

THREE-POINT FIELD GOALS MADE PER GAME
(Minimum 200 three-point field goals made)

Player, Team	Seasons	G	3FG	Avg.
Jeff Clement, Grinnell	1996-99	91	*516	*5.67
Ed Brands, Grinnell	1993-96	78	347	4.45
Steve Diekmann, Grinnell	1992-95	85	371	4.36
Steve Matthews, Emerson/Wentworth Inst.	1998-00	81	334	4.12
Chris Carideo, Widener	1992-95	103	402	3.90
Matt Garvey, Bates	1994-97	95	361	3.80
Billy Collins, Nichols	1992-95	92	331	3.60
Ray Wilson, UC Santa Cruz	1989-92	100	354	3.54
Chris Geruschat, Bethany (W.Va.)	1989-92	89	307	3.45
Mark Bedell, Fisk	1994-97	94	321	3.41
Chris Hamilton, Blackburn	1988-91	101	334	3.31
Jeff Jones, Lycoming	1987-89	71	232	3.27
Willie Chandler, Misericordia	2000-03	110	346	3.15
Darrel Lewis, Lincoln (Pa.)	1996-99	86	265	3.08
Jim Durrell, Colby-Sawyer	1991-94	100	308	3.08
Jason Valant, Colorado Col.	1990-93	103	315	3.06
Scott Fitch, Geneseo St.	1990-91, 93-94	109	332	3.05
Everett Foxx, Ferrum	1989-92	104	315	3.03
Josh Estelle, Wabash	1997-00	109	328	3.01
Nevada Smith, Bethany (W.Va.)	1999-02	105	313	2.98
Ryan Knuppel, Elmhurst	1998-01	102	303	2.97
Perry Junius, Allegheny	1988-91	93	275	2.96
David Bailey, Concordia (Ill.)	1992-95	94	277	2.95

*record

Photo by St. Lawrence Sports Information

Aaron Marshall of St. Lawrence led the nation in field-goal percentage last season.

DIVISION III

THREE-POINT FIELD-GOAL PERCENTAGE
(Minimum 200 three-point field goals made)

Player, Team	Seasons	G	3FG	3FGA	Pct.
Jeff Seifriz, Wis.-Whitewater	1987-89	85	217	423	*51.3
Chris Peterson, Eureka	1991-94	78	215	421	51.1
Everett Foxx, Ferrum	1989-92	104	315	630	50.0
Brad Alberts, Ripon	1989-92	95	277	563	49.2
Jeff Jonos, Lycoming	1987-89	71	232	472	49.2
Troy Greenlee, DePauw	1988-91	106	232	473	49.0
David Todd, Pomona-Pitzer	1987-90	84	212	439	48.3
Al Callejas, Scranton	1998-01	90	225	466	48.3

*record

FREE-THROW PERCENTAGE
(Minimum 250 free throws made)

Player, Team	Seasons	G	FT	FTA	Pct.
Andy Enfield, Johns Hopkins	1988-91	108	431	466	*92.5
Korey Coon, Ill. Wesleyan	1997-00	109	449	492	91.3
Ryan Knuppel, Elmhurst	1998-01	102	288	317	90.9
Doug Brown, Elizabethtown	1976-80	96	252	279	90.3
Al Callejas, Scranton	1998-01	90	333	372	89.5
Tim McGraw, Hartwick	1985-88	107	330	371	88.9
Eric Jacobs, Wilkes & Scranton	1984-87	106	303	343	88.3
John Luisi, Suffolk	1999-02	105	265	300	88.3
Charles Nenick, Scranton	1994-97	98	259	294	88.1
Todd Reinhardt, Wartburg	1988-91	105	283	322	87.9
Jeff Thomas, King's (Pa.)	1989-92	110	466	532	87.6
Brian Andrews, Alfred	1984-87	101	306	350	87.4
Matt Freesemann, Wartburg	1994-96	73	297	340	87.4
Dave Jannuzzi, Wilkes	1997-99, 2001	112	425	487	87.3
Eric Elliott, Hope	1988-91	103	350	403	86.8
Chad Onofrio, Tufts	1993-96	100	329	379	86.8
Pat Pruitt, Albright	1989-92	87	261	301	86.7
Ryan Billet, Elizabethtown	1995-98	98	434	501	86.6
Mike Johnson, Wis.-Eau Claire	1989-91	89	421	486	86.6
Sean Fleming, Clark (Mass.)	2000-03	109	371	429	86.6
Ron Barczak, Kalamazoo	1988-91	98	360	416	86.5
Scott Smith, Salisbury	1981-85	106	290	336	86.3
Brad Howe, Capital	1997-00	100	239	277	86.3
Rick Alspach, North Park	1997-00	100	283	328	86.3

*record

REBOUND AVERAGE
(Minimum 900 rebounds)

Player, Team	Seasons	G	Reb.	Avg.
Larry Parker, Plattsburgh St.	1975-78	85	1,482	*17.4
Charles Greer, Thomas	1975-77	58	926	16.0
Willie Parr, LeMoyne-Owen	1974-76	76	1,182	15.6
Michael Smith, Hamilton	1989-92	107	*1,628	15.2
Dave Kufeld, Yeshiva	1977-80	81	1,222	15.1
Ed Owens, Hampden-Sydney	1977-80	77	1,160	15.1
Kevin Clark, Clark (Mass.)	1978-81	101	1,450	14.4
Mark Veenstra, Calvin	1974-77	89	1,260	14.2

*record

ASSISTS

Player, Team	Seasons	G	Ast.
Tennyson Whitted, Ramapo	2000-03	108	*917
Steve Artis, Chris. Newport	1990-93	112	909
Phil Dixon, Shenandoah	1993-96	103	889
David Genovese, Mt. St. Vincent	1992-95	107	800
Andre Bolton, Chris. Newport	1993-96	109	737
Tim Gaspar, Mass.-Dartmouth	2000-03	97	690
Matt Lucero, Austin	1998-01	99	677
Brian Nigro, Mt. St. Vincent	1997-00	99	674
Greg Dunne, Nazareth	1996-99	106	671
Moses Jean-Pierre, Plymouth St.	1991-94	109	669
Mike Rhoades, Lebanon Valley	1992-95	114	668
Lance Andrews, N.J. Inst. of Tech.	1990-93	113	664
Dennis Jacobi, Bowdoin	1989-92	93	662
Tim Lawrence, Maryville (Tenn.)	1989-92	106	660
Pat Skerry, Tufts	1989-92	95	650
Eric Prendeville, Salisbury	1996-99	107	641
Eric Johnson, Coe	1989-92	90	637
John Snyder, King's (Pa.)	1989-92	107	631
Jason Saurbaugh, York (Pa.)	1997-00	101	624
Sammy Briggs, Catholic	1994-97	103	621
Anthony Robinson, Wittenberg	1993-96	117	618
Jerry Dennis, Otterbein	1989-92	118	613

*record

ASSIST AVERAGE
(Minimum 550 assists)

Player, Team	Seasons	G	Ast.	Avg.
Phil Dixon, Shenandoah	1993-96	103	889	*8.6
Tennyson Whitted, Ramapo	2000-03	108	*917	8.5
Steve Artis, Chris. Newport	1990-93	112	909	8.1
David Genovese, Mt. St. Vincent	1992-95	107	800	7.5
Kevin Root, Eureka	1989-91	81	579	7.1
Dennis Jacobi, Bowdoin	1989-92	93	662	7.1
Tim Gaspar, Mass.-Dartmouth	2000-03	97	690	7.1
Eric Johnson, Coe	1989-92	90	637	7.1
Nathan Reeves, York (N.Y.)	1994-97	81	572	7.1
Pat Skerry, Tufts	1989-92	95	650	6.8
Matt Lucero, Austin	1998-01	99	677	6.8
Brian Nigro, Mt. St. Vincent	1997-00	99	674	6.8
Andre Bolton, Chris. Newport	1993-96	109	737	6.8
Tony Wyzzard, Emerson-MCA	1992-95	90	604	6.7
Greg Dunne, Nazareth	1996-99	106	671	6.3
Tim Lawrence, Maryville (Tenn.)	1989-92	106	660	6.2
Jason Saurbaugh, York (Pa.)	1997-00	101	624	6.2
Kevin Clipperton, Upper Iowa	1994-97	99	610	6.2
Moses Jean-Pierre, Plymouth St.	1991-94	109	669	6.1
Paul Ferrell, Guilford	1991-94	99	607	6.1
Eric Prendeville, Salisbury	1996-99	107	641	6.0
Sammy Briggs, Catholic	1994-97	103	621	6.0

*record

BLOCKED SHOTS

Player, Team	Seasons	G	Blk.
Ira Nicholson, Mt. St. Vincent	1994-97	100	*576
Antoine Hyman, Keuka	1994-97	101	440
Andrew South, N.J. Inst. of Tech.	1993-95	80	344
Neil Edwards, York (N.Y.)	1998-00	55	337
Mike Mientus, Allentown	1994-97	87	324
Johnny Woods, Wesley	1999-02	78	319
Antonio Ramos, Clarke	2001-03	77	318
Terry Gray, Chris. Newport	2000-03	104	300
Jarriott Rook, Washington (Mo.)	2000-03	107	285
Jason Alexander, Catholic	1995-98	107	283
Jeremy Putman, Dubuque	1993-96	99	274
Matt Hilleary, Catholic	2000-03	118	273
Terry Thomas, Chris. Newport	1993-96	113	271
Ken LaFlamme, Emerson-MCA	1994-97	91	269
David Apple, Averett	1998-00	76	268
Don Overbeek, Hope	2000-03	100	264
Tory Black, N.J. Inst. of Tech.	1995-96	53	261
Kris Silveria, Salem St.	1995-98	112	254
Ryan Gorman, Wooster	1996-99	112	253
Tyrone Bennett, Methodist.	1994-97	101	253
Michael Lynch, Roger Williams	1998-01	106	248
Kyle McNamar, Curry	2000-03	93	243
Jon Wallenfelsz, Wis.-Eau Claire	1997-00	104	242
John Garber, Millsaps	1994-97	102	229
Arthur Hatch, Methodist#	2001-03	69	225

*record, #active player

BLOCKED-SHOT AVERAGE
(Minimum 175 blocked shots)

Player, Team	Seasons	G	Blk.	Avg.
Neil Edwards, York (N.Y.)	1998-00	55	337	*6.13
Ira Nicholson, Mt. St. Vincent	1994-97	100	576	5.76
Tory Black, N.J. Inst. of Tech.	1995-96	53	261	4.92
Antoine Hyman, Keuka	1994-97	101	440	4.36
Andrew South, N.J. Inst. of Tech.	1993-95	80	344	4.30
Antonio Ramos, Clarke	2001-03	77	318	4.13
Johnny Woods, Wesley	1999-02	78	319	4.09
Mike Mientus, Allentown	1994-97	87	324	3.72
Steve Butler, Chris. Newport	1997-00	55	196	3.56
David Apple, Averett	1998-00	76	268	3.53
Ken LaFlamme, Emerson-MCA	1994-97	91	269	2.96
Terry Gray, Chris. Newport	2000-03	104	300	2.88
Jeremy Putman, Dubuque	1993-96	99	274	2.77
Mike Brown, Clark (Mass.)	1997-00	71	195	2.75
Jarriott Rook, Washington (Mo.)	2000-03	107	285	2.66
Jason Alexander, Catholic	1995-98	107	283	2.64
Don Overbeek, Hope	2000-03	100	264	2.64
Kyle McNamar, Curry	2000-03	93	243	2.61
Robert Clyburn, Kean	1993-95	77	201	2.61
Tyrone Bennett, Methodist	1994-97	101	253	2.50
Jeff Manning, Curry	1993-95	74	184	2.49
Terry Thomas, Chris. Newport	1993-96	113	271	2.40

*record

STEALS

Player, Team	Seasons	G	Stl.
Tennyson Whitted, Ramapo	2000-03	108	*448
John Gallogly, Salve Regina	1995-98	98	413
Daniel Martinez, McMurry	1998-00	76	380
Ivo Moyano, Polytechnic (N.Y.)	1994-97	87	368
Eric Bell, New Paltz St.	1993-96	94	355
Scott Clarke, Utica	1993-96	96	346
Ricky Hollis, Brockport St.	1999-02	90	322
Greg Dean, Concordia-M'head	1995-97	75	307
Tom Roeder, St. Joseph's (N.Y.)	1999-02	98	303
Moses Jean-Pierre, Plymouth St.	1993-94	55	303
Joel Holstege, Hope	1995-98	118	301
Mario Thompson, Occidental	1999-01	71	300
Darrell Lewis, Lincoln (Pa.)	1996-99	86	298
Henry Shannon, Maryville (Mo.)	1996-99	106	292
B.J. Reilly, Montclair St.	1997-00	101	287
Damien Hunter, Alvernia	1995-98	110	287
Keith Poppor, Amherst	1993-96	98	283
Carl Cochran, Richard Stockton	1994-97	113	281
Kevin Weakly, Otterbein	1996-99	104	277
Terrence Stewart, Rowan	1993-96	113	277
Clarence Pierce, N.J. Inst. of Tech.	1993-96	102	273
Ben Hoffmann, Wis.-Platteville	1995-98	109	270
Dave Eshaya, Aurora	1995-98	101	265

*record

STEAL AVERAGE
(Minimum 175 steals)

Player, Team	Seasons	G	Stl.	Avg.
Moses Jean-Pierre, Plymouth St.	1993-94	55	303	*5.51
Daniel Martinez, McMurry	1998-00	76	380	5.00
Ivo Moyano, Polytechnic (N.Y.)	1994-97	87	368	4.23
Mario Thompson, Occidental	1999-01	71	300	4.23
John Gallogly, Salve Regina	1995-98	98	413	4.21
Tennyson Whitted, Ramapo	2000-03	108	*448	4.15
Greg Dean, Concordia-M'head	1995-97	75	307	4.09
Rodney Lusain, UC San Diego	1993-94	50	193	3.86
Eric Bell, New Paltz St.	1993-96	94	355	3.78
David Brown, Westfield St.	1993-95	53	193	3.64
Scott Clarke, Utica	1993-96	96	346	3.60
Ricky Hollis, Brockport St.	1999-02	90	322	3.58
Gerald Garlic, Goucher	1993-95	70	244	3.49
Darrel Lewis, Lincoln (Pa.)	1996-99	86	298	3.47
Shuron Woodyard, Villa Julie	1995-97	73	238	3.26
Shawn McCarthy, Hunter	1993-95	81	261	3.22
Carl Small, Cornell College	1993-95	69	222	3.22
Horace Jenkins, Wm. Paterson	1998-01	82	263	3.21
Tom Roeder, St. Joseph's (N.Y.)	1999-02	98	303	3.09
Deron Black, Allegheny	1993-96	78	240	3.08
Reuben Reyes, Salve Regina	1993-95	74	226	3.05
Ernie Peavy, Wis.-Platteville	1993-95	87	264	3.03

*record

Annual Individual Champions

Scoring Average

Season	Player, Team	G	FG	FT	Pts.	Avg.
1974	Dana Wilson, Husson	20	288	122	698	34.9
1975	Dwain Govan, Bishop	29	392	179	963	33.2
1976	Rickey Sutton, Lyndon St.	14	207	93	507	36.2
1977	Rickey Sutton, Lyndon St.	16	223	112	558	34.9
1978	John Atkins, Knoxville	25	340	103	783	31.3
1979	Scott Rogers, Kenyon	24	289	109	687	28.6
1980	Ray Buckland, Mass.-Boston	25	271	153	695	27.8
1981	Gerald Reece, William Penn	27	306	145	757	28.0
1982	Ashley Cooper, Ripon	22	256	89	601	27.3
1983	Shannon Lilly, Bishop	26	345	218	908	34.9
1984	Mark Van Valkenburg, Framingham St.	25	312	133	757	30.3
1985	Adam St. John, Maine Maritime	18	193	135	521	28.9
1986	John Saintignon, UC Santa Cruz	22	291	104	686	31.2

Season	Player, Team	G	FG	3FG	FT	Pts.	Avg.
1987	Rod Swartz, Hiram	23	232	78	133	675	29.3
1988	Matt Hancock, Colby	27	275	56	247	853	31.6
1989	Greg Grant, TCNJ	32	387	76	194	*1,044	32.6
1990	Grant Glover, Rust	23	235	1	164	635	27.6
1991	Andre Foreman, Salisbury	29	350	39	175	914	31.5
1992	Jeff deLaveaga, Cal Lutheran	28	258	122	187	825	29.5
1993	Dave Shaw, Drew	23	210	74	169	663	28.8
1994	Steve Diekmann, Grinnell	21	250	117	106	723	34.4
1995	Steve Diekmann, Grinnell	20	223	137	162	745	*37.3
1996	Ed Brands, Grinnell	24	260	158	136	814	33.9
1997	Mark Bedell, Fisk	19	177	97	88	539	28.4
1998	Jeff Clement, Grinnell	22	238	*186	84	746	33.9
1999	Jeff Clement, Grinnell	22	217	166	121	721	32.8
2000	Willie Chandler, Misericordia	27	249	92	114	704	26.1
2001	Willie Chandler, Misericordia	26	271	96	125	763	29.3
2002	Patrick Glover, Johnson St.	24	237	28	147	649	27.0
2003	Patrick Glover, Johnson St.	26	269	37	188	763	29.3

*record

Field-Goal Percentage

Season	Player, Team	G	FG	FGA	Pct.
1974	Fred Waldstein, Wartburg	28	163	248	65.7
1975	Dan Woodard, Elizabethtown	23	190	299	63.5
1976	Paul Merlis, Yeshiva	21	145	217	66.8
1977	Brent Cawelti, Trinity (Conn.)	20	107	164	65.2
1978	Earl Keith, Stony Brook	29	228	322	70.8
1979	Ed Owens, Hampden-Sydney	24	140	192	72.9
1980	E.D. Schechterley, Lynchburg	25	184	259	71.0
1981	Tony Rychlec, Mass. Maritime	25	233	311	74.9
1982	Pete Metzelaars, Wabash	28	271	360	75.3
1983	Mike Johnson, Drew	23	138	205	67.3
1984	Mark Van Valkenburg, Framingham St.	25	312	467	66.8
1985	Reinout Brugman, Muhlenberg	26	176	266	66.2
1986	Oliver Kyler, Frostburg St.	28	183	266	68.8
1987	Tim Ervin, Albion	21	127	194	65.5
1988	Matt Strong, Hope	27	163	232	70.3
1989	Kevin Ryan, TCNJ	32	246	345	71.3
1990	Bill Triplett, N.J. Inst. of Tech.	28	169	237	71.3
1991	Scott Baxter, Capital	26	164	226	72.6
1992	Brett Grebing, Redlands	23	125	176	71.0
1993	Jim Leibel, St. Thomas (Minn.)	28	141	202	69.8
1994	Travis Weiss, St. John's (Minn.)	26	160	209	*76.6
1995	Justin Wilkins, Neb. Wesleyan	28	163	237	68.8
1996	Jason Light, Emory & Henry	25	207	294	70.4
1997	Jason Hayes, Marietta	25	184	271	67.9
1998	Lonnie Walker, Alvernia	27	165	237	69.6
1999	Jason Nickerson, Va. Wesleyan	26	242	363	66.7
2000	Jack Jirak, Hampden-Sydney	28	147	220	66.8
2001	John Thomas, Fontbonne	22	157	223	70.4
2002	Omar Warthen, Neumann	27	135	202	66.8
2003	Aaron Marshall, St. Lawrence	27	206	305	67.5

*record

Three-Point Field Goals Made Per Game

Season	Player, Team	G	3FG	Avg.
1987	Scott Fearrin, MacMurray	25	96	3.8
1988	Jeff Jones, Lycoming	23	97	4.2
1989	Brad Block, Aurora	26	112	4.3
1990	Chris Hamilton, Blackburn	24	109	4.5
1991	Chris Jans, Loras	25	133	5.3
1992	Jeff deLaveaga, Cal Lutheran	28	122	4.4
1993	Mike Connelly, Catholic	27	111	4.1
1994	Steve Diekmann, Grinnell	21	117	5.6
1995	Steve Diekmann, Grinnell	20	137	6.8
1996	Ed Brands, Grinnell	24	158	6.6
1997	Jeff Clement, Grinnell	22	113	5.1
1998	Jeff Clement, Grinnell	22	*186	*8.5
1999	Jeff Clement, Grinnell	22	166	7.5
2000	Woody Piirto, Grinnell	20	87	4.3
2001	Nevada Smith, Bethany (W.Va.)	26	101	3.9
2002	Steve Nordlund, Grinnell	24	137	5.7
2003	Steve Nordlund, Grinnell	28	119	4.8

*record

DIVISION III

Three-Point Field-Goal Percentage

Season	Player, Team	G	3FG	3FGA	Pct.
1987	Chris Miles, N.J. Inst. of Tech.	26	41	65	63.1
1988	Ray Magee, Richard Stockton	26	41	71	57.7
1989	Reggie James, N.J. Inst. of Tech.	29	59	88	*67.0
1990	Matt Miota, Lawrence	22	33	54	61.1
1991	Mike Bachman, Alma	26	46	76	60.5
1992	John Kmack, Plattsburgh St.	26	44	84	52.4
1993	Brad Apple, Greensboro	26	49	91	53.8
1994	Trever George, Coast Guard	23	38	72	52.8
1995	Tony Frieden, Manchester	32	58	107	54.2
1996	Joey Bigler, John Carroll	27	54	111	48.6
1997	Andy Strommen, Chicago	27	49	93	52.7
1998	Pat Maloney, Catholic	29	59	114	51.8
1999	Al Callejas, Scranton	26	66	122	54.1
2000	Brett Lively, Mary Washington	20	40	78	51.3
2001	Bryan Bertola, Lake Forest	23	58	110	52.7
2002	Doug Schneider, Pitt.-Bradford	28	78	143	54.5
2003	Jeremy Currier, Endicott	28	74	144	51.4

*record

Free-Throw Percentage

Season	Player, Team	G	FT	FTA	Pct.
1974	Bruce Johnson, Plymouth St.	17	73	81	90.1
1975	Harold Howard, Austin	24	83	92	90.2
1976	Tim Mieure, Hamline	25	88	95	92.6
1977	Mike Scheib, Susquehanna	22	80	85	94.1
1978	Jerry Prestier, Baldwin-Wallace	25	125	134	93.3
1979	Joe Purcell, King's (Pa.)	26	66	71	93.0
1980	David Whiteside, UNC Greensboro	28	120	132	90.9
1981	Jim Cooney, Elmhurst	26	65	72	90.3
1982	Shannon Lilly, Bishop	22	142	153	92.8
1983	Mike Sain, Eureka	26	66	72	91.7
1984	Chris Genian, Redlands	24	71	78	91.0
1985	Bob Possehl, Coe	22	59	65	90.8
1986	Eric Jacobs, Scranton	29	81	87	93.1
1987	Chris Miles, N.J. Inst. of Tech.	26	70	76	92.1
1988	Jeff Bowers, Southern Me.	29	95	102	93.1
1989	Yudi Teichman, Yeshiva	21	119	125	95.2
1990	Todd Reinhardt, Wartburg	26	91	98	92.9
1991	Andy Enfield, Johns Hopkins	29	123	129	95.3
1992	Chris Carideo, Widener	26	80	84	95.2
1993	Jim Durrell, Colby-Sawyer	25	67	72	93.1
1994	Jason Prenevost, Middlebury	22	60	64	93.8
1995	Matt Freesemann, Wartburg	24	128	138	92.8
1996	Charlie Nanick, Scranton	25	96	103	93.2
1997	Mark Giovino, Babson	28	86	91	94.5
1998	Chanse Young, Manchester	25	65	68	95.6
1999	Ryan Eklund, Wis.-La Crosse	26	80	87	92.0
2000	Korey Coon, Ill. Wesleyan	25	157	163	*96.3
2001	Derrick Rogers, Averett	27	72	77	93.5
2002	Jason Luisi, Suffolk	28	87	94	92.6
2003	Nick Wilkins, Coe	26	66	69	95.7

*record

Rebound Average

Season	Player, Team	G	Reb.	Avg.
1974	Fred Petty, Southern N.H.	22	436	19.8
1975	Larry Parker, Plattsburgh St.	23	430	18.7
1976	Joe Manley, Bowie St.	29	*579	*20.0
1977	Larry Williams, Pratt	24	457	19.0
1978	John Jordan, Southern Me.	29	536	18.5
1979	Dave Kufeld, Yeshiva	20	355	17.8
1980	Dave Kufeld, Yeshiva	20	353	17.7
1981	Kevin Clark, Clark (Mass.)	27	465	17.2
1982	Len Washington, Mass.-Boston	23	361	15.7
1983	Luis Frias, Anna Maria	23	320	13.9
1984	Joe Weber, Aurora	27	370	13.7
1985	Albert Wells, Rust	22	326	14.8

Season	Player, Team	G	Reb.	Avg.
1986	Russell Thompson, Westfield St.	22	338	15.4
1987	Randy Gorniak, Penn St.-Behrend	25	410	16.4
1988	Mike Nelson, Hamilton	26	349	13.4
1989	Clinton Montford, Methodist	27	459	17.0
1990	Michael Stubbs, Trinity (Conn.)	22	398	18.1
1991	Mike Smith, Hamilton	27	435	16.1
1992	Jeff Black, Fitchburg St.	22	363	16.5
1993	Steve Lemmer, Hamilton	27	404	15.0
1994	Chris Sullivan, St. John Fisher	23	319	13.9
1995	Scott Suhr, Milwaukee Engr.	25	349	14.0
1996	Craig Jones, Rochester Inst.	26	363	14.0
1997	Lonnie Walker, Alvernia	32	430	13.4
1998	Adam Doll, Simpson	25	366	14.6
1999	Anthony Peeples, Montclair St.	24	345	14.4
2000	Jeff Gibbs, Otterbein	23	307	13.3
2001	Jeff Gibbs, Otterbein	25	390	15.6
2002	Jeff Gibbs, Otterbein	32	523	16.3
2003	Jed Johnson, Maine Maritime	25	414	16.6

*record

Assist Average

Season	Player, Team	G	Ast.	Avg.
1989	Robert James, Kean	27	*391	*13.5
1990	Albert Kirchner, Mt. St. Vincent	24	267	11.1
1991	Eric Johnson, Coe	24	238	9.9
1992	Edgar Loera, La Verne	23	202	8.8
1993	David Genovese, Mt. St. Vincent	27	237	8.8
1994	Phil Dixon, Shenandoah	26	253	9.7
1995	Joe Marcotte, N.J. Inst. of Tech.	30	292	9.7
1996	Andre Bolton, Chris. Newport	30	289	9.6
1997	Deshone Bond, Stillman	25	235	9.4
1998	David Rubin, Hobart	25	237	9.5
1999	Tim Kelly, Pacific Lutheran	25	214	8.6
2000	Daniel Martinez, McMurry	29	229	7.9
2001	Jimmy Driggs, Hamilton	25	213	8.5
2002	Tennyson Whitted, Ramapo	29	319	11.0
2003	Tennyson Whitted, Ramapo	30	253	8.4

*record

Blocked-Shot Average

Season	Player, Team	G	Stl.	Avg.
1993	Matt Cusano, Scranton	29	145	5.0
1994	Andrew South, N.J. Inst. of Tech.	27	128	4.7
1995	Ira Nicholson, Mt. St. Vincent	28	188	6.7
1996	Ira Nicholson, Mt. St. Vincent	27	163	6.0
1997	Tory Black, N.J. Inst. of Tech.	26	*198	*7.6
1998	Tony Seehase, Upper Iowa	23	89	3.9
1999	Neil Edwards, York (N.Y.)	26	144	5.5
2000	Neil Edwards, York (N.Y.)	26	193	7.4
2001	Johnny Woods, Wesley	22	101	4.6
2002	Kyle McNamar, Curry	25	107	4.3
2003	John Bunch, Lincoln (Pa.)	23	92	4.0

*record

Steal Average

Season	Player, Team	G	Stl.	Avg.
1993	Moses Jean-Pierre, Plymouth St.	25	114	4.6
1994	Moses Jean-Pierre, Plymouth St.	30	*189	*6.3
1995	Barry Aranoff, Yeshiva	22	121	5.5
1996	Purvis Presha, Stillman	25	144	5.8
1997	John Gallogly, Salve Regina	24	137	5.7
1998	John Gallogly, Salve Regina	23	121	5.3
1999	Mario Thompson, Occidental	24	114	4.8
2000	Daniel Martinez, McMurry	29	178	6.1
2001	Keith Darden, Concordia-Austin	24	111	4.6
2002	Tennyson Whitted, Ramapo	29	138	4.8
2003	Benny West, Howard Payne	24	99	4.1

*record

Annual Team Champions

Won-Lost Percentage

Season	Team	Won	Lost	Pct.
1974	Calvin	21	2	.913
1975	Calvin	22	1	.957
1976	Husson	25	1	.961
1977	Mass.-Boston	25	3	.893
1978	North Park	29	2	.935
1979	Stony Brook	24	3	.889
1980	Franklin Pierce	29	2	.935
1981	Potsdam St.	30	2	.938
1982	St. Andrews	27	3	.900
1983	Roanoke	31	2	.939
1984	Roanoke	27	2	.931
1985	Colby	22	3	.880
1986	Potsdam St.	32	0	1.000
1987	Potsdam St.	28	1	.966
1988	Scranton	29	3	.906
1989	TCNJ	30	2	.938
1990	Colby	26	1	.963
1991	Hamilton	26	1	.963
1992	Calvin	31	1	.969
1993	Rowan	29	2	.935
1994	Wittenberg	30	2	.938
1995	Wis.-Platteville	31	0	1.000
1996	Wilkes	28	2	.933
1997	Ill. Wesleyan	29	2	.935
1998	Wis.-Platteville	30	0	1.000
1999	Connecticut Col.	28	1	.966
2000	Calvin	30	2	.938
2001	Mass.-Dartmouth	25	3	.893
2002	Carthage	28	2	.933
2003	Williams	31	1	.969

Scoring Offense

Season	Team	G	W-L	Pts.	Avg.
1974	Bishop	26	14-12	2,527	97.2
1975	Bishop	29	25-4	2,932	101.1
1976	Husson	26	25-1	2,567	98.7
1977	Mercy	25	16-9	2,587	103.5
1978	Mercy	26	16-10	2,602	100.1
1979	Ashland	25	14-11	2,375	95.0
1980	Franklin Pierce	31	29-2	3,073	99.1
1981	Husson	23	20-3	2,173	94.5
1982	Husson	26	19-7	2,279	87.7
1983	Bishop	26	18-8	2,529	97.3
1984	St. Joseph's (Me.)	29	24-5	2,666	91.9
1985	St. Joseph's (Me.)	30	22-8	2,752	91.7
1986	St. Joseph's (Me.)	30	26-4	2,837	94.6
1987	Bishop	26	13-13	2,534	97.5
1988	St. Joseph's (Me.)	29	20-9	2,785	96.0
1989	Redlands	25	15-10	2,507	100.3
1990	Salisbury	27	14-13	2,822	104.5
1991	Redlands	26	15-11	2,726	104.8
1992	Redlands	25	18-7	2,510	100.4
1993	Salisbury	26	18-8	2,551	98.1
1994	Grinnell	21	13-8	2,297	109.4
1995	Grinnell	21	14-7	2,422	115.3
1996	Grinnell	25	17-8	2,587	103.5
1997	Grinnell	22	10-12	2,254	102.5
1998	Grinnell	22	10-12	2,434	110.6
1999	Grinnell	22	11-11	2,509	114.0
2000	Grinnell	21	6-15	2,175	103.6
2001	Grinnell	24	16-8	2,837	118.2
2002	Grinnell	24	12-12	2,997	*124.9
2003	Grinnell	25	19-6	*3,119	124.8

*record

Scoring Defense

Season	Team	G	W-L	Pts.	Avg.
1974	Fredonia St.	22	13-9	1,049	47.7
1975	Chicago	15	9-6	790	52.7
1976	Fredonia St.	23	10-13	1,223	53.2
1977	Hamline	30	22-8	1,560	52.0
1978	Widener	31	26-5	1,693	54.6
1979	Coast Guard	24	21-3	1,160	48.3

Season	Team	G	W-L	Pts.	Avg.
1980	John Jay	27	10-17	1,411	52.3
1981	Wis.-Stevens Point	26	19-7	1,394	53.6
1982	Wis.-Stevens Point	28	22-6	1,491	53.3
1983	Ohio Northern	26	18-8	1,379	53.0
1984	Wis.-Stevens Point	32	28-4	1,559	48.7
1985	Wis.-Stevens Point	30	25-3	1,438	47.9
1986	Widener	27	15-12	1,356	50.2
1987	Muskingum	27	16-11	1,454	53.9
1988	Ohio Northern	30	21-9	1,734	57.8
1989	Wooster	28	21-7	1,600	57.1
1990	Randolph-Macon	29	24-5	1,646	56.8
1991	Ohio Northern	27	14-13	1,508	55.9
1992	Wittenberg	29	23-6	1,651	56.9
1993	St. Thomas (Minn.)	28	19-9	1,599	57.1
1994	Yeshiva	22	12-10	1,308	59.5
1995	Johnson St.	26	15-11	1,559	60.0
1996	Upper Iowa	26	21-5	1,500	57.7
1997	Wis.-Platteville	27	24-3	1,283	*47.5
1998	Wis.-Platteville	30	30-0	1,552	51.7
1999	Rowan	27	25-2	1,549	57.4
2000	Baruch	28	19-9	1,639	58.5
2001	Cortland St.	28	21-7	1,678	59.9
2002	Babson	30	25-5	1,693	56.4
2003	Randolph-Macon	30	28-2	1,599	53.3

*record

Scoring Margin

Season	Team	Off.	Def.	Mar.
1974	Fisk	83.3	65.7	17.6
1975	Monmouth (Ill.)	83.9	66.0	17.9
1976	Husson	98.7	67.6	*31.1
1977	Husson	101.2	78.6	22.6
1978	Stony Brook	86.6	68.7	17.9
1979	North Park	84.4	67.3	17.1
1980	Franklin Pierce	99.1	76.5	22.6
1981	Husson	94.5	70.1	24.4
1982	Hope	83.9	70.0	13.8
1983	Trinity (Conn.)	79.8	61.4	18.4
1984	Wis.-Stevens Point	68.4	48.7	19.7
1985	Hope	85.4	66.0	19.4
1986	Potsdam St.	81.5	57.3	24.2
1987	N.J. Inst. of Tech.	90.8	63.9	26.9
1988	Cal St. San B'dino	89.4	69.4	20.0
1989	TCNJ	92.3	68.5	23.8
1990	Colby	94.7	71.9	22.8
1991	Hamilton	89.8	66.2	23.6
1992	N.J. Inst. of Tech.	95.0	73.4	21.6
1993	N.J. Inst. of Tech.	90.4	65.7	24.7
1994	Rowan	89.6	64.4	25.3
1995	Colby-Sawyer	94.4	71.7	22.6
1996	Cabrini	89.4	67.6	21.8
1997	Williams	83.6	62.5	21.0
1998	Wis.-Platteville	73.9	51.7	22.2
1999	Hampden-Sydney	84.2	62.3	21.9
2000	Hampden-Sydney	88.2	66.4	21.8
2001	Chapman	81.2	63.4	17.9
2002	Brockport St.	84.5	64.9	19.6
2003	Williams	83.1	62.4	20.7

*record

Field-Goal Percentage

Season	Team	FG	FGA	Pct.
1974	Muskingum	560	1,056	53.0
1975	Savannah St.	1,072	1,978	54.2
1976	Stony Brook	778	1,401	55.5
1977	Stony Brook	842	1,455	57.9
1978	Stony Brook	1,033	1,721	*60.0
1979	Stony Brook	980	1,651	59.4
1980	Framingham St.	924	1,613	57.3
1981	Averett	845	1,447	58.4
1982	Lebanon Valley	608	1,098	55.4
1983	Bishop	1,037	1,775	58.4
1984	Framingham St.	849	1,446	58.7
1985	Me.-Farmington	751	1,347	55.8
1986	Frostburg St.	971	1,747	55.6

DIVISION III

Season	Team	FG	FGA	Pct.
1987	N.J. Inst. of Tech.	969	1,799	53.9
1988	Rust	878	1,493	58.8
1989	Bridgewater (Va.)	650	1,181	55.0
1990	Wartburg	792	1,474	53.7
1991	Otterbein	1,104	2,050	53.9
1992	Bridgewater (Va.)	706	1,315	53.7
1993	St. John's (Minn.)	744	1,415	52.6
1994	Oglethorpe	774	1,491	51.9
1995	Simpson	892	1,627	54.8
1996	Simpson	946	1,749	54.1
1997	Neb. Wesleyan	968	1,834	52.8
1998	Ill. Wesleyan	843	1,546	54.5
1999	Lebanon Valley	751	1,445	52.0
2000	Franklin	814	1,577	51.6
2001	St. John's (Minn.)	772	1,471	52.5
2002	Wis.-Oshkosh	784	1,500	52.3
2003	Wis.-Oshkosh	849	1,600	53.1

*record

Field-Goal Percentage Defense

Season	Team	FG	FGA	Pct.
1978	Grove City	589	1,477	39.9
1979	Coast Guard	464	1,172	39.6
1980	Calvin	552	1,364	40.5
1981	Wittenberg	670	1,651	40.6
1982	Tufts	622	1,505	41.3
1983	Trinity (Conn.)	580	1,408	41.2
1984	Widener	617	1,557	39.6
1985	Colby	679	1,712	39.7
1986	Widener	531	1,344	39.5
1987	Widener	608	1,636	37.2
1988	Rust	603	1,499	40.2
1989	Wooster	595	1,563	38.1
1990	Rochester	760	1,990	38.2
1991	Hamilton	679	1,771	38.3
1992	Scranton	589	1,547	38.1
1993	Scranton	659	1,806	36.5
1994	Lebanon Valley	708	1,925	36.8
1995	New Jersey City	702	1,897	37.0
1996	Bowdoin	569	1,482	38.4
1997	N.J. Inst. of Tech.	572	1,565	36.5
1998	Rhodes	552	1,488	37.1
1999	Grove City	533	1,469	36.3
2000	Baruch	608	1,689	*36.0
2001	Endicott	575	1,569	36.6
2002	Rowan	503	1,377	36.5
2003	Trinity (Tex.)	589	1,587	37.1

*record

Three-Point Field Goals Made Per Game

Season	Team	G	3FG	Avg.
1987	Grinnell	22	166	7.5
1988	Southern Me.	29	233	8.0
1989	Redlands	25	261	10.4
1990	Augsburg	25	266	10.6
1991	Redlands	26	307	11.8
1992	Catholic	26	335	12.9
1993	Anna Maria	27	302	11.2
1994	Grinnell	21	297	14.1
1995	Grinnell	21	368	17.5
1996	Grinnell	25	415	16.6
1997	Grinnell	22	367	16.7
1998	Grinnell	22	406	18.5
1999	Grinnell	22	436	19.8
2000	Grinnell	21	353	16.8
2001	Grinnell	24	443	18.5
2002	Grinnell	24	490	20.4
2003	Grinnell	25	*522	*20.9

*record

Three-Point Field-Goal Percentage

Season	Team	G	3FG	3FGA	Pct.
1987	Mass.-Dartmouth	28	102	198	51.5
1988	Richard Stockton	26	122	211	57.8
1989	N.J. Inst. of Tech.	29	124	200	*62.0
1990	Western New Eng.	26	85	167	50.9
1991	Ripon	26	154	331	46.5
1992	Dickinson	27	126	267	47.2
1993	DePauw	26	191	419	45.6
1994	Eureka	31	317	646	49.1
1995	Manchester	32	222	487	45.6
1996	John Carroll	27	169	388	43.6
1997	Williams	30	235	507	46.4
1998	Franklin	29	168	390	43.1
1999	Union (N.Y.)	25	233	512	45.5
2000	Franklin	28	195	467	41.8
2001	Albion	25	192	417	46.0
2002	Gordon	27	262	590	44.4
2003	Wis.-Oshkosh	32	229	532	43.0

*record

Free-Throw Percentage

Season	Team	FT	FTA	Pct.
1974	Lake Superior St.	369	461	80.0
1975	Muskingum	298	379	78.6
1976	Case Reserve	266	343	77.6
1977	Hamilton	491	640	76.7
1978	Case Reserve	278	351	79.2
1979	Marietta	364	460	79.1
1980	Denison	377	478	78.9
1981	Ripon	378	494	76.5
1982	Otterbein	458	589	77.8
1983	DePauw	368	475	77.5
1984	Redlands	426	534	79.8
1985	Wis.-Stevens Point	363	455	79.8
1986	Heidelberg	375	489	76.7
1987	Denison	442	560	78.9
1988	Capital	377	473	79.7
1989	Colby	464	585	79.3
1990	Colby	485	605	80.2
1991	Wartburg	565	711	79.5
1992	Thiel	393	491	80.0
1993	Colby	391	506	77.3
1994	Wheaton (Ill.)	455	572	79.5
1995	Baldwin-Wallace	454	582	78.0
1996	Anderson	454	592	76.7
1997	Ill. Wesleyan	616	790	78.0
1998	Wis.-Oshkosh	516	631	*81.8
1999	Carleton	423	540	78.3
2000	Ill. Wesleyan	426	543	78.5
2001	Franklin	570	713	79.9
2002	Moravian	407	512	79.5
2003	Wooster	543	685	79.3

*record

Rebound Margin

Season	Team	Off.	Def.	Mar.
1976	Bowie St.	54.0	37.5	16.5
1977	Husson	51.6	35.0	16.7
1978	Gallaudet	46.3	33.0	13.3
1979	St. Lawrence	43.2	28.7	14.5
1980	Elmira	41.4	28.7	12.7
1981	Clark (Mass.)	40.0	25.0	15.0
1982	Maryville (Mo.)	41.0	26.7	14.4
1983	Framingham St.	38.0	22.2	15.8
1984	New England Col.	43.3	29.3	14.0
1985	Bethel (Minn.)	45.0	32.2	12.8
1986	St. Joseph's (Me.)	43.7	29.5	14.2
1987	Elmira	40.6	29.3	11.3
1988	Cal St. San B'dino	46.6	29.7	16.9
1989	Yeshiva	49.8	34.6	15.2
1990	Bethel (Minn.)	42.2	30.3	12.0
1991	Hamilton	49.6	32.5	*17.0
1992	Bethel (Minn.)	42.3	31.0	11.3
1993	Eureka	33.9	22.2	11.7
1994	Maritime (N.Y.)	46.3	32.3	14.1
1995	Wittenberg	43.1	29.2	13.9
1996	Cabrini	47.9	34.7	13.1
1997	Rochester Inst.	42.8	31.9	10.8
1998	Chris. Newport	47.5	33.7	13.9
1999	Rensselaer	41.5	29.8	11.7
2000	Albright	41.3	29.6	11.7
2001	Wittenberg	44.7	30.7	14.0
2002	Wittenberg	42.5	30.1	12.4
2003	Williams	43.7	31.1	12.6

*record

2003 Most-Improved Teams

School (Coach)	2003	2002	*Games Improved
1. Mary Washington (Rod Wood)	24-5	10-16	12½
2. Rhode Island Col. (Mike Kelly)	13-13	1-24	11½
3. Ursinus (Kevin Small)	21-7	8-16	11
4. Scranton (Carl Danzig)	24-6	12-13	9½
5. Hamline (Tom Gilles)	12-13	3-22	9
6. Lawrence (John Tharp)	18-6	9-14	8½
7. Elms (Ed Silva)	14-12	6-20	8

School (Coach)	2003	2002	*Games Improved
7. Ill. Wesleyan (Scott Trost)	22-6	12-12	8
7. John Carroll (Mike Moran)	22-7	12-13	8
7. St. John Fisher (Rob Kornaker)	21-5	13-13	8
7. Whittier (Rock Carter)	17-8	9-16	8
7. Worcester St. (Dave Lindberg)	17-11	8-18	8

To determine games improved, add the difference in victories between the two seasons to the difference in losses, then divide by two.

All-Time Winningest Teams

Includes records as a senior college only; minimum 10 seasons of competition. Postseason games are included.

Percentage

Team	Yrs.	Won	Lost	Pct.
1. Wittenberg	92	1,458	600	.708
2. Cabrini	23	452	191	.703
3. Colby-Sawyer	14	239	106	.693
4. St. Joseph's (Me.)	32	572	274	.676
5. New Jersey City	68	749	367	.671
6. Calvin	83	1,122	551	.671
7. Hope	97	1,280	649	.664
8. Chris. Newport	36	624	323	.659
9. Defiance	56	934	486	.658
10. Wis.-Eau Claire	87	*1,223	644	.655
11. Richard Stockton	31	534	287	.650
12. Williams	102	1,205	648	.650
13. Wooster	102	1,342	728	.648
14. Staten Island	26	468	254	.648
15. Ill. Wesleyan	93	1,353	770	.637
16. Roanoke	90	1,192	679	.637
17. St. Thomas (Minn.)	99	1,333	773	.633
18. New York U.	85	1,069	645	.624
19. St. John Fisher	40	606	369	.622
20. Mass.-Dartmouth	37	595	368	.618
21. Wartburg	67	988	614	.617
22. Augsburg	44	683	434	.611
23. Hartwick	73	940	603	.609
24. Wis.-Stevens Point	104	1,169	751	.609
25. Springfield	94	1,249	804	.608
26. Colby	64	896	587	.604
27. Beloit	96	1,093	717	.604
28. Augustana (Ill.)	98	1,199	792	.602
29. Buffalo St.	74	954	631	.602
30. Randolph-Macon	90	1,212	810	.599

*Includes one tie.

Victories

Team	Yrs.	Won	Lost	Pct.
1. Wittenberg	92	1,458	600	.708
2. Ill. Wesleyan	93	1,353	770	.637
3. Wooster	102	1,342	728	.648
4. St. Thomas (Minn.)	99	1,333	773	.633
5. Hope	97	1,280	649	.664
6. Neb. Wesleyan	98	1,267	847	.599
7. Springfield	94	1,249	804	.608
8. Wis.-Eau Claire	87	*1,223	644	.655
9. Randolph-Macon	90	1,212	810	.599
10. Scranton	86	1,208	816	.597
11. Gust. Adolphus	92	1,206	857	.585
12. Williams	102	1,205	648	.650
13. Augustana (Ill.)	98	1,199	792	.602
14. Roanoke	90	1,192	679	.637
15. Wheaton (Ill.)	103	1,174	930	.558
16. Wis.-Stevens Point	104	1,169	751	.609
17. Willamette	79	1,146	859	.572
18. Hamline	93	1,138	852	.572
19. Loras	95	1,130	892	.559

Team	Yrs.	Won	Lost	Pct.
20. Muskingum	99	1,129	850	.570
21. Frank. & Marsh.	99	1,124	799	.585
22. Calvin	83	1,122	551	.671
23. Mount Union	106	1,116	936	.544
24. Capital	97	1,111	751	.597
25. DePauw	97	**1,110	867	.561
26. Rochester	102	1,105	823	.573
27. Hampden-Sydney	92	1,102	842	.567
28. Beloit	96	1,093	717	.604
29. Ohio Wesleyan	98	1,092	993	.524
30. Albright	96	1,090	971	.529
30. Millikin	96	1,090	921	.542

*Includes one tie.   **Includes two ties.

Winningest Teams of the 2000s

PERCENTAGE
(Minimum three seasons as NCAA member)

Team	Yrs.	Won	Lost	Pct.
1. Hampden-Sydney	4	101	17	.856
1. Wooster	4	101	17	.856
3. Chris. Newport	4	97	17	.851
4. Catholic	4	102	18	.850
5. Washington (Mo.)	4	89	16	.848
6. Carthage	4	93	17	.845
7. Buena Vista	4	98	18	.845
8. Williams	4	94	18	.839
9. Maryville (Tenn.)	4	93	20	.823
10. Hanover	4	87	20	.813
11. McMurry	4	89	21	.809
12. Wis.-Stevens Point	4	88	22	.800
12. Wittenberg	4	88	22	.800
14. St. Thomas (Minn.)	4	86	22	.796
15. Salem St.	4	93	24	.795
16. Frank. & Marsh.	4	92	24	.793
17. Calvin	4	89	24	.788
18. Amherst	4	87	24	.784
19. Mississippi Col.	4	82	24	.774
20. Clark (Mass.)	4	87	27	.763
20. Wm. Paterson	4	87	27	.763
22. Colby-Sawyer	4	82	26	.759
23. Gust. Adolphus	4	86	28	.754
24. DePauw	4	78	26	.750
24. Pitt.-Bradford	3	63	21	.750
26. Lewis & Clark	4	81	28	.743
27. Chapman	4	74	26	.740
28. Brockport St.	4	87	31	.737
29. Chicago	4	77	28	.733
30. Trinity (Tex.)	4	76	28	.731

VICTORIES
(Minimum three seasons as NCAA member)

Team	Yrs.	Won	Lost	Pct.
1. Catholic	4	102	18	.850
2. Hampden-Sydney	4	101	17	.856
2. Wooster	4	101	17	.856
4. Buena Vista	4	98	18	.845
5. Chris. Newport	4	97	17	.851
6. Williams	4	94	18	.839

DIVISION III

Team	Yrs.	Won	Lost	Pct.
7. Carthage	4	93	17	.845
7. Maryville (Tenn.)	4	93	20	.823
7. Salem St.	4	93	24	.795
10. Frank. & Marsh.	4	92	24	.793
11. Washington (Mo.)	4	89	16	.848
11. McMurry	4	89	21	.809
11. Calvin	4	89	24	.788
14. Wis.-Stevens Point	4	88	22	.800
14. Wittenberg	4	88	22	.800
16. Hanover	4	87	20	.813
16. Amherst	4	87	24	.784
16. Clark (Mass.)	4	87	27	.763
16. Wm. Paterson	4	87	27	.763
16. Brockport St.	4	87	31	.737
21. St. Thomas (Minn.)	4	86	22	.796
21. Gust. Adolphus	4	86	28	.754
23. Merchant Marine	4	84	33	.718
24. Mississippi Col.	4	82	24	.774
24. Colby-Sawyer	4	82	26	.759
24. Wis.-Oshkosh	4	82	33	.713
27. Lewis & Clark	4	81	28	.743
28. Randolph-Macon	4	81	30	.730
29. Elizabethtown	4	80	30	.727
30. Wartburg	4	79	31	.718
30. Alvernia	4	79	35	.693

All-Time Won-Lost Records

(No Minimum Seasons of Competition)

Team	First Year	Yrs.	Won	Lost	Pct.
Albion	1898	92	944	835	.531
Albright	1901	96	1,090	971	.529
Alfred	1921	81	703	921	.433
Allegheny	1896	108	1,016	854	.543
Alma	1911	92	835	952	.467
Alvernia	1976	28	442	333	.570
Amherst	1902	102	948	673	.585
Anderson (Ind.)	1931	72	872	855	.505
Augsburg	1960	44	683	434	.611
Augustana (Ill.)	1901	98	1,199	792	.602
Aurora	1928	73	765	803	.488
Baldwin-Wallace	1907	96	979	990	.497
Beloit	1906	96	1,093	717	.604
Benedictine (Ill.)	1966	37	513	426	.546
Bethany (W.Va.)	1905	95	730	1,018	.418
Bethel (Minn.)	1947	57	636	681	.483
Bluffton	1915	88	734	1,056	.410
Bridgewater St.	1907	98	744	799	.482
Bridgewater (Va.)	1903	82	757	910	.454
Brockport St.	1929	71	785	684	.534
Buffalo St.	1926	74	954	631	.602
Cabrini	1981	23	452	191	.703
Cal Lutheran	1962	42	505	625	.447
Caltech	1919	84	303	1,146	.209
Calvin	1920	83	1,122	551	.671
Capital	1907	97	1,111	751	.597
Carleton	1909	94	1,025	813	.558
Carnegie Mellon	1907	96	765	1,157	.398
Carroll (Wis.)	1956	48	444	689	.392
Carthage	1907	95	916	1,035	.470
Case Reserve	1902	102	1,053	862	.550
Catholic	1910	92	1,030	973	.514
Central (Iowa)	1924	80	839	841	.499
Chicago	1903	99	1,008	983	.506
Chris. Newport	1968	36	624	323	.659
CCNY	1905	98	965	915	.513
Claremont-M-S.	1959	45	586	547	.517
Clarkson	1930	74	592	904	.396
Coast Guard	1926	78	652	853	.433
Colby	1938	64	896	587	.604
Colby-Sawyer	1991	14	239	106	.693
Colorado Col.	1915	89	736	955	.435
Concordia (Ill.)	1924	80	765	903	.459
Connecticut Col.	1970	34	355	339	.512
Cornell College	1910	94	864	903	.489
Cortland St.	1926	78	807	726	.526
Curry	1967	38	318	572	.357
Dallas	1917	30	188	423	.308
Defiance	1948	56	934	486	.658
Delaware Valley	1949	54	370	811	.313

Team	First Year	Yrs.	Won	Lost	Pct.
DePauw	1904	97	1,110	867	.561
DeSales	1969	35	390	464	.457
Dickinson	1900	93	805	921	.466
Drew	1930	72	540	853	.388
Dubuque	1915	89	815	911	.472
Eastern Conn. St.	1941	63	650	648	.501
Eusl. Mennonite	1967	37	309	578	.348
Edgewood	1972	28	401	296	.575
Elizabethtown	1927	75	829	835	.498
Elmhurst	1925	79	683	943	.420
Elmira	1971	33	430	395	.521
Emory	1987	17	195	231	.458
Emory & Henry	1927	72	755	830	.476
Eureka	1920	82	921	818	.530
FDU-Florham	1959	45	502	522	.490
Franklin	1907	97	1,036	913	.532
Frank. & Marsh.	1900	99	1,124	799	.585
Fredonia St.	1935	65	640	734	.466
Frostburg St.	1936	61	663	714	.481
Gallaudet	1904	100	516	1,272	.289
Geneseo St.	1915	85	725	769	.485
Gettysburg	1901	100	1,057	961	.524
Goucher	1991	13	188	151	.555
Grove City	1898	99	1,087	868	.556
Guilford	1906	89	791	954	.453
Gust. Adolphus	1904	92	1,206	857	.585
Gwynedd-Mercy	1993	11	102	146	.411
Hamilton	1899	91	896	670	.572
Hamline	1910	93	1,138	852	.572
Hampden-Sydney	1909	92	1,102	842	.567
Hanover	1901	98	1,030	862	.544
Hartwick	1928	73	940	603	.609
Heidelberg	1903	97	834	1,001	.454
Hobart	1902	93	637	970	.396
Hope	1901	97	1,280	649	.664
Hunter	1953	49	599	559	.517
Ill. Wesleyan	1910	93	1,353	770	.637
Ithaca	1930	73	896	648	.580
John Carroll	1920	82	825	848	.493
Johns Hopkins	1920	78	711	853	.455
Johnson & Wales	1996	8	69	137	.335
Juniata	1905	99	734	1,089	.403
Kalamazoo	1907	96	1,031	867	.543
Kean	1930	65	680	792	.462
Keene St.	1926	75	658	800	.451
King's (Pa.)	1947	57	733	636	.535
Knox	1909	94	852	838	.504
Lake Erie	1988	16	87	314	.217
Lakeland	1934	70	1,030	783	.568
Lawrence	1904	100	759	919	.452
Lebanon Valley	1904	100	908	884	.507
Loras	1909	95	1,130	892	.559
Luther	1905	99	562	455	.553
Lycoming	1949	55	594	642	.481
Lynchburg	1957	47	484	683	.415
Manhattanville	1976	28	378	357	.514
Marian (Wis.)	1973	31	413	373	.525
Marietta	1902	99	914	1,008	.476
Mary Washington	1975	29	297	432	.407
Marymount (Va.)	1988	16	195	221	.469
Maryville (Tenn.)	1903	100	1,036	855	.548
Maryville (Mo.)	1977	27	291	412	.414
Mass.-Boston	1981	23	239	346	.409
Mass.-Dartmouth	1967	37	595	368	.618
McDaniel	1922	81	656	1,059	.383
McMurry	1923	78	914	870	.512
Merchant Marine	1946	58	600	760	.441
Messiah	1962	42	445	516	.463
Millikin	1904	96	1,090	921	.542
Millsaps	1912	92	778	1,108	.413
Mississippi Col.	1909	91	1,012	860	.541
Monmouth (Ill.)	1900	103	1,076	835	.563
Montclair St.	1928	74	945	744	.560
Moravian	1936	62	736	705	.511
Mt. St. Vincent	1981	22	324	233	.582
Mount Union	1896	106	1,116	936	.544
Muhlenberg	1901	96	1,078	941	.534
Muskingum	1903	99	1,129	850	.570
Nazareth	1978	26	398	271	.595
Neb. Wesleyan	1906	98	1,267	847	.599
New Jersey City	1935	68	749	367	.671
New York U.	1906	85	1,069	645	.624
Nichols	1959	45	396	627	.387

Team	First Year	Yrs.	Won	Lost	Pct.	Team	First Year	Yrs.	Won	Lost	Pct.
N.C. Wesleyan	1964	40	462	488	.486	Susquehanna	1902	101	845	1,001	.458
North Central	1948	56	524	821	.390	Swarthmore	1902	102	736	1,081	.405
North Park	1959	45	677	460	.595	Thiel	1917	86	511	1,073	.323
Oberlin	1903	100	711	1,027	.409	Trinity (Conn.)	1914	90	907	701	.564
Occidental	1981	23	290	296	.495	Tufts	1912	92	942	864	.522
Ohio Northern	1911	91	1,075	821	.567	Upper Iowa	1916	88	794	872	.477
Ohio Wesleyan	1906	98	1,092	993	.524	Wabash	1897	107	1,062	932	.533
Otterbein	1903	100	1,066	861	.553	Wartburg	1936	67	988	614	.617
Pacific (Ore.)	1911	93	800	1,166	.407	Washington (Md.)	1914	91	960	877	.523
Pacific Lutheran	1939	63	941	695	.575	Washington (Mo.)	1905	97	971	842	.536
Pitt.-Bradford	1980	24	326	312	.511	Wash. & Jeff.	1913	91	857	796	.518
Plattsburgh St.	1926	74	605	624	.492	Wash. & Lee	1907	85	1,010	975	.509
Plymouth St.	1948	56	705	552	.561	Wentworth Inst.	1984	19	174	300	.367
Randolph-Macon	1910	90	1,212	810	.599	Wesleyan (Conn.)	1902	102	941	841	.528
Redlands	1917	86	921	824	.528	Western Conn. St.	1947	57	639	619	.508
Rensselaer	1897	106	865	902	.490	Western New Eng.	1966	35	451	469	.490
Richard Stockton	1973	31	534	287	.650	Westfield St.	1951	53	582	626	.482
Ripon	1898	105	1,037	784	.569	Westminster (Mo.)	1909	88	862	950	.476
Roanoke	1911	90	1,192	679	.637	Wheaton (Ill.)	1901	103	1,174	930	.558
Rochester	1902	102	1,105	823	.573	Wheaton (Mass.)	1989	15	175	185	.486
Rochester Inst.	1916	83	888	785	.531	Widener	1906	95	1,012	761	.571
Roger Williams	1973	30	222	347	.390	Wilkes	1947	57	679	652	.510
Rose-Hulman	1901	81	832	781	.516	Willamette	1925	79	1,146	859	.572
Rowan	1923	61	838	585	.589	Wm. Paterson	1939	61	789	712	.526
St. John Fisher	1964	40	606	369	.622	Williams	1901	102	1,205	648	.650
St. John's (Minn.)	1903	101	976	974	.501	Wilmington (Ohio)	1917	86	760	1,037	.423
St. Joseph's (Me.)	1972	32	572	274	.676	Wis.-Eau Claire	1917	87	1,223	644	.655
St. Mary's (Md.)	1967	37	399	537	.426	Wis.-Oshkosh	1899	105	1,013	894	.531
St. Norbert	1917	85	828	754	.523	Wis.-Platteville	1905	92	1,071	735	.593
St. Thomas (Minn.)	1905	99	1,333	773	.633	Wis.-Stevens Point	1897	104	1,169	751	.609
Salisbury	1963	41	497	515	.491	Wis.-Stout	1907	97	857	916	.483
Salve Regina	1975	29	266	359	.426	Wis.-Whitewater	1902	93	981	799	.551
Scranton	1917	86	1,208	816	.597	Wittenberg	1912	92	1,458	600	.708
Sewanee	1927	77	656	840	.439	Wooster	1901	102	1,342	728	.648
Shenandoah	1975	29	325	414	.440	Worcester St.	1950	53	583	628	.481
Simpson	1901	101	1,037	986	.513	WPI	1903	93	761	918	.453
Southern Me.	1923	86	770	653	.541	Yeshiva	1936	67	592	736	.446
Springfield	1906	94	1,249	804	.608	York (Pa.)	1970	34	391	471	.454
Staten Island	1978	26	468	254	.648						
Stevens Tech	1917	87	656	744	.469						

*Includes one tie.   **Includes two ties.

DIVISION III

Individual Collegiate Records

Individual Collegiate Records

Individual collegiate leaders are determined by comparing the best records in all three divisions in equivalent categories. Included are players whose careers were split between two divisions (e.g., Dwight Lamar of Louisiana-Lafayette or Howard Shockley of Salisbury).

Single-Game Records

POINTS

Pts.	Div.	Player, Team vs. Opponent	Date
113	II	Clarence "Bevo" Francis, Rio Grande vs. Hillsdale	Feb. 2, 1954
100	I	Frank Selvy, Furman vs. Newberry	Feb. 13, 1954
85	I	Paul Arizin, Villanova vs. Philadelphia NAMC	Feb. 12, 1949
84	II	Clarence "Bevo" Francis, Rio Grande vs. Alliance	1954
82	II	Clarence "Bevo" Francis, Rio Grande vs. Bluffton	1954
81	I	Freeman Williams, Portland St. vs. Rocky Mountain	Feb. 3, 1978
80	II	Paul Crissman, Southern Cal Col. vs. Pacific Christian	Feb. 18, 1966
77	III	Jeff Clement, Grinnell vs. Illinois Col.	Feb. 18, 1998
77	II	William English, Winston-Salem vs. Fayetteville St.	Feb. 19, 1968
75	II	Travis Grant, Kentucky St. vs. Northwood	1970
73	I	Bill Mlkvy, Temple vs. Wilkes	Mar. 3, 1951
72	II	Nate DeLong, Wis.-River Falls vs. Winona St.	Feb. 24, 1948
72	II	Lloyd Brown, Aquinas vs. Cleary	1953
72	II	Clarence "Bevo" Francis, Rio Grande vs. Calif. (Pa.)	1953
72	II	John McElroy, Youngstown St. vs. Wayne St. (Mich.)	Feb. 26, 1969
72	I	Kevin Bradshaw, U.S. Int'l vs. Loyola Marymount	Jan. 5, 1991
71	II	Clayborn Jones, L.A. Pacific vs. L.A. Baptist	Jan. 30, 1965
71	I	Freeman Williams, Portland St. vs. Southern Ore.	Feb. 9, 1977
70	II	Paul Wilcox, Davis & Elkins vs. Glenville St.	1959
70	II	Bo Clark, UCF vs. Fla. Memorial	Jan. 31, 1977
69	II	Clarence "Bevo" Francis, Rio Grande vs. Wilberforce	1953
69	II	Clarence Burks, St. Augustine's vs. St. Paul's	1955
69	I	Pete Maravich, LSU vs. Alabama	Feb. 7, 1970
69	II	John Rinka, Kenyon vs. Wooster	Dec. 9, 1969
69	III	Steve Diekmann, Grinnell vs. Simpson	Nov. 19, 1994
68	II	Florindo Vieira, Quinnipiac vs. Brooklyn Poly	Feb. 13, 1957
68	II	Wayne Proffitt, Lynchburg vs. Charlotte	Feb. 5, 1966
68	II	Earl Monroe, Winston-Salem vs. Fayetteville St.	Jan. 6, 1967
68	I	Calvin Murphy, Niagara vs. Syracuse	Dec. 7, 1968

Charlotte's Demon Brown made 137 three-pointers in 2002-03, second best in Division I.

Photo by Wade Bruton/Charlotte Sports Information

FIELD-GOAL PERCENTAGE
(Minimum 13 field goals made)

Pct.	Div.	Player, Team vs. Opponent (FG-FGA)	Date
100	II	Lance Berwald, North Dakota St. vs. Augustana (S.D.) (20 of 20)	Feb. 17, 1984
100	III	Jason Light, Emory & Henry vs. King (Tenn.) (18 of 18)	Dec. 2, 1995
100	I	Clifford Rozier, Louisville vs. Eastern Ky. (15 of 15)	Dec. 11, 1993
100	II	Derrick Scott, Calif. (Pa.) vs. Columbia Union (14 of 14)	Dec. 6, 1995
100	I	Dan Henderson, Arkansas St. vs. Ga. Southern (14 of 14)	Feb. 26, 1976
100	I	Cornelius Holden, Louisville vs. Southern Miss. (14 of 14)	Mar. 3, 1990
100	I	Dana Jones, Pepperdine vs. Boise St. (14 of 14)	Nov. 30, 1991
100	III	Waverly Yates, Clark (Mass.) vs. Suffolk (14 of 14)	Feb. 10, 1993
100	II	Derrick Freeman, Indiana (Pa.) vs. Clarion (13 of 13)	Feb. 17, 1996
100	I	Ben Handlogten, Western Mich. vs. Toledo (13 of 13)	Jan. 27, 1996
100	II	Ralfs Jansons, St. Rose vs. Concordia (N.Y.) (13 of 13)	Jan. 13, 1996
100	I	Ted Guzek, Butler vs. Michigan (13 of 13)	Dec. 15, 1956
100	I	Rick Dean, Syracuse vs. Colgate (13 of 13)	Feb. 14, 1966
100	I	Gary Lechman, Gonzaga vs. Portland St. (13 of 13)	Jan. 21, 1967
100	I	Kevin King, Charlotte vs. South Ala. (13 of 13)	Feb. 20, 1978
100	I	Vernon Smith, Texas A&M vs. Alas. Anchorage (13 of 13)	Nov. 26, 1978
100	I	Steve Johnson, Oregon St. vs. Hawaii-Hilo (13 of 13)	Dec. 5, 1979
100	I	Antoine Carr, Wichita St. vs. Abilene Christian (13 of 13)	Nov. 28, 1980
100	III	Rich Lengieza, Nichols vs. Mass.-Dartmouth (13 of 13)	Feb. 22, 1981
100	I	Doug Hashley, Montana St. vs. Idaho St. (13 of 13)	Feb. 5, 1982
100	I	Brad Daugherty, North Carolina vs. UCLA (13 of 13)	Nov. 24, 1985
100	III	Bruce Merklinger, Susquehanna vs. Drew (13 of 13)	Jan. 22, 1986
100	III	Antonio Randolph, Averett vs. Methodist (13 of 13)	Jan. 26, 1991
100	III	Pat Holland, Randolph-Macon vs. East. Mennonite (13 of 13)	Feb. 9, 1991
100	I	Ricky Butler, UC Irvine vs. Cal St. Fullerton (13 of 13)	Feb. 21, 1991
100	I	Rafael Solis, Brooklyn vs. Wagner (13 of 13)	Dec. 11, 1991
100	III	Todd Seifferlein, DePauw vs. Franklin (13 of 13)	Jan. 18, 1992
100	I	Mate Milisa, Long Beach St. vs. Cal St. Monterey (13 of 13)	Dec. 22, 1999
100	I	Nathan Blessen, South Dakota vs. Neb.-Omaha (13 of 13)	Jan. 9, 2000

THREE-POINT FIELD GOALS MADE

3FG	Div.	Player, Team vs. Opponent	Date
19	III	Jeff Clement, Grinnell vs. Illinois Col.	Feb. 18, 1998
17	III	Jeff Clement, Grinnell vs. Clarke	Dec. 3, 1997
16	II	Markus Hallgrimson, Mont. St.-Billings vs. Western N.M.	Feb. 9, 2000
16	III	Jeff Clement, Grinnell vs. Lawrence	Feb. 21, 1998
16	III	Jeff Clement, Grinnell vs. Monmouth (Ill.)	Feb. 8, 1997
15	I	Keith Veney, Marshall vs. Morehead St.	Dec. 14, 1996
14	I	Ronald Blackshear, Marshall vs. Akron	Mar. 1, 2002
14	II	Antonio Harris, LeMoyne-Owen vs. Savannah St.	Feb. 6, 1999
14	III	Ed Brands, Grinnell vs. Ripon	Feb. 24, 1996
14	I	Dave Jamerson, Ohio vs. Col. of Charleston	Dec. 21, 1989
14	I	Askia Jones, Kansas St. vs. Fresno St.	Mar. 24, 1994
14	II	Andy Schmidtmann, Wis.-Parkside vs. Lakeland	Feb. 14, 1989
14	III	Steve Diekmann, Grinnell vs. Illinois Col.	Feb. 18, 1994
14	III	Steve Diekmann, Grinnell vs. Simpson	Nov. 19, 1994
13	II	Markus Hallgrimson, Mont. St.-Billings vs. Western N.M.	Feb. 26, 2000
13	II	Markus Hallgrimson, Mont. St.-Billings vs. Chaminade	Feb. 5, 2000
13	II	Rodney Thomas, IUPUI vs. Wilberforce	Feb. 24, 1997
13	II	Danny Lewis, Wayne St. (Mich.) vs. Michigan Tech	Feb. 20, 1993
13	III	Eric Ochel, Sewanee vs. Emory	Feb. 22, 1995

REBOUNDS

Reb.	Div.	Player, Team vs. Opponent	Date
51	I	Bill Chambers, William & Mary vs. Virginia	Feb. 14, 1953
46	II	Tom Hart, Middlebury vs. Trinity (Conn.)	Feb. 5, 1955
46	II	Tom Hart, Middlebury vs. Clarkson	Feb. 12, 1955
45	II	William Henrikson, Windham vs. New England Col.	Feb. 4, 1970
44	II	Charles McCullough, Loyola (Md.) vs. McDaniel	Feb. 17, 1955
44	II	Norman Rokeach, Long Island vs. Brooklyn Poly	Dec. 28, 1963
43	I	Charlie Slack, Marshall vs. Morris Harvey	Jan. 12, 1954
43	II	Bob Bessoir, Scranton vs. King's (Pa.)	Mar. 5, 1955
42	I	Tom Heinsohn, Holy Cross vs. Boston College	Mar. 1, 1955
42	II	Larry Gooding, St. Augustine's vs. Shaw	Jan. 12, 1974
41	II	Richard Kross, American Int'l vs. Springfield	Feb. 19, 1958
40	II	Ellerbe Neal, Wofford vs. Presbyterian	Jan. 3, 1953
40	I	Art Quimby, Connecticut vs. Boston U.	Jan. 11, 1955
40	II	Donnie Fowler, Wofford vs. Mercer	Jan. 22, 1955
40	II	Charlie Harrison, N.C. A&T vs. Johnson Smith	Feb. 8, 1958

Reb.	Div.	Player, Team vs. Opponent	Date
40	II	Anthony Romano, Willimantic St. vs. Fitchburg St.	Jan. 5, 1963
40	II	Ed Halicki, Monmouth vs. Southeastern	Dec. 4, 1970
39	II	Maurice Stokes, St. Francis (Pa.) vs. John Carroll	Jan. 28, 1955
39	II	Roger Lotchin, Millikin vs. Lake Forest	Feb. 11, 1956
39	II	Joe Cole, Southwest Tex. St. vs. Tex. Lutheran	Dec. 10, 1956
39	I	Dave DeBusschere, Detroit vs. Central Mich.	Jan. 30, 1960
39	I	Keith Swagerty, Pacific (Cal.) vs. UC Santa Barb.	Mar. 5, 1965
39	II	Curtis Pritchett, St. Augustine vs. St. Paul's	Jan. 24, 1970
38		14 tied	

(Since 1973)

Reb.	Div.	Player, Team vs. Opponent	Date
42	II	Larry Gooding, St. Augustine's vs. Shaw	Jan. 12, 1974
36	III	Mark Veenstra, Calvin vs. Colorado St.-Pueblo	Feb. 3, 1976
36	III	Clinton Montford, Methodist vs. Warren Wilson	Jan. 21, 1989
35	I	Larry Abney, Fresno St. vs. Southern Methodist	Feb. 17, 2000
35	III	Ayal Hod, Yeshiva vs. Vassar	Feb. 22, 1989
34	I	David Vaughn, Oral Roberts vs. Brandeis	Jan. 8, 1973
34	II	Major Jones, Albany St. (Ga.) vs. Valdosta St.	Jan. 23, 1975
34	II	Herman Harris, Mississippi Val. vs. Texas Southern	Jan. 12, 1976
34	III	Walt Edwards, Husson vs. Me.-Farmington	Feb. 24, 1976
33	II	Joe Dombrowski, St. Anselm vs. New Hampshire	Dec. 8, 1974
33	II	Lee Roy Williams, Cal Poly Pomona vs. Wheaton (Ill.)	Dec. 15, 1973
33	III	Willie Parr, LeMoyne-Owen vs. Southern U.	Jan. 10, 1976
33	III	Larry Williams, Pratt vs. Mercy	Jan. 22, 1977
32	II	Marvin Webster, Morgan St. vs. South Carolina St.	Dec. 8, 1973
32	II	Earl Williams, Winston-Salem vs. N.C. Central	Dec. 13, 1973
32	III	Fred Petty, Southern N.H. vs. Curry	Jan. 28, 1974
32	II	George Wilson, Union (Ky.) vs. Southwestern	1974
32	II	Tony DuCros, Regis vs. Neb. Wesleyan	Feb. 28, 1975
32	I	Durand Macklin, LSU vs. Tulane	Nov. 26, 1976
32	II	Robert Clements, Jacksonville vs. Shorter	Jan. 12, 1977
32	I	Jervaughn Scales, Southern U. vs. Grambling St.	Feb. 7, 1994
31	I	Pete Harris, Stephen F. Austin vs. Texas A&M	Jan. 22, 1973
31	I	Jim Bradley, Northern Ill. vs. Wis.-Milwaukee	Feb. 19, 1973
31	III	John Humphrie, Swarthmore vs. Ursinus	Dec. 8, 1973
31	II	Roy Smith, Kentucky St. vs. Union (Ky.)	Feb. 10, 1975
31	I	Larry Parker, Plattsburgh St. vs. Clarkson	Jan. 19, 1976
31	I	Calvin Natt, Northeast La. vs. Ga. Southern	Dec. 29, 1976
31	II	Charles Wode, Mississippi Val. vs. Miss. Industrial	Dec. 10, 1977
31	III	Jon Ford, Norwich vs. Johnson St.	Feb. 16, 1982

ASSISTS

Ast.	Div.	Player, Team vs. Opponent	Date
26	III	Robert James, Kean vs. N.J. Inst. of Tech	Mar. 11, 1989
25	II	Ali Baaqar, Morris Brown vs. Albany St. (Ga.)	Jan. 26, 1991
25	II	Adrian Hutt, Metro St. vs. Sacramento St.	Feb. 9, 1991
24	II	Steve Ray, Bridgeport vs. Sacred Heart	Jan. 25, 1989
24	II	Steve Ray, Bridgeport vs. New Haven	Feb. 8, 1989
24	III	Adam Dzierzynski, Chapman vs. Amer. Indian Bible	Feb. 9, 1995
23	II	Todd Chappell, Texas Wesleyan vs. Texas Lutheran	Feb. 12, 2000
23	II	Steve Ray, Bridgeport vs. St. Anselm	Nov. 26, 1989
23	II	Jeff Duvall, Oakland City vs. St. Meinrad	Dec. 3, 1991
22	I	Tony Fairley, Charleston So. vs. Armstrong Atlantic	Feb. 9, 1987
22	I	Avery Johnson, Southern U. vs. Texas Southern	Jan. 25, 1988
22	I	Sherman Douglas, Syracuse vs. Providence	Jan. 28, 1989
22	II	Antonio Whitley, St. Augustine's vs. Shaw	Feb. 1, 1992
22	II	Ernest Jenkins, N.M. Highlands vs. Panhandle St.	Jan. 29, 1994
21	I	Mark Wade, UNLV vs. Navy	Dec. 29, 1986
21	I	Kelvin Scarborough, New Mexico vs. Hawaii	Feb. 13, 1987
21	I	Anthony Manuel, Bradley vs. UC Irvine	Dec. 19, 1987
21	I	Avery Johnson, Southern U. vs. Alabama St.	Jan. 16, 1988
21	III	Ron Torgalski, Hamilton vs. Vassar	Jan. 28, 1989
21	III	Mark Cottom, Ferrum vs. Concord	Dec. 15, 1990
21	II	Candice Pickens, Calif. (Pa.) vs. Slippery Rock	Feb. 8, 1995

BLOCKED SHOTS

Blk.	Div.	Player, Team vs. Opponent	Date
16	III	Tory Black, N.J. Inst. of Tech vs. Polytechnic (N.Y.)	Feb. 5, 1997
15	III	Johnny Woods, Wesley vs. Salisbury	Feb. 14, 2000
15	III	Antoine Hyman, Keuka vs. Hobart	Feb. 21, 1996
15	III	Erick Lidecis, Maritime (N.Y.) vs. Stevens Tech	Nov. 30, 1993
15	II	Mark Hensel, Pitt.-Johnstown vs. Slippery Rock	Jan. 22, 1994
15	III	Roy Woods, Fontbonne vs. MacMurray	Jan. 26, 1995
15	III	Ira Nicholson, Mt. St. Vincent vs. Stevens Tech	Nov. 27, 1994
14	III	Johnny Woods, Wesley vs. Eastern	Jan. 17, 2001
14	III	Neil Edwards, York (N.Y.) vs. Lehman	Feb. 12, 2000
14	I	Loren Woods, Arizona vs. Oregon	Feb. 3, 2000
14	I	Roy Rogers, Alabama vs. Georgia	Feb. 10, 1996
14	I	Victorlus Payne, Lane vs. Talladega	Jan. 26, 1996
14	I	David Robinson, Navy vs. UNC Wilmington	Jan. 4, 1986
14	I	Shawn Bradley, Brigham Young vs. Eastern Ky.	Dec. 7, 1990
14	II	Maurice Barnett, Elizabeth City St. vs. Bowie St.	Feb. 3, 1994
14	III	Andrew South, N.J. Inst. of Tech vs. Stevens Tech	Feb. 14, 1994

Blk.	Div.	Player, Team vs. Opponent	Date
13	I	Wojciech Myrda, La.-Monroe vs. Texas-San Antonio	Jan. 17, 2002
13	I	Kyle Davis, Auburn vs. Miami (Fla.)	Mar. 14, 2001
13	I	D'or Fischer, Northwestern St. vs. Southwest Tex. St.	Jan. 22, 2001
13	III	Neil Edwards, York (N.Y.) vs. Brooklyn	Feb. 22, 2000
13	III	Antoine Hyman, Keuka vs. Hobart	Jan. 8, 1997
13	III	Damon Avinger, CCNY vs. St. Joseph's (N.Y.)	Jan. 7, 1996
13	I	Kevin Roberson, Vermont vs. New Hampshire	Jan. 9, 1992
13	I	Jim McIlvaine, Marquette vs. Northeastern Ill.	Dec. 9, 1992
13	II	Mark Hensel, Pitt.-Johnstown vs. Wheeling Jesuit	Jan. 31, 1994
13	I	Keith Closs, Central Conn. St. vs. St. Francis (Pa.)	Dec. 21, 1994

STEALS

Stl.	Div.	Player, Team vs. Opponent	Date
17	II	Antonio Walls, Alabama A&M vs. Albany St. (Ga.)	Jan. 5, 1998
17	II	Matt Newton, Principia vs. Harris-Stowe	Jan. 4, 1994
14	III	Moses Jean-Pierre, Plymouth St. vs. Rivier	Dec. 7, 1993
13	III	Daniel Martinez, McMurry vs. Concordia (Tex.)	Feb. 3, 2000
13	III	Todd Lange, Pomona-Pitzer vs. LaSierra	Jan. 7, 1999
13	III	John Gallogly, Salve Regina vs. Roger Williams	Feb. 10, 1997
13	I	Mookie Blaylock, Oklahoma vs. Centenary (La.)	Dec. 12, 1987
13	I	Mookie Blaylock, Oklahoma vs. Loyola Marymount	Dec. 17, 1988
12	I	Jehiel Lewis, Navy vs. Bucknell	Jan. 12, 2002
12	I	Greedy Daniels, TCU vs. Ark.-Pine Bluff	Dec. 30, 2000
12	II	Terrence Baxter, Pfeiffer vs. Livingstone	Nov. 22, 2000
12	III	Greg Brown, Albertus Magnus vs. Rivier	Feb. 3, 2000
12	III	Daniel Martinez, McMurry vs. Ozarks (Ark.)	Dec. 2, 1999
12	I	Richard Duncan, Middle Tenn. vs. Eastern Ky.	Feb. 20, 1999
12	II	Derrick Brown, Davis & Elkins vs. Ohio Valley	Feb. 9, 1999
12	II	Marche' Bearad, Ark.-Monticello vs. Christian Bros.	Feb. 8, 1999
12	II	Freddy Conyers, Mass.-Boston vs. Westfield St.	Dec. 10, 1998
12	III	Mario Thompson, Occidental vs. LIFE Bible	Nov. 21, 1998
12	III	Deron Black, Allegheny vs. Case Reserve	Jan. 17, 1996
12	III	Jamal Elliott, Haverford vs. Gwynedd Mercy	Jan. 15, 1996
12	I	Kenny Robertson, Cleveland St. vs. Wagner	Dec. 3, 1988
12	III	Moses Jean-Pierre, Plymouth St. vs. Rhode Island Col.	Jan. 23, 1993
12	I	Terry Evans, Oklahoma vs. Florida A&M	Jan. 27, 1993
12	III	David Brown, Westfield St. vs. Albertus Magnus	Jan. 8, 1994
12	III	Barry Aranoff, Yeshiva vs. Purchase St.	Feb. 13, 1995

Season Records

(Based on qualifiers for annual statistical championship)

POINTS

Player, Team (Division)	Season	G	FG	3FG	FT	Pts.
Pete Maravich, LSU (I)	1970	31	522	—	337	1,381
Earl Monroe, Winston-Salem (II)	1967	32	509	—	311	1,329
Travis Grant, Kentucky St. (II)	1972	33	539	—	226	1,304
Clarence "Bevo" Francis, Rio Grande (II)	1954	27	444	—	367	1,255
Bill Reigel, McNeese St. (II)	1956	36	425	—	370	1,220
Elvin Hayes, Houston (I)	1968	33	519	—	176	1,214
Frank Selvy, Furman (I)	1954	29	427	—	355	1,209
Pete Maravich, LSU (I)	1969	26	433	—	282	1,148
Pete Maravich, LSU (I)	1968	26	432	—	274	1,138
Bo Kimble, Loyola Marymount (I)	1990	32	404	92	231	1,131
Hersey Hawkins, Bradley (I)	1988	31	377	87	284	1,125
Austin Carr, Notre Dame (I)	1970	29	444	—	218	1,106
Austin Carr, Notre Dame (I)	1971	29	430	—	241	1,101
Otis Birdsong, Houston (I)	1977	36	452	—	186	1,090
Dwight Lamar, La.-Lafayette (I)	1972	29	429	—	196	1,054
Kevin Bradshaw, U.S. Int'l (I)	1991	28	358	60	278	1,054
Dwight Lamar, La.-Lafayette (II)	1971	29	424	—	196	1,044
Greg Grant, TCNJ (III)	1989	32	387	76	194	1,044
Dave Russell, Shepherd (III)	1975	32	394	—	249	1,037
Glenn Robinson, Purdue (I)	1994	34	368	79	215	1,030
Oscar Robertson, Cincinnati (I)	1958	28	352	—	280	984
Oscar Robertson, Cincinnati (I)	1959	30	331	—	316	978
Rick Barry, Miami (Fla.) (I)	1965	26	340	—	221	973
Larry Bird, Indiana St. (I)	1979	34	376	—	221	973
Dennis Scott, Georgia Tech (I)	1990	35	336	137	161	970

SCORING AVERAGE

Player, Team (Division)	Season	G	FG	3FG	FT	Pts.	Avg.
Clarence "Bevo" Francis, Rio Grande (II)	1954	27	444	—	367	1,255	46.5
Pete Maravich, LSU (I)	1970	31	522	—	337	1,381	44.5
Pete Maravich, LSU (I)	1969	26	433	—	282	1,148	44.2
Pete Maravich, LSU (I)	1968	26	432	—	274	1,138	43.8
Earl Glass, Miss. Industrial (II)	1963	19	322	—	171	815	42.9
Frank Selvy, Furman (I)	1954	29	427	—	355	1,209	41.7
Earl Monroe, Winston-Salem (II)	1967	32	509	—	311	1,329	41.5
John Rinka, Kenyon (II)	1970	23	354	—	234	942	41.0

Player, Team (Division)	Season	G	FG	3FG	FT	Pts.	Avg.
Willie Shaw, Lane (II)	1964	18	303	—	121	727	40.4
Johnny Neumann, Mississippi (I)	1971	23	366	—	191	923	40.1
Travis Grant, Kentucky St. (II)	1972	33	539	—	226	1,304	39.5
Thales McReynolds, Miles (II)	1965	18	294	—	118	706	39.2
Bob Johnson, Fitchburg St. (II)	1963	18	213	—	277	703	39.1
Roger Kuss, Wis.-River Falls (II)	1953	21	291	—	235	817	38.9
Freeman Williams, Portland St. (I)	1977	26	417	—	176	1,010	38.8
Billy McGill, Utah (I)	1962	26	394	—	221	1,009	38.8
Calvin Murphy, Niagara (I)	1968	24	337	—	242	916	38.2
Austin Carr, Notre Dame (I)	1970	29	444	—	218	1,106	38.1
Austin Carr, Notre Dame (I)	1971	29	430	—	241	1,101	38.0
Kevin Bradshaw, U.S. Int'l (I)	1991	28	358	60	278	1,054	37.6
Rick Barry, Miami (Fla.) (I)	1965	26	340	—	221	973	37.4
Steve Diekmann, Grinnell (III)	1995	20	223	137	162	745	37.3
Florindo Vieira, Quinnipiac (II)	1954	14	191	—	138	520	37.1
Elvin Hayes, Houston (I)	1968	33	519	—	176	1,214	36.8
Marshall Rogers, Tex.-Pan American (I)	1976	25	361	—	197	919	36.8

FIELD-GOAL PERCENTAGE

Player, Team (Division)	Season	G	FG	FGA	Pct.
Travis Weiss, St. John's (Minn.) (III)	1994	26	160	209	76.6
Pete Metzelaars, Wabash (III)	1982	28	271	360	75.3
Todd Linder, Tampa (II)	1987	32	282	375	75.2
Maurice Stafford, North Ala. (II)	1984	34	198	264	75.0
Tony Rychlec, Mass. Maritime (III)	1981	25	233	311	74.9
Matthew Cornegay, Tuskegee (II)	1982	29	208	278	74.8
Steve Johnson, Oregon St. (I)	1981	28	235	315	74.6
Brian Moten, West Ga. (II)	1992	26	141	192	73.4
Ed Phillips, Alabama A&M (II)	1968	22	154	210	73.3
Tony Rychlec, Mass. Maritime (III)	1982	20	193	264	73.1
Russ Newman, Menlo (III)	1991	26	130	178	73.0
Ed Owens, Hampden-Sydney (III)	1979	24	140	192	72.9
Ray Strozier, Central Mo. St. (II)	1980	28	142	195	72.8
Harold Booker, Cheyney (II)	1965	24	144	198	72.7
Chad Scott, Calif. (Pa.) (II)	1994	30	178	245	72.7
Scott Baxter, Capital (III)	1991	26	164	226	72.6
Maurice Woods, Potsdam St. (III)	1982	30	203	280	72.5
Tom Schurfranz, Bellarmine (II)	1991	30	245	339	72.3
Marv Lewis, Southampton (II)	1969	24	271	375	72.3
Earl Keith, Stony Brook (III)	1979	24	164	227	72.2
Louis Newsome, North Ala. (II)	1988	29	192	266	72.2
Pete Metzelaars, Wabash (III)	1981	25	204	283	72.1
Ed Phillips, Alabama A&M (II)	1971	24	159	221	71.9
Jon Rosner, Yeshiva (III)	1991	22	141	196	71.9
Gregg Northington, Alabama St. (II)	1971	26	324	451	71.8
Pete Metzelaars, Wabash (III)	1979	24	122	170	71.8

THREE-POINT FIELD GOALS MADE

Player, Team (Division)	Season	G	3FG
Jeff Clement, Grinnell (III)	1998	22	186
Alex Williams, Sacramento St. (II)	1988	30	167
Jeff Clement, Grinnell (III)	1999	22	166
Markus Hallgrimson, Mont. St.-Billings (II)	2000	26	160
Ed Brands, Grinnell (III)	1996	24	158
Darrin Fitzgerald, Butler (I)	1987	28	158
Freddie Banks, UNLV (I)	1987	39	152
Eric Kline, Northern St. (II)	1994	33	148
Eric Kline, Northern St. (II)	1995	30	148
Randy Rutherford, Oklahoma St. (I)	1995	37	146
Chris Peterson, Eureka (III)	1994	31	145
Terrence Woods, Florida A&M (I)	2003	28	139
Shawn Pughsley, Central Okla. (II)	1998	32	139
Demon Brown, Charlotte (I)	2003	29	137
Dennis Scott, Georgia Tech (I)	1990	35	137
Steve Diekmann, Grinnell (III)	1995	20	137
Steve Nordlund, Grinnell (III)	2002	24	137
Rashad Phillips, Detroit (I)	2001	35	136
Jed Bedford, Columbus St. (II)	2003	32	135
Reece Gliko, Mont. St.-Billings (II)	1997	28	135
Ray Gutierrez, Calif. (Pa.) (II)	1993	27	135
Jason Garrow, Augustana (S.D.) (II)	1992	27	135
Troy Hudson, Southern Ill. (I)	1997	30	134
Markus Hallgrimson, Mont. St.-Billings (II)	1999	28	133
Chris Jans, Loras (III)	1991	25	133

THREE-POINT FIELD GOALS MADE PER GAME

Player, Team (Division)	Season	G	3FG	Avg.
Jeff Clement, Grinnell (III)	1998	22	186	8.45
Jeff Clement, Grinnell (III)	1999	22	166	7.55
Steve Diekmann, Grinnell (III)	1995	20	137	6.85
Ed Brands, Grinnell (III)	1996	24	158	6.58
Ed Brands, Grinnell (III)	1995	20	129	6.45

Player, Team (Division)	Season	G	3FG	Avg.
Markus Hallgrimson, Mont. St.-Billings (II)	2000	26	160	6.15
Steve Nordlund, Grinnell (III)	2002	24	137	5.71
Darrin Fitzgerald, Butler (I)	1987	28	158	5.64
Steve Diekmann, Grinnell (III)	1994	21	117	5.57
Alex Williams, Sacramento St. (II)	1988	30	167	5.57
Chris Jans, Loras (III)	1991	25	133	5.32
Woody Piirto, Grinnell (III)	1999	22	117	5.32
Jeff Clement, Grinnell (III)	1997	22	113	5.14
Mark Bedell, Fisk (III)	1997	19	97	5.11
Jason Garrow, Augustana (S.D.) (II)	1992	27	135	5.00
David Bailey, Concordia (Ill.) (III)	1994	24	120	5.00
Terrence Woods, Florida A&M (I)	2003	28	139	4.96
Eric Kline, Northern St. (II)	1995	30	148	4.93
Ray Gutierrez, Calif. (Pa.) (II)	1993	29	142	4.90
Steve Brown, West Ala. (II)	2000	26	126	4.85
Antonio Harris, LeMoyne-Owen (II)	1999	26	126	4.85
Kwame Morton, Clarion (II)	1994	26	126	4.85
Reece Gliko, Mont. St.-Billings (II)	1997	28	135	4.82
Steve Nordlund, Grinnell (III)	2003	25	119	4.76
Markus Hallgrimson, Mont. St.-Billings (II)	1999	28	133	4.75

THREE-POINT FIELD-GOAL PERCENTAGE

Player, Team (Division)	Season	G	3FG	3FGA	Pct.
Reggie James, N.J. Inst. of Tech (III)	1989	29	59	88	67.0
Ray Lee, Hampton (II)	1988	24	39	60	65.0
Glenn Tropf, Holy Cross (I)	1988	29	52	82	63.4
Sean Wightman, Western Mich. (I)	1992	30	48	76	63.2
Chris Miles, N.J. Inst. of Tech (III)	1987	26	41	65	63.1
Steve Hood, Winston-Salem (II)	1988	28	42	67	62.7
Chris Miles, N.J. Inst. of Tech (III)	1989	29	46	75	61.3
Matt Miota, Lawrence (III)	1990	22	33	54	61.1
Mike Bachman, Alma (III)	1991	26	46	76	60.5
Mark Wiley, Fort Hays St. (II)	1990	29	49	81	60.5
Aaron Fehler, Oakland City (II)	1995	26	73	121	60.3
Keith Jennings, East Tenn. St. (I)	1991	33	84	142	59.2
Aaron Baker, Mississippi Col. (II)	1989	27	69	117	59.0
Dave Calloway, Monmouth (I)	1989	28	48	82	58.5
Walter Hurd, Johnson Smith (II)	1989	27	49	84	58.3
Matt Hopson, Oakland City (II)	1996	31	84	145	57.9
Ray Magee, Richard Stockton (III)	1988	26	41	71	57.7
Keith Orchard, Whitman (III)	1988	26	42	73	57.5
Jon Bryant, St. Cloud St. (II)	1996	27	54	94	57.4
Adam Harness, Oakland City (II)	1997	26	39	68	57.4
Steve Kerr, Arizona (I)	1988	38	114	199	57.3
Reginald Jones, Prairie View (I)	1987	28	64	112	57.1
Brian O'Donnell, Rutgers-Camden (III)	1988	24	65	114	57.0
Eric Harris, Bishop (III)	1987	26	91	160	56.9
Rick Brown, Muskingum (III)	1988	30	71	125	56.8

FREE-THROW PERCENTAGE

Player, Team (Division)	Season	G	FT	FTA	Pct.
Paul Cluxton, Northern Ky. (II)	1997	35	94	94	100.0
Korey Coon, Ill. Wesleyan (III)	2000	25	157	163	96.3
Craig Collins, Penn St. (I)	1985	27	94	98	95.9
Nick Wilkins, Coe (III)	2003	26	66	69	95.7
Chanse Young, Manchester (III)	1998	25	65	68	95.6
Tomas Rimkus, Pace (II)	1997	25	65	68	95.6
Andy Enfield, Johns Hopkins (III)	1991	29	123	129	95.3
Chris Carideo, Eureka (III)	1992	26	80	84	95.2
Yudi Teichman, Yeshiva (III)	1989	21	119	125	95.2
Steve Drabyn, Belmont (I)	2003	29	78	82	95.1
Rod Foster, UCLA (I)	1982	27	95	100	95.0
C.J. Cowgill, Chaminade (II)	2001	22	113	119	95.0
Clay McKnight, Pacific (Cal.) (I)	2000	24	74	78	94.9
Matt Logie, Lehigh (I)	2003	28	91	96	94.8
Brett Davis, Wis.-Oshkosh (III)	1998	27	72	76	94.7
Mark Giovino, Babson (III)	1997	28	86	91	94.5
Kent Andrews, McNeese St. (II)	1968	24	85	90	94.4
Billy Newton, Morgan St. (II)	1976	28	85	90	94.4
Carlos Gibson, Marshall (I)	1978	28	84	89	94.4
Danny Basile, Marist (I)	1994	27	84	89	94.4
Mike Sanders, Northern Colo. (II)	1987	28	82	87	94.3
Jim Barton, Dartmouth (I)	1986	26	65	69	94.2
Gary Buchanan, Villanova (I)	2001	31	97	103	94.2
Mike Scheib, Susquehanna (III)	1977	22	80	85	94.1
Curtis Small, Southampton (II)	2002	29	109	116	94.0

REBOUNDS

Player, Team (Division)	Season	G	Reb.
Elmore Smith, Kentucky St. (II)	1972	33	799
Marvin Webster, Morgan St. (II)	1974	33	740
Walt Dukes, Seton Hall (I)	1953	33	734
Maurice Stokes, St. Francis (Pa.) (II)	1955	28	726
Frank Stronczek, American Int'l (II)	1966	26	717

Player, Team (Division)	Season	G	Reb.
Maurice Stokes, St. Francis (Pa.) (II)	1954	26	689
Jim Ahrens, Buena Vista (II)	1962	28	682
Elmore Smith, Kentucky St. (II)	1970	30	682
R.C. Owens, Albertson (II)	1954	25	677
Wilbert Jones, Albany St. (Ga.) (II)	1969	28	670
Leroy Wright, Pacific (Cal.) (I)	1959	26	652
Tom Gola, La Salle (I)	1954	30	652
Jim Smith, Steubenville (II)	1957	26	651
Marvin Webster, Morgan St. (II)	1973	28	650
Tom Hart, Middlebury (II)	1955	22	649
Charlie Tyra, Louisville (I)	1956	29	645
Jackie Jackson, Virginia Union (II)	1961	26	641
Vincent White, Savannah St. (II)	1972	29	633
Paul Silas, Creighton (I)	1964	29	631
Bill Thieben, Hofstra (II)	1955	26	627
Lucious Jackson, Tex.-Pan American (II)	1963	32	626
Elvin Hayes, Houston (I)	1968	33	624
Vincent White, Savannah St. (II)	1970	27	624
Artis Gilmore, Jacksonville (I)	1970	28	621
Bill Thieben, Hofstra (II)	1954	24	620
Tom Hart, Middlebury (II)	1956	21	620

(Since 1973)

Player, Team (Division)	Season	G	Reb.
Marvin Webster, Morgan St. (II)	1974	33	740
Marvin Webster, Morgan St. (II)	1973	28	650
Major Jones, Albany St. (Ga.) (II)	1975	27	608
Marvin Barnes, Providence (I)	1974	32	597
Joe Manley, Bowie St. (III)	1976	29	579
Marvin Barnes, Providence (I)	1973	30	571
Earl Williams, Winston-Salem (II)	1974	26	553
John Jordan, Southern Me. (III)	1978	29	536
Charles Oakley, Virginia Union (III)	1985	31	535
Lawrence Johnson, Prairie View (II)	1974	23	519
Andre Means, Sacred Heart (II)	1977	32	516
Major Jones, Albany St. (Ga.) (II)	1975	25	513
Kermit Washington, American (I)	1973	25	511
Bill Walton, UCLA (I)	1973	30	506
Larry Bird, Indiana St. (I)	1979	34	505
Harvey Jones, Alabama St. (II)	1974	28	503
Larry Kenon, Memphis (I)	1973	30	501
Akeem Olajuwon, Houston (I)	1984	37	500
Andre Means, Sacred Heart (II)	1978	30	493
Ricky Mahorn, Hampton (II)	1980	31	490
Rob Roesch, Staten Island (II)	1989	31	482
Howard Shockley, Salisbury (III)	1974	27	482
Keith Woolfolk, Upper Iowa (III)	1978	26	479
Leonard Robinson, Tennessee St. (II)	1974	28	478
Major Jones, Albany St. (Ga.) (II)	1976	24	475

REBOUND AVERAGE

Player, Team (Division)	Season	G	Reb.	Avg.
Tom Hart, Middlebury (II)	1956	21	620	29.5
Tom Hart, Middlebury (II)	1955	22	649	29.5
Frank Stronczek, American Int'l (II)	1966	26	717	27.6
R.C. Owens, Albertson (II)	1954	25	677	27.1
Maurice Stokes, St. Francis (Pa.) (II)	1954	26	689	26.5
Ellerbe Neal, Wofford (II)	1953	23	609	26.5
Roman Turmon, Clark Atlanta (II)	1954	23	602	26.2
Pat Callahan, Lewis (II)	1955	20	523	26.2
Hank Brown, Mass.-Lowell (II)	1966	19	496	26.1
Maurice Stokes, St. Francis (Pa.) (II)	1955	28	726	25.9
Bill Thieben, Hofstra (II)	1954	24	620	25.8
Dean Sandifer, Lakeland (II)	1965	23	592	25.7
Charlie Slack, Marshall (I)	1955	21	538	25.6
Charles Wrinn, Trinity (Conn.) (II)	1952	19	486	25.6
Leroy Wright, Pacific (Cal.) (I)	1959	26	652	25.1
Jim Smith, Steubenville (II)	1957	26	651	25.0
Marv Becker, Widener (II)	1958	18	450	25.0
Tony Williams, St. Francis (Me.) (II)	1971	24	599	25.0
Ernie Brock, Virginia (II)	1964	24	597	24.9
Russell Jackson, Southern U. (II)	1970	22	544	24.7
Gerry Govan, St. Mary's (Kan.) (II)	1963	18	445	24.7
Merv Shorr, CCNY (II)	1954	18	444	24.7
Art Quimby, Connecticut (I)	1955	25	611	24.4
Charlie Slack, Marshall (I)	1956	22	520	23.6
Ed Conlin, Fordham (I)	1953	26	612	23.5

Player, Team (Division)	Season	G	Reb.	Avg.

(Since 1973)

Player, Team (Division)	Season	G	Reb.	Avg.
Marvin Webster, Morgan St. (II)	1973	28	650	23.2
Lawrence Johnson, Prairie View (II)	1974	23	519	22.6
Major Jones, Albany St. (Ga.) (II)	1975	27	608	22.5
Marvin Webster, Morgan St. (II)	1974	33	740	22.4
Earl Williams, Winston-Salem (II)	1974	26	553	21.3
Major Jones, Albany St. (Ga.) (II)	1975	25	513	20.5

Player, Team (Division)	Season	G	Reb.	Avg.
Kermit Washington, American (I)	1973	25	511	20.4
Larry Gooding, St. Augustine's (II)	1974	22	443	20.1
Joe Manley, Bowie St. (III)	1976	29	579	20.0
Fred Petty, Southern N.H. (III)	1974	22	436	19.8
Major Jones, Albany St. (Ga.) (II)	1976	24	475	19.8
Larry Williams, Pratt (III)	1977	24	457	19.0
Marvin Barnes, Providence (I)	1973	30	571	19.0
Calvin Robinson, Mississippi Val. (II)	1976	23	432	18.8
Larry Williams, Pratt (III)	1977	17	318	18.7
Larry Parker, Plattsburgh St. (III)	1975	23	430	18.7
Marvin Barnes, Providence (I)	1974	32	597	18.7
Charles Greer, Thomas (III)	1977	17	318	18.7
John Jordan, Southern Me. (III)	1978	29	536	18.5
Keith Woolfolk, Upper Iowa (III)	1978	26	479	18.4
Michael Stubbs, Trinity (Conn.) (III)	1990	22	398	18.1
Mike Taylor, Pratt (III)	1978	23	414	18.0
Harvey Jones, Alabama St. (II)	1974	28	503	18.0
Walt Edwards, Husson (III)	1976	26	467	18.0
Scott Mountz, Calif. (Pa.) (II)	1978	24	431	18.0

ASSISTS

Player, Team (Division)	Season	G	Ast.
Mark Wade, UNLV (I)	1987	38	406
Steve Ray, Bridgeport (II)	1989	32	400
Avery Johnson, Southern U. (I)	1988	30	399
Robert James, Kean (III)	1989	29	391
Steve Ray, Bridgeport (II)	1990	33	385
Anthony Manuel, Bradley (I)	1988	31	373
Tony Smith, Pfeiffer (II)	1992	35	349
Avery Johnson, Southern U. (I)	1987	31	333
Mark Jackson, St. John's (N.Y.) (I)	1986	32	328
Sherman Douglas, Syracuse (I)	1989	38	326
Tennyson Whitted, Ramapo (III)	2002	29	319
Greg Anthony, UNLV (I)	1991	35	310
Sam Crawford, New Mexico St. (I)	1993	34	310
Reid Gettys, Houston (I)	1984	37	309
Jim Ferrer, Bentley (II)	1989	31	309
Rob Paternostro, Southern N.H. (II)	1995	33	309
Carl Golson, Loyola (Ill.) (I)	1985	33	305
Craig Neal, Georgia Tech (I)	1988	32	303
Keith Jennings, East Tenn. St. (I)	1991	33	301
Brian Gregory, Oakland (II)	1989	28	300
Doug Gottlieb, Oklahoma St. (I)	1999	34	299
Chris Corchiani, North Carolina St. (I)	1991	31	299
Charles Jordan, Erskine (II)	1992	34	298
Keith Jennings, East Tenn. St. (I)	1990	34	297
Ricky Spicer, Wis.-Whitewater (III)	1989	31	295

ASSIST AVERAGE

Player, Team (Division)	Season	G	Ast.	Avg.
Robert James, Kean (III)	1989	29	391	13.48
Avery Johnson, Southern U. (I)	1988	30	399	13.30
Steve Ray, Bridgeport (II)	1989	32	400	12.50
Anthony Manuel, Bradley (I)	1988	31	373	12.03
Steve Ray, Bridgeport (II)	1990	33	385	11.66
Demetri Beekman, Assumption (II)	1993	23	264	11.47
Albert Kirchner, Mt. St. Vincent (III)	1990	24	267	11.12
Tennyson Whitted, Ramapo (III)	2002	29	319	11.00
Ernest Jenkins, N.M. Highlands (II)	1995	27	291	10.78
Avery Johnson, Southern U. (I)	1987	31	333	10.74
Brian Gregory, Oakland (II)	1989	28	300	10.71
Mark Wade, UNLV (I)	1987	38	406	10.68
Ron Torgalski, Hamilton (III)	1989	26	275	10.57
Brent Schremp, Slippery Rock (II)	1995	25	259	10.36
Louis Adams, Rust (III)	1989	22	227	10.31
Ernest Jenkins, N.M. Highlands (II)	1994	27	277	10.31
Adrian Hutt, Metro St. (II)	1991	28	285	10.17
Nelson Haggerty, Baylor (I)	1995	28	284	10.14
Tony Smith, Pfeiffer (II)	1992	35	349	9.97
Jim Ferrer, Bentley (II)	1989	31	309	9.96
Glenn Williams, Holy Cross (I)	1989	28	278	9.92
Eric Johnson, Coe (III)	1991	24	238	9.91
Todd Chappell, Texas Wesleyan (II)	2000	27	263	9.74
Joe Marcotte, N.J. Inst. of Tech (III)	1995	30	292	9.73
Phil Dixon, Shenandoah (III)	1994	26	253	9.73

BLOCKED SHOTS

Player, Team (Division)	Season	G	Blk.
David Robinson, Navy (I)	1986	35	207
Tory Black, N.J. Inst. of Tech (III)	1997	26	198
Neil Edwards, York (N.Y.) (III)	2000	26	193
Ira Nicholson, Mt. St. Vincent (III)	1995	28	188
Adonal Foyle, Colgate (I)	1997	28	180
Keith Closs, Central Conn. St. (I)	1996	28	178

Player, Team (Division)	Season	G	Blk.
Shawn Bradley, Brigham Young (I)	1991	34	177
Wojciech Mydra, La.-Monroe (I)	2002	32	172
Alonzo Mourning, Georgetown (I)	1989	34	169
Adonal Foyle, Colgate (I)	1996	29	165
Ira Nicholson, Mt. St. Vincent (III)	1996	27	163
Ken Johnson, Ohio St. (I)	2000	30	161
Alonzo Mourning, Georgetown (I)	1992	32	160
James Doyle, Concord (II)	1998	30	157
Shaquille O'Neal, LSU (I)	1992	30	157
Emeka Okafor, Connecticut (I)	2003	33	156
Roy Rogers, Alabama (I)	1996	32	156
Antonio Harvey, Pfeiffer (II)	1993	29	155
Ira Nicholson, Mt. St. Vincent (III)	1997	24	151
Dikembe Mutombo, Georgetown (I)	1991	32	151
Antoine Hyman, Keuka (III)	1997	26	148
Tarvis Williams, Hampton (I)	2001	32	147
Adonal Foyle, Colgate (I)	1995	30	147
Matt Cusano, Scranton (III)	1993	29	145
Wojciech Myrda, La.-Monroe (I)	2000	28	144
Neil Edwards, York (N.Y.) (III)	1999	26	144
David Robinson, Navy (I)	1987	32	144
Theo Ratliff, Wyoming (I)	1995	28	144

BLOCKED-SHOT AVERAGE

Player, Team (Division)	Season	G	Blk.	Avg.
Tory Black, N.J. Inst. of Tech (III)	1997	26	198	7.62
Neil Edwards, York (N.Y.) (III)	2000	26	193	7.42
Ira Nicholson, Mt. St. Vincent (III)	1995	28	188	6.71
Adonal Foyle, Colgate (I)	1997	28	180	6.43
Keith Closs, Central Conn. St. (I)	1996	28	178	6.36
Ira Nicholson, Mt. St. Vincent (III)	1997	24	151	6.29
Ira Nicholson, Mt. St. Vincent (III)	1996	27	163	6.04
David Robinson, Navy (I)	1986	35	207	5.91
Antoine Hyman, Keuka (III)	1997	26	148	5.69
Adonal Foyle, Colgate (I)	1996	29	165	5.69
Neil Edwards, York (N.Y.) (III)	1999	26	144	5.54
Johnny Woods, Wesley (III)	2000	24	132	5.50
Wojciech Mydra, La.-Monroe (I)	2002	32	172	5.38
Ken Johnson, Ohio St. (I)	2000	30	161	5.37
Keith Closs, Central Conn. St. (I)	1995	26	139	5.35
Antonio Harvey, Pfeiffer (II)	1993	29	155	5.34
Antoine Hyman, Keuka (III)	1996	25	131	5.24
James Doyle, Concord (II)	1998	30	157	5.23
Shaquille O'Neal, LSU (I)	1992	30	157	5.23
Shawn Bradley, Brigham Young (I)	1991	34	177	5.21
Wojciech Myrda, La.-Monroe (I)	2000	28	144	5.14
Theo Ratliff, Wyoming (I)	1995	28	144	5.14
Cedric Lewis, Maryland (I)	1991	28	143	5.11
Joe Henderson, Hunter (III)	1999	22	112	5.09
John Burke, Southampton (II)	1996	28	142	5.07

STEALS

Player, Team (Division)	Season	G	Stl.
Moses Jean-Pierre, Plymouth St. (III)	1994	30	189
Daniel Martinez, McMurry (III)	2000	29	178
Desmond Cambridge, Alabama A&M (I)	2002	29	160
Mookie Blaylock, Oklahoma (I)	1988	39	150
Purvis Presha, Stillman (III)	1996	25	144
Aldwin Ware, Florida A&M (I)	1988	29	142
John Linehan, Providence (I)	2002	31	139
J.R. Gamble, Queens (N.C.) (II)	2001	32	139
Darron Brittman, Chicago St. (I)	1986	28	139
Tennyson Whitted, Ramapo (III)	2002	29	138
Nadav Henefeld, Connecticut (I)	1990	37	138
Matt Newton, Principia (III)	1994	25	138
John Gallogly, Salve Regina (III)	1997	24	137
Mookie Blaylock, Oklahoma (I)	1989	35	131
Ronn McMahon, Eastern Wash. (I)	1990	29	130
Wayne Copeland, Lynn (II)	2000	26	129
Greg Dean, Concordia-M'head (III)	1997	23	126
Scott Clarke, Utica (III)	1995	24	126
Wayne Copeland, Lynn (II)	1999	31	125
Allen Iverson, Georgetown (I)	1996	37	124
Marty Johnson, Towson (I)	1988	30	124
Eric Coley, Tulsa (I)	2000	37	123
Deron Black, Allegheny (III)	1996	27	123
Terrance Gist, S.C.-Spartanburg (II)	1998	29	122
Devlin Herring, Pitt.-Johnstown (II)	1997	27	122
David Brown, Westfield St. (III)	1994	25	122

STEAL AVERAGE

Player, Team (Division)	Season	G	Stl.	Avg.
Moses Jean-Pierre, Plymouth St. (III)	1994	30	189	6.30
Daniel Martinez, McMurry (III)	2000	29	178	6.14
Purvis Presha, Stillman (III)	1996	25	144	5.76
John Gallogly, Salve Regina (III)	1997	24	137	5.71
Matt Newton, Principia (III)	1994	25	138	5.52
Desmond Cambridge, Alabama A&M (I)	2002	29	160	5.52
Barry Aranoff, Yeshiva (III)	1995	22	121	5.50
Greg Dean, Concordia-M'head (III)	1997	23	126	5.48
John Gallogly, Salve Regina (III)	1998	23	121	5.26
Scott Clarke, Utica (III)	1995	24	126	5.25
Darron Brittman, Chicago St. (I)	1986	28	139	4.96
Wayne Copeland, Lynn (II)	2000	26	129	4.96
Joel Heckendorf, Martin Luther (III)	1996	17	84	4.94
Aldwin Ware, Florida A&M (I)	1988	29	142	4.90
David Brown, Westfield St. (III)	1994	25	122	4.88
Ivo Moyano, Polytechnic (N.Y.) (III)	1994	19	91	4.78
Tennyson Whitted, Ramapo (III)	2002	29	138	4.76
Mario Thompson, Occidental (III)	1999	24	114	4.75
Keith Darden, Concordia-Austin (III)	2001	24	111	4.63
Moses Jean-Pierre, Plymouth St. (III)	1993	25	114	4.56
Deron Black, Allegheny (III)	1996	27	123	4.56
Scott Clark, Utica (III)	1996	26	118	4.54
John Morris, Bluefield St. (II)	1994	23	104	4.52
Devlin Herring, Pitt.-Johnstown (II)	1997	27	122	4.52
John Linehan, Providence (I)	2002	31	139	4.48
Ronn McMahon, Eastern Wash. (I)	1990	29	130	4.48
Ricky Hollis, Brockport St. (III)	2000	27	121	4.48

Career Records

POINTS

Player, Team (Division)	Last Season	Yrs.	G	FG	3FG	FT	Pts.
Travis Grant, Kentucky St. (II)	1972	4	121	1,760	—	525	4,045
Bob Hopkins, Grambling (II)	1956	4	126	1,403	—	953	3,759
Pete Maravich, LSU (I)	1970	3	83	1,387	—	893	3,667
Dwight Lamar, La.-Lafayette (II & I)	1973	4	112	1,445	—	603	3,493
Tony Smith, Pfeiffer (II)	1992	4	126	1,150	431	619	3,350
Earnest Lee, Clark Atlanta (II)	1987	4	115	1,270	35	723	3,298
Joe Miller, Alderson-Broaddus (II)	1957	4	129	1,082	—	1,130	3,294
John Rinka, Kenyon (II)	1970	4	99	1,261	—	729	3,251
Freeman Williams, Portland St. (I)	1978	4	106	1,369	—	511	3,249
Lionel Simmons, La Salle (I)	1990	4	131	1,244	56	673	3,217
Dick Barnett, Tennessee St. (II)	1959	4	136	1,312	—	585	3,209
Alphonso Ford, Mississippi Val. (I)	1993	4	109	1,121	333	590	3,165
Willie Scott, Alabama St. (II)	1969	4	103	1,277	—	601	3,155
Harry Kelly, Texas Southern (I)	1983	4	110	1,234	—	598	3,066
Johnnie Allen, Bethune-Cookman (II)	1969	4	111	1,306	—	446	3,058
Bennie Swain, Texas Southern (II)	1958	4	137	1,157	—	694	3,008
Hersey Hawkins, Bradley (I)	1988	4	125	1,100	118	690	3,008
Rich Fuqua, Oral Roberts (II & I)	1973	4	111	1,273	—	458	3,004
Lambert Shell, Bridgeport (II)	1992	4	132	1,102	22	775	3,001
Oscar Robertson, Cincinnati (I)	1960	3	88	1,052	—	869	2,973
Carl Hartman, Alderson-Broaddus (II)	1955	4	118	1,124	—	711	2,959
Danny Manning, Kansas (I)	1988	4	147	1,216	10	509	2,951
Andre Foreman, Salisbury (III)	1992	5	109	1,141	68	592	2,940
Earl Monroe, Winston-Salem (II)	1967	4	110	1,158	—	619	2,935
Alfredrick Hughes, Loyola (Ill.) (I)	1985	4	120	1,226	—	462	2,914

SCORING AVERAGE
(Minimum 1,500 points)

Player, Team (Division)	Last Season	Yrs.	G	FG	3FG	FT	Pts.	Avg.
Pete Maravich, LSU (I)	1970	3	83	1,387	—	893	3,667	44.2
Austin Carr, Notre Dame (I)	1971	3	74	1,017	—	526	2,560	34.6
Oscar Robertson, Cincinnati (I)	1960	3	88	1,052	—	869	2,973	33.8
Travis Grant, Kentucky St. (II)	1972	4	121	1,760	—	525	4,045	33.4
Calvin Murphy, Niagara (I)	1970	3	77	947	—	654	2,548	33.1
John Rinka, Kenyon (II)	1970	4	99	1,261	—	729	3,251	32.8
Dwain Govan, Bishop (III)	1975	2	55	750	—	305	1,805	32.8
Florindo Vieira, Quinnipiac (II)	1957	4	69	761	—	741	2,263	32.8
Dwight Lamar, La.-Lafayette (I)	1973	2	57	768	—	326	1,862	32.7
Frank Selvy, Furman (I)	1954	3	78	922	—	694	2,538	32.5
Rick Mount, Purdue (I)	1970	3	72	910	—	503	2,323	32.3
Darrell Floyd, Furman (I)	1956	3	71	868	—	545	2,281	32.1
Nick Werkman, Seton Hall (I)	1964	3	71	812	—	649	2,273	32.0
Willie Humes, Idaho St. (I)	1971	2	48	565	—	380	1,510	31.5
William Averitt, Pepperdine (I)	1973	2	48	615	—	311	1,541	31.4
Elgin Baylor, Albertson & Seattle (I)	1958	3	80	956	—	588	2,500	31.3
Willie Shaw, Lane (II)	1964	4	76	960	—	459	2,379	31.3
Mike Davis, Virginia Union (II)	1969	4	89	1,014	—	730	2,758	31.0
Elvin Hayes, Houston (I)	1968	3	93	1,215	—	454	2,884	31.0
Freeman Williams, Portland St. (I)	1978	4	106	1,369	—	511	3,249	30.7
Willie Scott, Alabama St. (II)	1969	4	103	1,277	—	601	3,155	30.6
Dave Russell, Shepherd (III)	1975	2	60	710	—	413	1,833	30.6

Player, Team (Division)	Last Season	Yrs.	G	FG	3FG	FT	Pts.	Avg.
Larry Bird, Indiana St. (I)	1979	3	94	1,154	—	542	2,850	30.3
Carlos Knox, IUPUI (II)	1998	4	85	832	208	684	2,556	30.1
George Gilmore, Chaminade (II)	1992	2	51	485	174	387	1,531	30.0

FIELD-GOAL PERCENTAGE
(Minimum 400 field goals)

Player, Team (Division)	Last Season	Yrs.	G	FG	FGA	Pct.
Tony Rychlec, Mass. Maritime (III)	1983	3	55	509	692	73.6
Pete Metzelaars, Wabash (III)	1982	4	103	784	1,083	72.4
Todd Linder, Tampa (II)	1987	4	122	909	1,284	70.8
Tom Schurfranz, Bellarmine (II)	1992	4	112	742	1,057	70.2
Chad Scott, Calif. (Pa.) (II)	1994	4	115	465	664	70.0
Ricky Nedd, Appalachian St. (I)	1994	4	113	412	597	69.0
Ed Phillips, Alabama A&M (II)	1971	4	95	610	885	68.9
Stephen Scheffler, Purdue (I)	1990	4	110	408	596	68.5
Ulysses Hackett, S.C.-Spartanburg (II)	1992	3	90	824	1,213	67.9
Larry Tucker, Lewis (II)	1983	3	84	677	994	67.8
Steve Johnson, Oregon St. (I)	1981	4	116	828	1,222	67.8
Michael Bradley, Kentucky & Villanova (I)	2001	4	100	441	651	67.7
Otis Evans, Wayne St. (Mich.) (II)	1992	4	106	472	697	67.7
Maurice Woods, Potsdam St. (III)	1982	3	93	559	829	67.4
Matthew Cornegay, Tuskegee (II)	1982	4	105	524	783	66.9
Earl Keith, Stony Brook (III)	1979	4	94	777	1,161	66.9
Murray Brown, Florida St. (I)	1980	4	106	566	847	66.8
Ray Strozier, Central Mo. St. (II)	1981	4	110	563	843	66.8
Dennis Edwards, Fort Hays St. (II)	1995	2	59	666	998	66.7
James Morris, Central Okla. (II)	1993	4	76	532	798	66.7
Dan Rush, Bridgewater (Va.) (III)	1995	4	102	712	1,069	66.6
Lee Campbell, Middle Tenn. & Southwest Mo. St. (I)	1990	3	88	411	618	66.5
Warren Kidd, Middle Tenn. (I)	1993	3	83	496	747	66.4
Todd MacCulloch, Washington (I)	1999	4	115	702	1,058	66.4
Joe Senser, West Chester (II)	1979	4	96	476	719	66.2
Lance Berwald, North Dakota St. (II)	1984	2	58	475	717	66.2

THREE-POINT FIELD GOALS

Player, Team (Division)	Last Season	Yrs.	G	3FG
Jeff Clement, Grinnell (III)	1999	4	91	516
Steve Moyer, Gannon (II)	1999	4	112	442
Tony Smith, Pfeiffer (II)	1992	4	126	431
Curtis Staples, Virginia (I)	1998	4	122	413
Kwame Morton, Clarion (II)	1994	4	105	411
Keith Veney, Lamar & Marshall (I)	1997	4	111	409
Chris Carideo, Widener (III)	1995	4	103	402
Doug Day, Radford (I)	1993	4	117	401
Gary Duda, Merrimack (II)	1992	4	122	389
Ronnie Schmitz, UMKC (I)	1993	4	112	378
Mark Alberts, Akron (I)	1993	4	107	375
Brett Blizzard, UNC Wilmington (I)	2003	4	125	371
Kyle Korver, Creighton (I)	2003	4	128	371
Markus Hallgrimson, Mont. St.-Billings (II)	2000	3	82	371
Steve Diekmann, Grinnell (III)	1995	4	85	371
Pat Bradley, Arkansas (I)	1999	4	132	366
Bryce Drew, Valparaiso (I)	1998	4	121	364
Jeff Fryer, Loyola Marymount (I)	1990	4	112	363
Matt Garvey, Bates (III)	1997	4	95	361
Columbus Parker, Johnson Smith (II)	1993	4	115	354
Gary Paul, Indianapolis (II)	1990	4	111	354
Ray Wilson, UC Santa Cruz (III)	1992	4	100	354
Matt Miller, Drury (II)	2002	4	106	351
Dennis Scott, Georgia Tech (I)	1990	3	99	351
Travis Tuttle, North Dakota (II)	1997	4	108	350

THREE-POINT FIELD GOALS PER GAME
(Minimum 200 three-point field goals)

Player, Team (Division)	Last Season	Yrs.	G	3FG	Avg.
Jeff Clement, Grinnell (III)	1999	4	91	516	5.67
Antonio Harris, LeMoyne-Owen (II)	1999	2	52	245	4.71
Timothy Pollard, Mississippi Val. (I)	1989	2	56	256	4.57
Markus Hallgrimson, Mont. St.-Billings (II)	2000	3	82	371	4.52
Ed Brands, Grinnell (III)	1996	4	78	347	4.45
Steve Diekmann, Grinnell (III)	1995	4	85	371	4.36
Sydney Grider, La.-Lafayette (I)	1990	2	58	253	4.36
Alex Williams, Sacramento St. (I)	1988	2	58	247	4.26
Tommie Spearman, Columbus St. (II)	1995	2	56	233	4.16
Reece Gliko, Mont. St.-Billings (II)	1997	2	56	231	4.13
Steve Matthews, Emerson (III)/Wentworth Inst. (III)	2000	3	81	334	4.12
Danny Phillips, Mont. St.-Billings (II)	2002	2	55	222	4.03
Brian Merriweather, Tex.-Pan American (I)	2001	3	84	332	3.95
Steve Moyer, Gannon (II)	1999	4	112	442	3.95
Kwame Morton, Clarion (II)	1994	4	105	411	3.91

Maryland's Steve Blake ranks among the top 10 in career assists.

Player, Team (Division)	Last Season	Yrs.	G	3FG	Avg.
Chris Carideo, Widener (III)	1995	4	103	402	3.90
Josh Heard, Tennessee Tech (I)	2000	2	55	210	3.82
Matt Garvey, Bates (III)	1997	4	95	361	3.80
Shawn Williams, Central Okla. (II)	1991	3	57	212	3.72
Zoderick Green, Central Okla. (II)	1995	3	57	212	3.72
Kareem Townes, La Salle (I)	1995	3	81	300	3.70
Keith Veney, Lamar & Marshall (I)	1997	4	111	409	3.68
Mike Sinclair, Bowie St. (II)	1989	3	82	299	3.65
Tai Crutchfield, Philadelphia (II)	2001	2	58	210	3.62
Dave Mooney, Coastal Caro. (I)	1988	2	56	202	3.61

THREE-POINT FIELD-GOAL PERCENTAGE
(Minimum 200 three-point field goals)

Player, Team (Division)	Last Season	Yrs.	G	3FG	3FGA	Pct.
Scott Martin, Rollins (II)	1991	4	104	236	460	51.3
Jeff Seifriz, Wis.-Whitewater (III)	1989	3	85	217	423	51.3
Chris Peterson, Eureka (III)	1994	4	78	215	421	51.1
Todd Woelfle, Oakland City (II)	1998	4	103	210	412	51.0
Everett Foxx, Ferrum (III)	1992	4	104	315	630	50.0
Tony Bennett, Wis.-Green Bay (I)	1992	4	118	290	584	49.7
Matt Markle, Shippensburg (II)	1992	4	101	202	408	49.5
Keith Jennings, East Tenn. St. (I)	1991	4	127	223	452	49.3
Brad Alberts, Ripon (III)	1992	4	95	277	563	49.2
Jeff Jones, Lycoming (III)	1989	3	71	232	472	49.2
Troy Greenlee, DePauw (III)	1991	4	106	232	473	49.0
Paul Cluxton, Northern Ky. (II)	1997	4	122	303	619	48.9
Lance Gelnett, Millersville (II)	1992	4	109	266	547	48.6
David Todd, Pomona-Pitzer (III)	1990	4	84	212	439	48.3
Al Callejas, Scranton (III)	2001	4	90	225	466	48.3
Antonio Harris, LeMoyne-Owen (II)	1999	2	52	245	510	48.0
Jason Bullock, Indiana (Pa.) (II)	1995	4	88	235	491	47.9
Matt Ripaldi, Southern N.H. (II)	1995	4	95	205	431	47.6
Kirk Manns, Michigan St. (I)	1990	4	120	212	446	47.5
Tim Locum, Wisconsin (I)	1991	4	118	227	481	47.2
Mark Willey, Fort Hays St. (II)	1992	4	117	224	478	46.9
David Olson, Eastern Ill. (I)	1992	4	111	262	562	46.6
Todd Bowden, Randolph-Macon (III)	1989	3	84	229	491	46.6
Ross Land, Northern Ariz. (I)	2000	4	117	308	664	46.4
Dan Dickau, Washington (I) & Gonzaga (I)	2002	4	97	215	465	46.2

FREE-THROW PERCENTAGE
(Minimum 300 free throws made)

Player, Team (Division)	Last Season	Yrs.	G	FT	FTA	Pct.
Andy Enfield, Johns Hopkins (III)	1991	4	108	431	466	92.5
Gary Buchanan, Villanova (I)	2003	4	122	324	355	91.3
Korey Coon, Ill. Wesleyan (III)	2000	4	109	449	492	91.3
Greg Starrick, Kentucky & Southern Ill. (I)	1972	4	72	341	375	90.9
Ryan Knuppel, Elmhurst (III)	2001	4	102	288	317	90.9
Jack Moore, Nebraska (I)	1982	4	105	446	495	90.1
Steve Henson, Kansas St. (I)	1990	4	127	361	401	90.0
Steve Alford, Indiana (I)	1987	4	125	535	596	89.8
Bob Lloyd, Rutgers (I)	1967	3	77	543	605	89.8
Jim Barton, Dartmouth (I)	1989	4	104	394	440	89.5
Al Callejas, Scranton (III)	2001	4	90	333	372	89.5
Dave Reynolds, Davis & Elkins (II)	1989	4	107	383	429	89.3
Tommy Boyer, Arkansas (I)	1963	3	70	315	353	89.2
Kyle Korver, Creighton (I)	2003	4	128	312	350	89.1
Tim McGraw, Hartwick (III)	1988	4	107	330	371	88.9

Player, Team (Division)	Last Season	Yrs.	G	FT	FTA	Pct.
Rob Robbins, New Mexico (I)	1991	4	133	309	348	88.8
Brent Jolly, Tennessee Tech (I)	2003	4	123	347	391	88.7
Marcus Wilson, Evansville (I)	1999	4	119	455	513	88.7
Sean Miller, Pittsburgh (I)	1992	4	128	317	358	88.5
Ron Perry, Holy Cross (I)	1980	4	109	680	768	88.5
Joe Crispin, Penn. St.	2001	4	127	448	506	88.5
Joe Dykstra, Western Ill. (I)	1983	4	117	587	663	88.5
Michael Shue, Lock Haven (II)	1997	4	92	354	400	88.5
Mike Joseph, Bucknell (I)	1990	4	115	397	449	88.4
Kyle Macy, Purdue & Kentucky (I)	1980	5	125	416	471	88.3
Eric Jacobs, Wilkes & Scranton (III)	1987	4	106	303	343	88.3

REBOUNDS

Player, Team (Division)	Last Season	Yrs.	G	Reb.
Jim Smith, Steubenville (II)	1958	4	112	2,334
Marvin Webster, Morgan St. (II)	1975	4	114	2,267
Tom Gola, La Salle (I)	1955	4	118	2,201
Major Jones, Albany St. (Ga.) (II)	1976	4	105	2,052
Joe Holup, George Washington (I)	1956	4	104	2,030
Charles Hardnett, Grambling (II)	1962	4	117	1,983
Jim Ahrens, Buena Vista (II)	1962	4	95	1,977
Elmore Smith, Kentucky St. (II)	1971	3	85	1,917
Charlie Slack, Marshall (I)	1956	4	88	1,916
Zelmo Beaty, Prairie View (II)	1962	4	97	1,916
Ed Conlin, Fordham (I)	1955	4	102	1,884
Hal Booker, Cheyney (II)	1969	4	103	1,882
Bill Thieben, Hofstra (I)	1956	3	76	1,837
Maurice Stokes, St. Francis (Pa.) (II)	1955	3	72	1,812
Dickie Hemric, Wake Forest (I)	1955	4	104	1,802
Paul Silas, Creighton (I)	1964	3	81	1,751
James Morgan, Md.-Eastern Shore (II)	1970	4	95	1,747
Tom Hart, Middlebury (II)	1956	3	63	1,738
Joe Casey, Boston St. (II)	1969	4	102	1,733
Art Quimby, Connecticut (I)	1955	4	80	1,716
Jerry Harper, Alabama (I)	1956	4	93	1,688
Jeff Cohen, William & Mary (I)	1961	4	103	1,679
Steve Hamilton, Morehead St. (I)	1958	4	102	1,675
Herb Lake, Youngstown St. (II)	1959	4	95	1,638
Jim Fay, St. Ambrose (II)	1953	4	95	1,633

(For careers beginning in 1973 or after)

Player, Team (Division)	Last Season	Yrs.	G	Reb.
Major Jones, Albany St. (Ga.) (II)	1976	4	105	2,052
Michael Smith, Hamilton (III)	1992	4	107	1,628
Tim Duncan, Wake Forest (I)	1997	4	128	1,570
Derrick Coleman, Syracuse (I)	1990	4	143	1,537
Malik Rose, Drexel (I)	1996	4	120	1,514
Ralph Sampson, Virginia (I)	1983	4	132	1,511
John Jordan, Southern Me. (III)	1981	4	105	1,504
Clemon Johnson, Florida A&M (II)	1978	4	109	1,494
Wayne Robertson, Southern N.H. (II)	1994	4	127	1,487
Larry Parker, Plattsburgh St. (III)	1978	4	85	1,482
Carlos Terry, Winston-Salem (II)	1978	4	117	1,467
Pete Padgett, Nevada (I)	1976	4	104	1,464
Kevin Clark, Clark (Mass.) (III)	1981	4	101	1,450
James Hector, American Int'l (II)	1994	4	115	1,446
Lionel Simmons, La Salle (I)	1990	4	131	1,429
Anthony Bonner, St. Louis (I)	1990	4	133	1,424
E.D. Schecterly, Lynchburg (III)	1980	4	104	1,404
Jeff Covington, Youngstown St. (II)	1978	4	106	1,381
Tyrone Hill, Xavier (I)	1990	4	126	1,380
Larry Sheets, East. Mennonite (III)	1983	4	105	1,378
Popeye Jones, Murray St. (I)	1992	4	123	1,374
Michael Brooks, La Salle (I)	1980	4	114	1,372
John Ebeling, Fla. Southern (II)	1982	4	127	1,362
Xavier McDaniel, Wichita St. (I)	1985	4	117	1,359
John Irving, Arizona & Hofstra (I)	1977	4	103	1,348

REBOUND AVERAGE
(Minimum 800 rebounds)

Player, Team (Division)	Last Season	Yrs.	G	Reb.	Avg.
Tom Hart, Middlebury (II)	1956	3	63	1,738	27.6
Maurice Stokes, St. Francis (Pa.) (II)	1955	3	72	1,812	25.2
Frank Stronczek, American Int'l (II)	1967	3	62	1,549	25.0
Bill Thieben, Hofstra (I)	1956	3	76	1,837	24.2
Hank Brown, Mass.-Lowell (II)	1967	3	49	1,129	23.0
Artis Gilmore, Jacksonville (I)	1970	2	54	1,224	22.7
Elmore Smith, Kentucky St. (II)	1971	3	85	1,917	22.6
Charles Wrinn, Trinity (Conn.) (II)	1953	3	53	1,176	22.2
Roman Turmon, Clark Atlanta (II)	1954	3	60	1,312	21.9
Charlie Slack, Marshall (I)	1956	4	88	1,916	21.8
Tony Missere, Pratt (II)	1968	3	62	1,348	21.7
Ron Horton, Delaware St. (II)	1968	3	64	1,384	21.6
Paul Silas, Creighton (I)	1964	3	81	1,751	21.6

Player, Team (Division)	Last Season	Yrs.	G	Reb.	Avg.
Leroy Wright, Pacific (Cal.) (I)	1960	3	67	1,442	21.5
Art Quimby, Connecticut (I)	1955	4	80	1,716	21.5
Walt Dukes, Seton Hall (I)	1953	2	59	1,247	21.1
Jim Smith, Steubenville (II)	1958	4	112	2,334	20.8
Jim Ahrens, Buena Vista (II)	1962	4	95	1,977	20.8
Bob Brandes, Upsala (II)	1962	3	74	1,520	20.5
Jackie Jackson, Virginia Union (II)	1961	3	66	1,351	20.5
Bill Russell, San Francisco (I)	1956	3	79	1,606	20.3
Kermit Washington, American (I)	1973	3	73	1,478	20.2
Julius Erving, Massachusetts (I)	1971	2	52	1,049	20.2
Frank Hunter, Northland (II)	1962	4	79	1,581	20.0
Marvin Webster, Morgan St. (II)	1975	4	114	2,267	19.9

(For careers beginning in 1973 or after)

Player, Team (Division)	Last Season	Yrs.	G	Reb.	Avg.
Major Jones, Albany St. (Ga.) (II)	1976	4	105	2,052	19.5
Larry Parker, Plattsburgh St. (III)	1978	4	85	1,482	17.4
Howard Shockley, Salisbury (III & II)	1976	3	76	1,299	17.1
Andre Means, Sacred Heart (II)	1978	2	62	1,009	16.3
Charles Greer, Thomas (III)	1977	3	58	926	16.0
Willie Parr, LeMoyne-Owen (III)	1976	3	76	1,182	15.6
Glenn Mosley, Seton Hall (I)	1977	4	83	1,263	15.2
Michael Smith, Hamilton (III)	1992	4	107	1,628	15.2
Dave Kufeld, Yeshiva (III)	1980	4	81	1,222	15.1
Ed Owens, Hampden-Sydney (III)	1980	4	77	1,160	15.1
Tony Rychlec, Mass. Maritime (III)	1983	3	55	812	14.8
Bill Campion, Manhattan (I)	1975	3	74	1,070	14.5
John Jordan, Southern Me. (III)	1981	4	105	1,504	14.4
Kevin Clark, Clark (Mass.) (III)	1981	4	101	1,450	14.4
Antonio Garcia, Ky. Wesleyan (II)	1999	2	70	997	14.2
Mark Veenstra, Calvin (III)	1977	4	89	1,260	14.2
Pete Padgett, Nevada (I)	1976	4	104	1,464	14.1
Rob Roesch, Staten Island (III)	1989	2	61	850	13.9
Clemon Johnson, Florida A&M (II)	1978	4	109	1,494	13.7
Larry Johnson, Ark.-Little Rock (I)	1978	3	69	944	13.7
Carlo DeTommaso, Rhode Island Col. (III)	1976	3	72	984	13.7
Bob Warner, Maine (I)	1976	4	96	1,304	13.6
Shaquille O'Neal, LSU (I)	1992	3	90	1,217	13.5
Cornelius Cash, Bowling Green (I)	1975	3	79	1,068	13.5
E.D. Schecterly, Lynchburg (III)	1980	4	104	1,404	13.5
Ira Terrell, Southern Methodist (I)	1976	3	80	1,077	13.5

ASSISTS

Player, Team (Division)	Last Season	Yrs.	G	Ast.
Bobby Hurley, Duke (I)	1993	4	140	1,076
Demetri Beekman, Assumption (II)	1993	4	119	1,044
Chris Corchiani, North Carolina St. (I)	1991	4	124	1,038
Ed Cota, North Carolina (I)	2000	4	138	1,030
Keith Jennings, East Tenn. St. (I)	1991	4	127	983
Steve Blake, Maryland (I)	2003	4	138	972
Sherman Douglas, Syracuse (I)	1989	4	138	960
Tony Miller, Marquette (I)	1995	4	123	956
Greg Anthony, Portland/UNLV (I)	1991	4	138	950
Doug Gottlieb, Notre Dame & Oklahoma St. (I)	2000	4	124	947
Gary Payton, Oregon St. (I)	1990	4	120	938
Adam Kaufman, Edinboro (II)	2001	4	116	936
Rob Paternostro, Southern N.H. (II)	1995	4	129	919
Tennyson Whitted, Ramapo (III)	2003	4	108	917
Steve Artis, Chris. Newport (III)	1993	4	112	909
Orlando Smart, San Francisco (I)	1994	4	116	902
Andre LaFleur, Northeastern (I)	1987	4	128	894
Chico Fletcher, Arkansas St. (I)	2000	4	114	893
Phil Dixon, Shenandoah (III)	1996	4	103	889
Jim Les, Bradley (I)	1986	4	118	884
Frank Smith, Old Dominion (I)	1988	4	120	883
Gallagher Driscoll, St. Rose (II)	1992	4	121	878
Taurence Chisholm, Delaware (I)	1988	4	110	877
Grayson Marshall, Clemson (I)	1988	4	122	857
Anthony Manuel, Bradley (I)	1989	4	108	855

ASSIST AVERAGE
(Minimum 550 assists)

Player, Team (Division)	Last Season	Yrs.	G	Ast.	Avg.
Steve Ray, Bridgeport (II)	1990	2	65	785	12.08
Avery Johnson, Southern U. (I)	1988	2	61	732	12.00
Sam Crawford, New Mexico St. (I)	1993	2	67	592	8.84
Mark Wade, Oklahoma & UNLV (I)	1987	3	79	693	8.77
Demetri Beekman, Assumption (II)	1993	4	119	1,044	8.77
Phil Dixon, Shenandoah (III)	1996	4	103	889	8.63
Tennyson Whitted, Ramapo (III)	2003	4	108	917	8.49
Chris Corchiani, North Carolina St. (I)	1991	4	124	1,038	8.37
Ernest Jenkins, N.M. Highlands (II)	1995	4	84	699	8.32
Steve Artis, Chris. Newport (III)	1993	4	112	909	8.12
Adam Kaufman, Edinboro (II)	2001	4	116	936	8.07

Player, Team (Division)	Last Season	Yrs.	G	Ast.	Avg.
Taurence Chisholm, Delaware (I)	1988	4	110	877	7.97
Van Usher, Tennessee Tech (I)	1992	3	85	676	7.95
Anthony Manuel, Bradley (I)	1989	4	108	855	7.92
Mark Benson, Tex. A&M-Kingsville (II)	1991	3	86	674	7.84
Chico Fletcher, Arkansas St. (I)	2000	4	114	893	7.83
Pat Madden, Jacksonville St. (II)	1991	3	88	688	7.82
Gary Payton, Oregon St. (I)	1990	4	120	938	7.82
Orlando Smart, San Francisco (I)	1994	4	116	902	7.78
Tony Miller, Marquette (I)	1995	4	123	956	7.77
Keith Jennings, East Tenn. St. (I)	1991	4	127	983	7.74
Dan Ward, St. Cloud St. (II)	1995	4	100	774	7.74
Bobby Hurley, Duke (I)	1993	4	140	1,076	7.69
Doug Gottlieb, Notre Dame & Oklahoma St. (I)	2000	4	124	947	7.63
Chuck Evans, Old Dominion & Mississippi St. (I)	1993	3	85	648	7.62

BLOCKED SHOTS

Player, Team (Division)	Last Season	Yrs.	G	Blk.
Ira Nicholson, Mt. St. Vincent (III)	1997	4	100	576
Wojciech Mydra, La.-Monroe (I)	2002	4	115	535
Adonal Foyle, Colgate (I)	1997	3	87	492
Tim Duncan, Wake Forest (I)	1997	4	128	481
Alonzo Mourning, Georgetown (I)	1992	4	120	453
Tarvis Williams, Hampton (III)	2001	4	114	452
Ken Johnson, Ohio St. (I)	2001	4	127	444
Antoine Hyman, Keuka (III)	1997	4	101	440
Lorenzo Coleman, Tennessee Tech (I)	1997	4	113	437
Calvin Booth, Penn St. (I)	1999	4	114	428
Troy Murphy, Notre Dame (I)	2001	3	94	425
Theo Ratliff, Wyoming (I)	1995	4	111	425
Etan Thomas, Syracuse (I)	2000	4	122	424
Rodney Blake, St. Joseph's (I)	1988	4	116	419
James Doyle, Concord (II)	1998	4	120	416
Shaquille O'Neal, LSU (I)	1992	3	90	412
Kevin Roberson, Vermont (I)	1992	4	112	409
Derek Moore, S.C.-Aiken (II)	1999	4	102	408
Jim McIlvaine, Marquette (I)	1994	4	118	399
Tim Perry, Temple (I)	1988	4	130	392
Jason Lawson, Villanova (I)	1997	4	131	375
Pervis Ellison, Louisville (I)	1989	4	136	374
Peter Aluma, Liberty (I)	1997	4	119	366
Acie Earl, Iowa (I)	1993	3	116	365
Jerome James, Florida A&M (I)	1998	3	81	363

BLOCKED-SHOT AVERAGE
(Minimum 200 blocked shots)

Player, Team (Division)	Last Season	Yrs.	G	Blk.	Avg.
Neil Edwards, York (N.Y.) (III)	2000	3	55	337	6.13
Ira Nicholson, Mt. St. Vincent (III)	1997	4	100	576	5.76
Adonal Foyle, Colgate (I)	1997	3	87	492	5.66
David Robinson, Navy (I)	1987	2	67	351	5.24
Wojciech Mydra, La.-Monroe (I)	2002	4	115	535	4.65
Shaquille O'Neal, LSU (I)	1992	3	90	412	4.58
Troy Murphy, Notre Dame (I)	2001	3	94	425	4.52
Jerome James, Florida A&M (I)	1998	3	81	363	4.48
Antoine Hyman, Keuka (III)	1997	4	101	440	4.36
Andrew South, N.J. Inst. of Tech (III)	1995	4	80	344	4.30
Antonio Ramos, Clarke (III)	2003	3	77	318	4.13
Justin Rowe, Maine (I)	2003	2	55	226	4.11
Johnny Woods, Wesley (III)	2002	4	78	319	4.09
Derek Moore, S.C.-Aiken (II)	1999	4	102	408	4.00
Tarvis Williams, Hampton (III)	2001	4	114	452	3.96
Lorenzo Coleman, Tennessee Tech (I)	1997	4	113	437	3.87
Theo Ratliff, Wyoming (I)	1995	4	111	425	3.83
John Burke, Southampton (II)	1996	2	54	205	3.80
Alonzo Mourning, Georgetown (I)	1992	4	120	453	3.78

Player, Team (Division)	Last Season	Yrs.	G	Blk.	Avg.
Kino Outlaw, Mount Olive (II)	1996	3	81	305	3.77
Calvin Booth, Penn St. (I)	1999	4	114	428	3.75
Mike Mientus, Allentown (III)	1997	4	87	324	3.72
Tarvis Williams, Hampton (I)	2000	3	82	305	3.72
Lorenzo Williams, Stetson (I)	1991	2	63	234	3.71
Vonzell McGrew, Mo. Western St. (II)	1995	3	57	211	3.70

STEALS

Player, Team (Division)	Last Season	Yrs.	G	Stl.
Tennyson Whitted, Ramapo (III)	2003	4	108	448
John Gallogly, Salve Regina (III)	1998	4	98	413
John Linehan, Providence (I)	2002	5	122	385
Eddin Santiago, Mo. Southern St. (II)	2002	4	117	383
Daniel Martinez, McMurry (III)	2000	3	76	380
Eric Murdock, Providence (I)	1991	4	117	376
Ivo Moyano, Polytechnic (N.Y.) (III)	1997	4	87	368
Pepe Sanchez, Temple (I)	2000	4	116	365
Oronn Brown, Clarion (II)	1997	4	106	361
Robert Campbell, Armstrong Atlantic (II)	2001	4	118	357
Eric Bell, New Paltz St. (III)	1996	4	94	355
Cookie Belcher, Nebraska (I)	2001	5	131	353
Kevin Braswell, Georgetown (I)	2002	4	128	349
Bonzi Wells, Ball St. (I)	1998	4	116	347
Scott Clarke, Utica (III)	1996	4	96	346
Marcus Best, Winston-Salem (II)	2002	4	119	345
Gerald Walker, San Francisco (I)	1996	4	111	344
Johnny Rhodes, Maryland (I)	1996	4	122	344
Michael Anderson, Drexel (I)	1988	4	115	341
Kenny Robertson, Cleveland St. (I)	1990	4	119	341
Keith Jennings, East Tenn. St. (I)	1991	4	127	334
Juan Dixon, Maryland (I)	2002	4	141	333
Devlin Herring, Pitt.-Johnstown (II)	1998	4	106	333
Desmond Cambridge, Alabama A&M (I)	2002	3	84	330
Jason Hart, Syracuse (I)	2000	4	132	329
Greg Anthony, Portland & UNLV (I)	1991	4	138	329

STEAL AVERAGE
(Minimum 200 steals)

Player, Team (Division)	Last Season	Yrs.	G	Stl.	Avg.
Moses Jean-Pierre, Plymouth St. (III)	1994	2	55	303	5.51
Daniel Martinez, McMurry (III)	2000	3	76	380	5.00
Wayne Copeland, Lynn (II)	2000	2	57	254	4.46
Ivo Moyano, Polytechnic (N.Y.) (III)	1997	4	87	368	4.23
Mario Thompson, Occidental (III)	2001	3	71	300	4.23
John Gallogly, Salve Regina (III)	1998	4	98	413	4.21
Tennyson Whitted, Ramapo (III)	2003	4	108	448	4.15
Greg Dean, Concordia-M'head (III)	1997	3	75	307	4.09
Desmond Cambridge, Alabama A&M (I)	2002	3	84	330	3.93
Mookie Blaylock, Oklahoma (I)	1989	2	74	281	3.80
Eric Bell, New Paltz St. (III)	1996	4	94	355	3.78
Scott Clarke, Utica (III)	1996	4	96	346	3.60
Ricky Hollis, Brockport St. (III)	2002	4	90	322	3.58
Ronn McMahon, Eastern Wash. (I)	1990	3	64	225	3.52
Gerald Garlic, Goucher (III)	1995	3	70	244	3.49
Darrel Lewis, Lincoln (Pa.) (III)	1999	4	86	298	3.47
Oronn Brown, Clarion (II)	1997	4	106	361	3.41
Patrick Herron, Winston-Salem (II)	1995	3	78	263	3.37
David Clark, Bluefield St. (II)	1996	3	83	278	3.35
Eddin Santiago, Mo. Southern St. (II)	2002	4	117	383	3.27
Shuron Woodyard, Villa Julie (III)	1997	3	73	238	3.26
Shawn McCartney, Hunter (III)	1995	3	81	261	3.22
Carl Small, Cornell College (III)	1995	3	69	222	3.22
Eric Murdock, Providence (I)	1991	4	117	376	3.21
Ken Francis, Molloy (II)	1995	3	81	260	3.21

INDIVIDUAL COLLEGIATE

Award Winners

Division I Consensus All-America Selections

By Season

1929
Charley Hyatt, Pittsburgh; Joe Schaaf, Pennsylvania; Charles Murphy, Purdue; Vern Corbin, California; Thomas Churchill, Oklahoma; John Thompson, Montana St.

1930
Charley Hyatt, Pittsburgh; Charles Murphy, Purdue; Branch McCracken, Indiana; John Thompson, Montana St.; Frank Ward, Montana St.; John Wooden, Purdue.

1931
John Wooden, Purdue; Joe Reiff, Northwestern; George Gregory, Columbia; Wes Fesler, Ohio St.; Elwood Romney, Brigham Young.

1932
Forest Sale, Kentucky; Ed Krause, Notre Dame; John Wooden, Purdue; Louis Berger, Maryland; Les Witte, Wyoming.

1933
Forest Sale, Kentucky; Don Smith, Pittsburgh; Elliott Loughlin, Navy; Joe Reiff, Northwestern; Ed Krause, Notre Dame; Jerry Nemer, Southern California

1934
Claire Cribbs, Pittsburgh; Ed Krause, Notre Dame; Les Witte, Wyoming; Hal Lee, Washington; Norman Cottom, Purdue.

1935
Jack Gray, Texas; Lee Guttero, Southern California; Claire Cribbs, Pittsburgh; Bud Browning, Oklahoma; Leroy Edwards, Kentucky.

1936
Bob Kessler, Purdue; Paul Nowak, Notre Dame; Hank Luisetti, Stanford; Vern Huffman, Indiana; John Moir, Notre Dame; Ike Poole, Arkansas; Bill Kinner, Utah.

1937
Hank Luisetti, Stanford; Paul Nowak, Notre Dame; Jules Bender, Long Island; John Moir, Notre Dame; Jewell Young, Purdue.

1938
Hank Luisetti, Stanford; John Moir, Notre Dame; Fred Pralle, Kansas; Jewell Young, Purdue; Paul Nowak, Notre Dame; Meyer Bloom, Temple.

1939
First Team—Irving Torgoff, Long Island; Urgel Wintermute, Oregon; Chet Jaworski, Rhode Island; Ernie Andres, Indiana; Jimmy Hull, Ohio St.

Second Team—Bob Calihan, Detroit; Michael Novak, Loyola (Ill.); Bernard Opper, Kentucky; Robert Anet, Oregon; Bob Hassmiller, Fordham.

1940
First Team—Ralph Vaughn, Southern California; John Dick, Oregon; Bill Hapac, Illinois; George Glamack, North Carolina; Gus Broberg, Dartmouth.

Second Team—Jack Harvey, Colorado; Marvin Huffman, Indiana; James McNatt, Oklahoma; Jesse Renick, Oklahoma St.

1941
First Team—Gus Broberg, Dartmouth; John Adams, Arkansas; Howard Engleman, Kansas; George Glamack, North Carolina; Gene Englund, Wisconsin.

Second Team—Frank Baumholtz, Ohio; Paul Lindeman, Washington St.; Oscar Schechtman, Long Island; Robert Kinney, Rice; Stan Modzelewski, Rhode Island.

1942
First Team—John Kotz, Wisconsin; Price Brookfield, West Tex. A&M; Bob Kinney, Rice; Andrew Phillip, Illinois; Robert Davies, Seton Hall.

Second Team—Robert Doll, Colorado; Wilfred Doerner, Evansville; Donald Burness, Stanford; George Munroe, Dartmouth; Stan Modzelewski, Rhode Island; John Mandic, Oregon St.

1943
First Team—Andrew Phillip, Illinois; George Senesky, St. Joseph's; Ken Sailors, Wyoming; Harry Boykoff, St. John's (N.Y.); Charles Black, Kansas; Ed Beisser, Creighton; William Closs, Rice.

Second Team—Gerald Tucker, Oklahoma; Bob Rensberger, Notre Dame; Gene Rock, Southern California; John Kotz, Wisconsin; Otto Graham, Northwestern; Gale Bishop, Washington St.

1944
First Team—George Mikan, DePaul; Audley Brindley, Dartmouth; Otto Graham, Northwestern; Robert Brannum, Kentucky; Alva Paine, Oklahoma; Robert Kurland, Oklahoma St.; Leo Klier, Notre Dame.

Second Team—Arnold Ferrin, Utah; Dale Hall, Army; Don Grate, Ohio St.; Bob Dille, Valparaiso; William Henry, Rice; Dick Triptow, DePaul.

1945
First Team—George Mikan, DePaul; Robert Kurland, Oklahoma St.; Arnold Ferrin, Utah; Walton Kirk, Illinois; William Hassett, Notre Dame; William Henry, Rice; Howard Dallmar, Pennsylvania; Wyndol Gray, Bowling Green.

Second Team—Richard Ives, Iowa; Vince Hanson, Washington St.; Dale Hall, Army; Max Norris, Northwestern; Don Grate, Ohio St.; Herb Wilkinson, Iowa.

1946
First Team—George Mikan, DePaul; Robert Kurland, Oklahoma St.; Leo Klier, Notre Dame; Max Norris, Northwestern; Sid Tanenbaum, New York U.

Second Team—Jack Parkinson, Kentucky; John Dillon, North Carolina; Ken Sailors, Wyoming; Charles Black, Kansas; Tony Lavelli, Yale; William Hassett, Notre Dame.

1947
First Team—Ralph Beard, Kentucky; Gerald Tucker, Oklahoma; Alex Groza, Kentucky; Sid Tanenbaum, New York U.; Ralph Hamilton, Indiana.

Second Team—George Kaftan, Holy Cross; John Hargis, Texas; Don Barksdale, UCLA; Arnold Ferrin, Utah; Andrew Phillip, Illinois; Ed Koffenberger, Duke; Vern Gardner, Utah.

1948
First Team—Murray Wier, Iowa, 5-9, Muscatine, Iowa; Ed Macauley, St. Louis, 6-8, St. Louis; Jim McIntyre, Minnesota, 6-10, Minneapolis; Kevin O'Shea, Notre Dame, 6-1, San Francisco; Ralph Beard, Kentucky, 5-10, Louisville, Ky.

Second Team—Dick Dickey, North Carolina St.; Arnold Ferrin, Utah; Alex Groza, Kentucky; Harold Haskins, Hamline; George Kaftan, Holy Cross; Duane Klueh, Indiana St.; Tony Lavelli, Yale; Jack Nichols, Washington; Andy Wolfe, California.

1949
First Team—Tony Lavelli, Yale, 6-3, Somerville, Mass.; Vince Boryla, Denver, 6-5, East Chicago, Ind.; Ed Macauley, St. Louis, 6-8, St. Louis; Alex Groza, Kentucky, 6-7, Martin's Ferry, Ohio; Ralph Beard, Kentucky, 5-10, Louisville, Ky.

Second Team—Bill Erickson, Illinois; Vern Gardner, Utah; Wallace Jones, Kentucky; Jim McIntyre, Minnesota; Ernie Vandeweghe, Colgate.

1950
First Team—Dick Schnittker, Ohio St., 6-5, Sandusky, Ohio; Bob Cousy, Holy Cross, 6-1, St. Albans, N.Y.; Paul Arizin, Villanova, 6-3, Philadelphia; Paul Unruh, Bradley, 6-4, Toulon, Ill.; Bill Sharman, Southern California, 6-2, Porterville, Calif.

Second Team—Charles Cooper, Duquesne; Don Lofgran, San Francisco; Kevin O'Shea, Notre Dame; Don Rehfeldt, Wisconsin; Sherman White, Long Island.

1951
First Team—Bill Mlkvy, Temple, 6-4, Palmerton, Pa.; Sam Ranzino, North Carolina St., 6-1, Gary, Ind.; Bill Spivey, Kentucky, 7-0, Macon, Ga.; Clyde Lovellette, Kansas, 6-9, Terre Haute, Ind.; Gene Melchiorre, Bradley, 5-8, Highland Park, Ill.

Second Team—Ernie Barrett, Kansas St.; Bill Garrett, Indiana; Dick Groat, Duke; Mel Hutchins, Brigham Young; Gale McArthur, Oklahoma St.

1952
First Team—Cliff Hagan, Kentucky, 6-4, Owensboro, Ky.; Rod Fletcher, Illinois, 6-4, Champaign, Ill.; Chuck Darling, Iowa, 6-8, Denver; Clyde Lovellette, Kansas, 6-9, Terre Haute, Ind.; Dick Groat, Duke, 6-0, Swissvale, Pa.

Second Team—Bob Houbregs, Washington; Don Meineke, Dayton; Johnny O'Brien, Seattle; Mark Workman, West Virginia; Bob Zawoluk, St. John's (N.Y.).

1953
First Team—Ernie Beck, Pennsylvania, 6-4, Philadelphia; Bob Houbregs, Washington, 6-7, Seattle; Walt Dukes, Seton Hall, 6-11, Rochester, N.Y.; Tom Gola, La Salle, 6-6, Philadelphia; Johnny O'Brien, Seattle, 5-8, South Amboy, N.J.

Second Team—Dick Knostman, Kansas St.; Bob Pettit, LSU; Joe Richey, Brigham Young; Don Schlundt, Indiana; Frank Selvy, Furman.

1954
First Team—Frank Selvy, Furman, 6-3, Corbin, Ky.; Tom Gola, La Salle, 6-6, Philadelphia; Don Schlundt, Indiana, 6-10, South Bend, Ind.; Bob Pettit, LSU, 6-9, Baton Rouge, La.; Cliff Hagan, Kentucky, 6-4, Owensboro, Ky.

Second Team—Bob Leonard, Indiana; Tom Marshall, Western Ky.; Bob Mattick, Oklahoma St.; Frank Ramsey, Kentucky; Dick Ricketts, Duquesne.

1955
First Team—Tom Gola, La Salle, 6-6, Philadelphia; Dick Ricketts, Duquesne, 6-8, Pottstown, Pa.; Bill Russell, San Francisco, 6-9, Oakland, Calif.; Si Green, Duquesne, 6-3, Brooklyn, N.Y.; Dick Garmaker, Minnesota, 6-3, Hibbing, Minn.

Second Team—Darrell Floyd, Furman; Robin Freeman, Ohio St.; Dickie Hemric, Wake Forest; Don Schlundt, Indiana; Ron Shavlik, North Carolina St.

1956
First Team—Tom Heinsohn, Holy Cross, 6-7, Union City, N.J.; Ron Shavlik, North Carolina St., 6-9, Denver; Bill Russell, San Francisco, 6-9, Oakland, Calif.; Si Green, Duquesne, 6-3, Brooklyn, N.Y.; Robin Freeman, Ohio St., 5-11, Cincinnati.

Second Team—Bob Burrow, Kentucky; Darrell Floyd, Furman; Rod Hundley, West Virginia; K.C. Jones, San Francisco; Willie Naulls, UCLA; Bill Uhl, Dayton.

1957
First Team—Rod Hundley, West Virginia, 6-4, Charleston, W. Va.; Lenny Rosenbluth, North Carolina, 6-5, New York; Jim Krebs, Southern Methodist, 6-8, Webster Groves, Mo.; Wilt Chamberlain, Kansas, 7-0, Philadelphia; Charlie Tyra, Louisville, 6-8, Louisville, Ky.; Chet Forte, Columbia, 5-9, Hackensack, N.J.

Second Team—Elgin Baylor, Seattle; Frank Howard, Ohio St.; Guy Rodgers, Temple; Gary Thompson, Iowa St.; Grady Wallace, South Carolina

1958

First Team—Bob Boozer, Kansas St., 6-8, Omaha, Neb.; Elgin Baylor, Seattle, 6-6, Washington, D.C.; Wilt Chamberlain, Kansas, 7-0, Philadelphia; Oscar Robertson, Cincinnati, 6-5, Indianapolis; Guy Rodgers, Temple, 6-0, Philadelphia; Don Hennon, Pittsburgh, 5-9, Wampum, Pa.

Second Team—Pete Brennan, North Carolina; Archie Dees, Indiana; Dave Gambee, Oregon St.; Mike Farmer, San Francisco; Bailey Howell, Mississippi St.

1959

First Team—Bailey Howell, Mississippi St., 6-7, Middleton, Tenn.; Bob Boozer, Kansas St., 6-8, Omaha, Neb.; Oscar Robertson, Cincinnati, 6-5, Indianapolis; Jerry West, West Virginia, 6-3, Cabin Creek, W.Va.; Johnny Cox, Kentucky, 6-4, Hazard, Ky.

Second Team—Leo Byrd, Marshall; Johnny Green, Michigan St.; Tom Hawkins, Notre Dame; Don Hennon, Pittsburgh; Alan Seiden, St. John's (N.Y.).

1960

First Team—Oscar Robertson, Cincinnati, 6-5, Indianapolis; Jerry West, West Virginia, 6-3, Cabin Creek, W.Va.; Jerry Lucas, Ohio St., 6-8, Middletown, Ohio; Darrall Imhoff, California, 6-10, Alhambra, Calif.; Tom Stith, St. Bonaventure, 6-5, Brooklyn, N.Y.

Second Team—Terry Dischinger, Purdue; Tony Jackson, St. John's (N.Y.); Roger Kaiser, Georgia Tech; Lee Shaffer, North Carolina; Len Wilkens, Providence.

1961

First Team—Jerry Lucas, Ohio St., 6-8, Middletown, Ohio; Tom Stith, St. Bonaventure, 6-5, Brooklyn, N.Y.; Terry Dischinger, Purdue, 6-7, Terre Haute, Ind.; Roger Kaiser, Georgia Tech, 6-1, Dale, Ind.; Chet Walker, Bradley, 6-6, Benton Harbor, Mich.

Second Team—Walt Bellamy, Indiana; Frank Burgess, Gonzaga; Tony Jackson, St. John's (N.Y.); Billy McGill, Utah; Larry Siegfried, Ohio St.

1962

First Team—Jerry Lucas, Ohio St., 6-8, Middletown, Ohio; Len Chappell, Wake Forest, 6-8, Portage Area, Pa.; Billy McGill, Utah, 6-9, Los Angeles; Terry Dischinger, Purdue, 6-7, Terre Haute, Ind.; Chet Walker, Bradley, 6-6, Benton Harbor, Mich.

Second Team—Jack Foley, Holy Cross; John Havlicek, Ohio St.; Art Heyman, Duke; Cotton Nash, Kentucky; John Rudometkin, Southern California; Rod Thorn, West Virginia

1963

First Team—Art Heyman, Duke, 6-5, Rockville Center, N.Y.; Ron Bonham, Cincinnati, 6-5, Muncie, Ind.; Barry Kramer, New York U., 6-4, Schenectady, N.Y.; Jerry Harkness, Loyola (Ill.), 6-3, New York; Tom Thacker, Cincinnati, 6-2, Covington, Ky.

Second Team—Gary Bradds, Ohio St.; Bill Green, Colorado St.; Cotton Nash, Kentucky; Rod Thorn, West Virginia; Nate Thurmond, Bowling Green.

1964

First Team—Bill Bradley, Princeton, 6-5, Crystal City, Mo.; Dave Stallworth, Wichita St., 6-7, Dallas; Gary Bradds, Ohio St., 6-8, Jamestown, Ohio; Walt Hazzard, UCLA, 6-2, Philadelphia; Cotton Nash, Kentucky, 6-5, Leominster, Mass.

Second Team—Ron Bonham, Cincinnati; Mel Counts, Oregon St.; Fred Hetzel, Davidson; Jeff Mullins, Duke; Cazzie Russell, Michigan.

1965

First Team—Bill Bradley, Princeton, 6-5, Crystal City, Mo.; Rick Barry, Miami (Fla.), 6-7, Roselle Park, N.J.; Fred Hetzel, Davidson, 6-8, Washington, D.C.; Cazzie Russell, Michigan, 6-5, Chicago; Gail Goodrich, UCLA, 6-1, North Hollywood, Calif.

Second Team—Bill Buntin, Michigan; Wayne Estes, Utah St.; Clyde Lee, Vanderbilt; Dave Schellhase, Purdue; Dave Stallworth, Wichita St.

1966

First Team—Dave Bing, Syracuse, 6-3, Washington, D.C.; Dave Schellhase, Purdue, 6-4, Evansville, Ind.; Clyde Lee, Vanderbilt, 6-9, Nashville, Tenn.; Cazzie Russell, Michigan, 6-5, Chicago; Jim Walker, Providence, 6-3, Boston.

Second Team—Lou Dampier, Kentucky; Matt Guokas, St. Joseph's; Jack Marin, Duke; Dick Snyder, Davidson; Bob Verga, Duke; Walt Wesley, Kansas.

1967

First Team—Lew Alcindor, UCLA, 7-2, New York; Elvin Hayes, Houston, 6-8, Rayville, La.; Wes Unseld, Louisville, 6-8, Louisville, Ky.; Jim Walker, Providence, 6-3, Boston; Clem Haskins, Western Ky., 6-3, Campbellsville, Ky.; Bob Lloyd, Rutgers, 6-1, Upper Darby, Pa.; Bob Verga, Duke, 6-0, Sea Girt, N.J.

Second Team—Mel Daniels, New Mexico; Sonny Dove, St. John's (N.Y.); Larry Miller, North Carolina; Don May, Dayton; Lou Dampier, Kentucky.

1968

First Team—Wes Unseld, Louisville, 6-8, Louisville, Ky.; Elvin Hayes, Houston, 6-8, Rayville, La.; Lew Alcindor, UCLA, 7-2, New York; Pete Maravich, LSU, 6-5, Raleigh, N.C.; Larry Miller, North Carolina, 6-4, Catasauga, Pa.

Second Team—Lucius Allen, UCLA; Bob Lanier, St. Bonaventure; Don May, Dayton; Calvin Murphy, Niagara; Jo Jo White, Kansas.

1969

First Team—Lew Alcindor, UCLA, 7-2, New York; Spencer Haywood, Detroit, 6-8, Detroit; Pete Maravich, LSU, 6-5, Raleigh, N.C.; Rick Mount, Purdue, 6-4, Lebanon, Ind.; Calvin Murphy, Niagara, 5-10, Norwalk, Conn.

Second Team—Dan Issel, Kentucky; Mike Maloy, Davidson; Bud Ogden, Santa Clara; Charlie Scott, North Carolina; Jo Jo White, Kansas.

1970

First Team—Pete Maravich, LSU, 6-5, Raleigh, N.C.; Rick Mount, Purdue, 6-4, Lebanon, Ind.; Bob Lanier, St. Bonaventure, 6-11, Buffalo, N.Y.; Dan Issel, Kentucky, 6-9, Batavia, Ill.; Calvin Murphy, Niagara, 5-10, Norwalk, Conn.

Second Team—Austin Carr, Notre Dame; Jim Collins, New Mexico St.; John Roche, South Carolina; Charlie Scott, North Carolina; Sidney Wicks, UCLA.

1971

First Team—Austin Carr, Notre Dame, 6-3, Washington, D.C.; Sidney Wicks, UCLA, 6-8, Los Angeles; Artis Gilmore, Jacksonville, 7-2, Dothan, Ala.; Dean Meminger, Marquette, 6-1, New York; Jim McDaniels, Western Ky., 7-0, Scottsville, Ky.

Second Team—John Roche, South Carolina; Johnny Neumann, Mississippi; Ken Durrett, La Salle; Howard Porter, Villanova; Curtis Rowe, UCLA.

1972

First Team—Bill Walton, UCLA, 6-11, La Mesa, Calif.; Dwight Lamar, La.-Lafayette, 6-1, Columbus, Ohio; Ed Ratleff, Long Beach St., 6-6, Columbus, Ohio; Bob McAdoo, North Carolina, 6-8, Greensboro, N.C.; Tom Riker, South Carolina, 6-10, Oyster Bay, N.Y.; Jim Chones, Marquette, 6-11, Racine, Wis.; Henry Bibby, UCLA, 6-1, Franklinton, N.C.

Second Team—Barry Parkhill, Virginia; Jim Price, Louisville; Bud Stallworth, Kansas; Henry Willmore, Michigan; Rich Fuqua, Oral Roberts.

1973

First Team—Doug Collins, Illinois St., 6-6, Benton, Ill.; Ed Ratleff, Long Beach St., 6-6, Columbus, Ohio; Dwight Lamar, La.-Lafayette, 6-1, Columbus, Ohio; Bill Walton, UCLA, 6-11, La Mesa, Calif.; Ernie DiGregorio, Providence, 6-0, North Providence, R.I.; David Thompson, North Carolina St., 6-4, Shelby, N.C.; Keith Wilkes, UCLA, 6-6, Santa Barbara, Calif.

1974

First Team—Keith Wilkes, UCLA, 6-6, Santa Barbara, Calif.; John Shumate, Notre Dame, 6-9, Elizabeth, N.J.; Bill Walton, UCLA, 6-11, La Mesa, Calif.; David Thompson, North Carolina St., 6-4, Shelby, N.C.; Marvin Barnes, Providence, 6-9, Providence, R.I.

Second Team—Len Elmore, Maryland; Bobby Jones, North Carolina; Bill Knight, Pittsburgh; Larry Fogle, Canisius; Campy Russell, Michigan.

1975

First Team—David Thompson, North Carolina St., 6-4, Shelby, N.C.; Adrian Dantley, Notre Dame, 6-5, Washington, D.C.; Scott May, Indiana, 6-7, Sandusky, Ohio; John Lucas, Maryland, 6-4, Durham, N.C.; Dave Meyers, UCLA, 6-8, La Habra, Calif.

Second Team—Luther Burden, Utah; Kevin Grevey, Kentucky; Leon Douglas, Alabama; Gus Williams, Southern California; Ron Lee, Oregon.

1976

First Team—Scott May, Indiana, 6-7, Sandusky, Ohio; Richard Washington, UCLA, 6-10, Portland, Ore.; John Lucas, Maryland, 6-4, Durham, N.C.; Kent Benson, Indiana, 6-11, New Castle, Ind.; Adrian Dantley, Notre Dame, 6-5, Washington, D.C.

Second Team—Mitch Kupchak, North Carolina; Phil Sellers, Rutgers; Phil Ford, North Carolina; Earl Tatum, Marquette; Bernard King, Tennessee.

1977

First Team—Otis Birdsong, Houston, 6-4, Winter Haven, Fla.; Marques Johnson, UCLA, 6-7, Los Angeles; Kent Benson, Indiana, 6-11, New Castle, Ind.; Rickey Green, Michigan, 6-2, Chicago; Phil Ford, North Carolina, 6-2, Rocky Mount, N.C.; Bernard King, Tennessee, 6-7, Brooklyn, N.Y.

Second Team—Phil Hubbard, Michigan; Mychal Thompson, Minnesota; Ernie Grunfeld, Tennessee; Greg Ballard, Oregon; Rod Griffin, Wake Forest; Butch Lee, Marquette; Bill Cartwright, San Francisco.

1978

First Team—Phil Ford, North Carolina, 6-2, Rocky Mount, N.C.; Butch Lee, Marquette, 6-2, Bronx, N.Y.; David Greenwood, UCLA, 6-9, Los Angeles; Mychal Thompson, Minnesota, 6-10, Nassau, Bahamas; Larry Bird, Indiana St., 6-9, French Lick, Ind.

Second Team—Jack Givens, Kentucky; Freeman Williams, Portland St.; Rick Robey, Kentucky; Ron Brewer, Arkansas; Rod Griffin, Wake Forest.

1979

First Team—Larry Bird, Indiana St., 6-9, French Lick, Ind.; David Greenwood, UCLA, 6-9, Los Angeles; Earvin Johnson, Michigan St., 6-8, Lansing, Mich.; Sidney Moncrief, Arkansas, 6-4, Little Rock, Ark.; Mike Gminski, Duke, 6-11, Monroe, Conn.

Second Team—Bill Cartwright, San Francisco; Calvin Natt, Northeast La.; Kelly Tripucka, Notre Dame; Mike O'Koren, North Carolina; Jim Spanarkel, Duke; Jim Paxson, Dayton; Sly Williams, Rhode Island.

1980

First Team—Mark Aguirre, DePaul, 6-7, Chicago; Michael Brooks, La Salle, 6-7, Philadelphia; Joe Barry Carroll, Purdue, 7-1, Denver; Kyle Macy, Kentucky, 6-3, Peru, Ind.; Darrell Griffith, Louisville, 6-4, Louisville, Ky.

Second Team—Albert King, Maryland; Mike Gminski, Duke; Mike O'Koren, North Carolina; Sam Worthen, Marquette; Kelvin Ransey, Ohio St.

1981

First Team—Mark Aguirre, DePaul, 6-7, Chicago; Danny Ainge, Brigham Young, 6-5, Eugene, Ore.; Steve Johnson, Oregon St., 6-11, San Bernardino, Calif.; Ralph

Sampson, Virginia, 7-4, Harrisonburg, Va.; Isiah Thomas, Indiana, 6-1, Chicago.

Second Team—Sam Bowie, Kentucky; Jeff Lamp, Virginia; Durand Macklin, LSU; Kelly Tripucka, Notre Dame; Danny Vranes, Utah; Al Wood, North Carolina

1982

First Team—Terry Cummings, DePaul, 6-9, Chicago; Quintin Dailey, San Francisco, 6-4, Baltimore; Eric Floyd, Georgetown, 6-3, Gastonia, N.C.; Ralph Sampson, Virginia, 7-4, Harrisonburg, Va.; James Worthy, North Carolina, 6-9, Gastonia, N.C.

Second Team—Dale Ellis, Tennessee; Kevin Magee, UC Irvine; John Paxson, Notre Dame; Sam Perkins, North Carolina; Paul Pressey, Tulsa.

1983

First Team—Dale Ellis, Tennessee, 6-7, Marietta, Ga.; Patrick Ewing, Georgetown, 7-0, Cambridge, Mass.; Michael Jordan, North Carolina, 6-6, Wilmington, N.C.; Sam Perkins, North Carolina, 6-9, Latham, N.Y.; Ralph Sampson, Virginia, 7-4, Harrisonburg, Va.; Wayman Tisdale, Oklahoma, 6-9, Tulsa, Okla.; Keith Lee, Memphis, 6-9, West Memphis, Ark.

Second Team—Clyde Drexler, Houston; John Paxson, Notre Dame; Steve Stipanovich, Missouri; Jon Sundvold, Missouri; Darrell Walker, Arkansas; Sidney Green, UNLV; Randy Wittman, Indiana.

1984

First Team—Wayman Tisdale, Oklahoma, 6-9, Tulsa, Okla.; Sam Perkins, North Carolina, 6-10, Latham, N.Y.; Patrick Ewing, Georgetown, 7-0, Cambridge, Mass.; Akeem Olajuwon, Houston, 7-0, Lagos, Nigeria; Michael Jordan, North Carolina, 6-5, Wilmington, N.C.

Second Team—Chris Mullin, St. John's (N.Y.); Devin Durrant, Brigham Young; Leon Wood, Cal St. Fullerton; Keith Lee, Memphis; Melvin Turpin, Kentucky; Michael Cage, San Diego St.

1985

First Team—Wayman Tisdale, Oklahoma, 6-9, Tulsa, Okla.; Patrick Ewing, Georgetown, 7-0, Cambridge, Mass.; Keith Lee, Memphis, 6-10, West Memphis, Ark.; Chris Mullin, St. John's (N.Y.), 6-6, Brooklyn, N.Y.; Xavier McDaniel, Wichita St., 6-7, Columbia, S.C.; Johnny Dawkins, Duke, 6-2, Washington, D.C.

Second Team—Kenny Walker, Kentucky; Jon Koncak, Southern Methodist; Len Bias, Maryland; Mark Price, Georgia Tech; Dwayne Washington, Syracuse.

1986

First Team—Len Bias, Maryland, 6-8, Landover, Md.; Kenny Walker, Kentucky, 6-8, Roberta, Ga.; Walter Berry, St. John's (N.Y.), 6-8, Bronx, N.Y.; Johnny Dawkins, Duke, 6-2, Washington, D.C.; Steve Alford, Indiana, 6-2, New Castle, Ind.

Second Team—Dell Curry, Virginia Tech; Brad Daugherty, North Carolina; Danny Manning, Kansas; Ron Harper, Miami (Ohio); Scott Skiles, Michigan St.; David Robinson, Navy.

1987

First Team—David Robinson, Navy, 7-1, Woodbridge, Va.; Danny Manning, Kansas, 6-11, Lawrence, Kan.; Reggie Williams, Georgetown, 6-7, Baltimore; Steve Alford, Indiana, 6-2, New Castle, Ind.; Kenny Smith, North Carolina, 6-3, Queens, N.Y.

Second Team—Armon Gilliam, UNLV; Dennis Hopson, Ohio St.; Mark Jackson, St. John's (N.Y.); Ken Norman, Illinois; Horace Grant, Clemson.

1988

First Team—Gary Grant, Michigan, 6-3, Canton, Ohio; Hersey Hawkins, Bradley, 6-3, Chicago; J.R. Reid, North Carolina, 6-9, Virginia Beach, Va.; Sean Elliott, Arizona, 6-8, Tucson, Ariz.; Danny Manning, Kansas, 6-11, Lawrence, Kan.

Second Team—Mark Macon, Temple; Rony Seikaly, Syracuse; Danny Ferry, Duke; Jerome Lane, Pittsburgh; Mitch Richmond, Kansas St.; Michael Smith, Brigham Young.

1989

First Team—Sean Elliott, Arizona, 6-8, Sr., Tucson, Ariz.; Pervis Ellison, Louisville, 6-9, Sr., Savannah, Ga.; Danny Ferry, Duke, 6-10, Sr., Bowie, Md.; Chris Jackson, LSU, 6-1, Fr., Gulfport, Miss.; Stacey King, Oklahoma, 6-11, Sr., Lawton, Okla.

Second Team—Mookie Blaylock, Oklahoma, 6-1, Sr.; Sherman Douglas, Syracuse, 6-0, Sr.; Jay Edwards, Indiana, 6-4, So.; Todd Lichti, Stanford, 6-4, Sr.; Glen Rice, Michigan, 6-7, Sr.; Lionel Simmons, La Salle, 6-6, Jr.

1990

First Team—Derrick Coleman, Syracuse, 6-10, Sr., Detroit; Chris Jackson, LSU, 6-1, So., Gulfport, Miss.; Larry Johnson, UNLV, 6-7, Jr., Dallas; Gary Payton, Oregon St., 6-3, Sr., Oakland, Calif.; Lionel Simmons, La Salle, 6-6, Sr., Philadelphia.

Second Team—Hank Gathers, Loyola Marymount, 6-7, Sr.; Kendall Gill, Illinois, 6-5, Sr.; Bo Kimble, Loyola Marymount, 6-5, Sr.; Alonzo Mourning, Georgetown, 6-10, So.; Rumeal Robinson, Michigan, 6-2, Sr.; Dennis Scott, Georgia Tech, 6-8, Jr.; Doug Smith, Missouri, 6-10, Jr.

1991

First Team—Kenny Anderson, Georgia Tech, 6-2, So., Rego Park, N.Y.; Jim Jackson, Ohio St., 6-6, So., Toledo, Ohio; Larry Johnson, UNLV, 6-7, Sr., Dallas; Shaquille O'Neal, LSU, 7-1, So., San Antonio, Texas; Billy Owens, Syracuse, 6-9, Jr., Carlisle, Pa.

Second Team—Stacey Augmon, UNLV, 6-8, Sr.; Keith Jennings, East Tenn. St., 5-7, Sr.; Christian Laettner, Duke, 6-11, Jr.; Eric Murdock, Providence, 6-2, Sr.; Steve Smith, Michigan St., 6-6, Sr.

1992

First Team—Jim Jackson, Ohio St., 6-6, Jr., Toledo, Ohio; Christian Laettner, Duke, 6-11, Sr., Angola, N.Y.; Harold Miner, Southern California, 6-5, Jr., Inglewood, Calif.; Alonzo Mourning, Georgetown, 6-10, Sr., Chesapeake, Va.; Shaquille O'Neal, LSU, 7-1, Jr., San Antonio, Texas.

Second Team—Byron Houston, Oklahoma St., 6-7, Sr.; Don MacLean, UCLA, 6-10, Sr.; Anthony Peeler, Missouri, 6-4, Sr.; Malik Sealy, St. John's (N.Y.), 6-7, Sr.; Walt Williams, Maryland, 6-8, Sr.

1993

First Team—Calbert Cheaney, Indiana, 6-7, Sr., Evansville, Ind.; Anfernee Hardaway, Memphis, 6-7, Jr., Memphis, Tenn.; Bobby Hurley, Duke, 6-0, Sr., Jersey City, N.J.; Jamal Mashburn, Kentucky, 6-8, Jr., New York; Chris Webber, Michigan, 6-9, So., Detroit.

Second Team—Terry Dehere, Seton Hall, 6-3, Sr.; Grant Hill, Duke, 6-7, Jr.; Billy McCaffrey, Vanderbilt, 6-3, Jr.; Eric Montross, North Carolina, 7-0, Jr.; J.R. Rider, UNLV, 6-7, Sr.; Glenn Robinson, Purdue, 6-9, So.; Rodney Rogers, Wake Forest, 6-8, Jr.

1994

First Team—Grant Hill, Duke, 6-8, Sr., Reston, Va.; Jason Kidd, California, 6-4, So., Oakland, Calif.; Donyell Marshall, Connecticut, 6-9, Jr., Reading, Pa.; Glenn Robinson, Purdue, 6-8, Jr., Gary, Ind.; Clifford Rozier, Louisville, 6-9, Jr., Bradenton, Fla.

Second Team—Melvin Booker, Missouri, 6-2, Sr.; Eric Montross, North Carolina, 7-0, Sr.; Lamond Murray, California, 6-7, Jr.; Khalid Reeves, Arizona, 6-2, Sr.; Jalen Rose, Michigan, 6-8, Jr.; Corliss Williamson, Arkansas, 6-7, So.

1995

First Team—Ed O'Bannon, UCLA, 6-8, Sr., Lakewood, Calif.; Shawn Respert, Michigan St., 6-3, Sr., Detroit; Joe

Smith, Maryland, 6-10, So., Norfolk, Va.; Jerry Stackhouse, North Carolina, 6-6, So., Kingston, N.C.; Damon Stoudamire, Arizona, 6-10, Sr., Portland, Ore.

Second Team—Randolph Childress, Wake Forest, 6-2, Sr.; Kerry Kittles, Villanova, 6-5, Jr.; Lou Roe, Massachusetts, 6-7, Sr.; Rasheed Wallace, North Carolina, 6-10, So.; Corliss Williamson, Arkansas, 6-7, Jr.

1996

First Team—Ray Allen, Connecticut, 6-5, Jr., Dalzell, S.C.; Marcus Camby, Massachusetts, 6-11, Jr., Hartford, Conn.; Tony Delk, Kentucky, 6-1, Sr., Brownsville, Tenn.; Tim Duncan, Wake Forest, 6-10, Jr., St. Croix, Virgin Islands; Allen Iverson, Georgetown, 6-1, So., Hampton, Va.; Kerry Kittles, Villanova, 6-5, Sr., New Orleans.

Second Team—Danny Fortson, Cincinnati, 6-7, So.; Keith Van Horn, Utah, 6-9, Jr.; Jacque Vaughn, Kansas, 6-1, Jr.; John Wallace, Syracuse, 6-8, Sr.; Lorenzen Wright, Memphis, 6-11, So.

1997

First Team—Tim Duncan, Wake Forest, 6-10, Sr., St. Croix, Virgin Islands; Danny Fortson, Cincinnati, 6-7, Jr., Pittsburgh; Raef LaFrentz, Kansas, 6-11, Jr., Monona, Ia.; Ron Mercer, Kentucky, 6-7, So., Nashville, Tenn.; Keith Van Horn, Utah, 6-9, Sr., Diamond Bar, Calif.

Second Team—Chauncey Billups, Colorado, 6-3, So.; Bobby Jackson, Minnesota, 6-1, Sr.; Antawn Jamison, North Carolina, 6-9, So.; Brevin Knight, Stanford, 5-10, Sr.; Jacque Vaughn, Kansas, 6-1, Sr.

1998

First Team—Mike Bibby, Arizona, 6-2, So., Phoenix, Ariz.; Antawn Jamison, North Carolina, 6-9, Jr., Charlotte, N.C.; Raef LaFrentz, Kansas, 6-11, Sr., Monona, Ia.; Paul Pierce, Kansas, 6-7, Jr., Inglewood, Calif.; Miles Simon, Arizona, 6-5, Sr., Fullerton, Calif.

Second Team—Vince Carter, North Carolina, 6-6, Jr.; Mateen Cleaves, Michigan St., 6-2, So.; Pat Garrity, Notre Dame, 6-9, Sr.; Richard Hamilton, Connecticut, 6-6, So.; Ansu Sesay, Mississippi, 6-9, Sr.

1999

First Team—Elton Brand, Duke, 6-8, So., Peekskill, N.Y.; Mateen Cleaves, Michigan St., 6-2, Jr., Flint, Mich.; Richard Hamilton, Connecticut, 6-6, Jr., Coatesville, Pa.; Andre Miller, Utah, 6-2, Sr., Los Angeles; Jason Terry, Arizona, 6-2, Sr., Seattle.

Second Team—Evan Eschmeyer, Northwestern, 6-11, Sr.; Steve Francis, Maryland, 6-3, Jr.; Trajan Langdon, Duke, 6-3, Sr.; Chris Porter, Auburn, 6-7, Jr.; Wally Szczerbiak, Miami (Ohio), 6-8, Sr.

2000

First Team—Chris Carrawell, Duke, 6-6, Sr., St. Louis; Marcus Fizer, Iowa St., Jr., Arcadia, La.; A.J. Guyton, Indiana, 6-1, Sr., Peoria, Ill.; Kenyon Martin, Cincinnati, 6-9, Sr., Dallas, Tex.; Chris Mihm, Texas, 7-0, Jr., Austin, Tex.; Troy Murphy, Notre Dame, 6-10, So., Morristown, N.J.

Second Team—Courtney Alexander, Fresno St., 6-6, Sr.; Shane Battier, Duke, 6-8, Jr.; Mateen Cleaves, Michigan St., 6-2, Sr.; Scoonie Penn, Ohio St., 5-10, Sr.; Morrison Peterson, Michigan St., 6-6, Sr.; Stromile Swift, LSU, 6-9, So.

2001

First Team—Shane Battier, Duke, 6-8, Sr., Birmingham, Mich.; Joseph Forte, North Carolina, 6-4, So., Greenbelt, Md.; Casey Jacobsen, Stanford, 6-6, So., Glendora, Calif.; Troy Murphy, Notre Dame, 6-10, Jr., Morristown, N.J.; Jason Williams, Duke, 6-2, So., Plainfield, N.J.

Second Team—Troy Bell, Boston College, 6-1, So.; Michael Bradley, Villanova, 6-10, Jr.; Tayshaun Prince, Kentucky, 6-9, Jr.; Jason Richardson, Michigan St., 6-6, So.; Jamaal Tinsley, Iowa St., 6-3 Sr.

2002

First Team—Juan Dixon, Maryland, 6-3, Sr., Baltimore, Md.; Dan Dickau, Gonzaga, 6-1, Sr., Vancouver, Wash.; Drew Gooden, Kansas, 6-10, Jr., Richmond, Calif.; Steve Logan, Cincinnati, 6-1, Sr., Cleveland, Ohio; Jason Williams, Duke, 6-2, Jr., Plainfield, N.J.

Second Team—Sam Clancy, Southern California, 6-7, Sr.; Mike Dunleavy, Duke, 6-9, Jr.; Casey Jacobsen, Stanford, 6-6, Jr.; Jared Jeffries, Indiana, 6-10, So.; David West, Xavier, 6-8, Jr.

2003

First Team—Nick Collison, Kansas, 6-9, Sr., Iowa Falls, Iowa; T.J. Ford, Texas, 5-10, So., Houston, Tex.; Josh Howard, Wake Forest, 6-6, Sr., Winston-Salem, N.C.; Dwyane Wade, Marquette, 6-4, Jr., Robbins, Ill.; David West, Xavier, 6-9, Sr., Garner, N.C.

Second Team—Carmelo Anthony, Syracuse, 6-8, Fr.; Troy Bell, Boston College, 6-1, Sr.; Jason Gardner, Arizona, 5-10, Sr.; Kyle Korver, Creighton, 6-7, Sr.; Hollis Price, Oklahoma, 6-1, Sr.

Teams used for consensus selections:

Helms Foundation—1929-48
Converse Yearbook—1932-48
College Humor Magazine—1929-33, 1936
Christy Walsh Syndicate—1929-30
Literary Digest Magazine—1934
Madison Square Garden—1937-42
Omaha World Newspaper—1937
Newspaper Enterprises Assn.—1938, 1953-63
Colliers (Basketball Coaches)—1939, 1949-56
Pic Magazine—1942-44
Argosy Magazine—1945
True Magazine—1946-47
International News Service—1950-58
Look Magazine—1949-63
United Press International—1949-96
Sporting News—1943-46, 1997-2003
The Associated Press—1948-2003
National Association of Basketball Coaches—1957-2003
U.S. Basketball Writers Association—1960-2003

Consensus First-Team All-Americans By Team

ARIZONA
1988—Sean Elliott
1989—Sean Elliott
1995—Damon Stoudamire
1998—Mike Bibby
Miles Simon
1999—Jason Terry

ARKANSAS
1936—Ike Poole
1941—John Adams
1979—Sidney Moncrief

BOWLING GREEN
1945—Wyndol Gray

BRADLEY
1950—Paul Unruh
1951—Gene Melchiorre
1961—Chet Walker
1962—Chet Walker
1988—Hersey Hawkins

BRIGHAM YOUNG
1931—Elwood Romney
1981—Danny Ainge

CALIFORNIA
1929—Vern Corbin
1960—Darrall Imhoff
1994—Jason Kidd

CINCINNATI
1958—Oscar Robertson
1959—Oscar Robertson
1960—Oscar Robertson
1963—Ron Bonham
Tom Thacker
1997—Danny Fortson
2000—Kenyon Martin
2002—Steve Logan

COLUMBIA
1931—George Gregory
1957—Chet Forte

CONNECTICUT
1994—Donyell Marshall
1996—Ray Allen
1999—Richard Hamilton

CREIGHTON
1943—Ed Beisser

DARTMOUTH
1940—Gus Broberg
1941—Gus Broberg
1944—Audley Brindley

DAVIDSON
1965—Fred Hetzel

DENVER
1949—Vince Boryla

DEPAUL
1944—George Mikan
1945—George Mikan
1946—George Mikan
1980—Mark Aguirre
1981—Mark Aguirre
1982—Terry Cummings

DETROIT
1969—Spencer Haywood

DUKE
1952—Dick Groat
1963—Art Heyman
1967—Bob Verga
1979—Mike Gminski
1985—Johnny Dawkins
1986—Johnny Dawkins
1989—Danny Ferry
1992—Christian Laettner
1993—Bobby Hurley
1994—Grant Hill
1999—Elton Brand
2000—Chris Carrawell
2001—Shane Battier
Jason Williams
2002—Jason Williams

DUQUESNE
1955—Dick Ricketts
Si Green
1956—Si Green

FURMAN
1954—Frank Selvy

GEORGETOWN
1982—Eric Floyd
1983—Patrick Ewing
1984—Patrick Ewing
1985—Patrick Ewing
1987—Reggie Williams
1992—Alonzo Mourning
1996—Allen Iverson

GEORGIA TECH
1961—Roger Kaiser
1991—Kenny Anderson

GONZAGA
2002—Dan Dickau

HOLY CROSS
1950—Bob Cousy
1956—Tom Heinsohn

HOUSTON
1967—Elvin Hayes
1968—Elvin Hayes
1977—Otis Birdsong
1984—Akeem Olajuwon

ILLINOIS
1940—Bill Hapac
1942—Andrew Phillip
1943—Andrew Phillip
1945—Walton Kirk
1952—Rod Fletcher

ILLINOIS ST.
1973—Doug Collins

INDIANA
1930—Branch McCracken
1936—Vern Huffman
1939—Ernie Andres
1947—Ralph Hamilton
1954—Don Schlundt
1975—Scott May
1976—Scott May
Kent Benson
1977—Kent Benson
1981—Isiah Thomas
1986—Steve Alford
1987—Steve Alford
1993—Calbert Cheaney
2000—A.J. Guyton

INDIANA ST.
1978—Larry Bird
1979—Larry Bird

IOWA
1948—Murray Wier
1952—Chuck Darling

IOWA ST.
2000—Marcus Fizer

JACKSONVILLE
1971—Artis Gilmore

KANSAS
1938—Fred Pralle
1941—Howard Engleman
1943—Charles Black
1951—Clyde Lovellette
1952—Clyde Lovellette
1957—Wilt Chamberlain
1958—Wilt Chamberlain
1987—Danny Manning
1988—Danny Manning
1997—Raef LaFrentz
1998—Raef LaFrentz
Paul Pierce
2002—Drew Gooden
2003—Nick Collison

KANSAS ST.
1958—Bob Boozer
1959—Bob Boozer

KENTUCKY
1932—Forest Sale
1933—Forest Sale
1935—Leroy Edwards
1944—Robert Brannum
1947—Ralph Beard
Alex Groza
1948—Ralph Beard
1949—Ralph Beard
Alex Groza
1951—Bill Spivey
1952—Cliff Hagan
1954—Cliff Hagan
1959—Johnny Cox
1964—Cotton Nash

LA.-LAFAYETTE
1972—Dwight Lamar
1973—Dwight Lamar

LA SALLE
1953—Tom Gola
1954—Tom Gola
1955—Tom Gola
1980—Michael Brooks
1990—Lionel Simmons

LONG BEACH ST.
1972—Ed Ratleff
1973—Ed Ratleff

LONG ISLAND
1937—Jules Bender
1939—Irving Torgoff

LSU
1954—Bob Pettit
1968—Pete Maravich
1969—Pete Maravich
1970—Pete Maravich
1989—Chris Jackson
1990—Chris Jackson
1991—Shaquille O'Neal
1992—Shaquille O'Neal

LOUISVILLE
1957—Charlie Tyra
1967—Wes Unseld
1968—Wes Unseld
1980—Darrell Griffith
1989—Pervis Ellison
1994—Clifford Rozier

LOYOLA (ILL.)
1963—Jerry Harkness

MARQUETTE
1971—Dean Meminger
1972—Jim Chones
1978—Butch Lee
2003—Dwayne Wade

MARYLAND
1932—Louis Berger
1975—John Lucas
1976—John Lucas
1986—Len Bias
1995—Joe Smith
2002—Juan Dixon

MASSACHUSETTS
1996—Marcus Camby

MEMPHIS
1983—Keith Lee
1985—Keith Lee
1993—Anfernee Hardaway

MIAMI (FLA.)
1965—Rick Barry

1970—Dan Issel
1970—Dan Issel
1980—Kyle Macy
1986—Kenny Walker
1993—Jamal Mashburn
1996—Tony Delk
1997—Ron Mercer

MICHIGAN
1965—Cazzie Russell
1966—Cazzie Russell
1977—Rickey Green
1988—Gary Grant
1993—Chris Webber

MICHIGAN ST.
1979—Earvin Johnson
1995—Shawn Respert
1999—Mateen Cleaves

MINNESOTA
1948—Jim McIntyre
1955—Dick Garmaker
1978—Mychal Thompson

MISSISSIPPI ST.
1959—Bailey Howell

MONTANA ST.
1929—John Thompson
1930—John Thompson
        Frank Ward

NAVY
1933—Elliott Loughlin
1987—David Robinson

UNLV
1990—Larry Johnson
1991—Larry Johnson

NEW YORK U.
1946—Sid Tanenbaum
1947—Sid Tanenbaum
1963—Barry Kramer

NIAGARA
1969—Calvin Murphy
1970—Calvin Murphy

NORTH CAROLINA
1940—George Glamack
1941—George Glamack
1957—Lenny Rosenbluth
1968—Larry Miller
1972—Bob McAdoo
1977—Phil Ford
1978—Phil Ford
1982—James Worthy
1983—Michael Jordan
        Sam Perkins
1984—Michael Jordan
        Sam Perkins
1987—Kenny Smith
1988—J.R. Reid
1995—Jerry Stackhouse
1998—Antawn Jamison
2001—Joseph Forte

NORTH CAROLINA ST.
1951—Sam Ranzino
1956—Ron Shavlik
1973—David Thompson
1974—David Thompson
1975—David Thompson

NORTHWESTERN
1931—Joe Reiff
1933—Joe Reiff
1944—Otto Graham
1946—Max Norris

NOTRE DAME
1932—Ed Krause
1933—Ed Krause
1934—Ed Krause
1936—Paul Nowak
        John Moir
1937—Paul Nowak
        John Moir
1938—Paul Nowak
        John Moir
1944—Leo Klier
1945—William Hassett
1946—Leo Klier
1948—Kevin O'Shea
1971—Austin Carr
1974—John Shumate
1975—Adrian Dantley

1976—Adrian Dantley
2000—Troy Murphy
2001—Troy Murphy

OHIO ST.
1931—Wes Fesler
1939—Jimmy Hull
1950—Dick Schnittker
1956—Robin Freeman
1960—Jerry Lucas
1961—Jerry Lucas
1962—Jerry Lucas
1964—Gary Bradds
1991—Jim Jackson
1992—Jim Jackson

OKLAHOMA
1929—Thomas Churchill
1935—Bud Browning
1944—Alva Paine
1947—Gerald Tucker
1983—Wayman Tisdale
1984—Wayman Tisdale
1985—Wayman Tisdale
1989—Stacey King

OKLAHOMA ST.
1944—Robert Kurland
1945—Robert Kurland
1946—Robert Kurland

OREGON
1939—Urgel Wintermute
1940—John Dick

OREGON ST.
1981—Steve Johnson
1990—Gary Payton

PENNSYLVANIA
1929—Joe Schaaf
1945—Howard Dallmar
1953—Ernie Beck

PITTSBURGH
1929—Charley Hyatt
1930—Charley Hyatt
1933—Don Smith
1934—Claire Cribbs
1935—Claire Cribbs
1958—Don Hennon

PRINCETON
1964—Bill Bradley
1965—Bill Bradley

PROVIDENCE
1966—Jim Walker
1967—Jim Walker
1973—Ernie DiGregorio
1974—Marvin Barnes

PURDUE
1929—Charles Murphy
1930—Charles Murphy
        John Wooden
1931—John Wooden
1932—John Wooden
1934—Norman Cottom
1936—Bob Kessler
1937—Jewell Young
1938—Jewell Young
1961—Terry Dischinger
1962—Terry Dischinger
1966—Dave Schellhase
1969—Rick Mount
1970—Rick Mount
1980—Joe Barry Carroll
1994—Glenn Robinson

RHODE ISLAND
1939—Chet Jaworski

RICE
1942—Bob Kinney
1943—William Closs
1945—William Henry

RUTGERS
1967—Bob Lloyd

ST. BONAVENTURE
1960—Tom Stith
1961—Tom Stith
1970—Bob Lanier

ST. JOHN'S (N.Y.)
1943—Harry Boykoff
1985—Chris Mullin
1986—Walter Berry

ST. JOSEPH'S
1943—George Senesky

ST. LOUIS
1948—Ed Macauley
1949—Ed Macauley

SAN FRANCISCO
1955—Bill Russell
1956—Bill Russell
1982—Quintin Dailey

SEATTLE
1953—Johnny O'Brien
1958—Elgin Baylor

SETON HALL
1942—Robert Davies
1953—Walt Dukes

SOUTH CAROLINA
1972—Tom Riker

SOUTHERN CALIFORNIA
1933—Jerry Nemer
1935—Lee Guttero
1940—Ralph Vaughn
1950—Bill Sharman
1992—Harold Miner

SOUTHERN METHODIST
1957—Jim Krebs

STANFORD
1936—Hank Luisetti
1937—Hank Luisetti
1938—Hank Luisetti
2001—Casey Jacobsen

SYRACUSE
1966—Dave Bing
1990—Derrick Coleman
1991—Billy Owens

TEMPLE
1938—Meyer Bloom
1951—Bill Mlkvy
1958—Guy Rodgers

TENNESSEE
1977—Bernard King
1983—Dale Ellis

TEXAS
1935—Jack Gray
2000—Chris Mihm
2003—T.J. Ford

UCLA
1964—Walt Hazzard
1965—Gail Goodrich
1967—Lew Alcindor
1968—Lew Alcindor
1969—Lew Alcindor
1971—Sidney Wicks
1972—Bill Walton
        Henry Bibby
1973—Bill Walton
        Keith Wilkes
1974—Bill Walton
        Keith Wilkes
1975—Dave Meyers
1976—Richard Washington
1977—Marques Johnson
1978—David Greenwood
1979—David Greenwood
1995—Ed O'Bannon

UTAH
1936—Bill Kinner
1945—Arnold Ferrin
1962—Billy McGill
1997—Keith Van Horn

1999—Andre Miller

VANDERBILT
1966—Clyde Lee

VILLANOVA
1950—Paul Arizin
1996—Kerry Kittles

VIRGINIA
1981—Ralph Sampson
1982—Ralph Sampson
1983—Ralph Sampson

WAKE FOREST
1962—Len Chappell
1996—Tim Duncan
1997—Tim Duncan
2003—Josh Howard

WASHINGTON
1934—Hal Lee
1953—Bob Houbregs

WEST TEX. A&M
1942—Price Brookfield

WEST VIRGINIA
1957—Rod Hundley
1959—Jerry West
1960—Jerry West

WESTERN KY.
1967—Clem Haskins
1971—Jim McDaniels

WICHITA ST.
1964—Dave Stallworth
1985—Xavier McDaniel

WISCONSIN
1941—Gene Englund
1942—John Kotz

WYOMING
1932—Les Witte
1934—Les Witte
1943—Ken Sailors

XAVIER
2003—David West

YALE
1949—Tony Lavelli

Team Leaders In Consensus First-Team All-Americans

(Ranked on total number of selections)

Team	No.	Players
Kentucky	20	15
Notre Dame	19	10
UCLA	18	12
North Carolina	17	13
Purdue	16	10
Duke	15	12
Indiana	14	11
Kansas	14	10
Ohio St.	10	7
Cincinnati	8	6
Oklahoma	8	6
LSU	8	4
Georgetown	7	5
Arizona	6	5
Louisville	6	5
Maryland	6	5
Pittsburgh	6	4
DePaul	6	3
Southern California	5	5
Utah	5	5
Bradley	5	4
Illinois	5	4
La Salle	5	3
Michigan	5	3
North Carolina St.	5	3

Division I Academic All-Americans By Team

AIR FORCE
1968—Cliff Parsons
1970—Jim Cooper
1978—Tom Schneeberger

AMERICAN
1972—Kermit Washington
1973—Kermit Washington
1987—Patrick Witting

ARIZONA
1976—Bob Elliott
1977—Bob Elliott

ARIZONA ST.
1964—Art Becker
1999—Bobby Lazor

ARKANSAS
1978—Jim Counce

ARMY
1964—Mike Silliman

BALL ST.
2002—Patrick Jackson

BAYLOR
1996—Doug Brandt
1997—Doug Brandt

BELMONT
2002—Wes Burtner
2003—Adam Mark

BOSTON COLLEGE
1968—Terry Driscoll

BRIGHAM YOUNG
1980—Danny Ainge
1981—Danny Ainge
1983—Devin Durrant
1984—Devin Durrant
1987—Michael Smith
1988—Michael Smith
1989—Michael Smith
1990—Andy Toolson

BROWN
1986—Jim Turner

BUCKNELL
1999—Valter Karavanic

CALIFORNIA
1987—David Butler

CENTRAL MICH.
1993—Sander Scott

COL. OF CHARLESTON
2000—Jody Lumpkin
2001—Jody Lumpkin

CINCINNATI
1967—Mike Rolf

CLEVELAND ST.
1973—Pat Lyons

COLGATE
1997—Adonal Foyle

CONNECTICUT
1967—Wes Bialosuknia
2003—Emeka Okafor

CREIGHTON
1964—Paul Silas
1978—Rick Apke

DARTMOUTH
1984—Paul Anderson
1996—Seamus Lonergan

DAVIDSON
1988—Derek Rucker

DAYTON
1979—Jim Paxson
1981—Mike Kanieski
1982—Mike Kanieski

DENVER
2003—Brett Starkey

DEPAUL
1991—Stephen Howard
1992—Stephen Howard

DUKE
1963—Jay Buckley
1964—Jay Buckley
1971—Dick DeVenzio
1972—Gary Melchionni
1975—Bob Fleischer
1978—Mike Gminski
        Jim Spanarkel
1979—Mike Gminski
        Jim Spanarkel
1980—Mike Gminski
2000—Shane Battier
2001—Shane Battier

DUQUESNE
1969—Bill Zopf
1970—Bill Zopf

EVANSVILLE
1989—Scott Haffner
2003—Clint Cuffle

FAIRLEIGH DICKINSON
1978—John Jorgensen

FLORIDA
2002—Matt Bonner
2003—Matt Bonner

FORDHAM
1975—Darryl Brown

GEORGE WASHINGTON
1976—Pat Tallent
1986—Steve Frick

GEORGIA
1988—Alec Kessler
1989—Alec Kessler
1990—Alec Kessler

GEORGIA TECH
1964—Jim Caldwell
1969—Rich Yunkus
1970—Rich Yunkus
1971—Rich Yunkus
1998—Matt Harpring

GONZAGA
1984—Bryce McPhee
        John Stockton
1985—Bryce McPhee
1992—Jarrod Davis
1993—Jeff Brown
1994—Jeff Brown
2002—Dan Dickau

HARVARD
1985—Joe Carrabino
1987—Arne Duncan

HOLY CROSS
1969—Ed Siudut
1978—Ronnie Perry
1979—Ronnie Perry
1980—Ronnie Perry
1991—Jim Nairus

ILLINOIS
1968—Dave Scholz
1969—Dave Scholz
1971—Rich Howatt
1974—Rick Schmidt
1975—Rick Schmidt

ILLINOIS ST.
1973—Doug Collins

INDIANA
1964—Dick Van Arsdale
1965—Dick Van Arsdale
1965—Tom Van Arsdale
1973—John Ritter
1974—Steve Green
1975—Steve Green
1976—Kent Benson
1977—Kent Benson
1978—Wayne Radford
1982—Randy Wittman
1983—Randy Wittman
1985—Uwe Blab
1989—Joe Hillman

IOWA ST.
1995—Fred Hoiberg

JACKSONVILLE
1971—Vaughan Wedeking
1983—Maurice Roulhac

KANSAS
1971—Bud Stallworth
1974—Tom Kivisto
1977—Ken Koenigs
        Chris Barnthouse
1978—Ken Koenigs
1979—Darnell Valentine
1980—Darnell Valentine
1981—Darnell Valentine
1982—David Magley
1996—Jacque Vaughn
1997—Jerod Haase
        Jacque Vaughn
1999—Ryan Robertson

KANSAS ST.
1968—Earl Seyfert
1982—Tim Jankovich
        Ed Nealy

KENTUCKY
1966—Lou Dampier
1967—Lou Dampier
1969—Larry Conley
1970—Dan Issel
        Mike Pratt
1971—Mike Casey
1975—Bob Guyette
        Jimmy Dan Conner
1979—Kyle Macy

LA SALLE
1977—Tony DiLeo
1988—Tim Legler
1992—Jack Hurd

LAMAR
1999—Matt Sundblad

LEWIS
1989—Jamie Martin

LOUISVILLE
1976—Phil Bond

LOYOLA MARYMOUNT
1973—Steve Smith

MANHATTAN
1990—Peter Runge

MARQUETTE
1982—Marc Marotta
1983—Marc Marotta
1984—Marc Marotta

MARSHALL
1972—Mike D'Antoni
1973—Mike D'Antoni

MARYLAND
1972—Tom McMillen
1973—Tom McMillen
1974—Tom McMillen
1991—Matt Roe

MIAMI (OHIO)
1993—Craig Michaelis

MICHIGAN
1976—Steve Grote
1981—Marty Bodnar

MICHIGAN ST.
1970—Ralph Simpson
1979—Greg Kelser

MISSISSIPPI
1975—Dave Shepherd

MISSOURI
1983—Steve Stipanovich

MONTANA
1981—Craig Zanon
1985—Larry Krystkowiak
1986—Larry Krystkowiak

MURRAY ST.
1985—Mike Lahm

NEBRASKA
1984—John Matzke

UNLV
1983—Danny Tarkanian
1984—Danny Tarkanian

NEW MEXICO
1969—Ron Becker
1970—Ron Becker

NEW MEXICO ST.
2001—Eric Channing
2002—Eric Channing

NORTH CAROLINA
1965—Billy Cunningham
1970—Charlie Scott
1972—Dennis Wuycik
        Steve Previs
1976—Tommy LaGarde
1986—Steve Hale
1994—Eric Montross

UNC GREENSBORO
2001—Nathan Jameson

NORTH CAROLINA ST.
1984—Terry Gannon
1985—Terry Gannon
1995—Todd Fuller
1996—Todd Fuller

NORTHEASTERN
1977—David Caligaris
1978—David Caligaris

NORTHERN ILL.
1984—Tim Dillion
1998—T.J. Lux
2000—T.J. Lux

NORTHERN IOWA
1984—Randy Kraayenbrink

NORTHWESTERN
1967—Jim Burns
1980—Mike Campbell
1987—Shon Morris
1988—Shon Morris

NOTRE DAME
1967—Bob Arnzen
1968—Bob Arnzen
1969—Bob Arnzen
1974—Gary Novak
1979—Kelly Tripucka
1980—Rich Branning
1982—John Paxson
1983—John Paxson
1997—Pat Garrity
1998—Pat Garrity

OHIO
1971—Craig Love
1977—Steve Skaggs
1990—Dave Jamerson

OHIO ST.
1968—Bill Hosket

OKLAHOMA
1974—Alvan Adams
1975—Alvan Adams
1980—Terry Stotts

OKLAHOMA ST.
1964—Gary Hassmann
1969—Joe Smith

PACIFIC (CAL.)
1967—Keith Swagerty

PENNSYLVANIA
1972—Robert Morse

PENN ST.
1994—John Amaechi
1995—John Amaechi

PRINCETON
1965—Bill Bradley
1991—Kit Mueller

PURDUE
1965—Dave Schellhase
1966—Dave Schellhase
1972—Robert Ford
1981—Brian Walker
1982—Keith Edmonson
1983—Steve Reid
1985—Steve Reid

RADFORD
1998—Corey Reed

RICE
1994—Adam Peakes

ST. FRANCIS (PA.)
1990—Michael Iuzzolino
1991—Michael Iuzzolino

ST. LOUIS
1968—Rich Niemann
1994—Scott Highmark
1995—Scott Highmark

SAN DIEGO ST.
1976—Steve Copp

SANTA CLARA
1968—Dennis Awtrey
1969—Dennis Awtrey
1970—Dennis Awtrey

SIENA
1985—Doug Peotzch
1992—Bruce Schroeder

SOUTH CAROLINA
1970—John Roche
1971—John Roche

SOUTHERN ILL.
1976—Mike Glenn
1977—Mike Glenn

SOUTHERN METHODIST
1977—Pete Lodwick

STANFORD
2000—Mark Madsen

SYRACUSE
1981—Dan Schayes

TENNESSEE
1968—Bill Justus
1993—Lang Wiseman

TEXAS
1979—Jim Krivacs

TEXAS A&M
1964—Bill Robinette

UTEP
2000—Brandon Wolfram
2001—Brandon Wolfram

TULSA
1999—Michael Ruffin

UCLA
1967—Mike Warren
1969—Kenny Heitz
1971—Sidney Wicks
1972—Bill Walton
    Keith Wilkes
    Greg Lee

1973—Bill Walton
    Keith Wilkes
    Greg Lee
1974—Bill Walton
    Keith Wilkes
    Greg Lee
1975—Ralph Drollinger
1977—Marques Johnson
1979—Kiki Vandeweghe
1980—Kiki Vandeweghe
1995—George Zidek

UTAH
1970—Mike Newlin
1971—Mike Newlin
1977—Jeff Jonas
1998—Michael Doleac

UTAH ST.
1964—Gary Watts
1980—Dean Hunger
1982—Larry Bergeson
1996—Eric Franson

VANDERBILT
1975—Jeff Fosnes
1976—Jeff Fosnes
1993—Bruce Elder

VILLANOVA
1973—Tom Inglesby
1982—John Pinone
1983—John Pinone
1986—Harold Jensen
1987—Harold Jensen

VIRGINIA
1976—Wally Walker
1981—Jeff Lamp
    Lee Raker

VMI
1980—Andy Kolesar
1981—Andy Kolesar

WASHINGTON
1982—Dave Henley

WASHINGTON ST.
1989—Brian Quinnett

WEBER ST.
1985—Randy Worster

WICHITA ST.
1967—Jamie Thompson
1969—Ron Mendell

WILLIAM & MARY
1985—Keith Cieplicki

WISCONSIN
1974—Dan Anderson

WIS.-GREEN BAY
1992—Tony Bennett

Division I Player Of The Year

Season	United Press International	The Associated Press	U.S. Basketball Writers Assn.	Wooden Award	Nat'l Assn. of Basketball Coaches	Naismith Award	Frances Pomeroy Naismith Award
1955	Tom Gola La Salle						
1956	Bill Russell San Francisco						
1957	Chet Forte Columbia						
1958	Oscar Robertson Cincinnati						
1959	Oscar Robertson Cincinnati		Oscar Robertson Cincinnati				
1960	Oscar Robertson Cincinnati		Oscar Robertson Cincinnati				
1961	Jerry Lucas Ohio St.	Jerry Lucas Ohio St.	Jerry Lucas Ohio St.				
1962	Jerry Lucas Ohio St.	Jerry Lucas Ohio St.	Jerry Lucas Ohio St.				
1963	Art Heyman Duke	Art Heyman Duke	Art Heyman Duke				
1964	Gary Bradds Ohio St.	Gary Bradds Ohio St.	Walt Hazzard UCLA				
1965	Bill Bradley Princeton	Bill Bradley Princeton	Bill Bradley Princeton				
1966	Cazzie Russell Michigan	Cazzie Russell Michigan	Cazzie Russell Michigan				
1967	Lew Alcindor UCLA	Lew Alcindor UCLA	Lew Alcindor UCLA				
1968	Elvin Hayes Houston	Elvin Hayes Houston	Elvin Hayes Houston				
1969	Lew Alcindor UCLA	Lew Alcindor UCLA	Lew Alcindor UCLA			Lew Alcindor UCLA	Billy Keller Purdue
1970	Pete Maravich LSU	Pete Maravich LSU	Pete Maravich LSU			Pete Maravich LSU	John Rinka Kenyon

Season	United Press International	The Associated Press	U.S. Basketball Writers Assn.	Wooden Award	Nat'l Assn. of Basketball Coaches	Naismith Award	Frances Pomeroy Naismith Award
1971	Austin Carr Notre Dame	Austin Carr Notre Dame	Sidney Wicks UCLA			Austin Carr Notre Dame	Charlie Johnson California
1972	Bill Walton UCLA	Bill Walton UCLA	Bill Walton UCLA			Bill Walton UCLA	Scott Martin Oklahoma
1973	Bill Walton UCLA	Bill Walton UCLA	Bill Walton UCLA			Bill Walton UCLA	Bobby Sherwin Army
1974	Bill Walton UCLA	David Thompson North Carolina St.	Bill Walton UCLA			Bill Walton UCLA	Mike Robinson Michigan St.
1975	David Thompson North Carolina St.	David Thompson North Carolina St.	David Thompson North Carolina St.		David Thompson North Carolina St.	David Thompson North Carolina St.	Monty Towe North Carolina St.
1976	Scott May Indiana	Scott May Indiana	Adrian Dantley Notre Dame		Scott May Indiana	Scott May Indiana	Frank Algia St. John's (N.Y.)
1977	Marques Johnson UCLA	Marques Johnson UCLA	Marques Johnson UCLA	Marques Johnson UCLA	Marques Johnson UCLA	Marques Johnson UCLA	Jeff Jonas Utah
1978	Butch Lee Marquette	Butch Lee Marquette	Phil Ford North Carolina	Phil Ford North Carolina	Phil Ford North Carolina	Butch Lee Marquette	Mike Schib Susquehanna
1979	Larry Bird Indiana St.	Larry Bird Indiana St.	Larry Bird Indiana St.	Larry Bird Indiana St.	Larry Bird Indiana St.	Larry Bird Indiana St.	Alton Byrd Columbia
1980	Mark Aguirre DePaul	Mark Aguirre DePaul	Mark Aguirre DePaul	Darrell Griffith Louisville	Michael Brooks La Salle	Mark Aguirre DePaul	Jim Sweeney Boston College
1981	Ralph Sampson Virginia	Ralph Sampson Virginia	Ralph Sampson Virginia	Danny Ainge Brigham Young	Danny Ainge Brigham Young	Ralph Sampson Virginia	Terry Adolph West Tex. A&M
1982	Ralph Sampson Virginia	Ralph Sampson Virginia	Ralph Sampson Virginia	Ralph Sampson Virginia	Ralph Sampson Virginia	Ralph Sampson Virginia	Jack Moore Nebraska
1983	Ralph Sampson Virginia	Ralph Sampson Virginia	Ralph Sampson Virginia	Ralph Sampson Virginia	Ralph Sampson Virginia	Ralph Sampson Virginia	Ray McCallum Ball St.
1984	Michael Jordan North Carolina	Michael Jordan North Carolina	Michael Jordan North Carolina	Michael Jordan North Carolina	Michael Jordan North Carolina	Michael Jordan North Carolina	Ricky Stokes Virginia
1985	Chris Mullin St. John's (N.Y.)	Patrick Ewing Georgetown	Chris Mullin St. John's (N.Y.)	Chris Mullin St. John's (N.Y.)	Patrick Ewing Georgetown	Patrick Ewing Georgetown	Bubba Jennings Texas Tech
1986	Walter Berry St. John's (N.Y.)	Walter Berry St. John's (N.Y.)	Walter Berry St. John's (N.Y.)	Walter Berry St. John's (N.Y.)	Walter Berry St. John's (N.Y.)	Johnny Dawkins Duke	Jim Les Bradley
1987	David Robinson Navy	David Robinson Navy	David Robinson Navy	David Robinson Navy	David Robinson Navy	David Robinson Navy	Tyrone Bogues Wake Forest
1988	Hersey Hawkins Bradley	Hersey Hawkins Bradley	Hersey Hawkins Bradley	Danny Manning Kansas	Danny Manning Kansas	Danny Manning Kansas	Jerry Johnson Fla. Southern
1989	Danny Ferry Duke	Sean Elliott Arizona	Danny Ferry Duke	Sean Elliott Arizona	Sean Elliott Arizona	Danny Ferry Duke	Tim Hardaway UTEP
1990	Lionel Simmons La Salle	Lionel Simmons La Salle	Lionel Simmons La Salle	Lionel Simmons La Salle	Lionel Simmons La Salle	Lionel Simmons La Salle	Boo Harvey St. John's (N.Y.)
1991	Shaquille O'Neal LSU	Shaquille O'Neal LSU	Larry Johnson UNLV	Larry Johnson UNLV	Larry Johnson UNLV	Larry Johnson UNLV	Keith Jennings East Tenn. St.
1992	Jim Jackson Ohio St.	Christian Laettner Duke	Christian Laettner Duke	Christian Laettner Duke	Christian Laettner Duke	Christian Laettner Duke	Tony Bennett Wis.-Green Bay
1993	Calbert Cheaney Indiana	Calbert Cheaney Indiana	Calbert Cheaney Indiana	Calbert Cheaney Indiana	Calbert Cheaney Indiana	Calbert Cheaney Indiana	Sam Crawford New Mexico S.
1994	Glenn Robinson Purdue	Glenn Robinson Purdue	Glenn Robinson Purdue	Glenn Robinson Purdue	Glenn Robinson Purdue	Glenn Robinson Purdue	Greg Brown Evansville
1995	Joe Smith Maryland	Joe Smith Maryland	Ed O'Bannon UCLA	Ed O'Bannon UCLA	Shawn Respert Michigan St.	Joe Smith Maryland	Tyus Edney UCLA
1996	Marcus Camby Massachusetts	Marcus Camby Massachusetts	Marcus Camby Massachusetts	Marcus Camby Massachusetts	Marcus Camby Massachusetts	Marcus Camby Massachusetts	Eddie Benton Vermont
1997		Tim Duncan Wake Forest	Tim Duncan Wake Forest	Tim Duncan Wake Forest	Tim Duncan Wake Forest	Tim Duncan Wake Forest	Kent McCausland Iowa
1998		Antawn Jamison North Carolina	Antawn Jamison North Carolina	Antawn Jamison North Carolina	Antawn Jamison North Carolina	Antawn Jamison North Carolina	Earl Boykins Eastern Mich.
1999		Elton Brand Duke	Elton Brand Duke	Elton Brand Duke	Elton Brand Duke	Elton Brand Duke	Shawnta Rogers George Washington
2000		Kenyon Martin Cincinnati	Kenyon Martin Cincinnati	Kenyon Martin Cincinnati	Kenyon Martin Cincinnati	Kenyon Martin Cincinnati	Scoonie Penn Ohio St.
2001		Shane Battier Duke	Shane Battier Duke	Shane Battier Duke	Jason Williams Duke	Shane Battier Duke	Rashad Phillips Detriot
2002		Jason Williams Duke	Jason Williams Duke	Jason Williams Duke	Jason Williams Duke Drew Gooden Kansas	Jason Williams Duke	Steve Logan Cincinnati
2003		David West Xavier	David West Xavier	T.J. Ford Texas	Nick Collison Kansas	T.J. Ford Texas	Jason Gardner Arizona

Note: The Francis Pomeroy Naismith Award is given to the top player who is less than 6 feet tall.

Basketball Times Player of the Year: 1982-Ralph Sampson, Virginia; 1983-Ralph Sampson, Virginia; 1984-Akeem Olajuwon, Houston; 1985-Patrick Ewing, Georgetown; 1986-Scott Skiles, Michigan St.; 1987-Kenny Smith, North Carolina; 1988-Hersey Hawkins, Bradley; 1989-Sean Elliot, Arizona; 1990-Derrick Coleman, Syracuse; 1991-Larry Johnson, UNLV; 1992-Christian Laettner, Duke; 1993-Jamaal Mashburn, Kentucky; 1994-Glenn Robinson, Purdue; 1995-Ed O'Bannon, UCLA; 1996-Marcus Camby, Massachusetts; 1997-Tim Duncan, Wake Forest; 1998-Antawn Jamison, North Carolina; 1999-Jason Terry, Arizona; 2000-Kenyon Martin, Cincinnati; 2001-Shane Battier, Duke; 2002-Jason Williams, Duke; 2003-David West, Xavier.

Defensive Player of the Year: 1987-Tommy Amaker, Duke; 1988-Billy King, Duke; 1989-Stacey Augmon, UNLV; 1990-Stacey Augmon, UNLV; 1991-Stacey Augmon, UNLV; 1992-Alonzo Mourning, Georgetown; 1993-Grant Hill, Duke; 1994-Jim McIlvaine, Marquette; 1995-Tim Duncan, Wake Forest; 1996-Tim Duncan, Wake Forest; 1997-Tim Duncan, Wake Forest; 1998-Steve Wojciechowski, Duke; 1999-Shane Battier, Duke; 2000-Kenyon Martin, Cincinatti & Shane Battier, Duke; 2001-Shane Battier, Duke; 2002-John Linehan, Providence; 2003-Emeka Okafor, Connecticut.

Division II & III Player Of The Year

The Divisions II and III Player of the Year are chosen by the National Association of Basketball Coaches (NABC).

	Division II	**Division III**
1983	Earl Jones, Dist. of Columbia	Leroy Witherspoon, Potsdam St.
1984	Earl Jones, Dist. of Columbia	Leroy Witherspoon, Potsdam St.
1985	Charles Oakley, Virginia Union	Tim Casey, Wittenberg
1986	Todd Linder, Tampa	Dick Hempy, Otterbein
1987	Ralph Talley, Norfolk St.	Brendan Mitchell, Potsdam St.
1988	Jerry Johnson, Fla. Southern	Scott Tedder, Ohio Wesleyan
1989	Kris Kearney, Fla. Southern	Greg Grant, TCNJ
1990	A.J. English, Virginia Union	Matt Hancock, Colby
1991	Corey Crowder, Ky. Wesleyan	Brad Baldridge, Wittenberg
1992	Eric Manuel, Oklahoma City	Andre Foreman, Salisbury
1993	Alex Wright, Central Okla.	Steve Hondred, Calvin
1994	Derrick Johnson, Virginia Union	Scott Fitch, Geneseo St.
1995	Stan Gourard, Southern Ind.	D'Artis Jones, Ohio Northern
1996	Stan Gourard, Southern Ind.	David Benter, Hanover
1997	Kebu Stewart, Cal St. Bakersfield	Bryan Crabtree, Ill. Wesleyan
1998	Joe Newton, Central Okla.	Mike Nogelo, Williams
1999	Antonio Garica, Ky. Wesleyan	Merrill Berunson, Wis.-Platteville
2000	Ajumu Gaines, Charleston (W.Va.)	Aaron Winkle, Calvin
2001	Colin Ducharme, Longwood	Horace Jenkins, Wm. Paterson
2002	Ronald Murray, Shaw	Jeff Gibbs, Otterbein
2003	Marlon Parmer, Ky. Wesleyan	Bryan Nelson, Williams

Divisions II and III First-Team All-Americans By Team

Current Division I member denoted by (*). Non-NCAA member denoted by (†).

ABILENE CHRISTIAN
1968—John Godfrey

ADELPHI
2001—Ryan McCormack

AKRON*
1967—Bill Turner
1972—Len Paul

ALA.-HUNTSVILLE
1978—Tony Vann

ALAS. ANCHORAGE
1987—Jesse Jackson
1987—Hansi Gnad
1989—Michael Johnson
1990—Todd Fisher

ALBANY ST. (GA.)
1975—Major Jones

ALCORN ST.*
1976—John McGill

ALFRED
2001—Devon Downing

AMERICAN*
1960—Willie Jones

AMERICAN INT'L
1969—Greg Hill
1970—Greg Hill
2002—Malik Moore

AMHERST
1970—Dave Auten
1971—James Rehnquist
2003—Steve Zieja

ARKANSAS ST.*
1965—Jerry Rook

ARMSTRONG ATLANTIC
1975—Ike Williams

ASSUMPTION
1970—Jake Jones
1971—Jake Jones
1973—Mike Boylan
1974—John Grochowalski
1975—John Grochowalski
1976—Bill Wurm

AUGUSTANA (ILL.)
1973—John Laing

BABSON
1992—Jim Pierrakos

BENTLEY
1974—Brian Hammel
1975—Brian Hammel

BISHOP
1983—Shannon Lilly

BRIDGEPORT
1969—Gary Baum
1976—Lee Hollerbach
1985—Manute Bol
1991—Lambert Shell
1992—Lambert Shell
1995—Lamont Jones

BRIDGEWATER (VA.)
1995—Dan Rush
2002—Kyle Williford

BYU-HAWAII
2000—David Evans

BROCKPORT ST.
2002—Mike Medbury

BRYANT
1981—Ernie DeWitt

CALIF. (PA.)
1993—Ray Gutierrez

UC RIVERSIDE*
1989—Maurice Pullum

CAL ST. BAKERSFIELD
1996—Kebu Stewart
1997—Kebu Stewart

CALVIN
1993—Steve Honderd
2000—Aaron Winkle

CAMERON
1974—Jerry Davenport

CARLETON
1993—Gerrick Monroe

CARTHAGE
2002—Antoine McDaniel

CENTENARY (LA.)*
1957—Milt Williams

CENTRAL CONN. ST.*
1969—Howie Dickenman

UCF*
1979—Bo Clark
1980—Bo Clark

CENTRAL MO. ST.
1981—Bill Fennelly
1985—Ron Nunnelly
1991—Armando Becker

CENTRAL OKLA.
1993—Alex Wright
1997—Tyrone Hopkins
1998—Joe Newton

CENTRAL WASHINGTON
1999—Eddie Robinson

CENTRAL WASHINGTON
1967—Mel Cox

CHARLESTON (W.VA.)
2000—Ajamu Gaines

CHATTANOOGA*
1977—Wayne Golden

CHEYNEY
1979—Andrew Fields
1981—George Melton
1982—George Melton

CHICAGO
2003—Derek Reich

CHRIS. NEWPORT
1991—Lamont Strothers
2001—Antoine Sinclair

CLAREMONT-M-S
1992—Chris Greene

CLARION
1994—Kwame Morton

CLARK (MASS.)
1980—Kevin Clark
1981—Kevin Clark
1988—Kermit Sharp

COLBY
1977—Paul Harvey
1978—Paul Harvey
1989—Matt Hancock
1990—Matt Hancock

CORTLAND ST.
2000—Tom Williams

DAVIS & ELKINS
1959—Paul Wilcox

DELTA ST.
1969—Sammy Little
DEPAUW
1987—David Galle
DIST. COLUMBIA
1982—Earl Jones
1983—Earl Jones
Michael Britt
1984—Earl Jones
EASTERN MICH.*
1971—Ken McIntosh
1972—George Gervin
EDINBORO
1996—Tyrone Mason
2002—Kenny Tate
ELMHURST
2001—Ryan Knuppel
EMORY
1990—Tim Garrett
EVANSVILLE*
1959—Hugh Ahlering
1960—Ed Smallwood
1965—Jerry Sloan
Larry Humes
1966—Larry Humes
FLA. SOUTHERN
1981—John Ebeling
1982—John Ebeling
1988—Jerry Johnson
Kris Kearney
1989—Kris Kearney
1990—Donolly Tyrell
FORT HAYS ST.
1997—Alonzo Goldston
FRAMINGHAM ST.
1984—Mark Van Valkenburg
FRANKLIN
1999—Jason Sibley
FRANK. & MARSH.
1992—Will Lasky
1996—Jeremiah Henry
2000—Alex Kraft
GANNON
1985—Butch Warner
1998—Troy Nesmith
GENESEO ST.
1994—Scott Fitch
GEORGETOWN (KY.)†
1964—Cecil Tuttle
GRAMBLING*
1961—Charles Hardnett
1962—Charles Hardnett
1964—Willis Reed
1966—Johnny Comeaux
1976—Larry Wright
GRAND CANYON
1976—Bayard Forest
GRAND VALLEY ST.
1997—Joe Modderman
GUILFORD
1968—Bob Kauffman
1975—Lloyd Free
HAMILTON
1977—Cedric Oliver
1978—Cedric Oliver
1979—Cedric Oliver
1987—John Cavanaugh
1998—Mike Schantz
1999—Michael Schantz
2003—Joe Finley
HAMPDEN-SYDNEY
1992—Russell Turner
2000—T.J. Grimes
HANOVER
1996—David Benter
HARTFORD*
1979—Mark Noon

HARTWICK
1977—Dana Gahres
1983—Tim O'Brien
HAVERFORD
1977—Dick Vioth
HENDERSON ST.
2002—Niki Arinze
HOPE
1984—Chip Henry
1998—Joel Holstege
ILLINOIS ST.*
1968—Jerry McGreal
ILL. WESLEYAN
1977—Jack Sikma
1989—Jeff Kuehl
1995—Chris Simich
1997—Bryan Crabtree
1998—Brent Niebrugge
2000—Korey Coon
INDIANA (PA.)
1995—Derrick Freeman
IUPUI*
1996—Carlos Knox
INDIANA ST.*
1968—Jerry Newsome
ITHACA
2000—Pat Britton
JACKSON ST.*
1974—Eugene Short
1975—Eugene Short
1977—Purvis Short
JACKSONVILLE*
1962—Roger Strickland
1963—Roger Strickland
JOHNSON SMITH
2001—Wiyle Perry
KEAN
1993—Fred Drains
KEENE ST.
2001—Chris Coates
KENTUCKY ST.
1971—Travis Grant
Elmore Smith
1972—Travis Grant
1975—Gerald Cunningham
1977—Gerald Cunningham
KY. WESLEYAN
1957—Mason Cope
1967—Sam Smith
1968—Dallas Thornton
1969—George Tinsley
1984—Rod Drake
Dwight Higgs
1988—J.B. Brown
1990—Corey Crowder
1991—Corey Crowder
1995—Willis Cheaney
1998—Antonio Garcia
1999—Antonio Garcia
Dana Williams
2000—LeRoy John
2001—Lorico Duncan
2002—Ronald Evans
KENYON
1969—John Rinka
1970—John Rinka
1979—Scott Rogers
1980—Scott Rogers
LEBANON VALLEY
1995—Mike Rhodes
1997—Andy Panko
1998—Andy Panko
1999—Andy Panko
LEWIS & CLARK†
1963—Jim Boutin
1964—Jim Boutin
1999—Andy Panko

LINCOLN (MO.)
1978—Harold Robertson
LIPSCOMB*
1988—Phillip Hutcheson
1989—Phillip Hutcheson
1990—Phillip Hutcheson
1992—John Pierce
LONG ISLAND*
1968—Luther Green
Larry Newbold
LONGWOOD
1984—Jerome Kersey
2001—Colin Ducharme
LOUISIANA COLLEGE†
1979—Paul Poe
LOUISIANA TECH*
1973—Mike Green
LA.-LAFAYETTE*
1965—Dean Church
1970—Marvin Winkler
1971—Dwight Lamar
MAINE*
1961—Tom Chappelle
MASS.-DARTMOUTH
1993—Steve Haynes
MASS.-LOWELL
1989—Leo Parent
MERCHANT MARINE
1990—Kevin D'Arcy
MERRIMACK
1977—Ed Murphy
1978—Ed Murphy
Dana Skinner
1983—Joe Dickson
METHODIST
1997—Jason Childers
MICHIGAN TECH
2003—Matt Cameron
MINN. DULUTH
1977—Bob Bone
MISERICORDIA
2003—Willie Chandler
MO.-ST. LOUIS
1977—Bob Bone
MONTCLAIR ST.
1999—Anthony Peoples
MORGAN ST.
1974—Marvin Webster
1975—Marvin Webster
1999—Tim West
MT. ST. MARY'S*
1957—Jack Sullivan
MOUNT UNION
1997—Aaron Shipp
MUHLENBERG
2002—Mark Lesko
MUSKINGUM
1992—Andy Moore
NEB.-OMAHA
1992—Phil Cartwright
NEB. WESLEYAN
1986—Dana Janssen
NEW HAVEN
1988—Herb Watkins
N.J. INST. OF TECH.
1996—Clarence Pierce
TCNJ
1988—Greg Grant
1989—Greg Grant
NEW JERSEY CITY
1979—Brett Wyatt
NEW ORLEANS*
1971—Xavier Webster
NYIT
1980—Kelvin Hicks

NICHOLLS ST.*
1978—Larry Wilson
NORFOLK ST.
1979—Ken Evans
1984—David Pope
1987—Ralph Talley
1995—Corey Williams
NORTH ALA.
1980—Otis Boddie
N.C. WESLEYAN
1999—Marquis McDougald
NORTH DAKOTA
1966—Phil Jackson
1967—Phil Jackson
1991—Dave Vonesh
1993—Scott Guldseth
2003—Jerome Beasley
NORTH DAKOTA ST.
1960—Marvin Bachmeier
NORTH PARK
1979—Mike Harper
1980—Mike Harper
1981—Mike Thomas
NORTHEASTERN ST.
2003—Jon Shepherd
NORTHERN MICH.
1987—Bill Harris
2000—Cory Brathol
NORTHWOOD
1973—Fred Smile
OHIO NORTHERN
1982—Stan Mories
1995—D'Artis Jones
2001—Kris Oberdick
OHIO WESLEYAN
1987—Scott Tedder
1988—Scott Tedder
OKLAHOMA CITY†
1992—Eric Manuel
OLD DOMINION*
1972—Dave Twardzik
1974—Joel Copeland
1976—Wilson Washington
OTTERBEIN
1966—Don Carlos
1982—Ron Stewart
1983—Ron Stewart
1985—Dick Hempy
1986—Dick Hempy
1987—Dick Hempy
1991—James Bradley
1994—Nick Gutman
1999—Kevin Weakley
2002—Jeff Gibbs
PACIFIC LUTHERAN
1959—Chuck Curtis
PFEIFFER
1992—Tony Smith
PHILADELPHIA U.
1976—Emory Sammons
1977—Emory Sammons
PLYMOUTH ST.
1994—Moses Jean-Pierre
1999—Adam DeChristopher
POTSDAM ST.
1980—Derrick Rowland
1981—Derrick Rowland
1982—Maurice Woods
1983—Leroy Witherspoon
1984—Leroy Witherspoon
1986—Roosevelt Bullock
1986—Brendan Mitchell
1987—Brendan Mitchell
1988—Steve Babiarz
1989—Steve Babiarz
PRAIRIE VIEW*
1962—Zelmo Beaty
PUGET SOUND
1979—Joe Leonard

QUEENS (N.C.)
1998—Soce Faye

RAMAPO
2003—Charles Ransom

RANDOLPH-MACON
1983—Bryan Vacca
2003—Jared Mills

RICHARD STOCKTON
1997—Carl Cochrane

ROANOKE
1972—Hal Johnston
1973—Jay Piccola
1974—Jay Piccola
1983—Gerald Holmes
1984—Reggie Thomas
1985—Reggie Thomas
1994—Hilliary Scott

ROCHESTER
1991—Chris Fite
1992—Chris Fite

ROCHESTER INST.
1996—Craig Jones
1997—Craig Jones

ROWAN
1998—Rob Scott

RUTGERS-CAMDEN
2002—Brian Turner

SACRED HEART*
1972—Ed Czernota
1978—Hector Olivencia
        Andre Means
1982—Keith Bennett
1983—Keith Bennett
1986—Roger Younger
1993—Darrin Robinson

ST. CLOUD ST.
1957—Vern Baggenstoss
1986—Kevin Catron

ST. JOSEPH'S (IND.)
1960—Bobby Williams

ST. MICHAEL'S
1965—Richie Tarrant

ST. NORBERT
1963—Mike Wisneski

SALEM (W.VA.)†
1976—Archie Talley

SALEM ST.
2000—Tishaun Jenkins

SALISBURY
1991—Andre Foreman
1992—Andre Foreman

SAM HOUSTON ST.*
1973—James Lister

SCRANTON
1963—Bill Witaconis
1977—Irvin Johnson
1978—Irvin Johnson

1984—Bill Bessoir
1985—Bill Bessoir
1993—Matt Cusano

SEWANEE
1998—Ryan Harrigan

SHAW
2002—Ronald Murray

SHENANDOAH
1996—Phil Dixon

SLIPPERY ROCK
1991—Myron Brown

SOUTH DAKOTA
1958—Jim Daniels

SOUTH DAKOTA ST.
1961—Don Jacobsen
1964—Tom Black

SOUTHEASTERN OKLA.
1957—Jim Spivey

SOUTHERN ILL.*
1966—George McNeil
1967—Walt Frazier

SOUTHERN IND.
1995—Stan Gouard
1996—Stan Gouard

SOUTHERN N.H.
2003—Sotirios Karapostolou

SPRINGFIELD
1970—Dennis Clark
1986—Ivan Olivares

STEPHEN F. AUSTIN*
1970—Surry Oliver

STETSON*
1970—Ernie Killum

STEUBENVILLE†
1958—Jim Smith

STONEHILL
1979—Bill Zolga
1980—Bill Zolga
1982—Bob Reitz

STONY BROOK*
1979—Earl Keith

SUSQUEHANNA
1986—Dan Harnum

TAMPA
1985—Todd Linder
1986—Todd Linder
1987—Todd Linder
1994—DeCarlo Deveaux

TENNESSEE ST.*
1958—Dick Barnett
1959—Dick Barnett
1971—Ted McClain
1972—Lloyd Neal
1974—Leonard Robinson

TEX.-PAN AMERICAN*
1964—Lucious Jackson
1968—Otto Moore

TEXAS SOUTHERN*
1958—Bennie Swain
1977—Alonzo Bradley

TEXAS ST.*
1959—Charles Sharp
1960—Charles Sharp

THOMAS MORE
1996—Rick Hughes

TRINITY (TEX.)
1968—Larry Jeffries
1969—Larry Jeffries
2002—Colin Tabb

TROY ST.*
1993—Terry McCord

TUFTS
1995—Chris McMahon

UPSALA
1981—Steve Keenan
1982—Steve Keenan

VIRGINIA UNION
1985—Charles Oakley
1990—A.J. English
1994—Derrick Johnson
        Warren Peebles
1996—Ben Wallace
1998—Marquise Newbie

WABASH
1982—Pete Metzelaars

WASHBURN
1994—Clarence Tyson
1997—Dan Buie
2001—Ewan Auguste

WASH. & LEE
1978—Pat Dennis

WAYNE ST. (NEB.)
1999—Tyler Johnson

WEST CHESTER
2003—Ramzee Stanton

WEST GA.
1974—Clarence Walker

WESTERN CARO.*
1968—Henry Logan

WESTMINSTER (PA.)†
1962—Ron Galbreath

WESTMINSTER (UTAH)†
1969—Ken Hall

WHEATON (ILL.)
1958—Mel Peterson

WIDENER
1978—Dennis James
1988—Lou Stevens

WILKES
2001—Dave Jannuzzi

WM. PATERSON
2000—Horace Jenkins
2001—Horace Jenkins

WILLIAMS
1961—Bob Mahland
1962—Bob Mahland
1996—Mike Nogelo
1997—Mike Nogelo
1998—Mike Nogelo

WINSTON-SALEM
1967—Earl Monroe
1980—Reginald Gaines

WIS.-EAU CLAIRE
1972—Mike Ratliff

WIS.-GREEN BAY*
1978—Tom Anderson
1979—Ron Ripley

WIS.-OSHKOSH
1996—Dennis Ruedinger
2002—Tim Dworak

WIS.-PARKSIDE
1976—Gary Cole

WIS.-PLATTEVILLE
1992—T.J. Van Wie
1998—Ben Hoffmann
1999—Merrill Brunson

WIS.-RIVER FALLS
2003—Richard Melzer

WIS.-STEVENS POINT
1985—Terry Porter
2000—Brant Bailey

WIS.-SUPERIOR
2001—Vince Thomas

WIS.-WHITEWATER
1990—Ricky Spicer
1994—Ty Evans
1997—James Stewart

WOOSTER
2003—Bryan Nelson

WITTENBERG
1961—George Fisher
1963—Al Thrasher
1980—Brian Agler
1981—Tyrone Curtis
1985—Tim Casey
1989—Steve Allison
1990—Brad Baldridge
1991—Brad Baldridge

WRIGHT ST.
1981—Rodney Benson
1986—Mark Vest

XAVIER (LA.)†
1973—Bruce Seals

YOUNGSTOWN ST.*
1977—Jeff Covington
1978—Jeff Covington

Divisions II and III Academic All-Americans By Team

Teams used for selections:
AP Little All-America—1957-79
NABC College Division—1967-76
NABC Divisions II, III—1977-2003

ABILENE CHRISTIAN
1999—Jared Mosley

AKRON
1972—Wil Schwarzinger

ALBANY (N.Y.)
1988—John Carmello

ALBION
1979—John Nibert

ALDERSON-BROADDUS
2002—Kevyn McBride

ARKANSAS TECH
1990—Gray Townsend

1994—David Bevis
1995—David Bevis

ASHLAND
1967—Jim Basista
1970—Jay Franson

ASSUMPTION
1967—George Ridick

AUGUSTANA (ILL.)
1973—Bruce Hamming
1974—Bruce Hamming
1975—Bruce Hamming
1979—Glen Heiden

AUGUSTANA (S.D.)
1974—John Ritterbusch
1975—John Ritterbusch

BALDWIN-WALLACE
1985—Bob Scelza

BARRINGTON
1982—Shawn Smith

BATES
1983—Herb Taylor
1984—Herb Taylor

BEMIDJI ST.
1976—Steve Vogel
1977—Steve Vogel
1978—Steve Vogel
2003—Royce Bryan

BENTLEY
1980—Joe Betley

BETHEL (MINN.)
1994—Jason Mekelburg

BLOOMSBURG
1978—Steve Bright

BRANDEIS
1978—John Martin

BRIAR CLIFF
1989—Chad Neubrand

BRIDGEWATER (VA.)
1985—Sean O'Connell

BRYAN
1981—Dean Ropp

C.W. POST
1973—Ed Fields

CALIF. (PA.)
1993—Raymond Guttierez

CAL LUTHERAN
1983—Bill Burgess

UC DAVIS
1970—Tom Cupps
1983—Preston Neumayr

UC RIVERSIDE
1971—Kirby Gordon

CALVIN
1992—Steve Honderd
1993—Steve Honderd
1994—Chris Knoester

CAPITAL
1973—Charles Gashill

CARNEGIE MELLON
1973—Mike Wegener
1979—Larry Hufnagel
1980—Larry Hufnagel

CASE RESERVE
1996—Jim Fox
1997—Jim Fox

CASTLETON ST.
1985—Bryan DeLoatch

CATHOLIC
1997—Jeremy Borys

UCF
1982—Jimmie Farrell

CENTRAL MICH.
1967—John Berends
1971—Mike Hackett

CENTRAL ST. (OHIO)
1971—Sterling Quant

CHADRON ST.
1992—Josh Robinson

CLAREMONT-M-S
2002—Bob Donlan

COAST GUARD
1971—Ken Bicknell

COLORADO MINES
1991—Daniel McKeon
1991—Hank Prey

COLORADO ST.-PUEBLO
1972—Jim Von Loh

CORNELL COLLEGE
1974—Randy Kuhlman

1977—Dick Grant
1978—Robert Wisco
1979—Robert Wisco
1987—Jeff Fleming

DAVID LIPSCOMB
1989—Phil Hutcheson
1990—Phil Hutcheson
1992—Jerry Meyer

DELTA ST.
1972—Larry MaGee

DENISON
1967—Bill Druckemiller
1970—Charles Claggett
1987—Kevin Locke
1988—Kevin Locke
1997—Casey Chroust

DENVER
1987—Joe Fisher

DEPAUW
1970—Richard Tharp
1973—Gordon Pittenger
1987—David Galle

DICKINSON
1971—Lloyd Bonner
1981—David Freysinger
1982—David Freysinger

DREXEL
1967—Joe Hertrich

ELMHURST
2001—Ryan Knuppel

ELON
1988—Brian Branson
1988—Steve Page
1998—Christopher Kiger

EMBRY-RIDDLE
2001—Kyle Mas

EMORY
2000—Neil Bhutta

FORT HAYS ST.
1978—Mike Pauls

FORT LEWIS
1998—Ryan Ostrom

FRANK. & MARSH.
2000—Jerome Maiatico

GETTYSBURG
1975—Jeffrey Clark

GRINNELL
1976—John Haigh
1994—Steve Diekmann
1995—Steve Diekmann
1996—Ed Brands

GROVE CITY
1979—Mike Donahoe
1984—Curt Silverling
1985—Curt Silverling

GUST. ADOLPHUS
1983—Mark Hanson

HAMILTON
1978—John Klauberg

HAMLINE
1986—Paul Westling
1989—John Banovetz

HAMPDEN-SYDNEY
1992—Russell Turner

HARDING
1985—Kenneth Collins
1986—Kenneth Collins

HOWARD PAYNE
1973—Garland Bullock
1974—Garland Bullock

ILL. WESLEYAN
1972—Dean Gravlin
1973—Dean Gravlin
1975—Jack Sikma
Bob Spear
1976—Jack Sikma

Bob Spear
1977—Jack Sikma
Bob Spear
1979—Al Black
1981—Greg Yess
1982—Greg Yess
1987—Brian Coderre
1999—Korey Coon
2000—Korey Coon

INCARNATE WORD
1993—Randy Henderson

JAMES MADISON
1976—Sherman Dillard

JAMESTOWN
1980—Pete Anderson
1981—Pete Anderson

JOHN CARROLL
1999—Mark Heidorf

JOHNS HOPKINS
1991—Andy Enfield

KENYON
1970—John Rinka
1977—Tim Appleton
1985—Chris Coe Russell

LAGRANGE
1980—Todd Whitsitt

LIBERTY
1980—Karl Hess

LUTHER
1981—Doug Kintzinger
1982—Doug Kintzinger

MACMURRAY
1970—Tom Peters

MARIAN
2002—Scott Jaeger

MARIETTA
1982—Rick Clark
1983—Rick Clark

MARYVILLE (MO.)
2003—Kevin Bartow

MASS.-LOWELL
1970—Alfred Spinell
1984—John Paganetti

MIT
1980—Ray Nagem
1991—David Tomlinson

MCDANIEL
1983—Douglas Pinto
1985—David Malin

MCGILL
1983—Willie Hinz

MCNEESE ST.
1972—David Wallace

MERRIMACK
1983—Joseph Dickson
1984—Joseph Dickson

MICHIGAN TECH
1981—Russ VanDuine
1985—Wayne Helmila
2003—J.T. Luginski

MILLIKIN
1977—Roy Mosser
Dale Wills
1978—Gregg Finigan
1979—Rich Rames
Gary Jackson
1980—Gary Jackson
1981—Gary Jackson
1989—Brian Horst

MILWAUKEE ENGR.
1983—Jeffrey Brezovar

MINN. ST. MANKATO
1997—David Kruse

MO.-ROLLA
1984—Todd Wentz

MO.-ST. LOUIS
1975—Bobby Bone
1976—Bobby Bone
1977—Bobby Bone

MONMOUTH (ILL.)
1990—S. Juan Mitchell

MOORHEAD ST.
1996—Brett Beeson

MOUNT UNION
1971—Jim Howell

MUHLENBERG
1979—Greg Campisi
1981—Dan Barletta

NEB.-KEARNEY
1974—Tom Kropp
1975—Tom Kropp

NEB.-OMAHA
1981—Jim Gregory

NEB. WESLEYAN
1984—Kevin Cook
1986—Kevin Cook
1995—Justin Wilkins
1997—Kipp Kissinger
1998—Kipp Kissinger

UNC ASHEVILLE
1974—Randy Pallas

NORTHERN COLO.
1967—Dennis Colson

OBERLIN
1971—Vic Guerrieri
1972—Vic Guerrieri

OHIO NORTHERN
2001—Kris Oberdick

OHIO WESLEYAN
1990—Mark Slayman
1998—John Camillus

OLD DOMINION
1974—Gray Eubank
1975—Gray Eubank

OTTERBEIN
1980—Mike Cochran

PACIFIC LUTHERAN
1967—Doug Leeland

POINT PARK
1986—Richard Condo

RIPON
1999—Bret Van Dyken

ROCHESTER
1984—Joe Augustine

ROCKFORD
1976—John Morrissey
1977—John Morrissey

ROSE-HULMAN
2002—Christopher Unton

ST. JOHN'S (MINN.)
1995—Joe Deignan

ST. JOSEPH'S (IND.)
1975—James Thordsen

ST. LEO
1977—Ralph Nelson

ST. THOMAS (FLA.)
1976—Arthur Collins
1977—Mike LaPrete

ST. THOMAS (MINN.)
1967—Dan Hansard
1978—Terry Fleming

SCRANTON
1983—Michael Banas
1984—Michael Banas
1985—Dan Polacheck
1993—Matt Cusano

SHIPPENSBURG
1979—John Whitmer
1981—Brian Cozzens
1982—Brian Cozzens

SIMPSON
2002—Jesse Harris
2003—Jesse Harris

SLIPPERY ROCK
1971—Robert Wiegand
1979—Mike Hardy
1983—John Samsa
1995—Mark Metzka

SOUTH DAKOTA
1970—Bill Hamer
1975—Rick Nissen
1976—Rick Nissen
1978—Jeff Nannen
1980—Jeff Nannen
1985—Rob Swanhorst

SOUTH DAKOTA ST.
1971—Jim Higgins
1972—Jim Higgins

SOUTHERN N.H.
2003—Brian Larrabee

SUSQUEHANNA
1986—Donald Harnum
1994—Tres Wolf

TENNESSEE TEMPLE
1977—Dan Smith

1978—Dan Smith

TRINITY (CONN.)
1996—Keith Wolff

TRUMAN
1984—Mark Campbell
1999—Jason Reinberg
2000—Jason Reinberg

UNION (N.Y.)
1970—Jim Tedisco

VIRGINIA TECH
1968—Ted Ware

WABASH
1973—Joe Haklin

WARTBURG
1971—Dave Platte
1972—Dave Platte
1974—Fred Waldstein
1990—Dan Nettleton
1991—Dan Nettleton

WASHBURN
2001—Ewan Auguste

WASHINGTON (MO.)
1988—Paul Jackson

WASH. & JEFF.
1980—David Damico

WENTWORTH INST.
2000—Kevin Hanlon

WESLEYAN (CONN.)
1972—James Akin
1974—Rich Fairbrother
1982—Steven Maizes

WESTERN ST.
1970—Michael Adams
1973—Rod Smith

WESTMINSTER (PA.)
1967—John Fontanella

WILKES
2001—Dave Jannuzzi

WM. PATERSON
2001—Horace Jenkins

WIS.-EAU CLAIRE
1972—Steven Johnson
1975—Ken Kaiser
1976—Ken Kaiser

WIS.-GREEN BAY
1974—Tom Jones

WIS.-OSHKOSH
1998—Joe Imhoff

WIS.-PLATTEVILLE
1992—T.J. Van Wie
1993—T.J. Van Wie

WIS.-SUPERIOR
2001—Vince Thomas

WITTENBERG
1967—Jim Appleby

WPI
1996—James Naughton

NCAA Postgraduate Scholarship Winners By Team

ABILENE CHRISTIAN
1999—Jared Mosley

AIR FORCE
1970—James Cooper
1973—Thomas Blase
1974—Richard Nickelson
1978—Thomas Schneeberger
1992—Brent Roberts
1993—Brad Boyer

UAB
1999—Damon Cobb

ALBANY (N.Y.)
1988—John Carmello

ALLEGHENY
1976—Robert Del Greco

ALLENTOWN
1985—George Bilicic Jr.

ALMA
1976—Stuart TenHoor

AMERICAN
1973—Kermit Washington
1998—Nathan Smith

ARIZONA
1988—Steve Kerr
1991—Matt Muehlebach

ARIZONA ST.
1965—Dennis Dairman

ARKANSAS ST.
1975—J.H. Williams

ARMY
1965—John Ritch III
1972—Edward Mueller
1973—Robert Sherwin Jr.
1985—Randall Cozzens
1994—David Ardayfio

ASSUMPTION
1975—Paul Brennan
1977—William Wurm

AUBURN
1976—Gary Redding

AUGUSTANA (ILL.)
1975—Bruce Hamming

AUGUSTANA (S.D.)
1975—Neil Klutman
1992—Jason Garrow

BALL ST.
1989—Richard Hall

BATES
1984—Herbert Taylor

BAYLOR
1997—Doug Brandt

BELLARMINE
1992—Tom Schurfranz
2001—Ronald Brooks

BENTLEY
1980—Joseph Betley

BOSTON COLLEGE
1967—William Wolters
1970—Thomas Veronneau
1972—James Phelan
1980—James Sweeney
1995—Marc Molinsky

BOWDOIN
1966—Howard Pease

BOWLING GREEN
1965—Robert Dwors

BRANDEIS
1972—Donald Fishman
1978—John Martin

BRIDGEWATER (VA.)
1970—Frederick Wampler

BRIGHAM YOUNG
1966—Richard Nemelka
1983—Gregory Kite
1984—Devin Durrant
1987—Brent Stephenson
1989—Michael Smith
1990—Andy Toolson
1991—Steve Schreiner

BYU-HAWAII
2000—David Evans

BROWN
1972—Arnold Berman
1997—Jade Newburn

BUENA VISTA
2000—Landon Roth

BUTLER
1977—Wayne Burris
1991—John Karaffa

CALIFORNIA
1987—David Butler

UC DAVIS
1970—Thomas Cupps
1977—Mark Ford
1983—Preston Neumayr
1991—Matt Cordova

UC IRVINE
1975—Carl Baker

UC RIVERSIDE
1975—Randy Burnett

UC SAN DIEGO
1997—Matt Aune

UC SANTA BARB.
1973—Robert Schachter
1993—Michael Meyer

CALIF. (PA.)
1984—William Belko

CAL POLY POMONA
1978—Thomas Ispas

CAL ST. DOM. HILLS
1987—John Nojima

CAL ST. STANISLAUS
1983—Richard Thompson

CALTECH
1966—Alden Holford
1967—James Pearson
1968—James Stanley
1971—Thomas Heinz

CALVIN
1977—Mark Veenstra
1993—Steve Honderd

CARLETON
1969—Thomas Weaver
1982—James Tolf
1999—Joshua Wilhelm

CARNEGIE MELLON
1980—Lawrence Hufnagel

CASE RESERVE
1971—Mark Estes

CATHOLIC
1972—Joseph Good
1997—Jeremy Borys

CENTRAL (IOWA)
1973—Dana Snoap
1980—Jeffrey Verhoef

CENTRAL MICH.
1993—Sander Scott

CENTRE
1985—Thomas Cowens

CHAPMAN
1970—Anthony Mason

CHICAGO
1969—Dennis Waldon

1974—Gerald Clark
1985—Keith Libert

CINCINNATI
1977—Gary Yoder

CLAREMONT-M-S
1972—Jeffrey Naslund

CLARION
1973—Joseph Sebestyen

CLEMSON
1967—James Sutherland
1980—Robert Conrad Jr.
1999—Tom Wideman

COE
1965—Gary Schlarbaum

COLBY
1972—Matthew Zweig

COLGATE
1999—Ben Wandtke

COLORADO
1966—Charles Gardner
1985—Alex Stivrins

COLORADO MINES
1991—Hank Prey
1994—Todd Kenyon

COLORADO ST.
1986—Richard Strong Jr.

COLUMBIA
1968—William Ames

CORNELL COLLEGE
1967—David Crow
1979—Robert Wisco
1981—Eric Reitan
1987—Jefferson Fleming
1994—Abram Tubbs
      Chad Reed

CREIGHTON
1971—Dennis Bresnahan Jr.
1978—Richard Apke

DARTMOUTH
1968—Joseph Colgan
1976—William Healey
1984—Paul Anderson
1997—Sea Lonergan

DAVIDSON
1969—Wayne Huckel
1983—Clifford Tribus

DAYTON
1979—Jim Paxson
1985—Larry Schellenberg

DELAWARE
1978—Brian Downie

DENISON
1968—William Druckemiller Jr.
1988—Kevin Locke
1993—Kevin Frye
1997—Casey Chroust
1999—John Rusnak

DENVER
1968—Richard Callahan
2000—Tyler Church

DEPAUL
1992—Stephen Howard

DEPAUW
1969—Thomas McCormick
1970—Richard Tharp
1973—Gordon Pittenger
1986—Phillip Wendel

DICKINSON
1982—David Freysinger
1987—Michael Erdos

DREW
1989—Joe Novak

DUKE
1975—Robert Fleischer

EASTERN WASH.
2000—Ryan Hansen

ELON
1998—Christopher Kiger

EMORY
1993—Kevin Felner
1999—Lewis Satterwhite
2000—Neil Bhutta

EVANSVILLE
1989—Scott Haffner

FAIRLEIGH DICKINSON
1978—John Jorgensen
1993—Kevin Conway

FLORIDA
1970—Andrew Owens Jr.
1973—Anthony Miller
2003—Matthew Bonner

FLA. SOUTHERN
1969—Richard Lewis
1979—Larry Tucker
1989—Kris Kearney

FORT LEWIS
1998—Ryan Ostrom

FRANKLIN
1994—David Dunkle

FRANK. & MARSH.
2000—Jerome Maiatico

GEORGE WASHINGTON
1976—Pat Tallent
1987—Steve Frick

GEORGETOWN
1968—Bruce Stinebrickner

GEORGIA
1965—McCarthy Crenshaw Jr.
1987—Chad Kessler
1990—Alec Kessler

GEORGIA TECH
1998—Matt Harping

GONZAGA
1992—Jarrod Davis
1994—Jeff Brown
1996—Jon Kinloch

GRAMBLING
1983—William Hobdy

GRINNELL
1968—James Schwartz
1976—John Haigh

HAMILTON
1969—Brooks McCuen
1978—John Klauberg

HAMLINE
1989—John Banovetz

HAMPDEN-SYDNEY
1983—Christopher Kelly
1999—David Hobbs

HARVARD
1979—Glenn Fine

HAVERFORD
1966—Hunter Rawlings III
1967—Michael Bratman
1977—Richard Voith

HIRAM
1977—Edwin Niehaus

HOLY CROSS
1969—Edward Siudut
1977—William Doran Jr.
1979—John O'Connor
1980—Ronnie Perry

HOUSTON BAPTIST
1985—Albert Almanza

IDAHO
1967—Michael Wicks

IDAHO ST.
1993—Corey Bruce

ILLINOIS
1971—Rich Howat

ILLINOIS ST.
1988—Jeffrey Harris
1998—Dan Muller

ILLINOIS TECH
1969—Eric Wilson

ILL. WESLEYAN
1988—Brian Coderre
2000—Korey Coon

INDIANA
1975—Steven Green
1982—Randy Wittman
1985—Uwe Blab

INDIANA ST.
1972—Danny Bush
1981—Steven Reed

IOWA
1966—Dennis Pauling
1976—G. Scott Thompson
1981—Steven Waite
1998—Jess Settles

IOWA ST.
1989—Marc Urquhart

ITHACA
1973—David Hollowell

JACKSONVILLE
1971—Vaughn Wedeking
1983—Maurice Roulhac
1986—Thomas Terrell

JAMES MADISON
1978—Sherman Dillard

JAMESTOWN
1981—Peter Anderson

JOHNS HOPKINS
1965—Robert Smith
1975—Andrew Schreiber
1991—Andy Enfield
1992—Jay Gangemi
1997—Matt Gorman
1998—Greg Roehrig

KALAMAZOO
1965—Thomas Nicolai
1973—James Van Sweden
1979—David Dame
1982—John Schelske
1996—Jeremy Cole

KANSAS
1974—Thomas Kivisto
1978—Kenneth Koenigs
1997—Jerod Haase
1999—Ryan Robertson
      T.J. Pugh

KANSAS ST.
1968—Earl Seyfert

KENT ST.
1994—Rodney Koch
2002—Demetric Shaw

KENTUCKY
1975—Robert Guyette
1996—Mark Pope

KENYON
1995—Jamie Harless

KING'S (PA.)
1981—James Shea

KNOX
1965—James Jepson

LA SALLE
1992—John Hurd

LA VERNE
2001—Kevin Gustafson

LAFAYETTE
1972—Joseph Mottola
1980—Robert Falconiero
1991—Bruce Stankavage
1994—Keith Brazzo

LAKE FOREST
1968—Frederick Broda

LAMAR
1970—James Nicholson
1999—Matt Sundblad

LEWIS
1989—James Martin

LONG BEACH ST.
1990—Tyrone Mitchell

LORAS
1971—Patrick Lillis
1972—John Buri

LOUISVILLE
1977—Phillip Bond

LOYOLA MARYMOUNT
1973—Stephen Smith

LOYOLA (MD.)
1979—John Vogt

LUTHER
1968—David Mueller
1974—Timothy O'Neill
1982—Douglas Kintzinger
1986—Scott Sawyer

MAINE
1990—Dean Smith

MARQUETTE
1984—Marc Marotta

MARSHALL
1973—Michael D'Antoni
1997—John Brannen

MARYLAND
1974—Tom McMillen
1981—Gregory Manning
1991—Matt Roe

MASS.-LOWELL
1970—Alfred Spinell Jr.

MARYVILLE (MO.)
2003—Kevin Bartow

MIT
1966—John Mazola
1967—Robert Hardt
1968—David Jansson
1971—Bruce Wheeler
1991—David Tomlinson

MCDANIEL
1983—Douglas Pinto

MCNEESE ST.
1978—John Rudd

MIAMI (OHIO)
1982—George Sweigert

MICHIGAN
1981—Martin Bodnar
1993—Rob Pelinka

MICHIGAN TECH
1978—Michael Trewhella
1981—Russell Van Duine

MIDDLEBURY
1975—David Pentkowski
1982—Paul Righi

MINNESOTA
1970—Michael Regenfuss

MINN. MORRIS
1997—Todd Hanson

MINN. ST. MANKATO
1997—David Kruse

MISSISSIPPI ST.
1976—Richard Knarr

MISSOURI
1972—Gregory Flaker

MO.-ROLLA
1977—Ross Klie

MO.-ST. LOUIS
1977—Robert Bone

MONMOUTH (ILL.)
1992—Steve Swanson

MONTANA
1968—Gregory Hanson

1981—Craig Zanon
1986—Larry Krystkowiak
1992—Daren Engellant
1995—Jeremy Lake

MONTANA ST.
1988—Ray Willis Jr.
1996—Nico Harrison

MOORHEAD ST.
1980—Kevin Mulder
1996—Brett Beeson

MORNINGSIDE
1986—John Kelzenberg

MT. ST. MARY'S
1976—Richard Kidwell

MUHLENBERG
1976—Glenn Salo

MUSKINGUM
1974—Gary Ferber
1983—Myron Dulkoski Jr.

NAVY
1979—Kevin Sinnett
1984—Clifford Maurer
1995—Wesley Cooper

NEBRASKA
1972—Alan Nissen
1986—John Matzke
1987—William Jackman
1991—Beau Reid

NEB.-OMAHA
1981—James Gregory

NEB. WESLEYAN
1995—Justin Wilkins
1998—Kipp Kissinger

UNLV
1984—Danny Tarkanian

NEW MEXICO
1973—Breck Roberts

NEW YORK POLY
1968—Charles Privalsky

NEW YORK U.
1996—Greg Belinfanti

NORTH CAROLINA
1966—Robert Bennett Jr.
1974—John O'Donnell
1977—Bruce Buckley
1986—Steve Hale
1995—Pearce Landry

UNC GREENSBORO
2001—Nathan Jameson

UNC WILMINGTON
1997—Bill Mayew

NORTH CAROLINA ST.
1966—Peter Coker
1985—Terrence Gannon
1996—Todd Fuller

NORTH DAKOTA ST.
1989—Joe Regnier
2000—Jason Retzlaff

NORTHEASTERN
1978—David Caligaris

NORTHERN ARIZ.
1979—Troy Hudson

NORTHERN COLO.
1968—Dennis Colson
1990—Toby Moser

NORTHERN ILL.
1984—Timothy Dillion
2000—A.J. Lux

NORTHERN IOWA
1979—Michael Kemp

NORTHERN KY.
2000—Kevin Listerman

NORTHWEST MO. ST.
1989—Robert Sundell

NORTHWESTERN
1973—Richard Sund

1980—Michael Campbell
1990—Walker Lambiotte
1994—Kevin Rankin

NORTHWOOD
1999—Jeremy Piggott

NOTRE DAME
1969—Robert Arnzen
1974—Gary Novak
1983—John Paxson
1998—Pat Garrity

OAKLAND
1990—Brian Gregory

OBERLIN
1972—Victor Guerrieri

OCCIDENTAL
1973—Douglas McAdam
1981—Miles Glidden
1996—John Pike

OGLETHORPE
1992—David Fischer

OHIO
1967—John Hamilton
1968—Wayne Young
1979—Steven Skaggs

OHIO ST.
1968—Wilmer Hosket

OKLAHOMA
1972—Scott Martin
1975—Robert Pritchard
1980—Terry Stotts
1988—Dave Sieger

OKLAHOMA CITY
1967—Gary Gray

OKLAHOMA ST.
1965—Gary Hassmann
1969—Joseph Smith

OLD DOMINION
1975—Gray Eubank

OLIVET
1999—Jeff Bell

OREGON
1971—William Drozdiak
1988—Keith Balderston
2000—Adrian Smith

OREGON ST.
1967—Edward Fredenburg

PACIFIC (CAL.)
1967—Bruce Parsons Jr.
1979—Terence Carney
1986—Richard Anema
1992—Delano Demps

PENNSYLVANIA
1972—Robert Morse

PENN ST.
1982—Michael Edelman
1995—John Amaechi

PITTSBURGH
1976—Thomas Richards
1986—Joseph David
1992—Darren Morningstar

POMONA-PITZER
1966—Gordon Schloming
1970—Douglas Covey
1986—David Di Cesaris

PORTLAND ST.
1966—John Nelson

PRINCETON
1969—Christopher Thomforde
1997—Sydney Johnson

PRINCIPIA
1979—William Kelsey

PUGET SOUND
1974—Richard Brown

PURDUE
1971—George Faerber

1981—Brian Walker

RADFORD
1998—Corey Reed

REDLANDS
1990—Robert Stone

REGIS (COLO.)
1988—John Nilles
1994—Pat Holloway

RENSSELAER
1967—Kurt Hollasch

RHODES
1994—Greg Gonda
1996—Scott Brown

RICE
1995—Adam Peakes
2001—Michael Wilks

RICHMOND
1986—John Davis Jr.

RIPON
1978—Ludwig Wurtz
1999—Bret Van Dyken

ROANOKE
2000—Paris Butler

ROLLINS
1993—David Wolf

RUTGERS
1985—Stephen Perry

ST. ANSELM
1980—Sean Canning

ST. FRANCIS (PA.)
1997—Eric Shaner

ST. JOHN FISHER
1997—Eric Shaner

ST. JOHN'S (N.Y.)
1981—Frank Gilroy

ST. JOSEPH'S (IND.)
1975—James Thordsen

ST. JOSEPH'S
1966—Charles McKenna

ST. LAWRENCE
1969—Philip McWhorter

ST. LEO
1981—Kevin McDonald

ST. LOUIS
1967—John Kilo
1995—Scott Highmark

ST. MARY'S (CAL.)
1980—Calvin Wood
1999—Eric Schraeder

ST. NORBERT
1987—Andris Arians

ST. OLAF
1966—Eric Grimsrud
1971—David Finholt

ST. THOMAS (MINN.)
1967—Daniel Hansard
1995—John Tauer

SAN DIEGO
1978—Michael Strode

SAN DIEGO ST.
1976—Steven Copp

SAN FRANCISCO
1990—Joel DeBortoli

SANTA CLARA
1994—Peter Eisenrich

SCRANTON
1974—Joseph Cantafio
1984—Michael Banas
1985—Daniel Polacheck
1988—John Andrejko
1993—Matt Cusano

SEATTLE PACIFIC
1997—Geoffrey Ping

SETON HALL
1969—John Suminski

SEWANEE
1967—Thomas Ward Jr.
1976—Henry Hoffman Jr.
1982—James Sherman
1998—Ryan Harrigan

SIENA
1992—Bruce Schroeder

SIMPSON
1980—John Hines
1995—David Otte
2003—Jesse Harris

SLIPPERY ROCK
1975—Clyde Long

SOUTH ALA.
1998—Toby Madison

SOUTH DAKOTA
1976—Rick Nissen
2001—Jeremy Kudera

SOUTH DAKOTA ST.
1973—David Thomas
1997—Jason Sempsrott
2000—Casey Estling

SOUTH FLA.
1992—Radenko Dobras

SOUTHERN CALIFORNIA
1974—Daniel Anderson
1975—John Lambert

SOUTHERN ILL.
1977—Michael Glenn

SOUTHERN METHODIST
1977—Peter Lodwick

SOUTHERN UTAH
1991—Peter Johnson
1993—Richard Barton

SOUTHWEST MO. ST.
1971—Tillman Williams

STANFORD
1976—Edward Schweitzer
1980—Kimberly Belton
2000—Mark Madsen

SUSQUEHANNA
1986—Donald Harnum
1994—Lloyd Wolf

SWARTHMORE
1965—Cavin Wright
1987—Michael Dell

SYRACUSE
1981—Dan Schayes
1998—Marius Janulis

TENNESSEE
1993—Lang Wiseman

TENN.-MARTIN
1976—Michael Baker

TEXAS
1974—Harry Larrabee
1979—Jim Krivacs

TEXAS A&M
1970—James Heitmann

TEXAS-ARLINGTON
1980—Paul Renfor

TCU
1970—Jeffrey Harp
1981—Larry Frevert

TEX.-PAN AMERICAN
1976—Jesus Guerra Jr.

TEXAS TECH
1985—Brooks Jennings Jr.
1986—Tobin Doda

TOLEDO
1967—William Backensto
1980—Timothy Selgo

TRANSYLVANIA
1972—Robert Jobe Jr.
1980—Lawrence Kopczyk

TRINITY (CONN.)
1971—Howard Greenblatt
1996—Keith Wolff

TRINITY (TEX.)
1975—Phillip Miller

TRUMAN
2000—Jason Reinberg

TUFTS
1981—Scott Brown

TULSA
1999—Michael Ruffin

UCLA
1969—Kenneth Heitz
1971—George Schofield
1980—Kiki Vandeweghe
1995—George Zidek

UTAH
1968—Lyndon MacKay
1971—Michael Newlin
1977—Jeffrey Jonas
1998—Drew Hansen

UTAH ST.
1996—Eric Franson

VANDERBILT
1976—Jeffrey Fosnes

VILLANOVA
1983—John Pinone

VIRGINIA
1973—James Hobgood

VMI
1969—John Mitchell
1971—Jan Essenburg
1977—William Bynum III
1981—Andrew Kolesar
1987—Gay Elmore Jr.
1996—Bobby Prince

VIRGINIA TECH
1972—Robert McNeer

WABASH
1976—Len Fulkerson

WAKE FOREST
1969—Jerry Montgomery
1994—Marcus Blucas
1996—Rusty LaRue

WARTBURG
1972—David Platte
1974—Fred Waldstein
1991—Dan Nettleton

WASHINGTON
1970—Vincent Stone
1974—Raymond Price
1987—Rodney Ripley

WASHINGTON (MD.)
1979—Joseph Wilson
1990—Tim Keehan
1998—Bradd Burkhart

WASHINGTON (MO.)
1991—Jed Bargen

WASH. & JEFF.
1970—Terry Evans
1981—David Damico

WASH. & LEE
1983—Brian Hanson
1984—John Graves

WEBER ST.
1980—Mark Mattos
1985—Kent Hagan

WESLEYAN (CONN.)
1973—Brad Rogers
1974—Richard Fairbrother
1977—Steve Malinowski
1982—Steven Maizes
1985—Gregory Porydzy

WESTERN CARO.
1982—Gregory Dennis
1987—Richard Rogers

WESTERN ILL.
1984—Todd Hutcheson

WESTMINSTER (PA.)
1967—John Fontanella

WHEATON (ILL.)
1995—Nathan Frank

WHITTIER
1977—Rodney Snook

WICHITA ST.
1969—Ronald Mendell
1991—Paul Guffrovich

WIDENER
1983—Louis DeRogatis

WILLIAM & MARY
1985—Keith Cieplicki

WILLIAMS
1965—Edgar Coolidge III
1986—Timothy Walsh

WISCONSIN
1987—Rodney Ripley

WIS.-OSHKOSH
1998—Joe Imhoff

WIS.-PLATTEVILLE
1993—T.J. Van Wie

WIS.-STEVENS POINT
1983—John Mack

WITTENBERG
1984—Jay Ferguson
1996—Scott Schwartz

WOOSTER
1995—Scott Meech

WRIGHT ST.
1978—Alan McGee

XAVIER
1975—Peter Accetta
8191—Gary Massa

YALE
1967—Richard Johnson
1968—Robert McCallum Jr.

Florida's Matt Bonner was a 2003 Postgraduate Scholarship winner.

Richard Melzer of Wisconsin-River Falls was a Division II first-team All-American in 2003.

Coaching Records

All-Division Coaching Records

Some of the won-lost records included in this coaches section have been adjusted because of action by the NCAA Council or the NCAA Executive Committee to forfeit particular regular-season games or vacate particular NCAA Tournament games.

Coaches With At Least 500 Career Wins

(This list includes all coaches who have won at least 500 games regardless of classification with a minimum 10 head coaching seasons at NCAA schools.)

Coach (Alma Mater), Teams Coached, Tenure	Yrs.	Won	Lost	Pct.
1. Dean Smith (Kansas 1953) North Carolina 1962-97	36	879	254	.776
2. Adolph Rupp (Kansas 1923) Kentucky 1931-52, 54-72...	41	876	190	.822
3. Jim Phelan (La Salle 1951) Mt. St. Mary's 1955-2003.....	49	830	524	.613
4. Clarence Gaines (Morgan St. 1945) Winston-Salem 1947-93	47	828	447	.649
5. Jerry Johnson (Fayetteville St. 1951) LeMoyne-Owen 1959-2003*	45	812	400	.670
6. Bob Knight (Ohio St. 1962) Army 1966-71, Indiana 72-2000, Texas Tech 02-03*	37	809	311	.722
7. Lefty Driesell (Duke 1954) Davidson 1961-69, Maryland 70-86, James Madison 89-97, Georgia St. 98-2003	42	800	409	.662
8. Don Meyer (Northern Colo. 1967) Hamline 1973-75, Lipscomb 76-99, Northern St. 2000-03*	31	769	262	.746
9. Henry Iba [Westminster (Mo.) 1928] Northwest Mo. St. 1930-33, Colorado St. 34, Oklahoma St. 35-70	41	764	339	.693
10. Lou Henson (New Mexico St. 1955) Hardin-Simmons 1963-66, Illinois 76-96, New Mexico St. 67-75, 98-2003*	39	762	386	.664
11. Ed Diddle (Centre 1921) Western Ky. 1923-64	42	759	302	.715
12. Phog Allen (Kansas 1906) Baker 1906-08, Haskell 09, Central Mo. St. 13-19, Kansas 08-09, 20-56....	48	746	264	.739
12. Herb Magee (Philadelphia U. 1963) Philadelphia U. 1968-2003*	36	746	289	.721
14. Jerry Tarkanian (Fresno St. 1955) Long Beach St. 1969-73, UNLV 74-92, Fresno St. 96-2002	31	729	201	.784
15. Norm Stewart (Missouri 1956) Northern Iowa 1962-67, Missouri 68-99	38	728	374	.661
16. Eddie Sutton (Oklahoma St. 1958) Creighton 1970-74, Arkansas 75-85, Kentucky 86-89, Oklahoma St. 91-2003*	33	724	288	.715
16. Ray Meyer (Notre Dame 1938) DePaul 1943-84	42	724	354	.672
18. Don Haskins (Oklahoma St. 1952) UTEP 1962-99	38	719	353	.671
19. Dick Sauers (Slippery Rock 1951) Albany (N.Y.) 1956-87, 89-97	41	702	330	.680
20. John Chaney (Bethune-Cookman 1955) Cheyney 1973-82, Temple 83-2003*	31	693	269	.720
21. Lute Olson (Augsburg 1956) Long Beach St. 1974, Iowa 75-83, Arizona 84-2003*	30	690	240	.742
22. Denny Crum (UCLA 1958) Louisville 1972-01	30	675	295	.696
23. Dennis Bridges (Ill. Wesleyan 1961) Ill. Wesleyan 1966-01	36	666	320	.675
24. John Wooden (Purdue 1932) Indiana St. 1947-48, UCLA 49-75	29	664	162	.804
25. Mike Krzyzewski (Army 1969) Army 1976-80, Duke 81-2003*	28	663	234	.739
26. Ralph Miller (Kansas 1942) Wichita St. 1952-64, Iowa 65-70, Oregon St. 71-89	38	657	382	.632
27. Marv Harshman (Pacific Lutheran 1942) Pacific Lutheran 1946-58, Washington St. 59-71, Washington 72-85	40	654	449	.593
28. Jim Boeheim (Syracuse 1966) Syracuse 1977-2003*......	27	653	226	.743
29. Glenn Robinson (West Chester 1967) Frank. & Marsh. 1972-2003*	32	648	231	.737
30. Jim Calhoun (American Int'l 1968) Northeastern 1973-86, Connecticut 87-2003*	31	647	296	.686
30. Gene Bartow (Truman 1953) Central Mo. St. 1962-64, Valparaiso 65-70, Memphis 71-74, Illinois 75, UCLA 76-77, UAB 79-96	34	647	353	.647
32. Ed Adams (Tuskegee 1934) N.C. Central 1935-36, Tuskegee 37-49, Texas Southern 50-58	24	643	153	.808
33. John Lance (Pittsburg St. 1918) Southwestern Okla. 1919-22, Pittsburg St. 23-34, 36-63	44	632	340	.650
34. Ken Anderson (Wis.-Eau Claire 1955) Wis.-Eau Claire 1969-95	27	631	152	.806
35. Cam Henderson (Salem 1917) Muskingum 1920-23, Davis & Elkins 24-35, Marshall 36-55	36	630	243	.722
35. Ed Messbarger (Northwest Mo. St. 1956) Benedictine Hts. 1958-60, Dallas 61-63, St. Mary's (Tex.) 64-78, Angelo St. 79-98	41	630	518	.549
37. Norm Sloan (North Carolina St. 1951) Presbyterian 1952-55, Citadel 57-60, Florida 61-66, North Carolina St. 67-80, Florida 81-89	37	624	393	.614
38. Dean Nicholson (Central Wash. 1950) Central Wash. 1965-90	26	620	199	.757
39. Jim Smith (Marquette 1956) St. John's (Minn.) 1965-2003*	39	618	411	.601
40. Jerry Steele (Wake Forest 1961) Guilford 1963-70, High Point 73-2003	39	609	486	.556
41. Hugh Durham (Florida St. 1959) Florida St. 1967-78, Georgia 79-95, Jacksonville 98-2003*	35	604	401	.601
42. Slats Gill (Oregon St. 1924) Oregon St. 1929-64	36	599	393	.604
43. Abe Lemons (Oklahoma City 1949) Oklahoma City 1956-73, Tex.-Pan American 74-76, Texas 77-82, Oklahoma City 84-90	34	597	344	.634
44. John Thompson (Providence 1964) Georgetown 1973-99	27	596	239	.714
45. Billy Tubbs (Lamar 1958) Southwestern (Tex.) 1972-73, Lamar 77-80, Oklahoma 81-94, TCU 95-2002, Lamar 04*	28	595	297	.667
46. Guy Lewis (Houston 1947) Houston 1957-86	30	592	279	.680
47. Joe Hutton (Carleton 1924) Hamline 1932-65	34	591	207	.741
48. Dom Rosselli (Geneva 1939) Youngstown St. 1941-42, 47-82	38	590	387	.604
49. Dave Robbins (Catawba 1966) Virginia Union 1979-2003*	25	583	167	.777
49. Tom Murphy (Springfield 1960) Hamilton 1971-2003* ...	33	583	254	.697
51. Dan McCarrell (North Park 1961) North Park 1968-84, Minn. St. Mankato 85-2001	34	579	347	.625
52. Fred Hobdy (Grambling 1949) Grambling 1957-86	30	571	287	.666
53. Eldon Miller (Wittenberg 1961) Wittenberg 1963-70, Western Mich. 71-76, Ohio St. 77-86, Northern Iowa 87-98	36	568	419	.575
54. Davey Whitney (Kentucky St. 1953) Texas Southern 1965-69, Alcorn St. 70-89, 97-2003	32	566	356	.614
55. Gale Catlett (West Virginia 1963) Cincinnati 1973-78, West Virginia 79-2002	30	565	325	.635
56. Rudy Marisa (Penn St. 1956) Waynesburg 1970-03	34	563	300	.652
56. Gary Colson (Lipscomb 1956) Valdosta St. 1959-68, Pepperdine 69-79, New Mexico 81-88, Fresno St. 91-95	34	563	385	.594
58. John Kresse [St. John's (N.Y.) 1964] Col. of Charleston 1980-2002	23	560	143	.797
59. Bob Chipman (Kansas St. 1973) Washburn 1980-03*...	24	559	192	.744
59. Charles Chronister (East Stroudsburg 1963) Bloomsburg 1972-2002	31	559	288	.660
61. Tony Hinkle (Chicago 1921) Butler 1927-42, 46-70	41	558	392	.587
62. Bill Knapton (Wis.-La Crosse 1952) Beloit 1958-97	40	555	344	.617
63. Bob Bessoir (Scranton 1955) Scranton 1973-2001	29	554	263	.678
64. Glenn Wilkes (Mercer 1950) Stetson 1958-93	36	551	436	.558
65. Frank McGuire [St. John's (N.Y.) 1936] St. John's (N.Y.) 1948-52, North Carolina 53-61, South Carolina 65-80	30	549	236	.699
65. Bruce Webster (Rutgers 1959) Bridgeport 1966-99	34	549	405	.575
67. Dick Reynolds (Otterbein 1965) Otterbein 1973-2003*...	31	546	300	.645
68. Tom Davis (Wis.-Platteville 1960) Lafayette 1972-77, Boston College 78-82, Stanford 83-86, Iowa 87-99, Drake 2004*	28	543	290	.652
69. Chet Kammerer (Grace (Ind.) 1964) Grace (Ind.) 1966-75, Westmont 76-92	27	542	261	.675
70. Jerry Slocum [King's (N.Y.) 1975] Nyack 1976-87, Geneva 1988-96, Gannon 97-2003*	28	540	306	.638
71. Bob Davis [Georgetown (Ky.) 1950] High Point 1951-53, Georgetown (Ky.) 54-73, Auburn 74-78	28	538	277	.660
72. C. Alan Rowe (Villanova 1953) Widener 1966-98	33	536	324	.623
73. Harry Miller (Eastern N.M. 1951) Western St. 1953-58, Fresno St. 61-65, Eastern N.M. 66-70, North Texas 71, Wichita St. 72-78, Stephen F. Austin 79-88	34	534	374	.588
74. Bill C. Foster (Carson-Newman 1958) Shorter 1963-67, Charlotte 71-75, Clemson 76-84, Miami (Fla.) 86-90, Virginia Tech 92-97	30	532	325	.621
75. Dick Whitmore (Bowdoin 1965) Colby 1971-2001, 03*	32	531	252	.678
76. Tom Penders (Connecticut 1967) Tufts 1972-74, Columbia 75-78, Fordham 79-86, Rhode Island 87-88, Texas 89-98, George Washington 99-2001	30	527	361	.593
77. Lou Carnesecca [St. John's (N.Y.) 1946] St. John's (N.Y.) 1966-70, 74-92	24	526	200	.725
77. Dave Bliss (Cornell 1965) Oklahoma 1976-80, Southern Methodist 81-88, New Mexico 89-99, Baylor 2000-03	28	526	328	.616
79. Pete Carril (Lafayette 1952) Lehigh 1967, Princeton 68-96	30	525	273	.658
79. Gene Mehaffey (Southern Methodist 1954) Carson-Newman 1968-78, Ohio Wesleyan 80-99	31	525	384	.578
81. Tom Young (Maryland 1958) Catholic 1959-67, American 70-73, Rutgers 74-85, Old Dominion 86-91	31	524	328	.615

Coach (Alma Mater), Teams Coached, Tenure	Yrs.	Won	Lost	Pct.
81. Ben Jobe (Fisk 1956) Talladega 1965-67, Alabama St. 68, South Carolina St. 69-73, Denver 79-80, Alabama A&M 83-86, Southern U. 87-96, Tuskegee 97-2000,Southern U. 02-03	31	524	333	.611
83. Fred Enke (Minnesota 1921) Louisville 1924-25, Arizona 26-61	38	523	344	.603
84. Cliff Ellis (Florida St. 1968) South Ala. 1976-84, Clemson 85-94, Auburn 95-2003*	28	520	323	.617
85. Bob Huggins (West Virginia 1977) Walsh 1981-83, Akron 85-89, Cincinnati 90-2003*	22	517	184	.738
85. Mike Montgomery (Long Beach St. 1968) Montana 1979-86, Stanford 87-2003*	25	517	242	.681
87. Rollie Massimino (Vermont 1956) Stony Brook 1970-71, Villanova 74-92, UNLV 93-94, Cleveland St. 97-2003	30	515	391	.568
88. Arad McCutchan (Evansville 1934) Evansville 1947-77	31	514	314	.621
88. Jim Burson (Muskingum 1963) Muskingum 1968-2003*	36	514	400	.562
88. Jim Gudger (Western Caro. 1942) Western Caro. 1951-69, Tex. A&M-Commerce 70-83	33	514	415	.553
88. Arthur McAfee (Wichita St. 1951) Lane 1961, Mississippi Val. 62, Lincoln (Mo.) 63, Bishop 64-65, Morehouse 66-2000	40	514	512	.501
92. Paul Webb (William & Mary 1951) Randolph-Macon 1957-75, Old Dominion 76-85	29	511	257	.665
93. Lewis Levick (Drake 1950) Wartburg 1966-93	28	510	225	.694
93. Aubrey Bonham (Northern Iowa 1927) Whittier 1938-43 & 46-68	29	510	285	.642
95. Nolan Richardson (UTEP 1965) Tulsa 1981-85, Arkansas 86-2002	22	509	207	.711
95. Larry Hunter (Ohio 1971) Wittenberg 1977-89, Ohio 90-2001	25	509	224	.694
95. C.M. Newton (Kentucky 1952) Transylvania 1956-64, 66-68, Alabama 69-80, Vanderbilt 82-89	32	509	375	.576

Coach (Alma Mater), Teams Coached, Tenure	Yrs.	Won	Lost	Pct.
98. Hec Edmundson (Idaho 1909) Idaho 1917-18, Washington 21-47	29	508	204	.713
99. Gene Keady (Kansas St. 1958) Western Ky. 1979-80, Purdue 81-2003*	25	507	271	.652
99. Don DeVoe (Ohio St. 1964) Virginia Tech 1972-76, Wyoming 77-78, Tennessee 79-89, Florida 90, Navy 93-2003*	30	507	366	.581
101. Leo Nicholson (Washington 1925) Central Wash. 1930-43 & 46-64	33	505	281	.642
101. Homer Drew (William Jewell 1966) Bethel (Ind.) 1977-87, Ind.-South Bend 88, Valparaiso 89-02, 04*	26	505	306	.623
101. Gerald Stockton (Oklahoma St. 1953) Sul Ross St. 1967-68, Midwestern St. 71-94	26	505	363	.582
104. Harold Anderson (Otterbein 1924) Toledo 1935-42, Bowling Green 43-63	29	504	226	.690
105. Jerry Welsh (Ithaca 1958) Potsdam St. 1969-69, 71-91, Iona 92-95	26	502	205	.710
105. Gary Williams (Maryland 1968) American 1979-82, Boston College 83-86, Ohio St. 87-89, Maryland 90-2003*	25	502	281	.641
107. Ed Martin (N.C. A&T 1951) South Carolina St. 1956-68, Tennessee St. 69-85	30	501	253	.664
107. Bobby Vaughan (Virginia St. 1948) Elizabeth City St. 1952-66, 68-86	34	501	363	.580
109. Glenn Van Wieren (Hope 1964) Hope 1978-2003*	26	500	174	.742
109. Ed Douma (Calvin 1966) Alma 1974, Lake Superior St. 75-78, Kent St. 79-82, UNC Greensboro 83-84, Calvin 85-96, Hillsdale 99-2003*	28	500	248	.668

*active

Division I Coaching Records

Winningest Active Coaches

(Minimum five years as a Division I head coach; includes record at four-year U.S. colleges only.)

BY PERCENTAGE

No.	Coach	Team	Yrs.	Won	Lost	Pct.
1.	Roy Williams	North Carolina	15	418	101	.805
2.	Jim Boeheim	Syracuse	27	653	226	.743
3.	Lute Olson	Arizona	30	690	240	.742
4.	Rick Majerus	Utah	19	407	142	.741
5.	Mike Krzyzewski	Duke	28	663	234	.739
6.	Bob Huggins	Cincinnati	22	517	184	.738
7.	Rick Pitino	Louisville	17	396	144	.733
8.	Tubby Smith	Kentucky	12	288	109	.725
9.	Bob Knight	Texas Tech	37	809	311	.722
10.	John Chaney	Temple	31	693	269	.720
11.	John Calipari	Memphis	11	260	101	.720
12.	Eddie Sutton	Oklahoma St.	33	724	288	.715
13.	Tom Izzo	Michigan St.	8	189	78	.708
14.	Pat Douglass	UC Irvine	22	471	196	.706
15.	Skip Prosser	Wake Forest	8	175	77	.694
16.	Jim Calhoun	Connecticut	31	647	296	.686
17.	Mike Montgomery	Stanford	25	517	242	.681
18.	Billy Tubbs	Lamar	28	595	297	.667
19.	Mike Brey	Notre Dame	8	165	83	.665
20.	Tevester Anderson	Jackson St.	5	103	52	.665
21.	Dick Bennett	Washington St.	21	401	203	.664
22.	Lou Henson	New Mexico St.	39	762	386	.664
23.	Bill Self	Kansas	10	207	105	.663
24.	John Giannini	Maine	14	273	139	.663
25.	Billy Donovan	Florida	9	183	94	.661
26.	Mark Gottfried	Alabama	8	167	86	.660
27.	Pete Gillen	Virginia	16	325	168	.659
28.	Steve McClain	Wyoming	5	100	52	.658
29.	Bruce Weber	Illinois	5	103	54	.656
30.	Gregg Marshall	Winthrop	5	99	52	.656
31.	Fran Dunphy	Pennsylvania	14	253	135	.652
32.	Tom Davis	Drake	28	543	290	.652
33.	Gene Keady	Purdue	25	507	271	.652
34.	Charles Spoonhour	UNLV	18	361	193	.652
35.	Stew Morrill	Utah St.	17	336	180	.651
36.	Dennis Felton	Georgia	5	100	54	.649
37.	Jeff Lebo	Chattanooga	5	96	52	.649
38.	Mike Jarvis	St. John's (N.Y.)	18	361	198	.646
39.	Gary Williams	Maryland	25	502	281	.641
40.	Bill Carmody	Northwestern	7	131	74	.639
41.	Bobby Lutz	Charlotte	14	273	155	.638
42.	Buzz Peterson	Tennessee	7	137	78	.637
43.	Rick Barnes	Texas	16	318	184	.633
44.	Perry Watson	Detroit	10	194	113	.632
45.	Kelvin Sampson	Oklahoma	20	391	228	.632
46.	Blaine Taylor	Old Dominion	9	166	97	.631
47.	Ben Howland	UCLA	9	168	99	.629
48.	Steve Alford	Iowa	12	229	135	.629
49.	Keith Richard	Louisiana Tech	5	91	54	.628
50.	John Beilein	West Virginia	21	386	230	.627
51.	Tic Price	McNeese St.	7	129	77	.626
52.	Rick Stansbury	Mississippi St.	5	100	60	.625
53.	Rod Barnes	Mississippi	5	100	61	.621
54.	Cliff Ellis	Auburn	28	520	323	.617
55.	Dan Monson	Minnesota	6	119	74	.617
56.	Paul Hewitt	Georgia Tech	6	114	71	.616
57.	Tim Welsh	Providence	8	151	95	.614
58.	Bill Herrion	East Caro.	12	215	136	.613
59.	Bob Williams	UC Santa Barb.	15	265	168	.612
60.	Jessie Evans	La.-Lafayette	6	112	72	.609
61.	Mike Deane	Wagner	19	342	220	.609
62.	Royce Waltman	Indiana St.	16	276	178	.608
63.	Dana Altman	Creighton	14	258	167	.607
64.	Phil Martelli	St. Joseph's	8	149	97	.606
65.	Herb Sendek	North Carolina St.	10	190	124	.605
66.	Craig Esherick	Georgetown	5	90	59	.604
67.	Kevin Stallings	Vanderbilt	10	185	122	.603
68.	Dave Odom	South Carolina	17	311	206	.602
69.	Hugh Durham	Jacksonville	35	604	401	.601

COACHING RECORDS

(Coaches with fewer than five years as a Division I head coach; includes record at four-year U.S. colleges only.)

No. Coach	Team	Yrs.	Won	Lost	Pct.
1. Bruce Pearl	Wis.-Milwaukee	11	271	67	.802
2. Duane Reboul	Birmingham-So.	14	347	94	.787
3. Bo Ryan	Wisconsin	19	426	124	.775
4. Jim Ferry	Long Island	5	111	37	.750
5. Tony Shaver	William & Mary	17	358	121	.747
6. Bart Lundy	High Point	5	115	40	.742
7. Danny Kaspar	Stephen F. Austin	12	262	92	.740
8. L. Vann Pettaway	Alabama A&M	17	353	150	.702

No. Coach	Team	Yrs.	Won	Lost	Pct.
9. Bob Hoffman	Tex.-Pan American	13	296	142	.676
10. Jeff Price	Ga. Southern	10	197	96	.672
11. Larry Reynolds	Long Beach St.	6	115	57	.669
12. John Masi	UC Riverside	24	442	233	.655
13. Rick Byrd	Belmont	22	438	248	.638
14. Brad Soderberg	St. Louis	9	147	87	.628
15. Greg Jackson	Delaware St.	12	199	122	.620
16. Greg McDermott	Northern Iowa	9	156	96	.619
17. Dale Layer	Colorado St.	12	214	133	.617

BY VICTORIES

No. Coach, Team	Won
1. Bob Knight, Texas Tech	809
2. Lou Henson, New Mexico St.	762
3. Eddie Sutton, Oklahoma St.	724
4. John Chaney, Temple	693
5. Lute Olson, Arizona	690
6. Mike Krzyzewski, Duke	663
7. Jim Boeheim, Syracuse	653
8. Jim Calhoun, Connecticut	647
9. Hugh Durham, Jacksonville	604
10. Billy Tubbs, Lamar	595
11. Tom Davis, Drake	543
12. Cliff Ellis, Auburn	520
13. Bob Huggins, Cincinnati	517
13. Mike Montgomery, Stanford	517
15. Gene Keady, Purdue	507
15. Don DeVoe, Navy	507
17. Gary Williams, Maryland	502
18. Ben Braun, California	477
19. Pat Douglass, UC Irvine	471
20. Roy Williams, North Carolina	418
21. Rick Majerus, Utah	407
22. Pat Kennedy, Montana	406
23. Dick Bennett, Washington St.	401
24. Rick Pitino, Louisville	396
25. Kelvin Sampson, Oklahoma	391
26. John Beilein, West Virginia	386

No. Coach, Team	Won
26. Danny Nee, Duquesne	386
28. Mike Vining, La.-Monroe	381
29. Charles Spoonhour, UNLV	361
29. Mike Jarvis, St. John's (N.Y.)	361
31. Don Maestri, Troy St.	358
32. Jim O'Brien, Ohio St.	354
33. Nick Macarchuk, Stony Brook	352
34. Rick Samuels, Eastern Ill.	345
35. Mike Deane, Wagner	342
36. Gary Garner, Southeast Mo. St.	340
37. Stew Morrill, Utah St.	336
38. Pete Gillen, Virginia	325
39. Tom Green, Fairleigh Dickinson	321
40. Rick Barnes, Texas	318
41. Dave Odom, South Carolina	311
42. Dave Magarity, Marist	307
43. Jim Crews, Army	299
44. Jim Larranaga, George Mason	297
45. Jim Boone, Eastern Mich.	295
46. Tubby Smith, Kentucky	288
47. Bob Thomason, Pacific (Cal.)	287
48. Ron Fang Mitchell, Coppin St.	286
49. Dave Loos, Austin Peay	280
50. Riley Wallace, Hawaii	277
51. Royce Waltman, Indiana St.	276
51. Cy Alexander, Tennessee St.	276

No. Coach, Team	Won
53. John Giannini, Maine	273
53. Bobby Lutz, Charlotte	273
55. Rob Spivery, Alabama St.	272
56. Lafayette Stribling, Mississippi Val.	270
57. Tom Brennan, Vermont	269
58. Steve Aggers, Loyola Marymount	268
59. Bob Williams, UC Santa Barb.	265
60. Jim Wooldridge, Kansas St.	265
61. John Calipari, Memphis	260
62. Dana Altman, Creighton	258
63. Oliver Purnell, Clemson	256
64. Steve Lappas, Massachusetts	254
65. Fran Dunphy, Pennsylvania	253
66. Tom Sullivan, UMBC	252
67. Frank Sullivan, Harvard	251
68. Mike Dement, Southern Methodist	250
69. Perry Clark, Miami (Fla.)	236
69. Al Skinner, Boston College	236
71. Barry Collier, Nebraska	234
72. Jim Baron, Rhode Island	233
73. Steve Alford, Iowa	229
73. Pat Flannery, Bucknell	229
75. Dan Hipsher, Akron	225
76. Bob McKillop, Davidson	222
77. Ralph Willard, Holy Cross	220
78. Bill Herrion, East Caro.	215

No. Coach, Team	Won
79. Leonard Hamilton, Florida St.	214
80. Seth Greenberg, Virginia Tech	213
81. Charlie Coles, Miami (Ohio)	212
81. Frankie Allen, Howard	212
83. Bill Self, Kansas	207
83. Ernie Kent, Oregon	207
85. Mick Durham, Montana St.	203

(Coaches with fewer than five years as a Division I head coach; includes record at four-year U.S. colleges only.)

No. Coach, Team	Won
1. John Masi, UC Riverside	442
2. Rick Byrd, Belmont	438
3. Bo Ryan, Wisconsin	426
4. Dave Bike, Sacred Heart	400
5. Tony Shaver, William & Mary	358
6. L. Vann Pettaway, Alabama A&M	353
7. Duane Reboul, Birmingham-So.	347
8. Greg Kampe, Oakland	321
9. Rick Scruggs, Gardner-Webb	309
10. Bob Hoffman, Tex.-Pan American	296
11. Bruce Pearl, Wis.-Milwaukee	271
12. Danny Kaspar, Stephen F. Austin	262
13. Dale Layer, Colorado St.	214

Winningest Coaches All-Time

(Minimum 10 head coaching seasons in Division I)

BY PERCENTAGE

Coach, team coached & tenure	Yrs.	Won	Lost	Pct.
1. Clair Bee, Rider 1929-31, Long Island 32-43, 46-51	21	412	87	.826
2. Adolph Rupp, Kentucky 1931-72	41	876	190	.822
3. Roy Williams, Kansas 1989-03, North Carolina 2004*	15	418	101	.805
4. John Wooden, Indiana St. 1947-48, UCLA 49-75	29	664	162	.804
5. John Kresse, Col. of Charleston 1980-2002	23	560	143	.797
6. Jerry Tarkanian, Long Beach St. 1969-73, UNLV 74-92, Fresno St. 96-2002	31	729	201	.784
7. Dean Smith, North Carolina 1962-97	36	879	254	.776
8. George Keogan, Wis.-Superior 1913-14, St. Louis 16, St. Thomas (Minn.) 18, Allegheny 19, Valparaiso 20-21, Notre Dame 24-43	27	418	125	.769
9. Jack Ramsay, St. Joseph's 1956-66	11	231	71	.765
10. Frank Keaney, Rhode Island 1921-48	28	401	124	.764
11. Vic Bubas, Duke 1960-69	10	213	67	.761
12. Harry Fisher, Columbia 07-16, St. John's (N.Y.) 10, Army 07, 22-23, 25	13	171	54	.760
13. Chick Davies, Duquesne 1925-43, 47-48	21	314	106	.748
14. Ray Mears, Wittenberg 1957-62, Tennessee 63-77	21	399	135	.747
15. Jim Boeheim, Syracuse 1977-03*	27	653	226	.743
16. Lute Olson, Long Beach St. 1974, Iowa 75-83, Arizona 84-2003*	30	690	240	.742
17. Rick Majerus, Marquette 1984-86, Ball St. 88-89, Utah 90-2003*	19	407	142	.741
18. Mike Krzyzewski, Army 1976-80, Duke 81-2003*	28	663	234	.739
19. Al McGuire, Belmont Abbey 1958-64, Marquette 65-77	20	405	143	.739
20. Phog Allen, Baker 1906-08, Haskell 09, Central Mo. St. 13-19, Kansas 08-09, 20-56	50	746	264	.739
21. Everett Case, North Carolina St. 1947-65	19	377	134	.738
22. Bob Huggins, Walsh 1981-83, Akron 85-89, Cincinnati 90-2003*	22	517	184	.738
23. Arthur Schabinger, Ottawa 1917-20, Emporia St. 21-22, Creighton 23-35	19	245	88	.736
24. Doc Meanwell, Wisconsin 1912-17, 21-34, Missouri 18, 20.	22	280	101	.735
25. Rick Pitino, Boston U. 1979-83, Providence 86-87, Kentucky 90-97, Louisville 2002-03*	17	396	144	.733
26. Lew Andreas, Syracuse 1925-50	25	358	135	.726
27. Tubby Smith, Tulsa 1992-95, Georgia 96-97, Kentucky 98-2003*	12	288	109	.725
28. Lou Carnesecca, St. John's (N.Y.) 1966-70, 74-92	24	526	200	.725
29. Fred Schaus, West Virginia 1955-60, Purdue 73-78	12	251	96	.723
30. Bob Knight, Army 1966-71, Indiana 72-2000, Texas Tech 02-03*	37	809	311	.722
31. Cam Henderson, Muskingum 1920-23, Davis & Elkins 24-35, Marshall 36-55	36	630	243	.722

Coach, team coached & tenure	Yrs.	Won	Lost	Pct.
32. John Chaney, Cheyney 1973-82, Temple 83-2003*	31	693	269	.720
33. John Calipari, Massachusetts 1989-96, Memphis 2001-03*	11	260	101	.720
34. Joe Lapchick, St. John's (N.Y.) 1937-47, 57-65	20	334	130	.720
35. Hugh Greer, Connecticut 1947-63	17	286	112	.719
36. Dudey Moore, Duquesne 1949-58, La Salle 59-63	15	270	107	.716
37. Eddie Sutton, Creighton 1970-74, Arkansas 75-85, Kentucky 86-89, Oklahoma St. 91-2003*	33	724	288	.715
38. Ed Diddle, Western Ky. 1923-64	42	759	302	.715
39. Tom Blackburn, Dayton 1948-64	17	352	141	.714
40. John Lawther, Westminster (Pa.) 1927-36, Penn St. 37-49	23	317	127	.714
41. John Thompson, Georgetown 1973-99	27	596	239	.714
42. Lee Rose, Transylvania 1965-65, 69-75, Charlotte 76-78, Purdue 79-80, South Fla. 81-86	19	384	154	.714
43. Hec Edmundson, Idaho 1917-18, Washington 21-47 ..	29	508	204	.713
44. Nolan Richardson, Tulsa 1981-85, Arkansas 86-2002 ..	22	509	207	.711
45. Pat Page, Chicago 1913-20, Butler 21-26	14	243	99	.711
46. Piggy Lambert, Purdue 1917, 19-45	29	371	152	.709
47. Peck Hickman, Louisville 1945-67	23	443	183	.708
48. Joe B. Hall, Regis (Colo.) 1960-64, Central Mo. St. 65, Kentucky 73-85	19	373	156	.705
49. Frank McGuire, St. John's (N.Y.) 1948-52, North Carolina 53-61, South Carolina 65-80	30	549	236	.699
50. Boyd Grant, Fresno St. 1978-86, Colorado St. 88-91 ..	13	275	120	.696
51. Denny Crum, Louisville 1972-01	30	675	295	.696
52. Douglas Mills, Illinois 1937-47	11	151	66	.696
53. Larry Hunter, Wittenberg 1977-89, Ohio 90-2001	25	509	224	.694
54. Honey Russell, Seton Hall 1937-43, 50-60, Manhattan 46	19	310	137	.694
55. Henry Iba, Northwest Mo. St. 1930-33, Colorado 34, Oklahoma St. 35-70	41	764	339	.693
56. Larry Weise, St. Bonaventure 1962-73	12	202	90	.692
57. Gene Smithson, Illinois St. 1976-78, Wichita St. 79-86	11	221	99	.691
58. Harold Anderson, Toledo 1935-42, Bowling Green 43-63	29	504	226	.690
59. Nat Holman, CCNY 1920-52, 55-56, 59-60	37	423	190	.690
60. E.J. Stewart, Purdue 1909, Oregon St. 12-16, Texas 24-27	10	140	64	.686
61. Jim Calhoun, Northeastern 1973-86, Connecticut 87-2003*	31	647	296	.686
62. Dana Kirk, Tampa 1967-71, Va. Commonwealth 77-79, Memphis 80-86	15	281	131	.682
63. Mike Montgomery, Montana 1979-86, Stanford 87-2003*	25	517	242	.681
64. Guy Lewis, Houston 1957-86	30	592	279	.680
65. John Oldham, Tennessee Tech 1956-64, Western Ky. 65-71	16	260	123	.679
66. Harry Combes, Illinois 1948-67	20	316	150	.678
67. Digger Phelps, Fordham 1971, Notre Dame 72-91	21	419	200	.677
68. Bob King, New Mexico 1963-72, Indiana St. 76-78	13	236	113	.676
69. Hubert Read, Western Mich. 1922-49	28	358	173	.674
70. Jack Gardner, Kansas St. 1940-42, 47-53, Utah 54-71	28	486	235	.674
71. Roy Skinner, Vanderbilt 1959-59, 62-76	16	278	135	.673
72. Alex Severence, Villanova 1937-61	25	413	201	.673
73. Ray Meyer, DePaul 1943-84	42	724	354	.672
74. Don Haskins, UTEP 1962-99	38	719	353	.671
75. Neil McCarthy, Weber St. 1976-85, New Mexico St. 86-97	21	426	209	.671
76. Don Corbett, Lincoln (Mo.) 1972-79, N.C. A&T 80-93 .	22	413	204	.669
77. Ozzie Cowles, Carleton 1925-30, Wis.-River Falls 33-36, Dartmouth 37-43, 45-46, Michigan 47-48, Minnesota 49-59	32	421	208	.669
78. Billy Tubbs, Southwestern (Tex.) 1972-73, Lamar 77-80, Oklahoma 81-94, TCU 95-2002, Lamar 04*	28	595	297	.667
79. Jack Gray, Texas 1937-42, 46-51	12	194	97	.667
80. Jim Harrick, Pepperdine 1980-88, UCLA 89-96, Rhode Island 98-99, Georgia 2000-03	23	470	235	.667
81. Charles Moir, Virginia Tech 1977-87	20	392	196	.667
82. Harold Bradley, Hartwick 1948-50, Duke 51-59, Texas 60-67	20	337	169	.666
83. Wimp Sanderson, Alabama 1981-92, Ark.-Little Rock 95-99	17	352	177	.665
84. Dick Bennett, Wis.-Stevens Point 1981-85, Wis.-Green Bay 86-95, Wisconsin 1996-2001, Washington St. 04*	21	401	203	.664
85. Lou Henson, Hardin-Simmons 1963-66, New Mexico St. 67-75, Illinois 76-96, New Mexico St. 98-2003*	39	762	386	.664
86. Bill Self, Oral Roberts 1994-97, Tulsa 98-2000, Illinois 01-03, Kansas 04*	10	207	105	.663
87. Lefty Driesell, Davidson 1961-69, Maryland 70-86, James Madison 89-97, Georgia St. 98-2003	42	800	409	.662
88. Branch McCracken, Ball St. 1931-38, Indiana 39-43, 47-65	32	450	231	.661
89. Norm Stewart, Northern Iowa 1962-67, Missouri 68-99	38	728	374	.661
90. Dave Gavitt, Dartmouth 1968-69, Providence 70-79	12	227	117	.660

Marquette coach Tom Crean led the Golden Eagles to their first Final Four appearance since 1977 last season.

Coach, team coached & tenure	Yrs.	Won	Lost	Pct.
91. Terry Holland, Davidson 1970-74, Virginia 75-90	21	418	216	.659
92. Pete Gillen, Xavier 1986-94, Providence 95-98, Virginia 99-2003*	16	325	168	.659
93. Harry Litwack, Temple 1953-73	21	373	193	.659
94. Pete Carril, Lehigh 1967, Princeton 68-96	30	525	273	.658
95. Pete Newell, San Francisco 1947-50, Michigan St. 51-54, California 55-60	14	234	123	.655
96. Dick Tarrant, Richmond 1982-93	12	239	126	.655
97. Jack Kraft, Villanova 1962-73, Rhode Island 74-81	20	361	191	.654
98. Fred Taylor, Ohio St. 1959-76	18	297	158	.653
99. Jack Hartman, Southern Ill. 1963-70, Kansas St. 71-86	24	437	233	.652
100. Paul Evans, St. Lawrence 1974-80, Navy 81-86, Pittsburgh 87-94	21	390	208	.652
101. Eddie Hickey, Creighton 1936-43, 47, St. Louis 48-58, Marquette 59-64	26	433	231	.652
102. Fran Dunphy, Pennsylvania 1990-03*	14	253	135	.652
103. George King, Charleston (W.Va.) 1957, West Virginia 61-65, Purdue 66-72	13	223	119	.652
104. Tom Davis, Lafayette 1972-77, Boston College 78-82, Stanford 83-86, Iowa 87-99, Drake 2004*	28	543	290	.652
105. Gene Keady, Western Ky. 1979-80, Purdue 81-2003*	25	507	271	.652
106. Charles Spoonhour, Southwest Mo. St. 1984-92, St. Louis 93-99, UNLV 2002-03*	18	361	193	.652
107. Leonard Palmer, CCNY 1907-16	10	71	38	.651
108. Stew Morrill, Montana 1987-91, Colorado St. 92-98, Utah St. 99-2003*	17	336	180	.651

*active

BY VICTORIES

(Minimum 10 head coaching seasons in Division I)

Coach	Wins
1. Dean Smith	879
2. Adolph Rupp	876
3. Jim Phelan, Mt. St. Mary's 1955-03	830
4. Bob Knight*	809
5. Lefty Driesell	800
6. Henry Iba	764
7. Lou Henson*	762
8. Ed Diddle	759
9. Phog Allen	746
10. Jerry Tarkanian	729
11. Norm Stewart	728
12. Eddie Sutton*	724
12. Ray Meyer	724

Coach	Wins
14. Don Haskins	719
15. John Chaney*	693
16. Lute Olson*	690
17. Denny Crum	675
18. John Wooden	664
19. Mike Krzyzewski*	663
20. Ralph Miller, Wichita St. 1952-64, Iowa 65-70, Oregon St. 71-89	657
21. Marv Harshman, Pacific Lutheran 1946-58, Washington St. 59-71, Washington 72-85	654
22. Jim Boeheim*	653
23. Gene Bartow	647
23. Jim Calhoun*	647
25. Cam Henderson	630
26. Norm Sloan, Presbyterian 1952-55, Citadel 57-60, North Carolina St. 67-80, Florida 61-66, 81-89	624
27. Hugh Durham, Florida St. 1967-78, Georgia 79-95, Jacksonville 98-2003*	604
28. Slats Gill, Oregon St. 1929-64	599
29. Abe Lemons, Oklahoma City 1956-73, 84-90, Tex.-Pan American 74-76, Texas 77-82	597
30. John Thompson	596
31. Billy Tubbs*	595
32. Guy Lewis	592
33. Eldon Miller, Wittenberg 1963-70, Western Mich. 71-76, Ohio St. 77-86, Northern Iowa 87-98	568
34. Davey Whitney, Texas Southern 1965-69, Alcorn St. 70-89, 97-2003	566
35. Gale Catlett, Cincinnati 1973-78, West Virginia 79-2002	565
36. Gary Colson, Valdosta St. 1959-68, Pepperdine 69-79, New Mexico 81-88, Fresno St. 91-95	563
37. John Kresse	560
38. Tony Hinkle, Butler 1927-42, 46-70	558
39. Glenn Wilkes, Stetson 1958-93	551
40. Frank McGuire	549
41. Tom Davis*	543
42. Harry Miller, Western St.1953-58, Fresno St. 61-65, Eastern N.M. 66-70, North Texas 71, Wichita St. 72-78, Stephen F. Austin 79-88	534
43. Bill C. Foster, Shorter 1963-67, Charlotte 71-75, Clemson 76-84, Miami (Fla.) 86-90, Virginia Tech 92-97	532
44. Tom Penders, Tufts 1972-74, Columbia 75-78, Fordham 79-86, Rhode Island 87-88, Texas 89-98, George Washington 99-2001	527
45. Lou Carnesecca	526
45. Dave Bliss, Oklahoma 1976-80, Southern Methodist 81-88, New Mexico 89-99, Baylor 2000-03	526
47. Pete Carril	525
48. Ben Jobe, Talladega 1965-67, Alabama St. 68, South Carolina St. 69-73, Denver 79-80, Alabama A&M 83-86, Tuskegee 97-2000, Southern U. 1987-96, 2002-03	524
48. Tom Young, Catholic 1959-67, American 70-73, Rutgers 74-85, Old Dominion 86-91	524
50. Fred Enke, Louisville 1924-25, Arizona 26-61	523
51. Cliff Ellis, South Ala. 1976-84, Clemson 85-94, Auburn 95-2004*	520
52. Bob Huggins*	517
52. Mike Montgomery*	517
54. Rollie Massimino, Stony Brook 1970-71, Villanova 74-92, UNLV 93-94, Cleveland St. 97-2003	515
55. C.M. Newton, Transylvania 1956-64, 66-68, Alabama 69-80, Vanderbilt 82-89	509
55. Larry Hunter	509
55. Nolan Richardson	509
58. Hec Edmundson	508
59. Don DeVoe, Virginia Tech 1972-76, Wyoming 77-78, Tennessee 79-89, Florida 90, Navy 93-2004*	507
59. Gene Keady*	507
61. Homer Drew, Bethel (Ind.) 1977-87, Ind.-South Bend 88, Valparaiso 89-2002*	505
62. Harold Anderson	504
63. Gary Williams, American 1979-82, Boston College 83-86, Ohio St. 87-89, Maryland 90-2004*	502
64. Cal Luther, DePauw 1955-58, Murray St. 59-73, Longwood 82-90, Tenn.-Martin 92-99, Bethel (Tenn.) 2000	500
65. Bill Reinhart, Oregon 1924-35, George Washington 36-66	498
66. Everett Shelton, Phillips (Okla.) 1924-26, Wyoming 40-43, 45-59, Sacramento St. 60-68	495
66. Jack Friel, Washington St. 1929-58	495
66. Ned Wulk, Xavier 1952-57, Arizona St. 58-82	495
69. Jack Gardner	486
70. Bob Hallberg, St. Xavier 1972-77, Chicago St. 78-87, Ill.-Chicago 88-96	484
71. Butch Van Breda Kolff, Lafayette 1952-55, 85-88, Princeton 63-67, New Orleans 78-79, Hofstra 56-62, 89-94	482
72. Ben Braun, Siena Heights 1978-85, Eastern Mich. 86-96, California 97-2004*	477
73. Jim Harrick	470
74. Bill E. Foster, Bloomsburg 1961-63, Rutgers 64-71, Utah 72-74, Duke 75-80, South Carolina 81-86, Northwestern 87-93	467
75. Johnny Orr, Massachusetts 1964-66, Michigan 69-80, Iowa St. 81-94	466
76. Taps Gallagher, Niagara 1932-43, 47-65	465

Coach	Wins
77. George Blaney, Stonehill 1968-69, Dartmouth 70-72, Holy Cross 73-94, Seton Hall 95-97	459
78. Bobby Cremins, Appalachian St. 1976-81, Georgia Tech 82-2000	454
79. Tex Winter, Marquette 1952-53, Kansas St. 54-68, Washington 69-71, Northwestern 74-78, Long Beach St. 79-83	453
80. Branch McCracken	450
81. Nibs Price, California 1925-54	449
82. Dale Brown, LSU 1973 97	448
83. Peck Hickman	443
83. Shelby Metcalf, Texas A&M 1964-90	443
85. Don Donoher, Dayton 1965-89	437
85. Jack Hartman	437
87. Eddie Hickey	433
88. Howard Hobson, Southern Ore. 1933-35, Oregon 36-47, Yale 48-56	431
89. Neil McCarthy	426
90. Nat Holman	423
91. Ozzie Cowles	421
92. Murray Arnold, Birmingham-So. 1971-78, Chattanooga 80-85, Western Ky. 87-90, Stetson 98-2001	420
93. Digger Phelps	419
94. George Keogan	418
94. Jud Heathcote, Montana 1972-76, Michigan St. 77-95	418
94. Sam Barry	418
94. Roy Williams*	418
94. Terry Holland	418
99. Alex Severence	413
99. Don Corbett	413
101. Clair Bee	412
102. Howard Cann, New York U. 1924-58	409
103. Rick Majerus*	407
104. Pat Kennedy*	406
105. Al McGuire	405
106. Dick Bennett*	401
106. Frank Keaney	401

*active

Division I Active Coaches Listed by School

Coach	School	Yr	W	L	Pct.
Joe Scott	Air Force	3	29	56	.341
Dan Hipsher	Akron	14	225	167	.574
Mark Gottfried	Alabama	8	167	86	.660
L. Vann Pettaway	Alabama A&M	17	353	150	.702
Rob Spivery	Alabama St.	17	272	251	.520
Will Brown	Albany (N.Y.)	2	14	34	.292
Samuel West	Alcorn St.	0	0	0	.000
Jeff Jones	American	11	187	150	.555
Houston Fancher	Appalachian St.	3	40	48	.455
Lute Olson	Arizona	30	690	240	.742
Rob Evans	Arizona St.	11	166	153	.520
Steve Shields	Ark.-Little Rock	0	0	0	.000
Van Holt	Ark.-Pine Bluff	1	4	24	.143
Stan Heath	Arkansas	2	39	25	.609
Dickey Nutt	Arkansas St.	8	117	113	.509
Jim Crews	Army	18	299	231	.564
Cliff Ellis	Auburn	28	520	323	.617
Dave Loos	Austin Peay	17	280	234	.545
Tim Buckley	Ball St.	7	103	94	.523
Scott Drew	Baylor	1	20	11	.645
Rick Byrd	Belmont	23	441	271	.619
Clifford Reed	Bethune-Cookman	2	14	26	.350
Al Walker	Binghamton	15	179	217	.452
Duane Reboul	Birmingham-So.	14	347	94	.787
Greg Graham	Boise St.	2	31	21	.596
Al Skinner	Boston College	15	236	211	.528
Dennis Wolff	Boston U.	11	179	136	.568
Dan Dakich	Bowling Green	6	102	73	.583
Jim Les	Bradley	1	12	18	.400
Steve Cleveland	Brigham Young	6	108	78	.581
Glen Miller	Brown	10	152	111	.578
Pat Flannery	Bucknell	14	229	164	.583
Reggie Witherspoon	Buffalo	4	24	85	.220
Todd Lickliter	Butler	2	53	12	.815
Kevin Bromley	Cal Poly	3	35	38	.479
Bob Burton	Cal St. Fullerton	0	0	0	.000
Bobby Braswell	Cal St. Northridge	7	111	94	.541
Ben Braun	California	26	477	322	.597
Robbie Laing	Campbell	0	0	0	.000
Mike MacDonald	Canisius	6	78	95	.451
Kevin Johnson	Centenary (La.)	4	46	64	.418
Howie Dickenman	Central Conn. St.	7	112	92	.549

Coach	School	Yr	W	L	Pct.
Jay Smith	Central Mich.	7	98	100	.495
Jim Platt	Charleston So.	7	91	110	.453
Bobby Lutz	Charlotte	14	273	155	.638
Jeff Lebo	Chattanooga	5	96	52	.649
Kevin Jones	Chicago St.	0	0	0	.000
Bob Huggins	Cincinnati	22	517	184	.738
Pat Dennis	Citadel	11	129	174	.426
Oliver Purnell	Clemson	15	256	191	.573
Mike Garland	Cleveland St.	0	0	0	.000
Pete Strickland	Coastal Caro.	5	46	93	.331
Tom Herrion	Col. of Charleston	1	25	8	.758
Emmett Davis	Colgate	5	71	70	.504
Ricardo Patton	Colorado	8	125	103	.548
Dale Layer	Colorado St.	12	214	133	.617
Joe Jones	Columbia	0	0	0	.000
Jim Calhoun	Connecticut	31	647	296	.686
Ron Fang Mitchell	Coppin St.	17	286	214	.572
Steve Donahue	Cornell	3	21	60	.259
Dana Altman	Creighton	14	258	167	.607
Dave Faucher	Dartmouth	12	133	183	.421
Bob McKillop	Davidson	14	222	181	.551
Brian Gregory	Dayton	0	0	0	.000
David Henderson	Delaware	3	49	40	.551
Greg Jackson	Delaware St.	12	199	122	.620
Terry Carroll	Denver	2	25	35	.417
Dave Leitao	DePaul	3	38	48	.442
Perry Watson	Detroit	10	194	113	.632
Tom Davis	Drake	28	543	290	.652
Bruiser Flint	Drexel	7	119	98	.548
Mike Krzyzewski	Duke	28	663	234	.739
Danny Nee	Duquesne	23	386	319	.548
Bill Herrion	East Caro.	12	215	136	.613
Murry Bartow	East Tenn. St.	6	103	83	.554
Rick Samuels	Eastern Ill.	24	345	329	.512
Travis Ford	Eastern Ky.	6	83	96	.464
Jim Boone	Eastern Mich.	17	295	200	.596
Ray Giacoletti	Eastern Wash.	6	100	70	.588
Ernie Nestor	Elon	5	68	81	.456
Steve Merfeld	Evansville	6	102	73	.583
Tim O'Toole	Fairfield	5	69	75	.479
Tom Green	Fairleigh Dickinson	20	321	255	.557
Sidney Green	Fla. Atlantic	8	84	145	.367
Billy Donovan	Florida	9	183	94	.661
Mike Gillespie	Florida A&M	2	26	31	.456
Donnie Marsh	Florida Int'l	8	101	116	.465
Leonard Hamilton	Florida St.	15	214	225	.487
Dereck Whittenburg	Fordham	4	67	50	.573
Ray Lopes	Fresno St.	1	20	8	.714
Larry Davis	Furman	6	76	101	.429
Jeff Price	Ga. Southern	10	197	96	.672
Rick Scruggs	Gardner-Webb	17	309	212	.593
Jim Larranaga	George Mason	19	297	244	.549
Karl Hobbs	George Washington	2	24	33	.421
Craig Esherick	Georgetown	5	90	59	.604
Dennis Felton	Georgia	5	100	54	.649
Michael Perry	Georgia St.	1	10	9	.526
Paul Hewitt	Georgia Tech	6	114	71	.616
Mark Few	Gonzaga	4	105	29	.784
Larry Wright	Grambling	4	30	85	.261
Bobby Collins	Hampton	1	19	11	.633
Larry Harrison	Hartford	3	34	55	.382
Frank Sullivan	Harvard	19	251	263	.488
Riley Wallace	Hawaii	18	277	243	.533
Bart Lundy	High Point	5	115	40	.742
Tom Pecora	Hofstra	2	20	41	.328
Ralph Willard	Holy Cross	13	220	170	.564
Ray McCallum	Houston	10	161	131	.551
Frankie Allen	Howard	16	212	249	.460
Leonard Perry	Idaho	2	22	34	.393
Doug Oliver	Idaho St.	5	53	84	.387
Jimmy Collins	Ill.-Chicago	7	107	101	.514
Bruce Weber	Illinois	5	103	54	.656
Porter Moser	Illinois St.	3	54	34	.614
Mike Davis	Indiana	3	67	38	.638
Royce Waltman	Indiana St.	16	276	178	.608
Jeff Ruland	Iona	5	88	65	.575
Steve Alford	Iowa	12	229	135	.629
Wayne Morgan	Iowa St.	6	91	84	.520
Doug Noll	IPFW	11	166	188	.469
Ron Hunter	IUPUI	9	135	124	.521
Tevester Anderson	Jackson St.	5	103	52	.665
Hugh Durham	Jacksonville	35	604	401	.601
Mike LaPlante	Jacksonville St.	3	42	45	.483
Sherman Dillard	James Madison	9	115	136	.458

Coach	School	Yr	W	L	Pct.
Bill Self	Kansas	10	207	105	.663
Jim Wooldridge	Kansas St.	16	265	199	.571
Jim Christian	Kent St.	1	21	10	.677
Tubby Smith	Kentucky	12	269	100	.729
Billy Hahn	La Salle	2	27	34	.443
Jessie Evans	La.-Lafayette	6	112	72	.609
Mike Vining	La.-Monroe	22	381	265	.590
Fran O'Hanlon	Lafayette	8	123	107	.535
Billy Tubbs	Lamar	28	595	297	.667
Billy Taylor	Lehigh	1	16	12	.571
Randy Dunton	Liberty	2	25	32	.439
Scott Sanderson	Lipscomb	3	35	48	.422
Larry Reynolds	Long Beach St.	6	115	57	.669
Jim Ferry	Long Island	5	111	37	.750
Keith Richard	Louisiana Tech	5	91	54	.628
Rick Pitino	Louisville	17	396	144	.733
Larry Farmer	Loyola (Ill.)	11	157	159	.497
Scott Hicks	Loyola (Md.)	11	146	165	.469
Steve Aggers	Loyola Marymount	19	268	281	.488
John Brady	LSU	12	191	158	.547
John Giannini	Maine	14	273	139	.663
Bobby Gonzalez	Manhattan	4	69	46	.600
Dave Magarity	Marist	22	307	313	.495
Tom Crean	Marquette	4	83	41	.669
Ron Jirsa	Marshall	2	35	30	.538
Gary Williams	Maryland	25	502	281	.641
Steve Lappas	Massachusetts	15	254	206	.552
Tic Price	McNeese St.	7	129	77	.626
Thomas C. Trotter	Md.-East. Shore	3	28	57	.329
John Calipari	Memphis	11	260	101	.720
Mark Slonaker	Mercer	7	68	128	.347
Perry Clark	Miami (Fla.)	14	236	183	.563
Charlie Coles	Miami (Ohio)	13	212	177	.545
Tommy Amaker	Michigan	6	96	86	.527
Tom Izzo	Michigan St.	8	189	78	.708
Kermit Davis Jr.	Middle Tenn.	5	87	64	.576
Dan Monson	Minnesota	6	119	74	.617
Rod Barnes	Mississippi	5	100	61	.621
Rick Stansbury	Mississippi St.	5	100	60	.625
Lafayette Stribling	Mississippi Val.	20	270	296	.477
Quin Snyder	Missouri	4	84	49	.632
Dave Calloway	Monmouth	6	74	82	.474
Pat Kennedy	Montana	23	406	293	.581
Mick Durham	Montana St.	13	203	171	.543
Kyle Macy	Morehead St.	6	75	92	.449
Butch Beard	Morgan St.	6	55	116	.322
Milan Brown	Mt. St. Mary's	0	0	0	.000
Mick Cronin	Murray St.	0	0	0	.000
Jerry Eaves	N.C. A&T	0	0	0	.000
Don DeVoe	Navy	30	507	366	.581
Barry Collier	Nebraska	14	234	182	.563
Trent Johnson	Nevada	4	54	65	.454
Phil Rowe	New Hampshire	17	198	243	.449
Ritchie McKay	New Mexico	7	93	107	.465
Lou Henson	New Mexico St.	39	762	386	.664
Monte Towe	New Orleans	2	30	28	.517
Joe Mihalich	Niagara	5	84	63	.571
Ricky Blanton	Nicholls St.	1	3	25	.107
Dwight Freeman	Norfolk St.	5	60	80	.429
Roy Williams	North Carolina	15	418	101	.805
Herb Sendek	North Carolina St.	10	190	124	.605
Johnny Jones	North Texas	3	37	51	.420
Ron Everhart	Northeastern	9	115	140	.451
Mike Adras	Northern Ariz.	4	64	52	.552
Rob Judson	Northern Ill.	2	29	30	.492
Greg McDermott	Northern Iowa	9	156	96	.619
Bill Carmody	Northwestern	7	131	74	.639
Mike McConathy	Northwestern St.	4	55	65	.458
Mike Brey	Notre Dame	8	165	83	.665
Greg Kampe	Oakland	19	321	222	.591
Tim O'Shea	Ohio	2	31	27	.534
Jim O'Brien	Ohio St.	21	354	289	.551
Kelvin Sampson	Oklahoma	20	391	228	.632
Eddie Sutton	Oklahoma St.	33	724	288	.715
Blaine Taylor	Old Dominion	9	166	97	.631
Scott Sutton	Oral Roberts	4	58	60	.492
Ernie Kent	Oregon	12	207	148	.583
Jay John	Oregon St.	1	13	15	.464
Bob Thomason	Pacific (Cal.)	18	287	227	.558
Ed DeChellis	Penn St.	7	105	93	.530
Fran Dunphy	Pennsylvania	14	253	135	.652
Paul Westphal	Pepperdine	4	100	40	.714
Jamie Dixon	Pittsburgh	0	0	0	.000
Michael Holton	Portland	2	17	41	.293

Coach	School	Yr	W	L	Pct.
Heath Schroyer	Portland St.	1	5	22	.185
Jerry Francis	Prairie View	1	17	12	.586
John Thompson III	Princeton	3	48	34	.585
Tim Welsh	Providence	8	151	95	.614
Gene Keady	Purdue	25	507	271	.652
Joe DeSantis	Quinnipiac	7	73	120	.378
Byron Samuels	Radford	3	27	56	.325
Jim Baron	Rhode Island	16	233	234	.499
Willis Wilson	Rice	11	146	165	.469
Jerry Wainwright	Richmond	9	151	117	.563
Don Harnum	Rider	6	91	79	.535
Mark Schmidt	Robert Morris	2	22	35	.386
Gary Waters	Rutgers	7	122	89	.578
Jerome Jenkins	Sacramento St.	3	26	58	.310
Dave Bike	Sacred Heart	25	400	332	.546
Bob Marlin	Sam Houston St.	5	85	57	.599
Jimmy Tillette	Samford	6	102	73	.583
Brad Holland	San Diego	11	167	142	.540
Steve Fisher	San Diego St.	10	160	116	.580
Philip Mathews	San Francisco	8	122	109	.528
Phil Johnson	San Jose St.	2	19	37	.339
Dick Davey	Santa Clara	11	186	132	.585
Ed Daniels Jr.	Savannah St.	1	3	24	.111
Louis Orr	Seton Hall	3	49	42	.538
Rob Lanier	Siena	2	38	30	.559
John Pelphrey	South Ala.	1	14	14	.500
Dave Odom	South Carolina	17	311	206	.602
Ben Betts Jr.	South Carolina St.	0	0	0	.000
Robert McCullum	South Fla.	3	44	45	.494
Gary Garner	Southeast Mo. St.	20	340	246	.580
Billy Kennedy	Southeastern La.	6	60	108	.357
Henry Bibby	Southern California	8	117	102	.534
Matt Painter	Southern Ill.	0	0	0	.000
Mike Dement	Southern Methodist	17	250	228	.523
James Green	Southern Miss.	7	110	96	.534
Michael Grant	Southern U.	7	126	94	.573
Bill Evans	Southern Utah	12	160	156	.506
Barry Hinson	Southwest Mo. St.	6	106	77	.579
Dennis Nutt	Southwest Tex. St.	3	42	43	.494
Anthony Solomon	St. Bonaventure	0	0	0	.000
Ron Ganulin	St. Francis (N.Y.)	14	186	202	.479
Bobby Jones	St. Francis (Pa.)	4	39	71	.355
Mike Jarvis	St. John's (N.Y.)	18	361	198	.646
Phil Martelli	St. Joseph's	8	149	97	.606
Brad Soderberg	St. Louis	9	147	87	.628
Randy Bennett	St. Mary's (Cal.)	2	24	35	.407
Bob Leckie	St. Peter's	3	18	67	.212
Mike Montgomery	Stanford	25	517	242	.681
Danny Kaspar	Stephen F. Austin	12	262	92	.740
Derek Waugh	Stetson	3	30	44	.405
Nick Macarchuk	Stony Brook	26	352	391	.474
Jim Boeheim	Syracuse	27	653	226	.743
Neil Dougherty	TCU	1	9	19	.321
John Chaney	Temple	31	693	269	.720
Bret Campbell	Tenn.-Martin	4	49	65	.430
Buzz Peterson	Tennessee	7	137	78	.637
Cy Alexander	Tennessee St.	16	276	200	.580
Mike Sutton	Tennessee Tech	1	20	12	.625
Ronnie Arrow	Tex. A&M-Corp. Chris.	12	167	150	.527
Bob Hoffman	Tex.-Pan American	13	296	142	.676
Rick Barnes	Texas	16	318	184	.633
Melvin Watkins	Texas A&M	7	95	111	.461
Ronnie Courtney	Texas Southern	2	29	30	.492
Bob Knight	Texas Tech	37	809	311	.722
Eddie McCarter	Texas-Arlington	11	135	168	.446
Tim Carter	Texas-San Antonio	9	126	124	.504
Stan Joplin	Toledo	7	116	89	.566
Michael Hunt	Towson	2	15	42	.263
Don Maestri	Troy St.	21	358	240	.599
Shawn Finney	Tulane	3	39	51	.433
John Phillips	Tulsa	2	50	17	.746
Mike Anderson	UAB	1	21	13	.618
Pat Douglass	UC Irvine	22	471	196	.706
John Masi	UC Riverside	24	442	233	.655
Bob Williams	UC Santa Barb.	15	265	168	.612
Kirk Speraw	UCF	10	146	148	.497
Ben Howland	UCLA	9	168	99	.629
Tom Sullivan	UMBC	18	252	250	.502
Rich Zvosec	UMKC	11	130	179	.421
Eddie Biedenbach	UNC Asheville	10	131	152	.463
Fran McCaffery	UNC Greensboro	7	110	97	.531
Brad Brownell	UNC Wilmington	1	24	7	.774
Charles Spoonhour	UNLV	18	361	193	.652
Rick Majerus	Utah	19	407	142	.741

Coach	School	Yr	W	L	Pct.
Stew Morrill	Utah St.	17	336	180	.651
Billy Gillispie	UTEP	1	6	24	.200
Jeff Capel III	Va. Commonwealth	1	18	10	.643
Homer Drew	Valparaiso	26	505	306	.623
Kevin Stallings	Vanderbilt	10	185	122	.603
Tom Brennan	Vermont	26	315	394	.444
Jay Wright	Villanova	9	156	114	.578
Pete Gillen	Virginia	16	325	168	.659
Seth Greenberg	Virginia Tech	13	213	170	.556
Bart Bellairs	VMI	11	122	178	.407
Mike Deane	Wagner	19	342	220	.609
Skip Prosser	Wake Forest	8	175	77	.694
Lorenzo Romar	Washington	7	103	105	.495
Dick Bennett	Washington St.	21	401	203	.664
Joe Cravens	Weber St.	8	131	94	.582
John Beilein	West Virginia	21	386	230	.627
Steve Shurina	Western Caro.	3	27	60	.310
Derek Thomas	Western Ill.	0	0	0	.000
Darrin Horn	Western Ky.	0	0	0	.000
Steve Hawkins	Western Mich.	0	0	0	.000
Mark Turgeon	Wichita St.	5	67	75	.472
Tony Shaver	William & Mary	17	358	121	.747
Gregg Marshall	Winthrop	5	99	52	.656
Tod Kowalczyk	Wis.-Green Bay	1	10	20	.333
Bruce Pearl	Wis.-Milwaukee	11	271	67	.802
Bo Ryan	Wisconsin	19	426	124	.775
Mike Young	Wofford	1	14	15	.483
Paul Biancardi	Wright St.	0	0	0	.000
Steve McClain	Wyoming	5	100	52	.658
Thad Matta	Xavier	3	76	20	.792
James Jones	Yale	4	52	61	.460
John Robic	Youngstown St.	4	45	70	.391

Fastest To Milestone Wins

(Head coaches with at least half their seasons at Division I.)

FASTEST TO 100 WINS

Rk. Name, School	Games	Won	Lost	Pct.	Season	Year
1. Doc Meanwell, Wisconsin & Missouri	109	100	9	.917	7th	1918
2. Buck Freeman, St. John's (N.Y.)	110	100	10	.909	5th	1932
3. Adolph Rupp, Kentucky	116	100	16	.862	6th	1936
4. Jim Boeheim, Syracuse	117	100	17	.855	4th	1980
4. Jerry Tarkanian, Long Beach St.	117	100	17	.855	5th	1973
6. Everett Case, North Carolina St.	120	100	20	.833	4th	1950
6. Fred Taylor, Ohio St.	120	100	20	.833	5th	1963
7. Lew Andreas, Syracuse	122	100	22	.820	7th	1931
7. Denny Crum, Louisville	122	100	22	.820	5th	1976
7. Everett Dean, Carleton & Indiana	122	100	22	.820	7th	1929
11. Clair Bee, Rider & Long Island	123	100	23	.813	5th	1934
12. Don Haskins, UTEP	125	100	25	.800	5th	1966
12. Nat Holman, CCNY	125	100	25	.800	10th	1929
12. Buster Sheary, Holy Cross	125	100	25	.800	5th	1953
15. Mark Few, Gonzaga	126	100	26	.794	4th	2003
15. Tony Hinkle, Butler	126	100	26	.794	7th	1933
15. Ray Meyer, DePaul	126	100	26	.794	6th	1948
18. Harry Combes, Illinois	127	100	27	.787	6th	1953
18. Peck Hickman, Louisville	127	100	27	.787	5th	1949
20. Vic Bubas, Duke	128	100	28	.781	5th	1964
21. Hugh Greer, Connecticut	129	100	29	.775	6th	1952
21. Roy Williams, Kansas	129	100	29	.775	4th	1992
23. Speedy Morris, La Salle	130	100	30	.769	4th	1990
23. Fred Schaus, West Virginia	130	100	30	.769	5th	1959
23. Clifford Wells, Tulane	130	100	30	.769	6th	1951
26. Harry Fisher, Columbia	131	100	31	.763	10th	1916
26. Joseph Lapchick, St. John's (N.Y.)	131	100	31	.763	7th	1943
26. Nolan Richardson, Tulsa	131	100	31	.763	5th	1985
29. Gale Catlett, Cincinnati	132	100	32	.758	5th	1977
29. Jack Ramsay, St. Joseph's	132	100	32	.758	5th	1960
29. Bruce Stewart, West Virginia Wesleyan & Middle Tenn.	132	100	32	.758	4th	1986
32. Lou Carnesecca, St. John's (N.Y.)	134	100	34	.746	5th	1970
32. Frank McGuire, St. John's (N.Y.)	134	100	34	.746	5th	1952
32. Dudey Moore, Duquesne	134	100	34	.746	5th	1953
35. Ben Carnevale, North Carolina & Navy	135	100	35	.741	6th	1950
35. John Wooden, Indiana St. & UCLA	135	100	35	.741	5th	1951

FASTEST TO 200 WINS

Rk. Name, School	Games	Won	Lost	Pct.	Season	Year
1. Clair Bee, Rider & Long Island ..	231	200	31	.866	12th	1938
2. Jerry Tarkanian, Long Beach St. & UNLV	234	200	34	.855	9th	1977
3. Everett Case, North Carolina St.	250	200	50	.800	9th	1954
4. Harold Anderson, Toledo & Bowling Green	251	200	51	.797	10th	1945
4. Lew Andreas, Syracuse	251	200	51	.797	14th	1939
4. Nat Holman, CCNY	251	200	51	.797	18th	1937
4. Adolph Rupp, Kentucky	251	200	51	.797	13th	1943
8. Henry Iba, Northwest Mo. St., Colorado & Oklahoma St.	252	200	52	.794	10th	1939
8. Roy Williams, Kansas	252	200	52	.794	8th	1996
10. Vic Bubas, Duke	254	200	54	.787	10th	1969
10. Denny Crum, Louisville............	254	200	54	.787	9th	1980
10. Doc Meanwell, Missouri & Wisconsin	254	200	54	.787	15th	1927
13. Hec Edmundson, Washington ..	261	200	61	.766	13th	1931
13. Hugh Greer, Connecticut	261	200	61	.766	11th	1957
15. George Keogan, Wis.-Superior, St. Louis, St. Thomas (Minn.), Allegheny, Valparaiso & Notre Dame	263	200	63	.760	14th	1930
15. Joseph Lapchick, St. John's (N.Y.)	263	200	63	.760	13th	1958
17. Jack Ramsay, St. Joseph's	264	200	64	.758	10th	1965
18. Peck Hickman, Louisville	265	200	65	.755	10th	1954
19. Jim Boeheim, Syracuse	266	200	66	.752	9th	1985
19. Fred Schaus, West Virginia & Purdue	266	200	66	.752	10th	1976
21. Don Haskins, UTEP	269	200	69	.743	11th	1972
22. Bob Knight, Army & Indiana	270	200	70	.741	11th	1976
23. Lou Carnesecca, St. John's (N.Y.)	271	200	71	.738	10th	1978
23. Harry Combes, Illinois	271	200	71	.738	12th	1959
23. Arthur Schabinger, Ottawa, Emporia St. & Creighton	271	200	71	.738	16th	1932
26. Dudey Moore, Duquesne	272	200	72	.735	11th	1959
27. Pete Gillen, Xavier	273	200	73	.733	9th	1994
28. Tom Blackburn, Dayton	274	200	74	.730	10th	1957
29. Chick Davies, Duquesne	275	200	75	.727	15th	1939
29. Boyd Grant, Fresno St. & Colorado St.	275	200	75	.727	10th	1988

FASTEST TO 300 WINS

Rk. Name, School	Games	Won	Lost	Pct.	Season	Year
1. Clair Bee, Rider & Long Island	344	300	44	.872	15th	1943
2. Adolph Rupp, Kentucky	366	300	66	.820	17th	1947
3. Jerry Tarkanian, Long Beach St. & UNLV	370	300	70	.811	13th	1982
3. Roy Williams, Kansas	370	300	70	.811	11th	1999
5. Everett Case, North Carolina St.	377	300	77	.796	13th	1959
6. Harold Anderson, Toledo & Bowling Green	378	300	78	.794	14th	1949
7. Denny Crum, Louisville	382	300	82	.785	13th	1984
7. Henry Iba, Northwest Mo. St., Colorado & Oklahoma St.	382	300	82	.785	15th	1944
9. Hec Edmundson, Washington	392	300	92	.765	18th	1936
10. Jim Boeheim, Syracuse..............	393	300	93	.763	13th	1989
10. Frank Keaney, Rhode Island	393	300	93	.763	24th	1944
12. George Keogan, Wis.-Superior, St. Louis, St. Thomas (Minn.), Allegheny, Valparaiso & Notre Dame	394	300	94	.761	20th	1936
13. Ray Mears, Wittenberg & Tennessee	395	300	95	.759	16th	1972
14. Piggy Lambert, Purdue	397	300	97	.756	23rd	1940
15. Lew Andreas, Syracuse	400	300	100	.750	23rd	1947
15. Chick Davies, Duquesne	400	300	100	.750	21st	1948
17. John Lawther, Westminster (Pa.) & Penn St.	402	300	102	.746	21st	1947
18. Nolan Richardson, Tulsa & Arkansas	404	300	104	.743	13th	1993
19. Peck Hickman, Louisville..............	405	300	105	.741	15th	1959
20. Dean Smith, North Carolina........	406	300	106	.739	15th	1976
20. Eddie Sutton, Creighton & Arkansas	406	300	106	.739	15th	1984
22. Bob Knight, Army & Indiana	407	300	107	.737	15th	1980
22. John Thompson, Georgetown	407	300	107	.737	14th	1986
24. Nat Holman, CCNY	408	300	108	.735	27th	1946
25. Rick Majerus, Marquette, Ball St. & Utah	409	300	109	.733	14th	1998

FASTEST TO 400 WINS

Rk. Name, School	Games	Won	Lost	Pct.	Season	Year
1. Adolph Rupp, Kentucky	477	400	77	.839	20th	1950
2. Clair Bee, Rider & Long Island ..	483	400	83	.828	21st	1951
3. Jerry Tarkanian, Long Beach St. & UNLV	492	400	92	.813	17th	1985
4. Roy Williams, Kansas	496	400	96	.806	15th	2003
5. Henry Iba, Northwest Mo. St., Colorado & Oklahoma St.	500	400	100	.800	19th	1948
6. Frank Keaney, Rhode Island	521	400	121	.768	28th	1948
7. Phog Allen, Baker, Haskell, Central Mo. St. & Kansas	522	400	122	.766	29th	1935
7. George Keogan, Wis.-Superior, St. Louis, St. Thomas (Minn.), Allegheny, Valparaiso & Notre Dame	522	400	122	.766	26th	1942
9. Jim Boeheim, Syracuse	527	400	127	.759	17th	1993
10. Dean Smith, North Carolina......	531	400	131	.753	19th	1980
11. Lou Carnesecca, St. John's (N.Y.)	535	400	135	.748	18th	1986
11. John Thompson, Georgetown	535	400	135	.748	18th	1990
13. Denny Crum, Louisville............	536	400	136	.746	17th	1988
13. Ed Diddle, Western Ky.	536	400	136	.746	24th	1946
13. Nolan Richardson, Tulsa & Arkansas	536	400	136	.746	17th	1997
16. Rick Majerus, Marquette, Ball St. & Utah..................................	538	400	138	.743	19th	2003
17. Nat Holman, CCNY	539	400	139	.742	32nd	1952
18. Eddie Sutton, Creighton, Arkansas & Kentucky	541	400	141	.739	19th	1988
19. Al McGuire, Belmont Abbey & Marquette	542	400	142	.738	20th	1977
20. Bob Knight, Army & Indiana	545	400	145	.734	20th	1985
21. Bob Huggins, Walsh, Akron & Cincinnati	548	400	148	.730	19th	1999
21. John Wooden, Indiana St. & UCLA	548	400	148	.730	20th	1966

FASTEST TO 500 WINS

Rk. Name, School	Games	Won	Lost	Pct.	Season	Year
1. Adolph Rupp, Kentucky	583	500	83	.858	23rd	1955
2. Jerry Tarkanian, Long Beach St. & UNLV	604	500	104	.828	20th	1988
3. Henry Iba, Northwest Mo. St., Colorado & Oklahoma St.	631	500	131	.792	23rd	1952
4. Phog Allen, Baker, Haskell, Central Mo. St. & Kansas	646	500	146	.774	34th	1940
5. John Wooden, Indiana St. & UCLA	652	500	152	.767	24th	1970
6. Dean Smith, North Carolina......	653	500	153	.766	23rd	1984
7. John Chaney, Cheyney & Temple	662	500	162	.755	22nd	1994
8. Ed Diddle, Western Ky.	667	500	167	.750	28th	1950
9. Jim Boeheim, Syracuse	669	500	169	.747	21st	1997
10. Bob Huggins, Walsh, Akron & Cincinnati	671	500	171	.745	21st	2002
11. Lou Carnesecca, St. John's (N.Y.)	683	500	183	.732	23rd	1991
11. Bob Knight, Army & Indiana	683	500	183	.732	24th	1989
13. Eddie Sutton, Creighton, Arkansas, Kentucky & Oklahoma St.	685	500	185	.730	23rd	1993
13. John Thompson, Georgetown	685	500	185	.730	22nd	1994
15. Denny Crum, Louisville..............	687	500	187	.728	22nd	1993
16. Lute Olson, Long Beach St., Iowa & Arizona	690	500	190	.725	23rd	1996
17. Nolan Richardson, Tulsa & Arkansas	695	500	195	.719	22nd	2002
18. Frank McGuire, St. John's (N.Y.)	699	500	199	.715	27th	1977

FASTEST TO 600 WINS

Rk. Name, School	Games	Won	Lost	Pct.	Season	Year
1. Adolph Rupp, Kentucky	704	600	104	.852	27th	1959
2. Jerry Tarkanian, Long Beach St. & UNLV	720	600	120	.833	24th	1992
3. John Wooden, Indiana St. & UCLA	755	600	155	.795	27th	1973
4. Dean Smith, North Carolina......	773	600	173	.776	26th	1987
5. Henry Iba, Northwest Mo. St., Colorado & Oklahoma St.	775	600	175	.774	29th	1958
6. Phog Allen, Baker, Haskell, Central Mo. St. & Kansas	780	600	180	.769	41st	1947
7. Ed Diddle, Western Ky.	790	600	190	.759	32nd	1954
8. Jim Boeheim, Syracuse	807	600	207	.743	25th	2001
9. Bob Knight, Army & Indiana	812	600	212	.739	27th	1993
10. Lute Olson, Long Beach St., Iowa & Arizona	815	600	215	.736	27th	2000
11. John Chaney, Cheyney & Temple	816	600	216	.735	27th	1999
12. Mike Krzyzewski, Army & Duke	823	600	223	.729	26th	2001
13. Denny Crum, Louisville............	825	600	225	.727	26th	1997
14. Cam Henderson, Muskingum, Davis & Elkins, & Marshall........	830	600	230	.723	34th	1953
15. Eddie Sutton, Creighton, Arkansas, Kentucky & Oklahoma St.	837	600	237	.717	28th	1998

FASTEST TO 700 WINS

Rk. Name, School	Games	Won	Lost	Pct.	Season	Year
1. Adolph Rupp, Kentucky	836	700	136	.837	32nd	1964
2. Jerry Tarkanian, Long Beach St., UNLV & Fresno St.	876	700	176	.799	29th	2000

Rk. Name, School	Games	Won	Lost	Pct.	Season	Year
3. Dean Smith, North Carolina	904	700	204	.774	30th	1991
4. Phog Allen, Baker, Haskell, Central Mo. St. & Kansas	938	700	238	.746	47th	1953
5. Ed Diddle, Western Ky.	946	700	246	.740	28th	1960
6. Henry Iba, Northwest Mo. St., Colorado & Oklahoma St.	951	700	251	.736	35th	1964
7. Bob Knight, Army & Indiana	956	700	256	.732	32nd	1997
8. Eddie Sutton, Creighton, Arkansas, Kentucky & Oklahoma St.	975	700	275	.718	32nd	2002
9. Don Haskins, UTEP	1,029	700	329	.680	37th	1998
10. Lou Henson, Hardin-Simmons, Illinois & New Mexico St.	1,046	700	346	.669	36th	2000
11. Lefty Driesell, Davidson, Maryland, James Madison & Georgia St.	1,048	700	348	.668	37th	1999
12. Ray Meyer, DePaul	1,051	700	351	.666	52nd	1984
13. Norm Stewart, Northern Iowa & Missouri	1,055	700	355	.664	36th	1998

FASTEST TO 800 WINS

Rk. Name, School	Games	Won	Lost	Pct.	Season	Year
1. Adolph Rupp, Kentucky	972	800	172	.823	37th	1969
2. Dean Smith, North Carolina	1,029	800	229	.777	33rd	1994
3. Bob Knight, Army, Indiana & Texas Tech	1,102	800	302	.726	37nd	2003

Top 10 Best Career Starts By Percentage

(Head coaches with at least half of their seasons at Division I)

1 SEASON

Coach, Team	Season	W	L	Pct.
Norman Shepard, North Carolina	1924	23	0	1.000
Bill Hodges, Indiana St.	1979	33	1	.970
Tom Gola, La Salle	1969	23	1	.958
Lou Rossini, Columbia	1951	21	1	.955
Earl Brown, Dartmouth	1944	19	2	.905
Phil Johnson, Weber St.	1969	27	3	.900
Bill Guthridge, North Carolina	1998	34	4	.895
Gary Cunningham, UCLA	1978	25	3	.893
Bob Davies, Seton Hall	1947	24	3	.889
Jerry Tarkanian, Long Beach St.	1969	23	3	.885

2 SEASONS

Coach, Team	Seasons	W	L	Pct.
Lew Andreas, Syracuse	1925-26	33	3	.917
Bill Carmody, Princeton	1997-98	51	6	.895
Everett Case, North Carolina St.	1947-48	55	8	.873
Buck Freeman, St. John's (N.Y.)	1928-29	41	6	.872
Gary Cunningham, UCLA	1978-79	50	8	.862
Nibs Price, California	1925-26	25	4	.862
Denny Crum, Louisville	1972-73	49	8	.860
Adolph Rupp, Kentucky	1931-32	30	5	.857
Jerry Tarkanian, Long Beach St.	1969-70	47	8	.855
John Castellani, Seattle	1957-58	45	9	.833

3 SEASONS

Coach, Team	Seasons	W	L	Pct.
Nibs Price, California	1925-27	38	4	.905
Buck Freeman, St. John's (N.Y.)	1928-30	64	7	.901
Lew Andreas, Syracuse	1925-27	48	7	.873
Adolph Rupp, Kentucky	1931-33	51	8	.864
Jerry Tarkanian, Long Beach St.	1969-71	69	12	.852
Jim Boeheim, Syracuse	1977-79	74	14	.841
Bill Carmody, Princeton	1997-99	73	14	.841
Everett Case, North Carolina St.	1947-49	80	16	.833
Ben Carnevale, North Carolina & Navy	1945-47	68	14	.829
Phil Johnson, Weber St.	1969-71	68	16	.810

4 SEASONS

Coach, Team	Seasons	W	L	Pct.
Buck Freeman, St. John's (N.Y.)	1928-31	85	8	.914
Adolph Rupp, Kentucky	1931-34	67	9	.882
Jerry Tarkanian, Long Beach St.	1969-72	92	15	.860
Jim Boeheim, Syracuse	1977-80	100	18	.847
Fred Taylor, Ohio St.	1959-62	89	17	.840
Everett Case, North Carolina St.	1947-50	107	22	.829
Nibs Price, California	1925-28	47	10	.825
Nat Holman, CCNY	1920-23	46	10	.821
Denny Crum, Louisville	1972-75	98	22	.817
Lew Andreas, Syracuse	1925-28	58	13	.817

5 SEASONS

Coach, Team	Seasons	W	L	Pct.
Buck Freeman, St. John's (N.Y.)	1928-32	107	12	.899
Adolph Rupp, Kentucky	1931-35	86	11	.887
Jerry Tarkanian, Long Beach St. & UNLV	1969-73	116	17	.872
Nat Holman, CCNY	1920-24	58	11	.841
Fred Taylor, Ohio St.	1959-63	109	21	.838
Nibs Price, California	1925-29	64	13	.831
Everett Case, North Carolina St.	1947-51	137	29	.825
Buster Sheary, Holy Cross	1949-53	110	27	.803
Jim Boeheim, Syracuse	1977-81	122	30	.803
Lew Andreas, Syracuse	1925-29	69	17	.802

6 SEASONS

Coach, Team	Seasons	W	L	Pct.
Buck Freeman, St. John's (N.Y.)	1928-33	130	16	.890
Adolph Rupp, Kentucky	1931-36	101	17	.856
Jerry Tarkanian, Long Beach St. & UNLV	1969-74	136	23	.855
Nat Holman, CCNY	1920-25	70	13	.843
Buster Sheary, Holy Cross	1949-54	136	29	.824
Lew Andreas, Syracuse	1925-30	87	19	.821
Everett Dean, Carleton & Indiana	1922-27	82	18	.820
Clair Bee, Rider & Long Island	1929-34	101	23	.815
Fred Taylor, Ohio St.	1959-64	125	29	.812
Everett Case, North Carolina St.	1947-52	161	39	.805

7 SEASONS

Coach, Team	Seasons	W	L	Pct.
Buck Freeman, St. John's (N.Y.)	1928-34	146	19	.885
Jerry Tarkanian, Long Beach St. & UNLV	1969-75	160	28	.851
Adolph Rupp, Kentucky	1931-37	118	22	.843
Clair Bee, Rider & Long Island	1929-35	125	25	.833
Everett Dean, Carleton & Indiana	1922-28	97	20	.829
Lew Andreas, Syracuse	1925-31	103	23	.817
Nat Holman, CCNY	1920-26	79	18	.814
Buster Sheary, Holy Cross	1949-55	155	36	.812
Everett Case, North Carolina St.	1947-53	187	45	.806
Vic Bubas, Duke	1960-66	158	39	.802

8 SEASONS

Coach, Team	Seasons	W	L	Pct.
Jerry Tarkanian, Long Beach St. & UNLV	1969-76	189	30	.863
Clair Bee, Rider & Long Island	1929-36	150	25	.857
Buck Freeman, St. John's (N.Y.)	1928-35	159	27	.855
Adolph Rupp, Kentucky	1931-38	131	27	.829
Nat Holman, CCNY	1920-27	88	21	.807
Everett Case, North Carolina St.	1947-54	213	52	.804
Hugh Greer, Connecticut	1947-54	151	38	.799
Lew Andreas, Syracuse	1925-32	116	30	.795
Roy Williams, Kansas	1989-96	213	56	.792
Henry Iba, Northwest Mo. St., Colorado & Oklahoma St.	1930-37	157	42	.789

9 SEASONS

Coach, Team	Seasons	W	L	Pct.
Jerry Tarkanian, Long Beach St. & UNLV	1969-77	218	33	.869
Clair Bee, Rider & Long Island	1929-37	177	28	.863
Buck Freeman, St. John's (N.Y.)	1928-36	177	31	.851
Adolph Rupp, Kentucky	1931-39	147	31	.826
Everett Case, North Carolina St.	1947-55	241	56	.811
Roy Williams, Kansas	1989-97	247	58	.810
Lew Andreas, Syracuse	1925-33	130	32	.802
Henry Iba, Northwest Mo. St., Colorado & Oklahoma St.	1930-38	182	45	.802
Denny Crum, Louisville	1972-80	219	55	.799
Hugh Greer, Connecticut	1947-55	171	43	.799

10 SEASONS

Coach, Team	Seasons	W	L	Pct.
Clair Bee, Rider & Long Island	1929-38	200	32	.862
Jerry Tarkanian, Long Beach St. & UNLV	1969-78	238	41	.853
Roy Williams, Kansas	1989-98	282	62	.820
Everett Case, North Carolina St.	1947-56	265	60	.815
Adolph Rupp, Kentucky	1931-40	162	37	.814
Lew Andreas, Syracuse	1925-34	145	34	.810
Henry Iba, Northwest Mo. St., Colorado & Oklahoma St.	1930-39	201	53	.791
Denny Crum, Louisville	1972-81	240	64	.789
Harold Anderson, Toledo & Bowling Green	1935-44	182	50	.784
Nat Holman, CCNY	1920-29	108	30	.783

11 SEASONS

Coach, Team	Seasons	W	L	Pct.
Clair Bee, Rider & Long Island	1929-39	223	32	.875
Jerry Tarkanian, Long Beach St. & UNLV	1969-79	259	49	.841
Lew Andreas, Syracuse	1925-35	160	36	.816
Roy Williams, Kansas	1989-99	305	72	.809
Henry Iba, Northwest Mo. St., Colorado & Oklahoma St.	1930-40	227	56	.802
Adolph Rupp, Kentucky	1931-41	179	45	.799
Everett Case, North Carolina St.	1947-57	280	71	.798
Harold Anderson, Toledo & Bowling Green	1935-45	206	54	.792
Nat Holman, CCNY	1920-30	119	33	.783
Denny Crum, Louisville	1972-82	263	74	.780

12 SEASONS

Coach, Team	Seasons	W	L	Pct.
Clair Bee, Rider & Long Island	1929-40	242	36	.871
Jerry Tarkanian, Long Beach St. & UNLV	1969-80	282	58	.829
Lew Andreas, Syracuse	1925-36	172	41	.806
Roy Williams, Kansas	1989-2000	329	82	.800
Harold Anderson, Toledo & Bowling Green	1935-46	233	59	.798
Henry Iba, Northwest Mo. St., Colorado & Oklahoma St.	1930-41	245	63	.795
Adolph Rupp, Kentucky	1931-42	198	51	.795
Everett Case, North Carolina St.	1947-58	298	77	.795
Denny Crum, Louisville	1972-83	295	78	.791
Joe Mullaney, Norwich & Providence	1955-66	243	68	.781

13 SEASONS

Coach, Team	Seasons	W	L	Pct.
Clair Bee, Rider & Long Island	1929-41	267	38	.875
Jerry Tarkanian, Long Beach St. & UNLV	1969-81	298	70	.810
Lew Andreas, Syracuse	1925-37	185	45	.804
Roy Williams, Kansas	1989-2001	355	89	.800
Harold Anderson, Toledo & Bowling Green	1935-47	261	66	.798
Everett Case, North Carolina St.	1947-59	320	81	.798
Nat Holman, CCNY	1920-32	147	38	.795
Henry Iba, Northwest Mo. St., Colorado & Oklahoma St.	1930-42	265	69	.793
Adolph Rupp, Kentucky	1931-43	215	57	.790
Denny Crum, Louisville	1972-84	319	89	.782

14 SEASONS

Coach, Team	Seasons	W	L	Pct.
Clair Bee, Rider & Long Island	1929-42	291	41	.877
Roy Williams, Kansas	1989-2002	388	93	.807
Nat Holman, CCNY	1920-33	160	39	.804
Harold Anderson, Toledo & Bowling Green	1935-48	288	72	.800
Jerry Tarkanian, Long Beach St. & UNLV	1969-82	318	80	.799
Adolph Rupp, Kentucky	1931-44	234	59	.799
Lew Andreas, Syracuse	1925-38	198	50	.798
Henry Iba, Northwest Mo. St., Colorado & Oklahoma St.	1930-43	279	79	.779
Everett Case, North Carolina St.	1947-60	331	96	.775
Jim Boeheim, Syracuse	1977-90	343	108	.761

15 SEASONS

Coach, Team	Seasons	W	L	Pct.
Clair Bee, Rider & Long Island	1929-43	304	47	.866
Nat Holman, CCNY	1920-34	174	40	.813
Jerry Tarkanian, Long Beach St. & UNLV	1969-83	346	83	.807
Roy Williams, Kansas	1989-2003	418	101	.805
Adolph Rupp, Kentucky	1931-45	256	63	.803
Harold Anderson, Toledo & Bowling Green	1935-49	312	79	.798
Lew Andreas, Syracuse	1925-39	212	54	.797
Henry Iba, Northwest Mo. St., Colorado & Oklahoma St.	1930-44	306	85	.783
Everett Case, North Carolina St.	1947-61	347	105	.768
Denny Crum, Louisville	1972-86	370	114	.764
Jim Boeheim, Syracuse	1977-91	369	114	.764

16 SEASONS

Coach, Team	Seasons	W	L	Pct.
Clair Bee, Rider & Long Island	1929-43, 46	318	56	.850
Adolph Rupp, Kentucky	1931-46	284	65	.814
Jerry Tarkanian, Long Beach St. & UNLV	1969-84	375	89	.808
Nat Holman, CCNY	1920-35	184	46	.800
Henry Iba, Northwest Mo. St., Colorado & Oklahoma St.	1930-45	333	89	.789
Harold Anderson, Toledo & Bowling Green	1935-50	331	90	.786
Lew Andreas, Syracuse	1925-40	222	62	.782
Everett Case, North Carolina St.	1947-62	358	111	.763
Ray Mears, Wittenberg & Tennessee	1957-72	306	97	.759
Jim Boeheim, Syracuse	1977-92	391	124	.759

17 SEASONS

Coach, Team	Seasons	W	L	Pct.
Clair Bee, Rider & Long Island	1929-43, 46-47	335	61	.850
Adolph Rupp, Kentucky	1931-47	318	68	.824
Jerry Tarkanian, Long Beach St. & UNLV	1969-85	403	93	.813
Henry Iba, Northwest Mo. St., Colorado & Oklahoma St.	1930-46	364	91	.800
Nat Holman, CCNY	1920-36	194	50	.795
Harold Anderson, Toledo & Bowling Green	1935-51	341	94	.784
Lew Andreas, Syracuse	1925-41	236	67	.779
Jim Boeheim, Syracuse	1977-93	411	133	.756
Joseph Lapchick, St. John's (N.Y.)	1937-47, 57-62	291	95	.754
Ray Mears, Wittenberg & Tennessee	1957-73	321	106	.752

18 SEASONS

Coach, Team	Seasons	W	L	Pct.
Clair Bee, Rider & Long Island	1929-43, 46-48	352	65	.844
Adolph Rupp, Kentucky	1931-48	354	71	.833
Jerry Tarkanian, Long Beach St. & UNLV	1969-86	436	98	.816
Henry Iba, Northwest Mo. St., Colorado & Oklahoma St.	1930-47	388	99	.797
Nat Holman, CCNY	1920-37	204	56	.785
Harold Anderson, Toledo & Bowling Green	1935-52	358	104	.775
Lew Andreas, Syracuse	1925-42	251	73	.775
Jim Boeheim, Syracuse	1977-94	434	140	.756
Dean Smith, North Carolina	1962-79	386	127	.752
John Thompson, Georgetown	1973-90	423	142	.749

19 SEASONS

Coach, Team	Seasons	W	L	Pct.
Adolph Rupp, Kentucky	1931-49	386	73	.841
Clair Bee, Rider & Long Island	1929-43, 46-49	370	77	.828
Jerry Tarkanian, Long Beach St. & UNLV	1969-87	473	100	.825
Henry Iba, Northwest Mo. St., Colorado & Oklahoma St.	1930-48	415	103	.801
Nat Holman, CCNY	1920-38	217	59	.786
Lew Andreas, Syracuse	1925-43	259	83	.757
Harold Anderson, Toledo & Bowling Green	1935-53	370	119	.757
Jim Boeheim, Syracuse	1977-95	454	150	.752
Dean Smith, North Carolina	1962-80	407	135	.751
Frank Keaney, Rhode Island	1922-40	244	82	.748
Denny Crum, Louisville	1972-90	463	156	.748

20 SEASONS

Coach, Team	Seasons	W	L	Pct.
Adolph Rupp, Kentucky	1931-50	411	78	.840
Clair Bee, Rider & Long Island	1929-43, 46-50	390	82	.826
Jerry Tarkanian, Long Beach St. & UNLV	1969-88	501	106	.825
Henry Iba, Northwest Mo. St., Colorado & Oklahoma St.	1930-49	438	108	.802

Kentucky's Adolph Rupp is listed at or near the top of most lists of statistical coaching leaders.

Photo by Rich Clarkson/NCAA Photos

COACHING RECORDS

Coach, Team	Seasons	W	L	Pct.
Phog Allen, Baker, Kansas, Haskell, Central Mo. St. & Kansas	1906-09, 13-28	325	89	.785
Nat Holman, CCNY	1920-39	228	65	.778
John Chaney, Cheyney & Temple	1973-92	458	143	.762
Frank Keaney, Rhode Island	1922-41	265	86	.755
Harold Anderson, Toledo & Bowling Green	1935-54	387	126	.754
Dean Smith, North Carolina	1962-81	436	143	.753

21 SEASONS

Coach, Team	Seasons	W	L	Pct.
Adolph Rupp, Kentucky	1931-51	443	80	.847
Clair Bee, Rider & Long Island	1929-43, 46-51	410	86	.827
Jerry Tarkanian, Long Beach St. & UNLV	1969-89	530	114	.823
Henry Iba, Northwest Mo. St., Colorado & Oklahoma St.	1930-50	456	117	.796
Nat Holman, CCNY	1920-40	236	73	.764
Dean Smith, North Carolina	1962-82	468	145	.763
Phog Allen, Baker, Kansas, Haskell, Central Mo. St. & Kansas	1906-09, 13-29	328	104	.759
Frank Keaney, Rhode Island	1922-42	283	90	.759
John Chaney, Cheyney & Temple	1973-93	478	156	.754
Chick Davies, Duquesne	1925-40, 47-48	314	106	.748

22 SEASONS

Coach, Team	Seasons	W	L	Pct.
Adolph Rupp, Kentucky	1931-52	472	83	.850
Jerry Tarkanian, Long Beach St. & UNLV	1969-90	565	119	.826
Henry Iba, Northwest Mo. St., Colorado & Oklahoma St.	1930-51	485	123	.798
Nat Holman, CCNY	1920-41	253	78	.764
Dean Smith, North Carolina	1962-83	496	153	.764
Frank Keaney, Rhode Island	1922-43	299	93	.763
Phog Allen, Baker, Kansas, Haskell, Central Mo. St. & Kansas	1906-09, 13-30	342	108	.760
John Wooden, Indiana St. & UCLA	1947-68	464	151	.754
John Chaney, Cheyney & Temple	1973-94	501	164	.753
Lew Andreas, Syracuse	1925-47	308	105	.746

23 SEASONS

Coach, Team	Seasons	W	L	Pct.
Adolph Rupp, Kentucky	1931-52, 54	497	83	.857
Jerry Tarkanian, Long Beach St. & UNLV	1969-91	599	120	.833
Henry Iba, Northwest Mo. St., Colorado & Oklahoma St.	1930-52	504	131	.794
Dean Smith, North Carolina	1962-84	524	156	.771
Nat Holman, CCNY	1920-42	269	81	.769
John Wooden, Indiana St. & UCLA	1947-69	493	152	.764
Phog Allen, Baker, Kansas, Haskell, Central Mo. St. & Kansas	1906-09, 13-31	357	111	.763
Frank Keaney, Rhode Island	1922-44	313	99	.760
John Chaney, Cheyney & Temple	1973-95	520	175	.748
Ed Diddle, Western Ky.	1923-45	395	134	.747

24 SEASONS

Coach, Team	Seasons	W	L	Pct.
Adolph Rupp, Kentucky	1931-52, 54-55	520	86	.858
Jerry Tarkanian, Long Beach St. & UNLV	1969-92	625	122	.837
Henry Iba, Northwest Mo. St., Colorado & Oklahoma St.	1930-53	527	138	.792
John Wooden, Indiana St. & UCLA	1947-70	521	154	.772
Dean Smith, North Carolina	1962-85	551	165	.770
Frank Keaney, Rhode Island	1922-45	333	104	.762
Phog Allen, Baker, Kansas, Haskell, Central Mo. St. & Kansas	1906-09, 13-32	370	116	.761
Nat Holman, CCNY	1920-43	277	91	.753
Jim Boeheim, Syracuse	1977-2000	575	199	.743
Bob Knight, Army & Indiana	1966-89	514	187	.733

25 SEASONS

Coach, Team	Seasons	W	L	Pct.
Adolph Rupp, Kentucky	1931-52, 54-56	540	92	.854
Jerry Tarkanian, Long Beach St., UNLV & Fresno St.	1969-92, 96	647	133	.829
Henry Iba, Northwest Mo. St., Colorado & Oklahoma St.	1930-54	551	143	.794
John Wooden, Indiana St. & UCLA	1947-71	550	155	.780
Dean Smith, North Carolina	1962-86	579	171	.772
Frank Keaney, Rhode Island	1922-46	354	107	.768
Phog Allen, Baker, Kansas, Haskell, Central Mo. St. & Kansas	1906-09, 13-33	383	120	.761
Jim Boeheim, Syracuse	1977-2001	600	208	.743
John Chaney, Cheyney & Temple	1973-97	560	199	.738
Nat Holman, CCNY	1920-44	283	102	.735
Ed Diddle, Western Ky.	1923-47	435	157	.735

26 SEASONS

Coach, Team	Seasons	W	L	Pct.
Adolph Rupp, Kentucky	1931-52, 54-57	563	97	.853
Jerry Tarkanian, Long Beach St., UNLV & Fresno St.	1969-92, 96-97	667	145	.821
John Wooden, Indiana St. & UCLA	1947-72	580	155	.789
Henry Iba, Northwest Mo. St., Colorado & Oklahoma St.	1930-55	563	156	.783
Dean Smith, North Carolina	1962-87	611	175	.777
Frank Keaney, Rhode Island	1922-47	371	110	.771
Phog Allen, Baker, Kansas, Haskell, Central Mo. St. & Kansas	1906-09, 13-34	399	121	.767
Ed Diddle, Western Ky.	1923-48	463	159	.744
Jim Boeheim, Syracuse	1977-2002	623	221	.738
John Chaney, Cheyney & Temple	1973-98	581	208	.736
Nat Holman, CCNY	1920-45	295	106	.736

27 SEASONS

Coach, Team	Seasons	W	L	Pct.
Adolph Rupp, Kentucky	1931-52, 54-58	586	103	.851
Jerry Tarkanian, Long Beach St., UNLV & Fresno St.	1969-92, 96-98	688	158	.813
John Wooden, Indiana St. & UCLA	1947-73	610	155	.797
Henry Iba, Northwest Mo. St., Colorado & Oklahoma St.	1930-56	581	165	.779
Dean Smith, North Carolina	1962-88	638	182	.778
Frank Keaney, Rhode Island	1922-48	387	117	.768
Phog Allen, Baker, Kansas, Haskell, Central Mo. St. & Kansas	1906-09, 13-35	414	126	.767
Ed Diddle, Western Ky.	1923-49	488	163	.750
Jim Boeheim, Syracuse	1977-2003	653	226	.743
Nat Holman, CCNY	1920-46	309	110	.737
Bob Knight, Army & Indiana	1966-92	588	210	.737

28 SEASONS

Coach, Team	Seasons	W	L	Pct.
Adolph Rupp, Kentucky	1931-52, 54-59	610	106	.852
Jerry Tarkanian, Long Beach St., UNLV & Fresno St.	1969-92, 96-99	689	170	.802
John Wooden, Indiana St. & UCLA	1947-74	636	159	.800
Dean Smith, North Carolina	1962-89	667	190	.778
Henry Iba, Northwest Mo. St., Colorado & Oklahoma St.	1930-57	598	174	.775
Phog Allen, Baker, Kansas, Haskell, Central Mo. St. & Kansas	1906-09, 13-36	435	128	.773
Ed Diddle, Western Ky.	1923-50	513	169	.752
Bob Knight, Army & Indiana	1966-93	619	214	.743
Mike Krzyzewski, Army & Duke	1976-2003	663	234	.739
Lute Olson, Long Beach St., Iowa & Arizona	1974-2001	638	226	.738
Nat Holman, CCNY	1920-47	326	116	.738

29 SEASONS

Coach, Team	Seasons	W	L	Pct.
Adolph Rupp, Kentucky	1931-52, 54-60	628	113	.848
John Wooden, Indiana St. & UCLA	1947-75	664	162	.804
Jerry Tarkanian, Long Beach St., UNLV & Fresno St.	1969-92, 96-2000	701	179	.797
Phog Allen, Baker, Kansas, Haskell, Central Mo. St. & Kansas	1906-09, 13-37	450	132	.773
Henry Iba, Northwest Mo. St., Colorado & Oklahoma St.	1930-58	619	182	.773
Dean Smith, North Carolina	1962-90	688	203	.772
Ed Diddle, Western Ky.	1923-51	532	179	.748
Nat Holman, CCNY	1920-48	344	119	.743
Bob Knight, Army & Indiana	1966-94	640	223	.742
Lute Olson, Long Beach St., Iowa & Arizona	1974-2002	662	236	.737

30 SEASONS

Coach, Team	Seasons	W	L	Pct.
Adolph Rupp, Kentucky	1931-52, 54-61	647	122	.841
Jerry Tarkanian, Long Beach St., UNLV & Fresno St.	1969-92, 96-2001	710	186	.792
Phog Allen, Baker, Kansas, Haskell, Central Mo. St. & Kansas	1906-09, 13-38	468	134	.777
Dean Smith, North Carolina	1962-91	717	209	.774
Henry Iba, Northwest Mo. St., Colorado & Oklahoma St.	1930-59	630	196	.763
Ed Diddle, Western Ky.	1923-52	558	184	.752
Lute Olson, Long Beach St., Iowa & Arizona	1974-2003	690	240	.742
Nat Holman, CCNY	1920-49	361	127	.740
Bob Knight, Army & Indiana	1966-95	659	235	.737
John Chaney, Cheyney & Temple	1973-2002	675	253	.727

31 SEASONS

Coach, Team	Seasons	W	L	Pct.
Adolph Rupp, Kentucky	1931-52, 54-62	670	125	.843
Jerry Tarkanian, Long Beach St., UNLV & Fresno St.	1969-92, 96-2000	729	201	.784
Phog Allen, Baker, Kansas, Haskell, Central Mo. St. & Kansas	1906-09, 13-39	481	141	.773
Dean Smith, North Carolina	1962-92	740	219	.772
Ed Diddle, Western Ky.	1923-53	583	190	.754
Henry Iba, Northwest Mo. St., Colorado & Oklahoma St.	1930-60	640	211	.752
Nat Holman, CCNY	1920-50	385	132	.745
Bob Knight, Army & Indiana	1966-96	678	247	.733
John Chaney, Cheyney & Temple,	1973-2003	693	269	.720
Eddie Sutton, Creighton, Arkansas, Kentucky & Oklahoma St.	1970-89, 91-2001	679	269	.716

32 SEASONS

Coach, Team	Seasons	W	L	Pct.
Adolph Rupp, Kentucky	1931-52, 54-63	686	134	.837
Dean Smith, North Carolina	1962-93	774	223	.776
Phog Allen, Baker, Kansas, Haskell, Central Mo. St. & Kansas	1906-09, 13-40	500	147	.773
Ed Diddle, Western Ky.	1923-54	612	193	.760
Henry Iba, Northwest Mo. St., Colorado & Oklahoma St.	1930-61	655	221	.748
Nat Holman, CCNY	1920-51	397	139	.741
Bob Knight, Army & Indiana	1966-97	700	258	.731
Eddie Sutton, Creighton, Arkansas, Kentucky & Oklahoma St.	1970-89, 91-2002	702	278	.716
Don Haskins, UTEP	1962-93	627	276	.694
Lefty Driesell, Davidson, Maryland & James Madison	1961-86, 89-94	641	289	.689

33 SEASONS

Coach, Team	Seasons	W	L	Pct.
Adolph Rupp, Kentucky	1931-52, 54-64	707	140	.835
Dean Smith, North Carolina	1962-94	802	230	.777
Phog Allen, Baker, Kansas, Haskell, Central Mo. St. & Kansas	1906-09, 13-41	512	153	.770
Ed Diddle, Western Ky.	1923-55	630	203	.756
Henry Iba, Northwest Mo. St., Colorado & Oklahoma St.	1930-62	669	232	.743
Nat Holman, CCNY	1920-52	405	150	.730
Bob Knight, Army & Indiana	1966-98	720	270	.727
Eddie Sutton, Creighton, Arkansas, Kentucky & Oklahoma St.	1970-89, 91-2003	724	288	.715
Don Haskins, UTEP	1962-94	645	288	.691
Lefty Driesell, Davidson, Maryland & James Madison	1961-86, 89-95	657	302	.685

34 SEASONS

Coach, Team	Seasons	W	L	Pct.
Adolph Rupp, Kentucky	1931-52, 54-65	722	150	.828
Dean Smith, North Carolina	1962-95	830	236	.779
Phog Allen, Baker, Kansas, Haskell, Central Mo. St. & Kansas	1906-09, 13-42	529	158	.770
Ed Diddle, Western Ky.	1923-56	646	215	.750
Henry Iba, Northwest Mo. St., Colorado & Oklahoma St.	1930-63	685	241	.740
Bob Knight, Army & Indiana	1966-99	743	281	.726
Nat Holman, CCNY	1920-52, 55	413	160	.721
Don Haskins, UTEP	1962-95	665	298	.691
Lefty Driesell, Davidson, Maryland & James Madison	1961-86, 89-96	667	322	.674
Norm Stewart, Northern Iowa & Missouri	1962-95	660	319	.674

35 SEASONS

Coach, Team	Seasons	W	L	Pct.
Adolph Rupp, Kentucky	1931-52, 54-66	749	152	.831
Dean Smith, North Carolina	1962-96	851	247	.775
Phog Allen, Baker, Kansas, Haskell, Central Mo. St. & Kansas	1906-09, 13-43	551	164	.771
Ed Diddle, Western Ky.	1923-57	663	224	.747
Henry Iba, Northwest Mo. St., Colorado & Oklahoma St.	1930-64	700	251	.736
Bob Knight, Army & Indiana	1966-2000	764	289	.726
Nat Holman, CCNY	1920-52, 55-56	417	174	.706
Don Haskins, UTEP	1962-96	678	313	.684
Lefty Driesell, Davidson, Maryland & James Madison	1961-86, 89-97	683	335	.671
Norm Stewart, Northern Iowa & Missouri	1962-96	678	334	.670

36 SEASONS

Coach, Team	Seasons	W	L	Pct.
Adolph Rupp, Kentucky	1931-52, 54-67	762	165	.822
Dean Smith, North Carolina	1962-97	879	254	.776
Phog Allen, Baker, Kansas, Haskell, Central Mo. St. & Kansas	1906-09, 13-44	568	173	.767
Ed Diddle, Western Ky.	1923-58	677	235	.742
Henry Iba, Northwest Mo. St., Colorado & Oklahoma St.	1930-65	720	258	.736
Bob Knight, Army, Indiana & Texas Tech	1966-2000, 02	787	298	.725
Nat Holman, CCNY	1920-52, 55-56, 59	423	186	.695
Don Haskins, UTEP	1962-97	691	351	.679
Lou Henson, Hardin-Simmons, New Mexico St., Illinois & New Mexico St.	1963-96, 99-2000	708	351	.669
Lefty Driesell, Davidson, Maryland, James Madison & Georgia St.	1961-86, 89-98	699	347	.668

37 SEASONS

Coach, Team	Seasons	W	L	Pct.
Adolph Rupp, Kentucky	1931-52, 54-68	784	170	.822
Phog Allen, Baker, Kansas, Haskell, Central Mo. St. & Kansas	1906-09, 13-45	580	178	.765
Ed Diddle, Western Ky.	1923-59	693	245	.739
Bob Knight, Army, Indiana & Texas Tech	1966-2000, 02-03	809	311	.722
Henry Iba, Northwest Mo. St., Colorado & Oklahoma St.	1930-66	724	279	.722
Nat Holman, CCNY	1920-52, 55-56, 59-60	423	190	.690
Don Haskins, UTEP	1962-98	703	341	.673
Lefty Driesell, Davidson, Maryland, James Madison & Georgia St.	1961-86, 89-99	716	360	.665
Lou Henson, Hardin-Simmons, New Mexico St., Illinois & New Mexico St.	1963-96, 99-2001	722	365	.664
Norm Stewart, Northern Iowa & Missouri	1962-98	711	366	.660

38 SEASONS

Coach, Team	Seasons	W	L	Pct.
Adolph Rupp, Kentucky	1931-52, 54-69	807	175	.822
Phog Allen, Baker, Kansas, Haskell, Central Mo. St. & Kansas	1906-09, 13-46	599	180	.769
Ed Diddle, Western Ky.	1923-60	714	252	.739
Henry Iba, Northwest Mo. St., Colorado & Oklahoma St.	1930-67	731	297	.711
Don Haskins, UTEP	1962-99	719	353	.671
Lefty Driesell, Davidson, Maryland, James Madison & Georgia St.	1961-86, 89-2000	733	372	.663
Lou Henson, Hardin-Simmons, New Mexico St., Illinois & New Mexico St.	1963-96, 99-2002	742	377	.663
Norm Stewart, Northern Iowa & Missouri	1962-99	731	375	.661
Ray Meyer, DePaul	1943-80	623	335	.650
Ralph Miller, Wichita St., Iowa & Oregon St.	1952-89	657	382	.632

39 SEASONS

Coach, Team	Seasons	W	L	Pct.
Adolph Rupp, Kentucky	1931-52, 54-70	833	177	.825
Phog Allen, Baker, Kansas, Haskell, Central Mo. St. & Kansas	1906-09, 13-47	607	185	.766
Ed Diddle, Western Ky.	1923-61	732	260	.740
Henry Iba, Northwest Mo. St., Colorado & Oklahoma St.	1930-68	741	313	.703
Lefty Driesell, Davidson, Maryland, James Madison & Georgia St.	1961-86, 89-2001	762	377	.669
Ray Meyer, DePaul	1943-81	650	337	.659
Lou Henson, Hardin-Simmons, New Mexico St., Illinois & New Mexico St.	1963-96, 99-2003	762	386	.664
Tony Hinkle, Butler	1927-42, 46-68	531	367	.591
Marv Harshman, Pacific Lutheran, Washington St. & Washington	1946-84	632	439	.590

40 SEASONS

Coach, Team	Seasons	W	L	Pct.
Adolph Rupp, Kentucky	1931-52, 54-71	855	183	.824
Phog Allen, Baker, Kansas, Haskell, Central Mo. St. & Kansas	1906-09, 13-48	616	200	.755
Ed Diddle, Western Ky.	1923-62	749	270	.735
Henry Iba, Northwest Mo. St., Colorado & Oklahoma St.	1930-69	753	326	.698
Lefty Driesell, Davidson, Maryland, James Madison & Georgia St.	1961-86, 89-2002	782	388	.668
Ray Meyer, DePaul	1943-82	676	339	.666
Marv Harshman, Pacific Lutheran, Washington St. & Washington	1946-85	654	449	.593
Tony Hinkle, Butler	1927-42, 46-69	542	382	.587

41 SEASONS

Coach, Team	Seasons	W	L	Pct.
Adolph Rupp, Kentucky	1931-52, 54-72	876	190	.822
Phog Allen, Baker, Kansas, Haskell, Central Mo. St. & Kansas	1906-09, 13-49	628	212	.748
Ed Diddle, Western Ky.	1923-63	754	286	.725
Henry Iba, Northwest Mo. St., Colorado & Oklahoma St.	1930-70	767	338	.694
Ray Meyer, DePaul	1943-83	697	351	.665
Lefty Driesell, Davidson, Maryland, James Madison & Georgia St.	1961-86, 89-2003	800	409	.662
Tony Hinkle, Butler	1927-42, 46-70	557	393	.586

42 SEASONS

Coach, Team	Seasons	W	L	Pct.
Phog Allen, Baker, Kansas, Haskell, Central Mo. St. & Kansas	1906-09, 13-50	642	223	.742
Ed Diddle, Western Ky.	1923-64	759	302	.715
Ray Meyer, DePaul	1943-84	724	354	.672

Top 10 Best Career Starts By Wins

(Head coaches with at least half their seasons at Division I)

1 SEASON

Coach, Team	Season	W	L	Pct.
Bill Guthridge, North Carolina	1998	34	4	.895
Bill Hodges, Indiana St.	1979	33	1	.970
Stan Heath, Kent St.	2002	30	6	.833
John Warren, Oregon	1945	30	13	.698
Phil Johnson, Weber St.	1969	27	3	.900
Blaine Taylor, Montana	1992	27	4	.871
Tevester Anderson, Murray St.	1999	27	6	.818
John Phillips, Tulsa	2002	27	7	.794
Jim Boeheim, Syracuse	1977	26	4	.867
Everett Case, North Carolina St.	1947	26	5	.839
Denny Crum, Louisville	1972	26	5	.839
Pete Herrmann, Navy	1987	26	6	.813
Todd Lickliter, Butler	2002	26	6	.813
Nolan Richardson, Tulsa	1981	26	7	.788
Dick Hunsaker, Ball St.	1990	26	7	.788
Larry Finch, Memphis	1987	26	8	.765
Mark Few, Gonzaga	2000	26	9	.743

2 SEASONS

Coach, Team	Seasons	W	L	Pct.
Bill Guthridge, North Carolina	1998-99	58	14	.806
Everett Case, North Carolina St.	1947-48	55	8	.873
Todd Lickliter, Butler	2002-03	53	12	.815
Ben Carnevale, North Carolina	1945-46	52	11	.825
Mark Few, Gonzaga	2000-01	52	16	.765
Don Monson, Gonzaga	1998-99	52	17	.754
Bill Carmody, Princeton	1997-98	51	6	.895
Gary Cunningham, UCLA	1978-79	50	8	.862
Kermit Davis Jr., Idaho	1989-90	50	12	.806
Nolan Richardson, Tulsa	1981-82	50	13	.794
Thad Matta, Butler & Xavier	2001-02	50	14	.781
Tevester Anderson, Murray St.	1999-2000	50	15	.769
John Phillips, Tulsa	2002-03	50	17	.746
Stan Watts, Brigham Young	1950-51	50	21	.704

3 SEASONS

Coach, Team	Seasons	W	L	Pct.
Mark Few, Gonzaga	2000-02	81	20	.802
Everett Case, North Carolina St.	1947-49	80	16	.833
Bill Guthridge, North Carolina	1998-2000	80	28	.741
Thad Matta, Butler & Xavier	2001-03	76	20	.792
Roy Williams, Kansas	1989-91	76	25	.752
Jim Boeheim, Syracuse	1977-79	74	14	.841
Bill Carmody, Princeton	1997-99	73	14	.839
Jerry Tarkanian, Long Beach St.	1969-71	71	13	.845
Dick Hunsaker, Ball St.	1990-92	71	26	.732
Denny Crum, Louisville	1972-74	70	19	.787
Don Donoher, Dayton	1965-67	70	19	.787
Pat Foster, Lamar	1981-83	70	20	.777
Pete Gillen, Xavier	1986-88	70	22	.761
Tim Welsh, Iona	1996-98	70	22	.761
Randy Ayers, Ohio St.	1990-92	70	23	.753
Steve Lavin, UCLA	1997-99	70	26	.729
Speedy Morris, La Salle	1987-89	70	29	.707

4 SEASONS

Coach, Team	Seasons	W	L	Pct.
Everett Case, North Carolina St.	1947-50	107	22	.829
Mark Few, Gonzaga	2000-03	105	29	.784
Bruce Stewart, West Va. Wesleyan & Middle Tenn.	1983-86	104	34	.754
Roy Williams, Kansas	1989-92	103	30	.774
Jim Boeheim, Syracuse	1977-80	100	18	.847
Speedy Morris, La Salle	1987-90	100	31	.763
Paul Westphal, Grand Canyon & Pepperdine	1987-88, 2002-03	100	40	.714
Denny Crum, Louisville	1972-75	98	22	.817
Dick Hunsaker, Ball St.	1990-93	97	34	.740
Jerry Tarkanian, Long Beach St.	1969-72	96	17	.850
Pat Foster, Lamar	1981-84	96	25	.793
Nolan Richardson, Tulsa	1981-84	96	29	.768

5 SEASONS

Coach, Team	Seasons	W	L	Pct.
Everett Case, North Carolina St.	1947-51	137	29	.825
Roy Williams, Kansas	1989-93	132	37	.781
Bruce Stewart, West Va. Wesleyan & Middle Tenn.	1983-87	126	41	.754
Forddy Anderson, Drake & Bradley	1947-51	123	42	.745
Jerry Tarkanian, Long Beach St. & UNLV	1969-73	122	20	.859
Jim Boeheim, Syracuse	1977-81	122	30	.803
Fred Schaus, West Virginia	1955-59	120	32	.789
Larry Brown, UCLA & Kansas	1980-81, 84-86	120	38	.759
Tom Izzo, Michigan St.	1996-2000	120	48	.714
Nolan Richardson, Tulsa	1981-85	119	37	.763
Speedy Morris, La Salle	1987-91	119	41	.744
Pete Gillen, Xavier	1986-90	119	39	.753

6 SEASONS

Coach, Team	Seasons	W	L	Pct.
Everett Case, North Carolina St.	1947-52	161	39	.805
Roy Williams, Kansas	1989-94	159	45	.779
Bruce Stewart, West Va. Wesleyan & Middle Tenn.	1983-88	149	52	.741
Tom Izzo, Michigan St.	1996-2001	148	53	.736
Fred Schaus, West Virginia	1955-60	146	37	.798
Larry Brown, UCLA & Kansas	1980-81, 84-87	145	49	.747
Jerry Tarkanian, Long Beach St. & UNLV	1969-74	142	26	.845
Pete Gillen, Xavier	1986-91	141	49	.742
Forddy Anderson, Drake & Bradley	1947-52	140	54	.722
Denny Crum, Louisville	1972-77	139	37	.790
Speedy Morris, La Salle	1987-92	139	52	.728

7 SEASONS

Coach, Team	Seasons	W	L	Pct.
Everett Case, North Carolina St.	1947-53	187	45	.806
Roy Williams, Kansas	1989-95	184	51	.783
Larry Brown, UCLA & Kansas	1980-81, 84-88	172	60	.741
Bruce Stewart, West Va. Wesleyan & Middle Tenn.	1983-89	172	60	.741
Tom Izzo, Michigan St.	1996-2002	167	65	.720
Denny Crum, Louisville	1972-78	162	44	.786
Howard Hobson, Southern Ore. & Oregon	1933-39	162	48	.771
Fred Schaus, West Virginia & Purdue	1955-60, 73	161	46	.778
Jerry Tarkanian, Long Beach St. & UNLV	1969-75	160	28	.851
Jim Boeheim, Syracuse	1977-83	159	53	.750
Tubby Smith, Tulsa, Georgia & Kentucky	1992-98	159	66	.707

8 SEASONS

Coach, Team	Seasons	W	L	Pct.
Everett Case, North Carolina St.	1947-54	213	52	.804
Roy Williams, Kansas	1989-96	213	56	.792
Jerry Tarkanian, Long Beach St. & UNLV	1969-76	189	30	.863
John Calipari, Massachusetts	1989-96	189	70	.730
Tom Izzo, Michigan St.	1996-2003	189	78	.708
Tubby Smith, Tulsa, Georgia & Kentucky	1992-99	187	75	.714
Denny Crum, Louisville	1972-79	186	52	.782
Bruce Stewart, West Va. Wesleyan & Middle Tenn.	1983-90	184	75	.710
Fred Schaus, West Virginia & Purdue	1955-60, 73-74	182	55	.768
Jim Boeheim, Syracuse	1977-84	182	62	.745

9 SEASONS

Coach, Team	Seasons	W	L	Pct.
Roy Williams, Kansas	1989-97	247	58	.810
Everett Case, North Carolina St.	1947-55	241	56	.811
Denny Crum, Louisville	1972-80	219	55	.799
Jerry Tarkanian, Long Beach St. & UNLV	1969-77	218	33	.869
John Calipari, Massachusetts & Memphis	1989-96 2001	210	85	.712
Tubby Smith, Tulsa, Georgia & Kentucky	1992-2000	210	85	.712
Jim Boeheim, Syracuse	1977-85	204	71	.742
Fred Schaus, West Virginia & Purdue	1955-60, 73-75	199	66	.751
Howard Hobson, Southern Ore. & Oregon	1933-41	199	78	.718
Vic Bubas, Duke	1960-68	198	54	.786
Tom Blackburn, Dayton	1948-56	198	74	.728

10 SEASONS

Coach, Team	Seasons	W	L	Pct.
Roy Williams, Kansas	1989-98	282	62	.820
Everett Case, North Carolina St.	1947-56	265	60	.815
Denny Crum, Louisville	1972-81	240	64	.789
Jerry Tarkanian, Long Beach St. & UNLV	1969-78	238	41	.853
John Calipari, Massachusetts & Memphis	1989-96, 2001-02	237	94	.716
Tubby Smith, Tulsa, Georgia & Kentucky	1992-2001	234	95	.711
Jim Boeheim, Syracuse	1977-86	230	77	.749
Nolan Richardson, Tulsa & Arkansas	1981-90	226	88	.720
Pete Gillen, Xavier & Providence	1986-95	219	88	.713
Tom Blackburn, Dayton	1948-57	217	83	.723

11 SEASONS

Coach, Team	Seasons	W	L	Pct.
Roy Williams, Kansas	1989-99	305	72	.809
Everett Case, North Carolina St.	1947-57	280	71	.798
Denny Crum, Louisville	1972-82	263	74	.780
Jim Boeheim, Syracuse	1977-87	261	84	.757
Nolan Richardson, Tulsa & Arkansas	1981-91	260	92	.739
John Calipari, Massachusetts & Memphis	1989-96 2001-03	260	101	.720
Jerry Tarkanian, Long Beach St. & UNLV	1969-79	259	49	.841
Tubby Smith, Tulsa, Georgia & Kentucky	1992-2002	256	105	.709
Tom Blackburn, Dayton	1948-58	242	87	.736
Boyd Grant, Fresno St. & Colorado St.	1978-86, 88-89	239	97	.711
Wimp Sanderson, Alabama	1981-91	239	109	.687

12 SEASONS

Coach, Team	Seasons	W	L	Pct.
Roy Williams, Kansas	1989-2000	329	82	.800
Everett Case, North Carolina St.	1947-58	298	77	.795
Denny Crum, Louisville	1972-83	295	78	.791
Tubby Smith, Tulsa, Georgia & Kentucky	1992-2003	288	109	.725
Jim Boeheim, Syracuse	1977-88	287	93	.755
Nolan Richardson, Tulsa & Arkansas	1981-92	286	100	.741
Jerry Tarkanian, Long Beach St. & UNLV	1969-80	282	58	.829
Wimp Sanderson, Alabama	1981-92	265	118	.692
John Thompson, Georgetown	1973-84	262	104	.716
Bob Huggins, Walsh, Akron & Cincinnati	1981-93	262	108	.708
Pete Gillen, Xavier & Providence	1986-97	261	112	.700

13 SEASONS

Coach, Team	Seasons	W	L	Pct.
Roy Williams, Kansas	1989-2001	355	89	.800
Everett Case, North Carolina St.	1947-59	320	81	.798
Denny Crum, Louisville	1972-84	319	89	.782
Jim Boeheim, Syracuse	1977-89	317	101	.758
Nolan Richardson, Tulsa & Arkansas	1981-93	308	109	.739
Jerry Tarkanian, Long Beach St. & UNLV	1969-81	298	70	.810
John Thompson, Georgetown	1973-85	297	107	.735
Bob Huggins, Walsh, Akron & Cincinnati	1981-94	284	118	.706
Rick Pitino, Boston U., Providence & Kentucky	1979-83, 86-87, 90-95	283	117	.708
Wimp Sanderson, Alabama & Ark.-Little Rock	1981-92, 95	282	130	.684
Rick Majerus, Marquette, Ball St. & Utah	1984-86, 88-97	279	107	.723

14 SEASONS

Coach, Team	Seasons	W	L	Pct.
Roy Williams, Kansas	1989-2002	388	93	.807
Jim Boeheim, Syracuse	1977-90	343	108	.761
Nolan Richardson, Tulsa & Arkansas	1981-94	339	112	.752
Denny Crum, Louisville	1972-85	338	107	.760
Everett Case, North Carolina St.	1947-60	331	96	.775
John Thompson, Georgetown	1973-86	321	115	.736
Jerry Tarkanian, Long Beach St. & UNLV	1969-82	318	80	.799
Rick Pitino, Boston U., Providence & Kentucky	1979-83, 86-87, 90-96	317	119	.727
Rick Majerus, Marquette, Ball St. & Utah	1984-86, 88-98	309	111	.736
Bob Huggins, Walsh, Akron & Cincinnati	1981-95	307	129	.704

15 SEASONS

Coach, Team	Seasons	W	L	Pct.
Roy Williams, Kansas	1989-2003	418	101	.805
Nolan Richardson, Tulsa & Arkansas	1981-95	371	119	.757
Denny Crum, Louisville	1972-86	370	114	.764
Jim Boeheim, Syracuse	1977-91	369	114	.764
Rick Pitino, Boston U., Providence & Kentucky	1979-83, 86-87, 90-97	352	124	.739
John Thompson, Georgetown	1973-87	350	120	.745
Everett Case, North Carolina St.	1947-61	347	105	.768
Jerry Tarkanian, Long Beach St. & UNLV	1969-83	346	83	.807
Rick Majerus, Marquette, Ball St. & Utah	1984-86, 88-99	337	116	.744
Billy Tubbs, Southwest Tex. St., Lamar & Oklahoma	1972-73, 77-89	336	148	.694

16 SEASONS

Coach, Team	Seasons	W	L	Pct.
Jim Boeheim, Syracuse	1977-92	391	124	.759
Nolan Richardson, Tulsa & Arkansas	1981-96	391	132	.748
Denny Crum, Louisville	1972-87	388	128	.752
Jerry Tarkanian, Long Beach St. & UNLV	1969-84	375	89	.808
Rick Pitino, Boston U., Providence, Kentucky & Louisville	1979-83, 86-87, 90-97, 2002	371	137	.730
John Thompson, Georgetown	1973-88	370	130	.740
Billy Tubbs, Southwest Tex. St., Lamar & Oklahoma	1972-73, 77-90	363	153	.703
Bob Huggins, Walsh, Akron & Cincinnati	1981-97	361	142	.718
Rick Majerus, Marquette, Ball St. & Utah	1984-86, 88-2000	360	125	.742
Everett Case, North Carolina St.	1947-62	358	111	.763

17 SEASONS

Coach, Team	Seasons	W	L	Pct.
Denny Crum, Louisville	1972-88	412	139	.748
Jim Boeheim, Syracuse	1977-93	411	133	.756
Nolan Richardson, Tulsa & Arkansas	1981-97	409	146	.737
Jerry Tarkanian, Long Beach St. & UNLV	1969-85	403	93	.813
John Thompson, Georgetown	1973-89	399	135	.747
Rick Pitino, Boston U., Providence, Kentucky & Louisville	1979-83, 86-87, 90-97, 2002-03	396	144	.733
Bob Huggins, Walsh, Akron & Cincinnati	1981-98	388	148	.724
Billy Tubbs, Southwest Tex. St., Lamar & Oklahoma	1972-73, 77-91	383	168	.695
Eddie Sutton, Creighton, Arkansas & Kentucky	1970-86	374	129	.744
Lou Carnesecca, St. John's (N.Y.)	1966-70, 74-85	371	131	.739

18 SEASONS

Coach, Team	Seasons	W	L	Pct.
Jerry Tarkanian, Long Beach St. & UNLV	1969-86	436	98	.816
Denny Crum, Louisville	1972-89	436	148	.747
Jim Boeheim, Syracuse	1977-94	434	140	.756
Nolan Richardson, Tulsa & Arkansas	1981-98	433	155	.736
John Thompson, Georgetown	1973-90	423	142	.749
Bob Huggins, Walsh, Akron & Cincinnati	1981-99	415	154	.729
Billy Tubbs, Southwest Tex. St., Lamar & Oklahoma	1972-73, 77-92	404	177	.695
Lou Carnesecca, St. John's (N.Y.)	1966-70, 74-86	402	136	.747
Mike Krzyzewski, Army & Duke	1976-93	394	177	.690
Eddie Sutton, Creighton, Arkansas & Kentucky	1970-87	392	140	.740

19 SEASONS

Coach, Team	Seasons	W	L	Pct.
Jerry Tarkanian, Long Beach St. & UNLV	1969-87	473	100	.825
Denny Crum, Louisville	1972-90	463	156	.748
Nolan Richardson, Tulsa & Arkansas	1981-99	456	166	.733
Jim Boeheim, Syracuse	1977-95	454	150	.752
Bob Huggins, Walsh, Akron & Cincinnati	1981-2000	444	158	.738
John Thompson, Georgetown	1973-91	442	155	.740
Billy Tubbs, Southwest Tex. St., Lamar & Oklahoma	1972-73, 77-93	424	189	.692
Lou Carnesecca, St. John's (N.Y.)	1966-70, 74-87	423	145	.745
Mike Krzyzewski, Army & Duke	1976-94	422	183	.698
Eddie Sutton, Creighton, Arkansas & Kentucky	1970-88	417	145	.742

20 SEASONS

Coach, Team	Seasons	W	L	Pct.
Jerry Tarkanian, Long Beach St. & UNLV	1969-88	501	106	.825
Jim Boeheim, Syracuse	1977-96	483	159	.752
Denny Crum, Louisville	1972-91	477	172	.735

Coach, Team	Seasons	W	L	Pct.
Nolan Richardson, Tulsa & Arkansas	1981-2000	475	181	.724
Bob Huggins, Walsh, Akron & Cincinnati...........	1981-2001	469	168	.736
John Thompson, Georgetown	1973-92	464	165	.738
John Chaney, Cheyney & Temple	1973-92	458	143	.762
Lou Carnesecca, St. John's (N.Y.)	1966-70, 74-88	440	157	.737
Billy Tubbs, Southwest Tex. St., Lamar & Oklahoma...	1972-73, 77-94	439	202	.685
Henry Iba, Northwest Mo. St., Colorado & Oklahoma St.	1930-49	438	108	.802

21 SEASONS

Coach, Team	Seasons	W	L	Pct.
Jerry Tarkanian, Long Beach St. & UNLV............	1969-89	530	114	.823
Jim Boeheim, Syracuse....................................	1977-97	502	172	.745
Bob Huggins, Walsh, Akron & Cincinnati...........	1981-2002	500	172	.744
Denny Crum, Louisville...................................	1972-92	496	183	.730
Nolan Richardson, Tulsa & Arkansas	1981-2001	495	192	.721
John Thompson, Georgetown	1973-93	484	178	.731
John Chaney, Cheyney & Temple	1973-93	478	156	.754
Dean Smith, North Carolina............................	1962-82	468	145	.763
Lou Carnesecca, St. John's (N.Y.)	1966-70, 74-89	460	170	.730
Lute Olson, Long Beach St., Iowa & Arizona	1974-94	458	179	.719

22 SEASONS

Coach, Team	Seasons	W	L	Pct.
Jerry Tarkanian, Long Beach St. & UNLV............	1969-90	565	119	.826
Jim Boeheim, Syracuse....................................	1977-98	528	181	.745
Denny Crum, Louisville...................................	1972-93	518	192	.730
Bob Huggins, Walsh, Akron & Cincinnati...........	1981-2003	517	184	.738
John Thompson, Georgetown	1973-94	503	190	.726
John Chaney, Cheyney & Temple	1973-94	501	164	.753
Dean Smith, North Carolina............................	1962-83	496	153	.764
Henry Iba, Northwest Mo. St., Colorado & Oklahoma St.	1930-51	485	123	.798
Lou Carnesecca, St. John's (N.Y.)	1966-70, 74-90	484	180	.729
Eddie Sutton, Creighton, Arkansas, Kentucky & Oklahoma St.	1970-89, 91-92	482	180	.728
Lute Olson, Long Beach St., Iowa & Arizona	1974-95	482	186	.722

23 SEASONS

Coach, Team	Seasons	W	L	Pct.
Jerry Tarkanian, Long Beach St. & UNLV............	1969-91	599	120	.833
Jim Boeheim, Syracuse....................................	1977-99	549	193	.740
Denny Crum, Louisville...................................	1972-94	546	198	.734
Dean Smith, North Carolina............................	1962-84	524	156	.771
John Thompson, Georgetown	1973-95	524	200	.724
John Chaney, Cheyney & Temple	1973-95	520	175	.748
Lute Olson, Long Beach St., Iowa & Arizona	1974-96	509	192	.726
Lou Carnesecca, St. John's (N.Y.)	1966-70, 74-91	507	189	.728
Mike Krzyzewski, Army & Duke	1976-98	505	212	.704
Henry Iba, Northwest Mo. St., Colorado & Oklahoma St.	1930-52	504	131	.794

24 SEASONS

Coach, Team	Seasons	W	L	Pct.
Jerry Tarkanian, Long Beach St. & UNLV............	1969-92	625	122	.837
Jim Boeheim, Syracuse....................................	1977-2000	575	199	.743
Denny Crum, Louisville...................................	1972-95	565	212	.727
John Thompson, Georgetown	1973-96	553	208	.727
Dean Smith, North Carolina............................	1962-85	551	165	.770
Mike Krzyzewski, Army & Duke	1976-99	542	214	.717
John Chaney, Cheyney & Temple	1973-96	540	188	.742
Lute Olson, Long Beach St., Iowa & Arizona	1974-97	534	201	.718
Henry Iba, Northwest Mo. St., Colorado & Oklahoma St.	1930-53	527	138	.792
Eddie Sutton, Creighton, Arkansas, Kentucky & Oklahoma St.	1970-89, 91-94	526	199	.726
Lou Carnesecca, St. John's (N.Y.)	1966-70, 74-92	526	200	.725

25 SEASONS

Coach, Team	Seasons	W	L	Pct.
Jerry Tarkanian, Long Beach St., UNLV & Fresno St.	1969-92, 96	647	133	.829
Jim Boeheim, Syracuse....................................	1977-2001	600	208	.743
Denny Crum, Louisville...................................	1972-96	587	224	.724
Dean Smith, North Carolina............................	1962-86	579	171	.772
John Thompson, Georgetown	1973-97	573	218	.724
Mike Krzyzewski, Army & Duke	1976-2000	571	219	.723
Lute Olson, Long Beach St., Iowa & Arizona	1974-98	564	206	.732
John Chaney, Cheyney & Temple	1973-97	560	199	.738
Eddie Sutton, Creighton, Arkansas, Kentucky & Oklahoma St.	1970-89, 91-95	553	209	.726
Henry Iba, Northwest Mo. St., Colorado & Oklahoma St.	1930-54	551	143	.794

26 SEASONS

Coach, Team	Seasons	W	L	Pct.
Jerry Tarkanian, Long Beach St., UNLV & Fresno St.	1969-92, 96-97	667	145	.821
Jim Boeheim, Syracuse....................................	1977-2002	623	221	.738
Denny Crum, Louisville...................................	1972-97	613	233	.725
Dean Smith, North Carolina............................	1962-87	611	175	.777
Mike Krzyzewski, Army & Duke	1976-2001	606	223	.731
John Thompson, Georgetown	1973-98	589	233	.717
Lute Olson, Long Beach St., Iowa & Arizona	1974-99	586	213	.733
John Chaney, Cheyney & Temple	1973-98	581	208	.736
John Wooden, Indiana St. & UCLA....................	1947-72	580	155	.789
Eddie Sutton, Creighton, Arkansas, Kentucky & Oklahoma St.	1970-89, 91-96	570	219	.722

27 SEASONS

Coach, Team	Seasons	W	L	Pct.
Jerry Tarkanian, Long Beach St., UNLV & Fresno St.	1969-92, 96-98	688	158	.813
Jim Boeheim, Syracuse....................................	1977-2003	653	226	.743
Dean Smith, North Carolina............................	1962-88	638	182	.778
Mike Krzyzewski, Army & Duke	1976-2002	637	227	.737
Denny Crum, Louisville...................................	1972-98	625	253	.712
Lute Olson, Long Beach St., Iowa & Arizona	1974-2000	613	220	.736
John Wooden, Indiana St. & UCLA....................	1947-73	610	155	.797
John Chaney, Cheyney & Temple	1973-99	605	219	.734
John Thompson, Georgetown	1973-99	596	239	.714
Bob Knight, Army & Indiana	1966-92	588	210	.737

28 SEASONS

Coach, Team	Seasons	W	L	Pct.
Jerry Tarkanian, Long Beach St.,UNLV & Fresno St.	1969-92, 96-99	689	170	.802
Dean Smith, North Carolina............................	1962-89	667	190	.778
Mike Krzyzewski, Army & Duke	1976-2003	663	234	.739
Denny Crum, Louisville...................................	1972-99	644	264	.709
Lute Olson, Long Beach St., Iowa & Arizona	1974-2001	638	226	.738
John Wooden, Indiana St. & UCLA....................	1947-74	636	159	.800
John Chaney, Cheyney & Temple	1973-2000	632	225	.737
Bob Knight, Army & Indiana	1966-93	619	214	.743
Adolph Rupp, Kentucky..................................	1931-52, 54-59	610	106	.852
Eddie Sutton, Creighton, Arkansas, Kentucky & Oklahoma St.	1970-89, 91-98	609	241	.716

29 SEASONS

Coach, Team	Seasons	W	L	Pct.
Jerry Tarkanian, Long Beach St., UNLV & Fresno St.	1969-92, 96-2000	701	179	.797
Dean Smith, North Carolina............................	1962-90	688	203	.772
John Wooden, Indiana St. & UCLA....................	1947-75	664	162	.804
Denny Crum, Louisville...................................	1972-2000	663	276	.706
Lute Olson, Long Beach St., Iowa & Arizona	1974-2002	662	236	.737
John Chaney, Cheyney & Temple	1973-2001	656	238	.734
Bob Knight, Army & Indiana	1966-94	640	223	.742
Eddie Sutton, Creighton, Arkansas, Kentucky & Oklahoma St.	1970-89, 91-99	632	252	.715
Adolph Rupp, Kentucky..................................	1931-52, 54-60	628	113	.848
Henry Iba, Northwest Mo. St., Colorado & Oklahoma St.	1930-58	619	182	.773

30 SEASONS

Coach, Team	Seasons	W	L	Pct.
Dean Smith, North Carolina............................	1962-91	717	209	.774
Jerry Tarkanian, Long Beach St., UNLV & Fresno St.	1969-92, 96-2001	710	186	.792
Lute Olson, Long Beach St., Iowa & Arizona	1974-2003	690	240	.742
John Chaney, Cheyney & Temple	1973-2002	675	253	.727
Denny Crum, Louisville...................................	1972-2001	675	295	.696
Bob Knight, Army & Indiana	1966-95	659	235	.737
Eddie Sutton, Creighton, Arkansas, Kentucky & Oklahoma St.	1970-89, 91-2000	659	259	.718
Adolph Rupp, Kentucky..................................	1931-52, 54-61	647	122	.841
Henry Iba, Northwest Mo. St., Colorado & Oklahoma St.	1930-59	630	196	.763
Jim Calhoun, Northeastern & Connecticut...........	1973-2002	624	286	.686

31 SEASONS

Coach, Team	Seasons	W	L	Pct.
Dean Smith, North Carolina............................	1962-92	740	219	.772
Jerry Tarkanian, Long Beach St., UNLV, & Fresno St.	1969-92, 96-2002	729	201	.784
John Chaney, Cheyney & Temple	1973-2003	693	269	.720
Bob Knight, Army & Indiana	1966-96	679	246	.734

Coach, Team	Seasons	W	L	Pct.
Eddie Sutton, Creighton, Arkansas, Kentucky & Oklahoma St.	1970-89, 91-2001	679	269	.716
Adolph Rupp, Kentucky	1931-52, 54-62	670	125	.843
Jim Calhoun, Northeastern & Connecticut	1973-2003	647	296	.686
Henry Iba, Northwest Mo. St., Colorado & Oklahoma St.	1930-60	640	211	.752
Lefty Driesell, Davidson, Maryland & James Madison	1961-86, 89-93	621	279	.690
Lou Henson, Hardin-Simmons, New Mexico St. & Illinois	1963-93	609	295	.674

32 SEASONS

Coach, Team	Seasons	W	L	Pct.
Dean Smith, North Carolina	1962-93	774	223	.776
Eddie Sutton, Creighton, Arkansas, Kentucky & Oklahoma St.	1970-89, 91-2002	702	278	.716
Bob Knight, Army & Indiana	1966-97	701	257	.732
Adolph Rupp, Kentucky	1931-52, 54-63	686	134	.837
Henry Iba, Northwest Mo. St., Colorado & Oklahoma St.	1930-61	655	221	.748
Lefty Driesell, Davidson, Maryland & James Madison	1961-86, 89-94	641	289	.689
Don Haskins, UTEP	1962-93	627	276	.694
Lou Henson, Hardin-Simmons, New Mexico St. & Illinois	1963-94	626	306	.672
Gene Bartow, Central Mo. St., Valparaiso, Memphis, Illinois, UCLA, & UAB	1962-77, 78-94	617	323	.656
Ed Diddle, Western Ky.	1923-54	612	193	.760
Norm Stewart, Northern Iowa & Missouri	1962-93	612	306	.667

33 SEASONS

Coach, Team	Seasons	W	L	Pct.
Dean Smith, North Carolina	1962-94	802	230	.777
Eddie Sutton, Creighton, Arkansas, Kentucky & Oklahoma St.	1970-89, 91-2003	724	288	.715
Bob Knight, Army & Indiana	1966-98	721	269	.728
Adolph Rupp, Kentucky	1931-52, 54-64	707	140	.835
Henry Iba, Northwest Mo. St., Colorado & Oklahoma St.	1930-62	669	232	.743
Lefty Driesell, Davidson, Maryland & James Madison	1961-86, 89-95	657	302	.685
Don Haskins, UTEP	1962-94	645	288	.691
Lou Henson, Hardin-Simmons, New Mexico St. & Illinois	1963-95	645	318	.670
Norm Stewart, Northern Iowa & Missouri	1962-94	640	310	.674
Gene Bartow, Central Mo. St., Valparaiso, Memphis, Illinois, UCLA, & UAB	1962-77, 78-95	631	339	.651

34 SEASONS

Coach, Team	Seasons	W	L	Pct.
Dean Smith, North Carolina	1962-95	830	236	.779
Bob Knight, Army & Indiana	1966-99	744	280	.727
Adolph Rupp, Kentucky	1931-52, 54-65	722	150	.828
Henry Iba, Northwest Mo. St., Colorado & Oklahoma St.	1930-63	685	241	.740
Lefty Driesell, Davidson, Maryland & James Madison	1961-86, 89-96	667	322	.674
Don Haskins, UTEP	1962-95	665	298	.691
Lou Henson, Hardin-Simmons, New Mexico St. & Illinois	1963-96	663	331	.667
Norm Stewart, Northern Iowa & Missouri	1962-95	660	319	.674
Ed Diddle, Western Ky.	1923-56	646	215	.750
Abe Lemons, Oklahoma City, Tex.-Pan American, Texas & Oklahoma City	1956-82, 84-90	597	344	.634

35 SEASONS

Coach, Team	Seasons	W	L	Pct.
Dean Smith, North Carolina	1962-96	851	247	.775
Bob Knight, Army & Indiana	1966-2000	764	289	.726
Adolph Rupp, Kentucky	1931-52, 54-66	749	152	.831
Henry Iba, Northwest Mo. St., Colorado & Oklahoma St.	1930-64	700	251	.736
Lou Henson, Hardin-Simmons, New Mexico St., Illinois & New Mexico St.	1963-96, 99	686	341	.668
Lefty Driesell, Davidson, Maryland & James Madison	1961-86, 89-97	683	335	.671
Don Haskins, UTEP	1962-96	678	313	.684
Norm Stewart, Northern Iowa & Missouri	1962-96	678	334	.670
Ed Diddle, Western Ky.	1923-57	663	224	.747
Hugh Durham, Florida St., Georgia & Jacksonville	1967-95, 98-2003	604	401	.601

36 SEASONS

Coach, Team	Seasons	W	L	Pct.
Dean Smith, North Carolina	1962-97	879	254	.776
Bob Knight, Army, Indiana & Texas Tech	1966-2000, 02	787	298	.725
Adolph Rupp, Kentucky	1931-52, 54-67	762	165	.822
Henry Iba, Northwest Mo. St., Colorado & Oklahoma St.	1930-65	720	258	.736
Lou Henson, Hardin-Simmons, New Mexico St., Illinois & New Mexico St.	1963-96, 99-2000	708	351	.669
Lefty Driesell, Davidson, Maryland, James Madison & Georgia St.	1961-86, 89-98	699	347	.668
Norm Stewart, Northern Iowa & Missouri	1962-97	694	351	.664
Don Haskins, UTEP	1962-97	691	327	.679
Ed Diddle, Western Ky.	1923-58	677	235	.742
Ralph Miller, Wichita St., Iowa & Oregon St.	1952-87	615	363	.629

37 SEASONS

Coach, Team	Seasons	W	L	Pct.
Bob Knight, Army, Indiana & Texas Tech	1966-2000, 02-03	809	311	.722
Adolph Rupp, Kentucky	1931-52, 54-68	784	170	.822
Henry Iba, Northwest Mo. St., Colorado & Oklahoma St.	1930-66	724	279	.722
Lou Henson, Hardin-Simmons, New Mexico St., Illinois & New Mexico St.	1963-96, 99-2001	722	365	.664
Lefty Driesell, Davidson, Maryland, James Madison & Georgia St.	1961-86, 89-99	716	360	.665
Norm Stewart, Northern Iowa & Missouri	1962-98	711	366	.660
Don Haskins, UTEP	1962-98	703	341	.673
Ed Diddle, Western Ky.	1923-59	693	245	.739
Ralph Miller, Wichita St., Iowa & Oregon St.	1952-88	635	374	.629
Norm Sloan, Presbyterian, Citadel, Florida, North Carolina St. & Florida	1952-55, 57-89	627	395	.614

38 SEASONS

Coach, Team	Seasons	W	L	Pct.
Adolph Rupp, Kentucky	1931-52, 54-69	807	175	.822
Lou Henson, Hardin-Simmons, New Mexico St., Illinois & New Mexico St.	1963-96, 99-2002	742	377	.663
Lefty Driesell, Davidson, Maryland, James Madison & Georgia St.	1961-86, 89-2000	733	372	.663
Henry Iba, Northwest Mo. St., Colorado & Oklahoma St.	1930-67	731	297	.711
Norm Stewart, Northern Iowa & Missouri	1962-99	731	375	.661
Don Haskins, UTEP	1962-99	719	353	.671
Ed Diddle, Western Ky.	1923-60	714	252	.739
Ralph Miller, Wichita St., Iowa & Oregon St.	1952-89	657	382	.632
Ray Meyer, DePaul	1943-80	623	335	.650
Marv Harshman, Pacific Lutheran, Washington St. & Washington	1946-83	608	432	.585

39 SEASONS

Coach, Team	Seasons	W	L	Pct.
Adolph Rupp, Kentucky	1931-52, 54-70	833	177	.825
Lefty Driesell, Davidson, Maryland, James Madison & Georgia St.	1961-86, 89-2001	762	377	.669
Lou Henson, Hardin-Simmons, New Mexico St., Illinois & New Mexico St.	1963-96, 99-2003	762	386	.664
Henry Iba, Northwest Mo. St., Colorado & Oklahoma St.	1930-68	741	313	.703
Ed Diddle, Western Ky.	1923-61	732	260	.740
Ray Meyer, DePaul	1943-81	650	337	.659
Marv Harshman, Pacific Lutheran, Washington St. & Washington	1946-84	632	439	.590
Phog Allen, Baker, Kansas, Haskell, Central Mo. St. & Kansas	1906-09, 13-47	607	185	.766
Tony Hinkle, Butler	1927-42, 46-68	531	367	.591

40 SEASONS

Coach, Team	Seasons	W	L	Pct.
Adolph Rupp, Kentucky	1931-52, 54-71	855	183	.824
Lefty Driesell, Davidson, Maryland, James Madison & Georgia St.	1961-86, 89-2002	782	388	.668
Henry Iba, Northwest Mo. St., Colorado & Oklahoma St.	1930-69	753	326	.698
Ed Diddle, Western Ky.	1923-62	749	270	.735
Ray Meyer, DePaul	1943-82	676	339	.666
Marv Harshman, Pacific Lutheran, Washington St. & Washington	1946-85	654	449	.593
Phog Allen, Baker, Kansas, Haskell, Central Mo. St. & Kansas	1906-09, 13-40	616	200	.755
Tony Hinkle, Butler	1927-42, 46-69	542	382	.587

COACHING RECORDS

41 SEASONS

Coach, Team	Seasons	W	L	Pct.
Adolph Rupp, Kentucky	1931-52, 54-72	876	190	.822
Lefty Driesell, Davidson, Maryland, James Madison & Georgia St.	1961-86 89-2003	800	409	.662
Henry Iba, Northwest Mo. St., Colorado & Oklahoma St.	1930-70	767	338	.694
Ed Diddle, Western Ky	1923-63	754	286	.725
Ray Meyer, DePaul	1943-83	697	351	.665
Phog Allen, Baker, Kansas, Haskell, Central Mo. St. & Kansas	1906-09, 13-49	628	212	.748
Tony Hinkle, Butler	1927-42, 46-70	557	393	.586

42 SEASONS

Coach, Team	Seasons	W	L	Pct.
Ed Diddle, Western Ky.	1923-64	759	302	.715
Ray Meyer, DePaul	1943-84	724	354	.672
Phog Allen, Baker, Kansas, Haskell, Central Mo. St. & Kansas	1906-09, 13-50	642	223	.742

Active Coaching Longevity Records

(Minimum five years as a Division I head coach)

MOST GAMES

No.	Coach, Team and Seasons
1,148	Lou Henson, Hardin-Simmons 1963-66, New Mexico St. 67-75, Illinois 76-96, New Mexico St. 98-2003
1,120	Bob Knight, Army 1966-71, Indiana 72-2000, Texas Tech 02-03
1,012	Eddie Sutton, Creighton 1970-74, Arkansas 75-85, Kentucky 86-89, Oklahoma St. 91-2003
1,005	Hugh Durham, Florida St. 1967-78, Georgia 79-95, Jacksonville 98-2003
962	John Chaney, Cheyney 1973-82, Temple 83-2003
943	Jim Calhoun, Northeastern 1973-86, Connecticut 87-2003
930	Lute Olson, Long Beach St. 1974, Iowa 75-83, Arizona 84-2003
897	Mike Krzyzewski, Army 1976-80, Duke 81-2003
892	Billy Tubbs, Southwestern (Tex.) 1972-73, Lamar 77-80, Oklahoma 81-94, TCU 95-2002, Lamar 2004
879	Jim Boeheim, Syracuse 1977-2003
873	Don DeVoe, Virginia Tech 1972-76, Wyoming 77-78, Tennessee 79-89, Florida 90, Navy 93-2003
843	Cliff Ellis, South Ala. 1976-84, Clemson 85-94, Auburn 95-2003
833	Tom Davis, Lafayette 1972-77, Boston College 78-82, Stanford 83-86, Iowa 87-99, Drake 2004
799	Ben Braun, Siena Heights 1978-85, Eastern Mich. 86-96, California 97-2003
783	Gary Williams, American 1979-82, Boston College 83-86, Ohio St. 87-89, Maryland 90-2003
778	Gene Keady, Western Ky. 1979-80, Purdue 81-2003
759	Mike Montgomery, Montana 1979-86, Stanford 87-2003
743	Nick Macarchuk, Canisius 1978-87, Fordham 88-99, Stony Brook 2000-03
705	Danny Nee, Ohio 1981-86, Nebraska 87-2000, Robert Morris 01, Duquesne 02-03
701	Bob Huggins, Walsh 1981-83, Akron 85-89, Cincinnati 90-2003

MOST SEASONS

No.	Coach, Team and Seasons
39	Lou Henson, Hardin-Simmons 1963-66, Illinois 76-96, New Mexico St. 67-75, 98-2003
37	Bob Knight, Army 1966-71, Indiana 72-2000, Texas Tech 02-03
35	Hugh Durham, Florida St. 1967-78, Georgia 79-95, Jacksonville 98-2003
33	Eddie Sutton, Creighton 1970-74, Arkansas 75-85, Kentucky 86-89, Oklahoma St. 91-2003
31	Jim Calhoun, Northeastern 1973-86, Connecticut 87-2003
31	John Chaney, Cheyney 1973-82, Temple 83-2003
30	Don DeVoe, Virginia Tech 1972-76, Wyoming 77-78, Tennessee 79-89, Florida 90, Navy 93-2003
30	Lute Olson, Long Beach St. 1974, Iowa 75-83, Arizona 84-2003
28	Billy Tubbs, Southwestern (Tex.) 1972-73, Lamar 77-80, Oklahoma 81-94, TCU 95-2002, Lamar 04
28	Cliff Ellis, South Ala. 1976-84, Clemson 85-94, Auburn 95-2003
28	Mike Krzyzewski, Army 1976-80, Duke 81-2003
28	Tom Davis, Lafayette 1972-77, Boston College 78-82, Stanford 83-86, Iowa 87-99, Drake 2004
27	Jim Boeheim, Syracuse 1977-2003
26	Ben Braun, Siena Heights 1978-85, Eastern Mich. 86-96, California 97-2003
26	Nick Macarchuk, Canisius 1978-87, Fordham 88-99, Stony Brook 2000-03
25	Gary Williams, American 1979-82, Boston College 83-86, Ohio St. 87-89, Maryland 90-2003
25	Gene Keady, Western Ky. 1979-80, Purdue 81-2003
25	Mike Montgomery, Montana 1979-86, Stanford 87-2003

No.	Coach, Team and Seasons
24	Rick Samuels, Iowa St. 1980, Eastern Ill. 81-2003
23	Danny Nee, Ohio 1981-86, Nebraska 87-2000, Robert Morris 02, Duquesne 03
23	Pat Kennedy, Iona 1981-86, Florida St. 87-97, DePaul 98-2002, Montana 03

MOST SEASONS WITH CURRENT SCHOOL

No.	Coach, Team and Seasons
27	Jim Boeheim, #Syracuse 1977-2003
23	Rick Samuels, Eastern Ill. 1981-2003
23	Gene Keady, Purdue 1981-2003
23	Mike Krzyzewski, Duke 1981-2003
22	Mike Vining, #La.-Monroe 1982-2003
21	Don Maestri, #Troy St. 1983-2003
21	John Chaney, Temple 1983-2003
20	Lafayette Stribling, #Mississippi Val. 1984-2003
20	Tom Green, #Fairleigh Dickinson 1984-2003
20	Lute Olson, Arizona 1984-2003
17	Ron Fang Mitchell, #Coppin St. 1987-2003
17	Dave Magarity, Marist 1987-2003
17	Tom Brennan, Vermont 1987-2003
17	Mike Montgomery, Stanford 1987-2003
17	Jim Calhoun, Connecticut 1987-2003
16	Riley Wallace, Hawaii 1988-2003
15	Bob Thomason, Pacific (Cal.) 1989-2003
14	Bob McKillop, #Davidson 1990-2003
14	Fran Dunphy, #Pennsylvania 1990-2003
14	Rick Majerus, Utah 1990-2003
14	Bob Huggins, Cincinnati 1990-2003
14	Gary Williams, Maryland 1990-2003

#has coached only at this school

MOST DIVISION I 20-WIN SEASONS

No.	Coach, Team and Seasons
25	Jim Boeheim, Syracuse 1977-2003
25	Bob Knight, Army 1966-71, Indiana 72-2000, Texas Tech 03
25	Lute Olson, Long Beach St. 1974, Iowa 75-83, Arizona 84-2003
23	Eddie Sutton, Creighton 1970-74, Arkansas 75-85, Kentucky 86-89, Oklahoma St. 91-2003
21	Lou Henson, Hardin-Simmons 1963, 65-66, Illinois 76-96, New Mexico St. 67-75, 99-2003
20	Mike Krzyzewski, Army 1976-80, Duke 81-2003
18	Jim Calhoun, Northeastern 1973-86, Connecticut 87-2003
16	Tom Davis, Lafayette 1972-77, Boston College 78-82, Stanford 83-86, Iowa 87-99, Drake
16	Bob Huggins, Akron 85-89, Cincinnati 90-2003
16	Mike Montgomery, Montana 1979-86, Stanford 87-2003
15	John Chaney, Temple 83-2003
14	Gene Keady, Western Ky. 1979-80, Purdue 81-2003
14	Gary Williams, American 1979-82, Boston College 83-86, Ohio St. 87-89, Maryland 91-2003
14	Roy Williams, Kansas 1989-2003, North Carolina
13	Rick Majerus, Marquette 1984-86, Ball St. 88-89, Utah 90-2003
12	Don DeVoe, Virginia Tech 1972-76, Wyoming 77-78, Tennessee 79-89, Florida 90, Navy 93-2003
12	Charles Spoonhour, Southwest Mo. St. 1984-92, St. Louis 93-99, UNLV 2002-03
11	Danny Nee, Ohio 1981-86, Nebraska 87-2000, Robert Morris 02, Duquesne 03
11	Rick Pitino, Boston U. 1979-83, Providence 86-87, Kentucky 90-97, Louisville 2003
10	Mike Jarvis, Boston U. 1986-90, Georgetown 91-98, St. John's (N.Y.) 99-2003
10	Pat Kennedy, Iona 1981-86, Florida St. 87-97, DePaul 98-2002, Montana 03
10	Tubby Smith, Tulsa 1992-95, Georgia 96-97, Kentucky 98-2003

MOST TEAMS

No.	Coach, Team and Seasons
5	John Beilein, Nazareth 1983, Le Moyne 84-92, Canisius 93-97, Richmond 98-2002, West Virginia 03
5	Tom Davis, Lafayette 1972-77, Boston College 78-82, Stanford 83-86, Iowa 87-99, Drake 2004
5	Mike Deane, Oswego St. 1981-82, Siena 87-94, Marquette 95-99, Lamar 2000-03, Wagner 04
5	Don DeVoe, Virginia Tech 1972-76, Wyoming 77-78, Tennessee 79-89, Florida 90, Navy 93-2003
4	Steve Aggers, Great Falls 1980-85, Wayne St. (Neb.) 86-90, Eastern Wash. 96-2000, Loyola Marymount 01-03
4	Rick Barnes, George Mason 1988, Providence 89-94, Clemson 95-98, Texas 99-2003
4	Dick Bennett, Wis.-Stevens Point 1981-85, Wis.-Green Bay 86-95, Wisconsin 96-2001, Washington St. 04

No.	Coach, Team and Seasons
4	Kermit Davis Jr., Idaho 1989-90, Texas A&M 91, Idaho 97, Middle Tenn. 2003-03
4	Gary Garner, Mo. Southern St. 1977, Drake 82-88, Fort Hays St. 92-97, Southeast Mo. St. 98-2003
4	Pat Kennedy, Iona 1981-86, Florida St. 87-97, DePaul 98-2002, Montana 03
4	Ritchie McKay, Portland St. 1997-98, Colorado St. 99-2000, Oregon St. 01-02, New Mexico 03
4	Danny Nee, Ohio 1981-86, Nebraska 87-2000, Robert Morris 01, Duquesne 02-03
4	Rick Pitino, Boston U. 1979-83, Providence 86-87, Kentucky 90-97, Louisville 02-03
4	Oliver Purnell, Radford 1989-91, Old Dominion 92-94, Dayton 95-2003, Clemson 04
4	Bill Self, Oral Roberts 1994-97, Tulsa 98-2000, Illinois 01-03, Kansas 04
4	Eddie Sutton, Creighton 1970-74, Arkansas 75-85, Kentucky 86-89, Oklahoma St. 91-2003
4	Billy Tubbs, Southwestern (Tex.) 1972-73, Oklahoma 81-94, TCU 95-2002, Lamar 1977-80, 2004
4	Al Walker, Colorado Col. 1989-93, Cornell 94-96, Chaminade 97-2000, Binghamton 01-03
4	Gary Williams, American 1979-82, Boston College 83-86, Ohio St. 87-89, Maryland 90-2003
4	Jim Wooldridge, Central Mo. St. 1986-91, Southwest Tex. St. 92-94, Louisiana Tech 95-98, Kansas St. 2001-03
4	Rich Zvosec, St. Francis (N.Y.) 1989-91, North Fla. 93-97, Millersville 98, UMKC 2002-03

All-Time Coaching Longevity Records

(Minimum 10 years as a Division I head coach)

MOST GAMES

No.	Coach, Team and Seasons
1,354	Jim Phelan, Mt. St. Mary's 1955-03
1,209	Lefty Driesell, Davidson 1961-69, Maryland 70-86, James Madison 89-97, Georgia St. 1998-2003
1,148	Lou Henson, Hardin-Simmons 1963-66, New Mexico St. 67-75, Illinois 76-96, New Mexico St. 98-2003*
1,133	Dean Smith, North Carolina 1962-97
1,120	Bob Knight, Army 1966-71, Indiana 72-2000, Texas Tech 02-03*
1,103	Henry Iba, Northwest Mo. St. 1930-33, Colorado 34, Oklahoma St. 35-70
1,103	Marv Harshman, Pacific Lutheran 1946-58, Washington St. 59-71, Washington 72-85
1,102	Norm Stewart, Northern Iowa 1962-67, Missouri 68-99
1,078	Ray Meyer, DePaul 1943-84
1,073	Don Haskins, UTEP 1962-99
1,066	Adolph Rupp, Kentucky 1931-72
1,061	Ed Diddle, Western Ky. 1923-64
1,039	Ralph Miller, Wichita St. 1952-64, Iowa 65-70, Oregon St. 71-89
1,012	Eddie Sutton, Creighton 1970-74, Arkansas 75-85, Kentucky 86-89, Oklahoma St. 91-2003*
1,010	Phog Allen, Baker 1906-08, Haskell 1909, Central Mo. St. 13-19, Kansas 1908-09, 20-56
1,005	Hugh Durham, Florida St. 1967-78, Georgia 79-95, Jacksonville 1998-2003*
1,000	Gene Bartow, Central Mo. St. 1962-64, Valparaiso 65-70, Memphis 71-74, Illinois 75, UCLA 76-77, UAB 79-96
994	Slats Gill, Oregon St. 1929-64
987	Eldon Miller, Wittenberg 1963-70, Western Mich. 71-76, Ohio St. 77-86, Northern Iowa 87-98
987	Glenn Wilkes, Stetson 1958-93

*active

MOST SEASONS

No.	Coach, Team and Seasons
48	Phog Allen, Baker 1906-08, Haskell 09, Central Mo. St. 13-19, Kansas 08-09, 20-56
49	Jim Phelan, Mt. St. Mary's 1955-03
42	Lefty Driesell, Davidson 1961-69, Maryland 70-86, James Madison 89-97, Georgia St. 98-2003
42	Ray Meyer, DePaul 1943-84
42	Ed Diddle, Western Ky. 1923-64
41	Henry Iba, Northwest Mo. St. 1930-33, Colorado 34, Oklahoma St. 35-70
41	Adolph Rupp, Kentucky 1931-72
41	Tony Hinkle, Butler 1927-42, 46-70
40	Marv Harshman, Pacific Lutheran 1946-58, Washington St. 59-71, Washington 72-85
39	Lou Henson, Hardin-Simmons 1963-66, Illinois 76-96, New Mexico St. 67-75, 98-2003*
39	Cal Luther, DePauw 1955-58, Murray St. 59-74, Longwood 82-90, Tenn.-Martin 91-99, Bethel (Tenn.) 2000
38	Norm Stewart, Northern Iowa 1962-67, Missouri 68-99
38	Don Haskins, UTEP 1962-99
38	Ralph Miller, Wichita St. 1952-64, Iowa 65-70, Oregon St. 71-89
38	Fred A. Enke, Louisville 1924-25, Arizona 26-61
37	Bob Knight, Army 1966-71, Indiana 72-2000, Texas Tech 02-03*
36	Dean Smith, North Carolina 1962-97
36	Slats Gill, Oregon St. 1929-64
36	Eldon Miller, Wittenberg 1963-70, Western Mich. 71-76, Ohio St. 77-86, Northern Iowa 87-98
35	Hugh Durham, Florida St. 1967-78, Georgia 79-95, Jacksonville 98-2003*

*active

MOST SEASONS AT ONE SCHOOL

No.	Coach, Team and Seasons
48	James Phelan, Mt. St. Mary's 1955-2002*
42	Ed Diddle, #Western Ky. 1923-64
42	Ray Meyer, #DePaul 1943-84
41	Tony Hinkle, #Butler 1927-42, 46-70
41	Adolph Rupp, #Kentucky 1931-72
39	Phog Allen, Kansas 1908-09 and 20-56
38	Don Haskins, #UTEP 1962-99
37	Nat Holman, #CCNY 1920-52 and 55-56 and 59-60
36	Fred Enke, Arizona 1926-61
36	Slats Gill, #Oregon St. 1929-64
36	Henry Iba, Oklahoma St. 1935-70
36	Dean Smith, #North Carolina 1962-97
36	Glenn Wilkes, #Stetson 1958-93
32	Norm Stewart, Missouri 1968-99
31	Taps Gallagher, #Niagara 1932-43 and 47-65
31	Cy McClairen, #Bethune-Cookman 1962-66 and 68-93
30	Denny Crum, #Louisville 1972-2001
30	Jack Friel, #Washington St. 1929-58
30	Guy Lewis, #Houston 1957-86
30	Nibs Price, #California 1925-54
29	Pete Carril, Princeton 1968-96
29	Bob Knight, Indiana 1972-2000
29	Piggy Lambert, #Purdue 1917 and 19-46
29	Harry Rabenhorst, #LSU 1926-42 and 46-57
28	Frank Keaney, #Rhode Island 1921-48
27	Hec Edmundson, Washington 1921-47
27	Frank Keaney, Rhode Island #1922-48
27	Shelby Metcalf, #Texas A&M 1964-90
27	Herbert Read, #Western Mich. 1923-49
27	John Wooden, UCLA 1949-75

*active; #has coached only at this school

MOST DIVISION I 20-WIN SEASONS

No.	Coach, Team and Seasons
30	Dean Smith, North Carolina 1962-97
29	Jerry Tarkanian, Long Beach St. 1969-73, UNLV 74-92, Fresno St. 96-2002
25	Jim Boeheim, Syracuse 1977-2003*
25	Bob Knight, Army 1966-71, Indiana 72-2000, Texas Tech 02-03*
25	Lute Olson, Long Beach St. 1974, Iowa 75-83, Arizona 84-2003*
23	Adolph Rupp, Kentucky 1931-72
23	Eddie Sutton, Creighton 1970-74, Arkansas 75-85, Kentucky 86-89, Oklahoma St. 1991-2003*
22	Lefty Driesell, Davidson 1961-69, Maryland 70-86, James Madison 89-97, Georgia St. 98-2003
21	Denny Crum, Louisville 1972-2001
21	Lou Henson, Hardin-Simmons 1963, 65-66, Illinois 76-96, New Mexico St. 67-75, 99-2003*
20	Mike Krzyzewski, Army 1976-80, Duke 81-2003*
19	John Thompson, Georgetown 1973-99
18	Jim Calhoun, Northeastern 1973-86, Connecticut 87-2003*
18	Lou Carnesecca, St. John's (N.Y.) 1966-70 and 74-92
18	Ed Diddle, Western Ky. 1923-64
18	Don Haskins, UTEP 1962-99
18	Henry Iba, Northwest Mo. St. 1930-33, Colorado 34, Okla. St. 35-70
18	Norm Stewart, Northern Iowa 1962-67, Missouri 68-99
18	Billy Tubbs, Lamar 77-80, Oklahoma 81-94, TCU 95-2002*
18	John Wooden, Indiana St. 1947-48, UCLA 49-75

*active

MOST TEAMS

No.	Coach, Team and Seasons
7	Ben Jobe, Talladega 1965-67, Alabama St. 68, South Carolina St. 69-73, Denver 79-80, Alabama A&M 83-86, Tuskegee 97-2000, Southern U. 1987-96, 2002*
7	Elmer Ripley, Wagner 1923-25, Georgetown 28-29, 39-43 and 47-49, Yale 30-35, Columbia 44-45, Notre Dame 46, John Carroll 50-51, Army 52-53
7	Bob Vanatta, Central Methodist 1943 and 48-50, Southwest Mo. St. 51-53, Army 54, Bradley 55-56, Memphis 57-62, Missouri 63-67, Delta St. 73
6	J.D. Barnett, Lenoir Rhyne 1970, High Point 71, Louisiana Tech 78-79, Va. Commonwealth 80-85, Tulsa 86-91, Northwestern St. 95-99

COACHING RECORDS

No.	Coach, Team and Seasons
6	Gene Bartow, Central Mo. St. 1962-64, Valparaiso 65-70, Memphis 71-74, Illinois 75, UCLA 76-77, UAB 79-96
6	Bill E. Foster, Bloomsburg 1961-63, Rutgers 64-71, Utah 72-74, Duke 75-80, South Carolina 81-86, Northwestern 87-93
6	Robert Hopkins, Prairie View 1965, Alcorn St. 67-69, Xavier (La.) 70-74, Southern U. 85-86, Grambling 87-89, Md.-East. Shore 91-92
6	Press Maravich, West Va. Wesleyan 1950, Davis & Elkins 51-52; Clemson 57-62, North Carolina St. 65-66, LSU 1967-72, Appalachian St. 73-75
6	Harry Miller, Western St. 1953-58, Fresno St. 61-65, Eastern N.M. 66-70, North Texas 71, Wichita St. 72-78, Stephen F. Austin 79-88
6	Tom Penders, Tufts 1972-74, Columbia 75-78, Fordham 79-86, Rhode Island 87-88, Texas 89-98, George Washington 99-2001
6	Hal Wissel, TCNJ 1965-67, Lafayette 68-71, Fordham 72-76, Fla. Southern 78-82, Charlotte 83-85, Springfield 87-90
5	John Beilein, Nazareth 1983, Le Moyne 84-92, Canisius 93-97, Richmond 99-2002, West Virginia*
5	Ozzie Cowles, Carleton 1925-30, Wis.-River Falls 34-36, Dartmouth 37-43 and 45-46, Michigan 47-48, Minnesota 49-59
5	Tom Davis, Lafayette 1972-77, Boston College 78-82, Stanford 83-86, Iowa 87-99, Drake 2004*

No.	Coach, Team and Seasons
5	Mike Deane, Oswego St. 1981-82, Siena 87-94, Marquette 95-99, Lamar 2000-03, Wagner 04*
5	Don DeVoe, Virginia Tech 1972-76, Wyoming 77-78, Tennessee 79-89, Florida 90, Navy 93-2002*
5	Bill C. Foster, Shorter 1963-67, Charlotte 71-75, Clemson 76-84, Miami (Fla.) 86-90, Virginia Tech 92-97
5	Ron Greene, Loyola (La.) 1968-69, New Orleans 70-77, Mississippi St. 78, Murray St. 79-85, Indiana St. 86-89
5	Blair Gullion, Earlham 1928-35, Tennessee 36-38, Cornell 39-42, Connecticut 46-47, Washington (Mo.) 48-59
5	Tates Locke, Army 1964-65, Miami (Ohio) 67-70, Clemson 71-75, Jacksonville 79-81, Indiana St. 91-94
5	Cal Luther, DePauw 1955-58, Murray St. 59-74, Longwood 82-90, Tenn.-Martin 91-99, Bethel (Tenn.) 2000
5	John Mauer, Kentucky 1928-30, Miami (Ohio) 31-38, Tennessee 39-47, Army 48-51, Florida 52-60
5	Gordon Stauffer, Washburn 1967, Indiana St. 68-75, IPFW 76-79, Geneva 80-81, Nicholls 82-90
5	Tex Winter, Marquette 1952-53, Kansas St. 54-68, Washington 69-71, Northwestern 74-78, Long Beach St. 79-83

*active

Division I Head Coaching Changes

Year	Teams	Chngs.	Pct.	1st Yr.	Year	Teams	Chngs.	Pct.	1st Yr.
1950	145	22	15.2	11	1962	178	15	8.4	14
1951	153	28	18.3	15	1963	178	24	13.5	15
1952	156	23	14.7	18	1964	179	23	12.8	17
1953	158	20	12.7	13	1965	182	15	8.2	8
1954	160	12	7.5	7	1966	182	24	13.2	20
1955	162	21	13.0	9	1967	185	33	17.8	18
1956	166	18	10.8	12	1968	189	26	13.8	16
1957	167	18	10.8	9	1969	193	29	15.0	19
1958	173	14	8.1	8	1970	196	29	14.8	17
1959	174	20	11.5	10	1971	203	30	14.8	17
1960	175	23	13.1	15	1972	210	37	17.6	21
1961	173	15	8.7	11	1973	216	38	17.6	24

Year	Teams	Chngs.	Pct.	1st Yr.	Year	Teams	Chngs.	Pct.	1st Yr.
1974	233	41	17.6	23	1989	293	42	14.3	24
1975	235	44	18.7	30	1990	292	54	18.5	29
1976	235	34	14.5	20	1991	295	41	13.9	16
1977	245	39	15.9	21	1992	298	39	13.1	15
1978	254	39	15.4	24	1993	298	34	11.4	15
1979	257	53	20.6	28	1994	301	33	11.0	17
1980	261	43	16.5	23	1995	302	58	19.2	28
1981	264	42	15.9	21	1996	305	42	13.8	31
1982	273	37	13.6	20	1997	305	52	17.0	29
1983	274	37	13.5	18	1998	306	63	20.6	31
1984	276	38	13.8	21	1999	310	45	14.5	30
1985	282	26	9.2	15	2000	318	55	17.3	27
1986	283	56	19.8	21	2001	318	53	16.7	31
1987	290	66	22.8	35	2002	321	47	14.6	22
1988	290	39	13.4	16	2003	325	44	13.5	29

Division I Coach of the Year

Season	United Press International	The Associated Press	U.S. Basketball Writers Assn.	National Assn. of Basketball Coaches	Naismith	The Sporting News	CBS/Chevrolet
1955	Phil Woolpert San Francisco						
1956	Phil Woolpert San Francisco						
1957	Frank McGuire North Carolina						
1958	Tex Winter Kansas St.						
1959	Adolph Rupp Kentucky		Eddie Hickey Marquette				
1960	Pete Newell California		Pete Newell California				
1961	Fred Taylor Ohio St.		Fred Taylor Ohio St.				
1962	Fred Taylor Ohio St.		Fred Taylor Ohio St.				
1963	Ed Jucker Cincinnati		Ed Jucker Cincinnati				
1964	John Wooden UCLA		John Wooden UCLA			John Wooden UCLA	
1965	Dave Strack Michigan		Bill van Breda Kolff Princeton				
1966	Adolph Rupp Kentucky		Adolph Rupp Kentucky			Adolph Rupp Kentucky	
1967	John Wooden UCLA	John Wooden UCLA	John Wooden UCLA			Jack Hartman Southern Ill.	
1968	Guy Lewis Houston	Guy Lewis Houston	Guy Lewis Houston			Guy Lewis Houston	
1969	John Wooden UCLA	John Wooden UCLA	Maury John Drake	John Wooden UCLA		John Wooden UCLA	
1970	John Wooden UCLA	John Wooden UCLA	John Wooden UCLA	John Wooden UCLA		Adolph Rupp Kentucky	

Season	United Press International	The Associated Press	U.S. Basketball Writers Assn.	National Assn. of Basketball Coaches	Naismith	The Sporting News	CBS/Chevrolet
1971	Al McGuire Marquette	Al McGuire Marquette	Al McGuire Marquette	Jack Kraft Villanova		Al McGuire Marquette	
1972	John Wooden UCLA	John Wooden UCLA	John Wooden UCLA	John Wooden UCLA		John Wooden UCLA	
1973	John Wooden UCLA	John Wooden UCLA	John Wooden UCLA	Gene Bartow Memphis		John Wooden UCLA	
1974	Digger Phelps Notre Dame	Norm Sloan North Carolina St.	Norm Sloan North Carolina St.	Al McGuire Marquette		Digger Phelps Notre Dame	
1975	Bob Knight Indiana	Bob Knight Indiana	Bob Knight Indiana	Bob Knight Indiana		Bob Knight Indiana	
1976	Tom Young Rutgers	Bob Knight Indiana	Bob Knight Indiana	Johnny Orr Michigan		Tom Young Rutgers	
1977	Bob Gaillard San Francisco	Bob Gaillard San Francisco	Eddie Sutton Arkansas	Dean Smith North Carolina		Lee Rose Charlotte	
1978	Eddie Sutton Arkansas	Eddie Sutton Arkansas	Ray Meyer DePaul	Bill Foster Duke Abe Lemons Texas		Bill Foster Duke	
1979	Bill Hodges Indiana St.	Bill Hodges Indiana St.	Dean Smith North Carolina	Ray Meyer DePaul		Bill Hodges Indiana St.	
1980	Ray Meyer DePaul	Ray Meyer DePaul	Ray Meyer DePaul	Lute Olson Iowa		Lute Olson Iowa	
1981	Ralph Miller Oregon St.	Ralph Miller Oregon St.	Ralph Miller Oregon St.	Ralph Miller Oregon St. Jack Hartman Kansas St.		Dale Brown LSU	Dale Brown LSU
1982	Norm Stewart Missouri	Ralph Miller Oregon St.	John Thompson Georgetown	Don Monson Idaho		Ralph Miller Oregon St.	Gene Keady Purdue
1983	Jerry Tarkanian UNLV	Guy Lewis Houston	Lou Carnesecca St. John's (N.Y.)	Lou Carnesecca St. John's (N.Y.)		Denny Crum Louisville	Lou Carnesecca St. John's (N.Y)
1984	Ray Meyer DePaul	Ray Meyer DePaul	Gene Keady Purdue	Marv Harshman Washington		John Thompson Georgetown	Gene Keady Purdue
1985	Lou Carnesecca St. John's (N.Y.)	Bill Frieder Michigan	Lou Carnesecca St. John's (N.Y.)	John Thompson Georgetown		Lou Carnesecca St. John's (N.Y.)	Dale Brown LSU
1986	Mike Krzyzewski Duke	Eddie Sutton Kentucky	Dick Versace Bradley	Eddie Sutton Kentucky		Denny Crum Louisville	Mike Krzyzewski Duke
1987	John Thompson Georgetown	Tom Davis Iowa	John Chaney Temple	Rick Pitino Providence	Bob Knight Indiana	Rick Pitino Providence	Joey Meyer DePaul
1988	John Chaney Temple	John Chaney Temple	John Chaney Temple	John Chaney Temple	Larry Brown Kansas	John Chaney Temple	John Chaney Temple
1989	Bob Knight Indiana	Bob Knight Indiana	Bob Knight Indiana	P.J. Carlesimo Seton Hall	Mike Krzyzewski Duke	P.J. Carlisemo Seton Hall	Lute Olson Arizona
1990	Jim Calhoun Connecticut	Jim Calhoun Connecticut	Roy Williams Kansas	Jud Heathcote Michigan St.	Bobby Cremins Georgia Tech	Jim Calhoun Connecticut	Jim Calhoun Connecticut
1991	Rick Majerus Utah	Randy Ayers Ohio St.	Randy Ayers Ohio St.	Mike Krzyzewski Duke	Randy Ayers Ohio St.	Rick Pitino Kentucky	Randy Ayers Ohio St.
1992	Perry Clark Tulane	Roy Williams Kansas	Perry Clark Tulane	George Raveling Southern California	Mike Krzyzewski Duke	Mike Krzyzewski Duke	George Raveling Southern California
1993	Eddie Fogler Vanderbilt	Eddie Fogler Vanderbilt	Eddie Fogler Vanderbilt	Eddie Fogler Vanderbilt	Dean Smith North Carolina	Eddie Fogler Vanderbilt	Eddie Fogler Vanderbilt
1994	Norm Stewart Missouri	Norm Stewart Missouri	Charlie Spoonhour St. Louis	Nolan Richardson Arkansas Gene Keady Purdue	Nolan Richardson Arkansas	Norm Stewart Missouri	Nolan Richardson Arkansas
1995	Leonard Hamilton Miami (Fla.)	Kelvin Sampson Oklahoma	Kelvin Sampson Oklahoma	Jim Harrick UCLA	Jim Harrick UCLA	Jud Heathcote Michigan St.	Gene Keady Purdue
1996	Gene Keady Purdue	Gene Keady Purdue	Gene Keady Purdue	John Calipari Massachusetts	John Calipari Massachusetts	John Calipari Massachusetts	Gene Keady Purdue
1997		Clem Haskins Minnesota	Clem Haskins Minnesota	Clem Haskins Minnesota	Roy Williams Kansas	Roy Williams Kansas	Clem Haskins Minnesota
1998		Tom Izzo Michigan St.	Tom Izzo Michigan St.	Bill Guthridge North Carolina	Bill Guthridge North Carolina	Bill Guthridge North Carolina	Bill Guthridge North Carolina
1999		Cliff Ellis Auburn	Cliff Ellis Auburn	Mike Krzyzewski Duke	Mike Krzyzewski Duke	Cliff Ellis Auburn	Cliff Ellis Auburn
2000		Larry Eustachy Iowa St.	Larry Eustachy Iowa St.	Gene Keady Purdue	Mike Montgomery Stanford	Bob Huggins Cincinnati Bill Self Tulsa	Mike Krzyzewski Duke
2001		Matt Doherty North Carolina	Al Skinner Boston College	Tom Izzo Michigan St.	Rod Barnes Mississippi	Al Skinner Boston College	Al Skinner Boston College
2002		Ben Howland Pittsburgh	Bob Howland Pittsburgh	Kelvin Sampson Oklahoma	Ben Howland Pittsburgh	Ben Howland Pittsburgh	Kelvin Sampson Oklahoma
2003		Tubby Smith Kentucky	Tubby Smith Kentucky	Tubby Smith Kentucky	Tubby Smith Kentucky	Tubby Smith Kentucky	Tubby Smith Kentucky

Basketball Times Coach of the Year: 1982-Gale Catlett, West Virginia; 1983-Lou Carnesecca, St. John's (N.Y.); 1984-Jerry Tarkanian, UNLV; 1985-Bobby Cremins, Georgia Tech; 1986-Mike Krzyzewski, Duke; 1987-Wimp Sanderson, Alabama; 1988-Lute Olson, Arizona; 1989-Bob Knight, Indiana; 1990-Rick Pitino, Kentucky; 1991-Rick Majerus, Utah; 1992-Steve Fisher, Michigan; 1993-Dean Smith, North Carolina; 1994-Norm Stewart, Missouri; 1995-Eddie Sutton, Oklahoma St.; 1996-John Calipari, Massachusetts; 1997-Mike Krzyzewski, Duke; 1998-Bob Huggins, Cincinnati; 1999-Tom Izzo, Michigan St.; 2000-Mike Montgomery, Stanford; 2001-Al Skinner, Boston College; 2002-Bob Knight, Texas Tech.; 2003-Tubby Smith, Kentucky.

Legends of Coaching Award: 1999-Dean Smith, North Carolina; 2000-Mike Krzyzewski, Duke; 2001-Lute Olson, Arizona; 2002-Denny Crum, Louisville; 2003-Roy Williams, Kansas.

Division II Coaching Records

Winningest Active Coaches

(Minimum five years as a head coach; includes record at four-year colleges only.)

BY PERCENTAGE

Coach, Team	Years	Won	Lost	Pct.
1. Ray Harper, Ky. Wesleyan	7	205	25	.891
2. Scott Nagy, South Dakota St.	8	183	52	.779
3. Dave Robbins, Virginia Union	25	583	167	.777
4. Rand Chappell, Central Ark.	8	198	62	.762
5. Don Meyer, Northern St.	31	769	262	.746
6. Bob Chipman, Washburn	24	559	192	.744
7. Mike Dunlap, Metro St.	11	246	88	.737
8. Henry Clark, Cal St. Bakersfield	6	124	45	.734
9. Brian Beaury, St. Rose	17	386	142	.731
10. Gordon Gibbons, Clayton St.	13	288	107	.729
11. Herb Magee, Philadelphia U.	36	746	289	.721
12. Rick Cooper, West Tex. A&M	16	351	137	.719
13. Tom Kropp, Neb.-Kearney	13	275	108	.718
14. Butch Haswell, Fairmont St.	10	208	83	.715
15. Richard Schmidt, Tampa	22	459	189	.708
16. Stan Spirou, Southern N.H.	18	384	158	.708
17. Dave Boots, South Dakota	21	409	179	.696
18. Brett Vincent, Alderson-Broaddus	7	138	64	.683
19. Kevin Luke, Michigan Tech	9	180	84	.682
20. Herman Meyer, St. Mary's (Tex.)	25	488	235	.675
21. Jerry Johnson, LeMoyne-Owen	45	812	400	.670
22. Ed Douma, Hillsdale	28	500	248	.668
23. Kevin Schlagel, St. Cloud St.	6	122	61	.667
24. Steve Rives, Delta St.	18	342	171	.667
25. Craig Carse, Mont. St.-Billings	12	227	115	.664
26. Lonn Reisman, Tarleton St.	15	293	150	.661
27. Tom Billeter, Augustana (S.D.)	5	97	50	.660
28. Greg Walcavich, Edinboro	22	407	212	.658
29. Ken Wagner, BYU-Hawaii	13	250	130	.658
30. Jim Baker, Catawba	9	166	88	.654
31. Dick DeLaney, West Chester	16	290	154	.653
32. Ken Shields, Northern Ky.	15	290	155	.652
33. Keith Dickson, St. Anselm	17	327	176	.650
34. Tom Galeazzi, C.W. Post	22	414	224	.649
35. Steve Tappmeyer, Northwest Mo. St.	15	277	152	.646
36. Herbert Greene, Columbus St.	24	442	243	.645
37. Greg Sparling, Central Wash.	9	149	83	.642
38. Jerry Slocum, Gannon	28	540	306	.638
39. Gary Stanfield, Drury	12	215	123	.636
40. Larry Gipson, Northeastern St.	11	203	116	.636
41. Fred Thompson, Millersville	5	88	51	.633
42. Brad Jackson, Western Wash.	18	336	200	.627
43. Rich Glas, North Dakota	25	443	263	.627
44. Jim Heaps, Mesa St.	7	120	72	.625
45. Steve Joyner, Johnson Smith	16	287	174	.623
46. Tim Miles, North Dakota St.	8	144	87	.623
47. Art Luptowski, American Int'l	14	251	153	.621
48. Joe Esposito, Angelo St.	5	87	53	.621
49. Terry Sellers, GC&SU	10	173	106	.620
50. Tom Ryan, Eckerd	7	123	76	.618
51. Tom O'Shea, St. Michael's	6	109	68	.616
52. Wayne Cobb, East Central	26	428	268	.615
53. Gary Tuell, Augusta St.	16	298	188	.613
54. Tom Smith, Mo. Western St.	28	490	311	.612
55. Tom Klusman, Rollins	23	393	252	.609
56. Charlie Bruns, Alas. Anchorage	10	166	107	.608
57. Ed Murphy, West Ga.	24	416	268	.608
58. Ron Righter, Clarion	17	273	177	.607
59. Bill Brown, Calif. (Pa.)	17	277	180	.606
60. Jim Harter, Pace	6	94	62	.603
61. Gregg Nibert, Presbyterian	14	248	164	.602
62. Joe Folda, Colorado St.-Pueblo	19	324	215	.601
63. Ron Spry, Paine	23	425	282	.601
64. Jay Lawson, Bentley	12	203	136	.599
65. Jeff Morgan, Harding	11	184	123	.599
66. Roger Lyons, Ashland	10	163	110	.597
67. Lonnie Porter, Regis (Colo.)	26	427	295	.591
68. Dave Davis, Pfeiffer	12	195	140	.582
69. Darren Metress, Belmont Abbey	7	115	83	.581
70. Leighton McCrary, Grand Canyon	13	213	154	.580

BY VICTORIES

(Minimum five years as a head coach; includes record at four-year colleges only.)

Coach, Team	Years	Won	Lost	Pct.
1. Jerry Johnson, LeMoyne-Owen	45	812	400	.670
2. Don Meyer, Northern St.	31	769	262	.746
3. Herb Magee, Philadelphia	36	746	289	.721
4. Dave Robbins, Virginia Union	25	583	167	.777
5. Bob Chipman, Washburn	24	559	192	.744
6. Jerry Slocum, Gannon	28	540	306	.638
7. Ed Douma, Hillsdale	28	500	248	.668
8. Tom Smith, Mo. Western St.	28	490	311	.612
9. Herman Meyer, St. Mary's (Tex.)	25	488	235	.675
10. Richard Schmidt, Tampa	22	459	189	.708
11. Oliver Jones, Tuskegee	31	444	411	.519
12. Rich Glas, North Dakota	25	443	263	.627
13. Herbert Greene, Columbus St.	24	442	243	.645
14. Wayne Cobb, East Central	26	428	268	.615
15. Lonnie Porter, Regis (Colo.)	26	427	295	.591
16. Ron Spry, Paine	23	425	282	.601
17. Ed Murphy, West Ga.	24	416	268	.608
18. Tom Galeazzi, C.W. Post	22	414	224	.649
19. Dave Boots, South Dakota	21	409	179	.696
20. Greg Walcavich, Edinboro	22	407	212	.658
21. Tom Klusman, Rollins	23	393	252	.609
22. Dave Yanai, Cal St. L.A.	26	391	310	.558
23. Brian Beaury, St. Rose	17	386	142	.731
24. Stan Spirou, Southern N.H.	18	384	158	.708
25. Gene Iba, Pittsburg St.	23	382	279	.578
26. Art Leary, Southern Conn. St.	25	357	351	.504
27. Rick Cooper, West Tex. A&M	16	351	137	.719
28. Steve Rives, Delta St.	18	342	171	.667
29. Brad Jackson, Western Wash.	18	336	200	.627
30. Bert Hammel, Merrimack	23	333	318	.512
31. Keith Dickson, St. Anselm	17	327	176	.650
32. Joe Folda, Colorado St.-Pueblo	19	324	215	.601
33. Gary Edwards, Indiana (Pa.)	19	319	234	.577
34. Tom Wood, Humboldt St.	22	314	291	.519
35. Terry Brown, Bluefield St.	24	313	378	.453
36. John Lentz, Lenoir-Rhyne	20	307	253	.548
37. Gary Tuell, Augusta St.	16	298	188	.613
38. Lonn Reisman, Tarleton St.	15	293	150	.661
39. Dick DeLaney, West Chester	16	290	154	.653
39. Ken Shields, Northern Ky.	15	290	155	.652
41. Gordon Gibbons, Clayton St.	13	288	107	.729
42. Stephen Joyner, Johnson Smith	16	287	174	.623
43. Steve Tappmeyer, Northwest Mo. St.	15	277	152	.646
43. Bill Brown, Calif. (Pa.)	17	277	180	.606
45. Tom Kropp, Neb.-Kearney	13	275	108	.718
45. Dean Ellis, Northern Mich.	17	275	204	.574
47. Ron Righter, Clarion	17	273	177	.607
48. Jim Whitesell, Lewis	16	254	187	.576
49. Art Luptowski, American Int'l	14	251	153	.621
50. Ken Wagner, BYU-Hawaii	13	250	130	.658
51. Gregg Nibert, Presbyterian	14	248	164	.602
52. Mike Dunlap, Metro St.	11	246	88	.737
53. Dan Schmotzer, Coker	16	233	193	.547
53. Rick Reedy, West Ala.	19	233	274	.460
55. Jay DeFruscio, Wheeling Jesuit	14	230	175	.568
55. Bob Hofman, Fort Lewis	15	230	194	.542
57. Prescott Smith, Cal St. Chico	16	229	216	.515
58. Al Sokaitis, Alas. Fairbanks	16	228	195	.539
59. Craig Carse, Mont. St.-Billings	12	227	115	.664
59. Dale Clayton, Carson-Newman	15	227	197	.535
61. Tom Ackerman, Assumption	18	226	266	.459
62. Robert Corn, Mo. Southern St.	14	223	171	.566
63. Steve Cox, Concord	14	221	186	.543
64. Gary Stanfield, Drury	12	215	123	.636
65. Leighton McCrary, Grand Canyon	13	213	154	.580
66. Butch Haswell, Fairmont St.	10	208	83	.715
67. Bob Rukavina, Pitt.-Johnstown	14	206	168	.551
68. Lennie Acuff, Ala.-Huntsville	12	205	158	.565
68. Ray Harper, Ky. Wesleyan	7	205	25	.891
70. Larry Gipson, Northeastern St.	11	203	113	.636
70. Jay Lawson, Bentley	12	203	136	.599

Winningest Coaches All-Time

(Minimum 10 head coaching seasons in Division II)

BY PERCENTAGE

Coach (Team coached, tenure)	Years	Won	Lost	Pct.
1. Walter Harris (Philadelphia 1954-65, 67)	13	240	56	.811
2. Dolph Stanley (Beloit 1946-57)	12	238	56	.810
3. Ed Adams (N.C. Central 1935-36, Tuskegee 37-49, Texas Southern 50-58)	24	643	153	.808
4. Dave Robbins (Virginia Union 1979-03)*	25	583	167	.777
5. Charles Christian (Norfolk St. 1974-90)	14	318	95	.770
6. Lucias Mitchell (Alabama St. 1964-67, Kentucky St. 68-75, Norfolk St. 79-81)	15	325	103	.759
7. Dean Nicholson (Central Wash. 1965-90)	26	620	199	.757
8. John Kochan (Millersville 1984-96)	13	285	96	.748
9. Bob Chipman (Washburn 1980-03)*	24	559	192	.744
10. Joe Hutton (Hamline 1932-65)	34	591	207	.741
11. Harry Good (Indianapolis 1929-43, Indiana 44-46)	18	230	81	.740
12. Rock Oglesby (Florida A&M 1951-70, 72)	21	386	138	.737
13. John McLendon Jr. (N.C. Central 1941-52, Hampton 53-54, Tennessee St. 55-59, Kentucky St. 64-66, Cleveland St. 67-69)	25	496	179	.735
14. Calvin Irvin (Johnson Smith 1948-51, North Caro. A&T 55-72)	22	397	144	.734
15. Brian Beaury (St. Rose 1987-03)*	17	386	142	.731
16. Gordon Gibbons (South Fla. 1980; Fla. Southern 91-00, Clayton St. 2002-03)*	13	288	107	.729
17. Garland Pinholster (Oglethorpe 1957-66)	10	180	68	.726
18. Herb Magee (Philadelphia U. 1968-03)*	36	746	289	.721
19. Rick Cooper (Wayland Baptist 1988-93; West Tex. A&M 94-03)*	16	351	137	.719
20. Tom Kropp (Neb.-Kearney 1991-03)*	13	275	108	.718
21. Butch Haswell (Fairmont St. 1994-03)*	10	208	83	.715
22. Ed Jucker (Merchant Marine 1946-47, Rensselaer 49-53, Cincinnati 61-65, Rollins 73-77)	17	266	109	.709
23. Richard Schmidt (Vanderbilt 1980-81, Tampa 84-03)*	22	459	189	.708
24. Stan Spirou (Southern N.H. 1986-03)*	18	384	158	.708
25. Al Shields (Bentley 1964-78)	15	257	107	.706
26. Pat Douglass (Mont. St.-Billings 1982-87, Cal St. Bakersfield 88-97, UC Irvine 99-03)*	22	471	196	.706
27. Lou D'Allesandro (Southern N.H. 1964-70, 73-75)	10	183	77	.704
28. Bill Boylan (Monmouth 1957-77)	21	368	155	.704
29. L. Vann Pettaway (Alabama A&M 1987-03)*	17	353	150	.702
30. Beryl Shipley (La.-Lafayette 1958-73)	16	296	129	.696
31. Dave Boots (Augsburg 1983-88, South Dakota 89-03)*	21	409	179	.696
32. Ernest Hole (Wooster 1927-58)	32	412	181	.695
33. Sam Cozen (Drexel 1953-68)	16	213	94	.694
34. Barney Steen (Calvin 1954-66)	13	189	84	.692
35. Ken Bone (Cal St. Stanislaus 1985, Seattle Pacific 91-02)	13	257	118	.685
36. Robert Rainey [Albany St. (Ga.) 1961-72]	12	243	112	.685
37. Dick Sauers [Albany (N.Y.) 1956-87, 89-97]	41	702	330	.680
38. Bill Jones (Florence St. 1973, North Ala. 74, Jacksonville St. 75-98)	26	477	226	.679
39. Danny Rose (Central Mich. 1938-43, 47-54)	14	176	84	.677
40. Dale Race (Milton 1976-79, Minn. Duluth 85-98)	18	363	177	.672
41. Russell Beichly (Akron 1941-59)	19	288	141	.671
42. Jerry Johnson (LeMoyne-Owen 1959-03)*	45	812	400	.670
43. William Lucas (Central St. 1961-74)	14	241	120	.668
44. Roger Kaiser (West Ga. 1971-90)	20	379	189	.667
45. Steve Rives (Louisiana Col. 1986, Delta St. 87-03)*	18	342	171	.667
46. Fred Hobdy (Grambling 1957-86)	30	571	287	.666
47. Paul Webb (Randolph-Macon 1957-75, Old Dominion 76-85)	29	511	257	.665
48. Ed Martin (South Carolina St. 1956-68, Tennessee St. 69-85)	30	501	253	.664
49. Marlowe Severson (St. Cloud St. 1959-69, Minn. St. Mankato 70-73)	15	250	127	.663
50. Don Zech (Puget Sound 1969-89)	21	386	197	.662
51. Malcolm Eiken (Buffalo 1947-56)	10	141	72	.662
52. Dave Buss (Wis.-Green Bay 1970-82, Long Beach St. 84, St. Olaf 88-94)	21	381	195	.661
53. Lonn Reisman (Tarleton St. 1989-03)*	15	293	150	.661
54. Charles Chronister (Bloomsburg 1972-02)	31	559	288	.660
55. Wayne Boultinghouse (Southern Ind. 1975-81; Ky. Wesleyan 91-96)	13	240	124	.659
56. Greg Walcavich (Birmingham-So. 1979-83, Rice 87, West Va. Wesleyan 88-89, Edinboro 90-03)*	22	407	212	.658
57. Donald Feeley (Sacred Heart 1966-78, Fairleigh Dickinson 81-83)	16	285	148	.658
58. Ron Shumate (Chattanooga 1973-79; Southeast Mo. St. 82-97)	23	445	232	.657
59. Boyd King (Truman 1947-71)	25	377	199	.655
60. John Masi (UC Riverside 1980-03)*	24	442	233	.655

Coach (Team coached, tenure)	Years	Won	Lost	Pct.
61. Ernie Wheeler (Cal Poly 1973-86, Mont. St.-Billings 89-91)	17	314	166	.654
62. Jim McDonald (Edinboro 1963-71, 73-75)	12	174	92	.654
63. Dick DeLaney (West Chester 1988-03)*	16	290	154	.653
64. Dick Peth (Denver 1986-97; Wartburg 98-03)*	18	329	175	.653
65. Jim Wink (Ferris St. 1960-79, 81)	21	337	179	.653
66. Joseph O'Brien (Assumption 1968-85)	18	322	172	.652
67. Ken Shields (Northern Ky. 1989-03)*	15	290	155	.652
68. Ed Steitz (Springfield 1957-66)	10	160	86	.650
69. John Lance (Southwestern Okla. 1919-22, Pittsburg St. 23-34, 36-63)	44	632	340	.650
70. Keith Dickson (St. Anselm 1987-03)*	17	327	176	.650

Active coaches

BY VICTORIES

(Minimum 10 head coaching seasons in Division II)

Coach (Team coached, tenure)	Years	Won	Lost	Pct.
1. Clarence "Big House" Gaines (Winston-Salem 1947-93)	47	828	447	.649
2. Jerry Johnson (LeMoyne-Owen 1959-03)*	45	812	400	.670
3. Herb Magee (Philadelphia 1968-03)*	36	746	289	.721
4. Dick Sauers [Albany (N.Y.) 1956-87, 89-97]	41	702	330	.680
5. Ed Adams (N.C. Central 1935-36, Tuskegee 37-49, Texas Southern 50-58)	24	643	153	.808
6. John Lance (Southwestern Okla. 1919-22, Pittsburg St. 23-34, 36-63)	44	632	340	.650
7. Ed Messbarger [Benedictine Hts. 1958-60, Dallas 61-63, St. Mary's (Tex.) 64-78, Angelo St. 79-98]	41	630	518	.549
8. Dean Nicholson (Central Wash. 1965-90)	26	620	199	.757
9. Dom Rosselli (Youngstown St. 1941-42, 47-82)	38	591	385	.606
10. Joe Hutton (Hamline 1932-65)	34	591	207	.741
11. Dave Robbins (Virginia Union 1979-03)*	25	583	167	.777
12. Dan McCarrell, (North Park 1968-84, Minn. St. Mankato 85-01)	34	579	347	.625
13. Fred Hobdy (Grambling 1957-86)	30	571	287	.666
14. Bob Chipman (Washburn 1980-03)*	24	559	192	.744
14. Charles Chronister (Bloomsburg 1972-02)	31	559	288	.660
16. Bill Knapton (Beloit 1958-97)	40	555	347	.615
17. Bruce Webster (Bridgeport 1966-99)	34	549	405	.575
18. Arthur McAfee (Lane 1961, Mississippi Val. 62, Lincoln [Mo.] 63, Bishop 64-65, Morehouse 66-00)	40	516	510	.503
19. Arar McCutchan (Evansville 1947-77)	31	514	314	.621
19. Jim Gudger (Western Caro. 1951-69, Tex. A&M-Commerce 70-83)	33	514	415	.553
21. Paul Webb (Randolph-Macon 1957-75, Old Dominion 76-85)	29	511	257	.665
22. Leo Nicholson (Central Wash. 1930-64)	33	505	281	.642
23. Bobby Vaughan (Elizabeth City St. 1952-66, 68-86)	34	501	363	.580
23. Ed Martin (South Carolina St. 1956-68, Tennessee St. 69-85)	30	501	253	.664
25. Will Renken (Bloomfield 1948-52, Albright 56-88)	38	497	466	.516
26. John McLendon Jr. (N.C. Central 1941-52, Hampton 53-54, Tennessee St. 55-59, Kentucky St. 64-66, Cleveland St. 67-69)	25	496	179	.735
27. Tom Smith (Central Mo. St. 1976-80, Valparaiso 81-88, Mo. Western St. 89-03)*	28	490	311	.612
28. Angus Nicoson (Indianapolis 1948-76)	29	482	274	.638
29. Hamlet Peterson, (Luther 1923-65)	43	481	356	.575
30. Bill Detrick (Central Conn. St. 1960-87, Coast Guard 90)	30	479	278	.633
31. Bill Jones (Florence St. 1973, North Ala. 74, Jacksonville St. 75-98)	26	477	226	.679
31. Aubrey Bonham (Whittier 1938-43 & 46-68)	27	477	262	.645
33. Dave Gunther [Wayne St. (Neb.) 1968-70, North Dakota 71-88, Buena Vista 94-95, Bemidji St. 96-01]	29	476	328	.592
34. Pat Douglass (Mont. St.-Billings 1982-87, Cal St. Bakersfield 88-97, UC Irvine 99-03)*	22	471	196	.706
35. Richard Schmidt (Vanderbilt 1980-81, Tampa 84-03)*	22	459	189	.708
35. Richard Meckfessel (Charleston (W.Va.) 1966-79, Mo.-St. Louis 83-99)	31	459	420	.522
35. Burt Kahn (Quinnipiac 1962-91)	30	459	355	.564
38. Jim Seward [Wayne St. (Neb.) 1975-78, Ashland 79-83, Kansas Newman 84-87, Central Okla. 88-02]	28	454	339	.573
39. Butch Raymond (Augsburg 1971-73, Minn. St. Mankato 74-84, St. Cloud St. 85-97)	27	447	302	.597
40. J.B. Scearce (North Ga. 1942-43, Cumberland 47, Ga. Southern 48-79)	26	447	244	.647
41. Ron Shumate (Chattanooga 1973-79; Southeast Mo. St. 82-97)	23	445	232	.657
42. Oliver Jones [Albany St. (Ga.) 1973-00, Tuskegee 01-03]*	31	444	411	.519
43. Rich Glas (Minn.-Morris 1975-79, Willamette 80-84, North Dakota 89-03)*	25	443	263	.627

COACHING RECORDS

Coach (Team coached, tenure)	Years	Won	Lost	Pct.
44. Herbert Greene (Aub.-Montgomery 1976-77, Columbus St. 82-03)*	24	442	243	.645
44. John Masi (UC Riverside 1980-03)*	24	442	233	.655
46. Tom Villemure (Detroit Business 1967, Grand Valley St. 73-96)	25	437	268	.620
47. James Dominey (Valdosta St. 1972-00)	29	436	343	.560
48. Hal Nunnally (Randolph-Macon 1976-99)	24	431	232	.650
48. Leonidas Epps (Clark Atlanta 1950-78)	29	431	291	.597
50. Ollie Gelston (New Jersey City 1960-67, Montclair St. 68-91)	32	429	347	.553
51. Lonnie Porter (Regis [Colo.] 1978-03)*	26	427	295	.591
52. Jim Harley (Eckerd 1964-96)	32	420	349	.546

Coach (Team coached, tenure)	Years	Won	Lost	Pct.
53. Irvin Peterson (Neb. Wesleyan 1949-51, 54-80)	30	419	314	.572
54. Tom Feely [St. Thomas (Minn.) 1955-80]	26	417	269	.608
55. Ed Murphy (West Ala. 1979-83, Delta St. 84-86, Mississippi 87-92, West Ga. 94-03)*	24	416	268	.608
56. Tom Galeazzi (C.W. Post 1982-03)*	22	414	224	.649
57. Ernest Hole (Wooster 1927-58)	32	412	181	.695
58. Dave Boots (Augsburg 1983-88, South Dakota 89-03)*	21	409	179	.696
59. Greg Walcavich (Birmingham-So. 1979-83, Rice 87, West Va. Wesleyan 88-89, Edinboro 90-03)*	22	407	212	.658
60. Dave Bike (Sacred Heart 1979-03)*	25	400	332	.546

*Active coaches

Division III Coaching Records

Winningest Active Coaches

(Minimum five years as a head coach; includes record at four-year colleges only.)

BY PERCENTAGE

Coach, Team	Years	Won	Lost	Pct.
1. Brian Meehan, Salem St.	7	160	39	.804
2. Brian VanHaaften, Buena Vista	7	150	43	.777
3. Jerry Rickrode, Wilkes	11	231	67	.775
4. Joe Cassidy, Rowan	7	143	45	.761
5. Jack Bennett, Wis.-Stevens Point	7	142	48	.747
6. Mike Jones, Mississippi Col.	15	303	103	.746
7. Bill Foti, Colby-Sawyer	11	220	75	.746
8. Glenn Van Wieren, Hope	26	500	174	.742
9. Steve Moore, Wooster	22	446	157	.740
10. Glenn Robinson, Frank. & Marsh.	32	648	231	.737
11. Mike Lonergan, Catholic	11	227	82	.735
12. Joe Campoli, Ohio Northern	11	221	81	.732
13. Bob Campbell, Western Conn. St.	19	378	140	.730
14. C. J. Woollum, Chris. Newport	19	391	145	.729
15. Mark Hanson, Gust. Adolphus	13	262	98	.728
16. Rick Simonds, St. Joseph's (Me.)	23	463	176	.725
17. Bosko Djurickovic, Carthage	17	332	128	.722
18. Brian Baptiste, Mass.-Dartmouth	20	396	153	.721
19. Bob Gillespie, Ripon	23	393	156	.716
20. Gerry Matthews, Richard Stockton	17	333	136	.710
21. John Dzik, Cabrini	23	453	192	.702
22. Stan Ogrodnik, Trinity (Conn.)	22	368	156	.702
23. Richard Bihr, Buffalo St.	23	426	184	.698
24. Tom Murphy, Hamilton	33	583	254	.697
25. Todd Raridon, Neb. Wesleyan	14	256	113	.694
26. Charles Brown, New Jersey City	21	404	182	.689
27. Jose Rebimas, Wm. Paterson	9	163	75	.685
28. Jamie Matthews, Manchester	5	91	42	.684
29. Randy Lambert, Maryville (Tenn.)	23	413	194	.680
30. Bob Gaillard, Lewis & Clark	22	414	195	.680
31. Joe Nesci, New York U.	15	260	123	.679
32. Dick Whitmore, Colby	32	531	252	.678
33. David Hixon, Amherst	26	439	209	.677
34. Page Moir, Roanoke	14	256	124	.674
35. James Lancaster, Aurora	9	156	76	.672
36. David Paulsen, Williams	9	166	81	.672
37. Steve Fritz, St. Thomas (Minn.)	23	411	201	.672
38. Nelson Whitmore, Brockport St.	5	95	47	.669
39. Bill Harris, Wheaton (Ill.)	18	330	164	.668
40. John McCloskey, Alvernia	11	206	104	.665
41. Cazzie Russell, SCAD	7	118	60	.663
42. Ron Holmes, McMurry	13	229	119	.658
43. Doug Pearson, Western New Eng.	5	88	46	.657
44. Ken Scalmanini, Claremont-M-S	5	80	42	.656
45. Ted Van Dellen, Wis.-Oshkosh	13	228	120	.655
46. Dick Peth, Wartburg	18	329	175	.653
47. Rudy Marisa, Waynesburg	34	563	300	.652
48. Mark Edwards, Washington (Mo.)	22	374	200	.652
49. Dave Niland, Penn St.-Behrend	9	158	85	.650
50. Bill Brown, Wittenberg	16	286	156	.647
51. Steve Brennan, Babson	8	142	78	.645
52. Dick Reynolds, Otterbein	31	546	300	.645
53. Kevin Vande Streek, Calvin	13	234	130	.643
54. Paul Phillips, Clark (Mass.)	17	293	164	.641
55. Bill Nelson, Johns Hopkins	23	383	215	.640
56. Brad McAlester, Lebanon Valley	9	156	88	.639
57. Gordie James, Willamette	16	279	159	.637
58. Chris Downs, St. Lawrence	6	103	59	.636
59. Mike Moran, John Carroll	11	188	108	.635
60. Bill Fenlon, DePauw	18	292	168	.635
61. Steve Larson, Edgewood	17	315	182	.634
62. Mike Bokosky, Chapman	11	172	100	.632
63. Mike Beitzel, Hanover	23	400	233	.632
64. Keith Bunkenburg, Benedictine (Ill.)	8	129	76	.629
65. Chuck McBreen, Ramapo	5	83	49	.629
66. John Scheinman, Plymouth St.	8	132	81	.620
67. Terry Glasgow, Monmouth (Ill.)	31	429	265	.618
68. Duane Davis, Mt. St. Mary (N.Y.)	8	133	83	.616
69. Herb Hilgeman, Rhodes	27	406	255	.614
70. Tom Palombo, Guilford	6	100	63	.613

BY VICTORIES

(Minimum five years as a head coach; includes record at four-year colleges only.)

Coach, Team	Years	Won	Lost	Pct.
1. Glenn Robinson, Frank. & Marsh.	32	648	231	.737
2. Jim Smith, St. John's (Minn.)	39	618	411	.601
3. Tom Murphy, Hamilton	33	583	254	.697
4. Rudy Marisa, Waynesburg	34	563	300	.652
5. Dick Reynolds, Otterbein	31	546	300	.645
6. Dick Whitmore, Colby	32	531	252	.678
7. Jim Burson, Muskingum	36	514	400	.562
8. Glenn Van Wieren, Hope	26	500	174	.742
9. Rick Simonds, St. Joseph's (Me.)	23	463	176	.725
9. Cliff Garrsion, Hendrix	31	463	376	.552
11. John Dzik, Cabrini	23	453	192	.702
12. Steve Moore, Wooster	22	446	157	.740
13. Jon Davison, Clarke	34	440	427	.507
14. David Hixon, Amherst	26	439	209	.677
15. Mike Turner, Albion	29	432	281	.606
16. Terry Glasgow, Monmouth (Ill.)	31	429	265	.618
17. Richard Bihr, Buffalo St.	23	426	184	.698
17. Mike Neer, Rochester	27	426	277	.606
19. Mac Petty, Wabash	30	421	326	.564
20. Lee McKinney, Fontbonne	25	419	290	.591
21. Bob Gaillard, Lewis & Clark	22	414	195	.680
22. Randy Lambert, Maryville (Tenn.)	23	413	194	.680
23. Steve Fritz, St. Thomas (Minn.)	23	411	201	.672
24. Herb Hilgeman, Rhodes	27	406	255	.614

Coach, Team	Years	Won	Lost	Pct.
25. Charles Brown, New Jersey City	21	404	182	.689
26. Mike Beitzel, Hanover	23	400	233	.632
27. Brian Baptiste, Mass.-Dartmouth	20	396	153	.721
27. Gary Smith, Redlands	32	396	423	.484
29. Bob Gillespie, Ripon	23	393	156	.716
30. C. J. Woollum, Chris. Newport	19	391	145	.729
31. Bill Nelson, Johns Hopkins	23	383	215	.640
31. Joe Ramsey, Blackburn	28	383	335	.533
33. Bob Campbell, Western Conn. St.	19	378	140	.730
33. Rees Johnson, North Park	27	378	364	.509
35. Mark Edwards, Washington (Mo.)	22	374	200	.652
36. Stan Ogrodnik, Trinity (Conn.)	22	368	156	.702
37. Bob McVean, Rochester Inst.	25	361	270	.572
38. Gerry Matthews, Richard Stockton	17	333	136	.710
39. Bosko Djurickovic, Carthage	17	332	128	.722
40. Jim Walker, Moravian	24	331	273	.548
40. Jeff Gamber, York (Pa.)	26	331	338	.495
42. Bill Harris, Wheaton (Ill.)	18	330	164	.668
42. Peter Barry, Coast Guard	21	330	241	.578
44. Dick Peth, Wartburg	18	329	175	.653
45. Steve Bankston, Baldwin-Wallace	23	326	283	.535
45. Bob Gay, MacMurray	28	326	388	.457
47. Kerry Prather, Franklin	20	320	218	.595
48. Steve Larson, Edgewood	17	315	182	.634
48. Bob Johnson, Emory & Henry	23	315	285	.525
50. Charlie Brock, Springfield	23	314	281	.528
51. Roger Kindel, FDU-Florham	26	313	324	.491
52. Mike Jones, Mississippi Col.	15	303	103	.746
52. Jonathon Halpert, Yeshiva	31	303	382	.442
54. Mike Griffin, Rensselaer	26	295	356	.453
55. Paul Phillips, Clark (Mass.)	17	293	164	.641
56. Bill Fenlon, DePauw	18	292	168	.635
57. Bill Brown, Wittenberg	16	286	156	.647
58. Rich Rider, Cal Lutheran	18	283	182	.609
59. Gordie James, Willamette	16	279	159	.637
60. Bill Leatherman, Bridgewater (Va.)	18	273	194	.585
61. Bruce Wilson, Simpson	18	266	198	.573
62. Ray Rankis, Baruch	20	263	261	.502
63. Mark Hanson, Gust. Adolphus	13	262	98	.728
64. Joe Nesci, New York U.	15	260	123	.679
65. Todd Raridon, Neb. Wesleyan	14	256	113	.694
65. Page Moir, Roanoke	14	256	124	.674
67. Guy Kalland, Carleton	19	246	231	.516
68. Charles Katsiaficas, Pomona-Pitzer	16	245	165	.598
69. Mike Daley, Nazareth	17	244	201	.548
70. Dave Madeira, Muhlenburg	16	241	164	.595

Winningest Coaches All-Time

(Minimum 10 head coaching seasons in Division III)

BY PERCENTAGE

Coach (Team coached, tenure)	Years	Won	Lost	Pct.
1. Jerry Rickrode (Wilkes 1993-03)*	11	231	67	.775
2. Bo Ryan (Wis.-Platteville 1985-99, Wis.-Milwaukee 00-01, Wisconsin 02-03)*	19	426	124	.775
3. Jim Borcherding [Augustana (Ill.) 1970-84]	15	313	100	.758
4. Harry Sheehy (Williams 1984-00)	17	324	104	.757
5. Tony Shaver (Hampden-Sydney 1987-03)*	17	358	121	.747
6. Bill Foti (Colby-Sawyer 1993-03)*	11	220	75	.746
7. Glenn Van Wieren (Hope 1978-03)*	26	500	174	.742
8. Steve Moore (Muhlenberg 1982-87, Wooster 88-03)*	22	446	157	.740
9. Glenn Robinson (Frank. & Marsh. 1972-03)*	32	648	231	.737
10. Mike Longeran (Catholic 1993-03)*	11	227	82	.735
11. Joe Campoli (Ohio Northern 1993-03)*	11	221	81	.732
12. Bob Campbell (Western Conn. St. 1985-03)*	19	378	140	.730
13. C.J. Woollum (Chris. Newport 85-03)*	19	391	145	.729
14. Mark Hanson [Gust. Adolphus 1991-03]*	13	262	98	.728
15. Rick Simonds [St. Joseph's (Me.) 1980-03]*	23	463	176	.725
16. Bosko Djurickovic (North Park 1985-94, Carthage 1997-03)*	17	332	128	.722
17. Brian Baptiste (Mass.-Dartmouth 1984-03)*	19	396	153	.721
18. Dave Darnall (Eureka 1975-94)	20	383	150	.719
19. Bob Gillespie (Ripon 1981-03)*	23	393	156	.716
20. Bob Ward (St. John Fisher 1988-01)	14	261	106	.711
21. James Catalano (N.J. Inst. of Tech. 1980-01)	22	431	176	.710
22. Jerry Welsh (Potsdam St. 1969, 71-91, Iona 92-95).	26	502	205	.710
23. Gerry Mathews (Richard Stockton 1987-03)*	17	333	136	.710
24. Dave Vander Meulen (Wis.-Whitewater 1979-01)....	23	440	182	.707
25. John Dzik (Cabrini 1981-03)*	23	453	192	.702

Coach (Team coached, tenure)	Years	Won	Lost	Pct.
26. Stan Ogrodnik (Trinity [Conn.] 1982-03)*	22	368	156	.702
27. Richard Bihr (Buffalo St. 1980-03)*	23	426	184	.698
28. John Reynders (Allegheny 1980-89)	10	180	78	.698
29. Tom Murphy (Hamilton 1971-03)*	33	583	254	.697
30. Lewis Levick (Wartburg 1966-93)	28	510	225	.694
31. Todd Raridon (Neb. Wesleyan 1990-03)*	14	256	113	.694
32. Jim Todd [Fitchburg St. 1978-79, Salem St. 88-96]...	11	207	93	.690
33. Charles Brown (New Jersey City 1983-03)*	21	404	182	.689
34. Randy Lambert [Maryville (Tenn.) 1981-03]*	23	413	194	.680
35. Joe Nesci (New York U. 1989-03)*	15	260	123	.679
36. Dick Whitmore (Colby 1971-01, 03)*	32	531	252	.678
37. Bob Bessoir (Scranton 1973-01)	29	554	263	.678
38. David Hixon (Amherst 1978-03)*	26	439	209	.677
39. Dennie Bridges (Ill. Wesleyan 1966-01)	36	666	320	.675
40. Page Moir (Roanoke 1990-03)*	14	256	124	.674
41. Steve Fritz [St. Thomas (Minn.) 1981-03]*	23	411	201	.672
42. Ed Douma [Alma 1974, Kent St. 79-82, Lake Superior St. 75-78, UNC Greensboro 83-85, Calvin 85-96, Hillsdale 99-03]*	28	500	248	.668
43. Bill Harris [King's (N.Y.) 86-91, Wheaton (Ill.) 92-03]*	18	330	164	.668
44. Naylond Hayes (Rust 1970-88)	18	338	169	.667
45. Ted Van Dellen (Wis.-Oshkosh 91-03)*	13	228	120	.655
46. Rudy Marisa (Waynesburg 1970-03)*	34	563	374	.652
47. Mark Edwards [Washington (Mo.) 82-03]*	22	374	200	.652
48. Nick Lambros (Hartwick 78-98)	21	352	191	.648
49. Bill Brown (Wooster 83, Kenyon 84-88, Wittenberg 94-04)	16	286	156	.647
50. Dick Reynolds (Otterbein 73-03)*	31	546	300	.645

BY VICTORIES

(Minimum 10 head coaching seasons in Division III)

Coach (Team coached, tenure)	Years	Won	Lost	Pct.
1. Dennie Bridges (Ill. Wesleyan 1966-01)	36	666	320	.675
2. Glenn Robinson (Frank. & Marsh. 1972-03)*	32	648	231	.737
3. Jim Smith [St. John's (Minn.) 1965-03]*	39	618	411	.601
4. Tom Murphy (Hamilton 1971-03)*	33	583	254	.697
5. Rudy Marisa (Waynesburg 1970-03)*	34	563	374	.652
6. Bill Knapton (Beloit 1958-97)	40	555	347	.615
7. Bob Bessoir (Scranton 1973-01)	29	554	263	.678
8. Dick Reynolds (Otterbein 73-03)*	31	546	300	.645
9. C. Alan Rowe (Widener 1966-98)	33	536	324	.623
10. Dick Whitmore (Colby 1971-01, 03)*	32	531	252	.678
11. Gene Mehaffey (Carson-Newman 1968-78, Ohio Wesleyan 80-99)	31	525	384	.578
12. Jim Burson (Muskingum 1968-03)*	36	514	400	.562
13. Lewis Levick (Wartburg 1966-93)	28	510	225	.694
14. Jerry Welsh (Potsdam St. 1969, 71-91, Iona 92-95).	26	502	205	.710
15. Glenn Van Wieren (Hope 1978-03)*	26	500	174	.742
15. Ed Douma (Alma 1974, Lake Superior St. 75-78, UNC Greensboro 83-96, Calvin 85-96, Hillsdale 99-03)*	28	500	248	.668
17. Rick Simonds [St. Joseph's (Me.) 1980-03]*	23	463	176	.725
17. Cliff Garrison (Hendrix 1973-03)*	31	463	376	.552
19. Verne Canfield (Wash. & Lee 1965-95)	31	460	337	.577
20. John Dzik (Cabrini 1981-03)*	23	453	192	.702
21. Steve Moore (Muhlenberg 1982-87, Wooster 88-03)*	22	446	157	.740
22. Leon Richardson (Ozarks (Mo.) 1956, Dubuque 58-59, Drury 60-65, William Penn 75-01)	36	444	442	.501
23. Dave Vander Meulen (Wis.-Whitewater 1979-01)	23	440	182	.707
23. Jon Davison (Dubuque 1967-93, Clarke 97-03)*	34	440	427	.507
25. David Hixon (Amherst 1978-03)*	26	439	209	.677
26. Mike Turner (Albion 1975-03)*	29	432	281	.606
27. James Catalano (N.J. Inst. of Tech. 1980-01)	22	431	176	.710
28. Ollie Gelston (New Jersey City 1960-67, Montclair St. 68-91)	32	429	347	.553
28. Terry Glasgow (Monmouth [Ill.] 1973-03)*	31	429	265	.618
30. Bo Ryan (Wis.-Platteville 1985-99, Wis.-Milwaukee 00-01, Wisconsin 02-03)*	19	426	124	.775
31. Mike Neer (Rochester 1977-03)*	27	426	277	.606
32. Richard Bihr (Buffalo St. 1980-03)*	23	426	184	.698
33. Mac Petty (Sewanee 1974-76, Wabash 77-03)*	30	421	326	.564
34. Lee McKinney (Mo. Baptist 1979-88, Fontbonne 89-03)*	25	419	290	.591
35. Randy Lambert [Maryville (Tenn.) 1981-03]*	23	413	194	.680
35. Don Smith (Elizabethtown 1955-64, Bucknell 65-72, Elizabethtown 73-88)	34	413	381	.520
37. Steve Fritz [St. Thomas (Minn.) 1981-03]*	23	411	201	.672
38. Herb Hilgeman (Rhodes 1977-03)*	27	406	255	.614
39. Charles Brown (New Jersey City 1983-03)*	21	404	182	.689
40. Mike Beitzel (Northern Ky. 1981-88, Hanover 89-03)*	23	400	233	.632

* Active coaches.

COACHING RECORDS

Championships

Division I Championship

2003 Results

OPENING ROUND

UNC Asheville 92, Texas Southern 84 (ot)

FIRST ROUND

Kentucky 95, IUPUI 64
Utah 60, Oregon 58
Wisconsin 81, Weber St. 74
Tulsa 84, Dayton 71
Missouri 72, Southern Ill. 71
Marquette 72, Holy Cross 68
Indiana 67, Alabama 62
Pittsburgh 87, Wagner 61
Arizona 80, Vermont 51
Gonzaga 74, Cincinnati 69
Notre Dame 70, Wis.-Milwaukee 69
Illinois 65, Western Ky. 60
Central Mich. 79, Creighton 73
Duke 67, Colorado St. 57
Arizona St. 84, Memphis 71
Kansas 64, Utah St. 61
Texas 82, UNC Asheville 61
Purdue 80, LSU 56
Connecticut 58, Brigham Young 53
Stanford 77, San Diego 69
Maryland 75, UNC Wilmington 73
Xavier 71, Troy St. 59
Michigan St. 79, Colorado 64
Florida 85, Sam Houston St. 55
Oklahoma 71, South Carolina St. 54
California 76, North Carolina St. 74 (ot)
Butler 47, Mississippi St. 46
Louisville 86, Austin Peay 64
Oklahoma St. 77, Pennsylvania 63
Syracuse 76, Manhattan 65
Auburn 65, St. Joseph's 63 (ot)
Wake Forest 76, East Tenn. St. 73

SECOND ROUND

Kentucky 74, Utah 54
Wisconsin 61, Tulsa 60
Marquette 101, Missouri 92 (ot)
Pittsburgh 74, Indiana 52

Syracuse's Hakim Warrick, shown against Kansas' Nick Collison, blocked a potential game-tying three-point attempt with 1.5 seconds left in the title game.

Photo by Rich Clarkson/NCAA photos

Arizona 96, Gonzaga 95 (2 ot)
Notre Dame 68, Illinois 60
Duke 86, Central Mich. 60
Kansas 108, Arizona St. 76
Texas 77, Purdue 67
Connecticut 85, Stanford 74
Maryland 77, Xavier 64
Michigan St. 68, Florida 46
Oklahoma 74, California 65
Butler 79, Louisville 71
Syracuse 68, Oklahoma St. 56
Auburn 68, Wake Forest 62

REGIONAL SEMIFINALS

Kentucky 63, Wisconsin 57
Marquette 77, Pittsburgh 74
Arizona 88, Notre Dame 71
Kansas 69, Duke 65
Texas 82, Connecticut 78
Michigan St. 60, Maryland 58
Oklahoma 65 vs. Butler 54
Syracuse 79, Auburn 78

REGIONAL FINALS

Marquette 83, Kentucky 69
Kansas 78, Arizona 75
Texas 85, Michigan St. 76
Syracuse 63, Oklahoma 47

SEMIFINALS

Kansas 94, Marquette 61
Syracuse 95, Texas 84

CHAMPIONSHIP

Syracuse 81, Kansas 78

Final Four Box Scores

SEMIFINALS

APRIL 5, AT NEW ORLEANS
Kansas 94, Marquette 61

Marquette	FG-FGA	FTM-FTA	RB	PF	TP
Todd Townsend	0-3	1-2	2	3	1
Travis Diener	1-11	2-2	1	2	5
Robert Jackson	6-12	3-4	9	1	15
Dwyane Wade	7-15	4-8	6	3	19
Scott Merritt	5-14	2-2	11	1	12
Steve Novak	1-7	0-0	3	2	2
Karon Bradley	1-7	0-0	1	1	3
Terry Sanders	1-1	0-0	4	3	2
Joe Chapman	0-3	0-0	0	1	0
Chris Grimm	1-1	0-0	1	0	2
Jared Sichting	0-0	0-0	0	0	0
Tony Gries	0-0	0-0	0	0	0
Team			1		
TOTALS	23-74	12-18	39	17	61

Kansas	FG-FGA	FTM-FTA	RB	PF	TP
Keith Langford	11-14	1-3	5	1	23
Aaron Miles	7-12	2-3	5	2	18
Nick Collison	6-7	0-0	15	2	12
Jeff Graves	2-4	1-4	9	4	5
Kirk Hinrich	6-13	3-4	1	1	18
Michael Lee	4-8	2-2	6	1	13
Bryant Nash	1-4	1-1	4	3	3
Jeff Hawkins	0-3	0-0	0	0	0
Stephen Vinson	0-2	0-0	1	1	0
Moulaye Niang	1-3	0-0	1	0	2
Brett Olson	0-1	0-0	2	0	0

Kansas	FG-FGA	FTM-FTA	RB	PF	TP
Christian Moody	0-0	0-0	2	0	0
Team			1		
TOTALS	38-71	10-17	52	15	94

Halftime: Kansas 59, Marquette 30. Three-point field goals: Marquette: 3-16 (Diener 1-5, Wade 1-1, Townsend 0-1, Novak 0-5, Bradley 1-3, Chapman 0-1); Kansas: 8-19 (Langford 0-1, Miles 2-4, Hinrich 3-7, Lee 3-3, Nash 0-1, Hawkins 0-2, Vinson 0-1). Officials: Mike Kitts, Tom Lopes, Karl Hess. Attendance: 54,432.

Syracuse 95, Texas 84

Syracuse	FG-FGA	FTM-FTA	RB	PF	TP
Carmelo Anthony	12-19	6-7	14	3	33
Gerry McNamara	6-12	4-4	3	2	19
Hakim Warrick	6-11	6-8	7	4	18
Craig Forth	0-0	2-4	4	5	2
Billy Edelin	2-6	1-2	3	2	5
Josh Pace	5-6	2-2	3	2	12
Jeremy McNeil	0-0	2-2	1	4	2
Kueth Duany	1-2	1-2	1	1	4
Team			1		
TOTALS	32-56	24-31	37	21	95

Texas	FG-FGA	FTM-FTA	RB	PF	TP
Brandon Mouton	9-23	2-2	3	3	25
T. J. Ford	3-8	5-6	4	4	12
Royal Ivey	1-8	2-2	0	3	4
James Thomas	4-7	5-11	9	3	13
Brad Buckman	6-6	2-5	7	5	14
Brian Boddicker	3-5	3-4	5	4	12
Sydmill Harris	1-5	0-0	0	1	3
Jason Klotz	0-0	1-2	1	2	1
Deginald Erskin	0-1	0-0	2	1	0
Terrell Ross	0-0	0-0	0	0	0
Team			3		
TOTALS	27-63	20-32	34	26	84

Halftime: Syracuse 48, Texas 45. Three-point field goals: Syracuse 7-13 (Anthony 3-4, McNamara 3-8, Duany 1-1); Texas 10-21 (Mouton 5-9, Ford 1-2, Ivey 0-1, Boddicker 3-4, Harris 1-5). Attendance: 54,432.

NATIONAL CHAMPIONSHIP

APRIL 7, AT NEW ORLEANS
Syracuse 81, Kansas 78

Syracuse	FG-FGA	FTM-FTA	RB	PF	TP
Carmelo Anthony	7-16	3-4	10	2	20
Gerry McNamara	6-13	0-0	0	2	18
Hakim Warrick	2-4	2-4	2	3	6
Billy Edelin	4-10	4-6	2	1	12
Craig Forth	3-4	0-1	3	5	6
Josh Pace	4-9	0-0	8	2	8
Kueth Duany	4-6	1-2	4	3	11
Jeremy McNeil	0-1	0-0	5	4	0
Team			2		
TOTALS	30-63	10-17	36	22	81

Kansas	FG-FGA	FTM-FTA	RB	PF	TP
Nick Collison	8-14	3-10	21	5	19
Kirk Hinrich	6-20	1-1	2	1	16
Jeff Graves	7-13	2-7	16	2	16
Aaron Miles	1-5	0-0	6	1	2
Keith Langford	7-9	5-10	2	5	19
Michael Lee	2-8	0-0	1	1	5
Bryant Nash	0-2	1-2	1	1	1
Team			3		
TOTALS	31-71	12-30	52	16	78

Halftime: Syracuse 53, Kansas 42. Three-point field goals: Syracuse 11-18 (Anthony 3-5, McNamara 6-10, Duany 2-3); Kansas 4-20 (Langford 0-1, Hinrich 3-12, Miles 0-2, Lee 1-5). Officials: Gerald Boudreaux, Reginald Cofer, Dick Cartmell. Attendance: 54,524.

Year-by-Year Results

Season	Champion	Score	Runner-Up	Third Place	Fourth Place
1939	Oregon	46-33	Ohio St.	+Oklahoma	+Villanova
1940	Indiana	60-42	Kansas	+Duquesne	+Southern California
1941	Wisconsin	39-34	Washington St.	+Pittsburgh	+Arkansas
1942	Stanford	53-38	Dartmouth	+Colorado	+Kentucky
1943	Wyoming	46-34	Georgetown	+Texas	+DePaul
1944	Utah	42-40 (ot)	Dartmouth	+Iowa St.	+Ohio St.
1945	Oklahoma St.	49-45	New York U.	+Arkansas	+Ohio St.
1946	Oklahoma St.	43-40	North Carolina	Ohio St.	California
1947	Holy Cross	58-47	Oklahoma	Texas	CCNY
1948	Kentucky	58-42	Baylor	Holy Cross	Kansas St.
1949	Kentucky	46-36	Oklahoma St.	Illinois	Oregon St.
1950	CCNY	71-68	Bradley	North Carolina St.	Baylor
1951	Kentucky	68-58	Kansas St.	Illinois	Oklahoma St.
1952	Kansas	80-63	St. John's (N.Y.)	Illinois	Santa Clara
1953	Indiana	69-68	Kansas	Washington	LSU
1954	La Salle	92-76	Bradley	Penn St.	Southern California
1955	San Francisco	77-63	La Salle	Colorado	Iowa
1956	San Francisco	83-71	Iowa	Temple	Southern Methodist
1957	North Carolina	54-53 (3ot)	Kansas	San Francisco	Michigan St.
1958	Kentucky	84-72	Seattle	Temple	Kansas St.
1959	California	71-70	West Virginia	Cincinnati	Louisville
1960	Ohio St.	75-55	California	Cincinnati	New York U.
1961	Cincinnati	70-65 (ot)	Ohio St.	* St. Joseph's	Utah
1962	Cincinnati	71-59	Ohio St.	Wake Forest	UCLA
1963	Loyola (Ill.)	60-58 (ot)	Cincinnati	Duke	Oregon St.
1964	UCLA	98-83	Duke	Michigan	Kansas St.
1965	UCLA	91-80	Michigan	Princeton	Wichita St.
1966	UTEP	72-65	Kentucky	Duke	Utah
1967	UCLA	79-64	Dayton	Houston	North Carolina
1968	UCLA	78-55	North Carolina	Ohio St.	Houston
1969	UCLA	92-72	Purdue	Drake	North Carolina
1970	UCLA	80-69	Jacksonville	New Mexico St.	St. Bonaventure
1971	UCLA	68-62	*Villanova	* Western Ky.	Kansas
1972	UCLA	81-76	Florida St.	North Carolina	Louisville
1973	UCLA	87-66	Memphis	Indiana	Providence
1974	North Carolina St.	76-64	Marquette	UCLA	Kansas
1975	UCLA	92-85	Kentucky	Louisville	Syracuse
1976	Indiana	86-68	Michigan	UCLA	Rutgers
1977	Marquette	67-59	North Carolina	UNLV	Charlotte
1978	Kentucky	94-88	Duke	Arkansas	Notre Dame
1979	Michigan St.	75-64	Indiana St.	DePaul	Pennsylvania
1980	Louisville	59-54	*UCLA	Purdue	Iowa
1981	Indiana	63-50	North Carolina	Virginia	LSU
1982	North Carolina	63-62	Georgetown	+Houston	+Louisville
1983	North Carolina St.	54-52	Houston	+Georgia	+Louisville
1984	Georgetown	84-75	Houston	+Kentucky	+Virginia
1985	Villanova	66-64	Georgetown	+St. John's (N.Y.)	+*Memphis
1986	Louisville	72-69	Duke	+Kansas	+LSU
1987	Indiana	74-73	Syracuse	+UNLV	+Providence
1988	Kansas	83-79	Oklahoma	+Arizona	+Duke
1989	Michigan	80-79 (ot)	Seton Hall	+Duke	+Illinois
1990	UNLV	103-73	Duke	+Arkansas	+Georgia Tech
1991	Duke	72-65	Kansas	+UNLV	+North Carolina
1992	Duke	71-51	Michigan	+Cincinnati	+Indiana
1993	North Carolina	77-71	Michigan	+Kansas	+Kentucky
1994	Arkansas	76-72	Duke	+Arizona	+Florida
1995	UCLA	89-78	Arkansas	+North Carolina	+Oklahoma St.
1996	Kentucky	76-67	Syracuse	+Massachusetts	+Mississippi St.
1997	Arizona	84-79 (ot)	Kentucky	+Minnesota	+North Carolina
1998	Kentucky	78-69	Utah	+North Carolina	+Stanford
1999	Connecticut	77-74	Duke	+Michigan St.	+Ohio St.
2000	Michigan St.	89-76	Florida	+North Carolina	+Wisconsin
2001	Duke	82-72	Arizona	+Maryland	+Michigan St.
2002	Maryland	64-52	Indiana	+Kansas	+Oklahoma
2003	Syracuse	81-78	Kansas	+Marquette	+Texas

*+tied for third place; *later vacated*

Season	Site of Finals	Coach of Champion	Outstanding Player Award
1939	Evanston, Ill.	Howard Hobson, Oregon	Jimmy Hull, Ohio St.
1940	Kansas City, Mo.	Branch McCracken, Indiana	Marvin Huffman, Indiana
1941	Kansas City, Mo.	Harold Foster, Wisconsin	John Kotz, Wisconsin
1942	Kansas City, Mo.	Everett Dean, Stanford	Howard Dallmar, Stanford
1943	New York City	Everett Shelton, Wyoming	Ken Sailors, Wyoming
1944	New York City	Vadal Peterson, Utah	Arnold Ferrin, Utah
1945	New York City	Henry Iba, Oklahoma St.	Bob Kurland, Oklahoma St.
1946	New York City	Henry Iba, Oklahoma St.	Bob Kurland, Oklahoma St.
1947	New York City	Alvin Julian, Holy Cross	George Kaftan, Holy Cross
1948	New York City	Adolph Rupp, Kentucky	Alex Groza, Kentucky
1949	Seattle	Adolph Rupp, Kentucky	Alex Groza, Kentucky
1950	New York City	Nat Holman, CCNY	Irwin Dambrot, CCNY
1951	Minneapolis	Adolph Rupp, Kentucky	Bill Spivey, Kentucky

Syracuse's Jeremy McNeil denies Kansas center Jeff Graves during the championship final.

Photo by Rich Clarkson/NCAA photos

CHAMPIONSHIPS

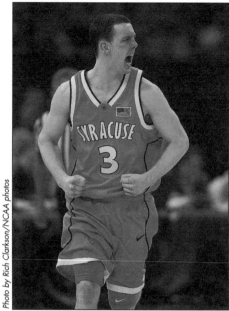

Photo by Rich Clarkson/NCAA photos

Gerry McNamara of Syracuse celebrates after one of his six treys in the title game.

Season	Site of Finals	Coach of Champion	Outstanding Player Award
1952	Seattle	Forrest Allen, Kansas	Clyde Lovellette, Kansas
1953	Kansas City, Mo.	Branch McCracken, Indiana	B.H. Born, Kansas
1954	Kansas City, Mo.	Kenneth Loeffler, La Salle	Tom Gola, La Salle
1955	Kansas City, Mo.	Phil Woolpert, San Francisco	Bill Russell, San Francisco
1956	Evanston, Ill.	Phil Woolpert, San Francisco	Hal Lear, Temple
1957	Kansas City, Mo.	Frank McGuire, North Carolina	Wilt Chamberlain, Kansas
1958	Louisville, Ky.	Adolph Rupp, Kentucky	Elgin Baylor, Seattle
1959	Louisville, Ky.	Pete Newell, California	Jerry West, West Virginia
1960	San Francisco	Fred Taylor, Ohio St.	Jerry Lucas, Ohio St.
1961	Kansas City, Mo.	Edwin Jucker, Cincinnati	Jerry Lucas, Ohio St.
1962	Louisville, Ky.	Edwin Jucker, Cincinnati	Paul Hogue, Cincinnati
1963	Louisville, Ky.	George Ireland, Loyola (Ill.)	Art Heyman, Duke
1964	Kansas City, Mo.	John Wooden, UCLA	Walt Hazzard, UCLA
1965	Portland, Ore.	John Wooden, UCLA	Bill Bradley, Princeton
1966	College Park, Md.	Don Haskins, UTEP	Jerry Chambers, Utah
1967	Louisville, Ky.	John Wooden, UCLA	Lew Alcindor, UCLA
1968	Los Angeles	John Wooden, UCLA	Lew Alcindor, UCLA
1969	Louisville, Ky.	John Wooden, UCLA	Lew Alcindor, UCLA
1970	College Park, Md.	John Wooden, UCLA	Sidney Wicks, UCLA
1971	Houston	John Wooden, UCLA	*Howard Porter, Villanova
1972	Los Angeles	John Wooden, UCLA	Bill Walton, UCLA
1973	St. Louis	John Wooden, UCLA	Bill Walton, UCLA
1974	Greensboro, N.C.	Norm Sloan, North Carolina St.	David Thompson, North Carolina St.
1975	San Diego	John Wooden, UCLA	Richard Washington, UCLA
1976	Philadelphia	Bob Knight, Indiana	Kent Benson, Indiana
1977	Atlanta	Al McGuire, Marquette	Butch Lee, Marquette
1978	St. Louis	Joe B. Hall, Kentucky	Jack Givens, Kentucky
1979	Salt Lake City	Jud Heathcote, Michigan St.	Earvin Johnson, Michigan St.
1980	Indianapolis	Denny Crum, Louisville	Darrell Griffith, Louisville
1981	Philadelphia	Bob Knight, Indiana	Isiah Thomas, Indiana
1982	New Orleans	Dean Smith, North Carolina	James Worthy, North Carolina
1983	Albuquerque, N.M.	Jim Valvano, North Carolina St.	Akeem Olajuwon, Houston
1984	Seattle	John Thompson, Georgetown	Patrick Ewing, Georgetown
1985	Lexington, Ky.	Rollie Massimino, Villanova	Ed Pinckney, Villanova
1986	Dallas	Denny Crum, Louisville	Pervis Ellison, Louisville
1987	New Orleans	Bob Knight, Indiana	Keith Smart, Indiana
1988	Kansas City, Mo.	Larry Brown, Kansas	Danny Manning, Kansas
1989	Seattle	Steve Fisher, Michigan	Glen Rice, Michigan
1990	Denver	Jerry Tarkanian, UNLV	Anderson Hunt, UNLV
1991	Indianapolis	Mike Krzyzewski, Duke	Christian Laettner, Duke
1992	Minneapolis	Mike Krzyzewski, Duke	Bobby Hurley, Duke
1993	New Orleans	Dean Smith, North Carolina	Donald Williams, North Carolina
1994	Charlotte, N.C.	Nolan Richardson, Arkansas	Corliss Williamson, Arkansas
1995	Seattle	Jim Harrick, UCLA	Ed O'Bannon, UCLA
1996	East Rutherford, N.J.	Rick Pitino, Kentucky	Tony Delk, Kentucky
1997	Indianapolis	Lute Olson, Arizona	Miles Simon, Arizona
1998	San Antonio	Tubby Smith, Kentucky	Jeff Sheppard, Kentucky
1999	St. Petersburg, Fla.	Jim Calhoun, Connecticut	Richard Hamilton, Connecticut
2000	Indianapolis	Tom Izzo, Michigan St.	Mateen Cleaves, Michigan St.
2001	Minneapolis	Mike Krzyzewski, Duke	Shane Battier, Duke
2002	Atlanta	Gary Williams, Maryland	Juan Dixon, Maryland
2003	New Orleans	Jim Boeheim	Carmelo Anthony, Syracuse

*later vacated

LEADING SCORER

Season	Player, Team	G	FG	FTM	Pts.	Avg.
1939	Jim Hull, Ohio St.	3	22	14	58	19.3
1940	Howard Engleman, Kansas	3	18	3	39	13.0
1941	John Adams, Arkansas	2	21	6	48	24.0
1942	Jim Pollard, Stanford	2	19	5	43	21.5
	Chet Palmer, Rice	2	20	3	43	21.5
1943	John Hargis, Texas	2	21	17	59	29.5
1944	Aud Brindley, Dartmouth	3	24	4	52	17.3
1945	Bob Kurland, Oklahoma St.	3	30	5	65	21.7
1946	Bob Kurland, Oklahoma St.	3	28	16	72	24.0
1947	George Kaftan, Holy Cross	3	25	13	63	21.0
1948	Alex Groza, Kentucky	3	23	8	54	18.0
1949	Alex Groza, Kentucky	3	31	20	82	27.3
1950	Sam Ranzino, North Carolina St.	3	25	25	75	25.0
1951	Don Sunderlage, Illinois	4	28	27	83	20.8
1952	Clyde Lovellette, Kansas	4	53	35	141	35.3
1953	Bob Houbregs, Washington	4	57	25	139	34.8
1954	Tom Gola, La Salle	5	38	38	114	22.8
1955	Bill Russell, San Francisco	5	49	20	118	23.6
1956	Hal Lear, Temple	5	63	34	160	32.0
1957	Len Rosenbluth, North Carolina	5	53	34	140	28.0
1958	Elgin Baylor, Seattle	5	48	39	135	27.0

Season	Player, Team	G	FG	FTM	Pts.	Avg.
1959	Jerry West, West Virginia	5	57	46	160	32.0
1960	Oscar Robertson, Cincinnati	4	47	28	122	30.5
1961	Billy McGill, Utah	4	49	21	119	29.8
1962	Len Chappell, Wake Forest	5	45	44	134	26.8
1963	Mel Counts, Oregon St.	5	50	23	123	24.6
1964	Jeff Mullins, Duke	4	50	16	116	29.0
1965	Bill Bradley, Princeton	5	65	47	177	35.4
1966	Jerry Chambers, Utah	4	55	33	143	35.8
1967	Elvin Hayes, Houston	5	57	14	128	25.6
1968	Elvin Hayes, Houston	5	70	27	167	33.4
1969	Rick Mount, Purdue	4	49	24	122	30.5
1970	Austin Carr, Notre Dame	3	68	22	158	52.7
1971	*Jim McDaniels, Western Ky.	5	61	25	147	29.4
	Austin Carr, Notre Dame	3	48	29	125	41.7
1972	Jim Price, Louisville	4	41	21	103	25.8
1973	Ernie DiGregorio, Providence	5	59	10	128	25.6
1974	David Thompson, North Carolina St.	4	38	21	97	24.3
1975	Jim Lee, Syracuse	5	51	17	119	23.8
1976	Scott May, Indiana	5	45	23	113	22.6
1977	Cedric Maxwell, Charlotte	5	39	45	123	24.6
1978	Mike Gminski, Duke	5	45	19	109	21.8
1979	Tony Price, Pennsylvania	6	58	26	142	23.7
1980	Joe Barry Carroll, Purdue	6	63	32	158	26.3

Season	Player, Team	G	FG	FTM	Pts.	Avg.
1981	Al Wood, North Carolina	5	44	21	109	21.8
1982	Rob Williams, Houston	5	30	28	88	17.6
1983	Dereck Whittenburg, North Carolina St.	6	47	26	120	20.0
1984	Roosevelt Chapman, Dayton	4	35	35	105	26.3
1985	Chris Mullin, St. John's (N.Y.)	5	39	32	110	22.0
1986	Johnny Dawkins, Duke	6	66	21	153	25.5

Season	Player, Team	G	FG	3FG	FTM	Pts.	Avg.
1987	Steve Alford, Indiana	6	42	21	33	138	23.0
	Rony Seikaly, Syracuse	6	87	0	32	138	23.0
1988	Danny Manning, Kansas	6	69	2	23	163	27.2
1989	Glen Rice, Michigan	6	75	27	7	184	30.7
1990	Dennis Scott, Georgia Tech	5	51	24	27	153	30.6
1991	Christian Laettner, Duke	6	37	2	49	125	20.8
1992	Christian Laettner, Duke	6	39	7	30	115	19.2
1993	Donald Williams, North Carolina	6	40	22	16	118	19.7
1994	Khalid Reeves, Arizona	5	45	8	39	137	27.4
1995	Corliss Williamson, Arkansas	6	49	0	27	125	20.8
1996	John Wallace, Syracuse	6	47	7	30	131	21.8
1997	Miles Simon, Arizona	6	42	10	38	132	22.0
1998	Michael Doleac, Utah	6	34	2	45	115	19.2
1999	Richard Hamilton, Connecticut	6	56	7	26	145	24.2
2000	Morris Peterson, Michigan St.	6	35	15	20	105	17.5
2001	Jason Williams, Duke	6	52	23	27	154	25.7
2002	Juan Dixon, Maryland	6	52	22	29	155	25.8
2003	Carmelo Anthony, Syracuse	6	47	10	17	121	20.2

*later vacated

SCORING AVERAGE

(Minimum: 50 percent of maximum tournament games)

Season	Player, Team	G	FG	FTM	Pts.	Avg.
1939	Jim Hull, Ohio St.	3	22	14	58	19.3
1940	Howard Engleman, Kansas	3	18	3	39	13.0
	Bob Kinney, Rice	2	12	2	26	13.0
1941	John Adams, Arkansas	2	21	6	48	24.0
1942	Chet Palmer, Rice	2	19	5	43	21.5
	Jim Pollard, Stanford	2	20	3	43	21.5
1943	John Hargis, Texas	2	21	17	59	29.5
1944	Nick Bozolich, Pepperdine	2	17	11	45	22.5
1945	Dick Wilkins, Oregon	2	19	6	44	22.0
1946	Bob Kurland, Oklahoma St.	3	28	16	72	24.0
1947	George Kaftan, Holy Cross	3	25	13	63	21.0
1948	Jack Nichols, Washington	2	13	13	39	19.5
1949	Alex Groza, Kentucky	3	31	20	82	27.3
1950	Sam Ranzino, North Carolina St.	3	25	25	75	25.0
1951	William Kukoy, North Carolina St.	3	25	19	69	23.0
1952	Clyde Lovellette, Kansas	4	53	35	141	35.3
1953	Bob Houbregs, Washington	4	57	25	139	34.8
1954	John Clune, Navy	3	30	19	79	26.3
1955	Terry Rand, Marquette	3	31	11	73	24.3
1956	Hal Lear, Temple	5	63	34	160	32.0
1957	Wilt Chamberlain, Kansas	4	40	41	121	30.3
1958	Wayne Embry, Miami (Ohio)	3	32	19	83	27.7
1959	Jerry West, West Virginia	5	57	46	160	32.0
1960	Jerry West, West Virginia	3	35	35	105	35.0
1961	Billy McGill, Utah	4	49	21	119	29.8
1962	Len Chappell, Wake Forest	5	45	44	134	26.8
1963	Barry Kramer, New York U.	3	31	28	100	33.3
1964	Jeff Mullins, Duke	4	50	16	116	29.0
1965	Bill Bradley, Princeton	5	57	47	147	35.4
1966	Jerry Chambers, Utah	4	55	33	143	35.8
1967	Lew Alcindor, UCLA	4	39	28	106	26.5
1968	Elvin Hayes, Houston	5	70	27	167	33.4
1969	Rick Mount, Purdue	4	49	24	122	30.5
1970	Austin Carr, Notre Dame	3	68	22	158	52.7
1971	Austin Carr, Notre Dame	3	48	29	125	41.7
1972	*Dwight Lamar, La.-Lafayette	4	41	18	100	33.3
	Jim Price, Louisville	4	41	21	103	25.8
1973	Larry Finch, Memphis	4	34	39	107	26.8
1974	John Shumate, Notre Dame	3	35	16	86	28.7
1975	Adrian Dantley, Notre Dame	3	29	34	92	30.7
1976	Willie Smith, Missouri	3	38	18	94	31.3
1977	Cedric Maxwell, Charlotte	5	39	45	123	24.6
1978	Dave Corzine, DePaul	3	33	16	82	27.3
1979	Larry Bird, Indiana St.	5	52	32	136	27.2
1980	Joe Barry Carroll, Purdue	6	63	32	158	26.3
1981	Al Wood, North Carolina	5	44	21	109	21.8
1982	Oliver Robinson, UAB	3	27	12	66	22.0
1983	Greg Stokes, Iowa	3	24	13	61	20.3
1984	Roosevelt Chapman, Dayton	4	35	35	105	26.3
1985	Kenny Walker, Kentucky	3	28	19	75	25.0
1986	David Robinson, Navy	4	35	40	110	27.5

Season	Player, Team	G	FG	3FG	FTM	Pts.	Avg.
1987	Fennis Dembo, Wyoming	3	25	11	23	84	28.0
1988	Danny Manning, Kansas	6	69	2	23	163	27.2

Season	Player, Team	G	FG	3FG	FTM	Pts.	Avg.
1989	Glen Rice, Michigan	6	75	27	7	184	30.7
1990	Bo Kimble, Loyola Marymount	4	51	15	26	143	35.8
1991	Terry Dehere, Seton Hall	4	34	12	17	97	24.3
1992	Jamal Mashburn, Kentucky	4	34	6	22	96	24.0
1993	Calbert Cheaney, Indiana	4	40	3	23	106	26.5
1994	Gary Collier, Tulsa	3	30	13	21	94	31.3
1995	Darryl Wilson, Mississippi St.	3	21	9	22	73	24.3
1996	Allen Iverson, Georgetown	4	38	12	23	111	27.8
1997	Dedric Willoughby, Iowa St.	3	24	14	12	74	24.7
1998	Khalid El-Amin, Connecticut	4	30	10	23	93	23.3
1999	Wally Szczerbiak, Miami (Ohio)	3	32	11	15	90	30.0
2000	Marcus Fizer, Iowa St.	4	32	2	14	80	20.0
2001	Jason Williams, Duke	6	52	23	27	154	25.7
2002	Caron Butler, Connecticut	4	32	8	34	106	26.5
2003	Dahntay Jones, Duke	3	25	8	16	74	24.7

*later vacated

CAREER SCORING

Player, Team (Seasons Competed)	G	FG	3FG	FTM	Pts.	Avg.
Christian Laettner, Duke (1989-92)	23	128	9	142	407	17.7
Elvin Hayes, Houston (1966-68)	13	152	—	54	358	27.5
Danny Manning, Kansas (1985-88)	16	140	2	46	328	20.5
Oscar Robertson, Cincinnati (1958-60)	10	117	—	90	324	32.4
Glen Rice, Michigan (1986-89)	13	128	35	17	308	23.7
Lew Alcindor, UCLA (1967-69)	12	115	—	74	304	25.3
Bill Bradley, Princeton (1963-65)	9	108	—	87	303	33.7
Corliss Williamson, Arkansas (1993-95)	15	123	0	57	303	20.2
Juan Dixon, Maryland (1999-2002)	16	99	38	58	294	18.4
Austin Carr, Notre Dame (1969-71)	7	117	—	55	289	41.3

SINGLE-GAME SCORING PERFORMANCES

Player, Team vs. Opponent, Season	Round	FG	3FG	FTM	Pts.
Austin Carr, Notre Dame vs. Ohio, 1970	1st	25	—	11	61
Bill Bradley, Princeton vs. Wichita St., 1965	N3d	22	—	14	58
Oscar Robertson, Cincinnati vs. Arkansas, 1958	R3d	21	—	14	56
Austin Carr, Notre Dame vs. Kentucky, 1970	RSF	22	—	8	52
Austin Carr, Notre Dame vs. TCU, 1971	1st	20	—	12	52
David Robinson, Navy vs. Michigan, 1987	1st	22	0	6	50
Elvin Hayes, Houston vs. Loyola (Ill.), 1968	1st	20	—	9	49
Hal Lear, Temple vs. Southern Methodist, 1956	N3d	17	—	14	48
Austin Carr, Notre Dame vs. Houston, 1971	R3d	17	—	13	47
Dave Corzine, DePaul vs. Louisville, 1978	RSF	18	—	10	46

[Key: 1st—first round; 2nd—second round; RSF—regional semifinal; RF—regional final; R3d—regional third place; N3d—national third place; CH—national championship.]

LEADING REBOUNDER

Season	Player, Team	G	Reb.	Avg.
1951	Bill Spivey, Kentucky	4	65	16.3
1957	John Green, Michigan St.	4	77	19.3
1958	Elgin Baylor, Seattle	5	91	18.2
1959	Jerry West, West Virginia	5	73	14.6
1960	Tom Sanders, New York U.	5	83	16.6
1961	Jerry Lucas, Ohio St.	4	73	18.3
1962	Len Chappell, Wake Forest	5	86	17.2
1963	Nate Thurmond, Bowling Green	3	70	23.3
	Vic Rouse, Loyola (Ill.)	5	70	14.0
1964	Paul Silas, Creighton	3	57	19.0
1965	Bill Bradley, Princeton	5	57	11.4
1966	Jerry Chambers, Utah	4	56	14.0
1967	Don May, Dayton	5	82	16.4
1968	Elvin Hayes, Houston	5	97	19.4
1969	Lew Alcindor, UCLA	4	64	16.0
1970	Artis Gilmore, Jacksonville	5	93	18.6
1971	*Clarence Glover, Western Ky.	5	89	17.8
	Sidney Wicks, UCLA	4	52	13.0
1972	Bill Walton, UCLA	4	64	16.0
1973	Bill Walton, UCLA	4	58	14.5
1974	Tom Burleson, North Carolina St.	4	61	15.3
1975	Richard Washington, UCLA	5	60	12.0
1976	Phil Hubbard, Michigan	5	61	12.2
1977	Cedric Maxwell, Charlotte	5	64	12.8
1978	Eugene Banks, Duke	5	50	10.0
1979	Larry Bird, Indiana St.	5	67	13.4
1980	Mike Sanders, UCLA	6	60	10.0
1981	Cliff Levingston, Wichita St.	4	53	13.3
1982	Clyde Drexler, Houston	5	42	8.4
1983	Akeem Olajuwon, Houston	5	65	13.0
1984	Akeem Olajuwon, Houston	5	57	11.4
1985	Ed Pinckney, Villanova	6	48	8.0
1986	Pervis Ellison, Louisville	6	57	9.5
1987	Derrick Coleman, Syracuse	6	73	12.2
1988	Danny Manning, Kansas	6	56	9.3
1989	Daryll Walker, Seton Hall	6	58	9.7
1990	Larry Johnson, UNLV	6	75	12.5

Season	Player, Team	G	Reb.	Avg.
1991	Larry Johnson, UNLV	5	51	10.2
1992	Chris Webber, Michigan	6	58	9.7
1993	Chris Webber, Michigan	6	68	11.3
1994	Cherokee Parks, Duke	6	55	9.2
1995	Ed O'Bannon, UCLA	6	54	9.0
1996	Tim Duncan, Wake Forest	4	52	13.0
1997	A. J. Bramlett, Arizona	6	62	10.3
1998	Antawn Jamison, North Carolina	5	63	12.6
1999	Elton Brand, Duke	6	55	9.2
2000	Brendan Haywood, North Carolina	5	48	9.6
2001	Shane Battier, Duke	6	61	10.2
2002	Drew Gooden, Kansas	5	61	12.2
2003	Nick Collison, Kansas	6	81	13.5

*later vacated

REBOUNDING AVERAGE

Season	Player, Team	G	Reb.	Avg.
1951	Bill Spivey, Kentucky	4	65	16.3
1957	John Green, Michigan St.	4	77	19.3
1958	Elgin Baylor, Seattle	5	91	18.2
1959	Oscar Robertson, Cincinnati	4	63	15.8
1960	Howard Jolliff, Ohio	3	64	21.3
1961	Jerry Lucas, Ohio St.	4	73	18.3
1962	Mel Counts, Oregon St.	3	53	17.7
1963	Nate Thurmond, Bowling Green	3	70	23.3
1964	Paul Silas, Creighton	3	57	19.0
1965	James Ware, Oklahoma City	3	55	18.3
1966	Elvin Hayes, Houston	3	50	16.7
1967	Don May, Dayton	5	82	16.4
1968	Elvin Hayes, Houston	5	97	19.4
1969	Lew Alcindor, UCLA	4	64	16.0
1970	Artis Gilmore, Jacksonville	5	93	18.6
1971	*Clarence Glover, Western Ky.	5	89	17.8
	Collis Jones, Notre Dame	3	49	16.3
1972	Bill Walton, UCLA	4	64	16.0
1973	Bill Walton, UCLA	4	58	14.5
1974	Marvin Barnes, Providence	3	51	17.0
1975	Mike Franklin, Cincinnati	3	49	16.3
1976	Al Fleming, Arizona	3	39	13.0
1977	Phil Hubbard, Michigan	3	45	15.0
1978	Greg Kelser, Michigan St.	3	37	12.3
1979	Larry Bird, Indiana St.	5	67	13.4
1980	Durand Macklin, LSU	3	31	10.3
1981	Cliff Levingston, Wichita St.	4	53	13.3
1982	Ed Pinckney, Villanova	3	30	10.0
1983	Akeem Olajuwon, Houston	5	65	13.0
1984	*Keith Lee, Memphis	3	37	12.3
	Akeem Olajuwon, Houston	5	57	11.4
1985	Karl Malone, Louisiana Tech	3	40	13.3
1986	David Robinson, Navy	4	47	11.8
1987	Derrick Coleman, Syracuse	6	73	12.2

Season	Player, Team	G	Reb.	Avg.
1988	Pervis Ellison, Louisville	3	33	11.0
1989	Pervis Ellison, Louisville	3	31	10.3
	Stacey King, Oklahoma	3	31	10.3
1990	Dale Davis, Clemson	3	44	14.7
1991	Byron Houston, Oklahoma St.	3	36	12.0
1992	Doug Edwards, Florida St.	3	32	10.7
1993	Chris Webber, Michigan	6	68	11.3
1994	Juwan Howard, Michigan	6	51	12.8
1995	Tim Duncan, Wake Forest	3	43	14.3
1996	Tim Duncan, Wake Forest	4	52	13.0
1997	Paul Pierce, Kansas	3	36	12.0
1998	Antawn Jamison, North Carolina	5	63	12.6
1999	Eduardo Najera, Oklahoma	3	35	11.7
2000	Eric Coley, Tulsa	4	43	10.8
2001	Dan Gadzuric, UCLA	3	36	12.0
2002	Drew Gooden, Kansas	5	61	12.2
2003	Nick Collison, Kansas	6	81	13.5

*later vacated

CAREER REBOUNDING

Player, Team (Seasons Competed)	G	Reb.	Avg.
Elvin Hayes, Houston (1966-68)	13	222	17.1
Lew Alcindor, UCLA (1967-69)	12	201	16.8
Jerry Lucas, Ohio St. (1960-62)	12	197	16.4
Bill Walton, UCLA (1972-74)	12	176	14.7
Christian Laettner, Duke (1989-92)	23	169	7.3
Tim Duncan, Wake Forest (1994-97)	11	165	15.0
Paul Hogue, Cincinnati (1960-62)	12	160	13.3
Sam Lacey, New Mexico St. (1968-70)	11	157	14.3
Derrick Coleman, Syracuse (1987-90)	14	155	11.1
Akeem Olajuwon, Houston (1982-84)	15	153	10.2

SINGLE-GAME REBOUNDING PERFORMANCES

Player, Team vs. Opponent, Season	Round	Reb.
Fred Cohen, Temple vs. Connecticut, 1956	RSF	34
Nate Thurmond, Bowling Green vs. Mississippi St., 1963	R3d	31
Jerry Lucas, Ohio St. vs. Kentucky, 1961	RF	30
Toby Kimball, Connecticut vs. St. Joseph's, 1965	1st	29
Elvin Hayes, Houston vs. Pacific (Cal.), 1966	R3d	28
Bill Russell, San Francisco vs. Iowa, 1956	CH	27
John Green, Michigan St. vs. Notre Dame, 1957	2nd	27
Paul Silas, Creighton vs. Oklahoma City, 1964	1st	27
Elvin Hayes, Houston vs. Loyola (Ill.), 1968	1st	27
Howard Jolliff, Ohio vs. Georgia Tech, 1960	RSF	26
Phil Hubbard, Michigan vs. Detroit, 1977	RSF	26

[Key: 1st—first round; 2nd—second round; RSF—regional semifinal; RF—regional final; R3d—regional third place; NSF—national semifinal; CH—national championship.]

INDIVIDUAL RECORDS

Single Game

POINTS
61—Austin Carr, Notre Dame vs. Ohio, SE 1st, 1970

POINTS BY TWO TEAMMATES
85—Austin Carr (61) and Collis Jones (24), Notre Dame vs. Ohio, SE 1st, 1970

POINTS BY TWO OPPOSING PLAYERS
96—Austin Carr (52), Notre Dame, and Dan Issel (44), Kentucky, SE RSF, 1970

FIELD GOALS
25—Austin Carr, Notre Dame vs. Ohio, SE 1st, 1970

FIELD GOALS ATTEMPTED
44—Austin Carr, Notre Dame vs. Ohio, SE 1st, 1970

FIELD-GOAL PERCENTAGE (Minimum 11 Made)
100% (11-11)—Kenny Walker, Kentucky vs. Western Ky., SE 2nd, 1986

THREE-POINT FIELD GOALS
11—Jeff Fryer, Loyola Marymount vs. Michigan, West 2nd, 1990

THREE-POINT FIELD GOALS ATTEMPTED
22—Jeff Fryer, Loyola Marymount vs. Arkansas, MW 1st, 1989

THREE-POINT FIELD-GOAL PERCENTAGE (Minimum 7 Made)
100% (8-8)—John Goldsberry, UNC Wilmington vs. Maryland, South 1st, 2003

FREE THROWS MADE
23—Bob Carney, Bradley vs. Colorado, MW RSF, 1954; Travis Mays, Texas vs. Georgia, MW 1st, 1990

FREE THROWS ATTEMPTED
27—David Robinson, Navy vs. Syracuse, East 2nd, 1986; Travis Mays, Texas vs. Georgia, MW 1st, 1990

FREE-THROW PERCENTAGE (Minimum 16 Made)
100% (16-16)—Bill Bradley, Princeton vs. St. Joseph's, East 1st, 1963; Fennis Dembo, Wyoming vs. UCLA, West 2nd, 1987

REBOUNDS
34—Fred Cohen, Temple vs. Connecticut, East RSF, 1956

ASSISTS
18—Mark Wade, UNLV vs. Indiana, NSF, 1987

BLOCKED SHOTS
11—Shaquille O'Neal, LSU vs. Brigham Young, West 1st, 1992

STEALS
8—Darrell Hawkins, Arkansas vs. Holy Cross, East 1st, 1993; Grant Hill, Duke vs. California, MW 2nd, 1993; Duane Clemens, Ball St. vs. UCLA, MW 1st, 2000

Series

(Three-game minimum for averages and percentages)

POINTS
184—Glen Rice, Michigan, 1989 (6 games)

SCORING AVERAGE
52.7—Austin Carr, Notre Dame, 1970 (158 points in 3 games)

FIELD GOALS
75—Glen Rice, Michigan, 1989 (6 games)

FIELD GOALS ATTEMPTED
138—*Jim McDaniels, Western Ky., 1971 (5 games)
137—Elvin Hayes, Houston, 1968 (5 games)

FIELD-GOAL PERCENTAGE (Minimum 5 Made Per Game)
78.8% (26-33)—Christian Laettner, Duke, 1989 (5 games)

THREE-POINT FIELD GOALS
27—Glen Rice, Michigan, 1989 (6 games)

THREE-POINT FIELD GOALS ATTEMPTED
66—Jason Williams, Duke, 2001 (6 games)

THREE-POINT FIELD-GOAL PERCENTAGE (Minimum 1.5 Made Per Game)
100% (6-6)—Ranzino Smith, North Carolina, 1987 (4 games)

FREE THROWS MADE
55—Bob Carney, Bradley, 1954 (5 games)

FREE THROWS ATTEMPTED
71—Jerry West, West Virginia, 1959 (5 games)

PERFECT FREE-THROW PERCENTAGE (Minimum 2.5 Made Per Game)
100% (35-35)—Arthur Lee, Stanford, 1998 (5 games)

REBOUNDS
97—Elvin Hayes, Houston, 1968 (5 games)

REBOUND AVERAGE
23.3—Nate Thurmond, Bowling Green, 1963 (70 rebounds in 3 games)

ASSISTS
61—Mark Wade, UNLV, 1987 (5 games)

BLOCKED SHOTS
24—Loren Woods, Arizona, 2001 (6 games)

STEALS
23—Mookie Blaylock, Oklahoma, 1988 (6 games)

Career

(Two-year minimum for averages and percentages)

POINTS
407—Christian Laettner, Duke, 1989-92 (23 games)

SCORING AVERAGE (Minimum 6 Games)
41.3—Austin Carr, Notre Dame, 1969-71 (289 points in 7 games)

FIELD GOALS
152—Elvin Hayes, Houston, 1966-68

FIELD GOALS ATTEMPTED
310—Elvin Hayes, Houston, 1966-68

FIELD-GOAL PERCENTAGE (Minimum 70 Made)
68.6% (109-159)—Bill Walton, UCLA, 1972-74

THREE-POINT FIELD GOALS
42—Bobby Hurley, Duke, 1990-93 (20 games)

THREE-POINT FIELD GOALS ATTEMPTED
112—Jason Williams, Duke, 2000-02 (12 games)

THREE-POINT FIELD-GOAL PERCENTAGE
(Minimum 30 made)
56.5% (35-62)—Glen Rice, Michigan, 1986-89 (13 games)
(Minimum 20 made)
65.0% (26-40)—William Scott, Kansas St., 1987-88 (5 games)

FREE THROWS MADE
142—Christian Laettner, Duke, 1989-92 (23 games)

FREE THROWS ATTEMPTED
167—Christian Laettner, Duke, 1989-92 (23 games)

FREE-THROW PERCENTAGE
(Minimum 50 made)
93.5% (58-62)—Arthur Lee, Stanford, 1996-99 (12 games)
(Minimum 30 made)
97.7% (42-43), Keith Van Horn, Utah, 1995-97 (8 games)

REBOUNDS
222—Elvin Hayes, Houston, 1966-68 (13 games)

REBOUNDING AVERAGE (Minimum 6 Games)
19.7—John Green, Michigan St., 1957-59 (118 rebounds in 6 games)

ASSISTS
145—Bobby Hurley, Duke, 1990-93 (20 games)

BLOCKED SHOTS
50—Tim Duncan, Wake Forest, 1994-97 (11 games)

STEALS
39—Grant Hill, Duke, 1991-94 (20 games)

GAMES PLAYED
23—Christian Laettner, Duke, 1989-92

TEAM RECORDS

Single Game

POINTS
149—Loyola Marymount vs. Michigan, West 2nd, 1990

FEWEST POINTS
20—North Carolina vs. Pittsburgh (26), East RF, 1941

WINNING MARGIN
69—Loyola (Ill.) (111) vs. Tennessee Tech (42), SE 1st, 1963

SMALLEST WINNING MARGIN
1—140 tied (most recent: three in 2001)

POINTS SCORED BY LOSING TEAM
120—Utah vs. *St. Joseph's (127), N3d, 1961 (4 ot)

FIELD GOALS
52—Iowa vs. Notre Dame, SE R3d, 1970

FEWEST FIELD GOALS
8—Springfield vs. Indiana, East 1st, 1940

FIELD GOALS ATTEMPTED
112—Marshall vs. La.-Lafayette, MW 1st, 1972

FIELD-GOAL PERCENTAGE
80.0% (28-35)—Oklahoma St. vs. Tulane, SE 2nd, 1992

LOWEST FIELD-GOAL PERCENTAGE
12.7% (8-63)—Springfield vs. Indiana, East RSF, 1940

THREE-POINT FIELD GOALS
21—Loyola Marymount vs. Michigan, West 2nd, 1990

THREE-POINT FIELD GOALS ATTEMPTED
43—St. Joseph's vs. Boston College, West 2nd, 1997 (ot)

THREE-POINT FIELD-GOAL PERCENTAGE (Minimum 7 Made)
88.9% (8-9)—Kansas St. vs. Georgia, West 1st, 1987

FREE THROWS MADE
43—Arizona vs. Illinois, MW RF, 2001

FREE THROWS ATTEMPTED
56—Arizona vs. Illinois, MW RF, 2001

HIGHEST FREE-THROW PERCENTAGE (Minimum 22 Made)
100% (22-22)—Fordham vs. South Carolina, East R3d, 1971

MOST REBOUNDS
86—Notre Dame vs. Tennessee Tech, SE 1st, 1958

LARGEST REBOUND MARGIN
42—Notre Dame (86) vs. Tennessee Tech (44), SE 1st, 1958

MOST ASSISTS
36—North Carolina vs. Loyola Marymount, West 2nd, 1988

MOST BLOCKED SHOTS
14—Kentucky vs. UCLA, South RSF, 1998

MOST STEALS
19—Providence vs. Austin Peay, SE 2nd, 1987; Connecticut vs. Boston U., East 1st, 1990

MOST PERSONAL FOULS
41—Dayton vs. Illinois, East RSF, 1952

MOST PLAYERS DISQUALIFIED
6—Kansas vs. Notre Dame, MW 1st, 1975; Illinois vs. Arizona, MW RF, 2001

Single Game, Both Teams

POINTS
264—Loyola Marymount (149) vs. Michigan (115), West 2nd, 1990

FEWEST POINTS
46—Pittsburgh (26) vs. North Carolina (20), East RF, 1941

FIELD GOALS
97—Iowa (52) vs. Notre Dame (45), SE R3d, 1970

FIELD GOALS ATTEMPTED
204—Utah (103) vs. *St. Joseph's (101), N3d, 1961 (4 ot)

THREE-POINT FIELD GOALS
28—Seton Hall (15) vs. Temple (13), East 2nd, 2000 (ot)

THREE-POINT FIELD GOALS IN REGULATION GAME
27—Wisconsin (15) vs. Missouri (12), West 2nd, 1994

THREE-POINT FIELD GOALS ATTEMPTED
66—UCLA (36) vs. Cincinnati (30), West 2nd, 2002

FREE THROWS MADE
69—Morehead St. (37) vs. Pittsburgh (32), SE 1st, 1957

FREE THROWS ATTEMPTED
105—Iowa (52) vs. Morehead St. (53), MW RSF, 1956

REBOUNDS
134—Marshall (68) vs. *La.-Lafayette (66), MW 1st, 1972

ASSISTS
58—UNLV (35) vs. Loyola Marymount (23), West RF, 1990

BLOCKED SHOTS
20—Kentucky (14) vs. UCLA (6), South RSF, 1998

STEALS
28—N.C. A&T (16) vs. Arkansas (12), MW 1st, 1994; Purdue (16) vs. Delaware (12), MW 1st, 1998; TCU (16) vs. Florida St. (12), MW 1st, 1998; Florida (15) vs. Weber St. (13), West 2nd, 1999

PERSONAL FOULS
68—Iowa (35) vs. Morehead St. (33), South RSF, 1956

Series

(Three-game minimum for averages and percentages)

POINTS
571—UNLV, 1990 (6 games)

SCORING AVERAGE
105.8—Loyola Marymount, 1990 (423 points in 4 games)

FIELD GOALS
218—UNLV, 1977 (5 games)

FIELD GOALS ATTEMPTED
442—*Western Ky., 1971 (5 games)
441—UNLV, 1977 (6 games)

FIELD-GOAL PERCENTAGE
60.4% (113-187)—North Carolina, 1975 (3 games)

THREE-POINT FIELD GOALS
60—Arkansas, 1995 (6 games); Duke, 2001 (6 games)

THREE-POINT FIELD GOALS ATTEMPTED
175—Duke, 2001 (6 games)

THREE-POINT FIELD-GOAL PERCENTAGE
(Minimum 30 made)
51.9% (40-77)—Kansas, 1993 (5 games)
(Minimum 12 made)
60.9% (14-23)—Indiana, 1995 (3 games)

FREE THROWS MADE
146—Bradley, 1954 (5 games)

CHAMPIONSHIPS

FREE THROWS ATTEMPTED
194—Bradley, 1954 (5 games)

FREE-THROW PERCENTAGE
87.0% (47-54)—St. John's (N.Y.), 1969 (3 games)

REBOUNDS
306—Houston, 1968 (5 games)

ASSISTS
143—Kentucky, 1996 (6 games)

BLOCKED SHOTS
48—Kentucky, 1998 (6 games)

STEALS
72—Oklahoma, 1988 (6 games)

PERSONAL FOULS
150—Pennsylvania, 1979 (6 games)

CH-National championship game
NSF-National semifinal game
N3d-National third-place game
RF-Regional final game

RSF-Regional semifinal game
R3d-Regional third-place game
2nd-Second-round game
1st-First-round game
Op-Opening-round game
East-East region
SE-Southeast/Mideast region
MW-Midwest region
West-West/Far West region

*later vacated

All-Time Division I Tournament Records

RECORD OF EACH TEAM COACH BY COACH
(288 Teams)

	Yrs.	Won	Lost	CH	2D	3d%	4th	RR
AIR FORCE								
Bob Spear (DePauw 1941) 1960, 62	2	0	2	0	0	0	0	0
TOTAL	2	0	2	0	0	0	0	0
AKRON								
Bob Huggins (West Virginia 1977) 1986	1	0	1	0	0	0	0	0
TOTAL	1	0	1	0	0	0	0	0
ALABAMA*								
C.M. Newton (Kentucky 1952) 1975, 76	2	1	2	0	0	0	0	0
Wimp Sanderson (North Ala. 1959) 1982, 83,84, 85, 86, 87, 89, 90, 91,92	10	12	10	0	0	0	0	0
David Hobbs (Va. Commonwealth 1971) 1994,95	2	2	2	0	0	0	0	0
Mark Gottfried (Alabama 1987) 2002, 03	2	1	2	0	0	0	0	0
TOTAL	16	16	16	0	0	0	0	0
ALABAMA ST.								
Rob Spivery (Ashland 1972) 2001	1	0	1	0	0	0	0	0
TOTAL	1	0	1	0	0	0	0	0
UAB								
Gene Bartow (Truman 1953) 1981, 82RR, 83,84, 85, 86, 87, 90, 94	9	6	9	0	0	0	0	1
Murry Bartow (UAB 1985) 1999	1	0	1	0	0	0	0	0
TOTAL	10	6	10	0	0	0	0	1
ALCORN ST.								
Davey L. Whitney (Kentucky St. 1953) 1980, 82, 83, 84, 99, 2002	6	3	6	0	0	0	0	0
TOTAL	6	3	6	0	0	0	0	0
APPALACHIAN ST.								
Bobby Cremins (South Carolina 1970) 1979	1	0	1	0	0	0	0	0
Buzz Peterson (North Carolina 1986) 2000	1	0	1	0	0	0	0	0
TOTAL	2	0	2	0	0	0	0	0
ARIZONA *								
Fred Enke (Minnesota 1921) 1951	1	0	1	0	0	0	0	0
Fred Snowden [Wayne St. (Mich.) 1958] 1976RR, 77	2	2	2	0	0	0	0	1
Luther "Lute" Olson (Augsburg 1957) 1985, 86, 87, 88-T3d, 89, 90, 91, 92, 93, 94-T3d, 95, 96, 97-CH, 98RR, 99, 2000, 01-2d, 02, 03RR	19	35	18	1	1	2	0	2
TOTAL	22	37	21	1	1	2	0	3
ARIZONA ST. *								
Ned Wulk (Wis.-La Crosse 1942) 1958, 61RR, 62, 63RR, 64, 73, 75RR, 80, 81	9	8	10	0	0	0	0	3
Bill Frieder (Michigan 1964) 1991, 95	2	3	2	0	0	0	0	0
Rob Evans (New Mexico St. 1968) 2003	1	1	1	0	0	0	0	0
TOTAL	12	12	13	0	0	0	0	3
ARKANSAS								
Eugene Lambert (Arkansas 1929) 1945-T3d, 49RR	2	2	2	0	0	1	0	1
Glen Rose (Arkansas 1928) 1941-T3d, 58	2	1	3	0	0	1	0	0
Eddie Sutton (Oklahoma St. 1958) 1977, 78-3d, 79RR,80, 81, 82, 83, 84, 85	9	10	9	0	0	1	0	1

	Yrs.	Won	Lost	CH	2D	3d%	4th	RR
Nolan Richardson (UTEP 1965) 1988, 89, 90-T3d, 91RR, 92, 93, 94-CH, 95-2d, 96, 98, 99, 2000, 01	13	26	12	1	1	1	0	1
TOTAL	26	39	26	1	1	4	0	3
ARKANSAS ST.								
Dickey Nutt (Oklahoma St. 1982) 1999	1	0	1	0	0	0	0	0
TOTAL	1	0	1	0	0	0	0	0
ARK.-LITTLE ROCK								
Mike Newell (Sam Houston St. 1973) 1986, 89, 90	3	1	3	0	0	0	0	0
TOTAL	3	1	3	0	0	0	0	0
AUBURN								
Sonny Smith (Milligan 1958) 1984, 85, 86RR, 87, 88	5	7	5	0	0	0	0	1
Cliff Ellis (Florida St. 1968) 1999, 2000, 03	3	5	3	0	0	0	0	0
TOTAL	8	12	8	0	0	0	0	1
AUSTIN PEAY*								
Lake Kelly (Ga. Tech 1956) 1973, 74, 87	3	2	4	0	0	0	0	0
Dave Loos (Memphis 1970) 1996, 2003	2	0	2	0	0	0	0	0
TOTAL	5	2	6	0	0	0	0	0
BALL ST.								
Steve Yoder (Ill. Wesleyan 1962) 1981	1	0	1	0	0	0	0	0
Al Brown (Purdue 1964) 1986	1	0	1	0	0	0	0	0
Rick Majerus (Marquette 1970) 1989	1	1	1	0	0	0	0	0
Dick Hunsaker (Weber St. 1977) 1990, 93	2	2	2	0	0	0	0	0
Ray McCallum (Ball St. 1983) 1995, 2000	2	0	2	0	0	0	0	0
TOTAL	7	3	7	0	0	0	0	0
BAYLOR								
R.E. "Bill" Henderson (Howard Payne 1925) 1946RR, 48-2d, 50-4th	3	3	5	0	1	0	1	1
Gene Iba (Tulsa 1963) 1988	1	0	1	0	0	0	0	0
TOTAL	4	3	6	0	1	0	1	1
BOISE ST.								
Doran "Bus" Connor (Idaho St. 1955) 1976	1	0	1	0	0	0	0	0
Bob Dye (Idaho St. 1962) 1988, 93, 94	3	0	3	0	0	0	0	0
TOTAL	4	0	4	0	0	0	0	0
BOSTON COLLEGE								
Donald Martin (Georgetown 1941) 1958	1	0	1	0	0	0	0	0
Bob Cousy (Holy Cross 1948) 1967RR, 68	2	2	2	0	0	0	0	1
Bob Zuffelato (Central Conn. St. 1959) 1975	1	1	2	0	0	0	0	0
Tom Davis (Wis.-Platteville 1960) 1981, 82RR	2	5	2	0	0	0	0	1
Gary Williams (Maryland 1967) 1983, 85	2	3	2	0	0	0	0	0
Jim O'Brien (Boston College 1971) 1994RR, 96, 97	3	5	3	0	0	0	0	1
Al Skinner (Massachusetts 1974) 2001, 02	2	1	2	0	0	0	0	0
TOTAL	13	17	14	0	0	0	0	3
BOSTON U.								
Matt Zunic (George Washington 1942) 1959RR	1	2	1	0	0	0	0	1
Rick Pitino (Massachusetts 1974) 1983	1	0	1	0	0	0	0	0
Mike Jarvis (Northeastern 1968) 1988, 90	2	0	2	0	0	0	0	0
Dennis Wolff (Connecticut 1978) 1997, 2002	2	0	2	0	0	0	0	0
TOTAL	6	2	6	0	0	0	0	1

	Yrs.	Won	Lost	CH	2D	3d%	4th	RR
BOWLING GREEN								
Harold Anderson (Otterbein 1924) 1959, 62, 63	3	1	4	0	0	0	0	0
Bill Fitch (Coe 1954) 1968	1	0	1	0	0	0	0	0
TOTAL	4	1	5	0	0	0	0	0
BRADLEY								
Forrest "Forddy" Anderson (Stanford 1942) 1950-2d, 54-2d	2	6	2	0	2	0	0	0
Bob Vanatta (Central Methodist 1945) 1955RR	1	2	1	0	0	0	0	1
Dick Versace (Wisconsin 1964) 1980, 86	2	1	2	0	0	0	0	0
Stan Albeck (Bradley 1955) 1988	1	0	1	0	0	0	0	0
Jim Molinari (Ill. Wesleyan 1977) 1996	1	0	1	0	0	0	0	0
TOTAL	7	9	7	0	2	0	0	1
BRIGHAM YOUNG								
Stan Watts (Brigham Young 1938) 1950RR, 51RR, 57, 65, 69, 71, 72	7	4	10	0	0	0	0	2
Frank Arnold (Idaho St. 1956) 1979, 80, 81RR	3	3	3	0	0	0	0	1
Ladell Andersen (Utah St. 1951) 1984, 87, 88	3	2	3	0	0	0	0	0
Roger Reid (Weber St. 1967) 1990, 91, 92, 93, 95	5	2	5	0	0	0	0	0
Steve Cleveland (UC Irvine 1976) 2001, 03	2	0	2	0	0	0	0	0
TOTAL	20	11	23	0	0	0	0	3
BROWN								
George Allen (West Virginia 1935) 1939RR	1	0	1	0	0	0	0	1
Mike Cingiser (Brown 1962) 1986	1	0	1	0	0	0	0	0
TOTAL	2	0	2	0	0	0	0	1
BUCKNELL								
Charles Woollum (William & Mary 1962) 1987, 89	2	0	2	0	0	0	0	0
TOTAL	2	0	2	0	0	0	0	0
BUTLER								
Paul "Tony" Hinkle (Chicago 1921) 1962	1	2	1	0	0	0	0	0
Barry Collier (Butler 1976) 1997, 98, 2000	3	0	3	0	0	0	0	0
Thad Matta (Butler 1990) 2001	1	1	1	0	0	0	0	0
Todd Lickliter (Butler 1979) 2003	1	2	1	0	0	0	0	0
TOTAL	6	5	6	0	0	0	0	0
CALIFORNIA*								
Clarence "Nibs" Price (California 1914) 1946-4th	1	1	2	0	0	0	1	0
Pete Newell (Loyola Marymount 1940) 1957RR, 58RR, 59-CH, 60-2d	4	10	3	1	1	0	0	2
Lou Campanelli (Montclair St. 1960) 1990	1	1	1	0	0	0	0	0
Todd Bozeman (Rhode Island 1986) 1993, 94, 96	3	2	3	0	0	0	0	0
Ben Braun (Wisconsin 1975) 1997, 2001, 02, 03	4	4	4	0	0	0	0	0
TOTAL	13	18	13	1	1	0	1	2
UC SANTA BARB.								
Jerry Pimm (Southern California 1961) 1988, 90	2	1	2	0	0	0	0	0
Bob Williams (San Jose St. 1975) 2002	1	0	1	0	0	0	0	0
TOTAL	3	1	3	0	0	0	0	0
CAL ST. FULLERTON								
Bob Dye (Idaho St. 1962) 1978RR	1	2	1	0	0	0	0	1
TOTAL	1	2	1	0	0	0	0	1
CAL ST. L.A.								
Bob Miller (Occidental 1953) 1974	1	0	1	0	0	0	0	0
TOTAL	1	0	1	0	0	0	0	0
CAL ST. NORTHRIDGE								
Bobby Braswell (Cal St. Northridge 1984) 2001	1	0	1	0	0	0	0	0
TOTAL	1	0	1	0	0	0	0	0
CAMPBELL								
Billy Lee (Barton 1971) 1992	1	0	1	0	0	0	0	0
TOTAL	1	0	1	0	0	0	0	0
CANISIUS								
Joseph Curran (Canisius 1943) 1955RR, 56RR, 57	3	6	3	0	0	0	0	2
John Beilein (Wheeling Jesuit 1975) 1996	1	0	1	0	0	0	0	0
TOTAL	4	6	4	0	0	0	0	2
CATHOLIC								
John Long (Catholic 1928) 1944RR	1	0	2	0	0	0	0	1
TOTAL	1	0	2	0	0	0	0	1

	Yrs.	Won	Lost	CH	2D	3d%	4th	RR
CENTRAL CONN. ST.								
Howie Dickenmann (Central Conn. St. 1970) 2000, 02	2	0	2	0	0	0	0	0
TOTAL	2	0	2	0	0	0	0	0
UCF								
Kirk Speraw (Iowa 1980) 1994, 96	2	0	2	0	0	0	0	0
TOTAL	2	0	2	0	0	0	0	0
CENTRAL MICH.								
Dick Parfitt (Central Mich. 1953) 1975, 77	2	2	2	0	0	0	0	0
Charlie Coles [Miami (Ohio) 1965] 1987	1	0	1	0	0	0	0	0
Jay Smith (Saginaw Valley 1984) 2003	1	1	1	0	0	0	0	0
TOTAL	4	3	4	0	0	0	0	0
COL. OF CHARLESTON								
John Kresse [St. John's (N.Y.) 1964] 1994, 97, 98, 99	4	1	4	0	0	0	0	0
TOTAL	4	1	4	0	0	0	0	0
CHARLESTON SO.								
Tom Conrad (Old Dominion 1979) 1997	1	0	1	0	0	0	0	0
TOTAL	1	0	1	0	0	0	0	0
CHARLOTTE								
Lee Rose (Transylvania 1958) 1977-4th	1	3	2	0	0	0	1	0
Jeff Mullins (Duke 1964) 1988, 92, 95	3	0	3	0	0	0	0	0
Melvin Watkins (Charlotte 1977) 1997, 98	2	2	2	0	0	0	0	0
Bob Lutz (Charlotte 1980) 1999, 2001, 02	3	2	3	0	0	0	0	0
TOTAL	9	7	10	0	0	0	1	0
CHATTANOOGA								
Murray Arnold (American 1960) 1981, 82, 83	3	1	3	0	0	0	0	0
Mack McCarthy (Virginia Tech 1974) 1988, 93, 94, 95, 97	5	2	5	0	0	0	0	0
TOTAL	8	3	8	0	0	0	0	0
CINCINNATI								
George Smith (Cincinnati 1935) 1958, 59-3d, 60-3d	3	7	3	0	0	2	0	0
Ed Jucker (Cincinnati 1940) 1961-CH, 62-CH, 63-2d	3	11	1	2	1	0	0	0
Tay Baker (Cincinnati 1950) 1966	1	0	2	0	0	0	0	0
Gale Catlett (West Virginia 1963) 1975, 76, 77	3	2	3	0	0	0	0	0
Bob Huggins (West Virginia 1977) 1992-T3d, 93RR, 94, 95,96RR, 97, 98, 99, 2000, 01, 02, 03	12	18	12	0	0	1	0	2
TOTAL	22	38	21	2	1	3	0	2
CCNY								
Nat Holman (Savage School of Phys. Ed. 1917) 1947-4th, 50-CH	2	4	2	1	0	0	1	0
TOTAL	2	4	2	1	0	0	1	0
CLEMSON*								
Bill C. Foster (Carson-Newman 1958) 1980RR	1	3	1	0	0	0	0	1
Cliff Ellis (Florida St. 1968) 1987, 89, 90	3	3	3	0	0	0	0	0
Rick Barnes (Lenoir-Rhyne 1977) 1996, 97, 98	3	2	3	0	0	0	0	0
TOTAL	7	8	7	0	0	0	0	1
CLEVELAND ST.								
Kevin Mackey (St. Anselm 1967) 1986	1	2	1	0	0	0	0	0
TOTAL	1	2	1	0	0	0	0	0
COASTAL CARO.								
Russ Bergman (LSU 1970) 1991, 93	2	0	2	0	0	0	0	0
TOTAL	2	0	2	0	0	0	0	0
COLGATE								
Jack Bruen (Catholic 1972) 1995, 96	2	0	2	0	0	0	0	0
TOTAL	2	0	2	0	0	0	0	0
COLORADO								
Forrest "Frosty" Cox (Kansas 1930) 1940RR, 42-T3d, 46RR	3	2	4	0	0	1	0	2
Horace "Bebe" Lee (Stanford 1938) 1954, 55-3d	2	3	3	0	0	1	0	0
Russell "Sox" Walseth (Colorado 1948) 1962RR, 63RR, 69	3	3	3	0	0	0	0	2
Ricardo Patton (Belmont 1980) 1997, 2003	2	1	2	0	0	0	0	0
TOTAL	10	9	12	0	0	2	0	4
COLORADO ST.								
Bill Strannigan (Wyoming 1941) 1954	1	0	2	0	0	0	0	0
Jim Williams (Utah St. 1947) 1963, 65, 66, 69RR	4	2	4	0	0	0	0	1
Boyd Grant (Colorado St. 1957) 1989, 90	2	1	2	0	0	0	0	0

	Yrs.	Won	Lost	CH	2D	3d%	4th	RR
Dale Layer (Eckerd 1979) 2003	1	0	1	0	0	0	0	0
TOTAL	8	3	9	0	0	0	0	1
COLUMBIA								
Gordon Ridings (Oregon 1929) 1948RR	1	0	2	0	0	0	0	1
Lou Rossini (Columbia 1948) 1951	1	0	1	0	0	0	0	0
John "Jack" Rohan (Columbia 1953) 1968	1	2	1	0	0	0	0	0
TOTAL	3	2	4	0	0	0	0	1
CONNECTICUT*								
Hugh Greer (Connecticut 1926) 1951, 54, 56, 57, 58, 59, 60	7	1	8	0	0	0	0	0
George Wigton (Ohio St. 1956) 1963 ...	1	0	1	0	0	0	0	0
Fred Shabel (Duke 1954) 1964RR, 65, 67	3	2	3	0	0	0	0	1
Donald "Dee" Rowe (Middlebury 1952) 1976	1	1	1	0	0	0	0	0
Dom Perno (Connecticut 1964) 1979	1	0	1	0	0	0	0	0
Jim Calhoun (American Int'l 1968) 1990RR, 91, 92, 94,95RR, 96, 98RR, 99-CH, 2000, 02RR, 03	11	28	10	1	0	0	0	4
TOTAL	24	32	24	1	0	0	0	5
COPPIN ST.								
Ron Mitchell (Edison 1984) 1990, 93, 97	3	1	3	0	0	0	0	0
TOTAL	3	1	3	0	0	0	0	0
CORNELL								
Royner Greene (Illinois 1929) 1954	1	0	2	0	0	0	0	0
Mike Dement (East Caro. 1976) 1988....	1	0	1	0	0	0	0	0
TOTAL	2	0	3	0	0	0	0	0
CREIGHTON								
Eddie Hickey (Creighton 1927) 1941RR	1	1	1	0	0	0	0	1
John "Red" McManus (St. Ambrose 1949) 1962, 64	2	3	3	0	0	0	0	0
Eddie Sutton (Oklahoma St. 1958) 1974	1	2	1	0	0	0	0	0
Tom Apke (Creighton 1965) 1975, 78, 81	3	0	3	0	0	0	0	0
Tony Barone (Duke 1968) 1989, 91.......	2	1	2	0	0	0	0	0
Dana Altman (Eastern N.M. 1980) 1999, 2000, 01, 02, 03	5	2	5	0	0	0	0	0
TOTAL	14	9	15	0	0	0	0	1
DARTMOUTH								
Osborne "Ozzie" Cowles (Carleton 1922) 1941RR, 42-2d, 43RR	3	4	3	0	1	0	0	2
Earl Brown (Notre Dame 1939) 1944-2d	1	2	1	0	1	0	0	0
Alvin "Doggie" Julian (Bucknell 1923) 1956, 58RR, 59	3	4	3	0	0	0	0	1
TOTAL	7	10	7	0	2	0	0	3
DAVIDSON								
Charles "Lefty" Driesell (Duke 1954) 1966, 68RR, 69RR	3	5	4	0	0	0	0	2
Terry Holland (Davidson 1964) 1970	1	0	1	0	0	0	0	0
Bobby Hussey (Appalachian St. 1962) 1986	1	0	1	0	0	0	0	0
Bob McKillop (Hofstra 1972) 1998, 2002	2	0	2	0	0	0	0	0
TOTAL	7	5	8	0	0	0	0	2
DAYTON								
Tom Blackburn [Wilmington (Ohio) 1931] 1952	1	1	1	0	0	0	0	0
Don Donoher (Dayton 1954) 1965, 66, 67-2d, 69, 70, 74, 84RR, 85........	8	11	10	0	1	0	0	1
Jim O'Brien (St. Joseph's 1974) 1990.....	1	1	1	0	0	0	0	0
Oliver Purnell (Old Dominion 1975) 2000, 03	2	0	2	0	0	0	0	0
TOTAL	12	13	14	0	1	0	0	1
DELAWARE								
Steve Steinwedel (Mississippi St. 1975) 1992, 93	2	0	2	0	0	0	0	0
Mike Brey (George Washington 1982) 1998, 99	2	0	2	0	0	0	0	0
TOTAL	4	0	4	0	0	0	0	0
DePAUL*								
Ray Meyer (Notre Dame 1938) 1943-T3d, 53, 56, 59, 60, 65, 76, 78RR, 79-3d, 80, 81, 82, 84	13	14	16	0	0	2	0	1
Joey Meyer (DePaul 1971) 1985, 86, 87, 88, 89, 92	7	6	7	0	0	0	0	0
Pat Kennedy [King's (Pa.) 1976] 2000 ...	1	0	1	0	0	0	0	0
TOTAL	21	20	24	0	0	2	0	1
DETROIT								
Robert Calihan (Detroit 1940) 1962.......	1	0	1	0	0	0	0	0
Dick Vitale (Seton Hall 1962) 1977........	1	1	1	0	0	0	0	0
Dave "Smokey" Gaines (LeMoyne-Owen 1963) 1979	1	0	1	0	0	0	0	0
Perry Watson (Eastern Mich. 1972) 1998, 99	2	2	2	0	0	0	0	0
TOTAL	5	3	5	0	0	0	0	0

	Yrs.	Won	Lost	CH	2D	3d%	4th	RR
DRAKE								
Maurice John (Central Mo. St. 1941) 1969-3d, 70RR, 71RR	3	5	3	0	0	1	0	2
TOTAL	3	5	3	0	0	1	0	2
DREXEL								
Eddie Burke (La Salle 1967) 1986	1	0	1	0	0	0	0	0
Bill Herrion (Merrimack 1981) 1994, 95, 96	3	1	3	0	0	0	0	0
TOTAL	4	1	4	0	0	0	0	0
DUKE								
Harold Bradley (Hartwick 1934) 1955 ...	1	0	1	0	0	0	0	0
Vic Bubas (North Carolina St. 1951) 1960RR, 63-3d, 64-2d, 66-3d.............	4	11	4	0	1	2	0	1
W.E. "Bill" Foster (Elizabethtown 1954) 1978-2d, 79, 80RR	3	6	3	0	1	0	0	1
Mike Krzyzewski (Army 1969) 1984, 85, 86-2d, 87, 88-T3d, 89-T3d, 90-2d, 91-CH, 92-CH, 93, 94-2d, 96, 97, 98RR, 99-2d, 2000, 01-CH, 02, 03 ...	19	60	16	3	4	2	0	1
TOTAL	27	77	24	3	6	4	0	3
DUQUESNE								
Charles "Chick" Davies (Duquesne 1934) 1940-T3d	1	1	1	0	0	1	0	0
Donald "Dudey" Moore (Duquesne 1934) 1952RR	1	1	1	0	0	0	0	1
John "Red" Manning (Duquesne 1951) 1969, 71	2	2	2	0	0	0	0	0
John Cinicola (Duquesne 1955) 1977	1	0	1	0	0	0	0	0
TOTAL	5	4	5	0	0	1	0	1
EAST CARO.								
Tom Quinn (Marshall 1954) 1972..........	1	0	1	0	0	0	0	0
Eddie Payne (Wake Forest 1973) 1993 ..	1	0	1	0	0	0	0	0
TOTAL	2	0	2	0	0	0	0	0
EAST TENN. ST.								
J. Madison Brooks (Louisiana Tech 1937) 1968	1	1	2	0	0	0	0	0
Les Robinson (North Carolina St. 1964) 1989, 90	2	0	2	0	0	0	0	0
Alan LeForce (Cumberland 1957) 1991, 92	2	1	2	0	0	0	0	0
Ed DeChellis (Penn St. 1982) 2003........	1	0	1	0	0	0	0	0
TOTAL	6	2	7	0	0	0	0	0
EASTERN ILL.								
Rick Samuels (Chadron St. 1971) 1992, 2001	2	0	2	0	0	0	0	0
TOTAL	2	0	2	0	0	0	0	0
EASTERN KY.								
Paul McBrayer (Kentucky 1930) 1953, 59	2	0	2	0	0	0	0	0
Jim Baechtold (Eastern Ky. 1952) 1965 ..	1	0	1	0	0	0	0	0
Guy Strong (Eastern Ky. 1955) 1972	1	0	1	0	0	0	0	0
Ed Byhre [Augustana (S.D.) 1966] 1979	1	0	1	0	0	0	0	0
TOTAL	5	0	5	0	0	0	0	0
EASTERN MICH.								
Ben Braun (Wisconsin 1975) 1988, 91, 96	3	3	3	0	0	0	0	0
Milton Barnes (Albion 1979) 1998.........	1	0	1	0	0	0	0	0
TOTAL	4	3	4	0	0	0	0	0
EVANSVILLE								
Dick Walters (Illinois St. 1969) 1982	1	0	1	0	0	0	0	0
Jim Crews (Indiana 1976) 1989, 92, 93, 99	4	1	4	0	0	0	0	0
TOTAL	5	1	5	0	0	0	0	0
FAIRFIELD								
Mitch Buonaguro (Boston College 1975) 1986, 87	2	0	2	0	0	0	0	0
Paul Cormier (New Hampshire 1973) 1997	1	0	1	0	0	0	0	0
TOTAL	3	0	3	0	0	0	0	0
FDU-TEANECK								
Tom Green (Syracuse 1971) 1985, 88, 98	3	0	3	0	0	0	0	0
TOTAL	3	0	3	0	0	0	0	0
FLORIDA*								
Norm Sloan (North Carolina St. 1951) 1987, 88, 89	3	3	3	0	0	0	0	0
Lon Kruger (Kansas St. 1974) 1994-T3d, 95	2	4	2	0	0	1	0	0
Billy Donovan (Providence 1987) 1999, 2000-2d, 01, 02, 03	5	9	5	0	1	0	0	0
TOTAL	10	16	10	0	1	1	0	0
FLORIDA A&M								
Mickey Clayton (Florida A&M 1975) 1999	1	0	1	0	0	0	0	0
TOTAL	1	0	1	0	0	0	0	0

	Yrs.	Won	Lost	CH	2D	3d%	4th	RR
FLORIDA ATLANTIC								
Sydney Green (UNLV 1983), 2002	1	0	1	0	0	0	0	0
TOTAL	1	0	1	0	0	0	0	0
FLORIDA INT'L								
Bob Weltlich (Ohio St. 1967) 1995	1	0	1	0	0	0	0	0
TOTAL	1	0	1	0	0	0	0	0
FLORIDA ST.								
Hugh Durham (Florida St. 1959) 1968, 72-2d, 78	3	4	3	0	1	0	0	0
Joe Williams (Southern Methodist 1956) 1980	1	1	1	0	0	0	0	0
Pat Kennedy [King's (Pa.) 1976] 1988, 89, 91, 92, 93RR	5	6	5	0	0	0	0	1
Steve Robinson (Radford 1981) 1998	1	1	1	0	0	0	0	0
TOTAL	10	12	10	0	1	0	0	1
FORDHAM								
John Bach (Fordham 1948) 1953, 54	2	0	2	0	0	0	0	0
Richard "Digger" Phelps (Rider 1963) 1971	1	2	1	0	0	0	0	0
Nick Macarchuk (Fairfield 1963) 1992	1	0	1	0	0	0	0	0
TOTAL	4	2	4	0	0	0	0	0
FRESNO ST.								
Boyd Grant (Colorado St. 1961) 1981, 82, 84	3	1	3	0	0	0	0	0
Jerry Tarkanian (Fresno St. 1956) 2000, 01	2	1	2	0	0	0	0	0
TOTAL	5	2	5	0	0	0	0	0
FURMAN								
Joe Williams (Southern Methodist 1956) 1971, 73, 74, 75, 78	5	1	6	0	0	0	0	0
Eddie Holbrook (Lenoir-Rhyne 1962) 1980	1	0	1	0	0	0	0	0
TOTAL	6	1	7	0	0	0	0	0
GEORGE MASON								
Ernie Nestor (Alderson-Broaddus 1968) 1989	1	0	1	0	0	0	0	0
Jim Larranaga (Providence 1971) 1999, 2001	2	0	2	0	0	0	0	0
TOTAL	3	0	3	0	0	0	0	0
GEORGE WASHINGTON								
Bill Reinhart (Oregon 1923) 1954, 61	2	0	2	0	0	0	0	0
Mike Jarvis (Northeastern 1968) 1993, 94, 96, 98	4	3	4	0	0	0	0	0
Tom Penders (Connecticut 1967) 1999	1	0	1	0	0	0	0	0
TOTAL	7	3	7	0	0	0	0	0
GEORGETOWN								
Elmer Ripley (No college) 1943-2d	1	2	1	0	1	0	0	0
John Thompson (Providence 1964) 1975, 76, 79, 80RR, 81, 82-2d, 83, 84-CH, 85-2d, 86, 87RR, 88, 89RR, 90, 91, 92, 94, 95, 96RR, 97	20	34	19	1	2	0	0	4
Craig Esherick (Georgetown 1978) 2001	1	2	1	0	0	0	0	0
TOTAL	22	38	21	1	3	0	0	4
GEORGIA*								
Hugh Durham (Florida St. 1959) 1983-T3d, 85, 87, 90, 91	5	4	5	0	0	1	0	0
Tubby Smith (High Point 1973) 1996, 97	2	2	2	0	0	0	0	0
Jim Harrick [Charleston (W.Va.) 1960] 2001, 02	2	1	2	0	0	0	0	0
TOTAL	9	7	9	0	0	1	0	0
GA. SOUTHERN								
Frank Kerns (Alabama 1957) 1983, 87, 92	3	0	3	0	0	0	0	0
TOTAL	3	0	3	0	0	0	0	0
GEORGIA ST.								
Bob Reinhart (Indiana 1961) 1991	1	0	1	0	0	0	0	0
Charles "Lefty" Driesell (Duke 1954) 2001	1	1	1	0	0	0	0	0
TOTAL	2	1	2	0	0	0	0	0
GEORGIA TECH								
John "Whack" Hyder (Georgia Tech 1937) 1960RR	1	1	1	0	0	0	0	1
Bobby Cremins (South Carolina 1970) 1985RR, 86, 87, 88, 89, 90-T3d, 91, 92, 93, 96	10	15	10	0	0	1	0	1
Paul Hewitt (St. John Fisher 1985) 2001	1	0	1	0	0	0	0	0
TOTAL	12	16	12	0	0	1	0	2
GONZAGA								
Dan Fitzgerald (Cal St. L.A. 1965) 1995	1	0	1	0	0	0	0	0
Dan Monson (Idaho 1985) 1999RR	1	3	1	0	0	0	0	1
Mark Few (Oregon 1987) 2000, 01, 02, 03	4	5	4	0	0	0	0	0
TOTAL	6	8	6	0	0	0	0	1

	Yrs.	Won	Lost	CH	2D	3d%	4th	RR
HAMPTON								
Steve Merfeld (Wis.-La Crosse 1984) 2001, 02	2	1	2	0	0	0	0	0
TOTAL	2	1	2	0	0	0	0	0
HARDIN-SIMMONS								
Bill Scott (Hardin-Simmons 1947) 1953, 57	2	0	2	0	0	0	0	0
TOTAL	2	0	2	0	0	0	0	0
HARVARD								
Floyd Stahl (Illinois 1926) 1946RR	1	0	2	0	0	0	0	1
TOTAL	1	0	2	0	0	0	0	1
HAWAII								
Ephraim "Red" Rocha (Oregon St. 1950) 1972	1	0	1	0	0	0	0	0
Riley Wallace [Centenary (La.) 1964] 1994, 2001, 02	3	0	3	0	0	0	0	0
TOTAL	4	0	4	0	0	0	0	0
HOFSTRA								
Roger Gaeckler (Gettysburg 1965) 1976, 77	2	0	2	0	0	0	0	0
Jay Wright (Bucknell 1983) 2000, 01	2	0	2	0	0	0	0	0
TOTAL	4	0	4	0	0	0	0	0
HOLY CROSS								
Alvin "Doggie" Julian (Bucknell 1923) 1947-CH, 48-3d	2	5	1	1	0	1	0	0
Lester "Buster" Sheary (Catholic 1933) 1950RR, 53RR	2	2	3	0	0	0	0	2
Roy Leenig [Trinity (Conn.) 1942] 1956	1	0	1	0	0	0	0	0
George Blaney (Holy Cross 1961) 1977, 80, 93	3	0	3	0	0	0	0	0
Ralph Willard (Holy Cross 1967) 2001, 02, 03	3	0	3	0	0	0	0	0
TOTAL	11	7	11	1	0	1	0	2
HOUSTON								
Alden Pasche (Rice 1932) 1956	1	0	2	0	0	0	0	0
Guy Lewis (Houston 1947) 1961, 65, 66, 67-3d, 68-4th, 70, 71, 72, 73, 78, 81, 82-T3d, 83-2d, 84-2d	14	26	18	0	2	2	1	0
Pat Foster (Arkansas 1961) 1987, 90, 92	3	0	3	0	0	0	0	0
TOTAL	18	26	23	0	2	2	1	0
HOUSTON BAPTIST								
Gene Iba (Tulsa 1963) 1984	1	0	1	0	0	0	0	0
TOTAL	1	0	1	0	0	0	0	0
HOWARD								
A.B. Williamson (N.C. A&T 1968) 1981[1]	0	1	0	0	0	0	0	0
Alfred "Butch" Beard (Louisville 1972) 1992	1	0	1	0	0	0	0	0
TOTAL	2	0	2	0	0	0	0	0
IDAHO								
Don Monson (Idaho 1955) 1981, 82	2	1	2	0	0	0	0	0
Kermit Davis Jr. (Mississippi St. 1982) 1989, 90	2	0	2	0	0	0	0	0
TOTAL	4	1	4	0	0	0	0	0
IDAHO ST.								
Steve Belko (Idaho 1939) 1953, 54, 55, 56	4	2	4	0	0	0	0	0
John Grayson (Oklahoma 1938) 1957, 58, 59	3	4	5	0	0	0	0	0
John Evans (Idaho 1948) 1960	1	0	1	0	0	0	0	0
Jim Killingsworth (Northeastern Okla. St. 1948) 1974, 77RR	2	2	2	0	0	0	0	1
Jim Boutin (Lewis & Clark 1964) 1987	1	0	1	0	0	0	0	0
TOTAL	11	8	13	0	0	0	0	1
ILLINOIS								
Doug Mills (Illinois 1930) 1942RR	1	0	2	0	0	0	0	1
Harry Combes (Illinois 1937) 1949-3d, 51-3d, 52-3d, 63RR	4	9	4	0	0	3	0	1
Lou Henson (New Mexico St. 1955) 1981, 83, 84RR, 85, 86, 87, 88, 89-T3d, 90, 93, 94, 95	12	12	12	0	0	1	0	1
Lon Kruger (Kansas St. 1974) 1997, 98 2000	3	3	3	0	0	0	0	0
Bill Self (Oklahoma St. 1985) 2001RR, 02, 03	3	6	3	0	0	0	0	1
TOTAL	23	30	24	0	0	4	0	4
ILLINOIS ST.								
Bob Donewald (Hanover 1964) 1983, 84, 85	3	2	3	0	0	0	0	0
Bob Bender (Duke 1980) 1990	1	0	1	0	0	0	0	0
Kevin Stallings (Purdue 1982) 1997, 98	2	1	2	0	0	0	0	0
TOTAL	6	3	6	0	0	0	0	0
ILL.-CHICAGO								
Jimmy Collins (New Mexico St. 1970) 1998, 2002	2	0	2	0	0	0	0	0
TOTAL	2	0	2	0	0	0	0	0

CHAMPIONSHIPS

	Yrs.	Won	Lost	CH	2D	3d%	4th	RR
INDIANA								
Branch McCracken (Indiana 1930) 1940-CH, 53-CH, 54, 58..........	4	9	2	2	0	0	0	0
Lou Watson (Indiana 1950) 1967	1	1	1	0	0	0	0	0
Bob Knight (Ohio St. 1962) 1973-3d, 75RR, 76-CH, 78, 80, 81-CH, 82, 83, 84RR, 86, 87-CH, 88, 89, 90, 91, 92-T3d, 93RR, 94, 95, 96, 97, 98, 99, 2000	24	42	21	3	0	2	0	3
Mike Davis (Alabama 1983) 2001, 02-2d, 03	3	6	3	0	1	0	0	0
TOTAL	32	58	27	5	1	2	0	3
IUPUI								
Ron Hunter [Miami (Ohio) 1986] 2003 ..	1	0	1	0	0	0	0	0
TOTAL	1	0	1	0	0	0	0	0
INDIANA ST.								
Bill Hodges (Marian 1970) 1979-2d	1	4	1	0	1	0	0	0
Royce Waltman (Slippery Rock 1964) 2000, 01	2	1	2	0	0	0	0	0
TOTAL	3	5	3	0	1	0	0	0
IONA*								
Jim Valvano (Rutgers 1967) 1979, 80	2	1	2	0	0	0	0	0
Pat Kennedy [King's (Pa.) 1976] 1984, 85	2	0	2	0	0	0	0	0
Tim Welsh (Potsdam St. 1984) 1998	1	0	1	0	0	0	0	0
Jeff Ruland (Iona 1991) 2000, 01	2	0	2	0	0	0	0	0
TOTAL	7	1	7	0	0	0	0	0
IOWA								
Frank "Bucky" O'Connor (Drake 1938) 1955-4th, 56-2d	2	5	3	0	1	0	1	0
Ralph Miller (Kansas 1942) 1970	1	1	1	0	0	0	0	0
Luther "Lute" Olson (Augsburg 1957) 1979, 80-4th, 81, 82, 83	5	7	6	0	0	0	1	0
George Raveling (Villanova 1960) 1985, 86	2	0	2	0	0	0	0	0
Tom Davis (Wis.-Platteville 1960) 1987RR, 88, 89, 91, 92, 93, 96, 97, 99	9	13	9	0	0	0	0	1
Steve Alford (Indiana 1987) 2001	1	1	1	0	0	0	0	0
TOTAL	20	27	22	0	1	0	2	1
IOWA ST.								
Louis Menze (Central Mo. St. 1928) 1944-T3d	1	1	1	0	0	1	0	0
Johnny Orr (Beloit 1949) 1985, 86, 88, 89, 92, 93	6	3	6	0	0	0	0	0
Tim Floyd (Louisiana Tech 1977) 1995, 96, 97	3	4	3	0	0	0	0	0
Larry Eustachy (Long Beach St. 1979) 2000RR, 01	2	3	2	0	0	0	0	1
TOTAL	12	11	12	0	0	1	0	1
JACKSON ST.								
Andy Stoglin (UTEP 1965) 1997, 2000 ..	2	0	2	0	0	0	0	0
TOTAL	2	0	2	0	0	0	0	0
JACKSONVILLE								
Joe Williams (Southern Methodist 1956) 1970-2d	1	4	1	0	1	0	0	0
Tom Wasdin (Florida 1957) 1971, 73	2	0	2	0	0	0	0	0
Tates Locke (Ohio Wesleyan 1959) 1979	1	0	1	0	0	0	0	0
Bob Wenzel (Rutgers 1971) 1986..........	1	0	1	0	0	0	0	0
TOTAL	5	4	5	0	1	0	0	0
JAMES MADISON								
Lou Campanelli (Montclair St. 1960) 1981, 82, 83	3	3	3	0	0	0	0	0
Charles "Lefty" Driesell (Duke 1954) 1994	1	0	1	0	0	0	0	0
TOTAL	4	3	4	0	0	0	0	0
KANSAS								
Forrest C. "Phog" Allen (Kansas 1906) 1940-2d, 42RR, 52-CH, 53-2d..........	4	10	3	1	2	0	0	1
Dick Harp (Kansas 1940) 1957-2d, 60RR	2	4	2	0	1	0	0	1
Ted Owens (Oklahoma 1951) 1966RR, 67, 71-4th, 74-4th, 75, 78, 81	7	8	9	0	0	0	2	1
Larry Brown (North Carolina 1963) 1984, 85, 86-T3d, 87, 88-CH	5	14	4	1	0	1	0	0
Roy Williams (North Carolina 1972) 1990, 91-2d, 92, 93-T3d, 94, 95, 96RR, 97, 98, 99, 2000, 01, 02-T3d, 03-2d	14	34	14	0	2	2	0	1
TOTAL	32	69	32	2	5	3	2	4
KANSAS ST.								
Jack Gardner (Southern California 1932) 1948-4th, 51-2d	2	4	3	0	1	0	1	0
Fred "Tex" Winter (Southern California 1947) 1956, 58-4th, 59RR, 61RR, 64-4th, 68	6	7	9	0	0	0	2	2
Lowell "Cotton" Fitzsimmons (Midwestern St. 1955) 1970	1	1	1	0	0	0	0	0
Jack Hartman (Oklahoma St. 1949) 1972RR, 73RR, 75RR, 77, 80, 81RR, 82	7	11	7	0	0	0	0	4
Lon Kruger (Kansas St. 1974) 1987, 88RR, 89, 90	4	4	4	0	0	0	0	1
Dana Altman (Eastern N.M. 1980) 1993	1	0	1	0	0	0	0	0
Tom Asbury (Wyoming 1967) 1996.......	1	0	1	0	0	0	0	0
TOTAL	22	27	26	0	1	0	3	7
KENT ST.								
Gary Waters (Ferris St. 1975) 1999, 2001	2	1	2	0	0	0	0	0
Stan Heath (Eastern Mich. 1988) 2002RR	1	3	1	0	0	0	0	1
TOTAL	3	4	3	0	0	0	0	1
KENTUCKY*								
Adolph Rupp (Kansas 1923) 1942-T3d, 45RR, 48-CH, 49-CH, 51-CH, 52RR, 55, 56RR, 57RR, 58-CH, 59, 61RR, 62RR, 64, 66-2d, 68RR, 69, 70RR, 71, 72RR	20	30	18	4	1	1	0	9
Joe B. Hall (Sewanee 1951) 1973RR, 75-2d, 77RR, 78-CH, 80, 81, 82, 83RR, 84-T3d, 85	10	20	9	1	1	1	0	3
Eddie Sutton (Oklahoma St. 1958) 1986RR, 87, 88	3	5	3	0	0	0	0	1
Rick Pitino (Massachusetts 1974) 1992RR, 93-T3d, 94, 95RR 96-CH, 97-2d	6	22	5	1	1	1	0	2
Tubby Smith (High Point 1973) 1998-CH, 99RR, 2000, 01, 02, 03RR	6	17	5	1	0	0	0	2
TOTAL	45	94	40	7	3	3	0	17
LA SALLE								
Ken Loeffler (Penn St. 1924) 1954-CH, 55-2d	2	9	1	1	1	0	0	0
Jim Harding (Iowa 1949) 1968	1	0	1	0	0	0	0	0
Paul Westhead (St. Joseph's 1961) 1975, 78	2	0	2	0	0	0	0	0
Dave "Lefty" Ervin (La Salle 1968) 1980, 83	2	1	2	0	0	0	0	0
Bill "Speedy" Morris (St. Joseph's 1973) 1988, 89, 90, 92	4	1	4	0	0	0	0	0
TOTAL	11	11	10	1	1	0	0	0
LAFAYETTE								
George Davidson (Lafayette 1951) 1957	1	0	2	0	0	0	0	0
Fran O'Hanlon (Villanova 1970) 1999, 2000	2	0	2	0	0	0	0	0
TOTAL	3	0	4	0	0	0	0	0
LAMAR								
Billy Tubbs (Lamar 1958) 1979, 80........	2	3	2	0	0	0	0	0
Pat Foster (Arkansas 1961) 1981, 83.....	2	2	2	0	0	0	0	0
Mike Deane (Potsdam St. 1974) 2000....	1	0	1	0	0	0	0	0
TOTAL	5	5	5	0	0	0	0	0
LEBANON VALLEY								
George "Rinso" Marquette (Lebanon Valley 1948) 1953	1	1	2	0	0	0	0	0
TOTAL	1	1	2	0	0	0	0	0
LEHIGH								
Tom Schneider (Bucknell 1969) 1985	1	0	1	0	0	0	0	0
Fran McCaffery (Pennsylvania 1982) 1988	1	0	1	0	0	0	0	0
TOTAL	2	0	2	0	0	0	0	0
LIBERTY								
Jeff Meyer (Taylor 1976) 1994	1	0	1	0	0	0	0	0
TOTAL	1	0	1	0	0	0	0	0
LONG BEACH ST.*								
Jerry Tarkanian (Fresno St. 1956) 1970, 71RR, 72RR, 73	4	7	5	0	0	0	0	2
Dwight Jones (Pepperdine 1965) 1977 ...	1	0	1	0	0	0	0	0
Seth Greenberg (FDU-Teaneck 1978) 1993, 95	2	0	2	0	0	0	0	0
TOTAL	7	7	8	0	0	0	0	2
LONG ISLAND								
Paul Lizzo (Northwest Mo. St. 1963) 1981, 84	2	0	2	0	0	0	0	0
Ray Haskins (Shaw 1972) 1997	1	0	1	0	0	0	0	0
TOTAL	3	0	3	0	0	0	0	0
LSU								
Harry Rabenhorst (Wake Forest 1921) 1953-4th, 54	2	2	4	0	0	0	1	0
Dale Brown (Minot St. 1957) 1979, 80RR, 81-4th, 84, 85, 86-T3d, 87RR, 88, 89, 90, 91, 92, 93	13	15	14	0	0	1	1	2
John Brady (Belhaven 1976) 2000, 03 ...	2	2	2	0	0	0	0	0
TOTAL	17	19	20	0	0	1	2	2
LOUISIANA TECH								
Andy Russo (Lake Forest 1970) 1984, 85	2	3	2	0	0	0	0	0

	Yrs.	Won	Lost	CH	2D	3d%	4th	RR
Tommy Joe Eagles (Louisiana Tech 1971) 1987, 89	2	1	2	0	0	0	0	0
Jerry Loyd (LeTourneau 1976) 1991	1	0	1	0	0	0	0	0
TOTAL	5	4	5	0	0	0	0	0
LA.-LAFAYETTE*								
Beryl Shipley (Delta St. 1951) 1972, 73	2	3	3	0	0	0	0	0
Bobby Paschal (Stetson 1964) 1982, 83	2	0	2	0	0	0	0	0
Marty Fletcher (Maryland 1973) 1992, 94	2	1	2	0	0	0	0	0
Jessie Evans (Eastern Mich. 1972) 2000 .	1	0	1	0	0	0	0	0
TOTAL	7	4	8	0	0	0	0	0
LA.-MONROE								
Mike Vining (La.-Monroe 1967) 1982, 86, 90, 91, 92, 93, 96	7	0	7	0	0	0	0	0
TOTAL	7	0	7	0	0	0	0	0
LOUISVILLE								
Bernard "Peck" Hickman (Western Ky. 1935) 1951, 59-4th, 61, 64, 67	5	5	7	0	0	0	1	0
John Dromo (John Carroll 1939) 1968 ...	1	1	1	0	0	0	0	0
Denny Crum (UCLA 1959) 1972-4th, 74, 75-3d, 77, 78, 79, 80-CH, 81, 82-T3d, 83-T3d, 84, 86-CH, 88, 89, 90, 92, 93, 94, 95, 96, 97RR, 99, 2000	23	42	23	2	0	3	1	1
Rick Pitino (Massachusetts 1974) 2003 ...	1	1	1	0	0	0	0	0
TOTAL	30	49	32	2	0	3	2	1
LOYOLA MARYMOUNT*								
William Donovan (Loyola Marymount 1950) 1961	1	1	1	0	0	0	0	0
Ron Jacobs (Southern California 1964) 1980	1	0	1	0	0	0	0	0
Paul Westhead (St. Joseph's 1961) 1988, 89, 90RR	3	4	3	0	0	0	0	1
TOTAL	5	5	5	0	0	0	0	1
LOYOLA (ILL.)								
George Ireland (Notre Dame 1936) 1963-CH, 64, 66, 68	4	7	3	1	0	0	0	0
Gene Sullivan (Notre Dame 1953) 1985	1	2	1	0	0	0	0	0
TOTAL	5	9	4	1	0	0	0	0
LOYOLA (LA.)								
Jim McCafferty [Loyola (La.) 1942] 1954, 57	2	0	2	0	0	0	0	0
Jim Harding (Iowa 1949) 1958	1	0	1	0	0	0	0	0
TOTAL	3	0	3	0	0	0	0	0
LOYOLA (MD.)								
Skip Prosser (Merchant Marine 1972) 1994	1	0	1	0	0	0	0	0
TOTAL	1	0	1	0	0	0	0	0
MANHATTAN								
Ken Norton (Long Island 1939) 1956, 58	2	1	3	0	0	0	0	0
Fran Fraschilla (Brooklyn 1980) 1993, 95	2	1	2	0	0	0	0	0
Bobby Gonzalez (Buffalo St. 1986) 2003	1	0	1	0	0	0	0	0
TOTAL	5	2	6	0	0	0	0	0
MARIST								
Matt Furjanic (Point Park 1973) 1986.....	1	0	1	0	0	0	0	0
Dave Magarity [St. Francis (Pa.) 1974] 1987	1	0	1	0	0	0	0	0
TOTAL	2	0	2	0	0	0	0	0
MARQUETTE								
Jack Nagle (Marquette 1940) 1955RR ...	1	2	1	0	0	0	0	1
Eddie Hickey (Creighton 1927) 1959, 61	2	1	3	0	0	0	0	0
Al McGuire [St. John's (N.Y.) 1951] 1968, 69RR, 71, 72, 73, 74-2d, 75, 76RR, 77-CH	9	20	9	1	1	0	0	2
Hank Raymonds (St. Louis 1948) 1978, 79, 80, 82, 83	5	2	5	0	0	0	0	0
Kevin O'Neill (McGill 1979) 1993, 94 ..	2	2	2	0	0	0	0	0
Mike Deane (Potsdam St. 1974) 1996, 97	2	1	2	0	0	0	0	0
Tom Crean (Central Mich. 1989) 2002, 03-T3d	2	4	2	0	0	1	0	0
TOTAL	23	32	24	1	1	1	0	3
MARSHALL*								
Jule Rivlin (Marshall 1940) 1956	1	0	1	0	0	0	0	0
Carl Tacy (Davis & Elkins 1956) 1972....	1	0	1	0	0	0	0	0
Rick Huckabay (Louisiana Tech 1967) 1984, 85, 87	3	0	3	0	0	0	0	0
TOTAL	5	0	5	0	0	0	0	0
MARYLAND*								
H.A. "Bud" Millikan (Oklahoma St. 1942) 1958	1	2	1	0	0	0	0	0
Charles "Lefty" Driesell (Duke 1954) 1973RR, 75RR, 80, 81, 83, 84, 85, 86	8	10	8	0	0	0	0	2

	Yrs.	Won	Lost	CH	2D	3d%	4th	RR
Bob Wade (Morgan St. 1967) 1988......	1	1	1	0	0	0	0	0
Gary Williams (Maryland 1967) 1994, 95, 96, 97, 98, 99, 2000, 01-T3d, 02-CH, 03	10	21	9	1	0	1	0	0
TOTAL	20	34	19	1	0	1	0	2
MASSACHUSETTS*								
Matt Zunic (George Washington 1942) 1962	1	0	1	0	0	0	0	0
John Calipari (Clarion 1982) 1992, 93, 94, 95RR, 96-T3d	5	11	5	0	0	1	0	1
James Flint (St. Joseph's 1987) 1997, 98	2	0	2	0	0	0	0	0
TOTAL	8	11	8	0	0	1	0	1
McNEESE ST.								
Steve Welch (Southeastern La. 1971) 1989	1	0	1	0	0	0	0	0
Tic Price (Virginia Tech 1979) 2002	1	0	1	0	0	0	0	0
TOTAL	2	0	2	0	0	0	0	0
MEMPHIS*								
Eugene Lambert (Arkansas 1929) 1955, 56	2	0	2	0	0	0	0	0
Bob Vanatta (Central Methodist 1945) 1962	1	0	1	0	0	0	0	0
Gene Bartow (Truman 1953) 1973-2d....	1	3	1	0	1	0	0	0
Wayne Yates (Memphis 1961) 1976......	1	0	1	0	0	0	0	0
Dana Kirk (Marshall 1960) 1982, 83, 84, 85-T3d, 86	5	9	5	0	0	1	0	0
Larry Finch (Memphis 1973) 1988, 89, 92RR, 93, 95, 96	6	6	6	0	0	0	0	1
John Calipari (Clarion 1982) 2003	1	0	1	0	0	0	0	0
TOTAL	17	18	17	0	1	1	0	1
MERCER								
Bill Bibb (Ky. Wesleyan 1957) 1981, 85	2	0	2	0	0	0	0	0
TOTAL	2	0	2	0	0	0	0	0
MIAMI (FLA.)								
Bruce Hale (Santa Clara 1941) 1960.....	1	0	1	0	0	0	0	0
Leonard Hamilton (Tenn.-Martin 1971) 1998, 99, 2000, 02	4	3	4	0	0	0	0	0
TOTAL	5	3	5	0	0	0	0	0
MIAMI (OHIO)								
Bill Rohr (Ohio Wesleyan 1940) 1953, 55, 57	3	0	3	0	0	0	0	0
Dick Shrider (Ohio 1948) 1958, 66.......	2	1	3	0	0	0	0	0
Tates Locke (Ohio Wesleyan 1959) 1969	1	1	2	0	0	0	0	0
Darrell Hedric [Miami (Ohio) 1955] 1971, 73, 78, 84	4	1	4	0	0	0	0	0
Jerry Peirson [Miami (Ohio) 1966] 1985, 86	2	0	2	0	0	0	0	0
Joby Wright (Indiana 1972) 1992	1	0	1	0	0	0	0	0
Herb Sendek (Carnegie Mellon 1985) 1995	1	1	1	0	0	0	0	0
Charlie Coles [Miami (Ohio) 1965] 1997, 99	2	2	2	0	0	0	0	0
TOTAL	16	6	18	0	0	0	0	0
MICHIGAN#*								
Osborne "Ozzie" Cowles (Carleton 1922) 1948RR	1	1	1	0	0	0	0	1
Dave Strack (Michigan 1946) 1964-3d, 65-2d, 66RR	3	7	3	0	1	1	0	1
Johnny Orr (Beloit 1949) 1974RR, 75, 76-2d, 77RR	4	7	4	0	1	0	0	2
Bill Frieder (Michigan 1964) 1985, 86, 87, 88	4	5	4	0	0	0	0	0
Steve Fisher (Illinois St. 1967) 1989-CH, 90, 92-2d, 93-2d, 94RR, 95, 96	7	20	6	1	2	0	0	1
Brian Ellerbe (Rutgers 1985) 1998	1	1	1	0	0	0	0	0
TOTAL	20	41	19	1	4	1	0	5
MICHIGAN ST.								
Forrest "Forddy" Anderson (Stanford 1942) 1957-4th, 59RR	2	3	3	0	0	0	1	1
George "Jud" Heathcote (Washington St. 1950) 1978RR, 79-CH, 85, 86, 90, 91, 92, 94, 95	9	14	8	1	0	0	0	1
Tom Izzo (Northern Mich. 1977) 1998, 99-T3d, 2000-CH, 01-T3d, 02, 03RR..	6	19	5	1	0	2	0	1
TOTAL	17	36	16	2	0	2	1	3
MIDDLE TENN.								
Jimmy Earle (Middle Tenn. 1959) 1975, 77	2	0	2	0	0	0	0	0
Stan Simpson (Ga. Southern 1961) 1982	1	1	1	0	0	0	0	0
Bruce Stewart (Jacksonville St. 1975) 1985, 87, 89	3	1	3	0	0	0	0	0
TOTAL	6	2	6	0	0	0	0	0
MINNESOTA*								
Bill Musselman (Wittenberg 1961) 1972.	1	1	1	0	0	0	0	0
Jim Dutcher (Michigan 1955) 1982........	1	1	1	0	0	0	0	0

	Yrs.	Won	Lost	CH	2D	3d%	4th	RR
Clem Haskins (Western Ky. 1967) 1989, 90RR, 94, 95, 97-T3d, 99	6	10	6	0	0	1	0	1
TOTAL	8	12	8	0	0	1	0	1
MISSISSIPPI								
Bob Weltlich (Ohio St. 1967) 1981	1	0	1	0	0	0	0	0
Rob Evans (New Mexico St. 1968) 1997, 98	2	0	2	0	0	0	0	0
Rod Barnes (Mississippi 1988) 1999, 2001, 02	3	3	3	0	0	0	0	0
TOTAL	6	3	6	0	0	0	0	0
MISSISSIPPI ST.								
James "Babe" McCarthy (Mississippi St. 1949) 1963	1	1	1	0	0	0	0	0
Richard Williams (Mississippi St. 1967) 1991, 95, 96-T3d	3	6	3	0	0	1	0	0
Rick Stansbury (Campbellsville 1982) 2002, 03	2	1	2	0	0	0	0	0
TOTAL	6	8	6	0	0	1	0	0
MISSISSIPPI VAL.								
Lafayette Stribling (Miss. Industrial 1957) 1986, 92, 96	3	0	3	0	0	0	0	0
TOTAL	3	0	3	0	0	0	0	0
MISSOURI#								
George Edwards (Missouri 1913) 1944RR	1	1	1	0	0	0	0	1
Norm Stewart (Missouri 1956) 1976RR, 78, 80, 81, 82 83, 86, 87, 88, 89, 90, 92, 93, 94RR, 95, 99	16	12	16	0	0	0	0	2
Quin Snyder (Duke 1989) 2000, 01, 02RR, 03	4	5	4	0	0	0	0	1
TOTAL	21	18	21	0	0	0	0	4
MONMOUTH								
Wayne Szoke (Maryland 1963) 1996	1	0	1	0	0	0	0	0
Dave Calloway [Monmouth 1991] 2001	1	0	1	0	0	0	0	0
TOTAL	2	0	2	0	0	0	0	0
MONTANA								
George "Jud" Heathcote (Washington St. 1950) 1975	1	1	2	0	0	0	0	0
Stew Morrill (Gonzaga 1974) 1991	1	0	1	0	0	0	0	0
Blaine Taylor (Montana 1982) 1992, 97	2	0	2	0	0	0	0	0
Don Holst (Northern Mont. 1975) 2002	1	0	1	0	0	0	0	0
TOTAL	5	1	6	0	0	0	0	0
MONTANA ST.								
John Breeden (Montana St. 1929) 1951	1	0	1	0	0	0	0	0
Stu Starner (Minn.-Morris 1965) 1986	1	0	1	0	0	0	0	0
Mike Durham (Montana St. 1979) 1996	1	0	1	0	0	0	0	0
TOTAL	3	0	3	0	0	0	0	0
MOREHEAD ST.								
Robert Laughlin (Morehead St. 1937) 1956, 57, 61	3	3	4	0	0	0	0	0
Wayne Martin (Morehead St. 1968) 1983, 84	2	1	2	0	0	0	0	0
TOTAL	5	4	6	0	0	0	0	0
MT. ST. MARY'S								
James Phelan (La Salle 1951) 1995, 99	2	0	2	0	0	0	0	0
TOTAL	2	0	2	0	0	0	0	0
MURRAY ST.								
Cal Luther (Valparaiso 1951) 1964, 69	2	0	2	0	0	0	0	0
Steve Newton (Indiana St. 1963) 1988, 90, 91	3	1	3	0	0	0	0	0
Scott Edgar (Pitt.-Johnstown 1978) 1992, 95	2	0	2	0	0	0	0	0
Mark Gottfried (Alabama 1987) 1997, 98	2	0	2	0	0	0	0	0
Tevester Anderson (Ark.-Pine Bluff 1962) 1999, 2002	2	0	2	0	0	0	0	0
TOTAL	11	1	11	0	0	0	0	0
NAVY								
Ben Carnevale (New York U. 1938) 1947RR, 53, 54RR, 59, 60	5	4	6	0	0	0	0	2
Paul Evans (Ithaca 1967) 1985, 86RR	2	4	2	0	0	0	0	1
Pete Herrmann (Geneseo St. 1970) 1987	1	0	1	0	0	0	0	0
Don DeVoe (Ohio St. 1964) 1994, 97, 98	3	0	3	0	0	0	0	0
TOTAL	11	8	12	0	0	0	0	3
NEBRASKA								
Moe Iba (Oklahoma St. 1962) 1986	1	0	1	0	0	0	0	0
Danny Nee (St. Marys of the Plains 1971) 1991, 92, 93, 94, 98	5	0	5	0	0	0	0	0
TOTAL	6	0	6	0	0	0	0	0
UNLV								
Jerry Tarkanian (Fresno St. 1956) 1975, 76, 77-3d, 83, 84, 85, 86, 87-T3d, 88, 89RR, 90-CH, 91-T3d	12	30	11	1	0	3	0	1
Bill Bayno (Sacred Heart 1985) 1998, 2000	2	0	2	0	0	0	0	0
TOTAL	14	30	13	1	0	3	0	1
NEVADA								
Sonny Allen (Marshall 1959) 1984, 85	2	0	2	0	0	0	0	0
TOTAL	2	0	2	0	0	0	0	0
NEW MEXICO								
Bob King (Iowa 1947) 1968	1	0	2	0	0	0	0	0
Norm Ellenberger (Butler 1955) 1974, 78	2	2	2	0	0	0	0	0
Dave Bliss (Cornell 1965) 1991, 93, 94, 96, 97, 98, 99	7	4	7	0	0	0	0	0
TOTAL	10	6	11	0	0	0	0	0
NEW MEXICO ST.*								
George McCarty (New Mexico St. 1950) 1952	1	0	2	0	0	0	0	0
Presley Askew (Southeastern Okla. 1930) 1959, 60	2	0	2	0	0	0	0	0
Ken Hayes (Northeastern St. 1956) 1979	1	0	1	0	0	0	0	0
Neil McCarthy (Sacramento St. 1965) 1990, 91, 92, 93, 94	5	3	5	0	0	0	0	0
Lou Henson (New Mexico St. 1955) 1967, 68, 69, 70-3d, 71, 75, 99	7	7	8	0	0	1	0	0
TOTAL	16	10	18	0	0	1	0	0
NEW ORLEANS								
Benny Dees (Wyoming 1958) 1987	1	1	1	0	0	0	0	0
Tim Floyd (Louisiana Tech 1977) 1991, 93	2	0	2	0	0	0	0	0
Tic Price (Virginia Tech 1979) 1996	1	0	1	0	0	0	0	0
TOTAL	4	1	4	0	0	0	0	0
NEW YORK U.								
Howard Cann (New York U. 1920) 1943RR, 45-2d, 46RR	3	3	4	0	1	0	0	2
Lou Rossini (Columbia 1948) 1960-4th, 62, 63	3	6	5	0	0	0	1	0
TOTAL	6	9	9	0	1	0	1	2
NIAGARA								
Frank Layden (Niagara 1955) 1970	1	1	2	0	0	0	0	0
TOTAL	1	1	2	0	0	0	0	0
NICHOLLS ST.								
Rickey Broussard (La.-Lafayette 1970) 1995, 98	2	0	2	0	0	0	0	0
TOTAL	2	0	2	0	0	0	0	0
NORTH CAROLINA								
Bill Lange (Wittenberg 1921) 1941RR	1	0	2	0	0	0	0	1
Ben Carnevale (New York U. 1938) 1946-2d	1	2	1	0	1	0	0	0
Frank McGuire [St. John's (N.Y.) 1936] 1957-CH, 59	2	5	1	1	0	0	0	0
Dean Smith (Kansas 1953) 1967-4th, 68-2d, 69-4th, 72-3d, 75 76, 77-2d, 78, 79, 80, 81-2d, 82-CH, 83RR, 84, 85RR 86, 87RR, 88RR, 89, 90, 91-T3d, 92, 93-CH, 94, 95-T3d, 96, 97-T3d	27	65	27	2	3	4	2	4
Bill Guthridge (Kansas 1963) 1998-T3d, 99, 2000-T3d	3	8	3	0	0	2	0	0
Matt Doherty (North Carolina 1984) 2001	1	1	1	0	0	0	0	0
TOTAL	35	81	35	3	4	6	2	5
N.C. A&T								
Don Corbett [Lincoln (Mo.) 1965] 1982, 83, 84, 85, 86, 87, 88	7	0	7	0	0	0	0	0
Jeff Capel (Fayetteville St. 1977) 1994	1	0	1	0	0	0	0	0
Roy Thomas (Baylor 1974) 1995	1	0	1	0	0	0	0	0
TOTAL	9	0	9	0	0	0	0	0
UNC ASHEVILLE								
Eddie Biedenback (North Carolina St. 1968) 2003	1	1	1	0	0	0	0	0
TOTAL	1	1	1	0	0	0	0	0
UNC GREENSBORO								
Randy Peele (Va. Wesleyan 1980) 1996	1	0	1	0	0	0	0	0
Fran McCaffery (Pennsylvania 1982) 2001	1	0	1	0	0	0	0	0
TOTAL	2	0	2	0	0	0	0	0
UNC WILMINGTON								
Jerry Wainwright (Colorado Col. 1968) 2000, 02	2	1	2	0	0	0	0	0
Brad Brownell (DePauw 1991) 2003	1	0	1	0	0	0	0	0
TOTAL	3	1	3	0	0	0	0	0
NORTH CAROLINA ST.*								
Everett Case (Wisconsin 1923) 1950-3d, 51RR, 52, 54, 56	5	6	6	0	0	1	0	1
Press Maravich (Davis & Elkins 1941) 1965	1	1	1	0	0	0	0	0
Norm Sloan (North Carolina St. 1951) 1970, 74-CH, 80	3	5	2	1	0	0	0	0

	Yrs.	Won	Lost	CH	2D	3d%	4th	RR
Jim Valvano (Rutgers 1967) 1982, 83-CH, 85RR, 86RR 87, 88, 89	7	14	6	1	0	0	0	2
Les Robinson (North Carolina St. 1964) 1991	1	1	1	0	0	0	0	0
Herb Sendek (Carnegie Mellon 1985) 2002, 03	2	1	2	0	0	0	0	0
TOTAL	19	28	18	2	0	1	0	3

NORTH TEXAS

	Yrs.	Won	Lost	CH	2D	3d%	4th	RR
Jimmy Gales (Alcorn St. 1963) 1988	1	0	1	0	0	0	0	0
TOTAL	1	0	1	0	0	0	0	0

NORTHEASTERN

	Yrs.	Won	Lost	CH	2D	3d%	4th	RR
Jim Calhoun (American Int'l 1966) 1981, 82, 84, 85, 86	5	3	5	0	0	0	0	0
Karl Fogel (Colby 1968) 1987, 91	2	0	2	0	0	0	0	0
TOTAL	7	3	7	0	0	0	0	0

NORTHERN ARIZ.

	Yrs.	Won	Lost	CH	2D	3d%	4th	RR
Ben Howland (Weber St. 1980) 1998	1	0	1	0	0	0	0	0
Mike Adras (UC Santa Barb. 1983) 2000	1	0	1	0	0	0	0	0
TOTAL	2	0	2	0	0	0	0	0

NORTHERN ILL.

	Yrs.	Won	Lost	CH	2D	3d%	4th	RR
John McDougal (Evansville 1950) 1982..	1	0	1	0	0	0	0	0
Jim Molinari (Ill. Wesleyan 1977) 1991	1	0	1	0	0	0	0	0
Brian Hammel (Bentley 1975) 1996	1	0	1	0	0	0	0	0
TOTAL	3	0	3	0	0	0	0	0

NORTHERN IOWA

	Yrs.	Won	Lost	CH	2D	3d%	4th	RR
Eldon Miller (Wittenberg 1961) 1990	1	1	1	0	0	0	0	0
TOTAL	1	1	1	0	0	0	0	0

NORTHWESTERN ST.

	Yrs.	Won	Lost	CH	2D	3d%	4th	RR
Mike McConathy (Louisiana Tech 1977) 2001	1	1	1	0	0	0	0	0
TOTAL	1	1	1	0	0	0	0	0

NOTRE DAME

	Yrs.	Won	Lost	CH	2D	3d%	4th	RR
John Jordan (Notre Dame 1935) 1953RR, 54RR, 57, 58RR, 60, 63	6	8	6	0	0	0	0	3
Johnny Dee (Notre Dame 1946) 1965, 69, 70, 71	4	2	6	0	0	0	0	0
Richard "Digger" Phelps (Rider 1963) 1974,75, 76, 77, 78-4th, 79RR, 80, 81, 85, 86, 87, 88, 89, 90	14	15	16	0	0	0	1	1
Mike Brey (George Washington 1982) 2001, 02, 03	3	4	3	0	0	0	0	0
TOTAL	27	29	31	0	0	0	1	4

OHIO

	Yrs.	Won	Lost	CH	2D	3d%	4th	RR
James Snyder (Ohio 1941) 1960, 61, 64RR, 65, 70, 72, 74	7	3	8	0	0	0	0	1
Danny Nee (St. Mary of the Plains 1971) 1983, 85	2	1	2	0	0	0	0	0
Larry Hunter (Ohio 1971) 1994	1	0	1	0	0	0	0	0
TOTAL	10	4	11	0	0	0	0	1

OHIO ST.

	Yrs.	Won	Lost	CH	2D	3d%	4th	RR
Harold Olsen (Wisconsin 1917) 1939-2d, 44-T3d, 45-T3d, 46-3d	4	6	4	0	1	3	0	0
William "Tippy" Dye (Ohio St. 1937) 1950RR	1	1	1	0	0	0	0	1
Fred Taylor (Ohio St. 1950) 1960-CH, 61-2d, 62-2d, 68-3d, 71RR..............	5	14	4	1	2	1	0	1
Eldon Miller (Wittenberg 1961) 1980, 82, 83, 85	4	3	4	0	0	0	0	0
Gary Williams (Maryland 1967) 1987...	1	1	1	0	0	0	0	0
Randy Ayers [Miami (Ohio) 1978] 1990, 91, 92RR	3	6	3	0	0	0	0	1
Jim O'Brien (Boston College 1971) 1999-T3d, 2000, 01, 02	4	6	4	0	0	1	0	0
TOTAL	22	37	21	1	3	5	0	3

OKLAHOMA

	Yrs.	Won	Lost	CH	2D	3d%	4th	RR
Bruce Drake (Oklahoma 1929) 1939-T3d, 43RR, 47-2d	3	4	3	0	1	1	0	1
Dave Bliss (Cornell 1965) 1979............	1	1	1	0	0	0	0	0
Billy Tubbs (Lamar 1958) 1983, 84, 85RR, 86, 87, 88-2d, 89, 90, 92	9	15	9	0	1	0	0	1
Kelvin Sampson (UNC Pembroke 1978) 1995, 96, 97, 98, 99, 2000, 01, 02-T3d, 03RR	9	10	9	0	0	1	0	1
TOTAL	22	30	22	0	2	2	0	3

OKLAHOMA CITY

	Yrs.	Won	Lost	CH	2D	3d%	4th	RR
Doyle Parrack (Oklahoma St. 1945) 1952, 53, 54, 55	4	1	5	0	0	0	0	0
A.E. "Abe" Lemons (Oklahoma City 1949) 1956RR, 57RR, 63, 64, 65, 66, 73	7	7	8	0	0	0	0	2
TOTAL	11	8	13	0	0	0	0	2

OKLAHOMA ST.

	Yrs.	Won	Lost	CH	2D	3d%	4th	RR
Henry Iba [Westminster (Mo.) 1928] 1945-CH, 46-CH, 49-2d, 51-4th, 53-RR, 54-RR, 58RR, 65RR	8	15	7	2	1	0	1	4
Paul Hansen (Oklahoma City 1950) 1983	1	0	1	0	0	0	0	0
Eddie Sutton (Oklahoma St. 1958) 1991, 92, 93, 94, 95-T3d, 98, 99, 2000RR, 01, 02, 03	11	16	11	0	0	1	0	1
TOTAL	20	31	19	2	1	1	1	5

OLD DOMINION

	Yrs.	Won	Lost	CH	2D	3d%	4th	RR
Paul Webb (William & Mary 1951) 1980, 82, 85	3	0	3	0	0	0	0	0
Tom Young (Maryland 1958) 1986	1	1	1	0	0	0	0	0
Oliver Purnell (Old Dominion 1975) 1992	1	0	1	0	0	0	0	0
Jeff Capel (Fayetteville St. 1977) 1995, 97	2	1	2	0	0	0	0	0
TOTAL	7	2	7	0	0	0	0	0

ORAL ROBERTS

	Yrs.	Won	Lost	CH	2D	3d%	4th	RR
Ken Trickey (Middle Tenn. 1954) 1974RR	1	2	1	0	0	0	0	1
Dick Acres (UC Santa Barb.) 1984.........	1	0	1	0	0	0	0	0
TOTAL	2	2	2	0	0	0	0	1

OREGON

	Yrs.	Won	Lost	CH	2D	3d%	4th	RR
Howard Hobson (Oregon 1926) 1939-CH	1	3	0	1	0	0	0	0
John Warren (Oregon 1928) 1945RR........	1	1	1	0	0	0	0	1
Steve Belko (Idaho 1939) 1960RR, 61 ...	2	2	2	0	0	0	0	1
Jerry Green (Appalachian St. 1968) 1995	1	0	1	0	0	0	0	0
Ernie Kent (Oregon 1977) 2000, 02RR, 03	3	3	3	0	0	0	0	1
TOTAL	8	9	7	1	0	0	0	3

OREGON ST.*

	Yrs.	Won	Lost	CH	2D	3d%	4th	RR
Amory "Slats" Gill (Oregon St. 1925) 1947RR, 49-4th, 55RR, 62RR, 63-4th, 64	6	8	8	0	0	0	2	3
Paul Valenti (Oregon St. 1942) 1966RR	1	1	1	0	0	0	0	1
Ralph Miller (Kansas 1942) 1975, 80, 81, 82RR, 84, 85, 88, 89	8	3	9	0	0	0	0	1
Jim Anderson (Oregon St. 1959) 1990...	1	0	1	0	0	0	0	0
TOTAL	16	12	19	0	0	0	2	5

PACIFIC (CAL.)

	Yrs.	Won	Lost	CH	2D	3d%	4th	RR
Dick Edwards (Culver-Stockton 1952) 1966, 67RR, 71	3	2	4	0	0	0	0	1
Stan Morrison (California 1962) 1979 ...	1	0	1	0	0	0	0	0
Bob Thomason [Pacific (Cal.) 1971] 1997	1	0	1	0	0	0	0	0
TOTAL	5	2	6	0	0	0	0	1

PENN ST.

	Yrs.	Won	Lost	CH	2D	3d%	4th	RR
John Lawther [Westminster (Pa.) 1919] 1942RR	1	1	1	0	0	0	0	1
Elmer Gross (Penn St. 1942) 1952, 54-3d	2	4	3	0	0	1	0	0
John Egli (Penn St. 1947) 1955, 65	2	1	3	0	0	0	0	0
Bruce Parkhill (Lock Haven 1971) 1991..	1	1	1	0	0	0	0	0
Jerry Dunn (George Mason 1980) 1996, 2001	2	2	2	0	0	0	0	0
TOTAL	9	9	11	0	0	1	0	1

PENNSYLVANIA

	Yrs.	Won	Lost	CH	2D	3d%	4th	RR
Howard "Howie" Dallmar (Stanford 1948) 1953	1	1	1	0	0	0	0	0
Dick Harter (Pennsylvania 1953) 1970, 71RR	2	2	2	0	0	0	0	1
Chuck Daly (Bloomsburg 1953) 1972RR, 73, 74, 75	4	3	5	0	0	0	0	1
Bob Weinhauer (Cortland St. 1961) 1978, 79-4th, 80, 82	4	6	5	0	0	0	1	0
Craig Littlepage (Pennsylvania 1973) 1985	1	0	1	0	0	0	0	0
Tom Schneider (Bucknell 1969) 1987 ...	1	0	1	0	0	0	0	0
Fran Dunphy (La Salle 1970) 1993, 94, 95, 99, 2000, 02, 03	7	1	7	0	0	0	0	0
TOTAL	20	13	22	0	0	0	1	2

PEPPERDINE

	Yrs.	Won	Lost	CH	2D	3d%	4th	RR
Al Duer (Emporia St. 1929) 1944RR.......	1	0	2	0	0	0	0	1
R.L. "Duck" Dowell (Northwest Mo. St. 1933) 1962	1	1	1	0	0	0	0	0
Gary Colson (David Lipscomb 1956) 1976, 79	2	2	2	0	0	0	0	0
Jim Harrick [Charleston (W.Va.) 1960] 1982, 83, 85, 86	4	1	4	0	0	0	0	0
Tom Asbury (Wyoming 1967) 1991, 92, 94	3	0	3	0	0	0	0	0
Jan van Breda Kolff (Vanderbilt 1974) 2000	1	1	1	0	0	0	0	0
Paul Westphal (Southern California 1972) 2002	1	0	1	0	0	0	0	0
TOTAL	13	5	14	0	0	0	0	1

PITTSBURGH

	Yrs.	Won	Lost	CH	2D	3d%	4th	RR
Henry Carlson (Pittsburgh 1917) 1941-T3d	1	1	1	0	0	1	0	0
Bob Timmons (Pittsburgh 1933) 1957, 58, 63	3	1	4	0	0	0	0	0

	Yrs.	Won	Lost	CH	2D	3d%	4th	RR
Charles "Buzz" Ridl [Westminster (Pa.) 1942] 1974RR	1	2	1	0	0	0	0	1
Roy Chipman (Maine 1961) 1981, 82, 85	3	1	3	0	0	0	0	0
Paul Evans (Ithaca 1967) 1987, 88, 89, 91, 93	5	3	5	0	0	0	0	0
Ben Howland (Weber St. 1980) 2002, 03	2	4	2	0	0	0	0	0
TOTAL	15	12	16	0	0	1	0	1
PORTLAND								
Al Negratti (Seton Hall 1943) 1959	1	0	1	0	0	0	0	0
Rob Chavez (Mesa St. 1980) 1996	1	0	1	0	0	0	0	0
TOTAL	2	0	2	0	0	0	0	0
PRAIRIE VIEW								
Elwood Plummer (Jackson St. 1966) 1998	1	0	1	0	0	0	0	0
TOTAL	1	0	1	0	0	0	0	0
PRINCETON#								
Franklin Cappon (Michigan 1924) 1952, 55, 60	3	0	5	0	0	0	0	0
J.L. "Jake" McCandless (Princeton 1951) 1961	1	1	2	0	0	0	0	0
Butch van Breda Kolff (Princeton 1947) 1963, 64, 65-3d, 67	4	7	5	0	0	1	0	0
Pete Carril (Lafayette 1952) 1969, 76, 77, 81, 83, 84, 89, 90, 91, 92, 96	11	4	11	0	0	0	0	0
Bill Carmody [Union (N.Y.) 1975] 1997, 98	2	1	2	0	0	0	0	0
John Thompson III (Princeton 1989) 2001	1	0	1	0	0	0	0	0
TOTAL	22	13	26	0	0	1	0	0
PROVIDENCE								
Joe Mullaney (Holy Cross 1949) 1964, 65RR, 66	3	2	3	0	0	0	0	1
Dave Gavitt (Dartmouth 1959) 1972, 73-4th, 74, 77, 78	5	5	6	0	0	0	1	0
Rick Pitino (Massachusetts 1974) 1987 tie-3d	1	4	1	0	0	1	0	0
Rick Barnes (Lenior-Rhyne 1977) 1989, 90, 94	3	0	3	0	0	0	0	0
Pete Gillen (Fairfield 1968) 1997RR	1	3	1	0	0	0	0	1
Tim Welsh (Potsdam St. 1984) 2001	1	0	1	0	0	0	0	0
TOTAL	14	14	15	0	0	1	1	2
PURDUE								
George King [Charleston (W.Va.) 1950] 1969-2d	1	3	1	0	1	0	0	0
Fred Schaus (West Virginia 1949) 1977	1	0	1	0	0	0	0	0
Lee Rose (Transylvania 1958) 1980-3d	1	5	1	0	0	1	0	0
Gene Keady (Kansas St. 1958) 1983, 84, 85, 86, 87, 88, 90, 91, 93, 94RR, 95, 96, 97, 98, 99, 2000RR, 03	17	19	17	0	0	0	0	2
TOTAL	20	27	20	0	1	1	0	2
RADFORD								
Ron Bradley (Eastern Nazarene 1973) 1998	1	0	1	0	0	0	0	0
TOTAL	1	0	1	0	0	0	0	0
RHODE ISLAND								
Ernie Calverley (Rhode Island 1946) 1961, 66	2	0	2	0	0	0	0	0
Jack Kraft (St. Joseph's 1942) 1978	1	0	1	0	0	0	0	0
Tom Penders (Connecticut 1967) 1988	1	2	1	0	0	0	0	0
Al Skinner (Massachusetts 1974) 1993, 97	2	1	2	0	0	0	0	0
Jim Harrick [Charleston (W.Va.) 1960] 1998, 99	2	3	2	0	0	0	0	1
TOTAL	8	6	8	0	0	0	0	1
RICE								
Byron "Buster" Brannon (TCU 1933) 1940RR, 42RR	2	1	3	0	0	0	0	2
Don Suman (Rice 1944) 1954	1	1	1	0	0	0	0	0
Don Knodel [Miami (Ohio) 1953] 1970	1	0	1	0	0	0	0	0
TOTAL	4	2	5	0	0	0	0	2
RICHMOND								
Dick Tarrant (Fordham 1951) 1984, 86, 88, 90, 91	5	5	5	0	0	0	0	0
John Beilein (Wheeling Jesuit 1975) 1998	1	1	1	0	0	0	0	0
TOTAL	6	6	6	0	0	0	0	0
RIDER								
John Carpenter (Penn St. 1958) 1984	1	0	1	0	0	0	0	0
Kevin Bannon (St. Peter's 1979) 1993, 94	2	0	2	0	0	0	0	0
TOTAL	3	0	3	0	0	0	0	0
ROBERT MORRIS								
Matt Furjanic (Point Park 1973) 1982, 83	2	1	2	0	0	0	0	0
Jarrett Durham (Duquesne 1971) 1989, 90, 92	3	0	3	0	0	0	0	0
TOTAL	5	1	5	0	0	0	0	0

	Yrs.	Won	Lost	CH	2D	3d%	4th	RR
RUTGERS								
Tom Young (Maryland 1958) 1975, 76-4th, 79, 83	4	5	5	0	0	0	1	0
Bob Wenzel (Rutgers 1971) 1989, 91	2	0	2	0	0	0	0	0
TOTAL	6	5	7	0	0	0	1	0
ST. BONAVENTURE								
Eddie Donovan (St. Bonaventure 1950) 1961	1	2	1	0	0	0	0	0
Larry Weise (St. Bonaventure 1958) 1968, 70-4th	2	4	4	0	0	0	1	0
Jim Satalin (St. Bonaventure 1969) 1978	1	0	1	0	0	0	0	0
Jim Baron (St. Bonaventure 1977) 2000	1	0	1	0	0	0	0	0
TOTAL	5	6	7	0	0	0	1	0
ST. FRANCIS (PA.)								
Jim Baron (St. Bonaventure 1977) 1991	1	0	1	0	0	0	0	0
TOTAL	1	0	1	0	0	0	0	0
ST. JOHN'S (N.Y.)								
Frank McGuire [St. John's (N.Y.) 1936] 1951RR, 52-2d	2	5	2	0	1	0	0	1
Joe Lapchick (No college) 1961	1	0	1	0	0	0	0	0
Frank Mulzoff [St. John's (N.Y.) 1951] 1973	1	0	1	0	0	0	0	0
Lou Carnesecca [St. John's (N.Y.) 1946] 1967, 68, 69, 76, 77, 78, 79RR, 80, 82, 83, 84, 85-T3d, 86, 87, 88, 90, 91RR, 92	18	17	20	0	0	1	0	2
Brian Mahoney (Manhattan 1971) 1993	1	1	1	0	0	0	0	0
Fran Fraschilla (Brooklyn 1980) 1998	1	0	1	0	0	0	0	0
Mike Jarvis (Northeastern 1968) 1999RR, 2000, 02	3	4	3	0	0	0	0	1
TOTAL	27	27	29	0	1	1	0	4
ST. JOSEPH'S*								
John "Jack" Ramsay (St. Joseph's 1949) 1959, 60, 61-3d, 62, 63RR, 65, 66	7	8	11	0	0	1	0	1
John "Jack" McKinney (St. Joseph's 1957) 1969, 71, 73, 74	4	0	4	0	0	0	0	0
Jim Lynam (St. Joseph's 1964) 1981RR	1	3	1	0	0	0	0	1
Jim Boyle (St. Joseph's 1964) 1982, 86	2	1	2	0	0	0	0	0
Phil Martelli (Widener 1976) 1997, 2001, 03	3	3	3	0	0	0	0	0
TOTAL	17	15	21	0	0	1	0	2
ST. LOUIS								
Eddie Hickey (Creighton 1927) 1952RR, 57	2	1	3	0	0	0	0	1
Charlie Spoonhour (School of Ozarks 1961) 1994, 95, 98	3	2	3	0	0	0	0	0
Lorenzo Romar (Washington 1980) 2000	1	0	1	0	0	0	0	0
TOTAL	6	3	7	0	0	0	0	1
ST. MARY'S (CAL.)								
James Weaver (DePaul 1947) 1959RR	1	1	1	0	0	0	0	1
Lynn Nance (Washington 1965) 1989	1	0	1	0	0	0	0	0
Ernie Kent (Oregon 1977) 1997	1	0	1	0	0	0	0	0
TOTAL	3	1	3	0	0	0	0	1
ST. PETER'S								
Ted Fiore (Seton Hall 1962) 1991, 95	2	0	2	0	0	0	0	0
TOTAL	2	0	2	0	0	0	0	0
SAM HOUSTON ST.								
Bob Marlin (Mississippi St. 1981) 2003	1	0	1	0	0	0	0	0
TOTAL	1	0	1	0	0	0	0	0
SAMFORD								
Jimmy Tillette (Our Lady of Holy Cross 1975) 1999, 2000	2	0	2	0	0	0	0	0
TOTAL	2	0	2	0	0	0	0	0
SAN DIEGO								
Jim Brovelli (San Francisco 1964) 1984	1	0	1	0	0	0	0	0
Hank Egan (Navy 1960) 1987	1	0	1	0	0	0	0	0
Brad Holland (UCLA 1979) 2003	1	0	1	0	0	0	0	0
TOTAL	3	0	3	0	0	0	0	0
SAN DIEGO ST.								
Tim Vezie (Denver 1967) 1975, 76	2	0	2	0	0	0	0	0
Dave "Smokey" Gaines (LeMoyne-Owen 1963) 1985	1	0	1	0	0	0	0	0
Steve Fisher (Illinois St. 1967) 2002	1	0	1	0	0	0	0	0
TOTAL	4	0	4	0	0	0	0	0
SAN FRANCISCO								
Phil Woolpert (Loyola Marymount 1940) 1955-CH, 56-CH, 57-3d, 58	4	13	2	2	0	1	0	0
Peter Peletta (Sacramento St. 1950) 1963, 64RR, 65RR	3	3	3	0	0	0	0	2
Bob Gaillard (San Francisco 1962) 1972, 73RR, 74RR, 77, 78	5	4	5	0	0	0	0	2
Dan Belluomini (San Francisco 1964) 1979	1	1	1	0	0	0	0	0
Peter Barry (San Francisco 1970) 1981, 82	2	0	2	0	0	0	0	0
Phil Mathews (UC Irvine 1972) 1998	1	0	1	0	0	0	0	0
TOTAL	16	21	14	2	0	1	0	4

	Yrs.	Won	Lost	CH	2D	3d%	4th	RR
SAN JOSE ST.								
Walter McPherson (San Jose St. 1940) 1951	1	0	1	0	0	0	0	0
Bill Berry (Michigan St. 1965) 1980	1	0	1	0	0	0	0	0
Stan Morrison (California 1962) 1996	1	0	1	0	0	0	0	0
TOTAL	3	0	3	0	0	0	0	0
SANTA CLARA								
Bob Feerick (Santa Clara 1941) 1952-4th, 53RR, 54RR, 60	4	6	6	0	0	0	1	2
Dick Garibaldi (Santa Clara 1957) 1968RR, 69RR, 70	3	3	3	0	0	0	0	2
Carroll Williams (San Jose St. 1955) 1987	1	0	1	0	0	0	0	0
Dick Davey [Pacific (Cal.) 1964] 1993, 95, 96	3	2	3	0	0	0	0	0
TOTAL	11	11	13	0	0	0	1	4
SEATTLE#								
Al Brightman [Charleston (W.Va.)] 1953, 54, 55, 56	4	4	6	0	0	0	0	0
John Castellani (Notre Dame 1952) 1958-2d	1	4	1	0	1	0	0	0
Vince Cazzetta (Arnold 1950) 1961, 62	2	0	2	0	0	0	0	0
Clair Markey (Seattle 1963) 1963	1	0	1	0	0	0	0	0
Bob Boyd (Southern California 1953) 1964	1	2	1	0	0	0	0	0
Lionel Purcell (UC Santa Barb. 1952) 1967	1	0	1	0	0	0	0	0
Morris Buckwalter (Utah 1956) 1969	1	0	1	0	0	0	0	0
TOTAL	11	10	13	0	1	0	0	0
SETON HALL								
P. J. Carlesimo (Fordham 1971) 1988, 89-2d, 91RR, 92, 93, 94	6	12	6	0	1	0	0	1
Tommy Amaker (Duke 1987) 2000	1	2	1	0	0	0	0	0
TOTAL	7	14	7	0	1	0	0	1
SIENA								
Mike Deane (Potsdam St. 1974) 1989	1	1	1	0	0	0	0	0
Paul Hewitt (St. John Fisher 1985) 1999	1	0	1	0	0	0	0	0
Rob Lanier (St. Bonaventure 1990) 2002	1	1	1	0	0	0	0	0
TOTAL	3	2	3	0	0	0	0	0
SOUTH ALA.								
Cliff Ellis (Florida St. 1968) 1979, 80	2	0	2	0	0	0	0	0
Ronnie Arrow (Texas St. 1969) 1989, 91	2	1	2	0	0	0	0	0
Bill Musselman (Wittenberg 1962) 1997	1	0	1	0	0	0	0	0
Bob Weltlich (Ohio St. 1967) 1998	1	0	1	0	0	0	0	0
TOTAL	6	1	6	0	0	0	0	0
SOUTH CAROLINA								
Frank McGuire [St. John's (N.Y.) 1936] 1971, 72, 73, 74	4	4	5	0	0	0	0	0
George Felton (South Carolina 1975) 1989	1	0	1	0	0	0	0	0
Eddie Fogler (North Carolina 1970) 1997, 98	2	0	2	0	0	0	0	0
TOTAL	7	4	8	0	0	0	0	0
SOUTH CAROLINA ST.								
Cy Alexander (Catawba 1975) 1989, 96, 98, 2000, 03	5	0	5	0	0	0	0	0
TOTAL	5	0	5	0	0	0	0	0
SOUTH FLA.								
Bobby Paschal (Stetson 1964) 1990, 92	2	0	2	0	0	0	0	0
TOTAL	2	0	2	0	0	0	0	0
SOUTHEAST MO. ST.								
Gary Garner (Missouri 1965) 2000	1	0	1	0	0	0	0	0
TOTAL	1	0	1	0	0	0	0	0
SOUTHERN U.								
Carl Stewart (Grambling 1954) 1981	1	0	1	0	0	0	0	0
Robert Hopkins (Grambling 1956) 1985	1	0	1	0	0	0	0	0
Ben Jobe (Fisk 1956) 1987, 88, 89, 93	4	1	4	0	0	0	0	0
TOTAL	6	1	6	0	0	0	0	0
SOUTHERN CALIFORNIA								
Justin "Sam" Barry (Lawrence 13) 1940-T3d	1	1	1	0	0	1	0	0
Forrest Twogood (Iowa 1929) 1954-4th, 60, 61	3	3	5	0	0	0	1	0
Bob Boyd (Southern California 1953) 1979	1	1	1	0	0	0	0	0
Stan Morrison (California 1962) 1982, 85	2	0	2	0	0	0	0	0
George Raveling (Villanova 1960) 1991, 92	2	1	2	0	0	0	0	0
Henry Bibby (UCLA 1972) 1997, 2001RR, 02	3	3	3	0	0	0	0	1
TOTAL	12	9	14	0	0	1	1	1
SOUTHERN ILL.								
Paul Lambert (William Jewell 1956) 1977	1	1	1	0	0	0	0	0
Rich Herrin (McKendree 1956) 1993, 94, 95	3	0	3	0	0	0	0	0
Bruce Weber (Wis.-Milwaukee 1978) 2002, 03	2	2	2	0	0	0	0	0
TOTAL	6	3	6	0	0	0	0	0
SOUTHERN METHODIST								
E.O. "Doc" Hayes (North Texas 1927) 1955, 56-4th, 57, 65, 66, 67RR	6	7	8	0	0	0	1	1
Dave Bliss (Cornell 1965) 1984, 85, 88	3	3	3	0	0	0	0	0
John Shumate (Notre Dame 1974) 1993	1	0	1	0	0	0	0	0
TOTAL	10	10	12	0	0	0	1	1
SOUTHERN MISS.								
M.K. Turk (Livingston 1964) 1990, 91	2	0	2	0	0	0	0	0
TOTAL	2	0	2	0	0	0	0	0
SOUTHERN UTAH								
Bill Evans (Southern Utah 1972) 2001	1	0	1	0	0	0	0	0
TOTAL	1	0	1	0	0	0	0	0
SOUTHWEST MO. ST.								
Charlie Spoonhour (School of Ozarks 1961) 1987, 88, 89, 90, 92	5	1	5	0	0	0	0	0
Steve Alford (Indiana 1987) 1999	1	2	1	0	0	0	0	0
TOTAL	6	3	6	0	0	0	0	0
SPRINGFIELD								
Ed Hickox (Ohio Wesleyan 1905) 1940RR	1	0	1	0	0	0	0	1
TOTAL	1	0	1	0	0	0	0	1
STANFORD								
Everett Dean (Indiana 1921) 1942-CH	1	3	0	1	0	0	0	0
Mike Montgomery (Long Beach St. 1968) 1989, 92, 95, 96, 97, 98-T3d, 99, 2000, 01RR, 02, 03	11	15	11	0	0	1	0	1
TOTAL	12	18	11	1	0	1	0	1
SYRACUSE								
Marc Guley (Syracuse 1936) 1957RR	1	2	1	0	0	0	0	1
Fred Lewis (Eastern Ky. 1946) 1966RR	1	1	1	0	0	0	0	1
Roy Danforth (Southern Miss. 1962) 1973, 74, 75-4th, 76	4	5	5	0	0	0	1	0
Jim Boeheim (Syracuse 1966) 1977, 78, 79, 80, 83, 84, 85, 86, 87-2d, 89RR, 90, 91, 92, 94, 95, 96-2d, 98, 99, 2000, 01, 03-CH	22	38	21	1	2	0	0	1
TOTAL	28	46	28	1	2	0	1	3
TEMPLE								
Josh Cody (Vanderbilt 1920) 1944RR	1	1	1	0	0	0	0	1
Harry Litwack (Temple 1930) 1956-3d, 58-3d, 64, 67, 70, 72	6	7	6	0	0	2	0	0
Don Casey (Temple 1970) 1979	1	0	1	0	0	0	0	0
John Chaney (Bethune-Cookman 1955) 1984, 85, 86, 87, 88RR, 90, 91RR, 92, 93RR, 94, 95, 96, 97, 98, 99RR, 2000, 01RR	17	23	17	0	0	0	0	5
TOTAL	25	31	25	0	0	2	0	6
TENNESSEE								
Ramon "Ray" Mears [Miami (Ohio) 1949] 1967, 76, 77	3	0	4	0	0	0	0	0
Don DeVoe (Ohio St. 1964) 1979, 80, 81, 82, 83, 89	6	5	6	0	0	0	0	0
Jerry Green (Appalachian St. 1968) 1998, 99, 2000, 01	4	3	4	0	0	0	0	0
TOTAL	13	8	14	0	0	0	0	0
TENNESSEE ST.								
Frankie Allen (Roanoke 1971) 1993, 94	2	0	2	0	0	0	0	0
TOTAL	2	0	2	0	0	0	0	0
TENNESSEE TECH								
Johnny Oldham (Western Ky. 1948) 1958, 63	2	0	2	0	0	0	0	0
TOTAL	2	0	2	0	0	0	0	0
TEXAS								
H.C. "Bully" Gilstrap (Texas 1922) 1943-T3d	1	1	1	0	0	1	0	0
Jack Gray (Texas 1935) 1939RR, 47-3d	2	2	3	0	0	1	0	1
Harold Bradley (Hartwick 1934) 1960, 63	2	2	3	0	0	0	0	0
Leon Black (Texas 1953) 1972, 74	2	1	3	0	0	0	0	0
A.E. "Abe" Lemons (Oklahoma City 1949) 1979	1	0	1	0	0	0	0	0
Tom Penders (Connecticut 1967) 1989, 90RR, 91, 92, 94, 95, 96, 97	8	10	8	0	0	0	0	1
Rick Barnes (Lenior-Rhyne 1977) 1999, 2000, 01, 02, 03-T3d	5	7	5	0	0	1	0	0
TOTAL	21	23	24	0	0	3	0	2
TEXAS A&M								
John Floyd (Oklahoma St. 1941) 1951	1	0	1	0	0	0	0	0
Shelby Metcalf (Tex. A&M-Commerce 1953) 1964, 69, 75, 80, 87	5	3	6	0	0	0	0	0
TOTAL	6	3	7	0	0	0	0	0

CHAMPIONSHIPS

	Yrs.	Won	Lost	CH	2D	3d%	4th	RR
TCU								
Byron "Buster" Brannon (TCU 1933) 1952, 53, 59	3	3	3	0	0	0	0	0
Johnny Swaim (TCU 1953) 1968RR, 71	2	1	2	0	0	0	0	1
Jim Killingsworth (Northeastern Okla. St. 1948) 1987	1	1	1	0	0	0	0	0
Billy Tubbs (Lamar 1958) 1998	1	0	1	0	0	0	0	0
TOTAL	7	5	7	0	0	0	0	1
TEXAS-SAN ANTONIO								
Ken Burmeister [St. Mary's (Tex.) 1971] 1988	1	0	1	0	0	0	0	0
Tim Carter (Kansas 1979) 1999	1	0	1	0	0	0	0	0
TOTAL	2	0	2	0	0	0	0	0
TEXAS SOUTHERN								
Robert Moreland (Tougaloo 1962) 1990, 94, 95	3	0	3	0	0	0	0	0
Ronnie Courtney (McMurry 1981) 2003	1	0	1	0	0	0	0	0
TOTAL	4	0	4	0	0	0	0	0
TEXAS ST.								
Jim Wooldridge (Louisiana Tech 1977) 1994	1	0	1	0	0	0	0	0
Mike Miller (Tex. A&M-Commerce 1987) 1997	1	0	1	0	0	0	0	0
TOTAL	2	0	2	0	0	0	0	0
TEXAS TECH								
Polk Robison (Texas Tech 1935) 1954, 56, 61	3	1	3	0	0	0	0	0
Gene Gibson (Texas Tech 1950) 1962	1	1	2	0	0	0	0	0
Gerald Myers (Texas Tech 1959) 1973, 76, 85, 86	4	1	4	0	0	0	0	0
James Dickey (Central Ark. 1976) 1993, 96	2	2	2	0	0	0	0	0
Bob Knight (Ohio St. 1962) 2002	1	0	1	0	0	0	0	0
TOTAL	11	5	12	0	0	0	0	0
TOLEDO								
Jerry Bush [St. John's (N.Y.) 1938] 1954	1	0	1	0	0	0	0	0
Bob Nichols (Toledo 1953) 1967, 79, 80	3	1	3	0	0	0	0	0
TOTAL	4	1	4	0	0	0	0	0
TOWSON								
Terry Truax (Maryland 1968) 1990, 91	2	0	2	0	0	0	0	0
TOTAL	2	0	2	0	0	0	0	0
TRINITY (TEX.)								
Bob Polk (Evansville 1939) 1969	1	0	1	0	0	0	0	0
TOTAL	1	0	1	0	0	0	0	0
TROY ST.								
Don Maestri (Southern Miss. 1968) 2003	1	0	1	0	0	0	0	0
TOTAL	1	0	1	0	0	0	0	1
TUFTS								
Richard Cochran (Tufts 1934) 1945RR	1	0	2	0	0	0	0	1
TOTAL	1	0	2	0	0	0	0	1
TULANE								
Perry Clark (Gettysburg 1974) 1992, 93, 95	3	3	3	0	0	0	0	0
TOTAL	3	3	3	0	0	0	0	0
TULSA								
Clarence Iba (Panhandle St. 1936) 1955	1	1	1	0	0	0	0	0
Nolan Richardson (UTEP 1965) 1982, 84, 85	3	0	3	0	0	0	0	0
J.D. Barnett (Winona St. 1966) 1986, 87	2	0	2	0	0	0	0	0
Tubby Smith (High Point 1973) 1994, 95	2	4	2	0	0	0	0	0
Steve Robinson (Radford 1981) 1996, 97	2	1	2	0	0	0	0	0
Bill Self (Oklahoma St. 1985) 1999, 2000RR	2	4	2	0	0	0	0	1
John Phillips (Oklahoma St. 1973) 2002, 03	2	2	2	0	0	0	0	0
TOTAL	14	12	14	0	0	0	0	1
UCLA*								
John Wooden (Purdue 1932) 1950RR, 52, 56, 62-4th, 63, 64-CH, 65-CH, 67-CH, 68-CH, 69-CH, 70-CH, 71-CH, 72-CH, 73-CH, 74-3d, 75-CH	16	47	10	10	0	1	1	1
Gene Bartow (Truman 1953) 1976-3d, 77	2	5	2	0	0	1	0	0
Gary Cunningham (UCLA 1962) 1978, 79RR	2	3	2	0	0	0	0	1
Larry Brown (North Carolina 1963) 1980-2d, 81	2	5	2	0	1	0	0	0
Larry Farmer (UCLA 1973) 1983	1	0	1	0	0	0	0	0
Walt Hazzard (UCLA 1964) 1987	1	1	1	0	0	0	0	0
Jim Harrick [Charleston (W.Va.) 1960] 1989, 90, 91, 92RR, 93, 94, 95-CH, 96	8	13	7	1	0	0	0	1
Steve Lavin (Chapman 1988) 1997RR, 98, 99, 2000, 01, 02	6	11	6	0	0	0	0	1
TOTAL	38	85	31	11	1	2	1	4
UTAH								
Vadal Petersen (Utah 1920) 1944-CH, 45RR	2	3	2	1	0	0	0	1
Jack Gardner (Southern California 1932) 1955, 56RR, 59, 60, 61-4th, 66-4th	6	8	9	0	0	0	2	1
Jerry Pimm (Southern California 1960) 1977, 78, 79, 81, 83	5	5	5	0	0	0	0	0
Lynn Archibald (Fresno St. 1968) 1986	1	0	1	0	0	0	0	0
Rick Majerus (Marquette 1970) 1991, 93, 95, 96, 97RR, 98-2d, 99, 2000, 02, 03	10	17	10	0	1	0	0	1
TOTAL	24	33	27	1	1	0	2	3
UTAH ST.								
E.L. "Dick" Romney (Utah 1917) 1939RR	1	1	1	0	0	0	0	1
Ladell Andersen (Utah St. 1951) 1962, 63, 64, 70RR, 71	5	4	7	0	0	0	0	1
Gordon "Dutch" Belnap (Utah St. 1958) 1975, 79	2	0	2	0	0	0	0	0
Rod Tueller (Utah St. 1959) 1980, 83, 88	3	0	3	0	0	0	0	0
Larry Eustachy (Long Beach St. 1979) 1998	1	0	1	0	0	0	0	0
Steve Morrill (Gonzaga 1974) 2000, 01, 03	3	1	3	0	0	0	0	0
TOTAL	15	6	17	0	0	0	0	2
UTEP								
Don Haskins (Oklahoma St. 1953) 1963, 64, 66-CH, 67, 70, 75, 84, 85, 86, 87, 88, 89, 90, 92	14	14	13	1	0	0	0	0
TOTAL	14	14	13	1	0	0	0	0
VALPARAISO								
Homer Drew (William Jewell 1966) 1996, 97, 98, 99, 2000, 02	6	2	6	0	0	0	0	0
TOTAL	6	2	6	0	0	0	0	0
VANDERBILT								
Roy Skinner (Presbyterian 1952) 1965RR, 74	2	1	3	0	0	0	0	1
C.M. Newton (Kentucky 1952) 1988, 89	2	2	2	0	0	0	0	0
Eddie Fogler (North Carolina 1970) 1991, 93	2	2	2	0	0	0	0	0
Jan van Breda Kolff (Vanderbilt 1974) 1997	1	0	1	0	0	0	0	0
TOTAL	7	5	8	0	0	0	0	1
VERMONT								
Tom Brennan (Georgia 1971) 2003	1	0	1	0	0	0	0	0
TOTAL	1	0	1	0	0	0	0	0
VILLANOVA*								
Alex Severance (Villanova 1929) 1939-T3d, 49RR, 51, 55	4	4	4	0	0	1	0	1
Jack Kraft (St. Joseph's 1942) 1962RR, 64, 69, 70RR, 71-2d, 72	6	11	7	0	1	0	0	2
Rollie Massimino (Vermont 1956) 1978RR, 80, 81, 82RR, 83RR, 84, 85-CH, 86, 88RR, 90, 91	11	20	10	1	0	0	0	4
Steve Lappas (CCNY 1977) 1995, 96, 97, 99	4	2	4	0	0	0	0	0
TOTAL	25	37	25	1	1	1	0	7
VIRGINIA								
Terry Holland (Davidson 1964) 1976, 81-3d, 82, 83RR, 84-T3d, 86, 87, 89RR, 90	9	15	9	0	0	2	0	2
Jeff Jones (Virginia 1982) 1991, 93, 94, 95RR, 97	5	6	5	0	0	0	0	1
Pete Gillen (Fairfield 1968) 2001	1	0	1	0	0	0	0	0
TOTAL	15	21	15	0	0	2	0	3
VA. COMMONWEALTH								
J.D. Barnett (Winona St. 1966) 1980, 81, 83, 84, 85	5	4	5	0	0	0	0	0
Sonny Smith (Milligan 1958) 1996	1	0	1	0	0	0	0	0
TOTAL	6	4	6	0	0	0	0	0
VMI								
Louis "Weenie" Miller (Richmond 1947) 1964	1	0	1	0	0	0	0	0
Bill Blair (VMI 1964) 1976RR	1	2	1	0	0	0	0	1
Charlie Schmaus (VMI 1966) 1977	1	1	1	0	0	0	0	0
TOTAL	3	3	3	0	0	0	0	1
VIRGINIA TECH								
Howard Shannon (Kansas St. 1948) 1967RR	1	2	1	0	0	0	0	1
Don DeVoe (Ohio St. 1964) 1976	1	0	1	0	0	0	0	0
Charles Moir (Appalachian St. 1952) 1979, 80, 85, 86	4	2	4	0	0	0	0	0
Bill C. Foster (Carson-Newman 1958) 1996	1	1	1	0	0	0	0	0
TOTAL	7	5	7	0	0	0	0	1

	Yrs.	Won	Lost	CH	2D	3d%	4th	RR
WAGNER								
Derek Whittenburg (North Carolina St. 1984) 2003	1	0	1	0	0	0	0	0
TOTAL	1	0	1	0	0	0	0	0
WAKE FOREST								
Murray Greason (Wake Forest 1926) 1939RR, 53	2	1	2	0	0	0	0	1
Horace "Bones" McKinney (North Carolina 1946) 1961RR, 62-3d	2	6	2	0	0	1	0	1
Carl Tacy (Davis & Elkins 1956) 1977RR, 81, 82, 84RR	4	5	4	0	0	0	0	2
Dave Odom (Guilford 1965) 1991, 92, 93, 94, 95, 96RR, 97, 2001	8	10	8	0	0	0	0	1
Skip Prosser (Merchant Marine 1972) 2002, 03	2	2	2	0	0	0	0	0
TOTAL	18	24	18	0	0	1	0	5
WASHINGTON								
Clarence "Hec" Edmundson (Idaho 1909) 1943RR	1	0	2	0	0	0	0	1
Art McLarney (Washington St. 1932) 1948RR	1	1	1	0	0	0	0	1
William "Tippy" Dye (Ohio St. 1937) 1951RR, 53-3d	2	5	2	0	0	1	0	1
Marv Harshman (Pacific Lutheran 1942) 1976, 84, 85	3	2	3	0	0	0	0	0
Andy Russo (Lake Forest 1970) 1986	1	0	1	0	0	0	0	0
Bob Bender (Duke 1980) 1998, 99	2	2	2	0	0	0	0	0
TOTAL	10	10	11	0	0	1	0	3
WASHINGTON ST.								
Jack Friel (Washington St. 1923) 1941-2d	1	2	1	0	1	0	0	0
George Raveling (Villanova 1960) 1980, 83	2	1	2	0	0	0	0	0
Kelvin Sampson (UNC Pembroke 1978) 1994	1	0	1	0	0	0	0	0
TOTAL	4	3	4	0	1	0	0	0
WAYNE ST. (MICH.)								
Joel Mason (Western Mich. 1936) 1956.	1	1	2	0	0	0	0	0
TOTAL	1	1	2	0	0	0	0	0
WEBER ST.								
Dick Motta (Utah St. 1953) 1968	1	0	1	0	0	0	0	0
Phil Johnson (Utah St. 1953) 1969, 70, 71	3	2	3	0	0	0	0	0
Gene Visscher (Weber St. 1966) 1972, 73	2	1	3	0	0	0	0	0
Neil McCarthy (Sacramento St. 1965) 1978, 79, 80, 83	4	1	4	0	0	0	0	0
Ron Abegglen (Brigham Young 1962) 1995, 99	2	2	2	0	0	0	0	0
Joe Cravens (Tex.-Arlington 1977) 2003 .	1	0	1	0	0	0	0	0
TOTAL	13	6	14	0	0	0	0	0
WEST TEXAS A&M								
W.A. "Gus" Miller (West Texas A&M 1927) 1955	1	0	1	0	0	0	0	0
TOTAL	1	0	1	0	0	0	0	0
WEST VIRGINIA								
Fred Schaus (West Virginia 1949) 1955, 56, 57, 58, 59-2d, 60	6	6	6	0	1	0	0	0
George King [Charleston (W.Va.) 1950] 1962, 63, 65	3	2	3	0	0	0	0	0
Raymond "Bucky" Waters (North Carolina St. 1957) 1967	1	0	1	0	0	0	0	0
Gale Catlett (West Virginia 1963) 1982, 83, 84, 86, 87, 89, 92, 98	8	5	8	0	0	0	0	0
TOTAL	18	13	18	0	1	0	0	0
WESTERN CARO.								
Phil Hopkins (Gardner-Webb 1972) 1996	1	0	1	0	0	0	0	0
TOTAL	1	0	1	0	0	0	0	0
WESTERN KY.*								
Ed Diddle (Centre 1921) 1940RR, 60, 62	3	3	4	0	0	0	0	1
Johnny Oldham (Western Ky. 1948) 1966, 67, 70, 71-3d	4	6	4	0	0	1	0	0
Jim Richards (Western Ky. 1959) 1976, 78	2	1	2	0	0	0	0	0
Gene Keady (Kansas St. 1958) 1980	1	0	1	0	0	0	0	0
Clem Haskins (Western Ky. 1967) 1981, 86	2	1	2	0	0	0	0	0
Murray Arnold (American 1960) 1987	1	1	1	0	0	0	0	0
Ralph Willard (Holy Cross 1967) 1993, 94	2	2	2	0	0	0	0	0
Matt Kilcullen (Lehman 1976) 1995	1	1	1	0	0	0	0	0

	Yrs.	Won	Lost	CH	2D	3d%	4th	RR
Dennis Felton (Howard 1985) 2001, 02, 03	3	0	3	0	0	0	0	0
TOTAL	19	15	20	0	0	1	0	1
WESTERN MICH.								
Eldon Miller (Wittenberg 1961) 1976	1	1	1	0	0	0	0	0
Bob Donewald (Hanover 1964) 1998	1	1	1	0	0	0	0	0
TOTAL	2	2	2	0	0	0	0	0
WICHITA ST.								
Ralph Miller (Kansas 1942) 1964RR	1	1	1	0	0	0	0	1
Gary Thompson (Wichita St. 1954) 1965-4th	1	2	2	0	0	0	1	0
Harry Miller (Eastern N.M. 1951) 1976	1	0	1	0	0	0	0	0
Gene Smithson (North Central 1961) 1981RR, 85	2	3	2	0	0	0	0	1
Eddie Fogler (North Carolina 1970) 1987, 88	2	0	2	0	0	0	0	0
TOTAL	7	6	8	0	0	0	1	2
WILLIAMS								
Alex Shaw (Michigan 1932) 1955	1	0	1	0	0	0	0	0
TOTAL	1	0	1	0	0	0	0	0
WINTHROP								
Gregg Marshall (Randolph-Macon 1985) 1999, 2000, 01, 02	4	0	4	0	0	0	0	0
TOTAL	4	0	4	0	0	0	0	0
WISCONSIN								
Harold "Bud" Foster (Wisconsin 1930) 1941-CH, 47RR	2	4	1	1	0	0	0	1
Stu Jackson (Seattle 1978) 1994	1	1	1	0	0	0	0	0
Dick Bennett (Ripon 1965) 1997, 99, 2000-T-3d	3	4	3	0	0	1	0	0
Brad Soderberg (Wis.-Stevens Point 1985) 2001	1	0	1	0	0	0	0	0
Bo Ryan (Wilkes 1969) 2002, 03	2	3	2	0	0	0	0	0
TOTAL	9	12	8	1	0	1	0	1
WIS.-GREEN BAY								
Dick Bennett (Ripon 1965) 1991, 94, 95	3	1	3	0	0	0	0	0
Mike Heideman (Wis.-La Crosse 1971) 1996	1	0	1	0	0	0	0	0
TOTAL	4	1	4	0	0	0	0	0
WIS.-MILWAUKEE								
Bruce Pearl (Boston College 1982) 2003	1	0	1	0	0	0	0	0
TOTAL	1	0	1	0	0	0	0	0
WRIGHT ST.								
Ralph Underhill (Tennessee Tech 1964) 1993	1	0	1	0	0	0	0	0
TOTAL	1	0	1	0	0	0	0	0
WYOMING								
Everett Shelton (Phillips 1923) 1941RR, 43-CH, 47RR, 48RR, 49RR, 52RR, 53, 58	8	4	12	1	0	0	0	5
Bill Strannigan (Wyoming 1941) 1967	1	0	2	0	0	0	0	0
Jim Brandenburg (Colorado St. 1958) 1981, 82, 87	3	4	3	0	0	0	0	0
Benny Dees (Wyoming 1958) 1988	1	0	1	0	0	0	0	0
Steve McClain (Chadron St. 1984) 2002	1	1	1	0	0	0	0	0
TOTAL	14	9	19	1	0	0	0	5
XAVIER								
Jim McCafferty [Loyola (La.) 1942] 1961	1	0	1	0	0	0	0	0
Bob Staak (Connecticut 1971) 1983	1	0	1	0	0	0	0	0
Pete Gillen (Fairfield 1968) 1986, 87, 88, 89, 90, 91, 93	7	5	7	0	0	0	0	0
Skip Prosser (Merchant Marine 1972) 1995, 97, 98, 2001	4	1	4	0	0	0	0	0
Thad Matta (Butler 1990) 2002, 03	2	2	2	0	0	0	0	0
TOTAL	15	8	15	0	0	0	0	0
YALE								
Howard Hobson (Oregon 1926) 1949RR	1	0	2	0	0	0	0	1
Joe Vancisin (Dartmouth 1944) 1957, 62	2	0	2	0	0	0	0	0
TOTAL	3	0	4	0	0	0	0	1

%National 3d-place games did not start until 1946 and ended with 1981; in other years, two teams tied for third and both listed this column. RR Regional runner-up, or one victory from Final Four, thus in the top eight.

NOTES ON TEAMS AND COACHES:
MICHIGAN: Steve Fisher coached Michigan in the 1989 tournament; Bill Freider was the coach during the regular season.
MISSOURI: Rich Daly coached Missouri in the 1989 tournament due to Norm Stewart's illness; Missouri credits the entire 1989 season to Stewart.
PRINCETON: J.L. McCandless coached Princeton in the 1961 tournament; Franklin Cappon suffered a heart attack 11 games into the season; Princeton credits the1961 regular season to Cappon and the postseason to McCandless.
SEATTLE: Clair Markey coached Seattle in the 1963 tournament due to Vince Cazetta's resignation.

* TEAMS VACATING NCAA TOURNAMENT ACTION

Teams	Years	Record	Placing	Conference
Alabama	1987	2-1		Southeastern
Arizona	1999	0-1		Pacific 10
Arizona St.	1995	2-1		Pacific 10
Austin Peay	1973	1-2		Ohio Valley
California	1996	0-1		Pacific 10
Clemson	1990	2-1		Atlantic Coast
Connecticut	1996	2-1		Big East
DePaul	1986-89	6-4		Independent
Fresno St.	2000	0-1		Western Athletic
Florida	1987-88	3-2		Southeastern
Georgia	1985	1-1		Southeastern
Iona	1980	1-1		Independent
Kentucky	1988	2-1		Southeastern
Long Beach St.	1971-73	6-3	2 RR	Pacific Coast
La.-Lafayette	1972-73	3-3		Southland
Loyola Marymount	1980	0-1		West Coast
Marshall	1987	0-1		Southern
Maryland	1988	1-1		Atlantic Coast
Massachusetts	1996	4-1	3d	Atlantic 10
Memphis	1982-86	9-5	3d	Metro
Michigan	1992-93, 96, 98	10-4	2 2d	Big Ten
Minnesota	1972, 94-95, 97	6-4	3d	Big Ten
Missouri	1994	3-1	RR	Big Eight
New Mexico St.	1992-94	3-3		Big West
North Carolina St.	1987-88	0-2		Atlantic Coast
Oregon St.	1980-82	2-3	RR	Pacific 10
Purdue	1996	1-1		Big Ten
St. Joseph's	1961	3-1	3d	Middle Atlantic
Texas Tech	1996	2-1		Southwest
UCLA	1980, 99	5-2	2d	Pacific 10
Villanova	1971	4-1	2d	Independent
Western Ky.	1971	4-1	3d	Ohio Valley
31 schools	54 years	88-56	4 2d, 5 3d, 4 RR	

Official NCAA Records	Yrs	Won	Lost	CH	2d	3d	4th	RR
Alabama	15	14	15	0	0	0	0	0
Arizona	21	37	20	1	1	2	0	2
Arizona St.	11	10	12	0	0	0	0	3
Austin Peay	4	1	4	0	0	0	0	0
California	12	18	12	1	1	0	1	2
Clemson	6	6	6	0	0	0	0	1
Connecticut	23	30	23	1	0	0	0	5
DePaul	17	14	20	0	0	2	0	1
Florida	8	13	8	0	0	1	0	0
Fresno St.	4	2	4	0	0	0	0	0
Georgia	8	6	8	0	0	1	0	0
Iona	6	0	6	0	0	0	0	0
Kentucky	44	92	39	7	3	3	0	16
Long Beach St.	4	1	5	0	0	0	0	0
La.-Lafayette	5	1	5	0	0	0	0	0
Loyola Marymount	4	5	4	0	0	0	0	1
Marshall	4	0	4	0	0	0	0	0
Maryland	19	33	18	1	0	1	0	2
Massachusetts	7	7	7	0	0	0	0	1
Memphis	12	9	12	0	1	0	0	1
Michigan	16	31	15	1	2	1	0	5
Minnesota	4	6	4	0	0	0	0	1
Missouri	20	15	20	0	0	0	0	3
New Mexico St.	13	7	15	0	0	1	0	0
North Carolina St.	17	28	16	2	0	1	0	3
Oregon St.	13	10	16	0	0	0	2	4
Purdue	19	26	19	0	1	1	0	2
St. Joseph's	16	12	20	0	0	0	0	0
Texas Tech	10	3	11	0	0	0	0	0
UCLA	36	80	29	11	0	2	1	4
Villanova	24	33	24	1	0	1	0	7
Western Ky.	18	11	19	0	0	0	0	1

Final Four All-Tournament Teams

(First player listed on each team was the outstanding player in the Final Four)

1939— Not chosen.

1940— Marvin Huffman, Indiana
Howard Engleman, Kansas
Bob Allen, Kansas
Jay McCreary, Indiana
William Menke, Indiana

1941-51— Not chosen.

1952— Clyde Lovellette, Kansas
Bob Zawoluk, St. John's (N.Y.)
John Kerr, Illinois
Ron MacGilvray, St. John's (N.Y.)
Dean Kelley, Kansas

1953— B.H. Born, Kansas
Bob Houbregs, Washington
Bob Leonard, Indiana
Dean Kelley, Kansas
Don Schlundt, Indiana

1954— Tom Gola, La Salle
Chuck Singley, La Salle
Jesse Arnelle, Penn St.
Roy Irvin, Southern California
Bob Carney, Bradley

1955— Bill Russell, San Francisco
Tom Gola, La Salle
K.C. Jones, San Francisco
Jim Ranglos, Colorado
Carl Cain, Iowa

1956— Hal Lear, Temple
Bill Russell, San Francisco
Carl Cain, Iowa
Hal Perry, San Francisco
Bill Logan, Iowa

1957— Wilt Chamberlain, Kansas
Len Rosenbluth, North Carolina
John Green, Michigan St.
Gene Brown, San Francisco
Pete Brennan, North Carolina

1958— Elgin Baylor, Seattle
John Cox, Kentucky
Guy Rodgers, Temple
Charley Brown, Seattle
Vern Hatton, Kentucky

1959— Jerry West, West Virginia
Oscar Robertson, Cincinnati
Darrall Imhoff, California
Don Goldstein, Louisville
Denny Fitzpatrick, California

1960— Jerry Lucas, Ohio St.
Oscar Robertson, Cincinnati
Mel Nowell, Ohio St.
Darrall Imhoff, California
Tom Sanders, New York U.

1961— Jerry Lucas, Ohio St.
Bob Wiesenhahn, Cincinnati
Larry Siegfried, Ohio St.
Carl Bouldin, Cincinnati
Vacated†

1962— Paul Hogue, Cincinnati
Jerry Lucas, Ohio St.
Tom Thacker, Cincinnati
John Havlicek, Ohio St.
Len Chappell, Wake Forest

1963— Art Heyman, Duke
Tom Thacker, Cincinnati
Les Hunter, Loyola (Ill.)
George Wilson, Cincinnati
Ron Bonham, Cincinnati

1964— Walt Hazzard, UCLA
Jeff Mullins, Duke
Bill Buntin, Michigan
Willie Murrell, Kansas St.
Gail Goodrich, UCLA

1965— Bill Bradley, Princeton
Gail Goodrich, UCLA
Cazzie Russell, Michigan
Edgar Lacey, UCLA
Kenny Washington, UCLA

1966— Jerry Chambers, Utah
Pat Riley, Kentucky
Jack Marin, Duke
Louie Dampier, Kentucky
Bobby Joe Hill, UTEP

1967— Lew Alcindor, UCLA
Don May, Dayton
Mike Warren, UCLA
Elvin Hayes, Houston
Lucius Allen, UCLA

1968— Lew Alcindor, UCLA
Lynn Shackelford, UCLA
Mike Warren, UCLA
Lucius Allen, UCLA
Larry Miller, North Carolina

1969— Lew Alcindor, UCLA
Rick Mount, Purdue
Charlie Scott, North Carolina
Willie McCarter, Drake
John Vallely, UCLA

1970— Sidney Wicks, UCLA
Jimmy Collins, New Mexico St.
John Vallely, UCLA
Artis Gilmore, Jacksonville
Curtis Rowe, UCLA

1971— Vacated†
Vacated†
Vacated†
Steve Patterson, UCLA
Sidney Wicks, UCLA

1972— Bill Walton, UCLA
Keith Wilkes, UCLA
Bob McAdoo, North Carolina
Jim Price, Louisville
Ron King, Florida St.

1973— Bill Walton, UCLA
Steve Downing, Indiana
Ernie DiGregorio, Providence
Larry Finch, Memphis
Larry Kenon, Memphis

1974— David Thompson, North Carolina St.
Bill Walton, UCLA
Tom Burleson, North Carolina St.
Monte Towe, North Carolina St.
Maurice Lucas, Marquette

1975— Richard Washington, UCLA
Kevin Grevey, Kentucky
Dave Myers, UCLA
Allen Murphy, Louisville
Jim Lee, Syracuse

1976— Kent Benson, Indiana
Scott May, Indiana
Rickey Green, Michigan
Marques Johnson, UCLA
Tom Abernethy, Indiana

1977— Butch Lee, Marquette
Mike O'Koren, North Carolina
Cedric Maxwell, Charlotte
Bo Ellis, Marquette
Walter Davis, North Carolina
Jerome Whitehead, Marquette

1978— Jack Givens, Kentucky
Ron Brewer, Arkansas
Mike Gminski, Duke
Rick Robey, Kentucky
Jim Spanarkel, Duke

1979— Earvin Johnson, Michigan St.
Greg Kelser, Michigan St.
Larry Bird, Indiana St.
Mark Aguirre, DePaul
Gary Garland, DePaul

1980— Darrell Griffith, Louisville
Vacated†
Joe Barry Carroll, Purdue
Vacated†
Rodney McCray, Louisville

1981— Isiah Thomas, Indiana
Jeff Lamp, Virginia
Jim Thomas, Indiana
Landon Turner, Indiana
Al Wood, North Carolina

1982— James Worthy, North Carolina
Patrick Ewing, Georgetown
Eric Floyd, Georgetown
Michael Jordan, North Carolina
Sam Perkins, North Carolina

1983— Akeem Olajuwon, Houston
Thurl Bailey, North Carolina St.
Sidney Lowe, North Carolina St.
Milt Wagner, Louisville
Dereck Whittenburg, North Carolina St.

1984— Patrick Ewing, Georgetown
Michael Graham, Georgetown
Akeem Olajuwon, Houston
Michael Young, Houston
Alvin Franklin, Houston

1985— Patrick Ewing, Georgetown
Ed Pinckney, Villanova
Dwayne McClain, Villanova
Harold Jensen, Villanova
Gary McLain, Villanova

1986— Pervis Ellison, Louisville
Billy Thompson, Louisville
Johnny Dawkins, Duke
Mark Alarie, Duke
Tommy Amaker, Duke

1987— Keith Smart, Indiana
Sherman Douglas, Syracuse
Derrick Coleman, Syracuse
Armon Gilliam, UNLV
Steve Alford, Indiana

1988— Danny Manning, Kansas
Milt Newton, Kansas
Stacey King, Oklahoma
Dave Sieger, Oklahoma
Sean Elliott, Arizona

1989— Glen Rice, Michigan
Rumeal Robinson, Michigan
Danny Ferry, Duke
Gerald Greene, Seton Hall
John Morton, Seton Hall

1990— Anderson Hunt, UNLV
Stacey Augmon, UNLV
Larry Johnson, UNLV
Phil Henderson, Duke
Dennis Scott, Georgia Tech

1991— Christian Laettner, Duke
Bobby Hurley, Duke
Bill McCaffrey, Duke
Mark Randall, Kansas
Anderson Hunt, UNLV

1992— Bobby Hurley, Duke
Grant Hill, Duke
Christian Laettner, Duke
Jalen Rose, Michigan
Chris Webber, Michigan

1993— Donald Williams, North Carolina
Eric Montross, North Carolina
George Lynch, North Carolina
Chris Webber, Michigan
Jamal Mashburn, Kentucky

1994— Corliss Williamson, Arkansas
Corey Beck, Arkansas
Scotty Thurman, Arkansas
Grant Hill, Duke
Antonio Lang, Duke

1995— Ed O'Bannon, UCLA
Toby Bailey, UCLA
Corliss Williamson, Arkansas
Clint McDaniel, Arkansas
Bryant Reeves, Oklahoma St.

1996— Tony Delk, Kentucky
Ron Mercer, Kentucky
Marcus Camby, Massachusetts
Todd Burgan, Syracuse
John Wallace, Syracuse

1997— Miles Simon, Arizona
Mike Bibby, Arizona
Ron Mercer, Kentucky
Scott Padgett, Kentucky
Bobby Jackson, Minnesota

1998— Jeff Sheppard, Kentucky
Scott Padgett, Kentucky
Arthur Lee, Stanford
Michael Doleac, Utah
Andre Miller, Utah

1999— Richard Hamilton, Connecticut
Khalid El-Amin, Connecticut
Ricky Moore, Connecticut
Elton Brand, Duke
Trajan Langdon, Duke

2000— Mateen Cleaves, Michigan St.
Udonis Haslem, Florida
Charlie Bell, Michigan St.
A.J. Granger, Michigan St.
Morris Peterson, Michigan St.

2001— Shane Battier, Duke
Mike Dunleavy, Duke
Richard Jefferson, Arizona
Jason Williams, Duke
Loren Woods, Arizona

2002— Juan Dixon, Maryland
Lonny Baxter, Maryland
Chris Wilcox, Maryland
Dane Fife, Indiana
Kyle Hornsby, Indiana

2003— Carmelo Anthony, Syracuse
Gerry McNamara, Syracuse
Nick Collison, Kansas
Kirk Hinrich, Kansas
Keith Langford, Kansas

†These student-athletes and the teams they represented were declared ineligible after the tournament. Under NCAA rules, the teams' and student-athletes' records were deleted and the teams' places in the final standings were vacated: 1961—John Egan, St. Joseph's; 1971—Howard Porter, Villanova; Hank Siemiontkowski, Villanova; Jim McDaniels, Western Kentucky; 1980—Kiki Vandeweghe, UCLA; Rod Foster, UCLA.

National Invitation Tournament Year-by-Year Results

Season	Champion	Score	Runner-Up	Third Place	Fourth Place
1938	Temple	60-36	Colorado	Oklahoma St.	New York U.
1939	Long Island	44-32	Loyola (Ill.)	Bradley	St. John's (N.Y.)
1940	Colorado	51-40	Duquesne	Oklahoma St.	DePaul
1941	Long Island	56-42	Ohio	CCNY	Seton Hall
1942	West Virginia	47-45	Western Ky.	Creighton	Toledo
1943	St. John's (N.Y.)	48-27	Toledo	Wash. & Jeff.	Fordham
1944	St. John's (N.Y.)	47-39	DePaul	Kentucky	Oklahoma St.
1945	DePaul	71-54	Bowling Green	St. John's (N.Y.)	Rhode Island
1946	Kentucky	46-45	Rhode Island	West Virginia	Muhlenberg
1947	Utah	49-45	Kentucky	North Carolina St.	West Virginia
1948	St. Louis	65-52	New York U.	Western Ky.	DePaul
1949	San Francisco	48-47	Loyola (Ill.)	Bowling Green	Bradley
1950	CCNY	69-61	Bradley	St. John's (N.Y.)	Duquesne
1951	Brigham Young	62-43	Dayton	St. John's (N.Y.)	Seton Hall
1952	La Salle	75-64	Dayton	St. Bonaventure	Duquesne
1953	Seton Hall	58-46	St. John's (N.Y.)	Duquesne	Manhattan
1954	Holy Cross	71-62	Duquesne	Niagara	Western Ky.
1955	Duquesne	70-58	Dayton	Cincinnati	St. Francis (Pa.)
1956	Louisville	93-80	Dayton	St. Joseph's	St. Francis (N.Y.)
1957	Bradley	84-83	Memphis	Tampa	St. Bonaventure
1958	Xavier	78-74(ot)	Dayton	St. Bonaventure	St. John's (N.Y.)
1959	St. John's (N.Y.)	76-71(ot)	Bradley	New York U.	Providence

CHAMPIONSHIPS

Season	Champion	Score	Runner-Up	Third Place	Fourth Place
1960	Bradley	88-72	Providence	Utah St.	St. Bonaventure
1961	Providence	62-59	St. Louis	Holy Cross	Dayton
1962	Dayton	73-67	St. John's (N.Y.)	Loyola (Ill.)	Duquesne
1963	Providence	81-66	Canisius	Marquette	Villanova
1964	Bradley	86-54	New Mexico	Army	New York U.
1965	St. John's (N.Y.)	55-51	Villanova	Army	New York U.
1966	Brigham Young	97-84	New York U.	Villanova	Army
1967	Southern Ill.	71-56	Marquette	Rutgers	Marshall
1968	Dayton	61-48	Kansas	Notre Dame	St. Peter's
1969	Temple	89-76	Boston College	Tennessee	Army
1970	Marquette	65-53	St. John's (N.Y.)	Army	LSU
1971	North Carolina	84-66	Georgia Tech	St. Bonaventure	Duke
1972	Maryland	100-69	Niagara	Jacksonville	St. John's (N.Y.)
1973	Virginia Tech	92-91(ot)	Notre Dame	North Carolina	Alabama
1974	Purdue	87-81	Utah	Boston College	Jacksonville
1975	Princeton	80-69	Providence	Oregon	St. John's (N.Y.)
1976	Kentucky	81-76	Charlotte	North Carolina St.	Providence
1977	St. Bonaventure	94-91	Houston	Villanova	Alabama
1978	Texas	101-93	North Carolina St.	Rutgers	Georgetown
1979	Indiana	53-52	Purdue	Alabama	Ohio St.
1980	Virginia	58-55	Minnesota	Illinois	UNLV
1981	Tulsa	86-84(ot)	Syracuse	Purdue	West Virginia
1982	Bradley	67-58	Purdue	+Georgia	+Oklahoma
1983	Fresno St.	69-60	DePaul	+Nebraska	+Wake Forest
1984	Michigan	83-63	Notre Dame	Virginia Tech	La.-Lafayette
1985	UCLA	65-62	Indiana	Tennessee	Louisville
1986	Ohio St.	73-63	Wyoming	Louisiana Tech	Florida
1987	Southern Miss.	84-80	La Salle	Nebraska	Ark.-Little Rock
1988	Connecticut	72-67	Ohio St.	Colorado St.	Boston College
1989	St. John's (N.Y.)	73-65	St. Louis	UAB	Michigan St.
1990	Vanderbilt	74-72	St. Louis	Penn St.	New Mexico
1991	Stanford	78-72	Oklahoma	Colorado	Massachusetts
1992	Virginia	81-76	Notre Dame	Utah	Florida
1993	Minnesota	92-61	Georgetown	UAB	Providence
1994	Villanova	80-73	Vanderbilt	Siena	Kansas St.
1995	Virginia Tech	65-64(ot)	Marquette	Penn St.	Canisius
1996	Nebraska	60-56	St. Joseph's	Tulane	Alabama
1997	Michigan	82-73	Florida St.	Connecticut	Arkansas
1998	Minnesota	79-72	Penn St.	Georgia	Fresno St.
1999	California	61-60	Clemson	Xavier	Oregon
2000	Wake Forest	71-61	Notre Dame	Penn St.	North Carolina St.
2001	Tulsa	79-60	Alabama	Memphis	Detroit
2002	Memphis	72-62	South Carolina	Syracuse	Temple
2003	St. John's (N.Y.)	70-67	Georgetown	Minnesota	Texas Tech

+tied for third place

POSTSEASON CHARITY GAME

During World War II, the American Red Cross sponsored a basketball game to raise money for the war effort. The game featured that year's NCAA champion versus the NIT champion.

Season	Winner	Score	Loser	Site
1943	Wyoming (NCAA champion)	52-47(ot)	St. John's (N.Y.) (NIT champion)	New York
1944	Utah (NCAA champion)	43-36	St. John's (N.Y.) (NIT champion)	New York
1945	Oklahoma St. (NCAA champion)	52-44	DePaul (NIT champion)	New York

NABC All-Star Game Results

Season	Winner	Score	MVP	Winning Coach	Losing Coach	Attendance
1963	East	77-70	Art Heyman, Duke	Harold Anderson	Cliff Wells	9,000
1964	West	79-78	Willie Murrell, Kansas St.	Slats Gill	Jack Gardner	9,700
1965	West	87-74	Gail Goodrich, UCLA	Doggie Julian	Joe Lapchick	7,000
1966	East	126-99	Cazzie Russell, Michigan	Taps Gallagher	Forrest Twogood	8,000
1967	East	102-93	Sonny Dove, St. John's (N.Y.)	Ben Carnevale	Everest Shelton	7,300
1968	West	95-88	Pete Maravich, LSU	Phog Allen & Tex Winter	Art Schabinger & John Bach	14,500
1969	East	104-80	Neal Walk, Florida	Tony Hinkle	Branch McCracken	6,100
1970	East	116-102	Charlie Scott, North Carolina	Nat Holman	Bud Foster	14,756
1971	East	106-104 (ot)	Jim McDaniels, Western Ky.	Dutch Lonborg	Vadal Peterson	13,178
1972	East	96-91 (ot)	Billy Shepard, Butler	Howard Hobson	Henry Iba	7,856
1973	West	98-94	Jim Brewer, Minnesota	Stan Watts	Adolph Rupp	8,609
1974	East	105-85	Marvin Barnes, Providence	Harry Litwack	John Hyder	8,396
1975	West	110-89	Gus Williams, Southern California	Bruce Drake	Eddie Hickey	NA
1976	West	101-98	Chuckie Williams, Kansas St.	Marv Harshman	Dean Smith	5,951
1977	East	114-93	Ernie Grunfeld, Tennessee	Bob Knight	Johnny Orr	6,537
1978	East	93-87	Butch Lee, Marquette	Frank McGuire	Al McGuire	4,275
1979	East	114-109	Greg Deane, Utah	Joe B. Hall	Bill Foster	7,472
1980	East	88-79	Mike O'Koren, North Carolina	Bill Hodges	Jud Heathcote	7,600
1981	West	99-97	Danny Ainge, Brigham Young	Larry Brown	Denny Crum	3,116
1982	West	102-68	Ricky Frazier, Missouri	Dale Brown	Bob Knight	3,965
1983	West	99-94	Darrell Walker, Arkansas	John Thompson	Dean Smith	4,178
1984	West	111-77	Fred Reynolds, UTEP	Marv Harshman	Jim Valvano	4,126
1985	West	97-90	Lorenzo Charles, North Carolina St.	Guy Lewis	Joe B. Hall	10,464
1986	West	94-92	David Wingate, Georgetown	Rollie Massimino	Lou Carnesecca	7,009
1987	West	92-91	David Robinson, Navy	Denny Crum	Mike Krzyzewski	8,041
1988	East	97-91	David Rivers, Notre Dame	Jim Boeheim	Jerry Tarkanian	8,528
1989	West	150-111	Tim Hardaway, UTEP	Lute Olson	Billy Tubbs	7,541
1990	East	127-126	Travis Mays, Texas	P.J. Carlesimo	Steve Fisher	7,161
1991	West	122-113	Jimmy Oliver, Purdue	Nolan Richardson	Bobby Cremins	8,000
1992	West	117-93	Doug Christie, Pepperdine	Roy Williams	Clem Haskins	10,344
1993	West	104-95	Ervin Johnson, New Orleans	Bob Huggins	Mike Krzyzewski	6,604
1994	East	77-73	Charlie Ward, Florida St.	Clarence "Bighouse" Gaines	Guy Lewis	6,500
1995	West	117-88	Fred Hoiberg, Iowa St.	Lute Olson	Lon Kruger	7,900
1996	East	99-92	Danetri Hill, Florida	Eddie Sutton	Jim Harrick	5,500
1997	East	105-94	James Collins, Florida St.	Jim Boeheim	Norm Stewart	6,019
1998	East	102-89	Felipe Lopez, St. John's (N.Y.)	Clem Haskins	Steve Lavin	8,998
1999	West	93-86	Doug Swenson, Creighton	Rick Majerus	Tubby Smith	6,753

Year	Score NABC-Opp.	NABC MVP	NABC Coach	Opponent	Attendance
2000	80-82	Kenyon Jones, San Francisco	Jim Calhoun	Harlem Globetrotters	8,000
2001	63-75	Kyle Hill, Eastern Mich.	Gene Keady	Harlem Globetrotters	15,253
2002	86-76	Tony Akins, Georgia Tech	Tom Izzo	Harlem Globetrotters	8,758
2003	85-87 (ot)	Dahntay Jones, Duke	Gary Williams	Harlem Globetrotters	14,844

Game Sites: 1963-67—Lexington, Kentucky; 1968-70—Indianapolis, Indiana; 1971-74—Dayton, Ohio; 1975-77—Tulsa, Ok.; 1978-present—same city as the NCAA Final Four.

CHAMPIONSHIPS

Division II Championship

2003 Results

FIRST ROUND
Mass.-Lowell 91, St. Rose 68
Bridgeport 64, Adelphi 56
New Haven 76, Southern N.H. 71
C.W. Post 81, Assumption 75 (ot)
Presbyterian 71, Columbus St. 59
Shaw 72, Johnson Smith 58
Kennesaw St. 74, Virginia Union 65
Bowie St. 88, Lenoir-Rhyne 82
Cal St. Bakersfield 50, BYU-Hawaii 41
Cal Poly Pomona 80, Alas. Fairbanks 76
Humboldt St. 102, Hawaii-Hilo 81
Cal St. San B'dino 86, Sonoma St. 58
Michigan Tech 90, Indianapolis 75
Southern Ind. 82, Lewis 63
Findlay 80, Northern Ky. 76
*Ky. Wesleyan 81, Gannon 74
Queens (N.C.) 72, West Chester 58
Salem Int'l 76, Calif. (Pa.) 73
Millersville 62, Belmont Abbey 56
Barton 81, Alderson-Broaddus 76
Rollins 76, Ala.-Huntsville 61
Eckerd 83, Morehouse 66
Delta St. 72, Fla. Southern 70
Henderson St. 67, Harding 59
Tarleton St. 56, St. Mary's (Tex.) 43
Northwest Mo. St. 71, Mo. Western St. 61
Washburn 75, West Tex. A&M 73
Northeastern St. 78, Central Okla. 67
Neb.-Kearney 72, Minn. Duluth 67
South Dakota St. 84, Fort Hays St. 78
Metro St. 85, Fort Lewis 63
St. Cloud St. 74, North Dakota 69

SECOND ROUND
Mass.-Lowell 86, Bridgeport 73
C.W. Post 78, New Haven 61
Presbyterian 77, Shaw 58
Bowie St. 95, Kennesaw St. 70
Cal Poly Pomona 62, Cal St. Bakersfield 49
Cal St. San B'dino 80, Humboldt St. 68
Southern Ind. 74, Michigan Tech 71
*Ky. Wesleyan 83, Findlay 66
Queens (N.C.) 100, Salem Int'l 87
Millersville 80, Barton 63
Eckerd 74, Rollins 70
Henderson St. 67, Delta St. 60
Tarleton St. 73, Northwest Mo. St. 58
Northeastern St. 64, Washburn 59
Neb.-Kearney 86, South Dakota St. 85
Metro St. 75, St. Cloud St. 63

REGIONAL FINALS
Mass.-Lowell 69, C.W. Post 59
Bowie St. 67, Presbyterian 53
Cal Poly Pomona 91, Cal St. San B'dino 84 (2 ot)
*Ky. Wesleyan 95, Southern Ind. 91
Queens (N.C.) 94, Millersville 77
Eckerd 85, Henderson St. 75
Northeastern St. 56, Tarleton St. 46
Neb.-Kearney 94, Metro St. 87 (2ot)

QUARTERFINALS
Bowie St. 72, Mass.-Lowell 62
*Ky. Wesleyan 85, Cal Poly Pomona 60
Queens (N.C.) 99, Eckerd 78
Northeastern St. 94, Neb.-Kearney 75

SEMIFINALS
*Ky. Wesleyan 84, Bowie St. 64
Northeastern St. 84, Queens (N.C.) 69

CHAMPIONSHIP
Northeastern St. 75, *Ky. Wesleyan 64

*Ky. Wesleyan's participation vacated.

Box Scores

SEMIFINALS
MARCH 27, AT LAKELAND, FLORIDA
Ky. Wesleyan 84, Bowie St. 64

Bowie St.	FG-FGA	FTM-FTA	RB	PF	TP
Tim Washington	4-14	1-2	5	5	9
Stephen Moss-Kelley	5-12	3-4	3	4	15
Jon Smith	6-8	0-0	8	2	12
Cornelius McMurray	3-12	4-5	8	1	12
Omarr Smith	4-9	0-0	1	2	10
Jamar Wood	0-1	1-2	0	1	1
Allen Van Norden	1-2	0-0	1	1	2
Shawn Hampton	0-1	0-1	6	2	0
Shaun Ross	0-0	1-2	0	0	1
Gabe Como	0-1	0-0	0	0	0
Donte Wright-Nelson	0-0	0-0	0	0	0
Arthur Lewis	1-3	0-0	2	3	2
Nathaniel Fields	0-2	0-0	2	1	0
Team			4		
TOTALS	24-66	10-16	40	22	64

Ky. Wesleyan	FG-FGA	FTM-FTA	RB	PF	TP
Dewayne Rogers	2-2	2-2	5	1	8
Thad Key	3-5	0-0	4	2	6
Eugene Dabney	11-17	6-7	8	0	28
Marlon Parmer	6-17	10-13	9	2	24
Huggy Dye	1-6	0-0	0	4	2
Damon Garris	4-7	1-1	6	4	9
Ryan West	0-0	0-0	1	0	0
Bobby Zuerner	2-8	0-0	2	3	5
Matt Enos	0-0	2-2	0	0	2
John Foster	0-0	0-0	1	0	0
Haven Mosley	0-0	0-0	0	0	0
Trey Ferguson	0-2	0-0	2	1	0
Eric Freeman	0-1	0-0	1	2	0
Dean Smith	0-1	0-0	2	1	0
Team			2		
TOTALS	29-66	21-25	43	20	84

Halftime: Ky. Wesleyan 39, Bowie St. 36. Three-point field goals: Bowie St. 6-21 (Moss-Kelley 2-6, J. Smith 0-1, McMurray 2-7, O. Smith 2-4, Van Norden 0-1, Como 0-1, Lewis 0-1); Ky. Wesleyan 5-19 (Rogers 2-2, Parmer 2-7, Dye 0-3, Zuerner 1-5, Ferguson 0-2). Officials: Mike Stephens, Bobby Pultz, Chris Rastatter. Attendance: 1,261.

Northeastern St. 84, Queens (N.C.) 69

Queens (N.C.)	FG-FGA	FTM-FTA	RB	PF	TP
Chris Benson	6-14	1-1	4	5	17
Spencer Ross	5-17	2-2	4	0	12
Carlos Andrade	5-10	0-0	4	5	12
Moustapha Diouf	8-12	0-1	11	2	16
Kendrick Harris	1-2	0-0	3	1	3
Shane Thorson	0-0	0-0	0	0	0
Hector Valenzuela	2-3	0-0	3	2	4
Guillermo Rausch	0-1	0-0	0	1	0
Juwaun Seegars	0-0	0-0	0	0	0
Anthony Thomas	1-5	0-0	3	4	3
Zachary English	1-3	0-0	2	0	2
Team			1		
TOTALS	29-67	3-4	35	20	69

Northeastern St.	FG-FGA	FTM-FTA	RB	PF	TP
Darnell Hinson	6-11	1-2	5	4	18
Shon Robinson	5-15	1-2	8	1	15
Reggie Battee	5-8	1-4	8	1	11
Justin Barkley	0-4	3-5	8	2	3
Jon Shepherd	5-7	0-0	6	3	10
Derek Cline	5-10	3-4	0	0	16
Ty Merchant	0-0	0-0	0	0	0
Shiloh Shores	4-5	3-3	4	1	11
Jeff Whitehead	0-0	0-0	1	1	0
Team			1		
TOTALS	30-60	12-20	41	13	84

Halftime: Northeastern St. 43, Queens (N.C.) 26. Three-point field goals: Queens (N.C.) 8-27 (Benson 4-12, Ross 0-3, Andrade 2-6, Harris 1-1, Thomas 1-5); Northeastern St. 12-24 (Hinson 5-7, Robinson 4-8, Battee 0-1, Barkley 0-2, Cline 3-6). Officials: Gary Vaughn, Bill Stock, Steve Morris. Attendance: 1,261.

CHAMPIONSHIP
MARCH 29, AT LAKELAND, FLORIDA
Northeastern St. 75, Ky. Wesleyan 64

Northeastern St.	FG-FGA	FTM-FTA	RB	PF	TP
Reggie Battee	1-3	0-1	7	2	2
Justin Barkley	2-3	1-1	12	2	7
Jon Shepherd	3-10	0-2	6	3	6
Darnell Hinson	6-9	4-5	5	3	19
Shon Robinson	6-17	11-13	1	2	26
Derek Cline	3-10	3-4	1	1	12
Ty Merchant	0-0	1-2	0	0	1
Shiloh Shores	1-3	0-0	1	1	2
Jeff Whitehead	0-0	0-1	2	0	0
Team			2		
TOTALS	22-55	20-29	37	14	75

Ky. Wesleyan	FG-FGA	FTM-FTA	RB	PF	TP
Dewayne Rogers	0-2	0-0	6	2	0
Thad Key	1-5	1-2	2	2	3
Eugene Dabney	4-7	1-2	7	4	9
Marlon Parmer	6-12	4-9	8	4	17
Huggy Dye	3-9	0-0	2	5	7
Damon Garris	5-9	0-0	7	4	10
Bobby Zuerner	5-9	0-0	1	5	14
John Foster	1-1	0-0	1	1	2
Trey Ferguson	1-2	0-0	0	0	2
Eric Freeman	0-1	0-0	0	0	0
Dean Smith	0-0	0-0	0	0	0
Team			2		
Totals	26-57	6-13	36	27	64

Halftime: Tied at 25. Three-point field goals: Northeastern St. 11-23 (Barkley 2-2, Hinson 3-4, Robinson 3-10, Cline 3-7); Ky. Wesleyan 6-17 (Rogers 0-1, Parmer 1-3, Dye 1-5, Zuerner 4-6, Ferguson 0-1, Freeman 0-1). Disqualifications: Dye, Zuerner. Officials: Mike Stephens, Bobby Pultz, Chris Rastatter. Attendance: 2,378.

Year-by-Year Results

Season	Champion	Score	Runner-Up	Third Place	Fourth Place
1957	Wheaton (Ill.)	89-65	Ky. Wesleyan	Mt. St. Mary's	Cal St. Los Angeles
1958	South Dakota	75-53	St. Michael's	Evansville	Wheaton (Ill.)
1959	Evansville	83-67	Southwest Mo. St.	N.C. A&T	Cal St. Los Angeles
1960	Evansville	90-69	Chapman	Ky. Wesleyan	Cornell College
1961	Wittenberg	42-38	Southeast Mo. St.	South Dakota St.	Mt. St. Mary's
1962	Mt. St. Mary's	58-57(ot)	Sacramento St.	Southern Ill.	Neb. Wesleyan
1963	South Dakota St.	44-42	Wittenberg	Oglethorpe	Southern Ill.
1964	Evansville	72-59	Akron	N.C. A&T	Northern Iowa
1965	Evansville	85-82(ot)	Southern Ill.	North Dakota	St. Michael's
1966	Ky. Wesleyan	54-51	Southern Ill.	Akron	North Dakota
1967	Winston-Salem	77-74	Southwest Mo. St.	Ky. Wesleyan	Illinois St.
1968	Ky. Wesleyan	63-52	Indiana St.	Trinity (Tex.)	Ashland
1969	Ky. Wesleyan	75-71	Southwest Mo. St.	**American Int'l	Ashland
1970	Philadelphia U.	76-65	Tennessee St.	UC Riverside	Buffalo St.
1971	Evansville	97-82	Old Dominion	**La.-Lafayette	Ky. Wesleyan
1972	Roanoke	84-72	Akron	Tennessee St.	Eastern Mich.
1973	Ky. Wesleyan	78-76(ot)	Tennessee St.	Assumption	Brockport St.
1974	Morgan St.	67-52	Southwest Mo. St.	Assumption	New Orleans
1975	Old Dominion	76-74	New Orleans	Assumption	Chattanooga
1976	Puget Sound	83-74	Chattanooga	Eastern Ill.	Old Dominion
1977	Chattanooga	71-62	Randolph-Macon	North Ala.	Sacred Heart
1978	Cheyney	47-40	Wis.-Green Bay	Eastern Ill.	UCF
1979	North Ala.	64-50	Wis.-Green Bay	Cheyney	Bridgeport
1980	Virginia Union	80-74	New York Tech	Fla. Southern	North Ala.
1981	Fla. Southern	73-68	Mt. St. Mary's	Cal Poly	Wis.-Green Bay
1982	Dist. Columbia	73-63	Fla. Southern	Ky. Wesleyan	Cal St. Bakersfield
1983	Wright St.	92-73	Dist. Columbia	*Cal St. Bakersfield	*Morningside
1984	Central Mo. St.	81-77	St. Augustine's	*Ky. Wesleyan	*North Ala.
1985	Jacksonville St.	74-73	South Dakota St.	*Ky. Wesleyan	*Mt. St. Mary's
1986	Sacred Heart	93-87	Southeast Mo. St.	*Cheyney	*Fla. Southern
1987	Ky. Wesleyan	92-74	Gannon	*Delta St.	*Mont. St.-Billings
1988	Mass.-Lowell	75-72	Alas. Anchorage	Fla. Southern	Troy St.
1989	N.C. Central	73-46	Southeast Mo. St.	UC Riverside	Jacksonville St.
1990	Ky. Wesleyan	93-79	Cal St. Bakersfield	North Dakota	Morehouse
1991	North Ala.	79-72	Bridgeport	*Cal St. Bakersfield	*Virginia Union
1992	Virginia Union	100-75	Bridgeport	*Cal St. Bakersfield	*Calif. (Pa.)
1993	Cal St. Bakersfield	85-72	Troy St.	*Wayne St. (Mich.)	*New Hamp. Col.
1994	Cal St. Bakersfield	92-86	Southern Ind.	*Washburn	*New Hamp. Col.
1995	Southern Ind.	71-63	UC Riverside	*Norfolk St.	*Indiana (Pa.)
1996	Fort Hays St.	70-63	Northern Ky.	*Virginia Union	*Calif. (Pa.)
1997	Cal St. Bakersfield	57-56	Northern Ky.	*Salem Int'l	*Lynn
1998	UC Davis	83-77	Ky. Wesleyan	*Virginia Union	*St. Rose
1999	Ky. Wesleyan	75-60	Metro St.	*Truman	*Fla. Southern
2000	Metro St.	97-99	Ky. Wesleyan	*Mo. Southern St.	*Seattle Pacific
2001	Ky. Wesleyan	72-63	Washburn	Western Wash.	Tampa
2002	Metro St.	80-72	Ky. Wesleyan	Shaw	Indiana (Pa.)
2003	Northeastern St.	75-64	**Ky. Wesleyan	*Queens (N.C.)	*Bowie St.

*Indicates tied for third. **Student-athletes representing American International in 1969, La.-Lafayette in 1971 and Ky. Wesleyan in 2003 were declared ineligible after the tournament. Under NCAA rules, the teams' and ineligible student-athletes' records were deleted, and the teams' places in the final standings were vacated.

Season	Site of Finals	Coach of Champion	Outstanding Player Award
1957	Evansville, Ind.	Lee Pfund, Wheaton (Ill.)	Mel Peterson, Wheaton (Ill.)
1958	Evansville, Ind.	Duane Clodfelter, South Dakota	Ed Smallwood, Evansville
1959	Evansville, Ind.	Arad McCutchan, Evansville	Hugh Ahlering, Evansville
1960	Evansville, Ind.	Arad McCutchan, Evansville	Ed Smallwood, Evansville
1961	Evansville, Ind.	Ray Mears, Wittenberg	Don Jacobsen, South Dakota St.
1962	Evansville, Ind.	James Phelan, Mt. St. Mary's	Ron Rohrer, Sacramento St.
1963	Evansville, Ind.	Jim Iverson, South Dakota St.	Wayne Rasmussen, South Dakota St.
1964	Evansville, Ind.	Arad McCutchan, Evansville	Jerry Sloan, Evansville
1965	Evansville, Ind.	Arad McCutchan, Evansville	Jerry Sloan, Evansville
1966	Evansville, Ind.	Guy Strong, Ky. Wesleyan	Sam Smith, Ky. Wesleyan
1967	Evansville, Ind.	C.E. Gaines, Winston-Salem	Earl Monroe, Winston-Salem
1968	Evansville, Ind.	Bob Daniels, Ky. Wesleyan	Jerry Newsom, Indiana St.
1969	Evansville, Ind.	Bob Daniels, Ky. Wesleyan	George Tinsley, Ky. Wesleyan
1970	Evansville, Ind.	Herb Magee, Philadelphia U.	Ted McClain, Tennessee St.
1971	Evansville, Ind.	Arad McCutchan, Evansville	Don Buse, Evansville
1972	Evansville, Ind.	Charles Moir, Roanoke	Hal Johnston, Roanoke
1973	Evansville, Ind.	Bob Jones, Ky. Wesleyan	Mike Williams, Ky. Wesleyan
1974	Evansville, Ind.	Nathaniel Frazier, Morgan St.	Marvin Webster, Morgan St.
1975	Evansville, Ind.	Sonny Allen, Old Dominion	Wilson Washington, Old Dominion
1976	Evansville, Ind.	Don Zech, Puget Sound	Curt Peterson, Puget Sound
1977	Springfield, Mass.	Ron Shumate, Chattanooga	Wayne Golden, Chattanooga
1978	Springfield, Mo.	John Chaney, Cheyney	Andrew Fields, Cheyney
1979	Springfield, Mo.	Bill Jones, North Ala.	Perry Oden, North Ala.
1980	Springfield, Mass.	Dave Robbins, Virginia Union	Keith Valentine, Virginia Union
1981	Springfield, Mass.	Hal Wissel, Fla. Southern	John Ebeling, Fla. Southern
1982	Springfield, Mass.	Wil Jones, Dist. Columbia	Michael Britt, Dist. Columbia
1983	Springfield, Mass.	Ralph Underhill, Wright St.	Gary Monroe, Wright St.
1984	Springfield, Mass.	Lynn Nance, Central Mo. St.	Ron Nunnelly, Central Mo. St.
1985	Springfield, Mass.	Bill Jones, Jacksonville St.	Mark Tetzlaff, South Dakota St.

Darnell Hinson's defensive work helped the Northeastern State guard win 2003 MOP honors.

Northeastern State's Justin Barkley and coach Larry Gipson celebrate after Barkley sank a three-pointer and drew a foul in the title game.

CHAMPIONSHIPS

Season	Site of Finals	Coach of Champion	Outstanding Player Award
1986	Springfield, Mass.	Dave Bike, Sacred Heart	Roger Younger, Sacred Heart
1987	Springfield, Mass.	Wayne Chapman, Ky. Wesleyan	Sam Smith, Ky. Wesleyan
1988	Springfield, Mass.	Don Doucette, Mass.-Lowell	Leo Parent, Mass.-Lowell
1989	Springfield, Mass.	Michael Bernard, N.C. Central	Miles Clarke, N.C. Central
1990	Springfield, Mass.	Wayne Chapman, Ky. Wesleyan	Wade Green, Cal St. Bakersfield
1991	Springfield, Mass.	Gary Elliott, North Ala.	Lambert Shell, Bridgeport
1992	Springfield, Mass.	Dave Robbins, Virginia Union	Derrick Johnson, Virginia Union
1993	Springfield, Mass.	Pat Douglass, Cal St. Bakersfield	Tyrone Davis, Cal St. Bakersfield
1994	Springfield, Mass.	Pat Douglass, Cal St. Bakersfield	Stan Gouard, Southern Ind.
1995	Louisville, Ky.	Bruce Pearl, Southern Ind.	William Wilson, UC Riverside
1996	Louisville, Ky.	Gary Garner, Fort Hays St.	Sherick Simpson, Fort Hays St.
1997	Louisville, Ky.	Pat Douglass, Cal St. Bakersfield	Kebu Stewart, Cal St. Bakersfield
1998	Louisville, Ky.	Bob Williams, Ky. Wesleyan	Antonio Garcia, Ky. Wesleyan
1999	Louisville, Ky.	Bob Williams, Ky. Wesleyan	Antonio Garcia, Ky. Wesleyan
2000	Louisville, Ky.	Mike Dunlap, Metro St.	DeMarcos Anzures, Metro St.
2001	Bakersfield, Calif.	Ray Harper, Ky. Wesleyan	Lorico Duncan, Ky. Wesleyan
2002	Evansville, Ind.	Mike Dunlap, Metro St.	Patrick Mutombo, Metro St.
2003	Lakeland, Fla.	Larry Gipson, Northeastern St.	Darnell Hinson, Northeastern St.

Individual Records

(Three-game minimum for series records and percentages)

POINTS, GAME
54—Willie Jones, American (91) vs. Evansville (101), 1960; Bill Fennelly, Central Mo. St. (112) vs. Jacksonville St. (91), 1980.

POINTS, TOURNAMENT
185—Jack Sullivan, Mt. St. Mary's, 1957 (36 vs. CCNY, 48 vs. N.C. Central, 39 vs. Rider, 19 vs. Ky. Wesleyan, 43 vs. Cal. St. Los Angeles).

FIELD GOALS, GAME
22—Phil Jackson, North Dakota (107) vs. Parsons (56), 1967.

FIELD GOALS, TOURNAMENT
71—Jack Sullivan, Mt. St. Mary's, 1957 (14 vs. CCNY, 19 vs. N.C. Central, 16 vs. Rider, 8 vs. Ky. Wesleyan, 14 vs. Cal. St. Los Angeles).

THREE-POINT FIELD GOALS, GAME
11—Kenny Warren, Cal St. Bakersfield (98) vs. Grand Canyon (68), 1993.

THREE-POINT FIELD GOALS, TOURNAMENT
22—Kenny Warren, Cal St. Bakersfield, 1993 (11 vs. Grand Canyon, 3 vs. Alas. Anchorage, 5 vs. N.C. Central, 1 vs. Wayne St. [Mich.], 2 vs. Troy St.).

FREE THROWS MADE, GAME
24—Dave Twardzik, Old Dominion (102) vs. Norfolk St. (97), 1971.

FREE THROWS MADE, TOURNAMENT
55—Don Jacobsen, South Dakota St., 1961 (9 vs. Cornell College, 22 vs. Prairie View, 9 vs. UC Santa Barb., 11 vs. Southeast Mo. St., 4 vs. Mt. St. Mary's).

HIGHEST FREE-THROW PERCENTAGE, GAME (Minimum 18 Made)
100.0%—Ralph Talley, Norfolk St. (70) vs. Virginia Union (60), 1986 (18-18).

ASSISTS, GAME
20—Steve Ray, Bridgeport (132) vs. Stonehill (127) (ot), 1989.

ASSISTS, TOURNAMENT
49—Tyrone Tate, Southern Ind., 1994 (8 vs. Ky. Wesleyan, 3 vs. Wayne St. [Mich.], 16 vs. South Dakota, 16 vs. New Hamp. Col., 6 vs. Cal St. Bakersfield).

REBOUNDS, TOURNAMENT (SINCE 1968)
99—Marvin Webster, Morgan St., 1974 (5 games).

Team Records

(Three-game minimum for tournament records and percentages)

POINTS, GAME
132—Bridgeport vs. Stonehill (127) (ot), 1989; Central Okla. vs. Washburn (114), 1992.

POINTS, TOURNAMENT
567—Southern Ind., 1995 (95 vs. Hillsdale, 102 vs. Ky. Wesleyan, 102 vs. Northern Ky., 108 vs. New Hamp. Col., 89 vs. Norfolk St., 71 vs. UC Riverside).

FIELD GOALS, GAME
54—Bentley (129) vs. Stonehill (118), 1989.

FIELD GOALS, TOURNAMENT
198—Southern Ind., 1995 (37 vs. Hillsdale, 37 vs. Ky. Wesleyan, 34 vs. Northern Ky., 40 vs. New Hamp. Col., 26 vs. Norfolk St., 24 vs. UC Riverside).

THREE-POINT FIELD GOALS, GAME
23—Troy St. (126) vs. New Hamp. Col (123), 1993.

THREE-POINT FIELD GOALS, TOURNAMENT
57—Troy St., 1993 (9 vs. Fla. Southern, 14 vs. Delta St., 6 vs. Washburn, 23 vs. New Hamp. Col., 5 vs. Cal St. Bakersfield).

FREE THROWS MADE, GAME
46—Evansville (110) vs. N.C. A&T (92), 1959.

FREE THROWS MADE, TOURNAMENT
142—Mt. St. Mary's, 1957.

ASSISTS, GAME
36—Troy St. (126) vs. New Hamp. Col. (123), 1993.

ASSISTS, TOURNAMENT
120—North Dakota, 1990.

All-Tournament Teams

*Most Outstanding Player.
#Participation voided by action of the NCAA Council.

1957
*Mel Peterson, Wheaton (Ill.)
Jack Sullivan, Mt. St. Mary's
Mason Cope, Ky. Wesleyan
Bob Whitehead, Wheaton (Ill.)
Jim Daniels, South Dakota

1958
*Ed Smallwood, Evansville
Jim Browne, St. Michael's
Jim Daniels, South Dakota

Mel Peterson, Wheaton (Ill.)
Dick Zeitler, St. Michael's

1959
*Hugh Ahlering, Evansville
Joe Cotton, N.C. A&T
Jack Israel, Southwest Mo. St.
Paul Benes, Hope
Leo Hill, Cal St. Los Angeles

1960
*Ed Smallwood, Evansville
Dale Wise, Evansville
Tom Cooke, Chapman
Gary Auten, Ky. Wesleyan
William Jones, American

1961
*Don Jacobsen, South Dakota St.
John O'Reilly, Mt. St. Mary's
George Fisher, Wittenberg
Vivan Reed, Southeast Mo. St.
Carl Ritter, Southeast Mo. St.

1962
*Ron Rohrer, Sacramento St.
Jim Mumford, Neb. Wesleyan
Ed Spila, Southern Ill.
John O'Reilly, Mt. St. Mary's
Ed Pfeiffer, Mt. St. Mary's

1963
*Wayne Rasmussen, South Dakota St.
Tom Black, South Dakota St.
Bob Cherry, Wittenberg
Bill Fisher, Wittenberg
Al Thrasher, Wittenberg

1964
*Jerry Sloan, Evansville
Maurice McHartley, N.C. A&T
Larry Humes, Evansville
Bill Stevens, Akron
Buster Briley, Evansville

1965
*Jerry Sloan, Evansville
Richard Tarrant, St. Michael's
Walt Frazier, Southern Ill.
George McNeil, Southern Ill.
Larry Humes, Evansville

1966
*Sam Smith, Ky. Wesleyan
Clarence Smith, Southern Ill.
George McNeil, Southern Ill.
David Lee, Southern Ill.
Phil Jackson, North Dakota

1967
*Earl Monroe, Winston-Salem
Lou Shepherd, Southwest Mo. St.
Sam Smith, Ky. Wesleyan
Danny Bolden, Southwest Mo. St.
Dallas Thornton, Ky. Wesleyan

1968
*Jerry Newsom, Indiana St.
Larry Jeffries, Trinity (Tex.)
George Tinsley, Ky. Wesleyan
Fred Hardman, Indiana St.
Dallas Thornton, Ky. Wesleyan

1969
*George Tinsley, Ky. Wesleyan
Curtis Perry, Southwest Mo. St.
Tommy Hobgood, Ky. Wesleyan
Mert Bancroft, Southwest Mo. St.
Bob Rutherford, American Int'l

1970
*Ted McClain, Tennessee St.
Randy Smith, Buffalo St.
Carl Poole, Philadelphia U.
Howard Lee, UC Riverside
John Pierantozzi, Philadelphia U.

1971
*Don Buse, Evansville
#Dwight Lamar, La.-Lafayette
Rick Coffey, Evansville
John Duncan, Ky. Wesleyan
Skip Noble, Old Dominion

1972
*Hal Johnston, Roanoke
Leonard Robinson, Tennessee St.
Lloyd Neal, Tennessee St.
Jay Piccola, Roanoke
Len Paul, Akron

1973
*Mike Williams, Ky. Wesleyan
Ron Gilliam, Brockport St.
Mike Boylan, Assumption
Leonard Robinson, Tennessee St.
Roger Zornes, Ky. Wesleyan

1974
*Marvin Webster, Morgan St.
John Grochowalski, Assumption
Randy Magers, Southwest Mo. St.
William Doolittle, Southwest Mo. St.
Alvin O'Neal, Morgan St.

1975
*Wilson Washington, Old Dominion
Wilbur Holland, New Orleans
John Grochowalski, Assumption
Joey Caruthers, Old Dominion
Paul Brennan, Assumption

1976
*Curt Peterson, Puget Sound
Wayne Golden, Chattanooga
Jeff Fuhrmann, Old Dominion
Jeff Furry, Eastern Ill.
Brant Gibler, Puget Sound

1977
*Wayne Golden, Chattanooga
Joe Allen, Randolph-Macon
Otis Boddie, North Ala.
William Gordon, Chattanooga
Hector Olivencia, Sacred Heart

1978
*Andrew Fields, Cheyney
Kenneth Hynson, Cheyney
Tom Anderson, Wis.-Green Bay
Charlie Thomas, Eastern Ill.
Jerry Prather, UCF

1979
*Perry Oden, North Ala.
Carlton Hurdle, Bridgeport

Ron Ripley, Wis.-Green Bay
Ron Darby, North Ala.
Rory Lindgren, Wis.-Green Bay

1980
*Keith Valentine, Virginia Union
Larry Holmes, Virginia Union
Bobby Jones, New York Tech
John Ebeling, Fla. Southern
Johnny Buckmon, North Ala.

1981
*John Ebeling, Fla. Southern
Mike Hayes, Fla. Southern
Durelle Lewis, Mt. St. Mary's
Jim Rowe, Mt. St. Mary's
Jay Bruchak, Mt. St. Mary's

1982
*Michael Britt, Dist. Columbia
John Ebeling, Fla. Southern
Dwight Higgs, Ky. Wesleyan
Earl Jones, Dist. Columbia
Wayne McDaniel, Cal St. Bakersfield

1983
*Gary Monroe, Wright St.
Anthony Bias, Wright St.
Fred Moore, Wright St.
Earl Jones, Dist. Columbia
Michael Britt, Dist. Columbia

1984
*Ron Nunnelly, Central Mo. St.
Brian Pesko, Central Mo. St.
Kenneth Bannister, St. Augustine's
Rod Drake, Ky. Wesleyan
Robert Harris, North Ala.

1985
*Mark Tetzlaff, South Dakota St.
Dave Bennett, Ky. Wesleyan
Melvin Allen, Jacksonville St.
Robert Spurgeon, Jacksonville St.
Darryle Edwards, Mt. St. Mary's

1986
*Roger Younger, Sacred Heart
Kevin Stevens, Sacred Heart
Keith Johnson, Sacred Heart
Riley Ellis, Southeast Mo. St.
Ronny Rankin, Southeast Mo. St.

1987
*Sam Smith, Ky. Wesleyan
Andra Whitlow, Ky. Wesleyan
John Worth, Ky. Wesleyan
Mike Runski, Gannon
Jerome Johnson, Mont. St.-Billings

1988
*Leo Parent, Mass.-Lowell
Bobby Licare, Mass.-Lowell
Averian Parrish, Alas. Anchorage
Jerry Johnson, Fla. Southern
Darryl Thomas, Troy St.

1989
*Miles Clarke, N.C. Central
Dominique Stephens, N.C. Central
Antoine Sifford, N.C. Central
Earnest Taylor, Southeast Mo. St.
Maurice Pullum, UC Riverside

1990
*Wade Green, Cal St. Bakersfield
LeRoy Ellis, Ky. Wesleyan
Corey Crowder, Ky. Wesleyan
Dave Vonesh, North Dakota
Vincent Mitchell, Ky. Wesleyan

1991
*Lambert Shell, Bridgeport
Pat Morris, Bridgeport
Fred Stafford, North Ala.
Allen Williams, North Ala.
Carl Wilmer, North Ala.

1992
*Derrick Johnson, Virginia Union
Reggie Jones, Virginia Union
Winston Jones, Bridgeport
Steve Wills, Bridgeport
Kenney Toomer, Calif. (Pa.)

1993
*Tyrone Davis, Cal St. Bakersfield
Roheen Oats, Cal St. Bakersfield
Terry McCord, Troy St.
Wayne Robertson, New Hamp. Col.
Danny Lewis, Wayne St. (Mich.)

1994
*Stan Gouard, Southern Ind.
Kenny Warren, Cal St. Bakersfield
Reggie Phillips, Cal St. Bakersfield
Roheen Oats, Cal St. Bakersfield
Tyrone Tate, Southern Ind.

1995
*William Wilson, UC Riverside
Brian Huebner, Southern Ind.
Chad Gilbert, Southern Ind.
Boo Purdom, UC Riverside
Corey Williams, Norfolk St.

1996
*Sherick Simpson, Fort Hays St.
Paul Cluxton, Northern Ky.
LaRon Moore, Northern Ky.
Alonzo Goldston, Fort Hays St.
Kebu Stewart, Cal St. Bakersfield

1997
*Kebu Stewart, Cal St. Bakersfield
Cliff Clinton, Northern Ky.
Paul Cluxton, Northern Ky.
Shannon Minor, Northern Ky.
Terrance Springer, Salem Int'l

1998
*Antonio Garcia, Ky. Wesleyan
Dana Williams, Ky. Wesleyan
Jason Cox, Ky. Wesleyan
Dante Ross, Ky. Wesleyan
William Davis, Virginia Union

1999
*Antonio Garcia, Ky. Wesleyan
Dana Williams, Ky. Wesleyan
Lee Barlow, Metro St.
DeMarcos Anzures, Metro St.
Innocent Kere, Fla. Southern

2000
*DeMarcos Anzures, Metro St.
Kane Oakley, Metro St.
John Bynum, Metro St.
Lee Barlow, Metro St.
Lorico Duncan, Ky. Wesleyan

2001
*Lorico Duncan, Ky. Wesleyan
Marshall Sanders, Ky. Wesleyan
Ewan Auguste, Washburn
Ryan Murphy, Washburn
Sylvere Bryan, Washburn

2002
*Patrick Mutombo, Metro St.
Clayton Smith, Metro St.
Chris Landry, Ky. Wesleyan
Ronald Evans, Ky. Wesleyan
Ronald Murray, Shaw

2003
*Darnell Hinson, Northeastern St.
Shon Robinson, Northeastern St.
Derek Cline, Northeastern St.
Marlon Parmer, Ky. Wesleyan
Eugene Dabney, Ky. Wesleyan

#The participation of Dwight Lamar (Louisiana-Lafayette)
in the 1971 tournament was voided by action of the
NCAA Council.

CHAMPIONSHIPS

Division III Championship

2003 Results

FIRST ROUND
Alvernia 58, Mary Washington 53
Wis.-Oshkosh 78, Milwaukee Engr. 56
SCAD 66, Chris. Newport 61
Ill. Wesleyan 79, Blackburn 59
Buena Vista 96, Illinois Col. 66
Aurora 67, Trinity (Tex.) 66
Gust. Adolphus 65, Whitworth 55
Maryville (Tenn.) 70, Mississippi Col. 58
Salem St. 81, St. Joseph's (Me.) 76
Hamilton 93, Colby-Sawyer 68
Southern Vt. 63, Lasell 60
Western Conn. St. 84, Clark (Mass.) 82
Scranton 58, Buffalo St. 56
John Carroll 85, Pitt.-Bradford 65
Merchant Marine 63, CCNY 57
Montclair St. 74, Elizabethtown 69

SECOND ROUND
Randolph-Macon 72, Alvernia 69 (ot)
Wis.-Oshkosh 84, Hope 77
Hampden-Sydney 56, SCAD 54
Ill. Wesleyan 85, Washington (Mo.) 73
Buena Vista 84, Rockford 72
Occidental 80, Aurora 61
Gust. Adolphus 75, Wis.-Stevens Point 62
Hanover 68, Maryville (Tenn.) 64
Williams 94, Salem St. 67
Hamilton 72, St. John Fisher 68
Amherst 84, Southern Vt. 60
Rochester 73, Western Conn. St. 62
Scranton 77, Ursinus 75
Wooster 77, John Carroll 75
Ramapo 92, Merchant Marine 76
Montclair St. 95, Catholic 78

SECTIONAL SEMIFINALS
Wis.-Oshkosh 53, Randolph-Macon 47
Hampden-Sydney 76, Ill. Wesleyan 68
Occidental 67, Buena Vista 62
Gust. Adolphus 79, Hanover 66
Williams 76, Hamilton 65
Amherst 74, Rochester 68
Wooster 75, Scranton 64
Ramapo 89, Montclair St. 80

SECTIONAL CHAMPIONSHIPS
Hampden-Sydney 68, Wis.-Oshkosh 63
Gust. Adolphus 74, Occidental 56
Williams 91, Amherst 74
Wooster 68, Ramapo 64

SEMIFINALS
Williams 74, Wooster 72 (ot)
Gust. Adolphus 79, Hampden-Sydney 68

THIRD PLACE
Wooster 78, Hampden-Sydney 74

CHAMPIONSHIP
Williams 67, Gust. Adolphus 65

Box Scores

SEMIFINALS
MARCH 21, AT SALEM, VIRGINIA
Williams 74, Wooster 72 (ot)

Williams	FG-FGA	FTM-FTA	R	PF	TP
Michael Crotty	1-8	0-0	2	2	2
Jaris Cole	2-6	0-0	1	2	4
Chuck Abba	2-4	0-0	3	4	5
Benjamin Coffin	14-24	5-6	6	2	33
Drew DeMuth	5-10	1-2	9	4	11
Michael Graham	2-3	0-1	1	2	4
Andrew Newton	0-0	0-0	0	2	0
Tim Folan	4-10	1-3	4	3	11
Tucker Kain	1-4	0-0	1	1	2
Sumant Baht	1-2	0-0	0	0	2
Team			1		
Totals	32-71	7-11	28	22	74

Wooster	FG-FGA	FTM-FTA	R	PF	TP
Rodney Mitchell	3-8	0-0	5	0	7
Kyle Witucky	0-3	0-2	3	2	0
Matt Smith	1-2	2-2	3	3	4
Blake Mealer	2-4	0-0	0	3	5
Bryan Nelson	8-12	13-14	9	3	29
Ryan Snyder	2-2	2-2	1	1	8
Andrew Lilienthal	2-4	2-2	3	1	6
Matt Schlingman	6-9	1-2	7	2	13
Team			5		
Totals	24-44	20-24	36	15	72

Halftime: Wooster 34, Williams 32. End of regulation: Tied at 64. Three-point field goals: Williams 3-15 (Crotty 0-5, Cole 0-2, Abba 1-3, Folan 2-3, Kain 0-2); Wooster 4-9 (Mitchell 1-2, Mealer 1-2, Nelson 0-2, Snyder 2-2, Lilienthal 0-1). Officials: John Spears, Dennis Howard, Tom Stinnett. Attendance: 3,980.

Gust. Adolphus 79, Hampden-Sydney 68

Hampden-Sydney	FG-FGA	FTM-FTA	R	PF	TP
Brandon Randall	2-7	4-4	2	3	9
Jeff Monroe	6-15	3-4	4	1	17
Marcus Gregory	3-9	0-0	5	3	7
Lane Brooks	4-7	1-1	6	3	9
Jason Holman	3-3	0-0	3	1	6
Jay Patrick	0-2	0-0	0	3	0
Brian Gunn	0-1	0-0	0	0	0
Matt Rannals	0-0	0-0	0	0	0
Matt McKeag	1-3	2-2	0	4	5
David Willson	2-3	6-8	5	1	10
Andy Jackson	2-4	1-1	4	2	5
Team			2		
Totals	23-54	17-20	31	21	68

Gust. Adolphus	FG-FGA	FTM-FTA	R	PF	TP
Chris TeBrake	4-8	2-2	3	0	11
Eric Nelson	2-8	0-0	4	1	6
Brett Boese	3-3	3-5	3	2	9
Tim Brown	7-9	2-2	2	1	20
David Newell	3-7	1-1	7	5	7
Doug Espenson	10-17	4-7	8	2	24
Hans Sviggum	0-2	0-0	0	0	0
Adam Hoffarber	0-0	0-2	1	0	0
Trent Hollerich,	0-0	0-0	0	0	0
Adam TeBrake	0-0	0-0	0	0	0
Derek Nelson	1-1	0-2	1	5	2
Adam Thorson	0-0	0-0	0	0	0
Team			2		
Totals	30-55	12-21	31	16	79

Halftime: Gust. Adolphus 39, Hampden-Sydney 37. Three-point field goals: Hampden-Sydney 5-22 (Randall 1-4, Monroe 2-8, Gregory 1-4, Patrick 0-2, Gunn 0-1, McKeag 1-3); Gust. Adolphus 7-20 (C. TeBrake 1-3, Nelson 2-8, Brown 4-6, Espenson 0-3). Officials: Kevin O'Connell, Kevin McGoff, Chris Ogden. Attendance: 4,179.

THIRD PLACE
MARCH 22, AT SALEM, VIRGINIA
Wooster 78, Hampden-Sydney 74

Wooster	FG-FGA	FTM-FTA	R	PF	TP
Rodney Mitchell	3-6	4-4	3	0	11
Kyle Witucky	2-7	2-4	1	2	6
Matt Smith	5-8	0-0	3	4	14
Blake Mealer	2-7	0-0	5	3	4
Bryan Nelson	9-13	11-11	11	4	29
Ryan Snyder	1-2	2-2	2	2	5
Andrew Lilienthal	1-2	2-2	1	1	4
P.J. McCloud	1-1	0-0	2	3	2
Matt Schlingman	0-1	3-4	0	4	3
Team			4		
TOTALS	24-47	24-27	32	23	78

Hampden-Sydney	FG-FGA	FTM-FTA	R	PF	TP
Brandon Randall	1-4	0-0	0	5	2
Jeff Monroe	10-19	5-6	0	1	27
Marcus Gregory	3-8	0-0	3	1	7
David Willson	3-3	2-4	9	4	8
Lane Brooks	0-5	0-0	0	1	0
Jay Patrick	1-1	2-2	2	3	4
Brian Gunn	0-0	0-0	1	0	0
Matt Rannals	0-1	0-0	0	0	0
Matt McKeag	0-1	0-0	0	0	0
Andy Jackson	6-9	3-3	4	4	15
Jason Holman	4-6	2-3	4	2	10
Mike Thompson	0-0	1-2	0	1	1
Team			3		
TOTALS	28-57	15-20	26	22	74

Halftime: Wooster 40, Hampden-Sydney 28. Three-point field goals: Wooster 6-20 (Mitchell 1-2, Witucky 0-4, Smith 4-7, Mealer 0-3, Nelson 0-1, Snyder 1-2, Lilienthal 0-1); Hampden-Sydney (Randall 0-3, Monroe 2-6, Gregory 1-2, Rannals 0-1, McKeag 0-1). Officials: Ken Falkner, LeMar Simpson, Jim Czocher. Attendance: 3,867.

CHAMPIONSHIP
MARCH 22, AT SALEM, VIRGINIA
Williams 67, Gust. Adolphus 65

Williams	FG-FGA	FTM-FTA	R	PF	TP
Michael Crotty	1-6	0-0	3	1	2
Jaris Cole	3-7	0-0	3	2	6
Chuck Abba	2-6	3-4	5	4	7
Benjamin Coffin	4-12	3-6	8	4	11
Drew DeMuth	3-6	3-4	5	1	9
Andy Campbell	0-0	0-0	0	0	0
Michael Graham	3-8	2-4	2	3	9
Andrew Newton	0-1	0-0	0	0	0
Tim Folan	4-10	4-4	2	2	15
Tucker Kain	2-5	0-0	1	2	6
Sumant Baht	2-5	0-0	0	2	2
Team			4		
Totals	23-62	15-22	33	19	67

Gust. Adolphus	FG-FGA	FTM-FTA	R	PF	TP
Chris TeBrake	5-6	0-2	3	1	11
Eric Nelson	0-3	1-2	5	5	1
Brett Boese	1-2	0-0	1	5	2
Tim Brown	7-13	4-4	5	3	19
David Newell	1-4	2-2	4	2	4
Doug Espenson	5-7	3-4	10	2	13
Hans Sviggum	2-2	0-0	1	0	4
Derek Nelson	5-9	1-4	5	5	11
Adam Thorson	0-1	0-0	0	1	0
Team			2		
TOTALS	26-47	11-18	36	24	65

Halftime: Gust. Adolphus 30, Williams 27. Three-point field goals: Williams 6-24 (Crotty 0-3, Cole 0-1, Abba 0-4, Coffin 0-1, Graham 1-3, Folan 3-7, Kain 2-5); Gust. Adolphus 2-5 (C. TeBrake 1-1, Nelson 0-1, Brown 1-3). Officials: Brian Dorsey, Terence Murphy, John Regan. Attendance: 3,867.

Year-by-Year Results

Season	Champion	Score	Runner-Up	Third Place	Fourth Place
1975	LeMoyne-Owen	57-54	Rowan	Augustana (Ill.)	Brockport St.
1976	Scranton	60-57	Wittenberg	Augustana (Ill.)	Plattsburgh St.
1977	Wittenberg	79-66	Oneonta St.	Scranton	Hamline
1978	North Park	69-57	Widener	Albion	Stony Brook
1979	North Park	66-62	Potsdam St.	Frank. & Marsh.	Centre
1980	North Park	83-76	Upsala	Wittenberg	Longwood
1981	Potsdam St.	67-65(ot)	Augustana (Ill.)	Ursinus	Otterbein
1982	Wabash	83-62	Potsdam St.	Brooklyn	Cal St. Stanislaus
1983	Scranton	64-63	Wittenberg	Roanoke	Wis.-Whitewater
1984	Wis.-Whitewater	103-86	Clark (Mass.)	DePauw	Upsala
1985	North Park	72-71	Potsdam St.	Neb. Wesleyan	Widener
1986	Potsdam St.	76-73	LeMoyne-Owen	Neb. Wesleyan	New Jersey City
1987	North Park	106-100	Clark (Mass.)	Wittenberg	Richard Stockton
1988	Ohio Wesleyan	92-70	Scranton	Neb. Wesleyan	Hartwick
1989	Wis.-Whitewater	94-86	Col. of New Jersey	Southern Me.	Centre
1990	Rochester	43-42	DePauw	Washington (Md.)	Calvin
1991	Wis.-Platteville	81-74	Frank. & Marsh.	Otterbein	Ramapo
1992	Calvin	62-49	Rochester	Wis.-Platteville	New Jersey City
1993	Ohio Northern	71-68	Augustana (Ill.)	Rowan	Mass.-Dartmouth
1994	Lebanon Valley	66-59†	New York U.	Wittenberg	St. Thomas (Minn.)
1995	Wis.-Platteville	69-55	Manchester	Rowan	Trinity (Conn.)
1996	Rowan	100-93	Hope	Ill. Wesleyan	Frank. & Marsh.
1997	Ill. Wesleyan	89-86	Neb. Wesleyan	Williams	Alvernia
1998	Wis.-Platteville	69-56	Hope	Williams	Wilkes
1999	Wis.-Platteville	76-75(ot)	Hampden-Sydney	Connecticut Col.	Wm. Paterson
2000	Calvin	79-75	Wis-Eau Claire	Salem St.	Frank. & Marsh.
2001	Catholic	76-62	Wm. Paterson	Ill. Wesleyan	Ohio Northern
2002	Otterbein	102-83	Elizabethtown	Carthage	Rochester
2003	Williams	67-65	Gust. Adolphus	Wooster	Hampden-Sydney

Season	Site of Finals	Coach of Champion	Outstanding Player Award
1975	Reading, Pa.	Jerry Johnson, LeMoyne-Owen	Bob Newman, LeMoyne-Owen
1976	Reading, Pa.	Bob Bessoir, Scranton	Jack Maher, Scranton
1977	Rock Island, Ill.	Larry Hunter, Wittenberg	Rick White, Wittenberg
1978	Rock Island, Ill.	Dan McCarrell, North Park	Michael Harper, North Park
1979	Rock Island, Ill.	Dan McCarrell, North Park	Michael Harper, North Park
1980	Rock Island, Ill.	Dan McCarrell, North Park	Michael Thomas, North Park
1981	Rock Island, Ill.	Jerry Welsh, Potsdam St.	Maxwell Artis, Augustana (Ill.)
1982	Grand Rapids, Mich.	Mac Petty, Wabash	Pete Metzelaars, Wabash
1983	Grand Rapids, Mich.	Bob Bessoir, Scranton	Bill Bessoir, Scranton
1984	Grand Rapids, Mich.	Dave Vander Meulen, Wis.-Whitewater	Andre McKoy, Wis.-Whitewater
1985	Grand Rapids, Mich.	Bosco Djurickovic, North Park	Earnest Hubbard, North Park
1986	Grand Rapids, Mich.	Jerry Welsh, Potsdam St.	Roosevelt Bullock, Potsdam St.
1987	Grand Rapids, Mich.	Bosco Djurickovic, North Park	Michael Starks, North Park
1988	Grand Rapids, Mich.	Gene Mehaffey, Ohio Wesleyan	Scott Tedder, Ohio Wesleyan
1989	Springfield, Ohio	Dave Vander Meulen, Wis.-Whitewater	Greg Grant, Col. of New Jersey
1990	Springfield, Ohio	Mike Neer, Rochester	Chris Fite, Rochester
1991	Springfield, Ohio	Bo Ryan, Wis.-Platteville	Shawn Frison, Wis.-Platteville
1992	Springfield, Ohio	Ed Douma, Calvin	Steve Honderd, Calvin
1993	Buffalo, N.Y.	Joe Campoli, Ohio Northern	Kirk Anderson, Augustana (Ill.)
1994	Buffalo, N.Y.	Pat Flannery, Lebanon Valley	Mike Rhoades, Lebanon Valley Adam Crawford, New York U.
1995	Buffalo, N.Y.	Bo Ryan, Wis.-Platteville	Ernie Peavy, Wis.-Platteville
1996	Salem, Va.	John Giannini, Rowan	Terrence Stewart, Rowan
1997	Salem, Va.	Dennie Bridges, Ill. Wesleyan	Bryan Crabtree, Ill. Wesleyan
1998	Salem, Va.	Bo Ryan, Wis.-Platteville	Ben Hoffmann, Wis.-Platteville
1999	Salem, Va.	Bo Ryan, Wis.-Platteville	Merrill Brunson, Wis.-Platteville
2000	Salem, Va.	Kevin Vande Streek, Calvin	Sherm Carstensen, Calvin
2001	Salem, Va.	Mike Lonergan, Catholic	Pat Maloney, Catholic
2002	Salem, Va.	Dick Reynolds, Otterbein	Jeff Gibbs, Otterbein
2003	Salem, Va.	David Paulsen, Williams	Benjamin Coffin, Williams

Photo by Andres Alonso/NCAA Photos

Williams' Tim Folan blocks the shot of Eric Nelson of Gustavus Adolphus during the title game.

CHAMPIONSHIPS

Individual Records

(Minimum three games for series records.)

POINTS, GAME
49—Gerald Reece, William Penn (85) vs. North Park (81), 1981.

POINTS, TOURNAMENT
177—Michael Nogelo, Williams, 1998 (31 vs. Trinity [Conn.], 30 vs. Springfield, 25 vs. Hamilton, 35 vs. St. Lawrence, 18 vs. Wis.-Platteville, 38 vs. Wilkes).

SCORING AVERAGE, TOURNAMENT
36.3—Greg Grant, Col. of New Jersey, 1988 (40 vs. Bridgewater [Va.], 45 vs. Emory & Henry, 24 vs. Hartwick).

FIELD GOALS, GAME
21—Gerald Reece, William Penn (85) vs. North Park (81), 1981.

FIELD GOALS, TOURNAMENT
68—Greg Grant, Col. of New Jersey, 1989 (11 vs. Shenandoah, 11 vs. New Jersey City, 16 vs. Potsdam St., 16 vs. Southern Me., 14 vs. Wis.-Whitewater).

THREE-POINT FIELD GOALS, GAME
12—Kirk Anderson, Augustana (Ill.) (100) vs. Wis.-Platteville (86), 1993.

THREE-POINT FIELD GOALS, TOURNAMENT
35—Kirk Anderson, Augustana (Ill.), 1993 (4 vs. DePauw, 5 vs. Beloit, 4 vs. La Verne, 12 vs. Wis.-Platteville, 6 vs. Rowan, 4 vs. Ohio Northern).

FREE THROWS MADE, GAME
21—Tom Montsma, Calvin (88) vs. Wabash (76), 1980.

FREE THROWS MADE, TOURNAMENT
52—Daimen Hunter, Alvernia, 1997 (6 vs. Lebanon Valley, 14 vs. Goucher, 5 vs. Rochester Inst., 11 vs. Salisbury St., 0 vs. Ill. Wesleyan, 16 vs. Williams).

ASSISTS, GAME
20—Matt Nadelhoffer, Wheaton (Ill.) (131) vs. Grinnell (117), 1996.

ASSISTS, TOURNAMENT
62—Ricky Spicer, Wis.-Whitewater, 1989.

REBOUNDS, TOURNAMENT
83—Jeff Gibbs, Otterbein, 2002.

REBOUNDING AVERAGE, TOURNAMENT
16.6—Jeff Gibbs, Otterbein, 2002 (13 vs. Bethany (W.Va.), 6 vs. Randolph Macon, 24 vs. DePauw; 15 vs. Carthage; 25 vs. Elizabethtown).

Team Records

(Minimum three games for tournament records.)

POINTS, GAME
132—Ill. Wesleyan vs. Grinnell (91), 2001.

POINTS, TOURNAMENT
594—Rowan, 1996 (130 vs. York [N.Y.], 102 vs. New Jersey City, 85 vs. Williams, 98 vs. Richard Stockton, 79 vs. Ill. Wesleyan, 100 vs. Hope).

FIELD GOALS, GAME
52—Wheaton (Ill.) (131) vs. Grinnell (117), 1996.

FIELD GOALS, TOURNAMENT
206—Rowan, 1996 (45 vs. York [N.Y.], 31 vs. New Jersey City, 29 vs. Williams, 35 vs. Richard Stockton, 32 vs. Ill. Wesleyan, 34 vs. Hope).

THREE-POINT FIELD GOALS, GAME
22—Grinnell (117) vs. Wheaton (Ill.) (131), 1996.

THREE-POINT FIELD GOALS, TOURNAMENT
59—Augustana (Ill.), 1993 (6 vs. DePauw, 11 vs. Beloit, 11 vs. La Verne, 14 vs. Wis.-Platteville, 9 vs. Rowan, 8 vs. Ohio Northern).

FREE THROWS MADE, GAME
43—Capital (103) vs. Va. Wesleyan (93), 1982; Potsdam St. (91) vs. New Jersey City (89), 1986.

FREE THROWS MADE, TOURNAMENT
137—Catholic, 2001 (18 vs. CCNY; 11 vs. Widener; 18 vs. Brockport St.; 25 vs. Clark (Mass.); 33 vs. Ohio Northern; 32 vs. Wm. Paterson).

ASSISTS, GAME
34—Hampden-Sydney (105) vs. Greensboro (79), 1995.

ASSISTS, TOURNAMENT
136—Neb. Wesleyan, 1997 (25 vs. Buena Vista, 17 vs. Gust. Adolphus, 22 vs. Hope, 23 vs. Wis.-Stevens Point, 26 vs. Williams, 23 vs. Ill. Wesleyan).

All-Tournament Teams

Most Outstanding Player.

1975
*Robert Newman, LeMoyne-Owen
Clint Jackson, LeMoyne-Owen
Dan Panaggio, Brockport St.
Bruce Hamming, Augustana (Ill.)
Greg Ackles, Rowan

1976
*Jack Maher, Scranton
Tom Dunn, Wittenberg
Bob Heubner, Wittenberg
Ronnie Wright, Plattsburgh St.
Terry Lawrence, Augustana (Ill.)

1977
*Rick White, Wittenberg
Phil Smyczek, Hamline
Paul Miernicki, Scranton
Clyde Eberhardt, Wittenberg
Ralph Christian, Oneonta St.

1978
*Michael Harper, North Park
Dennis James, Widener
John Nibert, Albion
Earl Keith, Stony Brook
Tom Florentine, North Park

1979
*Michael Harper, North Park
Don Marsh, Frank. & Marsh.
Derrick Rowland, Potsdam St.
Michael Thomas, North Park
Modzel Greer, North Park

1980
*Michael Thomas, North Park
Ellonya Green, Upsala
Steve Keenan, Upsala
Tyronne Curtis, Wittenberg
Keith French, North Park

1981
*Max Artis, Augustana (Ill.)
Bill Rapier, Augustana (Ill.)
Ed Jachim, Potsdam St.
Derrick Rowland, Potsdam St.
Ron Stewart, Otterbein

1982
*Pete Metzelaars, Wabash
Doug Cornfoot, Cal St. Stanislaus
Rick Davis, Brooklyn
Merlin Nice, Wabash
Leroy Witherspoon, Potsdam St.
Maurice Woods, Potsdam St.

1983
*Bill Bessoir, Scranton
Mickey Banas, Scranton
Jay Ferguson, Wittenberg
Mark Linde, Wis.-Whitewater
Gerald Holmes, Roanoke

1984
*Andre McKoy, Wis.-Whitewater
Mark Linde, Wis.-Whitewater
James Gist, Upsala
Dan Trant, Clark (Mass.)
David Hathaway, DePauw

1985
*Earnest Hubbard, North Park
Justyne Monegain, North Park
Dana Janssen, Neb. Wesleyan
Brendan Mitchell, Potsdam St.
Lou Stevens, Widener

1986
*Roosevelt Bullock, Potsdam St.
Barry Stanton, Potsdam St.
Johnny Mayers, New Jersey City
Michael Neal, LeMoyne-Owen
Dana Janssen, Neb. Wesleyan

1987
*Michael Starks, North Park
Mike Barach, North Park
Steve Iannarino, Wittenberg
Kermit Sharp, Clark (Mass.)
Donald Ellison, Richard Stockton

1988
*Scott Tedder, Ohio Wesleyan
Lee Rowlinson, Ohio Wesleyan
J.P. Andrejko, Scranton
Charlie Burt, Neb. Wesleyan
Tim McGraw, Hartwick

1989
*Greg Grant, Col. of New Jersey
Danny Johnson, Centre
Jeff Bowers, Southern Me.
Ricky Spicer, Wis.-Whitewater
Elbert Gordon, Wis.-Whitewater
Jeff Seifriz, Wis.-Whitewater

1990
*Chris Fite, Rochester
Brett Crist, DePauw
Chris Brandt, Washington (Md.)
Brett Hecko, DePauw
Steve Honderd, Calvin

1991
*Shawn Frison, Wis.-Platteville
James Bradley, Otterbein
Robby Jeter, Wis.-Platteville
Will Lasky, Frank. & Marsh.
David Wilding, Frank. & Marsh.

1992
*Steve Honderd, Calvin
Matt Harrison, Calvin
Mike LeFebre, Calvin
Chris Fite, Rochester
Kyle Meeker, Rochester

1993
*Kirk Anderson, Augustana (Ill.)
Mark Gooden, Ohio Northern
Aaron Madry, Ohio Northern
Steven Haynes, Mass.-Dartmouth
Keith Wood, Rowan

1994
*Mike Rhoades, Lebanon Valley
*Adam Crawford, New York U.
Jonathan Gabriel, New York U.
John Harper, Lebanon Valley
Matt Croci, Wittenberg

1995
*Ernie Peavy, Wis.-Platteville
Brad Knoy, Manchester
Kyle Hupfer, Manchester
Aaron Lancaster, Wis.-Platteville
Charles Grasty, Rowan

1996
*Terrence Stewart, Rowan
Antwan Dasher, Rowan
Joel Holstege, Hope
Duane Bosma, Hope
Chris Simich, Ill. Wesleyan

1997
*Bryan Crabtree, Ill. Wesleyan
Korey Coon, Ill. Wesleyan
Mitch Mosser, Neb. Wesleyan

Damien Hunter, Alvernia
Michael Nogelo, Williams

1998
*Ben Hoffmann, Wis.-Platteville
Andre Dalton, Wis.-Platteville
Joel Holstege, Hope
Michael Nogelo, Williams
Dave Jannuzzi, Wilkes

1999
*Merrill Brunson, Wis.-Platteville
Mike Jones, Wis.-Platteville
T.J. Grimes, Hampden-Sydney
Jeremy Harris, Hampden-Sydney
Horace Jenkins, Wm. Paterson

2000
*Sherm Carstensen, Wis.-Eau Claire
Jeremy Veenstra, Calvin
Aaron Winkle, Calvin
Tishaun Jenkins, Salem St.
Alex Kraft, Frank. & Marsh.

2001
*Pat Maloney, Catholic
Matt Hilleary, Catholic
Horace Jenkins, Wm. Paterson
Chad Bostleman, Ohio Northern
Luke Kasten, Ill. Wesleyan

2002
*Jeff Gibbs, Otterbein
Kevin Shay, Otterbein
Bob Porambo, Elizabethtown
Seth Hauben Carthage
Jason Wiertel, Carthage

2003
*Benjamin Coffin, Williams
Michael Crotty, Williams
Doug Espenson, Gust. Adolphus
Jeff Monroe, Hampden-Sydney
Bryan Nelson, Wooster

CHAMPIONSHIPS

Statistical Leaders

2003 Division I Individual Leaders

Points Per Game

Rank Name, Team	Cl	G	FGM	3FG	FT	PTS	PPG
1. Ruben Douglas, New Mexico	Sr.	28	218	94	253	783	28.0
2. Henry Domercant, Eastern Ill.	Sr.	29	252	84	222	810	27.9
3. Mike Helms, Oakland	Jr.	28	241	74	196	752	26.9
4. Michael Watson, UMKC	Jr.	29	247	118	128	740	25.5
5. Troy Bell, Boston College	Sr.	31	224	106	227	781	25.2
6. Keydren Clark, St. Peter's	Fr.	29	231	109	151	722	24.9
7. Luis Flores, Manhattan	Jr.	30	231	56	221	739	24.6
8. Chris Williams, Ball St.	Sr.	30	226	64	220	736	24.5
9. #Mike Sweetney, Georgetown	Jr.	34	264	0	248	776	22.8
10. Kevin Martin, Western Caro.	So.	24	161	50	174	546	22.8
11. Willie Green, Detroit	Sr.	30	244	37	153	678	22.6
12. Ricky Minard, Morehead St.	Jr.	29	225	54	149	653	22.5
13. #Chris Kaman, Central Mich.	Jr.	31	244	0	206	694	22.4
14. Seth Doliboa, Wright St.	Jr.	28	217	67	124	625	22.3
15. Marcus Hatten, St. John's (N.Y.)	Sr.	34	277	56	146	756	22.2
16. #Carmelo Anthony, Syracuse	Fr.	35	277	56	168	778	22.2
17. Andrew Wisniewski, Centenary (La.)	Jr.	28	207	53	150	617	22.0
18. Andre Emmett, Texas Tech	Jr.	34	297	11	136	741	21.8
19. Ron Williamson, Howard	Sr.	30	197	104	152	650	21.7
20. Julius Jenkins, Ga. Southern	Sr.	27	213	74	84	584	21.6
21. Darshan Luckey, St. Francis (Pa.)	Fr.	28	201	46	157	605	21.6
22. #Dwyane Wade, Marquette	Jr.	33	251	14	194	710	21.5
23. Brandon Hunter, Ohio	Sr.	30	217	11	199	644	21.5
24. Jermaine Hall, Wagner	Sr.	32	273	7	133	686	21.4
25. Marques Green, St. Bonaventure	Jr.	27	182	94	116	574	21.3
26. Ron Slay, Tennessee	Sr.	29	211	43	151	616	21.2
27. Brett Blizzard, UNC Wilmington	Sr.	31	223	109	100	655	21.1
28. Antonio Gates, Kent St.	Sr.	31	231	15	163	640	20.6
29. Derrick Tarver, Akron	Jr.	28	192	54	140	578	20.6
30. Terrence Woods, Florida A&M	Jr.	28	168	139	100	575	20.5
31. Jermaine Boyette, Weber St.	Sr.	32	199	31	228	657	20.5
32. Shawn Hall, Appalachian St.	Sr.	28	189	103	92	573	20.5
Thomas Tee Trotter, Md.-East. Shore	Jr.	28	183	83	124	573	20.5
34. Joe Shipp, California	Sr.	31	241	40	110	632	20.4
35. #Ronald Blackshear, Marshall	Jr.	29	190	98	111	589	20.3
36. Marcus Banks, UNLV	Sr.	32	223	41	162	649	20.3
37. Quinton Ross, Southern Methodist	Sr.	30	191	42	184	608	20.3
38. Chris Monroe, George Washington	Sr.	29	172	59	184	587	20.2
39. Adam Hess, William & Mary	Jr.	28	191	68	114	564	20.1
40. Taylor Coppenrath, Vermont	So.	30	211	38	144	604	20.1
41. David West, Xavier	Sr.	32	213	9	209	644	20.1
42. Drew Schifino, West Virginia	So.	29	220	25	117	582	20.1
43. Brian Cook, Illinois	Sr.	30	202	27	168	599	20.0
44. Craig Smith, Boston College	Fr.	31	241	3	132	617	19.9
45. Vernard Hollins, Wright St.	Sr.	28	197	3	160	557	19.9
46. Jameer Nelson, St. Joseph's	Jr.	30	194	64	139	591	19.7
47. #Luke Ridnour, Oregon	Jr.	33	203	81	162	649	19.7
48. #Carl English, Hawaii	Jr.	31	198	89	122	607	19.6
49. Josh Howard, Wake Forest	Sr.	31	204	53	145	606	19.5
50. Ben Gordon, Connecticut	So.	33	211	80	143	645	19.5

#entered NBA draft

Field-Goal Percentage

Minimum 5 Field Goals Made per Game

Rank Name, Team	Cl	G	FGM	FGA	FG%
1. Adam Mark, Belmont	Jr.	28	199	297	67.0
2. Rickey White, Maine	Sr.	24	131	198	66.2
3. Matt Nelson, Colorado St.	So.	31	205	319	64.3
4. Armond Williams, Ill.-Chicago	Jr.	30	168	263	63.9
5. Michael Harris, Rice	So.	28	172	276	62.3
6. #Chris Kaman, Central Mich.	Jr.	31	244	392	62.2
7. David Gruber, Northern Iowa	Jr.	28	141	231	61.0
8. Ike Diogu, Arizona St.	Fr.	32	209	344	60.8
9. Omar Barlett, Jacksonville St.	Sr.	30	178	293	60.8
10. Jason Keep, San Diego	Sr.	30	195	323	60.4
11. Craig Smith, Boston College	Fr.	31	241	400	60.3
12. Juan Mendez, Niagara	So.	29	207	344	60.2
13. Chris Massie, Memphis	Sr.	23	151	251	60.2
14. Steve Smith, Iona	Jr.	28	147	245	60.0
15. Jackie Rogers, Massachusetts	Sr.	29	148	247	59.9
16. Cuthbert Victor, Murray St.	Jr.	29	170	285	59.6
17. Dylan Page, Wis.-Milwaukee	Jr.	32	209	351	59.5
18. Damien Kinloch, Tennessee Tech	Sr.	32	180	307	58.6
19. James Moore, New Mexico St.	Jr.	23	156	267	58.4
20. Scott Emerson, Mercer	Jr.	28	164	282	58.2

Rank Name, Team	Cl	G	FGM	FGA	FG%
21. Frank Bennett, Ga. Southern	Jr.	29	165	284	58.1
22. Emeka Okafor, Connecticut	So.	33	221	381	58.0
23. Joey Walker, Tenn.-Martin	Sr.	26	162	281	57.7
24. Jermaine Hall, Wagner	Sr.	32	273	475	57.5
25. Ashley Champion, Chattanooga	Jr.	30	170	296	57.4
26. Brandon Griffin, Southeast Mo. St.	Jr.	30	150	262	57.3
27. Danny Gathings, High Point	So.	24	190	333	57.1
28. Cortney Scott, Oakland	So.	23	130	228	57.0
29. Channing Frye, Arizona	So.	32	165	290	56.9
30. Chris Hester, Eastern Wash.	Sr.	31	163	289	56.4

#entered NBA draft

Three-Point Field Goals Per Game

Rank Name, Team	Cl	G	3FG	3PG
1. Terrence Woods, Florida A&M	Jr.	28	139	5.0
2. Demon Brown, Charlotte	Jr.	29	137	4.7
3. Michael Watson, UMKC	Jr.	29	118	4.1
4. Brad Boyd, La.-Lafayette	Jr.	27	104	3.9
5. Kyle Korver, Creighton	Sr.	34	129	3.8
6. Keydren Clark, St. Peter's	Fr.	29	109	3.8
7. Shawn Hall, Appalachian St.	Sr.	28	103	3.7
8. Chris Young, South Ala.	Jr.	28	99	3.5
9. Brett Blizzard, UNC Wilmington	Sr.	31	109	3.5
10. Earl Bullock, Tenn.-Martin	Jr.	28	98	3.5
11. Marques Green, St. Bonaventure	Jr.	27	94	3.5
12. Ron Williamson, Howard	Sr.	30	104	3.5
13. Maurice Riddick, Bethune-Cookman	Sr.	30	103	3.4
14. Troy Bell, Boston College	Sr.	31	106	3.4
15. Gary Buchanan, Villanova	Sr.	26	88	3.4
16. #Ronald Blackshear, Marshall	Jr.	29	98	3.4
17. Ruben Douglas, New Mexico	Sr.	28	94	3.4
18. David Bell, Montana	Sr.	30	98	3.3
19. Sharif Chambliss, Penn St.	Jr.	28	89	3.2
20. Earnest Crumbley, Fla. Atlantic	Jr.	28	88	3.1
21. Steve Drabyn, Belmont	Jr.	29	91	3.1
22. Maurice Carter, Robert Morris	So.	27	84	3.1
23. Kenny Taylor, Baylor	So.	28	87	3.1
24. Troy Wheless, Col. of Charleston	Sr.	33	102	3.1
25. Nick Moore, Toledo	Sr.	29	89	3.1
26. Brion Rush, Grambling	Fr.	30	91	3.0
27. Dedrick Dye, Wagner	Sr.	32	96	3.0
Jason Coleman, McNeese St.	Sr.	29	87	3.0
Tevoris Thompson, Arkansas St.	Jr.	28	84	3.0
30. Blake Stepp, Gonzaga	Jr.	33	98	3.0

#entered NBA draft

Three-Point Field-Goal Percentage

Minimum 2.5 3-Pt. Field Goals Made per Game

Rank Name, Team	Cl	G	3FG	3FGA	3FG%
1. Jeff Schiffner, Pennsylvania	Jr.	28	74	150	49.3
2. Kyle Korver, Creighton	Sr.	34	129	269	48.0
3. Terrence Woods, Florida A&M	Jr.	28	139	304	45.7
4. Chez Marks, Morehead St.	Sr.	29	82	180	45.6
5. Tyson Dorsey, Samford	Jr.	27	75	165	45.5
6. Tim Keller, Air Force	So.	28	78	173	45.1
7. Pat Carroll, St. Joseph's	So.	30	76	169	45.0
8. Dedrick Dye, Wagner	Sr.	32	96	217	44.2
9. Jimmy Boykin, Coppin St.	Jr.	28	72	163	44.2
10. Brett Blizzard, UNC Wilmington	Sr.	31	109	247	44.1
11. Ron Williamson, Howard	Sr.	30	104	237	43.9
12. Gilson DeJesus, Kansas St.	Sr.	30	80	183	43.7
13. Steve Drabyn, Belmont	Jr.	29	91	210	43.3
14. Hollis Price, Oklahoma	Sr.	34	94	217	43.3
15. James Davis, Oregon	Jr.	33	90	209	43.1
16. Dante Swanson, Tulsa	Sr.	32	89	207	43.0
17. Jimmy Tricco, Duquesne	Jr.	30	76	177	42.9
18. Kelly Golob, Northern Ariz.	Fr.	28	78	182	42.9
Keith Gamble, Alabama St.	Sr.	29	75	175	42.9
Terrence Johnson, Pepperdine	So.	28	72	168	42.9
21. Henry Domercant, Eastern Ill.	Sr.	29	84	198	42.4
22. Pete Conway, Montana St.	Sr.	27	69	163	42.3
23. Andy Birley, Colorado St.	Sr.	33	90	213	42.3
24. John Reimold, Bowling Green	So.	29	84	200	42.0
25. Attarrius Norwood, Mississippi Val.	Jr.	29	81	193	42.0
26. Brion Rush, Grambling	Fr.	30	91	217	41.9
27. Glenn Stokes, American	Sr.	30	85	203	41.9

Rank Name, Team	Cl	G	3FG	3FGA	3FG%
28. Omar-Seli Mance, Rice	Sr.	28	82	196	41.8
29. Julius Jenkins, Ga. Southern	Sr.	27	74	177	41.8
30. Troy Wheless, Col. of Charleston	Sr.	33	102	244	41.8

Free-Throw Percentage

Minimum 2.5 Free Throws Made per Game

Rank Name, Team	Cl	G	FT	FTA	FT%
1. Steve Drabyn, Belmont	Jr.	29	78	82	95.1
2. Matt Logie, Lehigh	Sr.	28	91	96	94.8
3 Hollis Price, Oklahoma	Sr.	34	130	140	92.9
4. Brian Dux, Canisius	Sr.	28	115	125	92.0
5. J.J. Redick, Duke	Fr.	33	102	111	91.9
6. Tim Parker, Chattanooga	Sr.	30	78	85	91.8
7. Dwayne Byfield, Monmouth	So.	28	72	79	91.1
8. Gerry McNamara, Syracuse	Fr.	35	90	99	90.9
9. Kyle Korver, Creighton	Sr.	34	109	120	90.8
10. Jeb Ivey, Portland St.	Sr.	27	69	76	90.8
11. Luis Flores, Manhattan	Jr.	30	221	245	90.2
12. David Bennett, Marist	Sr.	28	117	130	90.0
13. Tevoris Thompson, Arkansas St.	Jr.	28	71	79	89.9
14. Tori Harris, Alcorn St.	Sr.	28	88	99	88.9
15. #Ronald Blackshear, Marshall	Jr.	29	111	125	88.8
16. Kenneth Lowe, Purdue	Jr.	27	126	142	88.7
17. Terrence Woods, Florida A&M	Jr.	28	100	113	88.5
18. Charles Harris, Dartmouth	Sr.	27	69	78	88.5
19. Junior Blount, TCU	Sr.	28	114	129	88.4
20. Kevin Martin, Western Caro.	So.	24	174	197	88.3
21. #Luke Ridnour, Oregon	Jr.	33	162	184	88.0
Jason Kapono, UCLA	Sr.	29	81	92	88.0
23. Marques Green, St. Bonaventure	Jr.	27	116	132	87.9
24. Jake Sullivan, Iowa St.	Jr.	31	103	118	87.3
25. Dalron Johnson, UNLV	Sr.	32	122	140	87.1
26. Chris Thomas, Notre Dame	So.	34	135	155	87.1
Kevin Warzynski, Charleston So.	So.	28	81	93	87.1
28. Luke Jackson, Oregon	Jr.	32	130	150	86.7
29. Tim Pickett, Florida St.	Jr.	29	77	89	86.5
30. Nick Eppehimer, Marist	Sr.	29	115	133	86.5

#entered NBA draft

Rebounds Per Game

Rank Name, Team	Cl	G	REB	RPG
1. Brandon Hunter, Ohio	Sr.	30	378	12.6
2. Amien Hicks, Morris Brown	Sr.	24	298	12.4
3. Adam Sonn, Belmont	Sr.	29	352	12.1
4. #Chris Kaman, Central Mich.	Jr.	31	373	12.0
5. David West, Xavier	Sr.	32	379	11.8
6. Louis Truscott, Houston	Sr.	28	315	11.3
7. Emeka Okafor, Connecticut	So.	33	370	11.2
8. Kenny Adeleke, Hofstra	So.	29	320	11.0
James Singleton, Murray St.	Sr.	29	320	11.0
10. James Thomas, Texas	Jr.	33	363	11.0
11. Chris Massie, Memphis	Sr.	23	249	10.8
12. Brandon Griffin, Southeast Mo. St.	Jr.	30	314	10.5
13. Lawrence Roberts, Baylor	So.	26	271	10.4
14. Travis Watson, Virginia	Sr.	31	321	10.4
15. #Mike Sweetney, Georgetown	Jr.	34	352	10.4
16. Kirby Lemons, La.-Monroe	Sr.	28	285	10.2
17. Marcus Smallwood, Northern Ill.	Jr.	31	313	10.1
18. Nick Collison, Kansas	Sr.	38	380	10.0
19. #Carmelo Anthony, Syracuse	Fr.	35	349	10.0
20. Chris Jackson, New Mexico St.	Sr.	23	229	10.0
21. Ryan Gomes, Providence	So.	32	311	9.7
Brett Starkey, Denver	Jr.	32	311	9.7
23. Uche Nsonwu-Amadi, Wyoming	Sr.	27	259	9.6
24. Charles Gaines, Southern Miss.	Jr.	29	278	9.6
25. Arthur Johnson, Missouri	Jr.	33	316	9.6
26. Erwin Dudley, Alabama	Sr.	29	276	9.5
27. Boakai Lalugba, Bucknell	Sr.	29	275	9.5
28. Justin Rowe, Maine	Sr.	25	235	9.4
29. Jackson Vroman, Iowa St.	Jr.	31	291	9.4
30. Stephane Pelle, Colorado	Sr.	32	298	9.3

#entered NBA draft

Assists Per Game

Rank Name, Team	Cl	G	AST	APG
1. Martell Bailey, Ill.-Chicago	Jr.	30	244	8.1
2. Marques Green, St. Bonaventure	Jr.	27	216	8.0
3. #T.J. Ford, Texas	So.	33	254	7.7
4. Elliott Prasse-Freeman, Harvard	Sr.	27	207	7.7
5. Antawn Dobie, Long Island	Sr.	26	193	7.4
6. Richard Little, VMI	Jr.	30	216	7.2
7. Steve Blake, Maryland	Sr.	31	221	7.1
8. Chris Thomas, Notre Dame	So.	34	236	6.9
9. Raymond Felton, North Carolina	Fr.	35	236	6.7
10. #Luke Ridnour, Oregon	Jr.	33	218	6.6
11. Chris Duhon, Duke	Jr.	33	212	6.4
12. Aaron Miles, Kansas	So.	38	244	6.4
13. Jay Collins, Southern Utah	Sr.	28	178	6.4
14. Brandin Knight, Pittsburgh	Sr.	33	209	6.3
15. Jave Meade, Holy Cross	Jr.	31	193	6.2
16. Reggie Kohn, South Fla.	Sr.	29	180	6.2
17. Mark Campbell, Hawaii	Sr.	31	192	6.2
18. Kevin Roberts, Southeast Mo. St.	So.	29	179	6.2
Mike Slattery, Delaware	So.	29	179	6.2
20. T.J. Thompson, George Washington	So.	29	177	6.1
21. Robert Shannon, Sam Houston St.	Sr.	30	181	6.0
22. Blake Stepp, Gonzaga	Jr.	33	198	6.0
Ray Trowell, Chattanooga	Jr.	30	180	6.0
24. Jarrett Jack, Georgia Tech	Fr.	31	185	6.0
25. Patrick Sparks, Western Ky.	So.	33	195	5.9
26. Luke Spencer-Gardner, Oral Roberts	Jr.	28	164	5.9
27. Alvin Cruz, Niagara	So.	29	168	5.8
28. Tory Cavalieri, St. Francis (N.Y.)	So.	30	173	5.8
29. Edward Scott, Clemson	Sr.	28	161	5.8
30. Ashley Robinson, Mississippi Val.	Sr.	29	165	5.7

#entered NBA draft

Blocked Shots Per Game

Rank Name, Team	Cl	G	BLKS	BKPG
1. Emeka Okafor, Connecticut	So.	33	156	4.7
2. Nick Billings, Binghamton	So.	27	117	4.3
3. Justin Rowe, Maine	Sr.	25	105	4.2
4. Deng Gai, Fairfield	So.	25	96	3.8
5. Robert Battle, Drexel	Sr.	31	116	3.7
6. Kyle Davis, Auburn	Jr.	34	124	3.6
7. Kendrick Moore, Oral Roberts	Sr.	28	94	3.4
8. David Harrison, Colorado	So.	32	106	3.3
9. #Mike Sweetney, Georgetown	Jr.	34	109	3.2
10. #Chris Kaman, Central Mich.	Jr.	31	98	3.2
11. Marcus Douthit, Providence	Jr.	32	97	3.0
12. Herve Lamizana, Rutgers	Jr.	28	83	3.0
13. Tony Dixon, Towson	So.	28	81	2.9
14. Jeremy McNeil, Syracuse	Jr.	35	100	2.9
15. William McDonald, Grambling	Sr.	30	83	2.8
16. Eddy Fobbs, Sam Houston St.	Jr.	29	79	2.7
17. Andre Williams, Oklahoma St.	Sr.	32	85	2.7
18. Josh Lewis, Austin Peay	Jr.	31	82	2.6
19. Michael Southall, La.-Lafayette	So.	27	68	2.5
20. Rans Brempong, Western Caro.	Jr.	26	65	2.5
21. George Leach, Indiana	Jr.	32	79	2.5
22. Ryan Lewis, Jacksonville	Sr.	28	66	2.4
23. Mike Benton, Col. of Charleston	Jr.	32	74	2.3
24. Kevin Johnson, Tulsa	Sr.	33	76	2.3
25. Moussa Badiane, East Caro.	So.	27	62	2.3
26. Josh Grant, Winthrop	So.	29	66	2.3
Zakee Wadood, East Tenn. St.	Jr.	29	66	2.3
28. Wesley Duke, Mercer	Jr.	29	65	2.2
29. Jordan Cornette, Notre Dame	So.	34	75	2.2
30. #Chris Bosh, Georgia Tech	Fr.	31	67	2.2

#entered NBA draft

Steals Per Game

Rank Name, Team	Cl	G	ST	STPG
1. Alexis McMillan, Stetson	Sr.	22	87	4.0
2. Zakee Wadood, East Tenn. St.	Jr.	29	93	3.2
3. Jay Heard, Jacksonville St.	Sr.	30	95	3.2
4. Eric Bush, UAB	Sr.	34	106	3.1
5. Marcus Hatten, St. John's (N.Y.)	Sr.	34	100	2.9
6. Rawle Marshall, Oakland	So.	28	80	2.9
7. Marcus Banks, UNLV	Sr.	32	91	2.8

Rank Name, Team	Cl	G	ST	STPG
8. Tim Pickett, Florida St.	Jr.	29	82	2.8
9. Demetrice Williams, South Ala.	Sr.	28	76	2.7
10. Robby Collum, Western Mich.	Sr.	31	83	2.7
11. Edward O'Neil, Charleston So.	Jr.	25	66	2.6
12. Marques Green, St. Bonaventure	Jr.	27	71	2.6
13. Tyronn Mitchell, Northwestern St.	Fr.	27	70	2.6
14. Jeff Gloger, UC Irvine	Fr.	29	75	2.6
15. Andrew Wisniewski, Centenary (La.)	Jr.	28	72	2.6
16. Errick Craven, Southern California	So.	29	73	2.5
17. David Hawkins, Temple	Jr.	34	85	2.5
18. DaShawn Freeman, Sacramento St.	Fr.	29	70	2.4
19. Aaron Miles, Kansas	So.	38	91	2.4
20. Tim Smith, East Tenn. St.	Fr.	31	73	2.4
21. Tony Dobbins, Richmond	Jr.	29	68	2.3
22. Ashley Robinson, Mississippi Val.	Sr.	29	67	2.3
23. Marquis Daniels, Auburn	Sr.	34	78	2.3
24. Terry Conerway, Southwest Tex. St.	Jr.	28	64	2.3
25. Chakowby Hicks, Norfolk St.	So.	29	66	2.3
Keith Triplett, Toledo	Jr.	29	66	2.3
27. Troy Bell, Boston College	Sr.	31	70	2.3
28. David Sykes, Southwest Tex. St.	Sr.	29	65	2.2
29. Brett Blizzard, UNC Wilmington	Sr.	31	69	2.2
30. Garrett Richardson, Tennessee St.	Jr.	27	60	2.2

2003 Division I Game Highs

Individual Highs

POINTS

Rank Name, Team	Cl	vs. Opponent	Game Date	PTS
1. Michael Watson, UMKC	Jr.	Oral Roberts	2/22/03	54
2. Antawn Dobie, Long Island	Sr.	St. Francis (N.Y.)	2/22/03	53
3. Ron Williamson, Howard	Sr.	N.C. A&T	1/21/03	52
4. Richard Toussaint, Bethune-Cookman	Sr.	Morgan St.	3/11/03	49
5. Chris Williams, Ball St.	Sr.	Akron	1/04/03	48
Keydren Clark, St. Peter's	Fr.	Northern Ariz.	11/23/02	48
7. David West, Xavier	Sr.	Dayton	2/08/03	47
8. Henry Domercant, Eastern Ill.	Sr.	Tennessee Tech	3/01/03	46
Kevin Martin, Western Caro.	So.	Coastal Caro.	11/22/02	46
10. Marcus Hatten, St. John's (N.Y.)	Sr.	Rutgers	3/06/03	44
Chris Williams, Ball St.	Sr.	Central Mich.	2/19/03	44
Luis Flores, Manhattan	Jr.	Fairfield	1/23/03	44
Jason Kapono, UCLA	Sr.	Washington St.	1/04/03	44
Keydren Clark, St. Peter's	Fr.	St. Francis (N.Y.)	11/27/02	44
15. Ruben Douglas, New Mexico	Sr.	San Diego St.	2/24/03	43
Chris Kaman, Central Mich.	Jr.	Ball St.	2/19/03	43
Ruben Douglas, New Mexico	Sr.	Wyoming	2/15/03	43
Ricky Minard, Morehead St.	Jr.	Eastern Ky.	2/15/03	43
Derrick Tarver, Akron	Jr.	Central Mich.	2/08/03	43
Willie Green, Detroit	Sr.	Ill.-Chicago	1/27/03	43
Darius Rice, Miami (Fla.)	Jr.	Connecticut	1/20/03	43
Mike Helms, Oakland	Jr.	Texas Southern	12/27/02	43

FIELD-GOAL PERCENTAGE
Minimum 10 Made

Rank Name, Team	Cl	vs. Opponent	Game Date	FG%	FGM	FGA
1. Calvin Ento, Montana St.	Jr.	Dickinson St.	12/10/02	100.0	13	13
Ashley Champion, Chattanooga	Jr.	Samford	11/22/02	100.0	12	12
Matt Sheftic, Vermont	Jr.	Albany (N.Y.)	3/02/03	100.0	10	10
Jackson Atoyebi, Elon	So.	Coastal Caro.	2/26/03	100.0	10	10
James Singleton, Murray St.	Sr.	Tennessee St.	1/27/03	100.0	10	10
Michael Harris, Rice	So.	Louisiana Col.	12/30/02	100.0	10	10
Quantel Murphy, Drake	Fr.	Grinnell	12/11/02	100.0	10	10
Craig Smith, Boston College	Fr.	St. Bonaventure	12/04/02	100.0	10	10
Matt Schneiderman, Northern Iowa	Jr.	Wayne St. (Neb.)	11/25/02	100.0	10	10
10. Omar Barlett, Jacksonville St.	Sr.	Georgia St.	1/11/03	92.3	12	13
11. Andre Emmett, Texas Tech	Jr.	Iowa St.	2/10/03	91.7	11	12
Kevin Martin, Western Caro.	So.	UNC Greensboro	2/08/03	91.7	11	12
Johnny Hollingsworth, Akron	Jr.	Eastern Mich.	2/01/03	91.7	11	12
Clint Cuffle, Evansville	Jr.	Southern Ill.	1/08/03	91.7	11	12
Pops Mensah-Bonsu, George Washington	Fr.	Bucknell	11/30/02	91.7	11	12
Kevinn Pinkney, Nevada	So.	Weber St.	11/30/02	91.7	11	12
17. Torin Francis, Notre Dame	Fr.	Arizona	3/27/03	90.9	10	11
Adam Mark, Belmont	Jr.	Fisk	1/14/03	90.9	10	11
Andrew Feeley, UMBC	So.	St. Francis (Pa.)	1/13/03	90.9	10	11
Marvin Black, Marshall	Sr.	Western Caro.	12/20/02	90.9	10	11
David West, Xavier	Sr.	Ball St.	12/20/02	90.9	10	11
Scott Emerson, Mercer	Jr.	Morris Brown	12/10/02	90.9	10	11
Keith Triplett, Toledo	Jr.	Ohio	12/07/02	90.9	10	11
Kelly Golob, Northern Ariz.	Fr.	Northeastern	12/04/02	90.9	10	11
David Moss, Indiana St.	Fr.	Southeast Mo. St.	11/29/02	90.9	10	11
Allen Holcomb, Tex.-Pan American	Jr.	New Mexico St.	11/22/02	90.9	10	11
Brian Woodward, Rhode Island	Sr.	Northeastern	11/22/02	90.9	10	11

THREE-POINT FIELD GOALS MADE

Rank Name, Team	Cl	vs. Opponent	Game Date	3FG
1. Terrence Woods, Florida A&M	Jr.	Coppin St.	3/01/2003	12
2. Terrence Woods, Florida A&M	Jr.	N.C. A&T	2/01/2003	11
Ron Williamson, Howard	Sr.	N.C. A&T	1/21/2003	11
4. Chris Hill, Michigan St.	So.	Syracuse	2/23/2003	10
Michael Watson, UMKC	Jr.	Oral Roberts	2/22/2003	10
Keydren Clark, St. Peter's	Fr.	Northern Ariz.	11/23/2002	10
7. Rickey Paulding, Missouri	Jr.	Marquette	3/22/2003	9
Attarrius Norwood, Mississippi Val.	Jr.	Grambling	3/03/2003	9
Romain Sato, Xavier	Jr.	Rhode Island	2/15/2003	9
Michael Watson, UMKC	Jr.	Southern Utah	2/06/2003	9
Hollis Price, Oklahoma	Sr.	Iowa St.	1/18/2003	9
Kyle Korver, Creighton	Sr.	Evansville	1/15/2003	9
Demon Brown, Charlotte	Jr.	UAB	1/14/2003	9
Jason Kapono, UCLA	Sr.	Washington St.	1/04/2003	9
Aaron Bond, Northern Ariz.	Jr.	Tenn.-Martin	12/21/2002	9
Marcus Moore, Washington St.	Jr.	Gonzaga	12/07/2002	9
Tevoris Thompson, Arkansas St.	Jr.	Lyon	12/07/2002	9
Thomas Tee Trotter, Md.-East. Shore	Jr.	Cleveland St.	12/06/2002	9
Nick Zachery, Ark.-Little Rock	Jr.	Colorado St.	11/30/2002	9
Percell Coles, Cleveland St.	So.	Duquesne	11/27/2002	9
Brad Boyd, La.-Lafayette	Jr.	Mississippi St.	11/23/2002	9

THREE-POINT FIELD GOAL PERCENTAGE
Min. 7 3FGM

Rank Name, Team	Cl	vs. Opponent	Game Date	3FG%	3FG	3FGA
1. John Goldsberry, UNC Wilmington	Fr.	Maryland	3/21/03	100.0	8	8
James Singleton, Murray St.	Sr.	Eastern Ill.	2/13/03	100.0	8	8
Tyrone Green, N.C. A&T	Jr.	N.C. Central	1/19/03	100.0	7	7
Ezra Williams, Georgia	Sr.	LSU	1/05/03	100.0	7	7
Matt Walsh, Florida	Fr.	Miami (Fla.)	12/21/02	100.0	7	7
Felton Freeman, Sam Houston St.	Sr.	TCU	11/22/02	100.0	7	7
7. Jason Kapono, UCLA	Sr.	Washington St.	1/04/03	90.0	9	10
Aaron Bond, Northern Ariz.	Jr.	Tenn.-Martin	12/21/02	90.0	9	10
9. Darnell Archey, Butler	Sr.	Louisville	3/23/03	88.9	8	9
10. Tim Henderson, Jackson St.	Sr.	Grambling	1/25/03	87.5	7	8
Jon Beck, Arkansas St.	Sr.	Lyon	12/07/02	87.5	7	8
Andy Birley, Colorado St.	Jr.	Gardner-Webb	12/07/02	87.5	7	8
Hodari Mallory, Canisius	Sr.	Bucknell	12/03/02	87.5	7	8
14. Thomas Tee Trotter, Md.-East. Shore	Jr.	Cleveland St.	12/06/02	81.8	9	11
15. Kevin Criswell, Montana	Fr.	Southern Utah	12/30/02	80.0	8	10
16. Ron Williamson, Howard	Sr.	N.C. A&T	1/21/03	78.6	11	14
17. Nathan Doudney, Texas Tech	So.	Texas	3/14/03	77.8	7	9
Dwayne Broyles, James Madison	Jr.	Old Dominion	2/08/03	77.8	7	9
Dedrick Dye, Wagner	Jr.	Robert Morris	1/25/03	77.8	7	9
Steve Drabyn, Belmont	Jr.	Gardner-Webb	1/09/03	77.8	7	9
Omar Wellington, Sacred Heart	Jr.	Columbia	1/06/03	77.8	7	9
Desmon Farmer, Southern California	Jr.	Washington St.	1/02/03	77.8	7	9
Marques Green, St. Bonaventure	Jr.	Ohio	12/31/02	77.8	7	9
Tim Parker, Chattanooga	Sr.	Bradley	11/30/02	77.8	7	9
Percell Coles, Cleveland St.	So.	IPFW	11/27/02	77.8	7	9

FREE-THROW PERCENTAGE
Minimum 13 Free Throws Made

Rank Name, Team	Cl	vs. Opponent	Game Date	FT%	FT	FTA
1. Gabe Martin, Liberty	Jr.	Fla. Atlantic	12/20/02	100.0	18	18
Henry Domercant, Eastern Ill.	Sr.	Eastern Ky.	2/06/03	100.0	16	16
Luis Flores, Manhattan	Jr.	Iona	12/28/02	100.0	16	16
Darshan Luckey, St. Francis (Pa.)	Fr.	UMBC	2/13/03	100.0	14	14
Bryan Hopkins, Southern Methodist	Fr.	Boise St.	2/01/03	100.0	14	14
Alan Anderson, Michigan St.	So.	Ohio St.	1/09/03	100.0	14	14
Troy Bell, Boston College	Sr.	Harvard	12/22/02	100.0	14	14
Matt Walsh, Florida	Fr.	Miami (Fla.)	12/21/02	100.0	14	14
Ruben Douglas, New Mexico	Sr.	Northwestern St.	11/25/02	100.0	14	14
Kevin Martin, Western Caro.	So.	Coastal Caro.	11/22/02	100.0	14	14
Julius Barnes, Stanford	Sr.	Arizona St.	2/27/03	100.0	13	13
Tony Robertson, Connecticut	Sr.	Rutgers	2/19/03	100.0	13	13
D.J. Munir, Stony Brook	Jr.	Boston U.	2/11/03	100.0	13	13
Ron Williamson, Howard	Sr.	Hampton	2/10/03	100.0	13	13
Julius Barnes, Stanford	Sr.	Southern California	1/25/03	100.0	13	13
Marc Jackson, Utah	So.	Brigham Young	1/25/03	100.0	13	13
Kevin Martin, Western Caro.	So.	Ga. Southern	1/25/03	100.0	13	13
Troy Bell, Boston College	Sr.	North Carolina St.	1/16/03	100.0	13	13
Michael Haney, Eastern Ky.	So.	Eastern Ill.	1/11/03	100.0	13	13
Rashad Bell, Boston U.	So.	Albany (N.Y.)	1/08/03	100.0	13	13
Robert Battle, Drexel	Sr.	Niagara	12/21/02	100.0	13	13

REBOUNDS

Rank Name, Team	Cl	vs. Opponent	Game Date	REB
1. Brandon Hunter, Ohio	Sr.	Akron	1/08/03	26
2. Erroyl Bing, East Caro.	Jr.	South Fla.	1/25/03	24
Brandon Hunter, Ohio	Sr.	St. Bonaventure	12/31/02	24
4. Chris Jackson, New Mexico St.	Sr.	North Texas	2/01/03	23
Nick Collison, Kansas	Sr.	Texas	1/27/03	23
Willie Neal, Mississippi Val.	Sr.	Ark.-Pine Bluff	1/04/03	23
7. Chris Kaman, Central Mich.	Jr.	Ball St.	3/08/03	22
Justin Rowe, Maine	Sr.	Jacksonville St.	12/22/02	22
Cameron Echols, Ball St.	Jr.	Wright St.	12/07/02	22
10. Louis Truscott, Houston	Sr.	TCU	2/01/03	21
Demetrius Williams, Loyola (Ill.)	Jr.	Wis.-Milwaukee	2/01/03	21
Aaron Gill, Radford	Jr.	Winthrop	1/03/03	21
Chris Kaman, Central Mich.	Jr.	Michigan	12/03/02	21
Marcus Smallwood, Northern Ill.	Jr.	Loyola (Ill.)	11/27/02	21
Stephane Pelle, Colorado	Sr.	Stetson	11/24/02	21
16. Kenny Adeleke, Hofstra	So.	UNC Wilmington	2/15/03	20
Lawrence Roberts, Baylor	So.	Oklahoma St.	2/15/03	20
Brandon Hunter, Ohio	Sr.	Buffalo	2/08/03	20
Travis Watson, Virginia	Sr.	Wofford	1/02/03	20
Carlton Aaron, UMKC	So.	Youngstown St.	12/21/02	20
Amien Hicks, Morris Brown	Sr.	Tennessee St.	12/18/02	20
Kenny Adeleke, Hofstra	So.	Monmouth	12/07/02	20
Napoleon Rhodes, Middle Tenn.	Jr.	UNC Greensboro	11/30/02	20
Troy Godwin, Va. Commonwealth	Jr.	Western Ky.	11/26/02	20
Torin Francis, Notre Dame	Fr.	Bucknell	11/22/02	20
Danny Granger, Bradley	So.	Pepperdine	11/22/02	20

ASSISTS
Minimum 14 Assists

Rank Name, Team	Cl	vs. Opponent	Game Date	AST
1. Antawn Dobie, Long Island	Sr.	St. Francis (N.Y.)	12/15/02	17
Zakee Smith, Cal St. Fullerton	Jr.	Pepperdine	12/04/02	17
3. Malcolm Campbell, Alabama St.	Jr.	Mississippi Val.	2/10/03	16
Blake Stepp, Gonzaga	Jr.	Long Beach St.	12/20/02	16
5. Antawn Dobie, Long Island	Sr.	St. Francis (N.Y.)	2/22/03	15
Mike Slattery, Delaware	So.	William & Mary	2/01/03	15
Mike Slattery, Delaware	So.	UNC Greensboro	12/19/02	15
8. Marques Green, St. Bonaventure	Jr.	La Salle	1/18/03	14

BLOCKED SHOTS

Rank Name, Team	Cl	vs. Opponent	Game Date	BLKS
1. David Harrison, Colorado	So.	Nebraska	3/08/03	11
Jordan Cornette, Notre Dame	So.	Belmont	11/17/02	11
3. Nick Billings, Binghamton	So.	Northeastern	2/22/03	10
William McDonald, Grambling	Sr.	Prairie View	2/15/03	10
Nick Billings, Binghamton	So.	Boston U.	2/09/03	10
David Harrison, Colorado	So.	Stetson	11/24/02	10
7. Marcus Douthit, Providence	Jr.	Connecticut	3/05/03	9
Emeka Okafor, Connecticut	So.	St. John's (N.Y.)	2/22/03	9
Josh Grant, Winthrop	So.	Elon	1/04/03	9
Kendrick Moore, Oral Roberts	Sr.	Stephen F. Austin	12/14/02	9
Kyle Davis, Auburn	Jr.	Georgia St.	11/26/02	9

New Mexico's Ruben Douglas led the nation in scoring average last season.

Rank Name, Team	Cl	vs. Opponent	Game Date	BLKS
12. Jeremy McNeil, Syracuse	Jr.	Connecticut	3/14/03	8
Deng Gai, Fairfield	So.	St. Peter's	2/26/03	8
Herve Lamizana, Rutgers	Jr.	Seton Hall	2/25/03	8
Hiram Fuller, Fresno St.	Sr.	San Jose St.	2/19/03	8
Deng Gai, Fairfield	So.	Manhattan	2/13/03	8
Tony Dixon, Towson	So.	William & Mary	2/12/03	8
Nick Billings, Binghamton	So.	Vermont	2/02/03	8
Justin Rowe, Maine	Sr.	Hartford	2/02/03	8
Robert Battle, Drexel	Sr.	Old Dominion	1/29/03	8
Nick Billings, Binghamton	So.	Northeastern	1/29/03	8
Ronald Mickel, Centenary (La.)	Jr.	Lipscomb	1/25/03	8
Jackson Vroman, Iowa St.	Jr.	Nebraska	1/25/03	8
Chris Kaman, Central Mich.	Jr.	Toledo	1/22/03	8
Justin Rowe, Maine	Sr.	Northeastern	1/15/03	8
Jordan Cornette, Notre Dame	So.	Rutgers	1/14/03	8
Nick Billings, Binghamton	So.	St. Francis (N.Y.)	1/07/03	8
Kyle Davis, Auburn	Jr.	Southern Miss.	12/30/02	8
Robert Battle, Drexel	Sr.	Philadelphia U.	12/28/02	8
Eddy Fobbs, Sam Houston St.	Jr.	Lamar	12/28/02	8
Emeka Okafor, Connecticut	So.	Central Conn. St.	12/28/02	8
Justin Rowe, Maine	Sr.	Jacksonville St.	12/22/02	8
Tony Dixon, Towson	So.	Norfolk St.	12/14/02	8
William McDonald, Grambling	Sr.	Texas Col.	12/12/02	8
Justin Rowe, Maine	Sr.	Morgan St.	12/09/02	8
Torin Francis, Notre Dame	Fr.	Texas	12/08/02	8
Emeka Okafor, Connecticut	So.	Wagner	12/07/02	8
Kendrick Moore, Oral Roberts	Sr.	Wichita St.	11/30/02	8
Wesley Edwards, Fla. Atlantic	Jr.	Nova Southeastern	11/27/02	8
Emeka Okafor, Connecticut	So.	George Washington	11/25/02	8
Jordan Cornette, Notre Dame	So.	IUPUI	11/18/02	8

STEALS

Rank Name, Team	Cl	vs. Opponent	Game Date	ST
1. Marcus Hatten, St. John's (N.Y.)	Sr.	Syracuse	02/18/03	10
Joseph Frazier, Cal St. Northridge	So.	Bethany (Cal.)	12/07/02	10
Rawle Marshall, Oakland	So.	Texas A&M	12/02/02	10
4. Aaron Miles, Kansas	So.	Iowa St.	02/16/03	9
5. Matt Crenshaw, IUPUI	Jr.	Chicago St.	03/01/03	8
Joseph Frazier, Cal St. Northridge	So.	Cal Poly	02/13/03	8
Tony Dobbins, Richmond	Jr.	Massachusetts	02/12/03	8
Marcus Banks, UNLV	Sr.	Colorado St.	02/03/03	8
Errick Craven, Southern California	So.	Oregon	02/02/03	8
Alexis McMillan, Stetson	Sr.	Campbell	01/25/03	8
Alexis McMillan, Stetson	Sr.	Jacksonville	01/10/03	8
Marcus Banks, UNLV	Sr.	IPFW	1/02/03	8
Terry Conerway, Southwest Tex. St.	Jr.	Arkansas	12/21/02	8
Eric Bush, UAB	Sr.	Tex. A&M-Corp. Chris.	12/19/02	8
Mike Gale, Centenary (La.)	Jr.	Jarvis Christian	12/17/02	8
Tim Smith, East Tenn. St.	Fr.	Virginia-Wise	12/14/02	8
Jeremy Bishop, Quinnipiac	Sr.	Hofstra	12/01/02	8
A.J. Diggs, California	Jr.	Cleveland St.	11/30/02	8

2003 Division I Team Leaders

Won-Lost Percentage

Rank Name	W	L	Pct
1. Kentucky	32	4	88.9
2. Arizona	28	4	87.5
3. Syracuse	30	5	85.7
4. Creighton	29	5	85.3
5. Pittsburgh	28	5	84.8
6. Holy Cross	26	5	83.9
7. Butler	27	6	81.8
Marquette	27	6	81.8
9. Troy St.	26	6	81.3
Weber St.	26	6	81.3
Xavier	26	6	81.3
12. Wake Forest	25	6	80.6
13. Dayton	24	6	80.0
14. Oklahoma	27	7	79.4
15. Mercer	23	6	79.3
16. Kansas	30	8	78.9
17. Duke	26	7	78.8
Texas	26	7	78.8
19. Pennsylvania	22	6	78.6
20. Central Mich.	25	7	78.1
Louisville	25	7	78.1
Illinois	25	7	78.1
23. UNC Wilmington	24	7	77.4
Southern Ill.	24	7	77.4
25. Manhattan	23	7	76.7
Sam Houston St.	23	7	76.7
Memphis	23	7	76.7
St. Joseph's	23	7	76.7
29. Florida	25	8	75.8
Col. of Charleston	25	8	75.8
Utah	25	8	75.8

Scoring Offense

Rank Name	GM	W-L	PTS	PPG
1. Arizona	32	28-4	2,725	85.2
2. Appalachian St.	29	19-10	2,434	83.9
3. Kansas	38	30-8	3,141	82.7
4. East Tenn. St.	31	20-11	2,543	82.0
5. Louisville	32	25-7	2,612	81.6
6. Oregon	33	23-10	2,689	81.5
7. Morehead St.	29	20-9	2,355	81.2
8. Chattanooga	30	21-9	2,435	81.2
9. Duke	33	26-7	2,677	81.1
10. Davidson	27	17-10	2,180	80.7
11. Troy St.	32	26-6	2,556	79.9
12. Central Mich.	32	25-7	2,553	79.8
13. Maryland	31	21-10	2,472	79.7
14. Syracuse	35	30-5	2,785	79.6
15. St. Bonaventure	27	13-14	2,146	79.5
16. Connecticut	33	23-10	2,622	79.5
17. Boston College	31	19-12	2,462	79.4
18. Texas	33	26-7	2,618	79.3
19. Georgia	27	19-8	2,138	79.2
20. Notre Dame	34	24-10	2,692	79.2
21. Creighton	34	29-5	2,688	79.1
22. Eastern Mich.	28	14-14	2,210	78.9
23. Oakland	28	17-11	2,207	78.8
24. Akron	28	14-14	2,201	78.6
25. Marquette	33	27-6	2,589	78.5
26. Pepperdine	28	15-13	2,195	78.4
27. Mercer	29	23-6	2,271	78.3
28. Wake Forest	31	25-6	2,412	77.8
29. UAB	34	21-13	2,640	77.6
30. Eastern Ky.	28	11-17	2,172	77.6

Scoring Defense

Rank Name	GM	W-L	OPP PTS	OPP PPG
1. Air Force	28	12-16	1,596	57.0
2. Miami (Ohio)	28	13-15	1,643	58.7
3. Holy Cross	31	26-5	1,821	58.7
4. Bucknell	29	14-15	1,706	58.8
5. Pittsburgh	33	28-5	1,955	59.2
6. Wisconsin	32	24-8	1,899	59.3
7. St. Joseph's	30	23-7	1,784	59.5
8. Mississippi St.	31	21-10	1,852	59.7
9. Utah St.	33	24-9	1,979	60.0
10. Oklahoma	34	27-7	2,041	60.0
11. Pennsylvania	28	22-6	1,681	60.0
12. UNC Wilmington	31	24-7	1,863	60.1
13. Butler	33	27-6	1,986	60.2
14. Utah	33	25-8	1,991	60.3
15. UC Santa Barb.	32	18-14	1,931	60.3
16. George Mason	28	16-12	1,694	60.5
17. St. Louis	30	16-14	1,822	60.7
18. Michigan St.	35	22-13	2,143	61.2
19. Southwest Mo. St.	29	17-12	1,782	61.4
20. Illinois	32	25-7	1,970	61.6
21. Coppin St.	28	11-17	1,726	61.6
22. American	30	16-14	1,857	61.9
23. Cincinnati	29	17-12	1,796	61.9
24. Columbia	27	2-25	1,676	62.1
25. Princeton	27	16-11	1,677	62.1
26. Richmond	29	15-14	1,811	62.4
27. Delaware St.	27	15-12	1,690	62.6
28. Oklahoma St.	32	22-10	2,004	62.6
29. Texas-Arlington	29	16-13	1,819	62.7
30. Stephen F. Austin	29	21-8	1,823	62.9

Scoring Margin

Rank Name	W-L	PTS	PPG	OPP PTS	OPP PPG	SCR MAR
1. Kansas	30-8	3,141	82.7	2,541	66.9	15.8
2. Pittsburgh	28-5	2,473	74.9	1,955	59.2	15.7
3. Arizona	28-4	2,725	85.2	2,262	70.7	14.5
4. Creighton	29-5	2,688	79.1	2,202	64.8	14.3
5. Kentucky	32-4	2,782	77.3	2,309	64.1	13.1
6. Illinois	25-7	2,388	74.6	1,970	61.6	13.1
7. Maryland	21-10	2,472	79.7	2,069	66.7	13.0
8. Louisville	25-7	2,612	81.6	2,197	68.7	13.0
9. Holy Cross	26-5	2,180	70.3	1,821	58.7	11.6
10. Duke	26-7	2,677	81.1	2,298	69.6	11.5
11. Xavier	26-6	2,482	77.6	2,115	66.1	11.5
12. UNC Wilmington	24-7	2,214	71.4	1,863	60.1	11.3
13. Wisconsin	24-8	2,250	70.3	1,899	59.3	11.0
14. St. Joseph's	23-7	2,111	70.4	1,784	59.5	10.9
15. Florida	25-8	2,484	75.3	2,128	64.5	10.8
16. Oklahoma	27-7	2,392	70.4	2,041	60.0	10.3
17. Syracuse	30-5	2,785	79.6	2,435	69.6	10.0
Wake Forest	25-6	2,412	77.8	2,102	67.8	10.0
19. Pennsylvania	22-6	1,958	69.9	1,681	60.0	9.9
20. Mississippi St.	21-10	2,151	69.4	1,852	59.7	9.6
21. Texas	26-7	2,618	79.3	2,300	69.7	9.6
22. Davidson	17-10	2,180	80.7	1,920	71.1	9.6
23. Stephen F. Austin	21-8	2,099	72.4	1,823	62.9	9.5
24. LSU	21-11	2,326	72.7	2,030	63.4	9.3
25. Troy St.	26-6	2,556	79.9	2,262	70.7	9.2
26. Marquette	27-6	2,589	78.5	2,292	69.5	9.0
27. Gonzaga	24-9	2,558	77.5	2,279	69.1	8.5
28. Brigham Young	23-9	2,299	71.8	2,032	63.5	8.3
29. Connecticut	23-10	2,622	79.5	2,351	71.2	8.2
30. Tulsa	23-10	2,423	73.4	2,155	65.3	8.1

Field-Goal Percentage

Rank Name	GM	W-L	FGM	FGA	FG%
1. Morehead St.	29	20-9	854	1,674	51.0
2. Pittsburgh	33	28-5	893	1,766	50.6
3. Colorado St.	33	19-14	876	1,733	50.5
4. Central Mich.	32	25-7	864	1,714	50.4
5. Creighton	34	29-5	974	1,956	49.8
6. Kansas	38	30-8	1,182	2,393	49.4
7. Stephen F. Austin	29	21-8	753	1,534	49.1
8. Kentucky	36	32-4	1,026	2,102	48.8
9. Maine	30	14-16	827	1,697	48.7
10. Akron	28	14-14	761	1,562	48.7
11. Kent St.	31	21-10	848	1,741	48.7
12. Chattanooga	30	21-9	846	1,750	48.3
13. Evansville	28	12-16	670	1,386	48.3
14. Arizona St.	32	20-12	886	1,838	48.2
15. LSU	32	21-11	851	1,767	48.2
16. Marquette	33	27-6	901	1,871	48.2
17. Tennessee Tech	32	20-12	839	1,743	48.1
18. Air Force	28	12-16	536	1,114	48.1
19. Detroit	30	18-12	798	1,662	48.0
20. Illinois	32	25-7	859	1,793	47.9
21. Southern Utah	28	11-17	683	1,429	47.8
22. Florida	33	25-8	883	1,856	47.6
23. Syracuse	35	30-5	1,020	2,146	47.5
24. Butler	33	27-6	786	1,655	47.5
25. Marshall	29	14-15	737	1,555	47.4
26. Ill.-Chicago	30	21-9	834	1,763	47.3
27. Eastern Wash.	31	18-13	758	1,603	47.3
28. Centenary (La.)	28	14-14	752	1,592	47.2
29. Mercer	29	23-6	800	1,694	47.2
30. Princeton	27	16-11	637	1,349	47.2

Field-Goal Percentage Defense

Rank Name	GM	W-L	OPP FG	OPP FGA	OPP FG%
1. St. Joseph's	30	23-7	609	1,639	37.2
2. Illinois	32	25-7	657	1,741	37.7
3. Maryland	31	21-10	704	1,864	37.8
4. Connecticut	33	23-10	817	2,157	37.9
5. Syracuse	35	30-5	878	2,253	39.0
6. Pittsburgh	33	28-5	682	1,750	39.0
7. Florida St.	29	14-15	650	1,662	39.1
8. Sam Houston St.	30	23-7	676	1,727	39.1
9. Lamar	27	13-14	621	1,577	39.4
10. Oklahoma St.	32	22-10	699	1,775	39.4
11. Wake Forest	31	25-6	734	1,849	39.7
12. Davidson	27	17-10	673	1,694	39.7
13. Tulsa	33	23-10	771	1,940	39.7
14. Va. Commonwealth	28	18-10	685	1,723	39.8
15. South Fla.	29	15-14	696	1,744	39.9
16. Mississippi St.	31	21-10	670	1,672	40.1
17. Cincinnati	29	17-12	615	1,534	40.1
18. Kansas St.	30	13-17	689	1,718	40.1
19. Kansas	38	30-8	937	2,332	40.2
20. Colorado	32	20-12	813	2,020	40.2
21. Michigan St.	35	22-13	712	1,768	40.3
22. Boston U.	31	20-11	657	1,626	40.4
23. UNC Wilmington	31	24-7	655	1,621	40.4
24. Binghamton	27	14-13	629	1,552	40.5
25. Winthrop	30	20-10	671	1,655	40.5
26. Richmond	29	15-14	620	1,529	40.5
27. Alabama St.	29	14-15	628	1,546	40.6
28. Memphis	30	23-7	706	1,738	40.6
29. Holy Cross	31	26-5	644	1,585	40.6
30. Houston	28	8-20	681	1,676	40.6

Three-Point Field Goals Made Per Game

Rank Name	GM	W-L	3FG	3PG
1. Mississippi Val.	29	15-14	299	10.3
2. St. Bonaventure	27	13-14	271	10.0
3. Davidson	27	17-10	269	10.0
4. Troy St.	32	26-6	312	9.8
5. UMKC	29	9-20	272	9.4
6. Col. of Charleston	33	25-8	308	9.3
7. Samford	28	13-15	258	9.2
8. Baylor	28	14-14	254	9.1
9. Pennsylvania	28	22-6	251	9.0
10. Oregon	33	23-10	291	8.8

Rank Name	GM	W-L	3FG	3PG
11. American	30	16-14	263	8.8
12. Florida	33	25-8	287	8.7
13. Arkansas St.	28	13-15	241	8.6
14. Toledo	29	13-16	248	8.6
15. Washington St.	27	7-20	230	8.5
16. Louisville	32	25-7	272	8.5
17. Fairleigh Dickinson	29	15-14	246	8.5
18. Notre Dame	34	24-10	283	8.3
19. Butler	33	27-6	274	8.3
20. North Carolina	35	19-16	290	8.3
21. Florida A&M	29	17-12	240	8.3
Wofford	29	14-15	240	8.3
23. Dartmouth	27	8-19	221	8.2
24. Belmont	29	17-12	237	8.2
25. Princeton	27	16-11	220	8.1
26. Northern Ariz.	28	15-13	227	8.1
27. North Carolina St.	31	18-13	248	8.0
Southwest Tex. St.	29	17-12	232	8.0
29. St. Joseph's	30	23-7	239	8.0
30. Charlotte	29	13-16	231	8.0
Gardner-Webb	29	5-24	231	8.0

Three-Point Field-Goal Percentage

Minimum 5.0 made per game

Rank Name	GM	W-L	3FG	3FGA	3FG%
1. Illinois St.	29	8-21	188	427	44.0
2. Davidson	27	17-10	269	645	41.7
3. Pennsylvania	28	22-6	251	608	41.3
4. Ill.-Chicago	30	21-9	187	463	40.4
5. Southeast Mo. St.	30	11-19	212	529	40.1
6. Marquette	33	27-6	202	508	39.8
7. New Orleans	29	15-14	159	400	39.8
8. Arkansas St.	28	13-15	241	611	39.4
9. Morehead St.	29	20-9	179	454	39.4
10. Kent St.	31	21-10	229	582	39.3
11. Butler	33	27-6	274	699	39.2
12. Oklahoma	34	27-7	250	638	39.2
13. Evansville	28	12-16	164	419	39.1
14. Florida	33	25-8	287	735	39.0
15. Col. of Charleston	33	25-8	308	789	39.0
16. Central Mich.	32	25-7	224	574	39.0
17. Maryland	31	21-10	204	523	39.0
18. Southern Utah	28	11-17	172	441	39.0
19. Creighton	34	29-5	270	693	39.0
20. Florida A&M	29	17-12	240	618	38.8
21. Toledo	29	13-16	248	640	38.8
22. Northern Ariz.	28	15-13	227	586	38.7
23. Pepperdine	28	15-13	220	568	38.7
24. Southern Ill.	31	24-7	191	494	38.7
25. Oregon	33	23-10	291	753	38.6
26. Rice	29	19-10	182	471	38.6
27. Connecticut	33	23-10	196	508	38.6
28. Notre Dame	34	24-10	283	735	38.5
29. Wichita St.	30	18-12	211	549	38.4
30. Northern Ill.	31	17-14	195	509	38.3

Free-Throw Percentage

Rank Name	GM	W-L	FT	FTA	FT%
1. Manhattan	30	23-7	560	711	78.8
2. Providence	32	18-14	496	637	77.9
3. Marist	29	13-16	442	568	77.8
4. Davidson	27	17-10	413	531	77.8
5. Oregon	33	23-10	530	685	77.4
6. Marquette	33	27-6	585	759	77.1
7. North Carolina St.	31	18-13	488	634	77.0
8. Marshall	29	14-15	468	609	76.8
9. Eastern Ill.	29	14-15	453	590	76.8
10. Central Mich.	32	25-7	601	789	76.2
11. UNC Asheville	32	15-17	506	665	76.1
12. Notre Dame	34	24-10	575	756	76.1
13. Centenary (La.)	28	14-14	518	682	76.0
14. St. Bonaventure	27	13-14	369	486	75.9
15. Chattanooga	30	21-9	517	683	75.7
16. Morehead St.	29	20-9	468	619	75.6
17. Brigham Young	32	23-9	575	762	75.5
18. Western Caro.	28	9-19	439	583	75.3
19. Purdue	30	19-11	569	757	75.2

Rank Name	GM	W-L	FT	FTA	FT%
20. Wake Forest	31	25-6	611	813	75.2
21. Oral Roberts	28	18-10	530	706	75.1
22. Central Conn. St.	28	15-13	373	499	74.7
23. Stetson	26	6-20	395	529	74.7
24. Charleston So.	28	14-14	350	469	74.6
25. Xavier	32	26-6	576	772	74.6
26. Brown	29	17-12	527	708	74.4
27. Arkansas St.	28	13-15	455	612	74.3
28. Georgetown	34	19-15	649	874	74.3
29. Boston U.	31	20-11	440	593	74.2
30. UC Santa Barb.	32	18-14	455	614	74.1

Rebound Margin

Rank Name	W-L	REB	RPG	OPP REB	OPP RPG	REB MAR
1. Wake Forest	25-6	1,292	41.7	993	32.0	9.6
2. Kansas	30-8	1,589	41.8	1,288	33.9	7.9
3. Holy Cross	26-5	1,131	36.5	887	28.6	7.9
4. Vermont	21-12	1,295	39.2	1,052	31.9	7.4
5. Utah St.	24-9	1,154	35.0	923	28.0	7.0
6. Texas	26-7	1,386	42.0	1,158	35.1	6.9
7. DePaul	16-13	1,075	37.1	875	30.2	6.9
8. Davidson	17-10	1,110	41.1	926	34.3	6.8
9. Mercer	23-6	1,171	40.4	977	33.7	6.7
10. Pittsburgh	28-5	1,203	36.5	984	29.8	6.6
11. Arizona	28-4	1,374	42.9	1,169	36.5	6.4
12. Siena	21-11	1,269	39.7	1,068	33.4	6.3
13. Tennessee Tech	20-12	1,197	37.4	999	31.2	6.2
14. Mississippi St.	21-10	1,148	37.0	957	30.9	6.2
15. Hofstra	8-21	1,178	40.6	1,000	34.5	6.1
	Murray St.	17-12	1,097	37.8	919	31.7	6.1
17. Kentucky	32-4	1,324	36.8	1,114	30.9	5.8
18. Fresno St.	20-8	1,057	37.8	897	32.0	5.7
19. Gonzaga	24-9	1,234	37.4	1,046	31.7	5.7
20. Xavier	26-6	1,259	39.3	1,080	33.8	5.6
21. Michigan St.	22-13	1,226	35.0	1,034	29.5	5.5
22. Colorado	20-12	1,351	42.2	1,176	36.8	5.5
23. UCF	21-11	1,166	36.4	993	31.0	5.4
24. Arkansas	9-19	1,063	38.0	912	32.6	5.4
25. Connecticut	23-10	1,407	42.6	1,230	37.3	5.4
26. Stanford	24-9	1,279	38.8	1,107	33.5	5.2
27. George Mason	16-12	1,019	36.4	874	31.2	5.2
28. San Diego	18-12	1,147	38.2	997	33.2	5.0
29. San Diego St.	16-14	1,051	35.0	903	30.1	4.9
30. Tennessee	17-12	1,036	35.7	893	30.8	4.9

Assists Per Game

Rank Name	GM	W-L	AST	APG
1. Maryland	31	21-10	573	18.5
2. Illinois	32	25-7	575	18.0
3. Georgia	27	19-8	483	17.9
4. Pittsburgh	33	28-5	589	17.8
5. Southeast Mo. St.	30	11-19	535	17.8
6. Arizona	32	28-4	569	17.8
7. Kansas	38	30-8	653	17.2
8. Oregon	33	23-10	567	17.2
9. Valparaiso	31	20-11	529	17.1
10. Davidson	27	17-10	460	17.0
11. Belmont	29	17-12	493	17.0
12. Chattanooga	30	21-9	509	17.0
13. Mercer	29	23-6	492	17.0
14. Wis.-Milwaukee	32	24-8	542	16.9
15. Tenn.-Martin	28	14-14	474	16.9
16. Creighton	34	29-5	575	16.9
17. Boston College	31	19-12	522	16.8
18. Maine	30	14-16	505	16.8
19. Sam Houston St.	30	23-7	502	16.7
20. Tennessee Tech	32	20-12	533	16.7
21. San Diego	30	18-12	496	16.5
22. Louisville	32	25-7	529	16.5
23. Quinnipiac	29	17-12	479	16.5
24. Iona	29	17-12	477	16.4
25. Memphis	30	23-7	493	16.4
26. Florida	33	25-8	542	16.4
27. Notre Dame	34	24-10	558	16.4

Rank Name	GM	W-L	AST	APG
28. Murray St.	29	17-12	475	16.4
29. Hawaii	31	19-12	507	16.4
30. Xavier	32	26-6	523	16.3

Blocked Shots Per Game

Rank Name	GM	W-L	BLKS	BKPG
1. Connecticut	33	23-10	253	7.7
2. Syracuse	35	30-5	247	7.1
3. Colorado	32	20-12	214	6.7
4. Binghamton	27	14-13	176	6.5
5. Maryland	31	21-10	198	6.4
6. Georgetown	34	19-15	209	6.1
7. Minnesota	33	19-14	196	5.9
8. Sam Houston St.	30	23-7	174	5.8
9. Maine	30	14-16	169	5.6
10. Providence	32	18-14	179	5.6
11. Notre Dame	34	24-10	189	5.6
12. St. Joseph's	30	23-7	166	5.5
13. Iowa St.	31	17-14	170	5.5
14. Jacksonville	29	13-16	159	5.5
15. Duke	33	26-7	178	5.4
16. Fairfield	31	19-12	167	5.4
17. Oklahoma	34	27-7	171	5.3
18. Georgia Tech	31	16-15	164	5.3
19. Rutgers	28	12-16	147	5.3
20. Troy St.	32	26-6	167	5.2
21. Towson	28	4-24	145	5.2
22. Auburn	34	22-12	176	5.2
23. Winthrop	30	20-10	155	5.2
24. Indiana	34	21-13	175	5.1
25. Va. Commonwealth	28	18-10	142	5.1
26. Memphis	30	23-7	152	5.1
27. Kansas	38	30-8	192	5.1
28. East Tenn. St.	31	20-11	156	5.0
29. James Madison	30	13-17	150	5.0
30. Southern Methodist	30	17-13	149	5.0

Steals Per Game

Rank Name	GM	W-L	ST	STPG
1. UAB	34	21-13	394	11.6
2. East Tenn. St.	31	20-11	354	11.4
3. Stetson	26	6-20	282	10.8
4. Jacksonville St.	30	20-10	314	10.5
5. Maryland	31	21-10	322	10.4
6. Appalachian St.	29	19-10	299	10.3
7. Charleston So.	28	14-14	277	9.9
Jackson St.	28	10-18	277	9.9
9. Kansas	38	30-8	373	9.8
10. Miami (Fla.)	28	11-17	272	9.7
11. Southwest Tex. St.	29	17-12	281	9.7
12. Troy St.	32	26-6	309	9.7
13. Georgetown	34	19-15	328	9.6
14. Northeastern	31	16-15	299	9.6
15. St. John's (N.Y.)	34	21-13	327	9.6
16. Florida St.	29	14-15	273	9.4
17. Alabama A&M	27	8-19	254	9.4
18. Fla. Atlantic	28	7-21	263	9.4
19. Savannah St.	27	3-24	253	9.4
20. Tenn.-Martin	28	14-14	262	9.4
21. Centenary (La.)	28	14-14	259	9.3
22. Rutgers	28	12-16	258	9.2
23. Sacred Heart	29	8-21	267	9.2
Belmont	29	17-12	267	9.2
25. Southern California	30	13-17	276	9.2
26. Manhattan	30	23-7	275	9.2
27. Cal St. Northridge	29	14-15	265	9.1
28. UNC Wilmington	31	24-7	283	9.1
29. Stephen F. Austin	29	21-8	264	9.1
30. Temple	34	18-16	309	9.1

Turnovers Per Game

Rank Name	GM	W-L	TO	TOPG
1. Temple	34	18-16	336	9.9
2. Wisconsin	32	24-8	334	10.4
3. Cincinnati	29	17-12	307	10.6
4. Butler	33	27-6	353	10.7

STATISTICAL LEADERS

Rank	Name	GM	W-L	TO	TOPG
5.	St. Louis	30	16-14	328	10.9
6.	UNC Wilmington	31	24-7	352	11.4
7.	Air Force	28	12-16	320	11.4
8.	Texas Tech	35	22-13	402	11.5
9.	Indiana	34	21-13	392	11.5
10.	Georgia	27	19-8	312	11.6
11.	Miami (Ohio)	28	13-15	325	11.6
12.	Mississippi Val.	29	15-14	338	11.7
13.	Princeton	27	16-11	318	11.8
14.	Detroit	30	18-12	354	11.8
15.	New Mexico	28	10-18	331	11.8
16.	Oklahoma	34	27-7	412	12.1
17.	Richmond	29	15-14	352	12.1
18.	Utah St.	33	24-9	406	12.3
19.	Wright St.	28	10-18	345	12.3
20.	Dartmouth	27	8-19	333	12.3
21.	St. Bonaventure	27	13-14	335	12.4
22.	UMKC	29	9-20	360	12.4
23.	Akron	28	14-14	349	12.5
	William & Mary	28	12-16	349	12.5
25.	Ill.-Chicago	30	21-9	374	12.5

Rank	Name	GM	W-L	TO	TOPG
26.	UC Santa Barb.	32	18-14	399	12.5
27.	Southern Ill.	31	24-7	388	12.5
28.	Albany (N.Y.)	28	7-21	352	12.6
29.	Weber St.	32	26-6	403	12.6
30.	Xavier	32	26-6	407	12.7

Personal Fouls Per Game

Rank	Name	Fouls	W-L	GM	PFPG	DQ
1.	Wisconsin	478	24-8	32	14.9	4
2.	Central Conn. St.	435	15-13	28	15.5	10
3.	Xavier	500	26-6	32	15.6	6
4.	Coppin St.	440	11-17	28	15.7	13
5.	Baylor	441	14-14	28	15.8	7
6.	Vermont	520	21-12	33	15.8	7
7.	Mississippi St.	490	21-10	31	15.8	8
8.	Texas Tech	555	22-13	35	15.9	8
9.	West Virginia	460	14-15	29	15.9	11
10.	Albany (N.Y.)	445	7-21	28	15.9	12

Rank	Name	Fouls	W-L	GM	PFPG	DQ
11.	Montana St.	431	11-16	27	16.0	6
12.	Butler	528	27-6	33	16.0	10
	Utah St.	528	24-9	33	16.0	5
14.	William & Mary	450	12-16	28	16.1	11
15.	New Mexico St.	467	20-9	29	16.1	7
16.	Notre Dame	551	24-10	34	16.2	6
17.	Lafayette	470	13-16	29	16.2	10
18.	LSU	524	21-11	32	16.4	3
19.	Northern Iowa	459	11-17	29	16.4	6
20.	Temple	558	18-16	34	16.4	11
21.	Auburn	561	22-12	34	16.5	8
	Towson	462	4-24	28	16.5	9
23.	Jacksonville	480	13-16	29	16.6	14
24.	Campbell	447	5-22	27	16.6	13
25.	Idaho	464	13-15	28	16.6	13
	Oregon St.	464	13-15	28	16.6	8
27.	Troy St.	531	26-6	32	16.6	7
28.	Houston	465	8-20	28	16.6	11
29.	Texas-Arlington	482	16-13	29	16.6	11
30.	Kansas	633	30-8	38	16.7	16

2003 Division I Game Highs

Team Highs

POINTS

Rank	Name	vs. Opponent	Game Date	PTS	OPP PTS
1.	Drake	Grinnell	12/11/2002	162	110
2.	St. Francis (N.Y.)	Long Island	2/22/2003	142	140
3.	Long Island	St. Francis (N.Y.)	2/22/2003	140	142
4.	Centenary (La.)	Ark. Baptist	2/01/2003	124	75
5.	Arkansas St.	Lyon	12/07/2002	120	55
6.	Western Caro.	Toccoa Falls Inst.	11/23/2002	119	58
7.	Maine	Me.-Fort Kent	11/23/2002	118	61
8.	Troy St.	Stetson	2/27/2003	117	70
	Connecticut	UNC Asheville	12/21/2002	117	67
	La.-Lafayette	Louisiana Col.	12/11/2002	117	57
	Cal St. Northridge	Bethany (Cal.)	12/07/2002	117	51
12.	Tenn.-Martin	Bethel (Tenn.)	12/14/2002	116	57
	Connecticut	Sacred Heart	12/03/2002	116	78
	Troy St.	Knoxville	11/23/2002	116	74
15.	Kentucky	Tennessee St.	12/30/2002	115	87
	Eastern Mich.	Concordia (Mich.)	12/02/2002	115	80
17.	Wofford	Toccoa Falls Inst.	2/19/2003	114	61
	Davidson	Washington (Md.)	12/01/2002	114	51
19.	Central Mich.	Spring Arbor	12/30/2002	113	63
20.	LSU	Centenary (La.)	1/15/2003	112	65
	Ohio	Akron	1/08/2003	112	104
	Wyoming	Savannah St.	1/08/2003	112	77
	Marshall	Kentucky St.	11/25/2002	112	78
	Oral Roberts	Okla. Wesleyan	11/23/2002	112	66

FIELD-GOAL PERCENTAGE

Rank	Name	vs. Opponent	Game Date	FG%	FGM	FGA
1.	Southern Utah	Montana Tech	12/19/2002	78.0	32	41
2.	Stephen F. Austin	LeTourneau	11/26/2002	77.2	44	57
3.	Morehead St.	Asbury	11/30/2002	73.6	39	53
4.	Chattanooga	Appalachian St.	3/06/2003	72.3	34	47
5.	Delaware St.	Fairleigh Dickinson	12/07/2002	72.1	31	43
6.	Air Force	Colorado St.	2/15/2003	71.9	23	32
7.	Samford	Georgia St.	1/18/2003	70.5	31	44
8.	LSU	Centenary (La.)	1/15/2003	70.3	45	64
9.	Iona	Wagner	12/03/2002	70.0	35	50
10.	Montana St.	Dickinson St.	12/10/2002	69.8	37	53
11.	Centenary (La.)	Ark. Baptist	2/01/2003	69.6	48	69
12.	Oakland	Texas Southern	12/27/2002	69.1	38	55
13.	Wagner	St. Francis (Pa.)	2/03/2003	68.6	35	51
	Toledo	Wright St.	12/11/2002	68.6	35	51
15.	Auburn	Georgia St.	11/26/2002	68.3	41	60
16.	Drake	Grinnell	12/11/2002	68.2	60	88
	Long Beach St.	Cal St. Fullerton	2/06/2003	68.2	30	44
18.	Kansas	Arizona St.	3/22/2003	67.8	40	59
	Vermont	Sacred Heart	12/31/2002	67.8	40	59
20.	Air Force	Ga. Southern	1/01/2003	67.5	27	40

THREE-POINT FIELD GOALS MADE

Rank	Name	vs. Opponent	Game Date	3FG
1.	Arkansas St.	Lyon	12/07/2002	20
2.	Temple	Charlotte	12/04/2002	19
	Davidson	Wash. & Lee	11/30/2002	19
4.	Washington St.	Gonzaga	12/07/2002	18
	Air Force	Tex.-Pan American	12/05/2002	18
6.	LSU	Tennessee	3/01/2003	17
	Troy St.	Jacksonville	3/01/2003	17
	Va. Commonwealth	William & Mary	2/19/2003	17
	UMKC	Southern Utah	2/06/2003	17
	Charlotte	Appalachian St.	11/25/2002	17
	Troy St.	Knoxville	11/23/2002	17
12.	UMKC	Western Ill.	3/01/2003	16
	Florida A&M	Coppin St.	3/01/2003	16
	LSU	Auburn	2/26/2003	16
	Ga. Southern	Chattanooga	2/24/2003	16
	Temple	Fordham	2/23/2003	16
	Col. of Charleston	Chattanooga	2/22/2003	16
	Wofford	Toccoa Falls Inst.	2/19/2003	16
	Tex.-Pan American	Central Baptist	2/08/2003	16
	Delaware	William & Mary	2/01/2003	16
	UMKC	Southern Utah	1/11/2003	16
	Northern Ariz.	Southern Utah	1/04/2003	16
	Air Force	Ga. Southern	1/01/2003	16
	Ohio	St. Bonaventure	12/31/2002	16
	Oral Roberts	UMBC	12/30/2002	16
	Montana	Southern Utah	12/30/2002	16
	Denver	UMKC	12/03/2002	16
	Mississippi Val.	Delta St.	12/03/2002	16
	San Diego St.	UC San Diego	12/02/2002	16

THREE-POINT FIELD-GOAL PERCENTAGE
Minimum 10 3FGM

Rank	Name	vs. Opponent	Game Date	3FG%	3FG	3FGA
1.	Portland St.	Weber St.	1/30/2003	76.9	10	13
2.	Eastern Ill.	Evansville	11/30/2002	76.5	13	17
3.	Ill.-Chicago	Wright St.	1/29/2003	75.0	12	16
4.	Mercer	Jacksonville St.	2/06/2003	73.7	14	19
5.	Jacksonville St.	Campbell	1/04/2003	73.3	11	15
6.	Texas Tech	Texas	3/14/2003	71.4	10	14
	Rice	Navy	12/23/2002	71.4	10	14
	Evansville	Austin Peay	12/19/2002	71.4	10	14
9.	Seton Hall	Miami (Fla.)	1/18/2003	70.6	12	17
	Evansville	Southern Ill.	1/08/2003	70.6	12	17
	Southwest Mo. St.	Samford	12/06/2002	70.6	12	17
12.	Maine	Northeastern	1/15/2003	70.0	14	20
	Toledo	Detroit	12/14/2002	70.0	14	20
14.	Florida A&M	Delaware St.	2/08/2003	68.8	11	16
15.	Toledo	Ball St.	3/05/2003	68.4	13	19
	Connecticut	Providence	2/08/2003	68.4	13	19
17.	Davidson	Wash. & Lee	11/30/2002	67.9	19	28
18.	Arkansas St.	Lyon	12/07/2002	66.7	20	30
	Northern Ariz.	St. Peter's	11/23/2002	66.7	14	21
	Central Mich.	Northern Ill.	3/14/2003	66.7	12	18
	Florida	South Carolina	2/25/2003	66.7	12	18
	TCU	UAB	1/29/2003	66.7	12	18
	Fairleigh Dickinson	Wagner	1/16/2003	66.7	12	18
	Duquesne	George Mason	12/02/2002	66.7	12	18
	Ark.-Little Rock	Colorado St.	11/30/2002	66.7	12	18
	LSU	Vanderbilt	2/12/2003	66.7	10	15

Rank	Name	vs. Opponent	Game Date	3FG%	3FG	3FGA
	South Carolina St.	Norfolk St.	1/25/2003	66.7	10	15
	Towson	UNC Wilmington	1/22/2003	66.7	10	15
	Delaware St.	Bethune-Cookman	1/06/2003	66.7	10	15
	Eastern Ill.	Southeast Mo. St.	1/04/2003	66.7	10	15

FREE-THROW PERCENTAGE
Minimum 15 Made

Rank	Name	vs. Opponent	Game Date	FT%	FT	FTA
1.	Idaho	Cal St. Northridge	3/08/2003	100.0	24	24
	St. Francis (Pa.)	Youngstown St.	12/04/2002	100.0	21	21
	Oregon	Washington St.	1/25/2003	100.0	19	19
	Kentucky	Utah	3/23/2003	100.0	18	18
	Washington St.	Stanford	2/15/2003	100.0	18	18
	Georgia St.	Stetson	1/31/2003	100.0	18	18
	Boston U.	Albany (N.Y.)	1/08/2003	100.0	18	18
	UC Santa Barb.	Cal Poly	2/20/2003	100.0	16	16
	Ohio St.	Michigan	1/15/2003	100.0	16	16
	Providence	Brown	11/23/2002	100.0	16	16
	UC Irvine	Cal St. Fullerton	2/08/2003	100.0	15	15
	Centenary (La.)	Tex. A&M-Corp. Chris.	1/18/2003	100.0	15	15
	St. Bonaventure	Kent St.	12/21/2002	100.0	15	15
	Boston U.	Ohio	12/13/2002	100.0	15	15
	Tenn.-Martin	Missouri Valley	11/25/2002	100.0	15	15
16.	Michigan St.	Ohio St.	1/09/2003	96.7	29	30
17.	Connecticut	Rutgers	2/19/2003	96.2	25	26
18.	Marist	Iona	2/23/2003	95.8	23	24
	UNLV	Brigham Young	1/16/2003	95.8	23	24
20.	Oregon	Stanford	2/06/2003	95.7	22	23
	Notre Dame	Rutgers	1/14/2003	95.7	22	23

2004 Division I Top Returnees

Career Totals

MOST POINTS

Seniors

	Name	Ht.	Yrs.	G	FG	3FG	FT	Pts.	Avg.
1.	Michael Watson, UMKC	6-0	3	88	625	295	263	1,808	20.5
2.	Ricky Minard, Morehead St.	6-4	3	85	606	181	357	1,750	20.6
3.	Mike Helms, Oakland	6-0	3	86	533	133	420	1,619	18.8
4.	Andre Emmett, Texas Tech	6-5	3	94	622	38	273	1,555	16.5
5.	Jameer Nelson, St. Joseph's	6-0	3	93	469	156	341	1,435	15.4
6.	Romain Sato, Xavier	6-5	3	93	443	232	284	1,402	15.1
7.	Darius Rice, Miami (Fla.)	6-10	3	88	465	205	258	1,393	15.8
8.	Thomas Tee Trotter, Md.-East. Shore	5-11	3	80	433	206	311	1,383	17.3
9.	David Hawkins, Temple	6-4	3	98	470	139	289	1,368	15.4
10.	Phillip Gilbert, Bradley	6-3	3	89	471	180	230	1,352	15.2

Juniors

	Name	Ht.	Yrs.	G	FG	3FG	FT	Pts.	Avg.
1.	Kevin Martin, Western Caro.	6-7	2	52	357	123	328	1,165	22.4
2.	Chris Thomas, Notre Dame	6-1	2	67	371	156	255	1,153	17.2
3.	Taylor Coppenrath, Vermont	6-9	2	59	377	47	285	1,086	18.4
4.	Ben Gordon, Connecticut	6-2	2	67	351	142	228	1,072	16.0
5.	T.J. Sorrentine, Vermont	5-11	2	58	318	160	178	974	16.8
6.	Ryan Gomes, Providence	6-7	2	56	345	0	231	921	16.4
7.	Jerry Johnson, Rider	6-0	2	55	305	140	165	915	16.6
8.	Corey Santee, TCU	6-2	2	59	329	114	139	911	15.4
9.	Kenny Adeleke, Hofstra	6-8	2	61	362	1	176	901	14.8
10.	Julius Hodge, North Carolina St.	6-6	2	64	274	74	268	900	14.1

SCORING AVERAGE

Seniors (Min. 1,200 Pts.)

	Name	Ht.	Yrs.	G	FG	3FG	FT	Pts.	Avg.
1.	Luis Flores, Manhattan	6-2	2	59	411	95	385	1,302	22.1
2.	Ricky Minard, Morehead St.	6-4	3	85	606	181	357	1,750	20.6
3.	Michael Watson, UMKC	6-0	3	88	625	295	263	1,808	20.5
4.	Mike Helms, Oakland	6-0	3	86	533	133	420	1,619	18.8
5.	Thomas Tee Trotter, Md.-East. Shore	5-11	3	80	433	206	311	1,383	17.3
6.	Andre Emmett, Texas Tech	6-5	3	94	622	38	273	1,555	16.5
7.	Darius Rice Miami (Fla.)	6-10	3	88	465	205	258	1,393	15.8
8.	Jameer Nelson, St. Joseph's	6-0	3	93	469	156	341	1,435	15.4
9.	Luke McDonald, Drake	6-6	3	87	438	241	211	1,328	15.3
10.	Phillip Gilbert, Bradley	6-3	3	89	471	180	230	1,352	15.2

Juniors (Min. 800 Pts.)

	Name	Ht.	Yrs.	G	FG	3FG	FT	Pts.	Avg.
1.	Kevin Martin, Western Caro.	6-7	2	52	357	123	328	1,165	22.4
2.	Taylor Coppenrath, Vermont	6-9	2	59	377	47	285	1,086	18.4
3.	Chris Thomas, Notre Dame	6-1	2	67	371	156	255	1,153	17.2
4.	T.J. Sorrentine, Vermont	5-11	2	58	318	160	178	974	16.8
5.	Jerry Johnson, Rider	6-0	2	55	305	140	165	915	16.6
6.	Ryan Gomes, Providence	6-7	2	56	345	0	231	921	16.4
7.	Ben Gordon, Connecticut	6-2	2	67	351	142	228	1,072	16.0
8.	Lawrence Roberts, Mississippi St.	6-9	2	56	307	37	243	894	16.0
9.	Matt Nelson, Colorado St.	7-0	2	53	308	0	220	836	15.8
10.	Corey Santee, TCU	6-2	2	59	329	114	139	911	15.4

HIGHEST FIELD-GOAL PERCENTAGE

Seniors (Min. 300 FGM)

	Name	Ht.	Yrs.	G	FG	FGA	Pct.
1.	Adam Mark, Belmont	6-8	3	82	423	666	63.5
2.	James Moore, New Mexico St.	6-8	3	83	460	802	57.4
3.	Cuthbert Victor, Murray St.	6-5	3	89	391	685	57.1
4.	Adam Parada, UC Irvine	7-0	3	91	380	678	56.0
5.	Jerald Fields, East Tenn. St.	6-7	3	82	315	566	55.7
6.	Marcus Smallwood, Northern Ill.	6-6	3	86	362	659	54.9
7.	Frank Bennett, Ga. Southern	6-7	3	87	356	653	54.5
8.	Keith Waleskowski, Dayton	6-8	3	96	367	677	54.2
9.	Phil Martin, Hawaii	6-8	3	94	381	712	53.5
10.	Adrian Henning, Austin Peay	6-6	3	95	339	634	53.5

Juniors (Min. 240 FGM)

	Name	Ht.	Yrs.	G	FG	FGA	Pct.
1.	Matt Nelson, Colorado St.	7-0	2	53	308	487	63.2
2.	Michael Harris, Rice	6-6	2	57	326	545	59.8
3.	Juan Mendez, Niagara	6-7	2	61	321	544	59.0
4.	David Harrison, Colorado	7-0	2	59	303	518	58.5
5.	Emeka Okafor, Connecticut	6-9	2	67	326	559	58.3
6.	Channing Frye, Arizona	6-10	2	66	287	495	58.0
7.	Michael Southall, La.-Lafayette	6-10	2	58	287	501	57.3
8.	Ryan Gomes, Providence	6-7	2	56	345	633	54.5
9.	Hakim Warrick, Syracuse	6-8	2	70	292	536	54.5
10.	Marco Killingsworth, Auburn	6-7	2	62	260	479	54.3

STATISTICAL LEADERS

MOST THREE-POINT FIELD GOALS MADE PER GAME

Seniors (Min. 120 3FGM)

	Ht.	Yrs.	G	3FG	Avg.
1. Terrence Woods, Florida A&M	6-3	1	28	139	4.96
2. Demon Brown, Charlotte	6-1	2	59	202	3.42
3. Michael Watson, UMKC	6-0	3	88	295	3.35
4. Nick Zachery, Ark.-Little Rock	6-3	3	75	219	2.92
5. Luke McDonald, Drake	6-6	3	87	241	2.77
6. Thomas Tee Trotter, Md.-East. Shore	5-11	3	80	206	2.58
7. Morris Finley, UAB	5-11	2	64	160	2.50
7. Anthony Anderson, Massachusetts	5-11	2	58	145	2.50
9. Romain Sato, Xavier	6-5	3	93	232	2.49
10. Sharif Chambliss, Penn St.	6-0	3	79	195	2.47

Juniors (Min. 80 3FGM)

	Ht.	Yrs.	G	3FG	Avg.
1. John Reimold, Bowling Green	6-6	1	29	84	2.90
2. T.J. Sorrentine, Vermont	5-11	2	58	160	2.76
3. Jerry Johnson, Rider	6-0	2	55	140	2.55
4. Chris Hill, Michigan St.	6-3	2	66	161	2.44
5. Patrick Sparks, Western Ky.	6-1	2	65	155	2.38
6. Kevin Martin, Western Caro.	6-7	2	52	123	2.37
7. Chris Thomas, Notre Dame	6-1	2	67	156	2.33
8. Phil Goss, Drexel	6-1	2	59	135	2.29
9. Terrance Johnson, Pepperdine	6-5	2	59	133	2.25
10. Salim Stoudamire, Arizona	6-1	2	64	144	2.25

HIGHEST THREE-POINT FIELD-GOAL PERCENTAGE

Seniors (Min. 120 3FGM)

	Ht.	Yrs.	G	3FG	3FGA	Pct.
1. Terrence Woods, Florida A&M	6-3	1	28	139	304	45.7
2. Jake Sullivan, Iowa St.	6-1	3	90	188	423	44.4
3. Kyle Bankhead, Gonzaga	6-0	3	90	128	298	43.0
4. Jeff Schiffner, Pennsylvania	6-6	3	81	144	336	42.9
5. Steve Drabyn, Belmont	6-0	3	82	198	469	42.2
6. Nick Jacobson, Utah	6-4	3	94	188	446	42.2
7. Mark Bigelow, Brigham Young	6-7	2	62	128	305	42.0
8. Nick Zachery, Ark.-Little Rock	6-3	3	75	219	525	41.7
9. Eric Haut, Kent St.	6-0	3	92	126	303	41.6
10. Clint Cuffle, Evansville	6-6	3	82	125	305	41.0

Juniors (Min. 80 3FGM)

	Ht.	Yrs.	G	3FG	3FGA	Pct.
1. Salim Stoudamire, Arizona	6-1	2	64	144	321	44.9
2. Tim Keller, Air Force	6-3	2	56	110	252	43.7
3. Ronny Dawn, Marshall	6-3	2	59	80	189	42.3
4. Gregg Alexander, Illinois St.	6-4	2	60	119	282	42.2
5. Tim Begley, Pennsylvania	6-5	2	60	94	223	42.2
6. Thomas Kelati, Washington St.	6-5	2	54	80	190	42.1
7. Chris Hill, Michigan St.	6-3	2	66	161	383	42.0
8. John Reimold, Bowling Green	6-6	1	29	84	200	42.0
9. Ben Gordon, Connecticut	6-2	2	67	142	341	41.6
10. Mike McLaren, Dartmouth	6-3	2	54	118	284	41.5

FREE-THROW PERCENTAGE

Seniors (Min. 175 FTM)

	Ht.	Yrs.	G	FG	FGA	Pct.
1. Steve Drabyn, Belmont	6-0	3	82	180	196	91.8
2. Luis Flores, Manhattan	6-2	2	59	385	433	88.9
3. Jake Sullivan, Iowa St.	6-1	3	90	271	306	88.6
4. D.J. Munir, Stony Brook	6-3	2	48	193	220	87.7
5. Curtis Allen, Washington	6-0	3	86	178	203	87.7
6. Kenneth Lowe, Purdue	6-3	4	80	277	321	86.3
7. Luke McDonald, Drake	6-6	3	87	211	245	86.1
8. James Gillingham, Bradley	6-4	3	90	373	435	85.7
9. Marques Green, St. Bonaventure	5-7	3	85	270	315	85.7
10. Luke Jackson, Oregon	6-7	3	95	343	407	84.3

Juniors (Min. 110 FTM)

	Ht.	Yrs.	G	FG	FGA	Pct.
1. Salim Stoudamire, Arizona	6-1	2	64	173	195	88.7
2. Chris Thomas, Notre Dame	6-1	2	67	255	290	87.9
3. Kevin Martin, Western Caro.	6-7	2	52	328	383	85.6
4. Matt Rohde, Wis.-Green Bay	6-2	2	60	167	199	83.9
5. Tim Keller, Air Force	6-3	2	56	111	134	82.8
6. T.J. Sorrentine, Vermont	5-11	2	58	178	215	82.8
7. Jerry Johnson, Rider	6-0	2	55	165	200	82.5
8. Jared Jensen, Brigham Young	6-9	2	62	159	193	82.4
9. Darryl Peterson, Akron	6-5	2	59	173	211	82.0
10. Alan Anderson, Michigan St.	6-6	2	63	195	239	81.6

REBOUNDS

Seniors

	Ht.	Yrs.	G	Reb.	Avg.
1. James Thomas, Texas	6-8	3	101	886	8.77
2. Arthur Johnson, Missouri	6-9	3	102	859	8.42
3. Keith Waleskowski, Dayton	6-8	3	96	765	7.97
4. Ron Robinson, Central Conn. St.	6-7	3	87	759	8.72
5. Erroyl Bing, East Caro.	6-6	3	85	715	8.41
6. James Reaves, Niagara	6-8	3	86	712	8.28
7. Ellis Myles, Louisville	6-8	3	87	657	7.55
8. Andre Brown, DePaul	6-9	3	84	643	7.65
8. Kim Adams, Arkansas St.	6-8	3	88	643	7.31
10. Anthony Kann, Western Mich.	6-7	3	87	630	7.24

Juniors

	Ht.	Yrs.	G	Reb.	Avg.
1. Emeka Okafor, Connecticut	6-9	2	67	676	10.09
2. Kenny Adeleke, Hofstra	6-8	2	61	570	9.34
3. Lawrence Roberts, Mississippi St.	6-9	2	56	518	9.25
4. Ryan Gomes, Providence	6-7	2	56	499	8.91
5. Channing Frye, Arizona	6-10	2	66	471	7.14
6. Hakim Warrick, Syracuse	6-8	2	70	465	6.64
7. Juan Mendez, Niagara	6-7	2	61	454	7.44
8. Michael Harris, Rice	6-6	2	57	453	7.95
8. David Harrison, Colorado	7-0	2	59	453	7.68
10. Michael Southall, La.-Lafayette	6-10	2	58	437	7.53

REBOUNDS PER GAME

Seniors (Min. 500 Rebs.)

	Ht.	Yrs.	G	Reb.	Avg.
1. James Thomas, Texas	6-8	3	101	886	8.77
2. Ron Robinson, Central Conn. St.	6-7	3	87	759	8.72
3. Arthur Johnson, Missouri	6-9	3	102	859	8.42
4. Erroyl Bing, East Caro.	6-6	3	85	715	8.41
5. James Reaves, Niagara	6-8	3	86	712	8.28
6. Keith Waleskowski, Dayton	6-8	3	96	765	7.97
7. Andre Brown, DePaul	6-9	3	84	643	7.65
8. Ellis Myles, Louisville	6-8	3	87	657	7.55
9. Kim Adams, Arkansas St.	6-8	3	88	643	7.31
10. Anthony Kann, Western Mich.	6-7	3	87	630	7.24

Juniors (Min. 280 Rebs.)

	Ht.	Yrs.	G	Reb.	Avg.
1. Emeka Okafor, Connecticut	6-9	2	67	676	10.09
2. Kenny Adeleke, Hofstra	6-8	2	61	570	9.34
3. Lawrence Roberts, Mississippi St.	6-9	2	56	518	9.25
4. Ryan Gomes, Providence	6-7	2	56	499	8.91
5. Michael Harris, Rice	6-6	2	57	453	7.95
6. David Harrison, Colorado	7-0	2	59	453	7.68
7. Michael Southall, La.-Lafayette	6-10	2	58	437	7.53
8. Juan Mendez, Niagara	6-7	2	61	454	7.44
9. Danny Granger, Bradley	6-8	2	43	318	7.40
10. Channing Frye, Arizona	6-10	2	66	471	7.14

ASSISTS PER GAME

Seniors (Min. 280 Asts.)

	Ht.	Yrs.	G	Ast.	Avg.
1. Martell Bailey, Ill.-Chicago	5-10	2	64	406	6.34
2. Marques Green, St. Bonaventure	5-7	3	85	517	6.08
3. Jameer Nelson, St. Joseph's	6-0	3	93	543	5.84
4. Chris Duhon, Duke	6-1	3	107	594	5.55
5. Luke Spencer-Gardner, Oral Roberts	6-1	2	59	320	5.42
6. Antonio Burks, Memphis	6-0	2	61	322	5.28
7. Andre Barrett, Seton Hall	5-8	3	91	479	5.26
8. Richard Little, VMI	5-10	3	86	443	5.15
9. Taliek Brown, Connecticut	6-1	2	63	312	4.95
10. Jave Meade, Holy Cross	6-1	3	93	444	4.77

Juniors (Min. 150 Asts.)

	Ht.	Yrs.	G	Ast.	Avg.
1. Chris Thomas, Notre Dame	6-1	2	67	488	7.28
2. Aaron Miles, Kansas	6-1	2	75	496	6.61
3. Tory Cavalieri, St. Francis (N.Y.)	6-0	1	30	173	5.77
4. Corey Santee, TCU	6-2	2	59	321	5.44
5. T.J. Thompson, George Washington	5-11	2	57	294	5.16
6. Jason Forte, Brown	6-0	2	56	276	4.93
7. Patrick Sparks, Western Ky.	6-1	2	65	312	4.80
8. T.J. Sorrentine, Vermont	5-11	2	58	275	4.74
9. Mike Slattery, Delaware	6-0	2	59	273	4.63
10. Woody Souffrant, Hofstra	5-11	2	60	272	4.53

BLOCKED SHOTS PER GAME

Seniors (Min. 90 Blks.)

	Ht.	Yrs.	G	Blk.	Avg.
1. Kyle Davis, Auburn	6-10	3	88	285	3.24
2. Herve Lamizana, Rutgers	6-10	2	51	144	2.82
3. Rans Brempong, Western Caro.	6-8	3	85	224	2.64
4. Eddy Fobbs, Sam Houston St.	6-11	3	86	199	2.31
5. Marcus Douthit, Providence	6-10	3	93	203	2.18
6. Mike Benton, Col. of Charleston	6-9	2	60	129	2.15
7. Jeremy McNeil, Syracuse	6-8	3	99	209	2.11
8. Arthur Johnson, Missouri	6-9	3	102	197	1.93
9. Josh Lewis, Austin Peay	6-8	3	93	174	1.87
10. Gerrick Morris, South Fla.	6-10	3	87	155	1.78

Juniors (Min. 70 Blks.)

	Ht.	Yrs.	G	Blk.	Avg.
1. Emeka Okafor, Connecticut	6-9	2	67	294	4.39
2. Nick Billings, Binghamton	7-0	2	48	197	4.10
3. Deng Gai, Fairfield	6-9	2	54	211	3.91
4. Moussa Badiane, East Caro.	6-10	2	51	149	2.92
5. Michael Southall, La.-Lafayette	6-10	2	58	165	2.84
6. David Harrison, Colorado	7-0	2	59	140	2.37
7. Danny Granger, Bradley	6-8	2	43	89	2.07
8. Josh Grant, Winthrop	6-10	2	54	103	1.91
9. Tony Dixon, Towson	6-10	2	48	84	1.75
10. Channing Frye, Arizona	6-10	2	66	110	1.67

STEALS PER GAME

Seniors (Min. 120 Stls.)	Ht.	Yrs.	G	Stl.	Avg.
1. Marques Green, St. Bonaventure	5-7	3	85	218	2.56
2. Andrew Wisniewski, Centenary (La.)	6-3	2	55	128	2.33
3. Edward O'Neil, Charleston So.	5-11	2	54	125	2.31
4. Garrett Richardson, Tennessee St.	6-3	3	84	193	2.30
5. Ricky Minard, Morehead St.	6-4	3	85	185	2.18
6. Tony Dobbins, Richmond	6-4	2	64	138	2.16
7. Keith Triplett, Toledo	6-3	2	59	124	2.10
8. Chris Duhon, Duke	6-1	3	107	220	2.06
9. Jave Meade, Holy Cross	6-1	3	93	186	2.00
10. Demarcus Wilkins, Florida A&M	6-0	3	77	151	1.96

Juniors (Min. 70 Stls.)	Ht.	Yrs.	G	Stl.	Avg.
1. Rawle Marshall, Oakland	6-7	2	28	80	2.86
2. Carlos Morban, Florida Int'l	6-2	2	58	151	2.60
3. Errick Craven, Southern California	6-2	2	61	141	2.31
4. Aaron Miles, Kansas	6-1	2	75	151	2.01
5. Chris Thomas, Notre Dame	6-1	2	67	134	2.00
6. Ian Boylan, Cal St. Northridge	6-6	2	57	112	1.96
7. Jason Forte, Brown	6-0	2	56	106	1.89
8. Patrick Sparks, Western Ky.	6-1	2	65	119	1.83
9. Eddie Basden, Charlotte	6-5	2	59	103	1.75
10. Lawrence Roberts, Mississippi St.	6-9	2	56	96	1.71

2003 Division II Individual Leaders

Points Per Game

Rank Name, Team	Cl	G	FGM	3FG	FT	PTS	PPG
1. Ron Christy, Teikyo Post	Jr.	29	295	64	134	788	27.2
2. Alexus Foyle, BYU-Hawaii	Sr.	23	261	11	81	614	26.7
3. Jerome Beasley, North Dakota	Sr.	29	293	16	186	788	26.6
4. Tim Black, Barton	Sr.	28	215	63	221	714	25.5
5. Patrick Pope, St. Augustine's	Sr.	27	204	65	212	685	25.4
6. Ben Dewar, Lake Superior St.	Sr.	26	190	69	173	622	23.9
7. Spencer Ross, Queens (N.C.)	Jr.	33	256	56	220	788	23.9
8. Robbie Ballard, Emporia St.	Sr.	27	226	95	83	630	23.3
9. Wykeen Kelly, Salem Int'l	Sr.	30	216	91	168	691	23.0
10. Rod Edwards, Ouachita Baptist	Jr.	28	193	91	167	644	23.0
11. Phillip Godfrey, West Va. Tech	Jr.	29	241	94	85	661	22.8
12. Sean Kelly, Western Ore.	Jr.	27	226	61	102	615	22.8
13. Charles Stephens, Longwood	Jr.	29	249	18	141	657	22.7
14. Tommie King, South Dakota	Sr.	28	249	4	129	631	22.5
15. Austin Nichols, Humboldt St.	Jr.	29	214	49	175	652	22.5
16. Adrian Penland, Lander	Sr.	28	216	55	142	629	22.5
17. Marcus West, Mount Olive	Jr.	28	223	34	147	627	22.4
18. Byran Chapman, Fayetteville St.	Sr.	28	248	31	97	624	22.3
19. Brice Mills, West Liberty St.	Sr.	26	235	48	61	579	22.3
20. Stephen Bahl, Colorado Mines	Jr.	28	207	91	117	622	22.2
21. Ronald Johnson, Cal St. L.A.	Sr.	27	197	35	170	599	22.2
22. Flem Tucker, Albany St. (Ga.)	Jr.	27	180	33	204	597	22.1
23. Joe Hasz, Minn.-Crookston	Sr.	24	183	78	85	529	22.0
24. Robert Day, Western Ore.	Jr.	27	188	94	122	592	21.9
25. Derek Jones, Charleston (W.Va.)	Sr.	30	206	58	179	649	21.6
26. Denver TenBroek, North Dakota St.	Sr.	31	223	82	138	666	21.5
27. Rashiem Wright, Dist. Columbia	Sr.	26	204	7	143	558	21.5
28. Jason Wilkerson, East Central	Sr.	28	207	79	106	599	21.4
29. Ramzee Stanton, West Chester	Sr.	30	254	1	131	640	21.3
30. Yari Scott, Paine	Sr.	27	197	79	100	573	21.2
31. Scott Land, Cal St. Chico	So.	26	200	89	62	551	21.2
32. Lawrence Ramsey, III, St. Edward's	Sr.	27	192	45	141	570	21.1
33. Garland Ragler, Alderson-Broaddus	Sr.	32	263	41	101	668	20.9
34. Billy McDaniel, Ark.-Monticello	Fr.	27	222	31	88	563	20.9
35. Cedric Brooks, Pittsburg St.	Sr.	28	193	61	136	583	20.8
36. Marco Spears, Johnson Smith	Sr.	29	230	44	99	603	20.8
37. Phil Sellers, St. Rose	Sr.	25	208	1	99	516	20.6
38. Nick Svehla, Neb.-Kearney	Sr.	33	251	14	160	676	20.5
39. Tom Barlow, Bloomsburg	Sr.	22	153	33	108	447	20.3
40. William Brown, Tex. A&M-Kingsville	Jr.	27	200	72	75	547	20.3
41. Robbie Seabrook, Anderson (S.C.)	Sr.	26	177	109	63	526	20.2
42. Jerome LaGrange, Livingstone	Jr.	27	198	47	102	545	20.2
Raymond Strachan, Columbia Union	Sr.	27	217	2	109	545	20.2
44. Sotirios Karapostolou, Southern N.H.	Sr.	30	194	112	104	604	20.1
45. Bobby Burries, Cal St. San B'dino	Sr.	29	184	58	156	582	20.1
46. Marlon Parmer, Ky. Wesleyan	Sr.	35	218	60	201	697	19.9
47. Brian Atkins, Concord	Jr.	28	201	40	114	556	19.9
48. Djuan Hankins, Wingate	Sr.	27	180	64	111	535	19.8
49. Tim Washington, Bowie St.	Sr.	35	248	1	191	688	19.7
50. Peter Bullock, Alas. Anchorage	Jr.	27	191	12	134	528	19.6

Rebounds Per Game

Rank Name, Team	Cl	G	REB	RPG
1. Billy McDaniel, Ark.-Monticello	Fr.	27	345	12.8
2. Gordon James, Bridgeport	Jr.	30	379	12.6
3. Fred Hooks, Humboldt St.	Jr.	29	353	12.2
4. Brian Atkins, Concord	Jr.	28	320	11.4
5. Dwight Windom, Lincoln Memorial	Sr.	29	324	11.2
6. Kenyon Booker, Shaw	Sr.	30	333	11.1
7. Danny Jones, Tarleton St.	Sr.	33	364	11.0
8. Marcus West, Mount Olive	Jr.	28	306	10.9
9. Ramzee Stanton, West Chester	Sr.	30	326	10.9
10. Jayson Williams, Lane	Jr.	28	303	10.8
11. Jakim Donaldson, Edinboro	So.	27	291	10.8
12. Wayne Wallace, Virginia Union	Sr.	23	243	10.6
13. Peter Bullock, Alas. Anchorage	Jr.	27	285	10.6
14. Brian Robinson, Assumption	So.	31	327	10.5
15. Paul Tonkovich, Caldwell	Sr.	26	273	10.5
16. Jamey Richardson, Pittsburg St.	Jr.	28	290	10.4
17. Jason Williams, Alas. Fairbanks	Jr.	28	289	10.3
18. Dominic Calfori, UC Davis	Sr.	25	255	10.2
19. Reggie McKoy, Kennesaw St.	Jr.	33	333	10.1
20. Bilal Salaam, Kutztown	So.	28	274	9.8
21. Mike Palm, Western Wash.	Sr.	27	264	9.8
22. Jeff Weirsma, Erskine	Sr.	30	292	9.7
23. Maurice Brown, Saginaw Valley	Jr.	27	262	9.7
24. Matt Mlynarchek, Hillsdale	Sr.	28	270	9.6
25. Brian Westre, Mo.-Rolla	Jr.	26	250	9.6
26. Ryan Pitts, Lenoir-Rhyne	Jr.	30	284	9.5
27. Mike Campbell, Ashland	So.	27	254	9.4
28. Vomo Walker, LeMoyne-Owen	Sr.	28	263	9.4
29. Michael Beaton, Mercy	Sr.	26	244	9.4
30. LaMont Jones, East Stroudsburg	Jr.	26	243	9.3
31. Justin Leith, Merrimack	Jr.	27	252	9.3
32. Tim Washington, Bowie St.	Sr.	35	326	9.3
33. Kyle Jones, Felician	Jr.	29	270	9.3
34. Jaquan Bracey, Francis Marion	Jr.	27	250	9.3
35. Flagan Prince, Le Moyne	Sr.	29	267	9.2
36. Austin Collier, LeMoyne-Owen	Sr.	24	219	9.1
37. Aaron Davis, Southern Conn. St.	Sr.	25	228	9.1
38. Sidney Holmes, Lewis	Jr.	29	263	9.1
39. Jason Bauer, Grand Valley St.	Sr.	28	252	9.0
Raymond Strachan, Columbia Union	Sr.	27	243	9.0
41. Cerwin Thompson, Eckerd	Sr.	30	269	9.0
42. Shawn Moss, St. Paul's	So.	27	242	9.0
43. Jerome Beasley, North Dakota	Sr.	29	259	8.9

Rank Name, Team	Cl	G	REB	RPG
Demond Cowins, N.J. Inst. of Tech.	Jr.	29	259	8.9
45. Achille Ngounou, Tampa	Jr.	27	241	8.9
46. Jason Wright, Indianapolis	Jr.	28	249	8.9
47. Charles Stephens, Longwood	Jr.	29	257	8.9
48. Desmond Peoples, St. Augustine's	Jr.	27	239	8.9
49. Kurt Patik, Fort Lewis	Sr.	31	273	8.8
50. Ronald Thompson, Morehouse	Jr.	25	220	8.8

Blocked Shots Per Game

Rank Name, Team	Cl	G	BLKS	BKPG
1. Aaron Davis, Southern Conn. St.	Sr.	25	103	4.1
2. Bilal Salaam, Kutztown	So.	28	104	3.7
3. Moustapha Diouf, Queens (N.C.)	Jr.	33	116	3.5
4. Wayne Wallace, Virginia Union	Sr.	23	73	3.2
5. Avis Wyatt, Virginia St.	Jr.	28	84	3.0
6. Jeff Weirsma, Erskine	Sr.	30	88	2.9
7. Mike Williams, Bryant	So.	31	90	2.9
8. Anthony Greenup, Shaw	Jr.	30	85	2.8
9. Todd Williams, S.C.-Aiken	Jr.	25	67	2.7
10. Sam Grannum, West Chester	Jr.	30	78	2.6
11. Eugene Dabney, Ky. Wesleyan	Sr.	35	89	2.5
12. Matt Smith, Lander	Sr.	23	57	2.5
13. Jonas Pierre, Lincoln (Mo.)	Jr.	26	64	2.5
14. Desmond Peoples, St. Augustine's	Jr.	27	66	2.4
15. Jamey Richardson, Pittsburg St.	Jr.	28	66	2.4
Jason Williams, Alas. Fairbanks	Jr.	28	66	2.4
17. Drew DeMond, West Fla.	Sr.	24	55	2.3
18. Thaddeus Daggett, Tex. A&M-Commerce	Jr.	28	64	2.3
19. Steven Hankle, San Fran. St.	Sr.	26	58	2.2
20. Vincent Bridgewater, Tarleton St.	Sr.	28	62	2.2
21. Ryan Pitts, Lenoir-Rhyne	Jr.	30	66	2.2
22. Mike Phenizee, Clayton St.	Sr.	29	63	2.2
23. Jean-Noel Leuly, Fla. Southern	Sr.	31	67	2.2
24. Jon Smith, Bowie St.	Jr.	35	75	2.1
Adam Wetzel, Neb.-Omaha	Sr.	28	60	2.1
26. Barry Mitchell, West Virginia St.	Jr.	24	50	2.1
27. Zach Comer, West Va. Wesleyan	Fr.	26	54	2.1
28. Brian Robinson, Assumption	So.	31	64	2.1
29. Phil Sellers, St. Rose	Sr.	25	51	2.0
30. Jason Pritchett, Central Okla.	Sr.	29	58	2.0
Michael Beaton, Mercy	Sr.	26	52	2.0
32. Athanasios Souflias, Southern N.H.	Jr.	30	59	2.0
33. Terri Miller, Cal St. Bakersfield	Jr.	29	57	2.0
34. Mike Palm, Western Wash.	Sr.	27	53	2.0
35. Kevin Harrington, S.C.-Spartanburg	Jr.	29	56	1.9
36. Mike Campbell, Ashland	So.	27	52	1.9
37. Andrew Harlie, Okla. Panhandle	Jr.	26	50	1.9
38. David Boyd, Tuskegee	Jr.	28	52	1.9
39. Michal Davenport, Millersville	Jr.	32	58	1.8
40. Alex McLean, Queens (N.Y.)	Sr.	28	49	1.8
Austin Collier, LeMoyne-Owen	Sr.	24	42	1.8
42. Jason Schneeweis, Minn. Duluth	Sr.	31	54	1.7
43. Nate Block, Hawaii Pacific	Sr.	27	47	1.7
Kyle Stirmlinger, Mont. St.-Billings	Sr.	27	47	1.7
45. Brian Westre, Mo.-Rolla	Jr.	26	45	1.7
46. Chad France, Colorado St.-Pueblo	Jr.	28	47	1.7
Chris Northcross, Hillsdale	Jr.	28	47	1.7
48. Josh Morgan, Gannon	Sr.	30	50	1.7
49. Scott Melle, Mercyhurst	Sr.	27	44	1.6
50. Joshua Allen, Alderson-Broaddus	Jr.	32	52	1.6

Steals Per Game

Rank Name, Team	Cl	G	ST	STPG
1. Gerry McNair, C.W. Post	Jr.	30	103	3.4
2. Ian Wilson, Pace	Jr.	27	84	3.1
3. Brad Oleson, Alas. Fairbanks	So.	27	80	3.0
4. Te'Ron Reed, Cal St. San B'dino	Jr.	30	87	2.9
5. Patrick Pope, St. Augustine's	Sr.	27	78	2.9
6. Joe Hasz, Minn.-Crookston	Sr.	24	68	2.8
7. Joe Bakhoum, Okla. Panhandle	Sr.	25	70	2.8
8. Tyrone Smith, Elizabeth City St.	Jr.	28	78	2.8
9. Justin Shouse, Mercyhurst	Jr.	27	75	2.8
10. Shahar Golan, Assumption	Jr.	31	86	2.8
11. Clayton Smith, Metro St.	Sr.	33	91	2.8
12. Ismael Caro, New Haven	Jr.	31	85	2.7
13. Cedric Brooks, Pittsburg St.	Sr.	28	75	2.7
14. Edward Porter, Tex. A&M-Kingsville	Jr.	27	72	2.7
15. Rudy Williams, North Ala.	Sr.	28	74	2.6

Rank Name, Team	Cl	G	ST	STPG
16. Andrew Harding, Glenville St.	Jr.	29	76	2.6
17. Mike Tucker, Alderson-Broaddus	So.	26	68	2.6
18. Dana Jones, Mass.-Lowell	Jr.	33	86	2.6
Luke Kendall, Metro St.	Jr.	33	86	2.6
20. Matt Vaughn, Colo. Christian	So.	26	66	2.5
21. Cayce Cook, Colo. Christian	Sr.	27	68	2.5
22. Brandon Lee, Tarleton St.	Jr.	33	83	2.5
23. Eric Faber, Rollins	So.	32	80	2.5
Luqman Jaaber, Virginia Union	So.	28	70	2.5
Kirk Maher, Mercy	Sr.	26	65	2.5
26. Todd Henry, Tiffin	Jr.	27	67	2.5
27. Kendrick Wilson, Eckerd	Sr.	32	79	2.5
28. Marcus Clements, Bluefield St.	Jr.	28	69	2.5
29. David Rhone, West Tex. A&M	Sr.	31	76	2.5
30. Clayton Barker, N.J. Inst. of Tech.	Fr.	29	71	2.4
31. Austin Hansen, South Dakota St.	Sr.	31	75	2.4
32. Jared Bledsoe, Minn. St. Moorhead	Sr.	29	70	2.4
Chris Harriman, Augusta St.	Jr.	29	70	2.4
34. Chase Graves, St. Michael's	Fr.	27	65	2.4
35. Royce Bryan, Bemidji St.	Sr.	25	60	2.4
36. Tim Black, Barton	Sr.	28	67	2.4
Christopher Dunn, West Virginia St.	Fr.	28	67	2.4
Kevin Newsome, Shepherd	Sr.	28	67	2.4
Carlos Vanhook, Bluefield St.	Fr.	28	67	2.4
40. Ryan Stock, Southwest Baptist	Sr.	26	62	2.4
41. Jamar Love, Incarnate Word	Sr.	28	66	2.4
Ahmad Rasool, N.J. Inst. of Tech.	Sr.	28	66	2.4
43. Kendall Boyd, Fort Lewis	Sr.	31	73	2.4
44. Spencer Ross, Queens (N.C.)	Jr.	33	77	2.3
45. Dustin Pfeifer, Findlay	Fr.	31	72	2.3
46. Joe Hardin, Fairmont St.	Jr.	28	65	2.3
Shawn Ray, N.C. Central	Sr.	28	65	2.3
48. Cliff Green, Abilene Christian	Jr.	23	53	2.3
49. Peter Bullock, Alas. Anchorage	Jr.	27	62	2.3
50. Kurt Patik, Fort Lewis	Sr.	31	71	2.3

Assists Per Game

Rank Name, Team	Cl	G	AST	APG
1. Clayton Smith, Metro St.	Sr.	33	274	8.3
2. Wayne Hinton, Johnson Smith	Sr.	29	237	8.2
3. Marlon Parmer, Ky. Wesleyan	Sr.	35	286	8.2
4. Josh Mueller, South Dakota	So.	28	227	8.1
5. Jamie Holden, St. Joseph's (Ind.)	Jr.	26	207	8.0
6. Aaron Smith, Columbia Union	Sr.	27	194	7.2
7. Cornelius McMurray, Bowie St.	Sr.	33	228	6.9
8. Deshawn Bowman, Columbus St.	Jr.	31	206	6.6
9. Joe Bakhoum, Okla. Panhandle	Sr.	25	164	6.6
10. Ryan Luckman, Bloomsburg	Sr.	26	170	6.5
11. Shahar Golan, Assumption	Jr.	31	191	6.2
12. Te'Ron Reed, Cal St. San B'dino	Jr.	30	184	6.1
13. Rico Grier, Pfeiffer	So.	29	177	6.1
14. William Davison, Mont. St.-Billings	Sr.	27	164	6.1
Kevin Tyner, Western Ore.	Fr.	27	164	6.1
16. Ryan Stock, Southwest Baptist	Sr.	26	157	6.0
17. Cliff Green, Abilene Christian	Jr.	23	138	6.0
18. Bobby Murgo, Merrimack	Fr.	28	167	6.0
19. Dennis Springs, Ferris St.	Fr.	26	155	6.0
20. Todd Henry, Tiffin	Jr.	27	157	5.8
21. Carlos Perez, Mercy	Sr.	26	150	5.8
22. Shawn Opunui, BYU-Hawaii	Fr.	23	132	5.7
23. Ameer Watts, Mo. Southern St.	Jr.	29	166	5.7
24. Seth Hoying, West Liberty St.	Jr.	25	143	5.7
25. Kevin Newsome, Shepherd	Sr.	28	158	5.6
26. Camara Mintz, Gannon	Sr.	30	169	5.6
27. Adam Bliven, Adams St.	Jr.	28	155	5.5
28. Dustin Smith, Arkansas Tech	Sr.	27	149	5.5
29. Spencer Ross, Queens (N.C.)	Jr.	33	181	5.5
30. Larry Taylor, Mo. Western St.	Sr.	31	170	5.5
31. Alfred Sanchez, Colorado St.-Pueblo	Jr.	28	153	5.5
32. Jarron Hinton, Francis Marion	Jr.	27	145	5.4
33. Rob Thorpe, Le Moyne	Jr.	27	144	5.3
Jason Read, Ohio Valley	Jr.	21	112	5.3
35. Eric Dugans, S.C.-Aiken	Sr.	27	142	5.3
36. Thomas Vincent, Emporia St.	Jr.	27	141	5.2
37. Bilal Rodgers, Felician	Sr.	29	150	5.2
38. Nic Walters, Hawaii Pacific	Sr.	24	124	5.2
39. David Rhone, West Tex. A&M	Sr.	31	159	5.1
40. Jeff Brickus, Kutztown	Jr.	22	112	5.1
41. Ryan Earl, Longwood	Jr.	29	147	5.1
Joe Gaetano, North Fla.	Sr.	29	147	5.1
43. Leon Pursoo, Southampton	So.	26	131	5.0

Rank Name, Team	Cl	G	AST	APG
44. Chucky Fine, Salem Int'l	Sr.	31	156	5.0
45. Steve Smiley, Northern St.	Jr.	29	144	5.0
46. Christopher Dunn, West Virginia St.	Fr.	28	139	5.0
47. Brian Faulstich, Cal St. Chico	Jr.	27	134	5.0
48. Dashi Leon, Pitt.-Johnstown	Sr.	21	104	5.0
49. Demitrius Hunter, Lewis	Jr.	31	153	4.9
50. Eric Faber, Rollins	So.	32	157	4.9

Field-Goal Percentage

Min. 5 FGM/G

Rank Name, Team	Cl	G	FGM	FGA	FG%
1. Anthony Greenup, Shaw	Jr.	30	172	242	71.1
2. Maxie Stamps, Drury	Jr.	23	125	189	66.1
3. Jon Smith, Bowie St.	Jr.	35	201	306	65.7
4. Ramzee Stanton, West Chester	Sr.	30	254	402	63.2
5. Phil Sellers, St. Rose	Sr.	25	208	333	62.5
6. Josh Buettner, Michigan Tech	So.	32	187	302	61.9
7. Ronald Thompson, Morehouse	Jr.	25	125	202	61.9
8. Paul Tonkovich, Caldwell	Sr.	26	159	258	61.6
9. Jon Shepherd, Northeastern St.	Sr.	35	201	327	61.5
10. Demond Perris, Emporia St.	Jr.	28	150	246	61.0
11. Michael Beaton, Mercy	Sr.	26	173	285	60.7
12. J.T. Luginski, Michigan Tech	Sr.	32	241	398	60.6
13. Mike Gitt, Neb.-Kearney	Sr.	33	168	278	60.4
14. Damon Bailey, Mo. Western St.	Sr.	31	212	351	60.4
15. Sulaiman Muhammad, Caldwell	Sr.	25	149	247	60.3
16. Geoff Husted, Gannon	So.	29	156	260	60.0
17. Desmond Peoples, St. Augustine's	Jr.	27	184	309	59.5
18. David Siebrands, Augusta St.	Sr.	29	156	262	59.5
19. Flagan Prince, Le Moyne	Sr.	29	202	340	59.4
20. Jason Schneeweis, Minn. Duluth	Sr.	31	215	362	59.4
21. Garland Ragler, Alderson-Broaddus	Sr.	32	263	444	59.2
22. Chris Oliver, Sonoma St.	Sr.	22	110	186	59.1
23. Michah Davenport, Millersville	Jr.	32	173	293	59.0
24. Brian McNeil, Quincy	Sr.	28	141	240	58.8
25. Tommie King, South Dakota	Sr.	28	249	427	58.3
26. Jason Williams, Alas. Fairbanks	Jr.	28	162	279	58.1
27. Jaquan Bracey, Francis Marion	Jr.	27	143	247	57.9
Jason Jones, West Va. Wesleyan	Jr.	26	143	247	57.9
29. Brian Robinson, Assumption	So.	31	230	398	57.8
30. Cam Wattling, Northwest Nazarene	Jr.	26	136	237	57.4
31. Adam Wetzel, Neb.-Omaha	Sr.	28	158	276	57.2
32. Joshua Helm, Mercyhurst	Jr.	27	210	367	57.2
33. Leandro Maruoka, Hawaii Pacific	Sr.	27	153	268	57.1
34. Kyle Stirmlinger, Mont. St.-Billings	Sr.	27	154	270	57.0
35. Jason Pritchett, Central Okla.	Sr.	29	158	278	56.8
36. Demond Cowins, N.J. Inst. of Tech.	Jr.	29	195	344	56.7
37. Mike Palm, Western Wash.	Sr.	27	187	330	56.7
38. Kenny Mickens, Pfeiffer	Jr.	30	184	325	56.6
39. Charlie Caston, Tuskegee	Jr.	28	143	253	56.5
40. Reuben Statam, C.W. Post	Jr.	33	205	363	56.5
41. Aaron Davis, Southern Conn. St.	Sr.	25	136	241	56.4
42. Nick Svehla, Neb.-Kearney	Sr.	33	251	445	56.4
43. Corey Seegers, St. Joseph's (Ind.)	Jr.	27	212	376	56.4
44. Marcus West, Mount Olive	Jr.	28	223	396	56.3
45. Ben Mccain, St. Mary's (Tex.)	Fr.	30	170	302	56.3
46. Melroy McKelvey, Fort Hays St.	Sr.	31	196	349	56.2
47. Cedric Palmer, Eastern N.M.	Sr.	26	137	244	56.1
48. Brian Westre, Mo.-Rolla	Jr.	26	192	344	55.8
49. Rashiem Wright, Dist. Columbia	Sr.	26	204	366	55.7
50. Brian Tomko, Philadelphia U.	So.	28	164	295	55.6

Free-Throw Percentage

Minimum 2.5 Free Throws Made per Game

Rank Name, Team	Cl	G	FT	FTA	FT%
1. Aaron Farley, Harding	Sr.	30	137	146	93.8
2. Derek Paben, South Dakota	Jr.	28	78	85	91.8
3. Robbie Ballard, Emporia St.	Sr.	27	83	91	91.2
Drew Carlson, Minn. St. Mankato	Sr.	27	83	91	91.2
5. Germayne Forbes, West Ga.	Jr.	28	82	90	91.1
6. Rico Grier, Pfeiffer	So.	29	80	88	90.9
7. Kelvin Parker, Northwest Mo. St.	Jr.	31	96	106	90.6
8. Cris Brunson, Southern Ind.	So.	32	105	116	90.5
9. Jacob Fahl, Southwest Minn. St.	Sr.	28	113	125	90.4
10. Jamar Love, Incarnate Word	Sr.	28	111	123	90.2
11. Helgi Magnusson, Catawba	Fr.	28	98	109	89.9
12. Rod Edwards, Ouachita Baptist	Jr.	28	167	186	89.8
13. Kevin Knudson, Northern Colo.	Sr.	26	76	85	89.4
14. Jared McIntire, Oakland City	Sr.	26	100	112	89.3
15. Brian Colbert, Cameron	Sr.	26	133	149	89.3
16. Chris Brooks, Fla. Southern	Jr.	31	124	139	89.2
17. Eric Horvat, Mesa St.	Sr.	27	71	80	88.8
18. Brooks Miller, Hillsdale	Sr.	28	86	97	88.7
19. Jeremy Mcfall, Central Mo. St.	Jr.	28	78	88	88.6
20. Sean Nolen, Northern Colo.	Jr.	26	108	122	88.5
21. Matt Williams, Rollins	Sr.	32	100	113	88.5
22. Luke Kendall, Metro St.	Jr.	33	96	109	88.1
23. Anthony Parker, Saginaw Valley	So.	27	102	116	87.9
24. Elad Inbar, Mass.-Lowell	Jr.	33	122	139	87.8
25. Patrick Pope, St. Augustine's	Sr.	27	212	243	87.2
26. Spencer Ross, Queens (N.C.)	Jr.	33	220	253	87.0
27. Nemanja Kreckovic, Northwood	Fr.	26	72	83	86.7
28. Phillip Godfrey, West Va. Tech	Jr.	29	85	98	86.7
29. Brett Longpre', Mansfield	Jr.	29	130	150	86.7
30. Cornelius McMurray, Bowie St.	Sr.	33	97	112	86.6
31. Wayne Nelson, Adelphi	Sr.	31	142	164	86.6
32. Brad Oleson, Alas. Fairbanks	So.	27	106	123	86.2
33. Titus Miller, Wingate	Jr.	28	87	101	86.1
34. Stephen Dye, Alderson-Broaddus	So.	32	86	100	86.0
35. Bryant Latimer, S.C.-Aiken	Jr.	28	119	139	85.6
36. Kasey Ulin, Central Wash.	Jr.	27	105	123	85.4
37. Mike Nelson, Northern Ky.	So.	31	81	95	85.3
38. Paul Cordasco, Molloy	Jr.	28	86	101	85.1
Ron Heflin, SIU Edwardsville	Sr.	27	86	101	85.1
40. Chris Cosby, LeMoyne-Owen	Sr.	28	126	148	85.1
41. Fowzi Abdelsamad, UC Davis	So.	27	97	114	85.1
Patrick Mutombo, Metro St.	Sr.	33	97	114	85.1
43. Ron Jones, SIU Edwardsville	Jr.	27	74	87	85.1
44. Tommie King, South Dakota	Sr.	28	129	152	84.9
45. Stephen Bahl, Colorado Mines	Jr.	28	117	138	84.8
46. Ryan Murphy, Washburn	Sr.	32	110	130	84.6
47. Austin Nichols, Humboldt St.	Jr.	29	175	207	84.5
48. Seth Nelson, Neb.-Omaha	Sr.	28	98	116	84.5
49. Jimmie Hunt, Franklin Pierce	Jr.	29	125	148	84.5
50. Matt Cameron, Michigan Tech	Sr.	32	146	173	84.4

Three-Point Field-Goal Percentage

Minimum 2.5 3-Pt. Field Goals Made per Game

Rank Name, Team	Cl	G	3FG	3FGA	3FG%
1. Ben Nemmers, North Dakota St.	Jr.	30	83	159	52.2
2. Derek Fillmore, Northwood	So.	26	69	141	48.9
3. Jim Rhodes, Fort Hays St.	Sr.	31	78	160	48.8
4. Wykeen Kelly, Salem Int'l	Sr.	30	91	188	48.4
5. Derek Cline, Northeastern St.	Jr.	33	85	179	47.5
6. Adam Daley, Bemidji St.	Jr.	29	73	157	46.5
7. Clint Weddle, Oakland City	Jr.	26	86	185	46.5
8. Dustin Kelver, UC-Colo. Spgs.	So.	23	92	203	45.3
9. Tyson McGlaughlin, Findlay	So.	30	75	166	45.2
10. Scott Land, Cal St. Chico	So.	26	89	197	45.2
11. Mike Taylor, West Virginia St.	Jr.	29	93	209	44.5
12. Jovani Allen, Midwestern St.	Jr.	28	83	187	44.4
13. Zack Cole, Fort Lewis	Sr.	31	85	193	44.0
14. Rodney Lee, Abilene Christian	Jr.	27	87	198	43.9
15. Germaine Forbes, West Ga.	Jr.	28	86	196	43.9
16. Cameron Munoz, Mont. St.-Billings	Fr.	26	96	220	43.6
17. Ron Jones, SIU Edwardsville	Jr.	27	74	171	43.3
18. Brandon Jones, Tusculum	Jr.	28	73	169	43.2
19. William Brown, Tex. A&M-Kingsville	Jr.	27	72	167	43.1
20. Sean Nolen, Northern Colo.	Jr.	26	75	174	43.1
21. Darius Pope, Colorado St.-Pueblo	Sr.	28	77	180	42.8
22. Robbie Seabrook, Anderson (S.C.)	Sr.	26	109	255	42.7
23. Irving Roland, Southwestern Okla.	Sr.	26	70	164	42.7
24. Phillip Godfrey, West Va. Tech	Jr.	29	94	222	42.3
25. Robbie Ballard, Emporia St.	Sr.	27	95	225	42.2
26. Robert Day, Western Ore.	Jr.	27	94	225	41.8
27. Kevin Hatch, Fort Lewis	Sr.	31	105	252	41.7
28. Stephen Bahl, Colorado Mines	Jr.	28	91	220	41.4
29. Calvin Owen, Carson-Newman	Jr.	28	76	184	41.3
30. Chris Benson, Queens (N.C.)	Sr.	33	106	259	40.9
31. Stephen Moss-Kelley, Bowie St.	Sr.	35	95	233	40.8
32. Ryan Stefanski, Calif. (Pa.)	Sr.	34	100	246	40.7
33. Joe Hasz, Minn.-Crookston	Jr.	24	78	192	40.6
34. Brett Longpre', Mansfield	Jr.	29	75	185	40.5
35. Austin Hansen, South Dakota St.	Sr.	31	85	210	40.5
36. Matthew Hubbard, UNC Pembroke	Jr.	28	71	176	40.3
37. Ronald Donaldson, West Virginia St.	Jr.	29	93	231	40.3
38. Randy Mauldin, Lenoir-Rhyne	Jr.	30	81	202	40.1
39. Stephen Dye, Alderson-Broaddus	So.	32	106	265	40.0
40. Darryl Williams, Fort Valley St.	Sr.	29	83	208	39.9
41. Mike Kelsey, Northern Ky.	So.	31	81	203	39.9

Rank Name, Team	Cl	G	3FG	3FGA	3FG%
42. Ryan McCarthy, Northwest Nazarene	Fr.	26	65	163	39.9
43. Ronald Lewis, Mars Hill	Jr.	28	75	189	39.7
44. Torry Mitchell, Mercyhurst	Fr.	27	70	177	39.5
45. Shaun Taylor, Belmont Abbey	Sr.	31	78	198	39.4
46. Kerry Darting, Mo.-Rolla	Jr.	21	59	150	39.3
47. Cody Levinson, Augustana (S.D.)	Sr.	27	71	182	39.0
48. Rod Edwards, Ouachita Baptist	Jr.	28	91	234	38.9
49. Josh Mueller, South Dakota	So.	28	73	189	38.6
50. Sotirios Karapostolou, Southern N.H.	Sr.	30	112	290	38.6

Three-Point Field Goals Per Game

Rank Name, Team	Cl	G	3FG	3PG
1. Jed Bedford, Columbus St.	Jr.	32	135	4.2
2. Robbie Seabrook, Anderson (S.C.)	Sr.	26	109	4.2
3. Dustin Kelver, UC-Colo. Spgs.	So.	23	92	4.0
4. Sotirios Karapostolou, Southern N.H.	Sr.	30	112	3.7
5. Cameron Munoz, Mont. St.-Billings	Fr.	26	96	3.7
6. Tarvoris Uzoigwe, Henderson St.	So.	35	128	3.7
7. Robbie Ballard, Emporia St.	Sr.	27	95	3.5
8. Robert Day, Western Ore.	Jr.	27	94	3.5
9. John Davis, Albany St. (Ga.)	Sr.	28	97	3.5
10. Scott Land, Cal St. Chico	So.	26	89	3.4
11. Kevin Hatch, Fort Lewis	Sr.	31	105	3.4
12. Rollie Smith, Clarion	Sr.	29	97	3.3
13. Matt Luedtke, Colorado Mines	So.	28	93	3.3
14. Stephen Dye, Alderson-Broaddus	So.	32	106	3.3
15. Clint Weddle, Oakland City	Jr.	26	86	3.3
16. J.T. Hoying, West Liberty St.	Sr.	25	82	3.3
17. Jay Maynard, Winston-Salem	Jr.	29	95	3.3
18. Stephen Bahl, Colorado Mines	Jr.	28	91	3.3
Rod Edwards, Ouachita Baptist	Jr.	28	91	3.3

Rank Name, Team	Cl	G	3FG	3PG
Joe Hasz, Minn.-Crookston	Sr.	24	78	3.3
21. Phillip Godfrey, West Va. Tech	Jr.	29	94	3.2
22. Rodney Lee, Abilene Christian	Jr.	27	87	3.2
23. Chris Benson, Queens (N.C.)	Sr.	33	106	3.2
24. Ronald Donaldson, West Virginia St.	Sr.	29	93	3.2
Mike Taylor, West Virginia St.	Jr.	29	93	3.2
26. Germayne Forbes, West Ga.	Jr.	28	86	3.1
27. Wykeen Kelly, Salem Int'l	Sr.	30	91	3.0
28. Jovani Allen, Midwestern St.	Jr.	28	83	3.0
29. Ryan Stefanski, Calif. (Pa.)	Sr.	34	100	2.9
30. Yari Scott, Paine	Sr.	27	79	2.9
31. Kenneth Barrett, Okla. Panhandle	Fr.	26	75	2.9
Sean Nolen, Northern Colo.	Jr.	26	75	2.9
33. Darryl Williams, Fort Valley St.	Sr.	29	83	2.9
34. Dan Thompson, Mont. St.-Billings	Sr.	27	77	2.9
35. Jason Wilkerson, East Central	Sr.	28	79	2.8
36. Kerry Darting, Mo.-Rolla	Jr.	21	59	2.8
37. Joey Ramirez, Western N.M.	Sr.	26	73	2.8
38. Jamie Shannon, Lincoln Memorial	Sr.	29	81	2.8
39. Brandon Lee, Tarleton St.	Jr.	33	92	2.8
40. Brent Welton, Philadelphia U.	So.	27	75	2.8
41. Ben Nemmers, North Dakota St.	Jr.	30	83	2.8
42. Darius Pope, Colorado St.-Pueblo	Sr.	28	77	2.8
43. Zack Cole, Fort Lewis	Sr.	31	85	2.7
Austin Hansen, South Dakota St.	Sr.	31	85	2.7
45. Ron Jones, SIU Edwardsville	Jr.	27	74	2.7
46. Stephen Moss-Kelley, Bowie St.	Sr.	35	95	2.7
Calvin Owen, Carson-Newman	Sr.	28	76	2.7
48. Arturo Jones, Southwestern Okla.	Sr.	24	65	2.7
49. Randy Mauldin, Lenoir-Rhyne	Jr.	30	81	2.7
50. Irving Roland, Southwestern Okla.	Sr.	26	70	2.7

2003 Division II Game Highs

Individual Highs

POINTS

Rank Name, Team	Cl	vs. Opponent	Game Date	PTS
1. Ron Christy, Teikyo Post	Jr.	Nyack	2/13/03	50
2. Robbie Ballard, Emporia St.	Sr.	Northwest Mo. St.	1/29/03	49
3. Anthony Parker, Saginaw Valley	So.	Wayne St. (Mich.)	11/30/03	46
Austin Nichols, Humboldt St.	Jr.	Seattle Pacific	2/20/03	46
5. Justin Leith, Merrimack	Jr.	St. Rose	2/19/03	45
Ben Dewar, Lake Superior St.	Sr.	Northern Mich.	11/30/02	45
Idrion Nelson, Ark.-Monticello	Sr.	Arkansas Tech	1/06/02	45
8. Charles Hanks, Bemidji St.	Jr.	Winona St.	3/01/03	44
Tim Black, Barton	Sr.	Mount Olive	2/20/03	44
Wayne Bishop, East Stroudsburg	Jr.	Shippensburg	12/06/02	44
11. Nick Gibbs, St. Martin's	Sr.	Western Wash.	3/08/03	43
Dan Thompson, Mont. St.-Billings	Sr.	Nova Southeastern	3/07/03	43
Denver TenBroek, North Dakota St.	Sr.	Augustana (S.D.)	1/25/03	43
14. Ben Dewar, Lake Superior St.	Sr.	Finlandia	12/11/02	42
15. Spencer Ross, Queens (N.C.)	Jr.	Pfeiffer	2/27/03	41
Jerome Beasley, North Dakota	Sr.	Augustana (S.D.)	1/24/03	41
17. Joe Hasz, Minn.-Crookston	Sr.	Minn.-Morris	2/15/03	40
Alexus Foyle, BYU-Hawaii	Sr.	Hawaii-Hilo	1/31/03	40
Rashiem Wright, Dist. Columbia	Sr.	Kutztown	12/03/02	40

FIELD-GOAL PERCENTAGE
Minimum 10 made

Rank Name, Team	Cl	vs. Opponent	Game Date	FG%	FGM	FGA
1. Ricky Johnson, Fairmont St.	Jr.	Bluefield St.	2/08/03	100.0	10	10
2. Brian Robinson, Assumption	So.	Le Moyne	1/25/03	92.3	12	13
3. Ramzee Stanton, West Chester	Sr.	Millersville	2/15/03	91.7	11	12
Kelvin Parker, Northwest Mo. St.	Jr.	Mo. Southern St.	2/08/03	91.7	11	12
5. Jason Schneeweis, Minn. Duluth	Sr.	Northern St.	2/22/03	90.9	10	11
Darrell Redmond, Mo. Southern St.	Jr.	Northwest Mo. St.	2/08/03	90.9	10	11
Nana Gbewonyo, Henderson St.	Sr.	Ark.-Monticello	2/03/03	90.9	10	11
Justin Hassell, Mont. St.-Billings	Jr.	Western N.M.	2/01/03	90.9	10	11
Javier Salson, Bloomfield	Jr.	Phila. Sciences	1/30/03	90.9	10	11
Brian Westre, Mo.-Rolla	Jr.	Northwest Mo. St.	1/25/03	90.9	10	11
Arthur Trousdell, Southwest Baptist	Fr.	Mo.-Rolla	12/30/02	90.9	10	11
Shamar Green, Clarion	Fr.	Winston-Salem	11/23/02	90.9	10	11

THREE-POINT FIELD-GOAL PERCENTAGE
Minimum 7 made

Rank Name, Team	Cl	vs. Opponent	Game Date	3FG%	3FG	3FGA
1. Joe Hasz, Minn.-Crookston	Sr.	Minn.-Morris	2/15/03	90.9	10	11
2. Dusty Decker, Minn. Duluth	Jr.	Winona St.	1/25/03	90.0	9	10
3. Shawn Opunui, BYU-Hawaii	Fr.	St. Martin's	1/03/03	87.5	7	8
4. Scott Land, Cal St. Chico	So.	Cal Poly Pomona	1/10/03	80.0	8	10
Cody Levinson, Augustana (S.D.)	Sr.	Western St. (Colo.)	11/22/02	80.0	8	10
6. Cameron Munoz, Mont. St.-Billings	Fr.	Hawaii-Hilo	2/15/03	69.2	9	13
Billy Speer, Cal St. Bakersfield	Sr.	UC San Diego	1/04/03	69.2	9	13
Robbie Seabrook, Anderson (S.C.)	Sr.	St. Andrews	2/20/02	69.2	9	13
9. Adam Daley, Bemidji St.	Jr.	Concordia-St. Paul	2/28/03	66.7	8	12

Rank Name, Team	Cl	vs. Opponent	Game Date	FG%	FGM	FGA
Rod Edwards, Ouachita Baptist	Jr.	Southern Ark.	2/03/03	66.7	8	12
Robert Day, Western Ore.	Jr.	Central Wash.	1/16/03	66.7	8	12
Doug Barnes, Barton	Sr.	Lees-McRae	1/11/03	66.7	8	12
Sean Nolen, Northern Colo.	Jr.	Colo. Christian	12/07/02	66.7	8	12

FREE-THROW PERCENTAGE

Rank Name, Team	Cl	vs. Opponent	Game Date	FT%	FT	FTA
1. Brad Ayer, Bellarmine	Sr.	St. Joseph's (Ind.)	2/22/03	100	17	17
Jimmie Hunt, Franklin Pierce	Jr.	Bryant	2/15/03	100	17	17
Fowzi Abdelsamad, UC Davis	So.	Sonoma St.	1/03/03	100	17	17
Rod Edwards, Ouachita Baptist	Jr.	Central Ark.	1/09/02	100	15	15
Jared McIntire, Oakland City	Sr.	Montevallo	1/29/03	100	14	14
Sean Nolen, Northern Colo.	Jr.	Minn. St. Mankato	1/18/03	100	14	14
Eugene Dabney, Ky. Wesleyan	Sr.	Gannon	12/14/02	100	14	14
Will Gardner, Ala.-Huntsville	Jr.	Lane	11/22/02	100	14	14
Denver TenBroek, North Dakota St.	Sr.	South Dakota	3/07/03	100	13	13
Tyrone McCann, Glenville St.	Sr.	Salem Int'l	1/18/03	100	13	13
Anthony Frazier, Cheyney	Jr.	Clarion	1/11/03	100	13	13
Jason Bauer, Grand Valley St.	Sr.	Northwood	12/16/02	100	13	13
Jerett Skrifvars, Mont. St.-Billings	Sr.	Chadron St.	12/07/02	100	13	13
Rod Edwards, Ouachita Baptist	Jr.	Southern Ark.	1/06/02	100	13	13
Mike DeGruy, Henderson St.	Sr.	Eckerd	3/18/03	100	12	12
Ron Jones, SIU Edwardsville	Jr.	Bellarmine	3/01/03	100	12	12
Chris Smith, Alas. Fairbanks	Fr.	Humboldt St.	3/01/03	100	12	12
Robbie Ballard, Emporia St.	Sr.	Washburn	2/19/03	100	12	12
Yusef Aziz, Seattle Pacific	Sr.	Western Wash.	2/08/03	100	12	12
Josh Lavere, Concord	Fr.	Fairmont St.	1/20/03	100	12	12
Rollie Smith, Clarion	Sr.	Pitt.-Johnstown	1/18/03	100	12	12
Forrest Witt, St. Cloud St.	Sr.	South Dakota St.	1/11/03	100	12	12
Burton Lee, S.C.-Aiken	Jr.	Catawba	12/19/02	100	12	12
Brett Longpre', Mansfield	Sr.	Lycoming	12/18/02	100	12	12
Matt Cameron, Michigan Tech	Sr.	Minn. Duluth	12/11/02	100	12	12
Tommie King, South Dakota	Sr.	Bellevue	12/08/02	100	12	12
Brandon Moore, Kennesaw St.	Sr.	Clayton St.	11/27/02	100	12	12
Brad Oleson, Alas. Fairbanks	So.	Wis.-Green Bay	11/21/02	100	12	12

REBOUNDS

Rank Name, Team	Cl	vs. Opponent	Game Date	REB
1. Marcus West, Mount Olive	Jr.	Limestone	2/03/03	22
2. Billy McDaniel, Ark.-Monticello	Fr.	Xavier (La.)	1/03/03	21
Fred Hooks, Humboldt St.	Jr.	UC San Diego	12/28/02	21
Brian Robinson, Assumption	So.	Le Moyne	12/19/02	21
Brian Westre, Mo.-Rolla	Jr.	Harris-Stowe	12/07/02	21
6. Mike Palm, Western Wash.	Sr.	Central Wash.	3/05/03	20
Jason Williams, Alas. Fairbanks	Jr.	Humboldt St.	3/01/03	20
Marcus West, Mount Olive	Jr.	Lees-McRae	2/17/03	20
Maurice Brown, Saginaw Valley	Jr.	Madonna	12/07/02	20
Ryan Pitts, Lenoir-Rhyne	Jr.	Limestone	11/22/02	20

ASSISTS

Rank Name, Team	Cl	vs. Opponent	Game Date	AST
1. Kevin Griffin, Henderson St.	Sr.	Central Baptist	12/03/02	19
2. Chris Turner, Dist. Columbia	Sr.	Pitt.-Johnstown	2/08/03	17
3. Shane Alexander, Delta St.	Sr.	Ark. Baptist	1/18/03	16
4. Aaron Smith, Columbia Union	Sr.	Oakwood	1/18/03	15
Deshawn Bowman, Columbus St.	Jr.	Francis Marion	1/11/03	15
Rob Thorpe, Le Moyne	Jr.	Alderson-Broaddus	11/22/02	15
7. Maurice Cato, Seattle Pacific	Sr.	Humboldt St.	2/20/03	14
Marlon Parmer, Ky. Wesleyan	Sr.	St. Joseph's (Ind.)	2/20/03	14
Josh Mueller, South Dakota	So.	Minn. St. Mankato	2/13/03	14
Thomas Vincent, Emporia St.	Jr.	Washburn	1/22/03	14
Jamie Holden, St. Joseph's (Ind.)	Jr.	Bellarmine	1/02/03	14
Kevin Griffin, Henderson St.	Sr.	Delta St.	1/06/02	14
13. Ryan Stock, Southwest Baptist	Sr.	Truman	2/26/03	13
William Davison, Mont. St.-Billings	Sr.	Western N.M.	2/22/03	13
Josh Mueller, South Dakota	So.	Northern Colo.	2/08/03	13
Ryan Stock, Southwest Baptist	Sr.	Mo. Southern St.	2/01/03	13
Todd Henry, Tiffin	Jr.	Malone	1/28/03	13
Rico Grier, Pfeiffer	So.	Limestone	1/25/03	13
Bobby Murgo, Merrimack	Fr.	Felician	1/02/03	13
Jason Roscoe, Mansfield	Jr.	Lycoming	12/18/02	13
Pat Lynch, Bentley	Jr.	Franklin Pierce	12/04/02	13
Dennis Springs, Ferris St.	Fr.	Calvin	11/26/02	13
Dion Thompson, Dist. Columbia	Sr.	Indiana (Pa.)	11/26/02	13

BLOCKED SHOTS

Rank Name, Team	Cl	vs. Opponent	Game Date	BLKS
1. Bilal Salaam, Kutztown	So.	Dist. Columbia	12/03/02	11
Mike Williams, Bryant	So.	Le Moyne	12/01/02	11
3. Moustapha Diouf, Queens (N.C.)	Jr.	Coker	1/11/03	10
Bilal Salaam, Kutztown	So.	Indiana (Pa.)	1/04/03	10
Aaron Davis, Southern Conn. St.	Sr.	Pace	12/04/02	10
6. Brad Hawks, Tusculum	So.	Lander	12/29/02	8
Eugene Dabney, Ky. Wesleyan	Sr.	Southern Ark.	12/22/02	8

STEALS

Rank Name, Team	Cl	vs. Opponent	Game Date	ST
1. Beau Nobmann, BYU-Hawaii	Fr.	Western N.M.	3/01/03	10
2. Jeremy Robinson, Humboldt St.	Sr.	Alas. Anchorage	2/27/03	8
Alan Goff, Southern Ind.	Sr.	SIU Edwardsville	1/30/03	8
Shahar Golan, Assumption	Jr.	St. Michael's	1/29/03	8
Te'Ron Reed, Cal St. San B'dino	Jr.	UC San Diego	1/17/03	8

THREE-POINT FIELD GOALS MADE

Rank Name, Team	Cl	vs. Opponent	Game Date	3FG
1. Robbie Ballard, Emporia St.	Sr.	Northwest Mo. St.	1/29/2003	13
2. Cameron Munoz, Mont. St.-Billings	Fr.	Western N.M.	2/20/2003	12
3. Joe Hasz, Minn.-Crookston	Sr.	Minn.-Morris	2/15/2003	10
Cameron Munoz, Mont. St.-Billings	Fr.	Hawaii-Hilo	1/06/2003	10
5. Robbie Seabrook, Anderson (S.C.)	Sr.	St. Andrews	2/20/2003	9
Cameron Munoz, Mont. St.-Billings	Fr.	Hawaii-Hilo	2/15/2003	9
Ben Renzin, Pace	Jr.	Southern Conn. St.	1/29/2003	9
Dusty Decker, Minn. Duluth	Jr.	Winona St.	1/25/2003	9
Mark Drake, Alas. Anchorage	So.	St. Martin's	1/11/2003	9
Billy Speer, Cal St. Bakersfield	Sr.	UC San Diego	1/04/2003	9
Sotirios Karapostolou, Southern N.H.	Sr.	St. Michael's	12/10/2002	9
Eric Rohy, Minn.-Morris	So.	Mayville St.	11/23/2002	9

2003 Division II Team Leaders

Scoring Offense

Rank Name	GM	W-L	PTS	PPG
1. Pfeiffer	31	22-9	2,926	94.4
2. Mont. St.-Billings	27	18-9	2,412	89.3
3. Ky. Wesleyan	35	31-4	3,112	88.9
4. West Virginia St.	29	16-13	2,572	88.7
5. Queens (N.C.)	33	29-4	2,921	88.5
6. Harding	30	21-9	2,632	87.7
7. Charleston (W.Va.)	31	21-10	2,711	87.5
8. Neb.-Kearney	33	30-3	2,878	87.2
9. Wheeling Jesuit	30	22-8	2,614	87.1
10. Southern Ind.	32	25-7	2,784	87.0
11. Bemidji St.	29	17-12	2,508	86.5
12. BYU-Hawaii	23	19-4	1,972	85.7
13. Bellarmine	29	10-19	2,462	84.9
14. Salem Int'l.	31	25-6	2,619	84.5
15. South Dakota	28	19-9	2,357	84.2
16. Barton	28	22-6	2,354	84.1
17. Central Wash.	27	16-11	2,268	84.0
18. Fort Lewis	31	19-12	2,599	83.8
19. Bowie St.	35	30-5	2,931	83.7
20. Humboldt St.	29	23-6	2,425	83.6
21. Mount Olive	28	18-10	2,340	83.6
22. Emporia St.	28	16-12	2,338	83.5
23. Alderson-Broaddus	32	25-7	2,664	83.3
24. St. Cloud St.	30	26-4	2,469	82.3
St. Rose	30	19-11	2,469	82.3
26. Seattle Pacific	27	16-11	2,219	82.2
27. Chaminade	27	12-15	2,211	81.9
28. Wingate	29	18-11	2,372	81.8
29. Western Wash.	27	16-11	2,203	81.6
30. St. Joseph's (Ind.)	28	11-17	2,278	81.4
31. South Dakota St.	31	24-7	2,520	81.3
32. N.C. Central	29	16-13	2,357	81.3
33. Lane	28	13-15	2,275	81.3
34. Central Okla.	29	19-10	2,347	80.9
35. St. Augustine's	27	18-9	2,180	80.7
36. Limestone	27	10-17	2,178	80.7
37. Colorado Mines	28	18-10	2,256	80.6
38. Neb.-Omaha	30	20-10	2,415	80.5
39. North Dakota St.	31	20-11	2,493	80.4
40. Ashland	27	16-11	2,170	80.4
41. Tex. A&M-Commerce	28	16-12	2,250	80.4
42. Kentucky St.	29	13-16	2,328	80.3
43. Christian Bros.	29	18-11	2,323	80.1
44. Northern	29	20-9	2,307	79.6
45. Saginaw Valley	27	13-14	2,145	79.4
46. Johnson Smith	29	20-9	2,303	79.4
47. Michigan Tech	32	29-3	2,540	79.4
48. Fairmont St.	28	19-9	2,220	79.3
49. Hawaii-Hilo	28	18-10	2,219	79.3
50. Alas. Fairbanks	28	20-8	2,216	79.1

Scoring Defense

Rank Name	GM	W-L	OPP PTS	OPP PPG
1. Barry	28	18-10	1,490	53.2
2. Tarleton St.	33	29-4	1,885	57.1
3. Presbyterian	36	27-9	2,138	59.4
4. Metro St.	33	28-5	1,962	59.5
5. Rollins	32	26-6	1,914	59.8
6. Valdosta St.	26	19-7	1,578	60.7
7. Tampa	27	15-12	1,642	60.8
8. Northeastern St.	35	32-3	2,146	61.3
9. Tusculum	28	16-12	1,730	61.8
10. Erskine	30	14-16	1,865	62.2
11. Armstrong Atlantic	28	14-14	1,741	62.2
12. Calif. (Pa.)	34	25-9	2,121	62.4
13. Ala.-Huntsville	31	20-11	1,941	62.6
14. Mass.-Lowell	33	28-5	2,070	62.7
15. Cal St. San B'dino	30	23-7	1,883	62.8
16. Cal St. Bakersfield	29	20-9	1,827	63.0
17. Henderson St.	35	30-5	2,209	63.1
18. S.C.-Spartanburg	29	18-11	1,838	63.4
19. Southeastern Okla.	27	5-22	1,714	63.5
20. Cal Poly Pomona	31	23-8	1,970	63.5

Rank Name	GM	W-L	OPP PTS	OPP PPG
New Haven	31	21-10	1,970	63.5
22. Clarion	29	19-10	1,843	63.6
23. Incarnate Word	28	19-9	1,780	63.6
24. Sonoma St.	28	18-10	1,788	63.9
25. Shaw	30	21-9	1,918	63.9
26. Fla. Southern	31	26-5	1,987	64.1
27. Lincoln Memorial	29	19-10	1,864	64.3
28. Queens (N.Y.)	28	14-14	1,806	64.5
29. Caldwell	26	15-11	1,678	64.5
30. Francis Marion	27	13-14	1,746	64.7
31. Belmont Abbey	31	24-7	2,006	64.7
32. Adelphi	31	22-9	2,007	64.7
33. Lenoir-Rhyne	30	22-8	1,956	65.2
34. C.W. Post	33	25-8	2,154	65.3
35. Clayton St.	29	17-12	1,893	65.3
36. Philadelphia U.	28	16-12	1,834	65.5
37. Eckerd	32	25-7	2,106	65.8
38. GC&SU	27	14-13	1,782	66.0
39. Millersville	32	26-6	2,113	66.0
40. Michigan Tech	32	29-3	2,114	66.1
41. Slippery Rock	25	8-17	1,657	66.3
42. St. Mary's (Tex.)	30	17-13	1,989	66.3
43. American Int'l	28	9-19	1,862	66.5
44. Kennesaw St.	35	25-10	2,336	66.7
45. Lynn	28	15-13	1,876	67.0
46. Cal St. L.A.	27	9-18	1,816	67.3
47. Edinboro	28	17-11	1,885	67.3
48. West Ga.	28	19-9	1,887	67.4
49. Bryant	31	17-14	2,093	67.5
50. Washburn	32	26-6	2,168	67.8

Scoring Margin

Rank Name	W-L	PTS	PPG	OPP PTS	OPP PPG	SCR MAR
1. Ky. Wesleyan	31-4	3,112	88.9	2,543	72.7	16.3
2. Metro St.	28-5	2,495	75.6	1,962	59.5	16.2
3. Henderson St.	30-5	2,720	77.7	2,209	63.1	14.6
4. Queens (N.C.)	29-4	2,921	88.5	2,460	74.5	14.0
5. Harding	21-9	2,632	87.7	2,215	73.8	13.9
6. Cal St. San B'dino	23-7	2,298	76.6	1,883	62.8	13.8
7. Neb.-Kearney	30-3	2,878	87.2	2,434	73.8	13.5
8. Tarleton St.	29-4	2,326	70.5	1,885	57.1	13.4
9. Michigan Tech	29-3	2,540	79.4	2,114	66.1	13.3
10. Wheeling Jesuit	22-8	2,614	87.1	2,220	74.0	13.1
11. BYU-Hawaii	19-4	1,972	85.7	1,679	73.0	12.7
12. St. Cloud St.	26-4	2,469	82.3	2,101	70.0	12.3
13. Northeastern St.	32-3	2,556	73.0	2,146	61.3	11.7
14. Pfeiffer	22-9	2,926	94.4	2,564	82.7	11.7
15. Mass.-Lowell	28-5	2,455	74.4	2,070	62.7	11.7
16. Humboldt St.	23-6	2,425	83.6	2,100	72.4	11.2
17. Valdosta St.	19-7	1,868	71.8	1,578	60.7	11.2
18. Fla. Southern	26-5	2,326	75.0	1,987	64.1	10.9
19. Mo. Western St.	23-8	2,445	78.9	2,109	68.0	10.8
20. Millersville	26-6	2,454	76.7	2,113	66.0	10.7
21. Alderson-Broaddus	25-7	2,664	83.3	2,328	72.8	10.5
Eckerd	25-7	2,442	76.3	2,106	65.8	10.5
23. Mont. St.-Billings	18-9	2,412	89.3	2,131	78.9	10.4
24. South Dakota St.	24-7	2,520	81.3	2,201	71.0	10.3
25. Rollins	26-6	2,242	70.1	1,914	59.8	10.3
26. Fairmont St.	19-9	2,220	79.3	1,936	69.1	10.1

Rank Name	W-L	PTS	PPG	OPP PTS	OPP PPG	SCR MAR
27. Salem Int'l	25-6	2,619	84.5	2,313	74.6	9.9
28. Bemidji St.	17-12	2,508	86.5	2,222	76.6	9.9
29. Belmont Abbey	24-7	2,311	74.5	2,006	64.7	9.8
30. Southern Ind.	25-7	2,784	87.0	2,471	77.2	9.8
31. Bowie St.	30-5	2,931	83.7	2,589	74.0	9.8
32. Barton	22-6	2,354	84.1	2,081	74.3	9.8
33. Fort Hays St.	23-8	2,434	78.5	2,143	69.1	9.4
34. Cal St. Bakersfield	20-9	2,099	72.4	1,827	63.0	9.4
35. Lewis	23-8	2,444	78.8	2,154	69.5	9.4
36. C.W. Post	25-8	2,462	74.6	2,154	65.3	9.3
37. Washburn	26-6	2,466	77.1	2,168	67.8	9.3
38. Northern St.	20-9	2,307	79.6	2,045	70.5	9.0
39. Lenoir-Rhyne	22-8	2,226	74.2	1,956	65.2	9.0
40. Charleston (W.Va.)	21-10	2,711	87.5	2,454	79.2	8.3
41. Northwest Mo. St.	22-9	2,409	77.7	2,154	69.5	8.2
42. Findlay	23-8	2,453	79.1	2,204	71.1	8.0
43. North Dakota St.	20-11	2,493	80.4	2,245	72.4	8.0
44. West Chester	21-9	2,289	76.3	2,050	68.3	8.0
45. Adelphi	22-9	2,251	72.6	2,007	64.7	7.9
46. West Tex. A&M	21-10	2,354	75.9	2,112	68.1	7.8
47. Neb.-Omaha	20-10	2,415	80.5	2,184	72.8	7.7
48. South Dakota	19-9	2,357	84.2	2,144	76.6	7.6
49. Western Wash.	16-11	2,203	81.6	1,999	74.0	7.6
50. Calif. (Pa.)	25-9	2,377	69.9	2,121	62.4	7.5

Field-Goal Percentage

Rank Name	GM	W-L	FGM	FGA	FG%
1. Michigan Tech	32	29-3	920	1,740	52.9
2. Northeastern St.	35	32-3	863	1,679	51.4
3. Neb.-Kearney	33	30-3	1,069	2,089	51.2
4. BYU-Hawaii	23	19-4	722	1,419	50.9
5. Ky. Wesleyan	35	31-4	1,087	2,151	50.5
6. Salem Int'l	31	25-6	919	1,833	50.1
7. Colorado St.-Pueblo	28	17-11	762	1,526	49.9
8. Seattle Pacific	27	16-11	805	1,618	49.8
9. Johnson Smith	29	20-9	820	1,650	49.7
10. Pfeiffer	31	22-9	1,048	2,121	49.4
11. Alderson-Broaddus	32	25-7	953	1,930	49.4
12. Findlay	31	23-8	872	1,768	49.3
13. St. Mary's (Tex.)	30	17-13	806	1,637	49.2
14. Minn. Duluth	31	19-12	910	1,849	49.2
15. Northern Ky.	31	25-6	820	1,667	49.2
16. Southern Ind.	32	25-7	1,021	2,079	49.1
17. Harding	30	21-9	929	1,893	49.1
18. Metro St.	33	28-5	977	1,993	49.0
19. Neb.-Omaha	30	20-10	845	1,729	48.9
20. West Tex. A&M	31	21-10	803	1,645	48.8
21. Eastern N.M.	28	20-8	775	1,588	48.8
22. South Dakota	28	19-9	828	1,703	48.6
23. Mo. Western St.	31	23-8	895	1,843	48.6
24. Emporia St.	28	16-12	855	1,763	48.5
25. St. Cloud St.	30	26-4	875	1,805	48.5
26. Central Wash.	27	16-11	795	1,641	48.4
27. Fort Hays St.	31	23-8	882	1,822	48.4
28. Queens (N.C.)	33	29-4	1,030	2,135	48.2
29. Lewis	31	23-8	896	1,861	48.1
30. Chaminade	27	12-15	802	1,667	48.1
31. Cal St. Bakersfield	29	20-9	770	1,605	48.0
32. Bemidji St.	29	17-12	881	1,837	48.0
33. Humboldt St.	29	23-6	837	1,746	47.9
34. Henderson St.	35	30-5	969	2,023	47.9
35. Fort Lewis	31	19-12	882	1,842	47.9
36. West Va. Tech	29	11-18	848	1,774	47.8
37. Glenville St.	29	12-17	829	1,736	47.8
38. Eckerd	32	25-7	845	1,772	47.7

Rank Name	GM	W-L	FGM	FGA	FG%
39. Northern St.	29	20-9	813	1,710	47.5
40. Pittsburg St.	28	16-12	757	1,594	47.5
41. Bowie St.	35	30-5	1,013	2,134	47.5
42. Chadron St.	26	12-14	686	1,447	47.4
43. Barton	28	22-6	810	1,711	47.3
44. West Virginia St.	29	16-13	919	1,942	47.3
45. Mont. St.-Billings	27	18-9	827	1,748	47.3
46. West Fla.	27	16-11	722	1,527	47.3
47. Northern Colo.	26	11-15	676	1,432	47.2
48. West Chester	30	21-9	836	1,773	47.2
49. Western Wash.	27	16-11	778	1,650	47.2
50. Christian Bros.	29	18-11	827	1,755	47.1

Field-Goal Percentage Defense

Rank Name	GM	W-L	OPP FG	OPP FGA	OPP FG%
1. Tarleton St.	33	29-4	655	1,757	37.3
2. Fla. Southern	31	26-5	660	1,768	37.3
3. Henderson St.	35	30-5	781	2,066	37.8
4. Tusculum	28	16-12	583	1,529	38.1
5. Barry	28	18-10	512	1,334	38.4
6. Queens (N.C.)	33	29-4	875	2,241	39.0
7. Southern Conn. St.	27	9-18	689	1,763	39.1
8. Francis Marion	27	13-14	614	1,569	39.1
9. Lincoln Memorial	29	19-10	625	1,593	39.2
10. Cal St. San B'dino	30	23-7	661	1,681	39.3
11. Ky. Wesleyan	35	31-4	914	2,319	39.4
12. Valdosta St.	26	19-7	541	1,364	39.7
13. Bryant	31	17-14	741	1,868	39.7
14. Hawaii Pacific	27	17-10	723	1,818	39.8
15. Tampa	27	15-12	557	1,400	39.8
16. Queens (N.Y.)	28	14-14	648	1,627	39.8
17. Paine	27	10-17	633	1,583	40.0
18. Teikyo Post	29	19-10	720	1,797	40.1
19. Morehouse	31	23-8	762	1,897	40.2
20. Cal St. Bakersfield	29	20-9	604	1,503	40.2
21. Adelphi	31	22-9	670	1,667	40.2
22. Calif. (Pa.)	34	25-9	782	1,938	40.4
23. West Fla.	27	16-11	680	1,680	40.5
24. Clayton St.	29	17-12	624	1,538	40.6
25. Erskine	30	14-16	663	1,633	40.6
26. Rollins	32	26-6	692	1,704	40.6
27. Mass.-Lowell	33	28-5	717	1,764	40.6
28. Ala.-Huntsville	31	20-11	714	1,756	40.7
29. Delta St.	30	22-8	710	1,744	40.7
30. South Dakota St.	31	24-7	795	1,947	40.8
31. New Haven	31	21-10	669	1,637	40.9
32. Alderson-Broaddus	32	25-7	857	2,094	40.9
33. Bowie St.	35	30-5	973	2,376	41.0
34. Shaw	30	21-9	726	1,772	41.0
35. Benedict	24	11-13	574	1,401	41.0
36. Belmont Abbey	31	24-7	684	1,668	41.0
37. Indiana (Pa.)	27	16-11	595	1,450	41.0
38. St. Anselm	27	13-14	710	1,729	41.1
39. Caldwell	26	15-11	598	1,456	41.1
40. Presbyterian	36	27-9	758	1,843	41.1
41. Clarion	29	19-10	621	1,508	41.2
42. West Ga.	28	19-9	671	1,627	41.2
43. Edinboro	28	17-11	696	1,685	41.3
44. Millersville	32	26-6	760	1,838	41.3
45. Wheeling Jesuit	30	22-8	775	1,872	41.4
46. North Ala.	28	18-10	759	1,831	41.5
47. Michigan Tech	32	29-3	786	1,893	41.5
48. Mo. Southern St.	29	19-10	748	1,794	41.7
49. Tex. A&M-Commerce	28	16-12	736	1,765	41.7
50. Cal Poly Pomona	31	23-8	704	1,687	41.7

Free-Throw Percentage

Rank Name	GM	W-L	FT	FTA	FT%
1. South Dakota	28	19-9	452	566	79.9
2. Johnson Smith	29	20-9	442	568	77.8
3. St. Andrews	30	9-21	482	622	77.5
4. Bellarmine	29	10-19	518	673	77.0
5. Mesa St.	27	15-12	480	624	76.9
6. Harding	30	21-9	529	691	76.6
7. Michigan Tech	32	29-3	448	586	76.5
8. Southwest Minn. St.	28	17-11	415	543	76.4
9. St. Cloud St.	30	26-4	471	620	76.0
10. Neb.-Kearney	33	30-3	522	688	75.9
11. West Virginia St.	29	16-13	451	595	75.8
12. Southern Ind.	32	25-7	561	741	75.7
13. West Va. Tech	29	11-18	409	544	75.2
14. Queens (N.C.)	33	29-4	629	837	75.1
15. Ouachita Baptist	28	16-12	469	627	74.8
16. Eastern N.M.	28	20-8	560	749	74.8
17. Henderson St.	35	30-5	542	726	74.7
18. Franklin Pierce	29	14-15	437	586	74.6
19. Wheeling Jesuit	30	22-8	577	776	74.4
20. Gannon	30	20-10	468	630	74.3
21. Northwest Mo. St.	31	22-9	482	649	74.3
22. Sonoma St.	28	18-10	447	602	74.3
23. Southern N.H.	30	22-8	504	679	74.2
24. Alas. Fairbanks	28	20-8	434	585	74.2
25. Drury	28	11-17	548	739	74.2
26. Minn. St. Mankato	28	15-13	449	606	74.1
27. Fla. Southern	31	26-5	534	721	74.1
28. Assumption	31	20-11	379	512	74.0
29. Adelphi	31	22-9	535	723	74.0
30. St. Anselm	27	13-14	381	515	74.0
31. Saginaw Valley	27	13-14	406	549	74.0
32. Cameron	26	9-17	343	464	73.9
33. Pfeiffer	31	22-9	524	709	73.9
34. Cal St. L.A.	27	9-18	385	521	73.9
35. Lenoir-Rhyne	30	22-8	384	520	73.8
36. Ala.-Huntsville	31	20-11	462	626	73.8
37. Northwest Nazarene	26	5-21	402	545	73.8
38. Minn. St. Moorhead	29	19-10	440	597	73.7
39. Alderson-Broaddus	32	25-7	469	638	73.5
40. North Dakota St.	31	20-11	405	551	73.5
41. Washburn	32	26-6	555	757	73.3
42. Incarnate Word	28	19-9	427	583	73.2
43. Ky. Wesleyan	35	31-4	706	964	73.2
44. Western Wash.	27	16-11	503	687	73.2
45. Presbyterian	36	27-9	537	736	73.0
46. LeMoyne-Owen	28	14-14	516	708	72.9
47. Northern St.	29	20-9	405	556	72.8
48. Indianapolis	29	18-11	459	631	72.7
49. Ferris St.	26	11-15	352	484	72.7
50. Bridgeport	31	23-8	493	679	72.6

Three-Point Field-Goal Percentage

Minimum 5.0 made per game

Rank Name	GM	W-L	3FG	3FGA	3FG%
1. Michigan Tech	32	29-3	252	581	43.4
2. Oakland City	26	11-15	207	486	42.6
3. West Virginia St.	29	16-13	283	676	41.9
4. Northeastern St.	35	32-3	269	649	41.4
5. Salem Int'l	31	25-6	182	441	41.3
6. Cal St. Bakersfield	29	20-9	168	410	41.0
7. Seattle Pacific	27	16-11	173	423	40.9
8. Fort Lewis	31	19-12	328	802	40.9
9. North Dakota St.	31	20-11	284	695	40.9
10. Southwest Minn. St.	28	17-11	262	646	40.6
11. Cal St. Chico	27	18-9	226	558	40.5
12. Pfeiffer	31	22-9	306	756	40.5
13. UC-Colo. Spgs.	25	6-19	185	459	40.3
14. Minn. Duluth	31	19-12	243	603	40.3
15. Carson-Newman	28	19-9	224	556	40.3
16. Colorado St.-Pueblo	28	17-11	282	701	40.2
17. Johnson Smith	29	20-9	221	556	39.7
18. Central Wash.	27	16-11	199	501	39.7
19. Central Ark.	25	7-18	162	409	39.6
20. Northern Ky.	31	25-6	213	538	39.6
21. Pitt.-Johnstown	27	11-16	195	496	39.3
22. Western Ore.	27	15-12	274	697	39.3
23. Assumption	31	20-11	221	563	39.3
24. Abilene Christian	27	13-14	175	446	39.2
25. Neb.-Kearney	33	30-3	218	556	39.2
26. Lenoir-Rhyne	30	22-8	224	572	39.2
27. Bellarmine	29	10-19	230	588	39.1
28. Gannon	30	20-10	221	565	39.1
29. Northern Colo.	26	11-15	189	484	39.0
30. Lewis	31	23-8	244	626	39.0
31. Presbyterian	36	27-9	258	662	39.0
32. Emporia St.	28	16-12	245	631	38.8
33. West Va. Tech	29	11-18	188	486	38.7
34. West Tex. A&M	31	21-10	205	530	38.7
35. Fort Hays St.	31	23-8	185	479	38.6
36. Northern St.	29	20-9	276	715	38.6
37. Harding	30	21-9	245	635	38.6
38. Northwood	26	10-16	249	646	38.5
39. Alderson-Broaddus	32	25-7	289	751	38.5
40. Queens (N.C.)	33	29-4	232	603	38.5
41. Mesa St.	27	15-12	220	573	38.4
42. Mass.-Lowell	33	28-5	216	564	38.3
43. Indiana (Pa.)	27	16-11	184	481	38.3
44. Ky. Wesleyan	35	31-4	232	607	38.2
45. UC Davis	27	12-15	194	508	38.2
46. Ouachita Baptist	28	16-12	245	642	38.2
47. Barton	28	22-6	256	671	38.2
48. St. Cloud St.	30	26-4	248	652	38.0
49. Northwest Nazarene	26	5-21	154	405	38.0
50. Christian Bros.	29	18-11	234	616	38.0

Three-Point Field Goals Per Game

Rank Name	GM	W-L	3FG	3PG
1. Bemidji St.	29	17-12	338	11.7
2. Mont. St.-Billings	27	18-9	290	10.7
3. Fort Lewis	31	19-12	328	10.6
4. Colorado Mines	28	18-10	288	10.3
5. Anderson (S.C.)	28	9-19	286	10.2
6. Western Ore.	27	15-12	274	10.1
7. Colorado St.-Pueblo	28	17-11	282	10.1
8. Pfeiffer	31	22-9	306	9.9
9. West Virginia St.	29	16-13	283	9.8
10. Northwood	26	10-16	249	9.6
11. Northern St.	29	20-9	276	9.5
12. Southwest Minn. St.	28	17-11	262	9.4
13. St. Anselm	27	13-14	248	9.2
14. North Dakota St.	31	20-11	284	9.2
15. Barton	28	22-6	256	9.1
16. Alderson-Broaddus	32	25-7	289	9.0
17. South Dakota	28	19-9	249	8.9
18. West Ala.	27	7-20	237	8.8
19. Emporia St.	28	16-12	245	8.8
Ouachita Baptist	28	16-12	245	8.8
21. Winona St.	28	11-17	244	8.7
22. Limestone	27	10-17	232	8.6
23. Concordia-St. Paul	28	4-24	239	8.5
24. Columbus St.	32	27-5	273	8.5
25. Alas. Anchorage	27	13-14	229	8.5
26. Cal St. Chico	27	18-9	226	8.4
27. West Liberty St.	27	11-16	225	8.3
28. Hillsdale	28	16-12	233	8.3
29. St. Andrews	30	9-21	249	8.3
30. Northwest Mo. St.	31	22-9	257	8.3
31. St. Cloud St.	30	26-4	248	8.3
32. Grand Valley St.	28	14-14	231	8.3
Tusculum	28	16-12	231	8.3
34. Clarion	29	19-10	238	8.2
35. Ferris St.	26	11-15	213	8.2
36. Rollins	32	26-6	262	8.2
37. Harding	30	21-9	245	8.2
38. Lake Superior St.	27	12-15	220	8.1
Mesa St.	27	15-12	220	8.1
40. Southwestern Okla.	26	8-18	211	8.1
41. Christian Bros.	29	18-11	234	8.1
42. Northern Mich.	29	15-14	232	8.0
Carson-Newman	28	19-9	224	8.0
44. Oakland City	26	11-15	207	8.0
45. Bellarmine	29	10-19	230	7.9
46. Alas. Fairbanks	28	20-8	222	7.9
Mount Olive	28	18-10	222	7.9
48. Michigan Tech	32	29-3	252	7.9
49. Lewis	31	23-8	244	7.9
50. N.C. Central	29	16-13	228	7.9

STATISTICAL LEADERS

Rebound Margin

Rank Name	W-L	REB	RPG	OPP REB	OPP RPG	REB MAR
1. South Dakota St.	24-7	1,367	44.1	1,008	32.5	11.6
2. Teikyo Post	19-10	1,312	45.2	997	34.4	10.9
3. Ark.-Monticello	9-18	1,190	44.1	935	34.6	9.4
4. BYU-Hawaii	19-4	934	40.6	717	31.2	9.4
5. Washburn	26-6	1,262	39.4	971	30.3	9.1
6. Salem Int'l	25-6	1,246	40.2	965	31.1	9.1
7. Edinboro	17-11	1,183	42.3	934	33.4	8.9
8. Cal St. Bakersfield	20-9	1,086	37.4	844	29.1	8.3
9. Minn. Duluth	19-12	1,221	39.4	969	31.3	8.1
10. Fayetteville St.	11-17	1,094	39.1	869	31.0	8.0
11. Henderson St.	30-5	1,404	40.1	1,144	32.7	7.4
12. Tarleton St.	29-4	1,326	40.2	1,085	32.9	7.3
13. Longwood	15-14	1,106	38.1	899	31.0	7.1
14. Wheeling Jesuit	22-8	1,307	43.6	1,093	36.4	7.1
15. Francis Marion	13-14	1,078	39.9	888	32.9	7.0
16. Fla. Southern	26-5	1,239	40.0	1,023	33.0	7.0
17. Fort Hays St.	23-8	1,192	38.5	978	31.5	6.9
18. West Fla.	16-11	1,082	40.1	904	33.5	6.6
19. Southern Ind.	25-7	1,292	40.4	1,086	33.9	6.4
Michigan Tech	29-3	1,145	35.8	939	29.3	6.4
21. Queens (N.C.)	29-4	1,529	46.3	1,326	40.2	6.2
22. Humboldt St.	23-6	1,170	40.3	995	34.3	6.0
Clayton St.	17-12	1,139	39.3	964	33.2	6.0
24. Metro St.	28-5	1,117	33.8	923	28.0	5.9
25. Western Wash.	16-11	1,049	38.9	894	33.1	5.7
26. Eckerd	25-7	1,201	37.5	1,018	31.8	5.7
27. Valdosta St.	19-7	1,006	38.7	858	33.0	5.7
28. Mount Olive	18-10	1,214	43.4	1,055	37.7	5.7
29. Millersville	26-6	1,236	38.6	1,055	33.0	5.7
30. Queens (N.Y.)	14-14	1,084	38.7	927	33.1	5.6
31. Virginia Union	18-11	1,117	38.5	955	32.9	5.6
32. Ky. Wesleyan	31-4	1,455	41.6	1,267	36.2	5.4
33. Barry	18-10	944	33.7	794	28.4	5.4
34. C.W. Post	25-8	1,303	39.5	1,128	34.2	5.3
35. Belmont Abbey	24-7	1,174	37.9	1,011	32.6	5.3
36. Caldwell	15-11	957	36.8	823	31.7	5.2
37. Lewis	23-8	1,140	36.8	983	31.7	5.1
38. West Ga.	19-9	1,107	39.5	967	34.5	5.0
39. West Chester	21-9	1,175	39.2	1,027	34.2	4.9
40. Bentley	17-12	1,194	41.2	1,052	36.3	4.9
41. Eastern N.M.	20-8	991	35.4	856	30.6	4.8
42. Neb.-Omaha	20-10	1,126	37.5	997	33.2	4.3
43. Cal Poly Pomona	23-8	1,107	35.7	977	31.5	4.2
44. Bowie St.	30-5	1,447	41.3	1,301	37.2	4.2
45. Indiana (Pa.)	16-11	1,060	39.3	949	35.1	4.1
46. Calif. (Pa.)	25-9	1,235	36.3	1,100	32.4	4.0
47. Gannon	20-10	1,157	38.6	1,038	34.6	4.0
48. Drury	11-17	1,003	35.8	892	31.9	4.0
49. West Va. Tech	11-18	1,123	38.7	1,012	34.9	3.8
50. Pittsburg St.	16-12	1,049	37.5	944	33.7	3.8

Won-Lost Percentage

Rank Name	W	L	Pct
1. Northeastern St.	32	3	91.4
2. Neb.-Kearney	30	3	90.9
3. Michigan Tech	29	3	90.6
4. Ky. Wesleyan	31	4	88.6
5. Tarleton St.	29	4	87.9
Queens (N.C.)	29	4	87.9
7. St. Cloud St.	26	4	86.7
8. Bowie St.	30	5	85.7
Henderson St.	30	5	85.7
10. Mass.-Lowell	28	5	84.8
Metro St.	28	5	84.8
12. Columbus St.	27	5	84.4
13. Fla. Southern	26	5	83.9
14. BYU-Hawaii	19	4	82.6
15. Millersville	26	6	81.3
Washburn	26	6	81.3
Rollins	26	6	81.3
18. Northern Ky.	25	6	80.6
Salem Int'l.	25	6	80.6
20. Humboldt St.	23	6	79.3
21. Barton	22	6	78.6
22. Eckerd	25	7	78.1
Alderson-Broaddus	25	7	78.1
Southern Ind.	25	7	78.1
25. South Dakota St.	24	7	77.4
Belmont Abbey	24	7	77.4
27. Cal St. San B'dino	23	7	76.7
28. C.W. Post	25	8	75.8
29. Presbyterian	27	9	75.0
30. Bridgeport	23	8	74.2
Findlay	23	8	74.2
Mo. Western St.	23	8	74.2
Fort Hays St.	23	8	74.2
Cal Poly Pomona	23	8	74.2
Morehouse	23	8	74.2
Lewis	23	8	74.2
37. Calif. (Pa.)	25	9	73.5
38. Delta St.	22	8	73.3
Southern N.H.	22	8	73.3
Wheeling Jesuit	22	8	73.3
Lenoir-Rhyne	22	8	73.3
42. Dist. Columbia	19	7	73.1
Valdosta St.	19	7	73.1
44. Kennesaw St.	25	10	71.4
Alas. Fairbanks	20	8	71.4
Eastern N.M.	20	8	71.4
47. Adelphi	22	9	71.0
Pfeiffer	22	9	71.0
Northwest Mo. St.	22	9	71.0
50. Shaw	21	9	70.0
West Chester	21	9	70.0
Harding	21	9	70.0

Team Highs

POINTS

Rank Name	vs. Opponent	Game Date	PTS	OPP PTS
1. Mont. St.-Billings	Western N.M.	2/01/2003	146	73
2. Henderson St.	Central Baptist	1/03/2003	123	67
3. Wheeling Jesuit	Ohio-Zanesville	1/06/2003	121	58
4. North Dakota St.	Mayville St.	12/19/2002	120	71
West Virginia St.	Ohio Southern	12/16/2002	120	79
Ashland	Bellarmine	11/23/2002	120	115
7. Western Wash.	Puget Sound Chrst.	1/07/2003	119	49
Carson-Newman	Trevecca Nazarene	12/12/2002	119	85
9. Bemidji St.	Minn.-Morris	2/22/2003	118	70
Western Wash.	Northwest (Wash.)	12/30/2002	118	65
11. Northwest Nazarene	Walla Walla	1/14/2003	117	77
Wheeling Jesuit	Ohio Valley	12/30/2002	117	49
13. Bemidji St.	Minn.-Morris	1/17/2003	116	71
14. Southern Ind.	St. Joseph's (Ind.)	1/23/2003	115	108
Bellarmine	Ashland	11/23/2002	115	120
16. Mo. Southern St.	Messenger	2/17/2003	114	48
Bloomfield	Wilmington (Del.)	2/08/2003	114	96

FIELD-GOAL PERCENTAGE

Minimum 66%

Rank Name	vs. Opponent	Game Date	FG%	FGM	FGA
1. BYU-Hawaii	Western N.M.	1/14/2003	71.4	40	56
2. West Fla.	Edward Waters	1/13/2003	69.0	40	58
3. Minn. Duluth	Northwest Mo. St.	11/30/2002	68.6	35	51
4. Mass.-Lowell	Stonehill	2/11/2003	67.9	36	53
5. Ky. Wesleyan	Lewis	1/30/2003	67.9	38	56
6. Neb.-Omaha	North Dakota St.	1/02/2003	67.4	29	43
7. Michigan Tech	Findlay	1/18/2003	67.4	31	46
8. Calif. (Pa.)	Allegheny	12/14/2002	67.3	37	55
Le Moyne	Alderson-Broaddus	11/22/2002	67.3	37	55
10. Northwest Nazarene	Walla Walla	1/14/2003	67.2	45	67
11. Neb.-Omaha	Midland Lutheran	12/21/2002	66.7	40	60
12. Wheeling Jesuit	Ohio-Zanesville	1/06/2003	66.2	51	77
13. Lewis	Quincy	12/07/2002	66.0	33	50

THREE-POINT FIELD GOALS MADE

Rank Name	vs. Opponent	Game Date	3FG
1. Mont. St.-Billings	Western N.M.	2/20/2003	21
2. Bemidji St.	Concordia-St. Paul	2/28/2003	20
Northern Mich.	Northland	12/16/2002	20

Rank	Name	vs. Opponent	Game Date	3FG
4.	Bemidji St.	Minn.-Morris	1/17/2003	19
5.	Mass.-Lowell	Merrimack	2/08/2003	18
	Presbyterian	North Greenville	2/03/2003	18
	Emporia St.	Northwest Mo. St.	1/29/2003	18
	Carson-Newman	Trevecca Nazarene	12/12/2002	18
	Western Ore.	Western Baptist	11/30/2002	18
10.	Bemidji St.	Minn. St. Moorhead	3/08/2003	17
	Western Ore.	Humboldt St.	3/08/2003	17
	St. Anselm	St. Rose	2/25/2003	17
	Bemidji St.	Minn.-Morris	2/22/2003	17
	West Ala.	Montevallo	2/10/2003	17
	Bemidji St.	Minn.-Crookston	2/08/2003	17
	St. Anselm	Southern Conn. St.	2/05/2003	17
	Mont. St.-Billings	Western N.M.	2/01/2003	17
	Christian Bros.	Ark.-Monticello	1/30/2003	17
	Barton	Lees-McRae	1/11/2003	17
	Delta St.	Philander Smith	1/25/2002	17
21.	Southwest Minn. St.	Minn.-Morris	2/08/2003	16
	UC Davis	UC San Diego	1/25/2003	16
	West Virginia St.	Bluefield St.	1/13/2003	16
	Winona St.	Northern St.	12/30/2002	16
	North Dakota St.	Mayville St.	12/19/2002	16
	West Liberty St.	Ohio-Eastern	12/02/2002	16
	Winona St.	Fla. Southern	11/29/2002	16

THREE-POINT FIELD-GOAL PERCENTAGE

Minimum 10 made

Rank	Name	vs. Opponent	Game Date	3FG%	3FG	3FGA
1.	Mass.-Lowell	Merrimack	2/08/2003	75.0	18	24
2.	Wingate	Tusculum	2/01/2003	73.7	14	19
3.	Central Ark.	Southern Ark.	1/30/2003	71.4	10	14
4.	Lock Haven	Bloomsburg	1/04/2003	70.6	12	17
5.	Cal St. L.A.	Cal St. Bakersfield	2/28/2003	68.8	11	16
	S.C.-Aiken	North Fla.	1/29/2003	68.8	11	16
7.	Cal St. Chico	San Fran. St.	2/08/2003	68.4	13	19
8.	Calif. (Pa.)	Allegheny	12/14/2002	66.7	10	15
9.	Bemidji St.	Wis.-Superior	12/02/2002	65.0	13	20

Rank	Name	vs. Opponent	Game Date	3FG%	3FG	3FGA
10.	Central Ark.	Henderson St.	2/15/2003	64.7	11	17
	St. Rose	Franklin Pierce	1/14/2003	64.7	11	17
12.	Southwest Minn. St.	Minn.-Morris	2/08/2003	64.0	16	25

FREE-THROW PERCENTAGE

Minimum 15 made

Rank	Name	vs. Opponent	Game Date	FT%	FT	FTA
1.	Southern Ind.	Wis.-Parkside	1/25/2003	100.0	25	25
	South Dakota	Bellevue	12/08/2002	100.0	21	21
	Southwest Baptist	Missouri Valley	12/16/2002	100.0	20	20
	Ferris St.	Calvin	11/26/2002	100.0	18	18
	Neb.-Omaha	South Dakota	1/23/2003	100.0	16	16
	Western Ore.	Northwest Nazarene	1/11/2003	100.0	15	15
7.	Ark.-Monticello	Southern Ark.	2/20/2003	96.0	24	25
8.	Western N.M.	Adams St.	12/05/2002	95.8	23	24
9.	Bellarmine	Northern Ky.	12/07/2002	95.5	21	22
10.	North Dakota St.	South Dakota	3/04/2003	95.2	20	21
	South Dakota	St. Cloud St.	1/04/2003	95.2	20	21
	West Fla.	North Ala.	1/20/2002	95.2	20	21
13.	Henderson St.	Ark.-Monticello	2/06/2003	95.0	19	20
14.	UC Davis	San Fran. St.	2/07/2003	94.7	18	19
	St. Cloud St.	Minn. St. Mankato	2/06/2003	94.7	18	19
	Cal St. Bakersfield	Cal St. Stanislaus	12/11/2002	94.7	18	19
	Bellarmine	Mo.-St. Louis	11/30/2002	94.7	18	19
18.	Henderson St.	Bryant	12/16/2002	94.4	17	18
	Ferris St.	Olivet	12/14/2002	94.4	17	18
	Lander	Presbyterian	11/23/2002	94.4	17	18
	Ark.-Monticello	Central Ark.	2/24/2002	94.4	17	18
22.	Gannon	Mercyhurst	2/15/2003	94.1	16	17
	Mount Olive	Lees-McRae	1/18/2003	94.1	16	17
	Harding	Ark.-Little Rock	1/04/2003	94.1	16	17
25.	North Dakota St.	Augustana (S.D.)	1/25/2003	93.9	31	33
26.	Minn.-Crookston	Southwest Minn. St.	1/24/2003	93.8	15	16
27.	Neb.-Omaha	St. Cloud St.	3/08/2003	93.5	29	31
28.	Southwest Minn. St.	Bemidji St.	12/29/2002	93.1	27	29
29.	Northern Mich.	Ferris St.	2/08/2003	92.6	25	27

2003 Division III Individual Leaders

Points Per Game

Rank	Name, Team	Cl	G	FGM	3FG	FT	PTS	PPG
1.	Patrick Glover, Johnson St.	Sr.	26	269	37	188	763	29.3
2.	Rich Melzer, Wis.-River Falls	Jr.	26	284	0	163	731	28.1
3.	Willie Chandler, Misericordia	Sr.	28	251	93	135	730	26.1
4.	Derek Reich, Chicago	Sr.	25	221	38	156	636	25.4
5.	Adam Turner, Bard	Fr.	21	191	35	114	531	25.3
6.	Robert Hennigan, Emerson	Jr.	25	184	101	154	623	24.9
7.	Shawn Jones, Westfield St.	Sr.	25	215	43	141	614	24.6
8.	Rohan Russell, Johnson & Wales	Jr.	25	190	92	136	608	24.3
	Steve Wood, Grinnell	Jr.	25	206	60	136	608	24.3
10.	Ray Robinson, Waynesburg	Sr.	25	217	73	95	602	24.1
11.	Jason Levecque, Southern Me.	So.	23	194	45	112	545	23.7
12.	Andy O'Brien, York (Pa.)	Sr.	25	216	65	94	591	23.6
13.	Derek Suttles, MacMurray	Jr.	24	225	2	114	566	23.6
14.	Joel Kolmodin, Wheaton (Ill.)	Jr.	23	189	38	117	533	23.2
15.	Benny West, Howard Payne	Jr.	24	206	19	122	553	23.0
16.	Justin Call, Emory & Henry	Jr.	26	224	67	84	599	23.0
17.	Larry Bryant, Wesley	Sr.	25	185	53	144	567	22.7
18.	Tim Dworak, Wis.-Oshkosh	Sr.	32	283	24	135	725	22.7
19.	Jed Johnson, Maine Maritime	Sr.	25	226	17	90	559	22.4
20.	Matt Brennan, Anna Maria	Jr.	27	241	39	81	602	22.3
21.	Shuaib Abdur-Rahman, Lincoln (Pa.)	Jr.	23	186	46	91	509	22.1
22.	Jason Larson, Wis.-Eau Claire	Sr.	27	192	70	143	597	22.1
23.	Tom Engelbrecht, Martin Luther	Jr.	23	182	26	117	507	22.0
24.	Lucas Messer, Heidelberg	Jr.	26	196	20	160	572	22.0
25.	Zareh Avedian, Cal Lutheran	Jr.	25	210	26	103	549	22.0
26.	Matt Beacom, Pitt.-Bradford	Sr.	29	231	0	168	630	21.7
27.	Mike Leimeister, Bluffton	Sr.	26	202	29	130	563	21.7
28.	Bryan Depew, Whitworth	Jr.	27	209	15	149	582	21.6
29.	Michael Reich, Colorado Col.	So.	24	163	28	161	515	21.5
30.	Tom Carey, Suffolk	Sr.	26	203	58	91	555	21.3
31.	Hasheem Alexander, Salisbury	Sr.	25	173	74	112	532	21.3
32.	Joe Finley, Hamilton	Sr.	29	244	1	127	616	21.2
33.	Travis Schwab, Ohio Wesleyan	Jr.	26	199	22	130	550	21.2
34.	Kevin Buth, St. John's (Minn.)	Sr.	27	199	82	91	571	21.1
35.	Nate Maurer, Grove City	So.	27	206	42	112	566	21.0
	Robby Pridgen, Roanoke	Sr.	27	179	77	131	566	21.0
37.	Bryan Nelson, Wooster	Sr.	31	221	10	193	645	20.8
38.	Derek James, MacMurray	Sr.	24	148	80	123	499	20.8
	Kanem Johnson, Wesleyan (Conn.)	Jr.	24	197	0	105	499	20.8
40.	Dejuan Green, Chowan	Sr.	26	191	62	95	539	20.7
41.	Andy Gilbert, Bethel (Minn.)	Sr.	26	184	37	128	533	20.5
	Mike Majzun, Bethany (W.Va.)	Sr.	26	177	69	110	533	20.5
43.	Kris Hebert, Western New Eng.	Sr.	27	191	12	159	553	20.5
44.	Chris Jeffries, Washington (Mo.)	Sr.	26	206	0	120	532	20.5

Rank Name, Team	Cl	G	FGM	3FG	FT	PTS	PPG
45. Kari Hannula, St. Norbert	Sr.	23	164	47	94	469	20.6
46. Jebah Clayton, Medgar Evers	Jr.	21	149	31	99	428	20.4
47. Badou Gaye, Gwynedd-Mercy	So.	25	217	1	74	509	20.4
48. Glenn Mills, Mass. Liberal Arts	Sr.	25	140	52	175	507	20.3
49. Michael Bollman, Ozarks (Ark.)	Sr.	24	192	10	91	485	20.2
50. Charles Ranson, Ramapo	Jr.	30	204	108	88	604	20.1

Rebounds Per Game

Rank Name, Team	Cl	G	REB	RPG
1. Jed Johnson, Maine Maritime	Sr.	25	414	16.6
2. Joe Corbett, Hobart	Sr.	23	331	14.4
3. Anthony Fitzgerald, Villa Julie	Fr.	25	337	13.5
4. Darren Pugh, Lebanon Valley	Sr.	26	324	12.5
5. Jon Schwadron, Dickinson	Sr.	25	303	12.1
6. Derek Suttles, MacMurray	Jr.	24	284	11.8
7. Craig Coupe, Tufts	So.	25	285	11.4
8. Matt Beacom, Pitt.-Bradford	Sr.	29	328	11.3
9. Patrick Glover, Johnson St.	Sr.	26	294	11.3
10. Perry Davis, Buffalo St.	Jr.	27	303	11.2
11. Kyle McNamar, Curry	Sr.	25	280	11.2
12. Badou Gaye, Gwynedd-Mercy	So.	25	275	11.0
13. Chris Braier, Lawrence	Fr.	24	263	11.0
14. Greg Foster, Westminster (Pa.)	Sr.	27	294	10.9
15. Bobby Davison, TCNJ	Fr.	25	270	10.8
16. Dan Luciano, Ursinus	Sr.	28	295	10.5
17. John Smith, Staten Island	So.	26	273	10.5
18. Joe Howell, Fitchburg St.	Sr.	25	261	10.4
19. Matt Stackhouse, Lycoming	Jr.	26	271	10.4
20. Adam Turner, Bard	Fr.	21	218	10.4
21. Rob Smith, N.C. Wesleyan	Sr.	27	279	10.3
22. Joel Kolmodin, Wheaton (Ill.)	Jr.	23	233	10.1
23. Joel Blackwell, Hartwick	Sr.	25	253	10.1
24. Jared Hite, Rensselaer	Jr.	23	232	10.1
25. Robert Haney, Gallaudet	Fr.	26	260	10.0
26. Joe Smith, Hamilton	Jr.	29	289	10.0
27. Magen McNeil, Arcadia	Fr.	25	248	9.9
28. Raheim Lowery, Medgar Evers	Jr.	20	197	9.9
29. Billy Allen, Mass.-Boston	So.	26	254	9.8
30. David Bright, DeSales	So.	30	291	9.7
31. Kenneth Lane, Mt. St. Mary (N.Y.)	So.	30	290	9.7
32. Rich Melzer, Wis.-River Falls	Jr.	26	251	9.7
33. Seth Hauben, Rochester	So.	27	260	9.6
34. Joel Leichtnam, Castleton St.	Jr.	26	250	9.6
35. Joe Ringger, DePauw	Sr.	23	220	9.6
36. Derek Hoffman, Bethany (W.Va.)	Sr.	26	248	9.5
37. Bret Lamboley, Mass. Liberal Arts	Sr.	25	238	9.5
38. Scott Mahan, Wheaton (Mass.)	Jr.	28	266	9.5
39. Brandon Crawford, Oberlin	Fr.	25	237	9.5
C.J. Vose, St. Joseph's (Me.)	Sr.	25	237	9.5
41. Brian Weber, Concordia (Wis.)	Jr.	26	244	9.4
42. Steve Erfle, Ursinus	Sr.	28	262	9.4
43. Jayson Douthwright, Albertus Magnus	Sr.	28	261	9.3
44. Charles Simmons, Aurora	Jr.	30	278	9.3
45. Terry Gray, Chris. Newport	Sr.	29	268	9.2
46. Tommy Stolhandske, Texas Lutheran	So.	25	231	9.2
47. Tom Engelbrecht, Martin Luther	Jr.	23	212	9.2
48. Derek Reich, Chicago	Sr.	25	230	9.2
49. Brian O'Donnell, Scranton	So.	30	275	9.2
Kevin Bartow, Maryville (Mo.)	Sr.	24	220	9.2

Blocked Shots Per Game

Rank Name, Team	Cl	G	BLKS	BKPG
1. John Bunch, Lincoln (Pa.)	Fr.	23	92	4.0
2. Antonio Ramos, Clarke	Sr.	27	106	3.9
3. Kyle McNamar, Curry	Sr.	25	97	3.9
4. Steve Juskin, Frank. & Marsh.	Jr.	30	108	3.6
5. Sean Devins, Trinity (Tex.)	So.	29	101	3.5
6. Jayson Douthwright, Albertus Magnus	Sr.	28	95	3.4
7. Don Overbeek, Hope	Sr.	28	94	3.4
8. Rob Smith, N.C. Wesleyan	Sr.	27	90	3.3
9. Badou Gaye, Gwynedd-Mercy	So.	25	77	3.1
Rockland Owens, Sul Ross St.	So.	25	77	3.1
11. Terry Gray, Chris. Newport	Sr.	29	86	3.0
12. Greg Foster, Westminster (Pa.)	Sr.	27	80	3.0
13. Jesse Foote, Rochester Inst.	So.	22	64	2.9
14. Jarriot Rook, Washington (Mo.)	Sr.	26	71	2.7
15. Mike Machin, Drew	Sr.	24	65	2.7
16. Matt Hilleary, Catholic	Sr.	29	77	2.7
17. Pierre Bowery, Frostburg St.	Sr.	26	68	2.6

Rank Name, Team	Cl	G	BLKS	BKPG
18. Travis Jones, Bethel (Minn.)	So.	27	69	2.6
19. Walter Fowler, Susquehanna	Fr.	26	66	2.5
20. Aaron Holden, Muhlenberg	Sr.	23	58	2.5
21. Ben Howard, Mass. Liberal Arts	Sr.	25	60	2.4
22. Charles Simmons, Aurora	Jr.	30	71	2.4
23. Justin Foster, Howard Payne	Sr.	25	58	2.3
Nick Fusare, Linfield	Jr.	25	58	2.3
25. Tyler Putnam, Colby-Sawyer	Fr.	28	64	2.3
26. Ted Mulvagh, Worcester St.	Jr.	28	63	2.3
27. Adam Rue, Augustana (Ill.)	Sr.	25	56	2.2
28. Marvin Gray, York (N.Y.)	Jr.	23	51	2.2
29. Garrett Ingram, Illinois Col.	Sr.	25	55	2.2
30. Billy Allen, Mass.-Boston	So.	26	57	2.2
31. Jason Murren, Monmouth (Ill.)	So.	23	50	2.2
32. Rocco Cordato, Utica	So.	22	47	2.1
33. John Cowan, Marywood	Sr.	25	53	2.1
34. Matt Stackhouse, Lycoming	Jr.	26	55	2.1
35. Gary Etienne, Baruch	Jr.	30	63	2.1
36. Chinedu Ibeh, Rutgers-Newark	So.	25	52	2.1
37. Rich Melzer, Wis.-River Falls	Jr.	26	54	2.1
38. Scott Mahan, Wheaton (Mass.)	Jr.	28	58	2.1
39. David Bright, DeSales	So.	30	62	2.1
40. Corey Days, Trinity (Conn.)	Sr.	24	49	2.0
41. Dallin Wilson, Occidental	So.	25	50	2.0
42. Nick Ripple, St. John Fisher	Jr.	26	51	2.0
43. David Myrie, Wesleyan (Conn.)	Jr.	24	46	1.9
44. Paul Muenchow, Hamline	So.	25	47	1.9
45. Deodrick Sanders, Upper Iowa	Sr.	24	45	1.9
46. Sean Walsh, Mass.-Dartmouth	Sr.	27	50	1.9
47. Tillman Sims, Alvernia	Sr.	30	55	1.8
48. Joel Cornilsen, Loras	Sr.	26	47	1.8
Nick Kane, Franklin	Fr.	26	47	1.8
50. Craig Coupe, Tufts	So.	25	45	1.8

Steals Per Game

Rank Name, Team	Cl	G	ST	STPG
1. Benny West, Howard Payne	Jr.	24	99	4.1
2. Isiah Walker, Marywood	Jr.	25	100	4.0
3. Tennyson Whitted, Ramapo	Sr.	30	118	3.9
4. Marquis Jones, Utica	Sr.	25	95	3.8
5. John Alesi, Baruch	Sr.	29	105	3.6
6. Adam Harper, Amherst	Jr.	29	101	3.5
7. Nick Catanzarite, Allegheny	Sr.	28	94	3.4
8. Joshua Didick, Mount Ida	Jr.	26	87	3.3
9. Jason Fulford, Brooklyn	So.	26	85	3.3
10. Hugh Morrisey, Sul Ross St.	Jr.	25	79	3.2
11. Brendan Twomey, Mt. St. Mary (N.Y.)	Jr.	31	96	3.1
12. Cliff Foster, La Roche	Jr.	26	79	3.0
13. Jeff Mikos, Milwaukee Engr.	Fr.	29	87	3.0
14. Andy Albright, Lynchburg	Fr.	25	73	2.9
15. Delson Fleurmond, Becker	Fr.	20	56	2.8
16. Rahim Washington, Neumann	Sr.	28	76	2.7
Adam Turner, Bard	Fr.	21	57	2.7
18. David Bostick, Becker	Jr.	26	70	2.7
19. Brian Pelkey, Keuka	Jr.	19	51	2.7
20. Beau Henderson, Waynesburg	Sr.	25	67	2.7
Shawn Jones, Westfield St.	Sr.	25	67	2.7
22. Matt Chewning, Eastern Nazarene	Jr.	26	69	2.7
23. Travis DePree, Albion	So.	25	66	2.6
24. Joe Howell, Fitchburg St.	Sr.	25	65	2.6
25. Chris LaCasse, Endicott	Jr.	28	72	2.6
26. Brian Loftus, Elizabethtown	Sr.	27	69	2.6
27. Matt Moore, Hanover	So.	29	74	2.6
28. Matt Duffy, Haverford	Sr.	24	61	2.5
29. Glenn Mills, Mass. Liberal Arts	Sr.	25	63	2.5
30. Xzavier Williams, Albertus Magnus	Sr.	27	68	2.5
31. Collin Bray, Colby-Sawyer	Fr.	28	70	2.5
Justin Bryant, Johnson & Wales	Sr.	26	65	2.5
Femi Akinnagbe, Messiah	Jr.	20	50	2.5
34. Billy Hagan, Dickinson	Sr.	25	62	2.5
35. Erin Gram, Pacific (Ore.)	Jr.	19	47	2.5
36. Anthony Oglesby, Plymouth St.	So.	29	71	2.4
37. Amin Wright, Ramapo	So.	23	56	2.4
38. Andy Gilbert, Bethel (Minn.)	Jr.	26	63	2.4
Robert Haney, Gallaudet	Fr.	26	63	2.4
Travis Schellhammer, Olivet	Jr.	26	63	2.4
41. Bryant James, Westfield St.	Sr.	22	53	2.4
42. Victor Esquer, Cal Lutheran	Jr.	25	60	2.4
Larry Morales, Sul Ross St.	Jr.	25	60	2.4
44. Bilal McAfee, Widener	Jr.	23	55	2.4
45. Khayri Battle, Wm. Paterson	Jr.	26	62	2.4
46. Perry Davis, Buffalo St.	Jr.	27	64	2.4

Rank Name, Team	Cl	G	ST	STPG
47. Bryan Dlugolenski, Salve Regina	Sr.	25	59	2.4
Yarzue Slowon, Augsburg	So.	25	59	2.4
49. Willie Chandler, Misericordia	Sr.	28	66	2.4
50. Shuaib Abdur-Rahman, Lincoln (Pa.)	Jr.	23	54	2.3

Assists Per Game

Rank Name, Team	Cl	G	AST	APG
1. Tennyson Whitted, Ramapo	Sr.	30	253	8.4
2. Michael Crotty, Williams	Jr.	32	245	7.7
3. Jesse Farrell, Trinity (Conn.)	So.	24	176	7.3
4. Cliff Foster, La Roche	Jr.	26	173	6.7
5. Paul Russo, Emory & Henry	Sr.	26	171	6.6
6. Travis Magnusson, Me.-Farmington	Fr.	25	163	6.5
7. Evan Fowler, Mary Washington	Jr.	29	187	6.4
8. Labeeb Abdullah, SCAD	Sr.	26	167	6.4
9. Trevelle Boyd, East Tex. Baptist	Sr.	26	163	6.3
10. Tim Gaspar, Mass.-Dartmouth	Sr.	27	167	6.2
11. Beau Henderson, Waynesburg	Sr.	25	148	5.9
12. Matt Tabash, Washington (Mo.)	Sr.	26	149	5.7
Jeff Weld, Castleton St.	Sr.	26	149	5.7
14. Chris Zimmerman, Susquehanna	Jr.	23	131	5.7
15. Tyson Thompson, Shenandoah	Sr.	26	148	5.7
16. Seth McLane, York (Pa.)	Sr.	25	141	5.6
17. Andrew Fairman, Mount Union	Fr.	27	152	5.6
18. Jon Newland, Maine Maritime	Sr.	24	135	5.6
19. Aaron Kiffer, Pitt-Bradford	So.	29	163	5.6
20. Hugh Morrisey, Sul Ross St.	Jr.	25	140	5.6
21. Scott Christensen, Carleton	Sr.	26	145	5.6
Lorcan Precious, Hunter	Jr.	26	145	5.6
23. Bobby Jenkins, N.C. Wesleyan	Jr.	28	155	5.5
24. Michael Irwin, New York U.	Sr.	25	138	5.5
25. Drew Petefish, Illinois Col.	Sr.	26	143	5.5
26. Josh Polantz, Bethany (W.Va.)	Fr.	26	141	5.4
27. Robert McCants, Cazenovia	So.	26	139	5.3
28. Areum Chae, Aurora	Sr.	30	160	5.3
29. Adam Fischer, Fontbonne	Sr.	22	116	5.3
30. Tom Becker, Ripon	So.	19	100	5.3
31. Justin Underwood, St. Joseph's (Me.)	Sr.	24	126	5.3
32. Greg Leone, Hamilton	Jr.	25	131	5.2
33. Casey Bock, Western Conn. St.	Sr.	29	150	5.2
34. Erin Gram, Pacific (Ore.)	Jr.	19	98	5.2
35. Mike O'Connor, Western New Eng.	Sr.	27	139	5.1
36. Victor Esquer, Cal Lutheran	Sr.	25	128	5.1
37. Mike McGarvey, Ursinus	Fr.	28	143	5.1
38. Adam Dickman, Catholic	Jr.	29	148	5.1
39. Patrick McKenzie, St. John's (Minn.)	Jr.	27	137	5.1
40. Jeff Mikos, Milwaukee Engr.	Fr.	29	145	5.0
K.C. Granfield, Rhode Island Col.	Fr.	26	130	5.0
Yarzue Slowon, Augsburg	So.	25	125	5.0
43. Justin Bryant, Johnson & Wales	Sr.	26	129	5.0
Kyle Seyboth, Elms	So.	26	129	5.0
45. Tony Tibayan, Lake Erie	Jr.	26	128	4.9
46. Blake Brookman, Chris. Newport	So.	29	142	4.9
47. Kenny Stewart, Plymouth St.	Sr.	29	140	4.8
48. Lee Taylor, Lake Forest	Sr.	22	106	4.8
49. Collin Bray, Colby-Sawyer	Fr.	28	133	4.8
Josh Oxton, Endicott	Jr.	28	133	4.8

Field-Goal Percentage

Minimum 5.0 Field Goals Made Per Game

Rank Name, Team	Cl	G	FGM	FGA	FG%
1. Aaron Marshall, St. Lawrence	So.	27	206	305	67.5
2. Gian Paul Gonzalez, Messiah	Fr.	22	144	218	66.1
3. Ryan Hodges, Cal Lutheran	Jr.	25	129	197	65.5
4. Omar Warthen, Neumann	Sr.	29	149	229	65.1
5. John Thomas, Fontbonne	Sr.	25	128	198	64.6
6. Bryan Nelson, Wooster	Sr.	31	221	343	64.4
7. Tim Dworak, Wis.-Oshkosh	Sr.	32	283	446	63.5
8. Kwesi Liverpool, York (N.Y.)	Fr.	24	128	202	63.4
9. Keith Davis, SCAD	Jr.	27	206	327	63.0
10. Mark Gabriel, Haverford	So.	18	141	227	62.1
11. Andy Larkin, Rochester	Jr.	27	139	224	62.1
12. Theo Powell, Carthage	Jr.	25	131	212	61.8
13. Derek Elphick, Scranton	Sr.	30	202	328	61.6
14. Gavin Keohane, Occidental	Sr.	27	175	288	60.8
15. Jared Swanson, Concordia-M'head	Sr.	24	164	270	60.7
16. James Lewis, Rust	Jr.	25	149	246	60.6
17. Jason Kalsow, Wis.-Stevens Point	So.	28	142	237	59.9
18. Justin Foster, Howard Payne	Sr.	25	135	226	59.7
19. Dustin Arnold, Fredonia St.	Sr.	23	126	211	59.7
20. Chris Jeffries, Washington (Mo.)	Sr.	26	206	345	59.7
21. Steve Adams, Johns Hopkins	Sr.	26	158	265	59.6
22. Matt Stackhouse, Lycoming	Jr.	26	162	272	59.6
23. Adam Lewis, Milwaukee Engr.	Sr.	28	180	303	59.4
24. Benny West, Howard Payne	Jr.	24	206	350	58.9
25. Robert Jenkins, Dubuque	Sr.	25	133	226	58.8
26. Badou Gaye, Gwynedd-Mercy	So.	25	217	369	58.8
27. Russell Johnson, Potsdam St.	Sr.	27	152	259	58.7
28. Ryan Pehanick, Lynchburg	So.	23	142	242	58.7
29. Brian Weber, Concordia (Wis.)	Jr.	26	143	244	58.6
30. Brian McCauley, FDU-Florham	Sr.	25	184	314	58.6
31. Dan Luciano, Ursinus	Sr.	28	211	361	58.4
32. Thabo Letsebe, Goucher	Sr.	26	163	280	58.2
33. Aubrey Lewis-Beyers, Wis.-Whitewater	Sr.	28	179	309	57.9
34. Greg Foster, Westminster (Pa.)	Sr.	27	146	253	57.7
35. James Curren, Penn St.-Behrend	Jr.	29	192	333	57.7
36. Eric McDonald, Lake Forest	So.	23	153	266	57.5
37. Jared Mills, Randolph-Macon	Sr.	29	183	319	57.4
38. Matt Beacom, Pitt-Bradford	Sr.	29	231	403	57.3
39. Jon Tipton, Blackburn	Jr.	25	156	273	57.1
Aaron Minister, Otterbein	Jr.	26	136	238	57.1
41. Kanem Johnson, Wesleyan (Conn.)	Jr.	24	197	346	56.9
42. Thad Davis, Baldwin-Wallace	So.	26	165	290	56.9
43. Jarel Hall, Schreiner	So.	25	146	257	56.8
44. Jared Hite, Rensselaer	Jr.	23	142	250	56.8
45. Don Overbeek, Hope	Sr.	28	151	267	56.6
46. Jeremy Miklovic, Defiance	So.	26	164	290	56.6
47. Matt Moore, Hanover	So.	29	162	287	56.4
48. Sean Fleming, Clark (Mass.)	Sr.	24	150	266	56.4
49. Steve Erfle, Ursinus	Sr.	28	165	293	56.3
50. Matt Hilleary, Catholic	Sr.	29	202	359	56.3

Free-Throw Percentage

Minimum 2.5 Free Throws Made Per Game

Rank Name, Team	Cl	G	FT	FTA	FT%
1. Nick Wilkins, Coe	So.	26	66	69	95.7
2. Matt Larson, Linfield	So.	25	99	108	91.7
3. Sean Fleming, Clark (Mass.)	Sr.	24	109	120	90.8
4. Aaron Faulkner, St. Norbert	So.	23	77	85	90.6
5. Victor Garcia, Knox	Sr.	21	114	126	90.5
6. Steve King, Fontbonne	Sr.	24	81	90	90.0
7. Nick Bennett, Wis.-Stevens Point	So.	24	62	69	89.9
8. Brandon Constantine, Wm. Paterson	Jr.	25	77	86	89.5
9. Ryan Connor, Salem St.	Jr.	28	90	101	89.1
10. Bryan Nelson, Wooster	Sr.	31	193	218	88.5
11. Mike Kurdziel, Defiance	Sr.	27	137	155	88.4
12. Billy Lewis, Rockford	Sr.	28	91	103	88.3
Josh Oxton, Endicott	Jr.	28	91	103	88.3
14. Tennyson Whitted, Ramapo	Sr.	30	144	163	88.3
15. Austin Lutz, Rhodes	Jr.	19	67	76	88.2
16. Justin Clifford, Muskingum	Sr.	27	88	100	88.0
Doug Billet, Marywood	Sr.	25	66	75	88.0
Justin Rice, Salisbury	Fr.	26	66	75	88.0
19. Doug Sumner, Blackburn	Sr.	25	113	129	87.6
20. Brandon Hansen, Neb. Wesleyan	Jr.	25	84	96	87.5
Miles Sandgathe, Willamette	Jr.	26	84	96	87.5
22. Derek Yvon, Springfield	Fr.	26	89	102	87.3
23. Craig Biller, Juniata	Jr.	25	82	94	87.2
Keith Sudler, N.C. Wesleyan	Jr.	28	82	94	87.2
25. Ray Robinson, Waynesburg	Sr.	25	95	109	87.2
26. Craig Avallone, Catholic	Sr.	27	74	85	87.1
27. Dan Archambault, Wis.-Eau Claire	So.	27	113	130	86.9
28. Greg Leone, Hamilton	Jr.	25	65	75	86.7
Perry Young, Denison	Jr.	21	65	75	86.7
30. Rami Almetty, Rhodes	Fr.	25	77	89	86.5
31. Casey Stitzel, Widener	So.	25	63	73	86.3
32. Robby Pridgen, Roanoke	Sr.	27	131	152	86.2
33. Matt Formato, Kenyon	Fr.	23	98	114	86.0
34. Shawn McCormick, Baldwin-Wallace	Sr.	26	85	99	85.9
35. Jim Conrad, Ohio Northern	Jr.	26	90	105	85.7
36. Wayne Bosworth, Elmhurst	Jr.	25	82	96	85.4
37. Michael Grogan, John Carroll	So.	28	70	82	85.4
38. Ben Stewart, St. Mary's (Md.)	So.	26	75	88	85.2
39. Ricky Davis, Lakeland	Jr.	27	98	115	85.2
40. Casey Taggatz, Wis.-La Crosse	Jr.	26	80	94	85.1
41. Nick Catanzarite, Allegheny	Sr.	28	139	164	84.8
42. Josh Hanson, Hamline	Jr.	24	61	72	84.7
43. Jeremy Currier, Endicott	Jr.	28	72	85	84.7
Chad Tobin, Illinois Col.	Sr.	26	72	85	84.7
45. Matt Bahl, Colorado Col.	Jr.	24	77	91	84.6

STATISTICAL LEADERS

Rank Name, Team	Cl	G	FT	FTA	FT%
Colin Camacho, Washington (Md.)	So.	26	77	91	84.6
47. Victor Esquer, Cal Lutheran	Sr.	25	104	123	84.6
48. Rod Ceasar, East Tex. Baptist	Sr.	26	93	110	84.5
49. Carlos Heard, Chris. Newport	Sr.	29	76	90	84.4
50. Aaron Johnson, Lake Erie	Jr.	26	65	77	84.4

Rank Name, Team	Cl	G	3FG	3FGA	3FG%
48. Jimmy Evans, Nazareth	Sr.	28	86	219	39.3
49. Doug Schneider, Pitt.-Bradford	Sr.	29	86	221	38.9
50. Steve Nordlund, Grinnell	Jr.	25	119	306	38.9

Three-Point Field-Goal Percentage

Minimum 2.5 3-Pt. Field Goals Made per Game

Rank Name, Team	Cl	G	3FG	3FGA	3FG%
1. Jeremy Currier, Endicott	Jr.	28	74	144	51.4
2. Geoff Wing, Rockford	Jr.	28	99	194	51.0
3. Wayne Bosworth, Elmhurst	Jr.	25	75	150	50.0
4. Nate Collord, Wheaton (Ill.)	Sr.	25	79	159	49.7
5. Jeff Joss, Rochester	Sr.	27	81	165	49.1
6. Dave McNamara, Clark (Mass.)	Jr.	28	91	192	47.4
7. Eric Wiebers, Buena Vista	So.	27	81	171	47.4
8. Keith Letendre, Mt. St. Mary (N.Y.)	Fr.	31	83	176	47.2
9. Robby Pridgen, Roanoke	Sr.	27	77	168	45.8
10. Tim White, John Jay	So.	23	58	127	45.7
11. Jackiem Wright, Frank. & Marsh.	Jr.	30	90	199	45.2
12. Casey Stitzel, Widener	So.	25	79	175	45.1
13. Sean Manovill, Castleton St.	Jr.	26	74	165	44.8
14. Brandon Bushey, York (Pa.)	Fr.	25	65	145	44.8
15. Jason Larson, Wis.-Eau Claire	Sr.	27	70	159	44.0
16. Justin Call, Emory & Henry	Jr.	26	67	153	43.8
17. Danny Ginn, Bowdoin	Sr.	24	66	151	43.7
18. Matt Kukla, Wis.-River Falls	Jr.	26	73	169	43.2
19. Shane Manley, Thiel	Sr.	28	79	183	43.2
20. Rafael Cardoso, Salve Regina	Sr.	25	64	149	43.0
21. Keith Sudler, N.C. Wesleyan	Jr.	28	73	170	42.9
22. Jeff Loberger, Martin Luther	Sr.	23	61	143	42.7
23. Jay Reginato, Western Conn. St.	So.	29	80	188	42.6
24. Landon Lewis, Chapman	So.	25	82	193	42.5
25. Jon-David Byers, Lebanon Valley	So.	26	78	184	42.4
26. Ryan Tozer, Eastern	So.	26	85	201	42.3
27. Casey Taggatz, Wis.-La Crosse	Jr.	26	68	163	41.7
28. Kyle Burke, TCNJ	So.	24	87	209	41.6
29. Reggie Tillit, Fontbonne	Sr.	25	77	185	41.6
30. Marcus Harvey, Chapman	Sr.	23	66	159	41.5
31. Michael Stewart, Staten Island	So.	26	70	169	41.4
32. Chase Williams, Whitworth	Sr.	26	68	167	40.7
33. Michael Kuderer, Concordia (Ill.)	Sr.	26	83	204	40.7
34. Brendan Twomey, Mt. St. Mary (N.Y.)	Jr.	31	111	273	40.7
Derrick Clevenger, Hanover	Sr.	29	74	182	40.7
36. Chuck Cassidy, Cazenovia	Sr.	20	59	146	40.4
37. Scott Beebe, Gordon	Sr.	26	88	218	40.4
38. Evan Harlor, Lebanon Valley	Jr.	26	67	167	40.1
39. Mike King, Waynesburg	Jr.	19	48	120	40.0
40. Nick Griffiths, Susquehanna	Jr.	26	71	178	39.9
41. Brett Quayle, Albion	Sr.	27	76	191	39.8
42. Colin Camacho, Washington (Md.)	So.	26	66	166	39.8
43. Andrew Tsai, MIT	Jr.	25	75	189	39.7
44. Michael O'Steen, Oswego St.	Sr.	27	82	207	39.6
45. Brad Gerard, Mount Union	So.	27	87	220	39.5
46. Brian Pelkey, Keuka	Jr.	19	51	129	39.5
47. Jason Atwell, Centre	Jr.	27	79	201	39.3

Three-Point Field Goals Per Game

Rank Name, Team	Cl	G	3FG	3PG
1. Steve Nordlund, Grinnell	Jr.	25	119	4.8
2. Robert Hennigan, Emerson	Jr.	25	101	4.0
3. Jermaine Woods, Chris. Newport	Sr.	29	113	3.9
4. Jess Preifer, Wis. Lutheran	Jr.	27	102	3.8
5. Rohan Russell, Johnson & Wales	Jr.	25	92	3.7
6. Tommy Wesner, Lycoming	Sr.	26	95	3.7
7. Kyle Burke, TCNJ	So.	24	87	3.6
8. Charles Ranson, Ramapo	Jr.	30	108	3.6
9. Brendan Twomey, Mt. St. Mary (N.Y.)	Jr.	31	111	3.6
10. Geoff Wing, Rockford	Jr.	28	99	3.5
11. Scott Beebe, Gordon	Sr.	26	88	3.4
12. Derek James, MacMurray	Sr.	24	80	3.3
13. Willie Chandler, Misericordia	Sr.	28	93	3.3
14. Aaron Fries, Ohio Northern	Sr.	27	89	3.3
15. Landon Lewis, Chapman	So.	25	82	3.3
16. Ryan Tozer, Eastern	So.	26	85	3.3
17. Dave McNamara, Clark (Mass.)	Jr.	28	91	3.3
18. Brad Gerard, Mount Union	So.	27	87	3.2
19. Reggie Bowman, Knox	Jr.	23	74	3.2
20. Dennis Stanton, Ursinus	Jr.	28	90	3.2
21. Josh Burr, Oglethorpe	Fr.	19	61	3.2
22. Michael Kuderer, Concordia (Ill.)	Sr.	26	83	3.2
23. Nate Collord, Wheaton (Ill.)	Sr.	25	79	3.2
Casey Stitzel, Widener	So.	25	79	3.2
25. Reggie Tillit, Fontbonne	Sr.	25	77	3.1
26. Matt Kersten, Hiram	Sr.	26	80	3.1
27. Jimmy Evans, Nazareth	Sr.	28	86	3.1
28. Kevin Buth, St. John's (Minn.)	Sr.	27	82	3.0
Michael O'Steen, Oswego St.	Sr.	27	82	3.0
30. Jackiem Wright, Frank. & Marsh.	Jr.	30	90	3.0
Kevin Yanni, Hamilton	Sr.	28	84	3.0
Jeff Joss, Rochester	Sr.	27	81	3.0
Eric Wiebers, Buena Vista	So.	27	81	3.0
Steve Brooks, Adrian	Sr.	26	78	3.0
Jon-David Byers, Lebanon Valley	So.	26	78	3.0
Wayne Bosworth, Elmhurst	Jr.	25	75	3.0
Andrew Tsai, MIT	Jr.	25	75	3.0
38. Doug Schneider, Pitt.-Bradford	Sr.	29	86	3.0
39. Jacob Gomez, Maranatha Baptist	Jr.	28	83	3.0
40. Hasheem Alexander, Salisbury	Sr.	25	74	3.0
41. Chuck Cassidy, Cazenovia	Sr.	20	59	3.0
42. Trevor Walker, Clark (Mass.)	Jr.	28	82	2.9
43. Jason Atwell, Centre	Jr.	27	79	2.9
44. Matthew Brown, Grinnell	So.	25	73	2.9
Zach Carlson, Grinnell	Sr.	25	73	2.9
Ray Robinson, Waynesburg	Sr.	25	73	2.9
47. Justin Clifford, Muskingum	Sr.	27	78	2.9
48. Adam Gioia, Hilbert	So.	24	69	2.9
49. Marcus Harvey, Chapman	Sr.	23	66	2.9
50. Robby Pridgen, Roanoke	Sr.	27	77	2.9

2003 Division III Game Highs

Individual Highs

POINTS

Rank	Name, Team	Cl	vs. Opponent	Game Date	PTS
1.	Rich Melzer, Wis.-River Falls	Jr.	Wis.-La Crosse	1/29/03	54
2.	Chuck Cassidy, Cazenovia	Sr.	Hilbert	1/18/03	50
3.	Steve Wood, Grinnell	Jr.	Lawrence	1/25/03	48
4.	Justin Call, Emory & Henry	Jr.	Wash. & Lee	1/22/03	46
	Lucas Messer, Heidelberg		Urbana	12/18/02	46
6.	Karle Lacey, Stillman	Jr.	Concordia (Ala.)	2/18/03	45
	Chris Braier, Lawrence	Fr.	Grinnell	1/25/03	45
	Willie Chandler, Misericordia	..	Gwynedd-Mercy	1/25/03	45
	Adam Turner, Bard		Albany Pharmacy	12/03/02	45
10.	Adam Turner, Bard	Fr.	St. Joseph's (Brkln)	2/15/03	44
	Chuck Cassidy, Cazenovia	Sr.	LeTourneau	1/06/03	44
	Derek Reich, Chicago	Sr.	Southwestern (Tex.)	11/30/02	44
13.	Scott Huisman, Central (Iowa)	So.	Upper Iowa	1/28/03	43
	Cj Neely, Bates		Colby-Sawyer	1/14/03	43
15.	Jed Johnson, Maine Maritime	Sr.	Castleton St.	2/25/03	42
	Ray Robinson, Waynesburg	Sr.	Thiel	2/22/03	42
	Zareh Avedian, Cal Lutheran	Jr.	Redlands	2/19/03	42
	Mike Leimeister, Bluffton	..	Defiance	1/22/03	42
	Drew Carstens, Augustana (Ill.)	Jr.	Coe	11/27/02	42
20.	Jon-David Byers, Lebanon Valley	So.	Messiah	2/22/03	41
	Tom Carey, Suffolk	..	Emerson	2/06/03	41
22.	Tim Smallwood, Marywood	Fr.	Alvernia	2/20/03	40
	Mike Kurdziel, Defiance	..	Manchester	2/12/03	40
	Justin Call, Emory & Henry	Jr.	Bridgewater (Va.)	2/09/03	40
	Warren Walters, Hilbert	So.	Fredonia St.	1/30/03	40
	Tom Engelbrecht, Martin Luther	Jr.	Northwestern (Minn.)	1/14/03	40
	Sean Fleming, Clark (Mass.)	..	Southern Vt.	1/03/03	40
	Justin Clifford, Muskingum	Sr.	Malone	12/20/02	40
	Patrick Glover, Johnson St.	Sr.	Thomas	12/08/02	40

FIELD-GOAL PERCENTAGE
Minimum 10 made

Rank	Name, Team	Cl	vs. Opponent	Game Date	FG%	FGM	FGA
1.	Sean Scola, St. Joseph's (L.I.)	So.	Stevens Tech	2/01/03	100	10	10
	Matt Uthoff, Loras	Jr.	Dubuque	2/01/03	100	10	10
	Jared Mills, Randolph-Macon	Sr.	Roanoke	1/05/03	100	10	10
	Nicholas Smith, Wis.-Whitewater	Jr.	Coe	12/21/02	100	10	10
	Robert Jenkins, Dubuque	Sr.	Mt. Mercy	11/27/02	100	10	10
6.	Franklyn Beckford, Lake Forest	Fr.	Grinnell	2/15/03	94.4	17	18

THREE-POINT FIELD-GOAL PERCENTAGE
Minimum 7 made

Rank	Name, Team	Cl	vs. Opponent	Game Date	3FG%	3FG	3FGA
1.	Josh Richter, Simpson	Jr.	Dubuque	2/22/03	100	10	10
	Matt Uthoff, Loras	Jr.	Dubuque	2/01/03	100	8	8
3.	Matt Kukla, Wis.-River Falls	Jr.	Wis.-Platteville	1/18/03	88.9	8	9
4.	Derek Lovely, Southern Me.	So.	Eastern Conn. St.	2/22/03	87.5	7	8
	Tim Maddox, Cabrini	Sr.	Marywood	2/10/03	87.5	7	8
	Justin Call, Emory & Henry	Jr.	Wash. & Lee	1/22/03	87.5	7	8
	Julian Swartz, Carroll (Wis.)	So.	Concordia (Wis.)	1/13/03	87.5	7	8
	Mike Pamepinto, Waynesburg	Sr.	Ohio-Eastern	12/03/02	87.5	7	8
	Ian McClure, Wash. & Lee	So.	Southern Va.	12/02/02	87.5	7	8
10.	Adam Turner, Bard	Fr.	St. Joseph's (Brooklyn)	2/15/03	81.8	9	11
11.	Greg Caldwell, Whitman	Jr.	Lewis & Clark	1/24/03	80.0	8	10
12.	Jim Zinn, DeSales	Jr.	Scranton	2/15/03	77.8	7	9
	Nate Collord, Wheaton (Ill.)	Sr.	North Park	2/08/03	77.8	7	9
	Justin Call, Emory & Henry	Jr.	Averett	1/05/03	77.8	7	9
	Jason Atwell, Centre	Jr.	Ferrum	12/01/02	77.8	7	9
16.	Willie Chandler, Misericordia	Sr.	Villa Julie	2/20/03	75.0	9	12
	Robby Pridgen, Roanoke	Sr.	East. Mennonite	2/18/03	75.0	9	12
18.	Nik Rao, Stevens Tech	Sr.	Yeshiva	2/20/03	72.7	8	11
	Casey Stitzel, Widener	So.	Albright	2/18/03	72.7	8	11
20.	Ryan Hepp, Willamette	Sr.	Whitworth	3/01/03	70.0	7	10
	Daniel Tumis, Southwestern (Tex.)	Sr.	Oglethorpe	2/14/03	70.0	7	10
	Tim Smith, Randolph-Macon	Sr.	East. Mennonite	2/05/03	70.0	7	10
	Peter Warren, Va. Wesleyan	So.	Emory & Henry	2/02/03	70.0	7	10
	Derek Yvon, Springfield	Fr.	Eastern Conn. St.	1/16/03	70.0	7	10

Rank	Name, Team	Cl	vs. Opponent	Game Date	3FG%	3FG	3FGA
	Nick Griffiths, Susquehanna	Jr.	Marywood	12/02/02	70.0	7	10
26.	Matt Kersten, Hiram	Sr.	Ohio Wesleyan	2/01/03	69.2	9	13
27.	Chad Bostelman, Ohio Northern	Jr.	Baldwin-Wallace	2/15/03	66.7	8	12
	Jeff Dunn, Linfield	So.	Willamette	2/07/03	66.7	8	12
	Jason Fisher, Millikin	So.	Ind.-Northwest	1/22/03	66.7	8	12
	Billy Shivers, Redlands	Jr.	Caltech	1/18/03	66.7	8	12
	Brad Gerard, Mount Union	So.	Wilmington (Ohio)	1/11/03	66.7	8	12
	Justin Clifford, Muskingum	Sr.	Malone	12/20/02	66.7	8	12
	Aaron Fries, Ohio Northern	Sr.	Albion	11/30/02	66.7	8	12

FREE-THROW PERCENTAGE
Minimum 10 made

Rank	Name, Team	Cl	vs. Opponent	Game Date	FT%	FT	FTA
1.	Michael Reich, Colorado Col.	So.	Western St.	1/22/03	100	15	15
	Matt Moore, Hanover	So.	Anderson (Ind.)	2/22/03	100	14	14
	Andy Gilbert, Bethel (Minn.)	Sr.	St. John's (Minn.)	2/12/03	100	14	14
	Gary Payne, Wesley	Sr.	Washington (Md.)	1/30/03	100	14	14
	Mike Kurdziel, Defiance	Sr.	Manchester	1/08/03	100	14	14
	Lucas Messer, Heidelberg	Jr.	Urbana	12/18/02	100	14	14
	Mike Wilson, North Central	Fr.	Spring Arbor	12/13/02	100	14	14
	Gian Paul Gonzalez, Messiah	Fr.	Gettysburg	12/02/02	100	14	14
	Jason Levecque, Southern Me.	So.	Clark (Mass.)	1/04/03	100	13	13
	Antoine McDaniel, Carthage	Sr.	Ill. Wesleyan	2/22/03	100	12	12
	Ray Robinson, Waynesburg	Sr.	Thiel	2/22/03	100	12	12
	Rob Nenahlo, Lawrence	Sr.	Carroll (Wis.)	2/15/03	100	12	12
	Casey Taggatz, Wis.-La Crosse	Jr.	Wis.-Superior	2/08/03	100	12	12
	Jason Steege, Wartburg	Fr.	Upper Iowa	1/25/03	100	12	12
	Marty O'Hora, King's (Pa.)	Fr.	Lycoming	1/22/03	100	12	12
	Brian Fadden, Westminster (Pa.)	Fr.	Thiel	1/18/03	100	12	12
	Steve Wood, Grinnell	Jr.	St. Norbert	1/18/03	100	12	12
	Wes Cain, Rhodes		Sewanee	1/10/03	100	12	12
	Mike Majzun, Bethany (W.Va.)	Sr.	Merchant Marine	12/29/02	100	12	12
	Rashawn Allen, Emory	So.	SCAD	12/06/02	100	12	12

REBOUNDS

Rank	Name, Team	Cl	vs. Opponent	Game Date	REB
1.	Dallas Green, Stillman	Sr.	Oakwood	2/22/03	27
2.	Greg Foster, Westminster (Pa.)	..	Pitt.-Greensburg	2/03/03	24
	Anthony Fitzgerald, Villa Julie	Fr.	John Jay	1/04/03	24
4.	Jed Johnson, Maine Maritime	Sr.	Mount Ida	2/16/03	23
	Chris Braier, Lawrence	Fr.	Grinnell	1/25/03	23
	Jed Johnson, Maine Maritime	Sr.	Castleton St.	1/12/03	23
	Brian Weber, Concordia (Wis.)	Jr.	Wis. Lutheran	12/14/02	23
	John Smith, Staten Island	So.	St. Joseph's (L.I.)	12/07/02	23
	Jed Johnson, Maine Maritime	..	Unity	12/03/02	23
10.	Corrin Jackson, Elmira	Sr.	Alfred	2/14/03	22
	Darren Pugh, Lebanon Valley	..	Delaware Valley	1/11/03	22
12.	Jed Johnson, Maine Maritime	..	Lasell	3/01/03	21
	Perry Davis, Buffalo St.	Jr.	Oswego St.	2/28/03	21
	Jake Marcoux, Waynesburg	Sr.	Bethany (W.Va.)	2/25/03	21
	Jed Johnson, Maine Maritime	Sr.	Johnson St.	2/01/03	21
	Dallas Green, Stillman	Sr.	Knoxville	1/08/03	21
	Craig Coupe, Tufts	So.	Clark (Mass.)	12/07/02	21
	Matt Stackhouse, Lycoming	Jr.	Wilkes	12/04/02	21
	Anthony Fitzgerald, Villa Julie	Fr.	Gallaudet	11/26/02	21
20.	Demetrius DeJesus, Lasell	So.	Johnson St.	2/28/03	20
	Seth Hauben, Rochester	So.	Washington (Mo.)	2/23/03	20
	Jayson Douthwright, Albertus Magnus	Sr.	Johnson & Wales	2/15/03	20
	Craig Coupe, Tufts	So.	Middlebury	2/14/03	20
	James Lewis, Rust	Jr.	Oakwood	1/30/03	20
	Joel Leichtnam, Castleton St.	Jr.	Mount Ida	1/23/03	20
	Seth Hauben, Rochester	So.	Rochester Inst.	12/11/02	20
	Reggie Stovell, Tufts	So.	MIT	12/05/02	20

ASSISTS

Rank	Name, Team	Cl	vs. Opponent	Game Date	AST
1.	Beau Henderson, Waynesburg	Sr.	Lancaster Bible	2/05/03	15
	Song Cun, Occidental	Sr.	Redlands	1/15/03	15
	Hugh Morrisey, Sul Ross St.	Jr.	Howard Payne	12/14/02	15
	Jesse Farrell, Trinity (Conn.)	So.	Coast Guard	12/09/02	15

STATISTICAL LEADERS

Rank Name, Team	Cl	vs. Opponent	Game Date	AST
5. Areum Chae, Aurora	Sr.	Rockford	2/22/03	14
Michael Crotty, Williams	Jr.	Trinity (Conn.)	1/24/03	14
Tim Elwell, Maryville (Mo.)	Fr.	Principia	1/22/03	14
Trevelle Boyd, East Tex. Baptist	Sr.	Wiley	11/26/02	14
9. Michael Crotty, Williams	Jr.	Amherst	3/15/03	13
Kyle Miller, Oswego St.	Sr.	Plattsburgh St.	1/21/03	13
Labeeb Abdullah, SCAD	Sr.	Apprentice	1/18/03	13
Michael Irwin, New York U.	Sr.	Brooklyn	12/07/02	13
Nolan Larry, Wash. & Jeff.	Sr.	Medaille	12/06/02	13
Pat McCann, Stevens Tech	So.	Staten Island	11/23/02	13

BLOCKED SHOTS

Rank Name, Team	Cl	vs. Opponent	Game Date	BLKS
1. John Bunch, Lincoln (Pa.)	Fr.	Wilkes	1/20/03	14
2. Jayson Douthwright, Albertus Magnus	Sr.	Framingham St.	1/09/03	10
3. Garrett Ingram, Illinois Col.	Sr.	Lawrence	2/28/03	9
Sean Devins, Trinity (Tex.)	So.	Rose-Hulman	2/23/03	9
Charles Simmons, Aurora	Jr.	North Central	12/20/02	9
Pat Fitzsimons, Amherst	Sr.	Clark (Mass.)	12/03/02	9
7. Sean Devins, Trinity (Tex.)	So.	DePauw	2/21/03	8
Mike Machin, Drew	Sr.	Wilkes	2/08/03	8
Walter Fowler, Susquehanna	Jr.	Albright	1/18/03	8
Nate Templer, Wis.-Stout	Jr.	Wis.-Whitewater	1/18/03	8
Rockland Owens, Sul Ross St.	So.	Howard Payne	1/13/03	8
Steve Juskin, Frank. & Marsh.	Jr.	Lincoln (Pa.)	1/04/03	8
Antonio Ramos, Clarke	Sr.	Wis.-Platteville	12/30/02	8
Sean Devins, Trinity (Tex.)	So.	Lake Forest	12/29/02	8
Ryan Faulkner, Amherst	Sr.	Mass. Liberal Arts	11/26/02	8

STEALS

Rank Name, Team	Cl	vs. Opponent	Game Date	ST
1. Adam Harper, Amherst	Jr.	Worcester St.	12/10/02	11
2. Adam Harper, Amherst	Jr.	Salve Regina	1/06/03	10

Rank Name, Team	Cl	vs. Opponent	Game Date	ST
3. Jeff Mikos, Milwaukee Engr.	Fr.	Northland Bapt.	2/08/03	9
4. Andrew McCormack, Bard	Fr.	Hampshire	2/19/03	8
Kevin Herrington, Connecticut Col.	Sr.	Amherst	2/14/03	8
Ben Davey, New Paltz St.	Sr.	Vassar	2/11/03	8
Marquis Jones, Utica	Sr.	Elmira	2/08/03	8
Brian Pelkey, Keuka	Jr.	Practical Bible	1/23/03	8
Hugh Morrisey, Sul Ross St.	Jr.	Schreiner	1/16/03	8
Senator Barnes, LeTourneau	Fr.	Jarvis Christian	1/14/03	8
Nick Catanzarite, Allegheny	Sr.	Westminster (Pa.)	12/20/02	8
Tom Becker, Ripon	So.	Beloit	12/11/02	8
Scott Bierlink, Whitworth	Jr.	Alvernia	11/30/02	8
Randy Henderson, Utica/Rome	Jr.	Hamilton	11/25/02	8
Billy Johnson, Keuka	So.	St. John Fisher	11/24/02	8
Nick Leibham, Concordia (Wis.)	Fr.	Oberlin	11/22/02	8

THREE-POINT FIELD GOALS MADE

Rank Name, Team	Cl	vs. Opponent	Game Date	3FG
1. Tim Smallwood, Marywood	Fr.	Alvernia	2/20/03	12
Adam Fischer, Fontbonne	Sr.	Lincoln Chrst.	1/13/03	12
3. Ottmas Richards, Marietta	Sr.	Baldwin-Wallace	2/08/03	11
Tommy Wesner, Lycoming	Sr.	Lincoln (Pa.)	11/23/02	11
5. Josh Richter, Simpson	Jr.	Dubuque	2/22/03	10
Chuck Cassidy, Cazenovia	Sr.	Hilbert	1/18/03	10
Aaron Fries, Ohio Northern	Sr.	Wilmington (Ohio)	12/11/02	10
8. Willie Chandler, Misericordia	Sr.	Villa Julie	2/20/03	9
Robby Pridgen, Roanoke	Sr.	East. Mennonite	2/18/03	9
Reggie Bowman, Knox	Jr.	Monmouth (Ill.)	2/15/03	9
Adam Turner, Bard	Fr.	St. Joseph's (L.I.)	2/15/03	9
Matt Kersten, Hiram	Sr.	Ohio Wesleyan	2/01/03	9
Aaron Fries, Ohio Northern	Sr.	Walsh	12/30/02	9
Brendan Twomey, Mt. St. Mary (N.Y.)	Jr.	Purchase St.	11/26/02	9

2003 Division III Team Leaders

Scoring Offense

Rank Name	GM	W-L	PTS	PPG
1. Grinnell	25	19-6	3,119	124.8
2. Redlands	25	10-15	2,557	102.3
3. Sul Ross St.	25	19-6	2,194	87.8
4. Ramapo	30	26-4	2,615	87.2
5. East Tex. Baptist	26	17-9	2,266	87.2
6. Defiance	27	17-10	2,319	85.9
7. Howard Payne	25	17-8	2,141	85.6
8. Middlebury	25	15-10	2,127	85.1
9. Clark (Mass.)	28	21-7	2,374	84.8
10. Anderson (Ind.)	27	17-10	2,285	84.6
11. Cal Lutheran	25	16-9	2,108	84.3
12. Washington (Mo.)	26	24-2	2,187	84.1
13. York (Pa.)	25	13-12	2,097	83.9
14. Whittier	25	17-8	2,095	83.8
15. Emory & Henry	26	13-13	2,169	83.4
16. Linfield	25	16-9	2,084	83.4
Waynesburg	25	16-9	2,084	83.4
18. Elizabethtown	27	18-9	2,247	83.2
19. Williams	32	31-1	2,659	83.1
20. Western New Eng.	27	16-11	2,242	83.0
21. Hanover	29	27-2	2,408	83.0
22. Hope	28	23-5	2,321	82.9
23. Frank. & Marsh.	30	25-5	2,475	82.5
24. La Verne	25	16-9	2,058	82.3
25. Keene St.	30	22-8	2,468	82.3
26. Western Conn. St.	29	20-9	2,379	82.0
27. Salem St.	29	23-6	2,377	82.0
28. Ozarks (Ark.)	24	14-10	1,965	81.9
29. Allegheny	28	16-12	2,290	81.8
30. Amherst	29	24-5	2,364	81.5
31. Greenville	24	9-15	1,953	81.4
32. Lycoming	26	15-11	2,112	81.2
33. Ripon	24	15-9	1,949	81.2
34. Mt. St. Mary (N.Y.)	31	23-8	2,517	81.2
35. Johnson & Wales	26	13-13	2,108	81.1
36. Catholic	29	24-5	2,347	80.9
37. Chris. Newport	29	24-5	2,344	80.8
38. Plymouth St.	29	21-8	2,339	80.7
39. McMurry	27	18-9	2,177	80.6
40. Knox	23	9-14	1,853	80.6
41. Augustana (Ill.)	25	20-5	2,013	80.5
42. Emory	25	14-11	2,012	80.5
43. Mass.-Dartmouth	27	13-14	2,171	80.4
44. Buena Vista	31	27-4	2,491	80.4
45. Hampden-Sydney	32	28-4	2,571	80.3
46. Fontbonne	25	15-10	2,008	80.3
47. Albertus Magnus	28	18-10	2,245	80.2
48. Hamilton	29	23-6	2,325	80.2
49. Lasell	28	22-6	2,240	80.0
50. Calvin	26	16-10	2,076	79.8

Scoring Defense

Rank Name	GM	W-L	OPP PTS	OPP PPG
1. Randolph-Macon	30	28-2	1,599	53.3
2. Wis.-Stevens Point	28	24-4	1,582	56.5
3. Wm. Paterson	26	19-7	1,507	58.0
4. Penn St.-Behrend	29	20-9	1,689	58.2
5. Rochester	27	23-4	1,577	58.4
6. Trinity (Tex.)	29	21-8	1,726	59.5
7. Wis.-Oshkosh	32	25-7	1,936	60.5
8. Gust. Adolphus	33	26-7	1,997	60.5
9. Babson	30	26-4	1,817	60.6
10. Hampden-Sydney	32	28-4	1,953	61.0
11. MIT	26	16-10	1,606	61.8
12. Wooster	33	30-3	2,052	62.2
13. Carthage	25	19-6	1,556	62.2
14. Chapman	25	18-7	1,557	62.3
15. Lakeland	27	19-8	1,682	62.3

Scoring Defense (continued)

Rank Name	GM	W-L	OPP PTS	OPP PPG
16. Williams	32	31-1	1,997	62.4
17. Albion	27	22-5	1,686	62.4
18. SCAD	27	21-6	1,694	62.7
19. Wittenberg	26	20-6	1,632	62.8
20. Occidental	27	24-3	1,697	62.9
21. Willamette	26	19-7	1,637	63.0
22. Gordon	26	20-6	1,641	63.1
23. Rutgers-Newark	25	8-17	1,579	63.2
24. Capital	28	22-6	1,770	63.2
25. Cortland St.	25	5-20	1,589	63.6
26. Manhattanville	29	19-10	1,844	63.6
27. Washington (Mo.)	26	24-2	1,654	63.6
28. Cabrini	26	17-9	1,657	63.7
29. Pomona-Pitzer	25	9-16	1,595	63.8
30. Alvernia	30	21-9	1,915	63.8
31. Mississippi Col.	27	19-8	1,725	63.9
32. N.C. Wesleyan	28	18-10	1,790	63.9
33. Montclair St.	29	23-6	1,854	63.9
34. Frank. & Marsh.	30	25-5	1,923	64.1
35. Buffalo St.	28	19-9	1,798	64.2
36. St. Thomas (Minn.)	27	21-6	1,735	64.3
37. Whitworth	27	23-4	1,741	64.5
38. St. Joseph's (L.I.)	25	12-13	1,616	64.6
39. Claremont-M-S	25	15-10	1,618	64.7
40. DeSales	30	23-7	1,946	64.9
41. Clarkson	25	11-14	1,633	65.3
42. Mary Washington	29	24-5	1,899	65.5
43. Utica	25	10-15	1,643	65.7
44. Aurora	30	24-6	1,974	65.8
45. Richard Stockton	26	14-12	1,711	65.8
46. Colby-Sawyer	28	21-7	1,843	65.8
47. Potsdam St.	27	18-9	1,780	65.9
48. Edgewood	25	14-11	1,650	66.0
49. Baruch	30	25-5	1,981	66.0
50. Marietta	27	10-17	1,785	66.1

Scoring Margin

Rank Name	W-L	PTS	PPG	OPP PTS	OPP PPG	SCR MAR
1. Williams	31-1	2,659	83.1	1,997	62.4	20.7
2. Washington (Mo.)	24-2	2,187	84.1	1,654	63.6	20.5
3. Hampden-Sydney	28-4	2,571	80.3	1,953	61.0	19.3
4. Frank. & Marsh.	25-5	2,475	82.5	1,923	64.1	18.4
5. Randolph-Macon	28-2	2,129	71.0	1,599	53.3	17.7
6. Wooster	30-3	2,586	78.4	2,052	62.2	16.2
7. Hanover	27-2	2,408	83.0	1,942	67.0	16.1
8. Babson	26-4	2,295	76.5	1,817	60.6	15.9
9. Wis.-Stevens Point	24-4	2,020	72.1	1,582	56.5	15.6
10. Occidental	24-3	2,119	78.5	1,697	62.9	15.6
11. Hope	23-5	2,321	82.9	1,896	67.7	15.2
12. Amherst	24-5	2,364	81.5	1,928	66.5	15.0
13. Whitworth	23-4	2,136	79.1	1,741	64.5	14.6
14. Rochester	23-4	1,970	73.0	1,577	58.4	14.6
15. Whittier	17-8	2,095	83.8	1,745	69.8	14.0
16. Wis.-Oshkosh	25-7	2,380	74.4	1,936	60.5	13.9
17. Chris. Newport	24-5	2,344	80.8	1,943	67.0	13.8
18. Buena Vista	27-4	2,491	80.4	2,063	66.5	13.8
19. Albion	22-5	2,055	76.1	1,686	62.4	13.7
20. Catholic	24-5	2,347	80.9	1,958	67.5	13.4
21. Chapman	18-7	1,889	75.6	1,557	62.3	13.3
22. Wittenberg	20-6	1,966	75.6	1,632	62.8	12.8
23. Augustana (Ill.)	20-5	2,013	80.5	1,693	67.7	12.8
24. N.C. Wesleyan	18-10	2,145	76.6	1,790	63.9	12.7
25. Carthage	19-6	1,868	74.7	1,556	62.2	12.5
26. Clark (Mass.)	21-7	2,374	84.8	2,037	72.8	12.0
27. Ramapo	26-4	2,615	87.2	2,263	75.4	11.7
28. Sul Ross St.	19-6	2,194	87.8	1,912	76.5	11.3
29. Elizabethtown	18-9	2,247	83.2	1,943	72.0	11.3

Scoring Defense — Scoring Margin continued (middle column)

Rank Name	W-L	PTS	PPG	OPP PTS	OPP PPG	SCR MAR
30. John Carroll	22-7	2,283	78.7	1,964	67.7	11.0
Rowan	20-6	2,048	78.8	1,762	67.8	11.0
32. Mississippi Col.	19-8	2,019	74.8	1,725	63.9	10.9
33. Cal Lutheran	16-9	2,108	84.3	1,836	73.4	10.9
34. Gordon	20-6	1,923	74.0	1,641	63.1	10.8
35. St. Joseph's (Me.)	20-5	1,978	79.1	1,708	68.3	10.8
36. Gust. Adolphus	26-7	2,329	70.6	1,997	60.5	10.1
37. Hamilton	23-6	2,325	80.2	2,044	70.5	9.7
38. Baruch	25-5	2,270	75.7	1,981	66.0	9.6
39. Montclair St.	23-6	2,132	73.5	1,854	63.9	9.6
40. Lasell	22-6	2,240	80.0	1,972	70.4	9.6
41. Aurora	24-6	2,250	75.0	1,974	65.8	9.2
42. Ill. Wesleyan	22-6	2,165	77.3	1,908	68.1	9.2
43. Claremont-M-S	15-10	1,847	73.9	1,618	64.7	9.2
44. Keene St.	22-8	2,468	82.3	2,198	73.3	9.0
45. Rockford	24-4	2,144	76.6	1,893	67.6	9.0
46. Capital	22-6	2,019	72.1	1,770	63.2	8.9
47. Nazareth	22-6	2,201	78.6	1,954	69.8	8.8
Colby-Sawyer	21-7	2,090	74.6	1,843	65.8	8.8
49. Lawrence	18-6	1,902	79.3	1,692	70.5	8.8
50. Salem St.	23-6	2,377	82.0	2,128	73.4	8.6

Field-Goal Percentage

Rank Name	GM	W-L	FGM	FGA	FG%
1. Wis.-Oshkosh	32	25-7	849	1,600	53.1
2. Occidental	27	24-3	815	1,575	51.7
3. Cal Lutheran	25	16-9	753	1,465	51.4
4. Babson	30	26-4	847	1,664	50.9
5. Wooster	33	30-3	899	1,769	50.8
6. Grove City	27	18-9	751	1,491	50.4
7. Howard Payne	25	17-8	789	1,567	50.4
8. Carthage	25	19-6	684	1,361	50.3
9. Gust. Adolphus	33	26-7	867	1,730	50.1
10. Ill. Wesleyan	28	22-6	767	1,540	49.8
11. Hanover	29	27-2	878	1,772	49.5
12. Frank. & Marsh.	30	25-5	908	1,838	49.4
13. Buena Vista	31	27-4	897	1,816	49.4
14. Wis.-Stevens Point	28	24-4	711	1,446	49.2
15. St. Lawrence	27	17-10	780	1,587	49.1
16. Otterbein	26	15-11	703	1,432	49.1
17. Wis.-Whitewater	28	21-7	747	1,526	49.0
18. Whitworth	27	23-4	758	1,549	48.9
19. Hope	28	23-5	834	1,711	48.7
20. Elizabethtown	27	18-9	823	1,690	48.7
21. Baldwin-Wallace	26	13-13	710	1,463	48.5
22. Wis.-River Falls	26	16-10	697	1,439	48.4
23. Hampden-Sydney	32	28-4	971	2,005	48.4
24. Nazareth	28	22-6	831	1,716	48.4
25. Ursinus	28	21-7	767	1,584	48.4
26. Wittenberg	26	20-6	719	1,490	48.3
27. Randolph-Macon	30	28-2	789	1,641	48.1
28. Wartburg	28	21-7	697	1,450	48.1
29. Bluffton	26	10-16	685	1,426	48.0
30. Whittier	25	17-8	771	1,606	48.0
31. York (Pa.)	25	13-12	804	1,675	48.0
32. Lycoming	26	15-11	738	1,538	48.0
33. Illinois Col.	26	15-11	771	1,611	47.9
34. Trinity (Conn.)	24	15-9	710	1,485	47.8
35. Willamette	26	19-7	673	1,410	47.7
36. Wheaton (Ill.)	25	18-7	637	1,336	47.7
37. Rochester	27	23-4	739	1,550	47.7
38. Augustana (Ill.)	25	20-5	704	1,477	47.7
39. Amherst	29	24-5	867	1,823	47.6
40. Geneseo St.	25	12-13	585	1,231	47.5
41. Clark (Mass.)	28	21-7	843	1,776	47.5
42. Lake Forest	23	8-15	585	1,233	47.4
43. Union (N.Y.)	29	17-12	762	1,607	47.4
44. Denison	26	9-17	628	1,325	47.4
45. Millsaps	26	15-11	735	1,551	47.4
46. Rowan	26	20-6	750	1,587	47.3
47. Richard Stockton	26	14-12	696	1,473	47.3
48. Sul Ross St.	25	19-6	797	1,687	47.2
49. Scranton	30	24-6	769	1,628	47.2
50. DeSales	30	23-7	816	1,730	47.2

Field-Goal Percentage Defense

Rank Name	GM	W-L	OPP FG	OPP FGA	OPP FG%
1. Trinity (Tex.)	29	21-8	589	1,587	37.1
2. Randolph-Macon	30	28-2	564	1,500	37.6
3. Baruch	30	25-5	713	1,895	37.6
4. Centenary (N.J.)	24	9-15	597	1,586	37.6
5. Chris. Newport	29	24-5	693	1,832	37.8
6. Wis.-Stevens Point	28	24-4	548	1,448	37.8
7. SCAD	27	21-6	558	1,468	38.0
8. Washington (Mo.)	26	24-2	608	1,599	38.0
9. Mississippi Col.	27	19-8	601	1,567	38.4
10. Lebanon Valley	26	13-13	613	1,590	38.6
11. Maine Maritime	25	15-10	645	1,668	38.7
12. Wm. Paterson	26	19-7	476	1,230	38.7
13. Gordon	26	20-6	579	1,493	38.8
14. Rowan	26	20-6	612	1,574	38.9
15. Pomona-Pitzer	25	9-16	536	1,378	38.9
16. Occidental	27	24-3	622	1,592	39.1
17. Williams	32	31-1	700	1,791	39.1
18. MIT	26	16-10	559	1,430	39.1
19. Worcester St.	28	17-11	686	1,750	39.2
20. Claremont-M-S	25	15-10	554	1,411	39.3
21. Frank. & Marsh.	30	25-5	679	1,727	39.3
22. Catholic	29	24-5	706	1,790	39.4
23. Aurora	30	24-6	718	1,813	39.6
24. Colby-Sawyer	28	21-7	651	1,643	39.6
25. Montclair St.	29	23-6	691	1,743	39.6
26. St. Joseph's (L.I.)	25	12-13	572	1,440	39.7
27. Clarke	27	14-13	663	1,668	39.7
28. St. John Fisher	26	21-5	616	1,542	39.9
29. Wittenberg	26	20-6	563	1,408	40.0
30. Bard	21	8-13	532	1,328	40.1
31. Kalamazoo	24	18-6	569	1,416	40.2
32. Manhattanville	29	19-10	689	1,711	40.3
33. Elmira	25	12-13	613	1,522	40.3
34. St. Thomas (Minn.)	27	21-6	628	1,559	40.3
35. Lehman	28	15-13	698	1,732	40.3
36. Rutgers-Newark	25	8-17	558	1,383	40.3
37. Wabash	26	16-10	637	1,578	40.4
38. Wooster	33	30-3	720	1,783	40.4
39. Eastern	26	12-14	602	1,487	40.5
40. St. Joseph's (Me.)	25	20-5	628	1,551	40.5
41. Richard Stockton	26	14-12	611	1,509	40.5
42. Buena Vista	31	27-4	727	1,794	40.5
43. Augustana (Ill.)	25	20-5	580	1,431	40.5
44. Lakeland	27	19-8	574	1,416	40.5
45. Lincoln (Pa.)	24	9-15	623	1,536	40.6
46. Buffalo St.	28	19-9	652	1,605	40.6
47. Hampden-Sydney	32	28-4	719	1,765	40.7
48. Me.-Farmington	25	12-13	677	1,655	40.9
49. Kean	24	11-13	548	1,338	41.0
50. Rochester	27	23-4	582	1,418	41.0

Free-Throw Percentage

Rank Name	GM	W-L	FT	FTA	FT%
1. Wooster	33	30-3	543	685	79.3
2. Wis.-Oshkosh	32	25-7	453	572	79.2
3. Wartburg	28	21-7	501	645	77.7
4. Moravian	27	16-11	472	608	77.6
5. Blackburn	25	15-10	405	522	77.6
6. Wis.-Stevens Point	28	24-4	410	529	77.5
7. Wheaton (Ill.)	25	18-7	458	594	77.1
8. St. Norbert	23	12-11	338	439	77.0
9. Eureka	25	8-17	350	460	76.1
10. Knox	23	9-14	372	489	76.1
11. Colorado Col.	24	11-13	396	522	75.9
12. Connecticut Col.	23	7-16	247	327	75.5
13. Franklin	26	9-17	435	576	75.5
14. Wis.-Platteville	26	11-15	347	460	75.4
15. Albion	27	22-5	349	463	75.4
16. Kalamazoo	24	18-6	408	542	75.3
17. Ohio Northern	27	14-13	302	405	74.6
18. Otterbein	26	15-11	424	570	74.4
19. Webster	25	12-13	345	464	74.4
20. Oglethorpe	25	9-16	455	612	74.3
21. Baldwin-Wallace	26	13-13	361	486	74.3
22. Ripon	24	15-9	409	551	74.2

Rank Name	GM	W-L	FT	FTA	FT%
23. Emory	25	14-11	380	512	74.2
24. Catholic	29	24-5	514	693	74.2
25. Rhodes	25	10-15	402	542	74.2
26. Ohio Wesleyan	26	12-14	396	534	74.2
27. Ill. Wesleyan	28	22-6	421	568	74.1
28. Cal Lutheran	25	16-9	460	621	74.1
29. Carnegie Mellon	25	12-13	417	563	74.1
30. Adrian	26	12-14	331	447	74.0
31. Monmouth (Ill.)	23	5-18	265	358	74.0
32. Western New Eng.	27	16-11	472	638	74.0
33. Calvin	26	16-10	420	568	73.9
34. Juniata	25	13-12	384	520	73.8
35. Gettysburg	26	13-13	364	493	73.8
36. Rockford	28	24-4	403	546	73.8
37. MacMurray	24	9-15	388	526	73.8
38. Kenyon	25	3-22	345	469	73.6
39. Lakeland	27	19-8	410	558	73.5
40. Martin Luther	23	13-10	353	481	73.4
41. Defiance	27	17-10	490	668	73.4
42. Clark (Mass.)	28	21-7	410	559	73.3
43. Wis.-Stout	25	14-11	403	550	73.3
44. Grove City	27	18-9	402	549	73.2
45. Cornell College	27	16-11	432	591	73.1
46. Wash. & Jeff.	25	6-19	407	557	73.1
47. Coe	26	9-17	352	482	73.0
48. Thomas More	25	7-18	404	554	72.9
49. Hope	28	23-5	457	627	72.9
50. Trinity (Tex.)	29	21-8	352	483	72.9

Three-Point Field-Goal Percentage

Minimum 5.0 made per game

Rank Name	GM	W-L	3FG	3FGA	3FG%
1. Wis.-Oshkosh	32	25-7	229	532	43.0
2. Endicott	29	19-10	222	531	41.8
3. Rockford	28	24-4	259	622	41.6
4. Hope	28	23-5	196	473	41.4
5. Gordon	26	20-6	263	638	41.2
6. Frank. & Marsh.	30	25-5	201	488	41.2
7. Elmhurst	25	11-14	169	411	41.1
8. DeSales	30	23-7	240	587	40.9
9. Baldwin-Wallace	26	13-13	149	366	40.7
10. Rochester	27	23-4	153	377	40.6
11. Scranton	30	24-6	228	562	40.6
12. Widener	25	11-14	174	429	40.6
13. Clark (Mass.)	28	21-7	278	687	40.5
14. Babson	30	26-4	186	462	40.3
15. Wooster	33	30-3	245	610	40.2
16. Allegheny	28	16-12	236	592	39.9
17. Lebanon Valley	26	13-13	192	485	39.6
18. Gust. Adolphus	33	26-7	205	518	39.6
19. Ill. Wesleyan	28	22-6	210	531	39.5
20. Williams	32	31-1	293	741	39.5
21. Hamline	25	12-13	165	418	39.5
22. Westfield St.	26	15-11	172	437	39.4
23. Wesleyan (Conn.)	24	14-10	149	379	39.3
24. Carthage	25	19-6	145	369	39.3
25. Simpson	26	14-12	165	420	39.3
26. Whittier	25	17-8	202	516	39.1
27. Mt. St. Mary (N.Y.)	31	23-8	227	581	39.1
28. Martin Luther	23	13-10	203	520	39.0
29. Webster	25	12-13	188	483	38.9
Wis.-Stevens Point	28	24-4	188	483	38.9
31. La Verne	25	16-9	220	566	38.9
32. Wis.-Eau Claire	27	17-10	190	489	38.9
33. Chapman	25	18-7	202	521	38.8
34. Wheaton (Ill.)	25	18-7	164	423	38.8
35. Hanover	29	27-2	217	560	38.8
36. Lasell	28	22-6	153	395	38.7
37. Wis.-River Falls	26	16-10	153	396	38.6
38. Bates	25	16-9	184	478	38.5
39. Wartburg	28	21-7	198	515	38.4
40. Carroll (Wis.)	23	7-16	181	471	38.4
41. York (Pa.)	25	13-12	149	388	38.4
42. Potsdam St.	27	18-9	186	486	38.3
43. Geneseo St.	25	12-13	153	400	38.3
44. Rowan	26	20-6	165	433	38.1
45. Wittenberg	26	20-6	176	462	38.1
46. Franklin	26	9-17	140	368	38.0
47. Mount Union	27	18-9	141	371	38.0
48. Eastern	26	12-14	172	453	38.0
49. Albion	27	22-5	220	580	37.9
50. Maranatha Baptist	28	12-16	229	604	37.9

Three-Point Field Goals Per Game

Rank Name	GM	W-L	3FG	3FG%
1. Grinnell	25	19-6	522	20.9
2. Redlands	25	10-15	337	13.5
3. Connecticut Col.	23	7-16	259	11.3
4. Southern Me.	25	4-21	261	10.4
5. Knox	23	9-14	237	10.3
6. New England	26	9-17	267	10.3
7. Gordon	26	20-6	263	10.1
8. Johnson & Wales	26	13-13	262	10.1
9. Clark (Mass.)	28	21-7	278	9.9
10. LeTourneau	25	9-16	243	9.7
11. Fontbonne	25	15-10	237	9.5
12. Emory & Henry	26	13-13	244	9.4
13. Juniata	25	13-12	233	9.3
14. Rockford	28	24-4	259	9.3
15. Ramapo	30	26-4	277	9.2
16. Williams	32	31-1	293	9.2
17. Wis. Lutheran	27	9-18	247	9.1
18. Muskingum	27	11-16	245	9.1
19. Oglethorpe	25	9-16	225	9.0
20. TCNJ	25	13-12	224	9.0
21. Marywood	25	7-18	222	8.9
22. Martin Luther	23	13-10	203	8.8
23. La Verne	25	16-9	220	8.8
24. Washington (Md.)	26	10-16	224	8.6
25. Middlebury	25	15-10	213	8.5
26. Allegheny	28	16-12	236	8.4
27. Chris. Newport	29	24-5	244	8.4
28. Puget Sound	25	12-13	208	8.3
29. Anderson (Ind.)	27	17-10	221	8.2
30. Maranatha Baptist	28	12-16	229	8.2
31. Albion	27	22-5	220	8.1
32. Chapman	25	18-7	202	8.1
Rhodes	25	10-15	202	8.1
Whittier	25	17-8	202	8.1
35. Old Westbury	28	16-12	226	8.1
36. Waynesburg	25	16-9	201	8.0
37. Concordia (Ill.)	26	5-21	209	8.0
38. DeSales	30	23-7	240	8.0
39. Kenyon	25	3-22	198	7.9
40. Colorado Col.	24	11-13	190	7.9
41. Guilford	26	12-14	205	7.9
Cazenovia	26	11-15	205	7.9
43. Carroll (Wis.)	23	7-16	181	7.9
44. Bethel (Minn.)	27	15-12	212	7.9
45. Union (N.Y.)	29	17-12	227	7.8
46. Skidmore	24	12-12	187	7.8
47. Adrian	26	12-14	202	7.8
Coe	26	9-17	202	7.8
49. Emory	25	14-11	192	7.7
50. Endicott	29	19-10	222	7.7

Rebound Margin

Rank Name	W-L	REB	RPG	OPP REB	OPP RPG	REB MAR
1. Williams	31-1	1,397	43.7	994	31.1	12.6
2. Buena Vista	27-4	1,269	40.9	921	29.7	11.2
3. Rochester	23-4	1,016	37.6	727	26.9	10.7
4. St. Joseph's (Me.)	20-5	1,111	44.4	861	34.4	10.0
5. Wooster	30-3	1,210	36.7	913	27.7	9.0
6. DePauw	18-8	1,042	40.1	810	31.2	8.9
7. Wittenberg	20-6	1,004	38.6	781	30.0	8.6
8. Mississippi Col.	19-8	1,135	42.0	905	33.5	8.5
Grove City	18-9	1,018	37.7	788	29.2	8.5
10. Chapman	18-7	969	38.8	758	30.3	8.4
11. Hampden-Sydney	28-4	1,285	40.2	1,016	31.8	8.4
12. Wm. Paterson	19-7	964	37.1	747	28.7	8.3

Rank Name	W-L	REB	RPG	OPP REB	OPP RPG	REB MAR
13. Lawrence	18-6	990	41.3	791	33.0	8.3
14. Rowan	20-6	1,111	42.7	898	34.5	8.2
15. Frank. & Marsh.	25-5	1,223	40.8	982	32.7	8.0
16. Ursinus	21-7	1,160	41.4	940	33.6	7.9
17. King's (Pa.)	16-10	1,055	40.6	856	32.9	7.7
18. Merchant Marine	21-9	1,249	41.6	1,021	34.0	7.6
19. Lasell	22-6	1,083	38.7	872	31.1	7.5
20. CCNY	17-12	1,221	42.1	1,008	34.8	7.3
21. Hartwick	10-15	991	39.6	808	32.3	7.3
22. Claremont-M-S	15-10	979	39.2	800	32.0	7.2
23. Maine Maritime	15-10	1,104	44.2	927	37.1	7.1
24. Catholic	24-5	1,191	41.1	987	34.0	7.0
25. Dallas	18-7	1,058	42.3	886	35.4	6.9
26. Lycoming	15-11	1,076	41.4	908	34.9	6.5
27. Calvin	16-10	1,002	38.5	837	32.2	6.3
28. Hamilton	23-6	1,210	41.7	1,028	35.4	6.3
29. Capital	22-6	1,027	36.7	858	30.6	6.0
30. East Tex. Baptist	17-9	1,176	45.2	1,020	39.2	6.0
Hope	23-5	1,118	39.9	950	33.9	6.0
Tufts	12-13	1,089	43.6	939	37.6	6.0
33. Buffalo St.	19-9	1,170	41.8	1,006	35.9	5.9
34. Cornell College	16-11	1,008	37.3	853	31.6	5.7
35. Albion	22-5	966	35.8	817	30.3	5.5
36. Plymouth St.	21-8	1,214	41.9	1,054	36.3	5.5
37. Kalamazoo	18-6	935	39.0	806	33.6	5.4
38. Augustana (Ill.)	2 20-5	984	39.4	850	34.0	5.4
39. Wis.-Stevens Point	24-4	951	34.0	803	28.7	5.3
40. Simpson	14-12	1,038	39.9	901	34.7	5.3
41. Clarke	14-13	1,046	38.7	913	33.8	4.9
42. Gwynedd-Mercy	13-13	1,100	42.3	976	37.5	4.8
Cabrini	17-9	1,068	41.1	944	36.3	4.8
Lebanon Valley	13-13	1,022	39.3	898	34.5	4.8
45. Potsdam St.	18-9	965	35.7	839	31.1	4.7
46. Hanover	27-2	1,101	38.0	966	33.3	4.7
47. Denison	9-17	860	33.1	740	28.5	4.6
48. Linfield	16-9	1,030	41.2	916	36.6	4.6
49. Wis.-Eau Claire	17-10	912	33.8	789	29.2	4.6
50. Geneseo St.	12-13	871	34.8	759	30.4	4.5

Won-Lost Percentage

Rank Name	W	L	Pct
1. Williams	31	1	96.9
2. Randolph-Macon	28	2	93.3
3. Hanover	27	2	93.1
4. Washington (Mo.)	24	2	92.3
5. Wooster	30	3	90.9
6. Occidental	24	3	88.9
7. Hampden-Sydney	28	4	87.5
8. Buena Vista	27	4	87.1
9. Babson	26	4	86.7
Ramapo	26	4	86.7
11. Rockford	24	4	85.7
Wis.-Stevens Point	24	4	85.7
13. Rochester	23	4	85.2
Whitworth	23	4	85.2
15. Baruch	25	5	83.3
Frank. & Marsh.	25	5	83.3
17. Amherst	24	5	82.8
Mary Washington	24	5	82.8
Chris. Newport	24	5	82.8
Catholic	24	5	82.8
21. Hope	23	5	82.1
22. Albion	22	5	81.5
23. St. John Fisher	21	5	80.8
24. Aurora	24	6	80.0
Southern Vt.	24	6	80.0
Scranton	24	6	80.0
Augustana (Ill.)	20	5	80.0
St. Joseph's (Me.)	20	5	80.0
29. Hamilton	23	6	79.3

Rank	Name	W	L	Pct	Rank	Name	W	L	Pct	Rank	Name	W	L	Pct
	Montclair St.	23	6	79.3		SCAD	21	6	77.8		Pitt.-Bradford	22	7	75.9
	Salem St.	23	6	79.3	40.	Rowan	20	6	76.9	49.	Clark (Mass.)	21	7	75.0
32.	Gust. Adolphus	26	7	78.8		Gordon	20	6	76.9		Ursinus	21	7	75.0
33.	Capital	22	6	78.6		Wittenberg	20	6	76.9		Wis.-Whitewater	21	7	75.0
	Nazareth	22	6	78.6	43.	DeSales	23	7	76.7		Colby-Sawyer	21	7	75.0
	Ill. Wesleyan	22	6	78.6	44.	Carthage	19	6	76.0		Wartburg	21	7	75.0
	Lasell	22	6	78.6		Grinnell	19	6	76.0		Kalamazoo	21	7	75.0
37.	Wis.-Oshkosh	25	7	78.1		Sul Ross St.	19	6	76.0		Lawrence	21	7	75.0
38.	St. Thomas (Minn.)	21	6	77.8	47.	John Carroll	22	7	75.9					

Team Highs

POINTS

Rank	Name	vs. Opponent	Game Date	PTS	OPP PTS
1.	Grinnell	Martin Luther	11/23/2002	160	131
2.	Grinnell	William Penn	12/09/2002	153	117
3.	Grinnell	Lawrence	1/25/2003	150	149
4.	Lawrence	Grinnell	1/25/2003	149	150
5.	Grinnell	Mt. Mercy	12/14/2002	148	136
6.	Grinnell	Augsburg	11/29/2002	144	114
7.	Grinnell	Carroll (Wis.)	2/01/2003	143	128
8.	Grinnell	Ripon	2/08/2003	139	125
9.	Whittier	Redlands	2/01/2003	138	124
10.	Ripon	Grinnell	1/17/2003	137	130
11.	Redlands	Caltech	2/12/2003	136	68
12.	Mt. St. Mary (N.Y.)	Purchase St.	11/26/2002	134	73
13.	Redlands	La Sierra	12/12/2002	133	107
14.	Cal Lutheran	California Christian	1/11/2003	132	78
15.	Cazenovia	Hilbert	1/18/2003	131	88
	Martin Luther	Grinnell	11/23/2002	131	160
17.	Grinnell	Monmouth (Ill.)	2/04/2003	129	118
18.	Carroll (Wis.)	Grinnell	2/01/2003	128	143
19.	Ripon	Grinnell	2/08/2003	125	139
	Redlands	Maine-Fort Kent	1/09/2003	125	102
21.	Redlands	Whittier	2/01/2003	124	138
	Wesley	Washington (Md.)	1/30/2003	124	125
23.	Linfield	George Fox	1/21/2003	123	91
	Redlands	Caltech	1/18/2003	123	73
	Occidental	Redlands	1/15/2003	123	95
	Emory & Henry	Warren Wilson	11/26/2002	123	58
27.	Grinnell	Grand View	1/04/2003	122	120
	Redlands	Northland	1/03/2003	122	77
29.	Beloit	Grinnell	1/31/2003	120	108
	Fredonia St.	Hilbert	1/30/2003	120	92
	Whitworth	Redlands	12/06/2002	120	86
	East Tex. Baptist	Wiley	11/26/2002	120	64

FIELD-GOAL PERCENTAGE

Rank	Name	vs. Opponent	Game Date	FG%	FGM	FGA
1.	Albertus Magnus	Suffolk	2/20/2003	76.5	39	51
2.	Monmouth (Ill.)	Grinnell	2/04/2003	73.2	52	71
3.	Monmouth (Ill.)	Concordia (Ill.)	11/30/2002	73.1	38	52
4.	Benedictine (Ill.)	Wis. Lutheran	1/22/2002	72.5	50	69
5.	Lycoming	Shenandoah	1/07/2003	72.1	31	43
6.	St. Norbert	Grinnell	1/18/2003	71.4	40	56
7.	Mount Union	Ohio Northern	2/01/2003	70.8	34	48
8.	Penn St.-Behrend	Thiel	3/05/2003	70.2	33	47
9.	Rochester	Alfred	1/22/2002	69.1	38	55
10.	Carthage	Wis. Lutheran	12/07/2002	68.2	30	44
11.	Geneseo St.	Brockport St.	2/04/2003	67.6	23	34

THREE-POINT FIELD GOALS MADE

Rank	Name	vs. Opponent	Game Date	3FG
1.	Grinnell	Carroll (Wis.)	2/01/2003	31
	Grinnell	Augsburg	11/29/2002	31
3.	Grinnell	Ripon	1/17/2003	28
4.	Grinnell	Northwestern (Iowa)	11/30/2002	27
	Grinnell	Martin Luther	11/23/2002	27
6.	Grinnell	Ripon	2/08/2003	24
	Grinnell	Monmouth (Ill.)	2/04/2003	24
8.	Grinnell	St. Norbert	1/18/2003	22
	Redlands	Northland	1/03/2003	22
	Redlands	La Sierra	12/12/2002	22
11.	Redlands	Maine-Fort Kent	1/09/2003	21
12.	Southern Me.	St. Joseph's (Me.)	11/22/2003	20
	Southern Me.	Eastern Conn. St.	2/22/2003	20
	Grinnell	Lawrence	1/25/2003	20
	Oglethorpe	Warren Wilson	1/22/2003	20
	New England	Me.-Farmington	12/09/2002	20
17.	Grinnell	Beloit	1/31/2003	19
	Redlands	Caltech	1/18/2003	19
	Wis. Lutheran	Trinity Int'l	11/30/2002	19
20.	Grinnell	Ripon	2/28/2003	18
	Oglethorpe	Sewanee	2/23/2003	18
	Connecticut Col.	Mass.-Dartmouth	1/30/2003	18
	Fontbonne	Lincoln Chrst.	1/13/2003	18
	Grinnell	Grand View	1/04/2003	18
	Muskingum	Malone	12/20/2002	18
	Redlands	Swarthmore	11/22/2002	18
	Wittenberg	Alma	11/22/2002	18
28.	Simpson	Dubuque	2/22/2003	17
	Redlands	Claremont-M-S	2/15/2003	17
	Williams	Wesleyan (Conn.)	2/08/2003	17
	Marietta	Baldwin-Wallace	2/08/2003	17
	Chapman	Southwestern Aly God	1/24/2003	17
	Connecticut Col.	Coast Guard	1/20/2003	17
	Cazenovia	Hilbert	1/18/2003	17
	Connecticut Col.	Bates	1/18/2003	17
	Middlebury	Mass. Liberal Arts	1/16/2003	17
	Clark (Mass.)	Southern Me.	1/04/2003	17
	Ill. Wesleyan	Olivet Nazarene	12/14/2002	17
	John Carroll	Muskingum	12/11/2002	17
	Juniata	Messiah	12/04/2002	17

THREE-POINT FIELD-GOAL PERCENTAGE
Minimum 10 made

Rank	Name	vs. Opponent	Game Date	3FG%	3FG	3FGA
1.	Simpson	Dubuque	2/22/03	89.5	17	19
2.	Penn St.-Behrend	Thiel	3/05/03	81.3	13	16
3.	Bates	Connecticut Col.	1/18/03	76.9	10	13
	Plymouth St.	Me.-Farmington	11/23/02	76.9	10	13
5.	Bluffton	Transylvania	1/18/03	75.0	12	16
6.	Carroll (Wis.)	Concordia (Wis.)	1/13/03	71.4	15	21
	Va. Wesleyan	Randolph-Macon	1/18/03	71.4	10	14
8.	Randolph-Macon	Alfred	12/29/03	70.6	12	17
9.	Illinois Col.	Lake Forest	1/08/03	70.0	14	20
10.	Puget Sound	Pacific (Ore.)	2/15/03	68.8	11	16
	Wis.-Eau Claire	St. Scholastica	12/21/02	68.8	11	16
12.	DePauw	Rhodes	1/03/03	68.4	13	19
13.	Albertus Magnus	Suffolk	2/20/03	66.7	14	21
	Sewanee	Rhodes	2/14/03	66.7	10	15
	Wis.-Stout	Wis.-Superior	2/05/03	66.7	10	15
	Mount Union	Westminster (Pa.)	12/04/02	66.7	10	15

FREE-THROW PERCENTAGE
Minimum 15 made

Rank	Name	vs. Opponent	Game Date	FT%	FT	FTA
1.	Edgewood	Maranatha Baptist	2/20/2003	100.0	20	20
	Lake Erie	Penn St.-Altoona	2/15/2003	100.0	16	16
	Wis.-Stout	Wis.-La Crosse	2/12/2003	100.0	16	16

STATISTICAL LEADERS

Rank	Name	vs. Opponent	Game Date	FT%	FT	FTA	Rank	Name	vs. Opponent	Game Date	FT%	FT	FTA
	Occidental	Whittier	2/15/2003	100.0	15	15		George Fox	Dominican (Ill.)	12/07/2002	94.7	18	19
	Whitworth	Willamette	2/15/2003	100.0	15	15		Benedictine (Ill.)	Eureka	1/11/2002	94.7	18	19
	Wis.-River Falls	Marian (Wis.)	1/11/2003	100.0	15	15	21.	Wheaton (Mass.)	WPI	2/15/2003	94.4	17	18
	Wis.-Stevens Point	Viterbo	12/21/2002	100.0	15	15		Puget Sound	Willamette	1/31/2003	94.4	17	18
8.	Ill. Wesleyan	North Park	2/18/2003	97.2	35	36		Simpson	Luther	1/14/2003	94.4	17	18
9.	Lake Erie	Heidelberg	1/04/2003	96.2	25	26		Bowdoin	Southern Me.	12/02/2002	94.4	17	18
10.	Wash. & Jeff.	Thiel	1/22/2003	95.5	21	22		Aurora	St. Norbert	11/30/2002	94.4	17	18
	Wheaton (Ill.)	Gallaudet	1/07/2003	95.5	21	22	26.	Wilmington (Ohio)	Otterbein	2/20/2003	94.1	16	17
12.	Edgewood	SCAD	1/05/2003	95.2	20	21		Moravian	Messiah	2/08/2003	94.1	16	17
13.	Oneonta St.	Geneseo St.	2/01/2003	95.0	19	20		Wis.-Platteville	Wis.-Whitewater	1/29/2003	94.1	16	17
	Carnegie Mellon	Grove City	11/23/2002	95.0	19	20		Bowdoin	Wesleyan (Conn.)	1/25/2003	94.1	16	17
15.	Mount Union	Marietta	2/20/2003	94.7	18	19		St. Norbert	Lawrence	1/14/2003	94.1	16	17
	Geneseo St.	Plattsburgh St.	2/14/2003	94.7	18	19		Ripon	Lawrence	1/11/2003	94.1	16	17
	King's (Pa.)	Lycoming	1/22/2003	94.7	18	19		Southern Me.	Williams	1/03/2003	94.1	16	17
	Carleton	St. Mary's (Minn.)	1/06/2003	94.7	18	19							

Conferences

2003 Division I Conference Standings

AMERICA EAST CONFERENCE

Team	Conference W	L	Pct.	Full Season W	L	Pct.
Boston U.	13	3	.813	20	11	.645
Vermont #	11	5	.688	21	12	.636
Hartford	10	6	.625	16	13	.552
Binghamton	9	7	.563	14	13	.519
Maine	8	8	.500	14	16	.467
Northeastern	8	8	.500	16	15	.516
Stony Brook	7	9	.438	13	15	.464
Albany (N.Y.)	3	13	.188	7	21	.250
New Hampshire	3	13	.188	5	23	.179

ATLANTIC COAST CONFERENCE

Team	Conference W	L	Pct.	Full Season W	L	Pct.
Wake Forest	13	3	.813	25	6	.806
Maryland	11	5	.688	21	10	.677
Duke #	11	5	.688	26	7	.788
North Carolina St.	9	7	.563	18	13	.581
Georgia Tech	7	9	.438	16	15	.516
Virginia	6	10	.375	16	16	.500
North Carolina	6	10	.375	19	16	.543
Clemson	5	11	.313	15	13	.536
Florida St.	4	12	.250	14	15	.483

ATLANTIC SUN CONFERENCE

North Division	Conference W	L	Pct.	Full Season W	L	Pct.
Belmont	12	4	.750	17	12	.586
Jacksonville St.	10	6	.625	20	10	.667
Samford	9	7	.563	13	15	.464
Georgia St.	8	8	.500	14	15	.483
Gardner-Webb	2	14	.125	5	24	.172
Campbell	1	15	.063	5	22	.185

South Division	Conference W	L	Pct.	Full Season W	L	Pct.
Mercer	14	2	.875	23	6	.793
Troy St. #	14	2	.875	26	6	.813
UCF	11	5	.688	21	11	.656
Jacksonville	8	8	.500	13	16	.448
Stetson	4	12	.250	6	20	.231
Fla. Atlantic	3	13	.188	7	21	.250

ATLANTIC 10 CONFERENCE

East Division	Conference W	L	Pct.	Full Season W	L	Pct.
St. Joseph's	12	4	.750	23	7	.767
Temple	10	6	.625	18	16	.529
Rhode Island	10	6	.625	19	12	.613
Massachusetts	6	10	.375	11	18	.379
Fordham	3	13	.188	2	26	.071
*St. Bonaventure	1	15	.063	13	14	.481

* forfeited six conference games

West Division	Conference W	L	Pct.	Full Season W	L	Pct.
Xavier	15	1	.938	26	6	.813
Dayton #	14	2	.875	24	6	.800
Richmond	10	6	.625	15	14	.517
La Salle	6	10	.375	12	17	.414
George Washington	5	11	.313	12	17	.414
Duquesne	4	12	.250	9	21	.300

BIG EAST CONFERENCE

East Division	Conference W	L	Pct.	Full Season W	L	Pct.
Boston College	10	6	.625	19	12	.613
Connecticut	10	6	.625	23	10	.697
Providence	8	8	.500	18	14	.563
Villanova	8	8	.500	15	16	.484
St. John's (N.Y.)	7	9	.438	21	13	.618
Miami (Fla.)	4	12	.250	11	17	.393
Virginia Tech	4	12	.250	11	18	.379

West Division	Conference W	L	Pct.	Full Season W	L	Pct.
Syracuse	13	3	.813	30	5	.857
Pittsburgh #	13	3	.813	28	5	.848
Seton Hall	10	6	.625	17	13	.567
Notre Dame	10	6	.625	24	10	.706
Georgetown	6	10	.375	19	15	.559

West Division	Conference W	L	Pct.	Full Season W	L	Pct.
West Virginia	5	11	.313	14	15	.483
Rutgers	4	12	.250	12	16	.429

BIG SKY CONFERENCE

Team	Conference W	L	Pct.	Full Season W	L	Pct.
Weber St. #	14	0	1.000	26	6	.813
Eastern Wash.	9	5	.643	18	13	.581
Montana	7	7	.500	13	17	.433
Idaho St.	7	7	.500	15	14	.517
Northern Ariz.	6	8	.429	15	13	.536
Sacramento St.	5	9	.357	12	17	.414
Montana St.	5	9	.357	11	16	.407
Portland St.	3	11	.214	5	22	.185

BIG SOUTH CONFERENCE

Team	Conference W	L	Pct.	Full Season W	L	Pct.
Winthrop	11	3	.786	20	10	.667
Liberty	8	6	.571	14	15	.483
Charleston So.	8	6	.571	14	14	.500
Elon	8	6	.571	12	15	.444
UNC Asheville #	7	7	.500	17	14	.469
Radford	6	8	.429	10	20	.333
Coastal Caro.	5	9	.357	13	15	.464
High Point	3	11	.214	7	20	.259

BIG TEN CONFERENCE

Team	Conference W	L	Pct.	Full Season W	L	Pct.
Wisconsin	12	4	.750	24	8	.750
Illinois #	11	5	.688	25	7	.781
Purdue	10	6	.625	19	11	.633
Michigan St.	10	6	.625	22	13	.629
*Michigan	10	6	.625	17	13	.567
Indiana	8	8	.500	21	13	.618
Minnesota	8	8	.500	19	14	.576
Iowa	7	9	.438	17	14	.548
Ohio St.	7	9	.438	17	15	.531
Northwestern	3	13	.188	12	17	.414
Penn St.	2	14	.125	7	21	.250

* ineligible for NCAA tournament

BIG 12 CONFERENCE

Team	Conference W	L	Pct.	Full Season W	L	Pct.
Kansas	14	2	.875	30	8	.789
Texas	13	3	.813	26	7	.788
Oklahoma #	12	4	.750	27	7	.794
Oklahoma St.	10	6	.625	22	10	.688
Missouri	9	7	.563	22	11	.667
Colorado	9	7	.563	20	12	.625
Texas Tech	6	10	.375	22	13	.629
Texas A&M	6	10	.375	14	14	.500
Iowa St.	5	11	.313	17	14	.548
Baylor	5	11	.313	14	14	.500
Kansas St.	4	12	.250	13	17	.433
Nebraska	3	13	.188	11	19	.367

BIG WEST CONFERENCE

Team	Conference W	L	Pct.	Full Season W	L	Pct.
UC Santa Barb.	14	4	.778	18	14	.563
UC Irvine	13	5	.722	20	9	.690
Utah St. #	12	6	.667	24	9	.727
Cal Poly	10	8	.556	16	14	.533
Idaho	9	9	.500	13	15	.464
Cal St. Fullerton	8	10	.444	10	19	.345
Cal St. Northridge	8	10	.444	14	15	.483
Pacific (Cal.)	7	11	.389	12	16	.429
UC Riverside	5	13	.278	6	18	.250
Long Beach St.	4	14	.222	5	22	.185

COLONIAL ATHLETIC ASSOCIATION

Team	Conference W	L	Pct.	Full Season W	L	Pct.
UNC Wilmington #	15	3	.833	24	7	.774
Drexel	12	6	.667	19	12	.613
Va. Commonwealth	12	6	.667	18	10	.643

Team	Conference W	L	Pct.	Full Season W	L	Pct.
George Mason	11	7	.611	16	12	.571
Delaware	9	9	.500	15	14	.517
Old Dominion	9	9	.500	12	15	.444
James Madison	8	10	.444	13	17	.433
William & Mary	7	11	.389	12	16	.429
Hofstra	6	12	.333	8	21	.276
Towson	1	17	.056	4	24	.143

CONFERENCE USA

American Division Team	Conference W	L	Pct.	Full Season W	L	Pct.
Marquette	14	2	.875	27	6	.818
Louisville #	11	5	.688	25	7	.781
St. Louis	9	7	.563	16	14	.533
Cincinnati	9	7	.563	17	12	.586
DePaul	8	8	.500	16	13	.552
Charlotte	8	8	.500	13	16	.448
East Caro.	3	13	.188	12	15	.444

National Division	Conference W	L	Pct.	Full Season W	L	Pct.
Memphis	13	3	.813	23	7	.767
Tulane	8	8	.500	16	15	.516
UAB	8	8	.500	21	13	.618
South Fla.	7	9	.438	15	14	.517
Houston	6	10	.375	8	20	.286
Southern Miss.	5	11	.313	13	16	.448
TCU	3	13	.188	9	19	.321

HORIZON LEAGUE

Team	Conference W	L	Pct.	Full Season W	L	Pct.
Butler	14	2	.875	27	6	.818
Wis.-Milwaukee #	13	3	.813	24	8	.750
Ill.-Chicago	12	4	.750	21	9	.700
Detroit	9	7	.563	18	12	.600
Loyola (Ill.)	9	7	.563	15	16	.484
Wright St.	4	12	.250	10	18	.357
Wis.-Green Bay	4	12	.250	10	20	.333
Youngstown St.	4	12	.250	9	20	.310
Cleveland St.	3	13	.188	8	22	.267

IVY GROUP

Team	Conference W	L	Pct.	Full Season W	L	Pct.
Pennsylvania	14	0	1.000	22	6	.786
Brown	12	2	.857	17	12	.586
Princeton	10	4	.714	16	11	.593
Yale	8	6	.571	14	13	.519
Harvard	4	10	.286	12	15	.444
Cornell	4	10	.286	9	18	.333
Dartmouth	4	10	.286	8	19	.296
Columbia	0	14	.000	2	25	.074

METRO ATLANTIC ATHLETIC CONFERENCE

Team	Conference W	L	Pct.	Full Season W	L	Pct.
Manhattan #	14	4	.778	23	7	.767
Fairfield	13	5	.722	19	12	.613
Siena	12	6	.667	21	11	.656
Niagara	12	6	.667	17	12	.586
Iona	11	7	.611	17	12	.586
Marist	8	10	.444	13	16	.448
Rider	7	11	.389	12	16	.429
St. Peter's	6	12	.333	10	19	.345
Canisius	6	12	.333	10	18	.357
Loyola (Md.)	1	17	.056	4	24	.143

MID-AMERICAN CONFERENCE

East Division	Conference W	L	Pct.	Full Season W	L	Pct.
Kent St.	12	6	.667	21	10	.677
Miami (Ohio)	11	7	.611	13	15	.464
Akron	9	9	.500	14	14	.500
Marshall	9	9	.500	14	15	.483
Ohio	8	10	.444	14	16	.467
Buffalo	2	16	.111	5	23	.179

West Division	Conference W	L	Pct.	Full Season W	L	Pct.
Central Mich. #	14	4	.778	25	7	.781
Northern Ill.	11	7	.611	17	14	.548

West Division	Conference			Full Season		
	W	L	Pct.	W	L	Pct.
Western Mich.	10	8	.556	20	11	.645
Eastern Mich.	8	10	.444	14	14	.500
Ball St.	8	10	.444	13	17	.433
Bowling Green	8	10	.444	13	16	.448
Toledo	7	11	.389	13	16	.448

MID-CONTINENT CONFERENCE

Team	Conference			Full Season		
	W	L	Pct.	W	L	Pct.
Valparaiso	12	2	.857	20	11	.645
IUPUI #	10	4	.714	20	14	.588
Oakland	10	4	.714	17	11	.607
Oral Roberts	9	5	.643	18	10	.643
UMKC	7	7	.500	9	20	.310
Southern Utah	5	9	.357	11	17	.393
Western Ill.	3	11	.214	7	21	.250
Chicago St.	0	14	.000	3	27	.100

MID-EASTERN ATHLETIC CONFERENCE

Team	Conference			Full Season		
	W	L	Pct.	W	L	Pct.
South Carolina St. #.	15	3	.833	20	11	.645
Delaware St.	13	5	.722	15	12	.556
Hampton	13	5	.722	19	11	.633
Coppin St.	11	7	.611	11	17	.393
Florida A&M	11	7	.611	17	12	.586
Norfolk St.	10	8	.556	14	15	.483
Howard	9	9	.500	13	17	.433
Morgan St.	6	12	.333	7	22	.241
Bethune-Cookman	5	13	.278	8	22	.267
Md.-East. Shore	5	13	.278	5	23	.179
N.C. A&T	1	17	.056	1	26	.037

MISSOURI VALLEY CONFERENCE

Team	Conference			Full Season		
	W	L	Pct.	W	L	Pct.
Southern Ill.	16	2	.889	24	7	.774
Creighton #	15	3	.833	29	5	.853
Wichita St.	12	6	.667	18	12	.600
Southwest Mo. St.	12	6	.667	17	12	.586
Evansville	8	10	.444	12	16	.429
Bradley	8	10	.444	12	18	.400
Northern Iowa	7	11	.389	11	17	.393
Drake	5	13	.278	10	20	.333
Illinois St.	5	13	.278	8	21	.276
Indiana St.	2	16	.111	7	24	.226

MOUNTAIN WEST CONFERENCE

Team	Conference			Full Season		
	W	L	Pct.	W	L	Pct.
Utah	11	3	.786	25	8	.758
Brigham Young	11	3	.786	23	9	.719
Wyoming	8	6	.571	21	11	.656
UNLV	8	6	.571	21	11	.656
San Diego St.	6	8	.429	16	14	.533
Colorado St. #	5	9	.357	19	14	.576
New Mexico	4	10	.286	10	18	.357
Air Force	3	11	.214	12	16	.429

NORTHEAST CONFERENCE

Team	Conference			Full Season		
	W	L	Pct.	W	L	Pct.
Wagner #	14	4	.778	21	11	.656
Monmouth	13	5	.722	15	13	.536
Central Conn. St.	12	6	.667	15	13	.536
Quinnipiac	10	8	.556	17	12	.586
St. Francis (Pa.)	10	8	.556	14	14	.500
Fairleigh Dickinson	9	9	.500	15	14	.517
St. Francis (N.Y.)	9	9	.500	14	16	.467
Long Island	7	11	.389	9	19	.321
Robert Morris	7	11	.389	10	17	.370
Mt. St. Mary's	6	12	.333	11	16	.407
Sacred Heart	6	12	.333	8	21	.276
UMBC	5	13	.278	7	20	.259

OHIO VALLEY CONFERENCE

Team	Conference			Full Season		
	W	L	Pct.	W	L	Pct.
Austin Peay #	13	3	.813	23	8	.742
Morehead St.	13	3	.813	20	9	.690
Tennessee Tech	11	5	.688	20	12	.625
Murray St.	9	7	.563	17	12	.586
Eastern Ill.	9	7	.563	14	15	.483
Tenn.-Martin	7	9	.438	14	14	.500
Southeast Mo. St.	5	11	.313	11	19	.367
Eastern Ky.	5	11	.313	11	17	.393
Tennessee St.	0	16	.000	2	25	.074

PACIFIC-10 CONFERENCE

Team	Conference			Full Season		
	W	L	Pct.	W	L	Pct.
Arizona	17	1	.944	28	4	.875
Stanford	14	4	.778	24	9	.727
California	13	5	.722	22	9	.710
Arizona St.	11	7	.611	20	12	.625
Oregon #	10	8	.556	23	10	.697
Oregon St.	6	12	.333	13	15	.464
Southern California	6	12	.333	13	17	.433
UCLA	6	12	.333	10	19	.345
Washington	5	13	.278	10	17	.370
Washington St.	2	17	.105	7	20	.259

PATRIOT LEAGUE

Team	Conference			Full Season		
	W	L	Pct.	W	L	Pct.
Holy Cross #	13	1	.929	26	5	.839
American	9	5	.643	16	14	.533
Colgate	9	5	.643	14	14	.500
Lehigh	8	6	.571	16	12	.571
Bucknell	7	7	.500	14	15	.483
Lafayette	6	8	.429	13	16	.448
Navy	4	10	.286	8	20	.286
Army	0	14	.000	5	22	.185

SOUTHEASTERN CONFERENCE

Eastern Division	Conference			Full Season		
	W	L	Pct.	W	L	Pct.
Kentucky #	16	0	1.000	32	4	.889
Florida	12	4	.750	25	8	.758
*Georgia	11	5	.688	19	8	.704
Tennessee	9	7	.563	17	12	.586
South Carolina	5	11	.313	12	16	.429
Vanderbilt	3	13	.188	11	18	.379

* ineligible for NCAA tournament

Western Division	Conference			Full Season		
	W	L	Pct.	W	L	Pct.
Mississippi St.	9	7	.563	21	10	.677
Auburn	8	8	.500	22	12	.647
LSU	8	8	.500	21	11	.656
Alabama	7	9	.438	17	12	.586
Arkansas	4	12	.250	9	19	.321
Mississippi	4	12	.250	14	15	.483

SOUTHERN CONFERENCE

North Division	Conference			Full Season		
	W	L	Pct.	W	L	Pct.
East Tenn. St. #	11	5	.688	20	11	.645
Appalachian St.	11	5	.688	19	10	.655
Davidson	11	5	.688	17	10	.630
Western Caro.	6	10	.375	9	19	.321
VMI	3	13	.188	10	20	.333
UNC Greensboro	3	13	.188	7	22	.241

South Division	Conference			Full Season		
	W	L	Pct.	W	L	Pct.
Col. of Charleston	13	3	.813	25	8	.758
Chattanooga	11	5	.688	21	9	.700
Ga. Southern	8	8	.500	16	13	.552
Wofford	8	8	.500	14	15	.483
Furman	8	8	.500	14	17	.452
Citadel	3	13	.188	8	20	.286

SOUTHLAND CONFERENCE

Team	Conference			Full Season		
	W	L	Pct.	W	L	Pct.
Sam Houston St. #	17	3	.850	23	7	.767
Stephen F. Austin	16	4	.800	21	8	.724
Texas-Arlington	13	7	.650	16	13	.552
Texas St.	11	9	.550	17	12	.586
La.-Monroe	10	10	.500	12	16	.429
McNeese St.	10	10	.500	15	14	.517
Lamar	10	10	.500	13	14	.481
Southeastern La.	9	11	.450	11	16	.407
Texas-San Antonio	7	13	.350	10	17	.370
Northwestern St.	6	14	.300	6	21	.222
Nicholls St.	1	19	.050	3	25	.107

SOUTHWESTERN ATHLETIC CONFERENCE

Team	Conference			Full Season		
	W	L	Pct.	W	L	Pct.
Prairie View	14	4	.778	17	12	.586
Mississippi Val.	13	5	.722	15	14	.517
Texas Southern #	11	7	.611	18	13	.581
Alabama St.	11	7	.611	14	15	.483
Alcorn St.	10	8	.556	14	19	.424
Grambling	9	9	.500	12	18	.400
Jackson St.	9	9	.500	10	18	.357
Southern U.	5	13	.278	9	20	.310
Alabama A&M	4	14	.222	8	19	.296
Ark.-Pine Bluff	4	14	.222	4	24	.143

SUN BELT CONFERENCE

East Division	Conference			Full Season		
	W	L	Pct.	W	L	Pct.
Western Ky. #	12	2	.857	24	9	.727
Middle Tenn.	9	5	.643	16	14	.533
Ark.-Little Rock	8	6	.571	18	12	.600
Arkansas St.	6	8	.429	13	15	.464
Florida Int'l	1	13	.071	8	21	.276

West Division	Conference			Full Season		
	W	L	Pct.	W	L	Pct.
La.-Lafayette	12	3	.800	20	10	.667
New Mexico St.	9	6	.600	20	9	.690
Denver	7	8	.467	17	15	.531
New Orleans	7	8	.467	15	14	.517
South Ala.	7	8	.467	14	14	.500
North Texas	2	13	.133	7	21	.250

WEST COAST CONFERENCE

Team	Conference			Full Season		
	W	L	Pct.	W	L	Pct.
Gonzaga	12	2	.857	24	9	.727
San Diego #	10	4	.714	18	12	.600
San Francisco	9	5	.643	15	14	.517
Pepperdine	7	7	.500	15	13	.536
St. Mary's (Cal.)	6	8	.429	15	15	.500
Santa Clara	4	10	.286	13	15	.464
Portland	4	10	.286	11	17	.393
Loyola Marymount	4	10	.286	11	20	.355

WESTERN ATHLETIC CONFERENCE

Team	Conference			Full Season		
	W	L	Pct.	W	L	Pct.
*Fresno St.	13	5	.722	20	8	.714
Tulsa #	12	6	.667	23	10	.697
Southern Methodist	11	7	.611	17	13	.567
Nevada	11	7	.611	18	14	.563
Rice	11	7	.611	19	10	.655
Hawaii	9	9	.500	19	12	.613
Louisiana Tech	9	9	.500	12	15	.444
Boise St.	7	11	.389	13	16	.448
San Jose St.	4	14	.222	7	21	.250
UTEP	3	15	.167	6	24	.200

* ineligible for NCAA tournament

INDEPENDENTS

	W	L	Pct.
Centenary (La.)	14	14	.500
Tex. A&M-Corp. Chris.	14	15	.483
Tex.-Pan American	10	20	.333
IPFW	9	21	.300
Morris Brown	8	20	.286
Savannah St.	3	24	.111

PROVISIONALS

	W	L	Pct.
Birmingham-So.	19	9	.679
Lipscomb	8	20	.286

#won conference tournament

Division I Conference Champions Season By Season

Regular-season and conference tournament champions; No. refers to the number of teams in the conference or tournament.

AMERICA EAST CONFERENCE

Season	No.	Regular Season
1980	10	Boston U./Northeastern
1981	9	Northeastern
1982	9	Northeastern
1983	9	Boston U./New Hampshire
1984	8	Northeastern
1985	9	Northeastern/Canisius
1986	10	Northeastern
1987	10	Northeastern
1988	10	Siena
1989	10	Siena
1990	7	Northeastern
1991	6	Northeastern
1992	8	Delaware
1993	8	Drexel/Northeastern
1994	8	Drexel
1995	9	Drexel
1996	10	Drexel
1997	10	Boston U.
1998	10	Delaware/Boston U.
1999	10	Delaware/Drexel
2000	10	Hofstra
2001	10	Hofstra
2002	9	Boston U./Vermont
2003	9	Boston U.

Season	No.	Conference Tournament
1980	8	Holy Cross
1981	6	Northeastern
1982	6	Northeastern
1983	9	Boston U.
1984	8	Northeastern
1985	9	Northeastern
1986	10	Northeastern
1987	10	Northeastern
1988	10	Boston U.
1989	10	Siena
1990	7	Boston U.
1991	6	Northeastern
1992	8	Delaware
1993	8	Delaware
1994	8	Drexel
1995	9	Drexel
1996	10	Drexel
1997	10	Boston U.
1998	10	Delaware
1999	10	Delaware
2000	10	Hofstra
2001	10	Hofstra
2002	8	Boston U.
2003	8	Vermont

AMERICAN SOUTH CONFERENCE

Season	No.	Regular Season
1988	6	Louisiana Tech/New Orleans
1989	6	New Orleans
1990	6	Louisiana Tech/New Orleans
1991	7	New Orleans/Arkansas St.

Season	No.	Conference Tournament
1988	6	Louisiana Tech
1989	6	Louisiana Tech
1990	6	New Orleans
1991	7	Louisiana Tech

AMERICAN WEST CONFERENCE

Season	No.	Regular Season
1995	4	Southern Utah
1996	4	Cal Poly

Season	No.	Conference Tournament
1995	4	Southern Utah
1996	4	Southern Utah

ATLANTIC COAST CONFERENCE

Season	No.	Regular Season
1954	8	Duke
1955	8	North Carolina St.
1956	8	North Carolina St./North Carolina
1957	8	North Carolina
1958	8	Duke
1959	8	North Carolina St./North Carolina
1960	8	North Carolina
1961	8	North Carolina
1962	8	Wake Forest
1963	8	Duke
1964	8	Duke
1965	8	Duke
1966	8	Duke
1967	8	North Carolina
1968	8	North Carolina
1969	8	North Carolina
1970	8	South Carolina
1971	8	North Carolina
1972	7	North Carolina
1973	7	North Carolina St.
1974	7	North Carolina St.
1975	7	Maryland
1976	7	North Carolina
1977	7	North Carolina
1978	7	North Carolina
1979	7	Duke/North Carolina
1980	8	Maryland
1981	8	Virginia
1982	8	North Carolina/Virginia
1983	8	North Carolina/Virginia
1984	8	North Carolina
1985	8	Georgia Tech/North Carolina/North Carolina St.
1986	8	Duke
1987	8	North Carolina
1988	8	North Carolina
1989	8	North Carolina St.
1990	8	Clemson
1991	8	Duke
1992	9	Duke
1993	9	North Carolina
1994	9	Maryland/North Carolina/Virginia/Wake Forest
1995	9	Georgia Tech
1996	9	Duke
1997	9	Duke
1998	9	Duke
1999	9	Duke
2000	9	Duke
2001	9	Duke/North Carolina
2002	9	Maryland
2003	9	Wake Forest

Season	No.	Conference Tournament
1954	8	North Carolina St.
1955	8	North Carolina St.
1956	8	North Carolina St.
1957	8	North Carolina
1958	8	Maryland
1959	8	North Carolina St.
1960	8	Duke
1961	7	Wake Forest
1962	8	Wake Forest
1963	8	Duke
1964	8	Duke
1965	8	North Carolina St.
1966	8	Duke
1967	8	North Carolina
1968	8	North Carolina
1969	8	North Carolina
1970	8	North Carolina St.
1971	8	South Carolina
1972	7	North Carolina
1973	7	North Carolina St.
1974	7	North Carolina St.
1975	7	North Carolina St.
1976	7	Virginia
1977	7	North Carolina
1978	7	Duke
1979	7	North Carolina
1980	8	Duke
1981	8	North Carolina
1982	8	North Carolina
1983	8	North Carolina St.
1984	8	Maryland
1985	8	Georgia Tech
1986	8	Duke
1987	8	North Carolina St.
1988	8	Duke
1989	8	North Carolina
1990	8	Georgia Tech
1991	7	North Carolina
1992	9	Duke

Season	No.	Conference Tournament
1993	9	Georgia Tech
1994	9	North Carolina
1995	9	Wake Forest
1996	9	Wake Forest
1997	9	North Carolina
1998	9	North Carolina
1999	9	Duke
2000	9	Duke
2001	9	Duke
2002	9	Duke
2003	9	Duke

ATLANTIC SUN CONFERENCE

Season	No.	Regular Season
1979	8	La.-Monroe
1980	7	La.-Monroe
1981	9	Houston Baptist
1982	9	Ark.-Little Rock
1983	8	Ark.-Little Rock
1984	8	Houston Baptist
1985	8	Ga. Southern
1986	8	Ark.-Little Rock
1987	10	Ark.-Little Rock
1988	10	Ark.-Little Rock/Ga. Southern
1989	10	Ga. Southern
1990	9	Centenary (La.)
1991	8	Texas-San Antonio
1992	8	Ga. Southern
1993	7	Florida Int'l
1994	10	Col. of Charleston
1995	11	Col. of Charleston
1996	12	Col. of Charleston (East)/Samford (West)/Southeastern La. (West)
1997	12	Col. of Charleston (East)/Samford (West)
1998	12	Col. of Charleston (East)/Georgia St. (West)
1999	11	Samford
2000	10	Georgia St./Troy St.
2001	10	Georgia St.
2002	11	Georgia St./Troy St.
2003	12	Belmont (North)/Mercer (South)/Troy St. (South)

Season	No.	Conference Tournament
1979	6	La.-Monroe
1980	7	Centenary (La.)
1981	9	Mercer
1982	7	La.-Monroe
1983	8	Ga. Southern
1984	8	Houston Baptist
1985	8	Mercer
1986	8	Ark.-Little Rock
1987	8	Ga. Southern
1988	8	Texas-San Antonio
1989	8	Ark.-Little Rock
1990	8	Ark.-Little Rock
1991	8	Georgia St.
1992	8	Ga. Southern
1993		DNP
1994	8	UCF
1995	8	Florida Int'l
1996	8	UCF
1997	8	Col. of Charleston
1998	8	Col. of Charleston
1999	8	Samford
2000	10	Samford
2001	10	Georgia St.
2002	8	Fla. Atlantic
2003	8	Troy St.

ATLANTIC 10 CONFERENCE

Season	No.	Regular Season
1977	8	Rutgers (Eastern)/West Virginia (Western)/Penn St. (Western)
1978	8	Rutgers/Villanova
1979	8	Villanova
1980	8	Villanova/Duquesne/Rutgers
1981	8	Rhode Island/Duquesne
1982	8	West Virginia
1983	10	Rutgers (Eastern)/St. Bonaventure (Western)/West Virginia (Western)
1984	10	Temple
1985	10	West Virginia
1986	10	St. Joseph's
1987	10	Temple

Season	No.	Regular Season
1988	10	Temple
1989	10	West Virginia
1990	10	Temple
1991	10	Rutgers
1992	9	Massachusetts
1993	8	Massachusetts
1994	9	Massachusetts
1995	9	Massachusetts
1996	12	Massachusetts (East)/George Washington (West)/Virginia Tech (West)
1997	12	St. Joseph's (East)/Xavier (West)
1998	12	Temple (East)/Xavier (West)/George Washington (West)/Dayton (West)
1999	12	Temple (East)/George Washington (West)
2000	12	Temple (East)/Dayton (West)
2001	11	St. Joseph's
2002	12	Temple (East)/St. Joseph's (East)/Xavier (West)
2003	12	St. Joseph's (East)/Xavier (West)

Season	No.	Conference Tournament
1977	8	Duquesne
1978	8	Villanova
1979	8	Rutgers
1980	8	Villanova
1981	8	Pittsburgh
1982	8	Pittsburgh
1983	10	West Virginia
1984	10	West Virginia
1985	10	Temple
1986	10	St. Joseph's
1987	10	Temple
1988	10	Temple
1989	10	Rutgers
1990	10	Temple
1991	10	Penn St.
1992	9	Massachusetts
1993	8	Massachusetts
1994	9	Massachusetts
1995	9	Massachusetts
1996	12	Massachusetts
1997	12	St. Joseph's
1998	12	Xavier
1999	12	Rhode Island
2000	12	Temple
2001	11	Temple
2002	12	Xavier
2003	11	Dayton

BIG EAST CONFERENCE

Season	No.	Regular Season
1980	7	Syracuse/Georgetown/St. John's (N.Y.)
1981	8	Boston College
1982	8	Villanova
1983	9	Boston College/Villanova/St. John's (N.Y.)
1984	9	Georgetown
1985	9	St. John's (N.Y.)
1986	9	St. John's (N.Y.)/Syracuse
1987	9	Syracuse/Georgetown/Pittsburgh
1988	9	Pittsburgh
1989	9	Georgetown
1990	9	Connecticut/Syracuse
1991	9	Syracuse
1992	10	Seton Hall/Georgetown/St. John's (N.Y.)
1993	10	Seton Hall
1994	10	Connecticut
1995	10	Connecticut
1996	13	Georgetown (Big East 7)/Connecticut (Big East 6)
1997	13	Georgetown (Big East 7)/Villanova (Big East 6)/Boston College (Big East 6)
1998	13	Syracuse (Big East 7)/Connecticut (Big East 6)
1999	13	Connecticut
2000	13	Syracuse/Miami (Fla.)
2001	14	Boston College (East)/Notre Dame (West)
2002	14	Connecticut (East)/Pittsburgh (West)
2003	14	Boston College (East)/Connecticut (East)/Pittsburgh (West)/Syracuse (West)

Season	No.	Conference Tournament
1980	7	Georgetown
1981	8	Syracuse
1982	8	Georgetown
1983	9	St. John's (N.Y.)
1984	9	Georgetown
1985	9	Georgetown
1986	9	St. John's (N.Y.)
1987	9	Georgetown
1988	9	Syracuse
1989	9	Georgetown
1990	9	Connecticut
1991	9	Seton Hall
1992	10	Syracuse
1993	10	Seton Hall
1994	10	Providence
1995	10	Villanova
1996	13	Connecticut
1997	13	Boston College
1998	13	Connecticut
1999	13	Connecticut
2000	13	St. John's (N.Y.)
2001	12	Boston College
2002	12	Connecticut
2003	12	Pittsburgh

BIG EIGHT CONFERENCE

(Note: The Big Eight and Missouri Valley conferences share the same history from 1908-28.)

Season	No.	Regular Season
1908	6	Kansas
1909	6	Kansas
1910	6	Kansas
1911	5	Kansas
1912	6	Nebraska/Kansas
1913	6	Nebraska
1914	7	Kansas/Nebraska
1915	7	Kansas
1916	7	Nebraska
1917	7	Kansas St.
1918	7	Missouri
1919	8	Kansas St.
1920	8	Missouri
1921	9	Missouri
1922	9	Missouri/Kansas
1923	9	Kansas
1924	9	Kansas
1925	9	Kansas
1926	10	Kansas
1927	10	Kansas
1928	10	Oklahoma
1929	6	Oklahoma
1930	6	Missouri
1931	6	Kansas
1932	6	Kansas
1933	6	Kansas
1934	6	Kansas
1935	6	Iowa St.
1936	6	Kansas
1937	6	Kansas/Nebraska
1938	6	Kansas
1939	6	Missouri/Oklahoma
1940	6	Kansas/Missouri/Oklahoma
1941	6	Iowa St./Kansas
1942	6	Kansas/Oklahoma
1943	6	Kansas
1944	6	Iowa St./Oklahoma
1945	6	Iowa St.
1946	6	Kansas
1947	6	Oklahoma
1948	7	Kansas St.
1949	7	Nebraska/Oklahoma
1950	7	Kansas/Kansas St./Nebraska
1951	7	Kansas St.
1952	7	Kansas
1953	7	Kansas
1954	7	Kansas/Colorado
1955	7	Colorado
1956	7	Kansas St.
1957	7	Kansas
1958	7	Kansas St.
1959	8	Kansas St.
1960	8	Kansas/Kansas St.
1961	8	Kansas St.
1962	8	Colorado
1963	8	Colorado/Kansas St.
1964	8	Kansas St.
1965	8	Oklahoma St.
1966	8	Kansas
1967	8	Kansas
1968	8	Kansas St.
1969	8	Colorado
1970	8	Kansas St.
1971	8	Kansas

Season	No.	Regular Season
1972	8	Kansas St.
1973	8	Kansas St.
1974	8	Kansas
1975	8	Kansas
1976	8	Missouri
1977	8	Kansas St.
1978	8	Kansas
1979	8	Oklahoma
1980	8	Missouri
1981	8	Missouri
1982	8	Missouri
1983	8	Missouri
1984	8	Oklahoma
1985	8	Oklahoma
1986	8	Kansas
1987	8	Missouri
1988	8	Oklahoma
1989	8	Oklahoma
1990	8	Missouri
1991	8	Oklahoma St./Kansas
1992	8	Kansas
1993	8	Kansas
1994	8	Missouri
1995	8	Kansas
1996	8	Kansas

Season	No.	Conference Tournament
1977	8	Kansas St.
1978	8	Missouri
1979	8	Oklahoma
1980	8	Kansas St.
1981	8	Kansas
1982	8	Missouri
1983	8	Oklahoma St.
1984	8	Kansas
1985	8	Oklahoma
1986	8	Kansas
1987	8	Missouri
1988	8	Oklahoma
1989	8	Missouri
1990	8	Oklahoma
1991	8	Missouri
1992	8	Kansas
1993	8	Missouri
1994	8	Nebraska
1995	8	Oklahoma St.
1996	8	Iowa St.

BIG SKY CONFERENCE

Season	No.	Regular Season
1964	6	Montana St.
1965	6	Weber St.
1966	6	Weber St./Gonzaga
1967	6	Gonzaga/Montana St.
1968	6	Weber St.
1969	6	Weber St.
1970	6	Weber St.
1971	6	Weber St.
1972	8	Weber St.
1973	8	Weber St.
1974	8	Idaho St./Montana
1975	8	Montana
1976	8	Boise St./Weber St./Idaho St.
1977	8	Idaho St.
1978	8	Montana
1979	8	Weber St.
1980	8	Weber St.
1981	8	Idaho
1982	8	Idaho
1983	8	Weber St./Nevada
1984	8	Weber St.
1985	8	Nevada
1986	8	Northern Ariz./Montana
1987	8	Montana St.
1988	9	Boise St.
1989	9	Boise St./Idaho
1990	9	Idaho
1991	9	Montana
1992	9	Montana
1993	9	Idaho
1994	8	Weber St./Idaho St.
1995	8	Montana/Weber St.
1996	8	Montana St.
1997	9	Northern Ariz.
1998	9	Northern Ariz.
1999	9	Weber St.
2000	9	Montana/Eastern Wash.
2001	9	Cal St. Northridge
2002	9	Montana St.
2003	8	Weber St.

CONFERENCES

Season	No.	Conference Tournament
1976	8	Boise St.
1977	8	Idaho St.
1978	8	Weber St.
1979	8	Weber St.
1980	8	Weber St.
1981	8	Idaho
1982	8	Idaho
1983	8	Weber St.
1984	8	Nevada
1985	8	Nevada
1986	7	Montana St.
1987	8	Idaho St.
1988	9	Boise St.
1989	9	Idaho
1990	9	Idaho
1991	9	Montana
1992	6	Montana
1993	6	Boise St.
1994	6	Boise St.
1995	6	Weber St.
1996	6	Montana St.
1997	6	Montana
1998	6	Northern Ariz.
1999	6	Weber St.
2000	6	Northern Ariz.
2001	6	Cal St. Northridge
2002	6	Montana
2003	6	Weber St.

BIG SOUTH CONFERENCE

Season	No.	Regular Season
1986	8	Charleston So.
1987	8	Charleston So.
1988	7	Coastal Caro.
1989	7	Coastal Caro.
1990	7	Coastal Caro.
1991	8	Coastal Caro.
1992	8	Radford
1993	9	Towson
1994	10	Towson
1995	9	UNC Greensboro
1996	9	UNC Greensboro
1997	8	Liberty/UNC Asheville
1998	7	UNC Asheville
1999	6	Winthrop
2000	8	Radford
2001	8	Radford
2002	8	Winthrop/UNC Asheville
2003	8	Winthrop

Season	No.	Conference Tournament
1986	8	Charleston So.
1987	8	Charleston So.
1988	7	Winthrop
1989	7	UNC Asheville
1990	7	Coastal Caro.
1991	8	Coastal Caro.
1992	8	Campbell
1993	9	Coastal Caro.
1994	8	Liberty
1995	8	Charleston So.
1996	8	UNC Greensboro
1997	8	Charleston So.
1998	7	Radford
1999	6	Winthrop
2000	6	Winthrop
2001	6	Winthrop
2002	8	Winthrop
2003	8	UNC Asheville

BIG TEN CONFERENCE

Season	No.	Regular Season
1906	6	Minnesota
1907	5	Chicago/Minnesota/Wisconsin
1908	5	Chicago/Wisconsin
1909	8	Chicago
1910	8	Chicago
1911	8	Purdue/Minnesota
1912	8	Purdue/Wisconsin
1913	9	Wisconsin
1914	9	Wisconsin
1915	9	Illinois
1916	9	Wisconsin
1917	9	Minnesota/Illinois
1918	10	Wisconsin
1919	10	Minnesota
1920	10	Chicago
1921	10	Michigan/Wisconsin/Purdue
1922	10	Purdue
1923	10	Iowa/Wisconsin

Season	No.	Regular Season
1924	10	Wisconsin/Illinois/Chicago
1925	10	Ohio St.
1926	10	Purdue/Indiana/Michigan/Iowa
1927	10	Michigan
1928	10	Indiana/Purdue
1929	10	Wisconsin/Michigan
1930	10	Purdue
1931	10	Northwestern
1932	10	Purdue
1933	10	Northwestern/Ohio St.
1934	10	Purdue
1935	10	Purdue/Illinois/Wisconsin
1936	10	Indiana/Purdue
1937	10	Minnesota/Illinois
1938	10	Purdue
1939	10	Ohio St.
1940	10	Purdue
1941	10	Wisconsin
1942	10	Illinois
1943	10	Illinois
1944	10	Ohio St.
1945	10	Iowa
1946	10	Ohio St.
1947	9	Wisconsin
1948	9	Michigan
1949	9	Illinois
1950	9	Ohio St.
1951	10	Illinois
1952	10	Illinois
1953	10	Indiana
1954	10	Indiana
1955	10	Iowa
1956	10	Iowa
1957	10	Indiana/Michigan St.
1958	10	Indiana
1959	10	Michigan St.
1960	10	Ohio St.
1961	10	Ohio St.
1962	10	Ohio St.
1963	10	Ohio St./Illinois
1964	10	Michigan/Ohio St.
1965	10	Michigan
1966	10	Michigan
1967	10	Indiana/Michigan St.
1968	10	Ohio St./Iowa
1969	10	Purdue
1970	10	Iowa
1971	10	Ohio St.
1972	10	Minnesota
1973	10	Indiana
1974	10	Indiana/Michigan
1975	10	Indiana
1976	10	Indiana
1977	10	Michigan
1978	10	Michigan St.
1979	10	Michigan St./Purdue/Iowa
1980	10	Indiana
1981	10	Indiana
1982	10	Minnesota
1983	10	Indiana
1984	10	Illinois/Purdue
1985	10	Michigan
1986	10	Michigan
1987	10	Indiana/Purdue
1988	10	Purdue
1989	10	Indiana
1990	10	Michigan St.
1991	10	Ohio St./Indiana
1992	10	Ohio St.
1993	11	Indiana
1994	11	Purdue
1995	11	Purdue
1996	11	Purdue
1997	11	Minnesota
1998	11	Michigan St./Illinois
1999	11	Michigan St.
2000	11	Michigan St./Ohio St.
2001	11	Michigan St./Illinois
2002	11	Illinois/Ohio St./Indiana/Wisconsin
2003	11	Wisconsin

Season	No.	Conference Tournament
1998	11	Michigan
1999	11	Michigan St.
2000	11	Michigan St.
2001	11	Iowa
2002	11	Ohio St.
2003	11	Illinois

BIG 12 CONFERENCE

Season	No.	Regular Season
1997	12	Kansas
1998	12	Kansas
1999	12	Texas
2000	12	Iowa St.
2001	12	Iowa St.
2002	12	Kansas
2003	12	Kansas

Season	No.	Conference Tournament
1997	12	Kansas
1998	12	Kansas
1999	12	Kansas
2000	12	Iowa St.
2001	12	Oklahoma
2002	12	Oklahoma
2003	12	Oklahoma

BIG WEST CONFERENCE

Season	No.	Regular Season
1970	6	Long Beach St.
1971	6	Long Beach St.
1972	7	Long Beach St.
1973	7	Long Beach St.
1974	7	Long Beach St.
1975	6	Long Beach St.
1976	6	Long Beach St./Cal St. Fullerton
1977	7	Long Beach St./San Diego St.
1978	8	Fresno St./San Diego St.
1979	8	Pacific (Cal.)
1980	8	Utah St.
1981	8	Fresno St.
1982	8	Fresno St.
1983	9	UNLV
1984	10	UNLV
1985	10	UNLV
1986	10	UNLV
1987	10	UNLV
1988	10	UNLV
1989	10	UNLV
1990	10	UNLV
1991	10	UNLV
1992	10	UNLV
1993	10	New Mexico St.
1994	10	New Mexico St.
1995	10	Utah St.
1996	10	Long Beach St.
1997	12	Nevada (Eastern)/New Mexico St. (Eastern)/Utah St. (Eastern)/Pacific (Cal.) (Western)
1998	1	Utah St. (Eastern)/Pacific (Cal.) (Western)
1999	12	Boise St. (Eastern)/New Mexico St. (Eastern)/UC Santa Barb. (Western)
2000	12	Utah St. (Eastern)/Long Beach St. (Western)
2001	9	UC Irvine
2002	10	Utah St./UC Irvine
2003	10	UC Santa Barb.

Season	No.	Conference Tournament
1976	4	San Diego St.
1977	7	Long Beach St.
1978	7	Cal St. Fullerton
1979	8	Pacific (Cal.)
1980	7	San Jose St.
1981	7	Fresno St.
1982	7	Fresno St.
1983	8	UNLV
1984	8	Fresno St.
1985	8	UNLV
1986	8	UNLV
1987	8	UNLV
1988	10	Utah St.
1989	10	UNLV
1990	10	UNLV
1991	8	UNLV
1992	8	New Mexico St.
1993	8	Long Beach St.
1994	10	New Mexico St.
1995	10	Long Beach St.
1996	6	San Jose St.
1997	8	Pacific (Cal.)
1998	8	Utah St.
1999	8	New Mexico St.
2000	8	Utah St.
2001	8	Utah St.
2002	8	UC Santa Barb.
2003	8	Utah St.

BORDER CONFERENCE

Season	No.	Regular Season
1932	5	Arizona
1933	6	Texas Tech
1934	6	Texas Tech
1935	6	Texas Tech
1936	7	Arizona
1937	7	New Mexico St.
1938	7	New Mexico St.
1939	7	New Mexico St.
1940	7	New Mexico St.
1941		DNP
1942	9	West Tex. A&M
1943	8	West Tex. A&M
1944	4	Northern Ariz.
1945	9	New Mexico
1946	9	Arizona
1947	9	Arizona
1948	9	Arizona
1949	9	Arizona
1950	9	Arizona
1951	9	Arizona
1952	8	New Mexico St./West Tex. A&M
1953	8	Arizona/Hardin-Simmons
1954	7	Texas Tech
1955	7	Texas Tech/West Tex. A&M
1956	7	Texas Tech
1957	6	UTEP
1958	6	Arizona St.
1959	6	Arizona St./New Mexico St./UTEP
1960	6	New Mexico St.
1961	6	Arizona St./New Mexico St.
1962	5	Arizona St.

COLONIAL ATHLETIC ASSOCIATION

Season	No.	Regular Season
1983	6	William & Mary
1984	6	Richmond
1985	8	Navy/Richmond
1986	8	Navy
1987	8	Navy
1988	8	Richmond
1989	8	Richmond
1990	8	James Madison
1991	8	James Madison
1992	8	Richmond/James Madison
1993	8	James Madison/Old Dominion
1994	8	James Madison/Old Dominion
1995	8	Old Dominion
1996	9	Va. Commonwealth
1997	9	Old Dominion/UNC Wilmington
1998	9	William & Mary/UNC Wilmington
1999	9	George Mason
2000	9	James Madison/George Mason
2001	9	Richmond
2002	10	UNC Wilmington
2003	10	UNC Wilmington

Season	No.	Conference Tournament
1983	6	James Madison
1984	6	Richmond
1985	8	Navy
1986	8	Navy
1987	8	Navy
1988	8	Richmond
1989	8	George Mason
1990	8	Richmond
1991	8	Richmond
1992	8	Old Dominion
1993	8	East Caro.
1994	8	James Madison
1995	8	Old Dominion
1996	9	Va. Commonwealth
1997	9	Old Dominion
1998	9	Richmond
1999	9	George Mason
2000	9	UNC Wilmington
2001	6	George Mason
2002	10	UNC Wilmington
2003	10	UNC Wilmington

CONFERENCE USA

Season	No.	Regular Season
1996	11	Tulane (Red)/Memphis (White)/Cincinnati (Blue)
1997	12	Tulane (Red)/Memphis (White)/Charlotte (White)/Cincinnati (Blue)
1998	12	Cincinnati (American)/Memphis (National)
1999	12	Cincinnati (American)/UAB (National)
2000	12	Cincinnati (American)/Tulane (National)/South Fla. (National)
2001	12	Cincinnati (American)/Southern Miss. (National)
2002	14	Cincinnati (American)/Memphis (National)
2003	14	Marquette (American)/Memphis (National)

Season	No.	Conference Tournament
1996	11	Cincinnati
1997	12	Marquette
1998	12	Cincinnati
1999	12	Charlotte
2000	12	St. Louis
2001	12	Charlotte
2002	12	Cincinnati
2003	12	Louisville

EAST COAST CONFERENCE

Season	No.	Regular Season
1959	10	St. Joseph's
1960	10	St. Joseph's
1961	10	St. Joseph's
1962	10	St. Joseph's
1963	9	St. Joseph's
1964	8	Temple
1965	8	St. Joseph's
1966	10	St. Joseph's
1967	12	Temple
1968	11	La Salle
1969	12	Temple
1970	12	St. Joseph's (East)/Rider (West)/Lehigh (West)/Lafayette (West)
1971	13	St. Joseph's (East)/Lafayette (West)
1972	13	Temple (East)/Rider (West)
1973	13	St. Joseph's (East)/Lafayette (West)
1974	13	St. Joseph's (East)/La Salle (East)/Rider (West)
1975	12	American (East)/La Salle (East)/Lafayette (West)
1976	12	St. Joseph's (East)/Lafayette (West)
1977	12	Temple (East)/Hofstra (East)/Lafayette (West)
1978	12	La Salle (East)/Lafayette (West)
1979	12	Temple (East)/Bucknell (West)
1980	12	St. Joseph's (East)/Lafayette (West)
1981	12	American (East)/Lafayette (West)/Rider (West)
1982	12	Temple (East)/West Chester (West)
1983	10	American (East)/La Salle (East)/Hofstra (East)/Rider (West)
1984	9	Bucknell
1985	8	Bucknell
1986	8	Drexel
1987	8	Bucknell
1988	8	Lafayette
1989	8	Bucknell
1990	8	Towson/Hofstra/Lehigh
1991	7	Towson
1992	7	Hofstra
1993		DNP
1994	6	Troy St.

Season	No.	Conference Tournament
1975	12	La Salle
1976	12	Hofstra
1977	12	Hofstra
1978	12	La Salle
1979	12	Temple
1980	12	La Salle
1981	12	St. Joseph's
1982	12	St. Joseph's
1983	10	La Salle
1984	9	Rider
1985	8	Lehigh
1986	8	Drexel
1987	8	Bucknell
1988	8	Lehigh
1989	8	Bucknell
1990	8	Towson

EASTERN INTERCOLLEGIATE CONFERENCE

Season	No.	Regular Season
1933	5	Pittsburgh
1934	6	Pittsburgh
1935	5	Pittsburgh/West Virginia
1936	6	Carnegie Mellon/Pittsburgh
1937	6	Pittsburgh/Tempe
1938	6	Tempe
1939	6	Carnegie Mellon/Georgetown

GREAT MIDWEST CONFERENCE

Season	No.	Regular Season
1992	6	DePaul/Cincinnati
1993	6	Cincinnati
1994	7	Marquette
1995	7	Memphis

Season	No.	Conference Tournament
1992	6	Cincinnati
1993	6	Cincinnati
1994	7	Cincinnati
1995	7	Cincinnati

GULF STAR CONFERENCE

Season	No.	Regular Season
1985	6	Southeast La.
1986	6	Sam Houston St.
1987	6	Stephen F. Austin

HORIZON LEAGUE CONFERENCE

Season	No.	Regular Season
1980	6	Loyola (Ill.)
1981	7	Xavier
1982	7	Evansville
1983	8	Loyola (Ill.)
1984	8	Oral Roberts
1985	8	Loyola (Ill.)
1986	7	Xavier
1987	7	Evansville/Loyola (Ill.)
1988	6	Xavier
1989	7	Evansville
1990	8	Xavier
1991	8	Xavier
1992	6	Evansville
1993	8	Evansville/Xavier
1994	6	Xavier
1995	11	Xavier
1996	9	Wis.-Green Bay
1997	9	Butler
1998	8	Detroit/Ill.-Chicago
1999	8	Detroit
2000	8	Butler
2001	8	Butler
2002	8	Butler
2003	9	Butler

Season	No.	Conference Tournament
1980	6	Oral Roberts
1981	7	Oklahoma City
1982	7	Evansville
1983	8	Xavier
1984	8	Oral Roberts
1985	8	Loyola (Ill.)
1986	7	Xavier
1987	7	Xavier
1988	6	Xavier
1989	7	Evansville
1990	8	Dayton
1991	8	Xavier
1992	6	Evansville
1993	8	Evansville
1994	6	Detroit
1995	10	Wis.-Green Bay
1996	8	Northern Ill.
1997	9	Butler
1998	8	Butler
1999	8	Detroit
2000	8	Butler
2001	8	Butler
2002	9	Ill.-Chicago
2003	9	Wis.-Milwaukee

IVY GROUP

Season	No.	Regular Season
1902	5	Yale
1903	5	Yale
1904	6	Columbia
1905	5	Columbia
1906	6	Pennsylvania
1907	6	Yale
1908	5	Pennsylvania
1909-10		DNP
1911	5	Columbia
1912	6	Columbia
1913	5	Cornell
1914	6	Cornell/Columbia
1915	6	Yale
1916	6	Pennsylvania
1917	6	Yale
1918	6	Pennsylvania
1919	5	Pennsylvania
1920	6	Pennsylvania
1921	6	Pennsylvania
1922	6	Princeton
1923	6	Yale
1924	6	Cornell
1925	6	Princeton
1926	6	Columbia
1927	6	Dartmouth
1928	6	Pennsylvania
1929	6	Pennsylvania
1930	6	Columbia
1931	6	Columbia
1932	6	Princeton
1933	6	Yale
1934	7	Pennsylvania
1935	7	Pennsylvania
1936	7	Columbia
1937	7	Pennsylvania
1938	7	Dartmouth
1939	7	Dartmouth
1940	7	Dartmouth
1941	7	Dartmouth
1942	7	Dartmouth
1943	7	Dartmouth
1944	5	Dartmouth
1945	4	Pennsylvania
1946	5	Dartmouth
1947	7	Columbia
1948	7	Columbia
1949	7	Yale
1950	7	Princeton
1951	7	Columbia
1952	7	Princeton
1953	7	Pennsylvania
1954	8	Cornell
1955	8	Princeton
1956	8	Dartmouth
1957	8	Yale
1958	8	Dartmouth
1959	8	Dartmouth
1960	8	Princeton
1961	8	Princeton
1962	8	Yale
1963	8	Princeton
1964	8	Princeton
1965	8	Princeton
1966	8	Pennsylvania
1967	8	Princeton
1968	8	Columbia
1969	8	Princeton
1970	8	Pennsylvania
1971	8	Pennsylvania
1972	8	Pennsylvania
1973	8	Pennsylvania
1974	8	Pennsylvania
1975	8	Pennsylvania
1976	8	Princeton
1977	8	Princeton
1978	8	Pennsylvania
1979	8	Pennsylvania
1980	8	Pennsylvania
1981	8	Princeton
1982	8	Pennsylvania
1983	8	Princeton
1984	8	Pennsylvania
1985	8	Pennsylvania
1986	8	Brown
1987	8	Pennsylvania
1988	8	Cornell
1989	8	Princeton
1990	8	Princeton
1991	8	Princeton
1992	8	Princeton
1993	8	Pennsylvania
1994	8	Pennsylvania
1995	8	Pennsylvania
1996	8	Princeton
1997	8	Princeton
1998	8	Princeton
1999	8	Pennsylvania
2000	8	Pennsylvania
2001	8	Princeton
2002	8	Pennsylvania/Yale/Princeton
2003	8	Pennsylvania

METRO ATLANTIC ATHLETIC CONFERENCE

Season	No.	Regular Season
1982	6	St. Peter's
1983	6	Iona
1984	8	La Salle/St. Peter's/Iona
1985	8	Iona
1986	8	Fairfield
1987	8	St. Peter's
1988	8	La Salle
1989	8	La Salle
1990	12	Holy Cross (North)/La Salle (South)
1991	9	Siena
1992	9	Manhattan
1993	8	Manhattan
1994	8	Canisius
1995	8	Manhattan
1996	8	Fairfield/Iona
1997	8	Iona
1998	10	Iona
1999	10	Niagara/Siena
2000	10	Siena
2001	10	Iona/Siena/Niagara
2002	10	Marist/Rider
2003	10	Manhattan

Season	No.	Conference Tournament
1982	6	Fordham
1983	6	Fordham
1984	8	Iona
1985	8	Iona
1986	8	Fairfield
1987	8	Fairfield
1988	8	La Salle
1989	8	La Salle
1990	12	La Salle
1991	9	St. Peter's
1992	9	La Salle
1993	8	Manhattan
1994	8	Loyola (Md.)
1995	8	St. Peter's
1996	8	Canisius
1997	8	Fairfield
1998	10	Iona
1999	10	Siena
2000	10	Iona
2001	10	Iona
2002	10	Siena
2003	10	Manhattan

METROPOLITAN COLLEGIATE ATHLETIC CONFERENCE

Season	No.	Regular Season
1976	6	Tulane
1977	7	Louisville
1978	7	Florida St.
1979	7	Louisville
1980	7	Louisville
1981	7	Louisville
1982	7	Memphis
1983	7	Louisville
1984	8	Memphis/Louisville
1985	7	Memphis
1986	7	Louisville
1987	7	Louisville
1988	7	Louisville
1989	7	Florida St.
1990	8	Louisville
1991	8	Southern Miss.
1992	7	Tulane
1993	7	Louisville
1994	7	Louisville
1995	7	Charlotte

Season	No.	Conference Tournament
1976	6	Cincinnati
1977	7	Cincinnati
1978	7	Louisville
1979	7	Virginia Tech
1980	7	Louisville
1981	7	Louisville
1982	7	Memphis
1983	7	Louisville
1984	8	Memphis
1985	8	Memphis
1986	7	Louisville
1987	7	Memphis
1988	7	Louisville
1989	5	Louisville
1990	8	Louisville
1991	8	Florida St.
1992	7	Charlotte
1993	7	Louisville
1994	7	Louisville
1995	7	Louisville

METROPOLITAN NEW YORK CONFERENCE

Season	No.	Regular Season
1943	8	St. John's (N.Y.)
1944-45		DNP
1946	7	New York U./St. John's (N.Y.)
1947	7	St. John's (N.Y.)
1948	7	New York U.
1949	7	Manhattan/St. John's (N.Y.)
1950	7	CCNY
1951	7	St. John's (N.Y.)
1952	7	St. John's (N.Y.)
1953	7	Manhattan
1954	7	St. Francis (N.Y.)
1955	7	Manhattan
1956	7	St. Francis (N.Y.)
1957	7	New York U.
1958	7	St. John's (N.Y.)
1959	7	Manhattan
1960	7	New York U.
1961	7	St. John's (N.Y.)
1962	7	St. John's (N.Y.)
1963	7	Fordham

MID-AMERICAN ATHLETIC CONFERENCE

Season	No.	Regular Season
1947	5	Butler/Cincinnati
1948	6	Cincinnati
1949	6	Cincinnati
1950	6	Cincinnati
1951	5	Cincinnati
1952	7	Miami (Ohio)/Western Mich.
1953	7	Miami (Ohio)
1954	8	Toledo
1955	8	Miami (Ohio)
1956	7	Marshall
1957	7	Miami (Ohio)
1958	7	Miami (Ohio)
1959	7	Bowling Green
1960	7	Ohio
1961	7	Ohio
1962	7	Bowling Green
1963	7	Bowling Green
1964	7	Ohio
1965	7	Ohio
1966	7	Miami (Ohio)
1967	7	Toledo
1968	7	Bowling Green
1969	7	Miami (Ohio)
1970	6	Ohio
1971	6	Miami (Ohio)
1972	6	Ohio
1973	7	Miami (Ohio)
1974	7	Ohio
1975	8	Central Mich.
1976	10	Western Mich.
1977	10	Central Mich.
1978	10	Miami (Ohio)
1979	10	Toledo
1980	10	Toledo
1981	10	Ball St./Northern Ill./Toledo/Western Mich./Bowling Green
1982	10	Ball St.
1983	10	Bowling Green
1984	10	Miami (Ohio)
1985	10	Ohio

Season	No.	Regular Season
1986	10	Miami (Ohio)
1987	9	Central Mich.
1988	9	Eastern Mich.
1989	9	Ball St.
1990	9	Ball St.
1991	9	Eastern Mich.
1992	8	Miami (Ohio)
1993	10	Ball St./Miami (Ohio)
1994	10	Ohio
1995	10	Miami (Ohio)
1996	10	Eastern Mich.
1997	10	Bowling Green/Miami (Ohio)
1998	12	Akron (East)/Ball St. (West)
1999	13	Miami (Ohio)(East)/Toledo (West)
2000	13	Bowling Green (East)/ Ball St. (West)/Toledo (West)
2001	13	Kent St. (East)/ Central Mich. (West)
2002	13	Kent St. (East)/Ball St. (West)
2003	13	Kent St. (East)/Central Mich. (West)

Season	No.	Conference Tournament
1980	7	Toledo
1981	7	Ball St.
1982	7	Northern Ill.
1983	7	Ohio
1984	7	Miami (Ohio)
1985	7	Ohio
1986	7	Ball St.
1987	7	Central Mich.
1988	7	Eastern Mich.
1989	8	Ball St.
1990	8	Ball St.
1991	8	Eastern Mich.
1992	8	Miami (Ohio)
1993	10	Ball St.
1994	8	Ohio
1995	8	Ball St.
1996	8	Eastern Mich.
1997	8	Miami (Ohio)
1998	8	Eastern Mich.
1999	8	Kent St.
2000	13	Ball St.
2001	13	Kent St.
2002	13	Kent St.
2003	13	Central Mich.

MID-CONTINENT CONFERENCE

Season	No.	Regular Season
1983	8	Western Ill.
1984	8	Ill.-Chicago
1985	8	Cleveland St.
1986	8	Cleveland St.
1987	8	Southwest Mo. St.
1988	8	Southwest Mo. St.
1989	8	Southwest Mo. St.
1990	7	Southwest Mo. St.
1991	9	Northern Ill.
1992	9	Wis.-Green Bay
1993	9	Cleveland St.
1994	10	Wis.-Green Bay
1995	10	Valparaiso
1996	10	Valparaiso
1997	8	Valparaiso
1998	9	Valparaiso
1999	9	Valparaiso
2000	9	Oakland
2001	9	Southern Utah/Valparaiso
2002	8	Valparaiso
2003	8	Valparaiso

Season	No.	Conference Tournament
1984	8	Western Ill.
1985	8	Eastern Ill.
1986	8	Cleveland St.
1987	8	Southwest Mo. St.
1988		DNP
1989	7	Southwest Mo. St.
1990	7	Northern Iowa
1991	8	Wis.-Green Bay
1992	8	Eastern Ill.
1993	8	Wright St.
1994	8	Wis.-Green Bay
1995	6	Valparaiso
1996	8	Valparaiso
1997	8	Valparaiso
1998	7	Valpairaso
1999	7	Valparaiso
2000	7	Valparaiso
2001	8	Southern Utah

Season	No.	Conference Tournament
2002	8	Valparaiso
2003	8	IUPUI

MID-EASTERN ATHLETIC CONFERENCE

Season	No.	Regular Season
1972	7	N.C. A&T
1973	7	Md.-East. Shore
1974	7	Md.-East. Shore/Morgan St.
1975	7	N.C. A&T
1976	7	N.C. A&T/Morgan St.
1977	7	South Carolina St.
1978	7	N.C. A&T
1979	7	N.C. A&T
1980	7	Howard
1981	6	N.C. A&T
1982	7	N.C. A&T
1983	7	Howard
1984	6	N.C. A&T
1985	7	N.C. A&T
1986	8	N.C. A&T
1987	8	Howard
1988	9	N.C. A&T
1989	9	South Carolina St.
1990	9	Coppin St.
1991	9	Coppin St.
1992	9	N.C. A&T/Howard
1993	9	Coppin St.
1994	9	Coppin St.
1995	9	Coppin St.
1996	10	Coppin St./South Carolina St.
1997	10	Coppin St.
1998	11	Coppin St.
1999	11	Coppin St./South Carolina St.
2000	11	South Carolina St.
2001	11	Hampton/South Carolina St.
2002	11	Hampton
2003	11	South Carolina St.

Season	No.	Conference Tournament
1972	7	N.C. A&T
1973	7	N.C. A&T
1974	7	Md.-East. Shore
1975	7	N.C. A&T
1976	7	N.C. A&T
1977	7	Morgan St.
1978	7	N.C. A&T
1979	7	N.C. A&T
1980	7	Howard
1981	6	Howard
1982	7	N.C. A&T
1983	7	N.C. A&T
1984	6	N.C. A&T
1985	6	N.C. A&T
1986	6	N.C. A&T
1987	7	N.C. A&T
1988	7	N.C. A&T
1989	8	South Carolina St.
1990	8	Coppin St.
1991	9	Florida A&M
1992	9	Howard
1993	9	Coppin St.
1994	9	N.C. A&T
1995	9	N.C. A&T
1996	8	South Carolina St.
1997	9	Coppin St.
1998	9	South Carolina St.
1999	10	Florida A&M
2000	11	South Carolina St.
2001	11	Hampton
2002	11	Hampton
2003	11	South Carolina St.

MISSOURI VALLEY CONFERENCE

(Note: The Big Eight and Missouri Valley conferences share the same history from 1908-28.)

Season	No.	Regular Season
1908	6	Kansas
1909	6	Kansas
1910	6	Kansas
1911	5	Kansas
1912	6	Nebraska/Kansas
1913	6	Nebraska
1914	7	Kansas/Nebraska
1915	7	Kansas
1916	7	Nebraska
1917	7	Kansas St.
1918	7	Missouri

Season	No.	Regular Season
1919	8	Kansas St.
1920	8	Missouri
1921	9	Missouri
1922	9	Missouri/Kansas
1923	9	Kansas
1924	9	Kansas
1925	9	Kansas
1926	10	Kansas
1927	10	Kansas
1928	10	Oklahoma
1929	5	Washington (Mo.)
1930	5	Creighton/Washington (Mo.)
1931	5	Creighton/Oklahoma St.
1932	5	Creighton
1933	6	Butler
1934	6	Butler
1935	7	Creighton/Drake
1936	7	Creighton/Oklahoma St./Drake
1937	7	Oklahoma St.
1938	7	Oklahoma St.
1939	8	Oklahoma St./Drake
1940	7	Oklahoma St.
1941	7	Creighton
1942	6	Oklahoma St./Creighton
1943	6	Creighton
1944	4	Oklahoma St.
1945	5	Oklahoma St.
1946	7	Oklahoma St.
1947	7	St. Louis
1948	6	Oklahoma St.
1949	6	Oklahoma St.
1950	7	Bradley
1951	8	Oklahoma St.
1952	6	St. Louis
1953	6	Oklahoma St.
1954	6	Oklahoma St.
1955	6	Tulsa/St. Louis
1956	7	Houston
1957	8	St. Louis
1958	8	Cincinnati
1959	8	Cincinnati
1960	8	Cincinnati
1961	7	Cincinnati
1962	7	Bradley/Cincinnati
1963	7	Cincinnati
1964	7	Drake/Wichita St.
1965	8	Wichita St.
1966	8	Cincinnati
1967	8	Louisville
1968	9	Louisville
1969	9	Drake/Louisville
1970	9	Drake
1971	8	Drake/Louisville/St. Louis
1972	8	Memphis/Louisville
1973	10	Memphis
1974	9	Louisville
1975	8	Louisville
1976	7	Wichita St.
1977	7	Southern Ill./New Mexico St.
1978	9	Creighton
1979	9	Indiana St.
1980	9	Bradley
1981	9	Wichita St.
1982	10	Bradley
1983	10	Wichita St.
1984	9	Tulsa/Illinois St.
1985	9	Tulsa
1986	9	Bradley
1987	8	Tulsa
1988	8	Bradley
1989	8	Creighton
1990	8	Southern Ill.
1991	9	Creighton
1992	10	Southern Ill./Illinois St.
1993	10	Illinois St.
1994	10	Southern Ill./Tulsa
1995	11	Tulsa
1996	11	Bradley
1997	10	Illinois St.
1998	10	Illinois St.
1999	10	Evansville
2000	10	Indiana St.
2001	10	Creighton
2002	10	Southern Ill./Creighton
2003	10	Southern Ill.

Season	No.	Conference Tournament
1977	8	Southern Ill.
1978	9	Creighton
1979	8	Indiana St.

Season	No.	Conference Tournament
1980	8	Bradley
1981	8	Creighton
1982	8	Tulsa
1983	8	Illinois St.
1984	8	Tulsa
1985	8	Wichita St.
1986	8	Tulsa
1987	7	Wichita St.
1988	8	Bradley
1989	8	Creighton
1990	8	Illinois St.
1991	9	Creighton
1992	8	Southwest Mo. St.
1993	8	Southern Ill.
1994	8	Southern Ill.
1995	8	Southern Ill.
1996	8	Tulsa
1997	10	Illinois St.
1998	10	Illinois St.
1999	10	Creighton
2000	10	Creighton
2001	10	Indiana St.
2002	10	Creighton
2003	10	Creighton

MOUNTAIN STATES CONFERENCE

Season	No.	Regular Season
1938	7	Colorado/Utah
1939	7	Colorado
1940	7	Colorado
1941	7	Wyoming
1942	7	Colorado
1943	5	Wyoming
1944	7	Utah
1945	7	Utah
1946	7	Wyoming
1947	7	Wyoming
1948	6	Brigham Young
1949	6	Wyoming
1950	6	Brigham Young
1951	6	Brigham Young
1952	8	Wyoming
1953	8	Wyoming
1954	8	Colorado
1955	8	Utah
1956	8	Utah
1957	8	Brigham Young
1958	8	Wyoming
1959	8	Utah
1960	8	Utah
1961	8	Colorado St./Utah
1962	8	Utah

MOUNTAIN WEST

Season	No.	Regular Season
2000	8	UNLV/Utah
2001	8	Brigham Young/Wyoming/Utah
2002	8	Wyoming
2003	8	Brigham Young/Utah

Season	No.	Conference Tournament
2000	8	UNLV
2001	7	Brigham Young
2002	8	San Diego St.
2003	8	Colorado St.

NEW ENGLAND CONFERENCE

Season	No.	Regular Season
1938	5	Rhode Island
1939	5	Rhode Island
1940	5	Rhode Island
1941	5	Rhode Island
1942	5	Rhode Island
1943	5	Rhode Island
1944	4	Rhode Island
1945		DNP
1946	5	Rhode Island

NEW JERSEY-NEW YORK 7 CONFERENCE

Season	No.	Regular Season
1977	7	Columbia/Seton Hall
1978	7	Rutgers/St. John's (N.Y.)
1979	7	Rutgers

NORTHEAST CONFERENCE

Season	No.	Regular Season
1982	11	Fairleigh Dickinson (North)/Robert Morris (South)
1983	10	Long Island (North)/Robert Morris (South)
1984	9	Long Island/Robert Morris
1985	8	Marist
1986	9	Fairleigh Dickinson
1987	9	Marist
1988	9	Fairleigh Dickinson/Marist
1989	9	Robert Morris
1990	9	Robert Morris
1991	9	St. Francis (Pa.)/Fairleigh Dickinson
1992	9	Robert Morris
1993	10	Rider
1994	10	Rider
1995	10	Rider
1996	10	Mt. St. Mary's
1997	10	Long Island
1998	9	Long Island
1999	11	UMBC
2000	12	Central Conn. St.
2001	12	St. Francis (N.Y.)
2002	12	Central Conn. St.
2003	12	Wagner

Season	No.	Conference Tournament
1982	8	Robert Morris
1983	8	Robert Morris
1984	8	Long Island
1985	8	Fairleigh Dickinson
1986	8	Marist
1987	6	Marist
1988	6	Fairleigh Dickinson
1989	6	Robert Morris
1990	6	Robert Morris
1991	7	St. Francis (Pa.)
1992	9	Robert Morris
1993	10	Rider
1994	10	Rider
1995	10	Mt. St. Mary's
1996	10	Monmouth
1997	8	Long Island
1998	8	Fairleigh Dickinson
1999	8	Mt. St. Mary's
2000	8	Central Conn. St.
2001	7	Monmouth
2002	8	Central Conn. St.
2003	8	Wagner

OHIO VALLEY CONFERENCE

Season	No.	Regular Season
1949	8	Western Ky.
1950	7	Western Ky.
1951	7	Murray St.
1952	7	Morehead St.
1953	6	Eastern Ky.
1954	6	Western Ky.
1955	6	Western Ky.
1956	6	Morehead St./Tennessee Tech/Western Ky.
1957	6	Morehead St./Western Ky.
1958	7	Tennessee Tech
1959	7	Eastern Ky.
1960	7	Western Ky.
1961	7	Morehead St./Western Ky./Eastern Ky.
1962	6	Western Ky.
1963	7	Tennessee Tech/Morehead St.
1964	8	Murray St.
1965	8	Eastern Ky.
1966	8	Western Ky.
1967	8	Western Ky.
1968	8	East Tenn. St./Murray St.
1969	8	Murray St./Morehead St.
1970	8	Western Ky.
1971	8	Western Ky.
1972	8	Eastern Ky./Morehead St./Western Ky.
1973	8	Austin Peay
1974	8	Austin Peay/Morehead St.
1975	8	Middle Tenn.
1976	8	Western Ky.
1977	8	Austin Peay
1978	8	Middle Tenn./Eastern Ky.
1979	7	Eastern Ky.

Season	No.	Regular Season
1980	7	Western Ky./Murray St.
1981	8	Western Ky.
1982	8	Murray St./Western Ky.
1983	8	Murray St.
1984	8	Morehead St.
1985	8	Tennessee Tech
1986	8	Akron/Middle Tenn.
1987	8	Middle Tenn.
1988	8	Murray St.
1989	7	Middle Tenn./Murray St.
1990	7	Murray St.
1991	7	Murray St.
1992	8	Murray St.
1993	9	Tennessee St.
1994	9	Tennessee St.
1995	9	Murray St./Tennessee St.
1996	9	Murray St.
1997	10	Austin Peay/Murray St.
1998	10	Murray St.
1999	10	Murray St.
2000	10	Southeast Mo. St./Murray St.
2001	9	Tennessee Tech
2002	9	Tennessee Tech
2003	9	Austin Peay/Morehead St.

Season	No.	Conference Tournament
1949	8	Western Ky.
1950	7	Eastern Ky.
1951	7	Murray St.
1952	7	Western Ky.
1953	6	Western Ky.
1954	6	Western Ky.
1955	6	Eastern Ky.
1956-63		DNP
1964	8	Murray St.
1965	8	Western Ky.
1966	8	Western Ky.
1967	8	Tennessee Tech
1968-74		DNP
1975	4	Middle Tenn.
1976	8	Western Ky.
1977	4	Middle Tenn.
1978	4	Western Ky.
1979	4	Eastern Ky.
1980	4	Western Ky.
1981	4	Western Ky.
1982	4	Middle Tenn.
1983	4	Morehead St.
1984	4	Morehead St.
1985	7	Middle Tenn.
1986	7	Akron
1987	7	Austin Peay
1988	7	Murray St.
1989	7	Middle Tenn.
1990	7	Murray St.
1991	7	Murray St.
1992	7	Murray St.
1993	6	Tennessee St.
1994	7	Tennessee St.
1995	7	Murray St.
1996	7	Austin Peay
1997	8	Murray St.
1998	8	Murray St.
1999	8	Murray St.
2000	8	Southeast Mo. St.
2001	8	Eastern Ill.
2002	8	Murray St.
2003	8	Austin Peay

PACIFIC-10 CONFERENCE

Season	No.	Regular Season
1916	3	California/Oregon St.
1917	6	Washington St.
1918		DNP
1919	6	Oregon
1920	6	Stanford
1921	6	Stanford
1922	8	Idaho
1923	8	Idaho
1924	9	California
1925	8	California
1926	9	California
1927	9	California
1928	10	Southern California
1929	10	California
1930	9	Southern California
1931	9	Washington
1932	9	California

Season	No.	Regular Season
1933	9	Oregon St.
1934	9	Washington
1935	9	Southern California
1936	9	Stanford
1937	9	Stanford
1938	10	Stanford
1939	9	Oregon
1940	9	Southern California
1941	9	Washington St.
1942	9	Stanford
1943	9	Washington
1944	8	Washington (North)/California (South)
1945	8	Oregon (North)/UCLA (South)
1946	9	California
1947	9	Oregon St.
1948	9	Washington
1949	9	Oregon St.
1950	9	UCLA
1951	9	Washington
1952	9	UCLA
1953	9	Washington
1954	9	Southern California
1955	9	Oregon St.
1956	9	UCLA
1957	9	California
1958	9	Oregon St./California
1959	9	California
1960	5	California
1961	5	Southern California
1962	5	UCLA
1963	5	UCLA/Stanford
1964	6	UCLA
1965	8	UCLA
1966	8	Oregon St.
1967	8	UCLA
1968	8	UCLA
1969	8	UCLA
1970	8	UCLA
1971	8	UCLA
1972	8	UCLA
1973	8	UCLA
1974	8	UCLA
1975	8	UCLA
1976	8	UCLA
1977	8	UCLA
1978	8	UCLA
1979	10	UCLA
1980	10	Oregon St.
1981	10	Oregon St.
1982	10	Oregon St.
1983	10	UCLA
1984	10	Washington/Oregon St.
1985	10	Washington/Southern California
1986	10	Arizona
1987	10	UCLA
1988	10	Arizona
1989	10	Arizona
1990	10	Oregon St./Arizona
1991	10	Arizona
1992	10	UCLA
1993	10	Arizona
1994	10	Arizona
1995	10	UCLA
1996	10	UCLA
1997	10	UCLA
1998	10	Arizona
1999	10	Stanford
2000	10	Arizona/Stanford
2001	10	Stanford
2002	10	Oregon
2003	10	Arizona

Season	No.	Conference Tournament
1987	10	UCLA
1988	10	Arizona
1989	10	Arizona
1990	10	Arizona
1991-2001		DNP
2002	8	Arizona
2003	8	Oregon

PATRIOT LEAGUE

Season	No.	Regular Season
1991	7	Fordham
1992	8	Bucknell/Fordham
1993	8	Bucknell
1994	8	Navy/Fordham/Colgate/Holy Cross
1995	8	Bucknell/Colgate

Season	No.	Regular Season
1996	7	Colgate/Navy
1997	7	Navy
1998	7	Lafayette/Navy
1999	7	Lafayette
2000	7	Lafayette/Navy
2001	7	Holy Cross
2002	8	American
2003	8	Holy Cross

Season	No.	Conference Tournament
1991	7	Fordham
1992	8	Fordham
1993	8	Holy Cross
1994	8	Navy
1995	8	Colgate
1996	7	Colgate
1997	7	Navy
1998	7	Navy
1999	7	Lafayette
2000	7	Lafayette
2001	7	Holy Cross
2002	8	Holy Cross
2003	8	Holy Cross

ROCKY MOUNTAIN CONFERENCE

Season	No.	Regular Season
1922	6	Colorado Col.
1923	5	Colorado Col.
1924	6	Colorado Col.
1925	12	Colorado Col. (East)/Brigham Young (West)
1926	12	Colorado St. (East)/Utah (West)
1927	12	Colorado Col. (East)/Montana St. (West)
1928	12	Wyoming (East)/Montana St. (West)
1929	12	Colorado (East)/Montana St. (West)
1929	12	Colorado (East)/Montana St. (West)
1930	12	Colorado (East)/Montana St. (West)/Utah St. (West)
1931	12	Wyoming (East)/Utah (West)
1932	12	Wyoming (East)/Brigham Young (West)/Utah (West)
1933	12	Wyoming (East)/Colorado St. (East)/Brigham Young (West)/Utah (West)
1934	12	Wyoming (East)/Brigham Young (West)
1935	12	Northern Colo. (East)/Utah St. (West)
1936	12	Wyoming (East)/Utah (West)
1937	12	Denver (East)/Colorado (East)/Montana St. (West)/Utah (West)
1938	5	Montana St.
1939	5	Northern Colo.
1940	5	Northern Colo.
1941	5	Northern Colo.
1942	5	Northern Colo.
1943	3	Northern Colo.
1944	3	Colorado Col.
1945	3	Colorado Col.
1946	5	Colorado St.
1947	5	Montana St.
1948	4	Colorado St.
1949	5	Colorado St.
1950	6	Montana St.
1951	6	Montana St.
1952	6	Colorado St./Montana St.
1953	6	Idaho St.
1954	6	Idaho St.
1955	6	Idaho St.
1956	6	Idaho St.
1957	6	Idaho St.
1958	6	Idaho St.
1959	6	Idaho St.
1960	6	Idaho St.

SOUTHEASTERN CONFERENCE

Season	No.	Regular Season
1933	13	Kentucky
1934	13	Alabama
1935	13	LSU/Kentucky
1936	13	Tennessee
1937	13	Kentucky
1938	13	Georgia Tech
1939	13	Kentucky
1940	13	Kentucky

Season	No.	Regular Season
1941	12	Tennessee
1942	12	Kentucky
1943	12	Tennessee
1944	6	Kentucky
1945	12	Kentucky
1946	12	Kentucky
1947	12	Kentucky
1948	12	Kentucky
1949	12	Kentucky
1950	12	Kentucky
1951	12	Kentucky
1952	12	Kentucky
1953	11	LSU
1954	12	Kentucky/LSU
1955	12	Kentucky
1956	12	Alabama
1957	12	Kentucky
1958	12	Kentucky
1959	12	Mississippi St.
1960	12	Auburn
1961	12	Mississippi St.
1962	12	Mississippi St./Kentucky
1963	12	Mississippi St.
1964	12	Kentucky
1965	11	Vanderbilt
1966	11	Kentucky
1967	10	Tennessee
1968	10	Kentucky
1969	10	Kentucky
1970	10	Kentucky
1971	10	Kentucky
1972	10	Tennessee/Kentucky
1973	10	Kentucky
1974	10	Vanderbilt/Alabama
1975	10	Kentucky/Alabama
1976	10	Alabama
1977	10	Kentucky/Tennessee
1978	10	Kentucky
1979	10	LSU
1980	10	Kentucky
1981	10	LSU
1982	10	Kentucky/Tennessee
1983	10	Kentucky
1984	10	Kentucky
1985	10	LSU
1986	10	Kentucky
1987	10	Alabama
1988	10	Kentucky*
1989	10	Florida
1990	10	Georgia
1991	10	Mississippi St./LSU
1992	12	Kentucky (Eastern)/Arkansas (Western)
1993	12	Vanderbilt (Eastern)/Arkansas (Western)
1994	12	Florida (Eastern)/Kentucky (Eastern)/Arkansas (Western)
1995	12	Kentucky (Eastern)/Arkansas (Western)/Mississippi St. (Western)
1996	12	Kentucky (Eastern)/Mississippi St. (Western)
1997	12	South Carolina (Eastern)/Mississippi (Western)
1998	12	Kentucky (Eastern)/Mississippi (Western)
1999	12	Tennessee (Eastern)/Auburn (Western)
2000	12	Tennessee (Eastern)/Florida (Eastern)/Kentucky (Eastern)/LSU (Western)
2001	12	Florida (Eastern)/Kentucky (Eastern)/Mississippi (Western)
2002	12	Georgia (Eastern)/Kentucky (Eastern)/Florida (Eastern)/Alabama (Western)
2003	12	Kentucky (Eastern)/Mississippi St. (Western)

Season	No.	Conference Tournament
1933	13	Kentucky
1934	10	Alabama
1935		DNP
1936	9	Tennessee
1937	8	Kentucky
1938	11	Georgia Tech
1939	12	Kentucky
1940	12	Kentucky
1941	12	Tennessee
1942	12	Kentucky

Season	No.	Conference Tournament
1943	11	Tennessee
1944	6	Kentucky
1945	11	Kentucky
1946	12	Kentucky
1947	12	Kentucky
1948	12	Kentucky
1949	12	Kentucky
1950	12	Kentucky
1951	12	Vanderbilt
1952	12	Kentucky
1953-78		DNP
1979	10	Tennessee
1980	10	LSU
1981	10	Mississippi
1982	10	Alabama
1983	10	Georgia
1984	10	Kentucky
1985	10	Auburn
1986	10	Kentucky
1987	10	Alabama
1988	10	Kentucky*
1989	10	Alabama
1990	9	Alabama
1991	9	Alabama
1992	11	Kentucky
1993	12	Kentucky
1994	12	Kentucky
1995	12	Kentucky
1996	12	Mississippi St.
1997	12	Kentucky
1998	12	Kentucky
1999	12	Kentucky
2000	12	Arkansas
2001	12	Kentucky
2002	12	Mississippi St.
2003	11	Kentucky

*later vacated

SOUTHERN CONFERENCE

Season	No.	Regular Season
1922	13	Virginia
1923	19	North Carolina
1924	21	Tulane
1925	21	North Carolina
1926	22	Kentucky
1927	22	South Carolina
1928	22	Auburn
1929	23	Wash. & Lee
1930	23	Alabama
1931	22	Georgia
1932	23	Kentucky/Maryland
1933	10	South Carolina
1934	10	South Carolina
1935	10	North Carolina
1936	10	Wash. & Lee
1937	16	Wash. & Lee
1938	15	North Carolina
1939	15	Wake Forest
1940	15	Duke
1941	15	North Carolina
1942	16	Duke
1943	15	Duke
1944	12	North Carolina
1945	14	South Carolina
1946	16	North Carolina
1947	16	North Carolina St.
1948	16	North Carolina St.
1949	16	North Carolina St.
1950	16	North Carolina St.
1951	17	North Carolina St.
1952	17	West Virginia
1953	17	North Carolina St.
1954	10	George Washington
1955	10	West Virginia
1956	10	George Washington/West Virginia
1957	10	West Virginia
1958	10	West Virginia
1959	9	West Virginia
1960	9	Virginia Tech
1961	9	West Virginia
1962	9	West Virginia
1963	9	West Virginia
1964	9	Davidson
1965	10	Davidson
1966	9	Davidson
1967	9	West Virginia
1968	9	Davidson
1969	8	Davidson
1970	8	Davidson
1971	7	Davidson
1972	8	Davidson
1973	8	Davidson
1974	8	Furman
1975	8	Furman
1976	8	VMI
1977	10	Furman/VMI
1978	8	Appalachian St.
1979	9	Appalachian St.
1980	9	Furman
1981	9	Appalachian St./Davidson/Chattanooga
1982	9	Chattanooga
1983	9	Chattanooga
1984	9	Marshall
1985	9	Chattanooga
1986	9	Chattanooga
1987	9	Marshall
1988	9	Marshall
1989	8	Chattanooga
1990	8	East Tenn. St.
1991	8	East Tenn. St./Furman/Chattanooga
1992	8	East Tenn. St./Chattanooga
1993	10	Chattanooga
1994	10	Chattanooga
1995	10	Marshall (Northern)/Chattanooga (Southern)
1996	10	Davidson (Northern)/Western Caro. (Southern)
1997	10	Davidson (Northern)/Marshall (Northern)/Chattanooga (Southern)
1998	11	Appalachian St. (North)/Davidson (North)/Chattanooga (South)
1999	12	Appalachian St.(North)/Col. of Charleston (South)
2000	12	Appalachian St. (North)/Col. of Charleston (South)
2001	12	East Tenn. St. (North)/Col. of Charleston (South)
2002	12	Davidson (North)/UNC Greensboro (North)/East Tenn. St. (North)/Col. of Charleston (South)/Ga. Southern(South)/Chattanooga (South)
2003	12	Appalachian St. (North)/Davidson (North)/East Tenn. St. (North)/Col. of Charleston (South)

Season	No.	Conference Tournament
1921		Kentucky
1922	23	North Carolina
1923	22	Mississippi St.
1924	16	North Carolina
1925	17	North Carolina
1926	16	North Carolina
1927	14	Vanderbilt
1928	16	Mississippi
1929	16	North Carolina St.
1930	16	Alabama
1931	16	Maryland
1932	16	Georgia
1933	8	South Carolina
1934	8	Wash. & Lee
1935	8	North Carolina
1936	8	North Carolina
1937	8	Wash. & Lee
1938	8	Duke
1939	11	Clemson
1940	8	North Carolina
1941	8	Duke
1942	8	North Carolina
1943	8	George Washington
1944	8	Duke
1945	8	North Carolina
1946	8	Duke
1947	8	North Carolina St.
1948	10	North Carolina St.
1949	8	North Carolina St.
1950	8	North Carolina St.
1951	8	North Carolina St.
1952	8	North Carolina St.
1953	8	Wake Forest
1954	8	George Washington
1955	8	West Virginia
1956	8	West Virginia
1957	8	West Virginia
1958	8	West Virginia
1959	8	West Virginia
1960	8	West Virginia
1961	8	George Washington
1962	8	West Virginia
1963	8	West Virginia
1964	8	VMI
1965	8	West Virginia
1966	8	Davidson
1967	8	West Virginia
1968	8	Davidson
1969	8	Davidson
1970	8	Davidson
1971	7	Furman
1972	8	East Caro.
1973	8	Furman
1974	8	Furman
1975	8	Furman
1976	8	VMI
1977	7	VMI
1978	8	Furman
1979	8	Appalachian St.
1980	8	Furman
1981	8	Chattanooga
1982	8	Chattanooga
1983	8	Chattanooga
1984	8	Marshall
1985	8	Marshall
1986	8	Davidson
1987	8	Marshall
1988	8	Chattanooga
1989	8	East Tenn. St.
1990	8	East Tenn. St.
1991	8	East Tenn. St.
1992	8	East Tenn. St.
1993	10	Chattanooga
1994	10	Chattanooga
1995	10	Chattanooga
1996	9	Western Caro.
1997	10	Chattanooga
1998	10	Davidson
1999	12	Col. of Charleston
2000	12	Appalachian St.
2001	12	UNC Greensboro
2002	12	Davidson
2003	12	East Tenn. St.

SOUTHLAND CONFERENCE

Season	No.	Regular Season
1964	5	Lamar
1965	5	Abilene Christian/Arkansas St.
1966	5	Abilene Christian
1967	5	Arkansas St.
1968	5	Abilene Christian
1969	5	Trinity (Tex.)
1970	5	Lamar
1971	5	Arkansas St.
1972	7	Louisiana Tech
1973	7	Louisiana Tech
1974	3	Arkansas St.
1975	5	McNeese St.
1976	6	Louisiana Tech
1977	6	La.-Lafayette
1978	6	McNeese St./Lamar
1979	6	Lamar
1980	6	Lamar
1981	6	Lamar
1982	6	La.-Lafayette
1983	7	Lamar
1984	7	Lamar
1985	7	Louisiana Tech
1986	7	La.-Monroe
1987	6	Louisiana Tech
1988	8	North Texas
1989	8	North Texas
1990	8	La.-Monroe
1991	8	La.-Monroe
1992	10	Texas-San Antonio
1993	10	La.-Monroe
1994	10	La.-Monroe
1995	10	Nicholls St.
1996	10	La.-Monroe
1997	10	McNeese St./La.-Monroe/Texas St.
1998	10	Nicholls St.
1999	10	Texas St.
2000	11	Sam Houston St.
2001	11	McNeese St.
2002	11	McNeese St.
2003	11	Sam Houston St.

Season	No.	Conference Tournament
1981	6	Lamar
1982	5	La.-Lafayette
1983	7	Lamar
1984	7	Louisiana Tech
1985	7	Louisiana Tech

Season	No.	Conference Tournament
1986	7	La.-Monroe
1987	6	Louisiana Tech
1988	6	North Texas
1989	6	McNeese St.
1990	7	La.-Monroe
1991	4	La.-Monroe
1992	6	La.-Monroe
1993	6	La.-Monroe
1994	8	Texas St.
1995	8	Nicholls St.
1996	6	La.-Monroe
1997	6	Texas St.
1998	6	Nicholls St.
1999	6	Texas-San Antonio
2000	8	Lamar
2001	8	Northwestern St.
2002	6	McNeese St.
2003	6	Sam Houston St.

SOUTHWEST CONFERENCE

Season	No.	Regular Season
1915	5	Texas
1916	5	Texas
1917	3	Texas
1918	5	Rice
1919	5	Texas
1920	6	Texas A&M
1921	5	Texas A&M
1922	6	Texas A&M
1923	6	Texas A&M
1924	8	Texas
1925	8	Oklahoma St.
1926	7	Arkansas
1927	7	Arkansas
1928	7	Arkansas
1929	7	Arkansas
1930	7	Arkansas
1931	7	TCU
1932	7	Baylor
1933	7	Texas
1934	7	TCU
1935	7	Arkansas/Rice/Southern Methodist
1936	7	Arkansas
1937	7	Southern Methodist
1938	7	Arkansas
1939	7	Texas
1940	7	Rice
1941	7	Arkansas
1942	7	Rice/Arkansas
1943	7	Texas/Rice
1944	7	Arkansas/Rice
1945	7	Rice
1946	7	Baylor
1947	7	Texas
1948	7	Baylor
1949	7	Arkansas/Baylor/Rice
1950	7	Baylor/Arkansas
1951	7	Texas A&M/TCU/Texas
1952	7	TCU
1953	7	TCU
1954	7	Rice/Texas
1955	7	Southern Methodist
1956	7	Southern Methodist
1957	7	Southern Methodist
1958	8	Arkansas/Southern Methodist
1959	8	TCU
1960	8	Texas
1961	8	Texas Tech
1962	8	Southern Methodist/Texas Tech
1963	8	Texas
1964	8	Texas A&M
1965	8	Southern Methodist/Texas
1966	8	Southern Methodist
1967	8	Southern Methodist
1968	8	TCU
1969	8	Texas A&M
1970	8	Rice
1971	8	TCU
1972	8	Texas/Southern Methodist
1973	8	Texas Tech
1974	8	Texas
1975	8	Texas A&M
1976	9	Texas A&M
1977	9	Arkansas
1978	9	Texas/Arkansas
1979	9	Texas/Arkansas
1980	9	Texas A&M
1981	9	Arkansas

Season	No.	Regular Season
1982	9	Arkansas
1983	9	Houston
1984	9	Houston
1985	9	Texas Tech
1986	9	TCU/Texas/Texas A&M
1987	9	TCU
1988	9	Southern Methodist
1989	9	Arkansas
1990	9	Arkansas
1991	9	Arkansas
1992	8	Houston/Texas
1993	8	Southern Methodist
1994	8	Texas
1995	8	Texas/Texas Tech
1996	8	Texas Tech

Season	No.	Conference Tournament
1976	9	Texas Tech
1977	9	Arkansas
1978	9	Houston
1979	9	Arkansas
1980	9	Texas A&M
1981	9	Houston
1982	9	Arkansas
1983	9	Houston
1984	9	Houston
1985	8	Texas Tech
1986	8	Texas Tech
1987	8	Texas A&M
1988	8	Southern Methodist
1989	8	Arkansas
1990	8	Arkansas
1991	9	Arkansas
1992	8	Houston
1993	8	Texas Tech
1994	8	Texas
1995	7	Texas
1996	8	Texas Tech

SOUTHWESTERN ATHLETIC CONFERENCE

Season	No.	Regular Season
1957	6	Texas Southern
1958	6	Texas Southern
1959	8	Grambling
1960	8	Grambling
1961	8	Prairie View
1962	7	Prairie View
1963	8	Grambling
1964	8	Grambling/Jackson St.
1965	8	Southern U.
1966	8	Alcorn St./Grambling
1967	8	Alcorn St./Ark.-Pine Bluff/Grambling
1968	8	Alcorn St./Jackson St.
1969	8	Alcorn St.
1970	8	Jackson St.
1971	7	Grambling
1972	7	Grambling
1973	7	Alcorn St.
1974	7	Jackson St.
1975	7	Jackson St.
1976	7	Alcorn St.
1977	7	Texas Southern
1978	7	Jackson St./Southern U.
1979	7	Alcorn St.
1980	7	Alcorn St.
1981	7	Alcorn St./Southern U.
1982	7	Alcorn St./Jackson St.
1983	8	Texas Southern
1984	8	Alcorn St.
1985	8	Alcorn St.
1986	8	Alcorn St./Southern U.
1987	8	Grambling
1988	8	Southern U.
1989	8	Grambling/Southern U./Texas Southern
1990	8	Southern U.
1991	8	Jackson St.
1992	8	Mississippi Val./Texas Southern
1993	8	Jackson St.
1994	8	Texas Southern
1995	8	Texas Southern
1996	8	Jackson St./Mississippi Val.
1997	8	Mississippi Val.
1998	9	Texas Southern
1999	9	Alcorn St.
2000	10	Alcorn St.
2001	10	Alabama St.

Season	No.	Regular Season
2002	10	Alcorn St.
2003	10	Prairie View

Season	No.	Conference Tournament
1980	7	Alcorn St.
1981	7	Southern U.
1982	7	Alcorn St.
1983	7	Alcorn St.
1984	8	Alcorn St.
1985	4	Southern U.
1986	8	Mississippi Val.
1987	8	Southern U.
1988	8	Southern U.
1989	8	Southern U.
1990	8	Texas Southern
1991	8	Jackson St.
1992	8	Mississippi Val.
1993	8	Southern U.
1994	8	Texas Southern
1995	6	Texas Southern
1996	6	Mississippi Val.
1997	8	Jackson St.
1998	8	Prairie View
1999	8	Alcorn St.
2000	8	Jackson St.
2001	8	Alabama St.
2002	8	Alcorn St.
2003	8	Texas Southern

SUN BELT CONFERENCE

Season	No.	Regular Season
1977	6	Charlotte
1978	6	Charlotte
1979	6	South Ala.
1980	8	South Ala.
1981	7	Va. Commonwealth/South Ala./UAB
1982	6	UAB
1983	8	Va. Commonwealth/Old Dominion
1984	8	Va. Commonwealth
1985	8	Va. Commonwealth
1986	8	Old Dominion
1987	8	Western Ky.
1988	8	Charlotte
1989	8	South Ala.
1990	8	UAB
1991	8	South Ala.
1992	11	Louisiana Tech/La.-Lafayette
1993	10	New Orleans
1994	10	Western Ky.
1995	10	Western Ky.
1996	10	Ark.-Little Rock/New Orleans
1997	10	New Orleans/South Ala.
1998	10	South Ala./Arkansas St.
1999	8	Louisiana Tech
2000	9	La.-Lafayette/South Ala.
2001	12	Western Ky. (East)/South Ala. (West)
2002	11	Western Ky. (East)/La.-Lafayette (West)/New Mexico St. (West)
2003	12	Western Ky. (East)/La.-Lafayette (West)

Season	No.	Conference Tournament
1977	6	Charlotte
1978	6	New Orleans
1979	6	Jacksonville
1980	8	Va. Commonwealth
1981	7	Va. Commonwealth
1982	6	UAB
1983	8	UAB
1984	8	UAB
1985	8	Va. Commonwealth
1986	8	Jacksonville
1987	8	UAB
1988	8	Charlotte
1989	8	South Ala.
1990	8	South Fla.
1991	8	South Ala.
1992	11	La.-Lafayette
1993	9	Western Ky.
1994	10	La.-Lafayette
1995	10	Western Ky.
1996	10	New Orleans
1997	10	South Ala.
1998	10	South Ala.
1999	8	Arkansas St.
2000	9	La.-Lafayette
2001	11	Western Ky.

CONFERENCES

Season	No.	Conference Tournament
2002	11	Western Ky.
2003	11	Western Ky.

WEST COAST CONFERENCE

Season	No.	Regular Season
1953	5	Santa Clara
1954	5	Santa Clara
1955	5	San Francisco
1956	8	San Francisco
1957	8	San Francisco
1958	7	San Francisco
1959	7	St. Mary's (Cal.)
1960	7	Santa Clara
1961	7	Loyola Marymount
1962	7	Pepperdine
1963	7	San Francisco
1964	7	San Francisco
1965	8	San Francisco
1966	8	Pacific (Cal.)
1967	8	Pacific (Cal.)
1968	8	Santa Clara
1969	8	Santa Clara
1970	8	Santa Clara
1971	8	Pacific (Cal.)
1972	8	San Francisco
1973	8	San Francisco
1974	8	San Francisco
1975	8	UNLV
1976	7	Pepperdine
1977	8	San Francisco
1978	8	San Francisco
1979	8	San Francisco
1980	9	San Francisco/St. Mary's (Cal.)
1981	8	San Francisco/Pepperdine
1982	8	Pepperdine
1983	7	Pepperdine
1984	7	San Diego
1985	7	Pepperdine
1986	8	Pepperdine
1987	8	San Diego
1988	8	Loyola Marymount
1989	8	St. Mary's (Cal.)
1990	8	Loyola Marymount
1991	8	Pepperdine
1992	8	Pepperdine
1993	8	Pepperdine
1994	8	Gonzaga
1995	8	Santa Clara
1996	8	Gonzaga/Santa Clara
1997	8	St. Mary's (Cal.)/Santa Clara
1998	8	Gonzaga
1999	8	Gonzaga
2000	8	Pepperdine
2001	8	Gonzaga
2002	8	Gonzaga/Pepperdine
2003	8	Gonzaga

Season	No.	Conference Tournament
1987	8	Santa Clara
1988	8	Loyola Marymount
1989	8	Loyola Marymount
1990		DNP
1991	8	Pepperdine
1992	8	Pepperdine
1993	8	Santa Clara
1994	8	Pepperdine
1995	8	Gonzaga
1996	8	Portland
1997	8	St. Mary's (Cal.)
1998	8	San Francisco
1999	8	Gonzaga
2000	8	Gonzaga
2001	8	Gonzaga
2002	8	Gonzaga
2003	6	San Diego

WESTERN ATHLETIC CONFERENCE

Season	No.	Regular Season
1963	6	Arizona St.
1964	6	New Mexico/Arizona St.
1965	6	Brigham Young
1966	6	Utah
1967	6	Wyoming/Brigham Young
1968	6	New Mexico
1969	6	Brigham Young/Wyoming
1970	8	UTEP
1971	8	Brigham Young
1972	8	Brigham Young
1973	8	Arizona St.
1974	8	New Mexico
1975	8	Arizona St.
1976	8	Arizona
1977	8	Utah
1978	8	New Mexico
1979	7	Brigham Young
1980	8	Brigham Young
1981	9	Utah/Wyoming
1982	9	Wyoming
1983	9	UTEP/Utah
1984	9	UTEP
1985	9	UTEP
1986	9	Wyoming/UTEP/Utah
1987	9	UTEP
1988	9	Brigham Young
1989	9	Colorado St.
1990	9	Colorado St./Brigham Young
1991	9	Utah
1992	9	UTEP/Brigham Young
1993	10	Brigham Young/Utah
1994	10	New Mexico
1995	10	Utah
1996	10	Utah
1997	16	Fresno St. (Pacific)/Hawaii (Pacific)/Utah (Mountain)
1998	16	TCU (Pacific)/Utah (Mountain)
1999	16	UNLV (Mountain)/Tulsa (Mountain)/Utah (Pacific)
2000	8	Tulsa
2001	9	Fresno St.
2002	10	Hawaii/Tulsa
2003	10	Fresno St.

Season	No.	Conference Tournament
1984	9	UTEP
1985	9	San Diego St.
1986	9	UTEP
1987	9	Wyoming
1988	9	Wyoming
1989	9	UTEP
1990	9	UTEP
1991	9	Brigham Young
1992	8	Brigham Young
1993	10	New Mexico
1994	10	Hawaii
1995	10	Utah
1996	10	New Mexico
1997	12	Utah
1998	12	UNLV
1999	12	Utah
2000	8	Fresno St.
2001	9	Hawaii
2002	10	Hawaii
2003	9	Tulsa

WESTERN NEW YORK LITTLE THREE CONFERENCE

Season	No.	Regular Season
1947	3	Canisius
1948	3	Niagara
1949	3	Niagara
1950	3	Canisius/Niagara/St. Bonaventure
1951	3	St. Bonaventure
1952		DNP
1953	3	Niagara
1954	3	Niagara
1955	3	Niagara
1956	3	Canisius
1957	3	Canisius/St. Bonaventure
1958	3	St. Bonaventure

YANKEE CONFERENCE

Season	No.	Regular Season
1947	6	Vermont
1948	6	Connecticut
1949	6	Connecticut
1950	6	Rhode Island
1951	6	Connecticut
1952	6	Connecticut
1953	6	Connecticut
1954	6	Connecticut
1955	6	Connecticut
1956	6	Connecticut
1957	6	Connecticut
1958	6	Connecticut
1959	6	Connecticut
1960	6	Connecticut
1961	6	Rhode Island
1962	6	Massachusetts
1963	6	Connecticut
1964	6	Connecticut/Rhode Island
1965	6	Connecticut
1966	6	Connecticut/Rhode Island
1967	6	Connecticut
1968	6	Massachusetts/Rhode Island
1969	6	Massachusetts
1970	6	Connecticut/Massachusetts
1971	6	Massachusetts
1972	6	Rhode Island
1973	7	Massachusetts
1974	7	Massachusetts
1975	7	Massachusetts

INDEPENDENTS
(Best Record)

Season	No.	Regular Season
1946	30	Yale
1947	32	Duquesne
1948	40	Bradley
1949	34	Villanova
1950	36	Toledo
1951	37	Dayton
1952	42	Seton Hall
1953	42	Seattle
1954	39	Holy Cross/Seattle
1955	41	Marquette
1956	35	Temple
1957	32	Seattle
1958	29	Temple
1959	32	St. Bonaventure
1960	34	Providence
1961	35	Memphis
1962	34	Loyola (Ill.)
1963	47	Loyola (Ill.)
1964	51	UTEP
1965	45	Providence
1966	44	UTEP
1967	47	Boston College
1968	47	Houston
1969	47	Boston College
1970	52	Jacksonville
1971	55	Marquette
1972	59	Oral Roberts
1973	68	Providence
1974	73	Notre Dame
1975	79	Tex.-Pan American
1976	79	Rutgers
1977	73	UNLV
1978	70	DePaul
1979	68	Syracuse
1980	55	DePaul
1981	54	DePaul
1982	52	DePaul
1983	19	New Orleans
1984	19	DePaul
1985	22	Notre Dame
1986	17	Notre Dame
1987	18	DePaul
1988	18	Akron
1989	22	Akron
1990	19	Wright St.
1991	17	DePaul
1992	12	Penn St.
1993	14	Wis.-Milwaukee
1994	6	Southern Utah
1995	2	Notre Dame
1996	2	Oral Roberts
1997	3	Oral Roberts
1998	0	
1999	2	Denver
2000	5	Tex.-Pan American
2001	5	Stony Brook
2002	3	Tex.-Pan American
2003	6	Centenary (La.)

CONSECUTIVE REGULAR-SEASON WINNER

No.	Team	Conference	Seasons
13	UCLA	Pacific-10	1967-79
10	Connecticut	Yankee	1951-60
10	UNLV	Big West	1983-92
9	Kentucky	Southeastern	1944-52
8	Idaho St.	Rocky Mountain	1953-60
8	Long Beach St.	Big West	1970-77
7	Cincinnati	Conference USA	1996-2002
7	Coppin St.	Mid-Eastern	1993-99

CONFERENCES

No.	Team	Conference	Seasons
7	Dartmouth	Ivy	1938-44
7	Murray St.	Ohio Valley	1994-2000
7	Rhode Island	New England	1938-44
6	Arizona	Border	1946-51
6	Cincinnati	Missouri Valley	1958-63
6	Davidson	Southern	1968-73
6	Kansas	Missouri Valley	1922-27
6	Kentucky	Southeastern	1968-73
6	Pennsylvania	Ivy	1970-75
6	Weber St.	Big Sky	1968-73

CONSECUTIVE CONFERENCE TOURNAMENT WINNER

No.	Team	Conference	Seasons
7	Kentucky	Southeastern	1944-50
7	N.C. A&T	Mid-Eastern	1982-88
6	North Carolina St.	Southern	1947-52
6	Valparaiso	Mid-Continent	1995-2000
6	West Virginia	Southern	1955-60
5	Duke	Atlantic Coast	1999-2003
5	Massachusetts	Atlantic 10	1992-96
4	Arizona	Pacific-10	1988-90, 2002
4	Cincinnati	Great Midwest	1992-95
4	East Tenn. St.	Southern	1989-92
4	Gonzaga	West Coast	1999-2002
4	Kentucky	Southeastern	1992-95
4	La.-Monroe	Southland	1990-93
4	Northeastern	America East	1984-87
4	Winthrop	Big South	1999-2002
3	26 tied		

DIVISION I UNDEFEATED IN CONFERENCE PLAY

Minimum 6 conference games.

Year	Conference	Team	Conference W-L	Overall W-L
1904	Ivy	Columbia	10-0	14-0
1905	Ivy	Columbia	8-0	13-0
1908	Ivy	Pennsylvania	8-0	23-4
1908	Missouri Valley	Kansas	6-0	18-6
1909	Big Ten	Chicago	12-0	12-0
1912	Big Ten	Purdue	12-0	12-0
1912	Big Ten	Wisconsin	12-0	15-0
1912	Missouri Valley	Nebraska	8-0	14-1
1913	Big Ten	Wisconsin	12-0	14-1
1913	Missouri Valley	Nebraska	10-0	17-2
1914	Big Ten	Wisconsin	12-0	15-0
1914	Missouri Valley	Nebraska	7-0	15-3
1915	Big Ten	Illinois	12-0	16-0
1916	Big Ten	Wisconsin	12-0	20-1
1916	Missouri Valley	Nebraska	12-0	13-1
1916	Southwest	Texas	6-0	12-0
1920	Ivy	Pennsylvania	10-0	22-1
1920	Southwest	Texas A&M	16-0	19-0
1922	Pacific Coast	Idaho	7-0	19-1
1923	Missouri Valley	Kansas	16-0	17-1
1924	Southwest	Texas	20-0	23-0
1926	Pacific Coast	California	7-0	14-0
1927	Pacific Coast	California	7-0	13-0
1928	Missouri Valley	Oklahoma	18-0	18-0
1928	Southwest	Arkansas	12-0	19-1
1929	Big Six	Oklahoma	10-0	13-2
1929	Missouri Valley	Wash. (Mo.)	7-0	11-7
1929	Pacific Coast	California	11-0	17-3
1930	Big Ten	Purdue	10-0	13-2
1931	Ivy	Columbia	10-0	20-2
1932	Missouri Valley	Creighton	8-0	17-4
1934	Eastern Intercollegiate	Pittsburgh	8-0	18-4
1936	Big Six	Kansas	10-0	21-2
1936	Ivy	Columbia	12-0	19-3
1937	Ivy	Pennsylvania	12-0	17-3
1938	Border	New Mex. St.	18-0	22-3
1940	Missouri Valley	Oklahoma St.	12-0	26-3
1941	Southwest	Arkansas	12-0	20-3
1942	Border	West Texas St.	16-0	28-3
1943	Big Six	Kansas	10-0	22-6
1943	Big Ten	Illinois	12-0	17-1
1943	Border	West Texas St.	10-0	15-7

Year	Conference	Team	Conference W-L	Overall W-L
1943	Missouri Valley	Creighton	10-0	16-1
1944	Ivy	Dartmouth	8-0	19-2
1945	Border	New Mexico	12-0	14-2
1945	Southwest	Rice	12-0	20-1
1946	Big Six	Kansas	10-0	19-2
1946	Missouri Valley	Oklahoma St.	12-0	31-2
1947	Southwest	Texas	12-0	26-2
1948	Missouri Valley	Oklahoma St.	10-0	27-4
1948	Southeastern	Kentucky	9-0	36-3
1949	Southeastern	Kentucky	13-0	32-2
1951	Ivy	Columbia	12-0	22-1
1951	Southeastern	Kentucky	14-0	32-2
1952	Southeastern	Kentucky	14-0	29-3
1953	Rocky Mountain	Idaho St.	10-0	18-7
1953	Southeastern	LSU	13-0	22-3
1954	Southeastern	Kentucky	14-0	25-0
1954	Southeastern	LSU	14-0	20-5
1954	Southern	George Washington	10-0	23-3
1954	Yankee	Connecticut	7-0	23-3
1955	West Coast	San Francisco	12-0	28-1
1955	Yankee	Connecticut	7-0	20-5
1956	Pacific Coast	UCLA	16-0	22-6
1956	Southeastern	Alabama	14-0	21-3
1956	Southwest	Southern Methodist	12-0	25-4
1956	West Coast	San Francisco	14-0	29-0
1957	Atlantic Coast	North Carolina	14-0	32-0
1957	Rocky Mountain	Idaho St.	12-0	25-4
1957	Southern	West Virginia	12-0	25-5
1957	Yankee	Connecticut	8-0	17-8
1958	Mid-American	Miami (Ohio)	12-0	18-9
1958	Rocky Mountain	Idaho St.	10-0	22-6
1958	Southern	West Virginia	12-0	26-2
1958	West Coast	San Francisco	12-0	25-2
1958	Yankee	Connecticut	10-0	17-10
1959	Big Eight	Kansas St.	14-0	25-2
1959	Middle Atlantic	St. Joseph's	7-0	22-5
1959	Southern	West Virginia	11-0	29-5
1960	Rocky Mountain	Idaho St.	8-0	21-5
1961	Big Ten	Ohio St.	14-0	27-1
1961	Middle Atlantic	St. Joseph's	8-0	25-5
1962	Border	Arizona St.	8-0	23-4
1963	Atlantic Coast	Duke	14-0	27-3
1963	Middle Atlantic	St. Joseph's	8-0	23-5
1964	AAWU	UCLA	15-0	30-0
1964	West Coast	San Francisco	12-0	23-5
1965	AAWU	UCLA	14-0	28-2
1965	Southern	Davidson	12-0	24-2
1965	Yankee	Connecticut	10-0	23-3
1966	Ohio Valley	Western Ky.	14-0	25-3
1967	AAWU	UCLA	14-0	30-0
1967	West Coast	Pacific (Cal.)	14-0	24-4
1968	AAWU	UCLA	14-0	29-1
1969	Big Sky	Weber St.	15-0	27-3
1969	Ivy	Princeton	14-0	19-7
1969	Southern	Davidson	9-0	27-3
1970	Atlantic Coast	South Carolina	14-0	25-3
1970	Big Ten	Iowa	14-0	20-5
1970	Ivy	Princeton	14-0	25-2
1970	Ohio Valley	Western Ky.	14-0	22-3
1970	Pacific Coast	Long Beach St.	10-0	24-5
1970	Southern	Davidson	10-0	22-5
1971	Big Eight	Kansas	14-0	27-3
1971	Ivy	Pennsylvania	14-0	28-1
1971	Middle Atlantic (E)	St. Joseph's	6-0	19-9
1971	Pacific Coast	Long Beach St.	10-0	24-5
1971	Pacific-8	UCLA	14-0	29-1
1971	Yankee	Massachusetts	10-0	23-4
1972	Middle Atlantic (E)	Temple	6-0	23-8
1972	Pacific-8	UCLA	14-0	30-0
1972	Southland	La.-Lafayette	8-0	25-4
1973	Atlantic Coast	North Caro. St.	12-0	27-0
1973	Middle Atlantic (E)	St. Joseph's	6-0	22-6
1973	Pacific-8	UCLA	14-0	30-0
1973	Southland	La.-Lafayette	12-0	24-5
1974	Atlantic Coast	North Caro. St.	12-0	30-1

Year	Conference	Team	Conference W-L	Overall W-L
1974	Pacific Coast	Long Beach St.	12-0	24-2
1975	Big Ten	Indiana	18-0	31-1
1975	Southern	Furman	13-0	22-7
1976	Big Ten	Indiana	18-0	32-0
1976	Ivy	Princeton	14-0	22-5
1977	Southwest	Arkansas	16-0	26-2
1977	West Coast	San Francisco	14-0	29-2
1978	East Coast (W)	Lafayette	10-0	23-8
1978	Pacific-8	UCLA	14-0	25-3
1979	East Coast	Temple	13-0	25-4
1979	Missouri Valley	Indiana St.	16-0	33-1
1979	New Jersey-New York 7	Rutgers	6-0	22-9
1979	Southwestern	Alcorn St.	12-0	28-1
1979	Sun Belt	South Ala.	10-0	20-7
1980	Louisville	Metro	12-0	33-3
1980	Southwestern	Alcorn St.	12-0	28-2
1980	Trans America	La.-Monroe	6-0	17-11
1981	East Coast (E)	American	11-0	24-6
1982	East Coast	Temple	11-0	19-8
1982	West Coast	Pepperdine	14-0	22-7
1983	ECAC South	William & Mary	9-0	20-9
1983	Metro	Louisville	12-0	32-4
1983	Southwest	Houston	16-0	31-3
1984	Atlantic 10	Temple	18-0	26-5
1984	Atlantic Coast	North Carolina	14-0	28-3
1984	ECAC North Atlantic	Northeastern	14-0	27-5
1986	Missouri Valley	Bradley	16-0	32-3
1987	Atlantic Coast	North Carolina	14-0	32-4
1987	Gulf Star	Stephen F. Austin	10-0	22-6
1987	Pacific Coast	UNLV	18-0	37-2
1988	Atlantic 10	Temple	18-0	32-2
1988	Metro Atlantic	La Salle	14-0	24-10
1988	Mid-Eastern	N.C. A&T	16-0	26-3
1988	West Coast	Loyola Marymount	14-0	28-4
1990	Metro Atlantic	La Salle	16-0	30-2
1991	Big West	UNLV	18-0	34-1
1991	Ivy	Princeton	14-0	24-3
1992	Big West	UNLV	18-0	26-2
1992	North Atlantic	Delaware	14-0	27-4
1992	West Coast	Pepperdine	14-0	24-7
1993	Ivy	Pennsylvania	14-0	22-5
1993	Mid-Eastern	Coppin St.	16-0	22-8
1993	Sun Belt	New Orleans	16-0	26-4
1994	Big Eight	Missouri	14-0	28-4
1994	Ivy	Pennsylvania	14-0	25-3
1994	Mid-Eastern	Coppin St.	16-0	22-8
1995	American West	Southern Utah	6-0	17-11
1995	Ivy	Pennsylvania	14-0	22-6
1995	Midwestern	Xavier	14-0	23-5
1996	Midwestern	Wis.-G.B.	16-0	25-4
1996	Southeastern (E)	Kentucky	16-0	34-2
1996	Southern	Davidson	14-0	25-5
1996	Southwest	Texas Tech	14-0	30-2
1997	Ivy	Princeton	14-0	24-4
1997	Trans America (E)	Col. of Charleston	16-0	29-3
1998	Ivy	Princeton	14-0	27-2
1998	Western Athletic (P)	TCU	14-0	27-6
1999	Atlantic Coast	Duke	16-0	37-2
1999	Southern (S)	Col. of Charleston	16-0	28-3
1999	Western Athletic (P)	Utah	14-0	28-5
2000	Big West (E)	Utah St.	16-0	28-6
2000	Conference USA (A)	Cincinnati	16-0	29-4
2000	Ivy	Pennsylvania	14-0	21-8
2002	Big 12	Kansas	16-0	33-4
2003	Big Sky	Weber St.	14-0	26-6
2003	Ivy	Pennsylvania	14-0	22-6
2003	Southeastern	Kentucky	16-0	32-4

Division I Conference Alignment History

CHANGES FOR 2003-04

Team	Old Conference	New Conference
Birmingham-So.	new to Division I	Big South
Centenary (La.)	Independent	Mid-Continent
Elon	Big South	Southern
Jacksonville St.	Atlantic Sun	Ohio Valley
Lipcomb	new to Division I	Atlantic Sun
UMBC	Northeast	America East
Morris Brown	Independent	dropped Division I
Samford	Atlantic Sun	Ohio Valley
VMI	Southern	Big South

AMERICA EAST CONFERENCE (1980-present)
ECAC North (1980-82)
ECAC North Atlantic (1983-89)
North Atlantic (1990-96)
America East (1997-present)

Albany (N.Y.)	2002-present
Binghamton	2002-present
Boston U.	1980-present
Canisius	1980-89
Colgate	1980-90
Delaware	1992-2001
Drexel	1992-2001
Hartford	1986-present
Hofstra	1995-2001
Holy Cross	1980-83
Maine	1980-present
UMBC	2004-present
New Hampshire	1980-present
Niagara	1980-89
Northeastern	1980-present
Rhode Island	1980
Siena	1985-89
Stony Brook	2002-present
Towson	1996-2001
Vermont	1980-present

AMERICAN SOUTH CONFERENCE (1988-91)

Arkansas St.	1988-91
UCF	1991
Lamar	1988-91
Louisiana Tech	1988-91
New Orleans	1988-91
La.-Lafayette	1988-91
Tex.-Pan American	1988-91

AMERICAN WEST CONFERENCE (1995-96)

Cal Poly	1995-96
Cal St. Northridge	1995-96
Sacramento St.	1995-96
Southern Utah	1995-96

ATLANTIC COAST CONFERENCE (1954-present)

Clemson	1954-present
Duke	1954-present
Florida St.	1992-present
Georgia Tech	1980-present
Maryland	1954-present
North Carolina	1954-present
North Carolina St.	1954-present
South Carolina	1954-71
Virginia	1954-present
Wake Forest	1954-present

ATLANTIC SUN CONFERENCE (1979-present)
Trans America Athletic (1979-2001)

Ark.-Little Rock	1981-91
Belmont	2002-present
Campbell	1995-present
Centenary (La.)	1979-99
UCF	1993-present
Col. of Charleston	1993-98
Fla. Atlantic	1994-present
Florida Int'l	1992-98
Gardner-Webb	2003-present
Georgia Southern	1981-92
Georgia St.	1985-present
Hardin-Simmons	1979-89
Houston Baptist	1979-89
Jacksonville	1999-present
Jacksonville St.	1996-2003
Lipcomb	2004-present
Mercer	1979-present
Nicholls St.	1983-84
La.-Monroe	1979-82
Northwestern St.	1981-84
Oklahoma City	1979
Samford	1979-2003
Southeastern La.	1992-97
Stetson	1987-present
Tex.-Pan American	1979-80
Troy St.	1998-present

ATLANTIC 10 CONFERENCE (1977-present)
Eastern Collegiate Basketball League (1977-78)
Eastern AA (1979-82)
Eastern 8
Atlantic 10 (1983-present)

Dayton	1996-present
Duquesne	1977-92, 94-present
Fordham	1996-present
George Washington	1977-present
La Salle	1996-present
Massachusetts	1977-present
Penn St.	1977-79, 83-91
Pittsburgh	1977-82
Rhode Island	1981-present
Richmond	2002-present
Rutgers	1977-95
St. Bonaventure	1980-present
St. Joseph's	1983-present
Temple	1983-present
Villanova	1977-80
Virginia Tech	1996-2000
West Virginia	1977-95
Xavier	1996-present

BIG EAST CONFERENCE (1980-present)

Boston College	1980-present
Connecticut	1980-present
Georgetown	1980-present
Miami (Fla.)	1992-present
Notre Dame	1996-present
Pittsburgh	1983-present
Providence	1980-present
Rutgers	1996-present
St. John's (N.Y.)	1980-present
Seton Hall	1980-present
Syracuse	1980-present
Villanova	1981-present
Virginia Tech	2001-present
West Virginia	1996-present

BIG EIGHT CONFERENCE (1908-96)
Missouri Valley (1908-28)
Big Six (1929-47)
Big Seven (1948-58)
Big Eight (1959-96)

Colorado	1948-96
Drake	1908-28
Grinnell	1919-28
Iowa St.	1908-96
Kansas	1908-96
Kansas St.	1914-96
Missouri	1908-96
Nebraska	1908-19, 21-96
Oklahoma	1920-96
Oklahoma St.	1926-28, 59-96
Washington (Mo.)	1908-10, 12-28

BIG SKY CONFERENCE (1964-present)

Boise St.	1971-96
Cal St. Northridge	1997-2001
Eastern Wash.	1988-present
Gonzaga	1964-79
Idaho	1964-96
Idaho St.	1964-present
Montana	1964-present
Montana St.	1964-present
Nevada	1980-92
Northern Ariz.	1971-present
Portland St.	1999-present
Sacramento St.	1997-present
Weber St.	1964-present

BIG SOUTH CONFERENCE (1986-present)

Armstrong Atlantic	1986-87
Augusta St.	1986-91
Birmingham-So.	2004-present
Campbell	1986-94
Charleston So.	1986-present
Coastal Caro.	1986-present
Davidson	1991-92
Elon	2000-present
High Point	2000-present
Liberty	1992-present
UMBC	1993-98
UNC Asheville	1986-present
UNC Greensboro	1993-97
Radford	1986-present
Towson	1993-95
VMI	2004-present
Winthrop	1986-present

BIG TEN CONFERENCE (1895-present)
Intercollegiate Conference of Faculty Representatives
Western Intercollegiate
Big Nine (1947-48)
Big Ten (1912-46, 49-present)

Chicago	1895-46
Illinois	1895-present
Indiana	1899-present
Iowa	1899-present
Michigan	1895-present
Michigan St.	1949-present
Minnesota	1895-present
Northwestern	1895-present
Ohio St.	1912-present
Penn St.	1993-present
Purdue	1895-present
Wisconsin	1895-present

BIG 12 CONFERENCE (1997-present)

Baylor	1997-present
Colorado	1997-present
Iowa St.	1997-present
Kansas	1997-present
Kansas St.	1997-present
Missouri	1997-present
Nebraska	1997-present
Oklahoma	1997-present
Oklahoma St.	1997-present
Texas	1997-present
Texas A&M	1997-present
Texas Tech	1997-present

BIG WEST CONFERENCE (1970-present)
Pacific Coast (1970-88)
Big West (1989-present)

Boise St.	1997-2001
UC Irvine	1978-present
UC Riverside	2002-present
UC Santa Barb.	1970-74, 77-present
Cal Poly	1997-present

Cal St. Fullerton	1975-present
Cal St. Los Angeles	1970-74
Cal St. Northridge	2002-present
Fresno St.	1970-92
Idaho	1997-present
Long Beach St.	1970-present
Nevada	1993-2000
UNLV	1983-96
New Mexico St.	1984-2000
North Texas	1997-2000
Pacific (Cal.)	1972-present
San Diego St.	1970-78
San Jose St.	1970-96
Utah St.	1979-present

BORDER CONFERENCE
(1932-40, 42-62)

Arizona	1932-40, 42-61
Arizona St.	1932-40, 42-43, 44-62
Hardin-Simmons	1942-43, 45-62
New Mexico	1932-40, 42, 45-51
New Mexico St.	1932-40, 42-62
Northern Ariz.	1932-40, 42-53
Texas Tech	1933-40, 42-56
UTEP	1936-40, 42-43, 44-62
West Tex. A&M	1942-43, 45-62

COLONIAL ATHLETIC ASSOCIATION
(1983-present)

American	1985-2001
Delaware	2002-present
Drexel	2002-present
East Caro.	1983-2001
George Mason	1983-present
Hofstra	2002-present
James Madison	1983-present
Navy	1983-91
UNC Wilmington	1985-present
Old Dominion	1992-present
Richmond	1983-2001
Towson	2002-present
Va. Commonwealth	1996-present
William & Mary	1983-present

CONFERENCE USA
(1996-present)

UAB	1996-present
Charlotte	1996-present
Cincinnati	1996-present
DePaul	1996-present
East Caro.	2002-present
Houston	1997-present
Louisville	1996-present
Marquette	1996-present
Memphis	1996-present
St. Louis	1996-present
South Fla.	1996-present
Southern Miss.	1996-present
TCU	2002-present
Tulane	1996-present

EAST COAST CONFERENCE
(1959-92, 94)

Middle Atlantic (1959-74)
East Coast (1975-92, 94)

American	1967-84
Brooklyn	1992
Bucknell	1959-90
Buffalo	1992, 94
Central Conn. St.	1991-92, 94
Chicago St.	1994
Delaware	1959-91
Drexel	1959-91
Gettysburg	1959-74
Hofstra	1966-92, 94
Lafayette	1959-90
La Salle	1959-83
Lehigh	1959-90
UMBC	1991-92
Muhlenberg	1959-64
Northeastern Ill.	1994
Rider	1967-92
Rutgers	1959-62
St. Joseph's	1959-82
Temple	1959-82
Towson	1983-92

Troy St.	1994
West Chester	1966-67, 69-74

EASTERN INTERCOLLEGIATE CONFERENCE
(1933-39)

Bucknell	1934
Carnegie Mellon	1933-39
Georgetown	1933-39
Penn St.	1936-39
Pittsburgh	1933-39
Temple	1933-39
West Virginia	1933-39

GREAT MIDWEST CONFERENCE
(1992-95)

UAB	1992-95
Cincinnati	1992-95
Dayton	1994-95
DePaul	1992-95
Marquette	1992-95
Memphis	1992-95
St. Louis	1992-95

GULF STAR CONFERENCE
(1985-87)

Nicholls St.	1985-87
Northwestern St.	1985-87
Sam Houston St.	1985-87
Southeastern La.	1985-87
Stephen F. Austin	1985-87
Texas St.	1985-87

HORIZON LEAGUE
(1980-present)
Midwestern Collegiate (1980-2001)

Butler	1980-present
Cleveland St.	1995-present
Dayton	1989-93
Detroit	1981-present
Duquesne	1993
Evansville	1980-94
Ill.-Chicago	1995-present
La Salle	1993-95
Loyola (Ill.)	1980-present
Marquette	1990-91
Northern Ill.	1995-97
Oklahoma City	1980-85
Oral Roberts	1980-87
St. Louis	1983-91
Wis.-Green Bay	1995-present
Wis.-Milwaukee	1995-present
Wright St.	1995-present
Xavier	1980-95
Youngstown St.	2002-present

IVY GROUP
(1902-08, 11-18, 20-present)
Eastern Intercollegiate League

Brown	1954-present
Columbia	1902-08, 11-18, 20-present
Cornell	1902-08, 11-18, 20-present
Dartmouth	1912-18, 20-present
Harvard	1902-04, 06-07, 34-43, 47-present
Pennsylvania	1904-08, 11-18, 20-present
Princeton	1902-08, 11-18, 20-44, 46-present
Yale	1902-08, 11-18, 20-43, 47-present

METRO ATLANTIC ATHLETIC CONFERENCE
(1982-present)

Army	1982-90
Canisius	1990-present
Fairfield	1982-present
Fordham	1982-90
Holy Cross	1984-90
Iona	1982-present
La Salle	1984-92
Loyola (Md.)	1990-present
Manhattan	1982-present

Marist	1998-present
Niagara	1990-present
Rider	1998-present
St. Peter's	1982-present
Siena	1990-present

METROPOLITAN COLLEGIATE ATHLETIC CONFERENCE
(1976-95)

Charlotte	1992-95
Cincinnati	1976-91
Florida St.	1977-91
Georgia Tech	1976-78
Louisville	1976-95
Memphis	1976-91
St. Louis	1976-82
South Carolina	1984-91
South Fla.	1992-95
Southern Miss.	1983-95
Tulane	1976-85, 90-95
Va. Commonwealth	1992-95
Virginia Tech	1979-95

METROPOLITAN COLLEGIATE CONFERENCE (1966-69)

Fairleigh Dickinson	1966-69
Hofstra	1966-69
Iona	1966-69
Long Island	1966-69
Manhattan	1966-69
New York U.	1966-67
St. Peter's	1966-69
St. Francis (N.Y.)	1966-68
Seton Hall	1966-69
Wagner	1966-69

METROPOLITAN NEW YORK CONFERENCE (1943, 46-63)

CCNY	1943, 46-63
Brooklyn	1943, 46-63
Fordham	1943, 46-63
Hofstra	1943
Manhattan	1943, 46-63
New York U.	1943, 46-63
St. Francis (N.Y.)	1943, 46-63
St. John's (N.Y.)	1943, 46-63

MID-AMERICAN ATHLETIC CONFERENCE
(1947-present)

Akron	1993-present
Ball St.	1976-present
Bowling Green	1954-present
Buffalo	1999-present
Butler	1947-50
Central Mich.	1973-present
Cincinnati	1947-53
Eastern Mich.	1975-present
Kent St.	1952-present
Marshall	1954-69, 98-present
Miami (Ohio)	1948-present
Northern Ill.	1976-86, 98-present
Ohio	1947-present
Toledo	1952-present
Wayne St. (Mich.)	1947
Western Mich.	1948-present
Case Reserve	1947-55

MID-CONTINENT CONFERENCE
(1983-present)

Akron	1991-92
Buffalo	1995-98
Central Conn. St.	1995-97
Centenary (La.)	2004-present
Chicago St.	1995-present
Cleveland St.	1983-94
Eastern Ill.	1983-96
Ill.-Chicago	1983-94
IUPUI	1999-present
UMKC	1995-present
Northeastern Ill.	1995-98
Northern Ill.	1991-94
Northern Iowa	1983-91
Oakland	2000-present
Oral Roberts	1998-present

Southern Utah	1998-present
Southwest Mo. St.	1983-90
Troy St.	1995-97
Valparaiso	1983-present
Western Ill.	1983-present
Wis.-Green Bay	1983-94
Wis.-Milwaukee	1994
Wright St.	1992-94
Youngstown St.	1993-2001

MID-EASTERN ATHLETIC CONFERENCE (1972-present)

Bethune-Cookman	1981-present
Coppin St.	1986-present
Delaware St.	1972-87, 89-present
Florida A&M	1981-83, 88-present
Hampton	1996-present
Howard	1972-present
Md.-East. Shore	1972-79, 83-present
Morgan St.	1972-80, 85-present
Norfolk St.	1998-present
N.C. A&T	1972-present
N.C. Central	1972-80
South Carolina St.	1972-present

MISSOURI VALLEY CONFERENCE (1908-present)

Bradley	1949-51, 56-present
Butler	1933-34
Cincinnati	1958-70
Creighton	1928-43, 46-48, 78-present
Detroit	1950-57
Drake	1908-51, 57-present
Evansville	1995-present
Grinnell	1919-39
Houston	1951-60
Illinois St.	1982-present
Indiana St.	1978-present
Iowa St.	1908-28
Kansas	1908-28
Kansas St.	1914-28
Louisville	1965-75
Memphis	1968-73
Missouri	1908-28
Nebraska	1908-19, 21-28
New Mexico St.	1973-83
Northern Iowa	1992-present
North Texas	1958-75
Oklahoma	1920-28
Oklahoma St.	1926-57
St. Louis	1938-43, 45-74
Southern Ill.	1976-present
Southwest Mo. St.	1991-present
Tulsa	1935-96
Washburn	1935-41
Washington (Mo.)	1908-10, 12-47
West Tex. A&M	1973-86
Wichita St.	1946-present

MOUNTAIN STATES CONFERENCE (1911-43, 46-62)
Also known as:
Rocky Mountain (1911-37)
Big Seven (1938-43, 46-47)
Skyline Six (1948-51)
Skyline Eight (1952-62)
Mountain States (1938-43, 46-62)

Brigham Young	1924-42, 46-62
Colorado	1911-42, 46-47
Colorado Col.	1911-37
Colorado Mines	1911-37
Colorado St.	1911-22, 24-42, 46-62
Denver	1911-42, 46-62
Montana	1952-62
Montana St.	1925-37
New Mexico	1952-62
Northern Colo.	1925-37
Utah	1924-42, 46-62
Utah St.	1924-42, 46-62
Western St.	1925-37
Wyoming	1923-43, 46-62

MOUNTAIN WEST CONFERENCE (2000-present)

Air Force	2000-present
Brigham Young	2000-present

Colorado St.	2000-present
UNLV	2000-present
New Mexico	2000-present
San Diego St.	2000-present
Utah	2000-present
Wyoming	2000-present

NEW JERSEY-NEW YORK 7 CONFERENCE (1977-79)

Columbia	1977-79
Fordham	1977-79
Manhattan	1977-79
Princeton	1977-79
Rutgers	1977-79
St. John's (N.Y.)	1977-79
Seton Hall	1977-79

NORTHEAST CONFERENCE (1982-present)
ECAC Metro (1982-88)
Northeast (1989-present)

Baltimore	1982-83
Central Conn. St.	1998-present
Fairleigh Dickinson	1982-present
Long Island	1982-present
Loyola (Md.)	1982-89
Marist	1982-97
UMBC	1999-2003
Monmouth	1986-present
Mt. St. Mary's	1990-present
Quinnipiac	1999-present
Rider	1993-97
Robert Morris	1982-present
Sacred Heart	2000-present
St. Francis (N.Y.)	1982-present
St. Francis (Pa.)	1982-present
Siena	1982-84
Towson	1982
Wagner	1982-present

OHIO VALLEY CONFERENCE (1949-present)

Akron	1981-87
Austin Peay	1964-present
Eastern Ill.	1997-present
Eastern Ky.	1949-present
East Tenn. St.	1958-78
Evansville	1949-52
Jacksonville St.	2004-present
Louisville	1949
Marshall	1949-52
Middle Tenn.	1953-2000
Morehead St.	1949-present
Murray St.	1949-present
Samford	2004-present
Southeast Mo. St.	1992-present
Tenn.-Martin	1993-present
Tennessee St.	1988-present
Tennessee Tech	1949-present
Western Ky.	1949-82
Youngstown St.	1982-88

PACIFIC-10 CONFERENCE (1916-17, 19-present)
Pacific Coast (1916-59)
Big Five (1960-62)
Big Six (1963)
Athletic Association of Western Universities—AAWU (1963-68)
Pacific 8 (1969-78)
Pacific-10 (1979-present)

Arizona	1979-present
Arizona St.	1979-present
California	1916-17, 19-present
Idaho	1922-59
Montana	1924-29
Oregon	1917, 19-59, 65-present
Oregon St.	1916-17, 19-59, 65-present
Southern California	1922-24, 26-present
Stanford	1917, 19-43, 46-present
UCLA	1928-present
Washington	1916-17, 19-present
Washington St.	1917, 19-59, 64-present

PATRIOT LEAGUE (1991-present)

American	2002-present
Army	1991-present
Bucknell	1991-present
Colgate	1991-present
Fordham	1991-95
Holy Cross	1991-present
Lafayette	1991-present
Lehigh	1991-present
Navy	1992-present

SOUTHEASTERN CONFERENCE (1933-present)

Alabama	1933-43, 45-present
Arkansas	1992-present
Auburn	1933-43, 45-present
Florida	1933-43, 45-present
Georgia	1933-present
Georgia Tech	1933-64
Kentucky	1933-52, 54-present
LSU	1933-present
Mississippi	1933-43, 45-present
Mississippi St.	1933-43, 45-present
Sewanee	1933-40
South Carolina	1992-present
Tennessee	1933-43, 45-present
Tulane	1933-66
Vanderbilt	1933-present

SOUTHERN CONFERENCE (1922-present)
Southern Intercollegiate Athletic Association—SIAA (1895-1921)

Appalachian St.	1973-present
Alabama	1922-32
Auburn	1922-32
Col. of Charleston	1999-present
Chattanooga	1977-present
Citadel	1937-present
Clemson	1922-53
Davidson	1937-88, 93-present
Duke	1929-53
East Caro.	1966-77
East Tenn. St.	1979-present
Elon	2004-present
Florida	1923-32
Furman	1937-42, 45-present
George Washington	1942-43, 46-70
Georgia	1922-32
Ga. Southern	1993-present
Ga. Tech	1922-32
Kentucky	1922-32
LSU	1923-32
Marshall	1977-97
Maryland	1924-53
Mississippi	1923-32
Mississippi St.	1922-30, 32
North Carolina	1922-53
UNC Greensboro	1998-present
North Carolina St.	1922-53
Richmond	1937-76
South Carolina	1923-53
Sewanee	1924-32
Tennessee	1922-32
Tulane	1923-32
Vanderbilt	1923-32
Virginia	1922-37
VMI	1926-present
Virginia Tech	1922-65
Wake Forest	1937-43, 45-53
Wash. & Lee	1922-43, 46-58
West Virginia	1951-68
Western Caro.	1977-present
William & Mary	1937-77
Wofford	1998-present

SOUTHLAND CONFERENCE (1964-present)

Abilene Christian	1964-73
Arkansas St.	1964-87
Lamar	1964-87, 99-present
Louisiana Tech	1972-87
La.-Lafayette	1972-82
La.-Monroe	1983-present
McNeese St.	1973-present
Nicholls St.	1992-present

North Texas	1983-96
Northwestern St.	1988-present
Sam Houston St.	1988-present
Southeastern La.	1998-present
Southwest Tex. St.	1988-present
Stephen F. Austin	1988-present
Texas-Arlington	1964-86, 88-present
Texas-San Antonio	1992-present
Texas St.	1988-present
Trinity (Tex.)	1964-72

SOUTHWEST CONFERENCE (1915-96)

Arkansas	1924-91
Baylor	1915-96
Houston	1976-96
Oklahoma St.	1918, 22-25
Phillips	1920
Rice	1915-16, 18-96
Southern Methodist	1919-96
Southwestern (Tex.)	1915-16
Texas	1915-96
Texas A&M	1915-96
TCU	1924-96
Texas Tech	1958-96

SOUTHWESTERN ATHLETIC CONFERENCE (1978-present)

Alabama A&M	2000-present
Alabama St.	1983-present
Alcorn St.	1978-present
Ark.-Pine Bluff	1999-present
Grambling	1978-present
Jackson St.	1978-present
Mississippi Val.	1978-present
Prairie View	1978-present
Southern U.	1978-present
Texas Southern	1978-present

SUN BELT CONFERENCE (1977-present)

| UAB | 1980-91 |
| Ark.-Little Rock | 1992-present |

Arkansas St.	1992-present
UCF	1992
Charlotte	1977-91
Denver	2000-present
Florida Int'l	1999-present
Georgia St.	1977-81
Jacksonville	1977-98
Lamar	1992-98
La.-Lafayette	1992-present
Louisiana Tech	1992-2001
Middle Tenn.	2001-present
New Mexico St.	2001-present
New Orleans	1977-80, 92-present
North Texas	2001-present
Old Dominion	1983-91
South Ala.	1977-present
South Fla.	1977-91
Tex.-Pan American	1992-98
Va. Commonwealth	1980-91
Western Ky.	1983-present

WEST COAST CONFERENCE (1953-present)

UC Santa Barb.	1965-69
Fresno St.	1956-57
Gonzaga	1980-present
Loyola Marymount	1956-present
Nevada	1970-79
UNLV	1970-75
Pacific (Cal.)	1953-71
Pepperdine	1956-present
Portland	1977-present
St. Mary's (Cal.)	1953-present
San Diego	1980-present
San Francisco	1953-82, 86-present
San Jose St.	1953-69
Santa Clara	1953-present
Seattle	1972-80

WESTERN ATHLETIC CONFERENCE (1963-present)

Air Force	1981-99
Arizona	1963-78
Arizona St.	1963-78
Boise St.	2002-present

Brigham Young	1963-99
Colorado St.	1970-99
Fresno St.	1993-present
Hawaii	1980-99
Louisiana Tech	2002-present
Nevada	2001-present
UNLV	1997-99
New Mexico	1963-present
Rice	1997-99
San Diego St.	1979-present
San Jose St.	1997-present
Southern Methodist	1997-present
TCU	1997-2001
Tulsa	1997-present
UTEP	1970-present
Utah	1963-99
Wyoming	1963-99

WESTERN NEW YORK LITTLE THREE CONFERENCE (1947-51, 53-58)

Canisius	1947-51, 53-58
Niagara	1947-51, 53-58
St. Bonaventure	1947-51, 53-58

YANKEE CONFERENCE (1938-43, 46-76)

Boston U.	1973-76
Connecticut	1938-43, 46-76
Maine	1938-43, 46-76
Massachusetts	1947-76
New Hampshire	1938-43, 46-76
Northeastern	1938-43, 46
Rhode Island	1938-43, 46-76
Vermont	1947-76

Division I Alignment History

Abilene Christian	1971-73
Air Force	1958-present
Akron	1948-50, 1981-present
Alabama	1948-present
Alabama A&M	2000-present
Alabama St.	1983-present
UAB	1980-present
Albany (N.Y.)	2000-present
Alcorn St.	1978-present
American	1967-present
Appalachian St.	1974-present
Arizona	1948, 1951-present
Arizona St.	1951-present
Arkansas	1948-present
Ark.-Little Rock	1979-present
Ark.-Pine Bluff	1999-present
Arkansas St.	1971-present
Armstrong St.	1987
Army	1948-present
Auburn	1948-present
Augusta	1985-91
Austin Peay	1964-present
Baldwin-Wallace	1948-53
Ball St.	1972-present

Baltimore	1979-83
Baylor	1948-present
Belmont	2000-present
Bethune-Cookman	1981-present
Binghamton	2002-present
Birmingham-So.	2004-present
Boise St.	1972-present
Boston College	1948-present
Boston U.	1948-49, 1958-present
Bowling Green	1948-present
Bradley	1948-present
Brigham Young	1948-present
Brooklyn	1948-49, 1983-92
Brown	1948-present
Bucknell	1948-present
Buffalo	1974-77, 1992-present
Butler	1948-present
California	1948-present
UC Irvine	1978-present
UC Riverside	2002-present
UC Santa Barb.	1964-present
Cal Poly	1995-present
Cal St. Fullerton	1975-present
Cal St. L.A.	1971-75

Cal St. Northridge	1991-present
Campbell	1978-present
Canisius	1948-present
Case Reserve	1948-55
Catholic	1977-81
Centenary (La.)	1960-present
Central Conn. St.	1987-present
UCF	1985-present
Central Mich.	1974-present
Col. of Charleston	1992-present
Charleston So.	1975-present
Charlotte	1973-present
Chattanooga	1978-present
Chicago St.	1985-present
Cincinnati	1948-present
Citadel	1948-present
CCNY	1948-53
Clemson	1948-present
Cleveland St.	1973-present
Coastal Caro.	1987-present
Colgate	1948-present
Colorado	1948-present
Colorado St.	1948-present
Columbia	1948-present

School	Years
Connecticut	1948, 1952-present
Coppin St.	1986-present
Cornell	1948-present
Creighton	1948-56, 1960-present
Dartmouth	1948-present
Davidson	1948-present
Dayton	1948-present
Delaware	1958-present
Delaware St.	1974-present
Denver	1948-80, 1999-present
DePaul	1948-present
Detroit	1948-present
Drake	1948-present
Drexel	1974-present
Duke	1948-present
Duquesne	1948-present
East Caro.	1965-present
East Tenn. St.	1959-present
Eastern Ill.	1982-present
Eastern Ky.	1948, 1952-present
Eastern Mich.	1974-present
Eastern Wash.	1984-present
Elon	2000-present
Evansville	1978-present
Fairfield	1965-present
Fairleigh Dickinson	1968-present
Florida	1948-present
Florida A&M	1979-present
Fla. Atlantic	1994-present
Florida Int'l	1988-present
Florida St.	1957-present
Fordham	1948-present
Fresno St.	1956-58, 1971-present
Furman	1948-present
Gardner-Webb	2003-present
George Mason	1979-present
George Washington	1948-present
Georgetown	1948-present
Georgia	1948-present
Gettysburg	1948-51, 1959-73
Ga. Southern	1974-present
Georgia St.	1974-present
Georgia Tech	1948-present
Gonzaga	1953-present
Grambling	1978-present
Hamline	1948
Hampton	1996-present
Hardin-Simmons	1951-63, 1965-90
Hartford	1985-present
Harvard	1948-present
Hawaii	1971-present
High Point	2000-present
Hofstra	1967-present
Holy Cross	1948-present
Houston	1951-present
Houston Baptist	1974-89
Howard	1974-present
Idaho	1948-present
Idaho St.	1959-present
Illinois	1948-present
Ill.-Chicago	1982-present
Illinois St.	1972-present
Indiana	1948-present
Indiana St.	1948, 1972-present
IPFW	2003-present
IUPUI	1999-present
Iona	1954-present
Iowa	1948-present
Iowa St.	1948-present
Jackson St.	1978-present
Jacksonville	1967-present
Jacksonville St.	1996-present
James Madison	1977-present
John Carroll	1948-55
Kansas	1948-present
Kansas St.	1948-present
Kent St.	1948, 1952-present
Kentucky	1948-52, 1954-present
Ky. Wesleyan	1957-58
La Salle	1948-present
Lafayette	1948-present
Lamar	1970-present
Lawrence Tech	1948
Lehigh	1948-present
Liberty	1989-present

School	Years
Lipscomb	2004-present
Long Beach St.	1970-present
Long Island	1948-51, 1969-present
Lafayette	1972-73, 1976-present
La.-Monroe	1974-present
LSU	1948-present
Louisiana Tech	1974-present
Louisville	1948-present
Loyola Marymount	1950-present
Loyola (La.)	1952-53, 1955-72
Loyola (Ill.)	1948-present
Loyola (Md.)	1948-50, 1982-present
Maine	1962-present
Manhattan	1948-present
Marist	1982-present
Marquette	1948-present
Marshall	1948, 1954-present
Maryland	1948-present
UMBC	1987-present
Md.-East. Shore	1974-75, 1982-present
Massachusetts	1962-present
McNeese St.	1974-present
Memphis St.	1956-present
Mercer	1974-present
Miami (Fla.)	1949-53, 1955-71, 1986-present
Miami (Ohio)	1948-present
Michigan	1948-present
Michigan St.	1948-present
Middle Tenn.	1959-present
Minnesota	1948-present
Mississippi	1948-present
Mississippi St.	1948-present
Mississippi Val.	1980-present
Missouri	1948-present
UMKC	1990-present
Monmouth	1984-present
Montana	1948, 1952-present
Montana St.	1948, 1958-present
Morehead St.	1956-present
Morgan St.	1985-present
Morris Brown	2002-03
Mt. St. Mary's	1989-present
Muhlenberg	1948-63
Murray St.	1954-present
Navy	1948-present
Nebraska	1948-present
UNLV	1970-present
Nevada	1948, 1970-present
New Hampshire	1962-present
New Mexico	1951-present
New Mexico St.	1951-present
New Orleans	1976-present
New York U.	1948-71; 84
Niagara	1948-present
Nicholls St.	1981-present
Norfolk St.	1998-present
North Carolina	1948-present
UNC Asheville	1987-present
UNC Greensboro	1992-present
UNC Wilmington	1977-present
N.C. A&T	1974-present
North Carolina St.	1948-present
North Texas	1958-present
Northeastern	1973-present
Northeastern Ill.	1991-98
Northern Ariz.	1951-53, 1972-present
Northern Colo.	1974-78
Northern Ill.	1968-present
Northern Iowa	1981-present
Northwestern	1948-present
Northwestern La.	1977-present
Notre Dame	1948-present
Oakland	2000-present
Ohio	1948-present
Ohio St.	1948-present
Oklahoma	1948-present
Oklahoma City	1951-85
Oklahoma St.	1948-present
Old Dominion	1977-present
Oral Roberts	1972-89, 1994-present
Oregon	1948-present
Oregon St.	1948-present
Pacific (Cal.)	1954-present
Penn St.	1948-present

School	Years
Pennsylvania	1948-present
Pepperdine	1956-present
Pittsburgh	1948-present
Portland	1954-present
Portland St.	1973-81, 1999-present
Prairie View	1981-present
Princeton	1948-present
Providence	1949, 1958-present
Purdue	1948-present
Quinnipiac	1999-present
Radford	1985-present
Regis	1962-64
Rhode Island	1948-present
Rice	1948-present
Richmond	1948-present
Rider	1968-present
Robert Morris	1977-present
Rutgers	1948-present
Sacramento St.	1992-present
Sacred Heart	2000-present
St. Bonaventure	1948-present
St. Francis (N.Y.)	1948-present
St. Francis (Pa.)	1956-present
St. John's (N.Y.)	1948-present
St. Joseph's	1948-present
St. Louis	1948-present
St. Mary's (Cal.)	1948-present
St. Peter's	1965-present
Sam Houston St.	1987-present
Samford	1973-present
San Diego	1980-present
San Diego St.	1971-present
San Francisco	1948-82, 1986-present
San Jose St.	1953-present
Santa Clara	1948-present
Savannah St.	2003-present
Scranton	1948
Seattle	1953-80
Seton Hall	1948-present
Siena	1948-49, 1951-60, 1977-present
South Ala.	1972-present
South Carolina	1948-present
South Carolina St.	1974-present
South Fla.	1974-present
Southeast Mo. St.	1992-present
Southeastern La.	1981-89, 1991-present
Southern U.	1978-present
Southern California	1948-present
Southern Ill.	1968-present
Southern Methodist	1948-present
Southern Miss.	1969, 1973-present
Southern Utah St.	1989-present
Southwest Mo. St.	1983-present
Stanford	1948-present
Stephen F. Austin	1987-present
Stetson	1972-present
Stony Brook	2000-present
Syracuse	1948-present
Temple	1948-present
Tennessee	1948-present
Tenn.-Martin	1993-present
Tennessee St.	1978-present
Tennessee Tech	1956-present
Texas	1948-present
Texas-Arlington	1969-present
Texas A&M	1948-present
Tex. A&M-Corp. Chris.	1973, 2003-present
TCU	1948-present
Tex.-Pan American	1969-present
UTEP	1951-present
Texas-San Antonio	1982-present
Texas Southern	1978-present
Texas St.	1985-present
Texas Tech	1951-present
Texas Wesleyan	1948
Toledo	1948-present
Towson	1980-present
Trinity (Texas)	1971-73
Troy St.	1994-present
Tulane	1948-85, 1990-present
Tulsa	1948-present
UCLA	1948-present
U.S. Int'l	1982-91
Utah	1948-present

*#won conference tournament; *ineligible for conference championship*

Utah St.	1948-present
Utica	1982-87
Valparaiso	1948-58, 1977-present
Vanderbilt	1948-present
Vermont	1962-present
Villanova	1948-present
Virginia	1948-present
Va. Commonwealth	1974-present
VMI	1948-present
Virginia Tech	1948-present
Wagner	1977-present
Wake Forest	1948-present
Washington	1948-present

Washington (Mo.)	1948-50, 1954-60
Wash. & Lee	1948-59
Washington St.	1948-present
Wayne St. (Neb.)	1948-50
Weber St.	1964-present
West Chester	1974-82
West Texas	1951-86
West Virginia	1948-present
Western Caro.	1977-present
Western Ill.	1982-present
Western Ky.	1948-present
Western Mich.	1948-present

Wichita St.	1948-present
William & Mary	1948-present
Winthrop	1987-present
Wisconsin	1948-present
Wis.-Green Bay	1982-present
Wis.-Milwaukee	1974-80, 1991-present
Wofford	1996-present
Wright St.	1988-present
Wyoming	1948-present
Xavier	1948-present
Yale	1948-present
Youngstown St.	1948, 1982-present

2003 Division II Conference Standings

CALIFORNIA COLLEGIATE ATHLETIC ASSOCIATION

	Conference			Full Season		
Team	W	L	Pct.	W	L	Pct.
Cal St. San B'dino	19	3	.864	23	7	.767
Cal Poly Pomona	16	6	.727	23	8	.742
Cal St. Chico	15	7	.682	18	9	.667
Sonoma St.	15	7	.682	18	10	.643
Cal St. Bakersfield	14	8	.636	20	9	.690
Cal St. Stanislaus	13	9	.591	18	11	.621
UC Davis	9	13	.409	12	15	.444
San Fran. St.	9	13	.409	11	16	.407
Grand Canyon	7	15	.318	9	18	.333
UC San Diego	6	16	.273	7	20	.259
Cal St. L.A.	5	17	.227	9	18	.333
Cal St. Dom. Hills	4	18	.182	6	21	.222

CAROLINAS-VIRGINIA ATHLETIC CONFERENCE

	Conference			Full Season		
Team	W	L	Pct.	W	L	Pct.
Queens (N.C.)	18	2	.900	29	4	.879
Barton	17	3	.850	22	6	.786
Belmont Abbey	15	5	.750	24	7	.774
Pfeiffer	13	7	.650	22	9	.710
Mount Olive	13	7	.650	18	10	.643
Longwood	11	9	.550	15	14	.517
Limestone	10	10	.500	10	17	.370
Erskine	8	12	.400	14	16	.467
Anderson (S.C.)	7	13	.350	9	19	.321
St. Andrews	4	16	.200	9	21	.300
Coker	3	17	.150	5	21	.192
Lees-McRae	1	19	.050	2	29	.065

CENTRAL ATLANTIC ATHLETIC ASSOCIATION

	Conference			Full Season		
Eastern Division	W	L	Pct.	W	L	Pct.
N.J. Inst. of Tech.	16	4	.800	18	11	.621
Teikyo Post	15	5	.750	19	10	.655
Holy Family	14	6	.700	18	11	.621
Caldwell	13	6	.684	15	11	.577
Felician	11	9	.550	14	15	.483
University of the Sciences	10	9	.526	14	13	.519
Dominican (N.Y.)	10	9	.526	12	14	.462
Bloomfield	10	9	.526	11	15	.423
Nyack	7	13	.350	7	21	.250
Goldey Beacom	1	19	.050	1	23	.042
Wilmington	1	19	.050	1	27	.036

CENTRAL INTERCOLLEGIATE ATHLETIC ASSOCIATION

	Conference			Full Season		
East Division	W	L	Pct.	W	L	Pct.
Virginia Union	8	2	.800	18	11	.621
Bowie St.	7	3	.700	30	5	.857
Shaw	7	3	.700	21	9	.700
St. Paul's	4	6	.400	8	20	.286
Virginia St.	3	7	.300	8	20	.286
Elizabeth City St.	1	9	.100	9	19	.321
West Division						
St. Augustine's	8	2	.800	18	9	.667
N.C. Central	8	2	.800	16	13	.552
Johnson Smith	7	3	.700	20	9	.690
Winston-Salem	4	6	.400	15	14	.517
Fayetteville St.	3	7	.300	11	17	.393
Livingstone	0	10	.000	7	21	.250

GREAT LAKES INTERCOLLEGIATE ATHLETIC CONFERENCE

	Conference			Full Season		
North Division	W	L	Pct.	W	L	Pct.
Michigan Tech	17	1	.944	29	3	.906
Northern Mich.	10	8	.556	15	14	.517
Grand Valley St.	8	10	.444	14	14	.500
Saginaw Valley	7	11	.389	13	14	.481
Ferris St.	7	11	.389	11	15	.423
Lake Superior St.	6	12	.333	12	15	.444
Northwood	6	12	.333	10	16	.385
South Division						
Findlay	13	4	.765	23	8	.742
Gannon	11	6	.647	20	10	.667
Wayne St. (Mich.)	9	8	.529	13	14	.481
Ashland	8	9	.471	16	11	.593
Hillsdale	8	9	.471	16	12	.571
Mercyhurst	4	13	.235	12	15	.444

GREAT LAKES VALLEY CONFERENCE

	Conference			Full Season		
Team	W	L	Pct.	W	L	Pct.
Ky. Wesleyan	18	2	.900	26	3	.886
Northern Ky.	16	4	.800	25	6	.806
Southern Ind.	16	4	.800	25	7	.781
Lewis	14	6	.700	23	8	.742
Indianapolis	13	7	.650	18	11	.621
Wis.-Parkside	8	12	.400	13	15	.464
St. Joseph's (Ind.)	7	13	.350	11	17	.393
Quincy	5	15	.250	12	16	.429
Bellarmine	5	15	.250	10	19	.345

	Conference			Full Season		
Team	W	L	Pct.	W	L	Pct.
SIU Edwardsville	5	15	.250	9	18	.333
Mo.-St. Louis	2	18	.100	5	22	.185

GREAT NORTHWEST ATHLETIC CONFERENCE

	Conference			Full Season		
Team	W	L	Pct.	W	L	Pct.
Humboldt St.	13	5	.722	23	6	.793
Alas. Fairbanks	13	5	.722	20	8	.714
Seattle Pacific	12	6	.667	16	11	.593
Central Wash.	10	8	.556	16	11	.593
Western Wash.	10	8	.556	16	11	.593
Alas. Anchorage	10	8	.556	13	14	.481
Seattle	9	9	.500	16	11	.593
Western Ore.	8	10	.444	15	12	.556
Northwest Nazarene	3	15	.167	5	21	.192
St. Martin's	2	16	.111	2	26	.071

GULF SOUTH CONFERENCE

	Conference			Full Season		
East Division	W	L	Pct.	W	L	Pct.
Ala.-Huntsville	11	3	.786	20	11	.645
West Ga.	9	5	.643	19	9	.679
Lincoln Memorial	9	5	.643	19	10	.655
North Ala.	9	5	.643	18	10	.643
Valdosta St.	8	6	.571	19	7	.731
West Fla.	6	8	.429	16	11	.593
West Ala.	3	11	.214	7	20	.259
Montevallo	1	13	.071	4	25	.138
West Division						
Henderson St.	14	2	.875	30	5	.857
Delta St.	12	4	.750	22	8	.733
Harding	12	4	.750	21	9	.700
Ouachita Baptist	10	6	.625	16	12	.571
Christian Bros.	9	7	.563	18	11	.621
Central Ark.	5	11	.313	7	18	.280
Arkansas Tech	4	12	.250	11	16	.407
Ark.-Monticello	3	13	.188	9	18	.333
Southern Ark.	2	14	.125	6	21	.222

HEARTLAND CONFERENCE

	Conference			Full Season		
Team	W	L	Pct.	W	L	Pct.
St. Mary's (Tex.)	8	2	.800	17	13	.567
Rockhurst	7	3	.700	17	11	.607
Incarnate Word	6	4	.600	19	9	.679
Drury	5	5	.500	11	17	.393

Team	Conference W	L	Pct.	Full Season W	L	Pct.
Lincoln (Mo.)	4	6	.400	13	13	.500
St. Edward's	0	10	.000	4	23	.148
Okla. Panhandle	-	-	—	15	11	.577

LONE STAR CONFERENCE

North Division	Conference W	L	Pct.	Full Season W	L	Pct.
Northeastern St.	11	1	.917	32	3	.914
Tarleton St.	11	1	.917	29	4	.879
Central Okla.	8	4	.667	19	10	.655
East Central	4	8	.333	11	17	.393
Southwestern Okla.	4	8	.333	8	18	.308
Cameron	2	10	.167	9	17	.346
Southeastern Okla.	2	10	.167	5	22	.185
South Division						
Eastern N.M.	11	1	.917	20	8	.714
West Tex. A&M	8	4	.667	21	10	.677
Tex. A&M-Commerce	6	6	.500	16	12	.571
Midwestern St.	6	6	.500	10	18	.357
Angelo St.	4	8	.333	14	13	.519
Abilene Christian	4	8	.333	13	14	.481
Tex. A&M-Kingsville	3	9	.250	12	15	.444

MID-AMERICA INTERCOLLEGIATE ATHLETICS ASSOCIATION

Team	Conference W	L	Pct.	Full Season W	L	Pct.
Washburn	15	3	.833	26	6	.813
Mo. Western St.	12	6	.667	23	8	.742
Northwest Mo. St.	12	6	.667	22	9	.710
Emporia St.	12	6	.667	16	12	.571
Mo. Southern St.	10	8	.556	19	10	.655
Pittsburg St.	8	10	.444	16	12	.571
Mo.-Rolla	7	11	.389	12	15	.444
Southwest Baptist	6	12	.333	9	17	.346
Central Mo. St.	5	13	.278	12	16	.429
Truman	2	16	.111	7	20	.259

NEW YORK COLLEGIATE ATHLETIC CONFERENCE

Team	Conference W	L	Pct.	Full Season W	L	Pct.
C.W. Post	20	4	.833	25	8	.758
Bridgeport	18	6	.750	23	8	.742
Adelphi	18	6	.750	22	9	.710
New Haven	17	7	.708	21	10	.677
NYIT	15	9	.625	17	11	.607
Philadelphia U.	15	9	.625	16	12	.571
Queens (N.Y.)	12	12	.500	14	14	.500
Molloy	11	13	.458	13	15	.464
Southampton	11	13	.458	10	17	.370
Mercy	10	14	.417	10	16	.385
Dowling	5	19	.208	7	20	.259
St. Thomas Aquinas	2	21	.087	3	23	.115
Concordia (N.Y.)	1	22	.043	3	24	.111

NORTH CENTRAL CONFERENCE

Team	Conference W	L	Pct.	Full Season W	L	Pct.
St. Cloud St.	13	3	.813	26	4	.867
South Dakota St.	12	4	.750	24	7	.774
North Dakota	11	5	.688	20	9	.690
North Dakota St.	9	7	.563	20	11	.645
Neb.-Omaha	8	8	.500	20	10	.667
South Dakota	8	8	.500	19	9	.679
Minn. St. Mankato	6	10	.375	15	13	.536
Northern Colo.	3	13	.188	11	15	.423
Augustana (S.D.)	2	14	.125	11	16	.407

NORTHEAST-10 CONFERENCE

Team	Conference W	L	Pct.	Full Season W	L	Pct.
Mass.-Lowell	18	4	.818	28	5	.848
Southern N.H.	17	5	.773	22	8	.733
St. Rose	14	8	.636	19	11	.633
Pace	14	8	.636	16	12	.571
Assumption	13	9	.591	20	11	.645
Bentley	12	10	.545	17	12	.586
Le Moyne	12	10	.545	17	12	.586
Bryant	12	10	.545	17	14	.548
Franklin Pierce	11	11	.500	14	15	.483
St. Anselm	10	12	.455	13	14	.481
Merrimack	8	14	.364	11	17	.393
American Int'l	8	14	.364	9	19	.321
Southern Conn. St.	7	15	.318	9	18	.333
St. Michael's	6	16	.273	10	17	.370
Stonehill	3	19	.136	6	20	.231

NORTHERN SUN INTERCOLLEGIATE CONFERENCE

Team	Conference W	L	Pct.	Full Season W	L	Pct.
Northern St.	15	3	.833	20	9	.690
Southwest Minn. St.	13	5	.722	17	11	.607
Minn. Duluth	12	6	.667	19	12	.613
Bemidji St.	12	6	.667	17	12	.586
Wayne St. (Neb.)	11	7	.611	13	15	.464
Minn. St.-Moorhead	10	8	.556	19	10	.655
Winona St.	10	8	.556	11	17	.393
Concordia-St.Paul	4	14	.222	4	24	.143
Minn.-Crookston	3	15	.167	4	21	.160
Minn.-Morris	0	18	.000	2	25	.074

PACIFIC WEST CONFERENCE

Pacific Division	Conference W	L	Pct.	Full Season W	L	Pct.
BYU-Hawaii	13	2	.867	19	4	.826
Hawaii-Hilo	10	5	.667	18	10	.643
Mont. St.-Billings	8	7	.533	18	9	.667
Chaminade	7	8	.467	12	15	.444
Hawaii Pacific	6	9	.400	17	10	.630
Western N.M.	1	14	.067	3	23	.115

PEACH BELT ATHLETIC CONFERENCE

North Division	Conference W	L	Pct.	Full Season W	L	Pct.
Augusta St.	13	6	.684	18	11	.621
S.C.-Spartanburg	11	8	.579	18	11	.621
Francis Marion	8	11	.421	13	14	.481
S.C.-Aiken	4	15	.211	5	23	.179
Lander	4	15	.211	7	21	.250
UNC Pembroke	0	19	.000	0	28	.000
South Division						
Columbus St.	16	3	.842	27	5	.844
Kennesaw St.	14	5	.737	25	10	.714
Armstrong Atlantic	12	7	.632	14	14	.500
Clayton St.	11	8	.579	17	12	.586
North Fla.	11	8	.579	15	14	.517
GC&SU	10	9	.526	14	13	.519

PENNSYLVANIA STATE ATHLETIC CONFERENCE

Eastern Division	Conference W	L	Pct.	Full Season W	L	Pct.
Millersville	11	1	.917	26	6	.813
West Chester	9	3	.750	21	9	.700
Kutztown	9	4	.692	18	10	.643
Mansfield	6	6	.500	18	11	.621
Cheyney	4	8	.333	13	14	.481
East Stroudsburg	2	10	.167	8	18	.308
Bloomsburg	2	10	.167	6	20	.231
Western Division						
Calif. (Pa.)	10	2	.833	25	9	.735
Edinboro	8	4	.667	17	11	.607
Clarion	7	5	.583	19	10	.655
Lock Haven	6	6	.500	10	17	.370
Indiana (Pa.)	5	7	.417	16	11	.593
Shippensburg	4	8	.333	8	19	.296
Slippery Rock	2	10	.167	8	17	.320

ROCKY MOUNTAIN ATHLETIC CONFERENCE

East Division	Conference W	L	Pct.	Full Season W	L	Pct.
Neb.-Kearney	18	1	.947	30	3	.909
Metro St.	16	3	.842	28	5	.848
Fort Hays St.	13	6	.684	23	8	.742
Colorado Mines	12	7	.632	18	10	.643
Chadron St.	8	11	.421	12	14	.462
Colo.-Christian	6	13	.316	9	18	.333
Regis (Colo.)	5	14	.263	12	15	.444

West Division	Conference W	L	Pct.	Full Season W	L	Pct.
Fort Lewis	15	4	.789	19	12	.613
Mesa St.	11	8	.579	15	12	.556
Colorado St.-Pueblo	10	9	.526	17	11	.607
Adams St.	10	9	.526	13	15	.464
N.M. Highlands	5	14	.263	7	20	.259
UC-Colo. Spgs.	4	15	.211	6	19	.240
Western St.	0	19	.000	0	26	.000

SOUTH ATLANTIC CONFERENCE

Team	Conference W	L	Pct.	Full Season W	L	Pct.
Lenoir-Rhyne	10	4	.714	22	8	.733
Carson-Newman	10	4	.714	19	9	.679
Wingate	10	4	.714	18	11	.621
Presbyterian	9	5	.643	27	9	.750
Tusculum	7	7	.500	16	12	.571
Catawba	6	8	.429	11	17	.393
Mars Hill	3	11	.214	13	15	.464
Newberry	1	13	.071	4	22	.154

SOUTHERN INTERCOLLEGIATE ATHLETIC CONFERENCE

Eastern Division	Conference W	L	Pct.	Full Season W	L	Pct.
Morehouse	13	2	.867	23	8	.742
Benedict	8	7	.533	11	13	.458
Albany St. (Ga.)	7	8	.467	8	20	.286
Clark Atlanta	6	8	.429	7	21	.250
Fort Valley St.	5	10	.333	13	16	.448
Paine	5	10	.333	10	17	.370
Western Division						
Lane	9	6	.600	14	14	.500
Miles	9	6	.600	13	13	.500
LeMoyne-Owen	9	6	.600	14	14	.500
Kentucky St.	6	9	.400	13	16	.448
Tuskegee	6	9	.400	11	17	.393

SUNSHINE STATE CONFERENCE

Team	Conference W	L	Pct.	Full Season W	L	Pct.
Rollins	13	1	.929	26	6	.813
Fla. Southern	10	4	.714	26	5	.839
Eckerd	10	4	.714	25	7	.781
Barry	7	7	.500	18	10	.643
Lynn	7	7	.500	15	13	.536
Tampa	6	8	.429	15	12	.556
St. Leo	2	12	.143	7	21	.250
Florida Tech	1	13	.071	9	19	.321
Nova Southeastern	-	-	—	6	21	.222

WEST VIRGINIA INTERCOLLEGIATE ATHLETIC CONFERENCE

Team	Conference W	L	Pct.	Full Season W	L	Pct.
Salem Int'l	16	2	.889	25	6	.806
Alderson-Broaddus	15	3	.833	25	7	.781
Wheeling Jesuit	14	4	.778	22	8	.733
Charleston (W.Va.)	13	5	.722	21	10	.677
Fairmont St.	11	7	.611	19	9	.679
Glenville St.	10	8	.556	12	17	.414
West Virginia St.	9	9	.500	16	13	.552
West Liberty St.	9	9	.500	11	16	.407
Shepherd	8	10	.444	12	17	.414
West Va. Wesleyan	8	10	.444	9	17	.346
West Va. Tech	7	11	.389	11	18	.379
Concord	7	11	.389	10	18	.357
Davis & Elkins	4	14	.222	6	22	.214
Bluefield St.	3	15	.167	5	23	.179
Ohio Valley	1	17	.056	2	26	.071

DIVISION II INDEPENDENTS

Team	Full Season W	L	Pct.
Okla. Panhandle	5	22	.185
Dist. Columbia	19	7	.731
Oakland City	11	15	.423
Pitt.-Johnstown	11	16	.407
Tiffin	9	18	.333
Columbia Union	1	26	.037

2003 Division III Conference Standings

ALLEGHENY MOUNTAIN COLLEGIATE CONFERENCE

Team	Conference			Full Season		
	W	L	Pct.	W	L	Pct.
Penn. St.-Behrend	10	2	.833	20	9	.690
Pitt.-Bradford............	8	4	.667	22	7	.759
LaRoche	8	4	.667	14	12	.538
Lake Erie	6	6	.500	12	14	.462
Pitt.-Greensburg.......	5	7	.417	14	12	.538
Frostburg St.	5	7	.417	10	16	.385
Penn. St.-Altoona.....	0	12	.000	2	25	.074

AMERICAN SOUTHWEST CONFERENCE

East Division	Conference			Full Season		
	W	L	Pct.	W	L	Pct.
East Tex. Baptist.....	10	2	.833	17	9	.654
Mississippi Col........	9	3	.750	19	8	.704
Ozarks (Ark.)...........	7	5	.583	14	10	.583
Louisiana Col...........	6	6	.500	13	11	.542
LeTourneau	5	7	.417	9	16	.360
Texas-Dallas	3	9	.250	7	18	.280
Austin	2	10	.167	8	17	.320

West Division	Conference			Full Season		
	W	L	Pct.	W	L	Pct.
Sul Ross St.	12	2	.857	19	6	.760
McMurry.................	11	3	.786	18	9	.667
Howard Payne.........	10	4	.714	17	8	.680
Texas Lutheran	8	6	.571	12	13	.480
Mary Hardin-Baylor..	7	7	.500	13	12	.520
Concordia-Austin......	3	11	.214	4	21	.160
Schreiner	3	11	.214	2	23	.080
Hardin-Simmons.......	2	12	.143	5	20	.200

CAPITAL ATHLETIC CONFERENCE

Team	Conference			Full Season		
	W	L	Pct.	W	L	Pct.
Catholic	13	1	.929	24	5	.828
Mary Washington	11	3	.786	24	5	.828
Goucher	9	5	.643	16	10	.615
Marymount (Va.)	8	6	.571	14	12	.538
York (Pa.)	7	7	.500	13	12	.520
Salisbury	4	10	.286	6	20	.231
St. Mary's (Md.).......	3	11	.214	6	20	.231
Gallaudet................	1	13	.071	5	21	.192

CENTENNIAL CONFERENCE

East Division	Conference			Full Season		
	W	L	Pct.	W	L	Pct.
Ursinus...................	13	0	1.000	21	7	.750
Washington (Md.)....	6	7	.462	10	16	.385
Haverford...............	5	8	.385	10	14	.417
Swarthmore	5	8	.385	9	16	.360
Muhlenberg	4	9	.308	10	14	.417

West Division	Conference			Full Season		
	W	L	Pct.	W	L	Pct.
Frank. & Marsh.......	10	3	.769	25	5	.833
Johns Hopkins..........	9	4	.692	19	7	.731
Gettysburg..............	9	4	.692	13	13	.500
Dickinson	2	11	.154	8	17	.320
McDaniel	2	11	.154	5	20	.200

CITY UNIVERSITY OF NEW YORK ATHLETIC CONFERENCE

Team	Conference			Full Season		
	W	L	Pct.	W	L	Pct.
Baruch	10	3	.769	25	5	.833
CCNY	9	4	.692	17	12	.586
Staten Island............	9	4	.692	15	11	.577
Lehman	8	5	.615	15	13	.536
Hunter....................	7	6	.000	8	18	.308
York (N.Y.)	6	6	.500	10	15	.400
John Jay.................	6	7	.462	10	16	.385
Brooklyn	4	8	.333	8	18	.308
Medgar Evers	3	10	.231	6	20	.231
NYIT	2	11	.154	6	19	.240

COMMONWEALTH COAST CONFERENCE

North Division	Conference			Full Season		
	W	L	Pct.	W	L	Pct.
Endicott	14	2	.875	19	10	.655
Colby-Sawyer	13	3	.813	21	7	.750
Gordon	13	3	.813	20	6	.769
New England	5	11	.313	9	17	.346
Wentworth Inst.........	3	13	.188	5	19	.208
New England Col. ...	1	15	.063	3	22	.120

South Division	Conference			Full Season		
	W	L	Pct.	W	L	Pct.
Nichols	10	6	.625	14	13	.519
Anna Maria.............	9	7	.563	15	12	.556
Salve Regina	9	7	.563	11	14	.440
Curry	7	9	.438	10	15	.400
Eastern Nazarene	7	9	.438	9	17	.346
Roger Williams	5	11	.313	5	20	.200

DIXIE INTERCOLLEGIATE ATHLETIC CONFERENCE

Team	Conference			Full Season		
	W	L	Pct.	W	L	Pct.
Chris. Newport	12	2	.857	24	5	.828
Methodist	12	2	.857	17	10	.630
N.C. Wesleyan........	10	4	.714	18	10	.643
Greensboro	7	7	.500	11	14	.440
Shenandoah	5	9	.357	13	13	.500
Chowan	5	9	.357	8	18	.308
Ferrum	4	10	.286	7	19	.269
Averett..................	1	13	.071	2	23	.080

EMPIRE ATHLETIC ASSOCIATION

Team	Conference			Full Season		
	W	L	Pct.	W	L	Pct.
St. John Fisher..........	12	2	.857	21	5	.808
Nazareth	11	3	.786	22	6	.786
Rochester Inst.	10	4	.714	20	8	.714
Ithaca	8	6	.571	12	13	.480
Utica	5	9	.357	10	15	.400
Elmira	4	10	.286	12	13	.480
Hartwick	4	10	.286	10	15	.400
Alfred	2	12	.143	5	20	.200

GREAT NORTHEAST ATHLETIC CONFERENCE

Team	Conference			Full Season		
	W	L	Pct.	W	L	Pct.
Southern Vt.	16	2	.889	24	6	.800
Albertus Magnus	13	5	.722	18	10	.643
Western New Eng. ..	12	6	.667	16	11	.593
Johnson & Wales	11	7	.611	13	13	.500
Norwich..................	10	8	.556	14	11	.560
Suffolk...................	10	8	.556	12	14	.462
Emmanuel (Mass.)	7	11	.389	8	17	.320
Rivier	5	13	.278	7	19	.269
Emerson	4	14	.222	8	17	.320
Daniel Webster........	2	16	.111	3	22	.120

HEARTLAND COLLEGIATE ATHLETIC CONFERENCE

Team	Conference			Full Season		
	W	L	Pct.	W	L	Pct.
Hanover..................	13	1	.929	27	2	.931
Anderson (Ind.)	8	6	.571	17	10	.630
Manchester.............	8	6	.571	16	10	.615
Defiance	7	7	.500	17	10	.630
Transylvania	6	8	.429	12	12	.500
Mt. St. Joseph	5	9	.357	12	15	.444
Franklin	5	9	.357	9	17	.346
Bluffton..................	4	10	.286	10	16	.385

COLLEGE CONFERNCE OF ILLINOIS & WISCONSIN

Team	Conference			Full Season		
	W	L	Pct.	W	L	Pct.
Augustana (Ill.)........	11	3	.786	20	5	.800
Ill. Wesleyan	11	3	.786	22	6	.786
Carthage	11	3	.786	19	6	.760
Wheaton (Ill.)..........	9	5	.643	18	7	.720
Elmhurst.................	6	8	.429	11	14	.440
North Central	4	10	.286	8	17	.320
North Park..............	2	12	.143	12	13	.480
Millikin....................	2	12	.143	7	18	.280

IOWA INTERCOLLEGIATE ATHLETIC CONFERENCE

Team	Conference			Full Season		
	W	L	Pct.	W	L	Pct.
Buena Vista	16	2	.889	27	4	.871
Wartburg	14	4	.778	21	7	.750
Cornell College........	12	6	.667	16	11	.593
Loras	11	7	.611	17	10	.630
Simpson	9	9	.500	14	12	.538
Coe	9	9	.500	9	17	.346
Luther	8	10	.444	9	17	.346
Upper Iowa	5	13	.278	8	17	.320
Central (Iowa).........	5	13	.278	5	21	.192
Dubuque	1	17	.056	2	23	.080

LAKE MICHIGAN CONFERENCE

Team	Conference			Full Season		
	W	L	Pct.	W	L	Pct.
Lakeland	10	2	.833	19	8	.704
Edgewood	8	4	.667	14	11	.560
Wis. Lutheran	6	6	.500	9	18	.333
Concordia (Wis.)	5	7	.417	14	12	.538
Milwaukee Engr.......	5	7	.417	12	17	.414
Marian (Wis.)	5	7	.417	8	18	.308
Maranatha Baptist....	3	9	.250	12	16	.429

LITTLE EAST CONFERENCE

Team	Conference			Full Season		
	W	L	Pct.	W	L	Pct.
Western Conn. St.....	11	3	.786	20	9	.690
Keene St.	10	4	.714	22	8	.733
Plymouth St............	10	4	.714	21	8	.724
Mass.-Dartmouth	7	7	.500	13	14	.481
Rhode Island Col.....	5	9	.357	13	13	.500
Mass.-Boston...........	5	9	.357	11	15	.423
Eastern Conn. St.	5	9	.357	7	19	.269
Southern Me.	3	11	.214	4	21	.160

MASSACHUSETTS STATE COLLEGE ATHLETIC CONFERENCE

Team	Conference			Full Season		
	W	L	Pct.	W	L	Pct.
Salem St.................	10	2	.833	23	6	.793
Worcester St............	9	3	.750	17	11	.607
Westfield St.............	9	3	.750	15	11	.577
Bridgewater St.........	5	7	.417	11	15	.423
Fitchburg St.	5	7	.417	8	17	.320
Framingham St.........	3	9	.250	6	17	.261
Mass. Liberal Arts.....	1	11	.083	2	23	.080

MICHIGAN INTERCOLLEGIATE ATHLETIC ASSOCIATION

Team	Conference			Full Season		
	W	L	Pct.	W	L	Pct.
Hope	10	2	.833	23	5	.821
Albion	10	2	.833	22	5	.815
Kalamazoo	7	5	.583	18	6	.750
Calvin	7	5	.583	16	10	.615
Adrian	5	7	.417	12	14	.462
Olivet....................	3	9	.250	11	15	.423
Alma.....................	0	12	.000	1	23	.042

MIDDLE ATLANTIC CONFERENCE

Commonwealth League	Conference			Full Season		
	W	L	Pct.	W	L	Pct.
Susquehanna	11	3	.786	18	8	.692
Elizabethtown	10	4	.714	18	9	.667
Moravian	9	5	.643	16	11	.593
Lebanon Valley	8	6	.571	13	13	.500
Juniata	7	7	.500	13	12	.520
Widener	6	8	.429	11	14	.440
Albright	3	11	.214	4	19	.174
Messiah	2	12	.143	7	16	.304

Freedom League	Conference			Full Season		
	W	L	Pct.	W	L	Pct.
Scranton	11	3	.786	24	6	.800
DeSales	10	4	.714	23	7	.767
Lycoming	10	4	.714	15	11	.577
King's (Pa.)	9	5	.643	16	10	.615
Wilkes	8	6	.571	17	7	.708
FDU-Florham	4	10	.286	11	14	.440
Drew	4	10	.286	7	17	.292
Delaware Valley	0	14	.000	5	19	.208

MIDWEST CONFERENCE

Team	Conference			Full Season		
	W	L	Pct.	W	L	Pct.
Grinnell	13	3	.813	19	6	.760
Lawrence	12	4	.750	18	6	.750
Ripon	9	7	.563	15	9	.625
Illinois Col.	9	7	.563	15	11	.577
St. Norbert	9	7	.563	12	11	.522
Beloit	8	8	.500	10	13	.435
Lake Forest	7	9	.438	8	15	.348
Knox	6	10	.375	9	14	.391
Carroll (Wis.)	5	11	.313	7	16	.304
Monmouth (Ill.)	2	14	.125	5	18	.217

MINNESOTA INTERCOLLEGIATE ATHLETIC CONFERENCE

Team	Conference			Full Season		
	W	L	Pct.	W	L	Pct.
St. Thomas (Minn.)	16	4	.800	21	6	.778
Gust. Adolphus	15	5	.750	26	7	.788
Carleton	13	7	.650	16	10	.615
Bethel (Minn.)	12	8	.600	15	12	.556
St. Olaf	11	9	.550	15	11	.577
St. John's (Minn.)	10	10	.500	12	15	.444
Hamline	8	12	.400	12	13	.480
Augsburg	8	12	.400	11	14	.440
Concordia-M'head	8	12	.400	9	15	.375
Macalester	7	13	.350	9	16	.360
St. Mary's (Minn.)	2	18	.100	2	22	.083

NEW ENGLAND SMALL COLLEGE ATHLETIC CONFERENCE

Team	Conference			Full Season		
	W	L	Pct.	W	L	Pct.
Williams	8	1	.889	31	1	.969
Amherst	8	1	.889	24	5	.828
Trinity (Conn.)	5	4	.556	15	9	.625
Wesleyan (Conn.)	5	4	.556	14	10	.583
Tufts	5	4	.556	12	13	.480
Bates	4	5	.444	16	9	.640
Middlebury	4	5	.444	15	10	.600
Bowdoin	3	6	.333	10	14	.417
Colby	2	7	.222	6	16	.273
Connecticut Col.	1	8	.111	7	16	.304

NEW ENGLAND WOMEN'S & MEN'S ATHLETIC CONFERENCE

Team	Conference			Full Season		
	W	L	Pct.	W	L	Pct.
Clark (Mass.)	10	2	.833	21	7	.750
Babson	9	2	.818	26	4	.867
MIT	7	4	.636	16	10	.615
Wheaton (Mass.)	6	6	.500	19	10	.655
Springfield	4	8	.333	12	15	.444
Coast Guard	4	8	.333	9	15	.375
WPI	1	11	.083	7	18	.280

NEW JERSEY ATHLETIC CONFERENCE

Team	Conference			Full Season		
	W	L	Pct.	W	L	Pct.
Ramapo	17	1	.944	26	4	.867
Montclair St.	13	5	.722	23	6	.793
Rowan	13	5	.722	20	6	.769
Wm. Paterson	13	5	.722	19	7	.731
Richard Stockton	8	10	.444	14	12	.538
New Jersey City	8	10	.444	14	13	.519
Kean	7	11	.389	11	13	.458
TCNJ	6	12	.333	13	12	.520
Rutgers-Camden	3	15	.167	8	17	.320
Rutgers-Newark	2	16	.111	8	17	.320

NORTH COAST ATHLETIC CONFERENCE

Team	Conference			Full Season		
	W	L	Pct.	W	L	Pct.
Wooster	15	1	.938	30	3	.909
Wittenberg	14	2	.875	20	6	.769
Allegheny	10	6	.625	16	12	.571
Wabash	9	7	.563	16	10	.615
Earlham	8	8	.500	13	13	.500
Ohio Wesleyan	8	8	.500	12	14	.462
Denison	7	9	.438	9	17	.346
Hiram	4	12	.250	6	20	.231
Kenyon	3	13	.188	3	22	.120
Oberlin	2	14	.125	3	22	.120

NORTHEASTERN ATHLETIC CONFERENCE

Team	Conference			Full Season		
	W	L	Pct.	W	L	Pct.
Keuka	6	2	.750	13	10	.565
Cazenovia	6	2	.750	11	15	.423
D'Youville	4	4	.500	11	16	.407
Medaille	4	4	.500	6	20	.231
Hilbert	0	8	.000	1	23	.042

NORTHERN ILLINOIS-IOWA INTERCOLLEGIATE CONFERENCE

Team	Conference			Full Season		
	W	L	Pct.	W	L	Pct.
Rockford	12	0	1.000	24	4	.857
Aurora	10	2	.833	24	6	.800
Clarke	7	5	.583	14	13	.519
Benedictine (Ill.)	6	6	.500	14	13	.519
Eureka	3	9	.250	8	17	.320
Dominican (Ill.)	3	9	.250	7	19	.269
Concordia (Ill.)	1	11	.083	5	21	.192

NORTHWEST CONFERENCE OF INDEPENDENT COLLEGES

Team	Conference			Full Season		
	W	L	Pct.	W	L	Pct.
Whitworth	13	3	.813	23	4	.852
Willamette	12	4	.750	19	7	.731
Lewis & Clark	11	5	.688	16	10	.615
Linfield	9	7	.563	16	9	.640
Pacific (Ore.)	8	8	.500	11	14	.440
Puget Sound	7	9	.438	12	13	.480
Pacific Lutheran	7	9	.438	10	15	.400
Whitman	4	12	.250	7	18	.280
George Fox	1	15	.063	7	18	.280

OHIO ATHLETIC CONFERENCE

Team	Conference			Full Season		
	W	L	Pct.	W	L	Pct.
Capital	15	3	.833	22	6	.786
John Carroll	15	3	.833	22	7	.759
Mount Union	12	6	.667	18	9	.667
Otterbein	11	7	.611	15	11	.577
Ohio Northern	11	7	.611	14	13	.519
Baldwin-Wallace	9	9	.500	13	13	.500
Muskingum	6	12	.333	11	16	.407
Marietta	5	13	.278	10	17	.370
Heidelberg	4	14	.222	7	19	.269
Wilmington (Ohio)	2	16	.111	4	22	.154

OLD DOMINION ATHLETIC CONFERENCE

Team	Conference			Full Season		
	W	L	Pct.	W	L	Pct.
Randolph-Macon	17	1	.944	28	2	.933
Hampden-Sydney	17	1	.944	28	4	.875
Va. Wesleyan	12	6	.667	18	9	.667
Roanoke	11	7	.611	15	12	.556
Bridgewater (Va.)	8	10	.444	14	12	.538
Emory & Henry	8	10	.444	13	13	.500
Guilford	8	10	.444	12	14	.462
Wash. & Lee	5	13	.278	8	17	.320
Lynchburg	3	15	.167	6	19	.240
East. Mennonite	1	17	.056	3	22	.120

PENNSYLVANIA ATHLETIC CONFERENCE

Team	Conference			Full Season		
	W	L	Pct.	W	L	Pct.
Cabrini	12	4	.750	17	9	.654
Neumann	12	4	.750	18	11	.621
Alvernia	11	5	.688	21	9	.700
Misericordia	9	7	.563	16	12	.571
Gwynedd-Mercy	8	8	.500	13	13	.500
Eastern	7	9	.438	12	14	.462
Arcadia	6	10	.375	11	14	.440
Wesley	4	12	.250	7	18	.280
Marywood	3	13	.188	7	18	.280

PRESIDENTS' ATHLETIC CONFERENCE

Team	Conference			Full Season		
	W	L	Pct.	W	L	Pct.
Grove City	7	3	.700	18	9	.667
Thiel	7	3	.700	16	12	.571
Waynesburg	6	4	.600	16	9	.640
Westminster (Pa.)	4	6	.400	11	15	.423
Bethany (W.Va.)	3	7	.300	11	15	.423
Wash. & Jeff.	3	7	.300	6	19	.240

ST. LOUIS INTERCOLLEGIATE ATHLETIC CONFERENCE

Team	Conference			Full Season		
	W	L	Pct.	W	L	Pct.
Blackburn	11	3	.786	15	10	.600
Fontbonne	10	4	.714	15	10	.600
Webster	9	5	.643	12	13	.480
Principia	7	7	.500	13	12	.520
Maryville (Mo.)	6	8	.429	7	18	.280
MacMurray	5	9	.357	9	15	.375
Westminster (Mo.)	4	10	.286	12	13	.480
Greenville	4	10	.286	9	15	.375

SKYLINE CONFERENCE

Team	Conference			Full Season		
	W	L	Pct.	W	L	Pct.
Merchant Marine	13	3	.813	21	9	.700
Mt. St. Mary (N.Y.)	12	4	.750	23	8	.742
Manhattanville	12	4	.750	19	10	.655
Old Westbury	11	5	.688	16	12	.571
St. Joseph's (L.I.)	8	8	.500	12	13	.480
Stevens Tech	7	9	.438	7	19	.269
Mt. St. Vincent	4	12	.250	11	15	.423
Yeshiva	4	12	.250	8	17	.320
Maritime (N.Y.)	1	15	.063	3	23	.115

SOUTHERN CALIFORNIA INTER-COLLEGIATE ATHLETIC CONFERENCE

Team	Conference			Full Season		
	W	L	Pct.	W	L	Pct.
Occidental	14	0	1.000	24	3	.889
Cal Lutheran	10	4	.714	16	9	.640
Claremont-M-S	8	6	.571	15	10	.600
Whittier	7	7	.500	17	8	.680
La Verne	6	8	.429	16	9	.640
Pomona-Pitzer	6	8	.429	9	16	.360
Redlands	5	9	.357	10	15	.400
Caltech	0	14	.000	1	23	.042

SOUTHERN COLLEGIATE ATHLETIC CONFERENCE

Team	Conference			Full Season		
	W	L	Pct.	W	L	Pct.
DePauw	12	2	.857	18	8	.692
Trinity (Tex.)	11	3	.786	21	8	.724
Centre	10	4	.714	18	9	.667
Southwestern (Tex.)	10	4	.714	18	9	.667
Millsaps	7	7	.500	15	11	.577
Rose-Hulman	6	8	.429	9	17	.346
Sewanee	5	9	.357	8	17	.320
Rhodes	4	10	.286	10	15	.400
Oglethorpe	3	11	.214	9	16	.360
Hendrix	2	12	.143	7	17	.292

STATE UNIVERSITY OF NEW YORK ATHLETIC CONFERENCE

Team	Conference			Full Season		
	W	L	Pct.	W	L	Pct.
Potsdam St.	12	4	.750	18	9	.667
Buffalo St.	11	5	.688	19	9	.679
Utica/Rome	11	5	.688	17	10	.630
Oswego St.	11	5	.688	16	11	.593
Brockport St.	10	6	.625	16	12	.571
Fredonia St.	9	7	.563	13	12	.520
Oneonta St.	8	8	.500	11	14	.440
Geneseo St.	6	10	.375	12	13	.480
New Paltz St.	6	10	.375	11	17	.393
Cortland St.	3	13	.188	5	20	.200
Plattsburgh St.	1	15	.063	6	19	.240

UNIVERSITY ATHLETIC ASSOCIATION

Team	Conference			Full Season		
	W	L	Pct.	W	L	Pct.
Washington (Mo.)	13	1	.929	24	2	.923
Rochester	12	2	.857	23	4	.852
Chicago	11	3	.786	15	10	.600
Emory	6	8	.429	14	11	.560
Carnegie Mellon	5	9	.357	12	13	.480
Case Reserve	4	10	.286	7	18	.280
New York U.	3	11	.214	11	14	.440
Brandeis	2	12	.143	6	19	.240

UPSTATE COLLEGIATE ATHLETIC ASSOCIATION

Team	Conference			Full Season		
	W	L	Pct.	W	L	Pct.
Hamilton	11	3	.786	23	6	.793
Union (N.Y.)	10	4	.714	17	12	.586

Team	Conference			Full Season		
	W	L	Pct.	W	L	Pct.
St. Lawrence	9	5	.643	17	10	.630
Rensselaer	7	7	.500	13	13	.500
Hobart	7	7	.500	10	15	.400
Clarkson	6	8	.429	11	14	.440
Skidmore	5	9	.357	12	12	.500
Vassar	1	13	.071	6	19	.240

WISCONSIN INTERCOLLEGIATE ATHLETIC CONFERENCE

Team	Conference			Full Season		
	W	L	Pct.	W	L	Pct.
Wis.-Stevens Point	14	2	.875	24	4	.857
Wis.-Whitewater	11	5	.688	21	7	.750
Wis.-Oshkosh	10	6	.625	25	7	.781
Wis.-River Falls	10	6	.625	16	10	.615
Wis.-Stout	9	7	.563	14	11	.560
Wis.-Eau Claire	8	8	.500	17	10	.630
Wis.-Platteville	7	9	.438	11	15	.423
Wis.-La Crosse	2	14	.125	6	20	.231
Wis.-Superior	1	15	.063	5	20	.200

DIVISION III INDEPENDENTS

Team	Full Season		
	W	L	Pct.
Baptist Bible	18	12	.600
Bard	8	13	.381
Becker	8	18	.308
Castleton St.	5	21	.192
Centenary (N.J.)	9	15	.375
Chapman	18	7	.720
Colorado Col.	11	13	.458
Dallas	18	7	.720
Eastern Ore.	9	17	.346

Team	Full Season		
	W	L	Pct.
Elms	14	12	.538
Fisk	14	14	.500
Husson	23	6	.793
Johnson St.	10	16	.385
Lasell	22	6	.786
Lincoln (Pa.)	9	15	.375
Maine Maritime	15	10	.600
Martin Luther	13	10	.565
Me.-Farmington	12	13	.480
Mount Ida	8	18	.308
Neb. Wesleyan	14	11	.560
Newbury	12	12	.500
Northland	3	21	.125
Philadelphia Bible	15	12	.556
Polytechnic (N.Y.)	10	17	.370
Rust	12	13	.480
SCAD	21	6	.778
St. Joseph's (Me.)	20	5	.800
St. Scholastica	7	18	.280
Stillman	12	14	.462
Thomas	6	19	.240
Thomas More	7	18	.280
UC Santa Cruz	4	23	.148
Villa Julie	6	19	.240

Attendance Records

Attendance

2003 Attendance Summary

(For All NCAA Varsity Teams)

	Total Teams	Games or Sessions	2003 Attendance	Avg.	Change in Total	Change in Avg.
Home Attendance, NCAA Div. I	*325	*4,437	*22,737,432	5,125	720,709	72
NCAA Championship Tournament		*35	715,080	20,431	-5,353	-153
Other Div. I Neutral-Site Attendance		182	1,549,166	8,512	-213,289	1,229
NCAA DIVISION I TOTALS	***325**	***4,654**	***25,011,678**	**5,372**	**502,067**	**85**
Home Attendance, NCAA Division II	*269	*3,597	3,076,804	855	86,163	-33
Home Attendance, NCAA Division III	*373	*4,389	1,869,592	426	65,383	2
Neutral-Site Attendance for Divisions II & III		*219	*152,575	697	–	–
NCAA Division II Tournament Neutral Sites		18	13,384	744	–	–
NCAA Division III Tournament Neutral Sites		4	10,271	*2,568	–	–
NATIONAL TOTALS FOR 2003	***967**	***12,881**	***30,124,304**	**2,339**	**729,064**	**-34**

Record high. NOTES: The neutral-site attendance for Division II and III does not include any tournaments. The total attendance figures for the Division II Tournament were 51,054 for a 1,418 average over 36 sessions and the Division III Tournament figures were 66,379 for a 1,580 average over 42 sessions.

Division I Championship Tournament

Round	Site	Att.	Site	Att.	Site	Att.	Site	Att.
Opening Round	Dayton	7,711						
1st Round	Birmingham	14,242	Indianapolis	20,960	Oklahoma City	18,462	Spokane	11,171
	Birmingham	16,467	Indianapolis	21,250	Oklahoma City	18,462	Spokane	11,284
	Boston	17,962	Nashville	17,484	Salt Lake City	14,378	Tampa	17,024
	Boston	18,141	Nashville	17,484	Salt Lake City	14,568	Tampa	20,224
2nd Round	Birmingham	16,471	Indianapolis	25,767	Oklahoma City	18,462	Spokane	11,271
	Boston	18,389	Nashville	17,484	Salt Lake City	14,627	Tampa	21,304
Regional Semifinal	Albany	15,093	Anaheim	17,607	Minneapolis	28,168	San Antonio	33,009
Regional Final	Albany	15,207	Anaheim	17,439	Minneapolis	28,383	San Antonio	30,169

Final Four

National Semifinal	New Orleans	54,432
National Final	New Orleans	54,524
Final Four Total		108,956

Total Tournament Attendance	715,080
Average Per Session	20,431

All Division I Conferences

	Total Teams	Games or Sessions	Entire Season 2003 Attendance	Average	Change In Avg.	Conference Tournament Total Sessions	Total Attendance	Average
1. Big Ten	11	180	2,254,658	12,526	-836	5	90,292	18,058
2. Atlantic Coast	9	149	*1,719,813	11,542	851	5	111,115	22,223
3. Southeastern	12	192	2,132,439	11,106	199	6	98,495	16,416
4. Big 12	12	194	*1,961,380	*10,110	65	6	94,800	15,800
5. Mountain West	8	132	*1,279,630	*9,694	463	4	53,930	13,483
6. Big East	14	224	*2,107,630	9,409	730	6	116,472	19,412
7. Conference USA	14	219	1,831,233	8,362	-135	6	76,157	12,693
8. Pacific 10	10	154	1,213,734	7,881	-151	4	63,663	15,916
9. Missouri Valley	10	148	979,173	6,616	372	5	62,007	12,401
10. Atlantic 10	12	173	981,671	5,674	-71	7	52,823	7,546
11. Western Athletic	10	151	794,384	5,261	-46	5	22,073	4,415
12. Mid-American	13	178	665,578	3,739	-224	9	39,329	4,370
13. Horizon	9	119	433,545	3,643	105	6	24,056	4,009
14. Sun Belt	11	150	538,102	3,587	86	5	29,410	5,882
15. Colonial	10	135	469,395	3,477	8	5	22,488	4,498
16. Ohio Valley	9	123	393,263	3,197	274	6	18,359	3,060
17. Big Sky	8	102	319,317	3,131	428	4	24,868	6,217
18. Big West	10	133	368,876	2,774	36	4	12,212	3,053
19. Southern	12	166	419,318	2,526	245	6	24,895	4,149
20. Metro Atlantic	10	134	336,347	2,510	120	4	10,978	2,745
21. Mid-Continent	8	104	259,329	2,494	-136	4	13,395	3,349
22. Ivy	8	90	216,328	2,404	-59			
23. West Coast	8	110	247,462	2,250	-234	4	17,000	4,250
24. Mid-Eastern	11	135	*263,070	1,949	-63	9	34,101	3,789
25. Southwestern	10	123	222,640	1,810	10	6	14,446	2,408
26. Southland	11	145	247,668	1,708	-32	5	13,776	2,755
27. Patriot	8	106	180,893	1,707	10	3	9,879	3,293
28. Big South	8	102	161,358	1,582	499	6	16,450	2,742
29. Atlantic Sun #	12	143	209,136	1,462	160	4	8,018	2,005
30. America East	9	116	151,149	1,303	-67	4	5,610	1,403
31. Northeast	12	140	173,726	1,241	60	4	7,908	1,977
Independent#	6	63	83,839	1,331	-1,263			

Record high for that conference. # Different lineups in 2002.

NOTE: Entire season total attendance includes the conference tournaments.

Leading Division II Conferences

Rank	Division II	Total Teams	Games or Sessions	2003 Attendance	Average	Change In Avg.
1.	North Central	9	133	328,903	2,473	-78
2.	Mid-America	10	135	235,682	1,746	159
3.	CIAA	12	144	224,249	1,557	69
4.	Great Northwest	10	137	159,956	1,168	-12
5.	Great Lakes Valley	11	165	185,860	1,126	-120
6.	SIAC	11	131	145,275	1,109	-62
7.	Rocky Mountain	14	183	197,725	1,080	325
8.	Northern Sun	10	131	140,462	1,072	-97
9.	Lone Star	14	184	190,363	1,035	25
10.	Great Lakes Int'col.	13	177	154,113	871	44

Leading Division III Conferences

Rank	Division III	Total Teams	Games or Sessions	2003 Attendance	Average	Change In Avg.
1.	Michigan	8	76	79,798	1,050	-194
2.	Illinois & Wisconsin	8	91	89,532	984	4
3.	Wisconsin	9	110	89,660	815	4
4.	Ohio	10	120	82,254	685	-79
5.	Northwest	9	94	62,555	665	49
6.	North Coast	10	116	76,467	659	71
7.	Iowa	10	119	69,565	585	-10
8.	Minnesota	11	132	76,278	578	-29
9.	Middle Atlantic	16	194	111,519	575	41
10.	Presidents'	6	70	38,720	553	279

Leading Teams

DIVISION I

Rank	School	G	Attendance	Average
1.	Kentucky	13	289,526	22,271
2.	Syracuse	17	355,663	20,921
3.	Louisville	18	342,672	19,037
4.	North Carolina	18	336,384	18,688
5.	Maryland	16	281,057	17,566
6.	Wisconsin	17	287,818	16,930
7.	Memphis	16	266,283	16,643
8.	Indiana	12	198,321	16,527
9.	Kansas	16	260,800	16,300
10.	Ohio St.	16	256,914	16,057
11.	Marquette	16	248,851	15,553
12.	New Mexico	17	258,161	15,186
13.	Illinois	14	212,303	15,165
14.	Arkansas	16	236,638	14,790
15.	Michigan St.	16	236,144	14,759
16.	Arizona	15	218,427	14,562
17.	Brigham Young	14	202,556	14,468
18.	Tennessee	17	233,413	13,730
19.	North Carolina St.	16	217,012	13,563
20.	Iowa	18	238,233	13,235
21.	Connecticut	16	211,660	13,229
22.	South Carolina	15	194,112	12,941
23.	Minnesota	18	228,527	12,696
24.	Dayton	18	220,789	12,266
25.	Cincinnati	16	194,915	12,182
26.	Alabama	15	176,663	11,778
27.	UNLV	21	247,043	11,764
28.	Iowa St.	19	223,122	11,743
29.	Utah	16	184,295	11,518
30.	Missouri	15	170,894	11,393

2003 DIVISION I TEAM-BY-TEAM ATTENDANCE

Team	G	Attendance	Avg.
Air Force	13	30,105	2,316
Akron	15	37,394	2,493
Alabama	15	176,663	11,778
Alabama A&M	12	19,892	1,658
Alabama St.	13	37,554	2,889
Albany (N.Y.)	14	16,353	1,168
Alcorn St.	10	20,079	2,008
American	12	16,721	1,393
Appalachian St.	14	40,418	2,887
Arizona	15	218,427	14,562
Arizona St.	15	126,277	8,418
Ark.-Little Rock	13	50,102	3,854
Ark.-Pine Bluff	10	7,667	767
Arkansas	16	236,638	14,790
Arkansas St.	14	72,135	5,153
Army	13	13,426	1,033
Auburn	17	120,994	7,117
Austin Peay	14	40,343	2,882
Ball St.	14	78,343	5,596
Baylor	16	108,292	6,768
Belmont	11	9,396	854
Bethune-Cookman	11	11,015	1,001
Binghamton	12	21,479	1,790
Boise St.	16	66,264	4,142
Boston College	14	85,855	6,133
Boston U.	14	15,250	1,089
Bowling Green	12	32,213	2,684
Bradley	14	130,907	9,351
Brigham Young	14	202,556	14,468

Team	G	Attendance	Avg.
Brown	10	19,143	1,914
Bucknell	11	20,253	1,841
Buffalo	13	24,547	1,888
Butler	12	70,951	5,913
Cal Poly	13	35,598	2,738
Cal St. Fullerton	12	13,050	1,088
Cal St. Northridge	13	15,604	1,200
California	14	146,625	10,473
Campbell	13	10,095	777
Canisius	14	25,770	1,841
Centenary (La.)	10	13,321	1,332
Central Conn. St.	12	24,586	2,049
Central Mich.	13	43,855	3,373
Charleston So.	13	7,683	591
Charlotte	15	96,338	6,423
Chattanooga	14	61,594	4,400
Chicago St.	12	4,793	399
Cincinnati	16	194,915	12,182
Citadel	15	27,555	1,837
Clemson	17	120,600	7,094
Cleveland St.	13	23,694	1,823
Coastal Caro.	12	9,542	795
Col. of Charleston	14	47,062	3,362
Colgate	13	6,939	534
Colorado	15	102,875	6,858
Colorado St.	18	70,498	3,917
Columbia	10	12,511	1,251
Connecticut	16	211,660	13,229
Coppin St.	10	9,261	926
Cornell	12	17,251	1,438
Creighton	17	140,174	8,246
Dartmouth	13	13,135	1,010
Davidson	13	38,427	2,956
Dayton	18	220,789	12,266
Delaware	13	61,063	4,697
Delaware St.	11	17,240	1,567
Denver	13	18,945	1,457
DePaul	16	99,433	6,215
Detroit	13	33,796	2,600
Drake	13	51,598	3,969
Drexel	11	19,242	1,749
Duke	15	139,710	9,314
Duquesne	13	55,368	4,259
East Caro.	14	81,538	5,824
East Tenn. St.	13	49,365	3,797
Eastern Ill.	12	39,097	3,258
Eastern Ky.	14	34,650	2,475
Eastern Mich.	14	34,550	2,468
Eastern Wash.	11	29,098	2,645
Elon	12	10,576	881
Evansville	14	93,398	6,671
Fairfield	15	42,883	2,859
Fairleigh Dickinson	13	10,158	781
Fla. Atlantic	10	7,597	760
Florida	16	167,827	10,489
Florida A&M	13	30,117	2,317
Florida Int'l	14	9,372	669
Florida St.	16	102,146	6,384
Fordham	15	37,499	2,500
Fresno St.	15	147,176	9,812
Furman	15	22,648	1,510
Ga. Southern	13	21,797	1,677
Gardner-Webb	11	26,389	2,399
George Mason	13	43,511	3,347
George Washington	11	30,917	2,811
Georgetown	17	149,526	8,796

Team	G	Attendance	Avg.	Team	G	Attendance	Avg.
Georgia	13	128,146	9,857	New Orleans	14	19,233	1,374
Georgia St.	14	15,895	1,135	Niagara	12	17,096	1,425
Georgia Tech	15	128,481	8,565	Nicholls St.	11	6,218	565
Gonzaga	12	48,000	4,000	Norfolk St.	12	23,900	1,992
Grambling	11	15,643	1,422	North Carolina	18	336,384	18,688
Hampton	14	46,852	3,347	North Carolina St.	16	217,012	13,563
Hartford	12	17,087	1,424	North Texas	11	23,751	2,159
Harvard	13	14,576	1,121	Northeastern	13	9,137	703
Hawaii	16	117,621	7,351	Northern Ariz.	13	21,132	1,626
High Point	10	10,510	1,051	Northern Ill.	14	48,726	3,480
Hofstra	13	25,563	1,966	Northern Iowa	12	38,645	3,220
Holy Cross	13	39,131	3,010	Northwestern	17	70,038	4,120
Houston	13	49,500	3,808	Northwestern St.	12	18,263	1,522
Howard	10	12,598	1,260	Notre Dame	16	177,373	11,086
Idaho	14	30,439	2,174	Oakland	15	22,215	1,481
Idaho St.	12	29,102	2,425	Ohio	12	74,096	6,175
Ill.-Chicago	13	55,161	4,243	Ohio St.	16	256,914	16,057
Illinois	14	212,303	15,165	Oklahoma	16	180,248	11,266
Illinois St.	14	84,298	6,021	Oklahoma St.	15	168,738	11,249
Indiana	12	198,321	16,527	Old Dominion	14	82,742	5,910
Indiana St.	14	60,749	4,339	Oral Roberts	13	72,309	5,562
Iona	12	26,153	2,179	Oregon	16	140,660	8,791
Iowa	18	238,233	13,235	Oregon St.	14	86,923	6,209
Iowa St.	19	223,122	11,743	Pacific (Cal.)	14	44,626	3,188
IPFW	9	10,953	1,217	Penn St.	16	110,437	6,902
IUPUI	11	15,226	1,384	Pennsylvania	12	67,840	5,653
Jackson St.	10	19,585	1,959	Pepperdine	12	24,196	2,016
Jacksonville	12	10,696	891	Pittsburgh	16	174,917	10,932
Jacksonville St.	11	34,133	3,103	Portland	13	18,564	1,428
James Madison	13	48,438	3,726	Portland St.	13	17,487	1,345
Kansas	16	260,800	16,300	Prairie View	12	32,156	2,680
Kansas St.	16	114,510	7,157	Princeton	11	53,845	4,895
Kent St.	14	64,246	4,589	Providence	18	157,985	8,777
Kentucky	13	289,526	22,271	Purdue	15	158,281	10,552
La Salle	14	40,877	2,920	Quinnipiac	12	16,022	1,335
La.-Lafayette	11	62,370	5,670	Radford	11	30,411	2,765
La.-Monroe	12	16,937	1,411	Rhode Island	17	96,194	5,658
Lafayette	14	30,835	2,203	Rice	15	34,944	2,330
Lamar	13	43,389	3,338	Richmond	15	85,486	5,699
Lehigh	13	21,396	1,646	Rider	14	22,362	1,597
Liberty	16	44,027	2,752	Robert Morris	11	8,247	750
Long Beach St.	13	26,148	2,011	Rutgers	16	104,426	6,527
Long Island	10	6,375	638	Sacramento St.	12	13,186	1,099
Louisiana Tech	13	28,478	2,191	Sacred Heart	11	7,344	668
Louisville	18	342,672	19,037	Sam Houston St.	15	38,812	2,587
Loyola (Ill.)	12	36,114	3,010	Samford	11	20,463	1,860
Loyola (Md.)	13	5,493	423	San Diego	14	40,460	2,890
Loyola Marymount	13	21,789	1,676	San Diego St.	17	121,926	7,172
LSU	18	156,368	8,687	San Francisco	14	43,516	3,108
Maine	13	20,647	1,588	San Jose St.	13	15,435	1,187
Manhattan	9	17,011	1,890	Santa Clara	15	20,636	1,376
Marist	13	33,764	2,597	Savannah St.	10	7,364	736
Marquette	16	248,851	15,553	Seton Hall	16	122,115	7,632
Marshall	14	53,828	3,845	Siena	17	125,156	7,362
Maryland	16	281,057	17,566	South Ala.	14	51,277	3,663
Massachusetts	15	52,566	3,504	South Carolina	15	194,112	12,941
McNeese St.	13	21,400	1,646	South Carolina St.	10	13,900	1,390
Md.-East. Shore	12	17,030	1,419	South Fla.	15	60,677	4,045
Memphis	16	266,283	16,643	Southeast Mo. St.	13	55,349	4,258
Mercer	12	6,669	556	Southeastern La.	13	10,631	818
Miami (Fla.)	14	50,397	3,600	Southern California	15	77,921	5,195
Miami (Ohio)	13	47,975	3,690	Southern Ill.	14	91,940	6,567
Michigan	16	167,350	10,459	Southern Methodist	13	49,169	3,782
Michigan St.	16	236,144	14,759	Southern Miss.	14	47,027	3,359
Middle Tenn.	14	35,362	2,526	Southern U.	16	16,360	1,023
Minnesota	18	228,527	12,696	Southern Utah	13	28,378	2,183
Mississippi	16	78,822	4,926	Southwest Mo. St.	15	94,425	6,295
Mississippi St.	14	98,312	7,022	St. Bonaventure	10	57,934	5,793
Mississippi Val.	13	20,310	1,562	St. Francis (N.Y.)	9	5,380	598
Missouri	15	170,894	11,393	St. Francis (Pa.)	13	12,983	999
Monmouth	12	22,720	1,893	St. John's (N.Y.)	16	129,384	8,087
Montana	14	62,872	4,491	St. Joseph's	14	62,898	4,493
Montana St.	14	60,103	4,293	St. Louis	16	147,712	9,232
Morehead St.	15	49,563	3,304	St. Mary's (Cal.)	15	24,074	1,605
Morgan St.	13	15,844	1,219	St. Peter's	11	9,681	880
Morris Brown	10	10,598	1,060	Stanford	17	93,698	5,512
Mt. St. Mary's	11	15,893	1,445	Stephen F. Austin	16	33,891	2,118
Murray St.	14	56,316	4,023	Stetson	12	17,141	1,428
N.C. A&T	10	31,212	3,121	Stony Brook	15	18,175	1,212
Navy	15	26,313	1,754	Syracuse	17	355,663	20,921
Nebraska	15	121,179	8,079	TCU	14	67,692	4,835
Nevada	14	95,272	6,805	Temple	15	78,036	5,202
New Hampshire	10	8,759	876	Tenn.-Martin	13	38,058	2,928
New Mexico	17	258,161	15,186	Tennessee	17	233,413	13,730
New Mexico St.	14	101,297	7,236				

Team	G	Attendance	Avg.
Tennessee St.	12	29,810	2,484
Tennessee Tech	14	42,776	3,055
Tex. A&M-Corp. Chris.	13	19,284	1,483
Texas	14	156,378	11,170
Texas A&M	14	90,528	6,466
Texas-Arlington	13	12,991	999
Tex.-Pan American	11	22,319	2,029
Texas-San Antonio	12	16,038	1,337
Texas Southern	14	28,476	2,034
Texas St.	15	29,098	1,940
Texas Tech	17	169,016	9,942
Toledo	12	57,912	4,826
Towson	12	10,285	857
Troy St.	11	30,738	2,794
Tulane	17	32,355	1,903
Tulsa	17	131,502	7,735
UAB	16	70,763	4,423
UC Irvine	13	34,206	2,631
UC Riverside	11	12,712	1,156
UC Santa Barb.	12	32,879	2,740
UCF	13	16,377	1,260
UCLA	15	125,223	8,348
UMBC	10	17,168	1,717
UMKC	12	34,297	2,858
UNC Asheville	12	12,250	1,021
UNC Greensboro	12	13,515	1,126
UNC Wilmington	12	69,766	5,814
UNLV	21	247,043	11,764
Utah	16	184,295	11,518
Utah St.	14	111,402	7,957
UTEP	17	102,645	6,038
Va. Commonwealth	15	57,753	3,850
Valparaiso	13	56,891	4,376
Vanderbilt	16	153,123	9,570
Vermont	12	23,460	1,955
Villanova	13	111,593	8,584
Virginia	15	112,726	7,515
Virginia Tech	15	63,167	4,211
VMI	12	25,452	2,121
Wagner	15	25,148	1,677
Wake Forest	16	170,582	10,661
Washington	15	101,983	6,799
Washington St.	14	32,334	2,310
Weber St.	13	86,337	6,641
West Virginia	14	97,097	6,936
Western Caro.	13	21,545	1,657
Western Ill.	11	11,825	1,075
Western Ky.	16	87,562	5,473
Western Mich.	14	39,815	2,844
Wichita St.	16	131,032	8,190
William & Mary	14	28,544	2,039
Winthrop	15	35,086	2,339
Wis.-Green Bay	15	64,411	4,294
Wis.-Milwaukee	13	55,453	4,266
Wisconsin	17	287,818	16,930
Wofford	12	25,045	2,087
Wright St.	14	61,051	4,361
Wyoming	15	151,614	10,108
Xavier	15	152,664	10,178
Yale	9	18,027	2,003
Youngstown St.	13	30,828	2,371

PROVISIONAL SCHOOLS

Team	G	Attendance	Avg.
Birmingham-So.	14	10,551	753
Lipscomb	14	10,155	725

LARGEST DIVISION I AVERAGE ATTENDANCE INCREASE FROM PREVIOUS YEAR

Rank	School	G	2003 Avg.	2002 Avg.	Change in Avg.
1.	Brigham Young	16	14,468	8,630	5,838
2.	Pittsburgh	18	10,932	6,803	4,129
3.	South Carolina	18	12,941	9,041	3,900
4.	Syracuse	19	20,921	17,023	3,898
5.	Maryland	15	17,566	14,166	3,400
6.	Rhode Island	11	5,658	2,283	3,375
7.	Marquette	16	15,553	12,680	2,873
8.	Old Dominion	15	5,910	3,260	2,650
9.	North Carolina	16	18,688	16,319	2,369
10.	Alabama	17	11,778	9,834	1,944
11.	Weber St.	13	6,641	4,771	1,870
12.	Colorado	16	6,858	5,006	1,852
13.	La.-Lafayette	13	5,670	3,836	1,834

Rank	School	G	2003 Avg.	2002 Avg.	Change in Avg.
14.	South Ala.	15	3,663	1,910	1,753
15.	Creighton	15	8,246	6,613	1,633
16.	Georgia Tech	16	8,565	7,003	1,562
17.	Arizona St.	17	8,418	6,984	1,434
18.	DePaul	15	6,215	4,871	1,344
19.	Wis.-Green Bay	14	4,294	2,959	1,335
20.	Radford	12	2,765	1,431	1,334
21.	Mississippi St.	14	7,022	5,689	1,333
22.	Murray St.	15	4,023	2,737	1,286
23.	Villanova	19	8,584	7,325	1,259
24.	Kentucky	15	22,271	21,014	1,257
25.	UNLV	20	11,764	10,511	1,253
26.	Kansas St.	17	7,157	5,915	1,242
27.	East Caro.	15	5,824	4,603	1,221
28.	Northern Ill.	12	3,480	2,263	1,217
29.	Florida St.	16	6,384	5,178	1,206
30.	Texas	15	11,170	10,015	1,155
31.	Chattanooga	14	4,400	3,257	1,143
32.	Liberty	13	2,752	1,658	1,094
33.	East Tenn. St.	13	3,797	2,704	1,093
34.	Wis.-Milwaukee	13	4,266	3,226	1,040
35.	Jacksonville St.	11	3,103	2,078	1,025
36.	Holy Cross	12	3,010	1,990	1,020

DIVISION I ALL GAMES ATTENDANCE (HOME, ROAD, NEUTRAL)

Rk.	School	Attendance
1.	Syracuse	686,997
2.	Kansas	649,809
3.	Kentucky	644,596
4.	Michigan St.	566,814
5.	North Carolina	562,670
6.	Marquette	530,317
7.	Indiana	518,414
8.	Louisville	516,217
9.	Maryland	514,318
10.	Illinois	510,355
11.	Texas	488,617
12.	Wisconsin	487,245
13.	Ohio St.	469,620
14.	Connecticut	456,903
15.	Missouri	440,537
16.	Notre Dame	436,462
17.	Oklahoma	433,402
18.	Duke	430,391
19.	Pittsburgh	426,653
20.	Arizona	424,171
21.	North Carolina St.	422,939
22.	Memphis	414,270
23.	Florida	412,280
24.	Minnesota	400,426

DIVISION II

Rank	Division II	G/S	Attendance	Avg.
1.	Neb.-Kearney	19	72,950	3,839
2.	South Dakota St.	17	59,357	3,491
3.	North Dakota	14	47,924	3,423
4.	Ky. Wesleyan	17	55,800	3,282
5.	Northern St.	16	50,451	3,153
6.	St. Cloud St.	15	46,579	3,105
7.	North Dakota St.	17	48,770	2,868
8.	Washburn	14	37,595	2,685
9.	Virginia St.	12	31,820	2,651
10.	Pittsburg St.	13	34,302	2,638
11.	Harding	12	31,505	2,625
12.	Augustana (S.D.)	13	33,118	2,547
13.	South Dakota	16	40,531	2,533
14.	Shaw	12	30,234	2,519
15.	Southern Ind.	17	42,565	2,503
16.	Winston-Salem	14	32,944	2,353
17.	Bowie St.	15	33,617	2,241
18.	UC Davis	14	29,029	2,073
19.	Angelo St.	13	26,450	2,034
20.	Minn. St. Mankato	14	28,458	2,032
21.	Northwest Mo. St.	14	28,150	2,010
22.	Southwest St.	14	27,954	1,996
23.	Emporia St.	15	29,373	1,958
24.	Michigan Tech	16	31,210	1,950
25.	Alas. Anchorage	18	33,451	1,858
26.	Central Mo. St.	12	22,224	1,852
27.	Gannon	16	29,525	1,845
28.	Cal St. Bakersfield	16	28,314	1,769

Rank	Division II	G/S	Attendance	Avg.
29.	Mo. Western St.	15	26,310	1,754
30.	Fort Hays St.	16	27,541	1,721

DIVISION III

Rank	Division III	G/S	Attendance	Avg.
1.	Hope	11	26,211	2,383
2.	Ill. Wesleyan	12	27,160	2,263
3.	Calvin	12	22,043	1,904
4.	Wooster	18	29,179	1,621
5.	Otterbein	13	18,488	1,422
6.	Scranton	17	22,910	1,348
7.	Wheaton (Ill.)	10	13,270	1,327
8.	Wis.-Stevens Point	15	19,694	1,313
9.	Chris. Newport	15	18,657	1,244
10.	Capital	14	16,429	1,174
11.	Gust. Adolphus	13	15,118	1,163
12.	Carthage	12	13,455	1,121
13.	Buena Vista	16	17,749	1,109
14.	Wis.-Stout	9	9,956	1,106
15.	Whitworth	12	13,081	1,090
16.	Hamilton	14	14,456	1,033
17.	Willamette	12	11,548	962
18.	Hampden-Sydney	15	14,112	941
19.	Wis.-Eau Claire	13	12,093	930
20.	Wartburg	14	12,925	923
21.	Linfield	10	9,222	922
22.	Lycoming	12	10,955	913
23.	Pacific Lutheran	9	8,100	900
24.	Wittenberg	12	10,755	896
25.	Wis.-Platteville	10	8,869	887
26.	Stillman	10	8,850	885
27.	Keene St.	15	13,024	868
28.	Mississippi Col.	14	12,036	860
29.	King's (Pa.)	11	9,450	859
30.	North Park	11	9,385	853

Annual NCAA Attendance

ALL DIVISIONS

Season	Teams	Attendance	Per Game Average	Change in Avg.	
1977	717	23,324,040	2,710	—	—
1978	726	23,590,952	2,678	Down	32
1979	718	24,482,516	2,757	Up	79
1980	715	24,861,722	2,765	Up	8
1981	730	25,159,358	2,737	Down	28
1982	741	25,416,017	2,727	Down	10
1983	755	26,122,785	2,706	Down	21
1984	750	26,271,613	2,728	Up	22
1985	753	26,584,426	2,712	Down	16
1986	760	26,368,815	2,654	Down	58
1987	760	26,797,644	2,698	Up	44
1988	761	27,452,948	2,777	Up	79
1989	772	28,270,260	2,814	Up	37
1990	767	28,740,819	*2,860	Up	46
1991	796	29,249,583	2,796	Down	64
1992	813	29,378,161	2,747	Down	49
1993	831	28,527,348	2,703	Down	44
1994	858	28,390,491	2,604	Down	99
1995	868	28,548,158	2,581	Down	23
1996	866	28,225,352	2,563	Down	18
1997	865	27,738,284	2,508	Down	55
1998	895	28,031,879	2,445	Down	63
1999	926	28,505,428	2,401	Down	44
2000	932	29,024,876	2,410	Up	9
2001	937	28,949,093	2,392	Down	18
2002	936	29,395,240	2,373	Down	19
2003	*967	*30,124,304	2,339	Down	34

DIVISION I

Season	Teams	Attendance	Per Game Average	Change in Avg.	
1976	235	15,059,892	4,759	—	—
1977	245	16,469,250	5,021	Up	262
1978	254	17,669,080	5,124	Up	103
1979	257	18,649,383	5,271	Up	147
1980	261	19,052,743	5,217	Down	54
1981	264	19,355,690	5,131	Down	86
1982	273	19,789,706	5,191	Up	60
1983	274	20,488,437	5,212	Up	21
1984	276	20,715,426	5,243	Up	31
1985	282	21,394,261	5,258	Up	15

Season	Teams	Attendance	Per Game Average	Change in Avg.	
1986	283	21,244,519	5,175	Down	83
1987	290	21,756,709	5,205	Up	30
1988	290	22,463,476	5,443	Up	238
1989	293	23,059,429	5,565	Up	122
1990	292	23,581,823	5,721	Up	156
1991	295	23,777,437	*5,735	Up	14
1992	298	23,893,993	5,643	Down	92
1993	298	23,321,655	5,635	Down	8
1994	301	23,275,158	5,571	Down	64
1995	302	23,560,495	5,641	Up	70
1996	305	23,542,652	5,588	Down	53
1997	305	23,190,856	5,485	Down	103
1998	306	23,282,774	5,459	Down	26
1999	310	23,587,824	5,451	Down	8
2000	318	24,281,774	5,386	Down	65
2001	318	24,100,555	5,311	Down	75
2002	321	24,499,611	5,287	Down	24
2003	*325	*25,001,678	5,372	Up	85

DIVISION II

Season	Teams	Attendance	Per Game Average	Change in Avg.	
1977	177	*3,846,907	*1,811	—	—
1978	173	3,168,419	1,515	Down	296
1979	172	3,295,149	1,535	Up	20
1980	177	3,324,670	1,479	Down	56
1981	190	3,543,766	1,486	Up	7
1982	190	3,329,518	1,391	Down	95
1983	195	3,364,184	1,324	Down	67
1984	189	3,199,307	1,306	Down	18
1985	181	2,988,083	1,255	Down	51
1986	184	2,946,020	1,204	Down	51
1987	179	2,893,392	1,220	Up	16
1988	175	2,902,400	1,242	Up	22
1989	189	3,157,464	1,273	Up	31
1990	189	3,104,462	1,223	Down	50
1991	204	3,388,278	1,221	Down	2
1992	214	3,395,684	1,188	Down	33
1993	220	3,201,765	1,145	Down	43
1994	243	3,219,979	1,036	Down	109
1995	244	3,125,974	992	Down	44
1996	242	2,918,802	938	Down	54
1997	242	2,873,311	915	Down	23
1998	252	2,976,420	904	Down	8
1999	266	3,063,436	892	Down	15
2000	258	2,942,477	882	Down	10
2001	261	2,951,969	877	Down	5
2002	258	2,990,641	888	Up	11
2003	*269	3,076,804	855	Down	33

DIVISION III

Season	Teams	Attendance	Per Game Average	Change in Avg.	
1977	295	*2,881,400	*912	—	—
1978	299	2,632,678	816	Down	96
1979	289	2,427,688	770	Down	46
1980	277	2,387,142	783	Up	13
1981	276	2,132,000	693	Down	90
1982	278	2,183,895	711	Up	18
1983	286	2,148,736	685	Down	26
1984	286	2,233,340	701	Up	16
1985	290	2,081,452	629	Down	72
1986	293	2,053,693	615	Down	14
1987	291	2,021,459	606	Down	9
1988	296	1,970,823	583	Down	23
1989	290	1,935,058	573	Down	10
1990	286	1,939,795	581	Up	8
1991	297	1,967,087	564	Down	17
1992	301	1,962,598	553	Down	11
1993	313	1,883,283	531	Down	22
1994	314	1,741,867	493	Down	38
1995	322	1,802,301	487	Down	6
1996	319	1,730,357	472	Down	15
1997	318	1,626,240	444	Down	28
1998	337	1,736,409	447	Up	3
1999	350	1,824,391	446	Down	1
2000	356	1,750,621	426	Down	20
2001	358	1,846,043	444	Up	18
2002	357	1,804,209	424	Down	20
2003	*373	1,869,592	426	Up	2

*record

Annual Conference Attendance Champions

DIVISION I

Season	Conference	Teams	Attendance	P/G Avg.
1976	Atlantic Coast	7	863,082	9,590
1977	Big Ten	10	1,346,889	9,977
1978	Big Ten	10	1,539,589	11,238
1979	Big Ten	10	1,713,380	12,238
1980	Big Ten	10	1,877,048	12,189
1981	Big Ten	10	1,779,892	12,026
1982	Big Ten	10	1,688,834	11,810
1983	Big Ten	10	1,747,910	11,499
1984	Big Ten	10	1,774,140	12,069
1985	Big Ten	10	1,911,325	12,097
1986	Big Ten	10	1,908,629	11,929
1987	Big Ten	10	1,805,263	11,877
1988	Big Ten	10	1,925,617	12,423
1989	Big Ten	10	1,971,110	12,635
1990	Big Ten	10	2,017,407	*13,449
1991	Big Ten	10	2,042,836	13,095
1992	Big Ten	10	1,994,144	12,865
1993	Big Ten	11	2,163,693	12,728
1994	Big Ten	11	2,107,600	12,696
1995	Big Ten	11	2,058,763	12,708
1996	Big Ten	11	2,106,810	12,769
1997	Big Ten	11	2,004,893	12,376
1998	Big Ten	11	2,166,264	12,450
1999	Big Ten	11	2,204,556	13,361
2000	Big Ten	11	2,255,913	13,428
2001	Big Ten	11	*2,342,022	13,383
2002	Big Ten	11	2,258,255	13,362
2003	Big Ten	11	2,254,658	12,526

DIVISION II

Season	Conference	Teams	Attendance	P/G Avg.
1979	Central Intercollegiate	12	375,370	2,760
1980	Mid-Continent	5	189,193	2,782
1981	North Central Intercollegiate	8	312,410	2,840
1982	North Central Intercollegiate	8	290,995	2,622
1983	North Central Intercollegiate	8	356,777	2,567
1984	North Central Intercollegiate	10	392,154	2,801
1985	North Central Intercollegiate	10	380,087	2,639
1986	North Central Intercollegiate	10	379,701	2,601
1987	North Central Intercollegiate	10	393,940	2,626
1988	North Central Intercollegiate	10	413,956	2,797
1989	North Central Intercollegiate	10	438,403	2,923
1990	North Central Intercollegiate	10	436,292	2,889
1991	North Central Intercollegiate	10	438,746	2,868
1992	North Central Intercollegiate	10	*482,213	*3,014
1993	North Central Intercollegiate	10	408,624	2,919
1994	North Central Intercollegiate	10	362,572	2,627
1995	North Central Intercollegiate	10	382,042	2,497
1996	North Central Intercollegiate	10	341,119	2,336
1997	North Central Intercollegiate	10	319,703	2,160
1998	North Central Intercollegiate	10	315,918	2,225
1999	North Central Intercollegiate	10	299,228	2,050
2000	North Central Intercollegiate	10	300,257	2,114
2001	North Central Intercollegiate	10	300,822	2,118
2002	North Central Intercollegiate	10	369,858	2,551
2003	North Central Intercollegiate	9	328,903	2,473

DIVISION III

Season	Conference	Teams	Attendance	P/G Avg.
1990	Wisconsin State University	9	*170,276	*1,362
1991	Wisconsin State University	7	84,615	1,128
1992	Michigan Intercollegiate	7	89,549	1,163
1993	Michigan Intercollegiate	7	97,624	1,236
1994	Michigan Intercollegiate	7	97,418	1,203
1995	Michigan Intercollegiate	7	86,353	1,183
1996	Michigan Intercollegiate	7	80,376	1,058
1997	Michigan Intercollegiate	7	81,370	1,085
1998	Michigan Intercollegiate	8	91,267	941
1999	Michigan Intercollegiate	8	87,055	957
2000	Michigan Intercollegiate	8	111,310	1,091
2001	Michigan Intercollegiate	7	95,378	1,163
2002	Michigan Intercollegiate	7	98,263	1,244
2003	Michigan Intercollegiate	8	79,798	1,050

*record

Annual Team Attendance Champions

DIVISION I

Season	Champion	Games	Attendance	Avg.
1970	Illinois	11	157,206	14,291
1971	Illinois	11	177,408	16,128
1972	Brigham Young	12	261,815	21,818
1973	Brigham Young	14	260,102	18,579
1974	Brigham Young	10	162,510	16,251
1975	Minnesota	13	219,047	16,850
1976	Indiana	12	202,700	16,892
1977	Kentucky	14	312,527	22,323
1978	Kentucky	16	373,367	23,335
1979	Kentucky	15	351,042	23,403
1980	Kentucky	15	352,511	23,501
1981	Kentucky	15	354,996	23,666
1982	Kentucky	16	371,093	23,193
1983	Kentucky	15	356,776	23,785
1984	Kentucky	16	380,453	23,778
1985	Syracuse	15	388,049	25,870
1986	Syracuse	19	498,850	26,255
1987	Syracuse	19	474,214	24,959
1988	Syracuse	16	461,223	28,826
1989	Syracuse	19	*537,949	28,313
1990	Syracuse	16	478,686	*29,918
1991	Syracuse	17	497,179	29,246
1992	Syracuse	17	460,752	27,103
1993	Syracuse	16	405,620	25,351
1994	Syracuse	17	419,039	24,649
1995	Syracuse	16	387,925	24,245
1996	Kentucky	13	310,633	23,895
1997	Kentucky	13	309,457	23,804
1998	Kentucky	12	287,354	23,946
1999	Kentucky	13	303,771	23,367
2000	Kentucky	14	314,267	22,448
2001	Kentucky	12	261,435	21,786
2002	Kentucky	15	315,203	21,014
2003	Kentucky	13	289,526	22,271

DIVISION II

Season	Champion	Avg.
1977	Evansville	4,576
1978	Norfolk St.	4,226
1979	Norfolk St.	4,984
1980	Norfolk St.	4,917
1981	North Dakota St.	5,300
1982	North Dakota St.	4,385
1983	North Dakota St.	6,057
1984	Norfolk St.	*6,663
1985	Norfolk St.	6,116
1986	St. Cloud St.	4,539
1987	North Dakota St.	4,820
1988	Southeast Mo. St.	5,227
1989	Southeast Mo. St.	5,052
1990	Southeast Mo. St.	5,287
1991	Southeast Mo. St.	5,370
1992	North Dakota	4,943
1993	Alabama A&M	4,748
1994	South Dakota	4,852
1995	Alabama A&M	5,141
1996	South Dakota St.	4,945
1997	South Dakota St.	4,423
1998	South Dakota St.	5,350
1999	Ky. Wesleyan	4,247
2000	South Dakota St.	4,077
2001	Morehouse	4,404
2002	South Dakota St.	4,449
2003	Neb.-Kearney	3,839

*record

DIVISION III

Season	Champion	Avg.
1977	Scranton	2,707
1978	Calvin	3,630
1979	Savannah St.	2,870
1980	Savannah St.	2,917
1981	Potsdam St.	2,873
1982	Wis.-Stevens Point	2,929
1983	Augustana (Ill.)	3,033
1984	Hope	2,144
1985	Wis.-Stevens Point	2,313
1986	Calvin	2,570
1987	Concordia-M'head	2,869
1988	Calvin	2,627
1989	Calvin	2,544
1990	Calvin	2,622
1991	Hope	2,480
1992	Calvin	2,757
1993	Calvin	*4,018
1994	Calvin	2,734
1995	Calvin	2,792
1996	Hope	2,409
1997	Calvin	2,821
1998	Ill. Wesleyan	2,615
1999	Hope	2,440
2000	Calvin	3,496
2001	Calvin	3,369
2002	Calvin	2,893
2003	Hope	2,383

*record

Annual NCAA Tournament Attendance

DIVISION I

Season	Sess.	Attend.	P/G Avg.
1939	5	15,025	3,005
1940	5	36,880	7,376

Season	Sess.	Attend.	P/G Avg.
1941	5	48,055	9,611
1942	5	24,372	4,874
1943	5	56,876	11,375
1944	5	59,369	11,874
1945	5	67,780	13,556
1946	5	73,116	14,623
1947	5	72,959	14,592
1948	5	72,523	14,505
1949	5	66,077	13,215
1950	5	75,464	15,093
1951	9	110,645	12,294
1952	10	115,712	11,571
1953	14	127,149	9,082
1954	15	115,391	7,693
1955	15	116,983	7,799
1956	15	132,513	8,834
1957	14	108,891	7,778
1958	14	176,878	12,634
1959	14	161,809	11,558
1960	16	155,491	9,718
1961	14	169,520	12,109
1962	14	177,469	12,676
1963	14	153,065	10,933
1964	14	140,790	10,056
1965	13	140,673	10,821
1966	13	140,925	10,840
1967	14	159,570	11,398
1968	14	160,888	11,492
1969	15	165,712	11,047
1970	16	146,794	9,175
1971	16	207,200	12,950
1972	16	147,304	9,207
1973	16	163,160	10,198
1974	16	154,112	9,632
1975	18	183,857	10,214
1976	18	202,502	11,250
1977	18	241,610	13,423
1978	18	227,149	12,619
1979	22	262,101	11,914
1980	26	321,260	12,356
1981	26	347,414	13,362
1982	26	427,251	16,433
1983	28	364,356	13,013
1984	28	397,481	14,196
1985	34	422,519	12,427
1986	34	499,704	14,697
1987	34	654,744	19,257
1988	34	558,998	16,441
1989	34	613,242	18,037
1990	34	537,138	15,798
1991	34	665,707	19,580
1992	34	580,462	17,072
1993	34	707,719	20,815
1994	34	578,007	17,000
1995	34	539,440	15,866
1996	34	643,290	18,920
1997	34	634,584	18,664
1998	34	682,530	20,074
1999	34	*720,685	*21,197
2000	34	638,577	18,782
2001	35	596,075	17,031
2002	35	720,433	20,584
2003	35	715,080	20,431

DIVISION II

Season	Sess.	Attend.	P/G Avg.
1977	22	*87,602	*3,982
1978	22	83,058	3,775
1979	22	66,446	3,020
1980	22	50,649	2,302
1981	22	69,470	3,158
1982	22	67,925	3,088
1983	22	70,335	3,197
1984	22	81,388	3,699
1985	22	81,476	3,703
1986	22	71,083	3,231
1987	22	77,934	3,542
1988	22	72,462	3,294
1989	20	69,008	3,450
1990	20	64,212	3,211
1991	20	59,839	2,992
1992	20	60,629	3,031
1993	20	56,125	2,806
1994	20	60,511	3,026
1995	36	86,767	2,410
1996	28	65,882	2,353
1997	28	66,626	2,380
1998	28	59,946	2,141
1999	28	49,144	1,755
2000	28	50,130	1,790
2001	28	60,418	2,158
2002	28	60,258	2,152
2003	36	51,054	1,418

*record

DIVISION III

Season	Sess.	Attend.	P/G Avg.
1977	21	38,881	1,851
1978	21	37,717	1,796
1979	22	43,850	1,993
1980	22	46,518	2,114
1981	22	58,432	*2,656
1982	22	44,973	2,044
1983	22	51,093	2,322
1984	22	42,152	1,916
1985	22	39,154	1,780
1986	22	53,500	2,432
1987	22	48,150	2,189
1988	22	43,787	1,990
1989	28	49,301	1,761
1990	26	50,527	1,943
1991	34	56,942	1,675
1992	34	65,257	1,919
1993	34	49,675	1,461
1994	34	54,848	1,613
1995	59	*88,684	1,503
1996	58	87,437	1,508
1997	58	70,647	1,218
1998	42	63,330	1,508
1999	42	53,928	1,284
2000	42	62,527	1,489
2001	42	77,110	1,836
2002	46	74,437	1,618
2003	42	66,379	1,580

*record

Division I Attendance Records

SINGLE GAME (PAID)
68,112—LSU (87) vs. Notre Dame (64), Jan. 20, 1990, at Louisiana Superdome, New Orleans (regular-season game)

SINGLE GAME (TURNSTILE)
58,903—North Carolina (78) vs. Kansas (68) and Michigan (81) vs. Kentucky (78) (ot), Apr. 3, 1993 (NCAA semifinals), at Louisiana Superdome, New Orleans

HOME COURT, SINGLE GAME
33,071—Syracuse (83) vs. Rutgers (74), Mar. 9, 2003, at Carrier Dome, Syracuse, N.Y.

HOME-COURT AVERAGE, SEASON
29,918—Syracuse, 1990 (478,686 in 16 games at Carrier Dome)

HOME-COURT TOTAL, SEASON
537,949—Syracuse, 1989 (19 games)

FULL-SEASON AVERAGE, ALL GAMES (home, road, neutral, tournaments)
22,501—Syracuse, 1989 (855,053 in 38 games)

FULL-SEASON TOTAL, ALL GAMES (home, road, neutral, tournaments)
855,053—Syracuse, 1989 (38 games)

TOP 10 ATTENDANCE GAMES (PAID)*
68,112 —LSU (87) vs. Notre Dame (64), Jan. 20, 1990, at Louisiana Superdome, New Orleans

66,144 —LSU (82) vs. Georgetown (80), Jan. 28, 1989, at Louisiana Superdome, New Orleans

64,959 —Indiana (74) vs. Syracuse (73), Mar. 30, 1987 (NCAA final); Indiana (97) vs. UNLV (93) and Syracuse (77) vs. Providence (63), Mar. 28, 1987 (NCAA semifinals), at Louisiana Superdome, New Orleans

64,151 —North Carolina (77) vs. Michigan (71), Apr. 5, 1993 (NCAA final); North Carolina (78) vs. Kansas (68) and Michigan (81) vs. Kentucky (78) (ot), Apr. 3, 1993 (NCAA semifinals), at Louisiana Superdome, New Orleans

61,612 —North Carolina (63) vs. Georgetown (62), Mar. 29, 1982 (NCAA final); North Carolina (68) vs. Houston (63) and George

town (50) vs. Louisville (46), Mar. 27, 1982 (NCAA semifinals), at Louisiana Superdome, New Orleans

61,304—LSU (84) vs. Texas (83), Jan. 3, 1992, at Louisiana Superdome, New Orleans

54,524—Syracuse (81) vs. Kansas (78), Apr. 7, 2003 (NCAA final); Kansas (94) vs. Marquette (61) and Syracuse (95) vs. Texas (84), Apr. 5, 2003 (NCAA semifinals), at Louisiana Superdome, New Orleans (attendance for the semifinals was 54,432)

52,693—Houston (71) vs. UCLA (69), Jan. 20, 1968, at The Astrodome, Houston

52,647—Maryland (64) vs. Indiana (52), Apr. 1, 2002 (NCAA final); Maryland (97) vs. Kansas (88) and Indiana (73) vs. Oklahoma (64), Mar. 30, 2002 (NCAA semifinals), at Georgia Dome, Atlanta

50,379—Duke (71) vs. Michigan (51), Apr. 6, 1992 (NCAA final); Duke (81) vs. Indiana (78) and Michigan (76) vs. Cincinnati (72), Apr. 4, 1992 (NCAA semifinals), at Hubert H. Humphrey Metrodome, Minneapolis

Note: Figures for games at the Final Four include the media.

TOP FIVE ATTENDANCE GAMES (TURNSTILE)

58,903—North Carolina (78) vs. Kansas (68) and Michigan (81) vs. Kentucky (78) (ot), Apr. 3, 1993 (NCAA semifinals), at Louisiana Superdome, New Orleans

56,707—Indiana (74) vs. Syracuse (73), Mar. 30, 1987 (NCAA final), at Louisiana Superdome, New Orleans

56,264—North Carolina (77) vs. Michigan (71), Apr. 5, 1993 (NCAA final), at Louisiana Superdome, New Orleans

55,841—Indiana (97) vs. UNLV (93) and Syracuse (77) vs. Providence (63), Mar. 28, 1987 (NCAA semifinals), at Louisiana Superdome, New Orleans

54,321—LSU (82) vs. Georgetown (80), Jan. 28, 1989, at Louisiana Superdome, New Orleans

TOP 10 REGULAR-SEASON GAMES (PAID)

68,112—LSU (87) vs. Notre Dame (64), Jan. 20, 1990, at Louisiana Superdome, New Orleans

66,144—LSU (82) vs. Georgetown (80), Jan. 28, 1989, at Louisiana Superdome, New Orleans

61,304—LSU (84) vs. Texas (83), Jan. 3, 1992, at Louisiana Superdome, New Orleans

52,693—Houston (71) vs. UCLA (69), Jan. 20, 1968, at The Astrodome, Houston

45,214—Louisville (101) vs. Indiana (79) and Notre Dame (81) vs. Kentucky (65), Dec. 3, 1988, at RCA Dome, Indianapolis

43,601—Notre Dame (69) vs. Louisville (54) and Kentucky (82) vs. Indiana (76), Dec. 5, 1987, at RCA Dome, Indianapolis

41,071—Kentucky (89) vs. Indiana (82), Dec. 2, 1995, at RCA Dome, Indianapolis

40,128—Louisville (84) vs. Notre Dame (73) and Indiana (71) vs. Kentucky (69), Dec. 2, 1989, at RCA Dome, Indianapolis

38,504—Kentucky (75) vs. Indiana (72), Dec. 6, 1997, at RCA Dome, Indianapolis

38,194—Indiana (96) vs. Kentucky (84), Dec. 4, 1993, at RCA Dome, Indianapolis

33,071—Syracuse (83) vs. Rutgers (74), Mar. 9, 2003, at Carrier Dome, Syracuse, N.Y.

ON-CAMPUS REGULAR-SEASON, SINGLE GAME

33,048—Syracuse (62) vs. Georgetown (58), Mar. 3, 1991, at Carrier Dome, Syracuse, N.Y.

33,015—Syracuse (89) vs. Georgetown (87), Mar. 4, 1990 (ot), at Carrier Dome, Syracuse, N.Y.

32,996—Syracuse (68) vs. Georgetown (72), Feb. 23, 1992, at Carrier Dome, Syracuse, N.Y.

32,820—Syracuse (90) vs. Connecticut (86), Feb. 10, 1990, at Carrier Dome, Syracuse, N.Y.

32,763—Syracuse (89) vs. Pittsburgh (68), Feb. 24, 1991, at Carrier Dome, Syracuse, N.Y.

32,747—Syracuse (65) vs. Notre Dame (66), Feb. 17, 1990, at Carrier Dome, Syracuse, N.Y.

32,683—Syracuse (82) vs. Georgetown (76) (ot), Mar. 5, 1989, at Carrier Dome, Syracuse, N.Y.

32,633—Syracuse (78) vs. Seton Hall (64), Jan. 19, 1991, at Carrier Dome, Syracuse, N.Y.

32,602—Syracuse (71) vs. Georgetown (72), Feb. 22, 1987, at Carrier Dome, Syracuse, N.Y.

2003 Division I Attendance Single-Game Highs

REGULAR-SEASON

33,071—Syracuse (83) vs. Rutgers (74), Mar. 9, 2003, Carrier Dome, Syracuse, NY

32,116—Syracuse (82) vs. Notre Dame (80), Feb. 15, 2003, Carrier Dome, Syracuse, NY

32,055—Indiana (66) vs. Purdue (63), Dec. 14, 2003, RCA Dome, Indianapolis

30,303—Syracuse (67) vs. Pittsburgh (65), Feb. 1, 2003, Carrier Dome, Syracuse, NY

24,459—Kentucky (70) vs. Florida (55), Feb. 4, 2003, Rupp Arena, Lexington, KY

POSTSEASON

54,524—Syracuse (81) vs. Kansas (78), Apr. 7, 2003 (NCAA final); Kansas (94) vs. Marquette (61) and Syracuse (95) vs. Texas (84), Apr. 5, 2003 (NCAA semifinals), at Superdome, New Orleans (attendance for the semifinals was 54,432)

33,009—Texas (82) vs. Connecticut (78) and Michigan St. (60) vs. Maryland (58), Mar. 28, 2003 (South Region semifinals), at Alamodome, San Antonio (30,169 in final)

28,383—Marquette (83) vs. Kentucky (69), Mar. 29, 2003 (Midwest Region final), at Hubert H. Humphrey Metrodome, Minneapolis (28,168 in semifinals)

25,767—Marquette (101) vs. Missouri (92) and Notre Dame (68) vs. Illinois (60), Mar. 22, 2003 (NCAA second round), at RCA Dome, Indianapolis

23,745—Sessions 2, 3, 4 & 5, Mar. 14-16, 2003 (Atlantic Coast Conference Tournament), at Greensboro Coliseum, Greensboro, N.C.

Division II Attendance Records

PAID ATTENDANCE

21,786—Bowie St. (72) vs. Virginia Union (71), Mar. 1, 2003, at RBC Center, Raleigh, N.C. (Central Intercollegiate Athletic Association final; early rounds had crowds of 16,536, 15,786 and 11,761)

20,432—Shaw (82) vs. Johnson Smith (68), Mar. 2, 2002, at RBC Center, Raleigh, N.C. (Central Intercollegiate Athletic Association final; early rounds had crowds of 18,054, 17,827 and 14,386)

13,913—Evansville (93) vs. Ky. Wesleyan (87), Feb. 13, 1960, at Roberts Stadium, Evansville, Indiana

13,240—La.-Lafayette (105) vs. Ky. Wesleyan (83), Mar. 19, 1971, at Roberts Stadium, Evansville, Indiana (NCAA third place)

13,124—Evansville (97) vs. Old Dominion (82), Mar. 20, 1971, at Roberts Stadium, Evansville, Indiana (NCAA final)

Division III Attendance Records

PAID ATTENDANCE

11,442—Hope (70) vs. Calvin (56), Jan. 29, 1997, at Van Andel Arena, Grand Rapids, Michigan

Playing-Rules History

Dr. James Naismith's 13 Original Rules of Basketball

Photo from NCAA archives

1. The ball may be thrown in any direction with one or both hands.
2. The ball may be batted in any direction with one or both hands (never with the fist).
3. A player cannot run with the ball. The player must throw it from the spot on which he catches it, allowance to be made for a man who catches the ball when running at a good speed if he tries to stop.
4. The ball must be held in or between the hands; the arms or body must not be used for holding it.
5. No shouldering, holding, pushing, tripping, or striking in any way the person of an opponent shall be allowed; the first infringement of this rule by any player shall count as a foul, the second shall disqualify him until the next goal is made, or, if there was evident intent to injure the person, for the whole of the game, no substitute allowed.
6. A foul is striking at the ball with the fist, violation of Rules 3, 4, and such as described in Rule 5.
7. If either side makes three consecutive fouls, it shall count a goal for the opponents (consecutive means without the opponents in the mean time making a foul).
8. A goal shall be made when the ball is thrown or batted from the grounds into the basket and stays there, providing those defending the goal do not touch or disturb the goal. If the ball rests on the edges, and the opponent moves the basket, it shall count as a goal.
9. When the ball goes out of bounds, it shall be thrown into the field of play by the person first touching it. In case of a dispute, the umpire shall throw it straight into the field. The thrower-in is allowed five seconds; if he holds it longer, it shall go to the opponent. If any side persists in delaying the game, the umpire shall call a foul on that side.
10. The umpire shall be judge of the men and shall note the fouls and notify the referee when three consecutive fouls have been made. He shall have power to disqualify men according to Rule 5.
11. The referee shall be judge of the ball and shall decide when the ball is in play, in bounds, to which side it belongs, and shall keep the time. He shall decide when a goal has been made, and keep account of the goals with any other duties that are usually performed by a referee.
12. The time shall be two 15-minute halves, with five minutes' rest between.
13. The side making the most goals in that time shall be declared the winner. In case of a draw, the game may, by agreement of the captains, be continued until another goal is made.

Note: These original rules were published in January 1892 in the Springfield College school newspaper, The Triangle.

Important Rules Changes by Year

1891-92
• The 13 original rules of basketball are written by Dr. James Naismith in December 1891 in Springfield, Massachusetts.

1894-95
• The free-throw line is moved from 20 to 15 feet.

1895-96
• Points awarded for field goal changes from three to two, and points awarded for each succesful free throw from three points to one point.

1896-97
• Backboards are installed.

1900-01
• A dribbler may not shoot for a field goal and may dribble only once, and then with two hands.

1908-09
• A dribbler is permitted to shoot. The dribble is defined as the "continuous passage of the ball," making the double dribble illegal.
• A second official is added for games in an effort to curb the rough play.

1910-11
• Players are disqualified upon committing their fourth personal foul.
• No coaching is allowed during the progress of the game by anybody connected with either team. A warning is given for the first violation and a free throw is awarded after that.

1913-14
• The bottom of the net is left open.

1914-15
• College, YMCA and AAU rules are made the same.

1920-21
• A player can re-enter the game once. Before this rule, if a player left the game, he could not re-enter for the rest of the game.
• The backboards are moved 2 feet from the wall of the court. Before this rule, players would "climb" the padded wall to sink baskets.

1921-22
• Running with the ball changes from a foul to a violation.

1923-24
• The player fouled must shoot his own free throws. Before this rule, one person usually shot all his team's free throws.

1928-29
• The charging foul by the dribbler is introduced.

1930-31
• A held ball may be called when a closely guarded player is withholding the ball from play for five seconds. The result will be a jump ball.
• The maximum circumference of the ball is reduced from 32 to 31 inches, and the maximum weight from 23 to 22 ounces.

1932-33
• The 10-second center (division) line is introduced to reduce stalling.
• No player can stand in the free-throw lane with the ball for more than three seconds.

1933-34
• A player may re-enter the game twice.

1934-35
• The circumference of the ball again is reduced to between 29½ and 30¼ inches.

1935-36
- No offensive player can remain in the free-throw lane, with or without the ball, for more than three seconds.
- After a made free throw, the team scored upon shall put the ball in play at the end of the court where the goal had been scored.

1937-38
- The center jump after every goal scored is eliminated.

1938-39
- The ball will be thrown in from out of bounds at mid-court by the team shooting a free throw after a technical foul. Before, the ball was put into play with a center jump after a technical-foul free throw.
- The circumference of the ball is established as 30 inches.

1939-40
- Teams have the choice of whether to take a free throw or take the ball out of bounds at mid-court. If two or more free throws are awarded, this option applies to the last throw.
- The backboards are moved from 2 to 4 feet from the end line to permit freer movement under the basket.

1940-41
- Fan-shaped backboards are made legal.

1942-43
- Any player who is eligible to start an overtime period will be allowed an extra personal foul, increasing the total so disqualification is on the fifth foul.

1944-45
- Defensive goaltending is banned.
- Five personal fouls disqualify a player. An extra foul is not permitted in overtime games.
- Unlimited substitution is introduced.
- It becomes a violation for an offensive player to remain in the free-throw lane for more than three seconds.

1946-47
- Transparent backboards are authorized.

1947-48
- The clock is stopped on every dead ball the last three minutes of the second half and of every overtime period. This includes every time a goal is scored because the ball is considered dead until put into play again. (This rule was abolished in 1951.)

1948-49
- Coaches are allowed to speak to players during a timeout.

1951-52
- Games are to be played in four 10-minute quarters. Before this, games were played in two 20-minute halves.

1952-53
- Teams can no longer waive free throws in favor of taking the ball out of bounds.
- The one-and-one free-throw rule is introduced, although the bonus is used only if the first shot is missed. The rule will be in effect the entire game except the last three minutes, when every foul results in two free throws.

1954-55
- The one-and-one free throw is changed so that the bonus shot is given only if the first shot is made.
- Games are changed back to being played in two 20-minute halves.

1955-56
- The two-shot penalty in the last three minutes of the game is eliminated. The one-and-one is now in effect the entire game.

1956-57
- The free-throw lane is increased from 6 feet to 12 feet. On the lineup for a free throw, the two spaces adjacent to the end line must be occupied by opponents of the free-thrower. In the past, one space was marked "H" for a home team player to occupy, and across the lane the first space was marked "V" for a visiting team player to stand in.
- Grasping the basket is now classified as a technical foul under unsportsmanlike tactics.

1957-58
- Offensive goaltending is now banned, as an addition to the original 1945 rule.
- One free throw for each common foul is taken for the first six personal fouls by one team in each half, and the one-and-one is used thereafter.

- On uniforms, the use of the single digit numbers one and two and any digit greater than five is prohibited.
- A ball that passes over the backboard—either front to back or back to front—is considered out of bounds.

1964-65
- Coaches must remain seated on the bench except while the clock is stopped or to direct or encourage players on the court. This rule is to help keep coaches from inciting undesirable crowd reactions toward the officials.

1967-68
- The dunk is made illegal during the game and pregame warm-up.

1970-71
- During a jump ball, a nonjumper may not change his position from the time the official is ready to make the toss until after the ball has been touched.

1972-73
- The free throw on the first six common fouls each half by a team is eliminated.
- Players cannot attempt to create the false impression that they have been fouled in charging/guarding situations or while screening when the contact was only incidental. An official can charge the "actor" with a technical foul for unsportsmanlike conduct if, in the official's opinion, the actor is making a travesty of the game.
- Freshmen are eligible to play varsity basketball. This was the result of a change in the NCAA bylaws, not the basketball playing rules.

1973-74
- Officials may now penalize players for fouls occurring away from the ball, such as grabbing, holding and setting illegal screens.

1974-75
- During a jump ball, a non-jumper on the restraining circle may move around the circle after the ball has left the official's hands.
- A player charged with a foul is no longer required to raise his hand. (In 1978, however, it was strongly recommended that a player start raising his hand again.)

1976-77
- The dunk is made legal again.

1981-82
- The jump ball is used only at the beginning of the game and the start of each overtime. An alternating arrow will indicate possession in jump-ball situations during the game.
- All fouls charged to bench personnel shall be assessed to the head coach.

1982-83
- When the closely guarded five-second count is reached, it is no longer a jump-ball situation. It is a violation, and the ball is awarded to the defensive team out of bounds.

1983-84
- Two free throws are taken for each common foul committed within the last two minutes of the second half and the entire overtime period, if the bonus rule is in effect. (This rule was rescinded one month into the season.)

1984-85
- The coaching box is introduced, whereby a coach and all bench personnel must remain in the 28-foot-long coaching box unless seeking information from the scorers' table.

1985-86
- The 45-second clock is introduced. The team in control of the ball must now shoot for a goal within 45 seconds after it attains team control.
- If a shooter is fouled intentionally and the shot is missed, the penalty will be two shots and possession of the ball out of bounds to the team that was fouled.
- The head coach may stand throughout the game, while all other bench personnel must remain seated.

1986-87
- The three-point field goal is introduced and set at 19 feet 9 inches from the center of the basket.
- A coach may leave the confines of the bench at any time without penalty to correct a scorer's or timer's mistake. A technical foul is assessed if there is no mistake. (This was changed the next year to a timeout.) Also, a television replay may be used to prevent or rectify a scorer's or timer's mistake or a malfunction of the clock.

1987-88
- Each intentional personal foul carries a two-shot penalty plus possession of the ball.

1988-89
- Any squad member who participates in a fight will be ejected from the game and will be placed on probation. If that player participates in a second fight during the season, he will be suspended for one game. A third fight involving the same person results in suspension for the rest of the season including championship competition.

1990-91
- Beginning with the team's 10th personal foul in a half, two free throws are awarded for each common foul, except player-control fouls.
- Three free throws are awarded when a shooter is fouled during an unsuccessful three-point try.
- The fighting rule is amended. The first time any squad member or bench personnel participates in a fight he will be suspended for the team's next game. If that same person participates in a second fight, he will be suspended for the rest of the season, including championship competition.

1991-92
- Contact technical fouls count toward the five fouls for player disqualification and toward the team fouls in reaching bonus free-throw situations.
- The shot clock is reset when the ball strikes the basket ring, not when a shot leaves the shooter's hands as it had been ever since the rule was introduced in 1986.

1992-93
- Unsporting technical fouls, in addition to contact technical fouls, count toward the five fouls for player disqualification and toward the team fouls in reaching bonus free-throw situations.

1993-94
- The shot clock is reduced to 35 seconds from 45. The team in control of the ball must shoot for a goal within 35 seconds after it gains team control.
- A foul shall be ruled intentional if, while playing the ball, a player causes excessive contact with an opponent.
- The game clock will be stopped after successful field goals in the last minute of the game and the last minute of any overtime period with no substitution allowed.
- The five-second dribbling violation when closely guarded is eliminated.
- The rule concerning the use of profanity is expanded to include abusive and obscene language in an effort to curtail verbal misconduct by players and coaches.

1994-95
- The inner circle at mid-court is eliminated.
- Scoring is restricted to a tap-in when (3/10) (.3) of a second or less remain on the game clock or shot clock.
- The fighting and suspension rules are expanded to include coaches and team personnel.

1995-96
- All unsporting technical fouls charged to anyone on the bench count toward the team foul total.
- Teams are allowed one 20-second timeout per half. This was an experimental rule in the 1994-95 season.

1996-97
- Teams shall warm up and shoot at the end of the court farthest from their own bench for the first half. Previously, teams had the choice of baskets in the first half.

- In games not involving commercial electronic media, teams are entitled to four full-length timeouts and two 20-second timeouts per game. In games involving commercial electronic media, teams are entitled to two full-length timeouts and three 20-second timeouts per game.

1997-98
- The five-second dribbling violation when closely guarded is reinstated.
- Timeout requests can be made by a player on the court or by the head coach.

1998-99
- In a held-ball situation initiated by the defense, the ball shall be awarded to the defensive team. Previously, possession was awarded by the direction of the possession arrow.

1999-00
- Held-ball change from previous season rescinded.
- Twenty-second timeouts increased to 30 seconds in length. New electronic-media timeout format adopted.
- Uniform numbers one and two are permitted.
- Officials must consult courtside television monitors, when available, to judge whether a game-deciding last-second shot in the second half or any extra period counts. (This was passed during the season.)

2000-01
- Technical fouls divided into direct (two-shot penalty) and indirect (one-shot penalty) with ball returned to point of interruption.

2001-02
- Both direct and indirect technical fouls penalized by two shots and returned to point of interruption.
- Officials can check an official courtside monitor to determine if a try is a three- or two-point attempt, regardless of whether the try is successful.

2002-03
- Composite ball can be used without mutual consent of coaches.
- Two free-throw lane spaces closest to the free-thrower shall remain unoccupied.
- No free throws to offended team in bonus for personal fouls committed by team while in team control or in possession of the ball during a throw-in (team-control foul).

2003-04
- Officials may consult courtside monitor at end of either half or any extra period to determine: (1) if a field-goal try beat the horn; (2) whether a shot-clock violation at the end of the first half beat the horn; or, (3) whether a shot-clock violation that will determine the outcome of a game beat the horn. The officials also may use a courtside monitor to correct a timer's mistake or to determine if the game clock or shot clock expired at or near the end of a period.
- A team shall have control when a player of that team has disposal of the ball for a throw-in.

Important Rules Changes by Subject

Ball: 1930-31, The maximum circumference of the ball is reduced from 32 to 31 inches, and the maximum weight from 23 to 22 ounces. 1934-35, The circumference of the ball again is reduced to between 29 1/2 and 30 1/4 inches. 1938-39, The circumference of the ball is established as 30 inches. 2002-03, Mutual consent no longer needed for composite ball to be legal.

Basket Equipment: 1896-97, Backboards are installed. 1913-14, The bottom of the net is left open. 1920-21, The backboards are moved 2 feet from the wall of the court. Before this rule, players would "climb" the padded wall to sink baskets. 1939-40, The backboards are moved from 2 to 4 feet from the end line to permit freer movement under the basket. 1940-41, Fan-shaped backboards are made legal. 1946-47, Transparent backboards are authorized. 1957-58, A ball that passes over the backboard—either front to back or back to front—is considered out of bounds. 1996-97, Teams shall warm up and shoot at the end of the court farthest from their own bench for the first half. Previously, teams had the choice of baskets in the first half. 2002-03, For Division I, shot clocks had to be mounted and recessed on backboard, red warning light had to be added and game clock had to show 10th-of-a-second display. 2003-04, for Division II, shot clocks must be recessed and mounted.

Block/Charge: 1928-29, The charging foul by the dribbler is introduced. 1972-73, Players cannot attempt to create the false impression that they have been fouled in charging/guarding situations or while screening when the contact was only incidental. An official can charge the "actor" with a technical foul for unsportsmanlike conduct if, in the official's opinion, the actor is making a travesty of the game. 2002, Prior rule was deleted because of lack of use.

Clock Stoppage: 1947-48, The clock is stopped on every dead ball the last three minutes of the second half and of every extra period. This includes every time a goal is scored because the ball is considered dead until put into play again. (This rule was abolished in 1951.)

Closely Guarded: 1982-83, When the closely guarded five-second count is reached, it is no longer a jump-ball situation. It is a violation, and the ball is awarded to the defensive team out of bounds. 1993-94, The five-second dribbling violation when closely guarded is eliminated. 1997-98, The five-second dribbling violation when closely guarded is reinstated.

Coaching: 1910-11, No coaching is allowed during the progress of the game by anybody connected with either team. A warning is given for the first violation and a free throw is awarded after that. 1948-49, Coaches are allowed to speak to players during a timeout. 1964-65, Coaches must remain seated on the bench except while the clock is stopped or to direct or encourage players on the court. This rule is to help keep coaches from inciting undesirable crowd reactions toward the officials. 1984-85, The coaching box is introduced, whereby a coach and all bench personnel must remain in the 28-foot-long coaching box unless seeking information from the scorers' table. 1985-86, The head coach may stand throughout the game, while all other bench personnel must remain seated. 1986-87, A coach may leave the confines of the bench at any time without penalty to correct a scorer's or timer's mistake. A technical foul is assessed if there is no mistake. (This penalty was changed the next year to a timeout.) Also, a television replay may be used to prevent or rectify a scorer's or timer's mistake or a malfunction of the clock. 1994-95, The fighting and suspension rules are expanded to include coaches and team personnel. 1995-96, All unsporting technical fouls charged to anyone on the bench count toward the team foul total.

Dunk: 1967-68, The dunk is made illegal during the game and pregame warm-up. 1976-77, The dunk is made legal again but remains illegal during warm-up.

Field Goals: 1895-96, A field goal changes from three to two points, and free throws from three points to one point.

Fighting: 1988-89, Any squad member who participates in a fight will be ejected from the game and will be placed on probation. If that individual participates in a second fight during the season, he will be suspended for one game. A third fight involving the same person results in suspension for the rest of the season including championship competition. 1990-91, The fighting rule is amended. The first time any squad member or bench personnel participates in a fight he will be suspended for the team's next game. If that same person participates in a second fight, he will be suspended for the rest of the season, including championship competition. 1994-95, The fighting and suspension rules are expanded to include coaches and team personnel.

Fouling Out: 1910-11, Players are disqualified upon committing their fourth personal foul. 1942-43, Any player who is eligible to start an extra period will be allowed an extra personal foul, increasing the total so disqualification is on the fifth foul. 1944-45, Five personal fouls disqualify a player. An extra foul is not permitted in overtime games. 1991-92, Contact technical fouls count toward the five fouls for player disqualification and toward the team fouls in reaching bonus free-throw situations.

Free Throws: 1894-95, The free-throw line is moved from 20 to 15 feet. 1923-24, The player fouled must shoot his own free throws. Before this rule, one person usually shot all his team's free throws. 1935-36, After a made free throw, the team scored upon shall put the ball in play at the end of the court where the goal had been scored. 1939-40, Teams have the choice of whether to take a free throw or take the ball out of bounds at mid-court. If two or more free throws are awarded, this option applies to the last throw. 1952-53, Teams can no longer waive free throws in favor of taking the ball out of bounds. 1952-53, The one-and-one free-throw rule is introduced, although the bonus is used only if the first shot is missed. The rule will be in effect the entire game except the last three minutes, when every foul is two shots. 1954-55, The one-and-one free throw is changed so that the bonus shot is given only if the first shot is made. 1955-56, The two-shot penalty in the last three minutes of the game is eliminated. The one-and-one is now in effect the entire game. 1956-57, The free-throw lane is increased from 6 feet to 12 feet. On the lineup for a free throw, the two spaces adjacent to the end line must be occupied by opponents of the free thrower. In the past, one space was marked "H" for a home team player to occupy, and across the lane the first space was marked "V" for a visiting team player to stand in. 1957-58, One free throw for each common foul is taken for the first six personal fouls by one team in each half, and the one-and-one is used thereafter. 1972-73, The free throw on the first six common fouls each half by a team is eliminated. 1974-75, A player charged with a foul is no longer required to raise his hand. (In 1978, however, it was strongly recommended that a player start raising his hand again.) 1983-84, Two free throws are taken for each common foul committed within the last two minutes of the second half and the entire overtime period, if the bonus rule is in effect. (This rule was rescinded one month into the season.) 1985-86, If a shooter is fouled intentionally and the shot is missed, the penalty will be two shots and possession of the ball out of bounds to the team that was fouled. 1987-88, Each intentional personal foul carries a two-shot penalty plus possession of the ball. 1990-91, Beginning with the team's 10th personal foul in a half, two free throws are awarded for each common foul, except player-control fouls. 1990-91, Three free throws are awarded when a shooter is fouled during an unsuccessful three-point try. 1991-92, Contact technical fouls count toward the five fouls for player disqualification and toward the team fouls in reaching bonus free-throw situations. 1992-93, Unsporting technical fouls, in addition to contact technical fouls, count toward the five fouls for player disqualification and toward the team fouls in reaching bonus free-throw situations. 1995-96, All unsporting technical fouls charged to anyone on the bench count toward the team foul total. 2000-01, Number of players permitted on free-throw lane reduced from eight to six. 2002-03, Lane spaces closest to the free-thrower shall remain unoccupied.

Freshmen: 1972-73, Freshmen are eligible to play varsity basketball. This was the result of a change in the NCAA bylaws, not the basketball playing rules.

Goaltending/Basket Interference: 1944-45, Defensive goaltending is banned. 1957-58, Offensive goaltending is now banned, as an addition to the original 1945 rule.

Held Ball: 1930-31, A held ball may be called when a closely guarded player is withholding the ball from play for five seconds. The result will be a jump ball. 1998-99, In a held-ball situation initiated by the defense, the ball shall be awarded to the defensive team. Previously, possession was awarded by the direction of the possession arrow. This was rescinded the next season.

Intentional Foul: 1985-86, If a shooter is fouled intentionally and the shot is missed, the penalty will be two shots and possession of the ball out of bounds to the team that was fouled. 1987-88, Each intentional personal foul carries a two-shot penalty plus possession of the ball. 1993-94, A foul shall be ruled intentional if, while playing the ball, a player causes excessive contact with an opponent.

Jump Ball/Alternate Possession: 1930-31, A held ball may be called when a closely guarded player is withholding the ball from play for five seconds. The result will be a jump ball. 1937-38, The center jump after every goal scored is eliminated. 1970-71, During a jump ball, a non-jumper may not change his position from the time the official is ready to make the toss until after the ball has been touched. 1974-75, During a jump ball, a non-jumper on the restraining circle may move around it after the ball has left the official's hands. 1981-82, The jump ball is used only at the beginning of the game and the start of each extra period. An alternating arrow will indicate possession in held-ball situations during the game. 1994-95, The inner circle at mid-court is eliminated.

Lines: 1894-95, The free-throw line is moved from 20 to 15 feet. 1932-33, The 10-second center (division) line is introduced to reduce stalling. 1956-57, The free-throw lane is increased from 6 feet to 12 feet. On the lineup for a free throw, the two spaces adjacent to the end line must be occupied by opponents of the free-thrower. In the past, one space was marked "H" for a home team player to occupy, and across the lane the first space was marked "V" for a visiting team player to stand in. 1984-85, The coaching box is introduced, whereby a coach and all bench personnel must remain in the 28-foot-long coaching box unless seeking information from the scorers' table. 1986-87, The three-point field goal is introduced and set at 19 feet 9 inches from the center of the basket. 1994-95, The inner circle at mid-court is eliminated.

Officials: 1908-09, A second official is added for games in an effort to curb the rough play. 1977-78, The option of a third official is allowed.

Out of Bounds: 1957-58, A ball that passes over the backboard—either front to back or back to front—is considered out of bounds.

Overtime: 1942-43, Any player who is eligible to start an extra period will be allowed an extra personal foul, increasing the total so disqualification is on the fifth foul. 1944-45, An extra foul is not permitted in overtime games. 1993-94, The game clock will be stopped after successful field goals in the last minute of the game and the last minute of any extra period with no substitution allowed.

Periods: 1951-52, Games are to be played in four 10-minute quarters. Before this, games were played in two 20-minute halves. 1954-55, Games are changed back to being played in two 20-minute halves. 1996-97, Teams shall warm up and shoot at the end of the court farthest from their own bench for the first half. Previously, teams had the choice of baskets in the first half.

Rough Play: 1908-09, A second official is added for games in an effort to curb the rough play. 1939-40, Teams have the choice of whether to take a free throw or take the ball out of bounds at mid-court. If two or more free throws are awarded, this option applies to the last throw. 1952-53, Teams can no longer waive free throws in favor of taking the ball out of bounds. 1957-58, One free throw for each common foul is taken for the first six personal fouls by one team in each half, and the one-and-one is used thereafter. 1972-73, The free throw on the first six common fouls each half by a team is eliminated. 1973-74, Officials may now penalize players for fouls occurring away from the ball, such as grabbing, holding and setting illegal screens. 1974-75, A player charged with a foul is no longer required to raise his hand. (In 1978, however, it was strongly recommended that a player start raising his hand again.) 1983-84, Two free throws are taken for each common foul committed within the last two minutes of the second half and the entire overtime period, if the bonus rule is in effect. (This rule was rescinded one month into the season.) 1987-88, Each intentional personal foul carries a two-shot penalty plus possession of the ball. 1990-91, Beginning with the team's 10th personal foul in a half, two free throws are awarded for each common foul, except player-control fouls. 1991-92, Contact technical fouls count toward the five fouls for player disqualification and toward the team fouls in reaching bonus free-throw situations. 1992-93, Unsporting technical fouls, in addition to contact technical fouls, count toward the five fouls for player disqualification and toward the team fouls in reaching bonus free-throw situations. 1993-94, A foul shall be ruled intentional if, while playing the ball, a player causes excessive contact with an opponent. 2000-01, Number of players permitted on free-throw lane reduced from eight to six.

Shot Clock/Stalling: 1932-33, The 10-second center (division) line is introduced to reduce stalling. 1985-86, The 45-second clock is introduced. The team in control of the ball must now shoot for a goal within 45 seconds after it attains team control. 1991-92, The shot clock is reset when the ball strikes the basket ring, not when a shot leaves the shooter's hands as it had been ever since the rule was introduced in 1986. 1993-94, The shot clock is reduced to 35 seconds from 45. The team in control of the ball must shoot for a goal within 35 seconds after it gains team control. 1993-94, The game clock will be stopped after successful field goals in the last minute of the game and the last minute of any overtime period with no substitution allowed. Officials may consult courtside monitor at end of either half or any extra period to determine: (1) if a field-goal try beat the horn; (2) whether a shot-clock violation at the end of the first half beat the horn; or, (3) whether a shot-clock violation that will determine the outcome of a game beat the horn. The officials also may use a courtside monitor to correct a timer's mistake or to determine if the game clock or shot clock expired at or near the end of a period.

Shot in Closing Seconds: 1994-95, Scoring is restricted to a tap-in when 3/10 (.3) of a second or less remain on the game clock or shot clock. 1999-00, During the season, rules committee made rule that requires official to look at courtside monitor to decipher if a potential game-determining shot in the last second of the game or overtime should count. 2003-04, Officials may consult courtside monitor at end of either half or any extra period to determine: (1) if a field-goal try beat the horn; (2) whether a shot-clock violation at the end of the first half beat the horn; or, (3) whether a shot-clock violation that will determine the outcome of a game beat the horn. The officials also may use a courtside monitor to correct a timer's mistake or to determine if the game clock or shot clock expired at or near the end of a period.

Substitution: 1920-21, A player can re-enter the game once. Before this rule, if a player left the game, he could not re-enter for the rest of the game. 1933-34, A player may re-enter the game twice. 1944-45, Unlimited substitution is introduced. 1993-94, The game clock will be stopped after successful field goals in the last minute of the game and the last minute of any extra period with no substitution allowed.

Technical Fouls: 1938-39, The ball will be thrown in from out of bounds at mid-court by the team shooting a free throw after a technical foul. Before, the ball was put into play with a center jump after a technical-foul free throw. 1956-57, Grasping the basket is now classified as a technical foul under unsportsmanlike tactics. 1981-82, All fouls charged to bench personnel shall be assessed to the head coach. 1988-89, Any squad member who participates in a fight will be ejected from the game and will be placed on probation. If that player participates in a second fight during the season, he will be suspended for one game. A third fight involving the same person results in suspension for the rest of the season including championship competition. 1990-91, The fighting rule is amended. The first time any squad member or bench personnel participates in a fight he will be suspended for the team's next game. If that same person participates in a second fight, he will be suspended for the rest of the season, including championship competition. 1991-92, Contact technical fouls count toward the five fouls for player disqualification and toward the team fouls in reaching bonus free-throw situations. 1992-93, Unsporting technical fouls, in addition to contact technical fouls, count toward the five fouls for player disqualification and toward the team fouls in reaching bonus free-throw situations. 1993-94, The rule concerning the use of profanity is expanded to include abusive and obscene language in an effort to curtail verbal misconduct by players and coaches. 1994-95, The fighting and suspension rules are expanded to include coaches and team personnel. 2000-01, technical fouls divided into direct (two-shot penalty) and indirect (one-shot penalty) with ball returned to point of interruption. 2001-02, Both direct and indirect technical fouls penalized by two shots and return to point of interruption.

Television Replay: 1986-87, A coach may leave the confines of the bench at any time without penalty to correct a scorer's or timer's mistake. A technical foul is assessed if there is no mistake. (This was changed the next year to a timeout.) Also, a television replay may be used to prevent or rectify a scorer's or timer's mistake or a malfunction of the clock. 1999-00, Officials must consult courtside television monitors, when available, to judge whether a game-deciding last-second shot in the second half or any extra period counts. (This was passed during season.) 2001-02, Officials can check an official courtside monitor to determine if a try is a three- or two-point attempt, regardless of whether the try is successful. 2003-04, Officials may consult courtside monitor at end of either half or any extra period to determine: (1) if a field-goal try beat the horn; (2) whether a shot-clock violation at the end of the first half beat the horn; or, (3) whether a shot-clock violation that will determine the outcome of a game beat the horn. The officials also may use a courtside monitor to correct a timer's mistake or to determine if the game clock or shot clock expired at or near the end of a period.

Three Seconds: 1932-33, No player can stand in the free-throw lane with the ball more than three seconds. 1935-36, No offensive player can remain in the free-throw lane, with or without the ball, for more than three seconds. 1944-45, It becomes a violation for an offensive player to remain in the free-throw lane more than three seconds.

Three-Point Shot: 1986-87, The three-point field goal is introduced and set at 19 feet 9 inches from the center of the basket. 1990-91, Three free throws are awarded when a shooter is fouled during an unsuccessful three-point try.

Timeouts: 1948-49, Coaches are allowed to speak to players during a timeout. 1995-96, Teams are allowed one 20-second timeout per half. This was an experimental rule in the 1994-95 season. 1996-97, In games not involving commercial electronic media, teams are entitled to four full-length timeouts and two 20-second timeouts per game. In games involving commercial electronic media, teams are entitled to two full-length timeouts and three 20-second timeouts per game. 1997-98, Timeout requests can be made by a player on the court or by the head coach. 1999-00, Twenty-second timeouts increased to 30 seconds in length. New electronic-media timeout format adopted.

Traveling: 1900-01, A dribbler may not shoot for a field goal and may dribble only once, and then with two hands. 1908-09, A dribbler is permitted to shoot. The dribble is defined as the "continuous passage of the ball," making the double dribble illegal. 1921-22, Running with the ball changes from a foul to a violation.

Uniforms: 1957-58, On uniforms, the use of the single digit numbers one and two and any digit greater than five is prohibited. 1999-00, Uniform numbers one and two are permitted.

Basketball Rules Committee Secretary-Rules Editor Roster

Name	Affiliation	Years
Oswald Tower	non-NCAA	1939-59
John Bunn	Colorado St.	1960-67
Ed Steitz	Springfield	1967-91
Henry Nichols	Villanova	1992-96
Ed Bilik	Springfield	1997-present

Division I Basketball Rules Committee Chair Roster

Name	Affiliation	Years
H.H. Salmon Jr.	Princeton	1939-40
Floyd Rowe	non-NCAA	1941
James W. St. Clair	Southern Methodist	1942-44
E.J. Hickox	non-NCAA	1945, 1947
H.G. Olsen	Ohio St.	1946
George Edwards	Missouri	1948-51
Bruce Drake	Oklahoma	1952-55
Paul Hinkle	Butler	1956-59
H.E. Foster	Wisconsin	1960-65
Polk Robison	Texas Tech	1966
Norvall Neve	Atlantic Coast, Missouri Valley Conferences	1967-75
Richard Wilson	Amherst	1976
John Carpenter	Rider	1977-78
Jack Thurnblad	Carleton	1979-80
C.M. Newton	Alabama, Southeastern Conference	1981-85
James Dutcher	Minnesota	1986

Name	Affiliation	Years
Jerry Krause	Eastern Wash.	1987
Richard Sauers	Albany (N.Y.)	1988
Gene Bartow	UAB	1989-93
George Raveling	Southern California	1994-96
Larry Keating Jr.	Seton Hall	1997
Herb Kenny	Wesleyan (Conn.)	1998
Reggie Minton	Air Force	1999-2000
Roy Williams	Kansas	2001
Art Hyland	Big East Conference	2002-03
Willis Wilson	Rice	2004

Basketball Rules Committee Roster

Name	Affiliation	Years
Phog Allen	Kansas	1939-41
William Anderson	Lafayette	1951-54
Lewis Andreas	Syracuse	1946-49
Tom Apke	Creighton, Colorado	1979-84
Tim Autry	South Carolina St.	1998-2002
Joe Baker	Wis.-La Crosse	2003-present
Ralph Barkey	Sonoma St.	1996
Sam Barry	Southern California	1946-48
Justin Barry	Southern California	1949-51
Gene Bartow	Memphis, Illinois, UCLA, UAB	1974-78, 88-93
Steve Belko	Oregon	1966-69
John Bennington	St. Louis, Michigan St.	1960-65
Bill Berry	San Jose St.	1988-90
Ed Bilik	Springfield	1968-69, 72-78, 96-2002
Hoyt Brawner	Denver	1960-66
Charlie Brock	Springfield	2003-present
Clint Bryant	Augusta St.	1996-99

Name	Affiliation	Years
Tom Bryant	Centre	1996-98
John Bunn	Stanford, Springfield, Colorado St.	1939-40, 54-67
Clarence Burch	Lycoming	1979-82
Jim Burson	Muskingum	1987-92
L.C. Butler	Colorado St.	1951-53
E.M. Cameron	Duke	1956-61
John Carpenter	Rider	1973-78
Don Casey	Temple	1979-82
Dale Clayton	Carson-Newman	2003-present
Gary Colson	New Mexico, California	1986-92
Forrest Cox	Colorado	1940-44
Sumner A. Dole	Connecticut	1939-41
Bruce Drake	Oklahoma	1947-55
Joe Dean Jr.	Birmingham So.	2003-present
Ed Douma	Hillsdale	2001-present
James Dutcher	Minnesota	1983-86
W.H.H. Dye	Washington	1955-59
C.S. Edmundson	Washington	1941-45
George Edwards	Missouri	1942-51
Fred Enke	Arizona	1957-61
Wesley E. Fesler	Wesleyan (Conn.)	1944
Dan Fitzgerald	Gonzaga	1996-97
H.E. Foster	Wisconsin	1958-66
Clarence Gaines	Winston-Salem	1992-93
Jayson Gee	Charleston (W.Va.)	2001-03
Pete Gillen	Xavier	1993-97
Jack Gray	Texas	1951-52
Hugh Greer	Connecticut	1963
Jim Gudger	Tex. A&M-Commerce	1976, 78
Richard Harter	Pennsylvania	1972
Clem Haskins	Minnesota	1992-96
E.O. "Doc" Hayes	Southern Methodist	1967-69
R.E. Henderson	Baylor	1953-56
Paul Hinkle	Butler	1954-59
Howard Hobson	Yale	1952-55
Ron Holmes	McMurry	1999-2002
Art Hyland	Big East Conference	1998-2003
Henry Iba	Oklahoma St.	1952-54, 67-69
Clarence Iba	Tulsa	1956-59
George Ireland	Loyola (Ill.)	1963-66
Calvin Irvin	N.C. A&T	1979
Brad Jackson	Western Wash.	2004-present
Bill Jones	North Ala.	1985-91
Larry Keating, Jr.	Seton Hall	1994-97; 2003-present
Herb Kenny	Wesleyan (Conn.)	1993-98
William Knapton	Beloit	1981-86
Jack Kraft	Villanova	1968-69
Jerry Krause	Eastern Wash. St.	1976-78, 83-87
Mike Kryzyewski	Duke	1991
John Kundla	Minnesota	1968-69, 72-74
Eugene Lambert	Arkansas	1945-49
Dale Lash	Springfield	1942-43
Debora Lazorik	Marietta	1999-2002
Harry Litwack	Temple	1960-65
Edward P. Markey	St. Michael's	1992-95
Jack Martin	Lamar	1974-79
Rollie Massimino	UNLV	1993-95
Arthur McAfee	Morehouse	1975-80
Walter "Doc" Meanwell	Wisconsin	1939
Gene Mehaffey	Ohio Wesleyan	1993-98
Bill Menefee	Baylor	1972-73
Ray Meyer	DePaul	1979-82
Joey Meyer	DePaul	1993-95
Douglas Mills	Illinois	1947-53
Reggie Minton	Air Force	1997-2000

Name	Affiliation	Years
Mike Montgomery	Stanford	1997-2000
Gerald Myers	Texas Tech	1986-92
Norvall Neve	Atlantic Coast, Missouri Valley Conferences	1967-75
C.M. Newton	Alabama, Southeastern Conference	1981-85
Henry Nichols	Villanova	1992-96
Thomas Niland Jr.	Le Moyne	1985-91
Kenneth Norton	Manhattan	1955-59
Tom O'Connor	George Mason	1998-2003
Dave Odom	Wake Forest	2001-present
H.G. Olsen	Ohio St.	1940-46
Ray Oosting	Trinity College (Conn.)	1946-49, 51, 58-62
James Padgett	California, Nevada	1972-74
Curtis Parker	Centenary (La.)	1939-41
Ted Paulauskas	St. Anselm	1997-99
Richard H. Perry	UC Riverside	1992
Vadal Peterson	Utah	1945-48
Mac Petty	Wabash	1987-92
Digger Phelps	Notre Dame	1988-91
Jerry Pimm	Utah	1979-84
Clarence Price	California	1952-54
Jack Ramsay	St. Joseph's	1966-67
George Raveling	Southern California	1993-96
Lonn Reisman	Tarleton St.	2000-03
Polk Robison	Texas Tech	1962-66
Paul Rundell	San Francisco St.	1980-81
Adolph Rupp	Kentucky	1962-66
Andy Russo	Florida Tech, Lynn	1997-2000
H.H. Salmon Jr.	Princeton	1939-40
Richard Sauers	Albany (N.Y.)	1983-87
William Scanlon	Union (N.Y.)	1989-94
Norman Shepard	Davidson	1942-47
J. Dallas Shirley	Southern Conference	1984-87
Dean Smith	North Carolina	1967-69, 72-73
James W. St. Clair	Southern Methodist	1939-44
Floyd Stahl	Ohio St.	1956-57, 60-61
Ed Steitz	Springfield College	1959-91
Norm Stewart	Missouri	1985-91
Kenneth Stibler	Biscayne	1978-84
Eddie Sutton	Arkansas	1980-85
H. Jamison Swarts	Pennsylvania	1941-45
A.K. Tebell	Virginia	1948-52
John Thompson III	Princeton	2003-present
Jack Thurnblad	Carleton	1975-80
Alvin J. Van Wie	Wooster	1981-86
Bob Vanatta	Sunshine State Conference	1994-95
Kevin Vande Streek	Calvin	2003-present
M. Edward Wagner	California Collegiate Athletic Association	1976-79
Russell Walseth	Colorado	1972-75, 77-78
Perry Watson	Detroit	2002-present
Stanley Watts	Brigham Young	1954-57
Clifford Wells	Tulane	1953-56
Don White	Connecticut	1945
Vining William	Ouachita Baptist	1977
James Williams	Colorado St.	1972-78
Roy Williams	Kansas	1997-2000
Floyd Wilson	Harvard	1964-69
Richard Wilson	Amherst	1972-75
Willis Wilson	Rice	2001-present
Willard A. Witte	Wyoming	1939
John Wooden	UCLA	1961-64
Ned Wulk	Arizona St.	1968-69
Jim Zalacca	New Paltz St., Potsdam St.	1999-2002

PLAYING-RULES HISTORY

Division I Basketball Firsts

The First Time...

Playing rules were published:
January 1892 in the Springfield College school newspaper, The Triangle.

A game was played:
January 20, 1892, at the Training School of the International YMCA College, now known as Springfield College in Massachusetts.

A game was played in public:
March 11, 1892, at Springfield College. A crowd of 200 saw the students defeat the teachers, 5-1.

A full schedule of games was played by a college:
1894 when the University of Chicago compiled a 6-1 season record.

A game between two colleges was played:
February 9, 1895, when the Minnesota School of Agriculture defeated Hamline, 9-3. Nine players were allowed on the court at the same time for both teams.

A game between two colleges was played with five players on each team:
January 16, 1896, when Chicago defeated Iowa, 15-12, in Iowa City. Iowa's starting lineup was composed of a YMCA team that just happened to be university students.

A game between two true college teams with five players on a team was played:
1897 when Yale defeated Pennsylvania, 32-10.

A conference season was played:
1901-02 by the East League, known today as the Ivy Group.

A conference tournament was played:
1921 by the Southern Conference. Kentucky was the winner.

A consensus all-America team was selected:
1929. Members were Charley Hyatt, Pittsburgh; Joe Schaaf, Pennsylvania; Charles Murphy, Purdue; Vern Corbin, California; Thomas Churchill, Oklahoma; and John Thompson, Montana State.

The National Invitation Tournament was played:
1938 when Temple was the winner.

A college game was televised:
February 28, 1940, when Pittsburgh defeated Fordham, 50-37, at Madison Square Garden in New York City. In the second game, New York University defeated Georgetown, 50-27.

The three-point shot was used experimentally in a game:
February 7, 1945, Columbia defeated Fordham, 73-58. The three-point line was set at 21 feet from the basket and Columbia scored 11 "long goals" to Fordham's nine. Also, free-throwers had an option to take their shots from the regular 15-foot distance for one point or from 21 feet for two points. Eight "long fouls" were made during the game.

The 12-foot free-throw lane was used experimentally in a game:
February 7, 1945, Columbia defeated Fordham, 73-58 in the same game as mentioned above. The free-throw lane was widened from 6 feet to 12 for this game and the rule was adopted 11 years later.

An Associated Press poll was published:
1949, when St. Louis was ranked No. 1. By the end of the season, Kentucky had taken over the top spot.

NCAA Tournament Firsts

The first game:
March 17, 1939, when Villanova defeated Brown, 42-30, in Philadelphia.

The first championship game:
March 27, 1939, when Oregon defeated Ohio State, 46-33, in Evanston, Illinois.

The first time two teams from the same conference played in the NCAA tournament:
1944 when Iowa State and Missouri, both of the Big Six, played in the Western regional.

The first time four teams advanced to the final site:
1946 (North Carolina, Ohio State, Oklahoma State and California).

The first championship game televised:
1946 locally in New York City by WCBS-TV. Oklahoma State defeated North Carolina, 43-40. An estimated 500,000 watched the game on television.

The first repeat champion:
Oklahoma State followed its 1945 championship with a title in 1946.

First NCAA championship team to have an integrated roster of white and black players:
CCNY's 1950 squad is believed to be the first integrated championship team.

The first time conference champions qualified automatically:
1951.

The first time a conference champion qualified automatically for the NCAA tournament instead of the regular-season champion:
1952, North Carolina State finished second in the Southern Conference but won the conference postseason tournament.

The first time there were four regional sites:
1952.

The first time games were televised regionally:
1952.

The first time a Final Four was played on Friday and Saturday:
1954.

The first tournament championship game televised nationally:
1954 for a broadcast rights fee of $7,500.

The first time an undefeated team won the NCAA championship:
1956 when San Francisco went 29-0.

The first time two teams from the same state played in the NCAA title game:
1961 when Cincinnati defeated Ohio State, 70-65, in overtime.

The first championship team to start five African-Americans:
UTEP in 1966—Harry Flournoy, David Lattin, Bobby Joe Hill, Orsten Artis, Willie Cager.

The first time the Final Four was played on Thursday and Saturday:
1969.

The first time the Final Four was played on Saturday and Monday:
1973.

The first NCAA title game televised during prime time:
UCLA's win over Memphis in 1973 was televised by NBC.

The first time television rights totaled more than $1 million:
1973.

The first public draw for Final Four tickets:
1973 for the 1974 championship.

The first time teams other than the conference champion could be chosen at large from the same conference:
1975.

The first reference to the term "Final Four":
1975 Official Collegiate Basketball Guide, page 5 in national preview-review section written by Ed Chay of the Cleveland Plain Dealer. Chay wrote, "Outspoken Al McGuire of Marquette, whose team was one of the final four in Greensboro, was among several coaches who said it was good for college basketball that UCLA was finally beaten."

The first time two teams from the same conference played in the Final Four title game:
1976 when Indiana defeated Michigan, 86-68. Both teams were Big Ten members.

The first time the seeding process was used to align teams in the bracket:
1978.

The first reference to term "Final Four" is capitalized:
1978 Official Collegiate Basketball Guide (page 7, first line).

The first time all teams were seeded in the bracket:
1979.

The first public lottery for Final Four tickets:
1979.

The first time more than two teams from the same conference were allowed in the NCAA tournament:
1980.

The first time none of the No. 1 seeds in the NCAA tournament advanced to the Final Four:
1980.

The first time the Rating Percentage Index (RPI), a computer ranking system, was used as an aid in evaluating teams for at-large selections and seeding:
1981.

The first time two No. 1 seeds in the NCAA tournament advanced to the Final Four:
1981.

The first time a Final Four logo was produced that was specific to the site of the championship game:
1981, when the final game was played in Philadelphia and the logo included the Liberty Bell.

The first live television broadcast of the selection show announcing the NCAA tournament bracket:
1982.

The first time CBS was awarded the television rights for the NCAA tournament:
1982.

The first time a men's and women's team from the same school advanced to the Final Four in the same year:
1983, when both Georgia teams lost in the national semifinals.

The first time awards were presented to all participating teams in the NCAA championship tournament:
1984.

The first time 64 teams participated in the NCAA tournament:
1985.

The first time three teams from the same conference advanced to the Final Four:
1985, when Georgetown, St. John's (New York) and Villanova represented the Big East.

The first time all 64 NCAA tournament teams were subject to drug testing:
1987.

The first time neutral courts were used in all rounds of the NCAA tournament:
1989.

The first time all the Nos. 1 and 2 seeds in the NCAA tournament advanced to the Sweet Sixteen:
1989.

The first time a bearded coach advanced to the Final Four:
P.J. Carlesimo of Seton Hall in 1989.

The first time a minimum facility seating capacity of 12,000 for first and second rounds and regionals was established:
1993.

The first time three No. 1 seeds in the NCAA tournament advanced to the Final Four:
1993.

The first time two former Final Four most outstanding players returned to the Final Four:
1995, when North Carolina's Donald Williams (1993) and Arkansas' Corliss Williamson (1994) returned to the Final Four.

The first NCAA tournament MOP:
Marv Huffman of Indiana in 1940.

The first freshman named NCAA tournament MOP:
Arnie Ferrin of Utah in 1944.

The first two-time NCAA tournament MOP:
Bob Kurland of Oklahoma State in 1945 and 1946.

The first NCAA tournament MOP not to play on the national championship team:
B.H. Born of Kansas in 1953.

The first football Heisman Trophy winner to play in the Final Four:
Terry Baker of Oregon State in 1963.

The first three-time NCAA tournament MOP:
Lew Alcindor of UCLA in 1967, 1968 and 1969.

The first player to play for two teams in the Final Four championship game:
Bob Bender with Indiana 1976 and Duke 1978.

The first coach to win the NCAA title in his first year as a head coach:
Steve Fisher of Michigan in 1989.

The First Team(s)...

To win 30 games in a season:
Wyoming went 31-2 in 1943.

To win a football bowl game and the NCAA tournament title in the same academic year:
Oklahoma State won the Cotton Bowl and the NCAA championship in 1944-45.

To be ranked No. 1 in the final regular-season poll and go on to win the NCAA championship:
Kentucky ended the 1949 regular season ranked No. 1 and proceeded to win its second NCAA title.

To win the NCAA tournament and the NIT in the same year:
CCNY won both tournaments in 1950.

To play for the national championship in both football and basketball in the same academic year:
Oklahoma lost in both the Orange Bowl and the Final Four title game in 1987-88.

Representing the same school to be ranked No. 1 in the men's and women's polls:
Connecticut's men's and women's basketball programs were ranked No. 1 in their respective top 25 polls February 13, 1995.

The First Coach...

Who also happened to be the inventor of the game:
Dr. James Naismith invented the game in December 1891 at Springfield College in Massachusetts.

To lead his team to a finish among the final four teams in the nation in his first season as a head coach:
Ray Meyer of DePaul in 1943.

To be recognized as coach of the year:
Phil Woolpert of San Francisco was named the 1955 coach of the year by United Press International.

To take two different schools to the NCAA championship game:
Frank McGuire in 1957 with North Carolina after St. John's (New York) in 1952.

To win the NCAA championship after playing for an NCAA championship team:
Bob Knight coached Indiana to the championship in 1976 after playing for the 1960 Ohio State champions.

To take two different teams to the Final Four:
Forddy Anderson and Frank McGuire. Anderson—Bradley in 1950 (first year) and Michigan State in 1957; McGuire—St. John's (New York) (first year) in 1952 and North Carolina in 1957.

To take two different teams to the NCAA tournament:
Ben Carnevale—North Carolina in 1946 (first year) and Navy in 1947.

To take three different teams to the NCAA tournament:
Eddie Hickey—Creighton in 1941 (first year), Saint Louis in 1952 and Marquette in 1959.

To take four different teams to the NCAA tournament:
Eddie Sutton—Creighton in 1974 (first year), Arkansas in 1977, Kentucky in 1986 and Oklahoma State in 1991.

The First Player...

To be named consensus all-American three times:
John Wooden of Purdue from 1930-32.

To score 1,000 points in his career:
Christian Steinmetz of Wisconsin from 1903-05.

To score 50 points in one game:
Hank Luisetti of Stanford, who scored 50 in a win over Duquesne, January 1, 1938.

To popularize the jump shot:
Hank Luisetti of Stanford in 1936-38.

African-American to be named to the consensus all-America team:
Don Barksdale of UCLA in 1947.

To score 2,000 points in his career:
Jim Lacy of Loyola (Md.) scored 2,154 points in 1946-49.

To lead the nation in scoring during the regular season and play for the NCAA championship team in the same year:
Clyde Lovellette of Kansas in 1952.

To achieve 2,000 points and 2,000 rebounds in his career:
Tom Gola of La Salle scored 2,462 points and pulled down 2,201 rebounds in 1952-55.

To grab 50 rebounds in one game:
Bill Chambers of William and Mary brought down 51 boards against Virginia on February 14, 1953.

To grab 700 rebounds in a season:
Walt Dukes of Seton Hall brought down 734 boards during the 1953 season.

To score 100 points in a game:
Frank Selvy of Furman scored 100 points in a 149-95 victory over Newberry on February 13, 1954, in Greenville, South Carolina.

To score 1,000 points in a single season:
Frank Selvy of Furman scored 1,209 during the 1954 season.

To average 40 points a game for a season:
Frank Selvy of Furman averaged 41.7 points a game during the 1954 season.

To average 30 points a game for a career:
Frank Selvy of Furman averaged 32.5 points a game from 1952-54.

To average more than 20 points and 20 rebounds per game during his career:
Bill Russell of San Francisco from 1954-56. He averaged 20.7 points and 20.3 rebounds.

Recognized as the player of the year:
Tom Gola of La Salle was named the 1955 player of the year by United Press International.

To score 3,000 points in his career:
Pete Maravich of LSU scored 3,667 points from 1968-70.

To average 40 points a game for a career:
Pete Maravich of LSU averaged 44.2 points a game from 1968-70.

To lead the nation in scoring and rebounding in the same season:
Xavier McDaniel of Wichita State in 1985.

To make 400 three-point field goals in his career:
Doug Day of Radford hit 401 three-pointers from 1990-93.

PLAYING-RULES HISTORY

2003 Results, All Divisions

Photo by Brian Spurlock

2002-2003 Results—All Divisions

Following is an alphabetical listing of the 2002-03 season's game-by-game scores for the men's teams of the member colleges and universities of the National Collegiate Athletic Association.

Below each team's name and location appear the name of its 2002-03 head coach and his alma mater, where available. All other information is from the 2002-03 season. Divisional designation for each team is indicated in the upper right-hand corner of each listing.

Squares (■) indicate home games and daggers (†) indicate neutral-site games.

All records are restricted to varsity games between four-year college institutions.

The 2002-03 schedules and updated information can be found on the World Wide Web at www.ncaa.org.

ABILENE CHRISTIAN
Abilene, TX 79699 II

Coach: Klint Pleasant, Lipscomb 1998

2002-03 RESULTS (13-14)

75	Southeastern Okla. ■	63
81	Howard Payne ■	75
120	St. Edward's	78
58	Okla. Panhandle	81
69	Central Okla.	79
49	Northeastern St.	88
93	Dallas Christian ■	72
81	Ark.-Monticello †	79
85	St. Edward's ■	80
93	Sul Ross St. ■	87
63	East Central ■	55
90	Cameron	80
71	Southwestern Okla.	78
76	Angelo St. ■	85
58	Tarleton St.	81
82	Eastern N.M. ■	97
63	West Tex. A&M ■	79
73	Angelo St.	70
82	Midwestern St.	71
68	Tex. A&M-Commerce	74
68	Tex. A&M-Kingsville	77
76	Tex. A&M-Kingsville ■	74
78	Tex. A&M-Commerce ■	72
64	West Tex. A&M	79
74	Eastern N.M.	87
78	Okla. Panhandle ■	86
51	Midwestern St. ■	68

Nickname: Wildcats
Colors: Purple & White
Arena: Moody Coliseum
   Capacity: 4,600; Year Built: 1968
AD: Jared Mosley
SID: Lance Fleming

ADAMS ST.
Alamosa, CO 81102 II

Coach: Larry Mortensen, Adams St. 1988

2002-03 RESULTS (13-15)

61	Westminster (Utah) †	77
84	Augustana (S.D.) †	78
73	Northern Colo.	77
57	Okla. Panhandle	79
77	Western N.M.	78
54	Metro St.	72
67	Chadron St.	65
85	Okla. Panhandle ■	65
70	Regis (Colo.)	63
64	Neb.-Kearney	107
51	Fort Hays St.	70
59	Colorado Mines ■	66
73	Colo. Christian ■	66
84	Western N.M. ■	73
58	Colorado St.-Pueblo	61
94	N.M. Highlands ■	62
67	Colorado Col.	80
82	Western St. ■	66
63	UC-Colo. Spgs. ■	61
64	Fort Lewis ■	67
89	Mesa St. ■	83
73	Western St.	62
74	UC-Colo. Spgs.	67
83	Fort Lewis	91
63	Mesa St.	76
66	N.M. Highlands	69
87	Colorado St.-Pueblo ■	72
86	Neb.-Kearney	113

Nickname: Grizzlies
Colors: Green & White
Arena: Plachy Hall
   Capacity: 3,200; Year Built: 1960
AD: Jeff Geiser
SID: Chris Day

ADELPHI
Garden City, NY 11530 II

Coach: James Cosgrove, St. Anselm 1987

2002-03 RESULTS (22-9)

84	Bentley	73
65	Merrimack †	73
93	Bridgeport ■	68
62	C.W. Post	65
97	Concordia (N.Y.)	70
73	NYIT	77
66	Mass.-Lowell	81
56	Philadelphia U.	71
76	Queens (N.Y.) ■	59
66	St. Thomas Aquinas	42
73	Southampton ■	68
75	Molloy	68
86	Mercy	81
53	New Haven	73
67	Bridgeport	70
84	C.W. Post ■	76
82	Dowling	75
77	Philadelphia U. ■	61
57	Concordia (N.Y.)	44
59	NYIT	68
58	Queens (N.Y.)	46
83	St. Thomas Aquinas ■	59
84	Molloy ■	61
87	Southampton	66
78	Dowling ■	50
85	Mercy ■	63
73	New Haven ■	60
52	Queens (N.Y.) ■	49
74	Bridgeport †	69
70	C.W. Post	57
56	Bridgeport †	64

Nickname: Panthers
Colors: Black & Gold
Arena: Woodruff Hall
   Capacity: 800; Year Built: 1929
AD: Robert E. Hartwell
SID: Suzette Thweatt

ADRIAN
Adrian, MI 49221 III

Coach: Buck Riley, Southwestern Okla. 1967

2002-03 RESULTS (12-14)

82	Heidelberg ■	52
73	Ohio Wesleyan ■	88
62	Northwood	85
69	Oakland	88
84	Rochester College ■	73
86	St. Mary's (Mich.) ■	55
87	Palm Beach Atl.	84
59	Goucher †	65
80	Goshen	85
69	Bluffton ■	77
59	Hope ■	64
63	Albion	72
69	Olivet	87
67	Kalamazoo ■	65
68	Alma ■	60
55	Rochester College	52
61	Calvin	58
67	Hope	83
54	Albion ■	83
84	Olivet ■	79
51	Kalamazoo	67
75	Alma	56
73	Marygrove ■	57
76	Siena Heights ■	75
63	Calvin ■	77
59	Albion	65

Nickname: Bulldogs
Colors: Gold & Black
Arena: Merillat Center
   Capacity: 1,350; Year Built: 1990
AD: C. Henry Mensing
SID: Darcy Gifford

AIR FORCE
USAF Academy, CO 80840-5001
....I

Coach: Joe Scott, Princeton 1987

2002-03 RESULTS (12-16)

47	Louisville	65
72	Stetson ■	43
57	Arkansas St.	52
47	Tennessee Tech	60
65	Tex.-Pan American ■	44
70	Ga. Southern	56
85	Belmont ■	76
44	Oakland	61
59	UAB †	69
63	UTEP	45
78	Ga. Southern ■	40
56	Navy ■	43
56	Savannah St. ■	33
48	San Diego St. ■	63
49	Colorado St.	51
44	Wyoming	46
75	UNLV ■	71
35	Utah	45
33	Brigham Young	65
59	New Mexico	73
80	Colorado St. ■	75
57	Wyoming ■	64
53	San Diego St.	67
70	UNLV	74
43	Brigham Young ■	56
52	Utah ■	57
68	New Mexico ■	60
38	Utah †	42

Nickname: Falcons
Colors: Blue & Silver
Arena: Clune Arena
   Capacity: 6,002; Year Built: 1968
AD: Randall Spetman
SID: Jerry Cross

AKRON
Akron, OH 44325 I

Coach: Dan Hipsher, Bowling Green 1977

2002-03 RESULTS (14-14)

75	Wright St.	78
74	Capital ■	45
88	Oakland	84
65	Cleveland St. ■	68
82	James Madison	84
85	Iona ■	78
71	Niagara	77
97	Radford ■	64
84	Hampton ■	79
105	Ball St. ■	104
104	Ohio	112
89	Buffalo ■	71
60	Bowling Green	74
59	Miami (Ohio)	74
72	Kent St. ■	79
52	Western Mich.	68
101	Northern Ill.	100
96	Eastern Mich. ■	80
78	Toledo	67
92	Central Mich. ■	99
58	Marshall	74
53	Miami (Ohio) ■	55
84	Ohio	82
70	Central Mich.	69
85	Kent St.	70
79	Marshall ■	71
66	Buffalo	70
77	Ohio ■	79

Nickname: Zips
Colors: Blue & Gold
Arena: James A. Rhodes Arena
   Capacity: 5,942; Year Built: 1983
AD: Michael J. Thomas
SID: Gregg Bach

ALABAMA
Tuscaloosa, AL 35487 I

Coach: Mark Gottfried, Alabama 1987

2002-03 RESULTS (17-12)

68	Oklahoma †	62
82	Alabama St. ■	56
80	Middle Tenn. ■	65
54	Ohio St. †	48
89	UNC Greensboro ■	61
77	St. Bonaventure ■	68
72	Bowling Green †	63
69	Providence ■	61
82	Morehead St. ■	64
49	Utah	51
65	Xavier ■	58
61	Arkansas ■	51
69	Vanderbilt	70
68	Mississippi St. ■	62
68	Auburn	77
57	Mississippi	76
46	Kentucky ■	63
75	LSU ■	66
70	Arkansas	81
56	Florida	75
84	Auburn ■	68

69 Georgia ■ ...74
76 Tennessee ...71
55 Mississippi St. ...59
86 Mississippi ■ ...63
82 South Carolina ■ ...59
62 LSU ...66
69 Vanderbilt † ...82
62 Indiana † ...67

Nickname: Crimson Tide
Colors: Crimson & White
Arena: Coleman Coliseum
Capacity: 15,043; Year Built: 1968
AD: Mal Moore
SID: Becky Hopf

ALABAMA A&M
Normal, AL 35762 ...I

Coach: L. Vann Pettaway, Alabama A&M 1980
2002-03 RESULTS (8-19)
96 Tuskegee ■ ...79
40 Vanderbilt ...68
58 Mississippi St. ...100
75 South Carolina St. † ...88
97 Savannah St. ■ ...78
65 Morris Brown ...58
89 Florida A&M ...91
69 UAB ...91
74 Grambling ■ ...70
68 Jackson St. ■ ...82
81 Mississippi Val. ...91
66 Ark.-Pine Bluff ...65
52 Alabama St. ■ ...53
65 Alcorn St. ■ ...66
60 Southern U. ■ ...66
67 Texas Southern ...72
67 Prairie View ...79
72 Mississippi Val. ■ ...103
72 Ark.-Pine Bluff ■ ...54
74 Alabama St. ...85
92 Morris Brown ■ ...58
71 Alcorn St. ...79
93 Southern U. ...94
90 Texas Southern ■ ...82
75 Prairie View ■ ...76
62 Grambling ...63
72 Jackson St. ...81

Nickname: Bulldogs
Colors: Maroon & White
Arena: Elmore Health Science Building
Capacity: 6,000; Year Built: 1973
AD: James A. Martin Sr.
SID: Ashley Balch

ALABAMA ST.
Montgomery, AL 36101-0271 ...I

Coach: Rob Spivery, Ashland 1972
2002-03 RESULTS (14-15)
73 Furman † ...74
47 Texas-Arlington † ...59
56 Alabama ...82
58 Mississippi ...74
67 Florida A&M ...68
82 Georgia St. ...77
71 Troy St. ...80
79 Montevallo ■ ...61
58 Birmingham-So. ■ ...53
61 Troy St. ...81
70 Jackson St. ■ ...58
79 Grambling ■ ...70
43 Ark.-Pine Bluff ...33
73 Mississippi Val. ...67
53 Alabama A&M ...52
78 Southern U. ■ ...60
75 Alcorn St. ■ ...49
57 Prairie View ...63
52 Texas Southern ...58
57 Ark.-Pine Bluff ■ ...33

78 Mississippi Val. ■ ...79
85 Alabama A&M ■ ...74
54 Southern U. ...57
50 Alcorn St. ...69
54 Prairie View ■ ...60
68 Texas Southern ■ ...64
60 Jackson St. ...70
67 Grambling ...63
55 Alcorn St. ■ ...,58

Nickname: Hornets
Colors: Black & Gold
Arena: Joe L. Reed Acadome
Capacity: 8,000; Year Built: 1992
AD: Robert Spivery
SID: Ronnie Johnson

UAB
Birmingham, AL 35294-0110 ...I

Coach: Mike Anderson, Tulsa 1982
2002-03 RESULTS (21-13)
71 Birmingham-So. ■ ...53
92 Chattanooga ■ ...81
75 UNLV ...84
97 West Ala. ■ ...71
68 Richmond ...72
82 Nicholls St. ■ ...70
108 Tex. A&M-Corp. Chris. ■ ...74
91 Alabama A&M ■ ...69
69 Air Force † ...59
71 Columbia † ...42
52 Mississippi St. ■ ...68
79 South Fla. ...69
63 Houston ...50
58 Charlotte ■ ...78
84 Southern Miss. ■ ...71
72 Tulane ...75
84 TCU ■ ...82
80 Southern Miss. ...82
66 Tulane ■ ...71
85 South Fla. ■ ...67
70 Memphis ...94
88 TCU ...85
80 Houston ■ ...52
77 DePaul ...71
87 Marquette ...98
70 Cincinnati ...87
79 Memphis ■ ...90
85 Charlotte † ...61
83 Marquette † ...76
63 St. Louis † ...62
78 Louisville ...83
82 La.-Lafayette ■ ...80
80 Siena ...71
71 St. John's (N.Y.) ...79

Nickname: Blazers
Colors: Forest Green & Old Gold
Arena: Bartow Arena
Capacity: 8,500; Year Built: 1987
AD: Watson Brown
SID: Aaron Jordan

ALA.-HUNTSVILLE
Huntsville, AL 35899 ...II

Coach: Lennie Acuff, Shorter 1988
2002-03 RESULTS (20-11)
82 Lane † ...71
80 Harding † ...83
64 Miles † ...59
70 LeMoyne-Owen † ...65
75 Athens St. ...57
69 Reinhardt ■ ...66
51 Carson-Newman ■ ...61
65 Athens St. ■ ...69
71 Southern Ark. ■ ...50
72 Kennesaw St. ■ ...76
59 Berry ■ ...67
57 West Ga. ■ ...51
56 Oakland City ...61

64 Valdosta St. ...55
65 West Ala. ...58
80 Montevallo ■ ...64
62 West Fla. ...76
69 Lincoln Memorial ■ ...56
58 North Ala. ...53
54 West Ga. ...64
81 Oakland City ■ ...65
70 West Fla. ■ ...64
77 Valdosta St. ■ ...76
82 West Ala. ...65
46 Lincoln Memorial ...49
60 Montevallo ...58
64 North Ala. ■ ...56
63 Ouachita Baptist † ...60
60 Lincoln Memorial † ...56
39 Henderson St. † ...54
61 Rollins ...76

Nickname: Chargers
Colors: Royal Blue & White
Arena: Spragins Hall
Capacity: 2,000; Year Built: 1977
AD: James E. Harris
SID: Antoine Bell

ALAS. ANCHORAGE
Anchorage, AK 99508 ...II

Coach: Charlie Bruns, Eastern Wash. 1968
2002-03 RESULTS (13-14)
87 Lincoln Chrst. ■ ...79
80 Cardinal Stritch ...95
69 Oklahoma St. ...98
69 Wyoming ■ ...77
69 Montana ■ ...52
71 Northwest Nazarene ...56
59 Seattle ...71
81 Colorado Mines ■ ...83
78 Colorado Mines ■ ...95
84 Montevallo ...60
94 Christian Bros. ■ ...96
81 Central Wash. ■ ...74
102 St. Martin's ■ ...63
68 Seattle Pacific ...86
88 Western Wash. ...83
55 Alas. Fairbanks ...78
88 Humboldt St. ■ ...90
78 Western Ore. ...68
80 Central Wash. ...78
92 St. Martin's ...85
79 Western Wash. ■ ...77
90 Seattle Pacific ...84
70 Alas. Fairbanks ■ ...73
69 Humboldt St. ...86
64 Western Ore. ...71
85 Seattle ■ ...70
74 Northwest Nazarene ■ ...79

Nickname: Seawolves
Colors: Green & Gold
Arena: UAA Sports Center
Capacity: 1,450; Year Built: 1977
AD: Steve Cobb
SID: Nate Sagan

ALAS. FAIRBANKS
Fairbanks, AK 99775-7500 ...II

Coach: Al Sokaitis, North Adams St. 1976
2002-03 RESULTS (20-8)
98 Walla Walla ■ ...71
112 Walla Walla ■ ...77
78 Wis.-Green Bay ■ ...55
64 Nebraska ...61
77 Weber St. ■ ...65
78 Seattle ...58
67 Northwest Nazarene ...63
81 Hawaii Pacific ...90
51 Hawaii Pacific ...64

76 Christian Bros. † ...63
94 Montevallo † ...61
76 St. Martin's ■ ...66
62 Central Wash. ■ ...60
79 Western Wash. ...97
71 Seattle Pacific ...95
78 Alas. Anchorage ■ ...55
83 Western Ore. ■ ...67
86 Humboldt St. ■ ...83
84 St. Martin's ...64
82 Central Wash. ...106
86 Seattle Pacific ■ ...78
72 Western Wash. ■ ...83
73 Alas. Anchorage ...70
78 Western Ore. ...82
90 Humboldt St. ...76
83 Northwest Nazarene ■ ...69
81 Seattle ■ ...59
76 Cal Poly Pomona † ...80

Nickname: Nanooks
Colors: Blue & Gold
Arena: Patty Center
Capacity: 2,000; Year Built: 1962
AD: Cory M. Schwartz
SID: Scott Roselius

ALBANY ST. (GA.)
Albany, GA 31705 ...II

Coach: John Davis, Albany St. (Ga.) 1969
2002-03 RESULTS (8-20)
67 Clayton St. ■ ...72
58 GC&SU ...65
64 GC&SU ...79
65 Kentucky St. ■ ...76
63 Columbus St. ■ ...80
82 Kentucky St. ...89
92 Lane ...91
87 West Ga. ...94
55 Columbus St. ...76
62 Clayton St. ...76
55 West Ga. † ...69
68 Tuskegee ■ ...65
69 LeMoyne-Owen ■ ...70
63 Miles ...57
73 Clark Atlanta ...64
67 Morehouse ...76
75 Benedict ...89
65 Paine ...57
67 Tuskegee ...74
66 West Ga. ■ ...74
66 Fort Valley St. ■ ...64
76 LeMoyne-Owen ...78
56 Benedict ...57
63 Paine ■ ...50
68 Morehouse ■ ...70
73 Clark Atlanta ■ ...79
67 Fort Valley St. ...64
65 Tuskegee † ...68

Nickname: Golden Rams
Colors: Blue & Gold
Arena: HPER Gym Complex
Capacity: 4,000; Year Built: 1998
AD: John I. Davis
SID: Edythe Bradley

ALBANY (N.Y.)
Albany, NY 12222 ...I

Coach: Will Brown, Dowling 1995
2002-03 RESULTS (7-21)
75 Siena ...79
53 Bucknell ■ ...56
55 Notre Dame ...90
47 Army ...43
62 Long Island ■ ...78
69 Robert Morris ■ ...67
65 Quinnipiac ■ ...78
79 Syracuse ...109

75	Lafayette	83
61	Colgate ■	54
71	Maine	90
63	Boston U. ■	66
61	New Hampshire ■	58
53	Vermont ■	63
87	Stony Brook	92
59	Binghamton	86
85	Dartmouth ■	84
68	Hartford	80
80	Northeastern ■	89
50	Boston U.	78
71	Maine ■	82
82	Stony Brook ■	74
87	New Hampshire	79
59	Binghamton ■	76
53	Hartford ■	67
54	Northeastern	69
60	Vermont	69
62	Vermont †	81

Nickname: Great Danes
Colors: Purple & Gold
Arena: Recreation & Convocation Center
   Capacity: 5,000; Year Built: 1992
AD: Lee McElroy
SID: Brian DePasquale

ALBERTUS MAGNUS
New Haven, CT 06511-1189...III

Coach: Bob McMahon, Boston U. 1976
2002-03 RESULTS (18-10)
81	Western Conn. St.	97
72	Coast Guard	70
55	Rivier	74
73	Wesleyan (Conn.)	75
72	Framingham St. ■	68
82	Southern Vt. ■	81
83	Suffolk ■	71
86	Western New Eng.	80
88	Daniel Webster	70
80	Norwich	70
80	Emmanuel (Mass.)	77
81	Johnson & Wales	106
87	Emerson	76
108	Daniel Webster ■	86
77	Southern Vt.	86
85	Western New Eng. ■	69
95	Emmanuel (Mass.) ■	63
80	Rivier ■	58
67	Emerson	88
71	Eastern Conn. St.	69
93	Johnson & Wales ■	94
84	Westfield St.	92
102	Suffolk	99
72	Norwich ■	62
74	Emmanuel (Mass.) ■	71
85	Western New Eng.	79
73	Southern Vt. †	89
59	Endicott ■	89

Nickname: Falcons
Colors: Royal Blue & White
Arena: Cosgrove Marcus Messer Center
   Capacity: 700; Year Built: 1989
AD: Jay Moran
SID: Jeff Mills

ALBION
Albion, MI 49224 III

Coach: Mike Turner, Albion 1969
2002-03 RESULTS (22-5)
89	Medaille ■	45
85	Tri-State ■	78
62	Ohio Northern †	76
85	Oberlin ■	60
84	Madonna ■	59
49	Wartburg †	62
88	Rose-Hulman	61
85	Madonna	76

82	DePauw ■	64
86	Manchester	58
80	Embry-Riddle	72
95	Ursinus †	64
79	Alma	43
72	Adrian ■	63
76	Calvin	64
89	Marygrove ■	54
52	Hope ■	57
82	Kalamazoo	89
79	Olivet	68
66	Alma ■	44
83	Adrian	54
77	Calvin	69
69	Hope	65
72	Kalamazoo ■	64
76	Olivet	57
65	Adrian ■	59
48	Hope ■	61

Nickname: Britons
Colors: Purple & Gold
Arena: Kresge Gymnasium
   Capacity: 1,400; Year Built: 1925
AD: Peter M. Hart
SID: Bobby Lee

ALBRIGHT
Reading, PA 19612-5234.........III

Coach: Rick Ferry, Susquehanna 1985
2002-03 RESULTS (4-19)
89	Practical Bible ■	48
42	Randolph-Macon ■	66
83	Wilkes	90
59	Moravian ■	66
75	Messiah ■	71
74	Gwynedd-Mercy ■	86
57	Alvernia ■	75
81	Hamilton †	85
66	York (Pa.)	89
67	Lebanon Valley ■	64
80	Susquehanna	100
81	Villa Julie ■	93
70	Juniata	77
67	Elizabethtown ■	105
66	Widener	56
81	Messiah	95
54	DeSales ■	59
74	Moravian ■	84
54	Susquehanna ■	74
66	Lebanon Valley	88
74	Juniata ■	76
58	Widener ■	74
59	Elizabethtown	95

Nickname: Lions
Colors: Red & White
Arena: Bollman Center
   Capacity: 2,500; Year Built: 1950
AD: Sally Stetler
SID: Jeff Feiler

ALCORN ST.
Alcorn State, MS 39096-7500 ...I

Coach: Davey L. Whitney, Kentucky St. 1953
2002-03 RESULTS (14-19)
70	Southern Miss.	78
61	Baylor †	81
67	UTEP	53
72	Jacksonville St.	75
62	South Fla.	81
58	Ark.-Little Rock	68
67	Jacksonville St. ■	74
66	La.-Lafayette	99
50	Tennessee Tech †	62
68	Bradley †	95
74	Tex.-Pan American †	56
63	Kentucky	94
70	Prairie View ■	77

70	Texas Southern ■	71
72	Jackson St.	76
66	Grambling	83
76	Mississippi Val. ■	69
79	Ark.-Pine Bluff ■	50
66	Alabama A&M	65
49	Alabama St.	75
93	Southern U.	87
93	Jackson St. ■	91
88	Grambling ■	79
65	Mississippi Val.	73
74	Ark.-Pine Bluff	68
79	Alabama A&M ■	71
69	Alabama St. ■	50
63	Southern U.	62
69	Texas Southern	79
64	Prairie View	75
58	Alabama St.	55
71	Prairie View †	64
68	Texas Southern †	77

Nickname: Braves
Colors: Purple & Gold
Arena: Davey L. Whitney Complex
   Capacity: 7,000; Year Built: 1974
AD: Robert Raines
SID: Peter G. Forest

ALDERSON-BROADDUS
Philippi, WV 26416..................II

Coach: Greg Zimmerman, Alderson-Broaddus 1978
2002-03 RESULTS (25-7)
86	Le Moyne †	98
84	Mercy †	73
68	Franklin Pierce †	60
87	St. Paul's †	78
89	Ohio Valley ■	46
71	Pitt.-Johnstown ■	59
47	Clayton St. †	87
104	Mount Olive †	106
82	West Liberty St. ■	71
68	Salem Int'l ■	79
85	Ohio Valley	61
66	Wheeling Jesuit	75
81	Shepherd ■	66
87	Bluefield St. ■	71
86	West Va. Tech ■	81
90	West Virginia St.	69
69	Charleston (W.Va.)	82
91	Concord	68
81	Fairmont St.	64
88	Davis & Elkins	75
97	West Va. Wesleyan ■	62
90	Pitt.-Johnstown	65
97	Glenville St.	89
97	Davis & Elkins ■	60
83	West Va. Wesleyan	73
95	Shepherd	75
91	Glenville St. ■	76
102	Ohio Valley ■	72
73	Glenville St. †	68
78	Wheeling Jesuit †	76
75	Charleston (W.Va.)	62
76	Barton †	81

Nickname: Battlers
Colors: Blue, Gray & Gold
Arena: Rex Pyles Arena
   Capacity: 2,500; Year Built: 1968
AD: Jerrell D. Long
SID: Michelle Odai

ALFRED
Alfred, NY 14802....................III

Coach: Jay Murphy, Brockport St. 1981
2002-03 RESULTS (5-20)
40	Rochester	95
94	Fredonia St. †	87
75	Hilbert ■	59

70	Cortland St.	63
56	Potsdam St.	72
62	St. Lawrence	80
55	Randolph-Macon	93
60	Thiel †	79
69	Allegheny ■	88
62	Geneseo St.	83
72	Nazareth	83
55	Rochester Inst.	73
75	Pitt.-Bradford ■	79
62	Hartwick	59
56	Utica	69
65	St. John Fisher	94
63	Ithaca ■	74
77	Elmira ■	72
63	Rochester Inst. ■	80
76	Nazareth ■	89
62	Elmira	71
63	Ithaca	77
73	St. John Fisher ■	80
58	Utica ■	80
73	Hartwick ■	87

Nickname: Saxons
Colors: Purple & Gold
Arena: James A. McLane Physical
   Capacity: 3,200; Year Built: 1971
AD: James M. Moretti
SID: Mark Whitehouse

ALLEGHENY
Meadville, PA 16335 III

Coach: Rob Clune, Albany (N.Y.) 1981
2002-03 RESULTS (16-12)
84	Grove City †	87
96	Wash. & Jeff. ■	71
84	Juniata ■	91
78	Olivet ■	83
82	Thiel ■	81
66	Wittenberg	70
75	Calif. (Pa.)	82
70	Westminster (Pa.)	57
80	Earlham	60
63	Wabash ■	74
88	Alfred	69
52	Penn St.-Behrend ■	53
83	Kenyon	68
69	Wooster ■	80
86	Ohio Wesleyan	93
103	Hiram ■	94
83	Denison	88
98	Oberlin	81
66	Wittenberg ■	63
74	Wooster	97
94	Kenyon	79
99	Oberlin ■	60
87	Denison ■	61
109	Hiram	76
85	Ohio Wesleyan ■	81
92	Earlham ■	90
73	Wittenberg †	72
71	Wooster	93

Nickname: Gators
Colors: Blue & Gold
Arena: Wise Center
   Capacity: 1,000; Year Built: 1997
AD: Larry Lee
SID: Jeff Schaefer

ALMA
Alma, MI 48801 III

Coach: Ed Kohtala, Maine 1981
2002-03 RESULTS (1-24)
58	Wittenberg	99
59	John Carroll †	93
73	Spring Arbor	82
49	Cornerstone	94
56	Franklin	76
80	Ind.-Southeast †	108

61	Northwood	93
67	Elmhurst ■	83
75	Luther †	85
66	Manchester	69
56	Rochester College ■	92
93	St. Mary's (Mich.) ■	78
43	Albion ■	79
66	Kalamazoo	89
51	Hope	101
75	Olivet ■	95
60	Adrian ■	68
57	Calvin ■	87
44	Albion	66
68	Kalamazoo ■	86
79	Hope	108
77	Olivet	78
56	Adrian ■	75
72	Calvin	95
75	Hope	101

Nickname: Scots
Colors: Maroon & Cream
Arena: Cappaert Gymnasium
 Capacity: 3,000; Year Built: 1967
AD: James Cole
SID: Dave Girrard

ALVERNIA
Reading, PA 19607..................III

Coach: Jack McCloskey, Kutztown 1964
2002-03 RESULTS (21-9)

88	Salisbury ■	58
62	Geneseo St. ■	56
91	Cal Lutheran †	70
65	Whitworth †	80
63	Misericordia	54
92	Neumann ■	78
65	Eastern	66
55	Lebanon Valley ■	54
75	Albright ■	57
61	Frank. & Marsh. ■	101
82	Gettysburg ■	63
90	Arcadia ■	55
67	Wesley ■	57
60	Marywood	56
57	Gwynedd-Mercy	68
63	Cabrini ■	49
54	Cheyney	55
60	Neumann	73
71	Eastern ■	55
61	Misericordia ■	65
61	Wesley	58
61	Gwynedd-Mercy ■	70
61	Cabrini	53
85	Marywood ■	82
72	Arcadia	65
83	Eastern ■	56
67	Cabrini	63
80	Neumann	73
58	Mary Washington ■	53
69	Randolph-Macon	72

Nickname: Crusaders
Colors: Maroon & Gold
Arena: Physical Education Center
 Capacity: 1,500; Year Built: 1987
AD: John McCloskey
SID: Jon King

AMERICAN
Washington, DC 20016..............I

Coach: Jeff Jones, Virginia 1982
2002-03 RESULTS (16-14)

57	Missouri	72
79	UNC Greensboro	80
61	Virginia Tech	69
72	Liberty	67
73	Radford ■	49
61	Howard	58
65	Col. of Charleston	68

57	Fairfield	68
76	Elon	51
55	Wagner	69
81	George Washington ■	75
54	St. Francis (Pa.) ■	64
55	Pennsylvania	66
52	Bucknell	63
70	Navy	53
54	Lehigh	57
58	Colgate ■	55
72	Holy Cross ■	49
66	Lafayette	67
79	Army	64
70	Bucknell ■	56
64	Navy	61
69	Lehigh ■	59
66	Holy Cross	68
59	Colgate	60
77	Army ■	43
79	Lafayette ■	62
72	Navy †	57
74	Lafayette †	55
64	Holy Cross	72

Nickname: Eagles
Colors: AU Red & Blue
Arena: Bender Arena
 Capacity: 4,500; Year Built: 1988
AD: Tom George
SID: Shaun May

AMERICAN INT'L
Springfield, MA 01109-3189....II

Coach: Arthur Luptowski, Bloomsburg 1973
2002-03 RESULTS (9-19)

72	Mercyhurst	76
74	West Liberty St. †	60
59	Bentley	71
87	St. Michael's ■	80
46	Le Moyne ■	50
55	St. Anselm	53
83	Pace ■	59
69	Queens (N.Y.)	74
72	Merrimack ■	75
74	New Haven	81
78	Dowling ■	83
47	Southern Conn. St.	57
53	Assumption	68
69	Bryant ■	68
62	St. Rose	76
51	Mass.-Lowell	65
57	Southern N.H. ■	64
55	Franklin Pierce ■	68
58	St. Anselm ■	52
64	Le Moyne	76
67	St. Michael's	77
62	Bryant	70
76	Assumption ■	80
82	Southern N.H.	59
65	Mass.-Lowell ■	73
68	Franklin Pierce ■	56
56	Stonehill ■	37
51	Assumption	54

Nickname: Yellow Jackets
Colors: Gold, White & Black
Arena: Henry A. Butova Gym
 Capacity: 2,500; Year Built: 1965
AD: Robert E. Burke
SID: George Sylvester

AMHERST
Amherst, MA 01002................III

Coach: David Hixon, Amherst 1975
2002-03 RESULTS (24-5)

91	New England Col. ■	55
74	WPI ■	57
115	Mass. Liberal Arts	84
68	Clark (Mass.) ■	62

77	Springfield ■	56
100	Westfield St. ■	63
80	Worcester St.	62
69	Webber	77
92	Salve Regina ■	58
72	Western New Eng.	66
65	Williams	74
92	Wesleyan (Conn.)	77
92	Colby	62
86	Bowdoin	56
94	Lasell ■	65
90	Middlebury ■	60
67	Williams ■	61
66	Tufts	83
90	Bates	60
78	Trinity (Conn.)	73
78	Brandeis ■	50
79	Connecticut Col. ■	62
81	Wesleyan (Conn.) ■	72
78	Bowdoin ■	67
87	Wesleyan (Conn.)	73
70	Williams ■	74
84	Southern Vt. ■	60
74	Rochester †	68
75	Williams	91

Nickname: Lord Jeffs
Colors: Purple & White
Arena: LeFrak Gymnasium
 Capacity: 2,450; Year Built: 1986
AD: Peter J. Gooding
SID: Kevin Graber

ANDERSON (IND.)
Anderson, IN 46012-3495.......III

Coach: Denny Lehnus, Anderson 1965
2002-03 RESULTS (17-10)

104	Maryville (Mo.) ■	86
77	Webster ■	80
88	Ohio Dominican ■	86
90	Miami-Middletown ■	74
83	Cedarville ■	94
84	Defiance ■	79
84	Mt. St. Joseph	75
75	Manchester ■	60
96	Thomas More	69
113	Ind.-Northwest ■	54
86	Fla. Gulf Coast	90
81	Johnson & Wales (FL)	75
89	Bluffton ■	87
98	Transylvania ■	81
99	Franklin	90
83	Hanover	85
66	Mt. St. Joseph	67
90	Defiance	101
70	Manchester ■	65
84	Bluffton	93
101	Thomas More ■	76
85	Franklin	79
68	Transylvania	70
91	Hanover ■	93
70	Bluffton	58
70	Mt. St. Joseph †	63
60	Hanover	79

Nickname: Ravens
Colors: Orange & Black
Arena: O.C. Lewis Gym
 Capacity: 3,000; Year Built: 1962
AD: A. Barrett Bates
SID: Justin Bates

ANDERSON (S.C.)
Anderson, SC 29621................II

Coach: Doug Novak, Tennessee 1990
2002-03 RESULTS (9-19)

75	Charleston So.	77
77	Wingate	93
68	Mount Olive	76
51	Belmont Abbey ■	98

78	North Greenville ■	57
59	Michigan Tech †	90
59	Fort Lewis †	103
69	Emmanuel (Ga.) ■	56
56	Barton ■	68
72	Limestone ■	79
47	Presbyterian	61
79	Queens (N.C.)	105
73	Longwood ■	60
84	St. Andrews	77
75	Lees-McRae ■	61
70	Pfeiffer	92
63	Erskine	65
64	Coker ■	74
79	Mount Olive ■	83
80	Barton	85
53	Belmont Abbey ■	61
68	Queens (N.C.) ■	77
77	Longwood	73
88	St. Andrews ■	66
72	Limestone	56
84	Lees-McRae ■	50
92	Pfeiffer	97
37	Erskine	48

Nickname: Trojans
Colors: Gold & Black
Arena: Abney Athletic Center
 Capacity: 1,500; Year Built: 1979
AD: Robert G. Beville
SID: Cobb Oxford

ANGELO ST.
San Angelo, TX 76909 II

Coach: Joe Esposito, Marist 1988
2002-03 RESULTS (14-13)

89	Rhema ■	61
71	East Tex. Baptist ■	67
65	Incarnate Word	70
70	St. Edward's †	67
57	Northeastern St.	74
79	Central Okla.	97
107	Hillsdale Free Will ■	52
89	Mary Hardin-Baylor ■	75
64	Hawaii-Hilo ■	82
110	UC Santa Cruz †	59
78	East Central ■	52
83	Southeastern Okla. ■	58
69	Southwestern Okla.	57
71	Cameron	70
85	Abilene Christian	76
47	Tarleton St. ■	63
72	West Tex. A&M	80
90	Eastern N.M. ■	93
70	Abilene Christian ■	73
76	Midwestern St.	77
81	Tex. A&M-Kingsville.	80
83	Tex. A&M-Commerce	95
73	Tex. A&M-Commerce ■	68
82	Tex. A&M-Kingsville ■	67
88	Eastern N.M.	93
73	West Tex. A&M	84
79	Midwestern St. ■	84

Nickname: Rams
Colors: Blue & Gold
Arena: Junell Center/Stephens Arena
 Capacity: 5,500; Year Built: 2001
AD: Jerry Vandergriff
SID: M.L. Stark Hinkle

ANNA MARIA
Paxton, MA 01612-1198 III

Coach: David Shea, Anna Maria 1993
2002-03 RESULTS (15-12)

59	Suffolk †	92
73	Mount Ida †	84
81	Worcester St. ■	70
51	WPI ■	70
80	Becker	68

83	Thomas †	71
47	Newbury †	73
73	Fitchburg St.	72
78	Newbury	57
60	Eastern Nazarene	48
66	Roger Williams ■	62
81	Salve Regina	79
67	Eastern Nazarene ■	64
76	Endicott ■	86
72	New England ■	98
53	Curry	66
61	Roger Williams	80
69	Nichols ■	70
60	Wentworth Inst.	57
59	New England Col. ■	51
50	Gordon	73
82	Salve Regina ■	75
73	Nichols	71
69	Curry ■	65
57	Colby-Sawyer	70
75	Gordon ■	67
70	Endicott	81

Nickname: AMCATS
Colors: Royal Blue & White
Arena: Fuller Activities Center
  Capacity: 500; Year Built: 1986
AD: Leonard Smith
SID: Joseph Brady

APPALACHIAN ST.
Boone, NC 28608 ...I

Coach: Houston Fancher, Middle Tenn. 1988
2002-03 RESULTS (19-10)

104	Mars Hill ■	72
103	Charlotte ■	100
56	South Carolina	71
78	Marquette	101
80	Greensboro ■	47
87	Southern Methodist ■	65
62	Georgia	99
83	James Madison	76
85	Bluefield Col. ■	65
108	East Tenn. St. ■	94
91	UNC Greensboro ■	60
87	Ga. Southern	81
99	Gardner-Webb ■	98
107	Chattanooga	99
69	Western Caro.	70
85	VMI	68
83	Furman ■	67
82	Gardner-Webb	88
75	Citadel ■	65
99	Western Caro. ■	69
86	Davidson	99
83	VMI ■	64
96	Col. of Charleston ■	108
76	Wofford	72
81	Davidson ■	94
71	UNC Greensboro	68
78	East Tenn. St.	88
73	Citadel †	63
67	Chattanooga †	98

Nickname: Mountaineers
Colors: Black & Gold
Arena: Holmes Convocation Center
  Capacity: 8,325; Year Built: 2000
AD: Roachel Laney
SID: Kelby Siler

ARCADIA
Glenside, PA 19038-3295 ...III

Coach: Mike Doyle, Philadelphia 1988
2002-03 RESULTS (11-14)

52	Gettysburg	70
71	Villa Julie †	66
82	Muhlenberg ■	75
44	Richard Stockton	67
73	Marywood	78
59	Gwynedd-Mercy ■	62
55	Neumann	70
66	Widener ■	69
80	Delaware Valley ■	73
65	Swarthmore ■	61
55	Alvernia	90
89	Misericordia ■	77
69	Wesley ■	64
62	Cabrini	84
77	Wesley	69
59	DeSales	67
53	Gwynedd-Mercy	78
70	Marywood ■	67
76	Eastern	54
63	Misericordia	72
47	Cabrini ■	54
79	Neumann ■	70
66	Eastern ■	68
84	Phila. Bible	74
65	Alvernia	72

Nickname: Knights
Colors: Scarlet & Gray
Arena: Kuch Center
  Capacity: 1,500; Year Built: 1993
AD: Shirley M. Liddle
SID: Tom Carlin

ARIZONA
Tucson, AZ 85721-0096 ...I

Coach: Lute Olson, Augsburg 1956
2002-03 RESULTS (28-4)

107	Western Ky. ■	68
101	Northern Ariz. ■	66
91	St. Louis ■	58
89	San Diego St.	81
73	Texas ■	70
65	LSU	66
95	Davidson ■	69
85	Boston U. ■	71
81	Oregon	72
80	Oregon St.	65
82	Washington St. ■	69
79	Washington	61
81	Southern California	72
87	UCLA	52
71	Arizona St. ■	63
91	Kansas	74
77	Stanford ■	82
95	California ■	80
88	Washington	85
75	Washington St.	62
106	UCLA ■	70
86	Southern California	59
92	Arizona St.	72
88	California	75
72	Stanford	69
72	Oregon St. ■	60
88	Oregon	80
89	UCLA †	96
80	Vermont †	51
96	Gonzaga †	95
88	Notre Dame †	71
75	Kansas †	78

Nickname: Wildcats
Colors: Cardinal & Navy
Arena: McKale Center
  Capacity: 14,545; Year Built: 1973
AD: Jim Livengood
SID: Richard Paige

ARIZONA ST.
Tempe, AZ 85287-2505 ...I

Coach: Rob Evans, New Mexico St. 1968
2002-03 RESULTS (20-12)

59	Morehead St. ■	56
65	Kentucky †	82
101	Chaminade †	72
83	Utah †	79
85	Lafayette ■	62
60	Brigham Young ■	64
55	Utah	78
76	Nevada ■	63
70	Purdue †	53
79	Bucknell ■	52
75	Nebraska ■	63
67	Oregon St.	47
73	Oregon	94
89	Washington ■	57
96	Washington St. ■	55
75	UCLA	64
74	Southern California	76
63	Arizona	71
75	California ■	70
57	Stanford ■	58
87	Washington St.	54
79	Washington	77
108	Southern California ■	78
85	UCLA ■	69
72	Arizona ■	92
77	Stanford	88
72	California	80
91	Oregon ■	77
74	Oregon St. ■	64
82	Oregon †	83
84	Memphis †	71
76	Kansas †	108

Nickname: Sun Devils
Colors: Maroon & Gold
Arena: Wells Fargo Arena
  Capacity: 14,198; Year Built: 1974
AD: Eugene Smith
SID: Doug Tammaro

ARKANSAS
Fayetteville, AR 72701 ...I

Coach: Stan Heath, Eastern Mich. 1988
2002-03 RESULTS (9-19)

81	Jackson St. ■	44
64	Oral Roberts	76
60	Tulsa ■	61
66	Troy St.	74
58	Illinois †	62
72	Louisiana Tech ■	60
78	Sam Houston St. ■	67
70	Texas St.	60
75	Centenary (La.)	51
45	Oklahoma St.	71
67	Memphis ■	72
51	Alabama	61
37	Auburn ■	52
64	Georgia ■	81
73	LSU ■	65
54	Mississippi	73
66	Florida	77
81	Alabama ■	70
54	Mississippi St.	84
62	Tennessee	70
65	South Carolina	72
50	Kentucky	66
56	LSU	75
60	Vanderbilt	50
53	Mississippi St. ■	51
54	Auburn	69
54	Mississippi	64
56	LSU †	85

Nickname: Razorbacks
Colors: Cardinal & White
Arena: Bud Walton Arena
  Capacity: 19,200; Year Built: 1993
AD: J. Frank Broyles
SID: Robby Edwards

ARKANSAS ST.
State University, AR 72467 ...I

Coach: Dickey Nutt, Oklahoma St. 1982
2002-03 RESULTS (13-15)

83	Southeast Mo. St. ■	71
61	Samford	70
52	Air Force ■	57
67	Samford ■	68
120	Lyon ■	55
103	Lincoln (Mo.) ■	48
64	Southern Miss.	48
92	Ark.-Pine Bluff ■	49
65	Southwest Mo. St.	72
73	Toledo	90
54	Utah St.	72
71	UMKC †	56
58	Middle Tenn. ■	65
69	Western Ky. ■	77
68	Denver	82
68	North Texas	65
100	Tex. A&M-Corp. Chris ■	73
70	Ark.-Little Rock	77
68	New Orleans	70
83	South Ala.	63
86	Ark.-Little Rock ■	76
67	Florida Int'l	65
55	Middle Tenn.	79
63	Western Ky.	69
84	La.-Lafayette ■	72
67	New Mexico St. ■	82
85	Florida Int'l ■	65
76	Denver †	82

Nickname: Indians
Colors: Scarlet & Black
Arena: Convocation Center
  Capacity: 10,563; Year Built: 1987
AD: Dean Lee
SID: Bill Bowen

ARKANSAS TECH
Russellville, AR 72801-2222 ...II

Coach: Robert Thompson, Belhaven 1992
2002-03 RESULTS (11-16)

79	Central Baptist ■	67
79	Southwestern Okla. ■	68
66	Lincoln Memorial ■	61
64	Northeastern St. ■	84
66	Southwestern Okla.	82
90	Drury ■	75
75	Drury	94
96	Ark.-Monticello ■	91
83	Southern Ark. ■	73
62	Central Ark.	67
66	Christian Bros. ■	79
73	Williams Baptist	67
49	Ouachita Baptist	68
88	Ark. Baptist	103
81	Williams Baptist ■	65
70	Henderson St. ■	79
66	Harding	91
76	Delta St. ■	75
60	Ark.-Monticello	76
70	Southern Ark.	74
65	Central Ark. ■	59
60	Christian Bros.	74
55	Ouachita Baptist ■	75
112	Ark. Baptist ■	69
56	Henderson St.	99
71	Harding ■	94
56	Delta St.	84

Nickname: Wonder Boys
Colors: Green & Gold
Arena: Tucker Coliseum
  Capacity: 3,500; Year Built: 1976
AD: Joe Foley
SID: Larry Smith

ARK.-LITTLE ROCK
Little Rock, AR 72204................I

Coach: Porter Moser, Creighton 1990
2002-03 RESULTS (18-12)
65	Hawaii	81
56	Cal St. Fullerton †	43
82	Central Ark. ■	69
84	Colorado St. ■	75
49	Memphis	73
68	Alcorn St. ■	58
84	Minnesota	86
83	Ark.-Pine Bluff	71
81	Southeast Mo. St. ■	56
76	Prairie View ■	65
54	Southern Miss.	70
110	Pepperdine †	116
48	Portland St. †	41
82	Harding ■	80
66	Western Ky. ■	74
71	Middle Tenn. ■	62
88	North Texas	80
55	Denver	72
77	Arkansas St. ■	70
59	South Ala.	65
85	New Orleans ■	83
76	Arkansas St.	86
46	Florida Int'l	45
51	Western Ky.	70
74	Middle Tenn.	58
72	New Mexico St. ■	64
81	La.-Lafayette ■	85
67	Florida Int'l ■	62
74	North Texas †	73
61	New Mexico St. †	78

Nickname: Trojans
Colors: Maroon & Silver
Arena: Alltel Arena
  Capacity: 18,000; Year Built: 1999
AD: Chris Peterson
SID: Kevin Taukersley

ARK.-MONTICELLO
Monticello, AR 71656-3596......II

Coach: Mike Newell, Sam Houston St.
1973
2002-03 RESULTS (9-18)
86	LeMoyne-Owen †	98
76	Miles †	66
82	Lambuth ■	83
54	Cameron	68
64	Texas-Arlington	87
70	Bradley	107
94	Central Baptist ■	69
79	Abilene Christian †	81
74	Texas Col.	53
105	Central Baptist	77
76	Xavier (La.) ■	70
91	Arkansas Tech	96
65	Henderson St. ■	71
67	Harding	88
58	Delta St. ■	72
76	Southern Ark.	75
76	Central Ark. ■	90
65	Christian Bros.	84
73	Ouachita Baptist ■	72
76	Arkansas Tech ■	60
60	Henderson St.	89
71	Harding ■	84
71	Delta St.	98
76	Southern Ark. ■	54
68	Central Ark.	83
79	Christian Bros. ■	85
59	Ouachita Baptist	63

Nickname: Boll Weevils
Colors: Kelly Green & White
Arena: Steelman Fieldhouse
  Capacity: 2,600; Year Built: 1959
AD: Alvy Early
SID: Chris Pluto

ARK.-PINE BLUFF
Pine Bluff, AR 71601 I

Coach: Van Holt, Ark.-Pine Bluff 1965
2002-03 RESULTS (4-24)
75	Georgia Tech	113
54	Memphis	78
43	Illinois	96
49	Pittsburgh	89
39	Kansas St.	76
71	Ark.-Little Rock ■	83
49	Arkansas St.	92
42	Miami (Fla.)	79
38	Mississippi	71
46	Iowa St.	90
52	Mississippi Val. ■	72
33	Alabama St. ■	43
65	Alabama A&M ■	66
44	Southern U.	52
50	Alcorn St.	79
57	Texas Southern ■	74
57	Prairie View ■	72
63	Grambling	99
62	Jackson St.	58
33	Alabama St.	57
54	Alabama A&M ■	72
88	Southern U. ■	79
68	Alcorn St. ■	74
58	Texas Southern	54
53	Prairie View	66
63	Grambling ■	68
52	Jackson St. ■	50
68	Mississippi Val.	75

Nickname: Golden Lions
Colors: Black & Gold
Arena: K.L. Johnson HPER Complex
  Capacity: 4,500; Year Built: 1982
AD: Craig Curry
SID: Carl Whimper

ARMSTRONG ATLANTIC
Savannah, GA 31419-1997 II

Coach: Jeff Burkhamer, Alderson-
Broaddus 1984
2002-03 RESULTS (14-14)
74	Queens (N.C.) †	75
61	Eckerd	82
60	Fort Valley St.	66
60	Clayton St. ■	65
47	Presbyterian	53
76	Fort Valley St. ■	59
56	Eckerd ■	67
42	Lenoir-Rhyne ■	77
50	Francis Marion ■	48
69	Lander	58
62	S.C.-Spartanburg ■	63
77	UNC Pembroke ■	53
73	S.C.-Aiken	67
61	Columbus St.	77
56	Francis Marion	51
55	S.C.-Spartanburg ■	65
59	GC&SU	72
58	UNC Pembroke	40
55	Augusta St. ■	59
65	Kennesaw St. ■	61
64	North Fla.	71
62	Clayton St.	58
62	North Fla. ■	48
79	Columbus St. ■	62
81	GC&SU ■	67
63	Kennesaw St.	57
67	UNC Pembroke †	59
57	S.C.-Spartanburg †	61

Nickname: Pirates
Colors: Maroon & Gold
Arena: Alumni Arena
  Capacity: 5,000; Year Built: 1995
AD: Eddie Aenchbacher
SID: Chad Jackson

ARMY
West Point, NY 10996-2101......I

Coach: Jim Crews, Indiana 1976
2002-03 RESULTS (5-22)
53	Duke	101
54	Fairleigh Dickinson	76
77	NYCCT ■	31
75	Sacred Heart ■	73
44	Columbia	58
43	Albany (N.Y.) ■	47
59	Stony Brook	68
57	Marist	74
50	Cornell ■	69
63	Coast Guard ■	51
65	Fairleigh Dickinson ■	63
45	Holy Cross	61
59	Lafayette ■	73
58	Colgate	86
69	Yale ■	63
38	Bucknell	53
61	Lehigh	78
46	Navy ■	65
64	American ■	79
45	Holy Cross	53
43	Lafayette	57
58	Colgate ■	68
52	Lehigh ■	59
65	Bucknell ■	66
43	American	77
56	Navy	62
40	Holy Cross †	58

Nickname: Black Knights/Cadets
Colors: Black, Gold & Gray
Arena: Christl Arena
  Capacity: 5,043; Year Built: 1985
AD: Richard I. Greenspan
SID: Mike Albright

ASHLAND
Ashland, OH 44805................II

Coach: Roger Lyons, Ashland 1974
2002-03 RESULTS (16-11)
82	West Virginia St. †	75
120	Bellarmine	115
98	Malone ■	69
91	West Va. Wesleyan ■	81
74	Tiffin	65
104	Saginaw Valley ■	76
85	Northwood ■	65
86	Tiffin	67
56	Lincoln Memorial	70
90	Calumet Col. ■	72
88	Wilberforce ■	80
75	Northern Mich.	71
50	Michigan Tech	74
84	Lake Superior St.	59
89	Grand Valley St. ■	97
80	Ferris St. ■	77
82	Findlay ■	87
65	Wayne St. (Mich.) ■	68
66	Hillsdale	95
76	Gannon ■	67
81	Mercyhurst ■	63
78	Findlay	92
71	Hillsdale ■	81
88	Wayne St. (Mich.) ■	92
74	Mercyhurst	73
62	Gannon	88
75	Michigan Tech	91

Nickname: Eagles
Colors: Purple & Gold
Arena: Charles Kates Gym
  Capacity: 3,200; Year Built: 1967
AD: Bill Goldring
SID: Al King

ASSUMPTION
Worcester, MA 01609 II

Coach: Tom Ackerman, St. Vincent 1979
2002-03 RESULTS (20-11)
80	Philadelphia U. †	76
88	West Chester	75
69	Merrimack	75
70	St. Anselm ■	56
69	St. Michael's	66
89	St. Rose ■	87
78	Le Moyne	82
80	Stonehill ■	67
85	Daemen ■	50
91	Queens (N.Y.) ■	72
79	Southern Conn. St. ■	83
77	Pace	74
68	American Int'l ■	53
58	Bryant	51
83	Southern N.H. ■	51
67	Franklin Pierce	70
66	Mass.-Lowell	75
83	Le Moyne ■	75
92	St. Michael's ■	79
72	St. Anselm	79
71	Green Mountain	51
80	American Int'l	76
60	Bryant ■	64
64	Mass.-Lowell ■	62
73	Franklin Pierce ■	79
75	Southern N.H.	80
79	Bentley ■	76
54	American Int'l ■	51
94	Pace	72
67	Mass.-Lowell	77
75	C.W. Post †	81

Nickname: Greyhounds
Colors: Royal Blue & White
Arena: Andrew Laska Gym
  Capacity: 3,000; Year Built: 1962
AD: Rita M. Castagna
SID: Steve Morris

AUBURN
Auburn , AL 36849-5113...........I

Coach: Cliff Ellis, Florida St. 1968
2002-03 RESULTS (22-12)
81	Wofford ■	63
100	Georgia St. ■	71
70	Western Ky. †	89
77	Southeastern La.	47
85	South Carolina St. ■	65
82	Rutgers	70
72	Murray St. ■	53
54	Western Mich.	72
94	P.R.-Mayaguez	64
63	Denver †	58
94	Troy St. †	66
92	Southern Miss. ■	46
90	North Texas	65
62	Vanderbilt ■	59
52	Arkansas	37
67	South Carolina	60
77	Alabama ■	68
51	Kentucky	67
79	Georgia	85
57	Tennessee ■	60
77	Mississippi ■	71
56	LSU ■	54
68	Alabama	84
46	Mississippi St. ■	63
80	Mississippi	75
63	LSU	94
70	Florida ■	73
69	Arkansas ■	54
45	Mississippi St.	67
66	Tennessee †	53
58	Kentucky †	78
65	St. Joseph's †	63
68	Wake Forest †	62
78	Syracuse †	79

Nickname: Tigers
Colors: Burnt Orange & Navy Blue
Arena: Beard-Eaves-Memorial
   Capacity: 10,500; Year Built: 1969
AD: David E. Housel
SID: Chuck Gallina

AUGSBURG
Minneapolis, MN 55454..........III

Coach: Brian Ammann, Augsburg 1985
2002-03 RESULTS (11-14)
68	Crown ■	62
71	St. Scholastica	61
114	Grinnell †	144
97	Peru St. †	84
53	Gust. Adolphus ■	71
67	Carleton	77
72	Macalester ■	76
60	St. John's (Minn.)	66
53	Augustana (S.D.) ■	89
57	St. Thomas (Minn.) ■	75
71	Bethel (Minn.) ■	77
62	Hamline	58
70	St. Olaf ■	60
71	St. Mary's (Minn.)	64
74	Concordia-M'head	81
64	Gust. Adolphus	73
77	Carleton ■	62
79	Macalester	69
60	St. John's (Minn.) ■	59
67	St. Thomas (Minn.)	73
74	Bethel (Minn.)	62
69	Hamline ■	78
49	St. Olaf	69
62	St. Mary's (Minn.) ■	59
53	Concordia-M'head ■	72

Nickname: Auggies
Colors: Maroon & Gray
Arena: Si Melby Hall
   Capacity: 2,200; Year Built: 1961
AD: Paul Grauer
SID: Don Stoner

AUGUSTA ST.
Augusta, GA 30904................II

Coach: Gary Tuell, Louisville 1973
2002-03 RESULTS (18-11)
83	Carson-Newman	100
74	West Ga. ■	79
69	S.C.-Aiken ■	48
62	North Fla.	54
67	West Ga.	74
80	Winston-Salem	87
75	Belmont Abbey †	67
97	Catawba †	60
81	Winston-Salem ■	67
74	Paine ■	58
87	S.C.-Spartanburg ■	73
71	GC&SU ■	60
68	Columbus St.	71
63	Kennesaw St. ■	65
103	UNC Pembroke ■	56
83	Lander	65
64	Francis Marion	62
65	Columbus St. ■	68
58	Clayton St. ■	61
59	Armstrong Atlantic	55
68	S.C.-Spartanburg	63
69	UNC Pembroke	62
82	Lander ■	73
57	Kennesaw St.	81
88	Francis Marion ■	78
69	North Fla. ■	79
77	S.C.-Aiken	63
90	North Fla. †	75
49	Kennesaw St. †	69

Nickname: Jaguars
Colors: Royal Blue & White
Arena: ASU Athletic Complex

Capacity: 2,216; Year Built: 1991
AD: Clint Bryant
SID: John Bush

AUGUSTANA (ILL.)
Rock Island, IL 61201-2296......III

Coach: Grey Giovanine, Central Mo. St. 1981
2002-03 RESULTS (20-5)
84	Clarke	73
92	Coe ■	81
70	Rockford	73
88	St. Ambrose	66
104	Central (Iowa) ■	75
89	Cornell College ■	59
89	Mount St. Clare	66
96	Eureka ■	47
54	Sioux Falls †	70
106	William Penn †	82
66	North Central	59
62	Ill. Wesleyan	66
76	Elmhurst ■	73
69	Carthage	55
72	North Central ■	62
88	North Park ■	65
69	Benedictine (Ill.)	66
64	Wheaton (Ill.)	70
76	Millikin	55
80	Ill. Wesleyan ■	75
72	Elmhurst	58
69	Carthage ■	79
96	Wheaton (Ill.) ■	81
89	Millikin ■	59
93	North Park	78

Nickname: Vikings
Colors: Gold & Blue
Arena: Carver PE Center
   Capacity: 3,200; Year Built: 1971
AD: Gregory D. Wallace
SID: Dave Wrath

AUGUSTANA (S.D.)
Sioux Falls, SD 57197..............II

Coach: Perry Ford, Jamestown 1978
2002-03 RESULTS (11-16)
80	Western St.	64
78	Adams St. †	84
99	Minn.-Morris ■	54
74	Bemidji St. †	70
69	Colorado Mines †	77
76	Northern St. ■	70
88	Mt. Marty ■	86
91	York (Neb.) ■	62
74	Dakota Wesleyan	73
89	Northwestern (Minn.) ■	65
89	Augsburg	53
60	Minn. St. Mankato	61
65	St. Cloud St.	74
51	North Dakota	66
77	Northern Colo. ■	74
68	South Dakota ■	70
79	North Dakota ■	87
78	North Dakota St. ■	93
50	South Dakota St. ■	83
57	Minn. St. Mankato ■	78
59	North Dakota St.	74
55	St. Cloud St. ■	67
62	Neb.-Omaha	75
61	Northern Colo.	83
58	South Dakota St.	77
84	South Dakota	70
95	Neb.-Omaha ■	102

Nickname: Vikings
Colors: Navy & Yellow
Arena: Elmen Center
   Capacity: 4,000; Year Built: 1988
AD: Bill Gross
SID: Karen Madsen

AURORA
Aurora, IL 60506......................III

Coach: James Lancaster, Aurora 1986
2002-03 RESULTS (24-6)
96	Judson (Ill.) ■	84
80	Millikin ■	63
64	Franklin	74
67	St. Norbert †	63
83	Beloit	78
77	Webster	53
69	Trinity Int'l	57
84	Monmouth (Ill.) ■	66
58	Blackburn	63
81	North Central ■	69
77	Western Conn. St. †	65
75	Loras †	67
64	Rockford ■	70
95	Eureka	48
91	Dominican (Ill.) ■	48
81	Concordia (Ill.) ■	57
70	Clarke	56
69	Benedictine (Ill.)	58
72	Eastern Ill.	80
65	Rockford	85
82	Eureka ■	70
81	Dominican (Ill.)	73
66	Concordia (Ill.)	51
72	Clarke	69
82	Benedictine (Ill.) ■	64
85	Concordia (Ill.) ■	70
68	Clarke ■	62
68	Rockford	65
67	Trinity (Tex.)	66
61	Occidental	80

Nickname: Spartans
Colors: Royal Blue & White
Arena: Thornton Gymnasium
   Capacity: 2,200; Year Built: 1970
AD: Mark Walsh
SID: Lane Stahl

AUSTIN
Sherman, TX 75090-4440........III

Coach: Chris Oestreich, St. Mary-Plains 1988
2002-03 RESULTS (8-17)
60	Southwestern (Tex.)	82
47	Sam Houston St.	105
64	McMurry ■	59
65	Hardin-Simmons ■	61
81	Concordia-Austin	70
73	Mary Hardin-Baylor	77
61	Howard Payne ■	78
80	Sul Ross St. ■	81
72	Southwestern (Tex.) ■	76
73	Texas Lutheran	63
79	Schreiner	73
74	LeTourneau	80
78	East Tex. Baptist	82
75	Ozarks (Ark.) ■	96
54	Texas-Dallas ■	53
65	Dallas ■	73
55	Mississippi Col. ■	63
73	Louisiana Col. ■	88
64	Mississippi Col.	89
64	Louisiana Col.	91
74	LeTourneau ■	72
75	East Tex. Baptist ■	82
70	Ozarks (Ark.)	75
60	Texas-Dallas	86
72	Dallas	69

Nickname: Kangaroos
Colors: Crimson & Gold
Arena: Hughey Gym
   Capacity: 2,000; Year Built: 1949
AD: Timothy P. Millerick
SID: Chuck Sadowski

AUSTIN PEAY
Clarksville, TN 37044-4576.......I

Coach: Dave Loos, Memphis 1970
2002-03 RESULTS (23-8)
81	Memphis	80
90	Bluefield Col. ■	66
46	Missouri	81
46	Mississippi	74
86	Knoxville ■	63
76	Belmont ■	75
85	Evansville	95
79	Middle Tenn. ■	71
69	Wis.-Green Bay	74
77	Eastern Wash. †	69
82	Westminster (Mo.) ■	58
64	Tenn.-Martin ■	66
66	Murray St.	63
47	Tennessee Tech	66
87	Eastern Ill. ■	80
62	Southeast Mo. St. ■	49
64	Tenn.-Martin ■	56
66	Morehead St.	59
86	Eastern Ky.	77
82	Tennessee St.	57
72	Murray St. ■	69
71	Tennessee St. ■	56
58	Tennessee Tech ■	54
76	Eastern Ill.	80
63	Southeast Mo. St.	56
78	Eastern Ky. ■	64
76	Morehead St. ■	64
83	Eastern Ky. ■	80
59	Murray St. †	56
63	Tennessee Tech †	57
64	Louisville †	86

Nickname: Governors
Colors: Red & White
Arena: Winfield Dunn Center
   Capacity: 9,092; Year Built: 1975
AD: Dave Loos
SID: Brad Kirtley

AVERETT
Danville, VA 24541.................III

Coach: Kirk Chandler, Elon 1981
2002-03 RESULTS (2-23)
63	Washington (Md.) †	66
75	Daniel Webster †	64
64	Apprentice	82
67	Apprentice ■	92
59	Wabash	74
70	Kalamazoo †	102
80	Lynchburg	92
57	Wheaton (Mass.) ■	70
75	Emory & Henry	109
80	Lynchburg ■	85
78	Ferrum	83
52	Shenandoah ■	78
58	Chris. Newport	109
67	Greensboro	78
61	Methodist	95
72	Chowan	75
72	N.C. Wesleyan ■	97
85	Ferrum ■	77
56	Shenandoah	83
84	Chris. Newport ■	111
80	Greensboro ■	86
76	Methodist ■	98
78	Chowan	79
64	N.C. Wesleyan	79
64	Chris. Newport †	79

Nickname: Cougars
Colors: Navy & Gold
Arena: Grant Center
   Capacity: 2,000; Year Built: 1998
AD: Vesa Hiltunen
SID: Sam Ferguson

BABSON
Babson Park, MA 02457-0310 ... III

Coach: Steve Brennan, Bates 1987
2002-03 RESULTS (26-4)
89	Mount Ida ■	60
97	Suffolk ■	71
74	Colby	60
79	Tufts	76
81	Salem St.	75
93	Roger Williams ■	55
85	Emerson ■	57
59	Ripon †	74
60	Wis.-Superior †	46
78	Brandeis ■	44
73	Trinity (Conn.)	54
81	Bowdoin	58
63	Coast Guard	48
90	Suffolk	58
58	Clark (Mass.) ■	62
72	WPI	36
64	Springfield	50
77	Wheaton (Mass.) ■	54
69	MIT ■	53
79	Coast Guard ■	59
76	Springfield ■	61
73	WPI ■	62
77	Wheaton (Mass.)	58
63	Clark (Mass.)	72
81	WPI ■	60
98	Springfield †	68
76	Clark (Mass.) ■	84
71	MIT ■	63
78	Endicott ■	68
81	Keene St. ■	71

Nickname: Beavers
Colors: Green & White
Arena: Staake Gymnasium
   Capacity: 1,000; Year Built: 1989
AD: Frank Millerick
SID: Chris Buck

BALDWIN-WALLACE
Berea, OH 44017 III

Coach: Steve Bankson, Graceland (Iowa) 1963
2002-03 RESULTS (13-13)
94	Nazareth †	87
71	Mt. St. Joseph	74
73	Thiel	71
76	Bethany (W.Va.) ■	62
56	Otterbein	70
73	Wilmington (Ohio)	71
87	Mount Union ■	83
74	Marietta ■	63
83	Edgewood †	59
72	Linfield †	80
86	Ramapo †	93
44	Ohio Northern ■	65
59	Capital ■	71
63	John Carroll	69
78	Muskingum ■	64
67	Heidelberg	57
100	Wilmington (Ohio) ■	75
71	Mount Union	72
60	Muskingum	46
84	Heidelberg ■	89
101	Marietta	94
74	Ohio Northern	83
70	Capital	79
80	John Carroll ■	98
76	Otterbein ■	72
58	Mount Union	67

Nickname: Yellow Jackets
Colors: Brown & Gold
Arena: Ursprung Gymnasium
   Capacity: 2,800; Year Built: 1949
AD: Stephen Bankson
SID: Kevin Ruple

BALL ST.
Muncie, IN 47306 I

Coach: Tim Buckley, Bemidji St. 1986
2002-03 RESULTS (13-17)
72	Jacksonville St. †	64
67	Weber St. †	72
73	Nebraska †	65
45	Butler	71
85	IUPUI ■	69
66	Wright St. ■	59
76	Indiana St. ■	68
65	Dayton	80
58	Xavier	87
62	Indiana ■	76
104	Akron	105
57	Bowling Green	61
64	Northern Ill. ■	66
52	Western Mich. ■	71
77	Toledo ■	72
91	Eastern Mich.	90
56	Miami (Ohio)	58
96	Marshall ■	75
60	Northern Ill.	78
82	Ohio ■	68
78	Miami (Ohio) ■	70
83	Kent St. ■	75
80	Buffalo	68
92	Central Mich.	94
79	Western Ky.	84
94	Bowling Green ■	73
74	Western Mich.	86
64	Toledo	100
66	Central Mich. ■	86
81	Bowling Green ■	90

Nickname: Cardinals
Colors: Cardinal & White
Arena: Worthen Arena
   Capacity: 11,500; Year Built: 1992
AD: Lawrence R. Cunningham
SID: Chris Taylor

BAPTIST BIBLE (PA.)
Clarks Summit, PA 18411 III

Coach: Mike Show
2002-03 RESULTS (18-12)
80	Misericordia	87
91	Brooklyn †	72
81	Messiah	89
65	Hartwick	72
84	Lancaster Bible	62
71	Farmingdale St.	80
88	Centenary (N.J.)	96
60	Wilkes	97
77	Farmingdale St. ■	70
82	King's (Pa.) ■	97
60	Mt. Aloysius ■	49
66	Eastern	69
63	Phila. Bible ■	60
89	Washington Bible ■	41
97	Lancaster Bible ■	59
96	Practical Bible ■	49
103	Maryland Bible	82
113	Washington Bible ■	60
76	D'Youville	77
83	Maryland Bible ■	67
90	Valley Forge Chrst.	74
95	Practical Bible	79
51	Phila. Bible	89
66	Valley Forge Chrst. ■	37
82	Cazenovia ■	96
78	Valley Forge Chrst. †	71
73	Phila. Bible	72
66	Simpson (Cal.) †	71
95	Clearwater †	75
92	Ky. Christian †	81

Nickname: Defenders
Colors: Royal Blue & White
AD: James M. Huckaby

BARD
Annandale-On-Hudson, NY 12504-5000 III

Coach: Chris Wood, Plymouth St. 1989
2002-03 RESULTS (8-13)
21	Skidmore	86
68	Sarah Lawrence ■	50
77	Albany Pharmacy ■	70
103	Webb Inst.	30
61	Polytechnic (N.Y.)	74
66	Pratt	79
70	Boston Bapt. ■	43
70	Boston Bapt.	68
61	Me.-Augusta	92
58	Unity	66
77	Albany Pharmacy	64
62	Purchase St. ■	82
65	St. Joseph's (Brkln) ■	89
61	Berkeley ■	70
47	Vassar	83
98	Hampshire	35
68	Polytechnic (N.Y.) ■	96
62	Pratt	71
41	Purchase St.	69
81	St. Joseph's (Brkln)	94
79	Hampshire ■	42

Nickname: Raptors
Colors: White & Black
Arena: Stevenson Gym
   Capacity: 850; Year Built: 1988
AD: Kristen E. Hall
SID: Phillip Roloson

BARRY
Miami Shores, FL 33161 II

Coach: Cesar Odio, Fla. Southern 1981
2002-03 RESULTS (18-10)
85	P.R.-Mayaguez ■	67
58	Nova Southeastern ■	47
55	P.R.-Cayey	51
55	Fla. Gulf Coast ■	36
62	Fla. Memorial ■	41
69	Nova Southeastern	63
53	Fla. Memorial	41
80	P.R.-Cayey †	46
67	Franklin Pierce †	63
44	Indianapolis †	43
48	Bentley	61
43	St. Leo ■	48
55	Lynn ■	37
39	Tampa	44
76	Eckerd ■	79
48	St. Leo ■	43
50	Fla. Southern	57
67	Rollins	75
69	Florida Tech	62
63	Tampa ■	56
53	Eckerd	65
33	St. Leo	48
68	Fla. Southern ■	63
48	Rollins	52
63	Florida Tech ■	57
59	Lynn	47
64	Lynn †	50
37	Rollins †	48

Nickname: Buccaneers
Colors: Red, Black & Silver
Arena: Health & Sports Center
   Capacity: 1,500; Year Built: 1990
AD: Michael L. Covone
SID: Dennis Jezek Jr.

BARTON
Wilson, NC 27893-7000 II

Coach: Ron Lievense, St. Thomas (Minn.) 1981
2002-03 RESULTS (22-6)
95	Shippensburg	86
78	St. Rose †	73
100	Limestone ■	89
81	St. Paul's ■	75
71	Virginia St.	79
77	Virginia St. ■	58
68	Anderson (S.C.)	56
101	Lees-McRae ■	63
59	Erskine	45
93	Coker ■	61
88	Mount Olive	83
96	Pfeiffer	104
75	Belmont Abbey ■	46
83	Queens (N.C.) ■	90
102	Longwood	94
73	St. Andrews ■	60
107	Limestone	98
85	Anderson (S.C.) ■	80
89	Pfeiffer ■	67
66	Erskine	53
96	Mount Olive ■	89
86	Lees-McRae	61
89	Belmont Abbey	70
93	Coker	64
84	Queens (N.C.) ■	99
77	St. Andrews	80
81	Alderson-Broaddus †	76
63	Millersville †	80

Nickname: Bulldogs
Colors: Royal Blue & White
Arena: Wilson Gym
   Capacity: 2,500; Year Built: 1966
AD: Gary W. Hall
SID: John Hackney

BARUCH
New York, NY 10010-5585 III

Coach: Ray Rankis, Lehman 1976
2002-03 RESULTS (25-5)
78	Western Conn. St. †	75
77	Vassar	68
87	New Paltz St. ■	67
65	Farmingdale St. ■	63
70	Maritime (N.Y.)	58
76	Lehman	60
78	John Jay	65
88	Yeshiva	70
79	Susquehanna †	68
66	Montclair St.	75
69	New York U. ■	48
83	Hunter ■	74
68	Polytechnic (N.Y.)	41
73	CCNY	62
82	Medgar Evers ■	72
71	NYCCT	62
71	Staten Island ■	59
81	Brooklyn ■	54
81	Stevens Institute ■	64
71	Lehman ■	75
62	John Jay ■	64
85	CCNY ■	72
69	Hunter	76
73	York (N.Y.) ■	61
78	Brooklyn ■	60
79	Lehman ■	75
79	CCNY ■	84
81	Lehman ■	66
60	Manhattanville ■	56
90	Mt. St. Mary (N.Y.)	87

Nickname: Bearcats
Colors: Navy Blue and Columbia Blue
Arena: Baruch College ARC Arena
   Capacity: 800; Year Built: 2002

AD: William Eng
SID: Eric John Kloiber

BATES
Lewiston, ME 04240 III

Coach: Joe Reilly, Trinity (Conn.) 1991
2002-03 RESULTS (16-9)
78	Lyndon St. †	74
115	New England †	68
110	Southern Me. ■	77
85	Bowdoin	68
80	Me.-Fort Kent †	69
100	Mount Ida ■	57
78	CCNY †	60
75	Salem St.	85
95	Endicott ■	63
78	Gordon	74
55	Colby	63
98	Colby-Sawyer ■	95
69	Wesleyan (Conn.)	68
89	Connecticut Col.	79
68	Wentworth Inst.	60
88	Tufts ■	72
84	Me.-Farmington ■	74
67	Trinity (Conn.) ■	64
60	Amherst ■	90
64	Colby ■	68
59	Bowdoin ■	84
75	St. Joseph's (Me.)	81
55	Williams	76
72	Middlebury	85
69	Williams	85

Nickname: Bobcats
Colors: Garnet
Arena: Alumni Gymnasium
    Capacity: 750; Year Built: 1925
AD: Suzanne Coffey
SID: John Jordan

BAYLOR
Waco, TX 76798-7096.............I

Coach: Dave Bliss, Cornell 1965
2002-03 RESULTS (14-14)
81	Alcorn St. †	61
82	Northwestern St. ■	54
62	Houston †	60
92	Texas St. ■	71
64	TCU ■	72
79	La.-Monroe ■	74
65	Montana St. ■	56
58	Southern Methodist	66
82	North Texas ■	56
78	Tex.-Pan American ■	50
80	Mt. St. Mary's ■	47
69	Missouri	77
71	Texas	82
64	Texas Tech	80
64	Oklahoma St. ■	67
54	Oklahoma ■	67
70	Iowa St.	74
77	Texas A&M ■	69
42	Oklahoma	91
58	Kansas ■	79
74	Oklahoma St.	72
66	Kansas St.	57
78	Nebraska ■	64
64	Texas	82
59	Colorado ■	72
60	Texas A&M	79
74	Texas Tech ■	68
65	Texas Tech †	68

Nickname: Bears
Colors: Green & Gold
Arena: Ferrell Center
    Capacity: 10,284; Year Built: 1988
AD: Thomas I. Stanton
SID: Heath Nielsen

BECKER
Leicester, MA 01524 III

Coach: Adam Nelson, Boston College 1996
2002-03 RESULTS (8-18)
60	Rhode Island Col. †	81
63	New Paltz St. †	70
67	Nichols ■	86
60	Wentworth Inst.	70
68	Anna Maria ■	80
60	Eastern Nazarene ■	64
84	Mass. Liberal Arts	77
56	Gordon	85
85	Mount Ida ■	70
96	Castleton St. ■	72
86	Johnson St. ■	83
64	Elms	75
70	Maine Maritime ■	81
64	Westfield St. ■	100
89	Lasell ■	84
78	Newbury ■	80
84	Fitchburg St.	97
84	Johnson St.	86
81	Castleton St.	79
67	Lasell	96
63	Elms ■	70
93	Berkeley ■	78
72	Mount Ida	84
79	Newbury	72
56	Maine Maritime	69
71	Johnson St.	86

Nickname: Hawks
Colors: Royal Blue/White/Scarlet
Arena: Leicester Gymnasium
    Capacity: 500; Year Built: 1972
AD: Gene Alley
SID: Herb Whitworth

BELLARMINE
Louisville, KY 40205-0671.........II

Coach: Chris Pullem, Eastern Ky. 1995
2002-03 RESULTS (10-19)
70	Bryant †	74
74	Presbyterian †	84
77	Lake Superior St. †	86
103	Bluefield St. ■	68
115	Ashland	120
96	Ind.-Southeast ■	90
68	Mo.-St. Louis ■	77
82	Southern Ind. ■	80
85	Northern Ky. ■	106
92	Spalding ■	80
99	Oakland City	89
90	Kentucky St. ■	80
95	St. Joseph's (Ind.) ■	106
67	Wis.-Parkside	94
62	SIU Edwardsville ■	65
110	Quincy ■	101
82	Southern Ind.	107
77	Ky. Wesleyan ■	110
68	Northern Ky.	75
73	Indianapolis	82
100	Wis.-Parkside ■	95
88	Lewis ■	99
75	Quincy	77
78	Mo.-St. Louis	67
85	Ky. Wesleyan	89
97	Indianapolis ■	104
112	St. Joseph's (Ind.) ■	104
66	Lewis	91
76	SIU Edwardsville	84

Nickname: Knights
Colors: Scarlet & Silver
Arena: Knights Hall
    Capacity: 3,000; Year Built: 1960
AD: Rick Bagby
SID: Shannon Satterly

BELMONT
Nashville, TN 37212-3757 I

Coach: Rick Byrd, Tennessee 1976
2002-03 RESULTS (17-12)
48	Notre Dame	76
83	Brown †	77
71	Georgia	87
68	Navy ■	61
76	Air Force	85
75	Loyola (Ill.) ■	57
75	Austin Peay	76
61	Purdue	78
65	Valparaiso	83
61	East Tenn. St. †	71
88	Long Island †	75
52	Samford	51
103	Gardner-Webb	86
73	Campbell	63
79	Fisk ■	49
87	Jacksonville St. ■	69
66	Georgia St. ■	69
64	Troy St. ■	67
69	Mercer	67
60	UCF	58
76	Fla. Atlantic	69
84	Jacksonville ■	52
80	Stetson ■	85
72	Georgia St.	57
87	Jacksonville St.	92
74	Campbell ■	56
81	Gardner-Webb ■	73
72	Samford	64
58	Georgia St.	76

Nickname: Bruins
Colors: Red, White & Navy Blue
Arena: Municipal Auditorium
    Capacity: 8,354; Year Built: 1962
AD: Michael D. Strickland
SID: Matt Wilson

BELMONT ABBEY
Belmont, NC 28012-1802 II

Coach: Darren Metress, Belmont Abbey 1988
2002-03 RESULTS (24-7)
57	Bloomsburg †	55
81	Shepherd	64
76	Johnson Smith ■	60
77	St. Andrews	65
98	Anderson (S.C.)	51
67	Augusta St. †	75
66	S.C.-Aiken	57
82	Paine ■	65
78	Salem Int'l	72
79	Limestone ■	60
63	Mount Olive ■	66
86	Pfeiffer	80
51	Erskine ■	59
83	Coker	65
46	Barton	75
98	Lees-McRae ■	59
71	Queens (N.C.)	79
81	Longwood ■	45
79	St. Andrews ■	68
84	Limestone	75
61	Anderson (S.C.) ■	53
74	Pfeiffer ■	72
51	Erskine	49
81	Coker ■	55
86	Mount Olive	64
70	Barton ■	89
87	Lees-McRae	73
76	Longwood ■	64
94	St. Andrews †	63
73	Pfeiffer	68
56	Millersville †	62

Nickname: Crusaders
Colors: Red & White

Arena: The Wheeler Center
    Capacity: 1,500; Year Built: 1971
AD: Eliane Kebbe
SID: Matt Kline

BELOIT
Beloit, WI 53511-5595 III

Coach: Cecil Youngblood, Augustana (Ill.) 1976
2002-03 RESULTS (10-13)
75	Marian (Wis.)	69
71	Maranatha Baptist †	68
95	Rockford ■	106
75	Wis.-Whitewater ■	79
78	Aurora	83
51	Lawrence ■	73
57	Ripon ■	66
46	Wis.-Oshkosh	77
61	Ill. Wesleyan	76
73	Carroll (Wis.)	69
73	St. Norbert	71
96	Knox ■	89
67	Illinois Col. ■	68
56	Lake Forest	75
73	Monmouth (Ill.)	75
120	Grinnell ■	108
85	Lake Forest ■	88
68	St. Norbert ■	88
80	Illinois Col.	63
79	Carroll (Wis.) ■	77
82	Ripon	77
71	Lawrence	72
104	Knox	96

Nickname: Buccaneers
Colors: Navy Blue & Gold
Arena: Flood Arena
    Capacity: 2,250; Year Built: 1986
AD: Edward J. DeGeorge
SID: Keith Domke

BEMIDJI ST.
Bemidji, MN 56601-2699.........II

Coach: Jeff Guiot, Pittsburg St.
2002-03 RESULTS (17-12)
73	Valley City St.	64
78	Jamestown	82
81	Bethel (Minn.)	72
70	Augustana (S.D.) †	74
66	South Dakota St.	83
102	Wis.-Superior ■	56
84	St. Cloud St.	91
102	St. Scholastica ■	67
70	Michigan Tech ■	80
71	Wayne St. (Neb.)	78
59	Southwest Minn. St.	73
99	Minn.-Crookston	59
89	Minn. St. Moorhead ■	60
69	Minn. Duluth	86
116	Minn.-Morris	71
82	Northern St.	77
108	Winona St. ■	98
94	Concordia-St. Paul ■	84
83	Southwest Minn. St. ■	87
78	Wayne St. (Neb.) ■	88
91	Minn. St. Moorhead	68
85	Minn.-Crookston	88
90	Minn. Duluth ■	67
69	Northern St. ■	68
118	Minn.-Morris ■	70
95	Concordia-St. Paul	77
102	Winona St.	96
106	Winona St. ■	79
78	Minn. St. Moorhead †	79

Nickname: Beavers
Colors: Kelly Green & White
Arena: BSU Gymnasium
    Capacity: 2,000; Year Built: 1959

RESULTS   277

AD: Rick Goeb
SID: Andy Bartlett

BENEDICT
Columbia, SC 29204...............II

Coach: Freddrell Watson, Benedict 1998

2002-03 RESULTS (11-14)

74	Livingstone ■	81
62	Voorhees ■	53
77	Elizabeth City St. ■	69
49	Presbyterian ■	66
84	LeMoyne-Owen	92
66	Miles †	75
91	Kentucky St. ■	82
85	Lane ■	84
67	Tuskegee ■	66
80	Livingstone	89
79	Clark Atlanta	81
65	Morehouse	68
58	Fort Valley St. ■	47
89	Albany St. (Ga.) ■	75
62	Elizabeth City St.	76
64	LeMoyne-Owen	77
80	Allen	72
73	Clark Atlanta ■	59
72	Morehouse ■	91
63	Fort Valley St.	53
57	Albany St. (Ga.)	56
53	Fayetteville St. ■	65
55	Paine ■	62
71	Paine	85
65	LeMoyne-Owen †	79

Nickname: Tigers
Colors: Purple & Gold
AD: Willie Washington
SID: Frankie Jackson

BENEDICTINE (ILL.)
Lisle, IL 60532-0900 III

Coach: Keith Bunkenburg, Benedictine (Ill.) 1989

2002-03 RESULTS (14-13)

111	Wis. Lutheran	66
61	Simpson †	59
63	St. Mary's (Ind.) ■	62
85	North Central ■	71
68	Lake Forest	79
73	Chicago ■	67
63	Elmhurst	62
70	Concordia (Wis.)	83
65	Clarke	80
66	Wooster	74
60	Illinois Col. †	61
55	Lakeland ■	58
68	Dominican (Ill.)	66
87	Eureka ■	70
46	Illinois Tech	45
62	Rockford	63
73	Concordia (Ill.)	56
58	Aurora ■	69
54	Clarke ■	65
66	Augustana (Ill.) ■	69
66	Dominican (Ill.) ■	58
76	Eureka	71
71	Rockford ■	74
76	Concordia (Ill.)	66
64	Aurora	82
80	Dominican (Ill.) ■	64
51	Rockford	65

Nickname: Eagles
Colors: Red & White
Arena: Dan & Ada Rice Center
   Capacity: 2,000; Year Built: 1976
AD: Lynn O'Linski
SID: Jill Redmond

BENTLEY
Waltham, MA 02154-4705.......II

Coach: Jay Lawson, New Hampshire 1979

2002-03 RESULTS (17-12)

73	Adelphi ■	84
86	Lynn ■	79
71	American Int'l ■	59
77	Southern N.H. ■	82
86	Franklin Pierce ■	79
57	Mass.-Lowell	72
74	Bryant	69
61	Barry	48
74	Nova Southeastern	62
81	Stonehill ■	59
75	Merrimack	59
87	St. Michael's ■	77
79	St. Anselm ■	76
75	Le Moyne ■	80
53	Pace ■	55
89	Southern Conn. St. ■	76
76	St. Rose	95
71	New Haven ■	48
76	Stonehill	49
75	Merrimack ■	71
64	Mass.-Lowell ■	69
65	Franklin Pierce	77
72	Southern N.H. ■	74
102	St. Rose ■	86
74	Southern Conn. St.	64
65	Pace ■	69
76	Assumption	79
88	St. Anselm ■	76
70	Southern N.H.	83

Nickname: Falcons
Colors: Blue & Gold
Arena: Charles Dana PE Center
   Capacity: 2,600; Year Built: 1973
AD: Robert De Felice
SID: Dick Lipe

BETHANY (W.VA.)
Bethany, WV 26032-0417 III

Coach: Aaron Huffman, West Virginia 1997

2002-03 RESULTS (11-15)

69	N.C. Wesleyan †	95
63	Va. Wesleyan	90
91	Pitt.-Greensburg	93
71	Notre Dame (Ohio)	83
62	Baldwin-Wallace	76
91	Kenyon ■	90
85	Penn St.-Altoona ■	74
43	Frank. & Marsh.	108
81	Hiram ■	75
68	Elmira †	67
89	Merchant Marine †	83
81	La Roche ■	77
72	Apprentice ■	75
71	Grove City ■	77
83	Waynesburg ■	78
85	Wash. & Jeff.	88
63	Thiel	82
82	Westminster (Pa.) ■	84
105	Frostburg St.	99
102	Grove City	100
90	Waynesburg	97
101	Wash. & Jeff. ■	85
74	Thiel ■	89
74	Westminster (Pa.)	76
82	Waynesburg	74
77	Thiel	81

Nickname: Bison
Colors: Kelly Green & White
Arena: Hummel Field House
   Capacity: 1,400; Year Built: 1948
AD: Janice L. Forsty
SID: Brian Rose

BETHEL (MINN.)
St. Paul, MN 55112-6999........III

Coach: Bob Bjorklund, Minnesota 1973

2002-03 RESULTS (15-12)

92	Finlandia ■	69
87	Wis.-River Falls ■	89
72	Bemidji St. ■	81
66	Carleton	73
68	Macalester ■	60
73	St. Mary's (Minn.)	62
74	Hamline	71
73	Crown	63
61	Master's	74
79	Concordia-M'head	77
77	Augsburg	71
72	St. Olaf ■	64
68	St. John's (Minn.) ■	63
57	Gust. Adolphus ■	63
84	St. Thomas (Minn.) ■	71
73	Carleton ■	85
73	Macalester	68
84	St. Mary's (Minn.) ■	57
71	Hamline ■	72
87	Concordia-M'head ■	73
62	Augsburg ■	74
57	St. Olaf	70
95	St. John's (Minn.)	92
67	Gust. Adolphus ■	73
74	St. Thomas (Minn.)	84
82	St. Olaf ■	54
64	Gust. Adolphus	65

Nickname: Royals
Colors: Blue & Gold
Arena: Robertson PE Center
   Capacity: 2,000; Year Built: 1971
AD: David A. Klostreich
SID: Greg Peterson

BETHUNE-COOKMAN
Daytona Beach, FL 32114-3099.I

Coach: Clifford Reed, Bethune-Cookman 1991

2002-03 RESULTS (8-22)

64	Canisius	77
79	Iona	98
71	Florida A&M	69
52	Minnesota	79
55	La.-Lafayette	81
64	Florida	99
54	Wake Forest	96
47	Delaware St.	70
58	Howard ■	63
69	Md.-East. Shore ■	74
66	Savannah St.	54
49	Norfolk St.	59
72	Hampton	74
50	Savannah St. ■	60
69	Coppin St. ■	73
79	Morgan St. ■	71
64	South Carolina St.	87
78	N.C. A&T ■	69
63	Morris Brown	65
48	Delaware St. ■	43
68	Howard	96
57	Md.-East. Shore	48
48	Norfolk St. ■	61
69	Hampton ■	76
85	Morris Brown ■	66
55	Morgan St.	59
65	Coppin St.	70
66	Florida A&M ■	72
104	Morgan St. †	103
73	South Carolina St. †	75

Nickname: Wildcats
Colors: Maroon & Gold
Arena: Moore Gymnasium
   Capacity: 3,000; Year Built: 1953
AD: Lynn W. Thompson
SID: Charles D. Jackson

BINGHAMTON
Binghamton, NY 13902-6000....I

Coach: Al Walker, Brockport St. 1981

2002-03 RESULTS (14-13)

77	Lafayette ■	68
70	Columbia ■	42
75	Long Island	66
61	Dartmouth	67
74	Denver †	69
56	Iowa St.	86
58	Syracuse	94
53	Villanova	68
64	George Washington ■	68
80	New Hampshire ■	50
65	Boston U.	70
74	St. Francis (N.Y.) ■	62
64	Stony Brook ■	59
55	Hartford ■	52
64	Maine	79
86	Albany (N.Y.) ■	59
82	New Hampshire ■	71
48	Northeastern	59
61	Vermont ■	50
51	Hartford	65
82	Boston U. ■	85
54	Vermont	74
63	Maine ■	62
76	Albany (N.Y.)	59
66	Northeastern ■	54
70	Stony Brook	77
68	Tex. A&M-Corp. Chris	72

Nickname: Bearcats
Colors: Green & Black
Arena: West Gym
   Capacity: 2,275; Year Built: 1970
AD: Joel Thirer
SID: John Hartrick

BIRMINGHAM-SO.
Birmingham, AL 35254..............I

Coach: Duane Reboul, New Orleans 1972

2002-03 RESULTS (19-9)

53	UAB	71
64	South Ala.	77
108	Covenant ■	65
75	Stetson ■	59
86	Texas Col. ■	81
92	La.-Lafayette ■	86
47	Florida St.	56
60	Nicholls St. ■	47
53	Alabama St.	58
75	Robert Morris	73
64	Coastal Caro.	74
69	Charleston So.	61
83	Radford ■	65
67	Winthrop ■	74
88	UNC Asheville ■	71
64	High Point	60
64	Elon	52
70	Savannah St.	58
72	Liberty ■	55
59	Coastal Caro. ■	65
63	Charleston So. ■	60
68	UNC Asheville	82
63	Winthrop	67
76	Elon ■	67
63	High Point ■	62
53	Liberty	50
67	Radford	57
92	Savannah St. ■	75

Nickname: Panthers
Colors: Black & Gold
Arena: Bill Battle Coliseum
   Capacity: 1,800; Year Built: 1980
AD: Joe Dean Jr.
SID: Jason Falls

SCHEDULES/RESULTS

BLACKBURN
Carlinville, IL 62626 III

Coach: Joe Ramsey, Southern Ill. 1965
2002-03 RESULTS (15-10)

54	Wheaton (Ill.)	81
45	Eastern †	58
66	Ill.-Springfield	80
83	Millikin	78
63	Eureka	60
59	Robert Morris (Ill.) ■	52
63	Aurora ■	58
45	Washington (Mo.)	76
67	Ill.-Springfield ■	74
59	Hannibal-LaGrange ■	62
95	MacMurray ■	84
85	Greenville ■	71
83	Webster ■	66
76	Fontbonne	87
92	Maryville (Mo.) ■	73
83	Westminster (Mo.)	80
73	Principia	54
77	MacMurray ■	66
72	Greenville	77
57	Webster	61
66	Fontbonne ■	59
74	Maryville (Mo.)	62
75	Westminster (Mo.) ■	65
65	Principia ■	44
59	Ill. Wesleyan	79

Nickname: Battlin' Beavers
Colors: Scarlet & Black
Arena: Dawes Gymnasium
  Capacity: 500; Year Built: 1938
AD: Joe Ramsey
SID: Mary McNeely

BLOOMFIELD
Bloomfield, NJ 07003 II

Coach: Gerald Holmes
2002-03 RESULTS (11-15)

56	Millersville	83
55	Lock Haven †	66
67	Felician	72
85	Goldey-Beacom ■	60
77	Nyack ■	69
78	Teikyo Post ■	70
51	Clarion	68
98	Wilmington (Del.)	88
79	West Chester †	83
76	Molloy †	78
71	East Stroudsburg	53
64	Dist. Columbia †	66
96	Dominican (N.Y.)	98
75	N.J. Inst. of Tech. ■	78
78	Holy Family	75
70	Felician	84
84	Teikyo Post	86
89	Caldwell	94
85	Dominican (N.Y.) ■	82
87	Phila. Sciences	89
82	Goldey-Beacom	71
84	Nyack	80
114	Wilmington (Del.) ■	96
83	Holy Family ■	94
64	N.J. Inst. of Tech.	98
80	Phila. Sciences ■	69

Nickname: Deacons
Colors: Maroon & Gold
Arena: Bloomfield College Gymnasium
  Capacity: 750; Year Built: 1958
AD: Shelia Wooten
SID: Steve Patchett

BLOOMSBURG
Bloomsburg, PA 17815 II

Coach: Rich Mills, Fairleigh Dickinson
1984
2002-03 RESULTS (6-20)

55	Belmont Abbey †	57
83	Columbia Union †	69
90	Lycoming ■	80
74	Shepherd ■	77
78	Indiana (Pa.) ■	86
81	Shippensburg ■	70
62	Edinboro	76
60	Clarion	74
69	Lock Haven	85
55	Dist. Columbia	75
65	Slippery Rock ■	70
71	Calif. (Pa.) ■	84
62	Millersville	89
71	West Chester ■	78
64	Mansfield	73
75	East Stroudsburg	62
78	Kutztown	85
84	Pitt.-Johnstown ■	77
83	Cheyney ■	61
60	West Chester	70
67	Millersville ■	90
76	East Stroudsburg ■	92
70	Mansfield ■	71
87	Kutztown	88
92	Pitt.-Johnstown	95
72	Cheyney	83

Nickname: Huskies
Colors: Maroon & Gold
Arena: E.H. Nelson Fieldhouse
  Capacity: 3,000; Year Built: 1972
AD: Mary Gardner
SID: Tom McGuire

BLUEFIELD ST.
Bluefield, WV 24701-2198 II

Coach: Terry Brown, Bluefield St. 1975
2002-03 RESULTS (5-23)

68	Bellarmine	103
89	West Virginia St. †	90
81	West Virginia St. ■	106
90	Concord ■	76
76	Shawnee St. ■	71
67	Lincoln Memorial ■	75
66	Pikeville ■	113
64	Salem Int'l ■	94
72	Pikeville	95
85	Southern Va. ■	96
92	West Virginia St. ■	106
80	Concord	76
79	Charleston (W.Va.)	88
79	Ohio Valley ■	67
71	Alderson-Broaddus	87
78	West Va. Wesleyan	87
59	Shepherd ■	71
85	Glenville St. ■	73
56	West Va. Tech ■	71
65	Fairmont St. ■	91
74	Wheeling Jesuit	90
66	West Liberty St.	80
56	Concord ■	68
63	Davis & Elkins	67
79	West Va. Tech	105
84	West Virginia St.	122
71	Charleston (W.Va.) ■	83
67	Wheeling Jesuit	83

Nickname: Big Blues
Colors: Blue & Gold

Arena: Ned Shott Gymnasium
  Capacity: 1,500; Year Built: 1969
AD: Terry Brown
SID: Terry Brown

BLUFFTON
Bluffton, OH 45817-1196 III

Coach: Guy Neal, Bowling Green 1982
2002-03 RESULTS (10-16)

88	Ozarks (Ark.) †	90
60	North Cent. (Minn.) †	63
72	Earlham	68
94	Marygrove ■	70
81	Heidelberg ■	84
58	Manchester ■	71
70	Hanover	88
60	Mt. St. Joseph ■	67
78	Denison	74
86	Madonna ■	79
69	Muskingum ■	62
77	Adrian	69
53	Franklin	65
87	Anderson (Ind.)	89
75	Thomas More	89
93	Transylvania	83
97	Defiance ■	93
59	Hanover ■	74
73	Manchester	79
79	Mt. St. Joseph	76
93	Anderson (Ind.) ■	84
68	Franklin	87
66	Transylvania ■	76
72	Defiance	85
63	Thomas More ■	70
58	Anderson (Ind.)	70

Nickname: Beavers
Colors: Royal Purple & White
Arena: Founders Hall
  Capacity: 1,500; Year Built: 1952
AD: Carlin B. Carpenter
SID: Tim Stried

BOISE ST.
Boise, ID 83725-1020 I

Coach: Greg Graham, Oregon 1978
2002-03 RESULTS (13-16)

59	Eastern Ill. ■	73
74	Idaho St. ■	71
75	Idaho ■	67
52	Albertson ■	50
73	Southern Utah	71
61	Wyoming	74
75	Idaho	70
59	Eastern Wash. ■	65
59	Portland St. ■	51
65	Weber St. ■	66
58	San Jose St. ■	56
65	Hawaii ■	63
54	Fresno St.	61
61	Nevada	71
65	Rice ■	74
78	Tulsa ■	74
78	UTEP	85
76	Louisiana Tech	79
88	Southern Methodist	85
64	Nevada ■	67
52	Fresno St. ■	59
55	Tulsa	71
62	Rice	72
69	UTEP ■	52
58	Southern Methodist ■	66
74	Louisiana Tech ■	51
65	Hawaii	68

65	San Jose St.	47
58	Southern Methodist †	65

Nickname: Broncos
Colors: Orange & Blue
Arena: Pavilion
  Capacity: 12,200; Year Built: 1982
AD: Gene Bleymaier
SID: Brad Larrondo

BOSTON COLLEGE
Chestnut Hill, MA 02467-3861 ..I

Coach: Al Skinner, Massachusetts 1974
2002-03 RESULTS (19-12)

58	St. Joseph's ■	85
80	Boston U. ■	61
70	Holy Cross	71
105	St. Bonaventure ■	96
80	Massachusetts	62
85	Iowa St.	78
79	Stony Brook ■	61
84	Harvard ■	77
83	Kent St. †	86
80	Providence ■	93
67	Northeastern ■	72
74	Syracuse	82
93	North Carolina St.	81
75	West Virginia ■	70
83	Villanova	94
96	Notre Dame ■	101
95	Virginia Tech	71
95	Connecticut	71
84	St. John's (N.Y.) ■	82
75	Rutgers	75
80	Providence	69
76	Miami (Fla.) ■	65
87	Virginia Tech ■	69
81	St. John's (N.Y.)	63
72	Miami (Fla.)	68
92	Villanova ■	84
54	Connecticut ■	91
82	St. John's (N.Y.) †	75
48	Pittsburgh †	61
90	Fairfield	78
62	Temple	75

Nickname: Eagles
Colors: Maroon & Gold
Arena: Silvio O. Conte Forum
  Capacity: 8,606; Year Built: 1988
AD: Gene De Filippo
SID: Mike Enright

BOSTON U.
Boston, MA 02215 I

Coach: Dennis Wolff, Connecticut 1978
2002-03 RESULTS (20-11)

57	Stanford	61
66	Columbia ■	37
61	Boston College	80
65	Dartmouth ■	53
68	Harvard ■	61
49	St. Joseph's	71
55	George Washington ■	68
78	Ohio ■	57
56	Cleveland St.	70
84	Florida St. †	69
70	Arizona	85
70	Binghamton ■	65
66	Albany (N.Y.)	63
65	Vermont ■	62
81	Stony Brook ■	66
59	Hartford	58
94	New Hampshire	64

69	Northeastern ■	72
63	Maine	53
78	Albany (N.Y.) ■	50
85	Binghamton	82
67	Stony Brook	73
65	Hartford ■	59
65	Maine ■	54
53	Vermont	60
76	New Hampshire ■	62
76	Northeastern	65
75	New Hampshire ■	61
71	Northeastern ■	61
55	Vermont ■	56
57	St. John's (N.Y.)	62

Nickname: Terriers
Colors: Scarlet & White
Arena: Case Gym
  Capacity: 1,800; Year Built: 1971
AD: Gary Strickler
SID: Stephan Lemon

BOWDOIN
Brunswick, ME 04011 III

Coach: Tim Gilbride, Providence 1974
2002-03 RESULTS (10-14)

78	Wheaton (Mass.) †	82
72	Salve Regina †	71
98	New England	85
87	Southern Me. ■	59
68	Bates ■	85
95	Mount Ida ■	57
99	Me.-Presque Isle †	50
69	Colby-Sawyer	80
65	Plymouth St.	76
58	Babson ■	81
91	Colby ■	95
64	Trinity (Conn.) ■	78
56	Amherst ■	86
69	Maine Maritime ■	47
93	Connecticut Col. ■	72
76	Wesleyan (Conn.) ■	86
55	St. Joseph's (Me.)	70
59	Williams	96
80	Middlebury	82
65	Tufts	75
84	Bates	59
77	Me.-Farmington	73
86	Colby	61
67	Amherst	78

Nickname: Polar Bears
Colors: White
Arena: Morrell Gymnasium
  Capacity: 2,000; Year Built: 1965
AD: Jeffrey H. Ward
SID: Jac Coyne

BOWIE ST.
Bowie, MD 20715-9465 II

Coach: Luke D'Alessio, Catholic 1983
2002-03 RESULTS (30-5)

110	Glenville St. ■	68
76	Southern Conn. St. ■	63
70	Winston-Salem	65
91	St. Augustine's ■	80
95	Dist. Columbia ■	97
98	Cheyney ■	80
74	St. Paul's ■	70
85	Shepherd	66
90	Edinboro †	75
88	Gannon	87
74	Virginia St.	59
92	N.C. Central ■	76
81	Fayetteville St. ■	71
80	Shaw	72
94	Johnson Smith ■	76
91	Livingstone	78
90	Virginia Union	88
86	Columbia Union	67

83	Pitt.-Johnstown	81
88	Elizabeth City St. ■	81
96	Virginia Union ■	99
58	Shaw	61
94	Virginia St. ■	71
85	Columbia Union ■	77
72	St. Paul's	75
74	Elizabeth City St.	69
94	Southern Va. ■	65
65	Johnson Smith †	63
99	N.C. Central †	87
72	Virginia Union †	71
88	Lenoir-Rhyne †	82
95	Kennesaw St. †	70
67	Presbyterian †	53
72	Mass.-Lowell †	62
64	Ky. Wesleyan †	84

Nickname: Bulldogs
Colors: Black & Gold
Arena: A.C. Jordan Arena
  Capacity: 4,000; Year Built: 1973
AD: Charles Davis
SID: Scott Rouch

BOWLING GREEN
Bowling Green, OH 43403 I

Coach: Dan Dakich, Indiana 1985
2002-03 RESULTS (13-16)

61	Detroit	75
91	Tiffin ■	57
76	Buffalo	59
60	Northwestern	62
57	Michigan	83
63	Alabama †	72
75	Oakland ■	68
76	Urbana ■	48
80	Cleveland St. †	72
64	Northern Ill.	63
61	Ball St. ■	57
78	Kent St.	74
67	Eastern Mich.	73
74	Akron ■	60
58	Western Mich.	76
46	Northern Ill.	63
66	Ohio	60
71	Central Mich.	88
67	Kent St. ■	73
54	Marshall	56
59	Toledo	73
65	Western Mich. ■	67
72	Ill.-Chicago	83
73	Ball St.	94
51	Miami (Ohio) ■	48
73	Eastern Mich. ■	72
64	Toledo ■	68
90	Ball St.	81
70	Central Mich. †	87

Nickname: Falcons
Colors: Orange & Brown
Arena: Anderson Arena
  Capacity: 5,000; Year Built: 1960
AD: Paul Krebs
SID: J.D. Campbell

BRADLEY
Peoria, IL 61625 I

Coach: Jim Les, Bradley 1986
2002-03 RESULTS (12-18)

95	Pepperdine ■	81
84	Loyola (Ill.)	88
70	Chattanooga ■	82
107	Ark.-Monticello ■	70
70	Butler	75
83	UNLV ■	85
71	Central Mich.	74
73	IUPUI	75
69	Hawaii	90
95	Alcorn St. †	68

88	Chicago St. †	76
45	Southwest Mo. St.	67
58	Creighton	65
79	Evansville	93
72	Drake ■	57
71	Northern Iowa	56
63	Indiana St.	45
60	Wichita St. ■	64
72	Southern Ill.	75
74	Illinois St.	89
63	Indiana St. ■	51
65	Creighton	88
88	Illinois St. ■	76
77	Southern Ill.	73
80	Northern Iowa	84
52	Southwest Mo. St. ■	54
86	Wichita St.	77
51	Evansville ■	54
77	Drake	67
66	Wichita St. †	70

Nickname: Braves
Colors: Red & White
Arena: Carver Arena
  Capacity: 11,300; Year Built: 1982
AD: Kenneth E. Kavanagh
SID: Bobby Parker

BRANDEIS
Waltham, MA 02454-9110 III

Coach: Chris Ford, Villanova 1971
2002-03 RESULTS (6-19)

58	Potsdam St.	63
63	Old Westbury †	79
65	Wheaton (Mass.)	89
85	Suffolk ■	69
44	Babson	78
54	MIT	67
45	Rochester	67
51	Carnegie Mellon	54
69	WPI	56
71	New York U. ■	68
59	Case Reserve ■	56
79	Emory ■	93
72	Tufts	70
60	Washington (Mo.)	92
57	Chicago	73
77	Mount Ida ■	68
49	Chicago ■	82
62	Washington (Mo.) ■	99
50	Amherst	78
56	Carnegie Mellon ■	69
45	Rochester ■	59
67	Emory	81
68	Case Reserve	81
71	Emerson	75
78	New York U.	99

Nickname: Judges
Colors: Blue & White
Arena: Auerbach Arena
  Capacity: 2,500; Year Built: 1992
AD: Jeffrey W. Cohen
SID: Adam Levin

BRIDGEPORT
Bridgeport, CT 06601 II

Coach: Mike Ruane, Alvernia 1992
2002-03 RESULTS (23-8)

85	Teikyo Post ■	71
79	St. Anselm ■	65
68	Adelphi	93
85	Dowling	68
70	NYIT	79
64	C.W. Post	92
79	Philadelphia U. ■	65
89	Pace ■	76
76	Queens (N.Y.)	69
74	Concordia (N.Y.) ■	60
72	St. Thomas Aquinas ■	41

73	Southampton	77
92	Molloy ■	68
75	Mercy	62
70	Adelphi ■	67
88	C.W. Post	92
89	Dowling	52
78	Concordia (N.Y.)	60
87	NYIT ■	73
81	Queens (N.Y.) ■	67
62	St. Thomas Aquinas	48
72	Southampton ■	63
78	New Haven	74
80	Mercy ■	63
75	Philadelphia U.	73
75	Molloy	82
68	New Haven ■	63
68	NYIT ■	56
69	Adelphi †	74
64	Adelphi †	56
73	Mass.-Lowell	86

Nickname: Purple Knights
Colors: Purple & White
Arena: Harvey Hubbell Gym
  Capacity: 2,000; Year Built: 1963
AD: Joseph DiPuma
SID: Mike Ruane

BRIDGEWATER (VA.)
Bridgewater, VA 22812-1599 ...III

Coach: Bill Leatherman, Milligan 1966
2002-03 RESULTS (14-12)

79	Phila. Bible †	44
86	Southern Va. †	84
79	Phila. Sciences †	75
103	Maryland Bible †	68
71	Christendom	53
50	Randolph-Macon	75
81	Southern Va. ■	57
61	St. Vincent	78
74	East. Mennonite	66
53	Hampden-Sydney ■	86
68	Lynchburg	50
53	Va. Wesleyan	79
91	Emory & Henry	89
62	Guilford	67
72	Roanoke	84
87	East. Mennonite ■	62
66	Wash. & Lee	64
51	Hampden-Sydney	74
86	Lynchburg ■	75
80	Roanoke ■	82
72	Guilford	70
96	Emory & Henry	97
45	Randolph-Macon ■	78
65	Va. Wesleyan	69
72	Wash. & Lee	63
58	Hampden-Sydney †	82

Nickname: Eagles
Colors: Cardinal & Vegas Gold
Arena: Nininger Hall
  Capacity: 1,200; Year Built: 1957
AD: Curtis L. Kendall
SID: Steve Cox

BRIDGEWATER ST.
Bridgewater, MA 02325-9998 ...III

Coach: Joe Farroba, Mass.-Boston 1975
2002-03 RESULTS (11-15)

70	Nyack	68
83	East Stroudsburg †	69
64	Mount Ida ■	56
65	Mass.-Dartmouth ■	72
70	Curry	62
70	Wheaton (Mass.)	83
80	Linfield †	105
62	Edgewood †	77
71	Concordia (Ill.) †	73
70	Rhode Island Col.	83

79	Emmanuel (Mass.) ■	50
74	Westfield St. ■	71
70	Framingham St.	55
101	Mass. Liberal Arts ■	75
59	Mass.-Boston	71
51	Worcester St. ■	58
70	Salem St.	84
64	Fitchburg St.	69
62	Westfield St.	72
65	Framingham St. ■	68
95	Mass. Liberal Arts	72
59	Worcester St.	60
73	Salem St. ■	86
75	Fitchburg St. ■	68
82	Fitchburg St. ■	78
70	Salem St.	75

Nickname: Bears
Colors: Crimson & White
Arena: Dr. Adrian Tinsley Center
  Capacity: 1,000; Year Built: 2002
AD: John C. Harper
SID: Mike Holbrook

BRIGHAM YOUNG
Provo, UT 84602 I

Coach: Steve Cleveland, UC Irvine 1976
2002-03 RESULTS (23-9)

71	Toledo †	56
73	Kansas St. †	64
66	St. Bonaventure †	57
95	Rice ■	56
64	Arizona St.	60
64	Creighton	74
64	San Diego ■	49
66	Utah St. ■	56
69	UC Santa Barb. ■	56
72	San Francisco	84
93	Southern Utah ■	60
84	Pepperdine ■	68
65	Oklahoma St. †	78
69	Weber St. ■	75
77	Idaho St. ■	58
85	UNLV ■	77
80	San Diego St. ■	69
75	Utah ■	79
80	New Mexico ■	64
65	Air Force ■	33
74	Wyoming	66
77	Colorado St.	68
54	UNLV	61
66	San Diego St. ■	64
64	Utah	71
56	Air Force	43
91	New Mexico	81
69	Wyoming ■	50
67	Colorado St. ■	55
71	New Mexico †	56
80	Colorado St. †	86
53	Connecticut †	58

Nickname: Cougars
Colors: Blue, White & Tan
Arena: Marriott Center
  Capacity: 22,700; Year Built: 1971
AD: Q. Val Hale
SID: Brett Pyne

BYU-HAWAII
Laie, HI 96762-1294 II

Coach: Ken Wagner, Brigham Young 1979
2002-03 RESULTS (19-4)

103	Oakland City ■	75
65	Western Wash.	74
99	St. Martin's †	53
94	Fort Lewis ■	87
87	Kennesaw St. ■	73
83	Lees-McRae ■	56
84	St. Martin's ■	65

83	Hawaii Pacific ■	80
103	Western N.M.	62
83	Western N.M.	63
76	Mont. St.-Billings	86
84	Hawaii Pacific ■	76
101	Hawaii-Hilo ■	95
94	Chaminade	71
70	Hawaii Pacific	61
83	Hawaii-Hilo	78
61	Hawaii-Hilo	71
91	Mont. St.-Billings ■	78
103	Mont. St.-Billings ■	89
100	Western N.M. ■	68
91	Chaminade ■	80
93	Chaminade ■	88
41	Cal St. Bakersfield ■	50

Nickname: Seasiders
Colors: Crimson, Gray & Gold
Arena: Cannon Activities Center
  Capacity: 4,338; Year Built: 1981
AD: Randy Day
SID: Scott Lowe

BROCKPORT ST.
Brockport, NY 14420-2989 III

Coach: Nelson Whitmore, St. John Fisher 1992
2002-03 RESULTS (16-12)

80	Dominican (Ill.) †	58
77	Calvin	93
68	St. John Fisher	74
78	Plattsburgh St.	68
64	Potsdam St.	76
65	C.W. Post †	64
77	Le Moyne	72
96	St. Lawrence ■	89
77	Oswego St.	86
68	Utica/Rome ■	74
82	Rochester Inst. †	84
66	Roberts Wesleyan ■	83
99	Keuka †	62
89	Fredonia St. ■	75
105	Oneonta St. ■	90
82	New Paltz St. ■	85
77	Geneseo St.	81
76	Fredonia St.	62
104	Oswego St. ■	60
71	Buffalo St. ■	62
86	Potsdam St. ■	81
76	Cortland St. ■	65
69	Oneonta St.	79
63	Cortland St.	47
71	Geneseo St. ■	66
82	Utica/Rome ■	65
62	New Paltz St. †	64
70	Nazareth	74

Nickname: Golden Eagles
Colors: Green & Gold
Arena: Tuttle North Gym
  Capacity: 3,000; Year Built: 1973
AD: Linda J. Case
SID: Eric McDowell

BROOKLYN
Brooklyn, NY 11210-2889 III

Coach: Steve Podias, Fordham 1978
2002-03 RESULTS (8-18)

55	Marywood †	76
72	Baptist Bible (Pa.) †	91
85	Centenary (N.J.) ■	97
79	St. Joseph's (Brkln) ■	83
65	York (N.Y.)	81
61	New York U.	91
71	Staten Island ■	75
70	St. Joseph's (Brkln)	50
72	NYCCT ■	66
63	Elms	70
80	Medgar Evers	91

66	Lehman ■	73
57	Maritime (N.Y.)	77
58	John Jay	65
71	Hunter	69
54	Baruch	81
77	Yeshiva	83
86	York (N.Y.) ■	84
58	Staten Island	78
97	Medgar Evers ■	96
83	Berkeley ■	62
65	NYCCT	67
61	CCNY	94
82	Pratt	71
84	Medgar Evers ■	68
60	Baruch	78

Nickname: Bridges
Colors: Maroon & Gold
Arena: Roosevelt Gymnasium
  Capacity: 800; Year Built: 1935
AD: Bruce Filosa
SID: Alex Lang

BROWN
Providence, RI 02912 I

Coach: Glen Miller, Connecticut 1986
2002-03 RESULTS (17-12)

65	IUPUI †	66
77	Belmont †	83
64	Providence	83
69	Wagner	81
97	Navy	92
71	Ohio	75
56	Holy Cross ■	72
48	Rhode Island	67
75	Central Conn. St.	67
86	San Jose St.	75
63	St. Mary's (Cal.)	77
52	San Francisco	81
65	Rider ■	53
93	New Hampshire	76
78	Yale	66
94	Yale ■	84
70	Cornell	54
72	Columbia	59
91	Harvard ■	86
61	Dartmouth ■	53
80	Princeton	73
66	Pennsylvania	73
83	Columbia ■	70
70	Cornell ■	62
65	Pennsylvania ■	69
88	Princeton ■	74
79	Dartmouth	67
93	Harvard	80
73	Virginia	89

Nickname: Bears
Colors: Brown, Red & White
Arena: Pizzitola Sports Center
  Capacity: 3,100; Year Built: 1989
AD: David T. Roach
SID: Chris Humm

BRYANT
Smithfield, RI 02917-1284 II

Coach: Max Good, Eastern Ky. 1969
2002-03 RESULTS (17-14)

74	Bellarmine †	70
67	Henderson St. †	78
73	Columbus St. †	77
95	Southampton ■	72
64	Stonehill ■	54
53	Le Moyne	54
68	St. Anselm ■	77
89	St. Michael's ■	77
66	Southern Conn. St.	60
77	Dowling	84
69	Bentley ■	74
80	Molloy ■	55

64	West Chester ■	63
68	Pace	73
75	St. Rose ■	52
68	American Int'l	69
51	Assumption ■	58
76	Franklin Pierce ■	68
78	Mass.-Lowell ■	72
73	Southern N.H.	74
65	St. Michael's	60
69	St. Anselm	65
67	Le Moyne ■	69
70	American Int'l ■	62
100	Green Mountain	50
64	Assumption	60
85	Franklin Pierce	91
82	Southern N.H. ■	72
58	Mass.-Lowell	64
76	Merrimack	65
70	Franklin Pierce ■	74

Nickname: Bulldogs
Colors: Black, Gold & White
Arena: Bryant Athletic Center
  Capacity: 2,400; Year Built: 1971
AD: Dan Gavitt
SID: Chuck Sullivan

BUCKNELL
Lewisburg, PA 17837 I

Coach: Pat Flannery, Bucknell 1980
2002-03 RESULTS (14-15)

42	Notre Dame	73
56	Albany (N.Y.)	53
61	Columbia †	47
77	George Washington	80
67	Canisius ■	71
52	St. Francis (Pa.) ■	54
72	FDU-Florham ■	45
55	Penn St.	59
52	Arizona St.	79
67	UC Santa Barb. †	60
52	Niagara ■	63
66	Robert Morris ■	53
63	American ■	52
56	Lehigh ■	60
53	Navy	66
60	Cornell	64
53	Army ■	38
68	Lafayette ■	48
62	Colgate	42
47	Holy Cross	69
56	American	70
49	Lehigh	61
59	Navy ■	41
70	Lafayette	53
66	Army	65
43	Holy Cross ■	54
56	Colgate ■	64
52	Lehigh †	47
50	Holy Cross †	75

Nickname: Bison
Colors: Orange & Blue
Arena: Davis Gymnasium
  Capacity: 2,300; Year Built: 1938
AD: John P. Hardt
SID: Jon Terry

BUENA VISTA
Storm Lake, IA 50588-9990 III

Coach: Brian Van Haaften, Northwestern (Iowa)
2002-03 RESULTS (27-4)

90	St. Scholastica ■	56
79	Dordt	75
75	Briar Cliff †	64
65	Neb. Wesleyan	61
67	Wartburg ■	75
74	St. Thomas (Minn.) †	78
90	Wis. Lutheran †	64

82	Simpson ■	70
71	Central (Iowa) ■	63
64	Cornell College	66
81	Coe	69
107	Morningside ■	72
86	Loras ■	75
89	Dubuque ■	63
80	Upper Iowa ■	55
81	Luther	63
70	Central (Iowa)	54
74	Simpson	61
92	Coe ■	84
74	Cornell College ■	49
71	Wartburg	62
102	Dubuque	77
70	Loras	58
75	Luther ■	73
93	Upper Iowa ■	79
105	Central (Iowa) ■	57
70	Loras ■	65
72	Wartburg ■	70
96	Illinois Col. ■	66
84	Rockford	72
62	Occidental ■	67

Nickname: Beavers
Colors: Blue & Gold
Arena: Siebens Center
  Capacity: 4,000; Year Built: 1969
AD: Jan Travis
SID: Paul Misner

BUFFALO
Buffalo, NY 14260 I

Coach: Reggie Witherspoon, Empire St. 1995

2002-03 RESULTS (5-23)

72	Cornell ■	78
84	Chicago St. ■	53
65	Detroit	66
57	Rhode Island ■	48
59	Bowling Green	76
48	Youngstown St.	63
75	Niagara ■	64
65	Canisius	71
62	Northwestern	69
60	Penn St.	68
63	Marshall ■	69
71	Akron	89
68	Kent St. ■	69
73	Central Mich.	97
66	Ohio ■	72
77	Marshall	87
55	Miami (Ohio)	57
61	Northern Ill. ■	70
49	Ohio	61
90	Eastern Mich. ■	66
68	Ball St.	80
55	Kent St.	98
35	Miami (Ohio) ■	63
59	Toledo ■	66
78	Eastern Mich.	88
66	Western Mich.	87
70	Akron ■	66
64	Northern Ill.	81

Nickname: Bulls
Colors: Royal Blue & White
Arena: Alumni Arena
  Capacity: 8,500; Year Built: 1982
AD: William J. Maher
SID: Jon Fuller

BUFFALO ST.
Buffalo, NY 14222-1095 III

Coach: Richard Bihr, Buffalo St. 1969

2002-03 RESULTS (19-9)

75	Elmira ■	80
80	Cazenovia ■	63

89	Oneonta St.	59
74	New Paltz St.	64
64	Wilmington (Ohio) †	63
66	Scranton †	75
55	Penn St.-Behrend	58
65	D'Youville †	51
79	Hilbert ■	61
84	D'Youville ■	66
75	Potsdam St. ■	76
85	Plattsburgh St. ■	61
68	Cortland St.	56
82	Utica/Rome ■	72
88	Oswego St. ■	63
73	Geneseo St. ■	69
71	Plattsburgh St.	62
68	Fredonia St.	60
62	Brockport St.	71
77	Cortland St. ■	63
74	New Paltz St. ■	71
61	Fredonia St. ■	64
57	Oswego St.	75
68	Utica/Rome	71
81	Fredonia St. ■	64
67	Oswego St. †	62
73	New Paltz St. †	40
56	Scranton	58

Nickname: Bengals
Colors: Orange & Black
Arena: Sports Arena
  Capacity: 3,500; Year Built: 1991
AD: Jerry S. Boyes
SID: Jeff Ventura

BUTLER
Indianapolis, IN 46208-3485 I

Coach: Todd Lickliter, Butler 1979

2002-03 RESULTS (27-6)

69	IPFW †	53
60	Wayne St. (Mich.) ■	37
71	Ball St. ■	45
65	Indiana St.	45
77	Evansville	64
75	Bradley ■	70
59	Miami (Ohio)	42
68	St. Louis	46
67	Tex.-Pan American †	48
63	Western Ky. †	60
78	Hawaii	81
68	Ill.-Chicago	65
81	Loyola (Ill.) ■	74
76	Detroit ■	68
81	Wright St.	70
64	Youngstown St. ■	60
65	Wis.-Milwaukee	69
68	Wis.-Green Bay	53
60	Duke	80
73	Cleveland St. ■	57
61	Ill.-Chicago ■	47
63	Loyola (Ill.)	73
66	Detroit	63
79	Wright St. ■	64
69	Youngstown St.	60
79	Cleveland St.	75
58	Wis.-Green Bay ■	37
76	Wis.-Milwaukee ■	74
58	Detroit †	55
52	Wis.-Milwaukee	69
47	Mississippi St. †	46
79	Louisville †	71
54	Oklahoma †	65

Nickname: Bulldogs
Colors: Blue & White
Arena: Hinkle Fieldhouse
  Capacity: 11,043; Year Built: 1928
AD: John C. Parry
SID: Jim McGrath

C.W. POST
Brookville, NY 11548 II

Coach: Tom Galeazzi, Cortland St. 1961

2002-03 RESULTS (25-8)

72	New Haven ■	62
65	Adelphi ■	62
81	Dowling	83
87	Concordia (N.Y.) ■	48
92	Bridgeport	64
64	Brockport St. †	65
69	Roberts Wesleyan †	71
82	NYIT	62
67	Philadelphia U. ■	51
76	Queens (N.Y.)	72
69	St. Thomas Aquinas ■	47
83	Southampton	58
73	Molloy	65
81	Mercy	66
55	New Haven	69
92	Bridgeport ■	88
76	Adelphi	84
82	Southern Conn. St. ■	58
87	Dowling ■	62
66	Concordia (N.Y.)	53
73	NYIT ■	57
61	Philadelphia U.	64
59	Queens (N.Y.) ■	53
78	Southampton ■	64
66	St. Thomas Aquinas	56
78	Mercy ■	69
88	Molloy	81
88	Molloy ■	76
77	New Haven	69
57	Adelphi ■	70
81	Assumption †	75
78	New Haven †	61
59	Mass.-Lowell	69

Nickname: Pioneers
Colors: Green & Gold
Arena: Conolly Gym
  Capacity: 600; Year Built: 1960
AD: Vincent Salamone
SID: Brad Sullivan

CABRINI
Radnor, PA 19087-3698 III

Coach: John Dzik, West Chester 1972

2002-03 RESULTS (17-9)

69	Mary Washington †	74
72	Christendom †	48
83	LaGrange †	70
64	Wis.-River Falls †	67
61	D'Youville †	58
82	Villa Julie	73
67	Kean ■	62
69	Pitt.-Bradford ■	71
60	Misericordia ■	55
70	Gwynedd-Mercy	60
81	Wesley	78
66	Neumann	71
72	Eastern ■	68
84	Arcadia	62
49	Alvernia	63
77	Marywood ■	63
52	Widener	70
66	Gwynedd-Mercy ■	58
58	Neumann	57
66	Misericordia ■	69
83	Marywood	58
54	Arcadia	47
71	Wesley ■	63
53	Alvernia	61
66	Eastern	64
63	Alvernia ■	67

Nickname: Cavaliers
Colors: Royal Blue & White

Arena: Sacred Heart Gymnasium
  Capacity: 750; Year Built: 1958
AD: John L. Dzik
SID: Rich Schepis

CALDWELL
Caldwell, NJ 07006-6195.........II

Coach: Mark Corino, Kean

2002-03 RESULTS (15-11)

73	St. Michael's	79
71	Green Mountain †	55
61	Goldey-Beacom	42
50	Holy Family ■	56
64	Teikyo Post	55
71	Wilmington (Del.)	56
65	Pace	80
51	North Fla.	64
63	Grand Canyon	65
50	Tiffin †	49
64	Dominican (N.Y.) ■	50
53	N.J. Inst. of Tech. ■	46
70	Felician ■	53
59	Phila. Sciences ■	63
71	Nyack	61
103	Wilmington (Del.) ■	87
94	Bloomfield	89
70	Phila. Sciences	68
60	Teikyo Post ■	69
50	N.J. Inst. of Tech.	59
87	Dominican (N.Y.)	73
60	Felician	63
71	Goldey-Beacom ■	50
88	Nyack ■	78
72	Holy Family	79
67	Teikyo Post ■	89

Nickname: Cougars
Colors: Scarlet & Gold
Arena: George R. Newman
  Capacity: 1,800; Year Built: 2002
AD: Mark A. Corino
SID: Micheal Lamberti

CALIFORNIA
Berkeley, CA 94720 I

Coach: Ben Braun, Wisconsin 1975

2002-03 RESULTS (22-9)

76	New Mexico	68
73	Cleveland St.	64
80	Howard ■	70
73	Georgia †	78
67	UC Santa Barb. ■	60
84	Grambling ■	65
77	La.-Lafayette ■	61
67	Kansas †	80
77	San Francisco ■	70
72	Stanford	59
88	Oregon ■	72
78	Oregon St. ■	73
73	Washington	66
76	Washington St.	63
73	Southern California ■	68
80	UCLA ■	69
70	Arizona St.	72
80	Arizona	95
84	Oregon St.	71
86	Oregon	75
63	Washington St. ■	53
58	Washington ■	76
75	UCLA	76
84	Southern California	82
75	Arizona ■	88
80	Arizona St. ■	72
60	Stanford	72
69	Oregon St. †	46
62	Southern California †	79
76	North Carolina St. †	74
65	Oklahoma †	74

Nickname: Golden Bears
Colors: Blue & Gold
Arena: Haas Pavilion
 Capacity: 11,892; Year Built: 1999
AD: Stephen Gladstone
SID: Herb Benenson

UC DAVIS
Davis, CA 95616-8674 II

Coach: Brian Fogel, Sonoma St. 1989
2002-03 RESULTS (12-15)
62 Dominican (Cal.) ■ 65
89 Western Wash. ■.....................74
62 Regis (Colo.).........................63
84 Cal St. Monterey Bay 65
65 Cal St. Chico........................70
90 Cal St. Hayward ■.................74
67 Cal St. Chico........................70
91 Sonoma St............................84
56 San Fran. St..........................74
49 Cal St. San B'dino ■...............76
64 Cal Poly Pomona ■.................77
74 Cal St. Stanislaus 76
69 Cal St. Bakersfield 65
79 Grand Canyon ■.....................68
105 UC San Diego 100
92 Cal St. Dom. Hills ■..............98
76 Cal St. L.A. ■.........................54
68 San Fran. St. ■.......................66
59 Sonoma St. ■.........................67
43 Cal Poly Pomona 65
49 Cal St. San B'dino 93
58 Cal St. Bakersfield ■..............70
71 Cal St. Stanislaus ■................73
84 UC San Diego ■.....................85
67 Grand Canyon ■.....................64
69 Cal St. L.A............................54
64 Cal St. Dom. Hills 63

Nickname: Aggies
Colors: Yale Blue & Gold
Arena: Recreation Hall
 Capacity: 7,600; Year Built: 1977
AD: Greg Warzecka
SID: Bill Stevens

UC IRVINE
Irvine, CA 92697-4125 I

Coach: Pat Douglass, Pacific (Cal.) 1972
2002-03 RESULTS (20-9)
65 Oklahoma 87
62 Western Mich. † 73
74 Pepperdine 69
81 Loyola Marymount ■.............66
91 Pomona-Pitzer ■....................23
57 Stanford 84
62 St. Mary's (Cal.) 50
96 IPFW ■.................................79
87 Fla. Atlantic ■.......................70
69 Long Beach St. 52
65 Cal St. Fullerton 66
81 UC Riverside.........................77
75 Utah St. ■.............................73
58 Idaho 45
66 Pacific (Cal.).........................62
63 Cal St. Northridge 69
54 UC Santa Barb. ■...................70
68 Cal Poly ■.............................74
78 UC Riverside ■.......................61
72 Cal St. Fullerton ■..................52
59 Utah St. 58
65 Idaho 52
64 Cal St. Northridge ■...............57
78 Pacific (Cal.) ■.......................73
68 Cal Poly 62
51 UC Santa Barb. 67
95 Long Beach St. ■....................60
70 Cal St. Northridge † 64
55 Utah St. † 62

Nickname: Anteaters
Colors: Blue & Gold
Arena: Bren Events Center
 Capacity: 5,000; Year Built: 1987
AD: John Hauscarriague
SID: Bob Olson

UC RIVERSIDE
Riverside, CA 92521 I

Coach: John Masi, UC Riverside 1970
2002-03 RESULTS (6-18)
68 Southern California 81
64 San Diego 84
71 UC Santa Cruz ■.....................58
74 St. Mary's (Cal.) 79
62 San Diego 73
67 Oregon 108
49 UC Santa Barb. 65
77 Cal Poly 83
77 Long Beach St. 73
77 UC Irvine ■............................81
47 Cal St. Fullerton 41
58 Utah St.................................77
53 Idaho 56
71 Pacific (Cal.) 79
74 Cal St. Northridge ■...............71
61 UC Irvine 78
68 Long Beach St. 65
64 Cal St. Fullerton 74
64 Idaho ■................................68
72 Utah St. ■.............................65
70 Cal St. Northridge 78
65 Pacific (Cal.)..........................77
67 Cal Poly ■.............................86
55 UC Santa Barb. 70

Nickname: Highlanders
Colors: Blue & Gold
Arena: UCR Student Rec Center
 Capacity: 3,168; Year Built: 1994
AD: Stanley M. Morrison
SID: Ross French

UC SAN DIEGO
La Jolla, CA 92093-0531 II

Coach: Greg Lanthier, Pt. Loma
Nazarene 1987
2002-03 RESULTS (7-20)
57 San Diego St. 87
82 Grand Canyon ■....................69
70 Grand Canyon 87
62 San Diego 105
75 UC Santa Cruz ■....................70
83 Chaminade ■.........................89
58 Humboldt St. ■.....................100
42 Cal St. Stanislaus ■................73
58 Cal St. Bakersfield ■..............87
62 Cal St. Dom. Hills 57
72 Cal St. L.A. 55
44 Cal St. San B'dino ■...............73
62 Cal Poly Pomona 88
69 Cal St. Chico ■.......................92
100 UC Davis ■.........................105
53 Sonoma St. 70
63 San Fran. St. 71
50 Cal St. Bakersfield 67
68 Cal St. Stanislaus 79
55 Cal St. L.A. ■.........................66
71 Cal St. Dom. Hills ■...............59
41 Cal Poly Pomona 57
68 Cal St. San B'dino 88
85 UC Davis 84
82 Cal St. Chico 89
72 San Fran. St. ■.......................56
49 Sonoma St. ■.........................59

Nickname: Tritons
Colors: Blue & Gold
Arena: RIMAC Arena
 Capacity: 5,000; Year Built: 1995

AD: Earl W. Edwards
SID: Bill Gannon

UC SANTA BARB.
Santa Barbara, CA 93106.........I

Coach: Bob Williams, San Jose St. 1975
2002-03 RESULTS (18-14)
82 Weber St. † 91
66 Jacksonville St. † 73
84 Centenary (La.) † 69
70 San Francisco ■......................47
69 Southern California ■..............53
68 Pepperdine 72
60 California 67
56 Brigham Young 69
57 Nebraska † 60
60 Bucknell † 67
65 UC Riverside ■.......................49
55 Cal St. Fullerton ■..................57
62 Idaho 53
59 Utah St. 75
77 Cal St. Northridge ■...............59
67 Pacific (Cal.) ■.......................52
70 Cal Poly ■.............................61
70 UC Irvine 54
67 Long Beach St. 68
62 Utah St. ■.............................50
52 Idaho ■................................44
62 Pacific (Cal.) 52
67 Cal St. Northridge 58
63 Cal Poly 66
59 Detroit ■...............................75
70 Long Beach St. ■....................46
67 UC Irvine ■............................51
63 Cal St. Fullerton 60
70 UC Riverside..........................55
53 Pacific (Cal.) † 44
52 Cal Poly † 67
62 San Diego St. 67

Nickname: Gauchos
Colors: Blue & Gold
Arena: The Thunderdome
 Capacity: 6,000; Year Built: 1979
AD: Gary A. Cunningham
SID: Bill Mahoney

UC SANTA CRUZ
Santa Cruz, CA 95064 III

Coach: Bernard Thompson/Gordie
Johnson
2002-03 RESULTS (4-23)
58 San Fran. St. 87
60 Westmont ■...........................82
70 Santa Clara 93
76 Northern Ariz. 100
61 San Jose Christian ■................76
58 UC Riverside..........................71
70 UC San Diego 75
63 Pt. Loma Nazarene 75
51 Cal St. San B'dino 99
59 Angelo St. † 110
61 Westmont 93
60 Seattle Pacific 95
67 Seattle 87
60 Menlo 77
97 Bethany (Cal.) ■.....................63
67 Cal St. Monterey Bay 68
65 Notre Dame de Namur 68
82 Simpson (Cal.) 94
78 Holy Names 92
69 Dominican (Cal.) ■.................96
68 Cal St. Hayward ■..................75
67 Cal Maritime 63
80 Pacific Union ■.......................60
89 Bethany (Cal.) 92
59 Cal St. Monterey Bay ■...........73
66 Notre Dame de Namur ■.........75
79 Menlo ■................................74

Nickname: Banana Slugs
Colors: Blue & Gold
Arena: West Field House
 Capacity: 300
AD: Greg Harshaw
SID: Dorth Raphaely

CALIF. (PA.)
California, PA 15419 II

Coach: Bill Brown, Ohio 1974
2002-03 RESULTS (25-9)
62 Columbus St. † 64
68 Lake Superior St. † 49
56 Presbyterian † 61
74 West Va. Wesleyan ■..............40
81 Dist. Columbia ■....................75
76 Cheyney ■.............................69
56 Kutztown ■............................61
73 Geneva ■...............................50
82 Allegheny ■...........................75
97 Ohio Valley ■.........................54
67 Mansfield ■............................62
69 Fairmont St. † 55
62 Wheeling Jesuit 60
56 Millersville 67
64 West Chester 79
92 East Stroudsburg 84
84 Bloomsburg 71
72 Clarion ■...............................79
62 Indiana (Pa.) 51
70 Pitt.-Johnstown 54
75 Lock Haven ■.........................61
46 Shippensburg 45
58 Edinboro ■.............................44
78 Slippery Rock 75
78 Indiana (Pa.) ■.......................65
61 Clarion 63
60 Lock Haven 58
80 Shippensburg ■......................61
73 Slippery Rock ■......................55
73 Edinboro 59
63 Lock Haven ■.........................60
62 West Chester ■.......................60
74 Millersville ■..........................79
73 Salem Int'l † 76

Nickname: Vulcans
Colors: Red & Black
Arena: Hamer Hall
 Capacity: 2,500; Year Built: 1962
AD: Thomas G. Pucci
SID: David Smith

CAL LUTHERAN
Thousand Oaks, CA 91360-2787
....III

Coach: Rich Rider, Northeast Mo. St.
1968
2002-03 RESULTS (16-9)
107 Hope Int'l ■.........................64
70 Alvernia † 91
77 Clarke † 65
82 La Sierra ■.............................66
64 Cal St. L.A. ■.........................82
76 Westmont ■...........................93
100 West Coast Chrst. ■..............56
87 Bethany (Cal.) ■.....................99
81 Wartburg ■............................89
71 Chapman ■............................50
132 Cal Christian ■.....................78
96 La Verne 87
65 Pomona-Pitzer 60
99 Caltech ■...............................40
112 Redlands 65
82 Whittier ■..............................69
77 Occidental ■..........................80
75 Claremont-M-S 76
98 La Verne ■.............................92
72 Pomona-Pitzer ■....................63

87 Caltech ...45
102 Redlands ■ ...96
79 Whittier ...75
63 Occidental ...76
56 Claremont-M-S ■ ...79

Nickname: Kingsmen
Colors: Purple & Gold
Arena: CLU Gymnasium
Capacity: 500; Year Built: 1962
AD: Bruce Bryde
SID: Scott Flanders

CAL POLY
San Luis Obispo, CA 93407 I

Coach: Kevin Bromley, Colorado St. 1983

2002-03 RESULTS (16-14)
69 Colorado ...97
88 Notre Dame de Namur ■ ...74
62 San Diego St. ■ ...65
60 Oregon St. ...81
66 Sacramento St. ■ ...73
72 Loyola Marymount ■ ...70
75 New Orleans † ...89
73 Eastern Ill. † ...70
59 St. Mary's (Cal.) ...52
65 Cal St. Fullerton ■ ...44
83 UC Riverside ■ ...77
67 Utah St. ...81
50 Idaho ...66
75 Pacific (Cal.) ...72
54 Cal St. Northridge ■ ...73
61 UC Santa Barb. ...70
86 Long Beach St. ...71
74 UC Irvine ...68
65 Idaho ■ ...68
63 Utah St. ■ ...64
62 Cal St. Northridge ...59
67 Pacific (Cal.) ...64
66 UC Santa Barb. ■ ...63
62 UC Irvine ■ ...68
76 Long Beach St. ■ ...64
86 UC Riverside. ...67
85 Cal St. Fullerton ...88
54 Idaho † ...50
67 UC Santa Barb. † ...52
54 Utah St. † ...57

Nickname: Mustangs
Colors: Green & Gold
Arena: Robert A. Mott Gymnasium
Capacity: 3,032; Year Built: 1960
AD: John F. McCutcheon
SID: Brian Thurmond

CAL POLY POMONA
Pomona, CA 91768.................II

Coach: Greg Kamansky, UC San Diego 1988

2002-03 RESULTS (23-8)
75 St. Martin's † ...72
54 Western Wash. ...68
68 Cal St. San B'dino ■ ...64
61 Pt. Loma Nazarene ■ ...57
64 Cal St. San B'dino ...72
86 Vanguard ■ ...61
82 Mont. St.-Billings ■ ...66
55 Cal St. Dom. Hills ■ ...42
79 Cal St. L.A. ■ ...63
84 Cal St. Chico ...88
77 UC Davis ...64
86 Grand Canyon ...56
88 UC San Diego ...62
48 Sonoma St. ...62
71 San Fran. St. ■ ...53
72 Cal St. Bakersfield ■ ...65
68 Cal St. Stanislaus ■ ...54
84 Cal St. L.A. ...79
62 Cal St. Dom. Hills ...67

65 UC Davis ■ ...43
72 Cal St. Chico ...73
57 UC San Diego ■ ...41
63 Grand Canyon ■ ...56
55 San Fran. St. ...54
62 Sonoma St. ...60
68 Cal St. Stanislaus ...72
67 Cal St. Bakersfield ...62
80 Alas. Fairbanks † ...76
62 Cal St. Bakersfield † ...49
91 Cal St. San B'dino † ...84
60 Ky. Wesleyan † ...85

Nickname: Broncos
Colors: Green & Gold
Arena: Kellogg Gym
Capacity: 5,000; Year Built: 1966
AD: Dan Bridges
SID: Paul Helms

CAL ST. BAKERSFIELD
Bakersfield, CA 93311-1099.....II

Coach: Henry Clark, Mont. St.-Billings 1980

2002-03 RESULTS (20-9)
93 UC-Colo. Spgs. ■ ...66
88 Azusa Pacific ■ ...77
77 Cal St. Stanislaus ...70
102 Cal St. Hayward ■ ...64
66 Cal St. Stanislaus ...52
80 Holy Names ■ ...49
98 Central Wash. ■ ...86
70 Grand Canyon ...72
87 UC San Diego ...58
74 Sonoma St. ...81
72 San Fran. St. ...65
93 Cal St. Chico ■ ...79
65 UC Davis ■ ...69
60 Cal St. Dom. Hills ■ ...44
60 Cal St. L.A. ■ ...51
65 Cal Poly Pomona ...72
62 Cal St. San B'dino ...63
67 UC San Diego ■ ...50
76 Grand Canyon ■ ...63
66 San Fran. St. ■ ...56
53 Sonoma St. ...36
70 UC Davis ...58
60 Cal St. Chico ...65
68 Cal St. L.A. ...84
92 Cal St. Dom. Hills ...59
74 Cal St. San B'dino ■ ...68
62 Cal Poly Pomona ■ ...67
50 BYU-Hawaii ...41
49 Cal Poly Pomona † ...62

Nickname: Roadrunners
Colors: Blue & Gold
Arena: Centennial Garden
Capacity: 10,800; Year Built: 1998
AD: Rudy Carvajal
SID: Kevin Gilmore

CAL ST. CHICO
Chico, CA 95929....................II

Coach: Prescott Smith, Southwestern Okla. 1965

2002-03 RESULTS (18-9)
73 Dominican (Cal.) ■ ...64
69 Humboldt St. ■ ...87
70 UC Davis ■ ...65
102 Bethany (Cal.) ■ ...64
82 Holy Names ■ ...61
64 Oregon Tech ■ ...71
70 UC Davis ...67
72 San Fran. St. ...96
61 Sonoma St. ...74
88 Cal Poly Pomona ■ ...84
77 Cal St. San B'dino ■ ...108
79 Cal St. Bakersfield ...93
93 Cal St. Stanislaus ...82

92 UC San Diego ...69
71 Grand Canyon ...74
75 Cal St. L.A. ■ ...74
81 Cal St. Dom. Hills ■ ...78
70 Sonoma St. ...74
87 San Fran. St. ■ ...66
60 Cal St. San B'dino ...78
73 Cal Poly Pomona ...72
92 Cal St. Stanislaus ■ ...82
65 Cal St. Bakersfield ■ ...60
94 Grand Canyon ...79
89 UC San Diego ...82
97 Cal St. Dom. Hills ...72
81 Cal St. L.A. ...67

Nickname: Wildcats
Colors: Cardinal & White
Arena: Art Acker Gym
Capacity: 1,997; Year Built: 1962
AD: Anita S. Barker
SID: Teresa Clements

CAL ST. DOM. HILLS
Carson, CA 90747...................II

Coach: Larry Hauser, Chicago St. 1971

2002-03 RESULTS (6-21)
73 Vanguard ■ ...71
66 Cal Baptist ...89
53 Cal St. L.A. ■ ...52
53 Cal St. Monterey Bay ...66
54 Dominican (Cal.) ■ ...50
62 Cal St. L.A. ...67
68 Humboldt St. ■ ...105
50 Cal Poly Pomona ...55
57 UC San Diego ■ ...62
73 Grand Canyon ■ ...71
62 San Fran. St. ...75
47 Sonoma St. ...59
44 Cal St. Bakersfield ...60
63 Cal St. Stanislaus ...76
98 UC Davis ...92
78 Cal St. Chico ...81
58 Cal St. San B'dino ■ ...74
67 Cal Poly Pomona ■ ...62
54 Grand Canyon ...56
59 UC San Diego ...71
66 Sonoma St. ...69
67 San Fran. St. ...87
57 Cal St. Stanislaus ■ ...78
59 Cal St. Bakersfield ■ ...92
72 Cal St. Chico ■ ...97
63 UC Davis ■ ...64

Nickname: Toros
Colors: Cardinal Red & Gold
Arena: Torodome
Capacity: 4,200; Year Built: 1978
AD: Ron Prettyman
SID: Patrick Guillen

CAL ST. FULLERTON
Fullerton, CA 92834-6810.........I

Coach: Donny Daniels, Cal St. Fullerton 1977

2002-03 RESULTS (10-19)
76 Tex. A&M-Corp. Chris † ...83
43 Ark.-Little Rock † ...56
74 Morris Brown ■ ...56
87 Pepperdine ■ ...90
68 Loyola Marymount ...75
63 Southern California ...78
70 Idaho St. ■ ...79
62 Sacramento St. ...54
61 San Francisco ...75
44 Cal Poly ...65
57 UC Santa Barb. ...55
66 UC Irvine ...65
57 Long Beach St. ■ ...53
66 Idaho St. ...74

41 UC Riverside ■ ...47
49 Idaho ...56
60 Utah St. ...61
70 Cal St. Northridge ■ ...54
61 Pacific (Cal.) ■ ...62
73 Long Beach St. ...79
52 UC Irvine ...72
74 UC Riverside. ...64
41 Utah St. ■ ...62
62 Idaho ■ ...59
55 Pacific (Cal.) ...52
62 Cal St. Northridge ...70
60 UC Santa Barb. ■ ...63
88 Cal Poly ■ ...85
83 Utah St. † ...89

Nickname: Titans
Colors: Navy, Orange & White
Arena: Titan Gym
Capacity: 3,500; Year Built: 1964
AD: Brian Quinn
SID: Mel Franks

CAL ST. HAYWARD
Hayward, CA 94542...............III

Coach: Will Biggs, Cal St. Hayward 1988

2002-03 RESULTS (12-17)
70 Fresno Pacific † ...126
73 Menlo ...91
69 Chapman † ...64
48 Claremont-M-S † ...75
92 Redlands ...107
64 Cal St. Bakersfield ...102
74 UC Davis ...90
79 Pacific Lutheran ■ ...84
58 Willamette ...86
82 Wis. Lutheran ■ ...72
62 Pacific Union ...52
76 Simpson (Cal.) ...66
54 Holy Names ...63
46 Dominican (Cal.) ...58
60 Cal St. Maritime ■ ...61
95 Bethany (Cal.) ...80
56 Cal St. Monterey Bay ...63
75 UC Santa Cruz ...68
67 Notre Dame de Namur ■ ...71
71 Menlo ■ ...79
83 Simpson (Cal.) ...87
78 Holy Names ...86
52 Dominican (Cal.) ■ ...49
85 Cal St. Maritime ...74
72 Pacific Union ...55
65 Cal St. Monterey Bay † ...56
69 Menlo † ...63
63 Notre Dame de Namur † ...51
44 Bellevue ...76

Nickname: Pioneers
Colors: Red & White
Arena: Pioneer Gym
Capacity: 5,000; Year Built: 1967
AD: Debby De Angelis
SID: Marty Valdez

CAL ST. L.A.
Los Angeles, CA 90032-8240 ...II

Coach: Dave Yanai, Long Beach St. 1966

2002-03 RESULTS (9-18)
62 Christian Heritage ...48
77 Biola ...85
52 Cal St. Dom. Hills ...53
82 Cal Lutheran ■ ...64
78 Vanguard ...75
67 Cal St. Dom. Hills ■ ...62
75 Mont. St.-Billings ■ ...55
60 Cal St. San B'dino ...72
63 Cal Poly Pomona ...79
65 Grand Canyon ■ ...66

55	UC San Diego ■	72
49	Sonoma St.	54
67	San Fran. St. ■	64
74	Cal St. Stanislaus	82
51	Cal St. Bakersfield	60
74	Cal St. Chico	75
54	UC Davis	76
79	Cal Poly Pomona ■	84
61	Cal St. San B'dino ■	78
66	UC San Diego	55
54	Grand Canyon	58
56	San Fran. St.	66
60	Sonoma St.	69
84	Cal St. Bakersfield ■	68
60	Cal St. Stanislaus ■	46
54	UC Davis	69
67	Cal St. Chico ■	81

Nickname: Golden Eagles
Colors: Black & Gold
Arena: Eagles Nest
 Capacity: 5,000; Year Built: 1947
AD: Carol M. Dunn
SID: Chris Hughes

CAL ST. NORTHRIDGE
Northridge, CA 91330 I

Coach: Bobby Braswell, Cal St. Northridge 1984
2002-03 RESULTS (14-15)

65	Portland St.	69
67	Jacksonville †	55
77	Oregon	86
101	Howard ■	80
64	San Diego	61
117	Bethany (Cal.) ■	51
92	San Jose St. ■	67
74	Loyola Marymount ■	71
74	Southern Ill.	86
80	Washington	89
44	Utah St. ■	59
66	Idaho ■	73
59	Pacific (Cal.)	67
59	UC Santa Barb.	77
73	Cal Poly	54
85	Long Beach St. ■	77
69	UC Irvine ■	63
54	Cal St. Fullerton	70
71	UC Riverside	74
75	Pacific (Cal.) ■	67
59	Cal Poly ■	62
58	UC Santa Barb. ■	67
57	UC Irvine	64
77	Long Beach St.	71
78	UC Riverside ■	70
70	Cal St. Fullerton ■	62
58	Utah St.	69
86	Idaho	78
64	UC Irvine †	70

Nickname: Matadors
Colors: Red, White & Black
Arena: The Matadome
 Capacity: 1,600; Year Built: 1962
AD: Richard Dull
SID: Ryan Finney

CAL ST. SAN B'DINO
San Bernardino, CA 92407-2397
.....II

Coach: Jeff Oliver, Cal Poly 1995
2002-03 RESULTS (23-7)

60	Mont. St.-Billings	61
64	Cal Poly Pomona	68
73	South Dakota †	84
50	Tarleton St. †	53
72	Cal Poly Pomona ■	64
99	UC Santa Cruz ■	51
78	Hawaii-Hilo ■	59
72	Cal St. L.A. ■	60

62	Cal St. Dom. Hills ■	50
76	UC Davis	49
108	Cal St. Chico	77
73	UC San Diego	44
74	Grand Canyon	48
78	San Fran. St. ■	57
71	Sonoma St.	62
73	Cal St. Stanislaus	54
63	Cal St. Bakersfield ■	62
74	Cal St. Dom. Hills	58
78	Cal St. L.A.	61
78	Cal St. Chico ■	60
93	UC Davis ■	49
86	Grand Canyon	58
88	UC San Diego ■	68
78	Sonoma St.	69
77	San Fran. St.	67
68	Cal St. Bakersfield	74
82	Cal St. Stanislaus	99
86	Sonoma St. †	58
80	Humboldt St. †	68
84	Cal Poly Pomona †	91

Nickname: Coyotes
Colors: Columbia Blue & Black
Arena: Coussoulis Arena
 Capacity: 5,000; Year Built: 1995
AD: Nancy P. Simpson
SID: Mike Murphy

CAL ST. STANISLAUS
Turlock, CA 95382-0299 II

Coach: Mike Terpstra, Northwest Nazarene
2002-03 RESULTS (18-11)

74	Westmont ■	71
61	Fresno Pacific	77
79	Hawaii-Hilo	84
83	Chaminade	80
70	Cal St. Bakersfield ■	77
84	Fresno Pacific ■	60
52	Cal St. Bakersfield	66
85	Chaminade ■	66
74	Notre Dame de Namur ■	63
73	UC San Diego	42
62	Grand Canyon	70
94	San Fran. St.	88
65	Sonoma St.	64
76	UC Davis ■	74
82	Cal St. Chico ■	93
82	Cal St. L.A. ■	74
76	Cal St. Dom. Hills ■	63
54	Cal St. San B'dino	73
54	Cal Poly Pomona	68
63	Grand Canyon ■	55
79	UC San Diego ■	68
61	Sonoma St.	67
70	San Fran. St. ■	55
82	Cal St. Chico	92
73	UC Davis	71
78	Cal St. Dom. Hills	57
46	Cal St. L.A.	60
72	Cal Poly Pomona ■	68
99	Cal St. San B'dino ■	82

Nickname: Warriors
Colors: Red & Gold
Arena: Warrior Gym
 Capacity: 2,000; Year Built: 1978
AD: Milton E. Richards
SID: Hung P. Tsai

CALTECH
Pasadena, CA 91125 III

Coach: Gene Victor, Cal St. L.A. 1959
2002-03 RESULTS (1-23)

67	Cooper Union ■	66
47	La Sierra ■	64
39	La Sierra ■	49
64	West Coast Chrst. ■	78

44	Whitworth ■	100
39	San Jose Christian	78
63	Golden St. Baptist	79
24	Whitworth	108
57	S'western (Ariz.) ■	66
36	Chapman	94
27	Claremont-M-S	83
73	Redlands ■	123
40	Cal Lutheran	99
55	Whittier	97
33	Pomona-Pitzer ■	84
58	La Verne	90
45	Occidental	90
27	Claremont-M-S ■	85
68	Redlands	136
45	Cal Lutheran ■	87
44	Whittier ■	86
46	Pomona-Pitzer	84
43	La Verne	81
42	Occidental ■	96

Nickname: Beavers
Colors: Orange, Black, & White
Arena: Braun Athletic Center
 Capacity: 300; Year Built: 1992
AD: Timothy D. Downes
SID: Brent Reger

CALVIN
Grand Rapids, MI 49546-4388 III

Coach: Kevin Vande Streek, Dordt 1981
2002-03 RESULTS (16-11)

96	Grace Bible (Mich.) ■	67
93	Brockport St.	77
71	Ferris St.	92
73	Wis.-Eau Claire †	78
84	Johns Hopkins †	85
83	Wheaton (Ill.) ■	74
77	Tri-State	73
87	Grace Bible (Mich.) †	63
64	Taylor (Ind.) †	85
103	Malone †	66
89	Defiance	76
48	Aquinas	74
81	Kalamazoo ■	70
94	Olivet	72
64	Albion	76
74	Hope ■	70
87	Alma	57
58	Adrian ■	61
59	Kalamazoo	74
111	Olivet ■	89
69	Albion ■	77
76	Hope	92
88	Orchard Lake ■	55
95	Alma ■	72
77	Adrian	63
75	Olivet †	62
80	Hope †	81

Nickname: Knights
Colors: Maroon & Gold
Arena: Calvin Fieldhouse
 Capacity: 4,500; Year Built: 1965
AD: Marvin A. Zuidema
SID: Jeff Febus

CAMERON
Lawton, OK 73505-6377 II

Coach: Garrette Mantle, Southeastern Okla. 1988
2002-03 RESULTS (9-17)

101	Paul Quinn ■	58
67	Western N.M. ■	60
73	Sterling (Kan.) ■	50
68	Ark.-Monticello ■	54
79	Midwestern St. ■	69
82	Paul Quinn	68
49	Rollins †	66
79	Central Mo. St. †	72

61	Tex. A&M-Kingsville	80
77	Tex. A&M-Commerce	104
80	Abilene Christian ■	90
70	Angelo St. ■	71
62	Eastern N.M.	72
50	West Tex. A&M	82
71	Central Okla. ■	89
65	Northeastern St.	78
82	Southwestern Okla.	86
64	Tarleton St. ■	72
76	East Central	60
55	Southeastern Okla.	61
55	Central Okla.	75
60	Northeastern St. ■	71
62	Southwestern Okla. ■	64
54	Tarleton St.	76
65	East Central	76
67	Southeastern Okla. ■	65

Nickname: Aggies
Colors: Black & Gold
Arena: Aggie Gymnasium
 Capacity: 1,800; Year Built: 1958
AD: Sam Carroll
SID: Steve Doughty

CAMPBELL
Buies Creek, NC 27506 I

Coach: Billy Lee, Atlanta Christian 1971
2002-03 RESULTS (5-22)

65	Francis Marion ■	64
43	Old Dominion	72
65	Coastal Caro. ■	49
36	UNC Wilmington	68
89	UNC Asheville	99
99	High Point ■	80
61	East Caro. †	86
76	High Point	79
80	William & Mary ■	82
78	Jacksonville St.	82
59	Georgia St.	92
53	Samford ■	62
63	Belmont ■	73
55	Lipscomb	80
76	Gardner-Webb ■	74
51	Jacksonville	65
57	Stetson	69
62	Mercer ■	77
75	Troy St. ■	100
69	UCF	98
56	Fla. Atlantic	83
91	Lipscomb ■	90
69	Gardner-Webb	81
56	Belmont	74
44	Samford	63
72	Georgia St. ■	88
56	Jacksonville St. ■	68

Nickname: Fighting Camels
Colors: Orange & Black
Arena: Carter Gymnasium
 Capacity: 945; Year Built: 1953
AD: Stan Williamson
SID: Stan Cole

CANISIUS
Buffalo, NY 14208-1098 I

Coach: Mike MacDonald, St. Bonaventure 1988
2002-03 RESULTS (10-18)

77	Bethune-Cookman ■	64
63	St. Joseph's	70
89	Niagara	69
71	Bucknell	67
81	Siena	71
71	Buffalo ■	65
72	Morgan St. ■	46
57	St. Bonaventure ■	69
75	Notre Dame	93
69	Syracuse	87

54 Florida Int'l 57
73 Iona 82
78 Marist 83
71 Fairfield ■ 76
84 Siena ■ 77
73 St. Peter's ■ 66
63 Rider 65
79 Loyola (Md.) 65
61 Iona ■ 64
72 Manhattan ■ 75
68 Fairfield 72
65 Manhattan 79
68 Niagara ■ 71
76 Loyola (Md.) ■ 64
60 St. Peter's 79
68 Marist ■ 73
84 Rider ■ 74
63 Marist † 69

Nickname: Golden Griffins
Colors: Blue & Gold
Arena: Koessler Athletic Center
Capacity: 1,800; Year Built: 1969
AD: Timothy J. Dillon
SID: Marc Gignac

CAPITAL
Columbus, OH 43209-2394.....III

Coach: Damon Goodwin, Dayton 1986
2002-03 RESULTS (22-6)

65 Concordia-M'head ■ 53
75 Concordia (Wis.) ■ 66
45 Akron 74
72 Ohio Wesleyan ■ 64
65 Ohio Dominican 71
66 Ohio Northern ■ 57
64 John Carroll 74
89 Marietta ■ 56
67 Otterbein 63
63 Mt. St. Joseph 59
83 Denison ■ 73
74 Mount Union ■ 55
71 Baldwin-Wallace 59
75 Muskingum ■ 55
80 Heidelberg ■ 55
86 Wilmington (Ohio) 69
74 John Carroll 76
64 Marietta 53
87 Heidelberg 62
88 Wilmington (Ohio) ■ 60
72 Otterbein ■ 64
66 Mount Union 72
79 Baldwin-Wallace ■ 70
68 Muskingum 53
76 Ohio Northern 67
57 Muskingum ■ 40
62 Mount Union † 56
86 John Carroll † 94

Nickname: Crusaders
Colors: Purple & White
Arena: The Capital Center
Capacity: 2,100; Year Built: 2001
AD: Roger Welsh
SID: Leonard Reich

CARLETON
Northfield, MN 55057.............III

Coach: Guy Kalland, Concordia-M'head 1974
2002-03 RESULTS (16-10)

90 Crown ■ 48
81 Hawaii Pacific 85
77 Chaminade 90
73 Bethel (Minn.) ■ 66
77 Augsburg 67
62 Wis.-La Crosse ■ 60
72 St. Olaf 75
55 Concordia-M'head 54
68 Northwestern (Minn.) 61
76 Macalester 69
71 St. Mary's (Minn.) 60
78 Hamline 65
56 St. Thomas (Minn.) ■ 66
73 St. John's (Minn.) 77
78 Gust. Adolphus ■ 64
85 Bethel (Minn.) 73
62 Augsburg 77
69 St. Olaf 71
81 Macalester ■ 74
76 St. Mary's (Minn.) ■ 55
75 Concordia-M'head ■ 57
81 Hamline ■ 77
66 St. Thomas (Minn.) 71
78 St. John's (Minn.) ■ 70
54 Gust. Adolphus 76
58 St. John's (Minn.) 69

Nickname: Knights
Colors: Maize & Blue
Arena: West Gymnasium
Capacity: 1,850; Year Built: 1964
AD: Leon Lunder
SID: Eric Sieger

CARNEGIE MELLON
Pittsburgh, PA 15213-3890.......III

Coach: Tony Wingen, Springfield 1982
2002-03 RESULTS (11-14)

82 Wash. & Jeff. 71
70 Grove City † 87
92 Penn St.-Altoona ■ 67
76 Elmira ■ 66
55 Robert Morris 68
50 Rochester ■ 66
47 Wis.-Stevens Point ■ 69
85 Hiram ■ 80
85 Johns Hopkins ■ 97
60 New York U. ■ 57
54 Brandeis ■ 51
85 Wash. & Jeff. ■ 71
73 La Roche 65
63 Chicago 74
59 Washington (Mo.) 79
89 Emory ■ 76
82 Case Reserve ■ 58
79 Case Reserve 93
83 Emory 101
69 Brandeis 56
75 New York U. 92
57 Penn St.-Behrend ■ 63
63 Washington (Mo.) ■ 98
82 Chicago ■ 86
48 Rochester 78

Nickname: Tartans
Colors: Cardinal, White & Grey
Arena: Skibo Gymnasium
Capacity: 1,500; Year Built: 1924
AD: John H. Harvey
SID: Jon Surmacz

CARROLL (WIS.)
Waukesha, WI 53186-5593 III

Coach: David Schultz, Wis.-Oshkosh
2002-03 RESULTS (7-16)

66 Lakeland † 63
69 Milwaukee Engr. 65
70 North Park 93
56 Wis.-Whitewater 78
69 St. Norbert 81
63 Wis.-Stevens Point ■ 82
71 Carthage ■ 86
79 Ripon ■ 83
69 Beloit ■ 73
63 Concordia (Wis.) 85
80 Lake Forest 68
97 Monmouth (Ill.) ■ 76
94 Lawrence 87
125 Grinnell 133

87 Knox 95
86 Illinois Col. 68
128 Grinnell 143
90 Monmouth (Ill.) 83
62 Lake Forest 79
77 Beloit 79
77 Lawrence ■ 83
58 St. Norbert ■ 73
77 Ripon 81

Nickname: Pioneers
Colors: Orange & White
Arena: Van Male Fieldhouse
Capacity: 2,000; Year Built: 1965
AD: Kris Jacobsen
SID: Rick Mobley

CARSON-NEWMAN
Jefferson City, TN 37760...........II

Coach: Dale Clayton, Milligan 1973
2002-03 RESULTS (19-9)

100 Augusta St. ■ 83
72 Lincoln Memorial ■ 59
70 S.C.-Aiken 64
52 Lincoln Memorial 83
119 Trevecca Nazarene ■ 85
98 Bryan ■ 67
61 Ala.-Huntsville 51
78 Johnson Smith 84
69 GC&SU † 63
81 Columbus St. 82
53 S.C.-Aiken 52
79 Johnson Smith ■ 81
84 Wingate ■ 72
56 Mars Hill 53
79 Presbyterian ■ 75
66 Lenoir-Rhyne 69
61 Tusculum 58
64 Maryville (Tenn.) ■ 55
75 Newberry ■ 65
80 Catawba ■ 78
76 Wingate 77
70 Mars Hill ■ 59
70 Presbyterian 63
82 Lenoir-Rhyne ■ 74
63 Tusculum 72
62 Newberry 51
83 Catawba 86
52 Presbyterian † 69

Nickname: Eagles
Colors: Orange & Blue
Arena: Holt Fieldhouse
Capacity: 2,000; Year Built: 1961
AD: David W. Barger
SID: Marlin Curnutt

CARTHAGE
Kenosha, WI 53140 III

Coach: Bosko Djurickovic, North Park 1973
2002-03 RESULTS (19-6)

69 Concordia (Wis.) ■ 54
72 Olivet Nazarene 77
77 Milwaukee Engr. 63
77 Apprentice ■ 44
83 Wis. Lutheran ■ 57
86 Carroll (Wis.) 71
84 Maryville (Mo.) † 50
65 Hawaii Pacific 74
77 St. Xavier 78
77 Chicago 64
89 MacMurray ■ 46
80 North Central ■ 62
55 Augustana (Ill.) 69
62 Ill. Wesleyan 64
71 Elmhurst ■ 48
81 North Park 73
72 North Central 69
52 Wheaton (Ill.) 63

79 Millikin ■ 56
80 North Park 69
79 Augustana (Ill.) 69
78 Millikin 55
76 Elmhurst 53
75 Ill. Wesleyan ■ 64
72 Wheaton (Ill.) ■ 64

Nickname: Redmen
Colors: Red, White & Black
Arena: PE Center
Capacity: 2,500; Year Built: 1964
AD: Robert R. Bonn
SID: Steve Marovich

CASE RESERVE
Cleveland, OH 44106 III

Coach: Adam Hutchinson, Amherst 1993
2002-03 RESULTS (7-18)

40 Wooster 94
48 Muskingum † 58
59 Westminster (Pa.) ■ 56
55 Lake Erie † 65
71 Hiram † 83
93 Wash. & Jeff. ■ 82
46 Grove City 70
57 Wittenberg 72
88 York (Pa.) † 80
64 Scranton 92
90 Emory ■ 83
74 Thiel 85
33 Washington (Mo.) ■ 102
52 Chicago ■ 93
56 Brandeis 59
76 New York U. 82
63 Rochester 77
58 Carnegie Mellon 82
93 Carnegie Mellon ■ 79
77 Rochester ■ 81
69 Chicago 84
67 Washington (Mo.) 85
77 New York U. ■ 75
81 Brandeis ■ 68
64 Emory 81

Nickname: Spartans
Colors: Blue, Gray & White
Arena: Emerson PE Center
Capacity: 1,220; Year Built: 1958
AD: David M. Hutter
SID: Creg Jantz

CASTLETON ST.
Castleton, VT 05735 III

Coach: Ted Shipley, Lyndon St. 1987
2002-03 RESULTS (5-21)

84 Keene St. 112
85 Me.-Machias † 74
64 Middlebury ■ 94
61 Gordon 86
62 Skidmore 74
61 Johnson St. ■ 66
72 Salem St. 104
77 CCNY † 84
63 Lyndon St. 78
54 Maine Maritime 78
60 Lasell 66
72 Becker 96
55 Elms 62
84 Mount Ida 59
92 Lasell ■ 108
93 Johnson St. 74
83 St. Joseph's (Me.) ■ 103
80 Maine Maritime ■ 77
77 Oneonta St. 81
84 Elms 67
79 Becker ■ 81
68 Green Mountain 79
93 Plattsburgh St. 107

74 Plymouth St. ■ ...81
76 Mount Ida ■ ...94
73 Maine Maritime ...80

Nickname: Spartans
Colors: Green & White
Arena: Glenbrook
 Capacity: 1,000; Year Built: 1959
AD: Deanna Tyson
SID: Tim Barrett

CATAWBA
Salisbury, NC 28144-2488 II

Coach: Jim Baker, Catawba 1978
2002-03 RESULTS (11-17)
74 Elizabeth City St. ...63
67 Johnson Smith ...80
105 St. Augustine's ...101
79 Shaw ■ ...85
71 St. Paul's ■ ...74
76 Elizabeth City St. ■ ...79
82 Pfeiffer ...102
82 N.C. Central ■ ...80
65 S.C.-Aiken ...73
60 Augusta St. † ...97
61 N.C. Central ...63
85 St. Augustine's ■ ...77
82 St. Paul's ■ ...70
71 Lenoir-Rhyne ...75
70 Tusculum ■ ...84
76 Mars Hill ■ ...67
77 Wingate ...98
71 Newberry ■ ...48
70 Presbyterian ...81
78 Carson-Newman ...80
77 Lenoir-Rhyne ■ ...79
71 Tusculum ...81
78 Mars Hill ...72
99 Wingate ■ ...87
80 Newberry ...74
75 Presbyterian ■ ...77
86 Carson-Newman ■ ...83
91 Lenoir-Rhyne ...95

Nickname: Indians
Colors: Blue & White
Arena: Goodman Gym
 Capacity: 3,500; Year Built: 1970
AD: Dennis Davidson
SID: Jim Lewis

CATHOLIC
Washington, DC 20064 III

Coach: Mike Lonergan, Catholic 1988
2002-03 RESULTS (24-5)
79 Wm. Paterson ■ ...76
82 Haverford ...70
71 Scranton ...66
108 Villa Julie ■ ...68
82 Salisbury ...64
83 Gallaudet ...47
90 Ithaca ■ ...56
70 West Fla. ...91
107 Wash. & Jeff. ■ ...60
69 Gettysburg ■ ...57
83 McDaniel ■ ...67
81 N.C. Wesleyan ...69
69 Johns Hopkins ■ ...77
78 Mary Washington ■ ...60
71 Marymount (Va.) ...60
78 St. Mary's (Md.) ...64
83 Goucher ■ ...67
82 York (Pa.) ...77
93 Gallaudet ■ ...67
97 Salisbury ...85
96 Marymount (Va.) ■ ...59
62 Mary Washington ...58
103 York (Pa.) ■ ...65
86 St. Mary's (Md.) ■ ...61
75 Goucher ...88

65 Gallaudet ■ ...58
58 Marymount (Va.) ■ ...56
68 Mary Washington ■ ...70
78 Montclair St. ■ ...95

Nickname: Cardinals
Colors: Cardinal Red & Black
Arena: DuFour Center
 Capacity: 2,000; Year Built: 1985
AD: Robert J. Talbot
SID: Chris Panter

CAZENOVIA
Cazenovia, NY 13035 III

Coach: Todd Widrick, Le Moyne 1985
2002-03 RESULTS (11-15)
53 Marietta † ...67
63 Buffalo St. ...80
56 Nazareth ...80
73 Clarkson † ...65
86 Hobart ...94
80 Mt. Aloysius ■ ...79
78 Worcester St. ■ ...82
81 Mt. St. Joseph † ...82
68 Grove City † ...86
75 LeTourneau † ...93
71 Dallas ...74
83 Potsdam St. ■ ...86
64 Clarkson ■ ...61
83 Utica ...86
62 Utica/Rome ■ ...78
131 Hilbert ■ ...88
86 Mt. Aloysius ...81
83 Keuka ■ ...82
73 D'Youville ■ ...67
83 Medaille ...76
92 Hilbert ...83
76 Keuka ...82
69 Medaille ■ ...65
74 D'Youville ...75
96 Baptist Bible (Pa.) ...82
63 D'Youville † ...75

Nickname: Wildcats
Colors: Navy Blue & Gold
Arena: Schneweiss Athletic Center
 Capacity: 800; Year Built: 1988
AD: Marvin Christopher
SID: Todd Widrick

CENTENARY (LA.)
Shreveport, LA 71134-1188 I

Coach: Kevin Johnson, Tex.-Pan American 1988
2002-03 RESULTS (14-14)
45 Nebraska † ...68
48 Wis.-Green Bay † ...68
69 UC Santa Barb. † ...84
80 La.-Monroe ...65
64 Northwestern St. ■ ...63
75 Stephen F. Austin ...69
92 La.-Monroe ■ ...71
52 Western Mich. ...72
84 Jarvis Christian ■ ...71
69 Fresno St. ...70
51 Arkansas ...75
66 Texas A&M ...90
89 TCU ...102
58 Missouri ...88
94 Tex.-Pan American ■ ...84
83 Northwestern St. ...72
65 LSU ...112
92 Tex. A&M-Corp. Chris. ■ ...93
98 Texas-Dallas ...57
93 Lipscomb ■ ...82
96 Texas Col. ■ ...45
124 Ark. Baptist ■ ...75
84 Southern U. ...56
75 Lipscomb ...85
76 IPFW ■ ...61

76 IPFW ...90
69 Tex. A&M-Corp. Chris. ...73
78 Tex.-Pan American ...76

Nickname: Gentlemen
Colors: Maroon & White
Arena: Gold Dome
 Capacity: 3,000; Year Built: 1971
AD: David Bedard
SID: Jason Behenna

CENTENARY (N.J.)
Hackettstown, NJ 07840 III

Coach: Abe Kasbo, Seton Hall
2002-03 RESULTS (9-15)
54 Montclair St. ...94
70 D'Youville † ...69
97 Brooklyn ...85
83 Keuka ■ ...66
77 Medgar Evers ...88
96 Baptist Bible (Pa.) ■ ...88
72 Delaware Valley ...74
57 Rutgers-Newark ■ ...68
42 Lafayette ...97
79 Lehman ...80
74 Manhattanville ...85
69 Kean ■ ...83
64 St. Joseph's (L.I.) ...57
73 Penn St.-Altoona ■ ...68
62 NYCCT ...69
73 Old Westbury ■ ...69
77 Mt. St. Vincent ...79
43 Stony Brook ...89
52 Phila. Bible ...76
84 FDU-Florham ■ ...87
47 Farmingdale St. ...68
71 Stevens Institute ...67
86 Maritime (N.Y.) ■ ...82
81 Hunter ...82

Nickname: Cyclones
Colors: Blue & White
Arena: Reeves Center
 Capacity: 250; Year Built: 1954
AD: Diane Finnan
SID: Josh Huber

CENTRAL (IOWA)
Pella, IA 50219 III

Coach: Dan Mason, North Park 1983
2002-03 RESULTS (5-21)
74 Trinity Christian † ...77
79 Northwestern (Iowa) ...105
71 Iowa Wesleyan ...87
60 Luther ■ ...73
75 Augustana (Ill.) ...104
55 Wheaton (Ill.) ■ ...73
69 Dordt ...91
81 Wartburg ...74
63 Buena Vista ...71
66 Mt. Mercy ■ ...80
75 Simpson ...94
62 Upper Iowa ■ ...77
73 Cornell College ■ ...82
64 Coe ■ ...77
60 Loras ...68
74 Dubuque ...77
98 Upper Iowa ...90
54 Buena Vista ■ ...70
59 Wartburg ■ ...73
76 Simpson ■ ...70
52 Luther ...74
74 Coe ...64
73 Cornell College ...79
78 Dubuque ■ ...54
62 Loras ■ ...70
57 Buena Vista ...105

Nickname: Dutch
Colors: Red & White
Arena: Kuyper Gymnasium

Capacity: 3,000; Year Built: 1970
AD: Al Dorenkamp
SID: Larry Happel

CENTRAL ARK.
Conway, AR 72035-0001 II

Coach: Charles Hervey
2002-03 RESULTS (7-18)
105 St. Edward's ■ ...69
75 East Central ■ ...70
69 Ark.-Little Rock ...82
42 Northeastern St. † ...68
76 Lincoln Memorial † ...79
75 Central Okla. ■ ...95
63 St. Edward's ...75
54 Incarnate Word † ...70
79 Okla. Panhandle ...86
80 Christian Bros. ■ ...87
80 Ouachita Baptist ...90
67 Arkansas Tech ...62
45 Henderson St. ...75
97 Harding ■ ...105
69 Delta St. ...71
90 Ark.-Monticello ...76
88 Southern Ark. ■ ...70
96 Christian Bros. ...92
59 Ouachita Baptist ■ ...61
59 Arkansas Tech ...65
80 Henderson St. ■ ...96
74 Harding ...105
68 Delta St. ■ ...72
83 Ark.-Monticello ■ ...68
76 Southern Ark. ...77

Nickname: Bears
Colors: Purple & Gray
Arena: Jeff Farris Center
 Capacity: 6,500; Year Built: 1973
AD: Vance Strange
SID: Steve East

CENTRAL CONN. ST.
New Britain, CT 06050-4010 I

Coach: Howie Dickenman, Central Conn. St. 1970
2002-03 RESULTS (15-13)
77 St. Peter's ■ ...67
63 High Point ■ ...74
46 Massachusetts † ...45
70 Hartford † ...66
59 Yale † ...71
67 Brown ■ ...75
65 Connecticut ...93
58 Rhode Island ...77
76 Quinnipiac ...72
63 Loyola (Md.) ...65
62 Wagner ■ ...76
85 Sacred Heart ■ ...80
68 St. Francis (Pa.) ■ ...67
80 Robert Morris ■ ...74
68 Fairleigh Dickinson ...57
66 Monmouth ...71
80 Long Island ...70
71 St. Francis (N.Y.) ■ ...59
63 UMBC ...49
80 Mt. St. Mary's ■ ...66
55 St. Francis (N.Y.) ...78
61 Sacred Heart ...58
58 Wagner ...61
95 Long Island ■ ...53
66 Quinnipiac ■ ...68
66 UMBC ...60
56 Mt. St. Mary's ...60
62 St. Francis (N.Y.) † ...67

Nickname: Blue Devils
Colors: Blue & White
Arena: Detrick Gymnasium
 Capacity: 4,500; Year Built: 1965
AD: Charles Jones Jr.

SID: Thomas Pincince

UCF
Orlando, FL 32816-3555...........I

Coach: Kirk Speraw, Iowa 1980
2002-03 RESULTS (21-11)
56	Navy ■	68
94	Niagara ■	69
66	Tulane	61
72	Maine †	55
50	Indiana St. †	49
54	Florida A&M	55
82	Col. of Charleston ■	64
58	Tenn.-Martin ■	63
99	Chicago St.	83
68	Fla. Gulf Coast ■	63
51	Miami (Fla.) ■	62
64	Citadel ■	55
80	Fla. Atlantic ■	69
59	Kansas St.	71
76	Troy St.	61
63	Mercer ■	85
82	Stetson ■	70
72	Jacksonville ■	48
68	Jacksonville St.	66
81	Georgia St.	74
58	Belmont ■	60
58	Samford ■	52
98	Campbell ■	69
82	Gardner-Webb ■	59
75	Jacksonville	80
90	Stetson	82
72	Troy St. ■	77
66	Mercer ■	69
82	Fla. Atlantic	75
68	Jacksonville St. †	51
79	Mercer †	59
69	Troy St. †	80

Nickname: Golden Knights
Colors: Black & Gold
Arena: UCF Arena
 Capacity: 5,100; Year Built: 1991
AD: Steve Orsini
SID: Chris Showiak

CENTRAL MICH.
Mount Pleasant, MI 48859-0001 .I

Coach: Jay Smith, Saginaw Valley 1984
2002-03 RESULTS (25-7)
61	George Mason ■	58
74	Illinois St. ■	69
56	DePaul	92
85	Michigan	78
73	Drake ■	61
88	Marist	66
74	Bradley	71
51	Valparaiso	65
113	Spring Arbor ■	63
62	Miami (Ohio)	71
80	Western Mich.	75
87	Ohio ■	84
81	Marshall	78
97	Buffalo ■	73
83	Toledo ■	74
68	Eastern Mich.	84
78	Kent St.	82
88	Bowling Green ■	71
99	Akron	92
77	Western Mich. ■	58
66	Toledo	64
94	Ball St.	92
87	Northern Ill.	75
69	Akron ■	70
106	Eastern Mich. ■	89
73	Northern Ill. ■	57
86	Ball St.	66
87	Bowling Green †	70
94	Northern Ill. †	72
77	Kent St. †	67
79	Creighton †	73

60	Duke †	86

Nickname: Chippewas
Colors: Maroon & Gold
Arena: Rose Arena
 Capacity: 5,200; Year Built: 1973
AD: Herbert W. Deromedi
SID: Don Helinski

CENTRAL MO. ST.
Warrensburg, MO 64093 II

Coach: Kim Anderson, Missouri 1979
2002-03 RESULTS (12-16)
101	Monmouth (Ill.) ■	62
99	Westminster (Mo.) ■	65
78	Midwestern St. †	75
69	St. Mary's (Tex.)	66
70	Kansas	97
87	Lincoln (Mo.)	72
81	Drury †	79
72	Cameron †	79
75	Rockhurst ■	78
66	Truman ■	63
85	Mo. Western St.	90
53	Mo. Southern St. ■	56
61	Southwest Baptist	77
72	Mo.-Rolla ■	70
66	Washburn	83
56	Northwest Mo. St. ■	78
64	Emporia St. ■	69
76	Pittsburg St.	78
99	Mo. Western St. ■	87
57	Mo. Southern St.	72
84	Southwest Baptist ■	71
69	Mo.-Rolla	70
68	Washburn ■	74
59	Northwest Mo. St.	80
80	Emporia St.	97
85	Pittsburg St. ■	75
73	Truman	71
60	Washburn †	75

Nickname: Mules
Colors: Cardinal & Black
Arena: CMSU Multipurpose Building
 Capacity: 8,500; Year Built: 1976
AD: Jerry M. Hughes
SID: Bill Turnage

CENTRAL OKLA.
Edmond, OK 73034 II

Coach: Terry Evans, Oklahoma 1992
2002-03 RESULTS (19-10)
100	Oklahoma City ■	88
78	Mo.-Rolla †	83
59	Mo. Western St.	77
95	Central Ark.	75
79	Abilene Christian ■	69
97	Angelo St. ■	79
74	Washburn †	82
81	Central Wash. †	82
71	Eastern N.M.	65
79	West Tex. A&M	77
108	Drury ■	88
78	Midwestern St. ■	67
78	Tex. A&M-Kingsville	72
93	Tex. A&M-Commerce ■	82
89	Cameron	71
77	Southwestern Okla. ■	59
100	Drury	90
101	East Central	92
80	Southeastern Okla. ■	74
69	Northeastern St.	73
63	Tarleton St. ■	82
75	Cameron ■	55
67	Southwestern Okla.	60
100	East Central ■	86
60	Southeastern Okla.	54
68	Northeastern St. ■	72
77	Tarleton St.	85
84	West Tex. A&M	88

67	Northeastern St. †	78

Nickname: Bronchos
Colors: Bronze & Blue
Arena: Hamilton Field House
 Capacity: 3,000; Year Built: 1965
AD: John E. Wagnon
SID: Mike Kirk

CENTRAL WASH.
Ellensburg, WA 98926..............II

Coach: Greg Sparling, Central Wash. 1993
2002-03 RESULTS (16-11)
94	Northwest Nazarene †	72
81	Seattle Pacific	84
98	Western St. †	80
103	Fort Lewis †	101
71	Seattle Pacific ■	81
82	Western Wash. ■	61
70	Tarleton St. †	61
82	Central Okla. †	81
101	Puget Sound ■	60
73	Cal Baptist †	76
86	Cal St. Bakersfield	98
74	Alas. Anchorage	81
60	Alas. Fairbanks	62
78	Western Ore. ■	77
85	Humboldt St. ■	69
89	Seattle	91
96	Northwest Nazarene	84
77	St. Martin's	69
78	Alas. Anchorage ■	80
106	Alas. Fairbanks ■	82
59	Humboldt St.	80
103	Western Ore.	95
80	Northwest Nazarene ■	74
74	Seattle ■	71
80	St. Martin's ■	83
83	Western Wash.	87
105	Seattle Pacific	102

Nickname: Wildcats
Colors: Crimson & Black
Arena: Nicholson Pavilion
 Capacity: 3,500; Year Built: 1959
AD: Jack Bishop
SID: Jonathan Gordon

CENTRE
Danville, KY 40422-1394.........III

Coach: Greg Mason, Centre 1994
2002-03 RESULTS (18-9)
85	Ind. Wesleyan †	73
61	Asbury †	56
64	Maryville (Tenn.)	83
61	Mary Washington †	80
90	Ferrum †	64
70	Thomas More	81
97	Union (Ky.) ■	81
69	Brescia ■	63
61	Sewanee ■	57
75	Transylvania †	84
78	Hendrix ■	67
90	Rhodes ■	85
79	Oglethorpe	70
66	Millsaps	88
57	Rose-Hulman	38
61	DePauw ■	76
87	Thomas More ■	75
83	Sewanee	71
73	Southwestern (Tex.) ■	84
69	Trinity (Tex.) ■	75
66	Hendrix	56
81	Rhodes	72
83	Oglethorpe ■	65
90	Millsaps ■	73
82	Millsaps †	78
88	DePauw † †	74
54	Trinity (Tex.) † †	58

Nickname: Colonels
Colors: Gold & White
Arena: Alumni Memorial Gym Gymna
 Capacity: 1,800; Year Built: 1950
AD: Brian E. Chafin
SID: Ed Rall

CHADRON ST.
Chadron, NE 69337-2690........II

Coach: Dan Beebe, Chadron St. 1992
2002-03 RESULTS (12-14)
50	North Dakota St.	88
67	Minn. St. Moorhead †	78
84	South Dak. Tech ■	47
84	Black Hills St. †	73
70	South Dak. Tech	67
80	Colorado Col.	75
69	Mont. St.-Billings	103
59	Fort Lewis ■	66
65	Adams St. ■	67
100	Western St.	92
97	UC-Colo. Spgs.	92
91	Mesa St. ■	80
110	Colorado St.-Pueblo	106
81	N.M. Highlands	83
80	Fort Hays St.	90
73	Neb.-Kearney ■	83
49	Metro St.	80
60	Regis (Colo.)	65
73	Colorado Mines	72
72	Colo. Christian	75
58	Regis (Colo.) ■	55
50	Metro St. ■	77
92	Colorado Mines ■	82
77	Colo. Christian ■	72
75	Neb.-Kearney	92
63	Fort Hays St.	72

Nickname: Eagles
Colors: Cardinal & White
Arena: Armstrong
 Capacity: 3,200; Year Built: 1965
AD: Bradley Roy Smith
SID: Con Marshall

CHAMINADE
Honolulu, HI 96816-1578 II

Coach: Aaron Griess, Colorado Col. 1993
2002-03 RESULTS (12-15)
70	St. Mary's (Tex.) ■	75
72	Virginia †	86
72	Arizona St. †	101
55	Massachusetts †	69
90	Carleton ■	77
78	Kennesaw St. ■	83
71	Lees-McRae ■	69
80	Cal St. Stanislaus ■	83
84	Northwest Nazarene ■	68
89	UC San Diego	83
66	Cal St. Stanislaus	85
107	Fontbonne ■	40
89	Mont. St.-Billings ■	76
102	Western N.M. ■	87
99	Western N.M.	83
78	Hawaii-Hilo	72
87	Hawaii-Hilo	93
78	Hawaii Pacific	87
71	BYU-Hawaii	94
71	Mont. St.-Billings	87
83	Mont. St.-Billings	97
97	Western N.M.	79
73	Hawaii Pacific	85
95	Hawaii Pacific ■	87
86	Hawaii-Hilo ■	78
80	BYU-Hawaii	91
88	BYU-Hawaii	93

Nickname: Silverswords
Colors: Royal Blue & White
Arena: McCabe Gym

Capacity: 2,500
AD: Aaron Griess
SID: John Hemenway

CHAPMAN
Orange, CA 92866 III

Coach: Mike Bokosky, Fort Lewis 1978
2002-03 RESULTS (18-7)
90	West Coast Chrst. ■	68
69	Cal Maritime ■	64
65	Whittier ■	72
110	Redlands ■	99
64	Cal St. Hayward †	69
75	George Fox †	78
75	North Central †	73
72	West Coast Chrst.	58
64	Occidental ■	80
50	Claremont-M-S	68
50	Cal Lutheran ■	71
63	La Verne ■	68
94	Caltech ■	36
117	Cal Christian	71
89	Golden St. Baptist	50
63	San Jose Christian	39
59	La Sierra ■	44
90	S'western (Ariz.) ■	46
68	Vanguard ■	57
56	San Jose Christian ■	47
106	Cal Christian ■	76
66	West Coast Chrst. ■	53
88	Hope Int'l ■	65
60	La Sierra ■	50
86	S'western (Ariz.)	55

Nickname: Panthers
Colors: Cardinal & Gray
Arena: Hutton Sports Center
  Capacity: 2,400; Year Built: 1978
AD: David Currey
SID: Doug Aiken

COL. OF CHARLESTON
Charleston, SC 29424 I

Coach: Tom Herrion, Merrimack 1989
2002-03 RESULTS (25-8)
84	Charleston So. †	70
108	Webber ■	48
81	Wyoming †	72
66	Oklahoma St. †	58
71	Villanova †	69
91	S.C.-Aiken ■	59
64	UCF	82
66	Stetson	64
68	American ■	65
69	UNC Wilmington ■	78
78	UMBC ■	57
77	Howard ■	73
53	Vanderbilt	70
88	Wofford	79
68	Chattanooga ■	78
61	East Tenn. St.	65
78	Wofford ■	68
59	Furman ■	52
58	Citadel	44
81	VMI ■	56
84	Ga. Southern	79
71	UNC Greensboro ■	69
64	Furman	53
84	Citadel ■	75
108	Appalachian St.	96
79	Western Caro. ■	63
78	Chattanooga	79
94	Davidson	89
73	Ga. Southern ■	71
67	Ga. Southern †	53
55	East Tenn. St. †	64
71	Kent St.	66
64	Providence	69

Nickname: Cougars
Colors: Maroon & White
Arena: F. Mitchell Johnson Center
  Capacity: 3,500; Year Built: 1983
AD: Jerry I. Baker
SID: Tony Ciuffo

CHARLESTON (W.VA.)
Charleston, WV 25304 II

Coach: Jayson Gee, Charleston (W.Va.) 1988
2002-03 RESULTS (21-10)
99	Davis & Elkins †	58
64	Mount Olive	74
108	Ohio St. Lima	83
106	Southern Va. ■	75
84	Dist. Columbia †	73
84	Pitt.-Johnstown	81
88	Concord ■	71
81	Mont. St.-Billings	82
111	Rocky Mountain	122
89	West Va. Wesleyan	90
78	West Va. Tech	74
96	West Virginia St. ■	80
88	Bluefield St. ■	79
82	Salem Int'l ■	87
83	Davis & Elkins	71
90	Shepherd ■	82
104	Glenville St. ■	79
82	Alderson-Broaddus ■	69
64	West Va. Wesleyan ■	82
96	Concord	102
98	West Liberty St. ■	83
83	Fairmont St.	74
84	Wheeling Jesuit ■	96
93	West Virginia St.	98
85	West Va. Tech ■	83
80	Ohio Valley	57
83	Bluefield St.	71
83	Davis & Elkins ■	51
85	West Va. Tech ■	61
98	Salem Int'l ■	91
62	Alderson-Broaddus ■	75

Nickname: Golden Eagles
Colors: Maroon & Gold
Arena: Eddie King Gym
  Capacity: 2,500; Year Built: 1888
AD: Tom Nozica
SID: Drew Meighen

CHARLESTON SO.
Charleston, SC 29423-8087 I

Coach: Jim Platt, Concordia (Ill.) 1973
2002-03 RESULTS (14-14)
70	Col. of Charleston †	84
77	Anderson (S.C.) ■	75
68	Stetson	62
68	Citadel	56
69	Voorhees ■	48
53	Michigan	84
49	Tennessee	63
62	Florida	74
80	Georgia St. ■	75
66	Fairfield	64
66	William & Mary	72
61	Birmingham-So. ■	69
58	UNC Asheville	71
66	Elon	51
75	High Point	66
72	Coastal Caro.	69
78	Liberty ■	57
81	Radford ■	64
69	Winthrop ■	72
60	Birmingham-So.	63
61	High Point ■	56
50	Elon ■	57
48	Liberty	54
57	Radford	59

56	Winthrop	75
76	UNC Asheville ■	68
70	Coastal Caro. ■	66
62	Radford ■	65

Nickname: Buccaneers
Colors: Navy & Old Gold
Arena: CSU Fieldhouse
  Capacity: 1,500; Year Built: 1965
AD: Hank Small

CHARLOTTE
Charlotte, NC 28223 I

Coach: Bobby Lutz, Charlotte 1980
2002-03 RESULTS (13-16)
89	Long Beach St. ■	61
100	Appalachian St.	103
60	Richmond	64
91	Temple ■	80
56	Davidson	75
69	Miami (Fla.)	64
80	Southern Ill. ■	67
82	Loyola (Ill.) ■	69
74	Colorado	76
47	La.-Lafayette ■	68
60	Indiana	70
59	Louisville ■	80
83	East Caro. ■	62
78	UAB	58
64	Marquette ■	67
79	Cincinnati	83
62	St. Louis ■	55
64	South Fla.	67
59	Valparaiso ■	73
64	DePaul	72
59	Houston ■	55
74	Cincinnati ■	64
67	Marquette	75
71	East Caro.	66
77	Southern Miss. ■	68
58	DePaul ■	50
39	St. Louis	50
59	Louisville	100
61	UAB †	85

Nickname: 49ers
Colors: Green & White
Arena: Dale F. Halton Arena
  Capacity: 9,105; Year Built: 1996
AD: Judith W. Rose
SID: Thomas E. Whitestone

CHATTANOOGA
Chattanooga, TN 37403-2598 ..I

Coach: Jeff Lebo, North Carolina 1989
2002-03 RESULTS (21-9)
68	Samford	66
81	UAB	92
93	Tenn. Wesleyan ■	47
82	Bradley	70
75	Illinois St.	68
107	Milligan ■	57
66	Furman ■	49
84	Kent St. ■	89
77	Samford ■	68
87	Lipscomb ■	78
75	Weber St. ■	63
51	Cincinnati	81
72	UNC Greensboro †	56
78	Col. of Charleston	68
67	Davidson ■	63
99	Appalachian St. ■	107
71	Wofford	79
69	Furman	83
79	Citadel ■	64
99	East Tenn. St. ■	94
97	Ga. Southern ■	94
74	Citadel	67
83	Wofford ■	92

77	VMI	52
79	Col. of Charleston ■	78
97	Ga. Southern	99
83	Western Caro.	75
98	Appalachian St. †	67
77	VMI †	58
90	East Tenn. St. †	97

Nickname: Mocs
Colors: Navy Blue & Gold
Arena: The McKenzie Arena
  Capacity: 11,218; Year Built: 1982
AD: Steve Sloan
SID: Jeff Romero

CHEYNEY
Cheyney, PA 19319-0200 II

Coach: Robert Marshall, Cheyney 1980
2002-03 RESULTS (13-14)
65	St. Anselm †	89
71	Teikyo Post †	67
99	Lincoln (Pa.) †	56
69	Calif. (Pa.)	76
57	Slippery Rock	55
80	Bowie St.	98
84	Lock Haven	55
78	Shippensburg ■	67
79	Indiana (Pa.) ■	83
84	Clarion	79
57	Edinboro ■	60
74	Kutztown	77
58	Millersville ■	92
78	Mansfield	83
55	Alvernia ■	54
54	West Chester ■	65
74	East Stroudsburg ■	51
74	Phila. Sciences	77
61	Bloomsburg ■	83
63	Kutztown ■	48
84	Columbia Union ■	64
76	Mansfield ■	70
62	Millersville	66
77	West Chester	84
88	Columbia Union	85
83	Bloomsburg ■	72
82	East Stroudsburg	83

Nickname: Wolves
Colors: Blue & White
Arena: Cope Hall
  Capacity: 1,500; Year Built: 1961
AD: Eve Atkinson
SID: Lenn Margolis

CHICAGO
Chicago, IL 60637 III

Coach: Mike McGrath, DePauw 1992
2002-03 RESULTS (15-10)
93	Kenyon ■	58
84	Thiel ■	68
75	Wheaton (Ill.) ■	85
41	Trinity (Tex.)	53
66	Southwestern (Tex.) †	68
77	Ill. Wesleyan ■	69
67	Benedictine (Ill.)	73
66	Hope ■	84
59	Kalamazoo	73
66	Lake Forest ■	54
64	Carthage ■	77
56	Washington (Mo.) ■	75
75	Emory	71
93	Case Reserve	52
74	Carnegie Mellon ■	63
72	Rochester ■	60
83	New York U.	66
73	Brandeis	57
82	Brandeis	49
71	New York U.	66
84	Case Reserve ■	69

60	Emory ■	56
54	Rochester	71
86	Carnegie Mellon	82
50	Washington (Mo.)	85

Nickname: Maroons
Colors: Maroon & White
Arena: Henry Crown Field House
   Capacity: 1,500; Year Built: 1931
AD: Thomas Weingartner
SID: Dave Hilbert

CHICAGO ST.
Chicago, IL 60628-1598 I

Coach: Bo Ellis, Marquette 1977
2002-03 RESULTS (3-27)

53	Buffalo	84
65	Wichita St.	71
58	Wis.-Green Bay	69
61	Colorado	80
49	Denver	76
83	UCF ■	99
67	Northern Iowa ■	63
79	Texas Southern ■	74
56	Western Ky. †	63
57	Tex.-Pan American †	54
76	Bradley †	88
45	Wisconsin	73
70	UMKC ■	80
66	Oral Roberts ■	77
73	Wis.-Milwaukee ■	81
73	Western Ill.	75
48	Valparaiso	80
63	IPFW ■	67
64	Southern Utah	65
71	Oakland ■	90
69	IUPUI ■	89
48	Oral Roberts	78
56	UMKC	59
70	Valparaiso ■	81
73	Western Ill. ■	75
71	IPFW	75
54	Southern Utah ■	70
61	Oakland	64
55	IUPUI	67
62	Valparaiso †	82

Nickname: Cougars
Colors: Green & White
Arena: Jacoby Dickens Center
   Capacity: 2,500; Year Built: 1971
AD: Al Avant
SID: Mark Johnson

CHOWAN
Murfreesboro, NC 27855.........III

Coach: Jim Tribbett, Florida St. 1977
2002-03 RESULTS (8-18)

54	New Jersey City †	69
71	Wesley †	79
50	Randolph-Macon ■	83
87	Kenyon †	69
62	Marymount (Va.)	69
66	St. John Fisher †	79
73	Lincoln (Pa.) †	65
61	Piedmont ■	66
76	Villa Julie ■	73
49	Va. Wesleyan	59
57	Guilford	85
55	N.C. Wesleyan ■	72
45	Methodist ■	66
77	Greensboro	76
75	Chris. Newport ■	88
59	Shenandoah ■	41
75	Averett	72
51	Ferrum	58
45	N.C. Wesleyan	65
50	Methodist	64
49	Greensboro ■	75
39	Chris. Newport	75

53	Shenandoah	62
79	Averett ■	78
59	Ferrum	57
56	N.C. Wesleyan †	66

Nickname: Braves
Colors: Columbia Blue & White
Arena: Helms Center
   Capacity: 3,000; Year Built: 1979
AD: Debra P. Warren
SID: Meredith Davies Long

CHRISTIAN BROS.
Memphis, TN 38104 II

Coach: Mike Nienaber, Mississippi Col.
1976
2002-03 RESULTS (18-11)

81	Williams Baptist	65
55	West Fla. ■	57
73	LeMoyne-Owen ■	78
86	LeMoyne-Owen	65
63	Montevallo †	52
85	Central Baptist †	67
90	West Ala. ■	83
57	Middle Tenn.	74
63	Alas. Fairbanks †	76
96	Alas. Anchorage	94
98	Crichton	74
87	Central Ark.	80
84	West Ala.	59
86	Ouachita Baptist ■	79
79	Arkansas Tech ■	66
63	Henderson St. ■	70
80	Harding	85
71	Delta St. ■	73
84	Ark.-Monticello ■	65
75	Southern Ark.	69
92	Central Ark. ■	96
106	Crichton ■	93
65	Ouachita Baptist	72
74	Arkansas Tech ■	60
69	Henderson St.	82
107	Harding ■	101
67	Delta St.	76
85	Ark.-Monticello ■	79
102	Southern Ark. ■	81

Nickname: Buccaneers
Colors: Scarlet & Gray
Arena: De La Salle Gymnasium
   Capacity: 2,000; Year Built: 1951
AD: Michael Daush
SID: Keith Smith

CHRIS. NEWPORT
Newport News, VA
23606-2998............................III

Coach: C.J. Woollum, Ky. Wesleyan
1971
2002-03 RESULTS (24-5)

91	DeSales ■	69
65	Va. Wesleyan	70
82	Salisbury ■	79
101	Fisk ■	54
55	Randolph-Macon	63
82	Marymount (Va.)	69
66	SCAD ■	58
85	Frostburg St. †	73
94	Gwynedd-Mercy	75
72	Wheaton (Ill.) ■	70
109	Southern Va. ■	86
72	Shenandoah	46
79	Ferrum	70
109	Averett ■	58
88	Chowan	75
84	N.C. Wesleyan	77
64	Greensboro ■	52
73	Methodist ■	68
85	Shenandoah ■	59
76	Ferrum	62

111	Averett	84
75	Chowan ■	39
74	N.C. Wesleyan ■	63
73	Methodist	74
78	Greensboro	86
79	Averett †	64
94	Shenandoah	70
67	N.C. Wesleyan †	64
61	SCAD ■	66

Nickname: Captains
Colors: Blue & Silver
Arena: Freeman Center
   Capacity: 2,300; Year Built: 2000
AD: C. J. Woollum
SID: Francis Tommasino

CINCINNATI
Cincinnati, OH 45221-0021 I

Coach: Bob Huggins, West Virginia
1977
2002-03 RESULTS (17-12)

54	Tennessee Tech ■	48
80	Florida A&M ■	53
69	Dayton	75
76	Valparaiso ■	50
44	Xavier ■	50
65	La Salle ■	62
77	Oregon †	52
51	Clemson	58
66	Miami (Ohio) ■	54
81	Chattanooga ■	51
64	DePaul ■	56
83	TCU	72
66	St. Louis	56
77	Tulane ■	54
59	East Caro.	53
83	Charlotte ■	79
52	DePaul	56
76	Marquette ■	82
71	Louisville	77
61	Oklahoma St. ■	50
64	Charlotte	74
55	St. Louis ■	58
101	Louisville ■	80
53	East Caro. ■	52
48	Memphis	67
87	UAB ■	70
61	Marquette	70
61	Southern Miss. †	63
69	Gonzaga †	74

Nickname: Bearcats
Colors: Red & Black
Arena: Myrl Shoemaker Center
   Capacity: 13,176; Year Built: 1989
AD: Robert G. Goin
SID: Tom Hathaway

CITADEL
Charleston, SC 29409-6150 I

Coach: Pat Dennis, Wash. & Lee 1978
2002-03 RESULTS (8-20)

83	Webber ■	60
51	Navy	57
49	Maryland	97
56	Charleston So. ■	68
82	High Point ■	67
95	Oglethorpe ■	55
78	Southwestern (Tex.) ■	50
66	South Carolina St. ■	78
55	UCF ■	64
50	South Carolina	66
72	Davidson	86
88	Emmanuel (Ga.) ■	55
81	East Tenn. St.	87
54	Wofford ■	69
83	Western Caro. ■	69
67	Ga. Southern	66
44	Col. of Charleston ■	58

64	Chattanooga	79
65	Appalachian St.	75
69	Furman ■	55
67	Chattanooga	74
75	Col. of Charleston	84
66	UNC Greensboro ■	67
60	Furman	77
63	Ga. Southern ■	64
49	VMI ■	58
63	Wofford	75
63	Appalachian St. †	73

Nickname: Bulldogs
Colors: Blue & White
Arena: McAlister Field House
   Capacity: 6,000; Year Built: 1939
AD: Les Robinson
SID: Andy Solomon

CCNY
New York, NY 10031 III

Coach: Andre Stampfel, Baruch 1996
2002-03 RESULTS (17-12)

76	Rutgers-Camden †	69
63	Juniata	76
72	Lehman ■	62
90	Mt. St. Mary (N.Y.)	95
75	Hunter	82
76	St. Joseph's (L.I.) ■	69
63	Yeshiva	72
60	Bates †	78
84	Castleton St. †	77
107	Mt. St. Vincent ■	65
65	Merchant Marine ■	85
75	Clark (Mass.) ■	89
69	John Jay ■	74
62	Baruch ■	73
103	Medgar Evers ■	60
76	NYCCT	74
74	Staten Island ■	51
70	York (N.Y.) ■	58
54	Farmingdale St. ■	65
77	Lehman	73
79	Hunter ■	65
71	Purchase St. ■	54
72	Baruch	85
80	John Jay ■	64
94	Brooklyn ■	61
84	NYCCT †	64
79	York (N.Y.) †	68
84	Baruch	79
57	Merchant Marine	63

Nickname: Beavers
Colors: Lavender & Black
Arena: Nat Holman Gymnasium
   Capacity: 3,500; Year Built: 1972
AD: Robert Coleman
SID: Derrick Harrison

CLAREMONT-M-S
Claremont, CA 91711-6400.....III

Coach: Ken Scalmanini, Cal Poly
Pomona 1993
2002-03 RESULTS (15-10)

68	Vanguard ■	79
71	Lewis & Clark ■	78
63	Rensselaer ■	62
90	George Fox †	57
75	Cal St. Hayward †	48
62	Whitworth †	73
79	Menlo	76
49	Concordia (Cal.) ■	97
68	Chapman ■	50
72	La Sierra	47
80	Hope Int'l ■	56
83	Caltech ■	27
74	Whittier ■	53
95	Redlands	104
73	La Verne	75

62	Occidental ■	65
63	Pomona-Pitzer	55
76	Cal Lutheran ■	75
85	Caltech	27
73	Whittier	82
104	Redlands ■	106
84	La Verne ■	68
58	Occidental	62
61	Pomona-Pitzer ■	40
79	Cal Lutheran	56

Nickname: Stags
Colors: Maroon, Gold & White
Arena: Ducey Gymnasium
  Capacity: 1,200; Year Built: 1959
AD: Michael L. Sutton
SID: Kelly Beck

CLARION
Clarion, PA 16214 II

Coach: Ron Righter, St. Joseph's 1975
2002-03 RESULTS (19-10)

82	Point Park ■	68
63	Winston-Salem ■	46
58	Felician	53
75	Davis & Elkins	51
62	West Chester ■	71
73	Millersville ■	75
68	Bloomfield	51
73	East Stroudsburg ■	48
74	Bloomsburg ■	60
80	Davis & Elkins ■	37
87	Mansfield	82
79	Cheyney	84
64	Kutztown	61
79	Calif. (Pa.)	72
90	Pitt.-Johnstown ■	72
65	Slippery Rock ■	54
76	Indiana (Pa.) ■	72
50	Pitt.-Bradford ■	57
63	Lock Haven	60
66	Shippensburg ■	67
74	Edinboro ■	49
63	Calif. (Pa.) ■	61
63	Indiana (Pa.)	58
62	Slippery Rock	67
68	Lock Haven ■	70
43	Edinboro	57
96	Shippensburg	98
76	Edinboro	63
57	Millersville †	79

Nickname: Golden Eagles
Colors: Blue & Gold
Arena: W.S. Tippin Gymnasium
  Capacity: 4,000; Year Built: 1968
AD: Robert Carlson
SID: Rich Herman

CLARK ATLANTA
Atlanta, GA 30314 II

Coach: Larry Nolley, Clark (Ga.) 1981
2002-03 RESULTS (7-21)

80	Voorhees ■	86
60	West Ala. †	74
56	Xavier (La.)	71
58	Fla. Memorial ■	61
74	Livingstone ■	79
57	St. Augustine's ■	65
36	Miles ■	61
71	LeMoyne-Owen ■	87
74	Lane	79
91	Kentucky St.	87
68	Xavier (La.) ■	73
64	Albany St. (Ga.) ■	73
81	Benedict ■	79
65	Paine	60
81	Morris Brown †	84
84	Miles	95
70	Morehouse ■	103

95	Lane ■	68
94	Fort Valley St. ■	87
73	Tuskegee ■	75
78	Tuskegee	88
59	Benedict	73
63	Paine	58
82	Morris Brown	89
107	Fort Valley St.	112
79	Albany St. (Ga.)	73
59	Morehouse	67
81	Kentucky St. †	87

Nickname: Panthers
Colors: Red, Black & Grey
Arena: L.S. Epps Gym
  Capacity: 1,800
AD: Brenda Edmond
SID: Charles Ward

CLARK (MASS.)
Worcester, MA 01610-1477 III

Coach: Paul Phillips, Assumption 1976
2002-03 RESULTS (21-7)

102	Lehman †	72
96	Elizabethtown	103
62	Amherst	68
89	Tufts ■	77
92	Mass.-Boston	68
99	Wesleyan (Conn.) ■	82
91	Worcester St.	54
109	Southern Vt. †	112
101	Southern Me. †	88
89	CCNY	75
86	Wheaton (Mass.) ■	73
100	Salve Regina	70
62	Babson	58
66	MIT	71
79	Keene St.	68
71	WPI ■	50
85	Springfield	78
83	Coast Guard	61
83	WPI	75
77	Trinity (Conn.) ■	82
72	Wheaton (Mass.)	79
86	MIT ■	60
85	Coast Guard	47
83	Springfield ■	77
72	Babson ■	63
88	Wheaton (Mass.) ■	66
84	Babson ■	76
82	Western Conn. St. ■	84

Nickname: Cougars
Colors: Scarlet & White
Arena: Kneller Athletic Center
  Capacity: 2,000; Year Built: 1977
AD: Linda S. Moulton
SID: Joe Brady

CLARKE
Dubuque, IA 52001 III

Coach: Jon Davison, Dubuque 1961
2002-03 RESULTS (14-13)

73	Augustana (Ill.) ■	84
94	Wis. Lutheran	87
64	Whitworth †	68
65	Cal Lutheran †	77
82	Mt. Mercy	98
63	Cornell College	77
64	Upper Iowa	81
83	Mount St. Clare	70
80	Benedictine (Ill.) ■	65
75	Dubuque	71
57	Lakeland	61
54	Wis.-Platteville ■	43
74	Dominican (Ill.)	57
64	Marian (Wis.) ■	49
59	Rockford	66
75	Eureka ■	69
56	Aurora	70

51	Concordia (Ill.)	50
65	Benedictine (Ill.)	54
71	Dominican (Ill.)	63
62	Kendall	59
64	Rockford ■	71
73	Eureka	88
69	Aurora ■	72
52	Concordia (Ill.) ■	50
86	Eureka ■	67
62	Aurora	68

Nickname: Crusaders
Colors: Navy & Gold
Arena: Kehl Center
  Capacity: 900; Year Built: 1994
AD: Curt Long
SID: Jerry Hanson

CLARKSON
Potsdam, NY 13699-5830 III

Coach: Tobin Anderson, Wesley 1995
2002-03 RESULTS (11-14)

63	Old Westbury †	60
49	Potsdam St. ■	47
78	Plattsburgh St.	69
61	Williams ■	78
51	Potsdam St. ■	66
58	Mt. Aloysius †	66
65	Cazenovia †	73
63	Medaille	52
66	Oneonta St.	57
60	Keuka	66
61	Cazenovia	64
65	Hamilton	79
59	Hobart	75
54	Rensselaer ■	59
70	Vassar	57
59	St. Lawrence	56
72	Union (N.Y.) ■	81
65	Skidmore ■	67
63	Vassar	59
58	Rensselaer	56
71	St. Lawrence	76
66	Hobart ■	65
72	Hamilton ■	80
56	Skidmore	55
57	Union (N.Y.)	70

Nickname: Golden Knights
Colors: Green & Gold
Arena: Alumni Gymnasium
  Capacity: 2,000; Year Built: 1952
AD: Sean Frazier
SID: Tommy Szarka

CLAYTON ST.
Morrow, GA 30260 II

Coach: Gordon Gibbons, Springfield 1968
2002-03 RESULTS (17-12)

72	Albany St. (Ga.)	67
96	Southeastern Fla. ■	60
61	Kennesaw St. ■	74
89	UNC Pembroke	49
65	Armstrong Atlantic	60
79	West Ga. ■	45
76	Albany St. (Ga.) ■	62
70	Mobile	73
87	Alderson-Broaddus †	47
55	Rollins	60
82	S.C.-Aiken ■	67
68	S.C.-Spartanburg ■	57
68	GC&SU ■	69
73	North Fla. ■	71
62	Columbus St.	64
69	UNC Pembroke	47
70	Kennesaw St.	73
61	Augusta St.	58
62	Columbus St. ■	73
74	Francis Marion ■	66

67	GC&SU ■	81
58	Armstrong Atlantic ■	62
77	West Ga.	93
66	S.C.-Spartanburg	59
57	North Fla.	65
86	Lander ■	72
64	Francis Marion	61
79	S.C.-Aiken †	71
79	Columbus St.	87

Nickname: Lakers
Colors: Blue & Orange
Arena: Athletics Center
  Capacity: 2,000; Year Built: 1983
AD: Mason Barfield
SID: Gid Rowell

CLEMSON
Clemson, SC 29634 I

Coach: Larry Shyatt, Wooster 1973
2002-03 RESULTS (15-13)

79	Wofford ■	72
91	High Point †	65
79	Penn St. ■	70
73	Maine ■	61
71	Gardner-Webb ■	61
78	Liberty ■	65
78	Winthrop ■	61
58	Cincinnati ■	51
90	Coastal Caro. ■	63
71	Duke ■	89
75	Morris Brown ■	52
66	North Carolina	68
78	Virginia ■	77
59	Florida St.	60
47	Maryland ■	52
60	Wake Forest ■	81
56	North Carolina St.	78
69	Georgia Tech ■	67
55	Duke	65
59	South Carolina	76
80	North Carolina ■	77
73	Virginia	64
74	Florida St. ■	60
52	Maryland	91
68	Wake Forest	80
60	North Carolina St. ■	63
56	Georgia Tech	66
61	Florida St. †	72

Nickname: Tigers
Colors: Orange & Purple
Arena: Littlejohn Coliseum
  Capacity: 11,020; Year Built: 1968
AD: Terry Don Phillips
SID: Tim Bourret

CLEVELAND ST.
Cleveland, OH 44115-2440 I

Coach: Rollie Massimino, Vermont 1956
2002-03 RESULTS (8-22)

66	Fla. Atlantic †	71
78	IPFW †	71
63	Colorado St.	77
74	Duquesne	67
64	California ■	73
68	Akron	65
81	Md.-East. Shore ■	61
47	Michigan St.	79
68	Kent St. ■	91
74	IUPUI	90
70	Boston U. ■	56
72	Bowling Green †	80
66	Wis.-Green Bay ■	55
58	Wis.-Milwaukee ■	70
55	Youngstown St.	57
55	Wright St. ■	52
63	Ill.-Chicago	69
65	Loyola (Ill.)	77
51	Detroit ■	70

67	St. Bonaventure	81
57	Butler	73
56	Wis.-Green Bay	89
69	Wis.-Milwaukee	86
86	Youngstown St. ■	76
63	Wright St. ■	76
74	Ill.-Chicago ■	87
72	Loyola (Ill.) ■	77
75	Butler ■	79
55	Detroit	72
57	Loyola (Ill.)	69

Nickname: Vikings
Colors: Forest Green & White
Arena: Henry J. Goodman Arena
   Capacity: 13,610; Year Built: 1991
AD: Lee Reed
SID: Paulette Welch

COAST GUARD
New London, CT 06320-4195..III

Coach: Peter Barry, San Francisco 1970

2002-03 RESULTS (9-15)

60	Mt. St. Joseph	78
59	Nazareth †	74
70	Albertus Magnus ■	72
88	Nichols	61
62	Merchant Marine	60
64	Trinity (Conn.)	94
74	Rhode Island Col. ■	76
51	Army	63
73	Wentworth Inst.	60
48	Babson	63
59	MIT	67
81	Connecticut Col. ■	67
77	Springfield ■	62
52	WPI ■	55
61	Clark (Mass.)	83
65	Wheaton (Mass.)	88
59	Babson	79
53	MIT ■	60
70	Roger Williams ■	59
47	Clark (Mass.) ■	85
72	WPI	65
65	Springfield	64
75	Wheaton (Mass.) ■	68
67	Wheaton (Mass.)	83

Nickname: Bears
Colors: Blue & White
Arena: John Merriman Gymnasium
   Capacity: 2,400; Year Built: 1964
AD: Raymond Cieplik
SID: Jason Southard

COASTAL CARO.
Conway, SC 29528-6054..........I

Coach: Pete Strickland, Pittsburgh 1979

2002-03 RESULTS (13-15)

77	Western Caro.	72
45	Florida	88
68	South Carolina St.	53
49	Campbell	65
60	Georgetown	87
63	Navy ■	59
67	Newberry ■	48
82	East Tenn. St.	93
90	East Caro. ■	71
70	Lees-McRae ■	60
63	Clemson	90
74	Birmingham-So. ■	64
64	Winthrop	50
77	High Point	75
60	Elon	63
69	Charleston So. ■	72
73	Radford ■	77
54	Liberty ■	55
76	UNC Asheville	80
65	Birmingham-So.	59
72	Winthrop ■	66
89	High Point ■	71

58	Radford	65
73	Liberty	79
68	UNC Asheville ■	55
53	Elon ■	75
66	Charleston So.	70
61	Liberty	63

Nickname: Chanticleers
Colors: Coastal Green, Bronze & Black
Arena: Kimbel Arena
   Capacity: 1,037; Year Built: 1974
AD: Warren Koegel
SID: Wayne White

COE
Cedar Rapids, IA
52402-5092............................III

Coach: Brent Brase, Cornell College
1990

2002-03 RESULTS (9-17)

65	Iowa St.	87
81	Augustana (Ill.)	92
105	Dubuque ■	78
85	Washington (Mo.) ■	95
61	Wis.-Stevens Point	100
73	Wis.-Whitewater ■	83
84	Scranton †	85
77	Wilmington (Ohio) †	82
74	Upper Iowa	65
70	Luther	77
80	Wartburg ■	85
69	Buena Vista ■	81
70	Loras ■	71
68	Simpson	69
77	Central (Iowa)	64
88	Cornell College	79
61	Loras	70
56	Luther ■	55
80	Upper Iowa ■	61
84	Buena Vista	92
66	Wartburg	71
92	Dubuque	83
64	Central (Iowa) ■	74
83	Simpson ■	79
71	Cornell College ■	60
60	Cornell College	70

Nickname: Kohawks
Colors: Crimson & Gold
Arena: Moray L. Eby Fieldhouse
   Capacity: 2,600; Year Built: 1931
AD: John Chandler
SID: To be named

COKER
Hartsville, SC 29550................II

Coach: Dan Schmotzer, St. Edward's
1974

2002-03 RESULTS (5-21)

75	Mount Olive	90
79	Davis & Elkins †	46
72	Wingate	88
51	Pfeiffer ■	82
50	Francis Marion ■	70
50	UNC Pembroke	45
47	Erskine	62
72	Queens (N.C.)	81
76	Lees-McRae ■	60
86	Mount Olive ■	91
61	Barton	93
65	Belmont Abbey ■	83
64	Longwood ■	82
74	St. Andrews ■	72
73	Limestone ■	82
74	Anderson (S.C.)	64
89	Pfeiffer	91
58	Erskine ■	62
69	Lees-McRae	79
59	Mount Olive	97
55	Belmont Abbey	81

61	Queens (N.C.) ■	102
57	Longwood	69
64	Barton	93
54	St. Andrews	91
62	Longwood	67

Nickname: Cobras
Colors: Navy Blue & Gold
Arena: Timberlake-Lawton Gym
   Capacity: 750; Year Built: 1963
AD: C. Timothy Griggs
SID: Paul Lyon

COLBY
Waterville, ME 04901-8849.....III

Coach: Dick Whitmore, Bowdoin 1965

2002-03 RESULTS (6-16)

50	Husson †	67
103	Southern Me. †	90
60	Babson ■	74
53	Colby-Sawyer	74
57	Cal St. Monterey Bay	73
44	Dominican (Cal.) †	65
66	Southern Me. ■	69
80	Me.-Farmington	76
63	Bates ■	55
95	Bowdoin	91
68	Maine Maritime ■	73
62	Amherst ■	92
69	Trinity (Conn.) ■	71
59	Wesleyan (Conn.) ■	61
59	Connecticut Col. ■	57
67	Lasell	78
67	Middlebury	86
44	Williams	87
68	Bates	64
71	Tufts	89
63	Me.-Machias ■	79
61	Bowdoin ■	86

Nickname: Mules
Colors: Blue & Gray
Arena: Wadsworth Gymnasium
   Capacity: 2,500; Year Built: 1966
AD: Marcella K. Zalot
SID: Bill Sodoma

COLBY-SAWYER
New London, NH 03257.........III

Coach: Bill Foti, New Hampshire 1986

2002-03 RESULTS (21-7)

72	Me.-Farmington	83
67	Fisher †	64
66	Plymouth St. †	77
74	Colby ■	53
77	Wentworth Inst. ■	47
80	Bowdoin ■	69
77	Middlebury ■	71
63	Eastern Nazarene	51
95	Bates	98
69	Endicott	83
66	Nichols	74
95	New England	77
78	Worcester St. ■	72
70	Salve Regina ■	55
76	Gordon	66
75	New England Col. ■	47
69	Wentworth Inst.	57
54	Gordon ■	44
80	Endicott ■	68
105	New England ■	62
61	Roger Williams ■	67
80	Curry ■	72
83	New England Col.	59
70	Anna Maria ■	48
69	Salve Regina ■	48
78	Nichols	64
73	Endicott	65
68	Hamilton	93

Nickname: Chargers

Colors: Royal Blue and White
Arena: David L. Coffin Fieldhouse
   Capacity: 650; Year Built: 1991
AD: Deborah McGrath
SID: Adam Kamras

COLGATE
Hamilton, NY 13346-1304 I

Coach: Emmett Davis, St. Lawrence
1981

2002-03 RESULTS (14-14)

65	Marist	72
65	Eastern Mich. †	66
76	Cornell ■	58
92	Hobart ■	56
68	Syracuse	98
87	New Hampshire ■	68
70	Long Island ■	78
71	Harvard ■	76
54	Drexel ■	75
92	Hartwick ■	51
54	Albany (N.Y.) ■	61
54	Oral Roberts	78
64	Dartmouth	54
66	Lafayette ■	64
43	Holy Cross	86
86	Army ■	58
55	American	58
53	Navy	48
42	Bucknell ■	62
77	Lehigh ■	68
56	Lafayette	60
91	Holy Cross ■	92
68	Army	58
73	Navy ■	52
60	American ■	59
75	Lehigh	68
64	Bucknell	56
76	Lafayette †	89

Nickname: Raiders
Colors: Maroon, Gray & White
Arena: Cotterell Court
   Capacity: 3,091; Year Built: 1966
AD: Janet Little
SID: Bob Cornell

COLORADO
Boulder, CO 80309..................I

Coach: Ricardo Patton, Belmont 1980

2002-03 RESULTS (20-12)

97	Cal Poly ■	69
107	Stetson ■	74
71	New Mexico St.	75
70	Georgia ■	71
62	UMKC	59
80	Chicago St. ■	61
61	Rice	80
87	North Texas ■	71
75	La.-Lafayette †	56
76	Charlotte	74
76	Loyola (Ill.) †	72
80	Pennsylvania ■	57
93	Colorado St. ■	72
54	Oklahoma	69
69	Kansas St. ■	63
77	Nebraska ■	80
60	Kansas ■	59
56	Texas Tech ■	66
70	Missouri	73
93	Texas ■	80
84	Iowa St. ■	69
54	Kansas St.	62
98	Texas A&M ■	83
87	Kansas	94
89	Missouri ■	68
55	Iowa St.	81
72	Baylor ■	59
68	Oklahoma St. ■	56
84	Nebraska ■	69

77	Kansas St. †	76
59	Oklahoma †	74
64	Michigan St. †	79

Nickname: Buffaloes
Colors: Silver, Gold & Black
Arena: Coors Events/Conference Center
Capacity: 11,064; Year Built: 1979
AD: Richard A. Tharp
SID: David Plati

COLO. CHRISTIAN
Lakewood, CO 80226 II

Coach: Brannon Hays, Cal Lutheran 1993
2002-03 RESULTS (9-18)

62	UC-Colo. Spgs. †	65
53	Colorado St.-Pueblo	60
92	Hastings ■	79
71	Christian Heritage †	73
64	Pt. Loma Nazarene	79
75	Northern Colo.	83
102	UC-Colo. Spgs. ■	77
77	Western St. ■	65
83	Doane ■	73
89	Judson (Ill.) ■	57
77	Mesa St.	65
81	N.M. Highlands ■	73
75	Colorado St.-Pueblo ■	89
68	Fort Lewis	81
66	Adams St.	73
73	Colorado Mines	82
82	Regis (Colo.) ■	67
61	Neb.-Kearney	81
64	Fort Hays St.	104
41	Metro St. ■	54
75	Chadron St. ■	72
77	Neb.-Kearney ■	83
63	Fort Hays St. ■	70
61	Metro St.	78
72	Chadron St.	77
67	Colorado Mines ■	75
68	Regis (Colo.)	81

Nickname: Cougars
Colors: Blue & Gold
Arena: Cougar Fieldhouse
Capacity: 1,800; Year Built: 1990
AD: Lisa Parker
SID: Aimee Davison

COLORADO COL.
Colorado Springs, CO 80903 ..III

Coach: Mike McCubbin, Grinnell 1988
2002-03 RESULTS (11-13)

71	Puget Sound	85
59	Pacific Lutheran †	53
95	Hastings ■	77
62	Phila. Bible ■	64
109	Tufts ■	82
75	Chadron St. ■	80
78	UC-Colo. Spgs. ■	75
72	Neb. Wesleyan	76
57	Hastings	77
74	St. Mary's (Minn.) ■	66
75	Judson (Ill.) ■	77
89	Avila ■	68
62	Dallas	78
55	Huntingdon †	56
75	Hardin-Simmons	70
80	N.M. Highlands ■	88
62	Regis (Colo.)	83
93	Western St. ■	79
80	Adams St. ■	67
76	Fort Lewis	95
65	Dallas ■	71
91	Johnson & Wales (CO) ■	31
67	UC-Colo. Spgs.	69
64	Neb. Wesleyan ■	63

Nickname: Tigers

Colors: Black & Gold
Arena: J. Juan Reid Gymnasium
Capacity: 1,000; Year Built: 1970
AD: Joel Nielsen
SID: Dave Moross

COLORADO MINES
Golden, CO 80401 II

Coach: Pryor Orser, Eastern Mont. 1990
2002-03 RESULTS (18-10)

81	Northern Colo. ■	80
98	Mesa St. ■	93
112	Grand View ■	76
78	South Dakota St.	98
77	Augustana (S.D.) †	69
57	Northern Colo.	76
113	Western St. ■	94
90	UC-Colo. Spgs. ■	72
83	Alas. Anchorage	81
95	Alas. Anchorage	78
70	Mesa St.	66
78	Colorado St.-Pueblo ■	66
101	N.M. Highlands ■	80
66	Adams St.	59
93	Fort Lewis	86
82	Colo. Christian ■	73
77	Regis (Colo.) ■	70
72	Fort Hays St.	78
73	Neb.-Kearney	103
72	Chadron St. ■	73
60	Metro St. ■	63
87	Fort Hays St. ■	71
70	Neb.-Kearney ■	72
82	Chadron St.	92
63	Metro St.	91
75	Colo. Christian	67
82	Regis (Colo.)	67
69	Fort Hays St.	82

Nickname: Orediggers
Colors: Silver & Blue
Arena: Volk Gymnasium
Capacity: 1,000; Year Built: 1959
AD: Marvin L. Kay
SID: Greg Murphy

COLORADO ST.
Fort Collins, CO 80523-6011 I

Coach: Dale Layer, Eckerd 1979
2002-03 RESULTS (19-14)

80	IPFW ■	62
81	Fla. Atlantic ■	56
77	Cleveland St. ■	63
91	Tex. A&M-Kingsville ■	66
71	Southern Ill.	83
75	Ark.-Little Rock	84
82	West Ala. ■	50
90	Gardner-Webb ■	63
96	Denver ■	80
90	Washington St. ■	79
81	South Carolina ■	67
85	Prairie View ■	73
56	Purdue	84
82	South Fla. ■	70
72	Colorado	93
74	New Mexico ■	58
51	Air Force ■	49
77	Wyoming ■	79
72	San Diego St.	69
57	UNLV	90
66	Utah ■	71
68	Brigham Young ■	77
75	Air Force	80
72	New Mexico	82
60	Wyoming	62
67	UNLV ■	73
102	San Diego St. ■	89
66	Utah	65
55	Brigham Young	67
74	Wyoming †	71

86	Brigham Young †	80
62	UNLV	61
57	Duke †	67

Nickname: Rams
Colors: Green & Gold
Arena: Moby Arena
Capacity: 8,745; Year Built: 1966
AD: Jeffrey A. Hathaway
SID: Gary Ozzello

COLORADO ST.-PUEBLO
Pueblo, CO 81001-4901 II

Coach: Joe Folda, Northern Colo. 1966
2002-03 RESULTS (17-11)

83	Peru St.	69
60	Colo. Christian ■	53
70	Western N.M.	66
62	Minn. Duluth	77
80	Concordia-St. Paul †	73
79	Western N.M.	72
75	Regis (Colo.)	51
90	Hope Int'l ■	58
105	Judson (Ill.) ■	71
68	Neb.-Kearney	86
74	Fort Hays St.	71
66	Colorado Mines	78
89	Colo. Christian	75
106	Chadron St.	110
51	Metro St. ■	66
61	Adams St. ■	58
78	Fort Lewis	77
76	N.M. Highlands	83
49	Mesa St.	50
79	Western St.	76
66	UC-Colo. Spgs.	62
84	N.M. Highlands ■	63
61	Mesa St. ■	76
68	UC-Colo. Spgs. ■	62
102	Western St. ■	86
74	Fort Lewis	81
72	Adams St.	87
65	Fort Lewis	83

Nickname: Thunderwolves
Colors: Red & Blue
Arena: Massari Arena
Capacity: 5,000; Year Built: 1971
AD: Chris Gage
SID: To be named

UC-COLO. SPGS.
Colorado Springs, CO 80933-7150 II

Coach: Ed Pipes, Okla. Christian 1978
2002-03 RESULTS (6-19)

65	Colo. Christian †	62
64	Peru St. †	87
66	Cal St. Bakersfield	93
75	Colorado Col.	78
77	Colo. Christian	102
72	Colorado Mines	90
50	Metro St. ■	74
92	Chadron St.	97
57	Regis (Colo.)	80
80	Neb.-Kearney ■	96
50	Fort Hays St.	92
80	Western St. ■	78
53	Mesa St.	61
84	Fort Lewis	105
61	Adams St.	63
93	N.M. Highlands ■	76
62	Colorado St.-Pueblo	66
66	New Mexico St.	89
77	Fort Lewis ■	81
67	Adams St. ■	63
69	Colorado Col.	67
62	Colorado St.-Pueblo	68
89	N.M. Highlands	87
84	Western St.	78

67	Mesa St. ■	72

Nickname: Mountain Lions
Colors: Black & Gold
Arena: Lions Den
Capacity: 500; Year Built: 1988
AD: Ruben A. Cubero
SID: Doug Fitzgerald

COLUMBIA
New York, NY 10027.................I

Coach: Armond Hill, Princeton 1985
2002-03 RESULTS (2-25)

36	Rutgers	60
37	Boston U.	66
42	Binghamton	70
47	Bucknell †	61
48	Mt. St. Mary's †	57
56	Stony Brook ■	65
58	Army ■	44
51	Lehigh	67
55	UTEP	54
42	UAB †	71
52	Lafayette	61
58	Sacred Heart ■	59
47	Massachusetts	66
38	Cornell	51
53	Cornell ■	55
51	Yale	65
59	Brown ■	72
51	Princeton ■	68
40	Pennsylvania	47
63	Harvard	77
49	Dartmouth	63
70	Brown	83
59	Yale	71
36	Dartmouth ■	50
63	Harvard ■	66
39	Pennsylvania	63
40	Princeton	44

Nickname: Lions
Colors: Columbia Blue & White
Arena: Levien Gym
Capacity: 3,408; Year Built: 1974
AD: John A. Reeves
SID: Casey Taylor

COLUMBIA UNION
Takoma Park, MD 20912 II

Coach: Sandy Smith, Winston-Salem
2002-03 RESULTS (1-26)

59	Shepherd	84
69	Bloomsburg †	83
62	Kutztown	106
80	Fairmont St.	83
80	Pfeiffer ■	95
76	Kennesaw St.	94
59	West Ga.	64
65	Johnson Smith	92
71	Pfeiffer	114
69	Kutztown	91
66	Virginia St. ■	72
52	Winston-Salem	85
55	Dist. Columbia	73
58	Pitt.-Johnstown	85
84	Oakwood ■	103
67	Bowie St. ■	86
67	Virginia St.	91
43	Virginia Union	76
72	Oakwood	77
51	Virginia Union ■	71
58	Lincoln (Pa.) ■	65
64	Cheyney	84
77	Bowie St.	85
62	Lincoln (Pa.) ■	71
75	Pitt.-Johnstown ■	70
85	Cheyney ■	88
63	Dist. Columbia ■	78

Nickname: Pioneers

Colors: Blue & Gold
Arena: The Pit
   Capacity: 350; Year Built: 1954
AD: Brad Durby
SID: Donna Polk

COLUMBUS ST.
Columbus, GA 31907-5645......II

Coach: Herbert Greene, Auburn 1967
2002-03 RESULTS (27-5)

64	Calif. (Pa.) †	62
67	North Dakota St. †	81
77	Bryant †	73
72	Morehouse ■	67
97	Tuskegee ■	86
80	Albany St. (Ga.)	63
68	GC&SU	55
81	S.C.-Spartanburg ■	79
76	Albany St. (Ga.) ■	55
75	Shaw ■	61
82	Carson-Newman ■	81
73	Lander	65
91	Francis Marion ■	86
71	Augusta St. ■	68
81	North Fla.	80
77	Armstrong Atlantic ■	61
64	Clayton St.	62
65	S.C.-Aiken ■	49
68	Augusta St.	65
89	North Fla. ■	65
73	Clayton St. ■	62
88	S.C.-Aiken	71
77	Kennesaw St.	93
84	UNC Pembroke ■	56
97	GC&SU ■	92
62	Armstrong Atlantic	79
70	Kennesaw St. ■	63
71	Lander	76
87	Clayton St. ■	79
70	S.C.-Spartanburg ■	59
72	Kennesaw St. ■	56
59	Presbyterian ■	71

Nickname: Cougars
Colors: Red, White & Blue
Arena: Lumpkin Center
   Capacity: 4,500; Year Built: 2000
AD: Herbert Greene
SID: Mike Peacock

CONCORD
Athens, WV 24712 II

Coach: Steve Cox, Salem Int'l 1974
2002-03 RESULTS (10-18)

51	Lincoln Memorial	71
73	Indiana (Pa.) †	77
76	Bluefield St.	90
86	West Virginia St.	91
73	Elizabeth City St. †	69
77	St. Paul's †	84
71	Tusculum ■	82
71	Charleston (W.Va.)	88
61	Lincoln Memorial ■	59
45	Tusculum	57
83	West Va. Tech	96
77	Ohio Southern ■	57
76	Bluefield St. ■	80
80	Fairmont St. ■	76
72	Glenville St.	83
72	Davis & Elkins	75
72	West Va. Wesleyan ■	75
66	Shepherd ■	58
68	Alderson-Broaddus	91
102	Charleston (W.Va.)	96
62	Salem Int'l ■	79
68	West Liberty St.	82
73	Wheeling Jesuit	88
68	Bluefield St.	56
110	West Virginia St. ■	109

91	West Va. Tech ■	81
88	Ohio Valley ■	54
80	West Virginia St.	99

Nickname: Mountain Lions
Colors: Maroon & Gray
Arena: Carter Center
   Capacity: 2,000; Year Built: 1972
AD: Steven Lee
SID: Ernie Horn

CONCORDIA (ILL.)
River Forest, IL 60305-1499......III

Coach: Brian Miller, Wis.-Milwaukee 1987
2002-03 RESULTS (5-21)

77	North Park ■	86
56	Marian (Wis.) ■	52
82	Monmouth (Ill.)	103
73	Knox	97
49	Wheaton (Ill.)	73
63	Dominican (Ill.)	66
63	Edgewood †	80
54	Milwaukee Engr. †	66
63	Monmouth (Ill.) ■	45
39	Lewis-Clark St. †	79
67	Simpson †	87
73	Bridgewater St. †	71
71	Eureka	74
54	Rockford ■	81
57	Aurora	81
56	Benedictine (Ill.)	73
50	Clarke ■	51
61	Concordia (Neb.) †	86
70	Concordia (Mich.)	68
59	Eureka ■	61
71	Rockford	93
51	Aurora ■	66
63	Dominican (Ill.) ■	54
66	Benedictine (Ill.) ■	76
50	Clarke	52
70	Aurora	85

Nickname: Cougars
Colors: Maroon & Gold
Arena: Geisman Gymnasium
   Capacity: 2,200; Year Built: 1964
AD: Janet L. Fisher
SID: Jim Egan

CONCORDIA (N.Y.)
Bronxville, NY 10708 II

Coach: John Dwinell, Springfield 1981
2002-03 RESULTS (3-24)

88	Green Mountain †	55
64	St. Michael's	94
70	Molloy ■	83
60	New Haven ■	77
70	Adelphi ■	97
48	C.W. Post	87
76	Mercy ■	81
64	Philadelphia U. ■	93
60	Bridgeport	74
49	NYIT	70
59	Philadelphia U.	83
58	Queens (N.Y.)	71
80	St. Thomas Aquinas ■	90
51	Hartford	101
64	Molloy	75
54	Mercy	57
68	Dowling	80
42	New Haven	79
60	Bridgeport ■	78
44	Adelphi	57
53	C.W. Post ■	66
73	Dowling ■	53
65	NYIT ■	70
57	Queens (N.Y.) ■	62
70	Southampton	83

75	Southampton ■	73
50	St. Thomas Aquinas	64

Nickname: Clippers
Colors: Blue & Gold
Arena: Meyer Athletic Center
   Capacity: 1,000; Year Built: 1963
AD: Ivan Marquez
SID: Kris Zeiter

CONCORDIA (WIS.)
Mequon, WI 53097-2402........III

Coach: Pete Gnan, Minn. St. Mankato 1985
2002-03 RESULTS (14-12)

72	Oberlin †	55
66	Capital	75
54	Carthage	69
83	Webster †	81
75	Eureka	73
74	Rockford ■	83
84	Lakeland ■	68
99	Wis. Lutheran	81
83	Benedictine (Ill.) ■	70
72	St. Norbert	83
79	Marian (Wis.)	77
68	Tenn.-Martin	98
115	Concordia (Mo.)	45
70	Edgewood	69
85	Carroll (Wis.) ■	83
68	Milwaukee Engr. ■	66
64	Maranatha Baptist ■	66
106	Concordia (Mich.)	104
70	Concordia (Neb.) †	76
58	Lakeland	78
81	Wis. Lutheran ■	97
61	Marian (Wis.) ■	73
78	Maranatha Baptist	53
72	Milwaukee Engr.	68
55	Edgewood	93
67	Milwaukee Engr. ■	71

Nickname: Falcons
Colors: Royal Blue & White
Arena: Fieldhouse
   Capacity: 2,000; Year Built: 1989
AD: Robert M. Barnhill
SID: Rick Riehl

CONCORDIA-AUSTIN
Austin, TX 78705-2799 III

Coach: Jim Jost, Illinois
2002-03 RESULTS (4-21)

59	Houston Baptist	112
64	LeTourneau	84
82	East Tex. Baptist	103
70	Austin ■	81
79	Ozarks (Ark.) ■	81
80	St. Edward's	97
71	Mary Hardin-Baylor ■	70
53	Stephen F. Austin	96
75	Texas Wesleyan	98
73	Mississippi Col.	84
55	Louisiana Col.	70
69	Texas-Dallas ■	78
89	McMurry ■	81
78	Hardin-Simmons ■	69
73	Texas Lutheran ■	81
81	Schreiner	88
78	Mary Hardin-Baylor	82
78	Howard Payne ■	80
85	Sul Ross St. ■	103
61	Howard Payne	93
67	Sul Ross St.	79
56	McMurry	81
75	Hardin-Simmons	89
75	Texas Lutheran ■	86
81	Schreiner ■	77

Nickname: Tornados
Colors: Purple & White
Arena: Woltman Center
   Capacity: 1,600; Year Built: 1982
AD: Linda Lowery
SID: Jim Jost

CONCORDIA-M'HEAD
Moorhead, MN 56562-3597 ...III

Coach: Duane Siverson, Yankton 1978
2002-03 RESULTS (9-15)

53	Capital	65
75	Oberlin †	45
71	Briar Cliff	74
62	St. Olaf	67
63	Minn. St. Moorhead	70
65	Gust. Adolphus	88
60	St. John's (Minn.) ■	66
68	Macalester	71
54	Carleton	55
77	Bethel (Minn.) ■	79
59	St. Thomas (Minn.)	67
66	Hamline ■	54
81	Augsburg ■	74
71	St. Mary's (Minn.) ■	52
73	St. Olaf ■	64
58	Gust. Adolphus ■	76
71	St. John's (Minn.)	75
87	Macalester ■	74
73	Bethel (Minn.)	87
57	St. Thomas (Minn.) ■	68
57	Carleton	75
77	St. Mary's (Minn.) ■	73
7	Hamline	68
72	Augsburg	53

Nickname: Cobbers
Colors: Maroon & Gold
Arena: Memorial Auditorium
   Capacity: 3,500; Year Built: 1951
AD: Armin Pipho
SID: Jim Cella

CONCORDIA-ST. PAUL
St. Paul, MN 55104 II

Coach: Tom Smith, Valparaiso 1967
2002-03 RESULTS (4-24)

60	Fla. Southern †	67
62	Fla. Gulf Coast †	77
76	Northwest Mo. St. †	78
73	Colorado St.-Pueblo †	80
77	South Dakota St.	83
72	South Dakota ■	85
69	Minn. St. Mankato ■	71
44	Hamline	50
79	St. Cloud St.	93
60	Northern St. ■	78
86	Minn.-Morris ■	48
79	Winona St. ■	83
68	Southwest Minn. St.	85
77	Wayne St. (Neb.)	79
54	Minn. St. Moorhead ■	80
85	Minn.-Crookston ■	66
70	Minn. Duluth	84
84	Bemidji St.	94
92	Minn.-Morris	84
84	Northern St.	93
64	Winona St.	87
60	Wayne St. (Neb.) ■	80
60	Southwest Minn. St. ■	74
88	Minn.-Crookston	73
78	Minn. St. Moorhead	81
77	Bemidji St. ■	95
65	Minn. Duluth ■	74
65	Northern St.	99

Nickname: Golden Bears
Colors: Navy & Vegas Gold
AD: David Herbster
SID: To be named

CONNECTICUT

Storrs, CT 06269 I

Coach: Jim Calhoun, American Int'l 1968

2002-03 RESULTS (23-10)

91	Quinnipiac ■	72
67	George Washington ■	55
76	Vanderbilt	70
116	Sacred Heart ■	78
97	Wagner ■	85
59	Massachusetts ■	48
117	UNC Asheville ■	67
93	Central Conn. St. ■	65
95	St. Bonaventure ■	78
63	Oklahoma	73
83	Miami (Fla.) ■	80
83	Virginia Tech ■	65
65	North Carolina	68
76	Miami (Fla.)	77
74	Villanova ■	65
74	St. John's (N.Y.)	68
71	Boston College ■	95
74	Virginia Tech	95
84	Providence	68
75	Syracuse ■	61
70	Villanova	79
87	Rutgers ■	70
77	St. John's (N.Y.) ■	69
87	Notre Dame	79
67	Pittsburgh	71
70	Providence ■	76
91	Boston College	54
83	Seton Hall †	70
80	Syracuse †	67
56	Pittsburgh †	74
58	Brigham Young †	53
85	Stanford †	74
78	Texas †	82

Nickname: Huskies, UConn
Colors: National Flag Blue & White
Arena: Harry A.Gampel Pavilion
 Capacity: 10,027; Year Built: 1990
AD: Lew Perkins
SID: Kyle Muncy

CONNECTICUT COL.

New London, CT 06320-4196..III

Coach: Tom Satran, Connecticut Col. 1994

2002-03 RESULTS (7-16)

60	Haverford	47
46	Swarthmore	64
46	MIT ■	49
82	Roger Williams ■	52
70	Framingham St.	58
48	Lasell	69
67	Hunter	57
81	Salve Regina ■	67
54	Moravian	71
55	King's (Pa.) †	93
62	Tufts ■	90
79	Bates ■	89
67	Coast Guard	81
72	Bowdoin	93
57	Colby	59
81	John Jay ■	72
85	Mass.-Dartmouth ■	97
83	Wesleyan (Conn.)	84
61	Elms	75
55	Williams ■	83
84	Middlebury ■	64
62	Amherst	79
71	Trinity (Conn.) ■	82

Nickname: Camels
Colors: Royal Blue & White

Arena: Luce Fieldhouse/Gymnasium
 Capacity: 800; Year Built: 1984
AD: Stanton Ching
SID: Mike Salerno

COPPIN ST.

Baltimore, MD 21216-3698 I

Coach: Ron "Fang" Mitchell, Edison St. 1984

2002-03 RESULTS (11-17)

46	Marquette	64
55	Idaho St. †	63
51	Ohio St.	58
37	North Carolina St.	58
45	George Mason ■	68
73	Morgan St.	59
47	Oklahoma	69
47	Rider	66
53	Oregon St.	59
37	Illinois	63
68	N.C. A&T ■	41
54	South Carolina St.	67
47	Norfolk St.	57
70	Hampton	81
54	Delaware St. ■	46
73	Bethune-Cookman	69
74	Florida A&M	69
68	Howard ■	60
55	Md.-East. Shore	58
66	N.C. A&T	50
74	South Carolina St.	72
64	Norfolk St. ■	52
51	Hampton ■	65
65	Delaware St.	69
69	Florida A&M ■	73
70	Bethune-Cookman ■	65
59	Morgan St. ■	50
53	Florida A&M †	55

Nickname: Eagles
Colors: Royal Blue & Gold
Arena: Coppin Center
 Capacity: 1,720; Year Built: 1987
AD: Ronald "Fang" Mitchell
SID: David Popham

CORNELL

Ithaca, NY 14853 I

Coach: Steve Donahue, Ursinus 1984

2002-03 RESULTS (9-18)

78	Buffalo	72
58	Colgate	76
83	Ithaca ■	66
49	Lehigh	66
62	Syracuse	85
62	New Hampshire ■	78
59	La Salle	73
61	St. Francis (Pa.)	64
69	Army	50
80	Lafayette ■	73
55	Georgia Tech	81
52	Vermont ■	66
51	Columbia ■	38
64	Bucknell ■	60
55	Columbia	53
54	Brown ■	70
47	Yale ■	76
67	Pennsylvania ■	70
49	Princeton ■	67
56	Dartmouth	65
82	Harvard	69
52	Yale	70
62	Brown	70
68	Harvard ■	63
53	Dartmouth ■	70
61	Princeton	71
52	Pennsylvania	69

Nickname: Big Red
Colors: Carnelian Red & White
Arena: Newman Arena
 Capacity: 4,473; Year Built: 1989
AD: J. Andrew Noel
SID: Jeremy Hartigan

CORNELL COLLEGE

Mt. Vernon, IA 52314-1098 III

Coach: Ed Timm, Central (Iowa) 1985

2002-03 RESULTS (16-11)

51	Wis.-Eau Claire	64
74	Northland †	62
68	Mt. Mercy ■	76
61	Loras ■	55
77	Clarke ■	63
91	Iowa Wesleyan	98
59	Augustana (Ill.)	89
91	Mount St. Clare	64
60	Luther	51
66	Upper Iowa	84
66	Buena Vista ■	64
69	Wartburg ■	67
88	Dubuque ■	62
82	Central (Iowa)	73
80	Simpson ■	81
79	Coe ■	88
63	Dubuque	61
74	Upper Iowa ■	73
69	Luther ■	56
58	Wartburg	64
49	Buena Vista	74
77	Loras	66
85	Simpson	81
79	Central (Iowa) ■	73
60	Coe	71
70	Coe ■	60
67	Wartburg	77

Nickname: Rams
Colors: Purple & White
Arena: Cornell Fieldhouse
 Capacity: 2,500; Year Built: 1953
AD: Tina Hill
SID: Darren Miller

CORTLAND ST.

Cortland, NY 13045 III

Coach: Tom Spanbauer, Cortland St. 1983

2002-03 RESULTS (5-20)

52	New York U.	56
70	Roger Williams †	65
54	Elmira	56
60	Oneonta St. ■	65
64	Oswego St. ■	70
63	Alfred ■	70
70	Ithaca ■	72
52	Hartwick	57
55	St. Joseph's (Me.) †	73
70	Maritime (N.Y.) †	50
67	Utica/Rome ■	68
56	Buffalo St. ■	68
61	Geneseo St.	69
63	Fredonia St.	71
48	Rochester Inst. ■	55
75	Oswego St.	64
51	New Paltz St.	50
47	Potsdam St. ■	52
71	Plattsburgh St. ■	55
53	Oneonta St.	62
63	Buffalo St.	77
65	Brockport St.	76
53	Potsdam St.	68
47	Brockport St. ■	63
56	Fredonia St. ■	57

Nickname: Red Dragons
Colors: Red & White
Arena: Corey Gymnasium
 Capacity: 3,500; Year Built: 1973
AD: Joan Sitterly
SID: Fran Elia

CREIGHTON

Omaha, NE 68178-0001 I

Coach: Dana Altman, Eastern N.M. 1980

2002-03 RESULTS (29-5)

106	Texas-Arlington ■	50
82	Furman	57
99	IUPUI †	52
80	Notre Dame †	75
65	Northern Iowa	52
74	Brigham Young ■	64
101	Tennessee Tech ■	72
68	Delaware St. ■	48
81	Nebraska	73
93	Southeast Mo. St. ■	70
73	Xavier	75
84	Drake ■	63
65	Bradley	58
76	Illinois St.	57
93	Evansville ■	56
85	Southern Ill. ■	76
95	Illinois St. ■	82
66	Evansville	74
89	TCU ■	79
74	Indiana St.	46
88	Drake	68
84	Northern Iowa ■	75
88	Bradley ■	65
70	Southwest Mo. St. ■	67
74	Wichita St.	80
77	Indiana St. ■	54
67	Fresno St. ■	66
63	Southwest Mo. St.	58
62	Southern Ill.	70
86	Wichita St. ■	60
57	Indiana St. †	56
70	Wichita St. †	69
80	Southern Ill. †	56
73	Central Mich. †	79

Nickname: Bluejays
Colors: Blue & White
Arena: Omaha Civic Auditorium
 Capacity: 9,377; Year Built: 1954
AD: Bruce D. Rasmussen
SID: Rob Anderson

CURRY

Milton, MA 02186 III

Coach: Sean Casey, Keene St. 1993

2002-03 RESULTS (10-15)

78	Me.-Machias †	73
46	Keene St.	82
73	WPI ■	57
64	Lasell	74
62	Bridgewater St. ■	70
80	Endicott ■	81
59	Springfield	78
53	Northeastern	93
77	Tufts ■	87
67	Gordon ■	77
72	Newbury †	67
86	Roger Williams	77
89	Eastern Nazarene	94
64	Salve Regina	67
97	New England	95
71	New England Col.	66
93	Eastern Nazarene ■	65
66	Anna Maria ■	53
60	Nichols	68

87 Salve Regina ■ 70
72 Wentworth Inst. ■ 62
56 Nichols ■ 84
72 Colby-Sawyer 80
65 Anna Maria 69
58 Roger Williams ■ 68

Nickname: Colonels
Colors: Purple & White
Arena: Miller Gymnasium
    Capacity: 300; Year Built: 1952
AD: Steve Nelson
SID: Ken Golner

D'YOUVILLE
Buffalo, NY 14201 III

Coach: Gary Stanfield, John Brown 1969
2002-03 RESULTS (11-16)
71 Trinity (Conn.) † 79
69 Centenary (N.J.) † 70
65 Skidmore 66
61 Fredonia St. 77
58 Cabrini † 61
80 Maryland Bible † 71
61 York (N.Y.) † 57
58 Rochester Inst. 81
60 Rochester Inst. † 70
51 Buffalo St. † 65
67 Medaille † 64
66 Buffalo St. 84
61 Oswego St. 83
55 Keuka ■ 69
58 Geneseo St. ■ 62
49 Medaille ■ 47
70 Lake Erie ■ 63
67 Cazenovia 73
77 Baptist Bible (Pa.) ■ 76
57 Daemen ■ 68
55 Medaille 60
71 Hilbert 69
65 Keuka 72
75 Cazenovia ■ 74
71 Hilbert ■ 57
75 Cazenovia † 63
70 Keuka † 56

Nickname: Spartans
Colors: Red & Black
AD: Brian F. Miller
SID: To be named

DALLAS
Irving, TX 75062 III

Coach: Brian Stanfield, Drury 1990
2002-03 RESULTS (18-7)
90 Rhodes † 87
72 Hendrix 54
72 Washington (Mo.) 91
86 Fontbonne 93
72 Maryville (Mo.) † ■ 84
75 Southwestern (Tex.) ■ 63
64 Trinity (Tex.) 71
78 Millsaps ■ 74
69 Webster ■ 68
73 LeTourneau ■ 71
74 Hendrix ■ 64
66 Huntingdon 56
82 Sewanee ■ 65
78 Colorado Col. ■ 62
70 Huntingdon ■ 53
74 Cazenovia ■ 71
59 Millsaps 72
97 Rhema ■ 85
73 Austin 65
58 Southwestern (Tex.) 81
92 Johnson & Wales (Co.) 33
71 Colorado Col. 65
78 Dallas Christian 63

87 Mid-America Bible ■ 72
69 Austin ■ 72

Nickname: Crusaders
Colors: Navy & White
Arena: Maher Athletic Center
    Capacity: 1,000; Year Built: 1965
AD: Richard L. Strockbine
SID: Patty Danko

DANIEL WEBSTER
Nashua, NH 03063-1300........III

Coach: John Griffith, Southern Me. 1979
2002-03 RESULTS (3-22)
59 Wash. & Lee 79
64 Averett † 75
71 Elms 82
59 Johnson & Wales ■ 63
50 Emerson ■ 74
60 Newbury 87
82 New England 86
57 New England Col. ■ 58
59 Southern Vt. 85
70 Albertus Magnus ■ 88
70 Emmanuel (Mass.) 84
65 Western New Eng. 103
74 Suffolk ■ 82
77 Norwich 91
86 Albertus Magnus 108
91 Emerson 88
69 Rivier 79
78 Western New Eng. ■ 105
74 Johnson & Wales 101
46 Norwich ■ 63
86 Suffolk 82
70 Rivier ■ 84
81 Southern Vt. ■ 106
87 Hampshire 61
71 Emmanuel (Mass.) ■ 84

Nickname: Eagles
Colors: Navy & White, Red
Arena: Vagge Gymnasium
    Capacity: 600; Year Built: 1977
AD: John Griffith
SID: Greg Andruskevich

DARTMOUTH
Hanover, NH 03755 I

Coach: Dave Faucher, New Hampshire 1972
2002-03 RESULTS (8-19)
62 Lehigh 68
41 Vermont 62
53 Boston U. ■ 65
67 Binghamton ■ 61
85 WPI ■ 50
72 Quinnipiac ■ 81
44 Hartford 59
86 Stetson † 74
63 Furman 59
50 Harvard 67
54 Colgate ■ 64
68 Harvard ■ 69
57 New Hampshire ■ 62
43 Holy Cross 63
84 Albany (N.Y.) 85
50 Pennsylvania 73
52 Princeton 57
64 Yale 75
53 Brown 61
65 Cornell ■ 56
63 Columbia ■ 49
60 Princeton ■ 70
52 Pennsylvania ■ 67
50 Columbia 36
70 Cornell 53
67 Brown 79
50 Yale ■ 60

Nickname: Big Green
Colors: Green & White
Arena: Leede Arena
    Capacity: 2,100; Year Built: 1986
AD: Jo Ann Harper
SID: Kathy Slattery

DAVIDSON
Davidson, NC 28036 I

Coach: Bob McKillop, Hofstra 1972
2002-03 RESULTS (17-10)
80 Duke 95
69 Navy 61
105 Wash. & Lee ■ 48
114 Washington (Md.) ■ 51
75 Charlotte ■ 56
77 St. Bonaventure ■ 72
125 Wash. & Jeff. ■ 44
69 Arizona 95
66 Florida St. † 82
86 Citadel ■ 72
64 North Carolina 79
83 Western Caro. ■ 66
63 Chattanooga 67
65 Furman ■ 57
60 VMI 61
83 UNC Greensboro ■ 72
80 East Tenn. St. 71
67 Western Caro. 57
82 Wofford 98
99 Appalachian St. ■ 86
84 UNC Greensboro 77
72 East Tenn. St. ■ 87
85 Ga. Southern 76
94 Appalachian St. 81
89 Col. of Charleston ■ 94
84 VMI ■ 49
60 VMI † 66

Nickname: Wildcats
Colors: Red & Black
Arena: Belk Arena
    Capacity: 5,700; Year Built: 1989
AD: James E. Murphy III
SID: Rick Bender

DAVIS & ELKINS
Elkins, WV 26241-3996 II

Coach: Amrit Rayfield, Davis & Elkins 1997
2002-03 RESULTS (6-22)
58 Charleston (W.Va.) † 99
46 Coker † 79
66 Wheeling Jesuit ■ 88
51 Clarion ■ 75
64 Fairmont St. ■ 88
71 Dist. Columbia ■ 75
57 West Virginia St. 71
37 Clarion 80
77 Shepherd ■ 83
68 Fla. Gulf Coast ■ 79
82 Mt. Aloysius ■ 57
60 West Liberty St. 77
92 Ohio Valley 77
92 West Va. Wesleyan 97
71 Charleston (W.Va.) ■ 83
75 Concord ■ 72
82 Ohio Valley ■ 51
63 West Va. Tech 96
89 West Virginia St. 109
62 Salem Int'l 106
75 Alderson-Broaddus ■ 88
58 Glenville St. ■ 79
63 Shepherd 80
60 Alderson-Broaddus 97
67 Bluefield St. ■ 63
79 Glenville St. 93
80 West Va. Wesleyan ■ 75
51 Charleston (W.Va.) 83

Nickname: Big Green
Colors: Scarlet & White
Arena: Memorial Gymnasium
    Capacity: 1,875; Year Built: 1950
AD: Ralph Hill
SID: Ron Bratton

DAYTON
Dayton, OH 45469 I

Coach: Oliver Purnell, Old Dominion 1975
2002-03 RESULTS (24-6)
65 Delaware St. ■ 38
64 Evansville ■ 59
75 Cincinnati ■ 69
63 Miami (Ohio) 78
59 UNC Wilmington ■ 48
55 St. Louis 63
80 Ball St. ■ 65
71 Old Dominion 67
80 Villanova ■ 78
74 Duke 85
92 Marquette ■ 85
76 La Salle ■ 72
77 Duquesne ■ 72
66 Richmond ■ 53
71 George Washington 61
57 Temple 49
83 Massachusetts ■ 55
75 La Salle 70
76 Duquesne 75
77 Xavier 85
87 George Washington ■ 68
66 St. Joseph's ■ 56
70 Richmond 63
72 Xavier ■ 73
82 Rhode Island 70
69 Fordham 64
74 Rhode Island ■ 57
76 St. Joseph's ■ 73
79 Temple ■ 72
71 Tulsa † 84

Nickname: Flyers
Colors: Red & Blue
Arena: University of Dayton Arena
    Capacity: 13,266; Year Built: 1969
AD: Ted Kissell
SID: Doug Hauschild

DEPAUL
Chicago, IL 60614 I

Coach: Dave Leitao, Northeastern 1983
2002-03 RESULTS (16-13)
63 Northern Ill. 48
92 Central Mich. ■ 56
73 Fairfield ■ 45
73 Ohio ■ 65
71 Notre Dame 102
72 Florida Int'l 57
62 St. Joseph's 65
52 Seton Hall ■ 41
82 Western Caro. ■ 62
95 Loyola (Ill.) ■ 74
56 Cincinnati 64
70 UNLV ■ 75
71 TCU ■ 65
55 East Caro. 42
43 Louisville 71
51 Marquette 72
56 Cincinnati ■ 52
57 St. Louis 55
72 Charlotte ■ 64
60 Marquette ■ 73
74 Southern Miss. 69
77 East Caro. 63
61 St. Louis ■ 62
71 UAB 77

50	Charlotte	58
79	Louisville ■	76
65	Houston ■	59
74	South Fla. †	76
72	North Carolina	83

Nickname: Blue Demons
Colors: Blue & Scarlet
Arena: Allstate Arena
   Capacity: 17,500; Year Built: 1980
AD: Jean Lenti Ponsetto
SID: Scott Reed

DEPAUW
Greencastle, IN 46135.............III

Coach: Bill Fenlon, Northwestern 1979
2002-03 RESULTS (18-8)

64	Ill. Wesleyan †	77
46	Purdue-Calumet †	62
73	Wabash ■	62
90	Ind.-Southeast †	77
68	Franklin	59
58	Grace (Ind.) ■	64
64	Albion	82
69	Loras †	80
85	Western Conn. St. †	70
97	Rhodes	68
73	Hendrix	56
62	Earlham	53
83	Rose-Hulman ■	50
77	Trinity (Tex.) ■	51
86	Southwestern (Tex.) ■	90
86	Sewanee ■	67
76	Centre ■	61
78	Oglethorpe	68
71	Millsaps	65
101	Rhodes ■	81
98	Hendrix ■	63
63	Rose-Hulman	52
60	Trinity (Tex.)	76
67	Southwestern (Tex.)	63
74	Rhodes †	64
74	Centre †	88

Nickname: Tigers
Colors: Old Gold & Black
Arena: Neal Fieldhouse
   Capacity: 2,800; Year Built: 1982
AD: Page Cotton Jr.
SID: Bill Wagner

DEFIANCE
Defiance, OH 43512 III

Coach: Tom Palombo, Va. Wesleyan 1989
2002-03 RESULTS (17-10)

118	Marygrove ■	68
86	Mt. Vernon Naz. ■	97
78	Heidelberg	60
79	Anderson (Ind.)	84
90	Franklin ■	85
76	Hanover ■	80
96	Spring Arbor ■	78
92	Ohio Northern ■	90
76	Calvin	89
81	Methodist †	56
92	LaGrange	78
88	Manchester	80
86	Transylvania ■	79
82	Marygrove ■	80
74	Mt. St. Joseph ■	80
93	Bluffton	97
69	Franklin	91
101	Anderson (Ind.) ■	90
91	Hanover	107
83	Thomas More	77
72	Transylvania	77
88	Manchester ■	78
85	Bluffton ■	72
88	Thomas More ■	81

91	Franklin ■	84
71	Hanover	86
93	Mt. St. Joseph	77

Nickname: Yellow Jackets
Colors: Purple & Gold
Arena: Weaner Community Center
   Capacity: 1,800; Year Built: 1964
AD: Dick Kaiser
SID: Mike Partee

DELAWARE
Newark, DE 19716 I

Coach: David Henderson, Duke 1986
2002-03 RESULTS (15-14)

56	La Salle	73
87	Long Island ■	58
60	Pennsylvania ■	59
59	St. Joseph's	77
60	Rider ■	70
74	UNC Greensboro ■	71
87	Siena	78
66	Eastern Wash. †	56
82	Wis.-Green Bay	88
67	George Mason	77
69	James Madison	54
74	William & Mary	72
55	Va. Commonwealth ■	53
75	Old Dominion	74
62	UNC Wilmington ■	68
78	Drexel ■	83
74	Towson ■	60
62	Hofstra	64
91	William & Mary ■	57
63	George Mason	71
53	UNC Wilmington	71
74	James Madison ■	71
66	Va. Commonwealth	71
82	Hofstra ■	91
73	Old Dominion ■	63
56	Drexel	70
74	Towson	69
61	George Mason †	49
50	UNC Wilmington †	63

Nickname: Fightin' Blue Hens
Colors: Blue & Gold
Arena: Bob Carpenter Center
   Capacity: 5,000; Year Built: 1992
AD: Edgar N. Johnson
SID: Mike Hirschman

DELAWARE ST.
Dover, DE 19901 I

Coach: Greg Jackson, St. Paul's 1982
2002-03 RESULTS (15-12)

46	West Virginia	59
38	Dayton	65
57	Hartford	70
44	LSU	65
83	Fairleigh Dickinson ■	75
70	Wagner ■	63
48	Creighton	68
41	Rutgers	54
62	Florida A&M ■	55
70	Bethune-Cookman ■	47
60	N.C. A&T ■	50
53	South Carolina St.	81
46	Coppin St.	54
72	Morgan St.	80
56	Md.-East. Shore ■	46
70	Howard ■	61
71	Hampton	66
71	Norfolk St. ■	56
77	Florida A&M	97
43	Bethune-Cookman	48
76	N.C. A&T	53
83	South Carolina St. ■	78
69	Coppin St. ■	65
80	Morgan St. ■	53

70	Md.-East. Shore	57
59	Howard	56
65	Howard †	68

Nickname: Hornets
Colors: Red & Columbia Blue
Arena: Memorial Hall
   Capacity: 3,000; Year Built: 1982
AD: Hallie Gregory
SID: Dennis Jones

DELAWARE VALLEY
Doylestown, PA 18901-2699 III

Coach: Bill Dooley, Richmond 1983
2002-03 RESULTS (5-19)

61	Geneseo St. †	70
67	Salisbury †	65
47	Phila. Bible	78
52	Scranton	84
51	Lycoming	96
74	Centenary (N.J.) ■	72
67	McDaniel †	64
66	Villa Julie	65
57	Moravian ■	64
73	Arcadia	80
56	Lebanon Valley ■	71
54	King's (Pa.) ■	79
61	DeSales ■	62
83	Valley Forge Chrst.	73
63	Wilkes	87
63	Drew ■	79
61	FDU-Florham	69
74	Lycoming ■	92
64	Scranton ■	76
63	DeSales	87
42	King's (Pa.)	65
58	Wilkes ■	61
66	FDU-Florham ■	78
69	Drew	80

Nickname: Aggies
Colors: Green & Gold
Arena: James Work Gymnasium
   Capacity: 1,800; Year Built: 1969
AD: Frank Wolfgang
SID: Matthew Levy

DELTA ST.
Cleveland, MS 38733 II

Coach: Steve Rives, Mississippi Col. 1972
2002-03 RESULTS (22-8)

93	Miles ■	64
86	LeMoyne-Owen ■	71
93	William Carey ■	82
94	Mississippi Val. ■	91
61	SIU Edwardsville ■	50
64	Mississippi Val.	87
89	William Carey	70
64	Henderson St.	83
67	Harding ■	66
72	Ark.-Monticello	58
104	Ark. Baptist ■	75
96	Southern Ark.	64
71	Central Ark. ■	69
102	Philander Smith ■	82
73	Christian Bros.	71
63	Ouachita Baptist ■	69
75	Arkansas Tech	76
77	Henderson St. ■	65
71	Harding	90
64	Ark. Baptist	69
92	North Ala. ■	78
98	Ark.-Monticello ■	71
78	Southern Ark. ■	70
72	Central Ark.	68
76	Christian Bros. ■	67
60	Ouachita Baptist	50
84	Arkansas Tech †	56
76	Lincoln Memorial †	78

DENISON
Granville, OH 43023 III

Coach: Bob Ghiloni, Ohio St. 1981
2002-03 RESULTS (9-17)

62	Eureka †	47
64	Westminster (Mo.) †	67
60	Mt. St. Joseph	66
75	Rhodes	85
68	Hendrix †	67
63	Wooster	74
52	Wabash	72
66	Grove City ■	83
74	Bluffton	78
73	Capital	83
67	Ohio Wesleyan ■	76
50	Earlham	62
75	Hiram ■	74
48	Wittenberg ■	70
66	Oberlin	56
88	Allegheny ■	83
80	Kenyon	73
76	Wabash ■	78
74	Hiram	68
53	Earlham ■	58
70	La Roche	74
61	Kenyon ■	53
61	Allegheny	87
72	Oberlin ■	61
51	Wittenberg	75
74	Wittenberg	80

Nickname: Big Red
Colors: Red & White
Arena: Livingston Gymnasium
   Capacity: 3,500; Year Built: 1949
AD: Larry Scheiderer
SID: Craig Hicks

DENVER
Denver, CO 80208 I

Coach: Terry Carroll, Northern Iowa 1978
2002-03 RESULTS (17-15)

65	Wyoming	85
47	Montana	75
69	Eastern Wash. ■	48
83	UMKC ■	66
69	Binghamton †	74
75	Western Ill. †	48
80	Colorado St.	96
76	Chicago St. ■	49
79	James Madison †	72
58	Auburn †	63
49	Duquesne †	48
87	Drake ■	62
62	Montana ■	54
75	Nebraska	79
71	Florida Int'l	60
59	North Texas	55
82	Arkansas St. ■	68
72	Ark.-Little Rock ■	55
50	South Ala.	59
65	New Orleans	75
77	New Mexico St. ■	80
80	La.-Lafayette ■	95
72	Western Ky.	81
68	Middle Tenn. ■	80
69	La.-Lafayette	72
90	North Texas ■	84
77	South Ala. ■	50

72	Fla. Southern †	70
60	Henderson St. †	67

Nickname: Statesmen
Colors: Forest Green & White
Arena: Walter Sillers Coliseum
   Capacity: 4,000; Year Built: 1961
AD: James H. Jordan
SID: Fred Sington

68 New Orleans ■ 63
76 New Mexico St. 87
82 Arkansas St. † 76
72 La.-Lafayette † 68
59 Middle Tenn. † 83

Nickname: Pioneers
Colors: Crimson & Gold
Arena: Magness Arena
   Capacity: 7,200; Year Built: 1999
AD: M. Dianne Murphy
SID: Daniel Lust

DESALES
Center Valley, PA 18034-9568..III

Coach: Scott Coval, William & Mary 1986
2002-03 RESULTS (23-7)
69 Chris. Newport......91
73 Moravian 63
62 Misericordia ■ 47
76 FDU-Florham ■ 59
69 King's (Pa.)......60
82 Haverford ■ 65
77 Villa Julie 63
79 Dickinson ■ 71
78 Elizabethtown ■ 66
86 Muhlenberg ■ 63
90 Lancaster Bible 52
63 Wilkes ■ 62
62 Delaware Valley......61
53 Scranton ■ 57
72 Lycoming 77
67 Arcadia ■ 59
71 Drew 53
74 King's (Pa.) ■ 56
59 Albright......54
74 FDU-Florham 84
87 Delaware Valley ■ 63
72 Wilkes 82
85 Scranton 79
81 Drew ■ 67
75 Lycoming ■ 67
88 Lycoming 73
65 Scranton 72
81 Misericordia ■ 65
61 Penn St.-Behrend † 45
60 Frank. & Marsh......70

Nickname: Bulldogs
Colors: Navy Blue & Scarlet
Arena: Billera Hall
   Capacity: 1,000; Year Built: 1964
AD: Scott Coval
SID: B.J. Spigelmyer

DETROIT
Detroit, MI 48219-0900............I

Coach: Perry Watson, Eastern Mich. 1972
2002-03 RESULTS (18-12)
75 Bowling Green ■ 61
66 Buffalo 65
55 Western Mich. 71
70 Hillsdale ■ 50
72 Toledo 80
79 Western III. 60
62 La.-Lafayette † 68
79 Grambling † 52
60 Wyoming 74
72 Wis.-Milwaukee ■ 73
87 Wis.-Green Bay ■ 72
64 Wright St. 67
68 Butler 76
72 Loyola (III.) 54
74 III.-Chicago ■ 77
57 Youngstown St. 49
70 Cleveland St. 51
80 III.-Chicago 73
86 Western Ky. 65

DICKINSON
Carlisle, PA 17013...................III

Coach: Dennis Csensits, DeSales 1990
2002-03 RESULTS (8-17)
67 Gwynedd-Mercy ■ 78
81 Hunter ■ 68
39 Lebanon Valley 62
66 Elizabethtown 93
68 Shippensburg ■ 84
69 Ursinus ■ 72
97 York (Pa.) ■ 95
82 Susquehanna ■ 78
71 DeSales 79
86 Grove City † 65
73 Eastern 77
48 Swarthmore 63
68 McDaniel 70
68 Johns Hopkins 80
68 Frank. & Marsh. ■ 90
81 Juniata 80
54 Gettysburg ■ 62
57 Haverford ■ 66
83 Muhlenberg 76
79 Washington (Md.) 80
80 McDaniel ■ 64
65 Johns Hopkins ■ 75
48 Frank. & Marsh. 78
59 Gettysburg 74
81 Messiah ■ 69

Nickname: Red Devils
Colors: Red & White
Arena: Kline Center
   Capacity: 2,000; Year Built: 1980
AD: Leslie J. Poolman
SID: Charlie McGuire

DIST. COLUMBIA
Washington, DC 20008............II

Coach: Mike McLeese, Elizabeth City St. 1974
2002-03 RESULTS (19-7)
67 Edinboro † 62
75 Calif. (Pa.)......81
72 Indiana (Pa.) ■ 64
74 Kutztown 81
73 Charleston (W.Va.) † 84
75 Glenville St. † 66
97 Bowie St.......95
75 Davis & Elkins 71
72 St. Augustine's 75
90 Elizabeth City St. 77
89 West Va. Wesleyan ■ 64
76 Pitt.-Johnstown † 69
66 Bloomfield † 64
75 Bloomsburg 55
75 Virginia Union ■ 72
73 Columbia Union ■ 55
67 Virginia St. ■ 63
77 Virginia St. 67
69 Elizabeth City St. ■ 56

72 Indiana (Pa.) 88
93 Pitt.-Johnstown ■ 74
87 Lock Haven 67
83 Shepherd ■ 66
65 Virginia Union 77
77 Pitt.-Johnstown 80
78 Columbia Union 63

Nickname: Firebirds
Colors: Red & Yellow
Arena: Physical Activities Center
   Capacity: 3,000; Year Built: 1976
AD: Mike McLeese
SID: Bernard S. Payton

DOMINICAN (ILL.)
River Forest, IL 60305...............III

Coach: Mark White, Macalester 1984
2002-03 RESULTS (7-19)
58 Brockport St. † 80
64 Grace Bible (Mich.) † 68
55 III. Wesleyan 79
65 Calumet Col. 63
48 Illinois Tech ■ 49
98 Redlands 103
59 North Central † 58
73 George Fox † 82
66 Concordia (III.) ■ 63
76 Milwaukee Engr. ■ 85
56 Edgewood 68
63 Illinois Col. 61
57 Ohio Wesleyan † 55
57 Clarke 74
69 Elmhurst ■ 84
66 Benedictine (III.) ■ 68
48 Aurora 91
72 Rockford ■ 90
71 Eureka 60
63 Clarke ■ 71
58 Benedictine (III.) 66
73 Aurora ■ 81
54 Concordia (III.)......63
67 Rockford 82
78 Eureka ■ 74
64 Benedictine (III.) 80

Nickname: Stars
Colors: Royal Blue, Black & White
Arena: IGINI Sports Forum
   Capacity: 1,000; Year Built: 1985
AD: Barb Bolich
SID: Brian Gibboney

DOMINICAN (N.Y.)
Orangeburg , NY
10962-1299 II

Coach: Joe Clinton
2002-03 RESULTS (12-14)
65 Gannon ■ 74
86 Pace ■ 74
81 Concordia (Cal.) † 105
70 Azusa Pacific......93
75 N.J. Inst. of Tech. ■ 78
46 Holy Family 59
91 Goldey-Beacom 71
81 Phila. Sciences ■ 79
74 Felician 70
98 St. Rose ■ 108
50 Stonehill 71
50 Caldwell 64
98 Bloomfield ■ 96
90 Green Mountain ■ 74
61 N.J. Inst. of Tech. 71
88 Wilmington (Del.) ■ 58
73 Teikyo Post 83
82 Bloomfield 85
67 Nyack ■ 63
78 Holy Family ■ 76
73 Caldwell ■ 87
79 Goldey-Beacom 78

63 Felician ■ 75
83 Wilmington (Del.) 69
64 Nyack 60
84 Teikyo Post 98

Nickname: Chargers
Colors: Black & Red
AD: Joseph S. Clinton
SID: To be named

DOWLING
Oakdale, NY 11769 II

Coach: Mike Voyack, St. John's (N.Y.) 1995
2002-03 RESULTS (7-20)
68 St. Thomas Aquinas 61
61 Holy Cross 101
80 Mercy ■ 71
68 Bridgeport ■ 85
83 C.W. Post ■ 81
84 Bryant ■ 77
75 New Haven 98
83 American Int'l 78
85 NYIT ■ 88
76 Philadelphia U. 98
60 Queens (N.Y.) ■ 64
74 Southampton ■ 84
78 Molloy 88
65 Mercy 70
52 New Haven ■ 67
80 Concordia (N.Y.) ■ 68
52 Bridgeport 89
75 Adelphi ■ 82
62 C.W. Post. 87
53 Concordia (N.Y.) 73
75 NYIT 86
64 Philadelphia U. ■ 88
78 Southampton 83
65 St. Thomas Aquinas ■ 62
58 Queens (N.Y.) 72
50 Adelphi 78
103 Molloy 106

Nickname: Golden Lions
Colors: Navy & Vegas Gold
Arena: Lasalle Center
   Capacity: 1,500
AD: Robert Dranoff
SID: Chris Celano

DRAKE
Des Moines, IA 50311-4505......I

Coach: Kurt Kanaskie, La Salle 1980
2002-03 RESULTS (10-20)
74 Fla. Atlantic ■ 62
49 Iowa ■ 50
70 Hawaii-Hilo 50
61 Utah St. † 73
83 Vermont † 78
62 Northern III. 77
61 Central Mich. 73
162 Grinnell 110
72 Western III. ■ 62
55 Iowa St. 76
62 Denver 87
63 Southern III. 76
63 Creighton 84
72 Southwest Mo. St. ■ 74
75 Northern Iowa ■ 73
57 Bradley 72
68 Indiana St. ■ 54
61 Wichita St. 69
45 Southwest Mo. St. 65
68 Creighton ■ 88
64 Southern III. ■ 65
51 Evansville 62
62 Indiana St. 63
59 Illinois St. 48
70 Wichita St. ■ 80
81 Evansville 73

70 Illinois St. ■ ...63
48 Northern Iowa ...59
67 Bradley ■ ...77
62 Illinois St. † ...63

Nickname: Bulldogs
Colors: Blue & White
Arena: Drake Knapp Center
　Capacity: 7,002; Year Built: 1992
AD: Dave Blank
SID: Mike Mahon

DREW
Madison, NJ 07940 ...III

Coach: Mark Coleman, St. Lawrence 1983
2002-03 RESULTS (7-17)
66 Kean ■ ...76
67 Ursinus ■ ...92
76 Swarthmore ■ ...66
58 King's (Pa.) ■ ...65
71 Scranton ■ ...79
55 Moravian ...87
44 Hawaii-Hilo ...86
42 Hawaii Pacific ...66
74 Vassar ■ ...69
67 Lycoming ...75
66 Wilkes ...76
50 Haverford ...84
67 FDU-Florham ■ ...63
79 Delaware Valley ...63
53 DeSales ■ ...71
59 Scranton ...74
71 Ursinus ■ ...74
64 King's (Pa.) ...77
65 Wilkes ■ ...72
89 Lycoming ■ ...87
58 FDU-Florham ...64
67 DeSales ...81
80 Delaware Valley ■ ...69
75 Farmingdale St. ...70

Nickname: Rangers
Colors: Green & Blue
Arena: Baldwin Gym
　Capacity: 800; Year Built: 1958
AD: Connee Zotos
SID: Jennifer Brauner

DREXEL
Philadelphia, PA 19104 ...I

Coach: Bruiser Flint, St. Joseph's 1987
2002-03 RESULTS (19-12)
41 Villanova ...64
71 Pennsylvania ...62
73 Monmouth ...68
65 Lafayette ...47
37 St. Joseph's † ...50
78 Quinnipiac ...81
72 Niagara ...88
75 Colgate ■ ...54
78 Philadelphia U. ■ ...61
82 James Madison ...62
53 George Mason ...75
74 Va. Commonwealth ...73
86 UNC Wilmington ■ ...88
67 William & Mary ■ ...51
85 Towson ■ ...56
83 Delaware ...78
78 Hofstra ■ ...66
69 Old Dominion ...72
56 UNC Wilmington ...77
82 Hofstra ...76
76 Towson ...50
59 Va. Commonwealth ■ ...72
78 James Madison ■ ...67
62 Old Dominion ...57
78 William & Mary ...62
70 Delaware ■ ...56
55 George Mason ...57
61 Old Dominion † ...52

62 Va. Commonwealth † ...60
62 UNC Wilmington † ...70
59 Temple ...68

Nickname: Dragons
Colors: Navy Blue & Gold
Arena: Daskalakis Athletic Center
　Capacity: 2,300; Year Built: 1975
AD: Eric A. Zillmer
SID: Mike Tuberosa

DRURY
Springfield, MO 65802 ...II

Coach: Gary Stanfield, John Brown 1969
2002-03 RESULTS (11-17)
79 Neb.-Kearney ...103
85 Midwestern St. ■ ...82
85 Cal Baptist ■ ...101
77 Neb.-Kearney ...84
49 Southwest Baptist ...81
69 Truman ...66
79 Central Mo. St. † ...81
84 Northwest Mo. St. † ...90
65 Truman ■ ...78
75 Arkansas Tech ...90
94 Arkansas Tech ■ ...75
88 Central Okla. ...108
85 Okla. Panhandle ...81
100 St. Edward's ...99
61 St. Mary's (Tex.) ■ ...73
73 Incarnate Word ■ ...76
60 Oakland City ...73
61 Rockhurst ...63
90 Central Okla. ■ ...100
78 Lincoln (Mo.) ■ ...67
89 Okla. Panhandle ■ ...81
103 St. Edward's ...75
72 Incarnate Word ...73
62 St. Mary's (Tex.) ...69
76 Lincoln (Mo.) ...67
93 Rockhurst ...90
80 Oakland City ■ ...75
64 St. Mary's (Tex.) ...69

Nickname: Panthers
Colors: Scarlet & Gray
Arena: Weiser Gymnasium
　Capacity: 2,250; Year Built: 1948
AD: Edsel Matthews
SID: Dan Cashel

DUBUQUE
Dubuque, IA 52001 ...III

Coach: Paul Lusk, Southern Ill.
2002-03 RESULTS (2-23)
46 Wis.-Platteville ...78
71 Mt. Mercy ...89
88 Iowa Wesleyan ...96
78 Coe ...105
74 Knox ...79
71 Clarke ...75
61 Wis.-La Crosse ■ ...64
80 Mt. Mercy ■ ...79
70 Loras ...72
67 Upper Iowa ■ ...78
55 Luther ...67
62 Cornell College ...88
48 Wartburg ...96
63 Buena Vista ...89
51 Simpson ■ ...63
77 Central (Iowa) ...74
61 Cornell College ■ ...63
53 Loras ...88
63 Luther ...67
64 Upper Iowa ...85
83 Coe ■ ...92
77 Buena Vista ■ ...102
64 Wartburg ■ ...70
54 Central (Iowa) ...78
73 Simpson ...109

Nickname: Spartans
Colors: Blue & White
Arena: McCormick Gym
　Capacity: 1,500; Year Built: 1916
AD: Dan Runkle
SID: Jason Hughes

DUKE
Durham, NC 27708-0555 ...I

Coach: Mike Krzyzewski, Army 1969
2002-03 RESULTS (26-7)
101 Army ■ ...53
95 Davidson ■ ...80
84 UCLA † ...73
91 Ohio St. † ...76
81 Michigan ■ ...59
91 N.C. A&T ...57
85 Dayton ■ ...74
86 Fairfield ■ ...58
89 Clemson ...71
93 Georgetown ■ ...86
74 Wake Forest ■ ...55
104 Virginia ■ ...93
72 Maryland ...87
71 North Carolina St. ...80
91 Georgia Tech ■ ...71
80 Butler ■ ...60
70 Florida St. ...75
83 North Carolina ...74
65 Clemson ■ ...55
80 Wake Forest ...94
78 Virginia ...59
75 Maryland ■ ...70
79 North Carolina St. ■ ...68
77 Georgia Tech ...58
71 St. John's (N.Y.) ...72
72 Florida St. ■ ...56
79 North Carolina ...82
83 Virginia † ...76
75 North Carolina † ...63
84 North Carolina St. † ...77
67 Colorado St. † ...57
86 Central Mich. † ...60
65 Kansas † ...69

Nickname: Blue Devils
Colors: Royal Blue & White
Arena: Cameron Indoor Stadium
　Capacity: 9,314; Year Built: 1939
AD: Joe Alleva
SID: Jon Jackson

DUQUESNE
Pittsburgh, PA 15282 ...I

Coach: Danny Nee, St. Mary's Plains 1971
2002-03 RESULTS (9-21)
67 Pittsburgh ...82
86 West Virginia ■ ...82
67 Cleveland St. ■ ...74
39 Maryland ...89
72 George Mason ...79
63 Mt. St. Mary's ■ ...77
61 Youngstown St. ■ ...56
74 Sacred Heart † ...63
69 Troy St. † ...73
48 Denver † ...49
67 St. Francis (N.Y.) † ...57
71 Florida Int'l ...68
74 Md.-East. Shore ■ ...71
56 St. Joseph's ...76
61 Temple ■ ...54
72 Dayton ...77
69 Richmond ■ ...75
58 Xavier ...93
78 St. Bonaventure ■ ...86
47 Richmond ...84
58 George Washington ...68
75 Dayton ■ ...76

74 La Salle ■ ...82
74 Fordham ...65
78 George Washington ■ ...73
55 Massachusetts ...70
78 Xavier ■ ...80
66 La Salle ...71
71 Rhode Island ■ ...76
73 Rhode Island ...75

Nickname: Dukes
Colors: Red & Blue
Arena: A.J. Palumbo Center
　Capacity: 6,200; Year Built: 1988
AD: Brian Colleary
SID: Dave Saba

EARLHAM
Richmond, IN 47374 ...III

Coach: Jeff Justus, Rose-Hulman 1978
2002-03 RESULTS (13-13)
69 Rust † ...54
78 Sewanee ...68
68 Bluffton ■ ...72
64 Mt. St. Joseph ...77
54 Hanover ■ ...87
73 Wilmington (Ohio) ■ ...62
72 Oberlin ...60
73 Rose-Hulman ...63
82 Franklin ...76
60 Allegheny ...80
67 Hiram ...74
53 DePauw ■ ...62
62 Denison ...50
57 Wabash ...93
58 Wooster ■ ...75
84 Kenyon ...72
68 Ohio Wesleyan ■ ...60
46 Wittenberg ...82
66 Oberlin ■ ...57
77 Wabash ■ ...74
58 Denison ...53
39 Wittenberg ■ ...82
56 Ohio Wesleyan ...60
88 Kenyon ■ ...72
72 Wooster ...78
90 Allegheny ...92

Nickname: Quakers
Colors: Maroon & White
Arena: Schuckman Court
　Capacity: 1,800; Year Built: 1999
AD: Frank Carr
SID: Jon Mires

EAST CARO.
Greenville, NC 27858-4353 ...I

Coach: Bill Herrion, Merrimack 1981
2002-03 RESULTS (12-15)
65 Middle Tenn. ...63
65 Mississippi ■ ...58
66 William & Mary ■ ...51
89 Radford ...42
75 Old Dominion ...67
76 Virginia Tech ■ ...60
90 Mount Olive ■ ...62
56 George Mason ■ ...66
86 Campbell † ...61
71 Coastal Caro. ...90
73 Marquette ■ ...70
62 Charlotte ...83
70 Louisville ■ ...87
42 DePaul ...55
53 Cincinnati ■ ...59
68 South Fla. ■ ...62
48 Marquette ...80
56 Tulane ...67
49 Memphis ...73
60 Southern Miss. ■ ...57
42 St. Louis ...56
63 DePaul ■ ...77

66	Charlotte ■	71
52	Cincinnati	53
76	Louisville	82
48	St. Louis ■	58

Nickname: Pirates
Colors: Purple & Gold
Arena: Williams Arena at Minges
 Capacity: 8,000; Year Built: 1967
AD: Mike Hamrick
SID: Jody Jones

EAST CENTRAL
Ada, OK 74820 II

Coach: Wayne Cobb, Southeastern
 Okla. 1965, and Terry Shannon,
 Southeastern Okla. 1989
2002-03 RESULTS (11-17)

64	Southern Ark. †	76
70	Central Ark.	75
54	Sterling (Kan.) †	65
69	Western N.M. †	57
65	Tex. A&M-Commerce ■	79
77	Tex. A&M-Kingsville ■	75
82	Central Baptist ■	51
81	Hillsdale Free Will †	49
79	Mid-America Naz. †	77
52	Angelo St.	78
55	Abilene Christian	63
64	West Tex. A&M ■	79
57	Eastern N.M. ■	60
77	Central Baptist	62
73	Midwestern St.	71
65	Southeastern Okla.	61
63	Tarleton St. ■	65
92	Central Okla. ■	101
42	Northeastern St.	77
60	Cameron	76
89	Southwestern Okla. ■	68
45	Southeastern Okla. ■	60
53	Tarleton St.	92
86	Central Okla.	100
64	Northeastern St. ■	70
76	Cameron ■	65
75	Southwestern Okla.	71
79	Eastern N.M.	112

Nickname: Tigers
Colors: Orange & Black
Arena: Kerr Activities Center
 Capacity: 2,771; Year Built: 1973
AD: Tim Green
SID: Zac Underwood

EAST STROUDSBURG
East Stroudsburg, PA 18301 II

Coach: Jeff Wilson, East Stroudsburg,
 1986
2002-03 RESULTS (8-18)

75	Malone †	71
69	Bridgewater St. †	83
87	Felician ■	56
95	Shippensburg ■	98
55	Indiana (Pa.) ■	72
48	Clarion	73
54	Edinboro	55
53	Bloomfield ■	71
81	Pitt.-Johnstown ■	72
56	Lock Haven	65
84	Calif. (Pa.) ■	92
79	Slippery Rock ■	69
56	West Chester	81
57	Kutztown ■	71
62	Bloomsburg ■	75
55	Millersville	81
51	Cheyney	74
84	Goldey-Beacom ■	55
53	Mansfield ■	65
100	Nyack ■	67
67	West Chester ■	83

92	Bloomsburg	76
75	Kutztown	77
48	Millersville ■	71
73	Mansfield ■	81
83	Cheyney ■	82

Nickname: Warriors
Colors: Red & Black
Arena: Koehler Fieldhouse
 Capacity: 2,650; Year Built: 1967
AD: Joy M. Richman
SID: Peter Nevins

EAST TENN. ST.
Johnson City, TN 37614 I

Coach: Ed DeChellis, Penn St. 1982
2002-03 RESULTS (20-11)

104	Guilford ■	37
66	South Carolina	71
57	UNC Wilmington	78
75	Vanderbilt	86
87	UNC Asheville ■	69
106	Virginia-Wise ■	70
76	Virginia	84
93	Coastal Caro. ■	82
71	Belmont †	61
56	South Fla.	68
108	Juniata ■	57
96	UNC Greensboro ■	94
94	Appalachian St.	108
87	Citadel ■	81
65	Col. of Charleston ■	61
67	VMI	62
81	Wofford	61
71	Davidson ■	80
94	Chattanooga	99
93	VMI ■	76
83	Ga. Southern	87
89	Western Caro. ■	71
87	Davidson	72
75	UNC Greensboro	73
89	Western Caro.	86
71	Furman ■	84
88	Appalachian St. ■	78
80	Wofford †	75
64	Col. of Charleston †	55
97	Chattanooga †	90
73	Wake Forest †	76

Nickname: Buccaneers
Colors: Navy Blue & Old Gold
Arena: Memorial Center
 Capacity: 13,000; Year Built: 1977
AD: Dave Mullins
SID: Luke LeNoble

EAST TEX. BAPTIST
Marshall, TX 75670-1498 III

Coach: Bert West, East Tex. Baptist 1973
2002-03 RESULTS (17-9)

105	Mt. St. Mary (N.Y.) †	78
67	Angelo St.	71
120	Wiley	64
68	Mary Hardin-Baylor ■	73
103	Concordia-Austin ■	82
80	Wiley ■	68
106	Schreiner	91
81	Texas Lutheran	97
80	Hardin-Simmons ■	64
64	McMurry ■	70
87	Sul Ross St.	76
93	Howard Payne	100
77	Ozarks (Ark.) ■	80
82	Austin ■	78
106	Louisiana Col.	101
82	Mississippi Col.	76
78	LeTourneau	85
87	Houston Baptist	104
82	Texas-Dallas	79
78	Texas-Dallas	76

86	Ozarks (Ark.)	71
82	Austin	75
103	LeTourneau ■	83
101	Louisiana Col. ■	80
77	Mississippi Col. ■	72
91	McMurry ■	98

Nickname: Tigers
Colors: Blue & Gold
Arena: Ornelas Gymnasium
 Capacity: 1,700; Year Built: 1995
AD: Kent Reeves
SID: David Weaver

EASTERN
St. Davids, PA 19087-3696 III

Coach: Matt Nadelhoffer, Wheaton (Ill.)
 1998
2002-03 RESULTS (12-14)

57	Rose-Hulman †	59
58	Blackburn †	45
66	Ursinus ■	79
55	N.C. Wesleyan ■	52
55	Gwynedd-Mercy ■	68
62	Phila. Bible	75
66	Alvernia ■	65
73	Gordon	87
71	Messiah ■	64
77	Dickinson ■	73
69	Baptist Bible (Pa.)	66
70	Misericordia	76
68	Cabrini	72
68	Wesley ■	86
66	Neumann ■	77
66	Marywood	65
55	Alvernia	71
54	Arcadia ■	76
76	Gwynedd-Mercy	65
63	Neumann	71
63	Wesley	51
66	Misericordia ■	61
68	Arcadia	66
89	Marywood ■	69
64	Cabrini	66
56	Alvernia	83

Nickname: Eagles
Colors: Maroon & White
Arena: Eastern College Gym
 Capacity: 600
AD: Harry Gutelius
SID: Mark Birtwistle

EASTERN CONN. ST.
Willimantic, CT 06226 III

Coach: Bill Geitner, Hamilton 1987
2002-03 RESULTS (7-19)

78	Fitchburg St. ■	50
66	Salem St. ■	78
72	Trinity (Conn.)	68
92	Wesleyan (Conn.) ■	96
86	Rhode Island Col. ■	81
48	Worcester St.	64
60	Plymouth St.	75
47	Montclair St.	73
60	Susquehanna †	74
64	Endicott	74
43	Mass.-Boston	60
76	Mass.-Dartmouth ■	75
73	Springfield	91
72	Southern Me. ■	65
67	Keene St. ■	70
72	Westfield St.	87
63	Rhode Island Col.	60
63	Western Conn. St.	94
67	Plymouth St. ■	82
62	Mass.-Boston	64
58	Keene St.	87
69	Albertus Magnus ■	71
61	Mass.-Dartmouth	83

78	Western Conn. St. ■	77
74	Southern Me.	106
61	Keene St.	62

Nickname: Warriors
Colors: Blue & White
Arena: Geissler Gymnasium
 Capacity: 3,000; Year Built: 1974
AD: Joyce Wong
SID: Bob Molta

EASTERN ILL.
Charleston, IL 61920-3099 I

Coach: Rick Samuels, Chadron St. 1971
2002-03 RESULTS (14-15)

73	Boise St.	59
65	Florida	99
78	Ill.-Chicago	91
74	Marquette	97
94	Evansville ■	89
76	Western Ill. ■	63
57	Indiana St.	63
68	Illinois	80
65	Hawaii	81
70	Cal Poly †	73
90	Northern Ill. ■	75
85	Southeast Mo. St.	75
71	Morehead St.	75
85	Eastern Ky.	94
74	Murray St. ■	80
68	Tenn.-Martin ■	60
80	Austin Peay	87
80	Aurora ■	72
61	Tennessee Tech ■	69
96	Tennessee St. ■	67
85	Southeast Mo. St. ■	73
95	Eastern Ky. ■	76
75	Morehead St. ■	69
77	Murray St.	96
85	Tenn.-Martin	84
80	Austin Peay ■	76
88	Tennessee St.	75
84	Tennessee Tech	97
63	Murray St.	74

Nickname: Panthers
Colors: Blue & Gray
Arena: Lantz Arena
 Capacity: 5,300; Year Built: 1966
AD: Richard A. Mc Duffie
SID: Dave Kidwell

EASTERN KY.
Richmond, KY 40475-3101 I

Coach: Travis Ford, Kentucky 1994
2002-03 RESULTS (11-17)

106	Ky. Christian ■	71
87	Mt. St. Joseph ■	68
69	IPFW	76
74	Morris Brown	61
78	Shepherd ■	55
109	Ohio Wesleyan ■	56
63	Louisville	104
61	Wright St. †	75
73	Winthrop ■	84
60	Xavier	84
109	Tennessee St.	83
77	Southeast Mo. St. ■	93
94	Eastern Ill. ■	85
76	Tennessee Tech	93
50	Morehead St. ■	54
75	Tenn.-Martin	85
80	Murray St.	92
68	Morris Brown ■	64
77	Austin Peay ■	86
76	Eastern Ill.	95
79	Southeast Mo. St.	75
89	Tennessee St. ■	72
87	Morehead St.	88
68	Tennessee Tech ■	76

73	Murray St. ■	71
70	Tenn.-Martin ■	78
64	Austin Peay	78
80	Austin Peay	83

Nickname: Colonels
Colors: Maroon & White
Arena: McBrayer Arena
  Capacity: 6,500; Year Built: 1963
AD: Jack Lengyel
SID: Karl Park

EAST. MENNONITE
Harrisonburg, VA 22802 III

Coach: Tom Baker, East. Mennonite 1981

2002-03 RESULTS (3-22)

74	Southern Va. ■	76
66	Phila. Bible ■	64
41	Shenandoah	80
52	Longwood	87
44	Va. Wesleyan	66
51	St. Vincent †	94
87	Southern Va. †	84
57	VMI	100
39	Randolph-Macon ■	73
66	Bridgewater (Va.) ■	74
69	Lynchburg	86
51	Hampden-Sydney ■	85
72	Wash. & Lee ■	75
72	Guilford	80
73	Emory & Henry	94
62	Bridgewater (Va.)	87
71	Roanoke ■	92
74	Lynchburg	88
33	Hampden-Sydney ■	88
51	Randolph-Macon	89
100	Emory & Henry ■	88
79	Guilford ■	92
55	Va. Wesleyan ■	80
73	Wash. & Lee ■	76
74	Roanoke	93

Nickname: Royals
Colors: Royal Blue & White
Arena: University Gym
  Capacity: 1,800; Year Built: 1999
AD: Larry Martin
SID: Seth McGuffin

EASTERN MICH.
Ypsilanti, MI 48197 I

Coach: Jim Boone, West Va. St. 1981

2002-03 RESULTS (14-14)

64	Vermont †	71
66	Colgate †	65
99	Robert Morris ■	85
115	Concordia (Mich.) ■	80
97	Rochester College ■	48
78	Gardner-Webb ■	63
57	Michigan	85
81	Navy	89
85	Kent St.	88
94	Wis.-Green Bay ■	87
54	Western Mich.	87
73	Bowling Green ■	67
79	Northern Ill.	88
90	Ball St.	91
84	Central Mich. ■	68
58	Miami (Ohio) ■	73
80	Akron	96
90	Marshall ■	81
76	Toledo ■	72
66	Buffalo	90
68	Northern Ill. ■	70
76	Ohio	73
76	Toledo	73
80	Western Mich. ■	72
89	Central Mich.	106
88	Buffalo ■	78

72	Bowling Green	73
75	Marshall	83

Nickname: Eagles
Colors: Green & White
Arena: Convocation Center
  Capacity: 8,824; Year Built: 1998
AD: David L. Diles
SID: Jim Streeter

EASTERN NAZARENE
Quincy, MA 02170-2999 III

Coach: Corey Zink, Olivet Nazarene 1996

2002-03 RESULTS (9-17)

64	Gordon ■	65
52	Newbury ■	65
68	Rhode Island Col.	80
70	Mount Ida	87
64	Becker	60
56	Emerson	66
60	Worcester St. ■	69
51	Colby-Sawyer ■	63
48	Anna Maria	60
77	New England Col.	59
94	Curry ■	89
64	Anna Maria	67
65	Newbury	56
51	Roger Williams ■	49
65	Curry	93
70	Wentworth Inst. ■	58
70	Roger Williams	41
54	Salve Regina ■	68
66	Gordon	73
83	Nichols ■	82
56	Salve Regina	67
87	New England ■	66
61	Endicott	86
65	Nichols	66
58	MIT ■	69
86	Endicott	90

Nickname: Crusaders
Colors: Red & White
Arena: Lahue Center
  Capacity: 1,600; Year Built: 1973
AD: Nancy B. Detwiler
SID: Carolyn Morse

EASTERN N.M.
Portales, NM 88130 II

Coach: Shawn Scanlan, Kansas 1978

2002-03 RESULTS (20-8)

97	N.M. Highlands ■	68
70	Okla. Panhandle ■	75
83	Ouachita Baptist †	77
65	West Tex. A&M	82
65	Tarleton St.	67
87	N.M. Highlands †	81
68	Okla. Panhandle	76
83	Lubbock Chrst. ■	60
65	Central Okla.	71
75	Northeastern St. ■	82
57	Southeastern Okla.	55
60	East Central	57
72	Cameron ■	62
72	Southwestern Okla.	59
97	Abilene Christian	82
93	Angelo St.	90
87	Tex. A&M-Commerce ■	81
78	Tex. A&M-Kingsville ■	70
76	Midwestern St.	69
63	West Tex. A&M	69
88	Midwestern St. ■	74
85	West Tex. A&M	76
93	Angelo St. ■	88
87	Abilene Christian ■	74
99	Tex. A&M-Kingsville	95
74	Tex. A&M-Commerce	71
112	East Central ■	79

58	Tarleton St. ■	64

Nickname: Greyhounds
Colors: Green & Silver
Arena: Greyhound Arena
  Capacity: 4,800; Year Built: 1967
AD: Michael Maguire
SID: Robert McKinney

EASTERN ORE.
La Grande, OR 97850-2899 III

Coach: Art Furman, Minn. St. Mankato 1978

2002-03 RESULTS (9-17)

80	Western Ore.	88
81	Great Falls †	67
73	Carroll (Mont.)	69
83	Walla Walla ■	63
69	Western Ore.	88
65	Concordia (Ore.)	84
80	Western Baptist	88
68	Idaho St.	86
84	Northwest (Wash.) ■	82
82	Evergreen St. ■	86
89	Warner Pacific	101
79	Cascade	94
86	Oregon Tech ■	94
44	Southern Ore.	63
85	Western Baptist ■	77
91	Concordia (Ore.) ■	96
80	Albertson	104
94	Evergreen St.	88
68	Northwest (Wash.)	71
70	Cascade ■	80
81	Warner Pacific ■	76
93	Walla Walla	91
86	Southern Ore.	97
60	Oregon Tech	89
75	Albertson ■	72
41	Cascade	71

Nickname: Mountaineers
Colors: Navy Blue & Vegas Gold
Arena: Quinn Coliseum
  Capacity: 2,500
AD: Rob Cashell
SID: Sam Ghrist

EASTERN WASH.
Cheney, WA 99004 I

Coach: Ray Giacoletti, Minot St. 1984

2002-03 RESULTS (18-13)

55	Wisconsin	81
75	Winthrop †	61
75	San Diego St.	70
88	St. Mary's (Cal.) ■	80
48	Denver	69
89	Concordia (Ore.) ■	73
67	Idaho	62
62	Washington	58
65	Boise St.	59
64	Gonzaga †	67
56	Delaware †	66
69	Austin Peay †	77
60	Nebraska	63
89	Portland ■	74
72	Montana	62
65	Montana St.	51
76	Northern Ariz. ■	53
75	Sacramento St. ■	41
75	Portland St. ■	51
86	Idaho St.	88
61	Weber St.	74
78	Montana St. ■	74
87	Montana	72
71	Sacramento St.	77
78	Northern Ariz.	75
72	Portland St.	58
64	Weber St.	67
63	Idaho St. ■	65

76	Idaho St. †	67
57	Weber St.	60
71	Wyoming	78

Nickname: Eagles
Colors: Red & White
Arena: Reese Court
  Capacity: 5,000; Year Built: 1975
AD: Scott Barnes
SID: Dave Cook

ECKERD
St. Petersburg, FL 33711 II

Coach: Tom Ryan, Eckerd 1987

2002-03 RESULTS (25-7)

108	P.R.-Mayaguez ■	82
94	P.R.-Cayey	50
93	Winona St. ■	74
82	P.R.-Bayamon ■	73
82	Armstrong Atlantic ■	61
89	Winston-Salem ■	76
84	Tenn. Wesleyan †	58
80	Fla. Memorial ■	66
59	Nova Southeastern	72
67	Armstrong Atlantic	56
72	UNC Pembroke †	46
71	Mass.-Dartmouth ■	51
75	Tampa ■	39
65	Fla. Southern	75
79	Barry	76
80	Florida Tech ■	65
47	Rollins	82
88	St. Leo ■	59
70	Lynn	72
77	Fla. Southern	89
65	Barry ■	53
74	Florida Tech	55
84	Rollins ■	79
59	St. Leo	56
67	Lynn ■	62
57	Tampa	44
68	Fla. Southern	77
86	Tampa †	48
83	Morehouse †	66
74	Rollins	70
85	Henderson St. †	75
78	Queens (N.C.) †	99

Nickname: Tritons
Colors: Red, White & Black
Arena: McArthur Center
  Capacity: 1,300; Year Built: 1970
AD: George Meese
SID: Katherine Turnbow

EDGEWOOD
Madison, WI 53711-1998 III

Coach: Steven Larson, Wis.-Oshkosh 1974

2002-03 RESULTS (14-11)

80	Newport News ■	63
74	Wis.-Superior ■	66
54	Wis.-Oshkosh	70
51	Wis.-Stevens Point †	78
95	Wis. Lutheran	77
52	Lakeland	63
80	Concordia (Ill.) †	63
68	Dominican (Ill.)	56
59	Baldwin-Wallace †	83
77	Bridgewater St. †	62
66	Simpson †	80
76	Robert Morris (Ill.) ■	56
60	SCAD ■	69
69	Concordia (Wis.)	70
73	Marian (Wis.) ■	61
67	Maranatha Baptist	57
74	Milwaukee Engr.	60
48	Lakeland ■	58
92	Wis. Lutheran	66
65	Marian (Wis.)	60

55	Wis.-Platteville ■	69
70	Maranatha Baptist ■	59
50	Milwaukee Engr.	59
93	Concordia (Wis.) ■	55
79	Maranatha Baptist ■	90

Nickname: Eagles
Colors: Black, Red & White
Arena: Todd Wehr Edgedome
  Capacity: 1,000; Year Built: 1961
AD: G. Steven Larson
SID: Clare Hunter

EDINBORO
Edinboro, PA 16444-0001 II

Coach: Greg Walcavich, Rutgers 1973
2002-03 RESULTS (17-11)

62	Dist. Columbia †	67
65	West Va. Wesleyan †	55
60	Gannon ■	74
60	Mercyhurst ■	68
79	Millersville ■	70
60	West Chester ■	58
60	Mercyhurst ■	69
76	Bloomsburg ■	62
55	East Stroudsburg ■	54
75	Bowie St. †	90
89	West Liberty St. †	67
85	Mansfield ■	80
74	Lake Erie ■	67
72	Kutztown	81
60	Cheyney	57
90	Slippery Rock ■	67
74	Lock Haven ■	72
73	Indiana (Pa.) ■	71
70	Shippensburg ■	58
44	Calif. (Pa.) ■	58
49	Clarion	74
69	Lock Haven	66
66	Slippery Rock ■	60
71	Shippensburg	60
59	Indiana (Pa.)	88
57	Clarion ■	43
59	Calif. (Pa.) ■	73
63	Clarion ■	76

Nickname: Fighting Scots
Colors: Red & White
Arena: McComb Fieldhouse
  Capacity: 4,000; Year Built: 1970
AD: Bruce R. Baumgartner
SID: Bob Shreve

ELIZABETH CITY ST.
Elizabeth City, NC 27909 II

Coach: Shawn Walker, Elizabeth City St. 1994
2002-03 RESULTS (9-19)

63	Catawba ■	74
77	Allen ■	61
69	Mountain St. Univ. ■	81
69	Benedict	77
69	Concord †	73
79	Catawba	76
80	Wingate ■	72
71	Winston-Salem ■	77
77	Dist. Columbia ■	90
73	Johnson Smith	86
71	Mountain St. Univ.	107
46	Shaw	61
68	Virginia St. ■	40
81	St. Augustine's ■	69
75	Fayetteville St.	60
76	Benedict ■	62
61	Virginia Union ■	75
52	St. Paul's ■	53
81	Bowie St.	88
56	Dist. Columbia	69
51	Shaw ■	62
57	Livingstone ■	56

78	St. Paul's	86
97	N.C. Central	92
81	Virginia St.	87
69	Bowie St. ■	74
73	Virginia Union	86
79	Johnson Smith	88

Nickname: Vikings
Colors: Royal Blue & White
Arena: R.L. Vaughan Center
  Capacity: 5,000; Year Built: 1976
AD: Edward Mc Lean
SID: April Emory

ELIZABETHTOWN
Elizabethtown, PA 17022-2298 III

Coach: Robert Schlosser, East Stroudsburg 1977
2002-03 RESULTS (18-9)

112	King's (Pa.) ■	97
103	Clark (Mass.) ■	96
78	Frank. & Marsh. ■	81
93	Dickinson ■	66
55	Widener ■	72
105	Susquehanna ■	70
72	Scranton	75
77	Grove City †	52
66	DeSales	78
101	Haverford ■	78
88	Gettysburg ■	64
76	Shenandoah	86
70	Moravian	76
73	Juniata ■	58
69	Lebanon Valley	57
105	Albright	67
78	Messiah ■	66
90	Susquehanna ■	78
80	Widener ■	67
72	Juniata	81
97	Moravian ■	64
77	Lebanon Valley ■	79
83	Messiah	54
95	Albright ■	59
71	Moravian ■	62
92	Susquehanna	86
69	Montclair St.	74

Nickname: Blue Jays
Colors: Blue & Grey
Arena: Thompson Gymnasium
  Capacity: 2,200; Year Built: 1969
AD: Nancy J. Latimore
SID: Ian Showalter

ELMHURST
Elmhurst, IL 60126-3296...........III

Coach: Mark Scherer, Eureka 1983
2002-03 RESULTS (11-14)

52	Trinity (Tex.) †	58
78	Emory & Henry †	89
75	Maryville (Mo.) ■	89
53	St. Norbert	55
72	Fontbonne ■	68
62	Benedictine (Ill.) ■	63
70	Olivet Nazarene	62
83	Alma ■	67
52	Wooster ■	70
85	Manchester ■	62
84	Dominican (Ill.)	69
73	North Park	70
73	Augustana (Ill.)	76
72	North Central ■	73
73	Wheaton (Ill.) ■	78
48	Carthage	71
74	Millikin	63
74	Ill. Wesleyan ■	72
90	North Central	81
58	Augustana (Ill.) ■	72
81	Millikin ■	69
53	Carthage ■	76

61	Wheaton (Ill.)	72
83	North Park ■	69
65	Ill. Wesleyan	73

Nickname: Bluejays
Colors: Blue & White
Arena: R.A. Faganel Hall
  Capacity: 1,800; Year Built: 1983
AD: Christopher Ragsdale
SID: Hope Wagner

ELMIRA
Elmira, NY 14901 III

Coach: Pat Donnelly, Mansfield 1992
2002-03 RESULTS (12-13)

80	Buffalo St.	75
58	Marietta †	56
56	Cortland St. ■	54
68	Marietta †	53
66	Carnegie Mellon	76
57	Pitt.-Bradford	77
97	Lycoming ■	85
67	Bethany (W.Va.) †	68
76	Staten Island	67
66	Utica ■	58
74	Hartwick ■	65
48	Ithaca	73
66	Houghton	62
73	Lycoming	69
61	Nazareth ■	88
96	Rochester Inst. ■	79
82	St. John Fisher	84
72	Alfred	77
75	Hartwick	78
65	Utica	74
71	Alfred ■	62
65	St. John Fisher ■	78
58	Ithaca ■	88
67	Rochester Inst.	80
58	Nazareth	64

Nickname: Soaring Eagles
Colors: Purple & Gold
Arena: Speidel Gymnasium
  Capacity: 1,000; Year Built: 1995
AD: Patricia A. Thompson
SID: Pat Donnelly

ELMS
Chicopee, MA 01013-2839 III

Coach: Ed Silva, Eastern Conn. St.
2002-03 RESULTS (14-12)

70	Salem St. †	87
69	Fitchburg St. †	64
62	Westfield St. ■	56
82	Daniel Webster ■	71
59	Nichols	66
51	St. Joseph's (Me.)	68
63	Rensselaer †	79
66	Keuka ■	70
70	Brooklyn	63
83	Trinity (Conn.)	91
85	Mount Ida ■	57
81	Johnson St. ■	68
62	Castleton St. ■	55
75	Becker ■	64
75	Maine Maritime ■	63
53	Maine Maritime	61
54	Lasell	70
75	Connecticut Col. ■	61
67	Castleton St.	84
77	Johnson St.	71
70	Becker	63
58	Newbury ■	54
74	Lasell ■	80
69	Mount Ida	73
85	Mount Ida ■	77
67	Maine Maritime †	71

Nickname: Blazers
Colors: Green & Gold

Arena: Picknelly Arena
  Capacity: 481; Year Built: 1994
AD: Louise McCleary
SID: Kathleen Bantley

ELON
Elon, NC 27244-2010 I

Coach: Mark Simons, Aquinas 1972
2002-03 RESULTS (12-15)

67	Mercer ■	79
69	St. Mary's (Md.) ■	56
68	Md.-East. Shore	64
77	Bluefield Col. ■	68
58	UNC Greensboro	57
51	Northwestern	66
57	Marquette	89
51	American	76
59	Liberty	77
65	Winthrop	82
56	Wake Forest	98
51	Charleston So. ■	66
63	Coastal Caro. ■	60
60	Winthrop ■	67
52	Birmingham-So. ■	64
47	Georgia Tech	66
65	High Point ■	61
57	Radford	53
87	UNC Asheville	93
52	Liberty ■	54
57	Charleston So.	50
67	Birmingham-So.	76
75	UNC Asheville ■	72
84	Radford ■	74
75	Coastal Caro.	53
70	High Point	46
66	UNC Asheville ■	68

Nickname: Phoenix
Colors: Maroon & Gold
Arena: Koury Center/Alumni Gym
  Capacity: 1,768; Year Built: 1949
AD: Alan J. White
SID: Matt Eviston

EMERSON
Boston, MA 02116 III

Coach: Hank Smith, Franklin Pierce
2002-03 RESULTS (8-17)

76	Mass.-Boston ■	75
74	Daniel Webster	50
66	Eastern Nazarene ■	56
57	Babson	85
68	Wheaton (Mass.)	82
82	Wentworth Inst. ■	64
62	Rivier	73
70	Norwich ■	83
86	Johnson & Wales ■	103
95	Rivier ■	80
80	Western New Eng.	74
56	MIT	95
96	Southern Vt. ■	101
76	Albertus Magnus	87
65	Suffolk	100
88	Daniel Webster ■	91
65	Emmanuel (Mass.)	77
79	Suffolk ■	86
64	Norwich	72
88	Albertus Magnus ■	67
77	Johnson & Wales	81
63	Southern Vt.	66
77	Emmanuel (Mass.) ■	80
79	Western New Eng. ■	95
75	Brandeis ■	71

Nickname: Lions
Colors: Purple & Black
Arena: Wang YMCA
  Capacity: 1,200
AD: Rudy Keeling
SID: Michael Burns

EMMANUEL (MASS.)
Boston, MA 02115 III

Coach: Lance Tucker, Boston U. 1975

2002-03 RESULTS (8-17)

65	Moravian ■	76
78	Yeshiva ■	75
58	Newbury	76
81	Rivier ■	68
58	Lehman	88
101	Johnson & Wales	103
50	Bridgewater St.	79
55	Western New Eng.	72
56	Norwich	76
57	Southern Vt. ■	71
84	Daniel Webster ■	70
77	Albertus Magnus ■	80
79	Norwich ■	63
60	Suffolk	57
85	Mount Ida	88
68	Rivier	75
77	Emerson ■	65
63	Albertus Magnus	95
65	Western New Eng. ■	81
62	Johnson & Wales ■	75
73	Southern Vt.	94
61	Suffolk ■	81
80	Emerson	77
84	Daniel Webster	71
71	Albertus Magnus	74

Nickname: Saints
Colors: Navy Blue & Gold
Arena: Marian Hall Gymnasium
  Capacity: 450; Year Built: 1956
AD: Andy Yosinoff
SID: Alexis Mastronardi

EMORY
Atlanta, GA 30322 III

Coach: Brett Zuver, Lake Superior St. 1991

2002-03 RESULTS (14-11)

86	LaGrange ■	59
82	Maryville (Tenn.) ■	81
98	Sewanee ■	82
90	Oglethorpe ■	72
86	SCAD ■	69
82	LaGrange	74
93	Sewanee	82
80	Piedmont	88
74	Maryville (Tenn.)	91
83	Case Reserve	90
71	Chicago	75
84	Washington (Mo.) ■	96
81	New York U. ■	66
93	Brandeis	79
76	Carnegie Mellon	89
74	Rochester	92
64	Oglethorpe	78
67	Rochester ■	68
101	Carnegie Mellon ■	83
63	Washington (Mo.)	89
56	Chicago	60
81	Brandeis ■	67
83	New York U. ■	71
83	Stillman ■	78
81	Case Reserve ■	64

Nickname: Eagles
Colors: Blue & Gold
Arena: Woodruff PE Center
  Capacity: 2,000; Year Built: 1983
AD: Charles J. Gordon
SID: John Arenberg

EMORY & HENRY
Emory, VA 24327-0947 III

Coach: Bob Johnson, Dickinson 1968

2002-03 RESULTS (13-13)

84	Johns Hopkins	94
89	Elmhurst †	78
123	Warren Wilson	58
97	Ferrum ■	90
64	Mary Washington ■	83
76	Roanoke	90
90	Lynchburg	74
86	Guilford ■	84
67	Hampden-Sydney ■	102
109	Averett ■	75
69	Va. Wesleyan	80
57	Randolph-Macon	59
89	Bridgewater (Va.) ■	91
94	East. Mennonite ■	73
75	Wash. & Lee ■	73
76	Hampden-Sydney	116
99	Warren Wilson ■	48
76	Randolph-Macon ■	88
73	Va. Wesleyan ■	81
80	Wash. & Lee ■	67
88	East. Mennonite	100
97	Bridgewater (Va.)	96
83	Roanoke ■	63
79	Lynchburg ■	78
76	Guilford	81
73	Va. Wesleyan †	81

Nickname: Wasps
Colors: Blue & Gold
Arena: King Health & Physical Ed
  Capacity: 1,300; Year Built: 1970
AD: Fred Selfe
SID: Nathan Graybeal

EMPORIA ST.
Emporia, KS 66801-5087 II

Coach: David Moe, Texas Lutheran 1986

2002-03 RESULTS (16-12)

87	Southwestern (Kan.) ■	83
98	Ottawa	61
76	Central Methodist †	88
81	Mesa St.	90
68	Mesa St. ■	72
95	St. Mary's (Tex.) ■	86
98	Newman	95
61	Kansas	113
93	Fort Hays St. ■	96
61	Pittsburg St. ■	59
75	Mo.-Rolla ■	57
61	Mo. Western St.	80
94	Truman ■	61
71	Southwest Baptist	73
90	Mo. Southern St.	85
84	Washburn ■	63
69	Central Mo. St.	64
109	Northwest Mo. St. ■	89
69	Mo.-Rolla	76
87	Mo. Western St. ■	96
93	Truman	70
80	Southwest Baptist ■	72
104	Mo. Southern St. ■	90
77	Washburn	85
97	Central Mo. St. ■	80
82	Northwest Mo. St.	92
80	Pittsburg St.	75
98	Mo. Southern St. †	99

Nickname: Hornets
Colors: Old Gold & Black
Arena: White Auditorium
  Capacity: 5,000; Year Built: 1940
AD: Kent Weiser
SID: Don Weast

ENDICOTT
Beverly, MA 01915 III

Coach: Michael Plansky, Fairfield 1991

2002-03 RESULTS (19-10)

55	Williams	98
61	Lasell †	77
68	Keene St. ■	82
81	Curry	80
67	Wheaton (Mass.) ■	68
69	WPI	61
63	Bates	95
74	Eastern Conn. St. ■	64
70	Roger Williams	64
83	Colby-Sawyer ■	69
51	Gordon	68
49	Framingham St. ■	58
86	Anna Maria	76
94	Nichols ■	67
82	Wentworth Inst.	50
71	Salve Regina ■	59
107	New England	82
81	New England Col. ■	60
68	Colby-Sawyer	80
79	Gordon ■	67
91	New England Col.	59
86	Eastern Nazarene ■	61
76	Wentworth Inst. ■	62
102	New England	77
90	Eastern Nazarene ■	86
81	Anna Maria ■	70
65	Colby-Sawyer ■	73
89	Albertus Magnus	59
68	Babson	78

Nickname: Gulls
Colors: Blue, Kelly Green & White
Arena: Post Center Arena
  Capacity: 1,400; Year Built: 1999
AD: Larry R. Hiser
SID: To be named

ERSKINE
Due West, SC 29639 II

Coach: Mark Peeler, Sewanee 1984

2002-03 RESULTS (14-16)

65	Shorter †	55
53	Berry	55
57	Tusculum	70
62	Newberry ■	61
44	Presbyterian	55
81	Lees-McRae ■	66
62	Coker	47
69	Longwood ■	75
67	Mount Olive	77
45	Barton	59
59	Belmont Abbey	51
60	Queens (N.C.) ■	70
50	St. Andrews	54
56	Limestone	78
69	North Greenville	53
65	Anderson (S.C.) ■	63
78	Pfeiffer ■	88
73	Lees-McRae	69
62	Coker	58
71	Mount Olive ■	69
55	Allen ■	48
53	Barton ■	66
49	Belmont Abbey ■	51
52	Queens (N.C.)	58
58	Longwood	61
80	St. Andrews ■	55
67	Limestone ■	70
48	Anderson (S.C.) ■	37
71	Queens (N.C.)	66
59	Pfeiffer	80

Nickname: The Flying Fleet
Colors: Maroon & Gold
Arena: Galloway PE Center

  Capacity: 2,000; Year Built: 1980
AD: Joseph H. Sherer
SID: Thomas Holland

EUREKA
Eureka, IL 61530-1500..............III

Coach: Mike DeGeorge, Monmouth (Ill.) 1992

2002-03 RESULTS (8-17)

47	Denison †	62
117	Messenger †	57
87	Lake Forest ■	82
73	Concordia (Wis.) ■	75
104	Greenville ■	94
60	Blackburn	63
73	Millikin	76
57	Rockford	76
47	Augustana (Ill.)	96
65	Milwaukee Engr.	78
81	Marian (Wis.)	84
74	Concordia (Ill.) ■	71
48	Aurora	95
70	Benedictine (Ill.)	87
69	Clarke	75
86	Robert Morris (Ill.) ■	83
60	Dominican (Ill.) ■	71
72	Rockford ■	91
61	Concordia (Ill.)	59
70	Aurora	82
71	Benedictine (Ill.) ■	76
88	Clarke ■	73
81	Lincoln Chrst.	71
74	Dominican (Ill.)	78
67	Clarke	86

Nickname: Red Devils
Colors: Maroon & Gold
Arena: Reagan Gym
  Capacity: 2,200; Year Built: 1970
AD: Joe Barth
SID: Shelly Lindsey

EVANSVILLE
Evansville, IN 47722 I

Coach: Steve Merfeld, Wis.-La Crosse 1984

2002-03 RESULTS (12-16)

73	Ill.-Chicago ■	68
59	Dayton	64
89	Eastern Ill.	94
81	Western Ky. ■	76
64	Butler ■	77
95	Austin Peay ■	85
58	Murray St. ■	76
69	Mississippi	87
66	Miami (Ohio)	58
60	Indiana St.	86
84	Southern Ill.	90
93	Bradley ■	79
56	Creighton	93
51	Southwest Mo. St.	70
74	Creighton ■	66
85	Illinois St. ■	74
75	Wichita St. ■	74
61	Northern Iowa	63
58	Southwest Mo. St. ■	73
62	Drake	51
84	Wichita St.	89
83	Northern Iowa ■	63
61	Illinois St.	65
73	Drake ■	81
64	Southern Ill.	76
54	Bradley	51
77	Indiana St. ■	69
51	Southwest Mo. St. †	65

Nickname: Purple Aces
Colors: Purple, White & Orange
Arena: Roberts Stadium

Capacity: 12,144; Year Built: 1956
AD: Bill McGillis
SID: Bob Boxell

FAIRFIELD
Fairfield, CT 06430-5195 I

Coach: Tim O'Toole, Fairfield 1986
2002-03 RESULTS (19-12)
67	Harvard ■	69
68	St. John's (N.Y.) ■	81
69	UNC Wilmington ■	60
83	Iona ■	78
45	DePaul	73
86	Marist	77
68	American ■	57
91	Fordham	83
64	Charleston So.	66
58	Duke	86
59	Yale ■	57
72	Loyola (Md.) ■	60
66	Rider	59
76	Canisius	71
82	Iona	78
80	Siena	71
86	Manhattan ■	93
79	St. Peter's ■	57
71	Siena	74
72	Canisius ■	68
74	Niagara ■	85
70	Manhattan	68
67	Marist ■	56
56	Rider ■	58
79	Niagara	83
73	St. Peter's	71
69	Loyola (Md.)	51
68	St. Peter's †	60
67	Siena †	63
54	Manhattan †	69
78	Boston College ■	90

Nickname: Stags
Colors: Red & White
Arena: Arena at Harbor Yard
Capacity: 9,500; Year Built: 2001
AD: Eugene Doris
SID: Jack Jones

FAIRLEIGH DICKINSON
Teaneck, NJ 07666 I

Coach: Tom Green, Syracuse 1971
2002-03 RESULTS (15-14)
76	Army ■	54
91	Morgan St. ■	75
61	Loyola (Md.)	56
75	Delaware St.	83
78	St. Peter's ■	71
66	Minnesota	104
65	North Carolina St.	104
81	Hartford ■	80
72	Monmouth ■	75
63	Army	65
80	Long Island ■	73
76	St. Francis (N.Y.) ■	71
83	Wagner	79
62	Sacred Heart	74
57	Central Conn. St. ■	68
100	Quinnipiac ■	90
57	UMBC	63
81	Mt. St. Mary's	83
68	Wagner ■	62
82	Sacred Heart ■	73
83	Long Island	68
80	St. Francis (N.Y.)	85
56	Robert Morris	69
66	St. Francis (Pa.)	68
88	Robert Morris ■	80
75	St. Francis (Pa.) ■	73
59	Monmouth	68
63	Monmouth †	51
62	St. Francis (N.Y.) †	88

Nickname: Knights
Colors: Blue & Maroon
Arena: Rothman Center
Capacity: 5,000; Year Built: 1987
AD: David Langford
SID: Drew Brown

FDU-FLORHAM
Madison, NJ 07940 III

Coach: Roger Kindel, Seton Hall 1972
2002-03 RESULTS (11-14)
85	Medgar Evers †	60
77	Ramapo	95
60	Stevens Institute ■	46
59	DeSales	76
51	Wilkes ■	60
45	Bucknell	72
75	Staten Island	77
73	Hunter ■	64
66	NYCCT	64
43	Wm. Paterson ■	65
67	John Jay ■	49
63	Scranton	75
89	Purchase St.	69
62	Lycoming ■	65
63	Drew	67
56	King's (Pa.)	81
69	Delaware Valley ■	61
66	Wilkes	78
87	Centenary (N.J.)	84
84	DeSales ■	74
63	Lycoming	81
64	Scranton ■	79
64	Drew ■	58
78	Delaware Valley	66
48	King's (Pa.)	74

Nickname: Devils
Colors: Cardinal and Navy
Arena: Ferguson Recreation Center
Capacity: 3,000; Year Built: 1995
AD: William T. Klika
SID: Scott Giglio

FAIRMONT ST.
Fairmont, WV 26554 II

Coach: Butch Haswell, Fairmont St. 1973
2002-03 RESULTS (19-9)
109	Ohio St.-Newark ■	48
68	St. Paul's ■	60
83	Columbia Union ■	80
88	Davis & Elkins	64
80	Lock Haven ■	65
79	Shippensburg	63
55	Calif. (Pa.) †	69
95	Ohio Valley †	56
80	Wilberforce ■	60
77	Glenville St.	82
62	West Va. Wesleyan ■	58
79	Shepherd ■	72
80	Concord	80
86	Ohio Valley	41
114	Ohio-Eastern ■	65
70	Wheeling Jesuit ■	79
82	West Liberty St. ■	72
65	Salem Int'l	82
64	Alderson-Broaddus ■	81
91	Bluefield St.	65
74	Charleston (W.Va.) ■	83
81	West Virginia St. ■	66
86	West Va. Tech	85
85	Ohio Valley ■	63
74	Wheeling Jesuit	88
82	West Liberty St.	68
75	Salem Int'l ■	66
60	West Va. Tech ■	75

Nickname: Falcons
Colors: Maroon, White & Fairmont Gold
Arena: Joe Retton Arena
Capacity: 4,000; Year Built: 1978
AD: David W. Cooper
SID: Jim Brinkman

FARMINGDALE ST.
Farmingdale, NY 11735-1021 .III

Coach: Bill Musto, Lock Haven
2002-03 RESULTS (13-11)
49	Randolph-Macon †	72
85	Practical Bible †	69
58	Staten Island	65
63	Baruch	65
100	Medgar Evers ■	82
71	Mt. St. Mary (N.Y.)	78
80	Baptist Bible (Pa.) ■	71
93	Purchase St.	51
64	Maritime (N.Y.)	60
71	Rutgers-Camden ■	86
70	Baptist Bible (Pa.)	77
59	Oneonta St.	65
68	New Jersey City ■	82
63	Polytechnic (N.Y.)	59
68	Medgar Evers ■	65
73	Manhattanville	81
65	CCNY	54
77	Lancaster Bible ■	50
85	Old Westbury ■	71
69	NYCCT ■	52
68	Centenary (N.J.) ■	47
64	Lancaster Bible	82
64	Lincoln (Pa.)	50
70	Drew	75

Nickname: Rams
Colors: Green & White
AD: Michael Harrington
SID: To be named

FAYETTEVILLE ST.
Fayetteville, NC 28301-4298 II

Coach: Sam Hanger, Binghamton 1974
2002-03 RESULTS (11-17)
104	Wingate ■	108
91	St. Andrews	90
75	Methodist ■	71
78	Salem Int'l	99
74	Shaw ■	75
64	Salem Int'l	73
85	Wingate	77
65	Francis Marion	69
79	North Fla.	64
93	N.C. Central	94
58	Virginia Union	83
71	Bowie St.	81
75	Johnson Smith †	82
67	St. Augustine's	73
60	Elizabeth City St. ■	75
84	Livingstone	70
73	St. Paul's	62
65	Winston-Salem ■	64
55	Shaw	71
68	N.C. Central	69
75	St. Augustine's ■	83
65	Benedict	53
72	Winston-Salem	84
73	Johnson Smith	78
82	Virginia St. ■	66
87	Livingstone	83
61	St. Paul's †	52
75	N.C. Central †	85

Nickname: Broncos
Colors: Royal Blue & Lilly White
Arena: Capel Arena
Capacity: 4,000; Year Built: 1995
AD: William Carver
SID: Marion Crowe

FELICIAN
Lodi, NJ 07644 II

Coach: Matt O'Connor, Davidson 1991
2002-03 RESULTS (14-15)
63	Southern Conn. St. †	70
67	Glenville St. †	65
72	Bloomfield ■	67
53	Clarion	58
56	East Stroudsburg	87
84	Wilmington (Del.) ■	59
68	Nyack ■	58
72	St. Anselm ■	83
76	Goldey-Beacom	55
60	Dominican (N.Y.) ■	74
79	Merrimack	89
75	Phila. Sciences ■	68
60	Holy Family ■	72
83	Green Mountain	69
82	Teikyo Post	64
53	Caldwell	70
84	Bloomfield	70
70	N.J. Inst. of Tech.	75
67	Phila. Sciences	75
91	Goldey-Beacom ■	70
67	Nyack	70
73	N.J. Inst. of Tech. ■	81
63	Caldwell	60
86	Wilmington (Del.)	57
75	Dominican (N.Y.)	63
63	Teikyo Post ■	67
68	Holy Family	69
74	N.J. Inst. of Tech. †	68
70	Teikyo Post †	74

Nickname: Golden Falcons
Colors: Hunter Green & Gold
AD: Ben Di Nallo
SID: To be named

FERRIS ST.
Big Rapids, MI 49307-2295 II

Coach: Bill Sall, Calvin 1994
2002-03 RESULTS (11-15)
76	St. Joseph's (Ind.)	75
92	Calvin	71
72	Findlay ■	79
84	Aquinas	88
62	Gannon	73
70	Mercyhurst	62
109	Olivet	85
89	Lincoln (Mo.) †	70
71	Lewis	84
77	Hillsdale	94
65	Northern Ky. †	85
65	Hillsdale ■	64
71	Wayne St. (Mich.) ■	74
77	Ashland	80
73	Northwood ■	79
81	Grand Valley St.	57
67	Saginaw Valley	75
79	Lake Superior St.	85
82	Michigan Tech	98
74	Northern Mich. ■	63
85	Lake Superior St. ■	71
72	Northwood	82
64	Grand Valley St. ■	70
78	Saginaw Valley ■	65
77	Northern Mich.	66
53	Michigan Tech	81

Nickname: Bulldogs
Colors: Crimson & Gold
Arena: Jim Wink Arena
Capacity: 2,400; Year Built: 1999
AD: Tom Kirinovic
SID: Rob Bentley

FERRUM
Ferrum, VA 24088 III

Coach: Ed Wills, North Carolina 1994

2002-03 RESULTS (7-19)

58	Goucher †	76
92	Greensboro †	89
83	Lynchburg	80
90	Emory & Henry	97
64	Centre †	90
63	SCAD ■	78
74	Lynchburg ■	70
63	Richard Stockton †	70
79	Utica/Rome †	83
47	SCAD	76
83	Averett ■	78
70	Chris. Newport	79
49	Randolph-Macon	92
61	Shenandoah ■	59
45	Methodist	90
75	Greensboro	72
73	N.C. Wesleyan ■	88
58	Chowan ■	51
77	Averett	85
62	Chris. Newport ■	76
71	Shenandoah	91
58	Methodist ■	64
76	Greensboro ■	78
61	N.C. Wesleyan	72
57	Chowan	59
70	Methodist †	77

Nickname: Panthers
Colors: Black & Gold
Arena: Swartz Gymnasium
  Capacity: 1,200; Year Built: 1960
AD: T. Michael Kinder
SID: Gary Holden

FINDLAY
Findlay, OH 45840 II

Coach: Ron Niekamp, Miami (Ohio) 1972

2002-03 RESULTS (23-8)

62	Northern Ky.	70
94	Ohio Valley †	73
97	Tiffin ■	67
79	Ferris St.	72
78	Grand Valley St.	59
74	Huntington	70
84	North Ala. ■	78
78	Wilmington (Ohio) ■	52
72	Walsh ■	56
92	Point Park ■	60
80	Northwood	83
73	Saginaw Valley	70
78	Northern Mich. ■	63
87	Lake Superior St. ■	71
87	Ashland	82
61	Michigan Tech ■	78
80	Hillsdale	60
62	Wayne St. (Mich.)	70
76	Mercyhurst ■	67
76	Gannon ■	62
92	Ashland ■	78
80	Wayne St. (Mich.) ■	72
80	Hillsdale ■	65
86	Gannon	88
106	Mercyhurst	99
82	Grand Valley St. ■	84
75	Hillsdale ■	61
70	Gannon †	67
66	Michigan Tech	68
80	Northern Ky. †	76
66	Ky. Wesleyan †	83

Nickname: Oilers
Colors: Orange & Black
Arena: Croy Gym
  Capacity: 2,200; Year Built: 1969
AD: Steven Rackley
SID: Dave Leisering

FISK
Nashville, TN 37208-3051 III

Coach: Larry Glover, Fisk 1979

2002-03 RESULTS (6-8)

76	Stillman ■	70
69	Tennessee St.	65
80	St. Mary's (Md.) †	74
54	Chris. Newport	101
70	Hendrix	58
87	Lincoln (Pa.) †	56
62	Rowan	79
49	Belmont	79
59	Maryville (Tenn.)	86
73	SCAD	78
51	Lipscomb	82
55	Sewanee	66
72	Maryville (Tenn.) ■	79
68	Maryville (Tenn.) †	65

Nickname: Bulldogs
Colors: Blue & Gold
Arena: Johnson, Henderson Gym
  Capacity: 2,500; Year Built: 1950
AD: Larry Glover
SID: Kindell Stephens

FITCHBURG ST.
Fitchburg, MA 01420-2697 III

Coach: Jack Scott, Clark (Mass.) 1994

2002-03 RESULTS (8-17)

50	Eastern Conn. St.	78
64	Elms †	69
74	Mass.-Boston ■	82
73	Western New Eng.	92
74	Lasell ■	82
92	Fisher	98
83	Nichols	61
72	Anna Maria ■	73
68	Wheaton (Mass.)	82
72	Worcester St.	75
80	Salem St. ■	90
70	Mount Ida ■	61
69	Westfield St.	74
73	Framingham St. ■	58
92	Mass. Liberal Arts	59
69	Bridgewater St. ■	64
69	Worcester St. ■	80
97	Becker ■	84
65	Salem St.	90
72	Newbury	82
76	Westfield St. ■	87
77	Framingham St.	75
96	Mass. Liberal Arts ■	62
68	Bridgewater St.	75
78	Bridgewater St. ■	82

Nickname: Falcons
Colors: Green, Gold & White
Arena: Recreation Center
  Capacity: 1,000; Year Built: 2000
AD: Sue E. Lauder
SID: Rusty Eggen

FLORIDA
Gainesville, FL 32611 I

Coach: Billy Donovan, Providence 1987

2002-03 RESULTS (25-8)

76	Louisiana Tech ■	55
99	Eastern Ill. ■	65
88	Coastal Caro. ■	45
65	Stanford †	73
83	Kansas †	73
66	West Virginia †	68
58	Florida St.	57
68	South Fla. ■	52
69	Maryland	64
94	Miami (Fla.) †	93
74	Charleston So. ■	62
99	Bethune-Cookman ■	64
91	Florida A&M ■	58
74	Mississippi St.	66
66	Georgia ■	63
77	Tennessee ■	64
77	South Carolina	75
87	Vanderbilt ■	75
70	LSU	53
77	Arkansas ■	66
55	Kentucky	70
75	Alabama ■	56
74	Mississippi ■	55
59	Tennessee	66
77	New Orleans ■	48
77	Vanderbilt	74
96	South Carolina ■	63
73	Auburn	70
81	Georgia	82
67	Kentucky ■	69
61	LSU †	65
85	Sam Houston St. †	55
46	Michigan St. †	68

Nickname: Gators
Colors: Orange & Blue
Arena: Stephen C. O'Connell Center
  Capacity: 12,000; Year Built: 1980
AD: Jeremy Foley
SID: Steve McClain

FLORIDA A&M
Tallahassee, FL 32307 I

Coach: Mike Gillespie, DePaul 1974

2002-03 RESULTS (17-12)

70	Norfolk St.	65
64	Xavier	93
53	Cincinnati	80
68	Alabama St. ■	67
69	Bethune-Cookman ■	71
55	UCF ■	54
91	Alabama A&M ■	89
66	Oregon	107
58	Florida	91
55	Delaware St.	62
76	Morris Brown	65
92	Md.-East. Shore ■	89
75	Howard ■	64
76	Hampton	90
85	Morgan St. ■	65
69	Coppin St. ■	74
86	N.C. A&T ■	61
63	South Carolina St. ■	69
97	Delaware St. ■	77
88	Morris Brown ■	56
62	Md.-East. Shore	60
68	Howard	74
80	Hampton ■	83
72	Norfolk St. ■	62
73	Coppin St.	69
69	Morgan St.	56
72	Bethune-Cookman	66
55	Coppin St. †	53
66	South Carolina St. †	72

Nickname: Rattlers
Colors: Orange & Green
Arena: Gaither Athletic Center
  Capacity: 3,365; Year Built: 1963
SID: Alvin Hollins

FLA. ATLANTIC
Boca Raton, FL 33431-0991 I

Coach: Sidney Green, UNLV 1983

2002-03 RESULTS (7-21)

71	Cleveland St. †	66
56	Colorado St.	81
93	IPFW †	86
62	Drake	74
52	Iowa	79

FLORIDA INT'L
Miami, FL 33199 I

Coach: Donnie Marsh, Frank. & Marsh. 1979

2002-03 RESULTS (8-21)

60	Morris Brown ■	52
65	Iona	55
78	Fla. Gulf Coast ■	50
68	Princeton	65
63	George Washington ■	77
48	Wis.-Milwaukee †	61
54	Samford †	64
62	Massachusetts	67
57	DePaul	72
48	Washington	83
81	Radford ■	45
68	Duquesne ■	71
57	Canisius ■	54
91	North Texas	94
60	Denver ■	71
52	New Mexico St. ■	74
51	La.-Lafayette	64
43	Western Ky.	63
58	Middle Tenn.	60
65	Arkansas St. ■	67
45	Ark.-Little Rock ■	46
56	South Ala.	46
48	New Orleans	49
58	Western Ky. ■	71
70	Middle Tenn. ■	80
62	Ark.-Little Rock	67
65	Arkansas St.	85
62	New Orleans †	45
60	Western Ky.	71

Nickname: Golden Panthers
Colors: Blue & Gold
Arena: Golden Panther Arena
  Capacity: 5,000; Year Built: 1986
AD: Rick Mello
SID: Andrew LaPlant

FLA. SOUTHERN
Lakeland, FL 33801-5698 II

Coach: Tony Longa, UCF 1987

2002-03 RESULTS (26-5)

67	Concordia-St. Paul †	60
87	P.R.-Bayamon †	79
83	P.R.-Mayaguez ■	63

(Florida Int'l column, continued at top)

86	Nova Southeastern ■	60
74	Miami (Fla.) ■	73
72	Va. Commonwealth	90
57	James Madison	71
79	Liberty	84
75	San Diego St.	91
70	UC Irvine	87
69	UCF	80
72	Troy St.	77
79	Mercer	86
63	Jacksonville ■	74
71	Stetson ■	64
64	Georgia St.	66
77	Jacksonville St.	83
53	Samford ■	73
69	Belmont ■	76
59	Gardner-Webb	57
83	Campbell ■	56
78	Stetson	83
54	Jacksonville	89
72	Mercer ■	87
66	Troy St. ■	76
75	UCF ■	82

Nickname: Owls
Colors: Blue, Red & Grey
Arena: FAU Gymnasium
  Capacity: 5,000; Year Built: 1984
AD: Dick Young
SID: Katrina McCormack

80	P.R.-Bayamon ■	71
101	Winona St. ■	94
65	Embry-Riddle	55
92	Webber ■	58
95	Warner Southern ■	75
68	North Fla. ■	66
68	Mass.-Dartmouth ■	63
77	Wayne St. (Mich.) ■	63
63	Morehouse ■	60
83	Nova Southeastern	59
87	St. Leo	54
75	Eckerd	65
42	Tampa ■	37
69	Lynn	72
57	Barry	50
85	Florida Tech ■	73
65	Rollins	75
89	Eckerd ■	77
63	Tampa	40
73	Lynn ■	68
63	Barry	68
69	Florida Tech	48
63	Rollins ■	69
101	St. Leo ■	63
68	St. Leo ■	54
77	Eckerd ■	68
81	Rollins ■	68
70	Delta St. †	72

Nickname: Moccasins
Colors: Scarlet & White
Arena: Jenkins Field House
 Capacity: 2,500; Year Built: 1966
AD: Lois Webb
SID: Tim Carpenter

FLORIDA ST.
Tallahassee, FL 32306................I

Coach: Leonard Hamilton, Tenn.-Martin 1971
2002-03 RESULTS (14-15)

79	Savannah St. ■	46
83	Mercer ■	47
80	Iowa ■	67
57	Florida	58
72	Miami (Fla.) ■	55
56	Birmingham-So. ■	47
93	Stetson ■	76
48	North Carolina ■	69
69	Boston U. †	84
82	Davidson †	66
76	Virginia Tech	69
72	Tex. A&M-Corp. Chris ■	56
62	Maryland	89
74	Georgia Tech	81
63	North Carolina St. ■	70
60	Clemson ■	59
60	Wake Forest	71
72	Virginia	85
75	Duke ■	70
60	North Carolina	61
72	Maryland ■	74
71	Georgia Tech ■	64
60	North Carolina St.	71
60	Clemson	74
56	Wake Forest ■	60
73	Virginia ■	59
56	Duke	72
72	Clemson †	61
61	Wake Forest †	69

Nickname: Seminoles
Colors: Garnet & Gold
Arena: Leon County Civic Center
 Capacity: 12,200; Year Built: 1981
AD: David R. Hart Jr.
SID: Chuck Walsh

FLORIDA TECH
Melbourne, FL 32901................II

Coach: Kris Olson, Iowa St. 1994
2002-03 RESULTS (9-19)

46	Northwest Mo. St.	92
72	Truman †	84
77	P.R.-Mayaguez ■	73
98	Union (Ky.) †	70
58	West Fla.	87
64	Nova Southeastern ■	57
2	P.R.-Bayamon ■	0
47	Valdosta St.	78
90	Illinois Tech ■	52
67	Fla. Gulf Coast ■	69
57	Valdosta St. ■	55
64	Nova Southeastern	61
94	Webber	83
55	Rollins	70
60	St. Leo	61
63	Lynn ■	78
65	Eckerd	80
53	Tampa ■	60
73	Fla. Southern	85
62	Barry ■	69
70	St. Leo ■	61
47	Lynn	97
55	Eckerd ■	74
52	Tampa	72
48	Fla. Southern ■	69
57	Barry	63
55	Rollins ■	66
66	Rollins †	78

Nickname: Panthers
Colors: Crimson & Gray
Arena: Percy Hedgecock Gymnasium
 Capacity: 1,400; Year Built: 1964
AD: William K. Jurgens
SID: Dean Watson

FONTBONNE
St Louis, MO 63105-3098........III

Coach: Lee McKinney, Southeast Mo. St. 1960
2002-03 RESULTS (15-10)

93	Moody Bible	55
64	Loras †	84
74	Rose-Hulman ■	66
93	Dallas	86
81	Manchester ■	88
68	Elmhurst	72
83	St. Louis Christian ■	42
63	Ill. Wesleyan	87
58	Washburn	99
40	Chaminade	107
101	Lincoln Chrst. ■	58
66	Principia	72
104	Maryville (Mo.) ■	70
87	Blackburn †	76
82	MacMurray ■	73
105	Greenville	94
86	Westminster (Mo.)	75
87	Webster ■	81
81	Principia	69
71	Maryville (Mo.)	85
85	Westminster (Mo.) ■	70
59	Blackburn	66
82	MacMurray	92
110	Greenville	89
85	Webster	77

Nickname: Griffins
Colors: Purple & Gold
Arena: Dunham Student Activities
 Capacity: 1,800; Year Built: 1993
AD: Lee McKinney
SID: Lance Thornhill

FORDHAM
Bronx, NY 10458-5155............I

Coach: Bob Hill, Bowling Green 1971
2002-03 RESULTS (2-26)

79	William & Mary	76
51	Western Mich. ■	70
69	Siena ■	78
75	Northeastern	99
57	Manhattan ■	85
58	St. John's (N.Y.) ■	81
83	Rutgers	94
60	Northwestern	62
83	Fairfield ■	91
54	Holy Cross ■	87
64	Iona	67
80	Massachusetts ■	67
63	Rhode Island	75
70	St. Bonaventure ■	76
51	Temple	82
46	St. Joseph's	79
61	Xavier ■	75
68	Rhode Island ■	76
66	Massachusetts	76
61	La Salle	74
64	St. Joseph's ■	82
65	Duquesne ■	74
65	St. Bonaventure	83
77	Temple ■	99
64	Dayton	69
53	Richmond ■	60
61	George Washington	77
62	La Salle	74

Nickname: Rams
Colors: Maroon & White
Arena: Rose Hill Gym
 Capacity: 3,470; Year Built: 1926
AD: Francis X. Mc Laughlin
SID: Joe DiBari

FORT HAYS ST.
Hays, KS 67601......................II

Coach: Mark Johnson, Pittsburg St. 1993
2002-03 RESULTS (23-8)

75	Bethany (Kan.) ■	60
85	Baker ■	54
70	Bethel (Kan.)	62
82	Central Christian ■	45
72	Sterling (Kan.) ■	61
77	Mesa St. ■	81
96	Emporia St.	93
77	N.M. Highlands	60
71	Colorado St.-Pueblo	74
78	Okla. Panhandle ■	72
93	Fort Lewis ■	79
70	Adams St. ■	51
74	Okla. Panhandle	62
86	Western St.	82
92	UC-Colo. Spgs.	50
90	Chadron St.	80
60	Metro St.	72
78	Colorado Mines ■	72
104	Colo. Christian ■	64
72	Neb.-Kearney	78
85	Regis (Colo.) ■	65
71	Colorado Mines	87
70	Colo. Christian	63
89	Neb.-Kearney ■	75
67	Regis (Colo.)	60
63	Metro St. ■	64
72	Chadron St. ■	63
82	Colorado Mines ■	69
86	Neb.-Kearney †	82
69	Metro St. †	79
78	South Dakota St. †	84

Nickname: Tigers
Colors: Black & Gold
Arena: Gross Memorial Coliseum
 Capacity: 6,814; Year Built: 1973
AD: Thomas E. Spicer
SID: Steve Webster

FORT LEWIS
Durango, CO 81301-3999 II

Coach: Bob Hofman, Colorado 1974
2002-03 RESULTS (19-12)

98	Western N.M.	57
84	Westminster (Utah)	86
101	Central Wash. †	103
87	BYU-Hawaii	94
87	Hawaii Pacific	92
81	Hawaii-Hilo	89
66	Chadron St.	59
84	Metro St.	75
70	South Dakota St.	95
103	Anderson (S.C.) †	59
71	Regis (Colo.) ■	61
79	Fort Hays St.	93
85	Neb.-Kearney	91
81	Colo. Christian ■	68
86	Colorado Mines	93
97	N.M. Highlands	89
77	Colorado St.-Pueblo	78
105	UC-Colo. Spgs. ■	84
89	Western St. ■	77
67	Adams St.	64
95	Colorado Col.	76
62	Mesa St. ■	57
81	UC-Colo. Spgs.	77
114	Western St.	85
91	Adams St. ■	83
66	Mesa St.	49
81	Colorado St.-Pueblo	74
104	N.M. Highlands ■	59
83	Colorado St.-Pueblo ■	65
61	Metro St. †	76
63	Metro St. †	85

Nickname: Skyhawks
Colors: Navy Blue, Light Blue & Gold
Arena: FLC Fieldhouse
 Capacity: 2,750
AD: David L. Preszler
SID: To be named

FORT VALLEY ST.
Fort Valley, GA 31030 II

Coach: Michael Moore, Albany St. (Ga.) 1984
2002-03 RESULTS (13-16)

62	Tuskegee	76
68	Kentucky St. ■	72
66	Armstrong Atlantic ■	60
49	GC&SU	70
69	LeMoyne-Owen	60
61	GC&SU ■	54
59	Armstrong Atlantic	76
71	Claflin	73
87	Harding †	86
62	West Fla.	61
75	Miles ■	59
72	LeMoyne-Owen ■	69
60	Paine ■	59
47	Benedict	58
65	Paine	76
80	Tuskegee ■	74
87	Clark Atlanta	94
57	Morehouse	80
67	Miles	61
64	Albany St. (Ga.)	66
59	Claflin ■	68

53	Benedict ■	63
112	Clark Atlanta ■	107
77	Kentucky St.	82
83	Lane	79
56	Morehouse ■	73
64	Albany St. (Ga.) ■	67
77	Paine †	71
66	Morehouse †	73

Nickname: Wildcats
Colors: Royal Blue & Old Gold
Arena: George Woodward Gymnasium
   Capacity: 1,345; Year Built: 1959
AD: Gwendolyn Reeves
SID: Russell Boone

FRAMINGHAM ST.
Framingham, MA 01701-9101 ..III

Coach: Don Spellman
2002-03 RESULTS (6-17)

52	Lasell ■	77
49	Mass.-Boston	83
57	St. Joseph's (Me.) †	72
59	MIT ■	77
58	Connecticut Col. ■	70
66	Newbury	65
45	WPI	78
68	Albertus Magnus	72
75	Mass. Liberal Arts	82
55	Bridgewater St.	70
60	Worcester St.	61
58	Endicott	49
63	Salem St. ■	59
58	Fitchburg St.	73
65	Westfield St.	71
56	Roger Williams	53
77	Mass. Liberal Arts ■	35
68	Bridgewater St.	65
55	Worcester St. ■	60
48	Salem St.	82
75	Fitchburg St. ■	77
56	Westfield St. ■	59
67	Worcester St.	72

Nickname: Rams
Colors: Black & Gold
Arena: Dwight Gymnasium
   Capacity: 450
AD: Thomas M. Kelley
SID: Carey Williams

FRANCIS MARION
Florence, SC 29501-0547.........II

Coach: John Schweitz, Richmond 1988
2002-03 RESULTS (13-14)

64	Campbell	65
79	Paine	90
61	GC&SU ■	75
70	Allen ■	66
70	Coker	50
90	St. Andrews	81
68	Paine ■	57
69	Fayetteville St. ■	65
48	Armstrong Atlantic	50
50	North Fla.	71
86	Columbus St.	91
66	S.C.-Aiken	54
74	UNC Pembroke ■	47
79	Lander ■	51
51	Armstrong Atlantic ■	56
62	Augusta St. ■	64
65	S.C.-Spartanburg	54
71	GC&SU	73
68	UNC Pembroke ■	58
66	Clayton St.	74
66	S.C.-Spartanburg ■	64
58	Kennesaw St.	62
78	Lander	62
78	Augusta St.	88
71	S.C.-Aiken ■	58

61	Clayton St. ■	64
54	GC&SU †	56

Nickname: Patriots
Colors: Red, White & Blue
Arena: Smith University Center
   Capacity: 3,027; Year Built: 1974
AD: Murray Hartzler
SID: Michael G. Hawkins

FRANKLIN
Franklin, IN 46131 III

Coach: Kerry Prather, Indiana 1977
2002-03 RESULTS (9-17)

75	Berea	83
60	Wabash	83
74	Aurora ■	64
59	Wittenberg ■	69
71	Mt. St. Joseph ■	72
85	Defiance	90
76	Alma ■	56
59	DePauw ■	68
73	Millikin	72
76	Earlham ■	82
62	Rose-Hulman ■	63
79	Hanover ■	67
65	Bluffton	53
67	Manchester ■	68
90	Anderson (Ind.) ■	99
60	Transylvania ■	73
91	Defiance ■	69
80	Mt. St. Joseph	77
78	Thomas More	86
69	Hanover	82
90	Thomas More ■	80
87	Bluffton ■	68
79	Anderson (Ind.)	85
71	Manchester	75
77	Transylvania ■	81
84	Defiance	91

Nickname: Grizzlies
Colors: Navy Blue & Old Gold
Arena: Spurlock Center
   Capacity: 1,500; Year Built: 1975
AD: Kerry N. Prather
SID: Kevin Elixman

FRANK. & MARSH.
Lancaster, PA 17604-3003 III

Coach: Glenn Robinson, West Chester 1967
2002-03 RESULTS (25-5)

75	Methodist ■	80
93	Widener ■	68
81	Elizabethtown	78
72	Wesley	64
93	Muhlenberg ■	70
108	Bethany (W.Va.) ■	43
89	Hobart ■	74
112	St. Mary's (Md.) ■	67
91	Lincoln (Pa.) ■	60
82	Goucher ■	49
101	Alvernia	61
93	McDaniel	56
75	Lebanon Valley ■	70
82	Ursinus ■	83
63	Gettysburg ■	52
83	Lincoln (Pa.)	59
90	Dickinson	68
84	Johns Hopkins ■	57
86	Washington (Md.)	96
54	McDaniel ■	46
62	Swarthmore	45
68	Gettysburg	52
76	Haverford ■	66
78	Dickinson ■	48
65	Johns Hopkins	68
92	Washington (Md.) ■	62
88	Ursinus	96

79	Moravian ■	59
90	Neumann ■	66
70	DeSales ■	60

Nickname: Diplomats
Colors: Blue & White
Arena: Mayser Center
   Capacity: 3,000; Year Built: 1960
AD: Robert D. Bunnell
SID: Edward Haas

FRANKLIN PIERCE
Rindge, NH 03461 II

Coach: David Chadbourne, St. Joseph's (Me.) 1987
2002-03 RESULTS (14-15)

76	Southern N.H. ■	78
56	Mass.-Lowell ■	71
60	Alderson-Broaddus †	68
76	Salem Int'l	86
79	Bentley	86
74	Merrimack ■	65
58	Le Moyne ■	79
75	Lynn	60
63	Barry †	67
74	Nova Southeastern †	62
67	St. Anselm	77
78	St. Michael's	69
76	Pace	71
71	Southern Conn. St. ■	60
83	St. Rose	92
68	Bryant	76
70	Assumption ■	67
68	American Int'l	55
60	Mass.-Lowell	76
85	Southern N.H.	76
42	Stonehill	53
64	Stonehill ■	51
77	Bentley ■	65
59	Merrimack	68
91	Bryant ■	85
79	Assumption	73
56	American Int'l ■	68
74	Bryant	70
65	Mass.-Lowell	74

Nickname: Ravens
Colors: Crimson, Gray & Black
Arena: FPC Fieldhouse
   Capacity: 2,000; Year Built: 1967
AD: Bruce Kirsh
SID: Doug Monson

FREDONIA ST.
Fredonia, NY 14063................III

Coach: Kevin Moore, Brockport St. 1983
2002-03 RESULTS (13-12)

63	Texas Lutheran †	75
87	Alfred †	94
82	Geneseo St.	73
77	D'Youville ■	61
78	New Paltz St.	76
73	Oneonta St.	65
41	St. John Fisher	56
67	Medaille ■	66
73	Plattsburgh St. ■	86
61	Potsdam St. ■	64
53	Penn St.-Behrend	69
68	Oswego St. ■	80
71	Cortland St. ■	63
75	Brockport St.	89
120	Hilbert ■	92
74	Plattsburgh St.	73
60	Buffalo St.	68
62	Brockport St. ■	76
64	Utica/Rome	85
88	Pitt.-Bradford ■	82
62	Utica/Rome ■	45
64	Buffalo St.	61
52	Geneseo St. ■	50

57	Cortland St.	56
64	Buffalo St.	81

Nickname: Blue Devils
Colors: Blue & White
Arena: Steele Hall
   Capacity: 3,500; Year Built: 1983
AD: Gregory Prechtl
SID: Jerry Reilly

FRESNO ST.
Fresno, CA 93740-0048............I

Coach: Ray Lopes, Alberton 1987
2002-03 RESULTS (20-8)

65	Idaho St. ■	53
67	St. Mary's (Cal.) ■	65
70	Santa Clara ■	55
74	San Francisco	71
80	Pacific (Cal.) ■	60
61	Oklahoma St.	71
70	Centenary (La.) ■	69
66	Washington St.	69
91	Sacramento St. ■	53
74	Tulsa ■	65
71	Rice	70
61	Boise St. ■	54
84	UTEP ■	58
77	Hawaii	88
75	Southern Methodist	73
61	Louisiana Tech	60
56	Hawaii ■	55
59	San Jose St. ■	48
79	Nevada	92
76	UTEP	63
59	Boise St.	52
77	Louisiana Tech ■	80
76	Southern Methodist ■	56
74	San Jose St.	70
66	Creighton	67
107	Nevada ■	99
59	Tulsa	62
71	Rice	92

Nickname: Bulldogs
Colors: Bulldog Red & Blue
Arena: Selland Arena
   Capacity: 10,220; Year Built: 1966
AD: Scott Johnson
SID: Jake Bragonier

FROSTBURG ST.
Frostburg, MD 21532-1099......III

Coach: Webb Hatch, VMI 1969
2002-03 RESULTS (10-16)

88	Waynesburg ■	77
76	Indiana (Pa.) ■	93
65	Muskingum	73
59	Shenandoah	76
65	Westminster (Pa.) ■	72
73	Chris. Newport †	85
63	Gettysburg †	76
74	Wash. & Jeff. †	54
80	Grove City	74
82	Lake Erie	88
67	Pitt.-Greensburg	71
65	Penn St.-Behrend ■	60
65	Gallaudet	57
63	Penn St.-Altoona	49
66	Pitt.-Bradford	78
71	La Roche	80
69	Lake Erie ■	71
73	Waynesburg	83
99	Bethany (W.Va.) ■	105
58	Penn St.-Behrend	77
99	Pitt.-Greensburg ■	85
82	Mt. Aloysius	75
66	Pitt.-Bradford ■	84
86	Penn St.-Altoona	72
81	La Roche ■	79
81	Lake Erie	90

Nickname: Bobcats
Colors: Red, White & Black
Arena: Bobcat Arena
  Capacity: 3,600; Year Built: 1977
AD: Ralph Brewer
SID: Chris Starke

FURMAN
Greenville, SC 29613 I

Coach: Larry Davis, Asbury 1978
2002-03 RESULTS (14-17)

74	Alabama St. †	73
57	Creighton	82
66	James Madison ■	68
50	Notre Dame †	75
70	IUPUI †	62
81	St. Mary's (Md.) ■	44
64	Georgia St.	70
55	Memphis	72
83	Methodist ■	29
49	Chattanooga	66
76	Sewanee ■	56
63	Louisville	104
75	New Hampshire ■	52
59	Dartmouth ■	63
62	Georgia St. ■	73
64	Ga. Southern	71
59	Wofford ■	60
71	Western Caro. ■	67
57	Davidson	65
52	Col. of Charleston	59
83	Chattanooga ■	69
67	Appalachian St.	83
61	VMI ■	55
55	Citadel	69
53	Col. of Charleston ■	64
77	Ga. Southern ■	69
77	Citadel ■	60
69	Wofford	66
84	East Tenn. St.	71
78	UNC Greensboro ■	74
56	VMI †	62

Nickname: Paladins
Colors: Purple & White
Arena: Timmons Arena
  Capacity: 5,500; Year Built: 1997
AD: Gary Clark
SID: Hunter Reid

GALLAUDET
Washington, DC 20002-3695 ..III

Coach: James DeStefano, Gallaudet 1985
2002-03 RESULTS (5-21)

67	Susquehanna	80
48	Scranton †	70
75	Villa Julie ■	66
73	Maryland Bible ■	77
57	Phila. Sciences ■	81
90	York (Pa.) ■	91
47	Catholic ■	83
68	Wheaton (Ill.) ■	88
73	Maryland Bible	65
63	McDaniel	55
78	Salisbury	84
67	Goucher	80
57	Frostburg St.	65
68	Mary Washington ■	74
70	Marymount (Va.) ■	74
72	Washington (Md.)	70
84	St. Mary's (Md.) ■	92
67	Catholic	93
74	York (Pa.)	103
62	Goucher ■	80
76	Lincoln (Pa.) ■	84
76	Salisbury ■	81
70	Mary Washington ■	74
89	St. Mary's (Md.)	85

63	Marymount (Va.)	84
58	Catholic	65

Nickname: Bison
Colors: Buff & Blue
Arena: Field House
  Capacity: 1,892; Year Built: 1984
AD: James De Stefano
SID: Richard Coco

GANNON
Erie, PA 16541-0001 II

Coach: Jerry Slocum, King's (N.Y.) 1975
2002-03 RESULTS (20-10)

74	Dominican (N.Y.)	65
81	Holy Family †	73
74	Edinboro ■	60
88	Roberts Wesleyan ■	66
74	Brescia ■	50
73	Ferris St. ■	62
76	Grand Valley St. ■	67
100	Daemen ■	74
64	Ky. Wesleyan	85
98	Thiel ■	53
101	West Liberty St. ■	76
87	Bowie St. ■	88
65	Northern Mich.	77
73	Michigan Tech	74
83	Lake Superior St. ■	75
81	Northwood ■	76
64	Wayne St. (Mich.) ■	69
57	Hillsdale ■	53
76	Mercyhurst ■	73
67	Ashland ■	76
62	Findlay ■	76
76	Hillsdale	90
62	Wayne St. (Mich.)	59
92	Mercyhurst ■	68
88	Findlay ■	86
88	Ashland ■	62
78	Wayne St. (Mich.) ■	60
67	Findlay †	70
74	Ky. Wesleyan †	81

Nickname: Golden Knights
Colors: Maroon & Gold
Arena: Hammermill Center
  Capacity: 2,800; Year Built: 1949
AD: Dick Sukitsch
SID: Dan Teliski

GARDNER-WEBB
Boiling Springs, NC 28017 I

Coach: Rick Scruggs, Georgia 1979
2002-03 RESULTS (5-24)

69	Tennessee	71
82	St. Mary's (Md.) ■	74
66	Winthrop	68
53	Georgia Tech	75
63	Colorado St.	90
61	Clemson	71
65	Virginia	72
63	Eastern Mich.	78
63	Southern Methodist †	64
58	West Virginia †	75
53	Georgia St.	56
69	Jacksonville St.	88
86	Belmont ■	103
56	Samford ■	52
98	Appalachian St.	99
74	Campbell ■	76
63	Stetson	78
75	Jacksonville	87
88	Appalachian St. ■	82
60	Troy St. ■	61
64	Mercer ■	76
57	Fla. Atlantic ■	59
59	UCF	82
78	Winthrop ■	74

81	Campbell ■	69
54	Samford	63
73	Belmont	81
75	Jacksonville St. ■	83
58	Georgia St. ■	64

Nickname: Runnin' Bulldogs
Colors: Scarlet, White & Black
Arena: Paul Porter Arena
  Capacity: 5,000; Year Built: 1982
AD: Chuck Burch
SID: Thomas Goodwin

GENESEO ST.
Geneseo, NY 14454...............III

Coach: Steve Minton, Heidelberg 1986
2002-03 RESULTS (12-13)

70	Delaware Valley †	61
56	Alvernia	62
73	Fredonia St. ■	82
71	Oswego St. ■	74
85	Potsdam St.	61
75	Plattsburgh St.	59
61	Medaille ■	54
68	Ithaca	66
83	Alfred ■	62
53	New Paltz St.	63
59	St. John Fisher †	66
79	Keuka †	68
72	Roberts Wesleyan †	79
69	Cortland St. ■	61
62	D'Youville	58
69	Buffalo St.	73
55	New Paltz St. ■	69
71	Oneonta St. ■	80
81	Brockport St. ■	77
68	Utica/Rome	88
58	Oswego St.	61
67	Plattsburgh St. ■	57
77	Potsdam St. ■	64
50	Fredonia St.	52
66	Brockport St.	71

Nickname: Blue Knights
Colors: Navy Blue & White
Arena: Alumni Fieldhouse
  Capacity: 3,000; Year Built: 1973
AD: Marilyn Moore
SID: George Gagnier

GEORGE FOX
Newberg, OR 97132-2697 III

Coach: Mark Sundquist, Seattle Pacific 1989
2002-03 RESULTS (7-18)

79	Concordia (Ore.) ■	87
57	Claremont-M-S †	90
78	Chapman †	75
82	Dominican (Ill.) †	73
83	Puget Sound Chrst.	79
85	Northwest Chrst.	75
85	Warner Pacific	86
84	Whitman	85
78	Whitworth	88
85	Northwest Chrst. ■	76
67	Pacific (Ore.) ■	80
69	Lewis & Clark	105
66	Puget Sound ■	91
72	Pacific Lutheran ■	69
91	Linfield	123
60	Willamette	76
65	Whitman ■	71
61	Whitworth ■	73
82	Multnomah Bible	68
49	Lewis & Clark ■	80
68	Pacific (Ore.)	76
72	Puget Sound	90
76	Pacific Lutheran	95
82	Linfield ■	90
52	Willamette ■	59

Nickname: Bruins
Colors: Navy & Gold
Arena: Wheeler Sports Center/Miller Gym
  Capacity: 2,750; Year Built: 1977
AD: Craig Taylor
SID: Blair Cash

GEORGE MASON
Fairfax, VA 22030...................I

Coach: Jim Larranaga, Providence 1971
2002-03 RESULTS (16-12)

58	Central Mich.	61
74	Southern Ill.	83
49	Mississippi ■	56
79	Duquesne ■	72
68	Coppin St.	45
65	Niagara ■	45
66	East Caro.	56
55	Hartford ■	54
41	Pittsburgh	65
77	Delaware ■	67
75	Drexel ■	53
67	Hofstra	70
90	Towson	56
56	Va. Commonwealth ■	68
70	James Madison	76
46	Old Dominion	59
67	William & Mary ■	58
70	UNC Wilmington	58
76	Towson ■	54
71	Delaware	63
62	Va. Commonwealth	78
70	Hofstra ■	54
60	William & Mary	43
55	UNC Wilmington	75
52	James Madison ■	57
69	Old Dominion ■	52
57	Drexel	55
49	Delaware †	61

Nickname: Patriots
Colors: Green & Gold
Arena: Patriot Center
  Capacity: 10,000; Year Built: 1985
AD: Thomas J. O'Connor
SID: Carlton D. White

GEORGE WASHINGTON
Washington, DC 20052.............I

Coach: Karl Hobbs, Connecticut 1985
2002-03 RESULTS (12-17)

55	Connecticut	67
68	Mt. St. Mary's ■	54
80	Bucknell ■	77
77	Florida Int'l	63
92	Texas †	100
82	Maryland †	93
68	Boston U.	55
70	Towson	60
76	Old Dominion	84
68	Binghamton	64
75	American	81
65	Temple	68
49	La Salle	67
61	Dayton ■	71
57	Richmond	63
70	Massachusetts ■	75
74	St. Joseph's ■	68
68	Duquesne	58
68	Xavier ■	80
72	Rhode Island	77
68	Dayton	87
64	Richmond ■	50
73	Duquesne	78
76	La Salle ■	67
89	St. Bonaventure	94
70	Xavier	71
77	Fordham ■	61

85 Massachusetts...74
73 Xavier † ...78

Nickname: Colonials
Colors: Buff & Blue
Arena: Charles E. Smith Center
   Capacity: 5,000; Year Built: 1975
AD: Jack E. Kvancz
SID: Brad Bower

GEORGETOWN
Washington, DC 20057-1121 I

Coach: Craig Esherick, Georgetown 1978
2002-03 RESULTS (19-15)
99 Grambling ...46
80 James Madison ...60
81 Towson ...52
87 Coastal Caro. ...60
67 South Carolina ...59
84 Norfolk St. ...48
91 Howard ...66
75 Virginia ...79
85 VMI ...48
86 Duke ...93
84 West Virginia ...82
54 Seton Hall ...68
72 St. John's (N.Y.) ...77
76 Rutgers ...66
64 Pittsburgh ...65
82 Seton Hall ...93
92 Notre Dame ...93
80 Syracuse ...88
70 UCLA ...71
59 Rutgers ...66
85 Virginia Tech ...73
67 Pittsburgh ...82
74 Miami (Fla.) ...72
71 Providence ...56
84 Syracuse ...93
69 West Virginia ...67
80 Notre Dame ...86
46 Villanova † ...41
69 Syracuse † ...74
70 Tennessee ...60
67 Providence ...58
79 North Carolina ...74
88 Minnesota † ...74
67 St. John's (N.Y.) † ...70

Nickname: Hoyas
Colors: Blue & Gray
Arena: MCI Center
   Capacity: 20,600; Year Built: 1997
AD: Joseph C. Lang
SID: Bill Shapland

GEORGIA
Athens, GA 30602-1661 ...I

Coach: Jim Harrick, Charleston (W.Va.) 1960
2002-03 RESULTS (19-8)
71 Texas † ...77
87 Belmont ...71
77 Georgia Tech ...83
69 Minnesota ...72
71 Colorado ...70
78 California † ...73
95 Gonzaga † ...83
94 South Ala. ...82
99 Appalachian St. ...62
89 Wis.-Milwaukee ...69
79 Pittsburgh ...67
89 LSU ...63
63 Florida ...66
81 Arkansas ...64
81 Tennessee ...76
85 Auburn ...79
91 Vanderbilt ...94
67 Mississippi St. ...63

72 Tennessee ...78
67 Kentucky ...87
83 Vanderbilt ...70
74 Alabama ...69
79 South Carolina ...66
89 Mississippi ...82
66 Kentucky ...74
82 Florida ...81
60 South Carolina...55

Nickname: Bulldogs
Colors: Red & Black
Arena: Stegeman Coliseum
   Capacity: 10,523; Year Built: 1963
AD: Vincent J. Dooley
SID: Tim Hix

GC&SU
Milledgeville, GA 31061 ...II

Coach: Terry Sellers, Aub.-Montgomery 1976
2002-03 RESULTS (14-13)
65 Albany St. (Ga.) ...58
79 Albany St. (Ga.) ...64
75 Francis Marion ...61
55 Columbus St. ...68
70 Fort Valley St. ...49
54 Fort Valley St. ...61
63 Carson-Newman † ...69
47 Shaw † ...55
72 North Fla. ...61
82 UNC Pembroke ...45
60 Augusta St. ...71
69 Clayton St. ...68
65 Kennesaw St. ...76
63 North Fla. ...77
86 Lander ...63
72 Armstrong Atlantic ...59
73 Francis Marion ...71
65 S.C.-Spartanburg ...67
63 UNC Pembroke ...56
81 Clayton St. ...67
68 S.C.-Aiken ...64
92 Columbus St. ...97
63 Kennesaw St. ...73
67 Armstrong Atlantic ...81
49 S.C.-Spartanburg ...68
56 Francis Marion † ...54
66 Kennesaw St. † ...79

Nickname: Bobcats
Colors: Navy Blue & Hunter Green
Arena: Centennial Center
   Capacity: 4,071; Year Built: 1989
AD: Stan Aldridge
SID: Brad Muller

GA. SOUTHERN
Statesboro, GA 30460-8086 ...I

Coach: Jeff Price, Pikeville 1981
2002-03 RESULTS (16-13)
83 John Jay † ...60
91 Maine ...77
60 Vanderbilt ...96
112 North Ga. ...85
74 Savannah St. ...62
72 Mercer ...80
56 Air Force ...70
66 Spring Hill ...41
90 Wagner ...81
83 Savannah St. ...67
40 Air Force ...78
71 Furman ...64
91 VMI ...84
81 Appalachian St. ...87
83 UNC Greensboro ...78
66 Citadel ...67
87 Western Caro. ...82
70 Wofford ...73
79 Col. of Charleston ...84

94 Chattanooga ...97
87 East Tenn. St. ...83
69 Furman ...77
69 Wofford ...68
76 Davidson ...85
64 Citadel ...63
99 Chattanooga ...97
71 Col. of Charleston ...73
89 Western Caro. † ...81
53 Col. of Charleston † ...67

Nickname: Eagles
Colors: Blue & White
Arena: Hanner Fieldhouse
   Capacity: 4,378; Year Built: 1969
AD: Samuel Q. Baker
SID: Shawn Reed

GEORGIA ST.
Atlanta, GA 30303-3083 ...I

Coach: Lefty Driesell, Duke 1954
2002-03 RESULTS (14-15)
76 N.C. A&T † ...44
71 Auburn ...100
95 St. Andrews ...80
70 Furman ...64
77 Alabama St. ...82
68 South Ala. ...81
54 Mississippi St. † ...78
62 Oklahoma ...89
75 Charleston So. ...80
73 Furman ...62
56 Gardner-Webb ...53
92 Campbell ...59
76 Jacksonville St. ...89
107 Tennessee St. ...71
78 Samford ...80
69 Belmont ...66
66 Fla. Atlantic ...64
74 UCF ...81
78 Stetson ...71
81 Troy St. ...99
80 Mercer ...88
57 Belmont ...72
74 Samford ...78
71 Jacksonville ...69
76 Jacksonville St. ...78
88 Campbell ...72
64 Gardner-Webb ...58
76 Belmont ...58
61 Troy St. ...71

Nickname: Panthers
Colors: Blue, White & Red
Arena: GSU Sports Arena
   Capacity: 5,000; Year Built: 1972
AD: Greg Manning
SID: Charlie Taylor

GEORGIA TECH
Atlanta, GA 30332-0455 ...I

Coach: Paul Hewitt, St. John Fisher 1985
2002-03 RESULTS (16-15)
113 Ark.-Pine Bluff ...75
83 Georgia ...77
75 Gardner-Webb ...53
63 Minnesota ...64
67 Marist † ...53
69 Tennessee † ...70
88 Troy St. ...66
65 Syracuse ...92
77 Maryland ...84
66 Tulane ...80
81 Cornell ...55
85 North Carolina St. ...61
81 Florida St. ...74
66 Wake Forest ...73
66 Elon ...47
71 Duke ...91
88 North Carolina ...68

80 Virginia ...60
67 Clemson ...69
90 Maryland ...84
57 North Carolina St. ...63
64 Florida St. ...71
67 Wake Forest ...75
58 Duke ...77
66 North Carolina ...67
90 Virginia ...73
66 Clemson ...56
65 North Carolina St. † ...71
72 Ohio St. ...58
79 Iowa ...78
72 Texas Tech ...80

Nickname: Yellow Jackets
Colors: Old Gold, White, Navy Blue
Arena: Alexander Memorial Coliseum
   Capacity: 9,191; Year Built: 1956
AD: David T. Braine
SID: Mike Stamus

GETTYSBURG
Gettysburg, PA 17325-1668 ...III

Coach: George Petrie, Lebanon Valley 1972
2002-03 RESULTS (13-13)
70 Arcadia ...52
72 Lynchburg ...54
67 York (Pa.) ...71
69 Goucher ...78
52 Messiah ...76
83 Lincoln (Pa.) ...68
76 Washington (Md.) ...69
70 Johns Hopkins ...53
36 Navy ...85
73 Mt. Aloysius ...83
76 Frostburg St. † ...63
57 Catholic ...69
64 Elizabethtown ...88
64 Alvernia ...82
58 Muhlenberg ...48
52 Frank. & Marsh. ...63
59 McDaniel ...42
62 Dickinson ...54
71 Swarthmore ...64
36 Johns Hopkins ...60
62 Haverford ...57
52 Frank. & Marsh. ...68
68 McDaniel ...66
77 Ursinus ...91
74 Dickinson ...59
78 Johns Hopkins ...82

Nickname: Bullets
Colors: Orange & Blue
Arena: Bream Gymnasium
   Capacity: 3,000; Year Built: 1962
AD: David Wright
SID: Matt Daskivich

GLENVILLE ST.
Glenville, WV 26351 ...II

Coach: Chad Hankinson, West Virginia 1994
2002-03 RESULTS (12-17)
68 Bowie St. ...110
65 Felician † ...67
53 Pitt.-Johnstown ...74
66 Dist. Columbia † ...75
93 Ohio Southern ...65
66 Slippery Rock ...67
68 Southern N.H. † ...85
111 Wilmington (Del.) † ...74
67 NYIT ...72
99 Ohio Valley ...71
92 Fairmont St. ...77
69 Wheeling Jesuit ...74
81 Salem Int'l ...97
83 Concord ...72

76 West Virginia St. ■ ...78
79 Charleston (W.Va.) ...104
73 Bluefield St. ...85
75 West Va. Tech ■ ...70
71 West Liberty St. ...61
74 Shepherd ■ ...61
79 Davis & Elkins ...58
66 West Va. Wesleyan ...74
89 Alderson-Broaddus ■ ...97
69 Shepherd ...81
82 West Va. Wesleyan ■ ...74
93 Davis & Elkins ■ ...79
76 Alderson-Broaddus ...91
94 West Va. Wesleyan ■ ...81
68 Alderson-Broaddus † ...73

Nickname: Pioneers
Colors: Royal Blue & White
Arena: Jesse Lilly Gym
  Capacity: 1,600; Year Built: 1950
AD: Greg Bamberger
SID: Jodi Devereux

GOLDEY-BEACOM
Wilmington, DE 19808 II

Coach: Richard Casey, Temple 1989
2002-03 RESULTS (1-23)
60 Walsh † ...80
52 Holy Family ...79
42 Caldwell ■ ...61
53 West Chester ...86
60 Bloomfield ...85
56 Teikyo Post ...77
71 Dominican (N.Y.) ...91
55 Felician ■ ...76
71 Wilmington (Del.) ■ ...82
63 Phila. Sciences ...84
57 Nyack ...64
61 Kutztown ■ ...88
52 Holy Family ■ ...80
68 N.J. Inst. of Tech. ...91
70 Felician ...91
71 Bloomfield ■ ...82
55 East Stroudsburg ...84
78 Wilmington (Del.) ...65
78 Dominican (N.Y.) ■ ...79
50 Caldwell ...71
64 N.J. Inst. of Tech. ■ ...73
54 Teikyo Post ■ ...79
41 Nyack ■ ...75
78 Phila. Sciences ■ ...87

Nickname: Lightning
Colors: Navy, Gold & White
Arena: MBNA America Hall Gymnasium
  Capacity: 1,000; Year Built: 1998
AD: Chris Morgan
SID: Lynne Nathan

GONZAGA
Spokane, WA 99258-0066 I

Coach: Mark Few, Oregon 1987
2002-03 RESULTS (24-9)
69 Hofstra ■ ...61
71 Utah † ...52
75 Indiana † ...76
72 Kentucky † ...80
95 Washington ■ ...89
75 Montana ...67
110 Washington St. ...104
83 Georgia † ...95
69 North Carolina St. † ...60
90 Long Beach St. ■ ...55
67 Eastern Wash. † ...64
71 Stanford † ...81
78 St. Joseph's ■ ...79
87 Portland St. ...49
85 Loyola Marymount ■ ...73
92 Pepperdine ...72
56 St. Mary's (Cal.) ...53

66 San Francisco ...56
70 Portland ...67
89 San Diego ■ ...65
96 Santa Clara ■ ...62
78 Pepperdine ...63
74 Loyola Marymount ...80
73 St. Mary's (Cal.) ■ ...49
82 San Francisco ...71
68 Portland ■ ...72
69 Tulsa ...60
71 Santa Clara ...66
72 San Diego ...69
73 St. Mary's (Cal.) † ...52
63 San Diego ...72
74 Cincinnati † ...69
95 Arizona † ...96

Nickname: Bulldogs, Zags
Colors: Blue, White & Red
Arena: The Kennel
  Capacity: 4,000; Year Built: 1960
AD: Michael L. Roth
SID: Oliver Pierce

GORDON
Wenham, MA 01984-1899 III

Coach: Mike Schauer, Wheaton (Ill.) 1993
2002-03 RESULTS (20-7)
65 Eastern Nazarene ...64
82 Johnson & Wales † ...60
86 Castleton St. ■ ...61
82 Nichols ■ ...62
69 Salem St. ■ ...82
99 Mass. Liberal Arts ■ ...84
87 Eastern ■ ...73
74 Bates ■ ...78
77 Curry ...67
85 Becker ■ ...56
76 Wentworth Inst. ■ ...56
68 Salve Regina ...55
68 Endicott ■ ...51
70 Johnson St. ...69
51 Roger Williams ■ ...48
66 Colby-Sawyer ...76
96 New England ■ ...57
82 New England Col. ...55
44 Colby-Sawyer ...54
73 Eastern Nazarene ■ ...66
67 Endicott ...79
73 Anna Maria ■ ...50
66 Wentworth Inst. ...50
67 New England ...50
83 New England Col. ■ ...63
67 Anna Maria ...75
84 Keene St. ...89

Nickname: Fighting Scots
Colors: Blue & White
Arena: Bennett Center
  Capacity: 2,300; Year Built: 1996
AD: Joe Hakes
SID: Steve Leonard

GOUCHER
Towson, MD 21204-2794 III

Coach: Leonard Trevino, Texas Tech 1987
2002-03 RESULTS (16-10)
76 Ferrum † ...58
63 Roanoke ...64
53 Johns Hopkins ...67
78 Gettysburg ■ ...69
65 St. Mary's (Md.) ...61
69 Marymount (Va.) ...63
70 Apprentice ■ ...72
65 Union (N.Y.) ■ ...59
73 Northwestern Okla. † ...62
65 Adrian † ...59
49 Frank. & Marsh. ...82

77 Villa Julie ■ ...76
71 York (Pa.) ■ ...68
80 Gallaudet ■ ...67
67 Salisbury ...72
67 Catholic ...83
61 Mary Washington ...63
56 Marymount (Va.) ■ ...72
82 St. Mary's (Md.) ■ ...78
80 Gallaudet ...62
90 York (Pa.) ...76
75 Salisbury ...44
54 Mary Washington ■ ...57
88 Catholic ■ ...75
82 Salisbury ■ ...67
61 Mary Washington ...75

Nickname: Gophers
Colors: Blue & Gold
Arena: Sports/Recreation Center
  Capacity: 1,200; Year Built: 1991
AD: Geoffrey Miller
SID: Mike Sanders

GRAMBLING
Grambling, LA 71245 I

Coach: Larry Wright, Grambling 1982
2002-03 RESULTS (12-18)
46 Georgetown ...99
52 Oregon ...97
68 Jacksonville † ...82
95 Wiley ■ ...80
74 Texas Col. ...58
74 Northwestern St. ...71
54 St. Louis ...83
65 California ...84
52 Detroit † ...79
74 Marquette ...105
84 TCU ...103
70 Alabama A&M ...74
70 Alabama St. ...79
80 Southern U. ■ ...79
83 Alcorn St. ...66
71 Prairie View ...73
44 Texas Southern ...87
97 Jackson St. ■ ...95
99 Ark.-Pine Bluff ■ ...63
85 Mississippi Val. ■ ...77
68 Southern U. ...87
79 Alcorn St. ...88
61 Prairie View ■ ...74
69 Texas Southern ■ ...60
75 Jackson St. ...80
68 Ark.-Pine Bluff ...63
99 Mississippi Val. ...92
63 Alabama A&M ■ ...62
63 Alabama St. ■ ...67
78 Mississippi Val. ...90

Nickname: Tigers
Colors: Black & Gold
Arena: Tiger Memorial Gym
  Capacity: 4,500; Year Built: 1954
AD: Albert Dennis
SID: T. Scott Boatright

GRAND CANYON
Phoenix, AZ 85017 II

Coach: Leighton McCrary, Philander Smith 1974
2002-03 RESULTS (9-18)
69 St. Xavier ...75
70 St. Thomas (Minn.) ■ ...79
69 UC San Diego ...82
87 UC San Diego ■ ...70
78 Seattle ...77
65 Caldwell ■ ...63
69 Concordia (Neb.) ■ ...74
72 Cal St. Bakersfield ■ ...70
70 Cal St. Stanislaus ■ ...62
66 Cal St. L.A. ...65

71 Cal St. Dom. Hills ...73
56 Cal Poly Pomona ■ ...86
48 Cal St. San B'dino ■ ...74
68 UC Davis ...79
74 Cal St. Chico ■ ...71
71 San Fran. St. ...75
80 Sonoma St. ...85
55 Cal St. Stanislaus ...63
63 Cal St. Bakersfield ...76
56 Cal St. Dom. Hills ■ ...54
58 Cal St. L.A. ■ ...54
58 Cal St. San B'dino ...86
56 Cal Poly Pomona ...63
79 Cal St. Chico ...94
64 UC Davis ■ ...67
75 Sonoma St. ...83
80 San Fran. St. ■ ...86

Nickname: Antelopes
Colors: Purple & White
Arena: Antelope Gym
  Capacity: 2,000; Year Built: 1994
AD: John Pierson
SID: Rebecca Brutlag

GRAND VALLEY ST.
Allendale, MI 49401 II

Coach: Terry Smith, Michigan St. 1984
2002-03 RESULTS (14-14)
80 Indianapolis ...69
63 Lewis ...103
79 Finlandia ■ ...74
66 Aquinas † ...65
80 Hope † ...103
59 Findlay ■ ...78
63 Mercyhurst ...84
67 Gannon ...76
89 St. Joseph's (Ind.) ■ ...90
84 Northwood ...88
76 Rochester College ■ ...67
84 Wayne St. (Mich.) ■ ...66
74 Hillsdale ■ ...65
97 Ashland ...89
105 Mich.-Dearborn ■ ...62
57 Ferris St. ...81
73 Lake Superior St. ...87
103 Saginaw Valley ...93
59 Northern Mich. ■ ...62
64 Michigan Tech ■ ...76
74 Northwood ■ ...75
73 Lake Superior St. ■ ...63
70 Ferris St. ...64
76 Saginaw Valley ■ ...62
42 Michigan Tech ...40
73 Northern Mich. ...89
84 Findlay ...82
56 Northern Mich. ...69

Nickname: Lakers
Colors: Blue, Black & White
Arena: Grand Valley Field House
  Capacity: 4,010; Year Built: 1982
AD: Tim W. Selgo
SID: Tim Nott

GREEN MOUNTAIN
Poultney, VT 05764 II

Coach: Ken Tyler, William & Mary 1987
2002-03 RESULTS (10-14)
55 Concordia (N.Y.) † ...88
55 Caldwell † ...71
104 Paul Smith ■ ...83
54 Teikyo Post ■ ...86
80 St. Joseph (Vt.) ■ ...69
79 St. Joseph (Vt.) ...55
46 Stonehill ...69
69 Felician ...83
74 Dominican (N.Y.) ...90
63 St. Michael's ...91
80 Lyndon St. ...73

102 Paul Smith 88
69 Middlebury 99
78 Lyndon St. ■ 70
61 St. Joseph's (Me.) ■ 82
51 Assumption ■ 71
50 Bryant ■ 100
69 Teikyo Post. 90
79 Castleton St. ■ 68
93 Johnson St. ■ 87
69 St. Michael's ■ 87
82 St. Thomas (Tex.) ■ 79
79 Mich.-Dearborn 68
51 Holy Family 85

Nickname: Eagles
Colors: Green & Gold
AD: Christopher Gilmore
SID: To be named

GREENSBORO
Greensboro, NC 27401-1875 ..III

Coach: Lynn Ramage, West Liberty St. 1992
2002-03 RESULTS (11-14)
59 Roanoke 76
89 Ferrum † 92
84 Lynchburg ■ 66
69 Guilford † 65
58 Maryville (Tenn.) ■ 87
47 Appalachian St. 80
85 Southern Va. ■ 73
66 Wheaton (Mass.) ■ 50
63 Hampden-Sydney 81
72 Piedmont 77
58 Methodist ■ 61
72 N.C. Wesleyan 56
76 Chowan ■ 77
78 Averett ■ 67
72 Ferrum ■ 75
52 Chris. Newport 64
53 Shenandoah 66
57 Methodist 73
55 N.C. Wesleyan ■ 64
75 Chowan 49
86 Averett 80
78 Ferrum 76
76 Shenandoah ■ 50
86 Chris. Newport ■ 78
65 Shenandoah 67

Nickname: The Pride
Colors: Green, White & Silver
Arena: Hanes Gymnasium
   Capacity: 850; Year Built: 1964
AD: Kim A. Strable
SID: Bob Lowe

GREENVILLE
Greenville, IL 62246 III

Coach: George Barber, Asbury 1986
2002-03 RESULTS (9-15)
70 Marian (Ind.) 99
99 Barat † 105
74 McKendree 124
94 Eureka 104
98 St. Louis Christian ■ 67
94 Atlanta Christian ■ 90
72 SIU Edwardsville 82
68 Sanford Brown ■ 59
90 Knox 82
98 St. Louis Pharmacy 88
75 Westminster (Mo.) ■ 73
71 Blackburn 85
95 MacMurray ■ 86
70 Principia 75
69 Webster 95
94 Fontbonne ■ 105
75 Maryville (Mo.) 79
74 Westminster (Mo.) 76

77 Blackburn ■ 72
70 MacMurray ■ 81
81 Principia ■ 74
73 Webster ■ 92
89 Fontbonne 110
83 Maryville (Mo.) ■ 98

Nickname: Panthers
Colors: Orange & Black
Arena: H.J. Long Gymnasium
   Capacity: 2,000; Year Built: 1960
AD: Doug Faulkner
SID: B.J. Schneck

GRINNELL
Grinnell, IA 50112 III

Coach: David Arseneault, Colby 1976
2002-03 RESULTS (19-6)
160 Martin Luther ■ 131
144 Augsburg † 114
118 Northwestern (Iowa) 129
127 Lake Forest 114
153 William Penn ■ 117
110 Drake 162
148 Mt. Mercy 136
122 Grand View 120
108 Knox ■ 88
106 Illinois Col. 114
130 Ripon 137
124 St. Norbert 114
133 Carroll (Wis.) ■ 125
150 Lawrence ■ 149
108 Beloit 120
143 Carroll (Wis.) 128
141 Monmouth (Ill.) 102
118 St. Norbert ■ 106
139 Ripon ■ 125
93 Knox 80
94 Lake Forest ■ 85
129 Monmouth (Ill.) ■ 118
118 Illinois Col. 98
112 Ripon ■ 107
91 Illinois Col. ■ 101

Nickname: Pioneers
Colors: Scarlet & Black
Arena: Darby Gym
   Capacity: 1,250; Year Built: 1942
AD: Diane (Dee) Fairchild
SID: Jenny Wood

GROVE CITY
Grove City, PA 16127-2104 III

Coach: Steve Lamie, Grove City 1985
2002-03 RESULTS (18-9)
87 Allegheny † 84
87 Carnegie Mellon † 70
82 Penn St.-Behrend ■ 58
70 Case Reserve ■ 46
77 La Roche ■ 57
83 Denison 66
69 Otterbein 79
86 Cazenovia † 68
52 Elizabethtown † 77
65 Dickinson † 86
74 Frostburg St. ■ 80
74 Geneva 81
71 Medaille 59
77 Bethany (W.Va.) 71
75 Penn St.-Altoona ■ 62
72 Westminster (Pa.) ■ 47
63 Thiel 69
79 Waynesburg 77
76 Wash. & Jeff. ■ 70
100 Bethany (W.Va.) ■ 102
60 Westminster (Pa.) 53
76 Thiel ■ 79
89 Waynesburg ■ 74
86 Wash. & Jeff. 66

91 Westminster (Pa.) ■ 60
60 Thiel 59
61 Neumann ■ 75

Nickname: Wolverines
Colors: Crimson and White
Arena: College Arena
   Capacity: 1,800; Year Built: 1953
AD: Donald L. Lyle
SID: Joe Klimchak

GUILFORD
Greensboro, NC 27410-4173 ..III

Coach: Butch Estes, North Carolina 1971
2002-03 RESULTS (12-14)
37 East Tenn. St. 104
83 Marymount (Va.) 77
65 Greensboro † 69
57 Wash. & Lee 55
61 Hampden-Sydney 62
84 Emory & Henry 86
75 Atlanta Christian ■ 64
81 Lynchburg 90
85 Chowan ■ 57
61 Randolph-Macon 80
64 Va. Wesleyan 76
78 Roanoke 92
80 East. Mennonite ■ 72
67 Bridgewater (Va.) ■ 62
71 UNC Greensboro 83
92 Lynchburg 80
110 Roanoke Bible ■ 44
72 Va. Wesleyan ■ 60
50 Randolph-Macon ■ 52
72 Hampden-Sydney ■ 84
70 Bridgewater (Va.) 72
92 East. Mennonite 79
57 Wash. & Lee ■ 72
96 Roanoke ■ 74
81 Emory & Henry ■ 76
69 Roanoke † 91

Nickname: Quakers
Colors: Crimson & Gray
Arena: Ragan-Brown Field House
   Capacity: 2,500; Year Built: 1980
AD: Marion Kirby
SID: Dave Walters

GUST. ADOLPHUS
St. Peter, MN 56082-1498 III

Coach: Mark Hanson, Gust. Adolphus 1983
2002-03 RESULTS (26-7)
71 Luther 59
66 Martin Luther ■ 51
71 Augsburg 53
88 Concordia-M'head 65
67 St. Olaf ■ 53
77 Puget Sound † 72
58 Westmont † 59
91 La Verne 77
70 Hamline ■ 52
65 Macalester ■ 70
70 St. Thomas (Minn.) 74
92 St. Mary's (Minn.) ■ 57
56 St. John's (Minn.) 58
63 Bethel (Minn.) ■ 57
64 Carleton 78
73 Augsburg ■ 64
76 Concordia-M'head ■ 58
66 St. Olaf 59
81 Hamline 58
59 Macalester 57
51 St. Thomas (Minn.) ■ 53
73 St. Mary's (Minn.) 64
68 St. John's (Minn.) ■ 54
73 Bethel (Minn.) 67

76 Carleton ■ 54
65 Bethel (Minn.) ■ 64
62 St. Thomas (Minn.) 36
65 Whitworth 55
75 Wis.-Stevens Point 62
79 Hanover † 66
74 Occidental † 56
79 Hampden-Sydney † 68
65 Williams † 67

Nickname: Golden Gusties
Colors: Black & Gold
Arena: Gus Young Court
   Capacity: 3,000; Year Built: 1984
AD: Alan Molde
SID: Tim Kennedy

GWYNEDD-MERCY
Gwynedd Valley, PA 19437-0901
............III

Coach: John Baron, York (Pa.) 1995
2002-03 RESULTS (13-13)
78 Dickinson 67
61 Wilkes † 67
85 Widener ■ 83
68 Eastern 55
62 Arcadia 59
86 Albright ■ 74
102 Rowan 107
75 Chris. Newport 94
74 New Jersey City † 76
81 Ursinus 78
60 Cabrini 70
81 Swarthmore 69
92 Neumann ■ 93
74 Marywood 72
68 Alvernia ■ 57
69 Misericordia ■ 82
64 Wesley 61
78 Arcadia ■ 53
58 Cabrini 66
65 Misericordia 73
65 Eastern ■ 76
70 Alvernia 61
80 Marywood ■ 73
79 Neumann 84
60 Wesley ■ 71
74 Misericordia 76

Nickname: Griffins
Colors: Cardinal & Gold
Arena: Griffin Complex
   Capacity: 1,200; Year Built: 1991
AD: Keith Mondillo
SID: Paul Murphy

HAMILTON
Clinton, NY 13323 III

Coach: Tom Murphy, Springfield 1960
2002-03 RESULTS (23-6)
80 Utica/Rome 71
78 Utica ■ 68
88 Middlebury ■ 90
97 Hilbert ■ 40
82 Messiah † 61
86 N.C. Wesleyan † 79
85 Albright † 81
83 Asbury † 77
54 Williams 74
79 Clarkson ■ 65
84 St. Lawrence ■ 67
72 Union (N.Y.) 80
98 Skidmore 78
61 Hobart ■ 52
71 Rensselaer 62
81 Vassar 52
81 Skidmore ■ 70
85 Union (N.Y.) ■ 58

101	Hobart	103
75	St. Lawrence	78
80	Clarkson	72
72	Hartwick ■	57
79	Vassar ■	66
89	Rensselaer ■	87
83	Rensselaer ■	74
74	Union (N.Y.) ■	70
93	Colby-Sawyer ■	68
72	St. John Fisher	68
65	Williams	76

Nickname: Continentals
Colors: Buff & Blue
Arena: Margaret Bundy Scott Fiel
    Capacity: 2,500; Year Built: 1978
AD: Thomas Murphy/David Thompson
SID: Stephen Jaynes

HAMLINE
St. Paul, MN 55104 III

Coach: Tom Gilles, Iowa 1986
2002-03 RESULTS (12-13)

95	St. Scholastica ■	71
70	Crown	61
80	Northwestern (Minn.) ■	69
70	St. Mary's (Minn.) ■	83
64	St. John's (Minn.) ■	54
65	St. Thomas (Minn.)	75
71	Bethel (Minn.) ■	74
79	Martin Luther ■	81
50	Concordia-St. Paul ■	44
52	Gust. Adolphus	70
58	Augsburg ■	62
65	Carleton ■	78
54	Concordia-M'head	66
78	Macalester ■	80
74	St. Olaf	68
66	St. Mary's (Minn.)	60
76	St. John's (Minn.)	75
84	St. Thomas (Minn.) ■	68
72	Bethel (Minn.)	71
58	Gust. Adolphus ■	81
78	Augsburg	69
77	Carleton	81
68	Concordia-M'head ■	77
81	Macalester	73
60	St. Olaf ■	79

Nickname: Pipers
Colors: Red & Gray
Arena: Hutton Fieldhouse
    Capacity: 2,000
AD: Dan O'Brien
SID: Tom Gilles

HAMPDEN-SYDNEY
Hampden-Sydney, VA 23943 III

Coach: Tony Shaver, North Carolina 1976
2002-03 RESULTS (28-4)

111	Wesley ■	55
98	New Jersey City ■	65
80	Methodist ■	71
90	Lynchburg ■	58
62	Guilford ■	61
106	Hunter	69
117	Mass. Liberal Arts ■	52
102	Emory & Henry	67
81	Greensboro ■	63
86	Bridgewater (Va.) ■	53
85	East. Mennonite ■	51
52	Randolph-Macon ■	45
81	Roanoke ■	65
87	Wash. & Lee ■	48
68	Va. Wesleyan	54
116	Emory & Henry ■	76
83	Lynchburg	74
74	Bridgewater (Va.) ■	51
88	East. Mennonite	33

84	Guilford	72
67	Wash. & Lee ■	60
71	Roanoke	63
55	Randolph-Macon	66
83	Va. Wesleyan ■	68
82	Bridgewater (Va.) †	58
73	Va. Wesleyan ■	66
47	Randolph-Macon †	48
56	SCAD ■	54
76	Ill. Wesleyan †	68
68	Wis.-Oshkosh †	63
68	Gust. Adolphus †	79
74	Wooster †	78

Nickname: Tigers
Colors: Garnet & Gray
Arena: S. Douglas Fleet Gym
    Capacity: 2,500; Year Built: 1979
AD: Joseph E. Bush
SID: Dan McCormick

HAMPTON
Hampton, VA 23668 I

Coach: Bobby Collins, Eastern Ky. 1991
2002-03 RESULTS (19-11)

82	Western Ill. ■	59
61	Richmond ■	60
77	Old Dominion	70
72	Norfolk St. ■	62
85	Va. Commonwealth	90
79	Akron	84
62	Ohio St.	70
55	Md.-East. Shore	45
80	Howard	75
58	Maryland	108
91	Morgan St. ■	75
81	Coppin St. ■	75
90	Florida A&M ■	76
74	Bethune-Cookman ■	72
66	N.C. A&T	61
69	South Carolina St.	77
66	Delaware St. ■	71
62	William & Mary ■	64
70	Md.-East. Shore ■	54
65	Howard	75
75	Morgan St.	59
65	Coppin St.	51
83	Florida A&M	80
76	Bethune-Cookman	69
79	N.C. A&T	63
73	South Carolina St. ■	78
44	Norfolk St.	48
64	Norfolk St. †	62
73	Howard †	64
67	South Carolina St. †	72

Nickname: Pirates
Colors: Royal Blue & White
Arena: Convocation Center
    Capacity: 7,200; Year Built: 1993
AD: Malcolm Avery
SID: Patricia Harvey

HANOVER
Hanover, IN 47243-0108 III

Coach: Mike Beitzel, Wooster 1968
2002-03 RESULTS (27-2)

69	Webster †	49
105	Maryville (Mo.) †	69
82	Miami-Middletown ■	71
85	Oberlin	56
85	Ohio Northern ■	65
87	Earlham	54
88	Bluffton ■	70
80	Defiance	76
78	Rose-Hulman	46
86	Hobart †	62
83	Messiah †	74
67	Franklin	79
86	Transylvania ■	62

85	Manchester ■	54
103	Mt. St. Joseph	89
99	Thomas More	82
85	Anderson (Ind.) ■	83
74	Bluffton	59
107	Defiance ■	91
82	Franklin	69
74	Manchester	46
80	Transylvania	63
74	Thomas More	52
72	Mt. St. Joseph ■	56
93	Anderson (Ind.)	91
86	Defiance ■	71
79	Anderson (Ind.) ■	60
68	Maryville (Tenn.) †	64
66	Gust. Adolphus †	79

Nickname: Panthers
Colors: Red & Blue
Arena: John Collier Arena
    Capacity: 2,000; Year Built: 1995
AD: Lynn Hall
SID: To be named

HARDIN-SIMMONS
Abilene, TX 79698 III

Coach: Dylan Howard, UAB 1989
2002-03 RESULTS (5-20)

66	Texas-Dallas	64
71	Tex. Permian Basin	61
71	Ozarks (Ark.)	90
61	Austin	65
89	McMurry ■	100
43	Texas St.	89
53	Texas-Dallas ■	62
64	East Tex. Baptist	80
77	LeTourneau	66
70	Colorado Col. ■	75
68	Louisiana Col. ■	79
61	Mississippi Col. ■	69
63	Mary Hardin-Baylor	76
69	Concordia-Austin	78
85	Sul Ross St. ■	100
76	Howard Payne ■	84
68	Schreiner ■	61
69	Texas Lutheran ■	78
71	McMurry	75
66	Schreiner	70
55	Texas Lutheran	71
66	Mary Hardin-Baylor ■	72
89	Concordia-Austin ■	75
70	Sul Ross St.	101
65	Howard Payne	93

Nickname: Cowboys
Colors: Purple & Gold
Arena: Mabee Complex
    Capacity: 3,003; Year Built: 1979
AD: John Neese
SID: Chad Grubbs

HARDING
Searcy, AR 72149-0001 II

Coach: Jeff Morgan, West Tex. A&M 1989
2002-03 RESULTS (21-9)

105	Montevallo	84
83	Ala.-Huntsville †	80
111	Ark. Baptist ■	75
96	Central Baptist ■	59
95	Montevallo ■	66
87	Southwest Baptist	61
55	Louisiana Tech	76
86	Fort Valley St. †	87
107	Lane †	64
80	Ark.-Little Rock	82
66	Delta St.	67
106	Philander Smith ■	72
88	Ark.-Monticello †	67
95	Southern Ark. ■	71

105	Central Ark.	97
85	Christian Bros. ■	80
82	Ouachita Baptist	78
91	Arkansas Tech ■	66
75	Henderson St.	84
90	Delta St. ■	71
84	Ark.-Monticello	71
98	Southern Ark.	73
105	Central Ark. ■	74
101	Christian Bros.	107
94	Ouachita Baptist ■	72
94	Arkansas Tech	71
74	Henderson St. ■	77
88	North Ala. †	66
47	Henderson St. †	50
59	Henderson St. †	67

Nickname: Bisons
Colors: Black & Gold
Arena: Rhodes Fieldhouse
    Capacity: 3,000; Year Built: 1949
AD: Greg Harnden
SID: Scott Goode

HARTFORD
West Hartford, CT 06117-1599 ..I

Coach: Larry Harrison, Pittsburgh 1978
2002-03 RESULTS (16-13)

81	Long Island	76
70	Delaware St. ■	57
52	Oklahoma St.	65
52	Oklahoma	92
66	Central Conn. St. †	70
53	Holy Cross †	79
59	Dartmouth ■	44
54	George Mason	55
59	Md.-East. Shore	58
80	Fairleigh Dickinson	81
88	New Hampshire ■	84
68	Stony Brook	61
82	Northeastern ■	75
52	Binghamton	55
58	Boston U. ■	59
101	Concordia (N.Y.) ■	51
63	Vermont	55
80	Albany (N.Y.) ■	68
50	Northeastern	51
71	Maine	82
65	Binghamton ■	51
61	New Hampshire	72
59	Boston U.	65
72	Stony Brook ■	64
67	Albany (N.Y.)	53
64	Vermont †	61
70	Maine	58
59	Stony Brook †	47
51	Vermont †	67

Nickname: Hawks
Colors: Scarlet & White
Arena: The Chase Family Arena
    Capacity: 3,977; Year Built: 1990
AD: Patricia Meiser-McKnett
SID: David Longolucco

HARTWICK
Oneonta, NY 13820-4020 III

Coach: Tim McGraw, Hartwick 1988
2002-03 RESULTS (10-15)

96	Oneonta St.	93
75	Westfield St. †	73
71	St. Joseph's (L.I.) ■	54
72	Baptist Bible (Pa.) ■	65
64	Union (N.Y.) ■	74
51	Colgate	92
60	Scranton	81
92	York (Pa.) †	82
57	Cortland St. ■	52
48	Ithaca	71
65	Elmira	74

60	Utica	64
59	Alfred ■	62
71	St. John Fisher ■	73
53	Rochester Inst.	76
70	Nazareth	61
97	Skidmore	98
78	Elmira ■	75
61	Ithaca ■	83
67	Nazareth ■	74
88	Rochester Inst. ■	68
57	Hamilton	72
62	Utica ■	74
57	St. John Fisher ■	61
87	Alfred	73

Nickname: Hawks
Colors: Royal Blue & White
Arena: Binder PE Center
  Capacity: 1,800; Year Built: 1968
AD: Kenneth Kutler
SID: Mike Chilson

HARVARD
Boston, MA 02163-1012 I

Coach: Frank Sullivan, Westfield St.
1973
2002-03 RESULTS (12-15)

69	Fairfield	67
66	Holy Cross ■	71
56	Stony Brook	45
61	Boston U. ■	68
84	Lehigh ■	72
85	Rider	82
76	Colgate	71
71	Vermont ■	64
86	Mercer ■	74
77	Boston College	84
59	Richmond	86
67	VMI †	71
67	Dartmouth ■	50
93	Roanoke ■	88
69	Dartmouth	68
61	Princeton	67
59	Pennsylvania	75
86	Brown	91
68	Yale	73
77	Columbia ■	63
69	Cornell ■	82
66	Pennsylvania ■	82
66	Princeton ■	77
63	Cornell	68
66	Columbia	63
82	Yale ■	95
80	Brown ■	93

Nickname: Crimson
Colors: Crimson, Black & White
Arena: Lavietes Pavilion
  Capacity: 2,195; Year Built: 1926
AD: Robert L. Scalise
SID: John Veneziano

HAVERFORD
Haverford, PA 19041-1392 III

Coach: Michael Mucci, Villanova 1977
2002-03 RESULTS (10-14)

47	Connecticut Col. ■	60
105	Redlands †	82
70	Catholic	82
67	Union (N.Y.) ■	56
47	Johns Hopkins	58
65	DeSales	82
89	Ursinus ■	93
78	Elizabethtown	101
74	Lehigh	86
69	Stevens Institute	59
49	TCNJ	66
85	McDaniel ■	62
75	Muhlenberg	74
84	Drew ■	50

51	Lebanon Valley	47
76	Washington (Md.) ■	80
59	Swarthmore	45
66	Dickinson	57
52	Ursinus ■	76
57	Gettysburg ■	62
74	Muhlenberg ■	75
66	Frank. & Marsh.	76
72	Washington (Md.)	84
60	Swarthmore ■	44

Nickname: Fords
Colors: Scarlet & Black
Arena: Alumni Field House
  Capacity: 1,200; Year Built: 1957
AD: Gregory Kannerstein
SID: John Douglas

HAWAII
Honolulu, HI 96822-2370 I

Coach: Riley Wallace, Centenary (La.)
1964
2002-03 RESULTS (19-12)

81	Ark.-Little Rock ■	65
100	Tex. A&M-Corp. Chris ■	81
49	San Diego St.	60
81	Eastern Ill. ■	65
68	New Orleans ■	56
90	Bradley ■	69
74	Tennessee Tech ■	61
81	Butler	78
64	UTEP	52
63	Boise St.	65
72	Southern Methodist ■	55
57	Louisiana Tech ■	53
88	Fresno St. ■	77
67	San Jose St.	79
55	Fresno St.	56
65	Nevada	73
85	Rice ■	70
73	Tulsa	67
65	Louisiana Tech	66
69	Southern Methodist	78
54	San Jose St. ■	55
73	Nevada ■	71
79	Kent St.	78
51	Tulsa	76
58	Rice	75
68	Boise St. ■	65
77	UTEP ■	63
62	Rice †	61
56	Tulsa	66
85	UNLV	68
70	Minnesota	84

Nickname: Rainbow Warriors
Colors: Green, Black, Silver & White
Arena: Stan Sheriff Center
  Capacity: 10,031; Year Built: 1994
AD: Herman R. Frazier
SID: Derek Inouchi

HAWAII PACIFIC
Honolulu, HI 96813 II

Coach: Russell Dung, Chaminade 1979
2002-03 RESULTS (17-10)

83	St. Mary's (Tex.) ■	78
85	Carleton	81
63	Kennesaw St. ■	71
92	Fort Lewis ■	87
69	Northwest Nazarene ■	50
69	Pacific (Ore.) ■	57
90	Alas. Fairbanks ■	81
64	Alas. Fairbanks	51
96	Maryville (Mo.) ■	60
74	Carthage	65
84	St. Martin's ■	64
66	Drew	42
80	BYU-Hawaii	83
72	Mont. St.-Billings	71

81	Mont. St.-Billings	98
75	Western N.M.	81
76	BYU-Hawaii ■	84
87	Chaminade ■	78
67	Hawaii-Hilo	83
61	BYU-Hawaii ■	70
85	Chaminade	73
87	Chaminade	95
102	Western N.M. ■	70
100	Western N.M.	81
81	Mont. St.-Billings ■	70
66	Hawaii-Hilo ■	70
66	Hawaii-Hilo ■	97

Nickname: Sea Warriors
Colors: Columbia Blue, Kelly Green,
  White
Arena: Neal Blaisdell Center
  Capacity: 7,500
AD: Russell Dung
SID: Jarnett Lono

HAWAII-HILO
Hilo, HI 96720-4091 II

Coach: Jeff Law, Plattsburgh St. 1985
2002-03 RESULTS (18-10)

75	Oakland City †	73
50	Drake ■	70
69	Vermont	66
60	Utah St. ■	71
86	Lees-McRae ■	60
84	Cal St. Stanislaus ■	79
89	Fort Lewis ■	81
60	Hawaii Loa	73
82	Ouachita Baptist ■	80
82	Angelo St. †	64
59	Cal St. San B'dino	78
86	Drew ■	44
101	Mont. St.-Billings ■	91
86	Mont. St.-Billings ■	77
90	Western N.M. ■	66
72	Chaminade ■	78
93	Chaminade ■	87
95	BYU-Hawaii	101
83	Hawaii Pacific ■	67
81	Western N.M.	59
83	Western N.M.	76
78	Mont. St.-Billings	93
78	BYU-Hawaii ■	83
71	BYU-Hawaii ■	61
78	Chaminade	86
70	Hawaii Pacific	66
97	Hawaii Pacific	66
81	Humboldt St. †	102

Nickname: Vulcans
Colors: Red, White & Blue
Arena: Afook-Chinen Civic Center
  Capacity: 3,000; Year Built: 1955
AD: Kathleen McNally
SID: Kelly Leong

HEIDELBERG
Tiffin, OH 44883-2462 III

Coach: Duane Sheldon, Baldwin-Wallace
1993
2002-03 RESULTS (7-19)

52	Adrian	82
80	MacMurray †	74
60	Defiance ■	78
90	Urbana †	79
84	Bluffton	81
77	Otterbein ■	92
70	Wilmington (Ohio) ■	58
56	Muskingum	71
101	Urbana ■	102
45	Mount Union	65
69	Lake Erie	84
56	John Carroll ■	75
71	Marietta	75

54	Ohio Northern	62
55	Capital	80
57	Baldwin-Wallace ■	67
65	Muskingum ■	72
71	Otterbein	93
62	Capital ■	87
89	Baldwin-Wallace	84
74	Mount Union ■	65
46	John Carroll	65
56	Marietta	69
58	Ohio Northern ■	62
85	Wilmington (Ohio)	78
72	Marietta	78

Nickname: Berg
Colors: Red, Orange & Black
Arena: Seiberling Gymnasium
  Capacity: 1,900; Year Built: 1952
AD: Jerry McDonald
SID: Aaron Chimenti

HENDERSON ST.
Arkadelphia, AR 71999-0001 ...II

Coach: Rand Chappell, Southwest Mo.
St. 1985
2002-03 RESULTS (30-5)

62	Presbyterian †	48
78	Bryant †	67
64	North Dakota St. †	51
76	North Ala. ■	71
55	West Ga. ■	65
70	Southern Ind.	79
80	Jarvis Christian ■	48
106	Central Baptist ■	65
80	Philander Smith	69
99	Rhema ■	57
123	Central Baptist	67
83	Delta St. ■	64
71	Ark.-Monticello ■	65
75	Southern Ark.	54
75	Central Ark. ■	45
70	Christian Bros.	63
103	Ouachita Baptist ■	68
79	Arkansas Tech	70
100	Philander Smith ■	67
84	Harding ■	75
65	Delta St.	77
89	Ark.-Monticello ■	60
79	Southern Ark. ■	64
58	Southeastern Okla.	52
96	Central Ark.	80
82	Christian Bros. ■	69
69	Ouachita Baptist	73
99	Arkansas Tech ■	56
77	Harding	74
60	West Ga. †	56
50	Harding †	47
54	Ala.-Huntsville †	39
67	Harding †	59
67	Delta St. †	60
75	Eckerd †	85

Nickname: Reddies
Colors: Red & Gray
Arena: Wells Center
  Capacity: 2,100; Year Built: 1971
AD: Sam Goodwin
SID: Matt Bonnnette

HENDRIX
Conway, AR 72032-3080 III

Coach: Cliff Garrison, Central Ark. 1962
2002-03 RESULTS (7-17)

67	Bacone ■	66
54	Dallas ■	72
65	Westminster (Mo.) †	68
67	Denison ■	68
90	Crichton	76
58	Fisk ■	70
63	LeTourneau †	61

64 Dallas ...74
57 Rose-Hulman ■ ...75
56 DePauw ■ ...73
67 Centre ...78
51 Sewanee ...67
77 Crichton ...71
62 Rhodes ...66
67 Millsaps ■ ...58
74 Oglethorpe ■ ...76
62 Southwestern (Tex.) ...75
64 Trinity (Tex.) ...81
49 Rose-Hulman ...62
63 DePauw ...98
56 Centre ■ ...66
51 Sewanee ■ ...60
87 Central Baptist ■ ...66
70 Rhodes ■ ...59

Nickname: Warriors
Colors: Orange & Black
Arena: Ivan H. Grove
Capacity: 1,200; Year Built: 1961
AD: Danny Powell
SID: Jason Rhodes

HIGH POINT
High Point, NC 27262-3598 I

Coach: Jerry Steele, Wake Forest 1961
2002-03 RESULTS (7-20)
70 Northern Ariz. † ...65
74 Central Conn. St. ...63
65 Clemson † ...91
64 Kentucky ...84
67 Citadel ...82
75 Vanderbilt ...81
80 Campbell ...99
71 Washington St. † ...78
79 Campbell ■ ...76
81 UNC Greensboro ■ ...74
81 Radford ...67
70 Liberty ...74
75 Coastal Caro. ■ ...77
66 Charleston So. ■ ...75
60 Birmingham-So. ■ ...64
61 Elon ...65
60 UNC Asheville ■ ...64
59 Winthrop ...84
75 Radford ■ ...64
76 UNC Asheville ...78
56 Charleston So. ...61
71 Coastal Caro. ...89
70 Winthrop ■ ...86
62 Birmingham-So. ...63
72 Liberty ■ ...68
46 Elon ■ ...70
64 Winthrop ...80

Nickname: Panthers
Colors: Purple & White
Arena: Millis Center
Capacity: 2,565; Year Built: 1992
AD: Woody Gibson
SID: Lee Owen

HILBERT
Hamburg, NY 14075-1597 III

Coach: Rob deGrandpre
2002-03 RESULTS (1-23)
56 Penn St.-Behrend ...87
55 Hiram † ...93
59 Alfred ...75
54 Rochester Inst. ■ ...84
70 Roberts Wesleyan ...104
40 Hamilton ...97
73 Oswego St. ■ ...90
61 Nazareth ■ ...93
61 Buffalo St. ...79
72 Medaille † ...69
77 Hobart ...92
88 Cazenovia ...131

69 Medaille ■ ...74
78 Daemen ■ ...103
92 Fredonia St. ...120
60 Keuka ■ ...64
79 Thiel ■ ...85
83 Cazenovia ■ ...92
60 Pitt.-Bradford ...94
69 D'Youville ■ ...71
69 Keuka ...89
77 Medaille ...86
57 D'Youville ...71
70 Medaille ...74

Nickname: Hawks
Colors: Royal Blue & White
Arena: Brad Hafner Recreation Center
Capacity: 1,200; Year Built: 1973
AD: Richard Walsh
SID: Rob deGrandpre

HILLSDALE
Hillsdale, MI 49242-1298 II

Coach: Ed Douma, Calvin 1966
2002-03 RESULTS (16-12)
68 Northwood † ...67
84 Saginaw Valley † ...68
75 Mo. Western St. ...85
81 Mo.-Rolla † ...68
72 Saginaw Valley ...85
84 St. Francis (Ill.) ■ ...71
50 Detroit ...70
112 Mich.-Dearborn ■ ...76
94 Ferris St. ■ ...77
74 Northern Ky. ■ ...60
64 Ferris St. ...65
65 Grand Valley St. ...74
63 Michigan Tech ■ ...67
54 Northern Mich. ■ ...55
74 Lake Superior St. ■ ...71
53 Gannon ...57
64 Mercyhurst ...51
60 Findlay ■ ...80
95 Ashland ■ ...66
94 Tri-State ■ ...75
62 Wayne St. (Mich.) ...78
90 Gannon ■ ...76
86 Mercyhurst ■ ...83
81 Ashland ...71
65 Findlay ...80
87 Northwood ...68
87 Wayne St. (Mich.) ■ ...65
61 Findlay ...75

Nickname: Chargers
Colors: Royal Blue & White
Arena: Jesse Philips Arena
Capacity: 2,500; Year Built: 1989
AD: Michael J. Kovalchik
SID: Dennis Worden

HIRAM
Hiram, OH 44234-0067 III

Coach: Sean McDonnell, Boston College 1996
2002-03 RESULTS (6-20)
77 Notre Dame (Ohio) † ...86
93 Hilbert ■ ...55
65 John Carroll ...86
83 Case Reserve † ...71
68 Pitt.-Greensburg ...86
64 Ohio Wesleyan ■ ...76
68 Notre Dame (Ohio) ■ ...75
75 Bethany (W.Va.) ...81
80 Carnegie Mellon ...85
73 Wabash ■ ...85
74 Earlham ■ ...67
87 Thiel ...100
75 Wittenberg ...93
74 Denison ...75
101 Kenyon ■ ...91

94 Allegheny ...103
87 Oberlin ■ ...79
61 Wooster ■ ...94
81 Ohio Wesleyan ...79
68 Denison ■ ...74
62 Wittenberg ■ ...78
58 Wooster ...91
72 Kenyon ...89
76 Allegheny ■ ...109
66 Oberlin ...69
51 Wooster ...73

Nickname: Terriers
Colors: Blue and Red
Arena: Price Gymnasium
Capacity: 2,000; Year Built: 1959
AD: Thomas E. Mulligan
SID: Jason Tirotta

HOBART
Geneva, NY 14456 III

Coach: Richard Roche, Hobart 1987
2002-03 RESULTS (10-15)
56 Colgate ...92
62 Rochester ...79
56 Rochester Inst. ...58
94 Cazenovia ■ ...86
74 Frank. & Marsh. ...89
62 Hanover † ...86
71 Ursinus † ...75
53 Rochester ...69
92 Hilbert ■ ...77
79 St. Lawrence ■ ...66
75 Clarkson ■ ...59
68 Utica ■ ...62
83 Skidmore ...65
89 Union (N.Y.) ...93
52 Hamilton ...61
96 Vassar ...48
75 Rensselaer ...77
62 Union (N.Y.) ■ ...78
93 Skidmore ■ ...85
103 Hamilton ■ ...101
65 Clarkson ...66
64 St. Lawrence ...68
72 Ithaca ■ ...82
76 Rensselaer ■ ...83
98 Vassar ■ ...73

Nickname: Statesmen
Colors: Royal Purple and Orange
Arena: Bristol Gym
Capacity: 1,500; Year Built: 1965
AD: Michael J. Hanna
SID: Ken DeBolt

HOFSTRA
Hempstead, NY 11549 I

Coach: Tom Pecora, Adelphi 1983
2002-03 RESULTS (8-21)
61 Gonzaga ...69
56 St. Francis (N.Y.) † ...72
63 Lehigh ■ ...50
68 Quinnipiac ■ ...71
57 Monmouth ■ ...70
59 St. John's (N.Y.) ...84
52 Stony Brook ...65
75 Manhattan ■ ...93
64 St. Peter's † ...77
62 Va. Commonwealth ...71
47 UNC Wilmington ...71
70 George Mason ■ ...67
58 James Madison ■ ...65
54 Towson ...61
69 Old Dominion ...65
66 William & Mary ■ ...51
66 Drexel ...78
64 Delaware ■ ...62
69 James Madison ...75
76 Drexel ...82

69 William & Mary ■ ...79
54 George Mason ■ ...70
70 UNC Wilmington ■ ...74
91 Delaware ■ ...82
77 Va. Commonwealth ■ ...80
66 Towson ■ ...47
46 Old Dominion ...77
74 William & Mary † ...64
56 UNC Wilmington † ...76

Nickname: Pride
Colors: Gold, White and Blue
Arena: Hofstra Arena
Capacity: 5,124; Year Built: 1999
AD: Harry H. Royle
SID: Jeremy Kniffin

HOLY CROSS
Worcester, MA 01610-2395 I

Coach: Ralph Willard, Holy Cross 1967
2002-03 RESULTS (26-5)
57 Kansas ...81
101 Dowling ■ ...61
71 Harvard ...66
71 Boston College ■ ...70
72 Brown ...56
66 Yale † ...70
79 Hartford † ...53
84 UNC Asheville ■ ...53
63 Marist ...66
87 Fordham ...54
55 Princeton ■ ...54
83 Quinnipiac ...75
61 Army ■ ...45
86 Colgate ■ ...43
76 Lafayette ...70
63 Dartmouth ...43
76 Navy ...61
49 American ...72
63 Lehigh ■ ...39
69 Bucknell ■ ...47
53 Army ...45
92 Colgate ...91
73 Lafayette ■ ...65
68 American ■ ...66
63 Navy ■ ...42
54 Bucknell ...43
72 Lehigh ...64
58 Army † ...40
75 Bucknell † ...50
72 American ■ ...64
68 Marquette † ...72

Nickname: Crusaders
Colors: Royal Purple
Arena: Hart Recreation Center
Capacity: 3,600; Year Built: 1975
AD: Richard M. Regan Jr.
SID: Frank Mastrandrea

HOLY FAMILY
Philadelphia, PA 19114 II

Coach: Cliff Garrison, Central Ark. 1962
2002-03 RESULTS (18-12)
79 Pace † ...94
73 Gannon † ...81
79 Goldey-Beacom ■ ...52
87 Southern Va. ■ ...50
56 Caldwell ...50
59 Dominican (N.Y.) ■ ...46
100 Wilmington (Del.) ...71
79 Phila. Sciences ...72
55 Lee † ...98
60 King (Tenn.) † ...67
72 Millersville ■ ...66
66 Mansfield ...68
89 Teikyo Post ■ ...100
72 Felician ...60
77 Nyack ■ ...61
75 Bloomfield ■ ...78

79 N.J. Inst. of Tech. ■ ...61
80 Goldey-Beacom ...52
52 Teikyo Post ...70
89 Wilmington (Del.) ■ ...71
76 Dominican (N.Y.) ...78
88 Phila. Sciences ■ ...85
60 N.J. Inst. of Tech. ...61
76 Nyack ...93
94 Bloomfield ...83
79 Caldwell ■ ...72
69 Felician ■ ...68
85 Green Mountain ■ ...51
71 Phila. Sciences ■ ...69
68 Huntington † ...71

Nickname: Tigers
Colors: Blue & White
AD: Sandra Michael
SID: To be named

HOPE
Holland, MI 49422-9000 III

Coach: Glenn Van Wieren, Hope 1964
2002-03 RESULTS (23-5)
82 Northwestern (Minn.) ...79
79 Trinity Christian † ...66
80 Cornerstone † ...69
103 Grand Valley St. † ...80
91 Trinity Christian ■ ...64
96 St. Mary's (Mich.) † ...50
69 Aquinas ...76
94 Grace Bible (Mich.) ■ ...58
92 North Central ■ ...76
84 Chicago ...66
63 Edward Waters † ...54
69 Warner Southern ...87
64 Adrian ...59
101 Alma ■ ...51
70 Calvin ...74
57 Albion ■ ...52
99 Olivet ...90
100 Kalamazoo ■ ...35
83 Adrian ...67
108 Alma ...79
92 Calvin ■ ...76
65 Albion ■ ...69
90 Olivet ...73
70 Kalamazoo ...59
101 Alma ...75
81 Calvin † ...80
61 Albion ...48
77 Wis.-Oshkosh ■ ...84

Nickname: Flying Dutchmen
Colors: Blue & Orange
Arena: Holland Civic Center
Capacity: 2,550; Year Built: 1954
AD: Raymond E. Smith
SID: Tom Renner

HOUSTON
Houston, TX 77204 I

Coach: Ray McCallum, Ball St. 1983
2002-03 RESULTS (8-20)
75 Prairie View ■ ...78
53 Rice ...71
60 Baylor † ...62
56 UTEP ...47
60 Texas-Arlington ■ ...59
59 Texas St. ...68
61 San Diego St. ■ ...71
61 Washington ...85
48 Texas Tech ...62
56 La.-Lafayette ...72
51 LSU ...80
50 UAB ■ ...63
72 St. Louis ■ ...59
66 Memphis ...77
76 Southern Miss. † ...75

59 South Fla. ■ ...57
61 TCU ...56
58 Tulane ■ ...65
55 Louisville ■ ...81
55 Charlotte ...59
47 South Fla. ...62
46 Southern Miss. ...42
52 UAB ...80
52 Tulane ...56
75 TCU ■ ...57
56 Memphis ■ ...71
59 DePaul ...65
52 Tulane † ...74

Nickname: Cougars
Colors: Scarlet & White with Navy Trim
Arena: Hofheinz Pavilion
Capacity: 8,479; Year Built: 1969
AD: Dave Maggard
SID: Chris Burkhalter

HOWARD
Washington, DC 20059.............I

Coach: Frankie Allen, Roanoke 1971
2002-03 RESULTS (13-17)
68 St. Francis (Pa.) ...70
62 Radford ...58
80 Cal St. Northridge ...101
70 California ...80
67 St. Francis (N.Y.) ■ ...88
58 American ...61
66 Georgetown ...91
72 Oral Roberts † ...62
73 Col. of Charleston ...77
75 Hampton ...80
68 Norfolk St. ■ ...73
63 Bethune-Cookman ...58
64 Florida A&M ...75
80 South Carolina St. ■ ...85
107 N.C. A&T ■ ...70
61 Delaware St. ■ ...70
83 Md.-East. Shore ■ ...76
60 Coppin St. ...68
74 Morgan St. ■ ...53
88 Norfolk St. ...78
75 Hampton ...65
96 Bethune-Cookman ■ ...68
74 Florida A&M ■ ...68
81 South Carolina St. ...90
105 N.C. A&T ...81
56 Delaware St. ■ ...59
67 Md.-East. Shore ...73
71 Md.-East. Shore † ...69
68 Delaware St. † ...65
64 Hampton † ...73

Nickname: Bison
Colors: Blue, White & Red
Arena: Burr Gymnasium
Capacity: 2,700; Year Built: 1963
AD: Sondra Norrell-Thomas
SID: Edward Hill Jr.

HOWARD PAYNE
Brownwood, TX 76801 III

Coach: Charles Pattillo, Howard Payne 1965
2002-03 RESULTS (17-8)
75 Abilene Christian ...81
71 Wayland Baptist ...77
82 Texas-Dallas ...69
85 Mississippi Col. ■ ...70
90 Louisiana Col. ■ ...73
109 Sul Ross St. ■ ...110
68 Tex. A&M-Corp. Chris ...84
75 Midwestern St. ...105
78 Austin ...61
87 Ozarks (Ark.) ...64
114 LeTourneau ■ ...82

100 East Tex. Baptist ■ ...93
89 Sul Ross St. ...93
93 Texas Lutheran ...78
114 Schreiner ■ ...95
67 McMurry ...78
84 Hardin-Simmons ...76
80 Concordia-Austin ...78
74 Mary Hardin-Baylor ...64
93 Concordia-Austin ■ ...61
77 Mary Hardin-Baylor ■ ...74
71 Texas Lutheran ...78
98 Schreiner ...96
74 McMurry ...69
93 Hardin-Simmons ■ ...65

Nickname: Yellow Jackets
Colors: Gold & Blue
Arena: Brownwood Coliseum
Capacity: 5,000; Year Built: 1968
AD: Vance Gibson
SID: Nadir Dalleh

HUMBOLDT ST.
Arcata, CA 95521-8299 II

Coach: Tom Wood, UC Davis 1971
2002-03 RESULTS (23-6)
99 Holy Names ■ ...62
76 Westmont † ...69
87 Cal St. Chico ...69
90 Southern Ore. ...72
88 Western Ore. ■ ...78
78 San Fran. St. ■ ...77
87 Dominican (Cal.) ...69
100 UC San Diego ...58
105 Cal St. Dom. Hills ...68
85 Notre Dame de Namur ■ ...59
94 Northwest Nazarene ■ ...70
70 Seattle ■ ...56
69 St. Martin's ...62
69 Central Wash. ...85
76 Western Wash. ...69
80 Seattle Pacific ■ ...70
90 Alas. Anchorage ...88
83 Alas. Fairbanks ...86
86 Seattle ...60
72 Northwest Nazarene ...63
80 Central Wash. ■ ...59
80 St. Martin's ■ ...63
108 Seattle Pacific ...113
73 Western Wash. ...72
86 Alas. Anchorage ...69
76 Alas. Fairbanks ■ ...90
68 Western Ore. ...83
102 Hawaii-Hilo † ...81
68 Cal St. San B'dino † ...80

Nickname: Lumberjacks
Colors: Green & Gold
Arena: HSU East Gym
Capacity: 1,400; Year Built: 1956
AD: Dan Collen
SID: Dan Pambianco

HUNTER
New York, NY 10021 III

Coach: Bill Healy, St. Joseph's 1983
2002-03 RESULTS (8-18)
57 Wilkes † ...89
68 Dickinson ...81
51 John Jay ...64
70 Ursinus ...77
82 CCNY ■ ...75
70 Western Conn. St. ■ ...75
64 FDU-Florham ...73
69 Hampden-Sydney ...106
86 Medgar Evers † ...95
57 Connecticut Col. ■ ...67
79 Lehman ■ ...86
74 Baruch ...83

75 NYCCT ■ ...72
66 Staten Island ...75
65 New York U. ...90
66 York (N.Y.) ...41
69 Brooklyn ■ ...71
71 Manhattanville ■ ...77
80 John Jay ■ ...70
65 CCNY ...79
69 Lehman ...67
62 Trinity (Conn.) ...76
76 Baruch ■ ...69
90 Medgar Evers ...75
82 Centenary (N.J.) ■ ...81
75 Lehman † ...84

Nickname: Hawks
Colors: Purple, White & Gold
Arena: Hunter College Sportsplex
Capacity: 1,500; Year Built: 1985
AD: Terry Ann Wansart
SID: Damion Jones

HUSSON
Bangor, ME 04401 III

Coach: Warren Caruso
2002-03 RESULTS (20-5)
67 Colby † ...50
70 St. Joseph's (Me.) ...72
76 Me.-Farmington ...60
96 Me.-Fort Kent ...87
83 Me.-Presque Isle ...61
68 Maine ...100
92 Me.-Machias † ...65
72 Rivier † ...89
80 Siena Heights † ...69
111 St. Joseph (Vt.) ■ ...48
81 Fisher ...73
83 Me.-Farmington ■ ...88
81 St. Joseph's (Me.) ...70
86 Thomas ...59
86 Me.-Machias ...69
97 Me.-Presque Isle ■ ...50
79 Me.-Fort Kent ■ ...71
78 Maine Maritime ...57
96 St. Joseph (Vt.) ...60
82 Lyndon St. ...70
91 Thomas ■ ...62
54 St. Joseph's (Me.) ■ ...68
100 Me.-Machias ■ ...69
83 Fisher ...66
90 Lyndon St. ■ ...77

Nickname: Braves
Colors: Green & White
AD: Pamala S. Hennessey
SID: To be named

IDAHO
Moscow, ID 83843-2302 I

Coach: Leonard Perry, Idaho 1995
2002-03 RESULTS (13-15)
76 Oregon St. ...73
88 Western Mont. ■ ...60
67 Boise St. ...75
62 Washington St. ■ ...58
62 Eastern Wash. ...67
69 Montana ...81
70 Boise St. ■ ...75
68 Montana St. ...74
81 Sacramento St. ■ ...62
50 Pacific (Cal.) ...73
73 Cal St. Northridge ...66
53 UC Santa Barb. ■ ...62
66 Cal Poly ■ ...50
55 Long Beach St. ...59
45 UC Irvine ...58
56 Cal St. Fullerton ■ ...49
56 UC Riverside ■ ...53
56 Utah St. ■ ...60

(continued)

68	Cal Poly	65
44	UC Santa Barb.	52
75	Long Beach St. ■	67
52	UC Irvine ■	65
68	UC Riverside	64
59	Cal St. Fullerton	62
52	Utah St.	51
60	Pacific (Cal.) ■	55
78	Cal St. Northridge ■	86
50	Cal Poly †	54

Nickname: Vandals
Colors: Silver & Gold
Arena: Cowan Spectrum
Capacity: 7,000; Year Built: 1975
AD: Mike R. Bohn
SID: Becky Paull

IDAHO ST.
Pocatello, ID 83209 I

Coach: Doug Oliver, San Jose St. 1973
2002-03 RESULTS (15-14)

71	Texas-San Antonio †	76
63	Coppin St. †	55
71	Boise St.	74
53	Fresno St.	65
58	Sam Houston St. †	65
72	Menlo ■	56
79	Cal St. Fullerton	70
84	Tennessee Tech ■	72
86	Eastern Ore. ■	68
75	UMKC †	61
59	Utah St.	66
58	Brigham Young	77
74	Cal St. Fullerton ■	66
88	Montana ■	90
56	Montana St. ■	55
67	Sacramento St.	62
62	Northern Ariz.	65
88	Eastern Wash. ■	86
58	Portland St. ■	57
76	Weber St. ■	82
70	Weber St.	87
65	Montana St.	73
65	Montana	69
90	Northern Ariz. ■	76
90	Sacramento St. ■	83
69	Portland St.	77
65	Eastern Wash.	63
85	Northern Ariz. ■	74
67	Eastern Wash. †	76

Nickname: Bengals
Colors: Orange & Black
Arena: Reed Gymnasium
Capacity: 3,241; Year Built: 1951
AD: Howard L. Gauthier
SID: Frank Mercogliano

ILLINOIS
Champaign, IL 61820 I

Coach: Bill Self, Oklahoma St. 1985
2002-03 RESULTS (25-7)

90	Lehigh ■	56
96	Ark.-Pine Bluff ■	43
85	Western Ill. ■	56
92	North Carolina ■	65
62	Arkansas †	58
80	Eastern Ill. ■	68
70	Temple †	54
85	Missouri †	70
74	Memphis	77
63	Coppin St. ■	37
88	Oakland ■	53
76	Minnesota	70
69	Wisconsin ■	63
61	Iowa	68
66	Indiana	74
75	Purdue ■	62
75	Penn St.	63

(continued)

67	Michigan ■	60
65	Michigan St.	68
76	Ohio St.	57
61	Purdue	70
70	Michigan St. ■	40
73	Northwestern †	61
80	Indiana ■	54
82	Michigan	79
59	Wisconsin ■	60
84	Minnesota ■	60
94	Northwestern †	65
73	Indiana †	72
72	Ohio St. †	59
65	Western Ky. †	60
60	Notre Dame †	68

Nickname: Fighting Illini
Colors: Orange & Blue
Arena: Assembly Hall
Capacity: 16,450; Year Built: 1963
AD: Ronald E. Guenther
SID: Kent Brown

ILLINOIS COL.
Jacksonville, IL 62650-2299 III

Coach: Mike Worrell, Urbana 1986
2002-03 RESULTS (15-11)

78	Millikin	72
95	Sanford Brown	42
90	MacMurray ■	68
79	Knox ■	80
61	Dominican (Ill.) ■	63
65	Rose-Hulman ■	77
63	Kalamazoo †	78
61	Benedictine (Ill.) †	60
88	Lake Forest ■	62
114	Grinnell ■	106
68	Lawrence	75
68	Beloit	67
82	Monmouth (Ill.)	73
80	Ripon ■	72
78	St. Norbert ■	82
68	Carroll (Wis.)	86
59	Ripon	57
87	Knox	80
63	Beloit ■	80
70	Lawrence ■	69
71	Lake Forest	76
83	Monmouth (Ill.) ■	77
98	Grinnell	118
86	Lawrence †	77
101	Grinnell	91
66	Buena Vista	96

Nickname: Blueboys
Colors: Blue & White
Arena: Memorial Gymnasium
Capacity: 2,000; Year Built: 1951
AD: Gale F. Vaughn
SID: Jim Murphy

ILLINOIS ST.
Normal, IL 61790-2660 I

Coach: Tom Richardson, St. Xavier 1977
2002-03 RESULTS (8-21)

53	Utah St. ■	68
69	Central Mich.	74
65	Ill.-Chicago ■	78
68	Chattanooga ■	75
61	Kent St.	76
43	Western Ky.	63
74	Jacksonville ■	50
65	Northern Ill. ■	72
48	Southwest Mo. St. ■	76
65	Southern Ill.	74
64	Northern Iowa	66
57	Creighton ■	76
46	Southwest Mo. St.	60
66	Wichita St. ■	69
82	Creighton	95

(continued)

74	Evansville	85
76	Northern Iowa ■	71
89	Bradley ■	74
71	Wichita St.	85
60	Indiana St. ■	52
76	Bradley	88
48	Drake ■	59
65	Evansville ■	61
57	Marshall	53
63	Drake	70
80	Indiana St.	50
62	Southern Ill. ■	78
63	Drake †	62
63	Southern Ill. †	75

Nickname: Redbirds
Colors: Red & White
Arena: Redbird Arena
Capacity: 10,200; Year Built: 1989
AD: Perk Weisenburger
SID: Todd Kober

ILL. WESLEYAN
Bloomington, IL 61702-2900 III

Coach: Scott Trost, Minn.-Morris 1985
2002-03 RESULTS (22-6)

77	DePauw †	64
78	Wabash	64
79	Dominican (Ill.) ■	55
69	Chicago	77
75	Washington (Mo.) ■	88
104	Olivet Nazarene ■	67
87	Fontbonne	63
76	St. John's (Minn.) †	56
89	Wis.-Stout †	75
68	Neb. Wesleyan †	56
76	Beloit ■	61
66	Augustana (Ill.) ■	62
69	Millikin ■	54
62	Wheaton (Ill.)	55
64	Carthage ■	62
103	North Central	95
78	North Park ■	51
72	Elmhurst	74
75	Augustana (Ill.)	80
81	North Central ■	67
80	Wheaton (Ill.) ■	75
98	North Park	97
64	Carthage	75
70	Millikin	62
73	Elmhurst ■	65
79	Blackburn ■	59
85	Washington (Mo.)	73
68	Hampden-Sydney †	76

Nickname: Titans
Colors: Green & White
Arena: Shirk Center
Capacity: 2,680; Year Built: 1994
AD: Dennis Bridges
SID: Stew Salowitz

ILL.-CHICAGO
Chicago, IL 60608 I

Coach: Jimmy Collins, New Mexico St. 1970
2002-03 RESULTS (21-9)

68	Evansville	73
91	Eastern Ill. ■	78
78	Illinois St.	65
62	Indiana	91
73	Southern Ill. ■	71
73	Samford ■	45
70	Northwestern	53
78	Wis.-Green Bay	71
54	Indiana St. ■	57
77	Northern Ill.	45
65	Butler ■	68
102	Wis.-Milwaukee ■	92
69	Cleveland St. ■	63

(continued)

77	Detroit	74
81	Loyola (Ill.) ■	77
78	Youngstown St.	76
73	Detroit ■	80
89	Wright St.	76
81	Wis.-Green Bay ■	68
77	Wright St. ■	62
47	Butler	61
78	Wis.-Milwaukee ■	81
85	IPFW ■	64
87	Cleveland St.	74
83	Bowling Green ■	72
66	Loyola (Ill.)	65
73	Youngstown St. ■	47
79	Youngstown St. †	59
73	Wis.-Milwaukee	75
62	Western Mich.	63

Nickname: Flames
Colors: Navy Blue & Fire Engine Red
Arena: UIC Pavilion
Capacity: 9,200; Year Built: 1982
AD: James W. Schmidt
SID: Mike Cassidy

INCARNATE WORD
San Antonio, TX 78209 II

Coach: Al Grushkin, Oglethorpe 1975
2002-03 RESULTS (19-9)

55	Huston-Tillotson †	65
43	Tarleton St. ■	62
70	Angelo St. ■	65
73	Tex. A&M-Commerce ■	62
87	Midwestern St.	81
67	Ouachita Baptist †	62
70	Central Ark. †	54
63	Midwestern St.	60
56	Southeastern Okla. ■	45
108	Paul Quinn	74
68	Mo.-Rolla ■	49
76	Shippensburg ■	64
57	Tarleton St.	68
71	Lincoln (Mo.) ■	48
59	Rockhurst ■	55
76	Drury	73
85	St. Edward's ■	60
84	Okla. Panhandle	69
55	St. Mary's (Tex.) ■	70
60	Lincoln (Mo.)	63
71	Rockhurst	76
73	Drury ■	72
86	St. Edward's	71
77	Okla. Panhandle ■	84
79	Huston-Tillotson ■	60
45	St. Mary's (Tex.)	50
66	Rockhurst	61
47	St. Mary's (Tex.)	57

Nickname: Crusaders
Colors: Red, Black & White
Arena: McDermott Center
Capacity: 2,000; Year Built: 1990
AD: Mark Papich
SID: Wayne Witt

INDIANA
Bloomington, IN 47408-1590 I

Coach: Mike Davis, Thomas Edison, 1995
2002-03 RESULTS (21-13)

84	Massachusetts †	71
76	Gonzaga †	75
70	Virginia †	63
84	North Texas ■	58
80	Maryland †	74
91	Ill.-Chicago †	62
73	Vanderbilt ■	56
66	Purdue †	63
64	Kentucky †	70
64	Temple	71

76	Ball St. ■	62
70	Charlotte ■	60
78	Penn St. ■	65
69	Ohio St.	81
71	Northwestern ■	57
74	Illinois ■	66
69	Ohio St. ■	51
47	Purdue	69
54	Michigan St.	61
76	Louisville	95
61	Northwestern	74
62	Michigan St. ■	67
63	Michigan ■	49
59	Wisconsin	71
79	Iowa	63
54	Illinois	80
91	Iowa ■	88
74	Minnesota ■	70
66	Penn St.	74
77	Penn St. †	49
63	Michigan †	56
72	Illinois †	73
67	Alabama †	62
52	Pittsburgh †	74

Nickname: Hoosiers
Colors: Cream & Crimson
Arena: Assembly Hall
Capacity: 17,357; Year Built: 1971
AD: J. Terry Clapacs
SID: Jeff Fanter

INDIANA (PA.)
Indiana, PA 15705-1077 II

Coach: Gary Edwards, Va. Wesleyan 1979
2002-03 RESULTS (16-11)

73	Neumann †	63
93	Frostburg St.	76
64	Dist. Columbia	72
77	Concord †	73
83	West Virginia St. †	63
86	Bloomsburg	78
72	East Stroudsburg	55
74	Millersville ■	66
66	West Chester ■	82
77	Lycoming ■	66
69	Kutztown	80
83	Cheyney	79
65	Mansfield ■	74
69	Pitt.-Johnstown ■	44
63	Lock Haven	75
51	Calif. (Pa.) ■	62
71	Edinboro	73
72	Clarion	76
65	Slippery Rock ■	49
88	Dist. Columbia ■	72
90	Shippensburg	72
65	Calif. (Pa.)	78
81	Lock Haven ■	73
58	Clarion ■	63
88	Edinboro	59
72	Slippery Rock	66
82	Shippensburg	90

Nickname: Indians
Colors: Crimson & Gray
Arena: Memorial Field House
Capacity: 2,365; Year Built: 1966
AD: Frank J. Condino
SID: Michael Hoffman

INDIANA ST.
Terre Haute, IN 47809 I

Coach: Royce Waltman, Slippery Rock 1964
2002-03 RESULTS (7-24)

63	Youngstown St. ■	56
56	Valparaiso	81

68	Southeast Mo. St. †	55
59	Wis.-Milwaukee †	71
49	UCF †	50
45	Butler	65
63	Eastern Ill. ■	57
68	Ball St.	76
39	Murray St.	85
73	Ill.-Chicago ■	54
57	Wyoming ■	69
86	Evansville ■	60
55	Wichita St.	71
61	Southern Ill. ■	69
61	Northern Iowa	74
54	Drake	68
45	Bradley ■	63
48	Southern Ill.	60
46	Creighton ■	74
44	Southwest Mo. St. ■	48
51	Bradley	63
52	Illinois St.	60
63	Drake ■	62
51	Southwest Mo. St.	65
54	Creighton	77
63	Wichita St. ■	72
39	Northern Iowa ■	59
50	Illinois St.	80
69	Evansville	77
61	Northern Iowa †	60
56	Creighton †	57

Nickname: Sycamores
Colors: Blue & White
Arena: Hulman Center
Capacity: 10,200; Year Built: 1972
AD: Andrea Myers
SID: Kent Johnson

IPFW
Fort Wayne, IN 46805-1499 I

Coach: Doug Noll, Malone 1979
2002-03 RESULTS (9-21)

62	Colorado St.	80
71	Cleveland St. †	78
86	Fla. Atlantic †	93
53	Butler †	69
68	Oakland	95
76	Eastern Ky. ■	69
79	Lipscomb	73
66	New Mexico	91
78	Aquinas ■	84
62	Wyoming	73
46	Nebraska	63
71	Oregon St. ■	78
79	UC Irvine	96
58	San Diego St.	74
62	UNLV	74
86	IUPUI ■	80
59	Utah	76
73	Morehead St.	86
67	Chicago St.	63
71	Loyola (Ill.) ■	80
52	Middle Tenn.	71
54	Tex.-Pan American	59
70	Tex. A&M-Corp. Chris	68
65	Youngstown St. ■	63
61	Centenary (La.)	76
64	Ill.-Chicago	85
90	Centenary (La.) ■	76
75	Chicago St. ■	71
84	Wright St. ■	61
67	Maine	92

Nickname: Mastodons
Colors: Blue & White
Arena: Gates Sports Center
Capacity: 2,700; Year Built: 1981
AD: Mark A. Pope
SID: Michael Jewell

IUPUI
Indianapolis, IN 46202..............I

Coach: Ron Hunter, Miami (Ohio) 1986
2002-03 RESULTS (20-14)

66	Brown †	65
45	Notre Dame	89
79	St. Joseph's (Ind.) ■	58
52	Creighton †	99
62	Furman †	70
56	Northwestern	53
69	Ball St.	85
74	San Diego †	81
60	Middle Tenn. †	64
90	Cleveland St.	74
75	Bradley ■	73
98	Morehead St.	89
51	Western Mich. ■	75
79	Michigan	84
80	IPFW	86
96	Oakland ■	82
63	Oral Roberts	66
74	UMKC	65
62	Valparaiso ■	72
76	Western Ill. ■	62
56	Southern Utah	53
89	Chicago St.	69
77	Lipscomb ■	61
78	Oakland	79
73	UMKC ■	61
76	Oral Roberts ■	65
75	Western Ill.	59
71	Valparaiso	77
77	Southern Utah ■	58
67	Chicago St. ■	55
75	Western Ill. †	51
72	Southern Utah †	67
66	Valparaiso †	64
64	Kentucky †	95

Nickname: Jaguars
Colors: Red & Gold
Arena: IUPUI Gymnasium
Capacity: 2,000; Year Built: 1982
AD: Michael R. Moore
SID: Kevin Buerge

INDIANAPOLIS
Indianapolis, IN 46227-3697 II

Coach: Todd Sturgeon, DePauw 1988
2002-03 RESULTS (18-11)

69	Grand Valley St. ■	80
65	Southwest Baptist ■	57
91	SIU Edwardsville ■	82
74	Quincy ■	70
78	Southern Ind.	82
80	Ky. Wesleyan	87
92	Oakland City ■	81
76	Nova Southeastern †	62
75	Lynn	70
43	Barry †	44
73	Lock Haven	70
73	Northern Ky. ■	72
59	Wis.-Parkside ■	58
77	Lewis ■	68
84	Quincy	81
69	Mo.-St. Louis	54
67	Ky. Wesleyan ■	77
82	Bellarmine ■	73
91	St. Joseph's (Ind.) ■	79
76	Lewis	81
78	SIU Edwardsville	70
71	Mo.-St. Louis ■	67
63	Southern Ind.	78
104	Bellarmine	97
76	Northern Ky.	83
81	St. Joseph's (Ind.)	89
80	Wis.-Parkside	77
68	Lewis †	78
75	Michigan Tech	90

Nickname: Greyhounds
Colors: Crimson & Grey
Arena: Nicoson Hall
Capacity: 4,000; Year Built: 1960
AD: David J. Huffman
SID: Joe Gentry

IONA
New Rochelle, NY 10801 I

Coach: Jeff Ruland, Iona 1991
2002-03 RESULTS (17-12)

89	Lipscomb †	86
55	Florida Int'l	65
98	Bethune-Cookman ■	79
68	Rider ■	56
87	Wagner ■	81
78	Fairfield	83
78	Akron	85
68	Rhode Island ■	71
65	North Carolina †	56
63	Manhattan †	68
67	Fordham	64
87	St. Peter's	80
82	Canisius ■	73
55	Siena	65
86	Loyola (Md.) ■	74
78	Fairfield ■	82
88	Marist ■	74
64	Canisius	61
74	Niagara	86
92	Niagara ■	83
65	Siena ■	64
58	Rider	69
80	Manhattan ■	77
98	St. Peter's ■	89
74	Marist	75
82	Loyola (Md.)	45
58	Manhattan	69
62	Loyola (Md.) †	39
75	Niagara †	81

Nickname: Gaels
Colors: Maroon & Gold
Arena: Mulcahy Center
Capacity: 2,611; Year Built: 1974
AD: Shawn Brennan
SID: Mike Laprey

IOWA
Iowa City, IA 52242 I

Coach: Steve Alford, Indiana 1987
2002-03 RESULTS (17-14)

79	Fla. Atlantic ■	52
50	Drake	49
84	Tennessee St. ■	51
67	Florida St.	80
63	Montana St. ■	44
65	Southern Miss. ■	63
63	Northern Iowa ■	54
69	Iowa St.	73
87	Liberty ■	49
67	Tulsa	63
82	Missouri ■	88
68	Northwestern	63
68	Michigan St. ■	64
68	Illinois ■	61
61	Wisconsin	74
72	Ohio St. ■	83
72	Purdue	80
75	Penn St.	55
62	Michigan	70
64	Minnesota	77
84	Penn St. ■	71
63	Indiana ■	91
53	Wisconsin ■	61
71	Ohio St.	64
88	Indiana	91
54	Michigan St.	82

77	Northwestern ■	.61
64	Ohio St. †	.66
62	Valparaiso ■	.60
54	Iowa St.	.53
78	Georgia Tech ■	.79

Nickname: Hawkeyes
Colors: Old Gold & Black
Arena: Carver-Hawkeye Arena
    Capacity: 15,500; Year Built: 1983
AD: Robert A. Bowlsby
SID: Steve Roe

IOWA ST.
Ames, IA 50011 I

Coach: Larry Eustachy, Long Beach St.
2002-03 RESULTS (17-14)

87	Coe ■	.65
91	Mercer ■	.60
85	Jackson St. ■	.63
59	Western Ill. ■	.44
86	Binghamton ■	.56
78	Boston College ■	.85
73	Iowa	.69
79	Savannah St. ■	.59
76	Drake ■	.55
71	Northern Iowa	.64
90	Ark.-Pine Bluff ■	.46
54	Kansas ■	.83
50	Texas	.70
60	Oklahoma ■	.70
59	Missouri	.64
71	Nebraska ■	.61
55	Oklahoma St.	.68
74	Baylor ■	.70
69	Colorado	.84
73	Texas Tech ■	.88
51	Kansas	.70
54	Texas A&M	.66
64	Kansas St. ■	.61
81	Colorado ■	.55
63	Nebraska	.69
71	Missouri ■	.55
63	Kansas St.	.74
97	Texas A&M †	.70
74	Kansas †	.89
76	Wichita St. ■	.65
53	Iowa ■	.54

Nickname: Cyclones
Colors: Cardinal & Gold
Arena: James H. Hilton Coliseum
    Capacity: 14,092; Year Built: 1971
AD: Bruce Van De Velde
SID: Mike Green

ITHACA
Ithaca, NY 14850 III

Coach: Jim Mullins, Connecticut 1980
2002-03 RESULTS (12-13)

79	Lasell †	.76
71	Williams	.74
66	Cornell	.83
56	Catholic	.90
72	Cortland St.	.70
62	St. Lawrence	.73
52	Potsdam St.	.69
66	Geneseo St. ■	.68
53	Trinity (Conn.) ■	.68
71	Hartwick ■	.48
48	Utica ■	.39
73	Elmira ■	.48
54	Rochester Inst. ■	.68
67	Nazareth ■	.70
88	Oneonta St.	.55
74	Alfred ■	.63
85	St. John Fisher	.97
63	Utica	.54
83	Hartwick	.61
64	St. John Fisher ■	.67

77	Alfred ■	.63
82	Hobart ■	.72
88	Elmira	.58
53	Nazareth	.69
66	Rochester Inst.	.71

Nickname: Bombers
Colors: Blue & Gold
Arena: Ben Light Gymnasium
    Capacity: 2,500; Year Built: 1964
AD: Kristen Ford
SID: Mike Warwick

JACKSON ST.
Jackson, MS 39217 I

Coach: Andy Stoglin, UTEP 1965
2002-03 RESULTS (10-18)

44	Arkansas	.81
62	Southern Miss.	.80
79	New Orleans	.93
63	Iowa St.	.85
56	Mississippi St.	.71
63	Utah St. ■	.57
79	Stephen F. Austin	.103
68	Louisiana Tech	.73
70	Tulane	.94
58	Alabama St.	.70
82	Alabama A&M ■	.68
76	Alcorn St. ■	.72
86	Southern U. ■	.66
50	Texas Southern ■	.65
62	Prairie View	.65
95	Grambling	.97
71	Mississippi Val. ■	.73
58	Ark.-Pine Bluff ■	.62
91	Alcorn St.	.93
79	Southern U.	.72
80	Texas Southern ■	.63
75	Prairie View ■	.70
80	Grambling ■	.75
78	Mississippi Val.	.85
50	Ark.-Pine Bluff	.52
70	Alabama St. ■	.60
81	Alabama A&M ■	.72
66	Texas Southern	.68

Nickname: Tigers
Colors: Blue & White
Arena: Williams Athletics Center
    Capacity: 8,000; Year Built: 1981
AD: Roy E. Culberson
SID: Sam Jefferson

JACKSONVILLE
Jacksonville, FL 32211-3394 I

Coach: Hugh Durham, Florida St. 1959
2002-03 RESULTS (13-16)

85	St. Leo ■	.55
55	Cal St. Northridge †	.67
82	Grambling †	.68
60	Savannah St.	.47
65	Mississippi St.	.100
57	New Orleans	.90
61	Southern Miss. †	.62
55	Montana St. †	.64
76	South Carolina St. ■	.68
50	Illinois St.	.74
62	UNC Wilmington ■	.81
68	Troy St. ■	.70
68	Mercer ■	.71
75	Stetson	.71
73	Savannah St. ■	.53
74	Fla. Atlantic	.63
48	UCF	.72
65	Campbell ■	.51
87	Gardner-Webb ■	.75
57	Jacksonville St. ■	.56
52	Belmont	.84
43	Samford	.70
80	UCF ■	.75

89	Fla. Atlantic ■	.54
69	Georgia St.	.71
73	Stetson ■	.59
63	Mercer	.73
72	Troy St.	.94
57	Mercer †	.73

Nickname: Dolphins
Colors: Green & White
Arena: Swisher Gymnasium
    Capacity: 1,500; Year Built: 1953
AD: Thomas M. Seitz/Hugh Durham
SID: Jamie Zeitz

JACKSONVILLE ST.
Jacksonville, AL 36265-1602......I

Coach: Mike LaPlante, Maine 1989
2002-03 RESULTS (20-10)

64	Ball St. †	.72
73	UC Santa Barb. †	.66
75	Wis.-Green Bay †	.66
75	Alcorn St. ■	.72
101	Stetson ■	.82
74	Alcorn St.	.67
94	Me.-Machias †	.61
64	Maine	.68
52	Michigan St.	.76
82	Oakland	.76
82	Campbell ■	.78
88	Gardner-Webb ■	.69
89	Georgia St. ■	.76
69	Belmont	.87
62	Samford	.74
66	UCF ■	.68
83	Fla. Atlantic ■	.77
78	Savannah St.	.73
56	Jacksonville	.57
87	Savannah St. ■	.71
78	Mercer	.84
51	Troy St.	.71
84	Lipscomb ■	.60
74	Samford ■	.63
92	Belmont ■	.87
96	Lipscomb ■	.72
78	Georgia St.	.76
83	Gardner-Webb	.75
68	Campbell	.56
51	UCF †	.68

Nickname: Gamecocks
Colors: Red & White
Arena: Pete Mathews Coliseum
    Capacity: 5,500; Year Built: 1974
AD: Thomas M. Seitz
SID: Greg Seitz

JAMES MADISON
Harrisonburg, VA 22807............I

Coach: Sherman Dillard, James Madison 1978
2002-03 RESULTS (13-17)

68	Furman	.66
60	Georgetown	.80
67	West Virginia	.70
59	La Salle ■	.67
84	Akron ■	.82
71	Fla. Atlantic ■	.57
72	Denver †	.79
88	P.R.-Mayaguez ■	.58
66	Northeastern †	.69
76	Appalachian St. ■	.83
62	Drexel ■	.82
54	Delaware ■	.69
64	Towson	.51
65	Hofstra	.58
58	UNC Wilmington ■	.73
76	George Mason ■	.70
58	Va. Commonwealth	.65
56	Old Dominion	.74
59	William & Mary ■	.61

75	Hofstra ■	.69
62	UNC Wilmington	.73
74	Old Dominion ■	.66
71	Delaware	.74
67	Drexel	.78
87	Towson ■	.56
57	George Mason	.52
64	Va. Commonwealth ■	.63
72	William & Mary	.75
72	Towson †	.61
53	Va. Commonwealth †	.73

Nickname: Dukes
Colors: Purple & Gold
Arena: JMU Convocation Center
    Capacity: 7,156; Year Built: 1982
AD: Jeffrey T. Bourne
SID: Gary Michael

JOHN CARROLL
University Hgts., OH 44118-4581
....III

Coach: Mike Moran, Xavier 1973
2002-03 RESULTS (22-7)

58	Ohio Dominican †	.62
93	Alma †	.59
86	Hiram ■	.65
113	Lake Erie ■	.68
80	Marietta ■	.55
83	Muskingum	.88
74	Capital ■	.64
78	Wilmington (Ohio) ■	.49
69	Johns Hopkins †	.72
55	Misericordia †	.66
75	Heidelberg	.56
62	Ohio Northern	.77
69	Baldwin-Wallace ■	.63
87	Otterbein	.78
78	Mount Union ■	.63
76	Capital	.74
75	Muskingum ■	.71
84	Otterbein ■	.79
68	Mount Union	.72
85	Wilmington (Ohio)	.57
65	Heidelberg ■	.46
72	Ohio Northern ■	.57
98	Baldwin-Wallace ■	.80
70	Marietta	.66
90	Marietta ■	.76
86	Ohio Northern †	.73
94	Capital †	.86
85	Pitt.-Bradford ■	.65
75	Wooster	.77

Nickname: Blue Streaks
Colors: Blue & Gold
Arena: Tony DeCarlo Varsity Center
    Capacity: 2,250; Year Built: 1957
AD: Anthony J. DeCarlo
SID: Chris Wenzler

JOHN JAY
New York, NY 10019 III

Coach: Guy Rancourt, Western Conn. St. 1995
2002-03 RESULTS (10-16)

60	Ga. Southern †	.83
77	Me.-Fort Kent †	.93
66	Rutgers-Camden ■	.61
64	Hunter ■	.51
76	Vassar ■	.58
65	Baruch ■	.78
65	Merchant Marine	.71
38	Wm. Paterson ■	.59
68	Villa Julie	.81
69	McDaniel †	.75
49	FDU-Florham	.67
74	CCNY ■	.69
68	Lehman ■	.76
64	Staten Island ■	.72

61	York (N.Y.) ■	71
65	Brooklyn ■	58
60	Polytechnic (N.Y.)	45
72	Connecticut Col.	81
70	Hunter	80
64	Baruch	62
76	Purchase St.	62
77	Lehman	81
64	CCNY	80
73	NYCCT ■	69
79	Medgar Evers	61
61	NYCCT ■	66

Nickname: Bloodhounds
Colors: Blue & Gold
Arena: College Gym
　Capacity: 700; Year Built: 1989
AD: Susan Larkin
SID: Jerry Albig

JOHNS HOPKINS
Baltimore, MD 21218-2684......III

Coach: Bill Nelson, Brockport St. 1965

2002-03 RESULTS (19-7)

94	Emory & Henry ■	84
50	Trinity (Tex.) ■	48
67	Goucher ■	53
48	Rochester	72
85	Calvin †	84
66	Navy	61
58	Haverford ■	47
53	Gettysburg	70
72	John Carroll †	69
51	Springfield	76
97	Carnegie Mellon	85
77	Catholic	69
82	Washington (Md.) ■	69
80	Villa Julie	62
80	Dickinson ■	68
73	McDaniel	58
57	Frank. & Marsh.	84
63	Ursinus	79
60	Gettysburg ■	36
84	Muhlenberg ■	65
50	Swarthmore	71
75	Dickinson	65
65	McDaniel ■	37
68	Frank. & Marsh. ■	65
82	Gettysburg ■	78
62	Ursinus	78

Nickname: Blue Jays
Colors: Columbia Blue & Black
Arena: White Athletic Center
　Capacity: 1,200; Year Built: 1965
AD: Thomas P. Calder
SID: Ernie Larossa

JOHNSON & WALES
Providence, RI 02903 III

Coach: Todd Finn, Fitchburg St. 1993

2002-03 RESULTS (13-13)

88	Newbury †	67
60	Gordon †	82
63	Daniel Webster	59
74	Southern Vt. ■	76
61	Rhode Island Col.	76
81	Mass.-Dartmouth	99
88	Roger Williams	74
103	Emmanuel (Mass.) ■	101
71	Norwich ■	77
91	Rivier ■	82
103	Emerson	86
73	Western New Eng. ■	92
85	Suffolk ■	88
106	Albertus Magnus ■	81
93	Rivier	90
72	Norwich	59
71	Suffolk	77
78	Plymouth St.	97

101	Daniel Webster ■	74
75	Emmanuel (Mass.)	62
81	Emerson	77
94	Albertus Magnus	93
80	Salve Regina ■	85
89	Western New Eng.	95
71	Southern Vt.	81
56	Norwich ■	77

Nickname: Wildcats
Colors: Red, Gold & Royal Blue
Arena: Harborside Student Center
　Capacity: 1,500; Year Built: 1998
AD: John Parente
SID: Dave Bloss

JOHNSON SMITH
Charlotte, NC 28216...............II

Coach: Steve Joyner, Johnson Smith 1973

2002-03 RESULTS (20-9)

93	Allen ■	71
80	Catawba ■	67
60	Belmont Abbey	76
72	Millersville †	79
87	Mars Hill †	71
98	Lynn †	84
75	Queens (N.C.) †	87
97	Virginia Union	73
86	St. Paul's	77
84	Carson-Newman ■	78
86	Elizabeth City St. ■	73
92	Columbia Union ■	65
81	Carson-Newman	79
82	Fayetteville St. †	75
76	Bowie St.	94
113	Livingstone ■	80
60	Winston-Salem †	65
68	St. Augustine's ■	67
70	Winston-Salem	48
78	N.C. Central	84
91	Livingstone	72
76	Virginia St.	69
69	St. Augustine's	85
73	Shaw ■	66
78	Fayetteville St. ■	73
69	N.C. Central ■	68
88	Elizabeth City St. ■	79
63	Bowie St. †	65
58	Shaw	72

Nickname: Golden Bulls
Colors: Gold & Blue
Arena: Brayboy Gymnasium
　Capacity: 2,500; Year Built: 1961
AD: Henry White
SID: Kristene Brathwaite

JOHNSON ST.
Johnson, VT 05656-9464 III

Coach: Gregory Dixon

2002-03 RESULTS (10-16)

74	WPI †	84
77	New England Col. †	73
68	Plymouth St.	107
86	Norwich ■	93
60	Newbury †	70
84	Thomas †	65
96	Lyndon St. ■	82
66	Castleton St.	61
67	Plattsburgh St. ■	82
81	Maine Maritime	65
93	Middlebury ■	108
68	Elms	81
83	Becker	86
69	Gordon ■	70
80	Lasell ■	103
74	Castleton St. ■	93
79	Maine Maritime ■	74
70	Mount Ida ■	64

86	Becker ■	84
71	Elms ■	77
68	Mount Ida	81
87	Green Mountain	93
80	Lyndon St.	76
67	Lasell	95
86	Becker	71
65	Lasell	82

Nickname: Badgers
Colors: Green, Blue & White
Arena: Carter Gymnasium
　Capacity: 700; Year Built: 1965
AD: Barbara Lougee Fountain
SID: Gregory Dixon

JUNIATA
Huntingdon, PA 16652.............III

Coach: Greg Curley, Allegheny 1995

2002-03 RESULTS (13-12)

80	Penn St.-Altoona ■	53
76	CCNY ■	63
80	Penn St.-Altoona	61
91	Allegheny	84
82	Mount Union †	88
94	Messiah ■	73
71	Widener	66
63	York (Pa.)	77
57	East Tenn. St.	108
103	La Roche	97
87	Pitt.-Greensburg ■	90
84	Susquehanna ■	89
58	Elizabethtown	73
77	Albright	70
58	Moravian	75
80	Dickinson	81
68	Lebanon Valley	76
85	Widener ■	73
72	Messiah	60
81	Elizabethtown ■	72
56	Susquehanna	75
75	Villa Julie ■	60
76	Albright	74
58	Lebanon Valley ■	60
55	Moravian	76

Nickname: Eagles
Colors: Yale Blue & Old Gold
Arena: Kennedy Sports & Recreation Center
　Capacity: 1,500; Year Built: 1982
AD: Lawrence R. Bock
SID: Bub Parker

KALAMAZOO
Kalamazoo, MI 49006-3295....III

Coach: Rob Passage, Kalamazoo 1993

2002-03 RESULTS (18-6)

91	Lake Forest	88
64	Madonna ■	56
86	Goshen	73
70	Concordia (Mich.)	56
82	Marian (Ind.) †	91
102	Averett †	70
73	Chicago ■	59
78	Illinois Col. †	63
79	Wooster	72
71	Tri-State	58
70	Calvin	81
89	Alma ■	66
83	Mich.-Dearborn	54
65	Adrian	67
72	Olivet ■	65
89	Albion ■	82
35	Hope	100
74	Calvin ■	59
86	Alma	68
84	Mich.-Dearborn ■	62
67	Adrian ■	51
94	Olivet	76

| 64 | Albion | 72 |
| 59 | Hope ■ | 70 |

Nickname: Hornets
Colors: Orange & Black
Arena: Anderson Athletic Center
　Capacity: 2,000; Year Built: 1980
AD: Robert L. Kent
SID: Steve Wideen

KANSAS
Lawrence, KS 66045-8881 I

Coach: Roy Williams, North Carolina 1972

2002-03 RESULTS (30-8)

81	Holy Cross ■	57
105	UNC Greensboro ■	66
56	North Carolina †	67
73	Florida †	83
97	Central Mo. St. ■	70
78	Oregon †	84
89	Tulsa	80
113	Emporia St. ■	61
87	UCLA ■	70
80	California †	67
102	UNC Asheville ■	50
100	UMKC †	46
83	Iowa St.	54
92	Nebraska ■	59
98	Wyoming ■	70
81	Kansas St. ■	64
59	Colorado	60
74	Arizona ■	91
90	Texas ■	87
81	Nebraska	51
76	Missouri ■	70
82	Kansas St.	64
79	Baylor	58
70	Iowa St. ■	51
94	Colorado ■	87
70	Oklahoma	77
85	Texas A&M ■	45
79	Oklahoma St. ■	61
65	Texas Tech	56
79	Missouri	74
89	Iowa St. †	74
63	Missouri †	68
64	Utah St. †	61
108	Arizona St. †	76
69	Duke †	65
78	Arizona †	75
94	Marquette †	61
78	Syracuse †	81

Nickname: Jayhawks
Colors: Crimson & Blue
Arena: Allen Fieldhouse
　Capacity: 16,300; Year Built: 1955
AD: Allen Bohl
SID: Mitch Germann

KANSAS ST.
Manhattan, KS 66502-3355 I

Coach: Jim Wooldridge, Louisiana Tech 1977

2002-03 RESULTS (13-17)

64	Brigham Young †	73
50	Toledo †	58
82	Michigan †	71
55	Northwestern ■	59
76	Ark.-Pine Bluff ■	39
64	Wis.-Green Bay	68
102	Tex.-Pan American ■	68
79	Wichita St.	66
88	Lipscomb ■	64
90	Oregon St. ■	72
73	Monmouth ■	64
65	St. Louis ■	48
71	UCF ■	59
68	Texas Tech ■	44

                                    319

63	Colorado	69
64	Kansas	81
77	Nebraska ■	53
66	Texas A&M	79
89	Oklahoma ■	91
55	Oklahoma St.	63
64	Kansas	82
62	Colorado ■	54
63	Missouri	71
57	Baylor ■	66
61	Iowa St.	64
61	Nebraska	68
70	Missouri ■	77
60	Texas	74
74	Iowa St. ■	63
76	Colorado †	77

Nickname: Wildcats
Colors: Purple & White
Arena: Bramlage Coliseum
  Capacity: 13,500; Year Built: 1988
AD: Tim Weiser
SID: Garry Bowman

KEAN
Union, NJ 07083 III

Coach: Bruce Hamburger, Kean 1981
2002-03 RESULTS (11-13)

76	Drew	66
69	Springfield †	57
60	New Jersey City	59
71	Rowan	81
60	TCNJ ■	67
50	Wm. Paterson	63
84	Ramapo ■	68
62	Cabrini	67
97	Medgar Evers †	74
62	Scranton	65
73	Rutgers-Camden ■	51
83	Centenary (N.J.)	69
70	Rutgers-Newark	59
56	Montclair St. ■	74
59	Richard Stockton ■	62
51	Rowan ■	63
64	New Jersey City ■	57
60	Richard Stockton	61
66	Wm. Paterson ■	62
38	Montclair St.	59
70	Ramapo	102
74	TCNJ	56
76	Rutgers-Newark ■	79
77	Rutgers-Camden	83

Nickname: Cougars
Colors: Blue & Silver
Arena: D'Angola Gymnasium
  Capacity: 700; Year Built: 1958
AD: Glenn Hedden
SID: Jack McKiernan

KEENE ST.
Keene, NH 03435 III

Coach: Rob Colbert, Marist 1992
2002-03 RESULTS (22-8)

112	Castleton St. ■	84
82	Curry ■	46
82	Endicott ■	68
109	New England Col. †	58
73	Southern Vt.	72
87	Mass.-Boston	78
90	Southern Me.	67
45	Wis.-Superior †	37
77	Ripon †	84
83	Springfield ■	76
99	Rhode Island Col. ■	88
80	Western Conn. St.	85
84	Mass.-Dartmouth	94
70	Eastern Conn. St.	67
68	Clark (Mass.) ■	79
87	Mass.-Boston ■	65

62	Plymouth St. ■	65
95	Southern Me. ■	76
95	Tufts ■	79
80	Rhode Island Col.	73
87	Eastern Conn. St. ■	58
79	Lasell	74
80	Western Conn. St. ■	83
69	Plymouth St.	63
100	Mass.-Dartmouth ■	83
62	Eastern Conn. St. ■	61
76	Plymouth St. †	82
89	Gordon	84
95	Wheaton (Mass.) ■	90
71	Babson	81

Nickname: Owls
Colors: Red & White
Arena: Spaulding Gym
  Capacity: 2,100; Year Built: 1968
AD: John C. Ratliff
SID: Stuart Kaufman

KENNESAW ST.
Kennesaw, GA 30144-5591 II

Coach: Tony Ingle, Huntington 1976
2002-03 RESULTS (25-10)

84	Reinhardt ■	72
78	Tenn. Temple ■	65
74	Clayton St. ■	61
59	North Fla. ■	62
83	Chaminade	78
71	Hawaii Pacific	63
73	BYU-Hawaii	87
67	S.C.-Aiken	50
94	Columbia Union ■	76
94	Carver Bible ■	77
62	Middle Tenn.	66
76	Ala.-Huntsville	72
77	Montevallo ■	63
70	UNC Pembroke	62
85	Lander	68
65	Augusta St.	63
76	GC&SU ■	65
65	West Ga.	68
81	S.C.-Aiken	57
70	North Fla.	62
73	Clayton St. ■	70
56	S.C.-Spartanburg	66
69	Lander ■	63
61	Armstrong Atlantic	65
93	Columbus St. ■	77
62	Francis Marion ■	58
81	Augusta St. ■	57
73	GC&SU	63
63	Columbus St.	70
57	Armstrong Atlantic ■	63
79	GC&SU †	66
69	Augusta St. †	49
56	Columbus St.	72
74	Virginia Union †	65
70	Bowie St. †	95

Nickname: Fighting Owls
Colors: Black & Gold
Arena: Spec Landrum Centre
  Capacity: 1,008; Year Built: 1963
AD: Dave Waples
SID: Steve Ruthsatz

KENT ST.
Kent, OH 44242-0001 I

Coach: Jim Christian, Rhode Island 1988
2002-03 RESULTS (21-10)

93	Urbana ■	39
88	Southwest Mo. St. ■	84
82	Rhode Island	63
76	Illinois St. ■	61
91	Cleveland St.	68
89	Chattanooga	84
80	St. Bonaventure	93

86	Boston College †	83
88	Eastern Mich. ■	85
60	Miami (Ohio)	52
74	Bowling Green	78
69	Buffalo	68
71	Marshall ■	58
79	Akron	72
74	Toledo	69
82	Central Mich. ■	78
78	Western Mich.	71
70	Miami (Ohio) ■	60
73	Bowling Green	67
61	Northern Ill. ■	67
75	Ball St.	83
71	Ohio	74
98	Buffalo ■	55
78	Hawaii ■	79
67	Marshall	80
70	Akron ■	85
73	Ohio ■	62
79	Marshall †	57
73	Ohio †	70
67	Central Mich. †	77
66	Col. of Charleston ■	71

Nickname: Golden Flashes
Colors: Navy Blue & Gold
Arena: Memorial Athletic & Convocation Center
  Capacity: 6,327; Year Built: 1950
AD: Laing E. Kennedy
SID: Will Roleson

KENTUCKY
Lexington, KY 40506-0033 I

Coach: Tubby Smith, High Point 1973
2002-03 RESULTS (32-4)

82	Arizona St. †	65
61	Virginia †	75
80	Gonzaga †	72
84	High Point ■	64
98	North Carolina	81
76	Tulane	60
67	Michigan St. ■	71
70	Indiana †	64
63	Louisville	81
115	Tennessee St. ■	87
94	Alcorn St. ■	63
83	Ohio †	75
74	Tennessee	71
62	South Carolina ■	55
74	Vanderbilt	52
88	Notre Dame ■	73
67	Auburn ■	51
63	Alabama	46
87	South Carolina	69
70	Florida ■	55
80	Mississippi	62
87	Georgia ■	67
68	LSU ■	57
66	Arkansas	50
70	Mississippi St. ■	62
80	Tennessee ■	68
74	Georgia	66
106	Vanderbilt ■	44
69	Florida	67
81	Vanderbilt †	63
78	Auburn †	58
64	Mississippi St. †	57
95	IUPUI †	64
74	Utah †	54
63	Wisconsin †	57
69	Marquette †	83

Nickname: Wildcats
Colors: Blue & White
Arena: Rupp Arena
  Capacity: 23,000; Year Built: 1976
AD: Mitch S. Barnhart
SID: Brooks Downing

KENTUCKY ST.
Frankfort, KY 40601 II

Coach: Winston Bennett, Kentucky 1987
2002-03 RESULTS (13-16)

87	Ohio Valley †	57
65	Northern Ky.	90
78	Marshall	112
72	Fort Valley St.	68
76	Albany St. (Ga.)	65
83	Paine	77
89	Albany St. (Ga.) ■	82
82	Benedict	91
80	Paine	75
73	Wayne St. (Mich.)	89
80	Bellarmine	90
87	Clark Atlanta ■	91
81	West Va. Tech ■	67
83	West Virginia St.	67
78	LeMoyne-Owen	85
83	Miles	88
61	Lane	79
81	Central St. (Ohio)	96
81	Lane ■	82
104	Central St. (Ohio)	100
70	Western Ky.	104
78	Tuskegee	83
75	LeMoyne-Owen	69
82	Fort Valley St. ■	77
80	Miles ■	73
90	Morehouse	93
82	Tuskegee	93
87	Clark Atlanta †	81
80	Lane †	89

Nickname: Thorobreds
Colors: Green & Gold
Arena: William Exum HPER Center
  Capacity: 2,750; Year Built: 1994
AD: Derrick Ramsey
SID: Ron Braden

KY. WESLEYAN
Owensboro, KY 42302-1039 II

Coach: Ray Harper, Ky. Wesleyan 1985
2002-03 RESULTS (31-4)

105	Ill.-Springfield ■	73
73	Southern Ind. ■	61
73	Northern Ky. ■	74
87	Indianapolis ■	80
85	Gannon ■	64
74	Northern Mich. ■	58
93	Lincoln (Mo.) ■	61
101	Southern Ark. ■	75
106	Saginaw Valley ■	92
92	Lees-McRae ■	60
76	Wis.-Parkside	68
73	Lewis	96
102	Quincy ■	85
76	Mo.-St. Louis ■	51
110	Bellarmine ■	77
77	Indianapolis	67
109	St. Joseph's (Ind.)	83
109	Lewis ■	82
88	SIU Edwardsville ■	70
82	Mo.-St. Louis	54
80	Southern Ind.	84
89	Bellarmine	85
71	Northern Ky.	68
101	St. Joseph's (Ind.) ■	66
97	Wis.-Parkside ■	59
91	SIU Edwardsville	60
110	Quincy	93
102	Quincy †	86
79	Lewis †	84
81	Gannon †	74
83	Findlay †	66
95	Southern Ind. †	91
85	Cal Poly Pomona †	60
84	Bowie St. †	64
64	Northeastern St. †	75

Nickname: Panthers
Colors: Purple & White
Arena: Owensboro Sportscenter
  Capacity: 5,002; Year Built: 1949
AD: Larry E. Moore
SID: Roy Pickerill

KENYON
Gambier, OH 43022-9223 III

Coach: Dave Kunka, Ill. Wesleyan 1993
2002-03 RESULTS (3-22)
58	Chicago	93
68	St. John's (Minn.) †	72
69	Chowan †	87
83	Pitt.-Greensburg †	90
76	Mt. Vernon Naz.	95
58	Wooster ■	96
90	Bethany (W.Va.)	91
61	Muskingum †	91
84	Madonna †	97
66	Ohio Wesleyan	100
66	Wittenberg ■	81
68	Allegheny	83
69	Oberlin	67
91	Hiram	101
72	Earlham ■	84
61	Wabash	65
73	Denison ■	80
55	Wooster	92
93	Wash. & Jeff. ■	98
94	Oberlin ■	81
79	Allegheny ■	94
53	Denison	61
89	Hiram ■	72
72	Earlham	88
73	Wabash ■	81

Nickname: Lords
Colors: Purple & White
Arena: Tomsich Arena
  Capacity: 2,000; Year Built: 1981
AD: Peter Smith
SID: Marty Fuller

KEUKA
Keuka Park, NY 14478-0098 ...III

Coach: George Wunder, Rochester 1986
2002-03 RESULTS (13-10)
55	St. John Fisher	93
84	Oswego St. †	86
56	Nazareth	76
66	Centenary (N.J.)	83
70	Elms	66
66	Clarkson ■	60
69	Potsdam St. ■	63
50	Rochester †	75
68	Geneseo St. †	79
62	Brockport St. †	99
69	D'Youville	55
69	Practical Bible ■	62
54	Medaille	76
82	Cazenovia	83
64	Hilbert	60
82	Utica ■	62
77	Medaille ■	60
82	Cazenovia ■	76
89	Hilbert ■	69
72	D'Youville ■	65
76	Mt. Aloysius ■	70
77	Medaille ■	71
56	D'Youville †	70

Nickname: Storm
Colors: Green & Gold
Arena: Weed Physical Arts Center
  Capacity: 1,800; Year Built: 1973
AD: David M. Sweet
SID: Mike Damon

KING'S (PA.)
Wilkes-Barre, PA 18711-0801 ..III

Coach: J.P. Andrejko, Scranton 1988
2002-03 RESULTS (16-10)
97	Elizabethtown	112
56	Lehman †	36
69	Lincoln (Pa.)	57
65	Drew	58
60	DeSales ■	69
71	Muhlenberg ■	74
71	Marywood ■	60
66	Salisbury ■	50
83	Neumann ■	76
97	Baptist Bible (Pa.)	82
68	Muhlenberg †	69
93	Connecticut Col. †	55
79	Delaware Valley	54
86	Scranton ■	73
58	Misericordia	75
87	Lycoming ■	81
81	FDU-Florham ■	56
64	Wilkes	77
56	DeSales	74
77	Drew ■	64
71	Scranton	77
65	Delaware Valley ■	42
77	Lycoming	83
78	Wilkes ■	61
74	FDU-Florham	48
70	Scranton	71

Nickname: Monarchs
Colors: Red & Gold
Arena: Scandlon Gym
  Capacity: 3,200; Year Built: 1968
AD: Tom Baker
SID: Bob Ziadie

KNOX
Galesburg, IL 61401-4999 III

Coach: Tim Heimann, Knox 1970
2002-03 RESULTS (9-14)
82	MacMurray ■	78
72	William Penn ■	76
97	Concordia (Ill.) ■	73
79	Dubuque ■	74
79	Monmouth (Ill.)	65
80	Illinois Col.	79
75	Webber	94
71	Warner Southern	116
88	Grinnell	108
82	Greenville ■	90
89	Beloit	96
77	Ripon	87
70	Lake Forest	62
67	St. Norbert ■	73
95	Carroll (Wis.) ■	87
70	Lawrence	80
69	St. Norbert	67
80	Illinois Col. ■	87
80	Ripon ■	92
80	Grinnell ■	93
91	Monmouth (Ill.) ■	85
84	Lake Forest ■	88
96	Beloit ■	104

Nickname: Prairie Fire
Colors: Purple & Gold
Arena: Memorial Gym
  Capacity: 3,000; Year Built: 1951
AD: Dan Calandro
SID: Kevin Walden

KUTZTOWN
Kutztown, PA 19530-0721 II

Coach: Bernie Driscoll, Dickinson 1977
2002-03 RESULTS (18-10)
80	St. Rose †	82
70	Shippensburg	79
106	Columbia Union ■	62
81	Dist. Columbia ■	74
60	Slippery Rock ■	66
61	Calif. (Pa.) ■	56
75	Neumann ■	61
77	Lock Haven ■	66
80	Indiana (Pa.) ■	69
76	Shippensburg ■	68
91	Columbia Union	69
81	Edinboro ■	72
61	Clarion	64
79	Mansfield ■	76
77	Cheyney ■	74
88	Goldey-Beacom ■	61
71	East Stroudsburg	57
85	Bloomsburg	78
65	Millersville	87
79	West Chester ■	82
48	Cheyney	63
78	Mansfield	69
70	Phila. Sciences	82
77	East Stroudsburg ■	75
88	Bloomsburg ■	87
76	West Chester	71
66	Millersville ■	80
66	West Chester	74

Nickname: Golden Bears
Colors: Maroon & Gold
Arena: Keystone Hall
  Capacity: 4,000; Year Built: 1971
AD: Clark Yeager
SID: Josh Leiboff

LA ROCHE
Pittsburgh, PA 15237 III

Coach: Scott Lang, Clarion 1993
2002-03 RESULTS (14-12)
96	Wash. & Jeff. ■	85
67	Medaille	63
76	Thiel	87
81	Lake Erie ■	85
57	Grove City	77
84	Waynesburg	83
43	Wis.-Stevens Point ■	80
77	Bethany (W.Va.)	81
56	Westminster (Pa.) ■	69
97	Juniata ■	103
84	Wash. & Jeff.	80
62	Penn St.-Altoona	61
68	Pitt.-Bradford ■	79
65	Carnegie Mellon ■	73
81	Pitt.-Greensburg	73
50	Penn St.-Behrend	63
80	Frostburg St. ■	71
93	Mt. Aloysius ■	50
63	Lake Erie	59
74	Pitt.-Bradford	67
74	Denison ■	70
68	Penn St.-Altoona ■	59
75	Penn St.-Behrend ■	63
90	Pitt.-Greensburg ■	85
79	Frostburg St.	81
65	Penn St.-Altoona †	67

Nickname: Redhawks
Colors: Red & White
Arena: Kerr Fitness & Sports Center
  Capacity: 1,200; Year Built: 1993
AD: Jim Tinkey
SID: Scott Lang

LA SALLE
Philadelphia, PA 19141-1199 I

Coach: Billy Hahn, Maryland 1975
2002-03 RESULTS (12-17)
73	Delaware ■	56
70	Lafayette ■	66
80	Marist ■	97
67	James Madison	59
71	Villanova †	74
62	Cincinnati	65
63	Southern California	89
73	Cornell ■	59
82	Quinnipiac ■	71
83	Rutgers	75
72	Dayton	76
67	George Washington ■	49
47	Xavier	80
77	St. Bonaventure	87
78	Massachusetts ■	57
55	Richmond ■	62
66	Pennsylvania	79
70	Dayton ■	75
74	Fordham ■	61
82	Duquesne ■	74
65	Rhode Island	77
71	Xavier ■	93
67	George Washington	76
53	St. Joseph's ■	75
71	Duquesne ■	66
58	Temple	68
62	Richmond	75
74	Fordham ■	62
48	St. Joseph's †	68

Nickname: Explorers
Colors: Blue & Gold
Arena: Tom Gola Arena
  Capacity: 4,000; Year Built: 1972
AD: Thomas M. Brennan
SID: Kale Beers

LA VERNE
La Verne, CA 91750-4443 III

Coach: Terry Boesel, Oregon St. 1986
2002-03 RESULTS (16-9)
81	Cal Maritime †	72
96	S'western (Ariz.) †	65
83	La Sierra	45
98	Hope Int'l ■	68
87	La Sierra ■	80
94	Vanguard ■	83
94	Notre Dame de Namur ■	76
77	St. Scholastica ■	67
77	Gust. Adolphus ■	91
68	Chapman	63
80	West Coast Chrst.	69
87	Cal Lutheran ■	96
67	Occidental	78
55	Pomona-Pitzer	59
75	Claremont-M-S ■	73
97	Redlands ■	83
90	Caltech ■	58
93	Whittier ■	85
92	Cal Lutheran	98
89	Occidental ■	93
71	Pomona-Pitzer ■	66
68	Claremont-M-S	84
90	Redlands	95
81	Caltech ■	43
68	Whittier	82

Nickname: Leopards, Leos
Colors: Orange & Green
Arena: Student Center Gym
  Capacity: 900; Year Built: 1973
AD: Jimmy M. Paschal/Christopher Ragsdale
SID: Will Darity

LAFAYETTE
Easton, PA 18042.....................I

Coach: Fran O'Hanlon, Villanova 1970

2002-03 RESULTS (13-16)

68	Binghamton	77
66	La Salle	70
62	Arizona St.	85
47	Drexel ■	65
75	Princeton ■	89
87	Ursinus ■	70
64	St. Peter's	53
54	Massachusetts	52
83	Albany (N.Y.) ■	75
61	Columbia ■	52
73	Cornell	80
97	Centenary (N.J.) ■ ■	42
64	Colgate	66
73	Army	59
70	Holy Cross ■	76
66	Pennsylvania ■	76
73	Lehigh	85
48	Bucknell	68
67	American ■	66
70	Navy ■	52
60	Colgate ■	56
57	Army ■	43
65	Holy Cross ■	73
53	Bucknell ■	70
86	Lehigh ■	68
74	Navy	79
62	American	79
89	Colgate †	76
55	American †	74

Nickname: Leopards
Colors: Maroon & White
Arena: Kirby Sports Center
  Capacity: 3,500; Year Built: 1973
AD: Jeff Cohen/Bruce McCutcheon
SID: Phil LaBella

LAKE ERIE
Painesville, OH 44077.............III

Coach: James Dolan, Hiram 1959

2002-03 RESULTS (12-14)

54	Westminster (Pa.)	78
73	Pitt.-Bradford †	95
70	Medaille	65
65	Case Reserve †	55
68	John Carroll	113
74	Houghton ■	67
85	La Roche	81
80	Rochester Inst.	83
71	York (N.Y.) †	75
73	Notre Dame (Ohio) ■	59
84	Heidelberg ■	69
67	Edinboro	74
88	Frostburg St. ■	82
50	Penn St.-Behrend ■	60
93	Pitt.-Greensburg ■	96
76	Pitt.-Bradford	81
75	Penn St.-Altoona	60
63	D'Youville	70
71	Frostburg St.	69
59	La Roche ■	63
74	Pitt.-Greensburg	75
58	Penn St.-Behrend	67
73	Penn St.-Altoona ■	58
73	Pitt.-Bradford ■	67
90	Frostburg St. ■	81
44	Penn St.-Behrend	47

Nickname: Storm
Colors: Green & White
Arena: Lincoln Gym
  Capacity: 1,000; Year Built: 1978
AD: James Schweickert
SID: Justin Hamilton

LAKE FOREST
Lake Forest, IL 60045 III

Coach: Chris Conger, Wisconsin 1995

2002-03 RESULTS (8-15)

88	Kalamazoo ■	91
82	Eureka	87
66	Webster †	84
79	Benedictine (Ill.) ■	68
114	Grinnell ■	127
53	Trinity (Tex.) †	65
66	Southwestern (Tex.)	82
54	Chicago ■	66
62	Illinois Col.	88
64	Monmouth (Ill.)	61
68	Carroll (Wis.)	80
60	Lawrence	73
62	Knox ■	70
75	Beloit ■	56
62	Ripon ■	53
69	St. Norbert	71
88	Beloit	85
53	Lawrence ■	58
79	Carroll (Wis.) ■	62
76	Illinois Col. ■	71
85	Grinnell	94
88	Knox	84
61	Monmouth (Ill.) ■	71

Nickname: Foresters
Colors: Red & Black
Arena: Sports Center
  Capacity: 1,200; Year Built: 1968
AD: Jackie A. Slaats
SID: Mike Wajerski

LAKE SUPERIOR ST.
Sault Ste. Marie, MI 49783 II

Coach: Marty McDermott, North Dakota 1993

2002-03 RESULTS (12-15)

80	North Dakota St. †	83
49	Calif. (Pa.) †	68
86	Bellarmine †	77
75	Madonna	63
72	West Va. Tech	69
86	Northern Mich.	94
72	Michigan Tech	85
78	Finlandia ■	58
75	Finlandia †	78
92	St. Mary's (Mich.) ■	48
78	Mercyhurst ■	70
75	Gannon ■	83
59	Ashland ■	84
68	Wayne St. (Mich.)	74
71	Findlay	87
71	Hillsdale	85
75	Northland ■	47
77	Northwood ■	67
87	Grand Valley St. ■	73
85	Ferris St. ■	79
92	Saginaw Valley ■	79
78	Northwood ■	75
71	Ferris St.	85
63	Grand Valley St.	73
68	Michigan Tech ■	82
68	Northern Mich. ■	74
69	Saginaw Valley	80

Nickname: Lakers
Colors: Royal Blue & Gold
Arena: James Norris Center
  Capacity: 2,500; Year Built: 1976
AD: Bill Crawford
SID: Linda Bouvet

LAKELAND
Sheboygan, WI 53082-0359 ...III

Coach: Paul Combs, Ripon 1993

2002-03 RESULTS (19-8)

63	Carroll (Wis.) †	66
63	Lawrence †	73
80	Trinity Int'l ■	42
70	North Central ■	57
68	Concordia (Wis.)	84
63	Edgewood ■	52
78	Northland Bapt.	59
58	Wis.-Parkside	64
75	Wis.-La Crosse †	68
61	Clarke	57
68	Cardinal Stritch †	67
58	Benedictine (Ill.)	55
71	Viterbo ■	66
79	Wis. Lutheran ■	62
75	Marian (Wis.) ■	58
76	Rockford	83
61	Maranatha Baptist	55
56	Milwaukee Engr. ■	49
78	Concordia (Wis.) ■	58
58	Edgewood	48
69	Wis.-Whitewater ■	71
61	Wis. Lutheran	62
80	Marian (Wis.)	77
68	Maranatha Baptist ■	54
60	Milwaukee Engr. ■	50
60	Wis. Lutheran ■	55
87	Milwaukee Engr. ■	91

Nickname: Muskies
Colors: Navy & Gold
Arena: Todd Wehr Center
  Capacity: 1,500; Year Built: 1985
AD: Jane Bouche
SID: John Weber

LAMAR
Beaumont, TX 77710 I

Coach: Mike Deane, Potsdam St. 1974

2002-03 RESULTS (13-14)

69	Pacific (Cal.)	73
94	Tex. A&M-Corp. Chris ■	78
80	Texas Southern	87
45	Rice	62
86	Loyola (La.) ■	67
73	Wichita St.	92
67	Tex.-Pan American ■	63
47	Sam Houston St.	61
56	Nicholls St. ■	47
63	Southeastern La. ■	55
79	Texas-San Antonio	81
55	Texas St.	68
62	Stephen F. Austin	74
52	Texas-Arlington	50
79	Northwestern St. ■	63
81	La.-Monroe ■	56
58	Sam Houston St. ■	62
68	McNeese St. ■	65
74	Nicholls St.	62
57	Southeastern La.	67
53	Texas-San Antonio ■	61
64	Texas St. ■	53
73	Stephen F. Austin ■	77
60	Texas-Arlington ■	58
62	Northwestern St.	47
52	La.-Monroe	80
62	McNeese St.	72

Nickname: Cardinals
Colors: Red & White
Arena: Montagne Center
  Capacity: 10,080; Year Built: 1984
AD: Billy Tubbs
SID: Daucy Crizer

LANE
Jackson, TN 38301-4598..........II

Coach: J.L. Perry, Lane 1971

2002-03 RESULTS (13-15)

71	Ala.-Huntsville †	82
80	Montevallo	76
96	Rust	109
84	Paine ■	89
91	Albany St. (Ga.) ■	92
66	Paine	79
84	Benedict	85
90	West Fla.	99
64	Harding ■	107
79	Clark Atlanta ■	74
69	West Ala.	86
82	LeMoyne-Owen	86
74	Miles	68
95	Tuskegee	92
79	Kentucky St. ■	61
84	Morehouse ■	75
68	Clark Atlanta	95
66	Morehouse	73
82	Kentucky St.	81
79	North Ala.	84
92	Tuskegee ■	86
80	West Ala. ■	68
93	LeMoyne-Owen ■	91
88	Rust ■	77
79	Fort Valley St. ■	83
90	Miles ■	79
89	Kentucky St. †	80
89	Miles †	90

Nickname: Dragons
Colors: Cardinal Red & Royal Blue
Arena: J.F. Lane Center
  Capacity: 2,500; Year Built: 1974
AD: J.L. Perry
SID: William Head

LASELL
Newton, MA 02466 III

Coach: Chris Harvey, Worcester St. 1994

2002-03 RESULTS (22-6)

76	Ithaca †	79
77	Endicott †	61
77	Framingham St.	52
74	Curry ■	64
82	Fitchburg St.	74
77	Maine Maritime	62
69	Connecticut Col. ■	48
64	Westfield St.	59
70	Newbury ■	58
92	Mount Ida ■	80
66	Castleton St.	60
79	St. Joseph's (Me.)	85
65	Amherst	94
108	Castleton St.	92
103	Johnson St.	80
78	Colby ■	69
84	Becker	89
70	Elms ■	54
78	Western Conn. St. ■	69
99	Mount Ida	84
96	Becker ■	67
74	Keene St. ■	79
83	Maine Maritime ■	73
80	Elms	74
95	Johnson St. ■	67
82	Johnson St. ■	65
84	Maine Maritime ■	71
60	Southern Vt.	63

Nickname: Lasers
Colors: Columbia & Navy
Arena: Lasell Gymnasium
  Capacity: 300; Year Built: 1997
AD: Kristy Walter
SID: Jessica King

SCHEDULES/RESULTS

LAWRENCE
Appleton, WI 54912-0599 III

Coach: John Tharp, Beloit 1991

2002-03 RESULTS (18-6)

90	Milwaukee Engr.	77
73	Lakeland †	63
52	Wis.-Oshkosh ■	81
69	Marian (Wis.)	57
73	Beloit	51
82	Viterbo ■	53
120	Redlands	89
81	La Sierra	64
79	Ripon	64
57	St. Norbert ■	54
75	Illinois Col. ■	68
73	Lake Forest ■	60
87	Carroll (Wis.) ■	94
75	Monmouth (Ill.)	40
149	Grinnell ■	150
80	Knox ■	70
86	Monmouth (Ill.) ■	56
78	Ripon ■	72
58	Lake Forest	53
69	Illinois Col.	70
83	Carroll (Wis.)	77
72	Beloit ■	71
64	St. Norbert	72
77	Illinois Col. †	86

Nickname: Vikings
Colors: Blue & White
Arena: Alexander Gym
  Capacity: 1,000; Year Built: 1929
AD: Kimberly N. Tatro
SID: Joe Vanden Acker

LE MOYNE
Syracuse, NY 13214-1399 II

Coach: Steve Evans, Union (N.Y.) 1994

2002-03 RESULTS (17-12)

98	Alderson-Broaddus †	86
73	Pitt.-Johnstown	67
59	St. Rose ■	63
54	Bryant ■	53
50	American Int'l	46
79	Franklin Pierce	58
82	Assumption ■	78
76	Pace	77
84	Roberts Wesleyan ■	81
72	Brockport St. ■	77
71	Southern N.H. ■	83
59	Mass.-Lowell	74
74	Merrimack	75
68	Stonehill ■	60
80	Bentley ■	75
74	St. Anselm	72
87	St. Michael's ■	62
75	Assumption	83
76	American Int'l ■	64
69	Bryant	67
65	Pace ■	45
74	Southern Conn. St. ■	66
57	St. Rose	58
84	St. Anselm ■	88
80	St. Michael's	82
85	Medaille ■	62
75	Southern Conn. St.	91
85	Merrimack ■	74
88	St. Rose	94

Nickname: Dolphins
Colors: Green & Gold
Arena: Ted Grant Court
  Capacity: 2,000; Year Built: 1954
AD: Richard Rockwell
SID: Mike Donlin

LEBANON VALLEY
Annville, PA 17003-1400 III

Coach: Brad McAlester, Southampton 1975

2002-03 RESULTS (13-13)

65	TCNJ	75
78	NYCCT †	66
62	Dickinson ■	39
68	Ursinus	69
93	Susquehanna ■	62
81	Moravian ■	85
54	Alvernia	55
80	Utica/Rome ■	72
76	Richard Stockton ■	72
59	Lincoln (Pa.)	62
71	Delaware Valley	56
70	Frank. & Marsh.	75
64	Albright	67
68	Widener ■	77
57	Elizabethtown ■	69
47	Haverford ■	51
73	Messiah	50
76	Juniata ■	68
72	Moravian	78
65	Susquehanna	80
76	Widener ■	64
88	Albright ■	66
79	Elizabethtown	77
60	Juniata	58
85	Messiah ■	82
61	Susquehanna	73

Nickname: Flying Dutchmen
Colors: Blue, White & Red
Arena: Lynch Memorial Gymnasium
  Capacity: 1,400; Year Built: 1950
AD: Kathleen Tierney
SID: Braden Snyder

LEES-MCRAE
Banner Elk, NC 28604-0128 II

Coach: Randy Unger, Taylor 1976

2002-03 RESULTS (2-29)

56	Tusculum	90
87	Southern Va.	97
60	Hawaii-Hilo	86
69	Chaminade	71
56	BYU-Hawaii	83
48	Newberry ■	68
60	Coastal Caro.	70
60	Ky. Wesleyan	92
34	Tusculum	69
70	Southern Va. ■	69
66	Erskine	81
49	Longwood ■	75
63	Barton	101
60	Coker	76
50	St. Andrews ■	74
62	Mount Olive	96
89	Limestone ■	122
61	Anderson (S.C.) ■	75
59	Belmont Abbey	98
75	Pfeiffer	92
74	Queens (N.C.) ■	110
69	Erskine ■	73
62	Longwood	80
79	Coker ■	69
63	St. Andrews	77
64	Limestone	99
61	Barton ■	86
50	Anderson (S.C.)	84
63	Mount Olive ■	74
73	Belmont Abbey ■	87
78	Pfeiffer	110

Nickname: Bobcats
Colors: Forest Green & Gold
Arena: Williams Gym
  Capacity: 1,200; Year Built: 1975

AD: Ried Estus
SID: Barbara Russo

LEHIGH
Bethlehem, PA 18015-3089 I

Coach: Billy Taylor, Notre Dame 1995

2002-03 RESULTS (16-12)

68	Dartmouth ■	62
56	Illinois	90
83	Swarthmore ■	46
50	Hofstra	63
66	Tex.-Pan American †	52
66	Cornell ■	49
72	Harvard	84
67	Columbia ■	51
54	Stony Brook	48
62	Miami (Fla.)	68
68	Wagner	80
74	St. Francis (N.Y.) ■	68
86	Haverford ■	74
76	Navy	59
60	Bucknell ■	56
57	American ■	54
85	Lafayette ■	73
78	Army ■	61
39	Holy Cross	63
68	Colgate	77
68	Navy ■	46
61	Bucknell ■	49
59	American	69
59	Army	52
68	Lafayette	86
68	Colgate ■	75
64	Holy Cross ■	72
47	Bucknell †	52

Nickname: Mountain Hawks
Colors: Brown & White
Arena: Stabler Arena
  Capacity: 5,600; Year Built: 1979
AD: Joseph D. Sterrett
SID: Michael Garland Jr.

LEHMAN
Bronx, NY 10468-1589 III

Coach: Steve Schluman, Syracuse 1989

2002-03 RESULTS (15-13)

72	Clark (Mass.) †	102
36	King's (Pa.) †	56
62	CCNY	72
60	Baruch ■	76
81	Valley Forge Chrst.	75
88	Emmanuel (Mass.) ■	58
57	New Paltz St. ■	65
54	St. Joseph's (L.I.)	59
53	Wm. Paterson	79
71	TCNJ ■	80
86	Hunter	79
80	Centenary (N.J.) ■	79
73	Lincoln (Pa.) ■	57
76	John Jay	68
68	York (N.Y.) ■	53
73	Brooklyn	66
90	Medgar Evers	79
86	NYCCT ■	80
71	Purchase St.	62
73	CCNY ■	77
75	Baruch	71
67	Hunter ■	69
81	John Jay ■	77
69	Staten Island	84
74	Polytechnic (N.Y.) ■	62
84	Hunter †	75
75	Baruch	79
66	Baruch	81

Nickname: Lightning
Colors: Blue, Green & White
Arena: Lehman College APEX

Capacity: 1,000; Year Built: 1994
AD: Martin L. Zwiren
SID: Eric Harrison

LEMOYNE-OWEN
Memphis, TN 38126 II

Coach: Jerry C. Johnson, Fayetteville St. 1951

2002-03 RESULTS (14-14)

98	Ark.-Monticello †	86
71	Delta St.	86
78	Christian Bros. ■	73
75	North Ala.	89
65	Ala.-Huntsville †	70
65	Christian Bros.	86
92	Benedict ■	84
83	Paine ■	64
60	Fort Valley St. ■	69
87	Clark Atlanta	71
82	Morehouse	89
70	Albany St. (Ga.) ■	69
69	Fort Valley St.	72
86	Lane ■	82
85	Kentucky St. ■	78
71	Miles	81
93	Tuskegee	90
77	Benedict	64
56	Paine	62
45	Miles ■	48
85	Tuskegee ■	78
78	Albany St. (Ga.) ■	76
91	Lane	93
69	Kentucky St.	75
82	Morehouse ■	88
83	Rust ■	74
79	Benedict †	65
64	Morehouse †	66

Nickname: Magicians
Colors: Purple & Old Gold
Arena: Bruce Hall
  Capacity: 1,000; Year Built: 1954
AD: E. D. Wilkens
SID: Willie Patterson

LENOIR-RHYNE
Hickory, NC 28603 II

Coach: John Lentz, Lenoir-Rhyne 1974

2002-03 RESULTS (22-8)

92	Limestone †	64
65	S.C.-Spartanburg	68
68	Longwood ■	72
77	Virginia St. ■	63
68	Virginia St. ■	55
96	North Greenville ■	54
97	UNC Pembroke †	55
77	Armstrong Atlantic	42
67	Longwood	62
67	St. Augustine's †	82
67	Barber-Scotia †	54
75	Catawba	71
75	Newberry ■	59
60	Tusculum	69
69	Carson-Newman	66
47	Presbyterian	55
72	Wingate	71
65	Mars Hill ■	44
88	North Greenville	75
79	Catawba	77
64	Newberry	41
63	Tusculum ■	56
74	Carson-Newman	82
71	Presbyterian ■	61
67	Wingate ■	77
83	Mars Hill	63
95	Catawba ■	91
85	Wingate ■	77
71	Presbyterian ■	62
82	Bowie St. †	88

Nickname: Bears
Colors: Red (PMS 201) & Black
Arena: Shuford Memorial Gym
   Capacity: 3,200; Year Built: 1957
AD: Neill McGeachy
SID: Michael MacEachern

LETOURNEAU
Longview, TX 75607-7001........III

Coach: Bernie Balikian, Pt. Loma 1978
2002-03 RESULTS (9-16)
50	Stephen F. Austin	101
84	Concordia-Austin ■	64
58	Mary Hardin-Baylor ■	85
77	Texas Lutheran	72
92	Schreiner	69
71	Dallas	73
61	Hendrix †	63
81	McMurry ■	84
66	Hardin-Simmons ■	77
93	Cazenovia †	75
82	Howard Payne	114
70	Sul Ross St.	91
66	Jarvis Christian	73
80	Austin ■	74
79	Ozarks (Ark.) ■	81
54	Mississippi Col.	77
94	Louisiana Col.	99
85	East Tex. Baptist ■	78
72	Texas-Dallas ■	71
85	Texas-Dallas ■	82
72	Austin	74
86	Ozarks (Ark.)	74
83	East Tex. Baptist	103
55	Mississippi Col. ■	82
82	Louisiana Col. ■	94

Nickname: YellowJackets
Colors: Blue & Gold
Arena: Solheim Arena
   Capacity: 1,200; Year Built: 1996
AD: Bernie Balikian
SID: John E. Inman

LEWIS
Romeoville, IL 60446.................II

Coach: Jim Whitesell, Luther 1982
2002-03 RESULTS (23-8)
103	Grand Valley St. ■	63
73	Olivet Nazarene ■	62
72	St. Joseph's (Ind.)	74
68	Wis.-Parkside	61
75	SIU Edwardsville	64
85	Quincy	74
64	Winona St.	61
85	St. Francis (Ill.) ■	50
84	Ferris St. ■	71
80	Northwood	69
76	Southern Ind. ■	69
96	Ky. Wesleyan ■	73
71	Northern Ky.	83
68	Indianapolis	77
88	Wis.-Parkside ■	64
102	Judson (Ill.) ■	63
77	Quincy ■	62
68	Mo.-St. Louis ■	47
82	Ky. Wesleyan	109
99	Bellarmine	88
81	Indianapolis ■	76
78	St. Joseph's (Ind.) ■	66
89	SIU Edwardsville ■	70
54	Mo.-St. Louis	42
83	Southern Ind.	87
91	Bellarmine ■	66
72	Northern Ky. ■	76
78	Indianapolis †	68
84	Ky. Wesleyan †	79
55	Northern Ky. †	58
63	Southern Ind. †	82

Nickname: Flyers
Colors: Red & White
Arena: Neil Carey Arena
   Capacity: 855; Year Built: 1961
AD: Paul Ruddy
SID: Mickey Smith

LEWIS & CLARK
Portland, OR 97219-7899........III

Coach: Bob Gaillard, San Francisco 1962
2002-03 RESULTS (15-9)
73	N.C. Central †	86
60	Biola †	68
78	Claremont-M-S	71
73	Pomona-Pitzer	55
100	Evergreen St. ■	66
75	Ramapo ■	69
66	Linfield †	81
65	Pacific Lutheran ■	73
78	Puget Sound ■	69
70	Willamette ■	77
66	Pacific (Ore.) ■	63
72	Linfield	73
105	George Fox ■	69
102	Whitman ■	93
78	Whitworth ■	76
75	Pacific Lutheran	72
81	Puget Sound	72
94	Linfield ■	89
80	George Fox ■	49
65	Willamette	79
58	Pacific (Ore.) ■	46
49	Whitworth	60
80	Whitman	69
74	Willamette	79

Nickname: Pioneers
Colors: Orange & Black
Arena: Pamplin Sports Center
   Capacity: 2,300; Year Built: 1969
AD: Steve Wallo
SID: Kerry Kemper

LIBERTY
Lynchburg, VA 24502-2269 I

Coach: Randy Dunton, Baptist Bible 1984
2002-03 RESULTS (14-15)
54	VMI	68
62	William & Mary ■	61
80	New Hampshire ■	70
67	American ■	72
66	Western Caro. ■	63
77	VMI ■	69
74	McNeese St. ■	87
65	Clemson	78
84	Fla. Atlantic	79
49	Iowa	87
58	Virginia	77
77	Elon ■	59
80	UNC Asheville ■	81
74	High Point ■	70
64	Winthrop ■	74
81	Radford ■	66
57	Charleston So.	78
55	Coastal Caro.	54
55	Birmingham-So.	72
54	Elon	52
73	UNC Asheville ■	72
54	Charleston So. ■	48
79	Coastal Caro. ■	73
72	Winthrop	84
50	Birmingham-So. ■	53
68	High Point	72
56	Radford	81
63	Coastal Caro. ■	61
52	Radford ■	55

Nickname: Flames
Colors: Red, White & Blue
Arena: Vines Center
   Capacity: 9,000; Year Built: 1990
AD: Kim Graham
SID: Todd Wetmore

LIMESTONE
Gaffney, SC 29340-3799 II

Coach: Larry Epperly, Emory & Henry 1975
2002-03 RESULTS (10-17)
64	Lenoir-Rhyne †	92
71	Aub.-Montgomery †	83
65	S.C.-Spartanburg ■	72
89	Barton	100
81	Queens (N.C.)	96
80	Mars Hill ■	88
60	S.C.-Spartanburg	79
47	Mars Hill	59
60	Belmont Abbey ■	79
79	Anderson (S.C.)	72
75	Longwood	84
96	St. Andrews ■	93
122	Lees-McRae	89
118	Pfeiffer ■	115
78	Erskine ■	56
82	Coker	73
83	Mount Olive	90
98	Barton ■	107
75	Belmont Abbey ■	84
87	Queens (N.C.) ■	95
78	Longwood ■	72
86	St. Andrews	84
99	Lees-McRae ■	64
56	Anderson (S.C.) ■	72
89	Pfeiffer	108
70	Erskine	67
90	St. Andrews ■	93

Nickname: Saints
Colors: Blue, White & Gold
Arena: Timken Center
   Capacity: 1,500; Year Built: 1972
AD: Larry Epperly
SID: Fabian Fuentes

LINCOLN (MO.)
Jefferson City, MO 65102-0029..II

Coach: Bill Pope, Kansas 1988
2002-03 RESULTS (13-13)
79	Mo.-Rolla ■	54
58	Truman ■	47
61	Mo. Southern St. †	76
62	Pittsburg St.	88
72	Truman	65
72	Central Mo. St. ■	87
48	Arkansas St.	103
70	Ferris St. †	89
70	St. Francis (Ill.) †	67
61	Ky. Wesleyan	93
48	Incarnate Word	71
66	St. Mary's (Tex.)	67
70	Okla. Panhandle ■	77
81	St. Edward's ■	72
73	SIU Edwardsville ■	59
83	Robert Morris (Ill.) ■	58
67	Drury	78
60	Rockhurst ■	72
62	Mo.-St. Louis ■	55
63	Incarnate Word ■	60
75	St. Mary's (Tex.) ■	59
75	Okla. Panhandle	72
75	St. Edward's	58
67	Drury ■	76
64	Mo.-St. Louis	63
73	Rockhurst	87

Nickname: Blue Tigers
Colors: Navy Blue & White
Arena: Jason Gym

Capacity: 2,500; Year Built: 1958
AD: Patric Simon
SID: David Klopfer

LINCOLN (PA.)
Lincoln Univ., PA 19352 III

Coach: Robert Byars, Cheyney 1978
2002-03 RESULTS (8-16)
78	Lancaster Bible †	62
65	Lycoming	92
57	King's (Pa.) ■	69
56	Cheyney †	99
68	Gettysburg	83
86	Salisbury	97
65	Chowan †	73
56	Fisk †	87
51	Rutgers-Newark †	65
73	St. John Fisher †	72
60	Frank. & Marsh.	91
66	St. Mary's (Md.) ■	76
62	Lebanon Valley ■	59
57	Lehman	73
65	Wilkes	85
65	Wilkes ■	63
59	Frank. & Marsh. ■	83
74	Pitt.-Greensburg	75
77	Mt. Aloysius	72
65	Columbia Union	58
84	Gallaudet	76
54	Widener ■	60
71	Columbia Union ■	62
50	Farmingdale St. ■	64

Nickname: Lions
Colors: Orange & Blue
Arena: Manuel Rivero Hall
   Capacity: 3,000; Year Built: 1973
AD: Cyrus D. Jones
SID: To be named

LINCOLN MEMORIAL
Harrogate, TN 37752-1901 II

Coach: Jeff Tungate, Oakland 1993
2002-03 RESULTS (19-10)
59	Carson-Newman	72
71	Concord ■	51
61	Arkansas Tech	66
79	Central Ark. †	76
83	Carson-Newman ■	52
63	West Ala.	70
52	Tusculum	47
92	West Va. Tech ■	80
59	Concord	61
70	Ashland ■	56
71	Tusculum ■	54
74	Wilberforce ■	78
74	Calumet Col. †	48
75	Bluefield St.	67
68	West Ga. ■	62
62	North Ala.	65
65	Montevallo ■	60
58	Valdosta St.	64
85	West Fla. ■	72
80	North Ala. ■	66
95	West Ala. ■	75
56	Ala.-Huntsville ■	69
61	West Ga.	75
72	Montevallo	71
57	Valdosta St. ■	55
49	Ala.-Huntsville ■	46
72	West Fla.	70
78	Delta St. †	76
56	Ala.-Huntsville †	60

Nickname: Railsplitters
Colors: Blue & Gray
Arena: B. Frank Turner Arena
   Capacity: 5,009; Year Built: 1990
AD: R. Jack Bondurant
SID: Michael Peace

LINFIELD
Mc Minnville, OR 97128-6894 ..III

Coach: Larry Doty, Linfield 1978
2002-03 RESULTS (16-9)

75	Western Baptist ■	74
89	Warner Pacific ■	77
99	Southern Ore. †	94
79	Western Baptist †	75
66	Portland St.	84
75	Southern Ore.	90
105	Bridgewater St. †	80
81	Lewis & Clark †	66
80	Baldwin-Wallace †	72
84	Puget Sound ■	80
67	Willamette	87
73	Lewis & Clark ■	72
61	Whitworth	80
76	Whitman	83
123	George Fox ■	91
80	Pacific (Ore.) ■	74
80	Puget Sound	82
78	Pacific Lutheran	66
89	Lewis & Clark ■	94
83	Willamette ■	71
100	Whitworth ■	104
85	Whitman ■	74
90	George Fox	82
71	Pacific (Ore.)	73
95	Pacific Lutheran ■	88

Nickname: Wildcats
Colors: Purple & Red
Arena: Ted Wilson Gymnasium
   Capacity: 1,924; Year Built: 1989
AD: Scott Carnahan
SID: Kelly Bird

LIPSCOMB
Nashville, TN 37204-3951 I

Coach: Scott Sanderson
2002-03 RESULTS (8-20)

86	Iona †	89
65	Morris Brown	67
97	Milligan ■	61
77	Troy St.	95
73	IPFW ■	79
97	Tennessee St. ■	85
90	Tenn.-Martin ■	99
77	Troy St. ■	89
81	New Orleans ■	76
64	Kansas St.	88
73	Pepperdine	89
78	Chattanooga	87
71	Maine †	87
71	Sacramento St. ■	83
60	Nebraska	70
66	Savannah St.	76
68	Stetson	73
80	Campbell ■	55
69	Morris Brown ■	75
82	Centenary (La.)	93
82	Fisk ■	51
96	Savannah St. ■	73
61	IUPUI	77
85	Centenary (La.) ■	75
60	Jacksonville St. ■	84
90	Campbell	91
87	Stetson ■	64
72	Jacksonville St.	96

Nickname: Bisons
Colors: Purple & Gold
AD: Steve Potts
SID: To be named

LIVINGSTONE
Salisbury, NC 28144 II

Coach: Westley Gillum, Southern U. 1995
2002-03 RESULTS (7-21)

81	Benedict	74
79	Lander ■	75
79	Newberry ■	73
79	Clark Atlanta	74
57	Central St. (Ohio)	79
55	Mars Hill	70
65	Virginia St.	73
81	Queens (N.C.)	101
89	Benedict ■	80
88	Winston-Salem ■	79
53	Newberry	54
64	N.C. Central	73
80	Johnson Smith	113
78	Bowie St. ■	91
70	Fayetteville St.	84
61	Shaw ■	70
81	St. Paul's ■	82
72	Johnson Smith ■	91
56	Elizabeth City St.	57
81	N.C. Central ■	84
68	Winston-Salem	69
98	Brevard ■	69
82	St. Augustine's	106
80	Virginia Union ■	73
67	St. Augustine's ■	76
87	Brevard	97
83	Fayetteville St. ■	87
62	Shaw	73

Nickname: Blue Bears
Colors: Columbia Blue & Black
Arena: Trent Gymnasium
   Capacity: 1,500
AD: Clifton Huff
SID: Adrian Ferguson

LOCK HAVEN
Lock Haven, PA 17745 II

Coach: John Wilson, Washburn 1980
2002-03 RESULTS (10-17)

62	Virginia St. †	80
66	Bloomfield †	55
63	Mansfield	77
65	Fairmont St.	80
66	Kutztown	77
55	Cheyney ■	84
63	Southern Ind.	86
70	Indianapolis	73
85	Bloomsburg ■	69
65	East Stroudsburg ■	56
64	Millersville	81
62	West Chester	81
75	Indiana (Pa.) ■	63
72	Edinboro	74
78	Shippensburg	72
61	Calif. (Pa.)	75
60	Clarion ■	63
55	Slippery Rock ■	49
78	Pitt.-Johnstown ■	77
66	Edinboro ■	69
67	Dist. Columbia	87
73	Indiana (Pa.)	81
58	Calif. (Pa.) ■	60
79	Shippensburg ■	72
70	Clarion	68
55	Slippery Rock	50
60	Calif. (Pa.)	63

Nickname: Bald Eagles
Colors: Crimson & White
Arena: Thomas Field House
   Capacity: 2,000; Year Built: 1928
AD: Sharon E. Taylor
SID: Danielle Barney

LONG BEACH ST.
Long Beach, CA 90840-0118 I

Coach: Larry Reynolds, UC Riverside 1976
2002-03 RESULTS (5-22)

61	Charlotte	89
84	Cal St. Monterey Bay ■	73
63	Pepperdine ■	65
67	Southern Utah	79
58	UCLA	81
55	San Diego St. ■	64
68	Loyola Marymount	76
55	Gonzaga	90
49	Portland	54
52	UC Irvine ■	69
73	UC Riverside	77
53	Cal St. Fullerton	57
59	Idaho ■	55
55	Utah St. ■	63
77	Cal St. Northridge	85
60	Pacific (Cal.)	93
71	Cal Poly ■	86
68	UC Santa Barb. ■	67
79	Cal St. Fullerton ■	73
65	UC Riverside ■	68
67	Idaho	75
61	Utah St.	95
70	Pacific (Cal.) ■	61
71	Cal St. Northridge ■	77
46	UC Santa Barb.	70
64	Cal Poly	76
60	UC Irvine	95

Nickname: Forty Niners
Colors: Black & Gold
Arena: The Pyramid
   Capacity: 5,000; Year Built: 1994
AD: Bill S. Shumard
SID: Steve Janisch

LONG ISLAND
Brooklyn, NY 11201 I

Coach: Jim Ferry, Keene St. 1990
2002-03 RESULTS (9-19)

86	Virginia	90
76	Hartford	81
66	Binghamton ■	75
58	Delaware	87
78	Colgate	70
78	Albany (N.Y.)	62
89	St. Francis (N.Y.) ■	76
52	South Fla.	92
75	Belmont †	88
42	Northwestern	70
74	Monmouth ■	75
73	Fairleigh Dickinson	80
82	Mt. St. Mary's	69
76	UMBC	64
69	Mt. St. Mary's ■	72
73	UMBC ■	72
70	Central Conn. St. ■	80
69	Quinnipiac	80
98	St. Francis (Pa.)	94
99	Robert Morris	85
68	Fairleigh Dickinson ■	83
70	Monmouth	78
62	Quinnipiac ■	70
53	Central Conn. St.	95
140	St. Francis (N.Y.)	142
87	Wagner ■	71
73	Sacred Heart ■	79
66	Wagner	88

Nickname: Blackbirds
Colors: Black, Silver & Royal Blue
Arena: Schwartz Athletic Center
   Capacity: 1,000; Year Built: 1963
AD: John Suarez
SID: Greg Fox

LONGWOOD
Farmville, VA 23909-1899 II

Coach: Michael Leeder, Florida St. 1992
2002-03 RESULTS (15-14)

67	Mansfield	82
76	Stonehill †	80
72	Lenoir-Rhyne	68
87	East. Mennonite ■	52
76	Queens (N.C.) ■	72
75	St. Andrews	63
81	Virginia St.	78
62	Lenoir-Rhyne ■	67
58	St. Paul's ■	63
75	Lees-McRae ■	49
75	Erskine	69
84	Limestone ■	75
60	Anderson (S.C.)	73
83	Pfeiffer ■	99
82	Coker	64
81	Mount Olive ■	76
94	Barton ■	102
45	Belmont Abbey	81
63	Queens (N.C.)	81
80	Lees-McRae ■	62
79	St. Andrews ■	61
72	Limestone	78
73	Anderson (S.C.) ■	77
79	Pfeiffer	107
61	Erskine ■	58
69	Coker ■	57
63	Mount Olive	66
67	Coker ■	62
64	Belmont Abbey	76

Nickname: Lancers
Colors: Blue & White
Arena: Lancer Hall
   Capacity: 2,522; Year Built: 1980
AD: Rick Mazzuto
SID: Greg Prouty

LORAS
Dubuque, IA 52004-0178 III

Coach: Chad Walthall, Concordia-M'head 1991
2002-03 RESULTS (17-10)

84	Robert Morris (Ill.) †	72
84	Fontbonne †	64
56	St. Cloud St.	88
55	Cornell College	61
65	Mount St. Clare	53
83	Rockford ■	71
80	DePauw †	69
67	Aurora †	75
72	Dubuque	70
58	Luther ■	44
71	Upper Iowa ■	62
71	Coe	70
75	Buena Vista	86
70	Wartburg	79
68	Central (Iowa) ■	57
68	Simpson ■	57
70	Coe ■	61
88	Dubuque ■	53
70	Upper Iowa	72
67	Luther	63
66	Cornell College ■	77
69	Wartburg ■	72
58	Buena Vista ■	72
69	Simpson	68
70	Central (Iowa)	62
75	Simpson ■	57
65	Buena Vista	70

Nickname: Duhawks
Colors: Purple & Gold
Arena: Loras Fieldhouse
   Capacity: 1,200; Year Built: 1923
AD: Greg Capell
SID: Dave Beyer

LA.-LAFAYETTE
Lafayette, LA 70506....................I

Coach: Jessie Evans, Eastern Mich. 1972

2002-03 RESULTS (20-10)

79	Mississippi St.	76
74	McNeese St.	76
86	Birmingham-So.	92
117	Louisiana Col. ■	57
99	Alcorn St. ■	66
81	Bethune-Cookman ■	55
68	Detroit †	62
61	California	77
56	Colorado †	75
88	Loyola (Ill.) †	77
68	Charlotte	47
81	New Mexico St. ■	74
72	Houston	56
89	South Ala.	93
78	New Orleans	71
58	Providence	67
64	Florida Int'l ■	51
71	Middle Tenn. ■	65
89	North Texas	58
95	Denver	80
67	South Ala. ■	60
79	New Orleans ■	75
72	Denver	69
69	New Mexico St.	58
72	Arkansas St.	84
85	Ark.-Little Rock	81
94	North Texas ■	60
66	Western Ky. ■	69
68	Denver †	72
80	UAB	82

Nickname: Ragin' Cajuns
Colors: Vermilion & White
Arena: Cajundome
 Capacity: 12,800; Year Built: 1985
AD: Nelson Schexnayder Jr.
SID: Matt Hebert

LA.-MONROE
Monroe, LA 71209-3000...........I

Coach: Mike Vining, La.-Monroe 1967

2002-03 RESULTS (12-16)

65	Centenary (La.) ■	80
85	Tougaloo ■	80
71	Centenary (La.)	92
74	Baylor	79
90	TCU	79
57	Mississippi	80
66	Texas A&M	107
72	Stephen F. Austin ■	82
69	Nicholls St.	60
77	Texas ■	74
65	Texas-San Antonio ■	82
66	McNeese St.	81
75	Nicholls St. ■	52
74	Southeastern La.	67
66	Sam Houston St.	83
56	Lamar	81
58	McNeese St. ■	50
62	Texas-Arlington ■	78
86	Texas St.	102
71	Texas-San Antonio	61
75	Northwestern St.	63
70	Southeastern La. ■	58
78	Northwestern St. ■	83
78	Sam Houston St. ■	71
80	Lamar ■	52
58	Stephen F. Austin	66
84	Texas-Arlington	85
85	Texas St.	94

Nickname: Indians
Colors: Maroon & Gold
Arena: Fant-Ewing Coliseum
 Capacity: 8,000; Year Built: 1971

AD: Bruce Hanks
SID: Hank Largin

LOUISIANA COL.
Pineville, LA 71360-0001.........III

Coach: Gene Rushing

2002-03 RESULTS (13-12)

88	Pensacola Christian †	72
109	Concordia (Ala.) †	91
109	Schreiner ■	95
115	Texas Lutheran ■	83
66	Sul Ross St.	87
73	Howard Payne	90
57	La.-Lafayette	117
69	Rice	86
79	Mary Hardin-Baylor ■	76
70	Concordia-Austin ■	55
79	Hardin-Simmons	68
84	McMurry	92
95	Texas-Dallas	85
101	East Tex. Baptist ■	106
99	LeTourneau ■	94
74	Mississippi Col.	83
89	Ozarks (Ark.)	101
88	Austin	73
72	Ozarks (Ark.) ■	89
91	Austin ■	64
49	Mississippi Col. ■	61
87	Texas-Dallas ■	81
80	East Tex. Baptist	101
94	LeTourneau	82
81	Okla. Wesleyan	84

Nickname: Wildcats
Colors: Orange & Blue
AD: Sheila Johnson
SID: To be named

LSU
Baton Rouge, LA 70803.............I

Coach: John Brady, Belhaven 1976

2002-03 RESULTS (21-11)

68	Nicholls St. ■	24
71	South Ala. ■	62
77	Texas A&M †	79
65	Delaware St. ■	44
93	McNeese St. ■	72
95	Tex. A&M-Corp. Chris	60
75	Prairie View ■	49
66	Arizona ■	65
74	Tulane †	62
69	New Orleans ■	57
63	Georgia	89
80	Houston ■	51
85	Mississippi St. ■	72
112	Centenary (La.) ■	65
57	Mississippi ■	67
65	Arkansas	73
64	Mississippi St.	67
53	Florida ■	70
66	Alabama	75
71	South Carolina ■	58
54	Auburn	56
79	Vanderbilt ■	60
57	Kentucky	68
75	Arkansas ■	56
94	Auburn ■	63
88	Tennessee	67
77	Mississippi	64
66	Alabama ■	62
85	Arkansas †	56
65	Florida †	61
61	Mississippi St. †	76
56	Purdue †	80

Nickname: Fighting Tigers
Colors: Purple & Gold
Arena: Maravich Assembly Center
 Capacity: 14,164; Year Built: 1972

AD: Skip Bertman
SID: Michael Bonnette

LOUISIANA TECH
Ruston, LA 71272.....................I

Coach: Keith Richard, La.-Monroe 1982

2002-03 RESULTS (12-15)

55	Florida	76
77	Millsaps ■	49
38	Mississippi St.	78
60	Arkansas	72
76	Harding ■	55
73	Jackson St. ■	68
50	Texas	58
89	Southern Methodist ■	77
80	San Jose St. ■	67
53	Hawaii	57
67	Nevada ■	75
60	Fresno St. ■	61
61	Tulsa	68
92	Rice	93
79	Boise St. ■	76
73	UTEP ■	57
66	Hawaii ■	65
65	San Jose St. ■	60
93	Tulsa ■	82
80	Fresno St.	77
99	Nevada	97
63	Rice ■	65
71	Northern Iowa ■	76
57	UTEP	75
51	Boise St.	74
61	Southern Methodist	84
66	Nevada †	72

Nickname: Bulldogs
Colors: Red & Blue
Arena: Thomas Assembly Center
 Capacity: 8,000; Year Built: 1982
AD: Jim M. Oakes
SID: Chris Weego

LOUISVILLE
Louisville, KY 40292.................I

Coach: Rick Pitino, Massachusetts 1974

2002-03 RESULTS (25-7)

65	Air Force ■	47
84	Purdue †	86
90	South Ala. ■	79
91	Seton Hall	70
104	Eastern Ky. ■	63
89	Manhattan ■	62
104	Furman ■	63
81	Kentucky ■	63
72	Ohio St.	64
80	Charlotte	59
73	St. Louis ■	54
87	East Caro.	70
87	TCU ■	74
71	DePaul ■	43
72	Tennessee	69
94	Southern Miss.	65
95	Indiana ■	76
77	Cincinnati ■	71
81	Houston	55
58	St. Louis	59
73	Marquette	70
73	Memphis ■	80
80	Cincinnati	101
73	Marquette ■	78
82	East Caro. ■	76
76	DePaul	79
100	Charlotte ■	59
82	Tulane ■	66
78	Memphis	75
83	UAB ■	78
86	Austin Peay †	64
71	Butler †	79

Nickname: Cardinals
Colors: Red, Black & White
Arena: Freedom Hall
 Capacity: 18,865; Year Built: 1956
AD: Thomas M. Jurich
SID: Kenny Klein

LOYOLA (ILL.)
Chicago, IL 60611....................I

Coach: Larry Farmer, UCLA 1973

2002-03 RESULTS (15-16)

79	Loyola Marymount	85
88	Bradley ■	84
67	Northern Ill.	69
94	Tex. A&M-Corp. Chris	77
80	Valparaiso ■	62
86	UMKC ■	75
57	Belmont	75
54	Michigan St.	80
80	Wis.-Milwaukee	100
69	Charlotte	82
77	La.-Lafayette †	88
72	Colorado †	76
76	Youngstown St. ■	59
74	DePaul	95
67	Wright St. ■	56
74	Butler	81
74	Wis.-Green Bay	62
54	Detroit	72
77	Cleveland St. ■	65
77	Ill.-Chicago	81
80	IPFW	71
91	Wis.-Milwaukee ■	92
63	Youngstown St.	65
71	Wright St.	69
73	Butler ■	63
84	Wis.-Green Bay ■	73
76	Detroit ■	64
77	Cleveland St.	72
65	Ill.-Chicago ■	66
69	Cleveland St. ■	57
84	Detroit †	98

Nickname: Ramblers
Colors: Maroon & Gold
Arena: Joseph J. Gentile Center
 Capacity: 5,200; Year Built: 1996
AD: John Planek
SID: Bill Behrns

LOYOLA (MD.)
Baltimore, MD 21210...............I

Coach: Scott Hicks, Le Moyne 1988

2002-03 RESULTS (4-24)

83	Morgan St.	80
43	UMBC †	57
53	Manhattan	65
56	Fairleigh Dickinson ■	61
53	Niagara ■	60
62	UMBC ■	43
55	Mt. St. Mary's ■	58
56	Santa Clara	81
69	Northeastern	99
65	Central Conn. St. ■	63
60	Fairfield	72
58	St. Peter's	83
74	Iona	86
69	Marist ■	74
74	Rider ■	69
65	Siena	81
65	Canisius ■	79
54	St. Peter's ■	73
58	Maryland	85
65	Marist	72
58	Siena ■	75
64	Canisius	76
66	Niagara	79
44	Rider	50
49	Manhattan †	83

45	Iona ■	82
51	Fairfield ■	69
39	Iona †	62

Nickname: Greyhounds
Colors: Green & Grey
Arena: Reitz Arena
  Capacity: 3,000; Year Built: 1984
AD: Joseph Boylan
SID: David Rosenfeld

LOYOLA MARYMOUNT
Los Angeles, CA 90045-8235 I

Coach: Steve Aggers, Chadron St. 1971
2002-03 RESULTS (11-20)
85	Loyola (Ill.) ■	79
88	Sacramento St. ■	55
71	Villanova †	87
65	Montana †	62
65	Wyoming †	72
66	UC Irvine	81
75	Cal St. Fullerton ■	68
76	Long Beach St. ■	68
70	Cal Poly	72
71	Cal St. Northridge ■	74
68	Montana ■	75
71	Siena †	79
74	South Carolina St. †	69
69	San Diego St. ■	79
71	Pt. Loma Nazarene ■	73
73	Gonzaga	85
68	Portland	73
68	San Diego ■	82
75	Santa Clara ■	69
67	Pepperdine ■	70
60	St. Mary's (Cal.)	71
73	San Francisco	91
86	Portland ■	71
80	Gonzaga ■	74
73	Santa Clara	61
51	San Diego	73
71	Pepperdine	94
69	San Francisco ■	75
62	St. Mary's (Cal.) ■	67
65	Portland †	63
56	San Francisco †	70

Nickname: Lions
Colors: Crimson & Navy Blue
Arena: Albert Gersten Pavilion
  Capacity: 4,156; Year Built: 1982
AD: William S. Husak
SID: John Shaffer

LUTHER
Decorah, IA 52101-1045 III

Coach: Jeff Olinger, Luther 1985
2002-03 RESULTS (9-17)
59	Gust. Adolphus ■	71
56	St. Olaf	74
48	Wis.-La Crosse	72
73	Central (Iowa)	60
51	Mt. Mercy	75
60	Wis.-Oshkosh ■	72
36	Wooster †	59
85	Alma †	75
51	Cornell College ■	60
77	Coe ■	70
44	Loras	58
67	Dubuque	55
64	Simpson	76
54	Upper Iowa	51
55	Wartburg ■	80
63	Buena Vista ■	81
82	Simpson ■	74
55	Coe	56
56	Cornell College	69
67	Dubuque ■	63
63	Loras ■	67
74	Central (Iowa) ■	52

61	Upper Iowa ■	57
73	Buena Vista	75
48	Wartburg	58
47	Wartburg	65

Nickname: Norse
Colors: Blue & White
Arena: Luther Field House
  Capacity: 3,500; Year Built: 1964
AD: Joe Thompson
SID: Dave Blanchard

LYCOMING
Williamsport, PA 17701-5192 ..III

Coach: Terry Conrad, Bloomsburg 1983
2002-03 RESULTS (15-11)
105	Valley Forge Chrst. ■	73
92	Lincoln (Pa.) ■	65
80	Bloomsburg	90
82	Wilkes	80
96	Delaware Valley ■	51
85	Elmira	97
81	Mansfield	93
66	Indiana (Pa.)	77
104	Marymount (Va.) ■	90
96	Shenandoah ■	82
87	Susquehanna	92
75	Misericordia	72
75	Drew ■	67
65	FDU-Florham	62
69	Elmira ■	73
81	King's (Pa.)	87
77	DeSales ■	72
92	Scranton ■	69
92	Delaware Valley	74
67	Wilkes ■	66
81	FDU-Florham ■	63
87	Drew	89
83	King's (Pa.) ■	77
54	Scranton	83
67	DeSales	75
73	DeSales	88

Nickname: Warriors
Colors: Blue & Gold
Arena: Lamade Gymnasium
  Capacity: 2,300; Year Built: 1979
AD: Frank L. Girardi
SID: Robb Dietrich

LYNCHBURG
Lynchburg, VA 24501-3199 III

Coach: Andrew Miller, Kenyon 1995
2002-03 RESULTS (6-19)
73	Villa Julie †	63
54	Gettysburg	72
80	Ferrum ■	83
66	Greensboro	84
58	Hampden-Sydney	90
74	Emory & Henry	90
92	Averett ■	80
70	Ferrum	74
90	Guilford	81
61	Va. Wesleyan ■	70
85	Averett	80
86	East. Mennonite	69
50	Bridgewater (Va.) ■	68
51	Wash. & Lee ■	68
67	Roanoke ■	79
33	Randolph-Macon	59
80	Guilford ■	92
74	Hampden-Sydney ■	83
88	East. Mennonite ■	74
75	Bridgewater (Va.)	86
60	Va. Wesleyan	75
67	Roanoke	79
62	Wash. & Lee	63
78	Emory & Henry	79
65	Randolph-Macon ■	78

Nickname: Hornets
Colors: Grey & Crimson
Arena: Turner Gym
  Capacity: 2,400; Year Built: 1970
AD: Jack M. Toms
SID: Mike Carpenter

LYNN
Boca Raton, FL 33431 II

Coach: Andy Russo, Lake Forest 1970
2002-03 RESULTS (15-13)
69	Merrimack †	53
79	Bentley	86
75	P.R.-Mayaguez ■	59
78	Washburn ■	53
79	Wingate †	67
84	Johnson Smith †	98
94	St. Leo †	89
84	Fla. Memorial	65
60	Franklin Pierce ■	75
70	Indianapolis ■	75
93	P.R.-Cayey ■	62
82	Nova Southeastern	58
37	Barry	55
66	Rollins ■	71
78	Florida Tech	63
72	Fla. Southern	69
60	Nova Southeastern ■	61
76	St. Leo	72
62	Tampa	65
72	Eckerd ■	70
62	Rollins	78
97	Florida Tech ■	47
68	Fla. Southern	73
75	St. Leo	59
75	Tampa ■	63
62	Eckerd	67
47	Barry ■	59
50	Barry †	64

Nickname: Fighting Knights
Colors: Royal Blue & White
Arena: De Hoernle Center
  Capacity: 1,500; Year Built: 1993
AD: John McCarthy
SID: Jeff Schaly

MACALESTER
St. Paul, MN 55105 III

Coach: Curt Kietzer, St. Thomas (Minn.) 1988
2002-03 RESULTS (9-16)
67	Viterbo †	68
71	Upper Iowa †	65
73	Wis.-River Falls	86
60	Bethel (Minn.)	68
76	Augsburg	72
71	Concordia-M'head ■	68
71	St. Cloud St.	101
69	Northwestern (Minn.)	61
69	Carleton	76
70	Gust. Adolphus	65
66	St. Mary's (Minn.)	56
58	St. Thomas (Minn.)	61
63	St. Olaf	70
80	Hamline	78
84	St. John's (Minn.)	70
68	Bethel (Minn.) ■	73
69	Augsburg	79
74	Concordia-M'head	87
74	Carleton	81
57	Gust. Adolphus ■	59
75	St. Mary's (Minn.)	62
56	St. Thomas (Minn.) ■	67
69	St. Olaf ■	70
73	Hamline ■	81
64	St. John's (Minn.)	97

Nickname: Scots
Colors: Orange & Blue

Arena: Macalester Gymnasium
  Capacity: 600; Year Built: 1933
AD: Irvin Cross
SID: Andy Johnson

MACMURRAY
Jacksonville, IL 62650-2590 III

Coach: Bob Gay, MacMurray 1967
2002-03 RESULTS (9-16)
62	Ohio Wesleyan †	102
74	Heidelberg †	80
78	Knox	82
83	Millikin ■	75
73	Monmouth (Ill.) ■	75
68	Illinois Col.	90
89	Lincoln Chrst. ■	77
60	Washington (Mo.)	74
61	SCAD †	81
72	Robert Morris (Ill.) †	69
46	Carthage	89
84	Blackburn ■	95
71	Principia ■	68
86	Greenville	95
74	Webster ■	93
73	Fontbonne	82
80	Maryville (Mo.) ■	82
76	Westminster (Mo.) ■	96
66	Blackburn	77
73	Principia	81
81	Greenville ■	70
75	Webster	63
92	Fontbonne ■	82
97	Maryville (Mo.) ■	91
83	Westminster (Mo.)	81

Nickname: Highlanders
Colors: Scarlet & Navy
Arena: Bill Wall Gymnasium
  Capacity: 1,500; Year Built: 1975
AD: Robert E. Gay
SID: Andy Danner

MAINE
Orono, ME 04469-5747 I

Coach: John Giannini, North Central 1984
2002-03 RESULTS (14-16)
118	Me.-Fort Kent ■	61
77	Ga. Southern ■	91
65	Tulane	84
55	UCF †	72
63	Wis.-Milwaukee †	79
61	Clemson	73
82	Morgan St.	61
63	Rhode Island	69
100	Husson ■	68
68	Jacksonville St. ■	64
66	Weber St. †	69
87	Lipscomb †	71
62	Vermont	65
90	Albany (N.Y.) ■	71
64	New Hampshire	74
90	Northeastern	76
79	Binghamton ■	64
59	Vermont	65
79	Stony Brook	81
53	Boston U. ■	63
82	Hartford ■	71
77	New Hampshire ■	72
82	Albany (N.Y.)	71
75	Northeastern	55
62	Binghamton	63
62	Boston U.	65
74	Stony Brook ■	56
92	IPFW ■	67
58	Hartford	70
68	Northeastern †	71

Nickname: Black Bears
Colors: Blue & White

Arena: Alfond Arena
  Capacity: 5,712; Year Built: 1977
AD: Paul Bubb
SID: Julia Eberhart

MAINE MARITIME
Castine, ME 04421 III

Coach: Chris Murphy, Maine 1973
2002-03 RESULTS (15-10)

79	Me.-Augusta †	73
77	Thomas †	72
96	Unity ■	49
78	Me.-Machias ■	67
62	Lasell ■	77
73	Me.-Presque Isle ■	66
65	Johnson St. ■	81
78	Castleton St. ■	54
73	Colby	68
47	Bowdoin	69
63	Elms	75
81	Becker	70
61	Elms ■	53
74	Johnson St.	79
77	Castleton St.	80
57	Husson ■	78
80	Mount Ida ■	65
88	Thomas ■	67
73	Lasell	83
72	Mount Ida	62
49	Me.-Farmington	65
69	Becker ■	56
80	Castleton St. ■	73
71	Elms †	67
71	Lasell	84

Nickname: Mariners
Colors: Royal Blue & Gold
Arena: Margaret Chase Smith Gym
  Capacity: 1,000; Year Built: 1965
AD: William J. Mottola
SID: Katrina Dagan

ME.-FARMINGTON
Farmington, ME 04938 III

Coach: Dick Meader, Me.-Farmington 1968
2002-03 RESULTS (12-13)

83	Colby-Sawyer ■	72
65	Plymouth St. ■	83
59	St. Joseph's (Me.)	72
54	Me.-Machias ■	57
71	Thomas ■	54
105	New England ■	99
60	Husson ■	76
80	Lyndon St.	74
82	St. Joseph (Vt.) ■	71
76	Colby	80
76	Me.-Machias	81
87	Me.-Fort Kent	83
69	Me.-Presque Isle ■	71
88	Husson	83
62	Fisher ■	65
74	Bates	84
84	St. Joseph (Vt.) ■	57
73	Lyndon St. ■	69
95	Thomas	79
73	Bowdoin	77
51	Fisher	92
65	Maine Maritime ■	49
87	Me.-Presque Isle ■	71
72	Me.-Fort Kent ■	73
66	Lyndon St. ■	69

Nickname: Beavers
Colors: Maroon & White
Arena: Dearborn Gymnasium
  Capacity: 600; Year Built: 1963
AD: Julie Davis
SID: Gina DiCrocco

MANCHESTER
North Manchester, IN 46962....III

Coach: Jamie Matthews, Ball St. 1993
2002-03 RESULTS (16-10)

75	Goshen †	78
77	Wilmington (Ohio)	65
88	Maryville (Mo.) †	79
88	Fontbonne	81
71	Bluffton	58
82	Thomas More	62
60	Anderson (Ind.) ■	75
91	Transylvania	87
58	Albion ■	86
82	Oberlin ■	45
69	Alma ■	66
62	Elmhurst	85
80	Defiance ■	88
54	Hanover	85
68	Franklin	67
71	Ind.-Northwest	55
83	Mt. St. Joseph ■	71
80	Thomas More ■	71
79	Bluffton ■	73
77	Transylvania ■	72
65	Anderson (Ind.)	70
46	Hanover ■	74
78	Defiance	88
75	Franklin ■	71
94	Mt. St. Joseph	82
72	Mt. St. Joseph ■	80

Nickname: Spartans
Colors: Black & Gold
Arena: Stauffer Wolfe Arena
  Capacity: 1,700; Year Built: 1983
AD: Tom Jarman
SID: Doug Shoemaker

MANHATTAN
Riverdale, NY 10471 I

Coach: Bobby Gonzalez, Buffalo St. 1986
2002-03 RESULTS (23-7)

77	Sacred Heart †	62
65	Loyola (Md.) ■	53
85	Fordham	57
69	Yale †	70
76	Wright St. †	74
62	Louisville	89
72	St. Peter's ■	74
93	Hofstra	75
72	St. John's (N.Y.) †	65
68	Iona †	63
81	Marist	73
82	Siena ■	66
88	Niagara ■	71
76	Rider	66
86	St. Peter's	71
75	Rider ■	61
93	Fairfield	86
74	Seton Hall	70
71	Niagara	65
75	Canisius	72
74	Marist ■	53
79	Canisius ■	65
68	Fairfield ■	70
77	Iona	80
83	Loyola (Md.) †	49
68	Siena	72
69	Iona ■	58
82	Niagara †	81
69	Fairfield †	54
65	Syracuse †	76

Nickname: Jaspers
Colors: Kelly Green & White
Arena: Draddy Gymnasium
  Capacity: 3,000; Year Built: 1979
AD: Robert J. Byrnes
SID: Adrienne J. Mullikin

MANHATTANVILLE
Purchase, NY 10577 III

Coach: Brian Curtin, St. Michael's 1987
2002-03 RESULTS (19-10)

61	Rowan	90
64	Yeshiva	56
64	Old Westbury	61
64	Vassar	74
54	Staten Island ■	59
34	Quinnipiac	58
78	Mt. St. Vincent ■	59
67	St. Joseph's (L.I.) ■	73
72	Skidmore	67
71	Merchant Marine ■	58
85	Centenary (N.J.) ■	74
45	Mt. St. Mary (N.Y.) ■	46
70	Stevens Institute	59
57	Maritime (N.Y.)	52
76	Purchase St. ■	63
81	Farmingdale St. ■	73
77	Hunter	71
77	Merchant Marine	82
60	Yeshiva ■	57
53	St. Joseph's (L.I.)	43
71	Old Westbury ■	74
75	Mt. St. Mary (N.Y.)	69
73	Stevens Institute ■	63
91	Mt. St. Vincent	67
58	Maritime (N.Y.) ■	45
53	Stevens Institute ■	46
79	Mt. St. Mary (N.Y.)	81
67	Richard Stockton ■	64
56	Baruch	60

Nickname: Valiants
Colors: Red & White
Arena: Kennedy Gymnasium
  Capacity: 700; Year Built: 1947
AD: Gail A. Lozado
SID: Ken Johnson Jr.

MANSFIELD
Mansfield, PA 16933 II

Coach: Vince Alexander, Okla. Baptist 1989
2002-03 RESULTS (18-11)

82	Longwood ■	67
84	N.J. Inst. of Tech. ■	77
68	Daemen	70
92	Daemen ■	80
77	Lock Haven ■	63
68	N.J. Inst. of Tech.	59
93	Lycoming ■	81
75	Slippery Rock	57
62	Calif. (Pa.)	67
68	Holy Family	66
80	Edinboro ■	85
82	Clarion ■	87
74	Roberts Wesleyan ■	67
74	Indiana (Pa.)	65
90	Shippensburg	76
76	Kutztown	79
62	Millersville ■	70
73	Bloomsburg ■	64
83	Cheyney ■	78
60	West Chester	84
65	East Stroudsburg	53
81	Millersville	90
69	Kutztown ■	78
70	Cheyney	76
71	Bloomsburg	70
81	East Stroudsburg ■	73
72	West Chester ■	70
63	Millersville	83
83	N.J. Inst. of Tech. ■	73

Nickname: Mountaineers
Colors: Red & Black
Arena: Decker Gymnasium
  Capacity: 2,500; Year Built: 1970

AD: Roger N. Maisner
SID: Steve McCloskey

MARANATHA BAPTIST
Watertown, WI 53094 III

Coach: Jerry Terrill, Illinois St. 1964
2002-03 RESULTS (12-16)

66	Ripon †	83
68	Beloit †	71
80	Emmaus ■	61
80	Emmaus †	57
67	Grace Bible (Mich.) †	52
72	Milwaukee Engr.	69
72	Northland Bapt.	64
49	Viterbo ■	64
59	Marian (Wis.)	62
71	Lincoln Chrst. ■	52
57	Edgewood ■	67
66	Concordia (Wis.)	64
55	Lakeland ■	61
80	Wis. Lutheran	88
47	Marian (Wis.) ■	49
66	Moody Bible	55
53	Milwaukee Engr. ■	61
53	Concordia (Wis.) ■	78
59	Edgewood	70
54	Lakeland	68
76	Wis. Lutheran ■	87
90	Edgewood	79
62	Milwaukee Engr.	68
66	Northland Bapt. †	52
79	Lincoln Chrst. ■	45
72	Ky. Christian †	57
63	Mid-America Bible †	77
82	Simpson (Cal.) †	92

Nickname: Crusaders
Colors: Navy Blue & Gold
Arena: Willis Denny Gym
  Capacity: 1,000
AD: Terry Price
SID: Greg Wright

MARIAN (WIS.)
Fond Du Lac, WI 54935-4699..III

Coach: Mark Boyle, Wis.-Eau Claire 1978
2002-03 RESULTS (8-18)

69	Beloit ■	75
69	Ripon ■	82
52	Concordia (Ill.)	56
50	Wis.-Stevens Point ■	72
36	Wis.-Oshkosh ■	88
57	Lawrence	69
76	Illinois Tech ■	54
65	Milwaukee Engr.	61
65	Rockford ■	69
84	Eureka ■	81
77	Concordia (Wis.) ■	79
49	Clarke	64
62	Maranatha Baptist ■	59
60	Wis.-River Falls	96
61	Edgewood	73
58	Lakeland	75
62	Wis. Lutheran ■	60
68	Cardinal Stritch	99
49	Maranatha Baptist	47
65	Milwaukee Engr. ■	68
73	Concordia (Wis.)	61
60	Edgewood	65
77	Lakeland ■	80
54	Wis. Lutheran	63
84	Northland Bapt. ■	67
63	Wis. Lutheran	71

Nickname: Sabres
Colors: Blue, White & Scarlet
Arena: Sadoff Gym
  Capacity: 1,000; Year Built: 1982
AD: Doug Hammonds
SID: Chris Zills

SCHEDULES/RESULTS

MARIETTA
Marietta, OH 45750 III

Coach: Doug Foote, Morehead St. 1983

2002-03 RESULTS (10-17)

67	Cazenovia †	53
56	Elmira †	58
53	Elmira †	68
85	Penn St.-Altoona	51
72	Ohio Valley	65
55	John Carroll	80
51	Ohio Northern	72
56	Capital	89
63	Baldwin-Wallace	74
62	Notre Dame (Ohio) ■	50
42	SCAD ■	51
73	Otterbein ■	65
75	Heidelberg	71
60	Mount Union	69
71	Wilmington (Ohio) ■	40
54	Muskingum	58
46	Ohio Northern ■	63
53	Capital ■	64
34	Wilmington (Ohio)	57
71	Muskingum ■	60
94	Baldwin-Wallace ■	101
55	Otterbein	60
69	Heidelberg ■	56
68	Mount Union ■	78
66	John Carroll ■	70
78	Heidelberg ■	72
76	John Carroll	90

Nickname: Pioneers
Colors: Navy Blue & White
Arena: Ban Johnson Gymnasium
  Capacity: 1,457; Year Built: 1929
AD: Debora Lazorik
SID: Nicole Peloquin

MARIST
Poughkeepsie, NY 12601-1387 ... I

Coach: Dave Magarity, St. Francis (Pa.) 1974

2002-03 RESULTS (13-16)

72	Colgate ■	65
63	Vermont ■	66
97	La Salle	80
72	Rider	70
53	Georgia Tech †	67
77	Fairfield ■	86
66	Central Mich. ■	88
73	South Ala.	93
66	Holy Cross ■	63
74	Army ■	57
65	Northern Ariz.	68
73	Manhattan ■	81
68	Niagara ■	76
83	Canisius ■	78
74	Loyola (Md.)	69
74	Iona	88
68	Siena ■	81
60	Rider ■	73
79	Siena	74
53	Manhattan	74
72	Loyola (Md.) ■	65
68	St. Peter's	72
56	Fairfield	67
91	St. Peter's †	86
75	Iona ■	74
73	Canisius	68
87	Niagara	88
69	Canisius †	63
68	Siena †	70

Nickname: Red Foxes
Colors: Red & White
Arena: McCann Recreation Center
  Capacity: 3,944; Year Built: 1977
AD: Timothy S. Murray
SID: Jill Skotarczak

MARITIME (N.Y.)
Bronx, NY 10465 III

Coach: David Summa

2002-03 RESULTS (3-23)

61	Ramapo	114
81	Medgar Evers †	64
65	Polytechnic (N.Y.) ■	66
58	Baruch ■	70
76	Yeshiva ■	69
52	Mt. St. Vincent ■	72
60	Farmingdale St. ■	64
53	Merchant Marine	73
40	Union (N.Y.)	76
50	Cortland St. †	70
59	Old Westbury	66
63	Stevens Institute ■	64
47	St. Joseph's (L.I.)	68
77	Brooklyn ■	57
52	Manhattanville ■	57
44	Stevens Institute	70
75	Mt. St. Mary (N.Y.) ■	87
61	Old Westbury ■	75
58	Mt. St. Vincent	60
60	Yeshiva	62
57	Merchant Marine ■	66
52	St. Joseph's (L.I.) ■	66
82	Centenary (N.J.)	86
68	Mt. St. Mary (N.Y.)	106
45	Manhattanville	58
52	Yeshiva	68

Nickname: Privateers
Colors: Cardinal, Navy & White
Arena: Riesenberg Hall
  Capacity: 800; Year Built: 1964
AD: James Migli
SID: Damian Becker

MARQUETTE
Milwaukee, WI 53201-1881 I

Coach: Tom Crean, Central Mich. 1989

2002-03 RESULTS (27-6)

73	Villanova †	61
64	Coppin St. ■	46
80	Texas-San Antonio ■	68
97	Eastern Ill. ■	74
71	Notre Dame	92
101	Appalachian St. ■	78
63	Wisconsin ■	54
89	Elon ■	57
105	Grambling ■	74
70	East Caro.	73
85	Dayton	92
60	St. Louis	54
96	South Fla. ■	63
85	Tulane	73
67	Charlotte	64
72	DePaul ■	51
80	East Caro. ■	48
82	Cincinnati	76
68	St. Louis ■	64
68	Wake Forest ■	61
73	DePaul	60
70	Louisville ■	73
75	Charlotte ■	67
79	TCU	68
78	Louisville	73
98	UAB ■	87
70	Cincinnati ■	61
76	UAB †	83
72	Holy Cross †	68
101	Missouri †	92
77	Pittsburgh †	74
83	Kentucky †	69
61	Kansas †	94

Nickname: Golden Eagles
Colors: Blue & Gold
Arena: Bradley Center
  Capacity: 19,150; Year Built: 1988

AD: William L. Cords
SID: John Farina

MARS HILL
Mars Hill, NC 28754 II

Coach: Terry Rogers, Gardner-Webb 1971

2002-03 RESULTS (13-15)

72	Appalachian St.	104
52	Southern Wesleyan ■	50
100	North Greenville ■	75
71	Johnson Smith †	87
73	Wingate †	74
69	Newberry †	67
94	Montreat ■	90
70	Livingstone	55
88	Limestone ■	80
59	Limestone ■	47
64	Southern Wesleyan	54
79	Winston-Salem ■	70
60	Newberry	58
53	Carson-Newman ■	56
67	Catawba ■	76
69	North Greenville	57
60	Presbyterian ■	64
56	Wingate ■	78
63	Tusculum	66
44	Lenoir-Rhyne	65
78	Newberry ■	53
59	Carson-Newman	70
72	Catawba ■	78
56	Presbyterian	68
85	Wingate	100
65	Tusculum ■	57
63	Lenoir-Rhyne ■	83
80	Wingate	84

Nickname: Lions
Colors: Royal Blue & Gold
Arena: Stanford Arena
  Capacity: 2,300; Year Built: 1969
AD: David Riggins
SID: Rick Baker

MARSHALL
Huntington, WV 25755 I

Coach: Greg White, Marshall 1982

2002-03 RESULTS (14-15)

92	Niagara	90
112	Kentucky St. ■	78
56	Rutgers	75
75	Northern Ill.	57
90	Radford	65
100	Morehead St.	101
83	Western Caro. ■	68
58	Massachusetts	81
66	Western Mich.	54
69	Buffalo	63
79	Toledo ■	58
78	Central Mich. ■	81
58	Kent St.	71
61	West Virginia †	65
87	Buffalo ■	77
75	Ball St.	96
85	Ohio ■	87
81	Eastern Mich.	90
75	Western Mich.	79
56	Bowling Green ■	54
74	Akron ■	58
49	Miami (Ohio)	69
53	Illinois St. ■	57
80	Kent St. ■	67
65	Ohio	70
71	Akron	79
58	Miami (Ohio) ■	51
83	Eastern Mich. ■	75
57	Kent St. †	79

Nickname: Thundering Herd
Colors: Green & White

Arena: Henderson Center
  Capacity: 9,043; Year Built: 1981
AD: Bob Marcum
SID: Randy Burnside

MARTIN LUTHER
New Ulm, MN 56073-3965 III

Coach: James Unke, Martin Luther 1983

2002-03 RESULTS (13-10)

68	Minn.-Morris ■	70
131	Grinnell	160
68	Mt. Marty	78
51	Gust. Adolphus	66
52	Dordt ■	55
81	Hamline	79
75	Dordt †	74
81	Northwestern (Iowa)	100
85	Crown ■	54
79	Northwestern (Minn.)	82
63	Viterbo	76
80	Pillsbury	48
57	Northland ■	49
88	Crown ■	72
74	St. Scholastica ■	69
88	North Cent. (Minn.) ■	99
77	Northwestern (Minn.) ■	69
79	North Cent. (Minn.)	65
68	Northland	54
68	Presentation	50
78	Presentation ■	72
93	St. Scholastica	75
58	Presentation ■	59

Nickname: Knights
Colors: Black, Red & White
Arena: Luther Student Center
  Capacity: 1,500; Year Built: 1967
AD: James M. Unke
SID: Jeremy Belter

MARY HARDIN-BAYLOR
Belton, TX 76513 III

Coach: Ken DeWeese, Louisiana Col. 1969

2002-03 RESULTS (13-12)

71	Midwestern St.	84
63	Texas St.	84
73	East Tex. Baptist	68
85	LeTourneau	58
88	Ozarks (Ark.) ■	91
77	Austin ■	73
70	Concordia-Austin	71
85	Hillsdale Free Will †	36
75	Angelo St.	89
76	Louisiana Col.	79
56	Mississippi Col.	55
71	Texas-Dallas ■	55
76	Hardin-Simmons ■	63
74	McMurry ■	76
75	Schreiner	72
62	Texas Lutheran	71
82	Concordia-Austin ■	78
70	Sul Ross St. ■	66
64	Howard Payne ■	74
84	Sul Ross St.	95
74	Howard Payne	77
72	Hardin-Simmons	66
79	McMurry	80
104	Schreiner	80
92	Texas Lutheran ■	84

Nickname: Crusaders
Colors: Purple, Gold & White
Arena: Mabee Gym
  Capacity: 1,000; Year Built: 1957
AD: Ben Shipp
SID: Jon Wallin

MARY WASHINGTON
Fredericksburg, VA
22401-5358.............................III

Coach: Rod Wood, Randolph-Macon 1985
2002-03 RESULTS (24-5)
74	Cabrini †	69
52	Shenandoah	67
79	Christendom	48
80	Centre †	61
83	Emory & Henry	64
76	Marymount (Va.) ■	67
82	York (Pa.)	76
78	Washington (Md.)	74
69	Union (N.Y.) ■	54
91	Villa Julie ■	75
60	VMI	56
76	Wash. & Lee ■	50
60	Catholic	78
84	St. Mary's (Md.) ■	74
74	Gallaudet ■	68
72	Salisbury	58
63	Goucher ■	61
101	York (Pa.) ■	72
67	Marymount (Va.)	73
70	Villa Julie	68
58	Catholic	62
74	Gallaudet	70
57	Goucher	54
85	Salisbury ■	65
90	St. Mary's (Md.)	79
82	St. Mary's (Md.) ■	69
75	Goucher ■	61
70	Catholic	68
53	Alvernia	58

Nickname: Eagles
Colors: Navy, Gray & White
Arena: Goolrick Gymnasium
  Capacity: 800; Year Built: 1967
AD: Edward H. Hegmann
SID: Clint Often

MARYLAND
College Park, MD 20742 I

Coach: Gary Williams, Maryland 1968
2002-03 RESULTS (21-10)
64	Miami (Ohio) ■	49
97	Citadel ■	49
89	Duquesne ■	39
74	Indiana †	80
67	Notre Dame †	79
93	George Washington †	82
64	Florida ■	69
101	UMBC ■	60
84	Georgia Tech ■	77
79	Wagner ■	57
108	Hampton ■	58
89	Florida St. ■	62
72	Wake Forest	81
87	Duke ■	72
81	North Carolina	66
52	Clemson	47
75	North Carolina St. ■	60
85	Loyola (Md.) ■	58
78	Virginia	86
84	Georgia Tech	90
74	Florida St.	72
90	Wake Forest ■	67
70	Duke	75
96	North Carolina ■	56
91	Clemson ■	52
68	North Carolina St.	65
78	Virginia	80
72	North Carolina †	84
75	UNC Wilmington †	73
77	Xavier †	64
58	Michigan St. †	60

Nickname: Terps
Colors: Red, White, Black & Gold
Arena: Cole Field House
  Capacity: 14,500; Year Built: 1955
AD: Deborah A. Yow
SID: Kevin Messenger

UMBC
Baltimore, MD 21250 I

Coach: Tom Sullivan, Fordham 1972
2002-03 RESULTS (7-20)
86	Towson †	81
57	Loyola (Md.) †	43
68	Mt. St. Mary's ■	53
43	Loyola (Md.)	62
60	Villanova	72
54	Santa Clara ■	55
60	Maryland	101
57	Col. of Charleston	78
48	Oral Roberts †	68
43	Princeton	76
71	Robert Morris	77
68	St. Francis (Pa.)	73
73	St. Francis (N.Y.) ■	58
64	Long Island ■	76
72	Long Island	73
69	St. Francis (N.Y.)	66
63	Fairleigh Dickinson ■	57
74	Monmouth ■	80
49	Central Conn. St.	63
66	Quinnipiac	87
74	Mt. St. Mary's	82
64	St. Francis (Pa.) ■	72
58	Robert Morris ■	64
57	Sacred Heart ■	68
65	Wagner	76
60	Central Conn. St. ■	66
80	Quinnipiac ■	58

Nickname: Retrievers
Colors: Black, Gold & Red
Arena: RAC Arena
  Capacity: 4,024; Year Built: 1974
AD: Charles R. Brown
SID: Steve Levy

MD.-EAST. SHORE
Princess Anne, MD 21853-1299 ..I

Coach: Thomas C. Trotter, Wis.-Parkside 1985
2002-03 RESULTS (5-23)
36	Northwestern	56
64	Elon ■	68
63	New Mexico St.	81
61	Cleveland St.	81
40	Towson	65
62	Old Dominion	82
74	Robert Morris ■	93
58	Hartford ■	59
71	Duquesne	74
45	Hampton ■	55
51	Norfolk St. ■	78
89	Florida A&M	92
74	Bethune-Cookman ■	69
82	N.C. A&T ■	58
68	South Carolina St. ■	71
46	Delaware St.	56
76	Howard ■	83
69	Morgan St.	90
58	Coppin St. ■	55
54	Hampton	70
63	Norfolk St.	80
60	Florida A&M ■	62
48	Bethune-Cookman ■	57
91	N.C. A&T	79
58	South Carolina St.	78
57	Delaware St. ■	70
73	Howard ■	67
69	Howard †	71

Fighting Hawks / MARYMOUNT (VA.)

Nickname: Fighting Hawks
Colors: Maroon & Gray
Arena: Hytche Athletic Center
  Capacity: 5,500; Year Built: 1998
AD: Vivian L. Fuller
SID: G. Stan Bradley

MARYMOUNT (VA.)
Arlington, VA 22207-4299 III

Coach: Chuck Driesell, Maryland 1985
2002-03 RESULTS (14-12)
86	Widener †	73
92	Methodist †	80
77	Guilford	83
84	Pitt.-Greensburg ■	80
69	Chowan ■	62
67	Mary Washington	76
63	Goucher ■	69
74	Washington (Md.) ■	76
69	Chris. Newport ■	82
90	Lycoming	104
83	TCNJ	98
113	Villa Julie	95
77	St. Mary's (Md.) ■	78
60	Catholic ■	71
73	York (Pa.) ■	75
74	Gallaudet	70
101	Salisbury	72
72	Goucher	56
73	Mary Washington ■	67
59	Catholic	96
71	St. Mary's (Md.) ■	66
98	York (Pa.)	94
67	Salisbury ■	57
84	Gallaudet ■	63
82	York (Pa.) ■	78
56	Catholic	58

Nickname: Saints
Colors: Royal Blue & White
Arena: Verizon Sports Arena
  Capacity: 1,000; Year Built: 1999
AD: William Finney
SID: Judy Finney

MARYVILLE (MO.)
St. Louis, MO 63141-7299 III

Coach: Matt Rogers, Coe
2002-03 RESULTS (7-18)
86	Anderson (Ind.)	104
69	Hanover †	105
89	Elmhurst	75
79	Manchester †	88
84	Dallas †	72
87	Mo. Baptist ■	94
80	Rhodes	105
71	Millsaps †	86
60	Hawaii Pacific	96
50	Carthage †	84
62	Mo. Baptist	94
69	Webster ■	75
70	Fontbonne	104
96	Principia ■	71
72	Westminster (Mo.) ■	80
73	Blackburn	92
82	MacMurray ■	80
79	Greenville ■	75
70	Webster	75
85	Fontbonne ■	71
71	Principia	78
68	Westminster (Mo.)	76
62	Blackburn ■	74
91	MacMurray	97
98	Greenville	83

Nickname: Saints
Colors: Red & White
Arena: Moloney Arena
  Capacity: 3,000; Year Built: 1980
AD: Matt Rogers
SID: Kelly Edgar

MARYVILLE (TENN.)
Maryville, TN 37804-5907.......III

Coach: Randy Lambert, Maryville (Tenn.) 1976
2002-03 RESULTS (22-6)
76	Oglethorpe †	68
81	Emory	82
83	Centre ■	64
59	SCAD ■	64
95	Roanoke ■	67
100	Sewanee ■	78
87	Greensboro	58
72	Mount Union †	60
79	Roanoke	75
80	Piedmont	73
79	King (Tenn.) ■	71
91	Emory ■	74
73	Huntingdon	54
86	Fisk ■	59
95	Rust ■	80
58	SCAD	68
75	LaGrange ■	61
55	Carson-Newman	64
88	Piedmont ■	70
88	Rust	54
79	Fisk	72
92	Huntingdon ■	59
89	Oglethorpe	63
88	LaGrange	78
65	Fisk †	68
106	Thomas More ■	73
70	Mississippi Col. ■	58
64	Hanover	68

Nickname: Scots
Colors: Orange & Garnet
Arena: Boydson Baird Gymnasium
  Capacity: 2,000; Year Built: 1971
AD: Randy Lambert
SID: Eric S. Etchison

MARYWOOD
Scranton, PA 18509-1598 III

Coach: Eric Grundman, Binghamton 1992
2002-03 RESULTS (7-18)
76	Brooklyn †	55
62	Misericordia	90
60	Scranton ■	79
78	Susquehanna ■	85
62	Neumann	96
78	Arcadia ■	73
60	King's (Pa.)	71
63	Wilkes	67
64	Swarthmore ■	58
100	Penn St.-Altoona ■	79
91	Practical Bible	61
82	Wesley	100
72	Gwynedd-Mercy ■	74
56	Alvernia ■	60
77	Misericordia	73
63	Cabrini	77
65	Eastern ■	66
67	Arcadia	70
72	Neumann ■	75
58	Cabrini	83
80	Misericordia ■	97
73	Gwynedd-Mercy	80
69	Eastern	89
82	Alvernia	85
80	Wesley ■	70

Nickname: Pacers
Colors: Green & White
Arena: Health & Physical Education Center
  Capacity: 1,000
AD: Mary Jo Gunning
SID: Will Donohoe

MASSACHUSETTS
Amherst, MA 01003 I

Coach: Steve Lappas, CCNY 1977
2002-03 RESULTS (11-18)

71	Indiana †	84
53	Utah †	69
69	Chaminade †	55
45	Central Conn. St. †	46
62	Boston College ■	80
48	Connecticut	59
67	Florida Int'l ■	62
52	Lafayette ■	54
76	Rider ■	54
81	Marshall ■	58
68	North Carolina St. ■	56
67	Fordham	80
66	Columbia ■	47
47	St. Joseph's ■	76
53	Rhode Island ■	60
73	Xavier ■	86
57	La Salle	78
75	George Washington	70
55	Dayton	83
76	Fordham ■	66
45	Tennessee	71
50	Temple ■	61
54	Richmond ■	53
82	St. Bonaventure	76
70	Duquesne ■	55
46	Temple	88
58	Rhode Island	65
49	St. Joseph's ■	52
74	George Washington ■	85

Nickname: Minutemen
Colors: Maroon & White
Arena: Mullins Center
  Capacity: 9,493; Year Built: 1993
AD: Ian McCaw
SID: Nick Joos

MASS.-DARTMOUTH
North Dartmouth, MA 02747-2300 III

Coach: Brian Baptiste, American Int'l 1976
2002-03 RESULTS (13-14)

78	Salve Regina ■	56
79	Wheaton (Mass.) ■	85
84	Worcester St. ■	70
72	Bridgewater St.	65
79	Plymouth St. ■	84
99	Johnson & Wales	81
65	Western Conn. St.	90
63	Fla. Southern	68
51	Eckerd	71
78	Montclair St.	88
75	Southern Me.	63
75	Eastern Conn. St.	76
94	Keene St. ■	84
86	Mass.-Boston ■	88
71	Tufts ■	89
80	Plymouth St.	92
93	Rhode Island Col.	80
97	Connecticut Col.	85
94	Western Conn. St. ■	71
77	Salem St.	80
89	Southern Me. ■	76
57	Mass.-Boston	66
83	Eastern Conn. St. ■	61
101	Rhode Island Col. ■	90
83	Keene St.	100
88	Mass.-Boston ■	78
74	Western Conn. St.	77

Nickname: Corsairs
Colors: Blue, White & Gold
Arena: Tripp Athletic Center
  Capacity: 3,000; Year Built: 1972

AD: Robert W. Mullen
SID: William Gathright

MIT
Cambridge, MA 02139-7404...III

Coach: Larry Anderson, Rust 1987
2002-03 RESULTS (16-10)

46	Pomona-Pitzer †	59
87	Wesleyan (Conn.) †	76
49	Connecticut Col.	46
63	Suffolk	72
77	Framingham St.	59
67	Tufts ■	70
87	Polytechnic (N.Y.)	61
67	Brandeis ■	54
54	Rensselaer ■	50
61	Springfield	68
58	Salem St.	60
67	Coast Guard ■	59
71	Clark (Mass.) ■	66
95	Emerson ■	56
77	Wheaton (Mass.)	65
71	Newbury ■	65
69	WPI	59
53	Babson	69
51	Wheaton (Mass.)	71
60	Coast Guard	53
60	Clark (Mass.)	86
57	Springfield ■	50
53	WPI ■	44
69	Eastern Nazarene	58
55	Springfield	59
63	Babson	71

Nickname: Engineers
Colors: Cardinal & Gray
Arena: Rockwell Cage
  Capacity: 600
AD: Candace L. Royer
SID: Roger Crosley

MASS. LIBERAL ARTS
North Adams, MA 01247-4100 ..III

Coach: Darrell Skeeter, Davis & Elkins
2002-03 RESULTS (2-23)

74	Vassar	86
83	Western Conn. St. †	111
84	Amherst ■	115
57	Williams ■	107
84	Gordon	99
70	Medgar Evers †	62
52	Hampden-Sydney	117
82	Western New Eng. ■	85
69	Skidmore	94
77	Becker ■	84
82	Framingham St. ■	75
90	Middlebury	111
74	Newbury	85
75	Bridgewater St.	101
84	Worcester St.	88
84	Salem St.	105
59	Fitchburg St. ■	92
69	Westfield St. ■	94
35	Framingham St.	77
72	Bridgewater St.	95
65	Worcester St. ■	88
75	Salem St.	101
62	Fitchburg St.	96
75	Westfield St.	97
62	Westfield St.	95

Nickname: Trailblazers
Colors: Navy & Gold
Arena: Amsler Campus Center Gym
  Capacity: 2,500; Year Built: 1975
AD: Scott F. Nichols
SID: Deb Raber

MASS.-BOSTON
Boston, MA 02125 III

Coach: Charlie Titus, St. Michael's 1972
2002-03 RESULTS (11-15)

82	Fitchburg St.	74
83	Framingham St. ■	49
71	Wesleyan (Conn.) ■	78
75	Emerson	76
70	Suffolk	69
78	Keene St. ■	87
68	Clark (Mass.) ■	92
85	Salem St.	74
77	Rhode Island Col.	81
71	Wentworth Inst. ■	57
92	Tufts	95
60	Eastern Conn. St. ■	43
81	Plymouth St.	82
76	Western Conn. St. ■	66
88	Mass.-Dartmouth ■	86
71	Bridgewater St. ■	59
65	Keene St.	87
71	Southern Me. ■	73
62	Rhode Island Col. ■	74
71	WPI	73
64	Eastern Conn. St.	62
66	Mass.-Dartmouth ■	57
58	Plymouth St.	67
78	Southern Me.	80
74	Western Conn. St.	78
78	Mass.-Dartmouth	88

Nickname: Beacons
Colors: Blue & White
Arena: Clark Athletic Center
  Capacity: 3,500; Year Built: 1981
AD: Charlie Titus
SID: Alan Wickstrom

MASS.-LOWELL
Lowell, MA 01854 II

Coach: Ken Barer, George Washington 1988
2002-03 RESULTS (28-5)

71	Franklin Pierce	56
84	Merrimack ■	68
71	Stonehill	46
72	Bentley ■	57
50	St. Anselm	49
81	Adelphi ■	66
79	Teikyo Post †	73
74	Quincy	57
87	St. Michael's ■	68
74	Le Moyne ■	59
75	St. Rose	61
66	Pace	60
72	Southern Conn. St. ■	52
65	American Int'l ■	51
72	Bryant	78
75	Assumption ■	66
76	Franklin Pierce	60
81	Southampton	56
68	Southern N.H. ■	73
69	Bentley	64
107	Merrimack	75
90	Stonehill ■	44
62	Assumption	64
73	American Int'l	65
64	Bryant ■	58
61	Southern N.H.	74
74	Franklin Pierce	65
77	Assumption ■	67
77	Southern N.H. ■	66
91	St. Rose	68
86	Bridgeport ■	73
69	C.W. Post ■	59
62	Bowie St. †	72

Nickname: River Hawks
Colors: Red, White & Royal Blue
Arena: Costello Gymnasium

Capacity: 2,100; Year Built: 1960
AD: Dana K. Skinner
SID: Chris O'Donnell

MCMURRY
Abilene, TX 79697 III

Coach: Ron Holmes, McMurry 1977
2002-03 RESULTS (18-9)

87	Tex. Permian Basin ■	75
59	Austin	64
91	Ozarks (Ark.)	99
100	Hardin-Simmons	89
70	Texas-Dallas ■	73
90	Tex. Permian Basin	79
67	Southwestern (Tex.) ■	81
74	Trinity (Tex.) †	89
84	LeTourneau	81
70	East Tex. Baptist	64
80	Mississippi Col. ■	72
92	Louisiana Col. ■	84
81	Concordia-Austin	89
76	Mary Hardin-Baylor	74
78	Howard Payne ■	67
80	Sul Ross St. ■	78
78	Texas Lutheran ■	73
108	Schreiner ■	99
75	Hardin-Simmons ■	71
75	Texas Lutheran	72
97	Schreiner	89
81	Concordia-Austin ■	56
80	Mary Hardin-Baylor ■	79
69	Howard Payne	74
74	Sul Ross St.	101
98	East Tex. Baptist	91
63	Mississippi Col. †	83

Nickname: Indians
Colors: Maroon & White
Arena: Kimbrell Arena
  Capacity: 2,250; Year Built: 1973
AD: Steve Keenum
SID: Chris Myers

MCNEESE ST.
Lake Charles, LA 70609 I

Coach: Tic Price, Virginia Tech 1979
2002-03 RESULTS (15-14)

85	Texas Wesleyan ■	54
65	Mississippi St.	81
76	La.-Lafayette ■	74
102	Loyola (La.) ■	63
72	LSU	93
87	Liberty	74
59	Texas	97
74	Texas St. ■	64
78	Sam Houston St. ■	85
62	Texas-Arlington	74
69	Stephen F. Austin	79
71	Northwestern St. ■	56
81	La.-Monroe ■	66
53	Texas St.	91
66	Texas-San Antonio	51
75	Nicholls St.	70
50	La.-Monroe	58
65	Lamar	68
63	Stephen F. Austin	53
52	Texas-Arlington ■	56
70	Northwestern St.	57
72	Texas-San Antonio ■	66
67	Southeastern La.	74
71	Nicholls St. ■	50
78	Southeastern La. ■	81
66	Sam Houston St.	81
72	Lamar	84
78	Texas-Arlington	67
58	Sam Houston St.	64

Nickname: Cowboys
Colors: Blue & Gold
Arena: Burton Coliseum

Capacity: 8,000; Year Built: 1986
AD: Sonny Watkins
SID: Louis Bonnette

MEDAILLE
Buffalo, NY 14214-2695..........III

Coach: Richard Jacob, Eisenhower 1980
2002-03 RESULTS (6-20)

45	Albion	89
50	Otterbein †	96
65	Lake Erie ■	70
63	La Roche ■	67
74	Wash. & Jeff.	71
43	Waynesburg	104
54	Geneseo St. ■	61
52	Clarkson ■	63
66	Fredonia St. ■	67
64	D'Youville †	67
69	Hilbert †	72
59	Grove City ■	71
52	Oswego St.	69
74	Hilbert	69
76	Keuka ■	54
47	D'Youville	49
76	Cazenovia ■	83
60	Keuka	77
60	D'Youville ■	55
62	Utica/Rome	64
65	Cazenovia	69
86	Hilbert ■	77
50	Penn St.-Behrend	80
62	Le Moyne	85
74	Hilbert ■	70
71	Keuka	77

Nickname: Mavericks
Colors: Scarlet/Navy/White
Arena: Kevin I. Sullivan Campus Center
  Capacity: 500; Year Built: 1995
AD: Peter Jerebko
SID: Michael P. Carbery

MEDGAR EVERS
Brooklyn, NY 11225-2298 III

Coach: George Moore
2002-03 RESULTS (6-20)

60	FDU-Florham †	85
64	Maritime (N.Y.) †	81
68	York (N.Y.) ■	72
81	NYCCT ■	77
82	Farmingdale St.	100
73	NYCCT	61
88	Centenary (N.J.) ■	77
78	New Jersey City ■	117
62	Mass. Liberal Arts †	70
95	Hunter †	86
59	Pitt.-Bradford †	86
74	Kean †	97
68	Staten Island	76
91	Brooklyn ■	80
60	CCNY	103
72	Baruch	82
79	Lehman ■	90
65	Farmingdale St.	68
66	Purchase St.	67
47	York (N.Y.)	72
59	NYCCT	72
96	Brooklyn	97
76	Staten Island ■	69
75	Hunter ■	90
61	John Jay ■	79
68	Brooklyn	84

Nickname: Cougars
Colors: Gold & Black
Arena: Medgar Evers College Gym
  Capacity: 300; Year Built: 1971
AD: Roy Anderson
SID: To be named

MEMPHIS
Memphis, TN 38152-3370 I

Coach: John Calipari, Clarion 1982
2002-03 RESULTS (23-7)

70	Syracuse †	63
80	Austin Peay ■	81
78	Ark.-Pine Bluff ■	54
73	Ark.-Little Rock ■	49
72	Furman ■	55
78	Missouri	93
58	Mississippi ■	51
77	Illinois ■	74
67	Murray St. ■	60
72	Arkansas	67
72	Villanova ■	68
85	Tulane ■	73
67	Southern Miss.	84
74	South Fla. ■	75
77	Houston ■	66
66	St. Louis	69
80	Southern Miss. ■	62
73	East Caro. ■	49
84	TCU	69
58	Tulane	57
94	UAB ■	70
80	Louisville	73
73	South Fla.	66
88	TCU ■	64
67	Cincinnati ■	48
71	Houston	56
90	UAB	79
62	South Fla. †	56
75	Louisville	78
71	Arizona St. †	84

Nickname: Tigers
Colors: Blue & Gray
Arena: The Pyramid
  Capacity: 20,004; Year Built: 1991
AD: R.C. Johnson
SID: Ron Mears

MENLO
Atherton, CA 94027-4185 III

Coach: Keith Larsen, San Francisco St. 1985
2002-03 RESULTS (14-12)

83	Willamette ■	86
91	Cal St. Hayward ■	73
73	San Jose St.	98
82	Southern Ore.	66
70	Oregon Tech	100
56	Idaho St.	72
69	Westminster (Utah)	67
76	Claremont-M-S	79
79	La Sierra	63
111	Wis. Lutheran ■	116
77	UC Santa Cruz ■	60
77	Notre Dame de Namur ■	70
65	Cal St. Monterey Bay ■	70
101	Bethany (Cal.) ■	64
97	Cal St. Maritime ■	69
57	Dominican (Cal.) ■	69
93	Pacific Union	86
95	Simpson (Cal.) ■	82
65	Holy Names	81
79	Cal St. Hayward	71
69	Notre Dame de Namur	70
83	Cal St. Monterey Bay	70
116	Bethany (Cal.)	74
74	UC Santa Cruz	79
81	Holy Names †	78
63	Cal St. Hayward †	69

Nickname: Oaks
Colors: Navy Blue & White
Arena: Haynes-Prim Pavilion
  Capacity: 700; Year Built: 1981
AD: Keith Larsen
SID: Nicholas Enriquez

MERCER
Macon, GA 31207 I

Coach: Mark Slonaker, Georgia 1980
2002-03 RESULTS (23-6)

79	Elon	67
47	Florida St.	83
60	Iowa St.	91
85	Reinhardt ■	62
80	Ga. Southern ■	72
89	Morris Brown	67
74	Harvard	86
84	Savannah St.	66
86	Stetson	72
71	Jacksonville	68
86	Fla. Atlantic ■	79
85	UCF ■	63
61	Troy St.	89
86	UNC Asheville ■	62
74	Samford	68
67	Belmont ■	69
77	Campbell	62
76	Gardner-Webb ■	64
84	Jacksonville St. ■	78
88	Georgia St. ■	80
90	Morris Brown ■	83
83	Troy St. ■	80
97	Savannah St. ■	72
87	Fla. Atlantic	72
69	UCF	66
73	Jacksonville ■	63
101	Stetson ■	84
73	Jacksonville †	57
59	UCF †	79

Nickname: Bears
Colors: Orange & Black
Arena: Porter Gym
  Capacity: 500; Year Built: 1925
AD: Bobby A. Pope
SID: Kevin Coulombe

MERCHANT MARINE
Kings Point, NY 11024-1699....III

Coach: Chris Carideo, Widener 1996
2002-03 RESULTS (21-9)

77	Muskingum †	71
70	Wooster	93
93	Mt. St. Vincent ■	66
60	Coast Guard ■	62
65	New York U.	80
71	John Jay	65
71	Old Westbury ■	70
73	Maritime (N.Y.) ■	53
68	Staten Island	45
83	Bethany (W.Va.) †	89
52	Wm. Paterson ■	64
85	CCNY ■	65
58	Manhattanville	71
87	Stevens Institute ■	72
79	Yeshiva	50
80	Mt. St. Vincent	78
72	Mt. St. Mary (N.Y.) ■	65
64	Old Westbury	60
82	Manhattanville ■	77
81	Stevens Institute	82
66	Maritime (N.Y.)	57
69	St. Joseph's (L.I.)	75
73	Yeshiva	67
74	St. Joseph's (L.I.) ■	65
71	Mt. St. Mary (N.Y.)	64
74	Yeshiva ■	58
65	Old Westbury	61
65	Mt. St. Mary (N.Y.) ■	54
63	CCNY ■	57
76	Ramapo	92

Nickname: Mariners
Colors: Blue & Gray
Arena: O'Hara Hall
  Capacity: 1,200; Year Built: 1943

AD: Susan Petersen-Lubow
SID: Kim McNulty

MERCY
Dobbs Ferry, NY 10522............II

Coach: Steve Kelly, Fordham 1969
2002-03 RESULTS (10-16)

65	Pitt.-Johnstown	88
73	Alderson-Broaddus †	84
71	Dowling	80
71	NYIT	80
74	Queens (N.Y.) ■	66
63	St. Thomas Aquinas ■	47
81	Concordia (N.Y.)	76
73	Southampton	83
66	Molloy ■	72
51	New Haven	70
62	Bridgeport ■	75
81	Adelphi ■	86
66	C.W. Post ■	81
70	Dowling ■	65
57	Concordia (N.Y.) ■	54
77	NYIT ■	65
72	Philadelphia U. ■	57
61	Queens (N.Y.)	59
64	St. Thomas Aquinas	62
61	Southampton ■	70
74	Molloy	72
63	Bridgeport	80
47	New Haven ■	58
60	Philadelphia U.	83
69	C.W. Post	78
63	Adelphi	85

Nickname: Flyers
Colors: Blue & White
Arena: Westchester Community College
  Capacity: 2,000
AD: Neil D. Judge
SID: Steve Balsan

MERCYHURST
Erie, PA 16546........................II

Coach: Karl Fogel, Colby 1968
2002-03 RESULTS (12-15)

76	American Int'l ■	72
89	Pfeiffer ■	95
81	St. Joseph's (Ind.) ■	71
68	Edinboro	60
84	Grand Valley St. ■	63
62	Ferris St.	70
86	Roberts Wesleyan ■	78
102	Point Park ■	68
69	Edinboro ■	60
72	St. Martin's	56
79	Western Ore. †	75
63	St. Joseph's (Ind.)	77
85	Michigan Tech	89
70	Lake Superior St.	78
71	Northern Mich.	76
88	Northwood ■	65
91	Saginaw Valley ■	86
69	Wayne St. (Mich.) ■	61
51	Hillsdale ■	64
73	Gannon ■	76
67	Findlay	76
63	Ashland	81
57	Wayne St. (Mich.)	71
83	Hillsdale	86
68	Gannon	92
73	Ashland ■	74
99	Findlay ■	106

Nickname: Lakers
Colors: Blue & Green
Arena: Mercyhurst Athletic Center
  Capacity: 1,800; Year Built: 1978
AD: Peter J. Russo
SID: John Leisering

SCHEDULES/RESULTS

MERRIMACK
North Andover, MA 01845 II

Coach: Bert Hammel, Bentley 1973
2002-03 RESULTS (11-17)
53	lynn †	69
73	Adelphi †	65
75	Assumption ■	69
68	Mass.-Lowell	84
74	Southern N.H. ■	78
65	Franklin Pierce	74
62	Stonehill	61
75	American Int'l	72
64	Southern N.H. †	78
98	Wilmington (Del.) †	80
89	Felician ■	79
59	Bentley ■	75
75	Le Moyne ■	74
90	St. Michael's	100
76	St. Anselm	100
65	Southern Conn. St.	79
89	St. Rose ■	85
74	Pace ■	80
60	Stonehill ■	55
71	Bentley	75
48	Southern N.H.	73
75	Mass.-Lowell ■	107
68	Franklin Pierce ■	59
74	Pace	83
91	St. Rose	98
83	Southern Conn. St. ■	74
65	Bryant	76
74	Le Moyne	85

Nickname: Warriors
Colors: Navy Blue & Gold
Arena: Volpe Complex
  Capacity: 1,600; Year Built: 1972
AD: Chris Serino
SID: Devin Bigoness

MESA ST.
Grand Junction, CO 81501 II

Coach: Jim Heaps, Mesa St. 1982
2002-03 RESULTS (15-12)
81	Regis (Colo.) †	69
93	Colorado Mines	98
108	Central Methodist ■	79
90	Emporia St. ■	81
72	Emporia St.	68
81	Neb.-Omaha †	100
81	Fort Hays St.	77
61	Neb.-Kearney	95
74	Westminster (Utah)	80
66	Colorado Mines ■	70
65	Colo. Christian ■	77
52	Metro St.	85
80	Chadron St.	91
60	Regis (Colo.) ■	47
61	UC-Colo. Spgs. ■	53
99	Western St. ■	65
80	N.M. Highlands ■	67
50	Colorado St.-Pueblo ■	49
83	Adams St.	89
57	Fort Lewis	62
76	Colorado St.-Pueblo	61
72	N.M. Highlands	68
49	Fort Lewis ■	66
76	Adams St. ■	63
97	Western St.	86
72	UC-Colo. Spgs.	67
64	Metro St.	87

Nickname: Mavericks
Colors: Maroon, Gold & White
Arena: Brownson Arena
  Capacity: 2,500; Year Built: 1969
AD: Clarence Ross
SID: Tish Elliott

MESSIAH
Grantham, PA 17027 III

Coach: Dave Manzer, Mt. Vernon Naz. 1984
2002-03 RESULTS (7-17)
74	York (Pa.)	87
89	Baptist Bible (Pa.) ■	81
76	Gettysburg ■	52
73	Juniata	94
71	Albright	75
61	Hamilton †	82
74	Hanover †	83
91	Washington (Md.) ■	82
64	Eastern	71
72	Phila. Bible	51
71	Widener ■	62
92	Villa Julie	80
58	Moravian ■	82
59	Susquehanna	66
50	Lebanon Valley ■	73
66	Elizabethtown	78
95	Albright ■	81
60	Juniata ■	72
75	Moravian	89
59	Widener	79
91	Susquehanna ■	97
54	Elizabethtown ■	83
82	Lebanon Valley	85
69	Dickinson	81

Nickname: Falcons
Colors: Navy & White
Arena: Brubaker Auditorium
  Capacity: 1,800; Year Built: 1972
AD: Jerry Chaplin
SID: Scott Frey

METHODIST
Fayetteville, NC 28311-1420 ...III

Coach: David Smith, Methodist 1981
2002-03 RESULTS (17-10)
80	Frank. & Marsh.	75
80	Marymount (Va.) †	92
71	Fayetteville St.	75
73	Flagler †	91
75	Palm Beach Atl.	65
71	Hampden-Sydney ■	80
76	SCAD	64
29	Furman	83
56	Defiance †	81
86	Thomas More †	74
66	SCAD	72
61	Greensboro	58
66	Chowan	45
82	N.C. Wesleyan ■	66
90	Ferrum ■	45
95	Averett ■	61
74	Shenandoah	46
68	Chris. Newport	73
73	Greensboro ■	57
64	Chowan ■	50
78	N.C. Wesleyan	87
64	Ferrum	58
98	Averett	76
74	Chris. Newport ■	73
90	Shenandoah ■	81
77	Ferrum †	70
53	N.C. Wesleyan †	58

Nickname: Monarchs
Colors: Green & Gold
Arena: March F. Riddle Center
  Capacity: 1,200; Year Built: 1990
AD: Bob McEvoy
SID: Lee Glenn

METRO ST.
Denver, CO 80217-3362 II

Coach: Mike Dunlap, Loyola Marymount 1980
2002-03 RESULTS (28-5)
69	Western Ore.	70
75	St. Martin's †	66
93	Tex. A&M-Kingsville ■	58
93	Grand View ■	51
87	Holy Names	60
72	Adams St. ■	54
75	Fort Lewis ■	84
72	Notre Dame de Namur	46
65	San Fran. St.	48
60	Sonoma St.	54
74	UC-Colo. Spgs.	50
81	Western St. ■	55
85	Mesa St. ■	52
77	N.M. Highlands ■	52
66	Colorado St.-Pueblo	51
64	Neb.-Kearney ■	80
72	Fort Hays St. ■	60
65	Regis (Colo.) ■	40
80	Chadron St. ■	49
54	Colo. Christian	41
63	Colorado Mines	60
100	Regis (Colo.) ■	65
77	Chadron St.	50
78	Colo. Christian ■	61
91	Colorado Mines ■	63
64	Fort Hays St.	63
54	Neb.-Kearney	65
87	Mesa St. ■	64
76	Fort Lewis †	61
79	Fort Hays St. †	69
85	Fort Lewis †	63
75	St. Cloud St. †	63
87	Neb.-Kearney	94

Nickname: Roadrunners
Colors: Navy Blue & Burgundy
Arena: Auraria Events Center
  Capacity: 3,000; Year Built: 1970
AD: Joan M. McDermott
SID: Nick Garner

MIAMI (FLA.)
Coral Gables, FL 33146 I

Coach: Perry Clark, Gettysburg 1974
2002-03 RESULTS (11-17)
93	New Hampshire ■	58
78	Texas A&M	72
91	Savannah St. ■	57
73	Fla. Atlantic	74
55	Florida St.	72
64	Charlotte	69
79	Ark.-Pine Bluff ■	42
93	Florida †	94
62	UCF	51
68	Lehigh	62
64	North Carolina ■	61
63	West Virginia	68
80	Connecticut	83
53	Seton Hall	76
77	Connecticut ■	76
49	Syracuse ■	54
60	Providence ■	57
74	St. John's (N.Y.)	77
67	Villanova ■	72
85	Virginia Tech ■	65
65	Boston College	76
63	Providence	73
72	Georgetown ■	74
56	Villanova	75
68	Boston College ■	72
79	Virginia Tech	71
73	St. John's (N.Y.) ■	76
52	Seton Hall †	67

Nickname: Hurricanes
Colors: Orange, Green & White
Arena: Miami Arena
  Capacity: 15,388; Year Built: 1988
AD: Paul Dee
SID: Sam Henderson

MIAMI (OHIO)
Oxford, OH 45056 I

Coach: Charlie Coles, Miami (Ohio) 1965
2002-03 RESULTS (13-15)
46	Purdue	73
49	Maryland	64
65	Ohio Dominican ■	39
48	Wright St.	51
78	Dayton ■	63
44	Western Mich. ■	39
58	Xavier	68
42	Butler ■	59
54	Cincinnati	66
58	Evansville ■	66
71	Central Mich. ■	62
52	Kent St. ■	60
51	Toledo	61
77	Ohio	65
74	Akron ■	59
58	Ball St. ■	56
73	Eastern Mich.	58
57	Buffalo ■	55
60	Kent St.	70
70	Ball St.	78
69	Marshall ■	49
55	Akron	53
63	Buffalo	35
59	Northern Ill. ■	56
48	Bowling Green	51
56	Ohio ■	64
51	Marshall	58
55	Ohio †	65

Nickname: RedHawks
Colors: Red & White
Arena: Millett Hall
  Capacity: 9,200; Year Built: 1968
AD: Steve Snyder
SID: Angie Renninger

MICHIGAN
Ann Arbor, MI 48109-2201 I

Coach: Tommy Amaker, Duke 1987
2002-03 RESULTS (17-13)
68	St. Bonaventure †	89
53	Virginia Tech †	65
71	Kansas St. †	82
52	Western Mich. ■	56
78	Central Mich. ■	85
59	Duke	81
83	Bowling Green ■	57
84	Charleston So. ■	53
70	Vanderbilt ■	66
85	Eastern Mich. ■	57
81	UCLA	76
74	San Francisco ■	64
84	IUPUI ■	79
66	Wisconsin ■	65
66	Penn St. ■	53
61	Ohio St.	50
70	Northwestern	70
75	Minnesota ■	63
60	Michigan St. ■	58
60	Illinois	67
80	Minnesota	87
70	Iowa ■	62
49	Indiana	63
70	Ohio St. ■	54
78	Purdue	67
42	Wisconsin	73

79	Illinois ■	82
78	Penn St. ■	62
61	Purdue ■	69
56	Indiana †	63

Nickname: Wolverines
Colors: Maize & Blue
Arena: Crisler Arena
  Capacity: 13,562; Year Built: 1967
AD: William C. Martin
SID: Bruce Madej

MICHIGAN ST.
East Lansing, MI 48824-1025 I

Coach: Tom Izzo, Northern Mich. 1977
2002-03 RESULTS (22-13)
66	UNC Asheville ■	52
80	Montana †	60
73	Villanova †	81
61	Oklahoma St. †	64
82	Virginia ■	75
79	Cleveland St. ■	47
71	Kentucky	67
80	Loyola (Ill.) ■	54
65	South Fla. ■	56
76	Jacksonville St. ■	52
76	Toledo ■	81
58	Oklahoma †	60
66	Ohio St. ■	55
64	Iowa	68
60	Purdue	72
69	Minnesota	77
70	Penn St. ■	36
58	Michigan	60
61	Indiana ■	54
68	Illinois ■	65
67	Indiana	62
53	Wisconsin	64
64	Northwestern ■	51
40	Illinois	70
75	Syracuse ■	76
71	Minnesota ■	61
69	Purdue ■	61
82	Iowa ■	54
72	Ohio St.	58
54	Purdue †	42
54	Ohio St. †	55
79	Colorado †	64
68	Florida †	46
60	Maryland †	58
76	Texas †	85

Nickname: Spartans
Colors: Green & White
Arena: Breslin Events Center
  Capacity: 14,759; Year Built: 1989
AD: Ronald H. Mason
SID: Matt Larson

MICHIGAN TECH
Houghton, MI 49931-1295 II

Coach: Kevin Luke, Northern Mich. 1982
2002-03 RESULTS (29-3)
93	Wis.-Stout †	71
87	Winona St. †	69
85	Finlandia ■	57
85	Lake Superior St. ■	72
90	Southwest Minn. St.	77
78	Wayne St. (Neb.) †	59
81	Minn. Duluth ■	77
80	Bemidji St. ■	70
90	Anderson (S.C.) †	59
66	South Dakota St.	67
89	Mercyhurst ■	85
74	Gannon ■	73
74	Ashland ■	50
67	Hillsdale	63
70	Wayne St. (Mich.)	56
90	Saginaw Valley	55

78	Findlay ■	61
79	Northwood ■	73
70	Northern Mich. ■	63
98	Ferris St.	82
76	Grand Valley St.	64
91	Saginaw Valley ■	78
79	Northern Mich.	59
82	Lake Superior St.	68
79	Northwood	62
40	Grand Valley St. ■	42
81	Ferris St. ■	53
91	Ashland ■	75
68	Northern Mich. ■	59
68	Findlay ■	66
90	Indianapolis ■	75
71	Southern Ind. ■	74

Nickname: Huskies
Colors: Silver, Gold & Black
Arena: SDC Gymnasium
  Capacity: 3,200; Year Built: 1981
AD: Rick Yeo
SID: Wes Frahm

MIDDLE TENN.
Murfreesboro, TN 37132 I

Coach: Kermit Jr. Davis, Mississippi St. 1982
2002-03 RESULTS (16-14)
63	East Caro. ■	65
65	Alabama	80
87	Tenn.-Martin ■	77
58	UNC Greensboro	70
66	Tennessee Tech ■	70
56	Purdue	85
64	IUPUI †	60
72	Murray St. ■	79
74	Christian Bros. ■	57
71	Austin Peay	79
66	Kennesaw St. ■	62
64	Murray St.	76
69	Western Ky. ■	65
65	Arkansas St.	58
62	Ark.-Little Rock	71
53	South Ala.	64
77	New Orleans ■	60
70	New Mexico St.	68
65	La.-Lafayette	71
71	IPFW ■	52
60	Florida Int'l ■	58
76	North Texas ■	55
80	Denver	68
79	Arkansas St. ■	55
58	Ark.-Little Rock ■	74
80	Florida Int'l	70
75	Western Ky.	89
72	South Ala. †	69
83	Denver †	59
52	Western Ky.	64

Nickname: Blue Raiders
Colors: Royal Blue & White
Arena: Murphy Athletic Center
  Capacity: 11,520; Year Built: 1972
AD: James Donnelly
SID: Ryan Simmons

MIDDLEBURY
Middlebury, VT 05753 III

Coach: Jeff Brown, Vermont 1982
2002-03 RESULTS (15-10)
84	Southern Vt. ■	87
102	St. Joseph (Vt.) ■	61
84	Skidmore ■	70
94	Castleton St.	64
90	Hamilton	88
102	St. Joseph (Vt.) †	61
77	Norwich	60
81	Rensselaer ■	84
85	Norwich	74

71	Colby-Sawyer	77
108	Johnson St.	93
111	Mass. Liberal Arts ■	90
67	Williams	90
83	Union (N.Y.)	68
60	Amherst	90
69	Trinity (Conn.)	76
99	Green Mountain ■	69
86	Colby ■	67
82	Bowdoin ■	80
75	Vermont	111
98	Wesleyan (Conn.)	106
64	Connecticut Col.	84
89	Tufts ■	83
85	Bates ■	72
81	Tufts	89

Nickname: Panthers
Colors: Blue & White
Arena: Pepin Gymnasium
  Capacity: 1,200; Year Built: 1949
AD: Russell Reilly
SID: Brad Nadeau

MIDWESTERN ST.
Wichita Falls, TX 76308-2099 ...II

Coach: Greg Giddings, Midwestern St. 1985
2002-03 RESULTS (10-18)
84	Mary Hardin-Baylor ■	71
82	Drury	85
75	Central Mo. St. †	78
82	Montevallo †	62
81	Incarnate Word	87
69	Cameron	79
56	Southwestern Okla.	71
60	Incarnate Word ■	63
105	Howard Payne ■	75
60	Tarleton St. ■	72
74	St. Mary's (Tex.) ■	63
67	Central Okla.	78
48	Northeastern St.	92
68	Southeastern Okla. ■	48
71	East Central ■	73
82	Tex. A&M-Commerce	91
76	Tex. A&M-Kingsville	72
71	Abilene Christian ■	82
77	Angelo St. ■	76
69	Eastern N.M.	76
64	West Tex. A&M ■	67
83	West Tex. A&M	89
74	Eastern N.M.	88
96	Tex. A&M-Kingsville ■	100
92	Tex. A&M-Commerce ■	83
84	Angelo St.	79
68	Abilene Christian	51
62	Northeastern St.	64

Nickname: Indians
Colors: Maroon and Gold
Arena: D.L. Ligon Coliseum
  Capacity: 5,200; Year Built: 1969
AD: Jeff Ray
SID: Andy Austin

MILES
Birmingham, AL 35208 II

Coach: Roosevelt Sanders, Alabama St. 1973
2002-03 RESULTS (13-14)
64	Delta St.	93
66	Ark.-Monticello †	76
59	Ala.-Huntsville †	64
63	North Ala.	73
61	Paine	57
75	Benedict †	66
61	Clark Atlanta	36
80	Morehouse	77
59	Fort Valley St.	75
57	Albany St. (Ga.)	63

58	Paine	74
80	Stillman	78
68	Lane ■	74
88	Kentucky St. ■	83
95	Clark Atlanta ■	84
81	LeMoyne-Owen ■	71
63	Stillman ■	71
61	Fort Valley St. ■	67
48	LeMoyne-Owen	45
79	Tuskegee	77
76	Morehouse	86
73	Kentucky St.	80
79	Lane	90
82	Tuskegee ■	80
79	Tuskegee †	69
90	Lane †	89
65	Morehouse †	68

Nickname: Golden Bears
Colors: Purple & Gold
Arena: Knox-Windham Gym
  Capacity: 2,000; Year Built: 1949
AD: Augustus James
SID: LaTaiya Barnes

MILLERSVILLE
Millersville, PA 17551-0302 II

Coach: Fred Thompson, La.-Monroe 1990
2002-03 RESULTS (26-6)
83	Bloomfield ■	56
84	Virginia St. ■	62
79	Johnson Smith †	72
87	Virginia Union †	80
68	West Va. Wesleyan	49
74	Virginia Union ■	70
70	Edinboro	79
75	Clarion	73
66	Indiana (Pa.)	74
71	Shippensburg	78
66	Holy Family	72
67	Calif. (Pa.) ■	56
67	Slippery Rock ■	52
81	Lock Haven ■	64
89	Bloomsburg ■	62
70	Mansfield	62
92	Cheyney	58
51	West Chester	59
81	East Stroudsburg ■	55
87	Kutztown	65
90	Mansfield ■	81
90	Bloomsburg	67
89	West Chester ■	84
66	Cheyney	62
71	East Stroudsburg	48
80	Kutztown	66
83	Mansfield ■	63
79	Clarion †	57
79	Calif. (Pa.)	74
62	Belmont Abbey †	56
80	Barton †	63
77	Queens (N.C.)	94

Nickname: Marauders
Colors: Black & Gold
Arena: Pucillo Gymnasium
  Capacity: 3,000; Year Built: 1970
AD: Daniel N. Audette
SID: Greg Wright

MILLIKIN
Decatur, IL 62522-2084 III

Coach: Tim Littrell, Millikin 1977
2002-03 RESULTS (7-18)
72	Illinois Col. ■	78
63	Aurora	80
75	MacMurray	83
78	Blackburn ■	83
72	Webster ■	66
76	Eureka ■	73

72 Franklin ■ ...73
110 Redlands † ...106
64 Whittier ...84
76 North Park ...69
77 North Central ...78
54 Ill. Wesleyan ...69
82 Judson (Ill.) ■ ...81
92 North Park ...91
98 Ind.-Northwest ...68
58 Wheaton (Ill.) ■ ...74
63 Elmhurst ■ ...74
55 Augustana (Ill.) ■ ...76
56 Carthage ...79
64 Wheaton (Ill.) ...82
69 Elmhurst ...81
55 Carthage ...78
59 Augustana (Ill.) ...89
62 Ill. Wesleyan ■ ...70
79 North Central ■ ...81

Nickname: Big Blue
Colors: Royal Blue & White
Arena: Griswold Gymnasium
  Capacity: 4,080; Year Built: 1970
AD: Doug Neibuhr
SID: Julie Farr

MILLSAPS
Jackson, MS 39210 ...III

Coach: John Stroud, Mississippi 1980
2002-03 RESULTS (15-11)
49 Louisiana Tech ...77
98 Rhodes ■ ...77
68 Huntingdon ...57
77 Rust ...65
89 Crichton † ...76
86 Maryville (Mo.) † ...71
74 Dallas ...78
77 Webster † ...58
76 Rust ■ ...77
85 Oglethorpe ...74
69 Trinity (Tex.) ...76
68 Southwestern (Tex.) ...86
72 Dallas ■ ...59
68 Sewanee ...63
88 Centre ■ ...66
58 Hendrix ...67
91 Rhodes ...78
71 Rose-Hulman ■ ...48
65 DePauw ...71
86 Huntingdon ■ ...71
75 Oglethorpe ■ ...60
60 Trinity (Tex.) ...51
79 Southwestern (Tex.) ■ ...84
69 Sewanee ...73
73 Centre ...90
78 Centre † ...82

Nickname: Majors
Colors: Purple & White
Arena: Physical Activities Cente
  Capacity: 3,000; Year Built: 1974
AD: Ron Jurney
SID: Jeff Mitchell

MILWAUKEE ENGR.
Milwaukee, WI 53202-3109 ...III

Coach: Brian Good, Wisconsin 1993
2002-03 RESULTS (12-17)
77 Lawrence ■ ...90
65 Carroll (Wis.) ■ ...69
46 Wis.-Eau Claire ...73
63 Carthage ...77
81 North Park ...88
69 Maranatha Baptist ■ ...72
85 Dominican (Ill.) ...76
66 Concordia (Ill.) † ...54
61 Marian (Wis.) ■ ...65
78 Eureka ■ ...65
72 Rockford ■ ...76

68 North Central ...71
62 Wis.-La Crosse ■ ...82
79 Illinois Tech ...51
72 Wis. Lutheran ...79
66 Concordia (Wis.) ...68
60 Edgewood ...74
49 Lakeland ...56
77 Wis. Lutheran ■ ...63
68 Marian (Wis.) ...65
61 Maranatha Baptist ...53
83 Northland Bapt. ...63
68 Concordia (Wis.) ...72
59 Edgewood ■ ...50
50 Lakeland ...60
71 Concordia (Wis.) ...67
68 Maranatha Baptist ...62
91 Lakeland ...87
56 Wis.-Oshkosh ...78

Nickname: Raiders
Colors: Red & White
Arena: US Cellular Arena
  Capacity: 12,000
AD: Daniel I. Harris
SID: Mark Ostapina

MINNESOTA
Minneapolis, MN 55455 ...I

Coach: Dan Monson, Idaho 1985
2002-03 RESULTS (19-14)
87 UNC Asheville ■ ...81
72 Georgia ■ ...69
64 Georgia Tech ■ ...63
79 Bethune-Cookman ■ ...52
60 Nebraska ...80
86 Ark.-Little Rock ■ ...84
104 Fairleigh Dickinson ■ ...66
81 Oregon ...90
89 Texas Tech ■ ...99
85 Oral Roberts ■ ...80
79 Sacred Heart ■ ...46
70 Illinois ...76
50 Wisconsin ...66
77 Michigan St. ■ ...69
63 Michigan ...75
74 Northwestern ...57
76 Penn St. ...75
87 Michigan ...80
68 Ohio St. ...73
90 Purdue ■ ...68
77 Iowa ■ ...64
73 Northwestern ...61
77 Penn St. ■ ...62
61 Michigan St. ...71
61 Wisconsin ■ ...69
70 Indiana ...74
60 Illinois ...84
64 Northwestern † ...76
62 St. Louis ...52
84 Hawaii ■ ...70
63 Temple ...58
74 Georgetown † ...88
61 Texas Tech † ...71

Nickname: Golden Gophers
Colors: Maroon & Gold
Arena: Williams Arena
  Capacity: 14,625; Year Built: 1928
AD: Joel Maturi
SID: Bill Crumley

MINN. ST. MOORHEAD
Moorhead, MN 56563-2996 ...II

Coach: Stu Engen, Augsburg 1986
2002-03 RESULTS (19-10)
83 Northern Mich. † ...72
78 Chadron St. † ...67
88 Valley City St. ...63
70 Concordia-M'head ■ ...63
80 North Dakota ■ ...66

94 Mayville St. ■ ...74
82 Dakota Wesleyan ■ ...76
66 North Dakota St. ...70
93 Minn.-Crookston ■ ...79
71 Minn. Duluth ...67
60 Bemidji St. ...89
71 Northern St. ■ ...75
73 Minn.-Morris ■ ...48
80 Concordia-St. Paul ...54
77 Winona St. ...85
80 Wayne St. (Neb.) ■ ...65
75 Southwest Minn. St. ■ ...80
70 Minn.-Crookston ...64
68 Bemidji St. ■ ...91
72 Minn. Duluth ■ ...82
74 Minn.-Morris ...52
71 Northern St. ...91
86 Winona St. ...76
81 Concordia-St. Paul ■ ...78
51 Southwest Minn. St. ...64
61 Wayne St. (Neb.) ■ ...50
70 Southwest Minn. St. ...62
79 Bemidji St. † ...78
66 Minn. Duluth † ...71

Nickname: Dragons
Colors: Scarlet & White
Arena: Alex Nemzek Hall
  Capacity: 3,400; Year Built: 1960
AD: Katy Wilson
SID: Larry Scott

MINN. ST. MANKATO
Mankato, MN 56001 ...II

Coach: Matt Margenthaler, Western Ill. 1991
2002-03 RESULTS (15-13)
100 Winona St. ■ ...75
84 Wis.-Stout ■ ...80
83 Upper Iowa ■ ...69
83 Minn.-Crookston ...73
81 Minn. Duluth ...65
66 Wayne St. (Neb.) † ...55
53 Southwest Minn. St. ...70
71 Concordia-St. Paul ...69
71 Rockhurst ...86
80 Sioux Falls ■ ...67
104 Minn.-Morris ■ ...76
88 South Dakota St. ...90
61 Augustana (S.D.) ■ ...60
72 North Dakota ...81
67 North Dakota St. ...74
89 Neb.-Omaha ...83
73 Northern Colo. ...87
85 North Dakota St. ■ ...74
74 St. Cloud St. ■ ...83
78 Augustana (S.D.) ...57
60 St. Cloud St. ...86
72 North Dakota ...69
83 South Dakota ...94
55 Neb.-Omaha ...76
71 South Dakota St. ...93
58 Northern Colo. ...63
78 South Dakota ■ ...70
65 South Dakota St. ...79

Nickname: Mavericks
Colors: Purple & Gold
Arena: Bresnan Arena In Taylor Center
  Capacity: 4,521; Year Built: 2000
AD: Kevin Buisman
SID: Paul Allan

MINN.-CROOKSTON
Crookston, MN 56716-5001 ...II

Coach: Jeff Oseth, Minn. St. Moorhead
2002-03 RESULTS (4-21)
49 St. Cloud St. ...88
90 Mayville St. ■ ...93
73 Minn. St. Mankato ■ ...83

79 Mayville St. ...83
63 Morningside ...78
54 North Dakota St. ...80
79 North Dakota ■ ...72
79 Minn. St. Moorhead ...93
59 Bemidji St. ...99
61 Minn. Duluth ...90
83 Minn.-Morris ■ ...63
44 Northern St. ■ ...75
69 Winona St. ...79
66 Concordia-St. Paul ...85
89 Southwest Minn. St. ■ ...96
64 Wayne St. (Neb.) ■ ...79
64 Minn. St. Moorhead ■ ...70
68 Minn. Duluth ...73
88 Bemidji St. ■ ...85
56 Northern St. ...77
100 Minn.-Morris ...52
73 Concordia-St. Paul ■ ...88
74 Winona St. ...89
67 Wayne St. (Neb.) ...85
74 Southwest Minn. St. ...82

Nickname: Golden Eagle
Colors: Maroon & Gold
Arena: Lysaker Gym
  Capacity: 3,500; Year Built: 1970
AD: Lon Boike
SID: Nick Kornder

MINN. DULUTH
Duluth, MN 55812-2496 ...II

Coach: Gary Holquist, Milton 1979
2002-03 RESULTS (19-12)
70 Seattle Pacific ...80
85 Northwest Nazarene † ...55
77 Colorado St.-Pueblo ■ ...62
97 Northwest Mo. St. ...67
65 Minn. St. Mankato ...81
71 North Dakota St. ■ ...83
87 St. Scholastica ...62
77 Michigan Tech ...81
79 North Dakota ...96
78 Southwest Minn. St. ...82
83 Wayne St. (Neb.) ■ ...84
67 Minn. St. Moorhead ■ ...71
90 Minn.-Crookston ■ ...61
86 Bemidji St. ■ ...69
75 Northern St. ...79
70 Minn.-Morris ...68
84 Concordia-St. Paul ■ ...70
80 Winona St. ...59
68 Wayne St. (Neb.) ■ ...65
98 Southwest Minn. St. ■ ...91
73 Minn.-Crookston ...68
82 Minn. St. Moorhead ...72
67 Bemidji St. ...90
93 Minn.-Morris ■ ...47
85 Northern St. ■ ...89
79 Winona St. ...68
74 Concordia-St. Paul ...65
93 Wayne St. (Neb.) ■ ...63
68 Northern St. † ...65
71 Minn. St. Moorhead † ...66
67 Neb.-Kearney ...72

Nickname: Bulldogs
Colors: Maroon & Gold
Arena: Romano Gymnasium
  Capacity: 2,759; Year Built: 1953
AD: Robert Corran
SID: Troy Andre

MINN.-MORRIS
Morris, MN 56267 ...II

Coach: Paul Grove, Gust. Adolphus 1989
2002-03 RESULTS (2-25)
70 Martin Luther ...68
65 Mayville St. ■ ...90

54	Augustana (S.D.)	99
78	St. Scholastica	82
45	South Dakota	95
66	North Dakota ■	92
53	Crown	66
79	Northwestern (Minn.) ■	75
76	Minn. St. Mankato	104
67	Winona St.	81
48	Concordia-St. Paul	86
37	Southwest Minn. St. ■	68
58	Wayne St. (Neb.) ■	85
63	Minn.-Crookston	83
48	Minn. St. Moorhead	73
71	Bemidji St. ■	116
68	Minn. Duluth ■	70
62	Northern St.	82
84	Concordia-St. Paul ■	92
71	Winona St. ■	107
81	Wayne St. (Neb.)	84
40	Southwest Minn. St.	93
52	Minn. St. Moorhead ■	74
52	Minn.-Crookston ■	100
47	Minn. Duluth	93
70	Bemidji St.	118
51	Northern St. ■	70

Nickname: Cougars
Colors: Maroon & Gold
Arena: Physical Education Center
 Capacity: 3,500; Year Built: 1971
AD: Mark Fohl
SID: Brian Curtis

MISERICORDIA
Dallas, PA 18612......................III

Coach: David Martin, Wilkes 1990
2002-03 RESULTS (16-12)
87	Baptist Bible (Pa.)	80
90	Marywood ■	62
47	DeSales	62
54	Alvernia ■	63
96	Wesley ■	73
65	Muhlenberg	55
63	Springfield	65
66	John Carroll †	55
55	Cabrini	60
72	Lycoming ■	75
77	Arcadia	89
76	Eastern ■	70
75	King's (Pa.) ■	58
73	Marywood ■	77
82	Gwynedd-Mercy	69
67	Neumann	62
58	Wesley	63
73	Gwynedd-Mercy ■	65
65	Alvernia	61
69	Cabrini ■	66
72	Arcadia ■	63
97	Marywood	80
61	Eastern	66
91	Villa Julie	64
82	Neumann ■	83
76	Gwynedd-Mercy ■	74
65	Neumann	97
65	DeSales	81

Nickname: Cougars
Colors: Royal Blue & Gold
Arena: Anderson Sports-Health Center
 Capacity: 1,500; Year Built: 1992
AD: Michael W. Mould
SID: Scott Crispell

MISSISSIPPI
University, MS 38677 I

Coach: Rod Barnes, Mississippi 1988
2002-03 RESULTS (14-15)
58	East Caro.	65
74	Alabama St. ■	58

56	George Mason	49
74	Austin Peay ■	46
82	Va. Commonwealth ■	68
80	La.-Monroe ■	57
51	Memphis	58
63	Nicholls St. ■	52
87	Evansville ■	69
71	Ark.-Pine Bluff ■	38
57	Samford	49
49	South Carolina	55
64	Tennessee ■	66
67	LSU	57
76	Alabama ■	57
73	Arkansas ■	54
57	Mississippi St. ■	58
68	Vanderbilt	76
71	Auburn	77
62	Kentucky ■	80
55	Florida	74
64	Mississippi St.	68
75	Auburn ■	80
82	Georgia ■	89
63	Alabama	86
64	LSU ■	77
64	Arkansas	54
62	South Carolina †	56
64	Mississippi St. †	73

Nickname: Rebels
Colors: Red & Blue
Arena: C.M. "Tad" Smith Coliseum
 Capacity: 8,700; Year Built: 1966
AD: Pete Boone
SID: Lamar Chance

MISSISSIPPI COL.
Clinton, MS 39058 III

Coach: Don Lofton, Mississippi Col. 1978
2002-03 RESULTS (19-8)
82	Concordia (Ala.) ■	62
74	Pensacola Christian ■	46
68	Texas Lutheran ■	53
83	Schreiner ■	54
70	Howard Payne	85
67	Sul Ross St.	75
78	Stillman ■	62
84	Concordia-Austin ■	73
55	Mary Hardin-Baylor ■	56
72	McMurry	80
69	Hardin-Simmons	61
65	Texas-Dallas	59
110	Messenger ■	50
77	LeTourneau	54
76	East Tex. Baptist ■	82
83	Louisiana Col. ■	74
63	Austin	55
73	Ozarks (Ark.)	83
89	Austin ■	64
87	Ozarks (Ark.) ■	66
61	Louisiana Col.	49
63	Texas-Dallas ■	50
82	LeTourneau	55
72	East Tex. Baptist	77
75	Sul Ross St. †	67
83	McMurry †	63
58	Maryville (Tenn.)	70

Nickname: Choctaws
Colors: Blue & Gold
Arena: A.E. Wood Coliseum
 Capacity: 3,500; Year Built: 1979
AD: Mike Jones
SID: Chris Brooks

MISSISSIPPI ST.
Mississippi State, MS 39762-5509 I

Coach: Rick Stansbury, Campbellsville 1982
2002-03 RESULTS (21-10)
76	La.-Lafayette ■	79
81	McNeese St. ■	65
100	Jacksonville ■	65
100	Alabama A&M ■	58
71	Jackson St. ■	56
78	Louisiana Tech ■	38
71	Xavier †	61
78	Georgia St. †	54
54	Oklahoma †	45
85	South Ala. †	74
68	UAB	52
66	Florida ■	74
72	LSU	85
62	Alabama	68
64	South Carolina ■	48
67	LSU ■	64
58	Mississippi	57
63	Georgia	67
82	Vanderbilt ■	60
84	Arkansas ■	54
68	Mississippi ■	64
63	Auburn	46
62	Kentucky	70
59	Alabama ■	55
51	Arkansas	53
49	Tennessee	59
67	Auburn ■	45
73	Mississippi †	64
76	LSU †	61
57	Kentucky †	64
46	Butler †	47

Nickname: Bulldogs
Colors: Maroon & White
Arena: Humphrey Coliseum
 Capacity: 10,500; Year Built: 1975
AD: Larry Templeton
SID: David Rosinski

MISSISSIPPI VAL.
Itta Bena, MS 38941-1400 I

Coach: Lafayette Stribling, Miss. Industrial 1957
2002-03 RESULTS (15-14)
75	Wis.-Milwaukee	77
68	Tex.-Pan American	73
91	Delta St.	94
75	Oral Roberts ■	85
87	Delta St. ■	64
75	Wis.-Milwaukee ■	83
63	Oral Roberts	96
63	Santa Clara	70
56	Texas A&M †	65
72	Ark.-Pine Bluff	52
91	Alabama A&M ■	81
67	Alabama St. ■	73
69	Alcorn St.	76
72	Southern U.	59
87	Prairie View ■	68
75	Texas Southern ■	80
73	Jackson St.	71
77	Grambling	85
103	Alabama A&M	72
79	Alabama St.	78
73	Alcorn St. ■	65
77	Southern U. ■	69
75	Prairie View	72
72	Texas Southern	66
85	Jackson St. ■	78
92	Grambling ■	99
75	Ark.-Pine Bluff ■	68
90	Grambling †	78
72	Texas Southern †	73

Nickname: Delta Devils
Colors: Forest Green & White
Arena: Harrison HPER Complex
 Capacity: 6,000; Year Built: 1970
AD: Lonza C. Hardy
SID: Marlon J. Reed

MISSOURI
Columbia, MO 65211-1050......I

Coach: Quin Snyder, Duke 1989
2002-03 RESULTS (22-11)
72	American ■	57
81	Austin Peay ■	46
98	Sacramento St. ■	60
78	Southern California	72
88	Wis.-Green Bay ■	67
93	Memphis ■	78
70	Illinois †	85
65	Valparaiso ■	47
88	Iowa	82
88	Centenary (La.) ■	58
77	Baylor ■	69
69	Syracuse	76
56	Oklahoma St.	76
64	Iowa St. ■	59
55	Texas	76
63	Nebraska	56
73	Colorado ■	70
70	Kansas	76
82	Texas Tech ■	73
71	Texas A&M ■	73
71	Kansas St. ■	63
67	Nebraska ■	50
68	Colorado	89
67	Oklahoma ■	52
77	Kansas St.	70
55	Iowa St.	71
74	Kansas	79
70	Nebraska †	61
60	Oklahoma St. †	58
68	Kansas †	63
47	Oklahoma †	49
72	Southern Ill. †	71
92	Marquette †	101

Nickname: Tigers
Colors: Old Gold & Black
Arena: Hearnes Center
 Capacity: 13,545; Year Built: 1972
AD: Michael F. Alden
SID: Chad Moller

UMKC
Kansas City, MO 64110............I

Coach: Rich Zvosec, Defiance 1983
2002-03 RESULTS (9-20)
77	Robert Morris ■	83
60	Norfolk St.	61
66	Denver	83
59	Colorado ■	62
75	Loyola (Ill.)	86
58	Southeast Mo. St. ■	66
61	Oklahoma St.	85
71	Youngstown St. ■	59
61	Idaho St. †	75
56	Arkansas St. †	71
61	Monmouth ■	64
46	Kansas †	100
80	Chicago St. ■	70
78	Southern Utah	82
65	Oakland ■	86
65	IUPUI ■	74
65	Southwest Mo. St.	78
62	Oral Roberts ■	76
78	Western Ill.	71
71	Valparaiso	68
91	Southern Utah ■	69
59	Chicago St. ■	56

61	IUPUI	73
79	Oakland	100
91	Oral Roberts ■	86
63	Valparaiso	75
83	Western Ill. ■	79
76	Oral Roberts †	73
50	Valparaiso †	71

Nickname: Kangaroos
Colors: Blue & Gold
Arena: Municipal Auditorium
  Capacity: 9,827; Year Built: 1936
AD: Robert W. Thomas
SID: Pat Madden

MO.-ROLLA
Rolla, MO 65401 ...II

Coach: Dale Martin, Central Mo. St. 1976

2002-03 RESULTS (12-15)

54	Lincoln (Mo.)	79
86	Ozarks (Ark.) ■	71
83	Central Okla. †	78
68	Hillsdale †	81
91	Harris-Stowe	60
50	Mo.-St. Louis ■	44
89	St. Edward's	79
49	Incarnate Word	68
71	Southwest Baptist	67
57	Emporia St.	75
67	Pittsburg St. ■	69
51	Washburn	67
70	Central Mo. St.	72
68	Mo. Western St. ■	61
70	Truman ■	62
58	Northwest Mo. St.	70
65	Mo. Southern St. ■	61
76	Emporia St.	69
64	Pittsburg St.	78
71	Washburn ■	84
70	Central Mo. St.	69
64	Mo. Western St.	85
58	Truman	79
54	Northwest Mo. St. ■	75
56	Mo. Southern St.	71
86	Southwest Baptist ■	63
56	Mo. Western St. †	73

Nickname: Miners
Colors: Silver & Gold
Arena: Bullman Multi-Purpose
  Capacity: 4,550; Year Built: 1969
AD: Mark Mullin
SID: John Kean

MO.-ST. LOUIS
St. Louis, MO 63121-4499 ...II

Coach: Mark Bernsen, Mo.-St. Louis 1972

2002-03 RESULTS (5-22)

60	Rockhurst ■	64
82	Harris-Stowe	69
87	Ill.-Springfield ■	76
77	Bellarmine	68
54	Northern Ky.	73
76	St. Joseph's (Ind.) ■	70
48	Wis.-Parkside ■	60
65	Harris-Stowe ■	55
44	Mo.-Rolla	50
51	SIU Edwardsville	61
68	Quincy	82
61	Southern Ind.	85
51	Ky. Wesleyan	76
52	Northern Ky. ■	64
54	Indianapolis ■	69
53	Wis.-Parkside	56
47	Lewis	68
57	Quincy ■	68
55	Lincoln (Mo.)	62
54	Ky. Wesleyan ■	82
67	Bellarmine ■	78
67	Indianapolis	71
78	St. Joseph's (Ind.)	87
42	Lewis ■	54
61	SIU Edwardsville ■	63
63	Lincoln (Mo.) ■	64
75	Southern Ind. ■	90

Nickname: Rivermen
Colors: Red & Gold
Arena: Mark Twain Building
  Capacity: 4,736; Year Built: 1971
AD: Patricia A. Dolan
SID: Todd Addington

MO. SOUTHERN ST.
Joplin, MO 64801-1595 ...II

Coach: Robert Corn, Mo. Southern St. 1978

2002-03 RESULTS (19-10)

96	Philander Smith ■	56
75	Southwestern Okla. ■	64
66	Quincy	77
76	Lincoln (Mo.) †	61
87	Northwestern Okla. †	74
66	Southeastern Okla.	49
67	Rockhurst	62
73	Northeastern St. ■	56
53	Washburn	80
65	Southwest Baptist	80
56	Central Mo. St.	53
78	Northwest Mo. St. ■	75
74	Pittsburg St.	69
85	Emporia St. ■	90
91	Mo. Western St. ■	83
91	Truman	83
61	Mo.-Rolla	65
92	Southwest Baptist ■	80
72	Central Mo. St. ■	57
92	Northwest Mo. St.	93
80	Pittsburg St. ■	75
90	Emporia St.	104
114	Messenger ■	48
68	Mo. Western St.	82
75	Truman ■	73
71	Mo.-Rolla ■	56
91	Washburn	105
99	Emporia St. †	98
61	Washburn †	80

Nickname: Lions
Colors: Green & Gold
Arena: Leggett & Platt A.C.
  Capacity: 3,240; Year Built: 1999
AD: Sallie Beard
SID: J.R. Belew

MO. WESTERN ST.
St. Joseph, MO 64507 ...II

Coach: Tom Smith, Valparaiso 1967

2002-03 RESULTS (23-8)

101	William Jewell ■	61
80	Benedictine (Kan.) ■	37
85	Hillsdale ■	75
77	Central Okla.	59
69	Rockhurst	73
92	Manhattan Chrst. ■	48
70	Seattle Pacific †	65
73	St. Mary's (Tex.)	68
74	Northwest Mo. St.	80
90	Central Mo. St. ■	85
80	Emporia St. ■	61
57	Pittsburg St.	67
99	Truman ■	62
61	Mo.-Rolla	68
83	Mo. Southern St.	91
77	Southwest Baptist ■	66
68	Washburn	67
87	Central Mo. St.	99
96	Emporia St.	87
88	Pittsburg St. ■	86
81	Park ■	58
80	Truman	57
85	Mo.-Rolla ■	64
82	Mo. Southern St. ■	68
83	Southwest Baptist	58
65	Washburn ■	75
77	Northwest Mo. St. ■	65
73	Mo.-Rolla †	56
76	Northwest Mo. St. †	67
75	Washburn †	65
61	Northwest Mo. St. †	71

Nickname: Griffons
Colors: Black & Gold
Arena: MWSC Fieldhouse
  Capacity: 3,750; Year Built: 1981
AD: Mark Linder
SID: Brett King

MOLLOY
Rockville Centre, NY 11570-5002
...II

Coach: Charles Marquardt, St. Joseph's (Me.) 1986

2002-03 RESULTS (13-15)

53	Queens (N.Y.) ■	66
83	Concordia (N.Y.)	70
83	Pace	79
79	Philadelphia U.	78
74	Southampton	80
66	St. Thomas Aquinas	54
55	Bryant	80
78	Bloomfield †	76
72	Mercy	66
77	New Haven ■	84
68	Bridgeport	92
68	Adelphi ■	75
65	C.W. Post	73
88	Dowling ■	78
75	Concordia (N.Y.) ■	64
62	NYIT	92
57	Philadelphia U. ■	69
62	Queens (N.Y.)	71
72	St. Thomas Aquinas ■	67
81	Southampton	75
72	Mercy ■	74
59	New Haven	69
61	Adelphi	84
85	NYIT ■	70
82	Bridgeport	75
106	Dowling ■	103
81	C.W. Post ■	88
76	C.W. Post	88

Nickname: Lions
Colors: Maroon & White
Arena: Quealy Gymnasium
  Capacity: 400; Year Built: 1955
AD: Harold Herman
SID: Dan Drutz

MONMOUTH
West Long Branch, NJ 07764 ...I

Coach: Dave Calloway, Monmouth 1991

2002-03 RESULTS (15-13)

61	Rider	66
68	Drexel ■	73
57	Princeton	60
70	Hofstra	57
57	Seton Hall	67
63	St. Peter's ■	72
64	Kansas St.	73
64	UMKC	61
75	Fairleigh Dickinson	72
75	Long Island	74
80	St. Francis (N.Y.) ■	76
54	Pennsylvania †	98
45	Wagner ■	63
65	Sacred Heart	55
79	Quinnipiac ■	59
71	Central Conn. St.	66
58	Mt. St. Mary's	42
80	UMBC	74
73	Sacred Heart	53
53	Wagner	62
71	St. Francis (N.Y.)	81
78	Long Island ■	70
72	St. Francis (Pa.)	70
69	Robert Morris	67
68	St. Francis (Pa.) ■	76
59	Robert Morris ■	69
68	Fairleigh Dickinson	59
51	Fairleigh Dickinson †	63

Nickname: Hawks
Colors: Royal Blue & White
Arena: Boylan Gymnasium
  Capacity: 2,500; Year Built: 1965
AD: Marilyn A. McNeil
SID: Thomas Dick

MONMOUTH (ILL.)
Monmouth, IL 61462-1998 ...III

Coach: Terry Glasgow, Alma Mater 1966

2002-03 RESULTS (5-18)

62	Central Mo. St.	101
103	Concordia (Ill.) ■	82
98	William Penn ■	89
75	MacMurray	73
65	Knox	79
66	Aurora	84
45	Concordia (Ill.)	63
51	SIU Edwardsville	66
61	Lake Forest	64
49	St. Norbert	69
76	Carroll (Wis.)	97
73	Illinois Col.	82
40	Lawrence ■	75
75	Beloit	73
68	Ripon	81
56	Lawrence	86
102	Grinnell ■	141
83	Carroll (Wis.) ■	90
49	St. Norbert ■	66
85	Knox	91
118	Grinnell	129
77	Illinois Col.	83
71	Lake Forest	61

Nickname: Fighting Scots
Colors: Red & White
Arena: Glennie Gymnasium
  Capacity: 1,600; Year Built: 1982
AD: Terry L. Glasgow
SID: Barry McNamara, Dan Nolan

MONTANA
Missoula, MT 59812-1291 ...I

Coach: Pat Kennedy, Kings (Pa.) 1975

2002-03 RESULTS (13-17)

71	Northern Iowa ■	77
75	Denver ■	47
60	Michigan St. †	80
62	Loyola Marymount †	65
52	Alas. Anchorage	69
67	Gonzaga ■	75
66	Montana Tech ■	52
61	Washington St.	73
81	Idaho ■	69
70	Stanford	68
69	Pepperdine †	86
75	Loyola Marymount	68
81	Southern Utah	61
54	Denver	62
66	Purdue	84
62	Eastern Wash. ■	72

61	Portland St. ■	49
90	Idaho St.	88
73	Weber St.	97
58	Montana St.	62
93	Northern Ariz. ■	97
66	Sacramento St. ■	59
67	Portland St.	49
72	Eastern Wash.	87
72	Weber St. ■	75
69	Idaho St. ■	65
66	Montana St.	63
77	Sacramento St.	71
59	Northern Ariz.	69
75	Sacramento St. ■	88

Nickname: Grizzlies
Colors: Copper, Silver & Gold
Arena: Adams Center/Dahlberg Arena
  Capacity: 7,500; Year Built: 1953
AD: Wayne Hogan
SID: Dave Guffey

MONTANA ST.
Bozeman, MT 59717-3380........I

Coach: Mick Durham, Montana St. 1979
2002-03 RESULTS (11-16)

56	Washington	53
66	Santa Clara	69
64	Winthrop ■	67
90	Great Falls ■	57
44	Iowa	65
64	Jacksonville †	55
88	Dickinson St. ■	74
56	Baylor	65
74	Idaho	68
85	South Carolina St. ■	57
58	Siena ■	71
56	Wyoming ■	60
65	Portland ■	76
52	Portland St. ■	48
51	Eastern Wash. ■	65
70	Weber St. ■	78
55	Idaho St. ■	56
62	Montana	58
66	Sacramento St. ■	72
80	Northern Ariz. ■	66
74	Eastern Wash.	78
60	Portland St.	56
73	Idaho St. ■	65
58	Weber St. ■	70
63	Montana	66
71	Northern Ariz.	81
52	Sacramento St.	72

Nickname: Bobcats
Colors: Blue & Gold
Arena: Worthington Arena
  Capacity: 7,250; Year Built: 1956
AD: Peter Fields
SID: Bill Lamberty

MONT. ST.-BILLINGS
Billings, MT 59101-0298 II

Coach: Craig Carse, Bethany (W.Va.) 1978
2002-03 RESULTS (18-9)

61	Cal St. San B'dino ■	60
86	St. Martin's	77
101	Minot St. ■	79
103	Chadron St. ■	69
101	St. Martin's ■	83
82	Charleston (W.Va.) ■	81
55	Cal St. L.A.	75
66	Cal Poly Pomona	82
76	Chaminade	89
91	Hawaii-Hilo	101
77	Hawaii-Hilo	86
71	Hawaii Pacific ■	72
98	Hawaii Pacific ■	81

86	BYU-Hawaii ■	76
109	Western N.M. ■	91
146	Western N.M. ■	73
102	Great Falls ■	61
87	Chaminade ■	71
97	Chaminade ■	83
93	Hawaii-Hilo ■	78
111	Western N.M. ■	79
83	Western N.M.	73
78	BYU-Hawaii	91
89	BYU-Hawaii ■	103
70	Hawaii Pacific	81
106	Nova Southeastern ■	70
87	Nova Southeastern ■	66

Nickname: Yellowjackets
Colors: Cobalt Blue & Yellow
Arena: Alterowitz Gymnasium
  Capacity: 3,500; Year Built: 1961
AD: Gary R. Gray
SID: Travis Elam

MONTCLAIR ST.
Upper Montclair, NJ 07043 III

Coach: Ted Fiore, Seton Hall 1962
2002-03 RESULTS (23-6)

94	Centenary (N.J.) ■	54
64	Trinity (Conn.) ■	57
72	Rutgers-Newark	51
72	Richard Stockton	57
73	Rowan ■	67
72	New Jersey City	58
74	Rutgers-Camden	69
73	Eastern Conn. St. ■	47
75	Baruch ■	66
85	Staten Island	77
88	Mass.-Dartmouth ■	78
71	TCNJ ■	54
72	Wm. Paterson	75
74	Kean	56
81	Ramapo	84
76	Richard Stockton	70
67	Rutgers-Newark ■	46
54	Ramapo ■	64
77	New Jersey City ■	79
59	Kean ■	38
78	Rutgers-Camden ■	55
69	Rowan ■	76
45	Wm. Paterson ■	31
62	TCNJ	59
70	Wm. Paterson	66
86	Ramapo	84
74	Elizabethtown ■	69
95	Catholic	78
80	Ramapo †	89

Nickname: Red Hawks
Colors: Scarlet & White
Arena: Panzer Gymnasium
  Capacity: 1,200; Year Built: 1954
AD: Holly P. Gera
SID: Mike Scala

MONTEVALLO
Montevallo, AL 35115-6001......II

Coach: Jeff Daniels, Montevallo 1984
2002-03 RESULTS (4-25)

84	Harding ■	105
76	Lane ■	80
55	St. Mary's (Tex.)	100
62	Midwestern St. †	82
52	Christian Bros. †	63
66	Harding	95
61	Alabama St.	79
70	Southern Ark. †	59
79	Athens St. †	74
60	Alas. Anchorage	84
61	Alas. Fairbanks †	94
63	Kennesaw St.	77
69	West Fla. ■	67

60	Lincoln Memorial	65
54	West Ala.	71
59	West Ga.	77
55	Valdosta St. ■	68
64	Ala.-Huntsville	80
70	Oakland City ■	83
63	North Ala. ■	86
49	West Fla.	72
71	Lincoln Memorial ■	72
77	West Ala. ■	85
106	Carver Bible ■	71
59	West Ga.	66
65	Valdosta St.	74
70	Oakland City	86
58	Ala.-Huntsville ■	60
78	North Ala.	82

Nickname: Falcons
Colors: Purple & Gold
Arena: Myrick Hall
  Capacity: 1,500; Year Built: 1964
AD: Michael Cancilla
SID: Alfred Kojima

MORAVIAN
Bethlehem, PA 18018-6650......III

Coach: Jim Walker, Gettysburg 1965
2002-03 RESULTS (16-11)

76	Emmanuel (Mass.)	65
69	Palm Beach Atl. †	60
63	DeSales ■	73
66	Albright ■	59
85	Lebanon Valley	81
87	Drew ■	55
64	Delaware Valley	57
77	TCNJ	79
71	Connecticut Col. ■	54
53	Muhlenberg ■	60
76	Elizabethtown ■	70
55	Scranton	67
82	Messiah	58
76	Swarthmore	67
66	Widener ■	68
75	Juniata	58
73	Susquehanna	85
78	Lebanon Valley ■	72
65	Muhlenberg ■	58
84	Albright	74
89	Messiah ■	75
64	Elizabethtown	97
65	Widener	73
67	Susquehanna ■	73
76	Juniata ■	55
62	Elizabethtown	71
59	Frank. & Marsh.	79

Nickname: Greyhounds
Colors: Blue & Grey
Arena: Johnston Hall
  Capacity: 1,200; Year Built: 1952
AD: Paul R. Moyer
SID: Mark Fleming

MOREHEAD ST.
Morehead, KY 40351-1689.......I

Coach: Kyle Macy, Kentucky 1980
2002-03 RESULTS (20-9)

56	Arizona St.	59
100	Taylor (Ind.) ■	77
100	Asbury ■	54
74	Wright St.	80
98	Tex. A&M-Corp. Chris.	88
60	Ohio St.	74
101	Marshall ■	100
64	Alabama	82
89	IUPUI ■	98
93	Tennessee St.	42
72	Tennessee Tech	70
75	Eastern Ill. ■	71
77	Southeast Mo. St. ■	63

86	IPFW ■	73
54	Eastern Ky.	50
103	Tennessee St. ■	89
83	Murray St.	76
83	Tenn.-Martin	60
59	Austin Peay ■	66
88	Ky. Christian ■	39
79	Southeast Mo. St.	69
69	Eastern Ill.	75
97	Tennessee Tech ■	89
88	Eastern Ky. ■	87
104	Tenn.-Martin ■	76
77	Murray St. ■	74
64	Austin Peay	76
91	Southeast Mo. St. ■	84
71	Tennessee Tech †	88

Nickname: Eagles
Colors: Blue & Gold
Arena: Ellis T. Johnson Arena
  Capacity: 6,500; Year Built: 1981
AD: Chip Smith
SID: Randy Stacy

MOREHOUSE
Atlanta, GA 30314...................II

Coach: Grady Brewer, Morehouse 1980
2002-03 RESULTS (23-8)

67	Columbus St.	72
86	West Ga. ■	80
74	Texas Col. ■	81
69	Xavier (La.)	72
77	Miles ■	80
89	LeMoyne-Owen ■	82
68	Tampa	58
60	Fla. Southern	63
50	Shaw ■	68
82	Xavier (La.) ■	66
82	Tuskegee ■	81
76	Albany St. (Ga.) ■	67
68	Benedict ■	65
73	Paine ■	57
82	Tuskegee	72
75	Lane	84
103	Clark Atlanta	70
73	Lane ■	66
80	Fort Valley St. ■	57
67	Paine	66
91	Benedict	72
86	Miles	76
88	LeMoyne-Owen	82
70	Albany St. (Ga.)	68
93	Kentucky St. ■	90
73	Fort Valley St.	56
67	Clark Atlanta	59
73	Fort Valley St. †	66
66	LeMoyne-Owen †	64
68	Miles †	65
66	Eckerd †	83

Nickname: Tigers
Colors: Maroon & White
Arena: Olympic Arena
  Capacity: 6,000; Year Built: 1996
AD: Andre' Pattillo
SID: James Nix

MORGAN ST.
Baltimore, MD 21251 I

Coach: Butch Beard, Louisville 1972
2002-03 RESULTS (7-22)

80	Loyola (Md.) ■	83
53	Towson ■	67
75	Fairleigh Dickinson	91
59	Coppin St. ■	73
61	Maine	82
64	Virginia Tech	71
46	Canisius	72
62	Towson ■	59
66	William & Mary	73

65	Tex. A&M-Corp. Chris.	...98
83	Texas Southern †	...94
79	South Carolina St. ■	...81
87	N.C. A&T ■	...68
75	Hampton	...91
63	Norfolk St.	...66
80	Delaware St. ■	...72
65	Florida A&M	...85
71	Bethune-Cookman	...79
90	Md.-East. Shore ■	...69
53	Howard	...74
68	South Carolina St.	...78
89	N.C. A&T ■	...84
59	Hampton ■	...75
63	Norfolk St. ■	...60
53	Delaware St.	...80
59	Bethune-Cookman ■	...55
56	Florida A&M ■	...69
50	Coppin St.	...59
103	Bethune-Cookman †	...104

Nickname: Bears
Colors: Blue & Orange
Arena: Hill Field House
  Capacity: 6,500; Year Built: 1975
AD: David Y. Thomas
SID: Joseph McIver

MORRIS BROWN
Atlanta, GA 30314 ...I

Coach: Derek Thompson
2002-03 RESULTS (8-20)

52	Florida Int'l	...60
67	Lipscomb	...65
54	Southern California	...93
56	Cal St. Fullerton	...74
61	Eastern Ky. ■	...74
54	Winthrop	...62
56	Weber St. †	...65
67	Mercer ■	...89
58	Alabama A&M ■	...65
78	Tennessee St. ■	...87
48	Rutgers	...68
30	Tulane	...88
65	Florida A&M ■	...76
52	Clemson	...75
84	Clark Atlanta †	...81
75	Savannah St. ■	...59
75	Lipscomb	...69
73	Tennessee St.	...68
64	Eastern Ky.	...68
89	Clark Atlanta ■	...82
65	Bethune-Cookman ■	...63
56	Florida A&M	...88
83	Mercer	...90
58	Alabama A&M	...92
58	Savannah St.	...67
66	Bethune-Cookman	...85
72	Tex.-Pan American ■	...71
49	Southern U.	...77

Nickname: Wolverines
Colors: Purple & Black
Arena: John H. Lewis Gym
  Capacity: 3,000; Year Built: 1970
AD: Russell Ellington
SID: William C. Lindsey

MOUNT IDA
Newton Centre, MA 02459-3323
...III

Coach: Rico Cabral, Mass.-Boston 1976
2002-03 RESULTS (8-18)

60	Babson	...89
84	Anna Maria †	...73
56	Bridgewater St.	...64
87	Eastern Nazarene ■	...70
57	Bowdoin	...95
57	Bates	...100

76	New England Col. ■	...70
68	Wheaton (Mass.) ■	...76
80	Lasell	...92
57	Elms	...85
70	Becker	...85
61	Fitchburg St.	...70
59	Castleton St. ■	...84
53	Nichols	...81
51	Williams	...110
88	Emmanuel (Mass.) ■	...85
64	Johnson St.	...70
68	Brandeis	...77
84	Lasell ■	...99
65	Maine Maritime	...80
81	Johnson St. ■	...68
62	Maine Maritime	...72
84	Becker ■	...72
73	Elms ■	...69
94	Castleton St.	...76
77	Elms	...85

Nickname: Mustangs
Colors: Green & White
Arena: Mount Ida College Athletic Center
  Capacity: 500; Year Built: 1999
AD: Jacqueline Palmer
SID: Peter Centola

MOUNT OLIVE
Mount Olive, NC 28365 ...II

Coach: Bill Clingan, Northeastern St.
2002-03 RESULTS (18-10)

90	Coker ■	...75
74	Charleston (W.Va.) ■	...64
89	UNC Pembroke	...68
76	Anderson (S.C.) ■	...68
95	N.C. Central	...85
62	East Caro.	...90
71	Rollins	...92
106	Alderson-Broaddus †	...104
75	Pfeiffer	...84
66	Belmont Abbey	...63
77	Erskine ■	...67
91	Coker	...86
96	Lees-McRae ■	...62
83	Barton	...88
96	Queens (N.C.) ■	...94
76	Longwood	...81
85	St. Andrews	...80
90	Limestone ■	...83
83	Anderson (S.C.)	...79
113	Pfeiffer ■	...89
69	Erskine	...71
97	Coker	...59
89	Barton	...96
64	Belmont Abbey ■	...86
89	Queens (N.C.)	...95
74	Lees-McRae	...63
66	Longwood ■	...63
93	Pfeiffer	...109

Nickname: Trojans
Colors: Green & White
Arena: College Hall
  Capacity: 1,500; Year Built: 1987
AD: Allen M. Cassell
SID: Adam Pitterman

MT. ST. JOSEPH
Cincinnati, OH 45233-1672 ...III

Coach: Larry Cox, Hanover 1981
2002-03 RESULTS (12-15)

78	Coast Guard ■	...60
74	Baldwin-Wallace ■	...71
66	Denison ■	...60
68	Eastern Ky.	...87
77	Earlham ■	...64
72	Franklin	...71
75	Anderson (Ind.) ■	...84
67	Bluffton	...60

82	Cazenovia †	...81
67	Otterbein	...76
59	Capital ■	...63
71	Transylvania	...69
73	Thomas More ■	...64
52	SCAD	...69
89	Hanover ■	...103
80	Defiance	...74
71	Manchester	...83
67	Anderson (Ind.)	...66
77	Franklin ■	...80
76	Bluffton ■	...79
70	Transylvania ■	...72
67	Thomas More	...78
56	Hanover	...72
82	Manchester ■	...94
80	Manchester	...72
63	Anderson (Ind.) †	...70
77	Defiance ■	...93

Nickname: Lions
Colors: Blue & Gold
Arena: Harrington Center
  Capacity: 2,000; Year Built: 1998
AD: Steven F. Radcliffe
SID: Dane Neumeister

MT. ST. MARY (N.Y.)
Newburgh, NY 12550 ...III

Coach: Duane Davis, Albany (N.Y.) 1969
2002-03 RESULTS (23-8)

78	East Tex. Baptist †	...105
84	Rhema †	...71
134	Purchase St. ■	...73
95	CCNY ■	...90
91	NYCCT	...74
78	Farmingdale St. ■	...71
79	Yeshiva ■	...66
74	St. Joseph's (L.I.)	...66
81	Stevens Institute	...79
72	York (N.Y.)	...65
46	Manhattanville	...45
78	Old Westbury	...65
104	Mt. St. Vincent ■	...70
72	Yeshiva	...51
65	Merchant Marine	...72
84	Stevens Institute ■	...74
87	Maritime (N.Y.)	...75
75	Polytechnic (N.Y.)	...64
61	Vassar	...67
95	Mt. St. Vincent	...84
73	St. Joseph's (L.I.) ■	...70
69	Manhattanville	...75
79	Old Westbury ■	...87
106	Maritime (N.Y.) ■	...68
64	Merchant Marine ■	...71
98	Mt. St. Vincent	...75
81	Manhattanville	...79
54	Merchant Marine	...65
86	Staten Island ■	...67
87	New Jersey City ■	...86
87	Baruch	...90

Nickname: Blue Knights
Colors: Royal Blue & Gold
Arena: Kaplan Recreation Center
  Capacity: 1,500; Year Built: 1992
AD: John J. Wright
SID: Dan Twomey

MT. ST. MARY'S
Emmitsburg, MD 21727-7799 ...I

Coach: Jim Phelan, La Salle 1951
2002-03 RESULTS (11-16)

60	North Carolina St.	...84
54	George Washington	...68
57	Columbia †	...48
70	New Hampshire ■	...68
53	UMBC	...68

77	Duquesne	...63
58	Loyola (Md.)	...55
70	Navy ■	...69
64	Texas	...80
47	Baylor	...80
57	St. Francis (Pa.)	...76
57	Robert Morris	...73
69	Long Island	...82
69	St. Francis (N.Y.) ■	...58
72	Long Island	...69
54	St. Francis (N.Y.)	...73
42	Monmouth	...58
83	Fairleigh Dickinson ■	...81
82	Quinnipiac	...87
66	Central Conn. St.	...80
82	UMBC ■	...74
56	Robert Morris ■	...54
69	St. Francis (Pa.) ■	...79
55	Wagner	...57
70	Sacred Heart	...78
52	Quinnipiac ■	...63
60	Central Conn. St. ■	...56

Nickname: Mountaineers
Colors: Blue & White
Arena: Knott Arena
  Capacity: 3,196; Year Built: 1987
AD: Harold P. Menninger
SID: Mark Vandergrift

MT. ST. VINCENT
Riverdale, NY 10471-1093 ...III

Coach: Chuck Mancuso, Concordia (N.Y.) 1981
2002-03 RESULTS (11-15)

103	Pratt ■	...67
86	St. Joseph's (Brkln) ■	...63
66	Merchant Marine	...93
78	Old Westbury ■	...74
72	Maritime (N.Y.)	...52
71	Yeshiva	...90
59	Manhattanville	...78
65	CCNY	...107
102	Berkeley ■	...56
63	St. Joseph's (L.I.) ■	...83
84	Purchase St.	...74
70	Mt. St. Mary (N.Y.)	...104
73	Stevens Institute	...84
78	Merchant Marine ■	...80
79	Centenary (N.J.) ■	...77
90	St. Joseph's (Brkln)	...91
120	Pratt	...74
60	Maritime (N.Y.) ■	...58
84	Mt. St. Mary (N.Y.) ■	...95
61	Stevens Institute ■	...63
73	Old Westbury	...76
80	Polytechnic (N.Y.) ■	...76
67	St. Joseph's (L.I.)	...55
67	Manhattanville	...91
71	Yeshiva ■	...53
75	Mt. St. Mary (N.Y.)	...98

Nickname: Dolphins
Colors: Blue, White & Gold
Arena: Cardinal Hayes Gymnasium
  Capacity: 450; Year Built: 1910
AD: Chuck Mancuso

MOUNT UNION
Alliance, OH 44601 ...III

Coach: Lee Hood, Ohio Northern 1982
2002-03 RESULTS (18-9)

72	Thiel ■	...67
78	Olivet †	...61
88	Juniata †	...82
83	Westminster (Pa.) ■	...73
78	Muskingum ■	...64
73	Otterbein	...72
83	Baldwin-Wallace	...87
65	Heidelberg ■	...45

60	Maryville (Tenn.) †	72
72	Transylvania †	69
66	Wooster ■	93
55	Capital	74
74	Wilmington (Ohio) ■	71
69	Marietta ■	60
74	Ohio Northern ■	87
63	John Carroll ■	78
77	Otterbein ■	81
72	Baldwin-Wallace ■	71
80	Ohio Northern ■	69
72	John Carroll ■	68
65	Heidelberg ■	74
72	Capital ■	66
84	Wilmington (Ohio) ■	71
78	Marietta	68
58	Muskingum	56
67	Baldwin-Wallace ■	58
56	Capital †	62

Nickname: Purple Raiders
Colors: Purple & White
Arena: Timken PE Building
  Capacity: 2,300; Year Built: 1970
AD: Larry Kehres
SID: Michael De Matteis

MUHLENBERG
Allentown, PA 18104-5586 III

Coach: Dave Madeira, Concord 1969
2002-03 RESULTS (10-14)

78	Stevens Institute ■	66
69	Richard Stockton ■	79
75	Arcadia	82
82	Phila. Sciences ■	72
70	Frank. & Marsh.	93
74	King's (Pa.) ■	71
55	Misericordia ■	65
108	Widener	101
63	DeSales	86
69	King's (Pa.) †	68
60	Moravian	53
48	Gettysburg	58
74	Haverford ■	75
98	Washington (Md.)	101
79	Swarthmore	83
68	Ursinus ■	80
73	McDaniel ■	55
58	Moravian ■	65
76	Dickinson ■	83
65	Johns Hopkins	84
75	Haverford ■	74
66	Swarthmore ■	58
80	Washington (Md.) ■	76
69	Ursinus ■	76

Nickname: Mules
Colors: Cardinal & Grey
Arena: Memorial Hall
  Capacity: 3,529; Year Built: 1954
AD: Sam Beidleman
SID: Mike Falk

MURRAY ST.
Murray, KY 42071-3318............I

Coach: Tevester Anderson, Arkansas AM&N 1962
2002-03 RESULTS (17-12)

87	West Fla. ■	66
86	SIU Edwardsville ■	58
56	Southern Ill.	85
83	Western Ky. ■	72
53	Auburn	72
79	Middle Tenn.	72
85	Indiana St. ■	39
76	Evansville	58
60	Memphis	67
76	Middle Tenn. ■	64
54	Southern Miss.	56

64	Tennessee Tech ■	52
63	Austin Peay ■	66
80	Eastern Ill.	74
68	Southeast Mo. St.	78
76	Morehead St. ■	83
92	Eastern Ky. ■	80
93	Tennessee St.	75
89	Tenn.-Martin ■	70
83	Tennessee Tech	91
69	Austin Peay	72
96	Eastern Ill. ■	77
71	Southeast Mo. St. ■	65
71	Eastern Ky.	73
74	Morehead St.	77
100	Tennessee St. ■	79
80	Tenn.-Martin	59
74	Eastern Ill. ■	63
56	Austin Peay †	59

Nickname: Racers
Colors: Navy & Gold
Arena: Regional Special Events Center
  Capacity: 8,600; Year Built: 1998
AD: E. W. Dennison
SID: Steve Parker

MUSKINGUM
New Concord, OH 43762 III

Coach: Jim Burson, Muskingum 1963
2002-03 RESULTS (11-16)

71	Merchant Marine †	77
58	Case Reserve †	48
73	Frostburg St. ■	65
64	Mount Union ■	78
88	John Carroll ■	83
71	Heidelberg ■	56
95	Malone ■	86
58	Taylor (Ind.) ■	61
49	Ohio Northern ■	78
91	Kenyon †	61
62	Bluffton	69
56	Otterbein ■	64
55	Capital	75
64	Baldwin-Wallace	78
58	Marietta ■	54
72	Heidelberg	65
71	John Carroll ■	75
46	Baldwin-Wallace ■	60
60	Marietta	71
64	Ohio Northern ■	66
72	Wilmington (Ohio)	53
69	Wilmington (Ohio) ■	58
58	Otterbein	72
53	Capital ■	68
56	Mount Union	58
73	Wilmington (Ohio) ■	63
40	Capital	57

Nickname: Fighting Muskies
Colors: Black & Magenta
Arena: Muskingum Recreation Center
  Capacity: 3,000; Year Built: 1986
AD: Larry Shank
SID: Bobby Lee

MCDANIEL
Westminster, MD 21157-4390 ..III

Coach: Jay Dull, Iowa 1980
2002-03 RESULTS (5-20)

80	Maryland Bible ■	77
79	Valley Forge Chrst.	87
72	Mt. Aloysius ■	76
76	York (Pa.)	90
91	Swarthmore ■	81
84	Pitt.-Greensburg	91
52	TCNJ ■	70
64	Delaware Valley †	67
75	John Jay †	69
67	Catholic	83
56	Frank. & Marsh. ■	93

55	Gallaudet ■	63
62	Haverford ■	85
70	Dickinson ■	68
42	Gettysburg	59
58	Johns Hopkins ■	73
56	Villa Julie	57
69	Wash. & Lee ■	66
55	Muhlenberg	73
46	Frank. & Marsh.	54
49	Ursinus ■	65
64	Dickinson	80
66	Gettysburg ■	68
37	Johns Hopkins	65
65	Washington (Md.)	69

Nickname: Green Terror
Colors: Green & Gold
Arena: Gill P.E. Learning Center
  Capacity: 3,000; Year Built: 1984
AD: James M. Smith
SID: Steve Peed

NAVY
Annapolis, MD 21402-5000 I

Coach: Don DeVoe, Ohio St. 1964
2002-03 RESULTS (8-20)

68	UCF ■	56
57	Citadel ■	51
61	Davidson	69
92	Brown ■	97
61	Belmont	68
61	Johns Hopkins ■	66
59	Coastal Caro.	63
85	Gettysburg ■	36
52	Ohio	54
60	Rice ■	82
89	Eastern Mich. ■	81
69	Mt. St. Mary's ■	70
43	Air Force	56
59	Lehigh ■	76
53	American	70
66	Bucknell ■	53
61	Holy Cross ■	76
48	Colgate ■	53
65	Army ■	46
52	Lafayette	70
46	Lehigh	68
61	American	64
41	Bucknell	59
52	Colgate	73
42	Holy Cross	63
79	Lafayette ■	74
62	Army ■	56
57	American †	72

Nickname: Midshipmen
Colors: Navy Blue & Gold
Arena: Alumni Hall
  Capacity: 5,710; Year Built: 1991
AD: Chet Gladchuck
SID: Scott Strasemeier

NAZARETH
Rochester, NY 14618-3790 III

Coach: Mike Daley, St. Bonaventure 1966
2002-03 RESULTS (22-6)

87	Baldwin-Wallace †	94
74	Coast Guard †	59
62	Rochester	74
76	Keuka ■	56
80	Cazenovia ■	56
78	Mt. Aloysius ■	68
93	Hilbert	61
94	Oswego St. ■	60
83	Alfred ■	72
81	St. John Fisher ■	72
96	Roberts Wesleyan ■	85
88	Rochester Inst. †	85
70	Rochester †	59

88	Elmira	61
70	Ithaca	67
73	Utica ■	69
61	Hartwick ■	70
79	Rochester Inst. ■	81
82	St. John Fisher	89
89	Alfred	76
74	Hartwick ■	67
73	Utica	62
82	Rochester Inst.	80
69	Ithaca ■	53
64	Elmira ■	58
74	Brockport St. ■	70
85	St. Lawrence ■	72
76	Rochester Inst. †	78

Nickname: Golden Flyers
Colors: Purple & Gold
Arena: Robert A. Kidera Gym
  Capacity: 1,200; Year Built: 1976
AD: Peter Bothner
SID: Joe Seil

NEBRASKA
Lincoln, NE 68588 I

Coach: Barry Collier, Butler 1976
2002-03 RESULTS (11-19)

68	Centenary (La.) †	45
61	Alas. Fairbanks	64
65	Ball St. †	73
69	Texas-San Antonio ■	53
60	South Fla.	65
80	Minnesota ■	60
63	IPFW ■	46
73	Creighton ■	81
60	UC Santa Barb. †	57
63	Arizona St.	75
63	Eastern Wash. ■	60
79	Denver ■	75
70	Lipscomb ■	60
59	Kansas	92
52	Texas A&M ■	53
80	Colorado ■	77
53	Kansas St.	77
61	Iowa St.	71
56	Missouri ■	63
51	Kansas ■	81
49	Texas Tech	75
70	Oklahoma St. ■	77
63	Texas ■	75
50	Missouri	67
64	Baylor	78
68	Kansas St. ■	61
69	Iowa St. ■	63
51	Oklahoma	76
69	Colorado	84
61	Missouri †	70

Nickname: Cornhuskers, Huskers
Colors: Scarlet & Cream
Arena: Bob Devaney Sports Center
  Capacity: 13,500; Year Built: 1976
AD: Steven C. Pederson
SID: Jerry Trickie

NEB. WESLEYAN
Lincoln, NE 68504-2796 III

Coach: Todd Raridon, Hastings 1980
2002-03 RESULTS (14-11)

89	Illinois Tech †	41
88	Robert Morris (Ill.) †	53
80	Baker	60
61	Buena Vista ■	65
65	Hastings	70
69	Dordt	68
76	Colorado Col. ■	72
81	Wis.-Stout †	87
79	St. John's (Minn.) †	70
56	Ill. Wesleyan †	68
81	Doane ■	91

79	Mt. Marty	66
69	Concordia (Neb.) ■	67
84	Midland Lutheran	92
93	Dana	88
66	Briar Cliff ■	72
97	Hastings ■	75
77	Doane	72
62	Concordia (Neb.)	78
74	Northwestern (Iowa) ■	89
85	Midland Lutheran ■	78
69	Sioux Falls	88
75	Dakota Wesleyan	74
63	Colorado Col.	64
93	Dana ■	81

Nickname: Prairie Wolves
Colors: Gold, Brown & Black
Arena: Snyder Arena
    Capacity: 2,350; Year Built: 1995
AD: Ira Zeff
SID: Karl Skinner

NEB.-KEARNEY
Kearney, NE 68849.................II

Coach: Tom Kropp, Neb.-Kearney 1975
2002-03 RESULTS (30-3)
95	Hastings ■	75
103	Drury	79
73	Evangel †	69
84	Drury	77
84	Wayne St. (Neb.) ■	63
84	Neb.-Omaha ■	64
95	Mesa St. ■	61
94	Doane	69
86	Colorado St.-Pueblo	68
83	N.M. Highlands	66
107	Adams St. ■	64
91	Fort Lewis ■	85
96	UC-Colo. Spgs.	80
106	Western St.	84
80	Metro St.	64
83	Chadron St.	73
81	Colo. Christian ■	61
103	Colorado Mines ■	73
78	Fort Hays St.	72
74	Regis (Colo.) ■	62
117	Morningside ■	96
83	Colo. Christian	77
72	Colorado Mines	70
75	Fort Hays St.	89
72	Regis (Colo.)	59
92	Chadron St. ■	75
65	Metro St. ■	54
113	Adams St. ■	86
82	Fort Hays St. †	86
72	Minn. Duluth ■	67
86	South Dakota St. ■	85
94	Metro St. ■	87
75	Northeastern St. †	94

Nickname: Antelopes, Lopers
Colors: Royal Blue & Light Old Gold
Arena: Health & Sports Center
    Capacity: 6,000; Year Built: 1990
AD: Jon McBride
SID: Peter Yazvac

NEB.-OMAHA
Omaha, NE 68182 II

Coach: Kevin McKenna, Creighton 1993
2002-03 RESULTS (20-10)
79	Mary ■	58
74	Rockhurst ■	58
91	Bellevue ■	58
77	St. Mary's (Tex.) †	69
100	Mesa St. †	81
64	Neb.-Kearney	84
76	Wayne St. (Neb.) ■	61

79	Winona St. ■	62
102	Midland Lutheran ■	87
91	Hastings	66
76	North Dakota St. ■	74
67	North Dakota ■	69
94	Northern Colo.	62
83	Minn. St. Mankato	89
90	South Dakota St. ■	72
67	South Dakota	58
88	Northern Colo. ■	66
77	St. Cloud St.	88
69	North Dakota	72
94	Morningside ■	61
70	South Dakota	85
75	Augustana (S.D.) ■	62
76	Minn. St. Mankato ■	55
87	North Dakota St.	98
68	St. Cloud St. ■	85
60	South Dakota	83
102	Augustana (S.D.)	95
81	North Dakota	73
80	South Dakota St. †	65
78	St. Cloud St.	88

Nickname: Mavericks
Colors: Black & Crimson
Arena: UNO Fieldhouse
    Capacity: 3,500; Year Built: 1950
AD: Robert Danenhauer
SID: Gary Anderson

NEUMANN
Aston, PA 19014-1298 III

Coach: Brian Nugent, Temple 1993
2002-03 RESULTS (18-11)
63	Indiana (Pa.) †	73
78	Waynesburg †	54
80	Widener ■	73
64	N.C. Wesleyan ■	61
96	Marywood ■	62
78	Alvernia	92
68	Wesley	41
70	Arcadia ■	55
61	Kutztown	75
80	Embry-Riddle †	104
64	Williams †	97
87	Susquehanna †	61
76	King's (Pa.)	83
93	Gwynedd-Mercy	92
71	Cabrini ■	66
77	Eastern	66
62	Misericordia ■	67
73	Alvernia ■	60
90	Wesley ■	70
57	Cabrini	58
75	Marywood	72
71	Eastern ■	63
70	Arcadia	79
84	Gwynedd-Mercy ■	79
83	Misericordia	82
97	Misericordia ■	65
73	Alvernia ■	80
75	Grove City	61
66	Frank. & Marsh.	90

Nickname: Knights
Colors: Blue, Gold & White
Arena: Bruder Gym
    Capacity: 350; Year Built: 1985
AD: To be named
SID: To be named

NEVADA
Reno, NV 89557......................I

Coach: Trent Johnson, Boise St. 1983
2002-03 RESULTS (18-14)
75	San Diego	77
64	San Francisco	61
70	Weber St.	73

80	UNLV ■	82
83	Pacific (Cal.) ■	54
63	Arizona St.	76
62	Santa Clara	67
89	Seattle Pacific ■	80
88	Portland ■	79
81	San Diego ■	70
75	Rice	79
60	Tulsa	63
78	UTEP ■	66
71	Boise St.	61
75	Louisiana Tech	67
76	Southern Methodist	86
86	San Jose St. ■	59
73	Hawaii	65
92	Fresno St. ■	79
67	Boise St.	64
71	UTEP	64
82	Southern Methodist ■	64
97	Louisiana Tech ■	99
71	Hawaii ■	73
74	San Jose St.	66
99	Fresno St.	107
86	Rice ■	68
73	Tulsa ■	79
72	Louisiana Tech †	66
81	Southern Methodist †	66
64	Tulsa	75
54	Texas Tech	66

Nickname: Wolf Pack
Colors: Silver & Blue
Arena: Lawlor Events Center
    Capacity: 11,200; Year Built: 1983
AD: Chris Ault
SID: Jason D. Houston

UNLV
Las Vegas, NV 89154...............I

Coach: Charles Spoonhour, Ozarks 1961
2002-03 RESULTS (21-11)
69	Portland St. ■	54
84	UAB ■	75
82	Washington ■	61
82	Nevada	80
74	Wisconsin	91
85	Bradley	83
101	Tenn.-Martin ■	78
66	Stanford	77
70	West Virginia ■	67
79	Southern Methodist ■	78
74	IPFW ■	62
75	Santa Clara ■	53
75	DePaul	70
77	Brigham Young	85
63	Utah ■	66
71	Air Force	75
75	New Mexico	66
80	Wyoming ■	90
90	Colorado St. ■	57
73	Southern California ■	98
79	San Diego St.	64
61	Brigham Young ■	54
80	Utah	86
74	New Mexico ■	69
74	Air Force ■	70
73	Colorado St.	67
66	Wyoming	69
83	San Diego St. ■	72
83	San Diego St. ■	67
64	Utah ■	41
61	Colorado St. ■	62
68	Hawaii ■	85

Nickname: Runnin' Rebels
Colors: Scarlet & Gray
Arena: Thomas & Mack Center
    Capacity: 18,500; Year Built: 1983
AD: John Robinson
SID: Andy Grossman

NEW ENGLAND
Biddeford, ME 04005 III

Coach: David Labbe, Southern Me. 1993
2002-03 RESULTS (9-17)
83	Rivier	75
68	Bates †	115
85	Bowdoin ■	98
90	Southern Me.	79
86	Salve Regina ■	104
99	Me.-Farmington	105
86	Daniel Webster ■	82
59	St. Joseph's (Me.) ■	98
75	Plymouth St.	114
66	Nichols	80
113	New England Col.	80
69	Wentworth Inst. ■	63
77	Colby-Sawyer	95
79	Newbury	76
95	Curry ■	97
98	Anna Maria	72
57	Gordon	96
82	Endicott ■	107
68	Wentworth Inst.	70
80	Roger Williams ■	79
62	Colby-Sawyer	105
66	Eastern Nazarene	87
86	New England Col. ■	58
50	Gordon ■	67
77	Endicott	102
72	Nichols	76

Nickname: Nor'easters
Colors: Royal & Grey
Arena: Campus Center
    Capacity: 1,500; Year Built: 1989
AD: Karol L'heureux
SID: Curt Smyth

NEW ENGLAND COL.
Henniker, NH 03242-3293 III

Coach: Charles Mason, Concordia-Mont. 1991
2002-03 RESULTS (3-22)
55	Amherst	91
73	Johnson St. †	77
66	Rivier	72
58	Keene St. †	109
64	Roger Williams ■	67
70	Mount Ida	76
61	Thomas	63
48	Salve Regina	60
58	Daniel Webster	57
80	New England ■	113
59	Eastern Nazarene ■	77
67	Wentworth Inst. ■	73
56	Wentworth Inst.	54
66	Curry †	71
47	Colby-Sawyer	75
60	Nichols	69
55	Gordon ■	82
60	Endicott	81
57	Newbury ■	69
51	Anna Maria	59
59	Endicott ■	91
69	Hampshire ■	49
58	New England	86
59	Colby-Sawyer ■	83
63	Gordon	83

Nickname: Pilgrims
Colors: Scarlet & Royal Blue
Arena: Bridges Gym
    Capacity: 400; Year Built: 1965
AD: Lori Runksmeier
SID: Renee Hellert

NEW HAMPSHIRE
Durham, NH 03824 I

Coach: Phil Rowe, Plymouth St. 1974
2002-03 RESULTS (5-23)

58	Miami (Fla.)	93
55	Northwestern	81
70	Liberty ■	80
68	Mt. St. Mary's	70
68	Colgate	87
78	Cornell	62
36	Wisconsin	85
52	Furman	75
69	Stetson †	75
50	Binghamton ■	80
84	Hartford	88
74	Maine ■	64
58	Albany (N.Y.)	61
76	Brown ■	93
62	Dartmouth	57
58	Northeastern	81
64	Boston U. ■	94
71	Binghamton	82
75	Vermont ■	92
71	Stony Brook ■	77
72	Maine	77
61	Northeastern ■	75
72	Hartford ■	61
79	Albany (N.Y.) ■	87
68	Vermont	85
62	Boston U.	76
62	Stony Brook	55
61	Boston U.	75

Nickname: Wildcats
Colors: Blue & White
Arena: Lundholm Gymnasium
Capacity: 3,500; Year Built: 1961
AD: Marty Scarano
SID: Derek Leslie

NEW HAVEN
West Haven, CT 06516-1999 ...II

Coach: Jay Young, Marist 1986
2002-03 RESULTS (21-10)

62	C.W. Post	72
77	Concordia (N.Y.)	60
71	Philadelphia U.	80
71	Queens (N.Y.) ■	75
98	Dowling ■	75
81	American Int'l ■	74
67	NYIT ■	51
87	Southampton	68
84	Molloy	77
70	Mercy ■	51
59	Southern Conn. St. ■	56
62	Philadelphia U. ■	61
73	Adelphi ■	53
69	C.W. Post ■	55
67	Dowling	52
48	Bentley	71
79	Concordia (N.Y.) ■	42
57	NYIT	66
66	Queens (N.Y.)	52
82	St. Thomas Aquinas ■	54
66	St. Thomas Aquinas	46
74	Southampton	69
69	Molloy ■	59
74	Bridgeport ■	78
58	Mercy	47
63	Bridgeport	68
60	Adelphi	73
72	Philadelphia U. ■	59
69	C.W. Post	77
76	Southern N.H. †	71
61	C.W. Post †	78

Nickname: Chargers
Colors: Blue & Gold
Arena: Charger Gymnasium
Capacity: 3,500; Year Built: 1971

AD: Deborah Chin
SID: Jason Sullivan

NEW JERSEY CITY
Jersey City, NJ 07305-1597 III

Coach: Charles Brown, New Jersey City 1965
2002-03 RESULTS (14-13)

69	Chowan †	54
65	Hampden-Sydney	98
59	Kean ■	60
93	Stevens Institute ■	63
47	Wm. Paterson	71
50	Rutgers-Newark ■	68
58	Montclair St. ■	72
67	Richard Stockton ■	64
117	Medgar Evers	78
56	Wheaton (Ill.) †	70
76	Gwynedd-Mercy †	74
79	Rowan	66
82	Farmingdale St.	68
70	Ramapo ■	73
68	TCNJ	63
78	Rutgers-Camden	68
53	Wm. Paterson ■	68
57	Kean	64
66	Rutgers-Camden ■	64
79	Montclair St.	77
85	TCNJ ■	82
81	Richard Stockton	86
63	Rutgers-Newark ■	55
95	Ramapo	101
83	Rowan ■	97
70	Old Westbury ■	52
86	Mt. St. Mary (N.Y.)	87

Nickname: Gothic Knights
Colors: Green & Gold
Arena: Athletic & Fitness Center
Capacity: 2,000; Year Built: 1994
AD: Lawrence R. Schiner
SID: Ira Thor

N.J. INST. OF TECH.
Newark, NJ 07102 II

Coach: James Paul Casciano, Drexel 1974
2002-03 RESULTS (18-11)

70	Stonehill †	64
77	Mansfield	84
83	Nyack ■	71
88	Wilmington (Del.)	62
78	Dominican (N.Y.)	75
72	Shaw ■	84
59	Mansfield ■	68
42	Queens (N.Y.) †	56
76	Daemen †	81
75	Phila. Sciences ■	69
46	Caldwell	53
83	Teikyo Post ■	69
78	Bloomfield	75
71	Dominican (N.Y.) ■	61
61	Holy Family	79
75	Felician ■	70
91	Goldey-Beacom	68
91	Nyack	66
59	Caldwell ■	50
81	Felician	73
65	Teikyo Post	68
61	Holy Family ■	60
72	Phila. Sciences	74
73	Goldey-Beacom ■	64
98	Bloomfield ■	64
79	West Chester	76
105	Wilmington (Del.) ■	77
68	Felician †	74
73	Mansfield	83

Nickname: Highlanders
Colors: Scarlet & White

Arena: Entwistle Gym
Capacity: 1,500; Year Built: 1960
AD: Leonard Kaplan
SID: Mark Mentone

TCNJ
Ewing, NJ 08628-0718............III

Coach: John Castaldo, TCNJ 1982
2002-03 RESULTS (13-12)

75	Lebanon Valley ■	65
89	NYCCT ■	60
70	Rutgers-Camden ■	54
59	Wm. Paterson ■	62
86	Ramapo	95
67	Kean	60
43	Rowan	60
70	McDaniel	52
80	Lehman	71
98	Marymount (Va.) ■	83
79	Moravian ■	77
54	Montclair St.	71
66	Haverford ■	49
75	Richard Stockton ■	77
63	New Jersey City ■	68
59	Rutgers-Newark	51
70	Ramapo ■	84
76	Rutgers-Camden ■	70
74	Rutgers-Newark ■	44
67	Rowan	72
82	New Jersey City	85
58	Wm. Paterson	59
56	Kean ■	74
72	Richard Stockton	70
59	Montclair St. ■	62

Nickname: Lions
Colors: Blue & Gold
Arena: Packer Hall
Capacity: 1,200; Year Built: 1962
AD: Kevin A. McHugh
SID: Ann King

NEW MEXICO
Albuquerque, NM 87131 I

Coach: Ritchie McKay, Seattle Pacific 1987
2002-03 RESULTS (10-18)

68	California ■	76
60	Northwestern St. ■	56
58	New Mexico St.	59
90	Northeastern ■	88
91	IPFW ■	66
60	New Mexico St. ■	72
71	Texas Tech	98
57	Southern Utah ■	69
69	Portland St. ■	52
68	Pepperdine ■	88
64	Tennessee	71
59	Northern Ariz. ■	57
58	Colorado St.	74
81	Wyoming	85
107	Western N.M. ■	49
66	San Diego St. ■	62
66	UNLV ■	75
64	Brigham Young	80
68	Utah	78
73	Air Force ■	59
91	Wyoming ■	103
82	Colorado St. ■	72
69	UNLV	74
73	San Diego St.	89
76	Utah ■	69
81	Brigham Young ■	91
60	Air Force	68
56	Brigham Young †	71

Nickname: Lobos
Colors: Cherry & Silver
Arena: The Pit/Bob King Court
Capacity: 18,018; Year Built: 1966

AD: Rudy Davalos
SID: Greg Remington

N.M. HIGHLANDS
Las Vegas, NM 87701 II

Coach: Ed Manzanares, New Mexico
2002-03 RESULTS (7-20)

68	Eastern N.M.	97
66	UTEP	75
75	West Tex. A&M ■	85
80	Western N.M.	87
81	Eastern N.M. †	87
58	West Tex. A&M	91
61	Regis (Colo.)	65
81	Western N.M. ■	78
60	Fort Hays St. ■	77
66	Neb.-Kearney ■	83
73	Colo. Christian	81
80	Colorado Mines	101
88	Colorado Col.	80
52	Metro St.	77
83	Chadron St. ■	81
89	Fort Lewis ■	97
62	Adams St.	94
83	Colorado St.-Pueblo ■	76
67	Mesa St.	80
76	UC-Colo. Spgs.	93
90	Western St.	85
63	Colorado St.-Pueblo	84
68	Mesa St. ■	72
83	Western St. ■	63
87	UC-Colo. Spgs. ■	89
69	Adams St. ■	66
59	Fort Lewis	104

Nickname: Cowboys
Colors: Purple & White
Arena: Wilsom Complex
Capacity: 5,000; Year Built: 1986
AD: Dennis Francois
SID: William Maes

NEW MEXICO ST.
Las Cruces, NM 88003 I

Coach: Lou Henson, New Mexico St. 1955
2002-03 RESULTS (20-9)

62	Tex.-Pan American †	59
61	Tulsa †	71
75	Colorado ■	71
59	New Mexico ■	58
81	Md.-East. Shore ■	63
78	UTEP	65
72	New Mexico	60
80	UTEP ■	58
84	Texas Tech	85
66	Texas-Arlington ■	51
74	La.-Lafayette	81
55	New Orleans	65
84	South Ala.	70
74	Florida Int'l	52
64	Tex.-Pan American ■	50
68	Middle Tenn. ■	70
92	Western Ky. ■	82
80	Denver	77
75	North Texas	82
78	New Orleans ■	60
77	South Ala. ■	71
89	UC-Colo. Spgs. ■	66
58	La.-Lafayette ■	69
64	Ark.-Little Rock	72
82	Arkansas St.	67
87	Denver ■	76
80	North Texas ■	66
78	Ark.-Little Rock †	61
59	Western Ky.	78

Nickname: Aggies
Colors: Crimson & White
Arena: Pan American Center

Capacity: 13,071; Year Built: 1968
AD: Brian Faison
SID: Tyler Dunkel

NEW ORLEANS
New Orleans, LA 70148 I

Coach: Monte Towe, North Carolina St.
2002-03 RESULTS (15-14)
107	St. Leo ■	57
93	Jackson St. ■	79
65	Rollins ■	57
90	Jacksonville ■	57
80	Tulane ■	67
77	Southeastern La. ■	69
76	Lipscomb ■	81
81	Texas St.	92
89	Cal Poly †	75
56	Hawaii	68
57	LSU	69
70	South Ala. ■	61
65	New Mexico St. ■	55
71	La.-Lafayette	78
59	Western Ky.	78
60	Middle Tenn.	77
74	North Texas ■	62
75	Denver ■	65
70	Arkansas St. ■	68
83	Ark.-Little Rock	85
60	New Mexico St.	78
75	La.-Lafayette	79
49	Florida Int'l ■	48
48	Florida	77
76	North Texas	73
63	Denver	68
77	Tex. A&M-Corp. Chris. ■	63
58	South Ala.	61
45	Florida Int'l †	62

Nickname: Privateers
Colors: Royal Blue & Silver
Arena: Kiefer Lakefront Arena
　Capacity: 10,000; Year Built: 1983
AD: Jame W. Miller
SID: Bob Boyle

NEW PALTZ ST.
New Paltz, NY 12561-2499 III

Coach: Doug Pasquerella, Cortland St. 1996
2002-03 RESULTS (11-17)
41	Rutgers-Newark	59
70	Becker †	63
67	Baruch	87
46	New York U. ■	48
76	Fredonia St. ■	78
64	Buffalo St. ■	74
65	Lehman	57
46	Wm. Paterson ■	73
51	New York U.	86
63	Geneseo St. ■	53
62	Rowan	78
64	Oneonta St.	81
63	Potsdam St.	82
73	Plattsburgh St.	56
70	Utica/Rome ■	76
69	Geneseo St.	55
85	Brockport St.	82
50	Cortland St. ■	51
88	Oneonta St. ■	90
74	Vassar	64
58	Oswego St.	73
71	Buffalo St.	74
70	Utica/Rome	78
74	Potsdam St. ■	66
88	Plattsburgh St. ■	74
59	Potsdam St.	53
64	Brockport St. †	62
40	Buffalo St. †	73

Nickname: Hawks
Colors: Orange & Blue
Arena: Elting Gymnasium
　Capacity: 2,200; Year Built: 1964
AD: Tracey Ranieri/Stuart Robinson
SID: Mike Salerno

NYCCT
Brooklyn, NY 11201 III

Coach: Raymond Amalbert, Hunter 1976
2002-03 RESULTS (6-20)
66	Lebanon Valley †	78
60	TCNJ	89
71	Vassar ■	73
31	Army	77
88	Polytechnic (N.Y.)	59
77	Medgar Evers	81
74	Mt. St. Mary (N.Y.)	91
61	Medgar Evers ■	73
69	Staten Island	84
64	FDU-Florham ■	66
45	York (N.Y.)	52
66	Brooklyn	72
72	Hunter	75
74	CCNY ■	76
69	Centenary (N.J.)	62
62	Baruch ■	71
80	Lehman	86
70	St. Joseph's (Brkln)	66
59	Staten Island ■	65
72	Medgar Evers ■	59
68	York (N.Y.) ■	80
52	Farmingdale St.	69
67	Brooklyn ■	65
69	John Jay	73
66	John Jay	61
64	CCNY †	84

Nickname: Yellow Jackets
Colors: Royal Blue & Gold
AD: Ray Amalbert Jr
SID: To be named

NYIT
Old Westbury, NY 11568-8000 ..II

Coach: Sal Lagano, Hofstra 1988
2002-03 RESULTS (17-11)
72	Southampton ■	81
80	Mercy ■	71
79	Bridgeport ■	70
77	Adelphi ■	73
85	Wilmington (Del.) †	55
78	St. Rose	104
72	Glenville St. †	67
51	New Haven	67
62	C.W. Post ■	82
88	Dowling ■	85
70	Concordia (N.Y.) ■	49
58	Philadelphia U. ■	56
60	Queens (N.Y.) ■	55
71	St. Thomas Aquinas ■	55
65	Southampton	60
74	Molloy ■	62
65	Mercy	77
66	New Haven ■	57
73	Bridgeport	87
68	Adelphi ■	59
57	C.W. Post	73
86	Dowling ■	75
70	Concordia (N.Y.)	65
50	Philadelphia U.	77
70	Molloy	85
80	St. Thomas Aquinas ■	46
72	Queens (N.Y.)	75
56	Bridgeport	68

Nickname: Bears
Colors: Navy Blue
Arena: Recreation Hall

Capacity: 500; Year Built: 1955
AD: Clyde Doughty Jr.
SID: Ben Arcuri

NEW YORK U.
New York, NY 10012-1019 III

Coach: Joe Nesci, Brooklyn 1979
2002-03 RESULTS (12-13)
56	Cortland St. ■	52
74	Rensselaer ■	69
84	Southern Vt. ■	86
48	New Paltz St.	46
91	Brooklyn ■	61
80	Merchant Marine ■	65
67	St. Joseph's (L.I.) ■	55
48	Baruch	69
86	New Paltz St. ■	51
57	Carnegie Mellon	60
53	Rochester	85
79	Polytechnic (N.Y.)	49
68	Brandeis	71
90	Hunter ■	65
66	Emory ■	81
82	Case Reserve ■	76
66	Chicago	83
56	Washington (Mo.)	64
55	Washington (Mo.) ■	87
66	Chicago ■	71
58	Rochester ■	87
92	Carnegie Mellon ■	75
75	Case Reserve	77
71	Emory	83
99	Brandeis ■	78

Nickname: Violets
Colors: Purple & White
Arena: Coles Sports Center
　Capacity: 1,900; Year Built: 1981
AD: Christopher Bledsoe
SID: Jeffrey Bernstein

NEWBERRY
Newberry, SC 29108 II

Coach: David Conrady, Furman 1987
2002-03 RESULTS (4-22)
60	Lander ■	61
87	S.C.-Aiken ■	77
75	St. Andrews	81
73	Livingstone	79
66	St. Leo †	73
44	Allen †	65
67	Mars Hill ■	69
68	Lees-McRae	48
61	Erskine	62
48	Coastal Caro.	67
62	St. Andrews ■	70
58	Mars Hill	60
54	Livingstone ■	53
59	Lenoir-Rhyne	75
90	Wingate	93
59	Tusculum ■	44
48	Catawba	71
65	Carson-Newman	75
59	Presbyterian ■	82
53	Mars Hill	78
41	Lenoir-Rhyne ■	64
76	Wingate ■	87
62	Tusculum	81
74	Catawba ■	80
51	Carson-Newman	62
56	Presbyterian	68

Nickname: Indians
Colors: Scarlet & Gray
Arena: Eleazer Arena
　Capacity: 1,600; Year Built: 1981
AD: Andy Carter
SID: Ryan Rose

NIAGARA
Niagara Univ., NY 14109 I

Coach: Joe Mihalich, La Salle 1978
2002-03 RESULTS (17-12)
90	Marshall ■	92
69	UCF	94
69	Canisius ■	89
60	Loyola (Md.)	53
45	George Mason	65
64	Buffalo	75
77	Akron ■	71
88	Drexel ■	72
66	Youngstown St.	58
68	St. John's (N.Y.)	78
63	Bucknell †	52
76	Marist	68
71	Manhattan	88
73	Siena ■	78
89	St. Peter's ■	75
77	St. Peter's	70
74	Rider	68
65	Manhattan ■	71
86	Iona ■	74
76	Iona	92
85	Fairfield	74
71	Canisius	68
79	Loyola (Md.) ■	66
71	Siena	84
83	Fairfield ■	79
78	Rider ■	72
88	Marist ■	87
81	Iona †	75
81	Manhattan †	82

Nickname: Purple Eagles
Colors: Purple and White
Arena: Gallagher Center
　Capacity: 2,400; Year Built: 1949
AD: Michael J. Hermann
SID: Mark Vandergrift

NICHOLLS ST.
Thibodaux, LA 70310 I

Coach: Ricky Blanton, LSU 1992
2002-03 RESULTS (3-25)
24	LSU	68
36	Southern U. †	52
66	Loyola (La.) ■	53
35	Texas Tech	107
51	Southern U.	46
70	UAB	82
47	Birmingham-So.	60
52	Mississippi	63
60	Southeastern La. ■	68
60	La.-Monroe ■	69
47	Lamar	56
45	Sam Houston St.	84
39	Stephen F. Austin ■	66
59	Texas-Arlington ■	54
52	La.-Monroe	75
61	Northwestern St.	70
70	McNeese St.	75
54	Southeastern La.	58
48	Texas St. ■	52
81	Texas-San Antonio ■	83
62	Lamar ■	74
65	Sam Houston St. ■	76
56	Stephen F. Austin	84
46	Texas-Arlington	74
53	Northwestern St. ■	62
50	McNeese St.	71
59	Texas St.	72
60	Texas-San Antonio	79

Nickname: Colonels
Colors: Red & Gray
Arena: David Stopher Gymnasium
　Capacity: 3,800; Year Built: 1967
AD: Robert J. Bernardi
SID: Bobby Galinsky

NICHOLS
Dudley, MA 01571-5000 III

Coach: Dave Sokolnicki, Nichols 1997
2002-03 RESULTS (14-13)
60	Worcester St.	82
86	Becker	67
61	Coast Guard ■	88
66	Elms	59
62	Gordon	82
61	Fitchburg St. ■	83
56	Cal St. Monterey Bay	90
62	Dominican (Cal.) †	90
80	New England ■	66
68	Salve Regina ■	63
74	Colby-Sawyer ■	66
62	Roger Williams	58
81	Mount Ida ■	53
67	Endicott	94
68	Newbury	75
69	New England Col. ■	60
70	Anna Maria	69
68	Curry ■	60
42	Salve Regina	66
82	Eastern Nazarene	83
74	Roger Williams ■	64
84	Curry	56
71	Anna Maria ■	73
66	Eastern Nazarene ■	65
71	Wentworth Inst.	74
76	New England ■	72
64	Colby-Sawyer ■	78

Nickname: Bison
Colors: Green & White
Arena: Chalmers Field House
   Capacity: 800; Year Built: 2000
AD: Charlyn Robert
SID: Mike Serijan

NORFOLK ST.
Norfolk, VA 23504.....................I

Coach: Dwight Freeman, Western St.
1982
2002-03 RESULTS (14-15)
65	Florida A&M ■	70
74	Western Ill. ■	75
61	UMKC ■	60
51	Pittsburgh	96
62	Hampton	72
50	Towson	53
48	Georgetown	84
75	UNC Greensboro ■	70
70	VMI †	69
38	Richmond	67
78	Md.-East. Shore	51
73	Howard	68
57	Coppin St. ■	47
66	Morgan St. ■	63
59	Bethune-Cookman ■	49
64	South Carolina St.	76
83	N.C. A&T ■	60
56	Delaware St.	71
78	Howard ■	88
80	Md.-East. Shore ■	63
52	Coppin St.	64
60	Morgan St.	63
61	Bethune-Cookman	48
62	Florida A&M	72
63	South Carolina St. ■	61
54	N.C. A&T ■	61
48	Hampton ■	44
76	N.C. A&T †	55
62	Hampton †	64

Nickname: Spartans
Colors: Green & Gold
Arena: Echols Arena
   Capacity: 7,600; Year Built: 1982
AD: Orby Moss Jr.
SID: Glen Mason

NORTH ALA.
Florence, AL 35632-0001 II

Coach: Gary Elliott, Alabama 1970
2002-03 RESULTS (18-10)
71	Henderson St.	76
89	Ouachita Baptist	80
100	Stillman ■	69
89	LeMoyne-Owen ■	75
73	Miles ■	63
49	Valdosta St.	64
93	Tuskegee ■	87
78	Findlay	84
78	Virginia Union †	80
74	Winston-Salem	65
65	Lincoln Memorial ■	62
82	West Ala. ■	57
85	West Ga.	82
92	Athens St. ■	79
69	West Fla.	75
66	Lincoln Memorial	80
75	Valdosta St. ■	70
84	Lane	79
86	Montevallo	63
53	Ala.-Huntsville ■	58
81	West Ala.	72
86	West Ga. ■	84
78	Delta St.	92
72	West Fla. ■	65
95	Athens St.	78
82	Montevallo ■	78
56	Ala.-Huntsville	64
66	Harding †	88

Nickname: Lions
Colors: Purple & Gold
Arena: Flowers Hall
   Capacity: 3,500; Year Built: 1972
AD: Joel Erdmann
SID: Jeff Hodges

NORTH CAROLINA
Chapel Hill, NC 27515 I

Coach: Matt Doherty, North Carolina
1984
2002-03 RESULTS (19-16)
85	Penn St. ■	55
71	Rutgers ■	67
67	Old Dominion	59
67	Kansas †	56
74	Stanford †	57
65	Illinois	92
81	Kentucky ■	98
80	Vermont ■	54
69	Florida St.	48
56	Iona †	65
63	St. John's (N.Y.) †	59
61	Miami (Fla.)	64
79	Davidson ■	64
72	Virginia	79
68	Clemson ■	66
68	Connecticut ■	65
66	Maryland ■	81
77	North Carolina St.	86
68	Georgia Tech	88
75	Wake Forest ■	79
74	Duke	83
61	Florida St. ■	60
81	Virginia ■	67
77	Clemson	80
93	N.C. A&T ■	57
56	Maryland	96
67	North Carolina St. ■	75
67	Georgia Tech ■	66
60	Wake Forest	75
82	Duke ■	79
84	Maryland †	72
63	Duke †	75
83	DePaul ■	72
90	Wyoming ■	74
74	Georgetown ■	79

Nickname: Tar Heels
Colors: Carolina Blue & White
Arena: Smith Center
   Capacity: 21,750; Year Built: 1986
AD: Richard Baddour
SID: Steve Kirschner

N.C. A&T
Greensboro, NC 27411 I

Coach: Curtis Hunter, North Carolina
1987
2002-03 RESULTS (1-26)
44	Georgia St. †	76
58	Radford	67
48	Va. Commonwealth	76
63	North Carolina St.	101
57	Duke ■	91
64	Wake Forest	104
41	Coppin St.	68
68	Morgan St.	87
50	Delaware St. ■	60
58	Md.-East. Shore	82
72	N.C. Central †	74
70	Howard	107
61	Hampton ■	66
60	Norfolk St. ■	83
53	South Carolina St.	59
61	Florida A&M ■	86
69	Bethune-Cookman	78
50	Coppin St. ■	66
84	Morgan St. ■	89
53	Delaware St.	76
57	North Carolina	93
79	Md.-East. Shore ■	91
81	Howard ■	105
63	Hampton	79
61	Norfolk St.	54
74	South Carolina St. ■	77
55	Norfolk St. †	76

Nickname: Aggies
Colors: Blue & Gold
Arena: Ellis Corbett Sports Center
   Capacity: 6,700; Year Built: 1978
AD: Charles Davis
SID: Donal O. Ware

UNC ASHEVILLE
Asheville, NC 28804-3299 I

Coach: Eddie Biedenbach, North
Carolina St. 1968
2002-03 RESULTS (15-17)
52	Michigan St.	66
81	Minnesota	87
102	Montreat ■	73
77	Western Caro.	72
69	East Tenn. St.	87
99	Campbell ■	89
67	Connecticut	117
53	Holy Cross	84
64	Oklahoma	100
50	Kansas	102
81	Liberty ■	80
71	Charleston So. ■	58
68	Radford	74
71	Birmingham-So.	88
62	Mercer ■	86
62	Winthrop	65
64	High Point ■	60
80	Coastal Caro. ■	76
93	Elon	87
78	High Point	76
82	Birmingham-So. ■	68
72	Liberty	73
75	Radford ■	68
72	Elon	75
55	Coastal Caro.	68
68	Charleston So.	76
65	Winthrop ■	76

Nickname: Bulldogs
Colors: Royal Blue & White
Arena: Charlie Justice Center
   Capacity: 1,100; Year Built: 1963
AD: Joni Comstock
SID: Mike Gore

(UNC Asheville results continued)
68	Elon	66
81	Winthrop	80
85	Radford †	71
92	Texas Southern †	84
61	Texas †	82

N.C. CENTRAL
Durham, NC 27707 II

Coach: Phil Spence, North Carolina St.
1976
2002-03 RESULTS (16-13)
86	Lewis & Clark †	73
60	Seattle	62
60	Shaw ■	73
106	Pfeiffer ■	100
84	Virginia St.	76
85	Mount Olive	95
80	Catawba	82
88	Salem Int'l	89
83	West Va. Tech	90
85	Wingate ■	63
63	Catawba ■	61
94	Fayetteville St.	93
76	Bowie St.	92
91	St. Augustine's †	68
73	Livingstone	64
74	N.C. A&T †	72
66	Virginia Union	75
79	St. Augustine's ■	94
84	Johnson Smith ■	78
94	Winston-Salem	89
69	Fayetteville St. ■	68
84	Livingstone	81
92	Elizabeth City St. ■	97
82	Virginia Union	91
91	Winston-Salem	68
88	St. Paul's	69
68	Johnson Smith	69
85	Fayetteville St. †	75
87	Bowie St. †	99

Nickname: Eagles
Colors: Maroon & Gray
Arena: McLendon-McDougald Gym
   Capacity: 3,000; Year Built: 1955
AD: Lin Dawson
SID: Kyle Serba

UNC GREENSBORO
Greensboro, NC 27402-6170 ...I

Coach: Fran McCaffery, Pennsylvania
1982
2002-03 RESULTS (7-22)
84	Wagner ■	65
66	Kansas	105
80	American ■	79
70	Middle Tenn. ■	58
61	Alabama	89
54	West Virginia	64
65	Syracuse	92
57	Elon ■	58
71	Delaware	74
70	Norfolk St.	75
74	High Point	81
94	East Tenn. St.	96
56	Chattanooga †	72
60	Appalachian St.	91
76	VMI	57
78	Ga. Southern ■	83
83	Guilford ■	71
72	Davidson	83
62	Western Caro. ■	63
85	Wofford ■	79

69	Col. of Charleston	71
63	Western Caro.	75
77	Davidson ■	84
67	Citadel	66
73	East Tenn. St. ■	75
60	VMI	61
68	Appalachian St. ■	71
74	Furman	78
73	Wofford †	77

Nickname: Spartans
Colors: Gold, White & Navy
Arena: Michael B. Fleming Gym
  Capacity: 2,320; Year Built: 1989
AD: Nelson E. Bobb
SID: Jake Keys

UNC PEMBROKE
Pembroke, NC 28372-1510......II

Coach: Bryan Garmroth, West Ala. 1984
2002-03 RESULTS (0-28)

68	Mount Olive ■	89
49	Clayton St. ■	89
72	North Greenville ■	78
68	S.C.-Aiken	77
64	St. Andrews	77
45	Coker ■	50
55	Lenoir-Rhyne †	97
46	Eckerd †	72
47	East Caro.	93
65	Newport News ■	78
45	GC&SU	82
62	Kennesaw St. ■	70
53	Armstrong Atlantic	77
47	Francis Marion ■	74
56	Augusta St.	103
51	S.C.-Spartanburg	75
47	Clayton St.	69
63	Lander	66
40	Armstrong Atlantic ■	58
58	Francis Marion	68
56	GC&SU ■	63
62	Augusta St. ■	69
56	Columbus St.	84
54	S.C.-Aiken ■	71
52	Lander ■	71
40	S.C.-Spartanburg ■	72
55	North Fla. ■	76
59	Armstrong Atlantic †	67

Nickname: Braves
Colors: Black & Gold
Arena: Jones Athletic Complex
  Capacity: 3,000; Year Built: 1972
AD: Dan Kenney
SID: Pamela Mason

NORTH CAROLINA ST.
Raleigh, NC 27695-7001..........I

Coach: Herb Sendek, Carnegie Mellon 1985
2002-03 RESULTS (18-13)

84	Mt. St. Mary's ■	60
58	Coppin St. ■	37
74	Northwestern ■	49
76	South Carolina ■	64
101	N.C. A&T ■	63
60	Gonzaga †	69
104	Fairleigh Dickinson ■	65
86	Wofford ■	71
56	Massachusetts	68
75	Virginia ■	63
61	Georgia Tech	85
81	Boston College ■	93
70	Florida St.	63
80	Duke ■	71
86	North Carolina	77
60	Maryland	75
78	Clemson ■	56

58	Wake Forest	73
58	Virginia	61
63	Georgia Tech ■	57
54	Temple	76
71	Florida St. ■	60
68	Duke	79
75	North Carolina	67
65	Maryland ■	68
63	Clemson	60
72	Wake Forest ■	78
71	Georgia Tech †	65
87	Wake Forest †	83
77	Duke †	84
74	California †	76

Nickname: Wolfpack
Colors: Red & White
Arena: Raleigh Entertainment & Sports Center
  Capacity: 19,722; Year Built: 1999
AD: Lee G. Fowler
SID: Annabelle Vaughan

N.C. WESLEYAN
Rocky Mount, NC 27804 III

Coach: John Thompson, UNC Greensboro 1984
2002-03 RESULTS (18-10)

95	Bethany (W.Va.) †	69
81	Thomas More †	75
121	Roanoke Bible ■	36
61	Neumann	64
52	Eastern	55
76	Flagler ■	70
89	York (N.Y.) ■	52
65	Williams †	68
79	Hamilton †	86
69	Catholic †	81
123	Roanoke Bible	37
72	Chowan	55
56	Greensboro ■	72
66	Methodist ■	82
74	Shenandoah ■	43
77	Chris. Newport ■	84
88	Ferrum	73
97	Averett	72
65	Chowan ■	45
64	Greensboro	55
87	Methodist ■	78
86	Shenandoah	65
63	Chris. Newport	74
72	Ferrum ■	61
79	Averett ■	64
66	Chowan †	56
58	Methodist †	53
64	Chris. Newport †	67

Nickname: Battling Bishops
Colors: Royal Blue & Gold
Arena: Everett Gymnasium
  Capacity: 800; Year Built: 1960
AD: John M. Thompson
SID: Renny Taylor

UNC WILMINGTON
Wilmington, NC 28403-3297....I

Coach: Brad Brownell, DePauw 1991
2002-03 RESULTS (24-7)

76	Texas Tech	85
66	Texas-San Antonio	52
78	East Tenn. St. ■	57
60	Fairfield	69
48	Dayton	59
68	Campbell ■	36
71	Texas-San Antonio	60
78	Col. of Charleston	69
81	Jacksonville	62
71	Hofstra ■	47
57	Old Dominion	67
88	Drexel	86

73	James Madison	58
68	Delaware	62
85	Towson ■	53
81	Va. Commonwealth	50
58	George Mason	70
77	Drexel ■	56
73	James Madison ■	62
71	Delaware ■	53
68	Old Dominion	71
74	Hofstra	70
75	George Mason ■	55
75	Towson	51
72	William & Mary	48
80	Va. Commonwealth ■	63
60	William & Mary ■	49
76	Hofstra †	56
63	Delaware †	50
70	Drexel †	62
73	Maryland †	75

Nickname: Seahawks
Colors: Teal, Navy & Gold
Arena: Trask Coliseum
  Capacity: 6,100; Year Built: 1977
AD: Peggy Bradley-Doppes
SID: Joe Browning

NORTH CENTRAL
Naperville, IL 60566-7063 III

Coach: Benjy Taylor, Richmond 1989
2002-03 RESULTS (8-17)

92	North Cent. (Minn.) ■	72
81	Ozarks (Ark.) ■	78
71	Benedictine (Ill.)	85
57	Lakeland	70
73	Whitworth †	83
58	Dominican (Ill.) †	59
73	Chapman †	75
92	Spring Arbor †	84
76	Hope	92
69	Aurora	81
71	Milwaukee Engr. ■	68
59	Augustana (Ill.) ■	66
78	Millikin ■	77
62	Carthage	80
73	Elmhurst	72
62	Augustana (Ill.)	72
95	Ill. Wesleyan ■	103
69	Wheaton (Ill.)	77
69	Carthage ■	72
81	Elmhurst ■	90
67	Ill. Wesleyan	81
70	North Park ■	85
104	North Park	100
86	Wheaton (Ill.) ■	95
81	Millikin	79

Nickname: Cardinals
Colors: Cardinal & White
Arena: Gregory Arena
  Capacity: 3,000; Year Built: 1931
AD: Walter J. Johnson
SID: Kevin Juday

NORTH DAKOTA
Grand Forks, ND 58202...........II

Coach: Rich Glas, Bemidji St. 1970
2002-03 RESULTS (20-9)

85	St. Martin's †	70
99	Western Ore.	82
88	Jamestown ■	76
78	Southwest Minn. St. ■	74
66	Minn. St. Moorhead	80
92	Minn.-Morris	66
73	Northern St. ■	70
96	Minn. Duluth	79
101	Minot St. ■	56
72	Minn.-Crookston	79
100	Mary ■	58
78	South Dakota	79

69	Neb.-Omaha	67
81	Minn. St. Mankato ■	72
66	Augustana (S.D.) ■	51
76	St. Cloud St.	81
57	North Dakota St. ■	64
87	Augustana (S.D.)	79
70	South Dakota	73
70	Northern Colo.	58
72	Neb.-Omaha ■	69
68	South Dakota St. ■	61
69	Minn. St. Mankato	72
51	St. Cloud St.	73
88	South Dakota	73
72	Northern Colo.	63
97	North Dakota St.	92
73	Neb.-Omaha ■	81
69	St. Cloud St. †	74

Nickname: Fighting Sioux
Colors: Green & White
Arena: Hyslop Sports Center
  Capacity: 4,792; Year Built: 1951
AD: Roger Thomas
SID: Joel Carlson

NORTH DAKOTA ST.
Fargo, ND 58105-5600............II

Coach: Tim Miles, Mary 1989
2002-03 RESULTS (20-11)

83	Lake Superior St. †	80
81	Columbus St. †	67
51	Henderson St. †	64
88	Chadron St. ■	50
67	Northern Mich.	77
92	Wis.-Platteville ■	63
85	Northern St.	88
83	Minn. Duluth	71
80	Minn.-Crookston ■	54
70	Minn. St. Moorhead ■	66
120	Mayville St. ■	71
85	Valley City St. ■	67
74	Neb.-Omaha	76
74	Northern Colo.	71
75	South Dakota St. ■	77
74	Minn. St. Mankato	67
64	North Dakota	57
74	Minn. St. Mankato ■	85
93	Augustana (S.D.)	78
78	South Dakota ■	64
91	Northern Colo. ■	79
74	Augustana (S.D.) ■	59
66	South Dakota St.	85
86	St. Cloud St.	88
98	Neb.-Omaha ■	87
87	South Dakota	80
104	Trinity Bible (N.D.) ■	64
77	St. Cloud St. ■	79
92	North Dakota	97
67	South Dakota ■	59
60	St. Cloud St.	75

Nickname: Bison
Colors: Yellow & Green
Arena: Bison Sports Arena
  Capacity: 8,000; Year Built: 1970
AD: Gene Taylor
SID: George Ellis

NORTH FLA.
Jacksonville, FL 32224-2645......II

Coach: Matt Kilcullen, Lehman 1976
2002-03 RESULTS (15-14)

69	Edward Waters ■	66
93	Flagler ■	100
62	Kennesaw St.	59
54	Augusta St. ■	62
62	Valdosta St. ■	84
66	Fla. Southern	68
64	Caldwell	51
64	Fayetteville St. ■	79

61	GC&SU	72
71	Francis Marion ■	50
81	Lander ■	69
80	Columbus St. ■	81
71	Clayton St.	73
77	GC&SU ■	63
62	Kennesaw St. ■	70
81	Nova Southeastern ■	75
83	S.C.-Aiken	82
65	Columbus St.	89
76	S.C.-Aiken	70
80	Lander	64
60	Fla. Gulf Coast ■	78
71	Armstrong Atlantic ■	64
67	S.C.-Spartanburg ■	72
48	Armstrong Atlantic	62
65	Clayton St. ■	57
79	Augusta St.	69
76	UNC Pembroke	55
77	Lander †	68
75	Augusta St. †	90

Nickname: Ospreys
Colors: Navy Blue & Gray
Arena: UNF Arena
Capacity: 5,800; Year Built: 1993
AD: Richard E. Gropper
SID: B.J. Sohn

NORTH GREENVILLE
Tigerville, SC 29688 II

Coach: Tom Smith, Valparaiso 1967
2002-03 RESULTS (1-12)

41	Tusculum	92
75	Mars Hill	100
78	UNC Pembroke	72
81	Western Caro.	96
54	Lenoir-Rhyne	96
57	Anderson (S.C.)	78
72	Lander	80
53	Presbyterian	91
69	Tusculum ■	87
57	Mars Hill ■	69
53	Erskine	69
60	Presbyterian ■	88
75	Lenoir-Rhyne ■	88

Nickname: Mounties
Colors: Scarlet & Black
AD: Jan McDonald
SID: To be named

NORTH PARK
Chicago, IL 60625-4895 III

Coach: Rees Johnson, Winona St. 1965
2002-03 RESULTS (12-13)

86	Concordia (Ill.)	77
97	Calumet Col.	89
107	Wis. Lutheran †	94
66	Ripon	92
93	Carroll (Wis.) ■	70
88	Milwaukee Engr. ■	81
83	Wis. Lutheran †	77
79	Apprentice †	67
77	Robert Morris (Ill.)	60
73	Judson (Ill.)	59
69	Millikin ■	76
70	Elmhurst ■	73
64	Wheaton (Ill.)	78
91	Millikin	92
79	Robert Morris (Ill.) ■	64
65	Augustana (Ill.)	88
73	Carthage ■	81
51	Ill. Wesleyan	78
76	Wheaton (Ill.) ■	73
69	Carthage	80
85	North Central	70
97	Ill. Wesleyan ■	98
100	North Central	104
69	Elmhurst	83
78	Augustana (Ill.) ■	93

Nickname: Vikings
Colors: Blue & Gold
Arena: North Park Gymnasium
Capacity: 1,300; Year Built: 1958
AD: Jack Surridge
SID: Chris Nelson

NORTH TEXAS
Denton, TX 76203-6737 I

Coach: Johnny Jones, LSU 1985
2002-03 RESULTS (7-21)

81	Southwest Mo. St.	78
75	Southern Methodist	88
58	Indiana	84
76	Weber St. †	72
65	Winthrop	56
80	TCU	87
88	St. Edward's ■	41
60	Tennessee Tech	75
71	Colorado	87
82	Tex. A&M-Commerce ■	74
56	Baylor	82
65	Auburn	90
94	Florida Int'l	91
55	Denver	59
80	Ark.-Little Rock ■	88
65	Arkansas St. ■	68
62	New Orleans	74
71	South Ala.	76
58	La.-Lafayette ■	89
82	New Mexico St. ■	75
55	Middle Tenn.	76
70	Western Ky. ■	85
84	Denver	90
73	New Orleans ■	76
60	South Ala. ■	70
66	La.-Lafayette	94
66	New Mexico St.	80
73	Ark.-Little Rock †	74

Nickname: Mean Green
Colors: Green & White
Arena: Super Pit
Capacity: 10,032; Year Built: 1973
AD: Rick Villarreal
SID: Jerry Scott

NORTHEASTERN
Boston, MA 02115-5096 I

Coach: Ron Everhart, Virginia Tech 1985
2002-03 RESULTS (16-15)

82	Rhode Island ■	95
104	Suffolk ■	50
99	Fordham ■	75
88	New Mexico	90
56	Northern Ariz.	71
67	Penn St.	79
93	Curry ■	53
72	Troy St. †	89
91	Sacred Heart †	74
69	James Madison †	66
61	Providence	80
99	Loyola (Md.) ■	69
72	Boston College	67
81	Vermont	89
75	Hartford	82
76	Maine	90
81	New Hampshire ■	58
67	Stony Brook	72
72	Boston U.	69
59	Binghamton ■	48
51	Hartford †	50
89	Albany (N.Y.)	80
60	Stony Brook ■	78
75	New Hampshire	61
55	Maine	75
76	Vermont ■	59
54	Binghamton	66
69	Albany (N.Y.) ■	54
65	Boston U. ■	76
71	Maine †	68
61	Boston U.	71

Nickname: Huskies
Colors: Red & Black
Arena: Matthews Arena
Capacity: 6,000; Year Built: 1909
AD: David O'Brien
SID: Jack Grinold

NORTHEASTERN ST.
Tahlequah, OK 74464-2399 II

Coach: Larry Gipson, Heidelberg 1974
2002-03 RESULTS (32-3)

86	Bacone	69
68	Central Ark. †	42
84	Arkansas Tech	64
76	John Brown	63
74	Angelo St. ■	57
88	Abilene Christian ■	49
79	St. Mary's (Tex.)	75
56	Mo. Southern St.	73
75	West Tex. A&M	69
82	Eastern N.M.	75
71	Sterling (Kan.) ■	40
92	Midwestern St. ■	48
73	St. Mary's (Tex.) ■	61
71	Tex. A&M-Commerce	66
67	Tex. A&M-Kingsville	56
73	Southwestern Okla.	66
78	Cameron ■	65
59	Southeastern Okla.	48
77	East Central ■	42
73	Central Okla. ■	69
61	Tarleton St. ■	48
81	Southwestern Okla. ■	66
71	Cameron	60
75	Southeastern Okla.	62
70	East Central	64
72	Central Okla.	68
53	Tarleton St.	61
64	Midwestern St. ■	62
56	West Tex. A&M †	78
78	Central Okla. †	67
64	Washburn †	59
56	Tarleton St.	46
94	Neb.-Kearney †	75
84	Queens (N.C.) †	69
75	Ky. Wesleyan †	64

Nickname: Redmen
Colors: Green & White
Arena: Dobbins Fieldhouse
Capacity: 1,200; Year Built: 1954
AD: Eddie Griffin
SID: Matt Conley

NORTHERN ARIZ.
Flagstaff, AZ 86011-5400 I

Coach: Mike Adras, UC Santa Barb. 1983
2002-03 RESULTS (15-13)

65	High Point †	70
99	St. Peter's †	93
66	Arizona	101
100	UC Santa Cruz ■	76
71	Northeastern ■	56
74	Western St. ■	60
73	Southern Utah	56
67	UCLA	63
92	Tenn.-Martin ■	76
61	Portland	63
68	Marist ■	65
85	Southern Utah ■	68
57	New Mexico	59
81	Sacramento St. ■	85
53	Eastern Wash.	76
60	Portland St.	73
61	Weber St. ■	64
65	Idaho St. ■	62
97	Montana	93
66	Montana St.	80
63	Sacramento St.	45
75	Portland St. ■	64
75	Eastern Wash.	78
76	Idaho St.	90
64	Weber St.	79
81	Montana St. ■	71
69	Montana ■	59
74	Idaho St.	85

Nickname: Lumberjacks
Colors: Blue & Gold
Arena: Walkup Skydome
Capacity: 7,000; Year Built: 1977
AD: Steven P. Holton
SID: Steve Shaff

NORTHERN COLO.
Greeley, CO 80639 II

Coach: Craig Rasmuson, Ashland 1990
2002-03 RESULTS (11-15)

80	Colorado Mines	81
66	Regis (Colo.) †	71
77	Adams St. ■	73
83	Holy Names †	60
93	Grand View †	57
76	Colorado Mines ■	57
83	Colo. Christian ■	75
82	Western St.	48
87	Judson (Ill.) †	69
96	Hope Int'l †	62
70	St. Cloud St.	71
71	North Dakota St. ■	74
62	Neb.-Omaha	94
84	South Dakota ■	91
74	Augustana (S.D.)	77
87	Minn. St. Mankato ■	73
66	Neb.-Omaha	88
58	North Dakota	70
79	North Dakota St.	91
73	South Dakota	86
63	South Dakota St. ■	79
83	Augustana (S.D.) ■	61
67	St. Cloud St.	79
63	North Dakota ■	72
63	Minn. St. Mankato	58
65	South Dakota St.	76

Nickname: Bears
Colors: Blue & Gold
Arena: Butler Hancock Hall
Capacity: 4,500; Year Built: 1975
AD: James E. Fallis
SID: Colin McDonough

NORTHERN ILL.
De Kalb, IL 60115-2854 I

Coach: Rob Judson, Illinois 1980
2002-03 RESULTS (17-14)

56	Winthrop †	50
56	Wisconsin	84
48	DePaul ■	63
69	Loyola (Ill.) ■	67
67	Valparaiso	78
77	Drake ■	62
57	Marshall ■	75
83	South Fla.	84
72	Illinois St.	65
45	Ill.-Chicago ■	77
75	Eastern Ill.	90
63	Bowling Green ■	64
72	Toledo	65
66	Ball St.	64

68	Ohio	61
88	Eastern Mich. ■	79
63	Bowling Green	46
100	Akron	101
78	Ball St. ■	60
70	Buffalo	61
67	Kent St. ■	61
80	Ohio	53
70	Eastern Mich.	68
75	Central Mich.	87
56	Miami (Ohio)	59
85	Toledo ■	75
57	Central Mich.	73
67	Western Mich. ■	71
81	Buffalo ■	64
75	Western Mich. †	63
72	Central Mich. †	94

Nickname: Huskies
Colors: Cardinal & Black
Arena: Convocation Center
Capacity: 9,100; Year Built: 2002
AD: Cary Groth
SID: Michael Smoose

NORTHERN IOWA
Cedar Falls, IA 50614 I

Coach: Greg McDermott, Northern Iowa
2002-03 RESULTS (11-17)

77	Montana	71
71	Wayne St. (Neb.) ■	40
58	Siena	69
52	Creighton ■	65
54	Iowa	63
53	Utah	75
63	Chicago St.	67
81	Wis.-Green Bay ■	67
64	Iowa St. ■	71
55	Wichita St.	79
66	Illinois St. ■	64
73	Drake	75
74	Indiana St. ■	61
56	Bradley	71
78	Southern Ill. ■	88
53	Southwest Mo. St. ■	70
71	Illinois St.	76
63	Evansville ■	61
75	Creighton	84
80	Wichita St. ■	72
61	Southern Ill.	72
63	Evansville	83
84	Bradley ■	80
76	Louisiana Tech	71
59	Indiana St.	39
59	Drake	48
51	Southwest Mo. St.	52
60	Indiana St. †	61

Nickname: Panthers
Colors: Purple & Old Gold
Arena: UNI-Dome
Capacity: 10,000; Year Built: 1976
AD: Rick Hartzell
SID: Nancy Justis

NORTHERN KY.
Highland Heights, KY 41099 II

Coach: Ken Shields, Dayton 1964
2002-03 RESULTS (25-6)

70	Findlay ■	62
90	Kentucky St. ■	65
79	Thomas More	58
79	Quincy ■	68
73	Mo.-St. Louis ■	54
74	Ky. Wesleyan	73
106	Bellarmine	85
68	Ohio Northern ■	47
79	Wayne St. (Mich.) ■	66

85	Ferris St. †	65
60	Hillsdale	74
72	Indianapolis	73
100	St. Joseph's (Ind.)	99
83	Lewis ■	71
77	SIU Edwardsville ■	63
64	Mo.-St. Louis	52
82	Southern Ind.	87
75	Bellarmine ■	68
91	St. Joseph's (Ind.) ■	69
76	Wis.-Parkside	75
74	SIU Edwardsville	72
70	Quincy	66
85	Southern Ind. ■	87
68	Ky. Wesleyan ■	71
83	Indianapolis ■	76
66	Wis.-Parkside	64
76	Lewis	72
64	Wis.-Parkside †	55
84	Southern Ind.	82
58	Lewis †	55
76	Findlay †	80

Nickname: Norse
Colors: Gold, Black & White
Arena: Regents Hall
Capacity: 2,000; Year Built: 1972
AD: Jane Meier
SID: Don Owen

NORTHERN MICH.
Marquette, MI 49855-5391 II

Coach: Dean Ellis, Northern Mich. 1983
2002-03 RESULTS (15-14)

72	Minn. St. Moorhead †	83
77	North Dakota St.	67
108	Northland Bapt. ■	48
65	Wis.-Parkside	70
94	Lake Superior St.	86
52	St. Cloud St.	84
91	St. Norbert ■	79
92	Northland ■	44
58	Ky. Wesleyan	74
77	Gannon ■	65
71	Ashland	75
76	Mercyhurst ■	71
63	Findlay	78
55	Hillsdale	54
74	Wayne St. (Mich.)	64
64	Saginaw Valley	60
77	Northwood ■	72
63	Michigan Tech	70
62	Grand Valley St.	59
63	Ferris St.	74
77	Saginaw Valley ■	85
59	Michigan Tech ■	79
63	Northwood	70
74	Lake Superior St.	68
66	Ferris St. ■	77
89	Grand Valley St.	73
67	Wis.-Green Bay	72
69	Grand Valley St. ■	56
59	Michigan Tech	68

Nickname: Wildcats
Colors: Old Gold & Olive Green
Arena: Berry Events Center
Capacity: 4,000; Year Built: 1999
AD: Ken Godfrey
SID: Jim Pinar

NORTHERN ST.
Aberdeen, SD 57401 II

Coach: Don Meyer, Northern Colo. 1967
2002-03 RESULTS (20-9)

83	Huron ■	69
70	Sioux Falls ■	71

98	Dakota St. ■	62
88	North Dakota St. ■	85
70	Augustana (S.D.)	76
87	South Dakota	95
70	North Dakota	73
69	South Dakota St. ■	74
78	Concordia-St. Paul	60
97	Winona St.	103
69	Wayne St. (Neb.) ■	55
67	Southwest Minn. St. ■	60
75	Minn. St. Moorhead	71
75	Minn.-Crookston	44
79	Minn. Duluth	75
77	Bemidji St. ■	82
82	Minn.-Morris	62
72	Winona St. ■	70
93	Concordia-St. Paul ■	84
73	Southwest Minn. St.	61
76	Wayne St. (Neb.) ■	73
77	Minn.-Crookston ■	56
91	Minn. St. Moorhead ■	71
68	Bemidji St.	69
89	Minn. Duluth	85
100	Morningside ■	75
70	Minn.-Morris	51
99	Concordia-St. Paul ■	65
65	Minn. Duluth †	68

Nickname: Wolves
Colors: Maroon & Gold
Arena: Wachs Arena
Capacity: 8,057; Year Built: 1987
AD: Robert A. Olson
SID: Mike Lefler

NORTHWEST MO. ST.
Maryville, MO 64468-6001 II

Coach: Steve Tappmeyer,
Southeast Mo. St. 1979
2002-03 RESULTS (22-9)

92	Florida Tech ■	46
71	South Dakota St.	69
78	Concordia-St. Paul †	76
67	Minn. Duluth †	97
79	Peru St. ■	62
109	Calvary Bible ■	28
90	York (Neb.) ■	56
80	Rollins †	65
90	Drury ■	84
80	Mo. Western St.	74
67	Pittsburg St.	81
71	Truman	83
75	Mo. Southern St.	78
59	Washburn	58
84	Southwest Baptist ■	71
78	Central Mo. St.	56
70	Mo.-Rolla ■	58
89	Emporia St.	109
92	Pittsburg St. ■	64
60	Truman ■	56
93	Mo. Southern St. ■	92
52	Washburn	62
80	Southwest Baptist	74
80	Central Mo. St. ■	59
75	Mo.-Rolla	54
92	Emporia St. ■	82
65	Mo. Western St.	77
95	Pittsburg St. †	73
67	Mo. Western St. †	76
71	Mo. Western St. †	61
58	Tarleton St.	73

Nickname: Bearcats
Colors: Green & White
Arena: Bearcat Arena
Capacity: 2,500; Year Built: 1955
AD: Bob Boerigter
SID: Andy Seeley

NORTHWEST NAZARENE
Nampa, ID 83686 II

Coach: Ed Weidenbach, Northwest
Nazarene
2002-03 RESULTS (5-21)

72	Central Wash. †	94
55	Minn. Duluth †	85
75	Cascade ■	69
51	Warner Pacific ■	63
56	Alas. Anchorage ■	71
63	Alas. Fairbanks ■	67
68	Chaminade	84
50	Hawaii Pacific	69
51	Westminster (Utah) ■	60
70	Humboldt St.	94
75	Western Ore.	87
117	Walla Walla ■	77
85	Seattle	87
64	St. Martin's ■	55
84	Central Wash. ■	96
61	Western Wash.	80
58	Seattle Pacific	95
83	Western Ore. ■	93
63	Humboldt St. ■	72
61	Seattle ■	79
74	Central Wash.	80
71	St. Martin's	75
83	Seattle Pacific ■	76
80	Western Wash. ■	88
69	Alas. Fairbanks	83
79	Alas. Anchorage	74

Nickname: Crusaders
Colors: Red and Black
Arena: Montgomery Fieldhouse
Capacity: 3,500; Year Built: 1971
AD: Rich Sanders
SID: Gil Craker

NORTHWESTERN
Evanston, IL 60208 I

Coach: Bill Carmody, Union (N.Y.) 1975
2002-03 RESULTS (12-17)

56	Md.-East. Shore ■	36
81	New Hampshire ■	55
53	IUPUI ■	56
59	Kansas St.	55
49	North Carolina St.	74
62	Bowling Green ■	60
66	Elon ■	51
53	Ill.-Chicago ■	70
62	Fordham ■	60
69	Buffalo ■	62
70	Long Island ■	42
63	Iowa ■	68
68	Purdue	82
57	Indiana	71
70	Michigan ■	77
57	Minnesota	74
50	Wisconsin	69
52	Ohio St.	65
74	Indiana ■	61
59	Wisconsin ■	74
78	Purdue ■	67
51	Michigan St.	64
61	Minnesota ■	73
61	Illinois †	73
85	Penn St.	79
48	Ohio St. ■	52
61	Iowa	77
76	Minnesota †	64
65	Illinois †	94

Nickname: Wildcats
Colors: Purple & White
Arena: Welsh-Ryan Arena
Capacity: 8,117; Year Built: 1952
AD: Mark H. Murphy
SID: Michael Mahoney

NORTHWESTERN ST.
Natchitoches, LA 71497-0003....I

Coach: Mike McConathy, Louisiana Tech 1977
2002-03 RESULTS (6-21)

56	New Mexico	60
54	Baylor	82
63	Centenary (La.)	64
55	Wichita St.	74
51	Oklahoma St.	77
71	Grambling ■	74
49	Southeastern La.	51
76	Texas-San Antonio ■	67
62	Texas St. ■	71
56	McNeese St.	71
72	Centenary (La.) ■	83
65	Southeastern La. ■	59
70	Nicholls St. ■	61
63	Lamar	79
62	Sam Houston St.	76
66	Texas-Arlington ■	75
59	Stephen F. Austin ■	71
73	Texas-San Antonio	63
62	Texas St.	95
57	McNeese St. ■	70
63	La.-Monroe ■	75
62	Nicholls St.	53
83	La.-Monroe	78
47	Lamar ■	62
72	Sam Houston St. ■	83
50	Texas-Arlington	68
63	Stephen F. Austin	75

Nickname: Demons
Colors: Purple, White & Orange
Arena: Prather Coliseum
    Capacity: 4,300; Year Built: 1963
AD: Gregory S. Burke
SID: Doug Ireland

NORTHWOOD
Midland, MI 48640-2398 II

Coach: Bob Taylor, Arkansas Tech 1980
2002-03 RESULTS (10-16)

67	Hillsdale †	68
65	Wayne St. (Mich.)	69
85	Adrian ■	62
70	Wayne St. (Mich.) ■	86
65	Ashland	85
79	St. Joseph's (Ind.)	84
88	Grand Valley St. ■	84
93	Alma ■	61
98	St. Mary's (Mich.) ■	68
72	Rochester College ■	64
69	Lewis ■	80
83	Findlay ■	80
65	Mercyhurst	88
76	Gannon	81
79	Ferris St.	73
67	Lake Superior St. ■	77
72	Northern Mich.	77
73	Michigan Tech	79
69	Saginaw Valley ■	75
75	Lake Superior St.	78
75	Grand Valley St.	74
82	Ferris St. ■	72
70	Northern Mich. ■	63
62	Michigan Tech ■	79
68	Hillsdale ■	87
81	Saginaw Valley	82

Nickname: Timberwolves
Colors: Columbia Blue & White
Arena: E.W. Bennett Sports Center
    Capacity: 1,500; Year Built: 1979
AD: Pat Riepma
SID: Ryan Thompson

NORWICH
Northfield, VT 05663 III

Coach: Paul Booth, St. Joseph's (Vt.) 1983
2002-03 RESULTS (14-11)

65	Plattsburgh St.	63
93	Johnson St.	86
85	Lyndon St. ■	74
60	Middlebury ■	77
74	Middlebury ■	85
60	Southern Vt. ■	78
77	Johnson & Wales ■	71
83	Emerson	70
76	Emmanuel (Mass.) ■	56
65	Suffolk	63
70	Albertus Magnus ■	80
66	Rivier	57
63	Emmanuel (Mass.)	79
91	Daniel Webster ■	77
80	Western New Eng. ■	87
59	Johnson & Wales ■	72
38	Southern Vt.	58
72	Emerson ■	64
63	Daniel Webster ■	46
66	Rivier ■	57
53	Western New Eng.	78
76	Suffolk ■	61
62	Albertus Magnus	72
77	Johnson & Wales	56
57	Southern Vt. †	65

Nickname: Cadets
Colors: Maroon & Gold
Arena: Andrews Hall
    Capacity: 1,500; Year Built: 1980
AD: Anthony A. Mariano
SID: Todd Bamford

NOTRE DAME
Notre Dame, IN 46556 I

Coach: Mike Brey, George Washington 1982
2002-03 RESULTS (24-10)

76	Belmont ■	48
89	IUPUI ■	45
73	Bucknell ■	42
75	Furman ■	50
75	Creighton †	80
90	Albany (N.Y.) ■	55
92	Marquette ■	71
79	Maryland †	67
98	Texas †	92
102	DePaul ■	71
93	Canisius ■	75
76	Vanderbilt ■	63
55	Valparaiso †	53
55	Pittsburgh	72
74	Seton Hall ■	64
68	Rutgers ■	57
73	Kentucky	88
71	Providence	65
101	Boston College	96
88	West Virginia ■	69
93	Georgetown ■	92
72	Seton Hall	78
66	Pittsburgh ■	64
80	Syracuse	82
56	West Virginia	55
98	Virginia Tech ■	76
79	Connecticut ■	87
82	Rutgers	95
88	Syracuse ■	92
86	Georgetown	80
80	St. John's (N.Y.) †	83
70	Wis.-Milwaukee †	69
68	Illinois †	60
71	Arizona †	88

Nickname: Fighting Irish
Colors: Blue & Gold
Arena: Joyce Center

Capacity: 11,418; Year Built: 1968
AD: Kevin White
SID: Bernadette Cafarelli

NOVA SOUTHEASTERN
Fort Lauderdale, FL 33314.........II

Coach: Tony McAndrews, St. Ambrose 1966
2002-03 RESULTS (6-21)

60	South Fla.	99
71	P.R.-Rio Piedras †	64
47	Barry	58
60	Fla. Atlantic	86
49	West Fla.	70
85	Union (Ky.) †	70
57	Florida Tech	64
45	Rollins ■	60
63	Barry ■	69
72	Eckerd ■	59
62	Indianapolis †	76
60	P.R.-Cayey †	57
62	Franklin Pierce †	74
53	Valdosta St.	66
62	Bentley	74
61	Florida Tech ■	64
59	Fla. Southern ■	83
58	Lynn ■	82
62	West Fla. ■	87
53	Rollins	64
61	Lynn	60
75	North Fla.	81
72	Valdosta St. ■	83
79	St. Leo ■	60
46	St. Leo	60
70	Mont. St.-Billings	106
66	Mont. St.-Billings	87

Nickname: Knights
Colors: Navy Blue & Gold
AD: Michael Mominey
SID: Robert Prior

NYACK
Nyack, NY 10960-3698...........II

Coach: Don Meyer, Northern Colo. 1967
2002-03 RESULTS (7-21)

68	Bridgewater St. ■	70
68	Malone ■	94
44	Winthrop	86
52	Xavier (La.) †	67
49	Spring Hill	64
71	N.J. Inst. of Tech.	83
69	Bloomfield	77
58	Felician	68
87	Phila. Sciences ■	85
61	Daemen	94
94	Wilmington (Del.)	82
61	Holy Family	77
58	Teikyo Post ■	77
64	Goldey-Beacom ■	57
61	Caldwell ■	71
66	Phila. Sciences	89
100	Wilmington (Del.) ■	88
66	N.J. Inst. of Tech.	91
63	Dominican (N.Y.)	67
70	Felician ■	67
80	Bloomfield ■	84
67	East Stroudsburg	100
93	Holy Family ■	76
77	Teikyo Post	104
78	Caldwell	88
60	Dominican (N.Y.) ■	64
75	Goldey-Beacom	41
88	Morningside †	95

Nickname: Purple Pride
Colors: Purple & White
AD: Keith Davie
SID: To be named

OAKLAND
Rochester, MI 48309-4401.........I

Coach: Greg Kampe, Bowling Green 1978
2002-03 RESULTS (17-11)

107	Spring Arbor ■	72
95	IPFW ■	68
84	Akron ■	88
65	Texas A&M ■	71
88	Adrian ■	69
68	Bowling Green	75
61	Air Force ■	44
91	Texas Southern †	88
72	Tex. A&M-Corp. Chris	80
76	Jacksonville St. ■	82
53	Illinois	88
75	Youngstown St. ■	70
82	IUPUI	96
86	UMKC	65
75	Oral Roberts	88
75	Western Ill. ■	62
70	Valparaiso ■	72
87	Tex. A&M-Corp. Chris ■	74
90	Chicago St. ■	71
85	Southern Utah	83
79	IUPUI ■	78
78	Oral Roberts ■	57
100	UMKC ■	79
65	Valparaiso	81
89	Western Ill.	79
64	Chicago St.	61
92	Southern Utah ■	77
55	Southern Utah †	66

Nickname: Golden Grizzlies
Colors: Gold, Black & White
Arena: Athletic Center
    Capacity: 4,005; Year Built: 1998
AD: Jack G. Mehl
SID: Phil Hess

OAKLAND CITY
Oakland City, IN 47660-1099 ..II

Coach: John Hayes, Oakland City 1990
2002-03 RESULTS (11-15)

73	Hawaii-Hilo †	75
75	BYU-Hawaii	103
95	Hannibal-LaGrange ■	61
66	Southeast Mo. St.	88
88	Harris-Stowe ■	69
81	Indianapolis ■	92
70	Southern Ind.	98
89	Bellarmine ■	99
77	Saginaw Valley ■	85
66	SIU Edwardsville	68
86	Brescia ■	72
80	Ill.-Springfield	50
61	Ala.-Huntsville ■	56
72	Spalding	82
73	Drury ■	60
97	Wilberforce	88
86	St. Louis Christian ■	52
83	Montevallo	70
83	Brescia	92
60	Spalding ■	62
88	Ill.-Springfield ■	84
65	Ala.-Huntsville	81
86	Montevallo ■	70
67	Robert Morris (Ill.) ■	77
75	Drury	80
85	Crichton	102

Nickname: Mighty Oaks
Colors: Navy & White
Arena: Johnson Center
    Capacity: 1,600; Year Built: 1987
AD: Mike Sandifar
SID: Dan Durbin

SCHEDULES/RESULTS

OBERLIN
Oberlin, OH 44074 III

Coach: James Sullinger, Oberlin 1978
2002-03 RESULTS (3-22)
55	Concordia (Wis.) †	72
45	Concordia-M'head †	75
62	Notre Dame (Ohio)	74
56	Hanover	85
60	Albion †	85
60	Earlham	72
45	Manchester	82
47	Wilmington (Ohio) ■	68
43	Wittenberg	101
45	Wooster ■	86
48	Ohio Wesleyan	81
68	Wash. & Jeff.	79
67	Kenyon ■	69
45	Wabash	64
56	Denison ■	66
79	Hiram	87
52	Penn St.-Behrend ■	46
81	Allegheny ■	98
57	Earlham	66
81	Kenyon	94
61	Ohio Wesleyan ■	78
60	Allegheny	99
87	Wabash ■	78
61	Denison	72
69	Hiram ■	66

Nickname: Yeomen
Colors: Crimson & Gold
Arena: Philips Gymnasium
  Capacity: 1,800; Year Built: 1971
AD: George Andrews
SID: Scott Wargo

OCCIDENTAL
Los Angeles, CA 90041 III

Coach: Brian Newhall, Occidental 1983
2002-03 RESULTS (24-3)
77	S'western (Ariz.) †	51
88	West Coast Chrst. †	47
64	Azusa Pacific	77
87	La Sierra	45
89	Pacific Union ■	58
80	Chapman	64
83	Swarthmore ■	52
79	St. Joseph's (Me.) ■	60
69	La Sierra	70
98	Latin American Bible ■	54
123	Redlands	95
78	La Verne ■	67
66	Whittier ■	63
51	Pomona-Pitzer ■ †	49
65	Claremont-M-S	62
80	Cal Lutheran	77
90	Caltech ■	45
97	Redlands	96
93	La Verne	89
64	Whittier ■	61
61	Pomona-Pitzer	55
62	Claremont-M-S ■	58
76	Cal Lutheran ■	63
96	Caltech	42
80	Aurora ■	61
67	Buena Vista	62
56	Gust. Adolphus †	74

Nickname: Tigers
Colors: Orange & Black
Arena: Rush Gymnasium
  Capacity: 1,800; Year Built: 1967
AD: Dixon Farmer
SID: To be named

OGLETHORPE
Atlanta, GA 30319-2797 III

Coach: Jim Owen, Berry 1981
2002-03 RESULTS (9-16)
68	Maryville (Tenn.) †	76
65	LaGrange ■	71
72	Warren Wilson	41
72	Emory	90
85	Carver Bible ■	70
55	Citadel	95
84	Alice Lloyd ■	74
74	Millsaps ■	85
84	LaGrange	77
74	Southwestern (Tex.)	81
67	Trinity (Tex.)	71
70	Centre ■	79
73	Sewanee	71
96	Warren Wilson ■	63
63	Rhodes	72
76	Hendrix	74
68	DePauw ■	78
65	Rose-Hulman ■	74
78	Emory ■	64
60	Millsaps	75
63	Maryville (Tenn.) ■	89
70	Southwestern (Tex.) ■	88
51	Trinity (Tex.) ■	90
65	Centre	83
114	Sewanee	100

Nickname: Stormy Petrels
Colors: Black & Gold
Arena: Dorough Fieldhouse
  Capacity: 2,000; Year Built: 1962
AD: Bob Unger
SID: Jack Berkshire

OHIO
Athens, OH 45701 I

Coach: Tim O'Shea, Boston College 1984
2002-03 RESULTS (14-16)
68	Providence	91
75	Brown	71
71	Toledo	78
65	DePaul	73
57	Boston U.	78
54	Navy ■	52
51	Wisconsin	75
104	St. Bonaventure ■	101
75	Kentucky †	83
112	Akron ■	104
84	Central Mich.	87
61	Northern Ill. ■	68
65	Miami (Ohio) ■	77
72	Buffalo	66
60	Bowling Green ■	66
87	Marshall	85
68	Ball St.	82
61	Buffalo ■	49
53	Northern Ill.	80
74	Kent St. ■	71
73	Eastern Mich. ■	76
79	Western Mich. ■	72
82	Akron	84
78	Virginia ■	72
70	Marshall ■	65
64	Miami (Ohio)	56
62	Kent St.	73
79	Akron	77
65	Miami (Ohio) †	55
70	Kent St. †	73

Nickname: Bobcats
Colors: Hunter Green & White
Arena: Convocation Center
  Capacity: 13,000; Year Built: 1968
AD: Thomas C. Boeh
SID: Jim Stephan

OHIO NORTHERN
Ada, OH 45810 III

Coach: Joe Campoli, Rhode Island 1964
2002-03 RESULTS (14-13)
62	Wooster ■	63
76	Albion †	62
65	Hanover	85
57	Capital	66
58	Wilmington (Ohio)	61
72	Marietta	51
90	Defiance	92
47	Northern Ky.	68
82	Wittenberg ■	62
78	Muskingum ■	49
66	Walsh	75
65	Baldwin-Wallace	44
77	John Carroll ■	62
62	Heidelberg ■	54
87	Mount Union ■	74
61	Otterbein ■	74
63	Marietta	46
61	Wilmington (Ohio) ■	48
69	Mount Union	80
77	Otterbein	88
66	Muskingum	64
83	Baldwin-Wallace ■	74
57	John Carroll	72
62	Heidelberg	58
67	Capital ■	76
74	Otterbein	65
73	John Carroll †	86

Nickname: Polar Bears
Colors: Burnt Orange & Black
Arena: ONU Sports Center
  Capacity: 3,200; Year Built: 1975
AD: Thomas E. Simmons
SID: Tim Glon

OHIO ST.
Columbus, OH 43210 I

Coach: Jim O'Brien, Boston College 1971
2002-03 RESULTS (17-15)
58	Coppin St. ■	51
48	Alabama †	54
76	Duke †	91
71	Tennessee Tech ■	64
74	Morehead St. ■	60
49	Pittsburgh	69
71	Seton Hall ■	54
96	Radford ■	80
94	Tennessee St. ■	73
70	Hampton ■	62
64	Louisville ■	72
55	Michigan St.	66
81	Indiana ■	69
50	Michigan ■	61
52	Wisconsin ■	53
51	Indiana	69
83	Iowa ■	72
65	Purdue	70
65	Northwestern ■	52
73	Minnesota ■	68
57	Illinois	76
76	Penn St.	67
54	Michigan	70
52	Purdue ■	44
64	Iowa ■	71
52	Northwestern	48
58	Michigan St. ■	72
66	Iowa †	64
58	Wisconsin †	50
55	Michigan St. †	54
59	Illinois †	72
58	Georgia Tech	72

Nickname: Buckeyes
Colors: Scarlet & Gray

Arena: Value City Arena
  Capacity: 19,200; Year Built: 1998
AD: Ferdinand A. Geiger
SID: Dan Wallenberg

OHIO VALLEY
Vienna, WV 26104 II

Coach: Jason Dougherty, Ohio Valley 1997
2002-03 RESULTS (2-26)
57	Kentucky St. †	87
73	Findlay †	94
65	Marietta	72
96	Ohio-Zanesville ■	32
46	Alderson-Broaddus	89
54	Calif. (Pa.)	97
49	Wheeling Jesuit	117
56	Fairmont St. †	95
71	Glenville St.	99
57	West Va. Wesleyan	92
61	Alderson-Broaddus ■	85
77	Davis & Elkins ■	92
67	Bluefield St.	79
41	Fairmont St. ■	86
56	West Liberty St.	61
51	Davis & Elkins	82
72	Salem Int'l	85
54	Wheeling Jesuit	76
71	Shepherd ■	56
67	West Virginia St.	93
56	West Va. Tech ■	89
63	Fairmont St.	85
55	West Liberty St. ■	97
72	Salem Int'l	98
57	Charleston (W.Va.) ■	80
86	Wheeling Jesuit ■	90
54	Concord	88
72	Alderson-Broaddus	102

Nickname: Fighting Scots
Colors: Royal Blue & Red
AD: Ron Pavan
SID: To be named

OHIO WESLEYAN
Delaware, OH 43015 III

Coach: Michael DeWitt, Ohio Wesleyan 1987
2002-03 RESULTS (12-14)
102	MacMurray †	62
88	Adrian	73
64	Capital	72
76	Hiram	64
71	Ohio Dominican ■	78
56	Eastern Ky.	109
66	Rose-Hulman †	60
55	Dominican (Ill.) †	57
79	Thiel †	61
57	Randolph-Macon	83
100	Kenyon ■	66
76	Denison	67
81	Oberlin ■	48
64	Wittenberg ■	73
93	Allegheny ■	86
59	Wooster	70
60	Earlham	68
77	Wabash ■	53
79	Hiram ■	81
58	Wittenberg	68
78	Oberlin	61
54	Wabash	55
60	Earlham	56
60	Wooster ■	73
81	Allegheny	85
63	Wabash	69

Nickname: Battling Bishops
Colors: Red & Black
Arena: Branch Rickey Arena

Capacity: 2,300; Year Built: 1976
AD: John A. Martin
SID: Mark Beckenbach

OKLAHOMA
Norman, OK 73019..................I

Coach: Kelvin Sampson, UNC-Pembroke 1978
2002-03 RESULTS (27-7)

62	Alabama †	68
87	UC Irvine ■	65
82	Princeton ■	63
75	Prairie View ■	63
92	Hartford ■	52
69	Coppin St. ■	47
89	Georgia St. ■	62
45	Mississippi St. †	54
100	UNC Asheville ■	64
60	Michigan St. †	58
73	Connecticut ■	63
69	Colorado ■	54
46	Oklahoma St.	48
70	Iowa St.	60
69	Texas Tech ■	64
67	Baylor	54
75	Texas A&M ■	68
91	Kansas St.	89
91	Baylor ■	42
61	Texas	67
63	Texas Tech	58
64	Oklahoma St. ■	48
77	Kansas ■	70
52	Missouri	67
69	Texas A&M	64
76	Nebraska ■	51
71	Texas ■	76
74	Colorado †	59
67	Texas Tech †	60
49	Missouri †	47
71	South Carolina St. †	54
74	California †	65
65	Butler †	54
47	Syracuse †	63

Nickname: Sooners
Colors: Crimson & Cream
Arena: Lloyd Noble Center
  Capacity: 12,000; Year Built: 1975
AD: Joseph R. Castiglione
SID: Mike Houck

OKLA. PANHANDLE
Goodwell, OK 73939...............II

Coach: Charles Terry, Arkansas 1976
2002-03 RESULTS (15-11)

65	Lubbock Chrst.	57
85	Southwest Baptist ■	78
75	Eastern N.M.	70
79	Adams St. ■	57
81	Abilene Christian	58
44	West Tex. A&M	73
76	Eastern N.M.	68
65	Adams St.	85
79	West Tex. A&M ■	75
86	Central Ark.	79
86	Bethel (Kan.) ■	59
72	Fort Hays St.	78
81	Drury ■	85
62	Fort Hays St. ■	74
77	Lincoln (Mo.)	70
56	Rockhurst	74
59	St. Mary's (Tex.) ■	75
69	Incarnate Word ■	84
92	St. Edward's ■	88
81	Drury	89
72	Lincoln (Mo.) ■	75
93	Rockhurst	83
73	St. Mary's (Tex.)	98
84	Incarnate Word	77
86	Abilene Christian	78
90	St. Edward's	73

Nickname: Aggies
Colors: Navy & Red
Arena: Carl Williams Field House
  Capacity: 2,800; Year Built: 1909
AD: Wayne Stewart
SID: Jason Cronin

OKLAHOMA ST.
Stillwater, OK 74078-5070........I

Coach: Eddie Sutton, Oklahoma St. 1958
2002-03 RESULTS (22-10)

68	Yale ■	59
98	Alas. Anchorage	69
58	Col. of Charleston †	66
64	Michigan St. †	61
65	Hartford ■	52
77	Northwestern St. ■	51
71	Fresno St. ■	61
85	UMKC ■	61
68	Wichita St.	58
71	Arkansas ■	45
78	Brigham Young †	65
91	Tex. A&M-Corp. Chris ■	58
93	Texas A&M	76
48	Oklahoma ■	46
76	Missouri ■	56
67	Baylor	64
79	Texas Tech	70
68	Iowa St. ■	55
65	Texas	78
63	Kansas St. ■	55
50	Cincinnati	61
77	Nebraska	70
72	Baylor ■	74
48	Oklahoma	64
82	Texas ■	77
57	Texas Tech ■	62
61	Kansas	79
56	Colorado	68
77	Texas A&M ■	52
58	Missouri †	60
77	Pennsylvania †	63
56	Syracuse †	68

Nickname: Cowboys
Colors: Orange & Black
Arena: Gallagher-Iba Arena
  Capacity: 13,611; Year Built: 1938
AD: Terry Don Phillips/Harry Birdwell
SID: Mike Noteware

OLD DOMINION
Norfolk, VA 23529-0197..........I

Coach: Blaine Taylor, Montana 1982
2002-03 RESULTS (12-15)

59	North Carolina ■	67
72	Campbell ■	43
47	St. Joseph's	63
70	Hampton	77
67	East Caro. ■	75
82	Md.-East. Shore ■	62
67	Dayton ■	71
84	George Washington	76
67	Towson ■	56
64	Va. Commonwealth	73
67	UNC Wilmington	57
76	William & Mary ■	64
74	Delaware ■	75
65	Hofstra	69
59	George Mason ■	46
74	James Madison ■	56
72	Drexel	69
69	Va. Commonwealth ■	72
53	William & Mary	69
66	James Madison	74
71	UNC Wilmington ■	68
73	Towson	51
57	Drexel	62
63	Delaware	73
52	George Mason	69
77	Hofstra ■	46
52	Drexel †	61

Nickname: Monarchs
Colors: Slate Blue, Sky Blue, & Silver
Arena: Ted Constant Convocation Ctr.
  Capacity: 8,600; Year Built: 2002
AD: James Jarrett
SID: Carol Hudson

OLD WESTBURY
Old Westbury, NY 11568-0210III

Coach: Bernard Tomlin, Hofstra 1976
2002-03 RESULTS (16-12)

60	Clarkson †	63
79	Brandeis †	63
61	Manhattanville ■	64
75	St. Joseph's (L.I.) ■	72
74	Mt. St. Vincent	78
73	York (N.Y.) ■	65
70	Merchant Marine	71
59	Palm Beach Atl.	66
70	Bethel (Ind.) †	84
100	Purchase St.	60
75	Stevens Institute	46
66	Maritime (N.Y.) ■	59
65	Mt. St. Mary (N.Y.) ■	78
69	Centenary (N.J.)	73
82	St. Joseph's (L.I.)	68
60	Merchant Marine ■	64
86	Polytechnic (N.Y.)	57
75	Maritime (N.Y.)	61
71	Farmingdale St.	85
74	Manhattanville	71
76	Mt. St. Vincent ■	73
66	Yeshiva	57
87	Mt. St. Mary (N.Y.)	79
85	Yeshiva	71
64	Stevens Institute ■	61
64	St. Joseph's (L.I.) †	59
61	Merchant Marine	65
52	New Jersey City	70

Nickname: Panthers
Colors: Forest Green & White
Arena: Clark Center
  Capacity: 2,500; Year Built: 1981
AD: John Lonardo
SID: Matt Farrand

OLIVET
Olivet, MI 49076.....................III

Coach: Steve Hettinga, Olivet 1993
2002-03 RESULTS (11-15)

91	Wilmington (Ohio)	69
80	Goshen †	88
100	Tri-State ■	79
61	Mount Union †	78
83	Allegheny	78
98	Marygrove ■	77
77	Marian (Ind.) †	73
71	Spring Arbor	79
84	Mich.-Dearborn ■	66
85	Ferris St. ■	109
86	St. Mary's (Mich.) ■	83
88	Grace Bible (Mich.)	82
75	Concordia (Mich.)	85
72	Calvin	94
87	Adrian ■	69
95	Alma	75
65	Kalamazoo	72
90	Hope	99
68	Albion ■	79
89	Calvin	111
79	Adrian	84
78	Alma ■	77
76	Kalamazoo ■	94
73	Hope ■	90
57	Albion	76
62	Calvin	75

Nickname: Comets
Colors: Crimson & White
Arena: Upton Gymnasium
  Capacity: 1,500; Year Built: 1981
AD: Thomas Shaw
SID: Geoffrey Henson

ONEONTA ST.
Oneonta, NY 13820-4015.......III

Coach: Paul Clune, Rochester Inst. 1984
2002-03 RESULTS (11-14)

93	Hartwick ■	96
79	Purchase St. ■	63
65	Cortland St.	60
59	Buffalo St. ■	89
65	Fredonia St. ■	73
60	St. Lawrence ■	80
70	Utica	96
57	Clarkson	66
65	Farmingdale St.	59
62	Utica/Rome	75
74	Oswego St. ■	67
81	New Paltz St. ■	64
91	Plattsburgh St. ■	77
55	Potsdam St.	76
55	Ithaca	88
90	Brockport St.	105
80	Geneseo St.	71
81	Castleton St. ■	77
90	New Paltz St.	88
62	Cortland St. ■	53
57	Oswego St.	60
79	Brockport St. ■	69
63	Utica/Rome ■	66
61	Potsdam St. ■	80
72	Oswego St.	90

Nickname: Red Dragons
Colors: Red & White
Arena: Dewar Arena
  Capacity: 4,000; Year Built: 1999
AD: Steve Garner
SID: Geoff Hassard

ORAL ROBERTS
Tulsa, OK 74171.......................I

Coach: Scott Sutton, Oklahoma St. 1995
2002-03 RESULTS (18-10)

112	Okla. Wesleyan ■	66
76	Arkansas	64
76	Wichita St. ■	71
77	Tennessee St.	69
75	Southern Methodist ■	62
85	Mississippi Val.	75
68	Stephen F. Austin	71
80	Tulsa	90
96	Mississippi Val.	63
62	Howard †	72
68	UMBC †	48
80	Minnesota	85
78	Colgate	54
58	Southern Utah	73
77	Chicago St.	66
66	IUPUI ■	63
88	Oakland ■	75
76	UMKC	62
71	Valparaiso	84
87	Western Ill.	77
78	Chicago St. ■	48
86	Southern Utah ■	73
57	Oakland	78
65	IUPUI	76
86	UMKC ■	91

79	Western Ill. ■	58
89	Valparaiso ■	75
73	UMKC †	76

Nickname: Golden Eagles
Colors: Gold, Navy Blue & White
Arena: Mabee Center
   Capacity: 10,575; Year Built: 1972
AD: R. Michael Carter
SID: Cory Rogers

OREGON
Eugene, OR 97401 I

Coach: Ernie Kent, Oregon 1977
2002-03 RESULTS (23-10)

97	Grambling ■	52
86	Cal St. Northridge ■	77
88	Pacific (Cal.) ■	69
96	Portland ■	66
84	Kansas †	78
105	Pepperdine	90
52	Cincinnati †	77
107	Florida A&M ■	66
90	Minnesota ■	81
108	UC Riverside ■	67
72	Arizona	81
94	Arizona St. ■	73
72	California	88
57	Stanford	81
69	Portland St.	63
79	Oregon St. ■	68
91	Washington ■	66
76	Washington St. ■	66
96	UCLA	91
76	Southern California	91
79	Stanford ■	64
75	California ■	86
80	Oregon St.	63
89	Washington St.	70
66	Washington	78
79	Southern California ■	66
79	UCLA ■	48
77	Arizona St.	91
80	Arizona	88
83	Arizona St. †	82
75	UCLA †	74
74	Southern California †	66
58	Utah †	60

Nickname: Ducks
Colors: Green & Yellow
Arena: McArthur Court
   Capacity: 9,087; Year Built: 1927
AD: William Moos
SID: Greg Walker

OREGON ST.
Corvallis, OR 97331 I

Coach: Jay John, Arizona 1981
2002-03 RESULTS (13-15)

73	Idaho ■	76
81	Seattle ■	38
81	Cal Poly ■	60
71	Portland	64
62	Sacramento St.	49
53	Portland St. ■	50
78	IPFW	71
72	Kansas St.	90
59	Coppin St. ■	53
47	Arizona St. ■	67
65	Arizona	80
54	Stanford	57
73	California	78
68	Oregon	79
63	Washington St. ■	48
82	Washington ■	62
83	Southern California	74
83	UCLA	79
71	California ■	84
73	Stanford ■	84

63	Oregon ■	80
80	Washington	72
71	Washington St.	75
66	UCLA ■	69
61	Southern California ■	60
60	Arizona	72
64	Arizona St.	74
46	California †	69

Nickname: Beavers
Colors: Orange & Black
Arena: Gill Coliseum
   Capacity: 10,400; Year Built: 1950
AD: Mitch S. Barnhart/Robert J De
   Carolis
SID: Steve Fenk

OSWEGO ST.
Oswego, NY 13126 III

Coach: Kevin Broderick, Nazareth 1989
2002-03 RESULTS (16-11)

72	St. Lawrence †	83
86	Keuka †	84
74	Geneseo St.	71
70	Cortland St.	64
74	Utica/Rome ■	66
90	Hilbert	73
60	Nazareth	94
81	St. Lawrence ■	85
86	Brockport St ■	77
83	D'Youville ■	61
67	Oneonta St.	74
69	Medaille ■	52
90	Plattsburgh St. ■	75
80	Fredonia St.	68
63	Buffalo St.	88
50	Utica	75
64	Cortland St.	75
87	Potsdam St.	93
60	Brockport St.	104
61	Geneseo St. ■	58
73	New Paltz St. ■	58
60	Oneonta St. ■	57
74	Plattsburgh St.	66
75	Buffalo St. ■	57
90	Oneonta St. ■	72
62	Buffalo St. †	67
83	Union (N.Y.)	84

Nickname: Lakers
Colors: Hunter Green and Golden Yellow
Arena: Max Ziel Gymnasium
   Capacity: 3,500; Year Built: 1968
AD: Sandra Moore
SID: Lyle Fulton

OTTERBEIN
Westerville, OH 43081-2006 ...III

Coach: Dick Reynolds, Otterbein 1965
2002-03 RESULTS (15-11)

69	Tri-State †	73
96	Medaille †	50
82	Roanoke †	73
72	SCAD †	76
92	Heidelberg	77
70	Baldwin-Wallace ■	56
71	Wittenberg	79
72	Mount Union ■	73
63	Capital ■	67
79	Grove City ■	69
76	Mt. St. Joseph ■	67
65	Marietta	73
64	Muskingum	56
79	Wilmington (Ohio) ■	53
78	John Carroll ■	87
74	Ohio Northern	61
81	Mount Union	77
93	Heidelberg ■	71
79	John Carroll	84
88	Ohio Northern ■	77

64	Capital	72
60	Marietta ■	55
72	Muskingum ■	58
76	Wilmington (Ohio)	73
72	Baldwin-Wallace	76
65	Ohio Northern ■	74

Nickname: Cardinals
Colors: Tan & Cardinal
Arena: The Rike Center
   Capacity: 3,100; Year Built: 1974
AD: Richard E. Reynolds
SID: Ed Syguda

OUACHITA BAPTIST
Arkadelphia, AR 71998-0001 ...II

Coach: Charlie Schaef, Texas Tech 1993
2002-03 RESULTS (16-12)

75	West Ga. ■	65
80	North Ala. ■	89
77	Eastern N.M. †	83
78	Tex. Permian Basin †	51
85	Jarvis Christian ■	74
62	Incarnate Word †	67
69	St. Edward's	68
80	Hawaii-Hilo	82
76	Mid-America Naz. †	77
94	St. Edward's ■	86
93	Southern Ark.	79
90	Central Ark. ■	80
79	Christian Bros.	86
89	Rhema ■	63
68	Arkansas Tech	49
68	Henderson St.	103
78	Harding ■	82
69	Delta St.	63
72	Ark.-Monticello	73
78	Southern Ark. ■	52
61	Central Ark.	59
72	Christian Bros. ■	65
75	Arkansas Tech	55
73	Henderson St. ■	69
72	Harding	94
50	Delta St. ■	60
63	Ark.-Monticello ■	59
60	Ala.-Huntsville †	63

Nickname: Tigers
Colors: Purple & Gold
Arena: Vining Arena
   Capacity: 2,500; Year Built: 1966
AD: David R. Sharp
SID: Chris Babb

OZARKS (ARK.)
Clarksville, AR 72830-2880......III

Coach: Matt O'Connor, Davidson 1991
2002-03 RESULTS (14-10)

90	Bluffton †	88
78	North Central	81
71	Mo.-Rolla	86
90	Hardin-Simmons ■	71
99	McMurry ■	91
91	Mary Hardin-Baylor ■	88
81	Concordia-Austin	79
66	Southern Ark.	71
64	Howard Payne ■	87
83	Sul Ross St. ■	79
92	Schreiner	83
90	Texas Lutheran	92
80	East Tex. Baptist	77
81	LeTourneau	79
96	Austin	75
75	Texas-Dallas	83
101	Louisiana Col.	89
83	Mississippi Col. ■	73
89	Louisiana Col.	72
66	Mississippi Col.	87
71	East Tex. Baptist ■	86
74	LeTourneau ■	86

75	Austin ■	70
79	Texas-Dallas	90

Nickname: Eagles
Colors: Purple & Gold
Arena: Mabee Gym
   Capacity: 2,500
AD: Dave DeHart
SID: Josh Peppas

PACE
Pleasantville, NY 10570-2799 ...II

Coach: Jim Harter, Delaware 1982
2002-03 RESULTS (16-12)

94	Holy Family †	79
74	Dominican (N.Y.)	86
68	St. Anselm	66
79	Molloy ■	83
73	Southern Conn. St.	68
69	St. Rose	81
59	American Int'l	83
80	Caldwell	65
77	Le Moyne ■	76
76	Bridgeport	89
73	Bryant ■	68
74	Assumption ■	77
71	Franklin Pierce	76
60	Mass.-Lowell ■	66
82	Southern N.H.	71
55	Bentley ■	53
70	Stonehill ■	47
80	Merrimack	74
85	Southern Conn. St. ■	74
77	St. Rose	84
45	Le Moyne	65
93	St. Michael's ■	72
87	St. Anselm ■	83
83	Merrimack ■	74
82	Stonehill	57
69	Bentley	65
76	St. Michael's	95
72	Assumption ■	94

Nickname: Setters
Colors: Navy & Gold
Arena: Goldstein Athletics Center
   Capacity: 2,400; Year Built: 2002
AD: Joseph F. O'Donnell
SID: Brian Mundy

PACIFIC (CAL.)
Stockton, CA 95211 I

Coach: Bob Thomason, Pacific (Cal.)
1971
2002-03 RESULTS (12-16)

72	Santa Clara ■	78
73	Lamar ■	69
69	Oregon	88
54	Nevada	83
60	Fresno St.	80
75	San Francisco ■	59
70	San Jose St.	61
70	Western Ky. ■	57
62	St. Joseph's ■	50
73	Idaho ■	50
66	Utah St. ■	54
67	Cal St. Northridge ■	59
72	Cal Poly	75
52	UC Santa Barb.	67
62	UC Irvine ■	66
93	Long Beach St. ■	60
79	UC Riverside	71
62	Cal St. Fullerton	61
67	Cal St. Northridge	75
52	UC Santa Barb.	62
64	Cal Poly ■	67
61	Long Beach St.	70
73	UC Irvine	78
52	Cal St. Fullerton ■	55
77	UC Riverside ■	65

55	Idaho	60
70	Utah St.	75
44	UC Santa Barb. †	53

Nickname: Tigers
Colors: Orange & Black
Arena: A.G. Spanos Center
 Capacity: 6,150; Year Built: 1981
AD: Lynn King
SID: Mike Millerick

PACIFIC (ORE.)
Forest Grove, OR 97116-1797 ..III

Coach: Ken Schumann, George Fox 1981
2002-03 RESULTS (11-14)

68	Northwest Chrst.	51
42	Portland	70
62	Warner Pacific	66
101	Multnomah Bible ■	85
52	Cascade	59
56	Northwest Chrst. ■	67
91	Multnomah Bible	67
57	Hawaii Pacific	69
57	Whitworth	75
72	Whitman	58
63	Lewis & Clark ■	66
80	George Fox	67
69	Pacific Lutheran ■	62
71	Puget Sound ■	61
53	Willamette	70
74	Linfield	80
49	Cascade ■	51
55	Whitworth ■	65
75	Whitman ■	57
76	George Fox ■	68
46	Lewis & Clark	58
72	Pacific Lutheran	76
76	Puget Sound	90
69	Willamette ■	64
73	Linfield ■	71

Nickname: Boxers
Colors: Red, Black & White
Arena: Pacific Athletic Center
 Capacity: 2,500; Year Built: 1970
AD: Judy Sherman
SID: Blake Timm

PACIFIC LUTHERAN
Tacoma, WA 98447-0003 III

Coach: Dave Harshman, Washington St. 1970
2002-03 RESULTS (10-15)

84	Principia †	47
53	Colorado Col. †	59
79	Evergreen ■	74
63	Southern Ore.	65
56	Oregon Tech	80
73	Evergreen St.	79
65	Seattle	77
84	Cal St. Hayward	79
66	Wis.-Whitewater †	90
73	Lewis & Clark	65
37	Willamette	62
73	Whitworth ■	85
61	Whitman ■	47
62	Pacific (Ore.)	69
69	George Fox	72
49	Puget Sound ■	46
57	Willamette ■	54
72	Lewis & Clark ■	75
66	Linfield ■	78
50	Whitworth	66
63	Whitman	49
76	Pacific (Ore.) ■	72
95	George Fox ■	76
83	Puget Sound	89
88	Linfield	95

Nickname: Lutes
Colors: Black & Gold
Arena: Olson Auditorium
 Capacity: 3,200; Year Built: 1969
AD: Paul Hoseth
SID: Nick Dawson

PAINE
Augusta, GA 30901-3182 II

Coach: Ron Spry, Campbellsville 1975
2002-03 RESULTS (10-17)

90	Francis Marion ■	79
89	Lane	84
77	Kentucky St.	83
57	Miles	61
64	LeMoyne-Owen	83
79	Lane ■	66
75	Kentucky St. ■	80
57	Francis Marion	68
65	Belmont Abbey	82
58	Augusta St.	74
78	Tuskegee ■	72
74	Miles ■	58
59	Fort Valley St.	60
60	Clark Atlanta	65
57	Morehouse	73
76	Fort Valley St. ■	65
57	Albany St. (Ga.) ■	65
62	LeMoyne-Owen ■	56
86	Stillman ■	82
66	Morehouse ■	67
58	Clark Atlanta ■	63
66	Voorhees ■	68
50	Albany St. (Ga.)	63
62	Benedict	55
72	Tuskegee	75
85	Benedict ■	71
71	Fort Valley St. †	77

Nickname: Lions
Colors: Purple & White
Arena: Randall Carter Gymnasium
 Capacity: 1,200; Year Built: 1952
AD: Ronnie O. Spry
SID: Andre Kent-Bright

PENNSYLVANIA
Philadelphia, PA 19104-6322 I

Coach: Fran Dunphy, La Salle 1970
2002-03 RESULTS (22-6)

62	Penn St. ■	37
62	Drexel ■	71
59	Delaware	60
71	Temple ■	46
72	Villanova	58
71	Providence	74
57	Colorado	80
66	American ■	55
99	Southern California	61
98	Monmouth †	54
76	Lafayette	66
48	St. Joseph's	66
79	La Salle ■	66
73	Dartmouth ■	50
75	Harvard ■	59
70	Cornell ■	67
47	Columbia	40
65	Princeton ■	55
68	Yale ■	57
73	Brown ■	66
82	Harvard	66
67	Dartmouth	52
69	Brown	65
80	Yale	75
63	Columbia ■	39
69	Cornell ■	52
74	Princeton	67
63	Oklahoma St. †	77

Nickname: Quakers
Colors: Red & Blue
Arena: The Palestra
 Capacity: 8,722; Year Built: 1927
AD: Steve Bilsky
SID: Carla Shultzberg

PENN ST.
University Park, PA 16802..........I

Coach: Jerry Dunn, George Mason 1980
2002-03 RESULTS (7-21)

55	North Carolina	85
37	Pennsylvania	62
68	Yale ■	84
70	Clemson	79
60	Pittsburgh ■	82
63	Temple ■	65
79	Northeastern ■	67
59	Bucknell ■	55
74	St. Francis (Pa.) ■	55
76	Robert Morris ■	59
68	Buffalo ■	60
65	Indiana	78
53	Michigan	66
78	Purdue ■	82
36	Michigan St.	70
63	Illinois	75
75	Minnesota ■	76
55	Wisconsin	86
55	Iowa ■	75
67	Ohio St. ■	76
71	Iowa	84
58	Wisconsin ■	57
62	Minnesota	77
55	Purdue	79
79	Northwestern	85
62	Michigan ■	78
74	Indiana ■	66
49	Indiana †	77

Nickname: Nittany Lions
Colors: Blue & White
Arena: Bryce Jordan Center
 Capacity: 15,261; Year Built: 1996
AD: Timothy M. Curley
SID: Jeff Nelson

PENN ST.-ALTOONA
Altoona, PA 16601-3760 III

Coach: Armon Gilliam, UNLV 1988
2002-03 RESULTS (2-25)

53	Juniata	80
61	Rutgers-Camden †	91
61	Juniata ■	80
67	Carnegie Mellon	92
51	Marietta ■	85
70	Pitt.-Greensburg	84
74	Bethany (W.Va.)	85
53	Penn St.-Behrend ■	73
62	Waynesburg	69
79	Marywood	100
68	Waynesburg ■	72
61	La Roche ■	62
68	Centenary (N.J.)	73
62	Grove City	75
49	Frostburg St.	63
60	Lake Erie ■	75
56	Pitt.-Bradford ■	74
41	Penn St.-Behrend	50
90	Mt. Aloysius ■	82
52	Pitt.-Greensburg ■	63
56	Mt. Aloysius	58
59	La Roche	68
58	Lake Erie	73
72	Frostburg St. ■	86
59	Pitt.-Bradford	79
67	La Roche †	65
55	Pitt.-Bradford †	60

Nickname: Lions
Colors: Navy Blue & White
AD: Fredina M. Ingold/Fredina M. Ingold
SID: Brent Baird

PENN ST.-BEHREND
Erie, PA 16563-0101 III

Coach: Dave Niland, Le Moyne 1989
2002-03 RESULTS (20-9)

87	Hilbert ■	56
79	Notre Dame (Ohio) ■	47
58	Grove City	82
57	Wash. & Jeff. ■	59
82	Pitt.-Bradford ■	73
40	Westminster (Pa.)	54
73	Penn St.-Altoona	53
58	Buffalo St. ■	55
50	Rochester Inst. ■	41
53	Allegheny	52
67	Thiel ■	69
60	Lake Erie	50
60	Frostburg St.	65
69	Fredonia St. ■	53
63	La Roche ■	50
46	Oberlin	52
75	Pitt.-Greensburg ■	67
50	Penn St.-Altoona ■	41
62	Pitt.-Bradford	57
77	Frostburg St. ■	58
67	Lake Erie ■	58
63	La Roche	75
63	Carnegie Mellon	57
80	Medaille ■	50
76	Pitt.-Greensburg	71
47	Lake Erie ■	44
59	Pitt.-Bradford ■	62
99	Thiel ■	77
45	DeSales †	61

Nickname: Lions
Colors: Blue & White
Arena: Athletics & Recreation Cn
 Capacity: 1,600; Year Built: 2000
AD: Brian Streeter
SID: Paul Benim

PEPPERDINE
Malibu, CA 90263 I

Coach: Paul Westphal, Southern California 1972
2002-03 RESULTS (15-13)

81	Bradley	95
69	UC Irvine ■	74
65	Long Beach St.	63
90	Cal St. Fullerton	87
72	UC Santa Barb. ■	68
90	Oregon	105
83	Richmond †	77
86	Montana †	69
61	Utah	77
89	Lipscomb ■	73
116	Ark.-Little Rock †	110
88	New Mexico	68
68	Brigham Young	84
82	Portland	68
72	Gonzaga	92
73	Santa Clara ■	69
73	San Diego ■	88
70	Loyola Marymount	67
77	San Francisco	87
67	St. Mary's (Cal.)	74
63	Gonzaga ■	78
82	Portland ■	62
98	San Diego	93
61	Santa Clara	73
94	Loyola Marymount ■	71
72	St. Mary's (Cal.) ■	67
82	San Francisco ■	90
71	St. Mary's (Cal.) †	75

SCHEDULES/RESULTS

Nickname: Waves
Colors: Blue & Orange
Arena: Firestone Fieldhouse
 Capacity: 3,104; Year Built: 1973
AD: John G. Watson
SID: Michael Zapolski

PFEIFFER
Misenheimer, NC 28109-0960..II

Coach: Dave Davis, Elon 1971
2002-03 RESULTS (22-9)

102	West Liberty St. †	83
95	Mercyhurst	89
123	Brevard ■	67
100	N.C. Central ■	106
82	Coker ■	51
102	Catawba ■	82
95	Columbia Union	80
114	Columbia Union ■	71
84	Mount Olive ■	75
99	St. Andrews ■	52
80	Belmont Abbey ■	86
87	Queens (N.C.) ■	105
99	Longwood	83
104	Barton ■	96
115	Limestone	118
92	Anderson (S.C.) ■	70
92	Lees-McRae ■	75
88	Erskine	78
91	Coker	89
89	Mount Olive	113
67	Barton	89
72	Belmont Abbey ■	74
79	Queens (N.C.)	89
107	Longwood ■	79
91	St. Andrews	80
108	Limestone ■	89
97	Anderson (S.C.)	92
110	Lees-McRae ■	78
109	Mount Olive	93
80	Erskine ■	59
68	Belmont Abbey ■	73

Nickname: Falcons
Colors: Black & Gold
Arena: Merner Gymnasium
 Capacity: 2,500; Year Built: 1976
AD: Jeffrey H. Childress
SID: Liz Stojetz

PHILA. BIBLE
Langhorne, PA 19047-2990 III

Coach: Dick Beach
2002-03 RESULTS (15-12)

44	Bridgewater (Va.) †	79
64	East. Mennonite	66
78	Delaware Valley ■	47
64	Colorado Col.	62
72	Wabash †	80
76	Swarthmore ■	86
75	Eastern ■	62
56	Rowan ■	66
51	Messiah ■	72
83	Practical Bible ■	57
60	Baptist Bible (Pa.)	63
78	Washington Bible ■	38
87	Valley Forge Chrst. ■	70
83	Practical Bible	46
75	Lancaster Bible ■	60
76	Centenary (N.J.) ■	52
64	Villa Julie	78
77	Lancaster Bible	52
57	Rutgers-Camden	61
83	Washington Bible	65
85	Maryland Bible ■	69
67	Wesley	78
89	Baptist Bible (Pa.) ■	51
89	Valley Forge Chrst.	66
74	Arcadia ■	84

78	Lancaster Bible ■	62
72	Baptist Bible (Pa.) ■	73

Nickname: Crimson Eagles
Colors: Crimson & Black
AD: Richard Beach
SID: Carolyn Burgman

PHILA. SCIENCES
Philadelphia, PA 19104-4495....II

Coach: Jim Jost, Illinois
2002-03 RESULTS (14-13)

81	Wilmington (Del.) ■	74
75	Bridgewater (Va.) †	79
81	Gallaudet	57
72	Muhlenberg	82
72	Holy Family ■	79
79	Dominican (N.Y.)	81
85	Nyack	87
69	N.J. Inst. of Tech.	75
68	Felician	75
71	Teikyo Post	77
84	Goldey-Beacom ■	63
63	Caldwell	59
67	West Chester	88
89	Nyack ■	66
75	Felician ■	67
68	Caldwell ■	70
89	Bloomfield	87
77	Cheyney ■	74
85	Holy Family	88
86	Teikyo Post ■	78
74	N.J. Inst. of Tech. ■	72
81	Wilmington (Del.) ■	79
82	Kutztown	70
69	Bloomfield	80
87	Goldey-Beacom ■	78
86	Morningside †	77
69	Holy Family	71

Nickname: Devils
Colors: Cardinal & Silver
AD: Robert C. Morgan
SID: To be named

PHILADELPHIA U.
Philadelphia, PA 19144-5497....II

Coach: Herb Magee, Philadelphia U. 1963
2002-03 RESULTS (16-12)

76	Assumption †	80
91	Wilmington (Del.) †	74
64	St. Thomas Aquinas	43
78	Molloy ■	79
80	New Haven ■	71
93	Concordia (N.Y.)	64
65	Bridgeport	79
61	Drexel	78
71	Adelphi ■	56
51	C.W. Post	67
98	Dowling ■	76
83	Concordia (N.Y.) ■	59
56	NYIT	58
61	New Haven	62
72	Queens (N.Y.)	60
85	St. Thomas Aquinas ■	67
70	Southampton ■	60
69	Molloy	57
57	Mercy	72
61	Adelphi	77
64	C.W. Post ■	61
88	Dowling	64
77	NYIT ■	50
73	Bridgeport ■	75
83	Mercy ■	60
59	Queens (N.Y.) ■	64
71	Southampton	49
59	New Haven	72

Nickname: Rams
Colors: Maroon & Grey

Arena: Bucky Harris Gym
 Capacity: 1,000; Year Built: 1960
AD: Don DiJulia
SID: Tony Berich

PITTSBURG ST.
Pittsburg, KS 66762 II

Coach: Gene Iba, Tulsa 1963
2002-03 RESULTS (16-12)

81	Southwestern Okla. †	66
94	Philander Smith †	65
78	Mid-America Naz. ■	66
86	Northwestern Okla. ■	64
88	Lincoln (Mo.) ■	62
75	Rockhurst	69
109	Central Bible (Mo.) ■	64
66	St. Mary's (Tex.)	73
70	Seattle Pacific †	64
59	Emporia St.	61
81	Northwest Mo. St.	67
69	Mo.-Rolla	67
67	Mo. Western St.	57
69	Mo. Southern St.	74
77	Truman	74
65	Southwest Baptist	68
72	Washburn	73
78	Central Mo. St. ■	76
64	Northwest Mo. St.	92
78	Mo.-Rolla ■	64
86	Mo. Western St.	88
75	Mo. Southern St.	80
82	Truman ■	66
79	Southwest Baptist ■	65
77	Washburn	79
75	Central Mo. St.	85
75	Emporia St. ■	80
73	Northwest Mo. St. †	95

Nickname: Gorillas
Colors: Crimson & Gold
Arena: John Lance Arena
 Capacity: 6,500; Year Built: 1971
AD: Charles Broyles
SID: Dan Wilkes

PITTSBURGH
Pittsburgh, PA 15260 I

Coach: Ben Howland, Weber St. 1980
2002-03 RESULTS (28-5)

82	Duquesne ■	67
69	St. Francis (Pa.) ■	46
89	Ark.-Pine Bluff ■	49
96	Norfolk St. ■	51
82	Penn St.	60
89	Southeastern La. ■	55
69	Ohio St.	49
87	Rhode Island	71
65	George Mason ■	41
67	Georgia	79
85	Robert Morris ■	49
72	Notre Dame ■	55
70	Rutgers ■	63
80	West Virginia	61
73	Syracuse ■	60
65	Georgetown ■	64
65	Syracuse	67
68	Providence ■	61
64	Notre Dame	66
82	West Virginia ■	46
61	Seton Hall	73
82	Georgetown	67
86	Rutgers	65
75	Virginia Tech	62
71	Connecticut	67
86	Seton Hall ■	54
56	Villanova	54
67	Providence †	59
61	Boston College †	48
74	Connecticut †	56

87	Wagner †	61
74	Indiana †	52
74	Marquette †	77

Nickname: Panthers
Colors: Gold & Blue
Arena: Fitzgerald Field House
 Capacity: 6,798; Year Built: 1951
AD: Marc Boehm
SID: Melissa Androutsos

PITT.-BRADFORD
Bradford, PA 16701-2898 III

Coach: Andy Moore, Mansfield 1986
2002-03 RESULTS (22-7)

71	Geneva	76
95	Lake Erie †	73
71	Houghton	62
77	Elmira ■	57
73	Penn St.-Behrend	82
85	Thiel ■	72
86	Medgar Evers †	59
71	Cabrini	69
78	Mt. Aloysius	66
95	Pitt.-Greensburg ■	85
79	Westminster (Pa.) ■	75
79	Alfred	75
79	La Roche ■	68
81	Lake Erie ■	76
78	Frostburg St. ■	66
57	Clarion	50
74	Penn St.-Altoona	56
81	Pitt.-Greensburg	71
57	Penn St.-Behrend ■	62
67	La Roche ■	74
94	Hilbert ■	60
82	Fredonia ■	88
84	Frostburg St.	78
67	Lake Erie	73
79	Penn St.-Altoona	59
74	Pitt.-Greensburg ■	51
60	Penn St.-Altoona †	55
62	Penn St.-Behrend	59
65	John Carroll	85

Nickname: Panthers
Colors: Navy & Gold
Arena: Pitt Bradford Sport & Fitness
 Center
 Capacity: 1,500; Year Built: 2002
AD: Lori Mazza
SID: Greg Clark

PITT.-GREENSBURG
Greensburg, PA 15601-5898 ...III

Coach: Marcus Kahn, Redlands 1997
2002-03 RESULTS (14-12)

87	Mt. Aloysius	78
93	Bethany (W.Va.) ■	91
80	Marymount (Va.) ■	84
90	Kenyon †	83
86	Hiram ■	68
84	Penn St.-Altoona ■	70
81	Waynesburg ■	87
91	McDaniel ■	84
68	Thiel	91
108	Wash. & Jeff.	99
85	Pitt.-Bradford	95
90	Juniata	87
71	Frostburg St. ■	67
96	Lake Erie	93
73	La Roche ■	81
75	Lincoln (Pa.) ■	74
67	Penn St.-Behrend	75
71	Pitt.-Bradford ■	81
76	Westminster (Pa.) ■	72
63	Penn St.-Altoona	52
75	Lake Erie ■	74
85	Frostburg St.	99
63	Newport News ■	85

85 La Roche ...90
71 Penn St.-Behrend ■ ...76
51 Pitt.-Bradford ...74

Nickname: Bobcats
Colors: Navy Blue & Gold
Arena: Chambers Hall
Capacity: 500; Year Built: 1989
AD: Daniel Swalga
SID: Mark Katarski

PITT.-JOHNSTOWN
Johnstown, PA 15904-2990...II

Coach: Bob Rukavina, Indiana (Pa.) 1985
2002-03 RESULTS (11-16)
88 Mercy ■ ...65
67 Le Moyne ■ ...73
71 Brescia † ...86
80 Roberts Wesleyan † ...75
75 West Va. Wesleyan ...63
74 Glenville St. ■ ...53
81 Charleston (W.Va.) ■ ...84
59 Alderson-Broaddus ...71
83 Shepherd ■ ...75
69 Dist. Columbia † ...76
72 East Stroudsburg ...81
60 Shippensburg ...57
44 Indiana (Pa.) ...69
85 Columbia Union ■ ...58
72 Clarion ...90
54 Calif. (Pa.) ...70
81 Bowie St. ...83
78 Mt. Aloysius ...59
77 Bloomsburg ...84
77 Lock Haven ...78
73 Mt. Aloysius ■ ...62
74 Dist. Columbia ...93
65 Alderson-Broaddus ■ ...90
58 Slippery Rock ...60
80 Dist. Columbia ■ ...77
70 Columbia Union ...75
95 Bloomsburg ■ ...92

Nickname: Mountain Cats
Colors: Gold & Blue
Arena: Sports Center
Capacity: 2,400; Year Built: 1976
AD: Michael Castner
SID: Chris Caputo

PLATTSBURGH ST.
Plattsburgh, NY 12901...III

Coach: Ed Jones, Brockport St. 1973
2002-03 RESULTS (6-19)
63 Norwich ■ ...65
87 Paul Smith ■ ...66
69 Clarkson ■ ...78
79 Utica/Rome ...88
68 Brockport St. ■ ...78
59 Geneseo St. ■ ...75
81 Union (N.Y.) ...76
82 Johnson St. ...67
60 St. Lawrence ...79
86 Fredonia St. ...73
61 Buffalo St. ...85
75 Oswego St. ...90
77 Oneonta St. ■ ...91
56 New Paltz St. ■ ...73
67 Potsdam St. ...68
62 Buffalo St. ■ ...71
73 Fredonia St. ■ ...74
59 Utica/Rome ■ ...79
96 Paul Smith ■ ...85
55 Cortland St. ...71
82 Paul Smith ...86
57 Geneseo St. ...67
107 Castleton St. ■ ...93

66 Oswego St. ■ ...74
74 New Paltz St. ...88

Nickname: Cardinals
Colors: Cardinal Red & White
Arena: Memorial Hall Gymnasium
Capacity: 1,000; Year Built: 1961
AD: Pater Luguri
SID: Jeremy Agor

PLYMOUTH ST.
Plymouth, NH 03264-1595...III

Coach: John Scheinman, Marist 1984
2002-03 RESULTS (21-8)
90 Fisher † ...77
83 Me.-Farmington ...65
107 Johnson St. ■ ...68
77 Colby-Sawyer † ...66
71 Salem St. ...73
84 Mass.-Dartmouth ...79
95 Tufts ...87
75 Eastern Conn. St. ■ ...60
48 Fla. Gulf Coast ...84
114 New England ■ ...75
76 Bowdoin ...65
83 Western Conn. St. ...87
82 Mass.-Boston ■ ...81
86 Rhode Island Col. ...89
83 Southern Me. ...71
92 Mass.-Dartmouth ■ ...80
65 Keene St. ...62
82 Eastern Conn. St. ...67
97 Johnson & Wales ■ ...78
62 Western Conn. St. ■ ...80
80 Southern Me. ...77
67 Mass.-Boston ...58
63 Keene St. ■ ...69
81 Castleton St. ...74
78 Rhode Island Col. ■ ...75
90 Rhode Island Col. ■ ...75
82 Keene St. † ...76
63 Western Conn. St. ...65
83 Wheaton (Mass.) ■ ...86

Nickname: Panthers
Colors: Green & White
Arena: Foley Gymnasium
Capacity: 2,000; Year Built: 1969
AD: John Clark
SID: Kent Cherrington

POLYTECHNIC (N.Y.)
Brooklyn, NY 11201...III

Coach: Laddy Baldwin, Long Island 1974
2002-03 RESULTS (3-13)
66 Maritime (N.Y.) ...65
59 NYCCT ■ ...88
61 MIT ■ ...87
74 Bard ■ ...61
41 Baruch ■ ...68
49 New York U. ■ ...79
42 St. Joseph's (L.I.) ■ ...61
59 Farmingdale St. ■ ...63
50 Yeshiva ...65
45 John Jay ■ ...60
57 Old Westbury ■ ...86
64 Mt. St. Mary (N.Y.) ■ ...75
96 Bard ...68
42 Rutgers-Newark ...65
76 Mt. St. Vincent ...80
62 Lehman ...74

Nickname: Blue Jays
Colors: Blue & Gray
Arena: Poly Gym
Capacity: 500; Year Built: 1984
AD: Maureen Braziel
SID: John Stalzer

POMONA-PITZER
Claremont, CA 91711-6346...III

Coach: Charles Katsiaficas, Tufts 1984
2002-03 RESULTS (9-16)
59 MIT † ...46
44 Washington (Mo.) ...77
56 Rensselaer † ...71
55 Lewis & Clark ■ ...73
23 UC Irvine ...91
43 Biola ...53
72 St. Scholastica ■ ...61
47 St. Joseph's (Me.) † ...55
63 Swarthmore † ...72
56 Concordia (Cal.) ...85
67 La Sierra ...47
75 Whittier ...71
60 Cal Lutheran ■ ...65
59 La Verne ■ ...55
49 Occidental ...51
84 Caltech ...33
55 Claremont-M-S ■ ...63
92 Redlands ...91
48 Whittier ■ ...76
63 Cal Lutheran ...72
66 La Verne ...71
55 Occidental ■ ...61
84 Caltech ■ ...46
40 Claremont-M-S ...61
103 Redlands ■ ...78

Nickname: Sagehens
Colors: Blue, Orange & White
Arena: Voelkel Gymnasium
Capacity: 1,500; Year Built: 1989
AD: Charles Katsiaficas
SID: Ryan Witt

PORTLAND
Portland, OR 97203-5798...I

Coach: Michael Holton, UCLA 1983
2002-03 RESULTS (11-17)
70 Pacific (Ore.) ■ ...42
91 San Diego St. ■ ...86
66 Portland St. ■ ...54
66 Oregon ...96
64 Oregon St. ■ ...71
67 UCLA ...105
71 Weber St. ■ ...78
79 Nevada ...88
59 Portland St. ...50
63 Northern Ariz. ■ ...61
54 Long Beach St. ...49
74 Eastern Wash. ...89
76 Montana St. ...65
68 Pepperdine ■ ...82
73 Loyola Marymount ■ ...68
59 San Francisco ...73
54 St. Mary's (Cal.) ...69
67 Gonzaga ■ ...70
72 Santa Clara ...47
77 San Diego ■ ...78
71 Loyola Marymount ...86
62 Pepperdine ...82
55 San Francisco ■ ...72
59 St. Mary's (Cal.) ■ ...71
72 Gonzaga ...68
69 San Diego ...92
75 Santa Clara ...63
63 Loyola Marymount † ...65

Nickname: Pilots
Colors: Purple & White
Arena: Chiles Center
Capacity: 5,000; Year Built: 1984
AD: Joesph Etzel
SID: Loren Wohlgemuth

PORTLAND ST.
Portland, OR 97207-0751...I

Coach: Heath Schroyer, Armstrong St. 1995
2002-03 RESULTS (5-22)
69 Cal St. Northridge ■ ...65
54 UNLV ...69
54 Portland ...66
66 Cascade ■ ...71
51 St. Mary's (Cal.) ...75
84 Linfield ■ ...66
50 Oregon St. ...53
51 Boise St. ...59
50 Portland ■ ...59
52 New Mexico ...69
41 Ark.-Little Rock † ...48
49 Gonzaga ■ ...87
65 Sacramento St. ■ ...52
48 Montana St. ...52
49 Montana ...61
63 Oregon ■ ...69
73 Northern Ariz. ■ ...60
51 Eastern Wash. ...75
64 Weber St. ...77
57 Idaho St. ...58
49 Montana ...67
56 Montana St. ■ ...60
64 Northern Ariz. ...75
58 Sacramento St. ...72
58 Eastern Wash. ■ ...72
77 Idaho St. ■ ...69
73 Weber St. ■ ...83

Nickname: Vikings
Colors: Forest Green & White
Arena: Peter W. Stott Center
Capacity: 1,775; Year Built: 1967
AD: Tom Burman
SID: Mike Lund

POTSDAM ST.
Potsdam, NY 13676...III

Coach: Bill Mitchell, Michigan 1983
2002-03 RESULTS (18-9)
63 Brandeis ■ ...58
47 Clarkson ■ ...49
66 Clarkson ...51
61 Geneseo St. ■ ...85
76 Brockport St. ■ ...64
72 Alfred ■ ...56
69 Ithaca ■ ...52
86 Cazenovia ...83
63 Keuka ...69
110 Paul Smith ■ ...66
76 Buffalo St. ...75
64 Fredonia St. ...61
68 Utica/Rome ...58
82 New Paltz St. ■ ...63
76 Oneonta St. ■ ...55
68 Plattsburgh St. ■ ...67
93 Oswego St. ■ ...87
75 St. Lawrence ■ ...82
52 Cortland St. ...47
69 Utica/Rome ■ ...57
81 Brockport St. ...86
64 Geneseo St. ...77
68 Cortland St. ■ ...53
66 New Paltz St. ...74
80 Oneonta St. ...61
53 New Paltz St. ■ ...59
80 St. Lawrence ...85

Nickname: Bears
Colors: Maroon & Gray
Arena: Maxcy Hall
Capacity: 3,600; Year Built: 1972
AD: James Zalacca
SID: Boyd Jones

PRAIRIE VIEW
Prairie View, TX 77446 I

Coach: Jerry Francis, Ohio St. 1991
2002-03 RESULTS (17-12)
78	Houston	75
63	Oklahoma	75
78	Texas A&M ■	83
49	LSU	75
65	Ark.-Little Rock	76
55	Wyoming	85
73	Colorado St.	85
57	Rutgers	66
77	Alcorn St.	70
88	Southern U.	86
59	Texas Southern ■	57
73	Grambling ■	71
65	Jackson St. ■	62
68	Mississippi Val.	87
72	Ark.-Pine Bluff	57
63	Alabama St. ■	57
79	Alabama A&M ■	67
100	Texas Southern	104
80	Tex. A&M-Corp. Chris ■	76
74	Grambling	61
70	Jackson St.	75
72	Mississippi Val. ■	75
66	Ark.-Pine Bluff ■	53
60	Alabama St.	54
76	Alabama A&M	75
87	Southern U. ■	76
75	Alcorn St.	64
56	Southern U. ■	55
64	Alcorn St. †	71

Nickname: Panthers
Colors: Purple & Gold
Arena: William J. Nicks Building
  Capacity: 5,000; Year Built: 1968
AD: Charles McClelland
SID: Harlan Robinson

PRESBYTERIAN
Clinton, SC 29325-2998..........II

Coach: Gregg Nibert, Marietta 1979
2002-03 RESULTS (27-9)
48	Henderson St. †	62
84	Bellarmine †	74
61	Calif. (Pa.) †	56
69	S.C.-Aiken †	67
72	Lander †	66
66	Allen ■	40
58	Shaw	63
66	Benedict	49
79	Shenandoah	70
63	S.C.-Spartanburg	53
61	Lander	46
53	Armstrong Atlantic ■	47
91	North Greenville ■	53
55	Erskine ■	44
54	Tusculum	49
61	Anderson (S.C.) ■	47
60	Wingate ■	64
75	Carson-Newman	79
64	Mars Hill	60
55	Lenoir-Rhyne ■	47
81	Catawba ■	70
82	Newberry	59
88	North Greenville	60
52	Tusculum	43
80	Wingate	81
63	Carson-Newman ■	70
68	Mars Hill ■	56
61	Lenoir-Rhyne	71
77	Catawba	75
68	Newberry ■	56
61	Tusculum ■	54
69	Carson-Newman †	52
62	Lenoir-Rhyne	71
71	Columbus St.	59

77	Shaw †	58
53	Bowie St. †	67

Nickname: Blue Hose
Colors: Garnet & Blue
Arena: Ross E. Templeton Center
  Capacity: 2,500; Year Built: 1975
AD: Valerie Sheley
SID: Al Ansley

PRINCETON
Princeton, NJ 08544..................I

Coach: John Thompson III,
Princeton 1989
2002-03 RESULTS (16-11)
62	Western Mich. †	59
63	Oklahoma	82
65	Florida Int'l ■	68
60	Monmouth	57
89	Lafayette	75
70	Rutgers ■	76
59	Rider	62
54	Texas	57
76	Texas A&M †	62
71	Santa Clara	77
54	Holy Cross	55
76	UMBC ■	43
99	Ursinus ■	56
67	Harvard ■	61
57	Dartmouth ■	52
68	Columbia ■	51
67	Cornell	49
55	Pennsylvania	65
73	Brown ■	80
56	Yale ■	49
70	Dartmouth	60
67	Harvard	66
61	Yale	52
74	Brown	88
71	Cornell ■	61
44	Columbia ■	40
67	Pennsylvania ■	74

Nickname: Tigers
Colors: Orange & Black
Arena: Jadwin Gymnasium
  Capacity: 6,854; Year Built: 1969
AD: Gary Walters
SID: Jerry Price

PRINCIPIA
Elsah, IL 62028-9799 III

Coach: Garry Sprague, Principia 1986
2002-03 RESULTS (13-12)
47	Pacific Lutheran †	84
57	Puget Sound	83
81	Lincoln Chrst.	76
80	St. Louis Pharmacy	69
79	Manhattan Chrst. †	85
94	Kansas City Bible †	53
89	Sanford Brown †	54
58	SCAD †	70
69	Notre Dame (Ohio) †	78
72	Fontbonne ■	66
68	MacMurray	71
71	Maryville (Mo.)	96
75	Greenville	70
84	Westminster (Mo.)	65
67	Webster	76
99	Sanford Brown †	51
54	Blackburn ■	73
69	Fontbonne	81
78	St. Louis Christian	58
81	MacMurray ■	73
78	Maryville (Mo.) ■	71
74	Greenville	81
79	Westminster (Mo.) ■	77
81	Webster ■	78
44	Blackburn	65

Nickname: Panthers
Colors: Gold & Blue
Arena: Hay Field House
  Capacity: 1,000; Year Built: 1967
AD: Lenore Suarez
SID: Mary Ann Sprague

PROVIDENCE
Providence, RI 02918 I

Coach: Tim Welsh, Potsdam St. 1984
2002-03 RESULTS (18-14)
83	Brown ■	64
64	South Fla.	68
91	Ohio ■	68
71	Vermont ■	60
71	Rhode Island ■	73
84	Richmond ■	55
61	Alabama	69
80	Northeastern ■	61
74	Pennsylvania ■	71
93	Boston College	80
81	Siena	89
75	St. John's (N.Y.) ■	71
67	Villanova	81
67	La.-Lafayette ■	58
79	Virginia Tech	92
65	Notre Dame ■	71
57	Miami (Fla.)	60
89	Virginia Tech ■	58
61	Pittsburgh	68
68	Connecticut ■	84
69	Boston College ■	80
69	St. John's (N.Y.)	59
73	Miami (Fla.) ■	63
70	Villanova ■	60
56	Georgetown	71
76	Connecticut	70
64	Seton Hall ■	61
73	West Virginia †	50
59	Pittsburgh †	67
67	Richmond	49
69	Col. of Charleston ■	64
58	Georgetown ■	67

Nickname: Friars
Colors: Black, White & Silver
Arena: Dunkin' Donuts Center
  Capacity: 12,993; Year Built: 1972
AD: Robert Driscoll
SID: Arthur Parks

PUGET SOUND
Tacoma, WA 98416 III

Coach: Eric Bridgeland, Alabama
2002-03 RESULTS (12-13)
85	Colorado Col. ■	71
83	Principia	57
63	Western Wash.	102
84	Northwest (Wash.) ■	68
84	Montana Tech ■	53
64	Cascade	75
60	Central Wash.	101
72	Gust. Adolphus †	77
88	Mt. Marty †	71
80	Linfield	84
69	Lewis & Clark ■	78
78	Whitman ■	53
86	Whitworth ■	75
91	George Fox	66
61	Pacific (Ore.)	71
46	Pacific Lutheran	49
82	Linfield ■	80
58	Willamette ■	61
72	Lewis & Clark	81
71	Whitman	81
71	Whitworth	73
90	George Fox ■	72
90	Pacific (Ore.) ■	76
89	Pacific Lutheran ■	83
64	Willamette	71

Nickname: Loggers
Colors: Maroon & White
Arena: Memorial Arena
  Capacity: 4,000; Year Built: 1949
AD: Amy Hackett
SID: Robin Hamilton

PURDUE
West Lafayette, IN 47907-1031 .I

Coach: Gene Keady, Kansas St. 1958
2002-03 RESULTS (19-11)
73	Miami (Ohio) ■	46
86	Louisville †	84
59	Xavier	74
85	Middle Tenn. ■	56
95	San Diego ■	65
63	Indiana †	66
78	Belmont ■	61
53	Arizona St. †	70
87	Valparaiso ■	55
84	Colorado St. ■	56
84	Montana ■	66
82	Northwestern ■	68
72	Michigan St. ■	60
82	Penn St.	78
62	Illinois	75
69	Indiana ■	47
70	Ohio St. ■	65
80	Iowa	77
78	Wisconsin ■	60
68	Minnesota	90
67	Northwestern	78
70	Illinois ■	61
67	Michigan ■	78
44	Ohio St.	52
79	Penn St. ■	55
61	Michigan St.	69
69	Michigan	61
42	Michigan St. †	54
80	LSU †	56
67	Texas †	77

Nickname: Boilermakers
Colors: Old Gold & Black
Arena: Mackey Arena
  Capacity: 14,123; Year Built: 1967
AD: Morgan Burke
SID: Elliot Bloom

QUEENS (N.Y.)
Flushing, NY 11367.................II

Coach: Kyrk Peponakis, St. John's (N.Y.) 1988
2002-03 RESULTS (14-14)
66	Molloy	53
78	Southampton ■	75
66	Mercy	74
75	New Haven	71
64	St. Thomas Aquinas	59
74	American Int'l	69
56	N.J. Inst. of Tech. †	42
72	Assumption	91
69	Bridgeport ■	76
59	Adelphi ■	76
72	C.W. Post ■	76
64	Dowling	60
71	Concordia (N.Y.) ■	58
55	NYIT	60
60	Philadelphia U. ■	72
53	St. Thomas Aquinas ■	54
66	Southampton	55
71	Molloy ■	62
59	Mercy ■	61
52	New Haven ■	66
67	Bridgeport	81
46	Adelphi ■	58
53	C.W. Post	59
62	Concordia (N.Y.)	57
72	Dowling ■	58
64	Philadelphia U.	59

75	NYIT ■	72
49	Adelphi	52

Nickname: Knights
Colors: Blue & Silver
Arena: Fitzgerald Gymnasium
 Capacity: 3,000; Year Built: 1958
AD: Richard Wettan
SID: Neal Kaufer

QUEENS (N.C.)
Charlotte, NC 28274...............II

Coach: Bart Lundy, Winthrop 1994
2002-03 RESULTS (29-4)

117	Allen ■	66
75	Armstrong Atlantic †	74
81	Bayamon Central †	74
72	Longwood	76
91	Allen †	60
79	St. Leo	68
87	Johnson Smith †	75
96	Limestone ■	81
101	Livingstone ■	81
99	St. Andrews ■	67
81	Coker ■	72
105	Anderson (S.C.) ■	79
105	Pfeiffer	87
70	Erskine	60
94	Mount Olive	96
90	Barton ■	83
79	Belmont Abbey ■	71
110	Lees-McRae ■	74
81	Longwood	63
85	St. Andrews	72
95	Limestone	87
77	Anderson (S.C.)	68
89	Pfeiffer ■	79
58	Erskine ■	52
102	Coker	61
95	Mount Olive ■	89
99	Barton	84
66	Erskine	71
72	West Chester ■	58
100	Salem Int'l ■	87
94	Millersville ■	77
99	Eckerd †	78
69	Northeastern St. †	84

Nickname: Royals
Colors: Navy Blue and Gold
Arena: Ovens Athletic Center
 Capacity: 900; Year Built: 1989
AD: Jeannie King
SID: Scott Handback

QUINCY
Quincy, IL 62301-2699.............II

Coach: Mike Foster, Missouri 1981
2002-03 RESULTS (12-16)

77	Mo. Southern St. ■	66
68	Northern Ky.	79
70	Indianapolis	74
68	Wis.-Parkside ■	59
74	Lewis ■	85
97	Hannibal-LaGrange ■	64
76	Culver-Stockton ■	60
75	Olivet Nazarene ■	64
82	Truman	79
90	Ill.-Springfield ■	64
57	Mass.-Lowell ■	74
82	Mo.-St. Louis	68
85	Ky. Wesleyan	102
101	Bellarmine	110
81	Indianapolis ■	84
90	St. Joseph's (Ind.) ■	92
62	Lewis	77
72	SIU Edwardsville	65
68	Mo.-St. Louis	57
83	Southern Ind.	90
77	Bellarmine ■	75

66	Northern Ky. ■	70
74	St. Joseph's (Ind.)	76
50	Wis.-Parkside	70
76	SIU Edwardsville ■	69
69	Southern Ind. ■	82
93	Ky. Wesleyan ■	110
86	Ky. Wesleyan †	102

Nickname: Hawks
Colors: Brown, White & Gold
Arena: Pepsi Arena
 Capacity: 2,000; Year Built: 1950
AD: Patrick Atwell
SID: Ryan Dowd

QUINNIPIAC
Hamden, CT 06518-1940..........I

Coach: Joe DeSantis, Fairfield 1979
2002-03 RESULTS (17-12)

72	Connecticut	91
72	Tex.-Pan American †	62
71	Hofstra	68
58	Manhattanville ■	34
81	Drexel	78
81	Dartmouth	72
78	Albany (N.Y.)	65
71	La Salle	82
72	Central Conn. St. ■	76
75	Holy Cross ■	83
85	Sacred Heart ■	88
69	Wagner	91
90	Robert Morris ■	76
69	St. Francis (Pa.) ■	61
59	Monmouth	79
90	Fairleigh Dickinson	100
76	St. Francis (N.Y.)	91
80	Long Island ■	69
87	Mt. St. Mary's ■	82
87	UMBC ■	66
70	Wagner	74
78	Sacred Heart	69
70	Long Island	62
80	St. Francis (N.Y.) ■	61
68	Central Conn. St.	66
63	Mt. St. Mary's	52
58	UMBC	80
75	St. Francis (Pa.) †	57
54	Wagner	61

Nickname: Braves
Colors: Navy & Maize
Arena: Burt Kahn Court-Athletic Center
 Capacity: 1,500; Year Built: 1969
AD: Jack McDonald
SID: Al Carbone

RADFORD
Radford, VA 24142 I

Coach: Byron Samuels, UNC Asheville
1986
2002-03 RESULTS (10-20)

46	Richmond	92
64	William & Mary	63
58	Howard ■	62
67	N.C. A&T ■	58
42	East Caro.	89
49	American	73
65	Marshall	90
64	Akron	97
80	Ohio St.	96
45	Florida Int'l	81
63	St. Francis (N.Y.) †	69
64	Winthrop ■	55
67	High Point ■	81
65	Birmingham-So.	83
74	UNC Asheville ■	68
66	Liberty	81
77	Coastal Caro.	73
64	Charleston So.	81
53	Elon ■	57

64	High Point	75
61	Winthrop	82
68	UNC Asheville	75
65	Coastal Caro.	58
59	Charleston So. ■	57
74	Elon	84
57	Birmingham-So. ■	67
81	Liberty ■	56
65	Charleston So.	62
55	Liberty	52
71	UNC Asheville †	85

Nickname: Highlanders
Colors: Blue, Red, Green & White
Arena: Donald N. Dedmon Center
 Capacity: 5,000; Year Built: 1981
AD: Greig Denny
SID: Aaron Barter

RAMAPO
Mahwah, NJ 07430-1680 III

Coach: Chuck McBreen, Towson 1988
2002-03 RESULTS (26-4)

114	Maritime (N.Y.) ■	61
95	FDU-Florham	77
76	Wm. Paterson ■	57
95	TCNJ	86
93	Rutgers-Camden ■	77
85	Rutgers-Newark ■	70
68	Kean	84
95	Simpson †	81
69	Lewis & Clark †	75
93	Baldwin-Wallace †	86
105	Staten Island	74
99	York (N.Y.) ■	81
90	Richard Stockton	86
73	New Jersey City	70
96	Rowan ■	93
84	Montclair St. ■	81
84	TCNJ	70
71	Wm. Paterson	60
64	Montclair St.	54
70	Rutgers-Newark	55
90	Rowan	78
102	Kean ■	70
88	Rutgers-Camden	63
101	New Jersey City ■	95
86	Richard Stockton ■	79
100	Rowan ■	90
84	Montclair St. ■	86
92	Merchant Marine ■	76
89	Montclair St. †	80
64	Wooster	68

Nickname: Roadrunners
Colors: Maroon, Black & White
Arena: Ramapo Athletic Center
 Capacity: 1,800; Year Built: 1974
AD: Eugene Marshall
SID: Rachel McCann

RANDOLPH-MACON
Ashland, VA 23005 III

Coach: Mike Rhoades, Lebanon Valley
1995
2002-03 RESULTS (28-2)

72	Farmingdale St. †	49
66	Albright	42
83	Chowan	50
75	Bridgewater (Va.) ■	50
63	Chris. Newport ■	55
73	East. Mennonite	39
93	Alfred ■	55
83	Ohio Wesleyan	57
65	Wash. & Lee	41
61	Roanoke	59
80	Guilford ■	61
59	Emory & Henry	57
45	Hampden-Sydney	52
73	Va. Wesleyan	63

92	Ferrum ■	49
59	Lynchburg ■	33
74	Roanoke ■	66
71	Wash. & Lee ■	46
88	Emory & Henry ■	76
52	Guilford	50
89	East. Mennonite ■	51
69	Va. Wesleyan ■	49
78	Bridgewater (Va.)	45
66	Hampden-Sydney ■	55
78	Lynchburg	65
71	Wash. & Lee †	53
84	Roanoke †	62
48	Hampden-Sydney †	47
72	Alvernia	69
47	Wis.-Oshkosh ■	53

Nickname: Yellow Jackets
Colors: Lemon & Black
Arena: Crenshaw Gymnasium
 Capacity: 2,500; Year Built: 1963
AD: Kevin Eastman
SID: Ann Marie Schlottman

REDLANDS
Redlands, CA 92373-0999 III

Coach: Gary Smith, Redlands 1964
2002-03 RESULTS (10-15)

111	Swarthmore †	117
82	Haverford †	105
99	Chapman	110
103	Dominican (Ill.) ■	98
86	Whitworth ■	120
107	Cal St. Hayward ■	92
133	La Sierra	107
89	Lawrence ■	120
106	Millikin †	110
122	Northland †	77
125	Me.-Fort Kent ■	102
95	Occidental	123
123	Caltech	73
104	Claremont-M-S ■	95
65	Cal Lutheran ■	112
83	La Verne	97
124	Whittier ■	138
91	Pomona-Pitzer	92
96	Occidental ■	97
136	Caltech ■	68
106	Claremont-M-S	104
96	Cal Lutheran	102
95	La Verne ■	90
102	Whittier ■	108
78	Pomona-Pitzer	103

Nickname: Bulldogs
Colors: Maroon & Gray
Arena: Currier Gym
 Capacity: 1,200; Year Built: 1929
AD: Jeffrey Martinez
SID: Rachel Johnson

REGIS (COLO.)
Denver, CO 80221-1099..........II

Coach: Lonnie Porter, Adams St. 1965
2002-03 RESULTS (12-15)

69	Mesa St. ■	81
71	Northern Colo. †	66
73	Grand View ■	62
63	UC Davis ■	62
51	Colorado St.-Pueblo ■	75
65	N.M. Highlands ■	61
98	St. Mary's (Minn.) ■	64
112	Avila	74
79	Doane	59
61	Fort Lewis	71
63	Adams St.	70
89	Western St. ■	79
80	UC-Colo. Spgs. ■	57
83	Colorado Col. ■	62
47	Mesa St.	60

70	Colorado Mines	77
67	Colo. Christian	82
40	Metro St. ■	65
65	Chadron St. ■	60
62	Neb.-Kearney	74
65	Fort Hays St.	85
65	Metro St.	100
55	Chadron St.	58
60	Fort Hays St. ■	67
59	Neb.-Kearney ■	72
81	Colo. Christian ■	68
67	Colorado Mines ■	82

Nickname: Rangers
Colors: Navy Blue & Gold
Arena: Regis University Fieldhouse
Capacity: 2,500; Year Built: 1959
AD: Babara Schroeder
SID: Jeff Duggan

RENSSELAER

Troy, NY 12180-3590..............III

Coach: Mike Griffin, Columbia 1965

2002-03 RESULTS (13-13)

62	Roger Williams †	42
69	New York U.	74
71	Pomona-Pitzer †	56
62	Claremont-M-S	63
60	Worcester St. †	63
79	Elms †	63
67	Stevens Institute ■	57
84	Middlebury	81
77	Southern Vt. ■	70
50	MIT	54
49	Yale	100
57	Union (N.Y.) ■	59
63	Skidmore ■	72
72	Vassar	57
59	Clarkson	54
80	St. Lawrence	74
62	Hamilton ■	71
77	Hobart ■	75
89	St. Lawrence ■	92
56	Clarkson ■	58
63	Skidmore	73
91	Union (N.Y.)	86
77	Vassar ■	63
83	Hobart	76
87	Hamilton	89
74	Hamilton	83

Nickname: Engineers
Colors: Cherry & White
Arena: Robison Gymnasium
Capacity: 1,500; Year Built: 1920
AD: Ken Ralph
SID: Kevin Beattie

RHODE ISLAND

Kingston, RI 02881-1303...........I

Coach: Jim Baron, St. Bonaventure 1977

2002-03 RESULTS (19-12)

95	Northeastern	82
73	Southern California ■	71
48	Buffalo	57
63	Kent St. ■	82
73	Providence	71
67	Brown ■	48
69	Maine ■	63
71	Pittsburgh ■	87
71	Iona	68
77	Central Conn. St. ■	58
80	St. Bonaventure	88
81	Yale	69
75	Fordham ■	63
60	Massachusetts	53
58	St. Joseph's ■	57
68	Temple ■	71
76	Fordham	68
53	St. Joseph's	69
91	St. Bonaventure ■	85

77	George Washington ■	72
77	La Salle ■	65
70	Xavier	93
64	Temple	69
69	Richmond	70
70	Dayton ■	82
65	Massachusetts ■	58
76	Duquesne	71
75	Duquesne ■	73
57	Dayton	74
61	Seton Hall ■	60
53	Temple ■	61

Nickname: Rams
Colors: Light & Dark Blue & White
Arena: Ryan Center
Capacity: 7,800; Year Built: 2002
AD: Ronald Petro
SID: Mike Ballweg

RHODE ISLAND COL.

Providence, RI 02908...............III

Coach: Mike Kelly, St. Joseph's (Me.) 1993

2002-03 RESULTS (13-13)

81	Becker †	60
41	Rutgers-Newark	45
80	Eastern Nazarene ■	68
51	Stony Brook	95
81	Eastern Conn. St.	86
76	Johnson & Wales ■	61
76	Coast Guard	74
81	Mass.-Boston ■	77
84	St. Joseph (Conn.) ■	53
62	Newbury ■	51
83	Bridgewater St. ■	70
88	Keene St.	99
80	Southern Me.	68
89	Plymouth St. ■	86
75	Western Conn. St. ■	90
60	Eastern Conn. St. ■	63
80	Mass.-Dartmouth ■	93
74	Mass.-Boston	62
78	Salve Regina	85
74	Roger Williams ■	62
73	Keene St. ■	80
95	Western Conn. St.	105
92	Southern Me. ■	85
90	Mass.-Dartmouth	101
75	Plymouth St.	78
75	Plymouth St.	90

Nickname: Anchormen
Colors: Gold, White & Burgundy
Arena: Intercollegiate Athletic
Capacity: 8,000; Year Built: 1995
AD: Donald Tencher
SID: Scott Gibbons

RHODES

Memphis, TN 38112-1690.......III

Coach: Herb Hilgeman, Miami (Ohio) 1972

2002-03 RESULTS (10-15)

87	Dallas †	90
90	Bacone †	98
77	Millsaps	98
85	Denison ■	75
74	Westminster (Mo.) ■	73
86	Huntingdon ■	58
105	Maryville (Mo.) ■	80
98	Crichton ■	86
82	Rust	85
70	Huntingdon	62
68	DePauw ■	97
68	Rose-Hulman ■	58
81	Sewanee	73
85	Centre	90
66	Hendrix ■	62
72	Oglethorpe ■	63
78	Millsaps ■	91

53	Trinity (Tex.)	78
59	Southwestern (Tex.)	85
81	DePauw	101
70	Rose-Hulman	79
76	Sewanee ■	77
72	Centre ■	81
59	Hendrix	70
64	DePauw †	74

Nickname: Lynx
Colors: Red, Black & White
Arena: Mallory Gym
Capacity: 2,000
AD: Mike Clary
SID: Laura Whiteley

RICE

Houston, TX 77251-1892..........I

Coach: Willis Wilson, Rice 1982

2002-03 RESULTS (19-10)

72	Tulane ■	58
62	Stanford	79
71	Houston ■	53
56	Brigham Young	95
62	Lamar ■	45
106	St. Edward's ■	48
80	Colorado ■	61
82	Navy	60
86	Louisiana Col. ■	69
79	Nevada ■	75
70	Fresno St.	71
85	Tex.-Pan American	79
77	Tulsa ■	94
74	Boise St.	65
91	UTEP	63
83	Southern Methodist ■	89
93	Louisiana Tech ■	92
70	Hawaii	85
71	San Jose St.	66
56	Tulsa	79
72	UTEP ■	66
72	Boise St. ■	62
65	Louisiana Tech	63
63	Southern Methodist	73
65	San Jose St. ■	52
75	Hawaii ■	58
68	Nevada	86
92	Fresno St. ■	71
61	Hawaii †	62

Nickname: Owls
Colors: Blue & Gray
Arena: Autry Court
Capacity: 5,000; Year Built: 1950
AD: John May
SID: John Sullivan

RICHARD STOCKTON

Pomona, NJ 08240-0195.........III

Coach: Gerry Matthews, Kean 1965

2002-03 RESULTS (14-12)

78	Staten Island †	43
79	Muhlenberg	69
62	Rowan ■	63
67	Arcadia ■	44
57	Montclair St.	72
50	Wm. Paterson ■	59
69	Stevens Institute ■	54
69	Rutgers-Camden ■	59
64	New Jersey City	67
70	Ferrum †	63
72	Lebanon Valley	76
86	Ramapo ■	90
77	TCNJ	75
72	Rutgers-Newark ■	60
82	Purchase St. ■	37
62	Kean	59
70	Montclair St. ■	76
69	Rowan	81
61	Kean ■	60
73	Rutgers-Camden	62

78	Rutgers-Newark	69
86	New Jersey City ■	81
50	Wm. Paterson	67
70	TCNJ ■	72
79	Ramapo	86
64	Manhattanville	67

Nickname: Ospreys
Colors: Black, White & Red
Arena: Sports Center
Capacity: 3,000; Year Built: 2000
AD: Larry James
SID: Chris Rollman

RICHMOND

Richmond, VA 23173-1903........I

Coach: Jerry Wainwright, Colorado Col. 1968

2002-03 RESULTS (15-14)

92	Radford ■	46
60	Hampton	61
64	Charlotte ■	60
72	UAB ■	68
68	Va. Commonwealth	73
77	Pepperdine †	83
83	Stanford	69
55	Providence	84
86	Harvard ■	59
67	Norfolk St. ■	38
62	Wake Forest ■	68
67	Xavier	59
61	Temple ■	42
53	Dayton	66
75	Duquesne	69
63	George Washington ■	57
62	La Salle	55
84	Duquesne ■	47
52	Xavier ■	66
55	St. Bonaventure ■	61
53	Massachusetts	54
50	George Washington	64
63	Dayton ■	70
70	Rhode Island ■	69
59	St. Joseph's	75
60	Fordham	53
75	La Salle ■	62
52	Temple †	66
49	Providence ■	67

Nickname: Spiders
Colors: Red & Blue
Arena: Robins Center
Capacity: 9,171; Year Built: 1972
AD: Jim Miller
SID: Stacey Brann

RIDER

Lawrenceville, NJ 08648-3099...I

Coach: Don Harnum, Susquehanna 1986

2002-03 RESULTS (12-16)

66	Monmouth ■	61
56	Iona	68
68	Towson ■	56
70	Marist ■	72
82	Harvard ■	85
70	Delaware	60
62	Princeton ■	59
66	Coppin St. ■	47
54	Massachusetts	76
60	Seton Hall	75
53	Brown	65
59	Fairfield ■	66
66	Manhattan ■	76
69	Loyola (Md.)	74
61	Manhattan	75
65	Canisius ■	63
68	Niagara ■	74
73	Marist	60
80	St. Peter's ■	76
87	Siena	77

83 St. Peter's 86
69 Iona ■ 58
58 Fairfield 56
50 Loyola (Md.) ■ 44
61 Siena ■ 72
72 Niagara 78
74 Canisius 84
73 St. Peter's † 77

Nickname: Broncs
Colors: Cranberry & White
Arena: Alumni Gymnasium
  Capacity: 1,650; Year Built: 1959
AD: Curtis Blake
SID: Bud Focht

RIPON
Ripon, WI 54971 III

Coach: Bob Gillespie, Lewis 1971
2002-03 RESULTS (15-9)
83 Maranatha Baptist † 66
82 Marian (Wis.) 69
86 Trinity Int'l ■ 58
92 North Park ■ 66
66 Beloit 57
74 Babson † 59
84 Keene St. † 77
83 Carroll (Wis.) ■ 79
67 St. Norbert ■ 54
64 Lawrence ■ 79
59 Utah 75
137 Grinnell ■ 130
87 Knox ■ 77
72 Illinois Col. 80
53 Lake Forest 62
81 Monmouth (Ill.) ■ 68
57 Illinois Col. ■ 59
72 Lawrence 78
92 Knox 80
125 Grinnell 139
68 St. Norbert 67
77 Beloit ■ 82
81 Carroll (Wis.) ■ 77
107 Grinnell 112

Nickname: Red Hawks
Colors: Red & White
Arena: Storzer Center
  Capacity: 1,500; Year Built: 1967
AD: Robert Gillespie
SID: Ron Ernst

RIVIER
Nashua, NH 03060-5086 III

Coach: Dave Morissette, Plymouth St. 1994
2002-03 RESULTS (7-16)
75 New England ■ 83
72 New England Col. 66
68 Emmanuel (Mass.) 81
74 Albertus Magnus ■ 55
89 Husson † 72
73 Emerson 62
82 Johnson & Wales 91
55 St. Anselm 113
80 Emerson 95
57 Norwich ■ 66
66 Western New Eng. 78
90 Johnson & Wales ■ 93
47 Southern Vt. 83
75 Emmanuel (Mass.) ■ 68
79 Daniel Webster ■ 69
66 Southern Vt. ■ 68
58 Albertus Magnus 80
68 Suffolk 82
57 Norwich 66
84 Daniel Webster ■ 70
73 Suffolk ■ 83
66 Western New Eng. ■ 82
35 Southern Vt. 71

Nickname: Raiders
Colors: Blue & Gray
Arena: Muldoon Fitness Center
  Capacity: 300; Year Built: 1984
AD: Joanne Merrill
SID: To be named

ROANOKE
Salem, VA 24153 III

Coach: Page Moir, Virginia Tech 1984
2002-03 RESULTS (15-12)
76 Greensboro ■ 59
64 Goucher ■ 63
73 Otterbein † 82
67 Maryville (Tenn.) 95
90 Emory & Henry ■ 76
101 Transylvania 88
75 Maryville (Tenn.) ■ 79
63 Va. Wesleyan ■ 69
59 Randolph-Macon ■ 61
88 Harvard 93
65 Wash. & Lee ■ 53
92 Guilford 78
65 Hampden-Sydney 81
79 Lynchburg 67
84 Bridgewater (Va.) ■ 72
66 Randolph-Macon ■ 74
71 Va. Wesleyan 68
92 East. Mennonite 71
57 Wash. & Lee ■ 47
82 Bridgewater (Va.) 80
79 Lynchburg ■ 67
63 Hampden-Sydney ■ 71
63 Emory & Henry 83
74 Guilford 96
93 East. Mennonite ■ 74
91 Guilford † 69
62 Randolph-Macon † 84

Nickname: Maroons
Colors: Maroon & Gray
Arena: Bast Center
  Capacity: 2,000; Year Built: 1982
AD: Scott Allison
SID: Chris Cummings

ROBERT MORRIS
Moon Township, PA
15108-1189 I

Coach: Mark Schmidt, Boston College
2002-03 RESULTS (10-17)
83 UMKC 77
85 Eastern Mich. 99
68 Carnegie Mellon ■ 55
66 St. Francis (Pa.) 75
93 Md.-East. Shore 74
67 Albany (N.Y.) 69
73 Birmingham-So. ■ 75
59 Penn St. 76
49 Pittsburgh 85
53 Bucknell 66
77 UMBC ■ 71
73 Mt. St. Mary's ■ 67
76 Quinnipiac 90
74 Central Conn. St. 80
80 Wagner 101
77 Sacred Heart ■ 66
72 Wagner 77
66 Sacred Heart 74
72 St. Francis (N.Y.) ■ 77
85 Long Island 99
54 Mt. St. Mary's 56
64 UMBC 58
69 Fairleigh Dickinson ■ 56
67 Monmouth ■ 69
61 St. Francis (Pa.) ■ 58
80 Fairleigh Dickinson 88
69 Monmouth 59

Nickname: Colonials
Colors: Blue & White
Arena: Charles L. Sewall Center
  Capacity: 3,056; Year Built: 1985
AD: Susan Hofacre
SID: Jim Duzyk

ROCHESTER
Rochester, NY 14627-0296 III

Coach: Mike Neer, Wash. & Lee 1970
2002-03 RESULTS (23-4)
95 Alfred ■ 40
57 Texas Lutheran ■ 47
74 Nazareth ■ 62
72 Johns Hopkins ■ 48
66 Wis.-Eau Claire ■ 52
79 Hobart 62
66 Carnegie Mellon 50
64 Rochester Inst. ■ 52
69 Hobart ■ 53
67 Brandeis ■ 45
85 New York U. ■ 53
75 Keuka † 50
74 St. John Fisher † 43
59 Nazareth † 70
71 Washington (Mo.) 74
60 Chicago 72
77 Case Reserve ■ 63
92 Emory ■ 74
68 Emory 67
81 Case Reserve 77
87 New York U. 58
59 Brandeis ■ 45
71 Chicago ■ 54
83 Washington (Mo.) ■ 82
78 Carnegie Mellon ■ 48
73 Western Conn. St. ■ 62
68 Amherst † 74

Nickname: Yellowjackets
Colors: Yellow & Blue
Arena: Louis Alexander Palestra
  Capacity: 1,889; Year Built: 1930
AD: George VanderZwaag
SID: Dennis O'Donnell

ROCHESTER INST.
Rochester, NY 14623-5603 III

Coach: Bob McVean, Brockport St. 1969
2002-03 RESULTS (20-8)
84 Hilbert 54
58 Hobart ■ 56
52 Rochester 64
83 Lake Erie ■ 80
81 D'Youville ■ 58
70 D'Youville † 60
41 Penn St.-Behrend 50
65 St. John Fisher ■ 55
73 Alfred ■ 55
84 Brockport St. † 82
85 Nazareth † 88
68 St. John Fisher † 70
68 Ithaca 54
79 Elmira 96
55 Cortland St. 48
76 Hartwick ■ 53
81 Utica ■ 70
81 Nazareth 79
80 Alfred 63
78 St. John Fisher 91
73 Utica 52
68 Hartwick 88
80 Nazareth ■ 82
80 Elmira ■ 67
71 Ithaca ■ 66
84 Utica/Rome ■ 57
65 Union (N.Y.) † 62
78 Nazareth 76

Nickname: Tigers
Colors: Burnt Umber, Orange & White
Arena: Clark Memorial Gymnasium
  Capacity: 2,200; Year Built: 1968
AD: Janet Jones
SID: Jamie Joss

ROCKFORD
Rockford, IL 61108-2393 III

Coach: Bill Lavery, Monmouth (Ill.) 1990
2002-03 RESULTS (24-4)
71 Robert Morris (Ill.) ■ 49
82 Illinois Tech ■ 53
106 Beloit 95
65 Iowa Wesleyan 68
73 Augustana (Ill.) ■ 70
83 Concordia (Wis.) ■ 74
72 Rose-Hulman ■ 69
79 Wartburg † 77
70 Kendall ■ 61
76 Eureka ■ 57
71 Loras 83
69 Marian (Wis.) 65
76 Milwaukee Engr. 72
70 Aurora 64
81 Concordia (Ill.) 54
66 Clarke ■ 59
63 Benedictine (Ill.) 62
90 Dominican (Ill.) 72
83 Lakeland ■ 76
91 Eureka 72
85 Aurora ■ 65
93 Concordia (Ill.) ■ 71
71 Clarke 64
74 Benedictine (Ill.) 71
82 Dominican (Ill.) ■ 67
65 Benedictine (Ill.) ■ 51
65 Aurora 68
72 Buena Vista ■ 84

Nickname: Regents
Colors: Purple, White & Black
Arena: Seaver Center
  Capacity: 1,750; Year Built: 1964
AD: Kristyn King
SID: John Krueger

ROCKHURST
Kansas City, MO 64110-2561 ..II

Coach: Bill O'Connor, St. Benedict 1972
2002-03 RESULTS (17-11)
64 Mo.-St. Louis 60
78 William Jewell ■ 67
73 Morningside † 63
58 Neb.-Omaha 74
73 Mo. Western St. ■ 69
66 Washburn 85
69 Pittsburg St. ■ 75
62 Mo. Southern St. ■ 67
86 Minn. St. Mankato ■ 71
78 Central Mo. St. ■ 75
62 Western Ore. † 66
84 St. Martin's 71
75 Benedictine (Kan.) 37
58 St. Mary's (Tex.) 67
55 Incarnate Word 59
99 St. Edward's ■ 76
74 Okla. Panhandle ■ 56
60 Park 67
63 Drury ■ 61
64 Park ■ 59
72 Lincoln (Mo.) 60
71 St. Mary's (Tex.) ■ 68
76 Incarnate Word ■ 71
96 St. Edward's 79
83 Okla. Panhandle 93
90 Drury 93
87 Lincoln (Mo.) ■ 73
61 Incarnate Word ■ 66

Nickname: Hawks
Colors: Blue & White
Arena: Mason-Halpin Field House
   Capacity: 2,000; Year Built: 1938
AD: Frank Diskin
SID: Sid Bordman

ROGER WILLIAMS
Bristol, RI 02809 III

Coach: Mike Tully, Clark (Mass.) 1991
2002-03 RESULTS (5-20)
42	Rensselaer †	62
65	Cortland St. †	70
52	Connecticut Col.	82
67	New England Col.	64
55	Babson	93
59	Wheaton (Mass.) ■	75
74	Johnson & Wales ■	88
64	Endicott ■	70
77	Curry ■	86
62	Anna Maria	66
58	Nichols ■	62
48	Gordon ■	51
49	Eastern Nazarene	51
50	Salve Regina ■	60
53	Framingham St. ■	56
80	Anna Maria ■	61
41	Eastern Nazarene ■	70
62	Rhode Island Col.	74
79	New England	80
59	Coast Guard	70
64	Nichols	74
67	Colby-Sawyer ■	61
70	Wentworth Inst.	64
59	Salve Regina	64
68	Curry	58

Nickname: Hawks
Colors: Blue & Gold
Arena: Paolino Recreation Center
   Capacity: 3,000; Year Built: 1983
AD: George Kolb
SID: David Kemmy

ROLLINS
Winter Park, FL 32789 II

Coach: Tom Klusman, Rollins 1976
2002-03 RESULTS (26-6)
60	Stetson	67
76	P.R.-Cayey ■	56
80	P.R.-Mayaguez ■	58
65	P.R.-Rio Piedras ■	54
57	New Orleans	65
60	Nova Southeastern	45
86	Warner Southern ■	74
66	Cameron †	49
65	Northwest Mo. St. †	80
62	Wesley ■	55
92	Mount Olive ■	71
60	Clayton St. ■	55
70	Florida Tech ■	55
71	Lynn	66
64	Nova Southeastern ■	53
78	St. Leo ■	46
62	Tampa	48
82	Eckerd ■	47
75	Barry	67
75	Fla. Southern ■	65
78	Lynn ■	62
74	St. Leo	44
78	Tampa ■	63
79	Eckerd	84
52	Barry ■	48
69	Fla. Southern	63
66	Florida Tech	55
78	Florida Tech †	66
48	Barry †	37
68	Fla. Southern	81
76	Ala.-Huntsville ■	61
70	Eckerd ■	74

Nickname: Tars
Colors: Blue & Gold
Arena: Alfond Sports Center
   Capacity: 2,500; Year Built: 2000
AD: Phillip Roach
SID: Dean Hybl

ROSE-HULMAN
Terre Haute, IN 47803 III

Coach: Jim Shaw, Indiana 1982
2002-03 RESULTS (9-17)
59	Eastern †	57
59	Wheaton (Ill.) ■	76
66	Fontbonne	74
69	Rockford ■	72
61	Albion ■	88
63	Earlham ■	73
71	Robert Morris (Ill.) ■	74
46	Hanover ■	78
60	Ohio Wesleyan †	66
77	Illinois Col.	65
63	Franklin	62
75	Hendrix	57
58	Rhodes	68
50	DePauw	83
65	Southwestern (Tex.) ■	60
54	Trinity (Tex.) ■	59
38	Centre ■	57
72	Sewanee ■	67
48	Millsaps	71
74	Oglethorpe	65
62	Hendrix ■	49
79	Rhodes ■	70
52	DePauw ■	63
75	Southwestern (Tex.)	83
53	Trinity (Tex.) †	70
76	Southwestern (Tex.) †	86

Nickname: Fightin' Engineers
Colors: Old Rose & White
Arena: Hulbert Arena
   Capacity: 2,000; Year Built: 1997
AD: Greg Ruark
SID: Kevin Lanke

ROWAN
Glassboro, NJ 08028-1701......III

Coach: Joe Cassidy, St. Joseph's 1974
2002-03 RESULTS (20-6)
90	Manhattanville ■	61
63	Richard Stockton	62
117	Valley Forge Chrst. ■	68
81	Kean ■	71
67	Montclair St.	73
60	TCNJ ■	43
64	Rutgers-Newark ■	41
79	Fisk ■	62
107	Gwynedd-Mercy ■	102
66	Phila. Bible ■	56
66	New Jersey City ■	79
78	New Paltz St.	62
62	Rutgers-Camden ■	41
93	Ramapo ■	96
79	Wm. Paterson ■	55
63	Kean	51
81	Richard Stockton ■	69
66	Wm. Paterson	73
72	TCNJ	67
78	Ramapo ■	90
108	Yeshiva ■	54
65	Rutgers-Newark ■	63
76	Montclair St. ■	69
80	Rutgers-Camden ■	71
97	New Jersey City ■	83
90	Ramapo ■	100

Nickname: Profs
Colors: Brown & Gold
Arena: Esby Gym
   Capacity: 1,500; Year Built: 1963

AD: Joy Reighn
SID: Sheila Stevenson

RUST
Holly Springs, MS 38635 III

Coach: Rodney Stennis, Rust 1969
2002-03 RESULTS (4-9)
54	Earlham †	69
109	Lane ■	96
65	Millsaps ■	77
85	Rhodes ■	82
77	Millsaps	76
80	Maryville (Tenn.) ■	95
74	Stillman	84
60	SCAD	72
63	SCAD ■	82
54	Maryville (Tenn.) ■	88
115	Stillman ■	104
77	Lane	88
74	LeMoyne-Owen	83

Nickname: Bearcats
Colors: Blue & White
Arena: McMillan Multipurpose Ctr
   Capacity: 2,000; Year Built: 1971
AD: Ishmell Edwards
SID: To be named

RUTGERS
Piscataway, NJ 08854-8053 I

Coach: Gary Waters, Ferris St. 1957
2002-03 RESULTS (12-16)
60	Columbia ■	36
67	North Carolina	71
59	Temple	53
75	Marshall ■	56
70	Auburn	82
94	Fordham ■	83
76	Princeton	70
57	Virginia ■	61
68	Morris Brown ■	48
54	Delaware St. ■	41
66	Prairie View ■	57
75	La Salle ■	83
63	Pittsburgh ■	70
57	Notre Dame	68
89	Villanova ■	110
66	Georgetown	76
75	West Virginia	86
68	Syracuse ■	65
53	Seton Hall	58
75	Boston College ■	72
66	Georgetown ■	59
46	West Virginia ■	52
70	Connecticut	87
65	Pittsburgh	86
52	Seton Hall ■	62
95	Notre Dame ■	82
59	St. John's (N.J.)	75
74	Syracuse	83

Nickname: Scarlet Knights
Colors: Scarlet
Arena: Louis Brown Athletic Center
   Capacity: 8,500; Year Built: 1978
AD: Robert Mulcahy
SID: John Wooding

RUTGERS-CAMDEN
Camden, NJ 08102 III

Coach: Jim Flynn, St. Joseph's 1988
2002-03 RESULTS (8-17)
69	CCNY †	76
91	Penn St.-Altoona †	61
54	TCNJ ■	70
61	John Jay ■	66
70	Rutgers-Newark †	60

77	Ramapo	93
59	Richard Stockton ■	69
69	Montclair St. ■	74
73	York (N.Y.) ■	53
86	Farmingdale St.	71
51	Kean	73
88	Lancaster Bible	58
41	Rowan ■	62
59	Wm. Paterson	62
68	New Jersey City ■	78
54	Rutgers-Newark	51
70	TCNJ	76
64	New Jersey City	66
62	Richard Stockton	73
61	Phila. Bible	57
57	Wm. Paterson ■	66
55	Montclair St.	78
63	Ramapo ■	88
71	Rowan ■	80
83	Kean ■	77

Nickname: Scarlet Raptors
Colors: Scarlet & Silver
Arena: Rutgers Camden Gymnasium
   Capacity: 2,100; Year Built: 1973
AD: Edward Cialella
SID: Mike Ballard

RUTGERS-NEWARK
Newark, NJ 07102.................III

Coach: Joe Loughran, American Int'l
   1993
2002-03 RESULTS (8-17)
59	New Paltz St. ■	41
45	Rhode Island Col. ■	41
51	Montclair St. ■	72
60	Rutgers-Camden †	70
68	New Jersey City ■	50
70	Ramapo ■	85
41	Rowan	64
65	Lincoln (Pa.) †	51
68	Centenary (N.J.)	57
58	Purchase St.	44
59	Wm. Paterson	70
59	Kean ■	70
60	Richard Stockton	72
51	TCNJ ■	59
51	Rutgers-Camden ■	54
71	York (N.Y.) ■	75
46	Montclair St.	67
44	TCNJ	74
55	Ramapo ■	70
69	Richard Stockton ■	78
65	Polytechnic (N.Y.) ■	42
63	Rowan ■	65
55	New Jersey City	63
79	Kean	76
50	Wm. Paterson ■	69

Nickname: Scarlet Raiders
Colors: Scarlet
Arena: The Golden Dome
   Capacity: 2,000; Year Built: 1977
AD: John Adams
SID: John Stallings

SACRAMENTO ST.
Sacramento, CA 95819.............I

Coach: Jerome Jenkins, Regis 1990
2002-03 RESULTS (12-17)
55	Loyola Marymount	88
62	Dominican (Cal.) ■	47
68	Southern Utah	74
60	Missouri	98
62	San Francisco ■	57
73	Cal Poly	66
72	San Jose St. ■	70
49	Oregon St. ■	62
54	Cal St. Fullerton ■	62
62	Idaho	81

53	Fresno St.	91
83	Lipscomb	71
52	Portland St.	65
85	Northern Ariz.	81
84	Tex. A&M-Corp. Chris.	80
41	Eastern Wash.	75
62	Idaho St.	67
53	Weber St. ■	65
72	Montana St.	66
59	Montana	66
45	Northern Ariz. ■	63
77	Eastern Wash. ■	71
72	Portland St. ■	58
65	Weber St.	88
83	Idaho St.	90
71	Montana ■	77
72	Montana St. ■	52
88	Montana	75
60	Weber St.	82

Nickname: Hornets
Colors: Green & Gold
Arena: Hornet Gym
 Capacity: 1,300; Year Built: 1951
AD: Terry Wanless
SID: Brian Berger

SACRED HEART
Fairfield, CT 06432-1000 I

Coach: Dave Bike, Sacred Heart 1969
2002-03 RESULTS (8-21)

64	Stony Brook	75
62	Manhattan †	77
73	Army ■	75
78	Connecticut	116
69	Yale ■	88
63	Duquesne †	74
74	Northeastern †	91
77	P.R.-Mayaguez	64
75	Vermont	101
46	Minnesota	79
59	Columbia	58
63	Wagner ■	74
88	Quinnipiac	85
80	Central Conn. St.	85
74	Fairleigh Dickinson ■	62
55	Monmouth ■	65
64	St. Francis (Pa.)	70
66	Robert Morris	77
62	St. Francis (Pa.) ■	66
74	Robert Morris ■	66
53	Monmouth	73
73	Fairleigh Dickinson	82
58	Central Conn. St. ■	61
69	Quinnipiac ■	78
68	UMBC ■	57
78	Mt. St. Mary's ■	70
71	Wagner	79
92	St. Francis (N.Y.)	110
79	Long Island	73

Nickname: Pioneers
Colors: Scarlet & White
Arena: William H. Pitt Center
 Capacity: 2,000; Year Built: 1997
AD: Donald Cook
SID: Gene Gumbs

SAGINAW VALLEY
University Center, MI 48710-0001
....II

Coach: Dean Lockwood, Spring Arbor 1982
2002-03 RESULTS (13-14)

81	Wayne St. (Mich.)	93
68	Hillsdale †	84
88	Finlandia ■	64
107	Rochester College ■	70
100	Wayne St. (Mich.) ■	94
85	Hillsdale ■	72

76	Ashland	104
87	Madonna ■	70
58	Spring Arbor ■	51
86	St. Mary's (Mich.) ■	79
85	Oakland City	77
92	Ky. Wesleyan	106
70	Findlay ■	73
87	Gannon ■	108
86	Mercyhurst	91
55	Michigan Tech ■	90
60	Northern Mich. ■	64
75	Ferris St. ■	67
93	Grand Valley St. ■	103
75	Northwood	69
79	Lake Superior St.	92
78	Michigan Tech	91
85	Northern Mich.	77
62	Grand Valley St.	76
65	Ferris St.	78
80	Lake Superior St. ■	69
82	Northwood ■	81

Nickname: Cardinals
Colors: Red, White & Blue
Arena: James O'Neill Jr. Arena
 Capacity: 4,000; Year Built: 1989
AD: Griz Zimmermann
SID: Tom Waske

ST. ANDREWS
Laurinburg, NC 28352-5598.....II

Coach: Rob Perron, St. Andrews 1996
2002-03 RESULTS (9-21)

90	Fayetteville St. ■	91
81	Newberry ■	75
80	Georgia St.	95
65	Belmont Abbey ■	77
63	Longwood ■	75
77	UNC Pembroke ■	64
81	Francis Marion ■	90
39	Winthrop	74
70	Newberry	62
67	Queens (N.C.)	99
52	Pfeiffer	99
74	Lees-McRae	50
93	Limestone	96
77	Anderson (S.C.) ■	84
54	Erskine ■	50
72	Coker	74
80	Mount Olive ■	85
60	Barton	73
68	Belmont Abbey	79
72	Queens (N.C.) ■	85
61	Longwood	79
77	Lees-McRae ■	63
84	Limestone ■	86
66	Anderson (S.C.)	88
80	Pfeiffer ■	91
55	Erskine	80
91	Coker ■	54
93	Limestone	90
80	Barton	77
63	Belmont Abbey †	94

Nickname: Knights
Colors: Royal Blue & White
Arena: Harris Court
 Capacity: 1,400; Year Built: 1967
AD: Carl Ullrich
SID: Chris Mathes

ST. ANSELM
Manchester, NH 03102-1310 ...II

Coach: Keith Dickson, New Hampshire 1979
2002-03 RESULTS (13-14)

89	Cheyney †	65
65	Bridgeport	79
66	Pace ■	68
56	Assumption	70

77	Bryant	68
53	American Int'l ■	55
49	Mass.-Lowell ■	50
83	Felician	72
82	Southern Conn. St.	80
77	Franklin Pierce ■	67
81	Southern N.H.	92
68	Stonehill	55
76	Bentley	79
100	Merrimack ■	76
113	Rivier	55
72	Le Moyne	74
70	St. Michael's	71
52	American Int'l	58
65	Bryant ■	69
79	Assumption ■	72
93	Southern Conn. St. ■	60
91	St. Rose	100
83	Pace	87
88	Le Moyne	84
88	St. Michael's ■	62
101	St. Rose ■	90
76	Bentley	88

Nickname: Hawks
Colors: Blue & White
Arena: Stoutenburgh Gymnasium
 Capacity: 1,600; Year Built: 1961
AD: Edward Cannon
SID: Kurt Svoboda

ST. AUGUSTINE'S
Raleigh, NC 27610 II

Coach: Thomas Hargrove
2002-03 RESULTS (18-9)

88	Morris ■	81
91	St. Paul's	76
101	Catawba	105
80	Bowie St.	91
86	Central St. (Ohio)	81
65	Clark Atlanta	57
84	West Va. Tech ■	62
75	Dist. Columbia ■	72
77	Catawba	85
82	Lenoir-Rhyne †	67
77	Wingate	74
99	Winston-Salem ■	70
68	N.C. Central †	91
69	Elizabeth City St.	81
73	Fayetteville St. ■	67
67	Johnson Smith	68
94	N.C. Central	79
82	Virginia St.	61
80	Virginia Union ■	83
81	Winston-Salem	75
83	Fayetteville St.	75
85	Johnson Smith ■	69
106	Livingstone ■	82
76	Livingstone	67
53	Shaw	65
78	Shaw	63
80	Virginia Union †	81

Nickname: Falcons
Colors: Blue & White.
Arena: Emery Gymnasium
 Capacity: 1,000; Year Built: 1962
AD: George Williams
SID: Leon Carrington

ST. BONAVENTURE
St. Bonaventure, NY 14778 I

Coach: Jan van Breda Kolff, Vanderbilt 1974
2002-03 RESULTS (13-14)

91	Virginia Tech †	78
89	Michigan †	68
57	Brigham Young †	66
54	St. Louis †	56
96	Boston College	105

68	Alabama	77
72	Davidson	77
69	Canisius	57
93	Kent St. ■	80
94	Toledo ■	68
101	Ohio	104
78	Connecticut	95
88	Rhode Island ■	80
58	St. Joseph's ■	75
83	Xavier	99
76	Fordham	70
87	La Salle ■	77
86	Duquesne	78
81	Cleveland St. ■	67
77	Temple ■	96
85	Rhode Island	91
61	Richmond	55
76	Massachusetts ■	82
83	Fordham ■	65
72	St. Joseph's	76
94	George Washington ■	89
77	Temple	78

Nickname: Bonnies
Colors: Brown & White
Arena: Reilly Center
 Capacity: 6,000; Year Built: 1966
AD: Paul Grys
SID: Steve Mest

ST. CLOUD ST.
St. Cloud, MN 56301-4498 II

Coach: Kevin Schlagel, St. Cloud St. 1976
2002-03 RESULTS (26-5)

88	Minn.-Crookston ■	49
88	Loras ■	56
70	Washburn †	87
99	P.R.-Mayaguez †	44
91	Bemidji St.	84
84	Northern Mich. ■	52
83	Southwest Minn. St.	58
80	St. John's (Minn.)	61
93	Concordia-St. Paul ■	79
77	Wayne St. (Neb.)	57
101	Macalester	71
71	Northern Colo.	70
84	South Dakota	79
74	Augustana (S.D.) ■	65
94	South Dakota St. ■	89
81	North Dakota	76
57	South Dakota St.	80
83	Minn. St. Mankato	74
88	Neb.-Omaha ■	77
89	South Dakota ■	97
86	Minn. St. Mankato ■	60
67	Augustana (S.D.)	55
88	North Dakota St. ■	86
73	North Dakota ■	76
79	Northern Colo. ■	67
85	Neb.-Omaha	68
79	North Dakota St.	77
75	North Dakota St. ■	60
88	Neb.-Omaha ■	78
74	North Dakota †	69
63	Metro St. †	75

Nickname: Huskies
Colors: Cardinal Red & Black
Arena: Halenbeck Hall
 Capacity: 6,900; Year Built: 1965
AD: Morris Kurtz
SID: Anne Abicht

ST. EDWARD'S
Austin, TX 78704 II

Coach: Mike Jones, Angelo St.
2002-03 RESULTS (4-23)

69	Central Ark.	105
56	Southern Ark. †	81

78	Abilene Christian ■	120
86	Tex. A&M-Commerce †	113
67	Angelo St. †	70
75	Central Ark. ■	63
68	Ouachita Baptist ■	69
97	Concordia-Austin ■	80
41	North Texas	88
48	Rice	106
79	Mo.-Rolla ■	89
80	Abilene Christian	85
81	Tex. Permian Basin	76
86	Ouachita Baptist	94
82	Paul Quinn ■	79
99	Drury ■	100
76	Rockhurst	99
72	Lincoln (Mo.)	81
60	Incarnate Word	85
53	St. Mary's (Tex.) ■	83
88	Okla. Panhandle	92
75	Drury	103
79	Rockhurst ■	96
58	Lincoln (Mo.) ■	75
71	Incarnate Word ■	86
57	St. Mary's (Tex.)	81
73	Okla. Panhandle ■	90

Nickname: Hilltoppers
Colors: Navy & White
Arena: Recreation & Convocation Center
Capacity: 2,500; Year Built: 1989
AD: Debora Taylor
SID: Naveen Boppana

ST. FRANCIS (PA.)
Loretto, PA 15940-0600 ...I

Coach: Bobby Jones, Western Ky. 1984
2002-03 RESULTS (14-14)

70	Howard ■	68
46	Pittsburgh	69
59	VMI ■	76
70	Youngstown St. ■	56
54	Bucknell	57
75	Robert Morris ■	66
45	Western Ky.	80
55	Penn St.	74
64	Cornell	61
64	American	54
76	Mt. St. Mary's ■	57
73	UMBC ■	68
67	Central Conn. St.	68
61	Quinnipiac	69
70	Sacred Heart ■	64
72	Wagner ■	84
66	Sacred Heart	62
89	Wagner	102
94	Long Island ■	98
89	St. Francis (N.Y.) ■	72
72	UMBC	64
79	Mt. St. Mary's	69
70	Monmouth ■	72
68	Fairleigh Dickinson ■	66
58	Robert Morris	61
76	Monmouth	68
73	Fairleigh Dickinson	75
57	Quinnipiac †	75

Nickname: Red Flash
Colors: Red & White
Arena: Maurice Stokes Athletic Center
Capacity: 3,500; Year Built: 1972
AD: Jeffrey Eisen
SID: Pat Farabaugh

ST. FRANCIS (N.Y.)
Brooklyn Heights, NY 11201-4398 ...I

Coach: Ron Ganulin, Long Island 1968
2002-03 RESULTS (14-16)

72	Hofstra †	56
85	St. Peter's	94

76	Seton Hall	84
88	Howard	67
58	St. John's (N.Y.)	80
76	Long Island	89
57	Duquesne †	67
69	Radford †	63
68	Lehigh	74
62	Binghamton	74
76	Monmouth	80
71	Fairleigh Dickinson	76
58	UMBC	73
58	Mt. St. Mary's	69
73	Mt. St. Mary's ■	54
66	UMBC ■	69
91	Quinnipiac ■	76
59	Central Conn. St.	71
77	Robert Morris	72
72	St. Francis (Pa.)	89
78	Central Conn. St. ■	55
81	Monmouth	71
85	Fairleigh Dickinson ■	80
61	Quinnipiac	80
142	Long Island ■	140
110	Sacred Heart ■	92
96	Wagner ■	84
67	Central Conn. St. †	62
88	Fairleigh Dickinson †	62
61	Wagner	78

Nickname: Terriers
Colors: Red & Blue
Arena: Pope Physical Education Center
Capacity: 1,200; Year Built: 1971
AD: Edward Aquilone
SID: Jim Hoffman

ST. JOHN FISHER
Rochester, NY 14618 ...III

Coach: Rob Kornaker, Alfred
2002-03 RESULTS (21-5)

93	Keuka ■	55
97	St. Lawrence ■	87
74	Brockport St. ■	68
79	Chowan †	66
67	Salisbury	52
56	Fredonia St. ■	41
72	Lincoln (Pa.) †	73
70	St. Mary's (Md.) †	61
55	Rochester Inst.	65
72	Nazareth	81
66	Geneseo St. †	59
43	Rochester †	74
70	Rochester Inst. †	68
58	Utica	55
73	Hartwick	71
94	Alfred ■	65
84	Elmira ■	82
97	Ithaca ■	85
89	Nazareth ■	82
91	Rochester Inst. ■	78
67	Ithaca	64
78	Elmira	65
80	Alfred	73
61	Hartwick ■	57
79	Utica ■	70
68	Hamilton ■	72

Nickname: Cardinals
Colors: Cardinal & Gold
Arena: Manning-Napier Varsity Gym
Capacity: 1,200; Year Built: 1963
AD: Bob Ward
SID: Norm Kieffer

ST. JOHN'S (MINN.)
Collegeville, MN 56321 ...III

Coach: Jim Smith, Marquette 1956
2002-03 RESULTS (12-15)

67	Thiel †	71
72	Kenyon †	68

66	St. Thomas (Minn.) ■	56
54	Hamline	64
66	Concordia-M'head	60
66	Augsburg	60
61	St. Cloud St. ■	80
56	Ill. Wesleyan †	76
70	Neb. Wesleyan †	79
67	St. Mary's (Minn.)	72
66	St. Olaf	56
63	Bethel (Minn.)	68
58	Gust. Adolphus	56
77	Carleton	73
70	Macalester	84
60	St. Thomas (Minn.)	69
75	Hamline	76
75	Concordia-M'head	71
59	Augsburg	60
75	St. Olaf ■	70
72	St. Mary's (Minn.) ■	52
92	Bethel (Minn.) ■	95
54	Gust. Adolphus	68
70	Carleton	78
97	Macalester ■	64
69	Carleton	58
57	St. Thomas (Minn.)	60

Nickname: Johnnies
Colors: Cardinal & Blue
Arena: Sexton Arena
Capacity: 3,500; Year Built: 1974
AD: Jim Smith
SID: Michael Hemmesch

ST. JOHN'S (N.Y.)
Jamaica, NY 11439 ...I

Coach: Mike Jarvis, Northeastern 1968
2002-03 RESULTS (21-13)

68	Stony Brook ■	57
81	Fairfield	68
81	Fordham	58
80	St. Francis (N.Y.) ■	58
84	Hofstra	59
72	Wake Forest	84
65	Manhattan †	72
59	North Carolina †	63
78	Niagara	68
74	Seton Hall ■	66
71	Providence	75
80	UCLA	65
73	Villanova ■	82
77	Georgetown	72
62	Virginia Tech	59
68	Connecticut	74
77	Miami (Fla.)	74
82	Boston College	84
54	Virginia Tech ■	71
52	Villanova	50
59	Providence	69
60	Syracuse	66
69	Connecticut	77
63	Boston College ■	81
72	Duke	71
75	Rutgers ■	59
76	Miami (Fla.)	73
83	Notre Dame †	80
75	Boston College †	82
62	Boston U. ■	57
73	Virginia	63
79	UAB ■	71
64	Texas Tech †	63
70	Georgetown †	67

Nickname: Red Storm
Colors: Red & White
Arena: Alumni Hall
Capacity: 6,008; Year Built: 1961
AD: David Wegrzyn
SID: Dominic P. Scianna

ST. JOSEPH'S (IND.)
Rensselaer, IN 47978 ...II

Coach: Linc Darner, Purdue 1995
2002-03 RESULTS (11-17)

75	Ferris St. ■	76
58	IUPUI	79
71	Mercyhurst ■	81
74	Lewis ■	72
84	SIU Edwardsville ■	73
70	Mo.-St. Louis	76
83	Southern Ind.	100
84	Northwood ■	79
90	Grand Valley St.	89
100	Calumet Col.	68
77	Mercyhurst	63
106	Bellarmine ■	95
99	Northern Ky. ■	100
71	Wis.-Parkside ■	100
78	SIU Edwardsville	81
92	Quincy	90
108	Southern Ind.	115
83	Ky. Wesleyan ■	109
69	Northern Ky.	91
79	Indianapolis	91
54	Wis.-Parkside	77
66	Lewis	78
76	Quincy ■	74
87	Mo.-St. Louis	78
66	Ky. Wesleyan	101
104	Bellarmine	112
89	Indianapolis ■	81
85	Southern Ind.	91

Nickname: Pumas
Colors: Cardinal & Purple
Arena: Richard F. Scharf Fieldhouse
Capacity: 2,000; Year Built: 1941
AD: Bill Massoels
SID: Joe Danahey

ST. JOSEPH'S (L.I.)
Patchogue, NY 11772-2603 ...III

Coach: John Mateyko, American Int'l 1984
2002-03 RESULTS (12-13)

54	Hartwick	71
72	Old Westbury	75
69	CCNY	76
59	Lehman ■	54
66	Mt. St. Mary (N.Y.) ■	74
74	Yeshiva	79
55	New York U.	67
73	Manhattanville	67
83	Mt. St. Vincent	63
85	Stevens Institute ■	77
57	Centenary (N.J.) ■	64
68	Maritime (N.Y.)	47
61	Polytechnic (N.Y.)	42
68	Old Westbury ■	82
60	Yeshiva ■	49
69	Stevens Institute	80
69	Purchase St.	58
78	Pratt	52
43	Manhattanville	53
70	Mt. St. Mary (N.Y.)	73
75	Merchant Marine	69
66	Maritime (N.Y.)	52
55	Mt. St. Vincent ■	54
65	Merchant Marine	74
59	Old Westbury	64

Nickname: Golden Eagles
Colors: Blue & Gold
Arena: Danzi Athletic Center
Capacity: 1,500; Year Built: 1996
AD: Donald Lizak
SID: Frank Flandina

ST. JOSEPH'S (ME.)
Standish, ME 04084-5263 III

Coach: Rick Simonds, Southern Me. 1972

2002-03 RESULTS (20-5)

88	Southern Me. ■	86
72	Husson ■	70
72	Me.-Farmington ■	59
75	Wesleyan (Conn.) †	87
72	Framingham St. †	57
102	Lyndon St. ■	67
68	Elms ■	51
71	Worcester St. ■	69
98	New England ■	59
55	Pomona-Pitzer †	47
60	Occidental	79
73	Cortland St. †	55
62	Union (N.Y.)	80
89	Thomas	65
85	Lasell ■	79
84	Me.-Machias ■	56
70	Husson	81
70	Bowdoin ■	55
103	Castleton St.	83
82	Green Mountain	61
106	Southern Me.	92
81	Bates ■	75
68	Husson ■	54
96	Thomas ■	60
76	Salem St.	81

Nickname: Monks
Colors: Royal Blue & White
Arena: Harold Alfond Center
  Capacity: 1,500; Year Built: 1999
AD: David Roussel
SID: Rob Sanicola

ST. JOSEPH'S
Philadelphia, PA 19131-1395 I

Coach: Phil Martelli, Widener 1976

2002-03 RESULTS (23-7)

85	Boston College	58
70	Canisius	63
63	Old Dominion ■	47
71	Boston U. ■	49
50	Drexel †	37
77	Delaware ■	59
65	DePaul ■	62
50	Pacific (Cal.)	62
79	Gonzaga	78
76	Duquesne ■	56
75	St. Bonaventure	58
76	Massachusetts ■	47
65	Temple	55
57	Rhode Island	58
79	Fordham	46
66	Pennsylvania ■	48
68	George Washington	74
69	Rhode Island ■	53
92	Villanova ■	75
82	Fordham ■	64
78	Temple ■	59
56	Dayton	66
76	St. Bonaventure ■	72
75	La Salle ■	53
75	Richmond ■	59
80	Xavier ■	88
52	Massachusetts	49
68	La Salle †	48
73	Dayton	76
63	Auburn †	65

Nickname: Hawks
Colors: Crimson & Gray
Arena: Alumni Memorial Fieldhouse
  Capacity: 3,200; Year Built: 1949
AD: Don DiJulia
SID: Larry Dougherty

ST. LAWRENCE
Canton, NY 13617 III

Coach: Chris Downs, Oneonta St. 1991

2002-03 RESULTS (17-10)

83	Oswego St. †	72
87	St. John Fisher	97
54	Williams	89
80	Oneonta St.	60
73	Ithaca	62
80	Alfred ■	62
89	Brockport St.	96
85	Oswego St.	81
79	Plattsburgh St. ■	60
66	Hobart	79
67	Hamilton	84
77	Vassar ■	56
74	Rensselaer ■	80
56	Clarkson	59
90	Skidmore ■	79
73	Union (N.Y.) ■	71
82	Potsdam St.	75
92	Rensselaer	89
86	Vassar	76
76	Clarkson ■	71
78	Hamilton ■	75
68	Hobart ■	64
60	Union (N.Y.)	81
75	Skidmore	59
50	Union (N.Y.) †	52
85	Potsdam St. ■	80
72	Nazareth	85

Nickname: Saints
Colors: Scarlet & Brown
Arena: Burkman Gymnasium
  Capacity: 1,500; Year Built: 1970
AD: Margaret Strait
SID: Erin Thompson

ST. LEO
Saint Leo, FL 33574 II

Coach: Mike Madagan, Northern Ill. 1987

2002-03 RESULTS (7-21)

55	Jacksonville	85
57	New Orleans	107
66	P.R.-Cayey ■	60
56	Fla. Gulf Coast	71
73	Newberry †	66
68	Queens (N.C.) †	79
89	Lynn †	94
41	Valdosta St.	47
81	Fla. Gulf Coast ■	72
51	Valdosta St. ■	78
48	Barry	43
54	Fla. Southern ■	87
61	Florida Tech ■	60
46	Rollins	78
43	Barry	48
72	Lynn ■	76
59	Eckerd	88
39	Tampa ■	65
61	Florida Tech	70
44	Rollins ■	74
48	Barry ■	33
59	Lynn	75
60	Nova Southeastern	79
56	Eckerd ■	59
55	Tampa	74
63	Fla. Southern	101
60	Nova Southeastern ■	46
54	Fla. Southern	68

Nickname: Lions
Colors: Forest Green & Old Gold
Arena: Marion Bowman Center
  Capacity: 2,700; Year Built: 1970
AD: Franis Reidy
SID: Walter Riddle

ST. LOUIS
St. Louis, MO 63108 I

Coach: Brad Soderberg, Wis.-Stevens Point 1985

2002-03 RESULTS (16-14)

58	Tenn.-Martin ■	63
64	Southwest Mo. St. ■	72
56	St. Bonaventure †	54
58	Arizona	91
57	Tex.-Pan American ■	42
63	Dayton ■	55
83	Grambling ■	54
46	Butler	68
71	Southern Ill. ■	60
48	Kansas St.	65
75	West Virginia ■	45
54	Marquette ■	60
54	Louisville	73
56	Cincinnati ■	66
59	Houston	72
69	Memphis ■	66
55	Charlotte	62
65	DePaul ■	57
64	Marquette	68
64	South Fla.	71
59	Louisville ■	58
56	East Caro. ■	42
58	Cincinnati	55
62	DePaul	61
76	Tulane ■	74
50	Charlotte ■	39
58	East Caro.	48
69	Southern Miss. †	56
62	UAB †	63
52	Minnesota ■	62

Nickname: Billikens
Colors: Blue & White
Arena: Savvis Center
  Capacity: 20,000; Year Built: 1994
AD: Douglas Woolard
SID: Doug McIlhagga

ST. MARTIN'S
Lacey, WA 98503 II

Coach: Bob Grisham, Col. of Idaho 1976

2002-03 RESULTS (2-26)

70	North Dakota †	85
66	Metro St. †	75
77	Mont. St.-Billings ■	86
72	Cal Poly Pomona †	75
53	BYU-Hawaii †	99
64	Western Wash. ■	70
56	Seattle Pacific ■	79
83	Mont. St.-Billings	101
56	Mercyhurst ■	72
71	Rockhurst ■	84
65	BYU-Hawaii	84
64	Hawaii Pacific	84
66	Alas. Fairbanks	76
63	Alas. Anchorage	102
62	Humboldt St. ■	69
61	Western Ore.	63
55	Northwest Nazarene	64
64	Seattle	67
69	Central Wash. ■	77
64	Alas. Fairbanks ■	84
85	Alas. Anchorage ■	92
62	Western Ore.	77
63	Humboldt St.	80
64	Seattle ■	71
75	Northwest Nazarene ■	71
83	Central Wash.	80
61	Seattle Pacific	96
82	Western Wash.	93

Nickname: Saints
Colors: Red & White
Arena: SMC Pavillion

Capacity: 4,300; Year Built: 1965
AD: Robert Grisham
SID: Michael Ostlund

ST. MARY'S (CAL.)
Moraga, CA 94575 I

Coach: Randy Bennett, UC San Diego 1986

2002-03 RESULTS (15-15)

78	Holy Names ■	33
80	Eastern Wash.	88
75	Sam Houston St. †	66
65	Fresno St.	67
94	San Jose St. ■	62
75	Portland St. ■	51
58	Stanford	76
79	UC Riverside ■	74
50	UC Irvine ■	62
52	Cal Poly ■	59
77	Brown ■	63
66	Yale ■	56
59	Utah	65
68	San Francisco	62
53	Gonzaga ■	56
69	Portland	54
63	Santa Clara	66
71	Loyola Marymount ■	60
74	Pepperdine ■	67
69	San Diego	76
67	San Francisco ■	68
49	Gonzaga	73
71	Portland	59
57	San Diego ■	75
56	Santa Clara ■	57
67	Pepperdine	72
67	Loyola Marymount	62
65	Santa Clara †	51
75	Pepperdine †	71
52	Gonzaga †	73

Nickname: Gaels
Colors: Navy Blue & Red
Arena: McKeon Pavilion
  Capacity: 3,500; Year Built: 1978
AD: Carl Clapp
SID: Jason Santos

ST. MARY'S (MD.)
St. Mary's City, MD 20686 III

Coach: Alfred Johnson, Elizabeth City St. 1994

2002-03 RESULTS (6-20)

74	Gardner-Webb	82
56	Elon	69
44	Furman	81
74	Fisk †	80
68	Salisbury †	64
61	Goucher ■	65
67	Frank. & Marsh.	112
61	St. John Fisher †	70
76	Lincoln (Pa.)	66
77	Widener ■	62
73	Salisbury ■	76
78	Marymount (Va.) ■	77
74	Mary Washington	84
64	Catholic ■	78
65	York (Pa.) ■	84
78	Wilkes ■	84
92	Gallaudet	84
82	Salisbury	72
78	Goucher	82
68	SCAD	82
66	Marymount (Va.)	71
85	Gallaudet ■	89
61	Catholic	86
102	York (Pa.)	121
79	Mary Washington ■	90
69	Mary Washington	82

Nickname: Seahawks
Colors: Navy Blue & Old Gold
Arena: Somerset Gymnasium
　　Capacity: 1,420; Year Built: 1968
AD: Scott Devine
SID: Shawne McCoy

ST. MARY'S (MINN.)
Winona, MN 55987-1399......III

Coach: Bob Biebel, St. Mary's (Minn.) 1979
2002-03 RESULTS (2-22)
63	Wis.-La Crosse ■	66
83	Hamline	70
69	St. Olaf ■	79
62	Bethel (Minn.) ■	73
45	St. Thomas (Minn.) ■	65
64	Regis (Colo.)	98
66	Colorado Col.	74
72	St. John's (Minn.) ■	67
60	Carleton	71
56	Macalester ■	66
57	Gust. Adolphus	92
64	Augsburg ■	71
50	Wis.-Eau Claire ■	78
52	Concordia-M'head	71
60	Hamline ■	66
74	St. Olaf	89
57	Bethel (Minn.)	84
62	St. Thomas (Minn.) ■	65
55	Carleton	76
52	St. John's (Minn.)	72
62	Macalester	75
73	Concordia-M'head	77
64	Gust. Adolphus	73
59	Augsburg	62

Nickname: Cardinals
Colors: Scarlet, Red & White
Arena: St. Mary's Fieldhouse
　　Capacity: 3,500; Year Built: 1965
AD: Chris Kendall
SID: Donny Nadeau

ST. MARY'S (TEX.)
San Antonio, TX 78228-8572....II

Coach: Herman Meyer, St. Mary's (Tex.) 1965
2002-03 RESULTS (17-13)
75	Chaminade	70
78	Hawaii Pacific	83
100	Montevallo ■	55
66	Central Mo. St. ■	69
67	Texas-San Antonio	81
69	Neb.-Omaha †	77
86	Emporia St.	95
75	Northeastern St. ■	79
73	Pittsburg St. ■	66
68	Mo. Western St. ■	73
59	Tarleton St.	66
80	Shippensburg ■	68
63	Midwestern St.	74
67	Rockhurst ■	58
67	Lincoln (Mo.) ■	66
61	Northeastern St.	73
73	Drury	61
75	Okla. Panhandle	59
83	St. Edward's	53
100	Schreiner	58
70	Incarnate Word	55
68	Rockhurst	71
59	Lincoln (Mo.)	75
69	Drury ■	62
98	Okla. Panhandle ■	73
81	St. Edward's ■	57
50	Incarnate Word ■	45
69	Drury ■	64

57	Incarnate Word ■	47
43	Tarleton St.	56

Nickname: Rattlers
Colors: Blue & Gold
Arena: Bill Greehey Arena
　　Capacity: 3,500; Year Built: 2000
AD: Charlie Migl
SID: Steve Johnson

ST. MICHAEL'S
Colchester, VT 05439..............II

Coach: Tom O'Shea, Vermont 1986
2002-03 RESULTS (10-17)
79	Caldwell ■	73
94	Concordia (N.Y.) ■	64
64	Southern Conn. St. ■	65
80	American Int'l	87
66	Assumption ■	69
77	Bryant	89
83	Southern N.H. ■	86
89	St. Rose	94
56	Vermont	81
68	Mass.-Lowell	87
69	Franklin Pierce ■	78
77	Bentley	87
100	Merrimack ■	90
61	Stonehill	70
91	Green Mountain ■	63
71	St. Anselm ■	70
62	Le Moyne	87
60	Bryant ■	65
79	Assumption	92
77	American Int'l ■	67
95	St. Rose	97
72	Pace	93
82	Southern Conn. St.	76
87	Green Mountain	69
82	Le Moyne ■	80
62	St. Anselm	88
95	Pace ■	76

Nickname: Purple Knights
Colors: Purple & Gold
Arena: Ross Sports Center
　　Capacity: 2,500; Year Built: 1974
AD: Geraldine Knortz
SID: Angela Aja

ST. NORBERT
De Pere, WI 54115 III

Coach: Paul De Noble, Wis.-Oshkosh 1973
2002-03 RESULTS (12-11)
76	Wis.-Parkside	74
53	Wis.-Oshkosh	94
58	Wittenberg †	74
63	Aurora †	67
55	Elmhurst ■	53
81	Carroll (Wis.) ■	69
79	Northern Mich.	91
83	Concordia (Wis.) ■	72
54	Ripon	67
71	Beloit ■	73
54	Lawrence	57
69	Monmouth (Ill.) ■	49
114	Grinnell ■	124
73	Knox	67
82	Illinois Col.	78
71	Lake Forest ■	69
67	Knox	69
88	Beloit	68
106	Grinnell	118
66	Monmouth (Ill.)	49
67	Ripon	68
73	Carroll (Wis.)	58
72	Lawrence ■	64

Nickname: Green Knights
Colors: Dartmouth Green & Old Gold
Arena: Schuldes Sports Center
　　Capacity: 2,000; Year Built: 1979
AD: Donald Maslinski
SID: Dan Lukes

ST. OLAF
Northfield, MN 55057-1098 III

Coach: Dan Kosmoski, Minnesota 1980
2002-03 RESULTS (15-11)
72	Northland †	42
58	Wis.-Eau Claire	79
74	Luther ■	56
67	Concordia-M'head ■	62
84	Northwestern (Minn.)	71
79	St. Mary's (Minn.) ■	69
53	Gust. Adolphus	67
75	Carleton	72
81	Crown ■	66
56	St. John's (Minn.) ■	66
64	Bethel (Minn.) ■	72
60	Augsburg	70
70	Macalester ■	63
65	St. Thomas (Minn.)	74
68	Hamline	74
64	Concordia-M'head	73
89	St. Mary's (Minn.) ■	74
59	Gust. Adolphus ■	66
71	Carleton	69
70	St. John's (Minn.)	75
70	Bethel (Minn.) ■	57
69	Augsburg ■	49
70	Macalester	69
82	St. Thomas (Minn.) ■	80
79	Hamline	60
54	Bethel (Minn.)	82

Nickname: Oles
Colors: Black & Old Gold
Arena: Skoglund Athletic Center
　　Capacity: 3,000; Year Built: 1968
AD: Cindy Book
SID: Le Ann Finger

ST. PAUL'S
Lawrenceville, VA 23868...........II

Coach: Jerry Seale
2002-03 RESULTS (8-20)
62	Wheeling Jesuit †	79
60	Fairmont St.	68
76	St. Augustine's ■	91
66	Salem Int'l	93
78	Alderson-Broaddus †	87
79	Wingate	87
74	Catawba	71
84	Concord †	77
75	Barton	81
70	Bowie St.	74
77	Johnson Smith ■	86
70	Catawba	82
63	Longwood	58
74	Barber-Scotia	78
75	Virginia Union ■	85
67	Virginia Union	87
47	Winston-Salem ■	77
52	Shaw ■	79
62	Fayetteville St.	73
53	Elizabeth City St.	52
82	Livingstone ■	81
76	Virginia St. ■	79
66	Shaw	74
86	Elizabeth City St. ■	78
75	Bowie St.	72
69	N.C. Central ■	88
75	Virginia St.	74
52	Fayetteville St. †	61

Nickname: Tigers
Colors: Black & Orange
Arena: Taylor-Whitehead Gym
　　Capacity: 1,500; Year Built: 1965
AD: LeRoy Bacote
SID: April Emory

ST. PETER'S
Jersey City, NJ 07306................I

Coach: Bob Leckie, St. Peter's 1969
2002-03 RESULTS (10-19)
48	Xavier	87
67	Central Conn. St.	77
93	Northern Ariz. †	99
94	St. Francis (N.Y.) ■	85
63	Siena ■	81
71	Fairleigh Dickinson	78
72	Monmouth	63
53	Lafayette ■	64
74	Manhattan	72
77	Hofstra †	64
80	Iona ■	87
83	Loyola (Md.) ■	58
75	Niagara	89
71	Manhattan ■	86
66	Canisius	73
70	Niagara ■	77
57	Fairfield	79
73	Loyola (Md.)	54
76	Rider	80
86	Rider ■	83
80	Seton Hall	97
72	Marist ■	68
86	Marist †	91
89	Iona	98
79	Canisius ■	60
71	Fairfield ■	73
69	Siena	100
77	Rider †	73
60	Fairfield †	68

Nickname: Peacocks
Colors: Blue & White
Arena: Yanitelli Center
　　Capacity: 3,200; Year Built: 1975
AD: William Stein
SID: Tim Camp

ST. ROSE
Albany, NY 12203 II

Coach: Brian Beaury, St. Rose 1982
2002-03 RESULTS (19-11)
82	Kutztown †	80
73	Barton †	78
63	Le Moyne	59
72	Southern Conn. St. ■	68
81	Pace	69
94	St. Michael's ■	89
87	Assumption	89
108	Dominican (N.Y.) ■	98
104	NYIT ■	78
86	Southern N.H. ■	83
52	Bryant	75
61	Mass.-Lowell ■	75
93	Southern N.H.	97
92	Franklin Pierce ■	83
76	American Int'l ■	62
103	Stonehill	73
85	Merrimack ■	89
95	Bentley ■	76
58	Southern Conn. St.	83
84	Pace ■	77
97	St. Michael's	95
100	St. Anselm ■	91
58	Le Moyne ■	57
86	Bentley	102
98	Merrimack ■	91

63	Stonehill	53
90	St. Anselm	101
94	Le Moyne ■	88
66	Southern N.H.	73
68	Mass.-Lowell	91

Nickname: Golden Knights
Colors: Gold, White & Black
Arena: Activities Center
    Capacity: 500; Year Built: 1977
AD: Catherine Haker
SID: David Alexander

ST. SCHOLASTICA
Duluth, MN 55811-4199..........III

Coach: David Staniger, St. Scholastica
1992
2002-03 RESULTS (9-19)

71	Hamline	95
56	Buena Vista	90
61	Augsburg ■	71
82	Minn.-Morris ■	78
75	North Cent. (Minn.) ■	62
74	Cardinal Stritch	104
75	Viterbo	87
62	Minn. Duluth	87
67	Bemidji St.	102
58	Wis.-Superior	88
53	Wis.-Eau Claire ■	82
67	La Verne	77
61	Pomona-Pitzer	72
91	Presentation ■	77
88	Northwestern (Minn.) ■	100
77	North Cent. (Minn.)	80
74	Northland	49
80	Presentation	82
74	Crown ■	64
69	Martin Luther	74
69	Northwestern (Minn.)	82
74	Finlandia ■	92
68	Northland ■	52
71	Crown	62
75	Martin Luther ■	93
84	Northland †	78
66	Northwestern (Minn.) †	44
63	Presentation †	74

Nickname: Saints
Colors: Royal Blue & Gold
Arena: Reif Center
    Capacity: 1,500; Year Built: 1975
AD: Dana Moore
SID: Jen Walter

ST. THOMAS (MINN.)
St. Paul, MN 55105................III

Coach: Steve Fritz, St. Thomas (Minn.)
1971
2002-03 RESULTS (21-6)

56	Salem Int'l †	65
79	Grand Canyon	70
88	Northwestern (Minn.)	51
56	St. John's (Minn.)	66
75	Hamline ■	65
65	St. Mary's (Minn.) ■	45
78	Buena Vista †	74
77	Wis.-River Falls	72
75	Augsburg	57
67	Concordia-M'head ■	59
74	Gust. Adolphus ■	70
61	Macalester ■	58
66	Carleton	56
74	St. Olaf ■	65
71	Bethel (Minn.)	84
69	St. John's (Minn.) ■	60
68	Hamline	84
65	St. Mary's (Minn.)	62
73	Augsburg ■	67
68	Concordia-M'head	57
53	Gust. Adolphus	51

67	Macalester	56
71	Carleton ■	66
80	St. Olaf	82
84	Bethel (Minn.) ■	74
60	St. John's (Minn.) ■	57
36	Gust. Adolphus ■	62

Nickname: Tommies
Colors: Purple & Grey
Arena: Schoenecker Arena
    Capacity: 2,200; Year Built: 1982
AD: Stephen Fritz
SID: Gene McGivern

ST. THOMAS AQUINAS
Sparkill, NY 10976................II

Coach: Dennis O'Donnell,
St. John's (N.Y.) 1980
2002-03 RESULTS (3-23)

61	Dowling	68
66	Slippery Rock	75
70	St. Vincent	81
43	Philadelphia U. ■	64
47	Mercy	63
59	Queens (N.Y.) ■	64
54	Molloy	66
68	Southampton	76
41	Bridgeport	72
42	Adelphi ■	66
47	C.W. Post ■	69
90	Concordia (N.Y.)	80
55	NYIT ■	71
67	Philadelphia U.	85
54	Queens (N.Y.)	53
50	Southampton ■	76
67	Molloy	72
62	Mercy ■	64
54	New Haven	82
46	New Haven ■	66
48	Bridgeport ■	62
59	Adelphi	83
62	Dowling	65
56	C.W. Post ■	66
46	NYIT	80
64	Concordia (N.Y.)	50

Nickname: Spartans
Colors: Maroon & Gold
AD: Gerald Oswald
SID: To be named

SALEM INT'L
Salem, WV 26426................II

Coach: Danny Young, Grand Canyon
1990
2002-03 RESULTS (25-6)

65	St. Thomas (Minn.) †	56
79	St. Xavier †	84
93	St. Paul's ■	66
86	Franklin Pierce ■	76
99	Fayetteville St. ■	78
73	Fayetteville St.	64
76	Shaw ■	71
89	N.C. Central ■	88
72	Belmont Abbey ■	78
94	Bluefield St.	64
88	West Va. Wesleyan	77
79	Alderson-Broaddus ■	68
85	Shepherd ■	75
97	Glenville St. ■	81
87	Charleston (W.Va.)	82
65	West Liberty St. ■	78
77	Wheeling Jesuit ■	74
85	Ohio Valley ■	72
82	Fairmont St.	65
106	Davis & Elkins ■	62
79	Concord	62
80	West Virginia St. ■	78
97	West Va. Tech ■	82
82	West Liberty St.	69

99	Wheeling Jesuit ■	85
98	Ohio Valley ■	72
66	Fairmont St.	75
87	Shepherd †	60
91	Charleston (W.Va.)	98
76	Calif. (Pa.) †	73
87	Queens (N.C.)	100

Nickname: Tigers
Colors: Kelly Green & White
Arena: T. Edward Davis Gym
    Capacity: 1,620
AD: Don Appiarius
SID: David Zinn

SALEM ST.
Salem, MA 01970................III

Coach: Brian Meehan, Clark (Mass.)
1986
2002-03 RESULTS (23-6)

87	Elms †	70
78	Eastern Conn. St.	66
73	Plymouth St. ■	71
75	Babson ■	81
82	Gordon	69
74	Mass.-Boston ■	85
65	Springfield	91
104	Castleton St. ■	72
85	Bates ■	75
88	Tufts ■	78
60	MIT ■	58
90	Fitchburg St.	80
92	Westfield St. ■	76
59	Framingham St.	63
105	Mass. Liberal Arts	84
84	Bridgewater St. ■	70
88	Worcester St. ■	76
80	Mass.-Dartmouth	77
90	Fitchburg St. ■	65
75	Westfield St.	76
94	Southern Me.	76
82	Framingham St. ■	48
101	Mass. Liberal Arts ■	75
86	Bridgewater St.	73
81	Worcester St. ■	65
75	Bridgewater St.	70
76	Worcester St. ■	68
81	St. Joseph's (Me.) ■	76
67	Williams	94

Nickname: Vikings
Colors: Orange & Blue
Arena: O'Keefe Sports Center
    Capacity: 2,200; Year Built: 1976
AD: Timothy Shea
SID: Thomas Roundy

SALISBURY
Salisbury, MD 21801-6860......III

Coach: Steve Holmes, Plattsburgh St.
1983
2002-03 RESULTS (6-20)

58	Alvernia	88
65	Delaware Valley †	67
80	Washington (Md.) ■	70
79	Chris. Newport	82
64	St. Mary's (Md.) †	68
64	Catholic	82
97	Lincoln (Pa.) ■	86
52	St. John Fisher ■	67
68	Va. Wesleyan	79
50	King's (Pa.) ■	66
67	Susquehanna †	90
96	Southern Va. ■	98
76	St. Mary's (Md.)	73
84	Gallaudet ■	78
82	York (Pa.)	86
72	Goucher	67
58	Mary Washington	72
72	Marymount (Va.) ■	101

72	St. Mary's (Md.) ■	82
85	Catholic	97
57	York (Pa.) ■	82
81	Gallaudet	76
44	Goucher ■	75
57	Marymount (Va.)	67
65	Mary Washington	85
67	Goucher	82

Nickname: Sea Gulls
Colors: Maroon & Gold
Arena: Maggs Activities Center
    Capacity: 2,000; Year Built: 1977
AD: Michael Vienna
SID: Paul Ohanian

SALVE REGINA
Newport, RI 02840-4192........III

Coach: Sean Foster, Salve Regina 1997
2002-03 RESULTS (11-14)

56	Mass.-Dartmouth	78
71	Bowdoin †	72
66	Wheaton (Mass.) ■	69
104	New England	86
58	Amherst	92
67	Connecticut Col.	81
60	New England Col. ■	48
63	Nichols	68
70	Clark (Mass.) ■	100
55	Gordon ■	68
79	Anna Maria ■	81
67	Curry ■	64
55	Colby-Sawyer	70
79	Wentworth Inst. ■	57
60	Roger Williams ■	50
59	Endicott	71
85	Rhode Island Col. ■	78
68	Eastern Nazarene	54
66	Nichols ■	42
70	Curry	87
67	Eastern Nazarene ■	56
75	Anna Maria	82
85	Johnson & Wales	80
64	Roger Williams ■	59
48	Colby-Sawyer	69

Nickname: Seahawks
Colors: Blue, Green & White
Arena: Rogers Gymnasium
    Capacity: 4,000
AD: Del Malloy
SID: Ed Habershaw

SAM HOUSTON ST.
Huntsville, TX 77340................I

Coach: Bob Marlin, Mississippi St. 1981
2002-03 RESULTS (23-7)

81	TCU	91
105	Austin ■	47
66	St. Mary's (Cal.) †	75
65	Idaho St. †	58
67	Arkansas	78
87	Texas-Dallas ■	57
61	Lamar ■	47
85	McNeese St.	78
74	Southeastern La. ■	65
84	Nicholls St. ■	45
60	Texas St.	69
82	Texas-San Antonio	65
62	Texas-Arlington	60
70	Stephen F. Austin	77
83	La.-Monroe ■	66
76	Northwestern St. ■	62
62	Lamar	58
66	Tex. A&M-Corp. Chris. ■	59
74	Southeastern La.	69
76	Nicholls St.	65
79	Texas St. ■	71
72	Texas-San Antonio ■	50
56	Texas-Arlington ■	52

69	Stephen F. Austin ■	62
71	La.-Monroe	78
83	Northwestern St.	72
81	McNeese St. ■	66
64	McNeese St. ■	58
69	Stephen F. Austin ■	66
55	Florida †	85

Nickname: Bearkats
Colors: Orange & White
Arena: Johnson Coliseum
   Capacity: 6,110; Year Built: 1976
AD: Bobby Williams
SID: Paul Ridings

SAMFORD
Birmingham, AL 35229 I

Coach: Jimmy Tillette, Lady/Holy Cross 1975
2002-03 RESULTS (13-15)

66	Chattanooga ■	68
70	Arkansas St. ■	61
90	North Ga. ■	81
68	Arkansas St.	67
49	Southwest Mo. St.	80
64	Florida Int'l †	54
79	Valparaiso	87
45	Ill.-Chicago	73
68	Chattanooga	77
51	South Ala.	74
49	Mississippi	57
51	Belmont ■	52
62	Campbell	53
52	Gardner-Webb	56
80	Georgia St. ■	78
74	Jacksonville St. ■	62
68	Mercer	74
48	Troy St.	66
73	Fla. Atlantic	53
52	UCF	58
79	Stetson ■	71
70	Jacksonville ■	43
63	Jacksonville St.	74
78	Georgia St.	74
63	Gardner-Webb ■	54
63	Campbell ■	44
64	Belmont	72
54	Troy St. †	70

Nickname: Bulldogs
Colors: Red & Blue
Arena: Seibert Hall
   Capacity: 4,000; Year Built: 1957
AD: Bob Roller
SID: Craig Threlkeld

SAN DIEGO
San Diego, CA 92110-2492 I

Coach: Brad Holland, UCLA 1979
2002-03 RESULTS (18-12)

77	Nevada ■	75
86	UCLA	81
84	UC Riverside	64
61	Cal St. Northridge ■	64
81	IUPUI †	74
65	Purdue	95
49	Brigham Young	64
105	UC San Diego ■	62
73	UC Riverside ■	62
58	Utah ■	64
70	Nevada	81
82	Southern Methodist	88
72	San Diego St.	78
65	Santa Clara ■	67
82	Loyola Marymount	68
88	Pepperdine	73
74	San Francisco ■	69
65	Gonzaga	89
78	Portland	77
76	St. Mary's (Cal.) ■	69
78	Santa Clara	66

93	Pepperdine ■	98
73	Loyola Marymount ■	51
75	St. Mary's (Cal.)	57
81	San Francisco	63
92	Portland ■	69
69	Gonzaga ■	72
72	San Francisco ■	63
72	Gonzaga ■	63
69	Stanford †	77

Nickname: Toreros
Colors: Columbia Blue, Navy & White
Arena: Jenny Craig Pavilion
   Capacity: 5,100; Year Built: 2000
AD: Thomas Iannacone
SID: Ted Gosen

SAN DIEGO ST.
San Diego, CA 92182 I

Coach: Steve Fisher, Illinois St. 1967
2002-03 RESULTS (16-14)

70	Eastern Wash. ■	75
86	Portland	91
65	Cal Poly	62
87	UC San Diego ■	57
81	Arizona	89
64	Long Beach St.	55
60	Hawaii ■	49
71	Houston	61
91	Fla. Atlantic ■	75
74	IPFW ■	58
79	Loyola Marymount ■	69
63	Texas Tech	75
78	San Diego ■	72
63	Air Force	48
58	Utah ■	56
69	Brigham Young ■	80
62	New Mexico	66
69	Colorado St. ■	72
80	Wyoming ■	70
64	UNLV ■	79
62	Utah	76
64	Brigham Young	66
67	Air Force ■	53
89	New Mexico ■	73
86	Wyoming	73
89	Colorado St.	102
72	UNLV	83
67	UNLV	83
67	UC Santa Barb. ■	62
48	Texas Tech	57

Nickname: Aztecs
Colors: Scarlet & Black
Arena: Cox Arena
   Capacity: 12,414; Year Built: 1997
AD: Ellene Gibbs
SID: Mike May

SAN FRANCISCO
San Francisco, CA 94117-1080 ..I

Coach: Philip Mathews, UC Irvine 1972
2002-03 RESULTS (15-14)

51	Seton Hall	77
61	Nevada ■	64
47	UC Santa Barb.	70
82	Southern U.	71
57	Sacramento St.	62
71	Fresno St. ■	74
59	Pacific (Cal.)	75
73	Sonoma St. ■	59
84	Brigham Young ■	72
75	Cal St. Fullerton ■	61
70	California	77
64	Michigan	74
81	Brown	52
62	St. Mary's (Cal.)	68
73	Portland	59
56	Gonzaga	66
55	Santa Clara	52
69	San Diego	74

87	Pepperdine ■	77
91	Loyola Marymount ■	73
68	St. Mary's (Cal.)	67
72	Portland	55
71	Gonzaga	82
78	Santa Clara ■	65
63	San Diego	81
75	Loyola Marymount	69
90	Pepperdine	82
70	Loyola Marymount †	56
63	San Diego	72

Nickname: Dons
Colors: Green & Gold
Arena: War Memorial Gymnasium
   Capacity: 5,300; Year Built: 1958
AD: William Hogan
SID: Peter Simon

SAN FRAN. ST.
San Francisco, CA 94132 II

Coach: Charlie Thomas, Virginia Tech 1978
2002-03 RESULTS (11-16)

87	UC Santa Cruz ■	58
83	Dominican (Cal.) ■	76
68	Sonoma St. ■	59
70	Concordia (Cal.) ■	76
77	Humboldt St.	78
58	Sonoma St.	68
48	Metro St. ■	65
96	Cal St. Chico ■	72
74	UC Davis	56
88	Cal St. Stanislaus ■	94
65	Cal St. Bakersfield ■	72
75	Cal St. Dom. Hills	62
64	Cal St. L.A.	67
57	Cal St. San B'dino	78
53	Cal Poly Pomona	71
75	Grand Canyon ■	71
71	UC San Diego	63
66	UC Davis	68
66	Cal St. Chico	87
56	Cal St. Bakersfield	66
55	Cal St. Stanislaus	70
66	Cal St. L.A.	56
87	Cal St. Dom. Hills ■	67
54	Cal Poly Pomona ■	55
67	Cal St. San B'dino	77
56	UC San Diego	72
86	Grand Canyon	80

Nickname: Gators
Colors: Purple & Gold
Arena: SFSU Main Gym
   Capacity: 2,000; Year Built: 1949
AD: Michael Simpson
SID: Joe Danahey

SAN JOSE ST.
San Jose, CA 95192 I

Coach: Phil Johnson, East Central Okla. 1981
2002-03 RESULTS (7-21)

68	Washington St.	76
98	Menlo ■	73
71	Santa Clara	69
62	St. Mary's (Cal.)	94
70	Cal St. Monterey Bay ■	52
70	Sacramento St.	72
67	Cal St. Northridge	92
61	Pacific (Cal.) ■	70
75	Brown	86
56	Boise St.	58
68	UTEP	80
67	Louisiana Tech ■	80
72	Southern Methodist ■	79
79	Hawaii ■	67
59	Nevada	86
48	Fresno St.	59

58	Tulsa ■	57
66	Rice ■	71
69	Southern Methodist	82
60	Louisiana Tech	65
55	Hawaii	54
70	Fresno St. ■	74
66	Nevada ■	74
52	Rice	65
53	Tulsa	74
74	UTEP ■	73
47	Boise St. ■	65
80	UTEP †	86

Nickname: Spartans
Colors: Gold, White & Blue
Arena: The Event Center
   Capacity: 5,000; Year Built: 1989
AD: Charles Bell
SID: Lawrence Fan

SANTA CLARA
Santa Clara, CA 95053 I

Coach: Dick Davey, Pacific (Cal) 1964
2002-03 RESULTS (13-15)

78	Pacific (Cal.)	72
93	UC Santa Cruz ■	70
69	Montana St. ■	66
69	San Jose St. ■	71
55	Fresno St.	70
55	Washington	72
67	Nevada ■	62
55	UMBC	54
81	Loyola (Md.) ■	56
70	Mississippi Val. ■	63
77	Princeton ■	71
71	Wright St. ■	67
53	UNLV	75
67	San Diego	65
69	Pepperdine	73
69	Loyola Marymount	75
52	San Francisco ■	55
66	St. Mary's (Cal.) ■	63
66	San Diego ■	78
61	Loyola Marymount ■	73
73	Pepperdine ■	61
65	San Francisco	78
57	St. Mary's (Cal.)	56
66	Gonzaga ■	71
63	Portland ■	75
51	St. Mary's (Cal.) †	65

Nickname: Broncos
Colors: Santa Clara Red & White
Arena: Leavey Center
   Capacity: 5,000; Year Built: 1975
AD: Cheryl Levick
SID: Richard Kilwien

SCAD
Savannah, GA 31402-3146 III

Coach: Cazzie Russell, Michigan 1966
2002-03 RESULTS (21-6)

65	Huntingdon	62
64	Maryville (Tenn.)	59
76	Otterbein †	72
64	Methodist	76
69	Emory	86
78	Ferrum	63
70	Flagler	71
64	Southwestern (Tex.) ■	60
61	LaGrange	67
58	Chris. Newport	66
70	Principia †	58
51	Marietta	42
81	MacMurray †	61
69	Edgewood	60
72	Methodist ■	66
76	Ferrum ■	47

69	Mt. St. Joseph ■	52
80	Newport News ■	69
68	Maryville (Tenn.) ■	58
78	Fisk ■	73
72	Rust ■	60
83	Flagler ■	58
82	Rust	63
64	Newport News ■	60
82	St. Mary's (Md.) ■	68
66	Chris. Newport	61
54	Hampden-Sydney	56

Nickname: Bees
Colors: Black & Gold
Arena: Savannah Civic Center
  Capacity: 7,500; Year Built: 1974
AD: Jud Damon
SID: Michael MacEachern

SAVANNAH ST.
Savannah, GA 31404 I

Coach: Ed Daniels Jr., Marquette 1974
2002-03 RESULTS (3-24)

46	Florida St.	79
47	Jacksonville ■	60
57	Miami (Fla.)	91
62	Ga. Southern ■	74
78	Alabama A&M	97
59	Iowa St.	79
47	Tulane	103
67	Ga. Southern	83
66	Mercer ■	84
53	Tex. A&M-Corp. Chris. ■	80
33	Air Force	56
77	Wyoming	112
76	Lipscomb ■	66
53	Jacksonville	73
54	Bethune-Cookman ■	66
59	Morris Brown	75
60	Bethune-Cookman	50
58	Birmingham-So. ■	70
73	Jacksonville St. ■	78
73	Lipscomb	96
71	Jacksonville St.	87
77	Tex. A&M-Corp. Chris.	96
62	Tex.-Pan American	76
72	Mercer	97
39	Tex.-Pan American ■	45
67	Morris Brown ■	58
75	Birmingham-So.	92

Nickname: Tigers
Colors: Reflex Blue & Orange
Arena: Wiley Gym
  Capacity: 2,100; Year Built: 1964
AD: Hank Ford
SID: Lee Pearson

SCHREINER
Kerrville, TX 78028 III

Coach: Thirman Dimery
2002-03 RESULTS (2-23)

60	Texas Wesleyan	88
95	Louisiana Col.	109
54	Mississippi Col.	83
91	East Tex. Baptist ■	106
69	LeTourneau ■	92
74	Texas Lutheran	97
65	Tex.-Pan American	100
65	Wayland Baptist	100
82	Texas-Dallas	83
83	Texas Lutheran ■	89
83	Ozarks (Ark.) ■	92
73	Austin ■	79
61	Sul Ross St.	89
95	Howard Payne	114
72	Mary Hardin-Baylor	75
88	Concordia-Austin ■	81
58	St. Mary's (Tex.)	100
61	Hardin-Simmons	68

99	McMurry	108
70	Hardin-Simmons ■	66
89	McMurry ■	97
70	Sul Ross St. ■	95
96	Howard Payne ■	98
80	Mary Hardin-Baylor ■	104
77	Concordia-Austin	81

Nickname: Mountaineers
Colors: Maroon & White
AD: Barry Shaw
SID: Stacey Patsko

SCRANTON
Scranton, PA 18510 III

Coach: Carl Danzig, Baker 1987
2002-03 RESULTS (24-6)

70	Gallaudet †	48
71	Susquehanna	73
79	Marywood	60
66	Catholic ■	71
84	Delaware Valley ■	52
79	Drew	71
75	Elizabethtown ■	72
85	Coe †	84
75	Buffalo St. †	66
81	Hartwick ■	60
92	Case Reserve ■	64
65	Kean ■	62
75	FDU-Florham ■	63
67	Moravian ■	55
73	King's (Pa.) ■	86
57	DeSales	53
75	Wilkes ■	66
69	Lycoming	92
74	Drew ■	59
76	Delaware Valley	64
77	King's (Pa.) ■	71
79	FDU-Florham	64
79	DeSales ■	85
83	Lycoming ■	54
82	Wilkes	77
71	King's (Pa.) ■	70
72	DeSales ■	65
58	Buffalo St. ■	56
77	Ursinus ■	75
64	Wooster	75

Nickname: Royals
Colors: Purple & White
Arena: John Long Center
  Capacity: 2,800; Year Built: 1968
AD: Toby Lovecchio
SID: Kevin Southard

SEATTLE
Seattle, WA 98122-4340 II

Coach: Joe Callero, Central Wash. 1986
2002-03 RESULTS (16-11)

71	Biola ■	60
62	N.C. Central ■	60
38	Oregon St.	81
70	Seattle Pacific	64
58	Alas. Fairbanks ■	78
71	Alas. Anchorage ■	59
75	Evergreen St.	70
77	Grand Canyon	78
77	Pacific Lutheran ■	65
77	Rocky Mountain ■	67
87	UC Santa Cruz ■	67
89	Western Ore.	81
56	Humboldt St.	70
87	Northwest Nazarene ■	85
91	Central Wash.	89
67	St. Martin's ■	64
66	Seattle Pacific	80
73	Western Wash.	65
60	Humboldt St. ■	86
63	Western Ore. ■	73
79	Northwest Nazarene	61

71	St. Martin's	64
71	Central Wash.	74
80	Western Wash. ■	77
70	Seattle Pacific ■	84
70	Alas. Anchorage	85
59	Alas. Fairbanks	81

Nickname: Redhawks
Colors: Scarlet & White
AD: Todd Schilperoort
SID: To be named

SEATTLE PACIFIC
Seattle, WA 98119-1997 II

Coach: Jeff Hironaka, Eastern Ore. 1980
2002-03 RESULTS (16-11)

80	Minn. Duluth ■	70
84	Central Wash. ■	81
71	Warner Pacific ■	66
64	Seattle ■	70
81	Central Wash. ■	71
79	St. Martin's ■	56
65	Mo. Western St. †	70
64	Pittsburg St. †	70
80	Nevada	89
95	UC Santa Cruz ■	60
67	Rocky Mountain ■	83
76	Western Wash. ■	83
86	Alas. Anchorage ■	68
95	Alas. Fairbanks ■	71
88	Western Ore.	77
70	Humboldt St.	80
80	Seattle	66
95	Northwest Nazarene ■	58
80	Western Wash.	72
78	Alas. Fairbanks	86
84	Alas. Anchorage	90
113	Humboldt St. ■	108
86	Western Ore. ■	84
76	Northwest Nazarene	83
84	Seattle	70
96	St. Martin's ■	61
102	Central Wash. ■	105

Nickname: Falcons
Colors: Maroon & White
Arena: Brougham Pavilion
  Capacity: 2,650; Year Built: 1953
AD: Tom Box
SID: Frank MacDonald

SETON HALL
South Orange, NJ 07079 I

Coach: Louis Orr, Syracuse 1980
2002-03 RESULTS (17-13)

77	San Francisco ■	51
61	Texas †	78
84	St. Francis (N.Y.) ■	76
67	Monmouth ■	57
70	Louisville ■	91
54	Ohio St.	71
41	DePaul	52
71	Stony Brook ■	48
75	Rider ■	60
66	St. John's (N.Y.)	74
66	Syracuse ■	70
64	Notre Dame	74
68	Georgetown ■	54
76	Miami (Fla.) ■	53
65	Syracuse	83
70	Manhattan ■	74
93	Georgetown	82
58	Rutgers ■	53
78	Notre Dame ■	72
97	St. Peter's ■	80
73	Pittsburgh ■	61
68	West Virginia ■	64
62	Rutgers	52
57	Villanova ■	56
56	West Virginia ■	53

54	Pittsburgh	86
61	Providence	64
67	Miami (Fla.) †	52
70	Connecticut †	83
60	Rhode Island	61

Nickname: Pirates
Colors: Blue & White
Arena: Continental Airlines Arena
  Capacity: 20,029; Year Built: 1981
AD: Jeffrey Fogelson
SID: Marie Wozniak

SEWANEE
Sewanee, TN 37383-1000.......III

Coach: Joe Thoni, Sewanee 1979
2002-03 RESULTS (8-17)

79	Huntingdon ■	55
68	Earlham ■	78
82	Emory	98
78	Maryville (Tenn.)	100
82	Emory ■	93
56	Furman	76
65	Dallas	82
57	Huntingdon	58
57	Centre	61
73	Rhodes ■	81
73	Hendrix ■	51
63	Millsaps	68
71	Oglethorpe	73
67	DePauw	86
67	Rose-Hulman	72
99	Oakwood ■	69
71	Centre ■	83
66	Fisk ■	55
44	Trinity (Tex.) ■	66
111	Southwestern (Tex.) ■	108
77	Rhodes	76
60	Hendrix	51
73	Millsaps ■	69
100	Oglethorpe ■	114
60	Trinity (Tex.) †	75

Nickname: Tigers
Colors: Purple & White
Arena: Juhan Gymnasium
  Capacity: 1,000; Year Built: 1955
AD: Mark Webb
SID: Larry Dagenhart

SHAW
Raleigh, NC 27601 II

Coach: Michael Bernard, Kentucky St. 1970
2002-03 RESULTS (21-9)

78	Claflin ■	68
73	N.C. Central	60
63	Presbyterian ■	58
85	Catawba	79
75	Fayetteville St.	74
84	N.J. Inst. of Tech.	72
71	Salem Int'l	76
69	Tampa	58
61	Columbus St.	75
55	GC&SU †	47
68	Morehouse	50
61	Elizabeth City St. ■	46
72	Bowie St.	80
66	Virginia St. ■	75
66	Winston-Salem	70
79	St. Paul's	52
70	Livingstone	61
69	Virginia Union ■	65
71	Fayetteville St.	55
62	Elizabeth City St.	51
74	St. Paul's ■	66
61	Bowie St. ■	58
58	Virginia Union	73
66	Johnson Smith	73
75	Virginia St.	48

65 St. Augustine's ■ 53
73 Livingstone ■ 62
63 St. Augustine's ■ 78
72 Johnson Smith ■ 58
58 Presbyterian † 77

Nickname: Bears
Colors: Maroon & White
Arena: Spaulding Gym
  Capacity: 1,000; Year Built: 1946
AD: Alfonza Carter
SID: To be named

SHENANDOAH
Winchester, VA 22601 III

Coach: Robert Harris, Shenandoah 1991
2002-03 RESULTS (13-13)
71 Christendom ■ 47
67 Mary Washington ■ 52
80 East. Mennonite ■ 41
81 Southern Va. ■ 72
76 Frostburg St. ■ 59
70 Presbyterian 79
79 Southern Va. 64
82 Lycoming 96
86 Elizabethtown ■ 76
46 Chris. Newport ■ 72
78 Averett 52
59 Ferrum 61
43 N.C. Wesleyan 74
41 Chowan 59
71 Villa Julie 80
46 Methodist ■ 74
66 Greensboro ■ 53
59 Chris. Newport 85
83 Averett ■ 56
91 Ferrum ■ 71
65 N.C. Wesleyan ■ 86
62 Chowan 53
50 Greensboro 76
81 Methodist 90
67 Greensboro ■ 65
70 Chris. Newport ■ 94

Nickname: Hornets
Colors: Red, White & Midnight Blue
Arena: Shingleton Gymnasium
  Capacity: 680; Year Built: 1969
AD: John Hill
SID: Scott Musa

SHEPHERD
Shepherdstown, WV 25443-3210 II

Coach: Ken Tyler, William & Mary 1987
2002-03 RESULTS (12-17)
84 Columbia Union ■ 59
64 Belmont Abbey ■ 81
78 Shippensburg ■ 72
77 Bloomsburg 74
55 Eastern Ky. 78
75 Pitt.-Johnstown 83
66 Bowie St. ■ 85
83 Davis & Elkins 77
50 Newport News ■ 51
84 Wheeling Jesuit ■ 72
67 West Liberty St. ■ 71
75 Salem Int'l 85
72 Fairmont St. 79
66 Alderson-Broaddus 81
70 West Va. Tech ■ 72
82 Charleston (W.Va.) ■ 90
71 Bluefield St. 59
58 Concord 66
69 West Virginia St. ■ 66
56 Ohio Valley 71
61 Glenville St. 74
66 Dist. Columbia 83
80 Davis & Elkins ■ 63

87 West Va. Wesleyan ■ 73
81 Glenville St. ■ 69
75 Alderson-Broaddus ■ 95
81 West Va. Wesleyan ■ 72
82 West Liberty St. 76
60 Salem Int'l † 87

Nickname: Rams
Colors: Blue & Gold
Arena: Butcher Athletic Center
  Capacity: 3,500; Year Built: 1989
AD: Monte Cater
SID: Chip Ransom

SHIPPENSBURG
Shippensburg, PA 17257 II

Coach: Dave Springer, Ohio 1982
2002-03 RESULTS (8-19)
86 Barton ■ 95
79 Kutztown ■ 70
72 Shepherd 78
84 Dickinson 68
98 East Stroudsburg 95
70 Bloomsburg 81
63 Fairmont St. ■ 79
79 West Chester ■ 81
78 Millersville ■ 71
64 Incarnate Word 76
68 St. Mary's (Tex.) 80
67 Cheyney 78
68 Kutztown 76
57 Pitt.-Johnstown ■ 60
76 Mansfield 90
76 Slippery Rock 58
72 Lock Haven ■ 78
58 Edinboro 70
45 Calif. (Pa.) ■ 46
67 Clarion 66
72 Indiana (Pa.) 90
51 Slippery Rock ■ 62
60 Edinboro 71
72 Lock Haven 79
61 Calif. (Pa.) 80
90 Indiana (Pa.) ■ 82
98 Clarion ■ 96

Nickname: Red Raiders
Colors: Red & Blue
Arena: Heiges Field House
  Capacity: 2,768; Year Built: 1970
AD: Roberta Page
SID: John Alosi

SIENA
Loudonville, NY 12211-1462 I

Coach: Rob Lanier, St. Bonaventure 1990
2002-03 RESULTS (21-11)
79 Albany (N.Y.) ■ 75
78 Fordham 69
69 Northern Iowa ■ 58
55 Toledo 59
71 Canisius ■ 63
81 St. Peter's 63
78 Delaware ■ 87
88 Xavier ■ 96
79 Loyola Marymount † 71
71 Montana St. 58
89 Providence ■ 81
66 Manhattan 82
65 Iona ■ 55
78 Niagara 73
77 Canisius 84
71 Fairfield 80
81 Loyola (Md.) ■ 65
81 Marist 68
74 Fairfield 71
74 Marist ■ 79
77 Rider ■ 87
64 Iona 65

75 Loyola (Md.) 58
84 Niagara ■ 71
72 Rider 61
72 Manhattan ■ 68
100 St. Peter's ■ 69
70 Marist † 68
63 Fairfield † 67
74 Villanova 59
68 Western Mich. ■ 62
71 UAB ■ 80

Nickname: Saints
Colors: Green & Gold
Arena: Pepsi Arena
  Capacity: 15,500; Year Built: 1990
AD: John D'Argenio
SID: Jason Rich

SIMPSON
Indianola, IA 50125 III

Coach: Bruce Wilson, Simpson 1976
2002-03 RESULTS (14-12)
82 Wis.-Platteville † 72
59 Benedictine (Ill.) † 61
101 Graceland (Iowa) 74
86 Upper Iowa ■ 62
92 Grand View ■ 70
81 Ramapo † 95
87 Concordia (Ill.) † 67
80 Edgewood † 66
70 Buena Vista 82
73 Wartburg 65
94 Central (Iowa) 75
76 Luther ■ 64
69 Coe ■ 68
81 Cornell College ■ 80
63 Dubuque 51
57 Loras 68
74 Luther 82
68 Wartburg ■ 76
61 Buena Vista 74
70 Central (Iowa) 76
80 Upper Iowa 61
81 Cornell College 85
79 Coe 83
68 Loras 69
109 Dubuque ■ 73
57 Loras 75

Nickname: Storm
Colors: Red & Gold
Arena: Cowles Fieldhouse
  Capacity: 3,000; Year Built: 1976
AD: John Sirianni
SID: Matt Turk

SKIDMORE
Saratoga Springs, NY 12866 ...III

Coach: John Quattrocchi, Albany (N.Y.) 1973
2002-03 RESULTS (12-12)
86 Bard ■ 21
66 D'Youville ■ 65
70 Middlebury 84
105 Hampshire ■ 69
59 Wesleyan (Conn.) ■ 61
68 Utica 55
74 Castleton St. ■ 62
67 Manhattanville 72
94 Mass. Liberal Arts ■ 69
82 Union (N.Y.) 78
75 Vassar 46
72 Rensselaer 63
65 Hobart ■ 83
78 Hamilton 98
79 St. Lawrence 90
67 Clarkson 65
98 Hartwick ■ 97
70 Hamilton 81
85 Hobart 93

64 Union (N.Y.) 65
73 Rensselaer ■ 63
62 Vassar 63
55 Clarkson ■ 56
59 St. Lawrence ■ 75

Nickname: Thoroughbreds
Colors: Green, White & Gold
Arena: Sports & Recreation Center
  Capacity: 1,500; Year Built: 1982
AD: Jeff Segrave
SID: Bill Jones

SLIPPERY ROCK
Slippery Rock, PA 16057 II

Coach: John Marhefka, Hiram 1993
2002-03 RESULTS (8-17)
75 St. Thomas Aquinas ■ 66
52 Youngstown St. 73
82 Geneva 60
66 Kutztown ■ 60
55 Cheyney ■ 57
67 Glenville St. 66
57 Mansfield ■ 75
58 West Chester 69
52 Millersville 67
70 Bloomsburg 65
69 East Stroudsburg 79
67 Edinboro 90
58 Shippensburg ■ 68
54 Clarion 65
57 St. Vincent 62
49 Indiana (Pa.) 65
49 Lock Haven 55
75 Calif. (Pa.) 78
62 Shippensburg 51
60 Edinboro 66
60 Pitt.-Johnstown ■ 58
67 Clarion ■ 62
66 Indiana (Pa.) ■ 72
55 Calif. (Pa.) 73
50 Lock Haven ■ 55

Nickname: The Rock
Colors: Green & White
Arena: Morrow Field House
  Capacity: 3,000; Year Built: 1962
AD: Paul Lueken
SID: Bob McComas

SONOMA ST.
Rohnert Park, CA 94928-3609 ..II

Coach: Pat Fuscaldo, San Fran. St. 1983
2002-03 RESULTS (18-10)
80 Holy Names ■ 59
59 San Fran. St. 68
79 Holy Names ■ 55
61 Dominican (Cal.) ■ 57
68 San Fran. St. 58
59 San Francisco 73
54 Metro St. ■ 60
84 UC Davis ■ 91
74 Cal St. Chico ■ 61
81 Cal St. Bakersfield ■ 74
64 Cal St. Stanislaus ■ 65
54 Cal St. L.A. 49
59 Cal St. Dom. Hills 47
62 Cal Poly Pomona 48
62 Cal St. San B'dino 71
70 UC San Diego ■ 53
85 Grand Canyon ■ 80
74 Cal St. Chico 70
67 UC Davis 59
67 Cal St. Stanislaus 61
36 Cal St. Bakersfield 53
69 Cal St. Dom. Hills ■ 66
69 Cal St. L.A. ■ 60
69 Cal St. San B'dino ■ 78
60 Cal Poly Pomona ■ 62
83 Grand Canyon 75

| 59 | UC San Diego | 49 |
| 58 | Cal St. San B'dino † | 86 |

Nickname: Cossacks
Colors: Navy, Blue & White
Arena: Cossack Gymnasium
  Capacity: 1,800; Year Built: 1968
AD: William Fusco
SID: Mitch Cox

SOUTH ALA.
Mobile, AL 36688 I

Coach: John Pelphrey, Kentucky 1992
2002-03 RESULTS (14-14)

82	Southern U.	61
62	LSU	71
77	Birmingham-So. ■	64
78	Southern Miss.	89
92	North Ga. ■	67
79	Louisville	90
81	Georgia St. ■	68
82	Georgia	94
93	Marist ■	73
74	Samford ■	51
74	Mississippi St. ■	85
61	New Orleans	70
93	La.-Lafayette ■	89
70	New Mexico St. ■	84
64	Middle Tenn.	53
69	Western Ky.	85
59	Denver ■	50
76	North Texas	71
65	Ark.-Little Rock ■	59
63	Arkansas St.	83
60	La.-Lafayette	67
71	New Mexico St.	77
46	Florida Int'l ■	56
50	Denver	77
70	North Texas	60
123	William Carey ■	75
61	New Orleans	58
69	Middle Tenn. †	72

Nickname: Jaguars
Colors: Red, White and Blue
Arena: Mitchell Center
  Capacity: 10,000; Year Built: 1999
AD: Joseph Gottfried
SID: Matt Smith

SOUTH CAROLINA
Columbia, SC 29208 I

Coach: Dave Odom, Guilford 1965
2002-03 RESULTS (12-16)

71	East Tenn. St. ■	66
82	South Carolina St. ■	65
71	Appalachian St. ■	56
66	Temple	47
59	Georgetown	67
64	North Carolina St.	76
70	Wofford ■	59
63	Wyoming	77
67	Colorado St.	81
66	Citadel ■	50
55	Mississippi ■	49
55	Kentucky	62
60	Auburn ■	67
75	Florida ■	77
48	Mississippi St.	64
56	Tennessee	60
69	Kentucky ■	87
58	LSU	71
84	Vanderbilt	72
76	Clemson ■	59
72	Arkansas	65
77	Tennessee ■	63
66	Georgia	79
63	Florida	96
76	Vanderbilt ■	64
59	Alabama	82

| 55 | Georgia ■ | 60 |
| 56 | Mississippi † | 62 |

Nickname: Gamecocks
Colors: Garnet & Black
Arena: The Carolina Center
  Capacity: 18,000; Year Built: 2002
AD: Michael McGee
SID: Brian Binette

SOUTH CAROLINA ST.
Orangeburg, SC 29117-0001....I

Coach: Cy Alexander, Catawba 1975
2002-03 RESULTS (20-11)

53	Coastal Caro. ■	68
65	South Carolina	82
65	Auburn	85
88	Alabama A&M †	75
68	Jacksonville	76
57	Wake Forest	100
78	Citadel	66
57	Montana St.	85
69	Loyola Marymount †	74
81	Morgan St.	79
67	Coppin St.	54
81	Delaware St. ■	53
85	Howard	80
71	Md.-East. Shore	68
76	Norfolk St. ■	64
77	Hampton ■	69
59	N.C. A&T ■	53
87	Bethune-Cookman ■	64
69	Florida A&M ■	63
78	Morgan St. ■	68
72	Coppin St. ■	74
78	Delaware St.	83
90	Howard ■	81
78	Md.-East. Shore ■	58
61	Norfolk St.	63
78	Hampton	73
77	N.C. A&T	74
75	Bethune-Cookman †	73
72	Florida A&M †	66
72	Hampton †	67
54	Oklahoma †	71

Nickname: Bulldogs
Colors: Garnet & Blue
Arena: SHM Memorial Center
  Capacity: 3,200; Year Built: 1968
AD: Timothy Autry
SID: Bill Hamilton

S.C.-AIKEN
Aiken, SC 29801 II

Coach: Mike Roberts, Elon 1977
2002-03 RESULTS (5-23)

67	Presbyterian †	69
77	Newberry	87
64	Carson-Newman ■	70
48	Augusta St.	69
77	UNC Pembroke ■	68
59	Col. of Charleston	91
50	Kennesaw St.	67
73	Catawba ■	65
57	Belmont Abbey ■	66
52	Carson-Newman	53
82	Wingate	89
67	Clayton St.	82
54	Francis Marion ■	66
67	Armstrong Atlantic ■	73
41	S.C.-Spartanburg	62
57	Kennesaw St. ■	81
49	Columbus St.	65
82	North Fla.	83
61	Lander ■	62
70	North Fla.	76
71	Columbus St. ■	88
85	Lander	76
64	GC&SU	68

71	UNC Pembroke	54
94	S.C.-Spartanburg ■	82
58	Francis Marion	71
63	Augusta St. ■	77
71	Clayton St. †	79

Nickname: Pacers
Colors: Cardinal & White
Arena: The Courthouse
  Capacity: 2,500; Year Built: 1977
AD: Douglas Warrick
SID: Brad Fields

S.C.-SPARTANBURG
Spartanburg, SC 29303-4999...II

Coach: Eddie Payne, Wake Forest 1973
2002-03 RESULTS (18-11)

62	Aub.-Montgomery ■	50
68	Lenoir-Rhyne ■	65
72	Limestone	65
63	West Va. Tech	73
79	Columbus St.	81
53	Presbyterian ■	63
92	Edward Waters ■	80
79	Limestone ■	60
58	Tusculum ■	55
73	Augusta St.	87
63	Armstrong Atlantic ■	62
57	Clayton St. ■	68
80	Lander	67
62	S.C.-Aiken	41
75	UNC Pembroke ■	51
65	Armstrong Atlantic	55
54	Francis Marion	65
66	Kennesaw St. ■	56
67	GC&SU	65
63	Augusta St. ■	68
71	Lander ■	52
64	Francis Marion	66
72	North Fla.	67
59	Clayton St. ■	66
82	S.C.-Aiken	94
72	UNC Pembroke	40
68	GC&SU ■	49
61	Armstrong Atlantic †	57
59	Columbus St.	70

Nickname: Rifles
Colors: Green, White & Black
Arena: G.B. Hodge Center
  Capacity: 1,535; Year Built: 1973
AD: Michael Hall
SID: Bill English

SOUTH DAKOTA
Vermillion, SD 57069-2390.......II

Coach: David Boots, Augsburg 1979
2002-03 RESULTS (19-9)

88	Wayne St. (Neb.) ■	63
95	Minn.-Morris ■	45
100	William Penn ■	62
95	Northern St.	87
88	Bellevue ■	67
85	Concordia-St. Paul	72
84	Cal St. San B'dino †	73
95	Western Wash. †	86
98	Southwest Minn. St. ■	86
99	Jamestown ■	76
105	Midland Lutheran ■	86
79	North Dakota ■	78
79	St. Cloud St. ■	84
91	Northern Colo.	84
82	South Dakota St.	94
70	Augustana (S.D.) ■	68
58	Neb.-Omaha	67
64	North Dakota St.	78
97	St. Cloud St.	89
85	Neb.-Omaha ■	70
86	Northern Colo. ■	73
94	Minn. St. Mankato ■	83

88	South Dakota St. ■	69
73	North Dakota	88
80	North Dakota St. ■	87
70	Augustana (S.D.)	84
70	Minn. St. Mankato	78
59	North Dakota St.	67

Nickname: Coyotes
Colors: Vermillion & White
Arena: Dakotadome
  Capacity: 10,000; Year Built: 1979
AD: Kelly Higgins
SID: Dan Genzler

SOUTH DAKOTA ST.
Brookings, SD 57007...............II

Coach: Scott Nagy, Delta St. 1988
2002-03 RESULTS (24-7)

75	Truman †	54
69	Northwest Mo. St.	71
98	Colorado Mines ■	78
83	Bemidji St. ■	66
83	Concordia-St. Paul ■	77
103	Dakota Wesleyan ■	67
84	Sioux Falls ■	72
74	Northern St.	69
95	Finlandia ■	57
95	Fort Lewis ■	70
67	Michigan Tech ■	66
90	Minn. St. Mankato ■	88
77	North Dakota St.	75
89	St. Cloud St.	94
94	South Dakota ■	82
72	Neb.-Omaha	90
80	St. Cloud St. ■	57
73	North Dakota	70
83	Augustana (S.D.)	50
61	North Dakota	68
85	North Dakota St. ■	66
79	Northern Colo.	63
69	South Dakota	88
77	Augustana (S.D.) ■	58
93	Minn. St. Mankato ■	71
83	Neb.-Omaha ■	60
76	Northern Colo.	65
79	Minn. St. Mankato ■	65
65	Neb.-Omaha †	80
84	Fort Hays St. †	78
85	Neb.-Kearney	86

Nickname: Jackrabbits
Colors: Yellow & Blue
Arena: Frost Arena
  Capacity: 9,000; Year Built: 1973
AD: Fred Oien
SID: Ron Lenz

SOUTH FLA.
Tampa, FL 33620 I

Coach: Seth Greenberg, Fairleigh
Dickinson 1978
2002-03 RESULTS (15-14)

99	Nova Southeastern ■	60
68	Providence ■	64
81	Alcorn St. ■	62
65	Nebraska ■	60
52	Florida	68
68	Wright St.	69
84	Northern Ill. ■	83
56	Michigan St.	65
92	Long Island ■	52
68	East Tenn. St. ■	56
70	Colorado St.	82
69	UAB ■	79
63	Marquette	96
74	Southern Miss. ■	65
75	Memphis	74
62	East Caro.	68
57	Houston ■	59
67	Charlotte ■	64

71 TCU ■ ...67
71 St. Louis ■ ...64
67 UAB ...85
62 Houston ■ ...47
65 Tulane ...68
66 Memphis ■ ...73
62 Southern Miss. ...70
72 Tulane ...60
63 TCU ...75
76 DePaul † ...74
56 Memphis † ...62

Nickname: Bulls
Colors: Green & Gold
Arena: Sun Dome
  Capacity: 10,411; Year Built: 1979
AD: Lee Roy Selmon
SID: Michael Hogan

SOUTHAMPTON
Southampton, NY 11968 ...II

Coach: Charles Peck, St. John's (N.Y.) 1983
2002-03 RESULTS (10-17)
72 Bryant ...95
81 NYIT ...72
75 Queens (N.Y.) ...78
77 Southern Conn. St. ■ ...88
80 Molloy ...74
83 Mercy ■ ...73
76 St. Thomas Aquinas ■ ...68
68 New Haven ...87
77 Bridgeport ...73
68 Adelphi ...73
58 C.W. Post ■ ...83
84 Dowling ...74
60 NYIT ■ ...65
60 Philadelphia U. ...70
56 Mass.-Lowell ■ ...81
55 Queens (N.Y.) ■ ...66
76 St. Thomas Aquinas ...50
75 Molloy ■ ...81
70 Mercy ...61
69 New Haven ■ ...74
63 Bridgeport ...72
83 Dowling ■ ...78
64 C.W. Post ...78
66 Adelphi ■ ...87
83 Concordia (N.Y.) ■ ...70
73 Concordia (N.Y.) ...75
49 Philadelphia U. ...71

Nickname: Colonials
Colors: Blue & Gold
Arena: Southampton Gym
  Capacity: 1,500; Year Built: 1964
AD: Mary Topping
SID: Cindy Corwith

SOUTHEAST MO. ST.
Cape Girardeau, MO 63701-4799 ...I

Coach: Gary Garner, Missouri 1965
2002-03 RESULTS (11-19)
71 Arkansas St. ...83
82 Central Methodist ■ ...63
89 Wis.-Milwaukee † ...75
55 Indiana St. † ...68
60 Tulane ...81
88 Oakland City ■ ...66
69 Southern Ill. ■ ...85
66 UMKC ...58
56 Ark.-Little Rock ...81
70 Southwest Mo. St. ■ ...53
70 Creighton ...93
75 Eastern Ill. ■ ...85
93 Eastern Ky. ...77
63 Morehead St. ...77
80 Tenn.-Martin ■ ...88
78 Murray St. ■ ...68

75 Western Ill. ...84
49 Austin Peay ...62
87 Tennessee St. ■ ...67
75 Tennessee Tech ■ ...71
73 Eastern Ill. ...85
69 Morehead St. ■ ...79
75 Eastern Ky. ■ ...79
61 Tenn.-Martin ...77
65 Murray St. ...71
53 Western Ill. ■ ...52
56 Austin Peay ■ ...63
73 Tennessee Tech ...89
89 Tennessee St. ...82
84 Morehead St. ...91

Nickname: Indians
Colors: Red & White
Arena: Show Me Center
  Capacity: 7,000; Year Built: 1987
AD: Donald Kaverman
SID: Ron Hines

SOUTHEASTERN LA.
Hammond, LA 70402 ...I

Coach: Billy Kennedy, Southeastern La. 1986
2002-03 RESULTS (11-16)
58 Vanderbilt ...80
81 Troy St. ■ ...87
47 Auburn ...77
88 Belhaven ■ ...45
69 New Orleans ...77
55 Pittsburgh ...89
83 Loyola (La.) ■ ...56
68 Nicholls St. ...60
51 Northwestern St. ■ ...49
65 Sam Houston St. ...74
55 Lamar ...63
50 Texas-Arlington ■ ...65
55 Stephen F. Austin ■ ...58
59 Northwestern St. ...65
67 La.-Monroe ...74
58 Nicholls St. ■ ...54
72 Texas-San Antonio ■ ...53
82 Texas St. ■ ...77
69 Sam Houston St. ...74
67 Lamar ■ ...57
68 Texas-Arlington ...73
51 Stephen F. Austin ...67
58 La.-Monroe ■ ...70
74 McNeese St. ■ ...67
81 McNeese St. ...78
69 Texas-San Antonio ...80
75 Texas St. ...70

Nickname: Lions
Colors: Green & Gold
Arena: University Center
  Capacity: 7,500; Year Built: 1982
AD: Frank Pergolizzi
SID: Dart Volz

SOUTHEASTERN OKLA.
Durant, OK 74701-0609 ...II

Coach: Tony Robinson, Southeastern Okla. 1976
2002-03 RESULTS (5-22)
63 Abilene Christian ...75
78 Southwestern Aly God ■ ...37
68 Southern Ark. ■ ...61
49 Mo. Southern St. ...66
55 Tex. A&M-Kingsville ■ ...57
74 Tex. A&M-Commerce ■ ...80
66 Tex. A&M-Commerce ...69
70 Southern Ark. ...68
45 Incarnate Word ...56
60 Tex. A&M-Kingsville † ...69
58 Angelo St. ...83
55 Eastern N.M. ...57
55 West Tex. A&M ■ ...58

48 Midwestern St. ...68
61 East Central ■ ...65
49 Tarleton St. ...65
48 Northeastern St. ■ ...59
74 Central Okla. ...80
61 Cameron ■ ...55
60 East Central ...45
52 Henderson St. ■ ...58
47 Tarleton St. ■ ...62
62 Northeastern St. ...75
54 Central Okla. ...60
53 Southwestern Okla. ...59
53 Southwestern Okla. ■ ...60
65 Cameron ...67

Nickname: Savages
Colors: Blue & Gold
Arena: Bloomer Sullivan Gym
  Capacity: 2,000; Year Built: 1956
AD: Donald Parham
SID: Dave Wester

SOUTHERN ARK.
Magnolia, AR 71754 ...II

Coach: Brian Daugherty, Southern Ark. 1994
2002-03 RESULTS (6-21)
76 East Central † ...64
81 St. Edward's † ...56
78 Tex. A&M-Commerce ■ ...90
61 Southeastern Okla. ...68
60 Tex. A&M-Commerce ...65
68 Southeastern Okla. ■ ...70
71 Ozarks (Ark.) ■ ...66
59 Montevallo † ...70
50 Ala.-Huntsville ...71
75 Ky. Wesleyan ...101
73 Jarvis Christian ■ ...60
79 Ouachita Baptist ■ ...93
73 Arkansas Tech ...83
54 Henderson St. ■ ...75
71 Harding ...95
64 Delta St. ■ ...96
75 Ark.-Monticello ■ ...76
70 Central Ark. ...88
69 Christian Bros. ■ ...75
52 Ouachita Baptist ...78
74 Arkansas Tech ■ ...70
64 Henderson St. ...79
73 Harding ■ ...98
70 Delta St. ...78
54 Ark.-Monticello ...76
77 Central Ark. ■ ...76
81 Christian Bros. ...102

Nickname: Muleriders
Colors: Royal Blue & Old Gold
Arena: W.T. Watson Athletic Cent
  Capacity: 2,600; Year Built: 1962
AD: Jay Adcox
SID: Landon Stevens

SOUTHERN CALIFORNIA
Los Angeles, CA 90089-0602 ...I

Coach: Henry Bibby, UCLA 1972
2002-03 RESULTS (13-17)
81 UC Riverside ■ ...68
71 Rhode Island ...73
93 Morris Brown ■ ...54
53 UC Santa Barb. ...69
72 Missouri ...78
78 Cal St. Fullerton ■ ...63
89 La Salle ...63
97 Washington St. ...90
72 Washington ...76
80 UCLA ...
61 Pennsylvania ...99
72 Arizona ■ ...81
76 Arizona St. ■ ...74
68 California ...73

72 Stanford ...80
74 Oregon St. ■ ...83
91 Oregon ■ ...76
86 UCLA ■ ...85
98 UNLV ...73
78 Arizona St. ...108
59 Arizona ...86
67 Stanford ■ ...73
82 California ■ ...84
66 Oregon ...79
60 Oregon St. ...61
89 Washington ■ ...95
86 Washington St. ■ ...68
79 Stanford † ...74
79 California † ...62
66 Oregon † ...74

Nickname: Trojans
Colors: Cardinal & Gold
Arena: Los Angeles Sports Arena
  Capacity: 16,161; Year Built: 1959
AD: Mike Garrett
SID: Tim Tessalone

SOUTHERN CONN. ST.
New Haven, CT 06515 ...II

Coach: Art Leary, Quinnipiac 1971
2002-03 RESULTS (9-18)
70 Felician † ...63
63 Bowie St. ...76
65 St. Michael's ...64
68 St. Rose ...72
68 Pace ■ ...73
88 Southampton ...77
60 Bryant ■ ...66
80 St. Anselm ■ ...82
83 Assumption ...79
57 American Int'l ■ ...47
68 Southern N.H. ■ ...75
60 Franklin Pierce ...71
52 Mass.-Lowell ...72
56 New Haven ...59
79 Merrimack ■ ...65
76 Bentley ...89
63 Stonehill ...57
83 St. Rose ■ ...58
74 Pace ...85
58 C.W. Post ...82
60 St. Anselm ...93
66 Le Moyne ...74
76 St. Michael's ■ ...82
66 Stonehill ■ ...69
64 Bentley ...74
74 Merrimack ...83
91 Le Moyne ■ ...75

Nickname: Owls
Colors: Blue & White
Arena: James W. Moore Fieldhouse
  Capacity: 2,800; Year Built: 1973
AD: Darryl Rogers
SID: Richard Leddy

SIU EDWARDSVILLE
Edwardsville, IL 62026-1129 ...II

Coach: Marty Simmons, Evansville 1987
2002-03 RESULTS (9-18)
78 Ill.-Springfield ■ ...67
58 Murray St. ...86
82 Indianapolis ...91
73 St. Joseph's (Ind.) ...84
64 Lewis ...75
50 Delta St. ...61
82 Greenville (Ill.) ■ ...72
66 Monmouth (Ill.) ■ ...51
68 Oakland City ■ ...66
61 Mo.-St. Louis ■ ...51
77 Southern Ind. ■ ...90
65 Bellarmine ...62
63 Northern Ky. ...77

81 St. Joseph's (Ind.) ■ ...78
53 Wis.-Parkside ■ ...70
59 Lincoln (Mo.) ...73
65 Quincy ■ ...72
64 Southern Ind. ...95
70 Ky. Wesleyan ...88
72 Northern Ky. ■ ...74
70 Indianapolis ■ ...78
59 Wis.-Parkside ...73
70 Lewis ...89
69 Quincy ...76
63 Mo.-St. Louis ...61
60 Ky. Wesleyan ■ ...91
84 Bellarmine ■ ...76

Nickname: Cougars
Colors: Red & White
Arena: Sam Vadalabene Center
Capacity: 4,000; Year Built: 1984
AD: Bradley Hewitt
SID: Eric Hess

SOUTHERN ILL.
Carbondale, IL 62901-6620.......I

Coach: Bruce Weber, Wis.-Milwaukee 1978
2002-03 RESULTS (24-7)
83 George Mason ■ ...74
83 Colorado St. ■ ...71
85 Murray St. ■ ...56
85 Southeast Mo. St. ...69
71 Ill.-Chicago ...73
67 Charlotte ...80
86 Cal St. Northridge ■ ...74
60 St. Louis ...71
76 Drake ■ ...63
74 Illinois St. ...65
90 Evansville ...84
69 Indiana St. ...61
69 Wichita St. ■ ...64
76 Creighton ...85
88 Northern Iowa ...78
60 Indiana St. ■ ...48
75 Bradley ■ ...72
94 Wichita St. ...59
65 Drake ...64
76 Southwest Mo. St. ...75
72 Northern Iowa ■ ...61
73 Bradley ...77
74 Southwest Mo. St. ■ ...69
66 Wis.-Milwaukee ■ ...64
76 Evansville ■ ...64
70 Creighton ■ ...62
78 Illinois St. ...62
75 Illinois St. † ...63
64 Southwest Mo. St. † ...55
56 Creighton † ...80
71 Missouri † ...72

Nickname: Salukis
Colors: Maroon & White
Arena: The SIU Arena
Capacity: 10,014; Year Built: 1964
AD: Paul Kowalczyk
SID: Tom Weber

SOUTHERN IND.
Evansville, IN 47712-3534........II

Coach: Rick Herdes, Grace (Ind.) 1980
2002-03 RESULTS (25-7)
86 Wilberforce ■ ...79
79 Henderson St. ■ ...70
61 Ky. Wesleyan ■ ...73
80 Bellarmine ...82
82 Indianapolis ■ ...78
100 St. Joseph's (Ind.) ■ ...83
81 Western Wash. † ...72
84 Washburn † ...92
98 Oakland City ■ ...70
86 Lock Haven ■ ...63

69 Lewis ...76
90 SIU Edwardsville ...77
85 Mo.-St. Louis ■ ...61
107 Bellarmine ...82
87 Northern Ky. ■ ...82
115 St. Joseph's (Ind.) ...108
80 Wis.-Parkside ...72
95 SIU Edwardsville ■ ...64
90 Quincy ■ ...83
116 Ill.-Springfield ■ ...72
84 Ky. Wesleyan ...89
87 Northern Ky. ...85
78 Indianapolis ...63
85 Wis.-Parkside ■ ...70
87 Lewis ■ ...83
82 Quincy ...69
90 Mo.-St. Louis ...75
91 St. Joseph's (Ind.) ■ ...85
82 Northern Ky. ■ ...84
82 Lewis † ...63
74 Michigan Tech ...71
91 Ky. Wesleyan † ...95

Nickname: Screaming Eagles
Colors: Red, White & Blue
Arena: Physical Activities Center
Capacity: 3,300; Year Built: 1980
AD: Jon Mark Hall
SID: Ray Simmons

SOUTHERN ME.
Gorham, ME 04038 ...III

Coach: Dan Costigan, Maine 1985
2002-03 RESULTS (4-21)
86 St. Joseph's (Me.) ...88
90 Colby † ...103
77 Bates ...110
59 Bowdoin ...87
79 New England ■ ...90
80 Western Conn. St. ...90
67 Keene St. ■ ...90
62 Williams ...82
88 Clark (Mass.) † ...101
69 Colby ...66
63 Mass.-Dartmouth ...75
68 Rhode Island Col. ■ ...80
65 Eastern Conn. St. ...72
71 Plymouth St. ...83
73 Western Conn. St. ■ ...95
73 Mass.-Boston ...71
76 Keene St. ...95
92 St. Joseph's (Me.) ■ ...106
76 Mass.-Dartmouth ...89
77 Plymouth St. ■ ...80
76 Salem St. ■ ...94
85 Rhode Island Col. ...92
80 Mass.-Boston ■ ...78
106 Eastern Conn. St. ■ ...74
81 Western Conn. St. ...95

Nickname: Huskies
Colors: Crimson, Navy Blue & White
Arena: Warren G. Hill Gymnasium
Capacity: 1,400; Year Built: 1963
AD: Albert Bean Jr.
SID: B.L. Efring

SOUTHERN METHODIST
Dallas, TX 75275 ...I

Coach: Mike Dement, East Caro. 1976
2002-03 RESULTS (17-13)
87 TCU ...84
59 Texas Tech ...77
88 North Texas ■ ...75
62 Oral Roberts ...75
49 Wake Forest ...73
65 Appalachian St. ...87
66 Baylor ■ ...58
64 Gardner-Webb † ...63
78 UNLV ...79

88 San Diego ■ ...82
77 Louisiana Tech ...89
55 Hawaii ...72
79 San Jose St. ...72
73 Fresno St. ■ ...75
86 Nevada ■ ...76
89 Rice ...83
86 Tulsa ...84
80 UTEP ■ ...56
85 Boise St. ■ ...88
82 San Jose St. ■ ...69
78 Hawaii ■ ...69
64 Nevada ...82
56 Fresno St. ...76
70 Tulsa ■ ...77
73 Rice ■ ...63
66 Boise St. ...58
65 UTEP ...43
84 Louisiana Tech ■ ...61
65 Boise St. † ...58
66 Nevada † ...81

Nickname: Mustangs
Colors: Red & Blue
Arena: Moody Coliseum
Capacity: 8,998; Year Built: 1956
AD: James Copeland Jr.
SID: Brad Sutton

SOUTHERN MISS.
Hattiesburg, MS 39402 ...I

Coach: James Green, Mississippi 1983
2002-03 RESULTS (13-16)
78 Alcorn St. ■ ...70
80 Jackson St. ■ ...62
77 Troy St. ■ ...70
89 South Ala. ■ ...78
62 Jacksonville † ...61
63 Iowa ...65
48 Arkansas St. ■ ...64
54 Western Ky. ...64
70 Ark.-Little Rock ■ ...54
46 Auburn ...92
56 Murray St. ...54
72 TCU ■ ...64
84 Memphis ■ ...67
65 South Fla. ...74
71 UAB ...84
75 Houston † ...76
65 Louisville ...94
62 Memphis ...80
82 UAB ■ ...80
57 East Caro. ...60
78 TCU ...85
69 DePaul ■ ...74
42 Houston ...46
76 Tulane ...72
68 Charlotte ...77
70 South Fla. ■ ...62
61 Tulane ...74
63 Cincinnati † ...61
56 St. Louis † ...69

Nickname: Golden Eagles
Colors: Black & Gold
Arena: Reed Green Coliseum
Capacity: 8,095; Year Built: 1965
AD: Richard Giannini
SID: Mike Montoro

SOUTHERN N.H.
Manchester, NH 03106-1045 ...II

Coach: Stan Spirou, Keene St. 1974
2002-03 RESULTS (22-8)
78 Franklin Pierce ...76
82 Bentley ■ ...77
78 Merrimack ...74
73 Stonehill ■ ...64
86 St. Michael's ...83
85 Glenville St. † ...68

78 Merrimack † ...64
83 St. Rose ...86
83 Le Moyne ...71
92 St. Anselm ■ ...81
75 Southern Conn. St. ...68
97 St. Rose ■ ...93
71 Pace ■ ...82
51 Assumption ...83
64 American Int'l ...57
74 Bryant ■ ...73
77 Teikyo Post ...65
76 Franklin Pierce ■ ...85
73 Mass.-Lowell ...68
73 Merrimack ■ ...48
70 Stonehill ...64
74 Bentley ...72
59 American Int'l ■ ...82
72 Bryant ...82
80 Assumption ■ ...75
74 Mass.-Lowell ■ ...61
83 Bentley ...70
73 St. Rose ■ ...66
66 Mass.-Lowell ...77
71 New Haven † ...76

Nickname: Penmen
Colors: Blue & Gold
Arena: SNHU Fieldhouse
Capacity: 2,000; Year Built: 1980
AD: Joseph Polak
SID: Tom McDermott

SOUTHERN U.
Baton Rouge, LA 70813 ...I

Coach: Ben Jobe, Fisk 1956
2002-03 RESULTS (9-20)
61 South Ala. ■ ...82
52 Nicholls St. † ...36
71 San Francisco ...82
46 Nicholls St. ■ ...51
78 Tuskegee ■ ...67
59 Tex.-Pan American ■ ...65
61 Texas Southern ■ ...66
86 Prairie View ■ ...88
79 Grambling ...80
66 Jackson St. ...86
52 Ark.-Pine Bluff ■ ...44
59 Mississippi Val. ■ ...72
61 Tex.-Pan American ...71
60 Alabama St. ...78
66 Alabama A&M ...60
87 Alcorn St. ...93
56 Centenary (La.) ■ ...84
87 Grambling ■ ...68
72 Jackson St. ■ ...79
79 Ark.-Pine Bluff ...88
69 Mississippi Val. ...77
77 West Ala. ■ ...62
57 Alabama St. ■ ...54
94 Alabama A&M ■ ...93
62 Alcorn St. ■ ...63
77 Morris Brown ■ ...49
76 Prairie View ...87
65 Texas Southern ...79
55 Prairie View ...56

Nickname: Jaguars
Colors: Columbia Blue & Gold
Arena: Clark Activity Center
Capacity: 7,500; Year Built: 1976
AD: Floyd Kerr
SID: Kevin Manns

SOUTHERN UTAH
Cedar City, UT 84720 ...I

Coach: Bill Evans, Southern Utah 1972
2002-03 RESULTS (11-17)
47 Utah ...61
66 Washington St. ...72
74 Sacramento St. ■ ...68

Column 1 (continued results)

79	Long Beach St. ■	67
71	Boise St. ■	73
83	Montana St.-Northern ■	54
56	Northern Ariz. ■	73
77	Montana Tech ■	34
69	New Mexico	57
60	Brigham Young	93
61	Montana	81
68	Northern Ariz.	85
73	Oral Roberts ■	58
82	UMKC ■	78
44	Valparaiso	74
69	Western Ill.	74
65	Chicago St. ■	64
53	IUPUI ■	56
83	Oakland ■	85
69	UMKC	91
73	Oral Roberts	86
78	Western Ill. ■	75
61	Valparaiso ■	69
70	Chicago St. ■	54
58	IUPUI	77
77	Oakland	92
66	Oakland †	55
67	IUPUI †	72

Nickname: Thunderbirds
Colors: Scarlet & White
Arena: Centrum
  Capacity: 5,300; Year Built: 1985
AD: Thomas Douple
SID: Neil Gardner

SOUTHERN VT.
Bennington, VT 05201-9983.....III

Coach: Ryan Marks, Southern California 1993

2002-03 RESULTS (24-6)

87	Middlebury	84
86	New York U.	84
72	Keene St. ■	73
76	Johnson & Wales	74
75	Paul Smith	66
112	Clark (Mass.) †	109
55	Williams	84
70	Rensselaer	77
78	Norwich	60
81	Albertus Magnus	82
85	Daniel Webster ■	59
71	Emmanuel (Mass.)	57
88	Suffolk	86
101	Emerson	96
87	Western New Eng. ■	68
83	Rivier ■	47
86	Albertus Magnus ■	77
58	Norwich ■	38
68	Rivier	66
76	Suffolk ■	79
101	Western New Eng.	94
94	Emmanuel (Mass.) ■	73
66	Emerson ■	63
106	Daniel Webster	81
81	Johnson & Wales ■	71
71	Rivier ■	35
65	Norwich †	57
89	Albertus Magnus †	73
63	Lasell ■	60
60	Amherst	84

Nickname: Mountaineers
Colors: Green, White & Gold
Arena: Field House
  Capacity: 300; Year Built: 1991
AD: Scott Kilgallon
SID: To be named

SOUTHWEST BAPTIST
Bolivar, MO 65613 II

Coach: Darin Archer, Southwest Baptist 1991

2002-03 RESULTS (9-17)

59	West Tex. A&M †	76
78	Okla. Panhandle	85
57	Indianapolis	65
102	Harris-Stowe ■	74
81	Drury	49
75	Central Bible (Mo.) ■	64
61	Harding ■	87
88	Missouri Valley ■	77
67	Mo.-Rolla ■	71
80	Mo. Southern St. ■	65
67	Washburn	99
77	Central Mo. St. ■	61
73	Emporia St. ■	71
71	Northwest Mo. St. ■	84
68	Pittsburg St. ■	65
66	Mo. Western St.	77
79	Truman ■	65
80	Mo. Southern St.	92
55	Washburn ■	68
71	Central Mo. St.	84
72	Emporia St.	80
74	Northwest Mo. St. ■	80
65	Pittsburg St.	79
58	Mo. Western St. ■	83
79	Truman	88
63	Mo.-Rolla	86

Nickname: Bearcats
Colors: Purple & White
Arena: Davison Field House
  Capacity: 2,500; Year Built: 1963
AD: Jim Middleton
SID: Darin Archer

SOUTHWEST MO. ST.
Springfield, MO 65804 I

Coach: Barry Hinson, Oklahoma St. 1983

2002-03 RESULTS (17-12)

78	North Texas ■	81
72	St. Louis	64
84	Kent St.	88
80	Samford ■	49
77	Wis.-Milwaukee ■	86
46	Tulsa	62
72	Arkansas St. ■	65
53	Southeast Mo. St.	70
76	Illinois St.	48
67	Bradley ■	45
74	Drake	72
63	Wichita St.	67
60	Illinois St. ■	46
70	Evansville ■	51
78	UMKC ■	65
70	Northern Iowa	53
65	Drake ■	45
48	Indiana St.	44
73	Evansville	58
75	Southern Ill. ■	76
67	Creighton	70
65	Indiana St. ■	51
69	Southern Ill.	74
54	Bradley	52
58	Creighton ■	63
65	Wichita St. ■	71
52	Northern Iowa ■	51
65	Evansville †	51
55	Southern Ill. †	64

Nickname: Bears
Colors: Maroon & White
Arena: Hammons Student Center

Capacity: 8,846; Year Built: 1976
AD: Bill Rowe Jr.
SID: Mark Stillwell

SOUTHWEST MINN. ST.
Marshall, MN 56258...............II

Coach: Greg Stemen, Valley City St. 1988

2002-03 RESULTS (17-11)

78	Western Wash. †	87
78	Dominican (Cal.) †	62
74	North Dakota	78
87	Viterbo	47
77	Michigan Tech	90
70	Minn. St. Mankato ■	53
58	St. Cloud St. ■	83
81	Finlandia ■	50
86	South Dakota	98
82	Minn. Duluth ■	78
73	Bemidji St. ■	59
68	Minn.-Morris	37
60	Northern St.	67
85	Concordia-St. Paul ■	68
71	Winona St. ■	73
91	Wayne St. (Neb.) ■	75
96	Minn.-Crookston	89
80	Minn. St. Moorhead	75
87	Bemidji St.	83
91	Minn. Duluth	98
61	Northern St. ■	73
93	Minn.-Morris ■	40
77	Winona St.	72
74	Concordia-St. Paul	60
55	Wayne St. (Neb.)	70
64	Minn. St. Moorhead ■	51
82	Minn.-Crookston ■	74
62	Minn. St. Moorhead ■	70

Nickname: Mustangs
Colors: Brown & Gold
Arena: R/A Facility
  Capacity: 4,000; Year Built: 1996
AD: Butch Raymond
SID: Kelly Loft

SOUTHWESTERN (TEX.)
Georgetown, TX 78627-0770...III

Coach: Bill Raleigh, Muhlenberg 1988

2002-03 RESULTS (18-9)

82	Austin ■	60
86	Texas-Dallas	75
64	Washington (Mo.) †	70
68	Chicago †	66
63	Dallas	75
60	SCAD	64
50	Citadel	78
81	McMurry	67
82	Lake Forest ■	66
61	Trinity (Tex.)	62
76	Austin	72
81	Oglethorpe ■	74
86	Millsaps ■	68
60	Rose-Hulman	65
90	DePauw	86
60	Trinity (Tex.) ■	57
81	Dallas ■	58
75	Hendrix ■	62
85	Rhodes ■	59
84	Centre	73
108	Sewanee	111
88	Oglethorpe	70
84	Millsaps	79
83	Rose-Hulman ■	75
63	DePauw	67
86	Rose-Hulman †	76
59	Trinity (Tex.) †	70

Nickname: Pirates
Colors: Black & Yellow
Arena: Corbin J. Robertson Center
  Capacity: 1,800; Year Built: 1995
AD: Glada Munt
SID: Jim Shelton

SOUTHWESTERN OKLA.
Weatherford, OK 73096...........II

Coach: George Hauser, Central Okla. 1960

2002-03 RESULTS (8-18)

66	Pittsburg St. †	81
64	Mo. Southern St.	75
68	Arkansas Tech	79
70	Oklahoma City	72
82	Arkansas Tech ■	66
106	Mid-America Bible ■	72
71	Midwestern St. ■	56
68	Oklahoma City ■	69
81	Tex. A&M-Commerce	90
74	Tex. A&M-Kingsville	81
57	Angelo St.	69
78	Abilene Christian	71
69	West Tex. A&M	79
59	Eastern N.M.	72
66	Northeastern St. ■	73
59	Central Okla.	77
86	Cameron ■	82
74	Tarleton St.	85
68	East Central	89
66	Northeastern St. ■	81
60	Central Okla. ■	67
64	Cameron	62
60	Tarleton St. ■	74
59	Southeastern Okla. ■	53
60	Southeastern Okla.	53
71	East Central ■	75

Nickname: Bulldogs
Colors: Navy Blue & White
Arena: Rankin Williams Fieldhouse
  Capacity: 2,400; Year Built: 1957
AD: Cecil Perkins
SID: Matt Bush

SPRINGFIELD
Springfield, MA 01109-3797 ...III

Coach: Charlie Brock, Springfield 1976

2002-03 RESULTS (12-15)

73	Ursinus †	59
57	Kean †	69
77	Tufts	86
56	Amherst	77
81	Western New Eng. †	68
78	Curry ■	59
91	Salem St. ■	65
65	Misericordia ■	63
76	Johns Hopkins ■	51
76	Keene St.	83
82	Trinity (Conn.) ■	90
68	MIT ■	61
91	Eastern Conn. St. ■	73
62	Coast Guard	77
50	Babson ■	64
78	Clark (Mass.) ■	85
56	Wheaton (Mass.)	76
72	WPI	53
69	Williams ■	84
61	Babson	76
71	Wheaton (Mass.) ■	58
50	MIT	57
77	Clark (Mass.)	83
64	Coast Guard ■	65
79	WPI ■	55
59	MIT	55
68	Babson †	98

Nickname: The Pride
Colors: Maroon & White
Arena: Blake Arena
  Capacity: 2,000; Year Built: 1981
AD: Cathie Schweitzer
SID: John White

STANFORD
Stanford, CA 94305-2060 I

Coach: Mike Montgomery,
Long Beach St. 1968

2002-03 RESULTS (24-9)
61	Boston U. ■	57
63	Xavier ■	62
79	Rice ■	62
69	Florida †	65
57	North Carolina †	74
76	St. Mary's (Cal.) ■	58
68	Montana ■	70
69	Richmond ■	83
84	UC Irvine ■	57
77	UNLV ■	66
81	Gonzaga †	71
79	Yale ■	56
59	California	72
57	Oregon St. ■	54
81	Oregon ■	57
73	Washington St.	68
68	Washington	73
52	UCLA	51
80	Southern California ■	72
82	Arizona	77
58	Arizona St.	57
64	Oregon	79
84	Oregon St.	73
78	Washington ■	69
72	Washington St. ■	54
73	Southern California	67
93	UCLA	84
88	Arizona St. ■	77
69	Arizona ■	72
72	California ■	60
74	Southern California †	79
77	San Diego †	69
74	Connecticut †	85

Nickname: Cardinal
Colors: Cardinal & White
Arena: Maples Pavilion
  Capacity: 7,391; Year Built: 1968
AD: Ted Leland
SID: Bob Vazquez

STATEN ISLAND
Staten Island, NY 10314 III

Coach: Brian Gasper

2002-03 RESULTS (15-11)
43	Richard Stockton †	78
90	Stevens Institute †	88
65	Farmingdale St. ■	58
59	Manhattanville	54
77	St. Joseph's (Brkln) ■	60
75	Brooklyn	71
77	FDU-Florham ■	75
84	NYCCT	69
45	Merchant Marine ■	68
67	Elmira ■	76
77	Montclair St. ■	85
74	Ramapo	105
76	Medgar Evers ■	68
48	York (N.Y.)	54
72	John Jay	64
75	Hunter ■	66
51	CCNY	74
59	Baruch	71
65	NYCCT	59
78	Brooklyn ■	58
66	York (N.Y.) ■	55
69	Medgar Evers	76
84	Lehman ■	69

72	Purchase St.	64
57	York (N.Y.) †	68
67	Mt. St. Mary (N.Y.) ■	86

Nickname: Dolphins
Colors: Maroon & Columbia Blue
Arena: Sports & Recreation Center
  Capacity: 1,200; Year Built: 1995
AD: Harold Merritt
SID: Jason Fein

STEPHEN F. AUSTIN
Nacogdoches, TX 75962 I

Coach: Danny Kaspar, North Texas
1978

2002-03 RESULTS (21-8)
55	Texas	81
101	LeTourneau ■	50
69	Centenary (La.) ■	75
75	Texas Southern ■	80
71	Oral Roberts ■	68
96	Concordia-Austin ■	53
103	Jackson St. ■	79
82	La.-Monroe ■	72
66	Texas St. ■	58
79	McNeese St. ■	69
66	Nicholls St.	39
58	Southeastern La.	55
74	Lamar ■	62
77	Sam Houston St. ■	70
77	Texas-San Antonio ■	66
76	Texas-Arlington ■	62
71	Northwestern St.	59
52	Texas-Arlington	60
53	McNeese St.	63
84	Nicholls St. ■	56
67	Southeastern La. ■	51
77	Lamar	73
62	Sam Houston St.	69
76	Texas-San Antonio	45
58	Texas St.	60
66	La.-Monroe ■	58
75	Northwestern St. ■	63
67	Texas St. ■	58
66	Sam Houston St.	69

Nickname: Lumberjacks
Colors: Purple & White
Arena: William Johnson Coliseum
  Capacity: 7,200; Year Built: 1974
AD: Steve McCarty
SID: Rob Meyers

STETSON
De Land, FL 32720 I

Coach: Derek Waugh, Furman 1993

2002-03 RESULTS (7-20)
67	Rollins ■	60
74	Colorado	107
43	Air Force	72
62	Charleston So. ■	68
59	Birmingham-So.	75
82	Jacksonville St.	101
64	Col. of Charleston ■	66
76	Florida St.	93
74	Dartmouth †	86
75	New Hampshire †	69
72	Mercer ■	86
81	Troy St. ■	85
71	Jacksonville ■	75
73	Lipscomb ■	68
70	UCF	82
64	Fla. Atlantic	71
78	Gardner-Webb ■	63
69	Campbell ■	57
71	Georgia St. ■	78
71	Samford	79
85	Belmont	80
83	Fla. Atlantic ■	78
82	UCF ■	90
64	Lipscomb	87

59	Jacksonville	73
70	Troy St.	117
84	Mercer	101

Nickname: Hatters
Colors: Green & White
Arena: Edmunds Center
  Capacity: 5,000; Year Built: 1974
AD: Jeff Altier
SID: Jamie Bataille

STEVENS INSTITUTE
Hoboken, NJ 07030-5991 III

Coach: Stephen Hayn, Stony Brook
1991

2002-03 RESULTS (7-19)
66	Muhlenberg	78
88	Staten Island †	90
46	FDU-Florham	60
63	New Jersey City	93
56	Yeshiva	71
54	Richard Stockton ■	69
57	Rensselaer	67
79	Mt. St. Mary (N.Y.) ■	81
46	Old Westbury ■	75
77	St. Joseph's (L.I.)	85
59	Haverford ■	69
72	Merchant Marine	87
64	Maritime (N.Y.)	63
59	Manhattanville ■	70
84	Mt. St. Vincent ■	73
70	Maritime (N.Y.) ■	44
74	Mt. St. Mary (N.Y.)	84
64	Baruch	81
80	St. Joseph's (L.I.) ■	69
82	Merchant Marine ■	81
63	Mt. St. Vincent	61
67	Centenary (N.J.) ■	71
63	Manhattanville	73
82	Yeshiva ■	51
61	Old Westbury	64
46	Manhattanville	53

Nickname: Ducks
Colors: Red & Gray
Arena: Canavan Arena
  Capacity: 1,500; Year Built: 1994
AD: Russell Rogers
SID: Tracy King

STILLMAN
Tuscaloosa, AL 35403 III

Coach: Shawn Parks, Paine 1994

2002-03 RESULTS (12-14)
57	West Ala. ■	63
70	Fisk	76
69	North Ala.	100
72	Philander Smith ■	91
65	Xavier (La.)	89
72	Southern-N.O.	106
81	Belhaven ■	78
62	Mississippi Col.	78
97	Knoxville	95
78	Miles ■	80
84	Oakwood ■	70
82	West Ala.	81
84	Rust ■	74
71	Miles	63
90	Belhaven	87
82	Paine	86
84	Concordia (Ala.)	86
77	Philander Smith	75
104	Rust	115
77	Claflin	80
59	Knoxville	71
100	Claflin ■	92
131	Concordia (Ala.) ■	99
76	Xavier (La.) ■	75
94	Oakwood	76
78	Emory	83

Nickname: Tigers
Colors: Navy Blue & Old Gold
Arena: Birthright
  Capacity: 1,000; Year Built: 1954
AD: Richard Cosby
SID: Wesley Peterson

STONEHILL
Easton, MA 02357 II

Coach: Kevin O'Brien, Tufts 1979

2002-03 RESULTS (6-20)
64	N.J. Inst. of Tech. †	70
80	Longwood †	76
54	Bryant	64
46	Mass.-Lowell ■	71
64	Southern N.H.	73
61	Merrimack ■	62
69	Green Mountain	46
67	Assumption ■	80
71	Dominican (N.Y.) ■	50
59	Bentley	81
55	St. Anselm ■	68
60	Le Moyne	68
70	St. Michael's ■	61
73	St. Rose	103
47	Pace	70
57	Southern Conn. St. ■	63
55	Merrimack	60
49	Bentley ■	76
53	Franklin Pierce ■	42
51	Franklin Pierce	64
64	Southern N.H. ■	70
44	Mass.-Lowell	90
69	Southern Conn. St.	66
57	Pace ■	82
53	St. Rose ■	63
37	American Int'l	56

Nickname: Chieftains
Colors: Purple & White
Arena: Merkert Gymnasium
  Capacity: 2,200; Year Built: 1973
AD: Paula Sullivan
SID: Jim Seavey

STONY BROOK
Stony Brook, NY 11794.............I

Coach: Nick Macarchuk, Fairfield 1963

2002-03 RESULTS (13-15)
75	Sacred Heart ■	64
57	St. John's (N.Y.)	68
45	Harvard ■	56
95	Rhode Island Col. ■	51
65	Columbia	56
68	Army ■	59
61	Boston College	79
65	Hofstra ■	52
48	Lehigh ■	54
48	Seton Hall	71
47	Vermont	66
61	Hartford ■	68
59	Binghamton ■	64
66	Boston U.	81
92	Albany (N.Y.) ■	87
72	Northeastern ■	67
81	Maine ■	79
89	Centenary (N.J.) ■	43
77	New Hampshire	71
78	Northeastern	60
60	Vermont ■	66
73	Boston U. ■	67
74	Albany (N.Y.)	82
64	Hartford	66
56	Maine	74
77	Binghamton ■	70
55	New Hampshire ■	62
47	Hartford †	59

Nickname: Seawolves
Colors: Scarlet & Gray
Arena: USB Sports Complex

Capacity: 4,100; Year Built: 1990
AD: Sandra Weeden
SID: Rob Emmerich

SUFFOLK
Boston, MA 02114 III

Coach: Dennis McHugh, Salem St. 1990
2002-03 RESULTS (12-14)
92	Anna Maria †	.59
71	Babson	.97
50	Northeastern	.104
72	MIT ■	.63
69	Brandeis	.85
69	Mass.-Boston	.70
88	Western New Eng. ■	.74
71	Albertus Magnus	.83
58	Babson ■	.90
63	Norwich ■	.65
86	Southern Vt. ■	.88
88	Johnson & Wales	.85
82	Daniel Webster	.74
57	Emmanuel (Mass.) ■	.60
100	Emerson ■	.65
79	Western New Eng.	.102
77	Johnson & Wales ■	.71
86	Emerson	.79
79	Southern Vt.	.76
82	Rivier ■	.68
82	Daniel Webster ■	.86
81	Emmanuel (Mass.)	.61
61	Norwich	.76
99	Albertus Magnus ■	.102
83	Rivier	.73
62	Western New Eng.	.79

Nickname: Rams
Colors: Blue & Gold
Arena: Regan Gymnasium
   Capacity: 150; Year Built: 1991
AD: James Nelson
SID: Lou Connelly

SUL ROSS ST.
Alpine, TX 79832 III

Coach: Doug Davalos, Houston 1994
2002-03 RESULTS (19-6)
108	Tex. Permian Basin ■	.71
78	Texas-Dallas	.65
87	Louisiana Col. ■	.66
75	Mississippi Col. ■	.67
110	Howard Payne	.109
93	Tex. Permian Basin	.67
87	Abilene Christian	.93
81	Austin	.80
79	Ozarks (Ark.)	.83
76	East Tex. Baptist ■	.87
91	LeTourneau ■	.70
93	Howard Payne ■	.89
89	Schreiner ■	.61
95	Texas Lutheran ■	.78
100	Hardin-Simmons ■	.85
78	McMurry	.80
66	Mary Hardin-Baylor	.70
103	Concordia-Austin	.85
95	Mary Hardin-Baylor ■	.84
79	Concordia-Austin ■	.67
95	Schreiner	.70
67	Texas Lutheran	.66
101	Hardin-Simmons ■	.70
101	McMurry ■	.74
67	Mississippi Col. †	.75

Nickname: Lobos
Colors: Scarlet & Gray
AD: Kay Whitley
SID: To be named

SUSQUEHANNA
Selinsgrove, PA 17870-1025 III

Coach: Frank Marcinek, Penn St. 1981
2002-03 RESULTS (18-8)
80	Gallaudet ■	.67
73	Scranton ■	.71
85	Marywood	.78
62	Lebanon Valley	.93
70	Elizabethtown ■	.105
78	Dickinson	.82
68	Baruch †	.79
74	Eastern Conn. St. †	.60
61	Neumann †	.87
90	Salisbury †	.67
85	York (Pa.)	.89
92	Lycoming ■	.87
89	Juniata	.84
100	Albright ■	.80
66	Messiah ■	.59
78	Widener	.73
85	Moravian ■	.73
78	Elizabethtown	.90
80	Lebanon Valley ■	.65
74	Albright	.54
75	Juniata ■	.56
97	Messiah	.91
73	Moravian	.67
89	Widener ■	.85
73	Lebanon Valley ■	.61
86	Elizabethtown ■	.92

Nickname: Crusaders
Colors: Orange & Maroon
Arena: O.W. Houts Gymnasium
   Capacity: 1,800; Year Built: 1976
AD: Donald Harnum
SID: Jim Miller

SWARTHMORE
Swarthmore, PA 19081-1397 ...III

Coach: Lee Wimberly, Stanford 1968
2002-03 RESULTS (9-16)
117	Redlands † ■	.111
64	Connecticut Col. ■	.46
66	Drew	.76
46	Lehigh	.83
54	Union (N.Y.) ■	.61
86	Phila. Bible	.76
81	McDaniel	.91
82	Washington (Md.)	.65
52	Occidental	.83
72	Pomona-Pitzer †	.63
58	Marywood	.64
61	Arcadia	.65
69	Gwynedd-Mercy ■	.81
63	Dickinson ■	.48
67	Moravian ■	.76
51	Ursinus	.75
83	Muhlenberg ■	.79
45	Haverford ■	.59
64	Gettysburg	.71
67	Washington (Md.) ■	.61
45	Frank. & Marsh. ■	.62
71	Johns Hopkins ■	.50
48	Ursinus ■	.70
58	Muhlenberg	.66
44	Haverford	.60

Nickname: Garnet Tide
Colors: Garnet, Gray & White
Arena: Tarble Pavillion
   Capacity: 1,800; Year Built: 1978
AD: Robert Williams
SID: Mark Duzenski

SYRACUSE
Syracuse, NY 13244 I

Coach: Jim Boeheim, Syracuse 1966
2002-03 RESULTS (30-5)
63	Memphis †	.70
81	Valparaiso ■	.66
98	Colgate ■	.68
85	Cornell ■	.62
92	UNC Greensboro ■	.65
94	Binghamton ■	.58
92	Georgia Tech ■	.65
109	Albany (N.Y.) ■	.79
87	Canisius ■	.69
70	Seton Hall	.66
82	Boston College ■	.74
76	Missouri	.69
60	Pittsburgh	.73
83	Seton Hall ■	.65
54	Miami (Fla.)	.49
65	Rutgers	.68
67	Pittsburgh ■	.65
88	Georgetown	.80
94	West Virginia	.80
61	Connecticut	.75
82	Notre Dame ■	.80
66	St. John's (N.Y.) ■	.60
76	Michigan St.	.75
89	West Virginia ■	.51
93	Georgetown	.84
92	Notre Dame	.88
83	Rutgers ■	.74
74	Georgetown †	.69
67	Connecticut †	.80
76	Manhattan †	.65
68	Oklahoma St. †	.56
79	Auburn †	.78
63	Oklahoma †	.47
95	Texas †	.84
81	Kansas †	.78

Nickname: Orangemen
Colors: Orange
Arena: Carrier Dome
   Capacity: 33,000; Year Built: 1980
AD: John Crouthamel
SID: Pete Moore

TAMPA
Tampa, FL 33606-1490.............II

Coach: Richard Schmidt, Western Ky. 1964
2002-03 RESULTS (15-12)
67	P.R.-Rio Piedras ■	.55
64	P.R.-Cayey ■	.53
71	Winona St. ■	.69
83	P.R.-Bayamon ■	.60
76	P.R.-Mayaguez ■	.65
69	Fla. Gulf Coast ■	.76
69	West Fla.	.67
69	Fla. Gulf Coast ■	.61
58	Shaw ■	.69
59	Wayne St. (Mich.) ■	.54
58	Morehouse ■	.68
70	Worcester St. ■	.44
39	Eckerd	.75
44	Barry ■	.39
37	Fla. Southern	.42
48	Rollins ■	.62
60	Florida Tech	.53
65	Lynn ■	.62
65	St. Leo ■	.39
56	Barry	.63
40	Fla. Southern ■	.63
63	Rollins	.78
72	Florida Tech ■	.52
63	Lynn	.75
74	St. Leo ■	.55

| 44 | Eckerd ■ | .57 |
| 48 | Eckerd † | .86 |

Nickname: Spartans
Colors: Scarlet, Gold & Black
Arena: Martinez Sports Center
   Capacity: 3,432; Year Built: 1984
AD: Larry Marfise
SID: Gil Swalls

TARLETON ST.
Stephenville, TX 76401 II

Coach: Lonn Reisman, Pittsburg St. 1977
2002-03 RESULTS (29-4)
111	Hillsdale Free Will ■	.38
77	Jarvis Christian ■	.62
62	Incarnate Word	.43
93	Dallas Christian	.45
67	Eastern N.M. ■	.65
61	Central Wash. †	.70
53	Cal St. San B'dino †	.50
66	St. Mary's (Tex.)	.59
75	West Tex. A&M ■	.49
72	Midwestern St.	.60
68	Incarnate Word ■	.57
58	Tex. A&M-Kingsville ■	.55
71	Tex. A&M-Commerce ■	.58
81	Abilene Christian	.58
63	Angelo St.	.47
65	East Central	.63
65	Southeastern Okla. ■	.49
72	Cameron	.64
85	Southwestern Okla. ■	.74
82	Central Okla.	.63
48	Northeastern St.	.61
92	East Central ■	.53
62	Southeastern Okla.	.47
76	Cameron ■	.54
74	Southwestern Okla.	.60
85	Central Okla. ■	.77
61	Northeastern St. ■	.53
81	Tex. A&M-Commerce	.67
64	Eastern N.M.	.58
61	West Tex. A&M †	.69
56	St. Mary's (Tex.) ■	.43
73	Northwest Mo. St. ■	.58
46	Northeastern St. ■	.56

Nickname: Texans
Colors: Purple & White
Arena: Wisdom Gymnasium
   Capacity: 3,212; Year Built: 1970
AD: Lonn Reisman
SID: Stan Wagnon

TEIKYO POST
Waterbury, CT 06723 II

Coach: J.J. DeTemple, New Mexico 1991
2002-03 RESULTS (19-10)
71	Bridgeport	.85
67	Cheyney †	.71
86	Green Mountain	.54
55	Caldwell ■	.64
70	Bloomfield	.78
77	Goldey-Beacom ■	.56
73	Mass.-Lowell †	.79
66	Ill.-Springfield †	.77
104	Wilmington (Del.) ■	.81
100	Holy Family	.89
69	N.J. Inst. of Tech.	.83
77	Phila. Sciences ■	.71
64	Felician ■	.82
77	Nyack	.58
86	Bloomfield ■	.84
83	Dominican (N.Y.) ■	.73
70	Holy Family ■	.52
65	Southern N.H.	.77

69	Caldwell ■	60
87	Wilmington (Del.)	68
68	N.J. Inst. of Tech. ■	65
78	Phila. Sciences	86
90	Green Mountain ■	69
104	Nyack ■	77
79	Goldey-Beacom	54
67	Felician	63
98	Dominican (N.Y.)	84
89	Caldwell	67
74	Felician †	70

Nickname: Eagles
Colors: Hunter, Black & White
Arena: Drubner Center
  Capacity: 350; Year Built: 1972
AD: Daniel Mara
SID: Todd McEvoy

TEMPLE
Philadelphia, PA 19122 I

Coach: John Chaney, Bethune-Cookman 1955

2002-03 RESULTS (18-16)

53	Rutgers ■	59
76	Wake Forest	83
47	South Carolina	66
80	Charlotte	91
46	Pennsylvania	71
65	Penn St.	63
54	Illinois †	70
71	Indiana ■	64
62	Villanova	70
67	Wisconsin ■	80
68	George Washington ■	65
54	Duquesne	61
42	Richmond	61
55	St. Joseph's ■	65
82	Fordham	51
71	Rhode Island	68
49	Dayton ■	57
96	St. Bonaventure	77
61	Massachusetts	50
59	St. Joseph's	78
76	North Carolina St. ■	54
69	Rhode Island	64
99	Fordham	77
88	Massachusetts ■	46
78	St. Bonaventure ■	77
68	La Salle ■	58
65	Xavier	96
66	Richmond †	52
63	Xavier †	57
72	Dayton	79
68	Drexel ■	59
75	Boston College ■	62
61	Rhode Island	53
58	Minnesota ■	63

Nickname: Owls
Colors: Cherry & White
Arena: Liacouras Center
  Capacity: 10,206; Year Built: 1997
AD: William Bradshaw
SID: Chet Zukowski

TENNESSEE
Knoxville, TN 37996 I

Coach: Buzz Peterson, North Carolina 1986

2002-03 RESULTS (17-12)

71	Gardner-Webb ■	69
88	VMI ■	56
66	Texas A&M	83
70	Georgia Tech †	69
63	Charleston So. ■	49
62	West Virginia	65
79	Western Caro. ■	61
77	Tenn.-Martin ■	50
71	New Mexico ■	64

71	Kentucky ■	74
66	Mississippi	64
64	Florida	77
71	Vanderbilt ■	66
76	Georgia	81
69	Louisville ■	72
60	South Carolina ■	56
60	Auburn	57
71	Massachusetts ■	45
78	Georgia ■	72
70	Arkansas	62
66	Florida ■	59
63	South Carolina	77
71	Alabama ■	76
68	Kentucky	80
67	LSU ■	88
59	Mississippi St. ■	49
70	Vanderbilt	65
53	Auburn †	66
60	Georgetown ■	70

Nickname: Volunteers
Colors: Orange & White
Arena: Thompson-Boling Arena
  Capacity: 24,535; Year Built: 1987
AD: Douglas A. Dickey
SID: Craig Pinkerton

TENNESSEE ST.
Nashville, TN 37209-1561 I

Coach: Nolan Richardson III, Langston 1990, and Hosea Lewis

2002-03 RESULTS (2-25)

107	Trevecca Nazarene ■	94
65	Fisk ■	69
51	Iowa	84
69	Oral Roberts ■	77
85	Lipscomb	97
87	Morris Brown	78
72	UTEP	91
73	Ohio St.	94
87	Kentucky	115
42	Morehead St. ■	93
83	Eastern Ky. ■	109
86	Tenn.-Martin	104
71	Georgia St.	107
89	Morehead St.	103
68	Morris Brown ■	73
65	Tennessee Tech	91
75	Murray St.	93
67	Southeast Mo. St.	87
67	Eastern Ill.	96
57	Austin Peay ■	82
75	Tenn.-Martin ■	95
72	Eastern Ky.	89
56	Austin Peay	71
72	Tennessee Tech ■	101
79	Murray St.	100
75	Eastern Ill. ■	88
82	Southeast Mo. St. ■	89

Nickname: Tigers
Colors: Blue & White
Arena: Howard Gentry Complex
  Capacity: 10,500; Year Built: 1980
AD: Teresa Phillips
SID: Kindell Stephens

TENNESSEE TECH
Cookeville, TN 38505-0001 I

Coach: Mike Sutton, East Caro. 1978

2002-03 RESULTS (20-12)

48	Cincinnati	54
99	Milligan ■	67
85	Cumberland (Tenn.) ■	57
60	Air Force	47
70	Middle Tenn.	66
64	Ohio St.	71
72	Creighton	101
72	Idaho St.	84

75	North Texas ■	60
62	Alcorn St. †	50
61	Hawaii	74
51	Western Ky. †	74
70	Morehead St. ■	72
104	Bryan ■	48
52	Murray St.	64
93	Eastern Ky. ■	76
66	Austin Peay ■	47
82	Tenn.-Martin	77
91	Tennessee St. ■	65
69	Eastern Ill.	61
71	Southeast Mo. St.	75
91	Murray St. ■	83
87	Tenn.-Martin ■	77
89	Morehead St.	97
54	Austin Peay	58
76	Eastern Ky.	68
101	Tennessee St.	72
89	Southeast Mo. St. ■	73
97	Eastern Ill. ■	84
76	Tenn.-Martin ■	62
88	Morehead St. †	71
57	Austin Peay †	63

Nickname: Golden Eagles
Colors: Purple & Gold
Arena: Eblen Center
  Capacity: 10,150; Year Built: 1977
AD: Mike Hennigan
SID: Scott Wilson

TENN.-MARTIN
Martin, TN 38238-5021 I

Coach: Bret Campbell, Valdosta St. 1983

2002-03 RESULTS (14-14)

63	St. Louis	58
77	Missouri Valley ■	58
77	Middle Tenn.	87
72	Union (Tenn.)	60
99	Lipscomb	90
116	Bethel (Tenn.) ■	57
63	UCF ■	58
78	UNLV	101
76	Northern Ariz.	92
50	Tennessee	77
98	Concordia (Wis.) ■	68
66	Austin Peay ■	64
104	Tennessee St.	86
88	Southeast Mo. St.	80
60	Eastern Ill.	68
77	Tennessee Tech ■	82
85	Eastern Ky.	75
60	Morehead St. ■	83
56	Austin Peay	64
70	Murray St.	89
95	Tennessee St.	75
77	Tennessee Tech	87
77	Southeast Mo. St. ■	61
84	Eastern Ill. ■	85
76	Morehead St.	104
78	Eastern Ky.	70
59	Murray St. ■	80
62	Tennessee Tech	76

Nickname: Skyhawks
Colors: Orange, White & Royal Blue
Arena: Skyhawk Arena
  Capacity: 6,700; Year Built: 1978
AD: Phil Dane
SID: Joe Lofaro

TEXAS
Austin, TX 78712.....................I

Coach: Rick Barnes, Lenoir Rhyne 1977

2002-03 RESULTS (26-7)

77	Georgia †	71
81	Stephen F. Austin ■	55
76	Texas-Arlington ■	45

78	Seton Hall †	61
100	George Washington †	92
92	Notre Dame †	98
70	Arizona	73
97	McNeese St. ■	59
57	Princeton ■	54
58	Louisiana Tech ■	50
80	Mt. St. Mary's ■	64
70	Iowa St.	50
82	Baylor	71
89	Texas A&M ■	61
76	Missouri ■	55
87	Kansas	90
78	Oklahoma St. ■	65
80	Colorado	93
95	Texas A&M	87
67	Oklahoma	61
75	Nebraska	63
77	Texas Tech ■	65
77	Oklahoma St.	82
82	Baylor ■	64
76	Texas Tech	71
74	Kansas St. ■	60
76	Oklahoma	71
81	Texas Tech †	92
82	UNC Asheville †	61
77	Purdue †	67
82	Connecticut †	78
85	Michigan St. †	76
84	Syracuse †	95

Nickname: Longhorns
Colors: Burnt Orange & White
Arena: Frank Erwin Center
  Capacity: 16,079; Year Built: 1977
AD: DeLoss Dodds
SID: Scott McConnell

TEXAS A&M
College Station, TX 77843-1228 I

Coach: Melvin Watkins, Charlotte 1977

2002-03 RESULTS (14-14)

70	Texas Southern ■	55
72	Miami (Fla.)	78
79	LSU †	77
71	Oakland ■	65
83	Tennessee ■	66
83	Prairie View	78
75	Texas-San Antonio ■	80
107	La.-Monroe ■	66
62	Princeton †	76
65	Mississippi Val. †	56
90	Centenary (La.) ■	66
76	Oklahoma St. ■	93
53	Nebraska	52
61	Texas	89
79	Kansas St. ■	66
68	Oklahoma	75
64	Texas Tech ■	59
69	Baylor	77
87	Texas ■	95
73	Missouri ■	71
83	Colorado	98
66	Iowa St. ■	54
69	Texas Tech	70
45	Kansas	85
64	Oklahoma ■	69
79	Baylor ■	60
52	Oklahoma St.	77
70	Iowa St. †	97

Nickname: Aggies
Colors: Maroon & White
Arena: Reed Arena
  Capacity: 12,500; Year Built: 1998
AD: William Byrne Jr.
SID: Colin Killian

TEX. A&M-COMMERCE
Commerce, TX 75429-3011 II

Coach: Sam Walker, Sam Houston St. 1991
2002-03 RESULTS (16-12)
95	Jarvis Christian	78
110	Hillsdale Free Will †	46
90	Southern Ark.	78
113	St. Edward's †	86
62	Incarnate Word	73
65	Southern Ark. ■	60
79	East Central	65
80	Southeastern Okla.	74
69	Southeastern Okla. ■	66
74	North Texas	82
90	Southwestern Okla. ■	81
104	Cameron	77
79	Tex. A&M-Kingsville ■	76
58	Tarleton St.	71
85	Tex. A&M-Kingsville ■	72
66	Northeastern St. ■	71
82	Central Okla.	93
91	Midwestern St. ■	82
81	Eastern N.M.	87
81	West Tex. A&M	73
74	Abilene Christian ■	68
95	Angelo St. ■	83
68	Angelo St.	73
72	Abilene Christian	78
83	Midwestern St.	92
66	West Tex. A&M ■	77
71	Eastern N.M. ■	74
67	Tarleton St.	81

Nickname: Lions
Colors: Blue & Gold
Arena: A&M-C Field House
Capacity: 5,000; Year Built: 1950
AD: Paul Peak
SID: Bill Powers

TEX. A&M-CORP. CHRIS.
Corpus Christi, TX 78412..........I

Coach: Ronnie Arrow, Texas St. 1969
2002-03 RESULTS (14-15)
83	Cal St. Fullerton †	76
81	Hawaii	100
73	Trinity (Tex.) ■	49
78	Lamar	94
77	Loyola (Ill.) ■	94
88	Morehead St. ■	98
60	LSU	95
84	Howard Payne ■	68
74	UAB	108
98	Morgan St. ■	65
80	Oakland	72
80	Savannah St.	53
56	Florida St.	72
58	Oklahoma St.	91
80	Sacramento St. ■	84
93	Centenary (La.)	92
73	Arkansas St.	100
77	Tex.-Pan American ■	60
74	Oakland	87
59	Sam Houston St.	66
68	IPFW ■	70
95	Central Baptist ■	56
96	Savannah St. ■	77
76	Prairie View	80
58	Tex.-Pan American	54
77	UTEP	72
73	Centenary (La.) ■	69
63	New Orleans	77
72	Binghamton ■	68

Nickname: Islanders
Colors: Blue, Green & Silver
Arena: Circle K Court
Capacity: 3,500; Year Built: 1953
AD: Dan Viola
SID: John Gilger

TEX. A&M-KINGSVILLE
Kingsville, TX 78363 II

Coach: Pete Peterson, Southwestern Kansas 1979
2002-03 RESULTS (12-15)
77	Huston-Tillotson	65
66	Colorado St.	91
58	Metro St.	93
118	Houston Baptist	110
57	Southeastern Okla.	55
75	East Central	77
85	Texas Lutheran ■	58
104	Paul Quinn †	72
69	Southeastern Okla. †	60
93	Houston Baptist	102
80	Cameron ■	61
81	Southwestern Okla.	74
76	Tex. A&M-Commerce	79
55	Tarleton St.	58
72	Tex. A&M-Commerce ■	85
72	Central Okla. ■	78
56	Northeastern St.	67
72	Midwestern St. ■	76
72	West Tex. A&M	68
70	Eastern N.M.	78
80	Angelo St. ■	81
77	Abilene Christian	68
74	Abilene Christian	76
67	Angelo St.	82
100	Midwestern St.	96
95	Eastern N.M. ■	99
80	West Tex. A&M ■	76

Nickname: Javelinas
Colors: Blue & Gold
Arena: Steinke PE Center
Capacity: 4,000; Year Built: 1970
AD: Jill Wilson
SID: Fred Nuesch

TCU
Fort Worth, TX 76129-0001 I

Coach: Neil Dougherty, Cameron 1984
2002-03 RESULTS (9-19)
91	Sam Houston St. ■	81
84	Southern Methodist	87
86	Washington St. ■	83
66	Texas Tech ■	84
72	Baylor	64
87	North Texas	80
79	La.-Monroe ■	90
78	Va. Commonwealth	91
65	Tulsa	78
103	Grambling ■	84
102	Centenary (La.) ■	89
64	Southern Miss.	72
72	Cincinnati ■	83
65	DePaul	71
74	Louisville	87
93	Tulane	84
79	Creighton	89
82	UAB	84
56	Houston ■	61
67	South Fla.	71
69	Memphis ■	84
85	Southern Miss. ■	78
78	Tulane	84
85	UAB ■	88
68	Marquette ■	79
64	Memphis	88
57	Houston	75
75	South Fla. ■	63

Nickname: Horned Frogs
Colors: Purple & White
Arena: Daniel-Meyer Coliseum
Capacity: 7,166; Year Built: 1961
AD: Eric Hyman
SID: Steve Fink

TEXAS LUTHERAN
Seguin, TX 78155-5999 III

Coach: Tom Oswald, Texas-San Antonio 1996
2002-03 RESULTS (12-13)
75	Fredonia St. †	63
47	Rochester	57
53	Mississippi Col.	68
83	Louisiana Col.	115
72	LeTourneau ■	77
97	East Tex. Baptist ■	81
97	Schreiner ■	74
58	Tex. A&M-Kingsville	85
80	Houston Baptist	98
69	Texas-Dallas ■	67
89	Schreiner	83
63	Austin	73
92	Ozarks (Ark.) ■	90
78	Howard Payne	93
78	Sul Ross St.	95
81	Concordia-Austin ■	73
71	Mary Hardin-Baylor ■	62
73	McMurry	78
78	Hardin-Simmons	69
72	McMurry ■	75
71	Hardin-Simmons ■	55
78	Howard Payne ■	71
66	Sul Ross St. ■	67
86	Concordia-Austin	75
84	Mary Hardin-Baylor	92

Nickname: Bulldogs
Colors: Black & Gold
Arena: Memorial Gym
Capacity: 1,500; Year Built: 1952
AD: Bill Miller
SID: Tim Clark

TEXAS SOUTHERN
Houston, TX 77004....................I

Coach: Ronnie Courtney, McMurry 1981
2002-03 RESULTS (18-13)
55	Texas A&M	70
71	Texas St. ■	79
87	Lamar ■	80
80	Stephen F. Austin ■	75
58	Wisconsin	81
74	Chicago St.	79
88	Oakland †	91
94	Morgan St. †	83
66	Southern U.	61
71	Alcorn St.	70
57	Prairie View	59
78	Tex.-Pan American ■	75
65	Jackson St. ■	50
87	Grambling ■	44
74	Ark.-Pine Bluff	57
80	Mississippi Val.	75
72	Alabama A&M ■	67
58	Alabama St. ■	52
104	Prairie View ■	100
63	Jackson St.	80
60	Grambling	69
54	Ark.-Pine Bluff ■	58
66	Mississippi Val. ■	72
82	Alabama A&M	90
64	Alabama St.	68
79	Alcorn St. ■	69
79	Southern U. ■	65
68	Jackson St. ■	66
73	Mississippi Val. †	72
77	Alcorn St. †	68
84	UNC Asheville †	92

Nickname: Tigers
Colors: Maroon & Gray
Arena: Health & Physical Education Arena
Capacity: 8,100; Year Built: 1988
AD: Alois Blackwell
SID: Bambi Hall

TEXAS ST.
San Marcos, TX 78666-4615 I

Coach: Dennis Nutt, TCU 1986
2002-03 RESULTS (17-12)
84	Mary Hardin-Baylor ■	63
79	Texas Southern	71
71	Baylor	92
68	Houston ■	59
89	Hardin-Simmons ■	43
92	New Orleans ■	81
60	Arkansas	70
64	McNeese St.	74
58	Stephen F. Austin	66
74	La.-Monroe	77
71	Northwestern St.	62
69	Sam Houston St. ■	60
68	Lamar ■	55
91	McNeese St. ■	53
58	Texas-Arlington	53
85	Texas-San Antonio ■	76
52	Nicholls St.	48
77	Southeastern La.	82
102	La.-Monroe ■	86
95	Northwestern St. ■	62
71	Sam Houston St.	79
53	Lamar	64
73	Texas-San Antonio	83
47	Texas-Arlington ■	50
60	Stephen F. Austin ■	58
72	Nicholls St. ■	59
70	Southeastern La. ■	75
94	La.-Monroe ■	85
58	Stephen F. Austin	67

Nickname: Bobcats
Colors: Maroon & Gold
Arena: Strahan Coliseum
Capacity: 7,200; Year Built: 1979
AD: Greg LaFleur
SID: Tony Brubaker

TEXAS TECH
Lubbock, TX 79409-3021...........I

Coach: Bob Knight, Ohio St. 1962
2002-03 RESULTS (22-13)
85	UNC Wilmington ■	76
77	Southern Methodist ■	59
83	UTEP	60
84	TCU	66
107	Nicholls St. ■	35
62	Wyoming †	67
98	New Mexico ■	71
85	New Mexico St. ■	84
99	Minnesota	89
62	Houston ■	48
75	San Diego St.	63
44	Kansas St.	68
80	Baylor ■	64
64	Oklahoma	69
70	Oklahoma St. ■	79
66	Colorado ■	56
59	Texas A&M	64
75	Nebraska ■	49
73	Missouri	82
88	Iowa St.	73
58	Oklahoma ■	63
65	Texas	77
70	Texas A&M ■	69
62	Oklahoma St.	57
71	Texas ■	76
56	Kansas ■	65
68	Baylor	74
68	Baylor †	65
92	Texas †	81
66	Nevada ■	54
57	San Diego St. ■	48
80	Georgia Tech ■	72
63	St. John's (N.Y.) †	64
71	Minnesota †	61
60	Oklahoma †	67

Nickname:
Colors:

Nickname: Red Raiders
Colors: Scarlet & Black
Arena: United Spirit Arena
  Capacity: 15,050; Year Built: 1999
AD: Gerald Myers
SID: Randy Farley

TEXAS-ARLINGTON
Arlington, TX 76013 I

Coach: Eddie McCarter, UAB 1975
2002-03 RESULTS (16-13)

50	Creighton	106
59	Alabama St. †	47
74	Wichita St.	76
45	Texas	76
81	Texas Wesleyan ■	65
87	Ark.-Monticello ■	64
59	Houston	60
51	New Mexico St.	66
71	Texas-San Antonio ■	59
74	McNeese St. ■	62
65	Southeastern La.	50
54	Nicholls St.	59
60	Sam Houston St. ■	62
50	Lamar ■	52
53	Texas St.	58
62	Stephen F. Austin	76
75	Northwestern St.	66
78	La.-Monroe	62
60	Stephen F. Austin ■	52
56	McNeese St.	52
73	Southeastern La. ■	68
74	Nicholls St. ■	46
52	Sam Houston St.	56
58	Lamar	60
50	Texas St.	47
68	Texas-San Antonio	60
68	Northwestern St. ■	50
85	La.-Monroe ■	84
67	McNeese St. ■	78

Nickname: Mavericks
Colors: Royal Blue & White
Arena: Texas Hall
  Capacity: 4,200; Year Built: 1965
AD: Peter Carlon
SID: Mickey Seward

TEXAS-DALLAS
Richardson, TX 75083-0688 III

Coach: Terry Butterfield, Eckerd 1979
2002-03 RESULTS (7-18)

64	Hardin-Simmons ■	66
75	Southwestern (Tex.) ■	86
69	Howard Payne ■	82
65	Sul Ross St. ■	78
45	Trinity (Tex.)	64
62	Hardin-Simmons	53
73	McMurry	70
57	Sam Houston St.	87
67	Texas Lutheran ■	69
83	Schreiner ■	82
78	Concordia-Austin	69
55	Mary Hardin-Baylor	71
59	Mississippi Col. ■	65
85	Louisiana Col.	95
57	Centenary (La.)	98
53	Austin	54
83	Ozarks (Ark.)	75
71	LeTourneau	72
79	East Tex. Baptist	82
82	LeTourneau ■	85
76	East Tex. Baptist ■	78
50	Mississippi Col.	63
81	Louisiana Col.	87
86	Austin ■	60
90	Ozarks (Ark.) ■	79

Nickname: Comets
Colors: Forest Green & Orange

Arena: UTD Activity Center
  Capacity: 2,500; Year Built: 1998
AD: Mary Walters
SID: Tricia Hoffmann

UTEP
El Paso, TX 79968 I

Coach: Billy Gillispie, Texas St. 1983
2002-03 RESULTS (6-24)

75	N.M. Highlands ■	66
53	Alcorn St. ■	67
60	Texas Tech ■	83
47	Houston	56
65	New Mexico St. ■	78
58	New Mexico St.	80
91	Tennessee St. ■	72
54	Columbia ■	55
45	Air Force	63
52	Hawaii ■	64
80	San Jose St. ■	68
66	Nevada ■	78
58	Fresno St.	84
65	Tulsa ■	79
63	Rice ■	91
85	Boise St. ■	78
56	Southern Methodist ■	80
57	Louisiana Tech	73
63	Fresno St. ■	76
64	Nevada ■	71
66	Rice	72
58	Tulsa	81
72	Tex. A&M-Corp. Chris ■	77
52	Boise St.	69
75	Louisiana Tech ■	57
43	Southern Methodist ■	65
73	San Jose St.	74
63	Hawaii	77
86	San Jose St. †	80
47	Tulsa	81

Nickname: Miners
Colors: Dark Blue, Orange & Silver
Arena: Don Haskins Center
  Capacity: 11,500; Year Built: 1977
AD: Bob Stull
SID: Jeff Darby

TEX.-PAN AMERICAN
Edinburg, TX 78541 I

Coach: Bob Hoffman, Oklahoma Bapt. 1979
2002-03 RESULTS (10-20)

59	New Mexico St. †	62
50	Tulsa †	80
88	Concordia (Mich.) ■	55
73	Mississippi Val. ■	68
62	Quinnipiac †	72
52	Lehigh †	66
44	Air Force	65
42	St. Louis	57
68	Kansas St.	102
100	Schreiner ■	65
65	Southern U.	59
63	Lamar	67
48	Butler †	67
54	Chicago St. †	57
56	Alcorn St. †	74
50	Baylor	78
79	Rice ■	85
84	Centenary (La.)	94
75	Texas Southern	78
50	New Mexico St.	64
71	Southern U. ■	61
60	Tex. A&M-Corp. Chris	77
59	IPFW ■	54
100	Southwestern Aly God ■	63
105	Central Baptist ■	43
76	Savannah St. ■	62
54	Tex. A&M-Corp. Chris.■	58
45	Savannah St.	39

76	Centenary (La.) ■	78
71	Morris Brown	72

Nickname: Broncs
Colors: Forest Green, Burnt Orange & W
Arena: UTPA Fieldhouse
  Capacity: 4,000; Year Built: 1969
AD: William Weidner
SID: Dave Geringer

TEXAS-SAN ANTONIO
San Antonio, TX 78249-0691 I

Coach: Tim Carter, Kansas 1979
2002-03 RESULTS (10-17)

76	Idaho St. †	71
68	Marquette	80
52	UNC Wilmington ■	66
53	Nebraska	69
81	St. Mary's (Tex.) ■	67
80	Texas A&M	75
60	UNC Wilmington	71
59	Texas-Arlington	71
67	Northwestern St.	76
82	La.-Monroe	65
81	Lamar	79
65	Sam Houston St. ■	82
51	McNeese St. ■	66
66	Stephen F. Austin ■	77
76	Texas St.	85
53	Southeastern La.	72
83	Nicholls St.	81
63	Northwestern St. ■	73
61	La.-Monroe ■	71
61	Lamar	53
50	Sam Houston St.	72
66	McNeese St.	72
83	Texas St. ■	73
45	Stephen F. Austin	76
60	Texas-Arlington ■	68
80	Southeastern La. ■	69
79	Nicholls St. ■	60

Nickname: Roadrunners
Colors: Orange, Navy Blue & White
Arena: Convocation Center
  Capacity: 5,100; Year Built: 1971
AD: Lynn Hickey
SID: Rick Nixon

THIEL
Greenville, PA 16125 III

Coach: Mike Snell, Ohio 1985
2002-03 RESULTS (16-12)

71	St. John's (Minn.) †	67
68	Chicago	84
67	Mount Union	72
71	Baldwin-Wallace ■	73
87	La Roche ■	76
81	Allegheny	82
72	Pitt.-Bradford	85
53	Gannon	98
61	Ohio Wesleyan †	79
79	Alfred †	60
91	Pitt.-Greensburg ■	68
100	Hiram ■	87
69	Penn St.-Behrend	67
85	Case Reserve	74
82	Westminster (Pa.) ■	94
72	Wash. & Jeff.	89
69	Grove City ■	63
82	Bethany (W.Va.) ■	63
68	Waynesburg	84
85	Hilbert	79
78	Westminster (Pa.)	74
83	Wash. & Jeff.	64
79	Grove City	76
89	Bethany (W.Va.)	74
91	Waynesburg ■	88
81	Bethany (W.Va.) ■	77
59	Grove City ■	60

77	Penn St.-Behrend	99

Nickname: Tomcats
Colors: Navy Blue & Old Gold
Arena: Rissell-Beeghly Gymnasium
  Capacity: 1,000; Year Built: 1968
AD: Joe Schaly
SID: Kevin Fenstermacher

THOMAS MORE
Crestview Hills, KY 41017-3495..
III

Coach: Terry Connor, Thomas More 1992
2002-03 RESULTS (7-18)

64	Va. Wesleyan	60
75	N.C. Wesleyan †	81
58	Northern Ky. ■	79
74	Transylvania	87
62	Manchester ■	82
69	Anderson (Ind.) ■	96
81	Centre ■	70
71	Huntington ■	79
75	LaGrange	78
74	Methodist †	86
64	Mt. St. Joseph	73
89	Bluffton ■	75
82	Hanover	99
71	Manchester	80
82	Transylvania	81
75	Centre	87
86	Franklin ■	78
77	Defiance ■	83
80	Franklin	90
78	Mt. St. Joseph ■	67
76	Anderson (Ind.)	101
52	Hanover ■	74
81	Defiance	88
70	Bluffton	63
73	Maryville (Tenn.)	106

Nickname: Saints
Colors: Royal Blue, White & Silver
Arena: Connor Convocation Center
  Capacity: 1,500; Year Built: 1989
AD: Terry Connor
SID: Jason Eichelberger

TIFFIN
Tiffin, OH 44883-2161 II

Coach: Andre'as James, Tiffin 1999
2002-03 RESULTS (9-18)

67	Findlay	97
57	Bowling Green	91
65	Ashland	74
89	Urbana	92
75	Wilberforce ■	81
67	Ashland ■	86
64	Roberts Wesleyan ■	61
49	Caldwell †	50
69	Concordia (Neb.) †	87
59	Shawnee St. ■	75
68	Malone	66
62	Cedarville ■	74
77	Walsh ■	71
78	Ohio Dominican ■	92
64	Rio Grande	69
87	Mt. Vernon Naz.	78
63	Houghton ■	62
75	Malone ■	83
61	Urbana ■	59
82	Shawnee St.	65
69	Cedarville	72
73	Mt. Vernon Naz.	89
70	Ohio Dominican	76
65	Rio Grande ■	47
83	Walsh	75
75	Wilberforce	83
91	Daemen	94

Nickname: Dragons
Colors: Green & Gold
AD: Ian Day
SID: Shane O'Donnell

TOLEDO
Toledo, OH 43606 I

Coach: Stan Joplin, Toledo 1979
2002-03 RESULTS (13-16)
56	Brigham Young †	71
58	Kansas St. †	50
45	Virginia Tech †	58
61	Youngstown St.	69
59	Siena ■	55
78	Ohio ■	71
98	Wright St.	84
80	Detroit ■	72
90	Arkansas St. ■	73
68	St. Bonaventure ■	94
81	Michigan St.	76
65	Northern Ill. ■	72
58	Marshall	79
61	Miami (Ohio) ■	51
72	Ball St.	77
74	Central Mich.	83
69	Kent St. ■	74
75	Western Mich. ■	62
67	Akron	78
72	Eastern Mich.	76
73	Bowling Green ■	59
64	Central Mich. ■	66
64	Western Mich.	67
73	Eastern Mich. ■	76
66	Buffalo	59
75	Northern Ill.	85
100	Ball St. ■	64
68	Bowling Green	64
64	Western Mich.	78

Nickname: Rockets
Colors: Blue & Gold
Arena: John F. Savage Hall
  Capacity: 9,000; Year Built: 1976
AD: Michael O'Brien
SID: Steve Easton

TOWSON
Towson, MD 21252-0001 I

Coach: Michael Hunt, Furman 1985
2002-03 RESULTS (4-24)
81	UMBC †	86
67	Morgan St.	53
52	Georgetown	81
56	Rider	68
65	Md.-East. Shore ■	40
53	Norfolk St. ■	50
59	Morgan St.	62
60	George Washington ■	70
52	Virginia Tech	76
56	Old Dominion	67
55	William & Mary	74
51	James Madison ■	64
56	George Mason ■	90
61	Hofstra ■	54
56	Drexel	85
53	UNC Wilmington	85
60	Delaware	74
47	Va. Commonwealth ■	82
54	George Mason	76
60	Va. Commonwealth	97
50	Drexel ■	76
52	William & Mary ■	59
51	Old Dominion ■	73
56	James Madison	87
51	UNC Wilmington ■	75
47	Hofstra	66
69	Delaware ■	74
61	James Madison †	72

TRINITY (CONN.)
Hartford, CT 06106 III

Coach: Stan Ogrodnik, Providence 1963
2002-03 RESULTS (15-9)
79	D'Youville †	71
57	Montclair St.	64
68	Eastern Conn. St. ■	72
75	Western Conn. St.	71
73	Wesleyan (Conn.) †	76
91	Hampshire †	73
94	Coast Guard ■	64
85	Ursinus	80
68	Ithaca	53
54	Babson ■	73
90	Springfield	82
91	Elms ■	83
78	Bowdoin	64
71	Colby	69
72	Williams ■	87
76	Middlebury †	69
64	Bates	67
97	Tufts	77
82	Clark (Mass.)	77
73	Amherst ■	78
76	Hunter ■	62
80	Wesleyan (Conn.) ■	81
82	Connecticut Col.	71
76	Wesleyan (Conn.)	88

Nickname: Bantams
Colors: Blue & Gold
Arena: Oosting Gym
  Capacity: 2,000; Year Built: 1963
AD: Richard Hazelton
SID: David Kingsley

TRINITY (TEX.)
San Antonio, TX 78212-7200 ...III

Coach: Pat Cunningham, Kalamazoo 1974
2002-03 RESULTS (21-8)
58	Elmhurst †	52
48	Johns Hopkins	50
49	Tex. A&M-Corp. Chris	73
53	Chicago ■	41
65	Washington (Mo.) ■	68
71	Dallas ■	64
64	Texas-Dallas ■	45
72	Webster ■	63
65	Lake Forest †	53
89	McMurry †	74
62	Southwestern (Tex.) ■	61
53	St. Xavier ■	61
76	Millsaps ■	69
71	Oglethorpe ■	67
51	DePauw ■	77
59	Rose-Hulman ■	54
57	Southwestern (Tex.)	60
78	Rhodes ■	53
81	Hendrix ■	64
66	Sewanee ■	44
75	Centre ■	69
51	Millsaps	60
90	Oglethorpe	51
76	DePauw ■	60
70	Rose-Hulman	53
75	Sewanee †	60
70	Southwestern (Tex.) †	59
58	Centre †	54
66	Aurora ■	67

TROY ST.
Troy, AL 36082 I

Coach: Don Maestri, Southern Miss. 1968
2002-03 RESULTS (26-6)
116	Knoxville ■	74
87	Southeastern La.	81
70	Southern Miss.	77
95	Lipscomb ■	77
74	Arkansas	66
80	Alabama St.	71
89	Lipscomb	77
66	Georgia Tech	88
89	Northeastern †	72
73	Duquesne †	69
66	Auburn †	94
81	Alabama St. ■	61
70	Jacksonville	68
85	Stetson	81
77	Fla. Atlantic ■	72
61	UCF †	76
89	Mercer ■	61
67	Belmont	64
66	Samford ■	48
61	Gardner-Webb	60
100	Campbell	75
99	Georgia St. ■	81
71	Jacksonville St. ■	51
80	Mercer	83
77	UCF	72
76	Fla. Atlantic	66
117	Stetson ■	70
94	Jacksonville ■	72
70	Samford †	54
71	Georgia St.	61
80	UCF †	69
59	Xavier †	71

Nickname: Trojans
Colors: Cardinal & Black
Arena: Trojan Arena
  Capacity: 4,000; Year Built: 1964
AD: Johnny Williams
SID: Joel Lamp

TRUMAN
Kirksville, MO 63501-4221 II

Coach: Jack Schrader, Arizona St. 1975
2002-03 RESULTS (7-20)
54	South Dakota St. †	75
84	Florida Tech †	72
47	Lincoln (Mo.)	58
111	Central Christian ■	47
65	Lincoln (Mo.) ■	74
66	Drury ■	69
80	Hannibal-LaGrange ■	58
78	Drury	65
79	Quincy	82
63	Central Mo. St.	66
71	Washburn	80
83	Northwest Mo. St. ■	71
61	Emporia St.	94
62	Mo. Western St.	99
74	Pittsburg St. ■	77
62	Mo.-Rolla	70
83	Mo. Southern St. ■	91
65	Southwest Baptist	79
50	Washburn ■	77
56	Northwest Mo. St.	60
70	Emporia St. ■	93
57	Mo. Western St.	80

Nickname: Tigers
Colors: Gold, White & Black
Arena: Towson Center
  Capacity: 5,000; Year Built: 1976
AD: Wayne Edwards
SID: Peter Schlehr

Nickname: Tigers
Colors: Maroon & White
Arena: Earl C. Sams Gymnasium
  Capacity: 1,850; Year Built: 1992
AD: Robert King
SID: Justin Parker

66	Pittsburg St.	82
79	Mo.-Rolla ■	58
73	Mo. Southern St.	75
88	Southwest Baptist ■	79
71	Central Mo. St. ■	73

Nickname: Bulldogs
Colors: Purple & White
Arena: Pershing
  Capacity: 3,000; Year Built: 1959
AD: Jerry Wollmering
SID: Melissa Ware

TUFTS
Medford, MA 02155 III

Coach: Robert Sheldon, St. Lawrence 1977
2002-03 RESULTS (12-13)
86	Springfield ■	77
81	Wabash †	87
82	Colorado Col.	109
76	Babson ■	79
70	MIT	67
77	Clark (Mass.)	89
87	Plymouth St. ■	95
87	Curry	77
95	Mass.-Boston ■	92
78	Salem St.	88
90	Connecticut Col.	62
64	Wesleyan (Conn.)	57
95	Wheaton (Mass.)	82
89	Mass.-Dartmouth	71
72	Bates	88
70	Brandeis	72
83	Amherst ■	66
77	Trinity (Conn.) ■	97
79	Keene St. ■	95
75	Bowdoin ■	65
89	Colby ■	71
83	Middlebury	89
56	Williams	76
89	Middlebury ■	81
63	Williams †	64

Nickname: Jumbos
Colors: Brown & Blue
Arena: Cousens Gym
  Capacity: 1,000; Year Built: 1932
AD: Bill Gehling
SID: Paul Sweeney

TULANE
New Orleans, LA 70118 I

Coach: Shawn Finney, Fairmont St. 1985
2002-03 RESULTS (16-15)
58	Rice	72
74	Loyola (La.) ■	58
84	Maine ■	65
61	UCF	66
81	Southeast Mo. St. ■	60
67	New Orleans	80
46	Vanderbilt	66
60	Kentucky ■	76
103	Savannah St. ■	47
94	Jackson St. ■	70
62	LSU †	74
80	Georgia Tech ■	66
88	Morris Brown ■	30
73	Memphis ■	85
73	Marquette ■	85
54	Cincinnati	77
84	TCU	93
75	UAB ■	72
67	East Caro.	56
65	Houston	58
71	UAB	66
57	Memphis ■	58
84	TCU ■	78

68	South Fla. ■	65
72	Southern Miss.	76
56	Houston ■	52
74	St. Louis	76
60	South Fla.	72
74	Southern Miss. ■	61
74	Houston †	52
66	Louisville	82

Nickname: Green Wave
Colors: Olive Green & Sky Blue
Arena: Avron B. Fogelman Arena
  Capacity: 3,600; Year Built: 1933
AD: Rick Dickson
SID: John Sudsbury

TULSA
Tulsa, OK 74104-3189 I

Coach: John Phillips, Oklahoma St.
1973
2002-03 RESULTS (23-10)

71	New Mexico St. †	61
80	Tex.-Pan American †	50
61	Arkansas	60
80	Wichita St. ■	69
80	Kansas ■	89
62	Southwest Mo. St.	46
90	Oral Roberts ■	80
78	TCU	65
63	Iowa ■	67
65	Fresno St.	74
63	Nevada ■	60
94	Rice	77
79	UTEP	65
74	Boise St.	78
68	Louisiana Tech ■	61
84	Southern Methodist ■	86
57	San Jose St.	58
67	Hawaii	73
79	Rice ■	56
82	Louisiana Tech	93
71	Boise St. ■	55
81	UTEP ■	58
77	Southern Methodist	70
60	Gonzaga	69
76	Hawaii ■	51
74	San Jose St. ■	53
62	Fresno St. ■	59
79	Nevada	73
81	UTEP ■	47
66	Hawaii ■	56
75	Nevada ■	64
84	Dayton †	71
60	Wisconsin †	61

Nickname: Golden Hurricane
Colors: Old Gold, Royal Blue, Crimson
Arena: Donald W. Reynolds Center
  Capacity: 8,355; Year Built: 1998
AD: Judy MacLeod
SID: Don Tomkalski

TUSCULUM
Greeneville, TN 37743 II

Coach: Griff Mills, DePauw 1988
2002-03 RESULTS (16-12)

90	Lees-McRae	56
77	Montreat	82
92	North Greenville ■	41
70	Erskine ■	57
82	Concord	71
47	Lincoln Memorial ■	52
84	Montreat ■	69
54	Lincoln Memorial	71
69	Lander	51
69	Lees-McRae ■	34
55	S.C.-Spartanburg	58
57	Concord ■	45
49	Presbyterian	54
87	North Greenville	69

84	Catawba	70
69	Lenoir-Rhyne ■	60
44	Newberry	59
58	Carson-Newman ■	61
66	Mars Hill ■	63
55	Wingate	81
43	Presbyterian ■	52
81	Catawba ■	71
56	Lenoir-Rhyne	63
81	Newberry ■	62
72	Carson-Newman	63
57	Mars Hill	65
92	Wingate ■	89
54	Presbyterian	61

Nickname: Pioneers
Colors: Black & Orange
Arena: Alpine Arena
  Capacity: 2,000; Year Built: 1998
AD: Ed Hoffmeyer
SID: Dom Donnelly

TUSKEGEE
Tuskegee, AL 36088 II

Coach: Oliver Jones, Albany St. (Ga.)
1965
2002-03 RESULTS (11-17)

79	Alabama A&M	96
76	Fort Valley St. ■	62
86	Columbus St.	97
80	Xavier (La.)	77
80	West Ala.	62
87	North Ala.	93
67	Southern U.	78
65	Albany St. (Ga.)	68
66	Benedict	67
72	Paine	78
81	Morehouse	82
92	Lane ■	95
72	Morehouse ■	82
74	Fort Valley St.	80
74	Albany St. (Ga.) ■	67
90	LeMoyne-Owen ■	93
75	Clark Atlanta	73
88	Clark Atlanta ■	78
86	Lane	92
78	LeMoyne-Owen	85
83	Kentucky St.	78
77	Miles ■	79
102	West Ala. ■	76
75	Paine	72
93	Kentucky St. ■	82
80	Miles	82
68	Albany St. (Ga.) †	65
69	Miles †	79

Nickname: Golden Tigers
Colors: Crimson & Old Gold
Arena: James Center Arena
  Capacity: 5,000; Year Built: 1987
AD: Rick Comegy
SID: Arnold Houston

UCLA
Los Angeles, CA 90095-1405 I

Coach: Steve Lavin, Chapman 1988
2002-03 RESULTS (10-19)

81	San Diego ■	86
73	Duke †	84
81	Long Beach St. ■	58
105	Portland	67
63	Northern Ariz. ■	67
70	Kansas	87
76	Michigan ■	81
77	Washington	67
98	Washington St.	83
75	Southern California ■	80
65	St. John's (N.Y.) ■	80
64	Arizona St.	75
52	Arizona ■	87

51	Stanford	52
69	California	80
91	Oregon ■	96
79	Oregon St. ■	83
85	Southern California	86
71	Georgetown	70
70	Arizona	106
69	Arizona St.	85
76	California ■	75
84	Stanford ■	93
69	Oregon St.	66
48	Oregon	79
86	Washington St. ■	71
83	Washington ■	72
96	Arizona †	89
74	Oregon †	75

Nickname: Bruins
Colors: Blue & Gold
Arena: Pauley Pavilion
  Capacity: 12,819; Year Built: 1965
AD: Daniel Guerrero
SID: Marc Dellins

UNION (N.Y.)
Schenectady, NY 12308 III

Coach: Bob Montana, Brockport St.
1972
2002-03 RESULTS (17-12)

56	Haverford	67
61	Swarthmore	54
63	Utica	48
74	Hartwick	64
59	Goucher	65
54	Mary Washington	69
76	Plattsburgh St. ■	81
76	Maritime (N.Y.) ■	40
80	St. Joseph's (Me.) ■	62
78	Skidmore	82
59	Rensselaer	57
75	Vassar	58
68	Middlebury ■	83
80	Hamilton ■	72
93	Hobart ■	89
81	Clarkson	72
71	St. Lawrence	73
78	Hobart	62
58	Hamilton	85
65	Skidmore ■	64
88	Vassar ■	51
86	Rensselaer ■	91
62	Williams	67
81	St. Lawrence ■	60
70	Clarkson ■	57
52	St. Lawrence †	50
70	Hamilton	74
84	Oswego St. ■	83
62	Rochester Inst. †	65

Nickname: Dutchmen
Colors: Garnet
Arena: Memorial Field House
  Capacity: 3,000; Year Built: 1950
AD: Val Belmonte
SID: George Cuttita

UPPER IOWA
Fayette, IA 52142-1857 III

Coach: Dave Martin, Upper Iowa 1990
2002-03 RESULTS (8-17)

36	Wis.-Stevens Point	63
65	Macalester †	71
69	Minn. St. Mankato	83
62	Simpson	86
80	Mt. Mercy	78
78	Iowa Wesleyan ■	76
53	William Penn	56
81	Clarke ■	64
65	Coe ■	74
84	Cornell College ■	66

78	Dubuque	67
62	Loras	71
77	Central (Iowa)	62
51	Luther ■	54
55	Buena Vista ■	80
68	Wartburg ■	71
90	Central (Iowa) ■	98
73	Cornell College	74
61	Coe	80
72	Loras ■	70
85	Dubuque ■	64
61	Simpson ■	80
57	Luther	61
67	Wartburg	80
79	Buena Vista	93

Nickname: Peacocks
Colors: Columbia Blue & White
Arena: Dorman Memorial Gym
  Capacity: 2,000; Year Built: 1963
AD: Gil Cloud
SID: Brian Thiessen

URSINUS
Collegeville, PA 19426-1000 III

Coach: Kevin Small, St. Joseph's 1991
2002-03 RESULTS (21-7)

59	Springfield †	73
92	Drew	67
79	Eastern	66
69	Lebanon Valley	68
77	Hunter ■	70
72	Dickinson	69
93	Haverford	89
70	Lafayette	87
75	Hobart †	71
64	Albion †	95
80	Trinity (Conn.) ■	85
78	Gwynedd-Mercy ■	81
83	Frank. & Marsh.	82
95	Washington (Md.) ■	82
75	Swarthmore ■	51
56	Princeton	99
80	Muhlenberg	68
79	Johns Hopkins ■	63
74	Drew	71
76	Haverford ■	52
65	McDaniel	49
92	Washington (Md.)	79
70	Swarthmore	48
91	Gettysburg ■	77
76	Muhlenberg ■	69
78	Johns Hopkins	62
96	Frank. & Marsh. ■	88
75	Scranton	77

Nickname: Bears
Colors: Red, Old Gold & Black
Arena: D.L. Helfferich Hall
  Capacity: 2,500; Year Built: 1972
AD: Brian Thomas
SID: Bill Stiles

UTAH
Salt Lake City, UT 84112-9008 ... I

Coach: Rick Majerus, Marquette 1970
2002-03 RESULTS (25-8)

61	Southern Utah ■	47
52	Gonzaga †	71
69	Massachusetts †	53
79	Arizona St. †	83
72	Winthrop ■	42
78	Arizona St. ■	55
75	Northern Iowa ■	53
54	Utah St.	59
77	Pepperdine	61
64	San Diego	58
51	Alabama ■	49
72	Weber St. ■	58
65	St. Mary's (Cal.) ■ ■	59

76	IPFW ■	59
75	Ripon ■	59
56	San Diego St.	58
66	UNLV	63
79	Brigham Young	75
45	Air Force ■	35
78	New Mexico ■	68
71	Colorado St.	66
69	Wyoming	56
76	San Diego St. ■	62
86	UNLV ■	80
71	Brigham Young ■	64
69	New Mexico	76
57	Air Force	52
65	Colorado St. ■	66
86	Wyoming ■	70
42	Air Force †	38
41	UNLV	64
60	Oregon †	58
54	Kentucky †	74

Nickname: Utes
Colors: Crimson & White
Arena: Jon M. Huntsman Center
  Capacity: 15,000; Year Built: 1969
AD: Christopher Hill
SID: Mike Lageschulte

UTAH ST.
Logan, UT 84322-7400 I

Coach: Stew Morrill, Gonzaga 1974
2002-03 RESULTS (24-9)

68	Illinois St.	53
86	Whitman ■	52
62	Vermont †	59
73	Drake †	61
71	Hawaii-Hilo	60
57	Jackson St.	63
56	Brigham Young	66
59	Utah ■	54
66	Weber St. ■	64
72	Arkansas St. ■	54
66	Idaho St. ■	59
59	Cal St. Northridge	44
54	Pacific (Cal.)	66
81	Cal Poly	67
75	UC Santa Barb. ■	59
73	UC Irvine	75
63	Long Beach St.	55
77	UC Riverside ■	58
61	Cal St. Fullerton ■	60
60	Idaho	56
50	UC Santa Barb.	62
64	Cal Poly	63
58	UC Irvine ■	59
95	Long Beach St. ■	61
62	Cal St. Fullerton	41
65	UC Riverside	72
51	Idaho ■	52
69	Cal St. Northridge ■	58
75	Pacific (Cal.) ■	70
89	Cal St. Fullerton †	83
62	UC Irvine †	55
57	Cal Poly †	54
61	Kansas †	64

Nickname: Aggies
Colors: Navy Blue & White
Arena: Dee Glen Smith Spectrum
  Capacity: 10,270; Year Built: 1970
AD: Rance Pugmire
SID: Doug Hoffman

UTICA
Utica, NY 13502-4892 III

Coach: Andrew Goodemote,
  Albany (N.Y.) 1990
2002-03 RESULTS (10-15)

96	St. Joseph (Vt.) ■	54
73	Utica/Rome ■	54

68	Hamilton	78
48	Union (N.Y.) ■	63
55	Skidmore	68
96	Oneonta St. ■	70
56	Utica/Rome	58
58	Elmira	66
39	Ithaca	48
86	Cazenovia ■	83
64	Hartwick ■	60
62	Hobart	68
55	St. John Fisher ■	58
69	Alfred ■	56
75	Oswego St. ■	50
69	Nazareth	73
70	Rochester Inst.	81
62	Keuka	82
54	Ithaca	63
74	Elmira ■	65
52	Rochester Inst. ■	73
62	Nazareth ■	73
74	Hartwick	62
80	Alfred	58
70	St. John Fisher	79

Nickname: Pioneers
Colors: Navy Blue & Burnt Orange
Arena: Clark Athletic Center
  Capacity: 2,200; Year Built: 1970
AD: James Spartano
SID: Ryan Hyland

UTICA/ROME
Utica, NY 13504-3050 III

Coach: Kevin Grimmer, Hamilton 1982
2002-03 RESULTS (17-10)

77	Wentworth Inst. †	64
54	Utica	73
71	Hamilton ■	80
88	Plattsburgh St. ■	79
66	Oswego St.	74
72	Lebanon Valley	80
83	Ferrum †	79
58	Utica ■	56
74	Brockport St. ■	68
75	Oneonta St. ■	62
78	Cazenovia	62
68	Cortland St.	67
58	Potsdam St. ■	68
72	Buffalo St.	82
76	New Paltz St.	70
106	Paul Smith ■	65
79	Plattsburgh St.	59
88	Geneseo St. ■	68
85	Fredonia St. ■	64
57	Potsdam St.	69
64	Medaille ■	62
45	Fredonia St.	62
78	New Paltz St. ■	70
66	Oneonta St.	63
71	Buffalo St. ■	68
65	Brockport St. ■	82
57	Rochester Inst.	84

Nickname: Wildcats
Colors: Royal Blue & Grey
Arena: Campus Center Gym
  Capacity: 1,400; Year Built: 1987
AD: Kevin Grimmer
SID: Kevin Grimmer

VALDOSTA ST.
Valdosta, GA 31698 II

Coach: Jim Yarbrough, Florida St. 1987
2002-03 RESULTS (19-7)

91	P.R.-Cayey ■	57
95	Carver Bible ■	61
75	P.R.-Rio Piedras ■	59
64	North Ala. ■	49
79	Tenn. Wesleyan ■	60
76	Winston-Salem ■	61

47	St. Leo ■	41
84	North Fla. ■	62
78	Florida Tech ■	47
78	St. Leo	51
66	Nova Southeastern ■	53
55	Florida Tech	57
58	West Ga.	78
64	Lincoln Memorial ■	58
55	Ala.-Huntsville ■	64
68	Montevallo	55
69	West Fla. ■	62
70	North Ala.	75
78	West Ala. ■	65
83	Nova Southeastern	72
55	Lincoln Memorial	57
76	Ala.-Huntsville	77
74	Montevallo ■	65
73	West Fla.	51
95	West Ala.	75
62	West Ga.	66

Nickname: Blazers
Colors: Red & Black
Arena: The Complex
  Capacity: 5,350; Year Built: 1982
AD: Herb Reinhard
SID: Steve Roberts

VALPARAISO
Valparaiso, IN 46383-6493 I

Coach: Scott Drew, Butler 1993
2002-03 RESULTS (20-11)

66	Syracuse	81
81	Indiana St. ■	56
78	Northern Ill. ■	67
50	Cincinnati	76
62	Loyola (Ill.)	80
61	Wis.-Milwaukee	75
87	Samford	79
83	Belmont ■	65
65	Central Mich. ■	51
55	Purdue	87
47	Missouri	65
53	Notre Dame †	55
74	Western Ill. ■	57
74	Southern Utah ■	44
80	Chicago St. ■	48
72	IUPUI	62
72	Oakland	70
84	Oral Roberts ■	71
68	UMKC ■	71
73	Charlotte ■	59
74	Western Ill.	62
81	Chicago St.	70
69	Southern Utah	61
81	Oakland ■	65
77	IUPUI ■	71
75	UMKC	63
75	Oral Roberts	89
82	Chicago St. †	62
71	UMKC †	50
64	IUPUI †	66
60	Iowa	62

Nickname: Crusaders
Colors: Brown & Gold
Arena: Athletics-Recreation Center
  Capacity: 5,000; Year Built: 1984
AD: William Steinbrecher
SID: Bill Rogers

VANDERBILT
Nashville, TN 37212 I

Coach: Kevin Stallings, Purdue 1982
2002-03 RESULTS (11-18)

80	Southeastern La. ■	58
68	Alabama A&M ■	40
96	Ga. Southern ■	60
70	Connecticut ■	76
86	East Tenn. St. ■	75

66	Tulane ■	46
56	Indiana ■	73
81	High Point ■	75
66	Michigan	70
63	Notre Dame	76
70	Col. of Charleston ■	53
59	Auburn	62
70	Alabama ■	69
52	Kentucky ■	74
66	Tennessee	71
75	Florida	87
94	Georgia ■	91
76	Mississippi ■	68
60	Mississippi St.	82
72	South Carolina ■	84
60	LSU	79
70	Georgia	83
74	Florida ■	77
50	Arkansas ■	60
64	South Carolina	76
44	Kentucky	106
65	Tennessee ■	70
82	Alabama †	69
63	Kentucky †	81

Nickname: Commodores
Colors: Black & Gold
Arena: Memorial Gymnasium
  Capacity: 14,168; Year Built: 1952
AD: Todd Turner
SID: Brent Ross

VASSAR
Poughkeepsie, NY
12604-0750 III

Coach: Mike Dutton, New Hampshire
  1981
2002-03 RESULTS (6-19)

86	Mass. Liberal Arts ■	74
68	Baruch ■	77
73	NYCCT	71
74	Manhattanville ■	64
88	Westfield St.	93
58	John Jay	76
55	Wesleyan (Conn.) ■	77
69	Drew	74
46	Skidmore ■	75
58	Union (N.Y.) ■	75
57	Rensselaer ■	72
56	St. Lawrence	77
57	Clarkson	70
48	Hobart ■	96
52	Hamilton ■	78
67	Mt. St. Mary (N.Y.) ■	61
83	Bard ■	47
59	Clarkson ■	63
76	St. Lawrence ■	86
64	New Paltz St. ■	74
51	Union (N.Y.)	88
63	Skidmore	62
63	Rensselaer	77
66	Hamilton	79
73	Hobart	98

Nickname: Brewers
Colors: Burgundy & Gray
Arena: Athletic & Fitness Facility
  Capacity: 850; Year Built: 2000
AD: Andy Jennings
SID: Casey Hager

VERMONT
Burlington, VT 05405 I

Coach: Tom Brennan, Georgia 1971
2002-03 RESULTS (21-12)

71	Eastern Mich. †	64
66	Marist	63
62	Dartmouth ■	41
59	Utah St. †	62
66	Hawaii-Hilo	69

78	Drake †	83
60	Providence	71
64	Harvard	71
54	North Carolina	80
81	St. Michael's ■	56
101	Sacred Heart ■	75
65	Maine	62
66	Stony Brook ■	47
89	Northeastern	81
62	Boston U.	65
66	Cornell	52
63	Albany (N.Y.)	53
65	Maine	59
55	Hartford ■	63
92	New Hampshire	75
50	Binghamton	61
111	Middlebury ■	75
66	Stony Brook	60
74	Binghamton ■	54
59	Northeastern	76
85	New Hampshire ■	68
60	Boston U.	53
61	Hartford	64
69	Albany (N.Y.) ■	60
81	Albany (N.Y.) †	62
67	Hartford †	51
56	Boston U.	55
51	Arizona †	80

Nickname: Catamounts
Colors: Green & Gold
Arena: Roy L. Patrick Gymnasium
  Capacity: 3,200; Year Built: 1963
AD: Richard Farnham
SID: Gordon Woodworth

VILLA JULIE
Stevenson, MD 21153-9999 III

Coach: Brett Adams, York (Pa.) 1989
2002-03 RESULTS (6-19)

63	Lynchburg †	73
66	Arcadia †	71
66	Gallaudet	75
68	Catholic	108
82	Maryland Bible ■	65
73	Cabrini ■	82
71	Piedmont †	89
73	Chowan	76
75	Mary Washington	91
63	DeSales ■	77
81	John Jay	68
65	Delaware Valley ■	66
76	Goucher	77
80	Wheaton (Ill.) ■	92
95	Marymount (Va.)	113
80	Messiah ■	92
62	Johns Hopkins ■	80
93	Albright	81
57	McDaniel ■	56
80	Shenandoah ■	71
78	Phila. Bible ■	64
86	Washington (Md.)	101
68	Mary Washington ■	70
60	Juniata	75
64	Misericordia ■	91

Nickname: Mustangs
Colors: Green, Black & White
Arena: Villa Julie Student Union
  Capacity: 1,200; Year Built: 1997
AD: Brett Adams
SID: Mike Buchanan

VILLANOVA
Villanova, PA 19085-1674 I

Coach: Jay Wright, Bucknell 1983
2002-03 RESULTS (15-16)

61	Marquette †	73
64	Drexel ■	41

87	Loyola Marymount †	71
81	Michigan St. †	73
69	Col. of Charleston †	71
74	La Salle †	71
58	Pennsylvania ■	72
72	UMBC ■	60
78	Dayton	80
68	Binghamton ■	53
70	Temple ■	62
68	Memphis	72
92	Virginia Tech ■	81
81	Providence ■	67
82	St. John's (N.Y.)	73
110	Rutgers	89
94	Boston College ■	83
65	Connecticut	74
83	West Virginia ■	91
75	St. Joseph's	92
72	Miami (Fla.)	67
50	St. John's (N.Y.) ■	52
79	Connecticut	70
60	Providence	70
75	Miami (Fla.) ■	56
56	Seton Hall	57
63	Virginia Tech	88
84	Boston College	92
54	Pittsburgh ■	56
41	Georgetown †	46
59	Siena	74

Nickname: Wildcats
Colors: Blue & White
Arena: Pavilion
  Capacity: 6,500; Year Built: 1986
AD: Vincent Nicastro
SID: Mike Sheridan

VIRGINIA
Charlottesville, VA 22904-4821 ..I

Coach: Pete Gillen, Fairfield 1968
2002-03 RESULTS (16-16)

90	Long Island ■	86
86	Chaminade †	72
75	Kentucky †	61
63	Indiana †	70
75	Michigan St.	82
84	East Tenn. St. ■	76
72	Gardner-Webb ■	65
61	Rutgers	57
79	Georgetown ■	75
77	Liberty ■	58
87	Wofford ■	65
63	North Carolina St.	75
79	North Carolina	72
93	Duke	104
77	Clemson	78
55	Virginia Tech	73
85	Wake Forest ■	75
85	Florida St. ■	72
60	Georgia Tech	80
86	Maryland	78
61	North Carolina St. ■	58
67	North Carolina	81
59	Duke ■	78
64	Clemson ■	73
71	Wake Forest	75
72	Ohio	78
59	Florida St.	73
73	Georgia Tech ■	90
80	Maryland ■	78
76	Duke †	83
89	Brown	73
63	St. John's (N.Y.)	73

Nickname: Cavaliers
Colors: Orange & Blue
Arena: University Hall
  Capacity: 8,392; Year Built: 1965
AD: Craig Littlepage
SID: Rich Murray

VA. COMMONWEALTH
Richmond, VA 23284-3013........I

Coach: Jeff Capel III, Duke 1997
2002-03 RESULTS (18-10)

73	Western Ky.	80
72	Wagner	80
76	N.C. A&T ■	48
90	Fla. Atlantic ■	72
73	Richmond	68
68	Mississippi	82
90	Hampton ■	85
91	TCU ■	78
71	Hofstra ■	62
73	Old Dominion	64
73	Drexel ■	74
53	Delaware	55
68	George Mason	56
83	William & Mary ■	88
65	James Madison	58
50	UNC Wilmington ■	81
82	Towson	47
72	Old Dominion	69
97	Towson ■	60
78	George Mason ■	62
72	Drexel	59
71	Delaware	66
93	William & Mary ■	73
80	Hofstra	77
63	James Madison	64
63	UNC Wilmington	80
73	James Madison †	53
60	Drexel †	62

Nickname: Rams
Colors: Black & Gold
Arena: Stuart C. Siegel Center
  Capacity: 7,500; Year Built: 1999
AD: Richard Sander
SID: Josh Lehman

VMI
Lexington, VA 24450-0304 I

Coach: Bart Bellairs, Warren Wilson
1979
2002-03 RESULTS (10-20)

68	Liberty ■	54
56	Tennessee	88
76	St. Francis (Pa.)	59
66	Virginia Tech	71
77	Virginia-Wise ■	66
69	Liberty	77
100	East. Mennonite ■	57
56	Mary Washington ■	60
69	Norfolk St. †	70
71	Harvard †	67
48	Georgetown	85
56	Western Caro.	78
84	Ga. Southern ■	91
57	UNC Greensboro	76
62	East Tenn. St. ■	67
61	Davidson ■	60
68	Appalachian St. ■	85
56	Col. of Charleston	81
55	Furman	61
76	East Tenn. St.	93
93	Wofford ■	94
64	Appalachian St.	83
58	Western Caro. ■	61
52	Chattanooga	77
61	UNC Greensboro ■	60
58	Citadel	49
49	Davidson	84
62	Furman †	56
66	Davidson †	60
58	Chattanooga †	77

Nickname: Keydets
Colors: Red, White, Yellow
Arena: Cameron Hall
  Capacity: 5,029; Year Built: 1981

AD: Donald White
SID: Wade Branner

VIRGINIA ST.
Petersburg, VA 23806-0001 II

Coach: Robert Booker, Claflin 1964
2002-03 RESULTS (8-20)

80	Lock Haven †	62
62	Millersville	84
63	Lenoir-Rhyne ■	77
76	N.C. Central ■	84
55	Lenoir-Rhyne	68
78	Longwood	81
79	Barton ■	71
73	Livingstone	65
59	Bowie St. ■	74
58	Barton	77
72	Columbia Union	66
40	Elizabeth City St.	68
75	Shaw	66
63	Dist. Columbia	67
60	Virginia Union ■	72
59	Winston-Salem	63
67	Dist. Columbia ■	77
91	Columbia Union ■	67
61	St. Augustine's	82
79	St. Paul's	76
69	Johnson Smith	76
69	Virginia Union	87
71	Bowie St.	94
87	Elizabeth City St. ■	81
48	Shaw ■	75
66	Fayetteville St.	82
74	St. Paul's ■	75
49	Winston-Salem †	54

Nickname: Trojans
Colors: Orange & Navy Blue
Arena: Daniel Gymnasium
  Capacity: 3,454; Year Built: 1965
AD: Derek Carter
SID: Paul Williams

VIRGINIA TECH
Blacksburg, VA 24061 I

Coach: Ricky Stokes, Virginia 1984
2002-03 RESULTS (11-18)

78	St. Bonaventure †	91
65	Michigan †	53
58	Toledo †	45
69	American ■	61
77	Wofford ■	79
71	VMI ■	66
52	William & Mary ■	60
60	East Caro.	76
71	Morgan St. ■	64
54	Western Mich.	75
76	Towson ■	52
69	Florida St. ■	76
81	Villanova	92
65	Connecticut	83
92	Providence ■	79
73	Virginia ■	55
59	St. John's (N.Y.) ■	62
71	Boston College ■	95
58	Providence	89
95	Connecticut ■	74
71	St. John's (N.Y.)	54
65	Miami (Fla.)	85
73	Georgetown ■	85
69	Boston College	87
76	Notre Dame	98
62	Pittsburgh ■	75
88	Villanova ■	63
71	Miami (Fla.) ■	79
67	West Virginia	71

Nickname: Hokies
Colors: Burnt Orange & Maroon
Arena: Cassell Coliseum

Capacity: 10,052; Year Built: 1961
AD: James Weaver
SID: Bill Dyer

VIRGINIA UNION
Richmond, VA 23220-1790 II

Coach: Dave Robbins, Catawba 1966
2002-03 RESULTS (18-11)
80	Millersville ■	87
70	Millersville	74
73	Johnson Smith ■	97
76	Winston-Salem	81
80	North Ala. †	78
83	Fayetteville St. ■	58
72	Dist. Columbia	75
85	St. Paul's	75
87	St. Paul's ■	67
72	Virginia St.	60
88	Bowie St. ■	90
75	N.C. Central ■	66
75	Elizabeth City St.	61
65	Shaw	69
76	Columbia Union ■	43
83	St. Augustine's	80
99	Bowie St.	96
71	Columbia Union	51
87	Virginia St. ■	69
73	Shaw ■	58
77	Dist. Columbia ■	65
91	N.C. Central	82
73	Livingstone	80
73	Winston-Salem	76
86	Elizabeth City St. ■	73
81	Winston-Salem †	59
81	St. Augustine's †	80
71	Bowie St. †	72
65	Kennesaw St. †	74

Nickname: Panthers
Colors: Steel & Maroon
Arena: Arthur Ashe Athletic Center
   Capacity: 6,000; Year Built: 1982
AD: Michael Bailey
SID: Paul Williams

VA. WESLEYAN
Norfolk, VA 23502-5599 III

Coach: David Macedo, Wilkes 1996
2002-03 RESULTS (18-9)
60	Thomas More ■	64
90	Bethany (W.Va.) ■	63
70	Chris. Newport ■	65
66	East. Mennonite ■	44
79	Salisbury	68
59	Chowan ■	49
62	Newport News ■	58
69	Roanoke	63
70	Wash. & Lee	54
70	Lynchburg	61
80	Emory & Henry ■	69
76	Guilford ■	64
79	Bridgewater (Va.)	53
63	Randolph-Macon ■	73
54	Hampden-Sydney ■	68
71	Wash. & Lee ■	49
68	Roanoke ■	71
60	Apprentice	72
60	Guilford	72
81	Emory & Henry	73
75	Lynchburg ■	60
49	Randolph-Macon	69
80	East. Mennonite	55
69	Bridgewater (Va.) ■	65
68	Hampden-Sydney	83
81	Emory & Henry †	73
66	Hampden-Sydney †	73

Nickname: Blue Marlins
Colors: Navy Blue & Silver
Arena: Batten Center

Capacity: 1,400; Year Built: 2002
AD: Sonny Travis
SID: Joe Wasiluk

WABASH
Crawfordsville, IN 47933 III

Coach: Mac Petty, Tennessee 1968
2002-03 RESULTS (16-10)
77	Purdue-Calumet ■	54
64	Ill. Wesleyan ■	78
83	Franklin ■	60
87	Tufts †	81
80	Phila. Bible †	72
62	DePauw	73
72	Denison	52
74	Averett ■	59
67	Marian (Ind.) ■	53
85	Hiram	73
74	Allegheny	63
63	Wooster	76
93	Earlham ■	57
64	Oberlin ■	45
47	Wittenberg	62
65	Kenyon ■	61
53	Ohio Wesleyan	77
78	Denison	76
74	Earlham	77
69	Wooster ■	74
55	Ohio Wesleyan ■	54
78	Oberlin	87
86	Wittenberg ■	95
81	Kenyon	73
69	Ohio Wesleyan ■	63
66	Wooster	76

Nickname: Little Giants
Colors: Scarlet
Arena: Chadwick Court
   Capacity: 1,800; Year Built: 1917
AD: Vernon Memmert
SID: Brent Harris

WAGNER
Staten Island, NY 10301-4495...I

Coach: Dereck Whittenburg, North
Carolina St. 1984
2002-03 RESULTS (21-11)
65	UNC Greensboro	84
81	Brown ■	69
80	Va. Commonwealth	72
81	Iona	87
85	Connecticut	97
63	Delaware St.	70
81	Ga. Southern	90
69	American ■	55
80	Lehigh ■	68
57	Maryland	79
74	Sacred Heart	63
76	Central Conn. St.	67
91	Quinnipiac ■	69
79	Fairleigh Dickinson ■	83
63	Monmouth	45
101	Robert Morris ■	80
84	St. Francis (Pa.)	72
77	Robert Morris	72
102	St. Francis (Pa.) ■	89
62	Fairleigh Dickinson	68
62	Monmouth ■	53
74	Quinnipiac	70
61	Central Conn. St. ■	58
57	Mt. St. Mary's ■	55
76	UMBC ■	65
79	Sacred Heart ■	71
71	Long Island	87
84	St. Francis (N.Y.)	96
88	Long Island ■	66
61	Quinnipiac ■	54
78	St. Francis (N.Y.) ■	61
61	Pittsburgh †	87

Nickname: Seahawks
Colors: Green & White
Arena: Spiro Sports Center
   Capacity: 2,100; Year Built: 1999
AD: Walt Hameline
SID: Bob Balut

WAKE FOREST
Winston-Salem, NC 27109 I

Coach: Skip Prosser, Merchant Marine
1972
2002-03 RESULTS (25-6)
73	Yale ■	61
83	Temple ■	76
90	Wisconsin	80
73	Southern Methodist ■	49
84	St. John's (N.Y.) ■	72
100	South Carolina St. ■	57
104	N.C. A&T	64
96	Bethune-Cookman ■	54
68	Richmond	62
98	Elon ■	56
55	Duke	74
81	Maryland ■	72
73	Georgia Tech	66
75	Virginia	85
71	Florida St. ■	60
81	Clemson	60
79	North Carolina	75
73	North Carolina St. ■	58
61	Marquette	68
94	Duke ■	80
67	Maryland	90
75	Georgia Tech	67
75	Virginia ■	71
60	Florida St.	56
80	Clemson ■	68
75	North Carolina ■	60
78	North Carolina St.	72
69	Florida St. †	61
83	North Carolina St. †	87
76	East Tenn. St. †	73
62	Auburn †	68

Nickname: Demon Deacons
Colors: Old Gold & Black
Arena: Lawrence Joel Coliseum
   Capacity: 14,665; Year Built: 1989
AD: Ron Wellman
SID: Dean Buchan

WARTBURG
Waverly, IA 50677-1003 III

Coach: Dick Peth, Iowa 1981
2002-03 RESULTS (21-7)
96	St. Mary (Kan.) ■	78
76	Wis.-Whitewater ■	67
75	Buena Vista	67
62	Albion †	49
77	Rockford †	79
88	Iowa Wesleyan	86
75	Concordia (Cal.) †	101
89	Cal Lutheran	81
74	Central (Iowa) ■	81
65	Simpson ■	73
85	Coe	80
67	Cornell College	69
96	Dubuque ■	48
79	Loras ■	70
80	Luther	55
71	Upper Iowa	68
76	Simpson	68
73	Central (Iowa)	59
64	Cornell College ■	58
71	Coe	66
62	Buena Vista ■	71
72	Loras	69
70	Dubuque	64
80	Upper Iowa ■	67

58	Luther ■	48
65	Luther ■	47
77	Cornell College ■	67
70	Buena Vista	72

Nickname: Knights
Colors: Orange & Black
Arena: Knights Gym
   Capacity: 1,800; Year Built: 1949
AD: Gary Grace
SID: Mark Adkins

WASHBURN
Topeka, KS 66621 II

Coach: Bob Chipman, Kansas St. 1973
2002-03 RESULTS (26-6)
71	Baker ■	53
77	Evangel ■	69
87	St. Cloud St. †	70
53	Lynn	78
85	Rockhurst ■	66
87	Newman ■	86
82	Central Okla. †	74
92	Southern Ind. †	84
99	Fontbonne ■	58
80	Mo. Southern St.	53
80	Truman	71
99	Southwest Baptist ■	67
67	Mo.-Rolla ■	51
58	Northwest Mo. St.	59
83	Central Mo. St. ■	66
63	Emporia St.	84
73	Pittsburg St.	72
67	Mo. Western St. ■	68
77	Truman	50
68	Southwest Baptist	55
84	Mo.-Rolla	71
62	Northwest Mo. St. ■	52
74	Central Mo. St.	68
85	Emporia St. ■	77
79	Pittsburg St. ■	77
75	Mo. Western St.	65
105	Mo. Southern St. ■	91
75	Central Mo. St. †	60
80	Mo. Southern St. †	61
65	Mo. Western St. †	75
75	West Tex. A&M †	73
59	Northeastern †	64

Nickname: Ichabods
Colors: Yale Blue & White
Arena: Lee Arena
   Capacity: 4,298; Year Built: 1984
AD: Loren Ferre'
SID: Gene Cassell

WASHINGTON
Seattle, WA 98195...................I

Coach: Lorenzo Romar, Washington
1992
2002-03 RESULTS (10-17)
53	Montana St. ■	56
61	UNLV	82
89	Gonzaga	95
79	Wyoming ■	70
72	Santa Clara	55
58	Eastern Wash. ■	62
83	Florida Int'l ■	48
85	Houston	61
89	Cal St. Northridge ■	80
67	UCLA ■	77
76	Southern California ■	72
57	Arizona St.	89
61	Arizona	79
66	California ■	73
73	Stanford ■	68
66	Oregon	91
92	Oregon St.	82
81	Washington St. ■	67

85 Arizona ■ ...88
77 Arizona St. ■ ...79
69 Stanford ...78
53 California ...58
72 Oregon St. ■ ...80
78 Oregon ■ ...66
76 Washington St. ...98
95 Southern California ...89
72 UCLA ...83

Nickname: Huskies
Colors: Purple & Gold
Arena: Bank of America Arena
Capacity: 10,000; Year Built: 1927
AD: Barbara Hedges
SID: Dan Lepse

WASH. & JEFF.
Washington, PA 15301-4801 ...III

Coach: Tom Reiter, Wisconsin 1975
2002-03 RESULTS (6-19)
71 Carnegie Mellon ■ ...82
71 Allegheny ...96
85 La Roche ...96
82 Case Reserve ...93
59 Penn St.-Behrend ■ ...57
71 Medaille ■ ...74
44 Davidson ...125
60 Catholic ...107
54 Frostburg St. † ...74
99 Pitt.-Greensburg ■ ...108
80 La Roche ...84
79 Oberlin ■ ...68
71 Carnegie Mellon ...85
76 Waynesburg ...78
89 Thiel ■ ...72
88 Bethany (W.Va.) ■ ...85
74 Westminster (Pa.) ...90
70 Grove City ...76
98 Kenyon ...93
69 Waynesburg ■ ...76
64 Thiel ...83
85 Bethany (W.Va.) ...101
83 Westminster (Pa.) ■ ...81
66 Grove City ■ ...86
64 Westminster (Pa.) ...85

Nickname: Presidents
Colors: Red & Black
Arena: Henry Memorial Center
Capacity: 2,800; Year Built: 1970
AD: Rick Creehan
SID: Scott McGuinness

WASH. & LEE
Lexington, VA 24450 ...III

Coach: Jeff Lafave, Southern Conn. St. 1992
2002-03 RESULTS (8-17)
79 Daniel Webster ■ ...59
87 Washington (Md.) ■ ...72
48 Davidson ...105
69 Southern Va. ■ ...58
55 Guilford ...57
41 Randolph-Macon ■ ...65
54 Va. Wesleyan ■ ...70
53 Roanoke ■ ...65
50 Mary Washington ...76
75 East. Mennonite ...72
68 Lynchburg ...51
48 Hampden-Sydney ...87
73 Emory & Henry ■ ...75
49 Va. Wesleyan ...71
46 Randolph-Macon ...71
66 McDaniel ...69
64 Bridgewater (Va.) ■ ...66
47 Roanoke ...57
67 Emory & Henry ...80
60 Hampden-Sydney ...67
63 Lynchburg ■ ...62

72 Guilford ...57
76 East. Mennonite ■ ...73
63 Bridgewater (Va.) ...72
53 Randolph-Macon † ...71

Nickname: Generals
Colors: Royal Blue & White
Arena: Warner Center
Capacity: 2,500; Year Built: 1972
AD: Michael Walsh
SID: Brian Laubscher

WASHINGTON (MD.)
Chestertown, MD 21620-1197 ..III

Coach: Rob Nugent, Mass. Liberal Arts 1997
2002-03 RESULTS (10-16)
66 Averett † ...63
72 Wash. & Lee ...87
70 Salisbury ...80
51 Davidson ...114
69 Gettysburg ...76
76 Marymount (Va.) ...74
65 Swarthmore ■ ...82
74 Mary Washington ■ ...78
82 Messiah ...91
75 Westminster (Pa.) † ...77
69 Wilkes ...93
69 Johns Hopkins ...82
82 Ursinus ...95
101 Muhlenberg ■ ...98
80 Haverford ...76
70 Gallaudet ■ ...72
125 Wesley ...124
96 Frank. & Marsh. ■ ...86
101 Villa Julie ■ ...86
61 Swarthmore ...67
80 Dickinson ■ ...79
79 Ursinus ■ ...92
84 Haverford ■ ...72
76 Muhlenberg ...80
69 McDaniel ■ ...65
62 Frank. & Marsh. ...92

Nickname: Shoremen
Colors: Maroon & Black
Arena: Frank C. Russell Gymnasium at Cain Athletic Center
Capacity: 1,200; Year Built: 1957
AD: Bryan Matthews
SID: Phil Ticknor

WASHINGTON (MO.)
St. Louis, MO 63130-4899 ...III

Coach: Mark Edwards, Washington (Mo.) 1969
2002-03 RESULTS (24-2)
91 Wesleyan (Conn.) ■ ...63
77 Pomona-Pitzer ■ ...44
91 Dallas ■ ...72
70 Southwestern (Tex.) † ...64
68 Trinity (Tex.) ...65
95 Coe ...85
88 Ill. Wesleyan ...75
74 MacMurray ■ ...60
76 Blackburn ■ ...45
95 Webster ■ ...53
82 Wis. Lutheran ...81
75 Chicago ...56
102 Case Reserve ...33
96 Emory ...84
74 Rochester ...71
79 Carnegie Mellon ■ ...59
92 Brandeis ...60
64 New York U. ■ ...56
87 New York U. ...55
99 Brandeis ...62
89 Emory ...63
85 Case Reserve ■ ...67
98 Carnegie Mellon ...63

82 Rochester ...83
85 Chicago ■ ...50
73 Ill. Wesleyan ■ ...85

Nickname: Bears
Colors: Red & Green
Arena: WU Field House
Capacity: 3,000; Year Built: 1984
AD: John Schael
SID: Keith Jenkins

WASHINGTON ST.
Pullman, WA 99164-1602 ...I

Coach: Paul Graham, North Texas 1974
2002-03 RESULTS (7-20)
76 San Jose St. ■ ...68
72 Southern Utah ■ ...66
83 TCU ...86
58 Idaho ...62
104 Gonzaga ■ ...110
73 Montana ...61
79 Colorado St. ...90
78 High Point † ...71
69 Fresno St. ■ ...66
90 Southern California ■ ...97
83 UCLA ■ ...98
69 Arizona ■ ...82
55 Arizona St. ...96
68 Stanford ■ ...73
63 California ■ ...76
48 Oregon St. ...63
66 Oregon ...76
67 Washington ...81
54 Arizona St. ■ ...87
62 Arizona ...75
53 California ...63
54 Stanford ...72
70 Oregon ...89
75 Oregon St. ■ ...71
98 Washington ■ ...76
71 UCLA ...86
68 Southern California ...86

Nickname: Cougars
Colors: Crimson & Gray
Arena: Friel Court
Capacity: 12,058; Year Built: 1973
AD: James Sterk
SID: Rod Commons

WAYNE ST. (MICH.)
Detroit, MI 48202-3489 ...II

Coach: David Greer, Bowling Green 1987
2002-03 RESULTS (13-14)
93 Saginaw Valley ■ ...81
69 Northwood ■ ...65
37 Butler ...60
94 Saginaw Valley ...100
86 Northwood ...70
82 Central St. (Ohio) ■ ...74
89 Kentucky St. ...73
66 Northern Ky. ...79
54 Tampa ...59
63 Fla. Southern ...77
66 Grand Valley St. ...84
74 Ferris St. ...71
74 Lake Superior St. ■ ...68
56 Michigan Tech ...70
64 Northern Mich. ■ ...74
69 Gannon ...64
61 Mercyhurst ...69
68 Ashland ■ ...65
70 Findlay ■ ...62
74 Central St. (Ohio) ...81
78 Hillsdale ...62
71 Mercyhurst ■ ...57
59 Gannon ...62
72 Findlay ...80
92 Ashland ...88

65 Hillsdale ...87
60 Gannon ...78

Nickname: Warriors
Colors: Green & Gold
Arena: Matthaei Building
Capacity: 2,000; Year Built: 1966
AD: Robert Fournier
SID: Eva McGillivray

WAYNE ST. (NEB.)
Wayne, NE 68787-1172 ...II

Coach: Rico Burkett, North Dakota 1993
2002-03 RESULTS (13-15)
63 South Dakota ...88
40 Northern Iowa ...71
86 Mt. Marty ...74
63 Neb.-Kearney ...84
55 Minn. St. Mankato † ...66
59 Michigan Tech † ...78
72 Briar Cliff ...68
61 Neb.-Omaha ...76
57 St. Cloud St. ...77
78 Bemidji St. ■ ...71
84 Minn. Duluth ■ ...83
55 Northern St. ...69
85 Minn.-Morris ...58
67 Winona St. ■ ...80
79 Concordia-St. Paul ...77
75 Southwest Minn. St. ...91
65 Minn. St. Moorhead ■ ...80
79 Minn.-Crookston ...64
65 Minn. Duluth ...68
88 Bemidji St. ...78
84 Minn.-Morris ...81
73 Northern St. ■ ...76
80 Concordia-St. Paul ...60
71 Winona St. ...56
70 Southwest Minn. St. ■ ...55
85 Minn.-Crookston ■ ...67
50 Minn. St. Moorhead ■ ...61
63 Minn. Duluth ...93

Nickname: Wildcats
Colors: Black & Gold
Arena: Rice Auditorium
Capacity: 2,500; Year Built: 1960
AD: Todd Barry
SID: Jeremy Phillips

WAYNESBURG
Waynesburg, PA 15370 ...III

Coach: Rudy Marisa, Penn St. 1956
2002-03 RESULTS (16-9)
77 Frostburg St. ...88
54 Neumann † ...78
86 Wheeling Jesuit † ...102
109 Ohio-Eastern ■ ...91
104 Medaille ■ ...43
83 La Roche ...84
87 Pitt.-Greensburg ...81
96 Mt. Aloysius ...94
69 Penn St.-Altoona ■ ...62
93 Lancaster Bible ...44
72 Penn St.-Altoona ...68
78 Wash. & Jeff. ■ ...76
78 Bethany (W.Va.) ...83
80 Westminster (Pa.) ...75
77 Grove City ■ ...79
84 Thiel ■ ...68
83 Frostburg St. ■ ...73
104 Lancaster Bible ■ ...60
76 Wash. & Jeff. ...89
86 Notre Dame (Ohio) ■ ...79
97 Bethany (W.Va.) ■ ...90
75 Westminster (Pa.) ■ ...67
74 Grove City ...89
88 Thiel ...91
74 Bethany (W.Va.) ■ ...82

Nickname: Yellow Jackets
Colors: Orange & Black
Arena: Marisa Field House
 Capacity: 1,350; Year Built: 1985
AD: Rudy Marisa
SID: Justin Zackal

WEBER ST.
Ogden, UT 84408-2701 I

Coach: Joe Cravens, Texas-Arlington
1977
2002-03 RESULTS (26-6)
91	UC Santa Barb. †	82
72	Ball St. †	67
65	Alas. Fairbanks	77
94	Montana Tech ■	58
73	Nevada ■	70
72	North Texas †	76
65	Morris Brown †	56
78	Wis.-Green Bay ■	72
78	Portland	71
64	Utah St.	66
66	Boise St.	65
69	Maine †	66
63	Chattanooga	75
58	Utah	72
75	Brigham Young ■	69
78	Montana St. ■	70
97	Montana ■	73
64	Northern Ariz.	61
65	Sacramento St.	53
77	Portland St. ■	64
74	Eastern Wash. ■	61
82	Idaho St.	76
87	Idaho St. ■	70
75	Montana	72
70	Montana St.	58
88	Sacramento St. ■	65
79	Northern Ariz. ■	64
67	Eastern Wash.	64
83	Portland St.	73
82	Sacramento St. ■	60
60	Eastern Wash. ■	57
74	Wisconsin †	81

Nickname: Wildcats
Colors: Royal Purple & White
Arena: Dee Events Center
 Capacity: 12,000; Year Built: 1977
AD: John Johnson
SID: Brad Larsen

WEBSTER
Webster Groves, MO 63119 III

Coach: Chris Bunch, Lincoln Memorial
1988
2002-03 RESULTS (12-13)
49	Hanover †	69
80	Anderson (Ind.)	77
81	Concordia (Wis.) †	83
84	Lake Forest †	66
53	Aurora ■	77
66	Millikin	72
58	Millsaps †	77
68	Dallas	69
63	Trinity (Tex.)	72
53	Washington (Mo.)	95
93	Concordia (Mo.) ■	60
75	Maryville (Mo.)	69
87	Westminster (Mo.) ■	80
66	Blackburn	83
93	MacMurray ■	74
95	Greenville ■	69
76	Principia ■	67
81	Fontbonne	87
75	Maryville (Mo.) ■	70
78	Westminster (Mo.)	66
61	Blackburn ■	57
63	MacMurray ■	75

92	Greenville	73
78	Principia	81
77	Fontbonne ■	85

Nickname: Gorloks
Colors: Gold, Navy Blue & White
Arena: Grant Gym
 Capacity: 800; Year Built: 1992
AD: Thomas Hart
SID: Ryan Barke

WENTWORTH INST.
Boston, MA 02115 III

Coach: Harry McShane, Northeastern
1983
2002-03 RESULTS (5-19)
64	Utica/Rome †	77
78	St. Joseph (Vt.) †	71
70	Becker ■	60
47	Colby-Sawyer	77
57	Mass.-Boston	71
64	Emerson	82
60	Coast Guard ■	73
56	Gordon	76
63	New England	69
73	New England Col.	67
60	Bates ■	68
54	New England Col. ■	56
57	Salve Regina	79
50	Endicott ■	82
58	Eastern Nazarene	70
57	Colby-Sawyer ■	69
70	New England ■	68
57	Anna Maria ■	60
62	Newbury	64
62	Curry	72
50	Gordon ■	66
64	Roger Williams ■	70
62	Endicott	76
74	Nichols ■	71

Nickname: Leopards
Colors: Black & Gold
Arena: Tansey Gymnasium
 Capacity: 1,000; Year Built: 1970
AD: Lee Conrad
SID: Bill Gorman

WESLEY
Dover, DE 19901-3875 III

Coach: Chris Wentworth, Wesley 1994
2002-03 RESULTS (7-18)
55	Hampden-Sydney	111
79	Chowan †	71
64	Frank. & Marsh. ■	72
82	Lancaster Bible	65
73	Misericordia	96
41	Neumann ■	68
55	Rollins	62
75	Cornerstone †	122
62	Palm Beach Atl.	72
100	Marywood ■	82
78	Cabrini ■	81
57	Alvernia	67
64	Arcadia	68
86	Eastern	68
69	Arcadia ■	77
61	Gwynedd-Mercy ■	64
124	Washington (Md.)	125
63	Misericordia ■	58
70	Neumann	90
58	Alvernia ■	61
51	Eastern ■	63
78	Phila. Bible ■	67
63	Cabrini	71
71	Gwynedd-Mercy	60
70	Marywood	80

Nickname: Wolverines
Colors: Navy Blue & White

Arena: Jim and Shirley Wentworth
 Gymnasium
 Capacity: 800
AD: Michele Stabley
SID: Kristen Calore

WESLEYAN (CONN.)
Middletown, CT 06459 III

Coach: Gerry McDowell, Colby 1976
2002-03 RESULTS (14-10)
63	Washington (Mo.)	91
76	MIT †	87
97	Western New Eng.	88
87	St. Joseph's (Me.) †	75
78	Mass.-Boston	71
96	Eastern Conn. St.	92
76	Trinity (Conn.) †	73
61	Skidmore	59
82	Clark (Mass.)	99
75	Albertus Magnus ■	73
60	Williams	94
77	Vassar	55
77	Amherst ■	92
68	Bates ■	69
57	Tufts ■	64
61	Colby	59
86	Bowdoin	76
84	Connecticut Col. ■	83
106	Middlebury ■	98
71	Williams ■	98
81	Trinity (Conn.)	80
72	Amherst	81
88	Trinity (Conn.) ■	76
73	Amherst	87

Nickname: Cardinals
Colors: Red & Black
Arena: Alumni Athletic Building
 Capacity: 1,200; Year Built: 1931
AD: John Biddiscombe
SID: Brian Katten

WEST ALA.
Livingston, AL 35470.................II

Coach: Rick Reedy, Flagler 1977
2002-03 RESULTS (7-20)
63	Stillman	57
74	Clark Atlanta †	60
56	Texas Col. †	53
71	UAB	97
50	Colorado St.	82
62	Tuskegee ■	80
70	Lincoln Memorial ■	63
83	Christian Bros.	90
81	West Fla.	94
86	Lane ■	69
59	Christian Bros. ■	84
57	North Ala.	82
71	Montevallo ■	54
81	Stillman ■	82
58	Ala.-Huntsville	65
51	West Ga. ■	67
75	Lincoln Memorial	95
65	Valdosta St.	78
68	West Fla. ■	81
68	Lane	80
72	North Ala. ■	81
85	Montevallo	77
76	Tuskegee	102
65	Ala.-Huntsville ■	82
62	Southern U.	77
79	West Ga.	101
75	Valdosta St. ■	95

Nickname: Tigers
Colors: Red, White & Black
Arena: Pruitt Hall
 Capacity: 1,500; Year Built: 1962
AD: Curtis Outlaw
SID: Jason Hughes

WEST CHESTER
West Chester, PA 19383 II

Coach: Dick DeLaney, West Chester
1969
2002-03 RESULTS (21-9)
109	Wilmington (Del.) ■	76
75	Assumption	88
86	Goldey-Beacom ■	53
71	Clarion	62
58	Edinboro	60
81	Shippensburg	79
82	Indiana (Pa.)	66
83	Bloomfield †	79
63	Bryant	64
69	Slippery Rock ■	58
79	Calif. (Pa.) ■	64
85	Wheeling Jesuit ■	81
81	Lock Haven ■	62
81	East Stroudsburg ■	56
78	Bloomsburg	71
88	Phila. Sciences ■	67
59	Millersville ■	51
65	Cheyney	54
84	Mansfield ■	60
82	Kutztown	79
70	Bloomsburg ■	60
83	East Stroudsburg	67
84	Millersville	89
76	N.J. Inst. of Tech. ■	79
84	Cheyney ■	77
71	Kutztown ■	76
70	Mansfield	72
74	Kutztown ■	66
60	Calif. (Pa.)	62
58	Queens (N.C.)	72

Nickname: Golden Rams
Colors: Purple & Gold
Arena: Hollinger Field House
 Capacity: 2,500; Year Built: 1949
AD: Edward Matejkovic
SID: Tom DiCamillo

WEST FLA.
Pensacola, FL 32514.................II

Coach: Don Hogan, South Ala. 1981
2002-03 RESULTS (16-11)
66	Murray St.	87
57	Christian Bros.	55
98	Union (Tenn.) ■	60
70	Nova Southeastern ■	49
87	Florida Tech ■	58
69	West Ga.	67
67	Tampa	69
91	Catholic ■	70
98	Loyola (La.)	81
99	Lane ■	90
61	Fort Valley St. ■	62
94	West Ala. ■	81
67	Montevallo	69
87	Nova Southeastern	62
107	Edward Waters ■	85
72	Lincoln Memorial	85
75	North Ala. ■	69
62	Valdosta St.	69
76	Ala.-Huntsville ■	62
68	West Ga.	79
81	West Ala.	68
72	Montevallo ■	49
79	Fla. Gulf Coast ■	58
64	Ala.-Huntsville	70
65	North Ala.	72
51	Valdosta St. ■	73
70	Lincoln Memorial ■	72

Nickname: Argonauts
Colors: Blue & Green
Arena: UWF Field House
 Capacity: 3,000; Year Built: 1969

AD: Richard Berg
SID: Cara Lynn Teague

WEST GA.
Carrollton, GA 30118..............II

Coach: Ed Murphy, Hardin-Simmons 1964

2002-03 RESULTS (19-9)
65	Ouachita Baptist	75
65	Henderson St.	55
79	Augusta St.	74
80	Morehouse	86
67	West Fla.	69
94	Albany St. (Ga.) ■	87
74	Augusta St. ■	67
45	Clayton St.	79
64	Columbia Union ■	59
77	Mobile †	66
69	Albany St. (Ga.) †	55
62	Lincoln Memorial	68
78	Valdosta St. ■	58
51	Ala.-Huntsville	57
82	North Ala. ■	85
77	Montevallo	59
68	Kennesaw St. ■	65
67	West Ala.	51
74	Albany St. (Ga.)	66
79	West Fla. ■	68
75	Lincoln Memorial ■	61
64	Ala.-Huntsville ■	54
84	North Ala.	86
66	Montevallo ■	59
93	Clayton St. ■	77
101	West Ala. ■	79
66	Valdosta St.	62
56	Henderson St. †	60

Nickname: Braves
Colors: Blue & Red
Arena: HPE Building
  Capacity: 2,800; Year Built: 1965
AD: Edward Murphy
SID: Mitch Gray

WEST LIBERTY ST.
West Liberty, WV 26074...........II

Coach: Dan Petri, West Liberty St. 1968

2002-03 RESULTS (11-16)
83	Pfeiffer †	102
60	American Int'l †	74
116	Ohio-Eastern	75
71	Wheeling Jesuit †	68
76	Gannon	101
67	Edinboro †	89
71	Alderson-Broaddus	82
71	Shepherd	67
77	Davis & Elkins ■	60
87	West Va. Wesleyan ■	59
84	West Va. Tech	81
78	Salem Int'l	65
61	Ohio Valley ■	56
70	Point Park	81
72	Fairmont St.	82
74	Wheeling Jesuit ■	89
61	Glenville St.	71
83	Charleston (W.Va.)	98
68	Point Park ■	73
82	Concord ■	68
80	Bluefield St. ■	66
69	Salem Int'l ■	82
97	Ohio Valley	55
88	West Virginia St.	100
68	Fairmont St. ■	82
61	Wheeling Jesuit	91
76	Shepherd ■	82

Nickname: Hilltoppers
Colors: Gold & Black
Arena: ASRC
  Capacity: 1,200; Year Built: 2000

AD: James Watson
SID: Lynn Ullom

WEST TEX. A&M
Canyon, TX 79016-0999 II

Coach: Rick Cooper, Wayland Bapt. 1981

2002-03 RESULTS (21-10)
76	Southwest Baptist †	59
61	Lubbock Chrst. †	65
85	N.M. Highlands	75
93	Tex. Permian Basin ■	58
82	Eastern N.M.	65
73	Okla. Panhandle ■	44
91	N.M. Highlands ■	58
75	Okla. Panhandle	79
49	Tarleton St.	75
69	Northeastern St. ■	75
77	Central Okla.	79
79	East Central	64
58	Southeastern Okla.	55
79	Southwestern Okla.	69
82	Cameron ■	50
80	Angelo St.	72
79	Abilene Christian	63
68	Tex. A&M-Kingsville ■	72
73	Tex. A&M-Commerce ■	81
67	Midwestern St.	64
69	Eastern N.M. ■	63
89	Midwestern St. ■	83
76	Eastern N.M.	85
79	Abilene Christian ■	64
84	Angelo St. ■	73
77	Tex. A&M-Commerce	66
76	Tex. A&M-Kingsville	80
88	Central Okla. ■	84
78	Northeastern St. †	56
69	Tarleton St. †	61
73	Washburn †	75

Nickname: Buffaloes
Colors: Maroon & White
Arena: WTAMU Fieldhouse
  Capacity: 2,557; Year Built: 1951
AD: Ed Harris
SID: Paul Sweetgall

WEST VIRGINIA
Morgantown, WV 26507 I

Coach: John Beilein, Wheeling Jesuit 1975

2002-03 RESULTS (14-15)
59	Delaware St. ■	46
82	Duquesne	86
70	James Madison ■	67
68	Florida †	66
64	UNC Greensboro ■	54
79	Wofford	69
82	Western Caro. ■	55
65	Tennessee ■	62
67	UNLV	70
75	Gardner-Webb †	58
45	St. Louis	75
68	Miami (Fla.) ■	63
82	Georgetown	84
61	Pittsburgh ■	80
70	Boston College	75
65	Marshall †	61
86	Rutgers ■	75
69	Notre Dame	88
91	Villanova	83
80	Syracuse ■	94
46	Pittsburgh	82
52	Rutgers	46
55	Notre Dame ■	56
64	Seton Hall ■	68
51	Syracuse	89
53	Seton Hall	56
67	Georgetown ■	69

71	Virginia Tech ■	67
50	Providence †	73

Nickname: Mountaineers
Colors: Old Gold & Blue
Arena: WVU Coliseum
  Capacity: 14,000; Year Built: 1970
AD: Ed Pastilong
SID: Bryan Messerly

WEST VIRGINIA ST.
Institute, WV 25112-1000.........II

Coach: Bryan Poore, West Virginia St. 1987

2002-03 RESULTS (16-13)
75	Ashland †	82
90	Bluefield St. †	89
106	Bluefield St.	81
63	Indiana (Pa.) †	83
91	Concord	86
120	Ohio Southern ■	79
71	Davis & Elkins ■	57
67	Fla. Gulf Coast †	87
67	Kentucky St. ■	83
106	Bluefield St.	92
80	Charleston (W.Va.)	96
67	West Va. Tech ■	61
101	Wheeling Jesuit ■	87
81	West Va. Wesleyan	89
78	Glenville St.	76
112	Southern Va. ■	91
69	Alderson-Broaddus ■	90
109	Davis & Elkins ■	89
66	Shepherd	69
93	Ohio Valley ■	67
78	Salem Int'l	80
66	Fairmont St.	81
98	Charleston (W.Va.)	93
109	Concord	110
100	West Liberty St. ■	88
122	Bluefield St. ■	84
104	West Va. Tech	111
99	Concord ■	80
84	Wheeling Jesuit †	90

Nickname: Yellow Jackets
Colors: Old Gold & Black
Arena: Fleming Hall
  Capacity: 1,800; Year Built: 1942
AD: Bryce Castro
SID: Sean McAndrews

WEST VA. TECH
Montgomery, WV 25136..........II

Coach: Steve Tucker, Mississippi Col. 1980

2002-03 RESULTS (11-18)
56	Mountain St. Univ.	89
67	Barber-Scotia †	82
69	Lake Superior St. ■	72
73	S.C.-Spartanburg ■	63
62	St. Augustine's	84
80	Lincoln Memorial	92
90	N.C. Central ■	83
67	Kentucky St.	81
74	Charleston (W.Va.) ■	78
96	Concord ■	83
100	Southern Va. ■	83
61	West Virginia St.	67
81	West Liberty St. ■	84
72	Shepherd	70
81	Alderson-Broaddus	86
96	Davis & Elkins ■	63
89	West Va. Wesleyan ■	93
70	Glenville St.	75
71	Bluefield St.	56
66	Wheeling Jesuit ■	78
89	Ohio Valley	56
82	Salem Int'l	97
85	Fairmont St. ■	86

83	Charleston (W.Va.)	85
105	Bluefield St. ■	79
81	Concord	91
111	West Virginia St. ■	104
75	Fairmont St.	60
61	Charleston (W.Va.)	85

Nickname: Golden Bears
Colors: Blue & Gold
Arena: Tech Fieldhouse
  Capacity: 3,000; Year Built: 1968
AD: Michael Springston
SID: Chad Gabrich

WEST VA. WESLEYAN
Buckhannon, WV 26201...........II

Coach: Charles Miller, West Va. Wesleyan 1966

2002-03 RESULTS (9-17)
40	Calif. (Pa.)	74
55	Edinboro †	65
81	Ashland	91
49	Millersville ■	68
63	Pitt.-Johnstown ■	75
64	Dist. Columbia	89
90	Charleston (W.Va.)	89
77	Salem Int'l ■	88
92	Ohio Valley ■	57
58	Fairmont St.	62
59	West Liberty St.	87
97	Davis & Elkins ■	92
89	West Virginia St. ■	81
87	Bluefield St. ■	78
75	Concord	72
93	West Va. Tech	89
82	Charleston (W.Va.) ■	64
88	Wheeling Jesuit	91
62	Alderson-Broaddus	97
74	Glenville St. ■	66
73	Shepherd	87
74	Glenville St. ■	82
73	Alderson-Broaddus ■	83
75	Davis & Elkins	80
72	Shepherd ■	81
81	Glenville St.	94

Nickname: Bobcats
Colors: Orange & Black
Arena: Rockefeller Center
  Capacity: 3,400; Year Built: 1974
AD: George Klebez
SID: Beth Mecouch

WESTERN CARO.
Cullowhee, NC 28723 I

Coach: Steve Shurina, St. John's (N.Y.) 1988

2002-03 RESULTS (9-19)
72	Coastal Caro. ■	77
119	Toccoa Falls Inst. ■	58
94	Southeastern Fla. ■	55
72	UNC Asheville	77
63	Liberty	66
96	North Greenville ■	81
55	West Virginia	82
68	Marshall	83
61	Tennessee	79
62	DePaul	82
78	VMI ■	56
63	Reinhardt ■	64
66	Davidson	83
67	Furman	71
69	Citadel	83
70	Appalachian St. ■	69
82	Ga. Southern	87
63	UNC Greensboro	62
57	Davidson ■	67
69	Appalachian St.	99
75	UNC Greensboro ■	63
71	East Tenn. St.	89

61 VMI ...58
63 Col. of Charleston ...79
86 East Tenn. St. ...89
86 Wofford ...77
75 Chattanooga ...83
81 Ga. Southern † ...89

Nickname: Catamounts
Colors: Purple & Gold
Arena: Ramsey Center
Capacity: 7,826; Year Built: 1986
AD: Jeff Compher
SID: Mike Cawood

WESTERN CONN. ST.
Danbury, CT 06810 ...III

Coach: Bob Campbell, Connecticut 1972
2002-03 RESULTS (20-9)
75 Baruch † ...78
111 Mass. Liberal Arts † ...83
97 Albertus Magnus ...81
71 Trinity (Conn.) ...75
90 Southern Me. ...80
94 Westfield St. ...84
75 Hunter ...70
90 Mass.-Dartmouth ...65
65 Aurora † ...77
70 DePauw ...85
87 Plymouth St. ...83
85 Keene St. ...80
66 Mass.-Boston ...76
90 Rhode Island Col. ...75
95 Southern Me. ...73
94 Eastern Conn. St. ...63
71 Mass.-Dartmouth ...94
69 Lasell ...78
78 Newbury ...53
80 Plymouth St. ...62
105 Rhode Island Col. ...95
83 Keene St. ...80
77 Eastern Conn. St. ...78
78 Mass.-Boston ...74
95 Southern Me. ...81
77 Mass.-Dartmouth ...74
65 Plymouth St. ...63
84 Clark (Mass.) ...82
62 Rochester ...73

Nickname: Colonials
Colors: Dark Blue, Metallic Copper & White
Arena: Stephen Feldman Arena
Capacity: 2,100; Year Built: 1994
AD: Edward Farrington
SID: Scott Ames

WESTERN ILL.
Macomb, IL 61455 ...I

Coach: Jim Kerwin, Tulane 1964
2002-03 RESULTS (7-21)
75 Norfolk St. ...74
59 Hampton ...82
56 Illinois ...85
63 Eastern Ill. ...76
44 Iowa St. ...59
48 Denver † ...75
62 Drake ...72
60 Detroit ...79
97 Concordia (Mich.) ...78
56 Wichita St. ...74
110 St. Ambrose ...83
57 Valparaiso ...75
75 Chicago St. ...73
74 Southern Utah ...69
84 Southeast Mo. St. ...75
62 Oakland ...75
62 IUPUI ...76
71 UMKC ...78
77 Oral Roberts ...87

62 Valparaiso ...74
75 Southern Utah ...78
75 Chicago St. ...73
52 Southeast Mo. St. ...53
59 IUPUI ...75
79 Oakland ...89
58 Oral Roberts ...79
79 UMKC ...83
51 IUPUI † ...75

Nickname: Leathernecks
Colors: Purple & Gold
Arena: Western Hall
Capacity: 5,139; Year Built: 1964
AD: Tim Van Alstine
SID: Doug Smiley

WESTERN KY.
Bowling Green, KY 42101-3576 ...I

Coach: Dennis Felton, Howard 1985
2002-03 RESULTS (24-9)
68 Arizona ...107
80 Va. Commonwealth ...73
89 Auburn † ...70
76 Evansville ...81
72 Murray St. ...83
63 Illinois St. ...43
64 Southern Miss. ...54
80 St. Francis (Pa.) ...45
57 Pacific (Cal.) ...70
63 Chicago St. † ...56
60 Butler † ...63
74 Tennessee Tech † ...51
65 Middle Tenn. ...69
74 Ark.-Little Rock ...66
77 Arkansas St. ...69
78 New Orleans ...59
85 South Ala. ...69
82 New Mexico St. ...92
63 Florida Int'l ...43
65 Detroit ...86
104 Kentucky St. ...70
81 Denver ...77
85 North Texas ...70
70 Ark.-Little Rock ...51
69 Arkansas St. ...63
71 Florida Int'l ...58
84 Ball St. ...79
69 La.-Lafayette ...66
89 Middle Tenn. ...75
71 Florida Int'l ...60
78 New Mexico St. ...59
64 Middle Tenn. ...52
60 Illinois † ...65

Nickname: Hilltoppers
Colors: Red & White
Arena: E.A. Diddle Arena
Capacity: 8,100; Year Built: 1963
AD: Camden Wood Selig
SID: Paul Just

WESTERN MICH.
Kalamazoo, MI 49008 ...I

Coach: Robert McCullum, Birmingham-So. 1976
2002-03 RESULTS (20-11)
59 Princeton † ...62
73 UC Irvine † ...62
70 Fordham ...51
56 Michigan ...52
71 Detroit ...55
39 Miami (Ohio) ...44
72 Centenary (La.) ...52
72 Auburn ...54
75 Virginia Tech ...54
75 IUPUI ...51
54 Marshall ...66
75 Central Mich. ...80

87 Eastern Mich. ...54
71 Ball St. ...52
76 Bowling Green ...58
68 Akron ...52
62 Toledo ...75
71 Kent St. ...78
79 Marshall ...75
58 Central Mich. ...77
67 Bowling Green ...65
67 Toledo ...64
72 Ohio ...79
72 Eastern Mich. ...80
86 Ball St. ...74
87 Buffalo ...66
71 Northern Ill. ...67
78 Toledo ...64
63 Northern Ill. † ...75
63 Ill.-Chicago ...62
62 Siena ...68

Nickname: Broncos
Colors: Brown & Gold
Arena: University Arena
Capacity: 5,649; Year Built: 1957
AD: Kathy Beauregard
SID: Scott Kuykendall

WESTERN NEW ENG.
Springfield, MA 01119 ...III

Coach: Doug Pearson, Bridgeport 1967
2002-03 RESULTS (16-11)
88 Wesleyan (Conn.) ...97
92 Fitchburg St. ...73
89 Westfield St. † ...81
68 Springfield † ...81
67 WPI ...73
85 Mass. Liberal Arts ...82
66 Amherst ...72
74 Suffolk ...88
72 Emmanuel (Mass.) ...55
80 Albertus Magnus ...86
92 Johnson & Wales ...73
74 Emerson ...80
103 Daniel Webster ...65
78 Rivier ...66
68 Southern Vt. ...87
87 Norwich ...80
102 Suffolk ...79
69 Albertus Magnus ...85
105 Daniel Webster ...78
81 Emmanuel (Mass.) ...65
94 Southern Vt. ...101
78 Norwich ...53
95 Johnson & Wales ...89
95 Emerson ...79
82 Rivier ...66
79 Suffolk ...62
79 Albertus Magnus ...85

Nickname: Golden Bears
Colors: Royal Blue & Gold
Arena: Alumni Healthful Living Center
Capacity: 2,000; Year Built: 1993
AD: Michael Theulen
SID: Ken Cerino

WESTERN N.M.
Silver City, NM 88061 ...II

Coach: Joe Mondragon and Vernon Brazeal, Northern Ariz. 1998
2002-03 RESULTS (3-23)
57 Fort Lewis ...98
66 Colorado St.-Pueblo ...70
60 Cameron ...67
57 East Central † ...69
87 N.M. Highlands ...80
78 Adams St. ...77
72 Colorado St.-Pueblo ...79
78 N.M. Highlands ...81
87 Chaminade ...102

83 Chaminade ...99
66 Hawaii-Hilo ...90
62 BYU-Hawaii ...103
63 BYU-Hawaii ...83
81 Hawaii Pacific ...75
73 Adams St. ...84
49 New Mexico ...107
91 Mont. St.-Billings ...109
73 Mont. St.-Billings ...146
59 Hawaii-Hilo ...81
76 Hawaii-Hilo ...83
79 Chaminade ...97
79 Mont. St.-Billings ...111
73 Mont. St.-Billings ...83
70 Hawaii Pacific ...102
81 Hawaii Pacific ...100
68 BYU-Hawaii ...100

Nickname: Mustangs
Colors: Purple & Gold
Arena: Mustang Field House
Capacity: 2,000; Year Built: 1448
AD: Scott Woodard
SID: Alan Kirsch

WESTERN ORE.
Monmouth, OR 97361-1394 ...II

Coach: Tim Hills, Western Baptist 1968
2002-03 RESULTS (15-12)
70 Metro St. ...69
82 North Dakota ...99
88 Eastern Ore. ...80
92 Western Baptist ...58
88 Eastern Ore. ...69
78 Humboldt St. ...88
61 Willamette ...57
66 Rockhurst † ...62
75 Mercyhurst † ...79
77 Western Baptist ...71
81 Seattle ...89
87 Northwest Nazarene ...75
77 Central Wash. ...78
63 St. Martin's ...61
77 Seattle Pacific ...88
63 Western Wash. ...68
68 Alas. Fairbanks ...83
68 Alas. Anchorage ...78
93 Northwest Nazarene ...83
73 Seattle ...63
77 St. Martin's ...62
95 Central Wash. ...103
69 Western Wash. ...78
84 Seattle Pacific ...86
82 Alas. Fairbanks ...78
71 Alas. Anchorage ...64
83 Humboldt St. ...68

Nickname: Wolves
Colors: Crimson Red & White
Arena: Physical Education Building
Capacity: 2,473; Year Built: 1972
AD: Jon Carey
SID: Russ Blunck

WESTERN ST.
Gunnison, CO 81231 ...II

Coach: Steve Phillips, Western St. 1978
2002-03 RESULTS (0-26)
64 Augustana (S.D.) ...80
54 Westminster (Utah) ...86
80 Central Wash. † ...98
61 Westminster (Utah) ...86
60 Northern Ariz. ...74
94 Colorado Mines ...113
65 Colo. Christian ...77
48 Northern Colo. ...82
92 Chadron St. ...100
55 Metro St. ...81
79 Regis (Colo.) ...89
82 Fort Hays St. ...86

84	Neb.-Kearney ■	106
78	UC-Colo. Spgs.	80
79	Colorado Col.	93
65	Mesa St.	99
66	Adams St.	82
77	Fort Lewis	89
76	Colorado St.-Pueblo ■	79
85	N.M. Highlands ■	90
62	Adams St. ■	73
85	Fort Lewis ■	114
63	N.M. Highlands	83
86	Colorado St.-Pueblo	102
78	UC-Colo. Spgs. ■	84
86	Mesa St. ■	97

Nickname: Mountaineers
Colors: Crimson & Slate
Arena: Paul Wright Gymnasium
Capacity: 2,250; Year Built: 1951
AD: Greg Waggoner
SID: Chris Chase

WESTERN WASH.

Bellingham, WA 98225 II

Coach: Brad Jackson, Washington St. 1975

2002-03 RESULTS (16-11)

87	Southwest Minn. St. †	78
74	UC Davis	89
102	Puget Sound ■	63
74	BYU-Hawaii ■	65
68	Cal Poly Pomona ■	54
70	St. Martin's	64
61	Central Wash.	82
72	Southern Ind. †	81
86	South Dakota †	95
118	Northwest (Wash.) ■	65
119	Puget Sound Chrst. ■	49
83	Seattle Pacific	76
97	Alas. Fairbanks ■	79
83	Alas. Anchorage ■	88
69	Humboldt St.	76
68	Western Ore.	63
80	Northwest Nazarene ■	61
65	Seattle ■	73
72	Seattle Pacific ■	80
77	Alas. Anchorage	79
83	Alas. Fairbanks	72
78	Western Ore. ■	69
72	Humboldt St. ■	73
77	Seattle	80
88	Northwest Nazarene	80
87	Central Wash. ■	83
93	St. Martin's ■	82

Nickname: Vikings
Colors: Blue, Silver & White
Arena: Sam Carver Gymnasium
Capacity: 2,534; Year Built: 1961
AD: Lynda Goodrich
SID: Paul Madison

WESTFIELD ST.

Westfield, MA 01086-1630......III

Coach: Rich Sutter, St. Bonaventure 1984

2002-03 RESULTS (15-11)

90	Purchase St. †	57
73	Hartwick †	75
56	Elms	62
93	Vassar ■	88
81	Western New Eng. †	89
63	Amherst	100
84	Western Conn. St. ■	94
59	Lasell ■	64
62	WPI	77
71	Bridgewater St.	74
72	Worcester St. ■	81
76	Salem St.	92
87	Eastern Conn. St. ■	72
74	Fitchburg St. ■	69
100	Becker	64
71	Framingham St. ■	65
94	Mass. Liberal Arts	69
72	Bridgewater St. ■	62
79	Worcester St.	75
76	Salem St. ■	75
87	Fitchburg St.	76
92	Albertus Magnus ■	84
59	Framingham St.	56
97	Mass. Liberal Arts ■	75
95	Mass. Liberal Arts ■	62
71	Worcester St. †	79

Nickname: Owls
Colors: Blue & White
Arena: Parenzo Gym
Capacity: 400; Year Built: 1956
AD: Kenneth Magarian
SID: Mickey Curtis

WESTMINSTER (MO.)

Fulton, MO 65251-1299 III

Coach: Matt Mitchell, Arkansas 1987

2002-03 RESULTS (12-13)

105	Messenger ■	51
67	Denison ■	64
65	Central Mo. St.	99
68	Hendrix †	65
73	Rhodes	74
94	Kansas City Bible ■	54
88	Manhattan Chrst. ■	81
85	Robert Morris (Ill.) ■	75
58	Austin Peay	82
43	Calvary Bible ■	19
73	Greenville	75
80	Webster	87
69	Lincoln Chrst.	52
80	Maryville (Mo.)	72
65	Principia ■	84
80	Blackburn ■	83
75	Fontbonne ■	86
96	MacMurray	76
76	Greenville ■	74
66	Webster ■	78
70	Fontbonne	85
76	Maryville (Mo.) ■	68
77	Principia	79
65	Blackburn	75
81	MacMurray ■	83

Nickname: Blue Jays
Colors: Blue & White
Arena: Westminster Gym
Capacity: 1,200; Year Built: 1928
AD: Terry Logue
SID: Sean Wright

WESTMINSTER (PA.)

New Wilmington, PA 16172.....III

Coach: Jim Dafler, Capital 1971

2002-03 RESULTS (11-16)

78	Lake Erie ■	54
66	Geneva ■	70
56	Case Reserve	59
53	Wooster ■	64
73	Mount Union ■	83
72	Frostburg St. ■	65
54	Penn St.-Behrend ■	40
71	Mt. Aloysius	62
57	Allegheny ■	70
55	Geneva	68
69	La Roche	56
61	Wilkes	66
77	Washington (Md.) †	75
75	Pitt.-Bradford	79
94	Thiel	82
47	Grove City	72
75	Waynesburg ■	80
90	Wash. & Jeff. ■	74
84	Bethany (W.Va.)	82
72	Pitt.-Greensburg	76
74	Thiel ■	78
53	Grove City ■	60
67	Waynesburg	75
81	Wash. & Jeff.	83
76	Bethany (W.Va.) ■	74
85	Wash. & Jeff. ■	64
60	Grove City	91

Nickname: Titans
Colors: Navy Blue & White
Arena: Buzz Ridl Gymnasium
Capacity: 2,300; Year Built: 1950
AD: James Dafler
SID: Joe Onderko

WHEATON (ILL.)

Wheaton, IL 60187-5593.........III

Coach: Bill Harris, Gordon 1970

2002-03 RESULTS (18-7)

81	Blackburn ■	54
76	Rose-Hulman ■	59
85	Chicago	75
74	Calvin	83
73	Concordia (Ill.) ■	49
77	Asbury	71
73	Central (Iowa)	55
70	New Jersey City †	56
70	Chris. Newport	72
88	Gallaudet	68
92	Villa Julie	80
78	North Park ■	64
55	Ill. Wesleyan ■	62
78	Elmhurst	73
74	Millikin	58
77	North Central ■	69
70	Augustana (Ill.) ■	64
63	Carthage ■	52
73	North Park	76
82	Millikin ■	64
75	Ill. Wesleyan	80
81	Augustana (Ill.)	96
72	Elmhurst ■	61
95	North Central	86
64	Carthage	72

Nickname: Thunder
Colors: Orange & Blue
Arena: King Arena
Capacity: 2,650; Year Built: 2000
AD: Tony Ladd
SID: Brett Marhanka

WHEATON (MASS.)

Norton, MA 02766..................III

Coach: Brian Walmsley, Bentley 1988

2002-03 RESULTS (19-10)

82	Bowdoin †	78
85	Mass.-Dartmouth	79
89	Brandeis ■	65
69	Salve Regina	66
83	Bridgewater St. ■	70
68	Endicott	67
75	Roger Williams ■	59
70	Averett	57
50	Greensboro	66
82	Emerson ■	68
76	Mount Ida	68
82	Fitchburg St. ■	68
73	Clark (Mass.)	86
73	WPI ■	49
82	Tufts ■	95
65	MIT	77
54	Babson	77
76	Springfield ■	56
88	Coast Guard ■	65
71	MIT ■	51
79	Clark (Mass.) ■	72
58	Springfield	71
66	WPI	54
58	Babson ■	77
68	Coast Guard	75
83	Coast Guard ■	67
66	Clark (Mass.)	88
86	Plymouth St.	83
90	Keene St.	95

Nickname: Lyons
Colors: Royal & White
Arena: Emerson Gymnasium
Capacity: 850; Year Built: 1991
AD: Chad Yowell
SID: Scott Dietz

WHEELING JESUIT

Wheeling, WV 26003-6295 II

Coach: Jay DeFruscio, Ursinus 1982

2002-03 RESULTS (22-8)

79	St. Paul's †	62
111	Ohio St.-Newark †	58
88	Davis & Elkins	66
102	Waynesburg †	86
68	West Liberty St. †	71
115	Ohio-Eastern ■	94
117	Ohio Valley ■	49
60	Calif. (Pa.) ■	62
121	Ohio-Zanesville ■	58
81	West Chester	85
72	Shepherd	84
74	Glenville St. ■	69
75	Alderson-Broaddus ■	66
87	West Virginia St.	101
74	Salem Int'l ■	77
79	Fairmont St.	70
76	Ohio Valley ■	54
89	West Liberty St.	74
91	West Va. Wesleyan ■	88
78	West Va. Tech	66
90	Bluefield St. ■	74
88	Concord ■	73
96	Charleston (W.Va.)	84
85	Salem Int'l	99
88	Fairmont St. ■	74
90	Ohio Valley	86
91	West Liberty St. ■	61
83	Bluefield St. ■	67
90	West Virginia St. †	84
76	Alderson-Broaddus †	78

Nickname: Cardinals
Colors: Red & Gold
Arena: Alma McDonough Center
Capacity: 2,200; Year Built: 1990
AD: Jay DeFruscio
SID: Susie Levitt

WHITMAN

Walla Walla, WA 99362.........III

Coach: Skip Molitor, Gonzaga 1974

2002-03 RESULTS (7-18)

82	Union (Neb.) †	93
66	Oakwood †	62
55	Walla Walla	75
52	Utah St.	86
65	Warner Pacific †	72
55	Carroll (Mont.) ■	81
78	Great Falls	59
94	Montana St.-Northern	76
41	Christian Heritage	80
85	George Fox ■	84
58	Pacific (Ore.) ■	72
53	Puget Sound	78
47	Pacific Lutheran	61
61	Willamette ■	81
83	Linfield ■	76
55	Whitworth	88
93	Lewis & Clark	102
71	George Fox	65
57	Pacific (Ore.)	75

SCHEDULES/RESULTS

81	Puget Sound ■	71
49	Pacific Lutheran ■	63
49	Willamette	62
74	Linfield	85
58	Whitworth ■	82
69	Lewis & Clark ■	80

Nickname: Missionaries
Colors: Blue & Gold
Arena: Sherwood Center
  Capacity: 2,000; Year Built: 1968
AD: Travis Feezell
SID: Dave Holden

WHITTIER
Whittier, CA 90608-0634 III

Coach: Rock Carter, Whittier 1989
2002-03 RESULTS (17-8)
78	Notre Dame de Namur ■	83
87	Paul Smith ■	47
72	Chapman	65
86	La Sierra ■	68
88	Cal Maritime ■	55
95	Hope Int'l ■	62
85	La Sierra	65
88	Northland ■	74
84	Millikin ■	64
92	S'western (Ariz.) ■	63
94	West Coast Chrst. ■	54
71	Pomona-Pitzer ■	75
53	Claremont-M-S	74
63	Occidental ■	66
97	Caltech ■	55
69	Cal Lutheran ■	82
138	Redlands ■	124
85	La Verne	93
76	Pomona-Pitzer	48
82	Claremont-M-S ■	73
61	Occidental	64
86	Caltech	44
75	Cal Lutheran ■	79
108	Redlands	102
82	La Verne ■	68

Nickname: Poets
Colors: Purple & Gold
Arena: Graham Activity Center
  Capacity: 2,200; Year Built: 1979
AD: Wendall Jack
SID: Rock Carter

WHITWORTH
Spokane, WA 99251-2501 III

Coach: Jim Hayford, Azusa Pacific 1989
2002-03 RESULTS (23-4)
75	Carroll (Mont.) ■	71
68	Clarke †	64
80	Alvernia †	65
83	North Central †	73
120	Redlands	86
73	Claremont-M-S †	62
100	Caltech	44
85	Western Baptist ■	68
108	Caltech ■	24
75	Pacific (Ore.) ■	57
88	George Fox ■	78
85	Pacific Lutheran	73
75	Puget Sound	86
80	Linfield ■	61
66	Willamette ■	57
88	Whitman ■	55
76	Lewis & Clark	78
65	Pacific (Ore.)	55
73	George Fox	61
66	Pacific Lutheran ■	50
73	Puget Sound ■	71
104	Linfield	100
56	Willamette	66
82	Whitman	58

60	Lewis & Clark ■	49
77	Willamette ■	64
55	Gust. Adolphus	65

Nickname: Pirates
Colors: Crimson & Black
Arena: Whitworth Field House
  Capacity: 1,600; Year Built: 1960
AD: Scott McQuilkin
SID: Steve Flegel

WICHITA ST.
Wichita, KS 67260 I

Coach: Mark Turgeon, Kansas 1987
2002-03 RESULTS (18-12)
76	Texas-Arlington ■	74
71	Chicago St. ■	65
71	Oral Roberts	76
69	Tulsa	80
74	Northwestern St. ■	55
66	Kansas St. ■	79
92	Lamar ■	73
58	Oklahoma St. ■	68
74	Western Ill. ■	56
79	Northern Iowa ■	55
71	Indiana St. ■	55
67	Southwest Mo. St. ■	63
64	Southern Ill.	69
69	Illinois St.	66
69	Drake ■	61
64	Bradley	60
74	Evansville	75
59	Southern Ill. ■	94
85	Illinois St. ■	71
72	Northern Iowa	80
89	Evansville ■	84
80	Creighton ■	74
80	Drake	70
72	Indiana St.	63
77	Bradley ■	86
71	Southwest Mo. St.	65
60	Creighton	86
70	Bradley †	66
69	Creighton †	70
65	Iowa St.	76

Nickname: Shockers
Colors: Yellow & Black
Arena: Levitt Arena
  Capacity: 10,559; Year Built: 1955
AD: Jim Schaus
SID: Larry Rankin

WIDENER
Chester, PA 19013-5792 III

Coach: Dave Duda, Spring Garden 1988
2002-03 RESULTS (11-14)
73	Marymount (Va.) †	86
68	Frank. & Marsh.	93
73	Neumann	80
83	Gwynedd-Mercy	85
72	Elizabethtown	55
66	Juniata ■	71
81	Wilmington (Del.) ■	62
101	Muhlenberg ■	108
69	Arcadia	66
62	St. Mary's (Md.)	77
62	Messiah	71
96	Wilmington (Del.)	66
77	Lebanon Valley ■	68
68	Moravian	66
73	Susquehanna ■	78
56	Albright ■	66
70	Cabrini ■	52
73	Juniata	85
67	Elizabethtown ■	80
64	Lebanon Valley	76
79	Messiah ■	59

60	Lincoln (Pa.)	54
73	Moravian ■	65
74	Albright	58
85	Susquehanna	89

Nickname: Pioneers
Colors: Widener Blue & Gold
Arena: Schwartz Center
  Capacity: 1,500; Year Built: 1971
AD: William Zwaan
SID: Susan Fumagalli

WILKES
Wilkes-Barre, PA 18766 III

Coach: Jerry Rickrode, Skidmore 1985
2002-03 RESULTS (17-7)
89	Hunter †	57
67	Gwynedd-Mercy †	61
90	Albright ■	83
80	Lycoming ■	82
60	FDU-Florham	51
97	Baptist Bible (Pa.) ■	60
67	Marywood ■	63
66	Westminster (Pa.) ■	61
93	Washington (Md.) ■	69
85	Lincoln (Pa.) ■	65
62	DeSales	63
76	Drew ■	66
63	Lincoln (Pa.)	65
87	Delaware Valley ■	63
66	Scranton	75
84	St. Mary's (Md.)	78
77	King's (Pa.) ■	64
78	FDU-Florham ■	66
66	Lycoming	67
72	Drew	65
82	DeSales ■	72
61	Delaware Valley	58
61	King's (Pa.)	78
77	Scranton ■	82

Nickname: Colonels
Colors: Navy & Gold
Arena: Arnaud Marts Sports Center
  Capacity: 3,500; Year Built: 1988
AD: Addy Malatesta
SID: John Seitzinger

WILLAMETTE
Salem, OR 97301-3931 III

Coach: Gordie James, Cal Poly Pomona 1964
2002-03 RESULTS (19-7)
86	Menlo	83
66	Fresno Pacific †	58
80	Western Baptist ■	73
87	Southern Ore. ■	66
72	Warner Pacific ■	61
57	Western Ore.	61
55	Wis.-Whitewater †	60
86	Cal St. Hayward	58
62	Pacific Lutheran ■	37
77	Lewis & Clark	70
87	Linfield ■	67
81	Whitman	61
57	Whitworth ■	66
70	Pacific (Ore.) ■	53
76	George Fox ■	60
54	Pacific Lutheran	57
61	Puget Sound	58
71	Linfield	83
79	Lewis & Clark ■	65
62	Whitman ■	49
66	Whitworth	56
64	Pacific (Ore.)	69
59	George Fox	52
71	Puget Sound ■	64
79	Lewis & Clark ■	74
64	Whitworth	77

Nickname: Bearcats
Colors: Cardinal & Old Gold
Arena: Cone Fieldhouse
  Capacity: 2,600; Year Built: 1974
AD: Mark Majeski
SID: Cliff Voliva

WILLIAM & MARY
Williamsburg, VA 23187 I

Coach: Rick Boyages, Bowdoin 1985
2002-03 RESULTS (12-16)
76	Fordham ■	79
63	Radford ■	64
61	Liberty	62
51	East Caro.	66
60	Virginia Tech ■	52
73	Morgan St. ■	66
82	Campbell	80
72	Charleston So. ■	66
74	Towson ■	55
72	Delaware ■	74
64	Old Dominion	76
51	Drexel	67
88	Va. Commonwealth ■	83
51	Hofstra ■	66
58	George Mason	67
61	James Madison ■	59
57	Delaware	91
64	Hampton	62
69	Old Dominion ■	53
79	Hofstra	69
59	Towson	52
43	George Mason ■	60
73	Va. Commonwealth	93
62	Drexel ■	78
48	UNC Wilmington ■	72
75	James Madison ■	72
49	UNC Wilmington	60
64	Hofstra †	74

Nickname: Tribe
Colors: Green, Gold, Silver
Arena: William and Mary Hall
  Capacity: 8,600; Year Built: 1970
AD: Edward Driscoll Jr.
SID: Dan Wakely

WM. PATERSON
Wayne, NJ 07470-2152 III

Coach: Jose Rebimbas, Seton Hall 1990
2002-03 RESULTS (19-7)
76	Catholic	79
57	Ramapo	76
62	TCNJ ■	59
71	New Jersey City ■	47
59	Richard Stockton	50
63	Kean ■	50
79	Lehman ■	53
62	York (N.Y.)	59
59	John Jay	38
64	Merchant Marine	52
73	New Paltz St.	46
65	FDU-Florham	43
70	Rutgers-Newark ■	59
75	Montclair St.	72
62	Rutgers-Camden	59
55	Rowan	79
68	New Jersey City	53
60	Ramapo ■	71
73	Rowan ■	66
62	Kean	66
66	Rutgers-Camden	57
59	TCNJ	58
67	Richard Stockton ■	50
31	Montclair St.	45
69	Rutgers-Newark	50
66	Montclair St. ■	70

Nickname: Pioneers
Colors: Orange & Black
Arena: Rec Center
  Capacity: 4,000; Year Built: 1984
AD: Sabrina Grant
SID: Joe Martinelli

WILLIAMS
Williamstown, MA 01267 III

Coach: David Paulsen, Williams 1987
2002-03 RESULTS (31-1)

98	Endicott ■	55
74	Ithaca ■	71
89	St. Lawrence	54
78	Clarkson	61
107	Mass. Liberal Arts	57
68	N.C. Wesleyan †	65
97	Neumann †	64
82	Southern Me. ■	62
84	Southern Vt. ■	55
94	Wesleyan (Conn.) ■	60
74	Amherst ■	65
74	Hamilton ■	54
90	Middlebury	67
87	Trinity (Conn.)	72
61	Amherst	67
110	Mount Ida ■	51
96	Bowdoin ■	59
87	Colby ■	44
84	Springfield	69
83	Connecticut Col.	55
98	Wesleyan (Conn.)	71
76	Bates ■	55
76	Tufts ■	56
67	Union (N.Y.)	62
85	Bates ■	69
64	Tufts †	63
74	Amherst	70
94	Salem St. ■	67
76	Hamilton ■	65
91	Amherst ■	75
74	Wooster †	72
67	Gust. Adolphus †	65

Nickname: Ephs
Colors: Purple & Gold
Arena: Chandler Gymnasium
  Capacity: 2,900; Year Built: 1988
AD: Harry Sheehy
SID: Dick Quinn

WILMINGTON (DEL.)
New Castle, DE 19720 II

Coach: Jim Hayford, Azusa Pacific 1989
2002-03 RESULTS (1-26)

76	West Chester	109
74	Philadelphia U. †	91
74	Phila. Sciences	81
62	N.J. Inst. of Tech. ■	88
59	Felician	84
71	Holy Family ■	100
56	Caldwell	71
62	Widener	81
88	Bloomfield ■	98
55	NYIT †	85
74	Glenville St. †	111
80	Merrimack †	98
81	Teikyo Post	104
82	Goldey-Beacom	71
82	Nyack ■	94
66	Widener ■	96
58	Dominican (N.Y.)	88
87	Caldwell	103
88	Nyack	100
71	Holy Family	89
68	Teikyo Post ■	87
65	Goldey-Beacom ■	78
96	Bloomfield	114
57	Felician ■	86

79	Phila. Sciences ■	81
69	Dominican (N.Y.) ■	83
77	N.J. Inst. of Tech.	105

Nickname: Wildcats
Colors: Green & White
AD: Frank Aiello
SID: To be named

WILMINGTON (OHIO)
Wilmington, OH 45177 III

Coach: Scott Stemple, Ohio Northern 1985
2002-03 RESULTS (4-22)

69	Olivet ■	91
65	Manchester ■	77
62	Earlham	73
58	Heidelberg	70
61	Ohio Northern ■	58
71	Baldwin-Wallace ■	73
52	Findlay	78
49	John Carroll ■	78
63	Buffalo St. †	64
82	Coe †	77
68	Oberlin	47
71	Mount Union ■	74
53	Otterbein	79
40	Marietta	71
69	Capital ■	86
75	Baldwin-Wallace	100
48	Ohio Northern	61
57	Marietta ■	34
60	Capital	88
57	John Carroll ■	85
53	Muskingum ■	72
58	Muskingum	69
71	Mount Union	84
73	Otterbein ■	76
78	Heidelberg ■	85
63	Muskingum	73

Nickname: Quakers
Colors: Green & White
Arena: Hermann Court
  Capacity: 3,000; Year Built: 1966
AD: Terry Rupert
SID: Bill Salyer

WINGATE
Wingate, NC 28174 II

Coach: Parker Laketa, Kansas St. 1986
2002-03 RESULTS (18-11)

108	Fayetteville St.	104
88	Coker ■	72
93	Anderson (S.C.) ■	77
87	St. Paul's ■	79
67	Lynn †	79
74	Mars Hill †	73
83	Allen †	88
72	Elizabeth City St.	80
77	Fayetteville St. ■	85
63	N.C. Central	85
81	Barber-Scotia ■	72
74	St. Augustine's ■	77
89	S.C.-Aiken ■	82
72	Carson-Newman	84
64	Presbyterian	60
93	Newberry ■	90
98	Catawba ■	77
78	Mars Hill	56
71	Lenoir-Rhyne ■	72
81	Tusculum	55
77	Carson-Newman ■	76
81	Presbyterian ■	80
87	Newberry	76
87	Catawba	99
100	Mars Hill ■	85
77	Lenoir-Rhyne	67
89	Tusculum	92

84	Mars Hill ■	80
77	Lenoir-Rhyne	85

Nickname: Bulldogs
Colors: Navy Blue & Old Gold
Arena: Cuddy Arena
  Capacity: 2,300; Year Built: 1986
AD: Steve Poston
SID: David Sherwood

WINONA ST.
Winona, MN 55987-5838 II

Coach: Mike Leaf, St. Mary's (Minn.) 1983
2002-03 RESULTS (11-17)

75	Minn. St. Mankato	100
69	Michigan Tech †	87
69	Tampa	71
74	Eckerd	93
94	Fla. Southern	101
89	Viterbo	75
61	Wis.-Parkside ■	71
61	Lewis ■	64
62	Neb.-Omaha	79
81	Minn.-Morris	67
103	Northern St. ■	97
83	Concordia-St. Paul	79
80	Wayne St. (Neb.)	67
73	Southwest Minn. St.	71
79	Minn.-Crookston ■	69
85	Minn. St. Moorhead ■	77
98	Bemidji St.	108
59	Minn. Duluth	80
70	Northern St.	72
107	Minn.-Morris	71
87	Concordia-St. Paul ■	64
72	Southwest Minn. St. ■	77
56	Wayne St. (Neb.) ■	71
76	Minn. St. Moorhead	86
89	Minn.-Crookston	74
68	Minn. Duluth ■	79
96	Bemidji St. ■	102
79	Bemidji St.	106

Nickname: Warriors
Colors: Purple & White
Arena: McCown Gymnasium
  Capacity: 3,500; Year Built: 1973
AD: Larry Holstad
SID: Michael Herzberg

WINSTON-SALEM
Winston-Salem, NC 27110 II

Coach: Phillip Stitt, North Carolina 1979
2002-03 RESULTS (15-14)

80	Georgia Southwestern	75
46	Clarion	63
71	Lander ■	53
65	Bowie St. ■	70
76	Eckerd †	89
61	Valdosta St.	76
77	Elizabeth City St.	71
87	Augusta St. ■	80
67	Augusta St.	81
81	Virginia Union ■	76
65	North Ala. ■	74
70	St. Augustine's	99
70	Mars Hill ■	79
79	Livingstone ■	78
85	Columbia Union ■	52
70	Shaw	66
77	St. Paul's	47
65	Johnson Smith †	60
63	Virginia St. ■	59
48	Johnson Smith ■	70
64	Fayetteville St.	65
89	N.C. Central	94
75	St. Augustine's ■	81
69	Livingstone	68

84	Fayetteville St. ■	72
68	N.C. Central ■	91
76	Virginia Union	73
54	Virginia St. †	49
59	Virginia Union †	81

Nickname: Rams
Colors: Scarlet & White
Arena: C.E. Gaines Center
  Capacity: 3,100; Year Built: 1978
AD: Percy Caldwell
SID: Chris Zona (Niagara '98)

WINTHROP
Rock Hill, SC 29733 I

Coach: Gregg Marshall, Randolph-Macon 1985
2002-03 RESULTS (20-10)

50	Northern Ill. †	56
61	Eastern Wash. †	75
86	Nyack ■	44
68	Gardner-Webb ■	66
67	Montana St.	64
42	Utah	72
62	Morris Brown ■	54
56	North Texas ■	65
61	Clemson	78
84	Eastern Ky.	73
74	St. Andrews ■	39
55	Radford	64
82	Elon ■	65
50	Coastal Caro. ■	64
74	Birmingham-So.	67
74	Liberty	64
67	Elon	60
65	UNC Asheville ■	62
72	Charleston So.	69
84	High Point ■	59
82	Radford ■	61
66	Coastal Caro.	72
61	Birmingham-So. ■	63
74	Gardner-Webb	78
86	High Point	70
84	Liberty ■	72
75	Charleston So. ■	56
76	UNC Asheville	65
80	High Point ■	64
80	UNC Asheville ■	81

Nickname: Eagles
Colors: Garnet & Gold
Arena: Winthrop Coliseum
  Capacity: 6,100; Year Built: 1982
AD: Thomas Hickman
SID: Jack Frost

WISCONSIN
Madison, WI 53711 I

Coach: Bo Ryan, Wilkes 1969
2002-03 RESULTS (24-8)

81	Eastern Wash. ■	55
84	Northern Ill. ■	56
83	Wis.-Milwaukee ■	72
69	Wis.-Green Bay	52
80	Wake Forest ■	90
91	UNLV	74
85	New Hampshire ■	36
54	Marquette	63
81	Texas Southern ■	58
75	Ohio ■	51
80	Temple	67
73	Chicago St. ■	45
65	Michigan	66
63	Illinois	69
66	Minnesota ■	50
53	Ohio St.	52
74	Iowa ■	61
69	Northwestern ■	50
86	Penn St. ■	55

60 Purdue ... 78
74 Northwestern ... 59
64 Michigan St. ■ ... 53
71 Indiana ■ ... 59
57 Penn St. ... 58
61 Iowa ■ ... 53
73 Michigan ■ ... 42
69 Minnesota ... 61
60 Illinois ■ ... 59
50 Ohio St. † ... 58
81 Weber St. † ... 74
61 Tulsa † ... 60
57 Kentucky † ... 63

Nickname: Badgers
Colors: Cardinal & White
Arena: Kohl Center
  Capacity: 17,142; Year Built: 1998
AD: Pat Richter
SID: Brian Lucas

WIS. LUTHERAN
Milwaukee, WI 53226 III

Coach: Skip Noon, Martin Luther 1986
2002-03 RESULTS (9-18)
66 Benedictine (Ill.) ■ ... 111
60 Wis.-Platteville ■ ... 78
87 Clarke ■ ... 94
94 North Park † ... 107
93 Trinity Int'l † ... 80
77 Edgewood ... 95
77 North Park † ... 83
57 Carthage ... 83
81 Concordia (Wis.) ■ ... 99
61 Wis.-Whitewater ... 104
65 Wis.-River Falls ... 82
64 Buena Vista † ... 90
116 Menlo ... 111
72 Cal St. Hayward ... 82
81 Washington (Mo.) ■ ... 82
79 Milwaukee Engr. ■ ... 72
62 Lakeland ... 79
60 Marian (Wis.) ... 62
88 Maranatha Baptist ■ ... 80
63 Milwaukee Engr. ... 77
97 Concordia (Wis.) ... 81
66 Edgewood ■ ... 92
62 Lakeland ■ ... 61
63 Marian (Wis.) ■ ... 54
87 Maranatha Baptist ... 76
71 Marian (Wis.) ■ ... 63
55 Lakeland ... 60

Nickname: Warriors
Colors: Forest Green & White
Arena: The REX
  Capacity: 2,500; Year Built: 1992
AD: Edward Noon
SID: Cheryl Pasbrig

WIS.-EAU CLAIRE
Eau Claire, WI 54702-4004 III

Coach: Terry Gibbons, Wis.-Oshkosh 1983
2002-03 RESULTS (17-10)
64 Cornell College ■ ... 51
79 St. Olaf ■ ... 58
73 Milwaukee Engr. ■ ... 46
78 Calvin † ... 73
52 Rochester ... 66
72 Wis.-La Crosse ■ ... 68
80 Wis.-Stout ... 74
66 Wis.-Superior ■ ... 61
82 St. Scholastica ... 53
78 William Penn ■ ... 66
69 Sioux Falls ■ ... 54
57 Wis.-Stevens Point ■ ... 73
64 Wis.-River Falls ... 79
75 Wis.-Whitewater ... 84
70 Wis.-Oshkosh ■ ... 74

78 St. Mary's (Minn.) ... 50
62 Wis.-Platteville ... 67
81 Wis.-Stout ■ ... 85
73 Wis.-Superior ... 70
73 Wis.-Stevens Point ... 82
74 Wis.-La Crosse ... 64
77 Wis.-River Falls ■ ... 70
62 Wis.-Oshkosh ... 76
77 Wis.-Whitewater ■ ... 64
77 Wis.-Platteville ■ ... 65
68 Wis.-River Falls ... 65
69 Wis.-Whitewater ... 81

Nickname: Blugolds
Colors: Navy Blue & Old Gold
Arena: W.L. Zorn Arena
  Capacity: 2,450; Year Built: 1952
AD: Tim Petermann
SID: Tim Petermann

WIS.-GREEN BAY
Green Bay, WI 54311-7001 I

Coach: Tod Kowalczyk, Minn. Duluth 1989
2002-03 RESULTS (10-20)
55 Alas. Fairbanks ... 78
68 Centenary (La.) † ... 48
66 Jacksonville St. † ... 75
52 Wisconsin ... 69
69 Chicago St. ■ ... 58
68 Kansas St. ■ ... 64
67 Missouri ... 88
72 Weber St. ... 78
71 Ill.-Chicago ... 78
67 Northern Iowa ... 81
74 Austin Peay ■ ... 69
88 Delaware ■ ... 82
55 Cleveland St. ... 66
72 Detroit ... 87
87 Eastern Mich. ... 94
62 Loyola (Ill.) ■ ... 74
79 Wis.-Milwaukee ■ ... 68
69 Wright St. ■ ... 67
53 Butler ■ ... 68
76 Youngstown St. ... 77
68 Ill.-Chicago ... 81
89 Cleveland St. ■ ... 56
62 Detroit ■ ... 71
54 Wis.-Milwaukee ... 78
73 Loyola (Ill.) ... 84
69 Youngstown St. ■ ... 53
72 Northern Mich. ■ ... 67
37 Butler ... 58
74 Wright St. ... 77
61 Youngstown St. † ... 65

Nickname: Phoenix
Colors: Green, White & Red
Arena: Resch Center
  Capacity: 10,200; Year Built: 2002
AD: Ken Bothof
SID: Brian Nicol

WIS.-LA CROSSE
La Crosse, WI 54601 III

Coach: Brad Nadborne, DePauw 1981
2002-03 RESULTS (6-20)
66 St. Mary's (Minn.) ... 63
60 Viterbo ■ ... 68
72 Luther ■ ... 48
68 Wis.-Eau Claire ... 72
65 Wis.-Platteville ■ ... 57
60 Carleton ... 62
66 Wis.-River Falls ... 70
74 Briar Cliff ■ ... 78
68 Lakeland † ... 75
64 Dubuque ... 61
58 Tri-State † ... 64
82 Milwaukee Engr. ... 62
55 Wis.-Superior ■ ... 57

43 Wis.-Stevens Point ... 70
59 Wis.-Stout ... 88
44 Wis.-Oshkosh ■ ... 76
58 Wis.-Whitewater ... 74
58 Wis.-Platteville ... 71
65 Wis.-River Falls ■ ... 81
64 Wis.-Eau Claire ■ ... 74
82 Wis.-Superior ... 79
58 Wis.-Stout ... 63
39 Wis.-Stevens Point ■ ... 75
72 Wis.-Whitewater ■ ... 79
58 Wis.-Oshkosh ... 74
41 Wis.-Stevens Point ... 66

Nickname: Eagles
Colors: Maroon & Gray
Arena: Mitchell Hall
  Capacity: 2,880; Year Built: 1964
AD: Joe Baker
SID: David Johnson

WIS.-MILWAUKEE
Milwaukee, WI 53211 I

Coach: Bruce Pearl, Boston College 1982
2002-03 RESULTS (24-8)
72 Wisconsin ... 83
77 Mississippi Val. ■ ... 75
75 Southeast Mo. St. † ... 89
71 Indiana St. † ... 59
79 Maine † ... 63
61 Florida Int'l † ... 48
86 Southwest Mo. St. ... 77
75 Valparaiso ... 61
83 Mississippi Val. ... 75
84 Wis.-Parkside ■ ... 70
100 Loyola (Ill.) ■ ... 80
69 Georgia ... 89
73 Detroit ... 72
70 Cleveland St. ... 58
92 Ill.-Chicago ... 102
74 Youngstown St. ■ ... 56
81 Chicago St. ... 73
68 Wis.-Green Bay ... 79
69 Butler ■ ... 65
74 Wright St. ■ ... 59
92 Loyola (Ill.) ... 91
61 Detroit ■ ... 50
86 Cleveland St. ■ ... 69
78 Wis.-Green Bay ■ ... 54
81 Ill.-Chicago ... 78
86 Youngstown St. ... 61
64 Southern Ill. ... 66
98 Wright St. ... 65
74 Butler ... 76
75 Ill.-Chicago ... 73
69 Butler ■ ... 52
69 Notre Dame † ... 70

Nickname: Panthers
Colors: Black & Gold
Arena: Klotsche Center
  Capacity: 5,000; Year Built: 1977
AD: Bud Haidet
SID: Kevin O'Connor

WIS.-OSHKOSH
Oshkosh, WI 54901-8617 III

Coach: Ted Van Dellen, Wis.-Oshkosh 1978
2002-03 RESULTS (25-7)
94 St. Norbert ■ ... 53
81 Lawrence ... 52
70 Edgewood † ... 54
88 Marian (Wis.) ... 36
71 Wis.-Platteville ... 56
71 Wis.-River Falls ■ ... 79
72 Luther ... 60
80 Kendall ■ ... 66
77 Beloit ■ ... 46

79 Finlandia ■ ... 60
79 Barat ■ ... 63
55 Wis.-Stout ... 70
70 Wis.-Whitewater ■ ... 71
87 Wis.-Superior ■ ... 63
74 Wis.-Eau Claire ... 70
76 Wis.-La Crosse ... 44
63 Wis.-Stevens Point ■ ... 59
55 Wis.-River Falls ... 56
88 Wis.-Stout ... 64
75 Wis.-Platteville ■ ... 50
63 Wis.-Whitewater ... 70
76 Wis.-Eau Claire ■ ... 62
91 Wis.-Superior ... 57
60 Wis.-Stevens Point ... 79
74 Wis.-La Crosse ... 58
103 Wis.-Stout ... 70
62 Wis.-Stevens Point ... 57
68 Wis.-Whitewater ... 63
78 Milwaukee Engr. ■ ... 56
84 Hope ... 77
53 Randolph-Macon ... 47
63 Hampden-Sydney † ... 68

Nickname: Titans
Colors: Black, Gold & White
Arena: Kolf Sports Center
  Capacity: 5,800; Year Built: 1971
AD: Allen Ackerman
SID: Kennan Timm

WIS.-PARKSIDE
Kenosha, WI 53141-2000 II

Coach: Jeff Rutter, Winona St. 1988
2002-03 RESULTS (13-15)
74 St. Norbert ■ ... 76
94 Calumet Col. ■ ... 68
70 Northern Mich. ■ ... 65
61 Lewis ... 68
59 Quincy ... 68
60 Mo.-St. Louis ... 48
71 Winona St. ... 61
92 Ill.-Springfield ■ ... 66
70 Wis.-Milwaukee ... 84
64 Lakeland ■ ... 58
68 Ky. Wesleyan ■ ... 76
94 Bellarmine ... 67
58 Indianapolis ... 59
100 St. Joseph's (Ind.) ... 71
70 Lewis ... 88
70 SIU Edwardsville ... 53
56 Mo.-St. Louis ■ ... 53
72 Southern Ind. ■ ... 80
95 Bellarmine ... 100
75 Northern Ky. ... 76
77 St. Joseph's (Ind.) ■ ... 54
73 SIU Edwardsville ■ ... 59
70 Quincy ■ ... 50
70 Southern Ind. ... 85
59 Ky. Wesleyan ... 97
64 Northern Ky. ■ ... 66
77 Indianapolis ■ ... 80
55 Northern Ky. † ... 64

Nickname: Rangers
Colors: Green, White & Black
Arena: DeSimone Gymnasium
  Capacity: 2,120; Year Built: 1970
AD: David Williams
SID: Steve Kratochvil

WIS.-PLATTEVILLE
Platteville, WI 53818-3099 III

Coach: Todd Landrum, Ohio Northern 1973
2002-03 RESULTS (11-15)
72 Simpson † ... 82
78 Wis. Lutheran ■ ... 60
78 Dubuque ■ ... 46
63 North Dakota St. ... 92

56	Wis.-Oshkosh ■	71
57	Wis.-La Crosse	65
72	Wis.-Whitewater ■	70
70	St. Xavier ■	77
77	Tri-State †	64
80	Cardinal Stritch †	87
43	Clarke	54
54	Wis.-Superior	52
56	Wis.-Stevens Point	64
85	Wis.-Stout ■	87
70	Wis.-River Falls	77
67	Wis.-Eau Claire ■	62
71	Wis.-La Crosse ■	58
85	Wis.-Whitewater	75
72	Wis.-Superior	61
50	Wis.-Oshkosh	75
62	Wis.-Stevens Point ■	73
69	Edgewood	55
68	Wis.-Stout	66
65	Wis.-Eau Claire	77
72	Wis.-River Falls ■	78
61	Wis.-Whitewater	64

Nickname: Pioneers
Colors: Blue & Orange
Arena: Williams Fieldhouse
    Capacity: 2,300; Year Built: 1962
AD: Mark Molesworth
SID: Paul Erickson

WIS.-RIVER FALLS
River Falls, WI 54022 III

Coach: Rick Bowen, Indiana 1966
2002-03 RESULTS (16-10)

79	Northwestern (Minn.) †	60
89	Bethel (Minn.)	87
86	Macalester ■	73
77	Embry-Riddle	80
67	Cabrini †	64
63	Wis.-Stevens Point ■	71
79	Wis.-Oshkosh	71
70	Wis.-La Crosse ■	66
65	Viterbo	66
82	Wis. Lutheran ■	65
72	St. Thomas (Minn.) ■	77
75	Wis.-Whitewater	86
79	Wis.-Eau Claire	64
96	Marian (Wis.) ■	60
65	Wis.-Superior	56
77	Wis.-Platteville ■	70
79	Wis.-Stout ■	88
56	Wis.-Oshkosh ■	55
81	Wis.-La Crosse	65
63	Wis.-Whitewater ■	71
61	Wis.-Stevens Point	74
70	Wis.-Eau Claire	77
62	Wis.-Superior ■	56
92	Wis.-Stout	86
78	Wis.-Platteville	72
65	Wis.-Eau Claire ■	68

Nickname: Falcons
Colors: Red & White
Arena: Karges Center
    Capacity: 2,000; Year Built: 1958
AD: Rick Bowen
SID: Jim Thies

WIS.-STEVENS POINT
Stevens Point, WI 54481 III

Coach: Jack Bennett, Ripon 1971
2002-03 RESULTS (24-4)

63	Upper Iowa ■	36
66	Viterbo ■	56
72	Marian (Wis.)	50
78	Edgewood †	51
71	Wis.-River Falls	63
69	Wis.-Stout ■	64
100	Coe ■	61
82	Carroll (Wis.)	63

75	Viterbo ■	50
69	Carnegie Mellon	47
80	La Roche	43
73	Wis.-Eau Claire	57
64	Wis.-Platteville ■	56
70	Wis.-La Crosse ■	43
70	Wis.-Whitewater ■	80
69	Wis.-Superior ■	53
59	Wis.-Oshkosh	63
80	Wis.-Stout	59
82	Wis.-Eau Claire ■	73
74	Wis.-River Falls ■	61
73	Wis.-Platteville	62
71	Wis.-Whitewater ■	53
75	Wis.-La Crosse	39
79	Wis.-Oshkosh ■	60
71	Wis.-Superior	61
66	Wis.-La Crosse ■	41
57	Wis.-Oshkosh ■	62
62	Gust. Adolphus ■	75

Nickname: Pointers
Colors: Purple & Gold
Arena: Quandt Fieldhouse
    Capacity: 3,281; Year Built: 1969
AD: Frank O'Brien
SID: Jim Strick

WIS.-STOUT
Menomonie, WI 54751-0790 ...III

Coach: Ed Andrist, Wis.-Stout 1976
2002-03 RESULTS (14-11)

71	Michigan Tech †	93
80	Minn. St. Mankato	84
81	Northland	38
68	Wis.-Superior	48
74	Wis.-Eau Claire ■	80
64	Wis.-Stevens Point	69
59	Viterbo	51
75	Mary	66
87	Neb. Wesleyan †	81
75	Ill. Wesleyan †	89
70	Wis.-Oshkosh ■	55
94	Northwestern (Minn.) ■	54
87	Wis.-Platteville	85
88	Wis.-La Crosse ■	59
87	Wis.-Whitewater ■	77
88	Wis.-River Falls ■	79
85	Wis.-Eau Claire	81
59	Wis.-Stevens Point ■	80
64	Wis.-Oshkosh	88
94	Wis.-Superior ■	73
63	Wis.-La Crosse	58
66	Wis.-Platteville ■	68
86	Wis.-River Falls ■	92
58	Wis.-Whitewater	60
70	Wis.-Oshkosh	103

Nickname: Blue Devils
Colors: Navy & White
Arena: Johnson Fieldhouse
    Capacity: 1,900; Year Built: 1965
AD: Steve Terry
SID: Layne Pitt

WIS.-SUPERIOR
Superior, WI 54880-4500 III

Coach: Jeff Kaminsky, Grand Valley St.
    1985
2002-03 RESULTS (5-20)

76	Apprentice †	61
66	Edgewood	74
86	Northland ■	68
56	Bemidji St.	102
48	Wis.-Stout ■	68
48	Wis.-Whitewater	57
61	Wis.-Eau Claire	66
88	St. Scholastica ■	58
37	Keene St. †	45
46	Babson †	60

52	Wis.-Platteville ■	54
57	Wis.-La Crosse	55
63	Wis.-Oshkosh	87
66	Finlandia	69
56	Wis.-River Falls	65
53	Wis.-Stevens Point	69
73	Wis.-Whitewater ■	78
70	Wis.-Eau Claire ■	73
61	Wis.-Platteville	72
73	Wis.-Stout	94
79	Wis.-La Crosse ■	82
56	Wis.-River Falls	62
57	Wis.-Oshkosh ■	91
73	Finlandia ■	51
61	Wis.-Stevens Point ■	71

Nickname: Yellowjackets
Colors: Gold, Black, & White
Arena: Gates Fieldhouse
    Capacity: 2,500; Year Built: 1966
AD: Jeff Kaminsky
SID: Chris Vito

WIS.-WHITEWATER
Whitewater, WI 53190 III

Coach: Pat Miller, Michigan St. 1972
2002-03 RESULTS (21-7)

90	Lindenwood †	81
67	Wartburg	76
79	Beloit	75
78	Carroll (Wis.) ■	56
57	Wis.-Superior ■	48
70	Wis.-Platteville	72
104	Wis. Lutheran ■	61
83	Coe	73
60	Willamette †	55
90	Pacific Lutheran †	66
86	Wis.-River Falls ■	75
71	Wis.-Oshkosh	70
84	Wis.-Eau Claire ■	75
80	Wis.-Stevens Point ■	70
77	Wis.-Stout	87
74	Wis.-La Crosse ■	58
78	Wis.-Superior	73
75	Wis.-Platteville ■	85
71	Wis.-River Falls	63
70	Wis.-Oshkosh ■	63
53	Wis.-Stevens Point	71
64	Wis.-Eau Claire	77
79	Wis.-La Crosse	72
60	Wis.-Stout ■	58
64	Wis.-Platteville ■	61
81	Wis.-Eau Claire ■	69
63	Wis.-Oshkosh ■	68

Nickname: Warhawks
Colors: Purple & White
Arena: Williams Center
    Capacity: 3,000; Year Built: 1967
AD: Shawn Eichorst
SID: Tom Fick

WITTENBERG
Springfield, OH 45504 III

Coach: Bill L. Brown, Wittenberg 1973
2002-03 RESULTS (20-6)

99	Alma ■	58
75	Ohio Dominican ■	80
74	St. Norbert †	58
69	Franklin	59
66	Cedarville ■	67
70	Allegheny ■	66
79	Otterbein	71
62	Ohio Northern	82
72	Case Reserve	57
101	Oberlin ■	43
81	Kenyon	66
93	Hiram ■	75
73	Ohio Wesleyan	64

70	Denison	48
62	Wabash ■	47
64	Wooster	81
82	Earlham ■	46
63	Allegheny	66
68	Ohio Wesleyan ■	58
78	Hiram	62
82	Earlham	39
61	Wooster ■	55
95	Wabash	86
75	Denison ■	51
80	Denison ■	74
72	Allegheny †	73

Nickname: Tigers
Colors: Red & White
Arena: Health, PE & Rec Center
    Capacity: 3,000; Year Built: 1982
AD: Garnett Purnell
SID: Ryan Maurer

WOFFORD
Spartanburg, SC 29303-3663 I

Coach: Mike Young, Emory & Henry
    1986
2002-03 RESULTS (14-15)

63	Auburn	81
72	Clemson	79
80	Emmanuel (Ga.) ■	54
79	Virginia Tech	77
86	Virginia Intermont ■	56
69	West Virginia	79
59	South Carolina	70
89	King (Tenn.) ■	52
71	North Carolina St.	86
65	Virginia	87
79	Col. of Charleston	88
60	Furman	59
69	Citadel	54
68	Col. of Charleston	78
79	Chattanooga ■	71
61	East Tenn. St. ■	81
73	Ga. Southern ■	70
79	UNC Greensboro	85
98	Davidson ■	82
94	VMI	93
92	Chattanooga	83
68	Ga. Southern	69
72	Appalachian St. ■	76
114	Toccoa Falls Inst. ■	61
66	Furman	69
77	Western Caro.	86
75	Citadel ■	63
77	UNC Greensboro †	73
75	East Tenn. St. †	80

Nickname: Terriers
Colors: Old Gold & Black
Arena: Benjamin Johnson Arena
    Capacity: 3,500; Year Built: 1981
AD: Richard Johnson
SID: Mark Cohen

WOOSTER
Wooster, OH 44691 III

Coach: Steve Moore, Wittenberg 1974
2002-03 RESULTS (30-3)

94	Case Reserve ■	40
93	Merchant Marine ■	70
63	Ohio Northern	62
64	Westminster (Pa.) ■	53
74	Denison ■	63
96	Kenyon	58
59	Luther †	36
70	Elmhurst	52
74	Benedictine (Ill.) ■	66
72	Kalamazoo ■	79
93	Mount Union	66
86	Oberlin	45
76	Wabash ■	63

80	Allegheny	69
75	Earlham	58
70	Ohio Wesleyan ■	59
81	Wittenberg ■	64
94	Hiram	61
92	Kenyon ■	55
97	Allegheny ■	74
74	Wabash	69
91	Hiram ■	58
55	Wittenberg	61
73	Ohio Wesleyan	60
78	Earlham ■	72
73	Hiram ■	51
76	Wabash ■	66
93	Allegheny ■	71
77	John Carroll ■	75
75	Scranton	64
68	Ramapo ■	64
72	Williams †	74
78	Hampden-Sydney †	74

Nickname: Fighting Scots
Colors: Black & Old Gold
Arena: Timken Gymnasium
Capacity: 3,400; Year Built: 1968
AD: Keith Beckett
SID: Hugh Howard

WPI
Worcester, MA 01609 III

Coach: Chris Bartley, Mass.-Lowell 1994
2002-03 RESULTS (7-18)
84	Johnson St. †	74
57	Amherst	74
57	Curry	73
70	Anna Maria	51
61	Endicott ■	69
50	Dartmouth	85
73	Western New Eng.	67
78	Framingham St. ■	45
77	Westfield St. ■	62
68	Worcester St. ■	87
56	Brandeis ■	69
49	Wheaton (Mass.)	73
36	Babson	72
50	Clark (Mass.)	71
55	Coast Guard	52
59	MIT ■	69
53	Springfield ■	72
75	Clark (Mass.) ■	83
73	Mass.-Boston ■	71
62	Babson	73
54	Wheaton (Mass.) ■	66
65	Coast Guard ■	72
44	MIT	53
55	Springfield	79
60	Babson	81

Nickname: Engineers
Colors: Crimson & Gray
Arena: Harrington Auditorium
Capacity: 3,000; Year Built: 1967
AD: Dana Harmon
SID: Steve Raczynski

WORCESTER ST.
Worcester, MA 01602-2597.....III

Coach: Dave Lindberg, Worcester St. 1991
2002-03 RESULTS (17-11)
82	Nichols ■	60
70	Mass.-Dartmouth	84
70	Anna Maria	81
63	Rensselaer †	60
69	St. Joseph's (Me.)	71
62	Amherst ■	80
64	Eastern Conn. St. ■	48
82	Cazenovia	78
54	Clark (Mass.)	91
44	Tampa	70
69	Eastern Nazarene	60

87	WPI	68
75	Fitchburg St. ■	72
81	Westfield St.	72
61	Framingham St. ■	60
72	Colby-Sawyer	78
88	Mass. Liberal Arts ■	84
58	Bridgewater St.	51
76	Salem St. ■	88
80	Fitchburg St.	69
75	Westfield St. ■	79
60	Framingham St.	55
88	Mass. Liberal Arts	65
60	Bridgewater St. ■	59
65	Salem St.	81
72	Framingham St. ■	67
79	Westfield St. †	71
68	Salem St.	76

Nickname: Lancers
Colors: Royal Blue & Gold
Arena: Lancer Gymnasium
Capacity: 1,200; Year Built: 1953
AD: Susan Chapman
SID: Bruce Baker

WRIGHT ST.
Dayton, OH 45435-0001 I

Coach: Ed Schilling, Miami (Ohio) 1988
2002-03 RESULTS (10-18)
78	Akron ■	75
85	Cedarville ■	64
51	Miami (Ohio) ■	48
80	Morehead St. ■	74
59	Ball St.	66
84	Toledo ■	98
69	South Fla. ■	68
74	Manhattan †	76
75	Eastern Ky. †	61
67	Santa Clara	71
56	Loyola (Ill.)	67
67	Detroit ■	64
52	Cleveland St.	55
60	Youngstown St.	66
70	Butler ■	81
67	Wis.-Green Bay	69
59	Wis.-Milwaukee	74
76	Ill.-Chicago	89
80	Youngstown St. ■	68
62	Ill.-Chicago	77
69	Loyola (Ill.) ■	71
63	Detroit	68
76	Cleveland St. ■	63
64	Butler	79
61	IPFW	84
65	Wis.-Milwaukee ■	98
77	Wis.-Green Bay ■	74
61	Detroit	78

Nickname: Raiders
Colors: Green & Gold
Arena: Ervin J. Nutter Center
Capacity: 11,019; Year Built: 1990
AD: Michael Cusack
SID: Robert J. Noss

WYOMING
Laramie, WY 82071.................I

Coach: Steve McClain, Chadron St. 1984
2002-03 RESULTS (21-11)
85	Denver ■	65
72	Col. of Charleston †	81
77	Alas. Anchorage	69
72	Loyola Marymount †	65
70	Washington	79
73	Boise St. ■	61
73	IPFW ■	62
67	Texas Tech †	62
77	South Carolina ■	63
85	Prairie View ■	55

74	Detroit ■	60
69	Indiana St.	57
60	Montana St. ■	56
112	Savannah St. ■	77
70	Kansas	98
85	New Mexico ■	81
46	Air Force ■	44
79	Colorado St.	77
90	UNLV	80
70	San Diego St.	80
66	Brigham Young ■	74
56	Utah ■	69
103	New Mexico	91
64	Air Force	57
62	Colorado St. ■	60
73	San Diego St. ■	86
69	UNLV ■	66
50	Brigham Young	69
70	Utah	86
71	Colorado St. †	74
78	Eastern Wash. ■	71
74	North Carolina	90

Nickname: Cowboys
Colors: Brown & Gold
Arena: Arena-Auditorium
Capacity: 15,000; Year Built: 1982
AD: Lee Moon
SID: Tim Harkins

XAVIER
Cincinnati, OH 45207-7530 I

Coach: Thad Matta, Butler 1990
2002-03 RESULTS (26-6)
87	St. Peter's ■	48
62	Stanford	63
93	Florida A&M ■	64
74	Purdue ■	59
50	Cincinnati	44
68	Miami (Ohio) ■	58
61	Mississippi St. †	71
87	Ball St.	58
96	Siena	88
84	Eastern Ky. ■	60
75	Creighton ■	73
58	Alabama	65
59	Richmond ■	67
99	St. Bonaventure ■	83
80	La Salle ■	47
86	Massachusetts	73
93	Duquesne ■	58
75	Fordham	61
66	Richmond	52
80	George Washington	68
85	Dayton ■	77
93	Rhode Island ■	70
93	La Salle	71
73	Dayton	72
80	Duquesne	78
71	George Washington ■	70
88	St. Joseph's	80
96	Temple ■	65
78	George Washington †	73
57	Temple †	63
71	Troy St. †	59
64	Maryland †	77

Nickname: Musketeers
Colors: Blue, Gray & White
Arena: Cintas Center
Capacity: 10,250; Year Built: 2000
AD: Michael Bobinski
SID: Tom Eiser

YALE
New Haven, CT 06520-8216 I

Coach: James Jones, Albany (N.Y.) 1986
2002-03 RESULTS (14-13)
59	Oklahoma St.	68
61	Wake Forest	73
84	Penn St.	68

88	Sacred Heart	69
70	Manhattan †	69
70	Holy Cross †	66
71	Central Conn. St. †	59
56	Stanford	79
56	St. Mary's (Cal.)	66
57	Fairfield	59
69	Rhode Island ■	81
100	Rensselaer ■	49
66	Brown ■	78
63	Army	69
84	Brown	94
65	Columbia	51
76	Cornell	47
75	Dartmouth ■	64
73	Harvard ■	68
57	Pennsylvania	68
49	Princeton	56
70	Cornell ■	52
71	Columbia ■	59
52	Princeton ■	61
75	Pennsylvania ■	80
95	Harvard	82
60	Dartmouth	50

Nickname: Elis, Bulldogs
Colors: Yale Blue & White
Arena: John J. Lee Ampitheater
Capacity: 3,100; Year Built: 1932
AD: Thomas Beckett
SID: Tim Bennett

YESHIVA
New York, NY 10033-3201 III

Coach: Jonathan Halpert, Yeshiva 1966
2002-03 RESULTS (8-17)
51	Palm Beach Atl. †	73
75	Emmanuel (Mass.)	78
56	Manhattanville ■	64
71	Stevens Institute ■	56
69	Maritime (N.Y.)	76
66	Mt. St. Mary (N.Y.)	79
70	Baruch	88
90	Mt. St. Vincent ■	71
79	St. Joseph's (L.I.) ■	74
72	CCNY	63
50	Merchant Marine	79
51	Mt. St. Mary (N.Y.) ■	72
65	Polytechnic (N.Y.)	50
49	St. Joseph's (L.I.)	60
83	Brooklyn	77
57	Manhattanville	60
62	Maritime (N.Y.) ■	60
54	Rowan	108
57	Old Westbury	66
67	Merchant Marine ■	73
71	Old Westbury ■	85
51	Stevens Institute	82
53	Mt. St. Vincent	71
68	Maritime (N.Y.) ■	52
58	Merchant Marine	74

Nickname: Maccabees
Colors: Royal Blue & White
Arena: Max Stern Athletic Center
Capacity: 1,100; Year Built: 1985
AD: Richard Zerneck
SID: To be named

YORK (N.Y.)
Jamaica, NY 11451.................III

Coach: Ronald St. John, York (N.Y.) 1980
2002-03 RESULTS (10-15)
72	Medgar Evers	68
81	Brooklyn ■	65
63	Flagler	79
52	N.C. Wesleyan	89
65	Old Westbury	73
57	D'Youville †	61

75	Lake Erie †	71
53	Rutgers-Camden	73
59	Wm. Paterson ■	62
52	NYCCT ■	45
81	Ramapo	99
65	Mt. St. Mary (N.Y.) ■	72
54	Staten Island ■	48
53	Lehman	68
71	John Jay	61
41	Hunter ■	66
58	CCNY	70
75	Rutgers-Newark ■	71
72	Medgar Evers ■	47
84	Brooklyn	86
80	NYCCT	68
55	Staten Island	66
61	Baruch	73
68	Staten Island †	57
68	CCNY †	79

Nickname: Cardinals
Colors: Red & White
Arena: Health & P.E. Complex
  Capacity: 1,200; Year Built: 1990
AD: Linda Barley
SID: Darrin Ford

YORK (PA.)
York, PA 17405-7199 III

Coach: Jeff Gamber, Millersville 1968
2002-03 RESULTS (13-12)

87	Messiah ■	74
71	Gettysburg	67
90	McDaniel ■	76
91	Gallaudet	90
76	Mary Washington ■	82
95	Dickinson	97
77	Juniata ■	63
80	Case Reserve †	88
82	Hartwick †	92
89	Susquehanna ■	85
89	Asbury ■	95
89	Albright ■	66
68	Goucher	71
86	Salisbury ■	82
75	Marymount (Va.)	73
84	St. Mary's (Md.)	65
77	Catholic ■	82
72	Mary Washington	101
103	Gallaudet ■	74
82	Salisbury	57

76	Goucher ■	90
94	Marymount (Va.) ■	98
65	Catholic	103
121	St. Mary's (Md.) ■	102
78	Marymount (Va.)	82

Nickname: Spartans
Colors: Kelly Green & White
Arena: Wolf Gym
  Capacity: 1,200; Year Built: 1964
AD: Jeffrey Gamber
SID: Scott Guise

YOUNGSTOWN ST.
Youngstown, OH 44555-0001 ...I

Coach: John Robic, Denison 1986
2002-03 RESULTS (9-20)

56	Indiana St.	63
73	Slippery Rock ■	52
69	Toledo ■	61
56	St. Francis (Pa.)	70
63	Buffalo ■	48
84	Shawnee St. ■	69
56	Duquesne	61
59	UMKC	71

58	Niagara ■	66
59	Loyola (Ill.)	76
70	Oakland	75
57	Cleveland St. ■	55
56	Wis.-Milwaukee	74
66	Wright St. ■	60
60	Butler	64
49	Detroit ■	57
76	Ill.-Chicago ■	78
77	Wis.-Green Bay ■	76
68	Wright St.	80
65	Loyola (Ill.) ■	63
63	IPFW	65
76	Cleveland St.	86
61	Wis.-Milwaukee ■	86
53	Wis.-Green Bay	69
60	Butler ■	69
52	Detroit	86
47	Ill.-Chicago	73
65	Wis.-Green Bay ■	61
59	Ill.-Chicago †	79

Nickname: Penguins
Colors: Red & White
Arena: Beeghley Center
  Capacity: 6,500; Year Built: 1972
AD: Ron Strollo
SID: Trevor Parks

SCHEDULES/RESULTS